792

The
Bedford
Introduction
to Drama

This book is due for return on or before the last date shown below.

The Bedford Introduction to Drama

SECOND EDITION

Lee A. Jacobus
University of Connecticut

BEDFORD BOOKS of ST. MARTIN'S PRESS
BOSTON

For Bedford Books
Publisher: Charles H. Christensen
Associate Publisher/General Manager: Joan E. Feinberg
Managing Editor: Elizabeth M. Schaaf
Developmental Editor: Karen S. Henry
Production Editor: Lori Chong
Copyeditor: Barbara Flanagan
Photo Researcher: Martha Friedman
Text Design: Claire Seng-Niemoeller
Cover Design: Hannus Design Associates
Cover Photo: From the Royal Dramatic Theatre of Stockholm's 1987 production of *Hamlet* at the National Theatre in London, directed by Ingmar Bergman. Photo by Donald Cooper/Milton Keynes, England.

Library of Congress Catalog Card Number: 92–52513

Manufactured in the United States of America.

7   6   5   4

f   e   d   c

For information, write: St. Martin's Press, Inc.
175 Fifth Avenue, New York, NY 10010

Editorial Offices: Bedford Books *of* St. Martin's Press
29 Winchester Street, Boston, MA 02116

ISBN: 0–312–06655–4

Acknowledgments

Greek Drama

Figure 1. Theater at Epidaurus from *The Theatre of Dionysus in Athens* by Arthur Wallace Pickard-Cambridge. Reprinted by permission of Oxford University Press.

Acknowledgments and copyrights are continued at the back of the book on pages 1432–35, which constitute an extension of the copyright page.

Preface for Instructors

In its second edition, *The Bedford Introduction to Drama* remains first and foremost a collection of thirty-seven important plays — the most comprehensive anthology available — that have shaped dramatic literature from the time of the early Greek dramatists to the present. As before, the book incorporates a number of features that distinguish it from other introductions to drama. Most notably, it presents five major playwrights in greater than usual depth, with two plays each by Sophocles, Ibsen, Beckett, and Williams and three plays by Shakespeare. Commentaries by playwrights, directors, actors, and critics, thorough biographical and critical introductions, and photographs of recent productions offer drama students a unique opportunity to study and write about major figures in the development of drama.

The second edition also incorporates a number of features that distinguish it from the first edition. Fourteen plays are new to this edition, including Euripides' *Medea,* William Shakespeare's *The Tempest,* Thomas Middleton and William Rowley's *The Changeling,* Aphra Behn's *The Rover,* William Congreve's *The Way of the World,* Oscar Wilde's *The Importance of Being Earnest,* Bertolt Brecht's *Galileo,* Tennessee Williams's *Cat on a Hot Tin Roof,* Samuel Beckett's *Endgame* and *All That Fall,* Wole Soyinka's *The Strong Breed,* Sam Shepard's *Buried Child,* Brian Friel's *Dancing at Lughnasa,* and Suzan-Lori Parks's *The Death of the Last Black Man in the Whole Entire World.* William Shakespeare is now represented by three plays, and Tennessee Williams is treated in depth with two. Commentaries and interviews, limited in the first edition to playwrights treated in depth, are now available for twenty-three plays. Of the forty-nine commentaries, twenty-one are new. Further, the introductions to the playwrights and the historical introductions have all been strengthened and revised with the help of a team of expert reviewers. In addition to these changes, the second edition now uses the Rolf Fjelde translations of Ibsen's plays, which offer up-to-date, idiomatic American-English versions that are much more accurate as well as easier to read. Chekhov's *The Cherry Orchard* now appears in Ann Dunnigan's sprightly translation.

The second edition almost doubles the number of photographs in keeping with a greater emphasis on production and performance. The introduction to each play now reviews the performance history of the play from its first appearance to some of its most recent productions.

Another distinctive feature of *The Bedford Introduction to Drama* is the strong representation by contemporary playwrights. Important plays by Sam Shepard, Athol Fugard, Marsha Norman, and Brian Friel, among others, together with commentaries by and about these play-wrights — including interviews and critical studies — give students an exposure to contemporary drama unavailable in any other introductory text. Moreover, the range of plays by minority and women playwrights is broader than that in most other introductory texts: Aphra Behn's *The Rover*, Lady Gregory's *The Rising of the Moon*, Lorraine Hansberry's *A Raisin in the Sun*, Marsha Norman's *'night, Mother*, Suzan-Lori Parks's *The Death of the Last Black Man in the Whole Entire World*, and August Wilson's *Fences*. The second edition also includes *The Strong Breed* by Nobel Prize–winning Nigerian playwright Wole Soyinka.

The Bedford Introduction to Drama offers a succinct but thorough history of Western drama. Even when it appears most timeless, all drama (like, of course, all literature) is a product of a language, an era, and a complex range of political, social, and ethnic influences. *The Bedford Introduction* highlights such influences. A general introduction gives an overview of the great ages of drama, the major genres and elements, and the cultural value of drama. Throughout the book, introductions to significant periods of drama, the playwrights, and the plays focus on the cultural contexts of the plays and on their stage history.

For the second edition a group of reviewers, experts in particular fields of interest, examined the historical introductions for accuracy and comprehensiveness. Each of the introductions was revised with the re-views in mind. These reviewers were Michael Cadden, Princeton University; Mary Coogan, University of Colorado, Boulder; Anthony Graham-White, University of Illinois, Chicago; C. Fenno Hoffman, Rhode Island School of Design; Robert D. Hume, Pennsylvania State University; Paul G. Reeve, University of Houston, University Park; Laurence Senelick, Tufts University; and Timothy Wiles, Indiana University, Bloomington.

Finally, *The Bedford Introduction to Drama* is a complete resource book for the beginning student of drama. In the general introduction a discussion of the elements of drama defines important terms and con-cepts and demonstrates these concepts in action, drawing its examples from Lady Gregory's brief one-act play *The Rising of the Moon*.

Writing About Drama, a useful appendix, shows students possible approaches to commenting on dramatic literature and points the way to developing ideas that can result in probing essays. From prewriting to drafting and outlining, the process of writing about drama is illustrated by reference to Lady Gregory's play, and a sample essay on the play provides one example of drama criticism.

A second appendix, the Glossary of Dramatic Terms, defines concepts and terms clearly and concisely. When these terms are first introduced and defined in the text, they appear in small capital letters.

The Selected Bibliography, a third appendix, includes a list of reference works for the major periods of drama, the playwrights, and the plays by the five playwrights treated in depth. The cited general references, histories, biographies, critical studies, journal articles, reviews, and collections of plays are especially useful for research in drama.

While the book emphasizes the plays as texts to be read, a fourth appendix, the Selected List of Film, Video, and Audiocassette Resources, reinforces the element of performance. This list, accompanied by a list of distributors, can help instructors and students find an illuminating treatment of the plays in performance.

Acknowledgments

First, I would like to thank those who offered their advice on what to include in the first edition of this book: Jeff Glauner, Park College; Susan Smith, University of Pittsburgh; and Jordan Miller, University of Rhode Island. Second, I am grateful to those who read the introductions and commentaries in the first edition and who gave me the advantage of their knowledge and wisdom. G. Jennifer Wilson, University of California, Los Angeles; William Carroll, Boston University; Ronald Bryden, Graduate Centre for the Study of Drama, University of Toronto; Robert Dial, University of Akron; Jonnie Guerra, Mount Vernon College; and John Timpane, Lafayette College, were all unhesitating in offering suggestions and improvements.

For the second edition I am grateful to Keith Hull of the University of Wyoming for the warmth of his response to the book. Those who were especially helpful in preparing the second edition are Elias Abdou, Community College of Allegheny, Pittsburgh; Robert E. Aldridge, Kirkwood Community College; Katya Amato, Portland State University; Keith Appler, University of Illinois, Urbana; Nora Bicki, University of Illinois, Champaign; Reverend Doctor Nadean Bishop, Eastern Michigan University; François Bonneville, State University of New York, Albany; Michael Boudreau, University of Illinois, Urbana; David Bratt, Winona State University; Marianne Cooley, University of Houston, University Park; Walter Creed, University of Hawaii, Manoa; Mary Beth Culp, Marymount College; Merilee Cunningham, University of Houston; Joan D'Antoni, University of Louisville; Wayne G. Deahl, Eastern Wyoming College; Charlotte Doctor, Los Angeles Pierce College; Janet Dow, Western Connecticut State University; Jerry D. Eisenhour, Eastern Illinois University; Fred M. Fetrow, United States Naval Academy; Jane E. Fisher, Canisius College; Charles Frey, University of Washington; Robert

W. Funk, Eastern Illinois University; Stephen R. Grecco, Pennsylvania State University; L. W. Harrison, Santa Rosa Junior College; Dave Hartley, Central Florida Community College; Andrew Jay Hoffman, Central Connecticut State University; Claudia L. Johnson, Marquette University; Ellen Redding Kaler, University of Kansas; Harvey Kassebaum, Cuyahoga Community College; Dorothy Louise, Franklin and Marshall College; Annette McGregor, Purdue University; Jack Mahoney, Vincennes University; James Marlow, Southeastern Massachusetts University; Christy Minadeo, Eastern Michigan University; Carol A. Moore, Louisiana State University; Roark Mulligan, University of Oregon; Eric Pedersen, Butler County Community College; M. Bernice Pepke, Manatee Community College; Patrick Quade, Saint Olaf College; Carol Replogle, Loyola University, Chicago; William Reynolds, Hope College; Mark Rocha, California State University, Northridge; Matthew C. Roudane, Georgia State University; Dolores J. Sarafinski, Gannon University; Carol Scklenica, Marquette University; Rodney Simard, California State University, San Bernardino; James Stephens, Marquette University; Jeannie B. Thomas, University of Oregon; Gregory Ulmer, Kearney State College; Susan Vick, Worcester Polytechnic Institute; Linda Wells, Boston University; Keith Welsh, Webster University; Virginia West, Franklin and Marshall College; Paul Wood, Villanova University; and J. S. Wszalek, James Madison University.

I am especially grateful to have had the guidance of Charles Christensen, publisher of Bedford Books of St. Martin's Press. Chris Rutigliano, Melissa Cook, and Jane Betz helped with extensive editing responsibilities for the first edition; Virginia Creeden cleared the permissions for reprinting the plays and commentaries; and Carole Frohlich was instrumental in finding excellent photographs of key performances. For the second edition, Laura McCready did most of the hard work gathering information on production histories; Barbara Flanagan was an indefatigable copyeditor; Martha Friedman found wonderful new photographs; Jonathan Burns helped in production; David Gibbs updated and expanded the list of film, video, and audiocassette resources for teaching the plays; Julia Dubnoff gave sound advice about translations of Greek plays; George Scribner and Donna Dennison supervised the production of a handsome cover; and Lori Chong has my gratitude for being such an expert production editor. My greatest debt is to my editor, Karen S. Henry, whose expertise and creativity are unmatched. Without her, this would have been a lesser book. I also thank Jacqueline McCurry, Joseph Zwier, and Nevil Parker, my research assistants at the University of Connecticut, Storrs.

Contents

*The
Bedford
Introduction
to Drama*

Introduction: Thinking About Drama

What Is Drama?

DRAMA is the art of representing for the pleasure of others events that happened or that we imagine happening. The primary ingredients of drama are characters, represented by players; action, described by gestures and movement; thought, implied by dialogue and action; spectacle, represented by scenery and costume; and, finally, audiences, who respond to this complex mixture.

When we are in the theater, we see the actors, hear the lines, are aware of the setting, and sense the theatrical community of which we are a part. Even when reading a play, we should imagine actors speaking lines and visualize a setting in which those lines are spoken. Drama is an experience in which we participate on many levels simultaneously. On one level, we may believe that what we see is really happening; on another level, we know it is only make-believe. On one level we may be amused, but on another level we realize that serious statements about our society are being made. Drama both entertains and instructs.

When Aristotle wrote about drama in the *Poetics*, a work providing one of the earliest and most influential theories of drama, he began by explaining it as the imitation of an action (MIMESIS). Those analyzing his work have interpreted this statement in several ways. One interpretation is that drama imitates life. On the surface, such an observation may seem simple, even obvious. But on reflection, we begin to find complex significance in his comment. The drama of the Greeks, for example, with its intense mythic structure, its formidable speeches, and its profound actions, often seems larger than life or other than life. Yet we recognize characters saying words that we ourselves are capable of saying, doing things that we ourselves might do. The great Greek tragedies are certainly lifelike and certainly offer literary mirrors in which we can examine human nature. And the same is true of Greek comedies.

The relationship between drama and life has always been subtle and complex. In some plays, such as Luigi Pirandello's *Six Characters in Search of an Author*, it is one of the central issues. We begin our reading or viewing of most plays knowing that the dramatic experience is not absolutely real in the sense that, for example, the actor playing Hamlet does not truly die or truly see a ghost or truly frighten his mother. The play imitates those imagined actions, but when done properly it is realistic enough to make us fear, if only for a moment, that they could be real.

We see significance in the actions Hamlet imitates; his actions help us live our own lives more deeply, more intensely, because they give us insight into the possibilities of life. We are all restricted to living this life as ourselves; drama is one art form that helps us realize the potential of life, for both the good and the bad. In an important sense, we can share the experience of a character such as Hamlet when he soliloquizes over the question of whether it is better to die than to live in a world filled with sin and crime.

Drama and Ritual

Such imaginative participation is only a part of what we derive from drama. In its origins, drama probably evolved from ancient Egyptian and Greek rituals, ceremonies that were performed the same way again and again and were thought to have a propitious effect on the relationship between the people and their gods.

Scholars believe that in ancient Egypt some religious rituals evolved into repeated passion plays, such as those celebrating Isis and Osiris at the festivals in Abydos some three thousand years ago. Greek drama was first performed during yearly religious celebrations to the god Dionysus. The early Greek playwrights, such as Sophocles in *Oedipus Rex* and *Antigone*, emphasized the interaction between the will of the gods and the will of human beings, often pitting the truths of men and women against the truths of the gods. Such an emphasis suggests a high seriousness and perhaps a religious mission in the Greek tragedies.

The rebirth of drama in the Middle Ages — after the fall of Rome and the loss of classical artistic traditions — took place in the great cathedrals of Europe. It evolved from medieval religious ceremonies that helped the faithful understand more about their own moral predicament. *Everyman*, a late play in the medieval theater (it was written about 1500), concerns itself with the central issue of reward and punishment after this life because the soul is immortal.

Drama: The Illusion of Reality

From the beginning, drama has had the capacity to hold up an illusion of reality like the reflection in a mirror — we take the reality for granted while recognizing that it is nonetheless illusory. As we have seen, Aristotle described DRAMATIC ILLUSION as an imitation of an action. But unlike the reflection in a mirror, the action of most drama is not drawn from our actual experience of life, but from our potential or imagined experience. In the great Greek drama, the illusion includes the narratives of ancient myths that were thought to offer profound illumination. The interpretation of the myths by the Greek playwrights over a three-hundred-year period helped the Greek people participate in the myths, understand them, and apply their values to their daily lives.

Different ages have had different approaches to representing reality onstage. The Greeks felt that their plays were exceptionally realistic, and yet their actors spoke in verse and wore masks. The staging consisted of very little setting and no special costumes. Medieval drama was sometimes acted on pushwagons and carts, but the special machinery developed to suggest hellfire and the presence of devils was said to be so realistic as to be frightening. Elizabethan audiences were accustomed to actors occasionally speaking directly to the crowds at their feet near the apron of the stage. All Elizabethan plays were done in essentially contemporary clothing, often with no more scenery than the suggestion of it in the spoken descriptions of the players. The actors recited their lines in verse, except when the author had a particular reason to use prose, for example to imply that the speaker was of low social station. Yet Elizabethans reported that their theater was very much like life itself.

Shakespeare's *A Midsummer Night's Dream* is not an illusion of waking reality, but an illusion of the reality of dreams — or the unreality of dreams. Fairies, enchantments, an ass's head on the shoulders of a man — all these are presented as illusions, and we accept them. They inform the audience — in Shakespeare's day and in modern times — not by showing us ourselves in a mirror but by demonstrating that even fantastic realities have significance for us.

Certainly *A Midsummer Night's Dream* gives us insight into the profound range of human emotions. We learn about the pains of rejection when we see Helena longing for Demetrius, who in turn longs for Hermia. We learn about jealousy and possessiveness when we see Oberon cast a spell on his wife, Titania, over a dispute concerning a changeling. And we learn, too, about the worldly ambitions of the "rude mechanicals" who themselves put on a play whose reality they fear might frighten their audience. They solve the problem by reminding their audience that it is only a play and that they need not fear that reality will spoil their pleasure.

In modern drama the dramatic illusion of reality has grown to include not just the shape of an action, the events, and character but also the details of everyday life. In Bernard Shaw's *Major Barbara* we see Barbara in front of a Salvation Army band and we hear the music. When the action changes locale, the setting changes as well. Some contemporary playwrights make an effort to re-create a reality close to the one we live in. Some modern plays, like August Wilson's *Fences*, make a precise representation of reality a primary purpose, shaping the tone of the language to reflect the way modern people speak, re-creating contemporary reality in the setting, language, and other elements of the drama.

But describing a play as an illusion of reality in no way means that it represents the precise reality that we take for granted in our everyday experience. Rather, drama ranges widely and explores multiple realities, some of which may seem very close to our own and some of which may seem improbably removed from our everyday experience.

Seeing a Play Onstage

For an audience, drama is one of the most powerful artistic experiences. When we speak about participating in drama, we mean that as a member of the audience we become a part of the action that unfolds. This is a mysterious phenomenon.

When we see a play today we are usually seated in a darkened theater looking at a lighted stage. In ages past, this contrast was not the norm. Greek plays took place outdoors during the morning and the afternoon; most Elizabethan plays were staged outdoors in the afternoon; in the Renaissance, some plays began to be staged indoors with ingenious systems of lighting that involved candles and reflectors. In the early nineteenth century most theaters used gaslight onstage; electricity took over in the later part of the century, and its use has grown increasingly complex: In most large theaters today computerized lighting boards have replaced the Elizabethan candles.

Sitting in the darkness has made our experience of seeing Greek and Elizabethan plays much different for us than it was for the original audiences. We do not worry about being seen by the "right people" or about studying the quality of the audience, as people did during the Restoration in the late seventeenth century. The darkness isolates us from all except those who sit adjacent to us. Yet we instantly respond when others in the audience laugh, when they gasp, when they shift restlessly. We recognize in those moments that we are part of a larger community drawn together by theater and that we are all involved in the dramatic experience.

Theaters and Their Effect

Different kinds of theaters make differing demands on actors and audiences. Despite its huge size, the open ARENA style theater of the early Greeks brought the audience into a special kind of intimacy with the actors. The players came very close to the first rows of seats, and the acoustics permitted even a whisper onstage to be audible in the far seats. The Greek theater also imparted a sense of formality to the occasion of drama. For one thing, its regularity and circularity was accompanied by a relatively rigid seating plan. The officials and nobility sat in special seats. Then each section of the theater was given over to specific families, with the edges of the seating area devoted to travelers and strangers to the town. One knew one's place in the Greek theater. Its regularity gave the community a sense of order.

Medieval theater also gave its audiences a sense of community, both when it used playing areas called mansions inside the churches and when it used wagons wheeled about outside the churches in processions in the streets or outside the city walls. That the medieval theater repeated the same cycles of plays again and again for about two hundred years, to the delight of many European communities, tells us something about the stability of those communities. Their drama was integrated with their religion, and both helped them express their sense of belonging to the church and the community.

In some medieval performances the actors came into the audience, breaking the sense of distance or the illusion of separation. It is difficult for us to know how much participation and involvement in the action the medieval audience felt. Modern audiences have responded very well to productions of medieval plays such as *The Second Shepherds' Play*, *Noah's Flood*, and *Everyman*, and we have every reason to think that medieval audiences enjoyed their dramas immensely. The guilds that performed them took pride in making their plays as exciting and involving as possible.

The Elizabethan playhouse was a wooden structure providing an enclosed space around a courtyard open to the sky. A covered stage thrust into the courtyard. As in the Greek theater, the audience was arranged somewhat by social station. Around the stage, which was about five feet off the ground, stood the groundlings, those who paid least for their entrance. Then in covered galleries in the building itself sat patrons who paid extra for a seat. The effect of the enclosed structure was of a small, contained world. Actors were in the habit of speaking directly to members of the audience, and the audience rarely kept a polite silence. It was a busy, humming theater that generated intimacy and involvement between actors and audience.

The proscenium stage of the nineteenth century — and our century as well — distances the audience from the play, providing a clear frame (the PROSCENIUM) behind which the performers act out their scenes. This detachment is especially effective for plays that demand a high degree of realism because the effect of the proscenium is to make the audience feel it is witnessing the action as a silent observer, looking in as if through an imaginary fourth wall on a living room or other intimate space in which the action takes place. The proscenium arch gives the illusion that the actors are in a world of their own, unaware of the audience's presence.

In the twentieth century some of the virtues of the Greek arena theater, or THEATER IN THE ROUND, were rediscovered. Antonin Artaud in France developed a concept called the theater of cruelty, which essentially closed the gap between actor and audience. One of its purposes was to confront the members of the audience individually to make them feel uncomfortable and force them to deal with the primary issues of the drama itself.

Twentieth-century theater is eclectic. It uses thrust, arena, proscenium, and every other kind of stage already described. Some contemporary theater also converts nontheatrical space, such as warehouses, or city streets, into space for performance.

Reading a Play

Reading a play is a different experience from seeing it enacted. For one thing, readers do not have the benefit of the interpretations made by a director, actors, and scene designers in presenting a performance. These interpretations are all critical judgments based both on their ideas of how the play should be presented and on their insights into the meaning of the play.

A reading of a play is largely an idealized version of the play. The interpretation remains in our heads and is not translated to the stage. The dramatic effect of the staging is lost to us unless we make a genuine effort to visualize it and to understand its contribution to the dramatic experience. For a fuller experience of the drama when reading plays, one should keep in mind the historical period and the conventions of staging that are appropriate to the period and that are specified by the playwright.

Some plays were prepared by their authors for reading as well as staging, as evident in plays whose stage directions supply information that would be unavailable to an audience, such as the color of the characters' eyes, characters' secret motives, and other such details. Occasionally stage directions, such as those of Tennessee Williams, are written in a poetic prose that can be appreciated only by a reader.

It is not a certainty that seeing a play will produce an experience more "true" to the play's meaning than reading it. Every act of reading silently or speaking the lines aloud is an act of interpretation. No one can say which is the best interpretation. Each has its own merits, and the ideal is probably to read and see any play.

The Great Ages of Drama

Certain historical periods have produced great plays and great playwrights, although why some periods generate more dramatic activity than others is still a matter of conjecture for scholars examining the social, historical, and religious conditions of the times. Each of the great ages of drama has affected the way plays are written, acted, and staged in successive ages. Today, for example, drama borrows important elements from each earlier period.

Greek Drama

The Greeks of the fifth century B.C. are credited with the first masterful dramatic age, which lasted from the birth of Aeschylus (525? B.C.) to the death of Aristophanes (c. 385 B.C.). Their theaters were supported by public funds, and the playwrights competed for prizes during the great feasts of Dionysus. Sometimes as many as ten to fifteen thousand people sat in the theaters and watched with a sense of delight and awe as the actors played out their tales.

Theater was extremely important to the Greeks as a way of interpreting their relationships with their gods and of reinforcing their sense of community. All classes enjoyed it; they came early in the morning and spent the entire day in the theater. Drama for the Greeks was not mere escapism or entertainment, not a frill or a luxury. Connected as it was with religious festivals, it was a cultural necessity.

Sophocles' plays *Oedipus Rex* and *Antigone* are examples of the powerful tragedies that have transfixed audiences for centuries. Euripides, who succeeded Sophocles, was also a prize-winning tragedian. His *Trojan Women*, *Alcestis*, *Medea*, *Bacchae*, and *Elektra* are still performed and still exert an influence on today's drama. The same is true of Aeschylus, who preceded both and whose *Agamemnon*, *The Libation Bearers*, *The Eumenides*, and *Prometheus Bound* have all been among the most lasting of plays.

In addition to such great tragedians, the Greeks also produced the important comedians Aristophanes and Menander, whose work has been plundered for plays as diverse as a Shakespeare comedy and a Broadway musical. Aristophanes' *Lysistrata*, in which the Athenian and Spartan women agree to withhold sex from their husbands until the men promise to stop making war, is a powerful social comedy. Menander produced a more subtle type of comedy that made the culture laugh at itself. Both styles of comedy are the staple of popular entertainment even today. Menander's social comedies were the basis of the comedy of manners, in which society's ways of behavior are criticized. The comedy of manners is exemplified in William Congreve's eighteenth-century *The Way of the World* and even in situation comedies on contemporary television.

Roman Drama

The Romans became aware of Greek drama in the third century B.C. and began to import Greek actors and playwrights. Because of many social and cultural differences between the societies, however, drama never took a central role in the life of the average Roman. Seneca, who is now viewed as Rome's most important tragedian, almost certainly wrote his plays to be read rather than to be seen onstage.

Roman comedy produced two great playwrights, Plautus and Terence, who helped develop the STOCK (or type) CHARACTER, such as the skinflint or the prude, and used the device of mix-ups involving identical twins in their plays. Plautus was the great Roman comedian in the tradition of Menander's comedy of manners. Plautus's best-known plays are *The*

Braggart Warrior and *The Twin Menaechmi,* and during the Renaissance, when all European schoolchildren read Latin, his works were favorites.

Terence's work was praised during the Renaissance as being smoother, more elegant, and more polished and refined than Plautus's. In his own age Terence was less admired by the general populace but more admired by connoisseurs of drama. His best-known plays are rarely performed today: *The Woman of Andros, The Phormio,* and *The Brothers.*

Drama took its place beside many other forms of entertainment in Roman culture — sports events, spectacles, the slaughter of wild beasts, and mass sacrifices of Christians and others to animals. The Roman public, when it did attend plays, enjoyed farces and relatively coarse humor. The audiences for Plautus and Terence, aristocratic in taste, did not represent the cross section of the community that was typical of Greek audiences.

Medieval Drama

After the fall of Rome and the spread of the Goths and Visigoths across southern Europe in the fifth century, Europe experienced a total breakdown of the strong central government Rome had provided. When Rome fell, Greek and Roman culture virtually disappeared. The great classical texts went largely unread until the end of the medieval period in the fourteenth and fifteenth centuries. However, expressions of culture, including art forms such as drama, did not entirely disappear. During the medieval period the church's power and influence grew extensively and it tried to fill the gap left by the demise of the Roman Empire. The church became a focus of both religious and secular activity for people all over Europe.

After almost five centuries of relative inactivity, European drama was reborn in religious ceremonies in the great stone churches that dominate most European towns. It moved out of the churches by the twelfth century perhaps because its own demands outgrew its circumstances: It had become a competitor, not just an adjunct, of the religious ceremonies that had spawned it.

One reason that the medieval European communities regarded their drama so highly is that it was a direct expression of many of their concerns and values. The age was highly religious; in addition, the people who produced the plays were members of guilds whose personal pride was represented in their work. Their plays came to be called MYSTERY PLAYS because the trade that each guild represented was a special skill — a mystery to the average person.

Many of these plays told stories drawn from the Bible. The tales of Noah's Ark, Abraham and Isaac, and Samson and Delilah all had immense dramatic potential, and the mystery plays capitalized on that potential. Among them *The Second Shepherds' Play* and *Abraham and Isaac* are still performed regularly.

Most mystery plays were gathered into groups of plays called CYCLES dramatizing incidents from the Bible, among other sources. They were usually performed outdoors, at times on movable wagons that doubled as stages. The audience either moved from wagon to wagon to see each play in a cycle, or the wagons moved among the audience. The interaction of the players and the audience was often taken for granted, and the distance between players and audience was often collapsed.

By the fifteenth and sixteenth centuries, another form of play developed that was not associated with cycles or with the guilds. These were the MORALITY PLAYS, and their purpose was to touch on larger contemporary issues that had a moral overtone. *Everyman* is certainly the best known of the morality plays and was performed in many nations in translation.

Renaissance Drama

The revival of learning in the Renaissance, beginning in the fourteenth century, had considerable effect on drama because classical Greek and Roman plays were discovered and studied. In the academies in Italy, some experiments in re-creating Greek and Roman plays introduced music into drama. New theaters were built in Italy to produce these plays, and while they did not have lasting effects on the modern stage, they allow us to see how the Renaissance reconceived the classical stage. The late medieval traditions of the Italian theater's COMMEDIA DELL'ARTE, a stylized improvisational slapstick comedy performed by actors' guilds, began to move outside Italy into other European nations. The *commedia*'s stock characters, Harlequins and Pulcinellas, began to appear in many countries in Europe.

Elizabethan and Jacobean drama developed most fully during the fifty years from approximately 1590 to 1640. Audiences poured into the playhouses eager for plays about history and for the great tragedies of Christopher Marlowe, such as *Doctor Faustus*, and of Shakespeare, including *Macbeth, Hamlet, Othello, Julius Caesar,* and *King Lear*. But there were others as well: Middleton and Rowley's *The Changeling*, Cyril Tourneur's *Revenger's Tragedy*, and John Webster's *The White Devil* and his touching but gory *The Duchess of Malfi*.

The great comedies of the age came mostly from the pen of William Shakespeare: *A Midsummer Night's Dream, The Comedy of Errors, As You Like It, Much Ado About Nothing, The Taming of the Shrew,* and *Twelfth Night*. Many of these comedies derived from Italian originals, usually novellas or popular poems and sometimes comedies. But Shakespeare, of course, elevated and vastly improved everything he borrowed.

Ben Jonson, a playwright who was significantly influenced by the classical writers, was also well represented on the Elizabethan stage, with *Volpone, The Alchemist, Everyman in His Humour, Bartholomew Fair*, and other durable comedies. Jonson is also important for his contributions to the masque, an aristocratic entertainment that featured music, dance, and fantastic costuming.

The Elizabethan stage sometimes grew bloody, with playwrights and audiences showing a passion for tragedies that, like *Hamlet*, centered on revenge and often ended with most of the characters meeting a premature death. Elizabethan plays also show considerable variety, with many plays detailing the history of English kings and, therefore, the history of England. It was a theater of powerful effect, and contemporary diaries indicate that the audiences delighted in it.

Theaters in Shakespeare's day were built outside city limits in seamy neighborhoods near brothels and bear-baiting pits, where chained bears were set upon by large dogs for the crowd's amusement. Happily, the theaters' business was good; the plays were constructed of remarkable language that seems to have fascinated all social classes, since all flocked to the theater by the thousands.

Late Seventeenth- and Eighteenth-Century Drama

After the Puritan reign in England from 1649 to 1660, during which dramatic productions were almost nonexistent, the theater was suddenly revived. In 1660 Prince Charles was invited back from France to be king, thus beginning what was known in England as the Restoration. It was a gay, exciting period in stark contrast to the gray Puritan era. During the period new indoor theaters modeled on those in France were built, and a new generation of actors and actresses (women took part in plays for the first time in England) came forth to participate in the dramatic revival.

Since the early 1600s, French writers, interpreting Aristotle's description of Greek drama, had leaned toward development of a classical theater, which was supposed to observe the "unities" of time, place, and action: A play had one plot and one setting and covered the action of one day. In 1637 Pierre Corneille wrote *Le Cid* using relatively modern Spanish history as his theme and carefully following classical techniques. Jean-Baptiste Racine was Corneille's successor, and his plays became even more classical by centering on classical topics. His work includes *Andromache*, *Britannicus*, and possibly his best play, *Phaedra*. Racine ended the century in retirement from the stage, but he left a powerful legacy of classicism that reached well into the eighteenth century.

Molière, an actor and producer, was the best comedian of seventeenth-century France. Among his plays, *The Misanthrope* and several others are still produced regularly in the West. Molière was classical in his way, borrowing ancient comedy's technique of using type, or stock, characters in his social satires.

Among the most important playwrights of the new generation were Aphra Behn, the first professional English female writer, whose play *The Rover* was one of the most popular plays of the late seventeenth century, and William Congreve, whose best-known play, *The Way of the World*, is often still produced. The latter is a lively comedy that aimed to chasten as well as entertain Congreve's audiences.

The eighteenth century saw the tradition of the comedy of manners continued in Richard Brinsley Sheridan's *School for Scandal* and Oliver Goldsmith's *She Stoops to Conquer*. The drama of this period focuses on an analysis of social manners, and much of it is SATIRE, that is, drama that offers mild criticism of society and holds society up to comic ridicule. But underlying that ridicule is the relatively noble motive of reforming society. We can see some of that motive at work in the plays of Molière and Congreve.

During the eighteenth century, theater in France centered on the court and was in the control of a small coterie of snobbish people. The situation in England was not quite the same, although the audiences were snobbish and socially conscious. They went to the theater to be seen, and they often went in claques — groups of like-minded patrons who applauded or booed together to express their views. Theater was important, but attendance at it was like a material possession: something to be displayed for others to admire.

Nineteenth-Century Drama to the Turn of the Century

English playwrights alone produced more than thirty thousand plays during the nineteenth century. Most of the plays were sentimental, melodramatic, and dominated by a few very powerful actors, stars who often overwhelmed the works written for them. The audiences were quite different from those of the seventeenth and eighteenth centuries. The upwardly mobile urban middle classes and the moneyed factory and mill owners who had benefited economically from the industrial revolution demanded a drama that would entertain them.

The new audiences were not especially well educated, nor were they interested in plays that were intellectually demanding. Instead, they wanted escapist and sentimental entertainment that was easy to respond to and did not challenge their basic values. Revivals of old plays and adaptations of Shakespeare were also common in the age, with great stars like Edward Forrest and William Macready using the plays as platforms for overwhelming, and sometimes overbearing, performances. Gothic thrillers were especially popular, as were historical plays and melodramatic plays featuring a helpless heroine.

As an antidote to such a diet, the new Realist movement in literature, marked by the achievements of French novelists Émile Zola and Gustave Flaubert, finally struck the stage in the 1870s in plays by August Strindberg and Henrik Ibsen. These Scandinavians revolutionized Western drama and forced their audiences, who were by then more sophisticated and better prepared, to pay attention to important issues and deeper psychological concerns than earlier audiences had done.

Strindberg's *Miss Julie*, a psychological study, challenged social complacency based on class and social differences. Ibsen's *A Doll House* was a blow struck for feminism, but it did not amuse all audiences. Some were horrified at the thought that Nora Helmer was to be taken as seriously as her husband. Such a view was heretical, but it was also thrilling for a newly awakened European conscience. Those intellectuals and writers who responded positively to Ibsen, including Bernard Shaw, acted as the new conscience and began a move that soon transformed drama. Feminism is also a theme, but perhaps less directly, of Ibsen's *Hedda Gabler*, the story of a woman whose frustration at being cast into an inferior role contributes toward a destructive — and ultimately self-destructive — impulse. Both plays are acted in a physical setting that seems to be as ordinary as a nineteenth-century sitting room, with characters as small — and yet as large — as the people who watched them.

The Russian Anton Chekhov's plays *Three Sisters*, *Uncle Vanya*, and *The Cherry Orchard*, written at the turn of the twentieth century, are realistic as well, but they are also patient examinations of character rather than primarily problem plays, as were so many of Ibsen's successful dramas. Chekhov is aware of social change in Russia, especially the changes that revealed a hitherto repressed class of peasants evolving into landowners and merchants.

The Cherry Orchard is suffused with an overpowering sense of inevitability through which Chekhov depicts the conflict between the necessity for change and a nostalgia for the past. Lyubov Andreyevna and Gayev, who live a false life of aristocratic privilege without the means to support it, choose to perish rather than to work or to change. Their estate is built on slave labor and while it is beautiful, it must perish with them. We watch them with fascination as they struggle to understand the new values that the landowner and former peasant Lopakhin explains to them.

These plays introduced a modern realism of a kind that was quite rare in earlier drama. The melodrama of the earlier nineteenth century was especially satisfying to mass audiences because the good characters were very good, the bad characters were very bad, and justice was meted out at the end. But it is difficult in Chekhov to be sure who the heroes and villains are. Nothing is as clear-cut in these plays as it is in popular melodramas. Instead, Chekhov's plays are as complicated as life itself. Such difficulties of distinction have become the norm of the most important drama of the twentieth century.

Drama in the Early and Mid-Twentieth Century

The drama of the early twentieth century nurtured the seeds of nineteenth-century realism into bloom, but sometimes with innovations such as experiments with the expectations of its audiences. John Millington Synge, for example, used the techniques of realism in *Riders to the Sea*, which might best be described as peasant tragedy. Synge contradicted the expectation of audiences that tragedy should focus on those who are elevated in social station. Maurya, the peasant mother who loses the last of her sons in the course of the play, is as tragic a figure as any in modern drama.

Eugene O'Neill's *Desire Under the Elms* is another tragedy that features the ordinary citizen rather than the noble. This play, while not a peasant tragedy, focuses on New England farmers as tragic characters. Arthur Miller's *Death of a Salesman* uses a sense of inevitability within the world of the commercial salesman, the ordinary man. As in many other twentieth-century tragedies, the point is that the life of the ordinary man can be tragic just as Oedipus's life can be tragic.

Luigi Pirandello experiments with reality in *Six Characters in Search of an Author*, a play that has a distinctly absurd quality, since it expects us to accept the notion that the characters on the stage are waiting for an author to put them into a play. Pirandello plays with our sense of illusion and of expectation and realism to such an extent that he forces us to reexamine our concepts of reality.

Bertolt Brecht's *Galileo*, an example of what the playwright called EPIC DRAMA, explores the relationship of the scientist to the state and to scientific truth. Galileo, a hero for many, recanted his beliefs at the threat of torture and regards himself as anything but a hero in the play. After Brecht composed the play, the atomic bomb was dropped on Japan, and he revised it to reflect this disturbing example of science in the hands of the state. Playwrights around the world responded to events such as World War I, the Communist revolution, and the Great Depression by writing plays that no longer permitted audiences to sit comfortably and securely in darkened theaters. Brecht and other playwrights came out to get their audiences, to make them feel, to make them realize their true condition.

Samuel Beckett's dramatic career began with *Waiting for Godot*, which audiences interpreted as an examination of humans' eternal vigilance for the revelation of God or of some transcendent meaning in their lives. In the play, Godot never comes. Yet the characters do not give up hope. *Endgame*'s characters seem to be awaiting the end of the world: In the 1950s the shadow of nuclear extinction cast by the cold war dominated most people's imagination. Beckett's inquiries into absurdity in *All That Fall* center on human beings' relation to God and to their fellow human beings. *All That Fall* raises some of the same questions of meaning implied in *Waiting for Godot*.

Tennessee Williams examines a physically and psychically frail young woman's withdrawal from life in *The Glass Menagerie*. The play derives from personal experience: Williams's sister was such a woman. Personal experience may also inform his *Cat on a Hot Tin Roof*, which portrays themes of homosexuality and marital sexual tension — themes that were not openly discussed in contemporary American theater except in veiled mythic terms, in the manner, for example, of O'Neill's *Desire Under the Elms*.

Nigerian playwright Wole Soyinka, who won the Nobel Prize for literature in 1986, portrays the complex intersection of a person's past and the present in his play *The Strong Breed*, set in an African village reminiscent of the Greek *polis*. Indeed, he has experimented with Greek tragic forms in *The Bacchae of Euripides*, which is also set in Africa. Soyinka's insights into the nature of culture and drama provide us with a new way of reflecting on drama's power in our lives.

Modern dramatists from the turn of the century to the Korean War explored in many different directions and developed new approaches to themes of dramatic illusion as well as to questions concerning the relationship of an audience to the stage and the players.

Contemporary Drama

As we approach the twenty-first century, the stage is vibrant. Although the commercial theaters in England and America are beset by high costs, they are producing remarkable plays. In Latin America, Germany, and France, the theater is active and exciting. Poland produced unusual experimental drama in the 1960s. The former Soviet Union, too, produced a number of plays that have been given a worldwide currency.

The hallmark of many of these plays has been experimentalism. Caryl Churchill's *Cloud Nine* experiments with cross-gender and cross-race casting, insisting, for example, that some male characters be played by females and that black characters be played by white actors. Such casting fits her exploration of Victorian mores based on colonialism and sexual repression. Doubling — having one actor play two or more parts — is common in all ages of drama, but Churchill's approach is novel and intriguing.

Sam Shepard is well known as an actor in films, but he is also one of the most prolific contemporary playwrights. His Pulitzer Prize–winning *Buried Child* appears serene and calm on the surface — especially at first — but Shepard is a master at probing beneath apparently ordinary surfaces and finding both surprises and shock in what people take for granted. The family is Shepard's true subject, and his portrait of the family, with its various psychic disfigurements, provides us with surprising insights into contemporary life.

In *'night, Mother*, Marsha Norman portrays two women whose lives are constricted, limited, and painful. Thelma, the mother, is desperately trying to keep Jessie, her daughter, from committing suicide. But she fails. The structure of the play is traditional, but the material is experimental. The people in these modern plays would not be at ease in Ibsen's living rooms or Chekhov's cherry orchard. They are people who have been given a bad deal and who have given themselves a bad deal, and the drama compels us both to examine characters from whom we might otherwise turn away and to confront what those characters represent in our own lives.

Not all modern theater is experimental, however. August Wilson's *Fences* shows us the pain of life at the lower end of the economic ladder and in a form that is recognizably realistic and plausible. The play is set in the 1950s and focuses on Troy Maxon, a black man, and his relationship with his son and his wife. Tenement life is one subject of the play, but the most important subject is the courage it takes to keep going after tasting defeat. The entire drama develops within the bounds of conventional nineteenth-century realism.

Contemporary Audiences. Audiences in the late twentieth century are an interesting study. Most theatergoers are middle or upper class and urban. The easy availability of dramatic entertainment on television has changed the nature of live drama. To some extent commercial theater in America depends on the wealthy to fill theaters on Broadway. The "tired businessman" wants to be entertained. This is one reason why serious plays are often not performed on Broadway. But in light of such facts, it is striking to see that some plays of very high and lasting literary quality do reach Broadway.

Regional theaters, some of them extremely influential, have been springing up all over the world to provide a forum for new playwrights. Many of the new playwrights in this volume have had their work supported by regional theaters. Athol Fugard's plays have premiered at the Yale Repertory Company, as have August Wilson's plays. Marsha Norman's work was first produced by the Louisville Actor's Theatre. The Royal Court Theatre in London supported Harold Pinter and continues to support experimental writers such as Caryl Churchill today. All over the world, local theaters are producing adventurous theater.

Genres of Drama
Tragedy

Drama since the great age of the Greeks has taken several different forms. As we have seen, tragedies were one genre that pleased Greek audiences, and comedies pleased the Romans. In later ages, a blend of the comic and the tragic produced a hybrid genre: tragicomedy. In our time, unless a play is modeled on the Greek or Shakespearean tragedies, as is O'Neill's *Desire Under the Elms*, it is usually considered tragicomic rather than tragic. Our age still enjoys the kind of comedy that people laugh at, although most plays that are strictly comedy are frothy, temporarily entertaining, and not lasting.

TRAGEDY demands a specific worldview. Aristotle, in his *Poetics*, points out that the tragic hero or heroine should be noble of birth, perhaps a king like Oedipus or a princess like Antigone. This has often been interpreted to mean that the tragic hero or heroine should be more magnanimous, more daring, larger in spirit than the average person.

Modern tragedies have rediscovered tragic principles, and while Synge, O'Neill, and Miller rely on Aristotle's precepts, they have shown that in a modern society shorn of the distinctions between noble and peasant it is possible for audiences to see the greatness in all classes. This has given us a new way of orienting ourselves to the concept of fate; to HAMARTIA, the wrong act that leads people to a tragic end; and to the hero's or heroine's relationship to the social order.

Aristotle suggested that plot was the heart and soul of tragedy and that character came second. But most older tragedies take the name of the tragic hero or heroine as their title; such nomenclature signifies the importance that dramatists invested in their tragic characters. Yet they also heeded Aristotle's stipulation that tragic action should have one plot rather than the double or triple plots that often characterize comedies. (Shakespeare was soundly criticized in the eighteenth century for breaking this rule in his tragedies.) And they paid attention to the concept of PERIPETEIA, which specifies that the progress of the tragic characters sometimes leads them to a reversal: They get what they want, but what they want turns out to be destructive. Aristotle especially valued a plot in which the reversal takes place simultaneously with the recognition of the truth, or the shift from ignorance to awareness, as it does in Sophocles' *Oedipus Rex.*

Playwrights in the seventeenth and eighteenth centuries in France were especially interested in following classical precepts. They were certain that Greek tragedy and Greek comedy were the epitome of excellence in drama. They interpreted Aristotle's discussion of dramatic integrity to be a set of rules governing what became known as the dramatic UNITIES specifying one plot, a single action that takes place in one day, a single setting, and characters who remained the same throughout the play. Their reinterpretations of the unities were probably much stricter than Aristotle intended them.

Comedy

Two kinds of comedy developed among the ancient Greeks: OLD COMEDY, which resembles FARCE and often pokes fun at individuals with social and political power; and NEW COMEDY, which is a more suave, refined commentary on the condition of society.

Old Comedy survives in the masterful works of Aristophanes, such as *Lysistrata,* while New Comedy hearkens back to the lost plays of Menander and resurfaces in plays such as Molière's *The Misanthrope* and Bernard Shaw's *Major Barbara.* Both plays use humor but mix it with a serious level of social commentary. New Comedy has become the modern COMEDY OF MANNERS, which studies and sometimes ridicules modern society.

Comedy is not always funny. Chekhov thought *The Cherry Orchard* was a comedy, while his producer, the great Konstantin Stanislavsky, who trained actors to interpret his lines and who acted in other Chekhov plays, thought it was a tragedy. The argument may have centered on the ultimate effect of the play on its audiences, but it may also have centered on the question of laughter. There are laughs in *The Cherry Orchard,* but they usually come at the expense of a character or a social group. This is true, as well, of Samuel Beckett's *All That Fall.* We may laugh, but we also know that the play is at heart very serious.

This collection contains no sentimental comedies such as Neil Simon's *Biloxi Blues* — comedy that pulls a few heartstrings and provides many a belly laugh — although they are popular enough to be around us on television and on the stage. The durability of sentimental comedies, such as Lindsay and Crouse's *Life with Father*, which was a perennial crowd-pleaser in the 1940s, is not great. To be put on modern stages, such works need to be emotionally as well as socially updated. Despite this fact, however, sentimental comedy will always be with us. Today we need only turn on any television situation comedy to see sentimental comedy.

Tragicomedy

Since the early seventeenth century, serious plays have been called TRAGICOMEDIES when they do not adhere strictly to the structure of tragedy, which emphasizes the nobility of the hero or heroine, fate, the wrong action of the hero or heroine, and a resolution that includes death, exile, or a similar end. Many serious plays have these qualities, but they also have some of the qualities of comedy: a commentary on society, raucous behavior that draws laughs, and a relatively happy ending. Yet their darkness is such that we can hardly feel comfortable regarding them as comedies.

Plays such as Sam Shepard's *Buried Child* and Lorraine Hansberry's *A Raisin in the Sun* can be considered tragicomedy. Indeed, the modern temperament has especially relied on the mixture of comic and tragic elements for its most serious plays. Eugene O'Neill, Tennessee Williams, Harold Pinter, and Caryl Churchill have all been masters of tragicomedy.

In contemporary drama tragicomedy takes several forms. One is the play whose seriousness is relieved by comic moments; another is a play whose comic structure absorbs a tragic moment and continues to express affirmation. Yet another is the dark comedy whose sardonic humor leaves us wondering how we can laugh at something that is ultimately frightening. This is the case with some absurdist comedies, which insist that there is no meaning in events other than the meaning we invent for ourselves. Pinter's *The Dumb Waiter* and Beckett's *All That Fall* are such plays. They are funny yet sardonic, and when we laugh we do so uneasily.

Other genres of drama exist, although they are generally versions of tragedy, comedy, and tragicomedy. Improvisational theater, in which actors use no scripts and may switch roles at any moment, defies generic description. Musical comedies and operas are dramatic entertainments that have established their own genres related in some ways to the standard genres of drama.

Genre distinctions are useful primarily because they establish expectations in the minds of audiences with theatrical experience. Tragedies and comedies make different demands on an audience. As Marsha Norman says in explaining her "rules" of drama: You have to know in a play just what is at stake. Understanding the principles that have developed over the centuries to create the genres of drama helps us know what is at stake.

Elements of Drama

All plays share some basic elements with which playwrights and producers work: plots, characters, settings, dialogue, movement, and themes. In addition, many modern plays pay close attention to lighting, costuming, and props. When we respond to a play, we observe the elements of drama in action together, and the total experience is rich, complex, and subtle. Occasionally, we respond primarily to an individual element — the theme or characterization, for instance — but that is rare. Our awareness of the elements of drama is most useful when we are thinking analytically about a play and the way it affects us.

For the sake of discussion, we will consider the way the basic elements of drama function in Lady Gregory's one-act play *The Rising of the Moon* (which follows this section). It has all the elements we expect from drama, and it is both a brief and a very successful play.

Plot

PLOT is a term for the action of a drama. Plot implies that the ACTION has a shape and form that will ultimately prove satisfying to the audience. Generally, a carefully plotted play begins with EXPOSITION, an explanation of what happened before the play began and of how the characters arrived at their present situation. The play then continues, using SUSPENSE to build tension in the audience and in the characters and to develop further the pattern of RISING ACTION. The audience wonders what is going to happen, sees the characters set in motion, and then watches as certain questions implied by the drama are answered one by one. The action achieves its greatest tension as it moves to a point of CLIMAX, when a revelation is experienced, usually by the chief characters. Once the climax has been reached, the plot continues, sometimes very briefly, in a pattern of FALLING ACTION as the drama reaches its conclusion and the characters understand their circumstances and themselves better than they did at the beginning of the play.

The function of plot is to give action a form that helps us understand elements of the drama in relation to one another. Plays can have several interrelated plots or only one. Lady Gregory's *The Rising of the Moon* has one very simple plot: A police sergeant is sent out with two policemen to make sure a political rebel does not escape from the area. The effect of the single plot is that the entire play focuses intensely on the interaction between the rebel, disguised as a ballad singer, and the sergeant. The sergeant meets the rebel, listens to him sing ballads, and then recognizes in him certain qualities they share. The audience wonders if a reward of one hundred pounds will encourage the sergeant to arrest the ballad singer or if, instead, the ballad singer's sense that his cause is just will convince the sergeant to let him go. The climax of the action occurs when the sergeant's two policemen return, as the ballad singer hides behind a barrel, and ask if the sergeant has seen any signs of the rebel. Not until that moment does the audience know for sure what the sergeant will do. When he declares that he has not seen the rebel, the falling action begins. The rebel thanks the sergeant and takes his leave, and then the sergeant, left alone, appears to lament his loss of the reward.

Plots depend on CONFLICT between characters, and in *The Rising of the Moon* the conflict is very deep. It is built into the characters themselves, but it is also part of the institution of law that the sergeant serves and the ongoing struggle for justice that the ballad singer serves. This conflict, still evident today, was a very significant national issue in Ireland when the play was first produced in Dublin in 1907.

Lady Gregory works subtly with the conflict between the sergeant and the ballad singer, showing that although they are on completely opposite sides of the law — and of the important political issues — they are more alike than they are different. The ballad singer begins to sing the "Granuaile," a revolutionary song about England's unlawful dominance over Ireland through seven centuries, and when he leaves out a line, the sergeant supplies it. In that action the sergeant reveals that, although he is paid by the English to keep law and order, his roots lie with the Irish people. By his knowledge of the revolutionary songs he reveals his sympathies, and we are prepared to accept his willingness to let the ballad singer go free and to forfeit the substantial hundred-pound reward.

Characterization

Lady Gregory has effectively joined CHARACTER and conflict in *The Rising of the Moon*: As the conflict is revealed, the characters of the sergeant and the ballad singer are also revealed. At first the sergeant seems eager to get the reward, and he acts bossy with Policeman X and Policeman B. And when he first meets the ballad singer he seems demanding and policemanlike. It is only when he begins to sense who the ballad singer really is that he changes and reveals a deep, sympathetic streak.

Lady Gregory, in a note to the play, said that in Ireland when the play was first produced, those who wanted Ireland to become part of England were incensed to see a policeman portrayed so as to show his sympathies with rebels. Those who wished Ireland to become a separate nation from England were equally shocked to see a policeman portrayed so sympathetically.

The sergeant and the ballad singer are both major characters in the play, but it is not clear that either is the villain or the hero. When the play begins, the sergeant seems to be the hero because he represents the law and the ballad singer appears to be the villain because he has escaped from prison. But as the action develops, those characterizations change. What replaces them is an awareness of the complications that underlie the relationship between the law and the lawbreaker in some circumstances. This is part of the point of Lady Gregory's play.

Lady Gregory has given a very detailed portrait of both main characters, although in a one-act play she does not have enough space to be absolutely thorough in developing them. Yet we get an understanding of the personal ambitions of each character, and we understand both their relationship to Ireland and their particular allegiances as individuals. They speak with each other in enough detail to show that they understand each other, and when the ballad singer hides behind the barrel at the approach of the other two policemen, he indicates that he trusts the sergeant not to reveal him.

Policeman X and Policeman B are only sketched in. Yet their presence is important. It is with them that the sergeant reveals his official personality, and it is their presence at the end that represents the most important threat to the security of the ballad singer. However, we know little or nothing about them personally. They are characters who are functionaries, a little like Rosencrantz and Guildenstern in *Hamlet,* but without the differentiating characterizations that Shakespeare was able to give minor players in his full-length play.

The plays in this collection have some of the most remarkable characters ever created in literature. Tragedy usually demands highly complex characters, such as Oedipus, Antigone, Medea, Hamlet, and Willy Loman. We come to know them through their own words, through their interaction with other characters, through their expression of feelings, and through their presence onstage depicted in movement and gesture.

Characters in tragicomedies are individualized and complexly portrayed, such as Hedda Gabler, Miss Julie, Nora Helmer, and Maurya in *Riders to the Sea.* But just as effective in certain kinds of drama are characters drawn as types, such as Alceste, the misanthrope in Molière's play, and Everyman in medieval drama.

In many plays we see that the entire shape of the action derives from the characters, from their strengths and weaknesses. In such plays we do not feel that the action lies outside the characters and that they must live through an arbitrary sequence of events. Instead we feel that they create their own opportunities and problems.

Setting

The SETTING of a play includes many things. First, it refers to the time and place in which the action occurs. Second, it refers to the scenery, the physical elements that appear onstage to vivify the author's stage directions. In Lady Gregory's play, we have a dock with barrels to suggest the locale, and darkness to suggest night. These are very important details that influence the emotional reaction of the audience.

Some plays make use of very elaborate settings, as does August Wilson's *Fences,* which is produced with a detailed tenement back yard onstage. Others make use of very simple settings, such as the empty stage of Pirandello's *Six Characters in Search of an Author.*

Lady Gregory's setting derives from her inspiration for the play. She visited the quays — places where boats dock and leave with goods — as a young girl and imagined how someone might escape from the nearby prison and make his getaway "under a load of kelp" in one of the ships.

The quay represents the meeting of the land and water, and it represents the getaway, the possibility of freedom. The barrel is a symbol of trade, and the sergeant and the ballad singer sit on its top and trade the words of a revolutionary song with each other.

The title of the play provides another element of the setting: the moonlight. The night protects the ballad singer, and it permits the sergeant to bend his sworn principles a bit. The rising of the moon, as a rebel song suggests, signifies a change in society, the time when "the small shall rise up and the big shall fall down." Lady Gregory uses these elements in the play in a very effective way, interrelating them so that their significance becomes more and more apparent as the play progresses.

Dialogue   Plays depend for their unfolding on dialogue. The DIALOGUE is the verbal exchanges between the characters. Since there is no description or commentary on the action, as there is in most novels, the dialogue must tell the whole story. Fine playwrights have developed ways of revealing character, advancing action, and introducing themes by a highly efficient use of dialogue.

Dialogue is spoken by one character to another, who then responds. But sometimes, as in Shakespeare's *Hamlet*, a character delivers a SO-LILOQUY, in which he or she speaks alone onstage, as if speaking to himself or herself. Ordinarily, such speeches take on special importance because they are thought to be especially true. Characters, when they speak to each other, may well wish to deceive, but when they speak to themselves, they have no reason to say anything but the truth.

In *The Rising of the Moon* Lady Gregory has written an unusual form of dialogue that reveals a regional way of speech. Lady Gregory was Anglo-Irish, but she lived in the west of Ireland and was familiar with the speech patterns that the characters in this play would have used. She has been recognized for her ability to re-create the speech of the rural Irish, and passages such as the following are meant to reveal the peculiarities of the rhythms and syntax of English as it was spoken in Ireland at the turn of the century:

> SERGEANT: Is he as bad as that?
> MAN: He is then.
> SERGEANT: Do you tell me so?

Lady Gregory makes a considerable effort to create dialogue that is rich in local color as well as in spirit. John Millington Synge, whose dialogue in *Riders to the Sea* is also an effort to re-create the sounds and rhythms of rural Irish speech, once said: "In a good play every speech should be as fully flavored as a nut or apple, and such speeches cannot be written by anyone who works among people who have shut their lips on poetry." Lady Gregory, who produced the plays of Synge at the Abbey Theatre in Dublin, would certainly agree, as her dialogue in *The Rising of the Moon* amply shows.

Music

Lady Gregory introduces another, occasional dramatic element: music. In *The Rising of the Moon* the music is integral to the plot because it allows the ballad singer, by omitting a line of a rebel song, gradually to expose the sergeant's sympathies with the rebel cause. The sergeant is at first mindful of his duty and insists that the balladeer stop, but eventually he is captivated by the music. As the ballad singer continues, he sings a song containing the title of the play, and the audience or reader realizes that the title exposes the play's rebel sympathies.

Movement

We as readers or witnesses are energized by the movement of the characters in a play. As we read, stage directions inform us where the characters are, when they move, how they move, and perhaps even what the significance of their movement is. In modern plays the author may give many directions for the action; in earlier plays stage directions are few and often supplemented by those of a modern editor. In performance the movements that you see may well have been invented by the director, although the text of a play often requires certain actions, as in the ghost scene and final dueling scene in *Hamlet*. In some kinds of drama, such as musical comedy and the choruses of Greek drama, part of the action may be danced.

Lady Gregory moves the ballad singer and the sergeant in telling ways. They move physically closer to one another as they become closer in their thinking. Their movement seems to pivot around the barrel, and in one of the most charming moments of the play, they meet each other's eyes when the ballad singer sits on the barrel and comments on the way the sergeant is pacing back and forth. They then both sit on the barrel, facing in opposite directions, and share a pipe between them, almost as a peace offering.

Theme

The theme of a play is its message, its central concerns — in short, what it is about. It is by no means a simple thing to decide what the theme of a play is, and many plays contain several rather than just a single theme. Often, the search for a theme tempts us to oversimplify and to reduce a complex play to a relatively simple catchphrase.

Sophocles' *Antigone* focuses on the conflict between human law and the law of the gods when following both sets of laws seems to be impossible. Antigone wishes to honor the gods by burying her brother, but the law of Kreon decrees that he shall have no burial, since her brother is technically a traitor to the state. Similar themes are present in other Greek plays. *Hamlet* has many themes. On a very elementary level, the main theme of *Hamlet* is revenge. This is played out in the obligation of a son to avenge the murder of a father, even when the murderer is a kinsman. Another theme centers on corruption in the state of Denmark.

Lady Gregory's play has revolution as one theme. The rising of the moon is a sign for "the rising" or revolution of the people against their

English oppressors. The sergeant is an especially English emblem of oppression, because the police were established by an Englishman, Robert Peele. At one point the balladeer suggests a song, "The Peeler and the Goat," but rejects it because in slang a peeler is a policeman.

Another important theme in *The Rising of the Moon* is that of unity among the Irish people. The sergeant seems to be at an opposite pole from the ballad singer when the play opens. He is posting signs announcing a reward that he could well use, since he is a family man. But as the play proceeds, the sergeant moves closer in thought to the Irish people, represented by the rebel, the ballad singer.

Sometimes playwrights become anxious about readers and viewers missing their thematic intentions and reveal them in one or two speeches. Usually, a careful reader or viewer has already divined the theme, and the speeches are intrusive. But Lady Gregory is able to introduce thematic material in certain moments of dialogue, as in this comment by the sergeant, revealing that the police are necessary to prevent a revolution:

> SERGEANT: Well, we have to do our duty in the force. Haven't we the whole country depending on us to keep law and order? It's those that are down would be up and those that are up would be down, if it wasn't for us.

But the thematic material in *The Rising of the Moon* is spread evenly throughout, as is the case in most good plays.

In every play, the elements of drama will work differently, sometimes giving us the feeling that character is dominant over theme, or plot over character, or setting over both. Ordinarily, critics feel that character, plot, and theme are the most important elements of drama, while setting, dialogue, music, and movement come next. But in the best of dramas each has its importance and each balances the others. The plays in this collection strive for that harmony and most achieve it memorably.

Lady Gregory

Isabella Augusta Persse (1852–1932) was born in the west of Ireland. Her family was known as "ascendancy stock," that is, it was educated, wealthy, and Protestant living in a land that was largely uneducated, poverty-ridden, and Roman Catholic. A huge gulf ordinarily existed between the rich ascendancy families, who lived in great houses with considerable style, partaking of lavish hunts and balls and parties, and the impoverished Irish, who lived in one-room straw-roofed homes and worked the soil with primitive tools.

Lady Gregory took a strong interest in the Irish language, stimulated in part by a nurse who often spoke the language to her when she was a child. Her nurse was an important source of Irish folklore and a contact with the people who lived in the modest cottages around her family estate. It was extraordinary for any wealthy Protestant to pay attention to the language or the life of the poor laborers of the west of Ireland. Yet these are the very people who figure most importantly in the plays that Lady Gregory wrote in later life.

Isabella Persse met Sir William Gregory when she was on a family trip to Nice and Rome. They were actually neighbors in Ireland, although they were only slightly acquainted. They were married the following year, when she was twenty-eight and he was sixty-three. He was also of Irish ascendancy stock and had been a governor of Ceylon for many years before they met. Their marriage was apparently quite successful. Their son, Robert Gregory, was born in 1881. They used the family home, Coole Park, as a retreat for short periods, but most of their time was spent traveling and living in London, where Sir William was a trustee of the National Gallery of Art. W. B. Yeats, Bernard Shaw, and numerous other important literary figures spent time in Coole Park and its beautiful great house in the early part of the twentieth century.

Lady Gregory led a relatively conventional life until Sir William Gregory died in 1892. According to the laws of that time, the estate passed to her son, so she looked forward to a life of relatively modest circumstances. She set herself to finishing Sir William's memoirs and in the process found herself to be a gifted writer. She used some of her spare time to learn Irish well enough to talk with the old cottagers in the hills, where she went to gather folklore and old songs. W. B. Yeats and others had collected volumes of Irish stories and poems, but they did not know Irish well enough to authenticate what they heard. Lady Gregory published her Kiltartan tales (she had dubbed her neighborhood

Kiltartan) as a way of preserving the rapidly disappearing myths and stories that were still told around the hearth as a matter of course in rural Ireland.

She was already an accomplished writer when she met W. B. Yeats in 1894. Their meeting was of immense importance for the history of drama, since they decided to forge their complementary talents and abilities in creating an Irish theater. Their discussions included certain Irish neighbors, among them Edward Martyn, a Catholic whose early plays were very successful. They also talked with Dr. Edward Hyde, a mythographer and linguist and the first president of modern Ireland. Another neighbor who took part, the flamboyant George Moore, was a well-established novelist and playwright.

The group's first plays — Yeats's *The Countess Cathleen* and Martyn's *The Heather Field* — were performed on May 8 and 9, 1899, under the auspices of the Irish Literary Theatre in Dublin at the Ancient Concert Rooms. The Irish Literary Theatre was dedicated to producing plays by Irish playwrights on Irish themes, and when it became an immediate success the greatest problem the founders faced was finding more plays. Lady Gregory tried her own hand and discovered herself, at age fifty, to be a playwright.

Her ear for people's speech was unusually good — good enough that she was able to give the great poet Yeats lessons in dialogue and help him prepare his own plays for the stage. She collaborated with Yeats on *The Pot of Broth* in 1902, the year she wrote her first plays, *The Jackdaw* and *A Losing Game*. Her first produced play, *Twenty-Five*, was put on in 1903. By 1904, the group had rented the historic Abbey Theatre. Some of her plays were quite popular and were very successful even in later revivals: *Spreading the News* (1904); *Kincora* and *The White Cockade* (1905); and *Hyacinth Halvey*, *The Doctor in Spite of Himself*, *The Gaol Gate*, and *The Canavans* (all 1906). In the next year, there were troubles at the Abbey over John Millington Synge's *Playboy of the Western World*. Lady Gregory faced down a rioting audience protesting what she felt was excellent drama.

In 1918 her son, a World War I pilot, was shot down over Italy. The years that followed were to some extent years of struggle. Lady Gregory managed the Abbey Theatre, directed its affairs, and developed new playwrights, among them Sean O'Casey. During the Irish Civil War (1920–1922), she was physically threatened and eventually her family home, Roxborough, was burned. When she found that she had cancer in 1926, she made arrangements to sell Coole Park to the government with the agreement that she could remain there for life. She died in 1932, the writer of a large number of satisfying plays and the prime mover in the development of one of the century's most important literary theaters.

THE RISING
OF THE MOON

One of Lady Gregory's shortest but most popular plays, *The Rising of the Moon* is openly political in its themes. Lady Gregory had been writing plays only a short time, and she had been directing the Irish Literary Theatre when it became the Abbey Theatre Company and produced this play in 1907. Her interest in Irish politics developed, she said, when she was going through the papers of a distant relative of her husband. That man had been in the Castle, the offices of the English authorities given the task of ruling Ireland from Dublin. She said that the underhanded dealings that were revealed in those papers convinced her that Ireland should be a nation apart from England if justice were ever to be done.

In 1907 the question of union with England or separation and nationhood was on everyone's lips. Ireland was calm, and the people in Dublin were relatively prosperous and by no means readying for a fight or a revolution. Yet there had been a tradition of risings against the English dating back to the Elizabethan age and earlier. In 1907 the average Irish person would have thought that revolution was a thing of the past. But the fact was that it was less than ten years in the future. Certain organizations had been developing, notably the widespread Gaelic League and the less known Sinn Féin (We Ourselves), to promote both Irish lore, Irish language, and Irish culture. English was the dominant language in Ireland, since it was the language of commerce, but it tended to obliterate the Irish culture. So Lady Gregory's work with the Abbey Theatre, which was making one of the age's most important contributions to Irish culture, coincided with growing interest in the rest of Ireland in rediscovering its literary past.

The title *The Rising of the Moon* comes from a popular old rebel song that pointed to the rising of the moon as the signal for the rising of peoples against oppression. The main characters of the play represent the two opposing forces in Ireland: freedom and independence, personified by the ballad singer ("a Ragged Man"), and law and order, represented by the sergeant. The ballad singer is aligned with those who want to change the social structure of Ireland so that the people now on the bottom will be on top. The sergeant's job is to preserve the status quo and avoid such a turning of the tables.

In an important way, the sergeant and the ballad singer represent the two alternatives that face the modern Irish — now as in the past. One alternative is to accept the power of the English and be in their pay, like the sergeant; one would then be well fed and capable of supporting a family. The other alternative is to follow the revolutionary path of the ballad singer and risk prison, scorn, and impoverishment. The ballad singer is a ragged man because he has been totally reduced in circumstances by his political choices.

For Lady Gregory, this play was a serious political statement. She and W. B. Yeats — both aristocratic Protestant Irish — were sympathetic to the Irish revolutionary causes. They each wrote plays that struck a revolutionary note during this period. Neither truly expected a revolution, and when the Easter Uprising of 1916 was put down with considerable loss of life and immense destruction of central Dublin, Yeats lamented that his plays may have sent some young men to their deaths.

It is possible that if either Yeats or Lady Gregory had thought there would be a revolution they would not have written such plays. They opposed violence, but it was clear to some that violence was the only means by which Ireland would be made into a separate nation.

The success of *The Rising of the Moon* lies in Lady Gregory's exceptional ear for dialogue. She captures the way people speak, and she also manages to draw the characters of the sergeant and ballad singer so as to gain our sympathies for them both. In a remarkably economic fashion, she shapes the problem of politics in Ireland, characterizing the two polarities and revealing some of the complexities that face anyone who tries to understand them.

Lady Gregory (1852–1932)

THE RISING OF THE MOON
1907

Persons

SERGEANT	POLICEMAN B
POLICEMAN X	A RAGGED MAN

Scene: *Side of a quay in a seaport town. Some posts and chains. A large barrel. Enter three policemen. Moonlight.*

(*Sergeant, who is older than the others, crosses the stage to right and looks down steps. The others put down a pastepot and unroll a bundle of placards.*)

POLICEMAN B: I think this would be a good place to put up a notice. (*He points to barrel.*)

POLICEMAN X: Better ask him. (*Calls to Sergeant.*) Will this be a good place for a placard?

(*No answer.*)

POLICEMAN B: Will we put up a notice here on the barrel?

(*No answer.*)

SERGEANT: There's a flight of steps here that leads to the water. This is a place that should be minded well. If he got down here, his friends might have a boat to meet him; they might send it in here from outside.

POLICEMAN B: Would the barrel be a good place to put a notice up?

SERGEANT: It might; you can put it there.

(*They paste the notice up.*)

SERGEANT (*reading it*): Dark hair — dark eyes, smooth face, height five feet five — there's not much to take hold of in that — It's a pity I had no chance of seeing him before he broke out of jail. They say he's a wonder, that it's he makes all the plans for the whole organization. There isn't another man in Ireland would have broken jail the way he did. He must have some friends among the jailers.

POLICEMAN B: A hundred pounds is little enough for the Government to offer for him. You may be sure any man in the force that takes him will get promotion.

SERGEANT: I'll mind this place myself. I wouldn't wonder at all if he came this way. He might come slipping along there (*points to side of quay*), and his friends might be waiting for him there (*points down steps*), and once he got away it's little chance we'd have of finding him; it's maybe under a load of kelp he'd be in a fishing boat, and not one to help a married man that wants it to the reward.

POLICEMAN X: And if we get him itself, nothing but abuse on our heads for it from the people, and maybe from our own relations.

SERGEANT: Well, we have to do our duty in the force. Haven't we the whole country depending on us to keep law and order? It's those that are down would be up and those that are up would be down, if it wasn't for us. Well, hurry on, you have plenty of other places to placard yet, and come back here then to me. You can take the lantern. Don't be too long now. It's very lonesome here with nothing but the moon.

POLICEMAN B: It's a pity we can't stop with you. The Government should have brought more police into the town, with *him* in jail, and at assize° time too. Well, good luck to your watch.

(*They go out.*)

SERGEANT (*walks up and down once or twice and looks at placard*): A hundred pounds and promotion sure. There must be a great deal of spending in a hundred pounds. It's a pity some honest man not to be better of that.

(*A Ragged Man appears at left and tries to slip past. Sergeant suddenly turns.*)

SERGEANT: Where are you going?

MAN: I'm a poor ballad-singer, your honor. I thought to sell some of these (*holds out bundle of ballads*) to the sailors.

(*He goes on.*)

SERGEANT: Stop! Didn't I tell you to stop? You can't go on there.

MAN: Oh, very well. It's a hard thing to be poor. All the world's against the poor!

---

assize: Judicial inquest.

SERGEANT: Who are you?

MAN: You'd be as wise as myself if I told you, but I don't mind. I'm one Jimmy Walsh, a ballad-singer.

SERGEANT: Jimmy Walsh? I don't know that name.

MAN: Ah, sure, they know it well enough in Ennis. Were you ever in Ennis, sergeant?

SERGEANT: What brought you here?

MAN: Sure, it's to the assizes I came, thinking I might make a few shillings here or there. It's in the one train with the judges I came.

SERGEANT: Well, if you came so far, you may as well go farther, for you'll walk out of this.

MAN: I will, I will; I'll just go on where I was going.

(*Goes toward steps.*)

SERGEANT: Come back from those steps; no one has leave to pass down them tonight.

MAN: I'll just sit on the top of the steps till I see will some sailor buy a ballad off me that would give me my supper. They do be late going back to the ship. It's often I saw them in Cork carried down the quay in a handcart.

SERGEANT: Move on, I tell you. I won't have anyone lingering about the quay tonight.

MAN: Well, I'll go. It's the poor have the hard life! Maybe yourself might like one, sergeant. Here's a good sheet now. (*Turns one over.*) "Content and a pipe" — that's not much. "The Peeler and the goat" — you wouldn't like that. "Johnny Hart" — that's a lovely song.

SERGEANT: Move on.

MAN: Ah, wait till you hear it. (*Sings.*)
   There was a rich farmer's daughter lived near
      the town of Ross;
   She courted a Highland soldier, his name was
      Johnny Hart;
   Says the mother to her daughter, "I'll go
      distracted mad
   If you marry that Highland soldier dressed up in
      Highland plaid."

SERGEANT: Stop that noise.

(*Man wraps up his ballads and shuffles toward the steps.*)

SERGEANT: Where are you going?

MAN: Sure you told me to be going, and I am going.

SERGEANT: Don't be a fool. I didn't tell you to go that way; I told you to go back to the town.

MAN: Back to the town, is it?

SERGEANT (*taking him by the shoulder and shoving him before him*): Here, I'll show you the way. Be off with you. What are you stopping for?

MAN (*who has been keeping his eye on the notice, points to it*): I think I know what you're waiting for, sergeant.

SERGEANT: What's that to you?

MAN: And I know well the man you're waiting for — I know him well — I'll be going.

(*He shuffles on.*)

SERGEANT: You know him? Come back here. What sort is he?

MAN: Come back is it, sergeant? Do you want to have me killed?

SERGEANT: Why do you say that?

MAN: Never mind. I'm going. I wouldn't be in your shoes if the reward was ten times as much. (*Goes on off stage to left.*) Not if it was ten times as much.

SERGEANT (*rushing after him*): Come back here, come back. (*Drags him back.*) What sort is he? Where did you see him?

MAN: I saw him in my own place, in the County Clare. I tell you you wouldn't like to be looking at him. You'd be afraid to be in the one place with him. There isn't a weapon he doesn't know the use of, and as to strength, his muscles are as hard as that board (*slaps barrel*).

SERGEANT: Is he as bad as that?

MAN: He is then.

SERGEANT: Do you tell me so?

MAN: There was a poor man in our place, a sergeant from Ballyvaughan. — It was with a lump of stone he did it.

SERGEANT: I never heard of that.

MAN: And you wouldn't, sergeant. It's not everything that happens gets into the papers. And there was a policeman in plain clothes, too. . . . It is in Limerick he was. . . . It was after the time of the attack on the police barrack at Kilmallock. . . . Moonlight . . . just like this . . . waterside. . . . Nothing was known for certain.

SERGEANT: Do you say so? It's a terrible county to belong to.

MAN: That's so, indeed! You might be standing there, looking out that way, thinking you saw him coming up this side of the quay (*points*), and he might be coming up this other side (*points*), and he'd be on you before you knew where you were.

SERGEANT: It's a whole troop of police they ought to put here to stop a man like that.

MAN: But if you'd like me to stop with you, I could be looking down this side. I could be sitting up here on this barrel.

SERGEANT: And you know him well, too?

MAN: I'd know him a mile off, sergeant.

SERGEANT: But you wouldn't want to share the reward?

MAN: Is it a poor man like me, that has to be going the roads and singing in fairs, to have the name on him that he took a reward? But you don't want me. I'll be safer in the town.

SERGEANT: Well, you can stop.

MAN (*getting up on barrel*): All right, sergeant. I wonder, now, you're not tired out, sergeant, walking up and down the way you are.

SERGEANT: If I'm tired I'm used to it.

MAN: You might have hard work before you tonight yet. Take it easy while you can. There's plenty of room up here on the barrel, and you see farther when you're higher up.

SERGEANT: Maybe so. (*Gets up beside him on barrel, facing right. They sit back to back, looking different ways.*) You made me feel a bit queer with the way you talked.

MAN: Give me a match, sergeant (*he gives it and man lights pipe*); take a draw yourself? It'll quiet you. Wait now till I give you a light, but you needn't turn round. Don't take your eye off the quay for the life of you.

SERGEANT: Never fear, I won't. (*Lights pipe. They both smoke.*) Indeed it's a hard thing to be in the force, out at night and no thanks for it, for all the danger we're in. And it's little we get but abuse from the people, and no choice but to obey our orders, and never asked when a man is sent into danger, if you are a married man with a family.

MAN (*sings*): As through the hills I walked to view the hills and shamrock plain,
I stood awhile where nature smiles to view the rocks and streams,
On a matron fair I fixed my eyes beneath a fertile vale,
And she sang her song it was on the wrong of poor old Granuaile.

SERGEANT: Stop that; that's no song to be singing in these times.

MAN: Ah, sergeant, I was only singing to keep my heart up. It sinks when I think of him. To think of us two sitting here, and he creeping up the quay, maybe, to get to us.

SERGEANT: Are you keeping a good lookout?

MAN: I am; and for no reward too. Amn't I the foolish man? But when I saw a man in trouble, I never could help trying to get him out of it. What's that? Did something hit me?

(*Rubs his heart.*)

SERGEANT (*patting him on the shoulder*): You will get your reward in heaven.

MAN: I know that, I know that, sergeant, but life is precious.

SERGEANT: Well, you can sing if it gives you more courage.

MAN (*sings*): Her head was bare, her hands and feet with iron bands were bound,
Her pensive strain and plaintive wail mingles with the evening gale,

And the song she sang with mournful air, I am old Granuaile.
Her lips so sweet that monarchs kissed . . .

SERGEANT: That's not it. . . . "Her gown she wore was stained with gore." . . . That's it — you missed that.

MAN: You're right, sergeant, so it is; I missed it. (*Repeats line.*) But to think of a man like you knowing a song like that.

SERGEANT: There's many a thing a man might know and might not have any wish for.

MAN: Now, I daresay, sergeant, in your youth, you used to be sitting up on a wall, the way you are sitting up on this barrel now, and the other lads beside you, and you singing "Granuaile"? . . .

SERGEANT: I did then.

MAN: And the "Shan Van Vocht"? . . .

SERGEANT: I did then.

MAN: And the "Green on the Cape"?

SERGEANT: That was one of them.

MAN: And maybe the man you are watching for to-night used to be sitting on the wall, when he was young, and singing those same songs. . . . It's a queer world. . . .

SERGEANT: Whisht! . . . I think I see something coming. . . . It's only a dog.

MAN: And isn't it a queer world? . . . Maybe it's one of the boys you used to be singing with that time you will be arresting today or tomorrow, and sending into the dock. . . .

SERGEANT: That's true indeed.

MAN: And maybe one night, after you had been singing, if the other boys had told you some plan they had, some plan to free the country, you might have joined with them . . . and maybe it is you might be in trouble now.

SERGEANT: Well, who knows but I might? I had a great spirit in those days.

MAN: It's a queer world, sergeant, and it's little any mother knows when she sees her child creeping on the floor what might happen to it before it has gone through its life, or who will be who in the end.

SERGEANT: That's a queer thought now, and a true thought. Wait now till I think it out. . . . If it wasn't for the sense I have, and for my wife and family, and for me joining the force the time I did, it might be myself now would be after breaking jail and hiding in the dark, and it might be him that's hiding in the dark and that got out of jail would be sitting up here where I am on this barrel. . . . And it might be myself would be creeping up trying to make my escape from himself, and it might be himself would be keeping the law, and myself would be breaking it, and myself would be trying to put a bullet in

his head, or to take up a lump of stone the way you said he did . . . no, that myself did. . . . Oh! (*Gasps. After a pause.*) What's that? (*Grasps man's arm.*)

MAN (*jumps off barrel and listens, looking out over water*): It's nothing, sergeant.

SERGEANT: I thought it might be a boat. I had a notion there might be friends of his coming about the quays with a boat.

MAN: Sergeant, I am thinking it was with the people you were, and not with the law you were, when you were a young man.

SERGEANT: Well, if I was foolish then, that time's gone.

MAN: Maybe, sergeant, it comes into your head sometimes, in spite of your belt and your tunic, that it might have been as well for you to have followed Granuaile.

SERGEANT: It's no business of yours what I think.

MAN: Maybe, sergeant, you'll be on the side of the country yet.

SERGEANT (*gets off barrel*): Don't talk to me like that. I have my duties and I know them. (*Looks round.*) That was a boat; I hear the oars.

(*Goes to the steps and looks down.*)

MAN (*sings*): O, then, tell me, Shawn O'Farrell,
      Where the gathering is to be.
   In the old spot by the river
      Right well known to you and me!

SERGEANT: Stop that! Stop that, I tell you!

MAN (*sings louder*): One word more, for signal token,
      Whistle up the marching tune,
   With your pike upon your shoulder,
      At the Rising of the Moon.

SERGEANT: If you don't stop that, I'll arrest you.

(*A whistle from below answers, repeating the air.*)

SERGEANT: That's a signal. (*Stands between him and steps.*) You must not pass this way. . . . Step farther back. . . . Who are you? You are no ballad-singer.

MAN: You needn't ask who I am; that placard will tell you. (*Points to placard.*)

SERGEANT: You are the man I am looking for.

MAN (*takes off hat and wig. Sergeant seizes them*): I am. There's a hundred pounds on my head. There is a friend of mine below in a boat. He knows a safe place to bring me to.

SERGEANT (*looking still at hat and wig*): It's a pity! It's a pity. You deceived me. You deceived me well.

MAN: I am a friend of Granuaile. There is a hundred pounds on my head.

SERGEANT: It's a pity, it's a pity!

MAN: Will you let me pass, or must I make you let me?

SERGEANT: I am in the force. I will not let you pass.

MAN: I thought to do it with my tongue. (*Puts hand in breast.*) What is that?

VOICE OF POLICEMAN X (*outside*): Here, this is where we left him.

SERGEANT: It's my comrades coming.

MAN: You won't betray me . . . the friend of Granuaile. (*Slips behind barrel.*)

VOICE OF POLICEMAN B: That was the last of the placards.

POLICEMAN X (*as they come in*): If he makes his escape it won't be unknown he'll make it.

(*Sergeant puts hat and wig behind his back.*)

POLICEMAN B: Did anyone come this way?

SERGEANT (*after a pause*): No one.

POLICEMAN B: No one at all?

SERGEANT: No one at all.

POLICEMAN B: We had no orders to go back to the station; we can stop along with you.

SERGEANT: I don't want you. There is nothing for you to do here.

POLICEMAN B: You bade us to come back here and keep watch with you.

SERGEANT: I'd sooner be alone. Would any man come this way and you making all that talk? It is better the place to be quiet.

POLICEMAN B: Well, we'll leave you the lantern anyhow.

(*Hands it to him.*)

SERGEANT: I don't want it. Bring it with you.

POLICEMAN B: You might want it. There are clouds coming up and you have the darkness of the night before you yet. I'll leave it over here on the barrel. (*Goes to barrel.*)

SERGEANT: Bring it with you, I tell you. No more talk.

POLICEMAN B: Well, I thought it might be a comfort to you. I often think when I have it in my hand and can be flashing it about into every dark corner (*doing so*) that it's the same as being beside the fire at home, and the bits of bogwood blazing up now and again.

(*Flashes it about, now on the barrel, now on Sergeant.*)

SERGEANT (*furious*): Be off the two of you, yourselves and your lantern!

(*They go out. Man comes from behind barrel. He and Sergeant stand looking at one another.*)

SERGEANT: What are you waiting for?

MAN: For my hat, of course, and my wig. You wouldn't wish me to get my death of cold?

(*Sergeant gives them.*)

MAN (*going toward steps*): Well, good night, comrade, and thank you. You did me a good turn tonight, and I'm obliged to you. Maybe I'll be able to do as much for you when the small rise up and the big fall down . . . when we all change places at the Rising (*waves his hand and disappears*) of the Moon.

SERGEANT (*turning his back to audience and reading placard*): A hundred pounds reward! A hundred pounds! (*Turns toward audience.*) I wonder, now, am I as great a fool as I think I am?

Greek Drama

Origins of Greek Drama

Because our historical knowledge of Greek drama is limited by the available contemporary commentaries and by partial archaeological remains — in the form of ruined theaters — we do not know when Greek theater began or what its original impulses were. Our best information points to the year 534 B.C. as the beginning of the formal competitions among playwrights for coveted prizes that continued to be awarded for several centuries. However, Greek drama could not have burst forth in full maturity in a given year, as Athena was said to have burst forth from the head of Zeus as a mature adult. Drama must have had a childhood and models to influence it, and it must have developed slowly.

One source that may well have influenced the Greeks was the Egyptian civilization of the first millennium B.C. Egyptian culture was fully formed, brilliant, and complex. And while Egyptologists do not credit it with having a formal theater, certain ceremonies, repeated annually at major festivals, seem to have counterparts in later Greek rituals and drama. The most important and most impressive Egyptian ritual, described by some scholars as a passion play, concerned the dramatic story of Isis and Osiris and the treachery of Osiris's brother Set.

Nut, the sky goddess, married Isis and Osiris and declared Osiris to be the king of upper and lower Egypt, throwing Set into a jealous rage. Set plotted to kill Osiris and after careful planning fell upon him and threw him into the Nile, where he drowned. Isis searched for his body and found it in Byblos. But before she could give it a proper burial, Set found the body, tore it into fourteen pieces, and cast it about the kingdom. After great effort, Isis recovered the parts of her husband's body, reassembled it, and breathed life into it. In some versions of the myth Osiris made Isis pregnant. However, Osiris could not remain on earth and became a god of the underworld. Osiris's last resting place, reputed to be Abydos in Egypt, was for two thousand years the site of ritual dancing, music, and passion plays dramatizing the myths of death and rebirth that lay buried deep in the Egyptian imagination.

The closest Greek counterpart to Osiris was DIONYSUS, who inspired orgiastic celebrations that found their way into early Greek drama. Dionysus was an agricultural deity, the Greek god of wine and the symbol of life-giving power. In several myths he, like Osiris, was ritually killed and dismembered and his parts scattered through the land. These myths paralleled the agricultural cycle of death and disintegration during the winter, followed by cultivation and rebirth in the spring, and reinforced the Greeks' understanding of the meaning of birth, life, and death.

Drama developed in ancient Greece in close connection with the Dionysia, religious celebrations dedicated to Dionysus. Four Dionysiac celebrations were held each winter in Athens beginning at the grape harvest and culminating during the first wine tastings: the Rural Dionysia in December, the Lenaia in January, the Anthesteria in February, and the City Dionysia in March. Except for the Anthesteria, the festivals featured drama contests among playwrights, and some of the works performed in those competitions have endured through the centuries. Theories that connect the origins of drama with religion hypothesize that one function of the religious festivals within which the drama competitions took place was the ritual attempt to guarantee fertility and the growth of the crops, upon which the society depended.

The CITY DIONYSIA, the most lavish of the festivals, lasted about five days. It was open to non-Athenians and therefore offered Athenians the opportunity to show off their wealth, their glorious history, and their heroes, who were often honored in parades the day before the plays began. There is some question about what was presented on each day. Two days were probably taken up with dithyrambic contests among the ten tribes of Athens. Each tribe presented two choruses — one of men and one of boys — each singing a narrative lyric called a DITHYRAMB. A prize was awarded the best performers. Three days were devoted to contests among tragedians, most of whom worked for half the year on three tragedies and a SATYR PLAY, an erotic piece of comic relief that ended the day's performance. A tragedian's three plays sometimes shared related themes or myths, but often they did not. The tragedians wrote the plays, trained and rehearsed the actors, composed the music, and created setting, dances, costumes, and masks. Five comedies were also presented during the festival. The performances were paid for by wealthy Athenians as part of their civic duty. The great Greek plays thus were not commercial enterprises, but an important part of civic and religious festivals.

Special judges awarded prizes, usually basing their decisions on the merits of the dramas. First prize went to the tragedian whose four plays were most powerful and most beautifully conceived.

Figure 1. Theater at Epidaurus

The Greek Stage

At the center of the Greek theater was the round ORCHESTRA, where the chorus sang and danced (*orches* is Greek for "dance"). The audience, sometimes numbering fifteen thousand, sat in rising rows on three sides of the orchestra. Often the steep sides of a hill formed a natural amphitheater for Greek audiences. Eventually, on the rim of the orchestra, an oblong building called the SKENE, or scene house, developed as a space for the actors and a background for the action. The term PROS-KENION was sometimes used to refer to a raised stage in front of the *skene* where the actors performed. The theater at Epidaurus (Figure 1) was a model for the basic Greek theater plan.

Greek theaters were widely dispersed from Greece to present-day Turkey, to Sicily, and even to southern France. Wherever the Greeks developed new colonies and city-states, they built theaters. In many of the surviving theaters the acoustics are so fine that a human voice onstage can be heard as a whisper from any seat in the theater.

Perhaps the most spectacular dramatic device used by the Greek playwrights, the DEUS EX MACHINA ("a god from a machine"), was implemented onstage by means of elaborate booms or derricks. Actors were lowered onto the stage to enact the roles of Olympian gods intervening in the affairs of humans. Some commentators, such as Aristotle (384–322 B.C.), felt that the *deus ex machina* should be used only if the intercession of deities was in keeping with the character of the play. The last of the great Greek tragedians, Euripides (c. 480–c. 406 B.C.), used the device in almost half of his tragedies. In *Medea* Euripides uses a derrick to lift Medea to the roof of the *skene* and into her dragon chariot as a means of resolving the play's conflict. At the end of the play Medea is beyond her persecutors' reach and is headed for safety in another country. Modern dramatists use a form of *deus ex machina* when they rescue characters at the last moment by improbable accidents or strokes of luck. Usually, these are unsatisfying means of solving dramatic problems.

The evidence both in the drama itself and in writings contemporaneous with the plays suggests that attending the theater was usually breathtaking. Besides the complex and sophisticated machinery, playwrights used inventive and colorful costumes and expressive dances. Greek drama combined many arts to produce a truly spectacular experience.

Genres of Greek Drama
Tragedy

Greek tragedy focused on a person of noble birth who in some cases had risen to a great height and then fell precipitately. Tragedies showed humans at the mercy of MOIRA, their fate, which they only partly understood. One objective of Greek drama was to have the audience experience a CATHARSIS, which Aristotle describes as a purging or purifying of the emotions of pity and fear. According to the Greeks, these are emotions that a person associates with the fall of someone in a high social station, such as a king or queen. A central character, or PROTAGONIST, of noble birth was therefore an essential element to the playwright striving to evoke catharsis in an audience. Twentieth-century experiments with tragic figures who are ordinary people, such as John Millington Synge's *Riders to the Sea* and Arthur Miller's *Death of a Salesman*, as masterful as they are, would not have been tolerated by the Greeks. For the Greeks, tragedy could befall only the great.

The modern critic Kenneth Burke identified a pattern for Greek tragedies. The tragic figure — who usually provides the name of the play — experiences three stages of development: purpose, passion, and perception. The play begins with a purpose, such as finding the source of the plague in *Oedipus Rex*. Then as the path becomes tangled and events unfold, the tragic figure begins an extensive process of soul-searching and suffers an inner agony — the passion. The perception of the truth involves a fate that the tragic figure would rather not face. It might be death or, as in *Oedipus Rex*, exile. It always involves separation from the human community. For the Greeks, that was the greatest punishment.

According to Aristotle, the tragic hero's perception of the truth was the most intense moment in the drama. He called it ANAGNORISIS, or recognition. When it came at the same moment that the tragic figure's fortunes reversed — the PERIPETEIA — Aristotle felt that the tragedy was most fulfilling for the audience. This is the case in the fourth episode of *Oedipus Rex*. Aristotle's comments in his *Poetics* on the structure and effect of *Oedipus Rex* remain the most significant critical observations made by a contemporary on Greek theater. (See the excerpt from the *Poetics* on page 93.)

The Structure of Greek Tragedies. The earliest tragedies seem to have developed from the emotional, intense dithyrambs of the kind sung by Athenian choruses. The CHORUS in most tragedies numbered fifteen men. They were ordinary Athenians and usually represented the citizenry in the drama. They dressed simply, and their song was sometimes sung together, sometimes delivered by the chorus leader. Originally, there were no actors separate from the chorus.

According to legend, Thespis (sixth century B.C.) was the first actor — the first to step from the chorus to act in dialogue with it — thus creating the AGON, or dramatic confrontation. He won the first prize for tragedy in 534 B.C. As the only actor, he took several parts, wearing MASKS to distinguish the different characters. One actor was the norm in tragedies until Aeschylus (525?–456 B.C.), the first important Greek tragedian whose work survives, introduced a second, and then Sophocles (c. 496–c. 406 B.C.) added a third. (Only comedy used more: four actors.)

Like the actors, the members of the chorus wore masks. At first the masks were simple, but they became more ornate, often trimmed with hair and decorated with details that established the gender, age, or station of each character. The chorus and all the actors were male.

Eventually the structure of the plays became elaborated into a series of alternations between the characters' dialogue and the choral odes, with each speaking part developing the action or responding to it. Often crucial information furthering the action came from the mouth of a messenger, as in *Oedipus Rex*. The tragedies were structured in three parts: The PROLOGUE established the conflict; the episodes or agons developed the dramatic relationships between characters; and the EXODOS revealed the conclusion. Between these sections the chorus performed different songs: PARODOS while moving onto the stage and stasima while standing still. In some plays the chorus sang a choral ODE called the STROPHE as it moved from right to left. It sang the ANTISTROPHE while moving back to the right. The actors' episodes consisted of dialogue with each other and with the chorus. The scholar Bernhard Zimmerman has plotted the structure of *Oedipus Rex* in this fashion:

> *Prologue:* Dialogue with Oedipus, the Priests, and Kreon establishing that the plague afflicting Thebes will cease when Laios's murderer is found.
>
> *Parodos:* The opening hymn of the Chorus appealing to the gods.
>
> *First Episode:* Oedipus seeks the murderer; Teiresias says it is Oedipus.

First Stasimon: The Chorus supports Oedipus, disbelieving Teiresias.

Second Episode: Oedipus accuses Kreon of being in league with Teiresias and the real murderer. Iokaste pleads for Kreon and tells the oracle of Oedipus's birth and of the death of Laios at the fork of a road. Oedipus sends for the eyewitness of the murder.

Second Stasimon: The Chorus, in a song, grows agitated for Oedipus.

Third Episode: The messenger from Oedipus's "hometown" tells him that his adoptive father has died and is not his real father. Iokaste guesses the truth and Oedipus becomes deeply worried.

Third Stasimon: The Chorus delivers a reassuring, hopeful song.

Fourth Episode: Oedipus, the Shepherd, and the Messenger confront the facts and Oedipus experiences the turning point of the play: He realizes he is the murderer he seeks.

Fourth Stasimon: The Chorus sings of the illusion of human happiness.

Exodos: Iokaste kills herself; Oedipus puts out his eyes; the Chorus and Kreon try to decide the best future action.

As this brief structural outline of *Oedipus Rex* demonstrates, the chorus assumed an important part in the tragedies. In Aeschylus's *Agamemnon* it represents the elders of the community. In Sophocles' *Oedipus Rex* it is a group of concerned citizens who give Oedipus advice and make demands on him. In *Antigone* the chorus consists of men loyal to the state. In Euripides' *Medea* the chorus is a group of the important women of Corinth.

Satyr Plays

The drama competitions held regularly from 534 B.C. consisted usually of the work of three playwrights who each produced three tragedies and one satyr play, a form of comic relief. In a satyr play, the chorus dressed as satyrs, comic half-beast, half-man figures who cavorted with a PHALLUS, a mock penis, and engaged in riotous, almost slapstick antics. The characters were not psychologically developed, as they were in tragedy; the situations were not socially instructive, as they were in comedy. Rough-hewn and lighthearted, the satyr plays may have been a necessary antidote to the intensity of the tragedies.

Only one satyr play survives, perhaps an indication that the form was not as highly valued as tragedy. In Euripides' *Cyclops*, based on Odysseus's confrontation with the one-eyed giant who dined on a number of his men, Odysseus outwits the giant with the aid of a well-filled wineskin. The powers of Bacchus (Dionysus) are often alluded to, and drunkenness is a prime ingredient. The play is witty, entertaining, and brief. It might well have been the perfect way to end an otherwise serious drama festival.

memnon's death. In *Eumenides,* Orestes is hounded by the Furies, female goddesses who avenge crimes against kinship. Finally, the Athenian judges render a split decision in the case against Orestes, and Athena herself decides in favor of him. The power of this trilogy has established Aeschylus among the greatest of Greek dramatists.

Sophocles (c. 496–c. 406 B.C.) and Euripides (c. 480–c. 406 B.C.) — see the introductions to their plays — learned from Aeschylus and each other since they sometimes competed with one another. These three tragedians, along with Aristophanes, provide us with insight into the Greek dramatic imagination. They also reveal something of our common humanity, since their achievement — lost though it was for many centuries — shapes our current dramatic practice. The Greeks give us not only the beginnings of drama but the basis of drama. We build on it today whenever a play is written, whenever we witness a play.

Sophocles

Sophocles (c. 496–c. 406 B.C.) won more prizes than any other tragedian in the Greek drama competitions, and he never came in lower than second place. His first victory was against the grand old master Aeschylus in 468 B.C. Sophocles' last plays, which he wrote in his eighties, were among his greatest. We have fragments of some ninety plays or poems and seven complete tragedies, while records suggest that his output numbered something over a hundred twenty plays.

Sophocles lived in interesting times. He would have recalled the first defeat of the Persians in 490 B.C., when the news came by a messenger who had run twenty-six miles from Marathon to Athens. In his adolescence, Athens achieved its astonishing and decisive victory over the Persians at Salamis. His popularity as a tragedian and as a statesman coincided with the development of an imperial attitude in Athens. Athenian society honored the greatness of men like Aeschylus, Sophocles, Euripides, the historian Herodotus, and all the politicians and artists that Pericles drew to Athens for its rebuilding. It was a golden age shadowed by war.

Sophocles was both sociable and religious, serving as the priest of several religious cults. However, he was also a man of action, popular enough to be elected as one of Athens's twelve generals; he participated with Pericles in the Samian War (440–439 B.C.). His plays — especially *Antigone* (441 B.C.), which preceded his election to generalship — often have deep political concerns. One of his primary themes concerns the relation of the individual to the *polis*, the state itself. Since the Greeks valued the individual and at the same time regarded the *polis* as a sacred bulwark against a return to barbarism, conflicts between the individual and the *polis* were immensely painful.

When Sophocles began writing, he broke with an old tradition. From the time of Thespis (mid-sixth century B.C.), each playwright acted in his own plays. Aeschylus, from what we know, probably did so, but it is on record that Sophocles' voice was not strong enough to permit him to take a part in his plays. He played the lyre well enough to appear onstage, and he participated in a game of ball in one of his plays, but he did not appear as an actor. He also introduced innovations in the structure of his plays by reducing the size of the chorus from fifty to fifteen and by adding painted scenery, more props, and a third actor to the two that Aeschylus and other tragedians had used. Sophocles wrote some of his plays with specific actors in mind, much as Shakespeare, Molière, and many other first-rank playwrights have done.

Sophocles was a deep reader of the epics of Homer. Many of his plays derive from the *Iliad* or the *Odyssey*, although Sophocles always adapted the material of others to his own purposes. His nickname was the Attic Bee because he could investigate wonderful pieces of literature and always return with a useful idea. The approach he took to the structure of the play, measuring the effect of the rising action of complication and then ensuring that the moment of recognition occurred at the same time the falling action began, was thought, rightly, to demonstrate a skill of supreme elegance. Nowhere is this illustrated with more completeness than in *Oedipus Rex*.

The plays of Aeschylus, powerful though they are, do not have the same delicacy of construction as do Sophocles'. They are forceful but, in terms of structure, somewhat rude. The structure of the plays of Euripides, Sophocles' successor, was never as fully worked out, and when Aristotle discussed the nature of tragedy in his *Poetics*, it was to Sophocles he turned for a model, not to the other two master playwrights of the genre.

Besides the Oedipus trilogy, Sophocles' other surviving plays are *Philoctetes, Ajax, Trachiniae,* and *Elektra.*

OEDIPUS REX

Oedipus Rex is one of a group of three plays by Sophocles that treat the fate of Oedipus and his children. The plays were written over a period of thirty years: *Antigone* (first produced in 441 B.C.), *Oedipus Rex* (produced approximately fifteen years later, between 430 and 427 B.C.), and *Oedipus at Colonus* (produced in 401 B.C., after Sophocles' death). When these plays are produced together today, they are usually given in an order that follows the events of Oedipus's and Antigone's lives — *Oedipus Rex, Oedipus at Colonus,* and *Antigone* — almost like the trilogies that Athenian audiences often viewed at the drama competitions. In fact, they were never a unified trilogy, and one of Sophocles' distinctions is that he did not present as trilogies plays that were thematically related, as poets before him had done.

The original narratives of the Oedipus plays were known to Sophocles' audience — with the possible exception of the story of Antigone — and one of the special pleasures for the audience watching the action of *Oedipus Rex* was that they knew the outcome. They watched for the steps, the choices, that led Oedipus to his fate.

Oedipus Rex is the story of a noble man who seeks knowledge that in the end destroys him. His greatness is measured in part by the fact that the gods have prophesied his fate: The gods do not take interest in insignificant men. Before the action of the play begins, Oedipus has set out to discover whether he is truly the son of Polybos and Merope, the people who have raised him. He learns from the oracle of Apollo at Delphi, the most powerful interpreter of the voice and the will of the gods, that he will kill his father and marry his mother. His response is overwhelmingly human: He has seen his *moira,* his fate, and he cannot accept it. His reaction is to do everything he can, including leaving his homeland as quickly as possible, to avoid the possibility of killing Polybos and marrying Merope.

The Greek audience would have known that Oedipus was a descendant of Kadmos, founder of Thebes, who had sown the dragon teeth that produced the Spartoi (the sown men). Legend determined that the rulership of Thebes would be in dispute, with fraternal rivalry resembling that of the Spartoi, who fought and killed each other. This bloody legacy follows Oedipus, but it also reaches into all the plays of the trilogy. For example, in *Antigone* we learn that Antigone's brothers Polyneices and Eteocles killed each other in the shadow of the city walls. Thus the fate Oedipus attempts to avoid actually dooms most of the characters in the three plays, including his true father, Laios, and his daughter Antigone.

Sophocles develops the drama in terms of IRONY — the disjunction between what seems to be true and what is true. Knowing the outcome of the action, the audience savors the ironic moments from the beginning of the play to the end. Oedipus flees his homeland to avoid fulfilling the prophecy, only to run headlong into the fate foretold by the oracle. He unwittingly returns to his original home, Thebes, and to his parents, murdering Laios, his true father, at a crossroads on the way and marrying Iokaste, his true mother, and becoming king of Thebes. The blind seer Teiresias warns Oedipus not to pursue the truth but, in human fashion, Oedipus refuses to heed Teiresias's warnings. When the complete truth becomes clear to Oedipus, he physically blinds himself in horror and expiation. Like the blind Teiresias, Oedipus must now look inward for the truth, without the distractions of surface experiences.

The belief that the moral health of the ruler reflected directly on the security of the *polis* was widespread in Athenian Greece. Indeed, the Athenians regarded their state as fragile — like a human being whose health, physical and moral, could change suddenly. Because of the concern of the Greeks for the well-being of their state, the *polis* often figures in the tragedies. The Sophoclean Oedipus trilogy is usually called the Theban plays, a nomenclature that reminds us that the story of Oedipus can be read as the story of an individual or as the story of a state.

Oedipus Rex examines the tension between and interdependence of the individual and the state. The agricultural and ritual basis of the

Dionysian festivals — in which Greek drama developed — underscores the importance the Greeks attached to the individual's dependence on the state that feeds him and on the proper ways of doing things, whether planting and harvesting or worshiping the gods or living as part of a political entity.

The underlying conflict in the play is political. The political relationship of human beings to the gods, the arbiters of their fate, is dramatized in Oedipus's relationship with Teiresias. If he had his way, Oedipus might disregard Teiresias entirely. But Oedipus cannot command everything, even as ruler. His incomplete knowledge, despite his wisdom, is symptomatic of the limitations of every individual.

The contrast of Oedipus and Kreon, Iokaste's brother, is one of political style. Oedipus is a fully developed character who reveals himself as sympathetic but willful. He acts on his misunderstanding of the prophecy without reconsulting the oracle. He marries Iokaste and blinds himself without reconsulting the oracle. Kreon, who is much less complicated, never acts without consulting the oracle and thoughtfully reflecting on the oracle's message. Oedipus sometimes behaves tyrannically, and he appears eager for power. Kreon would take power only if forced to do so.

The depth of Sophocles' character development was unmatched, except by his contemporary Euripides, for almost fifteen hundred years. Sophocles' drama is one of psychological development. His audiences saw Oedipus as a model for human greatness but also as a model for the human capacity to fall from a great height. The play is about the limits of human knowledge; it is also about the limits and frailty of human happiness.

Oedipus Rex in Performance

Oedipus Rex has enjoyed great popularity since its first performance. The Greeks, who originally restricted their plays to one performance, eventually began to revive plays of the masters. Oedipus was one of the most popular. In modern times, performance has been almost constant since the seventeenth century. Great dramatists have produced it in their own adaptations — Corneille (1659), John Dryden (1679), Voltaire (1718), William Butler Yeats (1923), and Jean Cocteau (1931) — proving the durability of the themes and the adaptability of the play. The early American performances (beginning in 1881) were in Greek but soon gave way to English. Modern versions have been both very traditional, such as those developed by the Royal Shakespeare Company in the 1970s, and experimental, such as that of Peter Brook (1968). Brook's production began with a huge golden cube reflecting brilliant light like the sun and ended with the ritual unveiling of a giant phallus. John Gielgud played Oedipus and Irene Worth, all in black, played Iokaste. Currently Greek companies perform the play regularly in the theater of Dionysus in Athens as well as in Epidaurus and elsewhere.

Sophocles (*c. 496–c. 406* B.C.)

OEDIPUS REX

c. 430 B.C.

TRANSLATED BY DUDLEY FITTS AND ROBERT FITZGERALD

Characters

OEDIPUS, *King of Thebes, supposed son of Polybos and Merope, King and Queen of Corinth*
IOKASTE, *wife of Oedipus and widow of the late King Laios*
KREON, *brother of Iokaste, a prince of Thebes*
TEIRESIAS, *a blind seer who serves Apollo*
PRIEST
MESSENGER, *from Corinth*
SHEPHERD, *former servant of Laios*
SECOND MESSENGER, *from the palace*
CHORUS OF THEBAN ELDERS
CHORAGOS, *leader of the Chorus*
ANTIGONE *and* ISMENE, *young daughters of Oedipus and Iokaste. They appear in the Exodos but do not speak.*
SUPPLIANTS, GUARDS, SERVANTS

The Scene: *Before the palace of Oedipus, King of Thebes. A central door and two lateral doors open onto a platform which runs the length of the facade. On the platform, right and left, are altars; and three steps lead down into the orchestra, or chorus-ground. At the beginning of the action these steps are crowded by suppliants who have brought branches and chaplets of olive leaves and who sit in various attitudes of despair. Oedipus enters.*

PROLOGUE°

OEDIPUS: My children, generations of the living
   In the line of Kadmos,° nursed at his ancient
     hearth:
   Why have you strewn yourselves before these
     altars
   In supplication, with your boughs and garlands?
5   The breath of incense rises from the city
   With a sound of prayer and lamentation.

                             Children,
I would not have you speak through messengers,
And therefore I have come myself to hear you —
I, Oedipus, who bear the famous name.
(*To a Priest.*) You, there, since you are eldest in
   the company,   10
Speak for them all, tell me what preys upon you,
Whether you come in dread, or crave some
   blessing:
Tell me, and never doubt that I will help you
In every way I can; I should be heartless
Were I not moved to find you suppliant here.   15
PRIEST: Great Oedipus, O powerful king of Thebes!
   You see how all the ages of our people
   Cling to your altar steps: here are boys
   Who can barely stand alone, and here are priests
   By weight of age, as I am a priest of God,   20
   And young men chosen from those yet
     unmarried;
   As for the others, all that multitude,
   They wait with olive chaplets in the squares,
   At the two shrines of Pallas,° and where Apollo°
   Speaks in the glowing embers.
                  Your own eyes   25
   Must tell you: Thebes is tossed on a murdering
     sea
   And can not lift her head from the death surge.
   A rust consumes the buds and fruits of the
     earth;
   The herds are sick; children die unborn,
   And labor is vain. The god of plague and pyre   30
   Raids like detestable lightning through the city,
   And all the house of Kadmos is laid waste,
   All emptied, and all darkened: Death alone
   Battens upon the misery of Thebes.

   You are not one of the immortal gods, we
     know;   35
   Yet we have come to you to make our prayer
   As to the man surest in mortal ways
   And wisest in the ways of God. You saved us

[**Note:** The line numbers to the original Greek text are cited in brackets at the top of the page.]
Prologue: Portion of the play explaining the background and current action. **2. Kadmos:** Founder of Thebes.

24. Pallas: Pallas Athene, daughter of Zeus and goddess of wisdom. **Apollo:** Son of Zeus and god of the sun, of light and truth.

From the Sphinx,° that flinty singer, and the
   tribute
40   We paid to her so long; yet you were never
   Better informed than we, nor could we teach
   you:
   A god's touch, it seems, enabled you to help us.

   Therefore, O mighty power, we turn to you:
   Find us our safety, find us a remedy,
45   Whether by counsel of the gods or of men.
   A king of wisdom tested in the past
   Can act in a time of troubles, and act well.
   Noblest of men, restore
   Life to your city! Think how all men call you
50   Liberator for your boldness long ago;
   Ah, when your years of kingship are
     remembered,
   Let them not say *We rose, but later fell* —
   Keep the State from going down in the storm!
   Once, years ago, with happy augury,
55   You brought us fortune; be the same again!
   No man questions your power to rule the land:
   But rule over men, not over a dead city!
   Ships are only hulls, high walls are nothing,
   When no life moves in the empty passageways.
60 OEDIPUS: Poor children! You may be sure I know
   All that you longed for in your coming here.
   I know that you are deathly sick; and yet,
   Sick as you are, not one is as sick as I.
   Each of you suffers in himself alone
65   His anguish, not another's; but my spirit
   Groans for the city, for myself, for you.

   I was not sleeping, you are not waking me.
   No, I have been in tears for a long while
   And in my restless thought walked many ways.
70   In all my search I found one remedy,
   And I have adopted it: I have sent Kreon,
   Son of Menoikeus, brother of the queen,
   To Delphi,° Apollo's place of revelation,
   To learn there, if he can,
75   What act or pledge of mine may save the city.
   I have counted the days, and now, this very day,
   I am troubled, for he has overstayed his time.
   What is he doing? He has been gone too long.
   Yet whenever he comes back, I should do ill
80   Not to take any action the god orders.

---

39. Sphinx: A winged monster with the body of a lion and
the face of a woman, the Sphinx had tormented Thebes with
her riddle, killing those who could not solve it. When Oedipus solved the riddle, the Sphinx killed herself. **73. Delphi:**
Site of the oracle, source of religious authority and prophecy,
under the protection of Apollo.

PRIEST: It is a timely promise. At this instant
   They tell me Kreon is here.
OEDIPUS: O Lord Apollo!
   May his news be fair as his face is radiant!
PRIEST: Good news, I gather! he is crowned with
   bay,
   The chaplet is thick with berries.
OEDIPUS: We shall soon know; 85
   He is near enough to hear us now. (*Enter
   Kreon.*) O prince:
   Brother: son of Menoikeus:
   What answer do you bring us from the god?
KREON: A strong one. I can tell you, great
   afflictions
   Will turn out well, if they are taken well. 90
OEDIPUS: What was the oracle? These vague words
   Leave me still hanging between hope and fear.
KREON: Is it your pleasure to hear me with all
   these
   Gathered around us? I am prepared to speak,
   But should we not go in?
OEDIPUS: Speak to them all, 95
   It is for them I suffer, more than for myself.
KREON: Then I will tell you what I heard at Delphi.
   In plain words
   The god commands us to expel from the land of
   Thebes
   An old defilement we are sheltering. 100
   It is a deathly thing, beyond cure;
   We must not let it feed upon us longer.
OEDIPUS: What defilement? How shall we rid
   ourselves of it?
KREON: By exile or death, blood for blood. It was
   Murder that brought the plague-wind on the
   city. 105
OEDIPUS: Murder of whom? Surely the god has
   named him?
KREON: My Lord: Laios once ruled this land,
   Before you came to govern us.
OEDIPUS: I know;
   I learned of him from others; I never saw him.
KREON: He was murdered; and Apollo commands
   us now 110
   To take revenge upon whoever killed him.
OEDIPUS: Upon whom? Where are they? Where
   shall we find a clue
   To solve that crime, after so many years?
KREON: Here in this land, he said. Search reveals
   Things that escape an inattentive man. 11
OEDIPUS: Tell me: Was Laios murdered in his
   house,
   Or in the fields, or in some foreign country?
KREON: He said he planned to make a pilgrimage.
   He did not come home again.
OEDIPUS: And was there no one,

No witness, no companion, to tell what
120   happened?
KREON: They were all killed but one, and he got
        away
    So frightened that he could remember one thing
        only.
OEDIPUS: What was that one thing? One may be
        the key
    To everything, if we resolve to use it.
KREON: He said that a band of highwaymen
125   attacked them,
    Outnumbered them, and overwhelmed the king.
OEDIPUS: Strange, that a highwayman should be so
        daring—
    Unless some faction here bribed him to do it.
KREON: We thought of that. But after Laios' death
130   New troubles arose and we had no avenger.
OEDIPUS: What troubles could prevent your hunting
        down the killers?
KREON: The riddling Sphinx's song
    Made us deaf to all mysteries but her own.
OEDIPUS: Then once more I must bring what is
        dark to light.
135   It is most fitting that Apollo shows,
    As you do, this compunction for the dead.
    You shall see how I stand by you, as I should,
    Avenging this country and the god as well,
    And not as though it were for some distant
        friend,
140   But for my own sake, to be rid of evil.
    Whoever killed King Laios might — who
        knows? —
    Lay violent hands even on me — and soon.
    I act for the murdered king in my own interest.

    Come, then, my children: leave the altar steps,
    Lift up your olive boughs!
145   One of you go
    And summon the people of Kadmos to gather
        here.
    I will do all that I can; you may tell them that.
                                    (*Exit a Page.*)
    So, with the help of God,
    We shall be saved — or else indeed we are lost.
PRIEST: Let us rise, children. It was for this we
150   came,
    And now the king has promised it.
    Phoibos° has sent us an oracle; may he descend
    Himself to save us and drive out the plague.

(*Exeunt*° *Oedipus and Kreon into the palace by the
central door. The Priest and the Suppliants disperse*

152. Phoibos: Apollo. [S.D.] *Exeunt:* Latin for "they go
out."

*right and left. After a short pause the Chorus enters
the orchestra.*)

PARODOS° • *Strophe*° *1*

CHORUS: What is God singing in his profound
    Delphi of gold and shadow?
    What oracle for Thebes, the Sunwhipped city?
    Fear unjoints me, the roots of my heart tremble.
    Now I remember, O Healer, your power, and
        wonder: 5
    Will you send doom like a sudden cloud, or
        weave it
    Like nightfall of the past?
    Speak to me, tell me, O
    Child of golden Hope, immortal Voice.

Antistrophe° *1*

    Let me pray to Athene, the immortal daughter of
        Zeus,   10
    And to Artemis° her sister
    Who keeps her famous throne in the market
        ring,
    And to Apollo, archer from distant heaven —
    O gods, descend! Like three streams leap against
    The fires of our grief, the fires of darkness;   15
    Be swift to bring us rest!
    As in the old time from the brilliant house
    Of air you stepped to save us, come again!

Strophe 2

    Now our afflictions have no end,
    Now all our stricken host lies down   20
    And no man fights off death with his mind;
    The noble plowland bears no grain,
    And groaning mothers can not bear —
    See, how our lives like birds take wing,
    Like sparks that fly when a fire soars,   25
    To the shore of the god of evening.

Parodos: The song or ode chanted by the Chorus on their
entry.   **Strophe:** Song sung by the Chorus as they danced
from stage right to stage left.   **Antistrophe:** Song sung by
the Chorus following the Strophe, as they danced back from
stage left to stage right.   **11. Artemis:** The huntress, daughter of Zeus, twin sister of Apollo.

For the day ravages what the night spares —   40
Destroy our enemy, lord of the thunder!
Let him be riven by lightning from heaven!

Antistrophe 3

Phoibos Apollo, stretch the sun's bowstring,
That golden cord, until it sing for us,
Flashing arrows in heaven!
       Artemis, Huntress,   45
Race with flaring lights upon our mountains!
O scarlet god,° O golden-banded brow,
O Theban Bacchos in a storm of Maenads,°

(*Enter Oedipus, center.*)

Whirl upon Death, that all the Undying hate!
Come with blinding torches, come in joy!   50

SCENE 1

OEDIPUS: Is this your prayer? It may be answered.
 Come,
Listen to me, act as the crisis demands,
And you shall have relief from all these evils.

Until now I was a stranger to this tale,
As I had been a stranger to the crime.   5
Could I track down the murderer without a
 clue?
But now, friends,
As one who became a citizen after the murder,
I make this proclamation to all Thebans:
If any man knows by whose hand Laios, son of
 Labdakos,   10
Met his death, I direct that man to tell me
 everything,
No matter what he fears for having so long
 withheld it.
Let it stand as promised that no further trouble
Will come to him, but he may leave the land in
 safety.
Moreover: If anyone knows the murderer to be
 foreign,   15
Let him not keep silent: he shall have his reward
 from me.
However, if he does conceal it; if any man
Fearing for his friend or for himself disobeys this
 edict,

47. **scarlet god:** Bacchus, god of wine and revelry; also called
Dionysus. 48. **Maenads:** Female worshipers of Bacchus
(Dionysus).

Antistrophe 2

The plague burns on, it is pitiless,
Though pallid children laden with death
Lie unwept in the stony ways,
30 And old gray women by every path
Flock to the strand about the altars
There to strike their breasts and cry
Worship of Phoibos in wailing prayers:
Be kind, God's golden child!

Strophe 3

35 There are no swords in this attack by fire,
No shields, but we are ringed with cries.
Send the besieger plunging from our homes
Into the vast sea-room of the Atlantic
Or into the waves that foam eastward of
 Thrace —

FAR LEFT: Le Clanche Du Rand as Iokaste in Donald Sutherland and Robert Loper's production of *Oedipus Rex* at the 1975 Oregon Shakespeare Festival in Ashland. RIGHT: Philip L. Jones as the Shepherd. BELOW: Ted D'Arms as Oedipus with the Chorus. (Photos by Henry S. Kranzler.)

Hear what I propose to do:

20 I solemnly forbid the people of this country,
Where power and throne are mine, ever to
        receive that man
Or speak to him, no matter who he is, or let
        him
Join in sacrifice, lustration, or in prayer.
I decree that he be driven from every house,
Being, as he is, corruption itself to us: the
25   Delphic
Voice of Apollo has pronounced this revelation.
Thus I associate myself with the oracle
And take the side of the murdered king.

As for the criminal, I pray to God —
Whether it be a lurking thief, or one of a
30   number —
I pray that that man's life be consumed in evil
        and wretchedness.
And as for me, this curse applies no less
If it should turn out that the culprit is my guest
        here,
Sharing my hearth.
                                You have heard the penalty.
35 I lay it on you now to attend to this
For my sake, for Apollo's, for the sick
Sterile city that heaven has abandoned.
Suppose the oracle had given you no command:
Should this defilement go uncleansed for ever?
40 You should have found the murderer: your king,
A noble king, had been destroyed!
                                                Now I,
Having the power that he held before me,
Having his bed, begetting children there
Upon his wife, as he would have, had he
        lived —
Their son would have been my children's
45   brother,
If Laios had had luck in fatherhood!
(And now his bad fortune has struck him
        down) —
I say I take the son's part, just as though
I were his son, to press the fight for him
50 And see it won! I'll find the hand that brought
Death to Labdakos' and Polydoros' child,
Heir of Kadmos' and Agenor's line.°
And as for those who fail me,
May the gods deny them the fruit of the earth,
55 Fruit of the womb, and may they rot utterly!

51–52. **Labdakos, Polydoros, Kadmos, and Agenor:** Father,
grandfather, great-grandfather, and great-great-grandfather
of Laios.

Let them be wretched as we are wretched, and
        worse!

For you, for loyal Thebans, and for all
Who find my actions right, I pray the favor
Of justice, and of all the immortal gods.
CHORAGOS: Since I am under oath, my lord, I
        swear   60
I did not do the murder, I can not name
The murderer. Phoibos ordained the search;
Why did he not say who the culprit was?
OEDIPUS: An honest question. But no man in the
        world
Can make the gods do more than the gods will.   65
CHORAGOS: There is an alternative, I think —
OEDIPUS: Tell me.
Any or all, you must not fail to tell me.
CHORAGOS: A lord clairvoyant to the lord Apollo,
As we all know, is the skilled Teiresias.
One might learn much about this from him,
        Oedipus.   70
OEDIPUS: I am not wasting time:
Kreon spoke of this, and I have sent for him —
Twice, in fact; it is strange that he is not here.
CHORAGOS: The other matter — that old report —
        seems useless.
OEDIPUS: What was that? I am interested in all
        reports.   75
CHORAGOS: The king was said to have been killed
        by highwaymen.
OEDIPUS: I know. But we have no witnesses to that.
CHORAGOS: If the killer can feel a particle of dread,
Your curse will bring him out of hiding!
OEDIPUS: No.
The man who dared that act will fear no curse. 80

(*Enter the blind seer Teiresias, led by a Page.*)

CHORAGOS: But there is one man who may detect
        the criminal.
This is Teiresias, this is the holy prophet
In whom, alone of all men, truth was born.
OEDIPUS: Teiresias: seer: student of mysteries,
Of all that's taught and all that no man tells,   85
Secrets of Heaven and secrets of the earth:
Blind though you are, you know the city lies
Sick with plague; and from this plague, my lord,
We find that you alone can guard or save us.

Possibly you did not hear the messengers?   90
Apollo, when we sent to him,
Sent us back word that this great pestilence
Would lift, but only if we established clearly
The identity of those who murdered Laios.
They must be killed or exiled.

95   Can you use
Birdflight° or any art of divination
To purify yourself, and Thebes, and me
From this contagion? We are in your hands.
There is no fairer duty
100   Than that of helping others in distress.

TEIRESIAS: How dreadful knowledge of the truth can be
   When there's no help in truth! I knew this well,
   But did not act on it; else I should not have come.

OEDIPUS: What is troubling you? Why are your eyes so cold?

TEIRESIAS: Let me go home. Bear your own fate, and I'll
105   Bear mine. It is better so: trust what I say.

OEDIPUS: What you say is ungracious and unhelpful
   To your native country. Do not refuse to speak.

TEIRESIAS: When it comes to speech, your own is neither temperate
110   Nor opportune. I wish to be more prudent.

OEDIPUS: In God's name, we all beg you —

TEIRESIAS: You are all ignorant.
   No; I will never tell you what I know.
   Now it is my misery; then, it would be yours.

OEDIPUS: What! You do know something, and will not tell us?
115   You would betray us all and wreck the State?

TEIRESIAS: I do not intend to torture myself, or you.
   Why persist in asking? You will not persuade me.

OEDIPUS: What a wicked old man you are! You'd try a stone's
   Patience! Out with it! Have you no feeling at all?

TEIRESIAS: You call me unfeeling. If you could only
120   see
   The nature of your own feelings . . .

OEDIPUS: Why,
   Who would not feel as I do? Who could endure
   Your arrogance toward the city?

TEIRESIAS: What does it matter?
   Whether I speak or not, it is bound to come.

OEDIPUS: Then, if "it" is bound to come, you are
125   bound to tell me.

TEIRESIAS: No, I will not go on. Rage as you please.

OEDIPUS: Rage? Why not!
                          And I'll tell you what I think:
   You planned it, you had it done, you all but
   Killed him with your own hands: if you had eyes,

96. Birdflight: Prophets used the flight of birds to predict the future.

   I'd say the crime was yours, and yours alone.   130

TEIRESIAS: So? I charge you, then,
   Abide by the proclamation you have made:
   From this day forth
   Never speak again to these men or to me;
   You yourself are the pollution of this country.   135

OEDIPUS: You dare say that! Can you possibly think you have
   Some way of going free, after such insolence?

TEIRESIAS: I have gone free. It is the truth sustains me.

OEDIPUS: Who taught you shamelessness? It was not your craft.

TEIRESIAS: You did. You made me speak. I did not want to.   140

OEDIPUS: Speak what? Let me hear it again more clearly.

TEIRESIAS: Was it not clear before? Are you tempting me?

OEDIPUS: I did not understand it. Say it again.

TEIRESIAS: I say that you are the murderer whom you seek.

OEDIPUS: Now twice you have spat out infamy. You'll pay for it!   145

TEIRESIAS: Would you care for more? Do you wish to be really angry?

OEDIPUS: Say what you will. Whatever you say is worthless.

TEIRESIAS: I say you live in hideous shame with those
   Most dear to you. You can not see the evil.

OEDIPUS: Can you go on babbling like this for ever?   150

TEIRESIAS: I can, if there is power in truth.

OEDIPUS: There is:
   But not for you, not for you,
   You sightless, witless, senseless, mad old man!

TEIRESIAS: You are the madman. There is no one here
   Who will not curse you soon, as you curse me.   155

OEDIPUS: You child of total night! I would not touch you;
   Neither would any man who sees the sun.

TEIRESIAS: True: it is not from you my fate will come.
   That lies within Apollo's competence,
   As it is his concern.

OEDIPUS: Tell me, who made   160
   These fine discoveries? Kreon? or someone else?

TEIRESIAS: Kreon is no threat. You weave your own doom.

OEDIPUS: Wealth, power, craft of statemanship!
   Kingly position, everywhere admired!
   What savage envy is stored up against these,   165
   If Kreon, whom I trusted, Kreon my friend,

For this great office which the city once
Put in my hands unsought — if for this power
Kreon desires in secret to destroy me!

170 He has bought this decrepit fortune-teller, this
Collector of dirty pennies, this prophet fraud —
Why, he is no more clairvoyant than I am!
                                                    Tell us:
Has your mystic mummery ever approached the
     truth?
When that hellcat the Sphinx was performing
     here,
175 What help were you to these people?
Her magic was not for the first man who came
     along:
It demanded a real exorcist. Your birds —
What good were they? or the gods, for the
     matter of that?
But I came by,
180 Oedipus, the simple man, who knows nothing —
I thought it out for myself, no birds helped me!
And this is the man you think you can destroy,
That you may be close to Kreon when he's king!
Well, you and your friend Kreon, it seems to
     me,
185 Will suffer most. If you were not an old man,
You would have paid already for your plot.

CHORAGOS: We can not see that his words or yours
Have been spoken except in anger, Oedipus,
And of anger we have no need. How to
     accomplish
The god's will best: that is what most concerns
190 us.

TEIRESIAS: You are a king. But where argument's
     concerned
I am your man, as much a king as you.
I am not your servant, but Apollo's.
I have no need of Kreon or Kreon's name.

195 Listen to me. You mock my blindness, do you?
But I say that you, with both your eyes, are
     blind:
You can not see the wretchedness of your life,
Nor in whose house you live, no, nor with
     whom.
Who are your father and mother? Can you tell
     me?
200 You do not even know the blind wrongs
That you have done them, on earth and in the
     world below.
But the double lash of your parents' curse will
     whip you
Out of this land some day, with only night
Upon your precious eyes.

Your cries then — where will they not be heard? 205
What fastness of Kithairon° will not echo them?
And that bridal-descant of yours — you'll know
     it then,
The song they sang when you came here to
     Thebes
And found your misguided berthing.
All this, and more, that you can not guess at
     now,   210
Will bring you to yourself among your children.

Be angry, then. Curse Kreon. Curse my words.
I tell you, no man that walks upon the earth
Shall be rooted out more horribly than you.

OEDIPUS: Am I to bear this from him? —
     Damnation   215
Take you! Out of this place! Out of my sight!

TEIRESIAS: I would not have come at all if you had
     not asked me.

OEDIPUS: Could I have told that you'd talk
     nonsense, that
You'd come here to make a fool of yourself, and
     of me?

TEIRESIAS: A fool? Your parents thought me sane
     enough.   220

OEDIPUS: My parents again! — Wait: who were my
     parents?

TEIRESIAS: This day will give you a father, and
     break your heart.

OEDIPUS: Your infantile riddles! Your damned
     abracadabra!

TEIRESIAS: You were a great man once at solving
     riddles.

OEDIPUS: Mock me with that if you like; you will
     find it true.   225

TEIRESIAS: It was true enough. It brought about
     your ruin.

OEDIPUS: But if it saved this town?

TEIRESIAS (to the Page):   Boy, give me your hand.

OEDIPUS: Yes, boy; lead him away.
                              — While you are here
We can do nothing. Go; leave us in peace.

TEIRESIAS: I will go when I have said what I have
     to say.   230
How can you hurt me? And I tell you again:
The man you have been looking for all this time,
The damned man, the murderer of Laios,
That man is in Thebes. To your mind he is
     foreign-born,
But it will soon be shown that he is a Theban, 235
A revelation that will fail to please.

206. **Kithairon:** The mountain where Oedipus was abandoned as an infant.

A blind man,
Who has his eyes now; a penniless man, who is
   rich now;
And he will go tapping the strange earth with
   his staff.
To the children with whom he lives now he will
   be
240   Brother and father — the very same; to her
Who bore him, son and husband — the very
   same
Who came to his father's bed, wet with his
   father's blood.
Enough. Go think that over.
If later you find error in what I have said,
245   You may say that I have no skill in prophecy.

(*Exit Teiresias, led by his Page. Oedipus goes into the
palace.*)

ODE° 1 • *Strophe 1*

CHORUS: The Delphic stone of prophecies
       Remembers ancient regicide
       And a still bloody hand.
       That killer's hour of flight has come.
5   He must be stronger than riderless
       Coursers of untiring wind,
       For the son of Zeus° armed with his father's
          thunder
       Leaps in lightning after him;
       And the Furies° hold his track, the sad Furies.

Antistrophe 1

10   Holy Parnassos'°° peak of snow
       Flashes and blinds that secret man,
       That all shall hunt him down:
       Though he may roam the forest shade
       Like a bull gone wild from pasture
15   To rage through glooms of stone.
       Doom comes down on him; flight will not avail
          him;
       For the world's heart calls him desolate,
       And the immortal voices follow, for ever follow.

Ode: Song sung by the Chorus.   **7. son of Zeus:** Apollo.
9. Furies: Spirits called upon to avenge crimes, especially
against kin.   **10. Parnassos:** Mountain sacred to Apollo.

Strophe 2

But now a wilder thing is heard
From the old man skilled at hearing Fate in the
   wing-beat of a bird.   20
Bewildered as a blown bird, my soul hovers and
   can not find
Foothold in this debate, or any reason or rest of
   mind.
But no man ever brought — none can bring
Proof of strife between Thebes' royal house,
Labdakos' line, and the son of Polybos;°   25
And never until now has any man brought word
Of Laios' dark death staining Oedipus the King.

Antistrophe 2

Divine Zeus and Apollo hold
Perfect intelligence alone of all tales ever told;
And well though this diviner works, he works in
   his own night;   30
No man can judge that rough unknown or trust
   in second sight,
For wisdom changes hands among the wise.
Shall I believe my great lord criminal
At a raging word that a blind old man let fall?
I saw him, when the carrion woman° faced him
   of old,   35
Prove his heroic mind. These evil words are lies.

SCENE 2

KREON: Men of Thebes:
     I am told that heavy accusations
     Have been brought against me by King Oedipus.

     I am not the kind of man to bear this tamely.

     If in these present difficulties   5
     He holds me accountable for any harm to him
     Through anything I have said or done — why,
        then,
     I do not value life in this dishonor.
     It is not as though this rumor touched upon
     Some private indiscretion. The matter is grave.   10
     The fact is that I am being called disloyal
     To the State, to my fellow citizens, to my
        friends.

25. Polybos: King who adopted Oedipus.   **35. woman:** The
Sphinx.

CHORAGOS: He may have spoken in anger, not
    from his mind.
KREON: But did you not hear him say I was the
    one
15 Who seduced the old prophet into lying?
CHORAGOS: The thing was said; I do not know
    how seriously.
KREON: But you were watching him! Were his eyes
    steady?
    Did he look like a man in his right mind?
CHORAGOS: I do not know.
    I can not judge the behavior of great men.
    But here is the king himself.

(*Enter Oedipus.*)

20 OEDIPUS: So you dared come back.
    Why? How brazen of you to come to my house,
    You murderer!
                    Do you think I do not know
    That you plotted to kill me, plotted to steal my
    throne?
    Tell me, in God's name: am I coward, a fool,
    That you should dream you could accomplish
25   this?
    A fool who could not see your slippery game?
    A coward, not to fight back when I saw it?
    You are the fool, Kreon, are you not? hoping
    Without support or friends to get a throne?
    Thrones may be won or bought: you could do
30   neither.
    KREON: Now listen to me. You have talked; let me
        talk, too.
    You can not judge unless you know the facts.
    OEDIPUS: You speak well: there is one fact; but I
        find it hard
    To learn from the deadliest enemy I have.
35 KREON: That above all I must dispute with you.
    OEDIPUS: That above all I will not hear you deny.
    KREON: If you think there is anything good in
        being stubborn
    Against all reason, then I say you are wrong.
    OEDIPUS: If you think a man can sin against his
        own kind
40   And not be punished for it, I say you are mad.
    KREON: I agree. But tell me: what have I done to
        you?
    OEDIPUS: You advised me to send for that wizard,
        did you not?
    KREON: I did. I should do it again.
    OEDIPUS: Very well. Now tell me:
        How long has it been since Laios —
    KREON: What of Laios?
    OEDIPUS: Since he vanished in that onset by the
45   road?
    KREON: It was long ago, a long time.

OEDIPUS: And this prophet,
    Was he practicing here then?
KREON: He was; and with honor, as now.
OEDIPUS: Did he speak of me at that time?
KREON: He never did,
    At least, not when I was present.
OEDIPUS: But . . . the enquiry?
    I suppose you held one?
KREON: We did, but we learned nothing. 50
OEDIPUS: Why did the prophet not speak against
    me then?
KREON: I do not know; and I am the kind of man
    Who holds his tongue when he has no facts to
        go on.
OEDIPUS: There's one fact that you know, and you
    could tell it.
KREON: What fact is that? If I know it, you shall
    have it.   55
OEDIPUS: If he were not involved with you, he
    could not say
    That it was I who murdered Laios.
KREON: If he says that, you are the one that knows
    it! —
    But now it is my turn to question you.
OEDIPUS: Put your questions. I am no murderer.   60
KREON: First, then: You married my sister?
OEDIPUS: I married your sister.
KREON: And you rule the kingdom equally with her?
OEDIPUS: Everything that she wants she has from
    me.
KREON: And I am the third, equal to both of you?
OEDIPUS: That is why I call you a bad friend.   65
KREON: No. Reason it out, as I have done.
    Think of this first: would any sane man prefer
    Power, with all a king's anxieties,
    To that same power and the grace of sleep?
    Certainly not I.   70
    I have never longed for the king's power — only
        his rights.
    Would any wise man differ from me in this?
    As matters stand, I have my way in everything
    With your consent, and no responsibilities.
    If I were king, I should be a slave to policy.   75
    How could I desire a scepter more
    Than what is now mine — untroubled influence?
    No, I have not gone mad; I need no honors,
    Except those with the perquisites I have now.
    I am welcome everywhere; every man salutes me, 80
    And those who want your favor seek my ear,
    Since I know how to manage what they ask.
    Should I exchange this ease for that anxiety?
    Besides, no sober mind is treasonable.
    I hate anarchy   85
    And never would deal with any man who
        likes it.

Test what I have said. Go to the priestess
At Delphi, ask if I quoted her correctly.
And as for this other thing: if I am found
90 Guilty of treason with Teiresias,
Then sentence me to death. You have my word
It is a sentence I should cast my vote for —
But not without evidence!
                            You do wrong
When you take good men for bad, bad men for
   good.
95 A true friend thrown aside — why, life itself
Is not more precious!
                       In time you will know this well:
For time, and time alone, will show the just
   man,
Though scoundrels are discovered in a day.
CHORAGOS: This is well said, and a prudent man
   would ponder it.
100 Judgments too quickly formed are dangerous.
OEDIPUS: But is he not quick in his duplicity?
And shall I not be quick to parry him?
Would you have me stand still, hold my peace,
   and let
This man win everything, through my inaction?
KREON: And you want — what is it, then? To
105 banish me?
OEDIPUS: No, not exile. It is your death I want,
So that all the world may see what treason
   means.
KREON: You will persist, then? You will not believe
   me?
OEDIPUS: How can I believe you?
KREON: Then you are a fool.
OEDIPUS: To save myself?
110 KREON: In justice, think of me.
OEDIPUS: You are evil incarnate.
KREON: But suppose that you are wrong?
OEDIPUS: Still I must rule.
KREON: But not if you rule badly.
OEDIPUS: O city, city!
KREON: It is my city, too!
CHORAGOS: Now, my lords, be still. I see the
   queen,
115 Iokaste, coming from her palace chambers;
And it is time she came, for the sake of you
   both.
This dreadful quarrel can be resolved through
   her.

(*Enter Iokaste.*)

IOKASTE: Poor foolish men, what wicked din is this?
With Thebes sick to death, is it not shameful
120 That you should rake some private quarrel up?
(*To Oedipus.*) Come into the house.
                            — And you, Kreon, go now:

Let us have no more of this tumult over nothing.
KREON: Nothing? No, sister: what your husband
   plans for me
Is one of two great evils: exile or death.
OEDIPUS: He is right.
                     Why, woman I have caught him squarely 125
Plotting against my life.
KREON: No! Let me die
Accurst if ever I have wished you harm!
IOKASTE: Ah, believe it, Oedipus!
In the name of the gods, respect this oath of his
For my sake, for the sake of these people here!   130

Strophe 1

CHORAGOS: Open your mind to her, my lord. Be
   ruled by her, I beg you!
OEDIPUS: What would you have me do?
CHORAGOS: Respect Kreon's word. He has never
   spoken like a fool,
And now he has sworn an oath.
OEDIPUS: You know what you ask?
CHORAGOS: I do.
OEDIPUS: Speak on, then.
CHORAGOS: A friend so sworn should not be baited
   so,   135
In blind malice, and without final proof.
OEDIPUS: You are aware, I hope, that what you say
Means death for me, or exile at the least.

Strophe 2

CHORAGOS: No, I swear by Helios, first in heaven!
   May I die friendless and accurst,   140
The worst of deaths, if ever I meant that!
It is the withering fields
   That hurt my sick heart:
Must we bear all these ills,
And now your bad blood as well?   145
OEDIPUS: Then let him go. And let me die, if I
   must,
Or be driven by him in shame from the land of
   Thebes.
It is your unhappiness, and not his talk,
That touches me.
               As for him —
Wherever he goes, hatred will follow him.   150
KREON: Ugly in yielding, as you were ugly in rage!
   Natures like yours chiefly torment themselves.
OEDIPUS: Can you not go? Can you not leave me?
KREON: I can.
You do not know me; but the city knows me,
And in its eyes I am just, if not in yours.   155
                                    (*Exit Kreon.*)

Antistrophe 1

CHORAGOS: Lady Iokaste, did you not ask the King
    to go to his chambers?
IOKASTE: First tell me what has happened.
CHORAGOS: There was suspicion without evidence;
    yet it rankled
    As even false charges will.
IOKASTE: On both sides?
CHORAGOS: On both.
160 IOKASTE: But what was said?
CHORAGOS: Oh let it rest, let it be done with!
    Have we not suffered enough?
OEDIPUS: You see to what your decency has
    brought you:
    You have made difficulties where my heart saw
    none.

Antistrophe 2

CHORAGOS: Oedipus, it is not once only I have told
165   you —
    You must know I should count myself unwise
    To the point of madness, should I now forsake
    you —
    You, under whose hand,
        In the storm of another time,
170   Our dear land sailed out free.
    But now stand fast at the helm!
IOKASTE: In God's name, Oedipus, inform your wife
    as well:
    Why are you so set in this hard anger?
OEDIPUS: I will tell you, for none of these men
    deserves
175   My confidence as you do. It is Kreon's work,
    His treachery, his plotting against me.
IOKASTE: Go on, if you can make this clear to me.
OEDIPUS: He charges me with the murder of Laios.
IOKASTE: Has he some knowledge? Or does he
    speak from hearsay?
OEDIPUS: He would not commit himself to such a
180   charge,
    But he has brought in that damnable soothsayer
    To tell his story.
IOKASTE: Set your mind at rest.
    If it is a question of soothsayers, I tell you
    That you will find no man whose craft gives
    knowledge
    Of the unknowable.
185   Here is my proof:
    An oracle was reported to Laios once
    (I will not say from Phoibos himself, but from

His appointed ministers, at any rate)
That his doom would be death at the hands of
    his own son —
His son, born of his flesh and of mine!   190

Now, you remember the story: Laios was killed
By marauding strangers where three highways
    meet;
But his child had not been three days in this
    world
Before the king had pierced the baby's ankles
And left him to die on a lonely mountainside.   195

Thus, Apollo never caused that child
To kill his father, and it was not Laios' fate
To die at the hands of his son, as he had feared.
This is what prophets and prophecies are worth!
Have no dread of them.
                It is God himself   200
Who can show us what he wills, in his own
    way.
OEDIPUS: How strange a shadowy memory crossed
    my mind,
Just now while you were speaking; it chilled my
    heart.
IOKASTE: What do you mean? What memory do
    you speak of?
OEDIPUS: If I understand you, Laios was killed   205
    At a place where three roads meet.
IOKASTE: So it was said;
    We have no later story.
OEDIPUS: Where did it happen?
IOKASTE: Phokis, it is called: at a place where the
    Theban Way
    Divides into the roads toward Delphi and
    Daulia.
OEDIPUS: When?
IOKASTE: We had the news not long before
    you came   210
    And proved the right to your succession here.
OEDIPUS: Ah, what net has God been weaving for
    me?
IOKASTE: Oedipus! Why does this trouble you?
OEDIPUS: Do not ask me yet.
    First, tell me how Laios looked, and tell me
    How old he was.
IOKASTE: He was tall, his hair just touched   215
    With white; his form was not unlike your own.
OEDIPUS: I think that I myself may be accurst
    By my own ignorant edict.
IOKASTE: You speak strangely.
    It makes me tremble to look at you, my king.
OEDIPUS: I am not sure that the blind man can not
    see.   220

But I should know better if you were to tell
   me —
IOKASTE: Anything — though I dread to hear you
   ask it.
OEDIPUS: Was the king lightly escorted, or did he
   ride
With a large company, as a ruler should?
IOKASTE: There were five men with him in all: one
   was a herald;
And a single chariot, which he was driving.
OEDIPUS: Alas, that makes it plain enough!
                             But who —
Who told you how it happened?
IOKASTE: A household servant,
The only one to escape.
OEDIPUS: And is he still
A servant of ours?
IOKASTE: No; for when he came back at last
And found you enthroned in the place of the
   dead king,
He came to me, touched my hand with his, and
   begged
That I would send him away to the frontier
   district
Where only the shepherds go —
As far away from the city as I could send him.
I granted his prayer; for although the man was a
   slave,
He had earned more than this favor at my
   hands.
OEDIPUS: Can he be called back quickly?
IOKASTE: Easily.
But why?
OEDIPUS: I have taken too much upon myself
Without enquiry; therefore I wish to consult
   him.
IOKASTE: Then he shall come.
                  But am I not one also
To whom you might confide these fears of
   yours?
OEDIPUS: That is your right; it will not be denied
   you,
Now least of all; for I have reached a pitch
Of wild foreboding. Is there anyone
To whom I should sooner speak?

Polybos of Corinth is my father.
My mother is a Dorian: Merope.
I grew up chief among the men of Corinth
Until a strange thing happened —
Not worth my passion, it may be, but strange.
At a feast, a drunken man maundering in his
   cups
Cries out that I am not my father's son!

I contained myself that night, though I felt anger
And a sinking heart. The next day I visited
My father and mother, and questioned them.
   They stormed,
Calling it all the slanderous rant of a fool;
And this relieved me. Yet the suspicion
Remained always aching in my mind;
I knew there was talk; I could not rest;
And finally, saying nothing to my parents,
I went to the shrine at Delphi.

The god dismissed my question without reply;
He spoke of other things.
                    Some were clear,
Full of wretchedness, dreadful, unbearable:
As, that I should lie with my own mother, breed
Children from whom all men would turn their
   eyes;
And that I should be my father's murderer.

I heard all this, and fled. And from that day
Corinth to me was only in the stars
Descending in that quarter of the sky,
As I wandered farther and farther on my way
To a land where I should never see the evil
Sung by the oracle. And I came to this country
Where, so you say, King Laios was killed.

I will tell you all that happened there, my lady.
There were three highways
Coming together at a place I passed;
And there a herald came towards me, and a
   chariot
Drawn by horses, with a man such as you
   describe
Seated in it. The groom leading the horses
Forced me off the road at his lord's command;
But as this charioteer lurched over towards me
I struck him in my rage. The old man saw me
And brought his double goad down upon my
   head
As I came abreast.
               He was paid back, and more!
Swinging my club in this right hand I knocked
   him
Out of his car, and he rolled on the ground.
                    I killed him.

I killed them all.
Now if that stranger and Laios were — kin,
Where is a man more miserable than I?
More hated by the gods? Citizen and alien alike
Must never shelter me or speak to me —
I must be shunned by all.

                                    And I myself
295   Pronounced this malediction upon myself!

           Think of it: I have touched you with these
               hands,
           These hands that killed your husband. What
               defilement!

           Am I all evil, then? It must be so,
           Since I must flee from Thebes, yet never again
300   See my own countrymen, my own country,
           For fear of joining my mother in marriage
           And killing Polybos, my father.
                                        Ah,
           If I was created so, born to this fate,
           Who could deny the savagery of God?

305   O holy majesty of heavenly powers!
           May I never see that day! Never!
           Rather let me vanish from the race of men
           Than know the abomination destined me!
       CHORAGOS: We too, my lord, have felt dismay at
               this.
           But there is hope: you have yet to hear the
310   shepherd.
       OEDIPUS: Indeed, I fear no other hope is left me.
       IOKASTE: What do you hope from him when he
               comes?
       OEDIPUS: This much:
           If his account of the murder tallies with yours,
           Then I am cleared.
       IOKASTE: What was it that I said
           Of such importance?
315   OEDIPUS: Why, "marauders," you said,
           Killed the king, according to this man's story.
           If he maintains that still, if there were several,
           Clearly the guilt is not mine: I was alone.
           But if he says one man, singlehanded, did it,
320   Then the evidence all points to me.
       IOKASTE: You may be sure that he said there were
               several;
           And can he call back that story now? He can
               not.
           The whole city heard it as plainly as I.
           But suppose he alters some detail of it:
325   He can not ever show that Laios' death
           Fulfilled the oracle: for Apollo said
           My child was doomed to kill him; and my
               child —
           Poor baby! — it was my child that died first.

           No. From now on, where oracles are concerned,
330   I would not waste a second thought on any.
       OEDIPUS: You may be right.

                                     But come: let someone go
           For the shepherd at once. This matter must be
               settled.
       IOKASTE: I will send for him.
           I would not wish to cross you in anything,
           And surely not in this. — Let us go in.   335
                                  (Exeunt into the palace.)

ODE 2 · *Strophe 1*

CHORUS: Let me be reverent in the ways of right,
       Lowly the paths I journey on;
       Let all my words and actions keep
       The laws of the pure universe
       From highest Heaven handed down.   5
       For Heaven is their bright nurse,
       Those generations of the realms of light;
       Ah, never of mortal kind were they begot,
       Nor are they slaves of memory, lost in sleep:
       Their Father is greater than Time, and ages not.   10

Antistrophe 1

       The tyrant is a child of Pride
       Who drinks from his great sickening cup
       Recklessness and vanity,
       Until from his high crest headlong
       He plummets to the dust of hope.   15
       That strong man is not strong.
       But let no fair ambition be denied;
       May God protect the wrestler for the State
       In government, in comely policy,
       Who will fear God, and on his ordinance wait.   20

Strophe 2

       Haughtiness and the high hand of disdain
       Tempt and outrage God's holy law;
       And any mortal who dares hold
       No immortal Power in awe
       Will be caught up in a net of pain: 25
       The price for which his levity is sold.
       Let each man take due earnings, then,
       And keep his hands from holy things,
       And from blasphemy stand apart —
       Else the crackling blast of heaven   30
       Blows on his head, and on his desperate heart.
       Though fools will honor impious men,
       In their cities no tragic poet sings.

Antistrophe 2

Shall we lose faith in Delphi's obscurities,
35   We who have heard the world's core
Discredited, and the sacred wood
Of Zeus at Elis praised no more?
The deeds and the strange prophecies
Must make a pattern yet to be understood.
40   Zeus, if indeed you are lord of all,
Throned in light over night and day,
Mirror this in your endless mind:
Our masters call the oracle
Words on the wind, and the Delphic vision
    blind!
45   Their hearts no longer know Apollo,
And reverence for the gods has died away.

SCENE 3

(Enter Iokaste.)

IOKASTE: Princes of Thebes, it has occurred to me
To visit the altars of the gods, bearing
These branches as a suppliant, and this incense.
Our king is not himself: his noble soul
5   Is overwrought with fantasies of dread,
Else he would consider
The new prophecies in the light of the old.
He will listen to any voice that speaks disaster,
And my advice goes for nothing. *(She
    approaches the altar, right.)*
                                To you, then, Apollo,
Lycean lord, since you are nearest, I turn in
10   prayer
Receive these offerings, and grant us deliverance
From defilement. Our hearts are heavy with fear
When we see our leader distracted, as helpless
    sailors
Are terrified by the confusion of their helmsman.

(Enter Messenger.)

15   MESSENGER: Friends, no doubt you can direct me:
Where shall I find the house of Oedipus,
Or, better still, where is the king himself?
CHORAGOS: It is this very place, stranger; he is
    inside.
This is his wife and mother of his children.
20   MESSENGER: I wish her happiness in a happy house,
Blest in all the fulfillment of her marriage.
IOKASTE: I wish as much for you: your courtesy
Deserves a like good fortune. But now, tell me:
Why have you come? What have you to say to
    us?

MESSENGER: Good news, my lady, for your house
    and your husband.   25
IOKASTE: What news? Who sent you here?
MESSENGER: I am from Corinth.
The news I bring ought to mean joy for you,
Though it may be you will find some grief in it.
IOKASTE: What is it? How can it touch us in both
    ways?
MESSENGER: The word is that the people of the
    Isthmus   30
Intend to call Oedipus to be their king.
IOKASTE: But old King Polybos — is he not reigning
    still?
MESSENGER: No. Death holds him in his sepulchre.
IOKASTE: What are you saying? Polybos is dead?
MESSENGER: If I am not telling the truth, may I die
    myself.   35
IOKASTE *(to a Maidservant)*: Go in, go quickly; tell
    this to your master.
O riddlers of God's will, where are you now!
This was the man whom Oedipus, long ago,
Feared so, fled so, in dread of destroying him —
But it was another fate by which he died.   40

(Enter Oedipus, center.)

OEDIPUS: Dearest Iokaste, why have you sent for
    me?
IOKASTE: Listen to what this man says, and then tell
    me
What has become of the solemn prophecies.
OEDIPUS: Who is this man? What is his news for
    me?
IOKASTE: He has come from Corinth to announce
    your father's death!   45
OEDIPUS: Is it true, stranger? Tell me in your own
    words.
MESSENGER: I can not say it more clearly: the king
    is dead.
OEDIPUS: Was it by treason? Or by an attack of
    illness?
MESSENGER: A little thing brings old men to their
    rest.
OEDIPUS: It was sickness, then?
MESSENGER: Yes, and his many years. 50
OEDIPUS: Ah!
Why should a man respect the Pythian hearth,°
    or
Give heed to the birds that jangle above his
    head?
They prophesied that I should kill Polybos,
Kill my own father; but he is dead and buried,   55
And I am here — I never touched him, never,

---

52. **Pythian hearth:** Delphi.

Unless he died of grief for my departure,
And thus, in a sense, through me. No. Polybos
Has packed the oracles off with him
     underground.
They are empty words.

60 IOKASTE: Had I not told you so?
OEDIPUS: You had; it was my faint heart that
     betrayed me.
IOKASTE: From now on never think of those things
     again.
OEDIPUS: And yet — must I not fear my mother's
     bed?
IOKASTE: Why should anyone in this world be
     afraid,
65   Since Fate rules us and nothing can be foreseen?
A man should live only for the present day.

Have no more fear of sleeping with your
     mother:
How many men, in dreams, have lain with their
     mothers!
No reasonable man is troubled by such things.
70 OEDIPUS: That is true; only —
If only my mother were not still alive!
But she is alive. I can not help my dread.
IOKASTE: Yet this news of your father's death is
     wonderful.
OEDIPUS: Wonderful. But I fear the living woman.
MESSENGER: Tell me, who is this woman that you
75   fear?
OEDIPUS: It is Merope, man; the wife of King
     Polybos.
MESSENGER: Merope? Why should you be afraid of
     her?
OEDIPUS: An oracle of the gods, a dreadful saying.
MESSENGER: Can you tell me about it or are you
     sworn to silence?
80 OEDIPUS: I can tell you, and I will.
Apollo said through his prophet that I was the
     man
Who should marry his own mother, shed his
     father's blood
With his own hands. And so, for all these years
I have kept clear of Corinth, and no harm has
     come —
Though it would have been sweet to see my
85   parents again.
MESSENGER: And is this the fear that drove you out
     of Corinth?
OEDIPUS: Would you have me kill my father?
MESSENGER: As for that
You must be reassured by the news I gave you.
OEDIPUS: If you could reassure me, I would reward
     you.

MESSENGER: I had that in mind, I will confess: I
     thought   90
I could count on you when you returned to
     Corinth.
OEDIPUS: No: I will never go near my parents
     again.
MESSENGER: Ah, son, you still do not know what
     you are doing —
OEDIPUS: What do you mean? In the name of God
     tell me!
MESSENGER: — If these are your reasons for not
     going home.   95
OEDIPUS: I tell you, I fear the oracle may come
     true.
MESSENGER: And guilt may come upon you through
     your parents?
OEDIPUS: That is the dread that is always in my
     heart.
MESSENGER: Can you not see that all your fears are
     groundless?
OEDIPUS: Groundless? Am I not my parents' son?   100
MESSENGER: Polybos was not your father.
OEDIPUS: Not my father?
MESSENGER: No more your father than the man
     speaking to you.
OEDIPUS: But you are nothing to me!
MESSENGER: Neither was he.
OEDIPUS: Then why did he call me son?
MESSENGER: I will tell you:
Long ago he had you from my hands, as a gift.   105
OEDIPUS: Then how could he love me so, if I was
     not his?
MESSENGER: He had no children, and his heart
     turned to you.
OEDIPUS: What of you? Did you buy me? Did you
     find me by chance?
MESSENGER: I came upon you in the woody vales
     of Kithairon.
OEDIPUS: And what were you doing there?
MESSENGER: Tending my flocks. 110
OEDIPUS: A wandering shepherd?
MESSENGER: But your savior, son, that day.
OEDIPUS: From what did you save me?
MESSENGER: Your ankles should tell you that.
OEDIPUS: Ah, stranger, why do you speak of that
     childhood pain?
MESSENGER: I pulled the skewer that pinned your
     feet together.
OEDIPUS: I have had the mark as long as I can
     remember.   115
MESSENGER: That was why you were given the
     name you bear.
OEDIPUS: God! Was it my father or my mother who
     did it?

Tell me!
MESSENGER: I do not know. The man who
   gave you to me
   Can tell you better than I.
OEDIPUS: It was not you that found me, but
20   another?
MESSENGER: It was another shepherd gave you to
   me.
OEDIPUS: Who was he? Can you tell me who he
   was?
MESSENGER: I think he was said to be one of Laïos'
   people.
OEDIPUS: You mean the Laïos who was king here
   years ago?
MESSENGER: Yes; King Laïos; and the man was one
125   of his herdsmen.
OEDIPUS: Is he still alive? Can I see him?
MESSENGER: These men here
   Know best about such things.
OEDIPUS: Does anyone here
   Know this shepherd that he is talking about?
   Have you seen him in the fields, or in the town?
   If you have, tell me. It is time things were made
130   plain.
CHORAGOS: I think the man he means is that same
   shepherd
   You have already asked to see. Iokastê perhaps
   Could tell you something.
OEDIPUS: Do you know anything
   About him, Lady? Is he the man we have
   summoned?
   Is that the man this shepherd means?
135 IOKASTE: Why think of him?
   Forget this herdsman. Forget it all.
   This talk is a waste of time.
OEDIPUS: How can you say that,
   When the clues to my true birth are in my hands?
IOKASTE: For God's love, let us have no more
   questioning!
140   Is your life nothing to you?
   My own is pain enough for me to bear.
OEDIPUS: You need not worry. Suppose my mother
   a slave,
   And born of slaves: no baseness can touch you.
IOKASTE: Listen to me, I beg you: do not do this
   thing!
OEDIPUS: I will not listen; the truth must be made
145   known.
IOKASTE: Everything that I say is for your own
   good!
OEDIPUS: My own good
   Snaps my patience, then; I want none of it.
IOKASTE: You are fatally wrong! May you never
   learn who you are!

OEDIPUS: Go, one of you, and bring the shepherd
   here.
   Let us leave this woman to brag of her royal
   name.   150
IOKASTE: Ah, miserable!
   That is the only word I have for you now.
   That is the only word I can ever have.
              (*Exit into the palace.*)
CHORAGOS: Why has she left us, Oedipus? Why has
   she gone
   In such a passion of sorrow? I fear this silence: 155
   Something dreadful may come of it.
OEDIPUS: Let it come!
   However base my birth, I must know about it.
   The Queen, like a woman, is perhaps ashamed
   To think of my low origin. But I
   Am a child of Luck; I can not be dishonored.   160
   Luck is my mother; the passing months, my
   brothers,
   Have seen me rich and poor.
                 If this is so,
   How could I wish that I were someone else?
   How could I not be glad to know my birth?

ODE 3 • *Strophe*

CHORUS: If ever the coming time were known
   To my heart's pondering,
   Kithairon, now by Heaven I see the torches
   At the festival of the next full moon,
   And see the dance, and hear the choir sing   5
   A grace to your gentle shade:
   Mountain where Oedipus was found,
   O mountain guard of a noble race!
   May the god° who heals us lend his aid,
   And let that glory come to pass   10
   For our king's cradling-ground.

Antistrophe

Of the nymphs that flower beyond the years,
Who bore you,° royal child,
To Pan° of the hills or the timberline Apollo,
Cold in delight where the upland clears,   15

---

9. god: Apollo.   **13. Who bore you:** The Chorus is asking
if Oedipus is the son of an immortal nymph and a god: Pan,
Apollo, Hermes, or Dionysus.   **14. Pan:** God of nature,
forests, flocks, and shepherds, depicted as half-man and half-
goat.

Or Hermes° for whom Kyllene's° heights are
    piled?
Or flushed as evening cloud,
Great Dionysos,° roamer of mountains,
He — was it he who found you there,

20   And caught you up in his own proud
Arms from the sweet god-ravisher
Who laughed by the Muses'° fountains?

SCENE 4

OEDIPUS: Sirs: though I do not know the man,
    I think I see him coming, this shepherd we want:
    He is old, like our friend here, and the men
    Bringing him seem to be servants of my house.

5   But you can tell, if you have ever seen him.

(*Enter Shepherd escorted by Servants.*)

CHORAGOS: I know him, he was Laios' man. You
    can trust him.
OEDIPUS: Tell me first, you from Corinth: is this the
    shepherd
    We were discussing?
MESSENGER: This is the very man.
OEDIPUS (*to Shepherd*): Come here. No, look at me.
    You must answer

10   Everything I ask. — You belonged to Laios?
SHEPHERD: Yes: born his slave, brought up in his
    house.
OEDIPUS: Tell me: what kind of work did you do
    for him?
SHEPHERD: I was a shepherd of his, most of my life.
OEDIPUS: Where mainly did you go for pasturage?
SHEPHERD: Sometimes Kithairon, sometimes the hills

15   near-by.
OEDIPUS: Do you remember ever seeing this man
    out there?
SHEPHERD: What would he be doing there? This
    man?
OEDIPUS: This man standing here. Have you ever
    seen him before?
SHEPHERD: No. At least, not to my recollection.
MESSENGER: And that is not strange, my lord. But

20   I'll refresh
    His memory: he must remember when we two

16. **Hermes:** Son of Zeus, messenger of the gods.   **Kyllene:**
Mountain reputed to be the birthplace of Hermes; also the
center of a cult to Hermes.   18. **Dionysos:** (Dionysus) God
of wine around whom wild, orgiastic rituals developed; also
called Bacchus.   22. **Muses:** Nine sister goddesses who presided over poetry and music, art and sciences.

Spent three whole seasons together, March to
    September,
On Kithairon or thereabouts. He had two flocks;
I had one. Each autumn I'd drive mine home
And he would go back with his to Laios'
    sheepfold. —   25
Is this not true, just as I have described it?
SHEPHERD: True, yes; but it was all so long ago.
MESSENGER: Well, then: do you remember, back in
    those days,
That you gave me a baby boy to bring up as my
    own?
SHEPHERD: What if I did? What are you trying to
    say?   30
MESSENGER: King Oedipus was once that little
    child.
SHEPHERD: Damn you, hold your tongue!
OEDIPUS: No more of that!
    It is your tongue needs watching, not this man's.
SHEPHERD: My king, my master, what is it I have
    done wrong?
OEDIPUS: You have not answered his question about
    the boy.   35
SHEPHERD: He does not know . . . He is only
    making trouble . . .
OEDIPUS: Come, speak plainly, or it will go hard
    with you.
SHEPHERD: In God's name, do not torture an old
    man!
OEDIPUS: Come here, one of you; bind his arms
    behind him.
SHEPHERD: Unhappy king! What more do you wish
    to learn?   40
OEDIPUS: Did you give this man the child he speaks
    of?
SHEPHERD: I did.
    And I would to God I had died that very day.
OEDIPUS: You will die now unless you speak the
    truth.
SHEPHERD: Yet if I speak the truth, I am worse
    than dead.
OEDIPUS (*to Attendant*): He intends to draw it out,
    apparently —   45
SHEPHERD: No! I have told you already that I gave
    him the boy.
OEDIPUS: Where did you get him? From your
    house? From somewhere else?
SHEPHERD: Not from mine, no. A man gave him to
    me.
OEDIPUS: Is that man here? Whose house did he
    belong to?
SHEPHERD: For God's love, my king, do not ask me
    any more!   50
OEDIPUS: You are a dead man if I have to ask you
    again.

SHEPHERD: Then ... Then the child was from the
　palace of Laios.
OEDIPUS: A slave child? or a child of his own line?
SHEPHERD: Ah, I am on the brink of dreadful
　speech!
OEDIPUS: And I of dreadful hearing. Yet I must
55　hear.
SHEPHERD: If you must be told, then ...
　　　　　　　　They said it was Laios' child;
　But it is your wife who can tell you about that.
OEDIPUS: My wife — Did she give it to you?
SHEPHERD:　　　　　　My lord, she did.
OEDIPUS: Do you know why?
SHEPHERD:　　　　　I was told to get rid of it.
OEDIPUS: Oh heartless mother!
60 SHEPHERD:　　　　But in dread of prophecies ...
OEDIPUS: Tell me.
SHEPHERD:　　　It was said that the boy would
　kill his own father.
OEDIPUS: Then why did you give him over to this
　old man?
SHEPHERD: I pitied the baby, my king,
　And I thought that this man would take him far
　away
　To his own country.
65　　　　　He saved him — but for what a fate!
　For if you are what this man says you are,
　No man living is more wretched than Oedipus.
OEDIPUS: Ah God!
　It was true!
　　　　All the prophecies!
　　　　　　　　— Now,
70　O Light, may I look on you for the last time!
　I, Oedipus,
　Oedipus, damned in his birth, in his marriage
　damned,
　Damned in the blood he shed with his own
　hand!

(He rushes into the palace.)

ODE 4 • Strophe 1

CHORUS: Alas for the seed of men.
　What measure shall I give these generations
　That breathe on the void and are void
　And exist and do not exist?
5　Who bears more weight of joy
　Than mass of sunlight shifting in images,
　Or who shall make his thought stay on
　That down time drifts away?
　Your splendor is all fallen.
10　O naked brow of wrath and tears,
　O change of Oedipus!

I who saw your days call no man blest —
Your great days like ghosts gone.

Antistrophe 1

That mind was a strong bow.
Deep, how deep you drew it then, hard archer,　15
At a dim fearful range,
And brought dear glory down!
You overcame the stranger° —
The virgin with her hooking lion claws —
And though death sang, stood like a tower　20
To make pale Thebes take heart.
Fortress against our sorrow!
True king, giver of laws,
Majestic Oedipus!
No prince in Thebes had ever such renown,　25
No prince won such grace of power.

Strophe 2

And now of all men ever known
Most pitiful is this man's story:
His fortunes are most changed; his state
Fallen to a low slave's　30
Ground under bitter fate.
O Oedipus, most royal one!
The great door° that expelled you to the light
Gave at night — ah, gave night to your glory:
As to the father, to the fathering son.　35
All understood too late.
How could that queen whom Laios won,
The garden that he harrowed at his height,
Be silent when that act was done?

Antistrophe 2

But all eyes fail before time's eye,　40
All actions come to justice there.
Though never willed, though far down the deep
　past,
Your bed, your dread sirings,
Are brought to book at last.
Child by Laios doomed to die,　45
Then doomed to lose that fortunate little death,
Would God you never took breath in this air
That with my wailing lips I take to cry:
For I weep the world's outcast.
I was blind, and now I can tell why:　50

18. stranger: The Sphinx.　**33. door:** Iokaste's womb.

The Shepherd (Oliver Cliff) tells Oedipus (Kenneth Welsh) the truth about his birth in the Guthrie Theater Company's 1973 production directed by Michael Langham.

Asleep, for you had given ease of breath
To Thebes, while the false years went by.

EXODOS°

(*Enter, from the palace, Second Messenger.*)

SECOND MESSENGER: Elders of Thebes, most
        honored in this land,
    What horrors are yours to see and hear, what
        weight
    Of sorrow to be endured, if, true to your birth,
    You venerate the line of Labdakos!
 5   I think neither Istros nor Phasis, those great
        rivers,
    Could purify this place of all the evil
    It shelters now, or soon must bring to light —
    Evil not done unconsciously, but willed.

    The greatest griefs are those we cause ourselves.
CHORAGOS: Surely, friend, we have grief enough
10   already;
    What new sorrow do you mean?
SECOND MESSENGER: The queen is dead.
CHORAGOS: O miserable queen! But at whose
        hand?
SECOND MESSENGER: Her own.
    The full horror of what happened you can not
        know,
    For you did not see it; but I, who did, will tell
        you
15   As clearly as I can how she met her death.

    When she had left us,
    In passionate silence, passing through the court,
    She ran to her apartment in the house,
    Her hair clutched by the fingers of both hands.
    She closed the doors behind her; then, by that
20   bed
    Where long ago the fatal son was conceived —
    That son who should bring about his father's
        death —
    We heard her call upon Laios, dead so many
        years,
    And heard her wail for the double fruit of her
        marriage,
    A husband by her husband, children by her
25   child.

Exactly how she died I do not know:
For Oedipus burst in moaning and would not let
    us
Keep vigil to the end: it was by him
As he stormed about the room that our eyes
    were caught.
From one to another of us he went, begging a
    sword,   30
Hunting the wife who was not his wife, the
    mother
Whose womb had carried his own children and
    himself.
I do not know: it was none of us aided him,
But surely one of the gods was in control!
For with a dreadful cry   35
He hurled his weight, as though wrenched out of
    himself,
At the twin doors: the bolts gave, and he rushed
    in.
And there we saw her hanging, her body
    swaying
From the cruel cord she had noosed about her
    neck.
A great sob broke from him, heartbreaking to
    hear,   40
As he loosed the rope and lowered her to the
    ground.

I would blot out from my mind what happened
    next!
For the king ripped from her gown the golden
    brooches
That were her ornament, and raised them, and
    plunged them down
Straight into his own eyeballs, crying, "No more, 45
No more shall you look on the misery about me,
The horrors of my own doing! Too long you
    have known
The faces of those whom I should never have
    seen,
Too long been blind to those for whom I was
    searching!
From this hour, go in darkness!" And as he
    spoke,   50
He struck at his eyes — not once, but many
    times;
And the blood spattered his beard,
Bursting from his ruined sockets like red hail.

So from the unhappiness of two this evil has
    sprung,
A curse on the man and woman alike. The old   55
Happiness of the house of Labdakos
Was happiness enough: where is it today?
It is all wailing and ruin, disgrace, death — all

Exodos: Final scene.

The misery of mankind that has a name —
60   And it is wholly and for ever theirs.
CHORAGOS: Is he in agony still? Is there no rest for
            him?
SECOND MESSENGER: He is calling for someone to
            open the doors wide
        So that all the children of Kadmos may look
            upon
        His father's murderer, his mother's — no,
        I can not say it!
65   And then he will leave Thebes,
        Self-exiled, in order that the curse
        Which he himself pronounced may depart from
            the house.
        He is weak, and there is none to lead him,
        So terrible is his suffering.
                                    But you will see:
70   Look, the doors are opening; in a moment
        You will see a thing that would crush a heart of
            stone.

(*The central door is opened; Oedipus, blinded, is led
in.*)

CHORAGOS: Dreadful indeed for men to see.
        Never have my own eyes
        Looked on a sight so full of fear.

75   Oedipus!
        What madness came upon you, what demon
        Leaped on your life with heavier
        Punishment than a mortal man can bear?
        No: I can not even
80   Look at you, poor ruined one.
        And I would speak, question, ponder,
        If I were able. No.
        You make me shudder.
OEDIPUS: God. God.
85   Is there a sorrow greater?
        Where shall I find harbor in this world?
        My voice is hurled far on a dark wind.
        What has God done to me?
CHORAGOS: Too terrible to think of, or to see.

Strophe 1

90   OEDIPUS: O cloud of night,
        Never to be turned away: night coming on,
        I can not tell how: night like a shroud!
        My fair winds brought me here.
                                    O God. Again
        The pain of the spikes where I had sight,
95   The flooding pain
        Of memory, never to be gouged out.

CHORAGOS: This is not strange.
        You suffer it all twice over, remorse in pain,
        Pain in remorse.

Antistrophe 1

OEDIPUS: Ah dear friend   10●
        Are you faithful even yet, you alone?
        Are you still standing near me, will you stay
            here,
        Patient, to care for the blind?
                                    The blind man!
        Yet even blind I know who it is attends me,
        By the voice's tone —   10.
        Though my new darkness hide the comforter.
CHORAGOS: Oh fearful act!
        What god was it drove you to rake black
        Night across your eyes?

Strophe 2

OEDIPUS: Apollo. Apollo. Dear   11●
        Children, the god was Apollo.
        He brought my sick, sick fate upon me.
        But the blinding hand was my own!
        How could I bear to see
        When all my sight was horror everywhere?   11⁵
CHORAGOS: Everywhere; that is true.
OEDIPUS: And now what is left?
        Images? Love? A greeting even,
        Sweet to the senses? Is there anything?
        Ah, no, friends: lead me away.   12●
        Lead me away from Thebes.
                                Lead the great wreck
        And hell of Oedipus, whom the gods hate.
CHORAGOS: Your misery, you are not blind to that.
        Would God you had never found it out!

Antistrophe 2

OEDIPUS: Death take the man who unbound   125
        My feet on that hillside
        And delivered me from death to life! What life?
        If only I had died,
        This weight of monstrous doom
        Could not have dragged me and my darlings
            down.   13●
CHORAGOS: I would have wished the same.

OEDIPUS: Oh never to have come here
   With my father's blood upon me! Never
   To have been the man they call his mother's
      husband!
135 Oh accurst! Oh child of evil,
   To have entered that wretched bed —
                              the selfsame one!
   More primal than sin itself, this fell to me.
CHORAGOS: I do not know what words to offer
      you.
   You were better dead than alive and blind.
OEDIPUS: Do not counsel me any more. This
140   punishment
   That I have laid upon myself is just.
   If I had eyes,
   I do not know how I could bear the sight
   Of my father, when I came to the house of
      Death,
   Or my mother: for I have sinned against them
145   both
   So vilely that I could not make my peace
   By strangling my own life.
                     Or do you think my children,
   Born as they were born, would be sweet to my
      eyes?
   Ah never, never! Nor this town with its high
      walls,
   Nor the holy images of the gods.
150   For I,
   Thrice miserable! — Oedipus, noblest of all the
      line
   Of Kadmos, have condemned myself to enjoy
   These things no more, by my own malediction
   Expelling that man whom the gods declared
155   To be a defilement in the house of Laïos.
   After exposing the rankness of my own guilt,
   How could I look men frankly in the eyes?
   No, I swear it,
   If I could have stifled my hearing at its source,
160   I would have done it and made all this body
   A tight cell of misery, blank to light and sound:
   So I should have been safe in my dark mind
   Beyond external evil.
                     Ah Kithairon!
   Why did you shelter me? When I was cast upon
      you,
165   Why did I not die? Then I should never
   Have shown the world my execrable birth.

   Ah Polybos! Corinth, city that I believed
   The ancient seat of my ancestors: how fair
   I seemed, your child! And all the while this evil
   Was cancerous within me!
170   For I am sick
   In my own being, sick in my origin.

O three roads, dark ravine, woodland and way
Where three roads met; you, drinking my
   father's blood,
My own blood, spilled by my own hand: can
   you remember
The unspeakable things I did there, and the
   things   175
I went on from there to do?
                     O marriage, marriage!
The act that engendered me, and again the act
Performed by the son in the same bed —
                        Ah, the net
Of incest, mingling fathers, brothers, sons,
With brides, wives, mothers: the last evil   180
That can be known by men: no tongue can say
How evil!
         No. For the love of God, conceal me
Somewhere far from Thebes; or kill me; or hurl
   me
Into the sea, away from men's eyes for ever.

Come, lead me. You need not fear to touch me. 185
Of all men, I alone can bear this guilt.

(*Enter Kreon.*)

CHORAGOS: Kreon is here now. As to what you
      ask,
   He may decide the course to take. He only
   Is left to protect the city in your place.
OEDIPUS: Alas, how can I speak to him? What right
      have I   190
   To beg his courtesy whom I have deeply
      wronged?
KREON: I have not come to mock you, Oedipus,
   Or to reproach you, either.
   (*To Attendants.*)   — You, standing there:
   If you have lost all respect for man's dignity,
   At least respect the flame of Lord Helios: 195
   Do not allow this pollution to show itself
   Openly here, an affront to the earth
   And Heaven's rain and the light of day. No,
      take him
   Into the house as quickly as you can.
   For it is proper   200
   That only the close kindred see his grief.
OEDIPUS: I pray you in God's name, since your
      courtesy
   Ignores my dark expectation, visiting
   With mercy this man of all men most execrable:
   Give me what I ask — for your good, not for
      mine.   205
KREON: And what is it that you turn to me begging
      for?
OEDIPUS: Drive me out of this country as quickly as
      may be

To a place where no human voice can ever greet
me.
KREON: I should have done that before now —
only,
210 God's will had not been wholly revealed to me.
OEDIPUS: But his command is plain: the parricide
Must be destroyed. I am that evil man.
KREON: That is the sense of it, yes; but as things
are,
We had best discover clearly what is to be done.
OEDIPUS: You would learn more about a man like
215 me?
KREON: You are ready now to listen to the god.
OEDIPUS: I will listen. But it is to you
That I must turn for help. I beg you, hear me.

The woman is there —
220 Give her whatever funeral you think proper:
She is your sister.
— But let me go, Kreon!
Let me purge my father's Thebes of the pollution
Of my living here, and go out to the wild hills,
To Kithairon, that has won such fame with me,
The tomb my mother and father appointed for
225 me,
And let me die there, as they willed I should.
And yet I know
Death will not ever come to me through sickness
Or in any natural way: I have been preserved
230 For some unthinkable fate. But let that be.

As for my sons, you need not care for them.
They are men, they will find some way to live.
But my poor daughters, who have shared my
table,
Who never before have been parted from their
father —
235 Take care of them, Kreon; do this for me.

And will you let me touch them with my hands
A last time, and let us weep together?
Be kind, my lord,
Great prince, be kind!
Could I but touch them,
They would be mine again, as when I had my
240 eyes.

(*Enter Antigone and Ismene, attended.*)

Ah, God!
Is it my dearest children I hear weeping?
Has Kreon pitied me and sent my daughters?
KREON: Yes, Oedipus: I knew that they were dear
to you
In the old days, and know you must love them
245 still.

OEDIPUS: May God bless you for this — and be a
friendlier
Guardian to you than he has been to me!

Children, where are you?
Come quickly to my hands: they are your
brother's —
Hands that have brought your father's once clear
eyes 250
To this way of seeing —
Ah dearest ones,
I had neither sight nor knowledge then, your
father
By the woman who was the source of his own
life!
And I weep for you — having no strength to see
you — ,
I weep for you when I think of the bitterness 255
That men will visit upon you all your lives.
What homes, what festivals can you attend
Without being forced to depart again in tears?
And when you come to marriageable age,
Where is the man, my daughters, who would
dare 260
Risk the bane that lies on all my children?
Is there any evil wanting? Your father killed
His father; sowed the womb of her who bore
him;
Engendered you at the fount of his own
existence!
That is what they will say of you.

Then, whom 265
Can you ever marry? There are no bridegrooms
for you,
And your lives must wither away in sterile
dreaming.

O Kreon, son of Menoikeus!
You are the only father my daughters have,
Since we, their parents, are both of us gone for
ever. 270
They are your own blood: you will not let them
Fall into beggary and loneliness;
You will keep them from the miseries that are
mine!
Take pity on them; see, they are only children,
Friendless except for you. Promise me this, 275
Great prince, and give me your hand in token
of it.

(*Kreon clasps his right hand.*)

Children:
I could say much, if you could understand me,
But as it is, I have only this prayer for you:

80   Live where you can, be as happy as you can —
          Happier, please God, than God has made your
              father.
      KREON: Enough. You have wept enough. Now go
              within.
      OEDIPUS: I must; but it is hard.
      KREON: Time eases all things.
      OEDIPUS: You know my mind, then?
      KREON: Say what you desire.
      OEDIPUS: Send me from Thebes!
85   KREON: God grant that I may!
      OEDIPUS: But since God hates me . . .
      KREON: No, he will grant your wish.
      OEDIPUS: You promise?
      KREON: I can not speak beyond my knowledge.
      OEDIPUS: Then lead me in.
      KREON: Come now, and leave your children.
      OEDIPUS: No! Do not take them from me!

KREON: Think no longer
      That you are in command here, but rather think   290
      How, when you were, you served your own
          destruction.

(*Exeunt into the house all but the Chorus; the Choragos chants directly to the audience.*)

CHORAGOS: Men of Thebes: look upon Oedipus.

This is the king who solved the famous riddle
And towered up, most powerful of men.
No mortal eyes but looked on him with envy,   295
Yet in the end ruin swept over him.

Let every man in mankind's frailty
Consider his last day; and let none
Presume on his good fortune until he find
Life, at his death, a memory without pain.   300

ANTIGONE

Antigone was Sophocles' thirty-second play, produced in March 441 B.C., when he was in his mid-fifties. It drew a powerful response from its audience partly because it portrayed the conflict between two proud, willful people: Antigone, a daughter of Oedipus and Iokaste, and Kreon, Iokaste's brother and the king of Thebes. Another reason for its success was its portrayal of the individual's struggle against a tyrannical king. Athens had enjoyed thirty years of peace with its archrival Sparta, but it was moving slowly toward war, and the memory of previous tyrants — both good, like Peisistratus, and bad, like his son Hippias — remained in the minds of Sophocles' audience.

It has never been easy to see which of the two main characters is correct. Yet the play is named for Antigone, not for Kreon. Kreon's portrayal as a tyrant content to take up the state as his private property tells us that he is not to be fully trusted. At the same time, Antigone knows that the social mores of Thebes imply that a citizen must obey the ruler. Antigone's great courage makes the audience feel intense sympathy and admiration for her. She is a martyr to her beliefs, an ancient Joan of Arc.

The main conflict in *Antigone* centers on a distinction between law and justice, the conflict between a human law and a higher law. Kreon, the uncle of Antigone and Ismene, has made a decree: Polyneices, the brother of Antigone and Ismene, was guilty not only of killing his brother Eteocles but also of attacking the state and, like all traitors, will be denied a proper burial. When the action of the play begins, Antigone is determined to give her brother the burial that ancient tradition and her religious beliefs demand.

The opening dialogue with Ismene clarifies the important distinction between human law and the higher law on which Antigone says she must act. Ismene declares simply that she cannot go against the law of the citizens. Kreon has been willful in establishing the law, but it is nonetheless the law. Antigone, knowing full well the consequences of defying Kreon, nonetheless acts on her principles.

The complex conflict between Antigone and Kreon occurs on the level of citizen and ruler and on a personal level in the relationship between Haimon, Kreon's son, and his intended bride, Antigone. The antagonism between Kreon and Haimon begins slowly, as Haimon appears to yield to the will of his father, but culminates in Haimon's ultimate rejection of his father by choosing to join Antigone in death.

When Teiresias reveals a prophecy of death and punishment and begs Kreon, for the sake of the suffering Thebes, to rescind his decree and give Polyneices a proper burial, Kreon willfully continues to heed his own declarations rather than oracular wisdom or the pleas of others.

By the time Kreon accepts Teiresias's prophecy, it is too late: He has lost his son, and his wife has killed herself. Power not only has corrupted Kreon but has taken from him the people about whom he cared most. He emerges as an unyielding tyrant, guilty of making some of the same mistakes that haunted Oedipus.

Antigone emerges as a heroine who presses forward in the full conviction that she is right. She must honor her dead brother at all costs. Even if she must break the law of the state, she must answer to what she regards as a higher law. As she says early in the play, she has "dared the crime of piety." Yet she has within her the complexity of all humans: She in one sense acts in the knowledge that she is right but in another dares Kreon to punish her. She challenges Kreon so boldly that her every move, coupled with Kreon's pride, forces him to harden his position and set in motion the ultimate tragedy — the loss of all he holds dear. This is yet one more tragic irony in the Theban trilogy.

Antigone in Performance

Antigone was performed frequently in ancient Greece and in Rome. Since the eighteenth century it has been produced in Europe and the Western Hemisphere in more or less its original form and in various adaptations and rewritings. Jean Cocteau combined his version with music by Arthur Honegger in 1930. It was rewritten and produced by Walter Hasenclever in 1917 as a protest against the First World War and then in 1944 by Jean Anouilh as a protest against Nazi occupation of Paris during World War II (see the excerpt on page 108). The Royal Shakespeare Company produced *Antigone* along with all the surviving Greek tragedies during the 1970s. Bertolt Brecht's production of *Antigone* in 1948 introduced a Gestapo officer and Nazi brutality. Athol Fugard's *The Island* (1973) features a remarkable production of *Antigone* as a play within a play, produced by convicts in a South African island jail as a Christmas entertainment for their jailers and specially invited white guests. Fugard found, as have so many other adapters and producers, that the political power of *Antigone* leaps out for virtually all contemporary audiences.

Sophocles (*c. 496–c. 406 B.C.*)

ANTIGONE   *441 B.C.*

TRANSLATED BY DUDLEY FITTS AND ROBERT FITZGERALD

Characters

ANTIGONE, } *daughters of Oedipus*
ISMENE,
EURYDICE, *wife of Kreon*
KREON, *King of Thebes*
HAIMON, *son of Kreon*
TEIRESIAS, *a blind seer*
A SENTRY
A MESSENGER
CHORUS

Scene: *Before the palace of Kreon, King of Thebes. A central double door, and two lateral doors. A platform extends the length of the facade, and from this platform three steps lead down into the orchestra, or chorus-ground.*

Time: *Dawn of the day after the repulse of the Argive army from the assault on Thebes.*

PROLOGUE°

(*Antigone and Ismene enter from the central door of the palace.*)

ANTIGONE: Ismene, dear sister,
  You would think that we had already suffered
    enough
  For the curse on Oedipus.°

[*Note:* The line numbers to the original Greek text are cited in brackets at the top of the page.]
Prologue: Portion of the play explaining the background and current action.   **3. curse on Oedipus:** Oedipus, King of Thebes and the father of Antigone and Ismene, had been abandoned by his parents as an infant after the oracle foretold that he would one day kill his father and marry his mother. Rescued by a shepherd and raised by the king of Corinth, Oedipus returned years later to Thebes and unknowingly lived out the oracle's prophecy by killing Laios and marrying Iokaste. After his two sons, Eteocles and Polyneices, killed each other in combat, the throne went to Kreon, Iokaste's brother.

I cannot imagine any grief
That you and I have not gone through. And
  now —   5
Have they told you of the new decree of our
  King Kreon?
ISMENE: I have heard nothing: I know
  That two sisters lost two brothers, a double
    death
  In a single hour; and I know that the Argive
    army
  Fled in the night; but beyond this, nothing.   10
ANTIGONE: I thought so. And that is why I wanted
  you
  To come out here with me. There is something
    we must do.
ISMENE: Why do you speak so strangely?
ANTIGONE: Listen, Ismene:
  Kreon buried our brother Eteocles   15
  With military honors, gave him a soldier's
    funeral,
  And it was right that he should; but Polyneices,
  Who fought as bravely and died as miserably, —
  They say that Kreon has sworn
  No one shall bury him, no one mourn for him,   20
  But his body must lie in the fields, a sweet
    treasure
  For carrion birds to find as they search for food.
  That is what they say, and our good Kreon is
    coming here
  To announce it publicly; and the penalty —
  Stoning to death in the public square!
                                        There it is,   25
  And now you can prove what you are:
  A true sister, or a traitor to your family.
ISMENE: Antigone, you are mad! What could I
  possibly do?
ANTIGONE: You must decide whether you will help
  me or not.
ISMENE: I do not understand you. Help you in
  what?   30
ANTIGONE: Ismene, I am going to bury him. Will
  you come?
ISMENE: Bury him! You have just said the new law
  forbids it.

ANTIGONE: He is my brother. And he is your
    brother, too.
ISMENE: But think of the danger! Think what Kreon
    will do!
ANTIGONE: Kreon is not strong enough to stand in
35   my way.
ISMENE: Ah sister!
    Oedipus died, everyone hating him
    For what his own search brought to light, his
      eyes
    Ripped out by his own hand; and Iocaste died,
    His mother and wife at once: she twisted the
40   cords
    That strangled her life; and our two brothers
      died,
    Each killed by the other's sword. And we are
      left:
    But oh, Antigone,
    Think how much more terrible than these
    Our own death would be if we should go
45   against Kreon
    And do what he has forbidden! We are only
      women,
    We cannot fight with men, Antigone!
    The law is strong, we must give in to the law
    In this thing, and in worse. I beg the Dead
50   To forgive me, but I am helpless: I must yield
    To those in authority. And I think it is
      dangerous business
    To be always meddling.
ANTIGONE: If that is what you think,
    I should not want you, even if you asked to
      come.
    You have made your choice, you can be what
      you want to be.
55   But I will bury him; and if I must die,
    I say that this crime is holy: I shall lie down
    With him in death, and I shall be as dear
    To him as he to me.
              It is the dead,
    Not the living, who make the longest demands:
    We die for ever . . .
60   You may do as you like,
    Since apparently the laws of the gods mean
      nothing to you.
ISMENE: They mean a great deal to me; but I have
    no strength
    To break laws that were made for the public
      good.
ANTIGONE: That must be your excuse, I suppose.
    But as for me,
    I will bury the brother I love.
65 ISMENE: Antigone,
    I am so afraid for you!

ANTIGONE: You need not be:
    You have yourself to consider, after all.
ISMENE: But no one must hear of this, you must tell
    no one!
    I will keep it a secret, I promise!
ANTIGONE: O tell it! Tell everyone!
    Think how they'll hate you when it all comes
      out   70
    If they learn that you knew about it all the time!
ISMENE: So fiery! You should be cold with fear.
ANTIGONE: Perhaps. But I am doing only what I
    must.
ISMENE: But can you do it? I say that you cannot.
ANTIGONE: Very well: when my strength gives out,   75
    I shall do no more.
ISMENE: Impossible things should not be tried at all.
ANTIGONE: Go away, Ismene:
    I shall be hating you soon, and the dead will
      too,
    For your words are hateful. Leave me my foolish
      plan: 80
    I am not afraid of the danger; if it means death,
    It will not be the worst of deaths — death
      without honor.
ISMENE: Go then, if you feel that you must.
    You are unwise,
    But a loyal friend indeed to those who love you.   85

(*Exit into the palace. Antigone goes off, left. Enter
the Chorus.*)

PARODOS° • *Strophe° 1*

CHORUS: Now the long blade of the sun, lying
    Level east to west, touches with glory
    Thebes of the Seven Gates. Open, unlidded
    Eye of golden day! O marching light
    Across the eddy and rush of Dirce's stream,°   5
    Striking the white shields of the enemy
    Thrown headlong backward from the blaze of
      morning!
CHORAGOS:° Polyneices their commander
    Roused them with windy phrases,
    He the wild eagle screaming   10
    Insults above our land,
    His wings their shields of snow,
    His crest their marshalled helms.

Parodos: The song or ode chanted by the Chorus on their
entry. **Strophe:** Song sung by the Chorus as they danced
from stage right to stage left. **5. Dirce's stream:** River near
Thebes. **8. Choragos:** Leader of the Chorus.

RIGHT: Antigone (Martha Henry) reassures Ismene in the Repertory Theatre of Lincoln Center production of *Antigone* at the Vivian Beaumont Theatre, directed by John Hirsch in 1971. FAR RIGHT: Kreon (Philip Bosco), Antigone, and Haimon (David Birney).

Antistrophe° 1

CHORUS: Against our seven gates in a yawning ring
15   The famished spears came onward in the night;
      But before his jaws were sated with our blood,
      Or pinefire took the garland of our towers,
      He was thrown back, and as he turned, great
          Thebes —
      No tender victim for his noisy power —
20   Rose like a dragon behind him, shouting war.

Antistrophe: Song sung by the Chorus following the Strophe, as they danced back from stage left to stage right.

CHORAGOS: **For God hates utterly**
      The bray of bragging tongues;
      And when he beheld their smiling,
      Their swagger of golden helms,
      The frown of his thunder blasted   25
      Their first man from our walls.

Strophe 2

CHORUS: We heard his shout of triumph high in the
          air
      Turn to a scream; far out in a flaming arc

He fell with his windy torch, and the earth
    struck him.
30 And others storming in fury no less than his
    Found shock of death in the dusty joy of battle.
CHORAGOS: Seven captains at seven gates
    Yielded their clanging arms to the god
    That bends the battle-line and breaks it.
35 These two only, brothers in blood,
    Face to face in matchless rage,
    Mirroring each the other's death,
    Clashed in long combat.

Antistrophe 2

CHORUS: But now in the beautiful morning of
    victory
40 Let Thebes of the many chariots sing for joy!

With hearts for dancing we'll take leave of war:
Our temples shall be sweet with hymns of
    praise,
And the long nights shall echo with our chorus.

SCENE 1

CHORAGOS: But now at last our new King is
    coming:
  Kreon of Thebes, Menoikeus' son.
  In this auspicious dawn of his reign
  What are the new complexities
  That shifting Fate has woven for him?   5
  What is his counsel? Why has he summoned
  The old men to hear him?

(*Enter Kreon from the palace, center. He addresses the Chorus from the top step.*)

KREON: Gentlemen: I have the honor to inform you
that our Ship of State, which recent storms have
10   threatened to destroy, has come safely to harbor
at last, guided by the merciful wisdom of Heaven.
I have summoned you here this morning because
I know that I can depend upon you: your devotion
to King Laios was absolute; you never hesitated in
15   your duty to our late ruler Oedipus; and when
Oedipus died, your loyalty was transferred to his
children. Unfortunately, as you know, his two sons,
the princes Eteocles and Polyneices, have killed each
other in battle; and I, as the next in blood, have
20   succeeded to the full power of the throne.
    I am aware, of course, that no Ruler can expect
complete loyalty from his subjects until he has been
tested in office. Nevertheless, I say to you at the
very outset that I have nothing but contempt for
25   the kind of Governor who is afraid, for whatever
reason, to follow the course that he knows is best
for the State; and as for the man who sets private
friendship above the public welfare, — I have no
use for him, either. I call God to witness that if I
30   saw my country headed for ruin, I should not be
afraid to speak out plainly; and I need hardly remind
you that I would never have any dealings with an
enemy of the people. No one values friendship more
highly than I; but we must remember that friends
35   made at the risk of wrecking our Ship are not real
friends at all.
    These are my principles, at any rate, and that
is why I have made the following decision concerning
the sons of Oedipus: Eteocles, who died as a man
40   should die, fighting for his country, is to be buried
with full military honors, with all the ceremony
that is usual when the greatest heroes die; but his
brother Polyneices, who broke his exile to come
back with fire and sword against his native city
45   and the shrines of his fathers' gods, whose one idea
was to spill the blood of his blood and sell his own
people into slavery — Polyneices, I say, is to have
no burial: no man is to touch him or say the least
prayer for him; he shall lie on the plain, unburied;
50   and the birds and the scavenging dogs can do with
him whatever they like.
    This is my command, and you can see the wisdom
behind it. As long as I am King, no traitor is going
to be honored with the loyal man. But whoever
55   shows by word and deed that he is on the side of
the State, — he shall have my respect while he is
living and my reverence when he is dead.
CHORAGOS: If that is your will, Kreon son of
    Menoikeus,

You have the right to enforce it: we are yours.
KREON: That is my will. Take care that you do
    your part.   60
CHORAGOS: We are old men: let the younger ones
    carry it out.
KREON: I do not mean that: the sentries have been
    appointed.
CHORAGOS: Then what is it that you would have us
    do?
KREON: You will give no support to whoever
    breaks this law.
CHORAGOS: Only a crazy man is in love with
    death!   65
KREON: And death it is; yet money talks, and the
    wisest
    Have sometimes been known to count a few
    coins too many.

(*Enter Sentry from left.*)

SENTRY: I'll not say that I'm out of breath from running,
    King, because every time I stopped to think about
    what I have to tell you, I felt like going back. And   70
    all the time a voice kept saying, "You fool, don't
    you know you're walking straight into trouble?";
    and then another voice: "Yes, but if you let some-
    body else get the news to Kreon first, it will be
    even worse than that for you!" But good sense   75
    won out, at least I hope it was good sense, and
    here I am with a story that makes no sense at all;
    but I'll tell it anyhow, because, as they say, what's
    going to happen's going to happen and —
KREON: Come to the point. What have you to say?   80
SENTRY: I did not do it. I did not see who did it. You
    must not punish me for what someone else has
    done.
KREON: A comprehensive defense! More effective,
    perhaps,
    If I knew its purpose. Come: what is it?   85
SENTRY: A dreadful thing . . . I don't know how to
    put it —
KREON: Out with it!
SENTRY: Well, then;
    The dead man —
                            Polyneices —

(*Pause. The Sentry is overcome, fumbles for words.
Kreon waits impassively.*)

                                        out there —
                                        someone, —
    New dust on the slimy flesh!

(*Pause. No sign from Kreon.*)

    Someone has given it burial that way, and   90
    Gone . . .

(*Long pause. Kreon finally speaks with deadly control.*)

KREON: And the man who dared do this?
SENTRY: I swear I
   Do not know! You must believe me!
                                    Listen:
   The ground was dry, not a sign of digging, no,
   Not a wheeltrack in the dust, no trace of
95   anyone.
   It was when they relieved us this morning: and
      one of them,
   The corporal, pointed to it.
                           There it was,
   The strangest —
            Look:
   The body, just mounded over with light dust:
      you see?
00 Not buried really, but as if they'd covered it
   Just enough for the ghost's peace. And no sign
   Of dogs or any wild animal that had been there.

   And then what a scene there was! Every man of
      us
   Accusing the other: we all proved the other man
      did it,
05 We all had proof that we could not have done
      it.
   We were ready to take hot iron in our hands,
   Walk through fire, swear by all the gods,
   It was not I!
   I do not know who it was, but it was not I!

(*Kreon's rage has been mounting steadily, but the
Sentry is too intent upon his story to notice it.*)

   And then, when this came to nothing, someone
10   said
   A thing that silenced us and made us stare
   Down at the ground: you had to be told the
      news,
   And one of us had to do it! We threw the dice,
   And the bad luck fell to me. So here I am,
15 No happier to be here than you are to have me:
   Nobody likes the man who brings bad news.
CHORAGOS: I have been wondering, King: can it be
      that the gods have done this?
KREON (*furiously*): Stop!
20 Must you doddering wrecks
   Go out of your heads entirely? "The gods"!
   Intolerable!
   The gods favor this corpse? Why? How had he
      served them?
   Tried to loot their temples, burn their images,
25 Yes, and the whole State, and its laws with it!
   Is it your senile opinion that the gods love to
      honor bad men?
   A pious thought! —
                    No, from the very beginning

There have been those who have whispered
   together,
Stiff-necked anarchists, putting their heads
   together,
Scheming against me in alleys. These are the
   men,   130
And they have bribed my own guard to do this
   thing.
(*Sententiously.*) Money!
There's nothing in the world so demoralizing as
   money.
Down go your cities,
Homes gone, men gone, honest hearts corrupted, 135
Crookedness of all kinds, and all for money!
(*To Sentry.*)   But you —
I swear by God and by the throne of God,
The man who has done this thing shall pay for
   it!
Find that man, bring him here to me, or your
   death
Will be the least of your problems: I'll string
   you up   140
Alive, and there will be certain ways to make
   you
Discover your employer before you die;
And the process may teach you a lesson you
   seem to have missed:
The dearest profit is sometimes all too dear:
That depends on the source. Do you understand
   me?   145
A fortune won is often misfortune.
SENTRY: King, may I speak?
KREON: Your very voice distresses me.
SENTRY: Are you sure that it is my voice, and not
   your conscience?
KREON: By God, he wants to analyze me now!
SENTRY: It is not what I say, but what has been
   done, that hurts you.   150
KREON: You talk too much.
SENTRY: Maybe; but I've done nothing.
KREON: Sold your soul for some silver: that's all
   you've done.
SENTRY: How dreadful it is when the right judge
   judges wrong!
KREON: Your figures of speech
   May entertain you now; but unless you bring me
      the man,   155
   You will get little profit from them in the end.
                    (*Exit Kreon into the palace.*)
SENTRY: "Bring me the man" — !
   I'd like nothing better than bringing him the
      man!
   But bring him or not, you have seen the last of
      me here.
   At any rate, I am safe!   (*Exit Sentry.*) 160

ODE° 1 • Strophe 1

CHORUS: Numberless are the world's wonders, but
    none
More wonderful than man; the stormgray sea
Yields to his prows, the huge crests bear him
    high;
Earth, holy and inexhaustible, is graven
5   With shining furrows where his plows have gone
Year after year, the timeless labor of stallions.

Antistrophe 1

The lightboned birds and beasts that cling to
    cover,
The lithe fish lighting their reaches of dim water,
All are taken, tamed in the net of his mind;
The lion on the hill, the wild horse windy-
    maned,
10   Resign to him; and his blunt yoke has broken
The sultry shoulders of the mountain bull.

Strophe 2

Words also, and thought as rapid as air,
He fashions to his good use; statecraft is his,
And his the skill that deflects the arrows of
15   snow,
The spears of winter rain: from every wind
He has made himself secure — from all but one:
In the late wind of death he cannot stand.

Antistrophe 2

O clear intelligence, force beyond all measure!
20   O fate of man, working both good and evil!
When the laws are kept, how proudly his city
    stands!
When the laws are broken, what of his city
    then?
Never may the anarchic man find rest at my
    hearth,
Never be it said that my thoughts are his
    thoughts.

SCENE 2

(Reenter Sentry leading Antigone.)

CHORAGOS: What does this mean? Surely this
    captive woman

Ode: Song sung by the Chorus.

Is the Princess, Antigone. Why should she be
    taken?
SENTRY: Here is the one who did it! We caught her
    In the very act of burying him. — Where is
    Kreon?
CHORAGOS: Just coming from the house.

(Enter Kreon, center.)

KREON: What has happened?   5
    Why have you come back so soon?
SENTRY (expansively):   O King,
    A man should never be too sure of anything:
    I would have sworn
    That you'd not see me here again: your anger
    Frightened me so, and the things you threatened
        me with;   10
    But how could I tell then
    That I'd be able to solve the case so soon?
    No dice-throwing this time: I was only too glad
        to come!
    Here is this woman. She is the guilty one:
    We found her trying to bury him.   15
    Take her, then; question her; judge her as you
        will.
    I am through with the whole thing now, and
        glad of it.
KREON: But this is Antigone! Why have you
    brought her here?
SENTRY: She was burying him, I tell you!
KREON (severely):   Is this the truth?
SENTRY: I saw her with my own eyes. Can I say
    more?   20
KREON: The details: come, tell me quickly!
SENTRY: It was like this:
    After those terrible threats of yours, King,
    We went back and brushed the dust away from
        the body.
    The flesh was soft by now, and stinking,
    So we sat on a hill to windward and kept guard. 25
    No napping this time! We kept each other
        awake.
    But nothing happened until the white round sun
    Whirled in the center of the round sky over us:
    Then, suddenly,
    A storm of dust roared up from the earth, and
        the sky
    Went out, the plain vanished with all its trees   30
    In the stinging dark. We closed our eyes and
        endured it.
    The whirlwind lasted a long time, but it passed;
    And then we looked, and there was Antigone!
    I have seen   35
    A mother bird come back to a stripped nest,
        heard
    Her crying bitterly a broken note or two
    For the young ones stolen. Just so, when this girl

Found the bare corpse, and all her love's work
    wasted,
She wept, and cried on heaven to damn the
40   hands
That had done this thing.
                And then she brought more dust
And sprinkled wine three times for her brother's
    ghost.

We ran and took her at once. She was not
    afraid,
Not even when we charged her with what she
    had done.
She denied nothing.
45   And this was a comfort to me,
And some uneasiness: for it is a good thing
To escape from death, but it is no great pleasure
To bring death to a friend.
               Yet I always say
There is nothing so comfortable as your own
    safe skin!
50 KREON (*slowly, dangerously*): And you, Antigone,
You with your head hanging, — do you confess
    this thing?
ANTIGONE: I do. I deny nothing.
KREON (*to Sentry*):   You may go.
               (*Exit Sentry.*)
(*To Antigone.*) Tell me, tell me briefly:
Had you heard my proclamation touching this
    matter?
55 ANTIGONE: It was public. Could I help hearing it?
KREON: And yet you dared defy the law.
ANTIGONE: I dared.
It was not God's proclamation. That final Justice
That rules the world below makes no such laws.

Your edict, King, was strong,
60 But all your strength is weakness itself against
The immortal unrecorded laws of God.
They are not merely now: they were, and shall
    be,
Operative for ever, beyond man utterly.

I knew I must die, even without your decree:
65 I am only mortal. And if I must die
Now, before it is my time to die,
Surely this is no hardship: can anyone
Living, as I live, with evil all about me,
Think Death less than a friend? This death of
    mine
70 Is of no importance; but if I had left my brother
Lying in death unburied, I should have suffered.
Now I do not.
          You smile at me. Ah Kreon,
Think me a fool, if you like; but it may well be
That a fool convicts me of folly.

CHORAGOS: Like father, like daughter: both
    headstrong, deaf to reason!   75
    She has never learned to yield.
KREON: She has much to learn.
The inflexible heart breaks first, the toughest
    iron
Cracks first, and the wildest horses bend their
    necks
At the pull of the smallest curb.
               Pride? In a slave?
This girl is guilty of a double insolence,   80
Breaking the given laws and boasting of it.
Who is the man here,
She or I, if this crime goes unpunished?
Sister's child, or more than sister's child,
Or closer yet in blood — she and her sister   85
Win bitter death for this!
(*To Servants.*)   Go, some of you,
Arrest Ismene. I accuse her equally.
Bring her: you will find her sniffling in the house
    there.

Her mind's a traitor: crimes kept in the dark
Cry for light, and the guardian brain shudders;   90
But how much worse than this
Is brazen boasting of barefaced anarchy!
ANTIGONE: Kreon, what more do you want than
    my death?
KREON: Nothing.
That gives me everything.
ANTIGONE: Then I beg you: kill me.
This talking is a great weariness: your words   95
Are distasteful to me, and I am sure that mine
Seem so to you. And yet they should not seem
    so:
I should have praise and honor for what I have
    done.
All these men here would praise me
Were their lips not frozen shut with fear of you.   100
(*Bitterly.*) Ah the good fortune of kings,
Licensed to say and do whatever they please!
KREON: You are alone here in that opinion.
ANTIGONE: No, they are with me. But they keep
    their tongues in leash.
KREON: Maybe. But you are guilty, and they are
    not.   105
ANTIGONE: There is no guilt in reverence for the
    dead.
KREON: But Eteocles — was he not your brother
    too?
ANTIGONE: My brother too.
KREON: And you insult his memory?
ANTIGONE (*softly*): The dead man would not say
    that I insult it.
KREON: He would: for you honor a traitor as much
    as him.   110

TOP LEFT: Kreon (F. Murray Abraham) in a scene from the 1982 New York Shakespeare Festival production directed by Joseph Chaikin. BOTTOM LEFT: Antigone (Lisa Banes) steadfastly admitting her guilt. ABOVE: The Chorus urges Kreon to change his decree before it is too late.

ANTIGONE: His own brother, traitor or not, and
    equal in blood.
KREON: He made war on his country. Eteocles
    defended it.
ANTIGONE: Nevertheless, there are honors due all
    the dead.
KREON: But not the same for the wicked as for the
    just.
115 ANTIGONE: Ah Kreon, Kreon,
    Which of us can say what the gods hold wicked?
KREON: An enemy is an enemy, even dead.
ANTIGONE: It is my nature to join in love, not hate.

KREON (*finally losing patience*): Go join them then;
    if you must have your love,
    Find it in hell!   120
CHORAGOS: But see, Ismene comes:

(*Enter Ismene, guarded.*)

    Those tears are sisterly, the cloud
    That shadows her eyes rains down gentle
      sorrow.
KREON: You too, Ismene,
    Snake in my ordered house, sucking my blood   125
    Stealthily — and all the time I never knew
    That these two sisters were aiming at my throne!
                    Ismene,
    Do you confess your share in this crime, or deny
      it?
    Answer me.

130   ISMENE: Yes, if she will let me say so. I am guilty.
       ANTIGONE (*coldly*): No, Ismene. You have no right
            to say so.
          You would not help me, and I will not have you
            help me.
       ISMENE: But now I know what you meant; and I
            am here
          To join you, to take my share of punishment.
       ANTIGONE: The dead man and the gods who rule
135   the dead
          Know whose act this was. Words are not
            friends.
       ISMENE: Do you refuse me, Antigone? I want to die
            with you:
          I too have a duty that I must discharge to the
            dead.
       ANTIGONE: You shall not lessen my death by
            sharing it.
140   ISMENE: What do I care for life when you are dead?
       ANTIGONE: Ask Kreon. You're always hanging on
            his opinions.
       ISMENE: You are laughing at me. Why, Antigone?
       ANTIGONE: It's a joyless laughter, Ismene.
       ISMENE: But can I do nothing?
       ANTIGONE: Yes. Save yourself. I shall not envy you.
          There are those who will praise you; I shall have
145   honor, too.
       ISMENE: But we are equally guilty!
       ANTIGONE: No more, Ismene.
          You are alive, but I belong to Death.
       KREON (*to the Chorus*): Gentlemen, I beg you to
            observe these girls:
          One has just now lost her mind; the other,
150   It seems, has never had a mind at all.
       ISMENE: Grief teaches the steadiest minds to waver,
            King.
       KREON: Yours certainly did, when you assumed
            guilt with the guilty!
       ISMENE: But how could I go on living without her?
       KREON: You are.
          She is already dead.
       ISMENE: But your own son's bride!
       KREON: There are places enough for him to push
155   his plow.
          I want no wicked women for my sons!
       ISMENE: O dearest Haimon, how your father
            wrongs you!
       KREON: I've had enough of your childish talk of
            marriage!
       CHORAGOS: Do you really intend to steal this girl
            from your son?
       KREON: No; Death will do that for me.
160   CHORAGOS: Then she must die?
       KREON (*ironically*): You dazzle me.
                        — But enough of this talk!

(*To Guards.*) You, there, take them away and
     guard them well:
For they are but women, and even brave men
     run
When they see Death coming.
          (*Exeunt° Ismene, Antigone, and Guards.*)

ODE 2 • *Strophe 1*

CHORUS: Fortunate is the man who has never tasted
     God's vengeance!
   Where once the anger of heaven has struck, that
     house is shaken
For ever: damnation rises behind each child
Like a wave cresting out of the black northeast,
When the long darkness under sea roars up   5
And bursts drumming death upon the
     windwhipped sand.

Antistrophe 1

I have seen this gathering sorrow from time long
     past
Loom upon Oedipus' children: generation from
     generation
Takes the compulsive rage of the enemy god.
So lately this last flower of Oedipus' line   10
Drank the sunlight! but now a passionate word
And a handful of dust have closed up all its
     beauty.

Strophe 2

   What mortal arrogance
   Transcends the wrath of Zeus?
Sleep cannot lull him nor the effortless long
     months   15
Of the timeless gods: but he is young for ever,
And his house is the shining day of high
     Olympos.
   All that is and shall be,
   And all the past, is his.
No pride on earth is free of the curse of heaven.   20

Antistrophe 2

   The straying dreams of men
   May bring them ghosts of joy:
But as they drowse, the waking embers burn
     them;

[S.D.] *Exeunt:* Latin for "they go out."

Or they walk with fixed eyes, as blind men
    walk.
But the ancient wisdom speaks for our own
25   time:
    Fate works most for woe
    With Folly's fairest show.
Man's little pleasure is the spring of sorrow.

SCENE 3

CHORAGOS: But here is Haimon, King, the last of
    all your sons.
    Is it grief for Antigone that brings him here,
    And bitterness at being robbed of his bride?

(Enter Haimon.)

KREON: We shall soon see, and no need of diviners.
                              — Son,
5   You have heard my final judgment on that girl:
    Have you come here hating me, or have you
      come
    With deference and with love, whatever I do?
HAIMON: I am your son, father. You are my guide.
    You make things clear for me, and I obey you.
    No marriage means more to me than your
10   continuing wisdom.
KREON: Good. That is the way to behave:
    subordinate
    Everything else, my son, to your father's will.
    This is what a man prays for, that he may get
    Sons attentive and dutiful in his house,
15   Each one hating his father's enemies,
    Honoring his father's friends. But if his sons
    Fail him, if they turn out unprofitably,
    What has he fathered but trouble for himself
    And amusement for the malicious?
                              So you are right
20   Not to lose your head over this woman.
    Your pleasure with her would soon grow cold,
      Haimon,
    And then you'd have a hellcat in bed and
      elsewhere.
    Let her find her husband in Hell!
    Of all the people in this city, only she
25   Has had contempt for my law and broken it.

    Do you want me to show myself weak before
      the people?
    Or to break my sworn word? No, and I will
      not.
    The woman dies.
    I suppose she'll plead "family ties." Well, let her.
30   If I permit my own family to rebel,

How shall I earn the world's obedience?
Show me the man who keeps his house in hand,
He's fit for public authority.
                         I'll have no dealings
With lawbreakers, critics of the government:
Whoever is chosen to govern should be
    obeyed —   35
Must be obeyed, in all things, great and small,
Just and unjust! O Haimon,
The man who knows how to obey, and that
    man only,
Knows how to give commands when the time
    comes.
You can depend on him, no matter how fast   40
The spears come: he's a good soldier, he'll stick
    it out.
Anarchy, anarchy! Show me a greater evil!
This is why cities tumble and the great houses
    rain down,
This is what scatters armies!
No, no: good lives are made so by discipline.   45
We keep the laws then, and the lawmakers,
And no woman shall seduce us. If we must lose,
Let's lose to a man, at least! Is a woman
    stronger than we?
CHORAGOS: Unless time has rusted my wits,
    What you say, King, is said with point and
      dignity.   50
HAIMON *(boyishly earnest)*: Father:
    Reason is God's crowning gift to man, and you
      are right
    To warn me against losing mine. I cannot say —
    I hope that I shall never want to say! — that
      you
    Have reasoned badly. Yet there are other men   55
    Who can reason, too; and their opinions might
      be helpful.
    You are not in a position to know everything
    That people say or do, or what they feel:
    Your temper terrifies — everyone
    Will tell you only what you like to hear.   60
    But I, at any rate, can listen; and I have heard
      them
    Muttering and whispering in the dark about this
      girl.
    They say no woman has ever, so unreasonably,
    Died so shameful a death for a generous act:
    "She covered her brother's body. Is this
      indecent?   65
    She kept him from dogs and vultures. Is this a
      crime?
    Death? — She should have all the honor that we
      can give her!"

    This is the way they talk out there in the city.

You must believe me:

70 Nothing is closer to me than your happiness.
What could be closer? Must not any son
Value his father's fortune as his father does his?
I beg you, do not be unchangeable:
Do not believe that you alone can be right.

75 The man who thinks that,
The man who maintains that only he has the
    power
To reason correctly, the gift to speak, the
    soul —
A man like that, when you know him, turns out
    empty.
It is not reason never to yield to reason!

80 In flood time you can see how some trees bend,
And because they bend, even their twigs are safe,
While stubborn trees are torn up, roots and all.
And the same thing happens in sailing:
Make your sheet fast, never slacken, — and over
    you go,
Head over heels and under: and there's your
85   voyage.
Forget you are angry! Let yourself be moved!
I know I am young; but please let me say this:
The ideal condition
Would be, I admit, that men should be right by
    instinct;
90 But since we are all too likely to go astray,
The reasonable thing is to learn from those who
    can teach.
CHORAGOS: You will do well to listen to him, King,
If what he says is sensible. And you, Haimon,
Must listen to your father. — Both speak well.
KREON: You consider it right for a man of my
95   years and experience
To go to school to a boy?
HAIMON: It is not right
If I am wrong. But if I am young, and right,
What does my age matter?
KREON: You think it right to stand up for an
    anarchist?
100 HAIMON: Not at all. I pay no respect to criminals.
KREON: Then she is not a criminal?
HAIMON: The City would deny it, to a man.
KREON: And the City proposes to teach me how to
    rule?
HAIMON: Ah. Who is it that's talking like a boy
    now?
KREON: My voice is the one voice giving orders in
105   this City!
HAIMON: It is no City if it takes orders from one
    voice.
KREON: The State is the King!

HAIMON: Yes, if the State is a desert.
(*Pause.*)
KREON: This boy, it seems, has sold out to a
    woman.
HAIMON: If you are a woman: my concern is only
    for you.
KREON: So? Your "concern"! In a public brawl
    with your father!   110
HAIMON: How about you, in a public brawl with
    justice?
KREON: With justice, when all that I do is within
    my rights?
HAIMON: You have no right to trample on God's
    right.
KREON (*completely out of control*): Fool, adolescent
    fool! Taken in by a woman!
HAIMON: You'll never see me taken in by anything
    vile.   115
KREON: Every word you say is for her!
HAIMON (*quietly, darkly*):   And for you.
And for me. And for the gods under the earth.
KREON: You'll never marry her while she lives.
HAIMON: Then she must die. — But her death will
    cause another.
KREON: Another?   120
Have you lost your senses? Is this an open
    threat?
HAIMON: There is no threat in speaking to
    emptiness.
KREON: I swear you'll regret this superior tone of
    yours!
You are the empty one!
HAIMON: If you were not my father,
I'd say you were perverse.   125
KREON: You girl-struck fool, don't play at words
    with me!
HAIMON: I am sorry. You prefer silence.
KREON: Now, by God —
I swear, by all the gods in heaven above us,
You'll watch it, I swear you shall!
(*To the Servants.*)   Bring her out!
Bring the woman out! Let her die before his
    eyes!   130
Here, this instant, with her bridegroom beside
    her!
HAIMON: Not here, no; she will not die here, King.
And you will never see my face again.
Go on raving as long as you've a friend to
    endure you.   (*Exit Haimon.*)
CHORAGOS: Gone, gone.   135
Kreon, a young man in a rage is dangerous!
KREON: Let him do, or dream to do, more than a
    man can.

He shall not save these girls from death.
CHORAGOS:　　　　　　　　　These girls?
You have sentenced them both?
KREON:　　　　　　　　　No, you are right.
40　I will not kill the one whose hands are clean.
CHORAGOS: But Antigone?
KREON (*somberly*):　　　I will carry her far away
Out there in the wilderness, and lock her
Living in a vault of stone. She shall have food,
As the custom is, to absolve the State of her
death.
45　And there let her pray to the gods of hell:
They are her only gods:
Perhaps they will show her an escape from
death,
Or she may learn,
　　　　　　　though late,
That piety shown the dead is pity in vain.
　　　　　　　　　　　(*Exit Kreon.*)

ODE 3 • *Strophe*

CHORUS: Love, unconquerable
Waster of rich men, keeper
Of warm lights and all-night vigil
In the soft face of a girl:
5　Sea-wanderer, forest-visitor!
Even the pure Immortals cannot escape you,
And mortal man, in his one day's dusk,
Trembles before your glory.

Antistrophe

Surely you swerve upon ruin
10　The just man's consenting heart,
As here you have made bright anger
Strike between father and son —
And none has conquered but Love!
A girl's glance working the will of heaven:
15　Pleasure to her alone who mocks us,
Merciless Aphrodite.°

SCENE 4

CHORAGOS (*as Antigone enters guarded*): But I can
no longer stand in awe of this,
Nor, seeing what I see, keep back my tears.

16. Aphrodite: Goddess of love and beauty.

Here is Antigone, passing to that chamber
Where all find sleep at last.

Strophe 1

ANTIGONE: Look upon me, friends, and pity me　5
Turning back at the night's edge to say
Good-by to the sun that shines for me no
longer;
Now sleepy Death
Summons me down to Acheron,° that cold
shore:
There is no bridesong there, nor any music.　10
CHORUS: Yet not unpraised, not without a kind of
honor,
You walk at last into the underworld;
Untouched by sickness, broken by no sword.
What woman has ever found your way to death?

Antistrophe 1

ANTIGONE: How often I have heard the story of
Niobe,°　　　　　　　　　　　　　15
Tantalos' wretched daughter, how the stone
Clung fast about her, ivy-close: and they say
The rain falls endlessly
And sifting soft snow; her tears are never done.
I feel the loneliness of her death in mine.　20
CHORUS: But she was born of heaven, and you
Are woman, woman-born. If her death is yours,
A mortal woman's, is this not for you
Glory in our world and in the world beyond?

Strophe 2

ANTIGONE: You laugh at me. Ah, friends, friends,　25
Can you not wait until I am dead? O Thebes,
O men many-charioted, in love with Fortune,
Dear springs of Dirce, sacred Theban grove,
Be witnesses for me, denied all pity,
Unjustly judged! and think a word of love　30
For her whose path turns
Under dark earth, where there are no more
tears.

9. Acheron: River in Hades, domain of the dead. **15. Niobe:** When Niobe's many children (up to twenty in some accounts) were slain in punishment for their mother's boastfulness, Niobe was turned into a stone on Mount Sipylus. Her tears became the mountain's streams.

CHORUS: You have passed beyond human daring
         and come at last
   Into a place of stone where Justice sits.
35 I cannot tell
   What shape of your father's guilt appears in this.

Antistrophe 2

ANTIGONE: You have touched it at last: that bridal
         bed
   Unspeakable, horror of son and mother
         mingling:
   Their crime, infection of all our family!
40 O Oedipus, father and brother!
   Your marriage strikes from the grave to murder
         mine.
   I have been a stranger here in my own land:
   All my life
   The blasphemy of my birth has followed me.
15 CHORUS: Reverence is a virtue, but strength
   Lives in established law: that must prevail.
   You have made your choice,
   Your death is the doing of your conscious hand.

Epode°

ANTIGONE: Then let me go, since all your words
         are bitter,
50 And the very light of the sun is cold to me.
   Lead me to my vigil, where I must have
   Neither love nor lamentation; no song, but
         silence.

(*Kreon interrupts impatiently.*)

KREON: If dirges and planned lamentations could
         put off death,
   Men would be singing for ever.
   (*To the Servants.*)   Take her, go!
55 You know your orders: take her to the vault
   And leave her alone there. And if she lives or
         dies,
   That's her affair, not ours: our hands are clean.
ANTIGONE: O tomb, vaulted bride-bed in eternal
         rock,
   Soon I shall be with my own again
   Where Persephone° welcomes the thin ghosts
60   underground:
   And I shall see my father again, and you,
         mother,

Epode: Song sung by the Chorus while standing still after
singing the strophe and antistrophe. **60. Persephone:** Abducted by Pluto, god of the underworld, to be his queen.

And dearest Polyneices —
                       dearest indeed
   To me, since it was my hand
   That washed him clean and poured the ritual
         wine:
   And my reward is death before my time!   65

   And yet, as men's hearts know, I have done no
         wrong,
   I have not sinned before God. Or if I have,
   I shall know the truth in death. But if the guilt
   Lies upon Kreon who judged me, then, I pray,
   May his punishment equal my own.
CHORAGOS: O passionate heart, 70
   Unyielding, tormented still by the same winds!
KREON: Her guards shall have good cause to regret
         their delaying.
ANTIGONE: Ah! That voice is like the voice of
         death!
KREON: I can give you no reason to think you are
         mistaken.
ANTIGONE: Thebes, and you my fathers' gods,   75
   And rulers of Thebes, you see me now, the last
   Unhappy daughter of a line of kings,
   Your kings, led away to death. You will
         remember
   What things I suffer, and at what men's hands,
   Because I would not transgress the laws of
         heaven.   80
   (*To the Guards, simply.*) Come: let us wait no
         longer.   (*Exit Antigone, left, guarded.*)

ODE 4 • Strophe 1

CHORUS: All Danae's beauty was locked away
   In a brazen cell where the sunlight could not
         come:
   A small room still as any grave, enclosed her.
   Yet she was a princess too,
   And Zeus in a rain of gold poured love upon
         her.°   5
   O child, child,
   No power in wealth or war
   Or tough sea-blackened ships
   Can prevail against untiring Destiny!

1–5. All Danae's beauty . . . poured love upon her: Locked
away to prevent the fulfillment of a prophecy that she would
bear a son who would kill her father, Danae was nonetheless
impregnated by Zeus, who came to her in a shower of gold.
The prophecy was fulfilled by the son that came of their
union.

Antistrophe 1

10   And Dryas' son° also, that furious king,
     Bore the god's prisoning anger for his pride:
     Sealed up by Dionysos in deaf stone,
     His madness died among echoes.
     So at the last he learned what dreadful power
15   His tongue had mocked:
     For he had profaned the revels,
     And fired the wrath of the nine
     Implacable Sisters° that love the sound of the
        flute.

Strophe 2

     And old men tell a half-remembered tale
20   Of horror° where a dark ledge splits the sea
     And a double surf beats on the gray shores:
     How a king's new woman, sick
     With hatred for the queen he had imprisoned,
     Ripped out his two sons' eyes with her bloody
        hands
25   While grinning Ares° watched the shuttle plunge
     Four times: four blind wounds crying for
        revenge,

Antistrophe 2

     Crying, tears and blood mingled. — Piteously
        born,
     Those sons whose mother was of heavenly birth!
     Her father was the god of the North Wind
30   And she was cradled by gales,
     She raced with young colts on the glittering hills
     And walked untrammeled in the open light:
     But in her marriage deathless Fate found means
     To build a tomb like yours for all her joy.

SCENE 5

*(Enter blind Teiresias, led by a boy. The opening
speeches of Teiresias should be in singsong contrast
to the realistic lines of Kreon.)*

10. **Dryas' son:** King Lycurgus of Thrace, whom Dionysus,
god of wine, caused to be stricken with madness.
18. **Sisters:** The Muses, nine sister goddesses who presided
over poetry and music, arts and sciences.   **19–20. half-
remembered tale of horror:** The second wife of King Phineas
blinded the sons of his first wife, Cleopatra, whom Phineas
had imprisoned in a cave.   25. **Ares:** God of war.

TEIRESIAS: This is the way the blind man comes,
     Princes, Princes,
     Lockstep, two heads lit by the eyes of one.
KREON: What new thing have you to tell us, old
     Teiresias?
TEIRESIAS: I have much to tell you: listen to the
     prophet, Kreon.
KREON: I am not aware that I have ever failed to
     listen.   5
TERESIAS: Then you have done wisely, King, and
     ruled well.
KREON: I admit my debt to you. But what have
     you to say?
TERESIAS: This, Kreon: you stand once more on the
     edge of fate.
KREON: What do you mean? Your words are a
     kind of dread.
TEIRESIAS: Listen, Kreon: 10
     I was sitting in my chair of augury, at the place
     Where the birds gather about me. They were all
        a-chatter,
     As is their habit, when suddenly I heard
     A strange note in their jangling, a scream, a
     Whirring fury; I knew that they were fighting,   15
     Tearing each other, dying
     In a whirlwind of wings clashing. And I was
        afraid.
     I began the rites of burnt-offering at the altar,
     But Hephaistos° failed me: instead of bright
        flame,
     There was only the sputtering slime of the fat
        thigh-flesh   20
     Melting: the entrails dissolved in gray smoke,
     The bare bone burst from the welter. And no
        blaze!

     This was a sign from heaven. My boy described
        it,
     Seeing for me as I see for others.
     I tell you, Kreon, you yourself have brought   25
     This new calamity upon us. Our hearths and
        altars
     Are stained with the corruption of dogs and
        carrion birds
     That glut themselves on the corpse of Oedipus'
        son.
     The gods are deaf when we pray to them, their
        fire
     Recoils from our offering, their birds of omen   30
     Have no cry of comfort, for they are gorged
     With the thick blood of the dead.
                              O my son,

19. **Hephaistos:** God of fire.

These are no trifles! Think: all men make
  mistakes,
But a good man yields when he knows his
  course is wrong,
35 And repairs the evil. The only crime is pride.

Give in to the dead man, then: do not fight with
  a corpse —
What glory is it to kill a man who is dead?
Think, I beg you:
It is for your own good that I speak as I do.
40 You should be able to yield for your own good.
KREON: It seems that prophets have made me their
  especial province.
All my life long
I have been a kind of butt for the dull arrows
Of doddering fortune-tellers!
                            No, Teiresias:
If your birds — if the great eagles of God
45 himself
Should carry him stinking bit by bit to heaven,
I would not yield. I am not afraid of pollution:
No man can defile the gods.
                        Do what you will,
Go into business, make money, speculate
50 In India gold or that synthetic gold from Sardis,
Get rich otherwise than by my consent to bury
  him.
Teiresias, it is a sorry thing when a wise man
Sells his wisdom, lets out his words for hire!
TEIRESIAS: Ah Kreon! Is there no man left in the
  world —
KREON: To do what? — Come, let's have the
55 aphorism!
TEIRESIAS: No man who knows that wisdom
  outweighs any wealth?
KREON: As surely as bribes are baser than any
  baseness.
TEIRESIAS: You are sick, Kreon! You are deathly
  sick!
KREON: As you say: it is not my place to challenge
  a prophet.
TEIRESIAS: Yet you have said my prophecy is for
60 sale.
KREON: The generation of prophets has always
  loved gold.
TEIRESIAS: The generation of kings has always loved
  brass.
KREON: You forget yourself! You are speaking to
  your King.
TEIRESIAS: I know it. You are a king because of me.
KREON: You have a certain skill; but you have sold
65 out.
TEIRESIAS: King, you will drive me to words that —

KREON: Say them, say them!
Only remember: I will not pay you for them.
TEIRESIAS: No, you will find them too costly.
KREON: No doubt. Speak:
Whatever you say, you will not change my will.
TEIRESIAS: Then take this, and take it to heart!   70
The time is not far off when you shall pay back
Corpse for corpse, flesh of your own flesh.
You have thrust the child of this world into
  living night,
You have kept from the gods below the child
  that is theirs:
The one in a grave before her death, the other, 75
Dead, denied the grave. This is your crime:
And the Furies° and the dark gods of Hell
Are swift with terrible punishment for you.

Do you want to buy me now, Kreon?

                        Not many days,
And your house will be full of men and women
  weeping,   80
And curses will be hurled at you from far
Cities grieving for sons unburied, left to rot
Before the walls of Thebes.

These are my arrows, Kreon: they are all for
  you.

(To Boy.) But come, child: lead me home.   85
Let him waste his fine anger upon younger men.
Maybe he will learn at last
To control a wiser tongue in a better head.
                        (Exit Teiresias.)
CHORAGOS: The old man has gone, King, but his
  words
Remain to plague us. I am old, too,   90
But I cannot remember that he was ever false.
KREON: That is true. . . . It troubles me.
Oh it is hard to give in! but it is worse
To risk everything for stubborn pride.
CHORAGOS: Kreon: take my advice.
KREON: What shall I do? 95
CHORAGOS: Go quickly: free Antigone from her
  vault
And build a tomb for the body of Polyneices.
KREON: You would have me do this!
CHORAGOS: Kreon, yes!
And it must be done at once: God moves
Swiftly to cancel the folly of stubborn men.   100

77. Furies: Spirits called upon to avenge crimes, especially
those against kin.

KREON: It is hard to deny the heart! But I
    Will do it: I will not fight with destiny.
CHORAGOS: You must go yourself, you cannot leave
    it to others.
KREON: I will go.
           — Bring axes, servants:
105 Come with me to the tomb. I buried her, I
    Will set her free.
              Oh quickly!
  My mind misgives —
  The laws of the gods are mighty, and a man
    must serve them
  To the last day of his life!   (*Exit Kreon.*)

PAEAN° • *Strophe 1*

CHORAGOS: God of many names
CHORUS: O Iacchos
                       son
  of Kadmeian Semele
              O born of the Thunder!
  Guardian of the West
                Regent
  of Eleusis' plain
           O Prince of maenad Thebes
5 and the Dragon Field by rippling Ismenos:°

Antistrophe 1

CHORAGOS: God of many names
CHORUS: the flame of torches
  flares on our hills
          the nymphs of Iacchos
  dance at the spring of Castalia:°
  from the vine-close mountain
            come ah come in ivy:
  Evohe evohe!° sings through the streets of
10   Thebes

Paean: A song of praise or prayer. **1–5. God of many names . . . rippling Ismenos:** The following is a litany of names for Dionysus (Iacchos): He was son of Zeus ("Thunder") and Semele; he was honored in secret rites at Eleusis; and he was worshiped by the Maenads of Thebes. Kadmos, Semele's father, sowed dragon's teeth in a field beside the river Ismenos from which sprang warriors who became the first Thebans. **8. spring of Castalia:** A spring on Mount Parnassus used by priestesses of Dionysus in rites of purification. **10.** *Evohe evohe!:* Cry of the Maenads to Dionysus.

Strophe 2

CHORAGOS: God of many names
CHORUS: Iacchos of Thebes
  heavenly Child
         of Semele bride of the Thunderer!
  The shadow of plague is upon us:
                  come
  with clement feet
           oh come from Parnasos
  down the long slopes
         across the lamenting water   15

Antistrophe 2

CHORAGOS: Io° Fire! Chorister of the throbbing
    stars!
  O purest among the voices of the night!
  Thou son of God, blaze for us!
CHORUS: Come with choric rapture of circling
    Maenads
  Who cry *Io Iacche!*
           God of many names!   20

EXODOS°

(*Enter Messenger from left.*)

MESSENGER: Men of the line of Kadmos, you who
    live
  Near Amphion's citadel,°
               I cannot say
  Of any condition of human life "This is fixed,
  This is clearly good, or bad." Fate raises up,
  And Fate casts down the happy and unhappy
    alike: 5
  No man can foretell his Fate.
              Take the case of Kreon:
  Kreon was happy once, as I count happiness:
  Victorious in battle, sole governor of the land,
  Fortunate father of children nobly born.
  And now it has all gone from him! Who can say   10
  That a man is still alive when his life's joy fails?
  He is a walking dead man. Grant him rich,
  Let him live like a king in his great house:
  If his pleasure is gone, I would not give
  So much as the shadow of smoke for all he
    owns.   15

16. Io: "Hail!" **Exodos:** Final scene. **2. Amphion's citadel:** A name for Thebes.

CHORAGOS: Your words hint at sorrow: what is
    your news for us?
MESSENGER: They are dead. The living are guilty of
    their death.
CHORAGOS: Who is guilty? Who is dead? Speak!
MESSENGER: Haimon.
    Haimon is dead; and the hand that killed him
    Is his own hand.
20 CHORAGOS: His father's? or his own?
MESSENGER: His own, driven mad by the murder
    his father had done.
CHORAGOS: Teiresias, Teiresias, how clearly you
    saw it all!
MESSENGER: This is my news: you must draw what
    conclusions you can from it.
CHORAGOS: But look: Eurydice, our Queen:
25   Has she overheard us?

(Enter Eurydice from the palace, center.)

EURYDICE: I have heard something, friends:
    As I was unlocking the gate of Pallas'° shrine,
    For I needed her help today, I heard a voice
    Telling of some new sorrow. And I fainted
    There at the temple with all my maidens about
30   me.
    But speak again: whatever it is, I can bear it:
    Grief and I are no strangers.
MESSENGER: Dearest Lady,
    I will tell you plainly all that I have seen.
    I shall not try to comfort you: what is the use,
35 Since comfort could lie only in what is not true?
    The truth is always best.
                      I went with Kreon
    To the outer plain where Polyneices was lying,
    No friend to pity him, his body shredded by
        dogs.
    We made our prayers in that place to Hecate
    And Pluto,° that they would be merciful. And we
40   bathed
    The corpse with holy water, and we brought
    Fresh-broken branches to burn what was left of
        it,
    And upon the urn we heaped up a towering
        barrow
    Of the earth of his own land.
                      When we were done, we ran
    To the vault where Antigone lay on her couch of
45   stone.
    One of the servants had gone ahead,

27. **Pallas:** Pallas Athene, goddess of wisdom. 39–
40. **Hecate and Pluto:** Goddess of witchcraft and sorcery
and King of Hades, the underworld.

And while he was yet far off he heard a voice
Grieving within the chamber, and he came back
And told Kreon. And as the King went closer,
The air was full of wailing, the words lost,   50
And he begged us to make all haste. "Am I a
    prophet?"
He said, weeping, "And must I walk this road,
The saddest of all that I have gone before?
My son's voice calls me on. Oh quickly, quickly!
Look through the crevice there, and tell me   55
If it is Haimon, or some deception of the gods!"

We obeyed; and in the cavern's farthest corner
We saw her lying:
She had made a noose of her fine linen veil
And hanged herself. Haimon lay beside her,   60
His arms about her waist, lamenting her,
His love lost under ground, crying out
That his father had stolen her away from him.

When Kreon saw him the tears rushed to his
    eyes
And he called to him: "What have you done,
    child? speak to me.   65
What are you thinking that makes your eyes so
    strange?
O my son, my son, I come to you on my
    knees!"
But Haimon spat in his face. He said not a
    word,
Staring —
              And suddenly drew his sword
And lunged. Kreon shrank back, the blade
    missed; and the boy,   70
Desperate against himself, drove it half its length
Into his own side, and fell. And as he died
He gathered Antigone close in his arms again,
Choking, his blood bright red on her white
    cheek.
And now he lies dead with the dead, and she is
    his   75
At last, his bride in the house of the dead.
                (Exit Eurydice into the palace.)
CHORAGOS: She has left us without a word. What
    can this mean?
MESSENGER: It troubles me, too; yet she knows
    what is best,
Her grief is too great for public lamentation,
And doubtless she has gone to her chamber to
    weep   80
For her dead son, leading her maidens in his
    dirge.

(Pause.)

CHORAGOS: It may be so: but I fear this deep
　　silence.
MESSENGER: I will see what she is doing. I will go
　　in.　　　　　　(Exit Messenger into the palace.)

(Enter Kreon with attendants, bearing Haimon's body.)

CHORAGOS: But here is the king himself: oh look at
　　him,
85　　Bearing his own damnation in his arms.
KREON: Nothing you say can touch me any more.
　　My own blind heart has brought me
　　From darkness to final darkness. Here you see
　　The father murdering, the murdered son —
90　　And all my civic wisdom!

　　Haimon my son, so young, so young to die,
　　I was the fool, not you; and you died for me.
CHORAGOS: That is the truth; but you were late in
　　learning it.
KREON: This truth is hard to bear. Surely a god
95　　Has crushed me beneath the hugest weight of
　　heaven,
　　And driven me headlong a barbaric way
　　To trample out the thing I held most dear.

　　The pains that men will take to come to pain!

(Enter Messenger from the palace.)

MESSENGER: The burden you carry in your hands is
　　heavy,
　　But it is not all: you will find more in your
100　　house.
KREON: What burden worse than this shall I find
　　there?
MESSENGER: The Queen is dead.
KREON: O port of death, deaf world,
　　Is there no pity for me? And you, Angel of evil,
105　　I was dead, and your words are death again.
　　Is it true, boy? Can it be true?
　　Is my wife dead? Has death bred death?
MESSENGER: You can see for yourself.

(The doors are opened and the body of Eurydice is
disclosed within.)

KREON: Oh pity!
110　　All true, all true, and more than I can bear!
　　O my wife, my son!
MESSENGER: She stood before the altar, and her
　　heart
　　Welcomed the knife her own hand guided,

And a great cry burst from her lips for
　　Megareus° dead,
And for Haimon dead, her sons; and her last
　　breath　　　　　　　　　　　　　　　　115
Was a curse for their father, the murderer of her
　　sons.
And she fell, and the dark flowed in through her
　　closing eyes.
KREON: O God, I am sick with fear.
　　Are there no swords here? Has no one a blow
　　for me?
MESSENGER: Her curse is upon you for the deaths
　　of both.　　　　　　　　　　　　　　　　120
KREON: It is right that it should be. I alone am
　　guilty.
　　I know it, and I say it. Lead me in,
　　Quickly, friends.
　　I have neither life nor substance. Lead me in.
CHORAGOS: You are right, if there can be right in
　　so much wrong.　　　　　　　　　　　　　125
　　The briefest way is best in a world of sorrow.
KREON: Let it come,
　　Let death come quickly, and be kind to me.
　　I would not ever see the sun again.
CHORAGOS: All that will come when it will; but
　　we, meanwhile,　　　　　　　　　　　　　130
　　Have much to do. Leave the future to itself.
KREON: All my heart was in that prayer!
CHORAGOS: Then do not pray any more: the sky is
　　deaf.
KREON: Lead me away. I have been rash and
　　foolish.
　　I have killed my son and my wife.　　　　　135
　　I look for comfort; my comfort lies here dead.
　　Whatever my hands have touched has come to
　　nothing.
　　Fate has brought all my pride to a thought of
　　dust.

(As Kreon is being led into the house, the Choragos
advances and speaks directly to the audience.)

CHORAGOS: There is no happiness where there is no
　　wisdom;
　　No wisdom but in submission to the gods.　　140
　　Big words are always punished,
　　And proud men in old age learn to be wise.

114. Megareus: Son of Kreon and brother of Haimon, Megareus sacrificed himself in the unsuccessful attack upon Thebes, believing that his death was necessary to save Thebes.

COMMENTARIES

Critical comment on the plays of Sophocles has been rich and various and has spanned the centuries. We are especially fortunate to have a commentary from the great age of Greek thought in which Sophocles himself flourished. In *Oedipus Rex* Sophocles gave the philosopher Aristotle a perfect drama on which to build a theory of tragedy, and Aristotle's observations have remained the most influential comments made on drama in the West. In some ways they have established the function, limits, and purposes of drama. In the twentieth century, for instance, when Bertolt Brecht tried to create a new theory of the drama, he specifically described his ideas as an alternative to Aristotelian notions.

Sigmund Freud, while not a critic, saw in the Oedipus myth as interpreted by Sophocles a basic psychological phenomenon experienced by all people in their infancy. His Oedipus complex is now well established in psychology and in the popular imagination.

The extraordinary range of commentary on the Oedipus story is demonstrated nowhere more amazingly than in Claude Lévi-Strauss's structural reading of the myth, both in Sophocles' version and in other versions. Lévi-Strauss shows that a pattern emerges when certain actions in the play are placed side by side. If he is correct, his theory offers a way to interpret myths and to see why they were valued so highly by the Greeks in their drama.

Oliver Taplin's emphasis on the audience's emotional state during the performance of a Greek tragedy brings us back to the seminal comments of Aristotle. Tragedies were noted for their capacity to invoke pity and fear in the audience. Taplin helps us understand how an audience's emotional response can clarify our critical view of tragedy. Meanwhile, George Steiner expands our understanding not only of *Antigone*, but of a generally important aspect of Greek drama by exploring the sources and nature of the conflict in that play. Steiner establishes five constants, such as confrontations of men and women and of the individual and society, that help deepen our understanding of the action in *Antigone* and other Greek tragedies.

Jean Anouilh, a major French playwright in the mid-twentieth century, wrote a version of *Antigone* while Nazi Germany occupied Paris and much of France. The political content of the play takes on interesting meaning in light of his experience. The excerpt that appears here offers a modern interpretation of the struggle between Antigone and Kreon.

Aristotle (384–322 B.C.)

POETICS: COMEDY AND EPIC AND TRAGEDY   *Tr. 1967*

TRANSLATED BY GERALD F. ELSE

Aristotle was Plato's most brilliant student and the heir of his teaching mantle. He remained with Plato for twenty years and then began his own school, called the Lyceum. His extant work consists mainly of his lectures, which were recorded by his students and carefully preserved. Called his treatises, they have greatly influenced later thought and deal with almost every branch of philosophy, science, and the arts. His Poetics remains, more than two thousand years later, a document of immense importance for literary criticism. It provides insight into the theoretical basis of Greek tragedy and comedy, and it helps us see that the drama was significant enough in Greek intellectual life to warrant an examination by the most influential Greek minds.

Comedy

Comedy is, as we said it was, an imitation of persons who are inferior; not, however, going all the way to full villainy, but imitating the ugly, of which the ludicrous is one part. The ludicrous, that is, is a failing or a piece of ugliness which causes no pain or destruction; thus, to go on farther, the comic mask° is something ugly and distorted but painless.

Now the stages of development of tragedy, and the men who were responsible for them, have not escaped notice but comedy did escape notice in the beginning because it was not taken seriously. (In fact it was late in its history that the presiding magistrate officially "granted a chorus" to the comic poets; until then they were volunteers.) Thus comedy already possessed certain defining characteristics when the first "comic poets," so-called, appear in the record. Who gave it masks, or prologues, or troupes of actors and all that sort of thing is not known. The composing of plots came originally from Sicily; of the Athenian poets, Crates° was the first to abandon the lampooning mode and compose arguments, that is, plots, of a general nature.

Epic and Tragedy

Well then, epic poetry followed in the wake of tragedy up to the point of being a (1) good-sized (2) imitation (3) in verse (4) of people who are to be taken seriously; but in its having its verse unmixed with any other and being narrative in character, there they differ. Further, so far as its length is concerned tragedy tries as hard as it can to exist during a single daylight period, or to vary but little, while the epic is not limited in its time and so differs in that respect. Yet originally they used to do this in tragedies just as much as they did in epic poems.

---

the comic mask: Actors in Greek drama wore masks behind which they spoke their lines. The comic mask showed a smiling face; the tragic mask, a weeping face.

Crates: Greek actor and playwright (fl. 470 B.C.), credited by Aristotle with developing Greek comedy into a fully plotted, credible form. Aristophanes (450–c. 388 B.C.), another Greek comic playwright, says that Crates was the first to portray a drunkard onstage.

The constituent elements are partly identical and partly limited to tragedy. Hence anybody who knows about good and bad tragedy knows about epic also; for the elements that the epic possesses appertain to tragedy as well, but those of tragedy are not all found in the epic.

Tragedy and Its Six Constituent Elements

Our discussions of imitative poetry in hexameters,° and of comedy, will come later; at present let us deal with tragedy, recovering from what has been said so far the definition of its essential nature, as it was in development. Tragedy, then, is a process of imitating an action which has serious implications, is complete, and possesses magnitude; by means of language which has been made sensuously attractive, with each of its varieties found separately in the parts; enacted by the persons themselves and not presented through narrative; through a course of pity and fear completing the purification of tragic acts which have those emotional characteristics. By "language made sensuously attractive" I mean language that has rhythm and melody, and by "its varieties found separately" I mean the fact that certain parts of the play are carried on through spoken verses alone and others the other way around, through song.

Now first of all, since they perform the imitation through action (by acting it), the adornment of their visual appearance will perforce constitute some part of the making of tragedy; and song-composition and verbal expression also, for those are the media in which they perform the imitation. By "verbal expression" I mean the actual composition of the verses, and by "song-composition" something whose meaning is entirely clear.

Next, since it is an imitation of an action and is enacted by certain people who are performing the action, and since those people must necessarily have certain traits both of character and thought (for it is thanks to these two factors that we speak of people's actions also as having a defined character, and it is in accordance with their actions that all either succeed or fail); and since the imitation of the action is the plot, for by "plot" I mean here the structuring of the events, and by the "characters" that in accordance with which we say that the persons who are acting have a defined moral character, and by "thought" all the passages in which they attempt to prove some thesis or set forth an opinion — it follows of necessity, then, that tragedy as a whole has just six constituent elements, in relation to the essence that makes it a distinct species; and they are plot, characters, verbal expression, thought, visual adornment, and song-composition. For the elements by which they imitate are two (i.e., verbal expression and song-composition), the manner in which they imitate is one (visual adornment), the things they imitate are three (plot, characters, thought), and there is nothing more beyond these. These then are the constituent forms they use.

The Relative Importance of the Six Elements

The greatest of these elements is the structuring of the incidents. For tragedy is an imitation not of men but of a life, an action, and they have moral quality in accordance with their characters but are happy or unhappy in accordance with their actions; hence they are not active in order to imitate their characters,

---

hexameters: The first known metrical form for classical verse. Each line had six metrical feet, some of which were prescribed in advance. It is the meter used for epic poetry and for poetry designed to teach a lesson. The form has sometimes been used in comparatively modern poetry but rarely with success except in French.

but they include the characters along with the actions for the sake of the latter. Thus the structure of events, the plot, is the goal of tragedy, and the goal is the greatest thing of all.

Again: a tragedy cannot exist without a plot, but it can without characters: thus the tragedies of most of our modern poets are devoid of character, and in general many poets are like that; so also with the relationship between Zeuxis and Polygnotus,° among the painters: Polygnotus is a good portrayer of character, while Zeuxis's painting has no dimension of character at all.

Again: if one strings end to end speeches that are expressive of character and carefully worked in thought and expression, he still will not achieve the result which we said was the aim of tragedy; the job will be done much better by a tragedy that is more deficient in these other respects but has a plot, a structure of events. It is much the same case as with painting: the most beautiful pigments smeared on at random will not give as much pleasure as a black-and-white outline picture. Besides, the most powerful means tragedy has for swaying our feelings, namely the peripeties and recognitions,° are elements of plot.

Again: an indicative sign is that those who are beginning a poetic career manage to hit the mark in verbal expression and character portrayal sooner than they do in plot construction; and the same is true of practically all the earliest poets.

So plot is the basic principle, the heart and soul, as it were, of tragedy, and the characters come second: . . . it is the imitation of an action and imitates the persons primarily for the sake of their action.

Third in rank is thought. This is the ability to state the issues and appropriate points pertaining to a given topic, an ability which springs from the arts of politics and rhetoric; in fact the earlier poets made their characters talk "politically," the present-day poets rhetorically. But "character" is that kind of utterance which clearly reveals the bent of a man's moral choice (hence there is no character in that class of utterances in which there is nothing at all that the speaker is choosing or rejecting), while "thought" is the passages in which they try to prove that something is so or not so, or state some general principle.

Fourth is the verbal expression of the speeches. I mean by this the same thing that was said earlier, that the "verbal expression" is the conveyance of thought through language: a statement which has the same meaning whether one says "verses" or "speeches."

The song-composition of the remaining parts is the greatest of the sensuous attractions, and the visual adornment of the dramatic persons can have a strong emotional effect but is the least artistic element, the least connected with the poetic art; in fact the force of tragedy can be felt even without benefit of public performance and actors, while for the production of the visual effect the property man's art is even more decisive than that of the poets.

Zeuxis and Polygnotus: Zeuxis (fl. 420–390 B.C.) developed a method of painting in which the figures were rounded and apparently three-dimensional. Thus, he was an illusionistic painter, imitating life in a realistic style. Polygnotus (c. 470–440 B.C.) was famous as a painter, and his works were on the Akropolis as well as at Delphi. His draftsmanship was especially praised.

peripeties and recognitions: The turning-about of fortune and the recognition on the part of the tragic hero of the truth. This is, for Aristotle, a critical moment in the drama, especially if both events happen simultaneously, as they do in *Oedipus Rex*. It is quite possible for these moments to happen apart from one another.

General Principles
of the Tragic Plot

With these distinctions out of the way, let us next discuss what the structuring of the events should be like, since this is both the basic and the most important element in the tragic art. We have established, then, that tragedy is an imitation of an action which is complete and whole and has some magnitude (for there is also such a thing as a whole that has no magnitude). "Whole" is that which has beginning, middle, and end. "Beginning" is that which does not necessarily follow on something else, but after it something else naturally is or happens; "end," the other way around, is that which naturally follows on something else, either necessarily or for the most part, but nothing else after it; and "middle" that which naturally follows on something else and something else on it. So, then, well constructed plots should neither begin nor end at any chance point but follow the guidelines just laid down.

Furthermore, since the beautiful, whether a living creature or anything that is composed of parts, should not only have these in a fixed order to one another but also possess a definite size which does not depend on chance — for beauty depends on size and order; hence neither can a very tiny creature turn out to be beautiful (since our perception of it grows blurred as it approaches the period of imperceptibility) nor an excessively huge one (for then it cannot all be perceived at once and so its unity and wholeness are lost), if for example there were a creature a thousand miles long — so, just as in the case of living creatures they must have some size, but one that can be taken in a single view, so with plots: they should have length, but such that they are easy to remember. As to a limit of the length, the one is determined by the tragic competitions and the ordinary span of attention. (If they had to compete with a hundred tragedies they would compete by the water clock, as they say used to be done [?].) But the limit fixed by the very nature of the case is: the longer the plot, up to the point of still being perspicuous as a whole, the finer it is so far as size is concerned; or to put it in general terms, the length in which, with things happening in unbroken sequence, a shift takes place either probably or necessarily from bad to good fortune or from good to bad — that is an acceptable norm of length.

But a plot is not unified, as some people think, simply because it has to do with a single person. A large, indeed an indefinite number of things can happen to a given individual, some of which go to constitute no unified event; and in the same way there can be many acts of a given individual from which no single action emerges. Hence it seems clear that those poets are wrong who have composed *Heracleïds*, *Theseïds*, and the like. They think that since Heracles was a single person it follows that the plot will be single too. But Homer, superior as he is in all other respects, appears to have grasped this point well also, thanks either to art or nature, for in composing an *Odyssey* he did not incorporate into it everything that happened to the hero, for example how he was wounded on Mt. Parnassus° or how he feigned madness at the muster, neither of which events, by happening, made it at all necessary or probable that

---

Mt. Parnassus: A mountain in central Greece traditionally sacred to Apollo. In legend, Odysseus was wounded there, but the point Aristotle is making is that the writer of epics need not include every detail of his hero's life in a given work. Homer, in writing the *Odyssey*, was working with a hero, Odysseus, whose story had been legendary long before he began writing.

the other should happen. Instead, he composed the *Odyssey* — and the *Iliad* similarly — around a unified action of the kind we have been talking about.

A poetic imitation, then, ought to be unified in the same way as a single imitation in any other mimetic field, by having a single object: since the plot is an imitation of an action, the latter ought to be both unified and complete, and the component events ought to be so firmly compacted that if any one of them is shifted to another place, or removed, the whole is loosened up and dislocated; for an element whose addition or subtraction makes no perceptible extra difference is not really a part of the whole.

From what has been said it is also clear that the poet's job is not to report what has happened but what is likely to happen: that is, what is capable of happening according to the rule of probability or necessity. Thus the difference between the historian and the poet is not in their utterances being in verse or prose (it would be quite possible for Herodotus' work to be translated into verse, and it would not be any the less a history with verse than it is without it); the difference lies in the fact that the historian speaks of what has happened, the poet of the kind of thing that *can* happen. Hence also poetry is a more philosophical and serious business than history; for poetry speaks more of universals, history of particulars. "Universal" in this case is what kind of person is likely to do or say certain kinds of things, according to probability or necessity; that is what poetry aims at, although it gives its persons particular names afterward; while the "particular" is what Alcibiades did or what happened to him.

In the field of comedy this point has been grasped: our comic poets construct their plots on the basis of general probabilities and then assign names to the persons quite arbitrarily, instead of dealing with individuals as the old iambic poets° did. But in tragedy they still cling to the historically given names. The reason is that what is possible is persuasive; so what has not happened we are not yet ready to believe is possible, while what has happened is, we feel, obviously possible: for it would not have happened if it were impossible. Nevertheless, it is a fact that even in our tragedies, in some cases only one or two of the names are traditional, the rest being invented, and in some others none at all. It is so, for example, in Agathon's *Antheus* — the names in it are as fictional as the events — and it gives no less pleasure because of that. Hence the poets ought not to cling at all costs to the traditional plots, around which our tragedies are constructed. And in fact it is absurd to go searching for this kind of authentication, since even the familiar names are familiar to only a few in the audience and yet give the same kind of pleasure to all.

So from these considerations it is evident that the poet should be a maker of his plots more than of his verses, insofar as he is a poet by virtue of his imitations and what he imitates is actions. Hence even if it happens that he puts something that has actually taken place into poetry, he is none the less a poet; for there is nothing to prevent some of the things that have happened

---

old iambic poets: Aristotle may be referring to Archilochus (fl. 650 B.C.) and the iambic style he developed. The iamb is a metrical foot of two syllables, a short and a long syllable, and was the most popular metrical style before the time of Aristotle. "Dealing with individuals" implies using figures already known to the audience rather than figures whose names can be arbitrarily assigned because no one knows who they are.

from being the kind of things that can happen, and that is the sense in which he is their maker.

Simple and Complex Plots

Among simple plots and actions the episodic are the worst. By "episodic" plot I mean one in which there is no probability or necessity for the order in which the episodes follow one another. Such structures are composed by the bad poets because they are bad poets, but by the good poets because of the actors: in composing contest pieces for them, and stretching out the plot beyond its capacity, they are forced frequently to dislocate the sequence.

Furthermore, since the tragic imitation is not only of a complete action but also of events that are fearful and pathetic,° and these come about best when they come about contrary to one's expectation yet logically, one following from the other; that way they will be more productive of wonder than if they happen merely at random, by chance — because even among chance occurrences the ones people consider most marvelous are those that seem to have come about as if on purpose: for example the way the statue of Mitys at Argos killed the man who had been the cause of Mitys' death, by falling on him while he was attending the festival; it stands to reason, people think, that such things don't happen by chance — so plots of that sort cannot fail to be artistically superior.

Some plots are simple, others are complex; indeed the actions of which the plots are imitations already fall into these two categories. By "simple" action I mean one the development of which being continuous and unified in the manner stated above, the reversal comes without peripety or recognition, and by "complex" action one in which the reversal is continuous but with recognition or peripety or both. And these developments must grow out of the very structure of the plot itself, in such a way that on the basis of what has happened previously this particular outcome follows either by necessity or in accordance with probability; for there is a great difference in whether these events happen because of those or merely after them.

"Peripety" is a shift of what is being undertaken to the opposite in the way previously stated, and that in accordance with probability or necessity as we have just been saying; as for example in the *Oedipus* the man who has come, thinking that he will reassure Oedipus, that is, relieve him of his fear with respect to his mother, by revealing who he once was, brings about the opposite; and in the *Lynceus*, as he (Lynceus) is being led away with every prospect of being executed, and Danaus pursuing him with every prospect of doing the executing, it comes about as a result of the other things that have happened in the play that *he* is executed and Lynceus is saved. And "recognition" is, as indeed the name indicates, a shift from ignorance to awareness, pointing in the direction either of close blood ties or of hostility, of people who have previously been in a clearly marked state of happiness or unhappiness.

The finest recognition is one that happens at the same time as a peripety, as is the case with the one in the *Oedipus*. Naturally, there are also other kinds of recognition: it is possible for one to take place in the prescribed manner in

---

fearful and pathetic: Aristotle said that tragedy should evoke two emotions: terror and pity. The terror results from our realizing that what is happening to the hero might just as easily happen to us; the pity results from our human sympathy with a fellow sufferer. Therefore, the fearful and pathetic represent significant emotions appropriate to our witnessing drama.

relation to inanimate objects and chance occurrences, and it is possible to recognize whether a person has acted or not acted. But the form that is most integrally a part of the plot, the action, is the one aforesaid; for that kind of recognition combined with peripety will excite either pity or fear (and these are the kinds of action of which tragedy is an imitation according to our definition), because both good and bad fortune will also be most likely to follow that kind of event. Since, further, the recognition is a recognition of persons, some are of one person by the other one only (when it is already known who the "other one" is), but sometimes it is necessary for both persons to go through a recognition, as for example Iphigenia is recognized by her brother through the sending of the letter, but of him by Iphigenia another recognition is required.

These then are two elements of plot: peripety and recognition; third is the *pathos*. Of these, peripety and recognition have been discussed; a *pathos* is a destructive or painful act, such as deaths on stage, paroxysms of pain, woundings, and all that sort of thing.

Sigmund Freud (1856–1939)
THE OEDIPUS COMPLEX   *1900°*

Sigmund Freud is the most celebrated psychiatrist of the twentieth century and the father of psychoanalytic theory. His researches into the unconscious have changed the way we think about the human mind, and his explorations into the symbolic meaning of dreams have been widely regarded as a breakthrough in connecting the meaning of world myth to personal life.

In his Interpretation of Dreams *he turned to Sophocles' drama and developed his theories of the Oedipus complex, which explain that the desire to kill one parent and marry the other may be rooted in the deepest natural psychological development of the individual. The passage that follows provides insight not only into a psychological state that all humans may share but also into the way in which a man of Freud's temperament read and interpreted a great piece of literature. Like Sophocles himself, Freud believed that the myth underlying* Oedipus Rex *has a meaning and importance for all human beings.*

In my experience, which is already extensive, the chief part in the mental lives of all children who later become psychoneurotics is played by their parents. Being in love with the one parent and hating the other are among the essential constituents of the stock of psychical impulses which is formed at that time and which is of such importance in determining the symptoms of the later neurosis. It is not my belief, however, that psychoneurotics differ sharply in this respect from other human beings who remain normal — that they are able, that is, to create something absolutely new and peculiar to themselves. It is far more probable — and this is confirmed by occasional observations on normal children — that they are only distinguished by exhibiting on a magnified scale feelings of

1900: *Interpretation of Dreams* was first published in 1900 and updated regularly by Freud through eight editions.

love and hatred to their parents which occur less obviously and less intensely in the minds of most children.

This discovery is confirmed by a legend that has come down to us from classical antiquity: a legend whose profound and universal power to move can only be understood if the hypothesis I have put forward in regard to the psychology of children has an equally universal validity. What I have in mind is the legend of King Oedipus and Sophocles' drama which bears his name.

Oedipus, son of Laïus, King of Thebes, and of Jocasta, was exposed as an infant because an oracle had warned Laïus that the still unborn child would be his father's murderer. The child was rescued and grew up as a prince in an alien court, until, in doubts as to his origin, he too questioned the oracle and was warned to avoid his home since he was destined to murder his father and take his mother in marriage. On the road leading away from what he believed was his home, he met King Laïus and slew him in a sudden quarrel. He came next to Thebes and solved the riddle set him by the Sphinx who barred his way. Out of gratitude the Thebans made him their king and gave him Jocasta's hand in marriage. He reigned long in peace and honor, and she who, unknown to him, was his mother bore him two sons and two daughters. Then at last a plague broke out and the Thebans made inquiry once more of the oracle. It is at this point that Sophocles's tragedy opens. The messengers bring back the reply that the plague will cease when the murderer of Laïus has been driven from the land.

> But he, where is he? Where shall now be read
> The fading record of this ancient guilt?[1]

The action of the play consists in nothing other than the process of revealing, with cunning delays and ever-mounting excitement — a process that can be likened to the work of a psychoanalysis — that Oedipus himself is the murderer of Laïus, but further that he is the son of the murdered man and of Jocasta. Appalled at the abomination which he has unwittingly perpetrated, Oedipus blinds himself and forsakes his home. The oracle has been fulfilled.

Oedipus Rex is what is known as a tragedy of destiny. Its tragic effect is said to lie in the contrast between the supreme will of the gods and the vain attempts of mankind to escape the evil that threatens them. The lesson which, it is said, the deeply moved spectator should learn from the tragedy is submission to the divine will and realization of his own impotence. Modern dramatists have accordingly tried to achieve a similar tragic effect by weaving the same contrast into a plot invented by themselves. But the spectators have looked on unmoved while a curse or an oracle was fulfilled in spite of all the efforts of some innocent man: later tragedies of destiny have failed in their effect.

If *Oedipus Rex* moves a modern audience no less than it did the contemporary Greek one, the explanation can only be that its effect does not lie in the contrast between destiny and human will, but is to be looked for in the particular nature of the material on which that contrast is exemplified. There must be something which makes a voice within us ready to recognize the compelling force of destiny in the *Oedipus*, while we can dismiss as merely arbitrary such dispositions as are laid down in [Grillparzer's] *Die Ahnfrau* or other modern tragedies of

---

[1]Lewis Campbell's translation (1883), lines 108ff [Fitts/Fitzgerald, Prologue, lines 112–13].

destiny. And a factor of this kind is in fact involved in the story of King Oedipus. His destiny moves us only because it might have been ours — because the oracle laid the same curse upon us before our birth as upon him. It is the fate of all of us, perhaps, to direct our first sexual impulse toward our mother and our first hatred and our first murderous wish against our father. Our dreams convince us that that is so. King Oedipus, who slew his father Laïus and married his mother Jocasta, merely shows us the fulfillment of our own childhood wishes. But, more fortunate than he, we have meanwhile succeeded, in so far as we have not become psychoneurotics, in detaching our sexual impulses from our mothers and in forgetting our jealousy of our fathers. Here is one in whom these primeval wishes of our childhood have been fulfilled, and we shrink back from him with the whole force of the repression by which those wishes have since that time been held down within us. While the poet, as he unravels the past, brings to light the guilt of Oedipus, he is at the same time compelling us to recognize our own inner minds, in which those same impulses, though suppressed, are still to be found. The contrast with which the closing Chorus leaves us confronted —

> . . . Fix on Oedipus your eyes,
> Who resolved the dark enigma, noblest champion and most wise.
> Like a star his envied fortune mounted beaming far and wide:
> Now he sinks in seas of anguish, whelmed beneath a raging tide . . .[2]

— strikes as a warning at ourselves and our pride, at us who since our childhood have grown so wise and so mighty in our own eyes. Like Oedipus, we live in ignorance of these wishes, repugnant to morality, which have been forced upon us by Nature, and after their revelation we may all of us well seek to close our eyes to the scenes of our childhood.[3]

There is an unmistakable indication in the text of Sophocles' tragedy itself that the legend of Oedipus sprang from some primeval dream material which had as its content the distressing disturbance of a child's relation to his parents owing to the first stirrings of sexuality. At a point when Oedipus, though he is not yet enlightened, has begun to feel troubled by his recollection of the oracle, Jocasta consoles him by referring to a dream which many people dream, though, as she thinks, it has no meaning:

> Many a man ere now in dreams hath lain
> With her who bare him. He hath least annoy
> Who with such omens troubleth not his mind.[4]

[2]Lewis Campbell's translation, lines 1524ff [Fitts/Fitzgerald, Antistrophe 2, lines 292–96].

[3][*Footnote added by Freud in 1914 edition.*] None of the findings of psychoanalytic research has provoked such embittered denials, such fierce opposition — or such amusing contortions — on the part of critics as this indication of the childhood impulses toward incest which persist in the unconscious. An attempt has even been made recently to make out, in the face of all experience, that the incest should only be taken as "symbolic." — Ferenczi (1912) has proposed an ingenious "overinterpretation" of the Oedipus myth, based on a passage in one of Schopenhauer's letters. [*Added 1919.*] Later studies have shown that the "Oedipus complex," which was touched upon for the first time in the above paragraphs in the *Interpretation of Dreams*, throws a light of undreamt-of importance on the history of the human race and the evolution of religion and morality.

[4]Lewis Campbell's translation, lines 982ff [Fitts/Fitzgerald, Scene 3, lines 67–69].

Today, just as then, many men dream of having sexual relations with their mothers, and speak of the fact with indignation and astonishment. It is clearly the key to the tragedy and the complement to the dream of the dreamer's father being dead. The story of Oedipus is the reaction of the imagination to these two typical dreams. And just as these dreams, when dreamt by adults, are accompanied by feelings of repulsion, so too the legend must include horror and self-punishment. Its further modification originates once again in a misconceived secondary revision of the material, which has sought to exploit it for theological purposes. . . . The attempt to harmonize divine omnipotence with human responsibility must naturally fail in connection with this subject matter just as with any other.

Claude Lévi-Strauss (b. 1908)
From *The Structural Study of Myth* 1955

Claude Lévi-Strauss is one of a handful of modern anthropologists whose interests span the range of thought, culture, and understanding. His work has been of immense influence on French intellectual life and, by extension, on the intellectual life of our entire century. His works include Triste Tropiques *(translated as* A World on the Wane), *about his own experiences as an anthropologist;* Structural Anthropology, *about the ways in which the study of anthropology implies a study of the structure of thought; and* Mythologies, *a four-volume summation of his thought. The excerpt that follows is structuralist in scope in that it attempts to understand the myth of Oedipus by examining the patterns of repetition in the original narrative. By setting up a grid, Lévi-Strauss begins to sort out the implications of the myth and to seek a meaning that is not necessarily apparent in the chronological order of the narrative. He examines the myth diachronically — across the lines of time — and thereby sees a new range of implications, which he treats as the structural implications of the myth. His reading is complex, suggesting that the Oedipus myth is a vegetation myth explaining the origins of mankind. Lévi-Strauss gives us a new way to interpret the significance of literary myths.*

The time has come to give a concrete example of the method we propose. We will use the Oedipus myth which has the advantage of being well known to everybody and for which no preliminary explanation is therefore needed. By doing so, I am well aware that the Oedipus myth has only reached us under late forms and through literary transfigurations concerned more with esthetic and moral preoccupations than with religious or ritual ones, whatever these may have been. But as will be shown later, this apparently unsatisfactory situation will strengthen our demonstration rather than weaken it.

The myth will be treated as would be an orchestra score perversely presented as a unilinear series and where our task is to reestablish the correct disposition. As if, for instance, we were confronted with a sequence of the type: 1,2,4,7,8,2,3,4,6,8,1,4,5,7,8,1,2,5,7,3,4,5,6,8 . . . , the assignment being to put all the 1's together, all the 2's, the 3's, etc.; the result is a chart:

```
1   2       4           7   8
    2   3   4       6       8
1           4   5       7   8
1   2           5       7
        3   4   5
                    6       8
```

We will attempt to perform the same kind of operation on the Oedipus myth, trying out several dispositions. . . . Let us suppose, for the sake of argument, that the best arrangement is the following (although it might certainly be improved by the help of a specialist in Greek mythology):

Kadmos seeks his sister Europa ravished by Zeus.			
		Kadmos kills the dragon.	
	The Spartoi kill each other.		
			Labdacos (Laios's father) = *lame* (?).
	Oedipus kills his father Laios.		
			Laios (Oedipus's father) = *left-sided* (?).
		Oedipus kills the Sphinx.	
Oedipus marries his mother Jocasta.			
	Eteocles kills his brother Polyneices.		Oedipus = *swollen-foot* (?).
Antigone buries her brother Polyneices despite prohibition.			

Thus, we find ourselves confronted with four vertical columns each of which includes several relations belonging to the same bundle. Were we to *tell* the myth, we would disregard the columns and read the rows from left to right and from top to bottom. But if we want to *understand* the myth, then we will have to disregard one half of the diachronic° dimension (top to bottom) and read from left to right, column after column, each one being considered as a unit.

All the relations belonging to the same column exhibit one common feature which it is our task to unravel. For instance, all the events grouped in the first column on the left have something to do with blood relations which are overem-

---

diachronic: Not ordered linearly in time, but through time.

phasized, i.e. are subject to a more intimate treatment than they should be. Let us say, then, that the first column has as its common feature the *overrating of blood relations*. It is obvious that the second column expresses the same thing, but inverted: *underrating of blood relations*. The third column refers to monsters being slain. As to the fourth, a word of clarification is needed. The remarkable connotation of the surnames in Oedipus's father-line has often been noticed. However, linguists usually disregard it, since to them the only way to define the meaning of a term is to investigate all the contexts in which it appears, and personal names, precisely because they are used as such, are not accompanied by any context. With the method we propose to follow the objection disappears since the myth itself provides its own context. The meaningful fact is no longer to be looked for in the eventual sense of each name, but in the fact that all the names have a common feature: i.e., that they may eventually mean something and that all these hypothetical meanings (which may well remain hypothetical) exhibit a common feature, namely they refer *to difficulties to walk and to behave straight*.

What is then the relationship between the two columns on the right? Column three refers to monsters. The dragon is a chthonian° being which has to be killed in order that mankind be born from the earth; the Sphinx is a monster unwilling to permit men to live. The last unit reproduces the first one which has to do with the *autochthonous*° origin of mankind. Since the monsters are overcome by men, we may thus say that the common feature of the third column is *the denial of the autochthonous origin of man*.

This immediately helps us to understand the meaning of the fourth column. In mythology it is a universal character of men born from the earth that at the moment they emerge from the depth, they either cannot walk or do it clumsily. This is the case of the chthonian beings in the mythology of the Pueblo: Masauwu, who leads the emergence, and the chthonian Shumaikoli are lame ("bleeding-foot," "sore-foot"). The same happens to the Koskimo of the Kwakiutl after they have been swallowed by the chthonian monster, Tsiakish: when they returned to the surface of the earth "they limped forward or tripped sideways." Then the common feature of the fourth column is: *the persistence of the autochthonous origin of man*. It follows that column four is to column three as column one is to column two. The inability to connect two kinds of relationships is overcome (or rather replaced) by the positive statement that contradictory relationships are identical inasmuch as they are both self-contradictory in a similar way. Although this is still a provisional formulation of the structure of mythical thought, it is sufficient at this stage.

Turning back to the Oedipus myth, we may now see what it means. The myth has to do with the inability, for a culture which holds the belief that mankind is autochthonous . . . to find a satisfactory transition between this theory and the knowledge that human beings are actually born from the union of man and woman. Although the problem obviously cannot be solved, the Oedipus myth provides a kind of logical tool which, to phrase it coarsely, replaces the original problem: born from one or born from two? born from different or born from same? By a correlation of this type, the overrating of blood relations is to the underrating of blood relations as the attempt to escape

chthonian: From the underworld.
autochthonous: Native, aboriginal; in this case, born of the earth.

autochthony is to the impossibility to succeed in it. Although experience contradicts theory, social life verifies the cosmology by its similarity of structure. Hence cosmology is true.

Two remarks should be made at this stage.

In order to interpret the myth, we were able to leave aside a point which has until now worried the specialists, namely, that in the earlier (Homeric) versions of the Oedipus myth, some basic elements are lacking, such as Jocasta killing herself and Oedipus piercing his own eyes. These events do not alter the substance of the myth although they can easily be integrated, the first one as a new case of autodestruction (column three) while the second is another case of crippledness (column four). At the same time there is something significant in these additions since the shift from foot to head is to be correlated with the shift from: autochthonous origin negated to: self-destruction.

Thus, our method eliminates a problem which has been so far one of the main obstacles to the progress of mythological studies, namely, the quest for the *true* version, or the *earlier* one. On the contrary, we define the myth as consisting of all its versions; to put it otherwise: a myth remains the same as long as it is felt as such. A striking example is offered by the fact that our interpretation may take into account, and is certainly applicable to, the Freudian use of the Oedipus myth. Although the Freudian problem has ceased to be that of autochthony *versus* bisexual reproduction, it is still the problem of understanding how *one* can be born from *two:* how is it that we do not have only one procreator, but a mother plus a father? Therefore, not only Sophocles, but Freud himself, should be included among the recorded versions of the Oedipus myth on a par with earlier or seemingly more "authentic" versions.

Oliver Taplin (b. 1943)
EMOTION AND MEANING IN GREEK TRAGEDY   *1983*

Scholar Oliver Taplin focuses on one of Aristotle's concerns in his commentary on tragedy: the emotions aroused by drama. Taplin explores the argument that devalues an emotional response to tragedy, and then he considers the proposition that "tragedy is essentially the emotional experience of its audience."

It seems to me, then, that Gorgias° is right that tragedy is essentially the *emotional experience of its audience.* Whatever it tells us about the world is conveyed by means of these emotions. Plato agreed with Gorgias in this, but he disapproved of the process and regarded it as harmful. Aristotle agreed with him too, but, contrary to Plato, regarded it as beneficial and salutary. Plato's objection was that such emotions are not the province of the highest part of the soul, the intellectual part. This is the forefather of the error made by so many later critics who have not acknowledged the centrality of emotion in the communication of tragedy. They think that if tragedy is essentially an emotional

Gorgias: Greek orator and rhetorician (c. 483–376 B.C.).

experience, it must be *solely* that; and they think this because they assume that strong emotion is necessarily in opposition to thought, that the psychic activities are mutually exclusive. But is this right? Understanding, reason, learning, moral discrimination; these things are not, in my experience, incompatible with emotion (nor presumably in the experience of Gorgias and Aristotle): What is incompatible is cold insensibility. Whether or not emotion is inimical to such intellectual processes depends on the *circumstances in which it is aroused.*

The characteristic tragic emotions — pity, horror, fascination, indignation, and so forth — are felt in many other situations besides in the theater. Above all we suffer them in the face of the misfortunes of real life, of course. What distinguishes the experience of a great tragedy? For one thing, as already remarked, we feel for the fortunes of people who have no direct personal relation to us: While this does not decrease the intensity of the emotion, it affords us some distance and perspective. We can feel and at the same time observe from outside. But does this distinguish tragedy from other "contrived" emotional experiences (most of them tending to the anti-intellectual), for example an animal hunt, a football match, an encounter group, reading a thriller, or watching a horror movie? Well, the experience of tragedy is by no means a random series of sensations. Our emotional involvement has perspective and context at the same time, and not just in retrospect. Thus the events of the tragedy are in an ordered *sequence,* a sequence which gives shape and comprehensibility to what we feel. And, most important of all, the affairs of the characters which move us are given a moral setting which is argued and explored in the play. They act and suffer within situations of moral conflict, or social, intellectual, and theological conflict. The quality of the tragedy depends *both* on its power to arouse our emotions *and* on the setting of those emotions in a sequence of moral and intellectual complications which is set out and examined. Tragedy evokes our feelings for others, like much else; but it is distinguished by the order and significance it imparts to suffering. So if the audience is not moved, then the tragedy, however intellectual, is a total failure: If its passions are aroused, but in a thoughtless, amorphous way, then it is merely a bad tragedy, sensational, melodramatic.

Thus it is that our emotions in the theater, far from driving out thought and meaning, are indivisible from them: They are simultaneous and mutually dependent. The experience of tragedy can achieve this coherence in a way that the emotional experiences of real life generally cannot because they are too close, too cluttered with detail and partiality, to be seen in perspective. Tragedy makes us feel that we understand life in its tragic aspects. We have the sense that we can better sympathize with and cope with suffering, misfortune, and waste. It is this sense of understanding (not isolated pearls of wisdom) that is the "message" of a tragedy, that the great playwright imparts. This is well put in T. S. Eliot's essay "Shakespeare and the Stoicism of Seneca," where he argues that it is the quality of the emotional expression rather than the quality of the philosophy which makes literature great, which makes it "strong, true and informative . . . useful and beneficial in the sense in which poetry is useful and beneficial." "All great poetry," Eliot° writes, "gives the illusion of a view of life . . . for every precise emotion tends towards intellectual formulation."

T. S. Eliot: Poet and critic (1888–1965).

George Steiner (b. 1929)
PRINCIPAL CONSTANTS OF CONFLICT
IN *ANTIGONE*   1984

George Steiner's Antigones, *a study of the history of variations on the theme of Sophocles' play, uncovers a remarkable range of interpretation, especially in the relationship of Kreon and Antigone. In his analysis, Steiner establishes five constants of conflict that he feels are responsible for much of the power of the play.*

It has, I believe, been given to only one literary text to express all the principal constants of conflict in the condition of man. These constants are fivefold: the confrontation of men and of women; of age and of youth; of society and of the individual; of the living and the dead; of men and of god(s). The conflicts which come of these five orders of confrontation are not negotiable. Men and women, old and young, the individual and the community or state, the quick and the dead, mortals and immortals, define themselves in the conflictual process of defining each other. Self-definition and the agonistic recognition of "otherness" (of *l'autre*) across the threatened boundaries of self are indissociable. The polarities of masculinity and of femininity, of aging and of youth, of private autonomy and of social collectivity, of existence and mortality, of the human and the divine, can be crystallized only in adversative terms (whatever the many shades of accommodation between them). To arrive at oneself — the primordial journey — is to come up, polemically, against "the other." The boundary-conditions of the human person are those set by gender, by age, by community, by the cut between life and death, and by the potentials of accepted or denied encounter between the existential and the transcendent.

But "collision" is, of course, a monistic and, therefore, inadequate term. Equally decisive are those categories of reciprocal perception, of grappling with "otherness," that can be defined as erotic, filial, social, ritual, and metaphysical. Men and women, old and young, individual and *communitas*, living and deceased, mortals and gods, meet and mesh in contiguities of love, of kinship, of commonality and group-communion, of caring remembrance, of worship. Sex, the honeycomb of generations and of kinship, the social unit, the presentness of the departed in the weave of the living, the practices of religion, are the modes of enactment of ultimate ontological dualities. In essence, the constants of conflict and of positive intimacy are the same. When man and woman meet, they stand against each other as they stand close. Old and young seek in each other the pain of remembrance and the matching solace of futurity. Anarchic individuation seeks interaction with the compulsions of law, of collective cohesion in the body politic. The dead inhabit the living and, in turn, await their visit. The duel between men and god(s) is the most aggressively amorous known to experience. In the physics of man's being, fission is also fusion.

It is in lines 441–581 [pages 79–82] of Sophocles' *Antigone* that each of the five fundamental categories of man's definition and self-definition through conflict is realized, and that all five are at work in a single act of confrontation. No other moment that I know of, in either sacred or secular imagining, achieves this totality. Creon and Antigone clash as man and as woman. Creon is a mature, indeed an aging, man; Antigone's is the virginity of youth. Their fatal debate turns on the nature of the coexistence between private vision and public need, between ego and community. The imperatives of immanence, of the living in the [*polis*], πόλις, press on Creon; in Antigone, these imperatives encounter the no less exigent night-throng of the dead. No syllable spoken, no gesture made, in the dialogue of Antigone and Creon but has within it the manifold, perhaps duplicitous, nearness of the gods. . . .

That which has in it the seed of all drama is the meeting of a man and of a woman. No experience of which we have direct knowledge is more charged with the potential of collision. Being inalienably one, by virtue of the humanity which distances them from all other life-forms, man and woman are at the same time inalienably different. The spectrum of difference is, as we know, one of most subtle continuum. There are in every human being elements of masculinity and of femininity (each encounter, each conflict is, therefore, also a civil war within the hybrid self). But at some point along the continuum, most men and women crystallize their essential manhood or womanhood. This gathering of the partly divided self to itself, this composition of identity, determines the gap across which the energies of love and of hatred meet.

Jean Anouilh (b. 1910)
FROM *ANTIGONE*   1942

TRANSLATED BY LEWIS GALANTIÈRE

Jean Anouilh began writing plays in 1931. Some of his best-known works, in addition to Antigone, *are* Eurydice *(1941),* Orestes *(1942),* Medea *(1946),* Ring Round the Moon *(1947),* The Waltz of the Toreadors *(1951), and* The Lark *(1952), which is about Joan of Arc. Anouilh wrote* Antigone *in 1942 in occupied Paris and produced it with his wife in the title role in February 1944, when the Nazis controlled most of Europe. Kreon (spelled Creon in this excerpt) is more willing to compromise in Anouilh's version of the play, and for that reason some critics saw the play as pro-Nazi. But Anouilh's sympathies were with Antigone, who represented the anti-Nazi view of the Parisian Resistance. Throughout its early run, the play was an inspiration to the patriotic French.*

This excerpt begins when Ismene returns to accept some of the responsibility for Polyneices' burial and continues through the confrontation of Haimon (Haemon in this excerpt) and Kreon to the end of the play.

(*Ismene enters through arch.*)

ISMENE (*distraught*): Antigone!
ANTIGONE (*turns to Ismene*): You, too? What do you want?
ISMENE: Oh, forgive me, Antigone. I've come back. I'll be brave. I'll go with
   you now.
ANTIGONE: Where will you go with me?
ISMENE (*to Creon*): Creon! If you kill her, you'll have to kill me too.

ANTIGONE: Oh, no, Ismene. Not a bit of it. I die alone. You don't think I'm going to let you die with me after what I've been through? You don't deserve it.

ISMENE: If you die, I don't want to live. I don't want to be left behind, alone.

ANTIGONE: You chose life and I chose death. Now stop blubbering. You had your chance to come with me in the black night, creeping on your hands and knees. You had your chance to claw up the earth with your nails, as I did; to get yourself caught like a thief, as I did. And you refused it.

ISMENE: Not anymore. I'll do it alone tonight.

ANTIGONE (*turns round toward Creon*): You hear that, Creon? The thing is catching! Who knows but that lots of people will catch the disease from me! What are you waiting for? Call in your guards! Come on, Creon! Show a little courage! It only hurts for a minute! Come on, cook!

CREON (*turns toward arch and calls*): Guard!

(*Guards enter through arch.*)

ANTIGONE (*in a great cry of relief*): At last, Creon!

(*Chorus enters through left arch.*)

CREON (*to the Guards*): Take her away! (*Creon goes up on top step.*)

(*Guards grasp Antigone by her arms, turn and hustle her toward the arch, right, and exeunt.° Ismene mimes horror, backs away toward the arch, left, then turns and runs out through the arch. A long pause, as Creon moves slowly downstage.*)

CHORUS (*Behind Creon. Speaks in a deliberate voice*): You are out of your mind, Creon. What have you done?

CREON (*his back to Chorus*): She had to die.

CHORUS: You must not let Antigone die. We shall carry the scar of her death for centuries.

CREON: She insisted. No man on earth was strong enough to dissuade her. Death was her purpose, whether she knew it or not. Polynices was a mere pretext. When she had to give up that pretext, she found another one — that life and happiness were tawdry things and not worth possessing. She was bent upon only one thing: to reject life and to die.

CHORUS: She is a mere child, Creon.

CREON: What do you want me to do for her? Condemn her to live?

HAEMON (*calls from offstage*): Father! (*Haemon enters through arch, right. Creon turns toward him.*)

CREON: Haemon, forget Antigone. Forget her, my dearest boy.

HAEMON: How can you talk like that?

CREON (*grasps Haemon by the hands*): I did everything I could to save her, Haemon. I used every argument. I swear I did. The girl doesn't love you. She could have gone on living for you; but she refused. She wanted it this way; she wanted to die.

HAEMON: Father! The guards are dragging Antigone away! You've got to stop them! (*He breaks away from Creon.*)

CREON (*looks away from Haemon*): I can't stop them. It's too late. Antigone has spoken. The story is all over Thebes. I cannot save her now.

CHORUS: Creon, you must find a way. Lock her up. Say that she has gone out of her mind.

CREON: Everybody will know it isn't so. The nation will say that I am making an exception of her because my son loves her. I cannot.

CHORUS: You can still gain time and get her out of Thebes.

exeunt: Latin for "they go out."

CREON: The mob already knows the truth. It is howling for her blood. I can do nothing.

HAEMON: But, Father, you are master in Thebes!

CREON: I am master under the law. Not above the law.

HAEMON: You cannot let Antigone be taken from me. I am your son!

CREON: I cannot do anything else, my poor boy. She must die and you must live.

HAEMON: Live, you say! Live a life without Antigone? A life in which I am to go on admiring you as you busy yourself about your kingdom, make your persuasive speeches, strike your attitudes? Not without Antigone. I love Antigone. I will not live without Antigone!

CREON: Haemon — you will have to resign yourself to life without Antigone. (*He moves to left of Haemon*). Sooner or later there comes a day of sorrow in each man's life when he must cease to be a child and take up the burden of manhood. That day has come for you.

HAEMON (*backs away a step*): That giant strength, that courage. That massive god who used to pick me up in his arms and shelter me from shadows and monsters — was that you, Father? Was it of you I stood in awe? Was that man you?

CREON: For God's sake, Haemon, do not judge me! Not you, too!

HAEMON (*pleading now*): This is all a bad dream, Father. You are not yourself. It isn't true that we have been backed up against a wall, forced to surrender. We don't have to say *yes* to this terrible thing. You are still king. You are still the father I revered. You have no right to desert me, to shrink into nothingness. The world will be too bare, I shall be too alone in the world, if you force me to disown you.

CREON: The world *is* bare, Haemon, and you *are* alone. You must cease to think your father all-powerful. Look straight at me. See your father as he is. That is what it means to grow up and be a man.

HAEMON (*stares at Creon for a moment*): I tell you that I will not live without Antigone. (*Turns and goes quickly out through arch.*)

CHORUS: Creon, the boy will go mad.

CREON: Poor boy! He loves her.

CHORUS: Creon, the boy is wounded to death.

CREON: We are all wounded to death.

(*First Guard enters through arch, right, followed by Second and Third Guards pulling Antigone along with them.*)

FIRST GUARD: Sir, the people are crowding into the palace!

ANTIGONE: Creon, I don't want to see their faces. I don't want to hear them howl. You are going to kill me; let that be enough. I want to be alone until it is over.

CREON: Empty the palace! Guards at the gates!

(*Creon quickly crosses toward the arch; exit. Two Guards release Antigone; exeunt behind Creon. Chorus goes out through arch, left. The lighting dims so that only the area about the table is lighted. The cyclorama° is covered with a dark blue color. The scene is intended to suggest a prison cell, filled with shadows and dimly lit. Antigone moves to stool and sits. The First Guard stands upstage. He watches Antigone, and as she sits, he begins pacing slowly downstage, then upstage. A pause.*)

ANTIGONE (*turns and looks at the Guard*): It's you, is it?

GUARD: What do you mean, me?

cyclorama: Curved cloth or wall forming the back of many modern stage settings.

ANTIGONE: The last human face that I shall see. (*A pause as they look at each other, then Guard paces upstage, turns, and crosses behind table.*) Was it you that arrested me this morning?

GUARD: Yes, that was me.

ANTIGONE: You hurt me. There was no need for you to hurt me. Did I act as if I was trying to escape?

GUARD: Come on now, Miss. It was my business to bring you in. I did it. (*A pause. He paces to and fro upstage. Only the sound of his boots is heard.*)

ANTIGONE: How old are you?

GUARD: Thirty-nine.

ANTIGONE: Have you any children?

GUARD: Yes. Two.

ANTIGONE: Do you love your children?

GUARD: What's that got to do with you? (*A pause. He paces upstage and downstage.*)

ANTIGONE: How long have you been in the Guard?

GUARD: Since the war. I was in the army. Sergeant. Then I joined the Guard.

ANTIGONE: Does one have to have been an army sergeant to get into the Guard?

GUARD: Supposed to be. Either that or on special detail. But when they make you a guard, you lose your stripes.

ANTIGONE (*murmurs*): I see.

GUARD: Yes. Of course, if you're a guard, everybody knows you're something special; they know you're an old N.C.O.° Take pay, for instance. When you're a guard you get your pay, and on top of that you get six months' extra pay, to make sure you don't lose anything by not being a sergeant anymore. And of course you do better than that. You get a house, coal, rations, extras for the wife and kids. If you've got two kids, like me, you draw better than a sergeant.

ANTIGONE (*barely audible*): I see.

GUARD: That's why sergeants, now, they don't like guards. Maybe you noticed they try to make out they're better than us? Promotion, that's what it is. In the army, anybody can get promoted. All you need is good conduct. Now in the Guard, it's slow, and you have to know your business — like how to make out a report and the like of that. But when you're an N.C.O. in the Guard, you've got something that even a sergeant major ain't got. For instance —

ANTIGONE (*breaking him off*): Listen.

GUARD: Yes, Miss.

ANTIGONE: I'm going to die soon.

(*The Guard looks at her for a moment, then turns and moves away.*)

GUARD: For instance, people have a lot of respect for guards, they have. A guard may be a soldier, but he's kind of in the civil service, too.

ANTIGONE: Do you think it hurts to die?

GUARD: How would I know? Of course, if somebody sticks a saber in your guts and turns it round, it hurts.

ANTIGONE: How are they going to put me to death?

GUARD: Well, I'll tell you. I heard the proclamation all right. Wait a minute. How did it go now? (*He stares into space and recites from memory.*) "In order that our fair city shall not be pol-luted with her sinful blood, she shall be im-mured — immured." That means, they shove you in a cave and wall up the cave.

ANTIGONE: Alive?

N.C.O.: Noncommissioned officer, usually of a subordinate rank such as sergeant.

GUARD: Yes.... (*He moves away a few steps.*)

ANTIGONE (*murmurs*): O tomb! O bridal bed! Alone! (*Antigone sits there, a tiny figure in the middle of the stage. You would say she felt a little chilly. She wraps her arms round herself.*)

GUARD: Yes! Outside the southeast gate of the town. In the Cave of Hades. In broad daylight. Some detail, eh, for them that's on the job! First they thought maybe it was a job for the army. Now it looks like it's going to be the Guard. There's an outfit for you! Nothing the Guard can't do. No wonder the army's jealous.

ANTIGONE: A pair of animals.

GUARD: What do you mean, a pair of animals?

ANTIGONE: When the winds blow cold, all they need do is to press close against one another. I am all alone.

GUARD: Is there anything you want? I can send out for it, you know.

ANTIGONE: You are very kind. (*A pause. Antigone looks up at the Guard.*) Yes, there is something I want. I want you to give someone a letter from me, when I am dead.

GUARD: How's that again? A letter?

ANTIGONE: Yes, I want to write a letter; and I want you to give it to someone for me.

GUARD (*straightens up*): Now, wait a minute. Take it easy. It's as much as my job is worth to go handing out letters from prisoners.

ANTIGONE (*removes a ring from her finger and holds it out toward him*): I'll give you this ring if you will do it.

GUARD: Is it gold? (*He takes the ring from her.*)

ANTIGONE: Yes, it is gold.

GUARD (*shakes his head*): Uh-uh. No can do. Suppose they go through my pockets. I might get six months for a thing like that. (*He stares at the ring, then glances off right to make sure that he is not being watched.*) Listen, tell you what I'll do. You tell me what you want to say, and I'll write it down in my book. Then, afterwards, I'll tear out the pages and give them to the party, see? If it's in my handwriting, it's all right.

ANTIGONE (*winces*): In your handwriting? (*She shudders slightly.*) No. That would be awful. The poor darling! In your handwriting.

GUARD (*offers back the ring*): O.K. It's no skin off my nose.

ANTIGONE (*quickly*): Of course, of course. No, keep the ring. But hurry. Time is getting short. Where is your notebook? (*The Guard pockets the ring, takes his notebook and pencil from his pocket, puts his foot up on chair, and rests the notebook on his knee, licks his pencil.*) Ready? (*He nods.*) Write, now. "My darling . . ."

GUARD (*writes as he mutters*): The boyfriend, eh?

ANTIGONE: "My darling. I wanted to die, and perhaps you will not love me anymore . . ."

GUARD (*mutters as he writes*): ". . . will not love me anymore."

ANTIGONE: "Creon was right. It is terrible to die."

GUARD (*repeats as he writes*): ". . . terrible to die."

ANTIGONE: "And I don't even know what I am dying for. I am afraid . . ."

GUARD (*looks at her*): Wait a minute! How fast do you think I can write?

ANTIGONE (*takes hold of herself*): Where are you?

GUARD (*reads from his notebook*): "And I don't even know what I am dying for."

ANTIGONE: No. Scratch that out. Nobody must know that. They have no right to know. It's as if they saw me naked and touched me, after I was dead. Scratch it all out. Just write: "Forgive me."

GUARD (*looks at Antigone*): I cut out everything you said there at the end, and I put down, "Forgive me"?

ANTIGONE: Yes. "Forgive me, my darling. You would all have been so happy except for Antigone. I love you."

GUARD (*finishes the letter*): ". . . I love you." (*He looks at her.*) Is that all?

ANTIGONE: That's all.

GUARD (*straightens up, looks at notebook*): Damn funny letter.

ANTIGONE: I know.

GUARD (*looks at her*): Who is it to? (*A sudden roll of drums begins and continues until after Antigone's exit. The First Guard pockets the notebook and shouts at Antigone.*) O.K. That's enough out of you! Come on!

(*At the sound of the drum roll, Second and Third Guards enter through the arch. Antigone rises. Guards seize her and exeunt with her. The lighting moves up to suggest late afternoon. Chorus enters.*)

CHORUS: And now it is Creon's turn.

(*Messenger runs through the arch, right.*)

MESSENGER: The Queen . . . the Queen! Where is the Queen?

CHORUS: What do you want with the Queen? What have you to tell the Queen?

MESSENGER: News to break her heart. Antigone had just been thrust into the cave. They hadn't finished heaving the last block of stone into place when Creon and the rest heard a sudden moaning from the tomb. A hush fell over us all, for it was not the voice of Antigone. It was Haemon's voice that came forth from the tomb. Everybody looked at Creon; and he howled like a man demented: "Take away the stones! Take away the stones!" The slaves leaped at the wall of stones, and Creon worked with them, sweating and tearing at the blocks with his bleeding hands. Finally a narrow opening was forced, and into it slipped the smallest guard.

Antigone had hanged herself by the cord of her robe, by the red and golden twisted cord of her robe. The cord was round her neck like a child's collar. Haemon was on his knees, holding her in his arms and moaning, his face buried in her robe. More stones were removed, and Creon went into the tomb. He tried to raise Haemon to his feet. I could hear him begging Haemon to rise to his feet. Haemon was deaf to his father's voice, till suddenly he stood up of his own accord, his eyes dark and burning. Anguish was in his face, but it was the face of a little boy. He stared at his father. Then suddenly he struck him — hard; and he drew his sword. Creon leaped out of range. Haemon went on staring at him, his eyes full of contempt — a glance that was like a knife, and that Creon couldn't escape. The King stood trembling in the far corner of the tomb, and Haemon went on staring. Then, without a word, he stabbed himself and lay down beside Antigone, embracing her in a great pool of blood.

(*A pause as Creon and Page enter through arch on the Messenger's last words. Chorus and the Messenger both turn to look at Creon; then exit the Messenger through curtain.*)

CREON: I have had them laid out side by side. They are together at last, and at peace. Two lovers on the morrow of their bridal. Their work is done.

CHORUS: But not yours, Creon. You have still one thing to learn. Eurydice, the Queen, your wife —

CREON: A good woman. Always busy with her garden, her preserves, her sweaters — those sweaters she never stopped knitting for the poor. Strange, how the poor never stop needing sweaters. One would almost think that was all they needed.

CHORUS: The poor in Thebes are going to be cold this winter, Creon. When the Queen was told of her son's death, she waited carefully until she had finished her row, then put down her knitting calmly — as she did everything.

She went up to her room, her lavender-scented room, with its embroidered doilies and its pictures framed in plush; and there, Creon, she cut her throat. She is laid out now in one of those two old-fashioned twin beds, exactly where you went to her one night when she was still a maiden. Her smile is still the same, scarcely a shade more melancholy. And if it were not for that great red blot on the bed linen by her neck, one might think she was asleep.

CREON (*in a dull voice*): She, too. They are all asleep. (*Pause.*) It must be good to sleep.

CHORUS: And now you are alone, Creon.

CREON: Yes, all alone. (*To Page.*) My lad.

PAGE: Sir?

CREON: Listen to me. They don't know it, but the truth is, the work is there to be done, and a man can't fold his arms and refuse to do it. They say it's dirty work. But if we didn't do it, who would?

PAGE: I don't know, sir.

CREON: Of course you don't. You'll be lucky if you never find out. In a hurry to grow up, aren't you?

PAGE: Oh, yes, sir.

CREON: I shouldn't be if I were you. Never grow up if you can help it. (*He is lost in thought as the hour chimes.*) What time is it?

PAGE: Five o'clock, sir.

CREON: What have we on at five o'clock?

PAGE: Cabinet meeting, sir.

CREON: Cabinet meeting. Then we had better go along to it.

(*Exeunt Creon and Page slowly through arch, left, and Chorus moves downstage.*)

CHORUS: And there we are. It is quite true that if it had not been for Antigone they would all have been at peace. But that is over now. And they are all at peace. All those who were meant to die have died: those who believed one thing, those who believed the contrary thing, and even those who believed nothing at all, yet were caught up in the web without knowing why. All dead: stiff, useless, rotting. And those who have survived will now begin quietly to forget the dead: they won't remember who was who or which was which. It is all over. Antigone is calm tonight, and we shall never know the name of the fever that consumed her. She has played her part.

(*Three Guards enter, resume their places on steps as at the rise of the curtain, and begin to play cards.*)

A great melancholy wave of peace now settles down upon Thebes, upon the empty palace, upon Creon, who can now begin to wait for his own death. Only the guards are left, and none of this matters to them. It's no skin off their noses. They go on playing cards.

(*Chorus walks toward the arch, left, as the curtain falls.*)

Euripides

Euripides (c. 485–c. 406 B.C.), last of the great Greek tragedians, did not enjoy the personal popularity accorded Aeschylus and Sophocles, possibly because his work criticized Athenian politics and society. Moreover, he was not highly regarded because he broke away from the formality of language and theme of his predecessors.

Euripides was raised in Salamis, the island from which the Greeks decisively defeated the Persians in 480 B.C. This victory heralded the Periclean Age (c. 460–404 B.C.), when Athens enjoyed its greatest power. However, during that time the Athenians spent almost three decades fighting the Peloponnesian Wars (431–404 B.C.), which drained their energies and treasury, eventually relinquishing their dominance to Sparta. In such an environment, the officials and patriots of Athens were not delighted to view the work of someone who reminded them of their mistakes and questioned their values.

Euripides is especially noted for shifting the focus of dramatic events from the gods to humans. His drama has been called bourgeois because of his emphasis on individuals and the working of their wills. Influenced by the teaching of the Sophists, wandering professors who taught argument and philosophy, he agreed with Protagoras's principle "Man is the measure of all things." The ancients sometimes referred to Euripides as the philosopher of the stage.

One aspect of his dramatic critique of Greek culture was an unusual emphasis on women. Medea is the first thoroughly developed female character in Greek drama. She is treated as an independent woman, not as Jason's wife or as someone's mother. She is herself. Euripides seemed committed to establishing the equality of women and men. Athenians, intolerant of foreigners and women, felt both groups to be inferior to Greek aristocratic men. It is no wonder that of the twenty plays Euripides produced at the feasts of Dionysus only five won prizes.

Of his ninety-two plays, eighteen survive — more than twice as many as survive from any other Greek tragedian: *Alcestis* (438), *Medea* (431), *Hippolytus* (428), *Andromache* (426?), *Cyclops* (c. 423), *The Children of Heracles* (c. 430), *Heracles* (c. 417), *The Suppliants* (c. 422), *Hecuba* (c. 424), *The Trojan Women* (415), *Electra* (c. 417), *Iphigenia in Taurus* (c. 412), *Helen* (412), *Ion* (c. 411), *The Phoenician Women* (c. 412–408), *Orestes* (408), *The Bacchae* (405), and *Iphigenia in Aulis* (405). Another play, *Rhesus*, long attributed to Euripides, is now thought to have been written by an anonymous fourth-century B.C. playwright. Ten of Euripides' plays place women at their center.

Euripides advanced the stagecraft of Greek drama through innovations in his use of the *skene*. Instead of representing the front of a palace, the *skene* in Euripides' plays sometimes represented a peasant's hut, a rural shrine, or other common structure. He was interested in theatrical devices, especially machines that gave him the opportunity to achieve dramatic effects. His use of the *deus ex machina* — a crane or derrick that lifted actors in or out of the play — to resolve his dramas when his characters found themselves in impossible situations was almost his trademark. His choral odes, although beautiful, are sometimes considered detachable from the episodes of dramatic action. Moreover, his dialogue is more colloquial — closer to everyday speech — than dialogue found in other Greek tragedies. All these deviations from the dramatic norm emphasize the humanity in his plays and elevate human values over those of the gods.

Eighteen months before his death, Euripides left Athens for the court of King Archelaus in Macedon. His departure may have signaled his dissatisfaction with the politics of Athens, or it may have been prompted by the indifference of Athens to his talents. In any event, his works were performed long after his death and, ironically, his posthumous popularity dwarfed that of the other tragic playwrights.

MEDEA

Medea won third prize at the City Dionysia festival in 431 B.C., behind works by Euphorion, son of Aeschylus, and Sophocles. The play's emotional dimension and Medea's depth of feeling make her one of the most impressive characters in dramatic fiction.

In his first play, *The Daughters of Pelias* (454 B.C.), Euripides treated part of the well-known legend of Jason and Medea. On the order of his enemy, King Pelias of Iolcus, Jason sailed with the Argonauts to Colchis, and there, with the help of Medea's witchcraft, retrieved the Golden Fleece. Medea returned with Jason to Iolcus, where she convinced Pelias's daughters that they could restore their father's youth if they cut him into pieces and boiled the pieces with magic herbs, as she had done with a ram. However, when the daughters tried it, Medea gave them impotent herbs and Pelias died. Jason's Argonauts captured Iolcus, and Medea and Jason escaped to Corinth.

Euripides continued the tale in *Medea*. When the play opens, Jason and Medea are in exile in Corinth. Jason has decided to marry King

Creon's daughter Glauke, supposedly to guarantee the safety of his and Medea's children. Considering all the sacrifices she has made for Jason, Medea feels betrayed and cast aside for a younger woman. Medea's situation is painful. The Chorus recognizes the legality of Jason's decision to put aside his wife in favor of a younger woman. His motives might be interpreted as plausible and perhaps noble. Medea is Asiatic, a foreigner. By marrying Glauke Jason will impart noble status on his and Medea's children. By law he can maintain Medea as a concubine along with his wife. Medea knows this, but she rejects all of Jason's explanations. He assumes that she is merely sexually jealous of Glauke.

The themes of this tragedy are certainly accessible to modern audiences. As the critic G. M. A. Grube has pointed out, "The tragedy of *Medea* — of Love turning to hatred when betrayed, until the woman's whole soul is dominated by a lust for vengeance that overpowers even maternal love — is one which no modern reader should, in its essentials, find difficult to make his own." The modern audience, however, may take pause at Medea's revenge. She plans not only to rid Jason of his young bride but to kill Creon as well. And her vengeance does not stop there: She determines to kill those whom Jason most loves — their children — and to do it with a loving hand.

The exploration of Medea's feelings and her awareness of the gravity of her actions and their consequences set Euripides' work apart from that of other Greek tragedians. Euripides created many tragic heroines, and his sympathy for women marks his work from beginning to end. Unlike other playwrights working with the Medea legend, Euripides saves Medea from the punishment of Jason and the people of Corinth, employing the *deus ex machina,* in the form of the dragon chariot that lifts her above the *skene* beyond Jason's reach at the end of the play. She leaves him in an agony of grief.

Medea in Performance

Medea has one of the longest and most active production histories in all of drama. Not only did Alexander the Great produce the play in the fourth century, but the Roman playwright Seneca wrote his own version (60 A.D.), with a much less sympathetic Medea. Seneca's Jason is a reasonable man unfairly wronged by a witch. French and English productions and adaptations began in 1553 and have continued to the present. The French playwright Corneille wrote his version in 1634, and an English version of 1756 portrays Medea as insane.

Important modern productions began early in this century. The American actress Margaret Anglin was a sensation in the 1918 production, which established her as the greatest Medea up to her time. Hans Henny Jahnne adapted *Medea* for a production in Berlin in 1926. According to a review written at the time, Medea was portrayed by an older black actress whose magic potions kept Jason young while she aged. The poisoned robe Medea gave to her young rival had the power to turn the princess into an elderly woman "who gradually [grew] older and older and [decayed] into death and decomposition."

Judith Anderson made the role hers in 1947, in a version by the American poet Robinson Jeffers that played for almost a decade. In the 1982 production with John Gielgud as Jason and Zoe Caldwell as Medea, a much older Judith Anderson played the nurse and received extraordinary reviews. In 1974 Greek actress Irene Papas starred in New York in a colloquial English version. Important productions were staged in Russia in the 1960s. Countee Cullen very successfully produced the play in 1959 with a black Medea. In 1986, an all-male Kabuki version of *Medea* was presented at the Delacorte Theater in Central Park by the Japanese Toho Company under the direction of Yukio Ninagawa. A critic from the *New York Times* described the director's intentions: "Yukio Ninagawa, known for his productions of classical theater as avant-garde spectacle, aims in his work to create a universal theater that fuses the traditions of Japanese and Western culture in an expressive style of its own" (Jennifer Dunning, *New York Times*, Aug. 31, 1986). A *Boston Globe* critic praised the power of the Kabuki production: "This was a *Medea* of stunning theatrical imagery. Classical Corinthian order was gradually and relentlessly replaced by savage revenge and blood-stained chaos" (Lyn Gardner, *Boston Globe*, Aug. 29, 1986).

Euripides (c. 485–406 B.C.)

MEDEA   *431 B.C.*
TRANSLATED BY PAUL ROCHE

Characters

NURSE
TUTOR *to Medea's sons*
MEDEA, *Asiatic princess*
CHORUS *of Corinthian women*
CREON, *King of Corinth*
JASON, *husband of Medea*
AEGEUS, *King of Athens*
MESSENGER
TWO BOYS, *sons of Medea*
HANDMAIDS *of Medea*
ATTENDANTS AND GUARDS *for Creon and Aegeus*

Time and Setting: *It is midmorning outside Jason's house in Corinth. Ten years have passed since the*

Argonauts sailed home after finding the Golden Fleece. During that time, Jason and Medea [the Asian bride he brought back with him] have been living modestly in Corinth: models of an unassailable married life of devotion to each other and their children. But the news has just broken that Jason is to marry the daughter of the King of Corinth. [The exit on stage left leads to the town and royal palace, that on the right to the country.]

[Enter the Nurse from the house. She is an old woman who has looked after Medea from babyhood. Her face, the only part of her showing from the dark, heavy clothes that envelop her, is puckered with age and distress.]

PROLOGUE°

NURSE: Why did the winged oars of the Argo°
    ever weave between those gnashing blue
    fjords towards the land of Colchis?
    Why did the pines in the dells of Pelion°
5   ever fall to the axe and fill
    the rowing hands of heroes sent by Pelias°
    to fetch the Golden Fleece?
    My mistress, Medea, then
    never would have sailed to Iolcus° with its
        towers
10   or been struck to the heart with love of Jason.
    She never would have baited Pelias' daughters
    to the murder of their father°
    and be living here in Corinth° now
    with her husband and her children . . .
15   Ah, she has merited this city's good opinion,
    exile though she came,
    and was in everything Jason's perfect foil,
    being in marriage that saving thing:
    a wife who does not go against her man.

[*With a despairing glance toward the house.*]

20   Now everything has turned to hate,
    her passion to a plague.
    Jason has betrayed his sons and her,
    takes to bed a royal bride,
    Creon's daughter — the king of Corinth's.
25   Medea, spurned and desolate,
    breaks out in oaths,
    invokes the solemnest vows,
    calls the gods to witness
    how Jason has rewarded her.

[*Note:* The line numbers to the original Greek text are cited in brackets at the top of the page.]
[*Prologue:* Portion of the play explaining the background and current action. (The editor's notes are in brackets.)]
1. Argo: The ship in which Jason and his companions sailed on the quest for the Golden Fleece.   **4. Pelion:** a mountain in northern Greece.   **6. Pelias:** When Jason came to claim the kingdom of Iolcus, from which Pelias had expelled Jason's father, Pelias sent Jason to get the Golden Fleece. **9. Iolcus:** Town from which the Argonauts sailed.   **11– 12. She never . . . murder of their father:** Medea, a sorceress by reputation, tricked Pelias' daughters into cutting their father into pieces and boiling them, on the pretext that this would magically restore him to youth. Her revenge on Pelias, who had murdered Jason's father, Aeson, during Jason's absence on the quest for the Golden Fleece, was successful. **13. be living here in Corinth:** Jason and Medea were expelled from the kingdom [of Iolcus], and they took refuge in Corinth, a wealthy city and rival of Athens, located on the isthmus between the Peloponnese and Attica.

    She does not eat,   30
lies prostrate, slumped in anguish,
wastes away in day-long tears.
    Ever since she heard of Jason's perfidy
she has not raised her eyes
or looked up from the floor.   35
    She might be a rock or wave of the sea,
for all she heeds of sympathy from friends,
except sometimes to tilt her pale head away
and moan to herself about her father —
whom she loved —   40
and her country and the home she sacrificed°
to journey here
with a man — oh — who so disdains her now.
    Yes, now she knows
at a terrible first hand   45
what it is to miss one's native land.

[*She pauses; almost whispers the next words.*]

    She hates her sons.
    Takes no pleasure in their sight.
    I dread to think
of what is hatching in her mind.   50
    She is a fierce spirit:
takes no insult lying down.
    I know her well. She frightens me:°
a dangerous woman, and
anyone who crosses her   55
will not easily sing a song of triumph.
    But here come the boys after their run:
suspecting nothing of a mother's tragedy . . .
    Oh, it is true —
unhappy thoughts and youth never go together. 60

[*Enter Tutor with Two Boys, aged about eight and ten. Tutor is an old man, dressed loosely in an ocher-colored cloak. The boys are squeezed into shorts and have close-fitting woolen caps on their heads. They hang about in the background, laughing and talking, while the old man advances.*]

TUTOR [*with a half-teasing familiarity*]: Ah, Nurse!
    Faithful old appendage of my Lady's home,
    what are you doing here all forlorn,
    standing moaning to yourself outside the gates?

41. home she sacrificed: Medea had helped Jason take the Golden Fleece away from her own father's kingdom.   **53. She frightens me:** [The translator notes that he has omitted four lines bracketed by many editors as doubtful (lines 40– 43 in the original Greek text).] Dramatically they are certainly a mistake: *"I am frightened she will slip / into the palace unawares, / and in the nuptial bedroom / ram a sharp knife into Jason's side, / or even kill the King as well as bridegroom / and get herself a far worse doom."*

65   Does Medea really want to be left alone?
NURSE: Ah, dogged old pedagogue of Jason's sons,
        when a master's fortunes are struck down
        the heart of a faithful slave is stricken too.
        I am plunged in such a depth of grief
70   I came out here to tell the earth and sky
        Medea's catastrophe.
TUTOR: What! Has the poor woman not stopped
        her crying yet?
NURSE: Stopped! You amaze me.
        Her ordeal, far from halfway done,
75   hardly has begun.
TUTOR: Poor innocent fool — to be quite frank
        about our mistress —
        she knows little of the latest blow.
NURSE: Latest? What's that, old man?
        Don't keep it from me.
TUTOR: Nothing, nothing . . . I'm sorry I even
80   spoke.
NURSE: Come now, we're both slaves here, are we
        not?
        By your own gray beard, do not hold it back . . .
        I can keep a secret if I must.
TUTOR: Well, I'd gone to where the old dice-players
        sit,
85   near Pirene's sacred fountain,
        and there I overheard (pretending not to listen)
        someone say:
        "Creon, this country's king,
        is making plans to drive these boys from
        Corinth —
90   their mother too" —
        I don't know if the story's true.
        I hope that it is not.
NURSE: No, surely no?
        Jason would not let his sons be treated so,
95   however far he's parted from their mother.
TUTOR [grimly]: Old loves are left behind by new.
        That man is not this house's friend.
NURSE: We're all finished, then —
        if we ship this second wave
100   before we've bailed the first.
TUTOR: Now listen —
        this is not the time to let our mistress know.
        Just keep quiet about it — not a word.
NURSE [with an anguished glance over her shoulder,
        in a whisper]: Poor little boys,
        do you hear how much your father's worth to
105   you?
        I wish he were . . .

[Checks herself.]

        no, not dead, he is my master still . . .
        but, oh, what an enemy he's proved
        to those he should have loved!

TUTOR: What human being is not?   11
        Is this news to you,
        that every person's dearest neighbor is himself:
        some rightly so, some out of greed and
        selfishness.
        This father does not love his sons, but —
        his new wedding bed.   11
NURSE: Come along, boys, into the house.
        Everything is going to be all right.

[Dropping her voice.]

        Keep them away as much as you can.
        Do not let them near their mother.
        so long as she is in this deadly mood.   12
        Already I have caught her eyes on them:
        the eyes of a mad bull.
        There's something she is plotting
        and her fury won't lie down — this I know —
        until the lightning strikes and someone's felled.   12
        Let us hope it's enemies, not friends.

[A long-drawn-out sob — Medea's — is heard from
the house.]°

MEDEA: I am so unhappy — oh!
        the misery of it! I wish I were dead.
NURSE [hustling the children toward the door]:
        Listen — there . . . poor children, your mother,
        Raking her heart up, raking her rage.   13
        Quick, inside: into the house.
        Don't come anywhere near her sight.
        Don't approach. Beware, watch out
        For her savage mood, destructive spleen:
        Yes and her implacable will.   13
        Off with you now; hurry inside.
        Soon, I know, her fury will flare
        Out from the slowly gathering cloud
        What will she perpetrate then, I fear —
        Proud, importunate willful soul —   14
        So bitterly spurned.
                                    [Exeunt° Tutor and Boys.]

[A long-suppressed shout is heard from inside: Medea's voice.]

MEDEA: Oh, what misery! Oh, what pain!
        Cursed sons, and a mother for cursing!
        Death take you all — you and your father:
        The whole house wither.   14
NURSE [sobbing]: Oh, how it grieves me!
        Why make the sons
        share in their father's

126. The next 116 lines in the Greek [to the end of the
Parodos] are cast in a different meter, which [the translator]
transposed into the nearest English equivalent. [141. (S.D.)
Exeunt: Latin for "they go out."]

Guilt? Oh, why
150   should *they* be hated?
Poor young children, your danger appals me.
Ruthless is the temper of royalty:
Often commanding, seldom commanded;
Terribly slow to forgive and forget.
155 How much better to live among equals.
I want no part of greatness and glory:
Let me decline in a safe old age.
The very name of the "middle way"
Has health in it: is best for man.
160 Good never comes from overreaching,
And when it provokes the gods, it destroys
All the more thoroughly.

PARODOS OR ENTRY SONG

[*The Chorus of Corinthian women enters, full of apprehension and concern for Medea.*]

CHORUS: I heard her voice, I heard her shout,
      It was the most unhappy
Woman from Colchis — far from calm yet —
But tell me, old Nurse.
5 From the porch of the house, it moaned outside.
O women, I cannot delight
In the pain of Jason's house:
A house I have loved very well.
NURSE: House there is none: life of it gone.
10 The master is had . . . by a princess's bed.
The mistress in her boudoir pines.
There are no words her friends can find
To touch her disconsolate heart.
MEDEA [*in another spasm*]: Ahhh!
15 Cleave my brain with a flash from the sky.
What good is left for me in living?
Alas! Alas! Come Death, unloose
My life from a life I loathe.

[*Strophe*]°

CHORUS: Listen, O Zeus and Earth and Light
20   To the stricken tune of this plangent° wife.
      And you, loveless lady,
What yearning for love on a bed of delight
Could make you hurry to death, the night?
      Pray not for that.
25   If your husband has gone to adore
A new bride in his bed, why, this
Has often happened before.

[**Strophe:** Song sung by the Chorus as they danced from stage right to stage left.]   **20. plangent:** Lamenting.

Do not harrow your soul. For Zeus
Will succor your cause. What use
To lessen your life with grief   30
For a lost lord?
MEDEA [*from inside*]: O mighty Themis,° and
      Artemis, Queen,°
For all the fine vows I bound him with,
See what my hated husband has done.
Grant me to watch him, at last, with his bride,   35
Palace and all, crumble in ruin.
How dare they do to me what they have done!
O Father, my country, the land I abandoned,
Flagrantly killing my brother.°
NURSE: Hear what she says   40
      with her cry from the heart
To Themis and Zeus:
      (goddess of rights
And he whom mankind
      makes keeper of vows.)   45
Certainly soon
      in no small way
Her fury will play itself out.

[*Antistrophe*]°

CHORUS: If she would come out and, face to face,
      Listen to what we have to say,   50
      She might let go
This rampant anger, spite of soul.
I hope I never fail my friends.
So go, Nurse, entice her to come:
Say we are *with* her: we are her friends.   55
Hurry, before she does any harm
      To those inside . . .
Grief can swell to enormity.
NURSE [*walking to the door*]: I'll do my best, but
      am afraid
May *not* be able to persuade   60
      My Lady; and yet
I am glad to shoulder the burden;
Although she glares with a bull-mad gaze
(Or is it a lioness with her whelps)
When anyone comes or speaks or helps.   65

[*She turns at the door.*]

Oh, botchers and blunderers! Yes,
That's what they were, those artists of old:

32. Themis: Justice. **Artemis:** Guardian of women. Called Diana by the Romans. **39. killing my brother:** Medea slew her brother Absyrtus when she escaped with Jason and tossed him piecemeal over the side of the ship, knowing that their pursuers would stop to pick the pieces up. [**Antistrophe:** Song sung by the Chorus following the Strophe, as they danced back from stage left to stage right.]

Makers of music for life and joy,
For grand celebrations and groaning boards;
70 But, oh, nothing for sorrow and pain:
No music or song on hand-plucked lyre
   For the thing that brings death
And terrible endings to many a home.

   Oh, what a blessing is missed
75   by having no music for this!
   What a waste of it, then
     by singing in vain,
   When fullness at feasts
     is its own joy and gain.

                [*Exit Nurse into the house.*]
80 CHORUS: Deep is her sobbing from depths of pain:
Shrill the news her suffering brings
Of marriage betrayed, a love gone wrong.
   Outraged, she
         importunate prays
85 To Themis, the daughter of Zeus:
Keeper of vows, who sailed her through
   Those dangerous straits and the night
To Hellas° across the salt of the sea.

FIRST EPISODE

[*Medea enters from the house, colorfully, even opulently, dressed. She is wan and her eyes are red with weeping, but she is surprisingly calm and in control.*]

MEDEA: Women of Corinth, be indulgent, please:
I have obeyed you and come out.
   The charge of aloofness — as I know too
     well —
is something often leveled
5 at both the retiring and the busy man.
   He who chooses a quiet life
has this alleged against him too:
laziness and lack of spirit.
   Yes, public opinion has most shallow eyes.
10   People hate at sight
a harmless human being,
knowing nothing of the real man.
   I agree, of course,
that a foreigner should conform,
15 adapt to his society . . .
and a citizen is censurable no less
when too self-centered or uncouth
to avoid offending his companions.
   Nevertheless, I . . .

[*She breaks off with a pang.*]

88. **Hellas:** Greece.

I . . . out of a clear sky   20
have been struck a blow that breaks my heart.
   My friends, it is over.
   I want to die.
   Life has lost all point.
   The man who was my life   25
— and he knows it too —
has become for me beneath contempt.

[*She surveys the women.*]

   Of all the creatures that can feel and think,
we women are the worst-treated things alive.
   To begin with,   30
we bid the highest price in dowries
just to buy some man
to be dictator of our bodies . . .
   How that compounds the wrong!
   Then there is the terrifying risk: 35
Shall we get a good man or a bad?
   Divorce is a disgrace
(at least for women),
to repudiate the man, not possible.
   So, plunged into habits new to her,   40
conventions she has never known at home,
she has to guess like some clairvoyant
how to handle the man who shares her bed.
   And if we learn our lesson well
in this exacting role,   45
and our husband does not kick against the
     marriage yoke,
oh, ours is an enviable life!
   Otherwise, we are better dead.
   When a man gets bored with wife and home,
he simply roams abroad,   50
relieves the tedium of his spirit:
turns to a friend or finds his cronies.
   We women, on the other hand,
turn only to a single man.
   We live safe at home, they say.   55
   They do battle with the spear.
   How superficial!
I had rather stand my ground three times among
     the shields
than face a childbirth once.
   Anyway,   60
your case and mine are not the same.
   You have your city.
   You have your father's home.
   Life offers you the sweet fellowship of
     friends.
   I am alone,   65
without a city, wronged by a husband,
uprooted from a foreign land.
   I have no mother, brother, cousin;
am without a haven from this storm.

70   So, please, I ask you this:
  if I can find a way to pay my husband back —
  your silence.
    Woman, on the whole, is a timid thing:
75   the din of war, the flash of steel, unnerves her;
  but, wronged in love,
  there is no heart more murderous.
LEADER: As you wish, Medea.
  You have a score to settle with your lord.
  I do not wonder that you smart . . .
80   But, look, I see Creon coming:
  this country's king —
  bristling, I dare say, with new decisions.

[*Enter Creon with attendants. He is a bearded man
of about sixty, royally but modestly dressed. His face
wears a look of troubled resolution.*]

CREON: Go, Medea. Remove yourself.
  Get packing from this land.
85   I order you —
  you with your black-faced fury
  lowering against your lord.
    And take your brace of offspring with you;
  no dallying either.
90   I am here to see this order done,
  and until I've pushed you out and over the
      border,
  I'll not go home.
MEDEA: So.
  I am lost — crushed utterly.
95   My enemies let out the sail,
  while I have no place to disembark from doom.
    Nevertheless, hard-pressed as I am,
  I ask you this:
    For what reason, Creon, do you drive me
      out?
100 CREON: Fear:
  no need to camouflage the fact;
  I am afraid you'll deal my child some lethal
      blow . . .
  and many things conspire to make me fear.
    You are a woman of some knowledge,
105   versed in many an unsavory skill.
    Your husband's gone:
  your soul is raw with loss of love . . .
  and now it is reported that you threaten me:
  mean to hurt the father of the bride
110   and of course the bride and groom.
    That is what I want to guard against —
  an accident.
    Madam, better to be hated now by you
  than soften and pay later with regrets.
MEDEA [*exchanging a look with the Chorus*]:
115   Heaven help me!
  My reputation is a curse:

  This is not the only time it has done me lasting
    harm.
    Oh, let the perspicacious man
  keep his children from enlightenment —
  above the general run.   120
    It will earn them only
  the sneer of uselessness
  and the spiteful jealousy of fellow men.
    Bring education to the dolt
  and, far from being accounted wise,   125
  you will yourself be cast as dolt.
    Outshine a pundit of established fame
  and you become a byword of distaste.
  This precisely
  is what I have to face.   130
    Because I have a little knowledge,
  some are filled with jealousy,
  others think me secretive, and crazy.

    In point of fact, my knowledge
  does not amount to much.   135

[*She turns upon Creon eyes pathetic with innocence.*]

    But now I frighten *you*:
  do you think I'll strike some death-knell on your
    house?
  No, no: I am not like that.
    Creon, forget your fear:
  I have no criminal intent against a king.   140
    For how have *you* wronged me?
  You simply gave your virgin child
  to a suitor of your bent.
    No, it is my husband that I hate.
    You, I think, have acted prudently   145
  and even now I don't begrudge your enterprise
    success.
    Marry them both and blessings on you,
  only let me go on living in this land.
    Ill-used though I am, I shall keep quiet:
  I am overruled.   150
CREON: Reassuring talk,
  but it chills me to the marrow.
    What are you really hatching in your mind?
  I trust you, Madam,
  less even than I did before.   155
    The impassioned woman,
  like the impassioned man,
  is easier to watch than the crafty and the quiet.
    So, leave, I say, at once,
  and no speeches, please.   160
    My mind's made up.
    You are dangerous.
    All your cleverness
  shall not keep you here.
MEDEA: Please, I beg you — on my knees —   165

by your fresh young daughter-bride . . .
CREON: You waste your words.
  I am adamant.
MEDEA: Will you expel me—
170 heedless of my prayers?
CREON: I will. For I love you less
  than I love my home.
MEDEA: Ah, home! My own beloved country.
  What memories crowd upon me now!
175 CREON: Exactly: next to my own children,
  my country is *my* dearest love as well.
MEDEA: Love, did you say?
  It is a mighty curse.
CREON: In my opinion . . . that depends . . .
180 MEDEA: O Zeus, remember
  the author of this crime.
CREON: Go away — you poor deluded thing —
  rid me of my troubles.
MEDEA: The troubles are all mine:
185 I have a glut of them.
CREON [*turning on his heel*]: I'll call the servants:
  They'll put you out by force.
MEDEA [*clinging to him*]: No, not that . . . Creon,
  I have something else . . .
190 CREON: You seem determined, Madam,
  to make a nuisance of yourself.
MEDEA: No, I'll go into banishment . . .
  That is not what I beg you now.
CREON: Then, why not *go*, and let this land be rid
  of you?
195 MEDEA: Just let me stay this single day
  to arrange my exodus from here
  and make provision for my little sons —
  whose father cannot bring himself to care.
    Be kind to them.
200   You are a father too:
  you know what kindly feelings are.
    As for me,
  it means nothing to me
  whether I stay or go.
205   It's them I shed my tears for:
  their lot is hard.
CREON [*after a tussle with himself*]:
  My soul is not tyrannical enough.
  My heart has often let me down . . .
  So now, Medea,
210 though I know I take a false step:
  have it your own way.
    But let me warn you solemnly,
  if tomorrow's holy light
  sees you and your two children
215 still inside the borders of this realm,
  you die.
    Every word of this I mean.

Now, stay if you must; but one day only . . .
not long enough for you to perpetrate anything I
  dread.
                 [*Exit Creon.*]
CHORUS: Ill-starred woman,   220
  Oh, what a nightmare of anguish is on you!
  Whom will you turn to? Where will you turn?
  What country, what stranger, what home for a
    haven?
    Who will receive you?
  God has certainly steered you —   225
  Oh, my poor Medea —
  Into a sea-race of sorrows.
MEDEA [*turning on them with the gleam of
    revenge*]:
  In the center of disasters, yes,
  but all is far from lost — make no mistake —
  a test awaits the newlyweds,   230
  no little ordeal for the happy pair.

[*With a laugh of derision.*]

    Do you think I ever would have toadied to
      this man
  if nothing could be got from it, no gain, no
    tool?
    No, not one syllable,
  not a touch with my little finger.   235
    The fool!
    He could have scotched me with one stroke,
  flung me out;
  instead he lets me stay one extra day,
  to make three enemies three corpses: 240
  ha! father, daughter, and my husband.

[*She leans toward the Chorus.*]

    Friends,
  I can think of several ways to bring their death
    about.
    Which one shall I choose?
    Shall I set their house of honeymoon alight,   245
  or creep into the nuptial bower
  and plunge a sharp knife through their vitals?
    One thing makes me pause:
    if I am caught entering the palace, or red-
    handed,
  I die . . . and give my enemies the last laugh.   250
    No, there is a surer way,
  one more direct;
  for which I have a natural bent:
  death by poison.
  Yes, that is it.   25?

[*She walks, thinking.*]

    Well, suppose they are dead:

will any city take me in,
will any man afford me home in a country safe
        for living
and shield me from reprisals?
60   No, there is none.
I must postpone it, therefore, for a while
until some tower of strength appears for me;
then, through trickery and stealth,
I shall proceed with death by poison
65   What if I'm forced to go before it's done?
        Ah, then I shall seize a sword,
face certain death,
and with my own hands run them through.
        I shall not shrink from such a step,
270   by Hecate,° no: the goddess who abides
in the shrine of my inner hearth —
the one I reverence most of all the gods
and have chosen to abet me.
        Nobody breaks my heart —
75   with impunity.
        Their wedding I'll reduce
to agony and grief:
agony for having met and married,
and grief for having banished me.
80   Good!
Use your magic to the hilt.
Plot, Medea, devise your recipes:
advance to the deadly act that tests your
        courage.
        See your present plight:
285   laughed at by the seed of Sisyphus°
because of Jason's match?
        Never.
        Your father was a king:
his father, Helios the Sun . . .
290   be aware of *that*.
        Besides, you are a born woman:
feeble when it comes to the sublime,
marvelously inventive over crime.

FIRST CHORAL ODE°

*[The Chorus sings an ode about the topsy-turvy
changing standards of the world. Out of the turmoil*

270. **Hecate:** Identified with Artemis, and sometimes called
Persephone (Roman name: Proserpina), she was supposed to
preside over magic and witchcraft. [285. **seed of Sisyphus:**
Sisyphus, a king of Corinth, was punished in the otherworld
by being made to roll a boulder up a hill. As it approached
the top, the boulder would roll back down, creating a never-
ending task. To be a descendant of Sisyphus was considered
a disgrace by the ancients.] [**Ode:** Song sung by the
Chorus.]

*will come a new importance for women, and a new
reverence. Meanwhile, Medea is a harbinger of female
independence and vitality.]*

[*Strophe 1*]

        Back to their fountains
                the sacred rivers are falling;
        The cosmos and all morality
                turning to chaos.
        The mind of a man is nothing but fraud   5
                and his faith in the gods a delusion.
        One day the story will change:
                then shall the glory
                of women resound,
And reverence will come to the race of woman,   10
        Reversing at last the sad
                reputation of ladies.

[*Antistrophe 1*]

        The ballads of ages gone by
                that harped on the falseness
        Of women, will cease to be sung . . .   15
                If only Apollo,
        Prince of the lyric, had put
                in *our* hearts the invention
        Of music and songs for the lyre,
        Wouldn't I then have raised   20
                up a feminine paean
        To answer the epic of men?
Time in the roll of the ages has much to unfold
        Of the fortunes of women no less
                than the fortunes of men.   25

[*Strophe 2*]

        So you, Medea, sailing away
                from your father's house,
        Threading a passage with heart on fire
                through the jowls of the Euxine
        Cliffs° to inhabit a strange   30
                land where your bed is empty of man
        (The lover you lost, O heartbroken lady!)
        Now are chased from the realm,
                shamed and banned.

29–30. **Euxine Cliffs:** On the Black Sea.

[*Antistrophe 2*]

35   The joy of a bond is gone;
           and wide of the world of Hellas,
       All shame has flown —
           high in the sky and away.
       Bereft of a fatherly home,
40   Where can you sail for a haven against
       The storm, unfortunate woman —
           Your bed
       Royally quelled by another
           who queens it in your home?

SECOND EPISODE

[*Jason enters from the road that leads to the palace. He is a young-looking man, dressed in the swash-buckling cloak and plumed helmet of a captain in the King's Guards.*]

JASON [*embarrassed and exasperated*]:
       So ... this is not the first time
       I have seen irrevocable damage done
       by a barbarous rage.
       You could have stayed here,
5   in this land, in this house,
       had you submitted quietly to your ruler's plans.
           Instead, you ranted like a lunatic ...
       so now are banished.
       To me your tirade does not mean a thing:
10   go on declaiming what a monster Jason is.
           But when it comes to royalty,
       the princess and the king,
       count yourself lucky to be only banished.
           I have tried continuously to calm things
               down;
15   for I should like you to remain.
           But you, Madam,
       obstinate in folly,
       have continuously reviled our royalty,
           And so you are banished.
20   Yet, in spite of everything, I come, Medea,
       patient to the last with someone I am fond of,
       to do what I can to help.
           You and the children
       need not leave the country penniless
25   and unprovided for ...
       exile drags with it a chain of troubles.
           And hate me though you may,
       I cannot bring myself to wish you harm.
MEDEA: You criminal —
       an epithet too good for you ... such
30   inhumanity ...

so you come to me, do you,
you byword of aversion both in heaven and on
           earth,°
to me your own worst enemy?
    This is not courage.
    This is not being brave: 35
to look a victim in the eyes whom you've
           betrayed —
somebody you loved —
    This is a disease,
and the foulest that a man can have:
you are shameless.   40

[*With the thinnest of smiles.*]

    But you have done well to come:
I can unload some venom from my heart
and you can smart to hear it.
    To begin at the beginning,
yes, first things first: 45
    I saved your life —
as every son of Greece who stepped on board
           the *Argo* knows.
You were sent to yoke
the fire-breathing bulls
and sow the plot of death.   50
    Yes, I saved you, lit up life for you,
when I slew the guardian of the Golden Fleece,
that giant snake which hugged it, sleepless,
           coil on coil.
    I deserted my own father and my home   55
to come away with you to Iolcus by Mount
           Pelion,
full of zeal and very little sense.
    King Pelias, I killed,
a most horrid death —
perpetrated through his daughters —   60
and overturned their home.
    All this for you,
I even bore you sons — you most reprobate
           man —
just to be discarded for a new bride.
    Had you been childless,   65
this craving for another bedmate
might have been forgiven.
    But no: all faith in vows is shattered.
    I am baffled:
    Do you suppose the gods of old no longer
           rule?   70
    Or is it that mankind
now has different principles —
because your every vow to me, I'm sure you
           know,
is null and void.

32. Editors bracket this line as doubtful.

5   Curse this right hand of mine,
so often held by yours; —
and these knees of mine —
sullied to no purpose
by the grasp of a rotten man.
0   You turned my hopes to lies.
Come now, tell me frankly —
as if we were two friends,
as if you really were prepared to help
(and I hope the question makes you feel
        ashamed) —
5   where do I go from here?

[*With a bitter laugh*.]

Home to my father, perhaps,
and my native land,
both of whom I sacrificed for *you*?
Or to the poor deprived daughters of Pelias?
0   They would be overjoyed to entertain
their father's murderer.
Yes: this is how things stand.
Among my own friends
I am an execrated woman.
5   There was no call for me to hurt *them*,
but now I have a death-feud on my hands —
and all for you.
What a reward!
What a heroine you have made me
0   among the daughters of Hellas!
Lucky Medea, having *you*:
such a wonderful husband . . . and so loyal!
I leave this land displaced, expelled,
deprived of friends,
5   only my children with me, and alone.
What a charming record for our new
        bridegroom this:
"His own sons and the wife who saved him
are wayside beggars."

[*She breaks off and looks upward*.]

O Zeus, what made you give us
0   clear signs for telling
mere glitter from true gold,
but when we need to know
the base metal of a man
no stamp upon his flesh for telling counterfeit?
5 LEADER: How frightening is resentment
        how difficult to cure,
When lovers hurl past love
        at one another's hate.
JASON: I'll have to choose my words
0   with no uncommon skill, it seems . . .
like a good sailor riding out a storm,
if I am to sail close-sheeted, Madam,
through your lashing, dangerous tongue.

[*Folding his arms*.]

So, you pile up what you did for me
into pinnacles of grace.   125
Well, as far as I am concerned,
it was Aphrodite° and no one else in heaven or
        earth
who saved me on my voyage.
Your cleverness played a part, of course,
but I could underline, if I wanted to be
        ungenerous,   130
how it was infatuation, sheer shooting passion,
that drove you to save my life.
I shall not stress the point.
After all, your service did no harm.
But this I shall maintain: 135
that what you gained by saving me
was far more than you gave.

[*Holds up a hand to stop Medea from interrupting*.]

In the first place,
you have a home in Hellas
instead of some barbarian land.   140
You have known justice:
the benefit of laws which never yield to might;
have had your talents recognized all over Greece
and won renown.
For, were you living at the world's ends,   145
your name would not be known . . .
Oh, to me, houses crammed with gold,
and a sweeter song than Orpheus sang,
are nothing with no name.
But, enough discussion of my dangerous
        voyage: 150
an argument which *you* provoked.
Now to your vindictive challenge
of my royal marriage.
I'll show you, first, it was an act of common
        sense,
secondly, unselfish,   155
and, finally, a mark of my devotion
to you and all my family.

[*Medea gives a gasp of incredulity*.]

No, be still.
When I came here from the land of Iolcus,
frustrations crowding on my trail,   160
could I, a wretched fugitive,
have hit upon a greater stroke of luck
than marriage to the daughter of the king?
It was not — which cuts you to the quick —
that I was tired of your attractions   165

---

127. Aphrodite: Goddess of love, called Venus by the Romans.

and smitten with a longing for a new wife;
still less that I was out to multiply my offspring
(I am quite satisfied with the sons we have);
no, it was simply that I wanted above all
170   to let us live in comfort, not be poor . . .
    I know too well
how the pauper is avoided by his friends.
    I wanted our children to be reared
in a manner worthy of my ancestry,
175   and, begetting others, brothers for your sons,
knit them all together
into one close and happy family.
    What point was there for *you* to have more
      children?
    My intention was — and it seemed real
      gain —
180   to help the ones I have,
through those I hope to have.
    Was this such a wicked plan?
    You would not say so,
except through jealousy — that stinging jealousy
    of bed.
185   You women are all the same.
    If your love life goes all right,
everything is fine;
but once crossed in bed,
the liveliest and best that life can offer
190   might as well be wormwood.
    What we poor males really need
is a way of having babies on our own —
no females, please.
    Then the world would be
195   completely trouble free.
LEADER [*sternly*]: Jason, this speech of yours is
      plausible,
But say what you like, it is not right
To sacrifice your wife.
MEDEA [*with cold disdain*]:
    My outlook must be very different, then, from
      others.
200   To my mind a hypocrite who is too glib
only multiplies the danger that it puts him in:
the more he glozes° falsehood with his tongue,
the more confident and rash he grows.
    He ends by not being very clever.
205   So, you, toward me —
you'd better drop your specious pleading.
    One simple observation
lays the whole thing flat:
were you not a coward, it was your duty
210   to convince *me*; not go sneaking off to marry.
JASON: And you would have welcomed the
      suggestion, I am sure.

[**202. glozes:** Glosses over.]

Why, even now you can't contain your blazing
    rage.
MEDEA: *That* was not what governed you:
you felt your glory tarnished by an aging
    oriental wife.
JASON: Please, please believe me: 21
it was nothing to do with women —
my desire to make this match —
but as I have already said
to safeguard you and rear young princes
to be brothers to my sons . . .   22
so make our family solid.
MEDEA [*with a bitter laugh*]:
Haha! Solid happiness on the grave of love;
Prosperity with a secret sting . . .
O you gods — not for me — ever.
JASON [*earnestly*]: Please change your prayer to this   22
and make it reasonable:
    "May success not seem to me sad failure,
nor good fortune ever a disaster."
MEDEA: You go on mocking me: *you* have roof
    and shelter.
    I am deserted, flying for my life, alone.   23
JASON: *You* chose it. Blame no one else.
MEDEA: Did I? I was the one who wed and then
    betrayed?
JASON: No: you just swore a heap of filthy curses
    on the king.
MEDEA: Yes, and you shall find that *I* am the curse
that Fate has made to haunt you.   23
JASON: There's no point in talking any more with
    you.

[*Preparing to go.*]

Anything that you or the children want in exile,
let me know; I'd gladly furnish it,
or send letters of introduction for you
to friends abroad who will be kind.   24
    To turn this offer down, Medea,
is nothing short of madness.
    Forget your feelings of resentment:
let yourself be helped.
MEDEA [*spitting out the words*]:
Not your friends, not your things: 24
I would not touch anything of yours —
how dare you offer it!
    The presents of the wicked are pure poison.
JASON [*flinging his cloak about him*]:
In that case, heaven be my witness:
all my design to help you and your sons   25
is thwarted by your preference for evil.
    Your self-will cuts you off.
    Suffer then accordingly.

[*He begins to go.*]

MEDEA: Go then. Don't waste your passion here:

go to the fresh young virgin you can't wait
    for . . .
  Have her.
      [*As Jason exits, furious and embarrassed.*]
  And God grant
the match you make, you'll long to have
    unmade.

SECOND CHORAL ODE

[*The women of the Chorus, appalled by what has happened to Medea, speak of the dangers of love and the sufferings of exile.*]

[*Strophe 1*]

Love is a dangerous thing:
Loving without any limit.
Discredit and loss it can bring . . .
But, oh, if the goddess should visit
5   A love that is modest and right,
No god is so exquisite.
Great lady, aim not at me
Your gold and infallibly
Passion-tipped, poisoned delight.

[*Antistrophe 1*]

10 Stay me with innocent living;
Most beautiful gift of the gods.
Never let Cypris° the fierce
Queen of desire propel
My heart to a dissolute lust
15 From old to a new and another
Bed and a dissonant longing,
But test with a sweet eye for peace
The love-bonds of reverent women.

[*Strophe 2*]

O my country, my home, never let
20 Me lose my state and my city —
Living that desperate loss
so helpless and hard, without pity.
Death: I would bargain with death,
To die such a day to a finish.
25 For nothing is like the sorrow
Or supersedes the sadness
Of losing your native land.

12. **Cypris:** Aphrodite, goddess of love.

[*Antistrophe 2*]

LEADER: The thing is before my eyes.
  Learned from no rumor or lies:
  Medea without city or friends   30
  Nowhere where pity extends —
  Oh, how you must suffer! . . .
  Let a man rot in a charmless lot
  If he never unshutters his heart
  To the cleansing esteem of another.   35
  He'll not be my friend: no, never.

THIRD EPISODE

[*Enter Aegeus from the country. He is a man in his early middle years and dressed in traveling clothes. His open features — kindly but unimaginative — seem preoccupied. In his retinue are Noblemen and Servants.*]

AEGEUS [*stretching out his hands*]:
  Medea, all health and happiness . . .
and one can say a fairer thing when greeting
    friends?
MEDEA [*wanly*]: Health and happiness to you, good
    Aegeus,
wise Panidon's son . . . But where do you stem
    from?
AEGEUS: I have just left Apollo's ancient oracle at
    Delphi.   5
MEDEA: What — a pilgrim there — the nub of the
    world of prophecy?
AEGEUS: I went to ask for progeny — for a fruitful
    seed.
MEDEA [*suddenly interested*]:
  In the name of heaven! Have you been childless
  all this time?
AEGEUS: Childless, yes — by some design of
    heaven.   10
MEDEA: But with a wife . . . or have you never
    married?
AEGEUS: I am married. Yes, I have a wife who
    shares my bed.
MEDEA: And what did Apollo say about your
    having children?
AEGEUS: Something far too deep for me, a mere
    mortal, to unravel.
MEDEA: Am I allowed to know the god's reply?   15
AEGEUS: Certainly. It would take a mind like yours
    to fathom.
MEDEA: Tell me . . . what did he say . . . since you
    are allowed?
AEGEUS: Why, just this:

"Do not unstopper the wine-skin till . . ."°
MEDEA: Till you've done something — been
20   somewhere — special?
AEGEUS [*baffled*]: Until I'm back at home again.
MEDEA: Then why did you sail in here?
AEGEUS: There is a man called Pittheus, king of
        Troezen . . .
MEDEA: Yes, a son of Pelops: a very pious man,
        they say.
25 AEGEUS: I want to ask his help about this oracle.
MEDEA: Yes, a clever man, and an expert in such
        things.
AEGEUS: And of all my old battle cronies, my
        favorite.
MEDEA: Well, I hope that all your dreams come
        true.
AEGEUS: Medea, you look so pale, so sad. What is
        it?
MEDEA: My husband, Aegeus: he is the world's
30   most wicked man.
AEGEUS: You don't say? . . . Come, tell me all
        about your troubles.
MEDEA: He's set up a mistress to queen it in my
        home.
AEGEUS: Dear me! Would he really do a thing like
        that?
MEDEA: Yes, yes . . . And I am deposed — the one
        he loved.
AEGEUS: Did he fall in love . . . or is he just tired of
35   *you*?
MEDEA: In love — Ha — head over heels . . .
        flinging all fidelity to the winds.
AEGEUS: Let him get on with it . . . since he's as
        wicked as you say he is.
MEDEA: But it was with royalty he fell in love:
        a king's daughter.
40 AEGEUS: Eh? What king's daughter? Please go on.
MEDEA: Creon's, king of Corinth.
AEGEUS: In that case, Madam, it *is* serious.
        You have my sympathies.
MEDEA: It is the end. What is more, I am being
        banished.
AEGEUS: Banished? This is indeed a crowning
45   blow —
        but by whom?
MEDEA: Creon: he wants to banish me from
        Corinth.
AEGEUS: And Jason agrees? I find that monstrous.
MEDEA [*with fierce irony*]: Oh, he says he
        doesn't —
50 but he'll bear it bravely.

19. **"Do not . . . wine-skin"**: Probably "Do not have sexual
intercourse."

[*On her knees.*]

        Aegeus, I beg you,
by your beard,
by these knees of yours I clasp,
pity me, pity my unhappiness.
        Do not see me banished and alone,   55
let me come to Athens, shelter me,
accept me in your home.
        The gods will pay you back,
give you the children you so long to have,
surround your death with happiness.   60
        You do not guess how Providence has blessed
                you, meeting me.
        I mean to end your childlessness
and make your seed bear sons.

[*Almost in a whisper.*]

        I promise it. I know the drugs.
AEGEUS [*impressed*]: Medea, many reasons make me
        ready   65
to acquiesce in your request,
not least of all the gods;
then because you've given me — a promise:
promise of children . . .
oh, left to myself, I had all but given up.   70

[*Gently raising her.*]

        My proposition, then is this:
get yourself to Athens
and there, as is incumbent on me,
I shall do my utmost to protect you.
        However, I must tell you clearly,   75
I cannot take you with me out of Corinth,
but if you reach my palace on your own,
there you shall have full sanctuary
and to no one shall I give you up.
        So, by your own means you must leave this
                land: 80
I cannot risk offending the Corinthians —
who are also friends of mine.
MEDEA: As you say . . . but . . .
        if only you could promise it on oath,
it would make it all so . . . settled between us.   85
AEGEUS: Do you not trust me? What is the matter
        now?
MEDEA [*glancing nervously over her shoulders*]:
        I do trust you . . . but . . .
but I have my enemies.
        It isn't only Creon,
there is the house of Pelias too: 90
They'll want to prize me from your territories.
        If you are bound by oath
you will not give me up.
        But if you have only made a promise,
not sworn it to the gods,   95

there is always the chance that sheer diplomacy
will win you to their wishes.
    I have no weapons on my side,
on theirs is wealth and all the weight of royalty.
AEGEUS: You are very provident, Medea.
    However, if that is what you want,
I shall not go against it.
    In point of fact,
to swear an oath protects me too:
I can counter those who wish you ill
with a clear excuse;
and you of course, are well secured.
    So, name your deities.
MEDEA [in crystal-cold syllables]:
    Swear by the Earth on which you tread.
    Swear by the Sun, my father's father dread.
    Swear by every god and godhead.
AEGEUS: Yes, but what to do or not to do? Please
    say.
MEDEA: Never yourself to drive me from your land,
    and if an enemy of mine tries to drag me off,
    never while you live to let me go.
AEGEUS: I swear by the Earth and sacred light of
    the Sun
to abide by the words you have just pronounced.
MEDEA [relentlessly]:
    Good . . . but if you break your word — what
        penalty?
AEGEUS: The penalty for sacrilege.

[They clasp hands in silence.]

MEDEA: Go now and be glad. All is well.
    I shall come to Athens as quickly as I can,
    but first I have some work to do, to carry out a
        plan.

[As Aegeus is leaving.]

LEADER: We hope that Hermes, master of journeys,
    Will hasten you home safely to Athens:
    Home to the hope of your heart's desire,
        For, Aegeus, you are
        A most magnanimous man.
MEDEA [wheels round and faces the Chorus]:
    O Zeus and lady daughter, Justice,
    O resplendent Sun!
    And you my friends,
        At last we are on the road to vengeance
    and to our song of triumph. At last there is
        hope:
    we shall see my enemies put down.
        At the very point my plot could founder,
    this man opens up a port, an anchorage.
        So to Athens I shall go
    and moor to her fast towers.

[She beckons the women closer.]

Now I can unfold to you my whole design:
there is nothing sweet in it, as you will see.
    I send a servant of my house to Jason   140
asking him to come to me.
    He arrives
I tell him in the softest accents;
how I now agree;
how it all seems for the best: 145
his royal marriage, his sacrifice of me;
everything that he has planned is for the best.
    But I ask him to let my children stay . . .
with no intention — you understand —
of leaving any child of mine in a hostile place   150
for those who hate me to maltreat.
    No, this is just a device
for murdering the daughter of the king.
    I send them there with presents in their
        hands,
presents for the bride — as a kind of plea   155
against their banishment —
yes, a gown of gossamer and a diadem made of
        beaten gold.
    If she takes this finery and puts it on,
the girl will die in agony
and anyone who touches her;   160
so deadly are the poisons I shall steep the
        presents in.
    But now my whole tone changes:
a sob of pain for the next thing I must do.
    I kill my sons — my own —
no one shall snatch them from me.   165
    And when I have desolated Jason's house
        beyond recall,
I shall escape from here:
fly from the murder of my little ones,
my mission done.
    People that one hates, my friends,   170
must never have the last laugh.
    Well, so be it.
    What good is life to me?
I have no father, home, defense from danger.
    Oh, the mistake I made was when I left his
        house,   175
trusting the word of a man from Greece . . .
but he is going to pay the price.
    Never again alive
shall he see the sons he had by me,
nor any child by this new bride of his —   180
poor girl, who has to die a wretched death,
poisoned by me.
    Let no man think me insignificant or weak:
I am no meek martyr, no — quite the
        contrary —
relentless an enemy I make;   185
though kind enough to friends.
    Such is the genius of my life.

LEADER [*imploringly*]:
>   Though you have shared all this in confidence
>   with us, Medea,
>   and though I long to be of help,
190 we must uphold the laws of life:
>   and so I say to you: "You must not do it."
MEDEA: There is no other way.
>   And though I understand your sentiments,
>   *you* have not been through my agony.
LEADER: But, my lady, to kill your own two
195   sons . . . ?
MEDEA: It is the supreme way to hurt my husband.
LEADER: And it makes you the most desolate of
>   women.
MEDEA: Be that as it may.
>   Argument is now superfluous.

[*She turns to the Nurse, who has entered during the previous dialogue.*]

200   Nurse, when I need real loyalty
>   you are the one I always turn to.
>   Go now and fetch Jason here.
>   But as you are a woman
>   and a faithful servant of this house,
205 whisper no syllable of what I plan.

[*Exit Nurse, dragging her feet.*]

THIRD CHORAL ODE

[*The Women of Corinth desperately try to move Medea from her purpose. Does she imagine Athens, that blessed land, will welcome a murderess? Surely, she herself will flinch from the cold-blooded killing of her sons?*]

[*Strophe 1*]

>   The people of Athens are blest through the ages,
>   Seeds of the all-hallowed gods,
>   Born on a soil unravaged and holy,
>   They feed on the wide
5   Bright pastures of knowledge.
>   Lightly they walk through the crystal air
>   In a land where Harmonia,
>   Goldenly fair,
>   Once gave birth, they say, to the nine
10   Muses, the pure
>   Maids of Pieria.°

7–11. where Harmonia . . . Maids of Pieria: Harmonia, the balance of nature, and the genius of the people resulted in the cultivation of the arts. Pieria was a holy fountain in Boetia where the nine Muses were supposed to live.

[*Antistrophe 1*]

>   And out of the sweetly flowing currents
>   Of Cephisus,° they declare,
>   Aphrodite sprinkles the land
>   And fragrantly breathes   15
>   Delicate breezes.
>   Forever she sheds from the stream of her hair,
>   Plaited with roses,
>   Scented petals; and sends the Loves — the
>   Erotes —
>   To preside with Wisdom over the heart   20
>   And together prepare
>   The glories of art.

[*Strophe 2*]

>   How then shall a glorious city,
>   City of sacred rivers,
>   Host of the salutary guest,   25
>   Kindly take to the killer of children,
>   Harbor among them a murderess?
>   Think of how you are stabbing your sons.
>   Think, too, of the blood you assume.
>   Do not, please, we beg by your knees,   30
>   By everything and every means —
>   Murder your children.

[*Antistrophe 2*]

>   Where, when, will you find the mind,
>   The hand or the callous heart
>   Hardened enough to strike   35
>   These, yours — oh, heartless enough? —
>   How then will you see through your gaze
>   Swollen with tears as you sight your aim?
>   No, no, when your little ones kneel
>   Crying for mercy, you will not   40
>   Find the nerve, never be able,
>   To bloody your hands.

FOURTH EPISODE

[*Jason enters with the Nurse behind him. On his face is written apprehension mixed with hope; on hers, despair.*]

JASON: I have come, Medea, because you asked me.
>   I put myself at your disposal
>   even though you are against me.
>   What, Madam, can I do for you?

13. Cephisus: An Athenian river.

MEDEA [*in a small, contrite voice*]:
　　Jason please forgive me for all the things I
　　　　said.
　　Bear lightly with my outbursts, will you,
if only in remembrance of our great love
　　　　together.
　　I have been arguing with myself,
have taxed myself severely.
　　"You raving fool," I said,
"To antagonize those who want to do you good,
setting yourself against your rulers and your
　　　　husband.
　　His royal marriage
and his design to bring up brothers for your
　　　　sons
does you the greatest service that he could.
　　Why not calm yourself?
　　Are *you* suffering because the gods are good?
　　Have you no children of your own?
　　And are you not aware
you came as fugitive with not too many
　　　　friends?"
　　Such reflections made me realize
I have been out of my mind, hysterical.
　　Now I thank you.
　　Now I am convinced
that in securing us this benefit
you are the wise one, I the fool —
I who should have been your ally
and encouraged you.
　　Yes, I should have been at hand to help,
decked the bed, dressed the bride —
and been glad to do it . . .
　　But we women —
well, we are what we are: let's leave it at that!
　　Do not copy us in our perverseness
or try to get your own back, giving tit for tat.
　　I ask your pardon.
　　I admit to being wrong.
　　I've thought better of it now.

[*With an upsurge of put-on happiness.*]

　　Children, children, come out here,
out of the house.

[*The two Boys appear with their Tutor.*]

　　Come greet your father, hug him, join with
　　　　me
in loving, not resenting him.
　　Your mother's rancor's over.
　　There's peace between us: the fighting's done.
　　Come, take his hand.

[*As the children run into their father's arms.*]

　　O God, what a presentiment!

What an image looming in the dark!
JASON: My sons, my sons,°
　　if only you could go on living, go on loving,
　　with your arms stretched out like that to me
　　　　forever . . .
MEDEA [*choking*]: It breaks my heart;
　　I am far too prone to tears, too full of tears . . .
　　it is the sudden ending of my quarrel with your
　　　　father
　　which makes them flow.
　　A sight so touching . . .
　　　　it overflows.
LEADER: My eyes, too, are stinging,
　　but may this be the worst that is to come.
JASON [*gently releasing the Boys*]: I praise you now,
　　　　Medea,
　　and I did not blame you then.
　　It is natural for a woman to be enraged
when her husband goes off making second
　　　　marriages.
　　But now
　　you are in a better frame of mind
and, even if it took a little time,
realize the good points of this plan . . .
the decision is a level-headed woman's.

[*Turning to the children.*]

　　As for you, my boys,
your father has been far from idle
and, heaven willing, he has made
good settlements for you.
　　In time I shouldn't wonder
if you were not first citizens in Corinth —
along with your new brothers.

[*Laying his hands on their shoulders.*]

　　Grow up now fine fellows.
　　Your father and a kindly providence
have the rest in hand.
　　How I look toward the time
when you will be two strapping grown young
　　　　men,
trampling down my enemies.

[*Medea has averted her head and is sobbing. Her feelings, though genuine, are being used by her to further her next move.*]

　　But, Medea, what is this —

---

48. To my mind there is no doubt that this line and half the next (in the Greek) go to Jason, and not Medea as the manuscripts and editors have it. Otherwise, Medea's remark in 93 [930] makes no sense. The attempt to have it correspond to Jason's wish in 72 [916] does not work. [Translator's note.]

Line numbers in left margin: 5, 10, 15, 20, 25, 30, 35, 40, 45
Line numbers in right margin: 50, 55, 60, 65, 70, 75, 80

these dewy eyes, these tears;
your white face turned away
as if my words struck pain, not joy?
85 MEDEA: It is nothing.
I was just thinking of our sons.
JASON: Well, be of good heart now:
I shall see them through.
MEDEA: I will do my best . . . it isn't that I don't
believe you,
90 but you know how women weep.
JASON: I know, but don't be sad for *them* . . . why
should you?
MEDEA [*watching the tender look on Jason's face*]:
I am their mother.
When you prayed just now
for a long life for your sons,
95 a sudden sadness whispered: "Will this be?"
Well, that's one item only
of what I had to say.
The other thing is this:
Since the king has set his mind
100 on sending me away from Corinth,
and since I've come to recognize that this is best
(for I'd only be an obstacle to you,
living with the royal family here —
who think I am a menace to their house),
105 I shall take myself away, go into banishment.
But the children, please, I should like *them*
to grow up under your own hand.
Persuade Creon to let them stay.
JASON [*taken off his guard, but flattered*]:
I — I am not certain that I can:
110 it'll take a little trying.
MEDEA: But you could ask your wife to beg her
father
to let the two boys stay.
JASON [*reflecting*]: Why not? I think I can get her
to agree.
MEDEA: Of course you can:
115 if she's the slightest bit like any woman.
And here *I* can play a useful part.
I shall send her a present
more ravishingly beautiful, believe me,
than anything this age has seen:
a gown of gossamer and a diadem of beaten
120 gold.
These the boys shall carry them to her.

[*She claps her hands and two Maids appear.*]

Go quickly, one of you,
and bring the gorgeous presents here.

[*One of the Maids hurries into the house.*]

What a double delight
125 What a shower of happiness for her
to have you for a hero husband

and now these treasures which were handed
down
by my father's father — the glorious Sun.

[*The Maid comes back with two boxes. Medea turns to the Boys.*]

Boys, take hold of this wedding gift.
Carry it to the happy princess-bride.
Place it in her hands.
It is not the kind of present she'll despise.
JASON [*as the Boys step forward*]:
You foolish woman — why empty your
hands?
Do you think a royal wardrobe is in want,
or a palace short of gold?
Keep these things. Don't give them up.
If my wife values me at all,
my mere wish will have more weight than
things,
I'm sure of that.
MEDEA [*with an onrush of conviction*]: Do not
deny me.
Even the gods, they say, succumb to gifts,
and gold is stronger than the strongest wits.
She is lucky, *she* is blessed, *she* increases.
This exile I would barter for my babies
not just with gold but with my life.

[*Forcing the boxes into the Boys' hands.*]

Go, my sons, into the halls of wealth;
down on your knees and beg her —
this new wife of your father's, and my
mistress —
to let you stay in Corinth.
Most important of all,
see that she takes the precious things
into her own hands.

[*Packing them off.*]

Quick, now, go. Success be yours.
Come and tell me the good news.
Your mother waits with all ears.
[*Exeunt the Boys with their Tutor, followed by Jason.*]

FOURTH CHORAL ODE

[*The multimurders are imminent. Woe to the victims! Woe to the murderess!*]

[*Strophe 1*]

Now has the last hope gone of the children
living,
Gone and forever: they walk already to murder.

The bride is taking the golden diadem,
    Is taking the poison and doom.
5 Over her yellow hair her hands are fitting
    The decorated dying.

[*Antistrophe 1*]

The gorgeousness of the gossamer gown will
        win,
And the beaten gold of the diadem embrace her.
The bride is decked and ready to meet the dead.
10   The trap is lethally set:
Doomed miserable woman, doomed to fall in —
Ineluctably caught by Fate.

[*Strophe 2*]

And you who are groomed for a murder:
    Son-in-law of a king,
15   Jason unsuspecting —
Are to bring on your sons a demise, and a death
On your bride of a hideous kind.
    Unhappy man, how far
        You are falling.

[*Antistrophe 2*]

20   And you the unenviable mother,
        How I weep for your pain!
        Killer of children for
A vengeance of love that has gone, betrayed
By your man for another
25   Bride whom he sleeps beside
        In his wrong.

FIFTH EPISODE

[*The Tutor hurries in from the palace with the two
Boys.*]

TUTOR [*breathless with excitement*]: My lady, your
        boys —
    they won't be banished.
        And the princess, the bride —
    with her own hands —
5 she took your presents, oh, so gladly . . .
        Now the children's danger is over!

[*Baffled by Medea's grim reaction.*]

    Well I never! Isn't this good news?
    What so transfixes you?

[*Medea draws in her breath in a muffled cry of pain.*]

TUTOR: What I hear is out of tune with what I say.

[*Medea sighs deeply.*]

TUTOR: I thought I brought good news.   10
    What kind of news, I wonder, have I brought?
MEDEA: What you have brought, you have brought:
    the fault is not with you.
TUTOR: Why, my Lady, these shuttered eyes:
    these tears falling?   15
MEDEA: Oh, I am pressed, old friend — hard
        pressed:
    the gods and my own evil counsels.
TUTOR: Courage, dear mistress:
    Your sons will always bring you home.
MEDEA [*in a kind of trance*]:
    Home? . . . First I must send others there . . .
        Mercy!   20
TUTOR: You are not the only mother to be severed
        from her sons.
    We have to bear our own humanity —
        humanely.
MEDEA [*pressing his hand*]:
    I shall try . . . Now go inside
    and see to what the children need today.
                              [*Exit Tutor, worried.*]
MEDEA [*throwing out her arms toward the two
        Boys*]: My sons, my sons,   25
    you will have a city and a home
    far from me.
        I shall be left lonely,
    and you will live without your mother always.
        For I must go in exile to another land: 30
    never have my joy in you,
    or see your bright young progress;
    never deck your brides, your marriage beds,
    or light you radiant to your wedding day.

[*The Boys are now in her arms.*]

    Oh, what a blight my ruthlessness has been!   35
        How useless, little ones,
    my nursing all your growing up!
        How useless all the cares endured:
    the wearying solicitudes,
    the shooting agony of giving you your lives.   40
        And now, how miserably have dwindled
    my innumerable dreams of you:
    your loving comfort when I'm old,
    your own hands dressing me when I am dead —
    a passing every person might desire.   45
        Such sweet fancy vanishes
    and, wrenched from you instead,
    I shall drag my sad life out alone.

[*She cups their faces in her hands in turn.*]

    Your own dear eyes shall miss forever
    your poor mother's face —   50
    your way of life and hers utterly apart.

Oh, children,
do you let those eyes now stare their fill,
and your last smiles linger to the last?

[*She turns to the Chorus, panting.*]

55   O–h! What shall I do?
My heart dissolves
when I gaze into their bright irises . . .
No, I cannot do it.
Goodbye to my determination.
60   I shall take my boys away with me.
Why damage *them* in trying to hurt their
        father,
and only hurt myself twice over?
No, I cannot.
Goodbye to my decisions.

[*A pause, then she suddenly breaks away from the Boys.*]

65   What — what undermines me now?
Do I really mean to let my enemies go,
to laugh at me?
Steel yourself, Medea:
away with this cowardice, these arguments that
        melt.

[*Almost pushing them.*]

70   Go, Boys, into the house.

[*She turns to the Chorus grimly.*]

Anyone whose conscience will not let him
        stay
let him look to it: avoid my sacrifice . . .
this hand of mine shall never falter.

[*Another spasm of emotion grips her, and she runs
to the Boys as they reach the door.*]

No, no! Stop me, my heart:
75   we must not do this thing.
Let them go, you stricken woman,
spare your sons.
Let them live with you in Athens:
they will be your joy.

[*Throwing her arms round them again.*]

Ah! Not by all the haunting spirits of the
80   underworld,
shall I leave my children for my enemies to
        trample down.
No, never.°

82. [Translator has followed] editors [who] omit lines 1062
and 1063 [of the Greek text] as a melodramatic interpolation: "But they have to die, and since they must, / let it be
by the hands of her who gave them life."

[*With a sharp realization.*]

But — they have to die —
the whole thing is settled anyway . . .
Yes . . . the diadem is on her head . . .   85
the royal bride at this moment rots,
dying in her gown — I know it.

[*She turns to the Chorus as if to explain her second
impulsive embrace.*]

You see: the path I have to tread
is unutterably sad,
but the one I set these children on   90
is sadder still . . .
Therefore I desire to speak with them.

[*Seizing their hands.*]

Give me your right hands to kiss,
each of you, my little ones —
give them to your mother.   95

[*Covering their hands, their faces, their bodies, in
kisses.*]

How adorable — this hand — and this . . .
These lips — how very much adored!
And this face and form of childhood's
ingenuous nobility . . . how I bless you both . . .
not here — beyond . . .   100
every blessing here your father has despoiled.
So sweet . . . the mere touch of you:
the bloom of children's skin — so soft . . .
their breath — a perfect balm.

[*Gently releasing them; then almost savagely turning
her back.*]

Go, go . . . I cannot look at you.   105
I am in an agony, and lost.
[*The two Boys, weeping, hurry into the house.*]
The evil that I do, I understand full well,
But a passion drives me greater than my will.
Passion is the curse of man:
It wreaks the greatest ill.   110

FIFTH CHORAL ODE

[*If there can be a feminine philosophy of parenthood,
is its honest judgment likely to be that children are
worth it after all?*]

So often before
Have I gone toward concepts far too tenuous
And come upon questions far too deep

For the race of woman to try to unravel.
5   Nevertheless, even we women
Have a muse of our own, that ushers us in.
(Though, alas, not all) to the world of wisdom.
Perhaps you might find it one in a thousand.
It serves to inspire the talent of ladies,
10 And makes me able now to proclaim
That people without the function of parent
Are happier than begetters of offspring.
The childless man has no way of telling
Whether he misses a curse or a blessing.
15 Nevertheless, the childless person
Certainly misses many a burden.
I mark how the man with children growing
Sweetly at home is worn with worrying:
How to make sure they are properly fed,
20 How to leave them a livelihood.
And then after all to be in the dark:
Were all the worries worth it or not?
Were they a worthy or worthless lot?

     But now let me tell
25 Of the worst and saddest trait of all.
Suppose the children have quite a good life,
Reach their teenhood honest and fine,
What if a fate like Death the cruel
Carries them downward body and soul?
30 What is the use if after all
(On top of all those other ones)
The gods let loose this grief as well . . .
Just for the joy of having sons?

SIXTH EPISODE

[*Medea has been sitting during the Chorus. Now she leaps up as she catches sight of a man lunging breathlessly toward them from the street: the Messenger.*]

MEDEA: Somebody with news at last, my friends,
     And from the right direction.
          Yes, I see him:
one of Jason's men — panting as he hurries —
5   With some tremendous news of bad.

[*The Messenger — an official of the Bride's house — bursts in: hardly able to get his words out.*]

MESSENGER: Run, Medea, run!
     What — you have done . . . is . . . too
          unthinkable . . .
too awful . . .
     Seize whatever means you can . . .
10 sailing boat or chariot . . . Escape!

MEDEA: Run? Escape? Is it then so vital?
MESSENGER: Dead . . . They are this minute
          dead . . .
     the princess royal with her father —
     and through your poisons.
MEDEA: What a pretty word you bring —   15
     my benefactor, my friend forever!
MESSENGER [*recoiling*]: What are you saying,
          Madam?
     Are you in your right mind — not unhinged?
     A king's home a charnel house —
     and you rejoice? . . . Are you not afraid?   20
MEDEA: I have my ready answer too,
     so don't be hasty, friend,
     but tell me how they perished.
     An appalling death
     would give me double joy.   25
MESSENGER [*supports himself against a pillar as he
          begins to recollect an agonizing
          experience*]:
     We were so pleased to see your brace of boys
     come hand in hand to the bride's house with
          their father:
     for your ordeal had upset us servants greatly.
     The rumor went racing through the house
     that all was well again between your husband
          and yourself.   30
     Some of us kissed the children's hands,
     kissed their golden tops;
     and I in my enthusiasm even followed them
     to the women's wing.
          There, the mistress —   35
     I mean the one we have to honor now —
     had eyes so taken up with Jason
     she did not even see at first
     the two boys hand in hand.
          But when she did,   40
     a veil of scorn dropped over her eyes,
     she turned her lovely face away,
     bristling at your sons' intrusion.
          Your husband then began to woo her
     from her petulance and girlish tantrums, saying: 45
     "You must not hate your friends.
     Stop being hurt and turn your head around.
     Consider yours your husband's loved ones.
     Come, won't you take their presents
     and beseech your father   50
     to let these boys off banishment — just for me?"

[*Pauses and sits down hopelessly on a step.*]

     When she saw how exquisite the presents
          were,
     far from holding out on him,
     there was nothing she withheld:
     but gave in completely to her groom.   55

And hardly had your husband and your
    children
left the house
when she took the gorgeous robe and put it on,
and placed the golden circlet on her curls,
arranging the ringlets in the brightness of a
60   mirror
and smiling at her own dead image there.
    Then rising from her stool
she minced off through the halls
on dainty milk white toes,
65 wildly pleased with what she had received,
over and over again
running her eyes down the clear sweep to her
    heels.
    But all at once
a hideous spectacle took place.
70   Her color changed. She tottered back;
shuddered in every limb; was able just in time
to fall into a chair and not upon the floor.
    An old woman there, attending her,
thinking that perhaps the fierce possession of
    Pan°
75 or some other power was on her,
broke into a chant of wonder,
then saw the white froth spuming at her lips,
her eyeballs bulging all askew,
her skin quite leached of blood,
80 and changed her chanting to a yelp:
a wail of horror.
    A maid went dashing to the palace for her
    father,
another went to tell the fresh-wed groom
what was happening to his bride.
85   The whole house rang with footsteps running.
It took no longer than a sprinter takes
to go the hundred yards,
before the poor girl lay unconscious with her
    eyelids shut.
Then suddenly she rallied
90 and gave a curdling shriek,
fighting off a double nightmare.

[*He pauses, gulps, takes a deep breath.*]

    The golden diadem that clasped her head
burst into a voracious and uncanny flow of fire,
while the robe of gossamer your children gave
    her

74. **Pan:** The god of wild nature was supposed to be the
cause of seizures and sudden madness. Hence our word
panic.

began to eat her tender flesh away.   9!
    Streaming with flame,
she leapt up from her chair and fled,
tossing her mane of hair from side to side,
in a frantic bid to shake the diadem off.
    But its grip was adamant   1(
and the golden circlet held.
The more she tossed,
the more the fire flowed,
till, overwhelmed with pain,
she sank down to the floor —   1(
unrecognizable to all except her father —
her calm regard grotesquely twisted,
her sweet symmetry all shattered;
and from the crown of her head in molten clots
fire and blood dripped down together.
    The flesh curdled off her bones   1 1
like the teardrops congealing out of pines,
inexplicably dissolved by those ravening venoms.
    It was curious and horrible to see.
    No one dared to touch her body: 1 1
the warning was too obvious.
    But her father, unawares, poor man,
rushed headlong through the room,
flung himself lamenting on the body,
hugged and kissed it, sobbing out: 12
    "My stricken darling,
what evil power has done this to you,
who has made you dead
and left me, like some ancient tombstone,
    derelict?
O gods! . . . let me die with you, my daughter."   12
    But . . . but when he stopped . . .
from these outpourings —
these melancholy sobs . . .
and tried to lift his aged carcass up,
he found himself stuck fast —   13
clamped to the flimsy robe
like ivy to a laurel bole.
    A ghastly wrestling match ensued.
    He would try to raise a knee,
she would drag him back;   13
and when he took to force,
his own decrepit flesh
pulled off from the bone.
    At last, exhausted,
pathetically unable   14
to lift himself above the shambles,
he gave his spirit up.
    There they lie, corpse by corpse,
father and young daughter —
fit objects for our tears.   14

[*He rises, swaying.*]

To you, Medea . . . from me . . .
there are no words to say.
          Retribution? You yourself will know
the best escape . . .
though in my esteem — and not just for
          today —
50
the whole of life is shadow,
and I would even say:
the people who know best or seem to know,
the subtlest professors,
55
are the very ones who pay the dearest price.

[*Flinging his cloak about him.*]

          A happy human being? Ha, there's no such
              thing . . .
more prosperity, more success in one maybe:
but happier? . . . It does not make one happy.
                                        [*Exit Messenger.*]
LEADER: Justice personified this day
60
has brought on Jason's head
— oh, we have seen it! —
the richest retribution.
          But it is you we weep for,
poor blighted child of Creon,
65
walking through the gates of death
because you married Jason.
MEDEA [*in clear, cold tones*]:
          Now, friends, to complete this mission with
              dispatch:
to slay my children and hurry from this land.
I must not dawdle and betray my sons
70
to much more savage hands than mine to kill.
          There's no way out. They have to die.
And since they must,
let me be the one to cut them down:
the very one who gave them life!

[*She begins her walk to the door, almost like a sleep-
walker, talking to herself.*]

75
          Yes, heart, be steel.
          Why vacillate?
          The act is . . .
necessary as it is cruel and hard.
          Come, reluctant hand,
80
grip the sword — grip it, Medea:
cross your borderline of lifelong pain.
          Away this flinching!
          Away this longing:
consign to oblivion the love you had for them —
85
the children of your flesh.
          Even when you kill them they are dear . . .
oh, my sons! . . . I am in despair, despair.
[*Medea, with the Nurse mutely following in tears,
                    passes into the house.*]

SIXTH CHORAL ODE

[*The women pray desperately for something to stop
the imminent murder.*]

[*Strophe*]

          Come Earth, come sunshafts of the Sun,
          Behold this woman and withhold her
          From her laying scarlet fingers
          On the children of her blood.
          Gold of your gold are they begotten: 5
          Heinous is to spill this holy
          Ichor in the blood of mortals.
          Curb her, stop her, godborn Light, oh,
          Keep this house from murder! Keep it
          Never haunted by the Furies.°   10

[*Antistrophe*]

          Were those birth pangs wasted bearing:
          Children's birth pangs wasted birth?
          You, my lady, after sailing
          Safe between the dark blue clashing
          Gorges, will you hug a rankling   15
          Hatred to your heart, a loathsome
          Rage for murder and revenge?
          Those that spill the blood of family
          Stain themselves with heaven's anger,
          Haunt their homes with doom forever.   20

SEVENTH EPISODE OR DENOUEMENT

[*Cries are heard from inside the house.*]

FIRST WOMAN: A shout — listen — a shout from
          the boys.
FIRST BOY: O–h! What can we do? . . .
          Our mother is on us!
SECOND BOY: Brother, brother! . . . We're going to
          be killed.
SECOND WOMAN: That murderous relentless
          woman!   5
THIRD WOMAN: Shall we break in, snatch them
          from death?
FIRST BOY: Yes, by heaven . . . save us . . . help!
SECOND BOY: We're trapped, cornered . . . now . . .
          by her sword.

---

10. Furies: Ministers of the vengeance of the gods, employed
in punishing the guilty on earth as well as in the underworld.

[*As the Chorus beat on the barred doors, there are groans and cries, and presently a trickle of blood oozes from under the doors. The women watch it, fascinated.*]

CHORUS: Woman of stone, heart of iron,
10 Disconsolate woman, ready to kill
The seed of your hands with the hand that tilled.
One other only, one have I known
Murderously handle the fruit of her womb:
Ino the maniac, god-driven one,
15 Whom Zeus's wife drove out to roam —°
Desperate woman goaded to slaughter
The sons of her flesh, clean against nature.
She pitched from the precipice into the sea,
Fell where her foot fell into the ocean,
20 Dashing two infants to death with her own.
What ghastlier thing is left to be known?

Women, O women, in love and in pangs,
What ruin you've brought on us human beings!

[*Jason, breathless, his face twisted with hatred, bursts in with a troop of servants.*]

JASON: You women standing here outside this house,
25 is that she-ravager, Medea, still at home,
or has she fled?

[*He waits for a reply, but the women cower before the door.*]

Deep down in the earth let that woman hide,
or wing into the highest alcoves of the sky,
before she ever saves herself from justice by this royal house.
30 Does she think that she can kill
a princess and a country's king
and vanish with impunity?

[*He strides toward the door.*]

But it is my sons, not her, I fear for.
She, she shall be repaid
35 through her victims.
I have come to save my children's lives
from some enormous retribution by the family of the dead
for those enormities their mother did.

14–15. Ino the maniac ... out to roam: Ino, a daughter of Cadmus and Harmonia, tried to destroy her two stepchildren so that her own two children might ascend the throne. Pursued, in turn, by their father, her husband Athamas, she leapt into the sea with her two boys. This is Euripides' version.

LEADER: Jason, you poor optimistic man,
you still don't know the evils that have come — 40
or you would not say what you have said.
JASON: What? Does she mean to kill me too?
LEADER: Your sons are dead: murdered by their mother.
JASON [*reeling*]: What — did — you — say?
Oh, woman — my own wife — you kill me too. 45
LEADER [*as the women form an avenue to the door, and Jason sees for the first time the blood beginning to trickle down the steps*]:
Yes. Your children.
You cannot think of them as being alive.
JASON [*limply*]:
Where did she kill them . . . here . . . outside,
or was it in the house?
LEADER: Force these doors 50
and you will see your children in their blood.
JASON [*drawing his sword in a frenzy*]: Servants, on the double,
break these bolts,
force the hinges: let me see
the double homicide, 55
the murdered dead . . . and the murderess to die.

[*There is a rumbling sound, and out of a cloud above the house Medea appears in a chariot drawn by dragons. By her side are the dead bodies of the two Boys.*]

MEDEA [*in triumphant disdain*]:
Why this battering, this beating at the doors?
Are you looking for their bodies —
and for me who did this thing?
Save yourself the trouble. 60
If there's anything you want, then ask.
But me you shall not lay a hand upon.
This chariot, the Sun
— my father's father — gave me
to keep me safe against my enemies. 65
JASON [*hissing with revulsion*]:
You miserable, mephitic° woman!
Beyond abhorrence —
by me, the gods, the rest of men —
you could put your own sons to the sword,
the sons you bore, 70
and kill me too with childlessness . . .
Yet still look upon the sun, see the earth . . .
Be damned! . . .
At last I understand
what I never understood before, 75
when I took you from your foreign home to live in Greece,
the sheer wickedness of you,

[66. **mephitic:** Foul-smelling.]

the treachery to your father and the land that
     reared you.
    You are possessed
and the gods have unleashed the fiend in you on
    me;
on your own brother, too, cut down in his home
before you came aboard the sweet ship *Argo*'s
    hull.
    Your work already had begun.
    You married me, bore my sons,
and murdered them through jealousy of love.
    No woman in the whole of Hellas
would have dared so much;
yet you were the one I married,
not a girl from Greece.
    Oh, I married a tigress,
not a woman, not a wife,
and yoked myself to a hater and destroyer:
to a viciousness more fierce than any Tuscan
    Scylla.°

[*Turning away from the door in a gesture of helplessness.*]

    But why go on?
A million accusations would not make you wince:
you are shameless through and through . . .
you — you bloodstained ogress, infanticide . . .
    Hell take you!
    Leave me to mourn my destiny of pain:
my fresh young wedding without joy,
my sons begot and reared and lost —
never to be seen alive again.
MEDEA [*with acid imperiousness from the chariot*]:
    How tediously I could rebut you point by
    point!
    Zeus the Father knows
exactly what you got from me
and how you then behaved.
    I would not let you or your royal princess
set out wedded life aside,
make me cheap,
so that you could live in bliss;
or let that match-arranger, Creon,
dismiss me from the land without a fight.
    So, call me a tigress if you like,
or a Scylla haunting the Tyrrhenian shore,
I have done what I ought:
broken your own heart to the core.
JASON [*wheeling round to face her*]:
    You are in agony too:
you share my broken life.

MEDEA: It is worth the suffering
    since *you* cannot scoff.   120
JASON: Poor children, what a monster
    fate gave you for a mother!
MEDEA: Poor sons, what a disaster
    your selfish father was!
JASON: It was not *his* right hand   125
    that killed and struck them down.
MEDEA: No, it was his pride:
    the lust of his new love.
JASON: You think it right to murder
    just for a thwarted bed.   130
MEDEA: And do you think that a thwarted bed
    is trifling to a woman?
JASON: A modest woman, yes:
    to you the world's worst crime.
MEDEA [*pointing at the dead children*]:
    See, they are no more;   135
    I can hurt you too.
JASON: They'll live, I think,
    in your tormented brain.
MEDEA: The gods know who began
    this whole calamity.   140
JASON: Yes, the gods know well
    your pernicious heart.
MEDEA: Hate then: I spurn
    the wormwood from your lips.
JASON: As I do yours; so let us   145
    be rid of one another.
MEDEA: Yes, but on what terms?
    That's also what *I* want.
JASON: Let me have the boys —
    to mourn and bury them.   150
MEDEA: Never!
    My own hands shall bury them, they shall be
    carried
to the sanctuary of Hera on the Cape,
where no enemy shall ever do them harm
or violate their sepulchre.   155
    Here in Corinth, the land of Sisyphus,
I shall inaugurate a solemn festival°
with rites in perpetuity
to exorcise this murder.
    I myself shall go to Athens, land of
    Erechtheus,   160
to live with Aegeus, Pandion's son . . .
you to a paltry death that fits you well:
your skull smashed by a fragment of the *Argo*'s
    hull:
ironic ending to the saga of your love for me.

---

93. **Tuscan Scylla:** A monster that inhabited the straits between Italy and Sicily and snatched sailors off passing ships
and devoured them.

157. **solemn festival:** Similar ceremonies were still performed
at Corinth in Euripides' time.

THE EXODUS°

[*As the Chorus begin to form for the exodos march, the meter changes. Jason strides into the middle of the arena.*]

JASON: Murder is punished, and you'll be destroyed
    by the avenging phantoms of your children.
MEDEA: What power or divine one is ready to hear
    you:
    perjurer, liar, treacherous guest?
5 JASON: Vile, vile, murderess of little ones!
MEDEA: Go — go and bury your bride.
JASON: Broken I go: bereft of two sons.
MEDEA: You bemoan too soon: wait till you're old.
JASON: Dearest children!
10 MEDEA: Dear to their mother.
JASON: And so she slew them.
MEDEA: To get at your heart.
JASON: You did! You did! How I long to press
    my little children's lips to mine!
15 MEDEA: Now you are longing, now you call;
    you utterly turned from them before.
JASON: For the love of the gods, allow me this:
    to stroke my children's tender skin.
MEDEA: No, you shall not: you waste your words.

[**Exodus**: Final scene.]

JASON [*flinging out his arms*]: Zeus, do you hear
    how I'm at bay,   20
Dismissed by this ogress, odious woman,
Tigress besmirched with the blood of her young?
So I mourn and call on the gods while I may,
On the powers to witness how you have slain
My children, and now prevent my hands   25
From touching them, dead, interring their clay.
I'd rather they'd never been born to me
Than have lived to see you destroy them this
    day.

[*Before the end of these words, Medea, with a cold, vindictive smile, has moved off in the chariot. Jason staggers out of the arena.*]

ENVOI°

CHORUS: Wide is the range of Zeus on Olympus.
    Wide the surprise which the gods can bring:
    What was expected is never perfected,
    What was not, finds a way opened up . . .
    So ended this terrible thing.   5

[**Envoi**: Concluding remarks.]

Aristophanes

The best known of the Greek comic playwrights, Aristophanes (c. 448–c. 385 B.C.) lived through some of the most difficult times in Athenian history. He watched Athenian democracy fade and decay as factionalism and war took their toll on the strength of the city-state. By the time he died, Athens was caught up in a fierce struggle between supporters of democracy and supporters of oligarchy, government by a small group of leaders.

Aristophanes' plays are democratic in that they appealed to sophisticated and unsophisticated theatergoers alike. He enjoyed complex wordplay, but he also enjoyed spirited and rowdy comedy. Since his plays were often sharply critical of Athenian policies, his ability to make people laugh was essential to getting his message across. He was a practitioner of Old Comedy, an irreverent form that ridiculed and insulted prominent people and important institutions. By Aristophanes' time, Old Comedy had become fiercely satirical, especially concerning political matters. Since Aristophanes held strong opinions, he found satire an ideal form for his talents.

Of his more than thirty known plays, only eleven survive. They come from three main periods in his life, beginning, according to legend, when he was a young man, in 427 B.C. *The Acharnians* (425 B.C.), from his first period, focuses on the theme of peace. Dicaeopolis (whose name means "honest" or "good citizen") decides to make a separate peace after the Spartans have ravaged the Acharnian vineyards, for which the Acharnians vow revenge. Dicaeopolis explains that peace must begin as an individual decision. War, as Aristophanes saw it, was a corporate venture, and it was easier for an individual to make peace than it was for a group or a nation.

The Acharnians was followed by *The Peace* in 421 B.C., just before Sparta and Athens signed a treaty, and it seems clearly to have been written in support of the Athenian peace party, which had been growing powerful from the time of *The Acharnians* and whose cause had been aided by that play.

His second period was also dominated by the problems of war. Athens's ill-fated expedition to Sicily in violation of the Treaty of Nicias lies thematically beneath the surface of *The Birds* (414 B.C.), in which some citizens build Cloud-Cuckoo-Land to come between the world of humans and the world of the gods. *Lysistrata* (411 B.C.) is also from this period; its frank antiwar theme is related to the Sicilian wars and to the ultimately devastating Peloponnesian Wars. These wars were fought by Greek city-states in the areas south of Athens, the Peloponneus. The states had voluntarily contributed money to arm and support Athens against the Persians in 480 B.C. — resulting in the Athenian victory at Salamis. The states later became angry when Pericles, the Athenian leader, demanded that they continue giving contributions, much of which he used to fund the rebuilding of the Akropolis and other civic projects in Athens.

The other Greek city-states felt that Athens was becoming imperialistic and was overreaching itself. War broke out between the city-states in 431 B.C. and lasted for nearly thirty years. These struggles and the difficulties of conducting a costly, long-distance war in Sicily combined eventually to exhaust the Athenian resources of men and funds. Athens was soundly defeated in 405 B.C. and surrendered to Sparta in 404. Unfortunately, Aristophanes lived to see the Spartan ships at rest in the harbors of Athens's chief port, the Piraeus. And he saw, too, the destruction of the walls of the city, leaving it essentially defenseless.

Aristophanes' third and final period, from 393 B.C. to his death, includes *The Ecclesiazusae* (c. 392 B.C.) (translated as "The Women in Government"), in which women dress as men, find their way into parliament, and pass a new constitution. It is a highly topical play that points to the current situation in Athens and the people's general discontent and anxiety. The last part of *The Plutus*, written five years later, is an allegory about the god of wealth, who is eventually encouraged to make the just wealthy and the unjust poor.

Among the best known of Aristophanes' plays are several whose names refer to the disguises or costumes of the chorus, among them *The Knights*, *The Wasps*, and *The Frogs*. *The Frogs* (405 B.C.) is especially interesting for its focus on literary issues. It features a contest in the underworld between Aeschylus, who had been dead more than fifty years, and Euripides, who had just died at a relatively young age. Aristophanes uses the contest to make many enlightening comments about Greek tragedy and the skills of the two authors.

Even in his last period, Aristophanes was an innovative force in theater. His last surviving play virtually does away with the chorus as an important character in the action. His later plays resemble modern comedies partly because the chorus does not intrude in the action. His genius helped shape the coming developments in later comedy.

LYSISTRATA

At the time *Lysistrata* was written (411 B.C.), Athens had had a steady diet of war for more than twenty years. Political groups were actively trying to convince Athenian leaders to discontinue the policies that had alienated Athens from the other city-states that were once its supporters in the Delian League, the group that had funded Athens's struggle against the Persian threat. The Athenian leaders were conducting distant wars and overextending their resources, and Aristophanes opposed the imperialist attitudes that seemed to contradict the democratic spirit of only a generation earlier.

Lysistrata makes it clear that war was the central business of the nation at that time. The men encountered by the heroine Lysistrata (whose name means "disband the army") on the Akropolis — men who guard the national security and the national treasury — are old and decrepit. The young men are in the field, and no sooner is one campaign ended than another begins. As Kalonike tells Lysistrata, her man has been away for five months. Such periods of separation were common, and these women are fed up. Lysistrata has gathered them together to propose a scheme to bring peace and negotiate a treaty.

The scheme is preposterous, but, typical of Old Comedy, its very outrageousness is its source of strength, and in time the idea begins to seem almost reasonable: Lysistrata asks the women to refuse to engage in sex with their husbands until the men stop making war. The women also seize the Akropolis and hold the treasury hostage. Without the national treasury there can be no war. And because they are confident of getting the support of the larger community of women in other nations — who suffer as they do — they do not fear the consequences of their acts.

In amusing scenes generated by this situation Aristophanes pokes fun at both sexes. We hear the gossipy conversation of the women, all of whom arrive late to Lysistrata's meeting. The men are dependent, helpless, and ineffectual and cannot resist the takeover. When the truth begins to settle in, the men solicit their wives' attention with enormous erections protruding beneath their gowns. The double meanings to the conversations are a great source of humor, but Aristophanes also counted on the visual humor of ridiculous men roaming about with large, painful erections.

The wonderful scene (3) between Myrrhine and her husband Kinesias is predicated on the audience's seeing the agony of the husband whose wife constantly promises, and then reneges, in order to build his sexual excitement to a fever pitch. It is no wonder that Lysistrata can eventually bring the men to sign any treaties she wants.

This heterosexual hilarity is also balanced by a number of homosexual allusions. Kleisthenes, possibly a bisexual Athenian, stands ready to relieve some of the men's sexual discomfort, while Lysistrata admits that if the men do not come around, the women will have to satisfy their own needs. Such frankness is typical of Athenian comedy. But the main source of humor is in the unrelieved sexual needs of the helpless and hapless men.

Women dominate the action of the play. They see the stupidity and waste of the war and devise the plan that will end it. They also observe that they pay their taxes in babies and that they are the ones who suffer most. The suffering of women had been a major theme in the tragedies of Euripides, and everyone in Aristophanes' audience would have understood Lysistrata's motivation. The idea that a woman should keep her place is expressed by several characters. And since Athenian audiences would have agreed that women should not meddle in war or government, Aristophanes offered them a play that challenged them on many levels.

Aristophanes praises Lysistrata's ingenuity and her perseverance. When the other women want to give up the plan because of their own sexual needs, she holds firm. She demands that they stand by their resolve. The picture of the strong, independent, intelligent, and capable woman obviously pleased the Athenians, since they permitted this play to be performed more than once (an unusual practice). Lysistrata became a recognizable and admirable character in Athenian life.

The following translation of *Lysistrata* has several interesting features. It is divided into scenes, a practice not done in the original Greek. The strophe and antistrophe are speeches given by the chorus moving first in one direction and then in the opposite direction. Instead of having a chorus of elders, as in *Antigone*, Aristophanes uses two choruses — one of men and one of women — that are truly representative of the people: They are as divided and antagonistic as Sophocles' chorus is united and wise. The KORYPHAIOS (leader) of the men's chorus speaks alone, often in opposition to the koryphaios of the women's chorus.

The rhyming patterns of some of the songs are approximated in English, and the sense of dialect is maintained in the speech of Lampito, who represents a kind of country bumpkin. She is also very muscular from the workouts that she and all other Spartans engaged in, and when she is taunted for her physique Aristophanes reveals certain Athenian prejudices toward the Spartans.

Lysistrata in Performance

Lysistrata has enjoyed and still enjoys numerous productions, both on college and commercial stages. Because it is a bawdy play it has sometimes run into trouble. In New York in 1932, the police shut down a performance and sent out a warrant for the arrest of "Arthur" Aristophanes. In 1959 Dudley Fitts's translation (used here) was performed at the Phoenix Theater in New York with "women . . . wearing simulated breasts, tipped with sequins, and the ruttish old men stripped down to union suits." Hunter College's 1968 production used rock music, hippie beads, and headbands. Less controversial productions include the first modern version, by Maurice Donnay in Paris (1892), in which Lysistrata takes a general as a lover. The Moscow Art Theater produced a highly acclaimed version in 1923 and brought it to the United States in 1925. That version, modified by Gilbert Seldes (published with illustrations by Picasso), was produced throughout the 1930s. All-black versions of the play have been staged several times since 1938. It ranks among the favorites of classical drama.

Aristophanes (*c. 448–c. 385* B.C.)

LYSISTRATA   *411* B.C.

TRANSLATED BY DUDLEY FITTS

Persons Represented

LYSISTRATA,⎫
KALONIKE, ⎬ *Athenian women*
MYRRHINE, ⎭
LAMPITO, *a Spartan woman*
CHORUS
COMMISSIONER
KINESIAS, *husband of Myrrhine*
SPARTAN HERALD
SPARTAN AMBASSADOR
A SENTRY
[BABY SON OF KINESIAS
STRATYLLIS
SPARTANS
ATHENIANS]

Scene: *Athens. First, a public square; later, beneath the walls of the Akropolis;° later, a courtyard within the Akropolis.*

PROLOGUE°

(*Athens; a public square; early morning; Lysistrata alone.*)

LYSISTRATA: If someone had invited them to a
    festival —

Akropolis: Fortress of Athens, sacred to the goddess Athena.
Prologue: Portion of the play explaining the background and current action.

of Bacchos,° say; or to Pan's° shrine, or to
    Aphrodite's°
over at Kolias — , you couldn't get through the
    streets,
what with the drums and the dancing. But now,
not a woman in sight!
                                Except — oh, yes!   5

(*Enter Kalonike.*)

Here's one of my neighbors, at last. Good
    morning, Kalonike.
KALONIKE: Good morning, Lysistrata.
                                                        Darling,
    don't frown so! You'll ruin your face!
LYSISTRATA: Never mind my face.
    Kalonike,
    the way we women behave! Really, I don't
        blame the men   10
    for what they say about us.
KALONIKE: No; I imagine they're right.
LYSISTRATA: For example: I call a meeting
    to think out a most important matter — and
        what happens?
    The women all stay in bed!
KALONIKE: Oh, they'll be along.
    It's hard to get away, you know: a husband, a
        cook,   15
    a child . . . Home life can be *so* demanding!

---

2. Bacchos: (Bacchus) God of wine and the object of wild, orgiastic ritual and celebration; also called Dionysus.   **Pan:** God of nature, forests, flocks, and shepherds, depicted as half-man and half-goat. Pan was considered playful and lecherous.   **Aphrodite:** Goddess of love.

LYSISTRATA: What I have in mind is even more
  demanding.
KALONIKE: Tell me: what is it?
LYSISTRATA: It's big.
KALONIKE: Goodness! *How* big?
LYSISTRATA: Big enough for all of us.
KALONIKE: But we're not all here!
LYSISTRATA: We would be, if *that's* what was up!
20   No, Kalonike,
  this is something I've been turning over for
    nights,
  long sleepless nights.
KALONIKE: It must be getting worn down, then,
  if you've spent so much time on it.
LYSISTRATA: Worn down or not,
  it comes to this: Only we women can save
    Greece!
KALONIKE: Only we women? Poor Greece!
25 LYSISTRATA: Just the same,
  it's up to us. First, we must liquidate
  the Peloponnesians —
KALONIKE: Fun, fun!
LYSISTRATA: — and then the Boiotians.°
KALONIKE: Oh! But not those heavenly eels!
LYSISTRATA: You needn't worry.
  I'm not talking about eels. — But here's the
    point:
30 If we can get the women from those places —
  all those Boiotians and Peloponnesians —
  to join us women here, why, we can save
  all Greece!
KALONIKE: But dearest Lysistrata!
  How can women do a thing so austere, so
35 political? We belong at home. Our only armor's
  our perfumes, our saffron dresses and
  our pretty little shoes!
LYSISTRATA: Exactly. Those
  transparent dresses, the saffron, the
    perfume, those pretty shoes —
KALONIKE: Oh?
LYSISTRATA: Not a single man would lift
  his spear —
KALONIKE: I'll send my dress to the dyer's
40   tomorrow!
LYSISTRATA: — or grab a shield —
KALONIKE: The sweetest little negligee —
LYSISTRATA: — or haul out his sword.
KALONIKE: I know where
  I can buy the dreamiest sandals!
LYSISTRATA: Well, so you see. Now, shouldn't
  the women have come?
KALONIKE: Come? They should have *flown!*

27. **Boiotians:** Crude-mannered inhabitants of Boiotia, which
was noted for its seafood.

LYSISTRATA: Athenians are always late.
                        But imagine!   45
  There's no one here from the South Shore, or
    from Salamis.
KALONIKE: Things are hard over in Salamis, I
  swear.
  They have to get going at dawn.
LYSISTRATA: And nobody from Acharnai.
  I thought they'd be here hours ago.
KALONIKE: Well, you'll get
  that awful Theagenes woman: she'll be   50
  a sheet or so in the wind.
                    But look!
  Someone at last! Can you see who they are?

(*Enter Myrrhine and other women.*)

LYSISTRATA: They're from Anagyros.
KALONIKE: They certainly are.
  You'd know them anywhere, by the scent.
MYRRHINE: Sorry to be late, Lysistrata.
                        Oh come,   55
  don't scowl so. Say something!
LYSISTRATA: My dear Myrrhine,
  what is there to say? After all,
  you've been pretty casual about the whole thing.
MYRRHINE: Couldn't find
  my girdle in the dark, that's all.
                    But what *is*
  "the whole thing"?
KALONIKE: No, we've got to wait   60
  for those Boiotians and Peloponnesians.
LYSISTRATA: That's more like it. — But, look!
  Here's Lampito!

(*Enter Lampito with women from Sparta.*)

LYSISTRATA: Darling Lampito,
  how pretty you are today! What a nice color!
  Goodness, you look as though you could
    strangle a bull!   65
LAMPITO: Ah think Ah could! It's the work-out
  in the gym every day; and, of co'se that dance
    of ahs
  where y' kick yo' own tail.
KALONIKE: What an adorable figure!
LAMPITO: Lawdy, when y' touch me lahk that,
  Ah feel lahk a heifer at the altar!
LYSISTRATA: And this young lady?   70
  Where is she from?
LAMPITO: Boiotia. Social-Register type.
LYSISTRATA: Ah. "Boiotia of the fertile plain."
KALONIKE: And if you look,
  you'll find the fertile plain has just been mowed.
LYSISTRATA: And this lady?
LAMPITO: Hagh, wahd, handsome.
  She comes from Korinth.

KALONIKE: High and wide's the word for it.

75 LAMPITO: Which one of you
    called this heah meeting, and why?

LYSISTRATA: I did.

LAMPITO: Well, then, tell us:
    What's up?

MYRRHINE: Yes, darling, what *is* on your
    mind, after all?

LYSISTRATA: I'll tell you. — But first, one little
    question.

MYRRHINE: Well?

LYSISTRATA: It's your husbands. Fathers of your
    children. Doesn't it bother you
    that they're always off with the Army? I'll stake
80   my life,
    not one of you has a man in the house this
    minute!

KALONIKE: Mine's been in Thrace the last five
    months, keeping an eye
    on that General.

MYRRHINE: Mine's been in Pylos for seven.

LAMPITO: And mahn,
    whenever he gets a *discharge*, he goes raht back
85   with that li'l ole shield of his, and enlists again!

LYSISTRATA: And not the ghost of a lover to be
    found!
    From the very day the war began —
                   those Milesians!
    I could skin them alive!
              — I've not seen so much, even,
    as one of those leather consolation prizes. —
    But there! What's important is: If I've found a
90   way
    to end the war, are you with me?

MYRRHINE: I should *say* so!
    Even if I have to pawn my best dress and
    drink up the proceeds.

KALONIKE: Me, too! Even if they split me
    right up the middle, like a flounder.

LAMPITO: Ah'm shorely with you.
95   Ah'd crawl up Taygetos° on mah knees
    if that'd bring peace.

LYSISTRATA: All right, then; here it is:
    Women! Sisters!
    If we really want our men to make peace,
    we must be ready to give up —

MYRRHINE: Give up what?
    Quick, tell us!

LYSISTRATA: But *will* you?

100 MYRRHINE: We will, even if it kills us.

LYSISTRATA: Then we must give up going to bed
    with our men.

95. **Taygetos:** A mountain range.

(*Long silence.*)

    Oh? So now you're sorry? Won't look at me?
    Doubtful? Pale? All teary-eyed?
               But come: be frank with me.
    Will you do it, or not? Well? Will you do it?

MYRRHINE: I couldn't. No.
    Let the war go on.

KALONIKE: Nor I. Let the war go on.   105

LYSISTRATA: You, you little flounder,
    ready to be split up the middle?

KALONIKE: Lysistrata, no!
    I'd walk through fire for you — you *know* I
    would! — but don't
    ask us to give up *that*! Why, there's nothing like
    it!

LYSISTRATA: And you?

BOIOTIAN: No. I must say *I'd* rather walk
    through fire.   110

LYSISTRATA: What an utterly perverted sex we
    women are!
    No wonder poets write tragedies about us.
    There's only one thing we can think of.
                  But you from Sparta:
    if you stand by me, we may win yet! Will you?
    It means so much!

LAMPITO: Ah sweah, it means *too* much!   115
    By the Two Goddesses,° it does! Asking a girl
    to sleep — Heaven knows how long! — in a
    great big bed
    with nobody there but herself! But Ah'll stay
    with you!
    Peace comes first!

LYSISTRATA: Spoken like a true Spartan!

KALONIKE: But if —
               oh dear!
               — if we give up what you tell us to,   120
    will there *be* any peace?

LYSISTRATA: Why, mercy, of course there will!
    We'll just sit snug in our very thinnest gowns,
    perfumed and powdered from top to bottom,
    and those men
    simply won't stand still! And when we say No,
    they'll go out of their minds! And there's your
    peace.   125
    You can take my word for it.

LAMPITO: Ah seem to remember
    that Colonel Menelaos threw his sword away
    when he saw Helen's breast all bare.°

116. **Two Goddesses:** A woman's oath referring to Demeter, the earth goddess, and her daughter Persephone, who was associated with seasonal cycles of fertility. **127–28. Colonel Menelaos . . . Helen's breast:** Helen, wife of King Menelaos of Sparta, was abducted by Paris and taken to Troy. The incident led to the Trojan War.

KALONIKE: But, goodness me!
What if they just get up and leave us?
LYSISTRATA: In that case
130   we'll have to fall back on ourselves, I suppose.
But they won't.
KALONIKE: I must say that's not much help. But
what if they drag us into the bedroom?
LYSISTRATA: Hang on to the door.
KALONIKE: What if they slap us?
LYSISTRATA: If they do, you'd better give in.
But be sulky about it. Do I have to teach you
how?
You know there's no fun for men when they
135   have to force you.
There are millions of ways of getting them to see
reason.
Don't you worry: a man
doesn't like it unless the girl cooperates.
KALONIKE: I suppose so. Oh, all right. We'll go
along.
LYSISTRATA: Ah imagine us Spahtans can arrange a
140   peace. But you
Athenians! Why, you're just war-mongerers!
LYSISTRATA: Leave that to me.
I know how to make them listen.
LAMPITO: Ah don't see how.
After all, they've got their boats; and there's lots
of money
piled up in the Akropolis.
LYSISTRATA: The Akropolis? Darling,
145   we're taking over the Akropolis today!
That's the older women's job. All the rest of us
are going to the Citadel to sacrifice — you
understand me?
And once there, we're in for good!
LAMPITO: Whee! Up the rebels!
Ah can see you're a good strateegist.
LYSISTRATA: Well, then, Lampito,
150   what we have to do now is take a solemn oath.
LAMPITO: Say it. We'll sweah.
LYSISTRATA: This is it.
— But where's our Inner Guard?
— Look, Guard: you see this shield?
Put it down here. Now bring me the victim's
entrails.
KALONIKE: But the oath?
LYSISTRATA: You remember how in
Aischylos' *Seven*°
they killed a sheep and swore on a shield? Well,
155   then?

154. **Seven:** Aeschylus's *Seven Against Thebes,* which deals
with the war between the sons of Oedipus for the throne of
Thebes.

KALONIKE: But I don't see how you can swear for
peace on a shield.
LYSISTRATA: What else do you suggest?
KALONIKE: Why not a white horse?
We could swear by that.
LYSISTRATA: And where will you get
a white horse?
KALONIKE: I never thought of that. *What* can we
do?
LYSISTRATA: I have it!
Let's set this big black wine-bowl on the ground   160
and pour in a gallon or so of Thasian,° and
swear
not to add one drop of water.
LAMPITO: Ah lahk *that* oath!
LYSISTRATA: Bring the bowl and the wine-jug.
KALONIKE: Oh, what a simply *huge* one!
LYSISTRATA: Set it down. Girls, place your hands on
the gift-offering.
O Goddess of Persuasion! And thou, O Loving-
cup: 165
Look upon this our sacrifice, and
be gracious!
KALONIKE: See the blood spill out. How red and
pretty it is!
LAMPITO: And Ah must say it smells good.
MYRRHINE: Let me swear first!
KALONIKE: No, by Aphrodite, we'll match for it!   170
LYSISTRATA: Lampito: all of you women: come,
touch the bowl,
and repeat after me — remember, this is an
oath — :
I WILL HAVE NOTHING TO DO WITH MY
HUSBAND OR MY LOVER
KALONIKE: *I will have nothing to do with my
husband or my lover*
LYSISTRATA: THOUGH HE COME TO ME IN
PITIABLE CONDITION   175
KALONIKE: *Though he come to me in pitiable
condition*
(Oh Lysistrata! This is killing me!)
LYSISTRATA: IN MY HOUSE I WILL BE
UNTOUCHABLE
KALONIKE: *In my house I will be untouchable*
LYSISTRATA: IN MY THINNEST SAFFRON SILK   180
KALONIKE: *In my thinnest saffron silk*
LYSISTRATA: AND MAKE HIM LONG FOR ME.
KALONIKE: *And make him long for me.*
LYSISTRATA: I WILL NOT GIVE MYSELF
KALONIKE: *I will not give myself*   185
LYSISTRATA: AND IF HE CONSTRAINS ME

161. **Thasian:** Wine from Thasos.

KALONIKE: *And if he constrains me*
LYSISTRATA: I WILL BE COLD AS ICE AND
    NEVER MOVE
KALONIKE: *I will be cold as ice and never move*
LYSISTRATA: I WILL NOT LIFT MY SLIPPERS
    TOWARD THE CEILING
KALONIKE: *I will not lift my slippers toward the*
    ceiling
LYSISTRATA: OR CROUCH ON ALL FOURS LIKE
    THE LIONESS IN THE CARVING
KALONIKE: *Or crouch on all fours like the lioness*
    in the carving
LYSISTRATA: AND IF I KEEP THIS OATH LET ME
    DRINK FROM THIS BOWL
KALONIKE: *And if I keep this oath let me drink*
    from this bowl
LYSISTRATA: IF NOT, LET MY OWN BOWL BE
    FILLED WITH WATER.
KALONIKE: *If not, let my own bowl be filled with*
    water.
LYSISTRATA: You have all sworn?
MYRRHINE: We have.
LYSISTRATA: Then thus
    I sacrifice the victim.

(Drinks largely.)

KALONIKE: Save some for us!
    Here's to you, darling, and to you, and to you!

(Loud cries offstage.)

LAMPITO: What's all *that* whoozy-goozy?
LYSISTRATA: Just what I told you.
    The older women have taken the Akropolis.
    Now you, Lampito,
    rush back to Sparta. We'll take care of things
    here. Leave
    these girls here for hostages.
                    The rest of you,
    up to the Citadel: and mind you push in the
    bolts.
KALONIKE: But the men? Won't they be after us?
LYSISTRATA: Just you leave
    the men to me. There's not fire enough in the
    world,
    or threats either, to make me open these doors
    except on my own terms.
KALONIKE: I hope not, by Aphrodite!
    After all,
    we've got a reputation for bitchiness to live up
    to.   *(Exeunt.°)*

[S.D.] **Exeunt:** Latin for "they go out."

PARODOS:°
CHORAL EPISODE

(The hillside just under the Akropolis. Enter Chorus of Old Men with burning torches and braziers; much puffing and coughing.)

KORYPHAIOS(man):° Forward march, Drakes, old
    friend: never you mind
    that damn big log banging hell down on your
    back.

Strophe° 1

CHORUS(men): There's this to be said for longevity:
    You see things you thought that you'd never see.
        Look, Strymodoros, who would have thought
        it?   5
        We've caught it —
                   the New Femininity!
    The wives of our bosom, our board, our bed —
    Now, by the gods, they've gone ahead
    And taken the Citadel (Heaven knows why!),
    Profanèd the sacred statuar-y,   10
                     And barred the doors,
                     The subversive whores!
KORYPHAIOS(m): Shake a leg there, Philurgos, man:
    the Akropolis or bust!
    Put the kindling around here. We'll build one
    almighty big
    bonfire for the whole bunch of bitches, every last
    one;   15
    and the first we fry will be old Lykon's woman.

Antistrophe° 1

CHORUS(m): They're not going to give me the old
    horse-laugh!
    No, by Demeter, they won't pull this off!
        Think of Kleomenes: even he
        Didn't go free
                 till he brought me his stuff.   20
    A good man he was, all stinking and shaggy,
    Bare as an eel except for the bag he
    Covered his rear with. God, what a mess!

Parodos: The song or ode chanted by the Chorus on their entry. **Koryphaios:** Leader of the Chorus; also called *Choragos*. There are two Choruses and two Koryphaioi, one male and one female. **Strophe:** Song sung by the Chorus as they danced from stage right to stage left. **Antistrophe:** Song sung by the Chorus following the Strophe, as they danced back from stage left to stage right.

Never a bath in six years, I'd guess.

25   Pure Sparta, man!
                                              He also ran.

KORYPHAIOS(m): That was a siege, friends! Seventeen
       ranks strong
we slept at the Gate. And shall we not do as
       much
against these women, whom God and Euripides
       hate?
If we don't, I'll turn in my medals from

30   Marathon.

Strophe 2

CHORUS(m): Onward and upward! A little push,
       And we're there.
Ouch, my shoulders! I could wish
       For a pair

35   Of good strong oxen. Keep your eye
On the fire there, it mustn't die.
                                              Akh! Akh!
The smoke would make a cadaver cough!

Antistrophe 2

Holy Herakles, a hot spark

40   Bit my eye!
Damn this hellfire, damn this work!
       So say I.
Onward and upward just the same.
(Laches, remember the Goddess: for shame!)

45   Akh! Akh!
The smoke would make a cadaver cough!

KORYPHAIOS(m): At last (and let us give suitable
       thanks to God
for his infinite mercies) I have managed to bring
my personal flame to the common goal. It
       breathes, it lives.

50   Now, gentlemen, let us consider. Shall we insert
the torch, say, into the brazier, and thus extract
a kindling brand? And shall we then, do you
       think,
push on to the gate like valiant sheep? On the
       whole yes.
But I would have you consider this, too: if
       they —

55   I refer to the women — should refuse to open,
what then? Do we set the doors afire
and smoke them out? At ease, men. Meditate.
Akh, the smoke! Woof! What we really need

is the loan of a general or two from the Samos
       Command.°

60   At least we've got this lumber off our backs.
That's something. And now let's look to our fire.

O Pot, brave Brazier, touch my torch with
       flame!
Victory, Goddess, I invoke thy name!
Strike down these paradigms of female pride,
And we shall hang our trophies up inside.   65

(*Enter Chorus of Old Women on the walls of the
Akropolis, carrying jars of water.*)

KORYPHAIOS(woman): Smoke, girls, smoke! There's
       smoke all over the place!
Probably fire, too. Hurry, girls! Fire! Fire!

Strophe 1

CHORUS(women): Nikodike, run!
       Or Kalyke's done
To a turn, and poor Kritylla's   70
Smoked like a ham.
                              Damn
These old men! Are we too late?
I nearly died down at the place
Where we fill our jars:
       Slaves pushing and jostling —   75
       Such a hustling
I never saw in all my days.

Antistrophe 1

But here's water at last.
Haste, sisters, haste!
Slosh it on them, slosh it down,   80
The silly old wrecks!
                              Sex
Almighty! What they want's
A hot bath? Good. Send one down.
Athena of Athens town,
       Trito-born!° Helm of Gold!   85
       Cripple the old
Firemen! Help us help them drown!

(*The old men capture a woman, Stratyllis.*)

STRATYLLIS: Let me go! Let me go!
KORYPHAIOS(w):   You walking corpses,
       have you no shame?

---

59. Samos Command: Headquarters of the Athenian military.   **85. Trito-born:** Athena, goddess of wisdom, was said to have been born near Lake Tritonis, in Libya.

KORYPHAIOS^(m):   I wouldn't have believed it!
90   An army of women in the Akropolis!
KORYPHAIOS^(w): So we scare you, do we? Grandpa,
       you've seen
       only our pickets yet!
KORYPHAIOS^(m):   Hey, Phaidrias!
       Help me with the necks of these jabbering hens!
KORYPHAIOS^(w): Down with your pots, girls! We'll
       need both hands
       if these antiques attack us!
95   KORYPHAIOS^(m):   Want your face kicked in?
KORYPHAIOS^(w): Want your balls chewed off?
KORYPHAIOS^(m):   Look out! I've got a stick!
KORYPHAIOS^(w): You lay a half-inch of your stick on
       Stratyllis,
       and you'll never stick again!
KORYPHAIOS^(m): Fall apart!
KORYPHAIOS^(w):   I'll spit up your guts!
KORYPHAIOS^(m):   Euripides! Master!
       How well you knew women!
100 KORYPHAIOS^(w):   Listen to him, Rhodippe,
       up with the pots!
KORYPHAIOS^(m):   Demolition of God,
       what good are your pots?
KORYPHAIOS^(w):   You refugee from the tomb,
       what good is your fire?
KORYPHAIOS^(m):   Good enough to make a pyre
       to barbecue you!
KORYPHAIOS^(w): We'll squizzle your kindling!
KORYPHAIOS^(m): You think so?
105 KORYPHAIOS^(w):   Yah! Just hang around a while!
KORYPHAIOS^(m): Want a touch of my torch?
KORYPHAIOS^(w):   It needs a good soaping.
KORYPHAIOS^(m): How about you?
KORYPHAIOS^(w):   Soap for a senile bridegroom!
KORYPHAIOS^(m): Senile? Hold your trap
KORYPHAIOS^(w):   Just *you* try to hold it!
KORYPHAIOS^(m): The yammer of women!
KORYPHAIOS^(w):   Oh is that so?
110 You're not in the jury room now, you know.
KORYPHAIOS^(m): Gentlemen, I beg you, burn off that
       woman's hair!
KORYPHAIOS^(w): Let it come down!

(*They empty their pots on the men.*)

KORYPHAIOS^(m): What a way to drown!
KORYPHAIOS^(w):   Hot, hey?
KORYPHAIOS^(m):   Say,
       enough!
KORYPHAIOS^(w): Dandruff
115   needs watering. I'll make you
       nice and fresh.
KORYPHAIOS^(m):   For God's sake, you,
       hold off!

SCENE 1

(*Enter a Commissioner accompanied by four constables.*)

COMMISSIONER: These degenerate women! What a
       racket of little drums,
       what a yapping for Adonis° on every house-top!
       It's like the time in the Assembly when I was
       listening
       to a speech — out of order, as usual — by that
       fool
       Demostratos,° all about troops for Sicily,°   5
       that kind of nonsense —
                       and there was his wife
       trotting around in circles howling
       Alas for Adonis! —
                       and Demostratos insisting
       we must draft every last Zakynthian that can
       walk —
       and his wife up there on the roof,   10
       drunk as an owl, yowling
       Oh weep for Adonis! —
                       and that damned ox Demostratos
       mooing away through the rumpus. That's what
       we get
       for putting up with this wretched woman-
       business!
KORYPHAIOS^(m): Sir, you haven't heard the half of it.
       They laughed at us!   . 15
       Insulted us! They took pitchers of water
       and nearly drowned us! We're still wringing out
       our clothes,
       for all the world like unhousebroken brats.
COMMISSIONER: Serves you right, by Poseidon!
       Whose fault is it if these women-folk of ours   20
       get out of hand? We coddle them,
       we teach them to be wasteful and loose. You'll
       see a husband
       go into a jeweler's. "Look," he'll say,
       "jeweler," he'll say, "you remember that gold
       choker
       you made for my wife? Well, she went to a
       dance last night   25
       and broke the clasp. Now, I've got to go to
       Salamis,
       and can't be bothered. Run over to my house
       tonight,
       will you, and see if you can put it together for
       her."

2. Adonis: Fertility god, loved by Aphrodite.   **5. Demos-
tratos:** Athenian orator and politician.   **Sicily:** Reference to
the Sicilian Expedition (415–413 B.C.) in which Athens was
decisively defeated.

Or another one

30 goes to a cobbler — a good strong workman, too,
with an awl that was never meant for child's play. "Here,"
he'll tell him, "one of my wife's shoes is pinching
her little toe. Could you come up about noon
and stretch it out for her?"
                         Well, what do you expect?
35 Look at me, for example, I'm a Public Officer,
and it's one of my duties to pay off the sailors.
And where's the money? Up there in the Akropolis!
And those blasted women slam the door in my face!
But what are we waiting for?
                         — Look here, constable,
40 stop sniffing around for a tavern, and get us
some crowbars. We'll force their gates! As a matter of fact,
I'll do a little forcing myself.

(*Enter Lysistrata, above, with Myrrhine, Kalonike, and the Boiotian.*)

LYSISTRATA: No need of forcing.
Here I am, of my own accord. And all this talk
about locked doors — ! We don't need locked doors,
45 but just the least bit of common sense.
COMMISSIONER: Is that so, ma'am!
                         — Where's my constable?
                         — Constable,
arrest that woman, and tie her hands behind her.
LYSISTRATA: If he touches me, I swear by Artemis
there'll be one scamp dropped from the public pay-roll tomorrow!
COMMISSIONER: Well, constable? You're not afraid,
50   I suppose? Grab her,
two of you, around the middle!
KALONIKE: No, by Pandrosos!°
Lay a hand on her, and I'll jump on you so hard
your guts will come out the back door!
COMMISSIONER: That's what *you* think!
Where's the sergeant? — Here, you: tie up that trollop first,
the one with the pretty talk!
55 MYRRHINE: By the Moon-Goddess,°
just try! They'll have to scoop you up with a spoon!

---

51. Pandrosos: A woman's oath referring to one of the daughters of the founder of Athens. **55. Moon-Goddess:** Artemis, goddess of the hunt and of fertility, daughter of Zeus.

COMMISSIONER: Another one!
                         Officer, seize that woman!
                         I swear
I'll put an end to this riot!
BOIOTIAN: By the Taurian,°
one inch closer, you'll be one screaming bald-head!
COMMISSIONER: Lord, what a mess! And my constables seem ineffective.   60
But — women get the best of us? By God, no!
                         — Skythians!°
Close ranks and forward march!
LYSISTRATA: "Forward," indeed!
By the Two Goddesses, what's the sense in *that*?
They're up against four companies of women
armed from top to bottom.
COMMISSIONER: Forward, my Skythians! 65
LYSISTRATA: Forward, yourselves, dear comrades!
You grainlettucebeanseedmarket girls!
You garlicandonionbreadbakery girls!
Give it to 'em! Knock 'em down! Scratch 'em!
Tell 'em what you think of 'em!

(*General melee, the Skythians yield.*)

                         — Ah, that's enough! 70
Sound a retreat: good soldiers don't rob the dead.
COMMISSIONER: A nice day *this* has been for the police!
LYSISTRATA: Well, there you are. — Did you really think we women
would be driven like slaves? Maybe now you'll admit
that a woman knows something about spirit.
COMMISSIONER: Spirit enough, 75
especially spirits in bottles! Dear Lord Apollo!
KORYPHAIOS[(m)]: Your Honor, there's no use talking to them. Words
mean nothing whatever to wild animals like these.
Think of the sousing they gave us! and the water
was not, I believe, of the purest.   80
KORYPHAIOS[(w)]: You shouldn't have come after us.
And if you try it again,
you'll be one eye short! — Although, as a matter of fact,
what I like best is just to stay at home and read,
like a sweet little bride: never hurting a soul, no,
never going out. But if you *must* shake hornets' nests,   85
look out for the hornets.

---

58. Taurian: Reference to Artemis, who was said to have been worshiped in a cult at Taurica Chersonesos. **61. Skythians:** Athenian archers.

Strophe 1

CHORUS[m]: Of all the beasts that God hath
          wrought
     What monster's worse than woman?
     Who shall encompass with his thought
        Their guile unending? No man.

     They've seized the Heights, the Rock, the
          Shrine —
     But to what end? I wot not.
     Sure there's some clue to their design!
     Have you the key? I thought not.
KORYPHAIOS[m]: We might question them, I suppose.
     But I warn you, sir,
     don't believe anything you hear! It would be un-
          Athenian
     not to get to the bottom of this plot.
COMMISSIONER: Very well.
     My first question is this: Why, so help you God,
     did you bar the gates of the Akropolis?
LYSISTRATA: Why?
     To keep the money, of course. No money, no
          war.
COMMISSIONER: You think that money's the cause
     of war?
LYSISTRATA: I do.
     Money brought about that Peisandros° business
     and all the other attacks on the State. Well and
          good!
     They'll not get another cent here!
COMMISSIONER: And what will you do?
LYSISTRATA: What a question! From now on, we
     intend
     to control the Treasury.
COMMISSIONER: Control the Treasury!
LYSISTRATA: Why not? Does that seem strange?
     After all,
     we control our household budgets.
COMMISSIONER: But that's different!
LYSISTRATA: "Different"? What do you mean?
COMMISSIONER: I mean simply this:
     it's the Treasury that pays for National Defense.
LYSISTRATA: Unnecessary. We propose to abolish
     war.
COMMISSIONER: Good God. — And National
     Security?
LYSISTRATA: Leave that to us.
COMMISSIONER: You?
LYSISTRATA: Us.
COMMISSIONER: We're done for, then!

---

102. Peisandros: A politician who plotted against the Athenian democracy.

LYSISTRATA: Never mind.
     We women will save you in spite of yourselves.
COMMISSIONER: What nonsense!
LYSISTRATA: If you like. But you must accept it, like
     it or not.
COMMISSIONER: Why, this is downright subversion!
LYSISTRATA: Maybe it is.
     But we're going to save you, Judge.
COMMISSIONER: I don't *want* to be saved.
LYSISTRATA: Tut. The death-wish. All the more
     reason.
COMMISSIONER: But the idea of women bothering
     themselves about peace and war!
LYSISTRATA: Will you listen to me?
COMMISSIONER: Yes. But be brief, or I'll —
LYSISTRATA: This is no time for stupid threats.
COMMISSIONER: By the gods,
     I can't stand any more!
AN OLD WOMAN: Can't stand? Well, well.
COMMISSIONER: That's enough out of you, you old
     buzzard!
     Now, Lysistrata: tell me what you're thinking.
LYSISTRATA: Glad to.
                    Ever since this war began
     We women have been watching you men,
          agreeing with you,
     keeping our thoughts to ourselves. That doesn't
          mean
     we were happy: we weren't, for we saw how
          things were going;
     but we'd listen to you at dinner
     arguing this way and that.
                    — Oh you, and your big
     Top Secrets! —
                    And then we'd grin like little patriots
     (though goodness knows we didn't feel like
          grinning) and ask you:
     "Dear, did the Armistice come up in Assembly
          today?"
     And you'd say, "None of your business! Pipe
          down!" you'd say.
     And so we would.
AN OLD WOMAN: *I* wouldn't have, by God!
COMMISSIONER: You'd have taken a beating, then!
                              — Go on.
LYSISTRATA: Well, we'd be quiet. But then, you
     know, all at once
     you men would think up something worse than
          ever.
     Even *I* could see it was fatal. And, "Darling,"
          I'd say,
     "have you gone completely mad?" And my
          husband would look at me
     and say, "Wife, you've got your weaving to
          attend to.

Mind your tongue, if you don't want a slap.
  'War's
a man's affair!' "°
COMMISSIONER: Good words, and well pronounced.
LYSISTRATA: You're a fool if you think so.
                                    It was hard enough
145 to put up with all this banquet-hall strategy.
But then we'd hear you out in the public square:
"Nobody left for the draft-quota here in
  Athens?"
you'd say; and, "No," someone else would say,
  "not a man!"
And so we women decided to rescue Greece.
You might as well listen to us now: you'll have
150   to, later.
COMMISSIONER: *You* rescue Greece? Absurd.
LYSISTRATA: You're the absurd one.
COMMISSIONER: You expect me to take orders from
  a woman?
              I'd die first!
LYSISTRATA: Heavens, if that's what's bothering
  you, take my veil,
here, and wrap it around your poor head.
KALONIKE: Yes,
155 and you can have my market-basket, too.
Go home, tighten your girdle, do the washing,
  mind
your beans! "War's
a woman's affair!"
KORYPHAIOS[(w)]:   Ground pitchers! Close
  ranks!

Antistrophe

CHORUS[(w)]: This is a dance that I know well,
160   My knees shall never yield.
Wobble and creak I may, but still
  I'll keep the well-fought field.
Valor and grace march on before,
  Love prods us from behind.
165 Our slogan is EXCELSIOR,
  Our watchword SAVE MANKIND.
KORYPHAIOS[(w)]: Women, remember your
  grandmothers! Remember
that little old mother of yours, what a stinger
  she was!
On, on, never slacken. There's a strong wind
  astern!
LYSISTRATA: O Eros of delight! O Aphrodite!

Kyprian!°   17
If ever desire has drenched our breasts or
  dreamed
in our thighs, let it work so now on the men of
  Hellas°
that they shall tail us through the land, slaves,
  slaves
to Woman, Breaker of Armies!
COMMISSIONER: And if we do?
LYSISTRATA: Well, for one thing, we shan't have to
  watch you   17
going to market, a spear in one hand, and
  heaven knows
what in the other.
KALONIKE: Nicely said, by Aphrodite!
LYSISTRATA: As things stand now, you're neither
  men nor women.
Armor clanking with kitchen pans and pots —
You sound like a pack of Korybantes!°   18
COMMISSIONER: A man must do what a man must
  do.
LYSISTRATA: So I'm told.
But to see a General, complete with Gorgon-
  shield,
jingling along the dock to buy a couple of
  herrings!
KALONIKE: *I* saw a Captain the other day — lovely
  fellow he was,
nice curly hair — sitting on his horse; and —
  can you believe it? —   18
he'd just bought some soup, and was pouring it
  into his helmet!
And there was a soldier from Thrace
swishing his lance like something out of
  Euripides,
and the poor fruit-store woman got so scared
that she ran away and let him have his figs free! 19
COMMISSIONER: All this is beside the point.
                            Will you be so kind
as to tell me how you mean to save Greece?
LYSISTRATA: Of course.
Nothing could be simpler.
COMMISSIONER: I assure you, I'm all ears.
LYSISTRATA: Do you know anything about weaving?
Say the yarn gets tangled: we thread it   19
this way and that through the skein, up and
  down,
until it's free. And it's like that with war.
We'll send our envoys

170. **Kyprian:** Reference to Aphrodite's association with Cyprus (Kyprus), a place sacred to her and a center for her worship. 172. **Hellas:** Greece. 180. **Korybantes:** Priestesses of Cybele, a fertility goddess, who was celebrated in frenzied rituals accompanied by the beating of cymbals.

142–43. **'War's a man's affair!':** Quoted from Homer's *Iliad*, VI, 492, Hector's farewell to his wife, Andromache.

up and down, this way and that, all over
    Greece,
until it's finished.
200 COMMISSIONER: Yarn? Thread? Skein?
    Are you out of your mind? I tell you,
war is a serious business.
LYSISTRATA: So serious
    that I'd like to go on talking about weaving.
COMMISSIONER: All right. Go ahead.
LYSISTRATA: The first thing we have to do
205   is to wash our yarn, get the dirt out of it.
    You see? Isn't there too much dirt here in
      Athens?
    You must wash those men away.
                Then our spoiled wool —
    that's like your job-hunters, out for a life
    of no work and big pay. Back to the basket,
210   citizens or not, allies or not,
    or friendly immigrants.
                And your colonies?
    Hanks of wool lost in various places. Pull them
    together, weave them into one great whole,
    and our voters are clothed for ever.
COMMISSIONER: It would take a woman
    to reduce state questions to a matter of carding
215   and weaving.
LYSISTRATA: You fool! Who were the mothers
    whose sons sailed off
    to fight for Athens in Sicily?
COMMISSIONER: Enough!
    I beg you, do not call back those memories.
LYSISTRATA: And then,
    instead of the love that every woman needs,
    we have only our single beds, where we can
      dream
220   of our husbands off with the Army.
                Bad enough for wives!
    But what about our girls, getting older every
      day,
    and older, and no kisses?
COMMISSIONER: Men get older, too.
LYSISTRATA: Not in the same sense.
                A soldier's discharged,
225   and he may be bald and toothless, yet he'll find
    a pretty young thing to go to bed with.
                But a woman!
    Her beauty is gone with the first gray hair.
    She can spend her time
    consulting the oracles and the fortune-tellers,
230   but they'll never send her a husband.
COMMISSIONER: Still, if a man can rise to the
      occasion —
LYSISTRATA: Rise? Rise, yourself!

(Furiously.)

Go invest in a coffin!
                You've money enough.
                    I'll bake you
a cake for the Underworld.
                And here's your funeral
    wreath!

(She pours water upon him.)

MYRRHINE: And here's another!

(More water.)

KALONIKE: And here's   235
    my contribution!

(More water.)

LYSISTRATA: What are you waiting for?
    All aboard Styx Ferry!
                Charon's° calling for you!
    It's sailing-time: don't disrupt the schedule!
COMMISSIONER: The insolence of women! And to
    me!
    No, by God, I'll go back to town and show   240
    the rest of the Commission what might happen
    to them.   *(Exit Commissioner.)*
LYSISTRATA: Really, I suppose we should have laid
    out his corpse
on the doorstep, in the usual way.
                    But never mind.
We'll give him the rites of the dead tomorrow
    morning.
    (Exit Lysistrata with Myrrhine and Kalonike.)

PARABASIS:° CHORAL EPISODE • Ode° 1

KORYPHAIOS[(m)]: Sons of Liberty, awake! The day of
    glory is at hand.
CHORUS[(m)]: I smell tyranny afoot, I smell it rising
    from the land.
    I scent a trace of Hippias,° I sniff upon the
      breeze
    A dismal Spartan hogo that suggests King
      Kleisthenes.°
    Strip, strip for action, brothers!   5

237. Charon: The god who ferried the souls of the newly
dead across the river Styx to Hades. **Parabasis:** Section of
the play in which the author presented his own views through
the Koryphaios directly to the audience. The parabasis in
Lysistrata is shorter than those in Aristophanes' other works
and unusual in that the Koryphaios does not speak directly
for the author. **Ode:** Song sung by the Chorus.
3. Hippias: An Athenian tyrant. **4. Kleisthenes:** A bisexual
Athenian.

Our wives, aunts, sisters, mothers
Have sold us out: the streets are full of godless
    female rages.
Shall we stand by and let our women confiscate
    our wages?

                          [Epirrhema° 1]

KORYPHAIOS^(m): Gentlemen, it's a disgrace to
    Athens, a disgrace
to all that Athens stands for, if we allow these
10   grandmas
to jabber about spears and shields and making
    friends
with the Spartans. What's a Spartan? Give me a
    wild wolf
any day. No. They want the Tyranny back, I
    suppose.
Are we going to take that? No. Let us look like
15   the innocent serpent, but be the flower under it,
as the poet sings. And just to begin with,
I propose to poke a number of teeth
down the gullet of that harridan over there.

Antode° 1

KORYPHAIOS^(w): Oh, is that so? When you get
    home, your own mamma won't know you!
CHORUS^(w): Who do you think we are, you senile
20   bravos? Well, I'll show you.
I bore the sacred vessels in my eighth year,° and
    at ten
I was pounding out the barley for Athena
    Goddess;° then
They made me Little Bear
At the Brauronian Fair;°
I'd held the Holy Basket° by the time I was of
25   age,
The Blessed Dry Figs had adorned my plump
    decolletage.

                      [Antepirrhema° 1]

KORYPHAIOS^(w): A "disgrace to Athens," and I, just
    at the moment

I'm giving Athens the best advice she ever had?
Don't I pay taxes to the State? Yes, I pay them
in baby boys. And what do you contribute, 30
you impotent horrors? Nothing but waste: all
our Treasury,° dating back to the Persian Wars,
gone! rifled! And not a penny out of your
    pockets!
Well, then? Can you cough up an answer to
    that?
Look out for your own gullet, or you'll get a
    crack 35
from this old brogan that'll make your teeth see
    stars!

Ode 2

CHORUS^(m): Oh insolence!
Am I unmanned?
Incontinence!
Shall my scarred hand 40
Strike never a blow
To curb this flow-
ing female curse?

Leipsydrion!°
Shall I betray 45
The laurels won
On that great day?
Come, shake a leg,
Shed old age, beg
The years reverse! 50

                      [Epirrhema 2]

KORYPHAIOS^(m): Give them an inch, and we're done
    for! We'll have them
launching boats next and planning naval
    strategy,
sailing down on us like so many Artemisias.
Or maybe they have ideas about the cavalry.
That's fair enough, women are certainly good 55
in the saddle. Just look at Mikon's paintings,
all those Amazons wrestling with all those men!
On the whole, a straitjacket's their best uniform.

Antode 2

CHORUS^(w): Tangle with me,
And you'll get cramps. 60
Ferocity
's no use now, Gramps!

Epirrhema: A part of the parabasis spoken by the Koryphaios following an ode delivered by his or her half of the Chorus. **Antode:** Lyric song sung by half of the Chorus in response to the Ode sung by the other half. **21. eighth year:** Young girls between the ages of seven and eleven served in the temple of Athena in the Akropolis. **22. pounding out the barley for Athena Goddess:** At age ten a girl could be chosen to grind the sacred grain of Athena. **24. Brauronian Fair:** A ritual in the cult of Artemis, who is associated with wild beasts, in which young girls dressed up as bears and danced for the goddess. **25. Holy Basket:** In one ritual to Athena, young girls carried baskets of objects sacred to the goddess. **Antepirrhema:** The speech delivered by the second Koryphaios after the second half of the Chorus had sung an ode.

32. Treasury: Athenian politicians were raiding the funds that were collected by Athens to finance a war against Persia. **44. Leipsydrion:** A place where Athenian patriots had heroically fought.

By the Two,
I'll get through
65 To you wrecks yet!

I'll scramble your eggs,
I'll burn your beans,
With my two legs.
You'll see such scenes
70 As never yet
Your two eyes met.
A curse? You bet!

[Antepirrhema 2]

KORYPHAIOS^(w): If Lampito stands by me, and that
delicious Theban girl,
Ismenia — what good are *you?* You and your
seven
75 Resolutions! Resolutions? Rationing Boiotian eels
and making our girls go without them at
Hekate's° Feast!
That was statesmanship! And we'll have to put
up with it
and all the rest of your decrepit legislation
until some patriot — God give him strength! —
grabs you by the neck and kicks you off the
80 Rock.

SCENE 2

(Reenter Lysistrata and her lieutenants.)

KORYPHAIOS^(w) *(tragic tone): Great Queen, fair
Architect of our emprise,
Why lookst thou on us with foreboding eyes?*
LYSISTRATA: The behavior of these idiotic women!
There's something about the female temperament
that I can't bear!
KORYPHAIOS^(w):   What in the world do you
5   mean?
LYSISTRATA: Exactly what I say.
KORYPHAIOS^(w):   What dreadful thing has happened?
Come, tell us: we're all your friends.
LYSISTRATA: It isn't easy
to say it; yet, God knows, we can't hush it up.
KORYPHAIOS^(w): Well, then? Out with it!
LYSISTRATA: To put it bluntly,
we're dying to get laid.
10 KORYPHAIOS^(w):   Almighty God!
LYSISTRATA: Why bring God into it? — No, it's just
as I say.
I can't manage them any longer: they've gone
man-crazy,

76. **Hekate:** Patron of successful wars, object of a Boiotian
cult (later associated with sorcery).

they're all trying to get out.
                         Why, look:
one of them was sneaking out the back door
over there by Pan's cave; another   15
was sliding down the walls with rope and tackle;
another was climbing aboard a sparrow, ready
to take off
for the nearest brothel — I dragged *her* back by
the hair!
They're all finding some reason to leave.
                         Look there!
There goes another one.
                    — Just a minute, you! 20
Where are you off to so fast?
FIRST WOMAN: I've got to get home.
I've a lot of Milesian wool, and the worms are
spoiling it.
LYSISTRATA: Oh bother you and your worms! Get
back inside!
FIRST WOMAN: I'll be back right away, I swear I
will.
I just want to get it stretched out on my bed. 25
LYSISTRATA: You'll do no such thing. You'll stay
right here.
FIRST WOMAN: And my wool?
You want it ruined?
LYSISTRATA: Yes, for all I care.
SECOND WOMAN: Oh dear! My lovely new flax
from Amorgos —
I left it at home, all uncarded!
LYSISTRATA: Another one!
And all she wants is someone to card her flax. 30
Get back in there!
SECOND WOMAN: But I swear by the Moon-
Goddess,
the minute I get it done, I'll be back!
LYSISTRATA: I say No.
If you, why not all the other women as well?
THIRD WOMAN: O Lady Eileithyia!° Radiant
goddess! Thou
intercessor for women in childbirth! Stay, I pray
thee,   35
oh stay this parturition. Shall I pollute
a sacred spot?°
LYSISTRATA: And what's the matter with *you?*
THIRD WOMAN: I'm having a baby — any minute
now.
LYSISTRATA: But you weren't pregnant yesterday.
THIRD WOMAN: Well, I am today.
Let me go home for a midwife, Lysistrata: 40
there's not much time.

34. **Eileithyia:** Goddess of childbirth. 36–37. **pollute a sacred spot:** Giving birth on the Akropolis was forbidden because it was sacred ground.

LYSISTRATA: I never heard such nonsense.
What's that bulging under your cloak?
THIRD WOMAN: A little baby boy.
LYSISTRATA: It certainly isn't. But it's something
    hollow,
like a basin or — Why, it's the helmet of
    Athena!
And you said you were having a baby.
45 THIRD WOMAN: Well, I am! So there!
LYSISTRATA: Then why the helmet?
THIRD WOMAN: I was afraid that my pains
    might begin here in the Akropolis; and I wanted
    to drop my chick into it, just as the dear doves
    do.
LYSISTRATA: Lies! Evasions! — But at least one
    thing's clear:
you can't leave the place before your
50   purification.°
THIRD WOMAN: But I can't stay here in the
    Akropolis! Last night I dreamed
of the Snake.
FIRST WOMAN: And those horrible owls, the
    noise they make!
I can't get a bit of sleep; I'm just about dead.
LYSISTRATA: You useless girls, that's enough: Let's
    have no more lying.
Of course you want your men. But don't you
55   imagine
that they want you just as much? I'll give you
    my word,
their nights must be pretty hard.
                    Just stick it out!
A little patience, that's all, and our battle's won.
I have heard an Oracle. Should you like to hear
    it?
FIRST WOMAN: An Oracle? Yes, tell us!
60 LYSISTRATA: Here is what it says:
    WHEN SWALLOWS SHALL THE HOOPOE
        SHUN
        AND SPURN HIS HOT DESIRE,
    ZEUS WILL PERFECT WHAT THEY'VE
        BEGUN
        AND SET THE LOWER HIGHER.
65 FIRST WOMAN: Does that mean we'll be on top?
LYSISTRATA: BUT IF THE SWALLOWS SHALL
        FALL OUT
        AND TAKE THE HOOPOE'S BAIT,
    A CURSE MUST MARK THEIR HOUR OF
        DOUBT,
        INFAMY SEAL THEIR FATE.
THIRD WOMAN: I swear, *that* Oracle's all too clear.
70 FIRST WOMAN: Oh the dear gods!

50. purification: A ritual cleansing of a woman after
childbirth.

LYSISTRATA: Let's not be downhearted, girls. Back
    to our places!
The god has spoken. How can we possibly fail
    him?
    (*Exit Lysistrata with the dissident women.*)

CHORAL EPISODE • *Strophe*

CHORUS(m): I know a little story that I learned way
        back in school
    Goes like this:
    Once upon a time there was a young man —
        and no fool —
    Named Melanion; and his
    One aversi-on was marriage. He loathed the very
        thought.   5
    So he ran off to the hills, and in a special grot
    Raised a dog, and spent his days
    Hunting rabbits. And it says
    That he never never never did come home.
    It might be called a refuge *from* the womb.   10
    All right,
            all right,
                    all right!
    We're as bright as young Melanion, and we hate
    the very sight
    Of you women!
A MAN: How about a kiss, old lady?
A WOMAN: Here's an onion for your eye!   15
A MAN: A kick in the guts, then?
A WOMAN: Try, old bristle-tail, just try!
A MAN: Yet they say Myronides
    On hands and knees
    Looked just as shaggy fore and aft as I!   20

Antistrophe

CHORUS(w): Well, *I* know a little story, and it's just
        as good as yours.
    Goes like this:
    Once there was a man named Timon — a rough
        diamond, of course,
    And that whiskery face of his
    Looked like murder in the shrubbery. By God, he
        was a son   25
    Of the Furies, let me tell you! And what did he
        do but run
    From the world and all its ways,
    Cursing mankind! And it says
    That his choicest execrations as of then
    Were leveled almost wholly at *old* men.   30
    All right,
            all right,
                    all right!

But there's one thing about Timon: he could
    always stand the sight
of us women.
A WOMAN: How about a crack in the jaw, Pop?
35 A MAN: I can take it, Ma — no fear!
A WOMAN: How about a kick in the face?
A MAN: You'd reveal your old caboose?
A WOMAN: What I'd show,
    I'll have you know,
40   Is an instrument you're too far gone to use.

SCENE 3

(*Reenter Lysistrata.*)

LYSISTRATA: Oh, quick, girls, quick! Come here!
A WOMAN: What is it?
LYSISTRATA: A man.
    A man simply bulging with love.
                              O Kyprian Queen,°
    O Paphian, O Kythereian! Hear us and aid us!
A WOMAN: Where is this enemy?
LYSISTRATA: Over there, by Demeter's shrine.
A WOMAN: Damned if he isn't. But who *is* he?
5   MYRRHINE: My husband.
    Kinesias.
LYSISTRATA: Oh then, get busy! Tease him!
    Undermine him!
    Wreck him! Give him everything — kissing,
        tickling, nudging,
    whatever you generally torture him with — :
        give him everything
    except what we swore on the wine we would
        not give.
MYRRHINE: Trust me.
10 LYSISTRATA: I do. But I'll help you get him started.
    The rest of you women, stay back.

(*Enter Kinesias.*)

KINESIAS: Oh God! Oh my God!
    I'm stiff from lack of exercise. All I can do to
        stand up.
LYSISTRATA: Halt! Who are you, approaching our
        lines?
KINESIAS: Me? I.
LYSISTRATA: A man?
KINESIAS: You have eyes, haven't you?
LYSISTRATA: Go away.
KINESIAS: Who says so?
LYSISTRATA: Officer of the Day.

2. **Kyprian Queen:** Aphrodite.

KINESIAS: Officer, I beg you, 15
    by all the gods at once, bring Myrrhine out.
LYSISTRATA: Myrrhine? And who, my good sir, are
    you?
KINESIAS: Kinesias. Last name's Pennison. Her
    husband.
LYSISTRATA: Oh, of course. I beg your pardon.
    We're glad to see you.
    We've heard so much about you. Dearest
        Myrrhine   20
    is always talking about Kinesias — never nibbles
        an egg
    or an apple without saying
    "Here's to Kinesias!"
KINESIAS: Do you really mean it?
LYSISTRATA: I do.
    When we're discussing men, she always says
    "Well, after all, there's nobody like Kinesias!" 25
KINESIAS: Good God. — Well, then, please send her
        down here.
LYSISTRATA: And what do *I* get out of it?
KINESIAS: A standing promise.
LYSISTRATA: I'll take it up with her.
                              (*Exit Lysistrata.*)
KINESIAS: But be quick about it!
    Lord, what's life without a wife? Can't eat.
        Can't sleep.
    Every time I go home, the place is so empty, so 30
    insufferably sad. Love's killing me, Oh,
    hurry!

(*Enter Manes, a slave, with Kinesias's baby; the voice
of Myrrhine is heard offstage.*)

MYRRHINE: But of course I love him! Adore
        him — But no,
    he hates love. No. I won't go down.

(*Enter Myrrhine, above.*)

KINESIAS: Myrrhine!
    Darlingest Myrrhinette! Come down quick!
MYRRHINE: Certainly not.
KINESIAS: Not? But why, Myrrhine? 35
MYRRHINE: Why? You don't need me.
KINESIAS: Need you? My God, *look* at me!
MYRRHINE: So long!

(*Turns to go.*)

KINESIAS: Myrrhine, Myrrhine, Myrrhine!
    If not for my sake, for our child!

(*Pinches Baby.*)

                          — All right, you: pipe up!
BABY: Mummie! Mummie! Mummie!
KINESIAS: You hear that?
    Pitiful, I call it. Six days now   40

with never a bath; no food; enough to break
your heart!
MYRRHINE: My darlingest child! What a father *you*
acquired!
KINESIAS: At least come down for his sake.
MYRRHINE: I suppose I must.
Oh, this mother business!   (*Exit.*)
KINESIAS: How pretty she is! And younger!
The harder she treats me, the more bothered I
get.

(*Myrrhine enters, below.*)

45   MYRRHINE: Dearest child,
you're as sweet as your father's horrid. Give me
a kiss.
KINESIAS: Now don't you see how wrong it was to
get involved
in this scheming League of women? It's bad
for us both.
MYRRHINE: Keep your hands to yourself!
KINESIAS: But our house
going to rack and ruin?
MYRRHINE: *I don't care.*
50   KINESIAS: And your knitting
all torn to pieces by the chickens? Don't you
care?
MYRRHINE: Not at all.
KINESIAS: And our debt to Aphrodite?
Oh, *won't* you come back?
MYRRHINE: No. — At least, not until you
men
make a treaty and stop this war.
KINESIAS: Why, I suppose
that might be arranged.
55   MYRRHINE: Oh? Well, I suppose
I might come down then. But meanwhile,
I've sworn not to.
KINESIAS: Don't worry. — Now let's have fun.
MYRRHINE: No! Stop it! I said no!
                           — Although, of course,
I *do* love you.
KINESIAS: I know you do. Darling Myrrhine:
come, shall we?
MYRRHINE: Are you out of your mind? In front of
60   the child?
KINESIAS: Take him home, Manes.
                        (*Exit Manes with Baby.*)
                           There. He's gone.
                                    Come on!
There's nothing to stop us now.
MYRRHINE: You devil! But where?
KINESIAS: In Pan's cave. What could be snugger
than that?
MYRRHINE: But my purification before I go back to
the Citadel?

KINESIAS: Wash in the Klepsydra.°
MYRRHINE: And my oath?
KINESIAS: Leave the oath to me.   65
After all, I'm the man.
MYRRHINE: Well . . . if you say so.
                    I'll go find a bed.
KINESIAS: Oh, bother a bed! The ground's good
enough for me.
MYRRHINE: No. You're a bad man, but you deserve
something better than dirt.   (*Exit Myrrhine.*)
KINESIAS: What a love she is! And how thoughtful!

(*Reenter Myrrhine.*)

MYRRHINE: Here's your bed.
Now let me get my clothes off.
                      But, good horrors!   70
We haven't a mattress.
KINESIAS: Oh, forget the mattress!
MYRRHINE: No.
Just lying on blankets? Too sordid.
KINESIAS: Give me a kiss.
MYRRHINE: Just a second.   (*Exit Myrrhine.*)
KINESIAS: I swear, I'll explode!

(*Reenter Myrrhine.*)

MYRRHINE: Here's your mattress.
I'll just take my dress off.
                 But look —
where's our pillow?
KINESIAS: I don't *need* a pillow!
MYRRHINE: Well, *I* do.   75
                    (*Exit Myrrhine.*)
KINESIAS: I don't suppose even Herakles°
would stand for this!

(*Reenter Myrrhine.*)

MYRRHINE: There we are. Ups-a-daisy!
KINESIAS: So we are. Well, come to bed.
MYRRHINE: But I wonder:
is everything ready now?
KINESIAS: I can swear to that. Come, darling!
MYRRHINE: Just getting out of my girdle.
                    But remember, now,   80
what you promised about the treaty.
KINESIAS: Yes, yes, yes!
MYRRHINE: But no coverlet!
KINESIAS: Damn it, I'll be
your coverlet!
MYRRHINE: Be right back.   (*Exit Myrrhine.*)

65. **Klepsydra:** A water clock beneath the walls of the Akropolis. Kinesias's suggestion borders on blasphemy.
76. **Herakles:** Greek hero (Hercules) known for his Twelve
Labors.

KINESIAS: This girl and her coverlets
      will be the death of me.

(*Reenter Myrrhine.*)

MYRRHINE: Here we are. Up you go!
KINESIAS: Up? I've been up for ages.
85 MYRRHINE: Some perfume?
KINESIAS: No, by Apollo!
MYRRHINE: Yes, by Aphrodite!
      I don't care whether you want it or not.
                                    (*Exit Myrrhine.*)
KINESIAS: For love's sake, hurry!

(*Reenter Myrrhine.*)

MYRRHINE: Here, in your hand. Rub it right in.
KINESIAS: Never cared for perfume.
90   And this is particularly strong. Still, here goes.
MYRRHINE: What a nitwit I am! I brought you the
      Rhodian bottle.
KINESIAS: Forget it.
MYRRHINE: No trouble at all. You just wait here.
                                    (*Exit Myrrhine.*)
KINESIAS: God damn the man who invented
      perfume!

(*Reenter Myrrhine.*)

MYRRHINE: At last! The right bottle!
KINESIAS: I've got the rightest
95   bottle of all, and it's right here waiting for you.
      Darling, forget everything else. Do come to bed.
MYRRHINE: Just let me get my shoes off.
                              — And, by the way,
      you'll vote for the treaty?
KINESIAS: I'll think about it.
                                    (*Myrrhine runs away.*)
      There! That's done it! The damned woman,
00   she gets me all bothered, she half kills me,
      and off she runs! What'll I do? Where
      can I get laid?
                        — And you, little prodding pal,
      who's going to take care of *you*? No, you and I
      had better get down to old Foxdog's Nursing
      Clinic.
05 CHORUS[(m)]: Alas for the woes of man, alas
      Specifically for you.
      She's brought you to a pretty pass:
      What are you going to do?
      Split, heart! Sag, flesh! Proud spirit, crack!
10   Myrrhine's got you on your back.
KINESIAS: The agony, the protraction!
KORYPHAIOS[(m)]:   Friend,
      What woman's worth a damn?
      They bitch us all, world without end.
KINESIAS: Yet they're so damned sweet, man!
15 KORYPHAIOS[(m)]: Calamitous, that's what I say.

You should have learned that much today.
CHORUS[(m)]: O blessed Zeus, roll womankind.
      Up into one great ball;
      Blast them aloft on a high wind,
      And once there, let them fall.   120
      Down, down they'll come, the pretty dears,
      And split themselves on our thick spears.
                                    (*Exit Kinesias.*)

SCENE 4

(*Enter a Spartan Herald.*)

HERALD: Gentlemen, Ah beg you will be so kind
      as to direct me to the Central Committee.
      Ah have a communication.

(*Reenter Commissioner.*)

COMMISSIONER: Are you a man,
      or a fertility symbol?
HERALD: Ah refuse to answer that question!
      Ah'm a certified herald from Spahta, and Ah've
      come   5
      to talk about an ahmistice.
COMMISSIONER: Then why
      that spear under your cloak?
HERALD: Ah have no speah!
COMMISSIONER: You don't walk naturally, with
      your tunic
      poked out so. You have a tumor, maybe,
      or a hernia?
HERALD: You lost yo' mahnd, man?
COMMISSIONER: Well,   10
      something's up, I can see that. And I don't like
      it.
HERALD: Colonel, Ah resent this.
COMMISSIONER: So I see. But what *is* it?
HERALD: A staff
      with a message from Spahta.
COMMISSIONER: Oh, I know about those staffs.
      Well, then, man, speak out: How are things in
      Sparta?
HERALD: Hahd, Colonel, hahd! We're at a
      standstill.   15
      Cain't seem to think of anything but women.
COMMISSIONER: How curious! Tell me, do you
      Spartans think
      that maybe Pan's to blame?
HERALD: Pan? No, Lampito and her little naked
      friends.
      They won't let a man come nigh them.   20
COMMISSIONER: How are you handling it?
HERALD: Losing our mahnds,

if y' want to know, and walking around
   hunched over
lahk men carrying candles in a gale.
The women have swohn they'll have nothing to
   do with us
until we get a treaty.
25 COMMISSIONER: Yes. I know.
It's a general uprising, sir, in all parts of Greece.
But as for the answer —
        Sir: go back to Sparta
and have them send us your Armistice
   Commission.
I'll arrange things in Athens.
        And I may say
that my standing is good enough to make them
30   listen.
HERALD: A man after mah own haht! Seh, Ah
   thank you.   (*Exit Herald.*)

CHORAL EPISODE · *Strophe*

CHORUS[(m)]: Oh these women! Where will you find
   A slavering beast that's more unkind?
     Where's a hotter fire?
   Give me a panther, any day.
5   He's not so merciless as they,
     And panthers don't conspire.

Antistrophe

CHORUS[(w)]: We may be hard, you silly old ass,
   But who brought you to this stupid pass?
     You're the ones to blame.
10   Fighting with us, your oldest friends,
   Simply to serve your selfish ends —
     Really, you have no shame!
KORYPHAIOS[(m)]: No, I'm through with women for
   ever.
KORYPHAIOS[(w)]:   If you say so.
Still, you might put some clothes on. You look
   too absurd
standing around naked. Come, get into this
15   cloak.
KORYPHAIOS[(m)]: Thank you; you're right. I merely
   took it off
because I was in such a temper.
KORYPHAIOS[(w)]:   That's much better.
Now you resemble a man again.
       Why have you been so horrid?
And look: there's some sort of insect in your eye.
Shall I take it out?
20 KORYPHAIOS[(m)]:   An insect, is it? So that's

what's been bothering me. Lord, yes: take it out!
KORYPHAIOS[(w)]: You might be more polite.
      — But, heavens!
What an enormous mosquito!
KORYPHAIOS[(m)]:   You've saved my life.
That mosquito was drilling an artesian well
in my left eye.
KORYPHAIOS[(w)]:   Let me wipe   25
those tears away. — And now: one little kiss?
KORYPHAIOS[(m)]: No, no kisses.
KORYPHAIOS[(w)]: You're so difficult.
KORYPHAIOS[(m)]: You impossible women! How you
   do get around us!
The poet was right: Can't live with you, or
   without you.
But let's be friends.   30
And to celebrate, you might join us in an Ode.

Strophe 1

CHORUS[(m and w)]: Let it never be said
   That my tongue is malicious:
   Both by word and by deed
I would set an example that's noble and
   gracious.   35
   We've had sorrow and care
   Till we're sick of the tune.
   Is there anyone here
   Who would like a small loan?
     My purse is crammed,   40
     As you'll soon find;
And you needn't pay me back if the Peace gets
signed.

Strophe 2

   I've invited to lunch
   Some Karystian rips° —
   An esurient bunch,   45
But I've ordered a menu to water their lips.
   I can still make soup
   And slaughter a pig.
   You're all coming, I hope?
   But a bath first, I beg!   50
     Walk right up
     As though you owned the place,
And you'll get the front door slammed to in
   your face.

---

44. Karystian rips: The Karystians were allies of Athens but
were scorned for their primitive ways and loose morals.

SCENE 5

(*Enter Spartan Ambassador, with entourage.*)

KORYPHAIOS[m]: The Commission has arrived from
　　Sparta.
　　　　　　How oddly they're walking!
　　　　　　　　Gentlemen, welcome to Athens!
　　How is life in Lakonia?
AMBASSADOR:　　　　　Need we discuss that?
　　Simply use your eyes.
CHORUS[m]:　　　　　　The poor man's right:
　　　　　　　　What a sight!
5 AMBASSADOR:　　　　　　　　Words fail me.
　　But come, gentlemen, call in your
　　　　Commissioners,
　　and let's get down to a Peace.
CHORAGOS[m]:　　　　The state we're in! Can't bear
　　a stitch below the waist. It's a kind of pelvic
　　paralysis.
COMMISSIONER:　　　Won't somebody call
　　Lysistrata? — Gentlemen,
　　we're no better off than you.
10 AMBASSADOR:　　　　　So I see.
A SPARTAN: Seh, do y'all feel a certain strain
　　early in the morning?
AN ATHENIAN: I do, sir. It's worse than a strain.
　　A few more days, and there's nothing for us but
　　　　Kleisthenes,
　　that broken blossom.
CHORAGOS[m]:　　　But you'd better get dressed again.
　　You know these people going around Athens
15　　with chisels,
　　looking for statues of Hermes.°
ATHENIAN:　　　　　Sir, you are right.
SPARTAN: He certainly is! Ah'll put mah own
　　clothes back on.

(*Enter Athenian Commissioners.*)

COMMISSIONER: Gentlemen from Sparta, welcome.
　　This is a sorry business.
SPARTAN (*to one of his own group*): Colonel, we
　　got dressed just in time. Ah sweah,
　　if they'd seen us the way we were, there'd have
20　　been a new wah
　　between the states.
COMMISSIONER: Shall we call the meeting to order?
　　　　　　　　　　Now, Lakonians,
　　what's your proposal?

---

16. **statues of Hermes:** The usual representation of Hermes
was with an erect phallus. Statues of Hermes were scattered
through Athens and were attacked by vandals just before
the Sicilian Expedition.

AMBASSADOR:　　　We propose to consider peace.
COMMISSIONER: Good. That's on our minds, too.
　　　　　　　　— Summon Lysistrata.
　　We'll never get anywhere without her.
AMBASSADOR:　　　　　　Lysistrata? 25
　　Summon Lysis-*anybody*! Only, summon!
KORYPHAIOS[m]:　　　　No need to summon:
　　here she is, herself.

(*Enter Lysistrata.*)

COMMISSIONER:　　　Lysistrata! Lion of women!
　　This is your hour to be
　　hard and yielding, outspoken and shy, austere
　　　　and
　　gentle. You see here 30
　　the best brains of Hellas (confused, I admit,
　　by your devious charming) met as one man
　　to turn the future over to you.
LYSISTRATA:　　　　　　That's fair enough,
　　unless you men take it into your heads
　　to turn to each other instead of to us. But I'd
　　　　know 35
　　soon enough if you did.
　　　　　　　— Where is Reconciliation?
　　Go, some of you: bring her here.
　　　　　　　(*Exeunt two women.*)
　　　　　　　　　And now, women,
　　lead the Spartan delegates to me: not roughly
　　or insultingly, as our men handle them, but
　　　　gently,
　　politely, as ladies should. Take them by the
　　　　hand, 40
　　or by anything else if they won't give you their
　　hands.

(*The Spartans are escorted over.*)

　　There. — The Athenians next, by any convenient
　　handle.

(*The Athenians are escorted.*)

　　Stand there, please. — Now, all of you, listen to
　　me.

(*During the following speech the two women reenter,
carrying an enormous statue of a naked girl; this is
Reconciliation.*)

　　I'm only a woman, I know; but I've a mind,
　　and, I think, not a bad one: I owe it to my
　　　　father 45
　　and to listening to the local politicians.
　　So much for that.
　　　　　　　Now, gentlemen,
　　since I have you here, I intend to give you a
　　scolding.
　　We are all Greeks.

50　Must I remind you of Thermopylai,° of Olympia,
　　of Delphoi? names deep in all our hearts?
　　Are they not a common heritage?
　　　　　　　　　　　　　　　Yet you men
　　go raiding through the country from both sides,
　　Greek killing Greek, storming down Greek
　　　　cities —
55　and all the time the Barbarian across the sea
　　is waiting for his chance!
　　　　　　　　　— That's my first point.
AN ATHENIAN: Lord! I can hardly contain myself.
LYSISTRATA:　　　　　　　　As for you Spartans:
　　Was it so long ago that Perikleides°
　　came here to beg our help? I can see him still,
　　his gray face, his sombre gown. And what did
60　　he want?
　　An army from Athens. All Messene
　　was hot at your heels, and the sea-god splitting
　　　your land.
　　Well, Kimon and his men,
　　four thousand strong, marched out and saved all
　　　Sparta.
　　And what thanks do we get? You come back to
65　　murder us.
AN ATHENIAN: They're aggressors, Lysistrata!
A SPARTAN:　　　　　　　　　　Ah admit it.
　　When Ah look at those laigs, Ah sweah Ah'll
　　　aggress mahself!
LYSISTRATA: And you, Athenians: do you think
　　you're blameless?
70　Remember that bad time when we were helpless,
　　and an army came from Sparta,
　　　and that was the end of the Thessalian
　　　menace,
　　the end of Hippias and his allies.
　　　　　　　　　　And that was Sparta,
　　and only Sparta; but for Sparta, we'd be
　　cringing slaves today, not free Athenians.

(*From this point, the male responses are less to Lysistrata than to the statue.*)

A SPARTAN: A well shaped speech.
75　AN ATHENIAN:　　　　　Certainly it has its points.
LYSISTRATA: Why are we fighting each other? With
　　all this history
　　of favors given and taken, what stands in the
　　　way
　　of making peace?

---

50. **Thermopylai:** A narrow pass where, in 480 B.C., an army
of three hundred Spartans held out for three days against a
superior Persian force.　58. **Perikleides:** Spartan ambassador
to Athens who successfully urged Athenians to aid Sparta in
quelling a rebellion.

AMBASSADOR:　　　Spahta is ready, ma'am,
　　so long as we get that place back.
LYSISTRATA:　　　　　　　What place, man?
AMBASSADOR: Ah refer to Pylos.
COMMISSIONER:　　　　　Not a chance, by God!　80
LYSISTRATA: Give it to them, friend.
COMMISSIONER: But — what shall we have to
　　bargain with?
LYSISTRATA: Demand something in exchange.
COMMISSIONER:　　　　　Good idea. — Well, then:
　　Cockeville first, and the Happy Hills, and the
　　　country
　　between the Legs of Megara.
AMBASSADOR:　　　　　Mah government objects.
LYSISTRATA: Overruled. Why fuss about a pair of
　　legs?　　　　　　　　　　　　　　85

(*General assent. The statue is removed.*)

AN ATHENIAN: I want to get out of these clothes
　　and start my plowing.
A SPARTAN: Ah'll fertilize mahn first, by the
　　Heavenly Twins!
LYSISTRATA: And so you shall,
　　once you've made peace. If you are serious,
　　go, both of you, and talk with your allies.　90
COMMISSIONER: Too much talk already. No, we'll
　　stand together.
　　We've only one end in view. All that we want
　　is our women; and I speak for our allies.
AMBASSADOR: Mah government concurs.
AN ATHENIAN:　　　　　　So does Karystos.
LYSISTRATA: Good. — But before you come inside　95
　　to join your wives at supper, you must perform
　　the usual lustration. Then we'll open
　　our baskets for you, and all that we have is
　　yours.
　　But you must promise upright good behavior
　　from this day on. Then each man home with his
　　woman!　　　　　　　　　　　　　10[0]
AN ATHENIAN: Let's get it over with.
A SPARTAN:　　　　　　　Lead on. Ah follow.
AN ATHENIAN: Quick as a cat can wink!
　　　　　　　　(*Exeunt all but the Choruses.*)

Antistrophe 1

CHORUS[(w)]: Embroideries and
　　Twinkling ornaments and
　　Pretty dresses — I hand　　　　　　　　10[5]
　　Them all over to you, and with never a qualm.
　　They'll be nice for your daughters
　　On festival days
　　When the girls bring the Goddess
　　The ritual prize.　　　　　　　　　　11[0]

Come in, one and all:
Take what you will.
I've nothing here so tightly corked that you can't
make it spill.

Antistrophe 2

You may search my house,
But you'll not find
The least thing of use,
Unless your two eyes are keener than mine.
Your numberless brats
Are half starved? and your slaves?
Courage, grandpa! I've lots
Of grain left, and big loaves.
    I'll fill your guts,
    I'll go the whole hog;
But if you come too close to me, remember:
    'ware the dog!   (*Exeunt Choruses.*)

15

20

EXODOS°

(*A Drunken Citizen enters, approaches the gate, and is halted by a sentry.*)

CITIZEN: Open. The. Door.
SENTRY: Now, friend, just shove along!
    — So you want to sit down. If it weren't such
        an old joke,
    I'd tickle your tail with this torch. Just the sort
        of gag
    this audience appreciates.
CITIZEN: I. Stay. Right. Here.
SENTRY: Get away from there, or I'll scalp you!
    The gentlemen from Sparta
    are just coming back from dinner.

5

(*Exit Citizen; the general company reenters; the two Choruses now represent Spartans and Athenians.*)

A SPARTAN: Ah must say,
    Ah never tasted better grub.
AN ATHENIAN: And those Lakonians!
    They're gentlemen, by the Lord! Just goes to
        show,
    a drink to the wise is sufficient.
COMMISSIONER: And why not?
    A sober man's an ass.
    Men of Athens, mark my words: the only
        efficient
    Ambassador's a drunk Ambassador. Is that
        clear?

10

Exodos: Final scene.

Look: we go to Sparta,
and when we get there we're dead sober. The
    result?
Everyone cackling at everyone else. They make
    speeches;
and even if we understand, we get it all wrong
when we file our reports in Athens. But
    today — !
Everybody's happy. Couldn't tell the difference
between *Drink to Me Only* and
The Star-Spangled Athens.
                    What's a few lies,
washed down in good strong drink?

15

20

(*Reenter the Drunken Citizen.*)

SENTRY: God almighty,
    he's back again!
CITIZEN: I. Resume. My. Place.
A SPARTAN (*to an Athenian*): Ah beg yo', seh,
    take yo' instrument in yo' hand and play for us.
    Ah'm told
    yo' understand the in*tric*acies of the floot?
    Ah'd lahk to execute a song and dance
    in honor of Athens,
                    and, of cohse, of Spahta.
CITIZEN: Toot. On. Your. Flute.

25

(*The following song is a solo — an aria — accompanied by the flute. The Chorus of Spartans begins a slow dance.*)

A SPARTAN: O Memory,
    Let the Muse speak once more
    In my young voice. Sing glory.
    Sing Artemision's shore,
    Where Athens fluttered the Persians. *Alalai,*°
    Sing glory, that great
    Victory! Sing also
    Our Leonidas and his men,
    Those wild boars, sweat and blood
    Down in a red drench. Then, then
    The barbarians broke, though they had stood
    Numberless as the sands before!

30

35

40

O Artemis,
Virgin Goddess, whose darts
Flash in our forests: approve
This pact of peace and join our hearts,
From this day on, in love.
Huntress, descend!
LYSISTRATA: All that will come in time.
                    But now, Lakonians,
    take home your wives. Athenians, take yours.

45

34. *Alalai:* War cry.

Each man be kind to his woman; and you,
50　　　women
be equally kind. Never again, pray God,
shall we lose our way in such madness.
KORYPHAIOS^(Athenian):　　　　　　　　And now
　　　let's dance our joy.

(*From this point the dance becomes general.*)

CHORUS^(Athenian): Dance, you Graces
　　　　　　　　　　Artemis, dance
Dance, Phoibos,° Lord of dancing
55　　　　　　　　　　　　Dance,
In a scurry of Maenads,° Lord Dionysos
　　　　　　　　Dance, Zeus Thunderer
　　　　　Dance, Lady Hera°
Queen of the sky
　　　　　　　Dance, dance, all you gods
Dance witness everlasting of our pact
60 *Evohi Evohe*°
Dance for the dearest
　　　　　　　　the Bringer of Peace
Deathless Aphrodite!
COMMISSIONER: Now let us have another song from
　　　Sparta.
CHORUS^(Spartan): From Taygetos, from Taygetos,

---

55. **Phoibos:** Apollo, god of the sun.　56. **Maenads:** Female
worshipers of Bacchus (Dionysus).　57. **Hera:** Wife of Zeus.
60. *Evohi Evohe:* "Come forth! Come forth!" An orgiastic
cry associated with rituals of Bacchus.

Lakonian Muse, come down.　　　　　65
Sing to the Lord Apollo
Who rules Amyklai Town.

Sing Athena of the House of Brass!°
Sing Leda's Twins,° that chivalry
　　Resplendent on the shore　　　　70
Of our Eurotas; sing the girls
　　That dance along before:

Sparkling in dust their gleaming feet,
　　Their hair a Bacchant fire,
And Leda's daughter, thyrsos° raised,　　75
　　Leads their triumphant choir.

CHORUS^(S and A): *Evohé!*
　　　　　　Evohaí!
　　　　　　　　Evohé!
　　　　　　　　　　We pass
　　　　　Dancing
　　　　　　　dancing
　　　　　　　　　to greet
Athena of the House of Brass.

---

68. *House of Brass:* Temple to Athena on the Akropolis of
Sparta.　69. **Leda's Twins:** Leda, raped by Zeus, bore quad-
ruplets, two daughters (one of whom was Helen) and two
sons.　75. **thyrsos:** A staff twined with ivy and carried by
Bacchus and his followers.

Roman Drama

Roman drama has several sources, not all of them well understood. The first and most literary is Greek drama, but among the more curious are the indigenous sources, which are especially difficult to trace. The Etruscans, members of an old and obscure civilization in northern Italy that reached its height in the sixth century B.C. and that the Romans eventually absorbed, had developed an improvised song and dance that was very entertaining. The town of Atella provided another indigenous comic tradition known as the ATELLAN FARCE, a very broad and sometimes coarse popular comedy. Such entertainments may have been acted in open spaces or at fairs and at first probably did not demand a stage at all.

The Atellan farce is especially interesting for developments in later Roman drama and world drama. The characters in this farce seem to have been STOCK CHARACTERS, characters who are always recognizable and whose antics are predictable. The most common in the Atellan farce are Maccus the clown; Bucco the stupid, and probably fat, clown; Pappus the foolish or stubborn old man; and the hunchbacked, wily slave Dossennus. At first these pieces of drama were improvised to a repeatable pattern, often involving a master who tries to get his slave to do his bidding but who somehow ends up being made to look the fool by the cunning slave. When the farces began to develop in Rome, they were written down and played onstage.

The concept of the stock character is associated with the masters of Roman comedy, Plautus and Terence, who often adapted Greek plays and made them their own. The braggart warrior (*miles gloriosus*) was a stock character on the Roman stage, and he reappears in modern plays such as George Bernard Shaw's *Arms and the Man* and Sean O'Casey's *Juno and the Paycock*. The miser has been a mainstay in literature since Roman times and probably is best known today as

Scrooge in Dickens's *A Christmas Carol* and from Molière's *The Miser*. The parasite was Roman in origin and can be seen today in numerous television situation comedies (Frank in M*A*S*H is an example). The use of identical twins for comic effect is a Roman invention, and because it permitted a wide range of comic misunderstandings it has been used by many playwrights, including Shakespeare in *The Comedy of Errors*. The Roman use of masks made the device of identical twins much easier to employ than it is today.

The Greek Influence

According to legend, in 240 B.C., a former slave, Livius Andronicus, presented performances of his Latin translations of a Greek tragedy and a Greek comedy, giving the Romans their first real taste of Greek drama and literature. Livius soon earned his freedom, and his literary career became so firmly established that his translations from the Greek were standard in Rome for more than two hundred years. His translation of the *Odyssey* was the standard text through the time of Cicero (first century B.C.).

Roman comedy derived primarily from the New Comedy of Menander, although it could, like Aristophanes' Old Comedy, sometimes be risqué. There is no question that comedy was the most well attended, the most performed, and the most beloved of Rome's drama. That is not to say that the Romans produced no tragedies. They did, and the influence of Roman tragedy has been as long-lasting as that of comedy. However, the Roman people preferred to laugh rather than to feel the pity and terror of tragic emotion.

Just as the Greek plays developed in connection with festivals, the Roman plays became associated with games held several times a year. During the games, performances were offered on an average of five to eleven days. The Megalesian Games took place in early April, in honor of the Great Mother, the goddess Cybele, whose temple stood on the Palatine Hill. In late April the Floral Games were held in front of the temple of Flora on the Aventine Hill. The most important were the Roman Games in September and the Plebeian Games in November.

The Greek drama competitions had no counterpart among the Romans, for whom drama was not the primary entertainment during the festivals. Roman playwrights and actors were hired to put on performances to entertain and divert the audiences watching gladiator fights, chariot races, animal baiting, and other spectacles. The producer had to please the audience or lose his chance to supply more entertainment. In a sense, this has a modern parallel in television ratings. The Roman audience was impatient and had many other diversions.

Roman comedies were sometimes revisions or amalgamations of Greek plays. The themes and characters of Roman tragedies also derived from Greek originals. The Trojan War figured largely in Roman plays, and the characters who fought the wars were reworked into new situations and their agonies reinterpreted.

For costumes, the actors wore the Greek tunic (called a CHITON) and a long white cloak or mantle called the PALLIUM. Like the Greeks, the Romans wore low shoes, called the SOCK, for comedy, and shoes with an elevated sole, the BUSKIN, for tragedy. For plays that had a totally Roman setting and narrative, the actors wore the Roman toga. Eventually, Roman actors used traditional Greek masks that immediately identified the characters for the audience. (The question of whether the earliest Roman actors wore masks as well has not been resolved.) The younger Roman characters wore black wigs, older characters wore white wigs, and characters representing slaves wore red wigs.

One of the most intriguing questions concerning Roman plays is the importance of music in the drama. In Greek plays, the chorus took most of the responsibility for the music, but since the chorus did not play as large a role in Roman drama (and was absent entirely from some works), the Roman plays may have resembled musical comedies. The dialogue in some comedies turns the play over to an interlude of flute playing, indicating that there were times with no actor onstage, no spoken words, and no mimed action, but only a musician to entertain the audience.

The Roman Stage

In the third century B.C., the Romans began building wooden stages that could be taken down quickly and moved as necessary. Eventually, they built stone theaters following Greek plans but varying from the Greek model in a number of important respects. They were built on flat ground, not utilizing hillsides as the Greek theaters did. The influence of the Romans' early wooden stage remained in the permanent buildings in several ways. The Roman stage was elevated, and since there was little or no chorus, the orchestra, in which the chorus moved from place to place, was no longer needed. The SCAENA, or background, against which the action took place, was often three stories tall and was proportionally longer than the Greek *skene*. This wide but shallow stage was exploited by the playwrights, who often set their plays on a street with various houses, temples, and other buildings along it.

The space in front of the *scaena* was known as the PROSCAENA, from which the PROSCENIUM ARCH, which frames the stage and separates the actors from the audience, developed in later centuries. The action took place on the *proscaena*. The potential for the proscenium arch is evident in the plan of the Theater of Marcellus (Figure 2), where the sections to the left and the right of the stage already indicate a separation of the stage from the audience and already imply a frame.

As in the plan of the Theater of Marcellus, the *frons scaena* (the front wall) usually had three doors (some had only two), which were ordinarily established as doors of separate buildings, one a temple and

Figure 2. Theater of Marcellus

the others the homes of chief characters. These doors were active "participants" in the drama; it has been said that the most common line heard in a Roman play is a statement that the door is opening and someone is coming in. The standard Roman play takes great care to justify the entrances and exits of its characters, which indicates that the Roman audience expected more realism in their comedies and tragedies than did their Greek counterparts.

The *scaena frons,* the front of the theater, not only was several stories high but also was much more architecturally developed than the *skene* of the Greek theater. The typical Roman architectural devices of multiple arches, columns, and pilasters decorated the *scaena,* giving it a stately appearance. Like the Greek theater, the Roman theater used machinery that permitted actors to be moved through the air and to make entrances from the heavens. Unlike the Greek theater, many Roman theaters had curtains covering the front wall of the stage.

Roman Dramatists
Plautus

All surviving Roman comedy shows the influence of Greek originals. Plautus (254–184 B.C.) is among Rome's most famous playwrights and he may have been a member of a troupe that performed Atellan comedy. His middle name is Maccius (a form of Maccus, the clown of the farces), which may allude to the role he had habitually played. Tradition has it that he was in the theater for a good while before he began writing comedies. His first plays date from 205 B.C., about thirty-five years after Livius introduced Greek drama to the Romans. No one knows how many plays he wrote, and it has been common to assign many titles to him that have not been authenticated. About twenty-one plays exist that are thought to be his, the most famous of which are *Amphitryon*, *The Pot of Gold*, *The Captives*, *Curculio*, *The Braggart Warrior*, *The Rope*, and *The Twin Menaechmi*.

The last play is probably the best-known Roman comedy. It features Menaechmus from Syracuse, who goes to Epidamnus searching for his lost twin. There he meets people who mistake him for his brother: a cook; a prostitute; Sponge, a typical parasite; and even his brother's wife and father-in-law. The comedy uses all the confusions inherent in mistaken identity.

Plautus (254–184 B.C.)

FROM *THE TWIN MENAECHMI*   *c. 205–184* B.C.

TRANSLATED BY LIONEL CASSON

The Twin Menaechmi was the first ancient play to be translated into a modern language and put on the stage (1486 in Italy). It has been adapted by numerous modern playwrights, including Shakespeare in *The Comedy of Errors* and, more recently, Rodgers and Hart in *The Boys from Syracuse* (1938), a Broadway musical that ran for 235 performances. *Boys* has been revived numerous times and is still a popular summer theater play. The following scene from the beginning of act III of *The Twin Menaechmi* shows the parasite Sponge mistaking the identity of Menaechmus of Syracuse for that of his friend Menaechmus of Epidamnus. They have a great go-around over a dress in a typical mix-up of the kind that originated with Roman comedies and has been popular in farces and comedies ever since.

ACT III

SPONGE: I'm over thirty now, and never have I ever in all those years pulled a more damned fool stunt than the one I pulled today: There was this town meeting, and *I* had to dive in and come up right in the middle of it. While I'm standing there with my mouth open, Menaechmus sneaks off on me. I'll bet he's gone to his girlfriend. Perfectly willing to leave me behind, too!

(*Paces up and down a few times, shaking his head bitterly. Then, in a rage.*) Damn, damn, damn the fellow who first figured out town meetings! All they do is keep a busy man away from his business. Why don't people pick a panel of men of leisure for this kind of thing? Hold a roll call at each meeting and whoever doesn't answer gets fined on the spot. There are plenty of persons around who need only one meal a day; they don't have business hours to keep because they don't go after dinner invitations or give them out. They're the ones to fuss with town meetings and town elections. If that's how things were run, I wouldn't have lost my lunch today. He sure wanted me along, didn't he? I'll go in, anyway. There's still hope of leftovers to soothe my soul. (*He is about to go up to the door when it suddenly swings open and Menaechmus of Syracuse appears, standing on the threshold with a garland, a little askew, on his head; he is holding the dress and listening to Lovey who is chattering at him from inside. Sponge quickly backs off into a corner.*) What's this I see? Menaechmus — and he's leaving, garland and all! The table's been cleared! I sure came in time — in time to walk him home. Well, I'll watch what his game is, and then I'll go and have a word with him.

MENAECHMUS OF SYRACUSE (*to Lovey inside*): Take it easy, will you! I'll have it back to you today in plenty of time, altered and trimmed to perfection. (*Slyly.*) Believe me, you'll say it's not your dress; you won't know it any more.

SPONGE (*to the audience*): He's bringing the dress to the dressmaker. The dining's done, the drinks are down — and Sponge spent the lunch hour outside. God damn it, I'm not the man I think I am if I don't get even with him for this, but really even. You just watch. I'll give it to him, I will.

MENAECHMUS OF SYRACUSE (*closing the door and walking downstage; to the audience, jubilantly*): Good god, no one ever expected less — and got more blessings from heaven in one day than me. I dined, I wined, I wenched, and (*holding up the dress*) made off with this to which, from this moment on, she hereby forfeits all right, title, and interest.

SPONGE (*straining his ears, to the audience*): I can't make out what he's saying from back here. Is that full-belly talking about me and my right title and interest?

MENAECHMUS OF SYRACUSE (*to the audience*): She said I stole it from my wife and gave it to her. I saw she was mistaking me for someone else, so I promptly played it as if she and I were having a hot and heavy affair and began to yes her; I agreed right down the line to everything she said. Well, to make a long story short, I never had it so good for so little.

SPONGE (*clenching his fists, to the audience*): I'm going up to him. I'm itching to give him the works. (*Leaves his corner and strides belligerently toward Menaechmus.*)

MENAECHMUS OF SYRACUSE (*to the audience*): Someone coming up to me. Wonder who it is?

SPONGE (*roaring*): Well! You featherweight, you filth, you slime, you disgrace to the human race, you double-crossing good-for-nothing! What did I ever do to you that you had to ruin my life? You sure gave me the slip downtown a little while ago! You killed off the day all right — and held the funeral feast without me. Me who was coheir under the will! Where do you come off to do a thing like that!

MENAECHMUS OF SYRACUSE (*too pleased with life to lose his temper*): Mister, will you please tell me what business you and I have that gives you the right to use language like that to a stranger here, someone you never saw in your life? You hand me that talk and I'll hand you something you won't like.

SPONGE (*dancing with rage*): God damn it, you already have! I know god damned well you have!

MENAECHMUS OF SYRACUSE (*amused and curious*): What's your name, mister?

SPONGE (*as before*): Still making jokes, eh? As if you don't know my name!

MENAECHMUS OF SYRACUSE: So help me, so far as I know, I never heard of you or saw you till this minute. But I know one thing for sure: whoever you are, you'd better behave yourself and stop bothering me.

SPONGE (*taken aback for a minute*): Menaechmus! Wake up!

MENAECHMUS OF SYRACUSE (*genially*): Believe me, to the best of my knowledge, I am awake.

SPONGE: You don't know me?

MENAECHMUS OF SYRACUSE (*as before*): If I did, I wouldn't say I didn't.

SPONGE (*incredulously*): You don't know your own parasite?

MENAECHMUS OF SYRACUSE: Mister, it looks to me as if you've got bats in your belfry.

SPONGE (*shaken, but not convinced*): Tell me this: Didn't you steal that dress there from your wife today and give it to Lovey?

MENAECHMUS OF SYRACUSE: Good god, no! I don't have a wife, I never gave anything to any Lovey, and I never stole any dress. Are you in your right mind?

SPONGE (*aside, groaning*): A dead loss, the whole affair. (*To Menaechmus.*) But you came out of your house wearing the dress! I saw you myself!

MENAECHMUS OF SYRACUSE (*exploding*): Damn you! You think everybody's a pervert just because you are? I was wearing this dress? Is that what you're telling me?

SPONGE: I most certainly am.

MENAECHMUS OF SYRACUSE: Now you go straight to the one place fit for you! No — get yourself to the lunatic asylum; you're stark-raving mad.

SPONGE (*venomously*): God damn it, there's one thing nobody in the world is going to stop me from doing: I'm telling the whole story, exactly what happened, to your wife this minute. All these insults are going to boomerang back on your own head. Believe you me, you'll pay for eating that whole lunch yourself. (*Dashes into the house of Menaechmus of Epidamnus.*)

MENAECHMUS OF SYRACUSE (*throwing his arms wide, to the audience*): What's going on here? Must everyone I lay eyes on play games with me this way? Wait — I hear the door.

(*The door of Lovey's house opens, and one of her maids comes out holding a bracelet. She walks over to Menaechmus and, as he looks on blankly, hands it to him.*)

MAID: Menaechmus, Lovey says would you please do her a big favor and drop this at the jeweler's on your way? She wants you to give him an ounce of gold and have him make the whole bracelet over.

MENAECHMUS OF SYRACUSE (*with alacrity*): Tell her I'll not only take care of this but anything else she wants taken care of. Anything at all. (*He takes the piece and examines it absorbedly.*)

MAID (*watching him curiously, in surprise*): Don't you know what bracelet it is?

MENAECHMUS OF SYRACUSE: Frankly no — except that it's gold.

MAID: It's the one you told us you stole from your wife's jewel box when nobody was looking.

MENAECHMUS OF SYRACUSE (*forgetting himself, in high dudgeon*): I never did anything of the kind!

MAID: You mean you don't remember it? Well, if that's the case, you give it right back!

MENAECHMUS OF SYRACUSE (*after a few seconds of highly histrionic deep thought*): Wait a second. No, I *do* remember it. Of course — this is the one I gave her. Oh, and there's something else: Where are the armlets I gave her at the same time?

MAID (*puzzled*): You never gave her any armlets.

MENAECHMUS OF SYRACUSE (*quickly*): Right you are. This was all I gave her.

MAID: Shall I tell her you'll take care of it?

MENAECHMUS OF SYRACUSE: By all means, tell her. I'll take care of it, all right. I'll see she gets it back the same time she gets the dress back.

MAID (*going up to him and stroking his cheek*): Menaechmus dear, will you do me a favor too? Will you have some earrings made for me? Drop earrings, please; ten grams of gold in each. (*Meaningfully.*) It'll make me *so* glad to see you every time you come to the house.

MENAECHMUS OF SYRACUSE: Sure. (*With elaborate carelessness.*) Just give me the gold. I'll pay for the labor myself.

MAID: Please, you pay for the gold too. I'll make it up to you afterward.

MENAECHMUS OF SYRACUSE: No, you pay for the gold. I'll make it up to *you* afterward. Double.

MAID: I don't have the money.

MENAECHMUS OF SYRACUSE (*with a great air of magnanimity*): Well, any time you get it, you just let me have it.

MAID (*turning to go*): I'm going in now. Anything I can do for you?

MENAECHMUS OF SYRACUSE: Yes. Tell her I'll see to both things — (*sotto voce, to the audience*) that they get sold as quickly as possible for whatever they'll bring. (*As the maid starts walking toward the door.*) Has she gone in yet? (*Hearing a slam.*) Ah, she's in, the door's closed. (*Jubilantly.*) The lord loves me! I've had a helping hand from heaven! (*Suddenly looks about warily.*) But why hang around when I have the time and chance to get away from this (*jerking his thumb at Lovey's house*) pimping parlor here? Menaechmus! Get a move on, hit the road, forward march! I'll take off this garland and toss it to the left here (*doing so*). Then, if anyone tries to follow me, he'll think I went that way. Now I'll go and see if I can find my servant. I want to let him know all the blessings from heaven I've had.

(*He races off, stage right. The stage is now empty.*)

Terence

Terence (c. 190–159 B.C.) is said to have been a North African slave brought to Rome, where his master realized he was unusually intelligent and gifted. After he was freed, Terence took his place in Roman literary life and produced a body of six plays, all of which still exist: *The Woman of Andros, The Self-Tormentor, The Eunuch, The Phormio, The Mother-in-Law,* and *The Brothers.* Terence's plays are notable for including a subplot or secondary action — carefully kept under control — and for avoiding the technique of addressing the audience directly.

The Romans preferred Plautus's broad farcical humor to Terence's more carefully plotted, elegantly styled plays, and Terence needed special support to get his plays produced. A manager or producer worked with him on all his plays, and the musician who worked with him was a slave, Flaccus. Terence's productive life was relatively short. He died on a trip to Greece, apparently worrying over a piece of missing luggage said to have contained new plays.

Terence's situation was unusual: He had two wealthy Roman patrons who were interested in seeing the best Greek comedy brought to the Romans. Consequently, they paid for his productions and gave him more support than the average comic playwright could have expected. Terence was often accused of plagiarism and admitted that he adapted Greek plays so closely that they seemed to be little more than translations. However, his dramatic skills developed considerably from the beginning to the end of his work, contrasting sharply with the carelessness of Plautus. Terence was more than a translator, but he wrote at a time when Romans were interested in emulating the Greeks, and his fidelity to Greek originals was one of his strongest recommendations.

Terence (c. 190–159 B.C.)

FROM *THE BROTHERS*   *160 B.C.*

The ending of *The Brothers*, generally recognized as his masterpiece and certainly the most influential of his plays, involves Demea planning a reversal on his brother, Micio. Micio is a good, easygoing bachelor who wishes well for others. Demea has been a stern father to one of his sons, Ctesipho, and has tried to steer him in a direction other than the one Ctesipho wants to follow. Demea has entrusted the upbringing of his second son, Aeschinus, to his lenient brother, Micio. Both sons deceive both brothers and end up with the women they want rather than the women the brothers want for them. Meanwhile, Demea gives up and turns the tables on Micio and engineers his brother's marriage to Aeschinus's mother-in-law. In the process of all this Demea decides to adopt the gentle, easygoing ways of his brother and forsake his former stern behavior.

This play was adapted often in the seventeenth century by Marston, Beaumont and Fletcher, and others. Molière relied on it for his *School for Wives*. At least five plays were adapted from it for the English stage in the eighteenth century.

FROM ACT V

MICIO (*to Syrus, within*): My brother ordered it,° say ye! Where is he? . . . Hah, Brother, was it you who ordered this?
DEMEA: Yes, that I did! And in this and all things else I'm ready to do whatever may conduce to the uniting, serving, helping, and the joining together of both families.
AESCHINUS (*to Micio*): Pray, Sir, let it be so!
MICIO: Well, I've nothing to say against it.
DEMEA: Truth, 'tis no more than we are obliged to do. For first, she's your son's mother-in-law . . .
MICIO: What then?
DEMEA: A very virtuous and modest woman . . .
MICIO: So they say indeed.
DEMEA: Not weighed down by years . . .
MICIO: Not yet.
DEMEA: But past child-bearing: a lonesome woman whom nobody esteems . . .
MICIO (*aside*): What the Devil is he at?
DEMEA: . . . Therefore you ought to marry her; and you Aeschinus, should do what you can to bring this about.

My brother ordered it: Demea ordered the breaking down of a wall to allow the two families to communicate. In this way Demea imitates the good-naturedness of his brother, Micio, and traps him into marrying Aeschinus's mother-in-law.

MICIO: Who? I marry?

DEMEA: Yes, you.

MICIO: I, prithee?

DEMEA: Yes, you I say.

MICIO: Pho, you are fooling us, surely?

DEMEA (*to Aeschinus*): If thou hast any life in thee, persuade him to it.

AESCHINUS: Dear Father . . .

MICIO (*interrupting*): Blockhead! Dost thou take in earnest what he says?

DEMEA: 'Tis in vain to refuse; it can't be avoided.

MICIO: Pho, you are in your dotage!

AESCHINUS: Good Sir, let me win this one favor.

MICIO (*angrily*): Art out of thy wits, let me alone!

DEMEA: Come, come! Hearken for once to what your son says.

MICIO: Haven't ye played the fool enough yet? Shall I at threescore and five marry an old woman who's ready to drop into the grave? This is your wise counsel, is it?

AESCHINUS: Pray, Sir, do; I've promised you shall.

MICIO: You promised, with a mischief! Promise for thyself, thou chit!

DEMEA: Fie, fie! What if he had begged a greater favor from you?

MICIO: As if there were any greater favor than this!

DEMEA: Pray grant his request.

AESCHINUS: Good Sir, be not so hard-hearted.

DEMEA: Pho, promise him for once!

MICIO: Will ye never leave baiting me?

AESCHINUS: Not till I've prevailed, Sir.

MICIO: Truth, this is downright forcing a man.

DEMEA: Come, Micio, be good-natured and consent.

MICIO: Though this be the most damned, foolish, ridiculous whim, and the most averse to my nature that could possibly be, yet since you are so extremely set upon it, I'll humor ye for once.

AESCHINUS: That is excellent; I'm obliged to ye beyond measure.

DEMEA (*aside*): Well, what's next? . . . What shall I say next? This is as I'd have it. . . . What's more to be done?

(*To Micio.*)

Ho! There's Hegio our poor kinsman, and nearest relation; in truth, we ought in conscience to do something for him.

MICIO: What, pray?

DEMEA: There's a small plot of land in the suburbs, which you farm out — pray let's give him that to live on.

MICIO: A small one, say ye?

DEMEA: Though it were a great one, you might yet give it to him. He has been as good as a father to Pamphila; he's a very honest man, our kinsman, and you couldn't bestow it better. Besides, Brother, there's a certain proverb (none of my own, I assure you) which you so well and wisely made use of: "That age has always this ill effect of making us more worldly, as well as wiser." We should do well to avoid this scandal. 'Tis a true proverb, Brother, and ought to be held in mind.

MICIO: What's all this? . . . Well, so let it be, if he has need of it.

AESCHINUS: Brave Father, I vow!

DEMEA: Now you are my true brother, both in body and soul.

MICIO: I'm glad of it.

DEMEA (*aside, laughing*): I've stabbed him with his own weapons, i'fack!

(*Enter Syrus, with a pick-axe upon his shoulders.*)

SYRUS (*to Demea*): The job is done as ye ordered, Sir.

DEMEA: Thou art an honest lad. . . . And upon my conscience I think Syrus deserves his freedom.

MICIO: He, his freedom? For what exploit?

DEMEA: O, for a thousand.

SYRUS: O dear Mr. Demea, you are a rare gentleman, edad you are! You know I've looked after the young gentlemen from their cradles. I taught them, advised them, and instructed them all I possibly could.

DEMEA: Nothing more evident! Nay, more than that, he catered for them, pimped for them, and in the morning took care of a debauchee for them. These are no ordinary accomplishments, I can assure ye.

SYRUS: Your worship's very merry.

DEMEA: Besides, he was prime mover in buying this music-girl. It was he who managed the whole intrigue, and 'tis no more than justice to reward him, as an encouragement to others! In short, Aeschinus desires the same thing.

MICIO (*to Aeschinus*): Do you desire it too?

AESCHINUS: Yes, if you please, Sir.

MICIO: Since 'tis so, come hither, Syrus! Thou art a free man.

(*Syrus kneels down, Micio lays his hand on his head, and after that gives him a cuff on the ear.*)

SYRUS (*rising up*): Generously done! A thousand thanks to ye all, and to you, Mr. Demea.

DEMEA: I'm well satisfied.

AESCHINUS: And I too.

SYRUS: I won't question it, Sir. But I wish heartily my joy were more complete, that my poor spouse Phrygia might be made as free as I am.

DEMEA: Truth, she's a mighty good woman.

SYRUS: And your grandson's first foster-mother, too.

DEMEA: Faith, in good earnest, if for that, she deserves her freedom before any woman in the world.

MICIO: What! For that simple service?

DEMEA: Yes, indeed! In fine, I'll pay for her freedom myself.

SYRUS: God's blessing light upon your worship, and grant all your wishes.

MICIO: Syrus, thou hast made a good day's work of it.

DEMEA: Besides, Brother, it would be a deed of charity to lend him a little money to set up in business that he may face the world without fear. I undertake that he'll soon repay it.

MICIO: Not a penny-piece!

AESCHINUS: He's a very honest fellow, Sir.

SYRUS: Upon my word, I'll repay you the loan. Do but trust me!

AESCHINUS: Pray do, Sir.

MICIO: I'll consider the matter with care.

DEMEA: He shall pay ye, I'll see to that.

SYRUS (*to Demea*): Egad, you're the best man alive.

AESCHINUS: And the pleasantest in the world.

MICIO: What's the meaning of this, Brother? How comes this sudden change of humor? Why this gallant squandering and profusion?

DEMEA: I'll tell ye, Brother. These sons of yours don't reckon you a sweet-natured and pleasant man because you live as you should and do what is just and reasonable, but because you fawn upon them, cocker them up, and give them what they'll spend. Now, son Aeschinus, if you are dissatisfied with my course of life, because I wouldn't indulge you in all things, right or wrong, then I'll not trouble my head with you any further. Be free to squander, buy mistresses, and do what you will! But if you wish me to advise ye, and set ye up, and help ye too in matters of which your youth can give ye but little understanding — matters of which you are over-fond, and don't well consider — see, here I'm ready to stand by you.

AESCHINUS: Dear Sir, we commit ourselves wholly to your charge; for you know what's fitting to be done far better than we . . . But what will ye do for my brother Ctesipho?

DEMEA: Why, let him take the music-girl; and so bid adieu to general wenching.

AESCHINUS: That's very reasonable. (*To the spectators.*) Gentlemen, your favor!

(*Exeunt°* all.)

Seneca

The surviving Roman plays come from just three hands: Plautus, Terence, and Seneca (4 B.C.–65 A.D.). The comedies of Plautus are raucous, broad, and farcical; those of Terence are polished and carefully structured. Seneca wrote tragedies that were well known to Elizabethans such as Marlowe and Shakespeare, and it is clear that the Elizabethan Age found SENECAN TRAGEDY to be peculiarly suited to its own temperament.

Senecan tragedies were based on either Greek or Roman themes and included murder, bloodthirsty actions, horror of various kinds, ghosts, and long, bombastic speeches. Signs of Senecan influence can be seen in Elizabethan drama, with its taste for many of these devices; plays like *Hamlet* are notable for ending in a pool of blood, with most of the actors lying dead onstage. The theme of revenge was also prized by Seneca and, later, by the Elizabethans.

Seneca was not a professional theater person. He was wealthy and learned, a philosopher active in the government of Emperor Nero's Rome. His plays, most of which were adapted from Euripides, were probably written only to be read, or perhaps recited as was common at his time; there is no record of their having been performed. The Roman people thirsted for comedy and low-down farce but had much less taste for serious plays.

Ten plays attributed to Seneca exist, nine of which are surely his and one of which is only possibly his. His most famous are *Mad Hercules, The Phoenician Women, Medea, Phaedra, Agamemnon, Thyestes,* and *The Trojan Women.*

Seneca (4 B.C.–65 A.D.)

FROM *THYESTES*

TRANSLATED BY ELLA ISABEL HARRIS

Thyestes influenced a number of Elizabethan revenge tragedies such as Shakespeare's *Hamlet.* The story is gruesome even by modern standards. Thyestes seduces his brother Atreus's wife. When Atreus summons him to Atreus's home, he goes suspiciously, hoping to be able to see

[S.D.] *Exeunt:* Latin for "they go out."

his children. The banquet Atreus holds for Thyestes seems to signal reconciliation between the brothers. But when it is over, Atreus brings in the heads of Thyestes' children, revealing that Thyestes has just eaten their bodies in the feast. The second scene from act V — before Thyestes is told about the meal he has eaten — follows in its entirety. It shows Thyestes wrestling with himself in a passion of uncertainty. Thyestes' soliloquy is a psychological study of the effects of grief, care, uncertainty, and fear. Seneca's plays have many such soliloquys and their revelations of complex emotional states deeply impressed the age of Shakespeare.

ACT V • Scene II

(*Thyestes sits alone at the banquet table, half overcome with wine; he tries to sing and be gay, but some premonition of evil weighs upon him.*)

THYESTES (*to himself*): By long grief dulled, put by thy cares, my heart,
    Let fear and sorrow fly and bitter need,
    Companion of thy timorous banishment,
    And shame, hard burden of afflicted souls.
    Whence thou has fallen profits more to know
    Than whither; great is he who with firm step
    Moves on the plain when fallen from the height;
    He who, oppressed by sorrows numberless
    And driven from his realm, with unbent neck
    Carries his burdens, not degenerate
    Or conquered, who stands firm beneath the weight
    Of all his burdens, he is great indeed.
    Now scatter all the clouds of bitter fate,
    Put by all signs of thy unhappy days,
    In happy fortunes show a happy face,
    Forget the old Thyestes. Ah, this vice
    Still follows misery: never to trust
    In happy days; though better fortunes come,
    Those who have borne afflictions find it hard
    To joy in better days. What holds me back,
    Forbids me celebrate the festal tide?
    What cause of grief, arising causelessly,
    Bids me to weep? What art thou that forbids
    That I should crown my head with festal wreath?
    It does forbid, forbid! Upon my head
    The roses languish, and my hair that drips
    With ointment rises as with sudden fear,
    My face is wet with showers of tears that fall
    Unwillingly, and groans break off my song.
    Grief loves accustomed tears, the wretched feel
    That they must weep. I would be glad to make
    Most bitter lamentation, and to wail,
    And rend this robe with Tyrian purple dyed.
    My mind gives warning of some coming grief,
    Presages future ills. The storm that smites
    When all the sea is calm weighs heavily
    Upon the sailor. Fool! What grief, what storm,
    Dost thou conceive? Believe thy brother now.
    Be what it may, thou fearest now too late,
    Or causelessly. I do not wish to be

Unhappy, but vague terror smites my breast.
No cause is evident and yet my eyes
O'erflow with sudden tears. What can it be,
Or grief, or fear? Or has great pleasure tears?

The surviving Roman plays offer enough variety to give us an idea of what the drama achieved. Like so much of Roman culture, Roman drama rested in the shadow of Greek accomplishments. The Romans were responsible for maintaining the Greek texts, allowing us to see a great deal of their work. Although it may be true that much of the Roman drama that was produced no longer exists, what survives shows variety and high quality.

Medieval Drama

The Role of the Church

The medieval period in Europe (476–1500 A.D.) began with the collapse of Rome, a calamity of such magnitude that the years between then and the beginning of the Crusades in 1095 have been traditionally called the Dark Ages. Historians used this term to refer to their lack of knowledge about a time in which no great central powers organized society or established patterns of behavior and standards in the arts.

Drama, or at least records of it, all but disappeared. The major institution to profit from the fall of the Roman Empire was the church, which in the ninth and tenth centuries enjoyed considerable power and influence. Many bishops considered drama a godless activity, a distraction from the piety that the church demanded of its members. During the great age of cathedral building and the great ages of religious painting and religious music — from the seventh century to the thirteenth — drama was not officially approved. Therefore, it is a striking irony that the rebirth of drama in the Western world should have taken place in the heart of the great cathedrals, developing slowly and inconspicuously until it outgrew its beginnings.

The church may well have intended nothing more than the simple dramatization of its message. Or it is possible that the people may have craved drama, and the church's response could have been an attempt to answer their needs. In either event, the church could never have foreseen the outcome of adding a few moments of drama to the liturgy, the church services. LITURGICAL DRAMA began in the ninth century with TROPES, or embellishments, which were sung during parts of the Mass. The earliest known example of a trope, called the QUEM QUAERITIS ("Whom seek ye?"), grew out of the Easter Mass and was sung in a monastic settlement in Switzerland called St. Gall:

ANGEL: Whom seek ye in the sepulchre, O ye Christians?
THREE MARYS: Jesus of Nazareth, who was crucified, O ye Angels.

ANGEL: He is not here; he is risen as he has foretold.
Go, announce that he is risen from the sepulchre.

Some scholars think that in its earliest form this trope was sung by two monks in a dialogue pattern, one monk representing the three Marys at Christ's tomb and the other representing the angels. Tropes like the *Quem Quaeritis* evolved over the years to include a number of participants — monks, nuns, and choirboys — as the tropes spread from church to church throughout the Continent. These dramatic interpolations never became dramas separate from the Mass itself, although their success and popularity led to experiments with other dramatic sequences centering on moments in the Mass and in the life of Christ. The actors in these pieces did not think of themselves as specialists or professionals; they were simply monks or nuns who belonged to the church. The churchgoers obviously enjoyed the tropes, and more were created, despite the church's official position on drama.

In the twelfth century, for reasons that remain unclear, the church expelled the liturgical drama to the churchyard. It may be that the dramatic moments inside the church, which had begun to demand more elaborate equipment and settings, were too complex to remain in the spaces normally assigned them, or they may have begun to conflict with the liturgy of the Mass.

Mystery Plays

Once outside the church, the drama flourished and soon became independent, although its themes continued to be religious and its services were connected with religious festivals. In 1264, a new and important feast was added to the religious calendar by order of Pope Urban IV: Corpus Christi, celebrated beginning on the first Thursday after Trinity Sunday, about two months after Easter. The purpose of the feast was to celebrate the new doctrine declaring that the body of Christ was real and present in the Host taken by the faithful in the sacrament of Communion.

At first the feast of Corpus Christi was localized in Liège, Belgium. But in the fourteenth and fifteenth centuries it spread through papal decree and became one of the chief feasts of the church. Among other things, it featured a procession and pageant in which the Host was displayed publicly through the streets of a town. Because of the importance and excitement of this feast, entire communities took part in the celebration.

The craft guilds, professional organizations of workers involved in the same trade — carpenters, wool merchants, and so on — soon began competing with each other in producing plays that could be performed during the feast of Corpus Christi. Most of their plays derived from Bible stories and the life of Christ. Because the Bible is silent on many details of Christ's life, some plays invented new material and illuminated dark areas, thereby satisfying the intense curiosity medieval Christians had about events the Bible omitted.

The church did not ignore drama after it cast it out of the church buildings. Since the subject matter of the plays was wholeheartedly religious and since the plays had an obvious use as a teaching device for the historical moments of the Bible as well as for models of Christian behavior, they remained of considerable value to the church.

First performed by the clergy, these religious plays dramatized the mystery of Christ's Passion. Later the plays were produced by members of craft guilds, and they became known as CRAFT or MYSTERY PLAYS. Beginning in the medieval period, the word *mystery* was used to describe a skill or trade known only to a few who apprenticed and mastered its special techniques.

By the fifteenth century mystery plays and the feast of Corpus Christi were popular almost everywhere in Europe, and in England certain towns produced exceptionally elaborate cycles with unusually complex and ambitious plays. The CYCLES were groups of plays numbering from twenty-four to forty-eight. Four cycles have been preserved: the Chester, York, Towneley (Wakefield), and N-Town cycles, named for their towns of origin. N-Town plays were a generic version of plays that any town could take and use as its own, although the plays were originally written near Lincoln, according to the best current information.

The plays were performed again and again during annual holidays and feasts, and the texts were carefully preserved. Some of the plays are very short, such as *The Fall of Lucifer*. Others are more elaborate in length and complexity and resemble modern plays: *Noah*, from the Wakefield Cycle, which has been produced regularly in this century; *The Slaughter of Innocents*; and *The Second Shepherds' Play*, one of the most entertaining mystery plays.

The producers of the plays often had a sense of humor in their choice of subjects. For example, the Water-Drawers guild sponsored *Noah's Flood*, the Butchers (because they sold "flesh") *Temptation, The Woman Taken in Adultery*, and the Shipwrights *The Building of the Ark*.

Some of that sense of humor spilled over into the content of the plays as well. Among the best-known mystery plays is the somewhat farcical *The Second Shepherds' Play*, which is both funny and serious. It tells of a crafty shepherd named Mak who steals a lamb from his fellow shepherds and takes it home. His wife, Gill, then places it in a cradle and pretends it is her baby. Eventually the shepherds — who suspect Mak from the first — smoke out the fraud and give Mak a blanket-tossing for their trouble. But after they do so, they see a star in the heavens and turn their attention to the birth of baby Jesus, the Lamb of God. They join the Magi and come to pay homage to the Christ Child.

The easy way in which the profane elements of everyday life coexisted with the sacred in medieval times has long interested scholars. *The*

Second Shepherds' Play virtually breaks into two parts, the first dedicated to the wickedness of Mak and Gill and the horseplay of the shepherds. But once Mak has had his due reward, the play alters in tone and the sense of devotion to Christian teachings becomes uppermost. The fact that the mystery plays moved away from liturgical Latin and to the vernacular (local) language made such a juxtaposition of sacred and profane much more possible.

The dominance of the guilds in producing mystery plays suggests that guilds enjoyed increasing political power and authority. The guilds grew stronger and more influential — probably at the expense of the church. Some historians have seen this development as crucial to the growing secularization of the Middle Ages.

Morality Plays

MORALITY PLAYS were never part of any cycle but developed independently as moral tales in the late fourteenth or early fifteenth century on the Continent and in England. They do not illustrate moments in the Bible, nor do they describe the life of Christ or the saints. Instead, they describe the lives of everyday people facing the temptations of the world. The plays are careful to present a warning to the unwary that their souls are always in peril, that the devil is on constant watch, and that people must behave properly if they are to be saved.

One feature of morality plays is their reliance on ALLEGORY, a favorite medieval device. Allegory is the technique of giving abstract ideas or values a physical representation. In morality plays, abstractions such as goodness became characters in the drama. In modern times we sometimes use allegory in art, as when we represent justice as a blindfolded woman. Allegorically, justice acts impartially because she does not "see" any distinctions, such as those of rank or privilege, that characterize most people standing before a judge.

The use of allegory permitted medieval dramatists to personify abstract values such as sloth, greed, daintiness, vanity, strength, and hope by making them characters and placing them onstage in action. The dramatist specified symbols, clothing, and gestures appropriate to these abstract figures, thus helping the audience recognize the ideas the characters represented. The use of allegory was an extremely durable technique that carried over into medieval painting, printed books, and books of emblems, in which, for example, sloth would be shown as a man reclining lazily on a bed or greed would be represented as overwhelmingly fat and vanity as a figure completely absorbed in a mirror.

The central problem in the morality play was the salvation of human beings, represented by an individual's struggle to avoid sin and damnation and achieve freedom in the otherworld. As in *Everyman* (c. 1495), a late medieval play that is the best known of the morality plays, the subjects of these plays were usually abstract battles between certain vices and certain virtues for the possession of the human soul, a theme repeated in the Elizabethan age in Marlowe's *Doctor Faustus*.

In many ways, the morality play was a dramatized sermon designed to teach a moral lesson. It was marked by high seriousness and, often, gloominess. The use of allegory to represent abstract qualities allowed the didactic playwrights to draw clear-cut lines of moral force: Satan was always bad; angels were always good. The allegories were clear, direct, and apparent to all who witnessed the plays.

We do not have much knowledge of the origins of morality plays, and many of them are lost, but some that remain are occasionally performed and have some power: *The Pride of Life*, the earliest extant morality play; *The Castle of Perseverance*; *Wisdom*; *Mankind*; and *Everyman* are the best known. They all enjoyed a remarkable popularity in the latter part of the medieval period, all the way up to the early Renaissance.

The Medieval Stage

Relatively little commentary survives about the conventions of medieval staging, and some of it is contradictory. We know that, in the earliest years, after the tropes developed into full-blown religious scenes acted inside the cathedrals, certain sections of the church were devoted to specific short plays. These areas of the church became known as MANSIONS; each mansion represented a building or physical place known to the audience. The audience moved from one mansion to another, seeing play after play, accepting the dramatic reality of the events, characters, and locale associated with each mansion.

The tradition of moving from mansion to mansion inside the church carried over into the performances that took place later outside the church. Instead of mansions, movable wagons with raised stages provided the playing areas, called PAGEANTS. In some cases, the wagons moved to new audiences, and in others the wagons remained stationary and the audience moved from one to another. During the guild cycles, the pageants would move and the performers would give their plays at several locales so that many people could see them.

According to contemporary descriptions, drawings, and reconstructions, the pageant was often a flat surface drawn on wheels that had a wagon next to it. Their long sides touched. In some cases a figure could descend from an upper area as if from the clouds, or actors could descend from the pageants onto the audience's level to enact a descent into an underworld. The stage was, then, a raised platform visible to the audience below (Figure 3).

A curtain concealed a space, usually inside or below the wagon, for changing costumes. The actors used costumes and props, sometimes very elaborate and expensive, in an effort to make the drama realistic. Indeed, between the thirteenth and the sixteenth centuries, a number of

Figure 3. Pageant Wagon

theatrical effects were developed to please a large audience. For instance, in the morality and mystery plays the devils were often portrayed as frightening, grotesque, and sometimes even comic figures. They became crowd pleasers. A sensational element was developed in some of the plays in the craft cycles, especially those that involved the lives of the saints and martyrs, in which there were plenty of chances to portray horrifying tortures.

The prop that seems to have pleased the most audiences was a complex machine known as the MOUTH OF HELL, usually a large fish-shaped orifice from which smoke and explosions, fueled by gunpowder, belched constantly. The devils took great delight in stuffing their victims into these maws. According to a contemporary account, one of the machines required seventeen men to operate.

The level of realism achieved by medieval plays was at times startling. Numerous surviving illustrations show scenes that appear lifelike and authentic. In addition to visual realism, medieval plays involved a psychological level of participation on the part of both audience and actor. Sometimes they demanded that the actors suffer in accord with the characters they played. Some records attest to characters playing Christ on the cross having to be revived after their hearts stopped, and at least one Judas apparently was hanged just a little too long and had to be resuscitated.

The Actors

In the early days of liturgical drama, the actors in the tropes were monks and choirboys, and in the mystery plays they were drawn from the guilds. At first all the actors were male, but records show that eventually women took important roles.

The demands of more sophisticated plays encouraged the development of a kind of professionalism, although it seems unlikely that players in the cycles could have supported themselves on their earnings. Special skills became essential for the design and operation of complex stage machines and for the performance of acrobatics that were expected of certain characters, such as devils. As actors developed facility in delivering lines and writers found ways to incorporate more challenging elements in their plays, a professionalism no doubt arose even if actors and writers had few opportunities to earn a living on the stage.

By the second half of the sixteenth century, in the early Renaissance, groups of wandering actors were producing highly demanding and sophisticated plays, and writers such as Shakespeare were able to join them and make a living. When these professionals secured their own theaters, they had no problems filling them with good drama, with actors, and with an audience. The continuing growth and development of professionalism in the medieval theater account in large part for the power and appeal of much of the drama of the period.

Dramatic techniques developed in the medieval period were put to good use in the Renaissance theater. For example, the colorful and dramatic devil characters that stalked the mystery plays were transformed into sophisticated villains in Elizabethan drama. Mephistopheles behaves like a smooth Tudor lawyer in Marlowe's *Dr. Faustus*; Iago in *Othello* is suspected of having cloven hooves; De Flores in *The Changeling* acts without conscience. Perhaps one important difference is that the Elizabethan devil-villains are truly frightening, since they are so recognizably human in their villainy.

EVERYMAN

This late medieval play may have origins in northern Europe. A Flemish play, *Elckerlijk* ("Everyman"), dates from c. 1495, and the question of whether the English *Everyman* was translated from it or whether it is a translation of *Everyman* has not been settled. Both plays may have had a common origin in an unknown play. The English *Everyman* was produced frequently in the early years of the sixteenth century. Its drama was largely theological and its purposes were aimed at reform of the audience. One indication that entertainment was not the primary goal of this morality play is its lack of the comic moments that other plays, such as *The Second Shepherds' Play*, contain.

The author of the play may have been a priest. This assumption has long been common because the play has so much theological content and offers a moral message of the kind one might expect to hear from the pulpit. The theme of the play is fundamental: the inevitability of death. And for that reason, in part, the play continues to have a universal appeal. Modern productions may not give the audience a suitable medieval chill, but the message of the play is still relevant for everyone.

The medieval reliance on allegory is apparent in the naming of the characters in *Everyman*: Death, Kindred, Cousin, Goods, Knowledge, Strength, Beauty, and Everyman himself. Each character not only stands for a specific quality; he or she is that quality. The allegorical way of thinking derived from the medieval faith that everything in the world had a moral meaning. Morality plays depended on this belief and always clarified setting, characters, and circumstances according to their moral value. This was in keeping with the medieval belief that the soul was always in jeopardy and that life was a test of one's moral condition. When Everyman meets a character, the most important information about his or her moral value is communicated instantly in the name of the character. Characters in allegorical plays also reveal themselves through their costumes and props. The character Good Deeds is simply good deeds — there is no need for psychological development because the medieval audience had a full understanding of what good deeds meant and how Good Deeds as a character would behave.

The structure of *Everyman* resembles a journey. Everyman undertakes to see who among all his acquaintances will accompany him on his most important trip: to the grave and the judgment of God Almighty. Seeing life as a journey — or as part of a journey — was especially natural for the medieval mind, which had as models the popular and costly religious pilgrimages to holy shrines and to the Holy Land itself. If life on earth is only part of the journey of the soul, then the morality play helps to put it into clear perspective. This life is not, the play tells us, the most important part of the soul's existence.

At its core, *Everyman* has a profound commercial metaphor: Everyman is called to square accounts with God. The metaphor of accounting appears early in the play, when Everyman talks about his accounts and reckonings as if they appeared in a book that should go with him to heaven. His life will be examined and if he is found wanting, he will go into the fires of hell. If he has lived profitably from a moral viewpoint, he will enjoy life everlasting. The language of the play is heavily loaded with accounting metaphors that indicate it is the product of a society quite unlike that of the Greeks or the Romans. Such metaphors suggest that *Everyman* directs its message to ordinary people, for whom accounting was a significant concept. For the Greeks and Romans such a metaphor would have reduced the significance of actions whose consequences reached not only into future ages but as far as the gods.

Like many sermons, *Everyman* imparts a lesson that its auditors were expected to heed. Hence the key points of the play are repeated at the end by the Doctor. For moderns, didactic plays are sometimes tedious. For the medieval mind, they represented delightful ways of learning important messages.

Everyman in Performance

Very little is known about early productions of *Everyman*. It was produced in Holland and England for seventy-five years beginning in the mid-fifteenth century. The play disappeared from the stage for a few centuries, finally resurfacing in 1901 in a production under the auspices of the Elizabethan Stage Society in London, under the direction of William Poel. Poel designed the costumes and set, directed, and played at first the part of Death, and then when he got older, the part of God. Poel produced *Everyman* many times over the next fifteen years.

The 1901 production was followed by a 1902 revival in New York starring Edith Wynne Matthison and produced by Ben Greet, marking the play's first American performance. Greet continued producing *Everyman* for the next thirty-five years in both England and America.

Max Reinhardt, the legendary German director, saw Poel's production and decided to produce *Everyman* in Germany. The Austrian poet and playwright Hugo von Hofmannsthal wrote a new German adaptation, *Jedermann*, for Reinhardt. The adaptation features Everyman as a wealthy burgher, and central to the play is an ornate banquet scene in which Death appears. Hofmannsthal's German adaptation marked a shift in emphasis from the simpler and more personal English *Everyman* to the spectacular *Jedermann* that concentrates on a wealthy man's lustful life and his attempts to get into heaven. *Jedermann* was first produced in Berlin on December 1, 1911. In 1913 Reinhardt produced the play in Salzburg, Austria, at the Salzburg Cathedral square, and except for the years of World War II, Reinhardt's version of *Jedermann* has been performed regularly at the annual Salzburg Festival. The critic Brooks Atkinson found Reinhardt's production "nothing short of miraculous." In a review of Reinhardt's 1927 production, the critic Gilbert Gabriel found *Jedermann*, "crammed with splendors for the eye, largesse of bells and uplifting voices for the ear." A reviewer at the 1936 Salzburg Festival production of *Jedermann* wrote that the play "has everything but simplicity."

The popularity of the Reinhardt productions of *Jedermann* paved the way for numerous productions of *Everyman* over the years. The WPA (Works Projects Administration) held special Sunday church performances of *Everyman* in 1936. Other notable productions include a 1941 *Everyman* in New York performed by refugee actors from Europe, and a 1955 tour with college casts in New England and California. In 1922 a new English adaptation of the German *Jedermann* by Sir John Martin-Harvey was presented at Stratford-on-Avon. This production toured to London and New York in 1923. In 1936 Sir John's adaptation was performed at the Hollywood Bowl in California with Peggy Wood and Lionel Braham. Long popular with college and community groups, the play continues to be performed around the world.

Anonymous

EVERYMAN   *c. 1495*

EDITED BY A. C. CAWLEY

Characters

GOD	KNOWLEDGE
MESSENGER	CONFESSION
DEATH	BEAUTY
EVERYMAN	STRENGTH
FELLOWSHIP	DISCRETION
KINDRED	FIVE WITS
COUSIN	ANGEL
GOODS	DOCTOR
GOOD DEEDS	

Here beginneth a treatise how the high Father of Heaven sendeth Death to summon every creature to come and give account of their lives in this world, and is in manner of a moral play.

MESSENGER: I pray you all give your audience,
    And hear this matter with reverence,

By figure° a moral play:
The *Summoning of Everyman* called it is,
That of our lives and ending shows   5
How transitory we be all day.°
This matter is wondrous precious,
But the intent of it is more gracious,
And sweet to bear away.
The story saith: Man, in the beginning   10
Look well, and take good heed to the ending,
Be you never so gay!
Ye think sin in the beginning full sweet,
Which in the end causeth the soul to weep,
When the body lieth in clay.   15
Here shall you see how Fellowship and Jollity,
Both Strength, Pleasure, and Beauty,
Will fade from thee as flower in May;

3. **By figure:** In form.   6. **all day:** Always.

For ye shall hear how our Heaven King
20   Calleth Everyman to a general reckoning:
Give audience, and hear what he doth say.

(*Exit.*)

(*God speaketh.*)

GOD: I perceive, here in my majesty,
How that all creatures be to me unkind,°
Living without dread in worldly prosperity:
25   Of ghostly sight° the people be so blind,
Drowned in sin, they know me not for their
        God;
In worldly riches is all their mind,
They fear not my righteousness, the sharp rod.
My law that I showed, when I for them died,
They forget clean, and shedding of my blood
30   red;
I hanged between two, it cannot be denied;
To get them life I suffered to be dead;
I healed their feet, with thorns hurt was my
        head.
I could do no more than I did, truly;
35   And now I see the people do clean forsake me:
They use the seven deadly sins damnable,
As pride, covetise, wrath, and lechery
Now in the world be made commendable;
And thus they leave of angels the heavenly
        company.
40   Every man liveth so after his own pleasure,
And yet of their life they be nothing sure:
I see the more that I them forbear
The worse they be from year to year.
All that liveth appaireth° fast;
45   Therefore I will, in all the haste,
Have a reckoning of every man's person;
For, and° I leave the people thus alone
In their life and wicked tempests,
Verily they will become much worse than beasts;
50   For now one would by envy another up eat;
Charity they do all clean forget.
I hoped well that every man
In my glory should make his mansion,
And thereto I had them all elect;
55   But now I see, like traitors deject,°
They thank me not for the pleasure that I to
        them meant,
Nor yet for their being that I them have lent.
I proffered the people great multitude of mercy,
And few there be that asketh it heartily.
60   They be so cumbered with worldly riches
That needs on them I must do justice,

On every man living without fear.
Where art thou, Death, thou mighty messenger?

(*Enter Death.*)

DEATH: Almighty God, I am here at your will,
Your commandment to fulfill.   65
GOD: Go thou to Everyman,
And show him, in my name,
A pilgrimage he must on him take,
Which he in no wise may escape;
And that he bring with him a sure reckoning   70
Without delay or any tarrying.

(*God withdraws.*)

DEATH: Lord, I will in the world go run overall,
And cruelly outsearch both great and small;
Every man will I beset that liveth beastly
Out of God's laws, and dreadeth not folly.   75
He that loveth riches I will strike with my dart,
His sight to blind, and from heaven to
        depart° —
Except that alms be his good friend —
In hell for to dwell, world without end.
Lo, yonder I see Everyman walking.   80
Full little he thinketh on my coming;
His mind is on fleshly lusts and his treasure,
And great pain it shall cause him to endure
Before the Lord, Heaven King.

(*Enter Everyman.*)

Everyman, stand still! Whither art thou going   85
        Thus gaily? Hast thou thy Maker forget?
EVERYMAN: Why askest thou?
        Wouldest thou wit?°
DEATH: Yea, sir; I will show you:
In great haste I am sent to thee   90
From God out of his majesty.
EVERYMAN: What, sent to me?
DEATH: Yea, certainly.
Though thou have forget him here,
He thinketh on thee in the heavenly sphere,   95
As, ere we depart, thou shalt know.
EVERYMAN: What desireth God of me?
DEATH: That shall I show thee:
A reckoning he will needs have
Without any longer respite.   100
EVERYMAN: To give a reckoning longer leisure I
        crave;
This blind matter troubleth my wit.
DEATH: On thee thou must take a long journey;
Therefore thy book of count° with thee thou
        bring,

---

23. **unkind:** Ungrateful.   25. **ghostly sight:** Spiritual vision.
44. **appaireth:** Degenerates.   47. **and:** If.   55. **deject:**
Abject.

77. **depart:** Separate.   88. **wit:** Know.   104. **count:**
Account.

105   For turn° again thou cannot by no way.
And look thou be sure of thy reckoning,
For before God thou shalt answer, and show
Thy many bad deeds, and good but a few;
How thou hast spent thy life, and in what wise,

110   Before the chief Lord of paradise.
Have ado that we were in that way,°
For, wit thou well, thou shalt make none
    attorney.°
EVERYMAN: Full unready I am such reckoning to
    give.
I know thee not. What messenger art thou?

115 DEATH: I am Death, that no man dreadeth,°
For every man I rest,° and no man spareth;
For it is God's commandment
That all to me should be obedient.
EVERYMAN: O Death, thou comest when I had thee
    least in mind!

120   In thy power it lieth me to save;
Yet of my good° will I give thee, if thou will be
    kind:
Yea, a thousand pound shalt thou have,
And defer this matter till another day.
DEATH: Everyman, it may not be, by no way.

125   I set not by gold, silver, nor riches,
Ne by pope, emperor, king, duke, ne princes;
For, and I would receive gifts great,
All the world I might get;
But my custom is clean contrary.
I give thee no respite. Come hence, and not

130   tarry.
EVERYMAN: Alas, shall I have no longer respite?
I may say Death giveth no warning!
To think on thee, it maketh my heart sick,
For all unready is my book of reckoning.

135   But twelve year and I might have abiding,°
My counting-book I would make so clear
That my reckoning I should not need to fear.
Wherefore, Death, I pray thee, for God's mercy,
Spare me till I be provided of remedy.

140 DEATH: Thee availeth not to cry, weep, and pray;
But haste thee lightly that thou were gone that
    journey,°
And prove thy friends if thou can;
For, wit thou well, the tide abideth no man,
And in the world each living creature

145   For Adam's sin must die of nature.°

EVERYMAN: Death, if I should this pilgrimage take,
And my reckoning surely make,
Show me, for saint charity,°
Should I not come again shortly?
DEATH: No, Everyman; and thou be once there,   150
Thou mayst never more come here,
Trust me verily.
EVERYMAN: O gracious God in the high seat
    celestial,
Have mercy on me in this most need!
Shall I have no company from this vale
    terrestrial   155
Of mine acquaintance, that way me to lead?
DEATH: Yea, if any be so hardy
That would go with thee and bear thee
    company.
Hie thee that thou were gone to God's
    magnificence,
Thy reckoning to give before his presence.   160
What, weenest° thou thy life is given thee,
And thy worldly goods also?
EVERYMAN: I had wend° so, verily.
DEATH: Nay, nay; it was but lent thee;
For as soon as thou art go,   165
Another a while shall have it, and then go
    therefro,
Even as thou has done.
Everyman, thou art mad! Thou hast thy wits
    five,
And here on earth will not amend thy life;
For suddenly I do come.   170
EVERYMAN: O wretched caitiff,° whither shall I flee,
That I might scape this endless sorrow?
Now, gentle Death, spare me till to-morrow,
That I may amend me
With good advisement.   175
DEATH: Nay, thereto I will not consent,
Nor no man will I respite;
But to the heart suddenly I shall smite
Without any advisement.
And now out of thy sight I will me hie;   180
See thou make thee ready shortly,
For thou mayst say this is the day
That no man living may scape away.
          (Exit Death.)
EVERYMAN: Alas, I may well weep with sighs deep!
Now have I no manner of company   185
To help me in my journey, and me to keep;
And also my writing is full unready,
How shall I do now for to excuse me?
I would to God I had never be get!°

---

105. **turn:** Return.   111. **Have ado . . . that way:** Let us see about making that journey.   112. **none attorney:** No one [your] advocate.   115. **no man dreadeth:** Fears no man. 116. **rest:** Arrest.   121. **good:** Goods.   135. **But twelve year . . . abiding:** If I could stay for just twelve more years. 141. **But haste thee . . . that journey:** But set off quickly on your journey.   145. **of nature:** In the course of nature.

148. **for saint charity:** In the name of holy charity.   **161. weenest:** Suppose.   163. **wend:** Supposed.   171. **caitiff:** Captive.   189. **be get:** Been born.

90 To my soul a full great profit it had be;
For now I fear pains huge and great.
The time passeth. Lord, help, that all wrought!
For though I mourn it availeth nought.
The day passeth, and is almost ago;°
95 I wot not well what for to do.
To whom were I best my complaint to make?
What and I to Fellowship thereof spake,
And showed him of this sudden chance?
For in him is all mine affiance;°
00 We have in the world so many a day
Be good friends in sport and play.
I see him yonder, certainly.
I trust that he will bear me company;
Therefore to him will I speak to ease my sorrow.
05 Well met, good Fellowship, and good morrow!

(*Fellowship speaketh.*)

FELLOWSHIP: Everyman, good morrow, by this day!
Sir, why lookest thou so piteously?
If any thing be amiss, I pray thee me say,
That I may help to remedy.
10 EVERYMAN: Yea, good Fellowship, yea;
I am in great jeopardy.
FELLOWSHIP: My true friend, show to me your
mind;
I will not forsake thee to my life's end,
In the way of good company.
15 EVERYMAN: That was well spoken, and lovingly.
FELLOWSHIP: Sir, I must needs know your
heaviness;°
I have pity to see you in any distress.
If any have you wronged, ye shall revenged be,
Though I on the ground be slain for thee —
20 Though that I know before that I should die.
EVERYMAN: Verily, Fellowship, gramercy.°
FELLOWSHIP: Tush! by thy thanks I set not a straw.
Show me your grief, and say no more.
EVERYMAN: If I my heart should to you break,°
25 And then you to turn your mind from me,
And would not me comfort when ye hear me
speak,
Then should I ten times sorrier be.
FELLOWSHIP: Sir, I say as I will do indeed.
EVERYMAN: Then be you a good friend at need:
30 I have found you true herebefore.
FELLOWSHIP: And so ye shall evermore;
For, in faith, and thou go to hell,
I will not forsake thee by the way.
EVERYMAN: Ye speak like a good friend; I believe
you well.

I shall deserve° it, and I may. 235
FELLOWSHIP: I speak of no deserving, by this day!
For he that will say, and nothing do,
Is not worthy with good company to go;
Therefore show me the grief of your mind,
As to your friend most loving and kind. 240
EVERYMAN: I shall show you how it is:
Commanded I am to go a journey,
A long way, hard and dangerous,
And give a strait count, without delay,
Before the high Judge, Adonai.° 245
Wherefore, I pray you, bear me company,
As ye have promised, in this journey.
FELLOWSHIP: That is matter indeed.° Promise is
duty;
But, and I should take such a voyage on me,
I know it well, it should be to my pain; 250
Also it maketh me afeard, certain.
But let us take counsel here as well as we can,
For your words would fear a strong man.
EVERYMAN: Why, ye said if I had need
Ye would me never forsake, quick ne dead, 255
Though it were to hell, truly.
FELLOWSHIP: So I said, certainly,
But such pleasures be set aside, the sooth to say;
And also, if we took such a journey,
When should we come again? 260
EVERYMAN: Nay, never again, till the day of doom.
FELLOWSHIP: In faith, then will not I come there!
Who hath you these tidings brought?
EVERYMAN: Indeed, Death was with me here.
FELLOWSHIP: Now, by God that all hath bought,° 265
If Death were the messenger,
For no man that is living to-day
I will not go that loath journey —
Not for the father that begat me!
EVERYMAN: Ye promised otherwise, pardie.° 270
FELLOWSHIP: I wot well I said so, truly;
And yet if thou wilt eat, and drink, and make
good cheer,
Or haunt to women the lusty company,°
I would not forsake you while the day is clear,°
Trust me verily. 275
EVERYMAN: Yea, thereto ye would be ready!
To go to mirth, solace, and play,
Your mind will sooner apply,
Than to bear me company in my long journey.

---

235. **deserve:** Repay. 245. **Adonai:** Hebrew name for God.
248. **That is matter indeed:** That is a good reason indeed
[for asking me]. 265. **bought:** Redeemed. 270. **pardie:**
By God. 273. **haunt to women the lusty company:** Frequent
the lively company of women. 274. **while the day is clear:**
Until daybreak.

---

194. **ago:** Gone. 199. **affiance:** Trust. 216. **heaviness:**
Sorrow. 221. **gramercy:** Thanks. 224. **break:** Open.

FELLOWSHIP: Now, in good faith, I will not that
280   way.
      But and thou will murder, or any man kill,
      In that I will help thee with a good will.
EVERYMAN: O, that is a simple advice indeed.
      Gentle fellow, help me in my necessity!
285   We have loved long, and now I need;
      And now, gentle Fellowship, remember me.
FELLOWSHIP: Whether ye have loved me or no,
      By Saint John, I will not with thee go.
EVERYMAN: Yet, I pray thee, take the labor, and do
      so much for me
290   To bring me forward, for saint charity,
      And comfort me till I come without the town.
FELLOWSHIP: Nay, and thou would give me a new
      gown,
      I will not a foot with thee go;
      But, and thou had tarried, I would not have left
      thee so.
295   And as now God speed thee in thy journey,
      For from thee I will depart as fast as I may.
EVERYMAN: Whither away, Fellowship? Will thou
      forsake me?
FELLOWSHIP: Yea, by my fay!° To God I betake°
      thee.
EVERYMAN: Farewell, good Fellowship; for thee my
      heart is sore.
300   Adieu for ever! I shall see thee no more.
FELLOWSHIP: In faith, Everyman, farewell now at
      the ending;
      For you I will remember that parting is
      mourning.   (Exit Fellowship.)
EVERYMAN: Alack! shall we thus depart° indeed —
      Ah, Lady, help! — without any more comfort?
305   Lo, Fellowship forsaketh me in my most need.
      For help in this world whither shall I resort?
      Fellowship herebefore with me would merry
      make,
      And now little sorrow for me doth he take.
      It is said, "In prosperity men friends may find,
310   Which in adversity be full unkind."
      Now whither for succor shall I flee,
      Sith° that Fellowship hath forsaken me?
      To my kinsmen I will, truly,
      Praying them to help me in my necessity;
315   I believe that they will do so,
      For kind will creep where it may not go.°
      I will go say,° for yonder I see them.
      Where be ye now, my friends and kinsmen?

(Enter Kindred and Cousin.)

KINDRED: Here be we now at your commandment.
      Cousin, I pray you show us your intent   320
      In any wise, and do not spare.
COUSIN: Yea, Everyman, and to us declare
      If ye be disposed to go anywhither;
      For, wit you well, we will live and die together.
KINDRED: In wealth and woe we will with you
      hold,   325
      For over his kin a man may be bold.°
EVERYMAN: Gramercy, my friends and kinsmen
      kind.
      Now shall I show you the grief of my mind:
      I was commanded by a messenger,
      That is a high king's chief officer;   330
      He bade me go a pilgrimage, to my pain,
      And I know well I shall never come again;
      Also I must give a reckoning strait,
      For I have a great enemy° that hath me in wait,°
      Which intendeth me for to hinder.   335
KINDRED: What account is that which ye must
      render?
      That would I know.
EVERYMAN: Of all my works I must show
      How I have lived and my days spent;
      Also of ill deeds that I have used   340
      In my time, sith life was me lent;
      And of all virtues that I have refused.
      Therefore, I pray you, go thither with me
      To help to make mine account, for saint charity.
COUSIN: What, to go thither? Is that the matter?   345
      Nay, Everyman, I had liefer fast bread and
      water°
      All this five year and more.
EVERYMAN: Alas, that ever I was bore!
      For now shall I never be merry,
      If that you forsake me.   350
KINDRED: Ah, sir, what ye be a merry man!
      Take good heart to you, and make no moan.
      But one thing I warn you, by Saint Anne —
      As for me, ye shall go alone.
EVERYMAN: My Cousin, will you not with me go?   355
COUSIN: No, by our Lady! I have the cramp in my
      toe.
      Trust not to me, for, so God me speed,
      I will deceive you in your most need.
KINDRED: It availeth not us to tice.°   360
      Ye shall have my maid with all my heart;
      She loveth to go to feasts, there to be nice,°
      And to dance, and abroad to start:

298. fay: Faith.   betake: Commend.   303. depart: Part.
312. Sith: Since.   316. for kind will creep where it may not
go: For kinship will creep where it cannot walk, i.e., blood
is thicker than water.   317. say: Essay, try.

326. For over his kin . . . may be bold: For a man may be
sure of his kinsfolk.   334. enemy: Devil.   hath me in wait:
Has me under observation.   346. liefer fast bread and water:
Rather fast on bread and water.   359. tice: Entice.   361.
nice: Wanton.

I will give her leave to help you in that journey,
If that you and she may agree.
EVERYMAN: Now show me the very effect° of your
    mind: 365
Will you go with me, or abide behind?
KINDRED: Abide behind? Yea, that will I, and I
    may!
Therefore farewell till another day.
                         (*Exit Kindred.*)
EVERYMAN: How should I be merry or glad?
For fair promises men to me make,   370
But when I have most need they me forsake.
I am deceived; that maketh me sad.
COUSIN: Cousin Everyman, farewell now,
For verily I will not go with you.
Also of mine own an unready reckoning   375
I have to account; therefore I make tarrying.
Now God keep thee, for now I go.
                      (*Exit Cousin.*)
EVERYMAN: Ah, Jesus, is all come hereto?
Lo, fair words maketh fools fain;°
They promise, and nothing will do, certain.   380
My kinsmen promised me faithfully
For to abide with me steadfastly,
And now fast away do they flee:
Even so Fellowship promised me.
What friend were best me of to provide?°   385
I lose my time here longer to abide.
Yet in my mind a thing there is:
All my life I have loved riches;
If that my Good° now help me might,
He would make my heart full light.   390
I will speak to him in this distress —
Where art thou, my Goods and riches?

(*Goods speaks from a corner.*)

GOODS: Who calleth me? Everyman? What! hast
    thou haste?
I lie here in corners, trussed and piled so high,
And in chests I am locked so fast,   395
Also sacked in bags. Thou mayst see with thine
    eye
I cannot stir; in packs low I lie.
What would ye have? Lightly° me say.
EVERYMAN: Come hither, Good, in all the haste
    thou may,
For of counsel I must desire thee.   400
GOODS: Sir, and ye in the world have sorrow or
    adversity,
That can I help you to remedy shortly.
EVERYMAN: It is another disease that grieveth me;

In this world it is not, I tell thee so.
I am sent for, another way to go,   405
To give a strait count general
Before the highest Jupiter of all;
And all my life I have had joy and pleasure in
    thee,
Therefore, I pray thee, go with me;
For, peradventure, thou mayst before God
    Almighty   410
My reckoning help to clean and purify;
For it is said ever among
That money maketh all right that is wrong.
GOODS: Nay, Everyman, I sing another song.
I follow no man in such voyages;   415
For, and I went with thee,
Thou shouldst fare much the worse for me;
For because on me thou did set thy mind,
Thy reckoning I have made blotted and blind,
That thine account thou cannot make truly; 420
And that hast thou for the love of me.
EVERYMAN: That would grieve me full sore,
When I should come to that fearful answer.
Up, let us go thither together.
GOODS: Nay, not so! I am too brittle, I may not
    endure;   425
I will follow no man one foot, be ye sure.
EVERYMAN: Alas, I have thee loved, and had great
    pleasure
All my life-days on good and treasure.
GOODS: That is to thy damnation, without leasing,°
For my love is contrary to the love everlasting; 430
But if thou had me loved moderately during,
As to the poor to give part of me,
Then shouldst thou not in this dolor be,
Nor in this great sorrow and care.
EVERYMAN: Lo, now was I deceived ere I was ware, 435
And all I may wite° misspending of time.
GOODS: What, weenest thou that I am thine?
EVERYMAN: I had wend so.
GOODS: Nay, Everyman, I say no.
As for a while I was lent thee;   440
A season thou hast had me in prosperity.
My condition is man's soul to kill;
If I save one, a thousand I do spill.°
Weenest thou that I will follow thee?
Nay, not from this world, verily.   445
EVERYMAN: I had wend otherwise.
GOODS: Therefore to thy soul Good is a thief;
For when thou art dead, this is my guise —
Another to deceive in this same wise
As I have done thee, and all to his soul's
    reprief.°   450

---

365. effect: Tenor.   379. fain: Glad.   385. me of to provide: To provide myself with.   389. Good: Goods.   398. Lightly: Quickly.

429. without leasing: Without a lie, i.e., truly.   436. wite: Blame.   443. spill: Ruin.   450. reprief: Shame.

EVERYMAN: O false Good, cursed may thou be,
        Thou traitor to God, that hast deceived me
        And caught me in thy snare!
GOODS: Marry, thou brought thyself in care,
455   Whereof I am glad;
        I must needs laugh, I cannot be sad.
EVERYMAN: Ah, Good, thou hast had long my
            heartly love;
        I gave thee that which should be the Lord's
            above.
        But wilt thou not go with me indeed?
460   I pray thee truth to say.
GOODS: No, so God me speed!
        Therefore farewell, and have good day.
                                    (Exit Goods.)
EVERYMAN: O, to whom shall I make my moan
        For to go with me in that heavy journey?
465   First Fellowship said he would with me gone;
        His words were very pleasant and gay,
        But afterward he left me alone.
        Then spake I to my kinsmen, all in despair,
        And also they gave me words fair;
470   They lacked no fair speaking,
        But all forsook me in the ending.
        Then went I to my Goods, that I loved best,
        In hope to have comfort, but there had I least;
        For my Goods sharply did me tell
475   That he bringeth many into hell.
        Then of myself I was ashamed,
        And so I am worthy to be blamed;
        Thus may I well myself hate.
        Of whom shall I now counsel take?
480   I think that I shall never speed
        Till that I go to my Good Deed.
        But, alas, she is so weak
        That she can neither go nor speak;
        Yet will I venture on her now.
485   My Good Deeds, where be you?

(Good Deeds speaks from the ground.)

GOOD DEEDS: Here I lie, cold in the ground;
        Thy sins hath me sore bound,
        That I cannot stir.
EVERYMAN: O Good Deeds, I stand in fear!
490   I must you pray of counsel,
        For help now should come right well.°
GOOD DEEDS: Everyman, I have understanding
        That ye be summoned account to make
        Before Messias, of Jerusalem King;
        And you do by me,° that journey with you will I
495   take.

491. should come right well: Would be very welcome.   495.
by me: As I advise.

EVERYMAN: Therefore I come to you, my moan to
            make;
        I pray you that ye will go with me.
GOOD DEEDS: I would full fain, but I cannot stand,
            verily.
EVERYMAN: Why, is there anything on you fall?
GOOD DEEDS: Yea, sir, I may thank you of° all;   500
        If ye had perfectly cheered me,
        Your book of count full ready had be.
        Look, the books of your works and deeds eke!°
        Behold how they lie under the feet,
        To your soul's heaviness.   505
EVERYMAN: Our Lord Jesus help me!
        For one letter here I cannot see.
GOOD DEEDS: There is a blind reckoning in time of
            distress.
EVERYMAN: Good Deeds, I pray you help me in this
            need,
        Or else I am for ever damned indeed;   510
        Therefore help me to make reckoning
        Before the Redeemer of all thing,
        That King is, and was, and ever shall.
GOOD DEEDS: Everyman, I am sorry of your fall,
        And fain would I help you, and I were able.   515
EVERYMAN: Good Deeds, your counsel I pray you
            give me.
GOOD DEEDS: That shall I do verily;
        Though that on my feet I may not go,
        I have a sister that shall with you also,
        Called Knowledge, which shall with you abide, 520
        To help you to make that dreadful reckoning.

(Enter Knowledge.)

KNOWLEDGE: Everyman, I will go with thee, and be
            thy guide,
        In thy most need to go by thy side.
EVERYMAN: In good condition I am now in every
            thing,
        And am wholly content with this good thing,   525
        Thanked be God my creator.
GOOD DEEDS: And when she hath brought you
            there
        Where thou shalt heal thee of thy smart,
        Then go you with your reckoning and your
            Good Deeds together,
        For to make you joyful at heart   530
        Before the blessed Trinity.
EVERYMAN: My Good Deeds, gramercy!
        I am well content, certainly,
        With your words sweet.
KNOWLEDGE: Now go we together lovingly   535
        To Confession, that cleansing river.
EVERYMAN: For joy I weep; I would we were there!

500. of: For.   503. eke: Also.

But, I pray you, give me cognition
Where dwelleth that holy man, Confession.
40 KNOWLEDGE: In the house of salvation:
We shall find him in that place,
That shall us comfort, by God's grace.

(*Knowledge takes Everyman to Confession.*)

Lo, this is Confession. Kneel down and ask
mercy,
For he is in good conceit° with God Almighty.
EVERYMAN: O glorious fountain, that all
45 uncleanness doth clarify,
Wash from me the spots of vice unclean,
That on me no sin may be seen.
I come with Knowledge for my redemption,
Redempt with heart° and full contrition;
50 For I am commanded a pilgrimage to take,
And great accounts before God to make.
Now I pray you, Shrift, mother of salvation,
Help my Good Deeds for my piteous
exclamation.
CONFESSION: I know your sorrow well, Everyman.
55 Because with Knowledge ye come to me,
I will you comfort as well as I can,
And a precious jewel I will give thee,
Called penance, voider of adversity;
Therewith shall your body chastised be,
60 With abstinence and perseverance in God's
service.
Here shall you receive that scourge of me,
Which is penance strong that ye must endure,
To remember thy Savior was scourged for thee
With sharp scourges, and suffered it patiently;
65 So must thou, ere thou scape that painful
pilgrimage.
Knowledge, keep him in this voyage,
And by that time Good Deeds will be with thee.
But in any wise be siker° of mercy,
For your time draweth fast; and° ye will saved
be,
70 Ask God mercy, and he will grant truly.
When with the scourge of penance man doth
him bind,
The oil of forgiveness then shall he find.
EVERYMAN: Thanked be God for his gracious work!
For now I will my penance begin;
75 This hath rejoiced and lighted my heart,
Though the knots be painful and hard within.
KNOWLEDGE: Everyman, look your penance that ye
fulfill,
What pain that ever it to you be;

And Knowledge shall give you counsel at will
How your account ye shall make clearly.   580
EVERYMAN: O eternal God, O heavenly figure,
O way of righteousness, O goodly vision,
Which descended down in a virgin pure
Because he would every man redeem,
Which Adam forfeited by his disobedience: 585
O blessed Godhead, elect and high divine,
Forgive my grievous offense;
Here I cry thee mercy in this presence.°
O ghostly treasure, O ransomer and redeemer,
Of all the world hope and conductor,   590
Mirror of joy, and founder of mercy,
Which enlumineth heaven and earth thereby,
Hear my clamorous complaint, though it late be;
Receive my prayers, of thy benignity;
Though I be a sinner most abominable,   595
Yet let my name be written in Moses' table.°
O Mary, pray to the Maker of all thing,
Me for to help at my ending;
And save me from the power of my enemy,
For Death assaileth me strongly.   600
And, Lady, that I may by mean of thy prayer
Of your Son's glory to be partner,
By the means of his passion, I it crave;
I beseech you help my soul to save.
Knowledge, give me the scourge of penance;   605
My flesh therewith shall give acquittance:°
I will now begin, if God give me grace.
KNOWLEDGE: Everyman, God give you time and
space!
Thus I bequeath you in the hands of our
Saviour;
Now may you make your reckoning sure.   610
EVERYMAN: In the name of the Holy Trinity,
My body sore punished shall be:
Take this, body, for the sin of the flesh!

(*Scourges himself.*)

Also° thou delightest to go gay and fresh,
And in the way of damnation thou did me
bring,   615
Therefore suffer now strokes and punishing.
Now of penance I will wade the water clear,
To save me from purgatory, that sharp fire.

(*Good Deeds rises from the ground.*)

588. **in this presence**: In the presence of this company.   596.
Moses' table: Medieval theologians regarded the two tablets given to Moses on Mount Sinai as symbols of baptism and penance. Thus Everyman is asking to be numbered among those who have escaped damnation by doing penance for their sins.   606. **acquittance**: Satisfaction (as part of the sacrament of penance).   614. **Also**: As.

544. **conceit**: Esteem.   549. **heart**: Heartfelt.   568. **siker**: Sure.   569. **and**: If.

GOOD DEEDS: I thank God, now I can walk and go,
620   And am delivered of my sickness and woe.
        Therefore with Everyman I will go, and not
            spare;
        His good works I will help him to declare.
KNOWLEDGE: Now, Everyman, be merry and glad!
        Your Good Deeds cometh now; ye may not be
            sad.
625   Now is your Good Deeds whole and sound,
        Going upright upon the ground.
EVERYMAN: My heart is light, and shall be
            evermore;
        Now will I smite° faster than I did before.
GOOD DEEDS: Everyman, pilgrim, my special friend,
630   Blessed be thou without end;
        For thee is preparate the eternal glory.
        Ye have me made whole and sound,
        Therefore I will bide by thee in every stound.°
EVERYMAN: Welcome, my Good Deeds; now I hear
            thy voice,
635   I weep for very sweetness of love.
KNOWLEDGE: Be no more sad, but ever rejoice;
        God seeth thy living in his throne above.
        Put on this garment to thy behoof,°
        Which is wet with your tears,
640   Or else before God you may it miss,
        When ye to your journey's end come shall.
EVERYMAN: Gentle Knowledge, what do ye it call?
KNOWLEDGE: It is a garment of sorrow:
        From pain it will you borrow;°
645   Contrition it is,
        That geteth forgiveness;
        It pleaseth God passing well.
GOOD DEEDS: Everyman, will you wear it for your
            heal?°
EVERYMAN: Now blessed be Jesu, Mary's Son,
650   For now have I on true contrition.
        And let us go now without tarrying;
        Good Deeds, have we clear our reckoning?
GOOD DEEDS: Yea, indeed, I have it here.
EVERYMAN: Then I trust we need not fear;
655   Now, friends, let us not part in twain.
KNOWLEDGE: Nay, Everyman, that will we not,
            certain.
GOOD DEEDS: Yet must thou lead with thee
        Three persons of great might.
EVERYMAN: Who should they be?
660 GOOD DEEDS: Discretion and Strength they hight,°
        And thy Beauty may not abide behind.
KNOWLEDGE: Also ye must call to mind
        Your Five Wits as for your counsellors.

628. **smite:** Strike. 633. **stound:** Trial. 638. **behoof:** Advantage. 644. **borrow:** Release. 648. **heal:** Salvation.
660. **hight:** Are called.

GOOD DEEDS: You must have them ready at all
        hours.
EVERYMAN: How shall I get them hither?   66[5]
KNOWLEDGE: You must call them all together,
        And they will hear you incontinent.°
EVERYMAN: My friends, come hither and be
            present,
        Discretion, Strength, my Five Wits, and Beauty.

(*Enter Beauty, Strength, Discretion, and Five Wits.*)

BEAUTY: Here at your will we be all ready.   67[0]
        What will ye that we should do?
GOOD DEEDS: That ye would with Everyman go,
        And help him in his pilgrimage.
        Advise you, will ye with him or not in that
            voyage?
STRENGTH: We will bring him all thither,   67[5]
        To his help and comfort, ye may believe me.
DISCRETION: So will we go with him all together.
EVERYMAN: Almighty God, lofed° may thou be!
        I give thee laud that I have hither brought
        Strength, Discretion, Beauty, and Five Wits. Lack
            I nought.   68[0]
        And my Good Deeds, with Knowledge clear,
        All be in my company at my will here;
        I desire no more to my business.
STRENGTH: And I, Strength, will by you stand in
            distress,
        Though thou would in battle fight on the
            ground.   68[5]
FIVE WITS: And though it were through the world
            round,
        We will not depart for sweet ne sour.
BEAUTY: No more will I unto death's hour,
        Whatsoever thereof befall.
DISCRETION: Everyman, advise you first of all;   69[0]
        Go with a good advisement and deliberation.
        We all give you virtuous monition°
        That all shall be well.
EVERYMAN: My friends, harken what I will tell:
        I pray God reward you in his heavenly sphere. 69[5]
        Now harken, all that be here,
        For I will make my testament
        Here before you all present:
        In alms half my good I will give with my hands
            twain
        In the way of charity, with good intent,   70[0]
        And the other half still shall remain
        In queth,° to be returned there it ought to be.°

667. **incontinent:** Immediately. 678. **lofed:** Praised. 692.
monition: Forewarning. 702. **queth:** Bequest. **returned
there it ought to be:** This line probably refers to restitution,
that is, the restoration to its proper owner of unlawfully
acquired property.

This I do in despite of the fiend of hell,
To go quit out of his peril°
'05 Ever after and this day.
KNOWLEDGE: Everyman, harken what I say:
Go to priesthood, I you advise,
And receive of him in any wise°
The holy sacrament and ointment together.
10 Then shortly see ye turn again hither;
We will all abide you here.
FIVE WITS: Yea, Everyman, hie you that ye ready
were.
There is no emperor, king, duke, ne baron,
That of God hath commission
'15 As hath the least priest in the world being;
For of the blessed sacraments pure and benign
He beareth the keys, and thereof hath the cure°
For man's redemption — it is ever sure —
Which God for our soul's medicine
'20 Gave us out of his heart with great pine.°
Here in this transitory life, for thee and me,
The blessed sacraments seven there be:
Baptism, confirmation, with priesthood good,
And the sacrament of God's precious flesh and
blood,
Marriage, the holy extreme unction, and
25 penance;
These seven be good to have in remembrance,
Gracious sacraments of high divinity.
EVERYMAN: Fain would I receive that holy body,
And meekly to my ghostly father I will go.
FIVE WITS: Everyman, that is the best that ye can
'30 do.
God will you to salvation bring,
For priesthood exceedeth all other thing:
To us Holy Scripture they do teach,
And converteth man from sin heaven to reach;
'35 God hath to them more power given
Than to any angel that is in heaven.
With five words° he may consecrate,
God's body in flesh and blood to make,
And handleth his Maker between his hands.
'40 The priest bindeth and unbindeth all bands,
Both in earth and in heaven.
Thou ministers all the sacraments seven;
Though we kissed thy feet, thou were worthy;
Thou art surgeon that cureth sin deadly:
'45 No remedy we find under God
But all only priesthood.°

Everyman, God gave priests that dignity,
And setteth them in his stead among us to be;
Thus be they above angels in degree.

(*Everyman goes to the priest to receive the last
sacraments.*)

KNOWLEDGE: If priests be good, it is so, surely.   750
But when Jesus hanged on the cross with great
smart,
There he gave out of his blessed heart
The same sacrament in great torment:
He sold them not to us, that Lord omnipotent.
Therefore Saint Peter the apostle doth say   755
That Jesu's curse hath all they
Which God their Savior do buy or sell,
Or they for any money do take or tell.°
Sinful priests giveth the sinners example bad;
Their children sitteth by other men's fires, I have
heard,   760
And some haunteth women's company
With unclean life, as lusts of lechery:
These be with sin made blind.
FIVE WITS: I trust to God no such may we find;
Therefore let us priesthood honor,   765
And follow their doctrine for our souls' succor.
We be their sheep, and they shepherds be
By whom we all be kept in surety.
Peace, for yonder I see Everyman come,
Which hath made true satisfaction.   770
GOOD DEEDS: Methink it is he indeed.

(*Reenter Everyman.*)

EVERYMAN: Now Jesu be your alder speed!°
I have received the sacrament for my
redemption,
And then mine extreme unction:
Blessed be all they that counselled me to take it! 775
And now, friends, let us go without longer
respite;
I thank God that ye have tarried so long.
Now set each of you on this rood° your hand,
And shortly follow me:
I go before there I would be; God be our guide!   780
STRENGTH: Everyman, we will not from you go
Till ye have done this voyage long.
DISCRETION: I, Discretion, will bide by you also.
KNOWLEDGE: And though this pilgrimage be never
so strong,°
I will never part you fro.   785

704. **quit out of his peril:** Free out of his power.   708. **in any wise:** Without fail.   717. **cure:** Charge.   720. **pine:** Suffering.   737. **five words:** *Hoc est enim Corpus meum* ("For this is My Body," the words of the consecration of the Body of Christ at Mass).   746. **But all only priesthood:** Except only from the priesthood.

755–58. **Therefore Saint Peter . . . do take or tell:** Reference to the sin of simony, the selling of Church offices or benefits. **tell:** Count out, i.e., sell.   772. **your alder speed:** The helper of you all.   778. **rood:** Cross.   784. **strong:** Grievous.

STRENGTH: Everyman, I will be as sure by thee
      As ever I did by Judas Maccabee.°

(*Everyman comes to his grave.*)

EVERYMAN: Alas, I am so faint I may not stand;
      My limbs under me doth fold.
790   Friends, let us not turn again to this land,
      Not for all the world's gold;
      For into this cave must I creep
      And turn to earth, and there to sleep.
BEAUTY: What, into this grave? Alas!
EVERYMAN: Yea, there shall ye consume, more and
795   less.
BEAUTY: And what, should I smother here?
EVERYMAN: Yea, by my faith, and never more
         appear.
      In this world live no more we shall,
      But in heaven before the highest Lord of all.
800 BEAUTY: I cross out all this;° adieu, by Saint John!
      I take my cap in my lap,° and am gone.
EVERYMAN: What, Beauty, whither will ye?
BEAUTY: Peace, I am deaf; I look not behind me,
      Not and thou wouldest give me all the gold in
         thy chest.   (*Exit Beauty.*)
805 EVERYMAN: Alas, whereto may I trust?
      Beauty goeth fast away from me;
      She promised with me to live and die.
STRENGTH: Everyman, I will thee also forsake and
         deny;
      Thy game liketh° me not at all.
810 EVERYMAN: Why, then, ye will forsake me all?
      Sweet Strength, tarry a little space.
STRENGTH: Nay, sir, by the rood of grace!
      I will hie me from thee fast,
      Though thou weep till thy heart to-brast.°
815 EVERYMAN: Ye would ever bide by me, ye said.
STRENGTH: Yea, I have you far enough conveyed.
      Ye be old enough, I understand,
      Your pilgrimage to take on hand;
      I repent me that I hither came.
EVERYMAN: Strength, you to displease I am to
820   blame;
      Yet promise is debt, this ye well wot.
STRENGTH: In faith, I care not.
      Thou art but a fool to complain;
      You spend your speech and waste your brain.
825   Go thrust thee into the ground! (*Exit Strength.*)

787. Judas Maccabee: Judas Maccabeus, who overcame Syr-
ian domination and won religious freedom for the Jews in
165 B.C., believed that his strength came not from worldly
might but from heaven (1 Maccabees 3:19).   800. I cross
out all this: I cancel all this, i.e., my promise to stay with
you.   801. I take my cap in my lap: Doff my cap [so low
that it comes] into my lap.   809. liketh: Pleases.   814.
brast: Break.

EVERYMAN: I had wend surer I should you have
      found.
      He that trusteth in his Strength
      She him deceiveth at the length.
      Both Strength and Beauty forsaketh me;
      Yet they promised me fair and lovingly.   83●
DISCRETION: Everyman, I will after Strength be
      gone;
      As for me, I will leave you alone.
EVERYMAN: Why, Discretion, will ye forsake me?
DISCRETION: Yea, in faith, I will go from thee,
      For when Strength goeth before   83.
      I follow after evermore.
EVERYMAN: Yet, I pray thee, for the love of the
      Trinity,
      Look in my grave once piteously.
DISCRETION: Nay, so nigh will I not come;
      Farewell, every one!   (*Exit Discretion.*) 84●
EVERYMAN: O, all thing faileth, save God alone —
      Beauty, Strength, and Discretion;
      For when Death bloweth his blast,
      They all run from me full fast.
FIVE WITS: Everyman, my leave now of thee I take; 84.
      I will follow the other, for here I thee forsake.
EVERYMAN: Alas, then may I wail and weep,
      For I took you for my best friend.
FIVE WITS: I will no longer thee keep;
      Now farewell, and there an end.   85

         (*Exit Five Wits.*)

EVERYMAN: O Jesu, help! All hath forsaken me.
GOOD DEEDS: Nay, Everyman; I will bide with thee.
      I will not forsake thee indeed;
      Thou shalt find me a good friend at need.
EVERYMAN: Gramercy, Good Deeds! Now may I
      true friends see.   85
      They have forsaken me, every one;
      I loved them better than my Good Deeds alone.
      Knowledge, will ye forsake me also?
KNOWLEDGE: Yea, Everyman, when ye to Death
      shall go;
      But not yet, for no manner of danger.   86
EVERYMAN: Gramercy, Knowledge, with all my
      heart.
KNOWLEDGE: Nay, yet I will not from hence depart
      Till I see where ye shall become.
EVERYMAN: Methink, alas, that I must be gone
      To make my reckoning and my debts pay,   86
      For I see my time is nigh spent away.
      Take example, all ye that this do hear or see,
      How they that I loved best do forsake me,
      Except my Good Deeds that bideth truly.
GOOD DEEDS: All earthly things is but vanity: 87
      Beauty, Strength, and Discretion do man forsake,
      Foolish friends, and kinsmen, that fair spake —
      All fleeth save Good Deeds, and that am I.

EVERYMAN: Have mercy on me, God most mighty;
  And stand by me, thou mother and maid, holy
    Mary.   875
GOOD DEEDS: Fear not; I will speak for thee.
EVERYMAN: Here I cry God mercy.
GOOD DEEDS: Short our end, and minish our pain;
  Let us go and never come again.
EVERYMAN: Into thy hands, Lord, my soul I   880
    commend;
  Receive it, Lord, that it be not lost.
  As thou me boughtest, so me defend,
  And save me from the fiend's boast,
  That I may appear with that blessed host   885
  That shall be saved at the day of doom.
  In manus tuas, of mights most
  For ever, *commendo spiritum meum.*°

(*He sinks into his grave.*)

KNOWLEDGE: Now hath he suffered that we all
    shall endure;
  The Good Deeds shall make all sure.
  Now hath he made ending;   890
  Methinketh that I hear angels sing,
  And make great joy and melody
  Where Everyman's soul received shall be.
ANGEL: Come, excellent elect spouse, to Jesu!
  Hereabove thou shalt go   895
  Because of thy singular virtue.
  Now the soul is taken the body fro,
  Thy reckoning is crystal-clear.
  Now shalt thou into the heavenly sphere,

Unto the which all ye shall come   900
That liveth well before the day of doom.

(*Enter Doctor.*)

DOCTOR: This moral men may have in mind.
  Ye hearers, take it of worth, old and young,
  And forsake Pride, for he deceiveth you in the
    end;
  And remember Beauty, Five Wits, Strength, and
    Discretion,   905
  They all at the last do every man forsake,
  Save his Good Deeds there doth he take.
  But beware, for and they be small
  Before God, he hath no help at all;
  None excuse may be there for every man.   910
  Alas, how shall he do then?
  For after death amends may no man make,
  For then mercy and pity doth him forsake.
  If his reckoning be not clear when he doth
    come,
  God will say: *"Ite, maledicti, in ignem
    eternum."*°   915
  And he that hath his account whole and sound,
  High in heaven he shall be crowned;
  Unto which place God bring us all thither,
  That we may live body and soul together.
  Thereto help the Trinity!   920
  Amen, say ye, for saint charity.

Thus endeth this moral play of Everyman.

886–87. *In manus tuas . . . commendo spiritum meum:* Into your hands, most mighty One for ever, I commend my spirit.

915. *Ite, maledicti, in ignem eternum:* Depart, ye cursed, into everlasting fire.

Renaissance Drama

Italian Drama

The period following the Middle Ages in Europe, from about the fourteenth to the seventeenth century, is known as the *Renaissance*, a term meaning "rebirth." In this period, a shift away from medieval values and culture was motivated by a revival of classical learning; advances in physics, astronomy, and the biological sciences; the exploration of the "new world"; and political and economic developments. This shift was not abrupt, however; it was gradual, like a thaw. It began in the south, in Italy, in the late 1300s and moved northward through the activities of scholars, travelers, performers, and writers, until it reached England sometime late in the 1400s.

The Renaissance built on medieval culture and at the same time developed a secular understanding of the individual in society that eventually transformed this culture, long dominated by the Roman Catholic Church in many spheres — artistic, intellectual, and political, as well as spiritual. The transformation was influenced by the work of great writers, scholars, philosophers, and scientists such as Desiderius Erasmus (1466?–1536), Niccolò Machiavelli (1469–1527), Nicolaus Copernicus (1473–1543), Francis Bacon (1561–1626), and Galileo Galilei (1564–1642). In addition, the rise in power of the guilds and the increase in wealth of the successful Italian trading states, which produced large and influential families in cities such as Florence, Venice, Milan, and Genoa, contributed to the erosion of the church's power.

Italian scholars, following classical models, had begun in the last decades of the fourteenth century to center their studies on humanity and human achievements. This focus on human sciences, known as the humanities, became the chief concern of the most innovative thinkers of the day. Their interests were well served by the rediscovery of ancient Greek philosophical and scientific texts. Although ancient texts had been preserved in monasteries for centuries, knowledge of them was restricted.

A new demand for classical texts, fed by the Humanists' focus on ancient models as the source of wisdom and by their return to a liberal arts curriculum established by the Greeks, led to the wide dissemination of the works of Plato, Aristotle, Cicero, and important Greek dramatists during the Renaissance. The achievement of the ancients was an inspiration to Renaissance writers and reaffirmed their conviction that a study of the humanities was the key to transforming the old medieval attitudes into a new, dynamic worldview.

Vitruvius and the Rediscovery of Roman Design

Most medieval Italian theater depended on portable stages, but it was clear in the last decades of the fourteenth century that to present the newly rediscovered Roman or Greek plays, something more closely resembling the original Greek theater would be necessary. Fortunately, *The Ten Books of Architecture* (written c. 16–13 B.C.) of the great Roman architect Vitruvius (first century B.C.) was rediscovered in a manuscript in the monastery of St. Gall. It included detailed plans for the Greek-inspired Roman theater.

Using Vitruvius's designs, the Italians began building stages that were raised platforms with a FRONS SCAENA, the flat front wall used in the Roman theater. The earliest Italian woodcuts show the stages to be relatively simple with pillars supporting a roof or cover. Curtains stretched between the pillars permitted the actors to enter and exit. Usually three "doors" with names over each indicated the houses of specific characters.

The study of Roman architecture eventually produced, in 1585, one of the wonders of the Renaissance, the Olympic Theater (Teatro Olimpico) in Vicenza, designed by the great Renaissance architect Andrea Palladio (1508–1580), whose interpretation of Roman architecture was so compelling that it influenced architecture all over the world (Figure 4). The Olympic Theater, which has been preserved and is still used for performances, has an orchestra, a semicircular seating area, and a multistory *frons scaena*. But it also has several vistas of streets constructed in three-dimensional forced perspective running backwards from the *frons scaena*.

The Olympic Theater was built with an essentially conservative design. It worked well for Roman plays, but not for Renaissance plays, and so did not inspire new theater designs. Italian plays had begun to use scenery and painted backdrops that could be changed to suggest a change in location of the action. Carefully painted backdrops were also effective in increasing realism — one backdrop could immediately locate an action on a city street, while another could help shift the audience imaginatively to a woodland scene. These innovations were not possible on a Roman stage.

The development of vanishing-point perspective by the architect Filippo Brunelleschi (1377–1446), published by Leon Battista Alberti in

ABOVE: Figure 4. Designed by Andrea Palladio, the Teatro Olimpico (begun 1579) in Vicenza, Italy, was the first indoor theater of the Renaissance. The *scaena*'s openings produced an illusion of depth.

RIGHT: Figure 5. Perspective setting designed by Baldassare Peruzzi (1481–1536)

On Painting in 1435, helped revolutionize the design of theatrical backdrops. Earlier Renaissance painters had had no way to establish a firm sense of perspective on a flat surface, so all three-dimensional objects appeared flat; all space in a landscape or cityscape seemed shortened and unreal. The use of a single vanishing point — in which lines were lightly drawn from the edges of the canvas (or theatrical backdrop) so that they met in a single point in the center — made it possible to show buildings, trees, and figures in their proper proportion to one another (Figure 5). For the first time, Renaissance painters could achieve lifelike illusions on a flat surface.

The designer Sebastiano Serlio (1475–1554) used the vanishing-point technique, intensified by receding lines of tiles in the floor and on the painted backdrop. Serlio established all-purpose settings for comedy, tragedy, and satire. The rigidity of the backdrops for comedy and tragedy — both used a piazza, a small town square, ringed by stone buildings — restricted their use. But the setting for satire was rustic: trees, bushes, a couple of cottages. European theaters until the nineteenth century were equipped with sets of backdrops and wingpieces derived from his designs.

The most important and long-lasting development of Italian theater design in the mid-1500s was the PROSCENIUM ARCH, a "frame" that surrounds the stage, permitting the audience to look in on the scene, whether it be in a room or in a town square. The arch lent a finished touch to the theater, separating the action from the audience and distancing the actors. The proscenium arch is common in most theaters today.

Commedia dell'Arte

Renaissance Italy had two traditions of theater. *Commedia erudita* was learned, almost scholarly, in its interests in Roman staging and Roman plays. COMMEDIA DELL'ARTE was less reverent, more slapstick, and generally more popular. It is difficult, however, to say which was more influential on literature over the years. Each made its contribution.

In terms of acting and storytelling, the influence of the *commedia dell'arte* is almost unparalleled. The term means "comedy performed by professionals." The actors usually had grown up in performing families that made their living touring the countryside, performing at fairs and on feast days. From the early Renaissance through the eighteenth century, the *commedia dell'arte* entertained all of Europe and influenced comic theater in every nation.

The essence of *commedia dell'arte* was improvised scripts — a general narrative outline served as a basis, but the speeches were improvised on the spot (with some reliance on set elements and on experience with performing the same role many times). The principal characters were types who soon became familiar all over Europe: Pantalone, the often magisterial but miserly old man; Arlecchino (Harlequin), the cunning clown; Pulcinella, the Punch of Punch and Judy; Columbina, the innocent; the *zanni*, shrewd and shifty servants who usually invented complications and got their way; and a host of other STOCK CHARACTERS such as pedantic lawyers, a braggart captain, and a serving maid. Certain versions of general characters — such as Arlecchino, who began as a simple *zanni* — became famous and were copied in many countries. When Volpone calls Mosca a "Zany" near the end of Ben Jonson's *Volpone*, he reminds his audience that his characters are indebted to the *zanni* in *commedia dell'arte*. Knowing who the characters were even before the play began was a convenience that Renaissance audiences enjoyed.

The youthful lovers in the *commedia* did not require masks, but the old men, the *zanni*, and other characters all had masks that identified them and made them look, to modern eyes, rather grotesque. These masks survive today in the Venetian carnival and other celebrations. Stock characters thrive in popular comedies everywhere. Molière depended on them; later, Bernard Shaw and Sean O'Casey did as well. To a large extent, one of comedy's greatest sources of energy lies in the delight audiences have always taken in stock characters. Today hardly a situation comedy on television could survive without them.

The staging of *commedia dell'arte* was simple. It often took place in open air, but sometimes indoors in a more formal theatrical setting. Sometimes performers dispensed with the stage altogether and worked in marketplaces. Their scenarios were farcical crowd pleasers filled with buffoonery. They were based on the LAZZO and the BURLA. The *burla* was the general plot for any given performance, usually an elaborate comic action something like Abbott and Costello's "Who's on First?" routine. Abbott and Costello developed their routine for burlesque, a form of comedy popular in the first half of the twentieth century centering on broad gags, routines, and running jokes. Its name derives from *commedia dell'arte*'s *burla*. *Lazzi* were carefully planned comic routines that appeared to be spontaneous interruptions of the *burla*. Chevy

Chase's trademark pratfall as he enters a scene is a descendant of the sixteenth-century *lazzo*.

Elizabethan Drama

The reign of Queen Elizabeth I, 1558–1603, is known as the Elizabethan age in England. It was a period of discovery and prosperity as well as a period of great achievement in the arts, especially drama. Sir Francis Drake and Sir Walter Raleigh adventured across the Atlantic Ocean to the "New World," and England secured its economic future by defeating the invasion attempt of the Spanish Armada in 1588. England had become Protestant in the 1530s — one reason Catholic Spain felt it needed to subdue the nation.

Elizabethan England, especially after the defeat of the Armada, produced one of the great ages of drama, rivaling the great age of Greece. During this period, playwrights such as Christopher Marlowe (1564–1593), William Shakespeare (1564–1616), Ben Jonson (1572–1637), Inigo Jones (1573–1652), Thomas Kyd (1558–1594), John Marston (1576–1634), John Fletcher (1579–1625), John Webster (1580?–1625?), Thomas Middleton (1580?–1627), and John Ford (1586–1639) were drawing crowds by the thousands.

That the Elizabethans enjoyed plays with a moral basis is plain from the fact that so much of the great drama of the late 1500s and early 1600s is moral in character. However, early Elizabethan plays were less obviously moralistic than the then popular morality plays. They did not aim specifically to teach a moral lesson, although it is true that there are many lessons to be learned from Shakespeare and his contemporaries.

During Shakespeare's youth wandering players put on a number of plays from REPERTORY, their stock of three or four current plays they could perform. How many players there were or what their source of plays was, we do not know. Much of what we know comes directly from *Hamlet* and the appearance of the players who perform Hamlet's "Mouse-trap." What we learn there tells us that dramatic styles had developed in the English countryside and that theater was thriving.

The First Professional Companies

Although professional players' groups had long been licensed to perform in France and Italy, until the 1570s professional actors — those who had no other trade — did not enjoy favor in England. Such people could be arrested for vagrancy. The law, however, changed, and when it did the history of theater changed too. In 1576, James Burbage (father of the famous star of Shakespeare's plays, Richard Burbage) built the first building made specially for plays in England. It was called The Theatre.

Soon there were other theaters: the Swan (Figure 6), the Globe, the Rose, the Fortune, the Hope. The Globe was large enough to accommodate two to three thousand people. All of these theaters were open-air, so they could not be used in winter, and all were extraordinarily successful. Shakespeare, who was part owner of the Globe and, later,

Figure 6. The Swan Theatre as
copied from Johannes De Witt's
sixteenth-century drawing

of the second indoor Blackfriars Theatre, received money from the tickets
in the stalls, from his share as one of the actors in the company, and
from his role as chief playwright. He became rich enough to retire early
in splendid style in Stratford, his hometown. Few other Elizabethan
actors and playwrights had as much of a financial stake in their work
as did Shakespeare.

The Elizabethan Theater

The design of the Elizabethan theater is a matter of some speculation.
Many of the plays popular before the theaters were built were performed
in a square inn yard, with a balcony above. The audience looked out
their windows or stood in the yard. As a result, Elizabethan theaters

seem to have taken the inn yard structure as their basis. One location of the earliest English drama is the Inns of Court, essentially a college for law students in London, where students staged plays. The audience there would have been learned, bright, and imaginative. Indeed, the first English tragedy, *Gorboduc* by Thomas Sackville and Thomas Norton, was played at the Inner Temple, one of the Inns of Court, in 1562, before Marlowe and Shakespeare were born.

The shape of the early theaters was often octagonal on the outside and circular on the inside, like the bear pits in which bears, tied to stakes, were baited by dogs for the amusement of the audience. The stage was raised about five feet from the ground with levels of seating on both sides, in front, and in upper galleries. Approximately half the area over the stage was roofed and contained machinery to lower actors from the "heavens," and it was painted blue with stars to simulate the sky. In most cases the stage was approximately twenty-five by forty feet. Doors or curtained openings at the back of the stage served for entrances and exits, and at the back of the stage was a special room for costume changes. The stage may have contained a section that was normally curtained but that opened to reveal an interior, such as a bedroom. The existence of this feature is in considerable dispute, however.

The Elizabethan Audience

The entrance fee to the theaters was a penny, probably the equivalent of five to ten dollars in today's money. For another penny one could take a seat, probably on a bench, in one of the upper galleries. In some theaters more private spaces were available as well. A great many playgoers were satisfied to stand around the stage and were thus nicknamed "groundlings." Hamlet calls them the "understanding gentlemen of the ground." The more academic playwrights, Marlowe and Jonson, used the term to mean those who would not perfectly understand the significance of the plays.

Shakespeare and other Elizabethan playwrights expected a widely diverse audience. Audiences could be coarse, or they could be extraordinarily polished. Shakespeare had the gift, as did Marlowe and even Jonson in his comedies, to appeal to them all. Shakespeare's plays were given in public playhouses open to everyone. They were also given in university theaters, as in the case of *Macbeth*; Shakespeare's universality reveals itself in his appeal to many different kinds of people.

Women on the English Stage

Because women were not allowed to act on English stages, boys filled the parts of young female characters such as Juliet, Desdemona, and Ophelia. Interestingly, no contemporary commentator makes any complaint about having to put up with a boy playing the part of Juliet or any of Shakespeare's other love interests, such as Miranda in *The Tempest*, Ophelia in *Hamlet*, or even Queen Cleopatra. Older women, such as the Nurse in *Romeo and Juliet*, were played by some of the gifted male character actors of the company.

The Masque

The Elizabethan MASQUE was a special entertainment of royalty. It was a celebration that included a rudimentary plot, a great deal of singing and dancing, and magnificent costumes and lighting. Masques were performed only once, often to celebrate a royal marriage. Masque audiences participated in the dances and were usually delighted by complex machinery that lifted or lowered characters from the skies. The masque was devised in Italy in the 1570s by Count Giovanni Bardi, founder of the Florentine Camerata, a Renaissance group of theatergoers sponsored by Lorenzo de' Medici.

The geniuses of the masque are generally considered to have been Ben Jonson and Inigo Jones. Jones was the architect whose Banqueting Hall at Whitehall in London, which still stands, provided the setting for most of the great masques of the seventeenth century. Jonson and Jones worked together from 1605 to 1631 to produce a remarkable body of masques that today resemble the bones of a dinosaur: What we read on the page suggests in only the vaguest way what the presentation must have been like when the masques were mounted.

Because of the expenses of costuming and staging, masques were too costly to be produced more than once. The royal exchequer was frequently burdened in Queen Elizabeth's time, but more so after King James took the throne in 1603. Masque costumes were impressive, the scenery astounding, and the effects amazing. In all of this, the words — which are, after all, at the center of Shakespeare's plays as well as other plays of the period — were of least account. As a result of the emphasis on the machinery and designs — the work of Inigo Jones — Jonson abandoned his partnership in a huff, complaining that he could not compete with the scene painters and carpenters.

The emphasis on spectacle in the masques tells us something about the taste of the aristocrats, who enjoyed sumptuous foods, clothes, and amusements. Eventually, the more common audiences of the public theaters began demanding more and more spectacle, too. Their appetite was satisfied by masques inserted in the plays of Marston, Webster, and Shakespeare, whose masque in *The Tempest* is a delightful short tribute to the genre. An added device for achieving spectacular effects onstage was huge storm machines installed in the Globe. Some say that one reason Shakespeare wrote *The Tempest* was to take advantage of the new equipment. Foreign visitors described London theaters as gorgeous places of entertainment far surpassing their own. The quest for more intense spectacle eventually led to disaster in one theater. The Globe actually burned down in 1613 because a cannon in the roof above the stage misfired and brought the house down in real flames.

The royal demand for masques was unaffected, however. As Francis Bacon said in his essay "On Masques" (1625), "These things are but toys to come amongst such serious observations. But yet, since princes will have such things, it is better they should be graced with elegancy than daubed with cost. Dancing to song is a thing of great state and pleasure."

William Shakespeare

Despite the fact that Shakespeare wrote some thirty-seven plays, owned part of his theatrical company, acted in plays, and retired a relatively wealthy man in the city of his birth, there is much we do not know about him. His father was a glovemaker with pretentions to being a gentleman, and Shakespeare himself had his coat of arms placed on his home, New Place, which he purchased in part because it was one of the grandest buildings in Stratford. Church records indicate that he was born in April 1564 and that he died in April 1616, after having been retired from the stage for two or three years. We know that he married Anne Hathaway in 1582, when he was eighteen and she twenty-six; that he had a daughter Susanna and twins, Judith and Hamnet; and that Hamnet, his only son, died at age eleven. He has no direct descendants today.

We know very little about his education. We assume he went to the local grammar school, since as the son of a burgess he was eligible to attend for free. If he did so, he would have received a very strong education based on rhetoric and logic and the reading of classical literature. He would have been exposed to the comedies of Plautus and the tragedies of Seneca as well as the poetry of Virgil, Ovid, and a host of other, lesser writers.

A rumor has persisted that he spent some time as a Latin teacher, but that is uncertain. No evidence exists to suggest that Shakespeare went to a university, although his general learning and knowledge are so extraordinary and broad that generations of scholars have assumed that he was perhaps educated and then sent to the Inns of Court to study law. The lack of evidence to support any of these views has led some people to assume that his plays could not have been written by him but must have been written by someone with a considerable university education. However, no one in the Elizabethan theater had an education of the sort often proposed for Shakespeare. Marlowe and Ben Jonson were the most learned of Elizabethan playwrights, but they did not train as lawyers, and their work is quite different in character and feeling from that of Shakespeare.

One recent theory about Shakespeare's early years suggests that before he went to London to work in theater he had been a member of a wandering company of actors much like those who appear in *Hamlet*. It is an ingenious theory and has much to recommend it. For one thing, it would explain how Shakespeare could take the spotlight so quickly as to arouse the anger of more experienced London writers.

Shakespeare did not begin his career writing for the stage. He took a more conventional approach for the age and, because of his obvious skill as a poet, sought the support of an aristocratic patron, the Earl of Southampton. Southampton, like many wealthy and polished young courtiers, felt it a pleasant ornament to have under his sponsorship a poet whose works would be dedicated to him and would give him great credit. Shakespeare wrote sonnets apparently with Southampton in mind. And, hoping for preferment, he also wrote the long narrative poems *Venus and Adonis, The Rape of Lucrece,* and *The Phoenix and the Turtle.* However, Southampton eventually decided to become the patron of another poet, John Florio, an Italian who had translated Michel de Montaigne's *Essays.*

Shakespeare's response was to turn to the stage. His first plays were a considerable success: *King Henry VI* in three parts — three full-length plays. Satisfying London's taste for plays that told the history of England's tangled political past, Shakespeare wrote a lengthy series of plays ranging from *Richard II* through the two parts of *King Henry IV* to *Henry V* and won considerable renown. He was envied by competing playwrights. Audiences, however, were delighted. Francis Meres, in a famous book of the period called *Palladis Tamia: Wit's Treasury,* cites Shakespeare as the modern Plautus and Seneca, as the best in both comedy and tragedy. Meres says that by 1598 Shakespeare was known for a dozen plays. That his success was firm by this time is demonstrated by his having purchased his large house, New Place, in Stratford in 1597. He could not have done this without financial security.

In the next few years, Shakespeare made a number of interesting purchases of property in Stratford, and he also made deals with his own theater company to secure the rights to perform in London. These arrangements produced legal records that give us some of the clearest information we have concerning Shakespeare's activities during this period. His company was called the Lord Chamberlain's Men while Queen Elizabeth was alive but was renamed the King's Men by King James in the spring of 1603, less than two months after Elizabeth died. As the King's Men, Shakespeare's company had considerable power and success. His company sometimes performed plays for an audience that included King James, as in the first performance of *Macbeth.*

Shakespeare was successful as a writer of histories, comedies, and tragedies. He also wrote in another genre, known as romance because the plays are certainly not comedies or tragedies and because they often depend on supernatural or improbable elements. *Cymbeline, The Winter's Tale,* and *The Tempest* are the best known of Shakespeare's romances. They are late works and have a fascinating complexity.

When Shakespeare died on April 23, 1616, he was buried as a gentleman in the church in which he had been baptized in Stratford-upon-Avon. His will left most of his money and possessions to his two daughters, Judith and Susanna.

A Midsummer Night's Dream

A Midsummer Night's Dream (1595–1596) is an early comedy and one of Shakespeare's most beloved works. It is also one of his most imaginative plays, introducing us to the world of fairies and the realm of dreams. Romantic painters, such as Fuseli, have long found in this play a rich store of images that stretch far beyond the limits of the real world of everyday experience.

For Shakespeare, the fun of the play is in the ways in which the world of the fairies intersects with the world of real people, and we can interpret the play as a hint of what would happen if the world of dreams were to intersect with the world of real experience. The fact that these worlds are more alike than they are different gives Shakespeare the comic basis on which to work. He finds some new and amusing ways to interpret the device of mistaken identities.

The play is set in Athens, with Duke Theseus about to wed Hippolyta, the queen of the Amazons. Helena and Hermia are young women in love with Demetrius and Lysander, respectively. However, Demetrius wants to marry Hermia, and he has the blessing of Hermia's father. Hermia's refusal to follow her father's wishes drives her into the woods, where she is followed by both young men and Helena, who does not want to lose Demetrius.

The four young people find themselves in the world of the fairies, although the humans cannot see the fairies. Puck, an impish sprite, is ordered by Oberon, king of the fairies, to put a balm in Demetrius's eyes so he will fall in love with Helena, but Puck puts it in Lysander's eyes, and the plot backfires. Lysander is suddenly in love with Helena, and Hermia is confounded. Oberon, in the meantime, has had Puck place the same balm in the eyes of Titania, the queen of the fairies. She will fall in love with the first creature she sees when she awakes.

That creature is Bottom, the "rude mechanical" (ignorant artisan) whose head has been transformed into an ass's head. Such a trick opens up possibilities for wonderful comic elements. The richness of the illusions that operate onstage constantly draws us to the question of how we ever can know the truth of our own experiences, especially when some of them are dreams whose imaginative power is occasionally overwhelming.

Shakespeare plays here with some of the Aristotelian conventions of the drama, especially Aristotle's view that drama imitates life. One of the great comic devices in *A Midsummer Night's Dream* is the play within a play that Bottom, Quince, Snug, Flute, and Starveling are to put on before Theseus and Hippolyta. They tell the story of Pyramus and Thisby, lovers who lose each other because they misinterpret signs. It is "Merry and tragical! Tedious and brief!" But it is also a wonderful parody of what playwrights — including Shakespeare — often do when operating in the Aristotelian mode. The aim of the play is realism, yet the players are naive and inexperienced in drama; they do their best constantly to remind the audience that it is only a play.

The comic ineptness of the rude mechanicals' play needs no disclaimers of this sort, and the immediate audience — Theseus, Hippolyta, Demetrius, Helena, Lysander, and Hermia — is amused by the ardor of the players. The audience in the theater is also mightily amused at the antics of the mechanicals, which on the surface are simply funny and a wonderful pastiche of artless playacting.

Beneath the surface, something more serious is going on. Shakespeare is commenting on the entire function of drama in our lives. He constantly reminds us in this play that we are watching an illusion, even an illusion within an illusion, but he also convinces us that illusions teach us a great deal about reality. The real-world setting of *A Midsummer Night's Dream* — Athens — is quite improbable. The mechanicals all have obviously English names and are out of place in an Athenian pastoral setting. The play on the level of Athens is pure fantasy, with even more fantastic goings-on at the level of the fairy world. But fantasy nourishes us. It helps us interpret our own experiences by permitting us to distance ourselves from them and reflect on how they affect others. This is one of the deepest functions of drama.

As in most comedies, everything turns out exceptionally well — the way we would want it to. A multiple marriage, one of the delightful conventions of many comedies, ends the drama, and virtually everyone receives what she or he wanted. We are left with a sense of satisfaction because we, too, get our wish about how things should turn out. Puck, one of the greatest of Shakespeare's characters, turns out to be sympathetic and human in his feelings about people. And Bottom, a clown whose origins are certainly Greek and Roman, warms us with his generosity and caring toward others. Shakespeare promotes a remarkably warm view of humanity in this play, leaving us with a sense of delight and a glow that is rare even in comedy.

A Midsummer Night's Dream in Performance

A Midsummer Night's Dream has attracted many great directors in modern times, although in the late seventeenth and eighteenth centuries the play was adapted essentially as a vehicle for presenting the world of the fairies. It even became an opera in 1692. Ludwig Tieck engaged Mendelssohn to write incidental music for the play in Berlin in 1843, and their production was for many years the most influential post-Shakespearean adaptation. Beerbohm Tree's 1900 production in London's Savoy Theatre included real rabbits and many other highly realistic details, eventually playing to more than 220,000 patrons. After numerous adaptations, it was produced by Granville Barker in London from 1912 to 1914 in its original text, and in New York in 1915. The Old Vic's 1954 production was so lavish that it was staged at the Metropolitan Opera House in New York. Peter Brook played down the fairies and explored the play as a study of love. His 1970 production is well remembered for his having placed Oberon and Puck on trapezes set against a stark white background. He also used some costumes and other elements of *commedia dell'arte* to spark the comedy. The American Repertory Theatre's 1986 Boston production (see photos on pages 226–27) reflects the approach to staging that the Royal Shakespeare Company has taken in recent years. The themes of love and transformation inspire the players in a way that shows off the play's brilliance.

William Shakespeare (1564–1616)
A MIDSUMMER NIGHT'S DREAM   *c. 1596*

[Dramatis Personae

THESEUS, *Duke of Athens*
EGEUS, *father to Hermia*
LYSANDER, }
DEMETRIUS, } *in love with Hermia*
PHILOSTRATE, *Master of the Revels to Theseus*

QUINCE, *a carpenter*
SNUG, *a joiner*
BOTTOM, *a weaver*
FLUTE, *a bellows-mender*
SNOUT, *a tinker*
STARVELING, *a tailor*

HIPPOLYTA, *Queen of the Amazons, betrothed to Theseus*
HERMIA, *daughter to Egeus, in love with Lysander*
HELENA, *in love with Demetrius*

OBERON, *King of the Fairies*
TITANIA, *Queen of the Fairies*
PUCK, *or Robin Goodfellow*
PEASEBLOSSOM, }
COBWEB, }
MOTH, } *fairies*
MUSTARDSEED, }
Other FAIRIES *attending their king and queen*
ATTENDANTS *on Theseus and Hippolyta*

Scene: *Athens, and a wood near it.*]

[*ACT I • Scene I*]°

(*Enter Theseus, Hippolyta, [Philostrate,] with others.*)

THESEUS: Now, fair Hippolyta, our nuptial hour
    Draws on apace. Four happy days bring in
    Another moon; but, O, methinks, how slow
    This old moon wanes! She lingers° my desires,
    Like to a step-dame° or a dowager°   5
    Long withering out a young man's revenue.

Note: The text of *A Midsummer Night's Dream* has come down to us in different versions — such as the first quarto, the second quarto, and the first Folio. The copy of the text used here is largely drawn from the first quarto. Passages enclosed in square brackets are taken from one of the other versions.

I, I. **Location:** The palace of Theseus.   **4. lingers:** Lengthens, protects.   **5. step-dame:** Stepmother.   **dowager:** Widow with a jointure or dower [an estate or title from her deceased husband].

HIPPOLYTA: Four days will quickly steep themselves
    in night,
    Four nights will quickly dream away the time;
    And then the moon, like to a silver bow
10   New-bent in heaven, shall behold the night
    Of our solemnities.
THESEUS: Go, Philostrate,
    Stir up the Athenian youth to merriments,
    Awake the pert and nimble spirit of mirth,
    Turn melancholy forth to funerals;
15   The pale companion° is not for our pomp.°
                          [Exit Philostrate.]
    Hippolyta, I woo'd thee with my sword,°
    And won thy love doing thee injuries;
    But I will wed thee in another key,
    With pomp, with triumph,° and with reveling.

(*Enter Egeus and his daughter Hermia, and Lysander, and Demetrius.*)

20 EGEUS: Happy be Theseus, our renowned Duke!
THESEUS: Thanks, good Egeus. What's the news
    with thee?
EGEUS: Full of vexation come I, with complaint
    Against my child, my daughter Hermia.
    Stand forth, Demetrius. My noble lord,
25   This man hath my consent to marry her.
    Stand forth, Lysander. And, my gracious Duke,
    This man hath bewitch'd the bosom of my child.
    Thou, thou, Lysander, thou hast given her
      rhymes
    And interchang'd love tokens with my child.
30   Thou hast by moonlight at her window sung
    With feigning voice verses of feigning love,°
    And stol'n the impression of her fantasy,°
    With bracelets of thy hair, rings, gauds,°
      conceits,°
    Knacks,° trifles, nosegays, sweetmeats —
      messengers
35   Of strong prevailment in unhardened youth.
    With cunning hast thou filch'd my daughter's
      heart,
    Turn'd her obedience, which is due to me,
    To stubborn harshness. And, my gracious Duke,
    Be it so she will not here before your Grace
40   Consent to marry with Demetrius,

    I beg the ancient privilege of Athens:
    As she is mine, I may dispose of her,
    Which shall be either to this gentleman
    Or to her death, according to our law
    Immediately° provided in that case.   45
THESEUS: What say you, Hermia? Be advis'd, fair
    maid.
    To you your father should be as a god —
    One that compos'd your beauties, yea, and one
    To whom you are but as a form in wax
    By him imprinted and within his power   50
    To leave° the figure or disfigure° it.
    Demetrius is a worthy gentleman.
HERMIA: So is Lysander.
THESEUS: In himself he is;
    But in this kind,° wanting° your father's voice,°
    The other must be held the worthier.   55
HERMIA: I would my father look'd but with my
    eyes.
THESEUS: Rather your eyes must with his judgment
    look.
HERMIA: I do entreat your Grace to pardon me.
    I know not by what power I am made bold,
    Nor how it may concern° my modesty,   60
    In such a presence here to plead my thoughts;
    But I beseech your Grace that I may know
    The worst that may befall me in this case,
    If I refuse to wed Demetrius.
THESEUS: Either to die the death, or to abjure   65
    Forever the society of men.
    Therefore, fair Hermia, question your desires,
    Know of your youth, examine well your blood,°
    Whether, if you yield not to your father's choice,
    You can endure the livery° of a nun,   70
    For aye° to be in shady cloister mew'd,°
    To live a barren sister all your life,
    Chanting faint hymns to the cold fruitless moon.
    Thrice blessed they that master so their blood
    To undergo such maiden pilgrimage,   75
    But earthlier happy° is the rose distill'd,
    Than that which withering on the virgin thorn
    Grows, lives, and dies in single blessedness.
HERMIA: So will I grow, so live, so die, my lord,
    Ere I will yield my virgin patent° up   80
    Unto his lordship, whose unwished yoke
    My soul consents not to give sovereignty.
THESEUS: Take time to pause; and, by the next new
    moon —

---

15. companion: Fellow.   **pomp:** Ceremonial magnificence.
16. with my sword: In a military engagement against the
Amazons, when Hippolyta was taken captive.   **19. triumph:**
Public festivity.   **31. feigning:** (1) Counterfeiting, (2) faining,
desirous.   **32. And . . . fantasy:** And made her fall in love
with you (imprinting your image on her imagination) by
stealthy and dishonest means.   **33. gauds:** Playthings. **con-
ceits:** Fanciful trifles.   **34. Knacks:** Knickknacks.

45. Immediately: Expressly.   **51. leave:** Leave unaltered.
disfigure: Obliterate.   **54. kind:** Respect.   **wanting:** Lacking.   **voice:** Approval.   **60. concern:** Befit.   **68. blood:**
Passions.   **70. livery:** Habit.   **71. aye:** Ever.   **mew'd:** Shut
in (said of a hawk, poultry, etc.).   **76. earthlier happy:**
Happier as respects this world.   **80. patent:** Privilege.

The sealing-day betwixt my love and me,
85 For everlasting bond of fellowship —
Upon that day either prepare to die
For disobedience to your father's will,
Or° else to wed Demetrius, as he would,
Or on Diana's altar° to protest°
90 For aye austerity and single life.
DEMETRIUS: Relent, sweet Hermia, and, Lysander,
     yield
Thy crazed° title to my certain right.
LYSANDER: You have her father's love, Demetrius;
Let me have Hermia's. Do you marry him.
95 EGEUS: Scornful Lysander! True, he hath my love,
And what is mine my love shall render him.
And she is mine, and all my right of her
I do estate unto° Demetrius.
LYSANDER: I am, my lord, as well deriv'd° as he,
100 As well possess'd;° my love is more than his;
My fortunes every way as fairly° rank'd,
If not with vantage,° as Demetrius';
And, which is more than all these boasts can be,
I am belov'd of beauteous Hermia,
105 Why should not I then prosecute my right?
Demetrius, I'll avouch it to his head,°
Made love to Nedar's daughter, Helena,
And won her soul; and she, sweet lady, dotes,
Devoutly dotes, dotes in idolatry,
110 Upon this spotted° and inconstant man.
THESEUS: I must confess that I have heard so much,
And with Demetrius thought to have spoke
     thereof;
But, being over-full of self-affairs,
My mind did lose it. But, Demetrius, come,
115 And come, Egeus, you shall go with me;
I have some private schooling for you both.
For you, fair Hermia, look you arm° yourself
To fit your fancies° to your father's will;
Or else the law of Athens yields you up —
120 Which by no means we may extenuate° —
To death, or to a vow of single life.
Come, my Hippolyta. What cheer, my love?
Demetrius and Egeus, go° along.
I must employ you in some business
125 Against° our nuptial, and confer with you
Of something nearly that° concerns yourselves.

EGEUS: With duty and desire we follow you.
     (*Exeunt*° [*all but Lysander and Hermia*].)
LYSANDER: How now, my love, why is your cheek
     so pale?
How chance the roses there do fade so fast?
HERMIA: Belike° for want of rain, which I could
     well   130
Beteem° them from the tempest of my eyes.
LYSANDER: Ay me! For aught that I could ever
     read,
Could ever hear by tale or history,
The course of true love never did run smooth;
But either it was different in blood° —   135
HERMIA: O cross,° too high to be enthrall'd to low!
LYSANDER: Or else misgraffed° in respect of years —
HERMIA: O spite, too old to be engag'd to young!
LYSANDER: Or else it stood upon the choice of
     friends° —
HERMIA: O hell, to choose love by another's eyes! 140
LYSANDER: Or, if there were a sympathy in choice,
War, death, or sickness did lay siege to it,
Making it momentany° as a sound,
Swift as a shadow, short as any dream,
Brief as the lightning in the collied° night,   145
That, in a spleen,° unfolds° both heaven and
     earth,
And ere a man hath power to say "Behold!"
The jaws of darkness do devour it up.
So quick° bright things come to confusion.°
HERMIA: If then true lovers have been ever cross'd,° 150
It stands as an edict in destiny.
Then let us teach our trial patience,°
Because it is a customary cross,
As due to love as thoughts and dreams and
     sighs,
Wishes and tears, poor fancy's° followers.   155
LYSANDER: A good persuasion. Therefore, hear me,
     Hermia.
I have a widow aunt, a dowager
Of great revenue, and she hath no child.
From Athens is her house remote seven leagues;
And she respects° me as her only son.   160
There, gentle Hermia, may I marry thee,
And to that place the sharp Athenian law

---

88. **Or:** Either. 89. **Diana's altar:** Diana was a virgin goddess. **protest:** Vow. 92. **crazed:** Cracked, unsound. 98. **estate unto:** Settle or bestow upon. 99. **deriv'd:** Descended, i.e., "as well born." 100. **possess'd:** Endowed with wealth. 101. **fairly:** Handsomely. 102. **vantage:** Superiority. 106. **head:** Face. 110. **spotted:** Morally stained. 117. **look you arm:** Take care you prepare. 118. **fancies:** Likings, thoughts of love. 120. **extenuate:** Mitigate. 123. **go:** Come. 125. **Against:** In preparation for. 126. **nearly that:** That closely.

127. **[S.D.]** *Exeunt:* Latin for "they go out." 130. **Belike:** Very likely. 131. **Beteem:** Grant, afford. 135. **blood:** Hereditary station. 136. **cross:** Vexation. 137. **misgraffed:** Ill grafted, badly matched. 139. **friends:** Relatives. 143. **momentany:** Lasting but a moment. 145. **collied:** Blackened (as with coal dust), darkened. 146. **in a spleen:** In a swift impulse, in a violent flash. **unfolds:** Discloses. 149. **quick:** Quickly; or, perhaps, living, alive. **confusion:** Ruin. 150. **ever cross'd:** Always thwarted. 152. **teach . . . patience:** Teach ourselves patience in this trial. 155. **fancy's:** Amorous passion's. 160. **respects:** Regards.

Cannot pursue us. If thou lovest me, then,
Steal forth thy father's house tomorrow night;
165   And in the wood, a league without the town,
Where I did meet thee once with Helena
To do observance to a morn of May,°
There will I stay for thee.
HERMIA: My good Lysander!
I swear to thee, by Cupid's strongest bow,
170   By his best arrow with the golden head,°
By the simplicity° of Venus' doves,°
By that which knitteth souls and prospers loves,
And by that fire which burn'd the Carthage
    queen,
When the false Troyan° under sail was seen,
175   By all the vows that ever men have broke,
In number more than ever women spoke,
In that same place thou hast appointed me
Tomorrow truly will I meet with thee.
LYSANDER: Keep promise, love. Look, here comes
    Helena.

(*Enter Helena.*)

180   HERMIA: God speed fair° Helena, whither away?
HELENA: Call you me fair? That fair again unsay.
Demetrius loves your fair.° O happy fair!°
Your eyes are lodestars,° and your tongue's
    sweet air°
More tuneable° than lark to shepherd's ear
When wheat is green, when hawthorn buds
185   appear.
Sickness is catching. O, were favor° so,
Yours would I catch, fair Hermia, ere I go;
My ear should catch your voice, my eye your
    eye,
My tongue should catch your tongue's sweet
    melody.
190   Were the world mine, Demetrius being bated,°
The rest I'd give to be to you translated.°
O, teach me how you look, and with what art
You sway the motion° of Demetrius' heart.

---

167. do . . . May: Perform the ceremonies of May Day.
170. best arrow . . . golden head: Cupid's best gold-pointed
arrows were supposed to induce love, his blunt leaden arrows
aversion.   171. simplicity: Innocence.   doves: Those that
drew Venus's chariot.   173–74. by that fire . . . false
Troyan: Dido, Queen of Carthage, immolated herself on a
funeral pyre after having been deserted by the Trojan hero
Aeneas.   180. fair: Fair-complexioned (generally regarded
by the Elizabethans as more beautiful than dark-complexioned).   182. your fair: Your beauty (even though Hermia
is dark-complexioned).   happy fair: Lucky fair one.   183.
lodestars: Guiding stars.   air: Music.   184. tuneable: Tune-
ful, melodious.   186. favor: Appearance, looks.   190.
bated: Excepted.   191. translated: Transformed.   193. motion: Impulse.

HERMIA: I frown upon him, yet he loves me still.
HELENA: O that your frowns would teach my
    smiles such skill!   195
HERMIA: I give him curses, yet he gives me love.
HELENA: O that my prayers could such affection°
    move!°
HERMIA: The more I hate, the more he follows me.
HELENA: The more I love, the more he hateth me.
HERMIA: His folly, Helena, is no fault of mine.   200
HELENA: None, but your beauty. Would that fault
    were mine!
HERMIA: Take comfort. He no more shall see my
    face.
Lysander and myself will fly this place.
Before the time I did Lysander see,
Seem'd Athens as a paradise to me.   205
O, then, what graces in my love do dwell,
That he hath turn'd a heaven unto a hell!
LYSANDER: Helen, to you our minds we will unfold.
Tomorrow night, when Phoebe° doth behold
Her silver visage in the wat'ry glass,°   210
Decking with liquid pearl the bladed grass,
A time that lovers' flights doth still° conceal,
Through Athens' gates have we devis'd to steal.
HERMIA: And in the wood, where often you and I
Upon faint° primrose beds were wont to lie,   215
Emptying our bosoms of their counsel° sweet,
There my Lysander and myself shall meet;
And thence from Athens turn away our eyes,
To seek new friends and stranger companies.
Farewell, sweet playfellow. Pray thou for us,   220
And good luck grant thee thy Demetrius!
Keep word, Lysander. We must starve our sight
From lovers' food till morrow deep midnight.
LYSANDER: I will, my Hermia.   (*Exit Hermia.*)
                                Helena, adieu.
As you on him, Demetrius dote on you!   225
                                (*Exit Lysander.*)
HELENA: How happy some o'er other some can be!°
Through Athens I am thought as fair as she.
But what of that? Demetrius thinks not so;
He will not know what all but he do know.
And as he errs, doting on Hermia's eyes,   230
So I, admiring of° his qualities.
Things base and vile, holding no quantity,°
Love can transpose to form and dignity.
Love looks not with the eyes, but with the mind,
And therefore is wing'd Cupid painted blind.   235

---

197. affection: Passion.   move: Arouse.   209. Phoebe:
Diana, the moon.   210. glass: Mirror.   212. still: Always.
215. faint: Pale.   216. counsel: Secret thought.   226. o'er
. . . can be: Can be in comparison to some others.   231.
admiring of: Wondering at.   232. holding no quantity: Un-
substantial, unshapely.

And drop the liquor of it in her eyes.
The next thing then she waking looks upon,
Be it on lion, bear, or wolf, or bull,
On meddling monkey, or on busy ape,
She shall pursue it with the soul of love.
And ere I take this charm from off her sight,
As I can take it with another herb,
I'll make her render up her page to me.
But who comes here? I am invisible,
And I will overhear their conference.

(*Enter Demetrius, Helena following him.*)

DEMETRIUS: I love thee not, therefore pursue me
    not.
Where is Lysander and fair Hermia?
The one I'll slay, the other slayeth me.
Thou told'st me they were stol'n unto this
    wood;
And here am I, and wode° within this wood,
Because I cannot meet my Hermia.
Hence, get thee gone, and follow me no more.
HELENA: You draw me, you hard-hearted
    adamant;°
But yet you draw not iron, for my heart
Is true as steel. Leave° you your power to draw,
And I shall have no power to follow you.
DEMETRIUS: Do I entice you? Do I speak you fair?°
Or, rather, do I not in plainest truth
Tell you I do not nor I cannot love you?
HELENA: And even for that do I love you the more.
I am your spaniel; and, Demetrius,
The more you beat me, I will fawn on you.
Use me but as your spaniel, spurn me, strike me,
Neglect me, lose me; only give me leave,
Unworthy as I am, to follow you.
What worser place can I beg in your love —
And yet a place of high respect with me —
Than to be used as you use your dog?
DEMETRIUS: Tempt not too much the hatred of my
    spirit,
For I am sick when I do look on thee.
HELENA: And I am sick when I look not on you.
DEMETRIUS: You do impeach° your modesty too
    much
To leave the city and commit yourself
Into the hands of one that loves you not,
To trust the opportunity of night
And the ill counsel of a desert° place

With the rich worth of your virginity.
HELENA: Your virtue° is my privilege.° For that°   220
It is not night when I do see your face,
Therefore I think I am not in the night;
Nor doth this wood lack worlds of company,
For you in my respect° are all the world.
Then how can it be said I am alone,   225
When all the world is here to look on me?
DEMETRIUS: I'll run from thee and hide me in the
    brakes,°
And leave thee to the mercy of wild beasts.
HELENA: The wildest hath not such a heart as you.
Run when you will, the story shall be chang'd: 230
Apollo flies and Daphne holds the chase,°
The dove pursues the griffin,° the mild hind°
Makes speed to catch the tiger — bootless°
    speed,
When cowardice pursues and valor flies.
DEMETRIUS: I will not stay° thy questions.° Let me
    go!   235
Or if thou follow me, do not believe
But I shall do thee mischief in the wood.
HELENA: Ay, in the temple, in the town, the field,
You do me mischief. Fie, Demetrius!
Your wrongs do set a scandal on my sex.   240
We cannot fight for love, as men may do;
We should be woo'd and were not made to
    woo.
                              [*Exit Demetrius.*]
I'll follow thee and make a heaven of hell,
To die upon° the hand I love so well.   [*Exit.*]
OBERON: Fare thee well, nymph. Ere he do leave
    this grove,   245
Thou shalt fly him and he shall seek thy love.

(*Enter Puck.*)

Hast thou the flower there? Welcome, wanderer.
PUCK: Ay, there it is.   [*Offers the flower.*]
OBERON: I pray thee, give it me.
I know a bank where the wild thyme blows,°
Where oxlips° and the nodding violet grows,   250
Quite over-canopied with luscious woodbine,°

---

192. **wode:** Mad (pronounced "wood" and often spelled so). 195. **adamant:** Lodestone, magnet (with pun on *hard-hearted*, since adamant was also thought to be the hardest of all stones and was confused with the diamond). 197. **Leave:** Give up. 199. **fair:** Courteously. 214. **impeach:** Call into question. 218. **desert:** Deserted.

220. **virtue:** Goodness or power to attract. **privilege:** Safeguard, warrant. **For that:** Because. 224. **in my respect:** As far as I am concerned. 227. **brakes:** Thickets. 231. **Apollo . . . chase:** In the ancient myth, Daphne fled from Apollo and was saved from rape by being transformed into a laurel tree; here it is the female who *holds the chase*, or pursues, instead of the male. 232. **griffin:** A fabulous monster with the head of an eagle and the body of a lion. **hind:** Female deer. 233. **bootless:** Fruitless. 235. **stay:** Wait for. **questions:** Talk or argument. 244. **upon:** By. 249. **blows:** Blooms. 250. **oxlips:** Flowers resembling cowslip and primrose. 251. **woodbine:** Honeysuckle.

NEAR RIGHT: Oberon instructing Puck in the power of the "little western flower." BELOW: The young lovers in the American Repertory Theatre's 1986 production. FAR LEFT: Oberon with Titania upon his shoulder. FAR RIGHT: The rude mechanicals: Moonshine with Lion.

With sweet musk-roses° and with eglantine.°
There sleeps Titania sometime of the night,
Lull'd in these flowers with dances and delight;
And there the snake throws° her enamel'd skin,
Weed° wide enough to wrap a fairy in.
And with the juice of this I'll streak° her eyes,
And make her full of hateful fantasies.
Take thou some of it, and seek through this
    grove.

                                    [Gives some love-juice.]

A sweet Athenian lady is in love
With a disdainful youth. Anoint his eyes,
But do it when the next thing he espies
May be the lady. Thou shalt know the man
By the Athenian garments he hath on.

Effect it with some care, that he may prove   265
More fond on° her than she upon her love;
And look thou meet me ere the first cock crow.
PUCK: Fear not, my lord, your servant shall do so.
                                            (*Exeunt.*)

[*Scene II*]°

(*Enter Titania, Queen of Fairies, with her train.*)

TITANIA: Come, now a roundel° and a fairy song;
    Then, for the third part of a minute, hence —
    Some to kill cankers° in the musk-rose buds,
    Some war with rere-mice° for their leathern
        wings,

252. musk-roses: A kind of large, sweet-scented rose. eglantine: Sweetbriar, another kind of rose. 255. throws: Sloughs off, sheds. 256. Weed: Garment. 257. streak: Anoint, touch gently.

266. fond on: Doting on. II, II. Location: The wood. 1. roundel: Dance in a ring. 3. cankers: Cankerworms. 4. rere-mice: Bats.

To make my small elves coats, and some keep
5   back
The clamorous owl, that nightly hoots and
         wonders
At our quaint° spirits. Sing me now asleep.
Then to your offices and let me rest.

(*Fairies sing.*)

FIRST FAIRY: You spotted snakes with double°
         tongue,
10   Thorny hedgehogs, be not seen;
Newts° and blindworms, do no wrong,
         Come not near our fairy queen.
[*Chorus.*] Philomel,° with melody
         Sing in our sweet lullaby;
15   Lulla, lulla, lullaby, lulla, lulla, lullaby.
         Never harm,
         Nor spell nor charm,
         Come our lovely lady nigh.
         So, good night, with lullaby.
20   FIRST FAIRY: Weaving spiders, come not here;
         Hence, you long-legg'd spinners, hence!
         Beetles black, approach not near;
         Worm nor snail, do no offense.
[*Chorus.*] Philomel, with melody, etc.
25   SECOND FAIRY: Hence, away! Now all is well.
         One aloof stand sentinel.
                    [*Exeunt Fairies. Titania sleeps.*]

(*Enter Oberon [and squeezes the flower on Titania's
eyelids].*)

OBERON: What thou seest when thou dost wake,
         Do it for thy true-love take;
         Love and languish for his sake.
30   Be it ounce,° or cat, or bear,
         Pard,° or boar with bristled hair,
         In thy eye that shall appear
         When thou wak'st, it is thy dear
         Wake when some vile thing is near.   [*Exit.*]

(*Enter Lysander and Hermia.*)

LYSANDER: Fair love, you faint with wand'ring in
35   the wood;
         And to speak troth,° I have forgot our way.
         We'll rest us, Hermia, if you think it good,
         And tarry for the comfort of the day.

HERMIA: Be 't so, Lysander. Find you out a bed,
         For I upon this bank will rest my head.   4
LYSANDER: One turf shall serve as pillow for us
         both,
         One heart, one bed, two bosoms, and one troth.°
HERMIA: Nay, good Lysander; for my sake, my
         dear,
         Lie further off yet, do not lie so near.
LYSANDER: O, take the sense, sweet, of my
         innocence!°   4
         Love takes the meaning in love's conference.°
         I mean, that my heart unto yours is knit
         So that but one heart we can make of it;
         Two bosoms interchained with an oath —
         So then two bosoms and a single troth.   5
         Then by your side no bed-room me deny,
         For lying so, Hermia, I do not lie.°
HERMIA: Lysander riddles very prettily.
         Now much beshrew° my manners and my pride
         If Hermia meant to say Lysander lied.   5
         But, gentle friend, for love and courtesy
         Lie further off, in human° modesty;
         Such separation as may well be said
         Becomes a virtuous bachelor and a maid,
         So far be distant; and, good night, sweet friend.   6
         Thy love ne'er alter till thy sweet life end!
LYSANDER: Amen, amen, to that fair prayer, say I,
         And then end life when I end loyalty!
         Here is my bed. Sleep give thee all his rest!
HERMIA: With half that wish the wisher's eyes be
         press'd!°   6
                    [*They sleep, separated by a short distance.*]

(*Enter Puck.*)

PUCK: Through the forest have I gone,
         But Athenian found I none
         On whose eyes I might approve°
         This flower's force in stirring love.
         Night and silence. — Who is here?   7
         Weeds of Athens he doth wear.
         This is he, my master said,
         Despised the Athenian maid;
         And here the maiden, sleeping sound,
         On the dank and dirty ground.
         Pretty soul! She durst not lie
         Near this lack-love, this kill-courtesy.

---

7. **quaint:** Dainty.   9. **double:** Forked.   11. **Newts:** Water
lizards (considered poisonous, as were blindworms — small
snakes with tiny eyes — and spiders).   13. **Philomel:** The
nightingale. (Philomela, daughter of King Pandion, was
transformed into a nightingale, according to Ovid's *Metamorphoses*, after she had been raped by her sister Procne's
husband, Tereus.)   30. **ounce:** Lynx.   31. **Pard:** Leopard.
36. **troth:** Truth.

42. **troth:** Faith, troth-plight.   45. **take . . . innocence:** Interpret my intention as innocent.   46. **Love . . . conference:**
When lovers confer, love teaches each lover to interpret the
other's meaning lovingly.   52. **lie:** Tell a falsehood (with a
riddling pun on *lie*, recline).   54. **beshrew:** Curse (but mildly
meant).   57. **human:** Courteous.   65. **With . . . press'd:**
May we share your wish, so that your eyes too are *press'd*,
closed, in sleep.   68. **approve:** Test.

Churl, upon thy eyes I throw
All the power this charm doth owe.°
                    [*Applies the love-juice.*]
80 When thou wak'st, let love forbid
Sleep his seat on thy eyelid.
So awake when I am gone,
For I must now to Oberon.   (*Exit.*)

(*Enter Demetrius and Helena, running.*)

HELENA: Stay, though thou kill me, sweet
    Demetrius.
DEMETRIUS: I charge thee, hence, and do not haunt
85   me thus.
HELENA: O, wilt thou darkling° leave me? Do not
    so.
DEMETRIUS: Stay, on thy peril!° I alone will go.
                    [*Exit.*]
HELENA: O, I am out of breath in this fond° chase!
    The more my prayer, the lesser is my grace.°
90 Happy is Hermia, wheresoe'er she lies,°
    For she hath blessed and attractive eyes.
    How came her eyes so bright? Not with salt
    tears;
    If so, my eyes are oft'ner wash'd than hers.
    No, no, I am as ugly as a bear;
95 For beasts that meet me run away for fear.
    Therefore no marvel though Demetrius
    Do, as a monster, fly my presence thus.
    What wicked and dissembling glass of mine
    Made me compare with Hermia's sphery eyne?°
00 But who is here? Lysander, on the ground?
    Dead, or asleep? I see no blood, no wound.
    Lysander, if you live, good sir, awake.
LYSANDER [*awaking*]: And run through fire I will
    for thy sweet sake.
    Transparent° Helena! Nature shows art,
    That through thy bosom makes me see thy
05   heart.
    Where is Demetrius? O, how fit a word
    Is that vile name to perish on my sword!
HELENA: Do not say so, Lysander, say not so.
    What though he love your Hermia? Lord, what
    though?
10 Yet Hermia still loves you. Then be content.
LYSANDER: Content with Hermia? No! I do repent
    The tedious minutes I with her have spent.
    Not Hermia but Helena I love.
    Who will not change a raven for a dove?

The will of man is by his reason sway'd,   115
And reason says you are the worthier maid.
Things growing are not ripe until their season;
So I, being young, till now ripe not° to reason.
And touching° now the point° of human skill,°
Reason becomes the marshal to my will   120
And leads me to your eyes, where I o'erlook°
Love's stories written in love's richest book.
HELENA: Wherefore was I to this keen mockery
    born?
    When at your hands did I deserve this scorn?
    Is 't not enough, is 't not enough, young man,   125
    That I did never, no, nor never can,
    Deserve a sweet look from Demetrius' eye,
    But you must flout my insufficiency?
    Good troth,° you do me wrong, good sooth,°
    you do,
    In such disdainful manner me to woo.   130
    But fare you well. Perforce I must confess
    I thought you lord of° more true gentleness.°
    O, that a lady, of° one man refus'd,
    Should of another therefore be abus'd!°   (*Exit.*)
LYSANDER: She sees not Hermia. Hermia, sleep thou
    there,   135
    And never mayst thou come Lysander near!
    For as a surfeit of the sweetest things
    The deepest loathing to the stomach brings,
    Or as the heresies that men do leave
    Are hated most of those they did deceive,   140
    So thou, my surfeit and my heresy,
    Of all be hated, but the most of me!
    And, all my powers, address your love and
    might
    To honor Helen and to be her knight!   (*Exit.*)
HERMIA [*awaking*]: Help me, Lysander, help me!
    Do thy best   145
    To pluck this crawling serpent from my breast!
    Ay me, for pity! What a dream was here!
    Lysander, look how I do quake with fear.
    Methought a serpent eat° my heart away,
    And you sat smiling at his cruel prey.°   150
    Lysander! What, remov'd? Lysander! Lord!
    What, out of hearing? Gone? No sound, no
    word?
    Alack, where are you? Speak, an if you hear,
    Speak, of all loves!° I swoon almost with fear.
    No? Then I well perceive you are not nigh.   155

---

79. owe: Own.   **86. darkling:** In the dark.   **87. on thy peril:** On pain of danger to you if you don't obey me and stay.   **88. fond:** Doting.   **89. my grace:** The favor I obtain. **90. lies:** Dwells.   **99. sphery eyne:** Eyes as bright as stars in their spheres.   **104. Transparent:** (1) Radiant; (2) able to be seen through.

118. ripe not: (Am) not ripened.   **119. touching:** Reaching. **point:** Summit.   **skill:** Judgment.   **121. o'erlook:** Read. **129. Good troth, good sooth:** Indeed, truly.   **132. lord of:** Possessor of.   **gentleness:** Courtesy.   **133. of:** By.   **134. abus'd:** Ill treated.   **149. eat:** Ate (pronounced "et").   **150. prey:** Act of preying.   **154. of all loves:** For all love's sake.

Either death, or you, I'll find immediately.
        (*Exit.* [*Manet*° *Titania lying asleep.*])

[*ACT III • Scene I*]°

(*Enter the Clowns* [*Quince, Snug, Bottom, Flute, Snout, and Starveling*].)

BOTTOM: Are we all met?

QUINCE: Pat, pat; and here's a marvailes° convenient
    place for our rehearsal. This green plot shall be
    our stage, this hawthorn brake° our tiring-house,°
5   and we will do it in action as we will do it before
    the Duke.

BOTTOM: Peter Quince?

QUINCE: What sayest thou, bully° Bottom?

BOTTOM: There are things in this comedy of Pyramus
10 and Thisby that will never please. First, Pyramus
    must draw a sword to kill himself, which the ladies
    cannot abide. How answer you that?

SNOUT: By 'r lakin,° a parlous° fear.

STARVELING: I believe we must leave the killing out,
15 when all is done.°

BOTTOM: Not a whit. I have a device to make all well.
    Write me° a prologue; and let the prologue seem
    to say, we will do no harm with our swords and
    that Pyramus is not kill'd indeed; and, for the more
20 better assurance, tell them that I Pyramus am not
    Pyramus, but Bottom the weaver. This will put
    them out of fear.

QUINCE: Well, we will have such a prologue, and it
    shall be written in eight and six.°

25 BOTTOM: No, make it two more; let it be written in
    eight and eight.

SNOUT: Will not the ladies be afeard of the lion?

STARVELING: I fear it, I promise you.

BOTTOM: Masters, you ought to consider with your-
30 selves, to bring in — God shield us! — a lion among
    ladies,° is a most dreadful thing. For there is not
    a more fearful° wild-fowl than your lion living;
    and we ought to look to 't.

SNOUT: Therefore another prologue must tell he is not
    a lion.   35

BOTTOM: Nay, you must name his name, and half his
    face must be seen through the lion's neck, and he
    himself must speak through, saying thus, or to the
    same defect:° "Ladies" — or "Fair ladies — I would
    wish you" — or "I would request you" — or "I   40
    would entreat you — not to fear, not to tremble;
    my life for yours.° If you think I come hither as a
    lion, it were pity of my life.° No, I am no such
    thing; I am a man as other men are." And there
    indeed let him name his name, and tell them plainly 45
    he is Snug the joiner.

QUINCE: Well, it shall be so. But there is two hard
    things: that is, to bring the moonlight into a cham-
    ber; for, you know, Pyramus and Thisby meet by
    moonlight.   50

SNOUT: Doth the moon shine that night we play our
    play?

BOTTOM: A calendar, a calendar! Look in the almanac.
    Find out moonshine, find out moonshine.
                    [*They consult an almanac.*]

QUINCE: Yes, it doth shine that night.   55

BOTTOM: Why then may you leave a casement of the
    great chamber window, where we play, open, and
    the moon may shine in at the casement.

QUINCE: Ay; or else one must come in with a bush
    of thorns° and a lantern, and say he comes to   60
    disfigure,° or to present,° the person of Moonshine.
    Then there is another thing: we must have a wall
    in the great chamber; for Pyramus and Thisby, says
    the story, did talk through the chink of a wall.

SNOUT: You can never bring in a wall. What say you, 65
    Bottom?

BOTTOM: Some man or other must present Wall. And
    let him have some plaster, or some loam, or some
    rough-cast° about him, to signify wall; and let him
    hold his fingers thus, and through that cranny shall 70
    Pyramus and Thisby whisper.

QUINCE: If that may be, then all is well. Come, sit
    down, every mother's son, and rehearse your parts.
    Pyramus, you begin. When you have spoken your
    speech, enter into that brake, and so every one 75
    according to his cue.

(*Enter Robin* [*Puck*].)

---

156. [S.D.] *Manet:* Latin for "she remains."   **III, I. Location:**
Scene continues.   **2. marvailes:** Marvelous.   **4. brake:**
Thicket.   **tiring-house:** Attiring area, hence backstage.   **8.
bully:** Worthy, jolly, fine fellow.   **13. By 'r lakin:** By our
ladykin, the Virgin Mary.   **parlous:** Perilous.   **15. when
all is done:** When all is said and done.   **17. Write me:** Write
at my suggestion.   **24. eight and six:** Alternate lines of eight
and six syllables, a common ballad measure.   **30–31. lion
among ladies:** A contemporary pamphlet tells how at the
christening in 1594 of Prince Henry, eldest son of King James
VI of Scotland, later James I of England, a "blackmoor"
instead of a lion drew the triumphal chariot, since the lion's
presence might have "brought some fear to the nearest."
32. fearful: Fear-inspiring.

39. defect: Bottom's blunder for *effect.*   **42. my life for
yours:** I pledge my life to make your lives safe.   **43. it were
. . . life:** My life would be endangered.   **59–60. bush of
thorns:** Bundle of thornbush faggots (part of the accoutrements of the man in the moon, according to the popular
notions of the time, along with his lantern and his dog).
61. disfigure: Quince's blunder for *prefigure.*   **present:** Represent.   **69. rough-cast:** A mixture of lime and gravel used
to plaster the outside of buildings.

PUCK: What hempen° home-spuns have we
        swagg'ring here,
    So near the cradle of the Fairy Queen?
    What, a play toward?° I'll be an auditor;°
    An actor too perhaps, if I see cause.
QUINCE: Speak, Pyramus. Thisby, stand forth.
BOTTOM: "Thisby, the flowers of odious savors
        sweet," —
QUINCE: Odors, odors.
BOTTOM: — "Odors savors sweet;
    So hath thy breath, my dearest Thisby dear.
    But hark, a voice! Stay thou but here awhile,
    And by and by I will to thee appear."   (*Exit.*)
PUCK: A stranger Pyramus than e'er played here.°
                                           [*Exit.*]

FLUTE: Must I speak now?
QUINCE: Ay, marry, must you; for you must understand
    he goes but to see a noise that he heard, and is to
    come again.
FLUTE: "Most radiant Pyramus, most lily-white of
        hue,
    Of color like the red rose on triumphant brier,
    Most brisky juvenal° and eke° most lovely Jew,°
    As true as truest horse that yet would never tire.
    I'll meet thee, Pyramus, at Ninny's tomb."
QUINCE: "Ninus'° tomb," man. Why, you must not
    speak that yet. That you answer to Pyramus. You
    speak all your part at once, cues and all. Pyramus
    enter. Your cue is past; it is, "never tire."
FLUTE: O — "As true as truest horse, that yet
        would never tire."

[*Enter Puck, and Bottom as Pyramus with the ass
head.*]°

BOTTOM: "If I were fair,° Thisby, I were° only
        thine."
QUINCE: O monstrous! O strange! We are haunted.
    Pray, masters! Fly, masters! Help!
                    [*Exeunt Quince, Snug, Flute,
                        Snout, and Starveling.*]
PUCK: I'll follow you, I'll lead you about a round,°
    Through bog, through bush, through brake,
        through brier.
    Sometime a horse I'll be, sometime a hound,

A hog, a headless bear, sometime a fire;°
    And neigh, and bark, and grunt, and roar, and
        burn,   110
    Like horse, hound, hog, bear, fire, at every turn.
                                           (*Exit.*)
BOTTOM: Why do they run away? This is a knavery
    of them to make me afeard.

(*Enter Snout.*)

SNOUT: O Bottom, thou art chang'd! What do I see
    on thee?   115
BOTTOM: What do you see? You see an ass-head of
    your own, do you?   [*Exit Snout.*]

(*Enter Quince.*)

QUINCE: Bless thee, Bottom, bless thee! Thou art
    translated.°   (*Exit.*)
BOTTOM: I see their knavery. This is to make an ass   120
    of me, to fright me, if they could. But I will not
    stir from this place, do what they can. I will walk
    up and down here, and I will sing, that they shall
    hear I am not afraid.   [*Sings.*]
    The woosel cock° so black of hue,   125
        With orange-tawny bill,
    The throstle° with his note so true,
        The wren with little quill° —
TITANIA [*awaking*]: What angel wakes me from my
        flow'ry bed?
BOTTOM [*sings*]: The finch, the sparrow, and the
        lark,   130
    The plain-song° cuckoo grey,
        Whose note full many a man doth mark,
        And dares not answer nay° —
    For, indeed, who would set his wit to so foolish
    a bird? Who would give a bird the lie,° though   135
    he cry "cuckoo" never so?°
TITANIA: I pray thee, gentle mortal, sing again.
    Mine ear is much enamored of thy note;
    So is mine eye enthralled to thy shape;
    And thy fair virtue's force° perforce doth move
        me   140
    On the first view to say, to swear, I love thee.
BOTTOM: Methinks, mistress, you should have little
    reason for that. And yet, to say the truth, reason
    and love keep little company together nowadays.
    The more the pity that some honest neighbors will   145

---

77. **hempen:** Made of hemp, a rough fiber.   79. **toward:**
About to take place.   **auditor:** One who listens, i.e., part
of the audience.   88. **here:** In this theater (?).   95. **brisky
juvenal:** Brisk youth.   **eke:** Also.   **Jew:** Probably an absurd
repetition of the first syllable of *juvenal*.   98. **Ninus:** Mythical founder of Nineveh (whose wife, Semiramis, was supposed to have built the walls of Babylon where the story of
Pyramus and Thisby takes place).   102. [S.D.] **with the ass
head:** This stage direction, taken from the Folio, presumably
refers to a standard stage property.   103. **fair:** handsome.
were: Would be.   106. **about a round:** Roundabout.

---

109. **fire:** Will-o'-the-wisp.   119. **translated:** Transformed.
125. **woosel cock:** Male ousel or ouzel, blackbird.   127.
throstle: Song thrush.   128. **quill:** Literally, a reed pipe;
hence, the bird's piping song.   131. **plain-song:** Singing a
melody without variations.   133. **dares . . . nay:** Cannot
deny that he is a cuckold.   135. **give . . . lie:** Call the bird
a liar.   136. **never so:** Ever so much.   140. **thy . . . force:**
The power of your beauty.

not make them friends. Nay, I can gleek° upon
occasion.
TITANIA: Thou art as wise as thou art beautiful.
BOTTOM: Not so, neither. But if I had wit enough to
150   get out of this wood, I have enough to serve mine
own turn.°
TITANIA: Out of this wood do not desire to go.
Thou shalt remain here, whether thou wilt or
no.
I am a spirit of no common rate.°
155   The summer still° doth tend upon my state;°
And I do love thee. Therefore, go with me.
I'll give thee fairies to attend on thee,
And they shall fetch thee jewels from the deep,
And sing while thou on pressed flowers dost
sleep.
160   And I will purge thy mortal grossness so
That thou shalt like an airy spirit go.
Peaseblossom, Cobweb, Moth,° and
Mustardseed!

(*Enter four Fairies [Peaseblossom, Cobweb, Moth, and
Mustardseed]*.)

PEASEBLOSSOM: Ready.
COBWEB: And I.
MOTH: And I.
MUSTARDSEED: And I.
ALL: Where shall we go?
165   TITANIA: Be kind and courteous to this gentleman.
Hop in his walks and gambol in his eyes;
Feed him with apricocks and dewberries,
With purple grapes, green figs, and mulberries;
The honey-bags steal from the humble-bees,
170   And for night-tapers crop their waxen thighs
And light them at the fiery glow-worm's eyes,
To have my love to bed and to arise;
And pluck the wings from painted butterflies
To fan the moonbeams from his sleeping eyes.
175   Nod to him, elves, and do him courtesies.
PEASEBLOSSOM: Hail, mortal!
COBWEB: Hail!
MOTH: Hail!
MUSTARDSEED: Hail!
180   BOTTOM: I cry your worship's mercy, heartily. I beseech
your worship's name.
COBWEB: Cobweb.
BOTTOM: I shall desire you of more acquaintance,
good Master Cobweb. If I cut my finger, I shall
185   make bold with you.° Your name, honest gentleman?

PEASEBLOSSOM: Peaseblossom.
BOTTOM: I pray you, commend me to Mistress Squash,°
your mother, and to Master Peascod,° your father.
Good Master Peaseblossom, I shall desire you of
more acquaintance too. Your name, I beseech you,   19
sir?
MUSTARDSEED: Mustardseed.
BOTTOM: Good Master Mustardseed, I know your
patience° well. That same cowardly, giant-like ox-
beef hath devour'd many a gentleman of your house.   19
I promise you your kindred hath made my eyes
water ere now. I desire you of more acquaintance,
good Master Mustardseed.
TITANIA: Come wait upon him; lead him to my
bower.
The moon methinks looks with a wat'ry eye;   20
And when she weeps,° weeps every little flower,
Lamenting some enforced° chastity.
Tie up my lover's tongue, bring him silently.
                                        (*Exeunt.*)

[*Scene II*]°

(*Enter [Oberon,] King of Fairies.*)

OBERON: I wonder if Titania be awak'd;
Then, what it was that next came in her eye,
Which she must dote on in extremity.

([*Enter*] *Robin Goodfellow [Puck].*)

Here comes my messenger. How now, mad
spirit?
What night-rule° now about this haunted° grove?   5
PUCK: My mistress with a monster is in love.
Near to her close° and consecrated bower,
While she was in her dull° and sleeping hour,
A crew of patches,° rude mechanicals,°
That work for bread upon Athenian stalls,   10
Were met together to rehearse a play
Intended for great Theseus' nuptial day.
The shallowest thick-skin of that barren sort,°
Who Pyramus presented,° in their sport
Forsook his scene° and ent'red in a brake.   15
When I did him at this advantage take,

---

146. **gleek:** Scoff, jest.   150–51. **serve . . . turn:** Answer my
purpose.   154. **rate:** Rank, value.   155. **still:** Ever always.
doth . . . state: Waits upon me as part of my royal retinue.
162. **Moth:** Mote, speck. (The two words *moth* and *mote*
were pronounced alike.)   184–85. **If . . . you:** Cobwebs
were used to stanch bleeding.

187. **Squash:** Unripe pea pod.   188. **Peascod:** Ripe pea pod.
193–94. **your patience:** What you have endured.   201. **she
weeps:** I.e., she causes dew.   202. **enforced:** Forced, violated; or, possibly, constrained (since Titania at this moment
is hardly concerned about chastity).   III, II. **Location:** The
wood.   5. **night-rule:** Diversion for the night.   **haunted:**
Much frequented.   7. **close:** Secret, private.   8. **dull:**
Drowsy.   9. **patches:** Clowns, fools.   **rude mechanicals:**
Ignorant artisans.   13. **barren sort:** Stupid company or crew.
14. **presented:** Acted.   15. **scene:** Playing area.

An ass's nole° I fixed on his head.
Anon his Thisby must be answered,
And forth my mimic° comes. When they him
   spy,
As wild geese that the creeping fowler eye,
Or russet-pated choughs,° many in sort,°
Rising and cawing at the gun's report,
Sever° themselves and madly sweep the sky,
So, at his sight, away his fellows fly;
And, at our stamp, here o'er and o'er one falls;
He murder cries and help from Athens calls.
Their sense thus weak, lost with their fears thus
   strong,
Made senseless things begin to do them wrong,
For briers and thorns at their apparel snatch;
Some, sleeves — some, hats; from yielders all
   things catch.
I led them on in this distracted fear
And left sweet Pyramus translated there,
When in that moment, so it came to pass,
Titania wak'd and straightway lov'd an ass.
OBERON: This falls out better than I could devise.
But hast thou yet latch'd° the Athenian's eyes
With the love-juice, as I did bid thee do?
PUCK: I took him sleeping — that is finish'd too —
And the Athenian woman by his side,
That, when he wak'd, of force° she must be
   ey'd.

(*Enter Demetrius and Hermia.*)

OBERON: Stand close. This is the same Athenian.
PUCK: This is the woman, but not this the man.
                              [*They stand aside.*]
DEMETRIUS: O, why rebuke you him that loves you
   so?
Lay breath so bitter on your bitter foe.
HERMIA: Now I but chide; but I should use thee
   worse,
For thou, I fear, hast given me cause to curse.
If thou hast slain Lysander in his sleep,
Being o'er shoes in blood, plunge in the deep,
And kill me too.
The sun was not so true unto the day
As he to me. Would he have stolen away
From sleeping Hermia? I'll believe as soon
This whole° earth may be bor'd and that the
   moon
May through the center creep and so displease
Her brother's° noontide with th' Antipodes.°

It cannot be but thou has murd'red him;
So should a murderer look, so dead,° so grim.
DEMETRIUS: So should the murdered look, and so
   should I,
Pierc'd through the heart with your stern cruelty.
Yet you, the murderer, look as bright, as clear, 60
As yonder Venus in her glimmering sphere.
HERMIA: What's this to my Lysander? Where is he?
Ah, good Demetrius, wilt thou give him me?
DEMETRIUS: I had rather give his carcass to my
   hounds.
HERMIA: Out dog! Out cur! Thou driv'st me past
   the bounds   65
Of maiden's patience. Hast thou slain him, then?
Henceforth be never numb'red among men!
O, once tell true, tell true, even for my sake!
Durst thou have look'd upon him being awake,
And hast thou kill'd him sleeping? O brave
   touch!°   70
Could not a worm,° an adder, do so much?
An adder did it; for with doubler tongue
Than thine, thou serpent, never adder stung.
DEMETRIUS: You spend your passion° on a mispris'd
   mood.°
I am not guilty of Lysander's blood,   75
Nor is he dead, for aught that I can tell.
HERMIA: I pray thee, tell me then that he is well.
DEMETRIUS: An if I could, what should I get
   therefore?
HERMIA: A privilege never to see me more.
And from thy hated presence part I so.   80
See me no more, whether he be dead or no.
                                        (*Exit.*)
DEMETRIUS: There is no following her in this fierce
   vein.
Here therefore for a while I will remain.
So sorrow's heaviness doth heavier° grow
For debt that bankrupt° sleep doth sorrow owe;   85
Which now in some slight measure it will pay,
If for his tender here I make some stay.°
                           (*Lie down [and sleep].*)
OBERON: What hast thou done? Thou hast
   mistaken quite
And laid the love-juice on some true-love's sight.

17. **nole:** Noddle, head. 19. **mimic:** Burlesque actor. 21. **russet-pated choughs:** Gray-headed jackdaws. **in sort:** In a flock. 23. **Sever:** Scatter. 36. **latch'd:** Moistened, anointed. 40. **of force:** Perforce. 53. **whole:** Solid. 55. **Her brother's:** I.e., the sun's. **th' Antipodes:** The people on the opposite side of the earth.

57. **dead:** Deadly, or deathly pale. 70. **brave touch:** Noble exploit (said ironically). 71. **worm:** Serpent. 74. **passion:** Violent feelings. **mispris'd mood:** Anger based on misconception. 84. **heavier:** (1) Harder to bear, (2) drowsier. 85. **bankrupt:** Demetrius is saying that his sleepiness adds to the weariness caused by sorrow. 86–87. **Which . . . stay:** To a small extent I will be able to "pay back" and hence find some relief from sorrow, if I pause here a while (*make some stay*) while sleep "tenders" or offers itself by way of paying the debt owed to sorrow.

90 Of thy misprision° must perforce ensue
    Some true love turn'd and not a false turn'd
      true.
    PUCK: Then fate o'er-rules, that, one man holding
      troth,°
    A million fail, confounding oath on oath.°
    OBERON: About the wood go swifter than the wind,
95   And Helena of Athens look thou find.
    All fancy-sick° she is and pale of cheer°
    With sighs of love, that cost the fresh blood°
      dear.
    By some illusion see thou bring her here.
    I'll charm his eyes against she do appear.°
100 PUCK: I go, I go; look how I go
    Swifter than arrow from the Tartar's bow.°
                                              [*Exit.*]
    OBERON: Flower of this purple dye,
    Hit with Cupid's archery.
    Sink in apple of his eye.
      [*Applies love-juice to Demetrius' eyes.*]
105 When his love he doth espy,
    Let her shine as gloriously
    As the Venus of the sky.
    When thou wak'st, if she be by,
    Beg of her for remedy.

    (*Enter Puck.*)

110 PUCK: Captain of our fairy band,
    Helena is here at hand,
    And the youth, mistook by me,
    Pleading for a lover's fee.°
    Shall we their fond pageant° see?
115 Lord, what fools these mortals be!
    OBERON: Stand aside. The noise they make
    Will cause Demetrius to awake.
    PUCK: Then will two at once woo one;
    That must needs be sport alone;°
120 And those things do best please me
    That befall prepost'rously.°
                                       [*They stand aside.*]

    (*Enter Lysander and Helena.*)

    LYSANDER: Why should you think that I should
      woo in scorn?
    Scorn and derision never come in tears.

    Look when° I vow, I weep; and vows so born,
    In their nativity all truth appears.°   12
    How can these things in me seem scorn to you,
    Bearing the badge° of faith, to prove them true?
    HELENA: You do advance° your cunning more and
      more.
    When truth kills truth,° O devilish-holy fray!
    These vows are Hermia's. Will you give her
      o'er?   13
    Weigh oath with oath, and you will nothing
      weigh.
    Your vows to her and me, put in two scales,
    Will even weigh, and both as light as tales.°
    LYSANDER: I had no judgment when to her I swore.
    HELENA: Nor none, in my mind, now you give her
      o'er.   13
    LYSANDER: Demetrius loves her, and he loves not
      you.
    DEMETRIUS [*awaking*]: O Helen, goddess, nymph,
      perfect, divine!
    To what, my love, shall I compare thine eyne?
    Crystal is muddy. O, how ripe in show°
    Thy lips, those kissing cherries, tempting grow!   14
    That pure congealed white, high Taurus'° snow,
    Fann'd with the eastern wind, turns to a crow°
    When thou hold'st up thy hand. O, let me kiss
    This princess of pure white, this seal° of bliss!
    HELENA: O spite! O hell! I see you all are bent   14
    To set against me for your merriment.
    If you were civil and knew courtesy,
    You would not do me thus much injury.
    Can you not hate me, as I know you do,
    But you must join in souls to mock me too?   15
    If you were men, as men you are in show,
    You would not use a gentle lady so —
    To vow, and swear, and superpraise° my parts,°
    When I am sure you hate me with your hearts.
    You both are rivals, and love Hermia;   15
    And now both rivals, to mock Helena.
    A trim° exploit, a manly enterprise,
    To conjure tears up in a poor maid's eyes
    With your derision! None of noble sort
    Would so offend a virgin and extort°   16
    A poor soul's patience, all to make you sport.

---

90. misprision: Mistake.   92. troth: Faith.   93. confound-
ing . . . oath: Invalidating one oath with another.   96. fancy-
sick: Lovesick.   cheer: Face.   97. sighs . . . blood: An allusion to the physiological theory that each sigh costs the
heart a drop of blood.   99. against . . . appear: in anticipation of her coming.   101. Tartar's bow: Tartars were
famed for their skill with the bow.   113. fee: Privilege,
reward.   114. fond pageant: Foolish exhibition.   119.
alone: Unequaled.   121. prepost'rously: Out of the natural
order.

124. Look when: Whenever.   124–25. vows . . . appears:
Vows made by one who is weeping give evidence thereby of
their sincerity.   127. badge: Identifying device such as that
worn on servants' livery.   128. advance: Carry forward,
display.   129. truth kills truth: One of Lysander's vows
must invalidate the other.   133. tales: Lies.   139. show:
Appearance.   141. Taurus: A lofty mountain range in Asia
Minor.   142. turns to a crow: Seems black by contrast.
144. seal: Pledge.   153. superpraise: Overpraise.   parts:
Qualities.   157. trim: Pretty, fine (said ironically).   160.
extort: Twist, torture.

LYSANDER: You are unkind, Demetrius. Be not so;
For you love Hermia; this you know I know.
And here, with all good will, with all my heart,
In Hermia's love I yield you up my part;   65
And yours of Helena to me bequeath,
Whom I do love and will do till my death.
HELENA: Never did mockers waste more idle
breath.
DEMETRIUS: Lysander, keep thy Hermia; I will
none.°
If e'er I lov'd her, all that love is gone.   70
My heart to her but as guest-wise sojourn'd,
And now to Helen is it home return'd.
There to remain.
LYSANDER: Helen, it is not so.
DEMETRIUS: Disparage not the faith thou dost not
know,
Lest, to thy peril, thou aby° it dear.   75
Look where thy love comes; yonder is thy dear.

(Enter Hermia.)

HERMIA: Dark night, that from the eye his°
function takes,
The ear more quick of apprehension makes;
Wherein it doth impair the seeing sense,
It pays the hearing double recompense.   80
Thou art not by mine eye, Lysander, found;
Mine ear, I thank it, brought me to thy sound.
But why unkindly didst thou leave me so?
LYSANDER: Why should he stay, whom love doth
press to go?
HERMIA: What love could press Lysander from my
side?   85
LYSANDER: Lysander's love, that would not let him
bide,
Fair Helena, who more engilds the night
Than all yon fiery oes° and eyes of light.
Why seek'st thou me? Could not this make thee
know,
The hate I bear thee made me leave thee so?   90
HERMIA: You speak not as you think. It cannot be.
HELENA: Lo, she is one of this confederacy!
Now I perceive they have conjoin'd all three
To fashion this false sport, in spite of me.°
Injurious Hermia, most ungrateful maid!   95
Have you conspir'd, have you with these
contriv'd°
To bait° me with this foul derision?
Is all the counsel° that we two have shar'd,

The sisters' vows, the hours that we have spent,
When we have chid the hasty-footed time   200
For parting us — O, is all forgot?
All school-days friendship, childhood innocence?
We, Hermia, like two artificial° gods,
Have with our needles created both one flower,
Both on one sampler, sitting on one cushion,   205
Both warbling of one song, both in one key,
As if our hands, our sides, voices, and minds
Had been incorporate. So we grew together,
Like to a double cherry, seeming parted,
But yet an union in partition;   210
Two lovely° berries molded on one stem;
So, with two seeming bodies, but one heart;
Two of the first, like coats in heraldry,
Due but to one and crowned with one crest.°
And will you rent° our ancient love asunder,   215
To join with men in scorning your poor friend?
It is not friendly, 'tis not maidenly.
Our sex, as well as I, may chide you for it,
Though I alone do feel the injury.
HERMIA: I am amazed at your passionate words.   220
I scorn you not. It seems that you scorn me.
HELENA: Have you not set Lysander, as in scorn,
To follow me and praise my eyes and face?
And made your other love, Demetrius,
Who even but now did spurn me with his foot,   225
To call me goddess, nymph, divine and rare,
Precious, celestial? Wherefore speaks he this
To her he hates? And wherefore doth Lysander
Deny your love, so rich within his soul,
And tender° me, forsooth, affection,   230
But by your setting on, by your consent?
What though I be not so in grace° as you,
So hung upon with love, so fortunate,
But miserable most, to love unlov'd?
This you should pity rather than despise.   235
HERMIA: I understand not what you mean by this.
HELENA: Ay, do! Persever, counterfeit sad° looks,
Make mouths° upon° me when I turn my back,
Wink each at other, hold the sweet jest up.
This sport, well carried,° shall be chronicled.   240
If you have any pity, grace, or manners,
You would not make me such an argument.°
But fare ye well. 'Tis partly my own fault,
Which death, or absence, soon shall remedy.

---

169. will none: Wish none of her.   175. aby: Pay for.   177.
his: Its.   188. oes: Circles, orbs, stars.   194. in spite of
me: To vex me.   196. contriv'd: Plotted.   197. bait: Torment, as one sets on dogs to bait a bear.   198. counsel:
Confidential talk.

203. artificial: Skilled in art or creation.   211. lovely: Loving.   213–14. Two . . . crest: We have two separate bodies,
just as a coat of arms in heraldry can be represented twice
on a shield but surmounted by a single crest.   215. rent:
Rend.   230. tender: Offer.   232. grace: Favor.   237. sad:
Grave, serious.   238. mouths: Mows, faces, grimaces.
upon: At.   240. carried: Managed.   242. argument: Subject
for a jest.

245 LYSANDER: Stay, gentle Helena; hear my excuse,
　　My love, my life, my soul, fair Helena!
HELENA: O excellent!
HERMIA:　　　　　　Sweet, do not scorn her so.
DEMETRIUS: If she cannot entreat,° I can compel.
LYSANDER: Thou canst compel no more than she
　　　　entreat.
　　Thy threats have no more strength than her
250　　weak prayers.
　　Helen, I love thee, by my life, I do!
　　I swear by that which I will lose for thee,
　　To prove him false that says I love thee not.
DEMETRIUS: I say I love thee more than he can do.
LYSANDER: If thou say so, withdraw, and prove it
255　　too.
DEMETRIUS: Quick, come!
HERMIA:　　　　Lysander, whereto tends all this?
LYSANDER: Away, you Ethiope!°
　　　　　　[*He tries to break away from Hermia.*]
DEMETRIUS:　　　　No, no; he'll
　　Seem to break loose; take on as you would
　　　　follow,
　　But yet come not. You are a tame man, go!
LYSANDER: Hang off,° thou cat, thou burr! Vile
260　　thing, let loose,
　　Or I will shake thee from me like a serpent!
HERMIA: Why are you grown so rude? What
　　change is this,
　　Sweet love?
LYSANDER:　　Thy love? Out, tawny Tartar, out!
　　Out, loathed med'cine!° O hated potion, hence!
HERMIA: Do you not jest?
265 HELENA:　　　　　Yes, sooth,° and so do you.
LYSANDER: Demetrius, I will keep my word with
　　thee.
DEMETRIUS: I would I had your bond, for I perceive
　　A weak bond° holds you. I'll not trust your
　　word.
LYSANDER: What, should I hurt her, strike her, kill
　　her dead?
270　　Although I hate her, I'll not harm her so.
HERMIA: What, can you do me greater harm than
　　hate?
　　Hate me? Wherefore? O me, what news,° my
　　love?
　　Am not I Hermia? Are not you Lysander?
　　I am as fair now as I was erewhile.°

Since night you lov'd me; yet since night you left
　　me.　　　　　　　　　　　　　　　　　　　27
Why, then you left me — O, the gods forbid! —
In earnest, shall I say?
LYSANDER:　　　　Ay, by my life!
　　And never did desire to see thee more.
　　Therefore be out of hope, of question, of doubt;
　　Be certain, nothing truer. 'Tis no jest　　　　28
　　That I do hate thee and love Helena.
HERMIA: O me! You juggler! You cankerblossom!°
　　You thief of love! What, have you come by
　　　　night
　　And stol'n my love's heart from him?
HELENA:　　　　　　　　　　　Fine, i' faith!
　　Have you no modesty, no maiden shame,　　28
　　No touch of bashfulness? What, will you tear
　　Impatient answers from my gentle tongue?
　　Fie, fie! You counterfeit, you puppet,° you!
HERMIA: Puppet? Why so? Ay, that way goes the
　　game.
　　Now I perceive that she hath made compare　　29
　　Between our statures; she hath urg'd her height,
　　And with her personage, her tall personage,
　　Her height, forsooth, she hath prevail'd with
　　　　him.
　　And are you grown so high in his esteem,
　　Because I am so dwarfish and so low?　　　　29
　　How low am I, thou painted maypole? Speak!
　　How low am I? I am not yet so low
　　But that my nails can reach unto thine eyes.
　　　　　　[*She flails at Helena but is restrained.*]
HELENA: I pray you, though you mock me,
　　　　gentlemen,
　　Let her not hurt me. I was never curst;°　　　　30
　　I have no gift at all in shrewishness;
　　I am a right° maid for my cowardice.
　　Let her not strike me. You perhaps may think,
　　Because she is something° lower than myself,
　　That I can match her.
HERMIA:　　　　　　Lower! Hark, again!　　30
HELENA: Good Hermia, do not be so bitter with
　　me.
　　I evermore did love you, Hermia,
　　Did ever keep your counsels, never wrong'd you;
　　Save that, in love unto Demetrius,
　　I told him of your stealth° unto this wood.　　31
　　He followed you; for love I followed him.
　　But he hath chid me hence and threat'ned me
　　To strike me, spurn me, nay, to kill me too.
　　And now, so° you will let me quiet go,

---

248. **entreat:** Succeed by entreaty.　**257. Ethiope:** Referring to Hermia's relatively dark hair and complexion; see also *tawny Tartar* six lines later.　**260. Hang off:** Let go.　**264. med'cine:** Poison.　**265. sooth:** Truly.　**268. weak bond:** Hermia's arm (with a pun on *bond,* oath, in the previous line).　**272. what news:** What is the matter.　**274. erewhile:** Just now.

282. **cankerblossom:** Worm that destroys the flower bud (?).
288. **puppet:** (1) Counterfeit; (2) dwarfish woman (in reference to Hermia's smaller stature).　**300. curst:** Shrewish.
302. **right:** True.　**304. something:** Somewhat.　**310. stealth:** Stealing away.　**314. so:** If only.

15 To Athens will I bear my folly back
      And follow you no further. Let me go.
      You see how simple and how fond° I am.
HERMIA: Why, get you gone. Who is 't that hinders
      you?
HELENA: A foolish heart, that I leave here behind.
HERMIA: What, with Lysander?
20 HELENA: With Demetrius.
LYSANDER: Be not afraid; she shall not harm thee,
      Helena.
DEMETRIUS: No, sir, she shall not, though you take
      her part.
HELENA: O, when she is angry, she is keen and
      shrewd!°
      She was a vixen when she went to school;
25 And though she be but little, she is fierce.
HERMIA: "Little" again! Nothing but "low" and
      "little"!
      Why will you suffer her to flout me thus?
      Let me come to her.
LYSANDER: Get you gone, you dwarf!
      You minimus,° of hind'ring knot-grass° made!
      You bead, you acorn!
30 DEMETRIUS: You are too officious
      In her behalf that scorns your services.
      Let her alone. Speak not of Helena;
      Take not her part. For, if thou dost intend°
      Never so little show of love to her,
35 Thou shalt aby° it.
LYSANDER: Now she holds me not;
      Now follow, if thou dar'st, to try whose right,
      Of thine or mine, is most in Helena.   [Exit.]
DEMETRIUS: Follow? Nay, I'll go with thee, cheek
      by jowl.°
                          [Exit, following Lysander.]
HERMIA: You, mistress, all this coil° is 'long of°
      you.
      Nay, go not back.°
40 HELENA: I will not trust you, I,
      Nor longer stay in your curst company.
      Your hands than mine are quicker for a fray;
      My legs are longer, though, to run away. [Exit.]
HERMIA: I am amaz'd, and know not what to say.
                                      (Exit.)
45 OBERON: This is thy negligence. Still thou mistak'st,
      Or else committ'st thy knaveries willfully.
PUCK: Believe me, king of shadows, I mistook.
      Did not you tell me I should know the man

By the Athenian garments he had on?
And so far blameless proves my enterprise   350
That I have 'nointed an Athenian's eyes;
And so far am I glad it so did sort°
As this their jangling I esteem a sport.
OBERON: Thou see'st these lovers seek a place to
      fight.
Hie therefore, Robin, overcast the night;   355
The starry welkin° cover thou anon
With drooping fog as black as Acheron,°
And lead these testy rivals so astray
As° one come not within another's way.
Like to Lysander sometime frame thy tongue,   360
Then stir Demetrius up with bitter wrong;°
And sometime rail thou like Demetrius.
And from each other look thou lead them thus,
Till o'er their brows death-counterfeiting sleep
With leaden legs and batty° wings doth creep.   365
Then crush this herb° into Lysander's eye,
                          [Gives herb.]
Whose liquor hath this virtuous° property,
To take from thence all error with his° might
And make his eyeballs roll with wonted° sight.
When they next wake, all this derision°   370
Shall seem a dream and fruitless vision,
And back to Athens shall the lovers wend
With league whose date° till death shall never
      end.
Whiles I in this affair do thee employ,
I'll to my queen and beg her Indian boy;   375
And then I will her charmed eye release
From monster's view, and all things shall be
      peace.
PUCK: My fairy lord, this must be done with haste,
For night's swift dragons° cut the clouds full
      fast,
And yonder shines Aurora's harbinger,°   380
At whose approach, ghosts, wand'ring here and
      there,
Troop home to churchyards. Damned spirits all,
That in crossways and floods have burial,°
Already to their wormy beds are gone.

352. **sort:** Turn out.   356. **welkin:** Sky.   357. **Acheron:**
River of Hades (here representing Hades itself).   359. **As:**
That.   361. **wrong:** Insults.   365. **batty:** Batlike.   366.
this herb: The antidote (mentioned in II, I, 184) to love-in-
idleness.   367. **virtuous:** Efficacious.   368. **his:** Its.   369.
wonted: Accustomed.   370. **derision:** Laughable business.
373. **date:** Term of existence.   379. **dragons:** Supposed by
Shakespeare to be yoked to the car of the goddess of night.
380. **Aurora's harbinger:** The morning star, precursor of
dawn.   383. **crossways ... burial:** Those who had committed suicide were buried at crossways, with a stake driven
through them; those drowned, i.e., buried in floods or great
waters, were condemned to wander disconsolate for want
of burial rites.

317. **fond:** Foolish.   323. **shrewd:** Shrewish.   329. **mini-
mus:** Diminutive creature.   **knot-grass:** A weed, an infusion
of which was thought to stunt the growth.   333. **intend:**
Give sign of.   335. **aby:** Pay for.   338. **cheek by jowl:** Side
by side.   339. **coil:** Turmoil, dissension.   **'long of:** On account of.   340. **go not back:** Don't retreat. (Hermia is again
proposing a fight.)

385   For fear lest day should look their shames upon,
    They willfully themselves exile from light
    And must for aye° consort with black-brow'd
      night.
OBERON: But we are spirits of another sort.
    I with the Morning's love° have oft made sport,
390   And, like a forester,° the groves may tread
    Even till the eastern gate, all fiery-red,
    Opening on Neptune with fair blessed beams,
    Turns into yellow gold his salt green streams.
    But, notwithstanding, haste; make no delay.
395   We may effect this business yet ere day.   *[Exit.]*
PUCK: Up and down, up and down,
    I will lead them up and down.

I am fear'd in field and town.
Goblin, lead them up and down.
Here comes one.   400

(*Enter Lysander.*)

LYSANDER: Where art thou, proud Demetrius?
    Speak thou now.
PUCK [*mimicking Demetrius*]: Here, villain, drawn°
    and ready. Where art thou?
LYSANDER: I will be with thee straight.°
PUCK: Follow me, then,
    To plainer° ground.
    [*Lysander wanders about, following the voice.*]°

387. **for aye:** Forever.   **389. Morning's love:** Cephalus, a beautiful youth beloved by Aurora; or perhaps the goddess of the dawn herself.   **390. forester:** Keeper of a royal forest.

402. **drawn:** With drawn sword.   403. **straight:** Immediately.   404. **plainer:** Smoother.   404. [S.D.] ***Lysander wanders about:*** It is not clearly necessary that Lysander exit at this point; neither exit nor reentrance is indicated in the early texts.

RIGHT: Elizabeth McGovern as
Helena in the 1987 New York
Shakespeare Festival production
of *A Midsummer Night's
Dream*, directed by A. J.
Antoon. LEFT: F. Murray
Abraham (left) as Bottom,
playing Pyramus.

(*Enter Demetrius.*)

DEMETRIUS: Lysander! Speak again!
05   Thou runaway, thou coward, art thou fled?
    Speak! In some bush? Where dost thou hide thy
        head?
PUCK [*mimicking Lysander*]: Thou coward, art thou
        bragging to the stars,
    Telling the bushes that thou look'st for wars,
    And wilt not come? Come, recreant;° come, thou
        child,
10   I'll whip thee with a rod. He is defil'd
    That draws a sword on thee.
DEMETRIUS: Yea, art thou there?
PUCK: Follow my voice. We'll try° no manhood
    here.
                                    (*Exeunt.*)

[*Lysander returns.*]

LYSANDER: He goes before me and still dares me
    on.

When I come where he calls, then he is gone.
The villain is much lighter-heel'd than I.   415
I followed fast, but faster he did fly,
That fallen am I in dark uneven way,
And here will rest me. [*Lies down.*] Come, thou
    gentle day!
For if but once thou show me thy gray light,
I'll find Demetrius and revenge this spite. [*Sleeps.*] 420

([*Enter*] Robin [*Puck*] *and Demetrius.*)

PUCK: Ho, ho, ho! Coward, why com'st thou not?
DEMETRIUS: Abide me, if thou dar'st; for well I
    wot°
    Thou runn'st before me, shifting every place,
    And dar'st not stand nor look me in the face.
    Where art thou now?
PUCK: Come hither. I am here.   425
DEMETRIUS: Nay, then, thou mock'st me. Thou
    shalt buy° this dear,°
    If ever I thy face by daylight see.

---

409. **recreant:** Cowardly wretch.   412. **try:** Test.   422. **wot:** Know.   426. **buy:** Pay for.   **dear:** Dearly.

Now, go thy way. Faintness constraineth me
To measure out my length on this cold bed.
430 By day's approach look to be visited.
                                    [*Lies down and sleeps.*]

(*Enter Helena.*)

HELENA: O weary night, O long and tedious night,
Abate° thy hours! Shine, comforts, from the east,
That I may back to Athens by daylight,
From these that my poor company detest;
435 And sleep, that sometimes shuts up sorrow's eye,
Steal me awhile from mine own company.
                                  [*Lies down and*] *sleep*[*s*].

PUCK: Yet but three? Come one more;
Two of both kinds makes up four.
Here she comes, curst and sad.
440 Cupid is a knavish lad,
Thus to make poor females mad.

[*Enter Hermia.*]

HERMIA: Never so weary, never so in woe,
Bedabbled with the dew and torn with briers,
I can no further crawl, no further go;
445 My legs can keep no pace with my desires.
Here will I rest me till the break of day.
Heavens shield Lysander, if they mean a fray!
                                    [*Lies down and sleeps.*]

PUCK: On the ground
         Sleep sound.
450 I'll apply
         To your eye,
Gentle lover, remedy.
             [*Squeezing the juice on Lysander's eyes.*]
         When thou wak'st,
         Thou tak'st
455 True delight
         In the sight
Of thy former lady's eye;
And the country proverb known,
That every man should take his own,
460 In your waking shall be shown:
         Jack shall have Jill;
         Nought shall go ill;
The man shall have his mare again, and all shall
         be well.   [*Exit. Manent the four lovers.*]

[*ACT IV • Scene I*]°

(*Enter* [*Titania,*] *Queen of Fairies, and* [*Bottom the*]
Clown, and Fairies; and [*Oberon,*] *the King, behind
them.*)

432. Abate: Lessen, shorten.   IV, I. Location: Scene continues. The four lovers are still asleep onstage.

TITANIA: Come, sit thee down upon this flow'ry
         bed,
While I thy amiable° cheeks do coy,°
And stick musk-roses in thy sleek smooth head,
And kiss thy fair large ears, my gentle joy.
                                        [*They recline.*]
BOTTOM: Where's Peaseblossom?   5
PEASEBLOSSOM: Ready.
BOTTOM: Scratch my head, Peaseblossom. Where's
         Mounsieur Cobweb?
COBWEB: Ready.
BOTTOM: Mounsieur Cobweb, good mounsieur, get   10
         you your weapons in your hand, and kill me a red-
         hipp'd humble-bee on the top of a thistle; and,
         good mounsieur, bring me the honey-bag. Do not
         fret yourself too much in the action, mounsieur;
         and, good mounsieur, have a care the honey-bag   15
         break not; I would be loath to have you overflown
         with a honey-bag, signior. Where's Mounsieur
         Mustardseed?
MUSTARDSEED: Ready.
BOTTOM: Give me your neaf,° Mounsieur Mustardseed.   20
         Pray you, leave your curtsy,° good mounsieur.
MUSTARDSEED: What's your will?
BOTTOM: Nothing, good mounsieur, but to help Cav-
         alery° Cobweb° to scratch. I must to the barber's,
         mounsieur; for methinks I am marvailes hairy about   25
         the face; and I am such a tender ass, if my hair
         do but tickle me, I must scratch.
TITANIA: What, wilt thou hear some music, my
         sweet love?
BOTTOM: I have a reasonable good ear in music. Let's
         have the tongs and the bones.°   30
                           [*Music: tongs, rural music.*]°
TITANIA: Or say, sweet love, what thou desirest to
         eat.
BOTTOM: Truly, a peck of provender. I could munch
         your good dry oats. Methinks I have a great desire
         to a bottle° of hay. Good hay, sweet hay, hath no   35
         fellow.°
TITANIA: I have a venturous fairy that shall seek
         The squirrel's hoard, and fetch thee new nuts.
BOTTOM: I had rather have a handful or two of dried

2. amiable: Lovely.   coy: Caress.   20. neaf: Fist.   21. leave
your curtsy: Put on your hat.   23–24. Cavalery: Cavalier.
Form of address for a gentleman.   24. Cobweb: Seemingly
an error, since Cobweb has been sent to bring honey while
Peaseblossom has been asked to scratch.   30. tongs ...
bones: Instruments for rustic music. (The tongs were played
like a triangle, whereas the bones were held between the
fingers and used as clappers.)   30. [S.D.] *Music ... music*:
This stage direction is added from the Folio.   34. bottle:
Bundle.   35. fellow: Equal.

peas. But, I pray you, let none of your people stir
40 me. I have an exposition° of sleep come upon me.
TITANIA: Sleep thou, and I will wind thee in my
    arms.
    Fairies, be gone, and be all ways° away.
                                    [Exeunt fairies.]
    So doth the woodbine the sweet honeysuckle
45 Gently entwist; the female ivy so
    Enrings the barky fingers of the elm.
    Oh, how I love thee! How I dote on thee!
                                    [They sleep.]

(Enter Robin Goodfellow [Puck].)

OBERON [advancing]: Welcome, good Robin. See'st
    thou this sweet sight?
    Her dotage now I do begin to pity.
    For, meeting her of late behind the wood,
50 Seeking sweet favors° for this hateful fool,
    I did upbraid her and fall out with her.
    For she his hairy temples then had rounded
    With coronet of fresh and fragrant flowers;
    And that same dew, which sometime° on the
      buds
55 Was wont to swell like round and orient pearls,°
    Stood now within the pretty flouriets'° eyes
    Like tears that did their own disgrace bewail.
    When I had at my pleasure taunted her,
    And she in mild terms begg'd my patience,
60 I then did ask of her her changeling child;
    Which straight she gave me, and her fairy sent
    To bear him to my bower in fairy land.
    And, now I have the boy, I will undo
    This hateful imperfection of her eyes.
65 And, gentle Puck, take this transformed scalp
    From off the head of this Athenian swain,
    That, he awaking when the other° do,
    May all to Athens back again repair,
    And think no more of this night's accidents
70 But as the fierce vexation of a dream.
    But first I will release the Fairy Queen.
                          [Squeezes juice in her eyes.]
    Be as thou wast wont to be;
    See as thou wast wont to see.
    Dian's bud° o'er Cupid's flower
75 Hath such force and blessed power.
    Now, my Titania, wake you, my sweet queen.

TITANIA [waking]: My Oberon! What visions have I
    seen!
    Methought I was enamor'd of an ass.
OBERON: There lies your love.
TITANIA: How came these things to pass?
    O, how mine eyes do loathe his visage now!   80
OBERON: Silence awhile. Robin, take off this head.
    Titania, music call, and strike more dead
    Than common sleep of all these five° the sense.
TITANIA: Music, ho! Music, such as charmeth sleep!
                                          [Music.]
PUCK [removing the ass's head]: Now, when thou
    wak'st, with thine own fool's eyes peep.   85
OBERON: Sound, music! Come, my queen, take
    hands with me,
    And rock the ground whereon these sleepers be.
                                          [Dance.]
    Now thou and I are new in amity,
    And will tomorrow midnight solemnly°
    Dance in Duke Theseus' house triumphantly   90
    And bless it to all fair prosperity.
    There shall the pairs of faithful lovers be
    Wedded, with Theseus, all in jollity.
PUCK: Fairy King, attend, and mark:
    I do hear the morning lark.   95
OBERON: Then, my queen, in silence sad,°
    Trip we after night's shade.
    We the globe can compass soon,
    Swifter than the wand'ring moon.
TITANIA: Come, my lord, and in our flight   100
    Tell me how it came this night
    That I sleeping here was found
    With these mortals on the ground.   (Exeunt.)
                              (Wind horn [within].)

(Enter Theseus and all his train; [Hippolyta, Egeus].)

THESEUS: Go, one of you, find out the forester,
    For now our observation° is perform'd;   105
    And since we have the vaward° of the day,
    My love shall hear the music of my hounds.
    Uncouple in the western valley; let them go.
    Dispatch, I say, and find the forester.
                              [Exit an Attendant.]
    We will, fair queen, up to the mountain's top   110
    And mark the musical confusion
    Of hounds and echo in conjunction.
HIPPOLYTA: I was with Hercules and Cadmus° once,
    When in a wood of Crete they bay'd° the bear

---

40. exposition: Bottom's word for *disposition.* **42. all ways:**
In all directions. **50. favors:** I.e., gifts of flowers. **54.**
sometime: Formerly. **55. orient pearls:** The most beautiful
of all pearls, those coming from the Orient. **56. flouriets':**
Floweréts'. **67. other:** Others. **74. Dian's bud:** Perhaps
the flower of the *agnus castus* or chaste-tree, supposed to
preserve chastity; or perhaps referring simply to Oberon's
herb by which he can undo the effects of "Cupid's flower,"
the love-in-idleness of II, I, 166–68.

83. these five: I.e., the four lovers and Bottom. **89. sol-**
emnly: Ceremoniously. **96. sad:** Sober. **105. observation:**
Observance to a morn of May (I, I, 167). **106. vaward:**
Vanguard, i.e., earliest part. **113. Cadmus:** Mythical founder
of Thebes. (This story about him is unknown). **114. bay'd:**
Brought to bay.

115   With hounds of Sparta.° Never did I hear
         Such gallant chiding; for, besides the groves,
         The skies, the fountains, every region near
         Seem'd all one mutual cry. I never heard
         So musical a discord, such sweet thunder.
         THESEUS: My hounds are bred out of the Spartan
120   kind,
         So flew'd,° so sanded;° and their heads are hung
         With ears that sweep away the morning dew;
         Crook-knee'd, and dewlapp'd° like Thessalian
             bulls;
         Slow in pursuit, but match'd in mouth like bells,
125   Each under each.° A cry° more tuneable°
         Was never holla'd to, nor cheer'd with horn,
         In Crete, in Sparta, nor in Thessaly.
         Judge when you hear. [Sees the sleepers.] But,
             soft! What nymphs are these?
         EGEUS: My lord, this' my daughter here asleep;
130   And this, Lysander; this Demetrius is;
         This Helena, old Nedar's Helena.
         I wonder of their being here together.
         THESEUS: No doubt they rose up early to observe
         The rite of May, and, hearing our intent,
135   Came here in grace of our solemnity.°
         But speak, Egeus. Is not this the day
         That Hermia should give answer of her choice?
         EGEUS: It is, my lord.
         THESEUS: Go, bid the huntsmen wake them with
             their horns.

                          [Exit an Attendant.]

         (Shout within. Wind horns. They all start up.)

140   Good morrow, friends. Saint Valentine° is past.
         Begin these wood-birds but to couple now?
         LYSANDER: Pardon, my lord.   [They kneel.]
         THESEUS: I pray you all, stand up.
         I know you two are rival enemies;
         How comes this gentle concord in the world,
145   That hatred is so far from jealousy
         To sleep by hate and fear no enmity?
         LYSANDER: My lord, I shall reply amazedly,
         Half sleep, half waking; but as yet, I swear,
         I cannot truly say how I came here.
150   But, as I think — for truly would I speak,
         And now I do bethink me, so it is —

115. **hounds of Sparta:** Breed famous in antiquity for their hunting skill.   121. **So flew'd:** Similarly having large hanging chaps or fleshy covering of the jaw. **sanded:** Of sandy color. 123. **dewlapp'd:** Having pendulous folds of skin under the neck.   124–25. **match'd . . . under each:** Harmoniously matched in their various cries like a set of bells, from treble down to bass.   125. **cry:** Pack of hounds. **tuneable:** Well tuned, melodious.   135. **solemnity:** Observance of these same rites of May.   140. **Saint Valentine:** Birds were supposed to choose their mates on St. Valentine's Day.

         I came with Hermia hither. Our intent
         Was to be gone from Athens, where° we might,
         Without° the peril of the Athenian law —
         EGEUS: Enough, enough, my lord; you have enough.   155
         I beg the law, the law, upon his head.
         They would have stol'n away; they would,
             Demetrius,
         Thereby to have defeated you and me,
         You of your wife and me of my consent,
         Of my consent that she should be your wife.   160
         DEMETRIUS: My lord, fair Helen told me of their
             stealth,
         Of this their purpose hither to this wood,
         And I in fury hither followed them,
         Fair Helena in fancy following me.
         But, my good lord, I wot not by what power —   165
         But by some power it is — my love to Hermia,
         Melted as the snow, seems to me now
         As the remembrance of an idle gaud.°
         Which in my childhood I did dote upon;
         And all the faith, the virtue of my heart,   170
         The object and the pleasure of mine eye,
         Is only Helena. To her, my lord,
         Was I betroth'd ere I saw Hermia,
         But like a sickness did I loathe this food;
         But, as in health, come to my natural taste,   175
         Now I do wish it, love it, long for it,
         And will for evermore be true to it.
         THESEUS: Fair lovers, you are fortunately met.
         Of this discourse we more will hear anon.
         Egeus, I will overbear your will;   180
         For in the temple, by and by, with us
         These couples shall eternally be knit.
         And, for° the morning now is something° worn,
         Our purpos'd hunting shall be set aside.
         Away with us to Athens. Three and three,   185
         We'll hold a feast in great solemnity.
         Come, Hippolyta.
             [Exeunt Theseus, Hippolyta, Egeus, and train.]
         DEMETRIUS: These things seem small and
             undistinguishable,
         Like far-off mountains turned into clouds.
         HERMIA: Methinks I see these things with parted°
             eye,   190
         When every thing seems double.
         HELENA: So methinks;
         And I have found Demetrius like a jewel,
         Mine own, and not mine own.°

153. **where:** Wherever; or to where.   154. **Without:** Outside of, beyond.   168. **idle gaud:** Worthless trinket.   183. **for:** Since. **something:** Somewhat.   190. **parted:** Improperly focused.   192–93. **like . . . not mine own:** Like a jewel that one finds by chance and therefore possesses but cannot certainly consider one's own property.

DEMETRIUS: Are you sure
    That we are awake? It seems to me
95 That yet we sleep, we dream. Do not you think
    The Duke was here, and bid us follow him?
HERMIA: Yea, and my father.
HELENA: And Hippolyta.
LYSANDER: And he did bid us follow to the temple.
DEMETRIUS: Why, then, we are awake. Let's follow
    him,
00 And by the way let us recount our dreams.
                                        [*Exeunt.*]
BOTTOM [*awaking*]: When my cue comes, call me,
    and I will answer. My next is, "Most fair Pyramus."
    Heigh-ho! Peter Quince! Flute, the bellows-mender!
05 Snout, the tinker! Starveling! God's my life, stol'n
    hence, and left me asleep! I have had a most rare
    vision. I have had a dream, past the wit of man
    to say what dream it was. Man is but an ass, if
    he go about° to expound this dream. Methought
10 I was — there is no man can tell what. Methought
    I was — and methought I had — but man is but
    a patch'd° fool, if he will offer° to say what me-
    thought I had. The eye of man hath not heard, the
    ear of man hath not seen, man's hand is not able
15 to taste, his tongue to conceive, nor his heart to
    report, what my dream was. I will get Peter Quince
    to write a ballad of this dream. It shall be call'd
    "Bottom's Dream," because it hath no bottom; and
    I will sing it in the latter end of a play, before the
    Duke. Peradventure, to make it the more gracious,
20 I shall sing it at her° death.   [*Exit.*]

[*Scene II*]°

(*Enter Quince, Flute, [Snout, and Starveling].*)

QUINCE: Have you sent to Bottom's house? Is he come
    home yet?
STARVELING: He cannot be heard of. Out of doubt he
    is transported.°
5 FLUTE: If he come not, then the play is marr'd. It goes
    not forward, doth it?
QUINCE: It is not possible. You have not a man in all
    Athens able to discharge° Pyramus but he.
FLUTE: No, he hath simply the best wit of any handicraft
10 man in Athens.
QUINCE: Yea, and the best person too; and he is a
    very paramour for a sweet voice.

---

208. go about: Attempt.   **211. patch'd:** Wearing motley,
i.e., a dress of various colors.   **offer:** venture.   **220. her:**
Thisby's (?).   **IV, II. Location:** Athens, Quince's house (?).
4. transported: Carried off by fairies; or, possibly, transformed.   **8. discharge:** Perform.

FLUTE: You must say "paragon." A paramour is, God
    bless us, a thing of naught.

(*Enter Snug the Joiner.*)

SNUG: Masters, the Duke is coming from the temple,   15
    and there is two or three lords and ladies more
    married. If our sport had gone forward, we had
    all been made men.
FLUTE: O sweet bully Bottom! Thus hath he lost six-
    pence a day° during his life; he could not have   20
    scap'd sixpence a day. An the Duke had not given
    him sixpence a day for playing Pyramus, I'll be
    hang'd. He would have deserv'd it. Sixpence a day
    in Pyramus, or nothing.

(*Enter Bottom.*)

BOTTOM: Where are these lads? Where are these hearts?°   25
QUINCE: Bottom! O most courageous day! O most
    happy hour!
BOTTOM: Masters, I am to discourse wonders.° But
    ask me not what; for if I tell you, I am no true
    Athenian. I will tell you everything, right as it fell   30
    out.
QUINCE: Let us hear, sweet Bottom.
BOTTOM: Not a word of° me. All that I will tell you
    is, that the Duke hath din'd. Get your apparel
    together, good strings° to your beards, new ribands°   35
    to your pumps; meet presently° at the palace; every
    man look o'er his part; for the short and the long
    is, our play is preferr'd.° In any case, let Thisby
    have clean linen; and let not him that plays the
    lion pare his nails, for they shall hang out for the   40
    lion's claws. And, most dear actors, eat no onions
    nor garlic, for we are to utter sweet breath; and I
    do not doubt but to hear them say, it is a sweet
    comedy. No more words. Away! go, away!
                                        [*Exeunt.*]

[*ACT V • Scene I*]°

(*Enter Theseus, Hippolyta, and Philostrate, [Lords,
and Attendants].*)

HIPPOLYTA: 'Tis strange, my Theseus, that° these
    lovers speak of.
THESEUS: More strange than true. I never may°
    believe

19–20. sixpence a day: As a royal pension.   **25. hearts:**
Good fellows.   **28. am . . . wonders:** Have wonders to relate.
33. of: Out of.   **35. strings:** To attach the beards.   **ribands:**
ribbons.   **36. presently:** Immediately.   **38. preferr'd:** Selected for consideration.   **V, I. Location:** Athens. The palace
of Theseus.   **1. that:** That which.   **2. may:** Can.

These antic° fables, nor these fairy toys.°
Lovers and madmen have such seething brains,
5   Such shaping fantasies,° that apprehend
More than cool reason ever comprehends.
The lunatic, the lover, and the poet
Are of imagination all compact.°
One sees more devils than vast hell can hold;
10   That is the madman. The lover, all as frantic,
Sees Helen's° beauty in a brow of Egypt.°
The poet's eye, in a fine frenzy rolling,
Doth glance from heaven to earth, from earth to
      heaven;
And as imagination bodies forth
15   The forms of things unknown, the poet's pen
Turns them to shapes and gives to airy nothing
A local habitation and a name.
Such tricks hath strong imagination
That, if it would but apprehend some joy,
20   It comprehends some bringer° of that joy;
Or in the night, imagining some fear,°
How easy is a bush suppos'd a bear!
HIPPOLYTA: But all the story of the night told over,
And all their minds transfigur'd so together,
25   More witnesseth than fancy's images°
And grows to something of great constancy;°
But, howsoever,° strange and admirable.°

(*Enter lovers: Lysander, Demetrius, Hermia, and
Helena.*)

THESEUS: Here come the lovers, full of joy and
      mirth.
Joy, gentle friends! Joy and fresh days of love
Accompany your hearts!
30   LYSANDER: More than to us
Wait in your royal walks, your board, your bed!
THESEUS: Come now, what masques, what dances
      shall we have,
To wear away this long age of three hours
Between our after-supper and bed-time?
35   Where is our usual manager of mirth?
What revels are in hand? Is there no play,
To ease the anguish of a torturing hour?
Call Philostrate.
PHILOSTRATE: Here, mighty Theseus.

THESEUS: Say, what abridgement° have you for this
      evening?
What masque? What music? How shall we
      beguile   40
The lazy time, if not with some delight?
PHILOSTRATE: There is a brief° how many sports are
      ripe.
Make choice of which your Highness will see
      first.
                                        [*Giving a paper.*]
THESEUS [*reads*]: "The battle with the Centaurs,° to
      be sung
By an Athenian eunuch to the harp."   45
We'll none of that. That have I told my love,
In glory of my kinsman° Hercules.
[*Reads.*] "The riot of the tipsy Bacchanals,
Tearing the Thracian singer in their rage."°
That is an old device; and it was play'd   50
When I from Thebes came last a conqueror.
[*Reads.*] "The thrice three Muses mourning for
      the death
Of Learning, late decceas'd in beggary."°
That is some satire, keen and critical,
Not sorting with° a nuptial ceremony.   55
[*Reads.*] "A tedious brief scene of young
      Pyramus
And his love Thisby; very tragical mirth."
Merry and tragical? Tedious and brief?
That is, hot ice and wondrous strange° snow.
How shall we find the concord of this discord?   60
PHILOSTRATE: A play there is, my lord, some ten
      words long,
Which is as brief as I have known a play;
But by ten words, my lord, it is too long,
Which makes it tedious. For in all the play
There is not one word apt, one player fitted.   65
And tragical, my noble lord, it is,
For Pyramus therein doth kill himself.
Which, when I saw rehears'd, I must confess,

---

3. **antic**: Strange, grotesque (with additional punning sense of *antique*, ancient). **fairy toys**: Trifling stories about fairies. 5. **fantasies**: Imaginations. 8. **compact**: Formed, composed. 11. **Helen's**: Of Helen of Troy, pattern of beauty. **brow of Egypt**: Face of a gypsy. 20. **bringer**: Source. 21. **fear**: Object of fear. 25. **More . . . images**: Testifies to something more substantial than mere imaginings. 26. **constancy**: Certainty. 27. **howsoever**: In any case. **admirable**: A source of wonder.

39. **abridgement**: Pastime (to abridge or shorten the evening). 42. **brief**: Short written statement, list. 44. **"battle . . . Centaurs"**: Probably refers to the battle of the Centaurs and the Lapithae, when the Centaurs attempted to carry off Hippodamia, bride of Theseus's friend Pirothous. 47. **kinsman**: Plutarch's *Life of Theseus* states that Hercules and Theseus were near-kinsmen. Theseus is referring to a version of the battle of the Centaurs in which Hercules was said to be present. 48–49. **"The riot . . . rage"**: This was the story of the death of Orpheus, as told in *Metamorphoses*. 52–53. **"The thrice . . . beggary"**: Possibly an allusion to Spenser's *Teares of the Muses* (1591), though "satires" deploring the neglect of learning and the creative arts were commonplace. 55. **sorting with**: Befitting. 59. **strange**: Seemingly an error for some adjective that would contrast with *snow*, just as *hot* contrasts with *ice*.

Made mine eyes water; but more merry tears
70　The passion of loud laughter never shed.
THESEUS: What are they that do play it?
PHILOSTRATE: Hard-handed men that work in
　　Athens here,
　　Which never labor'd in their minds till now,
　　And now have toil'd° their unbreathed°
　　　memories
75　With this same play, against° your nuptial.
THESEUS: And we will hear it.
PHILOSTRATE:　　　　　　No, my noble lord,
　　It is not for you. I have heard it over,
　　And it is nothing, nothing in the world;
　　Unless you can find sport in their intents,
80　Extremely stretch'd° and conn'd° with cruel pain,
　　To do you service.
THESEUS:　　　　　I will hear that play;
　　For never anything can be amiss'
　　When simpleness and duty tender it.
　　Go, bring them in; and take your places, ladies.
　　　　　[Philostrate goes to summon the players.]
HIPPOLYTA: I love not to see wretchedness
85　　o'ercharg'd°
　　And duty in his service° perishing.
THESEUS: Why, gentle sweet, you shall see no such
　　thing.
HIPPOLYTA: He says they can do nothing in this
　　kind.°
THESEUS: The kinder we, to give them thanks for
　　nothing.
90　Our sport shall be to take what they mistake;
　　And what poor duty cannot do, noble respect
　　Takes it in might, not merit.°
　　Where I have come, great clerks° have purposed
　　To greet me with premeditated welcomes;
95　Where I have seen them shiver and look pale,
　　Make periods in the midst of sentences,
　　Throttle their practic'd accent° in their fears,
　　And in conclusion dumbly have broke off,
　　Not paying me a welcome. Trust me, sweet,
100　Out of this silence yet I pick'd a welcome;
　　And in the modesty of fearful duty
　　I read as much as from the rattling tongue
　　Of saucy and audacious eloquence.
　　Love, therefore, and tongue-tied simplicity
105　In least° speak most, to my capacity.°

[*Philostrate returns.*]

PHILOSTRATE: So please your Grace, the Prologue° is
　　address'd.°
THESEUS: Let him approach. [*Flourish of trumpets.*]

(*Enter the Prologue [Quince].*)

PROLOGUE: If we offend, it is with our good will.
　　That you should think, we come not to offend,
　　But with good will. To show our simple skill,　110
　　That is the true beginning of our end.
　　Consider, then, we come but in despite.
　　We do not come, as minding° to content you,
　　Our true intent is. All for your delight
　　We are not here. That you should here repent
　　　you,　　　　　　　　　　　　　　　　　　115
　　The actors are at hand; and, by their show,
　　You shall know all that you are like to know.
THESEUS: This fellow doth not stand upon points.°
LYSANDER: He hath rid his prologue like a rough°
　　colt; he knows not the stop.° A good moral, my　120
　　lord: it is not enough to speak, but to speak true.
HIPPOLYTA: Indeed he hath play'd on his prologue like
　　a child on a recorder;° a sound, but not in
　　government.°
THESEUS: His speech was like a tangled chain, nothing°　125
　　impair'd, but all disorder'd. Who is next?

(*Enter Pyramus and Thisby, and Wall, and Moon-shine, and Lion.*)

PROLOGUE: Gentles, perchance you wonder at this
　　show;
　　But wonder on, till truth make all things plain.
　　This man is Pyramus, if you would know;
　　This beauteous lady Thisby is certain.　　　　130
　　This man, with lime and rough-cast, doth
　　　present
　　Wall, that vile Wall which did these lovers
　　　sunder;
　　And through Wall's chink, poor souls, they are
　　　content
　　To whisper. At the which let no man wonder.
　　This man, with lantern, dog, and bush of thorn,　135
　　Presenteth Moonshine; for, if you will know,
　　By moonshine did these lovers think no scorn°

---

74. **toil'd:** Taxed. **unbreathed:** Unexercised. **75. against:** In preparation for. **80. stretch'd:** Strained. **conn'd:** Memorized. **85. wretchedness o'ercharg'd:** Incompetence overburdened. **86. his service:** Its attempt to serve. **88. kind:** Kind of thing. **92. Takes . . . merit:** Values it for the effort made rather than for the excellence achieved. **93. clerks:** Learned men. **97. practic'd accent:** Rehearsed speech; or usual way of speaking. **105. least:** Saying least. **to my capacity:** In my judgment and understanding.

106. **Prologue:** Speaker of the prologue. **address'd:** Ready. 113. **minding:** Intending. 118. **stand upon points:** (1) Heed niceties or small points, (2) pay attention to punctuation in his reading. (The humor of Quince's speech is in the blunders of its punctuation.) 119. **rough:** Unbroken. 120. **stop:** (1) The stopping of a colt by reining it in, (2) punctuation mark. 123. **recorder:** A wind instrument like a flute. 124. **government:** Control. 125. **nothing:** Not at all. 137. **think no scorn:** Think it no disgraceful matter.

To meet at Ninus' tomb, there, there to woo.
This grisly beast, which Lion hight° by name,
140 The trusty Thisby, coming first by night,
Did scare away, or rather did affright;
And, as she fled, her mantle she did fall,°
Which Lion vile with bloody mouth did stain.
Anon comes Pyramus, sweet youth and tall,°
145 And finds his trusty Thisby's mantle slain;
Whereat, with blade, with bloody blameful
      blade,
He bravely broach'd° his boiling bloody breast.
And Thisby, tarrying in mulberry shade,
His dagger drew, and died. For all the rest,
150 Let Lion, Moonshine, Wall, and lovers twain
At large° discourse, while here they do remain.
            (*Exeunt Lion, Thisby, and Moonshine.*)
THESEUS: I wonder if the lion be to speak.
DEMETRIUS: No wonder, my lord. One lion may, when
      many asses do.
155 WALL: In this same interlude it doth befall
That I, one Snout by name, present a wall;
And such a wall, as I would have you think,
That had in it a crannied hole or chink,
Through which the lovers, Pyramus and Thisby,
160 Did whisper often very secretly.
This loam, this rough-cast, and this stone doth
      show
That I am that same wall; the truth is so.
And this the cranny is, right and sinister,°
Through which the fearful lovers are to whisper.
165 THESEUS: Would you desire lime and hair to speak
      better?
DEMETRIUS: It is the wittiest partition° that ever I
      heard discourse, my lord.

[*Pyramus comes forward.*]

THESEUS: Pyramus draws near the wall. Silence!
PYRAMUS: O grim-look'd° night! O night with hue
170   so black!
O night, which ever art when day is not!
O night, O night! Alack, alack, alack,
I fear my Thisby's promise is forgot.
And thou, O wall, O sweet, O lovely wall,
That stand'st between her father's ground and
175   mine,
Thou wall, O wall, O sweet and lovely wall,
Show me thy chink, to blink through with mine
      eyne!   [*Wall holds up his fingers.*]

Thanks, courteous wall. Jove shield thee well for
      this!
But what see I? No Thisby do I see.
O wicked wall, through whom I see no bliss!   18(
Curs'd be thy stones for thus deceiving me!
THESEUS: The wall, methinks, being sensible,° should
      curse again.
PYRAMUS: No, in truth, sir, he should not. "Deceiving
      me" is Thisby's cue: she is to enter now, and I am   18!
      to spy her through the wall. You shall see, it will
      fall pat as I told you. Yonder she comes.

(*Enter Thisby.*)

THISBY: O wall, full often hast thou heard my
      moans,
For parting my fair Pyramus and me.
My cherry lips have often kiss'd thy stones,   19(
Thy stones with lime and hair knit up in thee.
PYRAMUS: I see a voice. Now will I to the chink,
To spy an° I can hear my Thisby's face.
Thisby!
THISBY: My love! Thou art my love, I think.   19!
PYRAMUS: Think what thou wilt, I am thy lover's
      grace;°
And, like Limander,° am I trusty still.
THISBY: And I like Helen,° till the Fates me kill.
PYRAMUS: Not Shafalus° to Procrus° was so true.
THISBY: As Shafalus to Procrus, I to you.   20(
PYRAMUS: O, kiss me through the hole of this vile
      wall!
THISBY: I kiss the wall's hole, not your lips at all.
PYRAMUS: Wilt thou at Ninny's tomb meet me
      straightway?
THISBY: 'Tide° life, 'tide death, I come without
      delay.
                    [*Exeunt Pyramus and Thisby.*]
WALL: Thus have I, Wall, my part discharged so;   20!
And, being done, thus Wall away doth go. [*Exit.*]
THESEUS: Now is the mural down between the two
      neighbors.
DEMETRIUS: No remedy, my lord, when walls are so
      willful to hear° without warning.°   21(
HIPPOLYTA: This is the silliest stuff that ever I heard.
THESESUS: The best in this kind° are but shadows;°
      and the worst are no worse, if imagination amend
      them.

---

139. **hight:** Is called.   142. **fall:** Let fall.   144. **tall:** Courageous.   147. **broach'd:** Stabbed.   151. **At large:** In full,
at length.   163. **right and sinister:** The right side of it and
the left (sinister); or running from right to left, horizontally.
167. **partition:** (1) Wall, (2) section of a learned treatise or
oration.   170. **grim-look'd:** Grim-looking.

182. **sensible:** Capable of feeling.   193. **an:** If.   196. **lover's
grace:** Gracious lover.   197. **Limander:** Blunder for *Lean-
der.*   198. **Helen:** Blunder for *Hero.*   199. **Shafalus, Procrus:** Blunders for *Cephalus* and *Procris,* also famous lovers.
204. **'Tide:** Betide, come.   210. **to hear:** As to hear.   **without warning:** Without warning the parents.   212. **in this
kind:** Of this sort.   **shadows:** Likenesses, representations.

15 HIPPOLYTA: It must be your imagination then, and not
   theirs.
   THESEUS: If we imagine no worse of them than they
   of themselves, they may pass for excellent men.
   Here come two noble beasts in, a man and a lion.

(Enter Lion and Moonshine.)

20 LION: You, ladies, you, whose gentle hearts do fear
   The smallest monstrous mouse that creeps on
   floor,
   May now perchance both quake and tremble
   here,
   When lion rough in wildest rage doth roar.
   Then know that I, as Snug the joiner, am
25 A lion fell,° nor else no lion's dam;
   For, if I should as lion come in strife
   Into this place, 'twere pity on my life.
   THESEUS: A very gentle beast, and of a good conscience.
   DEMETRIUS: The very best at a beast, my lord, that
30 e'er I saw.
   LYSANDER: This lion is a very fox for his valor.°
   THESEUS: True; and a goose for his discretion.°
   DEMETRIUS: Not so, my lord; for his valor cannot
   carry his discretion; and the fox carries the goose.
35 THESEUS: His discretion, I am sure, cannot carry his
   valor; for the goose carries not the fox. It is well.
   Leave it to his discretion, and let us listen to the
   moon.
   MOON: This lanthorn° doth the horned moon
   present —
40 DEMETRIUS: He should have worn the horns on his
   head.°
   THESEUS: He is no crescent, and his horns are invisible
   within the circumference.
   MOON: This lanthorn doth the horned moon
   present;
45 Myself the man i' th' moon do seem to be.
   THESEUS: This is the greatest error of all the rest. The
   man should be put into the lanthorn. How is it
   else the man i' th' moon?
   DEMETRIUS: He dares not come there for the° candle;
50 for, you see, it is already in snuff.°

---

225. lion fell: Fierce lion (with a play on the idea of *lion
skin*). **231. is . . . valor:** His valor consists of craftiness and
discretion. **232. goose . . . discretion:** As discreet as a goose,
that is, more foolish than discreet. **239. lanthorn:** This
original spelling may suggest a play on the *horn* of which
lanterns were made and also on a cuckold's horns; but the
spelling *lanthorn* is not used consistently for comic effect in
this play or elsewhere. In V, I, 135, for example, the word
is *lantern* in the original. **240–41. on his head:** As a sign
of cuckoldry. **249. for the:** Because of the. **250. in snuff:**
(1) Offended, (2) in need of snuffing.

HIPPOLYTA: I am aweary of this moon. Would he
   would change!
THESEUS: It appears, by his small light of discretion,
   that he is in the wane; but yet, in courtesy, in all
   reason, we must stay the time.   255
LYSANDER: Proceed, Moon.
MOON: All that I have to say is to tell you that the
   lanthorn is the moon, I, the man in the moon, this
   thorn-bush my thorn-bush, and this dog my dog.
DEMETRIUS: Why, all these should be in the lanthorn; 260
   for all these are in the moon. But silence! Here
   comes Thisby.

(Enter Thisby.)

THISBY: This is old Ninny's tomb. Where is my love?
LION [*roaring*]: Oh —   [*Thisby runs off.*]
DEMETRIUS: Well roar'd, Lion.   265
THESEUS: Well run, Thisby.
HIPPOLYTA: Well shone, Moon. Truly, the moon shines
   with a good grace.
      [*The Lion shakes Thisby's mantle, and exit.*]
THESEUS: Well mous'd,° Lion.
DEMETRIUS: And then came Pyramus.   270
LYSANDER: And so the lion vanish'd.

(Enter Pyramus.)

PYRAMUS: Sweet Moon, I thank thee for thy sunny
   beams;
   I thank thee, Moon, for shining now so bright;
   For, by thy gracious, golden, glittering gleams,
   I trust to take of truest Thisby sight.   275
      But stay, O spite!
      But mark, poor knight,
   What dreadful dole° is here!
      Eyes, do you see?
      How can it be?   280
   O dainty duck! O dear!
      Thy mantle good,
      What, stain'd with blood!
   Approach, ye Furies fell!°
      O Fates, come, come,   285
      Cut thread and thrum;°
   Quail,° crush, conclude, and quell!°
THESEUS: This passion, and the death of a dear friend,
   would go near to make a man look sad.°
HIPPOLYTA: Beshrew my heart, but I pity the man.   290
PYRAMUS: O wherefore, Nature, didst thou lions
   frame?

---

269. mous'd: Shaken. **278. dole:** Grievous event. **284.
fell:** Fierce. **286. thread and thrum:** The warp in weaving
and the loose end of the warp. **287. Quail:** Overpower.
quell: Kill, destroy. **288–89. This . . . sad:** If one had other
reason to grieve, one might be sad, but not from this absurd
portrayal of passion.

Since lion vile hath here deflow'r'd my dear,
Which is — no, no — which was the fairest
  dame
That liv'd, that lov'd, that lik'd, that look'd with
  cheer.°
295 Come, tears, confound,
Out, sword, and wound
The pap of Pyramus;
  Ay, that left pap,
  Where heart doth hop.   [*Stabs himself.*]
300 Thus die I, thus, thus, thus.
  Now am I dead,
  Now am I fled;
My soul is in the sky.
Tongue, lose thy light;
305   Moon, take thy flight.   [*Exit Moonshine.*]
Now die, die, die, die, die.   [*Dies.*]
DEMETRIUS: No die, but an ace,° for him; for he is
  but one.°
LYSANDER: Less than an ace, man; for he is dead, he
310 is nothing.
THESEUS: With the help of a surgeon he might yet
  recover, and yet prove an ass.°
HIPPOLYTA: How chance Moonshine is gone before
  Thisby comes back and finds her lover?
315 THESEUS: She will find him by starlight. Here she comes;
  and her passion ends the play.

[*Enter Thisby.*]

HIPPOLYTA: Methinks she should not use a long one
  for such a Pyramus. I hope she will be brief.
DEMETRIUS: A mote will turn the balance, which Pyr-
320 amus, which° Thisby, is the better: he for a man,
  God warr'nt us; she for a woman, God bless us.
LYSANDER: She hath spied him already with those
  sweet eyes.
DEMETRIUS: And thus she means,° videlicet:°
325 THISBY: Asleep, my love?
    What, dead, my dove?
  O Pyramus, arise!
    Speak, speak. Quite dumb?
  Dead, dead? A tomb
330 Must cover thy sweet eyes.
    These lily lips,
    This cherry nose,
  These yellow cowslip cheeks,
    Are gone, are gone!
335 Lovers, make moan.

His eyes were green as leeks.
  O Sisters Three,°
  Come, come to me,
With hands as pale as milk;
  Lay them in gore,   340
  Since you have shore°
With shears his thread of silk.
  Tongue, not a word.
  Come, trusty sword,
Come, blade, my breast imbrue!° [*Stabs herself.*] 345
  And farewell, friends.
  Thus Thisby ends.
Adieu, adieu, adieu.   [*Dies.*]
THESEUS: Moonshine and Lion are left to bury the
  dead.   350
DEMETRIUS: Ay, and Wall too.
BOTTOM [*starting up*]: No, I assure you; the wall is
  down that parted their fathers. Will it please you
  to see the epilogue, or to hear a Bergomask dance°
  between two of our company?   355
THESEUS: No epilogue, I pray you; for your play needs
  no excuse. Never excuse; for when the players are
  all dead, there need none to be blam'd. Marry, if
  he that writ it had play'd Pyramus and hang'd
  himself in Thisby's garter, it would have been a 360
  fine tragedy; and so it is, truly, and very notably
  discharg'd. But, come, your Bergomask. Let your
  epilogue alone.   [*A dance.*]
The iron tongue of midnight hath told° twelve.
Lovers, to bed; 'tis almost fairy time. 365
I fear we shall outsleep the coming morn
As much as we this night have overwatch'd.°
This palpable-gross° play hath well beguil'd
The heavy° gait of night. Sweet friends, to bed.
A fortnight hold we this solemnity, 370
In nightly revels and new jollity.   (*Exeunt.*)

(*Enter Puck*)

PUCK: Now the hungry lion roars,
  And the wolf behowls the moon;
Whilst the heavy ploughman snores,
  All with weary task fordone.° 375
Now the wasted brands° do glow,
  Whilst the screech-owl, screeching loud,
Puts the wretch that lies in woe
  In remembrance of a shroud.
Now it is the time of night 380
  That the graves, all gaping wide,

---

294. **cheer:** Countenance.   307. **ace:** The side of the die
featuring the single pip, or spot. (The pun is on *die* as a
singular of *dice*; Bottom's performance is not worth a whole
die but rather one single face of it, one small portion.)   308.
one: (1) An individual person, (2) unique.   312. **ass:** With
a pun on *ace*.   319–20. **which . . . which:** Whether . . . or.
324. **means:** Moans, laments. **videlicet:** To wit.

337. **Sisters Three:** The Fates.   341. **shore:** Shorn.   345.
imbrue: Stain with blood.   354. **Bergomask dance:** A rustic
dance named for Bergamo, a province in the state of Venice.
364. **told:** Counted, struck ("tolled").   367. **overwatch'd:**
Stayed up too late.   368. **palpable-gross:** obviously crude.
369. **heavy:** Drowsy, dull.   375. **fordone:** Exhausted.   376.
wasted brands: Burned-out logs.

Every one lets forth his sprite,°
  In the churchway paths to glide.
And we fairies, that do run
  By the triple Hecate's° team
From the presence of the sun,
  Following darkness like a dream,
Now are frolic.° Not a mouse
Shall disturb this hallowed house.
I am sent with broom before,
To sweep the dust behind° the door.

*(Enter [Oberon and Titania,] King and Queen of Fairies,
with all their train.)*

OBERON: Through the house give glimmering light,
  By the dead and drowsy fire;
Every elf and fairy sprite
  Hop as light as bird from brier;
And this ditty, after me,
Sing, and dance it trippingly.
TITANIA: First, rehearse your song by rote,
To each word a warbling note.
Hand in hand, with fairy grace,
Will we sing, and bless this place.
                               [Song and dance.]
OBERON: Now, until the break of day,
Through this house each fairy stray.
To the best bride-bed will we,
Which by us shall blessed be;
And the issue there create°
Ever shall be fortunate.
So shall all the couples three
Ever true in loving be;

And the blots of Nature's hand   410
Shall not in their issue stand;
Never mole, hare lip, nor scar,
Nor mark prodigious,° such as are
Despised in nativity,
Shall upon their children be.   415
With this field-dew consecrate,°
Every fairy take his gait,°
And each several° chamber bless,
Through this palace, with sweet peace;
And the owner of it blest   420
Ever shall in safety rest.
Trip away; make no stay;
Meet me all by break of day.
          (Exeunt [Oberon, Titania, and train].)
PUCK: If we shadows have offended,
  Think but this, and all is mended,   425
That you have but slumb'red here°
While these visions did appear.
And this weak and idle theme,
No more yielding but° a dream,
Gentles, do not reprehend.   430
If you pardon, we will mend.
And, as I am an honest Puck,
If we have unearnèd luck
Now to scape the serpent's tongue,°
We will make amends ere long;   435
Else the Puck a liar call.
So, good night unto you all.
Give me your hands,° if we be friends,
And Robin shall restore amends.   *[Exit.]*

382. **Every . . . sprite:** Every grave lets forth its ghost.   385. **triple Hecate's:** Hecate ruled in three capacities: as Luna or Cynthia in heaven, as Diana on earth, and as Proserpina in hell.   388. **frolic:** Merry.   391. **behind:** From behind. (Robin Goodfellow was a household spirit who helped good housemaids and punished lazy ones.)   406. **create:** Created.

413. **prodigious:** Monstrous, unnatural.   416. **consecrate:** Consecrated.   417. **take his gait:** Go his way.   418. **several:** Separate.   426. **That . . . here:** That it is a "midsummer night's dream."   429. **No . . . but:** Yielding no more than.   434. **serpent's tongue:** Hissing.   438. **Give . . . hands:** Applaud.

HAMLET

Hamlet (1600–1601), Shakespeare's boldest, most profound play, is a landmark in the poet's work. It coincides with the new century and the uncertainties of the last years of the old regime, brought to an end by the death of Queen Elizabeth in 1603. Until the very moment of her death, the succession was in doubt, but at her death she indicated that her cousin James of Scotland would take the throne. The new age was in many ways more complicated, more ambiguous, and more democratic than the old. It was also more dangerous.

Almost like a voyager returning to England after the death of Elizabeth, Hamlet returns to a Denmark and a court that he hardly recognizes, to a mother newly wed to his uncle and in many ways not the woman he remembers, and, finally, to a ghostly father who will not rest until the crimes against him are avenged. Like Marlowe's Faustus, Hamlet was a scholar at the University of Wittenberg, where he presumably had studied theology and therefore had a special knowledge of the world of the spirits. Perhaps he studied medicine and law as well. He gives evidence of knowing literature and having a taste for theater, just as he gives evidence of being physically ready with weapons when necessary.

Hamlet is also a melancholic. To the Elizabethan, *melancholic* did not mean depressed, although Hamlet dresses in black and still mourns for his father, even against the wishes of his uncle. The melancholic, rather, was introspective, thoughtful, perhaps world-weary, and possibly a touch sardonic. Above all things, he was an intellectual, a person of wide-ranging knowledge and intelligence, a reliable commentator with a probing mind.

Hamlet's broad intelligence and the penetrating introspection revealed in his soliloquies, such as his famous "To be, or not to be" meditation on suicide, make him a character with more psychological dimension, more "soul," than many people we know in life. In this sense the play is thoroughly modern; it satisfies our modern need to know the interior lives of characters who engage us onstage. Hamlet's range of feeling, his range of felt and expressed emotion, is impressive to any audience.

Hamlet is a revenge tragedy, a type of play that was especially appealing to the Elizabethans. Thomas Kyd's *The Spanish Tragedy* and John Marston's *Antonio's Revenge* were other very successful Elizabethan revenge tragedies. Shakespeare had written one earlier play that could be termed a revenge tragedy, *Titus Andronicus*, in 1594. Some characteristics of the revenge tragedy are the following:

The revenge of a relative's murder or rape

The revenge of a father by a son or vice versa

The appearance of a ghost

The hesitation or delay of the hero

The use of real or pretended insanity

Suicide

Political intrigue in a court

An able, scheming villain or spy

Philosophical soliloquies

Sensational use of horror (murder and gore onstage)

All these elements are present in *Hamlet*. But the play has other important qualities as well. The minor characters are developed in unexpected ways. Ophelia, the innocent, loving woman, becomes a touching figure in her own right when, unable to understand the nature of evil in the Danish court and driven to insanity by Hamlet's rejection of her and by her father's murder, she permits herself to sink to a watery death in a stream. Audiences are moved by her songs, her insane ramblings, and her devotion to her father as well as to Hamlet.

Characters such as Gertrude, Hamlet's mother, reveal a richness of psychology that sometimes startles us. Polonius, Ophelia's father, is virtually a stock character — the old, foolish philosopher — but he takes on special significance when he urges Ophelia to spy for him and when he ultimately dies at the hand of Hamlet. As Hamlet says, it was an unnecessary death for a "wretched, rash, intruding fool." But his son Laertes loved Polonius, and when he returns grief-stricken, with the support of the people, he, unlike Hamlet, is not about to hesitate a moment to get his revenge.

Hamlet's hesitation is linked with his reputation as a melancholic. Because he thinks things through so deeply, he does not act instantly, as does Laertes. Even when the ghost reveals himself as his father and tells him that he has been murdered and must be avenged, Hamlet fears that the apparition might be a dangerous fakery of the devil to lure him to murder.

Hamlet shows he can act swiftly — indeed, rashly. His killing of Polonius is a rash act. He thinks the man behind the tapestry is his uncle, since they are in his mother's bedroom and no other man but her husband has any right to be there. When Hamlet is sent to England with Rosencrantz and Guildenstern he quickly senses a plot, undoes it, leaps aboard a pirate ship, and negotiates his way home with alacrity. This is not the work of a man who cannot act. In the graveyard scene he acts just as impulsively as Laertes in leaping into Ophelia's grave.

Hamlet's talents exhibited in his welcoming of the players in act II show him to be an experienced theatergoer, one with some skills onstage. He is also a skilled writer, since his additions to *The Murder of Gonzago* convert that imaginary play into a "mousetrap" baited to catch the murderer of his father. In early Renaissance paintings, the mousetrap is a symbol for Jesus Christ, who catches the devil. The allusion would not have been lost on the Elizabethan audience, who would have seen Hamlet's psychological approach as being quite reasonable.

Emotions are of great importance to Hamlet. He feels deeply and he watches others to see what their feelings are. He knows that their demeanor may not reveal them as they are, so he must be a careful student of behavior. As he tells his mother, "I know not 'seems.'" What seems is only what is apparent; his procedure is always to penetrate the surfaces of things to know their reality, which is why he uses drama as an instrument to penetrate psychological surfaces.

A connection between Seneca's tragedies and the Elizabethan revenge tragedy has prompted some Shakespeare scholars to declare that Elizabethan tragedy is all Senecan in nature. What they mean is that Seneca's preference for magic and ghosts as well as his penchant for onstage gore and murder translated well to the Elizabethan stage. Seneca has Iokaste kill herself onstage by ripping open her abdomen, for instance, and many such bloody scenes were enacted on the Elizabethan stage. Perhaps, however, the best remnant of Seneca in Elizabethan drama is the rhetorical, almost bombastic speeches of the player in act II, scene II. The lengthy nature of such speeches and their invitation to share a tragic emotion are much in the Senecan mold.

Hamlet in Performance

Richard Burbage played Hamlet in its original 1604 production and continued playing the part into advanced age. *Hamlet* was staged on an English ship off the coast of Africa in 1607. The first American production was in 1759. When one thinks of productions of the play, one thinks of the great actors who played the role. Their names read like a "Who's Who" of acting: David Garrick (1717–1779), Edmund Kean (1789–1833), William Charles Macready (1793–1873), and Sir Henry Irving (1838–1905) were all identified with the role.

In the twentieth century, the two most dominating Hamlets have been John Gielgud and Laurence Olivier, who both acted for the Old Vic Theatre. To interpret the part, Olivier studied psychoanalyst Ernest Jones's essay on Hamlet's Oedipus complex. Jones was a disciple of Freud, who discussed Hamlet in his *Interpretation of Dreams* (see Commentary on p. 366). Paul Scofield, in Peter Brook's 1955 production, found the part so challenging that he said playing it "feels like trespassing." Christopher Plummer, Derek Jacobi, and Jonathan Pryce have played the part to acclaim from the 1950s to recent times. Richard Burton also played Hamlet in New York in 1964. Michael Pennington's version for the Royal Shakespeare Company's 1980 production (see photos on pages 288–89) was well received by both critics and audiences. Pennington felt that the part tested not only one's skill but one's character. He said, "When things go well you could do three performances a day and still be the last to leave the party, and at other times the part shakes you like a rat."

The major productions in the 1980s alone were astonishingly numerous: Christopher Walken for the American Shakespeare Festival in Stratford, Connecticut (1982); Roger Rees for the Royal Shakespeare Company in Stratford, England (1984); Kevin Kline for the New York Shakespeare Festival (1986); Ingmar Bergman's acclaimed production in Swedish (1988) in Sweden and New York; Daniel Day-Lewis for the National Theatre in London (1989); Austin Pendleton for the Riverside Shakespeare Company in New York (1989). There is no end in sight.

Hamlet has been the dream role not only of great actors but of great actresses as well. Sarah Bernhardt played Hamlet in the late nineteenth century, and Eva Le Gallienne, Siobhan McKenna, and Judith Anderson took on the part in the twentieth century. *Hamlet* has also given rise to numerous spin-offs, the best of which is Tom Stoppard's *Rosencrantz and Guildenstern Are Dead* (1967). Lee Blessing's *Fortinbras* (1991) is also an innovative retelling of the play from the point of view of a minor character — except this character becomes the king. Blessing's success suggests that *Hamlet* is rich enough and inspiring enough to generate numerous further redactions and interpretations.

William Shakespeare (1564–1616)

HAMLET, PRINCE OF DENMARK   *c. 1600*

[Dramatis Personae

CLAUDIUS, *King of Denmark*
HAMLET, *son to the late King Hamlet, and nephew to the present King*
POLONIUS, *Lord Chamberlain*
HORATIO, *friend to Hamlet*
LAERTES, *son to Polonius*
VOLTIMAND,
CORNELIUS,
ROSENCRANTZ,   } *courtiers*
GUILDENSTERN,
OSRIC,
GENTLEMAN,
PRIEST, OR DOCTOR OF DIVINITY
MARCELLUS, } *officers*
BERNARDO,
FRANCISCO, *a soldier*
REYNALDO, *servant to Polonius*
PLAYERS
TWO CLOWNS, *grave-diggers*
FORTINBRAS, *Prince of Norway*
CAPTAIN
ENGLISH AMBASSADORS

GERTRUDE, *Queen of Denmark, mother to Hamlet*
OPHELIA, *daughter to Polonius*

LORDS, LADIES, OFFICERS, SOLDIERS, SAILORS, MESSENGERS, AND OTHER ATTENDANTS
GHOST *of Hamlet's father*

Scene: *Denmark.*]

[ACT I • Scene I]°

(*Enter Bernardo and Francisco, two sentinels, [meeting].*)

BERNARDO: Who's there?
FRANCISCO: Nay, answer me.° Stand and unfold yourself.
BERNARDO: Long live the King!
FRANCISCO: Bernardo?
BERNARDO: He.   5
FRANCISCO: You come most carefully upon your hour.
BERNARDO: 'Tis now struck twelve. Get thee to bed, Francisco.
FRANCISCO: For this relief much thanks. 'Tis bitter cold,
    And I am sick at heart.
BERNARDO: Have you had quiet guard?
FRANCISCO: Not a mouse stirring.   10
BERNARDO: Well, good night.
    If you do meet Horatio and Marcellus,
    The rivals° of my watch, bid them make haste.

(*Enter Horatio and Marcellus.*)

Note: The text of *Hamlet* has come down to us in different versions — such as the first quarto, the second quarto, and the first Folio. The copy of the text used here is largely drawn from the second quarto. Passages enclosed in square brackets are taken from one of the other versions, in most cases the first Folio.   **I, I. Location:** Elsinore castle. A guard platform.   **2. me:** Francisco emphasizes that *he* is the sentry currently on watch.   **13. rivals:** Partners.

FRANCISCO: I think I hear them. Stand, ho! Who is
  there?
HORATIO: Friends to this ground.
15 MARCELLUS: And liegemen to the Dane.°
FRANCISCO: Give you° good night.
MARCELLUS: O, farewell, honest soldier.
  Who hath relieved you?
FRANCISCO: Bernardo hath my place.
  Give you good night. (*Exit Francisco.*)
MARCELLUS: Holla, Bernardo!
BERNARDO: Say,
  What, is Horatio there?
HORATIO: A piece of him.
BERNARDO: Welcome, Horatio. Welcome, good
20 Marcellus.
HORATIO: What, has this thing appear'd again
  tonight?
BERNARDO: I have seen nothing.
MARCELLUS: Horatio says 'tis but our fantasy,
  And will not let belief take hold of him
25 Touching this dreaded sight, twice seen of us.
  Therefore I have entreated him along
  With us to watch the minutes of this night,
  That if again this apparition come
  He may approve° our eyes and speak to it.
HORATIO: Tush, tush, 'twill not appear.
30 BERNARDO: Sit down awhile,
  And let us once again assail your ears,
  That are so fortified against our story,
  What we have two nights seen.
HORATIO: Well, sit we down,
  And let us hear Bernardo speak of this.
35 BERNARDO: Last night of all,
  When yond same star that's westward from the
    pole°
  Had made his° course t' illume that part of
    heaven
  Where now it burns, Marcellus and myself,
  The bell then beating one —

(*Enter Ghost.*)

MARCELLUS: Peace, break thee off! Look where it
40 comes again!
BERNARDO: In the same figure, like the King that's
  dead.
MARCELLUS: Thou art a scholar.° Speak to it,
  Horatio.
BERNARDO: Looks 'a° not like the King? Mark it,
  Horatio.

HORATIO: Most like. It harrows me with fear and
  wonder.
BERNARDO: It would be spoke to.
MARCELLUS: Speak to it,° Horatio. 45
HORATIO: What art thou that usurp'st this time of
  night,
  Together with that fair and warlike form
  In which the majesty of buried Denmark°
  Did sometimes° march? By heaven I charge thee
    speak!
MARCELLUS: It is offended.
BERNARDO: See, it stalks away. 50
HORATIO: Stay! Speak, speak. I charge thee, speak.
  (*Exit Ghost.*)
MARCELLUS: 'Tis gone, and will not answer.
BERNARDO: How now, Horatio? You tremble and
  look pale.
  Is not this something more than fantasy?
  What think you on 't? 55
HORATIO: Before my God, I might not this believe
  Without the sensible° and true avouch
  Of mine own eyes.
MARCELLUS: Is it not like the King?
HORATIO: As thou art to thyself.
  Such was the very armor he had on 60
  When he the ambitious Norway° combated.
  So frown'd he once when, in an angry parle,°
  He smote the sledded° Polacks° on the ice.
  'Tis strange.
MARCELLUS: Thus twice before, and jump° at this
  dead hour, 65
  With martial stalk hath he gone by our watch.
HORATIO: In what particular thought to work I
  know not,
  But, in the gross and scope° of mine opinion,
  This bodes some strange eruption to our state.
MARCELLUS: Good now,° sit down, and tell me, he
  that knows, 70
  Why this same strict and most observant watch
  So nightly toils° the subject° of the land,
  And why such daily cast° of brazen cannon,
  And foreign mart° for implements of war,
  Why such impress° of shipwrights, whose sore
    task 75

---

15. **liegemen to the Dane:** Men sworn to serve the Danish
king. 16. **Give you:** God give you. 29. **approve:** Cor-
roborate. 36. **pole:** Polestar. 37. **his:** Its. 42. **scholar:**
One learned in Latin and able to address spirits. 43. **'a:**
He.

45. **It . . . it:** A ghost could not speak until spoken to. 48.
buried Denmark: The buried king of Denmark. 49. **some-**
times: Formerly. 57. **sensible:** Confirmed by the senses.
61. **Norway:** King of Norway. 62. **parle:** Parley. 63.
sledded: Traveling on sleds. **Polacks:** Poles. 65. **jump:**
Exactly. 68. **gross and scope:** General view. 70. **Good**
now: An expression denoting entreaty or expostulation. 72.
toils: Causes to toil. **subject:** Subjects. 73. **cast:** Casting.
74. **mart:** Buying and selling. 75. **impress:** Impressment,
conscription.

Does not divide the Sunday from the week.
What might be toward,° that this sweaty haste
Doth make the night joint-laborer with the day?
Who is 't that can inform me?
HORATIO: That can I,
80 At least, the whisper goes so. Our last king,
Whose image even but now appear'd to us,
Was, as you know, by Fortinbras of Norway,
Thereto prick'd on° by a most emulate° pride,
Dar'd to the combat; in which our valiant
        Hamlet —
85 For so this side of our known world esteem'd
        him —
Did slay this Fortinbras; who, by a seal'd
        compact,
Well ratified by law and heraldry,
Did forfeit, with his life, all those his lands
Which he stood seiz'd° of, to the conqueror;
90 Against the° which a moi'ty competent°
Was gaged° by our king, which had return'd
To the inheritance of Fortinbras
Had he been vanquisher, as, by the same
        comart°
And carriage° of the article design'd,
95 His fell to Hamlet. Now, sir, young Fortinbras,
Of unimproved° mettle hot and full,
Hath in the skirts° of Norway here and there
Shark'd up° a list of lawless resolutes°
For food and diet° to some enterprise
00 That hath a stomach° in 't, which is no other —
As it doth well appear unto our state —
But to recover of us, by strong hand
And terms compulsatory, those foresaid lands
So by his father lost. And this, I take it,
05 Is the main motive of our preparations,
The source of this our watch, and the chief
        head°
Of this post-haste and romage° in the land.
BERNARDO: I think it be no other but e'en so.
Well may it sort° that this portentous figure
Comes armed through our watch so like the
        King
10 That was and is the question of these wars.

HORATIO: A mote° it is to trouble the mind's eye.
In the most high and palmy° state of Rome,
A little ere the mightiest Julius fell,
The graves stood tenantless and the sheeted°
        dead   115
Did squeak and gibber in the Roman streets;
As° stars with trains of fire and dews of blood,
Disasters° in the sun; and the moist star°
Upon whose influence Neptune's° empire stands°
Was sick almost to doomsday° with eclipse.   120
And even the like precurse° of fear'd events,
As harbingers° preceding still° the fates
And prologue to the omen° coming on,
Have heaven and earth together demonstrated
Unto our climatures° and countrymen.   125

(*Enter Ghost.*)

But soft, behold! Lo where it comes again!
I'll cross° it, though it blast me. Stay, illusion!
If thou hast any sound, or use of voice,
Speak to me!   (*It spreads his arms.*)
If there be any good thing to be done   130
That may to thee do ease and grace to me,
Speak to me!
If thou art privy to thy country's fate,
Which, happily,° foreknowing may avoid,
O, speak!   135
Or if thou hast uphoarded in thy life
Extorted treasure in the womb of earth,
For which, they say, you spirits oft walk in
        death,
                          (*The cock crows.*)
Speak of it. Stay, and speak! Stop it, Marcellus.
MARCELLUS: Shall I strike at it with my partisan?° 140
HORATIO: Do, if it will not stand. [*They strike at
        it.*]
BERNARDO: 'Tis here!
HORATIO: 'Tis here!
MARCELLUS: 'Tis gone.   [*Exit Ghost.*]
We do it wrong, being so majestical,
To offer it the show of violence;
For it is, as the air, invulnerable,   145
And our vain blows malicious mockery.

77. **toward:** in preparation.   83. **prick'd on:** incited.   **emulate:** Ambitious.   89. **seiz'd:** Possessed.   90. **Against the:**
In return for.   **moi'ty competent:** Sufficient portion.   91.
gaged: Engaged, pledged.   93. **comart:** Joint bargain (?).
94. **carriage:** Import, bearing.   96. **unimproved:** Not turned
to account (?) or untested (?).   97. **skirts:** Outlying regions,
outskirts.   98. **Shark'd up:** Got together in haphazard fashion.   **resolutes:** desperadoes.   99. **food and diet:** No pay
but their keep.   100. **stomach:** Relish of danger.   106.
head: Source.   107. **romage:** Bustle, commotion.   109.
sort: Suit.

112. **mote:** Speck of dust.   113. **palmy:** Flourishing.   115.
sheeted: Shrouded.   117. **As:** This abrupt transition suggests
that matter is possibly omitted between lines 116 and 117.
118. **Disasters:** Unfavorable signs of aspects.   **moist star:**
Moon, governing tides.   119. **Neptune:** God of the sea.
stands: Depends.   120. **sick . . . doomsday:** See Matt. 24:29
and Rev. 6:12.   121. **precurse:** Heralding, foreshadowing.
122. **harbingers:** Forerunners.   **still:** Continually.   123.
omen: Calamitous event.   125. **climatures:** Regions.   127.
cross: Meet, face directly.   134. **happily:** Haply, perchance.
140. **partisan:** Long-handled spear.

BERNARDO: It was about to speak when the cock
  crew.
HORATIO: And then it started like a guilty thing
  Upon a fearful summons. I have heard,
150 The cock, that is the trumpet to the morn,
  Doth with his lofty and shrill-sounding throat
  Awake the god of day, and, at his warning,
  Whether in sea or fire, in earth or air,
  Th' extravagant and erring° spirit hies
155 To his confine; and of the truth herein
  This present object made probation.°
MARCELLUS: It faded on the crowing of the cock.
  Some say that ever 'gainst° that season comes
  Wherein our Savior's birth is celebrated,
160 The bird of dawning singeth all night long,
  And then, they say, no spirit dare stir abroad;
  The nights are wholesome, then no planets
    strike,°
  No fairy takes,° nor witch hath power to charm,
  So hallowed and so gracious° is that time.
165 HORATIO: So have I heard and do in part believe it.
  But, look, the morn, in russet mantle clad,
  Walks o'er the dew of yon high eastward hill.
  Break we our watch up, and by my advice
  Let us impart what we have seen tonight
170 Unto young Hamlet; for, upon my life,
  This spirit, dumb to us, will speak to him.
  Do you consent we shall acquaint him with it,
  As needful in our loves, fitting our duty?
MARCELLUS: Let's do 't, I pray, and I this morning
    know
175 Where we shall find him most conveniently.
                            (*Exeunt.*)°

[*Scene II*]°

(*Flourish. Enter Claudius, King of Denmark, Gertrude
the Queen, Councilors, Polonius and his son Laertes,
Hamlet, cum aliis*° [*including Voltimand and Cornelius*].)

KING: Though yet of Hamlet our dear brother's
    death
  The memory be green, and that it us befitted
  To bear our hearts in grief and our whole
    kingdom
  To be contracted in one brow of woe,
5 Yet so far hath discretion fought with nature

That we with wisest sorrow think on him,
Together with remembrance of ourselves.
Therefore our sometime sister, now our queen,
Th' imperial jointress° to this warlike state,
Have we, as 'twere with a defeated joy —   10
With an auspicious and a dropping eye,
With mirth in funeral and with dirge in
  marriage,
In equal scale weighing delight and dole —
Taken to wife. Nor have we herein barr'd
Your better wisdoms, which have freely gone   15
With this affair along. For all, our thanks.
Now follows that you know° young Fortinbras,
Holding a weak supposal° of our worth,
Or thinking by our late dear brother's death
Our state to be disjoint and out of frame,   20
Colleagued with° this dream of his advantage,°
He hath not fail'd to pester us with message
Importing° the surrender of those lands
Lost by his father, with all bands° of law,
To our most valiant brother. So much for him.   25
Now for ourself and for this time of meeting.
Thus much the business is: we have here writ
To Norway, uncle of young Fortinbras —
Who, impotent and bed-rid, scarcely hears
Of this his nephew's purpose — to suppress   30
His° further gait° herein, in that the levies,
The lists, and full proportions are all made
Out of his subject;° and we here dispatch
You, good Cornelius, and you, Voltimand,
For bearers of this greeting to old Norway,   35
Giving to you no further personal power
To business with the King, more than the scope
Of these delated° articles allow. [*Gives a paper.*]
Farewell, and let your haste commend your duty.
CORNELIUS, VOLTIMAND: In that, and all things,
  will we show our duty.   40
KING: We doubt it nothing. Heartily farewell.
          [*Exit Voltimand and Cornelius.*]
And now, Laertes, what's the news with you?
You told us of some suit; what is 't, Laertes?
You cannot speak of reason to the Dane°
And lose your voice.° What wouldst thou beg,
  Laertes,   45

---

154. **extravagant and erring:** Wandering. (The words have
similar meaning.) 156. **probation:** Proof. 158. **'gainst:**
Just before. 162. **strike:** Exert evil influence. 163. **takes:**
Bewitches. 164. **gracious:** Full of goodness. 175. [S.D.]
Exeunt: Latin for "they go out." **I, II. Location:** The castle.
[S.D.] *cum aliis:* With others.

9. **jointress:** Woman possessed of a joint tenancy of an estate.
17. **know:** Be informed (that). 18. **weak supposal:** Low
estimate. 21. **Colleagued with:** Joined to, allied with.
dream . . . advantage: Illusory hope of success. 23. **Importing:** Pertaining to. 24. **bands:** Contracts. 31. **His:**
Fortinbras's. **gait:** Proceeding. 31–33. **in that . . . subject:**
Since the levying of troops and supplies is drawn entirely
from the King of Norway's own subjects. 38. **delated:**
Detailed. (Variant of *dilated.*) 44. **the Dane:** The Danish
King. 45. **lose your voice:** Waste your speech.

That shall not be my offer, not thy asking?
The head is not more native° to the heart,
The hand more instrumental° to the mouth,
Than is the throne of Denmark to thy father.
What wouldst thou have, Laertes?

50 LAERTES: My dread lord,
Your leave and favor to return to France,
From whence though willingly I came to Denmark
To show my duty in your coronation,
Yet now I must confess, that duty done,
55 My thoughts and wishes bend again toward France
And bow them to your gracious leave and pardon.°

KING: Have you your father's leave? What says Polonius?

POLONIUS: H'ath, my lord, wrung from me my slow leave
By laborsome petition, and at last
60 Upon his will I seal'd my hard° consent.
I do beseech you, give him leave to go.

KING: Take thy fair hour, Laertes. Time be thine,
And thy best graces spend it at thy will!
But now, my cousin° Hamlet, and my son —

HAMLET: A little more than kin, and less than kind.°
65

KING: How is it that the clouds still hang on you?

HAMLET: Not so, my lord. I am too much in the sun.°

QUEEN: Good Hamlet, cast thy nighted color off,
And let thine eye look like a friend on Denmark.
70 Do not forever with thy vailed° lids
Seek for thy noble father in the dust.
Thou know'st 'tis common,° all that lives must die,
Passing through nature to eternity.

HAMLET: Ay, madam, it is common.

QUEEN: If it be,
75 Why seems it so particular with thee?

HAMLET: Seems, madam! Nay, it is. I know not "seems."
'Tis not alone my inky cloak, good mother,
Nor customary suits of solemn black,

Nor windy suspiration of forc'd breath,
No, nor the fruitful° river in the eye,   80
Nor the dejected havior of the visage,
Together with all forms, moods, shapes of grief,
That can denote me truly. These indeed seem,
For they are actions that a man might play.
But I have that within which passes show;   85
These but the trappings and the suits of woe.

KING: 'Tis sweet and commendable in your nature, Hamlet,
To give these mourning duties to your father.
But you must know your father lost a father,
That father lost, lost his, and the survivor bound 90
In filial obligation for some term
To do obsequious° sorrow. But to persever°
In obstinate condolement° is a course
Of impious stubbornness. 'Tis unmanly grief.
It shows a will most incorrect to heaven,   95
A heart unfortified, a mind impatient,
An understanding simple and unschool'd.
For what we know must be and is as common
As any the most vulgar thing to sense,°
Why should we in our peevish opposition   100
Take it to heart? Fie, 'tis a fault to heaven,
A fault against the dead, a fault to nature,
To reason most absurd, whose common theme
Is death of fathers, and who still hath cried,
From the first corse° till he that died today, 105
"This must be so." We pray you, throw to earth
This unprevailing° woe, and think of us
As of a father; for let the world take note,
You are the most immediate° to our throne,
And with no less nobility of love   110
Than that which dearest father bears his son
Do I impart toward you. For your intent
In going back to school in Wittenberg,°
It is most retrograde° to our desire,
And we beseech you, bend you° to remain   115
Here in the cheer and comfort of our eye,
Our chiefest courtier, cousin, and our son.

QUEEN: Let not thy mother lose her prayers, Hamlet.
I pray thee stay with us, go not to Wittenberg.

HAMLET: I shall in all my best obey you, madam.   120

KING: Why, 'tis a loving and a fair reply.
Be as ourself in Denmark. Madam, come.
This gentle and unforc'd accord of Hamlet

---

47. **native:** Closely connected, related. 48. **instrumental:** Serviceable. 56. **leave and pardon:** Permission to depart. 60. **hard:** Reluctant. 64. **cousin:** Any kin not of the immediate family. 65. **A little . . . kind:** Closer than an ordinary nephew (since I am stepson), and yet more separated in natural feeling (with pun on *kind*, meaning affectionate and natural, lawful. This line is often read as an aside, but it need not be.) 67. **sun:** The sunshine of the King's royal favor (with pun on *son*). 70. **vailed:** Downcast. 72. **common:** Of universal occurrence. (But Hamlet plays on the sense of *vulgar* in line 74.)

80. **fruitful:** Abundant. 92. **obsequious:** Suited to obsequies or funerals. **persever:** Persevere. 93. **condolement:** Sorrowing. 99. **As . . . sense:** As the most ordinary experience. 105. **corse:** Corpse. 107. **unprevailing:** Unavailing. 109. **most immediate:** Next in succession. 113. **Wittenberg:** Famous German university founded in 1502. 114. **retrograde:** Contrary. 115. **bend you:** Incline yourself.

Sits smiling to my heart, in grace whereof
125 No jocund° health that Denmark drinks today
But the great cannon to the clouds shall tell,
And the King's rouse° the heaven shall bruit
again,°
Respeaking earthly thunder.° Come away.
(Flourish. Exeunt all but Hamlet.)
HAMLET: O, that this too too sullied° flesh would
melt,
130 Thaw, and resolve itself into a dew!
Or that the Everlasting had not fix'd
His canon° 'gainst self-slaughter! O God, God,
How weary, stale, flat, and unprofitable
Seem to me all the uses of this world!
135 Fie on 't, ah, fie! 'Tis an unweeded garden
That grows to seed. Things rank and gross in
nature
Possess it merely.° That it should come to this!
But two months dead — nay, not so much, not
two.
So excellent a king, that was to° this
140 Hyperion° to a satyr; so loving to my mother
That he might not beteem° the winds of heaven
Visit her face too roughly. Heaven and earth,
Must I remember? Why, she would hang on him
As if increase of appetite had grown
145 By what it fed on, and yet, within a month —
Let me not think on 't. Frailty, thy name is
woman! —
A little month, or ere those shoes were old
With which she followed my poor father's body,
Like Niobe,° all tears, why she, even she —
150 O God, a beast, that wants discourse of reason,°
Would have mourn'd longer — married with my
uncle,
My father's brother, but no more like my father
Than I to Hercules. Within a month,
Ere yet the salt of most unrighteous tears
155 Had left the flushing in her galled° eyes,
She married. O, most wicked speed, to post

With such dexterity to incestuous° sheets!
It is not nor it cannot come to good.
But break, my heart, for I must hold my tongue.

(Enter Horatio, Marcellus, and Bernardo.)

HORATIO: Hail to your lordship!
HAMLET: I am glad to see you well. 16
Horatio! — or I do forget myself.
HORATIO: The same, my lord, and your poor
servant ever.
HAMLET: Sir, my good friend; I'll change° that
name with you.
And what make° you from Wittenberg, Horatio?
Marcellus?   16
MARCELLUS: My good lord.
HAMLET: I am very glad to see you. [*To Bernardo.*]
Good even, sir. —
But what, in faith, make you from Wittenberg?
HORATIO: A truant disposition, good my lord.
HAMLET: I would not hear your enemy say so,   17
Nor shall you do my ear that violence
To make it truster of your own report
Against yourself. I know you are no truant.
But what is your affair in Elsinore?
We'll teach you to drink deep ere you depart.   17
HORATIO: My lord, I came to see your father's
funeral.
HAMLET: I prithee do not mock me, fellow student;
I think it was to see my mother's wedding.
HORATIO: Indeed, my lord, it followed hard° upon.
HAMLET: Thrift, thrift, Horatio! The funeral bak'd
meats   18
Did coldly furnish forth the marriage tables.
Would I had met my dearest° foe in heaven
Or° ever I had seen that day, Horatio!
My father! — Methinks I see my father.
HORATIO: Where, my lord?
HAMLET: In my mind's eye, Horatio. 18
HORATIO: I saw him once. 'A° was a goodly king.
HAMLET: 'A was a man, take him for all in all,
I shall not look upon his like again.
HORATIO: My lord, I think I saw him yesternight.
HAMLET: Saw? Who?   19
HORATIO: My lord, the King your father.
HAMLET: The King my father?
HORATIO: Season your admiration° for a while

125. **jocund:** Merry.   127. **rouse:** Draft of liquor.   **bruit again:** Loudly echo.   128. **thunder:** Of trumpet and kettledrum, sounded when the King drinks; see I, IV, 8–12. 129. **sullied:** Defiled. (The early quartos read *sallied*, the Folio *solid*.)   132. **canon:** Law.   137. **merely:** Completely.   139. **to:** In comparison to.   140. **Hyperion:** Titan sun-god, father of Helios.   141. **beteem:** Allow.   149. **Niobe:** Tantalus's daughter, Queen of Thebes, who boasted that she had more sons and daughters than Leto; for this, Apollo and Artemis, children of Leto, slew her fourteen children. She was turned by Zeus into a stone which continually dropped tears.   150. **wants . . . reason:** Lacks the faculty of reason.   155. **galled:** Irritated, inflamed.

157. **incestuous:** In Shakespeare's day, the marriage of a man like Claudius to his deceased brother's wife was considered incestuous.   163. **change:** Exchange (i.e., the name of friend).   164. **make:** Do.   179. **hard:** Close.   182. **dearest:** Direst.   183. **or:** Ere, before.   186. **'A:** he.   192. **Season your admiration:** Restrain your astonishment.

With an attent° ear, till I may deliver,
Upon the witness of these gentlemen,
This marvel to you.
95   HAMLET: For God's love, let me hear!
HORATIO: Two nights together had these gentlemen,
Marcellus and Bernardo, on their watch,
In the dead waste and middle of the night,
Been thus encount'red. A figure like your father,
00   Armed at point° exactly, cap-a-pe,°
Appears before them, and with solemn march
Goes slow and stately by them. Thrice he walk'd
By their oppress'd and fear-surprised eyes
Within his truncheon's° length, whilst they,
distill'd
05   Almost to jelly with the act° of fear,
Stand dumb and speak not to him. This to me
In dreadful secrecy impart they did,
And I with them the third night kept the watch,
Where, as they had delivered, both in time,
Form of the thing, each word made true and
10   good,
The apparition comes. I knew your father;
These hands are not more like.
HAMLET: But where was this?
MARCELLUS: My lord, upon the platform where we
watch.
HAMLET: Did you not speak to it?
HORATIO: My lord, I did,
15   But answer made it none. Yet once methought
It lifted up it° head and did address
Itself to motion, like as it would speak;
But even then the morning cock crew loud,
And at the sound it shrunk in haste away,
20   And vanish'd from our sight.
HAMLET: 'Tis very strange.
HORATIO: As I do live, my honor'd lord, 'tis true,
And we did think it writ down in our duty
To let you know of it.
HAMLET: Indeed, indeed, sirs. But this troubles me.
Hold you the watch tonight?
25   ALL: We do, my lord.
HAMLET: Arm'd, say you?
ALL: Arm'd, my lord.
HAMLET: From top to toe?
ALL: My lord, from head to foot.
HAMLET: Then saw you not his face?
30   HORATIO: O, yes, my lord. He wore his beaver° up.
HAMLET: What, looked he frowningly?

HORATIO: A countenance more
In sorrow than in anger.
HAMLET: Pale or red?
HORATIO: Nay, very pale.
HAMLET: And fix'd his eyes upon you?
HORATIO: Most constantly.
HAMLET: I would I had been there.
HORATIO: It would have much amaz'd you.   235
HAMLET: Very like, very like. Stay'd it long?
HORATIO: While one with moderate haste might
tell° a hundred.
MARCELLUS, BERNARDO: Longer, longer.
HORATIO: Not when I saw 't.
HAMLET: His beard was grizzl'd, — no?
HORATIO: It was, as I have seen it in his life,   240
A sable silver'd.°
HAMLET: I will watch tonight.
Perchance 'twill walk again.
HORATIO: I warr'nt it will.
HAMLET: If it assume my noble father's person,
I'll speak to it, though hell itself should gape
And bid me hold my peace. I pray you all,   245
If you have hitherto conceal'd this sight,
Let it be tenable° in your silence still,
And whatsomever else shall hap tonight,
Give it an understanding, but no tongue.
I will requite your loves. So, fare you well.   250
Upon the platform, 'twixt eleven and twelve,
I'll visit you.
ALL: Our duty to your honor.
HAMLET: Your loves, as mine to you. Farewell.
                    (*Exeunt [all but Hamlet].*)
My father's spirit in arms! All is not well.
I doubt° some foul play. Would the night were
come!   255
Till then sit still, my soul. Foul deeds will rise,
Though all the earth o'erwhelm them, to men's
eyes.
                                        (*Exit.*)

[*Scene III*]°

(*Enter Laertes and Ophelia, his sister.*)

LAERTES: My necessaries are embark'd. Farewell.
And, sister, as the winds give benefit
And convoy is assistant,° do not sleep
But let me hear from you.
OPHELIA: Do you doubt that?
LAERTES: For Hamlet, and the trifling of his favor,   5

---

193. **attent:** Attentive. 200. **at point:** Completely. **cap-a-pe:** From head to foot. 204. **truncheon:** Officer's staff. 205. **act:** Action, operation. 216. **it:** Its. 230. **beaver:** Visor on the helmet.

237. **tell:** Count. 241. **sable silver'd:** Black mixed with white. 247. **tenable:** Held tightly. 255. **doubt:** Suspect. I, III. **Location:** Polonius's chambers. 3. **convoy is assistant:** Means of conveyance are available.

Hold it a fashion and a toy in blood,°
A violet in the youth of primy° nature,
Forward,° not permanent, sweet, not lasting,
The perfume and suppliance° of a minute —
No more.
OPHELIA: No more but so?
10 LAERTES: Think it no more.
For nature crescent° does not grow alone
In thews° and bulk, but, as this temple° waxes,
The inward service of the mind and soul
Grows wide withal.° Perhaps he loves you now,
15 And now no soil° nor cautel° doth besmirch
The virtue of his will;° but you must fear,
His greatness weigh'd,° his will is not his own.
[For he himself is subject to his birth.]
He may not, as unvalued persons do,
20 Carve° for himself; for on his choice depends
The safety and health of this whole state,
And therefore must his choice be circumscrib'd
Unto the voice and yielding° of that body
Whereof he is the head. Then if he says he loves
you,
25 It fits your wisdom so far to believe it
As he in his particular act and place
May give his saying deed,° which is no further
Than the main voice of Denmark goes withal.
Then weigh what loss your honor may sustain
30 If with too credent° ear you list° his songs,
Or lose your heart, or your chaste treasure open
To his unmaster'd importunity.
Fear it, Ophelia, fear it, my dear sister,
And keep you in the rear of your affection,
35 Out of the shot° and danger of desire.
The chariest° maid is prodigal enough
If she unmask her beauty to the moon.
Virtue itself scapes not calumnious strokes.
The canker galls° the infants of the spring
40 Too oft before their buttons° be disclos'd,°
And in the morn and liquid dew° of youth
Contagious blastments° are most imminent.
Be wary then; best safety lies in fear.
Youth to itself rebels, though none else near.

OPHELIA: I shall the effect of this good lesson keep   45
As watchman to my heart. But, good my
brother,
Do not, as some ungracious pastors do,
Show me the steep and thorny way to heaven,
Whiles, like a puff'd° and reckless libertine,
Himself the primrose path of dalliance treads,   50
And recks° not his own rede.°

(Enter Polonius.)

LAERTES: O, fear me not.
I stay too long. But here my father comes.
A double blessing is a double° grace;
Occasion° smiles upon a second leave.
POLONIUS: Yet here, Laertes? Aboard, aboard, for
shame!   55
The wind sits in the shoulder of your sail,
And you are stay'd for. There — my blessing
with thee!
And these few precepts in thy memory
Look thou character.° Give thy thoughts no
tongue,
Nor any unproportion'd thought his° act.   60
Be thou familiar,° but by no means vulgar.°
Those friends thou hast, and their adoption
tried,°
Grapple them to thy soul with hoops of steel,
But do not dull thy palm with entertainment
Of each new-hatch'd, unfledg'd courage.° Beware   65
Of entrance to a quarrel, but, being in,
Bear't that° th' opposed may beware of thee.
Give every man thy ear, but few thy voice;
Take each man's censure,° but reserve thy
judgment.
Costly thy habit as thy purse can buy,   70
But not express'd in fancy; rich, not gaudy,
For the apparel oft proclaims the man,
And they in France of the best rank and station
Are of a most select and generous chief° in that.
Neither a borrower nor a lender be,   75
For loan oft loses both itself and friend,
And borrowing dulleth edge of husbandry.°
This above all: to thine own self be true,
And it must follow, as the night the day,
Thou canst not then be false to any man.
Farewell. My blessing season° this in thee!   80

---

6. **toy in blood:** Passing amorous fancy. 7. **primy:** In its prime, springtime. 8. **Forward:** Precocious. 9. **suppliance:** Supply, filler. 11. **crescent:** Growing, waxing. 12. **thews:** Bodily strength. **temple:** Body. 14. **Grows wide withal:** Grows along with it. 15. **soil:** Blemish. **cautel:** deceit. 16. **will:** desire. 17. **greatness weigh'd:** High position considered. 20. **Carve:** Choose pleasure. 23. **Voice and yielding:** Assent, approval. 27. **deed:** Effect. 30. **credent:** Credulous. **list:** Listen to. 35. **shot:** Range. 36. **chariest:** Most scrupulously modest. 39. **canker galls:** Cankerworm destroys. 40. **buttons:** Buds. **disclos'd:** Opened. 41. **liquid dew:** Time when dew is fresh. 42. **blastments:** Blights.

49. **puff'd:** Bloated. 51. **recks:** Heeds. **rede:** Counsel. 53. **double:** I.e., Laertes has already bidden his father goodby. 54. **Occasion:** Opportunity. 59. **character:** Inscribe. 60. **his:** Its. 61. **familiar:** Sociable. **vulgar:** common. 62. **tried:** Tested. 65. **courage:** Young man of spirit. 67. **Bear't that:** Manage it so that. 69. **censure:** Opinion, judgment. 74. **generous chief:** Noble eminence (?). 77. **husbandry:** Thrift. 81. **season:** Mature.

LAERTES: Most humbly do I take my leave, my
     lord.
POLONIUS: The time invests° you. Go, your servants
     tend.°
LAERTES: Farewell, Ophelia, and remember well
85   What I have said to you.
OPHELIA: 'Tis in my memory lock'd,
     And you yourself shall keep the key of it.
LAERTES: Farewell.   (*Exit Laertes.*)
POLONIUS: What is 't, Ophelia, he hath said to you?
OPHELIA: So please you, something touching the
90   Lord Hamlet.
POLONIUS: Marry,° well bethought.
     'Tis told me he hath very oft of late
     Given private time to you, and you yourself
     Have of your audience been most free and
        bounteous.
95   If it be so — as so 'tis put on° me,
     And that in way of caution — I must tell you
     You do not understand yourself so clearly
     As it behooves my daughter and your honor.
     What is between you? Give me up the truth.
OPHELIA: He hath, my lord, of late made many
00   tenders°
     Of his affection to me.
POLONIUS: Affection? Pooh! You speak like a green
        girl,
     Unsifted° in such perilous circumstance.
     Do you believe his tenders, as you call them?
OPHELIA: I do not know, my lord, what I should
05   think.
POLONIUS: Marry, I will teach you. Think yourself
        a baby
     That you have ta'en these tenders° for true pay,
     Which are not sterling.° Tender° yourself more
        dearly,
10   Or — not to crack the wind° of the poor phrase,
     Running it thus — you'll tender me a fool.°
OPHELIA: My lord, he hath importun'd me with
        love
     In honorable fashion.
POLONIUS: Ay, fashion° you may call it. Go to, go
        to.
OPHELIA: And hath given countenance° to his
        speech, my lord,

With almost all the holy vows of heaven.   115
POLONIUS: Ay, springes° to catch woodcocks.° I do
        know,
     When the blood burns, how prodigal the soul
     Lends the tongue vows. These blazes, daughter,
     Giving more light than heat, extinct in both
     Even in their promise, as it is a-making,   120
     You must not take for fire. From this time
     Be something scanter of your maiden presence.
     Set your entreatments° at a higher rate
     Than a command to parle.° For Lord Hamlet,
     Believe so much in him° that he is young,   125
     And with a larger tether may he walk
     Than may be given you. In few,° Ophelia,
     Do not believe his vows, for they are brokers,°
     Not of that dye° which their investments° show,
     But mere implorators° of unholy suits,   130
     Breathing° like sanctified and pious bawds,
     The better to beguile. This is for all:
     I would not, in plain terms, from this time forth
     Have you so slander° any moment leisure
     As to give words or talk with the Lord Hamlet.   135
     Look to 't, I charge you. Come your ways.
OPHELIA: I shall obey, my lord.   (*Exeunt.*)

[*Scene IV*]°

(*Enter Hamlet, Horatio, and Marcellus.*)

HAMLET: The air bites shrewdly; it is very cold.
HORATIO: It is a nipping and an eager air.
HAMLET: What hour now?
HORATIO: I think it lacks of twelve.
MARCELLUS: No, it is struck.
HORATIO: Indeed? I heard it not.
     It then draws near the season   5
     Wherein the spirit held his wont to walk.
        (*A flourish of trumpets, and two pieces° go off
                                            [within].*)
     What does this mean, my lord?

83. **invests:** Besieges. **tend:** Attend, wait. 91. **Marry:** By
the Virgin Mary (a mild oath). 95. **put on:** Impressed on,
told to. 100. **tenders:** Offers. 103. **Unsifted:** Untried.
107. **tenders:** With added meaning here of *promises to pay*.
108. **sterling:** Legal currency. **Tender:** Hold. 109. **crack
the wind:** Run it until it is broken, winded. 110. **tender
me a fool:** (1) Show yourself to me as a fool; (2) show me
up as a fool; (3) present me with a grandchild (*fool* was a
term of endearment for a child). 113. **fashion:** Mere form,
pretense. 114. **countenance:** Credit, support.

116. **springes:** Snares. **woodcocks:** Birds easily caught; here
used to connote gullibility. 123. **entreatments:** Negotiations
for surrender (a military term). 124. **parle:** Discuss terms
with the enemy. (Polonius urges his daughter, in the metaphor of military language, not to meet with Hamlet and
consider giving in to him merely because he requests an
interview.) 125. **so . . . him:** This much concerning him.
127. **In few:** Briefly. 128. **brokers:** Go-betweens, procurers.
129. **dye:** Color or sort. **investments:** Clothes (i.e., they
are not what they seem). 130. **mere implorators:** Out and
out solicitors. 131. **Breathing:** Speaking. 134. **slander:**
Bring disgrace or reproach upon. I, IV. **Location:** The guard
platform. 6. [S.D.] *pieces:* I.e., of ordnance, cannon.

HAMLET: The King doth wake° tonight and takes
    his rouse,°
    Keeps wassail,° and the swagg'ring up-spring°
      reels;
10   And as he drains his draughts of Rhenish° down,
    The kettle-drum and trumpet thus bray out
    The triumph of his pledge.°
HORATIO: Is it a custom?
HAMLET: Ay, marry, is 't,
    But to my mind, though I am native here
15   And to the manner° born, it is a custom
    More honor'd in the breach than the
      observance.°
    This heavy-headed revel east and west°
    Makes us traduc'd and tax'd of° other nations.
    They clepe° us drunkards, and with swinish
      phrase°
20   Soil our addition;° and indeed it takes
    From our achievements, though perform'd at
      height,°
    The pith and marrow of our attribute.
    So, oft it chances in particular men,
    That for some vicious mole of nature° in them,
25   As in their birth — wherein they are not guilty,
    Since nature cannot choose his° origin —
    By the o'ergrowth of some complexion,°
    Oft breaking down the pales° and forts of
      reason,
    Or by some habit that too much o'er-leavens°
30   The form of plausive° manners, that these men,
    Carrying, I say, the stamp of one defect,
    Being nature's livery,° or fortune's star,°
    Their virtues else, be they as pure as grace,
    As infinite as man may undergo,
35   Shall in the general censure take corruption
    From that particular fault. The dram of eale°

8. **wake:** Stay awake and hold revel. **rouse:** Carouse, drinking bout. 9. **wassail:** Carousal. **up-spring:** Wild German dance. 10. **Rhenish:** Rhine wine. 12. **triumph . . . pledge:** His feat in draining the wine in a single draft. 15. **manner:** Custom (of drinking). 16. **More . . . observance:** Better neglected than followed. 17. **east and west:** I.e., everywhere. 18. **tax'd of:** Censured by. 19. **clepe:** Call. **with swinish phrase:** By calling us swine. 20. **addition:** Reputation. 21. **at height:** Outstandingly. 24. **mole of nature:** Natural blemish in one's constitution. 26. **his:** Its. 27. **complexion:** Humor (i.e., one of the four humors or fluids thought to determine temperament). 28. **pales:** Palings, fences (as of a fortification). 29. **o'er-leavens:** Induces a change throughout (as yeast works in dough). 30. **plausive:** Pleasing. 32. **nature's livery:** Endowment from nature. **fortune's star:** Mark placed by fortune. 36. **dram of eale:** Small amount of evil (?).

    Doth all the noble substance of a doubt°
    To his own scandal.°

(Enter Ghost.)

HORATIO: Look, my lord, it comes!
HAMLET: Angels and ministers of grace defend us!
    Be thou a spirit of health° or goblin damn'd,   40
    Bring with thee airs from heaven or blasts from
      hell,
    Be thy intents wicked or charitable,
    Thou com'st in such a questionable° shape
    That I will speak to thee. I'll call thee Hamlet,
    King, father, royal Dane. O, answer me!   45
    Let me not burst in ignorance; but tell
    Why thy canoniz'd° bones, hearsed° in death,
    Have burst their cerements;° why the sepulcher
    Wherein we saw thee quietly interr'd
    Hath op'd his ponderous and marble jaws   50
    To cast thee up again. What may this mean,
    That thou, dead corse, again in complete steel
    Revisits thus the glimpses of the moon,°
    Making night hideous, and we fools of nature°
    So horridly to shake our disposition   55
    With thoughts beyond the reaches of our souls?
    Say, why is this? Wherefore? What should we
      do?

               ([Ghost] beckons [Hamlet].)

HORATIO: It beckons you to go away with it,
    As if it some impartment° did desire
    To you alone.
MARCELLUS: Look with what courteous action   60
    It waves you to a more removed ground.
    But do not go with it.
HORATIO: No, by no means.
HAMLET: It will not speak. Then I will follow it.
HORATIO: Do not, my lord.
HAMLET: Why, what should be the fear?
    I do not set my life at a pin's fee,°   65
    And for my soul, what can it do to that,
    Being a thing immortal as itself?
    It waves me forth again. I'll follow it.
HORATIO: What if it tempt you toward the flood,
    my lord,
    Or to the dreadful summit of the cliff   70

37. **of a doubt:** A famous crux, sometimes emended to *oft about* or *often dout*, i.e., often erase or do out, or to *antidote*, counteract. 38. **To . . . scandal:** To the disgrace of the whole enterprise. 40. **of health:** Of spiritual good. 43. **questionable:** Inviting question or conversation. 47. **canoniz'd:** Buried according to the canons of the church. **hearsed:** Coffined. 48. **cerements:** Grave-clothes. 53. **glimpses of the moon:** Earth by night. 54. **fools of nature:** Mere men, limited to natural knowledge. 59. **impartment:** Communication. 65. **fee:** Value.

That beetles o'er° his° base into the sea,
And there assume some other horrible form
Which might deprive your sovereignty of
  reason,°
And draw you into madness? Think of it.
75 The very place puts toys of desperation,°
Without more motive, into every brain
That looks so many fathoms to the sea
And hears it roar beneath.
HAMLET: It waves me still.
  Go on, I'll follow thee.
MARCELLUS: You shall not go, my lord.
                    [*They try to stop him.*]
80 HAMLET: Hold off your hands!
HORATIO: Be rul'd, you shall not go.
HAMLET: My fate cries out,
  And makes each petty artery° in this body
  As hardy as the Nemean lion's° nerve.°
  Still am I call'd. Unhand me, gentlemen.
  By heaven, I'll make a ghost of him that lets°
85   me!
  I say, away! Go on. I'll follow thee.
            (*Exeunt Ghost and Hamlet.*)
HORATIO: He waxes desperate with imagination.
MARCELLUS: Let's follow. 'Tis not fit thus to obey
  him.
HORATIO: Have after. To what issue° will this
  come?
MARCELLUS: Something is rotten in the state of
90   Denmark.
HORATIO: Heaven will direct it.°
MARCELLUS: Nay, let's follow him. (*Exeunt.*)

[*Scene V*]°

(*Enter Ghost and Hamlet.*)

HAMLET: Whither wilt thou lead me? Speak. I'll go
  no further.
GHOST: Mark me.
HAMLET: I will.
GHOST: My hour is almost come,
  When I to sulph'rous and tormenting flames
  Must render up myself.
HAMLET: Alas, poor ghost!

GHOST: Pity me not, but lend thy serious hearing   5
  To what I shall unfold.
HAMLET: Speak. I am bound to hear.
GHOST: So art thou to revenge, when thou shalt
  hear.
HAMLET: What?
GHOST: I am thy father's spirit,   10
  Doom'd for a certain term to walk the night,
  And for the day confin'd to fast° in fires,
  Till the foul crimes° done in my days of nature
  Are burnt and purg'd away. But that° I am
    forbid
  To tell the secrets of my prison-house,   15
  I could a tale unfold whose lightest word
  Would harrow up thy soul, freeze thy young
    blood,
  Make thy two eyes, like stars, start from their
    spheres,°
  Thy knotted and combined locks° to part,
  And each particular hair to stand an end,°   20
  Like quills upon the fearful porpentine.°
  But this eternal blazon° must not be
  To ears of flesh and blood. List, list, O, list!
  If thou didst ever thy dear father love —
HAMLET: O God!   25
GHOST: Revenge his foul and most unnatural
  murder.
HAMLET: Murder?
GHOST: Murder most foul, as in the best it is,
  But this most foul, strange, and unnatural.
HAMLET: Haste me to know 't, that I, with wings
  as swift   30
  As meditation or the thoughts of love,
  May sweep to my revenge.
GHOST: I find thee apt;
  And duller shouldst thou be than the fat weed
  That roots itself in ease on Lethe° wharf,°
  Wouldst thou not stir in this. Now, Hamlet,
    hear.   35
  'Tis given out that, sleeping in my orchard,
  A serpent stung me. So the whole ear of
    Denmark
  Is by a forged process° of my death

---

12. **fast:** Do penance. 13. **crimes:** Sins. 14. **But that:**
Were it not that. 18. **spheres:** Eye sockets, here compared
to the orbits or transparent revolving spheres in which, according to Ptolemaic astronomy, the heavenly bodies were
fixed. 19. **knotted ... locks:** Hair neatly arranged and
confined. 20. **an end:** on end. 21. **fearful porpentine:**
Frightened porcupine. 22. **eternal blazon:** Revelation of the
secrets of eternity. 34. **Lethe:** The river of forgetfulness in
Hades. **wharf:** Bank. 38. **forged process:** Falsified
account.

---

71. **beetles o'er:** Overhangs threateningly. **his:** Its. 73.
deprive ... reason: Take away the rule of reason over your
mind. 75. **toys of desperation:** Fancies of desperate acts,
i.e., suicide. 82. **artery:** Sinew. 83. **Nemean lion:** One of
the monsters slain by Hercules in his twelve labors. **nerve:**
Sinew. 85. **lets:** Hinders. 89. **issue:** Outcome. 91. **it:**
The outcome. **I, v. Location:** The battlements of the castle.

        Rankly abus'd.° But know, thou noble youth,
40   The serpent that did sting thy father's life
      Now wears his crown.
HAMLET: O my prophetic soul!
      My uncle!
GHOST: Ay, that incestuous, that adulterate° beast,
      With witchcraft of his wits, with traitorous
            gifts —
45   O wicked wit and gifts, that have the power
      So to seduce! — won to his shameful lust
      The will of my most seeming-virtuous queen.
      O Hamlet, what a falling-off was there!
      From me, whose love was of that dignity
50   That it went hand in hand even with the vow
      I made to her in marriage, and to decline
      Upon a wretch whose natural gifts were poor
      To those of mine!
      But virtue, as it never will be moved,
55   Though lewdness court it in a shape of heaven,°
      So lust, though to a radiant angel link'd,
      Will sate itself in a celestial bed,
      And prey on garbage.
      But, soft, methinks I scent the morning air.
60   Brief let me be. Sleeping within my orchard,
      My custom always of the afternoon,
      Upon my secure° hour thy uncle stole,
      With juice of cursed hebona° in a vial,
      And in the porches of my ears did pour
65   The leprous° distillment, whose effect
      Holds such an enmity with blood of man
      That swift as quicksilver it courses through
      The natural gates and alleys of the body,
      And with a sudden vigor it doth posset°
70   And curd, like eager° droppings into milk,
      The thin and wholesome blood. So did it mine,
      And a most instant tetter° bark'd° about,
      Most lazar-like,° with vile and loathsome crust,
      All my smooth body.
75   Thus was I, sleeping, by a brother's hand
      Of life, of crown, of queen, at once dispatch'd,°
      Cut off even in the blossoms of my sin,
      Unhous'led,° disappointed,° unanel'd,°

No reck'ning made, but sent to my account
With all my imperfections on my head.   80
O, horrible! O, horrible, most horrible!
If thou hast nature° in thee, bear it not.
Let not the royal bed of Denmark be
A couch for luxury° and damned incest.
But, howsomever thou pursues this act,   85
Taint not thy mind, nor let thy soul contrive
Against thy mother aught. Leave her to heaven
And to those thorns that in her bosom lodge,
To prick and sting her. Fare thee well at once.
The glow-worm shows the matin° to be near,   90
And 'gins to pale his uneffectual fire.°
Adieu, adieu, adieu! Remember me.   [Exit.]
HAMLET: O all you host of heaven! O earth! What
      else?
      And shall I couple° hell? O fie! Hold, hold, my
            heart,
      And you, my sinews, grow not instant old,   95
      But bear me stiffly up. Remember thee!
      Ay, thou poor ghost, whiles memory holds a
            seat
      In this distracted globe.° Remember thee!
      Yea, from the table° of my memory
      I'll wipe away all trivial fond° records,   100
      All saws° of books, all forms,° all pressures° past
      That youth and observation copied there,
      And thy commandment all alone shall live
      Within the book and volume of my brain,
      Unmix'd with baser matter. Yes, by heaven!   105
      O most pernicious woman!
      O villain, villain, smiling, damned villain!
      My tables — meet it is I set it down,
      That one may smile, and smile, and be a villain.
      At least I am sure it may be so in Denmark.   110
                                                 [Writing.]
      So, uncle, there you are. Now to my word;
      It is "Adieu, adieu! Remember me."
      I have sworn 't.

(Enter Horatio and Marcellus.)

HORATIO: My lord, my lord!
MARCELLUS: Lord Hamlet!
HORATIO: Heavens secure him!
HAMLET: So be it!
MARCELLUS: Illo, ho, ho, my lord!   115
HAMLET: Hillo, ho, ho,° boy! Come, bird, come.

---

39. **abus'd:** Deceived.   43. **adulterate:** Adulterous.   55.
shape of heaven: Heavenly form.   62. **secure:** Confident,
unsuspicious.   63. **hebona:** Poison. (The word seems to be
a form of *ebony*, though it is perhaps thought to be related
to *henbane*, a poison, or to *ebenus*, yew.)   65. **leprous:**
Causing leprosy-like disfigurement.   69. **posset:** Coagulate,
curdle.   70. **eager:** Sour, acid.   72. **tetter:** Eruption of scabs.
bark'd: Covered with a rough covering, like bark on a tree.
73. **lazar-like:** Leper-like.   76. **dispatch'd:** Suddenly deprived.   78. **Unhous'led:** Without having received the sacrament [of Holy Communion].   **disappointed:** Unready
(spiritually) for the last journey.   **unanel'd:** Without having
received extreme unction.

82. **nature:** The promptings of a son.   84. **luxury:** Lechery.
90. **matin:** Morning.   91. **uneffectual fire:** Cold light.   94.
couple: Add.   98. **globe:** Head.   99. **table:** Writing tablet.
100. **fond:** Foolish.   101. **saws:** Wise sayings.   **forms:** Images.   **pressures:** Impressions stamped.   117. **Hillo, ho, ho:**
A falconer's call to a hawk in air. Hamlet is playing upon
Marcellus's *Illo*, i.e., *halloo*.

MARCELLUS: How is 't, my noble lord?
HORATIO: What news, my lord?
HAMLET: O, wonderful!
HORATIO: Good my lord, tell it.
20 HAMLET: No, you will reveal it.
HORATIO: Not I, my lord, by heaven.
MARCELLUS: Nor I, my lord.
HAMLET: How say you, then, would heart of man
    once think it?
    But you'll be secret?
HORATIO, MARCELLUS: Ay, by heaven, my
    lord.
HAMLET: There's never a villain dwelling in all
    Denmark
25 But he's an arrant° knave.
HORATIO: There needs no ghost, my lord, come
    from the grave
    To tell us this.
HAMLET: Why, right, you are in the right.
    And so, without more circumstance° at all,
    I hold it fit that we shake hands and part,
    You, as your business and desire shall point
30   you —
    For every man hath business and desire,
    Such as it is — and for my own poor part,
    Look you, I'll go pray.
HORATIO: These are but wild and whirling words,
    my lord.
35 HAMLET: I am sorry they offend you, heartily;
    Yes, faith, heartily.
HORATIO: There's no offense, my lord.
HAMLET: Yes, by Saint Patrick,° but there is,
    Horatio,
    And much offense too. Touching this vision
    here,
    It is an honest° ghost, that let me tell you.
40   For your desire to know what is between us,
    O'ermaster 't as you may. And now, good
    friends,
    As you are friends, scholars, and soldiers,
    Give me one poor request.
HORATIO: What is 't, my lord? We will.
HAMLET: Never make known what you have seen
45   tonight.
HORATIO, MARCELLUS: My lord, we will not.
HAMLET: Nay, but swear 't.
HORATIO: In faith,
    My lord, not I.
MARCELLUS: Nor I, my lord, in faith.

HAMLET: Upon my sword.°   [*Holds out his sword.*]
MARCELLUS: We have sworn, my lord, already.
HAMLET: Indeed, upon my sword, indeed.
    (*Ghost cries under the stage.*)
GHOST: Swear.   150
HAMLET: Ha, ha, boy, say'st thou so? Art thou
    there, truepenny?°
    Come on, you hear this fellow in the cellarage.
    Consent to swear.
HORATIO: Propose the oath, my lord.
HAMLET: Never to speak of this that you have seen,
    Swear by my sword.   155
GHOST [*beneath*]: Swear.
HAMLET: Hic et ubique?° Then we'll shift our
    ground.
          [*He moves to another spot.*]
    Come hither, gentlemen,
    And lay your hands again upon my sword.
    Swear by my sword   160
    Never to speak of this that you have heard.
GHOST [*beneath*]: Swear by his sword.
HAMLET: Well said, old mole! Canst work i' th'
    earth so fast?
    A worthy pioner!° Once more remove, good
    friends.
               [*Moves again.*]
HORATIO: O day and night, but this is wondrous
    strange!   165
HAMLET: And therefore as a stranger give it
    welcome.
    There are more things in heaven and earth,
    Horatio,
    Than are dreamt of in your philosophy.°
    But come;
    Here, as before, never, so help you mercy,   170
    How strange or odd soe'er I bear myself —
    As I perchance hereafter shall think meet
    To put an antic° disposition on —
    That you, at such times seeing me, never shall,
    With arms encumb'red° thus, or this headshake,   175
    Or by pronouncing of some doubtful phrase,
    As "Well, well, we know," or "We could, an if°
    we would,"
    Or "If we list° to speak," or "There be, an if
    they might,"
    Or such ambiguous giving out,° to note°

---

125. **arrant:** Thoroughgoing.   128. **circumstance:** Ceremony.   137. **Saint Patrick:** The keeper of purgatory and
patron saint of all blunders and confusion.   139. **honest:**
I.e., a real ghost and not an evil spirit.

148. **sword:** The hilt in the form of a cross.   151. **truepenny:**
Honest old fellow.   157. **Hic et ubique:** Here and everywhere (Latin).   164. **pioner:** Pioneer, digger, miner.   168.
your philosophy: This subject called "natural philosophy"
or "science" that people talk about.   173. **antic:** Fantastic.
175. **encumb'red:** Folded or entwined.   177. **an if:** If.   178.
list: Were inclined.   179. **giving out:** Profession of knowledge.   **note:** Give a sign, indicate.

180   That you know aught of me — this do swear,
    So grace and mercy at your most need help you.
GHOST [*beneath*]: Swear.   [*They swear.*]
HAMLET: Rest, rest, perturbed spirit! So, gentlemen,
    With all my love I do commend me to you;
185   And what so poor a man as Hamlet is
    May do, t' express his love and friending to you,
    God willing, shall not lack. Let us go in
        together,
    And still° your fingers on your lips, I pray.
    The time is out of joint. O cursed spite,
190   That ever I was born to set it right!
           [*They wait for him to leave first.*]
    Nay, come, let's go together.   (*Exeunt.*)

[ACT II • *Scene I*]°

(*Enter old Polonius, with his man* [*Reynaldo*].)

POLONIUS: Give him this money and these notes,
    Reynaldo.
REYNALDO: I will, my lord.
POLONIUS: You shall do marvel's° wisely, good
    Reynaldo,
    Before you visit him, to make inquire
    Of his behavior.
5 REYNALDO: My lord, I did intend it.
POLONIUS: Marry, well said, very well said. Look
    you, sir,
    Inquire me first what Danskers° are in Paris,
    And how, and who, what means,° and where
        they keep,°
    What company, at what expense; and finding
10   By this encompassment° and drift° of question
    That they do know my son, come you more
        nearer
    Than your particular demands will touch it.°
    Take° you, as 'twere, some distant knowledge of
        him,
    As thus, "I know his father and his friends,
15   And in part him." Do you mark this, Reynaldo?
REYNALDO: Ay, very well, my lord.
POLONIUS: "And in part him, but," you may say,
    "not well.
    But, if 't be he I mean, he's very wild,

    Addicted so and so," and there put on° him
    What forgeries° you please — marry, none so
        rank   20
    As may dishonor, him take heed of that,
    But, sir, such wanton,° wild, and usual slips,
    As are companions noted and most known
    To youth and liberty.
REYNALDO: As gaming, my lord.
POLONIUS: Ay, or drinking, fencing, swearing,   25
    Quarreling, drabbing° — you may go so far.
REYNALDO: My lord, that would dishonor him.
POLONIUS: Faith, no, as you may season° it in the
    charge.
    You must not put another scandal on him
    That he is open to incontinency;°   30
    That's not my meaning. But breathe his faults so
        quaintly°
    That they may seem the taints of liberty,°
    The flash and outbreak of a fiery mind,
    A savageness in unreclaimed° blood,
    Of general assault.°
REYNALDO: But, my good lord —   35
POLONIUS: Wherefore should you do this?
REYNALDO: Ay, my lord,
    I would know that.
POLONIUS: Marry, sir, here's my drift,
    And, I believe, it is a fetch of wit.°
    You laying these slight sullies on my son,
    As 'twere a thing a little soil'd i' th' working,°   40
    Mark you,
    Your party in converse,° him you would sound,°
    Having ever° seen in the prenominate crimes°
    The youth you breathe° of guilty, be assur'd
    He closes with you in this consequence:°   45
    "Good sir," or so, or "friend," or "gentleman,"
    According to the phrase or the addition°
    Of man and country.
REYNALDO: Very good, my lord.
POLONIUS: And then, sir, does 'a this — 'a does —
    what was I about to say?
    By the mass, I was about to say something.   50

---

188. still: Always.   **II, I. Location:** Polonius's chambers. **3. marvel's:** Marvelous(ly).   **7. Danskers:** Danes.   **8. what means:** What wealth (they have). **keep:** Dwell.   **10. encompassment:** Roundabout talking. **drift:** Gradual approach or course.   **11–12. come . . . it:** You will find out more this way than by asking pointed questions (*particular demands*).   **13. Take:** Assume, pretend.

19. put on: Impute to.   **20. forgeries:** Invented tales.   **22. wanton:** Sportive, unrestrained.   **26. drabbing:** Whoring. **28. season:** Temper, soften.   **30. incontinency:** Habitual loose behavior.   **31. quaintly:** Delicately, ingeniously.   **32. taints of liberty:** Faults resulting from freedom.   **34. unreclaimed:** Untamed.   **35. general assault:** Tendency that assails all unrestrained youth.   **38. fetch of wit:** Clever trick. **40. soil'd i' th' working:** Shopworn.   **42. converse:** Conversation. **sound:** Sound out.   **43. Having ever:** If he has ever. **prenominate crimes:** Before-mentioned offenses.   **44. breathe:** Speak.   **45. closes . . . consequence:** Follows your lead in some fashion as follows.   **47. addition:** Title.

Where did I leave?

REYNALDO: At "closes in the consequence."

POLONIUS: At "closes in the consequence," ay,
    marry.
    He closes thus: "I know the gentleman;
    I saw him yesterday, or th' other day,
    Or then, or then, with such, or such, and, as
55   you say,
    There was 'a gaming, there o'ertook in 's rouse,°
    There falling out° at tennis," or perchance,
    "I saw him enter such a house of sale,"
    Videlicet,° a brothel, or so forth. See you now,
60 Your bait of falsehood takes this carp° of truth;
    And thus do we of wisdom and of reach,°
    With windlasses° and with assays of bias,°
    By indirections find directions° out.
    So by my former lecture and advice
65 Shall you my son. You have me, have you not?

REYNALDO: My lord, I have.

POLONIUS: God buy ye; fare ye well.

REYNALDO: Good my lord.

POLONIUS: Observe his inclination in yourself.°

REYNALDO: I shall, my lord.

POLONIUS: And let him ply° his music.

70 REYNALDO: Well, my lord.

POLONIUS: Farewell.   (*Exit Reynaldo.*)

(*Enter Ophelia.*)

                    How now, Ophelia, what's the matter?

OPHELIA: O, my lord, my lord, I have been so
    affrighted!

POLONIUS: With what, i' th' name of God?

OPHELIA: My lord, as I was sewing in my closet,°
75   Lord Hamlet, with his doublet° all unbrac'd,°
    No hat upon his head, his stockings fouled,
    Ungart'red, and down-gyved to his ankle,°
    Pale as his shirt, his knees knocking each other,
    And with a look so piteous in purport
80 As if he had been loosed out of hell
    To speak of horrors — he comes before me.

POLONIUS: Mad for thy love?

OPHELIA: My lord, I do not know,

But truly I do fear it.

POLONIUS: What said he?

OPHELIA: He took me by the wrist and held me
    hard.
    Then goes he to the length of all his arm,   85
    And, with his other hand thus o'er his brow,
    He falls to such perusal of my face
    As 'a would draw it. Long stay'd he so.
    At last, a little shaking of mine arm
    And thrice his head thus waving up and down,   90
    He rais'd a sigh so piteous and profound
    As it did seem to shatter all his bulk°
    And end his being. That done, he lets me go,
    And, with his head over his shoulder turn'd,
    He seem'd to find his way without his eyes,   95
    For out o' doors he went without their helps,
    And, to the last, bended their light on me.

POLONIUS: Come, go with me. I will go seek the
    King.
    This is the very ecstasy° of love,
    Whose violent property° fordoes° itself   100
    And leads the will to desperate undertakings
    As oft as any passion under heaven
    That does afflict our natures. I am sorry.
    What, have you given him any hard words of
    late?

OPHELIA: No, my good lord, but, as you did
    command,   105
    I did repel his letters and denied
    His access to me.

POLONIUS: That hath made him mad.
    I am sorry that with better heed and judgment
    I had not quoted° him. I fear'd he did but trifle
    And meant to wrack thee; but, beshrew my
    jealousy!°   110
    By heaven, it is as proper to our age°
    To cast beyond° ourselves in our opinions
    As it is common for the younger sort
    To lack discretion. Come, go we to the King.
    This must be known, which, being kept close,°
    might move   115
    More grief to hide than hate to utter love.°
    Come.   (*Exeunt.*)

---

56. **o'ertook in 's rouse:** Overcome by drink.   57. **falling out:** Quarreling.   59. **Videlicet:** Namely.   60. **carp:** A fish. 61. **reach:** Capacity, ability.   62. **windlasses:** Circuitous paths (literally, circuits made to head off the game in hunting).   **assays of bias:** Attempts through indirection (like the curving path of the bowling ball which is biased or weighted to one side).   63. **directions:** The way things really are.   68. **in yourself:** In your own person (as well as by asking questions).   70. **let him ply:** See that he continues to study.   74. **closet:** Private chamber.   75. **doublet:** Close-fitting jacket.   **unbrac'd:** Unfastened.   77. **down-gyved to his ankle:** Fallen to the ankles (like gyves or fetters).

92. **bulk:** Body.   99. **ecstasy:** Madness.   100. **property:** Nature.   **fordoes:** Destroys.   109. **quoted:** Observed. 110. **beshrew my jealousy:** A plague upon my suspicious nature.   111. **proper . . . age:** Characteristic of us (old) men. 112. **cast beyond:** Overshoot, miscalculate.   115. **close:** Secret.   115–16. **might . . . love:** Might cause more grief (to others) by hiding the knowledge of Hamlet's strange behavior to Ophelia than hatred by telling it.

[Scene II]°

(*Flourish. Enter King and Queen, Rosencrantz, and Guildenstern [with others].*)

KING: Welcome, dear Rosencrantz and
   Guildenstern.
   Moreover that° we much did long to see you,
   The need we have to use you did provoke
   Our hasty sending. Something have you heard
5 Of Hamlet's transformation — so call it,
   Sith° nor th' exterior nor° the inward man
   Resembles that° it was. What it should be,
   More than his father's death, that thus hath put
      him
   So much from th' understanding of himself,
10 I cannot dream of. I entreat you both
   That, being of so young days° brought up with
      him,
   And sith so neighbor'd to his youth and havior,
   That you vouchsafe your rest° here in our court
   Some little time, so by your companies
15 To draw him on to pleasures, and to gather
   So much as from occasion you may glean,
   Whether aught to us unknown afflicts him thus,
   That, open'd,° lies within our remedy.
QUEEN: Good gentlemen, he hath much talk'd of
      you,
20 And sure I am two men there is not living
   To whom he more adheres. If it will please you
   To show us so much gentry° and good will
   As to expend your time with us awhile
   For the supply and profit° of our hope,
25 Your visitation shall receive such thanks
   As fits a king's remembrance.
ROSENCRANTZ: Both your Majesties
   Might, by the sovereign power you have of us,
   Put your dread pleasures more into command
   Than to entreaty.
GUILDENSTERN: But we both obey,
30 And here give up ourselves in the full bent°
   To lay our service freely at your feet,
   To be commanded.
KING: Thanks, Rosencrantz and gentle
      Guildenstern.
QUEEN: Thanks, Guildenstern and gentle
      Rosencrantz.

And I beseech you instantly to visit   35
My too much changed son. Go, some of you,
And bring these gentlemen where Hamlet is.
GUILDENSTERN: Heavens make our presence and
      our practices
   Pleasant and helpful to him!
QUEEN: Ay, amen!
(*Exeunt Rosencrantz and Guildenstern [with some
                                    Attendants].*)

(*Enter Polonius.*)

POLONIUS: Th' ambassadors from Norway, my
      good lord,   40
   Are joyfully return'd.
KING: Thou still° hast been the father of good
      news.
POLONIUS: Have I, my lord? I assure my good liege
   I hold my duty, as I hold my soul,
   Both to my God and to my gracious king;   45
   And I do think, or else this brain of mine
   Hunts not the trail of policy so sure
   As it hath us'd to do, that I have found
   The very cause of Hamlet's lunacy.
KING: O, speak of that! That do I long to hear. 50
POLONIUS: Give first admittance to th' ambassadors.
   My news shall be the fruit° to that great feast.
KING: Thyself do grace to them, and bring them in.
                              (*Exit Polonius.*)
   He tells me, my dear Gertrude, he hath found
   The head and source of all your son's distemper. 55
QUEEN: I doubt° it is no other but the main,°
   His father's death, and our o'erhasty marriage.

(*Enter Ambassadors [Voltimand and Cornelius, with
Polonius].*)

KING: Well, we shall sift him. — Welcome, my
      good friends!
   Say, Voltimand, what from our brother Norway?
VOLTIMAND: Most fair return of greetings and
      desires.   60
   Upon our first,° he sent out to suppress
   His nephew's levies, which to him appear'd
   To be a preparation 'gainst the Polack,
   But, better look'd into, he truly found
   It was against your Highness. Whereat griev'd 65
   That so his sickness, age, and impotence
   Was falsely borne in hand,° sends out arrests
   On Fortinbras, which he, in brief, obeys,
   Receives rebuke from Norway, and in fine°

II, II. **Location:** The castle.   **2. Moreover that:** Besides the fact that.   **6. Sith:** Since.   **nor . . . nor:** Neither . . . nor.   **7. that:** What.   **11. of . . . days:** From such early youth.   **13. vouchsafe your rest:** Please to stay.   **18. open'd:** Revealed.   **22. gentry:** Courtesy.   **24. supply and profit:** Aid and successful outcome.   **30. in . . . bent:** To the utmost degree of our capacity.

42. still: Always.   **52. fruit:** Dessert.   **56. doubt:** Fear, suspect.   **main:** Chief point, principal concern.   **61. Upon our first:** At our first words on the business.   **67. borne in hand:** Deluded, taken advantage of.   **69. in fine:** In the end.

70 Makes vow before his uncle never more
To give th' assay° of arms against your Majesty.
Whereon old Norway, overcome with joy,
Gives him three score thousand crowns in
    annual fee,
And his commission to employ those soldiers,
75 So levied as before, against the Polack,
With an entreaty, herein further shown,
                        [*Giving a paper.*]
That it might please you to give quiet pass
Through your dominions for this enterprise,
On such regards of safety and allowance°
As therein are set down.
80 KING: It likes° us well;
And at our more consider'd° time we'll read,
Answer, and think upon this business.
Meantime we thank you for your well-took
    labor.
Go to your rest; at night we'll feast together.
Most welcome home!   (*Exeunt Ambassadors.*)
85 POLONIUS: This business is well ended.
My liege, and madam, to expostulate°
What majesty should be, what duty is,
Why day is day, night night, and time is time,
Were nothing but to waste night, day, and time.
90 Therefore, since brevity is the soul of wit,°
And tediousness the limbs and outward
    flourishes,
I will be brief. Your noble son is mad.
Mad call I it, for, to define true madness,
What is 't but to be nothing else but mad?
But let that go.
95 QUEEN: More matter, with less art.
POLONIUS: Madam, I swear I use no art at all.
That he is mad, 'tis true; 'tis true 'tis pity,
And pity 'tis 'tis true — a foolish figure,°
But farewell it, for I will use no art.
00 Mad let us grant him, then, and now remains
That we find out the cause of this effect,
Or rather say, the cause of this defect,
For this effect defective comes by cause.°
Thus it remains, and the remainder thus.
05 Perpend.°
I have a daughter — have while she is mine —
Who, in her duty and obedience, mark,
Hath given me this. Now gather, and surmise.
[*Reads the letter.*] "To the celestial and my
    soul's idol,

the most beautified Ophelia" —   110
That's an ill phrase, a vile phrase; "beautified" is
    a vile
phrase. But you shall hear. Thus: [*Reads.*]
"In her excellent white bosom, these, etc."
QUEEN: Came this from Hamlet to her?
POLONIUS: Good madam, stay awhile; I will be
    faithful.   115
                                      [*Reads.*]
"Doubt° thou the stars are fire,
    Doubt that the sun doth move,
Doubt truth to be a liar,
    But never doubt I love.
O dear Ophelia, I am ill at these numbers.° I have 120
not art to reckon° my groans. But that I love thee
best, O most best, believe it. Adieu.
        Thine evermore, most dear lady, whilst this
                machine° is to him, Hamlet."
This in obedience hath my daughter shown me,   125
And, more above,° hath his solicitings,
As they fell out° by time, by means, and place,
All given to mine ear.
KING: But how hath she
Receiv'd his love?
POLONIUS: What do you think of me?
KING: As of a man faithful and honorable.   130
POLONIUS: I would fain prove so. But what might
    you think,
When I had seen this hot love on the wing —
As I perceiv'd it, I must tell you that,
Before my daughter told me — what might you,
Or my dear Majesty your Queen here, think,   135
If I had play'd the desk or table-book,°
Or given my heart a winking,° mute and dumb,
Or look'd upon this love with idle sight?°
What might you think? No, I went round° to
    work,
And my young mistress thus I did bespeak:°   140
"Lord Hamlet is a prince, out of thy star;°
This must not be." And then I prescripts gave
    her,
That she should lock herself from his resort,
Admit no messengers, receive no tokens.
Which done, she took the fruits of my advice;   145
And he, repelled — a short tale to make —
Fell into a sadness, then into a fast,

71. **assay:** Trial.   79. **On . . . allowance:** With such pledges of safety and provisos.   80. **likes:** Pleases.   81. **consider'd:** Suitable for deliberation.   86. **expostulate:** Expound.   90. **wit:** Sound sense or judgment.   98. **figure:** Figure of speech.   103. **For . . . cause:** I.e., for this defective behavior, this madness has a cause.   105. **Perpend:** Consider.

116. **Doubt:** Suspect, question.   120. **ill . . . numbers:** Unskilled at writing verses.   121. **reckon:** (1) Count, (2) number metrically, scan.   124. **machine:** Body.   126. **more above:** Moreover.   127. **fell out:** Occurred.   136. **play'd . . . table-book:** Remained shut up, concealing the information.   137. **winking:** Closing of the eyes.   138. **with idle sight:** Complacently or uncomprehendingly.   139. **round:** Roundly, plainly.   140. **bespeak:** Address.   141. **out of thy star:** Above your sphere, position.

Thence to a watch,° thence into a weakness,
Thence to a lightness,° and, by this declension,°
150 Into the madness wherein now he raves,
And all we mourn for.
KING: Do you think this?
QUEEN: It may be, very like.
POLONIUS: Hath there been such a time — I would
    fain know that —
That I have positively said " 'Tis so,"
When it prov'd otherwise?
155 KING: Not that I know.
POLONIUS [*pointing to his head and shoulder*]: Take
    this from this, if this be otherwise.
If circumstances lead me, I will find
Where truth is hid, though it were hid indeed
Within the center.°
KING: How may we try it further?
POLONIUS: You know, sometimes he walks four
160   hours together
Here in the lobby.
QUEEN: So he does indeed.
POLONIUS: At such a time I'll loose my daughter to
    him.
Be you and I behind an arras° then.
Mark the encounter. If he love her not
165 And be not from his reason fall'n thereon,°
Let me be no assistant for a state,
But keep a farm and carters.
KING: We will try it.

(*Enter Hamlet [reading on a book].*)

QUEEN: But look where sadly the poor wretch
    comes reading.
POLONIUS: Away, I do beseech you both, away.
I'll board° him presently.
            (*Exeunt King and Queen [with Attendants].*)
170   O, give me leave.
How does my good Lord Hamlet?
HAMLET: Well, God-a-mercy.°
POLONIUS: Do you know me, my lord?
HAMLET: Excellent well. You are a fishmonger.°
175 POLONIUS: Not I, my lord.
HAMLET: Then I would you were so honest a man.
POLONIUS: Honest, my lord?
HAMLET: Ay, sir. To be honest, as this world goes, is
    to be one man pick'd out of ten thousand.
180 POLONIUS: That's very true, my lord.

HAMLET: For if the sun breed maggots in a dead dog,
    being a good kissing carrion° — Have you a
    daughter?
POLONIUS: I have, my lord.
HAMLET: Let her not walk i' th' sun.° Conception° is 185
    a blessing, but as your daughter may conceive,
    friend, look to 't.
POLONIUS [*aside*]: How say you by that? Still harping
    on my daughter. Yet he knew me not at first; 'a
    said I was a fishmonger. 'A is far gone. And truly 190
    in my youth I suff'red much extremity for love,
    very near this. I'll speak to him again. — What do
    you read, my lord?
HAMLET: Words, words, words.
POLONIUS: What is the matter,° my lord? 195
HAMLET: Between who?
POLONIUS: I mean, the matter that you read, my lord.
HAMLET: Slanders, sir; for the satirical rogue says here
    that old men have gray beards, that their faces are
    wrinkled, their eyes purging° thick amber and 200
    plum-tree gum, and that they have a plentiful lack
    of wit, together with most weak hams. All which,
    sir, though I most powerfully and potently believe,
    yet I hold it not honesty° to have it thus set down,
    for you yourself, sir, shall grow old as I am, if like 205
    a crab you could go backward.
POLONIUS [*aside*]: Though this be madness, yet there
    is method in 't. — Will you walk out of the air,
    my lord?
HAMLET: Into my grave. 210
POLONIUS: Indeed, that's out of the air. [*Aside.*] How
    pregnant° sometimes his replies are! A happiness°
    that often madness hits on, which reason and sanity
    could not so prosperously° be deliver'd of. I will
    leave him, [and suddenly contrive the means of 215
    meeting between him] and my daughter. — My
    honorable lord, I will most humbly take my leave
    of you.
HAMLET: You cannot, sir, take from me any thing
    that I will more willingly part withal — except my 220
    life, except my life, except my life.

(*Enter Guildenstern and Rosencrantz.*)

POLONIUS: Fare you well, my lord.
HAMLET: These tedious old fools!°

---

148. **watch:** State of sleeplessness. 149. **lightness:** Light-headedness. **declension:** Decline, deterioration. 159. **center:** Middle point of the earth (which is also the center of the Ptolemaic universe). 163. **arras:** Hanging, tapestry. 165. **thereon:** On that account. 170. **board:** Accost. 172. **God-a-mercy:** Thank you. 174. **fishmonger:** Fish merchant (with connotation of *bawd, procurer*[?]).

182. **good kissing carrion:** A good piece of flesh for kissing, or for the sun to kiss. 185. **i' th' sun:** With additional implication of the sunshine of princely favors. **Conception:** (1) Understanding, (2) pregnancy. 195. **matter:** Substance (but Hamlet plays on the sense of *basis for a dispute*). 200. **purging:** Discharging. 204. **honesty:** Decency. 212. **pregnant:** Full of meaning. **happiness:** Felicity of expression. 214. **prosperously:** Successfully. 223. **old fools:** I.e., old men like Polonius.

POLONIUS: You go to seek the Lord Hamlet; there he
25   is.
ROSENCRANTZ [to Polonius]: God save you, sir!
                                    [Exit Polonius.]
GUILDENSTERN: My honor'd lord!
ROSENCRANTZ: My most dear lord!
HAMLET: My excellent good friends! How dost thou,
30   Guildenstern? Ah, Rosencrantz! Good lads, how
      do you both?
ROSENCRANTZ: As the indifferent° children of the earth.
GUILDENSTERN: Happy in that we are not over-happy.
      On Fortune's cap we are not the very button.
35   HAMLET: Nor the soles of her shoe?
ROSENCRANTZ: Neither, my lord.
HAMLET: Then you live about her waist, or in the
      middle of her favors?
GUILDENSTERN: Faith, her privates° we.
40   HAMLET: In the secret parts of Fortune? O, most true;
      she is a strumpet.° What news?
ROSENCRANTZ: None, my lord, but the world's grown
      honest.
HAMLET: Then is doomsday near. But your news is
45   not true. [Let me question more in particular. What
      have you, my good friends, deserv'd at the hands
      of Fortune that she sends you to prison hither?
GUILDENSTERN: Prison, my lord?
HAMLET: Denmark's a prison.
50   ROSENCRANTZ: Then is the world one.
HAMLET: A goodly one, in which there are many con-
      fines,° wards,° and dungeons, Denmark being one
      o' th' worst.
ROSENCRANTZ: We think not so, my lord.
55   HAMLET: Why then 'tis none to you, for there is nothing
      either good or bad but thinking makes it so. To
      me it is a prison.
ROSENCRANTZ: Why then, your ambition makes it
      one. 'Tis too narrow for your mind.
60   HAMLET: O God, I could be bounded in a nutshell
      and count myself a king of infinite space, were it
      not that I have bad dreams.
GUILDENSTERN: Which dreams indeed are ambition,
      for the very substance of the ambitious° is merely
65   the shadow of a dream.
HAMLET: A dream itself is but a shadow.
ROSENCRANTZ: Truly, and I hold ambition of so airy
      and light a quality that it is but a shadow's shadow.

232. **indifferent:** Ordinary.   239. **privates:** Close acquaintances (with sexual pun on *private parts*).   241. **strumpet:**
Prostitute (a common epithet for indiscriminate Fortune; see
line 505, p. 276).   251–52. **confines:** Places of confinement.
252. **wards:** Cells.   264. **the very . . . ambitious:** That seemingly very substantial thing which the ambitious pursue.

HAMLET: Then are our beggars bodies,° and our mon-
      archs and outstretch'd° heroes the beggars' shadows.   270
      Shall we to th' court? For, by my fay,° I cannot
      reason.
ROSENCRANTZ, GUILDENSTERN: We'll wait upon° you.
HAMLET: No such matter. I will not sort° you with
      the rest of my servants, for, to speak to you like   275
      an honest man, I am most dreadfully attended.°]
      But, in the beaten way° of friendship, what make°
      you at Elsinore?
ROSENCRANTZ: To visit you, my lord, no other occasion.
HAMLET: Beggar that I am, I am even poor in thanks;   280
      but I thank you, and sure, dear friends, my thanks
      are too dear a halfpenny.° Were you not sent for?
      Is it your own inclining? Is it a free visitation?
      Come, come, deal justly with me. Come, come;
      nay, speak.   285
GUILDENSTERN: What should we say, my lord?
HAMLET: Why, anything, but to th' purpose. You were
      sent for; and there is a kind of confession in your
      looks which your modesties have not craft enough
      to color. I know the good King and Queen have   290
      sent for you.
ROSENCRANTZ: To what end, my lord?
HAMLET: That you must teach me. But let me conjure°
      you, by the rights of our fellowship, by the con-
      sonancy of our youth,° by the obligation of our   295
      ever-preserv'd love, and by what more dear a better
      proposer° could charge° you withal, be even° and
      direct with me, whether you were sent for, or no?
ROSENCRANTZ [aside to Guildenstern]: What say you?
HAMLET [aside]: Nay then, I have an eye of° you. —   300
      If you love me, hold not off.
GUILDENSTERN: My lord, we were sent for.
HAMLET: I will tell you why; so shall my anticipation
      prevent your discovery;° and your secrecy to the
      King and Queen molt no feather.° I have of late —   305
      but wherefore I know not — lost all my mirth,
      forgone all custom of exercises; and indeed it goes
      so heavily with my disposition that this goodly
      frame, the earth, seems to me a sterile promontory;
      this most excellent canopy, the air, look you, this   310

269. **bodies:** Solid substances rather than shadows (since
beggars are not ambitious).   270. **outstretch'd:** (1) Far-reaching in their ambition, (2) elongated as shadows.   271. **fay:**
Faith.   273. **wait upon:** Accompany, attend.   274. **sort:**
Class, associate.   276. **dreadfully attended:** Waited upon in
slovenly fashion.   277. **beaten way:** Familiar path.   **make:**
Do.   282. **dear a halfpenny:** Expensive at the price of a
halfpenny, i.e., of little worth.   293. **conjure:** Adjure, entreat.   294–95. **consonancy of our youth:** The fact that we
are of the same age.   296–97. **better proposer:** More skillful
propounder.   297. **charge:** Urge.   **even:** Straight, honest.
300. **of:** On.   304. **prevent your discovery:** Forestall your
disclosure.   305. **molt no feather:** Not diminish in the least.

brave° o'erhanging firmament, this majestical roof
fretted° with golden fire, why, it appeareth nothing
to me but a foul and pestilent congregation of
vapors. What a piece of work is a man! How noble
in reason, how infinite in faculties, in form and
moving how express° and admirable, in action how
like an angel, in apprehension how like a god! The
beauty of the world, the paragon of animals! And
yet, to me, what is this quintessence° of dust? Man
delights not me — no, nor woman neither, though
by your smiling you seem to say so.

315

320

ROSENCRANTZ: My lord, there was no such stuff in
my thoughts.
HAMLET: Why did you laugh then, when I said "man
delights not me"?
ROSENCRANTZ: To think, my lord, if you delight not
in man, what lenten entertainment° the players shall
receive from you. We coted° them on the way, and
hither are they coming, to offer you service.
HAMLET: He that plays the king shall be welcome;
his Majesty shall have tribute of me. The adventurous
knight shall use his foil and target,° the lover shall
not sigh gratis, the humorous man° shall end his

32

33

---

311. brave: Splendid.   **312. fretted:** Adorned (with fret-
work, as in a vaulted ceiling).   **316. express:** Well-framed
(?), exact (?).   **319. quintessence:** The fifth essence of ancient
philosophy, beyond earth, water, air, and fire, supposed to
be the substance of the heavenly bodies and to be latent in
all things.

327. lenten entertainment: Meager reception (appropriate to
Lent).   **328. coted:** Overtook and passed beyond.   **332.
foil and target:** Sword and shield.   **333. humorous man:**
Eccentric character, dominated by one trait or "humor."

LEFT: Hamlet returns to Denmark. Left to right, Voltemand (Jeremy Geidt), Gertrude (Christine Estabrook), Claudius (Mark Metcalf), Hamlet (Mark Rylance), and Laertes (Derek Smith) in the 1991 American Repertory Theatre production of *Hamlet*, directed by Ron Daniels.
RIGHT: The dumb-show sequence with Candy Buckley as the Player Queen.

35   part in peace, [the clown shall make those laugh whose lungs are tickle o' th' sere°], and the lady shall say her mind freely, or the blank verse shall halt° for 't. What players are they?

ROSENCRANTZ: Even those you were wont to take such delight in, the tragedians of the city.

40   HAMLET: How chances it they travel? Their residence,° both in reputation and profit, was better both ways.

ROSENCRANTZ: I think their inhibition° comes by the means of the innovation.°

HAMLET: Do they hold the same estimation they did when I was in the city? Are they so follow'd?

45   ROSENCRANTZ: No, indeed, are they not.

[HAMLET: How comes it? Do they grow rusty?

ROSENCRANTZ: Nay, their endeavor keeps in the wonted° pace. But there is, sir, an aery° of children,

little eyases,° that cry out on the top of question,°   350
and are most tyrannically° clapp'd for 't. These are now the fashion, and so berattle° the common stages° — so they call them — that many wearing rapiers° are afraid of goose-quills° and dare scarce come thither.   355

HAMLET: What, are they children? Who maintains 'em? How are they escoted?° Will they pursue the quality° no longer than they can sing?° Will they not say afterwards, if they should grow themselves to common° players — as it is most like, if their   360
means are no better — their writers do them wrong, to make them exclaim against their own succession?°

335. tickle o' th' sere: Easy on the trigger, ready to laugh easily. (*Sere* is part of a gunlock.)   **337. halt:** Limp.   **340. residence:** Remaining in one place, i.e., in the city.   **342. inhibition:** Formal prohibition (from acting plays in the city).   **343. innovation:** I.e., the new fashion in satirical plays performed by boy actors in the "private" theaters; or possibly a political uprising; or the strict limitations set on the theater in London in 1600.   **349. wonted:** Usual.   **aery:** Nest.

350. eyases: Young hawks.   **cry . . . question:** Speak shrilly, dominating the controversy (in decrying the public theaters).   **351. tyrannically:** Outrageous.   **352. berattle:** Berate.   **352–53. common stages:** Public theaters.   **353–54. many wearing rapiers:** Many men of fashion, who were afraid to patronize the common players for fear of being satirized by the poets who wrote for the children.   **354. goose-quills:** pens of satirists.   **357. escoted:** maintained.   **358. quality:** (Acting) profession.   **no longer . . . sing:** Only until their voices change.   **360. common:** Regular, adult.   **362. succession:** Future careers.

ROSENCRANTZ: Faith, there has been much to do° on both sides; and the nation holds it no sin to tarre° 365 them to controversy. There was, for a while, no money bid for argument° unless the poet and the player went to cuffs in the question.°

HAMLET: Is 't possible?

GUILDENSTERN: O, there has been much throwing 370 about of brains.

HAMLET: Do the boys carry it away?°

ROSENCRANTZ: Ay, that they do, my lord — Hercules and his load° too.°]

HAMLET: It is not very strange; for my uncle is King 375 of Denmark, and those that would make mouths° at him while my father liv'd, give twenty, forty, fifty, a hundred ducats° apiece for his picture in little.° 'Sblood,° there is something in this more than natural, if philosophy could find it out.

(*A flourish* [*of trumpets within*].)

380 GUILDENSTERN: There are the players.

HAMLET: Gentlemen, you are welcome to Elsinore. Your hands, come then. Th' appurtenance of welcome is fashion and ceremony. Let me comply° with you in this garb,° lest my extent° to the players, 385 which, I tell you, must show fairly outwards,° should more appear like entertainment° than yours. You are welcome. But my uncle-father and aunt-mother are deceiv'd.

GUILDENSTERN: In what, my dear lord?

390 HAMLET: I am but mad north-north-west.° When the wind is southerly I know a hawk from a handsaw.°

(*Enter Polonius.*)

POLONIUS: Well be with you, gentlemen!

HAMLET: Hark you, Guildenstern, and you too; at each ear a hearer. That great baby you see there 395 is not yet out of his swaddling-clouts.°

363. **to do:** Ado. 364. **tarre:** Set on (as dogs). 366. **argument:** Plot for a play. 367. **went . . . question:** Came to blows in the play itself. 371. **carry it away:** Win the day. 372–73. **Hercules . . . load:** Thought to be an allusion to the sign of the Globe Theatre, which was Hercules bearing the world on his shoulder. 347–73. **How . . . load too:** The passage, omitted from the early quartos, alludes to the so-called War of the Theatres, 1599–1602, the rivalry between the children companies and the adult actors. 375. **mouths:** Faces. 377. **ducats:** Gold coins. 377–78. **in little:** In miniature. 378. **'Sblood:** By His (God's, Christ's) blood. 383. **comply:** Observe the formalities of courtesy. 384. **garb:** Manner. **my extent:** The extent of my showing courtesy. 385. **show fairly outwards:** Look cordial to outward appearances. 386. **entertainment:** A (warm) reception. 390. **north-north-west:** Only partly, at times. 391. **hawk, handsaw:** Mattock (or *hack*) and a carpenter's cutting tool respectively; also birds, with a play on *hernshaw* or heron. 395. **swaddling-clouts:** Cloths in which to wrap a newborn baby.

ROSENCRANTZ: Happily° he is the second time come to them; for they say an old man is twice a child.

HAMLET: I will prophesy he comes to tell me of the players; mark it. — You say right, sir, o' Monday morning, 'twas then indeed. 400

POLONIUS: My lord, I have news to tell you.

HAMLET: My lord, I have news to tell you. When Roscius° was an actor in Rome —

POLONIUS: The actors are come hither, my lord.

HAMLET: Buzz,° buzz! 405

POLONIUS: Upon my honor —

HAMLET: Then came each actor on his ass —

POLONIUS: The best actors in the world, either for tragedy, comedy, history, pastoral, pastoral-comical, historical-pastoral, tragical-historical, tragical-comical-historical-pastoral, scene individable,° or 41 poem unlimited.° Seneca° cannot be too heavy, nor Plautus° too light. For the law of writ and the liberty,° these are the only men.

HAMLET: O Jephthah, judge of Israel,° what a treasure 41 hadst thou!

POLONIUS: What a treasure had he, my lord?

HAMLET: Why,
  "One fair daughter, and no more,
    The which he loved passing° well." 42

POLONIUS [*aside*]: Still on my daughter.

HAMLET: Am I not i' th' right, old Jephthah?

POLONIUS: If you call me Jephthah, my lord, I have a daughter that I love passing well.

HAMLET: Nay, that follows not. 42

POLONIUS: What follows, then, my lord?

HAMLET: Why,
  "As by lot, God wot,"°
  and then, you know,
  "It came to pass, as most like° it was." 43
  The first row° of the pious chanson° will show you
  more, for look where my abridgement° comes.

(*Enter the Players.*)

396. **Happily:** Haply, perhaps. 403. **Roscius:** A famous Roman actor who died in 62 B.C. 405. **Buzz:** An interjection used to denote stale news. 411. **scene individable:** A play observing the unity of place. 412. **poem unlimited:** A play disregarding the unities of time and place. **Seneca:** Writer of Latin tragedies. 413. **Plautus:** Writer of Latin comedy. 413–14. **law . . . liberty:** Dramatic composition both according to rules and without rules, i.e., "classical" and "romantic" dramas. 415. **Jephthah . . . Israel:** Jephthah had to sacrifice his daughter; see Judges 11. Hamlet goes on to quote from a ballad on the theme. 420. **passing:** Surpassingly. 428. **wot:** Knows. 430. **like:** Likely, probable. 431. **row:** Stanza. **chanson:** Ballad, song. 432. **my abridgement:** Something that cuts short my conversation; also, a diversion.

You are welcome, masters; welcome, all. I am glad
to see thee well. Welcome, good friends. O, old
friend! Why, thy face is valanc'd° since I saw thee
last. Com'st thou to beard° me in Denmark? What,
my young lady° and mistress? By 'r lady, your
ladyship is nearer to heaven than when I saw you
last, by the altitude of a chopine.° Pray God your
voice, like a piece of uncurrent° gold, be not crack'd
within the ring.° Masters, you are all welcome.
We'll e'en to 't like French falconers, fly at anything
we see. We'll have a speech straight.° Come, give
us a taste of your quality; come, a passionate speech.

FIRST PLAYER: What speech, my good lord?

HAMLET: I heard thee speak me a speech once, but it
was never acted, or, if it was, not above once, for
the play, I remember, pleas'd not the million; 'twas
caviary to the general.° But it was — as I receiv'd
it, and others, whose judgments in such matters cried
in the top of ° mine — an excellent play, well digested
in the scenes, set down with as much modesty as
cunning.° I remember one said there were no sallets°
in the lines to make the matter savory, nor no
matter in the phrase that might indict° the author
of affectation, but call'd it an honest method, as
wholesome as sweet, and by very much more handsome than fine.° One speech in 't I chiefly lov'd:
'twas Aeneas' tale to Dido, and thereabout of it
especially when he speaks of Priam's slaughter.° If
it live in your memory, begin at this line: let me
see, let me see —
"The rugged Pyrrhus,° like th' Hyrcanian
beast"° —
'Tis not so. It begins with Pyrrhus:
"The rugged Pyrrhus, he whose sable° arms,
Black as his purpose, did the night resemble

---

435. **valanc'd:** Fringed (with a beard).   436. **beard:** Confront (with obvious pun).   437. **young lady:** Boy playing
women's parts.   439. **chopine:** Thick-soled shoe of Italian
fashion.   440. **uncurrent:** Not passable as lawful coinage.
440–41. **crack'd . . . ring:** Changed from adolescent to male
voice, no longer suitable for women's roles. (Coins featured
rings enclosing the sovereign's head; if the coin was cracked
within this ring, it was unfit for currency.)   443. **straight:**
At once.   449. **caviary to the general:** Caviar to the multitude, i.e., a choice dish too elegant for coarse tastes.   450–
51. **cried in the top of:** Spoke with greater authority than.
453. **cunning:** Skill.   **sallets:** Salad, i.e., spicy improprieties.
455. **indict:** Convict.   458. **fine:** Elaborately ornamented,
showy.   460. **Priam's slaughter:** The slaying of the rule of
Troy, when the Greeks finally took the city.   463. **Pyrrhus:**
A Greek hero in the Trojan War, also known as Neopto-
lemus, son of Achilles.   **Hyrcanian beast:** I.e., the tiger. (See
Virgil, *Aeneid*, IV, 266; compare the whole speech with Marlowe's *Dido Queen of Carthage*, II, I, 214 ff.)   465. **sable:**
Black (for reasons of camouflage during the episode of the
Trojan horse).

When he lay couched in the ominous horse,°
Hath now this dread and black complexion
    smear'd
With heraldry more dismal.° Head to foot
Now is he total gules,° horridly trick'd°   470
With blood of fathers, mothers, daughters, sons,
Bak'd and impasted° with the parching streets,°
That lend a tyrannous and a damned light
To their lord's° murder. Roasted in wrath and
    fire,
And thus o'er-sized° with coagulate gore,   475
With eyes like carbuncles, the hellish Pyrrhus
Old grandsire Priam seeks."
So proceed you.

POLONIUS: 'Fore God, my lord, well spoken, with good
accent and good discretion.

FIRST PLAYER: "Anon he finds him   480
Striking too short at Greeks. His antique sword,
Rebellious to his arm, lies where it falls,
Repugnant° to command. Unequal match'd,
Pyrrhus at Priam drives, in rage strikes wide,
But with the whiff and wind of his fell° sword   485
Th' unnerved father falls. [Then senseless Ilium,°]
Seeming to feel this blow, with flaming top
Stoops to his° base, and with a hideous crash
Takes prisoner Pyrrhus' ear. For, lo! His sword,
Which was declining on the milky head   490
Of reverend Priam, seem'd i' th' air to stick.
So as a painted° tyrant Pyrrhus stood,
And, like a neutral to his will and matter,°
Did nothing.
But, as we often see, against° some storm,   495
A silence in the heavens, the rack° stand still,
The bold winds speechless, and the orb below
As hush as death, anon the dreadful thunder
Doth rend the region,° so, after Pyrrhus' pause,
Aroused vengeance sets him new a-work,   500
And never did the Cyclops'° hammers fall
On Mars's armor forg'd for proof eterne°
With less remorse than Pyrrhus' bleeding sword

---

467. **ominous horse:** Trojan horse, by which the Greeks
gained access to Troy.   469. **dismal:** Ill-omened.   470.
gules: Red (a heraldic term).   **trick'd:** Adorned, decorated.
472. **impasted:** Crusted, like a thick paste.   **with . . . streets:**
By the parching heat of the streets (because of the fires everywhere).   474. **their lord's:** Priam's.   475. **o'er-sized:** Covered as with size or glue.   483. **Repugnant:** Disobedient,
resistant.   485. **fell:** Cruel.   486. **senseless Ilium:** Insensate
Troy.   488. **his:** Its.   492. **painted:** Painted in a picture.
493. **like . . . matter:** As though poised indecisively between
his intention and its fulfillment.   495. **against:** Just before.
496. **rack:** Mass of clouds.   499. **region:** Sky.   501. **Cyclops:** Giant armor makers in the smithy of Vulcan.   502.
proof eterne: Eternal resistance to assault.

Now falls on Priam.

505   Out, out, thou strumpet Fortune! All you gods,
In general synod,° take away her power!
Break all the spokes and fellies° from her wheel,
And bowl the round nave° down the hill of heaven,
As low as to the fiends!"

510   POLONIUS: This is too long.

HAMLET: It shall to the barber's with your beard. —
Prithee say on. He's for a jig° or a tale of bawdry,
or he sleeps. Say on; come to Hecuba.°

FIRST PLAYER: "But who, ah woe! had seen the
mobled° queen" —

515   HAMLET: "The mobled queen?"

POLONIUS: That's good. "Mobled queen" is good.

FIRST PLAYER: "Run barefoot up and down,
threat'ning the flames
With bisson rheum,° a clout° upon that head
Where late the diadem stood, and for a robe,

520   About her lank and all o'er-teemed° loins,
A blanket, in the alarm of fear caught up —
Who this had seen, with tongue in venom steep'd,
'Gainst Fortune's state° would treason have pronounc'd.°
But if the gods themselves did see her then

525   When she saw Pyrrhus make malicious sport
In mincing with his sword her husband's limbs,
The instant burst of clamor that she made,
Unless things mortal move them not at all,
Would have made milch° the burning eyes of heaven,

530   And passion in the gods."

POLONIUS: Look whe'er° he has not turn'd his color
and has tears in 's eyes. Prithee, no more.

HAMLET: 'Tis well; I'll have thee speak out the rest
of this soon. Good my lord, will you see the players

535   well bestow'd?° Do you hear, let them be well us'd,
for they are the abstract° and brief chronicles of
the time. After your death you were better have a
bad epitaph than their ill report while you live.

POLONIUS: My lord, I will use them according to their

540   desert.

HAMLET: God's bodkin,° man, much better! Use every
man after his desert, and who shall scape whipping?

Use them after your own honor and dignity. The
less they deserve, the more merit is in your bounty.
Take them in.   54?

POLONIUS: Come, sirs.

HAMLET: Follow him, friends. We'll hear a play tomorrow. [*As they start to leave, Hamlet detains
the First Player.*] Dost thou hear me, old friend?
Can you play the Murder of Gonzago?   55?

FIRST PLAYER: Ay, my lord.

HAMLET: We'll ha 't tomorrow night. You could, for
need, study a speech of some dozen or sixteen lines,
which I would set down and insert in 't, could you
not?   55?

FIRST PLAYER: Ay, my lord.

HAMLET: Very well. Follow that lord, and look you
mock him not. — My good friends, I'll leave you
till night. You are welcome to Elsinore.
       (*Exeunt Polonius and Players.*)

ROSENCRANTZ: Good my lord!   56?
       (*Exeunt [Rosencrantz and Guildenstern].*)

HAMLET: Ay, so, God buy you. — Now I am alone.
O, what a rogue and peasant slave am I!
Is it not monstrous that this player here,
But in a fiction, in a dream of passion,
Could force his soul so to his own conceit°   56?
That from her working all his visage wann'd,°
Tears in his eyes, distraction in his aspect,
A broken voice, and his whole function suiting
With forms to his conceit?° And all for nothing!
For Hecuba!   570
What's Hecuba to him, or he to Hecuba,
That he should weep for her? What would he do,
Had he the motive and the cue for passion
That I have? He would drown the stage with tears
And cleave the general ear with horrid speech,   575
Make mad the guilty and appall the free,°
Confound the ignorant, and amaze indeed
The very faculties of eyes and ears. Yet I,
A dull and muddy-mettled° rascal, peak,°
Like John-a-dreams,° unpregnant of° my cause,   580
And can say nothing — no, not for a king
Upon whose property° and most dear life
A damn'd defeat was made. Am I a coward?
Who calls me villain? Breaks my pate across?
Plucks off my beard, and blows it in my face?   585

---

506. **synod:** Assembly.   507. **fellies:** Pieces of wood forming the rim of a wheel.   508. **nave:** Hub.   512. **jig:** Comic song and dance often given at the end of a play.   513. **Hecuba:** Wife of Priam.   514. **mobled:** Muffled.   518. **bisson rheum:** Blinding tears.   **clout:** Cloth.   520. **o'er-teemed:** Worn out with bearing children.   523. **state:** Rule, managing.   **pronounc'd:** Proclaimed.   529. **milch:** Milky, moist with tears.   531. **whe'er:** Whether.   535. **bestow'd:** Lodged.   536. **abstract:** Summary account.   541. **God's bodkin:** By God's (Christ's) little body, *bodykin* (not to be confused with *bodkin*, dagger).

565. **conceit:** Conception.   566. **wann'd:** Grew pale.   568–69. **his whole . . . conceit:** His whole being responded with actions to suit his thought.   576. **free:** Innocent.   579. **muddy-mettled:** Dull-spirited.   **peak:** Mope, pine.   580. **John-a-dreams:** Sleepy dreaming idler.   **unpregnant of:** Not quickened by.   582. **property:** The crown; perhaps also character, quality.

Tweaks me by the nose? Gives me the lie° i' th'
  throat,
As deep as to the lungs? Who does me this?
Ha, 'swounds, I should take it; for it cannot be
But I am pigeon-liver'd,° and lack gall
To make oppression bitter, or ere this
I should have fatted all the region kites°
With this slave's offal. Bloody, bawdy villain!
Remorseless, treacherous, lecherous, kindless°
  villain!
[O, vengeance!]
Why, what an ass am I! This is most brave,
That I, the son of a dear father murder'd,
Prompted to my revenge by heaven and hell,
Must, like a whore, unpack my heart with
  words,
And fall a-cursing, like a very drab,°
A stallion!° Fie upon 't, foh! About,° my brains!
Hum, I have heard
That guilty creatures sitting at a play
Have by the very cunning of the scene
Been struck so to the soul that presently°
They have proclaim'd their malefactions;
For murder, though it have no tongue, will
  speak
With most miraculous organ. I'll have these
  players
Play something like the murder of my father
Before mine uncle. I'll observe his looks;
I'll tent° him to the quick. If 'a do blench,°
I know my course. The spirit that I have seen
May be the devil, and the devil hath power
T' assume a pleasing shape; yea, and perhaps
Out of my weakness and my melancholy,
As he is very potent with such spirits,°
Abuses° me to damn me. I'll have grounds
More relative° than this. The play's the thing
Wherein I'll catch the conscience of the King.
                                        (*Exit.*)

[ACT III · Scene I]°

(*Enter King, Queen, Polonius, Ophelia, Rosencrantz, Guildenstern, Lords.*)

KING: And can you, by no drift of conference,°

Get from him why he puts on this confusion,
Grating so harshly all his days of quiet
With turbulent and dangerous lunacy?
ROSENCRANTZ: He does confess he feels himself
  distracted,   5
But from what cause 'a will by no means speak.
GUILDENSTERN: Nor do we find him forward° to be
  sounded,°
But with a crafty madness keeps aloof
When we would bring him on to some
  confession
Of his true state.
QUEEN: Did he receive you well?   10
ROSENCRANTZ: Most like a gentleman.
GUILDENSTERN: But with much forcing of his
  disposition.°
ROSENCRANTZ: Niggard of question,° but of our
  demands
Most free in his reply.
QUEEN: Did you assay° him
To any pastime?   15
ROSENCRANTZ: Madam, it so fell out that certain
  players
We o'er-raught° on the way. Of these we told
  him,
And there did seem in him a kind of joy
To hear of it. They are here about the court,
And, as I think, they have already order   20
This night to play before him.
POLONIUS: 'Tis most true,
And he beseech'd me to entreat your Majesties
To hear and see the matter.
KING: With all my heart, and it doth much content
  me
To hear him so inclin'd.   25
Good gentlemen, give him a further edge,°
And drive his purpose into these delights.
ROSENCRANTZ: We shall, my lord.
        (*Exeunt Rosencrantz and Guildenstern.*)
KING: Sweet Gertrude, leave us too,
For we have closely° sent for Hamlet hither,
That he, as 'twere by accident, may here   30
Affront° Ophelia.
Her father and myself, [lawful espials,°]
Will so bestow ourselves that seeing, unseen,
We may of their encounter frankly judge,
And gather by him, as he is behav'd,   35
If 't be th' affliction of his love or no
That thus he suffers for.
QUEEN: I shall obey you.

---

586. Gives me the lie: Calls me a liar.   **589. pigeon-liver'd:**
The pigeon or dove was popularly supposed to be mild because it secreted no gall.   **591. region kites:** Kites (birds of
prey) of the air, from the vicinity.   **593. kindless:** Unnatural.
599. drab: Prostitute.   **600. stallion:** Prostitute (male or
female). (Many editors follow the Folio reading of *scullion.*)
About: About it, to work.   **604. presently:** At once.   **610.
tent:** Probe.   **blench:** Quail, flinch.   **615. spirits:** Humors
(of melancholy).   **616. Abuses:** Deludes.   **617. relative:**
Closely related, pertinent.   **III, I. Location:** The castle.   **1.
drift of conference:** Direction of conversation.

7. forward: Willing.   **sounded:** Tested deeply.   **12. disposition:** Inclination.   **13. question:** Conversation.   **14. assay:** Try to win.   **17. o'er-raught:** Overtook and passed.
26. edge: Incitement.   **29. closely:** Privately.   **31. Affront:**
Confront, meet.   **32. espials:** Spies.

And for your part, Ophelia, I do wish
That your good beauties be the happy cause
Of Hamlet's wildness. So shall I hope your
virtues
40 Will bring him to his wonted way again,
To both your honors.
OPHELIA: Madam, I wish it may.
                                    [*Exit Queen.*]
POLONIUS: Ophelia, walk you here. — Gracious,° so
    please you,
We will bestow ourselves. [*To Ophelia.*] Read
    on this book,   [*Gives her a book.*]
45 That show of such an exercise° may color°
Your loneliness. We are oft to blame in this —
'Tis too much prov'd° — that with devotion's
    visage
And pious action we do sugar o'er
The devil himself.
50 KING [*aside*]: O, 'tis too true!
How smart a lash that speech doth give my
    conscience!
The harlot's cheek, beautied with plast'ring art,
Is not more ugly to° the thing° that helps it
Than is my deed to my most painted word.
55 O heavy burden!
POLONIUS: I hear him coming. Let's withdraw, my
    lord.   [*King and Polonius withdraw.*°]

(*Enter Hamlet.* [*Ophelia pretends to read a book.*])

HAMLET: To be, or not to be, that is the question:
Whether 'tis nobler in the mind to suffer
The slings and arrows of outrageous fortune,
60 Or to take arms against a sea of troubles,
And by opposing end them. To die, to sleep —
No more — and by a sleep to say we end
The heart-ache and the thousand natural shocks
That flesh is heir to. 'Tis a consummation
65 Devoutly to be wish'd. To die, to sleep;
To sleep, perchance to dream. Ay, there's the
    rub,°
For in that sleep of death what dreams may
    come
When we have shuffled° off this mortal coil,°
Must give us pause. There's the respect°

That makes calamity of so long life.°   70
For who would bear the whips and scorns of
    time,
Th' oppressor's wrong, the proud man's
    contumely,°
The pangs of despis'd° love, the law's delay,
The insolence of office,° and the spurns°
That patient merit of th' unworthy takes,   75
When he himself might his quietus° make
With a bare bodkin?° Who would fardels° bear,
To grunt and sweat under a weary life,
But that the dread of something after death,
The undiscover'd country from whose bourn°   80
No traveler returns, puzzles the will,
And makes us rather bear those ills we have
Than fly to others that we know not of?
Thus conscience does make cowards of us all
And thus the native hue° of resolution   85
Is sicklied o'er with the pale cast° of thought,
And enterprises of great pitch° and moment°
With this regard° their currents° turn awry,
And lose the name of action. — Soft you now,
The fair Ophelia. Nymph, in thy orisons°   90
Be all my sins remember'd.
OPHELIA: Good my lord,
How does your honor for this many a day?
HAMLET: I humbly thank you; well, well, well.
OPHELIA: My lord, I have remembrances of yours,
That I have longed long to re-deliver.
I pray you, now receive them.   [*Offers tokens.*]   95
HAMLET: No, not I, I never gave you aught.
OPHELIA: My honor'd lord, you know right well
    you did,
And with them words of so sweet breath
    compos'd
As made these things more rich. Their perfume
    lost,   100
Take these again, for to the noble mind
Rich gifts wax poor when givers prove unkind.
There, my lord.   [*Gives tokens.*]
HAMLET: Ha, ha! Are you honest?°
OPHELIA: My lord?   105
HAMLET: Are you fair?°
OPHELIA: What means your lordship?

43. **Gracious:** Your Grace (i.e., the King).   45. **exercise:** Act of devotion. (The book she reads is one of devotion.) **color:** Give a plausible appearance to.   47. **too much prov'd:** Too often shown to be true, too often practiced.   53. **to:** Compared to. **thing:** I.e., the cosmetic.   56. [S.D.] **withdraw:** The King and Polonius may retire behind an arras. The stage directions specify that they "enter" again near the end of the scene.   66. **rub:** Literally, an obstacle in the game of bowls.   68. **shuffled:** Sloughed, cast. **coil:** Turmoil.   69. **respect:** Consideration.

70. **of . . . life:** So long-lived.   72. **contumely:** Insolent abuse.   73. **despis'd:** Rejected.   74. **office:** Officialdom. **spurns:** Insults.   76. **quietus:** Acquittance; here, death.   77. **bodkin:** Dagger. **fardels:** Burdens.   80. **bourn:** Boundary.   85. **native hue:** Natural color, complexion.   86. **cast:** Shade of color.   87. **pitch:** Height (as of a falcon's flight). **moment:** Importance.   88. **regard:** Respect, consideration. **currents:** Courses.   90. **orisons:** Prayers.   104. **honest:** (1) Truthful, (2) chaste.   106. **fair:** (1) Beautiful, (2) just, honorable.

HAMLET: That if you be honest and fair, your honesty°
should admit no discourse° to your beauty.

10 OPHELIA: Could beauty, my lord, have better commerce°
than with honesty?

HAMLET: Ay, truly; for the power of beauty will sooner
transform honesty from what it is to a bawd than
the force of honesty can translate beauty into his
15 likeness. This was sometime° a paradox,° but now
the time° gives it proof. I did love you once.

OPHELIA: Indeed, my lord, you made me believe so.

HAMLET: You should not have believ'd me, for virtue
cannot so inoculate° our old stock but we shall
20 relish of it.° I lov'd you not.

OPHELIA: I was the more deceiv'd.

HAMLET: Get thee to a nunn'ry.° Why wouldst thou
be a breeder of sinners? I am myself indifferent
honest;° but yet I could accuse me of such things
25 that it were better my mother had not borne me:
I am very proud, revengeful, ambitious, with more
offenses at my beck° than I have thoughts to put
them in, imagination to give them shape, or time
to act them in. What should such fellows as I do
30 crawling between earth and heaven? We are arrant
knaves, all; believe none of us. Go thy ways to a
nunn'ry. Where's your father?

OPHELIA: At home, my lord.

HAMLET: Let the doors be shut upon him, that he
35 may play the fool nowhere but in 's own house.
Farewell.

OPHELIA: O, help him, you sweet heavens!

HAMLET: If thou dost marry, I'll give thee this plague
for thy dowry: be thou as chaste as ice, as pure as
40 snow, thou shalt not escape calumny. Get thee to
a nunn'ry, farewell. Or, if thou wilt needs marry,
marry a fool, for wise men know well enough what
monsters° you° make of them. To a nunn'ry, go,
and quickly too. Farewell.

45 OPHELIA: Heavenly powers, restore him!

HAMLET: I have heard of your paintings too, well
enough. God hath given you one face, and you
make yourselves another. You jig,° and amble, and
you lisp, you nickname God's creatures, and make

your wantonness your ignorance.° Go to, I'll no   150
more on 't; it hath made me mad. I say, we will
have no moe marriage. Those that are married
already — all but one — shall live. The rest shall
keep as they are. To a nunn'ry, go.   (*Exit.*)

OPHELIA: O, what a noble mind is here o'erthrown!   155
The courtier's, soldier's, scholar's, eye, tongue,
sword,
Th' expectancy and rose of the fair state,°
The glass of fashion and the mold of form,°
Th' observ'd of all observers,° quite, quite down!
And I, of ladies most deject and wretched,   160
That suck'd the honey of his music vows,
Now see that noble and most sovereign reason,
Like sweet bells jangled, out of time and harsh,
That unmatch'd form and feature of blown°
youth
Blasted with ecstasy.° O, woe is me,   165
T' have seen what I have seen, see what I see!

(*Enter King and Polonius.*)

KING: Love? His affections do not that way tend;
Nor what he spake, though it lack'd form a
little,
Was not like madness. There's something in his
soul,
O'er which his melancholy sits on brood,   170
And I do doubt° the hatch and the disclose°
Will be some danger; which for to prevent,
I have in quick determination
Thus set it down: he shall with speed to
England,
For the demand of° our neglected tribute.   175
Haply the seas and countries different
With variable° objects shall expel
This something-settled° matter in his heart,
Whereon his brains still beating puts him thus
From fashion of himself.° What think you on 't?   180

POLONIUS: It shall do well. But yet do I believe
The origin and commencement of his grief
Sprung from neglected love. — How now,
Ophelia?
You need not tell us what Lord Hamlet said;
We heard it all. — My lord, do as you please,   185

---

108. **your honesty:** Your chastity.   109. **discourse:** Familiar
dealings.   110. **commerce:** Dealings.   115. **sometime:** Formerly.   **paradox:** A view opposite to commonly held opinion.   116. **the time:** The present age.   119. **inoculate:** Graft,
be engrafted to.   119–20. **but . . . it:** That we do not still
have about us a taste of the old stock; i.e., retain our sin-
fulness.   122. **nunn'ry:** (1) Convent, (2) brothel.   123–24.
indifferent honest: Reasonably virtuous.   127. **beck:** Command.   143. **monsters:** An allusion to the horns of a cuckold.   **you:** You women.   148. **jig:** Dance and sing affectedly
and wantonly.

149–50. **make . . . ignorance:** Excuse your affection on the
grounds of your ignorance.   157. **Th' expectancy . . . state:**
The hope and ornament of the kingdom made fair (by him).
158. **The glass . . . form:** The mirror of fashion and the
pattern of courtly behavior.   159. **observ'd . . . observers:**
The center of attention and honor in the court.   164. **blown:**
Booming.   165. **ecstasy:** Madness.   171. **doubt:** Fear.   **disclose:** Disclosure.   175. **For . . . of:** To demand.   177.
variable: Various.   178. **something-settled:** Somewhat settled.   180. **From . . . himself:** Out of his natural manner.

But, if you hold it fit, after the play
Let his queen mother all alone entreat him
To show his grief. Let her be round° with him;
And I'll be plac'd, so please you, in the ear
190 Of all their conference. If she find him not,
To England send him, or confine him where
Your wisdom best shall think.
KING: It shall be so.
Madness in great ones must not unwatch'd go.

(Exeunt.)

[Scene II]°

(Enter Hamlet and three of the Players.)

HAMLET: Speak the speech, I pray you, as I pronounc'd
it to you, trippingly on the tongue. But if you
mouth it, as many of our players° do, I had as lief
the town-crier spoke my lines. Nor do not saw the
5 air too much with your hand, thus, but use all
gently; for in the very torrent, tempest, and, as I
may say, whirlwind of your passion, you must acquire and beget a temperance that may give it
smoothness. O, it offends me to the soul to hear
10 a robustious° periwig-pated° fellow tear a passion
to tatters, to very rags, to split the ears of the
groundlings,° who for the most part are capable
of° nothing but inexplicable dumb-shows and noise.
I would have such a fellow whipp'd for o'er-doing
15 Termagant.° It out-herods Herod.° Pray you, avoid
it.
FIRST PLAYER: I warrant your honor.
HAMLET: Be not too tame neither, but let your own
discretion be your tutor. Suit the action to the
20 word, the word to the action, with this special
observance, that you o'erstep not the modesty of
nature. For anything so o'erdone is from° the purpose
of playing, whose end, both at the first and now,
was and is, to hold, as 't were, the mirror up to
25 nature, to show virtue her feature, scorn her own
image, and the very age and body of the time his°
form and pressure.° Now this overdone, or come

tardy off,° though it makes the unskillful laugh,
cannot but make the judicious grieve, the censure
of which one° must in your allowance o'erweigh   30
a whole theater of others. O, there be players that
I have seen play, and heard others praise, and that
highly, not to speak it profanely, that, neither having
th' accent of Christians nor the gait of Christian,
pagan, nor man, have so strutted and bellow'd that   35
I have thought some of nature's journeymen° had
made men and not made them well, they imitated
humanity so abominably.
FIRST PLAYER: I hope we have reform'd that indiffer-
ently° with us, sir.   40
HAMLET: O, reform it altogether. And let those that
play your clowns speak no more than is set down
for them; for there be of them° that will themselves
laugh, to set on some quantity of barren° spectators
to laugh too, though in the mean time some necessary   45
question of the play be then to be consider'd. That's
villainous, and shows a most pitiful ambition in
the fool that uses it. Go, make you ready.

[Exeunt Players.]

(Enter Polonius, Guildenstern, and Rosencrantz.)

How now, my lord! Will the King hear this piece
of work?   50
POLONIUS: And the Queen too, and that presently.°
HAMLET: Bid the players make haste.

[Exit Polonius.]

Will you two help to hasten them?
ROSENCRANTZ: Ay, my lord.   *(Exeunt they two.)*
HAMLET: What ho, Horatio!

(Enter Horatio.)

HORATIO: Here, sweet lord, at your service.   55
HAMLET: Horatio, thou art e'en as just a man
As e'er my conversation cop'd withal.°
HORATIO: O, my dear lord —
HAMLET: Nay, do not think I flatter;
For what advancement may I hope from thee
That no revenue hast but thy good spirits,   60
To feed and clothe thee? Why should the poor
be flatter'd?
No, let the candied° tongue lick absurd pomp,
And crook the pregnant° hinges of the knee
Where thrift° may follow fawning. Dost thou
hear?

---

188. **round:** Blunt.   III, II. **Location:** The castle.   3. **our
players:** Indefinite use; i.e., *players nowadays.*   10. **robus-
tious:** Violent, boisterous.   **periwig-pated:** Wearing a wig.
12. **groundlings:** Spectators who paid least and stood in the
yard of the theater.   12–13. **capable of:** Susceptible of being
influenced by.   15. **Termagant:** A god of the Saracens; a
character in the St. Nicholas play, where one of his worshipers, leaving him in charge of goods, returns to find them
stolen; whereupon he beats the god or idol, which howls
vociferously.   **Herod:** Herod of Jewry. (A character in *The
Slaughter of the Innocents* and other cycle plays. The part
was played with great noise and fury.)   22. **from:** Contrary
to.   26. **his:** Its.   27. **pressure:** Stamp, impressed character.

27–28. **come tardy off:** Inadequately done.   29–30. **the
censure . . . one:** The judgment of even one of whom.   36.
journeymen: Laborers not yet masters in their trade.   39–
40. **indifferently:** Tolerably.   43. **of them:** Some among
them.   44. **barren:** I.e., of wit.   51. **presently:** At once.
57. **my . . . withal:** My contact with people provided opportunity for encounter with.   62. **candied:** Sugared, flattering.   63. **pregnant:** Compliant.   64. **thrift:** Profit.

65 Since my dear soul was mistress of her choice
And could of men distinguish her election,
Sh' hath seal'd thee for herself, for thou hast been
   As one, in suff'ring all, that suffers nothing,
A man that Fortune's buffets and rewards
70 Hast ta'en with equal thanks; and blest are those
Whose blood° and judgment are so well
   commeddled°
That they are not a pipe for Fortune's finger
To sound what stop° she please. Give me that
   man
That is not passion's slave, and I will wear him
75 In my heart's core, ay, in my heart of heart,
As I do thee. — Something too much of this. —
There is a play tonight before the King.
One scene of it comes near the circumstance
Which I have told thee of my father's death.
80 I prithee, when thou seest that act afoot,
Even with the very comment of thy soul°
Observe my uncle. If his occulted° guilt
Do not itself unkennel in one speech,
It is a damned° ghost that we have seen,
85 And my imaginations are as foul
As Vulcan's stithy.° Give him heedful note,
For I mine eyes will rivet to his face,
And after we will both our judgments join
In censure of his seeming.°
HORATIO: Well, my lord.
90 If 'a steal aught the whilst this play is playing,
And scape detecting, I will pay the theft.

([*Flourish.*] *Enter trumpets and kettledrums, King,
Queen, Polonius, Ophelia, [Rosencrantz, Guildenstern,
and other Lords, with Guards carrying torches*].)

HAMLET: They are coming to the play. I must be idle.
   Get you a place. [*The King, Queen, and courtiers
                              sit.*]

KING: How fares our cousin Hamlet?
95 HAMLET: Excellent, i' faith, of the chameleon's dish:°
   I eat the air, promise-cramm'd. You cannot feed
   capons so.
KING: I have nothing with° this answer, Hamlet. These
   words are not mine.°

HAMLET: No, nor mine now. [*To Polonius.*] My lord,   100
   you played once i' th' university, you say?
POLONIUS: That did I, my lord; and was accounted a
   good actor.
HAMLET: What did you enact?
POLONIUS: I did enact Julius Caesar. I was killed i'   105
   th' Capitol; Brutus kill'd me.
HAMLET: It was a brute part of him to kill so capital
   a calf there. Be the players ready?
ROSENCRANTZ: Ay, my lord; they stay upon your
   patience.   110
QUEEN: Come hither, my dear Hamlet, sit by me.
HAMLET: No, good mother, here's metal more attractive.
POLONIUS [*to the King*]: O, ho, do you mark that?
HAMLET: Lady, shall I lie in your lap?
                [*Lying down at Ophelia's feet.*]
OPHELIA: No, my lord.   115
[HAMLET: I mean, my head upon your lap?
OPHELIA: Ay, my lord.]
HAMLET: Do you think I meant country° matters?
OPHELIA: I think nothing, my lord.
HAMLET: That's a fair thought to lie between maids'   120
   legs.
OPHELIA: What is, my lord?
HAMLET: Nothing.
OPHELIA: You are merry, my lord.
HAMLET: Who, I?   125
OPHELIA: Ay, my lord.
HAMLET: O God, your only jig-maker.° What should
   a man do but be merry? For look you how cheerfully
   my mother looks, and my father died within 's°
   two hours.   130
OPHELIA: Nay, 'tis twice two months, my lord.
HAMLET: So long? Nay then, let the devil wear black,
   for I'll have a suit of sables.° O heavens! Die two
   months ago, and not forgotten yet? Then there's
   hope a great man's memory may outlive his life   135
   half a year. But, by 'r lady, 'a must build churches,
   then, or else shall 'a suffer not thinking on,° with
   the hobby-horse, whose epitaph is "For, O, for,
   O, the hobby-horse is forgot."°

(*The trumpets sound. Dumb show follows.*)

(*Enter a King and a Queen* [*very lovingly*]; *the Queen
embracing him, and he her.* [*She kneels and makes*

---

show of protestation unto him.] He takes her up, and
declines his head upon her neck. He lies him down
upon a bank of flowers. She, seeing him asleep, leaves
him. Anon comes in another man, takes off his crown,
kisses it, pours poison in the sleeper's ears, and leaves
him. The Queen returns; finds the King dead, makes
passionate action. The Poisoner, with some three or
four, come in again, seem to condole with her. The
dead body is carried away. The Poisoner woos the
Queen with gifts; she seems harsh awhile but in the
end accepts love.)

[Exeunt.]

140   OPHELIA: What means this, my lord?
    HAMLET: Marry, this' miching mallecho;° it means
      mischief.
    OPHELIA: Belike° this show imports the argument° of
      the play.

(Enter Prologue.)

145   HAMLET: We shall know by this fellow. The players
      cannot keep counsel;° they'll tell all.
    OPHELIA: Will 'a tell us what this show meant?
    HAMLET: Ay, or any show that you will show him.
      Be not you° asham'd to show, he'll not shame to
150   tell you what it means.
    OPHELIA: You are naught, you are naught.° I'll mark
      the play.
    PROLOGUE: For us, and for our tragedy,
      Here stooping° to your clemency,
155   We beg your hearing patiently.   *[Exit.]*
    HAMLET: Is this a prologue, or the posy of a ring?°
    OPHELIA: 'Tis brief, my lord.
    HAMLET: As woman's love.

(Enter [two Players as] King and Queen.)

    PLAYER KING: Full thirty times hath Phoebus' cart°
      gone round
160   Neptune's salt wash° and Tellus'° orbed ground,
      And thirty dozen moons with borrowed° sheen
      About the world have times twelve thirties been,
      Since love our hearts and Hymen° did our hands
      Unite commutual° in most sacred bands.
    PLAYER QUEEN: So many journeys may the sun and
165   moon

Make us again count o'er ere love be done!
But, woe is me, you are so sick of late,
So far from cheer and from your former state,
That I distrust you. Yet, though I distrust,°
    Discomfort you, my lord, it nothing° must.   170
For women's fear and love hold quantity;°
In neither aught, or in extremity.
Now, what my love is, proof° hath made you
    know,
And as my love is siz'd, my fear is so.
Where love is great, the littlest doubts are fear;   175
Where little fears grow great, great love grows
    there.
PLAYER KING: Faith, I must leave thee, love, and
    shortly too;
My operant° powers their functions leave to do.°
And thou shalt live in this fair world behind,
Honor'd, belov'd; and haply one as kind   180
For husband shalt thou —
PLAYER QUEEN: O, confound the rest!
Such love must needs be treason in my breast.
In second husband let me be accurst!
None wed the second but who kill'd the first.
HAMLET: Wormwood, wormwood.   185
PLAYER QUEEN: The instances° that second marriage
    move°
Are base respects of thrift,° but none of love.
A second time I kill my husband dead,
When second husband kisses me in bed.
PLAYER KING: I do believe you think what now you
    speak,   190
But what we do determine oft we break.
Purpose is but the slave to memory,°
Of violent birth, but poor validity,°
Which now, like fruit unripe, sticks on the tree,
But fall unshaken when they mellow be.   195
Most necessary 'tis that we forget
To pay ourselves what to ourselves is debt.°
What to ourselves in passion we propose,
The passion ending, doth the purpose lose.
The violence of either grief or joy   200
Their own enactures° with themselves destroy.
Where joy most revels, grief doth most lament;
Grief joys, joy grieves, on slender accident.

---

141. this' miching mallecho: This is sneaking mischief. **143. Belike:** Probably. **argument:** Plot. **146. counsel:** Secret. **149. Be not you:** If you are not. **151. naught:** Indecent. **154. stooping:** Bowing. **156. posy . . . ring:** Brief motto in verse inscribed in a ring. **159. Phoebus' cart:** The sun god's chariot. **160. salt wash:** The sea. **Tellus:** Goddess of the earth, of the *orbed ground.* **161. borrowed:** Reflected. **163. Hymen:** God of matrimony. **164. commutual:** Mutually.

169. distrust: Am anxious about. **170. nothing:** Not at all. **171. hold quantity:** Keep proportion with one another. **173. proof:** Experience. **178. operant:** Active. **leave to do:** Cease to perform. **186. instances:** Motives. **move:** Motivate. **187. base . . . thrift:** Ignoble considerations of material prosperity. **192. Purpose . . . memory:** Our good intentions are subject to forgetfulness. **193. validity:** Strength, durability. **196–97. Most . . . debt:** It's inevitable that in time we forget the obligations we have imposed on ourselves. **201. enactures:** Fulfillments.

This world is not for aye,° nor 'tis not strange
That even our loves should with our fortunes
    change;
For 'tis a question left us yet to prove,
Whether love lead fortune, or else fortune love.
The great man down, you mark his favorite flies;
The poor advanc'd makes friends of enemies.
And hitherto doth love on fortune tend;
For who not needs° shall never lack a friend,
And who in want° a hollow friend doth try,°
Directly seasons him° his enemy.
But, orderly to end where I begun,
Our wills and fates do so contrary run
That our devices still° are overthrown;
Our thoughts are ours, their ends° none of our
    own.
So think thou wilt no second husband wed,
But die thy thoughts when thy first lord is dead.
PLAYER QUEEN: Nor earth to me give food, nor
    heaven light,
Sport and repose lock from me day and night,
To desperation turn my trust and hope,
An anchor's cheer° in prison be my scope!°
Each opposite° that blanks° the face of joy
Meet what I would have well and it destroy!
Both here and hence° pursue me lasting strife,
If, once a widow, ever I be wife!
HAMLET: If she should break it now!
PLAYER KING: 'Tis deeply sworn. Sweet, leave me
    here awhile;
My spirits grow dull, and fain I would beguile
The tedious day with sleep.   [*Sleeps.*]
PLAYER QUEEN: Sleep rock thy brain,
And never come mischance between us twain!
                        [*Exit.*]
HAMLET: Madam, how like you this play?
QUEEN: The lady doth protest too much, methinks.
HAMLET: O, but she'll keep her word.
KING: Have you heard the argument?° Is there no
    offense in 't?
HAMLET: No, no, they do but jest, poison in jest; no
    offense i' th' world.
KING: What do you call the play?
HAMLET: "The Mouse-trap." Marry, how? Tropically.°

This play is the image of a murder done in Vienna.
Gonzago is the Duke's name; his wife, Baptista.
You shall see anon. 'Tis a knavish piece of work,
but what of that? Your Majesty, and we that have
free° souls, it touches us not. Let the gall'd jade°
winch,° our withers° are unwrung.°

(*Enter Lucianus.*)

This is one Lucianus, nephew to the King.
OPHELIA: You are as good as a chorus,° my lord.
HAMLET: I could interpret between you and your love,
    if I could see the puppets dallying.°
OPHELIA: You are keen, my lord, you are keen.
HAMLET: It would cost you a groaning to take off
    mine edge.
OPHELIA: Still better, and worse.°
HAMLET: So° you mistake° your husbands. Begin, mur-
    derer; leave thy damnable faces, and begin. Come,
    the croaking raven doth bellow for revenge.
LUCIANUS: Thoughts black, hands apt, drugs fit, and
    time agreeing,
Confederate season,° else no creature seeing,
Thou mixture rank, of midnight weeds collected,
With Hecate's ban° thrice blasted, thrice infected,
Thy natural magic and dire property
On wholesome life usurp immediately.
    [*Pours the poison into the sleeper's ears.*]
HAMLET: 'A poisons him i' th' garden for his estate.
    His name's Gonzago. The story is extant, and written
    in very choice Italian. You shall see anon how the
    murderer gets the love of Gonzago's wife.
                        [*Claudius rises.*]
OPHELIA: The King rises.
[HAMLET: What, frighted with false fire?°]
QUEEN: How fares my lord?
POLONIUS: Give o'er the play.
KING: Give me some light. Away!

---

246. **free:** Guiltless. **gall'd jade:** Horse whose hide is rubbed by saddle or harness. 247. **Winch:** Wince. **withers:** The part between the horse's shoulder blades. **unwrung:** Not rubbed sore. 249. **chorus:** In many Elizabethan plays the forthcoming action was explained by an actor known as the "chorus"; at a puppet show the actor who spoke the dialogue was known as an "interpreter," as indicated by the lines following. 251. **dallying:** With sexual suggestion, continued in *keen,* i.e., sexually aroused, *groaning,* i.e., moaning in pregnancy, and *edge,* i.e., sexual desire or impetuosity. 255. **Still . . . worse:** More keen-witted and less decorous. 256. **So:** even thus (in marriage). **mistake:** Mis-take, take erringly, falseheartedly. 260. **Confederate season:** The time and occasion conspiring (to assist the murderer). 262. **Hecate's ban:** The curse of Hecate, the goddess of witchcraft. 270. **false fire:** The blank discharge of a gun loaded with powder but not shot.

203. **aye:** Ever. 211. **who not needs:** He who is not in need (of wealth). 212. **who in want:** He who is in need. **try:** Test (his generosity). 213. **seasons him:** Ripens him into. 216. **devices still:** Intentions continually. 217. **ends:** Results. 223. **anchor's cheer:** Anchorite's or hermit's fare. **my scope:** The extent of my happiness. 224. **opposite:** Adverse thing. **blanks:** Causes to blanch or grow pale. 226. **hence:** In the life hereafter. 236. **argument:** Plot. 241. **Tropically:** Figuratively. (The first quarto reading, *trapically,* suggests a pun on *trap* in *Mouse-trap.*)

POLONIUS: Lights, lights, lights!
(*Exeunt all but Hamlet and Horatio.*)
275 HAMLET: "Why, let the strucken deer go weep,
The hart ungalled° play.
For some must watch,° while some must sleep;
Thus runs the world away."°
Would not this,° sir, and a forest of feathers° —
280 if the rest of my fortunes turn Turk with° me —
with two Provincial roses° on my raz'd° shoes, get
me a fellowship in a cry of players?°
HORATIO: Half a share.
HAMLET: A whole one, I.
285 "For thou dost know, O Damon dear,
This realm dismantled° was
Of Jove himself, and now reigns here
A very, very — pajock."°
HORATIO: You might have rhym'd.
290 HAMLET: O good Horatio, I'll take the ghost's word
for a thousand pound. Didst perceive?
HORATIO: Very well, my lord.
HAMLET: Upon the talk of pois'ning?
HORATIO: I did very well note him.
295 HAMLET: Ah, ha! Come, some music! Come, the
recorders!°
"For if the King like not the comedy,
Why then, belike, he likes it not, perdy"°
Come, some music!

(*Enter Rosencrantz and Guildenstern.*)

300 GUILDENSTERN: Good my lord, vouchsafe me a word
with you.
HAMLET: Sir, a whole history.
GUILDENSTERN: The King, sir —
HAMLET: Ay, sir, what of him?
305 GUILDENSTERN: Is in his retirement marvelous
distemp'red.
HAMLET: With drink, sir?
GUILDENSTERN: No, my lord, with choler.°
HAMLET: Your wisdom should show itself more richer

to signify this to the doctor, for for me to put him 310
to his purgation would perhaps plunge him into
more choler.
GUILDENSTERN: Good my lord, put your discourse into
some frame° and start not so wildly from my affair.
HAMLET: I am tame, sir. Pronounce. 315
GUILDENSTERN: The Queen, your mother, in most great
affliction of spirit, hath sent me to you.
HAMLET: You are welcome.
GUILDENSTERN: Nay, good my lord, this courtesy is
not of the right breed. If it shall please you to make 320
me a wholesome answer, I will do your mother's
commandment; if not, your pardon° and my return
shall be the end of my business.
HAMLET: Sir, I cannot.
ROSENCRANTZ: What, my lord? 325
HAMLET: Make you a wholesome answer; my wit's
diseas'd. But, sir, such answer as I can make, you
shall command, or rather, as you say, my mother.
Therefore no more, but to the matter. My mother,
you say — 330
ROSENCRANTZ: Then thus she says: your behavior hath
struck her into amazement and admiration.°
HAMLET: O wonderful son, that can so stonish a
mother! But is there no sequel at the heels of this
mother's admiration? Impart. 335
ROSENCRANTZ: She desires to speak with you in her
closet,° ere you go to bed.
HAMLET: We shall obey, were she ten times our mother.
Have you any further trade with us?
ROSENCRANTZ: My lord, you once did love me. 340
HAMLET: And do still, by these pickers and stealers.°
ROSENCRANTZ: Good my lord, what is your cause of
distemper? You do surely bar the door upon your
own liberty, if you deny your griefs to your friend.
HAMLET: Sir, I lack advancement. 345
ROSENCRANTZ: How can that be, when you have the
voice of the King himself for your succession in
Denmark?
HAMLET: Ay, sir, but "While the grass grows"° — the
proverb is something° musty. 350

(*Enter the Players with recorders.*)

O, the recorders! Let me see one. [*He takes a recorder.*] To withdraw° with you: why do you go

276. **ungalled:** Unafflicted.   277. **watch:** Remain awake.
275–78. **Why . . . away:** Probably from an old ballad, with
allusion to the popular belief that a wounded deer retires to
weep and die; cf. *As You Like It*, II, i, 66.   279. **this:** The
play.   **feathers:** Allusion to the plumes which Elizabethan
actors were fond of wearing.   280. **turn Turk with:** Turn
renegade against, go back on.   281. **Provincial roses:** Ro-
settes of ribbon like the roses of a part of France.   **raz'd:**
With ornamental slashing.   282. **fellowship . . . players:**
Partnership in a theatrical company.   286. **dismantled:**
Stripped, divested.   288. **pajock:** Peacock, a bird with a bad
reputation (here substituted for the obvious rhyme-word *ass*).
296. **recorders:** Wind instruments like the flute.   298. **perdy:**
A corruption of the French *par dieu*, by God.   308. **choler:**
Anger. (But Hamlet takes the word in its more basic humors
sense of *bilious disorder*.)

314. **frame:** Order.   322. **pardon:** Permission to depart.
332. **admiration:** Wonder.   337. **closet:** Private chamber.
341. **pickers and stealers:** Hands (so called from the cate-
chism, "to keep my hands from picking and stealing").   349.
While . . . grows: The rest of the proverb is "the silly horse
starves"; Hamlet may not live long enough to succeed to the
kingdom.   350. **something:** Somewhat.   352. **withdraw:**
Speak privately.

about to recover the wind° of me, as if you would
drive me into a toil?°

55 GUILDENSTERN: O, my lord, if my duty be too bold,
my love is too unmannerly.°

HAMLET: I do not well understand that. Will you play
upon this pipe?

GUILDENSTERN: My lord, I cannot.

60 HAMLET: I pray you.

GUILDENSTERN: Believe me, I cannot.

HAMLET: I do beseech you.

GUILDENSTERN: I know no touch of it, my lord.

HAMLET: It is as easy as lying. Govern these ventages°
65 with your fingers and thumb, give it breath with
your mouth, and it will discourse most eloquent
music. Look you, these are the stops.

GUILDENSTERN: But these cannot I command to any
utt'rance of harmony; I have not the skill.

70 HAMLET: Why, look you now, how unworthy a thing
you make of me! You would play upon me, you
would seem to know my stops, you would pluck
out the heart of my mystery, you would sound me
from my lowest note to the top of my compass,°
75 and there is much music, excellent voice, in this
little organ,° yet cannot you make it speak. 'Sblood,
do you think I am easier to be play'd on than a
pipe? Call me what instrument you will, though
you can fret° me, you cannot play upon me.

(Enter Polonius.)

80   God bless you, sir!

POLONIUS: My lord, the Queen would speak with you,
and presently.°

HAMLET: Do you see yonder cloud that's almost in
shape of a camel?

85 POLONIUS: By th' mass, and 'tis like a camel, indeed.

HAMLET: Methinks it is like a weasel.

POLONIUS: It is back'd like a weasel.

HAMLET: Or like a whale?

POLONIUS: Very like a whale.

90 HAMLET: Then I will come to my mother by and by.°
[*Aside.*] They fool me° to the top of my bent.° —
I will come by and by.

POLONIUS: I will say so.   [*Exit.*]

---

353. **recover the wind:** Get the windward side.   354. **toil:**
Snare.   355–56. **if . . . unmannerly:** If I am using an unmannerly boldness, it is my love which occasions it.   364.
ventages: Stops of the recorder.   374. **compass:** Range (of
voice).   376. **organ:** Musical instrument.   379. **fret:** Irritate
(with a quibble on *fret* meaning the piece of wood, gut, or
metal which regulates the fingering on an instrument).   382.
presently: At once.   390. **by and by:** Immediately.   391.
fool me: Make me play the fool.   **top of my bent:** Limit of
my ability or endurance (literally, the extent to which a bow
may be bent).

HAMLET: "By and by" is easily said. Leave me, friends.
                          [*Exeunt all but Hamlet.*]
'Tis now the very witching time° of night,   395
When churchyards yawn and hell itself breathes
    out
Contagion to this world. Now could I drink hot
    blood,
And do such bitter business as the day
Would quake to look on. Soft, now to my
    mother.
O heart, lose not thy nature! Let not ever   400
The soul of Nero° enter this firm bosom.
Let me be cruel, not unnatural;
I will speak daggers to her, but use none.
My tongue and soul in this be hypocrites:
How in my words somever° she be shent,°   405
To give them seals° never, my soul, consent!
                                          (*Exit.*)

[Scene III]°

(Enter King, Rosencrantz, and Guildenstern.)

KING: I like him not, nor stands it safe with us
To let his madness range. Therefore prepare you.
I your commission will forthwith dispatch,°
And he to England shall along with you.
The terms° of our estate° may not endure   5
Hazard so near 's as doth hourly grow
Out of his brows.°

GUILDENSTERN: We will ourselves provide.
Most holy and religious fear it is
To keep those many many bodies safe
That live and feed upon your Majesty.   10

ROSENCRANTZ: The single and peculiar° life is
    bound
With all the strength and armor of the mind
To keep itself from noyance,° but much more
That spirit upon whose weal depends and rests
The lives of many. The cess° of majesty   15
Dies not alone, but like a gulf° doth draw
What's near it with it; or it is a massy wheel
Fix'd on the summit of the highest mount,
To whose huge spokes ten thousand lesser things

---

395. **witching time:** Time when spells are cast and evil is
abroad.   401. **Nero:** Murderer of his mother, Agrippina.
405. **How . . . somever:** However much by my words.
shent: Rebuked.   406. **give them seals:** Confirm them with
deeds.   III. III. **Location:** The castle.   3. **dispatch:** Prepare,
cause to be drawn up.   5. **terms:** Condition, circumstances.
our estate: My royal position.   7. **brows:** Effronteries,
threatening frowns (?), brain (?).   11. **single and peculiar:**
Individual and private.   13. **noyance:** Harm.   15. **cess:**
Decease.   16. **gulf:** Whirlpool.

20   Are mortis'd and adjoin'd, which, when it falls,
     Each small annexment, petty consequence,
     Attends° the boist'rous ruin. Never alone
     Did the King sigh, but with a general groan.
KING: Arm° you, I pray you, to this speedy voyage,
25   For we will fetters put about this fear,
     Which now goes too free-footed.
ROSENCRANTZ: We will haste us.
     (Exeunt Gentlemen [Rosencrantz and Guildenstern].)

     (Enter Polonius.)

POLONIUS: My lord, he's going to his mother's
          closet.
     Behind the arras° I'll convey myself
     To hear the process.° I'll warrant she'll tax him
          home,°
30   And, as you said, and wisely was it said,
     'Tis meet that some more audience than a
          mother,
     Since nature makes them partial, should o'erhear
     The speech, of vantage.° Fare you well, my liege.
     I'll call upon you ere you go to bed,
     And tell you what I know.
35   KING: Thanks, dear my lord.
                              (Exit [Polonius].)
     O, my offense is rank, it smells to heaven;
     It hath the primal eldest curse° upon 't,
     A brother's murder. Pray can I not,
     Though inclination be as sharp as will.°
40   My stronger guilt defeats my strong intent,
     And, like a man to double business bound,
     I stand in pause where I shall first begin,
     And both neglect. What if this cursed hand
     Were thicker than itself with brother's blood,
45   Is there not rain enough in the sweet heavens
     To wash it white as snow? Whereto serves
          mercy
     But to confront the visage of offense?°
     And what's in prayer but this twofold force,
     To be forestalled° ere we come to fall,
50   Or pardon'd being down? Then I'll look up;
     My fault is past. But, O, what form of prayer

Can serve my turn? "Forgive me my foul
     murder"?
That cannot be, since I am still possess'd
Of those effects for which I did the murder,
My crown, mine own ambition, and my queen.   55
May one be pardon'd and retain th' offense?
In the corrupted currents° of this world
Offense's gilded hand° may shove by justice,
And oft 'tis seen the wicked prize° itself
Buys out the law. But 'tis not so above.   60
There is no shuffling,° there the action lies°
In his° true nature, and we ourselves compell'd,
Even to the teeth and forehead° of our faults,
To give in evidence. What then? What rests?°
Try what repentance can. What can it not?   65
Yet what can it, when one cannot repent?
O wretched state! O bosom black as death!
O limed° soul, that, struggling to be free,
Art more engag'd!° Help, angels! Make assay.°
Bow, stubborn knees, and heart with strings of
     steel,   70
Be soft as sinews of the new-born babe!
All may be well.
                              [He kneels.]

(Enter Hamlet [with sword drawn].)

HAMLET: Now might I do it pat,° now 'a is a-
          praying;
     And now I'll do 't. And so 'a goes to heaven;
     And so am I reveng'd. That would be scann'd:° 75
     A villain kills my father, and for that,
     I, his sole son, do this same villain send
     To heaven.
     Why, this is hire and salary, not revenge.
     'A took my father grossly,° full of bread,°   80
     With all his crimes broad blown,° as flush° as
          May;
     And how his audit° stands who knows save
          heaven?
     But in our circumstance and course° of thought,
     'Tis heavy with him. And am I then reveng'd,

22. Attends: Participates in.   24. Arm: Prepare.   28. arras:
Screen of tapestry placed around the walls of household
apartments. (On the Elizabethan stage, the arras was presumably over a door or discovery space in the tiring-house
facade.)   29. process: Proceedings.   tax him home: Reprove him severely.   33. of vantage: From an advantageous
place.   37. primal eldest curse: The curse of Cain, the first
murderer; he killed his brother Abel.   39. Though . . . will:
Though my desire is as strong as my determination.   46–
47. Whereto . . . offense: For what function does mercy serve
other than to undo the effects of sin?   49. forestalled: Prevented (from sinning).

57. currents: Courses.   58. gilded hand: Hand offering gold
as a bribe.   59. wicked prize: Prize won by wickedness.
61. shuffling: Escape by trickery.   the action lies: The accusation is made manifest, comes up for consideration (a
legal metaphor).   62. his: Its.   63. teeth and forehead: Face
to face, concealing nothing.   64. rests: Remains.   68.
limed: Caught as with birdlime, a sticky substance used to
ensnare birds.   69. engag'd: Embedded.   assay: Trial.   73.
pat: Opportunely.   75. would be scann'd: Needs to be
looked into.   80. grossly: Not spiritually prepared.   full
of bread: Enjoying his worldly pleasures. (See Ezek. 16:49.)
81. crimes broad blown: Sins in full bloom.   flush: Lusty.
82. audit: Account.   83. in . . . course: As we see it in our
mortal situation.

To take him in the purging of his soul,
When he is fit and season'd for his passage?
No!
Up, sword, and know thou a more horrid hent.°
                                   [*Puts up his sword.*]
When he is drunk asleep, or in his rage,
Or in th' incestuous pleasure of his bed,
At game a-swearing, or about some act
That has no relish of salvation in 't —
Then trip him, that his heels may kick at
   heaven,
And that his soul may be as damn'd and black
As hell, whereto it goes. My mother stays.
This physic° but prolongs thy sickly days. (*Exit.*)
KING: My words fly up, my thoughts remain below.
Words without thoughts never to heaven go.
                                   (*Exit.*)

[*Scene IV*]°

(*Enter [Queen] Gertrude and Polonius.*)

POLONIUS: 'A will come straight. Look you lay°
   home to him.
Tell him his pranks have been too broad° to
   bear with,
And that your Grace hath screen'd and stood
   between
Much heat° and him. I'll sconce° me even here.
Pray you, be round° [with him.
HAMLET (*within*): Mother, mother, mother!]
QUEEN: I'll warrant you, fear me not.
Withdraw, I hear him coming.
                   [*Polonius hides behind the arras.*]

(*Enter Hamlet.*)

HAMLET: Now, mother, what's the matter?
QUEEN: Hamlet, thou hast thy father° much
   offended.
HAMLET: Mother, you have my father much
   offended.
QUEEN: Come, come, you answer with an idle°
   tongue.
HAMLET: Go, go, you question with a wicked
   tongue.
QUEEN: Why, how now, Hamlet?
HAMLET: What's the matter now?

QUEEN: Have you forgot me?
HAMLET: No, by the rood,° not so: 15
You are the Queen, your husband's brother's
   wife,
And — would it were not so! — you are my
   mother.
QUEEN: Nay, then, I'll set those to you that can
   speak.
HAMLET: Come, come, and sit you down; you shall
   not budge.
You go not till I set you up a glass   20
Where you may see the inmost part of you.
QUEEN: What wilt thou do? Thou wilt not murder
   me?
Help, ho!
POLONIUS [*behind*]: What, ho! Help!
HAMLET [*drawing*]: How now? A rat? Dead, for a
   ducat, dead!   25
                   [*Makes a pass through the arras.*]
POLONIUS [*behind*]: O, I am slain! [*Falls and dies.*]
QUEEN: O me, what hast thou done?
HAMLET: Nay, I know not. Is it the King?
QUEEN: O, what a rash and bloody deed is this!
HAMLET: A bloody deed — almost as bad, good
   mother,
As kill a king, and marry with his brother.   30
QUEEN: As kill a king!
HAMLET: Ay, lady, it was my word.
         [*Parts the arras and discovers Polonius.*]
Thou wretched, rash, intruding fool, farewell!
I took thee for thy better. Take thy fortune.
Thou find'st to be too busy is some danger. —
Leave wringing of your hands. Peace, sit you
   down,   35
And let me wring your heart, for so I shall,
If it be made of penetrable stuff,
If damned custom° have not braz'd° it so
That it be proof° and bulwark against sense.°
QUEEN: What have I done, that thou dar'st wag thy
   tongue   40
In noise so rude against me?
HAMLET: Such an art
That blurs the grace and blush of modesty,
Calls virtue hypocrite, takes off the rose
From the fair forehead of an innocent love
And sets a blister° there, makes marriage-vows 45
As false as dicers' oaths. O, such a deed
As from the body of contraction° plucks
The very soul, and sweet religion° makes

---

88. **know . . . hent**: Await to be grasped by me on a more
horrid occasion.   96. **physic**: Purging (by prayer).   **III, IV.
Location**: The Queen's private chamber.   1. **lay**: Thrust (i.e.,
reprove him soundly).   2. **broad**: Unrestrained.   4. **Much
heat**: The King's anger.   **sconce**: Ensconce, hide.   5. **round**:
Blunt.   10. **thy father**: Your stepfather, Claudius.   12. **idle**:
Foolish.

15. **rood**: Cross.   38. **damned custom**: Habitual wickedness.
braz'd: Brazened, hardened.   39. **proof**: Armor.   **sense**:
Feeling.   45. **sets a blister**: Brands as a harlot.   47. **contraction**: The marriage contract.   48. **religion**: Religious
vows.

FAR LEFT: Michael Pennington as Hamlet. NEAR LEFT: A scene from the Royal Shakespeare Company's 1980 production. BELOW LEFT: Gertrude watches Laertes and Hamlet dueling. The poisoned cup is in the foreground. RIGHT: The grave-digger holds up Yorick's skull as Hamlet and Horatio (Tom Wilkinson) look on. BELOW RIGHT: Carol Royale as Ophelia with Hamlet in the nunnery scene.

A rhapsody° of words. Heaven's face does glow
50   O'er this solidity and compound mass
      With heated visage, as against the doom,
      Is thought-sick at the act.
QUEEN: Ay me, what act,°
      That roars so loud and thunders in the index?°
HAMLET: Look here, upon this picture, and on this,
55   The counterfeit presentment° of two brothers.
                              [*Shows her two likenesses.*]
      See, what a grace was seated on this brow:
      Hyperion's° curls, the front° of Jove himself,
      An eye like Mars, to threaten and command,
      A station° like the herald Mercury
60   New-lighted on a heaven-kissing hill —
      A combination and a form indeed,
      Where every god did seem to set his seal,
      To give the world assurance of a man.
      This was your husband. Look you now, what
         follows:
65   Here is your husband, like a mildew'd ear,°
      Blasting his wholesome brother. Have you eyes?
      Could you on this fair mountain leave to feed,
      And batten° on this moor?° Ha, have you eyes?
      You cannot call it love, for at your age
70   The heyday° in the blood is tame, it's humble,
      And waits upon the judgment, and what
         judgment
      Would step from this to this? Sense,° sure, you
         have,
      Else could you not have motion, but sure that
         sense
      Is apoplex'd,° for madness would not err,
75   Nor sense to ecstasy was ne'er so thrall'd
      But it reserv'd some quantity of choice
      To serve in such a difference. What devil was 't
      That thus hath cozen'd° you at hoodman-blind?°
      Eyes without feeling, feeling without sight,

Ears without hands or eyes, smelling sans° all,   80
      Or but a sickly part of one true sense
      Could not so mope.°
      O shame, where is thy blush? Rebellious hell,
      If thou canst mutine° in a matron's bones,
      To flaming youth let virtue be as wax,   85
      And melt in her own fire. Proclaim no shame
      When the compulsive ardor gives the charge,
      Since frost itself as actively doth burn,
      And reason panders will.°
QUEEN: O Hamlet, speak no more!   90
      Thou turn'st mine eyes into my very soul,
      And there I see such black and grained° spots
      As will not leave their tinct.°
HAMLET: Nay, but to live
      In the rank sweat of an enseamed° bed,
      Stew'd in corruption, honeying and making love 95
      Over the nasty sty —
QUEEN: O, speak to me no more.
      These words, like daggers, enter in my ears.
      No more, sweet Hamlet!
HAMLET: A murderer and a villain,
      A slave that is not twentieth part the tithe°   100
      Of your precedent° lord, a vice° of kings,
      A cutpurse of the empire and the rule,
      That from a shelf the precious diadem stole,
      And put it in his pocket!
QUEEN: No more!   105

(*Enter Ghost* [*in his nightgown*].)

HAMLET: A king of shreds and patches° —
      Save me, and hover o'er me with your wings,
      You heavenly guards! What would your gracious
         figure?
QUEEN: Alas, he's mad!
HAMLET: Do you not come your tardy son to
         chide,   110
      That, laps'd in time and passion,° lets go by
      Th' important° acting of your dread command?
      O, say!
GHOST: Do not forget. This visitation

---

49. **rhapsody:** Senseless string.   **49–52. Heaven's . . . act:**
Heaven's face flushes with anger to look down upon this
solid world, this compound mass, with hot face as though
the day of doom were near, and is thought-sick at the deed
(i.e., Gertrude's marriage).   53. **index:** Table of contents,
prelude, or preface.   55. **counterfeit presentment:** Portrayed
representation.   57. **Hyperion:** The sun god.   **front:** Brow.
59. **station:** Manner of standing.   65. **ear:** I.e., of grain.
68. **batten:** Gorge.   **moor:** Barren upland.   70. **heyday:**
State of excitement.   72. **Sense:** Perception through the five
senses (the functions of the middle or sensible soul).   74.
apoplex'd: Paralyzed. (Hamlet goes on to explain that without such a paralysis of will, mere madness would not so err,
nor would the five senses so enthrall themselves to *ecstasy*
or lunacy; even such deranged states of mind would be able
to make the obvious choice between Hamlet Senior and Claudius.)   78. **cozen'd:** Cheated.   **hoodman-blind:** Blindman's
buff.

80. **sans:** Without.   82. **mope:** Be dazed, act aimlessly.   84.
mutine: Mutiny.   **86–89. Proclaim . . . will:** Call it no
shameful business when the compelling ardor of youth delivers the attack, i.e., commits lechery, since the frost of
advanced age burns with as active a fire of lust and reason
perverts itself by fomenting lust rather than restraining it.
92. **grained:** Dyed in grain, indelible.   93. **tinct:** Color.   94.
enseamed: Laden with grease.   100. **tithe:** Tenth part.
101. **precedent:** Former (i.e., the elder Hamlet).   **vice:** Buf-
foon (a reference to the vice of the morality plays).   106.
shreds and patches: Motley, the traditional costume of the
clown or fool.   111. **laps'd . . . passion:** Having allowed
time to lapse and passion to cool.   112. **important:** Importunate, urgent.

15   Is but to whet thy almost blunted purpose.
      But, look, amazement° on thy mother sits.
      O, step between her and her fighting soul!
      Conceit° in weakest bodies strongest works.
      Speak to her, Hamlet.
      HAMLET: How is it with you, lady?
20 QUEEN: Alas, how is 't with you,
      That you do bend your eye on vacancy,
      And with th' incorporal° air do hold discourse?
      Forth at your eyes your spirits wildly peep,
      And, as the sleeping soldiers in th' alarm,
25   Your bedded° hair, like life in excrements,°
      Start up and stand an° end. O gentle son,
      Upon the heat and flame of thy distemper
      Sprinkle cool patience. Whereon do you look?
    HAMLET: On him, on him! Look you how pale he
          glares!
      His form and cause conjoin'd,° preaching to
30   stones,
      Would make them capable.° — Do not look
          upon me,
      Lest with this piteous action you convert
      My stern effects.° Then what I have to do
      Will want true color° — tears perchance for
          blood.
35 QUEEN: To whom do you speak this?
    HAMLET: Do you see nothing there?
    QUEEN: Nothing at all; yet all that is I see.
    HAMLET: Nor did you nothing hear?
    QUEEN: No, nothing but ourselves.
    HAMLET: Why, look you there, look how it steals
40   away!
      My father, in his habit° as he lived!
      Look, where he goes, even now, out at the
          portal!
                                    (*Exit Ghost.*)
    QUEEN: This is the very coinage of your brain.
      This bodiless creation ecstasy°
45   Is very cunning in.
    HAMLET: Ecstasy?
      My pulse, as yours, doth temperately keep time,
      And makes as healthful music. It is not madness
      That I have utter'd. Bring me to the test,
50   And I the matter will reword, which madness
      Would gambol° from. Mother, for love of grace,

116. **amazement:** Distraction.   118. **Conceit:** Imagination.
122. **incorporal:** Immaterial.   125. **bedded:** Laid in smooth
layers. **excrements:** Outgrowths.   126. **an:** On.   130. **His
... conjoin'd:** His appearance joined to his cause for speaking.   131. **capable:** Receptive.   132–33. **convert ... effects:**
Divert me from my stern duty.   134. **want true color:** Lack
plausibility so that (with a play on the normal sense of *color*)
I shall shed tears instead of blood.   141. **habit:** Dress.   144.
ecstasy: Madness.   151. **gambol:** Skip away.

      Lay not that flattering unction° to your soul
      That not your trespass but my madness speaks.
      It will but skin and film the ulcerous place,
      Whiles rank corruption, mining° all within,   155
      Infects unseen. Confess yourself to heaven,
      Repent what's past, avoid what is to come,
      And do not spread the compost° on the weeds
      To make them ranker. Forgive me this my
          virtue;°
      For in the fatness° of these pursy° times   160
      Virtue itself of vice must pardon beg,
      Yea, curb° and woo for leave° to do him good.
    QUEEN: O Hamlet, thou hast cleft my heart in
          twain.
    HAMLET: O, throw away the worser part of it,
      And live the purer with the other half.   165
      Good night. But go not to my uncle's bed;
      Assume a virtue, if you have it not.
      That monster, custom, who all sense doth eat,°
      Of habits devil,° is angel yet in this,
      That to the use of actions fair and good   170
      He likewise gives a frock or livery°
      That aptly is put on. Refrain tonight,
      And that shall lend a kind of easiness
      To the next abstinence; the next more easy;
      For use° almost can change the stamp of nature,   175
      And either° . . . the devil, or throw him out
      With wondrous potency. Once more, good night;
      And when you are desirous to be bless'd,°
      I'll blessing beg of you. For this same lord,
                        [*Pointing to Polonius.*]
      I do repent; but heaven hath pleas'd it so   180
      To punish me with this, and this with me,
      That I must be their scourge and minister.°
      I will bestow° him, and will answer well
      The death I gave him. So, again, good night.
      I must be cruel only to be kind.   185
      Thus bad begins and worse remains behind.°

152. **unction:** Ointment.   155. **mining:** Working under the
surface.   158. **compost:** Manure.   159. **this my virtue:** My
virtuous talk in reproving you.   160. **fatness:** Grossness.
pursy: Short-winded, corpulent.   162. **curb:** Bow, bend the
knee. **leave:** Permission.   168. **who ... eat:** Who consumes all proper or natural feeling.   169. **Of habits devil:**
Devil-like in prompting evil habits.   171. **livery:** An outer
appearance, a customary garb (and hence a predisposition
easily assumed in time of stress).   175. **use:** Habit.   176.
And either: A defective line usually emended by inserting the
word *master* after *either*, following the fourth quarto and
early editors.   178. **be bless'd:** Become blessed, i.e., repen-
tant.   182. **their scourge and minister:** Agent of heavenly
retribution. (By *scourge*, Hamlet also suggests that he himself
will eventually suffer punishment in the process of fulfilling
heaven's will.)   183. **bestow:** Stow, dispose of.   186. **behind:** To come.

One word more, good lady.
QUEEN: What shall I do?
HAMLET: Not this, by no means, that I bid you do:
      Let the bloat° king tempt you again to bed,
190   Pinch wanton on your cheek, call you his mouse,
      And let him, for a pair of reechy° kisses,
      Or paddling in your neck with his damn'd
          fingers,
      Make you to ravel all this matter out,
      That I essentially am not in madness,
      But mad in craft. 'Twere good° you let him
195   know,
      For who that's but a queen, fair, sober, wise,
      Would from a paddock,° from a bat, a gib,°
      Such dear concernings° hide? Who would do so?
      No, in despite of sense and secrecy,
200   Unpeg the basket° on the house's top,
      Let the birds fly, and, like the famous ape,°
      To try conclusions,° in the basket creep
      And break your own neck down.
QUEEN: Be thou assur'd, if words be made of
          breath,
205   And breath of life, I have no life to breathe
      What thou hast said to me.
HAMLET: I must to England; you know that?
QUEEN: Alack,
      I had forgot. 'Tis so concluded on.
HAMLET: There's letters seal'd, and my two school-
          fellows,
210   Whom I will trust as I will adders fang'd,
      They bear the mandate; they must sweep my
          way,°
      And marshal me to knavery. Let it work.
      For 'tis the sport to have the enginer°
      Hoist with° his own petar,° and 't shall go hard
215   But I will delve one yard below their mines,°
      And blow them at the moon. O, 'tis most sweet,
      When in one line two crafts° directly meet.
      This man shall set me packing.°

189. bloat: Bloated. 191. reechy: Dirty, filthy. 195. good:
Said ironically; also the following eight lines. 197. pad-
dock: Toad. gib: Tomcat. 198. dear concernings: Important affairs. 200. Unpeg the basket: Open the cage, i.e.,
let out the secret. 201. famous ape: In a story now lost.
202. conclusions: Experiments (in which the ape apparently
enters a cage from which birds have been released and then
tries to fly out of the cage as they have done, falling to his
death). 211. sweep my way: Go before me. 213. enginer:
Constructor of military contrivances. 214. Hoist with:
Blown up by. petar: Petard, an explosive used to blow in
a door or make a breach. 215. mines: Tunnels used in
warfare to undermine the enemy's emplacements; Hamlet
will countermine by going under their mines. 217. crafts:
Acts of guile, plots. 218. set me packing: Set me to making
schemes, and set me to lugging (him) and, also, send me off
in a hurry.

      I'll lug the guts into the neighbor room.
      Mother, good night indeed. This counselor   220
      Is now most still, most secret, and most grave,
      Who was in life a foolish prating knave.
      Come, sir, to draw toward an end° with you.
      Good night, mother.
              (Exeunt [severally, Hamlet dragging in
                      Polonius].)

[ACT IV • Scene I]°

(Enter King and Queen, with Rosencrantz and Guildenstern.)

KING: There's matter in these sighs, these profound
          heaves
      You must translate; 'tis fit we understand them.
      Where is your son?
QUEEN: Bestow this place on us a little while.
              [Exeunt Rosencrantz and Guildenstern.]
      Ah, mine own lord, what have I seen tonight!   5
KING: What, Gertrude? How does Hamlet?
QUEEN: Mad as the sea and wind when both
          contend
      Which is the mightier. In his lawless fit,
      Behind the arras hearing something stir,
      Whips out his rapier, cries, "A rat, a rat!"   10
      And, in this brainish apprehension,° kills
      The unseen good old man.
KING: O heavy deed!
      It had been so with us, had we been there.
      His liberty is full of threats to all —
      To you yourself, to us, to everyone.   15
      Alas, how shall this bloody deed be answer'd?
      It will be laid to us, whose providence°
      Should have kept short,° restrain'd, and out of
          haunt°
      This mad young man. But so much was our love
      We would not understand what was most fit,   20
      But, like the owner of a foul disease,
      To keep it from divulging,° let it feed
      Even on the pith of life. Where is he gone?
QUEEN: To draw apart the body he hath kill'd,
      O'er whom his very madness, like some ore°   25
      Among a mineral° of metals base,
      Shows itself pure: 'a weeps for what is done.
KING: O Gertrude, come away!
      The sun no sooner shall the mountains touch

223. draw . . . end: Finish up (with a pun on draw, pull).
IV, I. Location: The castle. 11. brainish apprehension:
Headstrong conception. 17. providence: Foresight. 18.
short: On a short tether. out of haunt: Secluded. 22.
divulging: Becoming evident. 25. ore: Vein of gold. 26.
mineral: Mine.

30   But we will ship him hence; and this vile deed
       We must, with all our majesty and skill,
       Both countenance and excuse. Ho, Guildenstern!

(Enter Rosencrantz and Guildenstern.)

       Friends both, go join you with some further aid.
       Hamlet in madness hath Polonius slain,
       And from his mother's closet hath he dragg'd
35   him.
       Go seek him out; speak fair, and bring the body
       Into the chapel. I pray you, haste in this.
                  [*Exeunt Rosencrantz and Guildenstern.*]
       Come, Gertrude, we'll call up our wisest friends
       And let them know both what we mean to do
40   And what's untimely done° . . . .
       Whose whisper o'er the world's diameter,°
       As level° as the cannon to his blank,°
       Transports his pois'ned shot, may miss our
           name,
       And hit the woundless° air. O, come away!
45   My soul is full of discord and dismay. (*Exeunt.*)

[*Scene II*]°

(Enter Hamlet.)

HAMLET: Safely stow'd.
[ROSENCRANTZ, GUILDENSTERN (*within*): Hamlet! Lord
    Hamlet!]
HAMLET: But soft, what noise? Who calls on Hamlet?
5   O, here they come.

(Enter Rosencrantz and Guildenstern.)

ROSENCRANTZ: What have you done, my lord, with
    the dead body?
HAMLET: Compounded it with dust, whereto 'tis
    kin.
ROSENCRANTZ: Tell us where 'tis, that we may take
    it thence
    And bear it to the chapel.
10   HAMLET: Do not believe it.
ROSENCRANTZ: Believe what?
HAMLET: That I can keep your counsel and not mine
    own. Besides, to be demanded of° a sponge, what
    replication° should be made by the son of a king?
15   ROSENCRANTZ: Take you me for a sponge, my lord?

HAMLET: Ay, sir, that soaks up the King's countenance,°
    his rewards, his authorities. But such officers do
    the King best service in the end. He keeps them,
    like an ape an apple, in the corner of his jaw, first
    mouth'd, to be last swallow'd. When he needs what   20
    you have glean'd, it is but squeezing you, and,
    sponge, you shall be dry again.
ROSENCRANTZ: I understand you not, my lord.
HAMLET: I am glad of it. A knavish speech sleeps in°
    a foolish ear.   25
ROSENCRANTZ: My lord, you must tell us where the
    body is, and go with us to the King.
HAMLET: The body is with the King, but the King is
    not with the body.° The King is a thing —
GUILDENSTERN: A thing, my lord?   30
HAMLET: Of nothing.° Bring me to him. [Hide fox,
    and all after.°]   (*Exeunt.*)

[*Scene III*]°

(Enter King, and two or three.)

KING: I have sent to seek him, and to find the
           body.
       How dangerous is it that this man goes loose!
       Yet must not we put the strong law on him.
       He's lov'd of the distracted° multitude,
       Who like not in their judgment, but their eyes,   5
       And where 'tis so, th' offender's scourge° is
           weigh'd,°
       But never the offense. To bear° all smooth and
           even,
       This sudden sending him away must seem
       Deliberate pause.° Diseases desperate grown
       By desperate appliance are reliev'd,   10
       Or not at all.

(Enter Rosencrantz, [Guildenstern,] and all the rest.)

           How now? What hath befall'n?
ROSENCRANTZ: Where the dead body is bestow'd,
    my lord,
       We cannot get from him.
KING: But where is he?

---

16. **countenance:** Favor.   24. **sleeps in:** Has no meaning to.
28–29. **The . . . body:** Perhaps alludes to the legal commonplace of "the king's two bodies," which drew a distinction between the sacred office of kingship and the particular mortal who possessed it at any given time.   31. **Of
nothing:** Of no account.   31–32. **Hide . . . after:** An old
signal cry in the game of hide-and-seek, suggesting that Hamlet now runs away from them.   IV, III. **Location:** The castle.
4. **distracted:** Fickle, unstable.   6. **scourge:** Punishment.
weigh'd: Taken into consideration.   7. **bear:** Manage.   9.
Deliberate pause: Carefully considered action.

---

40. **And . . . done:** A defective line; conjectures as to the
missing words include *so, haply, slander* (Capell and others);
for, haply, slander (Theobald and others).   41. **diameter:**
Extent from side to side.   42. **As level:** With as direct aim.
blank: White spot in the center of a target.   44. **woundless:**
Invulnerable.   IV, II. **Location:** The castle.   13. **demanded
of:** Questioned by.   14. **replication:** Reply.

ROSENCRANTZ: Without, my lord; guarded, to
     know your pleasure.
KING: Bring him before us.
15 ROSENCRANTZ: Ho! Bring in the lord.

(*They enter [with Hamlet].*)

KING: Now, Hamlet, where's Polonius?
HAMLET: At supper.
KING: At supper? Where?
HAMLET: Not where he eats, but where 'a is eaten. A
20   certain convocation of politic worms° are e'en at
     him. Your worm is your only emperor for diet.°
     We fat all creatures else to fat us, and we fat ourselves
     for maggots. Your fat king and your lean beggar
     is but variable service,° two dishes, but to one
25   table — that's the end.
KING: Alas, alas!
HAMLET: A man may fish with the worm that hath
     eat° of a king, and eat of the fish that hath fed of
     that worm.
30 KING: What dost thou mean by this?
HAMLET: Nothing but to show you how a king may
     go a progress° through the guts of a beggar.
KING: Where is Polonius?
HAMLET: In heaven. Send thither to see. If your mes-
35   senger find him not there, seek him i' th' other
     place yourself. But if indeed you find him not within
     this month, you shall nose him as you go up the
     stairs into the lobby.
KING [*to some Attendants*]: Go seek him there.
40 HAMLET: 'A will stay till you come.
                              [*Exit Attendants.*]
KING: Hamlet, this deed, for thine especial safety. —
     Which we do tender,° as we dearly° grieve
For that which thou hast done — must send
     thee hence
     [With fiery quickness.] Therefore prepare thyself.
45 The bark° is ready, and the wind at help,
Th' associates tend,° and everything is bent°
     For England.
HAMLET: For England!
KING: Ay, Hamlet.
50 HAMLET: Good.
KING: So is it, if thou knew'st our purposes.
HAMLET: I see a cherub° that sees them. But, come,
     for England! Farewell, dear mother.

KING: Thy loving father, Hamlet.
HAMLET: My mother. Father and mother is man and   55
     wife, man and wife is one flesh, and so, my mother.
     Come, for England!   (*Exit.*)
KING: Follow him at foot;° tempt him with speed
     aboard.
     Delay it not; I'll have him hence tonight.
     Away! For everything is seal'd and done   60
     That else leans on° th' affair. Pray you, make
     haste.
                          [*Exeunt all but the King.*]
     And, England,° if my love thou hold'st at aught —
     As my great power thereof may give thee sense,
     Since yet thy cicatrice° looks raw and red
     After the Danish sword, and thy free awe°   65
     Pays homage to us — thou mayst not coldly set°
     Our sovereign process,° which imports at full,
     By letters congruing° to that effect,
     The present° death of Hamlet. Do it, England,
     For like the hectic° in my blood he rages,   70
     And thou must cure me. Till I know 'tis done,
     Howe'er my haps,° my joys were ne'er begun.
                                          (*Exit.*)

[*Scene IV*]°

(*Enter Fortinbras with his Army over the stage.*)

FORTINBRAS: Go, captain, from me greet the Danish
     king.
     Tell him that, by his license,° Fortinbras
     Craves the conveyance° of a promis'd march
     Over his kingdom. You know the rendezvous.
     If that his Majesty would aught with us,   5
     We shall express our duty in his eye;°
     And let him know so.
CAPTAIN: I will do 't, my lord.
FORTINBRAS: Go softly° on.   [*Exeunt all but the
                                          Captain.*]

(*Enter Hamlet, Rosencrantz, [Guildenstern,] etc.*)

HAMLET: Good sir, whose powers° are these?
CAPTAIN: They are of Norway, sir.
HAMLET: How purposed, sir, I pray you?   10
CAPTAIN: Against some part of Poland.
HAMLET: Who commands them, sir?

20. **politic worms:** Crafty worms (suited to a master spy like
Polonius).   21. **diet:** Food, eating (with perhaps a punning
reference to the Diet of Worms, a famous convocation held
in 1521).   24. **variable service:** Different courses of a single
meal.   28. **eat:** Eaten (pronounced "et").   32. **progress:**
Royal journey of state.   42. **tender:** Regard, hold dear.
dearly: Intensely.   45. **bark:** Sailing vessel.   46. **tend:** Wait.
bent: In readiness.   52. **cherub:** Cherubim are angels of
knowledge.

58. **at foot:** Close behind, at heel.   61. **leans on:** Bears upon,
is related to.   62. **England:** King of England.   64. **cicatrice:**
Scar.   65. **free awe:** Voluntary show of respect.   66. **set:**
Esteem.   67. **process:** Command.   68. **congruing:** Agreeing.
69. **present:** Immediate.   70. **hectic:** Persistent fever.   72.
haps: Fortunes.   **IV, IV. Location:** The coast of Denmark.
2. **license:** Permission.   3. **conveyance:** Escort, convoy.   6.
eye: Presence.   8. **softly:** Slowly.   9. **powers:** Forces.

CAPTAIN: The nephew to old Norway, Fortinbras.
15 HAMLET: Goes it against the main° of Poland, sir,
    Or for some frontier?
CAPTAIN: Truly to speak, and with no addition,°
    We go to gain a little patch of ground
    That hath in it no profit but the name.
20   To pay° five ducats, five, I would not farm it;°
    Nor will it yield to Norway or the Pole
    A ranker° rate, should it be sold in fee.°
HAMLET: Why, then the Polack never will defend it.
CAPTAIN: Yes, it is already garrison'd.
HAMLET: Two thousand souls and twenty thousand
25   ducats
    Will not debate the question of this straw.°
    This is th' imposthume° of much wealth and
      peace,
    That inward breaks, and shows no cause
      without
    Why the man dies. I humbly thank you, sir.
CAPTAIN: God buy you, sir.   [Exit.]
30 ROSENCRANTZ: Will 't please you go, my lord?
HAMLET: I'll be with you straight. Go a little
    before.   [Exit all except Hamlet.]
    How all occasions do inform against° me,
    And spur my dull revenge! What is a man,
    If his chief good and market of° his time
35   Be but to sleep and feed? A beast, no more.
    Sure he that made us with such large discourse,°
    Looking before and after, gave us not
    That capability and god-like reason
    To fust° in us unus'd. Now, whether it be
40   Bestial oblivion,° or some craven scruple
    Of thinking too precisely on th' event° —
    A thought which, quarter'd, hath but one part
      wisdom
    And ever three parts coward — I do not know
    Why yet I live to say "This thing's to do,"
    Sith° I have cause and will and strength and
45   means
    To do 't. Examples gross° as earth exhort me:
    Witness this army of such mass and charge°
    Led by a delicate and tender prince,
    Whose spirit, with divine ambition puff'd
50   Makes mouths° at the invisible event,
    Exposing what is mortal and unsure

To all that fortune, death, and danger dare,
Even for an egg-shell. Rightly to be great
Is not to stir without great argument,
But greatly to find quarrel in a straw   55
When honor's at the stake. How stand I then,
That have a father kill'd, a mother stain'd,
Excitements of° my reason and my blood,
And let all sleep, while, to my shame, I see
The imminent death of twenty thousand men,   60
That, for a fantasy° and trick° of fame,
Go to their graves like beds, fight for a plot°
Whereon the numbers cannot try the cause,°
Which is not tomb enough and continent°
To hide the slain? O, from this time forth,   65
My thoughts be bloody, or be nothing worth!
                                         (Exit.)

[Scene V]°

(Enter Horatio, [Queen] Gertrude, and a Gentleman.)

QUEEN: I will not speak with her.
GENTLEMAN: She is importunate, indeed distract.
    Her mood will needs be pitied.
QUEEN: What would she have?
GENTLEMAN: She speaks much of her father, says
    she hears
    There's tricks° i' th' world, and hems, and beats
      her heart,°   5
    Spurns enviously at straws,° speaks things in
      doubt°
    That carry but half sense. Her speech is nothing,
    Yet the unshaped use° of it doth move
    The hearers to collection;° they yawn° at it,
    And botch° the words up fit to their own
      thoughts,   10
    Which, as her winks and nods and gestures
      yield° them,
    Indeed would make one think there might be
      thought,°
    Though nothing sure, yet much unhappily.
HORATIO: 'Twere good she were spoken with, for
    she may strew

15. main: Main part.   17. addition: Exaggeration.   20. To
pay: I.e., for a yearly rental of.   farm it: Take a lease of
it.   22. ranker: Higher.   in fee: Fee simple, outright.   26.
debate . . . straw: Settle this trifling matter.   27. impos-
thume: Abscess.   32. inform against: Denounce, betray;
take shape against.   34. market of: Profit of, compensation
for.   36. discourse: Power of reasoning.   39. fust: Grow
moldy.   40. oblivion: Forgetfulness.   41. event: Outcome.
45. Sith: Since.   46. gross: Obvious.   47. charge: Expense.
50. Makes mouths: Makes scornful faces.

58. Excitements of: Promptings by.   61. fantasy: Fanciful
caprice.   trick: Trifle.   62. plot: I.e., of ground.   63. Whereon . . . cause: On which there is insufficient room for the
soldiers needed to engage in a military contest.   64. continent: Receptacle, container.   IV, v. Location: The castle.
5. tricks: Deceptions.   heart: Breast.   6. Spurns . . . straws:
Kicks spitefully, takes offense at trifles.   in doubt: Obscurely.   8. unshaped use: Distracted manner.   9. collection: Inference, a guess at some sort of meaning.   yawn:
Wonder, grasp.   10. botch: Patch.   11. yield: Delivery,
bring forth (her words).   12. thought: Conjectured.

15   Dangerous conjectures in ill-breeding° minds.
        QUEEN: Let her come in.   [*Exit Gentlemen.*]
            [*Aside.*] To my sick soul, as sin's true nature is,
            Each toy° seems prologue to some great amiss.°
            So full of artless jealousy is guilt,
20   It spills itself in fearing to be spilt.°

(*Enter Ophelia [distracted].*)

        OPHELIA: Where is the beauteous majesty of
                Denmark?
        QUEEN: How now, Ophelia?
        OPHELIA (*she sings*): "How should I your true love
                know
                From another one?
25   By his cockle hat° and staff,
                And his sandal shoon."°
        QUEEN: Alas, sweet lady, what imports this song?
        OPHELIA: Say you? Nay, pray you, mark.
                "He is dead and gone, lady,   (*Song.*)
30   He is dead and gone;
                At his head a grass-green turf,
                At his heels a stone."
                O, ho!
        QUEEN: Nay, but Ophelia —
35   OPHELIA: Pray you mark.
                [*Sings.*] "White his shroud as the mountain
                snow" —

(*Enter King.*)

        QUEEN: Alas, look here, my lord.
        OPHELIA: "Larded° all with flowers   (*Song.*)
                Which bewept to the ground did not go
40   With true-love showers."
        KING: How do you, pretty lady?
        OPHELIA: Well, God 'ild° you! They say the owl° was
                a baker's daughter. Lord, we know what we are,
                but know not what we may be. God be at your
45   table!
        KING: Conceit° upon her father.
        OPHELIA: Pray let's have no words of this; but when
                they ask you what it means, say you this:
                "Tomorrow is Saint Valentine's° day.   (*Song.*)
50   All in the morning betime,

And I a maid at your window,
    To be your Valentine.
Then up he rose, and donn'd his clo'es,
    And dupp'd° the chamber-door,
Let in the maid, that out a maid   55
    Never departed more."
KING: Pretty Ophelia!
OPHELIA: Indeed, la, without an oath, I'll make an
    end on 't:
    [*Sings.*] "By Gis° and by Saint Charity,   60
        Alack, and fie for shame!
    Young men will do 't, if they come to 't;
        By Cock,° they are to blame.
    Quoth she, 'Before you tumbled me,
        You promised me to wed.'"   65
He answers:
    "'So would I ha' done, by yonder sun,
        An thou hadst not come to my bed.'"
KING: How long hath she been thus?
OPHELIA: I hope all will be well. We must be patient, 70
    but I cannot choose but weep, to think they would
    lay him i' th' cold ground. My brother shall know
    of it; and so I thank you for your good counsel.
    Come, my coach! Good night, ladies; good night,
    sweet ladies; good night, good night.   75
                                              [*Exit.*]
KING: Follow her close; give her good watch, I
    pray you.   [*Exit Horatio.*]
    O, this is the poison of deep grief; it springs
    All from her father's death — and now behold!
    O Gertrude, Gertrude,
    When sorrows come, they come not single spies,°   80
    But in battalions. First, her father slain;
    Next, your son gone, and he most violent author
    Of his own just remove; the people muddied,°
    Thick and unwholesome in their thoughts and
        whispers,
    For good Polonius' death; and we have done but
        greenly,°   85
    In hugger-mugger° to inter him; poor Ophelia
    Divided from herself and her fair judgment,
    Without the which we are pictures, or mere
        beasts;
    Last, and as much containing as all these,
    Her brother is in secret come from France,   90
    Feeds on his wonder, keeps himself in clouds,°
    And wants° not buzzers° to infect his ear
    With pestilent speeches of his father's death,

---

15. **ill-breeding:** Prone to suspect the worst. **18. toy:** Trifle.
amiss: Calamity. **19–20. So . . . spilt:** Guilt is so full of
suspicion that it unskillfully betrays itself in fearing betrayal.
25. cockle hat: Hat with cockleshell stuck in it as a sign that
the wearer had been a pilgrim to the shrine of St. James of
Compostella in Spain. **26. shoon:** Shoes. **38. Larded:**
Decorated. **42. God 'ild:** God yield or reward. **owl:** Refers to a legend about a baker's daughter who was turned
into an owl for refusing Jesus bread. **46. Conceit:** Brooding.
49. Valentine's: This song alludes to the belief that the first
girl seen by a man on the morning of this day was his
valentine or true love.

54. dupp'd: Opened. **60. Gis:** Jesus. **63. Cock:** A per-
version of *God* in oaths. **80. spies:** Scouts sent in advance
of the main force. **83. muddied:** Stirred up, confused. **85.
greenly:** Imprudently, foolishly. **86. hugger-mugger:** Secret
haste. **91. in clouds:** I.e., of suspicion and rumor. **92.
wants:** Lacks. **buzzers:** Gossipers, informers.

Wherein necessity, of matter beggar'd,°
Will nothing stick our person to arraign
In ear and ear.° O my dear Gertrude, this,
Like to a murd'ring-piece,° in many places
Gives me superfluous death.   (*A noise within.*)
[QUEEN: Alack, what noise is this?]

KING: Attend!
    Where are my Switzers?° Let them guard the
        door.

(*Enter a Messenger.*)

    What is the matter?
MESSENGER: Save yourself, my lord!
    The ocean, overpeering of his list,°
    Eats not the flats° with more impiteous° haste
    Than young Laertes, in a riotous head,°
    O'erbears your officers. The rabble call him lord,
    And, as° the world were now but to begin,
    Antiquity forgot, custom not known,
    The ratifiers and props° of every word,°
    They cry, "Choose we! Laertes shall be king!"
    Caps, hands, and tongues applaud it to the
        clouds,
    "Laertes shall be king, Laertes king!"
                                        (*A noise within.*)
QUEEN: How cheerfully on the false trail they cry!
    O, this is counter,° you false Danish dogs!

(*Enter Laertes with others.*)

KING: The doors are broke.
LAERTES: Where is this King? Sirs, stand you all
        without.
ALL: No, let's come in.
LAERTES: I pray you, give me leave.
ALL: We will, we will.
                    [*They retire without the door.*]
LAERTES: I thank you. Keep the door. O thou vile
        king,
    Give me my father!
QUEEN: Calmly, good Laertes.
                    [*She tries to hold him back.*]
LAERTES: That drop of blood that's calm proclaims
    me bastard,

Cries cuckold to my father, brands the harlot
Even here, between the chaste unsmirched brow
Of my true mother.
KING: What is the cause, Laertes,
    That thy rebellion looks so giant-like?   125
    Let him go, Gertrude. Do not fear our° person.
    There's such divinity doth hedge a king
    That treason can but peep to what it would,°
    Acts little of his will.° Tell me, Laertes,
    Why thou art thus incens'd. Let him go,
        Gertrude.   130
    Speak, man.
LAERTES: Where is my father?
KING: Dead.
QUEEN: But not by him.
KING: Let him demand his fill.
LAERTES: How came he dead? I'll not be juggled
    with.
    To hell, allegiance! Vows, to the blackest devil!
    Conscience and grace, to the profoundest pit! 135
    I dare damnation. To this point I stand,
    That both the worlds I give to negligence,°
    Let come what comes, only I'll be reveng'd
    Most throughly° for my father.
KING: Who shall stay you?
LAERTES: My will, not all the world's.° 140
    And for my means, I'll husband them so well,
    They shall go far with little.
KING: Good Laertes,
    If you desire to know the certainty
    Of your dear father, is 't writ in your revenge
    That, swoopstake,° you will draw both friend
        and foe,   145
    Winner and loser?
LAERTES: None but his enemies.
KING: Will you know them then?
LAERTES: To his good friends thus wide I'll ope my
        arms,
    And, like the kind life-rend'ring pelican,°
    Repast° them with my blood.
KING: Why, now you speak   150
    Like a good child and a true gentleman.
    That I am guiltless of your father's death,

94. **of matter beggar'd:** Unprovided with facts. 95–96. **Will . . . and ear:** Will not hesitate to accuse my (royal) person in everybody's ears. 97. **murd'ring-piece:** Cannon loaded so as to scatter its shot. 101. **Switzers:** Swiss guards, mercenaries. 103. **overpeering of his list:** Overflowing its shore. 104. **flats:** Flatlands near shore. **impiteous:** Pitiless. 105. **head:** Armed force. 107. **as:** As if. 109. **ratifiers and props:** Refer to *antiquity* and *custom*. **word:** Promise. 114. **counter:** A hunting term meaning to follow the trail in a direction opposite to that which the game has taken.

126. **fear our:** Fear for my. 128. **can . . . would:** Can only glance; as from far off or through a barrier, at what it would intend. 129. **Acts . . . will:** (But) performs little of what it intends. 137. **both . . . negligence:** Both this world and the next are of no consequence to me. 139. **throughly:** Thoroughly. 140. **My will . . . world's:** I'll stop (*stay*) when my will is accomplished, not for anyone else's. 145. **swoopstake:** Literally, taking all stakes on the gambling table at once, i.e., indiscriminately; *draw* is also a gambling term. 149. **pelican:** Refers to the belief that the female pelican fed its young with its own blood. 150. **Repast:** Feed.

And am most sensibly° in grief for it,
It shall as level° to your judgment 'pear
As day does to your eye.
155   (*A noise within:*) "Let her come in."
LAERTES: How now? What noise is that?

(*Enter Ophelia.*)

O heat, dry up my brains! Tears seven times salt
Burn out the sense and virtue° of mine eye!
By heaven, thy madness shall be paid with
   weight°
160   Till our scale turn the beam.° O rose of May!
Dear maid, kind sister, sweet Ophelia!
O heavens, is 't possible a young maid's wits
Should be as mortal as an old man's life?
[Nature is fine in° love, and where 'tis fine,
165   It sends some precious instance° of itself
After the thing it loves.°]
OPHELIA: "They bore him barefac'd on the bier;
                                     (*Song.*)
[Hey non nonny, nonny, hey nonny,]
And in his grave rain'd many a tear" —
170   Fare you well, my dove!
LAERTES: Hadst thou thy wits, and didst persuade°
   revenge,
It could not move thus.
OPHELIA: You must sing "A-down a-down,
And you call him a-down-a."
175   O, how the wheel° becomes it! It is the false steward°
that stole his master's daughter.
LAERTES: This nothing's more than matter.°
OPHELIA: There's rosemary,° that's for remembrance;
pray you, love, remember. And there is pansies,°
180   that's for thoughts.
LAERTES: A document° in madness, thoughts and re-
membrance fitted.
OPHELIA: There's fennel° for you, and columbines.°
There's rue° for you, and here's some for me; we
185   may call it herb of grace o' Sundays. You may

153. **sensibly**: Feelingly.   154. **level**: Plain.   158. **virtue**:
Faculty, power.   159. **paid with weight**: Repaid, avenged
equally or more.   160. **beam**: Crossbar of a balance.   164.
fine in: Refined by.   165. **instance**: Token.   166. **After . . .
loves**: Into the grave, along with Polonius.   171. **persuade**:
Argue cogently for.   175. **wheel**: Spinning wheel as accompaniment to the song, or refrain.   **false steward**: The story
is unknown.   177. **This . . . matter**: This seeming nonsense
is more meaningful than sane utterance.   178. **rosemary**:
Used as a symbol of remembrance both at weddings and at
funerals.   179. **pansies**: Emblems of love and courtship;
perhaps from French *pensées*, thoughts.   181. **document**:
Instruction, lesson.   183. **fennel**: Emblem of flattery.   **columbines**: Emblems of unchastity (?) or ingratitude (?).   184.
rue: Emblem of repentance; when mingled with holy water,
it was known as *herb of grace*.

wear your rue with a difference.° There's a daisy.°
I would give you some violets,° but they wither'd
all when my father died. They say 'a made a good
end —
[*Sings.*] "For bonny sweet Robin is all my joy."   19●
LAERTES: Thought° and affliction, passion, hell
   itself,
She turns to favor° and to prettiness.
OPHELIA: "And will 'a not come again?   (*Song.*)
And will 'a not come again?
   No, no, he is dead,   19
   Go to thy death-bed,
He never will come again.

"His beard was as white as snow,
All flaxen was his poll.°
   He is gone, he is gone,   20●
   And we cast away moan.
God 'a' mercy on his soul!
And of all Christians' souls, I pray God. God
   buy you.
                                     [*Exit.*]
LAERTES: Do you see this, O God?   20.
KING: Laertes, I must commune with your grief,
Or you deny me right. Go but apart,
Make choice of whom your wisest friends you
   will,
And they shall hear and judge 'twixt you and
   me.
If by direct or by collateral° hand
They find us touch'd,° we will our kingdom give,   21●
Our crown, our life, and all that we call ours,
To you in satisfaction; but if not,
Be you content to lend your patience to us,
And we shall jointly labor with your soul   21
To give it due content.
LAERTES: Let this be so.
His means of death, his obscure funeral —
No trophy,° sword, nor hatchment° o'er his
   bones,
No noble rite nor formal ostentation° —
Cry to be heard, as 'twere from heaven to earth,   22●
That I must call 't in question.
KING: So you shall;
And where th' offense is, let the great ax fall.
I pray you go with me.   (*Exeunt.*)

186. **with a difference**: Suggests that Ophelia and the Queen
have different causes of sorrow and repentance; perhaps with
a play on *rue* in the sense of ruth, pity.   **daisy**: Emblem of
dissembling, faithlessness.   187. **violets**: Emblems of faithfulness.   191. **Thought**: Melancholy.   192. **favor**: Grace.
199. **poll**: Head.   210. **collateral**: Indirect.   211. **us
touch'd**: Me implicated.   218. **trophy**: Memorial.   **hatch-
ment**: Tablet displaying the armorial bearings of a deceased
person.   219. **ostentation**: Ceremony.

[*Scene VI*]°

(*Enter Horatio and others.*)

HORATIO: What are they that would speak with me?
GENTLEMAN: Seafaring men, sir. They say they have
   letters for you.
HORATIO: Let them come in.   [*Exit Gentleman.*]
5   I do not know from what part of the world
   I should be greeted, if not from lord Hamlet.

(*Enter Sailors.*)

FIRST SAILOR: God bless you sir.
HORATIO: Let him bless thee too.
FIRST SAILOR: 'A shall, sir, an 't please him. There's
10   a letter for you, sir — it came from th' ambassador
   that was bound for England — if your name be
   Horatio, as I am let to know it is. [*Gives letter.*]
HORATIO [*reads*]: "Horatio, when thou shalt have overlook'd this, give these fellows some means° to the
15   King; they have letters for him. Ere we were
   two days old at sea, a pirate of very warlike ap-
   pointment° gave us chase. Finding ourselves too
   slow of sail, we put on a compell'd valor, and in
   the grapple I boarded them. On the instant they
20   got clear of our ship, so I alone became their prisoner.
   They have dealt with me like thieves of mercy,°
   but they knew what they did: I am to do a good
   turn for them. Let the King have the letters I have
   sent, and repair thou to me with as much speed
25   as thou wouldest fly death. I have words to speak
   in thine ear will make thee dumb; yet are they
   much too light for the bore° of the matter. These
   good fellows will bring thee where I am. Rosencrantz
   and Guildenstern hold their course for England.
30   Of them I have much to tell thee. Farewell.
               He that thou knowest thine, Hamlet."
   Come, I will give you way for these your letters,
   And do 't the speedier that you may direct me
   To him from whom you brought them. (*Exeunt.*)

[*Scene VII*]°

(*Enter King and Laertes.*)

KING: Now must your conscience my acquittance
      seal,°
   And you must put me in your heart for friend,
   Sith you have heard, and with a knowing ear,

That he which hath your noble father slain
Pursued my life.
LAERTES: It well appears. But tell me   5
   Why you proceeded not against these feats°
   So criminal and so capital° in nature,
   As by your safety, greatness, wisdom, all things
      else,
   You mainly° were stirr'd up.
KING: O, for two special reasons,
   Which may to you, perhaps, seem much
      unsinew'd,°   10
   But yet to me th' are strong. The Queen his
      mother
   Lives almost by his looks, and for myself —
   My virtue or my plague, be it either which —
   She's so conjunctive° to my life and soul
   That, as the star moves not but in his sphere,°   15
   I could not but by her. The other motive,
   Why to a public count° I might not go,
   Is the great love the general gender° bear him,
   Who, dipping all his faults in their affection,
   Would, like the spring° that turneth wood to
      stone,   20
   Convert his gyves° to graces, so that my arrows,
   Too slightly timber'd° for so loud° a wind,
   Would have reverted to my bow again
   And not where I had aim'd them.
LAERTES: And so have I a noble father lost,   25
   A sister driven into desp'rate terms,°
   Whose worth, if praises may go back° again,
   Stood challenger on mount° of all the age
   For her perfections. But my revenge will come.
KING: Break not your sleeps for that. You must not
      think   30
   That we are made of stuff so flat and dull
   That we can let our beard be shook with danger
   And think it pastime. You shortly shall hear
      more.
   I lov'd your father, and we love ourself;
   And that, I hope, will teach you to imagine —   35

(*Enter a Messenger with letters.*)

---

6. **feats:** Acts.   7. **capital:** Punishable by death.   9. **mainly:**
Greatly.   10. **unsinew'd:** Weak.   14. **conjunctive:** Closely
united.   15. **sphere:** The hollow sphere in which, according
to Ptolemaic astronomy, the planets moved.   17. **count:**
Account, reckoning.   18. **general gender:** Common people.
20. **spring:** A spring with such a concentration of lime that
it coats a piece of wood with limestone, in effect gilding it.
21. **gyves:** Fetters (which, gilded by the people's praise, would
look like badges of honor).   22. **slightly timber'd:** Light.
loud: Strong.   26. **terms:** State, condition.   27. **go back:**
Recall Ophelia's former virtues.   28. **on mount:** On high.

IV, VI. **Location:** The castle.   14. **means:** Means of access.
16–17. **appointment:** Equipage.   21. **thieves of mercy:** Merciful thieves.   27. **bore:** Caliber, i.e., importance.   IV, VII.
Location: The castle.   1. **my acquittance seal:** Confirm or
acknowledge my innocence.

[How now? What news?]
MESSENGER: [Letters, my lord, from Hamlet:]
   These to your Majesty, this to the Queen.
                                      [*Gives letters.*]
KING: From Hamlet? Who brought them?
MESSENGER: Sailors, my lord, they say; I saw them
   not.
   They were given me by Claudio. He receiv'd
40   them
   Of him that brought them.
KING: Laertes, you shall hear them.
   Leave us.   [*Exit Messenger.*]
   [*Reads.*] "High and mighty, you shall know I am
   set naked° on your kingdom. Tomorrow shall I beg
45 leave to see your kingly eyes, when I shall, first
   asking your pardon° thereunto, recount the occasion
   of my sudden and more strange return.   Hamlet."
   What should this mean? Are all the rest come back?
   Or is it some abuse,° and no such thing?
LAERTES: Know you the hand?
50 KING: 'Tis Hamlet's character.° "Naked!"
   And in a postscript here, he says "alone."
   Can you devise° me?
LAERTES: I am lost in it, my lord. But let him come.
   It warms the very sickness in my heart
55 That I shall live and tell him to his teeth,
   "Thus didst thou."
KING: If it be so, Laertes —
   As how should it be so? How otherwise?° —
   Will you be ruled by me?
LAERTES: Ay, my lord,
   So° you will not o'errule me to a peace.
60 KING: To thine own peace. If he be now returned,
   As checking at° his voyage, and that he means
   No more to undertake it, I will work him
   To an exploit, now ripe in my device,
   Under the which he shall not choose but fall;
   And for his death no wind of blame shall
65   breathe,
   But even his mother shall uncharge the practice°
   And call it accident.
LAERTES: My lord, I will be rul'd,
   The rather if you could devise it so
   That I might be the organ.°

KING: It falls right.
   You have been talk'd of since your travel much,   70
   And that in Hamlet's hearing, for a quality
   Wherein, they say, you shine. Your sum of
      parts°
   Did not together pluck such envy from him
   As did that one, and that, in my regard,
   Of the unworthiest siege.°   75
LAERTES: What part is that, my lord?
KING: A very riband in the cap of youth,
   Yet needful too, for youth no less becomes
   The light and careless livery that it wears
   Than settled age his sables° and his weeds,°   80
   Importing health° and graveness. Two months
      since
   Here was a gentleman of Normandy.
   I have seen myself, and serv'd against, the
      French,
   And they can well° on horseback, but this
      gallant
   Had witchcraft in 't; he grew unto his seat,   85
   And to such wondrous doing brought his horse
   As had he been incorps'd and demi-natured°
   With the brave beast. So far he topp'd° my
      thought
   That I, in forgery° of shapes and tricks,
   Come short of what he did.
LAERTES: A Norman was 't?   90
KING: A Norman.
LAERTES: Upon my life, Lamord.
KING: The very same.
LAERTES: I know him well. He is the brooch°
      indeed
   And gem of all the nation.
KING: He made confession° of you,   95
   And gave you such a masterly report
   For art and exercise in your defense,
   And for your rapier most especial,
   That he cried out, 'twould be a sight indeed,
   If one could match you. The scrimers° of their
      nation,   10
   He swore, had neither motion, guard, nor eye,
   If you oppos'd them. Sir, this report of his
   Did Hamlet so envenom with his envy
   That he could nothing do but wish and beg

---

44. naked: Destitute, unarmed, without following.   46. pardon: Permission.   49. abuse: Deceit.   50. character: Handwriting.   52. devise: Explain to.   57. As . . . otherwise:
How can this (Hamlet's return) be true? Yet how otherwise
than true (since we have the evidence of his letter).   59. So:
Provided that.   61. checking at: Turning aside from (like a
falcon leaving the quarry to fly at a chance bird).   66.
uncharge the practice: Acquit the stratagem of being a plot.
69. organ: Agent, instrument.

72. Your . . . parts: All your other virtues.   75. unworthiest
siege: Least important rank.   80. sables: Rich robes furred
with sable.   weeds: Garments.   81. Importing health: Indicating prosperity.   84. can well: Are skilled.   87. incorps'd and demi-natur'd: Of one body and nearly of one
nature (like the centaur).   88. topp'd: Surpassed.   89. forgery: Invention.   93. brooch: Ornament.   95. confession:
Admission of superiority.   100. scrimers: Fencers.

05 Your sudden coming o'er to play° with you.
     Now, out of this —
LAERTES: What out of this, my lord?
KING: Laertes, was your father dear to you?
     Or are you like the painting of a sorrow,
     A face without a heart?
LAERTES: Why ask you this?
KING: Not that I think you did not love your
10   father,
     But that I know love is begun by time,°
     And that I see, in passages of proof,°
     Time qualifies° the spark and fire of it.
     There lives within the very flame of love
15   A kind of wick or snuff° that will abate it,
     And nothing is at a like goodness still,°
     For goodness, growing to a plurisy,°
     Dies in his own too much.° That° we would do,
     We should do when we would; for this "would"
          changes
20   And hath abatements° and delays as many
     As there are tongues, are hands, are accidents,°
     And then this "should" is like a spendthrift's
          sigh,°
     That hurts by easing.° But, to the quick o' th'
          ulcer;
     Hamlet comes back. What would you undertake
25   To show yourself your father's son in deed
     More than in words?
LAERTES: To cut his throat i' th' church!
KING: No place, indeed, should murder
          sanctuarize;°
     Revenge should have no bounds. But, good
          Laertes,
     Will you do this,° keep close within your
          chamber.
30   Hamlet return'd shall know you are come home.
     We'll put on those° shall praise your excellence
     And set a double varnish on the fame
     The Frenchman gave you, bring you in fine°
          together,

And wager on your heads. He, being remiss,°
Most generous,° and free from all contriving,   135
Will not peruse the foils, so that, with ease,
Or with a little shuffling, you may choose
A sword unbated,° and in a pass of practice°
Requite him for your father.
LAERTES: I will do 't.
And for that purpose I'll anoint my sword.   140
I bought an unction° of a mountebank°
So mortal that, but dip a knife in it,
Where it draws blood no cataplasm° so rare,
Collected from all simples° that have virtue
Under the moon, can save the thing from death   145
That is but scratch'd withal. I'll touch my point
With this contagion, that, if I gall° him slightly,
It may be death.
KING: Let's further think of this,
Weigh what convenience both of time and means
May fit us to our shape.° If this should fail,   150
And that our drift look through our bad
     performance,°
'Twere better not assay'd. Therefore this project
Should have a back or second, that might hold
If this did blast in proof.° Soft, let me see.
We'll make a solemn wager on your cunnings —   155
I ha 't!
When in your motion you are hot and dry —
As° make your bouts more violent to that end —
And that he calls for drink, I'll have prepar'd
     him
A chalice for the nonce,° whereon but sipping,   160
If he by chance escape your venom'd stuck,°
Our purpose may hold there. [*A cry within.*] But
     stay, what noise?

(*Enter Queen.*)

QUEEN: One woe doth tread upon another's heel,
     So fast they follow. Your sister's drowned,
          Laertes.
LAERTES: Drown'd! O, where?   165
QUEEN: There is a willow grows askant° the brook,
     That shows his hoar° leaves in the glassy stream;
     Therewith fantastic garlands did she make

---

105. **play:** Fence.   111. **begun by time:** Subject to change.
112. **passages of proof:** Actual instances.   113. **qualifies:**
Weakens.   115. **snuff:** The charred part of a candlewick.
116. **nothing . . . still:** Nothing remains at a constant level
of perfection.   117. **plurisy:** Excess, plethora.   118. **in . . .
much:** Of its own excess.   **That:** That which.   120. **abate-
ments:** Diminutions.   121. **accidents:** Occurrences, incidents.   122. **spendthrift's sigh:** An allusion to the belief that
each sigh cost the heart a drop of blood.   123. **hurts by
easing:** Costs the heart blood even while it affords emotional
relief.   127. **sanctuarize:** Protect from punishment (alludes
to the right of sanctuary with which certain religious places
were invested).   129. **Will you do this:** If you wish to do
this.   131. **put on those:** Instigate those who.   133. **in fine:**
Finally.

134. **remiss:** Negligently unsuspicious.   135. **generous:** No-
ble-minded.   138. **unbated:** Not blunted, having no button.
pass of practice: Treacherous thrust.   141. **unction:** Ointment.   **mountebank:** Quack doctor.   143. **cataplasm:** Plaster or poultice.   144. **simples:** Herbs.   147. **gall:** Graze,
wound.   150. **shape:** Part that we propose to act.   151.
drift . . . performance: I.e., intention be disclosed by our
bungling.   154. **blast in proof:** Burst in the test (like a
cannon).   158. **As:** And you should.   160. **nonce:** Occasion.   161. **stuck:** Thrust (from *stoccado*, a fencing term).
166. **askant:** Aslant.   167. **hoar:** White or gray.

Of crow-flowers, nettles, daisies, and long
    purples°
170 That liberal° shepherds give a grosser name,
But our cold° maids do dead men's fingers call
    them.
There on the pendent boughs her crownet°
    weeds
Clamb'ring to hang, an envious sliver° broke,
When down her weedy° trophies and herself
Fell in the weeping brook. Her clothes spread
175   wide,
And mermaid-like awhile they bore her up,
Which time she chanted snatches of old lauds,°
As one incapable° of her own distress,
Or like a creature native and indued°
180 Unto that element. But long it could not be
Till that her garments, heavy with their drink,
Pull'd the poor wretch from her melodious lay
To muddy death.
LAERTES: Alas, then she is drown'd?
QUEEN: Drown'd, drown'd.
LAERTES: Too much of water hast thou, poor
185   Ophelia,
And therefore I forbid my tears. But yet
It is our trick;° nature her custom holds,
Let shame say what it will. [*He weeps.*] When
    these are gone,
The woman will be out.° Adieu, my lord.
190 I have a speech of fire, that fain would blaze,
But that this folly drowns it.   (*Exit.*)
KING: Let's follow, Gertrude.
How much I had to do to calm his rage!
Now fear I this will give it start again;
Therefore let's follow.   (*Exeunt.*)

[*ACT V • Scene I*]°

(*Enter two Clowns°* [*with spades, etc.*])

FIRST CLOWN: Is she to be buried in Christian burial
    when she willfully seeks her own salvation?
SECOND CLOWN: I tell thee she is; therefore make her
    grave straight.° The crowner° hath sat on her, and
5   finds it Christian burial.

169. **long purples:** Early purple orchids.   170. **liberal:** Free-spoken.   171. **cold:** Chaste.   172. **crownet:** Made into a chaplet or coronet.   173. **envious sliver:** Malicious branch. 174. **weedy:** I.e., of plants.   177. **lauds:** Hymns.   178. **incapable:** Lacking capacity to apprehend.   179. **indued:** Adapted by nature.   187. **It is our trick:** Weeping is our natural way (when sad).   188–89. **When . . . out:** When my tears are all shed, the woman in me will be expended, satisfied. V, I. **Location:** A churchyard. [S.D.] *Clowns:* Rustics.   4. **straight:** Straightway, immediately.   **crowner:** Coroner.

FIRST CLOWN: How can that be, unless she drown'd
    herself in her own defense?
SECOND CLOWN: Why, 'tis found so.
FIRST CLOWN: It must be "se offendendo";° it cannot
    be else. For here lies the point: if I drown myself 10
    wittingly, it argues an act, and an act hath three
    branches — it is to act, to do, and to perform.
    Argal,° she drown'd herself wittingly.
SECOND CLOWN: Nay, but hear you, goodman
    delver —   15
FIRST CLOWN: Give me leave. Here lies the water;
    good. Here stands the man; good. If the man go
    to this water, and drown himself, it is, will he,°
    nill he, he goes, mark you that. But if the water
    come to him and drown him, he drowns not himself. 20
    Argal, he that is not guilty of his own death shortens
    not his own life.
SECOND CLOWN: But is this law?
FIRST CLOWN: Ay, marry, is 't — crowner's quest°
    law.   25
SECOND CLOWN: Will you ha' the truth on 't? If this
    had not been a gentlewoman, she should have been
    buried out o' Christian burial.
FIRST CLOWN: Why, there thou say'st.° And the more
    pity that great folk should have count'nance° in 30
    this world to drown or hang themselves, more than
    their even-Christen.° Come, my spade. There is no
    ancient gentlemen but gard'ners, ditchers, and
    grave-makers. They hold up Adam's profession.
SECOND CLOWN: Was he a gentleman?   35
FIRST CLOWN: 'A was the first that ever bore arms.
[SECOND CLOWN: Why, he had none.
FIRST CLOWN: What, art a heathen? How dost thou
    understand the Scripture? The Scripture says "Adam
    digg'd." Could he dig without arms?] I'll put another 40
    question to thee. If thou answerest me not to the
    purpose, confess thyself° —
SECOND CLOWN: Go to.
FIRST CLOWN: What is he that builds stronger than
    either the mason, the shipwright, or the carpenter? 45
SECOND CLOWN: The gallows-maker, for that frame
    outlives a thousand tenants.
FIRST CLOWN: I like thy wit well, in good faith. The
    gallows does well; but how does it well? It does
    well to those that do ill. Now thou dost ill to say 50
    the gallows is built stronger than the church. Argal,
    the gallows may do well to thee. To 't again, come.

9. **se offendendo:** A comic mistake for *se defendendo,* used in verdicts of justifiable homicide.   13. **Argal:** Corruption of *ergo,* therefore.   18. **will he:** Will he not.   24. **quest:** Inquest.   29. **there you say'st:** That's right.   30. **count'nance:** Privilege.   32. **even-Christen:** Fellow Christian.   42. **confess thyself:** The saying continues, "and be hanged."

SECOND CLOWN: "Who builds stronger than a mason, a shipwright, or a carpenter?"

55 FIRST CLOWN: Ay, tell me that, and unyoke.°

SECOND CLOWN: Marry, now I can tell.

FIRST CLOWN: To 't.

SECOND CLOWN: Mass,° I cannot tell.

(Enter Hamlet and Horatio [at a distance].)

FIRST CLOWN: Cudgel thy brains no more about it, for
60 your dull ass will not mend his pace with beating;
and, when you are ask'd this question next, say
"a grave-maker." The houses he makes lasts till
doomsday. Go, get thee in, and fetch me a stoup°
of liquor.

[Exit Second Clown. First Clown digs.]
(Song.)

65 "In youth, when I did love, did love,°
Methought it was very sweet,
To contract — O — the time for — a — my
behove,°
O, methought there — a — was nothing — a
— meet."°

HAMLET: Has this fellow no feeling of his business,
70 that a sings at grave-making?

HORATIO: Custom hath made it in him a property of
easiness.°

HAMLET: 'Tis e'en so. The hand of little employment
hath the daintier sense.°

(Song.)

75 FIRST CLOWN: "But age, with his stealing steps,
Hath claw'd me in his clutch,
And hath shipped me into the land,°
As if I had never been such."

[Throws up a skull.]

HAMLET: That skull had a tongue in it, and could
80 sing once. How the knave jowls° it to the ground,
as if 'twere Cain's jaw-bone, that did the first murder! This might be the pate of a politician,° which
this ass now o'erreaches,° one that would circumvent God, might it not?

HORATIO: It might, my lord.   85

HAMLET: Or of a courtier, which could say "Good
morrow, sweet lord! How dost thou, sweet lord?"
This might be my Lord Such-a-one, that prais'd
my Lord Such-a-one's horse when 'a meant to beg
it, might it not?   90

HORATIO: Ay, my lord.

HAMLET: Why, e'en so, and now my Lady Worm's,
chapless,° and knock'd about the mazzard° with a
sexton's spade. Here's fine revolution,° an° we had
the trick to see 't. Did these bones cost no more   95
the breeding,° but to play at loggats° with them?
Mine ache to think on 't.

(Song.)

FIRST CLOWN: "A pick-axe, and a spade, a spade,
For and° a shrouding sheet;
O, a pit of clay for to be made   100
For such a guest is meet."

[Throws up another skull.]

HAMLET: There's another. Why may not that be the
skull of a lawyer? Where be his quiddities° now,
his quillities,° his cases, his tenures,° and his tricks?
Why does he suffer this mad knave now to knock 105
him about the sconce° with a dirty shovel, and will
not tell him of his action of battery? Hum! This
fellow might be in 's time a great buyer of land,
with his statutes, his recognizances,° his fines, his
double° vouchers,° his recoveries.° [Is this the fine 110
of his fines, and the recovery of his recoveries,] to
have his fine pate full of fine dirt?° Will his vouchers
vouch him no more of his purchases, and double
[ones too], than the length and breadth of a pair
of indentures?° The very conveyances° of his lands 115

---

55. unyoke: After this great effort you may unharness the
team of your wits.   **58. Mass:** By the Mass.   **63. stoup:**
Two-quart measure.   **65. In . . . love:** This and the two
following stanzas, with nonsensical variations, are from a
poem attributed to Lord Vaux and printed in *Tottel's Mis-
cellany* (1557). The *O* and *a* (for "ah") seemingly are the
grunts of the digger.   **67. To contract . . . behove:** To make
a betrothal agreement for my benefit (?).   **68. meet:** Suitable,
i.e., more suitable.   **71–72. property of easiness:** Something
he can do easily and without thinking.   **74. daintier sense:**
More delicate sense of feeling.   **77. into the land:** Toward
my grave (?) (but note the lack of rhyme in *steps, land*).
80. jowls: Dashes.   **82. politician:** Schemer, plotter.   **83.
o'erreaches:** Circumvents, gets the better of (with a quibble
on the literal sense).

93. chapless: Having no lower jaw.   **mazzard:** Head (literally, a drinking vessel).   **94. revolution:** Change.   **an:** If.
96. the breeding: In the breeding, raising.   **loggats:** A game
in which pieces of hardwood are thrown to lie as near as
possible to a stake.   **99. For and:** And moreover.   **103.
quiddities:** Subtleties, quibbles (from Latin *quid*, a thing).
104. quillities: Verbal niceties, subtle distinctions (variation
of *quiddities*).   **tenures:** The holding of a piece of property
or office, or the conditions or period of such holding.   **106.
sconce:** Head.   **109. statutes, recognizances:** Legal documents guaranteeing a debt by attaching land and property.
109–10. fines, recoveries: Ways of converting entailed estates
into "fee simple" or freehold.   **110. double:** Signed by two
signatories.   **vouchers:** Guarantees of the legality of a title
to real estate.   **110–12. fine of his fines . . . fine pate . . .
fine dirt:** End of his legal maneuvers . . . elegant head . . .
minutely sifted dirt.   **114–15. pair of indentures:** Legal document drawn up in duplicate on a single sheet and then cut
apart on a zigzag line so that each pair was uniquely matched.
(Hamlet may refer to two rows of teeth, or dentures.)   **115.
conveyances:** Deeds.

will scarcely lie in this box,° and must th' inheritor°
himself have no more, ha?

HORATIO: Not a jot more, my lord.

HAMLET: Is not parchment made of sheep-skins?

120 HORATIO: Ay, my lord, and of calf-skins too.

HAMLET: They are sheep and calves which seek out
assurance in that.° I will speak to this fellow. —
Whose grave's this, sirrah?°

FIRST CLOWN: Mine, sir.

125 [*Sings.*] "O, a pit of clay for to be made
[For such a guest is meet]."

HAMLET: I think it be thine, indeed, for thou liest
in 't.

FIRST CLOWN: You lie out on 't, sir, and therefore 'tis
130 not yours. For my part, I do not lie in 't, yet it is
mine.

HAMLET: Thou dost lie in 't, to be in 't and say it is
thine. 'Tis for the dead, not for the quick;° therefore
thou liest.

135 FIRST CLOWN: 'Tis a quick lie, sir; 'twill away again
from me to you.

HAMLET: What man dost thou dig it for?

FIRST CLOWN: For no man, sir.

HAMLET: What woman, then?

140 FIRST CLOWN: For none, neither.

HAMLET: Who is to be buried in 't?

FIRST CLOWN: One that was a woman, sir, but, rest
her soul, she's dead.

HAMLET: How absolute° the knave is! We must speak
145 by the card,° or equivocation° will undo us. By the
Lord, Horatio, this three years I have taken note
of it: the age is grown so pick'd° that the toe of
the peasant comes so near the heel of the courtier,
he galls his kibe.° How long hast thou been a grave-
150 maker?

FIRST CLOWN: Of all the days i' th' year, I came to
't that day that our last king Hamlet overcame
Fortinbras.

HAMLET: How long is that since?

155 FIRST CLOWN: Cannot you tell that? Every fool can
tell that. It was that very day that young Hamlet
was born — he that is mad, and sent into England.

HAMLET: Ay, marry, why was he sent into England?

FIRST CLOWN: Why, because 'a was mad. 'A shall
160 recover his wits there, or, if 'a do not, 'tis no great
matter there.

---

116. **this box:** The skull.   **inheritor:** Possessor, owner.
122. **assurance in that:** Safety in legal parchments.   123.
sirrah: Term of address to inferiors.   133. **quick:** Living.
144. **absolute:** Positive, decided.   145. **by the card:** By the
mariner's card on which the points of the compass were
marked, i.e., with precision.   **equivocation:** Ambiguity in
the use of terms.   147. **pick'd:** Refined, fastidious.   149.
galls his kibe: Chafes the courtier's chilblain (a swelling or
sore caused by cold).

HAMLET: Why?

FIRST CLOWN: 'Twill not be seen in him there. There
the men are as mad as he.

HAMLET: How came he mad?   165

FIRST CLOWN: Very strangely, they say.

HAMLET: How strangely?

FIRST CLOWN: Faith, e'en with losing his wits.

HAMLET: Upon what ground?

FIRST CLOWN: Why, here in Denmark. I have been   170
sexton here, man and boy, thirty years.

HAMLET: How long will a man lie i' th' earth ere he
rot?

FIRST CLOWN: Faith, if 'a be not rotten before 'a die
— as we have many pocky° corses [now-a-days],   175
that will scarce hold the laying in — 'a will last
you some eight year or nine year. A tanner will
last you nine year.

HAMLET: Why he more than another?

FIRST CLOWN: Why, sir, his hide is so tann'd with his   180
trade that 'a will keep out water a great while, and
your water is a sore decayer of your whoreson dead
body. [*Picks up a skull.*] Here's a skull now hath
lain you° i' th' earth three and twenty years.

HAMLET: Whose was it?   185

FIRST CLOWN: A whoreson mad fellow's it was. Whose
do you think it was?

HAMLET: Nay, I know not.

FIRST CLOWN: A pestilence on him for a mad rogue!
'A pour'd a flagon of Rhenish° on my head once.   190
This same skull, sir, was Yorick's skull, the King's
jester.

HAMLET: This?

FIRST CLOWN: E'en that.

HAMLET: [Let me see.] [*Takes the skull.*] Alas, poor   195
Yorick! I knew him, Horatio, a fellow of infinite
jest, of most excellent fancy. He hath borne me on
his back a thousand times; and now, how abhorr'd
in my imagination it is! My gorge rises at it. Here
hung those lips that I have kiss'd I know not how   200
oft. Where be your gibes now? Your gambols, your
songs, your flashes of merriment that were wont
to set the table on a roar? Not one now, to mock
your own grinning? Quite chap-fall'n?° Now get
you to my lady's chamber, and tell her, let her   205
paint an inch thick, to this favor° she must come;
make her laugh at that. Prithee, Horatio, tell me
one thing.

HORATIO: What's that, my lord?

HAMLET: Dost thou think Alexander look'd o' this   210
fashion i' th' earth?

---

175. **pocky:** Rotten, diseased (literally, with the pox, or syphilis).   184. **lain you:** Lain.   190. **Rhenish:** Rhine wine.
204. **chap-fall'n:** (1) Lacking the lower jaw, (2) dejected.
206. **favor:** Aspect, appearance.

HORATIO: E'en so.

HAMLET: And smelt so? Pah! [*Puts down the skull.*]

HORATIO: E'en so, my lord.

15 HAMLET: To what base uses we may return, Horatio!
Why may not imagination trace the noble dust of
Alexander, till a' find it stopping a bung-hole?

HORATIO: 'Twere to consider too curiously,° to consider
so.

20 HAMLET: No, faith, not a jot, but to follow him thither
with modesty° enough, and likelihood to lead it.
[As thus]: Alexander died, Alexander was buried,
Alexander returneth to dust; the dust is earth; of
earth we make loam;° and why of that loam, whereto
25 he was converted, might they not stop a beer-barrel?
Imperious° Caesar, dead and turn'd to clay,
Might stop a hole to keep the wind away.
O, that that earth which kept the world in awe
Should patch a wall t' expel the winter's flaw!°
30 But soft, but soft awhile! Here comes the King.

(*Enter King, Queen, Laertes, and the Corse [of Ophelia,
in procession, with Priest, Lords etc.].*)

The Queen, the courtiers. Who is this they follow?
And with such maimed rites? This doth betoken
The corse they follow did with desp'rate hand
Fordo it° own life. 'Twas of some estate.°
35 Couch° we awhile, and mark.
        [*He and Horatio conceal themselves.
        Ophelia's body is taken to the grave.*]

LAERTES: What ceremony else?

HAMLET [*to Horatio*]: That is Laertes, a very noble
youth. Mark.

LAERTES: What ceremony else?

PRIEST: Her obsequies have been as far enlarg'd
40 As we have warranty. Her death was doubtful,
And, but that great command o'ersways the
order,
She should in ground unsanctified been lodg'd
Till the last trumpet. For° charitable prayers,
Shards,° flints, and pebbles should be thrown on
her.
45 Yet here she is allow'd her virgin crants,°
Her maiden strewments,° and the bringing home
Of bell and burial.°

LAERTES: Must there no more be done?

PRIEST: No more be done.
We should profane the service of the dead
To sing a requiem and such rest to her   250
As to peace-parted souls.

LAERTES: Lay her i' th' earth,
And from her fair and unpolluted flesh
May violets° spring! I tell thee, churlish priest,
A minist'ring angel shall my sister be
When thou liest howling!

HAMLET [*to Horatio*]:   What, the fair Ophelia!   255

QUEEN [*scattering flowers*]: Sweets to the sweet!
Farewell.
I hoped thou shouldst have been my Hamlet's
wife.
I thought thy bride-bed to have deck'd, sweet
maid,
And not have strew'd thy grave.

LAERTES: O, treble woe
Fall ten times treble on that cursed head   260
Whose wicked deed thy most ingenious sense°
Depriv'd thee of! Hold off the earth awhile,
Till I have caught her once more in mine arms.
        [*Leaps into the grave and embraces Ophelia.*]
Now pile your dust upon the quick and dead,
Till of this flat a mountain you have made   265
T 'o'ertop old Pelion,° or the skyish head
Of blue Olympus.°

HAMLET [*coming forward*]: What is he whose grief
Bears such an emphasis, whose phrase of sorrow
Conjures the wand'ring stars,° and makes them
stand   270
Like wonder-wounded hearers? This is I,
Hamlet the Dane.°

LAERTES: The devil take thy soul!
        [*Grappling with him.*]

HAMLET: Thou pray'st not well.
I prithee, take thy fingers from my throat;
For, though I am not splenitive° and rash,   275
Yet have I in me something dangerous,
Which let thy wisdom fear. Hold off thy hand.

KING: Pluck them asunder.

QUEEN: Hamlet, Hamlet!

ALL: Gentlemen!

HORATIO: Good my lord, be quiet.
        [*Hamlet and Horatio are parted.*]

HAMLET: Why, I will fight with him upon this
theme   280
Until my eyelids will no longer wag.

---

218. **curiously:** Minutely.   221. **modesty:** Moderation.
224. **loam:** Clay mixture for brickmaking or other clay use.
226. **Imperious:** Imperial.   229. **flaw:** Gust of wind.   234.
Fordo it: Destroy its.   **estate:** Rank.   235. **Couch:** Hide,
lurk.   243. **For:** In place of.   244. **Shards:** Broken bits of
pottery.   245. **crants:** Garland.   246. **strewments:** Traditional strewing of flowers.   246–47. **bringing . . . burial:**
Laying to rest of the body in consecrated ground, to the
sound of the bell.

253. **violets:** See IV, v, 187 and note.   261. **ingenious sense:**
Mind endowed with finest qualities.   266, 267. **Pelion,
Olympus:** Mountains in the north of Thessaly; see also *Ossa*
at line 297.   270. **wand'ring stars:** Planets.   272. **the Dane:**
This title normally signifies the King; see I, I, 15 and note.
275. **splenitive:** Quick-tempered.

QUEEN: O my son, what theme?

HAMLET: I lov'd Ophelia. Forty thousand brothers
   Could not with all their quantity of love
285   Make up my sum. What wilt thou do for her?

KING: O, he is mad, Laertes.

QUEEN: For love of God, forbear him.

HAMLET: 'Swounds,° show me what thou't do.
   Woo 't° weep? Woo 't fight? Woo 't fast? Woo
   't tear thyself?
290   Woo 't drink up eisel?° Eat a crocodile?
   I'll do 't. Dost thou come here to whine?
   To outface me with leaping in her grave?
   Be buried quick° with her, and so will I.
   And, if thou prate of mountains, let them throw
295   Millions of acres on us, till our ground,
   Singeing his pate° against the burning zone,°
   Make Ossa° like a wart! Nay, an thou 'lt
   mouth,°
   I'll rant as well as thou.

QUEEN: This is mere° madness,
   And thus a while the fit will work on him;
300   Anon, as patient as the female dove
   When that her golden couplets° are disclos'd,°
   His silence will sit drooping.

HAMLET: Hear you, sir.
   What is the reason that you use me thus?
   I lov'd you ever. But it is no matter.
305   Let Hercules himself do what he may,
   The cat will mew, and dog will have his day.°

KING: I pray thee, good Horatio, wait upon him.
                            (*Exit Hamlet and Horatio.*)
   [*To Laertes.*] Strengthen your patience in° our
   last night's speech;
   We'll put the matter to the present push.° —
   Good Gertrude, set some watch over your
310   son. —
   This grave shall have a living° monument.
   An hour of quiet shortly shall we see;
   Till then, in patience our proceeding be. (*Exeunt.*)

---

288. 'Swounds: By His (Christ's) wounds.   **289. Woo 't:**
Wilt thou.   **290. eisel:** Vinegar.   **293. quick:** Alive.   **296.
his pate:** Its head, i.e., top.   **burning zone:** Sun's orbit.
297. Ossa: Another mountain in Thessaly. (In their war
against the Olympian gods, the giants attempted to heap
Ossa, Pelion, and Olympus on one another to scale heaven.)
mouth: Rant.   **298. mere:** Utter.   **301. golden couplets:**
Two baby pigeons, covered with yellow down.   **disclos'd:**
Hatched.   **305–6. Let . . . day:** Despite any blustering attempts at interference every person will sooner or later do
what he must do.   **308. in:** By recalling.   **309. present
push:** Immediate test.   **311. living:** Lasting; also refers (for
Laertes' benefit) to the plot against Hamlet.

[*Scene II*]°

(*Enter Hamlet and Horatio.*)

HAMLET: So much for this, sir; now shall you see
   the other.°
   You do remember all the circumstance?

HORATIO: Remember it, my lord!

HAMLET: Sir, in my heart there was a kind of
   fighting
   That would not let me sleep. Methought I lay   5
   Worse than the mutines° in the bilboes.° Rashly,°
   And prais'd be rashness for it — let us know,°
   Our indiscretion sometime serves us well
   When our deep plots do pall,° and that should
   learn° us
   There's a divinity that shapes our ends,   10
   Rough-hew° them how we will —

HORATIO: That is most certain.

HAMLET: Up from my cabin,
   My sea-gown scarf'd about me, in the dark
   Grop'd I to find out them, had my desire,
   Finger'd° their packet, and in fine° withdrew   15
   To mine own room again, making so bold,
   My fears forgetting manners, to unseal
   Their grand commission; where I found,
     Horatio —
   Ah, royal knavery! — an exact command,
   Larded° with many several sorts of reasons   20
   Importing° Denmark's health and England's too,
   With, ho, such bugs° and goblins in my life,°
   That, on the supervise,° no leisure bated,°
   No, not to stay the grinding of the axe,
   My head should be struck off.

HORATIO: Is 't possible?   25

HAMLET: Here's the commission; read it at more
   leisure.   [*Gives document.*]
   But wilt thou hear now how I did proceed?

HORATIO: I beseech you.

HAMLET: Being thus benetted round with villainies,
   Or I could make a prologue to my brains,
   They had begun the play.° I sat me down,   30

V, II. Location: The castle.   **1. see the other:** Hear the other
news.   **6. mutines:** Mutineers.   **bilboes:** Shackles.   **Rashly:**
On impulse (this adverb goes with lines 12ff.).   **7. know:**
Acknowledge.   **9. pall:** Fail.   **learn:** Teach.   **11. Rough-
hew:** Shape roughly.   **15. Finger'd:** Pilfered, pinched.   **in
fine:** Finally, in conclusion.   **20. Larded:** Enriched.   **21.
Importing:** Relating to.   **22. bugs:** Bugbears, hobgoblins.
in my life: To be feared if I were allowed to live.   **23.
supervise:** Reading.   **leisure bated:** Delay allowed.   **30–31.
Or . . . play:** Before I could consciously turn my brain to the
matter, it had started working on a plan. (*Or* means ere.)

Devis'd a new commission, wrote it fair.°
I once did hold it, as our statists° do,
A baseness° to write fair, and labor'd much
35   How to forget that learning, but, sir, now
It did me yeoman's° service. Wilt thou know
Th' effect° of what I wrote?

HORATIO: Ay, good my lord.

HAMLET: An earnest conjuration from the King,
As England was his faithful tributary,
As love between them like the palm might
40   flourish,
As peace should still her wheaten garland° wear
And stand a comma° 'tween their amities,
And many such-like as's° of great charge,°
That, on the view and knowing of these
          contents,
45   Without debatement further, more or less,
He should those bearers put to sudden death,
Not shriving time° allow'd.

HORATIO: How was this seal'd?

HAMLET: Why, even in that was heaven ordinant.°
I had my father's signet° in my purse,
50   Which was the model of that Danish seal;
Folded the writ up in the form of th' other,
Subscrib'd° it, gave 't th' impression,° plac'd it
          safely,
The changeling° never known. Now, the next
          day
Was our sea-fight, and what to this was sequent
55   Thou knowest already.

HORATIO: So Guildenstern and Rosencrantz go
          to 't.

HAMLET: [Why, man, they did make love to this
          employment.]
They are not near my conscience. Their defeat
Does by their own insinuation° grow.
60   'Tis dangerous when the baser nature comes
Between the pass° and fell° incensed points
Of mighty opposites.

HORATIO: Why, what a king is this!

HAMLET: Does it not, think thee, stand° me now
          upon —
He that hath killed my king and whor'd my
          mother,
Popp'd in between th' election° and my hopes,   65
Thrown out his angle° for my proper° life,
And with such coz'nage° — is 't not perfect
          conscience
[To quit° him with this arm? And is 't not to be
          damn'd
To let this canker° of our nature come
In further evil?   70

HORATIO: It must be shortly known to him from
          England
What is the issue of the business there.

HAMLET: It will be short. The interim is mine,
And a man's life 's no more than to say "One."°
But I am very sorry, good Horatio,   75
That to Laertes I forgot myself,
For by the image of my cause I see
The portraiture of his. I'll court his favors.
But, sure, the bravery° of his grief did put me
Into a tow'ring passion.

HORATIO: Peace, who comes here?]   80

(*Enter a Courtier [Osric].*)

OSRIC: Your lordship is right welcome back to
          Denmark.

HAMLET: I humbly thank you, sir. [*To Horatio.*] Dost
          know this water-fly?

HORATIO: No, my good lord.   85

HAMLET: Thy state is the more gracious, for 'tis a vice
          to know him. He hath much land, and fertile. Let
          a beast be lord of beasts, and his crib shall stand
          at the King's mess.° 'Tis a chough,° but, as I say,
          spacious in the possession of dirt.   90

OSRIC: Sweet lord, if your lordship were at leisure, I
          should impart a thing to you from his Majesty.

HAMLET: I will receive it, sir, with all diligence of
          spirit. Put your bonnet to his right use; 'tis for the
          head.   95

OSRIC: I thank your lordship, it is very hot.

---

32. **fair:** In a clear hand.   33. **statists:** Statesmen.   34.
baseness: Lower-class trait.   36. **yeoman's:** Substantial,
workmanlike.   37. **effect:** Purport.   41. **wheaten garland:**
Symbolic of fruitful agriculture, of peace.   42. **comma:** Indicating continuity, link.   43. **as's:** (1) The "whereases" of
formal document, (2) asses.   **charge:** (1) Import, (2) burden.
47. **shriving time:** Time for confession and absolution.   48.
ordinant: Directing.   49. **signet:** Small seal.   52. **Subscrib'd:** Signed.   **impression:** With a wax seal.   53. **changeling:** The substituted letter (literally, a fairy child substituted for a human one).   59. **insinuation:** Interference.   61.
pass: Thrust.   **fell:** Fierce.

63. **stand:** Become incumbent.   65. **election:** The Danish
monarch was "elected" by a small number of high-ranking
electors.   66. **angle:** Fishing line.   **proper:** Very.   67.
coz'nage: Trickery.   68. **quit:** Repay.   69. **canker:** Ulcer.
74. **a man's . . . "One":** To take a man's life requires no
more than to count to one as one duels.   79. **bravery:**
Bravado.   87–89. **Let . . . mess:** If a man, no matter how
beastlike, is as rich in possessions as Osric, he may eat at
the King's table.   89. **chough:** Chattering jackdaw.

HAMLET: No, believe me, 'tis very cold; the wind is northerly.

OSRIC: It is indifferent° cold, my lord, indeed.

100 HAMLET: But yet methinks it is very sultry and hot for my complexion.°

OSRIC: Exceedingly, my lord; it is very sultry, as 'twere — I cannot tell how. My lord, his Majesty bade me signify to you that 'a has laid a great wager

105 on your head. Sir, this is the matter —

HAMLET: I beseech you, remember —

[*Hamlet moves him to put on his hat.*]

OSRIC: Nay, good my lord; for my ease,° in good faith. Sir, here is newly come to court Laertes — believe me, an absolute gentleman, full of most

110 excellent differences,° of very soft society° and great showing.° Indeed, to speak feelingly° of him, he is the card° or calendar° of gentry,° for you shall find in him the continent of what part° a gentleman would see.

115 HAMLET: Sir, his definement° suffers no perdition° in you, though, I know, to divide him inventorially° would dozy° th' arithmetic of memory, and yet but yaw° neither° in respect of° his quick sail. But, in the verity of extolment,° I take him to be a soul

120 of great article,° and his infusion° of such dearth and rareness,° as, to make true diction° of him, his semblable° is his mirror, and who else would trace° him, his umbrage,° nothing more.

OSRIC: Your lordship speaks most infallibly of him.

125 HAMLET: The concernancy,° sir? Why do we wrap the gentleman in our more rawer breath?°

OSRIC: Sir?

HORATIO: Is 't not possible to understand in another tongue?° You will do 't,° sir, really.

HAMLET: What imports the nomination° of this 130 gentleman?

OSRIC: Of Laertes?

HORATIO [*to Hamlet*]: His purse is empty already; all 's golden words are spent.

HAMLET: Of him, sir. 135

OSRIC: I know you are not ignorant —

HAMLET: I would you did, sir; yet, in faith, if you did, it would not much approve° me. Well, sir?

OSRIC: You are not ignorant of what excellence Laertes is — 140

HAMLET: I dare not confess that, lest I should compare° with him in excellence; but to know a man well were to know himself.°

OSRIC: I mean, sir, for his weapon; but in the imputation laid on him by them,° in his meed° he's unfellow'd.° 14

HAMLET: What's his weapon?

OSRIC: Rapier and dagger.

HAMLET: That's two of his weapons — but well.

OSRIC: The King, sir, hath wager'd with him six Barbary horses, against the which he has impawn'd,° as I 15 take it, six French rapiers and poniards, with their assigns,° as girdle, hangers,° and so. Three of the carriages,° in faith, are very dear to fancy,° very responsive° to the hilts, most delicate° carriages, and of very liberal conceit.° 15

HAMLET: What call you the carriages?

HORATIO [*to Hamlet*]: I knew you must be edified by the margent° ere you had done.

OSRIC: The carriages, sir, are the hangers.

HAMLET: The phrase would be more germane to the 16 matter if we could carry a cannon by our sides; I would it might be hangers till then. But, on: six Barb'ry horses against six French swords, their as-

---

99. indifferent: Somewhat. **101. complexion:** Temperament. **107. for my ease:** A conventional reply declining the invitation to put his hat back on. **110. differences:** Special qualities. **soft society:** Agreeable manners. **110–11. great showing:** Distinguished appearance. **111. feelingly:** With just perception. **112. card:** Chart, map. **calendar:** Guide. **gentry:** Good breeding. **113. the continent . . . part:** One who contains in him all the qualities (a *continent* is that which contains). **115. definement:** Definition. (Hamlet proceeds to mock Osric by using his lofty diction back at him.) **perdition:** Loss, diminution. **116. divide him inventorially:** Enumerate his graces. **117. dozy:** Dizzy. **118. yaw:** To move unsteadily (said of a ship). **neither:** For all that. **in respect of:** In comparison with. **118–19. in . . . extolment:** In true praise (of him). **120. article:** Moment or importance. **infusion:** Essence, character imparted by nature. **120–21. dearth and rareness:** Rarity. **121. make true diction:** Speak truly. **122. semblable:** Only true likeness. **who . . . trace:** Any other person who would wish to follow. **123. umbrage:** Shadow. **125. concernancy:** Import, relevance. **126. breath:** Speech.

128–29. to understand . . . tongue: For Osric to understand when someone else speaks in his manner. (Horatio twits Osric for not being able to understand the kind of flowery speech he himself uses when Hamlet speaks in such a vein.) **129. You will do 't:** You can if you try. **130. nomination:** Naming. **138. approve:** Commend. **141. compare:** Seem to compete. **142–43. but . . . himself:** For, to recognize excellence in another man, one must know oneself. **144–45. imputation . . . them:** Reputation given him by others. **145. meed:** Merit. **unfellow'd:** Unmatched. **150. impawn'd:** Staked, wagered. **152. assigns:** Appurtenances. **hangers:** Straps on the sword belt (*girdle*) from which the sword hung. **153. carriages:** An affected way of saying *hangers*; literally, gun-carriages. **dear to fancy:** Fancifully designed, tasteful. **154. responsive:** Corresponding closely, matching. **delicate:** I.e., in workmanship. **155. liberal conceit:** Elaborate design. **158. margent:** Margin of a book, place for explanatory notes.

signs, and three liberal-conceited carriages; that's
the French bet against the Danish. Why is this
impawn'd, as you call it?

OSRIC: The King, sir, hath laid,° sir, that in a dozen
passes° between yourself and him, he shall not exceed
you three hits. He hath laid on twelve for nine,
and it would come to immediate trial, if your lordship
would vouchsafe the answer.

HAMLET: How if I answer no?

OSRIC: I mean, my lord, the opposition of your person
in trial.

HAMLET: Sir, I will walk here in the hall. If it please
his Majesty, it is the breathing time° of day with
me. Let the foils be brought, the gentleman willing,
and the King hold his purpose, I will win for him
an I can; if not, I will gain nothing but my shame
and the odd hits.

OSRIC: Shall I deliver you so?

HAMLET: To this effect, sir — after what flourish your
nature will.

OSRIC: I commend my duty to your lordship.

HAMLET: Yours, yours. [*Exit Osric.*] He does well to
commend it himself; there are no tongues else for
's turn.

HORATIO: This lapwing° runs away with the shell on
his head.

HAMLET: 'A did comply, sir, with his dug,° before 'a
suck'd it. Thus has he — and many more of the
same breed that I know the drossy° age dotes on
— only got the tune° of the time and, out of an
habit of encounter,° a kind of yesty° collection,°
which carries them through and through the most
fann'd and winnow'd° opinions; and do but blow
them to their trial, the bubbles are out.°

(*Enter a Lord.*)

LORD: My lord, his Majesty commended him to you
by young Osric, who brings back to him that you
attend him in the hall. He sends to know if your
pleasure hold to play with Laertes, or that you will
take longer time.

HAMLET: I am constant to my purposes; they follow
the King's pleasure. If his fitness speaks,° mine is
ready; now or whensoever, provided I be so able
as now.

LORD: The King and Queen and all are coming down.

HAMLET: In happy time.°

LORD: The Queen desires you to use some gentle en-
tertainment° to Laertes before you fall to play.

HAMLET: She well instructs me.   [*Exit Lord.*]

HORATIO: You will lose, my lord.

HAMLET: I do not think so. Since he went into France,
I have been in continual practice; I shall win at the
odds. But thou wouldst not think how ill all's here
about my heart; but it is no matter.

HORATIO: Nay, good my lord —

HAMLET: It is but foolery, but it is such a kind of
gain-giving,° as would perhaps trouble a woman.

HORATIO: If your mind dislike anything, obey it. I
will forestall their repair hither, and say you are
not fit.

HAMLET: Not a whit, we defy augury. There is special
providence in the fall of a sparrow. If it be now,
'tis not to come; if it be not to come, it will be
now; if it be not now; yet it will come. The readiness
is all. Since no man of aught he leaves knows what
is 't to leave betimes,° let be.

(*A table prepar'd. [Enter] trumpets, drums, and Officers
with cushions; King, Queen, [Osric,] and all the State;
foils, daggers, [and wine borne in;] and Laertes.*)

KING: Come, Hamlet, come, and take this hand
from me.
           [*The King puts Laertes' hand into Hamlet's.*]

HAMLET: Give me your pardon, sir. I have done
you wrong,
But pardon 't, as you are a gentleman.
This presence° knows,
And you must needs have heard, how I am
punish'd
With a sore distraction. What I have done
That might your nature, honor, and exception°
Roughly awake, I here proclaim was madness.
Was 't Hamlet wrong'd Laertes? Never Hamlet.
If Hamlet from himself be ta'en away,
And when he's not himself does wrong Laertes,

167. **laid:** Wagered. 168. **passes:** Bouts. (The odds of the betting are hard to explain. Possibly the King bets that Hamlet will win at least five out of twelve, at which point Laertes raises the odds against himself by betting he will win nine.) 176. **breathing time:** Exercise period. 188. **lapwing:** A bird that draws intruders away from its nest and was thought to run about when newly hatched with its head in the shell; a seeming reference to Osric's hat. 190. **comply ... dug:** Observe ceremonious formality toward his mother's teat. 192. **drossy:** Frivolous. 193. **tune:** Temper, mood, manner of speech. 194. **habit of encounter:** Demeanor of social intercourse. **yesty:** Yeasty, frothy. **collection:** I.e., of current phrases. 196. **fann'd and winnow'd:** Select and refined. 196–97. **blow ... out:** Put them to the test, and their ignorance is exposed.

204. **If ... speaks:** If his readiness answers to the time. 208. **In happy time:** A phrase of courtesy indicating acceptance. 209–10. **entertainment:** Greeting. 219. **gain-giving:** Misgiving. 227–28. **what ... betimes:** What is the best time to leave it. 232. **presence:** Royal assembly. 235. **exception:** Disapproval.

240 Then Hamlet does it not, Hamlet denies it.
Who does it, then? His madness. If 't be so,
Hamlet is of the faction that is wrong'd;
His madness is poor Hamlet's enemy.
[Sir, in this audience,]
245 Let my disclaiming from a purpos'd evil
Free me so far in your most generous thoughts
That I have shot my arrow o'er the house
And hurt my brother.
LAERTES: I am satisfied in nature,°
Whose motive in this case should stir me most
250 To my revenge. But in my terms of honor
I stand aloof, and will no reconcilement
Till by some elder masters of known honor
I have a voice° and precedent of peace
To keep my name ungor'd. But till that time,
255 I do receive your offer'd love like love,
And will not wrong it.
HAMLET: I embrace it freely,
And will this brothers' wager frankly play.
Give us the foils. Come on.
LAERTES: Come, one for me.
HAMLET: I'll be your foil,° Laertes. In mine
ignorance
260 Your skill shall, like a star i' th' darkest night,
Stick fiery off° indeed.
LAERTES: You mock me, sir.
HAMLET: No, by this hand.
KING: Give them the foils, young Osric. Cousin
Hamlet,
You know the wager?
HAMLET: Very well, my lord.
265 Your Grace has laid the odds o' th' weaker side.
KING: I do not fear it; I have seen you both.
But since he is better'd,° we have therefore odds.
LAERTES: This is too heavy, let me see another.
                        [Exchanges his foil for another.]
HAMLET: This likes me well. These foils have all a
length?
                              [They prepare to play.]
270 OSRIC: Ay, my good lord.
KING: Set me the stoups of wine upon that table.
If Hamlet give the first or second hit,
Or quit° in answer of the third exchange,
Let all the battlements their ordnance fire.
275 The King shall drink to Hamlet's better breath,

And in the cup an union° shall he throw,
Richer than that which four successive kings
In Denmark's crown have worn. Give me the
cups,
And let the kettle° to the trumpet speak,
The trumpet to the cannoneer without,   280
The cannons to the heavens, the heaven to earth,
"Now the King drinks to Hamlet." Come, begin.
                              (Trumpets the while.)
And you, the judges, bear a wary eye.
HAMLET: Come on sir.
LAERTES: Come, my lord. [They play. Hamlet scores   285
                                            a hit.]
HAMLET: One.
LAERTES: No.
HAMLET: Judgment.
OSRIC: A hit, a very palpable hit.
                    (Drum, trumpets, and shot. Flourish.
                                    A piece goes off.)
LAERTES: Well, again.
KING: Stay, give me drink. Hamlet, this pearl is
thine.   290
[He throws a pearl in Hamlet's cup and drinks.]
Here's to thy health. Give him the cup.
HAMLET: I'll play this bout first; set it by awhile.
Come. [They play.] Another hit; what say you?
LAERTES: A touch, a touch, I do confess 't.
KING: Our son shall win.
QUEEN: He's fat,° and scant of breath.   295
Here, Hamlet, take my napkin,° rub thy brows.
The Queen carouses° to thy fortune, Hamlet.
HAMLET: Good madam!
KING: Gertrude, do not drink.
QUEEN: I will, my lord; I pray you pardon me.   300
                                                      [Drinks.]
KING [aside]: It is the pois'ned cup. It is too late.
HAMLET: I dare not drink yet, madam; by and by.
QUEEN: Come, let me wipe thy face.
LAERTES [to King]: My lord, I'll hit him now.
KING: I do not think 't.
LAERTES [aside]: And yet it is almost against my
conscience.   305
HAMLET: Come, for the third, Laertes. You do but
dally.
I pray you, pass with your best violence;
I am afeard you make a wanton of me.°
LAERTES: Say you so? Come on.   [They play.]
OSRIC: Nothing, neither way.   310

---

248. in nature. As to my personal feelings.   253. voice:
Authoritative pronouncement.   259. foil: Thin metal background which sets a jewel off (with pun on the blunted rapier
for fencing).   261. Stick fiery off: Stand out brilliantly.
267. is better'd: Has improved; is the odds-on favorite.
273. quit: Repay (with a hit).

276. union: Pearl (so called, according to Pliny's *Natural
History*, IX, because pearls are *unique*, never identical).
279. kettle: Kettledrum.   295. fat: Not physically fit, out
of training.   296. napkin: Handkerchief: 297. carouses:
Drinks a toast.   308. make . . . me: Treat me like a spoiled
child, holding back to give me an advantage.

LAERTES: Have at you now!
    [*Laertes wounds Hamlet; then, in scuffling,*
they change rapiers,° and Hamlet wounds Laertes.]
KING: Part them! They are incens'd.
HAMLET: Nay, come, again.   [*The Queen falls.*]
OSRIC: Look to the Queen there, ho!
HORATIO: They bleed on both sides. How is it, my
    lord?
OSRIC: How is 't, Laertes?
LAERTES: Why, as a woodcock° to mine own
15   springe,° Osric;
    I am justly kill'd with mine own treachery.
HAMLET: How does the Queen?
KING: She swoons to see them bleed.
QUEEN: No, no, the drink, the drink — O my dear
    Hamlet —
    The drink, the drink! I am pois'ned.   [*Dies.*]
20 HAMLET: O villainy! Ho, let the door be lock'd!
    Treachery! Seek it out.   [*Laertes falls.*]
LAERTES: It is here, Hamlet. Hamlet, thou art slain.
    No med'cine in the world can do thee good;
    In thee there is not half an hour's life.
25   The treacherous instrument is in thy hand,
    Unbated° and envenom'd. The foul practice
    Hath turn'd itself on me. Lo, here I lie,
    Never to rise again. Thy mother's pois'ned.
    I can no more. The King, the King's to blame.
HAMLET: The point envenom'd too? Then, venom,
30   to thy work.   [*Stabs the King.*]
ALL: Treason! Treason!
KING: O, yet defend me, friends; I am but hurt.
HAMLET: Here, thou incestuous, murd'rous, damned
    Dane,
    [*He forces the King to drink*
    the poisoned cup.]
    Drink off this potion. Is thy union° here?
    Follow my mother.   [*King dies.*]
35 LAERTES: He is justly serv'd.
    It is a poison temper'd° by himself.
    Exchange forgiveness with me, noble Hamlet.
    Mine and my father's death come not upon thee,
    Nor thine on me!   [*Dies.*]
HAMLET: Heaven make thee free of it! I follow
40   thee.
    I am dead, Horatio. Wretched Queen, adieu!

---

311. [S.D.] *in scuffling, they change rapiers*: This stage direction occurs in the Folio. According to a widespread stage tradition, Hamlet receives a scratch, realizes that Laertes' sword is unbated, and accordingly forces an exchange.   **315. woodcock**: A bird, a type of stupidity or as a decoy. **springe**: Trap, snare.   **326. Unbated**: Not blunted with a button.   **334. union**: Pearl (see line 276; with grim puns on the word's other meanings: marriage, shared death[?]). **336. temper'd**: Mixed.

You that look pale and tremble at this chance,
That are but mutes° or audience to this act,
Had I but time — as this fell° sergeant,° Death,
Is strict in his arrest — O, I could tell you —   345
But let it be. Horatio, I am dead;
Thou livest. Report me and my cause aright
To the unsatisfied.
HORATIO: Never believe it.
    I am more an antique Roman° than a Dane.
    Here's yet some liquor left.
    [*He attempts to drink from the poisoned cup.*
    Hamlet prevents him.]
HAMLET: As th' art a man,   350
    Give me the cup! Let go! By heaven, I'll ha 't.
    O God, Horatio, what a wounded name,
    Things standing thus unknown, shall I leave
    behind me!
    If thou didst ever hold me in thy heart,
    Absent thee from felicity awhile,   355
    And in this harsh world draw thy breath in pain
    To tell my story.
    (*A march afar off* [*and a volley within*].)
    What warlike noise is this?
OSRIC: Young Fortinbras, with conquest come from
    Poland,
To the ambassadors of England gives
This warlike volley.
HAMLET: O, I die, Horatio!   360
    The potent poison quite o'ercrows° my spirit.
    I cannot live to hear the news from England,
    But I do prophesy th' election lights
    On Fortinbras. He has my dying voice.°
    So tell him, with th' occurrents° more and less   365
    Which have solicited° — the rest is silence.[*Dies.*]
HORATIO: Now cracks a noble heart. Good night,
    sweet prince;
    And flights of angels sing thee to thy rest!
    [*March within.*]
    Why does the drum come hither?

(*Enter Fortinbras, with the* [*English*] *Ambassadors* [*with drum, colors, and attendants*].)

FORTINBRAS: Where is this sight?
HORATIO: What is it you would see?   370
    If aught of woe or wonder, cease your search.
FORTINBRAS: This quarry° cries on havoc.° O proud
    Death,

---

343. **mutes**: Silent observers. **344. fell**: Cruel. **sergeant**: Sheriff's officer. **349. Roman**: It was the Roman custom to follow masters in death. **361. o'ercrows**: Triumphs over. **364. voice**: Vote. **365. occurrents**: Events, incidents. **366. solicited**: Moved, urged. **372. quarry**: Heap of dead. **cries on havoc**: Proclaims a general slaughter.

What feast is toward° in thine eternal cell,
That thou so many princes at a shot
So bloodily hast struck?

375 FIRST AMBASSADOR: The sight is dismal;
And our affairs from England come too late.
The ears are senseless that should give us
    hearing,
To tell him his commandment is fulfill'd,
That Rosencrantz and Guildenstern are dead.
Where should we have our thanks?

380 HORATIO: Not from his° mouth,
Had it th' ability of life to thank you.
He never gave commandment for their death.
But since, so jump° upon this bloody question,°
You from the Polack wars, and you from
    England,
385 Are here arriv'd, give order that these bodies
High on a stage° be placed to the view,
And let me speak to th' yet unknowing world
How these things came about. So shall you hear
Of carnal, bloody, and unnatural acts,
390 Of accidental judgments,° casual° slaughters,
Of deaths put on° by cunning and forc'd cause,
And, in this upshot, purposes mistook
Fall'n on th' inventors' heads. All this can I
Truly deliver.

373. toward: In preparation.   380. his: Claudius's.   383.
jump: Precisely.   question: Dispute.   386. stage: Platform.
390. judgments: Retributions.   casual: Occurring by chance.
391. put on: Instigated.

FORTINBRAS: Let us haste to hear it,
And call the noblest to the audience.   39
For me, with sorrow I embrace my fortune.
I have some rights of memory° in this kingdom,
Which now to claim my vantage° doth invite me.
HORATIO: Of that I shall have also cause to speak,
And from his mouth whose voice will draw on
    more.°   40
But let this same be presently° perform'd,
Even while men's minds are wild, lest more
    mischance
On° plots and errors happen.
FORTINBRAS: Let four captains
Bear Hamlet, like a soldier, to the stage,
For he was likely, had he been put on,°   40
To have prov'd most royal; and, for his
    passage,°
The soldiers' music and the rite of war
Speak loudly for him.
Take up the bodies. Such a sight as this
Becomes the field,° but here shows much amiss.   41
Go, bid the soldiers shoot.
    (*Exeunt* [*marching, bearing off the dead bodies;
                a peal of ordnance is shot off*].)

397. of memory: Traditional, remembered.   398. vantage:
Presence at this opportune moment.   400. voice . . . more:
Vote will influence still others.   401. presently: Immediately.
403. On: On the basis of.   405. put on: Invested in royal
office and so put to the test.   406. passage: Death.   410.
field: I.e., of battle.

THE TEMPEST

One of Shakespeare's most thought-provoking plays, *The Tempest*
helps bridge the gap between Renaissance Italy, Elizabethan England,
and the discoveries of the New World. The Virginia Company, an
investment group in which Shakespeare had an interest, sent a flotilla
of ships to Virginia in 1609. However, its flagship, carrying the governor-
to-be of Virginia, Sir Thomas Gates, was lost in a July storm and washed
up on Bermuda, then reputed to be the Isle of Devils. Admiral Sir George
Somers built new boats and, with Gates and the rest of the crew,
continued the journey, arriving in Jamestown in May 1610. All this
news was reported in England on the eve of Shakespeare's preparation

to write a new play for the Globe Theatre. The "still-vexed Bermudas" of *The Tempest* (not to mention its opening storm) establishes a clear connection with events current in the Elizabethan world of politics and adventure.

There is also a connection between Prospero, the philosopher-magician of *The Tempest*, and the most celebrated Elizabethan magician of the time, John Dee (1527–1608). One of the Renaissance's most learned mathematicians, he was also an astrologer. Queen Elizabeth consulted him when she wanted to have her horoscope cast. His fame as a necromancer — one who called the spirits to do his bidding — took him as far as Poland to perform magic. While he was there in 1583 an English mob, certain Dee was a dangerous wizard, destroyed his library, furnishings, and laboratories. He was known by reputation to the audiences of the original productions of *The Tempest*, which occurred in November 1611 and again in 1612–1613.

King James I, who was almost surely at its first performances at court, took a special interest in magic. The play was performed at festivities celebrating the marriage of James's daughter Elizabeth. The marriage of Miranda and Ferdinand paralleled this real-life marriage. Moreover, the masque that the spirits perform for Miranda and Ferdinand (act IV, scene I) served as a special wedding celebration, since masques were dedicated to Hymen, the god of marriage.

Apart from relying on current events, *The Tempest* is notable in that it is one of the few plays for which Shakespeare did not use an earlier source from fiction, drama, or history. The plot of the good duke being cast adrift by his evil brother and then ending on an island with his infant daughter and controlling it through his magic seems entirely original. Early critics saw the play as a moral excursion in which the power of good, after great trial, eventually overcomes evil. However, Shakespeare leaves a loose end at the conclusion of the play. While most of those who colluded to remove Prospero from his dukedom are contrite and ashamed — and express honest regret at their earlier actions — Prospero's brother Antonio remains unrepentant at the end. Prospero, who controls everyone on the island through his magic, forsakes magic when he declares that he will return to Milan, thus leaving himself potentially defenseless against a possible repetition of his brother's crimes. This detail emphasizes the island as a magical place, while reminding us of the existence of evil in the world of Renaissance politics.

The political aspect of the play hints at governmental neglect. Not only is Antonio hungry for power, but Prospero is neglectful of it. Some critics have suggested that Niccolò Machiavelli (1469–1527) may have provided some thematic underpinning for the play in his political treatise *The Prince*, which insists that a prince (or duke) should hold on to power by any means possible. Prospero, by spending his time cultivating magic, neglects his political duties and leaves the way open to his usurping brother.

Early Shakespeare critics would have been surprised by late twentieth-century interpretations of *The Tempest* that posit colonialism as one of the primary themes of the play. Connected as the play is with the colonizing efforts of the Virginia Company, such a reading is plausible. In these interpretations Prospero is not seen primarily as a benevolent father of Miranda or as a magnanimous and forgiving ruler who restores his uninvited guests to their previously "wrecked" ship. Instead, taking Caliban's island from him, putting Caliban into slavery, and demanding his obeisance cast Prospero as a representative of the Europeans who usurped the land of Native Americans and enslaved them.

Not all modern-day Shakespeareans accept any one of these critical approaches to the play. However, the play's richness of characterization, impressive theatricality, and complex range of themes definitely support a multiple critical perspective.

The Tempest in Performance

Modern productions of the play demonstrate its ability to respond to varieties of interpretation. Late nineteenth-century actors did not especially enjoy playing Prospero. Beerbohm Tree, one of the most important Shakespearean actors, produced *The Tempest* in the early 1900s, but he took the part of Caliban apparently because he enjoyed its ambiguity. He played a sympathetic Caliban.

John Gielgud has been the most durable Prospero of the twentieth century. He first played him at the Old Vic in 1930 and, more recently, in the 1991 film *Prospero's Books*. In 1957 he played in Peter Brook's first production, which emphasized the theme of revenge. After his second production (1963) Brook said that *The Tempest* "includes all the themes from [Shakespeare's] earlier work — kingship, inheritance, treachery, conscience, identity, love, music, God; he draws them together as if to find the key to it all, but there is no such key. There is no grand order and Prospero returns to Milan not bathed in tranquility, but a wreck."

Prospero was more like an Old Testament prophet than an Elizabethan magus. However, Peter Hall's 1974 production at London's National Theatre presented Gielgud in makeup that made him resemble John Dee. The emphasis on magic was clear and powerful. The numerous productions in Europe and the Americas in the last three decades of this century demonstrate the increasing power of the play. *The Tempest* seems to grow in our imagination rather than diminish.

William Shakespeare (1564–1616)
THE TEMPEST   *1611*

Names of the Actors

ALONSO, *King of Naples*
SEBASTIAN, *his brother*
PROSPERO, *the right Duke of Milan*
ANTONIO, *his brother, the usurping Duke of Milan*
FERDINAND, *son to the King of Naples*
GONZALO, *an honest old councillor*
ADRIAN, ⎱ *lords*
FRANCISCO, ⎰
CALIBAN, *a savage and deformed slave*
TRINCULO, *a jester*
STEPHANO, *a drunken butler*
MASTER, *of a ship*
BOATSWAIN
MARINERS

MIRANDA, *daughter to Prospero*

ARIEL, *an airy Spirit*
IRIS,
CERES,
JUNO, ⎫ *[presented by] Spirits*
NYMPHS,
REAPERS,

[*Other Spirits attending Prospero*]

Scene: *An uninhabited island*

ACT I • *Scene I°*

(*A tempestuous noise of thunder and lightning heard. Enter a Shipmaster and a Boatswain.*)

MASTER: Boatswain!
BOATSWAIN: Here, Master. What cheer?
MASTER: Good,° speak to the mariners. Fall to 't yarely,° or we run ourselves aground. Bestir, bestir!   (*Exit.*)

(*Enter Mariners.*)

BOATSWAIN: Heigh, my hearts! Cheerly,° cheerly, my hearts! Yare, yare! Take in the topsail. Tend° to

the Master's whistle. — Blow° till thou burst thy wind, if room enough!°

(*Enter Alonso, Sebastian, Antonio, Ferdinand, Gonzalo, and others.*)

ALONSO: Good Boatswain, have care. Where's the   10
Master? Play the men.°
BOATSWAIN: I pray now, keep° below.
ANTONIO: Where is the Master, Boatswain?
BOATSWAIN: Do you not hear him? You mar our labor. Keep° your cabins! You do assist the storm.   15
GONZALO: Nay, good,° be patient.
BOATSWAIN: When the sea is. Hence!° What cares these roarers° for the name of king? To cabin! Silence! Trouble us not.
GONZALO: Good, yet remember whom thou hast   20
aboard.
BOATSWAIN: None that I more love than myself. You are a councillor; if you can command these elements to silence and work the peace of the present,° we will not hand° a rope more. Use your authority.   25
If you cannot, give thanks you have lived so long and make yourself ready in your cabin for the mischance° of the hour, if it so hap.° — Cheerly, good hearts! — Out of our way, I say.   (*Exit.*)
GONZALO: I have great comfort from this fellow.   30
Methinks he hath no drowning mark upon him; his complexion is perfect gallows.° Stand fast, good Fate, to his hanging! Make the rope of his destiny our cable, for our own doth little advantage.° If he be not born to be hanged, our case is mis-   35
erable.°   (*Exeunt.*)°

---

8. Blow: Addressed to the wind.   **9. if room enough:** As long as we have sea room enough.   **11. Play the men:** Act like men (?) ply, urge the men to exert themselves (?).   **12. keep:** Stay.   **15. Keep:** Remain in.   **16. good:** Good fellow.   **17. Hence:** Get away.   **18. roarers:** Waves or winds, or both; spoken to as though they were "bullies" or "blusterers."   **24. work . . . present:** Bring calm to our present circumstances.   **25. hand:** Handle.   **28. mischance:** Misfortune.   **hap:** Happen.   **32. complexion . . . gallows:** Appearance shows he was born to be hanged (and therefore, according to the proverb, in no danger of drowning).   **34. our . . . advantage:** I.e., our own cable is of little benefit.   **35–36. case is miserable:** Circumstances are desperate.   **36. [S.D.] Exeunt:** Latin for "they go out."

---

5 I, I. **Location:** On board ship, off the island's coast.   3. **Good:** I.e., it's good you've come; or, my good fellow.   4. **yarely:** Nimbly.   6. **Cheerly:** Cheerily.   7. **Tend:** Attend.

(*Enter Boatswain.*)

BOATSWAIN: Down with the topmast! Yare! Lower,
    lower! Bring her to try wi' the main course.° (*A
    cry within.*) A plague upon this howling! They are
40 louder than the weather or our office.°

(*Enter Sebastian, Antonio, and Gonzalo.*)

    Yet again? What do you here? Shall we give o'er°
    and drown? Have you a mind to sink?
SEBASTIAN: A pox o' your throat, you bawling, blas-
    phemous, incharitable dog!
45 BOATSWAIN: Work you, then.
ANTONIO: Hang, cur! Hang, you whoreson, insolent
    noisemaker! We are less afraid to be drowned than
    thou art.
GONZALO: I'll warrant him for drowning,° though the
50 ship were no stronger than a nutshell and as leaky
    as an unstanched° wench.
BOATSWAIN: Lay her ahold,° ahold! Set her two
    courses.° Off to sea again! Lay her off!

(*Enter Mariners wet.*)

MARINERS: All lost! To prayers, to prayers! All lost!
                              [*Exeunt Mariners.*]
55 BOATSWAIN: What, must our mouths be cold?°
GONZALO: The King and Prince at prayers! Let's
    assist them,
    For our case is as theirs.
SEBASTIAN: I am out of patience.
ANTONIO: We are merely° cheated of our lives by
    drunkards.
    This wide-chapped° rascal! Would thou mightst
    lie drowning
60 The washing of ten tides!°
GONZALO: He'll be hanged yet,
    Though every drop of water swear against it
    And gape at wid'st° to glut° him.
(*A confused noise within.*)   "Mercy on us! —
"We split,° we split!" — "Farewell my wife and
    children!" —

"Farewell, brother!" — "We split, we split, we
    split!"
                              [*Exit Boatswain.*]
ANTONIO: Let's all sink wi' the King.   65
SEBASTIAN: Let's take leave of him.
                              (*Exit* [*with Antonio*].)
GONZALO: Now would I give a thousand furlongs
    of sea for an acre of barren ground: long heath,°
    brown furze,° anything. The wills above be
    done! But I would fain° die a dry death.   (*Exit.*) 70

Scene II°

(*Enter Prospero* [*in his magic cloak*] *and Miranda.*)

MIRANDA: If by your art,° my dearest father, you
    have
    Put the wild waters in this roar,° allay° them.
    The sky, it seems, would pour down stinking
        pitch,°
    But that the sea, mounting to th' welkin's
        cheek,°
    Dashes the fire out. O, I have suffered   5
    With those that I saw suffer! A brave° vessel,
    Who had, no doubt, some noble creature in her,
    Dashed all to pieces. O, the cry did knock
    Against my very heart! Poor souls, they perished.
    Had I been any god of power, I would   10
    Have sunk the sea within the earth or ere°
    It should the good ship so have swallowed and
    The freighting° souls within her.
PROSPERO: Be collected.°
    No more amazement.° Tell your piteous° heart
    There's no harm done.
MIRANDA: O, woe the day!
PROSPERO: No harm. 15
    I have done nothing but° in care of thee,
    Of thee, my dear one, thee, my daughter, who
    Art ignorant of what thou art, naught knowing
    Of whence I am, nor that I am more better°
    Than Prospero, master of a full° poor cell,   20

---

38. Bring . . . course: Sail her close to the wind by means
of the mainsail.   **40. our office:** I.e., the noise we make at
our work.   **41. give o'er:** Give up.   **49. warrant him for
drowning:** Guarantee that he will never be drowned.   **51.
unstanched:** Insatiable, loose, unrestrained.   **52. ahold:**
Ahull, close to the wind.   **53. courses:** Sails, i.e., foresail as
well as mainsail, set in an attempt to get the ship back out
into open water.   **55. must . . . cold:** I.e., must we drown
in the cold sea; or, let us heat up our mouths with liquor.
58. merely: Utterly.   **59. wide-chapped:** With mouth wide
open.   **59–60. lie . . . tides:** Pirates were hanged on the
shore and left until three tides had come in.   **62. at wid'st:**
Wide.   **glut:** Swallow.   **63. split:** Break apart.

68. heath: Heather.   **69. furze:** Gorse, a weed growing on
wasteland.   **70. fain:** Rather.   **I, II. Location:** The island.
Prospero's cell is visible, and on the Elizabethan stage it
presumably remains so throughout the play, although in
some scenes the convention of flexible distance allows us to
imagine characters in other parts of the island.   **1. art:**
Magic.   **2. roar:** Uproar.   **allay:** Pacify.   **3. pitch:** A thick,
viscous substance produced by boiling down tar or turpen-
tine.   **4. welkin's cheek:** Sky's face.   **6. brave:** Gallant,
splendid.   **11. or ere:** Before.   **13. freighting:** Forming the
cargo.   **collected:** Calm, composed.   **14. amazement:** Consternation.   **piteous:** Pitying.   **16. but:** Except.   **19. more
better:** Of higher rank.   **20. full:** Very.

And thy no greater father.
MIRANDA: More to know
Did never meddle° with my thoughts.
PROSPERO: 'Tis time
I should inform thee farther. Lend thy hand
And pluck my magic garment from me. So,
          [*Laying down his magic cloak and staff.*]
Lie there, my art. — Wipe thou thine eyes. Have
25 comfort.
The direful spectacle of the wreck,° which
          touched
The very virtue° of compassion in thee,
I have with such provision° in mine art
So safely ordered that there is no soul —
30 No, not so much perdition° as an hair
Betid° to any creature in the vessel
Which° thou heardst cry, which thou sawst sink.
          Sit down,
For thou must now know farther.
MIRANDA [*sitting*]:   You have often
Begun to tell me what I am, but stopped
35 And left me to a bootless inquisition,°
Concluding, "Stay, not yet."
PROSPERO: The hour's now come;
The very minute bids thee ope° thine ear.
Obey, and be attentive. Canst thou remember
A time before we came unto this cell?
I do not think thou canst, for then thou wast
40   not
Out° three years old.
MIRANDA: Certainly, sir, I can.
PROSPERO: By what? By any other house or person?
Of anything the image, tell me, that
Hath kept with thy remembrance.
MIRANDA: 'Tis far off,
45 And rather like a dream than an assurance
That my remembrance warrants.° Had I not
Four or five women once that tended° me?
PROSPERO: Thou hadst, and more, Miranda. But
          how is it
That this lives in thy mind? What seest thou else
50 In the dark backward and abysm of time?°
If thou rememberest aught° ere thou cam'st here,
How thou cam'st here thou mayst.
MIRANDA: But that I do not.
PROSPERO: Twelve year since, Miranda, twelve year
          since,

22. **meddle:** Mingle.   26. **wreck:** Shipwreck.   27. **virtue:** Essence.   28. **provision:** Foresight.   30. **perdition:** Loss. 31. **Betid:** Happened.   32. **Which:** Whom.   35. **bootless inquisition:** Profitless inquiry.   37. **ope:** Open.   41. **Out:** Fully.   45–46. **assurance . . . warrants:** Certainty that my memory guarantees.   47. **tended:** Attended, waited upon. 50. **backward . . . time:** Abyss of the past.   51. **aught:** Anything.

Thy father was the Duke of Milan and
A prince of power.
MIRANDA: Sir, are not you my father?   55
PROSPERO: Thy mother was a piece° of virtue, and
She said thou wast my daughter; and thy father
Was Duke of Milan, and his only heir
And princess no worse issued.°
MIRANDA: O the heavens!
What foul play had we, that we came from
          thence?   60
Or Blessèd was 't we did?
PROSPERO: Both, both, my girl.
By foul play, as thou sayst, were we heaved
          thence,
But blessedly holp° hither.
MIRANDA: O, my heart bleeds
To think o' the teen that I have turned you to,°
Which is from° my remembrance! Please you,
          farther.   65
PROSPERO: My brother and thy uncle, called
          Antonio —
I pray thee, mark me; that a brother should
Be so perfidious! — he whom next° thyself
Of all the world I loved, and to him put
The manage° of my state, as at that time   70
Through all the seigniories° it was the first,
And Prospero the prime° duke, being so reputed
In dignity, and for the liberal arts
Without a parallel; those being all my study,
The government I cast upon my brother   75
And to my state grew stranger,° being
          transported°
And rapt in secret studies. Thy false uncle —
Dost thou attend me?
MIRANDA: Sir, most heedfully.
PROSPERO: Being once perfected° how to grant suits,
How to deny them, who t' advance and who   80
To trash° for overtopping,° new created
The creatures° that were mine, I say, or changed
          'em,
Or else new formed 'em;° having both the key°

56. **piece:** Masterpiece, exemplar.   59. **no worse issued:** No less nobly born, descended.   63. **holp:** Helped.   64. **teen . . . to:** Trouble I've caused you to remember or put you to. 65. **from:** Out of.   68. **next:** Next to.   70. **manage:** Management, administration.   71. **seigniories:** City-states of northern Italy.   72. **prime:** Of highest rank.   76. **to . . . stranger:** Withdrew from my responsibilities as duke.   **transported:** Carried away.   79. **perfected:** Grown skillful.   81. **trash:** Check a hound by tying a cord or weight to its neck. **overtopping:** Running too far ahead of the pack; surmounting, exceeding one's authority.   82. **creatures:** Dependents. 82–83. **or changed . . . formed 'em:** Either changed their loyalties and duties or else created new ones.   83. **key:** (1) Key for unlocking, (2) tool for tuning stringed instruments.

Of officer and office, set all hearts i' the state
To what tune pleased his ear, that° now he was
The ivy which had hid my princely trunk
And sucked my verdure° out on 't.° Thou
    attend'st not.
MIRANDA: O, good sir, I do.
PROSPERO: I pray thee, mark me.
I, thus neglecting worldly ends, all dedicated
To closeness° and the bettering of my mind
With that which, but by being so retired,
O'erprized all popular rate,° in my false brother
Awaked an evil nature; and my trust,
Like a good parent,° did beget of° him
A falsehood in its contrary as great
As my trust was, which had indeed no limit,
A confidence sans° bound. He being thus lorded°
Not only with what my revenue yielded
But what my power might else° exact, like one
Who, having into° truth by telling of it,
Made such a sinner of his memory
To° credit his own lie,° he did believe
He was indeed the Duke, out o'° the substitution
And executing th' outward face of royalty°
With all prerogative. Hence his ambition
    growing —
Dost thou hear?
MIRANDA: Your tale, sir, would cure deafness.
PROSPERO: To have no screen between this part he
    played
And him he played it for,° he needs° will be
Absolute Milan.° Me, poor man, my library
Was dukedom large enough. Of temporal
    royalties°
He thinks me now incapable; confederates° —

So dry° he was for sway° — wi' the King of
    Naples
To give him° annual tribute, do him homage,
Subject his coronet to his° crown, and bend°
The dukedom yet° unbowed — alas, poor
    Milan! —
To most ignoble stooping.
MIRANDA: O the heavens!
PROSPERO: Mark his condition° and th' event,° then
    tell me
If this might be a brother.
MIRANDA: I should sin
To think but° nobly of my grandmother.
Good wombs have borne bad sons.
PROSPERO: Now the condition.
This King of Naples, being an enemy
To me inveterate, hearkens° my brother's suit,
Which was that he, in lieu o' the premises°
Of homage and I know not how much tribute,
Should presently extirpate° me and mine
Out of the dukedom and confer fair Milan,
With all the honors, on my brother. Whereon,
A treacherous army levied, one midnight
Fated to th' purpose did Antonio open
The gates of Milan, and, i' the dead of darkness,
The ministers for the purpose° hurried thence°
Me and thy crying self.
MIRANDA: Alack, for pity!
I, not remembering how I cried out then,
Will cry it o'er again. It is a hint°
That wrings° mine eyes to 't.
PROSPERO: Hear a little further,
And then I'll bring thee to the present business
Which now's upon 's, without the which this
    story
Were most impertinent.°
MIRANDA: Wherefore° did they not
That hour destroy us?
PROSPERO: Well demanded,° wench.°
My tale provokes that question. Dear, they durst
    not,
So dear the love my people bore me, nor set

85
90
95
100
105
110
115
120
125
130
135
140

---

85. that: So that. **87. verdure:** Vitality. **on 't:** Of it. **90. closeness:** Retirement, seclusion. **91–92. but . . . rate:** Simply because it was done in such seclusion, had a value not appreciated by popular opinion. **94. good parent:** Alludes to the proverb that good parents often bear bad children; see also line 120. **of:** In. **97. sans:** Without. **lorded:** Raised to lordship, with power and wealth. **99. else:** Otherwise, additionally. **100–2. Who . . . lie:** Who, by repeatedly telling the lie (that he was indeed Duke of Milan), made his memory such a confirmed sinner against truth that he began to believe his own lie. **into:** Unto, against. **To:** So as to. **103. out o':** As a result of. **104. And . . . royalty:** And (as a result of) his carrying out all the ceremonial functions of royalty. **107–8. To have . . . it for:** To have no separation or barrier between his role and himself. (Antonio wanted to act in his own person, not as substitute.) **108. needs:** Necessarily. **109. Absolute Milan:** Unconditional Duke of Milan. **110. temporal royalties:** Practical prerogatives and responsibilities of a sovereign. **111. confederates:** Conspires, allies himself.

112. dry: Thirsty. **sway:** Power. **113. him:** The King of Naples. **114. his . . . his:** Antonio's . . . the King of Naples's. **bend:** Make bow down. **115. yet:** Hitherto. **117. condition:** Pact. **event:** Outcome. **119. but:** Other than. **122. hearkens:** Listens to. **123. in . . . premises:** In return for the stipulation. **125. presently extirpate:** At once remove. **131. ministers . . . purpose:** Agents employed to do this. **thence:** From there. **134. hint:** Occasion. **135. wrings:** (1) Constraints, (2) wrings tears from. **138. impertinent:** Irrelevant. **Wherefore:** Why. **139. demanded:** Asked. **wench:** Here a term of endearment.

A mark so bloody° on the business, but
With colors fairer° painted their foul ends.
In few,° they hurried us aboard a bark,°
Bore us some leagues to sea, where they
    prepared
45 A rotten carcass of a butt,° not rigged,
Nor tackle,° sail, nor mast; the very rats
Instinctively have quit° it. There they hoist us,
To cry to th' sea that roared to us, to sigh
50 To th' winds whose pity, sighing back again,
Did us but loving wrong.°
MIRANDA: Alack, what trouble
    Was I then to you!
PROSPERO: O, a cherubin°
    Thou wast that did preserve me. Thou didst
        smile,
    Infusèd with a fortitude from heaven,
55 When I have decked° the sea with drops full salt,
    Under my burden groaned, which° raised in me
    An undergoing stomach,° to bear up
    Against what should ensue.
MIRANDA: How came we ashore?
60 PROSPERO: By Providence divine.
    Some food we had, and some fresh water, that
    A noble Neapolitan, Gonzalo,
    Out of his charity, who being then appointed
    Master of this design, did give us, with
65 Rich garments, linens, stuffs,° and necessaries,
    Which since have steaded much.° So, of his
        gentleness,
    Knowing I loved my books, he furnished me
    From mine own library with volumes that
    I prize above my dukedom.
MIRANDA: Would° I might
    But ever° see that man!
70 PROSPERO: Now I arise.
        [He puts on his magic cloak.]
    Sit still and hear the last of our sea sorrow.°
    Here in this island we arrived; and here
    Have I, thy schoolmaster, made thee more profit°

Than other princess'° can, that have more time
For vainer° hours and tutors not so careful. 175
MIRANDA: Heavens thank you for 't! And now, I
    pray you, sir —
    For still 'tis beating in my mind — your reason
    For raising this sea storm?
PROSPERO: Know thus far forth:
    By accident most strange, bountiful Fortune,
    Now my dear lady, hath mine enemies 180
    Brought to this shore; and by my prescience
    I find my zenith° doth depend upon
    A most auspicious star, whose influence°
    If now I court not, but omit,° my fortunes
    Will ever after droop. Here cease more
        questions. 185
    Thou art inclined to sleep. 'Tis a good dullness,°
    And give it way.° I know thou canst not choose.
        [Miranda sleeps.]
    Come away,° servant, come! I am ready now.
    Approach, my Ariel, come.

(Enter Ariel.)

ARIEL: All hail, great master, grave sir, hail! I come 190
    To answer thy best pleasure; be 't to fly,
    To swim, to dive into the fire, to ride
    On the curled clouds, to thy strong bidding task°
    Ariel and all his quality.°
PROSPERO: Hast thou, spirit,
    Performed to point° the tempest that I bade
        thee? 195
ARIEL: To every article.
    I boarded the King's ship. Now on the beak,°
    Now in the waist,° the deck,° in every cabin,
    I flamed amazement.° Sometimes I'd divide
    And burn in many places; on the topmast, 200
    The yards, and the bowsprit would I flame
        distinctly,°
    Then meet and join. Jove's lightning, the
        precursors
    O' the dreadful thunderclaps, more momentary
    And sight-outrunning° were not. The fire and
        cracks

141–42. set . . . bloody: Make obvious their murderous intent. (From the practice of marking with the blood of the
prey those who have participated in a successful hunt.) 143.
fairer: Apparently more attractive. 144. few: Few words.
bark: Ship. 146. butt: Cask, tub. 147. Nor tackle: Neither rigging (i.e., the pulleys and ropes designed for hoisting
sails). 148. quit: Abandoned. 151. loving wrong: I.e., the
winds pitied Prospero and Miranda though of necessity they
blew them from shore. 152. cherubin: Angel. 155.
decked: Covered (with salt tears); adorned. 156. which: So
I.e., the smile. 157. undergoing stomach: Courage to go
on. 165. stuffs: Supplies. 166. steaded much: Been of
much use. 169. Would: I wish. 170. But ever: Someday.
171. sea sorrow: Sorrowful adventure at sea. 173. more
profit: Profit more.

174. princess': Princesses. (Or the word may be princes,
referring to royal children both male and female.) 175.
vainer: More foolishly spent. 182. zenith: Height of fortune
(astrological term). 183. influence: Astrological power.
184. omit: Ignore. 186. dullness: Drowsiness. 187. give
it way: Let it happen (i.e., don't fight it). 188. Come away:
Come. 193. task: Make demands upon. 194. quality: (1)
Fellow spirits, (2) abilities. 195. to point: To the smallest
detail. 197. beak: Prow. 198. waist: Midships. deck:
Poop deck at the stern. 199. flamed amazement: Struck
terror in the guise of fire, i.e., Saint Elmo's fire. 201. distinctly: In different places. 204. sight-outrunning: Swifter
than sight.

205 Of sulfurous roaring the most mighty Neptune°
Seem to besiege and make his bold waves
 tremble,
Yea, his dread trident shake.
PROSPERO: My brave spirit!
Who was so firm, so constant, that this coil°
Would not infect his reason?
ARIEL: Not a soul
210 But felt a fever of the mad° and played
Some tricks of desperation. All but mariners
Plunged in the foaming brine and quit the vessel,
Then all afire with me. The King's son,
 Ferdinand,
With hair up-staring° — then like reeds, not
 hair —
Was the first man that leapt; cried, "Hell is
215 empty,
And all the devils are here!"
PROSPERO: Why, that's my spirit!
But was not this nigh shore?
ARIEL: Close by, my master.
PROSPERO: But are they, Ariel, safe?
ARIEL: Not a hair perished.
On their sustaining garments° not a blemish,
220 But fresher than before; and, as thou bad'st° me,
In troops° I have dispersed them 'bout the isle.
The King's son have I landed by himself,
Whom I left cooling of° the air with sighs
In an odd angle° of the isle, and sitting,
His arms in this sad knot.°   [He folds his arms.]
225 PROSPERO: Of the King's ship,
The mariners, say how thou hast disposed,
And all the rest o' the fleet.
ARIEL: Safely in harbor
Is the King's ship; in the deep nook,° where once
Thou calledst me up at midnight to fetch dew
230 From the still-vexed Bermudas,° there she's hid;
The mariners all under hatches stowed,
Who, with a charm joined to their suffered
 labor,°
I have left asleep. And for the rest o' the fleet,
Which I dispersed, they all have met again
235 And are upon the Mediterranean float°

Bound sadly home for Naples,
Supposing that they saw the King's ship wrecked
And his great person perish.
PROSPERO: Ariel, thy charge
Exactly is performed. But there's more work.
What is the time o' the day?
ARIEL: Past the mid season.°   24●
PROSPERO: At least two glasses.° The time twixt six
 and now
Must by us both be spent most preciously.
ARIEL: Is there more toil? Since thou dost give me
 pains,°
Let me remember° thee what thou hast
 promised,
Which is not yet performed me.
PROSPERO: How now? Moody?   24●
What is 't thou canst demand?
ARIEL: My liberty.
PROSPERO: Before the time be out? No more!
ARIEL: I prithee,
Remember I have done thee worthy service,
Told thee no lies, made thee no mistakings,
 served
Without or grudge or grumblings. Thou did
 promise   25●
To bate° me a full year.
PROSPERO: Dost thou forget
From what a torment I did free thee?
ARIEL: No.
PROSPERO: Thou dost, and think'st it much to tread
 the ooze
Of the salt deep,
To run upon the sharp wind of the north,   25●
To do me° business in the veins° o' the earth
When it is baked° with frost.
ARIEL: I do not, sir.
PROSPERO: Thou liest, malignant thing! Hast thou
 forgot
The foul witch Sycorax, who with age and envy°
Was grown into a hoop?° Hast thou forgot her?   26●
ARIEL: No, sir.
PROSPERO: Thou hast. Where was she born? Speak.
 Tell me.
ARIEL: Sir, in Algiers.
PROSPERO: O, was she so? I must
Once in a month recount what thou hast been,

---

205. **Neptune:** Roman god of the sea.   208. **coil:** Tumult.
210. **of the mad:** I.e., such as madmen feel.   214. **up-staring:**
Standing on end.   219. **sustaining garments:** Garments that
buoyed them up in the sea.   220. **bad'st:** Ordered.   221.
troops: Groups.   223. **cooling of:** Cooling.   224. **angle:**
Corner.   225. **sad knot:** Folded arms are indicative of mel-
ancholy.   228. **nook:** Bay.   230. **still-vexed Bermudas:**
Ever-stormy Bermudas. (Perhaps refers to the then-recent
Bermuda shipwreck [see page 313]. The Folio text reads
"Bermoothes.")   232. **with . . . labor:** By means of a spell
added to all the labor they have undergone.   235. **float:**
Sea.

240. **mid season:** Noon.   241. **glasses:** Hourglasses.   243.
pains: Labors.   244. **remember:** Remind.   251. **bate:** Re-
mit, deduct.   256. **do me:** Do for me.   **veins:** Veins of
minerals, or underground streams thought to be analogous
to the veins of the human body.   257. **baked:** Hardened.
259. **envy:** Malice.   260. **grown into a hoop:** I.e., so bent
over with age as to resemble a hoop.

Which thou forgett'st. This damned witch
65   Sycorax,
For mischiefs manifold and sorceries terrible
To enter human hearing, from Algiers,
Thou know'st, was banished. For one thing she
   did°
They would not take her life. Is not this true?
70 ARIEL: Ay, sir.
PROSPERO: This blue-eyed° hag was hither brought
   with child°
And here was left by the sailors. Thou, my slave,
As thou report'st thyself, was then her servant;
And, for° thou wast a spirit too delicate
75 To act her earthy and abhorred commands,
Refusing her grand hests,° she did confine thee,
By help of her more potent ministers
And in her most unmitigable rage,
Into a cloven pine, within which rift
80 Imprisoned thou didst painfully remain
A dozen years; within which space she died
And left thee there, where thou didst vent thy
   groans
As fast as mill wheels strike.° Then was this
   island —
Save° for the son that she did litter° here,
A freckled whelp,° hag-born° — not honored
85   with
A human shape.
ARIEL: Yes, Caliban her son.
PROSPERO: Dull thing, I say so:° he, that Caliban
Whom now I keep in service. Thou best know'st
What torment I did find thee in. Thy groans
90 Did make wolves howl, and penetrate the breasts
Of ever-angry bears. It was a torment
To lay upon the damned, which Sycorax
Could not again undo. It was mine art,
When I arrived and heard thee, that made gape°
The pine and let thee out.
95 ARIEL: I thank thee, master.
PROSPERO: If thou more murmur'st, I will rend an
   oak
And peg thee in his° knotty entrails till
Thou hast howled away twelve winters.

ARIEL: Pardon, master.
I will be correspondent° to command
And do my spriting° gently.°
PROSPERO: Do so, and after two days   300
I will discharge thee.
ARIEL: That's my noble master!
What shall I do? Say what? What shall I do?
PROSPERO: Go make thyself like a nymph o' the
   sea. Be subject
To no sight but thine and mine, invisible   305
To every eyeball else. Go take this shape
And hither come in 't. Go, hence with diligence!
                      (*Exit* [*Ariel*].)
Awake, dear heart, awake! Thou hast slept well.
Awake!
MIRANDA: The strangeness of your story put
Heaviness° in me.
PROSPERO: Shake it off. Come on,   310
We'll visit Caliban, my slave, who never
Yields us kind answer.
MIRANDA: 'Tis a villain, sir,
I do not love to look on.
PROSPERO: But, as 'tis,
We cannot miss° him. He does make our fire,
Fetch in our wood, and serves in offices°   315
That profit us. — What ho! Slave! Caliban!
Thou earth, thou! Speak.
CALIBAN (*within*):   There's wood enough within.
PROSPERO: Come forth, I say! There's other
   business for thee.
Come, thou tortoise! When?°

(*Enter Ariel like a water nymph.*)

Fine apparition! My quaint° Ariel,   320
Hark in thine ear.   [*He whispers.*]
ARIEL: My lord, it shall be done. (*Exit.*)
PROSPERO: Thou poisonous slave, got° by the devil
   himself
Upon thy wicked dam,° come forth!

(*Enter Caliban.*)

CALIBAN: As wicked° dew as e'er my mother
   brushed
With raven's feather from unwholesome fen°   325
Drop on you both! A southwest° blow on ye
And blister you all o'er!

---

268. **one . . . did:** Perhaps a reference to her pregnancy, for which her life would be spared. 271. **blue-eyed:** With dark circles under the eyes or with blue eyelids, implying pregnancy. **with child:** Pregnant. 274. **for:** Because. 276. **hests:** Commands. 283. **as mill wheels strike:** As the blades of a mill wheel strike the water. 284. **Save:** Except. **litter:** Give birth to. 285. **whelp:** Offspring (used of animals). **hag-born:** Born of a female demon. 287. **Dull . . . so:** I.e., exactly, that's what I said, you dullard. 294. **gape:** Open wide. 297. **his:** Its.

299. **correspondent:** Responsive, submissive. 300. **spriting:** Duties as a spirit. **gently:** Willingly, ungrudgingly. 310. **Heaviness:** Drowsiness. 314. **miss:** Do without. 315. **offices:** Functions, duties. 319. **When:** An exclamation of impatience. 320. **quaint:** Ingenious. 322. **got:** Begotten, sired. 323. **dam:** Mother (used of animals). 324. **wicked:** Mischievous, harmful. 325. **fen:** Marsh, bog. 326. **southwest:** I.e., wind thought to bring disease.

PROSPERO: For this, be sure, tonight thou shalt have
    cramps,
Side-stitches that shall pen thy breath up.
    Urchins°
330 Shall forth at vast° of night that they may work
All exercise on thee. Thou shalt be pinched
As thick as honeycomb,° each pinch more
    stinging
Than bees that made 'em.°
CALIBAN: I must eat my dinner.
This island's mine, by Sycorax my mother,
Which thou tak'st from me. When thou cam'st
335   first,
Thou strok'st me and made much of me,
    wouldst give me
Water with berries in 't, and teach me how
To name the bigger light, and how the less,°
That burn by day and night. And then I loved
    thee
340 And showed thee all the qualities o' th' isle,
The fresh springs, brine pits, barren place and
    fertile.
Cursed be I that did so! All the charms°
Of Sycorax, toads, beetles, bats, light on you!
For I am all the subjects that you have,
Which first was mine own king; and here you
345   sty° me
In this hard rock, whiles you do keep from me
The rest o' th' island.
PROSPERO: Thou most lying slave,
Whom stripes° may move, not kindness! I have
    used thee,
Filth as thou art, with humane° care, and lodged
    thee
350 In mine own cell, till thou didst seek to violate
The honor of my child.
CALIBAN: Oho, Oho! Would 't had been done!
Thou didst prevent me; I had peopled else°
This isle with Calibans.
MIRANDA: Abhorrèd slave,°

Which any print° of goodness wilt not take,   355
Being capable of all ill! I pitied thee,
Took pains to make thee speak, taught thee each
    hour
One thing or other. When thou didst not,
    savage,
Know thine own meaning, but wouldst gabble
    like
A thing most brutish, I endowed thy purposes°   360
With words that made them known. But thy vile
    race,°
Though thou didst learn, had that in 't which
    good natures
Could not abide to be with; therefore wast thou
Deservedly confined into this rock,
Who hadst deserved more than a prison.   365
CALIBAN: You taught me language, and my profit
    on 't
Is I know how to curse. The red plague° rid°
    you
For learning° me your language!
PROSPERO: Hagseed,° hence!
Fetch us in fuel, and be quick, thou'rt best,°
To answer other business.° Shrugg'st thou,
    malice?   370
If thou neglect'st or dost unwillingly
What I command, I'll rack thee with old°
    cramps,
Fill all thy bones with aches,° make thee roar
That beasts shall tremble at thy din.
CALIBAN: No, pray thee.
[Aside.] I must obey. His art is of such power   375
It would control my dam's god, Setebos,°
And make a vassal of him.
PROSPERO: So, slave, hence!
                    (Exit Caliban.)

(Enter Ferdinand; and Ariel, invisible,° playing and
singing. [Ferdinand does not see Prospero and
Miranda.])

---

329. **Urchins:** Hedgehogs; here, suggesting goblins in the guise of hedgehogs.   330. **vast:** Lengthy, desolate time. (Malignant spirits were thought to be restricted to the hours of darkness.)   332. **As thick as honeycomb:** I.e., all over, with as many pinches as a honeycomb has cells.   333. **'em:** I.e., the honeycomb.   338. **the bigger . . . less:** I.e., the sun and the moon. (See Genesis 1:16: "God then made two great lights: the greater light to rule the day, and the less light to rule the night.")   342. **charms:** Spells.   345. **sty:** Confine as in a sty.   348. **stripes:** Lashes.   349. **humane:** Not distinguished as a word from *human.*   353. **peopled else:** Otherwise populated.   354–65. **Abhorrèd . . . prison:** These lines are sometimes assigned by editors to Prospero.

355. **print:** Imprint, impression.   360. **purposes:** Meanings, desires.   361. **race:** Natural disposition; species, nature. 367. **red plague:** Plague characterized by red sores and evacuation of blood. **rid:** Destroy.   368. **learning:** Teaching. **Hagseed:** Offspring of a female demon.   369. **thou'rt best:** You'd be well advised.   370. **answer other business:** Perform other tasks.   372. **old:** Such as old people suffer; or, plenty of.   373. **aches:** Pronounced "aitches."   376. **Setebos:** A god of the Patagonians, named in Robert Eden's *History of Travel* (1577).   377. **[S.D.]** *Ariel, invisible:* Ariel wears a garment that by convention indicates he is invisible to the other characters.

(*Ariel's Song.*)

ARIEL: Come unto these yellow sands,
    And then take hands;
80 Curtsied when you have,° and kissed
    The wild waves whist,°
Foot it featly° here and there,
And, sweet sprites,° bear
The burden.° Hark, hark!
85   (*Burden, dispersedly*° [*within*].) Bow-wow.
  The watchdogs bark.
      [*Burden, dispersedly within*]. Bow-wow.
Hark, hark! I hear
The strain of strutting chanticleer
90   Cry Cock-a-diddle-dow.
FERDINAND: Where should this music be? I' th' air
  or th' earth?
It sounds no more; and sure it waits upon°
Some god o' th' island. Sitting on a bank,°
Weeping again the King my father's wreck,
95 This music crept by me upon the waters,
Allaying both their fury and my passion°
With its sweet air. Thence° I have followed it,
Or it hath drawn me rather. But 'tis gone.
No, it begins again.
                (*Ariel's Song.*)
00 ARIEL: Full fathom five thy father lies.
  Of his bones are coral made.
Those are pearls that were his eyes.
  Nothing of him that doth fade
But doth suffer a sea change
05 Into something rich and strange.
Sea nymphs hourly ring his knell.°
        (*Burden* [*within*].) Ding dong.
Hark, now I hear them, ding dong bell.
FERDINAND: The ditty does remember° my drowned
  father.
10 This is no mortal business, nor no sound
That the earth owes.° I hear it now above me.
PROSPERO [*to Miranda*]: The fringèd curtains of
  thine eye advance°
And say what thou seest yond.
MIRANDA: What is 't? A spirit?
Lord, how it looks about! Believe me, sir,

It carries a brave° form. But 'tis a spirit.   415
PROSPERO: No, wench, it eats and sleeps and hath
  such senses
As we have, such. This gallant which thou seest
Was in the wreck; and, but° he's something
  stained°
With grief, that's beauty's canker,° thou mightst
  call him
A goodly person. He hath lost his fellows   420
And strays about to find 'em.
MIRANDA: I might call him
A thing divine, for nothing natural
I ever saw so noble.
PROSPERO [*aside*]:   It goes on,° I see,
As my soul prompts it. — Spirit, fine spirit, I'll
  free thee
Within two days for this.
FERDINAND [*seeing Miranda*]: Most sure, the
  goddess   425
On whom these airs° attend! — Vouchsafe° my
  prayer
May know° if you remain° upon this island,
And that you will some good instruction give
How I may bear me° here. My prime° request,
Which I do last pronounce, is — O you
  wonder!° —   430
If you be maid or no?°
MIRANDA: No wonder, sir,
But certainly a maid.
FERDINAND: My language? Heavens!
I am the best° of them that speak this speech,
Were I but where 'tis spoken.
PROSPERO [*coming forward*]:   How? The best?
What wert thou if the King of Naples heard
  thee?   435
FERDINAND: A single° thing, as I am now, that
  wonders
To hear thee speak of Naples.° He does hear
  me,°
And that he does I weep.° Myself am Naples,

---

380. **Curtsied ... have:** When you have curtsied. 380–81.
kissed ... whist: Kissed the waves into silence, or kissed
while the waves are being hushed. 382. **Foot it featly:**
Dance nimbly. 383. **sprites:** Spirits. 384. **burden:** Refrain,
undersong. 385. [S.D.] *dispersedly*: From all directions, not
in unison. 392. **waits upon:** Serves, attends. 393. **bank:**
Sandbank. 396. **passion:** Grief. 397. **Thence:** From the
bank on which he sat. 406. **knell:** Announcement of a
death by the tolling of a bell. 409. **remember:** Commem-
orate. 411. **owes:** Owns. 412. **advance:** Raise.

415. **brave:** Excellent. 418. **but:** Except that. **something
stained:** Somewhat disfigured. 419. **canker:** Cankerworm
(feeding on buds and leaves). 423. **It goes on:** I.e., my plan
works. 426. **airs:** Songs. **Vouchsafe:** Grant. 427. **May
know:** I.e., that I may know. **remain:** Dwell. 429. **bear
me:** Conduct myself. **prime:** Chief. 430. **wonder:** Miranda's name means "to be wondered at." 431. **maid or
no:** I.e., a human maiden as opposed to a goddess or married
woman. 433. **best:** I.e., in birth. 436. **single:** (1) Solitary,
being at once King of Naples and myself, (2) feeble. 437,
438. **Naples:** The King of Naples. 437. **He does hear me:**
I.e., the King of Naples does hear my words, for I am King
of Naples. 438. **And ... weep:** I.e., and I weep at this
reminder that my father is seemingly dead, leaving me heir.

Who with mine eyes, never since at ebb,° beheld
The King my father wrecked.

440 MIRANDA: Alack, for mercy!
FERDINAND: Yes, faith, and all his lords, the Duke
     of Milan
And his brave son° being twain.
PROSPERO [*aside*]:   The Duke of Milan
     And his more braver° daughter could control
        thee,
     If now 'twere fit to do 't. At the first sight
445   They have changed eyes.° — Delicate Ariel,
     I'll set thee free for this. [*To Ferdinand*.] A
        word, good sir.
     I fear you have done yourself some wrong.° A
        word!
MIRANDA [*aside*]: Why speaks my father so
     ungently? This
Is the third man that e'er I saw, the first

That e'er I sighed for. Pity move my father   45
To be inclined my way!
FERDINAND: O, if a virgin,
And your affection not gone forth, I'll make you
The Queen of Naples.
PROSPERO: Soft, sir! One word more.
     [*Aside*.] They are both in either's° powers; but
        this swift business
     I must uneasy° make, lest too light winning   45
     Make the prize light.° [*To Ferdinand*.] One word
        more: I charge thee
     That thou attend° me. Thou dost here usurp
     The name thou ow'st° not, and hast put thyself
     Upon this island as a spy, to win it
     From me, the lord on 't.°
FERDINAND: No, as I am a man.   46
MIRANDA: There's nothing ill can dwell in such a
     temple.
If the ill spirit have so fair a house,

---

439. **at ebb:** I.e., dry, not weeping.   442. **son:** The only reference in the play to a son of Antonio.   443. **more braver:** More splendid.   **control:** Refute.   445. **changed eyes:** Exchanged amorous glances.   447. **done ... wrong:** I.e., spoken falsely.

454. **both in either's:** Each in the other's.   455. **uneasy:** Difficult.   455–56. **light ... light:** Easy ... cheap.   457. **attend:** Follow, obey.   458. **ow'st:** Ownest.   460. **on 't:** Of it.

RIGHT: Raul Julia as Prospero (right) and Rick Elice as Ariel in the 1981 New York Shakespeare Festival production of *The Tempest*, directed by Lee Breuer with Ruth Maleczech at the Delacorte Theatre. FAR RIGHT: Prospero with Ariel and his spirits.

Good things will strive to dwell with 't.°
PROSPERO: Follow me. —
  Speak not you for him; he's a traitor. — Come,
  I'll manacle thy neck and feet together.
  Seawater shalt thou drink; thy food shall be
  The fresh-brook mussels, withered roots, and
    husks
  Wherein the acorn cradled. Follow.
FERDINAND: No!
  I will resist such entertainment° till
  Mine enemy has more power.
            (*He draws and is charmed° from moving.*)

MIRANDA: O dear father,   470
  Make not too rash° a trial of him, for
  He's gentle,° and not fearful.°
PROSPERO: What, I say,
  My foot° my tutor? — Put thy sword up, traitor,
  Who mak'st a show but dar'st not strike, thy
    conscience
  Is so possessed with guilt. Come from thy ward,°   475
  For I can here disarm thee with this stick
  And make thy weapon drop.
                         [*He brandishes his staff.*]

---

463. **strive ... with 't:** I.e., expel the evil and occupy the *temple*, the body.   469. **entertainment:** Treatment.   470. **[S.D.] charmed:** Magically prevented.

471. **rash:** Harsh.   472. **gentle:** Well-born.   **fearful:** Frightening, dangerous; or, perhaps, cowardly.   473. **foot:** Subordinate. (Miranda, the foot, presumes to instruct Prospero, the head.)   475. **ward:** Defensive posture (in fencing).

MIRANDA [*trying to hinder him*]: Beseech you,
     father!
PROSPERO: Hence! Hang not on my garments.
MIRANDA: Sir, have pity!
     I'll be his surety.°
PROSPERO: Silence! One word more
     Shall make me chide thee, if not hate thee.
480   What,
     An advocate for an impostor? Hush!
     Thou think'st there is no more such shapes as
     he,
     Having seen but him and Caliban. Foolish
     wench,
     To° the most of men this is a Caliban,
     And they to him are angels.
485 MIRANDA: My affections
     Are then most humble; I have no ambition
     To see a goodlier man.
PROSPERO [*to Ferdinand*]: Come on, obey.
     Thy nerves° are in their infancy again
     And have no vigor in them.
FERDINAND: So they are.
490   My spirits,° as in a dream, are all bound up.
     My father's loss, the weakness which I feel,
     The wreck of all my friends, nor this man's
     threats
     To whom I am subdued, are but light° to me,
     Might I but through my prison once a day
495   Behold this maid. All corners else° o' th' earth
     Let liberty make use of; space enough
     Have I in such a prison.
PROSPERO [*aside*]: It works. [*To Ferdinand.*] Come
     on. — Thou hast done well, fine Ariel! [*To
     Ferdinand.*] Follow me.
     [*To Ariel.*] Hark what thou else shalt do me.°
MIRANDA [*to Ferdinand*]:   Be of comfort.
500   My father's of a better nature, sir,
     Than he appears by speech. This is unwonted°
     Which now came from him.
PROSPERO [*to Ariel*]:   Thou shalt be as free
     As mountain winds; but then° exactly do
     All points of my command.
ARIEL: To th' syllable.
PROSPERO [*to Ferdinand*]: Come, follow. [*To
505   Miranda.*] Speak not for him.
                                   (*Exeunt.*)

479. **surety:** Guarantee.   484. **To:** Compared to.   488.
nerves: Sinews.   490. **spirits:** Vital powers.   493. **light:**
Unimportant.   495. **corners else:** Other corners, regions.
499. **me:** For me.   501. **unwonted:** Unusual.   503. **then:**
Until then; or, if that is to be so.

ACT II • Scene 1°

(*Enter Alonso, Sebastian, Antonio, Gonzalo, Adrian,
Francisco, and others.*)

GONZALO [*to Alonso*]: Beseech you, sir, be merry.
     You have cause,
     So have we all, of joy, for our escape
     Is much beyond° our loss. Our hint of° woe
     Is common; every day some sailor's wife,
     The masters of some merchant, and the
     merchant°   5
     Have just° our theme of woe. But for the
     miracle,
     I mean our preservation, few in millions
     Can speak like us. Then wisely, good sir, weigh
     Our sorrow with° our comfort.
ALONSO: Prithee, peace.
SEBASTIAN [*to Antonio*]: He receives comfort like cold   10
     porridge.°
ANTONIO [*to Sebastian*]: The visitor° will not give him
     o'er° so.
SEBASTIAN: Look, he's winding up the watch of his
     wit; by and by it will strike.   15
GONZALO [*to Alonso*]: Sir —
SEBASTIAN [*to Antonio*]: One. Tell.°
GONZALO: When every grief is entertained
     That's offered, comes to th' entertainer° —
SEBASTIAN: A dollar.°   20
GONZALO: Dolor comes to him, indeed. You have
     spoken truer than you purposed.
SEBASTIAN: You have taken it wiselier than I meant
     you should.
GONZALO [*to Alonso*]: Therefore, my lord —   25
ANTONIO: Fie, what a spendthrift is he of his tongue!
ALONSO [*to Gonzalo*]: I prithee, spare.°
GONZALO: Well, I have done. But yet —
SEBASTIAN: He will be talking.

II, I. Location: Another part of the island.   **3. much beyond:**
More remarkable than.   **hint of:** Occasion for.   **5. masters
. . . the merchant:** Officers of some merchant vessel and the
merchant himself, the owner (or else the ship itself).   **6.
just:** Exactly.   **9. with:** Against.   **11. porridge:** With a pun
on *peace* (line 9) and *peas* or *pease*, a common ingredient
of porridge.   **12. visitor:** One taking nourishment and comfort to the sick, i.e., Gonzalo.   **12–13. give him o'er:** Abandon him.   **17. Tell:** Keep count.   **18–19. When . . . entertainer:** When every sorrow that presents itself is accepted
without resistance, there comes to the recipient.   **20. dollar:**
Widely circulated coin, the German thaler and the Spanish
piece of eight. (Sebastian puns on *entertainer* in the sense of
innkeeper; to Gonzalo, *dollar* suggests *dolor*, grief.)   **27.
spare:** Forbear, cease.

30 ANTONIO: Which, of he or Adrian, for a good wager,
    first begins to crow?°
SEBASTIAN: The old cock.°
ANTONIO: The cockerel.°
SEBASTIAN: Done. The wager?
35 ANTONIO: A laughter.°
SEBASTIAN: A match!°
ADRIAN: Though this island seem to be desert° —
ANTONIO: Ha, ha, ha!
SEBASTIAN: So, you're paid.°
40 ADRIAN: Uninhabitable and almost inaccessible —
SEBASTIAN: Yet —
ADRIAN: Yet —
ANTONIO: He could not miss 't.°
ADRIAN: It must needs be° of subtle, tender, and del-
45   icate temperance.°
ANTONIO: Temperance° was a delicate° wench.
SEBASTIAN: Ay, and a subtle,° as he most learnedly
    delivered.°
ADRIAN: The air breathes upon us here most sweetly.
50 SEBASTIAN: As if it had lungs, and rotten ones.
ANTONIO: Or as 'twere perfumed by a fen.
GONZALO: Here is everything advantageous to life.
ANTONIO: True, save° means to live.
SEBASTIAN: Of that there's none, or little.
55 GONZALO: How lush and lusty° the grass looks! How
    green!
ANTONIO: The ground indeed is tawny.°

SEBASTIAN: With an eye° of green in 't.
ANTONIO: He misses not much.
SEBASTIAN: No. He doth but° mistake the truth totally. 60
GONZALO: But the rarity of it is — which is indeed
    almost beyond credit —
SEBASTIAN: As many vouched° rarities are.
GONZALO: That our garments, being, as they were,
    drenched in the sea, hold notwithstanding their 65
    freshness and glosses, being rather new-dyed than
    stained with salt water.
ANTONIO: If but one of his pockets° could speak,
    would it not say he lies?
SEBASTIAN: Ay, or very falsely pocket up° his report.° 70
GONZALO: Methinks our garments are now as fresh
    as when we put them on first in Afric, at the mar-
    riage of the King's fair daughter Claribel to the
    King of Tunis.
SEBASTIAN: 'Twas a sweet marriage, and we prosper 75
    well in our return.
ADRIAN: Tunis was never graced before with such a
    paragon to° their queen.
GONZALO: Not since widow Dido's° time.
ANTONIO: Widow! A pox o' that! How came that 80
    "widow" in? Widow Dido!
SEBASTIAN: What if he had said "widower Aeneas"
    too? Good Lord, how you take° it!
ADRIAN: "Widow Dido" said you? You make me
    study of° that. She was of Carthage, not of Tunis. 85
GONZALO: This Tunis, sir, was Carthage.
ADRIAN: Carthage?
GONZALO: I assure you, Carthage.
ANTONIO: His word is more than the miraculous
    harp.° 90
SEBASTIAN: He hath raised the wall, and houses too.
ANTONIO: What impossible matter will he make easy
    next?

30–31. Which . . . crow: Which of the two, Gonzalo or Adrian, do you bet will speak (crow) first? **32. old cock:** I.e., Gonzalo. **33. cockerel:** I.e., Adrian. **35. laughter:** (1) Burst of laughter, (2) sitting of eggs. (When Adrian, the *cockerel*, begins to speak two lines later, Sebastian loses the bet. The Folio speech prefixes in lines 38–39 are here reversed so that Antonio enjoys his laugh as the prize for winning, as in the proverb "He who laughs last laughs best" or "He laughs that wins." The Folio assignment can work in the theater, however, if Sebastian pays for losing with a sardonic laugh of concession.) **36. A match:** A bargain; agreed. **37. desert:** Uninhabited. **39. you're paid:** I.e., you've had your laugh. **43. miss 't:** (1) Avoid saying "Yet," (2) miss the island. **44. must needs be:** Has to be. **45. temperance:** Mildness of climate. **46. Temperance:** A girl's name. **delicate:** Here it means "given to pleasure, voluptuous"; in line 44, "pleasant." (Antonio is evidently suggesting that *tender, and delicate temperance* sounds like a Puritan phrase, which Antonio then mocks by applying the words to a woman rather than an island. He began this bawdy comparison with a double entendre on *inaccessible,* line 40.) **47. subtle:** Here it means "tricky, sexually crafty"; in line 44, "delicate." **48. delivered:** Uttered. (Sebastian joins Antonio in baiting the Puritans with his use of the pious cant phrase *learnedly delivered.*) **53. save:** Except. **55. lusty:** Healthy. **57. tawny:** Dull brown, yellowish.

58. eye: Tinge, or spot (perhaps with reference to Gonzalo's eye or judgment). **60. but:** Merely. **63. vouched:** Certified. **68. pockets:** I.e., because they are muddy. **70. pocket up:** I.e., conceal, suppress; often used in the sense of "receive unprotestingly, fail to respond to a challenge." **his report:** Sebastian's jest is that the evidence of Gonzalo's soggy and sea-stained pockets would confute Gonzalo's speech and his reputation for truth telling. **78. to:** For. **79. widow Dido:** Queen of Carthage, deserted by Aeneas. (She was in fact a widow when Aeneas, a widower, met her, but Antonio may be amused at Gonzalo's prudish use of the term *widow* to describe a woman deserted by her lover.) **83. take:** Understand, respond to, interpret. **85. study of:** Think about. **89–90. miraculous harp:** Alludes to Amphion's harp, with which he raised the walls of Thebes; Gonzalo has exceeded that deed by creating a modern Carthage — walls *and houses* — mistakenly on the site of Tunis.

SEBASTIAN: I think he will carry this island home in
95   his pocket and give it his son for an apple.
ANTONIO: And, sowing the kernels° of it in the sea,
    bring forth more islands.
GONZALO: Ay.°
ANTONIO: Why, in good time.°
100 GONZALO [*to Alonso*]: Sir, we were talking° that our
    garments seem now as fresh as when we were at
    Tunis at the marriage of your daughter, who is
    now queen.
ANTONIO: And the rarest° that e'er came there.
105 SEBASTIAN: Bate,° I beseech you, widow Dido.
ANTONIO: O, widow Dido? Ay, widow Dido.
GONZALO: Is not, sir, my doublet° as fresh as the first
    day I wore it? I mean, in a sort.°
ANTONIO: That "sort"° was well fished for.
110 GONZALO: When I wore it at your daughter's
    marriage.
ALONSO: You cram these words into mine ears
    against
    The stomach° of my sense.° Would I had never
    Married° my daughter there! For, coming thence,
115 My son is lost and, in my rate,° she too,
    Who is so far from Italy removed
    I ne'er again shall see her. O thou mine heir
    Of Naples and of Milan, what strange fish
    Hath made his meal° on thee?
FRANCISCO: Sir, he may live.
120 I saw him beat the surges° under him
    And ride upon their backs. He trod the water,
    Whose enmity he flung aside, and breasted
    The surge most swoll'n that met him. His bold
    head
    'Bove the contentious waves he kept, and oared
125 Himself with his good arms in lusty° stroke
    To th' shore, that o'er his wave-worn basis
    bowed,°
    As° stooping to relieve him. I not° doubt

He came alive to land.°
ALONSO: No, no, he's gone.
SEBASTIAN [*to Alonso*]: Sir, you may thank yourself
    for this great loss,
    That° would not bless our Europe with your
    daughter,   13(
    But rather° loose° her to an African,
    Where she at least is banished from your eye,°
    Who hath cause to wet the grief on 't.°
ALONSO   Prithee, peace.
SEBASTIAN: You were kneeled to and importuned°
    otherwise
    By all of us, and the fair soul herself   13£
    Weighed between loathness and obedience at
    Which end o' the beam should bow.° We have
    lost your son,
    I fear, forever. Milan and Naples have
    More widows in them of this business' making°
    Than we bring men to comfort them.   14(
    The fault's your own.
ALONSO: So is the dear'st° o' the loss.
GONZALO: My lord Sebastian,
    The truth you speak doth lack some gentleness
    And time° to speak it in. You rub the sore   14£
    When you should bring the plaster.°
SEBASTIAN: Very well.
ANTONIO: And most chirurgeonly.°
GONZALO [*to Alonso*]:
    It is foul weather in us all, good sir,
    When you are cloudy.
SEBASTIAN [*to Antonio*]: Fowl° weather?
ANTONIO [*to Sebastian*]:   Very foul.   15(
GONZALO: Had I plantation° of this isle, my lord —
ANTONIO [*to Sebastian*]:
    He'd sow 't with nettle seed.
SEBASTIAN: Or docks,° or mallows.°

96. kernels: Seeds.   **98. Ay:** Gonzalo may be reasserting his point about Carthage, or he may be responding ironically to Antonio, who in turn answers sarcastically.   **99. in good time:** An expression of ironical acquiescence or amazement; i.e., "sure, right away."   **100. talking:** Saying.   **104. rarest:** Most remarkable, beautiful.   **105. Bate:** Abate, except, leave out. (Sebastian says, "Don't forget Dido," or "Let's have no more talk of Dido.")   **107. doublet:** Close-fitting jacket.   **108. in a sort:** In a way.   **109. "sort":** Antonio plays on the idea of drawing lots.   **112–13. against . . . sense:** I.e., against my will.   **stomach:** Appetite.   **114. Married:** Given in marriage.   **115. rate:** Estimation, opinion.   **119. made his meal:** Fed himself.   **120. surges:** Waves.   **125. lusty:** Vigorous.   **126. that . . . bowed:** I.e., that projected out over the base of the cliff that had been eroded by the surf, thus seeming to bend down toward the sea.   **127. As:** As if.   **I not:** I do not.

128. came . . . land: Reached land alive.   **130. That:** You who.   **131. rather:** Would rather.   **loose:** (1) Release, let loose, (2) lose.   **132. is banished from your eye:** Is not constantly before your eye to serve as a reproachful reminder of what you have done.   **133. Who . . . on 't:** I.e., your eye, which has good reason to weep because of this; or Claribel, who has good reason to weep for it.   **134. importuned:** Urged, implored.   **135–37. the fair . . . bow:** I.e., Claribel herself was poised uncertainly between unwillingness to marry and obedience to her father as to which end of the scale should sink, which should prevail.   **139. of . . . making:** On account of this marriage.   **142. dear'st:** Heaviest, most costly.   **145. time:** Appropriate time.   **146. plaster:** A medical application.   **147. chirurgeonly:** Like a skilled surgeon. (Antonio mocks Gonzalo's medical analogy of a *plaster* applied curatively to a wound.)   **150. Fowl:** With a pun on *foul*, returning to the imagery of lines 30–35.   **151. plantation:** Colonization (with subsequent wordplay on the literal meaning).   **152. docks, mallows:** Weeds used as antidotes for nettle stings.

GONZALO: And were the king on 't, what would I
    do?
SEBASTIAN: Scape° being drunk for want° of wine.
GONZALO: I' the commonwealth I would by
    contraries°
    Execute all things; for no kind of traffic°
    Would I admit; no name of magistrate;
    Letters° should not be known; riches, poverty,
    And use of service,° none; contract, succession,°
    Bourn,° bound of land,° tilth,° vineyard, none;
    No use of metal, corn,° or wine, or oil;
    No occupation; all men idle, all,
    And women too, but innocent and pure;
    No sovereignty —
SEBASTIAN: Yet he would be king on 't.
ANTONIO: The latter end of his commonwealth forgets
    the beginning.
GONZALO: All things in common nature should
    produce
    Without sweat or endeavor. Treason, felony,
    Sword, pike,° knife, gun, or need of any engine°
    Would I not have; but nature should bring forth,
    Of its own kind, all foison,° all abundance,
    To feed my innocent people.
SEBASTIAN: No marrying 'mong his subjects?
ANTONIO: None, man, all idle — whores and
    knaves.
GONZALO: I would with such perfection govern, sir,
    T' excel the Golden Age.°
SEBASTIAN: Save° His Majesty!
ANTONIO: Long live Gonzalo!
GONZALO: And — do you mark me, sir?
ALONSO: Prithee, no more. Thou dost talk nothing to
    me.
GONZALO: I do well believe Your Highness, and did
    it to minister occasion° to these gentlemen, who
    are of such sensible° and nimble lungs that they
    always use° to laugh at nothing.
ANTONIO: 'Twas you we laughed at.
GONZALO: Who in this kind of merry fooling am

nothing to you; so you may continue, and laugh   185
    at nothing still.
ANTONIO: What a blow was there given!
SEBASTIAN: An° it had not fallen flat-long.°
GONZALO: You are gentlemen of brave mettle:° you
    would lift the moon out of her sphere° if she would   190
    continue in it five weeks without changing.

(*Enter Ariel [invisible] playing solemn music.*)

SEBASTIAN: We would so, and then go a-batfowling.°
ANTONIO: Nay, good my lord, be not angry.
GONZALO: No, I warrant you, I will not adventure
    my discretion so weakly.° Will you laugh me   195
    asleep? For I am very heavy.°
ANTONIO: Go sleep, and hear us.°
        [*All sleep except Alonso, Sebastian, and
                            Antonio.*]
ALONSO: What, all so soon asleep? I wish mine
        eyes
Would, with themselves, shut up my thoughts.° I
        find
They are inclined to do so.
SEBASTIAN: Please you, sir,   200
    Do not omit° the heavy° offer of it.
    It seldom visits sorrow; when it doth,
    It is a comforter.
ANTONIO: We two, my lord,
    Will guard your person while you take your rest,
    And watch your safety.
ALONSO: Thank you. Wondrous heavy.   205
        [*Alonso sleeps. Exit Ariel.*]
SEBASTIAN: What a strange drowsiness possesses
    them!
ANTONIO: It is the quality o' the climate.
SEBASTIAN: Why
    Doth it not then our eyelids sink? I find not
    Myself disposed to sleep.
ANTONIO: Nor I. My spirits are nimble.

---

154. Scape: Escape. **want:** Lack. (Sebastian jokes sarcastically that this hypothetical ruler would be saved from dissipation only by the barrenness of the island.)   **155. by contraries:** By what is directly opposite to usual custom. **156. traffic:** Trade.   **158. Letters:** Learning.   **159. use of service:** Custom of employing servants. **succession:** Holding of property by right of inheritance.   **160. Bourn:** Boundaries. **bound of land:** Landmarks. **tilth:** Tillage of soil. **161. corn:** Grain.   **169. pike:** Lance. **engine:** Instrument of warfare.   **171. foison:** Plenty.   **176. the Golden Age:** The age, according to Hesiod, when Cronus, or Saturn, ruled the world; an age of innocence and abundance. **Save:** God save.   **180. minister occasion:** Furnish opportunity.   **181. sensible:** Sensitive.   **182. use:** Are accustomed.

188. An: If. **flat-long:** With the flat of the sword, i.e., ineffectually. (Compare "fallen flat.")   **189. mettle:** Temperament, courage. (The sense of *metal*, indistinguishable as a form from *mettle*, continues the metaphor of the sword.) **190. sphere:** Orbit. (Literally, one of the concentric zones occupied by planets in the Ptolemaic astronomy.)   **192. a-batfowling:** Hunting birds at night with lantern and *bat* or stick; also, gulling a simpleton. (Gonzalo is the simpleton, or fowl, and Sebastian will use the moon as his lantern.) **194–95. adventure . . . weakly:** Risk my reputation for discretion for so trivial a cause (by getting angry at these sarcastic fellows).   **196. heavy:** Sleepy.   **197. Go . . . us:** Let our laughing send you to sleep, or go to sleep and hear us laugh at you.   **199. Would . . . thoughts:** Would shut off my melancholy brooding when they close themselves in sleep. **201. omit:** Neglect. **heavy:** Drowsy.

210 They fell together all, as by consent,°
They dropped, as by a thunderstroke. What might,
Worthy Sebastian, O, what might — ? No more.
And yet methinks I see it in thy face,
What thou shouldst be. Th' occasion° speaks thee,° and
215 My strong imagination sees a crown
Dropping upon thy head.
SEBASTIAN: What, art thou waking?
ANTONIO: Do you not hear me speak?
SEBASTIAN: I do, and surely
It is a sleepy language, and thou speak'st
Out of thy sleep. What is it thou didst say?
220 This is a strange repose, to be asleep
With eyes wide open — standing, speaking, moving —
And yet so fast asleep.
ANTONIO: Noble Sebastian,
Thou lett'st thy fortune sleep — die, rather; wink'st°
Whiles thou art waking.
SEBASTIAN: Thou dost snore distinctly;°
225 There's meaning in thy snores.
ANTONIO: I am more serious than my custom. You
Must be so too, if heed° me; which to do
Trebles thee o'er.°
SEBASTIAN: Well, I am standing water.°
ANTONIO: I'll teach you how to flow.
SEBASTIAN: Do so. To ebb°
Hereditary sloth° instructs me.
230 ANTONIO: O,
If you but knew how you the purpose cherish
Whiles thus you mock it!° How, in stripping it,
You more invest° it! Ebbing men, indeed,
Most often do so near the bottom° run
By their own fear or sloth.

SEBASTIAN: Prithee, say on.   23
The setting° of thine eye and cheek proclaim
A matter° from thee, and a birth indeed
Which throes° thee much to yield.°
ANTONIO: Thus, sir:
Although this lord° of weak remembrance,° this
Who shall be of as little memory   24
When he is earthed,° hath here almost persuaded —
For he's a spirit of persuasion, only
Professes to persuade° — the King his son's alive,
'Tis as impossible that he's undrowned
As he that sleeps here swims.
SEBASTIAN: I have no hope   24
That he's undrowned.
ANTONIO: O, out of that "no hope"
What great hope have you! No hope that way° is
Another way so high a hope that even
Ambition cannot pierce a wink° beyond,
But doubt discovery there.° Will you grant with me   25
That Ferdinand is drowned?
SEBASTIAN: He's gone.
ANTONIO: Then tell me,
Who's the next heir of Naples?
SEBASTIAN: Claribel.
ANTONIO: She that is Queen of Tunis; she that dwells
Ten leagues beyond man's life;° she that from Naples
Can have no note,° unless the sun were post° —   2.
The man i' the moon's too slow — till newborn chins
Be rough and razorable;° she that from° whom
We all were sea-swallowed, though some cast° again,

210. **consent:** Common agreement.   214. **occasion:** Opportunity of the moment.   **speaks thee:** I.e., calls upon you, proclaims you usurper of Alonso's crown.   223. **wink'st:** (You) shut your eyes.   224. **distinctly:** Articulately.   227. **if heed:** If you heed.   228. **Trebles thee o'er:** Makes you three times as great and rich.   **standing water:** Water that neither ebbs nor flows, at a standstill.   229. **ebb:** Recede, decline.   230. **Hereditary sloth:** Natural laziness and the position of younger brother, one who cannot inherit.   231–32. **If . . . mock it:** I.e., if you only knew how much you really enhance the value of ambition even while your words mock your purpose.   232–33. **How . . . invest it:** I.e., how the more you speak flippantly of ambition, the more you in effect affirm it.   233. **invest:** Clothe. (Antonio's paradox is that by skeptically stripping away illusions Sebastian can see the essence of a situation and the opportunity it presents, or that by disclaiming and deriding his purpose Sebastian shows how he values it.)   234. **the bottom:** I.e., on which unadventurous men may go aground and miss the tide of fortune.

236. **setting:** Set expression (of earnestness).   237. **matter:** Matter of importance.   238. **throes:** Causes pain, as in giving birth.   **yield:** Give forth, speak about.   239. **this lord:** I.e., Gonzalo.   **remembrance:** (1) Power of remembering, (2) being remembered after his death.   241. **earthed:** Buried.   242–43. **only . . . persuade:** I.e., whose whole function (as a privy councilor) is to persuade.   247. **that way:** I.e., in regard to Ferdinand's being saved.   249–50. **Ambition . . . there:** Ambition itself cannot see any further than that hope (of the crown), but is unsure of itself in seeing even so far, is dazzled by daring to think so high.   249. **wink:** Glimpse.   254. **Ten . . . life:** I.e., it would take more than a lifetime to get there.   255. **note:** News, intimation.   **post:** Messenger.   257. **razorable:** Ready for shaving.   **from:** On our voyage from.   258. **cast:** Were disgorged (with a pun on *casting* of parts for a play).

And by that destiny to perform an act
Whereof what's past is prologue, what to come
In yours and my discharge.°   ₆₀
SEBASTIAN: What stuff is this? How say you?
'Tis true my brother's daughter's Queen of
   Tunis,
So is she heir of Naples, twixt which regions
There is some space.
ANTONIO: A space whose every cubit°   ₆₅
Seems to cry out, "How shall that Claribel
Measure us° back to Naples? Keep° in Tunis,
And let Sebastian wake."° Say this were death
That now hath seized them, why, they were no
   worse
Than now they are. There be° that can rule
   Naples   ₇₀
As well as he that sleeps, lords that can prate°
As amply and unnecessarily
As this Gonzalo. I myself could make
A chough of as deep chat.° O, that you bore
The mind that I do! What a sleep were this   ₇₅
For your advancement! Do you understand me?
SEBASTIAN: Methinks I do.
ANTONIO: And how does your
   content°
Tender° your own good fortune?
SEBASTIAN: I remember
You did supplant your brother Prospero.
ANTONIO: True.
And look how well my garments sit upon me,   ₈₀
Much feater° than before. My brother's servants
Were then my fellows. Now they are my men.
SEBASTIAN: But, for your conscience?
ANTONIO: Ay, sir, where lies that? If 'twere a kibe,°
'Twould put me to° my slipper; but I feel not   ₈₅
This deity in my bosom. Twenty consciences
That stand twixt me and Milan,° candied° be
   they
And melt ere they molest!° Here lies your
   brother,
No better than the earth he lies upon,

---

261. **discharge:** Performance.   265. **cubit:** Ancient measure of length, about twenty inches.   267. **Measure us:** I.e., traverse the cubits, find her way.   **Keep:** Stay (addressed to Claribel).   268. **wake:** I.e., to his good fortune.   270. **There be:** There are those.   271. **prate:** Speak foolishly.   273–74. **I . . . chat:** I could teach a jackdaw to talk as wisely, or, be such a garrulous talker myself.   277. **content:** Desire, inclination.   278. **Tender:** Regard, look after.   281. **feater:** More becomingly, fittingly.   284. **kibe:** Chilblain, here a sore on the heel.   285. **put me to:** Oblige me to wear.   287. **Milan:** The dukedom of Milan.   **candied:** Frozen, congealed in crystalline form.   **be they:** May they be.   288. **molest:** Interfere.

If he were that which now he's like — that's
   dead,   ₂₉₀
Whom I, with this obedient steel, three inches of
   it,
Can lay to bed forever; whiles you, doing thus,°
To the perpetual wink° for aye° might put
This ancient morsel, this Sir Prudence, who
Should not° upbraid our course. For all the rest,   ₂₉₅
They'll take suggestion° as a cat laps milk;
They'll tell the clock° to any business that
We say befits the hour.
SEBASTIAN: Thy case, dear friend,
Shall be my precedent. As thou gott'st Milan,
I'll come by Naples. Draw thy sword. One
   stroke   ₃₀₀
Shall free thee from the tribute° which thou
   payest,
And I the king shall love thee.
ANTONIO: Draw together;
And when I rear my hand, do you the like
To fall it° on Gonzalo.   [*They draw.*]
SEBASTIAN: O, but one word.
                       [*They talk apart.*]

(*Enter Ariel* [*invisible*], *with music and song.*)

ARIEL: My master through his art foresees the
   danger   ₃₀₅
That you, his friend, are in, and sends me
   forth —
For else his project dies — to keep them living.
             (*Sings in Gonzalo's ear.*)
While you here do snoring lie,
Open-eyed conspiracy
   His time° doth take.   ₃₁₀
If of life you keep a care,
Shake off slumber, and beware.
Awake, awake!
ANTONIO: Then let us both be sudden.°
GONZALO [*waking*]: Now, good angels preserve the
   King!   ₃₁₅
                   [*The others wake.*]
ALONSO: Why, how now, ho, awake? Why are you
   drawn?
Wherefore this ghastly looking?
GONZALO: What's the matter?
SEBASTIAN: Whiles we stood here securing° your
   repose,

---

292. **thus:** The actor makes a stabbing gesture.   293. **wink:** Sleep, closing of eyes.   **aye:** Ever.   295. **Should not:** Would not then be able to.   296. **take suggestion:** Respond to prompting.   297. **tell the clock:** I.e., agree, answer appropriately, chime.   301. **tribute:** See I, II, 113–24.   304. **fall it:** Let it fall.   310. **time:** Opportunity.   314. **sudden:** Quick.   318. **securing:** Standing guard over.

Even now, we heard a hollow burst of bellowing
320 Like bulls, or rather lions. Did 't not wake you?
It struck mine ear most terribly.
ALONSO: I heard nothing.
ANTONIO: O, 'twas a din to fright a monster's ear,
To make an earthquake! Sure it was the roar
Of a whole herd of lions.
325 ALONSO: Heard you this, Gonzalo?
GONZALO: Upon mine honor, sir, I heard a
      humming,
   And that a strange one too, which did awake
      me.
   I shaked you, sir, and cried.° As mine eyes
      opened,
   I saw their weapons drawn. There was a noise,
330 That's verily.° 'Tis best we stand upon our guard,
   Or that we quit this place. Let's draw our
      weapons.
ALONSO: Lead off this ground, and let's make
      further search
   For my poor son.
GONZALO: Heavens keep him from these
      beasts!
   For he is, sure, i' th' island.
ALONSO: Lead away.
ARIEL [aside]: Prospero my lord shall know what I
335   have done.
   So, King, go safely on to seek thy son.
                       (Exeunt [separately].)

Scene II°

(Enter Caliban with a burden of wood. A noise of
thunder heard.)

CALIBAN: All the infections that the sun sucks up
   From bogs, fens, flats,° on Prosper fall, and
      make him
   By inchmeal° a disease! His spirits hear me,
   And yet I needs must° curse. But they'll nor°
      pinch,
   Fright me with urchin shows,° pitch me i' the
5   mire,
   Nor lead me, like a firebrand,° in the dark
   Out of my way, unless he bid 'em. But
   For every trifle are they set upon me,
   Sometimes like apes, that mow° and chatter at
      me

And after bite me; then like hedgehogs, which   10
Lie tumbling in my barefoot way and mount
Their pricks at my footfall. Sometimes am I
All wound with° adders, who with cloven
      tongues
Do hiss me into madness.

(Enter Trinculo.)

                         Lo, now, lo!
Here comes a spirit of his, and to torment me   15
For bringing wood in slowly. I'll fall flat.
Perchance he will not mind° me. [He lies down.]
TRINCULO: Here's neither bush nor shrub to bear off°
any weather at all. And another storm brewing; I
hear it sing i' the wind. Yond same black cloud,   20
yond huge one, looks like a foul bombard° that
would shed his° liquor. If it should thunder as it
did before, I know not where to hide my head.
Yond same cloud cannot choose but fall by pailfuls.
[Seeing Caliban.] What have we here, a man or a   25
fish? Dead or alive? A fish, he smells like a fish; a
very ancient and fishlike smell; a kind of not-of-
the-newest Poor John.° A strange fish! Were I in
England now, as once I was, and had but this fish
painted,° not a holiday fool there but would give   30
a piece of silver. There would this monster make
a man.° Any strange beast there makes a man.
When they will not give a doit° to relieve a lame
beggar, they will lay out ten to see a dead Indian.
Legged like a man, and his fins like arms! Warm,   35
o' my troth!° I do now let loose my opinion, hold
it° no longer: this is no fish, but an islander, that
hath lately suffered° by a thunderbolt. [Thunder.]
Alas, the storm is come again! My best way is to
creep under his gaberdine.° There is no other shelter   40
hereabout. Misery acquaints a man with strange
bedfellows. I will here shroud° till the dregs° of the
storm be past.
                 [He creeps under Caliban's garment.]

(Enter Stephano, singing, [a bottle in his hand].)

STEPHANO: "I shall no more to sea, to sea,
      Here shall I die ashore —"   45
This is a very scurvy tune to sing at a man's funeral.

---

328. cried: Called out. 330. verily: True. II. II. Location:
Another part of the island. 2. flats: Swamps. 3. By inch-
meal: Inch by inch. 4. needs must: Have to. nor: neither.
5. urchin shows: Elvish apparitions shaped like hedgehogs.
6. like a firebrand: In the guise of a will-o'-the-wisp. 9.
mow: Make faces.

13. wound with: Entwined by. 17. mind: Notice. 18.
bear off: Keep off. 21. foul bombard: Dirty leather jug.
22. his: Its. 28. Poor John: Salted fish, type of poor fare.
30. painted: I.e., painted on a sign set up outside a booth
or tent at a fair. 31–32. make a man: (1) Make one's
fortune, (2) be indistinguishable from an Englishman. 33.
doit: Small coin. 36. o' my troth: By my faith. 36–37.
hold it: Hold it in. 38. suffered: I.e., died. 40. gaberdine:
Cloak, loose upper garment. 42. shroud: Take shelter.
dregs: Last remains (as in a bombard or jug, line 21).

Well, here's my comfort.   (*Drinks.*)

(*Sings.*)

"The master, the swabber,° the boatswain, and I,
    The gunner and his mate,
Loved Mall, Meg, and Marian, and Margery,
    But none of us cared for Kate.
        For she had a tongue with a tang,°
        Would cry to a sailor, 'Go hang!'
She loved not the savor of tar nor of pitch,
Yet a tailor might scratch her where'er she did itch.°
Then to sea, boys, and let her go hang!"

This is a scurvy tune too. But here's my comfort.
                    (*Drinks.*)

CALIBAN: Do not torment me!° O!

STEPHANO: What's the matter?° Have we devils here?
Do you put tricks upon 's° with savages and men
of Ind,° ha? I have not scaped drowning to be
afeard now of your four legs. For it hath been said,
"As proper° a man as ever went on four legs° cannot make him give ground"; and it shall be said
so again while Stephano breathes at° nostrils.

CALIBAN: This spirit torments me! O!

STEPHANO: This is some monster of the isle with four
legs, who hath got, as I take it, an ague.° Where
the devil should he learn° our language? I will give
him some relief, if it be but for that.° If I can
recover° him and keep him tame and get to Naples
with him, he's a present for any emperor that ever
trod on neat's leather.°

CALIBAN: Do not torment me, prithee. I'll bring my
wood home faster.

STEPHANO: He's in his fit now and does not talk after
the wisest.° He shall taste of my bottle. If he have
never drunk wine afore,° it will go near to° remove
his fit. If I can recover° him and keep him tame, I
will not take too much° for him. He shall pay for
him that hath° him,° and that soundly.

CALIBAN: Thou does me yet but little hurt; thou wilt
anon,° I know it by thy trembling. Now Prosper
works upon thee.

STEPHANO: Come on your ways. Open your mouth.   85
Here is that which will give language to you, cat.
Open your mouth.° This will shake your shaking,
I can tell you, and that soundly. [*Giving Caliban
a drink.*] You cannot tell who's your friend. Open
your chaps° again.   90

TRINCULO: I should know that voice. It should be —
but he is drowned, and these are devils. O, defend
me!

STEPHANO: Four legs and two voices — a most deli-
cate° monster! His forward voice now is to speak   95
well of his friend; his backward voice° is to utter
foul speeches and to detract. If all the wine in my
bottle will recover him,° I will help° his ague. Come.
[*Giving a drink.*] Amen! I will pour some in thy
other mouth.   100

TRINCULO: Stephano!

STEPHANO: Doth thy other mouth call me?° Mercy,
mercy! This is a devil, and no monster. I will leave
him. I have no long spoon.°

TRINCULO: Stephano! If thou beest Stephano, touch   105
me and speak to me, for I am Trinculo — be not
afeard — thy good friend Trinculo.

STEPHANO: If thou beest Trinculo, come forth. I'll pull
thee by the lesser legs. If any be Trinculo's legs,
these are they. [*Pulling him out.*] Thou art very   110
Trinculo indeed! How cam'st thou to be the siege°
of this mooncalf?° Can he vent° Trinculos?

TRINCULO: I took him to be killed with a thunderstroke. But art thou not drowned, Stephano? I hope
now thou art not drowned. Is the storm over-   115
blown?° I hid me under the dead mooncalf's gaberdine for fear of the storm. And art thou living,
Stephano? O Stephano, two Neapolitans scaped!
                    [*He capers with Stephano.*]

STEPHANO: Prithee, do not turn me about. My stomach is not constant.°   120

---

48. swabber: Crew member whose job is to wash the decks.
52. tang: Sting. **55. tailor . . . itch:** A dig at tailors for their
supposed effeminacy and a bawdy suggestion of satisfying a
sexual craving. **58. Do . . . me:** Caliban assumes that one
of Prospero's spirits has come to punish him. **59. What's
the matter:** What's going on here? **60. put tricks upon 's:**
Trick us with conjuring shows. **61. Ind:** India. **63. proper:**
Handsome. **four legs:** The conventional phrase would supply *two legs.* **65. at':** At the. **68. ague:** Fever. (Probably
both Caliban and Trinculo are quaking; see lines 58 and
83.) **69. should he learn:** Could he have learned. **70. for
that:** I.e., for knowing our language. **71. recover:** Restore.
73. neat's leather: Cowhide. **76–77. after the wisest:** In
the wisest fashion. **78. afore:** Before. **go near to:** Nearly.
79. recover: Restore. **79–80. I will . . . much:** I.e., no sum
can be too much. **80–81. He shall . . . hath him:** I.e.,
anyone who wants him will have to pay dearly for him.
81. hath: Possesses, receives.

83. anon: Presently. **86–87. cat . . . mouth:** Allusion to
the proverb "Good liquor will make a cat speak." **90.
chaps:** Jaws. **94–95. delicate:** Ingenious. **96. backward
voice:** Trinculo and Caliban are facing in opposite directions.
Stephano supposes the monster to have a rear end that can
emit *foul speeches* or foul-smelling wind at the monster's
other mouth, line 100. **97–98. If . . . him:** Even if it takes
all the wine in my bottle to cure him. **98. help:** Cure.
102. call me: I.e., call me by name, know supernaturally
who I am. **104. long spoon:** Allusion to the proverb "He
that sups with the devil has need of a long spoon." **111.
siege:** Excrement. **112. mooncalf:** Monstrous or misshapen
creature (whose deformity is caused by the malignant influence of the moon). **vent:** Excrete, defecate. **115–16.
overblown:** Blown over. **120. not constant:** Unsteady.

BELOW: Caliban (Avery Brooks), Stephano (Ernest Perry, Jr.), and Trinculo (Kelly Walters) in the 1987 Theatre for a New Audience production of *The Tempest*, directed by Julie Taymor. RIGHT: Avery Brooks as Caliban.

CALIBAN: These be fine things, an if° they be not
    spirits.
    That's a brave° god, and bears° celestial liquor.
    I will kneel to him.
STEPHANO: How didst thou scape? How cam'st thou
    hither? Swear by this bottle how thou cam'st hither.
    I escaped upon a butt of sack° which the sailors
    heaved o'erboard — by this bottle,° which I made
    of the bark of a tree with mine own hands since°
    I was cast ashore.
CALIBAN [*kneeling*]: I'll swear upon that bottle to be
    thy true subject, for the liquor is not earthly.
STEPHANO: Here. Swear then how thou escapedst.
TRINCULO: Swum ashore, man, like a duck. I can swim
    like a duck, I'll be sworn.
STEPHANO: Here, kiss the book.° Though thou canst
    swim like a duck, thou art made like a goose.
                         [*Giving him a drink.*]
TRINCULO: O Stephano, hast any more of this?
STEPHANO: The whole butt, man. My cellar is in a
    rock by the seaside, where my wine is hid. — How
    now, mooncalf? How does thine ague?
CALIBAN: Hast thou not dropped from heaven?
STEPHANO: Out o' the moon, I do assure thee. I was
    the man i' the moon when time was.°
CALIBAN: I have seen thee in her, and I do adore
    thee.
    My mistress showed me thee, and thy dog, and
    thy bush.°
STEPHANO: Come, swear to that. Kiss the book. I will
    furnish it anon with new contents. Swear.
                         [*Giving him a drink.*]
TRINCULO: By this good light,° this is a very shallow
    monster! I afeard of him? A very weak monster!
    The man i' the moon? A most poor credulous
    monster! Well drawn,° monster, in good sooth!°
CALIBAN [*to Stephano*]: I'll show thee every fertile
    inch o' th' island,
    And I will kiss thy foot. I prithee, be my god.
TRINCULO: By this light, a most perfidious and
    drunken monster! When 's god's asleep, he'll rob
    his bottle.°

CALIBAN: I'll kiss thy foot. I'll swear myself thy
    subject.
STEPHANO: Come on then. Down, and swear.
                         [*Caliban kneels.*]
TRINCULO: I shall laugh myself to death at this puppy-   160
    headed monster. A most scurvy monster! I could
    find in my heart to beat him —
STEPHANO: Come, kiss.
TRINCULO: But that the poor monster's in drink.° An
    abominable monster!   165
CALIBAN: I'll show thee the best springs. I'll pluck
    thee berries.
    I'll fish for thee and get thee wood enough.
    A plague upon the tyrant that I serve!
    I'll bear him no more sticks, but follow thee,
    Thou wondrous man.   170
TRINCULO: A most ridiculous monster, to make a won-
    der of a poor drunkard!
CALIBAN: I prithee, let me bring thee where crabs°
    grow;
    And I with my long nails will dig thee pignuts,°
    Show thee a jay's nest, and instruct thee how   175
    To snare the nimble marmoset.° I'll bring thee
    To clustering filberts, and sometimes I'll get thee
    Young scamels° from the rock. Wilt thou go
    with me?
STEPHANO: I prithee now, lead the way without any   180
    more talking. — Trinculo, the King and all our
    company else° being drowned, we will inherit°
    here. — Here, bear my bottle. — Fellow Trinculo,
    we'll fill him by and by again.
CALIBAN (*sings drunkenly*): Farewell, master, farewell,
    farewell!   185
TRINCULO: A howling monster; a drunken monster!
CALIBAN: No more dams I'll make for fish,
    Nor fetch in firing°
    At requiring,
    Nor scrape trenchering,° nor wash dish.   190
    'Ban, 'Ban, Ca-Caliban
    Has a new master. Get a new man!°
    Freedom, high-day!° High-day, freedom! Free-
    dom, high-day, freedom!
STEPHANO: O brave monster! Lead the way.   195
                            (*Exeunt.*)

---

121. an if: If.   **122. brave:** Fine, magnificent.   **bears:** He
carries.   **126. butt of sack:** Barrel of Canary wine.   **127.
by this bottle:** I.e., I swear by this bottle.   **128. since:** After.
135. book: I.e., bottle (but with ironic reference to the practice of kissing the Bible in swearing an oath; see *I'll be sworn*
in line 134).   **143. when time was:** Once upon a time.   **145.
dog . . . bush:** The man in the moon was popularly imagined
to have with him a dog and a bush of thorn.   **148. By . . .
light:** By God's light, by this good light from heaven.   **151.
Well drawn:** Well pulled (on the bottle).   **in good sooth:**
Truly, indeed.   **155–56. When . . . bottle:** I.e., Caliban
wouldn't even stop at robbing his god of his bottle if he
could catch him asleep.

164. in drink: Drunk.   **173. crabs:** Crab apples, or perhaps
crabs.   **174. pignuts:** earthnuts, edible tuberous roots.
176. marmoset: Small monkey.   **178. scamels:** Possibly *sea-
mews*, mentioned in Strachey's letter, or shellfish; or perhaps
from *squamelle*, furnished with little scales. Contemporary
French and Italian travel accounts report that the natives of
Patagonia in South America ate small fish described as *fort
scameux* and *squame*.   **181. else:** In addition, besides ourselves.   **inherit:** Take possession.   **188. firing:** Firewood.
190. trenchering: Trenchers, wooden plates.   **192. Get a
new man:** Addressed to Prospero.   **193. high-day:** Holiday.

ACT III • Scene 1°

(*Enter Ferdinand, bearing a log.*)

FERDINAND: There be some sports° are painful,° and
    their labor
  Delight in them sets off.° Some kinds of
    baseness°
  Are nobly undergone,° and most poor° matters
  Point to rich ends. This my mean° task
5 Would be as heavy to me as odious, but°
  The mistress which I serve quickens° what's dead
  And makes my labors pleasures. O, she is
  Ten times more gentle than her father's crabbèd,
  And he's composed of harshness. I must remove
10 Some thousands of these logs and pile them up,
  Upon a sore injunction.° My sweet mistress
  Weeps when she sees me work and says such
    baseness
  Had never like executor.° I forget;°
  But these sweet thoughts do even refresh my
    labors,
  Most busy lest when I do it.°

(*Enter Miranda; and Prospero* [*at a distance, unseen*].)

15 MIRANDA: Alas now, pray you,
  Work not so hard. I would the lightning had
  Burnt up those logs that you are enjoined° to
    pile!
  Pray, set it down and rest you. When this°
    burns,
  'Twill weep° for having wearied you. My father
20 Is hard at study. Pray now, rest yourself.
  He's safe for these° three hours.
FERDINAND: O most dear mistress,
  The sun will set before I shall discharge°
  What I must strive to do.
MIRANDA: If you'll sit down,
  I'll bear your logs the while. Pray, give me that.
  I'll carry it to the pile.

FERDINAND: No, precious creature, 25
  I had rather crack my sinews, break my back,
  Than you should such dishonor undergo
  While I sit lazy by.
MIRANDA: It would become me
  As well as it does you; and I should do it
  With much more ease, for my good will is to it, 30
  And yours it is against.
PROSPERO [*aside*]:   Poor worm, thou art infected!
  This visitation° shows it.
MIRANDA: You look wearily.
FERDINAND: No, noble mistress, 'tis fresh morning
    with me
  When you are by° at night. I do beseech you —
  Chiefly that I might set it in my prayers — 35
  What is your name?
MIRANDA: Miranda. — O my father,
  I have broke your hest° to say so.
FERDINAND: Admired Miranda!°
  Indeed the top of admiration, worth
  What's dearest° to the world! Full many a lady
  I have eyed with best regard,° and many a time 40
  The harmony of their tongues hath into bondage
  Brought my too diligent° ear. For several° virtues
  Have I liked several women, never any
  With so full soul but some defect in her
  Did quarrel with the noblest grace she owed° 45
  And put it to the foil.° But you, O you,
  So perfect and so peerless, are created
  Of° every creature's best!
MIRANDA: I do not know
  One of my sex; no woman's face remember,
  Save, from my glass, mine own. Nor have I seen 50
  More that I may call men than you, good friend,
  And my dear father. How features are abroad°
  I am skilless° of; but, by my modesty,°
  The jewel in my dower, I would not wish
  Any companion in the world but you; 55
  Nor can imagination form a shape,
  Besides yourself, to like of.° But I prattle
  Something° too wildly, and my father's precepts
  I therein do forget.
FERDINAND: I am in my condition°

III, I. **Location:** Before Prospero's cell. **1. sports:** Pastimes, activities. **painful:** Laborious. **1–2. and their . . . sets off:** I.e., but the pleasure we get from those pastimes compensates for the effort. **2. baseness:** Menial activity. **3. undergone:** Undertaken. **most poor:** Poorest. **4. mean:** Lowly. **5. but:** Were it not that. **6. quickens:** Gives life to. **11. sore injunction:** Severe command. **13. Had . . . executor:** I.e., was never before undertaken by one of my noble rank. **I forget:** I.e., I forget that I'm supposed to be working, or, I forget my happiness, oppressed by my labor. **15. Most . . . it:** I.e., least troubled by my labor, and most active in my thoughts, when I think of her (?). (The line may be in need of emendation.) **17. enjoined:** Commanded. **18. this:** I.e., the log. **19. weep:** I.e., exude resin. **21. these:** I.e., the next. **22. discharge:** Complete.

32. visitation: (1) Visit of the sick, (2) visitation of the plague, i.e., infection of love. **34. by:** Nearby. **37. hest:** Command. **Admired Miranda:** Her name means "to be admired or wondered at." **39. dearest:** Most treasured. **40. best regard:** Thoughtful and approving attention. **42. diligent:** Attentive. **several:** Various (also in line 43). **45. owed:** Owned. **46. put . . . foil:** (1) Overthrew it (as in wrestling), (2) served as a *foil*, or contrast, to set it off. **48. Of:** Out of. **52. How . . . abroad:** What people look like in other places. **53. skilless:** Ignorant. **modesty:** Virginity. **57. like of:** Be pleased with, be fond of. **58. Something:** Somewhat. **59. condition:** Rank.

60   A prince, Miranda; I do think, a king —
    I would, not so! — and would° no more endure
    This wooden slavery° than to suffer
    The flesh-fly° blow° my mouth. Hear my soul
      speak:
    The very instant that I saw you did
65   My heart fly to your service, there resides
    To make me slave to it, and for your sake
    Am I this patient log-man.
MIRANDA: Do you love me?
FERDINAND: O heaven, O earth, bear witness to this
      sound,
    And crown what I profess with kind event°
70   If I speak true! If hollowly,° invert°
    What best is boded° me to mischief!° I
    Beyond all limit of what° else i' the world
    Do love, prize, honor you.
MIRANDA: I am a fool
    I weep at what I am glad of.
PROSPERO [aside]:   Fair encounter
75   Of two most rare affections! Heavens rain grace
    On that which breeds between 'em!
FERDINAND: Wherefore weep you?
MIRANDA: At mine unworthiness, that dare not
      offer
    What I desire to give, and much less take
    What I shall die° to want.° But this is trifling,
80   And all the more it seeks to hide itself
    The bigger bulk it shows. Hence, bashful
      cunning,°
    And prompt me, plain and holy innocence!
    I am your wife, if you will marry me;
    If not, I'll die your maid.° To be your fellow°
85   You may deny me, but I'll be your servant
    Whether you will° or no.
FERDINAND: My mistress,° dearest,
    And I thus humble ever.
MIRANDA: My husband, then?
FERDINAND: Ay, with a heart as willing°
90   As bondage e'er of freedom. Here's my hand.
MIRANDA [clasping his hand]: And mine, with my
      heart in 't. And now farewell
    Till half an hour hence.

61. **would:** Wish (it were).   62. **wooden slavery:** Being compelled to carry wood.   63. **flesh-fly:** Insect that deposits its eggs in dead flesh. **blow:** Befoul with fly eggs.   69. **kind event:** Favorable outcome.   70. **hollowly:** Insincerely, falsely. **invert:** Turn.   71. **boded:** Destined for. **mischief:** Evil.   72. **what:** Whatever.   79. **die:** Probably with an unconscious sexual meaning that underlies all of lines 77–81. **want:** Lack.   81. **bashful cunning:** Coyness.   84. **maid:** Handmaiden, servant. **fellow:** Mate, equal.   86. **will:** Desire it. **My mistress:** I.e., the woman I adore and serve (not an illicit sexual partner).   89. **willing:** Desirous.

FERDINAND: A thousand thousand!°
    (Exeunt [Ferdinand and Miranda, separately].)
PROSPERO: So glad of this as they I cannot be,
    Who are surprised with all;° but my rejoicing
    At nothing can be more. I'll to my book,   95
    For yet ere suppertime must I perform
    Much business appertaining.°   (Exit.)

Scene II°

(Enter Caliban, Stephano, and Trinculo.)

STEPHANO: Tell not me. When the butt is out,° we
    will drink water, not a drop before. Therefore bear
    up and board 'em.° Servant monster, drink to me.
TRINCULO: Servant monster? The folly of° this island!
    They say there's but five upon this isle. We are   5
    three of them; if th' other two be brained° like us,
    the state totters.
STEPHANO: Drink, servant monster, when I bid thee.
    Thy eyes are almost set° in thy head.
              [Giving a drink.]
TRINCULO: Where should they be set° else? He were   10
    a brave° monster indeed if they were set in his tail.
STEPHANO: My man-monster hath drowned his tongue
    in sack. For my part, the sea cannot drown me. I
    swam, ere I could recover° the shore, five and thirty
    leagues° off and on.° By this light,° thou shalt be   15
    my lieutenant, monster, or my standard.°
TRINCULO: Your lieutenant, if you list.° He's no
    standard.°
STEPHANO: We'll not run,° Monsieur Monster.
TRINCULO: Nor go° neither, but you'll lie° like dogs   20
    and yet say nothing neither.
STEPHANO: Mooncalf, speak once in thy life, if thou
    beest a good mooncalf.

92. A thousand thousand: I.e., a thousand thousand farewells.   **94. with all:** By everything that has happened; or *withal*, with it.   **97. appertaining:** Related to this. **III, II. Location:** Another part of the island.   **1. out:** Empty.   **2–3. bear . . . 'em:** Stephano uses the terminology of maneuvering at sea and boarding a vessel under attack as a way of urging an assault on the liquor supply.   **4. folly of:** I.e., stupidity found on.   **6. be brained:** Are endowed with intelligence.   **9. set:** Fixed in a drunken stare; or sunk, like the sun.   **10. set:** Placed.   **11. brave:** Fine, splendid.   **14. recover:** Gain, reach.   **15. leagues:** Units of distance each equaling about three miles. **off and on:** Intermittently. **By this light:** An oath: by the light of the sun.   **16. standard:** Standard-bearer, ensign (as distinguished from *lieutenant*, lines 15–17.   **17. list:** Prefer.   **17–18. no standard:** I.e., not able to stand up.   **19. run:** (1) Retreat, (2) urinate (taking Trinculo's *standard*, line 17, in the old sense of "conduit."   **20. go:** Walk. **lie:** (1) Tell lies, (2) lie prostrate, (3) excrete.

CALIBAN: How does thy honor? Let me lick thy
    shoe.
25   I'll not serve him. He is not valiant.
TRINCULO: Thou liest, most ignorant monster, I am
    in case to jostle a constable.° Why, thou debauched
    fish, thou, was there ever man a coward that hath
    drunk so much sack° as I today? Wilt thou tell a
30   monstrous lie, being but half a fish and half a
    monster?
CALIBAN: Lo, how he mocks me! Wilt thou let him,
    my lord?
TRINCULO: "Lord," quoth he? That a monster should
    be such a natural!°
35 CALIBAN: Lo, lo, again! Bite him to death, I prithee.
STEPHANO: Trinculo, keep a good tongue in your head.
    If you prove a mutineer — the next tree!° The poor
    monster's my subject, and he shall not suffer
    indignity.
CALIBAN: I thank my noble lord. Wilt thou be
40   pleased
    To hearken once again to the suit I made to
    thee?
STEPHANO: Marry,° will I. Kneel and repeat it. I will
    stand, and so shall Trinculo.   [*Caliban kneels.*]

(*Enter Ariel, invisible.°*)

CALIBAN: As I told thee before, I am subject to a
    tyrant,
45   A sorcerer, that by his cunning hath
    Cheated me of the island.
ARIEL [*mimicking Trinculo*]: Thou liest.
CALIBAN: Thou liest, thou jesting monkey, thou!
    I would my valiant master would destroy thee.
    I do not lie.
50 STEPHANO: Trinculo, if you trouble him any more in
    's tale, by this hand, I will supplant° some of your
    teeth.
TRINCULO: Why, I said nothing.
STEPHANO: Mum, then, and no more. — Proceed.
55 CALIBAN: I say by sorcery he got this isle;
    From me he got it. If thy greatness will
    Revenge it on him — for I know thou dar'st,
    But this thing° dare not —
STEPHANO: That's most certain.
60 CALIBAN: Thou shalt be lord of it, and I'll serve
    thee.

STEPHANO: How now shall this be compassed?°
    Canst thou bring me to the party?
CALIBAN: Yea, yea, my lord. I'll yield him thee
    asleep,
    Where thou mayst knock a nail into his head.
ARIEL: Thou liest; thou canst not.   65
CALIBAN: What a pied ninny's° this! Thou scurvy
    patch!° —
    I do beseech thy greatness, give him blows
    And take his bottle from him. When that's gone
    He shall drink naught but brine, for I'll not
    show him
    Where the quick freshes° are.   70
STEPHANO: Trinculo, run into no further danger. In-
    terrupt the monster one word further° and, by this
    hand, I'll turn my mercy out o' doors° and make
    a stockfish° of thee.
TRINCULO: Why, what did I? I did nothing. I'll go   75
    farther off.°
STEPHANO: Didst thou not say he lied?
ARIEL: Thou liest.
STEPHANO: Do I so? Take thou that. [*He beats Trin-
    culo.*] As you like this, give me the lie° another   80
    time.
TRINCULO: I did not give the lie. Out o' your wits
    and hearing too? A pox o' your bottle! This can
    sack and drinking do. A murrain° on your monster,
    and the devil take your fingers!   85
CALIBAN: Ha, ha, ha!
STEPHANO: Now, forward with your tale. [*To
    Trinculo.*] Prithee, stand further off.
CALIBAN: Beat him enough. After a little time
    I'll beat him too.
STEPHANO: Stand farther. — Come, proceed.   90
CALIBAN: Why, as I told thee, 'tis a custom with
    him
    I' th' afternoon to sleep. There thou mayst brain
    him,
    Having first seized his books; or with a log
    Batter his skull, or paunch° him with a stake,
    Or cut his weasand° with thy knife. Remember   95
    First to possess his books, for without them
    He's but a sot,° as I am, nor hath not
    One spirit to command. They all do hate him
    As rootedly as I. Burn but his books.
    He has brave utensils° — for so he calls them —   100

Which, when he has a house, he'll deck withal.°
And that most deeply to consider is
The beauty of his daughter. He himself
Calls her a nonpareil. I never saw a woman
But only Sycorax my dam and she;   105
But she as far surpasseth Sycorax
As great'st does least.

STEPHANO: Is it so brave° a lass?

CALIBAN: Ay, lord. She will become° thy bed, I
warrant,
And bring thee forth brave brood.   110

STEPHANO: Monster, I will kill this man. His daughter and I will be king and queen — save Our
Graces! — and Trinculo and thyself shall be vice-
roys. Dost thou like the plot, Trinculo?

TRINCULO: Excellent.   115

STEPHANO: Give me thy hand. I am sorry I beat thee;
but, while thou liv'st, keep a good tongue in thy
head.

CALIBAN: Within this half hour will he be asleep.
Wilt thou destroy him then?   120

STEPHANO: Ay, on mine honor.

ARIEL [aside]: This will I tell my master.

CALIBAN: Thou mak'st me merry; I am full of
pleasure.
Let us be jocund.° Will you troll the catch°
You taught me but whilere?°   125

STEPHANO: At thy request, monster, I will do reason,
any reason.° Come on, Trinculo, let us sing.
(Sings.)
"Flout° 'em and scout° 'em
And scout 'em and flout 'em!
Thought is free."   130

CALIBAN: That's not the tune.
(Ariel plays the tune on a tabor° and pipe.)

STEPHANO: What is this same?

TRINCULO: This is the tune of our catch, played by
the picture of Nobody.°

STEPHANO: If thou beest a man, show thyself in thy   135
likeness. If thou beest a devil, take 't as thou list.°

TRINCULO: O, forgive me my sins!

STEPHANO: He that dies pays all debts. I defy thee.
Mercy upon us!

CALIBAN: Art thou afeard?   140

STEPHANO: No, monster, not I.

CALIBAN: Be not afeard. The isle is full of noises,
Sounds, and sweet airs, that give delight and
hurt not.
Sometimes a thousand twangling instruments
Will hum about mine ears, and sometimes voices   145
That, if I then had waked after long sleep,
Will make me sleep again; and then, in
dreaming,
The clouds methought would open and show
riches
Ready to drop upon me, that when I waked
I cried to dream° again.   150

STEPHANO: This will prove a brave kingdom to me,
where I shall have my music for nothing.

CALIBAN: When Prospero is destroyed.

STEPHANO: That shall be by and by.° I remember the
story.   155

TRINCULO: The sound is going away. Let's follow it,
and after do our work.

STEPHANO: Lead, monster; we'll follow. I would I
could see this taborer! He lays it on.°

TRINCULO: Wilt come? I'll follow Stephano.   160
(Exeunt [following Ariel's music].)

Scene III°

(Enter Alonso, Sebastian, Antonio, Gonzalo, Adrian,
Francisco, etc.)

GONZALO: By 'r lakin,° I can go no further, sir.
My old bones aches. Here's a maze trod indeed
Through forthrights and meanders!° By your
patience,
I needs must° rest me.

ALONSO: Old lord, I cannot blame thee,
Who am myself attached° with weariness,   5
To the dulling of my spirits.° Sit down and rest.
Even here I will put off my hope, and keep it
No longer for° my flatterer. He is drowned
Whom thus we stray to find, and the sea mocks
Our frustrate° search on land. Well, let him go.   10
[Alonso and Gonzalo sit.]

ANTONIO [aside to Sebastian]: I am right° glad that
he's so out of hope.°
Do not, for° one repulse, forgo the purpose

---

101. **deck withal:** Furnish it with.   108. **brave:** Splendid,
attractive.   109. **become:** Suit.   124. **jocund:** Jovial, merry.
troll the catch: Sing the round.   125. **but whilere:** Only a
short time ago.   126–27. **reason, any reason:** Anything reasonable.   128. **Flout:** Scoff at.   **scout:** Deride.   131. [S.D.]
tabor: Small drum.   134. **picture of Nobody:** Refers to a
familiar figure with head, arms, and legs but no trunk.   136.
take 't . . . list: I.e., take my defiance as you please, as best
you can.

150. **to dream:** Desirous of dreaming.   154. **by and by:**
Very soon.   159. **lays it on:** I.e., plays the drum skillfully
and energetically.   **III, III. Location:** Another part of the
island.   1. **By 'r lakin:** By our Ladykin, by our Lady.   3.
forthrights and meanders: Paths straight and crooked.   4.
needs must: Have to.   5. **attached:** Seized.   6. **To . . . spirits:** To the point of being dull-spirited.   8. **for:** As.   10.
frustrate: Frustrated.   11. **right:** Very.   **out of hope:** Despairing, discouraged.   12. **for:** Because of.

That you resolved t' effect.
SEBASTIAN [*to Antonio*]:   The next advantage
     Will we take throughly.°
ANTONIO [*to Sebastian*]:   Let it be tonight,
15   For, now° they are oppressed with travel,° they
     Will not, nor cannot, use° such vigilance
     As when they are fresh.
SEBASTIAN [*to Antonio*]:   I say tonight. No more.
                    (*Solemn and strange music; and
                    Prospero on the top,° invisible.*)
ALONSO: What harmony is this? My good friends,
     hark!
GONZALO: Marvelous sweet music!

(*Enter several strange shapes, bringing in a banquet,
and dance about it with gentle actions of salutations;
and, inviting the King, etc., to eat, they depart.*)

ALONSO: Give us kind keepers,° heavens! What
20   were these?
SEBASTIAN: A living° drollery.° Now I will believe
     That there are unicorns; that in Arabia
     There is one tree, the phoenix'° throne, one phoenix
     At this hour reigning there.
ANTONIO: I'll believe both;
25   And what does else want credit,° come to me
     And I'll be sworn 'tis true. Travelers ne'er did
     lie,
     Thou fools at home condemn 'em.
GONZALO: If in Naples
     I should report this now, would they believe me
     If I should say I saw such islanders?
30   For, certes,° these are people of the island,
     Who though they are of monstrous shape, yet
     note,
     Their manners are more gentle, kind, than of
     Our human generation you shall find
     Many, nay, almost any.
PROSPERO [*aside*]:   Honest lord,
     Thou hast said well, for some of you there
35   present
     Are worse than devils.
ALONSO: I cannot too much muse°
     Such shapes, such gesture, and such sound,
     expressing —

14. **throughly:** Thoroughly.   15. **now:** Now that.   **travel:**
Spelled *trauaile* in the Folio and carrying the sense of labor
as well as traveling.   16. **use:** Apply.   17. [S.D.] *on the
top:* At some high point of the tiring-house or the theater,
on a third level above the gallery.   20. **kind keepers:** Guardian angels.   21. **living:** With live actors.   **drollery:** Comic
entertainment, caricature, puppet show.   23. **phoenix:**
Mythical bird consumed to ashes every five to six hundred
years only to be renewed into another cycle.   25. **want
credit:** Lack credence.   30. **certes:** Certainly.   36. **muse:**
Wonder at.

Although they want° the use of tongue — a kind
     Of excellent dumb discourse.
PROSPERO [*aside*]:   Praise in departing.°
FRANCISCO: They vanished strangely.
SEBASTIAN: No matter, since   40
     They have left their viands° behind, for we have
     stomachs.°
     Will 't please you taste of what is here?
ALONSO: Not I.
GONZALO: Faith, sir, you need not fear. When we
     were boys,
     Who would believe that there were
     mountaineers°
     Dewlapped° like bulls, whose throats had
     hanging at 'em   45
     Wallets° of flesh? Or that there were such men
     Whose heads stood in their breasts?° Which now
     we find
     Each putter-out of five for one° will bring us
     Good warrant° of.
ALONSO: I will stand to° and feed,
     Although my last° — no matter, since I feel   50
     The best° is past. Brother, my lord the Duke,
     Stand to, and do as we.
                    [*They approach the table.*]

(*Thunder and lightning. Enter Ariel, like a harpy,°
claps his wings upon the table, and with a quaint
device° the banquet vanishes.°*)

ARIEL: You are three men of sin, whom Destiny —
     That hath to° instrument this lower world
     And what is in 't — the never-surfeited sea   55
     Hath caused to belch up you, and on this island
     Where man doth not inhabit, you 'mongst men
     Being most unfit to live. I have made you mad;
     And even with suchlike valor° men hang and
     drown

38. **want:** Lack.   39. **Praise in departing:** I.e., save your
praise until the end of the performance (proverbial).   41.
viands: Provisions.   **stomachs:** Appetites.   44. **mountain-
eers:** Mountain dwellers.   45. **Dewlapped:** Having a dew-
lap, or fold of skin hanging from the neck, like cattle.   46.
Wallets: Pendent folds of skin, wattles.   47. **in their breasts:**
I.e., like the Anthropophagi described in *Othello*, I, III, 146.
48. **putter-out . . . one:** One who invests money or gambles
on the risks of travel on the condition that, if he returns
safely, he is to receive five times the amount deposited; hence,
any traveler.   49. **Good warrant:** Assurance.   **stand to:**
Fall to; take the risk.   50. **Although my last:** Even if this
were to be my last meal.   51. **best:** Best part of life.   52.
[S.D.] *harpy:* A fabulous monster with a woman's face and
breasts and a vulture's body, supposed to be a minister of
divine vengeance.   *quaint device:* Ingenious stage contrivance.   *the banquet vanishes:* I.e., the food vanishes, the table
remains until line 82.   54. **to:** I.e., as its.   59. **suchlike
valor:** I.e., the reckless valor derived from madness.

Their proper° selves.   [*Alonso, Sebastian, and*
                               Antonio draw their swords.]
60   You fools! I and my fellows
Are ministers of Fate. The elements
Of whom° your swords are tempered° may as
     well
Wound the loud winds, or with bemocked-at°
     stabs
Kill the still-closing° waters, as diminish
One dowl° that's in my plume. My fellow
65   ministers
Are like° invulnerable. If° you could hurt,
Your swords are now too massy° for your
     strengths
And will not be uplifted. But remember —
For that's my business to you — that you three
70 From Milan did supplant good Prospero;
Exposed unto the sea, which hath requit° it,
Him and his innocent child; for which foul deed
The powers, delaying, not forgetting, have
Incensed the seas and shores, yea, all the
     creatures,
75 Against your peace. Thee of thy son, Alonso,
They have bereft; and do pronounce by me
Lingering perdition,° worse than any death
Can be at once, shall step by step attend
You and your ways; whose° wraths to guard
     you from —
80 Which here, in this most desolate isle, else° falls
Upon your heads — is nothing° but heart's
     sorrow
And a clear° life ensuing.

(*He vanishes in thunder; then, to soft music, enter the
shapes again, and dance, with mocks and mows,° and
carrying out the table.*)

PROSPERO: Bravely° the figure of this harpy hast
     thou
     Performed, my Ariel; a grace it had devouring.°

Of my instruction hast thou nothing bated.°   85
In what thou hadst to say. So,° with good life°
And observation strange,° my meaner° ministers
Their several kinds° have done. My high charms
     work,
And these mine enemies are all knit up
In their distractions. They now are in my power;   90
And in these fits I leave them, while I visit
Young Ferdinand, whom they suppose is
     drowned,
And his and mine loved darling.   [*Exit above.*]
GONZALO: I' the name of something holy, sir, why°
     stand you
In this strange stare?
ALONSO: O, it° is monstrous, monstrous!   95
Methought the billows° spoke and told me of it;
The winds did sing it to me, and the thunder,
That deep and dreadful organ pipe, pronounced
The name of Prosper; it did bass my trespass.°
Therfor° my son i' th' ooze is bedded; and   100
I'll seek him deeper than e'er plummet°
     sounded,°
And with him there lie mudded.   (*Exit.*)
SEBASTIAN: But one fiend at a time,
     I'll fight their legions o'er.°
ANTONIO: I'll be thy second.
     (*Exeunt [Sebastian and Antonio].*)
GONZALO: All three of them are desperate.° Their
     great guilt,   105
Like poison given to work a great time after,
Now 'gins to bite the spirits.° I do beseech you
That are of suppler joints, follow them swiftly
And hinder them from what this ecstasy°
May now provoke them to.
ADRIAN: Follow, I pray you.   110
     (*Exeunt omnes.°*)

---

60. **proper:** Own. 62. **whom:** Which. **tempered:** Composed and hardened. 63. **bemocked-at:** Scorned. 64. **still-closing:** Always closing again when parted. 65. **dowl:** Soft, fine feather. 66. **like:** Likewise, similarly. **If:** Even if. 67. **massy:** Heavy. 71. **requit:** Requited, avenged. 77. **perdition:** Ruin, destruction. 79. **whose:** Refers to the heavenly powers. 80. **else:** Otherwise. 81. **is nothing:** There is no way. 82. **clear:** Unspotted, innocent. [S.D.] *mocks and mows:* Mocking gestures and grimaces. 83. **Bravely:** Finely, dashingly. 84. **a grace . . . devouring:** I.e., you gracefully caused the banquet to disappear as if you had consumed it (with puns on *grace* meaning "gracefulness" and "a blessing on the meal" and on *devouring* meaning "a literal eating" and "an all-consuming or ravishing grace").

85. **bated:** Abated, omitted. 86. **So:** In the same fashion. **good life:** Faithful reproduction. 87. **observation strange:** Exceptional attention to detail. **meaner:** I.e., subordinate to Ariel. 88. **several kinds:** Individual parts. 94. **why:** Gonzalo was not addressed in Ariel's speech to the *three men of sin,* (line 53) and is not, as they are, in a maddened state; see lines 105–7. 95. **it:** I.e., my sin (also in line 96). 96. **billows:** Waves. 99. **bass my trespass:** Proclaim my trespass like a bass note in music. 100. **Therfor:** In consequence of that. 101. **plummet:** A lead weight attached to a line for testing depth. **sounded:** Probed, tested the depth of. 104. **o'er:** One after another. 105. **desperate:** Despairing and reckless. 107. **bite the spirits:** Sap their vital powers through anguish. 109. **ecstasy:** mad frenzy. 110. [S.D.] *omnes:* Latin for "all."

ACT IV • Scene I

(*Enter Prospero, Ferdinand, and Miranda.*)

PROSPERO: If I have too austerely° punished you,
    Your compensation makes amends, for I
    Have given you here a third° of mine own life,
    Or that for which I live; who once again
5   I tender to thy hand. All thy vexations°
    Were but my trials of thy love, and thou
    Hast strangely° stood the test. Here, afore
        Heaven,
    I ratify this my rich gift. O Ferdinand,
    Do not smile at me that I boast her off,°
10   For thou shalt find she will outstrip all praise
    And make it halt° behind her.
FERDINAND: I do believe it
    Against an oracle.°
PROSPERO: Then, as my gift and thine own
        acquisition
    Worthily purchased, take my daughter. But
15   If thou dost break her virgin-knot before
    All sanctimonious° ceremonies may
    With full and holy rite be ministered,
    No sweet aspersion° shall the heavens let fall
    To make this contract grow; but barren hate,
20   Sour-eyed disdain, and discord shall bestrew
    The union of your bed with weeds° so loathly
    That you shall hate it both. Therefore take heed,
    As Hymen's lamps shall light you.°
FERDINAND: As I hope
    For quiet days, fair issue,° and long life,
25   With such love as 'tis now, the murkiest den,
    The most opportune place, the strong'st
        suggestion°
    Our worser genius° can,° shall never melt
    Mine honor into lust, to° take away

    The edge° of that day's celebration
    When I shall think or° Phoebus' steeds are
        foundered°   30
    Or Night kept chained below.
PROSPERO: Fairly spoke.
    Sit then and talk with her. She is thine own.
    [*Ferdinand and Miranda sit and talk together.*]
    What,° Ariel! My industrious servant, Ariel!

(*Enter Ariel.*)

ARIEL: What would my potent master? Here I am.
PROSPERO: Thou and thy meaner fellows° your last
        service   35
    Did worthily perform, and I must use you
    In such another trick.° Go bring the rabble,°
    O'er whom I give thee power, here to this place.
    Incite them to quick motion, for I must
    Bestow upon the eyes of this young couple   40
    Some vanity° of mine art. It is my promise,
    And they expect it from me.
ARIEL: Presently?°
PROSPERO: Ay, with a twink.°
ARIEL: Before you can say "Come" and "Go,"
    And breathe twice, and cry "So, so,"   45
    Each one, tripping on his toe,
    Will be here with mop and mow.°
    Do you love me, master? No?
PROSPERO: Dearly, my delicate Ariel. Do not
        approach
    Till thou dost hear me call.
ARIEL: Well, I conceive.°   50
                                 (*Exit*)
PROSPERO: Look thou be true;° do not give
        dalliance
    Too much the rein. The strongest oaths are
        straw
    To the fire i' the blood. Be more abstemious,
    Or else good night° your vow!
FERDINAND: I warrant° you, sir,
    The white cold virgin snow upon my heart°   55
    Abates the ardor of my liver.°

IV, I. **Location:** Before Prospero's cell. **1. austerely:** Severely. **3. a third:** I.e., Miranda, into whose education Prospero has put a third of his life (?) or who represents a large part of what he cares about, along with his dukedom and his learned study (?). **5. vexations:** Torments. **7. strangely:** Extraordinarily. **9. boast her off:** I.e., praise her so; or perhaps an error for "boast of her"; the Folio reads "boast her of." **11. halt:** Limp. **12. Against an oracle:** I.e., even if an oracle should declare otherwise. **16. sanctimonious:** Sacred. **18. aspersion:** Dew, shower. **21. weeds:** In place of the flowers customarily strewn on the marriage bed. **23. As . . . you:** I.e., as you long for happiness and concord in your marriage. (Hymen was the Greek and Roman god of marriage; his symbolic torches, the wedding torches, were supposed to burn brightly for a happy marriage, smokily for a troubled one.) **24. issue:** Offspring. **26. suggestion:** Temptation. **27. worser genius:** Evil genius, or evil attendant spirit. **can:** Is capable of. **28. to:** So as to.

29. edge: Keen enjoyment, sexual ardor. **30. or:** either. **foundered:** Broken down, made lame. (Ferdinand will wait impatiently for the bridal night.) **33. What:** Now then. **35. meaner fellows:** Subordinates. **37. trick:** Device. **rabble:** Band, i.e., the *meaner fellows* of line 35. **41. vanity:** (1) Illusion, (2) trifle, (3) desire for admiration, conceit. **42. Presently:** Immediately. **43. with a twink:** In the twinkling of an eye, in an instant. **47. mop and mow:** Gestures and grimaces. **50. conceive:** Understand. **51. true:** True to your promise. **54. good night:** I.e., say good-bye to. **warrant:** Guarantee. **55. The white . . . heart:** I.e., the ideal of chastity and consciousness of Miranda's chaste innocence enshrined in my heart. **56. liver:** As the presumed seat of the passions.

PROSPERO: Well.
    Now come, my Ariel! Bring a corollary,°
    Rather than want° a spirit. Appear, and
      pertly!° —
    No tongue!° All eyes! Be silent.   (*Soft music.*)

(*Enter Iris.°*)

60 IRIS: Ceres,° most bounteous lady, thy rich leas°
    Of wheat, rye, barley, vetches,° oats, and peas;
    Thy turfy mountains, where live nibbling sheep,
    And flat meads° thatched with stover,° them to
      keep;
    Thy banks with pionèd and twillèd° brims,
65   Which spongy° April at thy hest betrims
    To make cold nymphs chaste crowns; and thy
      broom groves,°
    Whose shadow the dismissèd bachelor° loves,
    Being lass-lorn; thy poll-clipped° vineyard;
    And thy sea marge,° sterile and rocky hard,
    Where thou thyself dost air: the queen o' the
70   sky,°
    Whose watery arch° and messenger am I,
    Bids thee leave these, and with her sovereign
      grace,
           (*Juno descends°* [*slowly in her car*].)
    Here on this grass plot, in this very place,
    To come and sport. Her peacocks° fly amain.°
75   Approach, rich Ceres, her to entertain.°

(*Enter Ceres.*)

CERES: Hail, many-colored messenger, that ne'er
    Dost disobey the wife of Jupiter,
    Who with thy saffron° wings upon my flowers
    Diffusest honeydrops, refreshing showers,
80   And with each end of thy blue bow° dost crown
    My bosky° acres and my unshrubbed down,°

Rich scarf to my proud earth. Why hath thy
    queen
    Summoned me hither to this short-grassed green?
IRIS: A contract of true love to celebrate,
    And some donation freely to estate°   85
    On the blest lovers.
CERES: Tell me, heavenly bow,
    If Venus or her son,° as° thou dost know,
    Do now attend the Queen? Since they did plot
    The means that dusky° Dis my daughter got,°
    Her° and her blind boy's scandaled° company   90
    I have forsworn.
IRIS: Of her society°
    Be not afraid. I met her deity°
    Cutting the clouds towards Paphos,° and her son
    Dove-drawn° with her. Here thought they to
      have done°
    Some wanton charm° upon this man and maid,   95
    Whose vows are that no bed-right shall be paid
    Till Hymen's torch be lighted; but in vain.
    Mars's hot minion° is returned° again;
    Her waspish-headed° son has broke his arrows,
    Swears he will shoot no more, but play with
      sparrows°   100
    And be a boy right out.°

[*Juno alights.*]

CERES: Highest Queen of state,°
    Great Juno, comes; I know her by her gait.°
JUNO: How does my bounteous sister? Go with me
    To bless this twain, that they may prosperous be
    And honored in their issue.°   (*They sing.*)   105

JUNO: Honor, riches, marriage blessing,
    Long continuance, and increasing,
    Hourly joys be still° upon you!
    Juno sings her blessings on you.
CERES: Earth's increase, foison plenty,°   110
    Barns and garners° never empty,

---

57. **corollary:** Surplus, extra supply. 58. **want:** Lack.
pertly: Briskly. 59. **No tongue:** All the beholders are to be
silent (lest the spirits vanish). [S.D.] **Iris:** Goddess of the
rainbow and Juno's messenger. 60. **Ceres:** Goddess of the
generative power of nature. **leas:** Meadows. 61. **vetches:**
Plants for forage, fodder. 63. **meads:** Meadows. **stover:**
Winter fodder for cattle. 64. **pionèd and twillèd:** Undercut
by the swift current and protected by roots and branches
that tangle to form a barricade. 65. **spongy:** Wet. 66.
broom groves: Clumps of broom, gorse, yellow-flowered
shrub. 67. **dismissèd bachelor:** Rejected male lover. 68.
poll-clipped: Pruned, looped at the top, or *pole-clipped*,
hedged in with poles. 69. **sea marge:** Shore. 70. **queen
o' the sky:** I.e., Juno. 71. **watery arch:** Rainbow. 72.
[S.D.] **Juno descends:** I.e., starts her descent from the "heavens" above the stage (?). 74. **peacocks:** Birds sacred to
Juno and used to pull her chariot. **amain:** With full speed.
75. **entertain:** Receive. 78. **saffron:** Yellow. 80. **bow:** I.e.,
rainbow. 81. **bosky:** Wooded. **down:** Upland.

85. **estate:** Bestow. 87. **son:** I.e., Cupid. **as:** As far as.
89. **dusky:** Dark. **Dis . . . got:** Pluto, or *Dis*, god of the
infernal regions, carried off Persephone, daughter of Ceres,
to be his bride in Hades. 90. **Her:** I.e., Venus's. **scandaled:**
Scandalous. 91. **society:** Company. 92. **her deity:** I.e.,
Her Highness. 93. **Paphos:** Place on the island of Cyprus,
sacred to Venus. 94. **Dove-drawn:** Venus's chariot was
drawn by doves. **done:** Placed. 95. **wanton charm:** Lustful spell. 98. **Mars's hot minion:** I.e., Venus, the beloved
of Mars. **returned:** I.e., returned to Paphos. 99. **waspish-
headed:** Fiery, hotheaded, peevish. 100. **sparrows:** Supposed lustful, and sacred to Venus. 101. **right out:** Outright. **Highest . . . state:** Most majestic Queen. 102. **gait:**
I.e., majestic bearing. 105. **issue:** Offspring. 108. **still:**
Always. 110. **foison plenty:** Plentiful harvest. 111. **gar-
ners:** Granaries.

Vines with clustering bunches growing,
Plants with goodly burden bowing;

115   Spring come to you at the farthest
In the very end of harvest!°
Scarcity and want shall shun you;
Ceres' blessing so is on you.
FERDINAND: This is a most majestic vision, and
Harmonious charmingly.° May I be bold
To think these spirits?
120 PROSPERO: Spirits, which by mine art
I have from their confines called to enact
My present fancies.
FERDINAND: Let me live here ever!
So rare a wondered° father and a wife
Makes this place Paradise.
    (*Juno and Ceres whisper, and send Iris on
employment.*)
PROSPERO: Sweet now, silence!
125 Juno and Ceres whisper seriously;
There's something else to do. Hush and be mute,
Or else our spell is marred.
IRIS: You nymphs, called naiads,° of the windring°
brooks,
With your sedged° crowns and ever-harmless°
looks,
Leave your crisp° channels, and on this green
130 land
Answer your summons; Juno does command.
Come, temperate° nymphs, and help to celebrate
A contract of true love. Be not too late.

(*Enter certain nymphs.*)

You sunburnt sicklemen,° of August weary,°
135 Come hither from the furrow° and be merry.
Make holiday; your rye-straw hats put on,
And these fresh nymphs encounter° every one
In country footing.°

(*Enter certain reapers, properly° habited. They join
with the nymphs in a graceful dance, toward the end
whereof Prospero starts suddenly, and speaks; after
which, to a strange, hollow, and confused noise, they
heavily° vanish.*)

PROSPERO [*aside*]: I had forgot that foul conspiracy
Of the beast Caliban and his confederates   140
Against my life. The minute of their plot
Is almost come. [*To the Spirits.*] Well done!
Avoid;° no more!
FERDINAND [*to Miranda*]: This is strange. Your
father's in some passion
That works° him strongly.
MIRANDA: Never till this day
Saw I him touched with anger so distempered. 145
PROSPERO: You do look, my son, in a moved sort,°
As if you were dismayed. Be cheerful, sir.
Our revels° now are ended. These our actors,
As I foretold you, were all spirits and
Are melted into air, into thin air;   150
And, like the baseless° fabric of this vision,
The cloud-capped towers, the gorgeous palaces,
The solemn temples, the great globe° itself,
Yea, all which it inherit,° shall dissolve,
And, like this insubstantial pageant faded,
Leave not a rack° behind. We are such stuff 155
As dreams are made on,° and our little life
Is rounded° with a sleep. Sir, I am vexed.
Bear with° my weakness. My old brain is
troubled.
Be not disturbed with my infirmity.   160
If you be pleased, retire° into my cell
And there repose. A turn or two I'll walk
To still my beating° mind.
FERDINAND, MIRANDA: We wish your peace.
    (*Exeunt [Ferdinand and Miranda].*)
PROSPERO: Come with a thought!° I thank thee,
Ariel. Come.

(*Enter Ariel.*)

ARIEL: Thy thoughts I cleave° to. What's thy
pleasure?
PROSPERO: Spirit,   165
We must prepare to meet with Caliban.
ARIEL: Ay, my commander. When I presented°
Ceres,
I thought to have told thee of it, but I feared
Lest I might anger thee.

---

115. **In . . . harvest:** I.e., with no winter in between.   119. **charmingly:** Enchantingly.   123. **wondered:** Wonder-performing, wondrous.   128. **naiads:** Nymphs of springs, rivers, or lakes.   **windring:** wandering, winding (?).   129. **sedged:** Made of reeds.   **ever-harmless:** Ever-innocent.   130. **crisp:** Curled, rippled.   132. **temperate:** Chaste.   134. **sicklemen:** Harvesters, field workers who cut down grain and grass.   **weary:** I.e., weary of the hard work of the harvest.   135. **furrow:** I.e., plowed fields.   137. **encounter:** Join.   138. **country footing:** Country dancing.   [S.D.] *properly:* Suitably.   *heavily:* Slowly, dejectedly.

142. **Avoid:** Depart, withdraw.   144. **works:** Affects, agitates.   146. **moved sort:** Troubled state, condition.   148. **revels:** Entertainment, pageant.   151. **baseless:** Without substance.   153. **great globe:** With a glance at the Globe Theatre.   154. **which it inherit:** Who subsequently occupy it.   156. **rack:** Wisp of cloud.   157. **on:** Of.   158. **rounded:** Surrounded, or crowned, rounded off.   159. **with:** By.   161. **retire:** Withdraw, go.   163. **beating:** Agitated.   164. **with a thought:** I.e., on the instant, or summoned by my thought, no sooner thought of than here.   165. **cleave:** Cling, adhere.   167. **presented:** Acted the part of, or introduced.

PROSPERO: Say again, where didst thou leave these
⁷⁰   varlets?
ARIEL: I told you, sir, they were red-hot with
      drinking,
   So full of valor that they smote the air
   For breathing in their faces, beat the ground
   For kissing of their feet, yet always bending°
⁷⁵ Towards their project. Then I beat my tabor,
   At which, like unbacked° colts, they pricked
      their ears,
   Advanced° their eyelids, lifted up their noses
   As° they smelt music. So I charmed their ears
   That calflike they my lowing° followed through
⁸⁰ Toothed briers, sharp furzes, pricking gorse,° and
      thorns,
   Which entered their frail shins. At last I left
      them
   I' the filthy-mantled° pool beyond your cell,
   There dancing up to the chins, that the foul lake
   O'erstunk° their feet.
PROSPERO: This was well done, my bird.
⁸⁵ Thy shape invisible retain thou still.
   The trumpery° in my house, go bring it hither,
   For stale° to catch these thieves.
ARIEL: I go, I go. (Exit.)
PROSPERO: A devil, a born devil, on whose nature
   Nurture can never stick; on whom my pains,
⁹⁰ Humanely taken, all, all lost, quite lost!
   And as with age his body uglier grows,
   So his mind cankers.° I will plague them all,
   Even to roaring.

(Enter Ariel, loaden with glistering apparel, etc.)

                     Come, hang them on this line.°

([Ariel hangs up the showy finery; Prospero and Ariel
remain,° invisible.] Enter Caliban, Stephano, and Trinculo, all wet.)

CALIBAN: Pray you, tread softly, that the blind mole
      may
⁹⁵ Not hear a footfall. We now are near his cell.

STEPHANO: Monster, your fairy, which you say is a
   harmless fairy, has done little better than played
   the jack° with us.
TRINCULO: Monster, I do smell all horse piss, at which
   my nose is in great indignation.   ²⁰⁰
STEPHANO: So is mine. Do you hear, monster? If I
   should take a displeasure against you, look you —
TRINCULO: Thou wert but a lost monster.
CALIBAN: Good my lord, give me thy favor still.
   Be patient, for the prize I'll bring thee to   ²⁰⁵
   Shall hoodwink° this mischance.° Therefore
      speak softly.
   All's hushed as midnight yet.
TRINCULO: Ay, but to lose our bottles in the pool —
STEPHANO: There is not only disgrace and dishonor
   in that, monster, but an infinite loss.   ²¹⁰
TRINCULO: That's more to me than my wetting. Yet
   this is your harmless fairy, monster!
STEPHANO: I will fetch off my bottle, though I be o'er
   ears° for my labor.
CALIBAN: Prithee, my king, be quiet. Seest thou
      here,   ²¹⁵
   This is the mouth o' the cell. No noise, and
      enter.
   Do that good mischief which may make this
      island
   Thine own forever, and I thy Caliban
   For aye thy footlicker.
STEPHANO: Give me thy hand. I do begin to have   ²²⁰
   bloody thoughts.
TRINCULO [seeing the finery]: O King Stephano! O
   peer!° O worthy Stephano! Look what a wardrobe
   here is for thee!
CALIBAN: Let it alone, thou fool, it is but trash.   ²²⁵
TRINCULO: Oho, monster! We know what belongs to
   a frippery.° O King Stephano! [He takes a gown.]
STEPHANO: Put off° that gown, Trinculo. By this hand,
   I'll have that gown.
TRINCULO: Thy Grace shall have it.   ²³⁰
CALIBAN: The dropsy° drown this fool! What do
      you mean
   To dote thus on such luggage?° Let 't alone
   And do the murder first. If he awake,
   From toe to crown° he'll fill our skins with
      pinches,

174. bending: Aiming.   176. unbacked: Unbroken, unrid-
den.   177. Advanced: Lifted up.   178. As: As if.   179.
lowing: Mooing.   180. furzes . . . gorse: Prickly shrubs.
182. filthy-mantled: Covered with a slimy coating.   184.
O'erstunk: Smelled worse than, or caused to stink terribly.
186. trumpery: Cheap goods, the glistering apparel mentioned in the following stage direction.   187. stale: (1) Decoy, (2) out-of-fashion garments (with possible further suggestions of fit for a stale or prostitute, stale meaning "horse
piss," line 199, and steal, pronounced like stale).   192.
cankers: Festers, grows malignant.   193. line: Lime tree or
linden.   [S.D.] Prospero and Ariel remain: The staging is
uncertain. They may instead exit here and return with the
spirits at line 256.

198. jack: (1) Knave, (2) will-o'-the wisp.   206. hoodwink:
Cover up, make you not see (a hawking term).   mischance:
Mishap, misfortune.   213–14. o'er ears: I.e., totally submerged and perhaps drowned.   222–23. King . . . peer:
Alludes to the old ballad beginning "King Stephen was a
worthy peer."   227. frippery: Place where cast-off clothes
are sold.   228. Put off: Put down, or take off.   231. dropsy:
Disease characterized by the accumulation of fluid in the
connective tissue of the body.   232. luggage: Cumbersome
trash.   234. crown: Head.

235   Make us strange stuff.
STEPHANO: Be you quiet, monster. — Mistress line,°
is not this my jerkin?° [*He takes it down.*] Now is
the jerkin under the line.° Now, jerkin, you are
like° to lose your hair and prove a bald° jerkin.

236. **Mistress line:** Addressed to the linden or lime tree upon
which, at line 193, Ariel hung the *glistering apparel*.   237.
jerkin: Jacket made of leather.   238. **under the line:** Under
the lime tree (with punning sense of being south of the equi-
noctial line or equator; sailors on long voyages to the southern regions were popularly supposed to lose their hair from
scurvy or other diseases. Stephano also quibbles bawdily on
losing hair through syphilis, and in *Mistress* and *jerkin*).
239. **like:** Likely.   **bald:** (1) Hairless, napless, (2) meager.

TRINCULO: Do, do!° We steal by line and level,° an 't   240
like° Your Grace.
STEPHANO: I thank thee for that jest. Here's a garment
for 't. [*He gives a garment.*] Wit shall not go unrewarded while I am king of this country. "Steal by
line and level" is an excellent pass of pate.° There's   245
another garment for 't.

240. **Do, do:** I.e., bravo. (Said in response to the jesting or
to the taking of the jerkin, or both.)   **by line and level:** I.e.,
by means of plumb line and carpenter's level, methodically
(with pun on *line*, "lime tree," line 238, and *steal*, pronounced like *stale*, i.e., prostitute, continuing Stephano's
bawdy quibble).   240–41. **an 't like:** If it please.   245.
pass of pate: Sally of wit. (The metaphor is from fencing.)

RIGHT: Ferdinand (Boyd
Gaines) and Miranda (Frances
Conroy) in the 1981 Guthrie
Theater production of *The
Tempest*, directed by Liviu
Ciulei. FAR RIGHT: Prospero,
right front, reflects on his
handiwork in the masque scene
from *The Tempest*.

TRINCULO: Monster, come, put some lime° upon your
    fingers, and away with the rest.
CALIBAN: I will have none on 't. We shall lose our
    time,
    And all be turned to barnacles,° or to apes
    With foreheads villainous° low.
STEPHANO: Monster, lay to° your fingers. Help to bear

this° away where my hogshead° of wine is, or I'll
    turn you out of my kingdom. Go to,° carry this.
TRINCULO: And this.   255
STEPHANO: Ay, and this.
    [*They load Caliban with more and more garments.*]

(*A noise of hunters heard. Enter divers spirits, in shape
of dogs and hounds, hunting them about, Prospero
and Ariel setting them on.*)

PROSPERO: Hey, Mountain, hey!
ARIEL: Silver! There it goes, Silver!

247. lime: Birdlime, sticky substance (to give Caliban sticky
fingers).   **250. barnacles:** Barnacle geese, formerly supposed
to be hatched from seashells attached to trees and to fall
thence into the water; here evidently used, like *apes*, as types
of simpletons.   **251. villainous:** Miserably.   **252. lay to:**
Start using.

253. this: I.e., the *glistering apparel.*   **hogshead:** Large cask.
254. Go to: An expression of exhortation or remonstrance.

PROSPERO: Fury, Fury! There, Tyrant, there! Hark! Hark!

[*Caliban, Stephano, and Trinculo are driven out.*]

Go, charge my goblins that they grind their

260   joints

With dry° convulsions,° shorten up their sinews

With agèd° cramps, and more pinch-spotted make them

Than pard° or cat o' mountain.°

ARIEL: Hark, they roar!

PROSPERO: Let them be hunted soundly.° At this hour

265   Lies at my mercy all mine enemies.

Shortly shall all my labors end, and thou

Shalt have the air at freedom. For a little°

Follow, and do me service.   (*Exeunt.*)

ACT V • *Scene 1*°

(*Enter Prospero in his magic robes, [with his staff,] and Ariel.*)

PROSPERO: Now does my project gather to a head.

My charms crack° not, my spirits obey, and Time

Goes upright with his carriage.° How's the day?

ARIEL: On° the sixth hour, at which time, my lord,

You said our work should cease.

5 PROSPERO: I did say so,

When first I raised the tempest. Say, my spirit,

How fares the King and 's followers?

ARIEL: Confined together

In the same fashion as you gave in charge,

Just as you left them; all prisoners, sir,

10   In the line grove° which weather-fends° your cell.

They cannot budge till your release.° The King,

His brother, and yours abide all three distracted,°

And the remainder mourning over them,

Brim full of sorrow and dismay; but chiefly

Him that you termed, sir, the good old lord,

15   Gonzalo.

His tears runs down his beard like winter's drops

From eaves of reeds.° Your charm so strongly works 'em

That if you now beheld them your affections°

Would become tender.

PROSPERO: Dost thou think so, spirit?

ARIEL: Mine would, sir, were I human.

PROSPERO: And mine shall. 20

Hast thou, which art but air, a touch° a feeling

Of their afflictions, and shall not myself,

One of their kind, that relish all as sharply

Passion as they,° be kindlier° moved than thou art?

Though with their high wrongs I am struck to the quick,   25

Yet with my nobler reason 'gainst my fury

Do I take part. The rarer° action is

In virtue than in vengeance. They being penitent,

The sole drift of my purpose doth extend

Not a frown further. Go release them, Ariel.   30

My charms I'll break, their senses I'll restore,

And they shall be themselves.

ARIEL: I'll fetch them, sir.

                            (*Exit.*)

[*Prospero traces a charmed circle with his staff.*]

PROSPERO: Ye elves of hills, brooks, standing lakes, and groves,°

And ye that on the sands with printless foot

Do chase the ebbing Neptune, and do fly him   35

When he comes back; you demi-puppets° that

By moonshine do the green sour ringlets° make,

Whereof the ewe not bites; and you whose pastime

Is to make midnight mushrooms,° that rejoice

To hear the solemn curfew,° by whose aid,   40

Weak masters though ye be, I have bedimmed

The noontide sun, called forth the mutinous winds,

And twixt the green sea and the azured vault°

---

261. **dry:** Associated with age, arthritic (?). **convulsions:** Cramps. 262. **agèd:** Characteristic of old age. 263. **pard:** Panther or leopard. **cat o' mountain:** Wildcat. 264. **soundly:** Thoroughly. 267. **little:** Little while longer. V, I. **Location:** Before Prospero's cell. 2. **crack:** Collapse, fail. (The metaphor is probably alchemical, as in *project* and *gather to a head*, line 1.) 3. **his carriage:** Its burden. (Time is no longer heavily burdened and so can go *upright*, standing straight and unimpeded.) 4. **On:** Approaching. 10. **line grove:** Grove of lime trees. **weather-fends:** Protects from the weather. 11. **your release:** You release them. 12. **distracted:** Out of their wits.

17. **eaves of reeds:** Thatched roofs. 18. **affections:** Feelings. 21. **touch:** Sense, feeling. 23–24. **that . . . they:** I.e., I who am just as sensitive to suffering as they. 24. **kindlier:** (1) More sympathetically, (2) more naturally, humanly. 27. **rarer:** Nobler. 33–50. **Ye . . . art:** This famous passage is an embellished paraphrase of Golding's translation of Ovid's *Metamorphoses*, 7. 197–219. 36. **demi-puppets:** Puppets of half size, i.e., elves and fairies. 37. **green sour ringlets:** Fairy rings, circles in grass (actually produced by mushrooms). 39. **midnight mushrooms:** Mushrooms appearing overnight. 40. **curfew:** Evening bell, usually rung at nine o'clock, ushering in the time when spirits are abroad. 43. **the azured vault:** I.e., the sky.

Set roaring war; to the dread rattling thunder
45 Have I given fire,° and rifted,° Jove's stout oak
With his own bolt;° the strong-based
        promontory
Have I made shake, and by the spurs° plucked
        up
The pine and cedar; graves at my command
Have waked their sleepers, oped, and let 'em
        forth
50 By my so potent art. But this rough° magic
I here abjure, and when I have required°
Some heavenly music — which even now I do —
To work mine end upon their senses that°
This airy charm° is for, I'll break my staff,
55 Bury it certain fathoms in the earth,
And deeper than did ever plummet sound
I'll drown my book.   (*Solemn music.*)

(*Here enters Ariel before; then Alonso, with a frantic
gesture, attended by Gonzalo; Sebastian and Antonio
in like manner, attended by Adrian and Francisco.
They all enter the circle which Prospero had made,
and there stand charmed; which Prospero observing,
speaks.*)

    [*To Alonso.*] A solemn air,° and° the best
        comforter
    To an unsettled fancy,° cure thy brains,
60 Now useless, boiled within thy skull! [*To
        Sebastian and Antonio.*] There stand,
    For you are spell-stopped. —
    Holy Gonzalo, honorable man,
    Mine eyes, e'en sociable° to the show° of thine,
    Fall° fellowly drops. [*Aside.*] The charm dissolves
        apace,
65 And as the morning steals upon the night,
    Melting the darkness, so their rising senses
    Begin to chase the ignorant fumes° that mantle°
    Their clearer° reason. — O good Gonzalo,
    My true preserver, and a loyal sir
70 To him thou follow'st! I will pay thy graces°
    Home° both in word and deed. — Most cruelly
    Didst thou, Alonso, use me and my daughter.
    Thy brother was a furtherer° in the act. —

Thou art pinched° for 't now, Sebastian. [*To
    Antonio.*] Flesh and blood,
You, brother mine, that entertained ambition,   75
Expelled remorse° and nature,° whom,° with
    Sebastian,
Whose inward pinches therefore are most strong,
Would here have killed your king, I do forgive
    thee,
Unnatural though thou art. — Their
    understanding
Begins to swell, and the approaching tide   80
Will shortly fill the reasonable shore°
That now lies foul and muddy. Not one of them
That yet looks on me, or would know me. —
    Ariel,
Fetch me the hat and rapier in my cell.
[*Ariel goes to the cell and returns immediately.*]
I will discase° me and myself present   85
As I was sometime Milan.° Quickly, spirit!
Thou shalt ere long be free.
                (*Ariel sings and helps to attire him.*)
ARIEL: Where the bee sucks, there suck I.
    In a cowslip's bell I lie;
    There I couch° when owls do cry.   90
    On the bat's back I do fly
    After° summer merrily.
Merrily, merrily shall I live now
Under the blossom that hangs on the bough.
PROSPERO: Why, that's my dainty Ariel! I shall miss
    thee,   95
But yet thou shalt have freedom. So, so, so.°
To the King's ship, invisible as thou art!
There shalt thou find the mariners asleep
Under the hatches. The Master and the
    Boatswain
Being awake, enforce them to this place,   100
And presently,° I prithee.
ARIEL: I drink the air before me and return
Or ere° your pulse twice beat.   (*Exit.*)
GONZALO: All torment, trouble, wonder, and
    amazement
Inhabits here. Some heavenly power guide us   105
Out of this fearful° country!
PROSPERO: Behold, sir King,
    The wrongèd Duke of Milan, Prospero.
    For more assurance that a living prince

44–45. **to . . . fire:** I have discharged the dread rattling thunderbolt.   45. **rifted:** Riven, split.   46. **bolt:** Lightning bolt.
47. **spurs:** Roots.   50. **rough:** Violent.   51. **required:** Requested.   53. **their senses that:** The senses of those whom.
54. **airy charm:** I.e., music.   58. **air:** Song.   **and:** I.e., which
is.   59. **fancy:** Imagination.   63. **sociable:** Sympathetic.
show: Appearance.   64. **Fall:** Let fall.   67. **ignorant fumes:**
Fumes that render them incapable of comprehension.   **mantle:** Envelop.   68. **clearer:** Growing clearer.   70. **pay thy
graces:** Reward your favors.   71. **Home:** Fully.   73. **fur-
therer:** Accomplice.

74. **pinched:** Punished, afflicted.   76. **remorse:** Pity.   **nature:** Natural feeling.   **whom:** I.e., who.   81. **reasonable
shore:** Shores of reason, i.e., minds. (Their reason returns,
like the incoming tide.)   85. **discase:** Disrobe.   86. **As . . .
Milan:** In my former appearance as Duke of Milan.   90.
couch: Lie.   92. **After:** I.e., pursuing.   96. **So, so, so:** Expresses approval of Ariel's help as valet.   101. **presently:**
Immediately.   103. **Or ere:** Before.   106. **fearful:**
Frightening.

Does now speak to thee, I embrace thy body;
110   And to thee and thy company I bid
A hearty welcome.   [*Embracing him.*]
ALONSO: Whe'er thou be'st he or no,
Or some enchanted trifle° to abuse° me,
As late° I have been, I not know. Thy pulse
Beats as of flesh and blood; and, since I saw thee,
115   Th' affliction of my mind amends, with which
I fear a madness held me. This must crave° —
An if this be at all° — a most strange story.°
Thy dukedom I resign,° and do entreat
Thou pardon me my wrongs.° But how should Prospero
Be living, and be here?
120   PROSPERO [*to Gonzalo*]:   First, noble friend,
Let me embrace thine age,° whose honor cannot
Be measured or confined.   [*Embracing him.*]
GONZALO: Whether this be
Or be not, I'll not swear.
PROSPERO: You do yet taste
Some subtleties° o' th' isle, that will not let you
125   Believe things certain. Welcome, my friends all!
[*Aside to Sebastian and Antonio.*] But you, my
brace° of lords, were I so minded,
I here could pluck His Highness' frown upon you
And justify you° traitors. At this time
I will tell no tales.
SEBASTIAN: The devil speaks in him.
PROSPERO: No.
[*To Antonio.*] For you, most wicked sir, whom
130   to call brother
Would even infect my mouth, I do forgive
Thy rankest fault — all of them; and require
My dukedom of thee, which perforce° I know
Thou must restore.
ALONSO: If thou be'st Prospero,
135   Give us particulars of thy preservation,
How thou hast met us here, whom° three hours since
Were wrecked upon this shore; where I have lost —
How sharp the point of this remembrance is! —
My dear son Ferdinand.

PROSPERO: I am woe° for 't, sir.
ALONSO: Irreparable is the loss, and Patience   140
Says it is past her cure.
PROSPERO: I rather think
You have not sought her help, of whose soft grace°
For the like loss I have her sovereign° aid
And rest myself content.
ALONSO: You the like loss?
PROSPERO: As great to me as late,° and supportable   145
To make the dear loss, have I° means much weaker
Than you may call to comfort you; for I
Have lost my daughter.
ALONSO: A daughter?
O heavens, that they were living both in Naples,   150
The king and queen there! That° they were, I wish
Myself were mudded° in that oozy bed
Where my son lies. When did you lose your daughter?
PROSPERO: In this last tempest. I perceive these lords
At this encounter do so much admire°   155
That they devour their reason° and scarce think
Their eyes do offices of truth, their words
Are natural breath.° But, howsoever you have
Been jostled from your senses, know for certain
That I am Prospero and that very duke   160
Which was thrust forth of° Milan, who most strangely
Upon this shore, where you were wrecked, was landed
To be the lord on 't. No more yet of this,
For 'tis a chronicle of day by day,°
Not a relation for a breakfast nor   165
Befitting this first meeting. Welcome, sir.
This cell's my court. Here have I few attendants,
And subjects none abroad.° Pray you, look in.
My dukedom since you have given me again,
I will requite° you with as good a thing,   170
At least bring forth a wonder to content ye
As much as me my dukedom.

---

112. trifle: Trick of magic. abuse: Deceive. 113. late: Lately. 116. crave: Require. 117. An . . . all: If this is actually happening. story: I.e., explanation. 118. Thy . . . resign: Alonso made an arrangement with Antonio at the time of Prospero's banishment for Milan to pay tribute to Naples; see I, II, 113–27. 119. wrongs: Wrongdoings. 121. thine age: Your venerable self. 124. subtleties: Illusions, magical powers. 126. brace: Pair. 128. justify you: Prove you to be. 133. perforce: Necessarily. 136. whom: I.e., who.

139. woe: Sorry. 142. of . . . grace: By whose mercy. 143. sovereign: Efficacious. 145. late: Recent. 145–46. supportable . . . have I: To make the deeply felt loss bearable, I have. 151. That: So that. 152. mudded: Buried in the mud. 155. admire: Wonder. 156. devour their reason: I.e., are dumbfounded. 156–58. scarce . . . breath: Scarcely believe that their eyes inform them accurately what they see or that their words are naturally spoken. 161. of: From. 164. of day by day: Requiring days to tell. 168. abroad: Away from here, anywhere else. 170. requite: Repay.

(*Here Prospero discovers° Ferdinand and Miranda playing at chess.*)

MIRANDA: Sweet lord, you play me false.
FERDINAND: No, my dearest love,
75   I would not for the world.
MIRANDA: Yes, for a score of kingdoms you should
        wrangle,
      And I would call if fair play.°
ALONSO: If this prove
      A vision° of the island, one dear son
      Shall I twice lose.
SEBASTIAN: A most high miracle!
FERDINAND [*approaching his father*]:
80   Though the seas threaten, they are merciful;
      I have cursed them without cause.   [*He kneels.*]
ALONSO: Now all the blessings
      Of a glad father compass° thee about!
      Arise, and say how thou cam'st here.
                                [*Ferdinand rises.*]
MIRANDA: O, wonder!
      How many goodly creatures are there here!
      How beauteous mankind is! O, brave° new
85   world,
      That has such people in 't!
PROSPERO: 'Tis new to thee.
ALONSO: What is this maid with whom thou wast
        at play?
      Your eld'st° acquaintance cannot be three hours.
      Is she the goddess that hath severed us
      And brought us thus together?
90 FERDINAND: Sir, she is mortal;
      But by immortal Providence she's mine.
      I chose her when I could not ask my father
      For his advice, nor thought I had one. She
      Is daughter to this famous Duke of Milan,
95   Of whom so often I have heard renown
      But never saw before, of whom I have
      Received a second life; and second father
      This lady makes him to me.
ALONSO: I am hers.
      But O, how oddly will it sound that I
      Must ask my child forgiveness!
00 PROSPERO: There, sir, stop.

172. [S.D.] *discovers*: I.e., by opening a curtain, presumably rear stage.   176–77. **Yes . . . play**: I.e., yes, even if we were playing for twenty kingdoms, something less than the whole world, you would still contend mightily against me and play me false, and I would let you do it as though it were fair play; or, if you were to play not just for stakes but literally for kingdoms, my accusation of false play would be out of order in that your "wrangling" would be proper.   178. **vision**: Illusion.   182. **compass**: Encompass, embrace.   185. **brave**: Splendid, gorgeously appareled, handsome.   188. **eld'st**: Longest.

      Let us not burden our remembrances with
      A heaviness° that's gone.
GONZALO: I have inly° wept,
      Or should have spoke ere this. Look down, you
        gods,
      And on this couple drop a blessèd crown!
      For it is you that have chalked forth the way°   205
      Which brought us hither.
ALONSO: I say amen, Gonzalo!
GONZALO: Was Milan° thrust from Milan that his
        issue
      Should become kings of Naples? O, rejoice
      Beyond a common joy, and set it down
      With gold on lasting pillars: In one voyage   210
      Did Claribel her husband find at Tunis,
      And Ferdinand, her brother, found a wife
      Where he himself was lost; Prospero his
        dukedom
      In a poor isle; and all of us ourselves
      When no man was his own.°
ALONSO [*to Ferdinand and Miranda*]: Give me your
        hands.   215
      Let grief and sorrow still° embrace his° heart
      That° doth not wish you joy!
GONZALO: Be it so! Amen!

(*Enter Ariel, with the Master and Boatswain amazedly following.*)

      O, look, sir, look, sir! Here is more of us.
      I prophesied, if a gallows were on land,
      This fellow could not drown. — Now,
        blasphemy,°   220
      That swear'st grace o'erboard,° not an oath° on
        shore?
      Hast thou no mouth by land? What is the news?
BOATSWAIN: The best news is that we have safely
        found
      Our King and company; the next, our ship —
      Which, but three glasses° since, we gave out°
        split —   225
      Is tight and yare° and bravely° rigged as when
      We first put out to sea.
ARIEL [*aside to Prospero*]: Sir, all this service
      Have I done since I went.

202. **heaviness**: Sadness.   **inly**: Inwardly.   205. **chalked . . . way**: Marked as with a piece of chalk the pathway.   207. **Was Milan**: Was the Duke of Milan.   214–15. **all . . . own**: All of us have found ourselves and our sanity when we all had lost our senses.   216. **still**: Always.   **his**: That person's.   217. **That**: Who.   220. **blasphemy**: I.e., blasphemer.   221. **That . . . o'erboard**: I.e., you who banish heavenly grace from the ship by your blasphemies.   **not an oath**: Aren't you going to swear an oath.   225. **glasses**: I.e., hours.   **gave out**: Reported, professed to be.   226. **yare**: Ready.   **bravely**: Splendidly.

PROSPERO [*aside to Ariel*]: My tricksy° spirit!

ALONSO: These are not natural events; they strengthen°

230   From strange to stranger. Say, how came you hither?

BOATSWAIN: If I did think, sir, I were well awake,
I'd strive to tell you. We were dead of sleep,°
And — how we know not — all clapped under hatches,
Where but even now, with strange and several° noises

235   Of roaring, shrieking, howling, jingling chains,
And more diversity of sounds, all horrible,
We were awaked; straightway at liberty;
Where we, in all her trim, freshly beheld
Our royal, good, and gallant ship, our Master

240   Cap'ring to eye° her. On a trice,° so please you,
Even in a dream, were we divided from them°
And were brought moping° hither.

ARIEL [*aside to Prospero*]:   Was 't well done?

PROSPERO [*aside to Ariel*]: Bravely, my diligence.
Thou shalt be free.

ALONSO: This is as strange a maze as e'er men trod,

245   And there is in this business more than nature
Was ever conduct° of. Some oracle
Must rectify our knowledge.

PROSPERO: Sir, my liege,
Do not infest° your mind with beating on°
The strangeness of this business. At picked° leisure,

250   Which shall be shortly, single° I'll resolve° you,
Which to you shall seem probable,° of every
These° happened accidents,° till when, be cheerful
And think of each thing well.° [*Aside to Ariel.*]
Come hither, spirit.
Set Caliban and his companions free.
Untie the spell. [*Exit Ariel.*] How fares my

255   gracious sir?
There are yet missing of your company
Some few odd° lads that you remember not.

(*Enter Ariel, driving in Caliban, Stephano, and Trinculo in their stolen apparel.*)

STEPHANO: Every man shift° for all the rest,° and let no man take care for himself; for all is but fortune. Coraggio,° bully monster,° coraggio!   260

TRINCULO: If these be true spies° which I wear in my head, here's a goodly sight.

CALIBAN: O Setebos, these be brave° spirits indeed!
How fine° my master is! I am afraid
He will chastise me.   265

SEBASTIAN: Ha, ha!
What things are these, my lord Antonio?
Will money buy 'em?

ANTONIO: Very like. One of them
Is a plain fish, and no doubt marketable.

PROSPERO: Mark but the badges° of these men, my lords,   270
Then say if they be true.° This misshapen knave,
His mother was a witch, and one so strong
That could control the moon, make flows and ebbs,
And deal in her command without her power.°
These three have robbed me, and this demidevil —   275
For he's a bastard° one — had plotted with them
To take my life. Two of these fellows you
Must know and own.° This thing of darkness I
Acknowledge mine.

CALIBAN: I shall be pinched to death.

ALONSO: Is not this Stephano, my drunken butler?   280

SEBASTIAN: He is drunk now. Where had he wine?

ALONSO: And Trinculo is reeling ripe.° Where should they
Find this grand liquor that hath gilded° 'em?
[*To Trinculo.*] How cam'st thou in this pickle?°

TRINCULO: I have been in such a pickle since I saw   285
you last that, I fear me, will never out of my bones.
I shall not fear flyblowing.°

---

228. **tricksy:** Ingenious, sportive.   229. **strengthen:** Increase.   232. **dead of sleep:** Deep in sleep.   234. **several:** Different, diverse.   240. **Cap'ring to eye:** Dancing for joy to see.   **On a trice:** In an instant.   241. **them:** I.e., the other crew members.   242. **moping:** In a daze.   246. **conduct:** Guide, leader.   248. **infest:** Harass, disturb.   **beating on:** Worrying about.   249. **picked:** Chosen, convenient.   250. **single:** I.e., by my own human powers.   **resolve:** Satisfy, explain to.   251. **probable:** Explicable, plausible.   251–52. **of every These:** About every one of these.   252. **accidents:** Occurrences.   253. **well:** Favorably.   257. **odd:** Unaccounted for.

258. **shift:** Provide.   **for all the rest:** Stephano drunkenly gets wrong the saying "Every man for himself."   260. **Coraggio:** Courage.   **bully monster:** Gallant monster. (Ironical.)   261. **true spies:** Accurate observers (i.e., sharp eyes).   263. **brave:** Handsome.   264. **fine:** Splendidly attired.   270. **badges:** Emblems of cloth or silver worn on the arms of retainers. (Prospero refers here to the stolen clothes as emblems of their villainy.)   271. **true:** Honest.   274. **deal . . . power:** Wield the moon's power, either without her authority or beyond her influence.   276. **bastard:** Counterfeit.   278. **own:** Recognize, admit as belonging to you.   282. **reeling ripe:** Stumblingly drunk.   283. **gilded:** (1) Flushed, made drunk, (2) covered with gilt (suggesting the horse urine).   284. **pickle:** (1) Fix, predicament, (2) pickling brine (in this case, horse urine).   287. **flyblowing:** I.e., being fouled by fly eggs (from which he is saved by being pickled).

SEBASTIAN: Why, how now, Stephano?
STEPHANO: O, touch me not! I am not Stephano, but
    a cramp.
PROSPERO: You'd be king o' the isle, sirrah?°
STEPHANO: I should have been a sore° one, then.
ALONSO [pointing to Caliban]: This is a strange
    thing as e'er I looked on.
PROSPERO: He is as disproportioned in his manners
    As in his shape. — Go, sirrah, to my cell.
    Take with you your companions. As you look
    To have my pardon, trim° it handsomely.
CALIBAN: Ay, that I will; and I'll be wise hereafter
    And seek for grace. What a thrice-double ass
    Was I to take this drunkard for a god
    And worship this dull fool!
PROSPERO: Go to. Away!
ALONSO: Hence, and bestow your luggage where
    you found it.
SEBASTIAN: Or stole it, rather.
          [Exeunt Caliban, Stephano, and Trinculo.]
PROSPERO: Sir, I invite Your Highness and your
    train
    To my poor cell, where you shall take your rest
    For this one night; which, part of it, I'll waste°
    With such discourse as, I not doubt, shall make
    it
    Go quick away: the story of my life,
    And the particular accidents° gone by
    Since I came to this isle. And in the morn
    I'll bring you to your ship, and so to Naples,
    Where I have hope to see the nuptial
    Of these our dear-belovèd solemnized;
    And thence retire me° to my Milan, where
    Every third thought shall be my grave.
ALONSO: I long
    To hear the story of your life, which must
    Take° the ear strangely.
PROSPERO: I'll deliver° all;

And promise you calm seas, auspicious gales,
And sail so expeditious that shall catch
Your royal fleet far off. [Aside to Ariel.] My
    Ariel, chick,   320
That is thy charge. Then to the elements
Be free, and fare thou well! — Please you, draw
    near.°

                              (Exeunt omnes.)

EPILOGUE

(Spoken by Prospero.)

Now my charms are all o'erthrown,
And what strength I have 's mine own,
Which is most faint. Now, 'tis true,
I must be here confined by you
Or sent to Naples. Let me not,   5
Since I have my dukedom got
And pardoned the deceiver, dwell
In this bare island by your spell,
But release me from my bands°
With the help of your good hands.°   10
Gentle breath° of yours my sails
Must fill, or else my project fails,
Which was to please. Now I want°
Spirits to enforce,° art to enchant,
And my ending is despair   15
Unless I be relieved by prayer,°
Which pierces so that it assaults°
Mercy itself, and frees° all faults.
As you from crimes° would pardoned be,
Let your indulgence° set me free.   (Exit.)   20

291. sirrah: Standard form of address to an inferior, here
expressing reprimand.   292. sore: (1) Tyrannical, (2) sorry,
inept, (3) wracked by pain.   297. trim: Prepare, decorate.
306. waste: Spend.   309. accidents: Occurrences.   314.
retire me: Return.   317. Take: Take effect upon, enchant.
deliver: Declare, relate.

322. draw near: I.e., enter my cell.   9. bands: Bonds.   10.
hands: I.e., applause (the noise of which would break the
spell of silence).   11. Gentle breath: Favorable breeze (produced by hands clapping or favorable comment).   13. want:
Lack.   14. enforce: Control.   16. prayer: I.e., Prospero's
petition to the audience.   17. assaults: Rightfully gains the
attention of.   18. frees: Obtains forgiveness for.   19.
crimes: Sins.   20. indulgence: (1) Humoring, lenient approval, (2) remission of punishment for sin.

COMMENTARIES

Some of the finest critical commentary ever written has been devoted to the works of Shakespeare. From the seventeenth century to the present, critics have taken a considerable interest in the nuances of his work.

In the commentary on *A Midsummer Night's Dream* we find a wide range of responses to the work. Enid Welsford's comments are in a special context, that of the court masque, the rich entertainments that were designed to please royalty. As Welsford explains, there are many elements of the masque in *A Midsummer Night's Dream*.

In more specifically feminist observations, the critics Carol Thomas Neely and Linda Bamber show how assumptions regarding power in a male-female relationship affect our interpretation of the play. Their readings are fresh, exciting, and provocative.

Peter Brook, one of the most notable contemporary directors of Shakespeare and the producer of the most striking recent production of *A Midsummer Night's Dream* (1970), gives us a director's view of the play. He centers the discussion on love, which in many forms is at the heart of the play.

The modern era of criticism on Shakespeare probably begins with Samuel Taylor Coleridge, whose lectures on Shakespeare were instrumental in helping a generation of early-nineteenth-century theatergoers take the playwright much more seriously than they might have done. Coleridge reached a wide and generally popular audience, and he stands as one of the most influential critics of the last century. His work on *Hamlet* centers on the character of Hamlet and his problems in the play. Coleridge shows how Hamlet reveals himself both to us and to himself.

Sigmund Freud sees in *Hamlet* the seeds of the Oedipus complex that he had already identified in Sophocles' *Oedipus Rex*. The question of how one psychoanalyzes a literary character is perhaps best raised in Freud's essay. Later, Ernest Jones, a follower of Freud, wrote an entire book on Hamlet, analyzing him from the psychoanalytic perspective.

T. S. Eliot, speaking as a careful and noted student of Elizabethan and Jacobean drama, begins to point out some of the difficulties he sees with *Hamlet*. It is fascinating to see how great poets such as Coleridge and Eliot can approach the same play from such diverse points of view.

The anthropologist Laura Bohannan offers a fascinating perspective on *Hamlet* in her "Shakespeare in the Bush." She spent time in a remote African village where she participated in tribal celebrations, storytelling, and rituals. In an effort to demonstrate the universality of Shakespeare, she eventually began to explain the story to the elders of her village.

Certain there was only one way to correctly read the play, she found that the elders interpreted it in a surprisingly different way.

Stephen J. Greenblatt comments on the theme of colonialism in *The Tempest*. Caliban was on the island before Prospero arrived, and he complains that Prospero robbed him of what was his own. Shakespeare seems to have been well informed about the original inhabitants of the New World, and while many critics resist Greenblatt's interpretation his questions are worth considering.

Enid Welsford

MASQUE ELEMENTS IN *A MIDSUMMER NIGHT'S DREAM*   1927

Enid Welsford examines A Midsummer Night's Dream *from the point of view of its masque-like qualities. Shakespeare's* The Tempest *includes a masque and has certain scenic qualities that link it to that tradition, and so does* A Midsummer Night's Dream: *fantastic costumes, a remarkable fairy population that could be considered part of the antimasque, which was a parody of the masque itself. It often involved masquers dressed in grotesque animal costumes, making a loud racket, and dancing in erratic and fantastic gestures. Meant originally as a foul contrast to the magnificence of the masque, the antimasque became a favorite of the less conservative masquers.*

The only character study in *A Midsummer Night's Dream* is to be found in the portrayal of Bottom, Theseus, and perhaps Hippolyta. Even in drawing these characters Shakespeare was evidently influenced by the memory of pageants, complimentary speeches, and entertainments addressed by townspeople and humble folk to the Queen or to the nobility. A glance through Nichols's *Public Progresses* shows what innumerable lengthy speeches, what innumerable disguisings and shows, Elizabeth was obliged to bear with gracious demeanor. Her experiences were similar to those of Theseus:

> Where I have come, great clerks have purposed
> To greet me with premeditated welcomes;
> Where I have seen them shiver and look pale,
> Make periods in the midst of sentences,
> Throttle their practic'd accent in their fears,
> And, in conclusion, dumbly have broke off,
> Not paying me a welcome.

One Sunday afternoon, at Kenilworth Castle, Elizabeth and her court whiled away the time by watching the countrypeople at a Brideale and Morris Dance. Their amused kindly tolerance is just that of Theseus and the lovers toward the Athenian workmen. So that even in the most solid and dramatic parts of his play Shakespeare is only giving an idealized version of courtly and country revels and of the people that played a part in them.

In *A Midsummer Night's Dream* Bottom and his companions serve the same purpose as the antimasque in the courtly revels. It is true that Shakespeare's play was written before Ben Jonson had elaborated and defined the antimasque, but from the first grotesque dances were popular, and the principle of contrast was always latent in the masque. There is, however, a great difference between Jonson's and Shakespeare's management of foil and relief. In the antimasque the transition is sudden and the contrast complete, a method of composition effective enough in spectacle and ballet. But in a play, as Shakespeare well knew, the greatest beauty is gained through contrast when the difference is not obvious and striking, but rises out of a deep though unobstrusive resemblance. This could not be better illustrated than by the picture of Titania winding the ass-headed Bottom in her arms. Why is it that this is a pleasing picture, why is it that the rude mechanicals do not, as a matter of fact, disturb or sully Titania's "close and consecrated bower"? Malvolio° in Bottom's place would be repellent, yet Malvolio, regarded superficially, is less violently contrasted to the Fairy Queen than is Nick Bottom. Bottom with his ass's head is grotesquely hideous, and in ordinary life he is crude, raw, and very stupid. We have no reason to suppose that Malvolio was anything but a well-set-up, proper-looking man, spruce, well dressed, the perfect family butler. His mentality too is of a distinctly higher order than Bottom's. He fills a responsible position with credit, he follows a reasoned line of conduct, he thinks nobly of the soul. Two things alone he lacks (and that is why no self-respecting fay could ever kiss him) — humor and imagination. Malvolio is, therefore, the only character who cannot be included in the final harmony of *Twelfth Night*. Bottom and his fellows did perhaps lack humor (though the interview with the fairies suggests that Bottom had a smack of it), but in its place they possessed unreason. Imagination they did have, of the most simple, primal, childlike kind. It is their artistic ambition that lifts them out of the humdrum world and turns them into Midsummer Dreamers, and we have seen how cunningly Shakespeare extracts from their very stupidity romance and moonshine. But, indeed, grotesqueness and stupidity (of a certain kind) have a kinship with beauty. For these qualities usually imply a measure of spiritual freedom, they lead to at least a temporary relief from the tyranny of reason and from the pressure of the external world. In *A Midsummer Night's Dream* the dominance of the Lord of Misrule is not marked by coarse parody, but by the partial repeal of the laws of cause and effect. By delicate beauty, gentle mockery, and simple romantic foolishness our freedom is gained.

Carol Thomas Neely (b. 1939)
Broken Nuptials

1985

Carol Thomas Neely is interested in the problem of marriage in A Midsummer Night's Dream, *examining it not from the traditional point of view — which essentially accepted the status quo of the play and then ignored it — but from*

Malvolio: A character in Shakespeare's *Twelfth Night*.

a modernist point of view that brings into question the institution of marriage and how it functions in the play. She is interested in the relationships of Titania and Oberon, who "make up" during the play, and of Theseus and Hippolyta, whose own nuptials have been postponed for the while it takes the action of the play to unfold. Neely reminds us how much "coupling" there is in the play.

In *Midsummer Night's Dream* desire, symbolized by the operations of the fairy juice, is urgent, promiscuous, and threatening to women as well as to men. Its effects mock the protestations of constancy by Lysander and Demetrius and exaggerate the patriarchal possessiveness of Theseus and Oberon: "every man should take his own. . . . The man shall have his mare again, and all shall be well" (III, II). All is made well in part because the erratic or aggressive desires of the controlling men are "linger[ed]" (I, I) by the chaste constancy of Hermia and Helena and the poised detachment of Hippolyta, or tempered by the inconstancy of Titania with Bottom. Oberon, engineering this union, imagines it as an ugly, bestial coupling "with lion, bear, or wolf, or bull" (II, I), an apt punishment for Titania's multiple desires and intimacies. But from Titania's perspective (and ours) it is a comically fulfilling alternate nuptial — and was staged as such by Peter Brook,° complete with streamers, the wedding march, a plumed bower of bliss, and a waving phallus. The union is a respite for Titania from the conflicts of her hierarchical marriage. She and Bottom experience not animal lust but a blissful, sensual, symbiotic union, characterized, like that of mother and child, by mutual affection and a shared sense of effortless omnipotence. Their eroticism, the opposite of Oberon's bestial fantasies or Theseus's phallic wooing, is tenderly gynocentric:° "So doth the woodbine the sweet honeysuckle / Gently entwist; the female ivy so / Enrings the barky fingers of the elm" (IV, I). Although Titania disavows her "enamored" visions (IV, I), and Oberon misconstrues them, the couple's "amity" (IV, I) depends on that prior union: freed by it to relinquish her other love object, the Indian boy, to Oberon, Titania's submission generates in him the tenderness she craves.

While Theseus and Hippolyta await their nuptials, marital harmony is reestablished by Titania and Oberon, and the chaotic desires of the young lovers are sorted out. During the last-act interval between the weddings and their consummations, the violent potentials in love, sex, and marriage are comically incorporated in the rejected and enacted entertainments. "The battle with the centaurs" interrupted the wedding of Theseus's friend Pirithous when the drunken centaurs attacked the Lapiths to capture the bride; during "the riot of the tipsy Bacchanals," the Bacchantes tore Orpheus to pieces, enraged by his devotion to Eurydice and his scorn of other women. The Pyramus and Thisby play dramatizes a lovers' union aborted by parental obstructions, devouring lion, and the lovers' deaths. The play within the play's joining of parodic romance with bawdy innuendo brings into the festive conclusion the two dimensions of love — conventional romanticism and uncontrollable desire — which, converging, threatened but did not harm the couples in the forest and which facilitated the union of Titania and Bottom.

Peter Brook: Innovative British film and theater director (b. 1925). His *Midsummer Night's Dream* was produced in 1970.
gynocentric: Women-centered.

Linda Bamber (b. 1945)

ON *A MIDSUMMER NIGHT'S DREAM*   1982

The question of masculine and feminine is central to A Midsummer Night's
Dream. *Much of the action is precipitated by a power struggle between Titania
and Oberon, and the young Athenians who rush off to the woods are there
because a father has decided to oppose the will of his daughter regarding her
marriage. Linda Bamber is a feminist critic interested in examining the centers
of power in the play, particularly with an eye for what we accept as the natural
order of relationships. She shows that the action of the comedy is essentially
tied into questions of gender, which begin to become questions of genre.*

The best example [in Shakespeare] of the relationship between male dominance and the status quo comes in *A Midsummer Night's Dream,* which begins
with a rebellion of the feminine against the power of masculine authority. Hermia
refuses the man both Aegeus and Theseus order her to marry; her refusal sends
us off into the forest, beyond the power of the father and the masculine state.
Once in the forest, of course, we find the social situation metaphorically repeated
in this world of imagination and nature. The fairy king, Oberon, rules the forest.
His rule, too, is troubled by the rebellion of the feminine. Titania has refused
to give him her page, the child of a human friend who died in childbirth. But
by the end of the story Titania is conquered, the child relinquished, and order
restored. Even here the comic upheavals, whether we see them as May games
or bad dreams, are associated with an uprising of women. David P. Young has
pointed out how firmly this play connects order with masculine dominance and
the disruption of order with the rebellion of the feminine:

> It is appropriate that Theseus, as representative of daylight and right reason, should
> have subdued his bride-to-be to the rule of his masculine will. That is the natural
> order of things. It is equally appropriate that Oberon, as king of darkness and fantasy,
> should have lost control of his wife, and that the corresponding natural disorder
> described by Titania should ensue.[1]

The natural order, the status quo, is for men to rule women. When they fail
to do so, we have the exceptional situation, the festive, disruptive, disorderly
moment of comedy.

A Midsummer Night's Dream is actually an anomaly among the festive
comedies. It is unusual for the forces of the green world to be directed, as they
are here, by a masculine figure. Because the green world here is a partial
reproduction of the social world, the feminine is reduced to a kind of first cause
of the action while a masculine power directs it. In the other festive comedies
the feminine Other presides. She does not *command* the forces of the alternative
world, as Oberon does, but since she acts in harmony with these forces her
will and desire often prevail.

Where are we to bestow our sympathies? On the forces that make for the
disruption of the status quo and therefore for the plot? Or on the force that

---

[1]David P. Young, *Something of Great Constancy* (New Haven, CT: Yale UP, 1966),
183.

asserts itself against the disruption and reestablishes a workable social order? Of course we cannot choose. We can only say that in comedy we owe our holiday to such forces as the tendency of the feminine to rebel, whereas to the successful reassertion of masculine power we owe our everyday order. Shakespearean comedy endorses both sides. Holiday is, of course, the subject and the analogue of each play; but the plays always end in a return to everyday life. The optimistic reading of Shakespearean comedy says that everyday life is clarified and enriched by our holiday from it; according to the pessimistic reading the temporary subversion of the social order has revealed how much that order excludes, how high a price we pay for it. But whether our return to everyday life is a comfortable one or not, the return itself is the inevitable conclusion to the journey out.

Does this make the comedies sexist? Is the association of women with the disruption of the social order an unconscious and insulting projection? It seems to begin as such; but as the form of Shakespearean comedy develops, the Otherness of the feminine develops into as powerful a force in the drama as the social authority of the masculine Self. For the feminine in Shakespearean comedy begins as a shrew but develops into a comic heroine. The shrew's rebellion directly challenges masculine authority, whereas the comic heroine merely presides over areas of experience to which masculine authority is irrelevant. But the shrew is essentially powerless against the social system, whereas the comic heroine is in alliance with forces that can never be finally overcome. The shrew is defeated by the superior strength, physical and social, of a man, or by women who support the status quo. She provokes a battle of the sexes, and the outcome of this battle, from Shakespeare's point of view, is inevitable. The comic heroine, on the other hand, does not fight the system but merely surfaces, again and again, when and where the social system is temporarily subverted. The comic heroine does not actively resist the social and political hegemony° of the men, but as an irresistible version of the Other she successfully competes for our favor with the (masculine) representatives of the social Self. The development of the feminine from the shrew to the comic heroine indicates a certain consciousness on the author's part of sexual politics; and it indicates a desire, at least, to create conditions of sexual equality within the drama even while reflecting the unequal conditions of men and women in the society at large.

Peter Brook (b. 1925)

THE PLAY IS THE MESSAGE . . .   1987

When a distinguished director becomes a critic, we have the opportunity to understand a play from the point of view of one who has to make the play work in front of an audience. Brook's production of A Midsummer Night's

---

hegemony: Overriding authority.

Dream was a sensation in England and the United States in 1970. It featured absolutely white lighting, white sets, and actors in swings. Brook had analyzed the play in such a fashion that he saw love as its constant concern, "constantly repeated." He concluded that to present the play, the players must embody the concept of love. They must bring to the play their own realization of the play's themes — even to the point of seeing theater anew, like the mechanicals "who are touching an extraordinary world with the tips of their fingers, a world which transcends their daily experience and which fills them with wonder" — the effect of the love they bring to their task.

People have often asked me: "What is the theme of *A Midsummer Night's Dream?*" There is only one answer to that question, the same as one would give regarding a cup. The quality of a cup is its cupness. I say this by way of introduction, to show that if I lay so much stress on the dangers involved in trying to define the themes of the *Dream* it is because too many productions, too many attempts at visual interpretation are based on preconceived ideas, as if these had to be illustrated in some way. In my opinion we should first of all try to rediscover the play as a living thing; then we shall be able to analyze our discoveries. Once I have finished working on the play, I can begin to produce my theories. It was fortunate that I did not attempt to do so earlier because the play would not have yielded up its secrets.

At the center of the *Dream*, constantly repeated, we find the word "love." Everything comes back to this, even the structure of the play, even its music. The quality the play demands from its performers is to build up an atmosphere of love during the performance itself, so that this abstract idea — for the word "love" is in itself a complete abstraction — may become palpable. The play presents us with forms of love which become less and less blurred as it goes on. "Love" soon begins to resound like a musical scale and little by little we are introduced to its various modes and tones.

Love is, of course, a theme which touches all men. No one, not even the most hardened, the coldest, or the most despairing, is insensitive to it, even if he does not know what love is. Either his practical experience confirms its existence or he suffers from its absence, which is another way of recognizing that it exists. At every moment the play touches something which concerns everyone.

As this is theater, there must be conflicts, so this play about love is also a play about the opposite of love, love and its opposite force. We are brought to realize that love, liberty, and imagination are closely connected. Right at the beginning of the play, for example, the father in a long speech tries to obstruct his daughter's love and we are surprised that such a character, apparently a secondary role, should have so long a speech — until we discover the real importance of his words. What he says not only reflects a generation gap (a father opposing his daughter's love because he had intended her for someone else), it also explains the reasons for his feeling of suspicion toward the young man whom his daughter loves. He describes him as an individual prone to fantasy, led by his imagination — an unpardonable weakness in the father's eyes.

From this starting point we see, as in any of Shakespeare's plays, a confrontation. Here it is between love and its opposing qualities, between fantasy and solid common sense — caught in an endless series of mirrors. As usual, Shakespeare confuses the issue. If we asked someone's opinion on the father's point of view, he might say, for example, that "The father is in the wrong because he is against freedom of the imagination," a very widespread attitude today.

In this way, for most present-day audiences, the girl's father comes over as the classical father figure who misunderstands young people and their flights of fancy. But later on, we discover surprisingly that he is right, because the imaginative world in which this lover lives causes him to behave in a quite disgusting way toward the very same daughter: as soon as a drop of liquid falls into his eyes, acting as a drug which liberates natural tendencies, he not only jilts her but his love is transformed into violent hate. He uses words which might well be borrowed from *Measure for Measure,* denouncing the girl with the kind of vehemence that, in the Middle Ages, led people to burn one another at the stake. Yet at the end of the play we are once more in agreement with the Duke, who rejects the father in the name of love. The young man has now been transformed.

So we observe this game of love in a psychological and metaphysical context; we hear Titania's assertion that the opposition between herself and Oberon is fundamental, primordial. But Oberon's acts deny this, for he perceives that within their opposition a reconciliation is possible.

The play covers an extraordinarily broad range of universal forces and feelings in a mythical world, which suddenly changes, in the last part, into high society. We find ourselves back in the very real palace: and the same Shakespeare who, a few pages earlier, offered us a scene of pure fantasy between Titania and Oberon, where it would be absurd to ask prosaic questions like "Where does Oberon live?" or "When describing a queen like Titania did Shakespeare wish to express political ideas?," now takes us into a precise social environment. We are present at the meeting point of two worlds, that of the workmen and the court, the world of wealth and elegance, and alleged sensitivity, the world of people who have had the leisure to cultivate fine sentiments and are now shown as insensitive and even disgusting in their superior attitude toward the poor.

At the beginning of the court scene we see our former heroes, who have spent the entire play involved in the theme of love, and would no doubt be quite capable of giving academic lectures on the subject, suddenly finding themselves plunged into a context which has apparently nothing to do with love (with their own love, since all their problems have been solved). Now they are in the context of a relationship with each other and with another social class, and they are at a loss. They do not realize that here too scorn eliminates love.

We see how well Shakespeare has situated everything. Athens in the *Dream* resembles our Athens in the sixties: the workmen, as they state in the first scene, are very much afraid of the authorities; if they commit the slightest error they will be hanged, and there is nothing comical about that. Indeed, they risk hanging as soon as they shed their anonymity. At the same time they are irresistibly attracted by the carrot of "sixpence a day" which will enable them to escape poverty. Yet their real motive is neither glory nor adventure nor money (that is made very clear and should guide the actors who perform this scene). Those simple men who have only ever worked with their hands apply to the use of the imagination exactly the same quality of love which traditionally underlies the relationship between a craftsman and his tools. That is what gives these scenes both their strength and their comic quality. These craftsmen make efforts which are grotesque in one sense because they push awkwardness to its limit, but at another level they set themselves to their task with such love that the meaning of their clumsy efforts changes before our eyes.

The spectators can easily decide to adopt the same attitude as the courtiers: to find all this quite simply ridiculous; to laugh with the complacency of people who quite confidently mock the efforts of others. Yet the audience is invited to take a step back: to feel it cannot quite identify with the court, with people who are too grand and too unkind. Little by little, we come to see that the craftsmen, who behave with little understanding but who approach their new job with love, are discovering theater — an imaginary world for them, toward which they instinctively feel great respect. In fact, the "mechanicals" scene is often misinterpreted because the actors forget to look at theater through innocent eyes, they take a professional actor's views of good or bad acting, and in so doing they diminish the mystery and the sense of magic felt by these amateurs, who are touching an extraordinary world with the tips of their fingers, a world which transcends their daily experience and which fills them with wonder.

We see this quite clearly in the part of the boy who plays the girl, Thisby. At first sight this tough lad is irresistibly absurd, but by degrees, through his love for what he is doing, we discover what more is involved. In our production, the actor playing the part is a professional plumber, who only took to acting a short while ago. He well understands what is involved, what it means to feel this nameless and shapeless kind of love. This boy, himself new to theater, acts the part of someone who is new to theater. Through his conviction and his identification we discover that these awkward craftsmen, without knowing it, are teaching us a lesson — or it might be preferable to say that a lesson is being taught us through them. These craftsmen are able to make the connection between love for their trade and for a completely different task, whereas the courtiers are not capable of linking the love about which they talk so well with their simple role as spectators.

Nonetheless, little by little the courtiers become involved, even touched by the play within the play, and if one follows very closely what is there in the text we see that for a moment the situation is completely transformed. One of the central images of the play is a wall, which, at a given moment, vanishes. Its disappearance, to which Bottom draws our attention, is caused by an act of love. Shakespeare is showing us how love can pervade a situation and act as a transforming force.

The *Dream* touches lightly on the fundamental question of the transformations which may occur if certain things are better understood. It requires us to reflect on the nature of love. All the landscapes of love are thrown into relief, and we are given a particular social context through which the other situations can be measured. Through the subtlety of its language the play removes all kinds of barriers. It is therefore not a play which provokes resistance, or creates disturbance in the usual sense. Rival politicians could sit side by side at a performance of *A Midsummer Night's Dream* and each leave with the impression that the play fits his point of view perfectly. But if they give it a fine, sensitive attention they cannot fail to perceive a world just like their own, more and more riddled with contradictions and, like their own, waiting for that mysterious force, love, without which harmony will never return.

Samuel Taylor Coleridge (1772–1834)
ON HAMLET   1812

Samuel Taylor Coleridge was the first modern critic of Shakespeare to develop powerful, original readings of the great plays. He visited atheneums and lyceums (institutions promoting learning) on both sides of the Atlantic delivering his lectures on Shakespeare, and his interpretations stimulated a new age of thoughtful criticism. His lecture on Hamlet *includes a careful reading of difficult lines, but it also centers on questions of the relationship of Shakespeare to his creation. Further, the mental state of* Hamlet *becomes of central interest to Coleridge and a basis of much of his observation.*

The seeming inconsistencies in the conduct and character of Hamlet have long exercised the conjectural ingenuity of critics; and, as we are always loath to suppose that the cause of defective apprehension is in ourselves, the mystery has been too commonly explained by the very easy process of setting it down as in fact inexplicable, and by resolving the phenomenon into a misgrowth or *lusus* of the capricious and irregular genius of Shakespeare. The shallow and stupid arrogance of these vulgar and indolent decisions I would fain do my best to expose. I believe the character of Hamlet may be traced to Shakespeare's deep and accurate science in mental philosophy. Indeed, that this character must have some connection with the common fundamental laws of our nature may be assumed from the fact that Hamlet has been the darling of every country in which the literature of England has been fostered. In order to understand him, it is essential that we should reflect on the constitution of our own minds. Man is distinguished from the brute animals in proportion as thought prevails over sense: but in the healthy processes of the mind, a balance is constantly maintained between the impressions from outward objects and the inward operations of the intellect: — for if there be an overbalance in the contemplative faculty, man thereby becomes the creature of mere meditation, and loses his natural power of action. Now one of Shakespeare's modes of creating characters is to conceive any one intellectual or moral faculty in morbid excess, and then to place himself, Shakespeare, thus mutilated or diseased, under given circumstances. In Hamlet he seems to have wished to exemplify the moral necessity of a due balance between our attention to the objects of our senses, and our meditation on the workings of our minds, — an *equilibrium* between the real and the imaginary worlds. In Hamlet this balance is disturbed: his thoughts, and the images of his fancy, are far more vivid than his actual perceptions, and his very perceptions, instantly passing through the *medium* of his contemplations, acquire, as they pass, a form and a color not naturally their own. Hence we see a great, an almost enormous, intellectual activity, and a proportionate aversion to real action, consequent upon it, with all its symptoms and accompanying qualities. This character Shakespeare places in circumstances, under which it is obliged to act on the spur of the moment: — Hamlet is brave and careless of death; but he vacillates from sensibility, and procrastinates from thought, and loses the power of action in the energy of resolve. Thus it is that this tragedy presents a direct contrast to that of Macbeth; the one proceeds with the utmost slowness, the other with a crowded and breathless rapidity.

The effect of this overbalance of the imaginative power is beautifully illustrated in the everlasting broodings and superfluous activities of Hamlet's mind, which, unseated from its healthy relation, is constantly occupied with the world within, and abstracted from the world without, — giving substance to shadows, and throwing a mist over all commonplace actualities. It is the nature of thought to be indefinite; — definiteness belongs to external imagery alone. Hence it is that the sense of sublimity arises, not from the sight of an outward object, but from the beholder's reflection upon it; — not from the sensuous impression, but from the imaginative reflex. Few have seen a celebrated waterfall without feeling something akin to disappointment: it is only subsequently that the image comes back full into the mind, and brings with it a train of grand or beautiful associations. Hamlet feels this; his senses are in a state of trance, and he looks upon external things as hieroglyphics. His soliloquy —

Oh! that this too, too solid flesh would melt, &c.

springs from that craving after the indefinite — for that which is not — which most easily besets men of genius; and the self-delusion common to this temper of mind is finely exemplified in the character which Hamlet gives of himself: —

> — It can not be
> But I am pigeon-livered, and lack gall
> To make oppression bitter.

He mistakes the seeing his chains for the breaking of them, delays action till action is of no use, and dies the victim of mere circumstance and accident. . . .

Act I, scene IV. The unimportant conversation with which this scene opens is a proof of Shakespeare's minute knowledge of human nature. It is a well-established fact, that on the brink of any serious enterprise, or event of moment, men almost invariably endeavor to elude the pressure of their own thoughts by turning aside to trivial objects and familiar circumstances: thus this dialogue on the platform begins with remarks on the coldness of the air, and inquiries, obliquely connected, indeed, with the expected hour of the visitation, but thrown out in a seeming vacuity of topics, as to the striking of the clock and so forth. The same desire to escape from the impending thought is carried on in Hamlet's account of, and moralizing on, the Danish custom of wassailing: he runs off from the particular to the universal, and in his repugnance to personal and individual concerns, escapes, as it were, from himself in generalizations, and smothers the impatience and uneasy feelings of the moment in abstract reasoning. Besides this, another purpose is answered; — for by thus entangling the attention of the audience in the nice distinctions and parenthetical sentences of this speech of Hamlet's, Shakespeare takes them completely by surprise on the appearance of the Ghost, which comes upon them in all the suddenness of its visionary character. Indeed, no modern writer would have dared, like Shakespeare, to have preceded this last visitation by two distinct appearances, — or could have contrived that the third should rise upon the former two in impressiveness and solemnity of interest.

But in addition to all the other excellences of Hamlet's speech concerning the wassail-music — so finely revealing the predominant idealism, the ratiocinative° meditativeness, of his character — it has the advantage of giving nature

---

ratiocinative: Reasoned.

and probability to the impassioned continuity of the speech instantly directed to the Ghost. The *momentum* had been given to his mental activity; the full current of the thoughts and words had set in, and the very forgetfulness, in the fervor of his augmentation, of the purpose for which he was there, aided in preventing the appearance from benumbing the mind. Consequently, it acted as a new impulse, — a sudden stroke which increased the velocity of the body already in motion, whilst it altered the direction. The copresence of Horatio, Marcellus, and Bernardo is most judiciously contrived; for it renders the courage of Hamlet and his impetuous eloquence perfectly intelligible. The knowledge, — the unthought of consciousness, — the sensation, — of human auditors — of flesh and blood sympathists — acts as a support and a stimulation of *a tergo,* while the front of the mind, the whole consciousness of the speaker, is filled, yea, absorbed, by the apparition. Add too, that the apparition itself has by its previous appearances been brought nearer to a thing of this world. This accrescence° of objectivity in a Ghost that yet retains all its ghostly attributes and fearful subjectivity, is truly wonderful.

Act I, scene v. Hamlet's speech: —

O all you host of heaven! O earth! What else?
And shall I couple hell? —

I remember nothing equal to this burst unless it be the first speech of Prometheus in the Greek drama, after the exit of Vulcan and the two Afrites. But Shakespeare alone could have produced the vow of Hamlet to make his memory a blank of all maxims and generalized truths, that "observation had copied there," — followed immediately by the speaker noting down the generalized fact,

That one may smile, and smile, and be a villain!

MARCELLUS: Hillo, ho, ho, my lord!
HAMLET: Hillo, ho, ho, boy! come bird, come, &c.

This part of the scene after Hamlet's interview with the Ghost has been charged with an improbable eccentricity. But the truth is that after the mind has been stretched beyond its usual pitch and tone, it must either sink into exhaustion and inanity, or seek relief by change. It is thus well known, that persons conversant in deeds of cruelty contrive to escape from conscience by connecting something of the ludicrous with them, and by inventing grotesque terms and a certain technical phraseology to disguise the horror of their practices. Indeed, paradoxical as it may appear, the terrible by a law of the human mind always touches on the verge of the ludicrous. Both arise from the perception of something out of the common order of things — something, in fact, out of its place; and if from this we can abstract danger, the uncommonness will alone remain, and the sense of the ridiculous be excited. The close alliance of these opposites — they are not contraries — appears from the circumstance, that laughter is equally the expression of extreme anguish and horror as of joy: as there are tears of sorrow and tears of joy, so is there a laugh of terror and a laugh of merriment. These complex causes will naturally have produced in Hamlet the disposition to escape from his own feelings of the overwhelming and supernatural by a wild transition to the ludicrous, — a sort of cunning bravado, bordering on the flights of

accrescence: Accumulation or concentration.

delirium. For you may, perhaps, observe that Hamlet's wildness is but half false; he plays that subtle trick of pretending to act only when he is very near really being what he acts.

Sigmund Freud (1856–1939)
HAMLET'S SCRUPLES   1900°

Sigmund Freud is the most celebrated psychiatrist of the twentieth century. He was especially interested in Greek myth, as his comments on Oedipus Rex *suggest.* Hamlet *was another play that took on mythic proportions for him, in part because Freud saw in* Hamlet *the operation of his famous theory of the Oedipus complex. In the following excerpt, Freud examines not only the play but the circumstances of the play to see to what extent it fulfills his theory.*

Another of the great creations of tragic poetry, Shakespeare's *Hamlet,* has its roots in the same soil as *Oedipus Rex.* But the changed treatment of the same material reveals the whole difference in the mental life of these two widely separated epochs of civilization: the secular advance of repression in the emotional life of mankind. In the *Oedipus* the child's wishful fantasy that underlies it is brought into the open and realized as it would be in a dream. In *Hamlet* it remains repressed; and — just as in the case of a neurosis — we only learn of its existence from its inhibiting consequences. Strangely enough, the overwhelming effect produced by the more modern tragedy has turned out to be compatible with the fact that people have remained completely in the dark as to the hero's character. The play is built up on Hamlet's hesitations over fulfilling the task of revenge that is assigned to him; but its text offers no reasons or motives for these hesitations and an immense variety of attempts at interpreting them have failed to produce a result. According to the view which was originated by Goethe and is still the prevailing one today, Hamlet represents the type of man whose power of direct action is paralyzed by an excessive development of his intellect. (He is "sicklied o'er with the pale cast of thought.") According to another view, the dramatist has tried to portray a pathologically irresolute character which might be classed as neurasthenic. The plot of the drama shows us, however, that Hamlet is far from being represented as a person incapable of taking any action. We see him doing so on two occasions: first in a sudden outburst of temper, when he runs his sword through the eavesdropper behind the arras, and secondly in a premeditated and even crafty fashion, when, with all the callousness of a Renaissance prince, he sends the two courtiers to the death that had been planned for himself. What is it, then, that inhibits him in fulfilling the task set him by his father's ghost? The answer, once again, is that it is the peculiar nature of the task. Hamlet is able to do anything — except take vengeance on the man who did away with his father and took that father's place with his mother, the man who shows him the repressed wishes of his own

---

1900: Freud's *Interpretation of Dreams,* from which this excerpt is taken, was first published in 1900 and updated regularly by Freud through eight editions.

childhood realized. Thus the loathing which should drive him on to revenge is replaced in him by self-reproaches, by scruples of conscience, which remind him that he himself is literally no better than the sinner whom he is to punish. Here I have translated into conscious terms what was bound to remain unconscious in Hamlet's mind; and if anyone is inclined to call him a hysteric, I can only accept the fact as one that is implied by my interpretation. The distaste for sexuality expressed by Hamlet in his conversation with Ophelia fits in very well with this: the same distaste which was destined to take possession of the poet's mind more and more during the years that followed, and which reached its extreme expression in *Timon of Athens*. For it can of course only be the poet's own mind which confronts us in Hamlet. I observe in a book on Shakespeare by Georg Brandes (1896) a statement that *Hamlet* was written immediately after the death of Shakespeare's father (in 1601), that is, under the immediate impact of his bereavement and, as we may well assume, while his childhood feelings about his father had been freshly revived. It is known, too, that Shakespeare's own son who died at an early age bore the name of "Hamnet," which is identical with "Hamlet." Just as *Hamlet* deals with the relation of a son to his parents, so *Macbeth* (written at approximately the same period) is concerned with the subject of childlessness. But just as all neurotic symptoms, and, for that matter, dreams, are capable of being "overinterpreted" and indeed need to be, if they are to be fully understood, so all genuinely creative writings are the product of more than a single motive and more than a single impulse in the poet's mind, and are open to more than a single interpretation. In what I have written I have only attempted to interpret the deepest layer of impulses in the mind of the creative writer.

T. S. Eliot (1888–1965)
HAMLET AND HIS PROBLEMS   *1934*

> *T. S. Eliot was not only one of the most important poets of the modernist period in the twentieth century, but also an extremely interesting critic of Elizabethan literature. His several collections of essays have in some cases defined important critical terms that later readers have used to gain insight into great writers. One of those terms is developed here: the objective correlative, which Eliot feels is missing in* Hamlet. *His argument is provocative and revealing.*

Few critics have ever admitted that *Hamlet* the play is the primary problem, and Hamlet the character only secondary. And Hamlet the character has had an especial temptation for that most dangerous type of critic: the critic with a mind which is naturally of the creative order, but which through some weakness in creative power exercises itself in criticism instead. These minds often find in Hamlet a vicarious existence for their own artistic realization. Such a mind had Goethe, who made of Hamlet a Werther; and such had Coleridge who made of Hamlet a Coleridge; and probably neither of these men in writing about Hamlet remembered that his first business was to study a work of art. The kind of criticism that Goethe and Coleridge produced, in writing of Hamlet, is the most misleading kind possible. For they both possessed unquestionable critical insight, and both make their critical aberrations the more plausible by the substitution — of their own Hamlet for Shakespeare's — which their creative gift effects. We should be thankful that Walter Pater° did not fix his attention on this play.

Two writers of our time, Mr. J. M. Robertson and Professor Stoll of the University of Minnesota, have issued small books which can be praised for moving in the other direction. Mr. Stoll performs a service in recalling to our attention the labors of the critics of the seventeenth and eighteenth centuries, observing that

> they knew less about psychology than more recent Hamlet critics, but they were nearer in spirit to Shakespeare's art; and as they insisted on the importance of the effect of the whole rather than on the importance of the leading character, they were nearer, in their old-fashioned way, to the secret of dramatic art in general.

Qua work of art, the work of art cannot be interpreted; there is nothing to interpret; we can only criticize it according to standards, in comparison to other works of art; and for "interpretation" the chief task is the presentation of relevant historical facts which the reader is not assumed to know. Mr. Robertson points out, very pertinently, how critics have failed in their "interpretation" of *Hamlet* by ignoring what ought to be very obvious: that *Hamlet* is a stratification, that it represents the efforts of a series of men, each making what he could out of the work of his predecessors. The *Hamlet* of Shakespeare will appear to us very differently if, instead of treating the whole action of the play as due to Shakespeare's design, we perceive his *Hamlet* to be superposed upon much cruder material which persists even in the final form.

We know that there was an older play by Thomas Kyd, that extraordinary dramatic (if not poetic) genius who was in all probability the author of two plays so dissimilar as the *Spanish Tragedy* and *Arden of Feversham;* and what this play was like we can guess from three clues: from the *Spanish Tragedy* itself, from the tale of Belleforest upon which Kyd's *Hamlet* must have been based, and from a version acted in Germany in Shakespeare's lifetime which bears strong evidence of having been adapted from the earlier, not from the later, play. From these three sources it is clear that in the earlier play the motive was a revenge motive simply; that the action or delay is caused, as in the *Spanish Tragedy,* solely by the difficulty of assassinating a monarch surrounded by guards; and that the "madness" of Hamlet was feigned in order to escape suspicion, and successfully. In the final play of Shakespeare, on the other hand, there is a motive which is more important than that of revenge, and which explicitly "blunts" the latter; the delay in revenge is unexplained on grounds of necessity or expediency; and the effect of the "madness" is not to lull but to arouse the king's suspicion. The alteration is not complete enough, however, to be convincing. Furthermore, there are verbal parallels so close to the *Spanish Tragedy* as to leave no doubt that in places Shakespeare was merely *revising* the text of Kyd. And finally there are unexplained scenes — the Polonius-Laertes and the Polonius-Reynaldo scenes — for which there is little excuse; these scenes are not in the verse style of Kyd, and not beyond doubt in the style of Shake-

Walter Pater: English writer and critic (1839–1894). His writings were often over-elaborate.

speare. These Mr. Robertson believes to be scenes in the original play of Kyd reworked by a third hand, perhaps Chapman,° before Shakespeare touched the play. And he concludes, with very strong show of reason, that the original play of Kyd was, like certain other revenge plays, in two parts of five acts each. The upshot of Mr. Robertson's examination is, we believe, irrefragable: that Shakespeare's *Hamlet,* so far as it is Shakespeare's, is a play dealing with the effect of a mother's guilt upon her son, and that Shakespeare was unable to impose this motive successfully upon the "intractable" material of the old play.

Of the intractability there can be no doubt. So far from being Shakespeare's masterpiece, the play is most certainly an artistic failure. In several ways the play is puzzling, and disquieting as is none of the others. Of all the plays it is the longest and is possibly the one on which Shakespeare spent most pains; and yet he has left in it superfluous and inconsistent scenes which even hasty revision should have noticed. The versification is variable. Lines like

> Look, the morn, in russet mantle clad,
> Walks o'er the dew of yon high eastern hill,

are of the Shakespeare of *Romeo and Juliet.* The lines in act V, scene II,

> Sir, in my heart there was a kind of fighting
> That would not let me sleep . . .
> Up from my cabin,
> My sea-grown scarf'd about me, in the dark
> Grop'd I to find out them: had my desire;
> Finger'd their packet;

are of his quite mature. Both workmanship and thought are in an unstable position. We are surely justified in attributing the play, with that other profoundly interesting play of "intractable" material and astonishing versification, *Measure for Measure,* to a period of crisis, after which follow the tragic successes which culminate in *Coriolanus. Coriolanus* may be not as "interesting" as *Hamlet,* but it is, with *Antony and Cleopatra,* Shakespeare's most assured artistic success. And probably more people have thought *Hamlet* a work of art because they found it interesting, than have found it interesting because it is a work of art. It is the *Mona Lisa* of literature.

The grounds of *Hamlet*'s failure are not immediately obvious. Mr. Robertson is undoubtedly correct in concluding that the essential emotion of the play is the feeling of a son toward a guilty mother:

> [Hamlet's] tone is that of one who has suffered tortures on the score of his mother's degradation. . . . The guilt of a mother is an almost intolerable motive for drama, but it had to be maintained and emphasized to supply a psychological solution, or rather a hint of one.

This, however, is by no means the whole story. It is not merely the "guilt of a mother" that cannot be handled as Shakespeare handled the suspicion of Othello, the infatuation of Antony, or the pride of Coriolanus. The subject might conceivably have expanded into a tragedy like these, intelligible, self-complete, in the sunlight. *Hamlet,* like the sonnets, is full of some stuff that the writer could not drag to light, contemplate, or manipulate into art. And when we search for this feeling, we find it, as in the sonnets, very difficult to

Chapman: George Chapman (1559?–1634), Elizabethan poet and playwright.

localize. You cannot point to it in the speeches; indeed, if you examine the two famous soliloquies you see the versification of Shakespeare, but a content which might be claimed by another, perhaps by the author of the *Revenge of Bussy d'Ambois,*° act V, scene I. We find Shakespeare's Hamlet not in the action, not in any quotations that we might select, so much as in an unmistakable tone which is unmistakably not in the earlier play.

The only way of expressing emotion in the form of art is by finding an "objective correlative"; in other words, a set of objects, a situation, a chain of events which shall be the formula of that *particular* emotion; such that when the external facts, which must terminate in sensory experience, are given, the emotion is immediately evoked. If you examine any of Shakespeare's more successful tragedies, you will find this exact equivalence; you will find that the state of mind of Lady Macbeth walking in her sleep has been communicated to you by a skillful accumulation of imagined sensory impressions; the words of Macbeth on hearing of his wife's death strike us as if, given the sequence of events, these words were automatically released by the last event in the series. The artistic "inevitability" lies in this complete adequacy of the external to the emotion; and this is precisely what is deficient in *Hamlet*. Hamlet (the man) is dominated by an emotion which is inexpressible, because it is in *excess* of the facts as they appear. And the supposed identity of Hamlet with his author is genuine to this point: that Hamlet's bafflement at the absence of objective equivalent to his feelings is a prolongation of the bafflement of his creator in the face of his artistic problem. Hamlet is up against the difficulty that his disgust is occasioned by his mother, but that his mother is not an adequate equivalent for it; his disgust envelops and exceeds her. It is thus a feeling which he cannot understand; he cannot objectify it, and it therefore remains to poison life and obstruct action. None of the possible actions can satisfy it; and nothing that Shakespeare can do with the plot can express Hamlet for him. And it must be noticed that the very nature of the *données* of the problem precludes objective equivalence. To have heightened the criminality of Gertrude would have been to provide the formula for a totally different emotion in Hamlet; it is just *because* her character is so negative and insignificant that she arouses in Hamlet the feeling which she is incapable of representing.

The "madness" of Hamlet lay to Shakespeare's hand; in the earlier play a simple ruse, and to the end, we may presume, understood as a ruse by the audience. For Shakespeare it is less than madness and more than feigned. The levity of Hamlet, his repetition of phrase, his puns, are not part of a deliberate plan of dissimulation, but a form of emotional relief. In the character Hamlet it is the buffoonery of an emotion which can find no outlet in action; in the dramatist it is the buffoonery of an emotion which he cannot express in art. The intense feeling, ecstatic or terrible, without an object or exceeding its object, is something which every person of sensibility has known; it is doubtless a subject of study for pathologists. It often occurs in adolescence: the ordinary person puts these feelings to sleep, or trims down his feelings to fit the business world; the artist keeps them alive by his ability to intensify the world to his emotions. The Hamlet of Laforgue° is an adolescent; the Hamlet of Shakespeare

Revenge of Bussy d'Ambois: Tragedy (1610–1611) by George Chapman, dealing with the reluctance of Clement d'Ambois to avenge his brother's death.

Laforgue: Jules Laforgue (1860–1887), French poet who was an important influence on Eliot.

is not, he has not that explanation and excuse. We must simply admit that here
Shakespeare tackled a problem which proved too much for him. Why he attempted it at all is an insoluble puzzle; under compulsion of what experience
he attempted to express the inexpressibly horrible, we cannot ever know. We
need a great many facts in his biography; and we should like to know whether,
and when, and after or at the same time as what personal experience, he read
Montaigne's *Apologie de Raimond Sebond*. We should have, finally, to know
something which is by hypothesis unknowable, for we assume it to be an
experience which, in the manner indicated, exceeded the facts. We should have
to understand things which Shakespeare did not understand himself.

Laura Bohannan (*b. 1922*)
Shakespeare in the Bush   *1966*

*As an Oxford-trained anthropologist, Laura Bohannan felt she understood
the way in which* Hamlet *ought to be interpreted. She took the play along with
her to a remote African village and during an unexpected lull in her studies of
the villagers, she told the story to the village elders and found they understood
it very well indeed. However, what they understood totally surprised the
anthropologist.*

Just before I left Oxford for the Tiv in West Africa, conversation turned to
the season at Stratford. "You Americans," said a friend, "often have difficulty
with Shakespeare. He was, after all, a very English poet, and one can easily
misinterpret the universal by misunderstanding the particular."

I protested that human nature is pretty much the same the whole world over;
at least the general plot and motivation of the greater tragedies would always
be clear — everywhere — although some details of custom might have to be
explained and difficulties of translation might produce other slight changes. To
end an argument we could not conclude, my friend gave me a copy of *Hamlet*
to study in the African bush: It would, he hoped, lift my mind above its primitive
surroundings, and possibly I might, by prolonged meditation, achieve the grace
of correct interpretation.

It was my second field trip to the African tribe, and I thought myself ready
to live in one of its remote sections — an area difficult to cross even on foot.
I eventually settled on the hillock of a very knowledgeable old man, the head
of a homestead of some hundred and forty people, all of whom were either his
close relatives or their wives and children. Like the other elders of the vicinity,
the old man spent most of his time performing ceremonies seldom seen these
days in the more accessible parts of the tribe. I was delighted. Soon there would
be three months of enforced isolation and leisure, between the harvest that takes
place just before the rising of the swamps and the clearing of new farms when
the water goes down. Then, I thought, they would have even more time to
perform ceremonies and explain them to me.

I was quite mistaken. Most of the ceremonies demanded the presence of
elders from several homesteads. As the swamps rose, the old men found it too
difficult to walk from one homestead to the next, and the ceremonies gradually

ceased. As the swamps rose even higher, all activities but one came to an end. The women brewed beer from maize and millet. Men, women, and children sat on their hillocks and drank it.

People began to drink at dawn. By midmorning the whole homestead was singing, dancing, and drumming. When it rained, people had to sit inside their huts: There they drank and sang or they drank and told stories. In any case, by noon or before, I either had to join the party or retire to my own hut and my books. "One does not discuss serious matters when there is beer. Come, drink with us." Since I lacked their capacity for the thick native beer, I spent more and more time with *Hamlet*. Before the end of the second month, grace descended on me. I was quite sure that *Hamlet* had only one possible interpretation, and that one universally obvious.

Early every morning, in the hope of having some serious talk before the beer party, I used to call on the old man at his reception hut — a circle of posts supporting a thatched roof above a low mud wall to keep out wind and rain. One day I crawled through the low doorway and found most of the men of the homestead sitting huddled in their ragged cloths on stools, low plank beds, and reclining chairs, warming themselves against the chill of the rain around a smoky fire. In the center were three pots of beer. The party had started.

The old man greeted me cordially. "Sit down and drink." I accepted a large calabash full of beer, poured some into a small drinking gourd, and tossed it down. Then I poured some more into the same gourd for the man second in seniority to my host before I handed my calabash over to a young man for further distribution. Important people shouldn't ladle beer themselves.

"It is better like this," the old man said, looking at me approvingly and plucking at the thatch that had caught in my hair. "You should sit and drink with us more often. Your servants tell me that when you are not with us, you sit inside your hut looking at a paper."

The old man was acquainted with four kinds of "papers": tax receipts, bride price receipts, court fee receipts, and letters. The messenger who brought him letters from the chief used them mainly as a badge of office, for he always knew what was in them and told the old man. Personal letters for the few who had relatives in the government or mission stations were kept until someone went to a large market where there was a letter writer and reader. Since my arrival, letters were brought to me to be read. A few men also brought me bride price receipts, privately, with requests to change the figures to a higher sum. I found moral arguments were of no avail, since in-laws are fair game, and the technical hazards of forgery difficult to explain to an illiterate people. I did not wish them to think me silly enough to look at any such papers for days on end, and I hastily explained that my "paper" was one of the "things of long ago" of my country.

"Ah," said the old man. "Tell us."

I protested that I was not a storyteller. Storytelling is a skilled art among them; their standards are high, and the audiences critical — and vocal in their criticism. I protested in vain. This morning they wanted to hear a story while they drank. They threatened to tell me no more stories until I told them one of mine. Finally, the old man promised that no one would criticize my style "for we know you are struggling with our language." "But," put in one of the elders, "you must explain what we do not understand, as we do when we tell you our stories." Realizing that here was my chance to prove *Hamlet* universally intelligible, I agreed.

The old man handed me some more beer to help me on with my storytelling. Men filled their long wooden pipes and knocked coals from the fire to place in the pipe bowls; then, puffing contentedly, they sat back to listen. I began in the proper style, "Not yesterday, not yesterday, but long ago, a thing occurred. One night three men were keeping watch outside the homestead of the great chief, when suddenly they saw the former chief approach them."

"Why was he no longer their chief?"

"He was dead," I explained. "That is why they were troubled and afraid when they saw him."

"Impossible," began one of the elders, handing his pipe on to his neighbor, who interrupted, "Of course it wasn't the dead chief. It was an omen sent by a witch. Go on."

Slightly shaken, I continued. "One of these three was a man who knew things" — the closest translation for scholar, but unfortunately it also meant witch. The second elder looked triumphantly at the first. "So he spoke to the dead chief saying, 'Tell us what we must do so you may rest in your grave,' but the dead chief did not answer. He vanished, and they could see him no more. Then the man who knew things — his name was Horatio — said this event was the affair of the dead chief's son, Hamlet."

There was a general shaking of heads round the circle. "Had the dead chief no living brothers? Or was this son the chief?"

"No," I replied. "That is, he had one living brother who became the chief when the elder brother died."

The old man muttered: Such omens were matters for chiefs and elders, not for youngsters; no good could come of going behind a chief's back; clearly Horatio was not a man who knew things.

"Yes, he was," I insisted, shooing a chicken away from my beer. "In our country the son is next to the father. The dead chief's younger brother had become the great chief. He had also married his elder brother's widow only about a month after the funeral."

"He did well," the old man beamed and announced to the others," I told you that if we knew more about Europeans, we would find they really were very like us. In our country also," he added to me, "the younger brother marries the elder brother's widow and becomes the father of his children. Now, if your uncle, who married your widowed mother, is your father's full brother, then he will be a real father to you. Did Hamlet's father and uncle have one mother?"

His question barely penetrated my mind; I was too upset and thrown too far off balance by having one of the most important elements of *Hamlet* knocked straight out of the picture. Rather uncertainly I said that I thought they had the same mother, but I wasn't sure — the story didn't say. The old man told me severely that these genealogical details made all the difference and that when I got home I must ask the elders about it. He shouted out the door to one of his younger wives to bring his goatskin bag.

Determined to save what I could of the mother motif, I took a deep breath and began again. "The son Hamlet was very sad because his mother had married again so quickly. There was no need for her to do so, and it is our custom for a widow not to go to her next husband until she has mourned for two years."

"Two years is too long," objected the wife, who had appeared with the old man's battered goatskin bag. "Who will hoe your farms for you while you have no husband?"

"Hamlet," I retorted without thinking, "was old enough to hoe his mother's farms himself. There was no need for her to remarry." No one looked convinced. I gave up. "His mother and the great chief told Hamlet not to be sad, for the great chief himself would be a father to Hamlet. Furthermore, Hamlet would be the next chief: Therefore he must stay to learn the things of a chief. Hamlet agreed to remain, and all the rest went off to drink beer."

While I paused, perplexed at how to render Hamlet's disgusted soliloquy to an audience convinced that Claudius and Gertrude had behaved in the best possible manner, one of the younger men asked me who had married the other wives of the dead chief.

"He had no other wives," I told him.

"But a chief must have many wives! How else can he brew beer and prepare food for all his guests?"

I said firmly that in our country even chiefs had only one wife, that they had servants to do their work, and that they paid them from tax money.

It was better, they returned, for a chief to have many wives and sons who would help him hoe his farms and feed his people; then everyone loved the chief who gave much and took nothing — taxes were a bad thing.

I agreed with the last comment, but for the rest fell back on their favorite way of fobbing off my questions: "That is the way it is done, so that is how we do it."

I decided to skip the soliloquy. Even if Claudius was here thought quite right to marry his brother's widow, there remained the poison motif, and I knew they would disapprove of fratricide. More hopefully I resumed, "That night Hamlet kept watch with the three who had seen his dead father. The dead chief again appeared, and although the others were afraid, Hamlet followed his dead father off to one side. When they were alone, Hamlet's dead father spoke."

"Omens can't talk!" The old man was emphatic.

"Hamlet's dead father wasn't an omen. Seeing him might have been an omen, but he was not." My audience looked as confused as I sounded. "It *was* Hamlet's dead father. It was a thing we call a 'ghost.'" I had to use the English word, for unlike many of the neighboring tribes, these people didn't believe in the survival after death of any individuating part of the personality.

"What is a 'ghost'? An omen?"

"No, a 'ghost' is someone who is dead but who walks around and can talk, and people can hear him and see him but not touch him."

They objected. "One can touch zombis."

"No, no! It was not a dead body the witches had animated to sacrifice and eat. No one else made Hamlet's dead father walk. He did it himself."

"Dead men can't walk," protested my audience as one man.

I was quite willing to compromise. A 'ghost' is the dead man's shadow."

But again they objected. "Dead men cast no shadows."

"They do in my country," I snapped.

The old man quelled the babble of disbelief that arose immediately and told me with that insincere, but courteous, agreement one extends to the fancies of the young, ignorant, and superstitious, "No doubt in your country the dead can also walk without being zombis." From the depths of his bag he produced a withered fragment of kola nut, bit off one end to show it wasn't poisoned, and handed me the rest as a peace offering.

"Anyhow," I resumed, "Hamlet's dead father said that his own brother, the one who became chief, had poisoned him. He wanted Hamlet to avenge him. Hamlet believed this in his heart, for he did not like his father's brother." I took another swallow of beer. "In the country of the great chief, living in the same homestead, for it was a very large one, was an important elder who was often with the chief to advise and help him. His name was Polonius. Hamlet was courting his daughter, but her father and her brother . . . [I cast hastily about for some tribal analogy] warned her not to let Hamlet visit her when she was alone on her farm, for he would be a great chief and so could not marry her."

"Why not?" asked the wife, who had settled down on the edge of the old man's chair. He frowned at her for asking stupid questions and growled, "They lived in the same homestead."

"That was not the reason," I informed them. "Polonius was a stranger who lived in the homestead because he helped the chief, not because he was a relative."

"Then why couldn't Hamlet marry her?"

"He could have," I explained, "but Polonius didn't think he would. After all, Hamlet was a man of great importance who ought to marry a chief's daughter, for in his country a man could have only one wife. Polonius was afraid that if Hamlet made love to his daughter, then no one else would give a high price for her."

"That might be true," remarked one of the shrewder elders, "but a chief's son would give his mistress's father enough presents and patronage to more than make up the difference. Polonius sounds like a fool to me."

"Many people think he was," I agreed. "Meanwhile Polonius sent his son Laertes off to Paris to learn the things of that country, for it was the homestead of a very great chief indeed. Because he was afraid that Laertes might waste a lot of money on beer and women and gambling, or get into trouble by fighting, he sent one of his servants to Paris secretly, to spy out what Laertes was doing. One day Hamlet came upon Polonius's daughter Ophelia. He behaved so oddly he frightened her. Indeed" — I was fumbling for words to express the dubious quality of Hamlet's madness — "the chief and many others had also noticed that when Hamlet talked one could understand the words but not what they meant. Many people thought that he had become mad." My audience suddenly became much more attentive. "The great chief wanted to know what was wrong with Hamlet, so he sent for two of Hamlet's age mates [school friends would have taken long explanation] to talk to Hamlet and find out what troubled his heart. Hamlet, seeing that they had been bribed by the chief to betray him, told them nothing. Polonius, however, insisted that Hamlet was mad because he had been forbidden to see Ophelia, whom he loved."

"Why," inquired a bewildered voice, "should anyone bewitch Hamlet on that account?"

"Bewitch him?"

"Yes, only witchcraft can make anyone mad, unless, of course, one sees the beings that lurk in the forest."

I stopped being a storyteller, took out my notebook, and demanded to be told more about these two causes of madness. Even while they spoke and I jotted notes, I tried to calculate the effect of this new factor on the plot. Hamlet had not been exposed to the beings that lurk in the forests. Only his relatives in the male line could bewitch him. Barring relatives not mentioned by Shakespeare, it had to be Claudius who was attempting to harm him. And, of course, it was.

For the moment I staved off questions by saying that the great chief also refused to believe that Hamlet was mad for the love of Ophelia and nothing else. "He was sure that something much more important was troubling Hamlet's heart."

"Now Hamlet's age mates," I continued, "had brought with them a famous storyteller. Hamlet decided to have this man tell the chief and all his homestead a story about a man who had poisoned his brother because he desired his brother's wife and wished to be chief himself. Hamlet was sure the great chief could not hear the story without making a sign if he was indeed guilty, and then he would discover whether his dead father had told him the truth."

The old man interrupted, with deep cunning, "Why should a father lie to his son?" he asked.

I hedged: "Hamlet wasn't sure that it really was his dead father." It was impossible to say anything, in that language, about devil-inspired visions.

"You mean," he said, "it actually was an omen, and he knew witches sometimes send false ones. Hamlet was a fool not to go to one skilled in reading omens and divining the truth in the first place. A man-who-sees-the-truth could have told him how his father died, if he really had been poisoned, and if there was witchcraft in it; then Hamlet could have called the elders to settle the matter."

The shrewd elder ventured to disagree. "Because his father's brother was a great chief, one-who-sees-the-truth might therefore have been afraid to tell it. I think it was for that reason that a friend of Hamlet's father — a witch and an elder — sent an omen so his friend's son would know. Was the omen true?"

"Yes," I said, abandoning ghosts and the devil; a witch-sent omen it would have to be. "It was true, for when the storyteller was telling his tale before all the homestead, the great chief rose in fear. Afraid that Hamlet knew his secret he planned to have him killed."

The stage set of the next bit presented some difficulties of translation. I began cautiously. "The great chief told Hamlet's mother to find out from her son what he knew. But because a woman's children are always first in her heart, he had the important elder Polonius hide behind a cloth that hung against the wall of Hamlet's mother's sleeping hut. Hamlet started to scold his mother for what she had done."

There was a shocked murmur from everyone. A man should never scold his mother.

"She called out in fear, and Polonius moved behind the cloth. Shouting, 'A rat!' Hamlet took his machete and slashed through the cloth." I paused for dramatic effect. "He had killed Polonius!"

The old men looked at each other in supreme disgust. "That Polonius truly was a fool and a man who knew nothing! What child would not know enough to shout, 'It's me!'" With a pang, I remembered that these people are ardent hunters, always armed with bow, arrow, and machete; at the first rustle in the grass an arrow is aimed and ready, and the hunter shouts "Game!" If no human voice answers immediately, the arrow speeds on its way. Like a good hunter Hamlet had shouted, "A rat!"

I rushed in to save Polonius's reputation. "Polonius did speak. Hamlet heard him. But he thought it was the chief and wished to kill him to avenge his father. He had meant to kill him earlier that evening. . . ." I broke down, unable to describe to these pagans, who had no belief in individual afterlife, the difference between dying at one's prayers and dying "unhousell'd, disappointed, unaneled."

This time I had shocked my audience seriously. "For a man to raise his hand against his father's brother and the one who has become his father — that is a terrible thing. The elders ought to let such a man be bewitched."

I nibbled at my kola nut in some perplexity, then pointed out that after all the man had killed Hamlet's father.

"No," pronounced the old man, speaking less to me than to the young men sitting behind the elders. "If your father's brother has killed your father, you must appeal to your father's age mates; *they* may avenge him. No man may use violence against his senior relatives." Another thought struck him. "But if his father's brother had indeed been wicked enough to bewitch Hamlet and make him mad that would be a good story indeed, for it would be his fault that Hamlet, being mad, no longer had any sense and thus was ready to kill his father's brother."

There was a murmur of applause. *Hamlet* was again a good story to them, but it no longer seemed quite the same story to me. As I thought over the coming complications of plot and motive, I lost courage and decided to skim over dangerous ground quickly.

"The great chief," I went on, "was not sorry that Hamlet had killed Polonius. It gave him a reason to send Hamlet away, with his two treacherous age mates, with letters to a chief of a far country, saying that Hamlet should be killed. But Hamlet changed the writing on their papers, so that the chief killed his age mates instead." I encountered a reproachful glare from one of the men whom I had told undetectable forgery was not merely immoral but beyond human skill. I looked the other way.

"Before Hamlet could return, Laertes came back for his father's funeral. The great chief told him Hamlet had killed Polonius. Laertes swore to kill Hamlet because of this, and because his sister Ophelia, hearing her father had been killed by the man she loved, went mad and drowned in the river."

"Have you already forgotten what we told you?" The old man was reproachful. "One cannot take vengeance on a madman; Hamlet killed Polonius in his madness. As for the girl, she not only went mad, she was drowned. Only witches can make people drown. Water itself can't hurt anything. It is merely something one drinks and bathes in."

I began to get cross. "If you don't like the story, I'll stop."

The old man made soothing noises and himself poured me some more beer. "You tell the story well, and we are listening. But it is clear that the elders of your country have never told you what the story really means. No, don't interrupt! We believe you when you say your marriage customs are different, or your clothes and weapons. But people are the same everywhere; therefore, there are always witches and it is we, the elders, who know how witches work. We told you it was the great chief who wished to kill Hamlet, and now your own words have proved us right. Who were Ophelia's male relatives?"

"There were only her father and her brother." Hamlet was clearly out of my hands.

"There must have been many more; this also you must ask of your elders when you get back to your country. From what you tell us, since Polonius was dead, it must have been Laertes who killed Ophelia, although I do not see the reason for it."

We had emptied one pot of beer, and the old men argued the point with slightly tipsy interest. Finally one of them demanded of me, "What did the servant of Polonius say on his return?"

With difficulty I recollected Reynaldo and his mission. "I don't think he did return before Polonius was killed."

"Listen," said the elder, "and I will tell you how it was and how your story will go, then you may tell me if I am right. Polonius knew his son would get into trouble, and so he did. He had many fines to pay for fighting, and debts from gambling. But he had only two ways of getting money quickly. One was to marry off his sister at once, but it is difficult to find a man who will marry a woman desired by the son of a chief. For if the chief's heir commits adultery with your wife, what can you do? Only a fool calls a case against a man who will someday be his judge. Therefore Laertes had to take the second way: He killed his sister by witchcraft, drowning her so he could secretly sell her body to the witches."

I raised an objection. "They found her body and buried it. Indeed Laertes jumped into the grave to see his sister once more — so, you see, the body was truly there. Hamlet, who had just come back, jumped in after him."

"What did I tell you?" The elder appealed to the others. "Laertes was up to no good with his sister's body. Hamlet prevented him, because the chief's heir, like a chief, does not wish any other man to grow rich and powerful. Laertes would be angry, because he would have killed his sister without benefit to himself. In our country he would try to kill Hamlet for that reason. Is this not what happened?"

"More or less," I admitted. "When the great chief found Hamlet was still alive, he encouraged Laertes to try to kill Hamlet and arranged a fight with machetes between them. In the fight both the young men were wounded to death. Hamlet's mother drank the poisoned beer that the chief meant for Hamlet in case he won the fight. When he saw his mother die of poison, Hamlet, dying, managed to kill his father's brother with his machete."

"You see, I was right!" exclaimed the elder.

"That was a very good story," added the old man, "and you told it with very few mistakes. There was just one more error, at the very end. The poison Hamlet's mother drank was obviously meant for the survivor of the fight, whichever it was. If Laertes had won, the great chief would have poisoned him, for no one would know that he arranged Hamlet's death. Then, too, he need not fear Laertes' witchcraft; it takes a strong heart to kill one's only sister by witchcraft.

"Sometime," concluded the old man, gathering his ragged toga about him, "you must tell us some more stories of your country. We, who are elders, will instruct you in their true meaning, so that when you return to your own land your elders will see that you have not been sitting in the bush, but among those who know things and who have taught you wisdom."

C. Walter Hodges
HAMLET'S GHOST

The drawing below by C. Walter Hodges gives us an interesting possible reconstruction for the manner in which Hamlet's ghost could have entered and exited. We also get a good idea of the resources of the Elizabethan stage from his illustration.

Stephen J. Greenblatt (b. 1943)
THE TEMPEST AND THE NEW WORLD   *1990*

Modern criticism has posed the question Is The Tempest *concerned with issues of colonization or not? Greenblatt, in studying the history of the settling of the New World, raises interesting questions when he describes the dramatist as a colonist. By pointing to Shakespeare's own ambivalence on the matter, he reminds us how difficult the question of colonialism was even in the seventeenth century.*

The link between *The Tempest* and the New World has often been noted, as, for example, by Terence Hawkes who suggests, in his book *Shakespeare's Talking Animals*, that in creating Prospero, the playwright's imagination was fired by the resemblance he perceived between himself and a colonist. "A colonist," writes Hawkes,

> acts essentially as a dramatist. He imposes the "shape" of his own culture, *embodied in his speech*, on the new world, and makes that world recognizable, habitable, "natural," able to speak his language.

Conversely,

> the dramatist is metaphorically a colonist. His art penetrates new areas of experience, his language expands the boundaries of our culture, and makes the new territory over in its own image. His "raids on the inarticulate" open up new worlds for the imagination. (212)

The problem for critics has been to accommodate this perceived resemblance between dramatist and colonist with a revulsion that reaches from the political critiques of colonialism in our own century back to the moral outrage of Las Casas° and Montaigne.° Moreover, there are many aspects of the play itself that make colonialism a problematical model for the theatrical imagination: If *The Tempest* holds up a mirror to empire, Shakespeare would appear deeply ambivalent about using the reflected image as a representation of his own practice.

Caliban enters in act I, cursing Prospero and protesting bitterly: "This island's mine, by Sycorax my mother, / Which thou tak'st from me" (I, II, 333–34). When he first arrived, Prospero made much of Caliban, and Caliban, in turn, showed Prospero "all the qualities o'th'isle." But now, Caliban complains, "I am all the subjects that you have, / Which first was mine own King." Prospero replies angrily that he had treated Caliban "with human care" until he tried to rape Miranda, a charge Caliban does not deny. At this point, Miranda herself chimes in, with a speech Dryden and others have found disturbingly indelicate:

> Abhorrèd slave,
> Which any print of goodness wilt not take,
> Being capable of all ill! I pitied thee,

Las Casas: Bartolomé de Las Casas (1474–1566), bishop of Chiapa in Mexico, who became known as "the protector of the Indians."
Montaigne: Michel de Montaigne (1533–1592), author of one of the first works of anthropology, "Apology of Raymond Sebonde," to which Shakespeare alludes in *The Tempest.*

Took pains to make thee speak, taught thee each hour
One thing or other: when thou didst not, savage,
Know thine own meaning, but wouldst gabble like
A thing most brutish, I endow'd thy purposes
With words that made them known. But thy vile race,
Though thou didst learn, had that in't which good natures
Could not abide to be with; therefore wast thou
Deservedly confin'd into this rock,
Who hadst deserv'd more than a prison.   (I, II, 354–65)

To this, Caliban replies:

You taught me language, and my profit on't
Is I know how to curse. The red plague rid you
For learning me your language!   (I, II, 366–68)

Caliban's retort might be taken as self-indictment: Even with the gift of language, his nature is so debased that he can only learn to curse. But the lines refuse to mean this; what we experience instead is a sense of their devastating justness. Ugly, rude, savage, Caliban nevertheless achieves for an instant an absolute if intolerably bitter moral victory. There is no reply; only Prospero's command: "Hagseed, hence! / Fetch us in fuel," coupled with an ugly threat:

If thou neglect'st, or dost unwillingly
What I command, I'll rack thee with old cramps,
Fill all thy bones with aches, make thee roar
That beasts shall tremble at thy din.   (I, II, 371–74)

What makes this exchange so powerful, I think, is that Caliban is anything but a Noble Savage. Shakespeare does not shrink from the darkest European fantasies about the Wild Man; indeed he exaggerates them: Caliban is deformed, lecherous, evil-smelling, idle, treacherous, naive, drunken, rebellious, violent, and devil-worshipping. According to Prospero, he is not even human: a "born devil," "got by the devil himself / Upon thy wicked dam" (I, II, 322–23). *The Tempest* utterly rejects the uniformitarian view of the human race, the view that would later triumph in the Enlightenment and prevail in the West to this day. All men, the play seems to suggest, are *not* alike; strip away the adornments of culture and you will *not* reach a single human essence. If anything, *The Tempest* seems closer in spirit to the attitude of the present-day inhabitants of Java who, according to Clifford Geertz, quite flatly say, "To be human is to be Javanese."

And yet out of the midst of this attitude Caliban wins a momentary victory that is, quite simply, an assertion of inconsolable human pain and bitterness. And out of the midst of this attitude Prospero comes, at the end of the play, to say of Caliban, "this thing of darkness I / Acknowledge mine" (V, I, 275–76). Like Caliban's earlier reply, Prospero's words are ambiguous; they might be taken as a bare statement that the strange "demi-devil" is one of Prospero's party as opposed to Alonso's, or even that Caliban is Prospero's slave. But again the lines refuse to mean this: They acknowledge a deep, if entirely unsentimental, bond. By no means is Caliban accepted into the family of man; rather, he is claimed as Philoctetes° might claim his own festering wound. Perhaps, too, the

Philoctetes: Minor Greek hero and famous archer who was bitten by a snake and made lame.

word "acknowledge" implies some moral responsibility, as when the Lord, in the King James translation of Jeremiah, exhorts men to "acknowledge thine iniquity, that thou hast transgressed against the Lord thy God" (3:13). Certainly the Caliban of act V is in a very real sense Prospero's creature, and the bitter justness of his retort early in the play still casts a shadow at its close. With Prospero restored to his dukedom, the match of Ferdinand and Miranda blessed, Ariel freed to the elements, and even the wind and tides of the return voyage settled, Shakespeare leaves Caliban's fate naggingly unclear. Prospero has acknowledged a bond; that is all.

Thomas Middleton and William Rowley

Thomas Middleton (1580?–1627) spent two or three years at Oxford before going to London, where he seems to have become involved in the theater almost immediately. Little is known of his collaborator, William Rowley (1585?–1642?), for whom *The Changeling* is probably his best remembered work. Rowley seems to have collaborated with a number of playwrights, although he did not establish a substantial independent reputation for himself. Collaboration was perhaps more common than single authorship in the Renaissance. In many cases plays seem to have been written by small committees because success in the Elizabethan and Jacobean theater depended on producing a variety of plays very rapidly. Like Shakespeare, Middleton wrote many plays in his short life but, unlike Shakespeare, he wrote a good number of them in collaboration with other playwrights.

Middleton was known for satires, masques, comedies, tragedies, and tragicomedies. Twenty-two plays and twelve masques have been positively identified as his, with a number of other plays possibly his. The most successful of his plays are *A Mad World, My Masters*, a comedy (1606?); *A Trick to Catch the Old One*, a comedy (1607?); *A Chaste Maid in Cheapside*, a comedy (1611); *A Fair Quarrel*, a tragicomedy with Rowley (1615?/1617); *The Changeling*, with Rowley (1622), a tragicomedy; *A Game at Chess*, political satire (1624); and *Women Beware Women*, a tragedy (1625?/1627).

For reasons difficult for us to reconstruct, a passion for boy actors took hold of the London stage in the first decade of the seventeenth century, and Middleton established his career early with comedies written for boy actors at St. Paul's, one of the most important schools in central London. In addition to these successful works, he also wrote plays for Philip Henslowe, an important theatrical entrepreneur of the period. After 1608, he began to write masques and civic pageants such as *Entertainment at the Opening of the New River* (1613); *The Triumphs of Truth* (1613); *The Triumphs of Honour and Industry* (1617); *The Triumphs of Love and Antiquity* (1619); *An Invention for the Lord Mayor* (1622); *The Triumphs of Honour and Virtue* (1622); and *The Triumphs of Integrity* (1623). These entertainments eventually helped procure him a position as chronicler of the city. His pay was soon above ten pounds a year, a living, if meager, wage. The usual fee for writing a play was six pounds, so as a speedy and able writer he was able to supplement his income handily. Because he was industrious, he was much in demand in the second decade of the century.

Like other playwrights such as Ben Jonson, Middleton sometimes got into trouble for his dangerous political satire. *A Game at Chess* (1624), satirizing Diego Gondomar, the Spanish ambassador to England, proved especially troublesome for the British government. It was produced while King James I was abroad and was so popular that it enjoyed nine performances in nine days, something unusual for this time. When word reached King James, he banned the play, thus almost ending Middleton's career in the theater. The players in the company were called to account and examined but pleaded innocence on the grounds that the master of the revels, who controlled publication of plays, had approved the play. Middleton seems to have disappeared entirely for a period of time, but eventually he went back to playwriting.

Middleton's plays are marked by strong plots, sharp portraits of shady types that he may have known in everyday London life, and powerful language. His imagery is also unusually rich and carefully controlled, with great attention paid to minor characters and details. *The Changeling* is set in Valencia, Spain, which made the horror of events more comfortable for an English audience to accept. While the play is written in verse, its direct language is almost as idiomatic today as it was in Middleton's time. Middleton, many current critics feel, deserves to be thought of as a worthy competitor to Shakespeare. Surely the psychological drama inherent in his work makes him a modern-sounding student of the distortions that can take place in the human mind and the human heart.

THE CHANGELING

In folklore, the fairies sometimes exchanged a beautiful child for an ugly child who was an idiot, mad, or simply "touched." The concept of the changeling depends on substitution and doubleness.

The play *The Changeling* has a double plot written by double authors. Thomas Middleton wrote the tragic main plot: Beatrice-Joanna's plan to murder Alonzo de Piracquo, her father Vermandero's choice for a husband, and to marry Alsemero instead. This plot is filled with intrigue, lust, and horror. The comic subplot, written by William Rowley, features Antonio, the Changeling of the title, who pretends to be a fool so that he can be near Isabella, the wife of Alibius, the keeper of an insane asylum. Alibius, in a frenzy of jealousy, has locked his young wife in with the fools to keep her away from "eligible" men. Alibius is almost as mad with jealousy at the beginning of the play as Alsemero is at the end. *The Changeling* is tragicomic, a psychological study in paranoia, sexual pathology, and insanity.

Antonio changes himself into an idiot for sexual purposes: He loves Isabella. His friend Franciscus also pretends he is insane. The scenes in the madhouse, however extraordinary, were not unusual in Renaissance drama. William Rowley perhaps witnessed such scenes in London's asylum for the insane: Bethlehem (pronounced "Bedlam"). In contrast, Vermandero's castle is not a madhouse. However, his man De Flores (a pun on "deflower") is mad with sexual desire for Beatrice-Joanna and puts up with her abuse just to be near her. Beatrice-Joanna demonstrates her own madness by inviting De Flores to kill her legal fiancé, Piracquo. She seems sane enough, even to herself, but her behavior reveals her madness. In the main plot, Beatrice-Joanna (whose doubleness is characterized in her double name) is the changeling. Vermandero, whose life has been exemplary and whose nature is calm and untroubled, admits that he could not have expected such a child as she has become.

Beatrice-Joanna has a complex relationship with De Flores. In the beginning of the play she says she detests him. She characterizes him as an ugly beast and torments him with her hatred. But such a profound emotional reaction seems to hide a fascination. De Flores's ugliness is typical of the changeling child. Beatrice-Joanna, while reviling him outwardly, has inwardly fallen under his spell. When he kills Alonzo Piracquo (his name means "pure water"), De Flores returns the valuable jewel ring she had given Alonzo as a wedding token, along with Piracquo's finger. She is horrified and fascinated at the same time. The finger and ring symbolize sexual union, in this instance detached from a humanizing husbandly host. De Flores demands his reward, sexual satisfaction with Beatrice-Joanna, and he is not denied. Once she has been deflowered, she knows Alsemero will realize she is not a virgin. She then concocts the scheme of placing her maid Diaphanta (whose name means "veil") under the sheets with Alsemero on their wedding night. Once that ruse works, she instructs De Flores to kill Diaphanta so that the maid cannot reveal the truth.

Such madness controls Beatrice-Joanna at the end of the play until she will do virtually anything to save herself. In the last scene, written, like the first scene, by Rowley, De Flores and Beatrice-Joanna seem to be having intercourse in her bedroom while Alsemero tells Piracquo's brother that Antonio was the murderer:

BEATRICE (within): Oh, oh, oh!
ALSEMERO: Hark, 'tis coming to you.
DE FLORES (within): Nay, I'll along for company.
BEATRICE (within):   Oh, oh! (V, III, 139–40)

Their madness has become recklessness, and when they finally appear Beatrice-Joanna is wounded and about to die.

The main characters, while deeply disturbed mentally, conduct themselves as if they were normal. Our modern awareness of psychotic behavior has reinforced the frightening perception that madness, when it is dangerous, does not come in the shape of an Antonio or a Franciscus. It comes in the shape of a Beatrice-Joanna and a De Flores. More frightening is the thought that those who are most mad seem virtually unaware of their own madness. Madness substitutes for sanity, a change that creeps up on Beatrice-Joanna virtually without her awareness.

The Changeling in Performance

The earliest recorded performance of *The Changeling* was in 1624, and it was held in repertory by Queen Henrietta's Company until 1636. It was played frequently until 1688, when a long lapse occurred until 1930. The twentieth century, however, has made up for lost time, with more than forty productions in England, the United States, and elsewhere since 1950. Tony Richardson directed the play for the Royal Court Theatre in London in 1961, one of the most important modern productions. In London, Terry Hands's 1978 production for the Royal Shakespeare Company was visually powerful. Most of the actors were costumed in brilliant red vinyl and others in resonant black, symbolizing sexual passion and psychological darkness. Hands's production emphasized the duality of Beatrice-Joanna in an extreme fashion: She was represented in a cardboard cutout marrying Alsemero (in a silent scene) while she and De Flores copulated in the background. Robert Brustein's 1985 production at the American Repertory Theatre in Boston was powerful and favorably reviewed. Its set was dominated by a moon, whose changes reinforced the title of the play and reminded audiences of the relationship between change and lunacy.

Thomas Middleton (1570?–1627) *and William Rowley* (1585?–1642?)
THE CHANGELING
1622

Dramatis Personae

VERMANDERO, *father to Beatrice*
TOMAZO DE PIRACQUO, *a noble lord*
ALONZO DE PIRACQUO, *his brother, suitor to Beatrice*
ALSEMERO, *a nobleman, afterward married to Beatrice*
JASPERINO, *his friend*
ALIBIUS, *a jealous doctor*
LOLLIO, *his man*
PEDRO, *friend to Antonio*

ANTONIO, *the Changeling*
FRANCISCUS, *the counterfeit madman*
DE FLORES, *servant to Vermandero*
MADMEN
SERVANTS

BEATRICE[-JOANNA], *daughter to Vermandero*
DIAPHANTA, *her waiting-woman*
ISABELLA, *wife to Alibius*

The Scene: *Alligant.°*

ACT I · Scene I

(*Enter Alsemero.*)

ALSEMERO: 'Twas in the temple where I first beheld
    her,
  And now again the same; what omen yet
  Follows of that? None but imaginary.
  Why should my hopes or fate be timorous?
5 The place is holy, so is my intent:
  I love her beauties to the holy purpose,°
  And that, methinks, admits comparison
  With man's first creation, the place blest,°
  And is his right home back, if he achieve it.
10 The church hath first begun our interview,
  And that's the place must join us into one;
  So there's beginning and perfection too.

(*Enter Jasperino.*)

JASPERINO: Oh, sir, are you here? Come, the wind's
    fair with you,
  Y'are like to have a swift and pleasant passage.
15 ALSEMERO: Sure, y'are deceived, friend; 'tis contrary
  In my best judgment.
JASPERINO: What, for Malta?
  If you could buy a gale amongst the witches,
  They could not serve you such a lucky
    pennyworth
  As comes a' God's name.°
ALSEMERO: Even now I observ'd
20 The temple's vane° to turn full in my face;
  I know 'tis against me.
JASPERINO: Against you?
  Then you know not where you are.
ALSEMERO: Not well,
  indeed.
JASPERINO: Are you not well, sir?
ALSEMERO: Yes, Jasperino;
  Unless there be some hidden malady
  Within me, that I understand not.
25 JASPERINO: And that
  I begin to doubt,° sir. I never knew
  Your inclinations to travels at a pause
  With any cause to hinder it, till now.
  Ashore you were wont to call your servants up,
30 And help to trap your horses for the speed;°

Alligant: Alicante, a seaport on the east coast of Spain, about seventy-five miles due south of Valencia. **6. holy purpose:** Marriage. **8. the place blest:** Paradise. **19. a' God's name:** As God's gift, as opposed to forbidden bargains with the occult. **20. temple's vane:** The wind vane on the top of the church. **26. doubt:** Fear. **30. trap your horses for the speed:** "Harness your horses to hasten departure."

  At sea I have seen you weigh the anchor with
    'em,
  Hoist sails for fear to lose the foremost breath,
  Be in continual prayers for fair winds,
  And have you chang'd your orisons?
ALSEMERO: No, friend,
  I keep the same church, same devotion.   35
JASPERINO: Lover I'm sure y'are none, the stoic
  Was found in you long ago; your mother
  Nor best friends, who have set snares of beauty,
  Ay, and choice ones too, could never trap you
    that way.
  What might be the cause?
ALSEMERO: Lord, how violent   40
  Thou art! I was but meditating of
  Somewhat I heard within the temple.
JASPERINO: Is this violence? 'Tis but idleness
  Compar'd with your haste yesterday.
ALSEMERO: I'm all this while a-going, man.   45

(*Enter Servants.*)

JASPERINO: Backwards, I think sir. Look, your
  servants.
1 SERVANT: The seamen call; shall we board your
  trunks?
ALSEMERO: No, not today.
JASPERINO: 'Tis the critical° day, it seems, and the
  sign in Aquarius.°
2 SERVANT [*aside*]: We must not to sea today; this
  smoke will bring forth fire!°   50
ALSEMERO: Keep all on shore; I do not know the
  end
  (Which needs I must do) of an affair in hand
  Ere I can go to sea.
1 SERVANT: Well, your pleasure.
2 SERVANT [*aside*]: Let him e'en take his leisure
  too, we are safer on land.
                 (*Exeunt° Servants.*)

(*Enter Beatrice, Diaphanta, and Servants.*) [*Alsemero greets Beatrice and kisses her.*]

JASPERINO [*aside*]: How now! The laws of the Medes° 55
  are chang'd, sure! Salute a woman? He kisses too;
  wonderful! Where learnt he this? And does it perfectly too; in my conscience,° he ne'er rehears'd it
  before. Nay, go on, this will be stranger and better
  news at Valencia than if he had ransom'd half 60
  Greece from the Turk.°

---

49. critical: Astrologically crucial. **sign in Aquarius:** Aquarius, the Water-carrier, is the eleventh sign of the zodiac; hence, it is a favorable time for a sea voyage. **50. smoke . . . fire:** Proverbial, alluding to the saying "There's no smoke without fire." **54. [S.D.] Exeunt:** Latin for "They go out." **55. laws of the Medes:** Unchangeable laws (Dan. 6:8). **58. in my conscience:** On my word. **61. Greece from the Turk:** Greece was part of the Ottoman Empire from 1460 to 1830.

BEATRICE: You are a scholar, sir?
ALSEMERO: A weak one, lady.
BEATRICE: Which of the sciences is this love you
    speak of?
ALSEMERO: From your tongue, I take it to be
    music.
BEATRICE: You are skillful in't, can sing at first
65   sight.°
ALSEMERO: And I have show'd you all my skill at
    once.
    I want more words to express me further,
    And must be forc'd to repetition:
    I love you dearly.
BEATRICE: Be better advis'd, sir:
70   Our eyes are sentinels unto our judgments,
    And should give certain judgment what they see;
    But they are rash sometimes and tell us wonders
    Of common things, which, when our judgments
    find,
    They then can check the eyes and call them
    blind.
75 ALSEMERO: But I am further, lady; yesterday
    Was mine eyes' employment, and higher now
    They brought my judgment, where are both
    agreed.
    Both Houses then consenting,° 'tis agreed;
    Only there wants the confirmation
80   By the hand royal° — that's your part, lady.
BEATRICE: Oh, there's one above me,° sir. [Aside.]
    For five days past
    To be recall'd! Sure, mine eyes were mistaken,
    This was the man was meant me. That he
    should come
    So near his time, and miss it!
85 JASPERINO [aside]: We might have come by the car-
    riers° from Valencia, I see, and sav'd all our sea
    provision; we are at farthest,° sure. Methinks I
    should do something too: I meant to be a venturer
    in this voyage. Yonder's another vessel, I'll board
90   her; if she be lawful prize,° down goes her topsail!°
    [Approaches Diaphanta.]

(Enter De Flores.)

DE FLORES: Lady, your father —
BEATRICE: Is in health, I
    hope.
DE FLORES: Your eye shall instantly instruct you,
    lady.
    He's coming hitherward.
BEATRICE: What needed then
    Your duteous preface? I had rather
    He had come unexpected; you must stall°   95
    A good presence° with unnecessary blabbing;
    And how welcome for your part you are,
    I'm sure you know.
DE FLORES [aside]:   Will't never mend, this scorn,
    One side nor other? Must I be enjoin'd
    To follow still whilst she flies from me? Well,   100
    Fates do your worst, I'll please myself with sight
    Of her, at all opportunities,
    If but to spite her anger; I know she had
    Rather see me dead than living, and yet
    She knows no cause for't but a peevish will.   105
ALSEMERO: You seem'd displeas'd, lady, on the
    sudden.
BEATRICE: Your pardon, sir, 'tis my infirmity;
    Nor can I other reason render you
    Than his or hers, of some particular thing
    They must abandon as a deadly poison,   110
    Which to a thousand other tastes were
    wholesome;
    Such to mine eyes is that same fellow there,
    The same that report speaks of the basilisk.°
ALSEMERO: This is a frequent frailty in our nature;
    There's scarce a man among a thousand sound,°   115
    But hath his imperfection: one distastes
    The scent of roses, which to infinites°
    Most pleasing is, and odoriferous;
    One oil, the enemy of poison;
    Another wine, the cheerer of the heart,   120
    And lively refresher of the countenance.°
    Indeed, this fault, if so it be, is general;
    There's scarce a thing but is both lov'd and
    loath'd;
    Myself, I must confess, have the same frailty.
BEATRICE: And what may be your poison, sir? I am
    bold with you.   125
ALSEMERO: What might be your desire, perhaps, a
    cherry.

---

65. **sing at first sight:** I.e., "You can sight-read music / make
love at a first introduction" (see *Troilus and Cressida*, V, II,
9).   **78. Both Houses then consenting:** Both Houses of Parliament, Commons and Lords, senses and judgment, having
given their approval.   **80. hand royal:** The royal assent, as
to a parliamentary bill.   **81. one above me:** Above the
"royal" Beatrice is the ultimate, God-like authority of her
father.   **85–86. carriers:** Land transport.   **87. at farthest:**
At the limits of our journey.   **90. lawful prize:** I.e., a vessel
which no regulations prohibit him from capturing.   **down
goes her topsail:** The sign of a ship's surrender.

95. stall: Forestall / make stale (as in Massinger, *The Bashful
Lover*, IV, III, 42).   **96. a good presence:** I.e., the impressive
bearing of her father.   **113. basilisk:** A mythical beast able
to kill by a glance.   **115. thousand sound:** A thousand
healthy people.   **117. infinites:** An infinite number of people.
119–21. One oil . . . countenance: A reminiscence of Psalm
104:15.

BEATRICE: I am no enemy to any creature
   My memory has, but yon gentleman.
ALSEMERO: He does ill to tempt your sight, if he
   knew it.
30 BEATRICE: He cannot be ignorant of that, sir,
   I have not spar'd to tell him so; and I want
   To help myself,° since he's a gentleman
   In good respect° with my father, and follows
   him.
ALSEMERO: He's out of his place then now.
                         [*They talk apart.*]
35 JASPERINO: I am a mad wag, wench.
DIAPHANTA: So methinks; but for your comfort I can
   tell you, we have a doctor° in the city that undertakes the cure of such.
JASPERINO: Tush, I know what physic is best for the
40   state of mine own body.
DIAPHANTA: 'Tis scarce a well govern'd state, I believe.
JASPERINO: I could show thee such a thing with an
   ingredient that we two would compound together,
   and if it did not tame the maddest blood i' th' town
45   for two hours after, I'll ne'er profess physic again.
DIAPHANTA: A little poppy, sir, were good to cause
   you sleep.
JASPERINO: Poppy? I'll give thee a pop i' th' lips for
   that first, and begin there; [*Kisses her.*] poppy is
   one simple° indeed, and cuckoo (what you call't)°
50   another. I'll discover no more now, another time
   I'll show thee all.
BEATRICE: My father, sir.

(*Enter Vermandero and Servants.*)

VERMANDERO: Oh, Joanna, I came to
   meet thee;
   Your devotion's ended?
BEATRICE: For this time, sir.
   [*Aside.*] I shall change my saint,° I fear me; I
   find
55   A giddy turning in me. — Sir, this while
   I am beholding to this gentleman,
   Who left his own way to keep me company,
   And in discourse I find him much desirous
   To see your castle: he hath deserv'd it, sir,
   If ye please to grant it.
60 VERMANDERO: With all my heart, sir.
   Yet there's an article between,° I must know

Your country; we use not to give survey
   Of our chief strengths to strangers; our citadels
   Are plac'd conspicuous to outward view,
   On promonts' tops; but within are secrets.   165
ALSEMERO: A Valencian, sir.
VERMANDERO: A Valencian?
   That's native, sir; of what name, I beseech you?
ALSEMERO: Alsemero, sir.
VERMANDERO: Alsemero? Not the son
   Of John de Alsemero?
ALSEMERO: The same, sir.
VERMANDERO: My best love bids you welcome.
BEATRICE [*aside*]:   He
   was wont   170
   To call me so,° and then he speaks a most
   Unfeigned truth.
VERMANDERO: Oh, sir, I knew your father;
   We two were in acquaintance long ago,
   Before our chins were worth Iulan down,°
   And so continued till the stamp of time   175
   Had coin'd us into silver. Well, he's gone;
   A good soldier went with him.
ALSEMERO: You went together in that, sir.
VERMANDERO: No, by Saint Jacques,° I came
   behind him;
   Yet I have done somewhat too. An unhappy day   180
   Swallowed him at last at Gibraltar°
   In fight with those rebellious Hollanders,
   Was it not so?
ALSEMERO: Whose death I had reveng'd,
   Or follow'd him in fate, had not the late league°
   Prevented me.
VERMANDERO: Ay, ay, 'twas time to breathe.   185
   — Oh, Joanna, I should ha' told thee news,
   I saw Piracquo lately.
BEATRICE [*aside*]:   That's ill news.
VERMANDERO: He's hot preparing for his day of
   triumph;
   Thou must be a bride within this sevennight.
ALSEMERO [*aside*]:   Ha!
BEATRICE: Nay, good sir, be not so violent; with
   speed   190
   I cannot render satisfaction
   Unto the dear companion of my soul,
   Virginity, whom I thus long have liv'd with,

131–32. **I want . . . myself:** I lack the means to help myself.
133. **In good respect:** Held in esteem.   137. **doctor:** I.e.,
Alibius.   149. **simple:** Medicine from a single herb or plant;
hence, a medicinal herb.   **cuckoo (what you call't):** Cuckoo-
pint or wild arum, of phallic appearance.   154. **change my
saint:** Change the object of my religious adoration (to an
earthly one).   161. **article between:** A stipulation to be satisfied beforehand.

171. **To call me so:** I.e., "'my best love' is his customary
endearment to me, and he is most right in saying I bid
Alsemero welcome."   174. **Iulan down:** The first growth of
the beard, the epithet being derived from commentaries on
the name of Iulus Ascanius in *Aeneid*, I, 267.   179. **Saint
Jacques:** St. James the Greater, patron saint of Spain.   181.
Gibraltar: A Dutch victory over the Spanish fleet, April 25,
1607.   184. **late league:** The Treaty of the Hague, April 9,
1609, which provided for a twelve-year truce.

And part with it so rude and suddenly;
195 Can such friends divide, never to meet again,
Without a solemn farewell?
VERMANDERO: Tush, tush, there's a
    toy.°
ALSEMERO [aside]: I must now part, and never meet
    again
With any joy on earth. — Sir, your pardon,
My affairs call on me.
VERMANDERO: How, sir? By no means;
200 Not chang'd so soon, I hope. You must see my
    castle,
And her best entertainment, ere we part;
I shall think myself unkindly us'd else.
Come, come, let's on; I had good hope your stay
Had been a while with us in Alligant;
205 I might have bid you to my daughter's wedding.
ALSEMERO [aside]: He means to feast me, and
    poisons me beforehand.
— I should be dearly glad to be there, sir,
Did my occasions suit as I could wish.
BEATRICE: I shall be sorry if you be not there
210 When it is done, sir; — but not so suddenly.
VERMANDERO: I tell you, sir, the gentleman's
    complete,
A courtier and a gallant, enrich'd
With many fair and noble ornaments;
I would not change him for a son-in-law
215 For any he in Spain, the proudest he,
And we have great ones, that you know.
ALSEMERO: He's
    much
Bound to you, sir.
VERMANDERO: He shall be bound to me,
As fast as this tie can hold him; I'll want
My will else.
220 BEATRICE [aside]: I shall want mine if you do it.
VERMANDERO: But come, by the way I'll tell you
    more of him.
ALSEMERO [aside]: How shall I dare to venture in
    his castle,
When he discharges murderers° at the gate?
But I must on, for back I cannot go.
225 BEATRICE [aside]: Not this serpent gone yet?
                          [She drops her glove.]
VERMANDERO: Look, girl, thy glove's fall'n.
Stay, stay; — De Flores, help a little.
            [Exeunt Vermandero, Alsemero, Jasperino, and
                                        Servants.]

DE FLORES: Here, lady.
                          (Offers the glove.)°
BEATRICE: Mischief on your officious forwardness!
Who bade you stoop? They touch my hand no
    more.
There! For t'other's sake I part with this;
[Takes off the other glove and throws it down.]
Take 'em and draw thine own skin off with 'em. 230
            (Exeunt [Beatrice and Diaphanta].)
DE FLORES: Here's a favor come, with a mischief!°
    Now I know
She had rather wear my pelt tann'd in a pair
Of dancing pumps than I should thrust my
    fingers
Into her sockets here; I know she hates me,
Yet cannot choose but love her;   235
No matter; if but to vex her, I'll haunt her still;
Though I get nothing else, I'll have my will.
                          (Exit.)

Scene II

(*Enter Alibius and Lollio.*)

ALIBIUS: Lollio, I must trust thee with a secret,
    But thou must keep it.
LOLLIO: I was ever close to a secret,° sir.
ALIBIUS: The diligence that I have found in thee,
    The care and industry already past,   5
    Assures me of thy good continuance.
    Lollio, I have a wife.
LOLLIO: Fie, sir, 'tis too late to keep her secret,
    she's
    known to be married all the town and country
    over.
ALIBIUS: Thou goest too fast, my Lollio; that
    knowledge   10
    I allow no man can be barr'd it;
    But there is a knowledge which is nearer,
    Deeper, and sweeter, Lollio.
LOLLIO: Well, sir, let us handle that between you
    and I.
ALIBIUS: 'Tis that I go about, man. Lollio,   15
    My wife is young.
LOLLIO: So much the worse to be kept secret, sir.
ALIBIUS: Why, now thou meet'st the substance of
    the point;

196. toy: Either "a whim" or, referring to her virginity, "a thing of no worth."   223. murderers: Small cannon, charged with grapeshot. The phrase relates ironically to future events.

226. [S.D.] Offers the glove: Presumably the glove is dropped as a love token for Alsemero, but (with proleptic symbolism) it is retrieved by De Flores.   231. Here's . . . mischief: Here's a kindness or love token come with an accompanying ill wish.   3. close to a secret: Discreet about or good at searching out secrets.

I am old, Lollio.

20 LOLLIO: No, sir, 'tis I am old Lollio.

ALIBIUS: Yet why may not this concord and
    sympathize?
    Old trees and young plants often grow together,
    Well enough agreeing.

LOLLIO: Ay, sir, but the old trees raise themselves
25   higher and broader than the young plants.°

ALIBIUS: Shrewd application! There's the fear man;
    I would wear my ring° on my own finger;
    Whilst it is borrowed it is none of mine,
    But his that useth it.

LOLLIO: You must keep it on still then; if it but lie
30   by,
    One or other will be thrusting into't.

ALIBIUS: Thou conceiv'st me, Lollio; here thy
    watchful eye
    Must have employment; I cannot always be
    At home.

35 LOLLIO: I dare swear you cannot.

ALIBIUS: I must look out.°

LOLLIO: I know't; you must look out, 'tis every
    man's case.

ALIBIUS: Here, I do say, must thy employment be:
    To watch her treadings, and in my absence
40   Supply my place.

LOLLIO: I'll do my best, sir; yet surely I cannot see
    who you should have cause to be jealous of.

ALIBIUS: Thy reason for that, Lollio? 'Tis a comfort-
    able° question.

45 LOLLIO: We have but two sorts of people in the house,
    and both under the whip, that's fools and madmen;
    the one has not wit enough to be knaves, and the
    other not knavery enough to be fools.

ALIBIUS: Ay, those are all my patients, Lollio.
50   I do profess the cure of either sort;
    My trade, my living 'tis, I thrive by it;
    But here's the care that mixes with my thrift:
    The daily visitants,° that come to see
    My brainsick patients, I would not have
55   To see my wife: gallants I do observe
    Of quick enticing eyes, rich in habits,
    Of stature and proportion very comely:
    These are most shrewd temptations, Lollio.

LOLLIO: They may be easily answered, sir; if they come
60   to see the fools and madmen, you and I may serve
the turn, and let my mistress alone, she's of neither
sort.

ALIBIUS: 'Tis a good ward;° indeed, come they to
    see
    Our madmen or our fools, let 'em see no more
    Than what they come for; by that consequent°   65
    They must not see her, I'm sure she's no fool.

LOLLIO: And I'm sure she's no madman.

ALIBIUS: Hold that buckler fast, Lollio; my trust
    Is on thee, and I account it firm and strong.
    What hour is't, Lollio?   70

LOLLIO: Towards belly-hour, sir.

ALIBIUS: Dinner time? Thou mean'st twelve o'clock?

LOLLIO: Yes, sir, for every part has his hour: we wake
    at six and look about us, that's eye-hour; at seven
    we should pray, that's knee-hour; at eight walk,   75
    that's leg-hour; at nine gather flowers and pluck a
    rose,° that's nose-hour; at ten we drink, that's
    mouth-hour; at eleven lay about us for victuals,
    that's hand-hour; at twelve go to dinner, that's
    belly-hour.   80

ALIBIUS: Profoundly, Lollio! It will be long
    Ere all thy scholars learn this lesson, and
    I did look to have a new one ent'red; — stay,
    I think my expectation is come home.

(*Enter Pedro, and Antonio like an idiot.*)

PEDRO: Save you, sir; my business speaks itself,   85
    This sight takes off the labor of my tongue.

ALIBIUS: Ay, ay, sir, 'tis plain enough; you mean him
    for my patient.

PEDRO: And if your pains prove but commodious,° to
    give but some little strength to his sick and weak   90
    part of nature in him, these are but patterns° [*Gives
    him money.*] to show you of the whole pieces that
    will follow to you, beside the charge of diet, wash-
    ing, and other necessaries fully defrayed.

ALIBIUS: Believe it, sir, there shall no care be wanting.   95

LOLLIO: Sir, an officer in this place may deserve some-
    thing; the trouble will pass through my hands.

PEDRO: 'Tis fit something should come to your hands
    then, sir.   [*Gives him money.*]

LOLLIO: Yes, sir, 'tis I must keep him sweet,° and read   100
    to him. What is his name?

PEDRO: His name is Antonio; marry, we use but half
    to him, only Tony.°

LOLLIO: Tony, Tony; 'tis enough, and a very good
    name for a fool. — What's your name, Tony?   105

24–25. **the old trees . . . plants:** I.e., the old become "higher
and broader" by the addition of a cuckold's horns.   **27.
ring:** With an allusion to the female *pudendum,* continued
in the following lines; *finger* = penis.   **36. look out:** Travel
away from home; beware.   **43–44. comfortable:** Comforting.   **53. daily visitants:** Bethlehem Hospital and other mad-
houses were resorted to as places of entertainment.

63. ward: Fencing guard, defensive position.   **65. consequent:** Logical sequence.   **76–77. pluck a rose:** Urinate.
89. commodious: Effective.   **91. patterns:** Samples, i.e.,
small change as earnest of the high value coins to come.
100. sweet: Clean and sweet-smelling.   **103. Tony:** The
name became a synonym for "fool" during the seventeenth
century.

ANTONIO: He, he, he! Well, I thank you, cousin; he, he, he!

LOLLIO: Good boy! Hold up your head. He can laugh;°
I perceive by that he is no beast.

110 PEDRO: Well, sir,
If you can raise him but to any height,
Any degree of wit, might he attain,
(As I might say) to creep but on all four
Toward the chair of wit, or walk on crutches,
115 'Twould add an honor to your worthy pains,
And a great family might pray for you,
To which he should be heir, had he discretion
To claim and guide his own; assure you, sir,
He is a gentleman.

120 LOLLIO: Nay, there's nobody doubted that; at first
sight I knew him for a gentleman, he looks no
other yet.

PEDRO: Let him have good attendance and sweet
lodging.

125 LOLLIO: As good as my mistress lies in, sir; and as
you allow us time and means, we can raise him to
the higher degree of discretion.

PEDRO: Nay, there shall no cost want, sir.

LOLLIO: He will hardly be stretch'd up to the wit of
130 a magnifico.°

PEDRO: Oh, no, that's not to be expected, far shorter
will be enough.

LOLLIO: I'll warrant you [I] make him fit to bear office
in five weeks; I'll undertake to wind him up to the
135 wit of constable.°

PEDRO: If it be lower than that it might serve turn.

LOLLIO: No, fie, to level him with a headborough,°
beadle,° or watchman were but little better than
he is; constable I'll able him;° if he do come to be
140 a justice afterward, let him thank the keeper. Or
I'll go further with you; say I do bring him up to
my own pitch, say I make him as wise as myself.

PEDRO: Why, there I would have it.

LOLLIO: Well, go to; either I'll be as arrant a fool as
145 he, or he shall be as wise as I, and then I think
'twill serve his turn.

PEDRO: Nay, I do like thy wit passing well.

LOLLIO: Yes, you may; yet if I had not been a fool,

I had had more wit than I have too; remember
what state° you find me in. 15[0]

PEDRO: I will, and so leave you; your best cares, I
beseech you. (Exit Pedro.)

ALIBIUS: Take you none with you; leave 'em all with
us.

ANTONIO: Oh, my cousin's gone! Cousin, cousin, oh! 15[5]

LOLLIO: Peace, peace, Tony; you must not cry, child,
you must be whipp'd if you do. Your cousin is
here still; I am your cousin, Tony.

ANTONIO: He, he! Then I'll not cry, if thou be'st my
cousin; he, he, he! 16[0]

LOLLIO: I were best try his wit a little, that I may
know what form to place him in.

ALIBIUS: Ay, do, Lollio, do.

LOLLIO: I must ask him easy questions at first. —
Tony, how many true fingers has a tailor on his 16[5]
right hand?

ANTONIO: As many as on his left, cousin.

LOLLIO: Good; and how many on both?

ANTONIO: Two less than a deuce,° cousin.

LOLLIO: Very well answered. I come to you again, 17[0]
cousin Tony: how many fools goes to° a wise man?

ANTONIO: Forty in a day sometimes, cousin.

LOLLIO: Forty in a day? How prove you that?

ANTONIO: All that fall out among themselves, and go
to a lawyer to be made friends. 17[5]

LOLLIO: A parlous° fool! He must sit in the fourth
form at least, I perceive that. I come again, Tony:
how many knaves make an honest man?

ANTONIO: I know not that, cousin.

LOLLIO: No, the question is too hard for you. I'll tell 18[0]
you, cousin, there's three knaves may make an
honest man: a sergeant, a jailer, and a beadle; the
sergeant catches him, the jailer holds him and the
beadle lashes him; and if he be not honest then,
the hangman must cure him. 18[5]

ANTONIO: Ha, ha, ha! That's fine sport, cousin.

ALIBIUS: This was too deep a question for the fool,
Lollio.

LOLLIO: Yes, this might have serv'd yourself, though
I say't. Once more, and you shall go play, Tony. 1[90]

ANTONIO: Ay, play at push-pin,° cousin; ha, he!

LOLLIO: So thou shalt. Say how many fools are
here —

ANTONIO: Two, cousin, thou and I.

LOLLIO: Nay, y'are too forward there, Tony. Mark 1[95]

---

108. **laugh:** The capacity for laughter was one Aristotelian distinction between man and beast. 130. **magnifico:** A magistrate of Venice and, by transference, a person of high authority. 135. **constable:** Constables were proverbially stupid and were frequent butts in the drama. 137. **headborough:** A petty constable. 138. **beadle:** A minor parish official charged with keeping order in church, making announcements, etc.; or a minor legal official acting as court crier and messenger. 139. **able him:** Make him fit for.

169. **Two less than a deuce:** I.e., none, since tailors were proverbially dishonest. 171. **goes to:** Make up; visit. 176. **parlous:** Contracted from "perilous"; so, dangerously cunning. 191. **push-pin:** A child's game in which each player attempts to push his pin across that of another player; frequently a euphemism for sexual intercourse.

my question: how many fools and knaves are here?
A fool before a knave, a fool behind a knave,
between every two fools a knave; how many fools,
how many knaves?

00 ANTONIO: I never learnt so far, cousin.

ALIBIUS: Thou putt'st too hard questions to him,
Lollio.

LOLLIO: I'll make him understand it easily. Cousin,
stand there.

05 ANTONIO: Ay, cousin.

LOLLIO: Master, stand you next the fool.

ALIBIUS: Well, Lollio.

LOLLIO: Here's my place. Mark now, Tony, there a
fool before a knave.

10 ANTONIO: That's I, cousin.

LOLLIO: Here's a fool behind a knave, that's I; and
between us two fools there is a knave, that's my
master; 'tis but we three,° that's all.

ANTONIO: We three, we three, cousin.

(*Madmen within.*)

15 1 WITHIN: Put's head i' th' pillory, the bread's too
little.°

2 WITHIN: Fly, fly, and he catches the swallow.°

3 WITHIN: Give her more onion, or the devil put the
rope about her crag.°

20 LOLLIO: You may hear what time of day it is, the
chimes of Bedlam° goes.

ALIBIUS: Peace, peace, or the wire° comes!

3 WITHIN: Cat whore, cat whore, her permasant,° her
permasant!

25 ALIBIUS: Peace, I say! — Their hour's come, they must
be fed, Lollio.

LOLLIO: There's no hope of recovery of that Welsh
madman, was undone by a mouse that spoil'd him
a permasant; lost his wits for't.

30 ALIBIUS: Go to your charge, Lollio, I'll to mine.

LOLLIO: Go to your madmen's ward, let me alone
with your fools.°

---

213. **we three:** Probably an allusion to a sign showing two
idiots' heads with the inscription "We three, loggerheads be,"
the third being the spectator. **215–16. bread's too little:**
Probably a complaint against the keepers for undersupplying
the inmates. **217. Fly . . . swallow:** The Madman imagines
he has seen fulfilled the ironic proverb "Fly and you will
catch the swallow." **219. crag:** Neck. The rope is both a
rope of onions and the hangman's rope. **221. chimes of
Bedlam:** I.e., the noise of the insane, crying at feeding time.
Bedlam is a corruption of Bethlehem Hospital, but used of
any madhouse. **222. wire:** A whip of wire. **223. cat
whore, her permasant:** *Her* is stage Welsh for "my"; the
Welshman reviles his worthless she-cat for failing to protect
the cheese of which he was proverbially fond. **231–32.
madmen's . . . fools:** The insane and the congenital idiots.

ALIBIUS: And remember my last charge, Loilio.

(*Exit.*)

LOLLIO: Of which your patients do you think I am?
Come, Tony, you must amongst your school fel- 235
lows now; there's pretty scholars amongst 'em, I
can tell you, there's some of 'em at *stultus, stulta,
stultum.*°

ANTONIO: I would see the madmen, cousin, if they
would not bite me.   240

LOLLIO: No, they shall not bite thee, Tony.

ANTONIO: They bite when they are at dinner, do they
not, cuz?

LOLLIO: They bite at dinner, indeed, Tony. Well, I
hope to get credit by thee; I like thee the best of 245
all the scholars that ever I brought up, and thou
shalt prove a wise man, or I'll prove a fool myself.

(*Exeunt.*)

ACT II • *Scene 1*

(*Enter Beatrice and Jasperino severally.*°)

BEATRICE: Oh sir, I'm ready now for that fair
        service
    Which makes the name of friend sit glorious on
        you.
    Good angels and this conduct° be your guide;
        [*She gives a paper.*]
    Fitness of time and place is there set down, sir.

JASPERINO: The joy I shall return rewards my
        service.   (*Exit.*) 5

BEATRICE: How wise is Alsemero in his friend!
    It is a sign he makes his choice with judgment.
    Then I appear in nothing more approv'd
    Than making choice of him;
    For 'tis a principle, he that can choose   10
    That bosom well, who of his thoughts partakes,
    Proves most discreet in every choice he makes.
    Methinks I love now with the eyes of judgment,
    And see the way to merit, clearly see it.
    A true deserver like a diamond sparkles,   15
    In darkness you may see him, that's in absence,
    Which is the greatest darkness falls on love;
    Yet he is best discern'd then
    With intellectual eyesight. What's Piracquo
    My father spends his breath for? And his
        blessing   20

237–38. *stultus, stulta, stultum:* I.e., there are some who
have attained to the three genders of the Latin for "fool":
masculine, feminine — and neuter. II, I. [S.D.] *severally:*
From different directions. **3. conduct:** A pass, a paper with
directions.

Is only mine as I regard his name,°
Else it goes from me, and turns head° against
  me,
Transform'd into a curse. Some speedy way
Must be remem'bred; he's so forward too,
25 So urgent that way, scarce allows me breath
To speak to my new comforts.

(*Enter De Flores.*)

DE FLORES [*aside*]:   Yonder's she.
Whatever ails me? Now a'late especially,
I can as well be hang'd as refrain seeing her;
Some twenty times a day, nay, not so little,
30 Do I force errands, frame ways and excuses
To come into her sight, and I have small reason
  for't,
And less encouragement; for she baits me still
Every time worse than other, does profess herself
The cruellest enemy to my face in town,
35 At no hand° can abide the sight of me,
As if danger or ill-luck hung in my looks.
I must confess my face is bad enough,
But I know far worse has better fortune,
And not endur'd alone, but doted on:
And yet such pick-hair'd° faces, chins like
40   witches',
Here and there five hairs, whispering in a corner,
As if they grew in fear one of another,
Wrinkles like troughs, where swine-deformity
  swills
The tears of perjury that lie there like wash°
45 Fallen from the slimy and dishonest eye;
Yet such a one pluck'd sweets without restraint,
And has the grace of beauty to his sweet.°
Though my hard fate has thrust me out to
  servitude,
I tumbled into th' world a gentleman.
50 She turns her blessed eye upon me now,
And I'll endure all storms before I part with't.

21. as I regard his name: Either "my father's blessing is mine
only in so far as I respect my father's authority (name)" or
"in so far as I respect the family name (by marrying well)"
or "in so far as I heed the name of Piracquo alone." **22.
turns head:** Directs its power. Her father's blessing depends
on her marrying the man he has chosen; otherwise it will
turn into a curse. **35. At no hand:** On no account. **40.
pick-hair'd:** Perhaps "sparsely bearded," or "black-haired"
or "with bristly hair and beard." **44. wash:** Watery discharge. The perjured tears lie like a discharge in the crevasses
of a swinishly deformed face, as hogwash on a pig's snout,
and fall like swill into the mouth. **47. to his sweet:** Perhaps
"as his sweetheart." If "sweet" is used this early as a synonym for "dessert," the metaphor may be from dining: he
has the postprandial *grace* of Beauty as an accompaniment
to his final indulgence.

BEATRICE [*aside*]: Again!
— This ominous ill-fac'd fellow more disturbs
  me
Than all my other passions.
DE FLORES [*aside*]:   Now't begins again;
I'll stand this storm of hail though the stones
  pelt me.   55
BEATRICE: Thy business? What's thy business?
DE FLORES [*aside*]:   Soft
  and fair,
I cannot part so soon now.
BEATRICE [*aside*]:   The villain's fix'd!
— Thou standing toad-pool!°
DE FLORES [*aside*]:   The shower falls
  amain° now.
BEATRICE: Who sent thee? What's thy errand?
  Leave my sight.
DE FLORES: My lord your father charg'd me to
  deliver   60
A message to you.
BEATRICE: What, another since?°
Do't and be hang'd then, let me be rid of thee.
DE FLORES: True service merits mercy.
BEATRICE: What's thy message?
DE FLORES: Let beauty settle but in patience,
You shall hear all.
BEATRICE: A dallying, trifling torment! 65
DE FLORES: Signior Alonzo de Piracquo, lady,
Sole brother to Tomazo de Piracquo —
BEATRICE: Slave, when wilt make an end?
DE FLORES: Too soon
  I shall.
BEATRICE: What all this while of him?
DE FLORES: The said
  Alonzo,
With the foresaid Tomazo —
BEATRICE: Yet again? 70
DE FLORES: Is new alighted.
BEATRICE: Vengeance strike the
  news!
Thou thing most loath'd, what cause was there
  in this
To bring thee to my sight?
DE FLORES: My lord your father
Charg'd me to seek you out.
BEATRICE: Is there no other
To send his errand by?
DE FLORES: It seems 'tis my luck 75
To be i' th' way still.

58. standing toad-pool: Stagnant and foul water from which
toads and other reptiles were held to be bred by the operation
of the sun. Presumably De Flores suffers from a repulsive
skin disease. **amain:** With full force. **61. another since:**
I.e., in addition to the last, at I, I, 91ff.

BEATRICE: Get thee from me.
DE FLORES: So!
   [*Aside.*] Why, am not I an ass to devise ways
   Thus to be rail'd at? I must see her still!
   I shall have a mad qualm° within this hour
     again,
   I know't, and, like a common Garden-bull,°
   I do but take breath to be lugg'd° again.
   What this may bode I know not; I'll despair the
     less,
   Because there's daily precedents of bad faces
   Belov'd beyond all reason; these foul chops
   May come into favor one day 'mongst his
     fellows;
   Wrangling has prov'd the mistress of good
     pastime:
   As children cry themselves asleep, I ha' seen
   Women have chid° themselves abed to men.
                   (*Exit De Flores.*)
BEATRICE: I never see this fellow, but I think
   Of some harm toward me, danger's in my mind
     still;
   I scarce leave trembling of an hour after.
   The next good mood I find my father in,
   I'll get him quite discarded. Oh, I was
   Lost in this small disturbance, and forgot
   Affliction's fiercer torrent that now comes
   To bear down all my comforts.

(*Enter Vermandero, Alonzo, Tomazo.*)

VERMANDERO: Y'are both
   welcome,
   But an especial one belongs to you, sir,
   To whose most noble name our love presents
   The addition° of a son, our son Alonzo.
ALONZO: The treasury of honor° cannot bring forth
   A title I should more rejoice in, sir.
VERMANDERO: You have improv'd it well. —
   Daughter, prepare,
   The day will steal upon thee suddenly.
BEATRICE [*aside*]: Howe'er, I will be sure to keep
   the night,°
   If it should come so near me.
           [*Beatrice and Vermandero talk apart.*]
TOMAZO: Alonzo.
ALONZO: Brother?

TOMAZO: In troth I see small welcome in her eye.
ALONZO: Fie, you are too severe a censurer
   Of love in all points, there's no bringing on
     you;°
   If lovers should mark everything a fault,
   Affection would be like an ill-set book,   110
   Whose faults° might prove as big as half the
     volume.
BEATRICE: That's all I do entreat.
VERMANDERO: It is but
   reasonable;
   I'll see what my son says to't. — Son Alonzo,
   Here's a motion made but to reprieve
   A maidenhead three days longer; the request   115
   Is not far out of reason, for indeed
   The former time is pinching.
ALONZO: Though my joys
   Be set back so much time as I could wish
   They had been forward, yet since she desires it,
   The time is set as pleasing as before;   120
   I find no gladness wanting.
VERMANDERO: May I ever
   Meet it in that point still. Y'are nobly welcome,
   sirs.

        (*Exeunt Vermandero and Beatrice.*)
TOMAZO: So: did you mark the dullness of her
   parting now?
ALONZO: What dullness? Thou art so exceptious°
   still!
TOMAZO: Why, let it go then, I am but a fool   125
   To mark your harms so heedfully.
ALONZO: Where's the
   oversight?
TOMAZO: Come, your faith's cozen'd° in her,
   strongly cozen'd;
   Unsettle your affection with all speed
   Wisdom can bring it to, your peace is ruin'd
   else.
   Think what a torment 'tis to marry one   130
   Whose heart is leap'd into another's bosom:
   If ever pleasure she receive from thee,
   It comes not in thy name, or of thy gift;
   She lies but with another in thine arms,
   He the half-father unto all thy children   135
   In the conception; if he get 'em not,
   She helps to get 'em for him, in[s] his passions;°

---

79. qualm: Sudden attack of illness or faintness; here, a pang of lust.   **80. common Garden-bull:** An ordinary bull at the Paris Garden, Southwark, where bull-baiting took place. **81. lugg'd:** Teased, worried, baited.   **88. chid:** Chided, reproached.   **99. addition:** The additional title.   **100. treasury of honor:** The whole compendium of honorific titles. **104. keep the night:** Stay on watch during the night; keep the night to myself (denying Alonzo the consummation of his marriage).

108. there's no bringing on you: Perhaps "there's no way of making you take a more reasonable view." However, "to bring on" means "to excite sexually," so the phrase may mean "there's no persuading you to love."   **111. faults:** Printing errors.   **124. exceptious:** Given to making objections.   **127. cozened:** Cheated.   **137. in[s] his passions:** Takes in his passions (in her imagination).

And how dangerous
And shameful her restraint may go in time to,°
140   It is not to be thought on without sufferings.
ALONZO: You speak as if she lov'd some other,
     then.
TOMAZO: Do you apprehend so slowly?
ALONZO: Nay, and
     that
     Be your fear only, I am safe enough.
     Preserve your friendship and your counsel,
          brother,
145   For times of more distress; I should depart
     An enemy, a dangerous, deadly one,
     To any but thyself, that should but think
     She knew the meaning of inconstancy,
     Much less the use and practice; yet w'are
          friends.
150   Pray, let no more be urg'd; I can endure
     Much, till I meet an injury to her,
     Then I am not myself. Farewell, sweet brother;
     How much w'are bound to heaven to depart
          lovingly.   (Exit.)
TOMAZO: Why, here is love's tame madness; thus a
     man
155   Quickly steals into his vexation.   (Exit.)

Scene II

(*Enter Diaphanta and Alsemero.*)

DIAPHANTA: The place is my charge, you have kept
     your hour,
     And the reward of a just meeting bless you.
     I hear my lady coming; complete gentleman,
     I dare not be too busy with my praises,
     Th'are dangerous things to deal with.° (*Exit.*)
ALSEMERO: This goes
5   well;
     These women are the ladies' cabinets,
     Things of most precious trust are lock['d] into
          'em.

(*Enter Beatrice.*)

BEATRICE: I have within mine eye all my desires;
     Requests that holy prayers ascend heaven for,
10   And brings 'em down to furnish our defects,°

Come not more sweet to our necessities
Than thou unto my wishes.
ALSEMERO: W'are so like
     In our expressions, lady, that unless I borrow
     The same words, I shall never find their equals.
                                    [*Kisses her.*]
BEATRICE: How happy were this meeting, this
     embrace,   15
     If it were free from envy! This poor kiss,
     It has an enemy, a hateful one,
     That wishes poison to't; how well were I now
     If there were none such name known as
          Piracquo,
     Nor no such tie as the command of parents!   20
     I should be but too much blessed.
ALSEMERO: One good
     service
     Would strike off° both your fears, and I'll go
          near it too,
     Since you are so distress'd; remove the cause,
     The command ceases;° so there's two fears
          blown out
     With one and the same blast.
BEATRICE: Pray, let me find
     you,° sir.   25
     What might that service be, so strangely happy?
ALSEMERO: The honorablest piece 'bout man, valor.
     I'll send a challenge to Piracquo instantly.
BEATRICE: How? Call you that extinguishing of
     fear,
     When 'tis the only way to keep it flaming?   30
     Are not you ventured in the action,
     That's all my joys and comforts? Pray, no more,
          sir.
     Say you prevail'd, you're danger's and not mine
          then;
     The law would claim you from me, or obscurity
     Be made the grave to bury you alive.   35
     I'm glad these thoughts come forth; oh, keep not
          one
     Of this condition,° sir; here was a course
     Found to bring sorrow on her way to death;
     The tears would ne'er 'a' dried till dust had
          chok'd 'em.
     Blood-guiltiness becomes a fouler visage,   40
     [*Aside.*] And now I think on one. I was to
          blame,
     I ha' marr'd so good a market° with my scorn;

138–39. **And how dangerous . . . go in time to:** And what
dangerous and shameful consequences will eventually result
from restraining her.   4–5. **I dare not . . . deal with:** Diaphanta is fearful of Beatrice-Joanna's jealousy, though indicating her own interest in Alsemero.   10. **And brings . . .**
defects: And brings down from heaven providential gifts (the
answer to "requests") to supply our deficiencies and human
limitations.

22. **strike off:** The metaphor is of the removal of fetters.
23–24. **remove . . . ceases:** An allusion to a scholastic tag,
ablata causa, tollitur effectus, "remove the cause and the
effect ceases."   25. **let me find you:** Let me understand your
meaning.   36–37. **one / Of this condition:** One thought of
this type.   42. **marr'd so good a market:** Proverbial. By her
insults, she has spoiled a good opportunity.

'T had been done questionless. The ugliest
     creature
Creation fram'd for some use,° yet to see
I could not mark so much where it should be!
ALSEMERO: Lady —
BEATRICE [*aside*]: Why, men of art make much of
     poison,
Keep one to expel another; where was my art?
ALSEMERO: Lady, you hear not me.
BEATRICE: I do especially,
     sir;
The present times are not so sure of our side
As those hereafter may be; we must use 'em
     then
As thrifty fools their wealth, sparingly now,
Till the time opens.°
ALSEMERO: You teach wisdom, lady.
BEATRICE: Within there! Diaphanta!

(*Enter Diaphanta.*)

DIAPHANTA: Do you call,
     madam?
BEATRICE: Perfect your service, and conduct this
     gentleman
The private way you brought him.
DIAPHANTA: I shall,
     madam.
ALSEMERO: My love's as firm as love e'er built
     upon.
                    (*Exeunt Diaphanta and Alsemero.*)

(*Enter De Flores.*)

DE FLORES [*aside*]: I have watch'd this meeting, and
     do wonder much
What shall become of t'other; I'm sure both
Cannot be serv'd unless she transgress; happily°
Then I'll put in for one:° for if a woman
Fly from one point, from him she makes a
     husband,
She spreads and mounts then like arithmetic,
One, ten, a hundred, a thousand, ten thousand,
Proves in time sutler° to an army royal.
Now do I look to be most richly rail'd at,
Yet I must see her.
BEATRICE [*aside*]:   Why, put case I loath'd him
As much as youth and beauty hates a sepulchre,
Must I needs show it? Cannot I keep that secret

And serve my turn upon him?° — See, he's here.
— De Flores!
DE FLORES [*aside*]: Ha, I shall run mad with joy!   70
She call'd me fairly by my name, De Flores,
And neither rogue nor rascal.
BEATRICE: What ha' you done
To your face a'late? Y'have met with some good
     physician;
Y'have prun'd° yourself, methinks; you were not
     wont
To look so amorously.°
DE FLORES [*aside*]:   Not I;   75
'Tis the same physnomy, to a hair and pimple,
Which she call'd scurvy scarce an hour ago;
How is this?
BEATRICE: Come hither; nearer, man.
DE FLORES [*aside*]: I'm up to the chin in heaven!
BEATRICE: Turn, let me see.
Faugh, 'tis but the heat of the liver,° I perceiv't;   80
I thought it had been worse.
DE FLORES [*aside*]:   Her fingers touch'd
     me!
She smells all amber.°
BEATRICE: I'll make a water° for you shall cleanse
     this
Within a fortnight.
DE FLORES: With your own hands, lady?
BEATRICE: Yes, mine own, sir; in a work of cure   85
I'll trust no other.
DE FLORES [*aside*]:   'Tis half an act of pleasure
To hear her talk thus to me.
BEATRICE: When w'are us'd
To a hard face, 'tis not so unpleasing;
It mends still in opinion, hourly mends,
I see it by experience.
DE FLORES [*aside*]:   I was bless'd   90
To light upon this minute; I'll make use on't.
BEATRICE: Hardness becomes the visage of a man
     well,
It argues service, resolution, manhood,
If cause were of employment.
DE FLORES: 'Twould be soon
     seen,
If e'er your ladyship had cause to use it.   95
I would but wish the honor of a service
So happy as that mounts to.

---

44. **for some use:** This draws on the traditional doctrine that
everything in nature has some use or purpose, even the apparently dangerous.   52. **opens:** Proves more favorable.
59. **happily:** In that case.   60. **put in for one:** As with *serv'd*
in the previous line, the expression has a sexual innuendo
beyond the usual meaning of "apply for a share."   64.
sutler: Supplier to an army.

69. **serve my turn upon him:** Use him for my own purposes.
Beatrice accidentally and ironically picks up De Flores's
expression in line 59.   74. **prun'd:** Preened (as does a bird);
cut away deformities.   75. **amorously:** Fit to be loved.   80.
heat of the liver: The liver was traditionally the seat of violent
passions; the diagnosis is ironically appropriate.   82. **all
amber:** I.e., of ambergris, perfumed.   83. **water:** Medicinal
wash.

BEATRICE: We shall try you.
  — Oh, my De Flores!
DE FLORES [*aside*]: How's that? She calls me hers
  already, "my De Flores"!
  — You were about to sigh out somewhat,
100 madam?
BEATRICE: No, was I? I forgot. — Oh!
DE FLORES: There 'tis
  again,
  The very fellow on't.
BEATRICE: You are too quick, sir.
DE FLORES: There's no excuse for't now; I heard it
  twice, madam;
  That sigh would fain have utterance, take pity
  on't,
105 And lend it a free word; 'las, how it labors
  For liberty! I hear the murmur yet
  Beat at your bosom.
BEATRICE: Would creation —
DE FLORES: Ay, well said, that's it.
BEATRICE: Had form'd me
  man!
DE FLORES: Nay, that's not it.
BEATRICE: Oh, 'tis the soul of
  freedom!
110 I should not then be forc'd to marry one
  I hate beyond all depths; I should have power
  Then to oppose my loathings, nay, remove 'em
  For ever from my sight.
DE FLORES [*aside*]:   O blest occasion!°
  — Without change to your sex, you have your
  wishes.
  Claim so much man in me.
115 BEATRICE: In thee, De Flores?
  There's small cause for that.
DE FLORES: Put it not from me;
  It's a service that I kneel for to you.   [*Kneels.*]
BEATRICE: You are too violent to mean faithfully;°
  There's horror in my service, blood and danger;
  Can those be things to sue for?
120 DE FLORES: If you knew
  How sweet it were to me to be employed
  In any act of yours, you would say then
  I fail'd, and us'd not reverence enough
  When I receive the charge on't.
BEATRICE [*aside*]:   This is much,
  methinks;
125 Belike his wants are greedy, and to such
  Gold tastes like angels' food.° — Rise.

DE FLORES: I'll have the work first.
BEATRICE [*aside*]:   Possible his need
  Is strong upon him. — There's to encourage
  thee;   [*Gives him money.*]
  As thou art forward° and thy service dangerous,
  Thy reward shall be precious.
DE FLORES: That I have
  thought on;   13
  I have assur'd myself of that beforehand.
  And know it will be precious; the thought
  ravishes.°
BEATRICE: Then take him to thy fury!
DE FLORES: I thirst for
  him.
BEATRICE: Alonzo De Piracquo!
DE FLORES: His end's upon him; he shall be seen
  no more.   13
BEATRICE: How lovely now dost thou appear to
  me!
  Never was man dearlier rewarded.
DE FLORES: I do think of that.
BEATRICE: Be wondrous careful in the execution.
DE FLORES: Why, are not both our lives upon the
  cast?°   14
BEATRICE: Then I throw all my fears upon thy
  service.
DE FLORES: They ne'er shall rise to hurt you.
BEATRICE: When
  the deed's done,
  I'll furnish thee with all things for thy flight;
  Thou may'st live bravely in another country.
DE FLORES: Ay, ay, we'll talk of that hereafter.
BEATRICE [*aside*]:   I
  shall rid myself   14
  Of two inveterate loathings at one time,
  Piracquo, and his dog-face.°   (*Exit.*)
DE FLORES: Oh my blood!°
  Methinks I feel her in mine arms already,
  Her wanton fingers combing out this beard,
  And, being pleased, praising this bad face.   15
  Hunger and pleasure, they'll commend
  sometimes
  Slovenly dishes, and feed heartily on 'em,
  Nay, which is stranger, refuse daintier for 'em.
  Some women are odd feeders. — I'm too loud.

---

113. occasion: Opportunity.   118. to mean faithfully: To
intend honest service.   126. angels' food: The bread of
heaven, *panis angelorum*, given as manna to the Jews in the
wilderness, and in the New Testament associated with the
Body of Christ, the true "heavenly manna," distributed in
the Eucharist.

129. As thou art forward: To the degree that you are courageous and energetic.   132. ravishes: The choice of verb
indicates De Flores's expectation of subsequent events.   140.
cast: Throw of the dice.   147. his dog-face: An insulting
epithet applied to De Flores.   blood: Lust, sensual desire;
presumably, De Flores's pulses are racing. The blood was
taken to be both the vital fluid and also the seat of violent
animal passion.

55 Here comes the man goes supperless to bed,
    Yet shall not rise tomorrow to his dinner.

(*Enter Alonzo.*)

ALONZO: De Flores.
DE FLORES: My kind, honorable lord.
ALONZO: I am glad I ha' met with thee.
DE FLORES: Sir?
ALONZO: Thou
    canst show me
    The full strength of the castle?
DE FLORES: That I can, sir.
ALONZO: I much desire it.
DE FLORES: And if the ways and
60   straits°
    Of some of the passages be not too tedious for
      you,
    I will assure you, worth your time and sight, my
      lord.
ALONZO: Puh, that shall be no hindrance.
DE FLORES: I'm your
    servant then.
    'Tis now near dinner time; 'gainst your
      lordship's rising°
    I'll have the keys about me.
ALONZO: Thanks, kind De
65   Flores.
DE FLORES [*aside*]: He's safely thrust upon me
    beyond hopes.
                                    (*Exeunt.*)

ACT III • *Scene I*

(*Enter Alonzo and De Flores.*)
(*In the act-time° De Flores hides a naked rapier.*)

DE FLORES: Yes, here are all the keys. I was afraid,
    my lord,
    I'd wanted for the postern,° this is it.
    I've all, I've all, my lord: this for the sconce.°
ALONZO: 'Tis a most spacious and impregnable
    fort.
DE FLORES: You'll tell me more, my lord. This
    descent
5   Is somewhat narrow, we shall never pass
    Well with our weapons, they'll but trouble us.
ALONZO: Thou say'st true.
DE FLORES: Pray let me help your
    lordship.
ALONZO: 'Tis done. Thanks, kind De Flores.

DE FLORES: Here
    are hooks, my lord,
    To hang such things on purpose.
                        (*He hangs up the swords.*)
ALONZO: Lead, I'll follow
    thee.   10
        (*Exeunt at one door and enter at the other.*)

Scene II

DE FLORES: All this is nothing; you shall see anon
    A place you little dream on.°
ALONZO: I am glad
    I have this leisure; all your master's house
    Imagine I ha' taken a gondola.
DE FLORES: All but myself, sir [*Aside.*] which makes   5
    up my safety.
    My lord, I'll place you at a casement here
    Will show you the full strength of all the castle.
    Look, spend your eye awhile upon that object.
ALONZO: Here's rich variety, De Flores.
DE FLORES: Yes, sir.
ALONZO: Goodly munition.
DE FLORES: Ay, there's ordnance,
    sir,   10
    No bastard metal,° will ring you a peal like bells
    At great men's funerals. Keep your eye straight,
      my lord;
    Take special notice of that sconce before you,
    There you may dwell° awhile.
                            [*Takes up the rapier.*]
ALONZO: I am upon't.
DE FLORES: And so am I.   [*Stabs him.*]
ALONZO: De Flores! Oh, De Flores!   15
    Whose malice hast thou put on?
DE FLORES: Do you question
    A work of secrecy? I must silence you.
                                    [*Stabs him.*]
ALONZO: Oh, oh, oh!
DE FLORES: I must silence you.
                                    [*Stabs him.*]
    So here's an undertaking well accomplish'd.
    This vault serves to good use now. — Ha,
      what's that   20
    Threw sparkles in my eye? — oh, 'tis a diamond
    He wears upon his finger; it was well found,
    This will approve° the work. What, so fast on?

---

160. **straits:** Narrow passages.   164. **rising:** I.e., leaving the
table.   III, I. [S.D.] **act-time:** The interval between acts.   2.
postern: A side or back door.   3. **sconce:** A small fort or
earthwork.

2. **A place you little dream on:** The grave; but as so often
with Middleton, there is the further implication that hell also
waits.   11. **bastard metal:** I.e., metal with impurities, or
with another metal mixed with it.   14. **dwell:** Rest the eye
on; remain in (after the murder).   23. **approve:** Give proof
of.

Not part in death? I'll take a speedy course then,
Finger and all shall off. [*Cuts off the finger.*]° So
25   now I'll clear
The passages from all suspect° or fear.

                    (*Exit with body.*)

Scene III

(*Enter Isabella and Lollio.*)

ISABELLA: Why, sirrah? Whence have you
    commission
    To fetter the doors against me? If you
    Keep me in a cage, pray whistle to me,
    Let me be doing something.
5 LOLLIO: You shall be doing, if it please you; I'll whistle
    to you if you'll pipe after.°
ISABELLA: Is it your master's pleasure or your own,
    To keep me in this pinfold?°
LOLLIO: 'Tis for my master's pleasure, lest being taken
10 in another man's corn, you might be pounded° in
    another place.
ISABELLA: 'Tis very well, and he'll prove very wise.
LOLLIO: He says you have company enough in the
    house, if you please to be sociable, of all sorts of
15 people.
ISABELLA: Of all sorts? Why, here's none but fools
    and madmen.
LOLLIO: Very well; and where will you find any other,
    if you should go abroad? There's my master and
    I to boot too.
20 ISABELLA: Of either sort one, a madman and a fool.
LOLLIO: I would ev'n participate° of both then, if I
    were as you; I know y'are half mad already, be
    half foolish too.
ISABELLA: Y'are a brave, saucy rascal! Come on, sir,
25 Afford me then the pleasure of your bedlam;
    You were commending once today to me
    Your last-come lunatic: what a proper
    Body there was without brains to guide it,
    And what a pitiful delight appear'd
30 In that defect, as if your wisdom had found

A mirth in madness; pray, sir, let me partake,
    If there be such a pleasure.
LOLLIO: If I do not show you the handsomest, dis-
    creetest madman, one that I may call the under-
    standing madman, then say I am a fool.   35
ISABELLA: Well, a match,° I will say so.
LOLLIO: When you have a taste of the madman, you
    shall, if you please, see Fools' College, o' th' side;
    I seldom lock there, 'tis but shooting a bolt or two,°
    and you are amongst 'em. (*Exit. Enter presently.*) 40
    — Come on, sir, let me see how handsomely you'll
    behave yourself now.

(*Enter Franciscus.*)

FRANCISCUS: How sweetly she looks! Oh, but there's
    a wrinkle in her brow as deep as philosophy. An-
    acreon,° drink to my mistress's health, I'll pledge 45
    it; stay, stay, there's a spider in the cup!° No, 'tis
    but a grape-stone; swallow it, fear nothing, poet;
    so, so, lift higher.
ISABELLA: Alack, alack, 'tis too full of pity
    To be laugh'd at. How fell he mad? Canst thou
    tell?   50
LOLLIO: For love, mistress; he was a pretty poet too,
    and that set him forward first; the Muses then
    forsook him; he ran mad for a chambermaid, yet
    she was but a dwarf neither.
FRANCISCUS: Hail, bright Titania!   55
    Why stand'st thou idle on these flow'ry banks?
    Oberon° is dancing with his Dryades;
    I'll gather daisies, primrose, violets,
    And bind them in a verse of poesy.
LOLLIO: Not too near; you see your danger.   60
                     [*Shows the whip.*]
FRANCISCUS: Oh, hold thy hand, great Diomed!°
    Thou feed'st thy horses well, they shall obey
    thee;
    Get up, Bucephalus° kneels.   [*Kneels.*]

---

25. [S.D.] This emblematic detail was added by Middleton.
The cleaving of ring to finger attests the binding nature of
the betrothal contract, which only unnatural murder can cut
through; even then, the contract cannot be annulled. **26.
suspect:** Suspicion. **5–6. whistle . . . after:** He will whistle
if the caged bird will agree to sing. *Doing* is probably used
with obscene innuendo; so also *whistle* and *pipe*: Lollio is
making a covert advance. **8. pinfold:** Pen, pound. **10.
pounded:** Impounded; sexually pressed. **21. participate:**
Share in the nature of, take part in; another sly advance.

36. a match: A bargain. **39. shooting a bolt or two:** Pulling
back a bolt, probably with a punning reference to the proverb
"A fool's bolt is soon shot," and thus a covert insult to
Isabella. **44–45. Anacreon:** Pliny and others recount that
Anacreon choked to death on a grape-stone while drinking
a cup of wine. **46. there's a spider in the cup:** This alludes
to the folk belief that spiders were poisonous and that to
knowingly drink one meant death. **55–57. Titania . . .
Oberon:** King and Queen of Faery; Franciscus insinuates
that Alibius is enjoying himself with other "nymphs" and invites Isabella to solace herself with him. The names perhaps
derive from *A Midsummer Night's Dream.* **61. Diomed:**
King of the Bistonians in Thrace, who fed his horses on human
flesh. **63. Bucephalus:** The monstrous horse of Alexander,
which only he could ride; Lollio is invited to "mount."

LOLLIO: You see how I awe my flock; a shepherd has
    not his dog at more obedience.
ISABELLA: His conscience is unquiet; sure that was
    The cause of this. A proper gentleman.
FRANCISCUS: Come hither, Esculapius;° hide the
    poison.
LOLLIO: Well, 'tis hid.
               [Hides the whip. Franciscus rises.]
FRANCISCUS: Didst thou never hear of one Tiresias,°
    a famous poet?
LOLLIO: Yes, that kept tame wild geese.°
FRANCISCUS: That's he; I am the man.
LOLLIO: No!
FRANCISCUS: Yes, but make no words on't; I was a
    man seven years ago.
LOLLIO: A stripling I think you might.
FRANCISCUS: Now I'm a woman, all feminine.
LOLLIO: I would I might see that.
FRANCISCUS: Juno struck me blind.
LOLLIO: I'll ne'er believe that; for a woman, they say,
    has an eye° more than a man.
FRANCISCUS: I say she struck me blind.
LOLLIO: And Luna° made you mad; you have two
    trades to beg with.
FRANCISCUS: Luna is now big-bellied,° and there's
    room
    For both of us to ride with Hecate;°
    I'll drag thee up into her silver sphere,
    And there we'll kick the dog, and beat the
    bush,°
    That barks against the witches of the night;
    The swift lycanthropi° that walks the round,
    We'll tear their wolvish skins and save the sheep.
                    [He tries to seize Lollio.]
LOLLIO: Is't come to this? Nay then, my poison comes
    forth again. *[Shows the whip.]* Mad slave, indeed,
    abuse your keeper!
ISABELLA: I prithee, hence with him, now he grows
    dangerous.
FRANCISCUS (*sings*): *Sweet love, pity me.*
    Give me leave to lie° with thee.

LOLLIO: No, I'll see you wiser first; to your own
    kennel.
FRANCISCUS: No noise, she sleeps, draw all the
    curtains round;
    Let no soft sound molest the pretty soul
    But love, and love creeps in at a mousehole.°
LOLLIO: I would you would get into your hole!
                  (*Exit Franciscus.*)
    Now, mistress, I will bring you another sort, you
    shall be fool'd another while; Tony, come hither,
    Tony; look who's yonder, Tony.

(*Enter Antonio.*)

ANTONIO: Cousin, is it not my aunt?°
LOLLIO: Yes, 'tis one of 'em, Tony.
ANTONIO: He, he! How do you, uncle?
LOLLIO: Fear him not, mistress, 'tis a gentle nidget;°
    you may play with him, as safely with him as with
    his bauble.°
ISABELLA: How long has thou been a fool?
ANTONIO: Ever since I came hither, cousin.°
ISABELLA: Cousin? I'm none of thy cousins, fool.
LOLLIO: O mistress, fools have always so much wit
    as to claim their kindred.
MADMAN (*within*): Bounce, bounce, he falls, he
    falls!
ISABELLA: Hark you, your scholars in the upper
    room are out of order.
LOLLIO: Must I come among you there? Keep you the
    fool, mistress; I'll go up and play left-handed° Or-
    lando amongst the madmen.   (*Exit.*)
ISABELLA: Well, sir.
ANTONIO: 'Tis opportuneful now, sweet lady! Nay,
    Cast no amazing° eye upon this change.
ISABELLA: Ha!
ANTONIO: This shape of folly shrouds your dearest
    love,
    The truest servant to your powerful beauties,
    Whose magic had this force thus to transform
    me.
ISABELLA: You are a fine fool indeed.
ANTONIO: Oh, 'tis not
    strange:
    Love has an intellect that runs through all

---

68. **Esculapius:** The Greek god of medicine; hence an ironic epithet for the keeper of a madhouse. 70. **Tiresias:** Theban prophet who changed from a man to a woman and reverted seven years later. Juno struck him blind for revealing that women enjoyed sexual intercourse more than men. 71. **tame wild geese:** A cant term for prostitutes. 80. **eye:** I.e., the pudendum. 82. **Luna:** The moon, which makes mad the lunatic. Madness and blindness are two qualifications for begging. 84. **big-bellied:** Full moon; pregnant. 85. **Hecate:** Greek goddess of witchcraft and magic, regarded as an underworld manifestation of Diana/Artemis, goddess of the moon. 87. **kick . . . bush:** The dog and the bush belong to the man in the moon. 89. **lycanthropi:** Suffers from lycanthropia, a delusion in which the victim believes he is a wolf and acts accordingly. 96. *lie:* Have sexual intercourse.

101. **mousehole:** Also, the female pudendum. 106. **aunt:** There is the usual pun on the meaning "prostitute," "bawd." 109. **nidget:** Contracted from "an idiot," hence, fool. 111. **bauble:** Fool's stick surmounted by a carved head with asses' ears; penis. 113. **cousin:** Besides indicating a wide range of blood relationships, the word also covers those liaisons implied by the modern term "just good friends," hence Isabella's indignant repudiation. 120. **left-handed:** I.e., a poor substitute for Ariosto's hero in *Orlando Furioso* (Mad Orlando). 124. **amazing:** Amazed.

The scrutinous° sciences, and, like
A cunning poet, catches a quantity
Of every knowledge, yet brings all home
Into one mystery, into one secret
That he proceeds in.

135 ISABELLA: Y'are a parlous fool.
ANTONIO: No danger in me: I bring naught but
        love
And his soft-wounding shafts to strike you with.
Try but one arrow; if it hurt you,
I'll stand you twenty back in recompense.
                                    [*Kisses her.*]

ISABELLA: A forward fool too!
ANTONIO: This was love's
140   teaching:
A thousand ways° he fashion'd out my way,
And this I found the safest and [the] nearest
To tread the Galaxia° to my star.

ISABELLA: Profound, withal! Certain, you dream'd
        of this;
Love never taught it waking.
ANTONIO: Take no
145   acquaintance
Of these outward follies; there is within
A gentleman that loves you.

ISABELLA: When I see him,
I'll speak with him; so in the meantime keep
Your habit, it becomes you well enough.

150 As you are a gentleman, I'll not discover you;
That's all the favor that you must expect;
When you are weary, you may leave the school,
For all this while you have but play'd the fool.

(*Enter Lollio.*)

ANTONIO: And must again — He, he! I thank you,
        cousin;
155   I'll be your valentine tomorrow morning.
LOLLIO: How do you like the fool, mistress?
ISABELLA: Passing well, sir.
LOLLIO: Is he not witty, pretty well for a fool?
ISABELLA: If he hold on as he begins, he is like to
        come to something.°
160 LOLLIO: Ay, thank a good tutor; you may put him
        to't;° he begins to answer pretty hard questions.
        Tony, how many is five times six?
ANTONIO: Five times six is six times five.
LOLLIO: What arithmetician could have answer'd bet-
165   ter? How many is one hundred and seven?

131. scrutinous: Accurately examining, searching.   **141. thousand ways:** Love suggested a thousand schemes to achieve his desire.   **143. Galaxia:** The Milky Way.   **159. to come to something:** Not an indication that Antonio may hope, but an ironic comment: The "something" to which he may attain is probably the gallows.   **160–61. put him to't:** Test him.

ANTONIO: One hundred and seven is seven hundred
        and one, cousin.
LOLLIO: This is no wit to speak on; will you be rid
        of the fool now?
ISABELLA: By no means, let him stay a little.   17[0]
MADMAN (*within*): Catch there, catch the last couple
        in hell!°
LOLLIO: Again! Must I come amongst you? Would
        my master were come home! I am not able to
        govern both these wards together.   (*Exit.*)   17[5]
ANTONIO: Why should a minute of love's hour be
        lost?
ISABELLA: Fie, out again! I had rather you kept
        Your other posture; you become not your
            tongue
        When you speak from your clothes.°
ANTONIO: How can he
            freeze   18[0]
Lives near so sweet a warmth? Shall I alone
Walk through the orchard of the Hesperides,°
And cowardly not dare to pull an apple?
This with the red cheeks I must venter° for.
                                    [*Tries to kiss her.*]

(*Enter Lollio above.*)

ISABELLA: Take heed, there's giants° keep 'em.   18[5]
LOLLIO [*aside*]: How now, fool, are you good at that?
        Have you read Lipsius?° He's past *Ars Amandi*;°
        I believe I must put harder questions to him, I
        perceive that —
ISABELLA: You are bold without fear too.
ANTONIO: What
        should I fear,   19[0]
Having all joys about me? Do you smile,
And love shall play the wanton on your lip,
Meet and retire, retire and meet again;
Look you but cheerfully, and in your eyes
I shall behold mine own deformity,   19[5]
And dress myself up fairer; I know this shape

171–72. catch the last couple in hell: An allusion to "barley-brake," a game in which one couple occupies the middle ground ("hell") and attempts to catch other couples as they run through. Caught couples assist the original pair until the last couple has been drawn in.   **180. speak from your clothes:** Speak out of the part suggested by your fool's garb.   **182. orchard of the Hesperides:** A mythical orchard beyond the rim of the Western world, which bore golden apples.   **184. venter:** Venture.   **185. giants:** The orchard of the Hesperides was guarded by the Hesperides, daughters of Atlas and Hesperus, and by a hundred-headed dragon, Ladon, offspring of the Giant Python.   **187. Lipsius:** Justus Lipsius (1547–1606), a Neo-Stoic scholar and jurist whose name is here introduced solely for the pun.   ***Ars Amandi:*** Ovid's *Art of Love*, which Antonio appears to have mastered.

Becomes me not, but in those bright mirrors
I shall array me handsomely.
LOLLIO: Cuckoo,° cuckoo!
                                        (*Exit.*)

([*Enter*] *Madmen above, some as birds, others as
beasts.*)

ANTONIO: What are these?
ISABELLA: Of fear enough to part
  us;
  Yet they are but our schools of lunatics,
  That act their fantasies in any shapes
  Suiting their present thoughts; if sad, they cry;
  If mirth be their conceit, they laugh again.
  Sometimes they imitate the beasts and birds,
  Singing, or howling, braying, barking; all
  As their wild fancies prompt 'em.
                              [*Exeunt Madmen.*]

(*Enter Lollio.*)

ANTONIO: These are no
  fears.
ISABELLA: But here's a large one, my man.
ANTONIO: Ha, he! That's fine sport indeed, cousin.
LOLLIO: I would my master were come home, 'tis too
  much for one shepherd to govern two of these
  flocks; nor can I believe that one churchman can
  instruct two benefices° at once; there will be some
  incurable mad of the one side, and very fools on
  the other. Come, Tony.
ANTONIO: Prithee, cousin, let me stay here still.
LOLLIO: No, you must to your book now, you have
  play'd sufficiently.
ISABELLA: Your fool is grown wondrous witty.
LOLLIO: Well, I'll say nothing; but I do not think but
  he will put you down° one of these days.
                    (*Exeunt Lollio and Antonio.*)
ISABELLA: Here the restrained current might make
  breach,
  Spite of the watchful bankers;° would a woman
  stray,
  She need not gad abroad to seek her sin,
  It would be brought home one ways or other.
  The needle's point will to the fixed north:
  Such drawing arctics° women's beauties are.

(*Enter Lollio.*)

198. cuckoo: Lollio's cry implies that Alibius is being cuckolded.   212. instruct two benefices: An allusion to the common and much-resented practice of augmenting clerical sti-
pends by holding benefices in plurality.   220. put you down:
Overcome you by his intelligence; surmount you sexually.
222. bankers: Dyke builders.   226. drawing arctics: Mag-
netic poles that attract the compass needle.

LOLLIO: How dost thou, sweet rogue?
ISABELLA: How now?
LOLLIO: Come, there are degrees, one fool may be
  better than another.   230
ISABELLA: What's the matter?
LOLLIO: Nay, if thou giv'st thy mind to fool's-flesh,
  have at thee!   [*He tries to kiss her.*]
ISABELLA: You bold slave, you!
LOLLIO: I could follow now as t'other fool did: 235
  "What should I fear,
  Having all joys about me? Do you but smile,
  And love shall play the wanton on your lip,
  Meet and retire, retire and meet again;
  Look you but cheerfully, and in your eyes   240
  I shall behold my own deformity,
  And dress myself up fairer; I know this shape
  Becomes me not"
  — and so as it follows; but is not this the more
    foolish way?
  Come, sweet rogue; kiss me, my little
    Lacedemonian.°   245
  Let me fell how thy pulses beat; thou hast a thing
  about thee would do a man pleasure; I'll lay my
  hand on't.
ISABELLA: Sirrah, no more! I see you have
  discovered
  This love's knight-errant, who hath made
  adventure   250
  For purchase° of my love; be silent, mute,
  Mute as a statue, or his injunction
  For me enjoying, shall be to cut thy throat:
  I'll do it, though for no other purpose,
  And be sure he'll not refuse it.   255
LOLLIO: My share, that's all: I'll have my fool's part
  with you.
ISABELLA: No more! Your master.

(*Enter Alibius.*)

ALIBIUS: Sweet, how dost
  thou?
ISABELLA: Your bounden° servant, sir.
ALIBIUS: Fie, fie,
  sweetheart,
  No more of that.
ISABELLA: You were best lock me up.   260
ALIBIUS: In my arms and bosom, my sweet Isabella,
  I'll lock thee up most nearly. Lollio,
  We have employment, we have task in hand;
  At noble Vermandero's, our castle-captain,
  There is a nuptial to be solemniz'd   265
  (Beatrice-Joanna, his fair daughter, bride)

245. Lacedemonian: Literally, a Spartan; a reference to the
faithless Helen of Sparta.   251. purchase: Achieving.   259.
bounden: Duty-bound; imprisoned.

For which the gentleman hath bespoke our
   pains:
A mixture of our madmen and our fools,
To finish (as it were) and make the fag°

270 Of all the revels, the third night from the first;
Only an unexpected passage over,°
To make a frightful pleasure, that is all,
But not the all I aim at; could we so act it,
To teach it in a wild, distracted measure,

275 Though out of form and figure, breaking time's
   head,°
It were no matter; 'twould be heal'd again
In one age or other, if not in this.
This, this, Lollio, there's a good reward begun,
And will beget a bounty, be it known.

280 LOLLIO: This is easy, sir, I'll warrant you: you have
   about you fools and madmen that can dance very
   well; and 'tis no wonder your best dancers are not
   the wisest men; the reason is, with often jumping
   they jolt their brains down into their feet, that their

285 wits lie more in their heels than in their heads.
ALIBIUS: Honest Lollio, thou giv'st me a good
   reason,
   And a comfort in it.
ISABELLA: Y'ave a fine trade on't,
   Madmen and fools are a staple° commodity.
ALIBIUS: Oh, wife, we must eat, wear clothes, and
   live;

290 Just at the lawyer's haven° we arrive:
   By madmen and by fools we both do thrive.
                                   (*Exeunt.*)

Scene IV

(*Enter Vermandero, Alsemero, Jasperino, and Beatrice.*)

VERMANDERO: Valencia speaks so nobly of you, sir,
   I wish I had a daughter now for you.
ALSEMERO: The fellow of this creature were a
   partner
   For a king's love.
VERMANDERO: I had her fellow once, sir,

But Heaven has married her to joys eternal;   5
'Twere sin to wish her in this vale° again.
Come, sir, your friend and you shall see the
   pleasures
Which my health chiefly joys in.
ALSEMERO: I hear the beauty of this seat largely.°
VERMANDERO: It falls much short of that.
                    (*Exeunt. Manet° Beatrice.*)
BEATRICE: So, here's
   one step   10
Into my father's favor; time will fix him.
I have got him now the liberty of the house;
So wisdom by degrees works out her freedom;
And if that eye be dark'ned° that offends me,
(I wait but that eclipse) this gentleman   15
Shall soon shine glorious in my father's liking,
Through the refulgent virtue of my love.

(*Enter De Flores.*)

DE FLORES [*aside*]: My thoughts are at a banquet;
   for the deed,
I feel no weight in't, 'tis but light and cheap
For the sweet recompense that I set down for't.   20
BEATRICE: De Flores.
DE FLORES: Lady?
BEATRICE: Thy looks promise
   cheerfully.
DE FLORES: All things are answerable: time,
   circumstance,
   Your wishes, and my service.
BEATRICE: Is it done then?
DE FLORES: Piracquo is no more.
BEATRICE: My joys start at mine eyes; our sweet'st
   delights   25
   Are evermore born weeping.
DE FLORES: I've a token for you.
BEATRICE: For me?
DE FLORES: But it was sent somewhat
   unwillingly;
   I could not get the ring without the finger.°
                             [*He shows the finger.*]
BEATRICE: Bless me! What has thou done?
DE FLORES: Why, is
   that more
   Than killing the whole man? I cut his heart-
   strings.   30
A greedy hand thrust in a dish at court

---

269. **fag:** The conclusion.   271. **unexpected passage over:**
A sudden, brief eruption into the festivities.   275. **breaking
time's head:** Probably a musical variation on the proverbial
"breaking Priscian's head." Priscian was a celebrated Latin
grammarian, and the expression was widely used of committing a grammatical solecism; here the offense is against
musical time, for the "measure" is to be unrhythmic, irregular.   288. **staple:** Basic.   290. **lawyer's haven:** I.e., the
port of wealth, which lawyers achieve by exploiting the mad
and the foolish.

6. **vale:** I.e., the world as the "Valley of Tribulation," "vale
of tears."   9. **largely:** Extensively expressed; everywhere I
go.   10. [S.D.] **Manet:** Latin for "she remains."   14. **that
eye be dark'ned:** He be killed.   28. **I could not . . . finger:**
As at lines 37–38 of this scene, and earlier at III, II, 24, this
emblem signifies the indissolubility of the bond made between Alonzo and Beatrice. Betrothal was regarded by many
as the binding contract.

In a mistake hath had as much as this.°
BEATRICE: 'Tis the first token my father made me
    send him.
DE FLORES: And I made him send it back again
    For his last token; I was loath to leave it,
    And I'm sure dead men have no use of jewels.
    He was as loath to part with't, for it stuck
    As if the flesh and it were both one substance.°
BEATRICE: At the stag's fall the keeper° has his fees;
    'Tis soon applied: all dead men's fees are yours,
    sir.
    I pray, bury the finger, but the stone
    You may make use on shortly; the true value,
    Take't of my truth, is near three hundred ducats.
DE FLORES: 'Twill hardly buy a capcase° for one's
    conscience, though,
    To keep it from the worm,° as fine as 'tis.
    Well, being my fees, I'll take it;
    Great men have taught me that, or else my merit
    Would scorn the way on't.
BEATRICE: It might justly, sir;
    Why, thou mistak'st, De Flores, 'tis not given
    In state of recompense.
DE FLORES: No, I hope so, lady;
    You should soon witness my contempt to't then!
BEATRICE: Prithee, thou look'st as if thou wert
    offended.
DE FLORES: That were strange, lady; 'tis not
    possible
    My service should draw such a cause from you.
    Offended? Could you think so? That were much
    For one of my performance, and so warm
    Yet in my service.
BEATRICE: 'Twere misery in me to give you cause,
    sir.
DE FLORES: I know so much, it were so, misery
    In her most sharp condition.
BEATRICE: 'Tis resolv'd then;
    Look you, sir, here's three thousand golden
    florins:
    I have not meanly thought upon thy merit.
DE FLORES: What, salary? Now you move me!
BEATRICE: How,
    De Flores?

DE FLORES: Do you place me in the rank of
    verminous fellows,
    To destroy things for wages? Offer gold?
    The life blood of man! Is anything
    Valued too precious for my recompense?
BEATRICE: I understand thee not.
DE FLORES: I could ha' hir'd
    A journeyman° in murder at this rate,
    And mine own conscience might have [slept at
    ease]
    And have had the work brought home.
BEATRICE [*aside*]:   I'm in a
    labyrinth;
    What will content him? I would fain be rid of
    him.
    — I'll double the sum, sir.
DE FLORES: You take a course
    To double my vexation, that's the good you do.
BEATRICE [*aside*]: Bless me! I am now in worse
    plight than I was;
    I know not what will please him. — For my
    fear's sake,
    I prithee make away with all speed possible.
    And if thou be'st so modest not to name
    The sum that will content thee, paper blushes
    not;
    Send thy demand in writing, it shall follow thee.
    But prithee take thy flight.
DE FLORES: You must fly too then.
BEATRICE: I?
DE FLORES: I'll not stir a foot else.
BEATRICE: What's your
    meaning?
DE FLORES: Why, are not you as guilty, in, I'm
    sure,
    As deep as I? And we should stick together.
    Come, your fears counsel you but ill; my
    absence
    Would draw suspect° upon you instantly;
    There were no rescue for you.
BEATRICE [*aside*]:   He speaks home.
DE FLORES: Nor is it fit we two, engag'd so jointly,
    Should part and live asunder. [*Tries to kiss her.*]
BEATRICE: How now, sir?
    This shows not well.
DE FLORES: What makes your lip so
    strange?°
    This must not be betwixt us.
BEATRICE [*aside*]:   The man talks
    wildly.
DE FLORES: Come, kiss me with a zeal now.

---

32. as much as this: I.e., fingers have been lost in the rush of knives into a dish to secure a portion. **38. flesh ... substance:** The language alludes to the biblical doctrine that husband and wife become one flesh, a union symbolized here by the indivisibility of finger and betrothal ring. **39. keeper:** The warden of a game park had a right to the skin, head, and other parts of a deer, when killed. **44. capcase:** A wallet, protective cover, traveling bag. **45. worm:** I.e., the gnawings of remorse, with a probable further allusion to the sufferings of hell, "where their worm dieth not, and the fire is never quenched" (Mark 9:48).

69. journeyman: A day laborer, a professional. **86. suspect:** Suspicion. **90. strange:** Unfriendly.

BEATRICE [*aside*]:   Heaven,
    I doubt° him!
DE FLORES: I will not stand so long to beg 'em
    shortly.
BEATRICE: Take heed, De Flores, of forgetfulness,
    'Twill soon betray us.
95 DE FLORES: Take you heed first;
    Faith, y'are grown much forgetful, y'are to
    blame in't.
BEATRICE [*aside*]: He's bold, and I am blam'd for't!
DE FLORES: I
    have eas'd
    You of your trouble, think on't; I'm in pain,
    And must be eas'd of you; 'tis a charity;
100   Justice invites your blood to understand me.
BEATRICE: I dare not.
DE FLORES: Quickly!
BEATRICE: Oh, I never shall!
    Speak it yet further off that I may lose
    What has been spoken, and no sound remain
    on't.
    I would not hear so much offence again
    For such another deed.
105 DE FLORES: Soft, lady, soft;
    The last is not yet paid for. Oh, this act
    Has put me into spirit;° I was as greedy on't
    As the parch'd earth of moisture, when the
    clouds weep.
    Did you not mark, I wrought myself into't,°
    Nay, sued and kneel'd for't? Why was all that
110   pains took?
    You see I have thrown contempt upon your
    gold;
    Not that I want it [not] for I do piteously:
    In order° I will come unto't, and make use on't.
    But 'twas not held so precious to begin with,
115   For I place wealth after the heels of pleasure;
    And were I not resolv'd° in my belief
    That thy virginity were perfect in thee,
    I should but take my recompense with grudging,
    As if I had but half my hopes I agreed for.
BEATRICE: Why, 'tis impossible thou canst be so
120   wicked,
    Or shelter such a cunning cruelty,
    To make his death the murderer of my honor!
    Thy language is so bold and vicious,
    I cannot see which way I can forgive it
    With any modesty.
125 DE FLORES: Push, you forget yourself!
    A woman dipp'd in blood, and talk of modesty!

BEATRICE: Oh misery of sin! Would I had been
    bound
    Perpetually unto my living hate
    In that Piracquo, than to hear these words.
    Think but upon the distance that creation   13⬤
    Set 'twixt thy blood and mine, and keep thee
    there.
DE FLORES: Look but into your conscience, read me
    there,
    'Tis a true book, you'll find me there your equal.
    Push! Fly not to your birth, but settle you
    In what the act has made you, y'are no more
    now;   13⬤
    You must forget your parentage to me:°
    Y'are the deed's creature; by that name
    You lost your first condition,° and I challenge
    you,
    As peace and innocency has turn'd you out,
    And made you one with me.
BEATRICE: With thee, foul
    villain?   14⬤
DE FLORES: Yes, my fair murd'ress! Do you urge°
    me?
    Though thou writ'st maid, thou whore in thy
    affection!
    'Twas chang'd from thy first love, and that's a
    kind
    Of whoredom in thy heart; and he's chang'd°
    now,
    To bring thy second on, thy Alsemero,   14⬤
    Whom (by all sweets that ever darkness tasted)
    If I enjoy thee not, thou ne'er enjoy'st;
    I'll blast the hopes and joys of marriage,
    I'll confess all; my life I rate at nothing.
BEATRICE: De Flores!   15⬤
DE FLORES: I shall rest from all lovers' plagues
    then;
    I live in pain now: that shooting eye
    Will burn my heart to cinders.
BEATRICE: Oh, sir, hear me.
DE FLORES: She that in life and love refuses me,
    In death and shame my partner she shall be.   15⬤
BEATRICE [*kneels*]: Stay, hear me once for all; I
    make thee master
    Of all the wealth I have in gold and jewels;
    Let me go poor unto my bed with honor,
    And I am rich in all things.
DE FLORES: Let this silence thee:
    The wealth of all Valencia shall not buy   16⬤
    My pleasure from me;

---

92. **doubt:** Fear, suspect.   107. **spirit:** Courage; sexual desire.   109. **wrought myself into't:** I.e., worked to have the job given me.   113. **In order:** In due time.   116. **resolv'd:** Certain.

136. **parentage to me:** I.e., "You must forget your origins in dealing with me" or "You must forget your parents in favor of me."   138. **first condition:** Original innocence.   141. **urge:** Provoke.   144. **chang'd:** I.e., from life to death.

Can you weep Fate from its determin'd purpose?
So soon may [you] weep me.
BEATRICE: Vengeance begins;
    Murder, I see, is followed by more sins.
65 Was my creation in the womb so curs'd,
    It must engender with a viper first?°
DE FLORES: Come, rise, and shroud your blushes in
    my bosom;   [*Raises her.*]
    Silence is one of pleasure's best receipts;°
    Thy peace is wrought for ever in this yielding.
70 'Las, how the turtle° pants! Thou'lt love anon
    What thou so fear'st and faint'st to venture on.
                                        (*Exeunt.*)

ACT IV • *Scene I*

[*Dumb show.*]

(*Enter Gentlemen, Vermandero meeting them with
action of wonderment at the flight of Piracquo. Enter
Alsemero, with Jasperino and Gallants; Vermandero
points to him, the Gentlemen seeming to applaud the
choice. [Exeunt in procession Vermandero] Alsemero,
Jasperino, and Gentlemen; Beatrice the bride following in great state, accompanied with Diaphanta, Isabella, and other Gentlewomen; De Flores after all,
smiling at the accident;° Alonzo's ghost appears to De
Flores in the midst of his smile, startles him, showing
him the hand whose finger he had cut off. They pass
over in great solemnity.*)

(*Enter Beatrice.*)

BEATRICE: This fellow has undone me endlessly;°
    Never was bride so fearfully distress'd.
    The more I think upon th' ensuing night,
    And whom I am to cope with in embraces,
5   One who's ennobled both in blood and mind,
    So clear in understanding (that's my plague
        now),
    Before whose judgment will my fault appear
    Like malefactors' crimes before tribunals;
    There is no hiding on't — the more I dive
10 Into my own distress. How a wise man
    Stands for° a great calamity! There's no
        venturing
    Into his bed (what course soe'er I light upon)

Without my shame, which may grow up to
    danger;
He cannot but in justice strangle me
As I lie by him, as a cheater use me.   15
'Tis a precious craft° to play with a false die
Before a cunning gamester. Here's his closet,
The key left in't, and he abroad i'th' park;
Sure 'twas forgot; I'll be so bold as look in't.
                        [*She opens the closet.*]
Bless me! A right physician's closet 'tis,   20
Set round with vials; every one her mark too.
Sure he does practice physic for his own use,
Which may be safely call'd your great man's
    wisdom.°
What manuscript lies here? "The Book of
    Experiment,
Call'd *Secrets in Nature*."° So 'tis, 'tis so;   25
"How to know whether a woman be with child
    or no."
I hope I am not yet. If he should try though!
Let me see, folio forty-five. Here 'tis;
The leaf tuck'd down upon't, the place
    suspicious.
"If you would know whether a woman be with
    child or not,   30
Give her two spoonfuls of the white water in
    glass C."
— Where's that glass C? Oh, yonder, I see't
    now.
— "And if she be with child she sleeps full
    twelve hours after; if not, not."
None of that water comes into my belly;
I'll know you from a hundred. I could break you
    now,   35
Or turn you into milk, and so beguile
The master of the mystery, but I'll look to you.°
Ha! That which is next is ten times worse:
"How to know whether a woman be a maid or
    not."
If that should be applied, what would become of
    me?   40
Belike he has a strong faith of my purity,
That never yet made proof;° but this he calls
"A merry sleight, but true experiment, the author
Antonius Mizaldus. Give the party you suspect the

165–66. **Was my creation . . . viper first?:** Was a curse laid
on me in my mother's womb, condemning me to make love
with a hideous, unnatural being before I could do so with
a normal man? 168. **receipts:** Recipes. 170. **turtle:** Turtle-
dove, the proverbial love bird. **IV, I.** [S.D.] *accident:* Event.
1. **undone me endlessly:** Seduced me without remission; destroyed me eternally. 11. **Stands for:** Represents.

16. **precious craft:** Difficult and refined art; *die* = "dice."
23. **your great man's wisdom:** Because it protects the great
from poisoning.   25. *Secrets in Nature:* Extracts from *De
Arcanis Naturae* by Antonius Mizaldus (1520–1578). The
work does not contain these tests, but similar ones are found
in Mizaldus's *Centuriae IX. Memorabilium.* 37. **I'll look
to you:** I'll watch out for you. 42. **made proof:** Put to the
test.

45 quantity of a spoonful of the water in the glass M,
which, upon her that is a maid, makes three several°
effects: 'twill make her incontinently° gape, then
fall into a sudden sneezing, last into a violent laughing; else dull, heavy, and lumpish."
50 Where had I been?°
I fear it, yet 'tis seven hours to bedtime.

(Enter Diaphanta.)

DIAPHANTA: Cuds,° madam, are you here?
BEATRICE [*aside*]:   Seeing
that wench now,
A trick comes in my mind; 'tis a nice piece°
Gold cannot purchase. — I come hither, wench,
55 To look my lord.
DIAPHANTA [*aside*]: Would I had such a cause
To look him too! — Why, he's i' th' park,
madam.
BEATRICE: There let him be.
DIAPHANTA: Ay, madam, let him
compass
Whole parks and forests, as great rangers do;
60 At roosting time a little lodge can hold 'em.
Earth-conquering Alexander, that thought the
world
Too narrow for him, in the end had but his pit-
hole.°
BEATRICE: I fear thou art not modest, Diaphanta.
DIAPHANTA: Your thoughts are so unwilling to be
known, madam;
65 'Tis ever the bride's fashion towards bedtime
To set light by her joys, as if she ow'd° 'em not.
BEATRICE: Her joys? Her fears, thou would'st say.
DIAPHANTA: Fear
of what?
BEATRICE: Art thou a maid, and talk'st so to a
maid?
You leave a blushing business° behind,
Beshrew your heart for't!
DIAPHANTA: Do you mean good
70 sooth,° madam?
BEATRICE: Well, if I'd thought upon the fear at first,
Man should have been unknown.
DIAPHANTA: Is't possible?
BEATRICE: I will give a thousand ducats to that
woman

Would try what my fear were, and tell me true
Tomorrow, when she gets from't; as she likes, 75
I might perhaps be drawn to't.
DIAPHANTA: Are you in
earnest?
BEATRICE: Do you get the woman, then challenge
me,
And see if I'll fly from't; but I must tell you
This by the way, she must be a true maid,
Else there's no trial, my fears are not hers else. 80
DIAPHANTA: Nay, she that I would put into your
hands, madam,
Shall be a maid.
BEATRICE: You know I should be sham'd
else,
Because she lies° for me.
DIAPHANTA: 'Tis a strange humor;°
But are you serious still? Would you resign
Your first night's pleasure, and give money too? 85
BEATRICE: As willingly as live; [*Aside.*] alas, the
gold
Is but a by-bet° to wedge in the honor.
DIAPHANTA: I do not know how the world goes
abroad
For faith or honesty; there's both requir'd in
this.
Madam, what say you to me, and stray no
further? 90
I've a good mind, in troth, to earn your money.
BEATRICE: Y'are too quick,° I fear, to be a maid.
DIAPHANTA: How? Not a maid? Nay, then you
urge° me, madam;
Your honorable self is not a truer
With all your fears upon you —
BEATRICE [*aside*]:   Bad enough
then. 95
DIAPHANTA: Than I with all my lightsome joys
about me.
BEATRICE: I'm glad to hear't; then you dare put
your honesty
Upon an easy trial?
DIAPHANTA: Easy? Anything.
BEATRICE: I'll come to you straight.
                    [*Goes to the closet.*]
DIAPHANTA [*aside*]:   She will not
search me, will she,
Like the forewoman of a female jury?° 100

46. several: Different, clearly distinguished.   47. incontinently: Immediately and unrestrainedly.   50. Where had I
been: What would have happened to me (if I had not discovered this)?   52. Cuds: A mild oath, contracted from
"God save me."   53. nice piece: Scrupulous woman.   62.
pit-hole: The grave; the female pudendum.   66. ow'd:
Owned.   69. blushing business: I.e., she must already have
fallen to a man.   70. Do you mean good sooth: Are you
in earnest?

83. lies: Copulates; deceives.   humor: whim.   87. by-bet:
A side bet, an added inducement to get her to stake her
honor.   92. quick: Eager, lively; pregnant.   93. urge: Provoke.   100. forewoman of a female jury: This is probably
a reference to the notorious divorce action involving the
Countess of Essex in 1613, during which she was examined
by a panel of matrons.

BEATRICE: Glass M; ay, this is it. — Look,
    Diaphanta,
  You take no worse than I do.   [*Drinks.*]
DIAPHANTA: And in so doing,
  I will not question what 'tis, but take it. [*Drinks.*]
BEATRICE [*aside*]: Now if the experiment be true,
    'twill praise itself,
  And give me noble ease: — begins already;
                                   [*Diaphanta gapes.*]
  There's the first symptom; and what haste it
    makes
  To fall into the second, there by this time!
                                   [*Diaphanta sneezes.*]
  Most admirable° secret! On the contrary,
  It stirs me not a whit, which most concerns it.°
DIAPHANTA: Ha, ha, ha!
BEATRICE [*aside*]: Just in all things and in order,
  As if 'twere circumscrib'd;° one accident°
  Gives way unto another.
DIAPHANTA: Ha, ha, ha!
BEATRICE: How now, wench?
DIAPHANTA: Ha, ha, ha! I am so-so
    light
  At heart — ha, ha, ha! — so pleasurable.
  But one swig more, sweet madam.
BEATRICE: Ay, tomorrow;
  We shall have time to sit by't.
DIAPHANTA: Now I'm sad
    again.
BEATRICE [*aside*]: It lays itself° so gently, too! —
    Come, wench,
  Most honest Diaphanta I dare call thee now.
DIAPHANTA: Pray tell me, madam, what trick call
    you this?
BEATRICE: I'll tell thee all hereafter; we must study
  The carriage of this business.
DIAPHANTA: I shall carry't° well,
  Because I love the burthen.
BEATRICE: About midnight
  You must not fail to steal forth gently,
  That I may use the place.
DIAPHANTA: Oh, fear not, madam,
  I shall be cool by that time. — The bride's
    place,
  And with a thousand ducats! I'm for a justice
    now,
  I bring a portion° with me; I scorn small fools.
                                        (*Exeunt.*)

---

108. **admirable:** Wonderful.   109. **which most concerns it:**
Whose lack of virginity it is its function to detect.   112.
circumscrib'd: With its specific effects laid down for it.   **accident:** Symptom.   118. **lays itself:** Subsides, disperses its
own effects.   122. **carry't:** Perform; support in intercourse.
128. **portion:** A dowry, which will recommend her now to
a *big* fool, a justice.

Scene II

(*Enter Vermandero and Servant.*)

VERMANDERO: I tell you, knave, mine honor is in
    question,
  A thing till now free from suspicion,
  Nor ever was there cause. Who of my gentlemen
  Are absent? Tell me and truly how many and
    who.
SERVANT: Antonio, sir, and Franciscus.   5
VERMANDERO: When did they leave the castle?
SERVANT: Some ten days since, sir, the one
    intending to
  Briamata,° th' other for Valencia.
VERMANDERO: The time accuses 'em. A charge of
    murder
  Is brought within my castle gate, Piracquo's
    murder;   10
  I dare not answer faithfully° their absence.
  A strict command of apprehension
  Shall pursue 'em suddenly, and either wipe
  The stain off clear, or openly discover it.
  Provide me winged warrants for the purpose.   15
  See, I am set on° again.
                                   (*Exit Servant.*)

(*Enter Tomazo.*)

TOMAZO: I claim a brother of you.
VERMANDERO: Y'are too hot,
  Seek him not here.
TOMAZO: Yes, 'mongst your dearest
    bloods,
  If my peace find no fairer satisfaction;
  This is the place must yield account for him,   20
  For here I left him, and the hasty tie
  Of this snatch'd marriage gives strong testimony
  Of his most certain ruin.
VERMANDERO: Certain falsehood!
  This is the place indeed; his breach of faith
  Has too much marr'd both my abused love,   25
  The honorable love I reserv'd for him,
  And mock'd my daughter's joy; the prepar'd
    morning
  Blush'd at his infidelity; he left
  Contempt and scorn to throw upon those friends
  Whose belief hurt 'em.° Oh 'twas most ignoble   30
  To take his flight so unexpectedly,
  And throw such public wrongs on those that
    lov'd him.

---

8. **Briamata:** In Middleton's source, Vermandero's country
house ten leagues away.   11. **answer faithfully:** Account for
them confidently.   16. **set on:** Badgered, harassed.   30.
Whose belief hurt 'em: Whose trust in him caused them to
be injured.

TOMAZO: Then this is all your answer?

VERMANDERO: 'Tis too fair
  For one of his alliance;° and I warn you
  That this place no more see you.   (*Exit.*)

(*Enter De Flores.*)

35 TOMAZO: The best is,
  There is more ground to meet a man's revenge
      on.
  — Honest De Flores?

DE FLORES: That's my name indeed.
  Saw you the bride? Good sweet sir, which way
      took she?

TOMAZO: I have bless'd mine eyes from seeing such
  a false one.

DE FLORES [*aside*]: I'd fain get off, this man's not
40   for my company;
  I smell his brother's blood when I come near
      him.

TOMAZO: Come hither, kind and true one; I
      remember
  My brother lov'd thee well.

DE FLORES: Oh purely, dear sir!
  [*Aside.*] Methinks I am now again a-killing on
      him,
  He brings it so fresh to me.

TOMAZO: Thou canst guess,
45   sirrah
  (One honest friend has an instinct of jealousy°),
  At some foul guilty person?

DE FLORES: 'Las, sir,
  I am so charitable I think none
  Worse than myself. — You did not see the bride
      then?

TOMAZO: I prithee name her not. Is she not
50   wicked?

DE FLORES: No, no, a pretty, easy, round-pack'd
      sinner,°
  As your most ladies are, else you might think
  I flatter'd her; but, sir, at no hand wicked,
  Till th' are so old their chins and noses meet,
55 And they salute witches.° I am call'd, I think, sir.
  [*Aside.*] His company ev'n o'erlays my
      conscience.°   (*Exit.*)

TOMAZO: That De Flores has a wondrous honest
      heart;
  He'll bring it out in time, I'm assur'd on't.

Oh, here's the glorious master of the day's joy;
  'Twill not be long till he and I do reckon.   60

(*Enter Alsemero.*)

  Sir!

ALSEMERO: You are most welcome.

TOMAZO: You may call
      that word back;
  I do not think I am, nor wish to be.

ALSEMERO: 'Tis strange you found the way to this
      house then.

TOMAZO: Would I'd ne'er known the cause! I'm
      none of those, sir,
  That come to give you joy and swill your wine;   65
  'Tis a more precious liquor that must lay°
  The fiery thirst I bring.

ALSEMERO: Your words and you
  Appear to me great strangers.

TOMAZO: Time and our
      swords
  May make us more acquainted. This the
      business:
  I should have a brother in your place;   70
  How treachery and malice have dispos'd of him,
  I'm bound to inquire of him which holds his
      right,
  Which never could come fairly.

ALSEMERO: You must look
  To answer for that word, sir.

TOMAZO: Fear you not,
  I'll have it° ready drawn at our next meeting.   75
  Keep your day solemn.° Farewell, I disturb it
      not;
  I'll bear the smart with patience for a time.
                                        (*Exit.*)

ALSEMERO: 'Tis somewhat ominous this, a quarrel
      ent'red
  Upon this day. My innocence relieves me,

(*Enter Jasperino.*)

  I should be wondrous sad else. — Jasperino,   80
  I have news to tell thee, strange news.

JASPERINO: I ha' some
      too,
  I think as strange as yours; would I might keep
  Mine, so my faith and friendship might be kept
      in't!
  Faith, sir, dispense a little with my zeal,
  And let it cool in this.°

---

34. **alliance:** Family. 46. **jealousy:** Suspicion. 51. **round-pack'd sinner:** I.e., firm in her curves and solid with sin. 53–55. **at no hand . . . witches:** They are not really evil until they lose their looks in old age and consort with witches. 56. **o'erlays my conscience:** Oppresses my heart and mind.

66. **lay:** Allay. 75. **it:** I.e., his sword, which will be "drawn up" as a formal answer. 76. **Keep your day solemn:** Celebrate your wedding with due solemnity. 84–85. **dispense . . . this:** Free me from the obligations of warm friendship in this instance.

85 ALSEMERO: This puts me on,°
    And blames thee for thy slowness.
    JASPERINO: All may prove
        nothing;
        Only a friendly fear that leapt from me, sir.
    ALSEMERO: No question it may prove nothing; let's
        partake it, though.
    JASPERINO: 'Twas Diaphanta's chance (for to that
        wench
90   I pretend° honest love, and she deserves it)
        To leave me in a back part of the house,
        A place we chose for private conference;
        She was no sooner gone, but instantly
        I heard your bride's voice in the next room to
        me;
95   And, lending more attention, found De Flores
        Louder than she.
    ALSEMERO: De Flores? Thou art out° now.
    JASPERINO: You'll tell me more anon.
    ALSEMERO: Still I'll
        prevent thee:°
        The very sight of him is poison to her.
    JASPERINO: That made me stagger too, but
        Diaphanta
        At her return confirm'd it.
100 ALSEMERO: Diaphanta!
    JASPERINO: Then fell we both to listen, and words
        pass'd
        Like those that challenge interest° in a woman.
    ALSEMERO: Peace! quench thy zeal; 'tis dangerous
        to thy bosom.
    JASPERINO: Then truth is full of peril.
    ALSEMERO: Such truths
        are.
105   — Oh, were she the sole glory of the earth,
        Had eyes that could shoot fire into kings'
        breasts,
        And touch'd,° she sleeps not here! Yet I have
        time,
        Though night be near, to be resolv'd hereof;
        And prithee, do not weigh me by my passions.
    JASPERINO: I never weigh'd friend so.
    ALSEMERO: Done
110   charitably.
        That key will lead thee to a pretty secret
                                          [Gives key.]
        By a Chaldean° taught me, and I've [made]

---

85. puts me on: Excites my curiosity.   **90. pretend:** Offer.
96. out: Mistaken.   **97. Still I'll prevent thee:** I.e., I'll forestall further slanders by pointing out their inherent im-
plausibility.   **102. challenge interest:** Claim rights.   **107.
touch'd:** Tainted, corrupted.   **112. Chaldean:** A soothsayer
or astrologer, not necessarily a native of Chaldea, though
the term derives from descriptions of Chaldean practices in
the Book of Daniel.

        My study upon some. Bring from my closet
        A glass inscrib'd there with the letter M,
        And question not my purpose.
    JASPERINO: It shall be done,
        sir.   (Exit.) 115
    ALSEMERO: How can this hang together? Not an
        hour since,
        Her woman came pleading her lady's fears,
        Deliver'd her for the most timorous virgin
        That ever shrunk at man's name, and so modest,
        She charg'd her weep out her request to me   120
        That she might come obscurely° to my bosom.

    (Enter Beatrice.)

    BEATRICE [aside]: All things go well. My woman's
        preparing yonder
        For her sweet voyage, which grieves me to lose;
        Necessity compels it, I lose all else.
    ALSEMERO [aside]: Push! Modesty's shrine is set in
        yonder forehead.   125
        I cannot be too sure though. — My Joanna!
    BEATRICE: Sir, I was bold to weep a message to
        you;
        Pardon my modest fears.
    ALSEMERO [aside]:   The dove's not meeker;
        She's abus'd, questionless.

    (Enter Jasperino [with glass].)

                                  — Oh, are you come,
        sir?
    BEATRICE [aside]: The glass, upon my life! I see the
        letter.   130
    JASPERINO: Sir, this is M.
    ALSEMERO: 'Tis it.
    BEATRICE [aside]:   I am suspected.
    ALSEMERO: How fitly our bride comes to partake
        with us!
    BEATRICE: What is't, my lord?
    ALSEMERO: No hurt.
    BEATRICE: Sir, pardon
        me,
        I seldom taste of any composition.°
    ALSEMERO: But this, upon my warrant, you shall
        venture on.   135
    BEATRICE: I fear 'twill make me ill.
    ALSEMERO: Heaven forbid
        that!
    BEATRICE [aside]: I'm put now to my cunning; th'
        effects I know,
        If I can now but feign 'em handsomely.
                                          [She drinks.]

---

121. obscurely: In darkness.   **134. composition:** A made-
up drink.

ALSEMERO [*to Jasperino*]: It has that secret virtue, it
    ne'er miss'd, sir,
    Upon a virgin.

140 JASPERINO: Treble qualitied?

                  [*Beatrice gapes, then sneezes.*]

ALSEMERO: By all that's virtuous, it takes there,
    proceeds!

JASPERINO: This is the strangest trick to know a
    maid by.

BEATRICE: Ha, ha, ha!
    You have given me joy of heart to drink, my
    lord.

ALSEMERO: No, thou hast given me such joy of
145   heart
    That never can be blasted.

BEATRICE: What's the matter, sir?

ALSEMERO [*to Jasperino*]: See, now 'tis settled in a
    melancholy,
    Keep[s] both the time and method. — My
    Joanna,
    Chaste as the breath of Heaven, or morning's
    womb
    That brings the day forth, thus my love encloses
150   thee.

                      [*Embraces her.*]
                      (*Exeunt.*)

Scene III

(*Enter Isabella and Lollio.*)

ISABELLA: Oh heaven! Is this the waiting° moon?
    Does love turn fool, run mad, and all [at] once?
    Sirrah, here's a madman, akin to the fool too,
    A lunatic lover.

5 LOLLIO: No, no, not he I brought the letter from?

ISABELLA: Compare his inside with his out,° and tell
    me.   [*Gives him the letter.*]

LOLLIO: The out's mad, I'm sure of that; I had a taste
    on't. "To the bright Andromeda, chief chamber-
    maid to the Knight of the Sun, at the sign of
10   Scorpio, in the middle region, sent by the bellows-
    mender of Aeolus.° Pay the post." This is stark
    madness.

---

1. waiting: Attendant (?), lying-in-wait, ominous. **6. inside
with his out:** I.e., the contents of the letter with the cover;
his actual nature with his disguise. **8–11. Andromeda . . .
Aeolus:** Presumably Franciscus calls Isabella Andromeda because he intends to act as Perseus, rescuing her from the
dragon Alibius; *chambermaid* is an obvious pun, the *Knight
of the Sun* appears in Diego Ortunez de Calahorra, *The
Mirror of Princely Deeds and Knighthood*, translated from
the Spanish in nine parts (1578–1601); in astrology, *Scorpio*
governs the *middle region*, the privy parts; *Aeolus* is god of
the winds; bellows-makers are elsewhere in Middleton associated with bawds.

ISABELLA: Now mark the inside. [*Takes the letter.*]
    "Sweet lady, having now cast off this counterfeit
    cover of a madman, I appear to your best judgment 15
    a true and faithful lover of your beauty."

LOLLIO: He is mad still.

ISABELLA: "If any fault you find, chide those perfec-
    tions in you which have made me imperfect; 'tis
    the same sun that causeth to grow and enforceth 20
    to wither, —"

LOLLIO: Oh rogue!

ISABELLA: "— Shapes and transhapes, destroys and
    builds again; I come in winter to you dismantled
    of my proper ornaments; by the sweet splendor of 25
    your cheerful smiles, I spring and live a lover."

LOLLIO: Mad rascal still!

ISABELLA: "Tread him not under foot, that shall appear
    an honor to your bounties. I remain — mad till I
    speak with you, from whom I expect my cure — 30
    Yours all, or one beside himself, Franciscus."

LOLLIO: You are like to have a fine time on't; my
    master and I may give over our professions. I do
    not think but you can cure fools and madmen faster
    than we, with little pains too. 35

ISABELLA: Very likely.

LOLLIO: One thing I must tell you, mistress: you per-
    ceive that I am privy to your skill; if I find you
    minister once and set up the trade,° I put in for
    my thirds,° I shall be mad or fool else. 40

ISABELLA: The first place is thine, believe it, Lollio,
    If I do fall —

LOLLIO: I fall upon you.

ISABELLA: So.

LOLLIO: Well, I stand to my venture.° 45

ISABELLA: But thy counsel now, how shall I deal°
    with 'em?

LOLLIO: Why, do you mean to deal with 'em?

ISABELLA: Nay, the fair understanding,° how to use
    'em.

LOLLIO: Abuse 'em! That's the way to mad the fool,
    and make a fool of the madman, and then you use 50
    'em kindly.°

ISABELLA: 'Tis easy, I'll practice;° do thou observe it.

---

39. minister once and set up in the trade: Commit adultery
and become a whore. **40. thirds:** Third share, Isabella being
divided between him, Alibius, and Franciscus. "Thirds," was
the legal share of captures and certain fines (the remainder
being due to the crown) and the traditional portion of a
deceased husband's estate which was due to the wife. **45.
I stand to my venture:** I will abide by my fortune; a "ven-
turer" took a share in a commercial voyage's risks and expenses, receiving a commensurate portion of any profits.
46. deal: Cope; have intercourse with. **48. the fair understanding:** Interpret my words in a decent sense. **51. kindly:**
Kindly; according to their natures. **52. practice:** Execute a
plot or intrigue, involving deceit.

The key of thy wardrobe.
LOLLIO: There; fit yourself for 'em, and I'll fit 'em
55   both for you.   [*Gives her the key.*]
ISABELLA: Take thou no further notice than the
        outside.   (*Exit.*)
LOLLIO: Not an inch; I'll put you to the inside.°

(*Enter Alibius.*)

ALIBIUS: Lollio, art there? Will all be perfect,
        think'st thou?
        Tomorrow night, as if to close up the solemnity,
60   Vermandero expects us.
LOLLIO: I mistrust the madmen most; the fools will
        do well enough, I have taken pains with them.
ALIBIUS: Tush, they cannot miss; the more absurdity
        The more commends it, so no rough behaviors
65   Affright the ladies; they are nice things, thou
        know'st.
LOLLIO: You need not fear, sir; so long as we are
        there with our commanding pizzles,° they'll be as
        tame as the ladies themselves.
ALIBIUS: I will see them once more rehearse before
        they go.
70 LOLLIO: I was about it, sir; look you to the madmen's
        morris, and let me alone with the other. There is
        one or two that I mistrust their fooling; I'll instruct
        them, and then they shall rehearse the whole
        measure.
ALIBIUS: Do so; I'll see the music prepar'd. But
75   Lollio,
        By the way, how does my wife brook her
        restraint?
        Does she not grudge at it?
LOLLIO: So, so; she takes some pleasure in the house,
        she would abroad else. You must allow her a little
80   more length, she's kept too short.
ALIBIUS: She shall go along to Vermandero's with
        us;
        That will serve her for a month's liberty.
LOLLIO: What's that on your face, sir?
ALIBIUS: Where, Lollio? I see nothing.
85 LOLLIO: Cry you mercy, sir, 'tis your nose; it show'd
        like the trunk of a young elephant.°
ALIBIUS: Away, rascal! I'll prepare the music, Lollio.
                                        (*Exit Alibius.*)
LOLLIO: Do, sir, and I'll dance the whilst. Tony, where
        art thou, Tony?

(*Enter Antonio.*)

57. I'll put you to the inside: Obscene; *put to* = "have intercourse with." **67. pizzles:** Whips made from the dried penises of bulls. **86. elephant:** Perhaps a sign of a cuckold; more probably Lollio suggests Alibius is being led by the nose.

ANTONIO: Here, cousin; where art thou?   90
LOLLIO: Come, Tony, the footmanship I taught you.
ANTONIO: I had rather ride,° cousin.
LOLLIO: Ay, a whip take you; but I'll keep you out.
        Vault in; look you, Tony: fa, la, la, la, la.
                                        [*Dances.*]
ANTONIO: Fa, la, la, la, la.   [*Dances.*] 95
LOLLIO: There, an honor.°
ANTONIO: Is this an honor, cuz?   [*Bows.*]
LOLLIO: Yes, and it please your worship.
ANTONIO: Does honor bend in the hams,° cuz?
LOLLIO: Marry, does it, as low as worship, squireship, 100
        nay, yeomandry itself sometimes, from whence it
        first stiffened. There, rise, a caper.
ANTONIO: Caper after an honor, cuz?
LOLLIO: Very proper; for honor is but a caper,° rise[s]
        as fast and high, has a knee or two, and falls to th' 105
        ground again. You can remember your figure,° Tony?
                                        (*Exit.*)
ANTONIO: Yes, cousin; when I see thy figure, I can
        remember mine.

(*Enter Isabella, [like a madwoman].*)

ISABELLA: Hey, how he treads the air! Shough,
        shough, t'other way!
        He burns his wings else. Here's wax enough
        below,   110
        Icarus,° more than will be canceled° these
        eighteen moons.   [*Antonio falls.*]
        He's down, he's down! What a terrible fall he
        had!
        Stand up, thou son of Cretan Daedalus,
        And let us tread the lower labyrinth;°

92. ride: Also, "mount sexually." **96. honor:** A bow. **99. Does honor bend in the hams:** This is ostensibly an inquiry about the right execution of the bow, but with the punning query "Do those of high rank abase themselves so?" Lollio answers that those of high rank will demean themselves to officials, squires, even yeomen; but since there appears to be a pun on *bow in the hams* = "to copulate," Lollio may be suggesting that those of rank will stoop to low liaisons. **104. caper:** Leap; brief frolic. **106. figure:** Set of movements in dancing; appearance. **111. Icarus:** Son of Daedalus, who made him wings to fly with; but Icarus flew too near the sun and melted the wax that attached them to his shoulders. **canceled:** Used up (as sealing wax on deeds). **114. the lower labyrinth:** According to one version of the legend, Daedalus and Icarus were imprisoned in the labyrinth which Daedalus had constructed to hold the Minotaur, as a punishment for conniving at Ariadne's assistance to Theseus in killing the man-bull. Ariadne gave Theseus a ball of thread to mark his way into the maze and be the "clue" to guide him out. It has been suggested that the maze is a *lower* labyrinth as opposed to that of the sky; but it is more probable that Isabella makes a mock advance, inviting Antonio to "tread" with her the labyrinth of sexual love.

115 I'll bring thee to the clue.   [*Antonio rises.*]
ANTONIO: Prithee, cuz, let me alone.
ISABELLA: Art thou now drown'd?°
    About thy head I saw a heap of clouds,
    Wrapp'd like a Turkish turbant; on thy back
120 A crook'd chameleon-color'd rainbow hung
    Like a tiara° down unto thy hams.
    Let me suck out those billows in thy belly;°
    Hark how they roar and rumble in the straits!°
    Bless thee from the pirates.
125 ANTONIO: Pox upon you; let me alone!
ISABELLA: Why shouldst thou mount so high as
        Mercury,
    Unless thou hadst reversion of his place?°
    Stay in the moon with me, Endymion,°
    And we will rule these wild, rebellious waves,
130 That would have drown'd my love.
ANTONIO: I'll kick thee if again thou touch me,
    Thou nimble unshapen antic;° I am no fool,
    You bedlam!
ISABELLA: But you are, as sure as I am, mad.
    Have I put on this habit of a frantic,
135 With love as full of fury, to beguile
    The nimble eye of watchful jealousy,
    And am I thus rewarded?   [*She reveals herself.*]
ANTONIO: Ha, dearest beauty!
ISABELLA: No, I have no beauty now,
    Nor never had, but what was in my garments.
140 You, a quick-sighted lover? Come not near me!
    Keep your caparisons,° y'are aptly clad;
    I came a feigner to return stark mad.   (*Exit.*)

(*Enter Lollio.*)

ANTONIO: Stay, or I shall change condition,
    And become as you are.
145 LOLLIO: Why, Tony, whither now? Why, fool?
ANTONIO: Whose fool, usher° of idiots? You
        coxcomb!
    I have fool'd too much.
LOLLIO: You were best be mad another while then.
ANTONIO: So I am, stark mad; I have cause
        enough;

And I could throw the full effects on thee,   15
    And beat thee like a fury!
LOLLIO: Do not, do not; I shall not forbear° the gentleman under the fool, if you do; alas, I saw through
your fox-skin before now. Come, I can give you
comfort; my mistress loves you, and there is as   15
arrant a madman i' th' house as you are a fool,
your rival, whom she loves not; if after the masque
we can rid her of him, you earn her love, she says,
and the fool shall ride° her.
ANTONIO: May I believe thee?   16
LOLLIO: Yes, or you may choose whether you will or
no.
ANTONIO: She's eas'd° of him; I have a good
        quarrel on't.
LOLLIO: Well, keep your old station yet, and be quiet.
ANTONIO: Tell her I will deserve her love.   [*Exit.*]
LOLLIO: And you are like to have your desire.   16

(*Enter Franciscus.*)

FRANCISCUS (*sings*): "Down, down, down a-down a-
        down" and then with a horse-trick,°
    To kick Latona's° forehead, and break her
        bowstring.
LOLLIO: This is t'other counterfeit; I'll put him out of
his humor. [*Takes out letter and reads.*] "Sweet
lady, having now cast off this counterfeit cover of   17
a madman, I appear to your best judgment a true
and faithful lover of your beauty." — This is pretty
well for a madman.
FRANCISCUS: Ha! What's that?
LOLLIO: "Chide those perfections in you which [have]   17
made me imperfect."
FRANCISCUS: I am discover'd to the fool.
LOLLIO: I hope to discover the fool in you, ere I have
done with you. "Yours all, or one beside himself,
Franciscus." — This madman will mend sure.   18
FRANCISCUS: What do you read, sirrah?
LOLLIO: Your destiny, sir; you'll be hang'd for this
trick, and another that I know.°
FRANCISCUS: Art thou of counsel with thy mistress?
LOLLIO: Next her apron strings.   18
FRANCISCUS: Give me thy hand.

117–29. **drown'd**: There is a continuing reference to the
Icarian Sea, in which Icarus drowned.   121. **tiara**: A high
head-dress, sometimes a turban, which here has a tail hanging
down the back.   122. **suck out . . . belly**: Probably again
this is an indecent advance under the guise of insane allusion
to the legend.   123. **straits**: Narrows; intestines.   127. **reversion of his place**: The right of succeeding Mercury as
winged messenger of the gods.   128. **Endymion**: A beautiful
youth loved by Luna (the moon); Isabella imagines herself
the moon goddess controlling tides.   132. **antic**: Clown,
grotesque figure.   141. **caparisons**: The coverings of a horse
and (by transference) clothes on a human beast.   146. **usher**:
Doorkeeper, subordinate teacher.

152. **forbear**: Spare.   159. **ride**: Mount sexually.   162.
eas'd: There is a verbal parallel to the main plot (III, IV, 97–
99), which points both similarity and contrast between the
two actions.   166. **horse-trick**: Horseplay, prancing in imitation of a performing horse.   167. **Latona**: The mother
of Artemis/Diana, here confused with Artemis herself, commonly depicted as a huntress with a bow. Rowley may have
written *Latonia* = daughter of Latona.   182–83. **this trick
. . . know**: Fraud and the act of adultery.

LOLLIO: Stay, let me put yours° in my pocket first.
    [*Puts away the letter.*] Your hand is true, is it not?
    It will not pick? I partly fear it, because I think it
90 does lie.
FRANCISCUS: Not in a syllable.
LOLLIO: So; if you love my mistress so well as you
    have handled the matter here, you are like to be
    cur'd of your madness.
95 FRANCISCUS: And none but she can cure it.
LOLLIO: Well, I'll give you over then, and she shall
    cast your water° next.
FRANCISCUS: Take for thy pains past.
                           [*Gives him money.*]
LOLLIO: I shall deserve more, sir, I hope; my mistress
00 loves you, but must have some proof of your love
    to her.
FRANCISCUS: There I meet my wishes.
LOLLIO: That will not serve, you must meet her enemy
    and yours.
05 FRANCISCUS: He's dead already!
LOLLIO: Will you tell me that, and I parted but now
    with him?
FRANCISCUS: Show me the man.
LOLLIO: Ay, that's a right course now, see him before
10 you kill him in any case; and yet it needs not go
    so far neither, 'tis but a fool that haunts the house
    and my mistress in the shape of an idiot. Bang but
    his fool's coat well-favoredly,° and 'tis well.
FRANCISCUS: Soundly, soundly!
15 LOLLIO: Only reserve him till the masque be past; and
    if you find him not now in the dance yourself, I'll
    show you. In, in! My master!
FRANCISCUS: He handles him like a feather. Hey!
                           [*Exit dancing.*]

(*Enter Alibius.*)

ALIBIUS: Well said.° In a readiness, Lollio?
20 LOLLIO: Yes, sir.
ALIBIUS: Away then, and guide them in, Lollio;
    Entreat your mistress to see this sight.
    Hark, is there not one incurable fool
    That might be begg'd?° I have friends.
LOLLIO: I have him for you, one that shall deserve it
25 too.   [*Exit.*]
ALIBIUS: Good boy, Lollio.

187. yours: I.e., your hand(writing). Lollio pretends a fear
that the "hand" will pick his pocket if he places it there,
since the "hand" appears to express dishonest sentiments.
197. cast your water: Diagnose your ailment by analyzing
your urine.   **213. well-favoredly:** Soundly, severely.   **219.
Well said:** A stock commendation, meaning "well done."
224. That might be begg'd: That might be sought as a ward,
so as to enjoy as guardian the profits of his estate. In his
reply Lollio may be thinking of Alibius himself or of the
disguised lovers.

([*Enter Isabella, then Lollio with Madmen and Fools.*]
The Madmen and Fools dance.)

ALIBIUS: 'Tis perfect; well, fit but once these
    strains,°
  We shall have coin and credit for our pains.
                           (*Exeunt.*)

ACT V · *Scene 1*

(*Enter Beatrice. A clock strikes one.*)

BEATRICE: One struck, and yet she lies by't! Oh my
    fears!
  This strumpet serves her own ends, 'tis apparent
    now,
  Devours the pleasure with a greedy appetite,
  And never minds my honor or my peace,
  Makes havoc of my right. But she pays dearly
    for't: 5
  No trusting of her life with such a secret,
  That cannot rule her blood to keep her promise.
  Beside, I have some suspicion of her faith to me,
  Because I was suspected of my lord,
  And it must come from her. Hark! By my
    horrors,   10
  Another clock strikes two.   (*Strikes two.*)

(*Enter De Flores.*)

DE FLORES: Pist! Where are you?
BEATRICE: De Flores?
DE FLORES: Ay. Is she not come from him
    yet?
BEATRICE: As I am a living soul, not.
DE FLORES: Sure the devil
  Hath sow'd his itch within her. Who'd trust
  A waiting-woman?
BEATRICE: I must trust somebody.   15
DE FLORES: Push, they are termagants,°
  Especially when they fall upon their masters
  And have their ladies' first-fruits; th'are mad
    whelps,
  You cannot stave 'em off from game royal.°
    Then
  You are so harsh and hardy, ask no counsel;   20
  And I could have help'd you to a[n] apothecary's
    daughter,

227. fit but once these strains: Make the strains of the music
fit the mad antics of the dance, or only get the music ready.
16. termagant: A savage deity, supposedly worshiped by
Mohammedans and, by transference, a fierce, shrewish
woman.   **19. stave . . . royal:** Divert them from hunting
game which are a royal preserve.

Would have fall'n off before eleven, and
    thank['d] you too.
BEATRICE: Oh me, not yet? This whore forgets
    herself.
DE FLORES: The rascal fares so well. Look, y'are
    undone,
    The day-star, by this hand! See Phosphorus°
25   plain yonder.
BEATRICE: Advise me now to fall upon some ruin,°
    There is no counsel safe else.
DE FLORES: Peace, I ha't now;
    For we must force a rising, there's no remedy.
BEATRICE: How? Take heed of that.
DE FLORES: Tush, be you
    quiet,
    Or else give over all.
30 BEATRICE: Prithee, I ha' done then.
DE FLORES: This is my reach:° I'll set some part
    a-fire
    Of Diaphanta's chamber.
BEATRICE: How? Fire, sir?
    That may endanger the whole house.
DE FLORES: You talk of danger when your fame's
    on fire?
BEATRICE: That's true; do what thou wilt now.
35 DE FLORES: Push! I aim
    At a most rich success, strikes all dead sure:
    The chimney being a-fire, and some light parcels°
    Of the least danger in her chamber only,
    If Diaphanta should be met by chance then,
40   Far from her lodging (which is now suspicious),
    It would be thought her fears and affrights then
    Drove her to seek for succor; if not seen
    Or met at all, as that's the likeliest,
    For her own shame she'll hasten towards her
    lodging;
45   I will be ready with a piece° high-charg'd,
    As 'twere to cleanse the chimney. There, 'tis
    proper now,°
    But she shall be the mark.
BEATRICE: I'm forc'd to love thee
    now,
    'Cause thou provid'st so carefully for my honor.
DE FLORES: 'Slid, it concerns the safety of us both,
    Our pleasure and continuance.
BEATRICE: One word now,
50   prithee:
    How for the servants?

DE FLORES: I'll dispatch them,
    Some one way, some another in the hurry,
    For buckets, hooks, ladders. Fear not you;
    The deed shall find its time; and I've thought
    since
    Upon a safe conveyance for the body too.   55
    How this fire purifies wit! Watch you your
    minute.
BEATRICE: Fear keeps my soul upon't, I cannot
    stray from't.

(Enter Alonzo's Ghost.)

DE FLORES: Ha! What art thou that tak'st away the
    light
    'Twixt that star and me? I dread thee not.
    'Twas but a mist of conscience — all's clear
    again.   *(Exit.)*   60
BEATRICE: Who's that, De Flores? Bless me! It slides
    by!   *[Exit Ghost.]*
    Some ill thing haunts the house; 't has left
    behind it
    A shivering sweat upon me. I'm afraid now.
    This night hath been so tedious. Oh, this
    strumpet!
    Had she a thousand lives, he should not leave
    her   65
    Till he had destroy'd the last. — List! Oh my
    terrors!   *(Struck three o'clock.)*
    Three struck by Saint Sebastian's!
    ([Voice] within.) Fire, fire, fire!
BEATRICE: Already? How rare is that man's speed!
    How heartily he serves me! His face loathes°
    one,   70
    But look upon his care, who would not love
    him?
    The east is not more beauteous than his service.
    ([Voice] within.) Fire, fire, fire!

(Enter De Flores; Servants pass over, ring a bell.)

DE FLORES: Away, dispatch! Hooks, buckets,
    ladders! — that's well said;
    The fire bell rings, the chimney works; my
    charge;°   75
    The piece is ready.   *(Exit.)*
BEATRICE: Here's a man worth loving —

(Enter Diaphanta.)

    Oh, y'are a jewel.
DIAPHANTA: Pardon frailty, madam;
    In troth I was so well, I ev'n forgot myself.
BEATRICE: Y'have made trim work.
DIAPHANTA: What?

---

25. **day-star . . . Phosphorus:** In Greek, the morning star; in
Latin, Lucifer.   26. **to fall upon some ruin:** To happen upon
some desperate action or catastrophe.   31. **reach:** Plan.   37.
light parcels: Small items of insufficient body to cause a
serious fire.   45. **piece:** Fowling-piece, gun.   46. **There, 'tis
proper now:** The plan is now fit for execution.

70. **loathes:** Disgusts.   75. **charge:** Powder and shot for the
gun.

BEATRICE: Hie
  quickly to your chamber;
  Your reward follows you.
DIAPHANTA: I never made
  So sweet a bargain.   (*Exit.*)

(*Enter Alsemero.*)

ALSEMERO: O my dear Joanna
  Alas, art thou risen too? I was coming,
  My absolute treasure.
BEATRICE: When I miss'd you,
  I could not choose but follow.
ALSEMERO: Th'art all
  sweetness!
  The fire is not so dangerous.
BEATRICE: Think you so, sir?
ALSEMERO: I prithee tremble not; believe me, 'tis
  not.

(*Enter Vermandero and Jasperino.*)

VERMANDERO: Oh bless my house and me!
ALSEMERO: My lord
  your father.

(*Enter De Flores with a piece.*)

VERMANDERO: Knave, whither goes that piece?
DE FLORES: To
  scour the chimney.   (*Exit.*)
VERMANDERO: Oh, well said, well said;
  That fellow's good on all occasions.
BEATRICE: A wondrous necessary man, my lord.
VERMANDERO: He hath a ready wit, he's worth 'em
  all, sir;
  Dog at° a house of fire; I ha' seen him sing'd ere
  now.   (*The piece goes off.*)
  — Ha, there he goes.
BEATRICE: 'Tis done.
ALSEMERO: Come, sweet, to
  bed now;
  Alas, thou wilt get cold.
BEATRICE: Alas, the fear keeps that
  out;
  My heart will find no quiet till I hear
  How Diaphanta, my poor woman, fares;
  It is her chamber, sir, her lodging chamber.
VERMANDERO: How should the fire come there?
BEATRICE: As good a soul as ever lady
  countenanc'd,°
  But in her chamber negligent and heavy;°
  She 'scap'd a mine° twice.
VERMANDERO: Twice?

BEATRICE: Strangely° twice,
  sir.
VERMANDERO: Those sleepy sluts are dangerous in
  a house,
  And they be ne'er so good.

(*Enter De Flores.*)

DE FLORES: O poor virginity,
  Thou hast paid dearly for't!
VERMANDERO: Bless us! What's
  that?°
DE FLORES: A thing you all knew once —
  Diaphanta's burnt.
BEATRICE: My woman, oh my woman!
DE FLORES: Now the
  flames
  Are greedy of her; burnt, burnt, burnt to death,
  sir!
BEATRICE: Oh, my presaging soul!
ALSEMERO: Not a tear more;
  I charge you by the last embrace I gave you
  In bed before this rais'd us.
BEATRICE: Now you tie me;
  Were it my sister, now she gets no more.

(*Enter Servant.*)

VERMANDERO: How now?
SERVANT: All danger's past; you may now take your
  rests, my lords, the fire is throughly quench'd. —
  Ah, poor gentlewoman, how soon was she stifled!
BEATRICE: De Flores, what is left of her inter,
  And we as mourners all will follow her;
  I will entreat that honor to my servant,
  Ev'n of my lord himself.
ALSEMERO: Command it, sweetness.
BEATRICE: Which of you spied the fire first?
DE FLORES: 'Twas I,
  madam.
BEATRICE: And took such pains in't too? A double
  goodness!
  'Twere well he were rewarded.
VERMANDERO: He shall be;
  De Flores, call upon me.
ALSEMERO: And upon me, sir.
                    (*Exeunt [all except De Flores].*)
DE FLORES: Rewarded? Precious! Here's a trick
  beyond me;
  I see in all bouts both of sport° and wit,
  Always a woman strives for the last hit.   (*Exit.*)

80, 85, 90, 95, 100, 102, 105, 110, 115, 120, 125

93. Dog at: Skilled at.   **100. countenanc'd:** Patronized, employed.   **101. heavy:** Sluggish, slovenly.   **102. mine:** Catastrophe, violent conflagration.

102. Strangely: Surprisingly, miraculously.   **105. What's that:** Probably De Flores carried not Diaphanta's body (V, I, 55 makes that unlikely) but the charred remains of some still recognizable outer garment, one worn earlier by Diaphanta onstage.   **126. sport:** Physical amusement; sexual pleasure.

Scene II

(*Enter Tomazo.*)

TOMAZO: I cannot taste the benefits of life
    With the same relish I was wont to do.
    Man I grow weary of, and hold his fellowship
    A treacherous, bloody friendship; and because
5   I am ignorant in whom my wrath should settle,
    I must think all men villains, and the next
    I meet, whoe'er he be, the murderer
    Of my most worthy brother. — Ha! What's he?

(*Enter De Flores, passes over the stage.*)

    Oh, the fellow that some call honest De Flores;
10   But methinks honesty was hard bested°
    To come there for a lodging — as if a queen
    Should make her palace of a pest-house.°
    I find a contrariety in nature
    Betwixt that face and me: the least occasion
    Would give me game° upon him. Yet he's so
15   foul
    One would scarce touch [him] with a sword he
    loved
    And made account of;° so most deadly
    venomous,
    He would go near to poison any weapon
    That should draw blood on him; one must
    resolve
20   Never to use that sword again in fight,
    In way of honest manhood, that strikes him;
    Some river must devour't, 'twere not fit
    That any man should find it. — What, again?

(*Enter De Flores.*)

    He walks a' purpose by, sure, to choke me up,
    To infect my blood.
25 DE FLORES: My worthy noble lord.
  TOMAZO: Dost offer to come near and breathe upon
    me?   [*Strikes him.*]
  DE FLORES: A blow!   [*Draws his sword.*]
  TOMAZO: Yea, are you so prepar'd?
    I'll rather, like a soldier, die by th' sword.
                           [*Draws.*]
    Than like a politician by thy poison.
30 DE FLORES: Hold, my lord, as you are honorable.
  TOMAZO: All slaves that kill by poison are still
    cowards.
  DE FLORES [*aside*]: I cannot strike; I see his
    brother's wounds

---

10. **hard bested:** Hard put to it.   12. **pest-house:** Hospital
for those suffering from infectious diseases, especially plague.
15. **give me game:** Give me occasion for quarreling; *to be
in game* = "to be engaged in hunting."   17. **made account
of:** Valued.

    Fresh bleeding in his eye, as in a crystal.°
    — I will not question this; I know y'are noble;
    I take my injury with thanks given, sir,   35
    Like a wise lawyer; and as a favor
    Will wear it for the worthy hand that gave it.
    [*Aside.*] Why this from him that yesterday
    appear'd
    So strangely loving to me?
    Oh, but instinct is of a subtler strain;   40
    Guilt must not walk so near his lodge again;
    He came near me now.   (*Exit.*)
  TOMAZO: All league with mankind I renounce for
    ever,
    Till I find this murderer; not so much
    As common courtesy, but I'll lock up;   45
    For in the state of ignorance I live in,
    A brother may salute his brother's murderer,
    And wish good speed to th' villain in a greeting.

(*Enter Vermandero, Alibius and Isabella.*)

VERMANDERO: Noble Piracquo!
TOMAZO: Pray keep on your
    way, sir,
    I've nothing to say to you.
VERMANDERO: Comforts bless you,
    sir.   50
TOMAZO: I have forsworn compliment, in troth I
    have, sir;
    As you are merely man, I have not left
    A good wish for you, nor any here.
VERMANDERO: Unless you be so far in love with
    grief
    You will not part from't upon any terms,   55
    We bring that news will make a welcome for us.
TOMAZO: What news can that be?
VERMANDERO: Throw no
    scornful smile
    Upon the zeal I bring you, 'tis worth more, sir.
    Two of the chiefest men I kept about me
    I hide not from the law or your just vengeance.   60
TOMAZO: Ha!
VERMANDERO: To give your peace more ample
    satisfaction,
    Thank these discoverers.
TOMAZO: If you bring that calm,
    Name but the manner I shall ask forgiveness in
    For that contemptuous smile upon you;   65
    I'll perfect it with reverence that belongs
    Unto a sacred altar.   [*Kneels.*]
VERMANDERO: Good sir, rise;
    Why, now you overdo as much a' this hand
    As you fell short a' t'other. Speak, Alibius.

---

33. **crystal:** Crystal ball.

ALIBIUS: 'Twas my wife's fortune, as she is most
70   lucky
      At a discovery, to find out lately
      Within our hospital of fools and madmen
      Two counterfeits slipp'd into these disguises:
      Their names, Franciscus and Antonio.
VERMANDERO: Both mine, sir, and I ask no favor
75   for 'em.
ALIBIUS: Now that which draws suspicion to their
      habits,°
      The time of their disguisings agrees justly
      With the day of the murder.
TOMAZO: O blest revelation!
VERMANDERO: Nay more, nay more, sir (I'll not
      spare mine own
80   In way of justice), they both feign'd a journey
      To Briamata, and so wrought out their leaves.°
      My love was so abus'd in't.
TOMAZO: Time's too precious
      To run in waste now; you have brought a peace
      The riches of five kingdoms could not purchase.
85   Be my most happy conduct;° I thirst for 'em;
      Like subtle lightning will I wind about 'em,
      And melt their marrow in 'em.°
                              (*Exeunt.*)

Scene III

(*Enter Alsemero and Jasperino.*)

JASPERINO: Your confidence, I'm sure, is now of
      proof;°
      The prospect from the garden has show'd
      Enough for deep suspicion.
ALSEMERO: The black mask°
      That so continually was worn upon't
5   Condemns the face for ugly ere't be seen:
      Her despite to him, and so seeming bottomless.
JASPERINO: Touch it home° then; 'tis not a shallow
      probe
      Can search this ulcer soundly; I fear you'll find
      it

---

76. **habits:** Clothes.   81. **wrought out their leaves:** Cunningly obtained permission to go.   85. **conduct:** Guide.
86–87. **Like subtle lightning . . . in 'em:** Lightning was held capable of melting marrow without damaging the skin and so became an image for sudden, undetectable murder.   1. **of proof:** Impenetrable, like armor. However, from the context it is possible that the phrase here means "capable of being put to the test," "on trial."   3. **The black mask:** I.e., Beatrice's treacherous pretense of hatred for De Flores; the obvious superficial deceit suggests an underlying viciousness.
7. **Touch it home:** Get to the root of the matter, the quick of the ulcer.

Full of corruption. 'Tis fit I leave you;
She meets you opportunely from that walk;   10
She took the back door at his parting with her.
                              (*Exit Jasperino.*)
ALSEMERO: Did my fate wait for this unhappy
      stroke
      At my first sight of woman? — She's here.

(*Enter Beatrice.*)

BEATRICE: Alsemero!
ALSEMERO: How do you?
BEATRICE: How do I?
      Alas! How do you? You look not well.   15
ALSEMERO: You read me well enough, I am not
      well.
BEATRICE: Not well, sir? Is't in my power to better
      you?
ALSEMERO: Yes.
BEATRICE: Nay, then y'are cur'd again.
ALSEMERO: Pray resolve me one question, lady.
BEATRICE: If I
      can.
ALSEMERO: None can so sure. Are you honest?°   20
BEATRICE: Ha, ha, ha! That's a broad° question, my
      lord.
ALSEMERO: But that's not a modest answer, my
      lady.
      Do you laugh? My doubts are strong upon me.
BEATRICE: 'Tis innocence that smiles, and no rough
      brow
      Can take away the dimple in her cheek.   25
      Say I should strain a tear to fill the vault,°
      Which would you give the better faith to?
ALSEMERO: 'Twere but hypocrisy of a sadder color,
      But the same stuff. Neither your smiles nor tears
      Shall move or flatter me from my belief: 30
      You are a whore!
BEATRICE: What a horrid sound it hath!
      It blasts a beauty to deformity;
      Upon what face soever that breath falls,
      It strikes it ugly: oh, you have ruin'd
      What you can ne'er repair again.   35
ALSEMERO: I'll all demolish, and seek out truth
      within you,
      If there be any left. Let your sweet tongue
      Prevent your heart's rifling; there I'll ransack
      And tear out my suspicion.
BEATRICE: You may, sir,
      'Tis an easy passage. Yet, if you please,   40

---

20. **honest:** Chaste.   21. **broad:** Wide; coarse.   26. **strain a tear to fill the vault:** Produce enough water to fill the heavens.

Show me the ground° whereon you lost your
    love;
My spotless virtue may but tread on that
Before I perish.
ALSEMERO: Unanswerable!
A ground you cannot stand on; you fall down
45   Beneath all grace and goodness when you set
Your ticklish° heel on't; there was a visor°
O'er that cunning face, and that became you;
Now impudence in triumph rides upon't;
How comes this tender reconcilement else
'Twixt you and your despite, your rancorous
50   loathing,
De Flores? He that your eye was sore at sight
    of,
He's now become your arm's supporter,° your
    lip's saint!°
BEATRICE: Is there the cause?
ALSEMERO: Worse; your lust's
    devil,
Your adultery!
BEATRICE: Would any but yourself say that,
'Twould turn him to a villain.
55   ALSEMERO: 'Twas witness'd
By the counsel of your bosom, Diaphanta.
BEATRICE: Is your witness dead then?
ALSEMERO: 'Tis to be
    fear'd
It was the wages of her knowledge, poor soul;
She liv'd not long after the discovery.
BEATRICE: Then hear a story of not much less
60   horror
Than this your false suspicion is beguil'd with;
To your bed's scandal I stand up innocence,°
Which even the guilt of one black other deed
Will stand for proof of: your love has made me
A cruel murd'ress.
ALSEMERO: Ha!
65   BEATRICE: A bloody one;
I have kiss'd poison for't, strok'd a serpent:
That thing of hate, worthy in my esteem
Of no better employment, and him most worthy
To be so employ'd, I caus'd to murder
70   That innocent Piracquo, having no
Better means than that worst, to assure
Yourself to me.

---

41. **ground:** Foundation, basic reason. 46. **ticklish:** Wanton, lascivious. **visor:** Mask. 52. **arm's supporter:** Physical prop; but it is probable that there is an allusion to the grotesque figures who served as "supporters" to a coat of arms. **lip's saint:** I.e., that adored person to whom your lips pay devotion. The phrase ironically echoes Beatrice's proleptic comment on first meeting Alsemero, "I shall change my saint, I fear me" (I, I, 154). 62. **stand up innocence:** Probably a legal metaphor: "Against the scandalous charge that your bed is dishonored I maintain my innocence."

ALSEMERO: Oh, the place itself e'er since
Has crying been for vengeance, the temple
Where blood° and beauty first unlawfully
Fir'd their devotion, and quench'd the right one;° 75
'Twas in my fears at first, 'twill have it now.°
Oh, thou art all deform'd!
BEATRICE: Forget not, sir,
It for your sake was done; shall greater dangers
Make the less welcome?
ALSEMERO: Oh, thou shouldst have
    gone
A thousand leagues about° to have avoided 80
This dangerous bridge of blood; here we are
    lost.
BEATRICE: Remember I am true unto your bed.
ALSEMERO: The bed itself's a charnel, the sheets
    shrouds
For murdered carcasses. It must ask pause
What I must do in this; meantime you shall 85
Be my prisoner only. Enter my closet;
                  (Exit Beatrice.)
I'll be your keeper yet. Oh, in what part
Of this sad story shall I first begin? — Ha!

(Enter De Flores.)

This same fellow has put me in.° — De Flores!
DE FLORES: Noble Alsemero?
ALSEMERO: I can tell you 90
News, sir; my wife has her commended to you.
DE FLORES: That's news indeed, my lord; I think
    she would
Commend me to the gallows if she could,
She ever lov'd me so well. I thank her.
ALSEMERO: What's this blood upon your band,° De
    Flores? 95
DE FLORES: Blood? No, sure, 'twas wash'd since.
ALSEMERO: Since
    when, man?
DE FLORES: Since t'other day I got a knock
In a sword-and-dagger school. I think 'tis out.
ALSEMERO: Yes, 'tis almost out, but 'tis perceiv'd
    though.
I had forgot my message; this it is: 10⟨0⟩
What price goes murder?
DE FLORES: How sir?
ALSEMERO: I ask you, sir;
My wife's behindhand with° you, she tells me,
For a brave bloody blow you gave for her sake
Upon Piracquo.
DE FLORES: Upon? 'Twas quite through him,
    sure.

---

74. **blood:** Sexual desire. 75. **the right one:** I.e., religious zeal. 76. **'twill have it now:** The temple will have vengeance. 80. **about:** Around. She should have made a detour. 89. **put me in:** Given me the cue. 95. **band:** Collar. 102. **behindhand with:** Indebted to.

Has she confess'd it?
ALSEMERO: As sure as death to both of
05   you,
And much more than that.
DE FLORES: It could not be much
      more;
'Twas but one thing, and that — she's a whore.
ALSEMERO: It could not choose but follow. Oh
      cunning devils!
How should blind men know you from fair-fac'd
      saints?
BEATRICE (*within*): He lies, the villain does belie
10   me!
DE FLORES: Let me go to her, sir.
ALSEMERO: Nay, you shall to
      her.
      — Peace, crying crocodile,° your sounds are
      heard!
      — Take your prey to you, get you in to her, sir.
                              (*Exit De Flores.*)
I'll be your pander now; rehearse again
15   Your scene of lust, that you may be perfect
When you shall come to act it to the black
      audience
Where howls and gnashings shall be music to
      you.
Clip° your adult'ress freely, 'tis the pilot
Will guide you to the Mare Mortuum,°
20   Where you shall sink to fadoms bottomless.

(*Enter Vermandero, Alibius, Isabella, Tomazo, Franciscus, and Antonio.*)

VERMANDERO: Oh, Alsemero, I have a wonder for
      you.
ALSEMERO: No, sir, 'tis I, I have a wonder for you.
VERMANDERO: I have suspicion near as proof itself
For Piracquo's murder.
ALSEMERO: Sir, I have proof
25   Beyond suspicion for Piracquo's murder.
VERMANDERO: Beseech you, hear me; these two
      have been disguis'd
E'er since the deed was done.
ALSEMERO: I have two other
That were more close disguis'd than your two
      could be
E'er since the deed was done.
VERMANDERO: You'll hear me: these mine own
30   servants —
ALSEMERO: Hear me: those nearer than your
      servants,

That shall acquit them and prove them guiltless.
FRANCISCUS: That may be done with easy truth, sir.
TOMAZO: How is my cause bandied° through your
      delays!
'Tis urgent in blood and calls for haste.   135
Give me a brother alive or dead:
Alive, a wife with him; if dead, for both
A recompense for murder and adultery.°
BEATRICE (*within*): Oh, oh, oh!
ALSEMERO: Hark, 'tis coming to
      you.
DE FLORES (*within*): Nay, I'll along for company.
BEATRICE (*within*):   Oh, oh! 140
VERMANDERO: What horrid sounds are these?
ALSEMERO: Come forth, you twins of mischief.

(*Enter De Flores, bringing in Beatrice [wounded].*)

DE FLORES: Here we are; if you have any more
To say to us, speak quickly, I shall not
Give you the hearing else; I am so stout yet,   145
And so, I think, that broken rib of mankind.°
VERMANDERO: An host of enemies ent'red my
      citadel
Could not amaze like this: Joanna! Beatrice-
      Joanna!
BEATRICE: Oh, come not near me, sir, I shall defile
      you;
I am that of your blood was taken from you   150
For your better health;° look no more upon't,
But cast it to the ground regardlessly;
Let the common shewer° take it from distinction.
Beneath the stars, upon yon meteor°
Ever hung my fate, 'mongst things corruptible; 155
I ne'er could pluck it from him; my loathing
Was prophet to the rest, but ne'er believ'd;
Mine honor fell with him, and now my life.
Alsemero, I am a stranger to your bed.
Your bed was coz'ned on the nuptial night,   160
For which your false bride died.
ALSEMERO: Diaphanta!

---

112. **crying crocodile:** The crocodile was thought to shed hypocritical tears as it killed its victims. 118. **clip:** Embrace. 119. **Mare Mortuum:** Latin for the Dead Sea, which was thought to be bottomless; this, however, has suggested also the bottomless pit of hell, to which Beatrice will pilot De Flores, as did Charon over the Styx.

134. **bandied:** Tossed aside. 138. **adultery:** Rowley may carelessly have made Tomazo refer to Beatrice's liaison with De Flores, which he cannot know. But according to much Jacobean opinion, the formal contract with Alonzo was a binding marriage, as is symbolized in III, IV, 28, 37–38. Tomazo may regard the marriage to Alsemero as a form of adultery. 146. **broken rib of mankind:** Beatrice, a daughter of the primal Eve who was made from the rib of Adam (Man) in Genesis 2:21–23. 150–51. **your blood . . . health:** An allusion to the practice of bloodletting. 153. **common shewer:** Main drain. 154. **yon meteor:** I.e., De Flores. As opposed to the pure, fixed stars, meteors belonged to the sublunary world of corruption and decay; the influence of stars might be beneficent, but meteors were provoked by, or resulted in, evil.

DE FLORES: Yes, and the while I coupled with your
    mate
    At barley-brake;° now we are left in Hell.
VERMANDERO: We are all there, it circumscribes
    here.°
DE FLORES: I lov'd this woman in spite of her
165   heart;
    Her love I earn'd out of Piracquo's murder.
TOMAZO: Ha! my brother's murtherer?
DE FLORES: Yes, and her
    honor's prize
    Was my reward; I thank life for nothing
    But that pleasure; it was so sweet to me
170   That I have drunk up all, left none behind
    For any man to pledge me.
VERMANDERO: Horrid villain!
    Keep life in him for further tortures.
DE FLORES: No!
    I can prevent you; here's my penknife still;
    It is but one thread more. [*Stabs himself.*] —
    And now 'tis cut.
175   Make haste, Joanna, by that token° to thee;
    Canst not forget, so lately put in mind,
    I would not go to leave thee far behind.   (*Dies.*)
BEATRICE: Forgive me, Alsemero, all forgive;
    'Tis time to die when 'tis a shame to live. (*Dies.*)
VERMANDERO: Oh, my name is ent'red now in that
180   record°
    Where till this fatal hour 'twas never read.
ALSEMERO: Let it be blotted out; let your heart lose
    it,
    And it can never look you in the face,
    Nor tell a tale behind the back of life
185   To your dishonor; justice hath so right
    The guilty hit that innocence is quit
    By proclamation, and may joy again.°
    — Sir, you are sensible of what truth hath done;
    'Tis the best comfort that your grief can find.
190 TOMAZO: Sir, I am satisfied; my injuries
    Lie dead before me. I can exact no more,
    Unless my soul were loose, and could o'ertake
    Those black fugitives that are fled from thence,°
    To take a second vengeance; but there are
    wraths
195   Deeper than mine, 'tis to be fear'd, about 'em.

ALSEMERO: What an opacous° body had that moon
    That last chang'd on us! Here's beauty chang'd
    To ugly whoredom; here, servant obedience
    To a master-sin, imperious murder;
    I, a suppos'd husband, chang'd embraces   20
    With wantonness, but that was paid before;°
    Your change° is come too, from an ignorant
    wrath
    To knowing friendship. Are there any more
    on's?
ANTONIO: Yes, sir, I was chang'd too, from a little
    ass as I was to a great fool as I am, and had like   20
    to ha' been chang'd to the gallows, but that you
    know my innocence° always excuses me.
FRANCISCUS: I was chang'd from a little wit to be
    stark mad,
    Almost for the same purpose.
ISABELLA [*to Alibius*]:   Your change is still
    behind°
    But deserve best your transformation;   21
    You are a jealous coxcomb, keep schools of
    folly,
    And teach your scholars how to break your own
    head.°
ALIBIUS: I see all apparent, wife, and will change
    now
    Into a better husband, and never keep
    Scholars that shall be wiser than myself.   21
ALSEMERO: Sir, you have yet a son's duty living,
    Please you accept it. Let that your sorrow,
    As it goes from your eye, go from your heart;
    Man and his sorrow at the grave must part.

EPILOGUE

ALSEMERO: All we can do to comfort one another,
    To stay° a brother's sorrow for a brother,
    To dry a child from the kind father's eyes,
    Is to no purpose, it rather multiplies;°
    Your only smiles have power to cause relive   5
    The dead again, or in their rooms to give
    Brother a new brother, father a child;
    If these appear, all griefs are reconcil'd.
                   (*Exeunt omnes*°.)

163. **barley-brake:** See note on III, III, 171.   **163–64. Hell
. . . circumscribes here:** Vermandero continues the metaphor
of "barley-brake," seeing the whole cast as within the central
circle which indicates the limits of "hell."   **175. that token:**
I.e., the wound he has just given himself.   **180. record:** The
heavenly record which lists criminal actions.   **186–87. The
guilty . . . joy again:** The innocent are acquitted by public
proclamation of the truth.   **193. black fugitives . . . thence:**
I.e., the damned souls of Beatrice and De Flores which have
left the bodies which lie before Tomazo.

196. **opacous:** Darkened, obscured, and therefore malevolent
or of ill omen.   **201. wantonness . . . before:** I.e., Diaphanta,
whose adultery was paid by her murder.   **202. Your change:**
Tomazo's.   **207. innocence:** Guiltlessness . . . idiocy (idiots
not being held criminally responsible).   **209. still behind:**
Yet to come.   **212. break your own head:** I.e., with cuckold's horns.   **2. stay:** Check, solace.   **4. multiplies:** I.e.,
increases grief.   **8. [S.D.] omnes:** Latin for "all."

COMMENTARY

David L. Hirst
TRAGICOMEDY AND *THE CHANGELING*   1984

In this brief comment, Hirst reflects on the play's two plots. The effect of emphasizing the Rowley plot, as he points out, is to reduce the tragic effect of the play.

Middleton and Rowley's *The Changeling* (1622) brings the development from Marlowe full circle in that this play represents a conscious attempt to integrate a sequence of carefully worked-out comic scenes with the main tragic plot. Middleton's moral story (of the corruption of his heroine Beatrice-Joanna who gradually becomes more dependent on De Flores, the "wondrous necessary man," who has murdered her intended husband in order that she may marry Alsemero) is matched point by point by the comic invention of Rowley who presents a parody in which Alibius, a jealous old doctor, entrusts the virtue of his young wife to the care of his servant, Lollio. Here the subplot deals with an alien world of comic characters whose conduct in large part is governed by the conventions of the *commedia dell'arte*. It has the effect of throwing the action of Middleton's noble characters into ironic relief and making them all appear as mad as the inmates of Alibius's asylum. More recent productions of the play which have given due attention to the Rowley plot — or indeed have inverted the two by setting the main action in the asylum — have drawn attention to the satiric purpose of the play in its exposure of sin and guilt. The potentially tragic stature of the protagonists is further reduced by the careful drawing together of the two plots at the end and the pointed parallels made between them. Rather than finding the tragedy diminished by the subplot, however, we discover that the moral potential of the drama is extended by this harsh juxtaposition of serious and comic material.

Late Seventeenth- and Eighteenth-Century Drama

The Restoration: Rebirth of Drama

Theater in England continued to thrive after Shakespeare's death, with a host of successful playwrights, including John Webster (1580?–1638?), Francis Beaumont (c. 1584–1616) and his collaborator John Fletcher (1579–1625), Philip Massinger (1583–1640), Thomas Middleton (1580–1627), John Ford (1586–c. 1655), and James Shirley (1596–1666). All these playwrights were busy working independently or in collaboration. Fletcher was chosen official successor to Shakespeare at the Globe and furnished the theater with as many as four plays a year. But in 1642 long-standing religious and political conflicts between King Charles I and Parliament finally erupted into civil war, with the Parliament, under the influence of Puritanism, eventually winning.

The Puritans were religious extremists with narrow, specific values. They were essentially an emerging merchant class of well-to-do citizens who viewed the aristocracy as wastrels. Theater for them was associated with both the aristocracy and the low life. Theatergoing was synonymous with wasting time, since by then the theaters were often a focus for immoral activity and the neighborhoods around the theaters were as unsavory as any in England. Under the Puritan government, the theaters were totally closed in England for almost twenty years. They became disused and when the new king, Charles II, was crowned in 1660, those that had not been converted to other uses had become completely outmoded.

As fate would have it, Charles II was sent with his mother and brother to the Continent in the early stages of the civil war. When Charles I was beheaded, the future king and his family were in France, where they were in a position to see the remarkable achievements of French comedy and French classical tragedy. Charles II developed a taste for theater that accompanied him back to England. And when he returned in triumph to usher in the gay, exciting, and swashbuckling period known as the Restoration, he permitted favorites to build new theaters.

Theater on the Continent: Neoclassicism

Interaction between the leading European countries — England, Spain, and France — was sporadic at best in the seventeenth century because of intermittent wars among the nations, yet the development of theater in all three countries took similar turns throughout the early 1600s.

The Spanish developed, independently, a corral resembling the Elizabethan inn yard, in which they produced plays. This development may have been an accident of architecture — because of the widespread need for inns and for places to store horses — that permitted the symmetry of growth of the English Elizabethan and the Spanish Golden Age theaters.

The most important playwright of the Spanish theater was Lope de Vega (1562–1635), who is said to have written twelve hundred plays (seven hundred fifty survive). Many of them are relatively brief, and some are like the scenarios for the *commedia dell'arte*. But a good number are full-length and impressive works, such as *Fuente Ovejuna* (*The Sheep Well*), *The King, The Greatest Alcalde,* and *The Gardener's Dog.* Calderón (Pedro Calderón de la Barca, 1600–1681) became, on Lope de Vega's death, the reigning Spanish playwright. His *Life Is a Dream* is performed regularly throughout the world. Calderón became a priest in 1651 and wrote religious plays that occasionally got him into trouble with the Inquisition, an agency of the church that searched out and punished heresy. He was especially imaginative in his use of stage machinery and especially gifted in producing philosophical and poetic dialogue.

The French became aware of Spanish achievements in the theater in the 1630s, and Pierre Corneille (1606–1684), who emerged as France's leading playwright of the time, adapted a play by de Vega that became one of his most important plays, *Le Cid.*

By the time Charles II took up residence in France in the 1640s, the French had developed a suave, polished, and intellectually demanding approach to drama. Corneille and the neoclassicists were part of a large movement in European culture and the arts that tried to codify the achievement of the ancients and emulate them. Qualities such as harmony, symmetry, balance in everything structural. and clear moral themes were most in evidence. NEOCLASSICISM privileged thought over feeling, so the thematic material in neoclassical drama was very important. That material was sometimes political, reflecting the values of Augustan Rome — 27 B.C. to 17 A.D. — when Caesar Augustus lived and when it was appropriate to think in terms of subordinating the self to the interests of the state. Neoclassical dramatists focused on honor, moral integrity, self-sacrifice, and heroic political subjects.

An overstrict interpretation of Aristotelian concepts of the unities of time, place, character, and action became central to the art of playwriting. A school of critics arose who criticized by the rules. These "rules critics" demanded a perfect observance of the unities, that is, they wanted a play to have one plot, a single action that takes place in one day, and a single setting. In most cases the plays that satisfied them are now often thought of as static, cold, limited, and dull. Their perfection is seen today as rigid and emotionally icy.

Corneille eventually gave way to a much younger competitor, Jean Baptiste Racine (1639–1699), who brought the tradition of French tragedy to its fullest. Most of his plays are on classical subjects, beginning in 1667 with *Andromache,* continuing with *Britannicus* (1669), *Iphigenia* (1674), and *Mithridate* (1673), and ending in 1677 with his most famous and possibly best play, *Phaedra.*

Phaedra is a deeply passionate, moral play centering on the love of Phaedra for her stepson, Hippolytus. Venus is responsible for her incestuous love — which is the playwright's way of saying that Phaedra is impelled by the gods or by destiny, almost against her will.

The French stage, unlike the English, never substituted boys for female roles, and so plays such as *Phaedra* were opportunities for brilliant actresses. Phaedra, in particular, dominates the stage — she is a commanding and infinitely complex figure. It is no wonder that this play was a favorite of Sarah Bernhardt (1844–1923), one of France's greatest actresses.

French Comedy: Molière

At the same time that Racine commanded the tragic stage, Jean Baptiste Poquelin (1622–1673), known as Molière, began his dominance of the comic stage. He was aware of Racine's achievements and applauded them strongly. His career started with a family-run theater company that spent most of its time touring the countryside beyond Paris. The plays the company developed were obviously influenced by some of the stock characters and situations of the *commedia dell'arte,* but they also began to reflect Molière's own genius for composition.

King Louis XIV saw the company in 1658 and found it so much to his liking that he installed it in a theater and demanded to see more of its work. From that time until his death, Molière wrote, produced, and acted in one comedy after another, most of which have become part of the permanent repertoire of the French stage. Plays such as *The Misanthrope* (1666), *The Miser* (1669), *The Bourgeois Gentleman* (1670), *The Imaginary Invalid* (1673), and his satire on the theme of Puritanism, *Tartuffe* (1669), are also staged all over the world.

Theater in England: Restoration Comedy of Manners

When the theaters reopened in England in the 1660s with the return of Charles II, they needed new plays. Times had changed, England had suffered enormous upheaval, and the Puritan-dominated, theater-darkened past was quickly undone. The new age wanted glitter, excitement, sensuality, and dramatic dazzle. Tastes had changed. Audiences wanted upbeat comedies that poked fun at the stuffed shirts of society and at old-fashioned institutions and fashions.

Several important physical changes took effect immediately. The new stages were in indoor theaters using artificial light. They could be operated year-round, and the price for seats varied according to location. The middle-priced seats were in the orchestra before the proscenium-arched stage (Figure 7). The first-level boxes against the walls were most expensive, while the lowest-priced seats were in the upper ranges of the balconies.

The new indoor theaters were generally adapted from spaces designed for courtly events. They were rectangular, often twice as long as they were wide, and usually lighted by candles in chandeliers. The proscenium frame around the stage appeared in the new theaters. Behind its sides was kept the machinery that could lift objects and characters high into the air. Eventually, movable scenery and changeable painted backdrops helped the playwrights create their illusions, although some plays of the period could easily be performed on a bare stage.

Once English women were permitted to take part in theater, actresses appeared who commanded the stage immediately. The actresses of the period were bright, witty, and charming and were often the most important "draw" for seventeenth-century audiences. Nell Gwynne (1650–1687), one of the most famous actresses of her day and mistress to Charles II, became one of the legends of the English stage.

Among England's most notable playwrights from 1660 through the eighteenth century were Aphra Behn (1640–1689), the first professional woman playwright on the English stage and author of *The Rover*, one of the most frequently performed plays of the period; William Wycherley (1640–1716), whose *The Plain Dealer*, indebted to Molière, and *The Country Wife* are regarded as his best work; William Congreve (1670–1729), whose *The Way of the World* is justly famous; and Richard Brinsley Sheridan (1751–1816), whose *School for Scandal* is still bright, lively, and engaging for modern audiences.

The English playwrights produced a wide range of comedy, drawing on their understanding of their audience and their desire to entertain them with bright, gay, and witty work. The comedies of the period came to be known in the twentieth century as COMEDIES OF MANNERS because they reveal the foibles of the society that watched them. Society enjoyed laughing at itself. Although some of the English drama of the eighteenth century developed a moralistic tone and was often heavily classical, the earlier RESTORATION COMEDIES were less interested in reforming the society than in capitalizing on its faults.

Eighteenth-Century Drama

Eighteenth-century Europe absorbed much of the spirit of France and the French neoclassicists. England, like other European countries, began to see the effects of neoclassicism in the arts and literature. Emulation of classical art and classical values was common throughout Europe,

Figure 7. Conjectural
reconstruction of an early
Restoration theater. By Peter
Kahn, Cornell University.

and critics established standards of excellence in the arts to guarantee
quality.

The most famous name in eighteenth-century English drama is David
Garrick (1717–1779), the legendary actor and manager of the Drury
Lane Theatre. The theaters, including his own, often reworked French

drama and earlier English and Italian drama, but they began to develop a new SENTIMENTAL COMEDY to balance the neoclassical heroic tragedies of the period. It was a comedy in which the emotions of the audience were played on, manipulated, and exploited to arouse sympathy for the characters in the play.

Sentimental comedy flourished after 1760, but earlier than that Colley Cibber (1671–1757) is sometimes credited with beginning the sentimental comedy with his *Love's Last Shift* (1696). The play centers on Loveless, who wanders from his marriage only to find that his wife has disguised herself as a prostitute to win him back. As in all sentimental comedies, what the audience most wants is what it gets: a certain amount of tears, a contrasting amount of laughter, and a happy ending. Cibber was especially well known as an actor for his portrayal of fops, his way of poking satiric fun at his own society and its pretentions.

Sir Richard Steele (1672–1729) wrote one of the best known sentimental comedies in his *The Conscious Lovers* (1722). Steele's coauthor of *The Spectator,* Joseph Addison (1672–1719), also distinguished himself with his contribution to the heroic tragedy of the age, the long neoclassical *Cato* (1713). The most often played tragedy of its day, it was considered to be the finest example of the moral, heroic style. Today it is not a playable drama because the action is too slow, the speeches too long, and the theme too obscure, although it is a perfect model of what the age preferred in heroic tragedy.

The audiences at the time enjoyed bright, amusing comedies that often criticized wayward youth, overprotective parents, dishonest financial dealings, and social expectations. Their taste in tragedies veered toward a moralizing heroism that extolled the ideals of dedication to the values of the community and self-sacrifice on the part of the hero.

Molière

Molière (1622–1673, born Jean Baptiste Poquelin) came from a family attached to the glittering court of King Louis XIV, the Sun King. His father had purchased an appointment to the king and as a result both Molière and his family were familiar with the exciting court life of Paris. That is not to say that they were on intimate terms with the courtiers who surrounded the king. Molière's father was a furnisher and upholsterer to the king, so the family, while well-to-do and in a position of some power, was still apart from royalty and the privileged aristocracy.

Molière's education was exceptional. He went to Jesuit schools and spent more than five years at Collège de Clermont, which he left in 1641 having studied both the humanities and philosophy. His knowledge of philosophy was unusually deep and his background in the classics, including the classical philosophers, was exceptionally strong. He also took a degree in the law in 1641 at Orléans, but never practiced. His father's dream was that his son should inherit his appointment as furnisher to the king, thereby guaranteeing himself a comfortable future.

That, however, was not to be. Instead of following the law, Molière decided at the last minute to abandon his secure future, change his name so as not to scandalize his family, and take up a career in the theater. He began by joining a company of actors run by the Béjart family. They established a theater based in Paris called the Illustre Théâtre. It was run by Madeleine Béjart, with whom Molière had a professional relationship until she died in 1672. Eventually Molière began writing plays, but only after he had worked extensively as an actor.

The famed *commedia dell'arte* actor Tiberio Fiorillo, known as Scaramouche, was a close friend of Molière and may have been responsible for Molière's choice of a career in theater. Scaramouche may have been part of the Illustre Théâtre, or he may have acted in it on occasion. Unfortunately, the Illustre Théâtre lasted only a year. It was one of several Parisian theatrical groups, and none of them prospered.

Eventually the company went bankrupt in 1644, and Molière, forced to leave Paris for about thirteen years, played in the provinces and remote towns. Before he left he had to be bailed out of debtors' prison. What was left of the Béjart group merged with another company on tour, and Molière became director of that company. During this time he suffered most of the indignities typical of the traveling life, including impoverishment.

In October 1658 Louis XIV saw Molière's troupe acting in one of his comedies at the Louvre. The royal court was so impressed with what it saw that the king gave him the use of a theater. His work remained, until his death in 1673, immensely popular and controversial. He acted in his own plays, produced his own plays, and wrote a succession of major works that are still favorites.

Because other companies envied his success and favor with the king, a number of "scandals" arose around some of his plays. The first play to invite controversy was *The School for Wives* (1662), in which Arnolphe reacts in horror to the infidelities he sees in the wives all around him. He decides that his wife-to-be must be raised far from the world, where she will be ignorant of the wayward lives of the Parisians. A man who intends to seduce her tells Arnolphe (not knowing who he is) how he will get her out of Arnolphe's grasp. The play is highly comic, but groups of theatergoers protested that it was immoral and scandalous. In response Molière wrote *Criticism of the School for Wives* (1663), in which the debate over the play is enacted.

One of Molière's most popular plays, *Tartuffe* (written in 1664), concerns a religious hypocrite who weasels his way into a noble household and then goes about trying to seduce its mistress. Molière envisioned the religious con man as his target in this play, and the name *Tartuffe* became shorthand for a religious hypocrite. The name still implies hypocrisy in France.

A French church group, the Society of the Holy Sacrament, thought it saw itself being portrayed in the title role and protested that the play was totally immoral and offensive. Its condemnation of the play effectively prevented it from being performed. Molière tried rewriting it; but the Society would not approve its production.

The Society was dissolved in a restructuring of the French church in 1669, and *Tartuffe* was finally permitted to be played to large audiences. Theatergoers loved the play and found great amusement in the sly, lecherous rogue who completely beguiles Orgon, the man who thinks Tartuffe is a great saint and who introduces him into his household. In most modern productions, Tartuffe is played broadly, almost as a caricature or a clown. Audiences find him amusing, scabrous, and irresistible. They usually find the play irresistible as well, since it involves crafty maneuvering onstage and complicated deceptions.

Among Molière's other successes are *The Miser* (1668), *The Bourgeois Gentleman* (1670), and his final play, *The Imaginary Invalid* (1673). He had a bad cough for most of the last decade of his life, which onstage, he often made to seem the cough of the character he was playing. But it was genuine, and he died playing the title role of *The Imaginary Invalid*.

THE MISANTHROPE

The Misanthrope (1666) in its own age was not the most successful of Molière's plays, but it has certainly been one of the most produced of all the plays in his canon. It is typical of his work in that it derives from a close and careful observation of French life and French manners. Recently English-language audiences have been able to savor this play in Richard Wilbur's superb translation, which catches the sharpness of the French wit and the elegance of the verse — both hallmarks of French seventeenth-century drama.

In one sense the play is based on the type of improbability that marks Greek New Comedy: the romance of two very different people, Alceste, the misanthrope who speaks his mind and brashly tells people what he thinks of them, and Célimène, the coquette who rarely says what she thinks but who enjoys the attention of many suitors. She enjoys society and her capacity to dominate it. Alceste cannot abide society and its superficialities. At the end of the play he resolves to leave it.

One of the revelations of the play is that while Alceste and Célimène are different on the surface, beneath the surface they are similar. They are extreme types who behave extremely. Célimène carries coquetry to great lengths, leading on as many men as possible. Alceste is the epitome of a misanthrope, refusing to flatter people just to make them feel good. He says that he must tell the truth, and he does — even when it hurts, perhaps especially when it hurts. For him to fall in love with a coquette who must deceive those around her to keep herself at the center of attention is a wonderful comic irony. But beneath that irony lies the thought that Alceste himself may have flaws that are the opposites of Célimène's.

The ending of *The Misanthrope,* which avoids the marriage of the protagonists (a more typical ending of comedies), may have contributed to the disappointment of its initial audiences. Another comic playwright would have brought the two lovers together. But Molière chose a more complex and, for some, a less satisfying ending. While two secondary characters marry, the main characters — Alceste and Célimène — agree to disagree and decide to live separately after all. Molière leaves his audience simply hoping that the two will change their minds. But as the play ends, the audience has no real reason to expect that they will come together.

This is a very French drama. The society is elegant, formal, and mannered. Molière knows every character and reveals each one totally. The surface elegance of the verse is such that the manners of the society seem polished, artificial, and ritualistic without being especially deceptive. The deception in this play is not at the center of things; the play does not depend on mix-ups and misapprehensions for its success. This in itself gives us a rather intriguing hint about Molière's intentions. The theme of honesty is at the play's center, but it is no simple thing to decide, in a social situation such as these characters enjoy, exactly how honest honesty should be or when honesty is the best policy. Alceste has one view and Célimène has another.

Molière enjoys pitting the values of Célimène and Alceste against one another, but it is clear that he does not want to offer sweeping or simple solutions to their conflict. Instead, he is content to leave his audience thinking and wondering.

The Misanthrope in Performance

The first full production of *The Misanthrope* was on June 4, 1666, with Molière as Alceste and his wife as Célimène. Most of the players who joined them were aware that Alceste was modeled after Molière himself and that Molière was poking fun at himself. Molière made the part more comical than serious. The French Comédie française records some fifteen hundred performances of the play between 1680 and 1960, making it one of the most performed of all French comedies. Late in the eighteenth century actors began playing Alceste as a serious character, as he is played today.

The first important American production in English was by Richard Mansfield, who acted the part of Alceste in New York in 1905. The reviews noted that "his embodiment of Alceste is vibrant with pain. . . . He smiles, but it is always the smile of bitterness." Richard Wilbur's verse translation played in the tiny Theatre East in New York in 1956 while a French version with a French company played simultaneously at the Winter Garden on Broadway. Both productions were very successful. Wilbur's version has since played virtually all over America, with several productions in New York in the 1960s, 1970s, and 1980s. The West Side Repertory Theater performed it in modern black tie and tails in 1991, with James Jacobus as Alceste. *The Misanthrope* has also had innumerable college productions since Wilbur's translation, which has, at least in the United States, become the standard version.

Tony Harrison also translated the play for the British National Theatre in 1975. Alec McCowan was Alceste and Diana Rigg was Célimène, both playing to mixed reviews. However, the play was said to have "the brilliance of a tiara of diamonds."

Molière [*Jean Baptiste Poquelin*] (1622–1673)

THE MISANTHROPE   *1666*
TRANSLATED BY RICHARD WILBUR

Characters

ALCESTE, *in love with Célimène*
PHILINTE, *Alceste's friend*
ORONTE, *in love with Célimène*
CÉLIMÈNE, *Alceste's beloved*
ÉLIANTE, *Célimène's cousin*
ARSINOÉ, *a friend of Célimène's*
ACASTE }
CLITANDRE } *Marquesses*
BASQUE, *Célimène's servant*
A GUARD *of the Marshalsea*
DUBOIS, *Alceste's valet*

The scene throughout is in Célimène's house at Paris.

ACT I • *Scene I*   [*Philinte, Alceste.*]

PHILINTE: Now, what's got into you?
ALCESTE (*seated*):   Kindly leave me alone.
PHILINTE: Come, come, what is it? This lugubrious
   tone . . .
ALCESTE: Leave me, I said; you spoil my solitude.
PHILINTE: Oh, listen to me, now, and don't be
   rude.
ALCESTE: I choose to be rude, Sir, and to be hard
5   of hearing.
PHILINTE: These ugly moods of yours are not
   endearing;
   Friends though we are, I really must insist . . .
ALCESTE (*abruptly rising*): Friends? Friends, you
   say? Well, cross me off your list.
   I've been your friend till now, as you well know;
10   But after what I saw a moment ago
   I tell you flatly that our ways must part.
   I wish no place in a dishonest heart.
PHILINTE: Why, what have I done, Alceste? Is this
   quite just?
ALCESTE: My God, you ought to die of self-disgust.
15   I call your conduct inexcusable, Sir,
   And every man of honor will concur.
   I see you almost hug a man to death,
   Exclaim for joy until you're out of breath,
   And supplement these loving demonstrations
20   With endless offers, vows, and protestations;

Then when I ask you "Who was that?" I find
That you can barely bring his name to mind!
Once the man's back is turned, you cease to love
   him,
And speak with absolute indifference of him!
By God, I say it's base and scandalous   25
To falsify the heart's affections thus;
If I caught myself behaving in such a way,
I'd hang myself for shame, without delay.
PHILINTE: It hardly seems a hanging matter to me;
I hope that you will take it graciously   30
If I extend myself a slight reprieve,
And live a little longer, by your leave.
ALCESTE: How dare you joke about a crime so
   grave?
PHILINTE: What crime? How else are people to
   behave?
ALCESTE: I'd have them be sincere, and never part   35
With any word that isn't from the heart.
PHILINTE: When someone greets us with a show of
   pleasure,
It's but polite to give him equal measure,
Return his love the best that we know how,
And trade him offer for offer, vow for vow.   40
ALCESTE: No, no, this formula you'd have me
   follow,
However fashionable, is false and hollow,
And I despise the frenzied operations
Of all these barterers of protestations,
These lavishers of meaningless embraces,   45
These utterers of obliging commonplaces,
Who court and flatter everyone on earth
And praise the fool no less than the man of
   worth.
Should you rejoice that someone fondles you,
Offers his love and service, swears to be true,   50
And fills your ears with praises of your name,
When to the first damned fop he'll say the same?
No, no: no self-respecting heart would dream
Of prizing so promiscuous an esteem;
However high the praise, there's nothing worse   55
Than sharing honors with the universe.
Esteem is founded on comparison:
To honor all men is to honor none.
Since you embrace this indiscriminate vice,
Your friendship comes at far too cheap a price;   60

I spurn the easy tribute of a heart
Which will not set the worthy man apart:
I choose, Sir, to be chosen; and in fine,
The friend of mankind is no friend of mine.

65 PHILINTE: But in polite society, custom decrees
That we show certain outward courtesies. . . .
ALCESTE: Ah, no! we should condemn with all our
force
Such false and artificial intercourse.
Let men behave like men; let them display
70 Their inmost hearts in everything they say;
Let the heart speak, and let our sentiments
Not mask themselves in silly compliments.
PHILINTE: In certain cases it would be uncouth
And most absurd to speak the naked truth;
75 With all respect for your exalted notions,
It's often best to veil one's true emotions.
Wouldn't the social fabric come undone
If we were wholly frank with everyone?
Suppose you met with someone you couldn't
bear;
80 Would you inform him of it then and there?
ALCESTE: Yes.
PHILINTE: Then you'd tell old Emilie it's
pathetic
The way she daubs her features with cosmetic
And plays the gay coquette at sixty-four?
ALCESTE: I would.
PHILINTE: And you'd call Dorilas a bore,
85 And tell him every ear at court is lame
From hearing him brag about his noble name?
ALCESTE: Precisely.
PHILINTE: Ah, you're joking.
ALCESTE: Au contraire:°
In this regard there's none I'd choose to spare.
All are corrupt; there's nothing to be seen
90 In court or town but aggravates my spleen.°
I fall into deep gloom and melancholy
When I survey the scene of human folly,
Finding on every hand base flattery,
Injustice, fraud, self-interest, treachery. . . .
95 Ah, it's too much; mankind has grown so base,
I mean to break with the whole human race.
PHILINTE: This philosophic rage is a bit extreme;
You've no idea how comical you seem;
Indeed, we're like those brothers in the play
Called *School for Husbands*,° one of whom was
100   prey . . .

87. *Au contraire*: On the contrary.   90. spleen: A body
organ thought to be the seat of melancholy, one of the four
humors of medieval physiology.   100. *School for Husbands*:
A play by Molière (1661) in which two brothers, Sganarelle
and Ariste, are guardians of two orphan girls. Sganarelle
hopes to marry one of the girls, Isabelle, but she frees herself
by trickery from his domineering ways and marries someone
else.

ALCESTE: Enough, now! None of your stupid
similes.
PHILINTE: Then let's have no more tirades, if you
please.
The world won't change, whatever you say or
do;
And since plain speaking means so much to you,
I'll tell you plainly that by being frank   105
You've earned the reputation of a crank,
And that you're thought ridiculous when you
rage
And rant against the manners of the age.
ALCESTE: So much the better; just what I wish to
hear.
No news could be more grateful to my ear.   110
All men are so detestable in my eyes,
I should be sorry if they thought me wise.
PHILINTE: Your hatred's very sweeping, is it not?
ALCESTE: Quite right: I hate the whole degraded
lot.
PHILINTE: Must all poor human creatures be
embraced,   115
Without distinction, by your vast distaste?
Even in these bad times, there are surely a
few . . .
ALCESTE: No, I include all men in one dim view:
Some men I hate for being rogues: the others
I hate because they treat the rogues like
brothers,   120
And, lacking a virtuous scorn for what is vile,
Receive the villain with a complaisant smile.
Notice how tolerant people choose to be
Toward that bold rascal who's at law with me.
His social polish can't conceal his nature;   125
One sees at once that he's a treacherous
creature;
No one could possibly be taken in
By those soft speeches and that sugary grin.
The whole world knows the shady means by
which
The low-brow's grown so powerful and rich,   130
And risen to a rank so bright and high
That virtue can but blush, and merit sigh.
Whenever his name comes up in conversation,
None will defend his wretched reputation;
Call him knave, liar, scoundrel, and all the rest, 135
Each head will nod, and no one will protest.
And yet his smirk is seen in every house,
He's greeted everywhere with smiles and bows,
And when there's any honor that can be got
By pulling strings, he'll get it, like as not.   140
My God! It chills my heart to see the ways
Men come to terms with evil nowadays;
Sometimes, I swear, I'm moved to flee and find
Some desert land unfouled by humankind.
PHILINTE: Come, let's forget the follies of the times 145

And pardon mankind for its petty crimes;
Let's have an end of rantings and of railings,
And show some leniency toward human failings.
This world requires a pliant rectitude;
150 Too stern a virtue makes one stiff and rude;
Good sense views all extremes with detestation,
And bids us to be noble in moderation.
The rigid virtues of the ancient days
Are not for us; they jar with all our ways
155 And ask of us too lofty a perfection.
Wise men accept their times without objection,
And there's no greater folly, if you ask me,
Than trying to reform society.
Like you, I see each day a hundred and one
160 Unhandsome deeds that might be better done,
But still, for all the faults that meet my view,
I'm never known to storm and rave like you.
I take men as they are, or let them be,
And teach my soul to bear their frailty;
And whether in court or town, whatever the
165   scene,
My phlegm's° as philosophic as your spleen.
ALCESTE: This phlegm which you so eloquently
       commend,
   Does nothing ever rile it up, my friend?
   Suppose some man you trust should
       treacherously
170   Conspire to rob you of your property,
   And do his best to wreck your reputation?
   Wouldn't you feel a certain indignation?
PHILINTE: Why, no. These faults of which you so
       complain
   Are part of human nature, I maintain,
175   And it's no more a matter for disgust
   That men are knavish, selfish and unjust,
   Than that the vulture dines upon the dead,
   And wolves are furious, and apes ill-bred.
ALCESTE: Shall I see myself betrayed, robbed, torn
       to bits,
180   And not . . . Oh, let's be still and rest our wits.
   Enough of reasoning, now. I've had my fill.
PHILINTE: Indeed, you would do well, Sir, to be
       still.
   Rage less at your opponent, and give some
       thought
   To how you'll win this lawsuit that he's
       brought.
185 ALCESTE: I assure you I'll do nothing of the sort.
PHILINTE: Then who will plead your case before the
       court?
ALCESTE: Reason and right and justice will plead
       for me.

166. **phlegm:** In medieval physiology, the humor thought to
be cold and moist and to cause sluggishness.

PHILINTE: Oh, Lord. What judges do you plan to
       see?
ALCESTE: Why, none. The justice of my cause is
       clear.
PHILINTE: Of course, man; but there's politics to
       fear. . . .   19
ALCESTE: No, I refuse to lift a hand. That's flat.
   I'm either right, or wrong.
PHILINTE: Don't count on that.
ALCESTE: No, I'll do nothing.
PHILINTE: Your enemy's influence
   Is great, you know . . .
ALCESTE: That makes no difference.
PHILINTE: It will; you'll see.
ALCESTE: Must honor bow to guile?   19
   If so, I shall be proud to lose the trial.
PHILINTE: Oh, really . . .
ALCESTE: I'll discover by this case
   Whether or not men are sufficiently base
   And impudent and villainous and perverse
   To do me wrong before the universe.   20
PHILINTE: What a man!
ALCESTE: Oh, I could wish, whatever the cost,
   Just for the beauty of it, that my trial were lost.
PHILINTE: If people heard you talking so, Alceste,
   They'd split their sides. Your name would be a
       jest.
ALCESTE: So much the worse for jesters.
PHILINTE: May I enquire   20
   Whether this rectitude you so admire,
   And these hard virtues you're enamored of
   Are qualities of the lady whom you love?
   It much surprises me that you, who seem
   To view mankind with furious disesteem,   21
   Have yet found something to enchant your eyes
   Amidst a species which you so despise.
   And what is more amazing, I'm afraid,
   Is the most curious choice your heart has made.
   The honest Éliante is fond of you,   21
   Arsinoé, the prude, admires you too;
   And yet your spirit's been perversely led
   To choose the flighty Célimène instead,
   Whose brittle malice and coquettish ways
   So typify the manners of our days.   22
   How is it that the traits you most abhor
   Are bearable in this lady you adore?
   Are you so blind with love that you can't find
       them?
   Or do you contrive, in her case, not to mind
       them?
ALCESTE: My love for that young widow's not the
       kind   22
   That can't perceive defects; no, I'm not blind.
   I see her faults, despite my ardent love,
   And all I see I fervently reprove.

And yet I'm weak; for all her falsity,
30   That woman knows the art of pleasing me,
And though I never cease complaining of her,
I swear I cannot manage not to love her.
Her charm outweighs her faults; I can but aim
To cleanse her spirit in my love's pure flame.
35 PHILINTE: That's no small task; I wish you all
  success.
You think then that she loves you?
ALCESTE: Heavens, yes!
I wouldn't love her did she not love me.
PHILINTE: Well, if her taste for you is plain to see,
Why do these rivals cause you such despair?
ALCESTE: True love, Sir, is possessive, and cannot
40   bear
To share with all the world. I'm here today
To tell her she must send that mob away.
PHILINTE: If I were you, and had your choice to
  make,
Éliante, her cousin, would be the one I'd take;
45 That honest heart, which cares for you alone,
Would harmonize far better with your own.
ALCESTE: True, true: each day my reason tells me
  so;
But reason doesn't rule in love, you know.
PHILINTE: I fear some bitter sorrow is in store;
50   This love . . .

Scene II   [*Oronte, Alceste, Philinte.*]

ORONTE (*to Alceste*): The servants told me at the
  door
That Éliante and Célimène were out,
But when I heard, dear Sir, that you were about,
I came to say, without exaggeration,
5 That I hold you in the vastest admiration,
And that it's always been my dearest desire
To be the friend of one I so admire.
I hope to see my love of merit requited,
And you and I in friendship's bond united.
I'm sure you won't refuse — if I may be
10   frank —
A friend of my devotedness — and rank.

(*During this speech of Oronte's Alceste is abstracted
and seems unaware that he is being spoken to. He
only breaks off his reverie when Oronte says:*)

It was for you, if you please, that my words
  were intended.
ALCESTE: For me, Sir?
ORONTE: Yes, for you. You're not offended?
ALCESTE: By no means. But this much surprises
  me. . . .

The honor comes most unexpectedly. . . .   15
ORONTE: My high regard should not astonish you;
The whole world feels the same. It is your due.
ALCESTE: Sir . . .
ORONTE: Why, in all the State there isn't one
Can match your merits; they shine, Sir, like the
  sun.
ALCESTE: Sir . . .
ORONTE: You are higher in my estimation   20
Than all that's most illustrious in the nation.
ALCESTE: Sir . . .
ORONTE: If I lie, may heaven strike me dead!
To show you that I mean what I have said,
Permit me, Sir, to embrace you most sincerely,
And swear that I will prize our friendship dearly.   25
Give me your hand. And now, Sir, if you
  choose,
We'll make our vows.
ALCESTE: Sir . . .
ORONTE: What! You refuse?
ALCESTE: Sir, it's a very great honor you extend:
But friendship is a sacred thing, my friend;
It would be profanation to bestow   30
The name of friend on one you hardly know.
All parts are better played when well-rehearsed;
Let's put off friendship, and get acquainted first.
We may discover it would be unwise
To try to make our natures harmonize.   35
ORONTE: By heaven! You're sagacious to the core;
This speech has made me admire you even more.
Let time, then, bring us closer day by day;
Meanwhile, I shall be yours in every way.
If, for example, there should be anything   40
You wish at court, I'll mention it to the King.
I have his ear, of course; it's quite well known
That I am much in favor with the throne.
In short, I am your servant. And now, dear
  friend,
Since you have such fine judgment, I intend   45
To please you, if I can, with a small sonnet
I wrote not long ago. Please comment on it,
And tell me whether I ought to publish it.
ALCESTE: You must excuse me, Sir; I'm hardly fit
To judge such matters.
ORONTE: Why not?
ALCESTE: I am, I fear,   50
Inclined to be unfashionably sincere.
ORONTE: Just what I ask; I'd take no satisfaction
In anything but your sincere reaction.
I beg you not to dream of being kind.
ALCESTE: Since you desire it, Sir, I'll speak my
  mind.   55
ORONTE: *Sonnet*. It's a sonnet. . . . *Hope* . . . The
  poem's addressed
To a lady who wakened hopes within my breast.

Hope . . . this is not the pompous sort of thing,
Just modest little verses, with a tender ring.
ALCESTE: Well, we shall see.
60   ORONTE: *Hope* . . . I'm anxious to hear
Whether the style seems properly smooth and
clear,
And whether the choice of words is good or
bad.
ALCESTE: We'll see, we'll see.
ORONTE: Perhaps I ought to add
That it took me only a quarter-hour to write it.
65   ALCESTE: The time's irrelevant, Sir: kindly recite it.
ORONTE (*reading*): Hope comforts us awhile, 'tis
true,
Lulling our cares with careless laughter,
And yet such joy is full of rue,
My Phyllis, if nothing follows after.
PHILINTE: I'm charmed by this already; the style's
70   delightful.
ALCESTE (*sotto voce,*° *to Philinte*): How can you
say that? Why, the thing is frightful.
ORONTE: Your fair face smiled on me awhile,
But was it kindness so to enchant me?
'Twould have been fairer not to smile,
75   If hope was all you meant to grant me.
PHILINTE: What a clever thought! How handsomely
you phrase it!
ALCESTE (*sotto voce, to Philinte*): You know the
thing is trash. How dare you praise it?
ORONTE: If it's to be my passion's fate
Thus everlastingly to wait,
80   Then death will come to set me free:

For death is fairer than the fair;
Phyllis, to hope is to despair
When one must hope eternally.
PHILINTE: The close is exquisite — full of feeling
and grace.
ALCESTE (*sotto voce, aside*): Oh, blast the close;
85   you'd better close your face
Before you send your lying soul to hell.
PHILINTE: I can't remember a poem I've liked so
well.
ALCESTE (*sotto voce, aside*): Good Lord!
ORONTE (*to Philinte*):   I fear you're flattering
me a bit.
PHILINTE: Oh, no!
ALCESTE (*sotto voce, aside*):   What else d'you
call it, you hypocrite?
ORONTE (*to Alceste*): But you, Sir, keep your
90   promise now: don't shrink
From telling me sincerely what you think.

71. [S.D.] *sotto voce:* In a soft voice or stage whisper.

ALCESTE: Sir, these are delicate matters; we all
desire
To be told that we've the true poetic fire.
But once, to one whose name I shall not
mention,
I said, regarding some verse of his invention,   95
That gentlemen should rigorously control
That itch to write which often afflicts the soul;
That one should curb the heady inclination
To publicize one's little avocation;
And that in showing off one's works of art   100
One often plays a very clownish part.
ORONTE: Are you suggesting in a devious way
That I ought not . . .
ALCESTE: Oh, that I do not say.
Further, I told him that no fault is worse
Than that of writing frigid, lifeless verse,   105
And that the merest whisper of such a shame
Suffices to destroy a man's good name.
ORONTE: D'you mean to say my sonnet's dull and
trite?
ALCESTE: I don't say that. But I went on to cite
Numerous cases of once-respected men   110
Who came to grief by taking up the pen.
ORONTE: And am I like them? Do I write so
poorly?
ALCESTE: I don't say that. But I told this person,
"Surely
You're under no necessity to compose;
Why you should wish to publish, heaven knows.   115
There's no excuse for printing tedious rot
Unless one writes for bread, as you do not.
Resist temptation, then, I beg of you;
Conceal your pastimes from the public view;
And don't give up, on any provocation,   120
Your present high and courtly reputation,
To purchase at a greedy printer's shop
The name of silly author and scribbling fop."
These were the points I tried to make him see.
ORONTE: I sense that they are also aimed at me;   125
But now — about my sonnet — I'd like to be
told . . .
ALCESTE: Frankly, that sonnet should be
pigeonholed.
You've chosen the worst models to imitate.
The style's unnatural. Let me illustrate:
For example, Your fair face smiled on me
awhile,   130
Followed by, 'Twould have been fairer not to
smile!
Or this: such joy is full of rue;
Or this: For death is fairer than the fair;
Or, Phyllis, to hope is to despair
When one must hope eternally!   135
This artificial style, that's all the fashion,

Has neither taste, nor honesty, nor passion;
It's nothing but a sort of wordy play,
And nature never spoke in such a way.
40 What, in this shallow age, is not debased?
Our fathers, though less refined, had better taste;
I'd barter all that men admire today
For one old love song I shall try to say:
If the King had given me for my own
45 Paris, his citadel,
And I for that must leave alone
Her whom I love so well,
I'd say then to the Crown,
Take back your glittering town;
50 My darling is more fair, I swear,
My darling is more fair.
The rhyme's not rich, the style is rough and old,
But don't you see that it's the purest gold
Beside the tinsel nonsense now preferred,
55 And that there's passion in its every word?
If the King had given me for my own
Paris, his citadel,
And I for that must leave alone
Her whom I love so well,

60 I'd say then to the Crown,
Take back your glittering town;
My darling is more fair, I swear,
My darling is more fair.
There speaks a loving heart. (*To Philinte.*)
You're laughing, eh?
65 Laugh on, my precious wit. Whatever you say,
I hold that song's worth all the bibelots°
That people hail today with ah's and oh's.
ORONTE: And I maintain my sonnet's very good.
ALCESTE: It's not at all surprising that you should.
70 You have your reasons; permit me to have mine
For thinking that you cannot write a line.
ORONTE: Others have praised my sonnet to the
skies.
ALCESTE: I lack their art of telling pleasant lies.
ORONTE: You seem to think you've got no end of
wit.
ALCESTE: To praise your verse, I'd need still more
175 of it.
ORONTE: I'm not in need of your approval, Sir.
ALCESTE: That's good; you couldn't have it if you
were.
ORONTE: Come now, I'll lend you the subject of
my sonnet;
I'd like to see you try to improve upon it.
ALCESTE: I might, by chance, write something just
180 as shoddy;
But then I wouldn't show it to everybody.

166. bibelots: Trinkets.

ORONTE: You're most opinionated and conceited.
ALCESTE: Go find your flatterers, and be better
treated.
ORONTE: Look here, my little fellow, pray watch
your tone.
ALCESTE: My great big fellow, you'd better watch
your own.   185
PHILINTE (*stepping between them*): Oh, please,
please, gentlemen! This will never do.
ORONTE: The fault is mine, and I leave the field to
you.
I am your servant, Sir, in every way.
ALCESTE: And I, Sir, am your most abject valet.

Scene III   [*Philinte, Alceste.*]

PHILINTE: Well, as you see, sincerity in excess
Can get you into a very pretty mess;
Oronte was hungry for appreciation. . . .
ALCESTE: Don't speak to me.
PHILINTE: What?
ALCESTE: No more conversation.
PHILINTE: Really, now . . .
ALCESTE: Leave me alone.
PHILINTE: If I . . .
ALCESTE: Out of my sight! 5
PHILINTE: But what . . .
ALCESTE: I won't listen.
PHILINTE: But . . .
ALCESTE: Silence!
PHILINTE: Now, is it polite . . .
ALCESTE: By heaven, I've had enough. Don't follow
me.
PHILINTE: Ah, you're just joking. I'll keep you
company.

ACT II · *Scene I*   [*Alceste, Célimène.*]

ALCESTE: Shall I speak plainly, Madam? I confess
Your conduct gives me infinite distress,
And my resentment's grown too hot to smother.
Soon, I foresee, we'll break with one another.
If I said otherwise, I should deceive you;   5
Sooner or later, I shall be forced to leave you,
And if I swore that we shall never part,
I should misread the omens of my heart.
CÉLIMÈNE: You kindly saw me home, it would
appear,
So as to pour invectives in my ear.   10
ALCESTE: I've no desire to quarrel. But I deplore
Your inability to shut the door
On all these suitors who beset you so.
There's what annoys me, if you care to know.

CÉLIMÈNE: Is it my fault that all these men pursue
15   me?
    Am I to blame if they're attracted to me?
    And when they gently beg an audience,
    Ought I to take a stick and drive them hence?
ALCESTE: Madam, there's no necessity for a stick;
20   A less responsive heart would do the trick.
    Of your attractiveness I don't complain;
    But those your charms attract, you then detain
    By a most melting and receptive manner,
    And so enlist their hearts beneath your banner.
25   It's the agreeable hopes which you excite
    That keep these lovers round you day and night;
    Were they less liberally smiled upon,
    That sighing troop would very soon be gone.
    But tell me, Madam, why it is that lately
30   This man Clitandre interests you so greatly?
    Because of what high merits do you deem
    Him worthy of the honor of your esteem?
    Is it that your admiring glances linger
    On the splendidly long nail of his little finger?
35   Or do you share the general deep respect
    For the blond wig he chooses to affect?
    Are you in love with his embroidered hose?
    Do you adore his ribbons and his bows?
    Or is it that this paragon bewitches
40   Your tasteful eye with his vast German breeches?
    Perhaps his giggle, or his falsetto voice,
    Makes him the latest gallant of your choice?
CÉLIMÈNE: You're much mistaken to resent him so.
    Why I put up with him you surely know:
45   My lawsuit's very shortly to be tried,
    And I must have his influence on my side.
ALCESTE: Then lose your lawsuit, Madam, or let it
    drop;
    Don't torture me by humoring such a fop.
CÉLIMÈNE: You're jealous of the whole world, Sir.
ALCESTE: That's true,
50   Since the whole world is well-received by you.
CÉLIMÈNE: That my good nature is so unconfined
    Should serve to pacify your jealous mind;
    Were I to smile on one, and scorn the rest,
    Then you might have some cause to be
    distressed.
55 ALCESTE: Well, if I mustn't be jealous, tell me, then,
    Just how I'm better treated than other men.
CÉLIMÈNE: You know you have my love. Will that
    not do?
ALCESTE: What proof have I that what you say is
    true?
CÉLIMÈNE: I would expect, Sir, that my having said
    it
60   Might give the statement a sufficient credit.
ALCESTE: But how can I be sure that you don't tell
    The selfsame thing to other men as well?

CÉLIMÈNE: What a gallant speech! How flattering to
    me!
    What a sweet creature you make me out to be!
    Well then, to save you from the pangs of doubt, 65
    All that I've said I hereby cancel out;
    Now, none but yourself shall make a monkey of
    you:
    Are you content?
ALCESTE: Why, why am I doomed to love you?
    I swear that I shall bless the blissful hour
    When this poor heart's no longer in your power! 70
    I make no secret of it: I've done my best
    To exorcise this passion from my breast;
    But thus far all in vain; it will not go;
    It's for my sins that I must love you so.
CÉLIMÈNE: Your love for me is matchless, Sir; that's
    clear. 75
ALCESTE: Indeed, in all the world it has no peer;
    Words can't describe the nature of my passion,
    And no man ever loved in such a fashion.
CÉLIMÈNE: Yes, it's a brand-new fashion, I agree:
    You show your love by castigating me, 80
    And all your speeches are enraged and rude.
    I've never been so furiously wooed.
ALCESTE: Yet you could calm that fury, if you
    chose.
    Come, shall we bring our quarrels to a close?
    Let's speak with open hearts, then, and
    begin . . . 85

Scene II   [*Célimène, Alceste, Basque.*]

CÉLIMÈNE: What is it?
BASQUE: Acaste is here.
CÉLIMÈNE: Well, send him in.

Scene III   [*Célimène, Alceste.*]

ALCESTE: What! Shall we never be alone at all?
    You're always ready to receive a call,
    And you can't bear, for ten ticks of the clock,
    Not to keep open house for all who knock.
CÉLIMÈNE: I couldn't refuse him: he'd be most put
    out. 5
ALCESTE: Surely that's not worth worrying about.
CÉLIMÈNE: Acaste would never forgive me if he
    guessed
    That I consider him a dreadful pest.
ALCESTE: If he's a pest, why bother with him then?
CÉLIMÈNE: Heavens! One can't antagonize such
    men; 10
    Why, they're the chartered gossips of the court,
    And have a say in things of every sort.

One must receive them, and be full of charm;
They're no great help, but they can do you
   harm,
And though your influence be ever so great,
They're hardly the best people to alienate.
ALCESTE: I see, dear lady, that you could make a
   case
For putting up with the whole human race;
These friendships that you calculate so nicely ...

Scene IV [*Alceste, Célimène, Basque.*]

BASQUE: Madam, Clitandre is here as well.
ALCESTE: Precisely.
CÉLIMÈNE: Where are you going?
ALCESTE: Elsewhere.
CÉLIMÈNE: Stay.
ALCESTE: No, no.
CÉLIMÈNE: Stay, Sir.
ALCESTE: I can't.
CÉLIMÈNE: I wish it.
ALCESTE: No, I must go.
   I beg you, Madam, not to press the matter;
   You know I have no taste for idle chatter.
CÉLIMÈNE: Stay. I command you.
ALCESTE: No, I cannot stay.
CÉLIMÈNE: Very well; you have my leave to go
   away.

Scene V [*Éliante, Philinte, Acaste, Clitandre,
Alceste, Célimène, Basque.*]

ÉLIANTE (*to Célimène*): The Marquesses have kindly
   come to call.
   Were they announced?
CÉLIMÈNE: Yes. Basque, bring chairs for all.

(*Basque provides the chairs and exits.*)

   (*To Alceste.*) You haven't gone?
ALCESTE: No; and I shan't depart
   Till you decide who's foremost in your heart.
CÉLIMÈNE: Oh, hush.
ALCESTE: It's time to choose; take them, or me.
CÉLIMÈNE: You're mad.
ALCESTE: I'm not, as you shall shortly see.
CÉLIMÈNE: Oh?
ALCESTE: You'll decide.
CÉLIMÈNE: You're joking now, dear friend.
ALCESTE: No, no; you'll choose; my patience is at
   an end.
CLITANDRE: Madam, I come from court, where
   poor Cléonte
   Behaved like a perfect fool, as is his wont.

Has he no friend to counsel him, I wonder,
And teach him less unerringly to blunder?
CÉLIMÈNE: It's true, the man's a most accomplished
   dunce;
His gauche behavior charms the eye at once;
And every time one sees him, on my word,
His manner's grown a trifle more absurd.
ACASTE: Speaking of dunces, I've just now
   conversed
With old Damon, who's one of the very worst;
I stood a lifetime in the broiling sun
Before his dreary monologue was done.
CÉLIMÈNE: Oh, he's a wondrous talker, and has the
   power
To tell you nothing hour after hour:
If, by mistake, he ever came to the point,
The shock would put his jawbone out of joint.
ÉLIANTE (*to Philinte*): The conversation takes its
   usual turn,
And all our dear friends' ears will shortly burn.
CLITANDRE: Timante's a character, Madam.
CÉLIMÈNE: Isn't he, though?
A man of mystery from top to toe,
Who moves about in a romantic mist
On secret missions which do not exist.
His talk is full of eyebrows and grimaces;
How tired one gets of his momentous faces;
He's always whispering something confidential
Which turns out to be quite inconsequential;
Nothing's too slight for him to mystify;
He even whispers when he says "good-by."
ACASTE: Tell us about Géralde.
CÉLIMÈNE: That tiresome ass.
He mixes only with the titled class,
And fawns on dukes and princes, and is bored
With anyone who's not at least a lord.
The man's obsessed with rank, and his
   discourses
Are all of hounds and carriages and horses;
He uses Christian names with all the great,
And the word Milord, with him, is out of date.
CLITANDRE: He's very taken with Bélisc, I hear.
CÉLIMÈNE: She is the dreariest company, poor dear.
Whenever she comes to call, I grope about
To find some topic which will draw her out,
But, owing to her dry and faint replies,
The conversation wilts, and droops, and dies.
In vain one hopes to animate her face
By mentioning the ultimate commonplace;
But sun or shower, even hail or frost
Are matters she can instantly exhaust.
Meanwhile her visit, painful though it is,
Drags on and on through mute eternities,
And though you ask the time, and yawn, and
   yawn,

She sits there like a stone and won't be gone.
ACASTE: Now for Adraste.
CÉLIMÈNE: Oh, that conceited elf
60   Has a gigantic passion for himself;
He rails against the court, and cannot bear it
That none will recognize his hidden merit;
All honors given to others give offense
To his imaginary excellence.
65   CLITANDRE: What about young Cléon? His house, they say,
Is full of the best society, night and day.
CÉLIMÈNE: His cook has made him popular, not he:
It's Cléon's table that people come to see.
ÉLIANTE: He gives a splendid dinner, you must admit.
70   CÉLIMÈNE: But must he serve himself along with it?
For my taste, he's a most insipid dish
Whose presence sours the wine and spoils the fish.
PHILINTE: Damis, his uncle is admired no end.
What's your opinion, Madam?
CÉLIMÈNE: Why, he's my friend.
PHILINTE: He seems a decent fellow, and rather
75   clever.
CÉLIMÈNE: He works too hard at cleverness, however.
I hate to see him sweat and struggle so
To fill his conversation with *bons mots.*°
Since he's decided to become a wit
80   His taste's so pure that nothing pleases it;
He scolds at all the latest books and plays,
Thinking that wit must never stoop to praise,
That finding fault's a sign of intellect,
That all appreciation is abject,
85   And that by damning everything in sight
One shows oneself in a distinguished light.
He's scornful even of our conversations:
Their trivial nature sorely tries his patience;
He folds his arms, and stands above the battle,
90   And listens sadly to our childish prattle.
ACASTE: Wonderful, Madam! You've hit him off precisely.
CLITANDRE: No one can sketch a character so nicely.
ALCESTE: How bravely, Sirs, you cut and thrust at all
These absent fools, till one by one they fall:
95   But let one come in sight, and you'll at once
Embrace the man you lately called a dunce,
Telling him in a tone sincere and fervent
How proud you are to be his humble servant.
CLITANDRE: Why pick on us? *Madame's* been speaking, Sir.

78. *bons mots:* Clever remarks, witticisms.

And you should quarrel, if you must, with her.   10
ALCESTE: No, no, by God, the fault is yours, because
You lead her on with laughter and applause,
And make her think that she's the more delightful
The more her talk is scandalous and spiteful.
Oh, she would stoop to malice far, far less   10
If no such claque approved her cleverness.
It's flatterers like you whose foolish praise
Nourishes all the vices of these days.
PHILINTE: But why protest when someone ridicules
Those you'd condemn, yourself, as knaves or fools?   11
CÉLIMÈNE: Why, Sir? Because he loves to make a fuss.
You don't expect him to agree with us,
When there's an opportunity to express
His heaven-sent spirit of contrariness?
What other people think, he can't abide;   11
Whatever they say, he's on the other side;
He lives in deadly terror of agreeing;
'Twould make him seem an ordinary being.
Indeed, he's so in love with contradiction,
He'll turn against his most profound conviction   12
And with a furious eloquence deplore it,
If only someone else is speaking for it.
ALCESTE: Go on, dear lady, mock me as you please;
You have your audience in ecstasies.
PHILINTE: But what she says is true: you have a way   12
Of bridling at whatever people say;
Whether they praise or blame, your angry spirit
Is equally unsatisfied to hear it.
ALCESTE: Men, Sir, are always wrong, and that's the reason
That righteous anger's never out of season;   13
All that I hear in all their conversation
Is flattering praise or reckless condemnation.
CÉLIMÈNE: But . . .
ALCESTE: No, no, Madam, I am forced to state
That you have pleasures which I deprecate,
And that these others, here, are much to blame   13
For nourishing the faults which are your shame.
CLITANDRE: I shan't defend myself, Sir; but I vow
I'd thought this lady faultless until now.
ACASTE: I see her charms and graces, which are many;
But as for faults, I've never noticed any.   14
ALCESTE: I see them, Sir; and rather than ignore them,
I strenuously criticize her for them.
The more one loves, the more one should object
To every blemish, every least defect.
Were I this lady, I would soon get rid   14

Of lovers who approved of all I did,
And by their slack indulgence and applause
Endorsed my follies and excused my flaws.
CÉLIMÈNE: If all hearts beat according to your
    measure,
50 The dawn of love would be the end of pleasure;
And love would find its perfect consummation
In ecstasies of rage and reprobation.
ÉLIANTE: Love, as a rule, affects men otherwise,
And lovers rarely love to criticize.
55 They see their lady as a charming blur,
And find all things commendable in her.
If she has any blemish, fault, or shame,
They will redeem it by a pleasing name.
The pale-faced lady's lily-white, perforce;
60 The swarthy one's a sweet brunette, of course;
The spindly lady has a slender grace;
The fat one has a most majestic pace;
The plain one, with her dress in disarray,
They classify as *beauté négligée;*°
65 The hulking one's a goddess in their eyes,
The dwarf, a concentrate of Paradise;
The haughty lady has a noble mind;
The mean one's witty, and the dull one's kind;
The chatterbox has liveliness and verve,
70 The mute one has a virtuous reserve.
So lovers manage, in their passion's cause,
To love their ladies even for their flaws.
ALCESTE: But I still say . . .
CÉLIMÈNE: I think it would be nice
To stroll around the gallery once or twice.
What! You're not going, Sirs?
75 CLITANDRE AND ACASTE: No, Madam, no.
ALCESTE: You seem to be in terror lest they go.
Do what you will, Sirs; leave, or linger on,
But I shan't go till after you are gone.
ACASTE: I'm free to linger, unless I should perceive
80 *Madame* is tired, and wishes me to leave.
CLITANDRE: And as for me, I needn't go today
Until the hour of the King's *coucher.*°
CÉLIMÈNE (*to Alceste*): You're joking, surely?
ALCESTE: Not in the least; we'll see
Whether you'd rather part with them, or me.

Scene VI [*Alceste, Célimène, Éliante, Acaste,
Philinte, Clitandre, Basque.*]

BASQUE (*to Alceste*): Sir, there's a fellow here who
    bids me state
That he must see you, and that it can't wait.

164. *beauté négligée:* Slovenly beauty.   182. the King's
coucher: The King's bedtime, a ceremonial occasion.

ALCESTE: Tell him that I have no such pressing
    affairs.
BASQUE: It's a long tailcoat that this fellow wears,
With gold all over.
CÉLIMÈNE (*to Alceste*):   You'd best go down
    and see.   5
Or — have him enter.

Scene VII [*Alceste, Célimène, Éliante, Acaste,
Philinte, Clitandre, Guard.*]

ALCESTE (*confronting the Guard*):   Well, what
    do you want with me?
Come in, Sir.
GUARD: I've a word, Sir, for your ear.
ALCESTE: Speak it aloud, Sir; I shall strive to hear.
GUARD: The Marshals have instructed me to say
You must report to them without delay.   5
ALCESTE: Who? Me, Sir?
GUARD: Yes, Sir; you.
ALCESTE: But what do they want?
PHILINTE (*to Alceste*): To scotch your silly quarrel
    with Oronte.
CÉLIMÈNE (*to Philinte*): What quarrel?
PHILINTE: Oronte and he have fallen out
Over some verse he spoke his mind about;
The Marshals wish to arbitrate the matter.   10
ALCESTE: Never shall I equivocate or flatter!
PHILINTE: You'd best obey their summons; come,
    let's go.
ALCESTE: How can they mend our quarrel, I'd like
    to know?
Am I to make a cowardly retraction,
And praise those jingles to his satisfaction?   15
I'll not recant; I've judged that sonnet rightly.
It's bad.
PHILINTE: But you might say so more
    politely. . . .
ALCESTE: I'll not back down; his verses make me
    sick.
PHILINTE: If only you could be more politic!
But come, let's go.
ALCESTE: I'll go, but I won't unsay   20
A single word.
PHILINTE: Well, let's be on our way.
ALCESTE: Till I am ordered by my lord the King
To praise that poem, I shall say the thing
Is scandalous, by God, and that the poet
Ought to be hanged for having the nerve to
    show it.   25

(*To Clitandre and Acaste, who are laughing.*)

By heaven, Sirs, I really didn't know
That I was being humorous.

CÉLIMÈNE: Go, Sir, go;
Settle your business.
ALCESTE: I shall, and when I'm through,
I shall return to settle things with you.

ACT III • Scene I   [Clitandre, Acaste.]

CLITANDRE: Dear Marquess, how contented you
     appear;
     All things delight you, nothing mars your cheer.
     Can you, in perfect honesty, declare
     That you've a right to be so debonair?
5 ACASTE: By Jove, when I survey myself, I find
     No cause whatever for distress of mind.
     I'm young and rich; I can in modesty
     Lay claim to an exalted pedigree;
     And owing to my name and my condition
10   I shall not want for honors and position.
     Then as to courage, that most precious trait,
     I seem to have it, as was proved of late
     Upon the field of honor, where my bearing,
     They say, was very cool and rather daring.
15   I've wit, of course; and taste in such perfection
     That I can judge without the least reflection,
     And at the theater, which is my delight,
     Can make or break a play on opening night,
     And lead the crowd in hisses or bravos,
20   And generally be known as one who knows.
     I'm clever, handsome, gracefully polite;
     My waist is small, my teeth are strong and
          white;
     As for my dress, the world's astonished eyes
     Assure me that I bear away the prize.
25   I find myself in favor everywhere,
     Honored by men, and worshiped by the fair;
     And since these things are so, it seems to me
     I'm justified in my complacency.
     CLITANDRE: Well, if so many ladies hold you dear,
30   Why do you press a hopeless courtship here?
     ACASTE: Hopeless, you say? I'm not the sort of fool
     That likes his ladies difficult and cool.
     Men who are awkward, shy, and peasantish
     May pine for heartless beauties, if they wish,
35   Grovel before them, bear their cruelties,
     Woo them with tears and sighs and bended
          knees,
     And hope by dogged faithfulness to gain
     What their poor merits never could obtain.
     For men like me, however, it makes no sense
40   To love on trust, and foot the whole expense.
     Whatever any lady's merits be,
     I think, thank God, that I'm as choice as she;
     That if my heart is kind enough to burn
     For her, she owes me something in return;

And that in any proper love affair   45
The partners must invest an equal share.
CLITANDRE: You think, then, that our hostess
     favors you?
ACASTE: I've reason to believe that that is true.
CLITANDRE: How did you come to such a mad
     conclusion?
     You're blind, dear fellow. This is sheer delusion.   50
ACASTE: All right, then: I'm deluded and I'm blind.
CLITANDRE: Whatever put the notion in your mind?
ACASTE: Delusion.
CLITANDRE: What persuades you that you're
     right?
ACASTE: I'm blind.
CLITANDRE: But have you any proofs to cite?
ACASTE: I tell you I'm deluded.
CLITANDRE: Have you, then,   55
     Received some secret pledge from Célimène?
ACASTE: Oh, no: she scorns me.
CLITANDRE: Tell me the truth, I beg.
ACASTE: She just can't bear me.
CLITANDRE: Ah, don't pull my leg.
     Tell me what hope she's given you, I pray.
ACASTE: I'm hopeless, and it's you who win the
     day.   60
     She hates me thoroughly, and I'm so vexed
     I mean to hang myself on Tuesday next.
CLITANDRE: Dear Marquess, let us have an
     armistice
     And make a treaty. What do you say to this?
     If ever one of us can plainly prove   65
     That Célimène encourages his love,
     The other must abandon hope, and yield,
     And leave him in possession of the field.
ACASTE: Now, there's a bargain that appeals to me;
     With all my heart, dear Marquess, I agree.   70
     But hush.

Scene II   [Célimène, Acaste, Clitandre.]

CÉLIMÈNE: Still here?
CLITANDRE: 'Twas love that stayed our feet.
CÉLIMÈNE: I think I heard a carriage in the street.
     Whose is it? D'you know?

Scene III   [Célimène, Acaste, Clitandre, Basque.]

BASQUE: Arsinoé is here,
     Madame.
CÉLIMÈNE: Arsinoé, you say? Oh, dear.
BASQUE: Éliante is entertaining her below.
CÉLIMÈNE: What brings the creature here, I'd like
     to know?

ACASTE: They say she's dreadfully prudish, but in
5   fact
    I think her piety . . .
CÉLIMÈNE: It's all an act.
    At heart she's worldly, and her poor success
    In snaring men explains her prudishness.
    It breaks her heart to see the beaux and gallants
10   Engrossed by other women's charms and talents,
    And so she's always in a jealous rage
    Against the faulty standards of the age.
    She lets the world believe that she's a prude
    To justify her loveless solitude,
15   And strives to put a brand of moral shame
    On all the graces that she cannot claim.
    But still she'd love a lover; and Alceste
    Appears to be the one she'd love the best.
    His visits here are poison to her pride;
20   She seems to think I've lured him from her side;
    And everywhere, at court or in the town,
    The spiteful, envious woman runs me down.
    In short, she's just as stupid as can be,
    Vicious and arrogant in the last degree,
25   And . . .

Scene IV [*Arsinoé, Célimène, Clitandre, Acaste.*]

CÉLIMÈNE: Ah! What happy chance has
    brought you here?
    I've thought about you ever so much, my dear.
ARSINOÉ: I've come to tell you something you
    should know.
CÉLIMÈNE: How good of you to think of doing so!

(*Clitandre and Acaste go out, laughing.*)

Scene V [*Arsinoé, Célimène.*]

ARSINOÉ: It's just as well those gentlemen didn't
    tarry.
CÉLIMÈNE: Shall we sit down?
ARSINOÉ: That won't be necessary.
    Madam, the flame of friendship ought to burn
    Brightest in matters of the most concern,
5   And as there's nothing which concerns us more
    Than honor, I have hastened to your door
    To bring you, as your friend, some information
    About the status of your reputation.
    I visited, last night, some virtuous folk,
10   And, quite by chance, it was of you they spoke;
    There was, I fear, no tendency to praise
    Your light behavior and your dashing ways.
    The quantity of gentlemen you see

And your by now notorious coquetry
Were both so vehemently criticized   15
By everyone, that I was much surprised.
Of course, I needn't tell you where I stood;
I came to your defense as best I could,
Assured them you were harmless, and declared
Your soul was absolutely unimpaired.   20
But there are some things, you must realize,
One can't excuse, however hard one tries,
And I was forced at last into conceding
That your behavior, Madam, is misleading,
That it makes a bad impression, giving rise   25
To ugly gossip and obscene surmise,
And that if you were more *overtly* good,
You wouldn't be so much misunderstood.
Not that I think you've been unchaste — no!
    no!
The saints preserve me from a thought so low!   30
But mere good conscience never did suffice:
One must avoid the outward show of vice.
Madam, you're too intelligent, I'm sure,
To think my motives anything but pure
In offering you this counsel — which I do   35
Out of a zealous interest in you.
CÉLIMÈNE: Madam, I haven't taken you amiss;
    I'm very much obliged to you for this;
    And I'll at once discharge the obligation
    By telling you about *your* reputation.   40
    You've been so friendly as to let me know
    What certain people say of me, and so
    I mean to follow your benign example
    By offering you a somewhat similar sample.
    The other day, I went to an affair   45
    And found some most distinguished people there
    Discussing piety, both false and true.
    The conversation soon came round to you.
    Alas! Your prudery and bustling zeal
    Appeared to have a very slight appeal.   50
    Your affectation of a grave demeanor,
    Your endless talk of virtue and of honor,
    The aptitude of your suspicious mind
    For finding sin where there is none to find,
    Your towering self-esteem, that pitying face 55
    With which you contemplate the human race,
    Your sermonizings and your sharp aspersions
    On people's pure and innocent diversions —
    All these were mentioned, Madam, and, in fact,
    Were roundly and concertedly attacked.   60
    "What good," they said, "are all these outward
        shows,
    When everything belies her pious pose?
    She prays incessantly; but then, they say,
    She beats her maids and cheats them of their
        pay;
    She shows her zeal in every holy place,   65

But still she's vain enough to paint her face;
She holds that naked statues are immoral,
But with a naked *man* she'd have no quarrel."
Of course, I said to everybody there
70 That they were being viciously unfair;
But still they were disposed to criticize you,
And all agreed that someone should advise you
To leave the morals of the world alone,
And worry rather more about your own.
They felt that one's self-knowledge should be
75   great
Before one thinks of setting others straight;
That one should learn the art of living well
Before one threatens other men with hell,
And that the Church is best equipped, no doubt,
80 To guide our souls and root our vices out.
Madam, you're too intelligent, I'm sure,
To think my motives anything but pure
In offering you this counsel — which I do
Out of a zealous interest in you.
85 ARSINOÉ: I dared not hope for gratitude, but I
Did not expect so acid a reply;
I judge, since you've been so extremely tart,
That my good counsel pierced you to the heart.
CÉLIMÈNE: Far from it, Madam. Indeed, it seems to
      me
90 We ought to trade advice more frequently.
One's vision of oneself is so defective
That it would be an excellent corrective.
If you are willing, Madam, let's arrange
Shortly to have another frank exchange
95 In which we'll tell each other, *entre nous,*°
What you've heard tell of me, and I of you.
ARSINOÉ: Oh, people never censure you, my dear;
It's me they criticize. Or so I hear.
CÉLIMÈNE: Madam, I think we either blame or
      praise
100 According to our taste and length of days.
There is a time of life for coquetry,
And there's a season, too, for prudery.
When all one's charms are gone, it is, I'm sure,
Good strategy to be devout and pure:
105 It makes one seem a little less forsaken.
Some day, perhaps, I'll take the road you've
      taken.
Time brings all things. But I have time aplenty,
And see no cause to be a prude at twenty.
ARSINOÉ: You give your age in such a gloating tone
110 That one would think I was an ancient crone;
We're not so far apart, in sober truth,
That you can mock me with a boast of youth!

Madam, you baffle me. I wish I knew
What moves you to provoke me as you do.
CÉLIMÈNE: For my part, Madam, I should like to
      know   115
Why you abuse me everywhere you go.
Is it my fault, dear lady, that your hand
Is not, alas, in very great demand?
If men admire me, if they pay me court
And daily make me offers of the sort   120
You'd dearly love to have them make to you,
How can I help it? What would you have me
      do?
If what you want is lovers, please feel free
To take as many as you can from me.
ARSINOÉ: Oh, come. D'you think the world is
      losing sleep   125
Over the flock of lovers which you keep,
Or that we find it difficult to guess
What price you pay for their devotedness?
Surely you don't expect us to suppose
Mere merit could attract so many beaux?   130
It's not your virtue that they're dazzled by;
Nor is it virtuous love for which they sigh.
You're fooling no one, Madam; the world's not
      blind;
There's many a lady heaven has designed
To call men's noblest, tenderest feelings out,   135
Who has no lovers dogging her about;
From which it's plain that lovers nowadays
Must be acquired in bold and shameless ways,
And only pay one court for such reward
As modesty and virtue can't afford.   140
Then don't be quite so puffed up, if you please,
About your tawdry little victories;
Try, if you can, to be a shade less vain,
And treat the world with somewhat less disdain.
If one were envious of your amours,   145
One soon could have a following like yours;
Lovers are no great trouble to collect
If one prefers them to one's self-respect.
CÉLIMÈNE: Collect them then, my dear; I'd love to
      see
You demonstrate that charming theory;   150
Who knows, you might . . .
ARSINOÉ: Now, Madam, that will do;
It's time to end this trying interview.
My coach is late in coming to your door,
Or I'd have taken leave of you before.
CÉLIMÈNE: Oh, please don't feel that you must rush
      away;   155
I'd be delighted, Madam, if you'd stay.
However, lest my conversation bore you,
Let me provide some better company for you;
This gentleman, who comes most apropos,
Will please you more than I could do, I know.   160

---

95. *entre nous*: Between ourselves.

Scene VI [*Alceste, Célimène, Arsinoé.*]

CÉLIMÈNE: Alceste, I have a little note to write
    Which simply must go out before tonight;
    Please entertain *Madame;* I'm sure that she
    Will overlook my incivility.

Scene VII [*Alceste, Arsinoé.*]

ARSINOÉ: Well, Sir, our hostess graciously contrives
    For us to chat until my coach arrives;
    And I shall be forever in her debt
    For granting me this little *tête-à-tête.*°
5   We women very rightly give our hearts
    To men of noble character and parts,
    And your especial merits, dear Alceste,
    Have roused the deepest sympathy in my breast.
    Oh, how I wish they had sufficient sense
10   At court, to recognize your excellence!
    They wrong you greatly, Sir. How it must hurt you
    Never to be rewarded for your virtue!
ALCESTE: Why, Madam, what cause have I to feel aggrieved?
    What great and brilliant thing have I achieved?
15   What service have I rendered to the King
    That I should look to him for anything?
ARSINOÉ: Not everyone who's honored by the State
    Has done great services. A man must wait
    Till time and fortune offer him the chance.
20   Your merit, Sir, is obvious at a glance,
    And . . .
ALCESTE: Ah, forget my merit; I am not neglected.
    The court, I think, can hardly be expected
    To mine men's souls for merit, and unearth
    Our hidden virtues and our secret worth.
ARSINOÉ: *Some* virtues, though, are far too bright to hide;
25   Yours are acknowledged, Sir, on every side.
    Indeed, I've heard you warmly praised of late
    By persons of considerable weight.
ALCESTE: This fawning age has praise for everyone,
30   And all distinctions, Madam, are undone.
    All things have equal honor nowadays,
    And no one should be gratified by praise.
    To be admired, one only need exist,
    And every lackey's on the honors list.
35 ARSINOÉ: I only wish, Sir, that you had your eye
    On some position at court, however high;
    You'd only have to hint at such a notion

4. *tête-à-tête:* French for "head-to-head," in private conversation.

    For me to set the proper wheels in motion;
    I've certain friendships I'd be glad to use
    To get you any office you might choose.   40
ALCESTE: Madam, I fear that any such ambition
    Is wholly foreign to my disposition.
    The soul God gave me isn't of the sort
    That prospers in the weather of a court.
    It's all too obvious that I don't possess   45
    The virtues necessary for success.
    My one great talent is for speaking plain;
    I've never learned to flatter or to feign;
    And anyone so stupidly sincere
    Had best not seek a courtier's career.   50
    Outside the court, I know, one must dispense
    With honors, privilege, and influence;
    But still one gains the right, foregoing these,
    Not to be tortured by the wish to please.
    One needn't live in dread of snubs and slights,   55
    Nor praise the verse that every idiot writes,
    Nor humor silly Marquesses, nor bestow
    Politic sighs on Madam So-and-So.
ARSINOÉ: Forget the court, then; let the matter rest.
    But I've another cause to be distressed   60
    About your present situation, Sir.
    It's to your love affair that I refer.
    She whom you love, and who pretends to love you,
    Is, I regret to say, unworthy of you.
ALCESTE: Why, Madam? Can you seriously intend   65
    To make so grave a charge against your friend?
ARSINOÉ: Alas, I must. I've stood aside too long
    And let that lady do you grievous wrong;
    But now my debt to conscience shall be paid:
    I tell you that your love has been betrayed.   70
ALCESTE: I thank you, Madam; you're extremely kind.
    Such words are soothing to a lover's mind.
ARSINOÉ: Yes, though she *is* my friend, I say again
    You're very much too good for Célimène.
    She's wantonly misled you from the start.   75
ALCESTE: You may be right; who knows another's heart?
    But ask yourself if it's the part of charity
    To shake my soul with doubts of her sincerity.
ARSINOÉ: Well, if you'd rather be a dupe than doubt her,
    That's your affair. I'll say no more about her.   80
ALCESTE: Madam, you know that doubt and vague suspicion
    Are painful to a man in my position;
    It's most unkind to worry me this way
    Unless you've some real proof of what you say.
ARSINOÉ: Sir, say no more: all doubts shall be removed,   85
    And all that I've been saying shall be proved.

You've only to escort me home, and there
We'll look into the heart of this affair.
I've ocular evidence which will persuade you
90   Beyond a doubt, that Célimène's betrayed you.
Then, if you're saddened by that revelation,
Perhaps I can provide some consolation.

ACT IV • *Scene I* [*Éliante, Philinte.*]

PHILINTE: Madam, he acted like a stubborn child;
    I thought they never would be reconciled;
    In vain we reasoned, threatened, and appealed;
    He stood his ground and simply would not
        yield.
5   The Marshals, I feel sure, have never heard
    An argument so splendidly absurd.
    "No, gentlemen," said he, "I'll not retract.
    His verse is bad: extremely bad, in fact.
    Surely it does the man no harm to know it.
10   Does it disgrace him, not to be a poet?
    A gentleman may be respected still,
    Whether he writes a sonnet well or ill.
    That I dislike his verse should not offend him;
    In all that touches honor, I commend him;
15   He's noble, brave, and virtuous — but I fear
    He can't in truth be called a sonneteer.
    I'll gladly praise his wardrobe; I'll endorse
    His dancing, or the way he sits a horse;
    But, gentlemen, I cannot praise his rhyme.
20   In fact, it ought to be a capital crime
    For anyone so sadly unendowed
    To write a sonnet, and read the thing aloud."
    At length he fell into a gentler mood
    And, striking a concessive attitude,
25   He paid Oronte the following courtesies:
    "Sir, I regret that I'm so hard to please,
    And I'm profoundly sorry that your lyric
    Failed to provoke me to a panegyric."°
    After these curious words, the two embraced,
30   And then the hearing was adjourned — in haste.
ÉLIANTE: His conduct has been very singular lately;
    Still, I confess that I respect him greatly.
    The honesty in which he takes such pride
    Has — to my mind — its noble, heroic side.
35   In this false age, such candor seems outrageous;
    But I could wish that it were more contagious.
PHILINTE: What most intrigues me in our friend
      Alceste
    Is the grand passion that rages in his breast.
    The sullen humors he's compounded of
40   Should not, I think, dispose his heart to love;
    But since they do, it puzzles me still more
    That he should choose your cousin to adore.

28. panegyric: Elaborate praise.

ÉLIANTE: It does, indeed, belie the theory
    That love is born of gentle sympathy,
    And that the tender passion must be based   45
    On sweet accords of temper and of taste.
PHILINTE: Does she return his love, do you
      suppose?
ÉLIANTE: Ah, that's a difficult question, Sir. Who
      knows?
    How can we judge the truth of her devotion?
    Her heart's a stranger to its own emotion.   50
    Sometimes it thinks it loves, when no love's
      there;
    At other times it loves quite unaware.
PHILINTE: I rather think Alceste is in for more
    Distress and sorrow than he's bargained for;
    Were he of my mind, Madam, his affection   55
    Would turn in quite a different direction,
    And we would see him more responsive to
    The kind regard which he receives from you.
ÉLIANTE: Sir, I believe in frankness, and I'm
      inclined,
    In matters of the heart, to speak my mind.   60
    I don't oppose his love for her; indeed,
    I hope with all my heart that he'll succeed,
    And were it in my power, I'd rejoice
    In giving him the lady of his choice.
    But if, as happens frequently enough   65
    In love affairs, he meets with a rebuff —
    If Célimène should grant some rival's suit —
    I'd gladly play the role of substitute;
    Nor would his tender speeches please me less
    Because they'd once been made without success.   70
PHILINTE: Well, Madam, as for me, I don't oppose
    Your hopes in this affair; and heaven knows
    That in my conversations with the man
    I plead your cause as often as I can.
    But if those two should marry, and so remove   75
    All chance that he will offer you his love,
    Then I'll declare my own, and hope to see
    Your gracious favor pass from him to me.
    In short, should you be cheated of Alceste,
    I'd be most happy to be second best.   80
ÉLIANTE: Philinte, you're teasing.
PHILINTE: Ah, Madam, never fear;
    No words of mine were ever so sincere,
    And I shall live in fretful expectation
    Till I can make a fuller declaration.

Scene II [*Alceste, Éliante, Philinte.*]

ALCESTE: Avenge me, Madam! I must have
      satisfaction,
    Or this great wrong will drive me to distraction!
ÉLIANTE: Why, what's the matter? What's upset you
      so?

ALCESTE: Madam, I've had a mortal, mortal blow.
5   If Chaos repossessed the universe,
     I swear I'd not be shaken any worse.
     I'm ruined. . . . I can say no more. . . . My
          soul . . .
ÉLIANTE: Do try, Sir, to regain your self-control.
ALCESTE: Just heaven! Why were so much beauty
          and grace
10   Bestowed on one so vicious and so base?
ÉLIANTE: Once more, Sir, tell us. . . .
ALCESTE: My world has gone to wrack;
     I'm — I'm betrayed; she's stabbed me in the
          back:
     Yes, Célimène (who would have thought it of
          her?)
     Is false to me, and has another lover.
15 ÉLIANTE: Are you quite certain? Can you prove
          these things?
PHILINTE: Lovers are prey to wild imaginings
     And jealous fancies. No doubt there's some
          mistake. . . .
ALCESTE: Mind your own business, Sir, for heaven's
          sake.
     (To Éliante.) Madam, I have the proof that you
          demand
20   Here in my pocket, penned by her own hand.
     Yes, all the shameful evidence one could want
     Lies in this letter written to Oronte —
     Oronte! whom I felt sure she couldn't love,
     And hardly bothered to be jealous of.
25 PHILINTE: Still, in a letter, appearances may deceive;
     This may not be so bad as you believe.
ALCESTE: Once more I beg you, Sir, to let me be;
     Tend to your own affairs; leave mine to me.
ÉLIANTE: Compose yourself; this anguish that you
          feel . . .
30 ALCESTE: Is something, Madam, you alone can heal.
     My outraged heart, beside itself with grief,
     Appeals to you for comfort and relief.
     Avenge me on your cousin, whose unjust
     And faithless nature has deceived my trust;
35   Avenge a crime your pure soul must detest.
ÉLIANTE: But how, Sir?
ALCESTE: Madam, this heart within my breast
     Is yours; pray take it; redeem my heart from
          her,
     And so avenge me on my torturer.
     Let her be punished by the fond emotion,
40   The ardent love, the bottomless devotion,
     The faithful worship which this heart of mine
     Will offer up to yours as to a shrine.
ÉLIANTE: You have my sympathy, Sir, in all you
          suffer;
     Nor do I scorn the noble heart you offer;
45   But I suspect you'll soon be mollified,
     And this desire for vengeance will subside.

     When some belovèd hand has done us wrong
     We thirst for retribution — but not for long;
     However dark the deed that she's committed,
     A lovely culprit's very soon acquitted.   50
     Nothing's so stormy as an injured lover,
     And yet no storm so quickly passes over.
ALCESTE: No, Madam, no — this is no lovers' spat;
     I'll not forgive her; it's gone too far for that;
     My mind's made up; I'll kill myself before   55
     I waste my hopes upon her any more.
     Ah, here she is. My wrath intensifies.
     I shall confront her with her tricks and lies,
     And crush her utterly, and bring you then
     A heart no longer slave to Célimène.   60

Scene III   [*Célimène, Alceste.*]

ALCESTE (*aside*): Sweet heaven, help me to control
          my passion.
CÉLIMÈNE (*aside*): Oh, Lord. (*To Alceste.*) Why
          stand there staring in that fashion?
     And what d'you mean by those dramatic sighs,
     And that malignant glitter in your eyes?
ALCESTE: I mean that sins which cause the blood to
          freeze   5
     Look innocent beside your treacheries;
     That nothing Hell's or Heaven's wrath could do
     Ever produced so bad a thing as you.
CÉLIMÈNE: Your compliments were always sweet
          and pretty.
ALCESTE: Madam, it's not the moment to be witty.   10
     No, blush and hang your head; you've ample
          reason,
     Since I've the fullest evidence of your treason.
     Ah, this is what my sad heart prophesied;
     Now all my anxious fears are verified;
     My dark suspicion and my gloomy doubt   15
     Divined the truth, and now the truth is out.
     For all your trickery, I was not deceived;
     It was my bitter stars that I believed.
     But don't imagine that you'll go scot-free;
     You shan't misuse me with impunity.   20
     I know that love's irrational and blind;
     I know the heart's not subject to the mind,
     And can't be reasoned into beating faster;
     I know each soul is free to choose its master;
     Therefore had you but spoken from the heart,   25
     Rejecting my attention from the start,
     I'd have no grievance, or at any rate
     I could complain of nothing but my fate.
     Ah, but so falsely to encourage me —
     That was a treason and a treachery   30
     For which you cannot suffer too severely,
     And you shall pay for that behavior dearly.
     Yes, now I have no pity, not a shred;

My temper's out of hand; I've lost my head;
Shocked by the knowledge of your double-
35   dealings,
My reason can't restrain my savage feelings;
A righteous wrath deprives me of my senses,
And I won't answer for the consequences.
CÉLIMÈNE: What does this outburst mean? Will you
        please explain?
40   Have you, by any chance, gone quite insane?
ALCESTE: Yes, yes, I went insane the day I fell
A victim to your black and fatal spell,
Thinking to meet with some sincerity
Among the treacherous charms that beckoned
        me.
CÉLIMÈNE: Pooh. Of what treachery can you
45   complain?
ALCESTE: How sly you are, how cleverly you feign!
But you'll not victimize me any more.
Look: here's a document you've seen before.
This evidence, which I acquired today,
50 Leaves you, I think, without a thing to say.
CÉLIMÈNE: Is this what sent you into such a fit?
ALCESTE: You should be blushing at the sight of it.
CÉLIMÈNE: Ought I to blush? I truly don't see why.
ALCESTE: Ah, now you're being bold as well as sly;
Since there's no signature, perhaps you'll
55   claim . . .
CÉLIMÈNE: I wrote it, whether or not it bears my
        name.
ALCESTE: And you can view with equanimity
This proof of your disloyalty to me!
CÉLIMÈNE: Oh, don't be so outrageous and
        extreme.
ALCESTE: You take this matter lightly, it would
60   seem.
Was it no wrong to me, no shame to you,
That you should send Oronte this *billet-doux*?°
CÉLIMÈNE: Oronte! Who said it was for him?
ALCESTE: Why, those
Who brought me this example of your prose.
65 But what's the difference? If you wrote the letter
To someone else, it pleases me no better.
My grievance and your guilt remain the same.
CÉLIMÈNE: But need you rage, and need I blush for
        shame,
If this was written to a *woman* friend?
ALCESTE: Ah! Most ingenious. I'm impressed no
70   end;
And after that incredible evasion
Your guilt is clear. I need no more persuasion.
How dare you try so clumsy a deception?
D'you think I'm wholly wanting in perception?

62. *billet-doux*: Love letter.

Come, come, let's see how brazenly you'll try   75
To bolster up so palpable a lie:
Kindly construe this ardent closing section
As nothing more than sisterly affection!
Here, let me read it. Tell me, if you dare to,
That this is for a woman . . .
CÉLIMÈNE: I don't care to.   80
What right have you to badger and berate me,
And so high-handedly interrogate me?
ALCESTE: Now, don't be angry; all I ask of you
Is that you justify a phrase or two . . .
CÉLIMÈNE: No, I shall not. I utterly refuse,   85
And you may take those phrases as you choose.
ALCESTE: Just show me how this letter could be
        meant
For a woman's eyes, and I shall be content.
CÉLIMÈNE: No, no, it's for Oronte; you're perfectly
        right.
I welcome his attentions with delight,   90
I prize his character and his intellect,
And everything is just as you suspect.
Come, do your worst now; give your rage free
        rein;
But kindly cease to bicker and complain.
ALCESTE (*aside*): Good God! Could anything be
        more inhuman?   95
Was ever a heart so mangled by a woman?
When I complain of how she has betrayed me,
She bridles, and commences to upbraid me!
She tries my tortured patience to the limit;
She won't deny her guilt; she glories in it!   100
And yet my heart's too faint and cowardly
To break these chains of passion, and be free,
To scorn her as it should, and rise above
This unrewarded, mad, and bitter love.
(*To Célimène.*) Ah, traitress, in how confident a
        fashion   105
You take advantage of my helpless passion,
And use my weakness for your faithless charms
To make me once again throw down my arms!
But do at least deny this black transgression;
Take back that mocking and perverse confession;   110
Defend this letter and your innocence,
And I, poor fool, will aid in your defense.
Pretend, pretend, that you are just and true,
And I shall make myself believe in you.
CÉLIMÈNE: Oh, stop it. Don't be such a jealous
        dunce,   115
Or I shall leave off loving you at once.
Just why should I *pretend*? What could impel me
To stoop so low as that? And kindly tell me
Why, if I loved another, I shouldn't merely
Inform you of it, simply and sincerely!   120
I've told you where you stand, and that
        admission

Should altogether clear me of suspicion;
After so generous a guarantee,
What right have you to harbor doubts of me?
25 Since women are (from natural reticence)
Reluctant to declare their sentiments,
And since the honor of our sex requires
That we conceal our amorous desires,
Ought any man for whom such laws are broken
30 To question what the oracle has spoken?
Should he not rather feel an obligation
To trust that most obliging declaration?
Enough, now. Your suspicions quite disgust me;
Why should I love a man who doesn't trust me?
35 I cannot understand why I continue,
Fool that I am, to take an interest in you.
I ought to choose a man less prone to doubt,
And give you something to be vexed about.
ALCESTE: Ah, what a poor enchanted fool I am;
40 These gentle words, no doubt, were all a sham,
But destiny requires me to entrust
My happiness to you, and so I must.
I'll love you to the bitter end, and see
How false and treacherous you dare to be.
CÉLIMÈNE: No, you don't really love me as you
45   ought.
ALCESTE: I love you more than can be said or
        thought;
Indeed, I wish you were in such distress
That I might show my deep devotedness.
Yes, I could wish that you were wretchedly
        poor,
50 Unloved, uncherished, utterly obscure;
That fate had set you down upon the earth
Without possessions, rank, or gentle birth;
Then, by the offer of my heart, I might
Repair the great injustice of your plight;
55 I'd raise you from the dust, and proudly prove
The purity and vastness of my love.
CÉLIMÈNE: This is a strange benevolence indeed!
God grant that I may never be in need. . . .
Ah, here's Monsieur Dubois in quaint disguise.

Scene IV [*Célimène, Alceste, Dubois.*]

ALCESTE: Well, why this costume? Why those
        frightened eyes?
What ails you?
DUBOIS: Well, Sir, things are most mysterious.
ALCESTE: What do you mean?
DUBOIS: I fear they're very serious.
ALCESTE: What?
DUBOIS: Shall I speak more loudly?
ALCESTE: Yes; speak out.
DUBOIS: Isn't there someone here, Sir?

ALCESTE: Speak, you lout! 5
Stop wasting time.
DUBOIS: Sir, we must slip away.
ALCESTE: How's that?
DUBOIS: We must decamp without delay.
ALCESTE: Explain yourself.
DUBOIS: I tell you we must fly.
ALCESTE: What for?
DUBOIS: We mustn't pause to say good-by.
ALCESTE: Now what d'you mean by all of this,
        you clown?   10
DUBOIS: I mean, Sir, that we've got to leave this
        town.
ALCESTE: I'll tear you limb from limb and joint
        from joint
If you don't come more quickly to the point.
DUBOIS: Well, Sir, today a man in a black suit,
Who wore a black and ugly scowl to boot,   15
Left us a document scrawled in such a hand
As even Satan couldn't understand.
It bears upon your lawsuit, I don't doubt;
But all hell's devils couldn't make it out.
ALCESTE: Well, well, go on. What then? I fail to see 20
How this event obliges us to flee.
DUBOIS: Well, Sir, an hour later, hardly more,
A gentleman who's often called before
Came looking for you in an anxious way.
Not finding you, he asked me to convey   25
(Knowing I could be trusted with the same)
The following message. . . . Now, what *was* his
        name?
ALCESTE: Forget his name, you idiot. What did he
        say?
DUBOIS: Well, it was one of your friends, Sir,
        anyway.
He warned you to begone, and he suggested   30
That if you stay, you may well be arrested.
ALCESTE: What? Nothing more specific? Think,
        man, think!
DUBOIS: No, Sir. He had me bring him pen and
        ink,
And dashed you off a letter which, I'm sure,
Will render things distinctly less obscure.   35
ALCESTE: Well — let me have it!
CÉLIMÈNE: What *is* this all about?
ALCESTE: God knows; but I have hopes of finding
        out.
How long am I to wait, you blitherer?
DUBOIS (*after a protracted search for the letter*): I
        must have left it on your table, Sir.
ALCESTE: I ought to . . .
CÉLIMÈNE: No, no, keep your self-control; 40
Go find out what's behind his rigmarole.
ALCESTE: It seems that fate, no matter what I do,
Has sworn that I may not converse with you;

But, Madam, pray permit your faithful lover
45   To try once more before the day is over.

ACT V • *Scene I*   [*Alceste, Philinte.*]

ALCESTE: No, it's too much. My mind's made up, I
    tell you.
PHILINTE: Why should this blow, however hard,
    compel you . . .
ALCESTE: No, no, don't waste your breath in
    argument;
    Nothing you say will alter my intent;
5   This age is vile, and I've made up my mind
    To have no further commerce with mankind.
    Did not truth, honor, decency, and the laws
    Oppose my enemy and approve my cause?
    My claims were justified in all men's sight;
10   I put my trust in equity and right;
    Yet, to my horror and the world's disgrace,
    Justice is mocked, and I have lost my case!
    A scoundrel whose dishonesty is notorious
    Emerges from another lie victorious!
15   Honor and right condone his brazen fraud,
    While rectitude and decency applaud!
    Before his smirking face, the truth stands
    charmed,
    And virtue conquered, and the law disarmed!
    His crime is sanctioned by a court decree!
20   And not content with what he's done to me,
    The dog now seeks to ruin me by stating
    That I composed a book now circulating,
    A book so wholly criminal and vicious
    That even to speak its title is seditious!
25   Meanwhile Oronte, my rival, lends his credit
    To the same libelous tale, and helps to spread it!
    Oronte! a man of honor and of rank,
    With whom I've been entirely fair and frank;
    Who sought me out and forced me, willy-nilly,
30   To judge some verse I found extremely silly;
    And who, because I properly refused
    To flatter him, or see the truth abused,
    Abets my enemy in a rotten slander!
    There's the reward of honesty and candor!
35   The man will hate me to the end of time
    For failing to commend his wretched rhyme!
    And not this man alone, but all humanity
    Do what they do from interest and vanity;
    They prate of honor, truth, and righteousness,
40   But lie, betray, and swindle nonetheless.
    Come then: man's villainy is too much to bear;
    Let's leave this jungle and this jackal's lair.
    Yes! treacherous and savage race of men,
    You shall not look upon my face again.
45 PHILINTE: Oh, don't rush into exile prematurely;

Things aren't as dreadful as you make them,
    surely.
    It's rather obvious, since you're still at large,
    That people don't believe your enemy's charge.
    Indeed, his tale's so patently untrue
    That it may do more harm to him than you.   50
ALCESTE: Nothing could do that scoundrel any
    harm:
    His frank corruption is his greatest charm,
    And, far from hurting him, a further shame
    Would only serve to magnify his name.
PHILINTE: In any case, his bald prevarication   55
    Has done no injury to your reputation,
    And you may feel secure in that regard.
    As for your lawsuit, it should not be hard
    To have the case reopened, and contest
    This judgment . . .
ALCESTE: No, no, let the verdict rest.   60
    Whatever cruel penalty it may bring,
    I wouldn't have it changed for anything.
    It shows the times' injustice with such clarity
    That I shall pass it down to our posterity
    As a great proof and signal demonstration   65
    Of the black wickedness of this generation.
    It may cost twenty thousand francs; but I
    Shall pay their twenty thousand, and gain
    thereby
    The right to storm and rage at human evil,
    And send the race of mankind to the devil.   70
PHILINTE: Listen to me . . .
ALCESTE: Why? What can you possibly say?
    Don't argue, Sir; your labor's thrown away.
    Do you propose to offer lame excuses
    For men's behavior and the times' abuses?
PHILINTE: No, all you say I'll readily concede: 75
    This is a low, conniving age, indeed;
    Nothing but trickery prospers nowadays,
    And people ought to mend their shabby ways.
    Yes, man's a beastly creature; but must we then
    Abandon the society of men?   80
    Here in the world, each human frailty
    Provides occasion for philosophy,
    And that is virtue's noblest exercise;
    If honesty shone forth from all men's eyes,
    If every heart were frank and kind and just.   85
    What could our virtues do but gather dust
    (Since their employment is to help us bear
    The villainies of men without despair)?
    A heart well-armed with virtue can endure. . . .
ALCESTE: Sir, you're a matchless reasoner, to be
    sure;   90
    Your words are fine and full of cogency;
    But don't waste time and eloquence on me.
    My reason bids me go, for my own good.
    My tongue won't lie and flatter as it should;

God knows what frankness it might next
05   commit,
And what I'd suffer on account of it.
Pray let me wait for Célimène's return
In peace and quiet. I shall shortly learn,
00   By her response to what I have in view,
Whether her love for me is feigned or true.

PHILINTE: Till then, let's visit Éliante upstairs.

ALCESTE: No, I am too weighed down with somber
    cares.
Go to her, do; and leave me with my gloom
Here in the darkened corner of this room.

PHILINTE: Why, that's no sort of company, my
05   friend;
I'll see if Éliante will not descend.

Scene II   [*Célimène, Oronte, Alceste.*]

ORONTE: Yes, Madam, if you wish me to remain
    Your true and ardent lover, you must deign
    To give me some more positive assurance.
    All this suspense is quite beyond endurance.
5   If your heart shares the sweet desires of mine,
    Show me as much by some convincing sign;
    And here's the sign I urgently suggest:
    That you no longer tolerate Alceste,
    But sacrifice him to my love, and sever
10   All your relations with the man forever.

CÉLIMÈNE: Why do you suddenly dislike him so?
    You praised him to the skies not long ago.

ORONTE: Madam, that's not the point. I'm here to
    find
    Which way your tender feelings are inclined.
15   Choose, if you please, between Alceste and me,
    And I shall stay or go accordingly.

ALCESTE (*emerging from the corner*): Yes, Madam,
    choose; this gentleman's demand
    Is wholly just, and I support his stand.
    I too am true and ardent; I too am here
20   To ask you that you make your feelings clear.
    No more delays, now; no equivocation;
    The time has come to make your declaration.

ORONTE: Sir, I've no wish in any way to be
    An obstacle to your felicity.

ALCESTE: Sir, I've no wish to share her heart with
25   you;
    That may sound jealous, but at least it's true.

ORONTE: If, weighing us, she leans in your
    direction . . .

ALCESTE: If she regards you with the least
    affection . . .

ORONTE: I swear I'll yield her to you there and
    then.
30 ALCESTE: I swear I'll never see her face again.

ORONTE: Now, Madam, tell us what we've come to
    hear.

ALCESTE: Madam, speak openly and have no fear.

ORONTE: Just say which one is to remain your
    lover.

ALCESTE: Just name one name, and it will all be
    over.

ORONTE: What! Is it possible that you're
    undecided?   35

ALCESTE: What! Can your feelings possibly be
    divided?

CÉLIMÈNE: Enough: this inquisition's gone too far:
    How utterly unreasonable you are!
    Not that I couldn't make the choice with ease;
    My heart has no conflicting sympathies;   40
    I know full well which one of you I favor,
    And you'd not see me hesitate or waver.
    But how can you expect me to reveal
    So cruelly and bluntly what I feel?
    I think it altogether too unpleasant   45
    To choose between two men when both are
    present;
    One's heart has means more subtle and more
    kind
    Of letting its affections be divined,
    Nor need one be uncharitably plain
    To let a lover know he loves in vain.   50

ORONTE: No, no, speak plainly; I for one can stand
    it.
    I beg you to be frank.

ALCESTE: And I demand it.
    The simple truth is what I wish to know,
    And there's no need for softening the blow.
    You've made an art of pleasing everyone,   55
    But now your days of coquetry are done:
    You have no choice now, Madam, but to
    choose,
    For I'll know what to think if you refuse;
    I'll take your silence for a clear admission
    That I'm entitled to my worst suspicion.   60

ORONTE: I thank you for this ultimatum, Sir.
    And I may say I heartily concur.

CÉLIMÈNE: Really, this foolishness is very wearing:
    Must you be so unjust and overbearing?
    Haven't I told you why I must demur?   65
    Ah, here's Éliante; I'll put the case to her.

Scene III   [*Éliante, Philinte, Célimène, Oronte,*
Alceste.]

CÉLIMÈNE: Cousin, I'm being persecuted here
    By these two persons, who, it would appear,
    Will not be satisfied till I confess
    Which one I love the more, and which the less,

5   And tell the latter to his face that he
     Is henceforth banished from my company.
     Tell me, has ever such a thing been done?
ÉLIANTE: You'd best not turn to me; I'm not the
        one
     To back you in a matter of this kind:
10   I'm all for those who frankly speak their mind.
ORONTE: Madam, you'll search in vain for a
        defender.
ALCESTE: You're beaten, Madam, and may as well
        surrender.
ORONTE: Speak, speak, you must; and end this
        awful strain.
ALCESTE: Or don't, and your position will be plain.
ORONTE: A single word will close this painful
15   scene.
ALCESTE: But if you're silent, I'll know what you
        mean.

Scene IV   [*Arsinoé, Célimène, Éliante, Alceste,
Philinte, Acaste, Clitandre, Oronte.*]

ACASTE (*to Célimène*): Madam, with all due
        deference, we two
     Have come to pick a little bone with you.
CLITANDRE (*to Oronte and Alceste*): I'm glad you're
        present, Sirs, as you'll soon learn,
     Our business here is also your concern.
ARSINOÉ (*to Célimène*): Madam, I visit you so soon
5   again
     Only because of these two gentlemen,
     Who came to me indignant and aggrieved
     About a crime too base to be believed.
     Knowing your virtue, having such confidence in
        it,
10   I couldn't think you guilty for a minute,
     In spite of all their telling evidence;
     And, rising above our little difference,
     I've hastened here in friendship's name to see
     You clear yourself of this great calumny.
ACASTE: Yes, Madam, let us see with what
15   composure
     You'll manage to respond to this disclosure.
     You lately sent Clitandre this tender note.
CLITANDRE: And this one, for Acaste, you also
        wrote.
ACASTE (*to Oronte and Alceste*): You'll recognize
        this writing, Sirs, I think;
20   The lady is so free with pen and ink
     That you must know it all too well, I fear.
     But listen: this is something you should hear.

     "How absurd you are to condemn my light-
heartedness in society, and to accuse me of being
happiest in the company of others. Nothing could   25
be more unjust; and if you do not come to me
instantly and beg pardon for saying such a thing,
I shall never forgive you as long as I live. Our big
bumbling friend the Viscount . . ."

What a shame that he's not here.   30

     "Our big bumbling friend the Viscount, whose
name stands first in your complaint, is hardly a
man to my taste; and ever since the day I watched
him spend three-quarters of an hour spitting into
a well, so as to make circles in the water, I have   35
been unable to think highly of him. As for the little
Marquess . . ."

In all modesty, gentlemen, that is I.

     "As for the little Marquess, who sat squeezing
my hand for such a long while yesterday, I find   40
him in all respects the most trifling creature alive;
and the only things of value about him are his cape
and his sword. As for the man with the green
ribbons . . ."

(*To Alceste.*) It's your turn now, Sir.   45

     "As for the man with the green ribbons, he
amuses me now and then with his bluntness and
his bearish ill-humor; but there are many times
indeed when I think him the greatest bore in the
world. And as for the sonneteer . . ."   50

(*To Oronte.*) Here's your helping.

     "And as for the sonneteer, who has taken it into
his head to be witty, and insists on being an author
in the teeth of opinion, I simply cannot be bothered
to listen to him, and his prose wearies me quite as   55
much as his poetry. Be assured that I am not always
so well-entertained as you suppose; that I long for
your company, more than I dare to say, at all these
entertainments to which people drag me; and that
the presence of those one loves is the true and   60
perfect seasoning to all one's pleasures."

CLITANDRE: And now for me.

     "Clitandre, whom you mention, and who so
pesters me with his saccharine speeches, is the last
man on earth for whom I could feel any affection.   65
He is quite mad to suppose that I love him, and
so are you, to doubt that you are loved. Do come
to your senses; exchange your suppositions for his;
and visit me as often as possible, to help me bear
the annoyance of his unwelcome attentions."   70

It's sweet character that these letters show,
And what to call it, Madam, you well know.
Enough. We're off to make the world acquainted
With this sublime self-portrait that you've
     painted.
75 ACASTE: Madam, I'll make you no farewell oration;
No, you're not worthy of my indignation.
Far choicer hearts than yours, as you'll discover,
Would like this little Marquess for a lover.

Scene V   [*Célimène, Éliante, Arsinoé, Alceste,*
Oronte, Philinte.]

ORONTE: So! After all those loving letters you
     wrote,
You turn on me like this, and cut my throat!
And your dissembling, faithless heart, I find,
Has pledged itself by turns to all mankind!
5   How blind I've been! But now I clearly see;
I thank you, Madam, for enlightening me.
My heart is mine once more, and I'm content;
The loss of it shall be your punishment.
(*To Alceste.*) Sir, she is yours; I'll seek no more
     to stand
10   Between your wishes and this lady's hand.

Scene VI   [*Célimène, Éliante, Arsinoé, Alceste,*
Philinte.]

ARSINOÉ: (*to Célimène*): Madam, I'm forced to
     speak. I'm far too stirred
To keep my counsel, after what I've heard.
I'm shocked and staggered by your want of
     morals.
It's not my way to mix in others' quarrels;
5   But really, when this fine and noble spirit,
This man of honor and surpassing merit,
Laid down the offering of his heart before you,
How *could* you . . .
ALCESTE: Madam, permit me, I implore you,
To represent myself in this debate.
10   Don't bother, please, to be my advocate.
My heart, in any case, could not afford
To give your services their due reward;
And if I chose, for consolation's sake,
Some other lady, 'twould not be you I'd take.
ARSINOÉ: What makes you think you could, Sir?
15   And how dare you
Imply that I've been trying to ensnare you?
If you can for a moment entertain
Such flattering fancies, you're extremely vain.
I'm not so interested as you suppose
20   In Célimène's discarded gigolos.

Get rid of that absurd illusion, do.
Women like me are not for such as you.
Stay with this creature, to whom you're so
     attached;
I've never seen two people better matched.

Scene VII   [*Célimène, Éliante, Alceste, Philinte.*]

ALCESTE (*to Célimène*): Well, I've been still
     throughout this exposé,
Till everyone but me has said his say.
Come, have I shown sufficient self-restraint?
And may I now . . .
CÉLIMÈNE: Yes, make your just complaint.
Reproach me freely, call me what you will;   5
You've every right to say I've used you ill.
I've wronged you, I confess it; and in my shame
I'll make no effort to escape the blame.
The anger of those others I could despise;
My guilt toward you I sadly recognize.   10
Your wrath is wholly justified, I fear;
I know how culpable I must appear,
I know all things bespeak my treachery,
And that, in short, you've grounds for hating
     me.
Do so; I give you leave.
ALCESTE: Ah, traitress — how,   15
How should I cease to love you, even now?
Though mind and will were passionately bent
On hating you, my heart would not consent.
(*To Éliante and Philinte.*) Be witness to my
     madness, both of you;
See what infatuation drives one to;   20
But wait; my folly's only just begun,
And I shall prove to you before I'm done
How strange the human heart is, and how far
From rational we sorry creatures are.
(*To Célimène.*) Woman, I'm willing to forget
     your shame,   25
And clothe your treacheries in a sweeter name;
I'll call them youthful errors, instead of crimes,
And lay the blame on these corrupting times.
My one condition is that you agree
To share my chosen fate, and fly with me   30
To that wild, trackless, solitary place
In which I shall forget the human race.
Only by such a course can you atone
For those atrocious letters; by that alone
Can you remove my present horror of you,   35
And make it possible for me to love you.
CÉLIMÈNE: What! *I* renounce the world at my
     young age,
And die of boredom in some hermitage?
ALCESTE: Ah, if you really loved me as you ought,

40   You wouldn't give the world a moment's
            thought;
        Must you have me, and all the world beside?
CÉLIMÈNE: Alas, at twenty one is terrified
        Of solitude. I fear I lack the force
        And depth of soul to take so stern a course.
45   But if my hand in marriage will content you,
        Why, there's a plan which I might well consent
            to,
        And . . .
ALCESTE: No, I detest you now. I could excuse
        Everything else, but since you thus refuse
        To love me wholly, as a wife should do,
50   And see the world in me, as I in you,
        Go! I reject your hand, and disenthrall
        My heart from your enchantments, once for all.

Scene VIII [*Éliante, Alceste, Philinte.*]

ALCESTE (*to Éliante*): Madam, your virtuous beauty
            has no peer;
        Of all this world you only are sincere;
        I've long esteemed you highly, as you know;

        Permit me ever to esteem you so,
        And if I do not now request your hand,   5
        Forgive me, Madam, and try to understand.
        I feel unworthy of it; I sense that fate
        Does not intend me for the married state,
        That I should do you wrong by offering you
        My shattered heart's unhappy residue,   10
        And that in short . . .
ÉLIANTE: Your argument's well taken:
        Nor need you fear that I shall feel forsaken.
        Were I to offer him this hand of mine,
        Your friend Philinte, I think, would not decline.
PHILINTE: Ah, Madam, that's my heart's most
            cherished goal,   15
        For which I'd gladly give my life and soul.
ALCESTE (*to Eliante and Philinte*): May you be true
            to all you now profess,
        And so deserve unending happiness.
        Meanwhile, betrayed and wronged in everything,
        I'll flee this bitter world where vice is king,   20
        And seek some spot unpeopled and apart
        Where I'll be free to have an honest heart.
PHILINTE: Come, Madam, let's do everything we
            can
        To change the mind of this unhappy man.

COMMENTARY

Lionel Gossman (*b. 1929*)
ALCESTE'S LOVE FOR CÉLIMÈNE   1963

> *Gossman treats Alceste seriously as he attempts to clarify his motives for his unlikely infatuation with Célimène. Gossman suggests that Alceste is playing to the very people of fashion whom he affects to look down upon. Consequently he must conceal the real reasons for his love.*

In reality, Alceste's love for Célimène is neither super-rational (above all reason and all explanation) nor irrational (below all reason and explanation). It is quite simply a peculiar and contradictory fascination which goes by the name of love in the vocabulary of the Alcestes of the world. It *can* be explained, and the explanation reveals that far from being the sincere and spontaneous being he says he is, Alceste is as calculating as anyone else.

It is precisely because Célimène is the most sought after and *worldly* of women (to all *appearances* the most unsuitable for Alceste) that he falls in love with her. It is not Célimène that Alceste loves or desires. She is irrelevant *as a person* to his "love." It is the world that he seeks to reach and possess through her. To have at his feet this woman whom all the world admires and courts would be to win the recognition of the world for himself. Alceste's love is entirely mediated by those very "gens à la mode"° for whom he so loudly protests his contempt. He "loves" Célimène because she has what he wants — the admiration of the world — and cannot admit he wants, without at the same time admitting that he is not the free, frank, and independent person he wants to be admired as. The object of his desire is thus also his unavowed rival, and this *for the very same reason* that she is the object of his desire. While he protests his love for Célimène, Alceste must therefore conceal the real reason for this love by affecting to deplore her participation in the "false" society of the *gens à la mode* and to despise her charms and her popularity. The final break with Célimène strikingly illustrates the ambiguity that characterizes Alceste's entire relationship with her from the beginning. Alceste calls on witnesses to observe how superior and disinterested his love is compared to the love of the elegant suitors who have abandoned Célimène, while at the same time he affirms before them his own contempt for it as unworthy of him:

> *Vous voyez* ce que peut une indigne tendresse,
> Et je vous fais tous deux *témoins* de ma foiblesse.
> Mais, à vous dire vrai, ce n'est pas encor tout,
> Et *vous allez me voir* la pousser jusqu'au bout,
> *Montrer* que c'est à tort que sages on nous nomme,
> Et que dans tous les coeurs il est toujours de l'homme.
> [V, VII, 19–24][1]

Having once proved how different his love is from that of Célimène's frivolous and calculating suitors, however, Alceste is only too quick to use her unwillingness to follow him to his desert as an excuse to drop her. Célimène without her suitors can have no attraction for Alceste.

Those who fall for Alceste's argument about the irrationality of passion are his dupes. Alceste cannot accept in the front rank of his own consciousness, or admit to others, that his whole life is pure posturing before others, that he who claims to be sincere and spontaneous is as preoccupied with the public as anybody and as mediated by it as those whom he charges with acting parts for others. Is he not, after all, the only person in the world who does not posture, whose emotions spring directly from the heart and who speaks nothing but what he really thinks and feels? Alceste uses the myth of the irrationality of passion to hide from others and from himself a character that is every bit as cold and ungenerous as the characters of those he criticizes for their coldness and lack of generosity. . . .

Alceste's life is in an important sense a life not of participation but of demonstration. This is one way in which he differs from the tragic heroes of Racine. The scandalous contradiction between the ideal and the real, between being and appearance, between the world of absolute values and the world of contingent opportunities is at the heart of seventeenth-century tragedy. There is never any danger, however, that Alceste will share in the somber destinies of Racine's heroes. His world is far removed from theirs. He does not stake his

---

"gens à la mode": Fashionable people.
[1]V, IV, 1751–56 of original text; italics added by Gossman.

destiny, as Junie or Andromaque or Monime° does, on living an authentic life in a world of inauthenticity. The inauthenticity of the world is not a menace to him; on the contrary, it is the very source of all his satisfactions. It provides the basis for his own superiority and he spends his time not in a real struggle to reach authenticity, but in endless efforts to have his superiority recognized by the very world of inauthenticity which he affects to detest. The absence of value in the world becomes, with Alceste, a matter for personal self-congratulation. Far from threatening his existence, the world of lies and deceit founds it. He exhausts himself in theatrical gestures, because all his wrestling with the ideal and the real, all his disgust with the world's falseness, however painfully experienced subjectively, is, objectively viewed, nothing but vain, ineffectual, and deeply inauthentic posturing. He does not really suffer because life is full of pretense and selfishness, because men have made their lives so vain and stupid. He suffers because he cannot bear to be like others and because others refuse him the adulation which he wants from them. . . .

Alceste acts the part of an absolute, but no one accepts his absoluteness: He loses his lawsuit, he fails to make Célimène submit to him, and he is laughed at by the world at large. He is an absolute in the world of his own conceptualizing alone, and thither he withdraws to decide for himself the fate of all his battles. The desert to which Alceste has always thought of withdrawing and to which he makes as if to withdraw at the end of the comedy is the world of his own mind. In it there is nothing to contradict his absoluteness, but there is unfortunately nothing to confirm it either. Alceste's difficulty is that his absoluteness can be experienced as real only with reference to others. Withdrawal to the desert cannot therefore be a final solution. It can only be an *act*, just as his rejection of Philinte at the beginning of the play was an act. This withdrawal requires an audience to watch it; and this hermit seeks not to escape but to be pursued. Alceste's withdrawal is simply a pose. And this is the very marrow of Molière's play. Alceste literally *joue la comédie*.° He is perpetually play-acting, whether we think of his passion for Célimène or of his passion for justice, and in this respect he resembles Molière's other comic heroes.

Junie . . . Andromaque . . . Monime: Characters in plays by Racine.
joue la comédie: Play a sham part; play-act.

Aphra Behn

Although not technically the first English woman playwright, or the first woman to earn a living by her pen, Aphra Behn (c. 1640–1689) was the first notably successful woman playwright. She wrote twenty plays, several novels, among them *Oroonoko* (c. 1688), and *Poems on Several Occasions* (1684). She also published translations and edited volumes of poetry.

Behn grew up in an England governed by the Puritan Commonwealth. Throughout the 1650s Cromwell was Protector, and the theaters were closed. The Puritans were, in her eyes, dull, hypocritical, and repressive. Her allegiance was with the Stuarts, whose King Charles I was beheaded by order of Parliament in 1649. His sons, Charles and James, were forced into exile on the Continent, along with many Stuart courtiers, such as the gallants who appear in *The Rover*. When Charles II was restored to the throne in 1660, the period known as the Restoration began. Behn was twenty years old.

Very little is known of her, and much of that is guesswork based on her writing. For example, *Oroonoko* is a novel set in Surinam, which was a British colony when she visited there with members of her family in 1663–1664. Her father had been appointed Lieutenant-General of Surinam, but he died, and she returned to London after several months. She married Mr. Behn, possibly a Dutch merchant in England, who died two years later. She seems to have been persuaded by the writer Thomas Killigrew to become an English spy in Antwerp, where she resided during the great London fire of 1666, in which most of the town was burned to the ground. Her services were of such little value that she was not paid and ended up for a brief time in debtors' prison when she returned to England.

Once out of prison, she took advantage of her friendship with Thomas Betterton, who was a member of a theater company at Lincoln's Inn Fields. He played the lead in her first play, *The Forced Marriage* (1670), which ran successfully for six nights. The record for the first run of a play was thirteen nights. In 1670 Behn reached a mostly courtly audience, those politically aligned with Charles II or somehow involved in court politics.

Behn succeeded again with *The Amorous Prince* following *The Forced Marriage* in 1671. Those first two plays were wholly original, but she quickly resorted to the Shakespearean device of adapting the work of others. Like Shakespeare, she made considerable changes and constantly improved the material she borrowed. After the success of *The Rover* (1677), she was accused of plagiarism and answered the charge in the Postscript to the play. She did borrow some characters and details from Thomas Killigrew's *Thomaso; or, The Wanderer*, a closet drama, or play intended to be read, not staged (1654; published 1664), but, as she says in her Postscript, no one would have taken notice if her play were not so successful — and written by a woman. Playwrights commonly adapted earlier material because they had to produce many plays in a short time to earn a meager living.

The theme of her first play, loveless and unhappy marriages arranged by families, recurs throughout Behn's work. All we know about her own marriage is that it was brief; she did not remarry despite having long-term relationships. But she concerned herself with the fate of women in her society. A woman could not hope to marry if she were not a virgin. Once she was married, a woman's property became her husband's and her legal identity was melded with his. Consequently, she was at her husband's mercy since she had no recourse in law against any of his excesses.

However, the alternative to marriage was considered worse. If a woman was seduced, she could expect to lose her status and forsake marriage. As a result, she would be forced to earn her own living, a harsh prospect since women were not given the same education as men and could not take part in any of the professions. One fate of many such women was to become prostitutes. In the meantime, men pursued their goal of seduction, as they do in *The Rover* and other Behn plays, with no thought given to the welfare of the women they seduced. Furthermore, they frequently threatened women with rape if the women were uncompliant. The theme of rape echoes through Behn's plays. By necessity Behn had to appeal to a predominantly male audience, but even so she expresses some of her deeper concerns for the welfare of her sex. She exposes the unfairness and pain of arranged marriages and portrays women as complex and intelligent. Her work seems to bear the influence of Shakespeare's female characters, such as Helena and Hermia in *A Midsummer Night's Dream* and Beatrice in *Much Ado About Nothing*.

Behn's plays include *Abdelazer* (1676), *The Town Fop* (1676), *The Lucky Chance* (1686), and *The Emperor of the Moon* (1687). Her last play, *The Widow Ranter* (1689), produced posthumously, was a failure. But it is an interesting portrait of the settlement of the Virginias, based on her experience in the New World. The prefaces to Behn's plays treat important issues, such as the unequal education of women. She points out, however, that in playwriting the lack of education in Greek and Latin is no handicap. She reminds her readers that Shakespeare and Jonson did very well with limited education, and that "gownmen" (scholars) talked incessantly and to little account. What was needed for the stage was experience and a good ear, and Aphra Behn had both.

THE ROVER; OR, THE BANISHED CAVALIERS

The English rakes who swagger through this play are displaced Royalist cavaliers who lived perilously in exile during the Puritan Interregnum of the 1650s awaiting the restoration of Charles II to the throne. Their concerns in Naples are warlike and lusty. Their frequent dueling delighted the audiences of 1677 and caused *The Rover* to be one of Behn's best-received plays. However, beneath the brawling is a more serious struggle between the sexes.

It is pre-Lenten Carnival time in Naples, when all the people dress in masquerade. The players in *The Rover* disguise themselves — Hellena as a gypsy or a page, Belvile as Antonio, the others in costumes that make them unrecognizable — from the first act to the last. Such masquerading permits the young men and women to meet and talk without supervision. Among the characters, the most stable are Florinda and Belvile, who love each other from the beginning and who end up married despite the objections of Florinda's brother Pedro and their father, who has promised Florinda to Don Vincentio, a wealthy old man.

Behn's favorite theme of arranged or forced marriage thus surfaces quickly in this play, and much of the action involves its circumvention. However, another related theme also develops quickly: forcible rape. The Cavaliers, or rakes, treat women of lower social class as if they were whores. In this play Florinda faces rape not once, but twice. First Willmore, the Rover, treats her as "an errant harlot" and forces her to scream rape (III, v). When Frederick and Belvile intervene, he explains that he was drunk and not to blame. Florinda's second close call comes with Blunt. She runs into his apartment to escape discovery on the street, and Blunt decides to avenge his disgrace at the hands of Lucetta by raping Florinda — thus punishing the entire sex for his mishandling. This time Frederick, without knowing who Florinda is, decides he will help Blunt and rape her as well. When she gives them a ring that reveals her to be an aristocrat, a woman of quality, Frederick says, "'Twould anger us vilely to be trussed up for a rape upon a maid of quality, when we only believe we ruffle a harlot" (IV, v, 157–60).

These scenes are painful from our modern perspective and must have been painful to women in Behn's audience. However, part of her purpose is to point out that men treated women differently according to class. Aristocrats such as these cavaliers were sometimes willfully brutal with women in a lower class. Behn's purpose is to build sympathy for Florinda and, by extension, for all women who are treated viciously by men. It is conceivable that some men in the audiences of Behn's day might not have been conscious of her purpose, since they may have approved of behavior such as Blunt's and Frederick's.

Like Florinda, the other female characters in *The Rover* face obstacles with wit and resourcefulness, but not all the women are successful. Behn's portrait of the courtesan Angellica is laced with irony. Against her will and better judgment, Angellica finds herself falling in love with Willmore. When she takes Willmore as a lover without demanding from him the usual thousand crowns, her handmaid Moretta watches in horror, realizing her mistress is giving away something that she would normally sell at a dear price. Angellica is smitten by Willmore — just as Hellena is smitten by the same rover — but once Willmore enjoys Angellica's pleasures, he dismisses her from his mind. Angellica the courtesan knows that this is the way men relate to women. But Angellica the woman, who gave Willmore her "virgin heart," is as deceived as any woman could be.

Hellena, promised to the church as a nun by her father, begins the play revealing her plans to avoid the convent at all costs. Her brother Pedro does not say so, but he seems to expect that when she is in the convent he will have access to the three hundred thousand crowns her uncle has bequeathed her. Pedro attempts to force Hellena to "marry" the church in the same way he attempts to force Florinda to marry a man she does not love. Neither sister will have any of it.

The play centers more on the success of Florinda and Hellena than it does on Belvile or Willmore. Hellena, by virtue of her wit — which is equal to Willmore's — and her understanding of social realities, forces Willmore to submit to her will. He is all for making love, but she demands that Hymen, the god of marriage, be invoked before their lovemaking. When he tells her she should be content with love and not demand that they marry, she replies, "What shall I get? A cradle full of noise and mischief, with a pack of repentance at my back?" She is more than his match. The play ends with Florinda, Hellena, and Valeria all winning the husbands of their choice on their own terms.

The Rover; or, The Banished Cavaliers in Performance

King Charles II attended the March 24, 1677, production of *The Rover*, and successive royal performances were commanded in 1724 and 1729. Some seventy performances of the play took place between 1700 and 1725, and even more were recorded between 1726 and 1760. However, after 1790 the play was not produced for many decades.

Today's productions indicate a modern understanding of the play's feminist themes and its subtle wit-play between the sexes. The Folger Theater Group in Washington, D.C., produced the play in 1982, playing it broadly for its humor. Critics praised the play for its vitality but complained that the production overdid the "business" — stage gestures, movement, and action — and did not clearly deliver the lines. Christopher Reeve played Willmore in the Williamstown Theater production in 1987, with Kate Burton as Florinda. The director, John Rubinstein, moved the setting from Naples to the West Indies. One of the most interesting, although not wholly satisfying, productions was in 1986 by the Royal Shakespeare Company. Jeremy Irons played Willmore and Imogen Stubbs played Hellena. The director, John Barton, adapted the text using the earlier source play *Thomaso; or, The Wanderer* by Thomas Killigrew. Critics of the Royal Shakespeare production were struck by the modernity of Behn's play.

Aphra Behn (1640–1689)

THE ROVER; OR, THE BANISHED CAVALIERS

1677

PROLOGUE

Wits, like physicians, never can agree,
When of a different society.
And Rabel's drops° were never more cried down
By all the learned doctors of the town,
5   Than a new play whose author is unknown.
Nor can those doctors with more malice sue
(And powerful purses) the dissenting few,
Than those, with an insulting pride, do rail
At all who are not of their own cabal.°
10   If a young poet hit your humor right,
You judge him then out of revenge and spite.
So amongst men there are ridiculous elves,
Who monkeys hate for being too like themselves.
So that the reason of the grand debate
15   Why wit so oft is damned when good plays take,
Is that you censure as you love, or hate.
Thus like a learned conclave poets sit,
Catholic° judges both of sense and wit,
And damn or save as they themselves think fit.

Yet those who to others' faults are so severe,   20
Are not so perfect but themselves may err.
Some write correct, indeed, but then the whole
(Bating° their own dull stuff i'th' play) is stole:
As bees do suck from flowers their honeydew,
So they rob others striving to please you.   25
   Some write their characters genteel and fine,
But then they do so toil for every line,
That what to you does easy seem, and plain,
Is the hard issue of their laboring brain.
And some th' effects of all their pains, we see,   30
Is but to mimic good extempore.°
Others, by long converse about the town,
Have wit enough to write a lewd lampoon,
But their chief skill lies in a bawdy song.
In short, the only wit that's now in fashion,   35
Is but the gleanings of good conversation.
As for the author of this coming play,
I asked him what he thought fit I should say
In thanks for your good company today:
He called me fool, and said it was well known   40
You came not here for our sakes, but your own.

---

3. **Rabel's drops:** A patent medicine.   9. **cabal:** A small, secret political group.   18. **Catholic:** Having broad tastes or interests.

23. **Bating:** Leaving out.   31. **extempore:** A performance given without a script or rehearsal.

New plays are stuffed with wits, and with
deboches,°
That crowd and sweat like cits° in May-Day°
coaches.°

WRITTEN BY A PERSON OF QUALITY

The Actors' Names

[Men]
DON ANTONIO, *the Viceroy's son*
DON PEDRO, *a noble Spaniard, his friend*
BELVILE, *an English colonel in love with Florinda*
WILLMORE, *the Rover*
FREDERICK, *an English gentleman, and friend to
Belvile and Blunt*
BLUNT, *an English country gentleman*
STEPHANO, *servant to Don Pedro*
PHILIPPO, *Lucetta's gallant*
SANCHO, *pimp to Lucetta*
BISKEY *and* SEBASTIAN, *two bravos° to Angellica*
OFFICER *and* SOLDIERS
[DIEGO,] *Page to Don Antonio*

[Women]
FLORINDA, *sister to Don Pedro*
HELLENA, *a gay young woman designed for a nun,
and sister to Florinda*
VALERIA, *a kinswoman to Florinda*
ANGELLICA BIANCA, *a famous courtesan*
MORETTA, *her woman*
CALLIS, *governess to Florinda and Hellena*
LUCETTA, *a jilting wench*
SERVANTS, other MASQUERADERS, MEN and WOMEN

The Scene: *Naples, in Carnival time.*

ACT I • *Scene 1*

(*A Chamber. Enter Florinda and Hellena.*)

FLORINDA: What an impertinent thing is a young girl
bred in a nunnery! How full of questions! Prithee
no more, Hellena; I have told thee more than thou
understand'st already.

5 HELLENA: The more's my grief. I would fain know as
much as you, which makes me so inquisitive; nor
is't enough I know you're a lover, unless you tell
me too who 'tis you sigh for.

FLORINDA: When you're a lover I'll think you fit for
10 a secret of that nature.

HELLENA: 'Tis true, I never was a lover yet, but I
begin to have a shrewd guess what 'tis to be so,
and fancy it very pretty to sigh, and sing, and blush,
and wish, and dream and wish, and long and wish
to see the man, and when I do, look pale and 15
tremble, just as you did when my brother brought
home the fine English colonel to see you. What do
you call him? Don Belvile?

FLORINDA: Fie, Hellena.

HELLENA: That blush betrays you. I am sure 'tis so. 20
Or is it Don Antonio the Viceroy's son? Or perhaps
the rich old Don Vincentio, whom my father designs you for a husband? Why do you blush again?

FLORINDA: With indignation; and how near soever my
father thinks I am to marrying that hated object, 25
I shall let him see I understand better what's due
to my beauty, birth, and fortune, and more to my
soul, than to obey those unjust commands.

HELLENA: Now hang me, if I don't love thee for that
dear disobedience. I love mischief strangely, as 30
most of our sex do who are come to love nothing
else. But tell me, dear Florinda, don't you love that
fine *Anglese?*° For I vow, next to loving him myself,
'twill please me most that you do so, for he is so
gay and so handsome. 35

FLORINDA: Hellena, a maid designed for a nun ought
not to be so curious in a discourse of love.

HELLENA: And dost thou think that ever I'll be a nun?
Or at least till I'm so old I'm fit for nothing else?
Faith no, sister; and that which makes me long to 40
know whether you love Belvile, is because I hope
he has some mad companion or other that will
spoil my devotion. Nay, I'm resolved to provide
myself this Carnival, if there be e'er a handsome
proper fellow of my humor above ground,° though 45
I ask first.

FLORINDA: Prithee be not so wild.

HELLENA: Now you have provided yourself of a man
you take no care of poor me. Prithee tell me, what
dost thou see about me that is unfit for love? Have 50
I not a world of youth? A humor gay? A beauty
passable? A vigor desirable? Well shaped? Clean
limbed? Sweet breathed? And sense enough to
know how all these ought to be employed to the
best advantage? Yes, I do and will; therefore lay 55
aside your hopes of my fortune by my being a
devote,° and tell me how you came acquainted with
this Belvile. For I perceive you knew him before
he came to Naples.

FLORINDA: Yes, I knew him at the siege of Pamplona; 60

---

42. **deboches:** Orgies, debauches. 43. **cits:** Residents of
cities. **May-Day:** May 1, celebrated as a spring festival.
coaches: Carriages on parade during a May Day celebration.
[**The Actors' Names**] **bravos:** Villains, adventurers.

33. *Anglese:* The English colonel Belvile. 45. **above ground:**
In the real world (i.e., outside the convent). 57. **devote:**
Nun.

he was then a colonel of French horse,° who when the town was ransacked, nobly treated my brother and myself, preserving us from all insolences. And I must own, besides great obligations, I have I know not what that pleads kindly for him about my heart, and will suffer no other to enter. But see, my brother.

(*Enter Don Pedro, Stephano with a masking habit,*° *and Callis.*)

PEDRO: Good morrow, sister. Pray when saw you your lover Don Vincentio?

FLORINDA: I know not, sir. Callis, when was he here? For I consider it so little I know not when it was.

PEDRO: I have a command from my father here to tell you you ought not to despise him, a man of so vast a fortune, and such a passion for you. — Stephano, my things.

(*Puts on his masking habit.*)

FLORINDA: A passion for me? 'Tis more than e'er I saw, or he had a desire should be known. I hate Vincentio, sir, and I would not have a man so dear to me as my brother follow the ill customs of our country and make a slave of his sister. And, sir, my father's will I'm sure you may divert.

PEDRO: I know not how dear I am to you, but I wish only to be ranked in your esteem equal with the English colonel Belvile. Why do you frown and blush? Is there any guilt belongs to the name of that cavalier?

FLORINDA: I'll not deny I value Belvile. When I was exposed to such dangers as the licensed lust of common soldiers threatened when rage and conquest flew through the city, then Belvile, this criminal for my sake, threw himself into all dangers to save my honor. And will you not allow him my esteem?

PEDRO: Yes, pay him what you will in honor, but you must consider Don Vincentio's fortune, and the jointure° he'll make you.

FLORINDA: Let him consider my youth, beauty, and fortune, which ought not to be thrown away on his age and jointure.

PEDRO: 'Tis true, he's not so young and fine a gentleman as that Belvile. But what jewels will that cavalier present you with? Those of his eyes and heart?

HELLENA: And are not those better than any Don Vincentio has brought from the Indies?

PEDRO: Why, how now! Has your nunnery breeding taught you to understand the value of hearts and eyes?

HELLENA: Better than to believe Vincentio's deserve value from any woman. He may perhaps increase her bags, but not her family.°

PEDRO: This is fine! Go! Up to your devotion! You are not designed for the conversation of lovers.

HELLENA (*aside*): Nor saints yet a while, I hope. — Is't not enough you make a nun of me, but you must cast my sister away too, exposing her to a worse confinement than a religious life?

PEDRO: The girl's mad! It is a confinement to be carried into the country to an ancient villa belonging to the family of the Vincentios these five hundred years, and have no other prospect than that pleasing one of seeing all her own that meets her eyes: a fine air, large fields, and gardens where she may walk and gather flowers?

HELLENA: When, by moonlight? For I am sure she dares not encounter with the heat of the sun; that were a task only for Don Vincentio and his Indian breeding, who loves it in the dog days.° And if these be her daily divertissements,° what are those of the night? To lie in a wide moth-eaten bed-chamber with furniture in fashion in the reign of King Sancho the First;° the bed, that which his forefathers lived and died in.

PEDRO: Very well.

HELLENA: This apartment, new furbrushed° and fitted out for the young wife, he out of freedom makes his dressing room; and being a frugal and a jealous coxcomb,° instead of a valet to uncase° his feeble carcass, he desires you to do that office. Signs of favor, I'll assure you, and such as you must not hope for unless your woman be out of the way.

PEDRO: Have you done yet?

HELLENA: That honor being past, the giant stretches itself, yawns and sighs a belch or two loud as a musket, throws himself into bed, and expects you in his foul sheets; and ere you can get yourself undressed, calls you with a snore or two. And are not these fine blessings to a young lady?

PEDRO: Have you done yet?

HELLENA: And this man you must kiss, nay you must kiss none but him too, and nuzzle through his beard to find his lips. And this you must submit to for threescore years, and all for a jointure.

---

61. **of French horse:** In the French cavalry.   67. [S.D.] **masking habit:** Costume for the Carnival masquerades.   96. **jointure:** An estate given by a husband to a wife in lieu of her dowry.

109–110. **increase her bags . . . family:** Give her material goods but not enhance her family's standing.   127. **dog days:** The hot days of summer.   128. **divertissements:** Amusements.   131. **King Sancho the First:** King of Spain, probably Sancho I of Castile (970–1035).   134. **new furbrushed:** Refurbished.   137. **coxcomb:** Conceited person, fop.   **uncase:** Disrobe.

PEDRO: For all your character of Don Vincentio, she is as like to marry him as she was before.

155 HELLENA: Marry Don Vincentio! Hang me, such a wedlock would be worse than adultery with another man. I had rather see her in the *Hostel de Dieu,*° to waste her youth there in vows, and be a handmaid to lazars° and cripples, than to lose it

160   in such a marriage.

PEDRO: You have considered, sister, that Belvile has no fortune to bring you to; banished his country, despised at home, and pitied abroad.

HELLENA: What then? The Viceroy's son is better than

165   that old Sir Fifty. Don Vincentio! Don Indian! He thinks he's trading to Gambo° still, and would barter himself — that bell and bauble — for your youth and fortune.

PEDRO: Callis, take her hence and lock her up all this

170   Carnival, and at Lent she shall begin her everlasting penance in a monastery.

HELLENA: I care not; I had rather be a nun than be obliged to marry as you would have me if I were designed for't.

175 PEDRO: Do not fear the blessing of that choice. You shall be a nun.

HELLENA (*aside*): Shall I so? You may chance to be mistaken in my way of devotion. A nun! Yes, I am like to make a fine nun! I have an excellent humor

180   for a grate!° No, I'll have a saint of my own to pray to shortly, if I like any that dares venture on me.

PEDRO: Callis, make it your business to watch this wildcat. — As for you, Florinda, I've only tried

185   you all this while and urged my father's will; but mine is that you would love Antonio: He is brave and young, and all that can complete the happiness of a gallant maid. This absence of my father will give us opportunity to free you from Vincentio by

190   marrying here, which you must do tomorrow.

FLORINDA: Tomorrow!

PEDRO: Tomorrow, or 'twill be too late. 'Tis not my friendship to Antonio which makes me urge this, but love to thee and hatred to Vincentio; therefore

195   resolve upon tomorrow.

FLORINDA: Sir, I shall strive to do as shall become your sister.

PEDRO: I'll both believe and trust you. Adieu.

(*Exeunt*° *Pedro and Stephano.*)

157–58. *Hostel de Dieu*: Hospital operated by a group of nuns.   159. **lazars**: Lepers.   166. **Gambo**: British colony in West Africa.   180. **grate**: The grille covering the windows in a convent (i.e., the convent).   198. [S.D.] *Exeunt*: Latin for "they go out."

HELLENA: As becomes his sister! That is to be as 200 resolved your way as he is his.

(*Hellena goes to Callis.*)

FLORINDA: I ne'er till now perceived my ruin near. I've no defense against Antonio's love, For he has all the advantages of nature, The moving arguments of youth and fortune.

HELLENA: But hark you, Callis, you will not be so 205 cruel to lock me up indeed, will you?

CALLIS: I must obey the commands I have. Besides, do you consider what a life you are going to lead?

HELLENA: Yes, Callis, that of a nun; and till then I'll be indebted a world of prayers to you if you'll let 210 me now see what I never did, the divertissements of a Carnival.

CALLIS: What, go in masquerade? 'Twill be a fine farewell to the world, I take it. Pray what would you do there? 215

HELLENA: That which all the world does, as I am told: Be as mad as the rest and take all innocent freedoms. Sister, you'll go too, will you not? Come, prithee be not sad. We'll outwit twenty brothers if you'll be ruled by me. Come, put off this dull 220 humor with your clothes, and assume one as gay and as fantastic as the dress my cousin Valeria and I have provided, and let's ramble.

FLORINDA: Callis, will you give us leave to go?

CALLIS (*aside*): I have a youthful itch of going my- 225 self. — Madam, if I thought your brother might not know it, and I might wait on you; for by my troth I'll not trust young girls alone.

FLORINDA: Thou seest my brother's gone already, and thou shalt attend and watch us. 230

(*Enter Stephano.*)

STEPHANO: Madam, the habits are come, and your cousin Valeria is dressed and stays for you.

FLORINDA (*aside*): 'Tis well. I'll write a note, and if I chance to see Belvile and want an opportunity to speak to him, that shall let him know what I've 235 resolved in favor of him.

HELLENA: Come, let's in and dress us.   (*Exeunt.*)

Scene II

(*A long street. Enter Belvile, melancholy; Blunt and Frederick.*)

FREDERICK: Why, what the devil ails the colonel, in a time when all the world is gay to look like mere Lent thus? Hadst thou been long enough in Naples to have been in love, I should have sworn some such judgment had befallen thee. 5

BELVILE: No, I have made no new amours since I came to Naples.

FREDERICK: You have left none behind you in Paris?

BELVILE: Neither.

10 FREDERICK: I cannot divine the cause then, unless the old cause, the want of money.

BLUNT: And another old cause, the want of a wench. Would not that revive you?

BELVILE: You are mistaken, Ned.

15 BLUNT: Nay, 'adsheartlikins,° then thou'rt past cure.

FREDERICK: I have found it out: Thou hast renewed thy acquaintance with the lady that cost thee so many sighs at the siege of Pamplona — pox on't, what d'ye call her — her brother's a noble Span-
20 iard, nephew to the dead general. Florinda. Ay, Florinda. And will nothing serve thy turn but that damned virtuous woman, whom on my conscience thou lov'st in spite too, because thou seest little or no possibility of gaining her.

25 BELVILE: Thou art mistaken; I have int'rest enough in that lovely virgin's heart to make me proud and vain, were it not abated by the severity of a brother, who, perceiving my happiness —

FREDERICK: Has civilly forbid thee the house?

30 BELVILE: 'Tis so, to make way for a powerful rival, the Viceroy's son, who has the advantage of me in being a man of fortune, a Spaniard, and her broth-er's friend; which gives him liberty to make his court, whilst I have recourse only to letters and
35 distant looks from her window, which are as soft and kind as those which heaven sends down on penitents.

BLUNT: Heyday! 'Adsheartlikins, simile! By this light the man is quite spoiled. Fred, what the devil are
40 we made of that we cannot be thus concerned for a wench? 'Adsheartlikins, our Cupids are like the cooks of the camp: They can roast or boil a woman, but they have none of the fine tricks to set 'em off; no hogoes° to make the sauce pleasant
45 and the stomach sharp.

FREDERICK: I dare swear I have had a hundred as young, kind, and handsome as this Florinda; and dogs eat me if they were not as troublesome to me i'th' morning as they were welcome o'er night.

50 BLUNT: And yet I warrant he would not touch another woman if he might have her for nothing.

BELVILE: That's thy joy, a cheap whore.

BLUNT: Why, 'adsheartlikins, I love a frank soul. When did you ever hear of an honest woman that
55 took a man's money? I warrant 'em good ones. But gentlemen, you may be free; you have been kept so poor with parliaments and protectors that the little stock you have is not worth preserving.

But I thank my stars I had more grace than to
60 forfeit my estate by cavaliering.

BELVILE: Methinks only following the court should be sufficient to entitle 'em to that.

BLUNT: 'Adsheartlikins, they know I follow it to do it no good, unless they pick a hole in my coat for
65 lending you money now and then, which is a greater crime to my conscience, gentlemen, than to the commonwealth.

(*Enter Willmore.*)

WILLMORE: Ha! Dear Belvile! Noble colonel!

BELVILE: Willmore! Welcome ashore, my dear rover!
70 What happy wind blew us this good fortune?

WILLMORE: Let me salute my dear Fred, and then command me. — How is't, honest lad?

FREDERICK: Fair, sir, the old compliment, infinitely the better to see my dear mad Willmore again. Prithee,
75 why camest thou ashore? And where's the Prince?°

WILLMORE: He's well, and reigns still lord of the wat'ry element. I must aboard again within a day or two, and my business ashore was only to enjoy myself a little this Carnival.

80 BELVILE: Pray know our new friend, sir; he's but bash-ful, a raw traveler, but honest, stout, and one of us.   (*Embraces Blunt.*)

WILLMORE: That you esteem him gives him an int'rest here.

85 BLUNT: Your servant, sir.

WILLMORE: But well, faith, I'm glad to meet you again in a warm climate, where the kind sun has its godlike power still over the wine and women. Love and mirth are my business in Naples, and if I mis-
90 take not the place, here's an excellent market for chapmen° of my humor.

BELVILE: See, here be those kind merchants of love you look for.

(*Enter several men in masking habits, some playing on music, others dancing after; women dressed like courtesans, with papers pinned on their breasts, and baskets of flowers in their hands.*)

BLUNT: 'Adsheartlikins, what have we here?

FREDERICK: Now the game begins.   95

WILLMORE: Fine pretty creatures! May a stranger have leave to look and love? What's here? "Roses for every month"?   (*Reads the papers.*)

BLUNT: Roses for every month? What means that?

BELVILE: They are, or would have you think they're   100
courtesans, who here in Naples are to be hired by the month.

---

15. 'adsheartlikins: Expostulation equivalent to "As God loves us."   44. hogoes: Relishes.

75. Prince: Charles II, in exile on the Continent during the reign of Cromwell.   91. chapmen: Merchants, in this case merchants of love.

WILLMORE: Kind and obliging to inform us, pray
105 where do these roses grow? I would fain plant some
of 'em in a bed of mine.

WOMAN: Beware such roses, sir.

WILLMORE: A pox of fear: I'll be baked with thee
between a pair of sheets, and that's thy proper still;
so I might but strew such roses over me and under
110 me. Fair one, would you would give me leave to
gather at your bush this idle month; I would go
near to make somebody smell of it all the year
after.

BELVILE: And thou hast need of such a remedy, for
115 thou stink'st of tar and ropes' ends like a dock or
pesthouse.

(*The Woman puts herself into the hands of a*
man and exeunt.)

WILLMORE: Nay, nay, you shall not leave me so.

BELVILE: By all means use no violence here.

WILLMORE: Death! Just as I was going to be damnably
120 in love, to have her led off! I could pluck that rose
out of his hand, and even kiss the bed the bush
grew in.

FREDERICK: No friend to love like a long voyage at
sea.

125 BLUNT: Except a nunnery, Fred.

WILLMORE: Death! But will they not be kind? Quickly
be kind? Thou know'st I'm no tame sigher, but a
rampant lion of the forest.

(*Advances from the farther end of the scenes two men*
dressed all over with horns° of several sorts, making
grimaces at one another, with papers pinned on their
backs.)

BELVILE: Oh the fantastical rogues, how they're
130 dressed! 'Tis a satire against the whole sex.

WILLMORE: Is this a fruit that grows in this warm
country?

BELVILE: Yes, 'tis pretty to see these Italians start,
swell, and stab at the word cuckold, and yet
135 stumble at horns on every threshold.

WILLMORE: See what's on their back. (*Reads.*) "Flowers of every night." Ah, rogue! And more sweet
than roses of every month! This is a gardener of
Adam's own breeding.

(*They dance.*)

140 BELVILE: What think you of these grave people? Is a
wake in Essex half so mad or extravagant?

WILLMORE: I like their sober grave way; 'tis a kind
of legal authorized fornication, where the men are
not chid° for't, nor the women despised, as amongst

our dull English. Even the monsieurs° want that 145
part of good manners.

BELVILE: But here in Italy, a monsieur is the humblest
best-bred gentleman: Duels are so baffled by bravos
that an age shows not one but between a French-
man and a hangman, who is as much too hard for 150
him on the Piazza as they are for a Dutchman on
the New Bridge. But see, another crew.

(*Enter Florinda, Hellena, and Valeria, dressed like*
gypsies; Callis and Stephano, Lucetta, Philippo, and
Sancho in masquerade.)

HELLENA: Sister, there's your Englishman, and with
him a handsome proper fellow. I'll to him, and
instead of telling him his fortune, try my own. 155

WILLMORE: Gypsies, on my life. Sure these will prattle
if a man cross their hands.° (*Goes to Hellena.*) —
Dear, pretty, and, I hope, young devil, will you tell
an amorous stranger what luck he's like to have?

HELLENA: Have a care how you venture with me, sir, 160
lest I pick your pocket, which will more vex your
English humor than an Italian fortune will please
you.

WILLMORE: How the devil cam'st thou to know my
country and humor? 165

HELLENA: The first I guess by a certain forward impudence, which does not displease me at this time;
and the loss of your money will vex you because
I hope you have but very little to lose.

WILLMORE: Egad, child, thou'rt i'th' right; it is so 170
little I dare not offer it thee for a kindness. But
cannot you divine what other things of more value
I have about me that I would more willingly part
with?

HELLENA: Indeed no, that's the business of a witch, 175
and I am but a gypsy. Yet without looking in
your hand, I have a parlous° guess 'tis some foolish
heart you mean, an inconstant English heart, as
little worth stealing as your purse.

WILLMORE: Nay, then thou dost deal with the devil, 180
that's certain. Thou hast guessed as right as if thou
hadst been one of that number it has languished
for. I find you'll be better acquainted with it, nor
can you take it in a better time; for I am come
from sea, child, and Venus not being propitious to 185
me in her own element,° I have a world of love in
store. Would you would be good-natured and take
some on't° off my hands.

---

145. monsieurs: Frenchmen. **157. cross their hands:** Cross
their hands with silver: pay them to tell his fortune. **177.
parlous:** Dangerously cunning, clever (from *perilous*). **185–
86. Venus ... element:** Venus, the goddess of love, was
supposedly born from the foam of the sea. **188. on't:** Of
it.

128. [S.D.] horns: Emblem of the cuckold, a man whose
wife is unfaithful. **144. chid:** Chided, reproached.

HELLENA: Why, I could be inclined that way, but for
90   a foolish vow I am going to make to die a maid.
WILLMORE: Then thou art damned without redemption, and as I am a good Christian, I ought in
charity to divert so wicked a design. Therefore
prithee, dear creature, let me know quickly when
95   and where I shall begin to set a helping hand to
so good a work.
HELLENA: If you should prevail with my tender heart,
as I begin to fear you will, for you have horrible
loving eyes, there will be difficulty in't that you'll
00   hardly undergo for my sake.
WILLMORE: Faith, child, I have been bred in dangers,
and wear a sword that has been employed in a
worse cause than for a handsome kind woman.
Name the danger; let it be anything but a long
05   siege, and I'll undertake it.
HELLENA: Can you storm?
WILLMORE: Oh, most furiously.
HELLENA: What think you of a nunnery wall? For he
that wins me must gain that first.
10   WILLMORE: A nun! Oh, now I love thee for't! There's
no sinner like a young saint. Nay, now there's no
denying me; the old law had no curse to a woman
like dying a maid: Witness Jeptha's daughter.°
HELLENA: A very good text this, if well handled; and
15   I perceive, Father Captain, you would impose no
severe penance on her who were inclined to console
herself before she took orders.°
WILLMORE: If she be young and handsome.
HELLENA: Ay, there's it. But if she be not —
20   WILLMORE: By this hand, child, I have an implicit
faith, and dare venture on thee with all faults.
Besides, 'tis more meritorious to leave the world
when thou hast tasted and proved the pleasure on't.
Then 'twill be a virtue in thee, which now will be
225   pure ignorance.
HELLENA: I perceive, good Father Captain, you design
only to make me fit for heaven. But if, on the
contrary, you should quite divert me from it, and
bring me back to the world again, I should have
230   a new man to seek, I find. And what a grief that
will be; for when I begin, I fancy I shall love like
anything; I never tried yet.
WILLMORE: Egad, and that's kind! Prithee, dear creature, give me credit for a heart, for faith, I'm a

very honest fellow. Oh, I long to come first to the   235
banquet of love! And such a swinging appetite I
bring. Oh, I'm impatient. Thy lodging, sweetheart,
thy lodging, or I'm a dead man!
HELLENA: Why must we be either guilty of fornication
or murder if we converse with you men? And is   240
there no difference between leave to love me, and
leave to lie with me?
WILLMORE: Faith, child, they were made to go
together.
LUCETTA (*pointing to Blunt*): Are you sure this is   245
the man?
SANCHO: When did I mistake your game?
LUCETTA: This is a stranger, I know by his gazing; if
he be brisk he'll venture to follow me, and then,
if I understand my trade, he's mine. He's English,   250
too, and they say that's a sort of good-natured
loving people, and have generally so kind an opinion of themselves that a woman with any wit may
flatter 'em into any sort of fool she pleases.

(*She often passes by Blunt and gazes on him; he struts
and cocks, and walks and gazes on her.*)

BLUNT: 'Tis so, she is taken; I have beauties which   255
my false glass° at home did not discover.
FLORINDA (*aside*): This woman watches me so, I shall
get no opportunity to discover myself to him, and
so miss the intent of my coming. — [*To Belvile.*]
But as I was saying, sir, by this line you should be   260
a lover.   (*Looking in his hand.*)
BELVILE: I thought how right you guessed: All men
are in love, or pretend to be so. Come, let me go;
I'm weary of this fooling.   (*Walks away.*)
FLORINDA: I will not, sir, till you have confessed   265
whether the passion that you have vowed Florinda
be true or false.
                (*She holds him; he strives to get from her.*)
BELVILE: Florinda!   (*Turns quick toward her.*)
FLORINDA: Softly.
BELVILE: Thou hast nam'd one will fix me here forever.   270
FLORINDA: She'll be disappointed then, who expects
you this night at the garden gate. And if you fail
not, as — (*Looks on Callis, who observes 'em.*)
Let me see the other hand — you will go near to
do, she vows to die or make you happy.   275
BELVILE: What canst thou mean?
FLORINDA: That which I say. Farewell.
                        (*Offers to go.*)
BELVILE: O charming sibyl,° stay; complete that joy
which as it is will turn into distraction! Where must

---

213. Jeptha's daughter: To fulfill a vow, Jeptha sacrificed
his only child, a virgin daughter, whom he allowed to go
off to the mountains for two months to "bewail" her virginity
before he killed her. "And it became a custom in Israel that
the daughters of Israel went year by year to lament the
daughter of Jeptha . . . four days in the year" (Judges 11:39–
40).   **217. took orders:** Entered the convent.

256. false glass: Lying mirror.   **278. sibyl:** A female prophet;
fortune-teller.

280   I be? At the garden gate? I know it. At night, you
      say? I'll sooner forfeit heaven than disobey.

(*Enter Don Pedro and other maskers, and pass over the stage.*)

CALLIS: Madam, your brother's here.
FLORINDA: Take this to instruct you farther.
                              (*Gives him a letter, and goes off.*)
FREDERICK: Have a care, sir, what you promise; this
285   may be a trap laid by her brother to ruin you.
BELVILE: Do not disturb my happiness with doubts.
                              (*Opens the letter.*)
WILLMORE: My dear pretty creature, a thousand bless-
      ings on thee! Still in this habit, you say? And after
      dinner at this place?
290 HELLENA: Yes, if you will swear to keep your heart
      and not bestow it between this and that.
WILLMORE: By all the little gods of love, I swear; I'll
      leave it with you, and if you run away with it,
      those deities of justice will revenge me.
                    (*Exeunt all the women [except Lucetta].*)
295 FREDERICK: Do you know the hand?
BELVILE: 'Tis Florinda's.
      All blessings fall upon the virtuous maid.
FREDERICK: Nay, no idolatry; a sober sacrifice I'll al-
      low you.
300 BELVILE: Oh friends, the welcom'st news! The softest
      letter! Nay, you shall all see it. And could you now
      be serious, I might be made the happiest man the
      sun shines on!
WILLMORE: The reason of this mighty joy?
305 BELVILE: See how kindly she invites me to deliver her
      from the threatened violence of her brother. Will
      you not assist me?
WILLMORE: I know not what thou mean'st, but I'll
      make one at any mischief where a woman's con-
310   cerned. But she'll be grateful to us for the favor,
      will she not?
BELVILE: How mean you?
WILLMORE: How should I mean? Thou know'st
      there's but one way for a woman to oblige me.
315 BELVILE: Do not profane; the maid is nicely virtuous.
WILLMORE: Who, pox, then she's fit for nothing but
      a husband. Let her e'en go, colonel.
FREDERICK: Peace, she's the colonel's mistress, sir.
WILLMORE: Let her be the devil; if she be thy mistress,
320   I'll serve her. Name the way.
BELVILE: Read here this postscript.
                              (*Gives him a letter.*)
WILLMORE (*reads*): "At ten at night, at the garden
      gate, of which, if I cannot get the key, I will contrive
      a way over the wall. Come attended with a friend
325   or two." — Kind heart, if we three cannot weave
      a string to let her down a garden wall, 'twere pity
      but the hangman wove one for us all.

FREDERICK: Let her alone for that; your woman's wit,
      your fair kind woman, will outtrick a broker or
      a Jew, and contrive like a Jesuit° in chains. But   330
      see, Ned Blunt is stolen out after the lure of a
      damsel.   (*Exeunt Blunt and Lucetta.*)
BELVILE: So, he'll scarce find his way home again un-
      less we get him cried by the bellman in the market
      place. And 'twould sound prettily: "A lost English   335
      boy of thirty."
FREDERICK: I hope 'tis some common crafty sinner,
      one that will fit him. It may be she'll sell him for
      Peru:° The rogue's sturdy, and would work well
      in a mine. At least I hope she'll dress him for our   340
      mirth, cheat him of all, then have him well-
      favoredly banged, and turned out at midnight.
WILLMORE: Prithee what humor is he of, that you
      wish him so well?
BELVILE: Why, of an English elder brother's humor: 345
      educated in a nursery, with a maid to tend him till
      fifteen, and lies with his grandmother till he's of
      age; one that knows no pleasure beyond riding to
      the next fair, or going up to London with his right
      worshipful father in parliament time, wearing gay   350
      clothes, or making honorable love to his lady moth-
      er's laundry maid; gets drunk at a hunting match,
      and ten to one then gives some proofs of his prow-
      ess. A pox upon him, he's our banker, and has all
      our cash about him; and if he fail, we are all broke. 355
FREDERICK: Oh, let him alone for that matter; he's of
      a damned stingy quality that will secure our stock.
      I know not in what danger it were indeed if the
      jilt should pretend she's in love with him, for 'tis
      a kind believing coxcomb; otherwise, if he part   360
      with more than a piece of eight,° geld° him — for
      which offer he may chance to be beaten if she be
      a whore of the first rank.
BELVILE: Nay, the rogue will not be easily beaten; he's
      stout enough. Perhaps if they talk beyond his ca-   365
      pacity he may chance to exercise his courage upon
      some of them, else I'm sure they'll find it as difficult
      to beat as to please him.
WILLMORE: 'Tis a lucky devil to light upon so kind
      a wench!   370
FREDERICK: Thou hadst a great deal of talk with thy
      little gypsy; couldst thou do no good upon her?
      For mine was hardhearted.
WILLMORE: Hang her, she was some damned honest
      person of quality, I'm sure, she was so very free   375
      and witty. If her face be but answerable to her wit
      and humor, I would be bound to constancy this

---

330. **Jew . . . Jesuit:** Anti-Semitic and anti-Catholic attitudes of the time portrayed Jews and Jesuits as cunning and distrustful.   338–39. **sell him for Peru:** Sell him as a slave.   361. **piece of eight:** Spanish money.   **geld:** Castrate.

month to gain her. In the meantime, have you made
no kind acquaintance since you came to town? You
do not use to be honest° so long, gentlemen.

FREDERICK: Faith, love has kept us honest: We have
been all fir'd with a beauty newly come to town,
the famous Paduana° Angellica Bianca.

WILLMORE: What, the mistress of the dead Spanish
general?

BELVILE: Yes, she's now the only ador'd beauty of all
the youth in Naples, who put on all their charms
to appear lovely in her sight: Their coaches, liveries,
and themselves all gay as on a monarch's birthday
to attract the eyes of this fair charmer, while she
has the pleasure to behold all languish for her that
see her.

FREDERICK: 'Tis pretty to see with how much love the
men regard her, and how much envy the women.

WILLMORE: What gallant has she?

BELVILE: None; she's exposed to sale, and four days
in the week she's yours, for so much a month.

WILLMORE: The very thought of it quenches all manner of fire in me. Yet prithee, let's see her.

BELVILE: Let's first to dinner, and after that we'll pass
the day as you please. But at night ye must all be
at my devotion.

WILLMORE: I will not fail you.   [*Exeunt.*]

ACT II • *Scene 1*

(*The long street. Enter Belvile and Frederick in masking habits, and Willmore in his own clothes, with a
vizard° in his hand.*)

WILLMORE: But why thus disguised and muzzled?

BELVILE: Because whatever extravagances we commit
in these faces, our own may not be obliged to
answer 'em.

WILLMORE: I should have changed my eternal buff,°
too; but no matter, my little gypsy would not have
found me out then. For if she should change hers,
it is impossible I should know her unless I should
hear her prattle. A pox on't, I cannot get her out
of my head. Pray heaven, if ever I do see her again,
she prove damnably ugly, that I may fortify myself
against her tongue.

BELVILE: Have a care of love, for o' my conscience
she was not of a quality to give thee any hopes.

WILLMORE: Pox on 'em, why do they draw a man in
then? She has played with my heart so, that 'twill
never lie still till I have met with some kind wench

that will play the game out with me. Oh, for my
arms full of soft, white, kind woman — such as I
fancy Angellica.

BELVILE: This is her house, if you were but in stock
to get admittance. They have not dined yet; I perceive the picture is not out.°

(*Enter Blunt.*)

WILLMORE: I long to see the shadow of the fair substance; a man may gaze on that for nothing.

BLUNT: Colonel, thy hand. And thine, Fred. I have
been an ass, a deluded fool, a very coxcomb from
my birth till this hour, and heartily repent my little
faith.

BELVILE: What the devil's the matter with thee, Ned?

BLUNT: Oh, such a mistress, Fred! Such a girl!

WILLMORE: Ha! Where?

FREDERICK: Ay, where?

BLUNT: So fond, so amorous, so toying, and so fine!
And all for sheer love, ye rogue! Oh, how she
looked and kissed! And soothed my heart from my
bosom! I cannot think I was awake, and yet methinks I see and feel her charms still. Fred, try if
she have not left the taste of her balmy kisses upon
my lips.   (*Kisses him.*)

BELVILE: Ha! Ha! Ha!

WILLMORE: Death, man, where is she?

BLUNT: What a dog was I to stay in dull England so
long! How have I laughed at the colonel when he
sighed for love! But now the little archer° has revenged him! And by this one dart I can guess at
all his joys, which then I took for fancies, mere
dreams and fables. Well, I'm resolved to sell all in
Essex and plant here forever.

BELVILE: What a blessing 'tis, thou hast a mistress
thou dar'st boast of; for I know thy humor is rather
to have a proclaimed clap than a secret amour.

WILLMORE: Dost know her name?

BLUNT: Her name? No, 'adsheartlikins. What care I
for names? She's fair, young, brisk and kind, even
to ravishment! And what a pox care I for knowing
her by any other title?

WILLMORE: Didst give her anything?

BLUNT: Give her? Ha! Ha! Ha! Why, she's a person
of quality. That's a good one! Give her? 'Adsheartlikins, dost think such creatures are to be bought?
Or are we provided for such a purchase? Give her,
quoth ye? Why, she presented me with this bracelet
for the toy of a diamond I used to wear. No,
gentlemen, Ned Blunt is not everybody. She expects
me again tonight.

---

380. **honest:** Sexually inactive.   383. **Paduana:** Angellica
was born in Padua, Italy.   II. I. [S.D.] **vizard:** Face mask.
5. **buff:** Military coat made of buff (leather).

23. **picture is not out:** Hanging her picture outside the house
is a sign that she is open for business. (See lines 117–18
later in the scene.)   45. **little archer:** Cupid.

WILLMORE: Egad, that's well; we'll all go.

BLUNT: Not a soul! No, gentlemen, you are wits; I am a dull country rogue, I.

70 FREDERICK: Well, sir, for all your person of quality, I shall be very glad to understand your purse be secure; 'tis our whole estate at present, which we are loath to hazard in one bottom.° Come sir, unlade.

75 BLUNT: Take the necessary trifle useless now to me, that am beloved by such a gentlewoman. 'Adsheartlikins, money! Here, take mine too.

FREDERICK: No, keep that to be cozened,° that we may laugh.

80 WILLMORE: Cozened? Death! Would I could meet with one that would cozen me of all the love I could spare tonight.

FREDERICK: Pox, 'tis some common whore, upon my life.

85 BLUNT: A whore? Yes, with such clothes, such jewels, such a house, such furniture, and so attended! A whore!

BELVILE: Why yes, sir, they are whores, though they'll neither entertain you with drinking, swearing, or

90 bawdry; are whores in all those gay clothes and right° jewels; are whores with those great houses richly furnished with velvet beds, store of plate,° handsome attendance, and fine coaches; are whores, and errant° ones.

95 WILLMORE: Pox on't, where do these fine whores live?

BELVILE: Where no rogues in office, ycleped° constables, dare give 'em laws, nor the wine-inspired bullies of the town break their windows; yet they are whores though this Essex calf° believe 'em per-

100 sons of quality.

BLUNT: 'Adsheartlikins, y'are all fools. There are things about this Essex calf that shall take with the ladies, beyond all your wit and parts. This shape and size, gentlemen, are not to be despised; my

105 waist, too, tolerably long, with other inviting signs that shall be nameless.

WILLMORE: Egad, I believe he may have met with some person of quality that may be kind to him.

BELVILE: Dost thou perceive any such tempting things

110 about him that should make a fine woman, and of quality, pick him out from all mankind to throw away her youth and beauty upon; nay, and her dear heart, too? No, no, Angellica has raised the price too high.

WILLMORE: May she languish for mankind till she die, 11 and be damned for that one sin alone.

(*Enter two Bravos and hang up a great picture of Angellica's against the balcony, and two little ones at each side of the door.*)

BELVILE: See there the fair sign to the inn where a man may lodge that's fool enough to give her price.
(*Willmore gazes on the picture.*)

BLUNT: 'Adsheartlikins, gentlemen, what's this?

BELVILE: A famous courtesan, that's to be sold.   12

BLUNT: How? To be sold? Nay, then I have nothing to say to her. Sold? What impudence is practiced in this country; with what order and decency whoring's established here by virtue of the Inquisition!° Come, let's be gone; I'm sure we're no chapmen 12 for this commodity.

FREDERICK: Thou art none, I'm sure, unless thou couldst have her in thy bed at a price of a coach in the street.

WILLMORE: How wondrous fair she is! A thousand 13 crowns a month? By heaven, as many kingdoms were too little! A plague of this poverty, of which I ne'er complain but when it hinders my approach to beauty which virtue ne'er could purchase.
(*Turns from the picture.*)

BLUNT: What's this? (*Reads.*) "A thousand crowns a 13 month"! 'Adsheartlikins, here's a sum! Sure 'tis a mistake. — [*To one of the Bravos.*] Hark you, friend, does she take or give so much by the month?

FREDERICK: A thousand crowns! Why, 'tis a portion for the Infanta!°   14

BLUNT: Hark ye, friends, won't she trust?°

BRAVO: This is a trade, sir, that cannot live by credit.

(*Enter Don Pedro in masquerade, followed by Stephano.*)

BELVILE: See, here's more company; let's walk off a while.
(*Exeunt English;° Pedro reads.*)

PEDRO: Fetch me a thousand crowns; I never wished 14 to buy this beauty at an easier rate. (*Passes off.*)

(*Enter Angellica and Moretta in the balcony, and draw a silk curtain.*)

ANGELLICA: Prithee, what said those fellows to thee?

BRAVO: Madam, the first were admirers of beauty only, but no purchasers; they were merry with your

---

73. **hazard in one bottom:** Keep in one place, as in the hold (bottom) of a ship.   78. **cozened:** Cheated.   91. **right:** Real.   92. **plate:** Silverware.   94. **errant:** Unmitigated.   96. **ycleped:** Past participle of *clepe*: called.   99. **Essex calf:** Derogatory term meaning "fool," referring to Essex, England, Blunt's home.

124. **Inquisition:** The Spanish Inquisition (1478–1834) forced prostitutes out of Spain and into neighboring countries.   139–40. **portion for the Infanta:** Dowry for the Spanish princess.   141. **trust:** Extend credit for payment.   144. [S.D.] **English:** All the English characters.

50 price and picture, laughed at the sum, and so passed
off.

ANGELLICA: No matter, I'm not displeased with their
rallying; their wonder feeds my vanity, and he that
55 wishes but to buy gives me more pride than he
that gives my price can make my pleasure.

BRAVO: Madam, the last I knew through all his disguises to be Don Pedro, nephew to the general,
and who was with him in Pamplona.

ANGELLICA: Don Pedro? My old gallant's nephew?
60 When his uncle died he left him a vast sum of
money; it is he who was so in love with me at
Padua, and who used to make the general so
jealous.

MORETTA: Is this he that used to prance before our
65 window, and take such care to show himself an
amorous ass? If I am not mistaken, he is the likeliest
man to give your price.

ANGELLICA: The man is brave and generous, but of a
humor so uneasy and inconstant that the victory
70 over his heart is as soon lost as won; a slave that
can add little to the triumph of the conqueror. But
inconstancy's the sin of all mankind, therefore I'm
resolved that nothing but gold shall charm my
heart.

75 MORETTA: I'm glad on't; 'tis only interest that women
of our profession ought to consider, though I wonder what has kept you from that general disease
of our sex so long; I mean, that of being in love.

ANGELLICA: A kind but sullen star under which I had
80 the happiness to be born. Yet I have had no time
for love; the bravest and noblest of mankind have
purchased my favors at so dear a rate, as if no coin
but gold were current with our trade. But here's
Don Pedro again; fetch me my lute, for 'tis for him
85 or Don Antonio the Viceroy's son that I have
spread my nets.

(*Enter at one door Don Pedro, Stephano; Don Antonio and Diego [his page] at the other door, with
people following him in masquerade, antically attired,
some with music. They both go up to the picture.*)

ANTONIO: A thousand crowns! Had not the painter
flattered her, I should not think it dear.

PEDRO: Flattered her? By heaven, he cannot. I have
190 seen the original, nor is there one charm here more
than adorns her face and eyes; all this soft and
sweet, with a certain languishing air that no artist
can represent.

ANTONIO: What I heard of her beauty before had fired
195 my soul, but this confirmation of it has blown it
to a flame.

PEDRO: Ha!

PAGE: Sir, I have known you throw away a thousand
crowns on a worse face, and though y'are near

your marriage, you may venture a little love here; 200
Florinda will not miss it.

PEDRO (*aside*): Ha! Florinda! Sure 'tis Antonio.

ANTONIO: Florinda! Name not those distant joys;
there's not one thought of her will check my passion here. 205

PEDRO [*aside*]: Florinda scorned! (*A noise of a lute
above.*) And all my hopes defeated of the possession
of Angellica! (*Antonio gazes up.*) Her injuries, by
heaven, he shall not boast of!
(*Song to a lute above.*)

SONG
[I]
When Damon first began to love 210
He languished in a soft desire,
And knew not how the gods to move,
To lessen or increase his fire.
For Caelia in her charming eyes
Wore all love's sweets, and all his cruelties. 215

II
But as beneath a shade he lay,
Weaving of flowers for Caelia's hair,
She chanced to lead her flock that way,
And saw the am'rous shepherd there.
She gazed around upon the place, 220
And saw the grove, resembling night,
To all the joys of love invite,
Whilst guilty smiles and blushes dressed her face.
At this the bashful youth all transport grew,
And with kind force he taught the virgin how 225
To yield what all his sighs could never do.

(*Angellica throws open the curtains and bows to Antonio, who pulls off his vizard and bows and blows
up kisses. Pedro, unseen, looks in's face. [The curtains
close.]*)

ANTONIO: By heaven, she's charming fair!

PEDRO (*aside*): 'Tis he, the false Antonio!

ANTONIO (*to the Bravo*): Friend, where must I pay
my off'ring of love?
My thousand crowns I mean. 230

PEDRO: That off'ring I have designed to make,
And yours will come too late.

ANTONIO: Prithee begone; I shall grow angry else,
And then thou art not safe.

PEDRO: My anger may be fatal, sir, as yours, 235
And he that enters here may prove this truth.

ANTONIO: I know not who thou art, but I am sure
thou'rt worth my killing, for aiming at Angellica.
(*They draw and fight.*)

(*Enter Willmore and Blunt, who draw and part 'em.*)

BLUNT: 'Adsheartlikins, here's fine doings.

WILLMORE: Tilting for the wench, I'm sure. Nay, gad, 240
if that would win her I have as good a sword as

the best of ye. Put up, put up, and take another
time and place, for this is designed for lovers
only.   (*They all put up.*)

PEDRO: We are prevented; dare you meet me
245   tomorrow on the Molo?°
For I've a title to a better quarrel,
That of Florinda, in whose credulous heart
Thou'st made an int'rest, and destroyed my
hopes.

ANTONIO: Dare!
250   I'll meet thee there as early as the day.

PEDRO: We will come thus disguised, that whosoever
chance to get the better, he may escape unknown.

ANTONIO: It shall be so.
(*Exeunt Pedro and Stephano.*)
255   — Who should this rival be? Unless the English
colonel, of whom I've often heard Don Pedro
speak. It must be he, and time he were removed
who lays a claim to all my happiness.

(*Willmore, having gazed all this while on the picture[s], pulls down a little one.*)

WILLMORE: This posture's loose and negligent;
The sight on't would beget a warm desire
260   In souls whom impotence and age had chilled.
This must along with me.

BRAVO: What means this rudeness, sir? Restore the
picture.

ANTONIO: Ha! Rudeness committed to the fair An-
265   gellica! — Restore the picture, sir.

WILLMORE: Indeed I will not, sir.

ANTONIO: By heaven, but you shall.

WILLMORE: Nay, do not show your sword; if you do,
by this dear beauty, I will show mine too.

270   ANTONIO: What right can you pretend to't?

WILLMORE: That of possession, which I will maintain.
You, perhaps, have a thousand crowns to give for
the original.

ANTONIO: No matter, sir, you shall restore the picture.

([*The curtains open.*] *Angellica and Moretta above.*)

275   ANGELLICA: Oh, Moretta, what's the matter?

ANTONIO: Or leave your life behind.

WILLMORE: Death! You lie; I will do neither.

(*They fight. The Spaniards join with Antonio, Blunt
laying on like mad.*)

ANGELLICA: Hold, I command you, if for me you fight.
(*They leave off and bow.*)

WILLMORE [*aside*]: How heavenly fair she is! Ah,
280   plague of her price!

ANGELLICA: You sir, in buff, you that appear a soldier,
that first began this insolence —

245. **Molo:** Wharf.

WILLMORE: 'Tis true, I did so, if you call it insolence
for a man to preserve himself. I saw your charming
picture and was wounded; quite through my soul   285
each pointed beauty ran; and wanting a thousand
crowns to procure my remedy, I laid this little
picture to my bosom, which, if you cannot allow
me, I'll resign.

ANGELLICA: No, you may keep the trifle.   290

ANTONIO: You shall first ask me leave, and this.
(*Fight again as before.*)

(*Enter Belvile and Frederick, who join with the
English.*)

ANGELLICA: Hold! Will you ruin me? — Biskey! Sebastian! Part 'em!
(*The Spaniards are beaten off.*)

MORETTA: Oh, madam, we're undone. A pox upon
that rude fellow; he's set on to ruin us. We shall   295
never see good days again till all these fighting poor
rogues are sent to the galleys.

(*Enter Belvile, Blunt, Frederick, and Willmore with's
shirt bloody.*)

BLUNT: 'Adsheartlikins, beat me at this sport and I'll
ne'er wear sword more.

BELVILE (*to Willmore*): The devil's in thee for a mad   300
fellow; thou art always one at an unlucky adventure. Come, let's be gone whilst we're safe, and
remember these are Spaniards, a sort of people that
know how to revenge an affront.

FREDERICK: You bleed! I hope you are not wounded.   305

WILLMORE: Not much. A plague on your dons; if they
fight no better they'll ne'er recover Flanders.° What
the devil was't to them that I took down the
picture?

BLUNT: Took it! 'Adsheartlikins, we'll have the great   310
one too; 'tis ours by conquest. Prithee help me up
and I'll pull it down.

ANGELLICA [*to Willmore*]: Stay, sir, and ere you affront me farther let me know how you durst commit this outrage. To you I speak, sir, for you appear   315
a gentleman.

WILLMORE: To me, madam? — Gentlemen, your
servant.
(*Belvile stays him.°*)

BELVILE: Is the devil in thee? Dost know the danger
of ent'ring the house of an incensed courtesan?   320

WILLMORE: I thank you for your care, but there are
other matters in hand, there are, though we have
no great temptation. Death! Let me go!

307. **ne'er recover Flanders:** In 1659, the Spanish gave Flan-
ders, which had been part of the Spanish Netherlands, to
France as settlement to end a war.   318. [S.D.] *stays him*:
Keeps him from leaving.

25 FREDERICK: Yes, to your lodging if you will, but not
in here. Damn these gay harlots; by this hand I'll
have as sound and handsome a whore for a patacoon.° Death, man, she'll murder thee!

WILLMORE: Oh, fear me not. Shall I not venture where
30 a beauty calls? A lovely charming beauty! For fear
of danger? When, by heaven, there's none so great
as to long for her whilst I want money to purchase
her.

FREDERICK: Therefore 'tis loss of time unless you had
the thousand crowns to pay.

35 WILLMORE: It may be she may give a favor; at least
I shall have the pleasure of saluting her when I
enter and when I depart.

BELVILE: Pox, she'll as soon lie with thee as kiss thee,
and sooner stab than do either. You shall not go.

40 ANGELLICA: Fear not, sir, all I have to wound with is
my eyes.

BLUNT: Let him go. 'Adsheartlikins, I believe the
gentlewoman means well.

BELVILE: Well, take thy fortune; we'll expect you in
45 the next street. Farewell, fool, farewell.

WILLMORE: 'Bye, colonel.   (*Goes in.*)

FREDERICK: The rogue's stark mad for a wench.

                                                      (*Exeunt.*)

Scene II

(*A fine chamber. Enter Willmore, Angellica, and
Moretta.*)

ANGELLICA: Insolent sir, how durst you pull down my
picture?

WILLMORE: Rather, how durst you set it up to tempt
poor am'rous mortals with so much excellence,
5 which I find you have but too well consulted by
the unmerciful price you set upon't. Is all this
heaven of beauty shown to move despair in those
that cannot buy? And can you think th'effects of
that despair should be less extravagant than I have
10 shown?

ANGELLICA: I sent for you to ask my pardon, sir, not
to aggravate your crime. I thought I should have
seen you at my feet imploring it.

WILLMORE: You are deceived. I came to rail at you,
15 and rail such truths too, as shall let you see the
vanity of that pride which taught you how to set
such price on sin.
For such it is whilst that which is love's due
Is meanly bartered for.

20 ANGELLICA: Ha! Ha! Ha! Alas, good captain, what

pity 'tis your edifying doctrine will do no good
upon me. Moretta, fetch the gentleman a glass,°
and let him survey himself to see what charms he
has. — (*Aside, in a soft tone.*) And guess my
business.   25

MORETTA: He knows himself of old: I believe those
breeches and he have been acquainted ever since
he was beaten at Worcester.°

ANGELLICA: Nay, do not abuse the poor creature.

MORETTA: Good weather-beaten corporal, will you   30
march off? We have no need of your doctrine,
though you have of our charity. But at present we
have no scraps; we can afford no kindness for
God's sake. In fine, sirrah, the price is too high
i'th' mouth° for you, therefore troop, I say.   35

WILLMORE: Here, good forewoman of the shop, serve
me and I'll be gone.

MORETTA: Keep it to pay your laundress; your linen
stinks of the gun room. For here's no selling by
retail.   40

WILLMORE: Thou hast sold plenty of thy stale ware
at a cheap rate.

MORETTA: Ay, the more silly kind heart I, but this is
an age wherein beauty is at higher rates. In fine,
you know the price of this.   45

WILLMORE: I grant you 'tis here set down, a thousand
crowns a month. Pray, how much may come to
my share for a pistole?° Bawd, take your black
lead° and sum it up, that I may have a pistole's
worth of this vain gay thing, and I'll trouble you   50
no more.

MORETTA: Pox on him, he'll fret me to death! Abominable fellow, I tell thee we only sell by the whole
piece.

WILLMORE: 'Tis very hard, the whole cargo or noth-   55
ing. Faith, madam, my stock will not reach it; I
cannot be your chapman. Yet I have countrymen
in town, merchants of love like me; I'll see if they'll
put in for a share. We cannot lose much by it, and
what we have no use for, we'll sell upon the Fri-   60
day's mart at "Who gives more?" — I am studying,
madam, how to purchase you, though at present
I am unprovided of money.

ANGELLICA (*aside*): Sure this from any other man
would anger me; nor shall he know the conquest   65
he has made. — Poor angry man, how I despise
this railing.

WILLMORE: Yes, I am poor. But I'm a gentleman,

326–27. patacoon: Portuguese or Spanish coin of small
denomination.

22. glass: Mirror. **28. Worcester:** Charles II was routed by
Cromwell at Worcester in 1651 and was forced into exile
on the Continent. **34–35. high i'th' mouth:** High. **47–
48. how much . . . pistole:** How much will my pistole (a
Spanish coin) buy? **48–49. black lead:** Pencil.

And one that scorns this baseness which you
 practice.

70 Poor as I am I would not sell myself,
 No, not to gain your charming high-prized
 person.
 Though I admire you strangely for your beauty,
 Yet I contemn your mind.
 And yet I would at any rate enjoy you;
75 At your own rate; but cannot. See here
 The only sum I can command on earth:
 I know not where to eat when this is gone.
 Yet such a slave I am to love and beauty
 This last reserve I'll sacrifice to enjoy you.
80 Nay, do not frown, I know you're to be bought,
 And would be bought by me. By me,
 For a meaning trifling sum, if I could pay it
 down.
 Which happy knowledge I will still repeat,
 And lay it to my heart: It has a virtue in't,
 And soon will cure those wounds your eyes have
85 made.
 And yet, there's something so divinely powerful
 there —
 Nay, I will gaze, to let you see my strength.

(*Holds her, looks on her, and pauses and sighs.*)

By heav'n, bright creature, I would not for the
 world
 Thy fame were half so fair as is thy face.
                         (*Turns her away from him.*)
ANGELLICA (*aside*): His words go through me to the
90 very soul. —
 If you have nothing else to say to me —
WILLMORE: Yes, you shall hear how infamous you
 are —
 For which I do not hate thee —
 But that secures my heart, and all the flames it
 feels
95 Are but so many lusts:
 I know it by their sudden bold intrusion.
 The fire's impatient and betrays; 'tis false.
 For had it been the purer flame of love,
 I should have pined and languished at your feet,
100 Ere found the impudence to have discovered it.
 I now dare stand your scorn and your denial.
MORETTA: Sure she's bewitched, that she can stand
 thus tamely and hear his saucy railing. — Sirrah,
 will you be gone?
105 ANGELLICA (*to Moretta*): How dare you take this liberty! Withdraw! — Pray tell me, sir, are not you
 guilty of the same mercenary crime? When a lady
 is proposed to you for a wife, you never ask how
 fair, discreet, or virtuous she is, but what's her
110 fortune; which, if but small, you cry "She will not

do my business," and basely leave her, though she
 languish for you. Say, is not this as poor?
WILLMORE: It is a barbarous custom, which I will
 scorn to defend in our sex, and do despise in yours.
ANGELLICA: Thou'rt a brave fellow! Put up thy
 gold, and know,   115
 That were thy fortune as large as is thy soul,
 Thou shouldst not buy my love
 Couldst thou forget those mean effects of vanity
 Which set me out to sale,
 And as a lover prize my yielding joys.   120
 Canst thou believe they'll be entirely thine,
 Without considering they were mercenary?
WILLMORE: I cannot tell, I must bethink me first.
 (*Aside.*) Ha! Death, I'm going to believe her.
ANGELLICA: Prithee confirm that faith, or if thou
 canst not,   125
 Flatter me a little: 'Twill please me from thy
 mouth.
WILLMORE (*aside*): Curse on thy charming tongue!
 Dost thou return
 My feigned contempt with so much subtlety? —
 Thou'st found the easiest way into my heart,
 Though I yet know that all thou say'st is false. 130
                         (*Turning from her in rage.*)
ANGELLICA: By all that's good, 'tis real;
 I never loved before, though oft a mistress.
 Shall my first vows be slighted?
WILLMORE (*aside*): What can she mean?
ANGELLICA (*in an angry tone*): I find you cannot
 credit me.   135
WILLMORE: I know you take me for an errant ass,
 An ass that may be soothed into belief,
 And then be used at pleasure;
 But, madam, I have been so often cheated
 By perjured, soft, deluding hypocrites,   140
 That I've no faith left for the cozening sex,
 Especially for women of your trade.
ANGELLICA: The low esteem you have of me
 perhaps
May bring my heart again:
For I have pride that yet surmounts my love.   145
                         (*She turns with pride; he holds her.*)
WILLMORE: Throw off this pride, this enemy to
 bliss,
 And show the power of love: 'Tis with those
 arms
 I can be only vanquished, made a slave.
ANGELLICA: Is all my mighty expectation vanished?
 No, I will not hear thee talk; thou hast a charm   150
 In every word that draws my heart away,
 And all the thousand trophies I designed
 Thou hast undone. Why art thou soft?
 Thy looks are bravely rough, and meant for war.

55   Couldst thou not storm on still?
      I then perhaps had been as free as thou.
WILLMORE (*aside*): Death, how she throws her fire
      about my soul! —
    Take heed, fair creature, how you raise my
      hopes,
    Which once assumed pretends to all dominion:
60   There's not a joy thou hast in store
    I shall not then command.
    For which I'll pay you back my soul, my life!
    Come, let's begin th'account this happy minute!
ANGELLICA: And will you pay me then the price I
    ask?
WILLMORE: Oh, why dost thou draw me from an
65   awful worship,
    By showing thou art no divinity.
    Conceal the fiend, and show me all the angel!
    Keep me but ignorant, and I'll be devout
    And pay my vows forever at this shrine.
                (*Kneels and kisses her hand.*)
ANGELLICA: The pay I mean is but thy love for
70   mine.
    Can you give that?
WILLMORE: Entirely. Come, let's withdraw where I'll
    renew my vows, and breathe 'em with such ardor
    thou shalt not doubt my zeal.
75 ANGELLICA: Thou hast a power too strong to be
    resisted.
             (*Exeunt Willmore and Angellica.*)
MORETTA: Now my curse go with you! Is all our
    project fallen to this? To love the only enemy to
    our trade? Nay, to love such a shameroon;° a very
80   beggar; nay, a pirate beggar, whose business is to
    rifle and be gone; a no-purchase, no-pay tatter-
    demalion,° and English picaroon;° a rogue that
    fights for daily drink, and takes a pride in being
    loyally lousy? Oh, I could curse now, if I durst.
85   This is the fate of most whores.
     Trophies, which from believing fops we win,
     Are spoils to those who cozen us again. [*Exit.*]

ACT III · Scene I

(*A street. Enter Florinda, Valeria, Hellena, in antic°
different dresses from what they were in before; Callis
attending.*)

FLORINDA: I wonder what should make my brother
    in so ill a humor? I hope he has not found out our
    ramble this morning.

HELLENA: No, if he had, we should have heard on't
    at both ears, and have been mewed up° this after- 5
    noon, which I would not for the world should have
    happened. Hey ho, I'm as sad as a lover's lute.
VALERIA: Well, methinks we have learnt this trade of
    gypsies as readily as if we had been bred upon the
    road to Loretto;° and yet I did so fumble when I 10
    told the stranger his fortune that I was afraid I
    should have told my own and yours by mistake.
    But methinks Hellena has been very serious ever
    since.
FLORINDA: I would give my garters she were in love, 15
    to be revenged upon her for abusing me. How is't,
    Hellena?
HELLENA: Ah, would I had never seen my mad mon-
    sieur. And yet, for all your laughing, I am not in
    love. And yet this small acquaintance, o' my con- 20
    science, will never out of my head.
VALERIA: Ha! Ha! Ha! I laugh to think how thou art
    fitted with a lover, a fellow that I warrant loves
    every new face he sees.
HELLENA: Hum, he has not kept his word with me 25
    here, and may be taken up. That thought is not
    very pleasant to me. What the deuce should this
    be now that I feel?
VALERIA: What is't like?
HELLENA: Nay, the Lord knows, but if I should be 30
    hanged I cannot choose but be angry and afraid
    when I think that mad fellow should be in love
    with anybody but me. What to think of myself I
    know not: Would I could meet with some true
    damned gypsy, that I might know my fortune. 35
VALERIA: Know it! Why there's nothing so easy: Thou
    wilt love this wand'ring inconstant till thou find'st
    thyself hanged about his neck, and then be as mad
    to get free again.
FLORINDA: Yes, Valeria, we shall see her bestride his 40
    baggage horse and follow him to the campaign.
HELLENA: So, so, now you are provided for there's
    no care taken of poor me. But since you have set
    my heart a-wishing, I am resolved to know for
    what; I will not die of the pip,° so I will not. 45
FLORINDA: Art thou mad to talk so? Who will like
    thee well enough to have thee, that hears what a
    mad wench thou art?
HELLENA: Like me? I don't intend every he that likes
    me shall have me, but he that I like. I should have 50
    stayed in the nunnery still if I had liked my lady

---

179. shameroon: Shameful person. **181–82. tatterdemalion:** Ragamuffin. **182. picaroon:** Wandering rogue. **III.
I. [S.D.] antic:** Absurd, ludicrous, strange.

5. mewed up: Shut in, imprisoned. **10. Loretto:** Loreto is
an Italian town on the Adriatic coast, a destination for pil-
grims visiting the cottage of the Virgin Mary. **45. pip:** A
disease of poultry and birds, applied vaguely, usually hu-
morously, to various ailments in humans.

abbess as well as she liked me. No, I came thence not, as my wise brother imagines, to take an eternal farewell of the world, but to love and to be beloved; and I will be beloved, or I'll get one of your men, so I will.

VALERIA: Am I put into° the number of lovers?

HELLENA: You? Why, coz, I know thou'rt too good-natured to leave us in any design; thou wouldst venture a cast° though thou comest off a loser, especially with such a gamester. I observed your man, and your willing ear incline that way; and if you are not a lover, 'tis an art soon learnt — that I find. *(Sighs.)*

FLORINDA: I wonder how you learnt to love so easily. I had a thousand charms to meet my eyes and ears ere I could yield, and 'twas the knowledge of Belvile's merit, not the surprising person, took my soul. Thou art too rash, to give a heart at first sight.

HELLENA: Hang your considering lover! I never thought beyond the fancy that 'twas a very pretty, idle, silly kind of pleasure to pass one's time with: to write little soft nonsensical billets,° and with great difficulty and danger receive answers in which I shall have my beauty praised, my wit admired, though little or none, and have the vanity and power to know I am desirable. Then I have the more inclination that way because I am to be a nun, and so shall not be suspected to have any such earthly thoughts about me; but when I walk thus — and sigh thus — they'll think my mind's upon my monastery, and cry, "How happy 'tis she's so resolved." But not a word of man.

FLORINDA: What a mad creature's this!

HELLENA: I'll warrant, if my brother hears either of you sigh, he cries gravely, "I fear you have the indiscretion to be in love, but take heed of the honor of our house, and your own unspotted fame"; and so he conjures on till he has laid the soft winged god in your hearts, or broke the bird's nest.° But see, here comes your lover, but where's my inconstant? Let's step aside, and we may learn something.

(Go aside.)

(Enter Belvile, Frederick, and Blunt.)

BELVILE: What means this! The picture's taken in.

BLUNT: It may be the wench is good-natured, and will be kind gratis.° Your friend's a proper handsome fellow.

BELVILE: I rather think she has cut his throat and is fled; I am mad he should throw himself into dangers. Pox on't, I shall want him, too, at night. Let's knock and ask for him.

HELLENA: My heart goes a-pit, a-pat, for fear 'tis my man they talk of.

(Knock; Moretta above.)

MORETTA: What would you have?

BELVILE: Tell the stranger that entered here about two hours ago that his friends stay here for him.

MORETTA: A curse upon him for Moretta: Would he were at the devil! But he's coming to you.

(Enter Willmore.)

HELLENA: Ay, ay 'tis he. Oh, how this vexes me!

BELVILE: And how and how, dear lad, has fortune smiled? Are we to break her windows, or raise up altars to her, hah?

WILLMORE: Does not my fortune sit triumphant on my brow? Dost not see the little wanton god there all gay and smiling? Have I not an air about my face and eyes that distinguish me from the crowd of common lovers? By heaven, Cupid's quiver has not half so many darts as her eyes! Oh, such a *bona roba!*° To sleep in her arms is lying *in fresco,*° all perfumed air about me.

HELLENA *(aside)*: Here's fine encouragement for me to fool on!

WILLMORE: Hark'ee, where didst thou purchase that rich Canary° we drank today? Tell me, that I may adore the spigot and sacrifice to the butt.° The juice was divine; into which I must dip my rosary, and then bless all things that I would have bold or fortunate.

BELVILE: Well, sir, let's go take a bottle and hear the story of your success.

FREDERICK: Would not French wine do better?

WILLMORE: Damn the hungry balderdash!° Cheerful sack° has a generous virtue in't inspiring a successful confidence, gives eloquence to the tongue and vigor to the soul, and has in a few hours completed all my hopes and wishes! There's nothing left to raise a new desire in me. Come, let's be gay and wanton. And, gentlemen, study; study what you want, for here are friends that will supply gentlemen. [*Jingles gold.*] Hark what a charming sound they make! 'Tis he and she gold whilst here, and shall beget new pleasures every moment.

BLUNT: But hark'ee, sir, you are not married, are you?

---

57. **Am I put into:** Do you include me among?   60. **venture a cast:** Throw the dice.   74. **billets:** Brief letters, notes.   90–92. **laid . . . bird's nest:** Ruined your chances.   97. **gratis:** Free of charge.

120. *bona roba:* A courtesan.   *in fresco:* In the fresh air; out of doors.   125. **Canary:** A light sweet wine from the Canary Islands.   126. **butt:** Large wine cask.   133. **hungry balderdash:** Cheap mixture of liquor.   134. **sack:** Dry white Spanish wine.

45   WILLMORE: All the honey of matrimony but none of
         the sting, friend.
     BLUNT: 'Adsheartlikins, thou'rt a fortunate rogue!
     WILLMORE: I am so, sir: let these inform you! Ha,
         how sweetly they chime! Pox of poverty: It makes
50   a man a slave, makes wit and honor sneak. My
         soul grew lean and rusty for want of credit.
     BLUNT: 'Adsheartlikins, this I like well; it looks like
         my lucky bargain! Oh, how I long for the approach
         of my squire, that is to conduct me to her house
55   again. Why, here's two provided for!
     FREDERICK: By this light, y'are happy men.
     BLUNT: Fortune is pleased to smile on us, gentlemen,
         to smile on us.

     (Enter Sancho and pulls down Blunt by the sleeve;
     they go aside.)

     SANCHO: Sir, my lady expects you. She has removed
60   all that might oppose your will and pleasure, and
         is impatient till you come.
     BLUNT: Sir, I'll attend you. — Oh the happiest rogue!
         I'll take no leave, lest they either dog me or stay
         me.
                                 (Exit with Sancho.)
65   BELVILE: But then the little gypsy is forgot?
     WILLMORE: A mischief on thee for putting her into
         my thoughts! I had quite forgot her else, and this
         night's debauch had drunk her quite down.
     HELLENA: Had it so, good captain!
                                 (Claps him on the back.)
70   WILLMORE (aside): Ha! I hope she did not hear me!
     HELLENA: What, afraid of such a champion?
     WILLMORE: Oh, you're a fine lady of your word, are
         you not? To make a man languish a whole day —
     HELLENA: In tedious search of me.
75   WILLMORE: Egad, child, thou'rt in the right. Hadst
         thou seen what a melancholy dog I have been ever
         since I was a lover, how I have walked the streets
         like a Capuchin,° with my hands in my sleeves —
         faith, sweetheart, thou wouldst pity me.
80   HELLENA [aside]: Now if I should be hanged I can't
         be angry with him, he dissembles so heartily. —
         Alas, good captain, what pains you have taken;
         now were I ungrateful not to reward so true a
         servant.
85   WILLMORE: Poor soul, that's kindly said; I see thou
         barest a conscience. Come then, for a beginning
         show my thy dear face.
     HELLENA: I'm afraid, my small acquaintance, you have
         been staying that swinging stomach you boasted
90   of this morning. I then remember my little colla-

tion° would have gone down with you without the
sauce of a handsome face. Is your stomach so
queasy now?
WILLMORE: Faith, long fasting, child, spoils a man's
     appetite. Yet if you durst treat, I could so lay about   195
     me still —
HELLENA: And would you fall to before a priest says
     grace?
WILLMORE: O fie, fie, what an old out-of-fashioned
     thing hast thou named? Thou couldst not dash me   200
     more out of countenance shouldst thou show me
     an ugly face.

(Whilst he is seemingly courting Hellena, enter Angellica, Moretta, Biskey, and Sebastian, all in masquerade. Angellica sees Willmore and stares.)

ANGELLICA: Heavens, 'tis he! And passionately fond
     to see another woman!
MORETTA: What could you less expect from such a   205
     swaggerer?
ANGELLICA: Expect? As much as I paid him: a
         heart entire,
     Which I had pride enough to think when'er I
         gave,
     It would have raised the man above the vulgar,
     Made him all soul, and that all soft and
         constant.   210
HELLENA: You see, captain, how willing I am to be
     friends with you, till time and ill luck make us
     lovers; and ask you the question first rather than
     put your modesty to the blush by asking me. For
     alas, I know you captains are such strict men, and   215
     such severe observers of your vows to chastity, that
     'twill be hard to prevail with your tender con-
     science to marry a young willing maid.
WILLMORE: Do not abuse me, for fear I should take
     thee at thy word and marry thee indeed, which I'm   220
     sure will be revenge sufficient.
HELLENA: O' my conscience, that will be our destiny,
     because we are both of one humor: I am as in-
     constant as you, for I have considered, captain,
     that a handsome woman has a great deal to do   225
     whilst her face is good. For then is our harvest-
     time to gather friends, and should I in these days
     of my youth catch a fit of foolish constancy, I were
     undone: 'tis loitering by daylight in our great jour-
     ney. Therefore, I declare I'll allow but one year for   230
     love, one year for indifference, and one year for
     hate; and then go hang yourself, for I profess myself
     the gay, the kind, and the inconstant. The devil's
     in't if this won't please you!
WILLMORE: Oh, most damnably. I have a heart with   235

---

178. Capuchin: Franciscan monk.   190–91. **collation:** Snack.

a hole quite through it too; no prison mine, to keep
a mistress in.

ANGELLICA (*aside*): Perjured man! How I believe thee
now!

240 HELLENA: Well, I see our business as well as humors
are alike: yours to cozen as many maids as will
trust you, and I as many men as have faith. See if
I have not as desperate a lying look as you can
have for the heart of you. (*Pulls off her vizard; he
245 starts.*) How do you like it, captain?

WILLMORE: Like it! By heaven, I never saw so much
beauty! Oh, the charms of those sprightly black
eyes! That strangely fair face, full of smiles and
dimples! Those soft round melting cherry lips and
250 small even white teeth! Not to be expressed, but
silently adored! [*She replaces her mask.*] Oh, one
look more, and strike me dumb, or I shall repeat
nothing else till I'm mad.

(*He seems to court her to pull off her vizard; she
refuses.*)

ANGELLICA: I can endure no more. Nor is it fit to
255 interrupt him, for if I do, my jealousy has so destroyed my reason I shall undo him. Therefore I'll
retire, and you, Sebastian (*to one of her Bravos*),
follow that woman and learn who 'tis; while you
(*to the other Bravo*) tell the fugitive I would speak
260 to him instantly. (*Exit.*)

(*This while Florinda is talking to Belvile, who stands
sullenly; Frederick courting Valeria.*)

VALERIA [*to Belvile*]: Prithee, dear stranger, be not so
sullen, for though you have lost your love you see
my friend frankly offers you hers to play with in
the meantime.

265 BELVILE: Faith, madam, I am sorry I can't play at her
game.

FREDERICK [*to Valeria*]: Pray leave your intercession
and mind your own affair. They'll better agree
apart: He's a modest sigher in company, but alone
270 no woman 'scapes him.

FLORINDA [*aside*]: Sure he does but rally. Yet, if it
should be true? I'll tempt him farther. — Believe
me, noble stranger, I'm no common mistress. And
for a little proof on't, wear this jewel.° Nay, take
275 it, sir, 'tis right, and bills of exchange may sometimes miscarry.

BELVILE: Madam, why am I chose out of all mankind
to be the object of your bounty?

VALERIA: There's another civil question asked.

280 FREDERICK [*aside*]: Pox of's modesty; it spoils his own
markets and hinders mine.

FLORINDA: Sir, from my window I have often seen

274. jewel: A locket with her picture in it.

you, and women of my quality have so few opportunities for love that we ought to lose none.

FREDERICK [*to Valeria*]: Ay, this is something! Here's   28
a woman! When shall I be blest with so much
kindness from your fair mouth? — (*Aside to Belvile.*) Take the jewel, fool!

BELVILE: You tempt me strangely, madam, every
way —   29

FLORINDA (*aside*): So, if I find him false, my whole
repose is gone.

BELVILE: And but for a vow I've made to a very fair
lady, this goodness had subdued me.

FREDERICK [*aside to Belvile*]: Pox on't, be kind, in   29
pity to me be kind. For I am to thrive here but as
you treat her friend.

HELLENA: Tell me what you did in yonder house, and
I'll unmask.

WILLMORE: Yonder house? Oh, I went to a — to —   30
why, there's a friend of mine lives there.

HELLENA: What, a she or a he friend?

WILLMORE: A man, upon honor, a man. A she friend?
No, no, madam, you have done my business, I
thank you.   30

HELLENA: And was't your man friend that had more
darts in's eyes than Cupid carries in's whole budget
of arrows?

WILLMORE: So —

HELLENA: "Ah, such a *bona roba*! To be in her arms   31
is lying *in fresco*, all perfumed air about me." Was
this your man friend too?

WILLMORE: So —

HELLENA: That gave you the he and the she gold, that
begets young pleasures?   31

WILLMORE: Well, well, madam, then you can see there
are ladies in the world that will not be cruel. There
are, madam, there are.

HELLENA: And there be men, too, as fine, wild, inconstant fellows as yourself. There be, captain,   32
there be, if you go to that now. Therefore, I'm
resolved —

WILLMORE: Oh!

HELLENA: To see your face no more —

WILLMORE: Oh!   32

HELLENA: Till tomorrow.

WILLMORE: Egad, you frighted me.

HELLENA: Nor then neither, unless you'll swear never
to see that lady more.

WILLMORE: See her! Why, never to think of woman-   33
kind again.

HELLENA: Kneel and swear.
                    (*Kneels; she gives him her hand.*)

WILLMORE: I do, never to think, to see, to love, nor
lie, with any but thyself.

HELLENA: Kiss the book.   335

WILLMORE: Oh, most religiously. (*Kisses her hand.*)

HELLENA: Now what a wicked creature am I, to damn a proper fellow.

CALLIS (to *Florinda*): Madam, I'll stay no longer: 'tis
40   e'en dark.

FLORINDA [to *Belvile*]: However, sir, I'll leave this with you, that when I'm gone you may repent the opportunity you have lost by your modesty.

(*Gives him the jewel, which is her picture, and exit.
He gazes after her.*)

WILLMORE [to *Hellena*]: 'Twill be an age till tomor-
45   row, and till then I will most impatiently expect you. Adieu, my dear pretty angel.

(*Exeunt all the women.*)

BELVILE: Ha! Florinda's picture! 'Twas she herself. What a dull dog was I! I would have given the world for one minute's discourse with her.

50 FREDERICK: This comes of your modesty. Ah, pox o' your vow; 'twas ten to one but we had lost the jewel by't.

BELVILE: Willmore, the blessed'st opportunity lost! Florinda, friends, Florinda!

55 WILLMORE: Ah, rogue! Such black eyes! Such a face! Such a mouth! Such teeth! And so much wit!

BELVILE: All, all, and a thousand charms besides.

WILLMORE: Why, dost thou know her?

BELVILE: Know her! Ay, ay, and a pox take me with all my heart for being so modest.

60 WILLMORE: But hark'ee, friend of mine, are you my rival? And have I been only beating the bush all this while?

BELVILE: I understand thee not. I'm mad! See here —

(*Shows the picture.*)

65 WILLMORE: Ha! Whose picture's this? 'Tis a fine wench!

FREDERICK: The colonel's mistress, sir.

WILLMORE: Oh, oh, here. (*Gives the picture back.*) I
70   thought't had been another prize. Come, come, a bottle will set thee right again.

BELVILE: I am content to try, and by that time 'twill be late enough for our design.

WILLMORE: Agreed.

Love does all day the soul's great empire keep,
75   *But wine at night lulls the soft god asleep.*

(*Exeunt.*)

Scene II

(*Lucetta's house. Enter Blunt and Lucetta with a
light.*)

LUCETTA: Now we are safe and free: no fears of the coming home of my old jealous husband, which made me a little thoughtful when you came in first. But now love is all the business of my soul.

BLUNT: I am transported! — (*Aside.*) Pox on't, that 5
I had but some fine things to say to her, such as lovers use. I was a fool not to learn of Fred a little by heart before I came. Something I must say. — 'Adsheartlikins, sweet soul, I am not used to compliment, but I'm an honest gentleman, and thy 10 humble servant.

LUCETTA: I have nothing to pay for so great a favor, but such a love as cannot but be great, since at first sight of that sweet face and shape it made me your absolute captive. 15

BLUNT (*aside*): Kind heart, how prettily she talks! Egad, I'll show her husband a Spanish trick: Send him out of the world and marry her; she's damnably in love with me, and will ne'er mind settlements,° and so there's that saved. 20

LUCETTA: Well, sir, I'll go and undress me, and be with you instantly.

BLUNT: Make haste then, for 'adsheartlikins, dear soul, thou canst not guess at the pain of a longing lover when his joys are drawn within the compass 25 of a few minutes.

LUCETTA: You speak my sense, and I'll make haste to prove it. (*Exit.*)

BLUNT: 'Tis a rare girl, and this one night's enjoyment with her will be worth all the days I ever passed 30 in Essex. Would she would go with me into England, though to say truth, there's plenty of whores already. Put a pox on 'em, they are such mercenary prodigal whores that they want such a one as this, that's free and generous, to give 'em good ex- 35 amples. Why, what a house she has, how rich and fine!

(*Enter Sancho.*)

SANCHO: Sir, my lady has sent me to conduct you to her chamber.

BLUNT: Sir, I shall be proud to follow. — (*Aside.*) 40 Here's one of her servants too; 'adsheartlikins, by this garb and gravity he might be a justice of peace in Essex, and is but a pimp here.

(*Exeunt.*)

Scene III

(*The scene changes to a chamber with an alcove bed
in't, a table, etc.; Lucetta in bed. Enter Sancho and
Blunt, who takes the candle of Sancho at the door.*)

SANCHO: Sir, my commission reaches no farther.

19–20. will ne'er mind settlements: Won't require the gifts of property usually settled on a wife after marriage.

BLUNT: Sir, I'll excuse your compliment.

                                    [Exit Sancho.]

   — What, in bed, my sweet mistress?

LUCETTA: You see, I still outdo you in kindness.

5 BLUNT: And thou shalt see what haste I'll make to quit scores. Oh, the luckiest rogue!

                           (*He undresses himself.*)

LUCETTA: Should you be false or cruel now —

BLUNT: False! 'Adsheartlikins, what dost thou take me for, a Jew? An insensible heathen? A pox of thy
10 old jealous husband: An° he were dead, egad, sweet soul, it should be none of my fault if I did not marry thee.

LUCETTA: It never should be mine.

BLUNT: Good soul! I'm the fortunatest dog!

15 LUCETTA: Are you not undressed yet?

BLUNT: As much as my impatience will permit.

    (*Goes toward the bed in his shirt, drawers, etc.*)

LUCETTA: Hold, sir, put out the light; it may betray us else.

BLUNT: Anything; I need no other light but that of
20 thine eyes. — (*Aside.*) 'Adsheartlikins, there I think I had it.

          (*Puts out the candle; the bed descends; he
                        gropes about to find it.*)

Why, why, where am I got? What, not yet? Where are you, sweetest? — Ah, the rogue's silent now. A pretty love-trick this; how she'll laugh at me
25 anon! — You need not, my dear rogue, you need not! I'm all on fire already; come, come, now call me, in pity. — Sure I'm enchanted! I have been round the chamber, and can find neither woman nor bed. I locked the door; I'm sure she cannot go
30 that way, or if she could, the bed could not. — Enough, enough, my pretty wanton; do not carry the jest too far! (*Lights on a trap, and is let down.*) — Ha! Betrayed! Dogs! Rogues! Pimps! Help! Help!

(*Enter Lucetta, Philippo, and Sancho with a light.*)

35 PHILIPPO: Ha! Ha! Ha! He's dispatched finely.

LUCETTA: Now, sir, had I been coy, we had missed of this booty.

PHILIPPO: Nay, when I saw 'twas a substantial fool, I was mollified. But when you dote upon a sere-
40 nading coxcomb, upon a face, fine clothes, and a lute, it makes me rage.

LUCETTA: You know I was never guilty of that folly, my dear Philippo, but with yourself. But come, let's see what we have got by this.

45 PHILIPPO: A rich coat; sword and hat; these breeches, too, are well lined! See here, a gold watch! A purse — Ha! Gold! At least two hundred pis-

10. **An:** If.

toles! A bunch of diamond rings, and one with the family arms! A gold box, with a medal of his king, and his lady mother's picture! These were sacred 50 relics, believe me. See, the waistband of his breeches have a mine of gold — old queen Bess's!° We have a quarrel to her ever since eighty-eight,° and may therefore justify the theft: The Inquisition might have committed it. 55

LUCETTA: See, a bracelet of bowed gold! These his sisters tied about his arm at parting. But well, for all this, I fear his being a stranger may make a noise and hinder our trade with them hereafter.

PHILIPPO: That's our security: He is not only a stranger 60 to us, but to the country too. The common shore° into which he is descended, thou know'st, conducts him into another street, which this light will hinder him from ever finding again. He knows neither your name, nor that of the street where your house 65 is; nay, nor the way to his own lodgings.

LUCETTA: And art thou not an unmerciful rogue, not to afford him one night for all this? I should not have been such a Jew.

PHILIPPO: Blame me not, Lucetta, to keep as much 70 of thee as I can to myself. Come, that thought makes me wanton; let's to bed. — Sancho, lock up these.

    This is the fleece which fools do bear,
    Designed for witty men to shear.   (*Exeunt.*)

Scene IV

(*The scene changes, and discovers Blunt creeping out of a common shore; his face, etc., all dirty.*)

BLUNT (*climbing up*): Oh, Lord, I am got out at last, and, which is a miracle, without a clue. And now to damning and cursing! But if that would ease me, where shall I begin? With my fortune, myself, or the quean° that cozened me? What a dog was 5 I to believe in woman! Oh, coxcomb! Ignorant conceited coxcomb! To fancy she could be ena- mored with my person! At first sight enamored! Oh, I'm a cursed puppy! 'Tis plain, fool was writ upon my forehead! She perceived it; saw the Essex 10 calf there. For what allurements could there be in this countenance, which I can endure because I'm acquainted with it. Oh dull, silly dog, to be thus soothed into a cozening! Had I been drunk, I might fondly have credited the young quean; but as I was 15 in my right wits to be thus cheated, confirms it: I

52. **old queen Bess's:** Queen Elizabeth I (reigned 1558–1603).   53. **eighty-eight:** The year the Spanish Armada was defeated by the English (1588).   61. **common shore:** Sewer.   5. **quean:** Harlot, tramp.

am a dull believing English country fop. But my
comrades! Death and the devil, there's the worst
of all! Then a ballad will be sung tomorrow on the
Prado,° to a lousy tune of the enchanted squire and
the annihilated damsel. But Fred — that rogue —
and the colonel will abuse me beyond all Christian patience. Had she left me my clothes, I have
a bill of exchange at home would have saved my
credit. But now all hope is taken from me. Well,
I'll home, if I can find the way, with this consolation: that I am not the first kind believing coxcomb; but there are, gallants, many such good natures amongst ye.

> And though you've better arts to hide your
>   follies,
> 'Adsheartlikins, y'are all as errant cullies.°

(Exit.)

Scene V

*(Scene: the garden in the night. Enter Florinda in an
undress,° with a key and a little box.)*

FLORINDA: Well, thus far I'm in my way to happiness.
I have got myself free from Callis; my brother too,
I find by yonder light, is got into his cabinet,° and
thinks not of me; I have by good fortune got the
key of the garden back door. I'll open it to prevent
Belvile's knocking: A little noise will now alarm
my brother. Now am I as fearful as a young thief.
(Unlocks the door.) Hark! What noise is that? Oh,
'twas the wind that played amongst the boughs.
Belvile stays long, methinks; it's time. Stay, for fear
of a surprise, I'll hide these jewels in yonder
jasmine.   *(She goes to lay down the box.)*

(Enter Willmore, drunk.)

WILLMORE: What the devil is become of these fellows
Belvile and Frederick? They promised to stay at
the next corner for me, but who the devil knows
the corner of a full moon? Now, whereabouts am
I? Ha, what have we here? A garden! A very convenient place to sleep in. Ha! What has God sent
us here? A female! By this light, a woman! I'm a
dog if it be not a very wench!

FLORINDA: He's come! Ha! Who's there?

WILLMORE: Sweet soul, let me salute thy shoestring.

FLORINDA [*aside*]: 'Tis not my Belvile. Good heavens,
I know him not! — Who are you, and from whence
come you?

WILLMORE: Prithee, prithee, child, not so many hard
questions! Let is suffice I am here, child. Come,
come kiss me.

FLORINDA: Good gods! What luck is mine?

WILLMORE: Only good luck, child, parlous° good luck.
Come hither. — 'Tis a delicate shining wench. By
this hand, she's perfumed, and smells like any nosegay. — Prithee, dear soul, let's not play the fool
and lose time — precious time. For as Gad shall
save me, I'm as honest a fellow as breathes, though
I'm a little disguised° at present. Come, I say. Why,
thou mayst be free with me: I'll be very secret. I'll
not boast who 'twas obliged me, not I; for hang
me if I know thy name.

FLORINDA: Heavens! What a filthy beast is this!

WILLMORE: I am so, and thou ought'st the sooner to
lie with me for that reason. For look you, child,
there will be no sin in't, because 'twas neither designed nor premeditated: 'Tis pure accident on both
sides. That's a certain thing now. Indeed, should
I make love to you, and you vow fidelity, and swear
and lie till you believed and yielded — that were
to make it willful fornication, the crying sin of the
nation. Thou art, therefore, as thou art a good
Christian, obliged in conscience to deny me nothing. Now, come be kind without any more idle
prating.

FLORINDA: Oh, I am ruined! Wicked man, unhand
me!

WILLMORE: Wicked? Egad, child, a judge, were he
young and vigorous, and saw those eyes of thine,
would know 'twas they gave the first blow, the
first provocation. Come, prithee let's lose no time,
I say. This is a fine convenient place.

FLORINDA: Sir, let me go, I conjure° you, or I'll call
out.

WILLMORE: Ay, ay, you were best to call witness to
see how finely you treat me. Do!

FLORINDA: I'll cry murder, rape, or anything, if you
do not instantly let me go!

WILLMORE: A rape? Come, come, you lie, you baggage, you lie. What! I'll warrant you would fain
have the world believe now that you are not so
forward as I. No, not you. Why at this time of
night was your cobweb door set open, dear spider,
but to catch flies? Ha! Come, or I shall be damnably
angry. Why, what a coil° is here!

FLORINDA: Sir, can you think —

WILLMORE: That you would do't for nothing? Oh,

19–20. ballad . . . Prado: A song satirizing him will be sung
on the Prado, a fashionable promenade in Madrid, for common amusement.   **31. cullies:** A *cully* is one easily fooled;
a simpleton.   **III. v. [S.D.] undress:** Undergarment.   **3. cabinet:** Private room.

30. parlous: Excessively, with pun on *perilous*.   **36. disguised:** I.e., by liquor.   **60. conjure:** Entreat, implore.   **72. coil:** Noisy disturbance.

75 oh, I find what you would be at. Look here, here's a pistole for you. Here's a work indeed! Here, take it, I say!

FLORINDA: For heaven's sake, sir, as you're a gentleman —

80 WILLMORE: So now, now, she would be wheedling me for more! What, you will not take it then? You are resolved you will not? Come, come, take it or I'll put it up again, for look ye, I never give more. Why, how now, mistress, are you so high i'th'

85 mouth a pistole won't down with you? Ha! Why, what a work's here! In good time! Come, no struggling to be gone. But an y'are good at a dumb wrestle, I'm for ye. Look ye, I'm for ye.

(She struggles with him.)

(Enter Belvile and Frederick.)

BELVILE: The door is open. A pox of this mad fellow!

90 I'm angry that we've lost him; I durst have sworn he had followed us.

FREDERICK: But you were so hasty, colonel, to be gone.

FLORINDA: Help! Help! Murder! Help! Oh, I am ruined!

95 BELVILE: Ha! Sure that's Florinda's voice! (Comes up to them.) A man! — Villain, let go that lady!

(A noise; Willmore turns and draws; Frederick interposes.)

FLORINDA: Belvile! Heavens! My brother too is coming, and 'twill be impossible to escape. Belvile, I conjure you to walk under my chamber window,

100 from whence I'll give you some instructions what to do. This rude man has undone us. (Exit.)

WILLMORE: Belvile!

(Enter Pedro, Stephano, and other servants, with lights.)

PEDRO: I'm betrayed! Run, Stephano, and see if Florinda be safe.

(Exit Stephano.)

(They fight, and Pedro's party beats 'em out.)

105 — So, whoe'er they be, all is not well. I'll to Florinda's chamber. (Going out, meets Stephano.)

STEPHANO: You need not, sir: The poor lady's fast asleep, and thinks no harm. I would not awake her, sir, for fear of frighting her with your danger.

110 PEDRO: I'm glad she's there. — Rascals, how came the garden door open?

STEPHANO: That question comes too late, sir. Some of my fellow servants masquerading, I'll warrant.

PEDRO: Masquerading! A lewd custom to debauch our

115 youth! There's something more in this than I imagine. (Exeunt.)

Scene VI

(Scene changes to the street. Enter Belvile in rage, Frederick holding him, Willmore melancholy.)

WILLMORE: Why, how the devil should I know Florinda?

BELVILE: Ah, plague of your ignorance! If it had not been Florinda, must you be a beast? A brute? A senseless swine? 5

WILLMORE: Well, sir, you see I am endued° with patience: I can bear. Though egad, y'are very free with me, methinks. I was in good hopes the quarrel would have been on my side, for so uncivilly interrupting me. 10

BELVILE: Peace, brute, whilst thou'rt safe. Oh, I'm distracted!

WILLMORE: Nay, nay, I'm an unlucky dog, that's certain.

BELVILE: Ah, curse upon the star that ruled my birth, 15 or whatsoever other influence that makes me still so wretched.

WILLMORE: Thou break'st my heart with these complaints. There is no star in fault, no influence but sack, the cursed sack I drunk. 20

FREDERICK: Why, how the devil came you so drunk?

WILLMORE: Why, how the devil came you so sober?

BELVILE: A curse upon his thin skull, he was always beforehand that way.

FREDERICK: Prithee, dear colonel, forgive him; he's 25 sorry for his fault.

BELVILE: He's always so after he has done a mischief. A plague on all such brutes!

WILLMORE: By this light, I took her for an errant harlot. 30

BELVILE: Damn your debauched opinion! Tell me, sot, hadst thou so much sense and light about thee to distinguish her woman, and couldst not see something about her face and person to strike an awful reverence into thy soul? 35

WILLMORE: Faith no, I considered her as mere a woman as I could wish.

BELVILE: 'Sdeath, I have no patience. Draw, or I'll kill you!

WILLMORE: Let that alone till tomorrow, and if I set 40 not all right again, use your pleasure.

BELVILE: Tomorrow! Damn it,
The spiteful light will lead me to no happiness.
Tomorrow is Antonio's, and perhaps
Guides him to my undoing. Oh, that I could meet 45
This rival, this powerful fortunate!

6. **endued:** Endowed.

WILLMORE: What then?

BELVILE: Let thy own reason, or my rage, instruct thee.

WILLMORE: I shall be finely informed then, no doubt. Hear me, colonel, hear me; show me the man and I'll do his business.

BELVILE: I know him no more than thou, or if I did I should not need thy aid.

WILLMORE: This you say is Angellica's house; I promised the kind baggage to lie with her tonight.

(Offers to go in.)

(Enter Antonio and his Page. Antonio knocks on the hilt of's sword.)

ANTONIO: You paid the thousand crowns I directed?

PAGE: To the lady's old woman, sir, I did.

WILLMORE: Who the devil have we here?

BELVILE: I'll now plant myself under Florinda's window, and if I find no comfort there, I'll die.

(Exeunt Belvile and Frederick.)

(Enter Moretta.)

MORETTA: Page?

PAGE: Here's my lord.

WILLMORE: How is this? A picaroon going to board my frigate? — Here's one chase gun for you!

(Drawing his sword, justles Antonio, who turns and draws. They fight; Antonio falls.)

MORETTA: Oh, bless us! We're all undone!

(Runs in and shuts the door.)

PAGE: Help! Murder!

(Belvile returns at the noise of fighting.)

BELVILE: Ha! The mad rogue's engaged in some unlucky adventure again.

(Enter two or three Masqueraders.)

MASQUERADER: Ha! A man killed!

WILLMORE: How, a man killed? Then I'll go home to sleep.

(Puts up and reels out. Exeunt Masqueraders another way.)

BELVILE: Who should it be? Pray heaven the rogue is safe, for all my quarrel to him.

(As Belvile is groping about, enter an Officer and six Soldiers.)

SOLDIER: Who's there?

OFFICER: So, here's one dispatched. Secure the murderer.

BELVILE: Do not mistake my charity for murder! I came to his assistance! (Soldiers sieze on Belvile.)

OFFICER: That shall be tried, sir. St. Jago! Swords drawn in the Carnival time!   (Goes to Antonio.)

ANTONIO: Thy hand, prithee.

OFFICER: Ha! Don Antonio! Look well to the villain there. — How is it, sir?

ANTONIO: I'm hurt.

BELVILE: Has my humanity made me a criminal?

OFFICER: Away with him!

BELVILE: What a curst chance is this!

(Exeunt soldiers with Belvile.)

ANTONIO [aside]: This is the man that has set upon me twice. — (To the officer.) Carry him to my apartment till you have further orders from me.

(Exit Antonio, led.)

ACT IV • Scene I

(A fine room. Discovers Belvile as by dark alone.)

BELVILE: When shall I be weary of railing on fortune, who is resolved never to turn with smiles upon me? Two such defeats in one night none but the devil and that mad rogue could have contrived to have plagued me with. I am here a prisoner. But where, heaven knows. And if there be murder done, I can soon decide the fate of a stranger in a nation without mercy. Yet this is nothing to the torture my soul bows with when I think of losing my fair, my dear Florinda. Hark, my door opens. A light! A man, and seems of quality. Armed, too! Now shall I die like a dog, without defense.

(Enter Antonio in a nightgown, with a light; his arm in a scarf, and a sword under his arm. He sets the candle on the table.)

ANTONIO: Sir, I come to know what injuries I have done you, that could provoke you to so mean an action as to attack me basely without allowing time for my defense?

BELVILE: Sir, for a man in my circumstances to plead innocence would look like fear. But view me well, and you will find no marks of coward on me, nor anything that betrays that brutality you accuse me with.

ANTONIO: In vain, sir, you impose upon my sense. You are not only he who drew on me last night, but yesterday before the same house, that of Angellica. Yet there is something in your face and mien° that makes me wish I were mistaken.

BELVILE: I own I fought today in the defense of a friend of mine with whom you, if you're the same, and your party were first engaged. Perhaps you

26. mien: Demeanor, appearance.

30   think this crime enough to kill me; but if you do,
      I cannot fear you'll do it basely.
ANTONIO: No sir, I'll make you fit for a defense with
      this.   (*Gives him the sword.*)
BELVILE: This gallantry surprises me, nor know I
35   how to use this present, sir, against a man so brave.
ANTONIO: You shall not need. For know, I come to
      snatch you from a danger that is decreed against
      you: perhaps your life, or long imprisonment. And
      'twas with so much courage you offended, I cannot
40   see you punished.
BELVILE: How shall I pay this generosity?
ANTONIO: It had been safer to have killed another
      than have attempted me. To show your danger,
      sir, I'll let you know my quality: And 'tis the Vice-
45   roy's son whom you have wounded.
BELVILE: The Viceroy's son! — (*Aside.*) Death and
      confusion! Was this plague reserved to complete
      all the rest? Obliged by° him, the man of all the
      world I would destroy!
50   ANTONIO: You seem disordered, sir.
BELVILE: Yes, trust me, I am, and 'tis with pain that
      man receives such bounties who wants the power
      to pay 'em back again.
ANTONIO: To gallant spirits 'tis indeed uneasy, but
55   you may quickly overpay me, sir.
BELVILE (*aside*): Then I am well. Kind heaven, but set
      us even, that I may fight with him and keep my
      honor safe. — Oh, I'm impatient, sir, to be dis-
      counting the mighty debt I owe you. Command
60   me quickly.
ANTONIO: I have a quarrel with a rival, sir, about the
      maid we love.
BELVILE (*aside*): Death, 'tis Florinda he means! That
      thought destroys my reason, and I shall kill him.
65   ANTONIO: My rival, sir, is one has all the virtues man
      can boast of —
BELVILE (*aside*): Death, who should this be?
ANTONIO: He challenged me to meet him on the Molo
      as soon as day appeared, but last night's quarrel
70   has made my arm unfit to guide a sword.
BELVILE: I apprehend you, sir. You'd have me kill the
      man that lays a claim to the maid you speak of.
      I'll do't. I'll fly to do't!
ANTONIO: Sir, do you know her?
75   BELVILE: No, sir, but 'tis enough she is admired by
      you.
ANTONIO: Sir, I shall rob you of the glory on't, for
      you must fight under my name and dress.
BELVILE: That opinion must be strangely obliging that
80   makes you think I can personate the brave Antonio,
      whom I can but strive to imitate.

ANTONIO: You say too much to my advantage. Come,
      sir, the day appears that calls you forth. Within,
      sir, is the habit.°   (*Exit Antonio.*)
BELVILE: Fantastic fortune, thou deceitful light,   85
      That cheats the wearied traveler by night,
      Though on a precipice each step you tread,
      I am resolved to follow where you lead.   (*Exit.*)

Scene II

(*The Molo. Enter Florinda and Callis in masks, with
Stephano.*)

FLORINDA (*aside*): I'm dying with my fears: Belvile's
      not coming as I expected under my window makes
      me believe that all those fears are true. — Canst
      thou not tell with whom my brother fights?
STEPHANO: No, madam, they were both in masquerade.   5
      I was by when they challenged one another, and
      they had decided the quarrel then, but were
      prevented by some cavaliers; which made 'em
      put it off till now. But I am sure 'tis about you
      they fight.   10
FLORINDA (*aside*): Nay, then, 'tis with Belvile, for
      what other lover have I that dares fight for me
      except Antonio, and he is too much in favor with
      my brother. If it be he, for whom shall I direct my
      prayers to heaven?   15
STEPHANO: Madam, I must leave you, for if my master
      see me, I shall be hanged for being your conductor.
      I escaped narrowly for the excuse I made for you
      last night i'th' garden.
FLORINDA: I'll reward thee for't. Prithee, no more.   20
                                          (*Exit Stephano.*)

(*Enter Don Pedro in his masking habit.*)

PEDRO: Antonio's late today; the place will fill, and
      we may be prevented.   (*Walks about.*)
FLORINDA (*aside*): Antonio? Sure I heard amiss.
PEDRO: But who will not excuse a happy lover
      When soft fair arms confine the yielding neck,   25
      And the kind whisper languishingly breathes
      "Must you be gone so soon?"
      Sure I had dwelt forever on her bosom —
      But stay, he's here.

(*Enter Belvile dressed in Antonio's clothes.*)

FLORINDA [*aside*]: 'Tis not Belvile; half my fears are   30
      vanished.
PEDRO: Antonio!
BELVILE (*aside*): This must be he. — You're early, sir;
      I do not use to be outdone this way.

---

48. Obliged by: Favored by.

84. habit: Antonio's clothing.

35 PEDRO: The wretched, sir, are watchful, and 'tis
enough you've the advantage of me in Angellica.

BELVILE (*aside*): Angellica! Or° I've mistook my man,
or else Antonio! Can he forget his interest in Florinda and fight for common prize?

40 PEDRO: Come, sir, you know our terms.

BELVILE (*aside*): By heaven, not I. — No talking; I am
ready, sir.

> (*Offers to fight; Florinda runs in.*)

FLORINDA (*to Belvile*): Oh, hold! Whoe'er you be, I
do conjure you hold! If you strike here, I die!

45 PEDRO: Florinda!

BELVILE: Florinda imploring for my rival!

PEDRO: Away; this kindness is unseasonable.

> (*Puts her by; they fight; she runs in just as Belvile
> disarms Pedro.*)

FLORINDA: Who are you, sir, that dares deny my
prayers?

50 BELVILE: Thy prayers destroy him; if thou wouldst
preserve him, do that thou'rt unacquainted with,
and curse him.

> (*She holds him.*)

FLORINDA: By all you hold most dear, by her you
love,
I do conjure you, touch him not.

55 BELVILE: By her I love?
See, I obey, and at your feet resign
The useless trophy of my victory.

> (*Lays his sword at her feet.*)

PEDRO: Antonio, you've done enough to prove you
love Florinda.

60 BELVILE: Love Florinda! Does heaven love adoration,
prayer, or penitence? Love her? Here, sir, your
sword again.

> (*Snatches up the sword and gives it to him.*)
Upon this truth I'll fight my life away.

PEDRO: No, you've redeemed my sister, and my
65 friendship.

(*He gives him Florinda, and pulls off his vizard to
show his face, and puts it on again.*)

BELVILE: Don Pedro!

PEDRO: Can you resign your claims to other women,
and give your heart entirely to Florinda?

BELVILE: Entire, as dying saints' confessions are!
70 I can delay my happiness no longer:
This minute let me make Florinda mine.

PEDRO: This minute let it be. No time so proper: This
night my father will arrive from Rome, and possibly may hinder what we purpose.

75 FLORINDA: O, heavens! This minute?

(*Enter Masqueraders and pass over.*)

37. Or: Either.

BELVILE: Oh, do not ruin me!

PEDRO: The place begins to fill, and that we may not
be observed, do you walk off to St. Peter's church,
where I will meet you and conclude your happiness.

BELVILE: I'll meet you there. — (*Aside.*) If there be   80
no more saints' churches in Naples.

FLORINDA: Oh, stay, sir, and recall your hasty
doom!
Alas, I have not yet prepared my heart
To entertain so strange a guest.

PEDRO: Away; this silly modesty is assumed too late.   85

BELVILE: Heaven, madam, what do you do?

FLORINDA: Do? Despise the man that lays a tyrant's
claim
To what he ought to conquer by submission.

BELVILE: You do not know me. Move a little this way.

> (*Draws her aside.*)

FLORINDA: Yes, you may force me even to the altar,   90
But not the holy man that offers there
Shall force me to be thine.

> (*Pedro talks to Callis this while.*)

BELVILE: Oh, do not lose so blest an opportunity!

> (*Pulls off his vizard.*)
See, 'tis your Belvile, not Antonio,
Whom your mistaken scorn and anger ruins.   95

FLORINDA: Belvile!
Where was my soul it could not meet thy voice,
And take this knowledge in.

(*As they are talking, enter Willmore, finely dressed,
and Frederick.*)

WILLMORE: No intelligence? No news of Belvile yet?
Well, I am the most unlucky rascal in nature. Ha!   100
Am I deceived, or is it he? Look, Fred! 'Tis he, my
dear Belvile!

> (*Runs and embraces him; Belvile's vizard falls
> out on's hand.*)

BELVILE: Hell and confusion seize thee!

PEDRO: Ha! Belvile! I beg your pardon, sir.

> (*Takes Florinda from him.*)

BELVILE: Nay, touch her not. She's mine by
conquest, sir;   105
I won her by my sword.

WILLMORE: Didst thou so? And egad, child, we'll
keep her by the sword.

> (*Draws on Pedro; Belvile goes between.*)

BELVILE: Stand off!
Thou'rt so profanely lewd, so curst by heaven,
All quarrels thou espousest must be fatal.   110

WILLMORE: Nay, an you be so hot, my valor's coy,
And shall be courted when you want it next.

> (*Puts up his sword.*)

BELVILE (*to Pedro*): You know I ought to claim a
victor's right,
But you're the brother to divine Florinda,

115 To whom I'm such a slave. To purchase her
I durst not hurt the man she holds so dear.
PEDRO: 'Twas by Antonio's, not by Belvile's sword
This question should have been decided, sir.
I must confess much to your bravery's due,
120 Both now and when I met you last in arms;
But I am nicely punctual in my word,
As men of honor ought, and beg your pardon:
For this mistake another time shall clear.
(Aside to Florinda as they are going out.)
— This was some plot between you and Belvile,
125 But I'll prevent you.
[Exeunt Pedro and Florinda.]

(Belvile looks after her and begins to walk up and
down in rage.)

WILLMORE: Do not be modest now and lose the
woman. But if we shall fetch her back so —
BELVILE: Do not speak to me!
WILLMORE: Not speak to you? Egad, I'll speak to you,
130 and will be answered, too.
BELVILE: Will you, sir?
WILLMORE: I know I've done some mischief, but I'm
so dull a puppy that I'm the son of a whore if
I know how or where. Prithee inform my
135 understanding.
BELVILE: Leave me, I say, and leave me instantly!
WILLMORE: I will not leave you in this humor, nor
till I know my crime.
BELVILE: Death, I'll tell you, sir —
(Draws and runs at Willmore; he runs out, Belvile
after him; Frederick interposes.)

(Enter Angellica, Moretta, and Sebastian.)

140 ANGELLICA: Ha! Sebastian, is that not Willmore?
Haste! haste and bring him back.
[Exit Sebastian.]
FREDERICK [aside]: The colonel's mad: I never saw
him thus before. I'll after 'em lest he do some
mischief, for I am sure Willmore will not draw on
145 him.
(Exit.)
ANGELLICA: I am all rage! My first desires defeated!
For one for aught he knows that has no
Other merit than her quality,
Her being Don Pedro's sister. He loves her!
150 I know 'tis so. Dull, dull, insensible,
He will not see me now, though oft invited,
And broke his word last night. False perjured
man!
He that but yesterday fought for my favors,
And would have made his life a sacrifice
155 To've gained one night with me,
Must now be hired and courted to my arms.
MORETTA: I told you what would come on't, but
Moretta's an old doting fool. Why did you give
him five hundred crowns, but to set himself out

for other lovers? You should have kept him poor 160
if you had meant to have had any good from him.
ANGELLICA: Oh, name not such mean trifles! Had I
given
Him all my youth has earned from sin,
I had not lost a thought nor sigh upon't.
But I have given him my eternal rest, 165
My whole repose, my future joys, my heart!
My virgin heart, Moretta! Oh, 'tis gone!
MORETTA: Curse on him, here he comes. How fine
she has made him, too.

(Enter Willmore and Sebastian; Angellica turns and
walks away.)

WILLMORE: How now, turned shadow? 170
Fly when I pursue, and follow when I fly? (Sings.)
Stay, gentle shadow of my dove,
And tell me ere I go,
Whether the substance may not prove
A fleeting thing like you. 175
(As she turns she looks on him.)
There's a soft kind look remaining yet.
ANGELLICA: Well, sir, you may be gay: All happiness,
all joys pursue you still. Fortune's your slave, and
gives you every hour choice of new hearts and
beauties, till you are cloyed° with the repeated bliss 180
which others vainly languish for. But know, false
man, that I shall be revenged.
(Turns away in rage.)
WILLMORE: So, gad, there are of those faint-hearted
lovers, whom such a sharp lesson next their hearts
would make as impotent as fourscore.° Pox o' this 185
whining; my business is to laugh and love. A pox
on't, I hate your sullen lover: A man shall lose as
much time to put you in humor now as would
serve to gain a new woman.
ANGELLICA: I scorn to cool that fire I cannot raise, 190
Or do the drudgery of your virtuous mistress.
WILLMORE: A virtuous mistress? Death, what a thing
thou hast found out for me! Why, what the devil
should I do with a virtuous woman, a sort of ill-
natured creatures that take a pride to torment a 195
lover. Virtue is but an infirmity in woman, a disease
that renders even the handsome ungrateful; whilst
the ill-favored, for want of solicitations and address, only fancy themselves so. I have lain with a
woman of quality who has all the while been railing 200
at whores.
ANGELLICA: I will not answer for your mistress's
virtue,
Though she be young enough to know no guilt;
And I could wish you would persuade my heart

180. cloyed: Full to bursting.   185. as fourscore: As an
eighty-year-old.

'Twas the two hundred thousand crowns you
courted.

WILLMORE: Two hundred thousand crowns! What
story's this? What trick? What woman, ha?

ANGELLICA: How strange you make it. Have you forgot the creature you entertained on the Piazzo last
night?

WILLMORE (aside): Ha! My gypsy worth two hundred
thousand crowns! Oh, how I long to be with her!
Pox, I knew she was of quality.

ANGELLICA: False man! I see my ruin in thy face.
How many vows you breathed upon my bosom
Never to be unjust. Have you forgot so soon?

WILLMORE: Faith, no; I was just coming to repeat
'em. But here's a humor indeed would make a man
a saint. — (Aside.) Would she would be angry
enough to leave me, and command me not to wait
on her.

(Enter Hellena dressed in man's clothes.)

HELLENA: This must be Angellica: I know it by her
mumping° matron here. Ay, ay, 'tis she. My mad
captain's with her, too, for all his swearing. How
this unconstant humor makes me love him! — Pray,
good grave gentlewoman, is not this Angellica?

MORETTA: My too young sir, it is. — [Aside.] I hope
'tis one from Don Antonio. (Goes to Angellica.)

HELLENA (aside): Well, something I'll do to vex him
for this.

ANGELLICA: I will not speak with him. Am I in humor
to receive a lover?

WILLMORE: Not speak with him? Why, I'll be gone,
and wait your idler minutes. Can I show less obedience to the thing I love so fondly?

(Offers to go.)

ANGELLICA: A fine excuse this! Stay —

WILLMORE: And hinder your advantage? Should I repay your bounties so ungratefully?

ANGELLICA [to Hellena]: Come hither, boy. — [To
Willmore.] That I may let you see
How much above the advantages you name
I prize one minute's joy with you.

WILLMORE (impatient to be gone): Oh, you destroy
me with this endearment. — [Aside.] Death, how
shall I get away? — Madam, 'twill not be fit I
should be seen with you. Besides, it will not be
convenient. And I've a friend — that's dangerously
sick.

ANGELLICA: I see you're impatient. Yet you shall stay.

WILLMORE (aside): And miss my assignation with my
gypsy.

(Walks about impatiently; Moretta brings Hellena,
who addresses herself to Angellica.)

223. **mumping:** Moping.

HELLENA: Madam,
You'll hardly pardon my instrusion
When you shall know my business,
And I'm too young to tell my tale with art;
But there must be a wondrous store of goodness   255
Where so much beauty dwells.

ANGELLICA: A pretty advocate, whoever sent thee.
Prithee proceed.
(To Willmore, who is stealing off.)
— Nay, sir, you shall not go.

WILLMORE (aside): Then I shall lose my dear gypsy
forever. Pox on't, she stays me out of spite.   260

HELLENA: I am related to a lady, madam,
Young, rich, and nobly born, but has the fate
To be in love with a young English gentleman.
Strangely she loves him, at first sight she loved
him,
But did adore him when she heard him speak;   265
For he, she said, had charms in every word
That failed not to surprise, to wound and
conquer.

WILLMORE (aside): Ha! Egad, I hope this concerns
me.

ANGELLICA (aside): 'Tis my false man he means.
Would he were gone:
This praise will raise his pride, and ruin me.
(To Willmore.) — Well,   270
Since you are so impatient to be gone,
I will release you, sir.

WILLMORE (aside): Nay, then I'm sure 'twas me he
spoke of: This cannot be the effects of kindness in
her. — No, Madam, I've considered better on't,   275
and will not give you cause of jealousy.

ANGELLICA: But sir, I've business that —

WILLMORE: This shall not do; I know 'tis but to try
me.

ANGELLICA: Well, to your story, boy. — (Aside).   280
Though 'twill undo me.

HELLENA: With this addition to his other beauties,
He won her unresisting tender heart.
He vowed, and sighed, and swore he loved her
dearly;
And she believed the cunning flatterer,   285
And thought herself the happiest maid alive.
Today was the appointed time by both
To consummate their bliss:
The virgin, altar, and the priest were dressed;
And whilst she languished for th'expected
bridegroom,   290
She heard he paid his broken vows to you.

WILLMORE (aside): So, this is some dear rogue that's
in love with me, and this way lets me know it. Or,
if it be not me, he means someone whose place I
may supply.   295

ANGELLICA: Now I perceive
The cause of thy impatience to be gone,

And all the business of this glorious dress.
WILLMORE: Damn the young prater; I know not what
300   he means.
HELLENA: Madam,
    In your fair eyes I read too much concern
    To tell my further business.
ANGELLICA: Prithee, sweet youth, talk on: Thou
    mayst perhaps
305   Raise here a storm that may undo my passion,
    And then I'll grant thee anything.
HELLENA: Madam, 'tis to entreat you (oh
    unreasonable)
    You would not see this stranger.
    For if you do, she vows you are undone;
310   Though nature never made a man so excellent,
    And sure he 'ad been a god, but for inconstancy.
WILLMORE (aside): Ah, rogue, how finely he's in-
    structed! 'Tis plain, some woman that has seen me
    en passant.°
315 ANGELLICA: Oh, I shall burst with jealousy! Do you
    know the man you speak of?
HELLENA: Yes, madam, he used to be in buff and
    scarlet.
ANGELLICA (to Willmore): Thou false as hell, what
320   canst thou say to this?
WILLMORE: By heaven —
ANGELLICA: Hold, do not damn thyself —
HELLENA: Nor hope to be believed.
            (He walks about; they follow.)
ANGELLICA: Oh perjured man!
325   Is't thus you pay my generous passion back?
HELLENA: Why would you, sir, abuse my lady's faith?
ANGELLICA: And use me so unhumanely.
HELLENA: A maid so young, so innocent —
WILLMORE: Ah, young devil!
330 ANGELLICA: Dost thou not know thy life is in my
    power?
HELLENA: Or think my lady cannot be revenged?
WILLMORE (aside): So, so, the storm comes finely on.
ANGELLICA: Now thou art silent: Guilt has struck
    thee dumb.
335   Oh, hadst thou still been so, I'd lived in safety.
            (She turns away and weeps.)
WILLMORE (aside to Hellena): Sweetheart, the lady's
    name and house — quickly! I'm impatient to be
    with her.

(Looks toward Angellica to watch her turning, and
    as she comes towards them he meets her.)

HELLENA (aside): So, now is he for another woman.
340 WILLMORE: The impudent'st young thing in nature:
    I cannot persuade him out of his error, madam.

ANGELLICA: I know he's in the right; yet thou'st a
    tongue
    That would persuade him to deny his faith.
            (In rage walks away.)
WILLMORE (said softly to Hellena): Her name, her
    name, dear boy!
HELLENA: Have you forgot it, sir?
WILLMORE (aside): Oh, I perceive he's not to know
    I am a stranger to his lady. — Yes, yes, I do know,
    but I have forgot the — (Angellica turns.) — By
    heaven, such early confidence I never saw.
ANGELLICA: Did I not charge you with this mistress,
    sir?
    Which you denied, though I beheld your perjury.
    This little generosity of thine has rendered back
    my heart.   (Walks away.)
WILLMORE (to Hellena): So, you have made sweet
    work here, my little mischief. Look your lady
    be kind and good-natured now, or I shall have
    but a cursed bargain on't. (Angellica turns toward
    them.) — The rogue's bred up to mischief; art
    thou so great a fool to credit him?
ANGELLICA: Yes, I do, and you in vain impose upon
    me. Come hither, boy. Is not this he you spake of?
HELLENA: I think it is. I cannot swear, but I vow he
    has just such another lying lover's look.

(Hellena looks in his face; he gazes on her.)

WILLMORE (aside): Ha! Do I not know that face? By
    heaven, my little gypsy! What a dull dog was I:
    Had I but looked that way I'd known her. Are all
    my hopes of a new woman banished? — Egad, if
    I do not fit thee for this, hang me. — [To Angellica.]
    Madam, I have found out the plot.
HELLENA [aside]: Oh lord, what does he say? Am I
    discovered now?
WILLMORE: Do you see this young spark here?
HELLENA [aside]: He'll tell her who I am.
WILLMORE: Who do you think this is?
HELLENA [aside]: Ay, ay, he does know me. — Nay,
    dear captain, I am undone if you discover me.
WILLMORE: Nay, nay, no cogging;° she shall know
    what a precious mistress I have.
HELLENA: Will you be such a devil?
WILLMORE: Nay, nay, I'll teach you to spoil sport you
    will not make. — This small ambassador comes
    not from a person of quality, as you imagine and
    he says, but from a very errant gypsy: the talking'st,
    prating'st, canting'st little animal thou ever saw'st.
ANGELLICA: What news you tell me, that's the thing
    I mean.

---

314. *en passant*: In passing.   377. cogging: Fawning, coaxing.

HELLENA (*aside*): Would I were well off the place! If ever I go a-captain-hunting again —

WILLMORE: Mean that thing? That gypsy thing? Thou mayst as well be jealous of thy monkey or parrot as of her. A German motion° were worth a dozen of her, and a dream were a better enjoyment — a creature of a constitution fitter for heaven than man.

HELLENA (*aside*): Though I'm sure he lies, yet this vexes me.

ANGELLICA: You are mistaken: she's a Spanish woman made up of no such dull materials.

WILLMORE: Materials? Egad, an she be made of any that will either dispense or admit of love, I'll be bound to continence.

HELLENA (*aside to him*): Unreasonable man, do you think so?

WILLMORE: You may return, my little brazen head, and tell your lady, that till she be handsome enough to be beloved, or I dull enough to be religious, there will be small hopes of me.

ANGELLICA: Did you not promise, then, to marry her?

WILLMORE: Not I, by heaven.

ANGELLICA: You cannot undeceive my fears and torments, till you have vowed you will not marry her.

HELLENA (*aside*): If he swears that, he'll be revenged on me indeed for all my rogueries.

ANGELLICA: I know what arguments you'll bring against me: fortune and honor.

WILLMORE: Honor! I tell you, I hate it in your sex; and those that fancy themselves possessed of that foppery are the most impertinently troublesome of all womankind, and will transgress nine commandments to keep one. And to satisfy your jealousy, I swear —

HELLENA (*aside to him*): Oh, no swearing, dear captain.

WILLMORE: If it were possible I should ever be inclined to marry, it should be some kind young sinner: one that has generosity enough to give a favor handsomely to one that can ask it discreetly, one that has wit enough to manage an intrigue of love. Oh, how civil such a wench is to a man that does her the honor to marry her.

ANGELLICA: By heaven, there's no faith in anything he says.

(*Enter Sebastian.*)

SEBASTIAN: Madam, Don Antonio —

ANGELLICA: Come hither.

HELLENA [*aside*]: Ha! Antonio! He may be coming hither, and he'll certainly discover me. I'll therefore retire without a ceremony.   (*Exit Hellena.*)

ANGELLICA: I'll see him. Get my coach ready.

SEBASTIAN: It waits you, madam.

WILLMORE [*aside*]: This is lucky. — What, madam, now I may be gone and leave you to the enjoyment of my rival?

ANGELLICA: Dull man, that canst not see how ill, how poor,
That false dissimulation looks. Be gone,
And never let me see thy cozening face again,
Lest I relapse and kill thee.

WILLMORE: Yes, you can spare me now. Farewell, till you're in better humor. — [*Aside.*] I'm glad of this release. Now for my gypsy:
For though to worse we change, yet still we find
New joys, new charms, in a new miss that's kind.   (*Exit Willmore.*)

ANGELLICA: He's gone, and in this ague° of my soul
The shivering fit returns.
Oh, with what willing haste he took his leave,
As if the longed-for minute were arrived
Of some blest assignation.
In vain I have consulted all my charms,
In vain this beauty prized, in vain believed
My eyes could kindle any lasting fires;
I had forgot my name, my infamy,
And the reproach that honor lays on those
That dare pretend a sober passion here.
Nice reputation, though it leave behind
More virtues than inhabit where that dwells,
Yet that once gone, those virtues shine no more.
Then since I am not fit to be beloved,
I am resolved to think on a revenge
On him that soothed° me thus to my undoing.
(*Exeunt.*)

Scene III

(*A street. Enter Florinda and Valeria in habits different from what they have been seen in.*)

FLORINDA: We're happily escaped, and yet I tremble still.

VALERIA: A lover, and fear? Why, I am but half an one, and yet I have courage for any attempt. Would Hellena were here: I would fain have had her as deep in this mischief as we; she'll fare but ill else, I doubt.

FLORINDA: She pretended a visit to the Augustine nuns; but I believe some other design carried her out; pray heaven we light on her. Prithee, what didst do with Callis?

---

391. motion: Puppet show.

452. ague: Fever, accompanied by shivering.   **468. soothed:** Advised.

VALERIA: When I saw no reason would do good on her, I followed her into the wardrobe, and as she was looking for something in a great chest, I toppled her in by the heels, snatched the key of the apartment where you were confined, locked her in, and left her bawling for help.

FLORINDA: 'Tis well you resolve to follow my fortunes, for thou darest never appear at home again after such an action.

VALERIA: That's according as the young stranger and I shall agree. But to our business. I delivered your note to Belvile when I got out under pretense of going to mass. I found him at his lodging, and believe me it came seasonably, for never was man in so desperate a condition. I told him of your resolution of making your escape today if your brother would be absent long enough to permit you; if not, to die rather than be Antonio's.

FLORINDA: Thou should'st have told him I was confined to my chamber upon my brother's suspicion that the business on the Molo was a plot laid between him and I.

VALERIA: I said all this, and told him your brother was now gone to his devotion; and he resolves to visit every church till he find him, and not only undeceive him in that, but caress him so as shall delay his return home.

FLORINDA: Oh heavens! He's here, and Belvile with him, too.

(*They put on their vizards.*)

(*Enter Don Pedro, Belvile, Willmore; Belvile and Don Pedro seeming in serious discourse.*)

VALERIA: Walk boldly by them, and I'll come at a distance, lest he suspect us.
(*She walks by them and looks back on them.*)

WILLMORE: Ha! A woman, and of excellent mien!

PEDRO: She throws a kind look back on you.

WILLMORE: Death, 'tis a likely wench, and that kind look shall not be cast away. I'll follow her.

BELVILE: Prithee do not.

WILLMORE: Do not? By heavens, to the antipodies,° with such an invitation.
(*She goes out, and Willmore follows her.*)

BELVILE: 'Tis a mad fellow for a wench.

(*Enter Frederick.*)

FREDERICK: Oh, colonel, such news!

BELVILE: Prithee what?

FREDERICK: News that will make you laugh in spite of fortune.

BELVILE: What, Blunt has had some damned trick put upon him? Cheated, banged, or clapped?°

FREDERICK: Cheated, sir, rarely cheated of all but his shirt and drawers; the unconscionable whore too turned him out before consummation, so that, traversing the streets at midnight, the watch found him in this *fresco* and conducted him home. By heaven, 'tis such a sight, and yet I durst as well been hanged as laughed at him or pity him: He beats all that do but ask him a question, and is in such an humor.

PEDRO: Who is't has met with this ill usage, sir?

BELVILE: A friend of ours whom you must see for mirth's sake. — (*Aside.*) I'll employ him to give Florinda time for an escape.

PEDRO: What is he?

BELVILE: A young countryman of ours, one that has been educated at so plentiful a rate he yet ne'er knew the want of money; and 'twill be a great jest to see how simply he'll look without it. For my part, I'll lend him none: And the rogue know not how to put on a borrowing face and ask first, I'll let him see how good 'tis to play our parts whilst I play his. Prithee, Fred, do you go home and keep him in that posture till we come.   (*Exeunt.*)

(*Enter Florinda from the farther end of the scene, looking behind her.*)

FLORINDA: I am followed still. Ha! My brother too advancing this way! Good heavens defend me from being seen by him!   (*She goes off.*)

(*Enter Willmore, and after him Valeria, at a little distance.*)

WILLMORE: Ah, there she sails! She looks back as she were willing to be boarded; I'll warrant her prize.°
(*He goes out, Valeria following.*)

(*Enter Hellena, just as he goes out, with a page.*)

HELLENA: Ha, is not that my captain that has a woman in chase? 'Tis not Angellica. — Boy, follow those people at a distance, and bring me an account where they go in.   (*Exit Page.*)
— I'll find his haunts, and plague him everywhere. Ha! My brother!
(*Belvile, Willmore, Pedro cross the stage; Hellena runs off.*)

Scene IV

(*Scene changes to another street. Enter Florinda.*)

FLORINDA: What shall I do? My brother now pursues me. Will no kind power protect me from his tyr-

---

48. antipodies: Antipodes; parts of the earth diametrically opposite.   **56. clapped:** Given gonorrhea.

83. warrant her prize: Consider her worthy of pursuing.

anny? Ha! Here's a door open; I'll venture in, since nothing can be worse than to fall into his hands. My life and honor are at stake, and my necessity has no choice.   (*She goes in.*)

(*Enter Valeria, Hellena's Page peeping after Florinda.*)

PAGE: Here she went in; I shall remember this house.
                                   (*Exit Boy.*)

VALERIA: This is Belvile's lodging; she's gone in as readily as if she knew it. Ha! Here's that mad fellow again; I dare not venture in. I'll watch my opportunity.   (*Goes aside.*)

(*Enter Willmore, gazing about him.*)

WILLMORE: I have lost her hereabouts. Pox on't, she must not 'scape me so.   (*Goes out.*)

Scene V

(*Scene changes to Blunt's chamber, discovers him sitting on a couch in his shirt and drawers, reading.*)

BLUNT: So, now my mind's a little at peace, since I have resolved revenge. A pox on this tailor, though, for not bringing home the clothes I bespoke. And a pox of all poor cavaliers: A man can never keep a spare suit for 'em, and I shall have these rogues come in and find me naked, and then I'm undone. But I'm resolved to arm myself: The rascals shall not insult over me too much. (*Puts on an old rusty sword and buff belt.*) Now, how like a morris dancer° I am equipped! A fine ladylike whore to cheat me thus without affording me a kindness for my money! A pox light on her, I shall never be reconciled to the sex more; she has made me as faithless as a physician, as uncharitable as a churchman, and as ill-natured as a poet. Oh, how I'll use all womankind hereafter! What would I give to have one of 'em within my reach now! Any mortal thing in petticoats, kind fortune, send me, and I'll forgive thy last night's malice. — Here's a cursed book, too — a warning to all young travelers — that can instruct me how to prevent such mischiefs now 'tis too late. Well, 'tis a rare convenient thing to read a little now and then, as well as hawk and hunt.
                       (*Sits down again and reads.*)

(*Enter to him Florinda.*)

FLORINDA: This house is haunted, sure: 'Tis well furnished, and no living thing inhabits it. Ha! A man! Heavens, how he's attired! Sure 'tis some rope dan-

9–10. **morris dancer:** The morris dance is a lively dance performed by men wearing costumes and bells.

cer, or fencing master. I tremble now for fear, and yet I must venture now to speak to him. — Sir, if I may not interrupt your meditations —
                       (*He starts up and gazes.*)

BLUNT: Ha, what's here? Are my wishes granted? And is not that a she creature? 'Adsheartlikins, 'tis. — What wretched thing art thou, ha?

FLORINDA: Charitable sir, you've told yourself already what I am: a very wretched maid, forced by a strange unlucky accident to seek a safety here, and must be ruined if you do not grant it.

BLUNT: Ruined! Is there any ruin so inevitable as that which now threatens thee? Dost thou know, miserable woman, into what den of mischiefs thou art fallen; what abyss of confusion, ha? Dost not see something in my looks that frights thy guilty soul, and makes thee wish to change that shape of woman for any humble animal, or devil? For those were safer for thee, and less mischievous.

FLORINDA: Alas, what mean you, sir? I must confess, your looks have something in 'em makes me fear, but I beseech you, as you seem a gentleman, pity a harmless virgin that takes your house for sanctuary.

BLUNT: Talk on, talk on; and weep, too, till my faith return. Do, flatter me out of my senses again. A harmless virgin with a pox; as much one as t'other, 'adsheartlikins. Why, what the devil, can I not be safe in my house for you, not in my chamber? Nay, not even being naked too cannot secure me? This is an impudence greater than has invaded me yet. Come, no resistance.   (*Pulls her rudely.*)

FLORINDA: Dare you be so cruel?

BLUNT: Cruel? 'Adsheartlikins, as a galley slave, or a Spanish whore. Cruel? Yes, I will kiss and beat thee all over, kiss and see thee all over; thou shalt lie with me too, not that I care for the enjoyment, but to let thee see I have ta'en deliberated malice to thee, and will be revenged on one whore for the sins of another. I will smile and deceive thee; flatter thee, and beat thee; embrace thee and rob thee, as she did me; fawn on thee, and strip thee stark naked; then hang thee out at my window by the heels, with a paper of scurvy verses fastened to thy breast in praise of damnable women. Come, come, along.

FLORINDA: Alas, sir, must I be sacrificed for the crimes of the most infamous of my sex? I never understood the sins you name.

BLUNT: Do, persuade the fool you love him, or that one of you can be just or honest; tell me I was not an easy coxcomb, or any strange impossible tale: It will be believed sooner than thy false showers or protestations. A generation of damned hypocrites! To flatter my very clothes from my back! Dissembling witches! Are these the returns you

make an honest gentleman that trusts, believes, and
loves you? But if I be not even with you — Come
along, or I shall —   (*Pulls her again.*)

(*Enter Frederick.*)

85   FREDERICK: Ha, what's here to do?
BLUNT: 'Adsheartlikins, Fred, I am glad thou art come,
to be a witness of my dire revenge.
FREDERICK: What's this, a person of quality too, who
is upon the ramble° to supply the defects of some
90   grave impotent husband?
BLUNT: No, this has another pretense: Some very unfortunate accident brought her hither, to save a life
pursued by I know not who or why, and forced
to take sanctuary here at fool's haven. 'Adsheart-
95   likins, to me of all mankind for protection? Is the
ass to be cajoled again, think ye? No, young one,
no prayers or tears shall mitigate my rage; therefore
prepare for both my pleasures of enjoyment and
revenge. For I am resolved to make up my loss
100   here on thy body: I'll take it out in kindness and
in beating.
FREDERICK: Now, mistress of mine, what do you think
of this?
FLORINDA: I think he will not, dares not be so
105   barbarous.
FREDERICK: Have a care, Blunt, she fetched a deep
sigh; she is enamored with thy shirt and drawers.
She'll strip thee even of that; there are of her calling
such unconscionable baggages and such dexterous
110   thieves, they'll flea° a man and he shall ne'er miss
his skin till he feels the cold. There was a countryman of ours robbed of a row of teeth whilst he
was a-sleeping, which the jilt made him buy again
when he waked. You see, lady, how little reason
115   we have to trust you.
BLUNT: 'Adsheartlikins, why this is most abominable!
FLORINDA: Some such devils there may be, but by all
that's holy, I am none such. I entered here to save
a life in danger.
120   BLUNT: For no goodness, I'll warrant her.
FREDERICK: Faith, damsel, you had e'en confessed the
plain truth, for we are fellows not to be caught
twice in the same trap. Look on that wreck: a tight
vessel when he set out of haven, well trimmed and
125   laden. And see how a female picaroon of this island
of rogues has shattered him, and canst thou hope
for any mercy?
BLUNT: No, no, gentlewoman, come along; 'adsheartlikins, we must be better acquainted. — We'll both
130   lie with her, and then let me alone to bang her.

FREDERICK: I'm ready to serve you in matters of revenge that has a double pleasure in't.
BLUNT: Well said. — You hear, little one, how you
are condemned by public vote to the bed within;
there's no resisting your destiny, sweetheart.   135
                                        (*Pulls her.*)
FLORINDA: Stay, sir. I have seen you with Belvile, an
English cavalier. For his sake, use me kindly. You
know him, sir.
BLUNT: Belvile? Why yes, sweeting, we do know Belvile, and wish he were with us now. He's a cor-   140
morant at whore and bacon:° He'd have a limb or
two of thee, my virgin pullet. But 'tis no matter;
we'll leave him the bones to pick.
FLORINDA: Sir, if you have any esteem for that Belvile,
I conjure you to treat me with more gentleness;   145
he'll thank you for the justice.
FREDERICK: Hark'ee, Blunt, I doubt we are mistaken
in this matter.
FLORINDA: Sir, if you find me not worth Belvile's care,
use me as you please. And that you may think I   150
merit better treatment than you threaten, pray take
this present.
            (*Gives him a ring; he looks on it.*)
BLUNT: Hum, a diamond! Why, 'tis a wonderful virtue
now that lies in this ring, a mollifying virtue. 'Adsheartlikins, there's more persuasive rhetoric in't   155
than all her sex can utter.
FREDERICK: I begin to suspect something, and 'twould
anger us vilely to be trussed up for a rape upon a
maid of quality, when we only believe we ruffle a
harlot.   160
BLUNT: Thou art a credulous fellow, but 'adsheartlikins, I have no faith yet. Why, my saint prattled
as parlously as this does; she gave me a bracelet,
too, a devil on her! But I sent my man to sell it
today for necessaries, and it proved as counterfeit   165
as her vows of love.
FREDERICK: However, let it reprieve her till we see
Belvile.
BLUNT: That's hard, yet I will grant it.

(*Enter a Servant.*)

SERVANT: Oh, sir, the colonel is just come in with his   170
new friend and a Spaniard of quality, and talks of
having you to dinner with 'em.
BLUNT: 'Adsheartlikins, I'm undone! I would not see
'em for the world. Hark'ee, Fred, lock up the wench
in your chamber.   175
FREDERICK: Fear nothing, madam: Whate'er he threatens, you are safe whilst in my hands.
                (*Exeunt Frederick and Florinda.*)

---

89. **upon the ramble:** Rambling, wandering.   110. **flea:** Strip
off the skin (flay).

140–41. **cormorant . . . bacon:** Glutton for sex.

BLUNT: And sirrah, upon your life, say I am not at
home, or that I'm asleep, or — or — anything.
Away; I'll prevent their coming this way.
(*Locks the door, and exeunt.*)

ACT V

(*Blunt's chamber. After a great knocking as at his
chamber door, enter Blunt softly crossing the stage,
in his shirt and drawers as before.*)

[VOICES] (*call within*): Ned! Ned Blunt! Ned Blunt!
BLUNT: The rogues are up in arms. 'Adsheartlikins,
this villainous Frederick has betrayed me: They
have heard of my blessed fortune.
[VOICES] (*and knocking within*): Ned Blunt! Ned!
Ned!
BELVILE [*within*]: Why, he's dead, sir, without dispute
dead; he has not been seen today. Let's break open
the door. Here, boy —
BLUNT: Ha, break open the door? 'Adsheartlikins, that
mad fellow will be as good as his word.
BELVILE [*within*]: Boy, bring something to force the
door.
(*A great noise within, at the door again.*)
BLUNT: So, now must I speak in my own defense; I'll
try what rhetoric will do. — Hold, hold! What do
you mean, gentlemen, what do you mean?
BELVILE (*within*): Oh, rogue, art alive? Prithee open
the door and convince us.
BLUNT: Yes, I am alive, gentlemen, but at present a
little busy.
BELVILE (*within*): How, Blunt grown a man of business? Come, come, open and let's see this miracle.
BLUNT: No, no, no, no, gentlemen, 'tis no great business. But — I am — at — my devotion. 'Adsheartlikins, will you not allow a man time to pray?
BELVILE (*within*): Turned religious? A greater wonder
than the first! Therefore open quickly, or we shall
unhinge, we shall.
BLUNT [*aside*]: This won't do. — Why hark'ee, colonel, to tell you the truth, I am about a necessary
affair of life: I have a wench with me. You apprehend me? — The devil's in't if they be so uncivil
as to disturb me now.
WILLMORE [*within*]: How, a wench? Nay then, we
must enter and partake. No resistance. Unless it
be your lady of quality, and then we'll keep our
distance.
BLUNT: So, the business is out.
WILLMORE [*within*]: Come, come, lend's more hands
to the door. Now heave, all together. (*Breaks open
the door.*) So, well done, my boys.

(*Enter Belvile [and his Page], Willmore, Frederick, and
Pedro. Blunt looks simply, they all laugh at him; he
lays his hand on his sword, and comes up to
Willmore.*)

BLUNT: Hark'ee, sir, laugh out your laugh quickly,
d'ye hear, and be gone. I shall spoil your sport
else, 'adsheartlikins, sir. I shall. The jest has been
carried on too long. — (*Aside.*) A plague upon my
tailor!
WILLMORE: 'Sdeath, how the whore has dressed him!
Faith, sir, I'm sorry.
BLUNT: Are you so, sir? Keep't to yourself then, sir,
I advise you, d'ye hear, for I can as little endure
your pity as his mirth.
(*Lays his hand on's sword.*)
BELVILE: Indeed, Willmore, thou wert a little too rough
with Ned Blunt's mistress. Call a person of quality
whore, and one so young, so handsome, and so
eloquent? Ha, ha, he.
BLUNT: Hark'ee, sir, you know me, and know I can
be angry. Have a care, for 'adsheartlikins, I can
fight, too, I can, sir. Do you mark me? No more.
BELVILE: Why so peevish, good Ned? Some disappointments, I'll warrant. What, did the jealous
count, her husband, return just in the nick?
BLUNT: Or the devil, sir. (*They laugh.*) D'ye laugh?
Look ye settle me a good sober countenance, and
that quickly, too, or you shall know Ned Blunt is
not —
BELVILE: Not everybody, we know that.
BLUNT: Not an ass to be laughed at, sir.
WILLMORE: Unconscionable sinner! To bring a lover
so near his happiness — a vigorous passionate
lover — and then not only cheat him of his mov-
ables, but his very desires, too.
BELVILE: Ah, sir, a mistress is a trifle with Blunt; he'll
have a dozen the next time he looks abroad. His
eyes have charms not to be resisted; there needs
no more than to expose that taking person to the
view of the fair, and he leads 'em all in triumph.
PEDRO: Sir, though I'm a stranger to you, I am
ashamed at the rudeness of my nation; and could
you learn who did it, would assist you to make an
example of 'em.
BLUNT: Why ay, there's one speaks sense now, and
handsomely. And let me tell you, gentlemen, I
should not have showed myself like a jack pudding°
thus to have made you mirth, but that I have revenge within my power. For know, I have got into
my possession a female, who had better have fallen
under any curse than the ruin I design her. 'Adsheartlikins, she assaulted me here in my own lodg-

83. jack pudding: Clown.

90 ings, and had doubtless committed a rape upon me, had not this sword defended me.

FREDERICK: I know not that, but o' my conscience thou had ravished her, had she not redeemed herself with a ring. Let's see't, Blunt.

(*Blunt shows the ring.*)

BELVILE [*aside*]: Ha! The ring I gave Florinda when
95 we exchanged our vows! — Hark'ee, Blunt —

(*Goes to whisper to him.*)

WILLMORE: No whispering, good colonel, there's a woman in the case. No whispering.

BELVILE [*aside to Blunt*]: Hark'ee, fool, be advised, and conceal both the ring and the story for your
100 reputation's sake. Do not let people know what despised cullies we English are; to be cheated and abused by one whore, and another rather bribe thee than be kind to thee, is an infamy to our nation.

105 WILLMORE: Come, come, where's the wench? We'll see her; let her be what she will, we'll see her.

PEDRO: Ay, ay, let us see her. I can soon discover whether she be of quality, or for your diversion.

BLUNT: She's in Fred's custody.

110 WILLMORE: Come, come, the key —

(*To Frederick, who gives him the key; they are going.*)

BELVILE [*aside*]: Death, what shall I do? — Stay, gentlemen. — [*Aside.*] Yet if I hinder 'em, I shall discover all. — Hold, let's go one at once.° Give me the key.

115 WILLMORE: Nay, hold there, colonel, I'll go first.

FREDERICK: Nay, no dispute, Ned and I have the propriety of her.

WILLMORE: Damn propriety! Then we'll draw cuts. (*Belvile goes to whisper* [*to*] *Willmore.*) Nay, no
120 corruption, good colonel. Come, the longest sword carries her.

(*They all draw, forgetting Don Pedro, being a Spaniard, had the longest.*)

BLUNT: I yield up my interest to you, gentlemen, and that will be revenge sufficient.

WILLMORE (*to Pedro*): The wench is yours. — [*Aside.*]
125 Pox of his Toledo,° I had forgot that.

FREDERICK: Come, sir, I'll conduct you to the lady.

(*Exeunt Frederick and Pedro.*)

BELVILE (*aside*): To hinder him will certainly discover her. — Dost know, dull beast, what mischief thou hast done?

(*Willmore walking up and down, out of humor.*)

113. **one at once:** One after the other.   125. **Toledo:** His sword, which won the draw, was made in Toledo, Spain.

WILLMORE: Ay, ay, to trust our fortune to lots! A
130 devil on't, 'twas madness, that's the truth on't.

BELVILE: Oh, intolerable sot —

(*Enter Florinda running, masked, Pedro after her; Willmore gazing round her.*)

FLORINDA (*aside*): Good heaven defend me from discovery!

PEDRO: 'Tis but in vain to fly me; you're fallen to my
135 lot.

BELVILE [*aside*]: Sure she's undiscovered yet, but now I fear there is no way to bring her off.

WILLMORE [*aside*]: Why, what a pox, is not this my
140 woman, the same I followed but now?

(*Pedro talking to Florinda, who walks up and down.*)

PEDRO: As if I did not know ye, and your business here.

FLORINDA (*aside*): Good heaven, I fear he does indeed!

PEDRO: Come, pray be kind; I know you meant to be so when you entered here, for these are proper
145 gentlemen.

WILLMORE: But sir, perhaps the lady will not be imposed upon: She'll choose her man.

PEDRO: I am better bred than not to leave her choice
150 free.

(*Enter Valeria, and is surprised at sight of Don Pedro.*)

VALERIA (*aside*): Don Pedro here! There's no avoiding him.

FLORINDA (*aside*): Valeria! Then I'm undone.

VALERIA (*to Pedro, running to him*): Oh, I have found you, sir! The strangest accident — if I had
155 breath — to tell it.

PEDRO: Speak! Is Florinda safe? Hellena well?

VALERIA: Ay, ay, sir. Florinda is safe. — [*Aside.*] From any fears of you.

PEDRO: Why, where's Florinda? Speak!
160 VALERIA: Ay, where indeed, sir; I wish I could inform you. But to hold you no longer in doubt —

FLORINDA (*aside*): Oh, what will she say?

VALERIA: She's fled away in the habit — of one of her pages, sir. But Callis thinks you may retrieve
165 her yet, if you make haste away. She'll tell you, sir, the rest. — (*Aside.*) If you can find her out.

PEDRO: Dishonorable girl, she has undone my aim. — [*To Belvile.*] Sir, you see my necessity of leaving you, and I hope you'll pardon it. My sister,
170 I know, will make her flight to you; and if she do, I shall expect she should be rendered back.

BELVILE: I shall consult my love and honor, sir.

(*Exit Pedro.*)

FLORINDA (*to Valeria*): My dear preserver, let me embrace thee.
175 WILLMORE: What the devil's all this?

BLUNT: Mystery, by this light.

VALERIA: Come, come, make haste and get yourselves married quickly, for your brother will return again.

BELVILE: I'm so surprised with fears and joys, so amazed to find you here in safety, I can scarce persuade my heart into a faith of what I see.

WILLMORE: Hark'ee, colonel, is this that mistress who has cost you so many sighs, and me so many quarrels with you?

BELVILE: It is. — [*To Florinda.*] Pray give him the honor of your hand.

WILLMORE: Thus it must be received, then. (*Kneels and kisses her hand.*) And with it give your pardon, too.

FLORINDA: The friend to Belvile may command me anything.

WILLMORE (*aside*): Death, would I might; 'tis a surprising beauty.

BELVILE: Boy, run and fetch a father instantly.
(*Exit Boy.*)

FREDERICK: So, now do I stand like a dog, and have not a syllable to plead my own cause with. By this hand, madam, I was never thoroughly confounded before, nor shall I ever more dare look up with confidence, till you are pleased to pardon me.

FLORINDA: Sir, I'll be reconciled to you on one condition: that you'll follow the example of your friend in marrying a maid that does not hate you, and whose fortune, I believe, will not be unwelcome to you.

FREDERICK: Madam, had I no inclinations that way, I should obey your kind commands.

BELVILE: Who, Fred marry? He has so few inclinations for womankind that had he been possessed of paradise he might have continued there to this day, if no crime but love could have disinherited him.

FREDERICK: Oh, I do not use to boast of my intrigues.

BELVILE: Boast! Why, thou dost nothing but boast. And I dare swear, wert thou as innocent from the sin of the grape as thou art from the apple, thou might'st yet claim that right in Eden which our first parents lost by too much loving.

FREDERICK: I wish this lady would think me so modest a man.

VALERIA: She would be sorry then, and not like you half so well. And I should be loath to break my word with you, which was, that if your friend and mine agreed, it should be a match between you and I. (*She gives him her hand.*)

FREDERICK: Bear witness, colonel, 'tis a bargain.
(*Kisses her hand.*)

BLUNT (*to Florinda*): I have a pardon to beg, too; but 'adsheartlikins, I am so out of countenance that I'm a dog if I can say anything to purpose.

FLORINDA: Sir, I heartily forgive you all.

BLUNT: That's nobly said, sweet lady. — Belvile, 230 prithee present her her ring again, for I find I have not courage to approach her myself.
(*Gives him the ring; he gives it to Florinda.*)

(*Enter Boy.*)

BOY: Sir, I have brought the father that you sent for.
[*Exit Boy.*]

BELVILE: 'Tis well. And now, my dear Florinda, let's fly to complete that mighty joy we have so long 235 wished and sighed for. — Come, Fred, you'll follow?

FREDERICK: Your example, sir, 'twas ever my ambition in war, and must be so in love.

WILLMORE: And must not I see this juggling° knot 240 tied?

BELVILE: No, thou shalt do us better service and be our guard, lest Don Pedro's sudden return interrupt the ceremony.

WILLMORE: Content; I'll secure this pass. 245
(*Exeunt Belvile, Florinda, Frederick, and Valeria.*)

(*Enter Boy.*)

BOY (*to Willmore*): Sir, there's a lady without would speak to you.

WILLMORE: Conduct her in; I dare not quit my post.

BOY [*to Blunt*]: And sir, your tailor waits you in your chamber. 250

BLUNT: Some comfort yet: I shall not dance naked at the wedding.
(*Exeunt Blunt and Boy.*)

(*Enter again the Boy, conducting in Angellica in a masking habit and a vizard. Willmore runs to her.*)

WILLMORE [*aside*]: This can be none but my pretty gypsy. — Oh, I see you can follow as well as fly. Come, confess thyself the most malicious devil in 255 nature; you think you have done my business with Angellica —

ANGELLICA: Stand off, base villain!
(*She draws a pistol and holds it to his breast.*)

WILLMORE: Ha, 'tis not she! Who art thou, and what's thy business? 260

ANGELLICA: One thou hast injured, and who comes to kill thee for't.

WILLMORE: What the devil canst thou mean?

ANGELLICA: By all my hopes to kill thee —
(*Holds still the pistol to his breast; he going back, she following still.*)

WILLMORE: Prithee, on what acquaintance? For I 265 know thee not.

240. **juggling:** Based on trickery or deception.

ANGELLICA: Behold this face so lost to thy remembrance,   *(Pulls off her vizard.)*
And then call all thy sins about thy soul,
270   And let 'em die with thee.

WILLMORE: Angellica!

ANGELLICA: Yes, traitor! Does not thy guilty blood
run shivering through thy veins? Hast thou no horror at this sight, that tells thee thou hast not long
275   to boast thy shameful conquest?

WILLMORE: Faith, no, child. My blood keeps its old
ebbs and flows still, and that usual heat too, that
could oblige thee with a kindness, had I but
opportunity.

280 ANGELLICA: Devil! Dost wanton with my pain? Have
at thy heart!

WILLMORE: Hold, dear virago!° Hold thy hand a little;
I am not now at leisure to be killed. Hold and hear
me. — *(Aside.)* Death, I think she's in earnest.

285 ANGELLICA *(aside, turning from him)*: Oh, if I take
not heed, my coward heart will leave me to his
mercy. — What have you, sir, to say? — But should
I hear thee, thou'dst talk away all that is brave
about me, and I have vowed thy death by all that's
290   sacred.
        (Follows him with the pistol to his breast.)

WILLMORE: Why then, there's an end of a proper
handsome fellow, that might 'a lived to have done
good service yet. That's all I can say to't.

ANGELLICA *(pausingly)*: Yet — I would give thee time
295   for — penitence.

WILLMORE: Faith, child, I thank God I have ever took
care to lead a good, sober, hopeful life, and am of
a religion that teaches me to believe I shall depart
in peace.

300 ANGELLICA: So will the devil! Tell me,
How many poor believing fools thou hast
    undone?
How many hearts thou hast betrayed to ruin?
Yet these are little mischiefs to the ills
Thou'st taught mine to commit: Thou'st taught
    it love.

305 WILLMORE: Egad, 'twas shrewdly hurt the while.

ANGELLICA: Love, that has robbed it of its
    unconcern,
Of all that pride that taught me how to value it.
And in its room
A mean submissive passion was conveyed,
310   That made me humbly bow, which I ne'er did
To anything but heaven.

---

282. **virago:** A woman of great stature, strength, and
courage.

Thou, perjured man, didst this; and with thy
    oaths,
Which on thy knees thou didst devoutly make,
Softened my yielding heart, and then I was a
    slave.
Yet still had been content to've worn my chains,   315
Worn 'em with vanity and joy forever,
Hadst thou not broke those vows that put them
    on.
'Twas then I was undone.
    (All this while follows him with the pistol
        to his breast.)

WILLMORE: Broke my vows? Why, where hast thou
lived? Amongst the gods? For I never heard of   320
mortal man that has not broke a thousand vows.

ANGELLICA: Oh, impudence!

WILLMORE: Angellica, that beauty has been too long
tempting, not to have made a thousand lovers languish; who, in the amorous fever, no doubt have   325
sworn like me. Did they all die in that faith, still
adoring? I do not think they did.

ANGELLICA: No, faithless man; had I repaid their
vows, as I did thine, I would have killed the in-
grateful that had abandoned me.   330

WILLMORE: This old general has quite spoiled thee:
Nothing makes a woman so vain as being flattered.
Your old lover ever supplies the defects of age with
intolerable dotage, vast charge, and that which you
call constancy; and attributing all this to your own   335
merits, you domineer, and throw your favors in's
teeth, upbraiding him still with the defects of age,
and cuckold him as often as he deceives your expectations. But the gay, young, brisk lover, that
brings his equal fires, and can give you dart for   340
dart, you'll find will be as nice as you sometimes.

ANGELLICA: All this thou'st made me know, for
    which I hate thee.
Had I remained in innocent security,
I should have thought all men were born my
    slaves,
And worn my power like lightning in my eyes,   345
To have destroyed at pleasure when offended.
But when love held the mirror, the undeceiving
    glass
Reflected all the weakness of my soul, and made
    me know
My richest treasure being lost, my honor,
All the remaining spoil could not be worth   350
The conqueror's care or value.
Oh, how I fell, like a long-worshiped idol,
Discovering all the cheat.
Would not the incense and rich sacrifice
Which blind devotion offered at my altars   355
Have fallen to thee?

Why wouldst thou then destroy my fancied
    power?
WILLMORE: By heaven, thou'rt brave, and I admire
    thee strangely.
I wish I were that dull, that constant thing
Which thou wouldst have, and nature never
    meant me.
I must, like cheerful birds, sing in all groves,
And perch on every bough,
Billing the next kind she that flies to meet me;
Yet, after all, could build my nest with thee,
Thither repairing when I'd loved my round,
And still reserve a tributary flame.
To gain your credit, I'll pay you back your
    charity,
And be obliged for nothing but for love.
                  (Offers her a purse of gold.)
ANGELLICA: Oh, that thou wert in earnest!
So mean a thought of me
    Would turn my rage to scorn, and I should pity
    thee,
And give thee leave to live;
Which for the public safety of our sex,
And my own private injuries, I dare not do.
Prepare —   (Follows still, as before.)
I will no more be tempted with replies.
WILLMORE: Sure —
ANGELLICA: Another word will damn thee! I've heard
    thee talk too long.

(She follows him with the pistol ready to shoot; he
retires, still amazed. Enter Don Antonio, his arm in
a scarf, and lays hold on the pistol.)

ANTONIO: Ha! Angellica!
ANGELLICA: Antonio! What devil brought thee hither?
ANTONIO: Love and curiosity, seeing your coach at
    door. Let me disarm you of this unbecoming in-
    strument of death. (Takes away the pistol.)
    Amongst the number of your slaves was there not
    one worthy the honor to have fought your quar-
    rel? — [To Willmore.] Who are you, sir, that are
    so very wretched to merit death from her?
WILLMORE: One, sir, that could have made a better
    end of an amorous quarrel without you, than with
    you.
ANTONIO: Sure 'tis some rival. Ha! The very man took
    down her picture yesterday; the very same that set
    on me last night! Blessed opportunity —
                  (Offers to shoot him.)
ANGELLICA: Hold, you're mistaken, sir.
ANTONIO: By heaven, the very same! — Sir, what
    pretensions have you to this lady?
WILLMORE: Sir, I do not use to be examined, and am
    ill at all disputes but this —

(Draws; Antonio offers to shoot.)
ANGELLICA (to Willmore): Oh, hold! You see he's
    armed with certain death.
— And you, Antonio, I command you hold,
By all the passion you've so lately vowed me.

(Enter Don Pedro, sees Antonio, and stays.)

PEDRO (aside): Ha! Antonio! And Angellica!
ANTONIO: When I refuse obedience to your will,
May you destroy me with your mortal hate.
By all that's holy, I adore you so,
That even my rival, who has charms enough
To make him fall a victim to my jealousy,
Shall live; nay, and have leave to love on still.
PEDRO (aside): What's this I hear?
ANGELLICA (pointing to Willmore): Ah thus, 'twas
    thus he talked, and I believed.
Antonio, yesterday
I'd not have sold my interest in his heart
For all the sword has won and lost in battle.
— But now, to show my utmost of contempt,
I give thee life; which, if thou wouldst preserve,
Live where my eyes may never see thee more.
Live to undo someone whose soul may prove
So bravely constant to revenge my love.
        (Goes out. Antonio follows, but Pedro
                      pulls him back.)
PEDRO: Antonio, stay.
ANTONIO: Don Pedro!
PEDRO: What coward fear was that prevented thee
    from meeting me this morning on the Molo?
ANTONIO: Meet thee?
PEDRO: Yes, me; I was the man that dared thee to't.
ANTONIO: Hast thou so often seen me fight in war,
    to find no better cause to excuse my absence? I
    sent my sword and one to do thee right, finding
    myself uncapable to use a sword.
PEDRO: But 'twas Florinda's quarrel that we fought,
    and you, to show how little you esteemed her, sent
    me your rival, giving him your interest. But I have
    found the cause of this affront, and when I meet
    you fit for the dispute, I'll tell you my resentment.
ANTONIO: I shall be ready, sir, ere long, to do you
    reason.   (Exit Antonio.)
PEDRO: If I could find Florinda, now whilst my anger's
    high, I think I should be kind, and give her to
    Belvile in revenge.
WILLMORE: Faith, sir, I know not what you would
    do, but I believe the priest within has been so kind.
PEDRO: How? My sister married?
WILLMORE: I hope by this time he is, and bedded too,
    or he has not my longings about him.
PEDRO: Dares he do this? Does he not fear my power?
WILLMORE: Faith, not at all; if you will go in and

thank him for the favor he has done your sister,
so; if not, sir, my power's greater in this house
than yours: I have a damned surly crew here that
450　will keep you till the next tide, and then clap you
on board for prize. My ship lies but a league off
the Molo, and we shall show your donship a
damned Tramontana° rover's trick.

(Enter Belvile.)

BELVILE: This rogue's in some new mischief. Ha! Pedro
455　returned!
PEDRO: Colonel Belvile, I hear you have married my
sister.
BELVILE: You have heard truth then, sir.
PEDRO: Have I so? Then, sir, I wish you joy.
460　BELVILE: How?
PEDRO: By this embrace I do, and I am glad on't.
BELVILE: Are you in earnest?
PEDRO: By our long friendship and my obligations to
thee, I am; the sudden change I'll give you reasons
465　for anon. Come, lead me to my sister, that she may
know I now approve her choice.
　　　　　　　　　　　　　(Exit Belvile with Pedro.)

(Willmore goes to follow them. Enter Hellena, as before in boy's clothes, and pulls him back.)

WILLMORE: Ha! My gypsy! Now a thousand blessings
on thee for this kindness. Egad, child, I was e'en
in despair of ever seeing thee again; my friends are
470　all provided for within, each man his kind woman.
HELLENA: Ha! I thought they had served me some
such trick!
WILLMORE: And I was e'en resolved to go aboard,
and condemn myself to my lone cabin, and the
475　thoughts of thee.
HELLENA: And could you have left me behind? Would
you have been so ill natured?
WILLMORE: Why, 'twould have broke my heart, child.
But since we are met again, I defy foul weather to
480　part us.
HELLENA: And would you be a faithful friend now,
if a maid should trust you?
WILLMORE: For a friend I cannot promise: Thou art
of a form so excellent, a face and humor too good
485　for cold dull friendship. I am parlously afraid of
being in love, child; and you have not forgotten
how severely you have used me?
HELLENA: That's all one; such usage you must still
look for: to find out all your haunts, to rail at you
490　to all that love you, till I have made you love only
me in your own defense, because nobody else will
love you.

---

453. **Tramontana:** Region of Italy north of the Alps.

WILLMORE: But hast thou no better quality to recommend thyself by?
HELLENA: Faith, none, captain. Why, 'twill be the　49
greater charity to take me for thy mistress. I am a
lone child, a kind of orphan lover; and why I
should die a maid, and in a captain's hands too,
I do not understand.
WILLMORE: Egad, I was never clawed away with　5C
broadsides from any female before. Thou hast one
virtue I adore — good nature. I hate a coy demure
mistress, she's as troublesome as a colt; I'll break
none. No, give me a mad mistress when mewed,
and in flying, one I dare trust upon the wing, that　50
whilst she's kind will come to the lure.°
HELLENA: Nay, as kind as you will, good captain,
whilst it lasts. But let's lose no time.
WILLMORE: My time's as precious to me as thine can
be. Therefore, dear creature, since we are so well　51
agreed, let's retire to my chamber; and if ever thou
wert treated with such savory love! Come, my bed's
prepared for such a guest all clean and sweet as
thy fair self. I love to steal a dish and a bottle with
a friend, and hate long graces. Come, let's　51
retire and fall to.
HELLENA: 'Tis but getting my consent, and the business is soon done. Let but old gaffer Hymen° and
his priest say amen to't, and I dare lay my mother's
daughter by as proper a fellow as your father's　52
son, without fear or blushing.
WILLMORE: Hold, hold, no bug words,° child. Priest
and Hymen? Prithee add a hangman to 'em to make
up the consort. No, no, we'll have no vows but
love, child, nor witness but the lover: The kind　52
deity enjoins naught but love and enjoy. Hymen
and priest wait still upon portion and jointure; love
and beauty have their own ceremonies. Marriage
is as certain a bane to love as lending money is to
friendship. I'll neither ask nor give a vow, though　53
I could be content to turn gypsy and become a left-
handed bridegroom to have the pleasure of working that great miracle of making a maid a mother,
if you durst venture. 'Tis upse gypsy° that, and if
I miss I'll lose my labor.　　　　　　　　　　　　　53
HELLENA: And if you do not lose, what shall I get?
A cradle full of noise and mischief, with a pack of
repentance at my back? Can you teach me to weave
incle° to pass my time with? 'Tis upse gypsy that,
too.　　　　　　　　　　　　　　　　　　　　　54

505–506. **flying . . . lure:** I.e., one who will be faithful as
long as that doesn't interfere with her wishes.　518. **Hymen:**
God of marriage.　522. **bug words:** Words that inspire fear.
534. **upse gypsy:** Gypsy fashion.　539. **incle:** Linen yarn or
tape.

WILLMORE: I can teach thee to weave a true love's knot better.

HELLENA: So can my dog.

WILLMORE: Well, I see we are both upon our guards, and I see there's no way to conquer good nature but by yielding. Here, give me thy hand: One kiss, and I am thine.

HELLENA: One kiss! How like my page he speaks! I am resolved you shall have none, for asking such a sneaking sum. He that will be satisfied with one kiss will never die of that longing. Good friend single-kiss, is all your talking come to this? A kiss, a caudle!° Farewell, captain single-kiss.

(*Going out; he stays her.*)

WILLMORE: Nay, if we part so, let me die like a bird upon a bough, at the sheriff's charge. By heaven, both the Indies shall not buy thee from me. I adore thy humor and will marry thee, and we are so of one humor it must be a bargain. Give me thy hand. (*Kisses her hand.*) And now let the blind ones, love and fortune, do their worst.

HELLENA: Why, god-a-mercy, captain!

WILLMORE: But hark'ee: the bargain is now made, but is it not fit we should know each other's names, that when we have reason to curse one another hereafter, and people ask me who 'tis I give to the devil, I may at least be able to tell what family you came of?

HELLENA: Good reason, captain; and where I have cause, as I doubt not but I shall have plentiful, that I may know at whom to throw my — blessings, I beseech ye your name.

WILLMORE: I am called Robert the Constant.

HELLENA: A very fine name! Pray was it your faulkner° or butler that christened you? Do they not use to whistle when they call you?

WILLMORE: I hope you have a better, that a man may name without crossing himself — you are so merry with mine.

HELLENA: I am called Hellena the Inconstant.

(*Enter Pedro, Belvile, Florinda, Frederick, Valeria.*)

PEDRO: Ha! Hellena!

FLORINDA: Hellena!

HELLENA: The very same. Ha! My brother! Now, captain, show your love and courage; stand to your arms and defend me bravely, or I am lost forever.

PEDRO: What's this I hear? False girl, how came you hither, and what's your business? Speak!

(*Goes roughly to her.*)

WILLMORE: Hold off, sir; you have leave to parley° only.   (*Puts himself between.*)

HELLENA: I had e'en as good tell it, as you guess it. Faith, brother, my business is the same with all living creatures of my age: to love and be beloved — and here's the man.

PEDRO: Perfidious maid, hast thou deceived me too; deceived thyself and heaven?

HELLENA: 'Tis time enough to make my peace with that;
Be you but kind, let me alone with heaven.

PEDRO: Belvile, I did not expect this false play from you. Was't not enough you'd gain Florinda, which I pardoned, but your lewd friends too must be enriched with the spoils of a noble family?

BELVILE: Faith, sir, I am as much surprised at this as you can be. Yet, sir, my friends are gentlemen, and ought to be esteemed for their misfortunes, since they have the glory to suffer with the best of men and kings. 'Tis true, he's a rover of fortune, yet a prince aboard his little wooden world.

PEDRO: What's this to the maintenance of a woman of her birth and quality?

WILLMORE: Faith, sir, I can boast of nothing but a sword which does me right where'er I come, and has defended a worse cause than a woman's; and since I loved her before I either knew her birth or name, I must pursue my resolution and marry her.

PEDRO: And is all your holy intent of becoming a nun debauched into a desire of man?

HELLENA: Why, I have considered the matter, brother, and find the three hundred thousand crowns my uncle left me, and you cannot keep from me, will be better laid out in love than in religion, and turn to as good an account. Let most voices carry it: for heaven or the captain?

ALL CRY: A captain! A captain!

HELLENA: Look ye, sir, 'tis a clear case.

PEDRO: Oh, I am mad! — (*Aside.*) If I refuse, my life's in danger. — Come, there's one motive induces me. Take her; I shall now be free from fears of her honor. Guard it you now, if you can; I have been a slave to't long enough. (*Gives her to him.*)

WILLMORE: Faith, sir, I am of a nation that are of opinion a woman's honor is not worth guarding when she has a mind to part with it.

HELLENA: Well said, captain.

PEDRO (*to Valeria*): This was your plot, mistress, but I hope you have married one that will revenge my quarrel to you.

VALERIA: There's no altering destiny, sir.

---

553. **caudle:** A warm drink made of gruel and wine or ale, sweetened and spiced, given to the sick.   573. **faulkner:** Falconer, trainer of hawks.

587. **parley:** Speak or discuss.

PEDRO: Sooner than a woman's will; therefore I forgive you all, and wish you may get my father's
pardon as easily, which I fear.

(*Enter Blunt dressed in a Spanish habit, looking very ridiculous; his Man adjusting his band.*)

640   MAN: 'Tis very well, sir.

BLUNT: Well, sir! 'Adsheartlikins, I tell you 'tis damnable ill, sir. A Spanish habit! Good Lord! Could
the devil and my tailor devise no other punishment
for me but the mode of a nation I abominate?

645   BELVILE: What's the matter, Ned?

BLUNT: Pray view me round, and judge.

(*Turns round.*)

BELVILE: I must confess thou art a kind of an odd
figure.

BLUNT: In a Spanish habit with a vengeance! I had
650   rather be in the Inquisition for Judaism° than in
this doublet and breeches; a pillory were an easy
collar to this, three handfuls high; and these shoes,
too, are worse than the stocks, with the sole an
inch shorter than my foot. In fine, gentlemen, me-
655   thinks I look like a bag of bays° stuffed full of fool's
flesh.

BELVILE: Methinks 'tis well, and makes thee look e'en
cavalier. Come, sir, settle your face and salute our
friends. Lady —

660   BLUNT (*to Hellena*): Ha! Sayst thou so, my little rover?
Lady, if you be one, give me leave to kiss your
hand, and tell you, 'adsheartlikins, for all I look
so, I am your humble servant. A pox of my Spanish
habit!   (*Music is heard to play.*)

665   WILLMORE: Hark! What's this?

(*Enter Boy.*)

BOY: Sir, as the custom is, the gay people in masquerade, who make every man's house their own,
are coming up.

(*Enter several men and women in masking habits, with music; they put themselves in order and dance.*)

BLUNT: 'Adsheartlikins, would 'twere lawful to pull
670   off their false faces, that I might see if my doxy°
were not amongst 'em.

BELVILE (*to the maskers*): Ladies and gentlemen, since
you are come so *a propos,*° you must take a small
collation with us.

675   WILLMORE (*to Hellena*): Whilst we'll to the good man
within, who stays to give us a cast of his office.°

---

650. **Inquisition for Judaism:** The Spanish Inquisition, which persecuted heretics, Jews, and Muslims.   655. **bag of bays:** Spices wrapped in cloth and used for flavoring in cooking.   670. **doxy:** Mistress, prostitute.   673. *a propos:* In a timely fashion; appropriately.   676. **stays . . . office:** The priest waits to perform his office, i.e., to marry them.

Have you no trembling at the near approach?

HELLENA: No more than you have in an engagement
or a tempest.

WILLMORE: Egad, thou'rt a brave girl, and I admire   68
thy love and courage.
    *Lead on; no other dangers they can dread,
    Who venture in the storms o'th' marriage bed.*
                                              (*Exeunt.*)

EPILOGUE

The banished cavaliers! A roving blade!
A popish carnival! A masquerade!
The devil's in't if this will please the nation
In these our blessed times of reformation,
When conventickling° is so much in fashion.   5
And yet —
That mutinous tribe less factions do beget,
Than your continual differing in wit.
Your judgment's, as your passion's, a disease:
Nor muse nor miss your appetite can please;   10
You're grown as nice as queasy consciences,
Whose each convulsion, when the spirit moves,
Damns everything that maggot° disapproves.
    With canting° rule you would the stage refine,
And to dull method all our sense confine.   15
With th'insolence of commonwealths you rule,
Where each gay fop and politic grave fool
On monarch wit impose, without control.
As for the last, who seldom sees a play,
Unless it be the old Blackfriars° way;   20
Shaking his empty noddle o'er bamboo,°
He cries, "Good faith, these plays will never do!
Ah, sir, in my young days, what lofty wit,
What high-strained scenes of fighting there were
writ.
These are slight airy toys. But tell me, pray,   25
What has the House of Commons done today?"
Then shows his politics, to let you see
Of state affairs he'll judge as notably
As he can do of wit and poetry.
The younger sparks, who hither do resort,   30
Cry,
"Pox o' your genteel things! Give us more sport!
Damn me, I'm sure 'twill never please the court."
    Such fops are never pleased, unless the play
Be stuffed with fools as brisk and dull as they.   35

---

5. **conventickling:** A pun. A conventicle was a secret meeting of religious dissenters (those who were not members of the Church of England).   13. **maggot:** Conscience.   14. **canting:** Hypocritical.   20. **Blackfriars:** The Blackfriars Theatre (1576–1655), considered old-fashioned in Behn's time.   21. **o'er bamboo:** Over a cane, implying old age.

Such might the half-crown spare, and in a glass
At home behold a more accomplished ass.
Where they may set their cravats, wigs, and faces,
And practice all their buffoonry grimaces:
40 See how this huff becomes, this damny,° stare,
Which they at home may act because they dare,
But must with prudent caution do elsewhere.
Oh that our Nokes, or Tony Lee,° could show
A fop but half so much to th' life as you.

POSTSCRIPT

This play had been sooner in print, but for a report
about the town (made by some either very malicious
or very ignorant) that 'twas *Thomaso*° altered; which
made the booksellers fear some trouble from the pro-
5 prietor of that admirable play, which indeed has wit
enough to stock a poet, and is not to be pieced or
mended by any but the excellent author himself. That
I have stolen some hints from it, may be a proof that

I valued it more than to pretend to alter it, had I the
dexterity of some poets, who are not more expert in   10
stealing than in the art of concealing, and who even
that way outdo the Spartan boys.° I might have ap-
propriated all to myself; but I, vainly proud of my
judgment, hang out the sign of Angellica (the only
stolen object) to give notice where a great part of the   15
wit dwelt; though if the *Play of the Novella*° were as
well worth remembering as *Thomaso*, they might (bat-
ing° the name) have as well said I took it from thence.
I will only say the plot and business (not to boast
on't) is my own; as for the words and characters, I   20
leave the reader to judge and compare 'em with *Thomaso*, to whom I recommend the great entertainment
of reading it. Though had this succeeded ill, I should
have had no need of imploring that justice from the
critics, who are naturally so kind to any that pretend   25
to usurp their dominion, especially of our sex: They
would doubtless have given me the whole honor on't.
Therefore I will only say in English what the famous
Vergil does in Latin: I make verses, and others have
the fame.   30

40. **damny:** Damn me.   43. **Nokes . . . Lee:** The best low
comedians of the day. James Nokes performed in Thomas
Betterton's company.   3. ***Thomaso:*** Thomas Killigrew's
Thomaso; or, The Wanderer (1654; published 1664).

12. **Spartan boys:** Those who hid in the Trojan horse.   16.
Play of the Novella: *The Novella* (1632) by Richard Brome,
from which Behn borrowed several ideas.   17–18. **bating:**
Excepting.

COMMENTARIES

Virginia Woolf (1882–1941)
ON APHRA BEHN   *1929*

*Virginia Woolf was one of the foremost experimental writers of fiction in
the first half of the twentieth century. She is known for the novels* Mrs. Dalloway
(1925), To the Lighthouse (1927), *and* Orlando (1928) *and her essays, including*
A Room of One's Own (1929), *from which this excerpt comes. Woolf was one
of the first modern commentators to call attention to the extraordinary achievement of Aphra Behn.*

With Mrs. Behn we turn a very important corner on the road. We leave
behind, shut up in their parks among their folios, those solitary great ladies
who wrote without audience or criticism, for their own delight alone. We come

to town and rub shoulders with ordinary people in the streets. Mrs. Behn was a middle-class woman with all the plebeian virtues of humor, vitality, and courage; a woman forced by the death of her husband and some unfortunate adventures of her own to make her living by her wits. She had to work on equal terms with men. She made, by working very hard, enough to live on. The importance of that fact outweighs anything that she actually wrote, even the splendid "A Thousand Martyrs I Have Made," or "Love in Fantastic Triumph Sat," for here begins the freedom of the mind, or rather the possibility that in the course of time the mind will be free to write what it likes. For now that Aphra Behn had done it, girls could go to their parents and say, You need not give me an allowance; I can make money by my pen. Of course the answer for many years to come was, Yes, by living the life of Aphra Behn! Death would be better! and the door was slammed faster than ever. That profoundly interesting subject, the value that men set upon women's chastity and its effect upon their education, here suggests itself for discussion, and might provide an interesting book if any student at Girton or Newnham cared to go into the matter. Lady Dudley, sitting in diamonds among the midges of a Scottish moor, might serve for frontispiece. Lord Dudley, *The Times* said when Lady Dudley died the other day, "a man of cultivated taste and many accomplishments, was benevolent and bountiful, but whimsically despotic. He insisted upon his wife's wearing full dress, even at the remotest shooting-lodge in the Highlands; he loaded her with gorgeous jewels," and so on, "he gave her everything — always excepting any measure of responsibility." Then Lord Dudley had a stroke and she nursed him and ruled his estates with supreme competence for ever after. That whimsical despotism was in the nineteenth century too.

But to return. Aphra Behn proved that money could be made by writing at the sacrifice, perhaps, of certain agreeable qualities; and so by degrees writing became not merely a sign of folly and a distracted mind, but was of practical importance. A husband might die, or some disaster overtake the family. Hundreds of women began as the eighteenth century drew on to add to their pin money, or to come to the rescue of their families by making translations or writing the innumerable bad novels which have ceased to be recorded even in textbooks, but are to be picked up in the fourpenny boxes in the Charing Cross Road. The extreme activity of mind which showed itself in the later eighteenth century among women — the talking, and the meeting, the writing of essays on Shakespeare, the translating of the classics — was founded on the solid fact that women could make money by writing. Money dignifies what is frivolous if unpaid for. It might still be well to sneer at "blue stockings with an itch for scribbling," but it could not be denied that they could put money in their purses. Thus, towards the end of the eighteenth century a change came about which, if I were rewriting history, I should describe more fully and think of greater importance than the Crusades or the Wars of the Roses. The middle-class woman began to write. For if *Pride and Prejudice* matters, and *Middlemarch* and *Vilette* and *Wuthering Heights* matter, then it matters far more than I can prove in an hour's discourse that women generally, and not merely the lonely aristocrat shut up in her country house among her folios and her flatterers, took to writing. Without those forerunners, Jane Austen and the Brontës and George Eliot could no more have written than Shakespeare could have written without Marlowe, or Marlowe without Chaucer, or Chaucer without those forgotten poets who paved the ways and tamed the natural savagery of the tongue. For masterpieces are not single and solitary births; they are the outcome of many years of thinking in common, of thinking by the body of the people, so that the experience of the mass is behind the single voice. Jane Austen should have laid a wreath upon the grave of Fanny Burney, and George Eliot done homage to the robust shade of Eliza Carter — the valiant old woman who tied a bell to her bedstead in order that she might wake early and learn Greek. All women together ought to let flowers fall upon the tomb of Aphra Behn, which is, most scandalously but rather appropriately, in Westminster Abbey,° for it was she who earned them the right to speak their minds. It is she — shady and amorous as she was — who makes it not quite fantastic for me to say to you tonight: Earn five hundred a year by your wits.

Westminster Abbey: The burial place in London of British royalty as well as distinguished citizens, including, in the Poets' Corner, famous writers.

Elaine Hobby (b. 1956)
COURTSHIP AND MARRIAGE IN *THE ROVER*   1989

Elaine Hobby closely examines The Rover *to help us understand the conventions of romantic love in Aphra Behn's work. Her essay is especially enlightening on the questions of marriage and rape and the differences in the viewpoints of men and women characters in the play. Hobby examines the complexities implied in the characterization of Angellica, the courtesan.*

Commonly, Behn's plays feature at least two pairs of young lovers, whose attitudes to love and marriage serve as contrasting strategies in courtship. A common pattern is that of the "constant couple," who remain true to one another, and finally marry, despite parental opposition and, usually, confusions over one another's true identity and conduct. These lovers are not, however, idyllically well matched or perfectly happy. In *The Rover*, Florinda and Belvile are just such a constant couple. From the beginning they are in love with one another, and resolved to accept no other partner. Except for her stubbornness on this one issue, Florinda is all quiet obedience, failing to argue her case against an arranged marriage. Her passivity is no ideal. Twice in the course of the play she narrowly escapes being raped by the friends of her beloved, and on each occasion is only saved because her obvious high social class causes her attackers to hesitate, fearing retribution from her relatives. The second of these incidents is a nightmare scene where, seeking refuge in Blunt's house, she is regarded by him as the perfect target for his revenge against all women (and Lucetta in particular) for making fun of him. When Frederick, the play's great upholder of patriarchal morality, arrives, the two men agree to rape her.

BLUNT: We'll both lie with her, and then let me alone to bang her.
FREDERICK: I'm ready to serve you in matters of revenge that has a double
    pleasure in't. (IV, v, 129–32)

In a world where men can choose to rape a woman, any woman, for spite, there is no safety for the romantic heroine. In Behn's plays, as in her novels, rape or the threat of it is shown to be an almost routine masculine strategy to bully and manipulate women. In *The Amorous Prince,* Frederick threatens to rape Laura at knifepoint to humble her for scorning him, and in the same play Silvio threatens to rape his "sister" Cleonte. Sir Timothy Tawdrey in *The Town-Fopp,* when threatening to rape Phillis, tells her that old patriarchal lie: that all women want to be forcibly taken. Phillis's fate is the most terrible of all. Having no economic choices (like Philadelphia in Behn's novel *The Unfortunate Happy Lady*), she has no option but to marry her would-be rapist.

Setting out with a theme of courtship and marriage, Behn writes about rape and prostitution, constructing scenarios that show how closely connected these fates are for women. Where Florinda's reliance on "true love" for her salvation twice brings her to the brink of being raped, the courtesan Angellica Bianca in the same play is betrayed by her final inability to escape from the tempting lies of romance. Early in the play, she makes a cool assessment of women's position, explaining that she had opted to sell her body for the solid return of financial reward, rather than trusting to illusory male fidelity: "Nothing but gold shall charm my heart" (II, I, 173–74). She knows, too, that marriage for money is a no less mercenary affair than prostitution. Disaster arrives, however, because she has seriously misjudged the power structure of her society. She arrives in town hoping to captivate either the viceroy's son Don Antonio, or Don Pedro, the nephew of her deceased "protector." Had she been married to her old lover, Don Pedro would have been her kin, and had some social duty to support her. As it is, she is left to live on her wits and her transitory physical charms. When Willmore, the "rover" of the title, finally rejects her in favor of the wealthy virgin Hellena, she is forced to recognize that her chosen independence was illusory. In a world where men make the rules, her only salable item is her virginity. Having sold that in the wrong market, she is damned.

When Angellica falls hopelessly for the feckless Willmore, she wants to believe that love and romance can be dissociated from social and economic structures, that "true love" in her world can be above financial considerations. She calls on him to see things her way and, blinded by this desire, does not recognize that he is using her for his pleasure.

> ANGELLICA: Thou'rt a brave fellow! Put up thy gold, and know,
> That were thy fortune large as is thy soul,
> Thou shouldst not buy my love
> Couldst thou forget these mean effects of vanity
> Which set me out to sale,
> And as a lover prize my yielding joys.
> Canst thou believe they'll be entirely thine,
> Without considering they were mercenary? (II, II, 115–22)

In the course of the play, Willmore's repeated answer to this is a resounding "No." Having worshiped her beauty, tasted the pleasures of her body, and spent her money to attract a wealthier woman, he leaves her for a better catch.

Angellica is a troubling and uncomfortable figure in the play, disrupting the wit and airiness of scenes between Hellena and Willmore and undercutting the conventional "happy ending" of true lovers united. Realizing she has been betrayed by Willmore despite giving him "My virgin heart . . . Oh! 'tis gone!" (IV, II, 167) she plots her revenge "for the public safety of our sex" (V, 373). Trapping him at gunpoint she decides, however, to let him live: he is not worth the trouble of an execution: "But now, to show my utmost of contempt, / I give thee life" (V, 415–16). Through Willmore, she has learned that male protestations of devotion, and all their courtly love rhetoric, are for them just a game. There is no true power, no safety, for women. . . .

In many of Behn's plays, men's obsessions with their courtship conventions prevent them from understanding the women they address. Romance is a male invention, and women are jeopardized and often betrayed if they believe such declarations of undying passion. The task for the witty heroine who is at the center of many of Behn's plays, as Hellena is in *The Rover*, is to discover as much as possible about her man's true intentions, beneath his courtly facade. Willmore refers to both Angellica and to Hellena as his "angel" in high-flown rhetoric, but where Angellica is briefly fooled by this worship, Hellena is quite clear-sighted about the limit of his commitment. As far as possible, she takes control of her situation, disguising herself and playing parts, testing out and then capturing the man she has chosen. Disguised, she watches him court and promise fidelity to Angellica, and in a bitter but witty scene mocks him, throwing back at him the overblown promises she has heard him make (III, I). She has no interest in traditional courtship rituals, thinking them "a very pretty, idle, silly kind of pleasure to pass one's time with" (III, I, 72–73), but she is not deceived by Willmore's forthright arguments in favor of unfettered sensuality. She knows already what Angellica shows the audience: Marriage is a necessity for women, otherwise, as she challenges Willmore, "What shall I get? A cradle full of noise and mischief, with a pack of repentance at my back?" (V, 536–38).

She gets her man, but it is a tawdry victory and the audience knows it, with Angellica there to remind them. Willmore has shown himself to be insensitive, capricious, and dangerous to women, and there is no reason to imagine that he will be faithful to Hellena for longer than the month that he originally resolves to sacrifice to gain her. In *The Second Part of the Rover*, where Willmore again chooses between two women (and this time chooses the prostitute), it is revealed in passing that Hellena had died at sea within three months of the marriage.

The world of courtship and marriage depicted by Behn in these plays is a bleak one. Bright, witty women like Hellena use daring and imagination in a desperate attempt to evade the arranged marriages or confinements to nunneries destined them by their families. They race against time, trying their best to negotiate when all power lies in others' hands. None of the dashing young blades they choose and test out are admirable characters, but they seem preferable to a fool like Haunce van Ezel (in *The Dutch Lover*) or an odious tyrant like Octavio (in *The Feign'd Curtizans*). Woven in with the wit and humor, music and spectacle, are hard, sober women's truths about the debauchery of the Restoration court and its acolytes. Armed with wit and driven by necessity, like her heroines, Aphra Behn succeeded in dramatizing in marketable form the dilemmas that faced her and her sisters.

William Congreve

Although born in England, William Congreve (1670–1729) was educated in Ireland, first at Kilkenny School and then at Trinity College, Dublin. Jonathan Swift, who praised him in his poetry, was also at Kilkenny and Trinity during part of this time. They were lifelong friends and central figures in literary London. Later Congreve read law at the Middle Temple in London and was able to make good use of his legal training in several of his plays.

Congreve's literary career began with a novel, *Incognita* (1691), which he wrote in his teens. John Dryden praised the novel and later praised his plays. After Congreve's first play was produced, the poet Thomas Southerne named Congreve the likely inheritor of Dryden's crown as poet laureate, but Congreve's career as a playwright lasted only seven years. He left the stage after the production of *The Way of the World* (1700) ostensibly because of its cool reception. The play was not technically a failure, but it was not received with the enthusiasm Congreve thought it deserved.

His first play, *The Old Bachelor* (1693) was an immediate success and established him as an important playwright. Later in 1693 he produced his second play, *The Double Dealer*, which had a mixed reception. Dryden, in a letter, said, "The women thinke he has exposed their Bitchery too much and the Gentlemen are offended with him; for the discovery of their follyes: & the way of their Intrigues, under the notion of Friendship to their Ladyes Husbands." Maskwell, the double dealer, is a classic manipulator who forwards his own interests while damaging those of other characters. Congreve defended the play as a moral fable, and it was not until Queen Mary requested a command performance that the play was restored in the eyes of the public. *Love for Love* (1695) was for many years Congreve's most popular and best-liked play. It is the story of the worthy Valentine, who is about to lose an inheritance to a younger brother. In the end Valentine's intelligence wins out, and by pretending madness he secures his beloved, the wealthy heiress Angelica, as well as his own estate. Thomas Betterton, the acclaimed Restoration actor, played Valentine in the first performances; his theater company at Lincoln's Inn Field produced all of Congreve's work. John Gielgud played Valentine in London, opening on April 8, 1943, to considerable acclaim and continuing for 471 performances through World War II. Laurence Olivier and Lynn Redgrave played in the 1965 revival, also a success. Congreve's one tragedy, *The Mourning Bride*

(1697), was very successful although it has not been revived in the twentieth century.

After leaving the dramatic stage in 1700, Congreve spend the rest of his life writing occasional poetry, such as *A Pindarique Ode on the Victorious Progress of Her Majesties Arms* (1706), and libretti for several operas: *The Judgment of Paris* (1701), *A Hymn to Harmony* (1703), and *The Tears of Amarylis* (1703). He spent much of his later years as a retiring gentleman in the company of the duchess of Marlborough, with whom he probably had a child, Lady Mary Godolphin, who inherited his estate.

Like Aphra Behn, Congreve was buried in the Poet's Corner of Westminster Abbey. Critics in his time and in succeeding generations regarded his plays as among the purest examples of the English comic style of the late seventeenth century. *The Way of the World* has been especially singled out for praise because while it is witty, brisk, and amusing, it is pungent and serious at the core, with characters whose intelligence and essential worth help animate a drama that vies with the achievement of Molière.

THE WAY OF THE WORLD

The Way of the World (1700), Congreve's fifth and last play, has been his most enduring and — taking the long view — his most successful. It is an intellectual romp, with plot twists, disguises, and numerous complications. The names of the characters — Fainall, Mirabell, Wilful, Witwoud, Waitwell, and Petulant — indicate Congreve's use of stock or TYPE CHARACTERS, characters immediately recognizable for their stereotypical behavior and traits. However, he always moves beneath the surfaces of types and reveals a satisfying complexity. Type characters have been used to advantage in all ages of comic drama, especially in the English Restoration.

Congreve's genius shows up in his witty use of REPARTEE, or quick replies. He is a master of the one-liner and the RIPOSTE, a sharp return in speech. Wit was a rapier in the late seventeenth century, to be used for the amusement of those intelligent enough to follow the exchanges. Early on, Witwoud says, "A wit should no more be sincere than a

woman constant; one argues a decay of parts, as t'other of beauty."
Mirabell tells Mrs. Fainall, "You should have just so much disgust for
your husband as may be sufficient to make you relish your lover." Such
witty comment on early eighteenth-century marriage, once we get to
know Fainall and his essential viciousness, takes on a serious cast.

The plot of *The Way of the World* centers on marriage, adultery,
and family fortunes. Mirabell wishes to marry Millamant, who has
inherited six thousand pounds and will receive another six thousand
pounds if she marries in accord with the wishes of her aunt, Lady
Wishfort (an older woman "full of the vigor of fifty-five"). Lady Wishfort, however, feels betrayed by Mirabell, who pretended to love her
to get close to Millamant. Wishfort wants Millamant to marry Sir Wilfull
Witwoud, and Mirabell's efforts to make Lady Wishfort relent in this
wish are carried forth on a wave of deception, disguise, and comic mix-
ups. Mirabell and Millamant resemble traditional Shakespearean lovers
such as Petruchio and Katharine in *The Taming of the Shrew* and
Benedick and Beatrice in *Much Ado About Nothing*. However, they
also resemble Aphra Behn's Willmore and Hellena and Molière's Alceste
and Célimène. Millamant is every bit a match for Mirabell, and, as a
result, their comic scenes are intense and engaging even as they reveal
the limits of Congreve's society.

The "contract" scene in act IV, in which Millamant and Mirabell
discuss their intentions to marry, is both funny and very serious. Their
use of legal language in what is ostensibly a romantic situation is point-
edly ironic. Millamant is no starry-eyed bride. Once married, she knows
that all her possessions will belong to her husband; she will be like his
chattel, to do with as he pleases. Millamant has the advantage of studying the marriages around her and covenants in this scene for her
independence.

The villain in the play is Fainall. He is having an affair with Mrs.
Marwood but discovers she is seriously attracted to Mirabell. He is no
longer interested in her, but because she can expose him to his wife as
an adulterer he cannot turn away from her. Fainall's wife is Mrs. Wishfort's daughter, once married to a Mr. Languish who died. Before becoming involved with Fainall, Mrs. Fainall was Mirabell's mistress, but
when she feared she was pregnant, Mirabell arranged the hasty marriage
to Fainall, knowing that Fainall needed the widow's money and that
Mrs. Fainall needed the respectability of marriage. It turned out that
Mrs. Fainall was not pregnant and now regrets her marriage. In act II
when she asks Mirabell why she married, he responds: "Why do we
daily commit disagreeable and dangerous actions? To save that idol,
reputation." Of her husband Fainall, he says, "When you are weary of
him, you know your remedy." (The epigraph at the beginning of the
play warns us that adultery is the subject of the drama.) These circumstances demonstrate that Fainall, for all his villainy, is being used by

the Wishfort family for their ends almost as much as he is using them for his own.

Mirabell, like Fainall, is a manipulator. However, he is not a villain at heart. He respects Millamant and manages ultimately to find a way to undo Fainall's schemes to control Millamant's fortune. The play does not end with everyone happy, but with Mirabell and Millamant possessing the advantage and looking forward to marriage and children. Eventually all deceptions are revealed, the proper lovers are joined, and the complications are smoothed out. Because of its careful examination of the relationship between the sexes and of the impediments a sophisticated society can throw between them, *The Way of the World* is virtually a timeless comedy.

The Way of the World in Performance

After its initial poor reception, Alexander Pope praised *The Way of the World* as having "so much bullion in it as would serve to lace fifty modern comedies." It was revived relatively soon after 1701 in London and, according to theater historian Emmet Avery, it played 285 times in the eighteenth century. It was one of the first plays at the new Covent Garden Theatre on December 7, 1732, and is said to be the most produced English comedy ever since. It is manifestly a vehicle for female stars. The great actress Peggy Ashcroft, along with Dame Edith Evans, starred in the London production of 1942. The play has been done steadily in the United States since the 1920s. The Tyrone Guthrie Theater in Minneapolis produced it in 1965 to rave notices, with Jessica Tandy in the role of Lady Wishfort essentially stealing the show. Britain's Actor's Company brought it to the Brooklyn Academy in 1974, with the characters wearing cutaway formal clothes, top hats, and tails instead of eighteenth-century garb. The production used telephones and other modern conveniences to demonstrate that the play is not a museum piece. Robin Phillips's 1976 Stratford, Ontario, production was described as "nothing short of brilliant." Maggie Smith played Millamant several times in the 1980s, joining Jessica Tandy in her role as Lady Wishfort. Smith's breathless performance in the January 1985 London production underscored the fact that the role is ideal for a great comic actress. She made the play her own.

William Congreve (1670–1729)

THE WAY OF THE WORLD   *1700*

Audire est operae pretium, procedere recte
Qui moechis non vultis.   — HORACE, *Satires*°

— Metuat doti deprensa.°

PROLOGUE

(Spoken by Mr. Fainall.)

Of those few fools who with ill stars are curst,
Sure scribbling fools, call'd poets, fare the worst;
For they're a sort of fools which Fortune makes,
And after she has made 'em fools, forsakes.
5   With Nature's oafs 'tis quite a different case,
For Fortune favors all her idiot-race;
In her° own nest the cuckoo-eggs we find,
O'er which she broods to hatch the changeling-
        kind.°
No portion for her own she has to spare,
10   So much she dotes on her adopted care.
        Poets are bubbles,° by the town drawn in,
Suffer'd at first some trifling stakes to win;
But what unequal hazards do they run!
Each time they write, they venture all they've won;
The squire that's buttered° still, is sure to be
15   undone.
This author, heretofore, has found your favor,
But pleads no merit from his past behavior.
To build on that might prove a vain presumption,
Should grants to poets made admit resumption;

And in Parnassus° he must lose his seat,   20
If that be found a forfeited estate.
        He owns, with toil he wrought the following
        scenes,
But, if they're naught, ne'er spare him for his pains;
Damn him the more; have no commiseration
For dullness on mature deliberation.   25
He swears he'll not resent one hiss'd-off scene,
Nor, like those peevish wits, his play maintain,
Who, to assert their sense, your taste arraign.
Some plot we think he has, and some new thought;
Some humor too, no farce; but that's a fault.   30
Satire, he thinks, you ought not to expect;
For so reform'd a town who dares correct?
To please, this time, has been his sole pretense;
He'll not instruct, lest it should give offense.
Should he by chance a knave or fool expose,   35
That hurts none here, sure here are none of those.
In short, our play shall (with your leave to show it)
Give you one instance of a passive poet,
Who to your judgments yields all resignation;
So save or damn, after your own discretion.   40

Dramatis Personae

Men
FAINALL, *in love with Mrs. Marwood*
MIRABELL, *in love with Mrs. Millamant*
WITWOUD, }
PETULANT, } *followers of Mrs. Millamant*
SIR WILFULL WITWOUD, *half brother to Witwoud, and*
    nephew to Lady Wishfort
WAITWELL, *servant to Mirabell*

Women
LADY WISHFORT, *enemy to Mirabell, for having falsely*
    pretended love to her

[Epigraphs] *Audire . . . vultis*: Horace, *Satires* I.2.37–38. "Ye
that do not wish well to the proceedings of adulterers, it is
worth your while to hear how they are hampered on all
sides" (trans. Christopher Smart). *Metuat doti deprensa*:
Ibid., line 131. The context of the lines in which the epigraph
appears is "Nor am I apprehensive, while I am in her company, . . . lest the maid . . . should be in apprehension for
her limbs, *the detected wife for her portion* [dowry], I for
myself" (trans. Smart).   7. **her**: Fortune's.   8. **O'er which**
. . . changeling-kind: The cuckoo lays its eggs in the nests
of other birds to whom they are left to be hatched. The implication is that Fortune is favorable to fools.   11. **bubbles**:
Dupes.   15. **buttered**: Abundantly flattered.

20. **Parnassus**: The Greek mountain sacred to Apollo and
the Muses.

Mrs. MILLAMANT, *a fine lady, niece to Lady Wishfort, and loves Mirabell*

Mrs. MARWOOD, *friend to Mr. Fainall, and likes Mirabell*

Mrs. FAINALL, *daughter to Lady Wishfort, and wife to Fainall, formerly friend to Mirabell*

FOIBLE, *woman to Lady Wishfort*

MINCING, *woman to Mrs. Millamant*

BETTY, *waiting-maid at a chocolate-house*

PEG, *maid to Lady Wishfort*

DANCERS, FOOTMEN, *and* ATTENDANTS

Scene: *London. The time equal to that of the presentation.*

ACT I

(*A Chocolate-House. Mirabell and Fainall, rising from cards; Betty waiting.*)

MIRABELL: You are a fortunate man, Mr. Fainall.

FAINALL: Have we done?

MIRABELL: What you please. I'll play on to entertain you.

5 FAINALL: No, I'll give you your revenge another time, when you are not so indifferent; you are thinking of something else now, and play too negligently. The coldness of a losing gamester lessens the pleasure of the winner. I'd no more play with a man
10 that slighted his ill fortune than I'd make love to a woman who undervalued the loss of her reputation.

MIRABELL: You have a taste extremely delicate and are for refining on your pleasures.

15 FAINALL: Prithee, why so reserved? Something has put you out of humor.

MIRABELL: Not at all. I happen to be grave today, and you are gay; that's all.

FAINALL: Confess, Millamant and you quarreled last
20 night, after I left you; my fair cousin has some humors° that would tempt the patience of a Stoic.° What, some coxcomb° came in, and was well received by her, while you were by.

MIRABELL: Witwoud and Petulant, and what was
25 worse, her aunt, your wife's mother, my evil genius; or to sum up all in her own name, my old Lady Wishfort came in.

---

21. humors: Moods.   Stoic: One who subscribes to the Stoic school of philosophy, which teaches freedom from passion and indifference to pleasure and pain.   22. coxcomb: Conceited person, fop.

FAINALL: Oh, there it is then! She has a lasting passion for you, and with reason. What, then my wife was there?   30

MIRABELL: Yes, and Mrs. Marwood, and three or four more, whom I never saw before. Seeing me, they all put on their grave faces, whispered one another; then complained aloud of the vapors,° and after fell into a profound silence.   35

FAINALL: They had a mind to be rid of you.

MIRABELL: For which reason I resolved not to stir. At last the good old lady broke through her painful taciturnity with an invective against long visits. I would not have understood her, but Millamant   40 joining in the argument, I rose, and, with a constrained smile, told her, I thought nothing was so easy as to know when a visit began to be troublesome. She reddened, and I withdrew, without expecting° her reply.   45

FAINALL: You were to blame to resent what she spoke only in compliance with her aunt.

MIRABELL: She is more mistress of herself than to be under the necessity of such a resignation.

FAINALL: What? though half her fortune depends upon   50 her marrying with my lady's approbation?

MIRABELL: I was then in such a humor that I should have been better pleased if she had been less discreet.

FAINALL: Now I remember, I wonder not they were   55 weary of you. Last night was one of their cabal nights; they have 'em three times a week, and meet by turns at one another's apartments, where they come together like the coroner's inquest, to sit upon the murdered reputations of the week. You and I   60 are excluded; and it was once proposed that all the male sex should be excepted. But somebody moved that, to avoid scandal, there might be one man of the community; upon which motion Witwoud and Petulant were enrolled members.°   65

MIRABELL: And who may have been the foundress of this sect? My Lady Wishfort, I warrant, who publishes her detestation of mankind, and full of the vigor of fifty-five, declares for a friend° and ratafia,° and let posterity shift for itself, she'll breed no   70 more.

FAINALL: The discovery of your sham addresses to her, to conceal your love to her niece, has provoked this separation; had you dissembled better, things might have continued in the state of nature.   75

---

34. vapors: Boredom.   45. expecting: Awaiting.   64–65. Witwoud . . . members: The implication is that Witwoud and Petulant are but half-men.   69. friend: Lover. When applied to a lady, the word carries the meaning of "mistress." ratafia: Fruit-flavored liqueur.

MIRABELL: I did as much as man could, with any reasonable conscience; I proceeded to the very last act of flattery with her, and was guilty of a song in her commendation. Nay, I got a friend to put her into a lampoon, and compliment her with the imputation of an affair with a young fellow, which I carried so far that I told her the malicious town took notice that she was grown fat of a sudden; and when she lay in of a dropsy,° persuaded her she was reported to be in labor. The devil's in't, if an old woman is to be flattered further, unless a man should endeavor downright personally to debauch° her; and that my virtue forbade me. But for the discovery of this amour I am indebted to your friend, or your wife's friend, Mrs. Marwood.

FAINALL: What should provoke her to be your enemy, unless she has made you advances which you have slighted? Women do not easily forgive omissions of that nature.

MIRABELL: She was always civil to me till of late. I confess I am not one of those coxcombs who are apt to interpret a woman's good manners to her prejudice, and think that she who does not refuse 'em everything can refuse 'em nothing.

FAINALL: You are a gallant man, Mirabell; and though you may have cruelty enough not to satisfy a lady's longing, you have too much generosity not to be tender of her honor. Yet you speak with an indifference which seems to be affected, and confesses you are conscious of a negligence.

MIRABELL: You pursue the argument with a distrust that seems to be unaffected, and confesses you are conscious of a concern for which the lady is more indebted to you than is your wife.

FAINALL: Fie, fie, friend! If you grow censorious, I must leave you. I'll look upon the gamesters in the next room.

MIRABELL: Who are they?

FAINALL: Petulant and Witwoud. (*To Betty.*) Bring me some chocolate. (*Exit.*)

MIRABELL: Betty, what says your clock?

BETTY: Turned of the last canonical hour,° sir.
(*Exit.*)

MIRABELL: How pertinently the jade° answers me! (*Looking on his watch.*) Ha? almost one o'clock! O, y'are come!

(*Enter a Footman.*)

Well, is the grand affair over? You have been something tedious.

FOOTMAN: Sir, there's such coupling at Pancras° that they stand behind one another, as 'twere in a country dance. Ours was the last couple to lead up, and no hopes appearing of dispatch, besides the parson growing hoarse, we were afraid his lungs would have failed before it came to our turn; so we drove round to Duke's place,° and there they were riveted in a trice.°

MIRABELL: So, so, you are sure they are married.

FOOTMAN: Married and bedded, sir; I am witness.

MIRABELL: Have you the certificate?

FOOTMAN: Here it is, sir.

MIRABELL: Has the tailor brought Waitwell's clothes home, and the new liveries?

FOOTMAN: Yes, sir.

MIRABELL: That's well. Do you go home again, d'ye hear, and adjourn the consummation till further order; bid Waitwell shake his ears, and Dame Partlet° rustle up her feathers, and meet me at one o'clock by Rosamond's Pond,° that I may see her before she returns to her lady; and as you tender your ears, be secret.

(*Exit Footman.*)

(*Reenter Fainall and Betty.*)

FAINALL: Joy of your success, Mirabell; you look pleased.

MIRABELL: Aye, I have been engaged in a matter of some sort of mirth, which is not yet ripe for discovery. I am glad this is not a cabal night. I wonder, Fainall, that you who are married, and of consequence should be discreet, will suffer your wife to be of such a party.

FAINALL: Faith, I am not jealous. Besides, most who are engaged are women and relations; and for the men, they are of a kind too contemptible to give scandal.

MIRABELL: I am of another opinion. The greater the coxcomb, always the more the scandal; for a woman who is not a fool can have but one reason for associating with a man who is one.

FAINALL: Are you jealous as often as you see Witwoud entertained by Millamant?

MIRABELL: Of her understanding I am, if not of her person.

---

84. dropsy: An excessive accumulation of fluid in the body. **88. debauch:** Seduce. **117. canonical hour:** It was only during the canonical hours (eight in the morning to twelve noon) that marriages could be legally performed. **118. jade:** Derogatory term for a woman.

123. Pancras: St. Pancras Church, where marriages were performed without license and outside the canonical hours. **129. Duke's place:** St. James's Church, Aldgate. **129–30. riveted in a trice:** Married quickly. **140–41. Dame Partlet:** Refers to Foible, who has just been married to Waitwell. "Partlet" derives from Pertelote, the hen in Chaucer's "Nun's Priest's Tale." **142. Rosamond's Pond:** A lake in St. James's Park.

65 FAINALL: You do her wrong; for, to give her her due, she has wit.

MIRABELL: She has beauty enough to make any man think so, and complaisance enough not to contradict him who shall tell her so.

70 FAINALL: For a passionate lover, methinks you are a man somewhat too discerning in the failings of your mistress.

MIRABELL: And for a discerning man, somewhat too passionate a lover; for I like her with all her faults,
75 nay, like her for her faults. Her follies are so natural, or so artful, that they become her; and those affectations which in another woman would be odious, serve but to make her more agreeable. I'll tell thee, Fainall, she once used me with that in-
80 solence, that in revenge I took her to pieces, sifted° her, and separated her failings; I studied 'em, and got 'em by rote.° The catalogue was so large that I was not without hopes one day or other to hate her heartily: To which end I so used° myself to
85 think of 'em at length, contrary to my design and expectation, they gave me every hour less and less disturbance; till in a few days it became habitual to me to remember 'em without being displeased. They are now grown as familiar to me as
90 my own frailties; and in all probability, in a little time longer I shall like 'em as well.

FAINALL: Marry her, marry her! Be half as well acquainted with her charms as you are with her defects, and my life on't, you are your own man
95 again.

MIRABELL: Say you so?

FAINALL: Aye, aye, I have experience; I have a wife, and so forth.

(Enter a Messenger.)

MESSENGER: Is one Squire Witwoud here?

100 BETTY: Yes; what's your business?

MESSENGER: I have a letter for him, from his brother Sir Wilfull, which I am charged to deliver into his own hands.

BETTY: He's in the next room, friend; that way.

(Exit Messenger.)

105 MIRABELL: What, is the chief of that noble family in town, Sir Wilfull Witwoud?

FAINALL: He is expected today. Do you know him?

MIRABELL: I have seen him. He promises to be an extraordinary° person; I think you have the honor
110 to be related to him.

FAINALL: Yes, he is half brother to this Witwoud by a former wife, who was sister to my Lady Wishfort,

my wife's mother. If you marry Millamant, you must call cousins too.

215 MIRABELL: I had rather be his relation than his acquaintance.

FAINALL: He comes to town in order to equip himself for travel.

220 MIRABELL: For travel! Why the man that I mean is above forty.°

FAINALL: No matter for that; 'tis for the honor of England that all Europe should know we have blockheads of all ages.

225 MIRABELL: I wonder there is not an act of parliament to save the credit of the nation, and prohibit the exportation of fools.

FAINALL: By no means; 'tis better as 'tis. 'Tis better to trade with a little loss than to be quite eaten up
230 with being overstocked.

MIRABELL: Pray, are the follies of this knight-errant and those of the squire his brother anything related?

FAINALL: Not at all; Witwoud grows by the knight,
235 like a medlar grafted on a crab.° One will melt in your mouth, and t'other set your teeth on edge; one is all pulp, and the other all core.

MIRABELL: So one will be rotten before he be ripe, and the other will be rotten without ever being ripe at all.

240 FAINALL: Sir Wilfull is an odd mixture of bashfulness and obstinacy. But when he's drunk, he's as loving as the monster in *The Tempest*,° and much after the same manner. To give t'other his due, he has something of good nature and does not always
245 want wit.

MIRABELL: Not always; but as often as his memory fails him, and his commonplace° of comparisons. He is a fool with a good memory and some few scraps of other folks' wit. He is one whose con-
250 versation can never be approved, yet it is now and then to be endured. He has indeed one good quality, he is not exceptious;° for he so passionately affects the reputation of understanding raillery° that he will construe an affront into a jest and call
255 downright rudeness and ill language, satire and fire.

FAINALL: If you have a mind to finish his picture, you

---

220. above forty: It was customary for a gentleman of quality to make a "grand tour" of continental capitals in his early twenties.   234. medlar grafted on a crab: The medlar is like a crab apple and is edible only when it begins to decay. The crab apple is always sour.   242. the monster in *The Tempest*: Caliban (or Sycorax) in the adaptation of Shakespeare's play by John Dryden and Sir William Davenant (1667). 247. commonplace: Commonplace book; scrapbook.   252. exceptious: Inclined to take exceptions.   253. raillery: Good-humored ridicule; banter.

180. sifted: Examined closely.   182. by rote: In a mechanical way.   184. used: Accustomed.   209. extraordinary: Somewhat eccentric.

have an opportunity to do it at full length. Behold
the original!

(*Enter Witwoud.*)

WITWOUD: Afford me your compassion, my dears!
260 Pity me, Fainall! Mirabell, pity me!
MIRABELL: I do from my soul.
FAINALL: Why, what's the matter?
WITWOUD: No letters for me, Betty?
BETTY: Did not a messenger bring you one but now,
265 sir?
WITWOUD: Aye, but no other?
BETTY: No, sir.
WITWOUD: That's hard, that's very hard. A messenger,
a mule, a beast of burden! He has brought me a
270 letter from the fool my brother, as heavy as a
panegyric° in a funeral sermon, or a copy of com-
mendatory verses from one poet to another. And
what's worse, 'tis as sure a forerunner of the author
as an epistle dedicatory.
275 MIRABELL: A fool, and your brother, Witwoud!
WITWOUD: Aye, aye, my half brother. My half brother
he is, no nearer upon honor.
MIRABELL: Then 'tis possible he may be but half a
fool.
280 WITWOUD: Good, good, Mirabell, *le drôle!*° Good,
good; hang him, don't let's talk of him. Fainall,
how does your lady? Gad, I say anything in the
world to get this fellow out of my head. I beg
pardon that I should ask a man of pleasure and
285 the town a question at once so foreign and domestic.° But I talk like an old maid at a marriage,
I don't know what I say; but she's the best woman
in the world.°
FAINALL: 'Tis well you don't know what you say, or
290 else your commendation would go near to make
me either vain or jealous.
WITWOUD: No man in town lives well with a wife
but Fainall. Your judgment, Mirabell?
MIRABELL: You had better step and ask his wife, if
295 you would be credibly informed.
WITWOUD: Mirabell.
MIRABELL: Aye.
WITWOUD: My dear, I ask ten thousand pardons; gad,
I have forgot what I was going to say to you!
300 MIRABELL: I thank you heartily, heartily.

271. panegyric: Eulogy, especially involving elaborate praise.
280. *le drôle*: The wag.   285–86. foreign and domestic:
Since he knows (by gossip) that the Fainall marriage is not
working out very well, Witwoud plays on the words "foreign
and domestic."   287–88. best woman in the world: I.e.,
Mrs. Fainall. Witwoud realizes that he has blundered into a
rather delicate situation.

WITWOUD: No, but prithee excuse me; my memory
is such a memory.
MIRABELL: Have a care of such apologies, Witwoud;
for I never knew a fool but he affected to complain,
either of the spleen° or his memory.   305
FAINALL: What have you done with Petulant?
WITWOUD: He's reckoning his money — my money
it was. I have no luck today.
FAINALL: You may allow him to win of you at play,
for you are sure to be too hard for him at repartee;° 310
since you monopolize the wit that is between you,
the fortune must be his, of course.
MIRABELL: I don't find that Petulant confesses the
superiority of wit to be your talent, Witwoud.
WITWOUD: Come, come, you are malicious now, and 315
would breed debates. Petulant's my friend, and a
very honest fellow, and a very pretty fellow, and
has a smattering — faith and troth,° a pretty deal
of an odd sort of a small wit; nay, I'll do him
justice. I'm his friend, I won't wrong him. And if 320
he had any judgment in the world, he would not
be altogether contemptible. Come, come, don't detract from the merits of my friend.
FAINALL: You don't take your friend to be over-nicely
bred?   325
WITWOUD: No, no, hang him, the rogue has no manners at all, that I must own. No more breeding
than a bum-baily,° that I grant you. 'Tis pity, faith;
the fellow has fire and life.
MIRABELL: What, courage?   330
WITWOUD: Hum, faith I don't know as to that; I can't
say as to that. Yes, faith, in a controversy he'll
contradict anybody.
MIRABELL: Though 'twere a man whom he feared, or
a woman whom he loved.   335
WITWOUD: Well, well, he does not always think before
he speaks; we have all our failings. You are too
hard upon him, you are, faith. Let me excuse him.
I can defend most of his faults, except one or two.
One he has, that's the truth on't; if he were my 340
brother, I could not acquit him. That indeed I could
wish were otherwise.
MIRABELL: Aye, marry, what's that, Witwoud?
WITWOUD: Oh, pardon me! Expose the infirmities of
my friend? No, my dear, excuse me there.   345
FAINALL: What, I warrant he's unsincere, or 'tis some
such trifle.
WITWOUD: No, no, what if he be? 'Tis no matter for

305. spleen: Ill humor; peevishness.   310. repartee: Adroit-
ness and cleverness in making replies in conversation.   318.
troth: Loyalty, faithfulness.   328. bum-baily: An under-
bailiff, a minor court officer.

that; his wit will excuse that. A wit should no more
50 be sincere than a woman constant; one argues a
decay of parts,° as t'other of beauty.
MIRABELL: Maybe you think him too positive?
WITWOUD: No, no, his being positive is an incentive
to argument, and keeps up conversation.
55 FAINALL: Too illiterate?
WITWOUD: That! that's his happiness; his want of
learning gives him the more opportunities to show
his natural parts.
MIRABELL: He wants words?
60 WITWOUD: Aye, but I like him for that now; for his
want of words gives me the pleasure very often to
explain his meaning.
FAINALL: He's impudent?
WITWOUD: No, that's not it.
65 MIRABELL: Vain?
WITWOUD: No.
MIRABELL: What! he speaks unseasonable truths
sometimes, because he has not wit enough to invent
an evasion?
70 WITWOUD: Truths! ha! ha! ha! No, no; since you will
have it, I mean he never speaks truth at all, that's
all. He will lie like a chambermaid, or a woman
of quality's porter. Now that is a fault.

(*Enter a Coachman.*)

COACHMAN: Is Master Petulant here, mistress?
75 BETTY: Yes.
COACHMAN: Three gentlewomen in a coach would
speak with him.
FAINALL: O brave Petulant! Three!
BETTY: I'll tell him.
80 COACHMAN: You must bring two dishes of chocolate
and a glass of cinnamon-water.°
                    (*Exeunt°* Betty *and* Coachman.)
WITWOUD: That should be for two fasting strumpets,°
and a bawd troubled with wind.° Now you may
know what the three are.
85 MIRABELL: You are very free with your friend's
acquaintance.
WITWOUD: Aye, aye, friendship without freedom is as
dull as love without enjoyment, or wine without
toasting. But to tell you a secret, these are trulls°
90 whom he allows coach-hire, and something more,
by the week, to call on him once a day at public
places.
MIRABELL: How!

WITWOUD: You shall see how he won't go to 'em,
because there's no more company here to take no- 395
tice of him. Why, this is nothing to what he used
to do; before he found out this way, I have known
him call for himself.
FAINALL: Call for himself? What dost thou mean?
WITWOUD: Mean? Why, he would slip you out° of 400
this chocolate-house, just when you had been talking to him; as soon as your back was turned, whip,
he was gone! Then trip to his lodging, clap on a
hood and scarf, and a mask, slap into a hackney-
coach, and drive hither to the door again in a trice, 405
where he would send in for himself; that I mean,
call for himself, wait for himself. Nay, and what's
more, not finding himself, sometimes leave a letter
for himself.
MIRABELL: I confess this is something extraordinary. 410
I believe he waits for himself now, he is so long
a-coming. Oh! I ask his pardon.

(*Enter Petulant and Betty.*)

BETTY: Sir, the coach stays.
PETULANT: Well, well; I come. 'Sbud,° a man had as
good be a professed midwife as a professed whore- 415
master, at this rate! To be knocked up and raised
at all hours, and in all places! Pox on 'em, I won't
come! D'ye hear, tell 'em I won't come. Let 'em
snivel and cry their hearts out.
FAINALL: You are very cruel, Petulant. 420
PETULANT: All's one, let it pass. I have a humor to
be cruel.
MIRABELL: I hope they are not persons of condition°
that you use at this rate.
PETULANT: Condition! Condition's a dried fig, if I am 425
not in humor! By this hand, if they were your —
a — a — your what-d'ye-call-'ems themselves, they
must wait or rub off,° if I want appetite.°
MIRABELL: What-d'ye-call-'ems! What are they,
Witwoud? 430
WITWOUD: Empresses, my dear; by your what-d'ye-
call-'ems he means sultana queens.
PETULANT: Aye, Roxolanas.°
MIRABELL: Cry you mercy!
FAINALL: Witwoud says they are — 435
PETULANT: What does he say th'are?
WITWOUD: I? Fine ladies, I say.
PETULANT: Pass on, Witwoud. Harkee, by this light

---

351. **parts:** Personal endowments.   381. **cinnamon-water:**
A cordial of spirits, cinnamon, and hot water, prescribed to
aid digestion.   [S.D.] *Exeunt:* Latin for "they go out."
382. **strumpets:** Prostitutes.   383. **wind:** Air in the stomach
or bowels.   389. **trulls:** Women of easy virtue.

400. **slip you out:** Slip out.   414. **'Sbud:** "God's blood," a
mild oath.   423. **condition:** Social distinction.   428. **rub
off:** Go away.   **want appetite:** Lack desire for them.   433.
Roxolanas: Roxolana is the name of the Turkish sultana in
Davenant's *The Siege of Rhodes* (1656), one of the first
"heroic plays."

his relations: two co-heiresses his cousins, and an
440 old aunt, who loves caterwauling° better than a
conventicle.°

WITWOUD: Ha! ha! ha! I had a mind to see how the
rogue would come off. Ha! ha! ha! Gad, I can't
be angry with him, if he had said they were my
445 mother and my sisters.

MIRABELL: No!

WITWOUD: No; the rogue's wit and readiness of invention charm me. Dear Petulant!

BETTY: They are gone, sir, in great anger.

450 PETULANT: Enough, let 'em trundle. Anger helps complexion, saves paint.°

FAINALL: This continence is all dissembled; this is in
order to have something to brag of the next time
he makes court to Millamant, and swear he has
455 abandoned the whole sex for her sake.

MIRABELL: Have you not left off your impudent pretensions there yet? I shall cut your throat some
time or other, Petulant, about that business.

PETULANT: Aye, aye, let that pass. There are other
460 throats to be cut.

MIRABELL: Meaning mine, sir?

PETULANT: Not I. I mean nobody; I know nothing.
But there are uncles and nephews in the world,
and they may be rivals. What then? All's one for
465 that.

MIRABELL: How! harkee Petulant, come hither. Explain, or I shall call your interpreter.°

PETULANT: Explain! I know nothing. Why, you have
an uncle, have you not, lately come to town, and
470 lodges by my Lady Wishfort's?

MIRABELL: True.

PETULANT: Why, that's enough. You and he are not
friends; and if he should marry and have a child,
you may be disinherited, ha?

475 MIRABELL: Where hast thou stumbled upon all this
truth?

PETULANT: All's one for that; why, then say I know
something.

MIRABELL: Come, thou art an honest fellow, Petulant,
480 and shalt make love to my mistress, thou sha't,°
faith. What hast thou heard of my uncle?

PETULANT: I? Nothing I. If throats are to be cut, let
swords clash! Snug's the word;° I shrug and am
silent.

485 MIRABELL: Oh, raillery, raillery! Come, I know thou
art in the women's secrets. What, you're a cabalist;

I know you stayed at Millamant's last night, after
I went. Was there any mention made of my uncle
or me? Tell me. If thou hadst but good nature equal
to thy wit, Petulant, Tony Witwoud, who is now   490
thy competitor in fame, would show as dim by
thee as a dead whiting's° eye by a pearl of orient;°
he would no more be seen by thee than Mercury
is by the sun.° Come, I'm sure thou wo't° tell me.

PETULANT: If I do, will you grant me common sense   495
then for the future?

MIRABELL: Faith, I'll do what I can for thee, and I'll
pray that Heaven may grant it thee in the
meantime.

PETULANT: Well, harkee.   500

   (*Mirabell and Petulant talk apart.*)

FAINALL: Petulant and you both will find Mirabell as
warm a rival as a lover.

WITWOUD: Pshaw! pshaw! That she laughs at Petulant
is plain. And for my part, but that it is almost a
fashion to admire her, I should — Harkee, to tell   505
you a secret, but let it go no further; between
friends, I shall never break my heart for her.

FAINALL: How!

WITWOUD: She's handsome; but she's a sort of an
uncertain woman.   510

FAINALL: I thought you had died for her.

WITWOUD: Umh — no —

FAINALL: She has wit.

WITWOUD: 'Tis what she will hardly allow anybody
else. Now, demme,° I should hate that, if she were   515
as handsome as Cleopatra. Mirabell is not so sure
of her as he thinks for.

FAINALL: Why do you think so?

WITWOUD: We stayed pretty late there last night, and
heard something of an uncle to Mirabell, who is   520
lately come to town, and is between him and the
best part of his estate. Mirabell and he are at some
distance, as my Lady Wishfort has been told; and
you know she hates Mirabell worse than a Quaker
hates a parrot,° or than a fishmonger hates a hard   525
frost.° Whether this uncle has seen Mrs. Millamant
or not, I cannot say; but there were items of such
a treaty being in embryo, and if it should come to
life, poor Mirabell would be in some sort unfortunately fobbed,° i'faith.   530

---

440. **caterwauling:** Noisy quarreling.   441. **conventicle:** A meetinghouse of nonconformist religious sects, especially Presbyterians.   451. **paint:** Makeup.   467. **interpreter:** Possibly a second, as in a duel.   480. **sha't:** Slangy contraction for "shalt."   483. **Snug's the word:** In modern slang, "Mum's the word."

492. **whiting:** A kind of codfish.   **pearl of orient:** Said to be particularly brilliant.   493–94. **than Mercury is by the sun:** The planet nearest the sun and of very low magnitude.   494. **wo't:** Wilt.   515. **demme:** Contraction of "damn me."   524–25. **Quaker . . . parrot:** Parrots are proverbially known to swear.   525–26. **fishmonger . . . frost:** Fishmongers peddled fish and consequently hated very cold weather.   530. **fobbed:** Cheated.

FAINALL: 'Tis impossible Millamant should hearken to it.

WITWOUD: Faith, my dear, I can't tell; she's a woman, and a kind of a humorist.°

35 MIRABELL: And this° is the sum of what you could collect last night?

PETULANT: The quintessence. Maybe Witwoud knows more; he stayed longer. Besides, they never mind him; they say anything before him.

40 MIRABELL: I thought you had been the greatest favorite.

PETULANT: Aye, *tête à tête*,° but not in public, because I make remarks.

MIRABELL: You do?

45 PETULANT: Aye, aye, pox, I'm malicious, man! Now he's soft, you know; they are not in awe of him. The fellow's well bred; he's what you call a what-d'ye-call-'em, a fine gentleman; but he's silly withal.

MIRABELL: I thank you. I know as much as my curiosity requires. Fainall, are you for the Mall?°

50 FAINALL: Aye, I'll take a turn before dinner.

WITWOUD: Aye, we'll walk in the Park; the ladies talked of being there.

55 MIRABELL: I thought you were obliged to watch for your brother Sir Wilfull's arrival.

WITWOUD: No, no, he comes to his aunt's, my Lady Wishfort. Pox on him! I shall be troubled with him too; what shall I do with the fool?

60 PETULANT: Beg him for his estate, that I may beg you afterwards; and so have but one trouble with you both.

WITWOUD: O rare Petulant! Thou art as quick as fire in a frosty morning; thou shalt to the Mall with us, and we'll be very severe.

65 PETULANT: Enough, I'm in a humor to be severe.

MIRABELL: Are you? Pray then walk by yourselves: Let us not be accessory to your putting the ladies out of countenance with your senseless ribaldry,° which you roar out aloud as often as they pass by

70 you; and when you have made a handsome woman blush, then you think you have been severe.

PETULANT: What, what? Then let 'em either show their innocence by not understanding what they hear, or else show their discretion by not hearing what

75 they would not be thought to understand.

MIRABELL: But hast not thou then sense enough to know that thou oughtest to be most ashamed

thyself, when thou hast put another out of countenance?

580 PETULANT: Not I, by this hand! I always take blushing either for a sign of guilt or ill breeding.

MIRABELL: I confess you ought to think so. You are in the right, that you may plead the error of your judgment in defense of your practice.

585 Where modesty's ill manners, 'tis but fit
That impudence and malice pass for wit.

(*Exeunt.*)

ACT II

(*St. James's Park. Enter Mrs. Fainall and Mrs. Marwood.*)

MRS. FAINALL: Aye, aye, dear Marwood, if we will be happy, we must find the means in ourselves, and among ourselves. Men are ever in extremes, either doting or averse. While they are lovers, if

5 they have fire and sense, their jealousies are insupportable. And when they cease to love (we ought to think at least) they loathe; they look upon us with horror and distaste; they meet us like the ghosts of what we were, and as from such, fly from

10 us.

MRS. MARWOOD: True, 'tis an unhappy circumstance of life that love should ever die before us; and that the man so often should outlive the lover. But say what you will, 'tis better to be left than never to

15 have been loved. To pass our youth in dull indifference, to refuse the sweets of life because they once must leave us, is as preposterous as to wish to have been born old, because we one day must be old. For my part, my youth may wear and waste,

20 but it shall never rust in my possession.

MRS. FAINALL: Then it seems you dissemble an aversion to mankind, only in compliance to my mother's humor?

MRS. MARWOOD: Certainly. To be free,° I have no

25 taste of those insipid dry discourses with which our sex of force must entertain themselves, apart from men. We may affect endearments to each other, profess eternal friendships, and seem to dote like lovers; but 'tis not in our natures long to persevere.

30 Love will resume his empire in our breasts; and every heart, or soon or late, receive and readmit him as its lawful tyrant.

MRS. FAINALL: Bless me, how have I been deceived! Why, you profess a libertine!°

---

534. **humorist:** A moody or capricious person, hence unreliable.   535. **And this:** During the dialogue of Fainall and Witwoud, Mirabell and Petulant have been talking "apart." They now reenter the general dialogue.   542. *tête à tête*: Head to head.   550. **Mall:** A fashionable walk in St. James's Park.   568. **ribaldry:** Coarse behavior or language.

24. **free:** Frank.   34. **profess a libertine:** Speak as one who leads a loose, unconventional life.

35 MRS. MARWOOD: You see my friendship by my free-
    dom. Come, be as sincere, acknowledge that your
    sentiments agree with mine.
    MRS. FAINALL: Never!
    MRS. MARWOOD: You hate mankind?
40 MRS. FAINALL: Heartily, inveterately.
    MRS. MARWOOD: Your husband?
    MRS. FAINALL: Most transcendently; aye, though I say
    it, meritoriously.
    MRS. MARWOOD: Give me your hand upon it.
45 MRS. FAINALL: There.
    MRS. MARWOOD: I join with you; what I have said
    has been to try you.
    MRS. FAINALL: Is it possible? Dost thou hate those
    vipers, men?
50 MRS. MARWOOD: I have done hating 'em; and am
    now come to despise 'em; the next thing I have to
    do, is eternally to forget 'em.
    MRS. FAINALL: There spoke the spirit of an Amazon,
    a Penthesilea!°
55 MRS. MARWOOD: And yet I am thinking sometimes
    to carry my aversion further.
    MRS. FAINALL: How?
    MRS. MARWOOD: Faith, by marrying; if I could but
    find one that loved me very well and would be
60 thoroughly sensible of ill usage, I think I should
    do myself the violence of undergoing the ceremony.
    MRS. FAINALL: You would not make him a cuckold?
    MRS. MARWOOD: No, but I'd make him believe I did,
    and that's as bad.
65 MRS. FAINALL: Why had not you as good do it?
    MRS. MARWOOD: Oh, if he should ever discover it,
    he would then know the worst, and be out of his
    pain; but I would have him ever to continue upon
    the rack of fear and jealousy.
70 MRS. FAINALL: Ingenious mischief! Would thou wert
    married to Mirabell.
    MRS. MARWOOD: Would I were!
    MRS. FAINALL: You change color.
    MRS. MARWOOD: Because I hate him.
75 MRS. FAINALL: So do I; but I can hear him named.
    But what reason have you to hate him in particular?
    MRS. MARWOOD: I never loved him; he is, and always
    was, insufferably proud.
    MRS. FAINALL: By the reason you give for your aver-
80 sion, one would think it dissembled; for you have
    laid a fault to his charge of which his enemies must
    acquit him.
    MRS. MARWOOD: Oh, then it seems you are one of

54. Penthesilea: Queen of the Amazons, the mythical race
of women warriors. After befriending Priam following the
death of Hector, she was killed by Achilles, who fell in love
with her as she lay dying.

his favorable enemies. Methinks you look a little
pale, and now you flush again.   85
MRS. FAINALL: Do I? I think I am a little sick o' the
sudden.
MRS. MARWOOD: What ails you?
MRS. FAINALL: My husband. Don't you see him? He
turned short upon me unawares, and has almost   90
overcome me.

(Enter Fainall and Mirabell.)

MRS. MARWOOD: Ha! ha! ha! He comes opportunely
for you.
MRS. FAINALL: For you, for he has brought Mirabell
with him.   95
FAINALL: My dear!
MRS. FAINALL: My soul!
FAINALL: You don't look well today, child.
MRS. FAINALL: D'ye think so?
MIRABELL: He is the only man that does, madam.   100
MRS. FAINALL: The only man that would tell me so
at least; and the only man from whom I could hear
it without mortification.
FAINALL: O my dear, I am satisfied of your tenderness;
I know you cannot resent anything from me, es-   105
pecially what is in effect of my concern.
MRS. FAINALL: Mr. Mirabell, my mother interrupted
you in a pleasant relation last night; I would fain
hear it out.
MIRABELL: The persons concerned in that affair have 110
yet a tolerable reputation. I am afraid Mr. Fainall
will be censorious.
MRS. FAINALL: He has a humor more prevailing than
his curiosity and will willingly dispense with the
hearing of one scandalous story, to avoid giving   115
an occasion to make another by being seen to walk
with his wife. This way, Mr. Mirabell, and I dare
promise you will oblige us both.
               (Exeunt Mrs. Fainall and Mirabell.)
FAINALL: Excellent creature! Well, sure if I should live
to be rid of my wife, I should be a miserable man.   120
MRS. MARWOOD: Aye!
FAINALL: For having only that one hope, the accomplishment of it, of consequence, must put an end
to all my hopes; and what a wretch is he who must
survive his hopes! Nothing remains when that day 125
comes, but to sit down and weep like Alexander,°
when he wanted other worlds to conquer.
MRS. MARWOOD: Will you not follow 'em?
FAINALL: Faith, I think not.
MRS. MARWOOD: Pray let us; I have a reason.   130
FAINALL: You are not jealous?

126. Alexander: Alexander the Great (356–323 B.C.), the
powerful ruler and conqueror.

MRS. MARWOOD: Of whom?

FAINALL: Of Mirabell.

MRS. MARWOOD: If I am, is it inconsistent with my
love to you that I am tender of your honor?

FAINALL: You would intimate, then, as if there were
a fellow-feeling between my wife and him.

MRS. MARWOOD: I think she does not hate him to
that degree she would be thought.

FAINALL: But he, I fear, is too insensible.

MRS. MARWOOD: It may be you are deceived.

FAINALL: It may be so. I do now begin to apprehend
it.

MRS. MARWOOD: What?

FAINALL: That I have been deceived, madam, and you
are false.

MRS. MARWOOD: That I am false! What mean you?

FAINALL: To let you know I see through all your little
arts. Come, you both love him; and both have
equally dissembled your aversion. Your mutual
jealousies of one another have made you clash till
you have both struck fire. I have seen the warm
confession reddening on your cheeks and sparkling
from your eyes.

MRS. MARWOOD: You do me wrong.

FAINALL: I do not. 'Twas for my ease to oversee° and
willfully neglect the gross advances made him by
my wife; that by permitting her to be engaged, I
might continue unsuspected in my pleasures, and
take you oftener to my arms in full security. But
could you think, because the nodding husband
would not awake, that e'er the watchful lover slept?

MRS. MARWOOD: And wherewithal can you reproach
me?

FAINALL: With infidelity, with loving another, with
love of Mirabell.

MRS. MARWOOD: 'Tis false! I challenge you to show
an instance that can confirm your groundless accusation. I hate him.

FAINALL: And wherefore do you hate him? He is insensible, and your resentment follows his neglect.
An instance? The injuries you have done him are
a proof, your interposing in his love. What cause
had you to make discoveries of his pretended passion? to undeceive the credulous aunt, and be the
officious obstacle of his match with Millamant?

MRS. MARWOOD: My obligations to my lady urged
me; I had professed a friendship to her, and could
not see her easy nature so abused by that
dissembler.

FAINALL: What, was it conscience then? Professed a
friendship! Oh, the pious friendships of the female
sex!

MRS. MARWOOD: More tender, more sincere, and
more enduring, than all the vain and empty vows
of men, whether professing love to us, or mutual
faith to one another.

FAINALL: Ha! ha! ha! You are my wife's friend too.

MRS. MARWOOD: Shame and ingratitude! Do you reproach me? You, you upbraid me? Have I been
false to her, through strict fidelity to you, and sacrificed my friendship to keep my love inviolate?
And have you the baseness to charge me with the
guilt, unmindful of the merit? To you it should be
meritorious, that I have been vicious; and do you
reflect that guilt upon me, which should lie buried
in your bosom?

FAINALL: You misinterpret my reproof. I meant but
to remind you of the slight account you once could
make of strictest ties, when set in competition with
your love to me.

MRS. MARWOOD: 'Tis false; you urged it with deliberate malice! 'Twas spoke in scorn, and I never
will forgive it.

FAINALL: Your guilt, not your resentment, begets your
rage. If yet you loved, you could forgive a jealousy;
but you are stung to find that you are discovered.

MRS. MARWOOD: It shall be all discovered. You too
shall be discovered; be sure you shall. I can but be
exposed. If I do it myself, I shall prevent° your
baseness.

FAINALL: Why, what will you do?

MRS. MARWOOD: Disclose it to your wife; own what
has passed between us.

FAINALL: Frenzy!

MRS. MARWOOD: By all my wrongs I'll do't! I'll publish to the world the injuries you have done me,
both in my fame and fortune! With both I trusted
you, you bankrupt in honor, as indigent of wealth.

FAINALL: Your fame I have preserved. Your fortune
has been bestowed as the prodigality of your love
would have it, in pleasures which we both have
shared. Yet, had not you been false, I had ere this
repaid it. 'Tis true, had you permitted Mirabell
with Millamant to have stolen their marriage, my
lady had been incensed beyond all means of reconcilement; Millamant had forfeited the moiety°
of her fortune, which then would have descended
to my wife. And wherefore did I marry, but to
make lawful prize of a rich widow's wealth, and
squander it on love and you?

MRS. MARWOOD: Deceit and frivolous pretense!

FAINALL: Death, am I not married! What's pretense?
Am I not imprisoned, fettered? Have I not a wife?
nay a wife that was a widow, a young widow, a

---

156. oversee: Overlook.   **210. prevent:** Anticipate.   **227. moiety:** Half.

handsome widow; and would be again a widow, but that I have a heart of proof,° and something of a constitution to bustle through the ways of wedlock and this world! Will you yet be reconciled
240 to truth and me?

MRS. MARWOOD: Impossible. Truth and you are inconsistent. I hate you, and shall for ever.

FAINALL: For loving you?

MRS. MARWOOD: I loathe the name of love after such
245 usage; and next to the guilt with which you would asperse me, I scorn you most. Farewell!

FAINALL: Nay, we must not part thus.

MRS. MARWOOD: Let me go.

FAINALL: Come, I'm sorry.

250 MRS. MARWOOD: I care not, let me go, break my hands, do! I'd leave 'em to get loose.

FAINALL: I would not hurt you for the world. Have I no other hold to keep you here?

MRS. MARWOOD: Well, I have deserved it all.

255 FAINALL: You know I love you.

MRS. MARWOOD: Poor dissembling! Oh, that — well, it is not yet —

FAINALL: What? what is it not? what is it not yet? It is not yet too late —

260 MRS. MARWOOD: No, it is not yet too late; I have that comfort.

FAINALL: It is, to love another.

MRS. MARWOOD: But not to loathe, detest, abhor mankind, myself, and the whole treacherous world.

265 FAINALL: Nay, this is extravagance. Come, I ask your pardon. No tears. I was to blame; I could not love you and be easy in my doubts. Pray, forbear. I believe you. I'm convinced I've done you wrong; and any way, every way will make amends. I'll
270 hate my wife yet more, damn her! I'll part with her, rob her of all she's worth, and we'll retire somewhere, anywhere, to another world. I'll marry thee; be pacified. 'Sdeath,° they come; hide your face, your tears. You have a mask;° wear it a mo-
275 ment. This way, this way. Be persuaded.

(*Exeunt.*)

(*Reenter Mirabell and Mrs. Fainall.*)

MRS. FAINALL: They are here yet.

MIRABELL: They are turning into the other walk.

MRS. FAINALL: While I only hated my husband, I could bear to see him; but since I have despised him, he's
280 too offensive.

MIRABELL: Oh, you should hate with prudence.

MRS. FAINALL: Yes, for I have loved with indiscretion.

MIRABELL: You should have just so much disgust for your husband as may be sufficient to make you relish your lover.
28

MRS. FAINALL: You have been the cause that I have loved without bounds, and would you set limits to that aversion of which you have been the occasion? Why did you make me marry this man?

MIRABELL: Why do we daily commit disagreeable and 29 dangerous actions? To save that idol, reputation. If the familiarities of our loves had produced that consequence of which you were apprehensive, where could you have fixed a father's name with credit, but on a husband?° I knew Fainall to be a 29 man lavish of his morals, an interested and professing° friend, a false and a designing lover; yet one whose wit and outward fair behavior have gained a reputation with the town enough to make that woman stand excused who has suffered herself 3C to be won by his addresses. A better man ought not to have been sacrificed to the occasion; a worse had not answered to the purpose. When you are weary of him, you know your remedy.

MRS. FAINALL: I ought to stand in some degree of 3(credit with you, Mirabell.

MIRABELL: In justice to you, I have made you privy to my whole design, and put it in your power to ruin or advance my fortune.

MRS. FAINALL: Whom have you instructed to represent 3' your pretended uncle?

MIRABELL: Waitwell, my servant.

MRS. FAINALL: He is an humble servant° to Foible, my mother's woman, and may win her to your interest.
3'

MIRABELL: Care is taken for that. She is won and worn by this time. They were married this morning.

MRS. FAINALL: Who?

MIRABELL: Waitwell and Foible. I would not tempt my servant to betray me by trusting him too far. 3. If your mother, in hopes to ruin me, should consent to marry my pretended uncle, he might, like Mosca in *The Fox,*° stand upon terms;° so I made him sure beforehand.

---

237. **heart of proof:** A heart that is proof against such wishes. 273. **'Sdeath:** "God's death," an oath. 274. **mask:** Ladies' masks were fashionable and reputable except when worn at the theater, where they were construed as the mark of a loose woman.

292–95. **If the familiarities . . . husband:** Mirabell refers to his affair with Mrs. Fainall, after the death of her first husband, Mr. Languish, and prior to her marriage to Fainall. She feared that she was pregnant by Mirabell, and as a result Mirabell urged her marriage to Fainall. 296–97. **professing:** Self-interested and dissembling. 313. **servant:** Suitor. 322–23. **Mosca . . . Fox:** Mosca, the crafty servant in Ben Jonson's play *Volpone; or, The Fox* (1606). 323. **stand upon terms:** Insist upon the proper terms of a binding contract, as Mosca does in the denouement of the Jonson play.

MRS. FAINALL: So if my poor mother is caught in a contract, you will discover the imposture betimes, and release her by producing a certificate of her gallant's former marriage?

MIRABELL: Yes, upon condition that she consent to my marriage with her niece, and surrender the moiety of her fortune in her possession.°

MRS. FAINALL: She talked last night of endeavoring at a match between Millamant and your uncle.

MIRABELL: That was by Foible's direction, and my instruction, that she might seem to carry it more privately.°

MRS. FAINALL: Well, I have an opinion of your success, for I believe my lady will do anything to get a husband; and when she has this, which you have provided for her, I suppose she will submit to anything to get rid of him.

MIRABELL: Yes, I think the good lady would marry anything that resembled a man, though 'twere no more than what a butler could pinch out of a napkin.°

MRS. FAINALL: Female frailty! We must all come to it, if we live to be old and feel the craving of a false appetite when the true is decayed.

MIRABELL: An old woman's appetite is depraved like that of a girl. 'Tis the green sickness° of a second childhood; and, like the faint offer of a latter spring, serves but to usher in the fall, and withers in an affected bloom.

MRS. FAINALL: Here's your mistress.

(*Enter Mrs. Millamant, Witwoud, and Mincing.*)

MIRABELL: Here she comes, i'faith, full sail, with her fan spread and streamers out, and a shoal of fools for tenders.° Ha, no, I cry her mercy!

MRS. FAINALL: I see but one poor empty sculler;° and he tows her woman after him.

MIRABELL (*to Mrs. Millamant*): You seem to be unattended, madam. You used to have the *beau*

monde° throng after you, and a flock of gay, fine perukes° hovering round you.

WITWOUD: Like moths about a candle. I had like to have lost my comparison for want of breath.   365

MRS. MILLAMANT: Oh, I have denied myself airs today. I have walked as fast through the crowd —

WITWOUD: As a favorite just disgraced, and with as few followers.

MRS. MILLAMANT: Dear Mr. Witwoud, truce with   370 your similitudes;° for I'm as sick of 'em —

WITWOUD: As a physician of a good air. I cannot help it, madam, though 'tis against myself.

MRS. MILLAMANT: Yet again! Mincing, stand between me and his wit.   375

WITWOUD: Do, Mrs. Mincing, like a screen before a great fire. I confess I do blaze today; I am too bright.

MRS. FAINALL: But, dear Millamant, why were you so long?   380

MRS. MILLAMANT: Long! Lord, have I not made violent haste? I have asked every living thing I met for you; I have inquired after you, as after a new fashion.

WITWOUD: Madam, truce with your similitudes. No,   385 you met her husband, and did not ask him for her.

MIRABELL: By your leave, Witwoud, that were like inquiring after an old fashion, to ask a husband for his wife.

WITWOUD: Hum, a hit! a hit! a palpable hit!° I confess   390 it.

MRS. FAINALL: You were dressed before I came abroad.

MRS. MILLAMANT: Aye, that's true. Oh, but then I had — Mincing, what had I? Why was I so long?   395

MINCING: O mem,° your laship° stayed to peruse a pecket° of letters.

MRS. MILLAMANT: Oh, aye, letters; I had letters. I am persecuted with letters. I hate letters. Nobody knows how to write letters, and yet one has 'em,   400 one does not know why. They serve one to pin up one's hair.

WITWOUD: Is that the way? Pray, madam, do you pin up your hair with all your letters? I find I must keep copies.   405

MRS. MILLAMANT: Only with those in verse, Mr. Witwoud. I never pin up my hair with prose, I think I tried once, Mincing.

329–31. **condition that she ... possession:** Lady Wishfort has control of half of Mrs. Millamant's (her niece's) fortune, which Millamant will acquire upon her marriage, provided Lady Wishfort approves of the match; should Millamant marry without her aunt's approval, she forfeits the half of her fortune in trust.   335–36. **she might ... privately:** I.e., to allay any suspicions Lady Wishfort might have about the validity of Mirabell's "uncle."   344–45. **pinch out of a napkin:** It was fashionable to pinch table napkins into curious and fancy shapes.   350. **green sickness:** An anemia prevalent in adolescent girls, marked by a sallow yellow-green complexion.   357. **tenders:** Small boats that attend larger ships.   358. **sculler:** A man operating a rowboat; i.e., Witwoud.

361–62. **beau monde:** People of fashion.   363. **perukes:** Suitors, referring to the wigs worn by gentlemen of the period.   371. **similitudes:** Witwoud is a tireless (and tiresome) maker of comparisons, or similes. See "his commonplace [book] of comparisons" in act I.   390. **a palpable hit:** See Osric in *Hamlet*, V, II: "A hit, a very palpable hit."   396. **mem:** Madam. **laship:** Ladyship.   397. **pecket:** Packet.

MINCING: O mem, I shall never forget it.

410   MRS. MILLAMANT: Aye, poor Mincing tiffed° and tiffed all the morning.

MINCING: Till I had the cremp in my fingers, I'll vow, mem. And all to no purpose. But when your laship pins it up with poetry, it sits so pleasant the next

415   day as anything, and is so pure and so crips.°

WITWOUD: Indeed, so crips?

MINCING: You're such a critic, Mr. Witwoud.

MRS. MILLAMANT: Mirabell, did you take exceptions last night? Oh, aye, and went away. Now I think

420   on't, I'm angry. No, now I think on't, I'm pleased; for I believe I gave you some pain.

MIRABELL: Does that please you?

MRS. MILLAMANT: Infinitely; I love to give pain.

MIRABELL: You would affect a cruelty which is not

425   in your nature; your true vanity is in the power of pleasing.

MRS. MILLAMANT: Oh, I ask your pardon for that. One's cruelty is one's power; and when one parts with one's cruelty, one parts with one's power; and

430   when one has parted with that, I fancy one's old and ugly.

MIRABELL: Aye, aye, suffer your cruelty to ruin the object of your power, to destroy your lover, and then how vain, how lost a thing you'll be! Nay,

435   'tis true: You are no longer handsome when you've lost your lover; your beauty dies upon the instant. For beauty is the lover's gift; 'tis he bestows your charms, your glass is all a cheat. The ugly and the old, whom the looking-glass mortifies, yet after

440   commendation° can be flattered by it, and discover beauties in it; for that reflects our praises, rather than your face.

MRS. MILLAMANT: Oh, the vanity of these men! Fainall, d'ye hear him? If they did not commend us,

445   we were not handsome! Now, you must know they could not commend one, if one was not handsome. Beauty the lover's gift! Lord, what is a lover, that it can give? Why, one makes lovers as fast as one pleases, and they live as long as one pleases, and

450   they die as soon as one pleases; and then, if one pleases, one makes more.

WITWOUD: Very pretty. Why, you make no more of making of lovers, madam, than of making so many card matches.°

455   MRS. MILLAMANT: One no more owes one's beauty to a lover than one's wit to an echo. They can but reflect what we look and say; vain empty things if we are silent or unseen, and want a being.

MIRABELL: Yet to those two vain empty things you owe two° the greatest pleasures of your life.   46

MRS. MILLAMANT: How so?

MIRABELL: To your lover you owe the pleasure of hearing yourselves praised; and to an echo the pleasure of hearing yourselves talk.

WITWOUD: But I know a lady that loves talking so   46 incessantly, she won't give an echo fair play; she has that everlasting rotation of tongue, that an echo must wait till she dies, before it can catch her last words.

MRS. MILLAMANT: Oh, fiction! Fainall, let us leave   47 these men.

MIRABELL (*aside to Mrs. Fainall*): Draw off Witwoud.

MRS. FAINALL: Immediately. I have a word or two for Mr. Witwoud.

(*Exeunt Witwoud and Mrs. Fainall.*)

MIRABELL: I would beg a little private audience too.   47 You had the tyranny to deny me last night, though you knew I came to impart a secret to you that concerned my love.

MRS. MILLAMANT: You saw I was engaged.

MIRABELL: Unkind! You had the leisure to entertain   48 a herd of fools; things who visit you from their excessive idleness, bestowing on your easiness that time which is the encumbrance of their lives. How can you find delight in such society? It is impossible they should admire you; they are not capable. Or   48 if they were, it should be to you as a mortification, for sure to please a fool is some degree of folly.

MRS. MILLAMANT: I please myself. Besides, sometimes to converse with fools is for my health.

MIRABELL: Your health! Is there a worse disease than   49 the conversation of fools?

MRS. MILLAMANT: Yes, the vapors; fools are physic° for it, next to assafetida.°

MIRABELL: You are not in a course of fools?°

MRS. MILLAMANT: Mirabell, if you persist in this of-   49 fensive freedom, you'll displease me. I think I must resolve, after all, not to have you; we shan't agree.

MIRABELL: Not in our physic, it may be.

MRS. MILLAMANT: And yet our distemper,° in all like-lihood, will be the same; for we shall be sick of   5 one another. I shan't endure to be reprimanded nor instructed; 'tis so dull to act always by advice, and so tedious to be told of one's faults — I can't bear it. Well, I won't have you, Mirabell. I'm re-solved — I think — you may go. Ha! ha! ha! What   5 would you give that you could help loving me?

---

410. tiffed: Arranged.   415. crips: Crisp.   440. commen-dation: Praise.   454. card matches: Matches made from pieces of heavy paper tipped with sulfur.

460. two: Two of.   492. physic: Medicine.   493. assafe-tida: A gum resin prescribed by doctors as an antidote to "the vapors."   494. course of fools: Series of treatments. 499. distemper: Illness.

MIRABELL: I would give something that you did not know I could not help it.

MRS. MILLAMANT: Come, don't look grave then. Well, what do you say to me?

MIRABELL: I say that a man may as soon make a friend by his wit, or a fortune by his honesty, as win a woman with plain dealing° and sincerity.

MRS. MILLAMANT: Sententious Mirabell! Prithee, don't look with that violent and inflexible wise face, like Solomon at the dividing of the child° in an old tapestry hanging.

MIRABELL: You are merry, madam, but I would persuade you for a moment to be serious.

MRS. MILLAMANT: What, with that face? No, if you keep your countenance, 'tis impossible I should hold mine. Well, after all, there is something very moving in a lovesick face. Ha! ha! ha! Well, I won't laugh; don't be peevish. Heigho! now I'll be melancholy, as melancholy as a watchlight.° Well, Mirabell, if ever you will win me, woo me now. Nay, if you are so tedious, fare you well; I see they are walking away.

MIRABELL: Can you not find in the variety of your disposition one moment —

MRS. MILLAMANT: To hear you tell me Foible's married, and your plot like to speed? No.

MIRABELL: But how you came to know it —

MRS. MILLAMANT: Without the help of the devil, you can't imagine; unless she should tell me herself. Which of the two it may have been, I will leave you to consider; and when you have done thinking of that, think of me.

(Exeunt Mrs. Millamant with Mincing.)

MIRABELL: I have something more — Gone! Think of you! To think of a whirlwind, though 'twere in a whirlwind, were a case of more steady contemplation; a very tranquility of mind and mansion. A fellow that lives in a windmill has not a more whimsical dwelling than the heart of a man that is lodged in a woman. There is no point of the compass to which they cannot turn, and by which they are not turned; and by one as well as another; for motion, not method, is their occupation. To know this, and yet continue to be in love, is to be made wise from the dictates of reason, and yet persevere to play the fool by the force of instinct. Oh, here come my pair of turtles!° What, billing so sweetly? Is not Valentine's Day over with you yet?

(Enter Waitwell and Foible.)

Sirrah, Waitwell, why, sure you think you were married for your own recreation, and not for my conveniency.

WAITWELL: Your pardon, sir. With submission, we have indeed been solacing° in lawful delights; but still with an eye to business, sir. I have instructed her as well as I could. If she can take your directions as readily as my instructions, sir, your affairs are in a prosperous way.

MIRABELL: Give you joy, Mrs. Foible.

FOIBLE: O las, sir, I'm so ashamed! I'm afraid my lady has been in a thousand inquietudes for me. But I protest, sir, I made as much haste as I could.

WAITWELL: That she did indeed, sir. It was my fault that she did not make more.

MIRABELL: That I believe.

FOIBLE: But I told my lady as you instructed me, sir, that I had a prospect of seeing Sir Rowland, your uncle; and that I would put her ladyship's picture in my pocket to show him, which I'll be sure to say has made him so enamored of her beauty, that he burns with impatience to lie at her ladyship's feet and worship the original.

MIRABELL: Excellent Foible! Matrimony has made you eloquent in love.

WAITWELL: I think she has profited, sir. I think so.

FOIBLE: You have seen Madam Millamant, sir?

MIRABELL: Yes.

FOIBLE: I told her, sir, because I did not know that you might find an opportunity; she had so much company last night.

MIRABELL: Your diligence will merit more. In the meantime —   *(Gives money.)*

FOIBLE: O dear sir, your humble servant!

WAITWELL: Spouse.

MIRABELL: Stand off, sir, not a penny! Go on and prosper, Foible; the lease shall be made good and the farm stocked, if we succeed.°

FOIBLE: I don't question your generosity, sir; and you need not doubt of success. If you have no more commands, sir, I'll be gone; I'm sure my lady is at her toilet and can't dress till I come. Oh, dear, I'm

---

513. **plain dealing:** Honesty, frankness.   516. **Solomon . . . child:** The Old Testament Solomon, king of Israel, was known for his wisdom. When confronted with two women both claiming to be the mother of a newborn baby, Solomon said he would divide the baby in two and give one half to each woman. When one of the women told the king not to slay the baby but to let it live and give it whole to the other woman, Solomon declared the former woman the baby's true mother (I Kings 3:16–28).   525. **watchlight:** A small night candle.

552. **pair of turtles:** Turtle doves; lovers.   559. **solacing:** Taking pleasure.   591–92. **the lease . . . succeed:** I.e., "If our little plot succeeds, I'll be even more generous."

sure that (*looking out*) was Mrs. Marwood that
went by in a mask; if she has seen me with you,
I'm sure she'll tell my lady. I'll make haste home
600 and prevent her. Your servant, sir. B'w'y,°
Waitwell.   (*Exit.*)
WAITWELL: Sir Rowland, if you please. The jade's so
pert upon her preferment° she forgets herself.
MIRABELL: Come, sir, will you endeavor to forget
605 yourself, and transform into Sir Rowland?
WAITWELL: Why, sir, it will be impossible I should
remember myself. Married, knighted, and at-
tended° all in one day! 'Tis enough to make any
forget himself. The difficulty will be how to recover
610 my acquaintance and familiarity with my former
self, and fall from my transformation to a reformation into Waitwell. Nay, I shan't be quite the
same Waitwell neither; for, now I remember me,
I'm married and can't be my own man again.
      Aye, there's my grief; that's the sad change of
615 life,
      To lose my title, and yet keep my wife.
                                          (*Exeunt.*)

ACT III

(*A room in Lady Wishfort's house. Lady Wishfort at
her toilet, Peg waiting.*)

LADY WISHFORT: Merciful! no news of Foible yet?
PEG: No, madam.
LADY WISHFORT: I have no more patience. If I have
not fretted myself till I am pale again, there's no
5 veracity in me! Fetch me the red; the red, do you
hear, sweetheart? An arrant ash-color, as I'm a
person! Look you how this wench stirs! Why dost
thou not fetch me a little red? Didst thou not hear
me, mopus?°
10 PEG: The red ratafia° does your ladyship mean, or the
cherry-brandy?
LADY WISHFORT: Ratafia, fool! No, fool! Not the ratafia, fool! Grant me patience! I mean the Spanish
paper,° idiot; complexion, darling. Paint, paint,
15 paint; dost thou understand that, changeling,° dan-
gling thy hands like bobbins° before thee? Why
dost thou not stir, puppet? thou wooden thing
upon wires!
PEG: Lord, madam, your ladyship is so impatient! I

cannot come at the paint, madam; Mrs. Foible has 20
locked it up and carried the key with her.
LADY WISHFORT: A pox take you both! Fetch me the
cherry-brandy then. (*Exit Peg.*) I'm as pale and as
faint, I look like Mrs. Qualmsick, the curate's wife,
that's always breeding. Wench, come, come, 25
wench, what art thou doing? sipping? tasting? Save
thee, dost thou not know the bottle?

(*Reenter Peg with a bottle and china cup.*)

PEG: Madam, I was looking for a cup.
LADY WISHFORT: A cup, save thee! and what a cup
hast thou brought! Does thou take me for a fairy, 30
to drink out of an acorn? Why didst thou not bring
thy thimble? Hast thou ne'er a brass thimble clink-
ing in thy pocket with a bit of nutmeg? I warrant
thee. Come, fill, fill! So; again. (*One knocks.*) See
who that is. Set down the bottle first. Here, here, 35
under the table. What, wouldst thou go with the
bottle in thy hand, like a tapster?° As I'm a person,
this wench has lived in an inn upon the road, before
she came to me, like Maritornes the Asturian in
Don Quixote!° No Foible yet? 40
PEG: No, madam; Mrs. Marwood.
LADY WISHFORT: Oh, Marwood; let her come in.
Come in, good Marwood.

(*Enter Mrs. Marwood.*)

MRS. MARWOOD: I'm surprised to find your ladyship
in *déshabillé*° at this time of day. 45
LADY WISHFORT: Foible's a lost thing; has been
abroad since morning, and never heard of since.
MRS. MARWOOD: I saw her but now, as I came masked
through the park, in conference with Mirabell.
LADY WISHFORT: With Mirabell! You call my blood 50
into my face, with mentioning that traitor. She
durst not have the confidence! I sent her to negotiate an affair in which, if I'm detected, I'm undone. If that wheedling villain has wrought upon
Foible to detect me, I'm ruined. O my dear friend, 55
I'm a wretch of wretches if I'm detected.
MRS. MARWOOD: O madam, you cannot suspect Mrs.
Foible's integrity.
LADY WISHFORT: Oh, he carries poison in his tongue
that would corrupt integrity itself! If she has given 60
him an opportunity, she has as good as put her
integrity into his hands. Ah, dear Marwood, what's
integrity to an opportunity? Hark! I hear her! Go,
you thing, and send her in. (*Exit Peg.*) Dear friend,

---

600. B'w'y: A slurred form of "God be with you."   **603.
preferment:** Her advancement in the world; her new status
as a wife.   **607–08. attended:** Waited upon.   **9. mopus:**
Idiot; dull-witted girl.   **10. ratafia:** Fruit-flavored brandy.
13–14. Spanish paper: Cosmetic rouge.   **15. changeling:**
Simpleton.   **16. bobbins:** Spools of yarn.

37. tapster: A person who taps beer in a tavern.   **39–40.
Maritornes . . . Don Quixote:** In Cervantes's *Don Quixote*
(part I, chapter 16), Maritornes is an Austrian chambermaid
with whom the Don fancies himself in love.   **45. *déshabillé*:**
Casual attire.

65   retire into my closet,° that I may examine her with more freedom. You'll pardon me, dear friend; I can make bold with you. There are books over the chimney, Quarles° and Prynne,° and the *Short View of the Stage*,° with Bunyan's works,° to entertain
70   you.

(Exit Mrs. Marwood.)

(*Enter Foible.*)

  O Foible, where hast thou been? What hast thou been doing?

FOIBLE: Madam, I have seen the party.

LADY WISHFORT: But what hast thou done?

75 FOIBLE: Nay, 'tis your ladyship has done, and are to do; I have only promised. But a man so enamored, so transported! Well, if worshiping of pictures be a sin, poor Sir Rowland, I say.

LADY WISHFORT: The miniature has been counted like.
80   But hast thou not betrayed me, Foible? Hast thou not detected me to that faithless Mirabell? What hadst thou to do with him in the Park? Answer me, has he got nothing out of thee?

FOIBLE (*aside*): So the devil has been beforehand with
85   me. What shall I say? (*Aloud.*) Alas, madam, could I help it, if I met that confident thing? Was I in fault? If you had heard how he used me, and all upon your ladyship's account, I'm sure you would not suspect my fidelity. Nay, if that had been the
90   worst, I could have borne; but he had a fling at your ladyship too. And then I could not hold; but i'faith I gave him his own.

LADY WISHFORT: Me? what did the filthy fellow say?

FOIBLE: O madam! 'tis a shame to say what he said,
95   with his taunts and his fleers, tossing up his nose. "Humh!" says he. "What, you are a-hatching some plot," says he, "you are so early abroad, or catering," says he. "Ferreting for some disbanded° officer, I warrant. Half-pay is but thin subsistence,"
00   says he. "Well, what pension does your lady propose? Let me see," says he. "What, she must come down pretty deep now, she's superannuated,"° says he, "and —"

LADY WISHFORT: Ods° my life, I'll have him, I'll have
105   him murdered! I'll have him poisoned! Where does he eat? I'll marry a drawer° to have him poisoned in his wine! I'll send for Robin° from Locket's° immediately.

FOIBLE: Poison him? Poisoning's too good for him.
110   Starve him, madam, starve him; marry Sir Rowland, and get him disinherited. Oh, you would bless yourself to hear what he said!

LADY WISHFORT: A villain! "superannuated"!

FOIBLE: "Humh," says he. "I hear you are laying de-
115   signs against me too," says he, "and Mrs. Millamant is to marry my uncle" (he does not suspect a word of your ladyship); "but," says he, "I'll fit you for that." "I warrant you," says he. "I'll hamper you for that," says he. "You and your old
120   frippery° too," says he. "I'll handle you —"

LADY WISHFORT: Audacious villain! "handle" me; would he durst! "Frippery! old frippery!" Was there ever such a foul-mouthed fellow? I'll be married tomorrow; I'll be contracted tonight.

125 FOIBLE: The sooner the better, madam.

LADY WISHFORT: Will Sir Rowland be here, sayest thou? When, Foible?

FOIBLE: Incontinently,° madam. No new sheriff's wife expects the return of her husband after knighthood
130   with that impatience in which Sir Rowland burns for the dear hour of kissing your ladyship's hands after dinner.

LADY WISHFORT: "Frippery! superannuated! frippery!" I'll frippery the villain; I'll reduce him to
135   frippery and rags! A tatterdemalion!° I hope to see him hung with tatters, like a Long Lane penthouse° or a gibbet thief. A slander-mouthed railer! I warrant the spendthrift prodigal's in debt as much as the million lottery,° or the whole court upon a
140   birthday.° I'll spoil his credit with his tailor. Yes, he shall have my niece with her fortune, he shall!

FOIBLE: He! I hope to see him lodge in Ludgate° first,

---

65. closet: Private sitting room.   **68. Quarles:** Francis Quarles, devotional poet, author of *Emblems, Divine and Moral* (1635). **Prynne:** William Prynne, Puritan author of *Histrio-Mastix* (1633), an attack on the immorality of the stage. **68–69. Short View of the Stage:** By Jeremy Collier, an attack on "the Immorality and Profaneness of the English Stage" (1698), directly aimed at the earlier plays of Congreve. Dryden answered the censures of Collier in his Preface to the *Fables* (1700). **69. Bunyan's works:** John Bunyan, the great Puritan writer and preacher. A one-volume edition of the *Works of That Eminent Servant of Christ, Mr. John Bunyan* had appeared in 1692. **98. disbanded:** Discharged. **102. superannuated:** Old and infirm.

104. Ods: "God's."   **106. drawer:** One who draws wine or ale; a waiter.   **107. Robin:** Common name for a waiter. **Locket's:** A fashionable restaurant in Charing Cross.   **119–20. old frippery:** Old clothes, as applied to Lady Wishfort, "old clotheshorse."   **128. Incontinently:** Immediately, and with the added suggestion of passionate impatience.   **135. tatterdemalion:** Ragamuffin.   **136. Long Lane penthouse:** A shed with a sloping roof in Long Lane, a district famous for its shops of old and secondhand clothes.   **139. million lottery:** A wild scheme to raise a million pounds by the sale of lottery tickets.   **139–40. the whole ... birthday:** Since custom demanded gifts on such an occasion, a royal birthday was an expensive event.   **142. Ludgate:** The debtors' prison.

and angle into Blackfriars° for brass farthings with an old mitten.°

145 LADY WISHFORT: Aye, dear Foible; thank thee for that, dear Foible. He has put me out of all patience. I shall never recompose my features to receive Sir Rowland with any economy of face.° This wretch has fretted me that I am absolutely decayed. Look, 150 Foible.

FOIBLE: Your ladyship has frowned a little too rashly, indeed, madam. There are some cracks discernible in the white varnish.

LADY WISHFORT: Let me see the glass. "Cracks," say-155 est thou? Why I am arrantly fleaed;° I look like an old peeled wall. Thou must repair me, Foible, before Sir Rowland comes, or I shall never keep up to my picture.°

FOIBLE: I warrant you, madam, a little art once made 160 your picture like you; and now a little of the same art must make you like your picture. Your picture must sit for you, madam.

LADY WISHFORT: But art thou sure Sir Rowland will not fail to come? Or will 'a not fail when he does 165 come? Will he be importunate, Foible, and push? For if he should not be importunate, I shall never break decorums. I shall die with confusion, if I am forced to advance. Oh no, I can never advance! I shall swoon if he should expect advances. No, I 170 hope Sir Rowland is better bred than to put a lady to the necessity of breaking her forms. I won't be too coy neither. I won't give him despair; but a little disdain is not amiss, a little scorn is alluring.

FOIBLE: A little scorn becomes your ladyship.

175 LADY WISHFORT: Yes, but tenderness becomes me best, a sort of dyingness. You see that picture has a sort of a — ha, Foible? a swimmingness in the eyes. Yes, I'll look so. My niece affects it; but she wants features. Is Sir Rowland handsome? Let my 180 toilet be removed. I'll dress above. I'll receive Sir Rowland here. Is he handsome? Don't answer me. I won't know; I'll be surprised, I'll be taken by surprise.

FOIBLE: By storm, madam. Sir Rowland's a brisk man.

185 LADY WISHFORT: Is he! Oh, then he'll importune, if

he's a brisk man. I shall save decorums if Sir Rowland importunes. I have a mortal terror at the apprehension of offending against decorums. Oh, I'm glad he's a brisk man. Let my things be removed, good Foible. (*Exit.*) 190

(*Enter Mrs. Fainall.*)

MRS. FAINALL: O Foible, I have been in a fright, lest I should come too late! That devil Marwood saw you in the Park with Mirabell, and I'm afraid will discover it to my lady.

FOIBLE: Discover what, madam? 195

MRS. FAINALL: Nay, nay, put not on that strange face. I am privy to the whole design, and know that Waitwell, to whom thou wert this morning married, is to personate Mirabell's uncle, and as such, winning my lady, to involve her in those difficulties 200 from which Mirabell only must release her, by his making his conditions to have my cousin and her fortune left to her own disposal.

FOIBLE: O dear madam, I beg your pardon. It was not my confidence in your ladyship that was de- 205 ficient; but I thought the former good correspondence between your ladyship and Mr. Mirabell might have hindered his communicating this secret.

MRS. FAINALL: Dear Foible, forget that.

FOIBLE: O dear madam, Mr. Mirabell is such a sweet, 210 winning gentleman, but your ladyship is the pattern of generosity. Sweet lady, to be so good! Mr. Mirabell cannot choose but be grateful. I find your ladyship has his heart still. Now, madam, I can safely tell your ladyship our success. Mrs. Mar- 215 wood had told my lady; but I warrant I managed myself. I turned it all for the better. I told my lady that Mr. Mirabell railed at her. I laid horrid things to his charge, I'll vow; and my lady is so incensed that she'll be contracted to Sir Rowland tonight, 220 she says. I warrant I worked her up, that he may have her for asking for, as they say of a Welsh maidenhead.

MRS. FAINALL: O rare Foible!

FOIBLE: I beg your ladyship to acquaint Mr. Mirabell 225 of his success. I would be seen as little as possible to speak to him; besides, I believe Madam Marwood watches me. She has a month's mind;° but I know Mr. Mirabell can't abide her. (*Calls.*) John! Remove my lady's toilet. Madam, your servant. 230 My lady is so impatient, I fear she'll come for me if I stay.

MRS. FAINALL: I'll go with you up the back stairs, lest I should meet her. (*Exeunt.*)

(*Reenter Mrs. Marwood alone.*)

---

143. **angle into Blackfriars:** Ludgate Prison abutted on the precinct of Blackfriars, the area of London between Ludgate Hill and the river. 144. **old mitten:** It was the practice of Ludgate prisoners to beg money from passersby, probably by lowering an old mitten on a string from a high window. 148. **economy of face:** The sense is that Lady Wishfort has been so distressed by Foible's account of Mirabell's words that her makeup has been ruined, and the cosmetics necessary to make her face presentable to Sir Rowland will be very expensive. 155. **fleaed:** Flayed; skinned. 157–58. **keep . . . picture:** I.e., "look as lovely as I do in my picture."

228. **month's mind:** A longing, desire.

MRS. MARWOOD: Indeed, Mrs. Engine,° is it thus with you? Are you become a go-between of this importance? Yes, I shall watch you. Why, this wench is the *passe-partout*, a very master-key to everybody's strong-box. My friend Fainall,° have you carried it so swimmingly? I thought there was something in it; but it seems it's over with you.° Your loathing is not from a want of appetite then, but from a surfeit. Else you could never be so cool to fall from a principal to be an assistant; to procure for him! "A pattern of generosity," that I confess. Well, Mr. Fainall, you have met with your match. O man, man! woman, woman! the devil's an ass; if I were a painter, I would draw him like an idiot, a driveller with a bib and bells. Man should have his head and horns,° and woman the rest of him. Poor simple fiend! "Madam Marwood has a month's mind, but he can't abide her." 'Twere better for him you had not been his confessor in that affair, without° you could have kept his counsel closer. I shall not prove another "pattern of generosity." He has not obliged me to that with those excesses of himself; and now I'll have none of him. Here comes the good lady, panting ripe; with a heart full of hope, and a head full of care, like any chemist upon the day of projection.°

(*Reenter Lady Wishfort.*)

LADY WISHFORT: O dear Marwood, what shall I say for this rude forgetfulness? But my dear friend is all goodness.

MRS. MARWOOD: No apologies, dear madam. I have been very well entertained.

LADY WISHFORT: As I'm a person, I am in a very chaos to think I should so forget myself; but I have such an olio of affairs,° really I know not what to do. (*Calls.*) Foible! I expect my nephew, Sir Wilfull, every moment too. (*Calls.*) Why, Foible! He means to travel for improvement.

MRS. MARWOOD: Methinks Sir Wilfull should rather think of marrying than travelling at his years. I hear he is turned of forty.

LADY WISHFORT: Oh, he's in less danger of being spoiled by his travels. I am against my nephew's marrying too young. It will be time enough when he comes back and has acquired discretion to choose for himself.

MRS. MARWOOD: Methinks Mrs. Millamant and he would make a very fit match. He may travel afterwards. 'Tis a thing very usual with young gentlemen.

LADY WISHFORT: I promise you I have thought on't; and since 'tis your judgment, I'll think on't again. I assure you I will; I value your judgment extremely. On my word, I'll propose it.

(*Reenter Foible.*)

Come, come, Foible, I had forgot my nephew will be here before dinner. I must make haste.

FOIBLE: Mr. Witwoud and Mr. Petulant are come to dine with your ladyship.

LADY WISHFORT: Oh, dear, I can't appear till I am dressed. Dear Marwood, shall I be free with you again, and beg you to entertain 'em? I'll make all imaginable haste. Dear friend, excuse me.
                    (*Exeunt Lady Wishfort and Foible.*)

(*Enter Mrs. Millamant and Mincing.*)

MRS. MILLAMANT: Sure never anything was so unbred as that odious man! Marwood, your servant.

MRS. MARWOOD: You have a color; what's the matter?

MRS. MILLAMANT: That horrid fellow, Petulant, has provoked me into a flame. I have broke my fan. Mincing, lend me yours; is not all the powder out of my hair?

MRS. MARWOOD: No. What has he done?

MRS. MILLAMANT: Nay, he has done nothing; he has only talked. Nay, he has said nothing neither; but he has contradicted everything that has been said. For my part, I thought Witwoud and he would have quarreled.

MINCING: I vow, mem, I thought once they would have fit.°

MRS. MILLAMANT: Well, 'tis a lamentable thing, I swear, that one has not the liberty of choosing one's acquaintance as one does one's clothes.

MRS. MARWOOD: If we had that liberty, we should be as weary of one set of acquaintance, though never so good, as we are of one suit, though never so fine. A fool and a doily stuff° would now and then find days of grace, and be worn for variety.

MRS. MILLAMANT: I could consent to wear 'em, if they would wear alike; but fools never wear out,

235. **Mrs. Engine:** I.e., Foible, the agent of the plot, which Mrs. Marwood has discovered by eavesdropping on the discourse between Foible and Mrs. Fainall.   239. **Fainall:** Mrs. Fainall.   241. **it seems . . . you:** Among other things, Mrs. Marwood has learned of Mrs. Fainall's affair with Mirabell before her marriage to Fainall.   250. **horns:** The traditional sign of the cuckold, a man whose wife is unfaithful.   254. **without:** Unless.   260. **like any chemist . . . projection:** The comparison refers to the attempts of the alchemists to transmute base metals into gold. The "day of projection" is the last day of the experiment, when success or failure will be known.   268. **such an olio of affairs:** I.e., "such a number of things on my mind."

310. **fit:** Fought.   317. **doily stuff:** A coarse woolen material.

they are such *drap-de-Berry*° things! without one could give 'em to one's chambermaid after a day or two.

MRS. MARWOOD: 'Twere better so indeed. Or what
325   think you of the playhouse? A fine, gay, glossy fool should be given there, like a new masking habit, after the masquerade is over, and we have done with the disguise. For a fool's visit is always a disguise, and never admitted by a woman of wit,
330   but to blind° her affair with a lover of sense. If you would but appear barefaced now, and own Mirabell, you might as easily put off Petulant and Witwoud as your hood and scarf. And indeed 'tis time, for the town has found it; the secret is grown
335   too big for the pretense. 'Tis like Mrs. Primly's great belly; she may lace it down before, but it burnishes° on her hips. Indeed, Millamant, you can no more conceal it than my Lady Strammel can her face, that goodly face, which, in defiance of
340   her Rhenish-wine tea,° will not be comprehended in a mask.°

MRS. MILLAMANT: I'll take my death, Marwood, you are more censorious than a decayed beauty, or a discarded toast. Mincing, tell the men they may
345   come up. My aunt is not dressing here; their folly is less provoking than your malice. (*Exit Mincing.*) "The town has found it!" What has it found? That Mirabell loves me is no more a secret than it is a secret that you discovered it to my aunt, or than
350   the reason why you discovered it is a secret.

MRS. MARWOOD: You are nettled.°

MRS. MILLAMANT: You're mistaken. Ridiculous!

MRS. MARWOOD: Indeed, my dear, you'll tear another fan, if you don't mitigate those violent airs.

355   MRS. MILLAMANT: O silly! ha! ha! ha! I could laugh immoderately. Poor Mirabell! His constancy to me has quite destroyed his complaisance for all the world beside. I swear, I never enjoined it him to be so coy. If I had the vanity to think he would
360   obey me, I would command him to show more gallantry. 'Tis hardly well-bred to be so particular° on one hand, and so insensible on the other. But I despair to prevail, and so let him follow his own way, ha! ha! ha! Pardon me, dear creature, I must
365   laugh, ha! ha! ha! though I grant you 'tis a little barbarous, ha! ha! ha!

MRS. MARWOOD: What pity 'tis, so much fine raillery,

and delivered with so significant gesture, should be so unhappily directed to miscarry!

MRS. MILLAMANT: Ha? Dear creature, I ask your par-   370
don. I swear I did not mind you.°

MRS. MARWOOD: Mr. Mirabell and you both may think it a thing impossible, when I shall tell him by telling you —

MRS. MILLAMANT: Oh, dear, what? For it is the same   375
thing if I hear it, ha! ha! ha!

MRS. MARWOOD: That I detest him, hate him, madam.

MRS. MILLAMANT: O madam, why so do I. And yet the creature loves me, ha! ha! ha! How can one forbear laughing to think of it! I am a sibyl° if I   380
am not amazed to think what he can see in me. I'll take my death, I think you are handsomer and, within a year or two as young; if you could but stay for me, I should overtake you, but that cannot be. Well, that thought makes me melancholic.   385
Now, I'll be sad.

MRS. MARWOOD: Your merry note may be changed sooner than you think.

MRS. MILLAMANT: D'ye say so? Then I'm resolved I'll have a song to keep up my spirits.   390

(*Reenter Mincing.*)

MINCING: The gentlemen stay but to comb,° madam, and will wait on you.

MRS. MILLAMANT: Desire Mrs. —, that is in the next room, to sing the song I would have learnt yester-day. You shall hear it, madam, not that there's any   395
great matter in it, but 'tis agreeable to my humor.

(*Song.*)

[*Set by Mr. John Eccles.*]

I
Love's but the frailty of the mind,
    When 'tis not with ambition join'd;
A sickly flame, which, if not fed, expires,
And feeding, wastes in self-consuming fires.   400

II
'Tis not to wound a wanton boy
    Or am'rous youth, that gives the joy;
But 'tis the glory to have pierc'd a swain,
For whom inferior beauties sigh'd in vain.

III
Then I alone the conquest prize,
    When I insult a rival's eyes;   405
If there's delight in love, 'tis when I see
That heart, which others bleed for, bleed for me.

---

321. *drap-de-Berry*: Woolen cloth, probably coarse, from the French province of Berry.   330. blind: Camouflage.
337. burnishes: Is all the more evident.   340. Rhenish-wine tea: Rhenish white wine was supposed to reduce corpulence.
340–41. will not . . . mask: The sense is that the lady's face was so fat that no mask would fit it.   351. nettled: Annoyed.
361. particular: Attentive to one lady (i.e., Millamant).

371. I did not mind you: "I did not have you in mind."
380. sibyl: A female prophet or seer.   391. comb: I.e., comb their wigs.

(*Enter Petulant and Witwoud.*)

MRS. MILLAMANT: Is your animosity composed, gentlemen?

WITWOUD: Raillery, raillery, madam; we have no animosity. We hit off a little wit now and then, but no animosity. The falling-out of wits is like the falling-out of lovers; we agree in the main, like treble and bass. Ha, Petulant?

PETULANT: Aye, in the main, but when I have a humor to contradict.

WITWOUD: Aye, when he has a humor to contradict, then I contradict too. What, I know my cue. Then we contradict one another like two battledores; for contradictions beget one another like Jews.

PETULANT: If he says black's black, if I have a humor to say 'tis blue, let that pass; all's one for that. If I have a humor to prove it, it must be granted.

WITWOUD: Not positively must, but it may, it may.

PETULANT: Yes, it positively must, upon proof positive.

WITWOUD: Aye, upon proof positive it must; but upon proof presumptive it only may. That's a logical distinction now, madam.

MRS. MARWOOD: I perceive your debates are of importance and very learnedly handled.

PETULANT: Importance is one thing, and learning's another; but a debate's a debate, that I assert.

WITWOUD: Petulant's an enemy to learning; he relies altogether on his parts.

PETULANT: No, I'm no enemy to learning; it hurts not me.

MRS. MARWOOD: That's a sign indeed it's no enemy to you.

PETULANT: No, no, it's no enemy to anybody but them that have it.

MRS. MILLAMANT: Well, an illiterate man's my aversion; I wonder at the impudence of any illiterate man to offer to make love.

WITWOUD: That I confess I wonder at too.

MRS. MILLAMANT: Ah! to marry an ignorant that can hardly read or write!

PETULANT: Why should a man be any further from being married, though he can't read, than he is from being hanged? The ordinary's° paid for setting the psalm, and the parish priest for reading the ceremony. And for the rest which is to follow in both cases, a man may do it without book; so all's one for that.

MRS. MILLAMANT: D'ye hear the creature? Lord, here's company; I'll be gone.

(*Exeunt Mrs. Millamant and Mincing.*)

(*Enter Sir Wilfull Witwoud in a riding dress, and a Footman to Lady Wishfort.*)

WITWOUD: In the name of Bartlemew and his fair,° what have we here?

MRS. MARWOOD: 'Tis your brother, I fancy. Don't you know him?

WITWOUD: Not I. Yes, I think it is he. I've almost forgot him; I have not seen him since the Revolution.°

FOOTMAN (*to Sir Wilfull*): Sir, my lady's dressing. Here's company; if you please to walk in, in the meantime.

SIR WILFULL: Dressing! What, it's but morning here, I warrant, with you in London; we should count it towards afternoon in our parts, down in Shropshire. Why then, belike my aunt han't dined yet, ha, friend?

FOOTMAN: Your aunt, sir?

SIR WILFULL: My aunt, sir! Yes, my aunt, sir, and your lady, sir; your lady is my aunt, sir. Why, what, dost thou not know me, friend? Why, then send somebody hither that does. How long hast thou lived with thy lady, fellow, ha?

FOOTMAN: A week, sir; longer than anybody else in the house, except my lady's woman.

SIR WILFULL: Why then, belike thou dost not know thy lady, if thou seest her, ha, friend?

FOOTMAN: Why truly, sir, I cannot safely swear to her face in a morning, before she is dressed. 'Tis like I may give a shrewd guess at her by this time.

SIR WILFULL: Well, prithee try what thou canst do; if thou canst not guess, inquire her out, dost hear, fellow? And tell her, her nephew, Sir Wilfull Witwoud, is in the house.

FOOTMAN: I shall, sir.

SIR WILFULL: Hold ye, hear me, friend; a word with you in your ear. Prithee who are these gallants?

FOOTMAN: Really, sir, I can't tell; here come so many here, 'tis hard to know 'em all. (*Exit.*)

SIR WILFULL: Oons,° this fellow knows less than a starling;° I don't think 'a knows his own name.

MRS. MARWOOD: Mr. Witwoud, your brother is not behind-hand in forgetfulness; I fancy he has forgot you too.

---

451. ordinary's: The ordinary was the chaplain of a prison, who prepared criminals for death.

458. Bartlemew and his fair: Bartholomew Fair was held in August of each year at Smithfield. Since it was specially renowned for its sale of country cloths, Witwoud may here be referring to the inappropriateness of his brother's riding habit in a London drawing room. **464. Revolution:** The bloodless Revolution of 1688, which marked the defeat of James II and the accession to the throne of William and Mary. **495. Oons:** "God's wounds," an oath. **496. starling:** Proverbially a stupid bird.

500   WITWOUD: I hope so. The devil take him that remem-
       bers first, I say.
       SIR WILFULL: Save you, gentlemen and lady!
       MRS. MARWOOD: For shame, Mr. Witwoud; why
       won't you speak to him? And you, sir.
505   WITWOUD: Petulant, speak.
       PETULANT: And you, sir.
       SIR WILFULL: No offense, I hope.
                                    (Salutes Mrs. Marwood.)
       MRS. MARWOOD: No sure, sir.
       WITWOUD: This is a vile dog; I see that already. No
510   offense! Ha! ha! ha! to him; to him, Petulant,
       smoke° him.
       PETULANT: It seems as if you had come a journey, sir;
       hem, hem.   (Surveying him round.)
       SIR WILFULL: Very likely, sir, that it may seem so.
515   PETULANT: No offense, I hope, sir.
       WITWOUD: Smoke the boots, the boots; Petulant, the
       boots, ha! ha! ha!
       SIR WILFULL: Maybe not, sir; thereafter as 'tis meant,°
       sir.
520   PETULANT: Sir, I presume upon the information of
       your boots.
       SIR WILFULL: Why, 'tis like you may, sir. If you are
       not satisfied with the information of my boots, sir,
       if you will step to the stable, you may inquire
525   further of my horse, sir.
       PETULANT: Your horse, sir! Your horse is an ass, sir!
       SIR WILFULL: Do you speak by way of offense, sir?
       MRS. MARWOOD: The gentleman's merry, that's all
       sir. (Aside.) 'Slife,° we shall have a quarrel betwixt
530   an horse and an ass, before they find one another
       out. (Aloud.) You must not take anything amiss
       from your friends, sir. You are among your friends
       here, though it may be you don't know it. If I am
       not mistaken, you are Sir Wilfull Witwoud.
535   SIR WILFULL: Right, lady; I am Sir Wilfull Witwoud,
       so I write myself; no offense to anybody, I hope;
       and nephew to the Lady Wishfort of this mansion.
       MRS. MARWOOD: Don't you know this gentleman, sir?
       SIR WILFULL: Hum! What, sure 'tis not — yea by'r
540   Lady, but 'tis. 'Sheart° I know not whether 'tis or
       no. Yea, but 'tis, by the Wrekin.° Brother Antony!
       What, Tony, i'faith! What, dost thou not know
       me? By'r Lady, nor I thee, thou art so becravated°
       and so beperiwigged.° 'Sheart, why dost not speak?
545   Art thou o'erjoyed?

       WITWOUD: Odso, brother, is it you? Your servant,
       brother.
       SIR WILFULL: Your servant! Why, yours, sir. Your
       servant again, 'sheart, and your friend and servant
       to that, and a — (puff) and a flapdragon for your
       service,° sir! and a hare's foot, and a hare's scut°
       for your service, sir, an you be so cold and so
       courtly!
       WITWOUD: No offense, I hope, brother.
       SIR WILFULL: 'Sheart, sir, but there is, and much of-
       fense! A pox, is this your Inns o' Court° breeding,
       not to know your friends and your relations, your
       elders and your betters?
       WITWOUD: Why, brother Wilfull of Salop,° you may
       be as short as a Shrewsbury° cake, if you please.
       But I tell you 'tis not modish to know relations in
       town. You think you're in the country, where great
       lubberly° brothers slabber° and kiss one another
       when they meet, like a call of serjeants.° 'Tis not
       the fashion here; 'tis not indeed, dear brother.
       SIR WILFULL: The fashion's a fool; and you're a fop,
       dear brother. 'Sheart, I've suspected this. By'r Lady,
       I conjectured you were a fop, since you began to
       change the style of your letters, and write in a scrap
       of paper, gilt round the edges, no broader than a
       subpoena.° I might expect this when you left off,
       "Honored brother," and "hoping you are in good
       health," and so forth, to begin with a "Rat me,°
       knight, I'm so sick of a last night's debauch," ods
       heart, and then tell a familiar tale of a cock and
       a bull,° and a whore and a bottle, and so conclude.
       You could write news before you were out of your
       time,° when you lived with honest Pumple Nose,
       the attorney of Furnival's Inn;° you could entreat
       to be remembered then to your friends round the
       Wrekin. We could have gazettes, then, and Dawks's
       Letter,° and the Weekly Bill,° till of late days.

---

511. smoke: "To affront a stranger at his coming in" (Summers, Dictionary of the Canting Crew).   518. as 'tis meant:
"According to the way it is meant."   529. 'Slife: "God's
life."   540. 'Sheart: "God's heart."   541. Wrekin: A hill
in his native Shropshire.   543. becravated: Wearing a cravat,
or tie.   544. beperiwigged: Wearing a wig.

550–51. flapdragon . . . service: Derived from the game of
catching raisins out of burning brandy; meaning "a fig for
your service."   551. scut: Tail.   556. Inns o' Court: The
center of the legal world of London; used for the city itself.
Sir Wilfull, the country squire, simply asks if Witwoud's
rudeness is a mark of city manners.   559. Salop: Another
name for Shropshire.   560. Shrewsbury: The capital of
Shropshire.   563. lubberly: Loutish.   slabber: Slobber.
564. serjeants: When sergeants-at-law are admitted to the
bar.   571. subpoena: A legal summons.   573. "Rat me":
Contraction of the oath "May God rot me."   575–76. tale
. . . bull: A wildly exaggerated tale.   577–78. out of your
time: I.e., before he had finished his legal apprenticeship.
579. Furnival's Inn: One of the Inns of Court (Chancery)
attached to Lincoln's Inn.   581–82. Dawks's Letter: A
newsletter with a wide circulation in the provinces.   582.
Weekly Bill: It reported all deaths in and around London.

PETULANT: 'Slife, Witwoud, were you ever an attorney's clerk? of the family of the Furnivals? Ha! ha! ha!

WITWOUD: Aye, aye, but that was but for a while, not long, not long. Pshaw! I was not in my own power then; an orphan, and this fellow was my guardian. Aye, aye, I was glad to consent to that man to come to London. He had the disposal of me then. If I had not agreed to that, I might have been bound prentice to a felt maker in Shrewsbury; this fellow would have bound me to a maker of felts.

SIR WILFULL: 'Sheart, and better than to be bound to a maker of fops, where, I suppose, you have served your time; and now you may set up for yourself.

MRS. MARWOOD: You intend to travel, sir, as I'm informed.

SIR WILFULL: Belike I may, madam. I may chance to sail upon the salt seas, if my mind hold.

PETULANT: And the wind serve.

SIR WILFULL: Serve or not serve, I shan't ask license of you, sir; nor the weathercock your companion. I direct my discourse to the lady, sir. 'Tis like my aunt may have told you, madam. Yes, I have settled my concerns, I may say now, and am minded to see foreign parts. If an how that the peace° holds, whereby, that is, taxes abate.

MRS. MARWOOD: I thought you had designed for France at all adventures.°

SIR WILFULL: I can't tell that; 'tis like I may, and 'tis like I may not. I am somewhat dainty in making a resolution, because when I make it, I keep it. I don't stand shill I, shall I,° then; if I say't, I'll do't. But I have thoughts to tarry a small matter in town, to learn somewhat of your lingo first, before I cross the seas. I'd gladly have a spice of your French, as they say, whereby to hold discourse in foreign countries.

MRS. MARWOOD: Here's an academy in town for that use.

SIR WILFULL: There is? 'Tis like there may.

MRS. MARWOOD: No doubt you will return very much improved.

WITWOUD: Yes, refined, like a Dutch skipper from a whale-fishing.

(*Reenter Lady Wishfort with Fainall.*)

LADY WISHFORT: Nephew, you are welcome.

SIR WILFULL: Aunt, your servant.

FAINALL: Sir Wilfull, your most faithful servant.

SIR WILFULL: Cousin Fainall, give me your hand.

LADY WISHFORT: Cousin Witwoud, your servant; Mr. Petulant, your servant. Nephew, you are welcome again. Will you drink anything after your journey, nephew, before you eat? Dinner's almost ready.

SIR WILFULL: I'm very well, I thank you, aunt; however, I thank you for your courteous offer. 'Sheart I was afraid you would have been in the fashion too, and have remembered to have forgot your relations. Here's your cousin Tony; belike I mayn't call him brother for fear of offense.

LADY WISHFORT: O, he's a rallier,° nephew. My cousin's a wit; and your great wits always rally their best friends to choose.° When you have been abroad, nephew, you'll understand raillery better.
(*Fainall and Mrs. Marwood talk apart.*)

SIR WILFULL: Why then, let him hold his tongue in the meantime, and rail when that day comes.

(*Reenter Mincing.*)

MINCING: Mem, I come to acquaint your laship that dinner is impatient.

SIR WILFULL: Impatient? Why then, belike it won't stay till I pull off my boots. Sweetheart, can you help me to a pair of slippers? My man's with the horses, I warrant.

LADY WISHFORT: Fie, fie, nephew, you would not pull off your boots here. Go down into the hall; dinner shall stay for you. My nephew's a little unbred; you'll pardon him, madam. Gentlemen, will you walk? Marwood?

MRS. MARWOOD: I'll follow you, madam, before Sir Wilfull is ready.
(*Exeunt all but Mrs. Marwood and Fainall.*)

FAINALL: Why then, Foible's a bawd, an arrant, rank, match-making bawd. And I, it seems, am a husband, a rank husband; and my wife a very arrant, rank wife, all in the way of the world. 'Sdeath, to be a cuckold by anticipation, a cuckold in embryo!° Sure I was born with budding antlers, like a young satyr, or a citizen's child.° 'Sdeath! to be outwitted, to be outjilted, outmatrimonied! If I had kept my speed like a stag, 'twere somewhat; but to crawl after, with my horns, like a snail, and be outstripped by my wife, 'tis scurvy wedlock.

MRS. MARWOOD: Then shake it off. You have often

---

608. peace: The Treaty of Ryswick (1697), which temporarily terminated the war between France on the one hand and England and her Continental allies on the other. **611. at all adventures:** In any case. **615. shill I, shall I:** Shilly-shally. Sir Wilfull is saying that he is not an indecisive man.

642. rallier: A railer; one who delights in raillery, gentle mockery. **644. to choose:** As they like. **664–65. to be . . . embryo:** In their "talk apart," Mrs. Marwood has told Mr. Fainall what she has learned of his wife's affair with Mirabell before her marriage to Fainall. **667. citizen's child:** I.e., a cuckold's child. Many a child of an honest citizen was fathered by a gentleman of the town.

wished for an opportunity to part; and now you have it. But first prevent their plot; the half of Millamant's fortune is too considerable to be parted with, to a foe, to Mirabell.

FAINALL: Damn him! that had been mine, had you not made that fond° discovery. That had been forfeited, had they been married. My wife had added luster to my horns by that increase of fortune; I could have worn 'em tipped with gold, though my forehead had been furnished like a deputy lieutenant's hall.°

MRS. MARWOOD: They may prove a cap of maintenance° to you still, if you can away with° your wife. And she's no worse than when you had her. I dare swear she had given up her game before she was married.

FAINALL: Hum! that may be.

MRS. MARWOOD: You married her to keep you; and if you can contrive to have her keep you better than you expected, why should you not keep her longer than you intended?

FAINALL: The means, the means.

MRS. MARWOOD: Discover to my lady your wife's conduct; threaten to part with her. My lady loves her, and will come to any composition° to save her reputation. Take the opportunity of breaking it, just upon the discovery of this imposture. My lady will be enraged beyond bounds, and sacrifice niece and fortune and all, at that conjuncture. And let me alone to keep her warm; if she should flag in her part, I will not fail to prompt her.

FAINALL: Faith, this has an appearance.°

MRS. MARWOOD: I'm sorry I hinted to my lady to endeavor a match between Millamant and Sir Wilfull; that may be an obstacle.

FAINALL: Oh, for that matter leave me to manage him; I'll disable him for that. He will drink like a Dane;° after dinner, I'll set his hand in.°

MRS. MARWOOD: Well, how do you stand affected towards your lady?

FAINALL: Why, faith, I'm thinking of it. Let me see. I am married already, so that's over. My wife has played the jade with me; well, that's over too. I never loved her, or if I had, why, that would have been over too by this time. Jealous of her I cannot be, for I am certain; so there's an end of jealousy. Weary of her I am, and shall be. No, there's no end of that; no, no, that were too much to hope. Thus far concerning my repose; now for my reputation. As to my own, I married not for it, so that's out of the question. And as to my part in my wife's, why, she had parted with hers before; so bringing none to me, she can take none from me. 'Tis against all rule of play that I should lose to one who has not wherewithal to stake.

MRS. MARWOOD: Besides, you forget marriage is honorable.

FAINALL: Hum! Faith, and that's well thought on. Marriage is honorable, as you say; and if so, wherefore should cuckoldom be a discredit, being derived from so honorable a root?

MRS. MARWOOD: Nay, I know not; if the root be honorable, why not the branches?°

FAINALL: So, so; why, this point's clear. Well, how do we proceed?

MRS. MARWOOD: I will contrive a letter which shall be delivered to my lady at the time when that rascal who is to act Sir Rowland is with her. It shall come as from an unknown hand, for the less I appear to know of the truth, the better I can play the incendiary. Besides, I would not have Foible provoked if I could help it, because you know she knows some passages.° Nay, I expect all will come out; but let the mine be sprung first, and then I care not if I am discovered.

FAINALL: If the worst come to the worst, I'll turn my wife to grass,° I have already a deed of settlement of the best part of her estate, which I wheedled out of her; and that you shall partake at least.

MRS. MARWOOD: I hope you are convinced that I hate Mirabell now; you'll be no more jealous?

FAINALL: Jealous! No, by this kiss. Let husbands be jealous; but let the lover still believe. Or if he doubt, let it be only to endear his pleasure, and prepare the joy that follows, when he proves his mistress true. But let husbands' doubts convert to endless jealousy; or if they have belief, let it corrupt to superstition and blind credulity. I am single, and will herd no more with 'em. True, I wear the badge,

---

678. fond: Foolish.   682–83. forehead . . . hall: I.e., though he had been cuckolded as many times as there are antlers of stags and deer decorating the country mansion of a deputy lieutenant.   684–85. cap of maintenance: A term in heraldry. The coat of arms of a royal bastard sometimes included a cap with two points behind, like the horns of a cuckold. Mrs. Marwood puns on the word *maintenance* since she is insinuating that, armed with this new information concerning his wife, Fainall may be in a better position to blackmail Lady Wishfort to the amount of Millamant's fortune that she controls.   685. away with: Continue to tolerate.   697. come to any composition: Agree to anything.   704. an appearance: Possibilities.   709. drink like a Dane: The Danes were known as heavy drinkers.   710. I'll set . . . in: I.e., "I'll involve him in the plot."

735. branches: I.e., the cuckold's horns.   744–45. she knows some passages: I.e., Foible knows of Mrs. Marwood's affair with Mr. Fainall and may divulge it. Indeed, she does, in the denouement of act V.   748–49. turn . . . grass: Turn her out, as he would an animal to graze.

but I'll disown the order. And since I take my leave
of 'em, I care not if I leave 'em a common motto
to their common crest.

65   All husbands must or pain or shame endure;
        The wise too jealous are, fools too secure.

                                                    (*Exeunt.*)

ACT IV

([*Scene continues.*] *Enter Lady Wishfort and Foible.*)

LADY WISHFORT: Is Sir Rowland coming, sayest thou,
    Foible? and are things in order?
FOIBLE: Yes, madam, I have put wax-lights in the
    sconces, and placed the footmen in a row in the
5   hall, in their best liveries, with the coachman and
    postillion to fill up the equipage.
LADY WISHFORT: Have you pulvilled° the coachman
    and postillion, that they may not stink of the stable
    when Sir Rowland comes by?
10 FOIBLE: Yes, madam.
LADY WISHFORT: And are the dancers and the music
    ready, that he may be entertained in all points with
    correspondence to his passion?
FOIBLE: All is ready, madam.
15 LADY WISHFORT: And — well, and how do I look,
    Foible?
FOIBLE: Most killing well, madam.
LADY WISHFORT: Well, and how shall I receive him?
    In what figure shall I give his heart the first impres-
20 sion? There is a great deal in the first impression.
    Shall I sit? No, I won't sit, I'll walk; aye, I'll walk
    from the door upon his entrance; and then turn
    full upon him. No, that will be too sudden. I'll
    lie, aye, I'll lie down. I'll receive him in my little
25 dressing-room; there's a couch. Yes, yes, I'll
    give the first impression on a couch. I won't lie
    neither, but loll and lean upon one elbow; with
    one foot a little dangling off, jogging in a thought-
    ful way. Yes, and then as soon as he appears, start,
30 aye, start and be surprised, and rise to meet him
    in a pretty disorder. Yes, oh, nothing is more
    alluring than a levee° from a couch, in some
    confusion; it shows the foot to advantage, and fur-
    nishes with blushes and recomposing airs beyond
35 comparison. Hark! there's a coach.
FOIBLE: 'Tis he, madam.
LADY WISHFORT: Oh dear, has my nephew made his
    addresses to Millamant? I ordered him.

FOIBLE: Sir Wilfull is set in to drinking, madam, in
    the parlor.   40
LADY WISHFORT: Ods my life, I'll send him to her.
    Call her down, Foible; bring her hither. I'll send
    him as I go. When they are together, then come
    to me, Foible, that I may not be too long alone
    with Sir Rowland.   (*Exit.*)   45

(*Enter Mrs. Millamant and Mrs. Fainall.*)

FOIBLE: Madam, I stayed here to tell your ladyship
    that Mr. Mirabell has waited this half hour for an
    opportunity to talk with you, though my lady's
    orders were to leave you and Sir Wilfull together.
    Shall I tell Mr. Mirabell that you are at leisure? 50
MRS. MILLAMANT: No, what would the dear man
    have? I am thoughtful, and would amuse myself;
    bid him come another time.
        "There never yet was woman made,
        Nor shall, but to be curs'd."°   55
                            (*Repeating and walking about.*)
    That's hard!
MRS. FAINALL: You are very fond of Sir John Suckling
    today, Millamant, and the poets.
MRS. MILLAMANT: He? Aye, and filthy verses; so I
    am.   60
FOIBLE: Sir Wilfull is coming, madam. Shall I send
    Mr. Mirabell away?
MRS. MILLAMANT: Aye, if you please, Foible, send
    him away, or send him hither; just as you will,
    dear Foible. I think I'll see him; shall I? Aye, let 65
    the wretch come.
                                                    (*Exit Foible.*)
    "Thyrsis, a youth of the inspired train."°
                                                    (*Repeating.*)
    Dear Fainall, entertain Sir Wilfull. Thou hast
    philosophy to undergo° a fool; thou art married
    and hast patience. I would confer with my own   70
    thoughts.
MRS. FAINALL: I am obliged to you, that you would
    make me your proxy in this affair; but I have
    business of my own.

(*Enter Sir Wilfull.*)

    O Sir Wilfull, you are come at the critical instant. 75
    There's your mistress up to the ears in love and
    contemplation; pursue your point, now or never.
SIR WILFULL: Yes; my aunt will have it so. I would
    gladly have been encouraged with a bottle or two,

---

7. **pulvilled:** Scented with a sweet-smelling powder.   32.
levee: Rising.

54–55. **"There never ... curs'd":** The opening lines of a
poem by Sir John Suckling (1609–1642).   67. **"Thyrsis ...
train":** The first line of *The Story of Phoebus and Daphne,
Applied*, a poem by Edmund Waller (1606–1687), a poet
much admired by Dryden and renowned for the "sweetness"
of his verse.   69. **undergo:** Put up with.

80   because I'm somewhat wary at first, before I am
acquainted. (*This while Millamant walks about repeating to herself.*) But I hope, after a time, I shall
break my mind; that is, upon further acquaintance.
So for the present, cousin, I'll take my leave. If so
85   be you'll be so kind to make my excuse, I'll return
to my company.
MRS. FAINALL: Oh, fie, Sir Wilfull! What, you must
not be daunted.
SIR WILFULL: Daunted! No, that's not it. It is not so
90   much for that; for if so be that I set on't, I'll do't.
But only for the present; 'tis sufficient till further
acquaintance, that's all. Your servant.
MRS. FAINALL: Nay, I'll swear you shall never lose so
favorable an opportunity, if I can help it. I'll leave
95   you together and lock the door.   (*Exit.*)
SIR WILFULL: Nay, nay, cousin. I have forgot my
gloves. What d'ye do? 'Sheart, 'a has locked the
door indeed, I think. Nay, Cousin Fainall, open the
door! Pshaw, what a vixen trick is this? Nay,
100   now 'a has seen me too. Cousin, I made bold to
pass through as it were. I think this door's
enchanted!
MRS. MILLAMANT (*repeating*):
      "I prithee spare me, gentle boy,
      Press me no more for that slight toy —"°
105   SIR WILFULL: Anan?° Cousin, your servant.
MRS. MILLAMANT (*repeating*):
      "That foolish trifle of a heart —"
      Sir Wilfull!
SIR WILFULL: Yes. Your servant. No offense, I hope,
cousin.
MRS. MILLAMANT (*repeating*):
110   "I swear it will not do its part,
      Though thou dost thine, employ'st thy pow'r
      and art."
      Natural, easy Suckling!
SIR WILFULL: Anan? Suckling? No such suckling neither, cousin, nor stripling! I thank Heaven, I'm no
115   minor.
MRS. MILLAMANT: Ah, rustic! ruder than Gothic.°
SIR WILFULL: Well, well, I shall understand your lingo
one of these days, cousin; in the meanwhile I must
answer in plain English.
120   MRS. MILLAMANT: Have you any business with me,
Sir Wilfull?
SIR WILFULL: Not at present, cousin. Yes, I made bold
to see, to come and know if that how you were

disposed to fetch a walk this evening; if so be that
I might not be troublesome, I would have fought°   12
a walk with you.
MRS. MILLAMANT: A walk! What then?
SIR WILFULL: Nay, nothing. Only for the walk's sake,
that's all.
MRS. MILLAMANT: I nauseate walking; 'tis a country   13
diversion. I loathe the country and everything that
relates to it.
SIR WILFULL: Indeed! hah! Look ye, look ye, you do?
Nay, 'tis like you may. Here are choice of pastimes
here in town, as plays and the like; that must be   13
confessed indeed.
MRS. MILLAMANT: Ah, *l'étourdi!*° I hate the town
too.
SIR WILFULL: Dear heart, that's much. Hah! that you
should hate 'em both! Hah! 'tis like you may; there   14
are some can't relish the town, and others can't
away with the country. 'Tis like you may be one
of those, cousin.
MRS. MILLAMANT: Ha! ha! ha! Yes, 'tis like I may.
You have nothing further to say to me?   14
SIR WILFULL: Not at present, cousin. 'Tis like when I
have an opportunity to be more private, I may
break my mind in some measure. I conjecture you
partly guess — however, that's as time shall try;
but spare to speak and spare to speed,° as they say.   15
MRS. MILLAMANT: If it is of no great importance, Sir
Wilfull, you will oblige me to leave me; I have just
now a little business —
SIR WILFULL: Enough, enough, cousin, yes, yes, all a
case;° when you're disposed, when you're disposed.   15
Now's as well as another time; and another time
as well as now. All's one for that. Yes, yes, if your
concerns call you, there's no haste; it will keep
cold, as they say. Cousin, your servant. I think this
door's locked.   16
MRS. MILLAMANT: You may go this way, sir.
SIR WILFULL: Your servant; then with your leave I'll
return to my company.
MRS. MILLAMANT: Aye, aye; ha! ha! ha!
      "Like Phoebus sung the no less am'rous boy."°   16

(*Enter Mirabell.*)

MIRABELL: "Like Daphne, she, as lovely and as
      coy."°

103–104. "**I prithee . . . toy**": The first two lines of a "Song" by Suckling. The three lines quoted by Millamant in her next two speeches complete the first stanza of the poem.   105. **Anan**: "I beg your pardon."   116. **Gothic**: The Restoration and early eighteenth century considered the civilization of the Goths and "Gothic" art rude and barbarous.   125. **fought**: A provincial form of "fetched."   137. *l'étourdi*: The silly fellow.   150. **spare to speak . . . speed**: Proverb meaning "If you hold your tongue, you won't get along in the world."   154–55. **all a case**: Idiomatic for "It's all the same."   165. "**Like Phoebus . . . boy**": The third line of Waller's *Story of Phoebus and Daphne, Applied.*   166. "**Like Daphne . . . coy**": The fourth line of Waller's poem. Mirabell completes the couplet begun by Millamant.

Do you lock yourself up from me, to make my
search more curious?° Or is this pretty artifice contrived, to signify that here the chase must end and
170 my pursuit be crowned, for you can fly no further?

MRS. MILLAMANT: Vanity! No. I'll fly and be followed
to the last moment. Though I am upon the very
verge of matrimony, I expect you should solicit me
as much as if I were wavering at the grate of a
175 monastery, with one foot over the threshold. I'll
be solicited to the very last, nay, and afterwards.

MIRABELL: What, after the last?

MRS. MILLAMANT: Oh, I should think I was poor and
had nothing to bestow, if I were reduced to an
180 inglorious ease and freed from the agreeable fa-
tigues of solicitation.

MIRABELL: But do not you know that when favors are
conferred upon instant and tedious solicitation,
that they diminish in their value, and that both the
185 giver loses the grace, and the receiver lessens his
pleasure?

MRS. MILLAMANT: It may be in things of common
application; but never sure in love. Oh, I hate a
lover that can dare to think he draws a moment's
190 air independent on the bounty of his mistress.
There is not so impudent a thing in nature as the
saucy look of an assured man, confident of success.
The pedantic arrogance of a very husband has not
so pragmatical° an air. Ah! I'll never marry, unless
195 I am first made sure of my will and pleasure.

MIRABELL: Would you have 'em both before marriage?
Or will you be contented with the first now, and
stay for the other till after grace?

MRS. MILLAMANT: Ah! don't be impertinent. My dear
200 liberty, shall I leave thee? My faithful solitude, my
darling contemplation, must I bid you then adieu?
Ay-h adieu, my morning thoughts, agreeable wak-
ings, indolent slumbers, all ye *douceurs,*° ye *sommeils du matin,*° adieu. I can't do't, 'tis more than
205 impossible. Positively, Mirabell, I'll lie abed in a
morning as long as I please.

MIRABELL: Then I'll get up in a morning as early as
I please.

MRS. MILLAMANT: Ah! idle creature, get up when you
210 will. And d'ye hear, I won't be called names after
I'm married; positively I won't be called names.

MIRABELL: Names!

MRS. MILLAMANT: Aye, as wife, spouse, my dear, joy,
jewel, love, sweetheart, and the rest of that nau-
215 seous cant, in which men and their wives are so
fulsomely familiar; I shall never bear that. Good
Mirabell, don't let us be familiar or fond, nor kiss

before folks, like my Lady Fadler and Sir Francis;
nor go to Hyde Park together the first Sunday in
a new chariot, to provoke eyes and whispers, and   220
then never be seen there together again, as if we
were proud of one another the first week, and
ashamed of one another ever after. Let us never
visit together, nor go to a play together. But let us
be very strange and well-bred; let us be as strange   225
as if we had been married a great while, and as
well-bred as if we were not married at all.

MIRABELL: Have you any more conditions to offer?
Hitherto your demands are pretty reasonable.

MRS. MILLAMANT: Trifles! As liberty to pay and re-   230
ceive visits to and from whom I please; to write
and receive letters, without interrogatories° or wry
faces on your part; to wear what I please, and
choose conversation with regard only to my own
taste; to have no obligation upon me to converse   235
with wits that I don't like, because they are your
acquaintance, or to be intimate with fools, because
they may be your relations. Come to dinner when
I please; dine in my dressing-room when I'm out
of humor, without giving a reason. To have my   240
closet inviolate; to be sole empress of my tea-table,
which you must never presume to approach without first asking leave. And lastly, wherever I am,
you shall always knock at the door before you
come in. These articles subscribed, if I continue to   245
endure you a little longer, I may by degrees dwindle
into a wife.

MIRABELL: Your bill of fare is something advanced in
this latter account. Well, have I liberty to offer
conditions, that when you are dwindled into a wife,   250
I may not be beyond measure enlarged into a
husband?

MRS. MILLAMANT: You have free leave. Propose your
utmost; speak and spare not.

MIRABELL: I thank you. *Imprimis*° then, I covenant°   255
that your acquaintance be general; that you admit
no sworn confidante, or intimate of your own sex;
no she-friend to screen her affairs under your countenance, and tempt you to make trial of a mutual
secrecy. No decoy-duck to wheedle° you a fop,   260
scrambling° to the play in a mask; then bring you
home in a pretended fright, when you think you
shall be found out, and rail at me for missing the
play, and disappointing the frolic which you had
to pick me up and prove my constancy.   265

MRS. MILLAMANT: Detestable *imprimis!* I go to the
play in a mask!

---

168. curious: Difficult.   194. pragmatical: Officious.   203.
douceurs: Sweet pleasures.   203–204. sommeils du matin:
Morning sleep.

232. interrogatories: Prying questions.   255. *Imprimis:*
First.   covenant: Decree.   260. wheedle: Procure.   261.
scrambling: Going without suitable dignity.

MIRABELL: *Item,°* I article that you continue to like your own face, as long as I shall; and while it passes current with me, that you endeavor not to new-coin it. To which end, together with all vizards for the day, I prohibit all masks for the night, made of oiled skins and I know not what: hog's bones, hare's gall, pig water, and the marrow of a roasted cat.° In short, I forbid all commerce with the gentlewoman in What-d'ye-call-it Court. *Item,* I shut my doors against all bawds with baskets, and pennyworths of muslin, china, fans, atlases,° etc. *Item,* when you shall be breeding —

MRS. MILLAMANT: Ah! name it not.

MIRABELL: Which may be presumed, with a blessing on our endeavors —

MRS. MILLAMANT: Odious endeavors!

MIRABELL: I denounce against all strait-lacing, squeezing for a shape, till you mold my boy's head like a sugar-loaf, and instead of a man child, make me father to a crooked billet.° Lastly, to the dominion of the tea-table I submit, but with *proviso* that you exceed not in your province, but restrain yourself to native and simple tea-table drinks, as tea, chocolate, and coffee, as likewise to genuine and authorized tea-table talk, such as mending of fashions, spoiling reputations, railing at absent friends, and so forth; but that on no account you encroach upon the men's prerogative, and presume to drink healths, or toast fellows; for prevention of which, I banish all foreign forces, all auxiliaries to the tea-table, as orange brandy, all aniseed, cinnamon, citron, and Barbados waters, together with ratafia and the most noble spirit of clary.° But for cowslip wine, poppy water, and all dormitives,° those I allow. These *provisos* admitted, in other things I may prove a tractable and complying husband.

MRS. MILLAMANT: O horrid *provisos!* filthy strongwaters! I toast fellows, odious men! I hate your odious *provisos.*

MIRABELL: Then we're agreed. Shall I kiss your hand upon the contract? And here comes one to be a witness to the sealing of the deed.

(Reenter Mrs. Fainall.)

MRS. MILLAMANT: Fainall, what shall I do? Shall I have him? I think I must have him.

MRS. FAINALL: Aye, aye, take him, take him; what should you do?

MRS. MILLAMANT: Well then — I'll take my death

I'm in a horrid fright. Fainall, I shall never say it. Well — I think — I'll endure you.

MRS. FAINALL: Fie! fie! have him, have him, and tell him so in plain terms; for I am sure you have a mind to him.

MRS. MILLAMANT: Are you? I think I have; and the horrid man looks as if he thought so too. Well, you ridiculous thing you, I'll have you; I won't be kissed, nor I won't be thanked. Here, kiss my hand, though. So, hold your tongue now; don't say a word.

MRS. FAINALL: Mirabell, there's a necessity for your obedience; you have neither time to talk nor stay. My mother is coming; and in my conscience, if she should see you, would fall into fits and maybe not recover, time enough to return to Sir Rowland, who, as Foible tells me, is in a fair way to succeed. Therefore spare your ecstacies for another occasion, and slip down the back stairs, where Foible waits to consult you.

MRS. MILLAMANT: Aye, go, go. In the meantime I suppose you have said something to please me.

MIRABELL: I am all obedience.   *(Exit.)*

MRS. FAINALL: Yonder Sir Wilfull's drunk, and so noisy that my mother has been forced to leave Sir Rowland to appease him; but he answers her only with singing and drinking. What they may have done by this time I know not; but Petulant and he were upon quarreling as I came by.

MRS. MILLAMANT: Well, if Mirabell should not make a good husband, I am a lost thing; for I find I love him violently.

MRS. FAINALL: So it seems; for you mind not what's said to you. If you doubt him, you had best take up with Sir Wilfull.

MRS. MILLAMANT: How can you name that superannuated lubber? Foh!

(Enter Witwoud, from drinking.)

MRS. FAINALL: So, is the fray made up, that you have left 'em?

WITWOUD: Left 'em? I could stay no longer. I have laughed like ten christenings; I am tipsy with laughing. If I had stayed any longer I should have burst; I must have been let out and pieced in the sides like an unsized camlet.° Yes, yes, the fray is composed; my lady came in like a *noli prosequi*° and stopped the proceedings.

MRS. MILLAMANT: What was the dispute?

WITWOUD: That's the jest; there was no dispute. They

---

268. *Item:* In addition.   273–75. hog's bones . . . cat: All were ingredients in cosmetics.   278. atlases: A kind of satin.   287. billet: Stick.   298–300. orange brandy . . . clary: All these "auxiliaries" were cordials made of brandy and variously flavored.   301. dormitives: Sedatives.

358. unsized camlet: I.e., like a piece of unstiffened satin.
359. *noli prosequi:* A legal term meaning that the plaintiff does not wish to continue the prosecution.

could neither of 'em speak for rage, and so fell
asputtering at one another like two roasting apples.

(*Enter Petulant, drunk.*)

65   Now, Petulant? All's over, all's well? Gad, my head
begins to whim° it about. Why dost thou not speak?
Thou art both as drunk and as mute as a fish.

PETULANT: Look you, Mrs. Millamant, if you can love
me, dear nymph, say it, and that's the conclusion.
70   Pass on, or pass off; that's all.

WITWOUD: Thou hast uttered volumes, folios, in less
than *decimo sexto*,° my dear Lacedemonian.° Sirrah, Petulant, thou art an epitomizer of words.°

PETULANT: Witwoud, you are an annihilator of sense.

75   WITWOUD: Thou art a retailer of phrases and dost
deal in remnants of remnants, like a maker of pin-
cushions; thou art in truth (metaphorically speaking) a speaker of shorthand.

PETULANT: Thou art (without a figure) just one half
80   of an ass, and Baldwin° yonder, thy half brother,
is the rest. A Gemini° of asses split would make
just four of you.

WITWOUD: Thou dost bite, my dear mustard seed;
kiss me for that.

385   PETULANT: Stand off! I'll kiss no more males. I have
kissed your twin yonder in a humor of reconciliation, till he (*hiccup*) rises upon my stomach like
a radish.

MRS. MILLAMANT: Eh! filthy creature! What was the
390   quarrel?

PETULANT: There was no quarrel; there might have
been a quarrel.

WITWOUD: If there had been words enow between 'em
to have expressed provocation, they had gone to-
395   gether by the ears like a pair of castanets.

PETULANT: You were the quarrel.

MRS. MILLAMANT: Me!

PETULANT: If I have a humor to quarrel, I can make
less matters conclude premises. If you are not hand-
400   some, what then, if I have a humor to prove it? If
I shall have my reward, say so; if not, fight for
your face the next time yourself. I'll go sleep.

WITWOUD: Do, wrap thyself up like a wood louse,
and dream revenge; and hear me, if thou canst
405   learn to write by tomorrow morning, pen me a
challenge. I'll carry it for thee.

---

366. whim: Spin.   **372. *decimo sexto*:** A very tiny book.
Lacedemonian: Spartan. (The Spartans were known to be
very laconic people, that is, terse in their speech.)   **373.
thou art . . . words:** I.e., "You say much in few words."
380. Baldwin: The name of the ass in the medieval tale
Reynard the Fox.   **381. Gemini:** Matched pair of twins.
The constellation Gemini derives its name from the twin stars
Castor and Pollux.

PETULANT: Carry your mistress's monkey a spider! Go
flea dogs, and read romances! I'll go to bed to my
maid.   (*Exit.*)

MRS. FAINALL: He's horridly drunk. How came you   410
all in this pickle?

WITWOUD: A plot! a plot! to get rid of the knight.
Your husband's advice; but he sneaked off.

(*Reenter Sir Wilfull drunk, and Lady Wishfort.*)

LADY WISHFORT: Out upon't, out upon't! At years of
discretion, and comport yourself at this rantipole°   415
rate!

SIR WILFULL: No offense, aunt.

LADY WISHFORT: Offense? As I'm a person, I'm
ashamed of you. Fogh! how you stink of wine!
D'ye think my niece will ever endure such a bor-   420
achio!° you're an absolute borachio.

SIR WILFULL: Borachio!

LADY WISHFORT: At a time when you should commence an amour, and put your best foot foremost —   425

SIR WILFULL: 'Sheart, an you grutch° me your liquor,
make a bill. Give me more drink, and take my
purse.

(*Sings.*) "Prithee fill me the glass
    Till it laugh in my face,   430
With ale that is potent and mellow;
    He that whines for a lass
    Is an ignorant ass,
For a bumper has not its fellow."

But if you would have me marry my cousin, say   435
the word, and I'll do't. Wilfull will do't; that's the
word. Wilfull will do't; that's my crest. My motto
I have forgot.

LADY WISHFORT: My nephew's a little overtaken,°
cousin, but 'tis with drinking your health. O' my   440
word you are obliged to him.

SIR WILFULL: *In vino veritas*,° aunt. If I drunk your
health today, cousin, I am a borachio. But if you
have a mind to be married, say the word, and send
for the piper; Wilfull will do't. If not, dust it away,   445
and let's have t'other round. Tony! Ods-heart,
where's Tony? Tony's an honest fellow; but he spits
after a bumper, and that's a fault.

(*Sings.*) "We'll drink, and we'll never ha' done,
    boys,
    Put the glass then around with the sun, boys;   450

---

415. rantipole: Wild.   **420–21. borachio:** Spanish for "wine
bag," a drunkard. Shakespeare has a character named Borachio in *Much Ado About Nothing.*   **426. grutch:** Grudge.
439. overtaken: Overcome by drink.   **442. *In vino veritas*:**
"In wine (there is) truth."

> Let Apollo's example invite us;
>   For he's drunk every night,
>   And that makes him so bright,
> That he's able next morning to light us."

455 The sun's a good pimple,° an honest soaker; he has a cellar at your Antipodes.° If I travel, aunt, I touch at your Antipodes; your Antipodes are a good, rascally sort of topsy-turvy fellows. If I had a bumper, I'd stand upon my head and drink a

460 health to 'em. A match or no match, cousin, with the hard name. Aunt, Wilfull will do't. If she has her maidenhead, let her look to't; if she has not, let her keep her own counsel in the meantime, and cry out at the nine months' end.

465 MRS. MILLAMANT: Your pardon, madam, I can stay no longer. Sir Wilfull grows very powerful. Egh! how he smells! I shall be overcome if I stay. Come, cousin.

(Exeunt Mrs. Millamant and Mrs. Fainall.)

LADY WISHFORT: Smells! he would poison a tallow-

470 chandler° and his family! Beastly creature, I know not what to do with him. Travel, quotha! aye, travel, travel, get thee gone, get thee but far enough, to the Saracens, or the Tartars, or the Turks, for thou art not fit to live in a Christian common-

475 wealth, thou beastly pagan!

SIR WILFULL: Turks, no; no Turks, aunt; your Turks are infidels, and believe not in the grape. Your Mahometan, your Mussulman, is a dry stinkard.° No offense, aunt. My map says that your Turk is

480 not so honest a man as your Christian. I cannot find by the map that your mufti° is orthodox; whereby it is a plain case that orthodox is a hard word, aunt, and *(hiccup)* Greek for claret.

(Sings.) "To drink is a Christian diversion,

485 Unknown to the Turk or the Persian;
    Let Mahometan fools
    Live by heathenish rules,
And be damn'd over teacups and coffee!
    But let British lads sing,

490   Crown a health to the king,
And a fig for your sultan and sophy!"°

Ah, Tony!

(Enter Foible, and whispers [to] Lady Wishfort.)

LADY WISHFORT *(aside to Foible)*: Sir Rowland impatient? Good lack! what shall I do with this

beastly tumbril?° *(Aloud.)* Go lie down and sleep, 49▪ you sot! or, as I'm a person, I'll have you bastinadoed° with broomsticks. Call up the wenches with broomsticks.

(Exit Foible.)

SIR WILFULL: Ahey! Wenches, where are the wenches?

LADY WISHFORT: Dear Cousin Witwoud, get him 50▪ away, and you will bind me to you inviolably. I have an affair of moment that invades me with some precipitation. You will oblige me to all futurity.

WITWOUD: Come, knight. Pox on him, I don't know 50▪ what to say to him. Will you go to a cock match?

SIR WILFULL: With a wench, Tony? Is she a shakebag,° Sirrah? Let me bite your cheek° for that.

WITWOUD: Horrible! he has a breath like a bagpipe! Aye, aye, come, will you march, my Salopian?° 51▪

SIR WILFULL: Lead on, little Tony; I'll follow thee, my Anthony, my Tantony. Sirrah, thou shalt be my Tantony, and I'll be thy pig.°
    "And a fig for your sultan and sophy."

(Exit singing with Witwoud.)

LADY WISHFORT: This will never do. It will never make 51▪ a match; at least before he has been abroad.

(Enter Waitwell, disguised as Sir Rowland.)

> Dear Sir Rowland, I am confounded with confusion at the retrospection of my own rudeness! I have more pardons to ask than the Pope distributes in the Year of Jubilee.° But I hope, where there is 52▪ likely to be so near an alliance, we may unbend the severity of decorum, and dispense with a little ceremony.

WAITWELL: My impatience, madam, is the effect of my transport; and till I have the possession of your 52▪ adorable person, I am tantalized on the rack, and do but hang, madam, on the tenter° of expectation.

LADY WISHFORT: You have excess of gallantry, Sir Rowland, and press things to a conclusion with a most prevailing vehemence. But a day or two for 53▪ decency of marriage —

WAITWELL: For decency of funeral, madam! The delay will break my heart; or, if that should fail, I shall be poisoned. My nephew will get an inkling of my designs, and poison me — and I would willingly 535

---

455. pimple: Drinking companion.   **456. Antipodes:** The opposite end of the world, or its inhabitants.   **469–70. tallow-chandler:** Candle maker.   **478. dry stinkard:** A miserable nondrinker. Mohammedans drink neither wine nor spirits.   **481. mufti:** An expert in Mohammedan religious law.   **491. sophy:** A former title of the Persian shah.

495. tumbril: Dump-cart.   **496–97. bastinadoed:** Beaten. **507–08. shake-bag:** A term in cock fighting for a very game or sporting cock.   **508. bite your cheek:** I.e., "give you a big kiss."   **510. Salopian:** Shropshireman.   **513. pig:** In art and legend, the pig is associated with St. Anthony the Great. **520. Year of Jubilee:** The year (approximately every twenty-fifth) in which the Pope grants general remission from the penal consequences of sin.   **527. tenter:** A tenterhook.

starve him before I die; I would gladly go out of the world with that satisfaction. That would be some comfort to me, if I could but live so long as to be revenged on that unnatural viper.

540 LADY WISHFORT: Is he so unnatural, say you? Truly I would contribute much both to the saving of your life, and the accomplishment of your revenge. Not that I respect myself, though he has been a perfidious wretch to me.

545 WAITWELL: Perfidious to you!

LADY WISHFORT: O Sir Rowland, the hours that he has died away at my feet, the tears that he has shed, the oaths that he has sworn, the palpitations that he has felt, the trances and the tremblings, the 550 ardors and the ecstasies, the kneelings and the risings, the heart-heavings and the hand-gripings, the pangs and the pathetic regards of his protesting eyes! Oh, no memory can register!

WAITWELL: What, my rival! Is the rebel my rival? 'A 555 dies.

LADY WISHFORT: No, don't kill him at once, Sir Rowland; starve him gradually, inch by inch.

WAITWELL: I'll do't. In three weeks he shall be barefoot; in a month out at knees with begging an alms. 560 He shall starve upward and upward, till he has nothing living but his head, and then go out in a stink like a candle's end upon a save-all.°

LADY WISHFORT: Well, Sir Rowland, you have the way. You are no novice in the labyrinth of love; 565 you have the clue. But as I am a person, Sir Rowland, you must not attribute my yielding to any sinister appetite, or indigestion of widowhood; nor impute my complacency to any lethargy of continence. I hope you do not think me prone to any 570 iteration° of nuptials.

WAITWELL: Far be it from me —

LADY WISHFORT: If you do, I protest I must recede, or think that I have made a prostitution of decorums; but in the vehemence of compassion, and 575 to save the life of a person of so much importance —

WAITWELL: I esteem it so.

LADY WISHFORT: Or else you wrong my condescension.

580 WAITWELL: I do not, I do not!

LADY WISHFORT: Indeed you do.

WAITWELL: I do not, fair shrine of virtue!

LADY WISHFORT: If you think the least scruple of carnality° was an ingredient —

WAITWELL: Dear madam, no. You are all camphire° 585 and frankincense, all chastity and odor.

LADY WISHFORT: Or that —

(*Reenter Foible.*)

FOIBLE: Madam, the dancers are ready; and there's one with a letter, who must deliver it into your own hands. 590

LADY WISHFORT: Sir Rowland, will you give me leave? Think favorably, judge candidly, and conclude you have found a person who would suffer racks in honor's cause, dear Sir Rowland, and will wait on you incessantly.° (*Exit.*) 595

WAITWELL: Fie, fie! What a slavery have I undergone! Spouse, hast thou any cordial? I want spirits.

FOIBLE: What a washy° rogue art thou, to pant thus for a quarter of an hour's lying and swearing to a fine lady! 600

WAITWELL: Oh, she is the antidote to desire! Spouse, thou wilt fare the worse for't. I shall have no appetite to "iteration of nuptials" this eight-and-forty hours. By this hand I'd rather be a chair-man° in the dog days° than act Sir Rowland till this time 605 tomorrow!

(*Reenter Lady Wishfort, with a letter.*)

LADY WISHFORT: Call in the dancers. Sir Rowland, we'll sit, if you please, and see the entertainment. (*Dance.*) Now, with your permission, Sir Rowland, I will peruse my letter. I would open it in your 610 presence, because I would not make you uneasy. If it should make you uneasy, I would burn it — speak if it does — but you may see, the superscription is like a woman's hand.

FOIBLE (*aside to Waitwell*): By Heaven! Mrs. Mar- 615 wood's; I know it. My heart aches. Get it from her.

WAITWELL: A woman's hand? No, madam, that's no woman's hand; I see that already. That's somebody whose throat must be cut. 620

LADY WISHFORT: Nay, Sir Rowland, since you give me a proof of your passion by your jealousy, I promise you I'll make a return, by a frank communication. You shall see it; we'll open it together. Look you here. (*Reads.*) "Madam, though un- 625 known to you." Look you there; 'tis from nobody that I know. "I have that honor for your character, that I think myself obliged to let you know you

---

562. save-all: A device in a candlestick to ensure that the candle will be completely burned. 570. iteration: Repetition. The sense seems to be that Lady Wishfort hopes Sir Rowland will not suspect her of a willingness to marry just any man. 584. carnality: Sensuality, lust.

585. camphire: Camphor was believed to reduce sexual desire. 595. incessantly: Immediately. 598. washy: Weak. 604. chair-man: A sedan-chair carrier. 605. dog days: The sultriest days of the summer, a period of about six weeks beginning in early July.

are abused. He who pretends to be Sir Rowland
is a cheat and a rascal." Oh, heavens! what's this?

630

FOIBLE (*aside*): Unfortunate! all's ruined!

WAITWELL: How, how, let me see, let me see! (*Reading.*) "A rascal, and disguised and suborned° for
that imposture." O villainy! O villainy! "by the
contrivance of —"

635

LADY WISHFORT: I shall faint, I shall die, oh!

FOIBLE (*aside to Waitwell*): Say 'tis your nephew's
hand. Quickly, his plot, swear, swear it!

WAITWELL: Here's a villain! Madam, don't you perceive it? don't you see it?

640

LADY WISHFORT: Too well, too well! I have seen too
much.

WAITWELL: I told you at first I knew the hand. A
woman's hand? The rascal writes a sort of a large
hand, your Roman hand. I saw there was a throat
to be cut presently. If he were my son, as he is my
nephew, I'd pistol him!

645

FOIBLE: Oh, treachery! But are you sure, Sir Rowland,
it is his writing?

WAITWELL: Sure? Am I here? Do I live? Do I love this
pearl of India? I have twenty letters in my pocket
from him in the same character.°

650

LADY WISHFORT: How!

FOIBLE: Oh, what luck it is, Sir Rowland, that you
were present at this juncture! This was the business
that brought Mr. Mirabell disguised to Madam
Millamant this afternoon. I thought something was
contriving, when he stole by me and would have
hid his face.

655

LADY WISHFORT: How, how! I heard the villain was
in the house indeed; and now I remember, my niece
went away abruptly, when Sir Wilfull was to have
made his addresses.

660

FOIBLE: Then, then, madam, Mr. Mirabell waited for
her in her chamber, but I would not tell your ladyship to discompose° you when you were to receive
Sir Rowland.

665

WAITWELL: Enough, his date is short.

FOIBLE: No, good Sir Rowland, don't incur the law.

WAITWELL: Law? I care not for law. I can but die,
and 'tis in a good cause. My lady shall be satisfied
of my truth and innocence, though it cost me my
life.

670

LADY WISHFORT: No, dear Sir Rowland, don't fight;
if you should be killed, I must never show my face;
or hanged! Oh, consider my reputation, Sir Rowland! No, you shan't fight. I'll go in and examine
my niece; I'll make her confess. I conjure you, Sir
Rowland, by all your love, not to fight.

675

WAITWELL: I am charmed, madam; I obey. But some

680

proof you must let me give you; I'll go for a black
box, which contains the writings of my whole estate, and deliver that into your hands.

LADY WISHFORT: Aye, dear Sir Rowland, that will be
some comfort; bring the black box.

685

WAITWELL: And may I presume to bring a contract
to be signed this night? May I hope so far?

LADY WISHFORT: Bring what you will; but come alive,
pray come alive. Oh, this is a happy discovery!

WAITWELL: Dead or alive I'll come, and married we
will be in spite of treachery; aye, and get an heir
that shall defeat the last remaining glimpse of hope
in my abandoned nephew. Come, my buxom
widow.

690

Ere long you shall substantial proof receive,
That I'm an arrant knight —°

695

FOIBLE (*aside*):   Or arrant° knave.
                                       (*Exeunt.*)

ACT V

([*Scene continues.*] *Enter Lady Wishfort and Foible.*)

LADY WISHFORT: Out of my house, out of my house,
thou viper! thou serpent, that I have fostered! thou
bosom traitress, that I raised from nothing! Begone!
begone! begone! go! go! That I took from washing
of old gauze and weaving of dead hair, with a bleak
blue nose, over a chafing-dish of starved embers,
and dining behind a traverse rag,° in a shop no
bigger than a birdcage! Go, go! starve again, do,
do!

5

FOIBLE: Dear madam, I'll beg your pardon on my
knees.

10

LADY WISHFORT: Away! out! out! Go set up for yourself
again! Do, drive a trade, do, with your threepennyworth of small ware flaunting upon a packthread under a brandy-seller's bulk,° or against
a dead wall by a ballad-monger! Go, hang out an
old frisoneer-gorget,° with a yard of yellow colberteen° again. Do; an old gnawed mask, two rows
of pins, and a child's fiddle; a glass necklace with
the beads broken, and a quilted nightcap with one
ear. Go, go, drive a trade! These were your commodities, you treacherous trull! this was the merchandise you dealt in, when I took you into my
house, placed you next myself, and made you gov-

15

20

---

633. **suborned:** Bribed.   652. **character:** Handwriting.
666. **discompose:** Distress, upset.

696. **arrant knight:** I.e., a true knight-errant.   **arrant:** Downright.   7. **traverse rag:** A curtain or hanging that serves as a screen.   15. **bulk:** A booth where brandy is sold.   17. **frisoneer-gorget:** A kind of wimple, or head covering, made of coarse woolen cloth.   17–18. **colberteen:** A French lace of inferior quality.

ernante of my whole family! You have forgot this, have you, now you have feathered your nest?

FOIBLE: No, no, dear madam. Do but hear me; have but a moment's patience. I'll confess all. Mr. Mirabell seduced me; I am not the first that he has wheedled with his dissembling tongue. Your ladyship's own wisdom has been deluded by him; then how should I, a poor ignorant, defend myself? O madam, if you knew but what he promised me, and how he assured me your ladyship should come to no damage! Or else the wealth of the Indies should not have bribed me to conspire against so good, so sweet, so kind a lady as you have been to me.

LADY WISHFORT: "No damage"? What, to betray me, to marry me to a cast-servingman?° To make me a receptacle, a hospital for a decayed pimp? "No damage"? O thou frontless° impudence, more than a big-bellied actress!

FOIBLE: Pray do but hear me, madam; he could not marry your ladyship, madam. No indeed; his marriage was to have been void in law, for he was married to me first, to secure your ladyship. He could not have bedded your ladyship; for if he had consummated with your ladyship, he must have run the risk of the law and been put upon his clergy.° Yes indeed; I inquired of the law in that case before I would meddle or make.°

LADY WISHFORT: What, then I have been your property, have I? I have been convenient to you, it seems! While you were catering for Mirabell, I have been broker° for you? What, have you made a passive bawd of me? This exceeds all precedent; I am brought to fine uses, to become a botcher° of second-hand marriages between Abigails° and Andrews!° I'll couple you! Yes, I'll baste you together, you and your Philander!° I'll Duke's-Place you, as I'm a person! Your turtle is in custody already; you shall coo in the same cage, if there be constable or warrant in the parish.   (*Exit.*)

FOIBLE: Oh, that ever I was born! Oh, that I was ever married! A bride! aye, I shall be a Bridewell-bride.° Oh!

---

40. **cast-servingman:** A discharged servant.   42. **frontless:** Shameless.   50–51. **put upon his clergy:** Forced to plead benefit of clergy. Clergy (and, later, people who could read or write) could claim exemption from punishment imposed by a secular court.   52. **meddle or make:** A colloquialism for "get mixed up in this business."   56. **broker:** Marriage broker.   58. **botcher:** A maker or mender.   59. **Abigails:** A maidservant in Beaumont and Fletcher's play *The Scornful Lady.*   59–60. **Andrews:** A manservant in Fletcher and Massinger's *The Elder Brother.*   61. **Philander:** The lover in Beaumont and Fletcher's *The Laws of Candy.*   66. **Bridewell-bride:** Bridewell was a house of correction.

(*Enter Mrs. Fainall.*)

MRS. FAINALL: Poor Foible, what's the matter?

FOIBLE: O madam, my lady's gone for a constable. I shall be had to a justice, and put to Bridewell to beat hemp. Poor Waitwell's gone to prison already.

MRS. FAINALL: Have a good heart, Foible; Mirabell's gone to give security for him. This is all Marwood's and my husband's doing.

FOIBLE: Yes, yes, I know it, madam; she was in my lady's closet, and overheard all that you said to me before dinner. She sent the letter to my lady; and that missing effect, Mr. Fainall laid this plot to arrest Waitwell, when he pretended to go for the papers; and in the meantime Mrs. Marwood declared all to my lady.

MRS. FAINALL: Was there no mention made of me in the letter? My mother does not suspect my being in the confederacy? I fancy Marwood has not told her, though she has told my husband.

FOIBLE: Yes, madam; but my lady did not see that part. We stifled the letter before she read so far. Has that mischievous devil told Mr. Fainall of your ladyship then?

MRS. FAINALL: Aye, all's out, my affair with Mirabell, everything discovered. This is the last day of our living together; that's my comfort.

FOIBLE: Indeed, madam, and so 'tis a comfort if you knew all. He has been even with your ladyship; which I could have told you long enough since, but I love to keep peace and quietness by my good will. I had rather bring friends together than set 'em at distance. But Mrs. Marwood and he are nearer related than ever their parents thought for.

MRS. FAINALL: Sayest thou so, Foible? Canst thou prove this?

FOIBLE: I can take my oath of it, madam; so can Mrs. Mincing. We have had many a fair word from Madam Marwood, to conceal something that passed in our chamber one evening when you were at Hyde Park and we were thought to have gone awalking; but we went up unawares, though we were sworn to secrecy too. Madam Marwood took a book and swore us upon it, but it was but a book of poems. So long as it was not a Bible oath, we may break it with a safe conscience.

MRS. FAINALL: This discovery is the most opportune thing I could wish. Now, Mincing?

(*Enter Mincing.*)

MINCING: My lady° would speak with Mrs. Foible, mem. Mr. Mirabell is with her; he has set your spouse at liberty, Mrs. Foible, and would have you hide yourself in my lady's closet till my old lady's

---

114. **My lady:** I.e., Millamant.

anger is abated. Oh, my old lady is in a perilous passion at something Mr. Fainall has said; he
120 swears, and my old lady cries. There's a fearful hurricane, I vow. He says, mem, how that he'll have my lady's fortune made over to him, or he'll be divorced.

MRS. FAINALL: Does your lady or Mirabell know that?

125 MINCING: Yes, mem; they have sent me to see if Sir Wilfull be sober and to bring him to them. My lady is resolved to have him, I think, rather than lose such a vast sum as six thousand pound. Oh, come, Mrs. Foible, I hear my old lady.

130 MRS. FAINALL: Foible, you must tell Mincing that she must prepare to vouch° when I call her.

FOIBLE: Yes, yes, madam.

MINCING: O yes, mem, I'll vouch anything for your ladyship's service, be what it will.

(*Exeunt Mincing and Foible.*)

(*Reenter Lady Wishfort, with Mrs. Marwood.*)

135 LADY WISHFORT: O my dear friend, how can I enumerate the benefits that I have received from your goodness? To you I owe the timely discovery of the false vows of Mirabell; to you I owe the detection of the impostor, Sir Rowland. And now
140 you are become an intercessor with my son-in-law, to save the honor of my house, and compound for the frailties of my daughter. Well, friend, you are enough to reconcile me to the bad world, or else I would retire to deserts and solitudes, and feed
145 harmless sheep by groves and purling streams. Dear Marwood, let us leave the world, and retire by ourselves and be shepherdesses.

MRS. MARWOOD: Let us first dispatch the affair in hand, madam. We shall have leisure to think of
150 retirement afterwards. Here is one who is concerned in the treaty.

LADY WISHFORT: O daughter, daughter, is it possible thou shouldst be my child, bone of my bone, and flesh of my flesh, and, as I may say, another me,
155 and yet transgress the most minute particle of severe virtue? Is it possible you should lean aside to iniquity, who have been cast in the direct mold of virtue? I have not only been a mold but a pattern for you, and a model for you, after you were
160 brought into the world.

MRS. FAINALL: I don't understand your ladyship.

LADY WISHFORT: Not understand? Why, have you not been naught?° Have you not been sophisticated?° Not understand? Here I am ruined to compound°

---

131. **vouch:** Testify.   163. **naught:** Naughty, wicked.   **sophisticated:** Corrupted, debauched.   164. **compound:** Compensate. Lady Wishfort refers to Mr. Fainall's blackmailing tactics.

for your caprices and your cuckoldoms. I must 165 pawn my plate and my jewels, and ruin my niece, and all little enough.

MRS. FAINALL: I am wronged and abused, and so are you. 'Tis a false accusation, as false as hell, as false as your friend there, aye, or your friend's friend, 170 my false husband.

MRS. MARWOOD: My friend, Mrs. Fainall? Your husband my friend? What do you mean?

MRS. FAINALL: I know what I mean, madam, and so do you; and so shall the world at a time convenient. 175

MRS. MARWOOD: I am sorry to see you so passionate, madam. More temper° would look more like innocence. But I have done. I am sorry my zeal to serve your ladyship and family should admit of misconstruction, or make me liable to affronts. You 180 will pardon me, madam, if I meddle no more with an affair in which I am not personally concerned.

LADY WISHFORT: O dear friend, I am so ashamed that you should meet with such returns! (*To Mrs. Fainall.*) You ought to ask pardon on your knees, un- 185 grateful creature; she deserves more from you than all your life can accomplish. (*To Mrs. Marwood.*) Oh, don't leave me destitute in this perplexity! No, stick to me, my good genius.

MRS. FAINALL: I tell you, madam, you're abused. Stick 190 to you? Aye, like a leech, to suck your best blood; she'll drop off when she's full. Madam, you shan't pawn a bodkin,° nor part with a brass counter,° in composition for me. I defy 'em all. Let 'em prove their aspersions; I know my own innocence, and 195 dare stand a trial. (*Exit.*)

LADY WISHFORT: Why, if she should be innocent, if she should be wronged after all, ha? I don't know what to think; and, I promise you, her education has been unexceptionable.° I may say it; for I chiefly 200 made it my own care to initiate her very infancy in the rudiments of virtue, and to impress upon her tender years a young odium° and aversion to the very sight of men. Aye, friend, she would ha' shrieked if she had but seen a man, till she was in 205 her teens. As I'm a person 'tis true. She was never suffered to play with a male child, though but in coats; nay, her very babies° were of the feminine gender. Oh, she never looked a man in the face but her own father, or the chaplain, and him we 210 made a shift° to put upon her for a woman, by the help of his long garments and his sleek face, till she was going in her fifteen.°

---

177. **temper:** Temperateness.   193. **bodkin:** Needle or hairpin.   **brass counter:** A farthing (a quarter of a penny).   200. **unexceptionable:** Exemplary.   203. **odium:** Dislike.   208. **babies:** Dolls.   211. **made a shift:** Devised a plan.   213. **in her fifteen:** Into her fifteenth year.

MRS. MARWOOD: 'Twas much she should be deceived so long.

LADY WISHFORT: I warrant you, or she would never have borne to have been catechized by him; and have heard his long lectures against singing and dancing, and such debaucheries, and going to filthy plays and profane music meetings, where the lewd trebles squeak nothing but bawdy, and the basses roar blasphemy. Oh, she would have swooned at the sight or name of an obscene playbook! And can I think, after all this, that my daughter can be naught? What, a whore? and thought it excommunication to set her foot within the door of a playhouse! O dear friend, I can't believe it, no, no! As she says, let him prove it, let him prove it.

MRS. MARWOOD: Prove it, madam? What, and have your name prostituted in a public court? yours and your daughter's reputation worried at the bar by a pack of bawling lawyers? To be ushered in with an *Oyez*° of scandal, and have your case opened by an old fumbling lecher in a quoif° like a manmidwife; to bring your daughter's infamy to light; to be a theme for legal punsters and quibblers by the statute, and become a jest against a rule of court, where there is no precedent for a jest in any record, not even in Doomsday Book;° to discompose the gravity of the bench, and provoke naughty interrogatories in more naughty law Latin, while the good judge, tickled with the proceeding, simpers under a gray beard, and fidges° off and on his cushion as if he had swallowed cantharides,° or sat upon cow-itch!°

LADY WISHFORT: Oh, 'tis very hard!

MRS. MARWOOD: And then to have my young revelers of the Temple° take notes, like prentices at a conventicle;° and after, talk it over again in Commons,° or before drawers in an eating-house.

LADY WISHFORT: Worse and worse!

MRS. MARWOOD: Nay, this is nothing; if it would end here, 'twere well. But it must, after this, be consigned by the shorthand writers to the public press; and from thence be transferred to the hands, nay into the throats and lungs of hawkers,° with voices more licentious than the loud flounder-man's.° And this you must hear till you are stunned; nay, you must hear nothing else for some days.

LADY WISHFORT: Oh, 'tis insupportable! No, no, dear friend; make it up, make it up; aye, aye, I'll compound. I'll give up all, myself and my all, my niece and her all, anything, everything for composition.

MRS. MARWOOD: Nay, madam, I advise nothing; I only lay before you, as a friend, the inconveniencies which perhaps you have overseen. Here comes Mr. Fainall; if he will be satisfied to huddle up all in silence, I shall be glad. You must think I would rather congratulate than condole with you.

(Enter Fainall.)

LADY WISHFORT: Aye, aye, I do not doubt it, dear Marwood; no, no, I do not doubt it.

FAINALL: Well, madam, I have suffered myself to be overcome by the importunity of this lady, your friend, and am content you shall enjoy your own proper estate during life, on condition you oblige yourself never to marry, under such penalty as I think convenient.

LADY WISHFORT: Never to marry?

FAINALL: No more Sir Rowlands; the next imposture may not be so timely detected.

MRS. MARWOOD: That condition, I dare answer, my lady will consent to, without difficulty; she has already but too much experienced the perfidiousness of men. Besides, madam, when we retire to our pastoral solitude, we shall bid adieu to all other thoughts.

LADY WISHFORT: Aye, that's true; but in case of necessity, as of health, or some such emergency —

FAINALL: Oh, if you are prescribed marriage, you shall be considered; I will only reserve to myself the power to choose for you. If your physic be wholesome, it matters not who is your apothecary. Next, my wife shall settle on me the remainder of her fortune, not made over already; and for her maintenance depend entirely on my discretion.

LADY WISHFORT: This is most inhumanly savage, exceeding the barbarity of a Muscovite° husband.

FAINALL: I learned it from his Czarish majesty's retinue,° in a winter evening's conference over brandy and pepper, amongst other secrets of matrimony and policy, as they are at present practised in the northern hemisphere. But this must be agreed unto,

---

233. *Oyez:* The court crier's call for silence.   234. **quoif:** Coif, the lawyer's white cap.   239. **Doomsday Book:** A record of a survey of the lands of England made by order of William the Conqueror.   243. **fidges:** Fidgets.   244. **cantharides:** A powder made from dried beetles and used medicinally as a skin irritant.   245. **cow-itch:** Cowage, a plant that causes intense itching.   248. **Temple:** The courts of law.   248–49. **prentices at a conventicle:** It was customary for a Puritan master to require his apprentice to take notes on the Sunday sermon in the meetinghouse (conventicle).   249. **Commons:** The dining hall.   256. **hawkers:** Peddlers.

257. **flounder-man:** An actual flounder seller, well known to the Londoners of the day and noted for his "loud, but not unmusical" voice.   298. **Muscovite:** Russian.   299–300. **Czarish majesty's retinue:** Referring to Peter the Great's visit to England in 1697.

and that positively. Lastly, I will be endowed, in
305 right of my wife, with that six thousand pound,
which is the moiety of Mrs. Millamant's fortune
in your possession; and which she has forfeited (as
will appear by the last will and testament of your
deceased husband, Sir Jonathan Wishfort) by her
310 disobedience in contracting herself against your
consent or knowledge, and by refusing the offered
match with Sir Wilfull Witwoud, which you, like
a careful aunt, had provided for her.
LADY WISHFORT: My nephew was *non compos*,° and
315 could not make his addresses.
FAINALL: I come to make demands. I'll hear no
objections.
LADY WISHFORT: You will grant me time to consider?
FAINALL: Yes, while the instrument° is drawing, to
320 which you must set your hand till more sufficient
deeds can be perfected; which I will take care shall
be done with all possible speed. In the meanwhile
I will go for the said instrument, and till my return
you may balance this matter in your own
325 discretion.   (*Exit.*)
LADY WISHFORT: This insolence is beyond all precedent, all parallel; must I be subject to this merciless
villain?
MRS. MARWOOD: 'Tis severe indeed, madam, that you
330 should smart for your daughter's wantonness.
LADY WISHFORT: 'Twas against my consent that she
married this barbarian, but she would have him,
though her year° was not out. Ah! her first husband, my son Languish, would not have carried it
335 thus. Well, that was my choice, this is hers; she is
matched now with a witness.° I shall be mad! Dear
friend, is there no comfort for me? Must I live to
be confiscated at this rebel-rate?° Here come two
more of my Egyptian plagues° too.

(*Enter Mrs. Millamant and Sir Wilfull Witwoud.*)

340 SIR WILFULL: Aunt, your servant.
LADY WISHFORT: Out, caterpillar, call not me aunt!
I know thee not!
SIR WILFULL: I confess I have been a little in disguise,°
as they say. 'Sheart! and I'm sorry for't. What
345 would you have? I hope I committed no offense,
aunt, and if I did, I am willing to make satisfaction;
and what can a man say fairer? If I have broke

anything, I'll pay for't, an it cost a pound. And so
let that content for what's past, and make no more
words. For what's to come, to pleasure you I'm 350
willing to marry my cousin. So pray let's all be
friends; she and I are agreed upon the matter before
a witness.
LADY WISHFORT: How's this, dear niece? Have I any
comfort? Can this be true?   355
MRS. MILLAMANT: I am content to be a sacrifice to
your repose, madam; and to convince you that I
had no hand in the plot, as you were misinformed,
I have laid my commands on Mirabell to come in
person, and be a witness that I give my hand to 360
this flower of knighthood; and for the contract that
passed between Mirabell and me, I have obliged
him to make a resignation of it in your ladyship's
presence. He is without, and waits your leave for
admittance.   365
LADY WISHFORT: Well, I'll swear I am something revived at this testimony of your obedience; but I
cannot admit that traitor. I fear I cannot fortify
myself to support his appearance. He is as terrible
to me as a Gorgon;° if I see him, I fear I shall turn 370
to stone, petrify incessantly.
MRS. MILLAMANT: If you disoblige him, he may resent
your refusal, and insist upon the contract still. Then
'tis the last time he will be offensive to you.
LADY WISHFORT: Are you sure it will be the last time? 375
If I were sure of that! Shall I never see him again?
MRS. MILLAMANT: Sir Wilfull, you and he are to travel
together, are you not?
SIR WILFULL: 'Sheart, the gentleman's a civil gentleman, aunt; let him come in. Why, we are sworn 380
brothers and fellow travelers. We are to be Pylades
and Orestes,° he and I. He is to be my interpreter
in foreign parts. He has been overseas once already;
and with *proviso* that I marry my cousin, will cross
'em once again, only to bear me company. 'Sheart, 385
I'll call him in. An I set on't once, he shall come
in; and see who'll hinder him.
                    (*Goes to the door and hems.*)
MRS. MARWOOD: This is precious fooling, if it would
pass; but I'll know the bottom of it.
LADY WISHFORT: O dear Marwood, you are not 390
going?
MRS. MARWOOD: Not far, madam; I'll return
immediately.   (*Exit.*)

---

314. *non compos*: I.e., *non compos mentis*, not in his right
mind.   319. *instrument*: Formal agreement.   333. *her year*:
Period of mourning for her first husband.   336. *with a
witness*: Colloquialism meaning "with a vengeance."   337–
38. *must I live . . . rebel-rate*: The sense is "Must I live to
see my property and fortune confiscated in this piratical
fashion?"   339. *Egyptian plagues*: Referring to the plagues
of Egypt recorded in Exodus 7ff.   343. *disguise*: Drunk.

370. *Gorgon*: Any one of the three sisters in Greek legend
(Medusa was one) whose hair was wreathed with snakes and
whose glance turned the beholder to stone.   381–82. *Pylades and Orestes*: In Greek legend Pylades was the loyal
and trusted friend of Orestes, son of Agamemnon and
brother of Electra.

(*Reenter Sir Wilfull with Mirabell.*)

SIR WILFULL: Look up, man, I'll stand by you; 'sbud
and she do frown, she can't kill you; besides, harkee, she dare not frown desperately, because her
face is none of her own. 'Sheart, an she should,
her forehead would wrinkle like the coat of a cream
cheese; but mum for that, fellow traveler.

MIRABELL: If a deep sense of the many injuries I have
offered to so good a lady, with a sincere remorse
and a hearty contrition, can but obtain the least
glance of compassion, I am too happy. Ah, madam,
there was a time! But let it be forgotten. I confess
I have deservedly forfeited the high place I once
held, of sighing at your feet. Nay, kill me not, by
turning from me in disdain. I come not to plead
for favor; nay, not for pardon. I am a suppliant
only for pity. I am going where I shall never behold
you more.

SIR WILFULL: How, fellow traveler! You shall go by
yourself then.

MIRABELL: Let me be pitied first, and afterwards forgotten. I ask no more.

SIR WILFULL: By'r lady, a very reasonable request, and
will cost you nothing, aunt. Come, come, forgive
and forget, aunt; why, you must, an you are a
Christian.

MIRABELL: Consider, madam, in reality you could not
receive much prejudice; it was an innocent device,
though I confess it had a face of guiltiness. It was
at most an artifice which love contrived, and errors
which love produces have ever been accounted ve-
nial. At least think it is punishment enough that I
have lost what in my heart I hold most dear, that
to your cruel indignation I have offered up this
beauty, and with her my peace and quiet; nay, all
my hopes of future comfort.

SIR WILFULL: An he does not move me, would I may
never be o' the quorum!° An it were not as good
a deed as to drink, to give her to him again, I
would I might never take shipping! Aunt, if you
don't forgive quickly, I shall melt, I can tell you
that. My contract went no farther than a little
mouth-glue, and that's hardly dry; one doleful sigh
more from my fellow traveler, and 'tis dissolved.

LADY WISHFORT: Well, nephew, upon your account
— ah, he has a false insinuating tongue! Well, sir,
I will stifle my just resentment at my nephew's
request. I will endeavor what I can to forget, but
on *proviso* that you resign the contract with my
niece immediately.

MIRABELL: It is in writing, and with papers of concern;
but I have sent my servant for it, and will deliver

it to you, with all acknowledgments for your tran-   445
scendent goodness.

LADY WISHFORT (*aside*): Oh, he has witchcraft in his
eyes and tongue! When I did not see him, I could
have bribed a villain to his assassination; but his
appearance rakes the embers which have so long   450
lain smothered in my breast.

(*Reenter Fainall and Mrs. Marwood.*)

FAINALL: Your date of deliberation, madam, is expired. Here is the instrument; are you prepared to
sign?

LADY WISHFORT: If I were prepared, I am not em-   455
powered. My niece exerts a lawful claim, having
matched herself by my direction to Sir Wilfull.

FAINALL: That sham is too gross to pass on me, though
'tis imposed on you, madam.

MRS. MILLAMANT: Sir, I have given my consent.   460

MIRABELL: And, sir, I have resigned my pretensions.

SIR WILFULL: And, sir, I assert my right; and will
maintain it in defiance of you, sir, and of your
instrument. 'Sheart, an you talk of an instrument,
sir, I have an old fox° by my thigh shall hack your   465
instrument of ram vellum° to shreds, sir! It shall
not be sufficient for a *mittimus*° or a tailor's measure.° Therefore withdraw your instrument, sir, or,
by'r lady, I shall draw mine.

LADY WISHFORT: Hold, nephew, hold!   470

MRS. MILLAMANT: Good Sir Wilfull, respite° your
valor.

FAINALL: Indeed? Are you provided of your guard,
with your single beefeater° there? But I'm prepared
for you, and insist upon my first proposal. You   475
shall submit your own estate to my management
and absolutely make over my wife's to my sole use,
as pursuant to the purpose and tenor of this other
covenant. (*To Mrs. Millamant.*) I suppose, madam,
your consent is not requisite in this case; nor, Mr.   480
Mirabell, your resignation; nor, Sir Wilfull, your
right. You may draw your fox if you please, sir,
and make a Bear Garden° flourish somewhere
else; for here it will not avail. — This, my Lady
Wishfort, must be subscribed, or your darling   485
daughter's turned adrift, like a leaky hulk, to
sink or swim, as she and the current of this lewd
town can agree.

LADY WISHFORT: Is there no means, no remedy to

---

430. quorum: An indispensable member of the legal bench.

465. fox: Sword.   466. ram vellum: Parchment (made from
sheepskin).   467. *mittimus*: Legal term for a warrant of
commitment to prison.   467–68. tailor's measure: Tailors'
measurements were recorded on parchment.   471. respite:
Control.   474. beefeater: A guard of the Tower of London.
483. Bear Garden: Bear baiting was a popular amusement
in the London of the day, and the gardens in which it took
place were notorious for brawls and rowdy behavior.

490 stop my ruin? Ungrateful wretch! dost thou not owe thy being, thy subsistence, to my daughter's fortune?

FAINALL: I'll answer you when I have the rest of it in my possession.

495 MIRABELL (*to Lady Wishfort*): But that you would not accept of a remedy from my hands — I own I have not deserved you should owe any obligation to me; or else perhaps I could advise —

LADY WISHFORT: Oh, what? what? to save me and 500 my child from ruin, from want, I'll forgive all that's past; nay, I'll consent to anything to come, to be delivered from this tyranny.

MIRABELL: Aye, madam, but that is too late; my reward is intercepted. You have disposed of her who 505 only could have made me a compensation for all my services. But be it as it may, I am resolved I'll serve you; you shall not be wronged in this savage manner.

LADY WISHFORT: How! Dear Mr. Mirabell, can you 510 be so generous at last? But it is not possible. Harkee, I'll break my nephew's match; you shall have my niece yet, and all her fortune, if you can but save me from this imminent danger.

MIRABELL: Will you? I take you at your word. I ask 515 no more. I must have leave for two criminals to appear.

LADY WISHFORT: Aye, aye; anybody, anybody!

MIRABELL: Foible is one, and a penitent.

(*Reenter Mrs. Fainall, Foible, and Mincing.*)

MRS. MARWOOD (*to Fainall*): O my shame! (*Mirabell and* 520 *Lady Wishfort go to Mrs. Fainall and Foible.*) These corrupt things are brought hither to expose me.

FAINALL: If it must all come out, why let 'em know it; 'tis but the way of the world. That shall not urge me to relinquish or abate one tittle of my 525 terms; no, I will insist the more.

FOIBLE: Yes indeed, madam; I'll take my Bible oath of it.

MINCING: And so will I, mem.

LADY WISHFORT: O Marwood. Marwood, art thou 530 false? my friend deceive me? Hast thou been a wicked accomplice with that profligate man?

MRS. MARWOOD: Have you so much ingratitude and injustice, to give credit against your friend to the aspersions of two such mercenary trulls?

535 MINCING: "Mercenary," mem? I scorn your words. 'Tis true we found you and Mr. Fainall in the blue garret; by the same token, you swore us to secrecy upon Messalina's poems.° "Mercenary?" No, if we

would have been mercenary, we should have held our tongues; you would have bribed us sufficiently. 54[0]

FAINALL: Go, you are an insignificant thing! Well, what are you the better for this? Is this Mr. Mirabell's expedient? I'll be put off no longer. You thing, that was a wife, shall smart for this! I will not leave thee wherewithal to hide thy shame; your 54[5] body shall be naked as your reputation.

MRS. FAINALL: I despise you, and defy your malice! You have aspersed me wrongfully. I have proved your falsehood. Go, you and your treacherous — I will not name it, but starve together, perish! 55[0]

FAINALL: Not while you are worth a groat,° indeed, my dear. Madam, I'll be fooled no longer.

LADY WISHFORT: Ah, Mr. Mirabell, this is small comfort, the detection of this affair.

MIRABELL: Oh, in good time. Your leave for the other 55[5] offender and penitent to appear, madam.

(*Enter Waitwell, with a box of writings.*)

LADY WISHFORT: O Sir Rowland! Well, rascal?

WAITWELL: What your ladyship pleases. I have brought the black box at last, madam.

MIRABELL: Give it me. Madam, you remember your 56[0] promise.

LADY WISHFORT: Aye, dear sir.

MIRABELL: Where are the gentlemen?

WAITWELL: At hand, sir, rubbing their eyes; just risen from sleep. 56[5]

FAINALL: 'Sdeath, what's this to me? I'll not wait your private concerns.

(*Enter Petulant and Witwoud.*)

PETULANT: How now? What's the matter? Whose hand's out?°

WITWOUD: Heyday! what, are you all got together, 57[0] like players at the end of the last act?

MIRABELL: You may remember, gentlemen, I once requested your hands as witnesses to a certain parchment.

WITWOUD: Aye, I do; my hand I remember. Petulant 57[5] set his mark.

MIRABELL: You wrong him, his name is fairly written, as shall appear. You do not remember, gentlemen, anything of what that parchment contained?

(*Undoing the box.*)

WITWOUD: No. 58[0]

PETULANT: Not I. I writ. I read nothing.

MIRABELL: Very well; now you shall know. Madam, your promise.

LADY WISHFORT: Aye, aye, sir, upon my honor.

MIRABELL: Mr. Fainall, it is now time that you should 58[5] know that your lady, while she was at her own

---

538. **Messalina's poems:** Mincing means a volume of "miscellaneous" poems. Her mistake presents an amusing irony, since Messalina, the wife of the Roman Emperor Claudius, was notorious for her avarice, treachery, and dissoluteness.

551. **groat:** An old silver coin worth about fourpence. 568–69. **Whose hand's out:** "What is the trouble?"

disposal, and before you had by your insinuations
wheedled her out of a pretended settlement of the
greatest part of her fortune —

FAINALL: Sir! pretended!

MIRABELL: Yes, sir. I say that this lady, while a widow,
having it seems received some cautions respecting
your inconstancy and tyranny of temper, which
from her own partial opinion and fondness of you
she could never have suspected — she did, I say,
by the wholesome advice of friends and of sages
learned in the laws of this land, deliver this same
as her act and deed to me in trust, and to the uses
within mentioned. You may read if you please
(*holding out the parchment*), though perhaps what
is written on the back may serve your occasions.

FAINALL: Very likely, sir. What's here? Damnation!
(*Reads.*) "A deed of conveyance of the whole estate
real of Arabella Languish, widow, in trust to Edward Mirabell." Confusion!

MIRABELL: Even so, sir; 'tis the way of the world, sir,
of the widows of the world. I suppose this deed
may bear an elder° date than what you have obtained from your lady?

FAINALL: Perfidious fiend! Then thus I'll be revenged.
(*Offers to run at Mrs. Fainall.*)

SIR WILFULL: Hold, sir! Now you may make your
Bear Garden flourish somewhere else, sir.

FAINALL: Mirabell, you shall hear of this, sir; be sure
you shall. (*To Sir Wilfull.*) Let me pass, oaf!
(*Exit.*)

MRS. FAINALL (*to Mrs. Marwood*): Madam, you seem
to stifle your resentment; you had better give it
vent.

MRS. MARWOOD: Yes, it shall have vent, and to your
confusion; or I'll perish in the attempt.   (*Exit.*)

LADY WISHFORT: O daughter, daughter, 'tis plain thou
hast inherited thy mother's prudence.

MRS. FAINALL: Thank Mr. Mirabell, a cautious friend,
to whose advice all is owing.

LADY WISHFORT: Well, Mr. Mirabell, you have kept
your promise, and I must perform mine. First, I
pardon, for your sake, Sir Rowland there, and
Foible. The next thing is to break the matter
to my nephew, and how to do that —

MIRABELL: For that, madam, give yourself no trouble;
let me have your consent. Sir Wilfull is my friend;
he has had compassion upon lovers, and generously
engaged a volunteer° in this action, for our service,
and now designs to prosecute his travels.

SIR WILFULL: 'Sheart, aunt, I have no mind to marry.
My cousin's a fine lady, and the gentleman loves
her, and she loves him, and they deserve one another; my resolution is to see foreign parts. I have
set on't, and when I'm set on't, I must do't. And

if these two gentlemen would travel too, I think
they may be spared.

PETULANT: For my part, I say little; I think things are
best off or on.°

WITWOUD: Egad, I understand nothing of the matter;
I'm in a maze yet, like a dog in a dancing school.

LADY WISHFORT: Well, sir, take her, and with her all
the joy I can give you.

MRS. MILLAMANT: Why does not the man take me?
Would you have me give myself to you over again?

MIRABELL: Aye, and over and over again; (*kisses her
hand*) for I would have you as often as possibly I
can. Well, Heaven grant I love you not too well;
that's all my fear.

SIR WILFULL: 'Sheart, you'll have time enough to toy°
after you're married; or if you will toy now, let us
have a dance in the meantime, that we who are
not lovers may have some other employment besides looking on.

MIRABELL: With all my heart, dear Sir Wilfull. What
shall we do for music?

FOIBLE: Oh, sir, some that were provided for Sir Rowland's entertainment are yet within call.

(*A dance.*)

LADY WISHFORT: As I am a person, I can hold out
no longer. I have wasted my spirits so today already
that I am ready to sink under the fatigue; and I
cannot but have some fears upon me yet that my
son Fainall will pursue some desperate course.

MIRABELL: Madam, disquiet not yourself on that account; to my knowledge his circumstances are such,
he must of force° comply. For my part, I will contribute all that in me lies to a reunion; in the meantime, madam (*to Mrs. Fainall*), let me before these
witnesses restore to you this deed of trust; it may
be a means, well-managed, to make you live easily
together.

> From hence let those be warn'd, who mean to
>   wed,
> Lest mutual falsehood stain the bridal bed;
> For each deceiver to his cost may find,
> That marriage frauds too oft are paid in kind.
>   (*Exeunt omnes.*)°

EPILOGUE

(*Spoken by Mrs. Millamant.*)

After our Epilogue this crowd dismisses,
I'm thinking how this play'll be pull'd to pieces.
But pray consider, ere you doom its fall,

---

608. elder: Earlier.   **632. a volunteer:** As a volunteer.

641. off or on: One way or the other.   **653. toy:** Play.
669. of force: Of necessity.   **678. [S.D.]** *omnes*: Latin for
"all."

How hard a thing 'twould be to please you all.
5   There are some critics so with spleen diseas'd,
They scarcely come inclining to be pleas'd;
And sure he must have more than mortal skill,
Who pleases any one against his will.
Then, all bad poets we are sure are foes,
And how their number's swell'd the town well
10   knows;
In shoals I've mark'd 'em judging in the pit;
Though they're on no pretense for judgment fit,
But that they have been damn'd for want of wit.
Since when they, by their own offenses taught,
15   Set up for spies on plays, and finding fault.
Others there are whose malice we'd prevent;
Such who watch plays with scurrilous intent
To mark out who by characters are meant.
And though no perfect likeness they can trace,
20   Yet each pretends to know the copy'd face.
These with false glosses° feed their own ill nature,

21. **glosses:** Marginal notes.

And turn to libel what was meant a satire.°
May such malicious fops this fortune find,
To think themselves alone the fools design'd;
If any are so arrogantly vain,   25
To think they singly can support a scene,
And furnish fool enough to entertain.
For well the learn'd and the judicious know
That satire scorns to stoop so meanly low
As any one abstracted° fop to show.   30
For, as when painters form a matchless face,
They from each fair one catch some diff'rent grace;
And shining features in one portrait blend,
To which no single beauty must pretend;
So poets oft do in one piece expose   35
Whole *belles assemblées*° of coquettes and beaux.

21–22. **nature ... satire:** According to seventeenth-century pronunciation, "nature" and "satire" were good rhymes.   30. **abstracted:** Particular.   36. *belles assemblées*: Fine gatherings.

Nineteenth-Century Drama to the Turn of the Century

Technical Innovations

Technically, theaters changed more during the period between 1800 and 1900 than in any comparable earlier period. Lighting innovations, especially the introduction of gas jets, which permitted light to be dimmed or raised as needed, had a major effect beginning in the second decade of the century. Plays could now be staged conveniently in houses that could be gradually and entirely darkened. With gaslight onstage, selective lighting contributed to the emotional effect of plays and allowed actors to move deeper into the stage instead of playing important scenes on the apron. With the advent of changeable scenery, as in the Drottningholm Theater in Sweden, lighting devices were often placed behind the proscenium pillars and scenery so that actors were more visible when they stood within the proscenium. The changes did not take place overnight, but as new theaters were built in the early nineteenth century (and as older theaters were refurbished) the apron shrank and the front doors leading to it disappeared. That change reinforced the nineteenth-century practice of treating the proscenium opening as the "fourth wall" of a room.

Numerous other technical innovations were introduced into the new theaters, such as David Garrick's Drury Lane Theatre, which was rebuilt in 1812. Highly sophisticated machinery lifted actors from below the stage, and flies or fly galleries above the stage permitted scene changes and other dramatic alterations and effects. The technical resources of the modern theaters in Europe were extraordinary by midcentury.

Romantic Drama

The architectural and lighting changes were complex and uneven, but they resulted in changes in styles of acting, styles of plays, and their content. Early nineteenth-century English Romantic poets produced a variety of plays espousing a new philosophy of the individual, a philosophy of democracy, and a cry for personal liberation, but unfortunately their plays failed to capture the popular stage. William Wordsworth's *The Borderers* (1796–1797), concerning political struggles in the marches, the border between England and Scotland, was a failure. A recent production (1989) at Yale University revealed its static, declamatory nature. Even a play with an inherently dramatic subject such as *The Fall of Robespierre* (1794) by Robert Southey and Samuel Taylor Coleridge — concerning the violent excesses of the French Revolution of 1789 — could not stir popular audiences. John Keats wrote *Otho the Great* (1819) about a tenth-century dispute between brothers and a father and son. He hoped the great actor and producer Edmund Kean would want to produce the play, but he did not. Percy Bysshe Shelley wrote *The Cenci* (1819) when he was in Italy, hoping it would be produced on the stage, but it was not. The style of Shelley's play has been compared with that of the Elizabethan John Webster; its themes include violent death and insanity. George Gordon, Lord Byron, seems to be the only English Romantic writer able to produce a play that met with any success. *Manfred* (1817), a CLOSET DRAMA — a play meant to be read, not produced — presents a powerful portrait of a brooding intellect that could, in some ways, be compared with Hamlet. Allardyce Nicoll, the British drama historian and critic, has said of this and other Romantic plays that "audiences and readers familiar with *Lear* and *Macbeth* and *Othello* could not be expected to feel a thrill of wonder and delight in the contemplation of works so closely akin to these in general aim and yet so far removed from them in freshness of imaginative power."

French and German Romantic dramatists were more successful than their English counterparts. Johann Wolfgang von Goethe (1749–1832), one of Germany's most important playwrights, produced a number of successful plays in the late eighteenth century, but his *Faust* (1808, 1832), in two parts, had a scope and grandeur of concept that challenged the theaters of his day. The play opens in heaven, with Mephistopheles presenting his plan for tempting Faust; Faust signs over his soul to Mephistopheles in return for one moment of perfect joy. Faust was willing to risk all in his efforts to live life to its fullest, and despite his sins he was admired as a hero. Faust's self-analytic individualism, marked by a love of excess and a capacity for deep feeling and frightening intensity, has fascinated the German mind ever since Goethe introduced him.

Another important force in German theater was Johann Cristoph Friedrich von Schiller (1759–1805), whose early play *The Robbers* (1781) was written when he was twenty-two. This still popular (and still produced) play reminds English audiences of the legend of Robin Hood since its hero, Karl von Moor, is a robber admirable for his generosity and seriousness. His adversary is his evil brother, who dominates the castle, the emblem of local repressive political power. Schiller was a highly successful playwright throughout the late eighteenth century. In the early nineteenth century he produced several popular historical plays such as *Maria Stuart* (1800) on England's Queen Mary, the ill-fated sister of Queen Elizabeth I. *The Maid of Orleans* (1801) told the story of Joan of Arc, the French heroine who led her army to victory only to be burned at the stake to satisfy political and religious exigencies. Both plays evoke deep sympathy for their heroines and both have been noted for their sentimentality. His last play, *William Tell* (1804), like *The Robbers*, tells the story of a heroic individual's fight against the oppressive forces of an evil baron. Schiller made the story of William Tell universal, and his theatrical successes were soon known throughout Europe and the Americas.

Melodrama

MELODRAMA developed in Germany and France in the mid- and late eighteenth century. The *melo* in *melodrama* means song; incidental music was a hallmark of melodrama. In England certain regulations separated Covent Garden, Drury Lane, and the Haymarket — the three "major" theaters with exclusive licences to produce spoken drama — from the "minor" theaters, which had to produce musical plays such as burlettas, which resembled our comic operettas. Eventually they began to produce plays with spoken dialogue and accompanying music, heralding a new, popular style. Melodrama proved to be one of the most durable innovations of the late eighteenth century.

In Germany, August Friedrich Ferdinand von Kotzebue (1761–1819) and in France Guilbert de Pixérécourt (1773–1844) began the development of the melodramatic play. Many of these dramas used background music that altered according to the mood of the scene, a tradition that continues in popular films and on television. Nineteenth-century melodramas featured familiar crises: the virtuous maiden fallen into the hands of an unscrupulous landlord; the father who, lamenting over a portrait of his dead wife, discovers he is speaking to his — until then — lost daughter. Nineteenth-century melodramas had well-defined heroes, heroines, and villains. The plots were filled with surprises and unlikely twists designed to amaze and delight the audience. Most of the plays were explicitly sentimental, depending on a strong emotional appeal with clear-cut and relatively decisive endings.

The plays of both Kotzebue and Pixérécourt have not been popular in later ages, but they found a way to speak to their contemporary audiences and helped establish melodrama as a dominant style that endured for the first six decades of the nineteenth century. Kotzebue published thirty-six plays (twenty-two were produced) and enjoyed an immense popularity in England. His plays, translated into several languages, influenced later popular playwrights, who admired his ability to invent and resolve complex plot situations. An example of the ending of *La-Peyrouse* (1798) may provide a taste of the mode. The hero, cast ashore on a desert island, falls in love with the "savage" Malvina. When he rejoins his wife, Adelaide, he is presented with the problem of what to do with Malvina. Here is the women's solution:

> MALVINA (*turning affectionately, yet with trembling to Adelaide*): I have prayed for thee, and for myself — let us be sisters!
> ADELAIDE: Sisters! (*She remains some moments lost in thought.*) Sisters! Sweet girl, you have awakened a consoling idea in my bosom! Yes, we will be sisters, and this man shall be our brother! Share him we cannot, nor can either possess him singly. (*With enthusiasm.*) We, the sisters, will inhabit one hut, he shall dwell in another. We will educate our children, he shall assist us both — by day we will make but one family, at night we will separate — how say you? will you consent? . . . (*Extending her arms to La-Peyrouse.*) A sisterly embrace!

In France Pixérécourt produced a similar and highly successful drama that pleased his audiences. Not everyone was pleased, however. Goethe resigned his office from the Weimar Court Theatre when Pixérécourt's *The Dog of Montargis* was produced in 1816 because he did not want to be associated with any play that had a dog as its hero.

Not all these plays have been forgotten. Alexander Dumas's *La Dame aux camélias* (*Camille*) was a theatrical hit in 1852 and has remained popular ever since, inspiring the Verdi opera *La Traviata* (1853) and revivals and adaptations up to the present, including the British playwright Pam Gems's new feminist version (1987), which starred Kathleen Turner. Based on a woman Dumas knew in Paris, it is the story of a wealthy young man who falls in love with a courtesan, Marguerite Gauthier. Like Angellica in *The Rover*, she has manipulated men throughout her life, but now she is truly in love with Armand. The young man's father opposes the match, but even he is moved by the majesty of their love. Eventually the father faces Marguerite and persuades her that if she really loves his son, she will let him go since their union can bring nothing but harm to him. She then fabricates a contempt for Armand and dismisses him, broken-hearted. Later, after they have been separated and she has fallen deathly ill, Armand learns the truth and rushes to her. On her deathbed Armand professes his love as she dies in his arms.

In the United States, George Aiken produced another long-lasting and influential drama, *Uncle Tom's Cabin* (1852), based on Harriet Beecher Stowe's novel. Stowe, a prominent northern abolitionist, poured all her anger at slavery into her novel. Aiken's stage version played for three hundred nights in its first production and across the nation more than a quarter of a million times. Some of its characters — Uncle Tom, Little Eva, Sambo, Topsy, and Simon Legree — live on in the popular imagination, but despite the contemporary interest in Stowe and in this play, its paternalism, evidenced in its subtitle, "Life Among the Lowly," marks it of its age.

The Well-Made Play

Early in the nineteenth century, a man with an unusual theatrical gift for pleasing popular audiences began a career that spanned fifty successful years. Eugène Scribe (1791–1861) may have produced as many as four or five hundred plays. He employed collaborators and mined novels and stories for his plots, producing tragedies, comedies, opera libretti, and vaudeville one-act pieces. He quickly determined that the plot held the attention of the audience and that rambling character studies were of lesser interest. Consequently he developed a formula for dramatic action and made sure all his works fit into it. The result was the creation of a "factory" for making plays. Among the elements of Scribe's formula were the following:

1. A careful exposition telling the audience what the situation is, usually including one or more secrets to be revealed later.
2. Surprises, such as letters to be opened at a critical moment and identities to be revealed later.
3. Suspense that builds steadily throughout the play, usually sustained by cliff-hanging situations and characters who miss each other by way of carefully timed entrances and exits. At critical moments, characters lose important papers or misplace identifying jewelry, for instance.
4. A CLIMAX late in the play when the secrets are revealed and the hero confronts his antagonists and succeeds.
5. A DENOUEMENT, the resolution of the drama when all the loose ends are drawn together and explanations are made that render all the action plausible.

It should be evident from this description that the WELL-MADE PLAY still thrives, not only on the stage, but in films and on television. Scribe's emphasis on plot was sensational for his time, and his success was unrivaled. However, none of his plays have survived in contemporary performance, and one only, *Adrienne Lecouvreur* (1849), the story of a famous actress poisoned by a rival, is mentioned by critics as interesting because of its depth of characterization. Scribe was superficial and brilliant — a winning combination in theater at the time. He was followed by numerous imitators and helped set the stage for later developments in theater.

The Rise of Realism

Technical changes in theaters during the latter part of the nineteenth century continued at a rapid pace. Limelight was added to gas, and the result was bright, intense lighting onstage; in the last decades of the century electric light was introduced, beginning a new era in lighting design. Good lighting generally demanded detailed and authentic scenery; the dreamy light produced by gas often hid imperfections that were now impossible to disguise. The new Madison Square Theater

(1879) in New York was built with elevators that allowed its stage, complete with detailed and realistic scenery as well as actors, to be raised into position. European theaters had developed similar capacities.

In the 1840s accurate period costumes began to be the norm for historical plays. In the Elizabethan theater, contemporary clothing had been worn onstage, but by the mid-1800s costume designers were researching historical periods and producing costumes that aimed at historical accuracy.

In addition to offering lifelike scenery, lighting, and costumes, the theaters of the latter part of the century also featured plays whose circumstances and language were recognizable, contemporary, and believable. Even the sentimental melodramas seemed more realistic than productions of *King Lear* or *Macbeth*, plays that were still quite popular. The work of Scribe, including his historical plays, used a relatively prosaic everyday language. The situations may not seem absolutely lifelike to our eyes, but in their day they prepared the way for realism.

Changes in philosophy also contributed to the development of a realistic drama. Émile Zola (1840–1902) preached a doctrine of NATURALISM, demanding that drama avoid the artificiality of convoluted plot and urging a drama of natural, lifelike action. His naturalistic novel *Nana* (1880) focused on a courtesan whose life came to a terrifying end. The play *Thérèse Raquin* (1873), based on Zola's novel of the same name, told the story of a woman and her lover who murder her husband and then commit suicide out of a sense of mutual guilt. There are no twists, surprises, or even much suspense in the play. Zola's subjects seem to have been uniformly grim, and naturalism became associated with the darker side of life.

REALISM, which avoided mechanical "clockwork" plots with their artificially contrived conclusions, began in the later years of the eighteenth century (some scholars claim to see evidence of it even earlier, in the work of Middleton) and progressed steadily through to the end of the nineteenth century. In the realistic plays of Henrik Ibsen (1828–1906) and August Strindberg (1849–1912), the details of the setting, the costuming, and the circumstances of the action were so fully realized as to convince audiences that they were listening in on life itself. (See Figure 8 for an example of a realistic stage setting.)

In England, Oscar Wilde (1854–1900), poet, novelist, and playwright, offered an alternative to both melodrama and realistic drama near the end of the century. Wilde had spent much of his literary life promoting the philosophy of art for art's sake. He asserted that the pleasure of poetry was in its sounds, images, and thoughts. Poetry and drama did not serve religious, political, social, or even personal goals. For Wilde, art served itself. He was a conversationalist who provoked the Irish poet-playwright W. B. Yeats to declare that Wilde was the only person he ever heard who spoke complete, rounded sentences that sounded as if he had written and polished them the night before. His witticisms

Figure 8. Realistic setting in a 1941 production of Anton Chekhov's *The Cherry Orchard*.

were often barbed and vicious but always incisive and perceptive. He became famous for his bright, witty comedies. *The Importance of Being Earnest* (1895), sometimes wrongly accused of being about nothing, is the most performed of them. It is an unsentimental, witty, and sometimes brittle comedy that dissects English upper-class attitudes that most of his audience would have taken for granted.

Wilde competed with numerous comic playwrights in England and abroad, such as the enormously successful Arthur Wing Pinero (1855–1934) and W. S. Gilbert (1836–1911) in England and Georges Feydeau (1862–1921) in France, but none of them was able to manage the unusual combination of wit and seriousness that mark the achievement of Wilde. Perhaps the closest competitor Wilde had was Bernard Shaw (1856–1950), whose plays were also comic and serious, such as *Arms and the Man* (1894), *You Never Can Tell* (1898), and *Pygmalion* (1913). But Shaw is probably best known for his plays of ideas — plays in which an underlying idea or principle drives the action — such as *Mrs. Warren's Profession* (1898), *Man and Superman* (1903), and *Major Barbara* (1905). The nineteenth century ended with sparkling variety holding the stage.

Henrik Ibsen

Henrik Ibsen (1828–1906) slowly and painfully became the most influential modern dramatist using the new style of realism. Subjects that had been ignored on the stage became the center of his work. But his rise to fame was anything but direct. His family was extremely poor, and when he was young he worked in a drugstore in Grimstad, a seaport town in Norway. At seventeen he had an illegitimate child with a servant girl. At twenty-one, he wrote his first play, in verse. In 1850, at the age of twenty-two, he left Grimstad for Oslo (then called Christiana) to become a student, but within a year he joined the new National Theater and stayed for six years, writing and directing.

In the 1850s he wrote numerous plays that did not bring him recognition: *St. John's Eve* (1853), *Lady Inger of Østraat* (1855), *Olaf Liljekrans* (1857), and *The Vikings at Helgeland* (1857). In the early 1860s, with a wife and daughter to support, he went through a period of serious self-doubt and despair, and his first play in five years, *Love's Comedy* (1862), was turned down and not performed. Eventually, he got a job with the Christiana Theater and had a rare success with *The Pretenders* (1864), a historical play about thirteenth-century warriors vying for the vacant throne of Norway.

His breakthrough came with the publication in 1866 of the verse play *Brand*, which was written to be read and not performed. (It was first produced in 1885.) It is the portrait of a clergyman who takes the strictures of religion so seriously that he rejects the New Testament doctrine of love and accepts the Old Testament doctrine of the will of God. He destroys himself in the process and ends the play on a mountaintop in the Ice Church, facing an avalanche about to kill him. Out of the clouds comes the answer to his questions of whether love or will achieves salvation: "He is the God of Love." *Brand* made Ibsen famous. He followed it with another successful closet drama, *Peer Gynt* (1867), about a character, quite unlike Brand, who avoids the rigors of morality and ends up unable to know if he has been saved or condemned.

Despite these successes, Ibsen still struggled for recognition. It was not until 1877 that he had his first success in a play that experimented with the new realistic style of drama: *The Pillars of Society*, which probed behind the hypocrisies of Karsten Bernick, a merchant who prospers by all manner of double-dealing and betrayal of his relatives. Eventually he admits his crimes but instead of being punished is welcomed back into society and is more successful than ever. This play gave Ibsen a reputation in Germany, where it was frequently performed, and prepared him for his great successes. *A Doll House* (1879), which he wrote in Italy, came two years later. It was more fully realistic in style than *The Pillars of Society* and, while immensely successful in Scandinavia, it did not become widely known elsewhere for another ten years.

His next play, *Ghosts* (1881), was denounced violently because it dared to treat a subject that had been taboo on the stage: syphilis. *Ghosts* introduced a respectable family, the Alvings, who harbor the secret that the late father contracted the disease and passed it on to Oswald, his son. In addition, the theme of incest is suggested in the presence of Alving's illegitimate daughter, Regina, who falls in love with Oswald. This kind of material was so foreign to the late nineteenth-century stage that Ibsen was vilified and isolated by the literary community in Norway. He chose exile for a time in Rome, Amalfi, and Munich.

Ibsen's last years were filled with activity. He wrote some of his best-known plays in rapid succession: *An Enemy of the People* (1882), *The Wild Duck* (1884), *Hedda Gabler* (1890), *The Master Builder* (1892), and *John Gabriel Borkman* (1896). In 1891 he returned to live in Norway, where he died fifteen years later.

Ibsen was the most influential European dramatist in the late nineteenth century. He inspired emerging writers in the United States, Ireland, and many other nations. But his full influence was not felt until the early decades of the twentieth century, when other writers were able to spread the revolutionary doctrine that was implied in realism as practiced by Ibsen and Strindberg. Being direct, honest, and unsparing in treating character and theme became the normal mode of serious drama after Ibsen.

A DOLL HOUSE

Once Henrik Ibsen found his voice as a realist playwright, he began to develop plays centering on social problems and the problems of the individual struggling against the demands of society. In *A Doll House* (1879) he focused on the repression of women. It was a subject that deeply offended conservatives and was very much on the minds of progressive and liberal Scandinavians. It was therefore a rather daring theme. The play opens with the dutiful, eager wife Nora Helmer twittering like a lark and nattering like a squirrel pleasing her husband,

Torvald. Helmer is himself so concerned with propriety as to leave a modern audience almost breathless with alarm and amusement. As far as he is concerned, Nora is only a woman, an empty-headed ornament in a house designed to keep his life functioning smoothly.

Nora is portrayed as a macaroon-eating, sweet-toothed creature looking for ways to please her husband. When she reveals that she borrowed the money that took them to Italy for a year to save her husband's life, she shows us that she is made of much stronger stuff than anyone has given her credit for. Yet the manner in which she borrowed the money is technically criminal because she had to forge her father's signature, and she now finds herself at the mercy of the lender, Nils Krogstad.

From a modern perspective, Nora's action seems daring and imaginative rather than merely illegal and surreptitious. Torvald Helmer's moralistic position is to us essentially stifling. He condemns Nora's father for a similar failure to secure proper signatures, just as he condemns Nils Krogstad for doing the same. He condemns people for their crimes without considering their circumstances or motives. He is moralistic rather than moral.

The atmosphere of the Helmer household is oppressive. Everything is set up to amuse Torvald, and he lacks any awareness that other people might be his equal. Early in the play Ibsen establishes Nora's longings: She explains that to pay back her loan she has had to take in copying work, and rather than resent her labor she observes that it made her feel wonderful, the way a man must feel. Ibsen said that his intention in the play was not primarily to promote the emancipation of women; it was to establish, as Ibsen's biographer Michael Meyer says, "that the primary duty of anyone was to find out who he or she really was and to become that person."

However, the play from the first was seen as addressing the problems of women, especially married women who were treated as their husbands' property. When the play was first performed, the slam of the door at Nora's leaving was much louder than it is today. It was shocking to late nineteenth-century society, which took Torvald Helmer's attitudes for granted. The first audiences probably were split in their opinions about Nora's actions. As Meyer reminds us, "No play had ever before contributed so momentously to the social debate, or been so widely and furiously discussed among people who were not normally interested in theatrical or even artistic matters." Although the critics in Copenhagen and England were very negative, the audiences were filled with curiosity and flocked to the theaters to see the play.

What the audiences saw was that once Nora is awakened, the kind of life Torvald imagines for her is death to Nora. Torvald cannot see how his self-absorbed concern and fear for his own social standing reveal his limitations and selfishness. Nora sees immediately the limits of his concern, and her only choice is to leave him so that she can grow morally and spiritually.

What she does and where she goes have been a matter of speculation since the play was first performed. Ibsen refused to encourage any specific conjecture. It is enough that she has the courage to leave. But the ending of the play bothered audiences as well as critics, and it was performed in Germany in 1880 with a happy ending that Ibsen himself wrote to forestall anyone else from doing so. The first German actress to play the part insisted that she would never leave her children and would not do the play as written. In the revised version, instead of leaving, Nora is led to the door of her children's room and falls weeping as the curtain goes down. The happy-ending version was played for a while in England and elsewhere. No one was satisfied with this ending, and eventually the play reverted to its original form.

Through the proscenium arch of the theater in Ibsen's day audiences were permitted to eavesdrop on themselves, since Ibsen clearly was analyzing their own mores. In a way the audience was looking at a dollhouse; but instead of containing miniature furniture and miniature people, it contained replicas of those watching. That very sense of intimacy, made possible by the late nineteenth-century theater, heightened the intensity of the play.

A Doll House in Performance

A Doll House was first produced in the Royal Theatre, Copenhagen, in December 1879, and despite its immediate success in Scandinavia and Germany, it took two years for it to appear elsewhere and ten years for it to appear in England and America in a complete and accurate text. Further, the early German version (February 1880), with Hedwig Niemann-Raabe as Nora, had to be revised with a happy ending because the actress refused to play the original ending. Fortunately, the "happy ending," in which Nora does not leave home, was not successful and Niemann-Raabe eventually played the part as written. An adaptation, also with the happy ending, titled *The Child Wife*, was produced in Milwaukee in 1882. While the first professional London production of the play in 1889 was successful with the public, it was attacked in the press for being "unnatural, immoral and, in its concluding scene, essentially undramatic." Among other things, Ibsen was being condemned for not providing a vibrant plot.

Among the memorable performances of the play was Ethel Barrymore's version in New York in 1905. Barrymore was praised for a brilliant interpretation of "the child wife." Ruth Gordon played the part to acclaim in 1937, as did Claire Bloom in 1971 on the stage and in 1973 in film. Jane Fonda played in Joseph Losey's film version of 1973. The Norwegian actress Liv Ullmann performed the role in Lincoln Center in 1975 and was praised as "the most enchanting," the "most honest" Nora that the critic Walter Kerr had seen. Other critics were less kind, but it was a successful run. The play is performed regularly in college and regional theaters in the United States and elsewhere.

Henrik Ibsen (1828–1906)

A DOLL HOUSE   *1879*

TRANSLATED BY ROLF FJELDE

The Characters

TORVALD HELMER, *a lawyer*
NORA, *his wife*
DR. RANK
MRS. LINDE
NILS KROGSTAD, *a bank clerk*
THE HELMERS' THREE SMALL CHILDREN
ANNE-MARIE, *their nurse*
HELENE, *a maid*
A DELIVERY BOY

The action takes place in Helmer's residence.

ACT I

(*A comfortable room, tastefully but not expensively furnished. A door to the right in the back wall leads to the entryway; another to the left leads to Helmer's study. Between these doors, a piano. Midway in the left-hand wall a door, and further back a window. Near the window a round table with an armchair and a small sofa. In the right-hand wall, toward the rear, a door, and nearer the foreground a porcelain stove with two armchairs and a rocking chair beside it. Between the stove and the side door, a small table. Engravings on the walls. An étagère° with china figures and other small art objects; a small bookcase with richly bound books; the floor carpeted; a fire burning in the stove. It is a winter day.*)

(*A bell rings in the entryway; shortly after we hear the door being unlocked. Nora comes into the room, humming happily to herself; she is wearing street clothes and carries an armload of packages, which she puts down on the table to the right. She has left the hall door open; and through it a Delivery Boy is seen, holding a Christmas tree and a basket, which he gives to the Maid who let them in.*)

NORA: Hide the tree well, Helene. The children mustn't get a glimpse of it till this evening, after

---

étagère: Cabinet with shelves.

it's trimmed. (*To the Delivery Boy, taking out her purse.*) How much?
DELIVERY BOY: Fifty, ma'am.
NORA: There's a crown. No, keep the change. (*The Boy thanks her and leaves. Nora shuts the door. She laughs softly to herself while taking off her street things. Drawing a bag of macaroons from her pocket, she eats a couple, then steals over and listens at her husband's study door.*) Yes, he's home. (*Hums again as she moves to the table right.*)
HELMER (*from the study*): Is that my little lark twittering out there?
NORA (*busy opening some packages*): Yes, it is.
HELMER: Is that my squirrel rummaging around?
NORA: Yes!
HELMER: When did my squirrel get in?
NORA: Just now. (*Putting the macaroon bag in her pocket and wiping her mouth.*) Do come in, Torvald, and see what I've bought.
HELMER: Can't be disturbed. (*After a moment he opens the door and peers in, pen in hand.*) Bought, you say? All that there? Has the little spendthrift been out throwing money around again?
NORA: Oh, but Torvald, this year we really should let ourselves go a bit. It's the first Christmas we haven't had to economize.
HELMER: But you know we can't go squandering.
NORA: Oh yes, Torvald, we can squander a little now. Can't we? Just a tiny, wee bit. Now that you've got a big salary and are going to make piles and piles of money.
HELMER: Yes — starting New Year's. But then it's a full three months till the raise comes through.
NORA: Pooh! We can borrow that long.
HELMER: Nora! (*Goes over and playfully takes her by the ear.*) Are your scatterbrains off again? What if today I borrowed a thousand crowns, and you squandered them over Christmas week, and then on New Year's Eve a roof tile fell on my head, and I lay there —
NORA (*putting her hand on his mouth*): Oh! Don't say such things!
HELMER: Yes, but what if it happened — then what?
NORA: If anything so awful happened, then it just wouldn't matter if I had debts or not.

HELMER: Well, but the people I'd borrowed from?

NORA: Them? Who cares about them! They're strangers.

HELMER: Nora, Nora, how like a woman! No, but seriously, Nora, you know what I think about that. No debts! Never borrow! Something of freedom's lost — and something of beauty, too — from a home that's founded on borrowing and debt. We've made a brave stand up to now, the two of us; and we'll go right on like that the little while we have to.

NORA (*going toward the stove*): Yes, whatever you say, Torvald.

HELMER (*following her*): Now, now, the little lark's wings mustn't droop. Come on, don't be a sulky squirrel. (*Taking out his wallet.*) Nora, guess what I have here.

NORA (*turning quickly*): Money!

HELMER: There, see. (*Hands her some notes.*) Good grief, I know how costs go up in a house at Christmastime.

NORA: Ten — twenty — thirty — forty. Oh, thank you, Torvald; I can manage no end on this.

HELMER: You really will have to.

NORA: Oh yes, I promise I will! But come here so I can show you everything I bought. And so cheap! Look, new clothes for Ivar here — and a sword. Here a horse and a trumpet for Bob. And a doll and a doll's bed here for Emmy; they're nothing much, but she'll tear them to bits in no time anyway. And here I have dress material and handkerchiefs for the maids. Old Anne-Marie really deserves something more.

HELMER: And what's in that package there?

NORA (*with a cry*): Torvald, no! You can't see that till tonight!

HELMER: I see. But tell me now, you little prodigal, what have you thought of for yourself?

NORA: For myself? Oh, I don't want anything at all.

HELMER: Of course you do. Tell me just what — within reason — you'd most like to have.

NORA: I honestly don't know. Oh, listen, Torvald —

HELMER: Well?

NORA (*fumbling at his coat buttons, without looking at him*): If you want to give me something, then maybe you could — you could —

HELMER: Come on, out with it.

NORA (*hurriedly*): You could give me money, Torvald. No more than you think you can spare; then one of these days I'll buy something with it.

HELMER: But Nora —

NORA: Oh, please, Torvald darling, do that! I beg you, please. Then I could hang the bills in pretty gilt paper on the Christmas tree. Wouldn't that be fun?

HELMER: What are those little birds called that always fly through their fortunes?

NORA: Oh yes, spendthrifts; I know all that. But let's do as I say, Torvald; then I'll have time to decide what I really need most. That's very sensible, isn't it?

HELMER (*smiling*): Yes, very — that is, if you actually hung onto the money I give you, and you actually used it to buy yourself something. But it goes for the house and for all sorts of foolish things, and then I only have to lay out some more.

NORA: Oh, but Torvald —

HELMER: Don't deny it, my dear little Nora. (*Putting his arm around her waist.*) Spendthrifts are sweet, but they use up a frightful amount of money. It's incredible what it costs a man to feed such birds.

NORA: Oh, how can you say that! Really, I save everything I can.

HELMER (*laughing*): Yes, that's the truth. Everything you can. But that's nothing at all.

NORA (*humming, with a smile of quiet satisfaction*): Hm, if you only knew what expenses we larks and squirrels have, Torvald.

HELMER: You're an odd little one. Exactly the way your father was. You're never at a loss for scaring up money; but the moment you have it, it runs right out through your fingers; you never know what you've done with it. Well, one takes you as you are. It's deep in your blood. Yes, these things are hereditary, Nora.

NORA: Ah, I could wish I'd inherited many of Papa's qualities.

HELMER: And I couldn't wish you anything but just what you are, my sweet little lark. But wait; it seems to me you have a very — what should I call it? — a very suspicious look today —

NORA: I do?

HELMER: You certainly do. Look me straight in the eye.

NORA (*looking at him*): Well?

HELMER (*shaking an admonitory finger*): Surely my sweet tooth hasn't been running riot in town today, has she?

NORA: No. Why do you imagine that?

HELMER: My sweet tooth really didn't make a little detour through the confectioner's?

NORA: No, I assure you, Torvald —

HELMER: Hasn't nibbled some pastry?

NORA: No, not at all.

HELMER: Not even munched a macaroon or two?

NORA: No, Torvald, I assure you, really —

HELMER: There, there now. Of course I'm only joking.

NORA (*going to the table, right*): You know I could never think of going against you.

HELMER: No, I understand that; and you *have* given

me your word. (*Going over to her.*) Well, you keep your little Christmas secrets to yourself, Nora darling. I expect they'll come to light this evening, when the tree is lit.

NORA: Did you remember to ask Dr. Rank?

HELMER: No. But there's no need for that; it's assumed he'll be dining with us. All the same, I'll ask him when he stops by here this morning. I've ordered some fine wine. Nora, you can't imagine how I'm looking forward to this evening.

NORA: So am I. And what fun for the children, Torvald!

HELMER: Ah, it's so gratifying to know that one's gotten a safe, secure job, and with a comfortable salary. It's a great satisfaction, isn't it?

NORA: Oh, it's wonderful!

HELMER: Remember last Christmas? Three whole weeks before, you shut yourself in every evening till long after midnight, making flowers for the Christmas tree, and all the other decorations to surprise us. Ugh, that was the dullest time I've ever lived through.

NORA: It wasn't at all dull for me.

HELMER (*smiling*): But the outcome *was* pretty sorry, Nora.

NORA: Oh, don't tease me with that again. How could I help it that the cat came in and tore everything to shreds.

HELMER: No, poor thing, you certainly couldn't. You wanted so much to please us all, and that's what counts. But it's just as well that the hard times are past.

NORA: Yes, it's really wonderful.

HELMER: Now I don't have to sit here alone, boring myself, and you don't have to tire your precious eyes and your fair little delicate hands —

NORA (*clapping her hands*): No, is it really true, Torvald, I don't have to? Oh, how wonderfully lovely to hear! (*Taking his arm.*) Now I'll tell you just how I've thought we should plan things. Right after Christmas — (*The doorbell rings.*) Oh, the bell. (*Straightening the room up a bit.*) Somebody would have to come. What a bore!

HELMER: I'm not at home to visitors, don't forget.

MAID (*from the hall doorway*): Ma'am, a lady to see you —

NORA: All right, let her come in.

MAID (*to Helmer*): And the doctor's just come too.

HELMER: Did he go right to my study?

MAID: Yes, he did.

(*Helmer goes into his room. The Maid shows in Mrs. Linde, dressed in traveling clothes, and shuts the door after her.*)

MRS. LINDE (*in a dispirited and somewhat hesitant voice*): Hello, Nora.

NORA (*uncertain*): Hello —

MRS. LINDE: You don't recognize me.

NORA: No, I don't know — but wait, I think — (*Exclaiming.*) What! Kristine! Is it really you?

MRS. LINDE: Yes, it's me.

NORA: Kristine! To think I didn't recognize you. But then, how could I? (*More quietly.*) How you've changed, Kristine!

MRS. LINDE: Yes, no doubt I have. In nine — ten long years.

NORA: Is it so long since we met! Yes, it's all of that. Oh, these last eight years have been a happy time, believe me. And so now you've come in to town, too. Made the long trip in the winter. That took courage.

MRS. LINDE: I just got here by ship this morning.

NORA: To enjoy yourself over Christmas, of course. Oh, how lovely! Yes, enjoy ourselves, we'll do that. But take your coat off. You're not still cold? (*Helping her.*) There now, let's get cozy here by the stove. No, the easy chair there! I'll take the rocker here. (*Seizing her hands.*) Yes, now you have your old look again; it was only in that first moment. You're a bit more pale, Kristine — and maybe a bit thinner.

MRS. LINDE: And much, much older, Nora.

NORA: Yes, perhaps a bit older; a tiny, tiny bit; not much at all. (*Stopping short; suddenly serious.*) Oh, but thoughtless me, to sit here, chattering away. Sweet, good Kristine, can you forgive me?

MRS. LINDE: What do you mean, Nora?

NORA (*softly*): Poor Kristine, you've become a widow.

MRS. LINDE: Yes, three years ago.

NORA: Oh, I knew it, of course; I read it in the papers. Oh, Kristine, you must believe me; I often thought of writing you then, but I kept postponing it, and something always interfered.

MRS. LINDE: Nora dear, I understand completely.

NORA: No, it was awful of me, Kristine. You poor thing, how much you must have gone through. And he left you nothing?

MRS. LINDE: No.

NORA: And no children?

MRS. LINDE: No.

NORA: Nothing at all, then?

MRS. LINDE: Not even a sense of loss to feed on.

NORA (*looking incredulously at her.*): But Kristine, how could that be?

MRS. LINDE (*smiling wearily and smoothing her hair*): Oh, sometimes it happens, Nora.

NORA: So completely alone. How terribly hard that must be for you. I have three lovely children. You can't see them now; they're out with the maid. But now you must tell me everything —

MRS. LINDE: No, no, no, tell me about yourself.

NORA: No, you begin. Today I don't want to be selfish. I want to think only of you today. But there *is* something I must tell you. Did you hear of the wonderful luck we had recently?

MRS. LINDE: No, what's that?

NORA: My husband's been made manager in the bank, just think!

MRS. LINDE: Your husband? How marvelous!

NORA: Isn't it? Being a lawyer is such an uncertain living, you know, especially if one won't touch any cases that aren't clean and decent. And of course Torvald would never do that, and I'm with him completely there. Oh, we're simply delighted, believe me! He'll join the bank right after New Year's and start getting a huge salary and lots of commissions. From now on we can live quite differently — just as we want. Oh, Kristine, I feel so light and happy! Won't it be lovely to have stacks of money and not a care in the world?

MRS. LINDE: Well, anyway, it would be lovely to have enough for necessities.

NORA: No, not just for necessities, but stacks and stacks of money!

MRS. LINDE (*smiling*): Nora, Nora, aren't you sensible yet? Back in school you were such a free spender.

NORA (*with a quiet laugh*): Yes, that's what Torvald still says. (*Shaking her finger.*) But "Nora, Nora" isn't as silly as you all think. Really, we've been in no position for me to go squandering. We've had to work, both of us.

MRS. LINDE: You too?

NORA: Yes, at odd jobs — needlework, crocheting, embroidery, and such — (*casually*) and other things too. You remember that Torvald left the department when we were married? There was no chance of promotion in his office, and of course he needed to earn more money. But that first year he drove himself terribly. He took on all kinds of extra work that kept him going morning and night. It wore him down, and then he fell deathly ill. The doctors said it was essential for him to travel south.

MRS. LINDE: Yes, didn't you spend a whole year in Italy?

NORA: That's right. It wasn't easy to get away, you know. Ivar had just been born. But of course we had to go. Oh, that was a beautiful trip, and it saved Torvald's life. But it cost a frightful sum, Kristine.

MRS. LINDE: I can well imagine.

NORA: Four thousand, eight hundred crowns it cost. That's really a lot of money.

MRS. LINDE: But it's lucky you had it when you needed it.

NORA: Well, as it was, we got it from Papa.

MRS. LINDE: I see. It was just about the time your father died.

NORA: Yes, just about then. And, you know, I couldn't make that trip out to nurse him. I had to stay here, expecting Ivar any moment, and with my poor sick Torvald to care for. Dearest Papa, I never saw him again, Kristine. Oh, that was the worst time I've known in all my marriage.

MRS. LINDE: I know how you loved him. And then you went off to Italy?

NORA: Yes. We had the means now, and the doctors urged us. So we left a month after.

MRS. LINDE: And your husband came back completely cured?

NORA: Sound as a drum!

MRS. LINDE: But — the doctor?

NORA: Who?

MRS. LINDE: I thought the maid said he was a doctor, the man who came in with me.

NORA: Yes, that was Dr. Rank — but he's not making a sick call. He's our closest friend, and he stops by at least once a day. No, Torvald hasn't had a sick moment since, and the children are fit and strong, and I am, too. (*Jumping up and clapping her hands.*) Oh, dear God, Kristine, what a lovely thing to live and be happy! But how disgusting of me — I'm talking of nothing but my own affairs. (*Sits on a stool close by Kristine, arms resting across her knees.*) Oh, don't be angry with me! Tell me, is it really true that you weren't in love with your husband? Why did you marry him, then?

MRS. LINDE: My mother was still alive, but bedridden and helpless — and I had my two younger brothers to look after. In all conscience, I didn't think I could turn him down.

NORA: No, you were right there. But was he rich at the time?

MRS. LINDE: He was very well off, I'd say. But the business was shaky, Nora. When he died, it all fell apart, and nothing was left.

NORA: And then —?

MRS. LINDE: Yes, so I had to scrape up a living with a little shop and a little teaching and whatever else I could find. The last three years have been like one endless workday without a rest for me. Now, it's over, Nora. My poor mother doesn't need me, for she's passed on. Nor the boys, either; they're working now and can take care of themselves.

NORA: How free you must feel —

MRS. LINDE: No — only unspeakably empty. Nothing to live for now. (*Standing up anxiously.*) That's why I couldn't take it any longer out in that desolate hole. Maybe here it'll be easier to find something to do and keep my mind occupied. If I could only be lucky enough to get a steady job, some office work —

NORA: Oh, but Kristine, that's so dreadfully tiring, and you already look so tired. It would be much better for you if you could go off to a bathing resort.

MRS. LINDE (*going toward the window*): I have no father to give me travel money, Nora.

NORA (*rising*): Oh, don't be angry with me.

MRS. LINDE (*going to her*): Nora dear, don't you be angry with me. The worst of my kind of situation is all the bitterness that's stored away. No one to work for, and yet you're always having to snap up your opportunities. You have to live; and so you grow selfish. When you told me the happy change in your lot, do you know I was delighted less for your sakes than for mine?

NORA: How so? Oh, I see. You think maybe Torvald could do something for you.

MRS. LINDE: Yes, that's what I thought.

NORA: And he will, Kristine! Just leave it to me; I'll bring it up so delicately — find something attractive to humor him with. Oh, I'm so eager to help you.

MRS. LINDE: How very kind of you, Nora, to be so concerned over me — doubly kind, considering you really know so little of life's burdens yourself.

NORA: I —? I know so little —?

MRS. LINDE (*smiling*): Well, my heavens — a little needlework and such — Nora, you're just a child.

NORA (*tossing her head and pacing the floor*): You don't have to act so superior.

MRS. LINDE: Oh?

NORA: You're just like the others. You all think I'm incapable of anything serious —

MRS. LINDE: Come now —

NORA: That I've never had to face the raw world.

MRS. LINDE: Nora dear, you've just been telling me all your troubles.

NORA: Hm! Trivial! (*Quietly.*) I haven't told you the big thing.

MRS. LINDE: Big thing? What do you mean?

NORA: You look down on me so, Kristine, but you shouldn't. You're proud that you worked so long and hard for your mother.

MRS. LINDE: I don't look down on a soul. But it *is* true: I'm proud — and happy, too — to think it was given to me to make my mother's last days almost free of care.

NORA: And you're also proud thinking of what you've done for your brothers.

MRS. LINDE: I feel I've a right to be.

NORA: I agree. But listen to this, Kristine — I've also got something to be proud and happy for.

MRS. LINDE: I don't doubt it. But whatever do you mean?

NORA: Not so loud. What if Torvald heard! He mustn't, not for anything in the world. Nobody must know, Kristine. No one but you.

MRS. LINDE: But what is it, then?

NORA: Come here. (*Drawing her down beside her on the sofa.*) It's true — I've also got something to be proud and happy for. I'm the one who saved Torvald's life.

MRS. LINDE: Saved —? Saved how?

NORA: I told you about the trip to Italy. Torvald never would have lived if he hadn't gone south —

MRS. LINDE: Of course; your father gave you the means —

NORA (*smiling*): That's what Torvald and all the rest think, but —

MRS. LINDE: But —?

NORA: Papa didn't give us a pin. I was the one who raised the money.

MRS. LINDE: You? That whole amount?

NORA: Four thousand, eight hundred crowns. What do you say to that?

MRS. LINDE: But Nora, how was it possible? Did you win the lottery?

NORA (*disdainfully*): The lottery? Pooh! No art to that.

MRS. LINDE: But where did you get it from then?

NORA (*humming, with a mysterious smile*): Hmm, tra-la-la-la.

MRS. LINDE: Because you couldn't have borrowed it.

NORA: No? Why not?

MRS. LINDE: A wife can't borrow without her husband's consent.

NORA (*tossing her head*): Oh, but a wife with a little business sense, a wife who knows how to manage —

MRS. LINDE: Nora, I simply don't understand —

NORA: You don't have to. Whoever said I *borrowed* the money? I could have gotten it other ways. (*Throwing herself back on the sofa.*) I could have gotten it from some admirer or other. After all, a girl with my ravishing appeal —

MRS. LINDE: You lunatic.

NORA: I'll bet you're eaten up with curiosity, Kristine.

MRS. LINDE: Now listen here, Nora — you haven't done something indiscreet?

NORA (*sitting up again*): Is it indiscreet to save your husband's life?

MRS. LINDE: I think it's indiscreet that without his knowledge you —

NORA: But that's the point: He mustn't know! My

Lord, can't you understand? He mustn't ever know the close call he had. It was to *me* the doctors came to say his life was in danger — that nothing could save him but a stay in the south. Didn't I try strategy then! I began talking about how lovely it would be for me to travel abroad like other young wives; I begged and I cried; I told him please to remember my condition, to be kind and indulge me; and then I dropped a hint that he could easily take out a loan. But at that, Kristine, he nearly exploded. He said I was frivolous, and it was his duty as man of the house not to indulge me in whims and fancies — as I think he called them. Aha, I thought, now you'll just have to be saved — and that's when I saw my chance.

MRS. LINDE: And your father never told Torvald the money wasn't from him?

NORA: No, never. Papa died right about then. I'd considered bringing him into my secret and begging him never to tell. But he was too sick at the time — and then, sadly, it didn't matter.

MRS. LINDE: And you've never confided in your husband since?

NORA: For heaven's sake, no! Are you serious? He's so strict on that subject. Besides — Torvald, with all his masculine pride — how painfully humiliating for him if he ever found out he was in debt to me. That would just ruin our relationship. Our beautiful, happy home would never be the same.

MRS. LINDE: Won't you ever tell him?

NORA (*thoughtfully, half smiling*): Yes — maybe sometime years from now, when I'm no longer so attractive. Don't laugh! I only mean when Torvald moves me less than now, when he stops enjoying my dancing and dressing up and reciting for him. Then it might be wise to have something in reserve — (*Breaking off.*) How ridiculous! That'll never happen — Well, Kristine, what do you think of my big secret? I'm capable of something too, hm? You can imagine, of course, how this thing hangs over me. It really hasn't been easy meeting the payments on time. In the business world there's what they call quarterly interest and what they call amortization, and these are always so terribly hard to manage. I've had to skimp a little here and there, wherever I could, you know. I could hardly spare anything from my house allowance, because Torvald has to live well. I couldn't let the children go poorly dressed; whatever I got for them, I felt I had to use up completely — the darlings!

MRS. LINDE: Poor Nora, so it had to come out of your own budget, then?

NORA: Yes, of course. But I was the one most responsible, too. Every time Torvald gave me money for new clothes and such, I never used more than half; always bought the simplest, cheapest outfits. It was a godsend that everything looks so well on me that Torvald never noticed. But it did weigh me down at times, Kristine. It *is* such a joy to wear fine things. You understand.

MRS. LINDE: Oh, of course.

NORA: And then I found other ways of making money. Last winter I was lucky enough to get a lot of copying to do. I locked myself in and sat writing every evening till late in the night. Ah, I was tired so often, dead tired. But still it was wonderful fun, sitting and working like that, earning money. It was almost like being a man.

MRS. LINDE: But how much have you paid off this way so far?

NORA: That's hard to say, exactly. These accounts, you know, aren't easy to figure. I only know that I've paid out all I could scrape together. Time and again I haven't known where to turn. (*Smiling.*) Then I'd sit here dreaming of a rich old gentleman who had fallen in love with me —

MRS. LINDE: What! Who is he?

NORA: Oh, really! And that he'd died, and when his will was opened, there in big letters it said, "All my fortune shall be paid over in cash, immediately, to that enchanting Mrs. Nora Helmer."

MRS. LINDE: But Nora dear — who *was* this gentleman?

NORA: Good grief, can't you understand? The old man never existed; that was only something I'd dream up time and again whenever I was at my wits' end for money. But it makes no difference now; the old fossil can go where he pleases for all I care; I don't need him or his will — because now I'm free. (*Jumping up.*) Oh, how lovely to think of that, Kristine! Carefree! To know you're carefree, utterly carefree; to be able to romp and play with the children, and to keep up a beautiful, charming home — everything just the way Torvald likes it! And think, spring is coming, with big blue skies. Maybe we can travel a little then. Maybe I'll see the ocean again. Oh yes, it *is* so marvelous to live and be happy!

(*The front doorbell rings.*)

MRS. LINDE (*rising*): There's the bell. It's probably best that I go.

NORA: No, stay. No one's expected. It must be for Torvald.

MAID (*from the hall doorway*): Excuse me, ma'am — there's a gentleman here to see Mr. Helmer, but I didn't know — since the doctor's with him —

NORA: Who is the gentleman?

KROGSTAD (*from the doorway*): It's me, Mrs. Helmer.

(*Mrs. Linde starts and turns away toward the window.*)

NORA (*stepping toward him, tense, her voice a whisper*): You? What is it? Why do you want to speak to my husband?

KROGSTAD: Bank business — after a fashion. I have a small job in the investment bank, and I hear now your husband is going to be our chief —

NORA: In other words, it's —

KROGSTAD: Just dry business, Mrs. Helmer. Nothing but that.

NORA: Yes, then please be good enough to step into the study. (*She nods indifferently as she sees him out by the hall door, the returns and begins stirring up the stove.*)

MRS. LINDE: Nora — who was that man?

NORA: That was a Mr. Krogstad — a lawyer.

MRS. LINDE: Then it really was him.

NORA: Do you know that person?

MRS. LINDE: I did once — many years ago. For a time he was a law clerk in our town.

NORA: Yes, he's been that.

MRS. LINDE: How he's changed.

NORA: I understand he had a very unhappy marriage.

MRS. LINDE: He's a widower now.

NORA: With a number of children. There now, it's burning. (*She closes the stove door and moves the rocker a bit to one side.*)

MRS. LINDE: They say he has a hand in all kinds of business.

NORA: Oh? That may be true; I wouldn't know. But let's not think about business. It's so dull.

(*Dr. Rank enters from Helmer's study.*)

RANK (*still in the doorway*): No, no, really — I don't want to intrude, I'd just as soon talk a little while with your wife. (*Shuts the door, then notices Mrs. Linde.*) Oh, beg pardon. I'm intruding here too.

NORA: No, not at all. (*Introducing him.*) Dr. Rank, Mrs. Linde.

RANK: Well now, that's a name much heard in this house. I believe I passed the lady on the stairs as I came.

MRS. LINDE: Yes, I take the stairs very slowly. They're rather hard on me.

RANK: Uh-hm, some touch of internal weakness?

MRS. LINDE: More overexertion, I'd say.

RANK: Nothing else? Then you're probably here in town to rest up in a round of parties?

MRS. LINDE: I'm here to look for work.

RANK: Is that the best cure for overexertion?

MRS. LINDE: One has to live, Doctor.

RANK: Yes, there's a common prejudice to that effect.

NORA: Oh, come on, Dr. Rank — you really do want to live yourself.

RANK: Yes, I really do. Wretched as I am, I'll gladly prolong my torment indefinitely. All my patients feel like that. And it's quite the same, too, with the morally sick. Right at this moment there's one of those moral invalids in there with Helmer —

MRS. LINDE (*softly*): Ah!

NORA: Who do you mean?

RANK: Oh, it's a lawyer, Krogstad, a type you wouldn't know. His character is rotten to the root — but even he began chattering all-importantly about how he had to *live*.

NORA: Oh? What did he want to talk to Torvald about?

RANK: I really don't know. I only heard something about the bank.

NORA: I didn't know that Krog — that this man Krogstad had anything to do with the bank.

RANK: Yes, he's gotten some kind of berth down there. (*To Mrs. Linde.*) I don't know if you also have, in your neck of the woods, a type of person who scuttles about breathlessly, sniffing out hints of moral corruption, and then maneuvers his victim into some sort of key position where he can keep an eye on him. It's the healthy these days that are out in the cold.

MRS. LINDE: All the same, it's the sick who most need to be taken in.

RANK (*with a shrug*): Yes, there we have it. That's the concept that's turning society into a sanatorium.

(*Nora, lost in her thoughts, breaks out into quiet laughter and claps her hands.*)

RANK: Why do you laugh at that? Do you have any real idea of what society is?

NORA: What do I care about dreary old society? I was laughing at something quite different — something terribly funny. Tell me, Doctor — is everyone who works in the bank dependent now on Torvald?

RANK: Is that what you find so terribly funny?

NORA (*smiling and humming*): Never mind, never mind! (*Pacing the floor.*) Yes, that's really immensely amusing: that we — that Torvald has so much power now over all those people. (*Taking the bag out of her pocket.*) Dr. Rank, a little macaroon on that?

RANK: See here, macaroons! I thought they were contraband here.

NORA: Yes, but these are some that Kristine gave me.

MRS. LINDE: What? I —?

NORA: Now, now, don't be afraid. You couldn't possibly know that Torvald had forbidden them. You see, he's worried they'll ruin my teeth. But hmp!

Just this once! Isn't that so, Dr. Rank? Help your-self! (*Puts a macaroon in his mouth.*) And you too, Kristine. And I'll also have one, only a little one — or two, at the most. (*Walking about again.*) Now I'm really tremendously happy. Now's there's just one last thing in the world that I have an enormous desire to do.

RANK: Well! And what's that?

NORA: It's something I have such a consuming desire to say so Torvald could hear.

RANK: And why can't you say it?

NORA: I don't dare. It's quite shocking.

MRS. LINDE: Shocking?

RANK: Well, then it isn't advisable. But in front of us you certainly can. What do you have such a desire to say so Torvald could hear?

NORA: I have such a huge desire to say — to hell and be damned!

RANK: Are you crazy?

MRS. LINDE: My goodness, Nora!

RANK: Go on, say it. Here he is.

NORA (*hiding the macaroon bag*): Shh, shh, shh!

(*Helmer comes in from his study, hat in hand, over-coat over his arm.*)

NORA (*going toward him*): Well, Torvald dear, are you through with him?

HELMER: Yes, he just left.

NORA: Let me introduce you — this is Kristine, who's arrived here in town.

HELMER: Kristine —? I'm sorry, but I don't know —

NORA: Mrs. Linde, Torvald dear. Mrs. Kristine Linde.

HELMER: Of course. A childhood friend of my wife's, no doubt?

MRS. LINDE: Yes, we knew each other in those days.

NORA: And just think, she made the long trip down here in order to talk with you.

HELMER: What's this?

MRS. LINDE: Well, not exactly —

NORA: You see, Kristine is remarkably clever in office work, and so she's terribly eager to come under a capable man's supervision and add more to what she already knows —

HELMER: Very wise, Mrs. Linde.

NORA: And then when she heard that you'd become a bank manager — the story was wired out to the papers — then she came in as fast as she could and — Really, Torvald, for my sake you can do a little something for Kristine, can't you?

HELMER: Yes, it's not at all impossible. Mrs. Linde, I suppose you're a widow?

MRS. LINDE: Yes.

HELMER: Any experience in office work?

MRS. LINDE: Yes, a good deal.

HELMER: Well, it's quite likely that I can make an opening for you —

NORA (*clapping her hands*): You see, you see!

HELMER: You've come at a lucky moment, Mrs. Linde.

MRS. LINDE: Oh, how can I thank you?

HELMER: Not necessary. (*Putting his overcoat on.*) But today you'll have to excuse me —

RANK: Wait, I'll go with you. (*He fetches his coat from the hall and warms it at the stove.*)

NORA: Don't stay out long, dear.

HELMER: An hour; no more.

NORA: Are you going too, Kristine?

MRS. LINDE (*putting on her winter garments*): Yes, I have to see about a room now.

HELMER: Then perhaps we can all walk together.

NORA (*helping her*): What a shame we're so cramped here, but it's quite impossible for us to —

MRS. LINDE: Oh, don't even think of it! Good-bye, Nora dear, and thanks for everything.

NORA: Good-bye for now. Of course you'll be back this evening. And you too, Dr. Rank. What? If you're well enough? Oh, you've got to be! Wrap up tight now.

(*In a ripple of small talk the company moves out into the hall; children's voices are heard outside on the steps.*)

NORA: There they are! There they are! (*She runs to open the door. The children come in with their nurse, Anne-Marie.*) Come in, come in! (*Bends down and kisses them.*) Oh, you darlings — ! Look at them, Kristine. Aren't they lovely!

RANK: No loitering in the draft here.

HELMER: Come, Mrs. Linde — this place is unbearable now for anyone but mothers.

(*Dr. Rank, Helmer, and Mrs. Linde go down the stairs. Anne-Marie goes into the living room with the children. Nora follows, after closing the hall door.*)

NORA: How fresh and strong you look. Oh, such red cheeks you have! Like apples and roses. (*The children interrupt her throughout the following.*) And it was so much fun? That's wonderful. Really? You pulled both Emmy and Bob on the sled? Imagine, all together! Yes, you're a clever boy, Ivar. Oh, let me hold her a bit, Anne-Marie. My sweet little doll baby! (*Takes the smallest from the nurse and dances with her.*) Yes, yes, Mama will dance with Bob as well. What? Did you throw snowballs? Oh, if I'd only been there! No, don't bother, Anne-Marie — I'll undress them myself. Oh yes, let me. It's such fun. Go in and rest; you look half frozen. There's hot coffee waiting for you on the stove. (*The nurse goes into the room to the left. Nora takes the children's winter things off, throwing them about, while the children talk to her all at once.*) Is that so? A big dog chased you? But it didn't bite? No, dogs never bite little, lovely doll babies. Don't peek in the packages, Ivar! What is it? Yes, wouldn't you like to know. No, no, it's an ugly something. Well? Shall we play? What shall we play? Hide-and-seek? Yes, let's play hide-and-seek. Bob must hide first. I must? Yes, let me hide first. (*Laughing and shouting, she and the children play in and out of the living room and the adjoining room to the right. At last Nora hides under the table. The children come storming in, search, but cannot find her, then hear her muffled laughter, dash over to the table, lift the cloth up and find her. Wild shouting. She creeps forward as if to scare them. More shouts. Meanwhile, a knock at the hall door; no one has noticed it. Now the door half opens, and Krogstad appears. He waits a moment; the game goes on.*)

KROGSTAD: Beg pardon, Mrs. Helmer —

NORA (*with a strangled cry, turning and scrambling to her knees*): Oh! What do you want?

KROGSTAD: Excuse me. The outer door was ajar; it must be someone forgot to shut it —

NORA (*rising*): My husband isn't home, Mr. Krogstad.

KROGSTAD: I know that.

NORA: Yes — then what do you want here?

KROGSTAD: A word with you.

NORA: With —? (*To the children, quietly.*) Go in to Anne-Marie. What? No, the strange man won't hurt Mama. When he's gone, we'll play some more. (*She leads the children into the room to the left and shuts the door after them. Then, tense and nervous:*) You want to speak to me?

KROGSTAD: Yes, I want to.

NORA: Today? But it's not yet the first of the month —

KROGSTAD: No, it's Christmas Eve. It's going to be up to you how merry a Christmas you have.

NORA: What is it you want? Today I absolutely can't —

KROGSTAD: We won't talk about that till later. This is something else. You do have a moment to spare, I suppose?

NORA: Oh yes, of course — I do, except —

KROGSTAD: Good. I was sitting over at Olsen's Restaurant when I saw your husband go down the street —

NORA: Yes?

KROGSTAD: With a lady.

NORA: Yes. So?

KROGSTAD: If you'll pardon my asking: Wasn't that lady a Mrs. Linde?

NORA: Yes.

KROGSTAD: Just now come into town?

NORA: Yes, today.

KROGSTAD: She's a good friend of yours?

NORA: Yes, she is. But I don't see —

KROGSTAD: I also knew her once.

NORA: I'm aware of that.

KROGSTAD: Oh? You know all about it. I thought so. Well, then let me ask you short and sweet: Is Mrs. Linde getting a job in the bank?

NORA: What makes you think you can cross-examine me, Mr. Krogstad — you, one of my husband's employees? But since you ask, you might as well know — yes, Mrs. Linde's going to be taken on at the bank. And I'm the one who spoke for her, Mr. Krogstad. Now you know.

KROGSTAD: So I guessed right.

NORA (*pacing up and down*): Oh, one does have a tiny bit of influence, I should hope. Just because I am a woman, don't think it means that — When one has a subordinate position, Mr. Krogstad, one really ought to be careful about pushing somebody who — hm —

KROGSTAD: Who has influence?

NORA: That's right.

KROGSTAD (*in a different tone*): Mrs. Helmer, would you be good enough to use your influence on my behalf?

NORA: What? What do you mean?

KROGSTAD: Would you please make sure that I keep my subordinate position in the bank?

NORA: What does that mean? Who's thinking of taking away your position?

KROGSTAD: Oh, don't play the innocent with me. I'm quite aware that your friend would hardly relish the chance of running into me again; and I'm also aware now whom I can thank for being turned out.

NORA: But I promise you —

KROGSTAD: Yes, yes, yes, to the point: There's still time, and I'm advising you to use your influence to prevent it.

NORA: But Mr. Krogstad, I have absolutely no influence.

KROGSTAD: You haven't? I thought you were just saying —

NORA: You shouldn't take me so literally. I! How can you believe that I have any such influence over my husband?

KROGSTAD: Oh, I've known your husband from our student days. I don't think the great bank manager's more steadfast than any other married man.

NORA: You speak insolently about my husband, and I'll show you the door.

KROGSTAD: The lady has spirit.

NORA: I'm not afraid of you any longer. After New Year's, I'll soon be done with the whole business.

KROGSTAD (*restraining himself*): Now listen to me, Mrs. Helmer. If necessary, I'll fight for my little job in the bank as if it were life itself.

NORA: Yes, so it seems.

KROGSTAD: It's not just a matter of income; that's the least of it. It's something else — All right, out with it! Look, this is the thing. You know, just like all the others, of course, that once, a good many years ago, I did something rather rash.

NORA: I've heard rumors to that effect.

KROGSTAD: The case never got into court; but all the same, every door was closed in my face from then on. So I took up those various activities you know about. I had to grab hold somewhere; and I dare say I haven't been among the worst. But now I want to drop all that. My boys are growing up. For their sakes, I'll have to win back as much respect as possible here in town. That job in the bank was like the first rung in my ladder. And now your husband wants to kick me right back down in the mud again.

NORA: But for heaven's sake, Mr. Krogstad, it's simply not in my power to help you.

KROGSTAD: That's because you haven't the will to — but I have the means to make you.

NORA: You certainly won't tell my husband that I owe you money?

KROGSTAD: Hm — what if I told him that?

NORA: That would be shameful of you. (*Nearly in tears.*) This secret — my joy and my pride — that he should learn it in such a crude and disgusting way — learn it from you. You'd expose me to the most horrible unpleasantness —

KROGSTAD: Only unpleasantness?

NORA (*vehemently*): But go on and try. It'll turn out the worse for you, because then my husband will really see what a crook you are, and then you'll *never* be able to hold your job.

KROGSTAD: I asked if it was just domestic unpleasantness you were afraid of?

NORA: If my husband finds out, then of course he'll pay what I owe at once, and then we'd be through with you for good.

KROGSTAD (*a step closer*): Listen, Mrs. Helmer — you've either got a very bad memory, or else no head at all for business. I'd better put you a little more in touch with the facts.

NORA: What do you mean?

KROGSTAD: When your husband was sick, you came to me for a loan of four thousand, eight hundred crowns.

NORA: Where else could I go?

KROGSTAD: I promised to get you that sum —

NORA: And you got it.

KROGSTAD: I promised to get you that sum, on certain conditions. You were so involved in your husband's illness, and so eager to finance your trip, that I guess you didn't think out all the details. It might just be a good idea to remind you. I promised you the money on the strength of a note I drew up.

NORA: Yes, and that I signed.

KROGSTAD: Right. But at the bottom I added some lines for your father to guarantee the loan. He was supposed to sign down there.

NORA: Supposed to? He did sign.

KROGSTAD: I left the date blank. In other words, your father would have dated his signature himself. Do you remember that?

NORA: Yes, I think —

KROGSTAD: Then I gave you the note for you to mail to your father. Isn't that so?

NORA: Yes.

KROGSTAD: And naturally you sent it at once — because only some five, six days later you brought me the note, properly signed. And with that, the money was yours.

NORA: Well, then; I've made my payments regularly, haven't I?

KROGSTAD: More or less. But — getting back to the point — those were hard times for you then, Mrs. Helmer.

NORA: Yes, they were.

KROGSTAD: Your father was very ill, I believe.

NORA: He was near the end.

KROGSTAD: He died soon after?

NORA: Yes.

KROGSTAD: Tell me, Mr. Helmer, do you happen to recall the date of your father's death? The day of the month, I mean.

NORA: Papa died the twenty-ninth of September.

KROGSTAD: That's quite correct; I've already looked into that. And now we come to a curious thing — (*taking out a paper*) which I simply cannot comprehend.

NORA: Curious thing? I don't know —

KROGSTAD: This is the curious thing: that your father co-signed the note for your loan three days after his death.

NORA: How —? I don't understand.

KROGSTAD: Your father died the twenty-ninth of September. But look. Here your father dated his signature October second. Isn't that curious, Mrs. Helmer? (*Nora is silent.*) Can you explain it to me? (*Nora remains silent.*) It's also remarkable that the words "October second" and the year aren't written in your father's hand, but rather in one that I think I know. Well, it's easy to understand. Your father forgot perhaps to date his signature, and then someone or other added it, a bit sloppily, before anyone knew of his death. There's nothing wrong in that. It all comes down to the signature. And there's no question about *that*, Mrs. Helmer. It really *was* your father who signed his own name here, wasn't it?

NORA (*after a short silence, throwing her head back and looking squarely at him*): No, it wasn't. *I* signed Papa's name.

KROGSTAD: Wait, now — are you fully aware that this is a dangerous confession?

NORA: Why? You'll soon get your money.

KROGSTAD: Let me ask you a question — why didn't you send the paper to your father?

NORA: That was impossible. Papa was so sick. If I'd asked him for his signature, I also would have had to tell him what the money was for. But I couldn't tell him, sick as he was, that my husband's life was in danger. That was just impossible.

KROGSTAD: Then it would have been better if you'd given up the trip abroad.

NORA: I couldn't possibly. The trip was to save my husband's life. I couldn't give that up.

KROGSTAD: But didn't you ever consider that this was a fraud against me?

NORA: I couldn't let myself be bothered by that. You weren't any concern of mine. I couldn't stand you,

ABOVE: Nora (Claire Bloom) is troubled as Helmer (Donald Madden) kisses her in Patrick Garland's 1971 production. BELOW: Helmer, Nora, and Mrs. Linde (Patricia Elliott) discuss the possibility of finding a suitable job for Mrs. Linde in the bank. FAR RIGHT: Krogstad (Robert Gerringer) explains the seriousness of her actions to Nora.

with all those cold complications you made, even though you knew how badly off my husband was.

KROGSTAD: Mrs. Helmer, obviously you haven't the vaguest idea of what you've involved yourself in. But I can tell you this: It was nothing more and nothing worse that I once did — and it wrecked my whole reputation.

NORA: You? Do you expect me to believe that you ever acted bravely to save your wife's life?

KROGSTAD: Laws don't inquire into motives.

NORA: Then they must be very poor laws.

KROGSTAD: Poor or not — if I introduce this paper in court, you'll be judged according to law.

NORA: This I refuse to believe. A daughter hasn't a right to protect her dying father from anxiety and care? A wife hasn't a right to save her husband's life? I don't know much about laws, but I'm sure that somewhere in the books these things are allowed. And you don't know anything about it — you who practice the law? You must be an awful lawyer, Mr. Krogstad.

KROGSTAD: Could be. But business — the kind of business we two are mixed up in — don't you think I know about that? All right. Do what you want now. But I'm telling you *this:* If I get shoved down a second time, you're going to keep me company. (*He bows and goes out through the hall.*)

NORA (*pensive for a moment, then tossing her head*): Oh, really! Trying to frighten me! I'm not so silly as all that. (*Begins gathering up the children's clothes, but soon stops.*) But —? No, but that's impossible! I did it out of love.

THE CHILDREN (*in the doorway, left*): Mama, that strange man's gone out the door.

NORA: Yes, yes, I know it. But don't tell anyone about the strange man. Do you hear? Not even Papa!

THE CHILDREN: No, Mama. But now will you play again?

NORA: No, not now.

THE CHILDREN: Oh, but Mama, you promised.

NORA: Yes, but I can't now. Go inside; I have too much to do. Go in, go in, my sweet darlings. (*She herds them gently back in the room and shuts the door after them. Settling on the sofa, she takes up a piece of embroidery and makes some stitches, but soon stops abruptly.*) No! (*Throws the work aside, rises, goes to the hall door and calls out.*) Helene! Let me have the tree in here. (*Goes to the table, left, opens the table drawer, and stops again.*) No, but that's utterly impossible!

MAID (*with the Christmas tree*): Where should I put it, ma'am?

NORA: There. The middle of the floor.

MAID: Should I bring anything else?

NORA: No, thanks. I have what I need.

(*The Maid, who has set the tree down, goes out.*)

NORA (*absorbed in trimming the tree*): Candles here — and flowers here. That terrible creature! Talk, talk, talk! There's nothing to it at all. The tree's going to be lovely. I'll do anything to please you Torvald. I'll sing for you, dance for you —

(*Helmer comes in from the hall, with a sheaf of papers under his arm.*)

NORA: Oh! You're back so soon?

HELMER: Yes. Has anyone been here?

NORA: Here? No.

HELMER: That's odd. I saw Krogstad leaving the front door.

NORA: So? Oh yes, that's true. Krogstad was here a moment.

HELMER: Nora, I can see by your face that he's been here, begging you to put in a good word for him.

NORA: Yes.

HELMER: And it was supposed to seem like your own idea? You were to hide it from me that he'd been here. He asked you that, too, didn't he?

NORA: Yes, Torvald, but —

HELMER: Nora, Nora, and you could fall for that? Talk with that sort of person and promise him anything? And then in the bargain, tell me an untruth.

NORA: An untruth —?

HELMER: Didn't you say that no one had been here? (*Wagging his finger.*) My little songbird must never do that again. A songbird needs a clean beak to warble with. No false notes. (*Putting his arm about her waist.*) That's the way it should be, isn't it? Yes, I'm sure of it. (*Releasing her.*) And so, enough of that. (*Sitting by the stove.*) Ah, how snug and cozy it is here. (*Leafing among his papers.*)

NORA (*busy with the tree, after a short pause*): Torvald!

HELMER: Yes.

NORA: I'm so much looking forward to the Stenborgs' costume party, day after tomorrow.

HELMER: And I can't wait to see what you'll surprise me with.

NORA: Oh, that stupid business!

HELMER: What?

NORA: I can't find anything that's right. Everything seems so ridiculous, so inane.

HELMER: So my little Nora's come to *that* recognition?

NORA (*going behind his chair, her arms resting on its back*): Are you very busy, Torvald?

HELMER: Oh —

NORA: What papers are those?

HELMER: Bank matters.

NORA: Already?

HELMER: I've gotten full authority from the retiring management to make all necessary changes in personnel and procedure. I'll need Christmas week for that. I want to have everything in order by New Year's.

HELMER: So that was the reason this poor Krogstad —

HELMER: Hm.

NORA (*still leaning on the chair and slowly stroking the nape of his neck*): If you weren't so very busy, I would have asked you an enormous favor, Torvald.

HELMER: Let's hear. What is it?

NORA: You know, there isn't anyone who has your good taste — and I want so much to look well at the costume party. Torvald, couldn't you take over and decide what I should be and plan my costume?

HELMER: Ah, is my stubborn little creature calling for a lifeguard?

NORA: Yes, Torvald, I can't get anywhere without your help.

HELMER: All right — I'll think it over. We'll hit on something.

NORA: Oh, how sweet of you. (*Goes to the tree again. Pause.*) Aren't the red flowers pretty —? But tell me, was it really such a crime that this Krogstad committed?

HELMER: Forgery. Do you have any idea what that means?

NORA: Couldn't he have done it out of need?

HELMER: Yes, or thoughtlessness, like so many others. I'm not so heartless that I'd condemn a man categorically for just one mistake.

NORA: No, of course not, Torvald!

HELMER: Plenty of men have redeemed themselves by openly confessing their crimes and taking their punishment.

NORA: Punishment —?

HELMER: But now Krogstad didn't go that way. He got himself out by sharp practices, and that's the real cause of his moral breakdown.

NORA: Do you really think that would —?

HELMER: Just imagine how a man with that sort of guilt in him has to lie and cheat and deceive on all sides, has to wear a mask even with the nearest and dearest he has, even with his own wife and children. And with the children, Nora — that's where it's most horrible.

NORA: Why?

HELMER: Because that kind of atmosphere of lies infects the whole life of a home. Every breath the children take in is filled with the germs of something degenerate.

NORA (*coming closer behind him*): Are you sure of that?

HELMER: Oh, I've seen it often enough as a lawyer. Almost everyone who goes bad early in life has a mother who's a chronic liar.

NORA: Why just — the mother?

HELMER: It's usually the mother's influence that's dominant, but the father's works in the same way, of course. Every lawyer is quite familiar with it. And still this Krogstad's been going home year in, year out, poisoning his own children with lies and pretense; that's why I call him morally lost. (*Reaching his hands out toward her.*) So my sweet little Nora must promise me never to plead his cause. Your hand on it. Come, come, what's this? Give me your hand. There, now. All settled. I can tell you it'd be impossible for me to work alongside of him. I literally feel physically revolted when I'm anywhere near such a person.

NORA (*withdraws her hand and goes to the other side*

of the Christmas tree): How hot it is here! And I've got so much to do.

HELMER (*getting up and gathering his papers*): Yes, and I have to think about getting some of these read through before dinner. I'll think about your costume, too. And something to hang on the tree in gilt paper, I may even see about that. (*Putting his hand on her head.*) Oh you, my darling little songbird. (*He goes into his study and closes the door after him.*)

NORA (*softly, after a silence*): Oh, really! It isn't so. It's impossible. It must be impossible.

ANNE-MARIE (*in the doorway left*): The children are begging so hard to come in to Mama.

NORA: No, no, no, don't let them in to me! You stay with them, Anne-Marie.

ANNE-MARIE: Of course, ma'am. (*Closes the door.*)

NORA (*pale with terror*): Hurt my children —! Poison my home? (*A moment's pause; then she tosses her head.*) That's not true. Never. Never in all the world.

ACT II

(*Same room. Beside the piano the Christmas tree now stands stripped of ornament, burned-down candle stubs on its ragged branches. Nora's street clothes lie on the sofa. Nora, alone in the room, moves restlessly about; at last she stops at the sofa and picks up her coat.*)

NORA (*dropping the coat again*): Someone's coming! (*Goes toward the door, listens.*) No — there's no one. Of course — nobody's coming today, Christmas Day — or tomorrow, either. But maybe — (*Opens the door and looks out.*) No, nothing in the mailbox. Quite empty. (*Coming forward.*) What nonsense! He won't do anything serious. Nothing terrible could happen. It's impossible. Why, I have three small children.

(*Anne-Marie, with a large carton, comes in from the room to the left.*)

ANNE-MARIE: Well, at last I found the box with the masquerade clothes.

NORA: Thanks. Put it on the table.

ANNE-MARIE (*does so*): But they're all pretty much of a mess.

NORA: Ahh! I'd love to rip them in a million pieces!

ANNE-MARIE: Oh, mercy, they can be fixed right up. Just a little patience.

NORA: Yes, I'll go get Mrs. Linde to help me.

ANNE-MARIE: Out again now? In this nasty weather? Miss Nora will catch cold — get sick.

NORA: Oh, worse things could happen — How are the children?

ANNE-MARIE: The poor mites are playing with their Christmas presents, but —

NORA: Do they ask for me much?

ANNE-MARIE: They're so used to having Mama around, you know.

NORA: Yes, but Anne-Marie, I *can't* be together with them as much as I was.

ANNE-MARIE: Well, small children get used to anything.

NORA: You think so? Do you think they'd forget their mother if she was gone for good?

ANNE-MARIE: Oh, mercy — gone for good!

NORA: Wait, tell me. Anne-Marie — I've wondered so often — how could you ever have the heart to give your child over to strangers?

ANNE-MARIE: But I had to, you know, to become little Nora's nurse.

NORA: Yes, but how could you *do* it?

ANNE-MARIE: When I could get such a good place? A girl who's poor and who's gotten in trouble is glad enough for that. Because that slippery fish, he didn't do a thing for me, you know.

NORA: But your daughter's surely forgotten you.

ANNE-MARIE: Oh, she certainly has not. She's written to me, both when she was confirmed and when she was married.

NORA (*clasping her about the neck*): You old Anne-Marie, you were a good mother for me when I was little.

ANNE-MARIE: Poor little Nora, with no other mother but me.

NORA: And if the babies didn't have one, then I know that you'd — What silly talk! (*Opening the carton.*) Go in to them. Now I'll have to — Tomorrow you can see how lovely I'll look.

ANNE-MARIE: Oh, there won't be anyone at the party as lovely as Miss Nora. (*She goes off into the room, left.*)

NORA (*begins unpacking the box, but soon throws it aside*): Oh, if I dared to go out. If only nobody would come. If only nothing would happen here while I'm out. What craziness — nobody's coming. Just don't think. This muff — needs a brushing. Beautiful gloves, beautiful gloves. Let it go. Let it go! One, two, three, four, five, six — (*With a cry.*) Oh, there they are! (*Poises to move toward the door, but remains irresolutely standing. Mrs. Linde enters from the hall, where she has removed her street clothes.*)

NORA: Oh, it's you, Kristine. There's no one else out there? How good that you've come.

MRS. LINDE: I hear you were up asking for me.

NORA: Yes, I just stopped by. There's something you really can help me with. Let's get settled on the sofa. Look, there's going to be a costume party tomorrow evening at the Stenborgs' right above us, and now Torvald wants me to go as a Neapolitan peasant girl and dance the tarantella that I learned in Capri.

MRS. LINDE: Really, are you giving a whole performance?

NORA: Torvald says yes, I should. See, here's the dress. Torvald had it made for me down there; but now it's all so tattered that I just don't know —

MRS. LINDE: Oh, we'll fix that up in no time. It's nothing more than the trimmings — they're a bit loose here and there. Needle and thread? Good, now we have what we need.

NORA: Oh, how sweet of you!

MRS. LINDE (*sewing*): So you'll be in disguise tomorrow, Nora. You know what? I'll stop by then for a moment and have a look at you all dressed up. But listen, I've absolutely forgotten to thank you for that pleasant evening yesterday.

NORA (*getting up and walking about*): I don't think it was as pleasant as usual yesterday. You should have come to town a bit sooner, Kristine — Yes, Torvald really knows how to give a home elegance and charm.

MRS. LINDE: And you do, too, if you ask me. You're not your father's daughter for nothing. But tell me, is Dr. Rank always so down in the mouth as yesterday?

NORA: No, that was quite an exception. But he goes around critically ill all the time — tuberculosis of the spine, poor man. You know, his father was a disgusting thing who kept mistresses and so on — and that's why the son's been sickly from birth.

MRS. LINDE (*lets her sewing fall to her lap*): But my dearest Nora, how do you know about such things?

NORA (*walking more jauntily*): Hmp! When you've had three children, then you've had a few visits from — from women who know something of medicine, and they tell you this and that.

MRS. LINDE (*resumes sewing; a short pause*): Does Dr. Rank come here every day?

NORA: Every blessed day. He's Torvald's best friend from childhood, and *my* good friend, too. Dr. Rank almost belongs to this house.

MRS. LINDE: But tell me — is he quite sincere? I mean, doesn't he rather enjoy flattering people?

NORA: Just the opposite. Why do you think that?

MRS. LINDE: When you introduced us yesterday, he was proclaiming that he'd often heard my name in this house; but later I noticed that your husband hadn't the slightest idea who I really was. So how could Dr. Rank —?

NORA: But it's all true, Kristine. You see, Torvald loves me beyond words, and, as he puts it, he'd like to keep me all to himself. For a long time he'd almost be jealous if I even mentioned any of my old friends back home. So of course I dropped that. But with Dr. Rank I talk a lot about such things, because he likes hearing about them.

MRS. LINDE: Now listen, Nora; in many ways you're still like a child. I'm a good deal older than you, with a little more experience. I'll tell you something: You ought to put an end to all this with Dr. Rank.

NORA: What should I put an end to?

MRS. LINDE: Both parts of it, I think. Yesterday you said something about a rich admirer who'd provide you with money —

NORA: Yes, one who doesn't exist — worse luck. So?

MRS. LINDE: Is Dr. Rank well off?

NORA: Yes, he is.

MRS. LINDE: With no dependents?

NORA: No, no one. But —

MRS. LINDE: And he's over here every day?

NORA: Yes, I told you that.

MRS. LINDE: How can a man of such refinement be so grasping?

NORA: I don't follow you at all.

MRS. LINDE: Now don't try to hide it, Nora. You think I can't guess who loaned you the forty-eight hundred crowns?

NORA: Are you out of your mind? How could you think such a thing! A friend of ours, who comes here every single day. What an intolerable situation that would have been!

MRS. LINDE: Then it really wasn't him.

NORA: No, absolutely not. It never even crossed my mind for a moment — And he had nothing to lend in those days; his inheritance came later.

MRS. LINDE: Well, I think that was a stroke of luck for you, Nora dear.

NORA: No, it never would have occurred to me to ask Dr. Rank — Still, I'm quite sure that if I had asked him —

MRS. LINDE: Which you won't, of course.

NORA: No, of course not. I can't see that I'd ever need to. But I'm quite positive that if I talked to Dr. Rank —

MRS. LINDE: Behind your husband's back?

NORA: I've got to clear up this other thing; *that's* also behind his back. I've *got* to clear it all up.

MRS. LINDE: Yes, I was saying that yesterday, but —

NORA (*pacing up and down*): A man handles these problems so much better than a woman —

MRS. LINDE: One's husband does, yes.

NORA: Nonsense. (*Stopping.*) When you pay everything you owe, then you get your note back, right?

MRS. LINDE: Yes, naturally.

NORA: And can rip it into a million pieces and burn it up — that filthy scrap of paper!

MRS. LINDE (*looking hard at her, laying her sewing aside, and rising slowly*): Nora, you're hiding something from me.

NORA: You can see it in my face?

MRS. LINDE: Something's happened to you since yesterday morning. Nora, what is it?

NORA (*hurrying toward her*): Kristine! (*Listening.*) Shh! Torvald's home. Look, go in with the children a while. Torvald can't bear all this snipping and stitching. Let Anne-Marie help you.

MRS. LINDE (*gathering up some of the things*): All right, but I'm not leaving here until we've talked this out. (*She disappears into the room, left, as Torvald enters from the hall.*)

NORA: Oh, how I've been waiting for you, Torvald dear.

HELMER: Was that the dressmaker?

NORA: No, that was Kristine. She's helping me fix up my costume. You know, it's going to be quite attractive.

HELMER: Yes, wasn't that a bright idea I had?

NORA: Brilliant! But then wasn't I good as well to give in to you?

HELMER: Good — because you give in to your husband's judgment? All right, you little goose, I know you didn't mean it like that. But I won't disturb you. You'll want to have a fitting, I suppose.

NORA: And you'll be working?

HELMER: Yes. (*Indicating a bundle of papers.*) See. I've been down to the bank. (*Starts toward his study.*)

NORA: Torvald.

HELMER (*stops*): Yes.

NORA: If your little squirrel begged you, with all her heart and soul, for something —?

HELMER: What's that?

NORA: Then would you do it?

HELMER: First, naturally, I'd have to know what it was.

NORA: Your squirrel would scamper about and do tricks, if you'd only be sweet and give in.

HELMER: Out with it.

NORA: Your lark would be singing high and low in every room —

HELMER: Come on, she does that anyway.

NORA: I'd be a wood nymph and dance for you in the moonlight.

HELMER: Nora — don't tell me it's that same business from this morning?

NORA (*coming closer*): Yes, Torvald, I beg you, please!

HELMER: And you actually have the nerve to drag that up again?

NORA: Yes, yes, you've got to give in to me; you *have* to let Krogstad keep his job in the bank.

HELMER: My dear Nora, I've slated his job for Mrs. Linde.

NORA: That's awfully kind of you. But you could just fire another clerk instead of Krogstad.

HELMER: This is the most incredible stubbornness! Because you go and give an impulsive promise to speak up for him, I'm expected to —

NORA: That's not the reason, Torvald. It's for your own sake. That man does writing for the worst papers; you said it yourself. He could do you any amount of harm. I'm scared to death of him —

HELMER: Ah, I understand. It's the old memories haunting you.

NORA: What do you mean by that?

HELMER: Of course, you're thinking about your father.

NORA: Yes, all right. Just remember how those nasty gossips wrote in the papers about Papa and slandered him so cruelly. I think they'd have had him dismissed if the department hadn't sent you up to investigate, and if you hadn't been so kind and open-minded toward him.

HELMER: My dear Nora, there's a notable difference between your father and me. Your father's official career was hardly above reproach. But mine is; and I hope it'll stay that way as long as I hold my position.

NORA: Oh, who can ever tell what vicious minds can invent? We could be so snug and happy now in our quiet, carefree home — you and I and the children, Torvald! That's why I'm pleading with you so —

HELMER: And just by pleading for him you make it impossible for me to keep him on. It's already known at the bank that I'm firing Krogstad. What if it's rumored around now that the new bank manager was vetoed by his wife —

NORA: Yes, what then —?

HELMER: Oh yes — as long as our little bundle of stubbornness gets her way —! I should go and make myself ridiculous in front of the whole office — give people the idea I can be swayed by all kinds of outside pressure. Oh, you can bet I'd feel the effects of that soon enough! Besides — there's something that rules Krogstad right out at the bank as long as I'm the manager.

NORA: What's that?

HELMER: His moral failings I could maybe overlook if I had to —

NORA: Yes, Torvald, why not?

HELMER: And I hear he's quite efficient on the job. But he was a crony of mine back in my teens — one of those rash friendships that crop up again and again to embarrass you later in life. Well, I might as well say it straight out: We're on a first-name basis. And that tactless fool makes no effort at all to hide it in front of others. Quite the contrary — he thinks that entitles him to take a familiar air around me, and so every other second he comes booming out with his, "Yes, Torvald!" and "Sure thing, Torvald!" I tell you, it's been excruciating for me. He's out to make my place in the bank unbearable.

NORA: Torvald, you can't be serious about all this.

HELMER: Oh no? Why not?

NORA: Because these are such petty considerations.

HELMER: What are you saying? Petty? You think I'm petty!

NORA: No, just the opposite, Torvald dear. That's exactly why —

HELMER: Never mind. You call my motives petty; then I might as well be just that. Petty! All right! We'll put a stop to this for good. (*Goes to the hall door and calls.*) Helene!

NORA: What do you want?

HELMER (*searching among his papers*): A decision. (*The Maid comes in.*) Look here; take this letter; go out with it at once. Get hold of a messenger and have him deliver it. Quick now. It's already addressed. Wait, here's some money.

MAID: Yes, sir. (*She leaves with the letter.*)

HELMER (*straightening his papers*): There, now, little Miss Willful.

NORA (*breathlessly*): Torvald, what was that letter?

HELMER: Krogstad's notice.

NORA: Call it back, Torvald! There's still time. Oh, Torvald, call it back! Do it for my sake — for your sake, for the children's sake! Do you hear, Torvald; do it! You don't know how this can harm us.

HELMER: Too late.

NORA: Yes, too late.

HELMER: Nora, dear, I can forgive you this panic, even though basically you're insulting me. Yes, you are! Or isn't it an insult to think that *I* should be afraid of a courtroom hack's revenge? But I forgive you anyway, because this shows so beautifully how much you love me. (*Takes her in his arms.*) This is the way it should be, my darling Nora. Whatever comes, you'll see: When it really counts, I have strength and courage enough as a man to take on the whole weight myself.

NORA (*terrified*): What do you mean by that?

HELMER: The whole weight, I said.

NORA (*resolutely*): No, never in all the world.

HELMER: Good. So we'll share it, Nora, as man and wife. That's as it should be. (*Fondling her.*) Are you happy now? There, there, there — not these frightened dove's eyes. It's nothing at all but empty

fantasies — Now you should run through your tarantella and practice your tambourine. I'll go to the inner office, and shut both doors, so I won't hear a thing; you can make all the noise you like. (*Turning in the doorway.*) And when Rank comes, just tell him where he can find me. (*He nods to her and goes with his papers into the study, closing the door.*)

NORA (*standing as though rooted, dazed with fright, in a whisper*): He really could do it. He will do it. He'll do it in spite of everything. No, not that, never, never! Anything but that! Escape! A way out — (*The doorbell rings.*) Dr. Rank! Anything but that! *Anything*, whatever it is! (*Her hands pass over her face, smoothing it; she pulls herself together, goes over and opens the hall door. Dr. Rank stands outside, hanging his fur coat up. During the following scene, it begins getting dark.*)

NORA: Hello, Dr. Rank. I recognized your ring. But you mustn't go in to Torvald yet; I believe he's working.

RANK: And you?

NORA: For you, I always have an hour to spare — you know that. (*He has entered, and she shuts the door after him.*)

RANK: Many thanks. I'll make use of these hours while I can.

NORA: What do you mean by that? While you can?

RANK: Does that disturb you?

NORA: Well, it's such an odd phrase. Is anything going to happen?

RANK: What's going to happen is what I've been expecting so long — but I honestly didn't think it would come so soon.

NORA (*gripping his arm*): What is it you've found out? Dr. Rank, you have to tell me!

RANK (*sitting by the stove*): It's all over with me. There's nothing to be done about it.

NORA (*breathing easier*): Is it you — then —?

RANK: Who else? There's no point in lying to one's self. I'm the most miserable of all my patients, Mrs. Helmer. These past few days I've been auditing my internal accounts. Bankrupt! Within a month I'll probably be laid out and rotting in the churchyard.

NORA: Oh, what a horrible thing to say.

RANK: The thing itself is horrible. But the worst of it is all the other horror before it's over. There's only one final examination left; when I'm finished with that, I'll know about when my disintegration will begin. There's something I want to say. Helmer with his sensitivity has such a sharp distaste for anything ugly. I don't want him near my sickroom.

NORA: Oh, but Dr. Rank —

RANK: I won't have him in there. Under no condition. I'll lock my door to him — As soon as I'm completely sure of the worst, I'll send you my calling card marked with a black cross, and you'll know then the wreck has started to come apart.

NORA: No, today you're completely unreasonable. And I wanted you so much to be in a really good humor.

RANK: With death up my sleeve? And then to suffer this way for somebody else's sins. Is there any justice in that? And in every single family, in some way or another, this inevitable retribution of nature goes on —

NORA (*her hands pressed over her ears*): Oh, stuff! Cheer up! Please — be gay!

RANK: Yes, I'd just as soon laugh at it all. My poor, innocent spine, serving time for my father's gay army days.

NORA (*by the table, left*): He was so infatuated with asparagus tips and pâté de foie gras, wasn't that it?

RANK: Yes — and with truffles.

NORA: Truffles, yes. And then with oysters, I suppose?

RANK: Yes, tons of oysters, naturally.

NORA: And then the port and champagne to go with it. It's so sad that all these delectable things have to strike at our bones.

RANK: Especially when they strike at the unhappy bones that never shared in the fun.

NORA: Ah, that's the saddest of all.

RANK (*looks searchingly at her*): Hm.

NORA (*after a moment*): Why did you smile?

RANK: No, it was you who laughed.

NORA: No, it was you who smiled, Dr. Rank!

RANK (*getting up*): You're even a bigger tease than I'd thought.

NORA: I'm full of wild ideas today.

RANK: That's obvious.

NORA (*putting both hands on his shoulders*): Dear, dear Dr. Rank, you'll never die for Torvald and me.

RANK: Oh, that loss you'll easily get over. Those who go away are soon forgotten.

NORA (*looks fearfully at him*): You believe that?

RANK: One makes new connections, and then —

NORA: Who makes new connections?

RANK: Both you and Torvald will when I'm gone. I'd say you're well under way already. What was that Mrs. Linde doing here last evening?

NORA: Oh, come — you can't be jealous of poor Kristine?

RANK: Oh yes, I am. She'll be my successor here in the house. When I'm down under, that woman will probably —

NORA: Shh! Not so loud. She's right in there.

RANK: Today as well. So you see.

NORA: Only to sew on my dress. Good gracious, how unreasonable you are. (*Sitting on the sofa.*) Be nice now, Dr. Rank. Tomorrow you'll see how beautifully I'll dance; and you can imagine then that I'm dancing only for you — yes, and of course for Torvald, too — that's understood. (*Takes various items out of the carton.*) Dr. Rank, sit over here and I'll show you something.

RANK (*sitting*): What's that?

NORA: Look here. Look.

RANK: Silk stockings.

NORA: Flesh-colored. Aren't they lovely? Now it's so dark here, but tomorrow — No, no, no, just look at the feet. Oh well, you might as well look at the rest.

RANK: Hm —

NORA: Why do you look so critical? Don't you believe they'll fit?

RANK: I've never had any chance to form an opinion on that.

NORA (*glancing at him a moment*): Shame on you. (*Hits him lightly on the ear with the stockings.*) That's for you. (*Puts them away again.*)

RANK: And what other splendors am I going to see now?

NORA: Not the least bit more, because you've been naughty. (*She hunts a little and rummages among her things.*)

RANK (*after a short silence*): When I sit here together with you like this, completely easy and open, then I don't know — I simply can't imagine — whatever would have become of me if I'd never come into this house.

NORA (*smiling*): Yes, I really think you feel completely at ease with us.

RANK (*more quietly, staring straight ahead*): And then to have to go away from it all —

NORA: Nonsense, you're not going away.

RANK (*his voice unchanged*): — and not even be able to leave some poor show of gratitude behind, scarcely a fleeting regret — no more than a vacant place that anyone can fill.

NORA: And if I asked you now for — No —

RANK: For what?

NORA: For a great proof of your friendship —

RANK: Yes, yes?

NORA: No, I mean — for an exceptionally big favor —

RANK: Would you really, for once, make me so happy?

NORA: Oh, you haven't the vaguest idea what it is.

RANK: All right, then tell me.

NORA: No, but I can't, Dr. Rank — it's all out of reason. It's advice and help, too — and a favor —

RANK: So much the better. I can't fathom what you're hinting at. Just speak out. Don't you trust me?

NORA: Of course. More than anyone else. You're my best and truest friend, I'm sure. That's why I want

RIGHT: Cheryl Campbell as
Nora in the 1981–1982 Royal
Shakespeare Company
production of *A Doll House.*
FAR RIGHT: Nora and Torvald
(Stephen Moore).

to talk to you. All right, then, Dr. Rank: There's
something you can help me prevent. You know
how deeply, how inexpressibly dearly Torvald
loves me; he'd never hesitate a second to give up
his life for me.

RANK (*leaning close to her*): Nora — do you think
he's the only one —

NORA (*with a slight start*): Who —?

RANK: Who'd gladly give up his life for you.

NORA (*heavily*): I see.

RANK: I swore to myself you should know this before
I'm gone. I'll never find a better chance. Yes, Nora,
now you know. And also you know now that you
can trust me beyond anyone else.

NORA (*rising, natural and calm*): Let me by.

RANK (*making room for her, but still sitting*): Nora —

NORA (*in the hall doorway*): Helene, bring the lamp
in. (*Goes over to the stove.*) Ah, dear Dr. Rank,
that was really mean of you.

RANK (*getting up*): That I've loved you just as deeply
as somebody else? Was *that* mean?

NORA: No, but that you came out and told me. That
was quite unnecessary —

RANK: What do you mean? Have you known —?

(*The Maid comes in with the lamp, sets it on the table,
and goes out again.*)

RANK: Nora — Mrs. Helmer — I'm asking you: Have
you known about it?

NORA: Oh, how can I tell what I know or don't know?
Really, I don't know what to say — Why did you
have to be so clumsy, Dr. Rank! Everything was
so good.

RANK: Well, in any case, you now have the knowledge
that my body and soul are at your command. So
won't you speak out?

NORA (*looking at him*): After that?

RANK: Please, just let me know what it is.

NORA: You can't know anything now.

RANK: I have to. You mustn't punish me like this.
Give me the chance to do whatever is humanly
possible for you.

NORA: Now there's nothing you can do for me. Besides, actually, I don't need any help. You'll see —
it's only my fantasies. That's what it is. Of course!
(*Sits in the rocker, looks at him, and smiles.*) What

a nice one you are, Dr. Rank. Aren't you a little bit ashamed, now that the lamp is here?

RANK: No, not exactly. But perhaps I'd better go — for good?

NORA: No, you certainly can't do that. You must come here just as you always have. You know Torvald can't do without you.

RANK: Yes, but *you?*

NORA: You know how much I enjoy it when you're here.

RANK: That's precisely what threw me off. You're a mystery to me. So many times I've felt you'd almost rather be with me than with Helmer.

NORA: Yes — you see, there are some people that one loves most and other people that one would almost prefer being with.

RANK: Yes, there's something to that.

NORA: When I was back home, of course I loved Papa most. But I always thought it was so much fun when I could sneak down to the maids' quarters, because they never tried to improve me, and it was always so amusing, the way they talked to each other.

RANK: Aha, so it's *their* place that I've filled.

NORA (*jumping up and going to him*): Oh, dear, sweet Dr. Rank, that's not what I meant at all. But you can understand that with Torvald it's just the same as with Papa —

(*The Maid enters from the hall.*)

MAID: Ma'am — please! (*She whispers to Nora and hands her a calling card.*)

NORA (*glancing at the card*): Ah! (*Slips it into her pocket.*)

RANK: Anything wrong?

NORA: No, no, not at all. It's only some — it's my new dress —

RANK: Really? But — there's your dress.

NORA: Oh, that. But this is another one — I ordered it — Torvald mustn't know —

RANK: Ah, now we have the big secret.

NORA: That's right. Just go in with him — he's back in the inner study. Keep him there as long as —

RANK: Don't worry. He won't get away. (*Goes into the study.*)

NORA (*to the Maid*): And he's standing waiting in the kitchen?

MAID: Yes, he came up by the back stairs.

NORA: But didn't you tell him somebody was here?

MAID: Yes, but that didn't do any good.

NORA: He won't leave?

MAID: No, he won't go till he's talked with you, ma'am.

NORA: Let him come in, then — but quietly. Helene, don't breathe a word about this. It's a surprise for my husband.

MAID: Yes, yes, I understand — (*Goes out.*)

NORA: This horror — it's going to happen. No, no, no, it can't happen, it mustn't. (*She goes and bolts Helmer's door. The Maid opens the hall door for Krogstad and shuts it behind him. He is dressed for travel in a fur coat, boots, and a fur cap.*)

NORA (*going toward him*): Talk softly. My husband's home.

KROGSTAD: Well, good for him.

NORA: What do you want?

KROGSTAD: Some information.

NORA: Hurry up, then. What is it?

KROGSTAD: You know, of course, that I got my notice.

NORA: I couldn't prevent it, Mr. Krogstad. I fought for you to the bitter end, but nothing worked.

KROGSTAD: Does your husband's love for you run so thin? He knows everything I can expose you to, and all the same he dares to —

NORA: How can you imagine he knows anything about this?

KROGSTAD: Ah, no — I can't imagine it either, now. It's not at all like my fine Torvald Helmer to have so much guts —

NORA: Mr. Krogstad, I demand respect for my husband!

KROGSTAD: Why, of course — all due respect. But since the lady's keeping it so carefully hidden, may I presume to ask if you're also a bit better informed than yesterday about what you've actually done?

NORA: More than you ever could teach me.

KROGSTAD: Yes, I *am* such an awful lawyer.

NORA: What is it you want from me?

KROGSTAD: Just a glimpse of how you are, Mrs. Helmer. I've been thinking about you all day long. A cashier, a night-court scribbler, a — well, a type like me also has a little of what they call a heart, you know.

NORA: Then show it. Think of my children.

KROGSTAD: Did you or your husband ever think of mine? But never mind. I simply wanted to tell you that you don't need to take this thing too seriously. For the present, I'm not proceeding with any action.

NORA: Oh no, really! Well — I knew that.

KROGSTAD: Everything can be settled in a friendly spirit. It doesn't have to get around town at all; it can stay just among us three.

NORA: My husband must never know anything of this.

KROGSTAD: How can you manage that? Perhaps you can pay me the balance?

NORA: No, not right now.

KROGSTAD: Or you know some way of raising the money in a day or two?

NORA: No way that I'm willing to use.

KROGSTAD: Well, it wouldn't have done you any good, anyway. If you stood in front of me with a fistful of bills, you still couldn't buy your signature back.

NORA: Then tell me what you're going to do with it.

KROGSTAD: I'll just hold onto it — keep it on file. There's no outsider who'll even get wind of it. So if you've been thinking of taking some desperate step —

NORA: I have.

KROGSTAD: Been thinking of running away from home —

NORA: I have!

KROGSTAD: Or even of something worse —

NORA: How could you guess that?

KROGSTAD: You can drop those thoughts.

NORA: How could you guess I was thinking of *that*?

KROGSTAD: Most of us think about *that* at first. I thought about it too, but I discovered I hadn't the courage —

NORA (*lifelessly*): I don't either.

KROGSTAD (*relieved*): That's true, you haven't the courage? You too?

NORA: I don't have it — I don't have it.

KROGSTAD: It would be terribly stupid, anyway. After that first storm at home blows out, why, then — I have here in my pocket a letter for your husband —

NORA: Telling everything?

KROGSTAD: As charitably as possible.

NORA (*quickly*): He mustn't ever get that letter. Tear it up. I'll find some way to get money.

KROGSTAD: Beg pardon, Mrs. Helmer, but I think I just told you —

NORA: Oh, I don't mean the money I owe you. Let me know how much you want from my husband, and I'll manage it.

KROGSTAD: I don't want any money from your husband.

NORA: What do you want, then?

KROGSTAD: I'll tell you what. I want to recoup, Mrs. Helmer; I want to get on in the world — and there's where your husband can help me. For a year and a half I've kept myself clean of anything disreputable — all that time struggling with the worst conditions; but I was satisfied, working my way up step by step. Now I've been written right off, and I'm just not in the mood to come crawling back. I tell you, I want to move on. I want to get back in the bank — in a better position. Your husband can set up a job for me —

NORA: He'll never do that!

KROGSTAD: He'll do it. I know him. He won't dare breathe a word of protest. And once I'm in there together with him, you just wait and see! Inside of a year, I'll be the manager's right-hand man. It'll be Nils Krogstad, not Torvald Helmer, who runs the bank.

NORA: You'll never see the day!

KROGSTAD: Maybe you think you can —

NORA: I have the courage now — for *that*.

KROGSTAD: Oh, you don't scare me. A smart, spoiled lady like you —

NORA: You'll see; you'll see!

KROGSTAD: Under the ice, maybe? Down in the freezing, coal-black water? There, till you float up in the spring, ugly unrecognizable, with your hair falling out —

NORA: You don't frighten me.

KROGSTAD: Nor do you frighten me. One doesn't do these things, Mrs. Helmer. Besides what good would it be? I'd still have him safe in my pocket.

NORA: Afterwards? When I'm no longer —?

KROGSTAD: Are you forgetting that *I'll* be in control then over your final reputation? (*Nora stands speechless, staring at him.*) Good; now I've warned you. Don't do anything stupid. When Helmer's read my letter, I'll be waiting for his reply. And bear in mind that it's your husband himself who's forced me back to my old ways. I'll never forgive him for that. Good-bye, Mrs. Helmer. (*He goes out through the hall.*)

NORA (*goes to the hall door, opens it a crack, and listens*): He's gone. Didn't leave the letter. Oh no, no, that's impossible too! (*Opening the door more and more.*) What's that? He's standing outside — not going downstairs. He's thinking it over? Maybe he'll —? (*A letter falls in the mailbox; then Krogstad's footsteps are heard, dying away down a flight of stairs. Nora gives a muffled cry and runs over toward the sofa table. A short pause.*) In the mailbox. (*Slips warily over to the hall door.*) It's lying there. Torvald, Torvald — now we're lost!

MRS. LINDE (*entering with the costume from the room, left*): There now, I can't see anything else to mend. Perhaps you'd like to try —

NORA (*in a hoarse whisper*): Kristine, come here.

MRS. LINDE (*tossing the dress on the sofa*): What's wrong? You look upset.

NORA: Come here. See that letter? There! Look — through the glass in the mailbox.

MRS. LINDE: Yes, yes, I see it.

NORA: That letter's from Krogstad —

MRS. LINDE: Nora — it's Krogstad who loaned you the money!

NORA: Yes, and now Torvald will find out everything.

MRS. LINDE: Believe me, Nora, it's best for both of you.

NORA: There's more you don't know. I forged a name.

MRS. LINDE: But for heaven's sake —?

NORA: I only want to tell you that, Kristine, so that you can be my witness.

MRS. LINDE: Witness? Why should I —?

NORA: If I should go out of my mind — it could easily happen —

MRS. LINDE: Nora!

NORA: Or anything else occurred — so I couldn't be present here —

MRS. LINDE: Nora, Nora, you aren't yourself at all!

NORA: And someone should try to take on the whole weight, all of the guilt, you follow me —

MRS. LINDE: Yes, of course, but why do you think —?

NORA: Then you're the witness that it isn't true, Kristine. I'm very much myself; my mind right now is perfectly clear; and I'm telling you: Nobody else has known about this; I alone did everything. Remember that.

MRS. LINDE: I will. But I don't understand all this.

NORA: Oh, how could you ever understand it? It's the miracle now that's going to take place.

MRS. LINDE: The miracle?

NORA: Yes, the miracle. But it's so awful, Kristine. It mustn't take place, not for anything in the world.

MRS. LINDE: I'm going right over and talk with Krogstad.

NORA: Don't go near him; he'll do you some terrible harm!

MRS. LINDE: There was a time once when he'd gladly have done anything for me.

NORA: He?

MRS. LINDE: Where does he live?

NORA: Oh, how do I know? Yes. (*Searches in her pocket.*) Here's his card. But the letter, the letter —!

HELMER (*from the study, knocking on the door*): Nora!

NORA (*with a cry of fear*): Oh! What is it? What do you want?

HELMER: Now, now, don't be so frightened. We're not coming in. You locked the door — are you trying on the dress?

NORA: Yes, I'm trying it. I'll look just beautiful, Torvald.

MRS. LINDE (*who has read the card*): He's living right around the corner.

NORA: Yes, but what's the use? We're lost. The letter's in the box.

MRS. LINDE: And your husband has the key?

NORA: Yes, always.

MRS. LINDE: Krogstad can ask for his letter back unread; he can find some excuse —

NORA: But it's just this time that Torvald usually —

MRS. LINDE: Stall him. Keep him in there. I'll be back as quick as I can. (*She hurries out through the hall entrance.*)

NORA (*goes to Helmer's door, opens it, and peers in*): Torvald!

HELMER (*from the inner study*): Well — does one dare set foot in one's own living room at last? Come on, Rank, now we'll get a look — (*In the doorway.*) But what's this?

NORA: What, Torvald dear?

HELMER: Rank had me expecting some grand masquerade.

RANK (*in the doorway*): That was my impression, but I must have been wrong.

NORA: No one can admire me in my splendor — not till tomorrow.

HELMER: But Nora dear, you look so exhausted. Have you practiced too hard?

NORA: No, I haven't practiced at all yet.

HELMER: You know, it's necessary —

NORA: Oh, it's absolutely necessary, Torvald. But I can't get anywhere without your help. I've forgotten the whole thing completely.

HELMER: Ah, we'll soon take care of that.

NORA: Yes, take care of me, Torvald, please! Promise me that? Oh, I'm so nervous. That big party — You must give up everything this evening for me. No business — don't even touch your pen. Yes? Dear Torvald, promise?

HELMER: It's a promise. Tonight I'm totally at your service — you little helpless thing. Hm — but first there's one thing I want to — (*Goes toward the hall door.*)

NORA: What are you looking for?

HELMER: Just to see if there's any mail.

NORA: No, no, don't do that, Torvald!

HELMER: Now what?

NORA: Torvald, please. There isn't any.

HELMER: Let me look, though. (*Starts out. Nora, at the piano, strikes the first notes of the tarantella. Helmer, at the door, stops.*) Aha!

NORA: I can't dance tomorrow if I don't practice with you.

HELMER (*going over to her*): Nora dea, are you really so frightened?

NORA: Yes, so terribly frightened. Let me practice right now; there's still time before dinner. Oh, sit down and play for me, Torvald. Direct me. Teach me, the way you always have.

HELMER: Gladly, if it's what you want. (*Sits at the piano.*)

NORA (*snatches the tambourine up from the box, then a long, varicolored shawl, which she throws around herself, whereupon she springs forward and cries out*): Play for me now! Now I'll dance!

(*Helmer plays and Nora dances. Rank stands behind Helmer at the piano and looks on.*)

HELMER (*as he plays*): Slower. Slow down.

NORA: Can't change it.

HELMER: Not so violent, Nora!

NORA: Has to be just like this.

HELMER (*stopping*): No, no, that won't do at all.

NORA (*laughing and swinging her tambourine*): Isn't that what I told you?

RANK: Let me play for her.

HELMER (*getting up*): Yes, go on. I can teach her more easily then.

(*Rank sits at the piano and plays; Nora dances more and more wildly. Helmer has stationed himself by the stove and repeatedly gives her directions; she seems not to hear them; her hair loosens and falls over her shoulders; she does not notice, but goes on dancing. Mrs. Linde enters.*)

MRS. LINDE (*standing dumbfounded at the door*): Ah —!

NORA (*still dancing*): See what fun, Kristine!

HELMER: But Nora darling, you dance as if your life were at stake.

NORA: And it is.

HELMER: Rank, stop! This is pure madness. Stop it, I say!

(*Rank breaks off playing, and Nora halts abruptly*).

HELMER (*going over to her*): I never would have believed it. You've forgotten everything I taught you.

NORA (*throwing away the tambourine*): You see for yourself.

HELMER: Well, there's certainly room for instruction here.

NORA: Yes, you see how important it is. You've got to teach me to the very last minute. Promise me that, Torvald?

HELMER: You can bet on it.

NORA: You mustn't, either today or tomorrow, think about anything else but me; you mustn't open any letters — or the mailbox —

HELMER: Ah, it's still the fear of that man —

NORA: Oh yes, yes, that too.

HELMER: Nora, it's written all over you — there's already a letter from him out there.

NORA: I don't know. I guess so. But you mustn't read such things now; there mustn't be anything ugly between us before it's all over.

RANK (*quietly to Helmer*): You shouldn't deny her.

HELMER (*putting his arm around her*): The child can have her way. But tomorrow night, after you've danced —

NORA: Then you'll be free.

MAID (*in the doorway, right*): Ma'am, dinner is served.

NORA: We'll be wanting champagne, Helene.

MAID: Very good, ma'am. (*Goes out.*)

HELMER: So — a regular banquet, hm?

NORA: Yes, a banquet — champagne till daybreak! (*Calling out.*) And some macaroons, Helene. Heaps of them — just this once.

HELMER (*taking her hands*): Now, now, now — no hysterics. Be my own little lark again.

NORA: Oh, I will soon enough. But go on in — and you, Dr. Rank. Kristine, help me put up my hair.

RANK (*whispering, as they go*): There's nothing wrong — really wrong, is there?

HELMER: Oh, of course not. It's nothing more than this childish anxiety I was telling you about. (*They go out, right.*)

NORA: Well?

MRS. LINDE: Left town.

NORA: I could see by your face.

MRS. LINDE: He'll be home tomorrow evening. I wrote him a note.

NORA: You shouldn't have. Don't try to stop anything now. After all, it's a wonderful joy, this waiting here for the miracle.

MRS. LINDE: What is it you're waiting for?

NORA: Oh, you can't understand that. Go in to them; I'll be along in a moment.

(*Mrs. Linde goes into the dining room. Nora stands a short while as if composing herself; then she looks at her watch.*)

NORA: Five. Seven hours to midnight. Twenty-four hours to the midnight after, and then the tarantella's done. Seven and twenty-four? Thirty-one hours to live.

HELMER (*in the doorway, right*): What's become of the little lark?

NORA (*going toward him with open arms*): Here's your lark!

ACT III

(*Same scene. The table, with chairs around it, has been moved to the center of the room. A lamp on the table is lit. The hall door stands open. Dance music drifts down from the floor above. Mrs. Linde sits at the table, absently paging through a book, trying to read, but apparently unable to focus her thoughts.*

Once or twice she pauses, tensely listening for a sound at the outer entrance.)

MRS. LINDE (*glancing at her watch*): Not yet — and there's hardly any time left. If only he's not — (*Listening again.*) Ah, there is is. (*She goes out in the hall and cautiously opens the outer door. Quiety footsteps are heard on the stairs. She whispers.*) Come in. Nobody's here.

KROGSTAD (*in the doorway*): I found a note from you at home. What's back of all this?

MRS. LINDE: I just *had* to talk to you.

KROGSTAD: Oh? And it just *had* to be here in this house?

MRS. LINDE: At my place it was impossible; my room hasn't a private entrance. Come in; we're all alone. The maid's asleep, and the Helmers are at the dance upstairs.

KROGSTAD (*entering the room*): Well, well, the Helmers are dancing tonight? Really?

MRS. LINDE: Yes, why not?

KROGSTAD: How true — why not?

MRS. LINDE: All right, Krogstad, let's talk.

KROGSTAD: Do we two have anything more to talk about?

MRS. LINDE: We have a great deal to talk about.

KROGSTAD: I wouldn't have thought so.

MRS. LINDE: No, because you've never understood me, really.

KROGSTAD: Was there anything more to understand — except what's all too common in life? A calculating woman throws over a man the moment a better catch comes by.

MRS. LINDE: You think I'm so thoroughly calculating? You think I broke it off lightly?

KROGSTAD: Didn't you?

MRS. LINDE: Nils — is that what you really thought?

KROGSTAD: If you cared, then why did you write me the way you did?

MRS. LINDE: What else could I do? If I had to break off with you, then it was my job as well to root out everything you felt for me.

KROGSTAD (*wringing his hands*): So that was it. And this — all this, simply for money!

MRS. LINDE: Don't forget I had a helpless mother and two small brothers. We couldn't wait for you, Nils; you had such a long road ahead of you then.

KROGSTAD: That may be; but you still hadn't the right to abandon me for somebody else's sake.

MRS. LINDE: Yes — I don't know. So many, many times I've asked myself if I did have that right.

KROGSTAD (*more softly*): When I lost you, it was as if all the solid ground dissolved from under my feet. Look at me; I'm a half-drowned man now, hanging onto a wreck.

MRS. LINDE: Help may be near.

KROGSTAD: It was near — but then you came and blocked it off.

MRS. LINDE: Without my knowing it, Nils. Today for the first time I learned that it's you I'm replacing at the bank.

KROGSTAD: All right — I believe you. But now that you know, will you step aside?

MRS. LINDE: No, because that wouldn't benefit you in the slightest.

KROGSTAD: Not "benefit" me, hm! I'd step aside anyway.

MRS. LINDE: I've learned to be realistic. Life and hard, bitter necessity have taught me that.

KROGSTAD: And life's taught me never to trust fine phrases.

MRS. LINDE: Then life's taught you a very sound thing. But you do have to trust in actions, don't you?

KROGSTAD: What does that mean?

MRS. LINDE: You said you were hanging on like a half-drowned man to a wreck.

KROGSTAD: I've good reason to say that.

MRS. LINDE: I'm also like a half-drowned woman on a wreck. No one to suffer with; no one to care for.

KROGSTAD: You made your choice.

MRS. LINDE: There wasn't any choice then.

KROGSTAD: So — what of it?

MRS. LINDE: Nils, if only we two shipwrecked people could reach across to each other.

KROGSTAD: What are you saying?

MRS. LINDE: Two on one wreck are at least better off than each on his own.

KROGSTAD: Kristine!

MRS. LINDE: Why do you think I came into town?

KROGSTAD: Did you really have some thought of me?

MRS. LINDE: I have to work to go on living. All my born days, as long as I can remember, I've worked, and it's been my best and my only joy. But now I'm completely alone in the world; it frightens me to be so empty and lost. To work for yourself — there's no joy in that. Nils, give me something — someone to work for.

KROGSTAD: I don't believe all this. It's just some hysterical feminine urge to go out and make a noble sacrifice.

MRS. LINDE: Have you ever found me to be hysterical?

KROGSTAD: Can you honestly mean this? Tell me — do you know everything about my past?

MRS. LINDE: Yes.

KROGSTAD: And you know what they think I'm worth around here.

MRS. LINDE: From what you were saying before, it would seem that with me you could have been another person.

KROGSTAD: I'm positive of that.

MRS. LINDE: Couldn't it happen still?

KROGSTAD: Kristine — you're saying this in all seriousness? Yes, you are! I can see it in you. And do you really have the courage, then —?

MRS. LINDE: I need to have someone to care for; and your children need a mother. We both need each other. Nils, I have faith that you're good at heart — I'll risk everything together with you.

KROGSTAD (*gripping her hands*): Kristine, thank you, thank you — Now I know I can win back a place in their eyes. Yes — but I forgot —

MRS. LINDE (*listening*): Shh! The tarantella. Go now! Go on!

KROGSTAD: Why? What is it?

MRS. LINDE: Hear the dance up there? When that's over, they'll be coming down.

KROGSTAD: Oh, then I'll go. But — it's all pointless. Of course, you don't know the move I made against the Helmers.

MRS. LINDE: Yes, Nils, I know.

KROGSTAD: And all the same, you have the courage to —?

MRS. LINDE: I know how far despair can drive a man like you.

KROGSTAD: Oh, if I only could take it all back.

MRS. LINDE: You easily could — your letter's still lying in the mailbox.

KROGSTAD: Are you sure of that?

MRS. LINDE: Positive. But —

KROGSTAD (*looks at her searchingly*): Is that the meaning of it, then? You'll save your friend at any price. Tell me straight out. Is that it?

MRS. LINDE: Nils — anyone who's sold herself for somebody else once isn't going to do it again.

KROGSTAD: I'll demand my letter back.

MRS. LINDE: No, no.

KROGSTAD: Yes, of course. I'll stay here till Helmer comes down; I'll tell him to give me my letter again — that it only involves my dismissal — that he shouldn't read it —

MRS. LINDE: No, Nils, don't call the letter back.

KROGSTAD: But wasn't that exactly why you wrote me to come here?

MRS. LINDE: Yes, in that first panic. But it's been a whole day and night since then, and in that time I've seen such incredible things in this house. Helmer's got to learn everything; this dreadful secret has to be aired; those two have to come to a full understanding; all these lies and evasions can't go on.

KROGSTAD: Well, then, if you want to chance it. But at least there's one thing I can do, and do right away —

MRS. LINDE (*listening*): Go now, go, quick! The dance is over. We're not safe another second.

KROGSTAD: I'll wait for you downstairs.

MRS. LINDE: Yes, please do; take me home.

KROGSTAD: I can't believe it; I've never been so happy. (*He leaves by way of the outer door; the door between the room and the hall stays open.*)

MRS. LINDE (*straightening up a bit and getting together her street clothes*): How different now! How different! Someone to work for, to live for — a home to build. Well, it is worth the try! Oh, if they'd only come! (*Listening.*) Ah, there they are. Bundle up. (*She picks up her hat and coat. Nora's and Helmer's voices can be heard outside; a key turns in the lock, and Helmer brings Nora into the hall almost by force. She is wearing the Italian costume with a large black shawl about her; he has on evening dress, with a black domino open over it.*)

NORA (*struggling in the doorway*): No, no, no, not inside! I'm going up again. I don't want to leave so soon.

HELMER: But Nora dear —

NORA: Oh, I beg you, please, Torvald. From the bottom of my heart, *please* — only an hour more!

HELMER: Not a single minute, Nora darling. You know our agreement. Come on, in we go; you'll catch cold out here. (*In spite of her resistance, he gently draws her into the room.*)

MRS. LINDE: Good evening.

NORA: Kristine!

HELMER: Why, Mrs. Linde — are you here so late?

MRS. LINDE: Yes, I'm sorry, but I did want to see Nora in costume.

NORA: Have you been sitting here, waiting for me?

MRS. LINDE: Yes. I didn't come early enough; you were all upstairs; and then I thought I really couldn't leave without seeing you.

HELMER (*removing Nora's shawl*): Yes, take a good look. She's worth looking at, I can tell you that, Mrs. Linde. Isn't she lovely?

MRS. LINDE: Yes, I should say —

HELMER: A dream of loveliness, isn't she? That's what everyone thought at the party, too. But she's horribly stubborn — this sweet little thing. What's to be done with her? Can you imagine, I almost had to use force to pry her away.

NORA: Oh, Torvald, you're going to regret you didn't indulge me, even for just a half hour more.

HELMER: There, you see. She danced her tarantella and got a tumultuous hand — which was well earned, although the performance may have been a bit too naturalistic — I mean it rather overstepped the proprieties of art. But never mind — what's important is, she made a success, an overwhelming success. You think I could let her stay on after that and spoil the effect? Oh no; I took my lovely little

Capri girl — my capricious little Capri girl, I should say — took her under my arm; one quick tour of the ballroom, a curtsy to every side, and then — as they say in novels — the beautiful vision disappeared. An exit should always be effective, Mrs. Linde, but that's what I can't get Nora to grasp. Phew, It's hot in here. (*Flings the domino on a chair and opens the door to his room.*) Why's it dark in here? Oh yes, of course. Excuse me. (*He goes in and lights a couple of candles.*)

NORA (*in a sharp, breathless whisper*): So?

MRS. LINDE (*quietly*): I talked with him.

NORA: And —?

MRS. LINDE: Nora — you must tell your husband everything.

NORA (*dully*): I knew it.

MRS. LINDE: You've got nothing to fear from Krogstad, but you have to speak out.

NORA: I won't tell.

MRS. LINDE: Then the letter will.

NORA: Thanks, Kristine. I know now what's to be done. Shh!

HELMER (*reentering*): Well, then, Mrs. Linde — have you admired her?

MRS. LINDE: Yes, and now I'll say good night.

HELMER: Oh, come, so soon? Is this yours, this knitting?

MRS. LINDE: Yes, thanks. I nearly forgot it.

HELMER: Do you knit, then?

MRS. LINDE: Oh yes.

HELMER: You know what? You should embroider instead.

MRS. LINDE: Really? Why?

HELMER: Yes, because it's a lot prettier. See here, one holds the embroidery so, in the left hand, and then one guides the needle with the right — so — in an easy, sweeping curve — right?

MRS. LINDE: Yes, I guess that's —

HELMER: But, on the other hand, knitting — it can never be anything but ugly. Look, see here, the arms tucked in, the knitting needles going up and down — there's something Chinese about it. Ah, that was really a glorious champagne they served.

MRS. LINDE: Yes, good night, Nora, and don't be stubborn anymore.

HELMER: Well put, Mrs. Linde!

MRS. LINDE: Good night, Mr. Helmer.

HELMER (*accompanying her to the door*): Good night, good night. I hope you get home all right. I'd be very happy to — but you don't have far to go. Good night, good night. (*She leaves. He shuts the door after her and returns.*) There, now, at last we got her out the door. She's a deadly bore, that creature.

NORA: Aren't you pretty tired, Torvald?

HELMER: No, not a bit.

NORA: You're not sleepy?

HELMER: Not at all. On the contrary, I'm feeling quite exhilarated. But you? Yes, you really look tired and sleepy.

NORA: Yes, I'm very tired. Soon now I'll sleep.

HELMER: See! You see! I was right all along that we shouldn't stay longer.

NORA: Whatever you do is always right.

HELMER (*kissing her brow*): Now my little lark talks sense. Say, did you notice what a time Rank was having tonight?

NORA: Oh, was he? I didn't get to speak with him.

HELMER: I scarcely did either, but it's a long time since I've seen him in such high spirits. (*Gazes at her a moment, then comes nearer her.*) Hm — it's marvelous, though, to be back home again — to be completely alone with you. Oh, you bewitchingly lovely young woman!

NORA: Torvald, don't look at me like that!

HELMER: Can't I look at my richest treasure? At all that beauty that's mine, mine alone — completely and utterly.

NORA (*moving around to the other side of the table*): You mustn't talk to me that way tonight.

HELMER (*following her*): The tarantella is still in your blood. I can see — and it makes you even more enticing. Listen. The guests are beginning to go. (*Dropping his voice.*) Nora — it'll soon be quiet through this whole house.

NORA: Yes, I hope so.

HELMER: You do, don't you, my love? Do you realize — when I'm out at a party like this with you — do you know why I talk to you so little, and keep such a distance away; just send you a stolen look now and then — you know why I do it? It's because I'm imagining then that you're my secret darling, my secret young bride-to-be, and that no one suspects there's anything between us.

NORA: Yes, yes; oh, yes, I know you're always thinking of me.

HELMER: And then when we leave and I place the shawl over those fine young rounded shoulders — over that wonderful curving neck — then I pretend that you're my young bride, that we're just coming from the wedding, that for the first time I'm bringing you into my house — that for the first time I'm alone with you — completely alone with you, your trembling young beauty! All this evening I've longed for nothing but you. When I saw you turn and sway in the tarantella — my blood was pounding till I couldn't stand it — that's why I brought you down here so early —

NORA: Go away, Torvald! Leave me alone. I don't want all this.

HELMER: What do you mean? Nora, you're teasing me. You will, won't you? Aren't I your husband —?

(*A knock at the outside door.*)

NORA (*startled*): What's that?

HELMER (*going toward the hall*): Who is it?

RANK (*outside*): It's me. May I come in a moment?

HELMER (*with quiet irritation*): Oh, what does he want now? (*Aloud.*) Hold on. (*Goes and opens the door.*) Oh, how nice that you didn't just pass us by!

RANK: I thought I heard your voice, and then I wanted so badly to have a look in. (*Lightly glancing about.*) Ah, me, these old familiar haunts. You have it snug and cozy in here, you two.

HELMER: You seemed to be having it pretty cozy upstairs, too.

RANK: Absolutely. Why shouldn't I? Why not take in everything in life? As much as you can, anyway, and as long as you can. The wine was superb —

HELMER: The champagne especially.

RANK: You noticed that too? It's amazing how much I could guzzle down.

NORA: Torvald also drank a lot of champagne this evening.

RANK: Oh?

NORA: Yes, and that always makes him so entertaining.

RANK: Well, why shouldn't one have a pleasant evening after a well-spent day?

HELMER: Well spent? I'm afraid I can't claim that.

RANK (*slapping him on the back*): But I can, you see!

NORA: Dr. Rank, you must have done some scientific research today.

RANK: Quite so.

HELMER: Come now — little Nora talking about scientific research!

NORA: And can I congratulate you on the results?

RANK: Indeed you may.

NORA: Then they were good?

RANK: The best possible for both doctor and patient — certainty.

NORA (*quickly and searchingly*): Certainty?

RANK: Complete certainty. So don't I owe myself a gay evening afterwards?

NORA: Yes, you're right, Dr. Rank.

HELMER: I'm with you — just so long as you don't have to suffer for it in the morning.

RANK: Well, one never gets something for nothing in life.

NORA: Dr. Rank — are you very fond of masquerade parties?

RANK: Yes, if there's a good array of odd disguises —

NORA: Tell me, what should we two go as at the next masquerade?

HELMER: You little featherhead — already thinking of the next!

RANK: We two? I'll tell you what: You must go as Charmed Life —

HELMER: Yes, but find a costume for that!

RANK: Your wife can appear just as she looks every day.

HELMER: That was nicely put. But don't you know what you're going to be?

RANK: Yes, Helmer, I've made up my mind.

HELMER: Well?

RANK: At the next masquerade I'm going to be invisible.

HELMER: That's a funny idea.

RANK: They say there's a hat — black, huge — have you never heard of the hat that makes you invisible? You put it on, and then no one on earth can see you.

HELMER (*suppressing a smile*): Ah, of course.

RANK: But I'm quite forgetting what I came for. Helmer, give me a cigar, one of the dark Havanas.

HELMER: With the greatest pleasure. (*Holds out his case.*)

RANK: Thanks. (*Takes one and cuts off the tip.*)

NORA (*striking a match*): Let me give you a light.

RANK: Thank you. (*She holds the match for him; he lights the cigar.*) And now good-bye.

HELMER: Good-bye, good-bye, old friend.

NORA: Sleep well, Doctor.

RANK: Thanks for that wish.

NORA: Wish me the same.

RANK: You? All right, if you like — Sleep well. And thanks for the light. (*He nods to them both and leaves.*)

HELMER (*his voice subdued*): He's been drinking heavily.

NORA (*absently*): Could be. (*Helmer takes his keys from his pocket and goes out in the hall.*) Torvald — what are you after?

HELMER: Got to empty the mailbox; it's nearly full. There won't be room for the morning papers.

NORA: Are you working tonight?

HELMER: You know I'm not. Why — what this? Someone's been at the lock.

NORA: At the lock —?

HELMER: Yes, I'm positive. What do you suppose — ? I can't imagine one of the maids —? Here's a broken hairpin. Nora, it's yours —

NORA (*quickly*): Then it must be the children —

HELMER: You'd better break them of that. Hm, hm — well, opened it after all. (*Takes the contents out and calls into the kitchen.*) Helene! Helene, would you put out the lamp in the hall. (*He returns to the room, shutting the hall door, then displays the handful of mail.*) Look how it's piled up. (*Sorting through them.*) Now what's this?

NORA (*at the window*): The letter! Oh, Torvald, no!

HELMER: Two calling cards — from Rank.

NORA: From Dr. Rank?

HELMER (*examining them*): "Dr. Rank, Consulting Physician." They were on top. He must have dropped them in as he left.

NORA: Is there anything on them?

HELMER: There's a black cross over the name. See? That's a gruesome notion. He could almost be announcing his own death.

NORA: That's just what he's doing.

HELMER: What! You've heard something? Something he's told you?

NORA: Yes. That when those cards came, he'd be taking his leave of us. He'll shut himself in now and die.

HELMER: Ah, my poor friend! Of course I knew he wouldn't be here much longer. But so soon — And then to hide himself away like a wounded animal.

NORA: If it has to happen, then it's best it happens in silence — don't you think so, Torvald?

HELMER (*pacing up and down*): He's grown right into our lives. I simply can't imagine him gone. He with his suffering and loneliness — like a dark cloud setting off our sunlit happiness. Well, maybe it's best this way. For him, at least. (*Standing still.*) And maybe for us too, Nora. Now we're thrown back on each other, completely. (*Embracing her.*) Oh you, my darling wife, how can I hold you close enough? You know what, Nora — time and again I've wished you were in some terrible danger, just so I could stake my life and soul and everything, for your sake.

NORA (*tearing herself away, her voice firm and decisive*): Now you must read your mail, Torvald.

HELMER: No, no, not tonight. I want to stay with you, dearest.

NORA: With a dying friend on your mind?

HELMER: You're right. We've both had a shock. There's ugliness between us — these thoughts of death and corruption. We'll have to get free of them first. Until then — we'll stay apart.

NORA (*clinging about his neck*): Torvald — good night! Good night!

HELMER (*kissing her on the cheek*): Good night, little songbird. Sleep well, Nora. I'll be reading my mail now. (*He takes the letters into his room and shuts the door after him.*)

NORA (*with bewildered glances, groping about, seizing Helmer's domino, throwing it around her, and speaking in short, hoarse, broken whispers*): Never see him again. Never, never. (*Putting her shawl over her head.*) Never see the children either — them, too. Never, never. Oh, the freezing black water! The depths — down — Oh, I wish it were over — He has it now; he's reading it — now. Oh no, no, not yet. Torvald, good-bye, you and the children — (*She starts for the hall; as she does, Helmer throws open his door and stands with an open letter in his hand.*)

HELMER: Nora!

NORA (*screams*): Oh —!

HELMER: What is this? You know what's in this letter?

NORA: Yes, I know. Let me go! Let me out!

HELMER (*holding her back*): Where are you going?

NORA (*struggling to break loose*): You can't save me, Torvald!

HELMER (*slumping back*): True! Then it's true what he writes? How horrible! No, no, it's impossible — it can't be true.

NORA: It *is* true. I've loved you more than all this world.

HELMER: Ah, none of your slippery tricks.

NORA (*taking one step toward him*): Torvald —!

HELMER: What *is* this you've blundered into!

NORA: Just let me loose. You're not going to suffer for my sake. You're not going to take on my guilt.

HELMER: No more playacting. (*Locks the hall door.*) You stay right here and give me a reckoning. You understand what you've done? Answer! You understand?

NORA (*looking squarely at him, her face hardening*): Yes. I'm beginning to understand everything now.

HELMER (*striding about*): Oh, what an awful awakening! In all these eight years — she who was my pride and joy — a hypocrite, a liar — worse, worse — a criminal! How infinitely disgusting it all is! The shame! (*Nora says nothing and goes on looking straight at him. He stops in front of her.*) I should have suspected something of the kind. I should have known. All your father's flimsy values — Be still! All your father's flimsy values have come out in you. No religion, no morals, no sense of duty — Oh, how I'm punished for letting him off! I did it for your sake, and you repay me like this.

NORA: Yes, like this.

HELMER: Now you've wrecked all my happiness — ruined my whole future. Oh, it's awful to think of. I'm in a cheap little grafter's hands; he can do anything he wants with me, ask for anything, play with me like a puppet — and I can't breathe a word. I'll be swept down miserably into the depths on account of a featherbrained woman.

NORA: When I'm gone from this world, you'll be free.

HELMER: Oh, quit posing. Your father had a mess of those speeches too. What good would that ever do

me if you were gone from this world, as you say? Not the slightest. He can still make the whole thing known; and if he does, I could be falsely suspected as your accomplice. They might even think that I was behind it — that I put you up to it. And all that I can thank you for — you that I've coddled the whole of our marriage. Can you see now what you've done to me?

NORA (*icily calm*): Yes.

HELMER: It's so incredible, I just can't grasp it. But we'll have to patch up whatever we can. Take off the shawl. I said, take it off! I've got to appease him somehow or other. The thing has to be hushed up at any cost. And as for you and me, it's got to seem like everything between us is just as it was — to the outside world, that is. You'll go right on living in this house, of course. But you can't be allowed to bring up the children; I don't dare trust you with them — Oh, to have to say this to someone I've loved so much! Well, that's done with. From now on happiness doesn't matter; all that matters is saving the bits and pieces, the appearance — (*The doorbell rings. Helmer starts.*) What's that? And so late. Maybe the worst —? You think he'd —? Hide, Nora! Say you're sick. (*Nora remains standing motionless. Helmer goes and opens the door.*)

MAID (*half dressed, in the hall*): A letter for Mrs. Helmer.

HELMER: I'll take it. (*Snatches the letter and shuts the door.*) Yes, it's from him. You don't get it; I'm reading it myself.

NORA: Then read it.

HELMER (*by the lamp*): I hardly dare. We may be ruined, you and I. But — I've got to know. (*Rips open the letter, skims through a few lines, glances at an enclosure, then cries out joyfully.*) Nora! (*Nora looks inquiringly at him.*) Nora! Wait — better check it again — Yes, yes, it's true. I'm saved. Nora, I'm saved!

NORA: And I?

HELMER: You too, of course. We're both saved, both of us. Look. He's sent back your note. He says he's sorry and ashamed — that a happy development in his life — oh, who cares what he says! Nora, we're saved! No one can hurt you. Oh, Nora, Nora — but first, this ugliness all has to go. Let me see — (*Takes a look at the note.*) No, I don't want to see it; I want the whole thing to fade like a dream. (*Tears the note and both letters to pieces, throws them into the stove and watches them burn.*) There — now there's nothing left — He wrote that since Christmas Eve you — Oh, they must have been three terrible days for you, Nora.

NORA: I fought a hard fight.

HELMER: And suffered pain and saw no escape but — No, we're not going to dwell on anything unpleasant. We'll just be grateful and keep on repeating: It's over now, it's over! You hear me, Nora? You don't seem to realize — it's over. What's it mean — that frozen look? Oh, poor little Nora, I understand. You can't believe I've forgiven you. But I have, Nora; I swear I have. I know that what you did, you did out of love for me.

NORA: That's true.

HELMER: You loved me the way a wife ought to love her husband. It's simply the means that you couldn't judge. But you think I love you any the less for not knowing how to handle your affairs? No, no — just lean on me; I'll guide you and teach you. I wouldn't be a man if this feminine helplessness didn't make you twice as attractive to me. You mustn't mind those sharp words I said — that was all in the first confusion of thinking my world had collapsed. I've forgiven you, Nora; I swear I've forgiven you.

NORA: My thanks for your forgiveness. (*She goes out through the door, right.*)

HELMER: No, wait — (*Peers in.*) What are you doing in there?

NORA (*inside*): Getting out of my costume.

HELMER (*by the open door*): Yes, do that. Try to calm yourself and collect your thoughts again, my frightened little songbird. You can rest easy now; I've got wide wings to shelter you with. (*Walking about close by the door.*) How snug and nice our home is, Nora. You're safe here; I'll keep you like a hunted dove I've rescued out of a hawk's claws. I'll bring peace to your poor, shuddering heart. Gradually it'll happen, Nora; you'll see. Tomorrow all this will look different to you; then everything will be as it was. I won't have to go on repeating I forgive you; you'll feel it for yourself. How can you imagine I'd ever conceivably want to disown you — or even blame you in any way? Ah, you don't know a man's heart, Nora. For a man there's something indescribably sweet and satisfying in knowing he's forgiven his wife — and forgiven her out of a full and open heart. It's as if she belongs to him in two ways now: In a sense he's given her fresh into the world again, and she's become his wife and his child as well. From now on that's what you'll be to me — you little, bewildered, helpless thing. Don't be afraid of anything, Nora; just open your heart to me, and I'll be conscience and will to you both — (*Nora enters in her regular clothes.*) What's this? Not in bed? You've changed your dress?

NORA: Yes, Torvald, I've changed my dress.

HELMER: But why now, so late?

NORA: Tonight I'm not sleeping.

HELMER: But Nora dear —

NORA (*looking at her watch*): It's still not so very late. Sit down, Torvald; we have a lot to talk over. (*She sits at one side of the table.*)

HELMER: Nora — what is this? That hard expression —

NORA: Sit down. This'll take some time. I have a lot to say.

HELMER (*sitting at the table directly opposite her*): You worry me, Nora. And I don't understand you.

NORA: No, that's exactly it. You don't understand me. And I've never understood you either — until tonight. No, don't interrupt. You can just listen to what I say. We're closing out accounts, Torvald.

HELMER: How do you mean that?

NORA (*after a short pause*): Doesn't anything strike you about our sitting here like this?

HELMER: What's that?

NORA: We've been married now eight years. Doesn't it occur to you that this is the first time we two, you and I, man and wife, have ever talked seriously together?

HELMER: What do you mean — seriously?

NORA: In eight whole years — longer even — right from our first acquaintance, we've never exchanged a serious word on any serious thing.

HELMER: You mean I should constantly go and involve you in problems you couldn't possibly help me with?

NORA: I'm not talking of problems. I'm saying that we've never sat down seriously together and tried to get to the bottom of anything.

HELMER: But dearest, what good would that ever do you?

NORA: That's the point right there: You've never understood me. I've been wronged greatly, Torvald — first by Papa, and then by you.

HELMER: What! By us — the two people who've loved you more than anyone else?

NORA (*shaking her head*): You never loved me. You've thought it fun to be in love with me, that's all.

HELMER: Nora, what a thing to say!

NORA: Yes, it's true now, Torvald. When I lived at home with Papa, he told me all his opinions, so I had the same ones too; or if they were different I hid them, since he wouldn't have cared for that. He used to call me his doll-child, and he played with me the way I played with my dolls. Then I came into your house —

HELMER: How can you speak of our marriage like that?

NORA (*unperturbed*): I mean, then I went from Papa's hands into yours. You arranged everything to your own taste, and so I got the same taste as you — or I pretended to; I can't remember. I guess a little of both, first one, then the other. Now when I look back, it seems as if I'd lived here like a beggar — just from hand to mouth. I've lived by doing tricks for you, Torvald. But that's the way you wanted it. It's a great sin what you and Papa did to me. You're to blame that nothing's become of me.

HELMER: Nora, how unfair and ungrateful you are! Haven't you been happy here?

NORA: No, never. I thought so — but I never have.

HELMER: Not — not happy!

NORA: No, only lighthearted. And you've always been so kind to me. But our home's been nothing but a playpen. I've been your doll-wife here, just as at home I was Papa's doll-child. And in turn the children have been my dolls. I thought it was fun when you played with me, just as they thought it fun when I played with them. That's been our marriage, Torvald.

HELMER: There's some truth in what you're saying — under all the raving exaggeration. But it'll all be different after this. Playtime's over; now for the schooling.

NORA: Whose schooling — mine or the children's?

HELMER: Both yours and the children's, dearest.

NORA: Oh, Torvald, you're not the man to teach me to be a good wife to you.

HELMER: And you can say that?

NORA: And I — how am I equipped to bring up children?

HELMER: Nora!

NORA: Didn't you say a moment ago that that was no job to trust me with?

HELMER: In a flare of temper! Why fasten on that?

NORA: Yes, but you were so very right. I'm not up to the job. There's another job I have to do first. I have to try to educate myself. You can't help me with that. I've got to do it alone. And that's why I'm leaving you now.

HELMER (*jumping up*): What's that?

NORA: I have to stand completely alone, if I'm ever going to discover myself and the world out there. So I can't go on living with you.

HELMER: Nora, Nora!

NORA: I want to leave right away. Kristine should put me up for the night —

HELMER: You're insane! You've no right! I forbid you!

NORA: From here on, there's no use forbidding me anything. I'll take with me whatever is mine. I don't want a thing from you, either now or later.

HELMER: What kind of madness is this!

NORA: Tomorrow I'm going home — I mean, home where I came from. It'll be easier up there to find something to do.

HELMER: Oh, you blind, incompetent child!

NORA: I must learn to be competent, Torvald.

HELMER: Abandon your home, your husband, your children! And you're not even thinking what people will say.

NORA: I can't be concerned about that. I only know how essential this is.

HELMER: Oh, it's outrageous. So you'll run out like this on your most sacred vows.

NORA: What do you think are my most sacred vows?

HELMER: And I have to tell you that! Aren't they your duties to your husband and children?

NORA: I have other duties equally sacred.

HELMER: That isn't true. What duties are they?

NORA: Duties to myself.

HELMER: Before all else, you're a wife and a mother.

NORA: I don't believe in that anymore. I believe that, before all else, I'm a human being, no less than you — or anyway, I ought to try to become one. I know the majority thinks you're right, Torvald, and plenty of books agree with you, too. But I can't go on believing what the majority says, or what's written in books. I have to think over these things myself and try to understand them.

HELMER: Why can't you understand your place in your own home? On a point like that, isn't there one everlasting guide you can turn to? Where's your religion?

NORA: Oh, Torvald, I'm really not sure what religion is.

HELMER: What —?

NORA: I only know what the minister said when I was confirmed. He told me religion was this thing and that. When I get clear and away by myself, I'll go into that problem too. I'll see if what the minister said was right, or, in any case, if it's right for me.

HELMER: A young woman your age shouldn't talk like that. If religion can't move you, I can try to rouse your conscience. You do have some moral feeling? Or, tell me — has that gone too?

NORA: It's not easy to answer that, Torvald. I simply don't know. I'm all confused about these things. I just know I see them so differently from you. I find out for one thing, that's the law's not at all what I'd thought — but I can't get it through my head that the law is fair. A woman hasn't a right to protect her dying father or save her husband's life! I can't believe that.

HELMER: You talk like a child. You don't know anything of the world you live in.

NORA: No, I don't. But now I'll begin to learn for myself. I'll try to discover who's right, the world or I.

HELMER: Nora, you're sick; you've got a fever. I almost think you're out of your head.

NORA: I've never felt more clearheaded and sure in my life.

HELMER: And — clearheaded and sure — you're leaving your husband and children?

NORA: Yes.

HELMER: Then there's only one possible reason.

NORA: What?

HELMER: You no longer love me.

NORA: No. That's exactly it.

HELMER: Nora! You can't be serious!

NORA: Oh, this is so hard, Torvald — you've been so kind to me always. But I can't help it. I don't love you anymore.

HELMER (*struggling for composure*): Are you also clearheaded and sure about that?

NORA: Yes, completely. That's why I can't go on staying here.

HELMER: Can you tell me what I did to lose your love?

NORA: Yes, I can tell you. It was this evening when the miraculous thing didn't come — then I knew you weren't the man I'd imagined.

HELMER: Be more explicit; I don't follow you.

NORA: I've waited now so patiently eight long years — for, my Lord, I know miracles don't come every day. Then this crisis broke over me, and such a certainty filled me: *Now* the miraculous event would occur. While Krogstad's letter was lying out there, I never for an instant dreamed that you could give in to his terms. I was so utterly sure you'd say to him: Go on, tell your tale to the whole wide world. And when he'd done that —

HELMER: Yes, what then? When I'd delivered my own wife into shame and disgrace —!

NORA: When he'd done that, I was so utterly sure that you'd step forward, take the blame on yourself and say: I am the guilty one.

HELMER: Nora —!

NORA: You're thinking I'd never accept such a sacrifice from you? No, of course not. But what good would my protests be against you? That was the miracle I was waiting for, in terror and hope. And to stave that off, I would have taken my life.

HELMER: I'd gladly work for you day and night, Nora — and take on pain and deprivation. But there's no one who gives up honor for love.

NORA: Millions of women have done just that.

HELMER: Oh, you think and talk like a silly child.

NORA: Perhaps. But you neither think nor talk like the man I could join myself to. When your big fright was over — and it wasn't from any threat against me, only for what might damage you — when all the danger was past, for you it was just as if nothing had happened. I was exactly the same, your little lark, your doll, that you'd have to handle with double care now that I'd turned out so brittle and frail. (*Gets up.*) Torvald — in that instant it dawned on me that for eight years I've been living here with a stranger, and that I'd even conceived three children — oh, I can't stand the thought of it! I could tear myself to bits.

HELMER (*heavily*): I see. There's a gulf that's opened between us — that's clear. Oh, but Nora, can't we bridge it somehow?

NORA: The way I am now, I'm no wife for you.

HELMER: I have the strength to make myself over.

NORA: Maybe — if your doll gets taken away.

HELMER: But to part! To part from you! No, Nora, no — I can't imagine it.

NORA (*going out, right*): All the more reason why it has to be. (*She reenters with her coat and a small overnight bag, which she puts on a chair by the table.*)

HELMER: Nora, Nora, not now! Wait till tomorrow.

NORA: I can't spend the night in a strange man's room.

HELMER: But couldn't we live here like brother and sister —

NORA: You know very well how long that would last. (*Throws her shawl about her.*) Good-bye, Torvald. I won't look in on the children. I know they're in better hands than mine. The way I am now, I'm no use to them.

HELMER: But someday, Nora — someday —?

NORA: How can I tell? I haven't the least idea what'll become of me.

HELMER: But you're my wife, now and wherever you go.

NORA: Listen, Torvald — I've heard that when a wife deserts her husband's house just as I'm doing, then the law frees him from all responsibility. In any case, I'm freeing you from being responsible. Don't feel yourself bound, any more than I will. There has to be absolute freedom for us both. Here, take your ring back. Give me mine.

HELMER: That too?

NORA: That too.

HELMER: There it is.

NORA: Good. Well, now it's all over. I'm putting the keys here. The maids know all about keeping up the house — better than I do. Tomorrow, after I've left town, Kristine will stop by to pack up everything that's mine from home. I'd like those things shipped up to me.

HELMER: Over! All over! Nora, won't you ever think about me?

NORA: I'm sure I'll think of you often, and about the children and the house here.

HELMER: May I write you?

NORA: No — never. You're not to do that.

HELMER: Oh, but let me send you —

NORA: Nothing. Nothing.

HELMER: Or help you if you need it.

NORA: No. I accept nothing from strangers.

HELMER: Nora — can I never be more than a stranger to you?

NORA (*picking up the overnight bag*): Ah, Torvald — it would take the greatest miracle of all —

HELMER: Tell me the greatest miracle!

NORA: You and I both would have to transform ourselves to the point that — Oh, Torvald, I've stopped believing in miracles.

HELMER: But I'll believe. Tell me! Transform ourselves to the point that —?

NORA: That our living together could be a true marriage. (*She goes out down the hall.*)

HELMER (*sinks down on a chair by the door, face buried in his hands*): Nora! Nora! (*Looking about and rising.*) Empty. She's gone. (*A sudden hope leaps in him.*) The greatest miracle —?

(*From below, the sound of a door slamming shut.*)

HEDDA GABLER

Hedda Gabler (1890) is today Ibsen's most produced and perhaps his most respected play. But when it was first performed, it provoked a more uniformly negative response than any of his other plays. Critics were alarmed at the depressing environment that Ibsen created, and some Scandinavians were especially annoyed by the sense that Ibsen was condemning their entire society. The critics denounced the play "as a base escape of moral sewage gas" and Hedda herself as "acrawl with the foulest passions of humanity."

Hedda Gabler is an intense, powerful woman living in a world totally dominated by men. She is herself dominated by her memory of her father, the General, a man of action whose pistols she now uses to amuse herself. What she enjoys is something of the General's prerogative: the shaping of the destiny of men, especially the manner of their death. But her rejection of anything she deems bourgeois, including sex, which seems to repulse her, drives her to reject the baby she may or may not be about to have and to lure Eilert Løvborg to her only to destroy him.

She wants to be an independent woman just as her father was independent and free. She chooses marriage not because she wants to give herself to George Tesman but because she anticipates, on the strength of his expectations of a professorship, a life of comfort and influence. The play opens on Hedda's return from her wedding trip abroad, with the question of whether or not she is pregnant. Hedda is not interested in children or domesticity. We realize that Hedda and Tesman's marriage is bound for failure, but Tesman cannot see the truth about her.

Eilert Løvborg, Hedda's friend before she married, is also Tesman's professional rival. Løvborg has the fire and genius needed to be truly distinguished — unlike Tesman, who is most comfortable gathering material for other people's books. But Løvborg is intemperate. He does everything to excess, including drinking. Hedda drives Løvborg to drink after he has been "renovated" by her friend Mrs. Elvsted. This is only one way in which Hedda's cruelty is revealed. She abuses the innocent Aunt Julia and actually burns Løvborg's book because it was created in part by Mrs. Elvsted and is therefore their "baby."

Hedda is a frustrated woman who cannot satisfy herself in the stifling society she hoped to dominate. To ensure that Løvborg commits suicide in an elegant, romantic way, she gives him one of the General's pistols, but her dreams for a romantic shot in the temple are shattered when Judge Brack reveals that Løvborg actually died miserably in a brothel from a pistol discharging into his "stomach — more or less."

Hedda watches on as Mrs. Elvsted and Tesman team up to rewrite Løvborg's lost book, and when she turns from them she discovers that she has lost all her independence. Judge Brack knows about the pistol, and it is clear that the price of silence is her becoming his mistress.

Hedda's fate has been variously interpreted. Is she a worthwhile character? Is her behavior excusable because she is a woman in a society that will value her not for what she can do but only for who she is? Is her fate determined by the fact that as a woman she cannot live the life she knows she should? Hedda does some frightful things in the play, but how are we to take her? She is clearly larger than anyone else in the play, and certainly more interesting. The men are all weak: Tesman is tied to his aunt's apron strings; Løvborg cannot control himself; and Brack is corrupt. Mrs. Elvsted is a sympathetic character, but her ambition is to be nothing more than a helpmate. None of these fates would satisfy Hedda, and so she takes the action she does at the end of the play.

The sense in which this is a realistic play is qualified by Ibsen's adherence to most of the standards of classical theater. The characters, plot, and setting are established according to the Scribean principles of the well-made play, and the effort to maintain a sense that the play is a "slice of life" seems minimal. The play is structured in four acts, and its rhythms resemble those of a tragedy. There is no attempt to raise issues that are especially shocking to the society or the audiences, as Ibsen had done, for instance, in dealing with syphilis in his play *Ghosts*.

The way we are to interpret Hedda is complicated by some facts that we know about the composition of the play. When Ibsen was writing it, he was himself an unfulfilled husband, with a profoundly repressed sex life. But he was also famous and as a result attracted a great many young women who were interested in him sexually. One of these, Emilie Bardach, age eighteen, fell in love with him, and he with her. They agreed to go off together, but soon Ibsen had second thoughts. He was afraid to take the chance of happiness when it was finally offered.

Ibsen's biographer, Michael Meyer, in a commentary on the play refers to Hedda Gabler as "a merciless self-portrait of Ibsen in skirts." The psychologist Arne Duve has argued that Hedda is a portrait of Ibsen's "repressed and crippled emotional life." Whether this biographical interpretation is fully warranted is difficult to say, but if it is true, then the character of Hedda and our interpretation of the play are intensely complicated.

Hedda Gabler in Performance

Hedda Gabler debuted in Munich in January 1891 and then played elsewhere in Germany, Scandinavia, and England that year. However, it was not received well. The public and the press called the play incoherent and unpleasant, feeling Hedda to be evil. The French audiences jeered the first performances in Paris. The play withstood its unfavorable reception and was eventually a worldwide success. In February 1899 the great theorist of acting Konstantin Stanislavsky played the part of Løvborg in the Moscow Arts Theatre's first production of an Ibsen play.

Blanche Bates first played Hedda Gabler in the United States in Philadelphia in 1904, and the reviews read as if they deplored a real woman when they spoke about Hedda's "degeneracy." Its performance in New York in 1918 met with critical attacks and the accusation that it was essentially meaningless. Critical taste changed, however, and by 1948 it was praised because it proved itself resistant to being dated or old-fashioned.

Ingmar Bergman's 1968 Stockholm production moved to England in 1970 with Maggie Smith as an "icily aware" Hedda. Bergman, an eminent filmmaker, divided the stage in two so that characters, especially Hedda, could exit from a scene but linger at a doorway to eavesdrop over the other characters' conversations. One critic said, "At times the drama seems to be taking place in different levels of the mind."

Trevor Nunn's production at the National Theater in Washington, D.C., in 1975 relied on Glenda Jackson as Hedda, but critics complained that she played the part as if it were comedic. No such complaints were raised, however, when Nunn's production was made into a film (1976), which won Jackson a nomination for an Academy Award.

Henrik Ibsen (1828–1906)

HEDDA GABLER   *1890*

TRANSLATED BY ROLF FJELDE

The Characters

GEORGE TESMAN, *research fellow in cultural history*
HEDDA TESMAN, *his wife*
MISS JULIANA TESMAN, *his aunt*
MRS. ELVSTED
JUDGE BRACK
EILERT LØVBORG
BERTA, *the Tesmans' maid*

The action takes place in Tesman's residence in the fashionable part of town.

ACT I

(*A large, attractively furnished drawing room, decorated in dark colors. In the rear wall, a wide doorway with curtains drawn back. The doorway opens into a smaller room in the same style as the drawing room. In the right wall of the front room, a folding door that leads to the hall. In the left wall opposite, a glass door, with curtains similarly drawn back. Through the panes one can see part of an overhanging veranda and trees in autumn colors. In the foreground is an oval table, with tablecloth and chairs around it. By the right wall, a wide, dark porcelain stove, a high-backed armchair, a cushioned footstool, and two taborets.° In the right-hand corner, a settee with a small round table in front. Nearer, on the left and slightly out from the wall, a piano. On either side of the doorway in back, étagères° with terra cotta and majolica ornaments. Against the back wall of the inner room, a sofa, a table, and a couple of chairs can be seen. Above this sofa hangs a portrait of a handsome, elderly man in a general's uniform. Over the table, a hanging lamp with an opalescent glass shade. A number of bouquets of flowers are placed about the drawing room in vases and glasses. Others lie on the tables. The floors in both rooms are covered with thick car-*

taborets: Stools without back or arms.
étagères: Cabinets with shelves.

pets. Morning light. The sun shines in through the glass door.)

(*Miss Juliana Tesman, wearing a hat and carrying a parasol, comes in from the hall, followed by Berta, who holds a bouquet wrapped in paper. Miss Tesman is a lady around sixty-five with a kind and good-natured look, nicely but simply dressed in a gray tailored suit. Berta is a maid somewhat past middle age, with a plain and rather provincial appearance.*)

MISS TESMAN (*stops close by the door, listens, and says softly*): Goodness, I don't think they're even up yet!

BERTA (*also softly*): That's just what I said, Miss Juliana. Remember how late the steamer got in last night. Yes, and afterward! My gracious, how much the young bride had to unpack before she could get to bed.

MISS TESMAN: Well, then — let them enjoy a good rest. But they must have some of this fresh morning air when they do come down. (*She goes to the glass door and opens it wide.*)

BERTA (*by the table, perplexed, with the bouquet in her hand*): I swear there isn't a bit of space left. I think I'll have to put it here, miss. (*Places the bouquet on the piano.*)

MISS TESMAN: So now you have a new mistress, Berta dear. Lord knows it was misery for me to give you up.

BERTA (*on the verge of tears*): And for me, miss! What can I say? All those many blessed years I've been in your service, you and Miss Rina.

MISS TESMAN: We must take it calmly, Berta. There's really nothing else to do. George needs you here in this house, you know that. You've looked after him since he was a little boy.

BERTA: Yes, but miss, I'm all the time thinking of her, lying at home. Poor thing — completely helpless. And with that new maid! She'll never take proper care of an invalid, that one.

MISS TESMAN: Oh, I'll manage to teach her. And most of it, you know, I'll do myself. So you mustn't be worrying over my poor sister.

BERTA: Well, but there's something else too, miss. I'm really so afraid I won't please the young mistress.

MISS TESMAN: Oh, well — there might be something or other at first —

BERTA: Because she's so very particular.

MISS TESMAN: Well, of course. General Gabler's daughter. What a life she had in the general's day! Remember seeing her out with her father — how she'd go galloping past in that long black riding outfit, with a feather in her hat?

BERTA: Oh yes — I remember! But I never would have dreamed then that she and George Tesman would make a match of it.

MISS TESMAN: Nor I either. But now, Berta — before I forget: From now on, you mustn't say George Tesman. You must call him Doctor Tesman.

BERTA: Yes, the young mistress said the same thing — last night, right after they came in the door. Is that true then, miss?

MISS TESMAN: Yes, absolutely. Think of it, Berta — they gave him his doctor's degree. Abroad, that is — on this trip, you know. I hadn't heard one word about it, till he told me down on the pier.

BERTA: Well, he's clever enough to be anything. But I never thought he'd go in for curing people.

MISS TESMAN: No, he wasn't made that kind of doctor. (Nods significantly.) But as a matter of fact, you may soon now have something still greater to call him.

BERTA: Oh, really! What's that, miss?

MISS TESMAN (smiling): Hm, wouldn't you like to know! (Moved.) Ah, dear God — if only my poor brother could look up from his grave and see what his little boy has become! (Glancing about.) But what's this, Berta? Why, you've taken all the slipcovers off the furniture —?

BERTA: Madam told me to. She doesn't like covers on chairs, she said.

MISS TESMAN: Are they going to make this their regular living room, then?

BERTA: It seems so — with her. For his part — the doctor — he said nothing.

(George Tesman enters the inner room from the right, singing to himself and carrying an empty, unstrapped suitcase. He is a youngish-looking man of thirty-three, medium sized, with an open, round, cheerful face, blond hair and beard. He is somewhat carelessly dressed in comfortable lounging clothes.)

MISS TESMAN: Good morning, good morning, George!

TESMAN (in the doorway): Aunt Julie! Dear Aunt Julie! (Goes over and warmly shakes her hand.) Way out here — so early in the day — uh?

MISS TESMAN: Yes, you know I simply had to look in on you a moment.

TESMAN: And that without a decent night's sleep.

MISS TESMAN: Oh, that's nothing at all to me.

TESMAN: Well, then you did get home all right from the pier? Uh?

MISS TESMAN: Why, of course I did — thank goodness. Judge Brack was good enough to see me right to my door.

TESMAN: We were sorry we couldn't drive you up. But you saw for yourself — Hedda had all those boxes to bring along.

MISS TESMAN: Yes, that was quite something, the number of boxes she had.

BERTA (to Tesman): Should I go in and ask Mrs. Tesman if there's anything I can help her with?

TESMAN: No, thanks, Berta — don't bother. She said she'd ring if she needed anything.

BERTA (going off toward the right): All right.

TESMAN: But wait now — you can take this suitcase with you.

BERTA (taking it): I'll put it away in the attic. (She goes out by the hall door.)

TESMAN: Just think, Aunt Julie — I had that whole suitcase stuffed full of notes. You just can't imagine all I've managed to find, rummaging through archives. Marvelous old documents that nobody knew existed —

MISS TESMAN: Yes, you've really not wasted any time on your wedding trip, George.

TESMAN: I certainly haven't. But do take your hat off, Auntie. Here — let me help you — uh?

MISS TESMAN (as he does so): Goodness — this is exactly as if you were still back at home with us.

TESMAN (turning the hat in his hand and studying it from all sides): My — what elegant hats you go in for!

MISS TESMAN: I bought that for Hedda's sake.

TESMAN: For Hedda's sake? Uh?

MISS TESMAN: Yes, so Hedda wouldn't feel ashamed of me if we walked down the street together.

TESMAN (patting her cheek): You think of everything, Aunt Julie! (Laying the hat on a chair by the table.) So — look, suppose we sit down on the sofa and have a little chat till Hedda comes. (They settle themselves. She puts her parasol on the corner of the sofa.)

MISS TESMAN (takes both of his hands and gazes at him): How wonderful it is having you here, right before my eyes again, George! You — dear Jochum's own boy!

TESMAN: And for me too, to see you again, Aunt Julie! You, who've been father and mother to me both.

MISS TESMAN: Yes, I'm sure you'll always keep a place in your heart for your old aunts.

TESMAN: But Auntie Rina — hm? Isn't she any better?

MISS TESMAN: Oh no — we can hardly expect that she'll ever be better, poor thing. She lies there, just as she has all these years. May God let me keep her a little while longer! Because otherwise, George, I don't know what I'd do with my life. The more so now, when I don't have you to look after.

TESMAN (*patting her on the back*): There, there, there —

MISS TESMAN (*suddenly changing her tone*): No, but to think of it, that now you're a married man! And that it was *you* who carried off Hedda Gabler. The beautiful Hedda Gabler! Imagine! She, who always had so many admirers!

TESMAN (*hums a little and smiles complacently*): Yes, I rather suspect I have several friends who'd like to trade places with me.

MISS TESMAN: And then to have such a wedding trip! Five — almost six months —

TESMAN: Well, remember, I used it for research, too. All those libraries I had to check — and so many books to read!

MISS TESMAN: Yes, no doubt. (*More confidentially; lowering her voice.*) But now listen, George — isn't there something — something special you have to tell me?

TESMAN: From the trip?

MISS TESMAN: Yes.

TESMAN: No, I can't think of anything beyond what I wrote in my letters. I got my doctor's degree down there — but I told you that yesterday.

MISS TESMAN: Yes, of course. But I mean — whether you have any kind of — expectations —?

TESMAN: Expectations?

MISS TESMAN: My goodness, George — I'm your old aunt!

TESMAN: Why, naturally I have expectations.

MISS TESMAN: Ah!

TESMAN: I have every expectation in the world of becoming a professor shortly.

MISS TESMAN: Oh, a professor, yes —

TESMAN: Or I might as well say, I'm sure of it. But, Aunt Julie — you know that perfectly well yourself.

MISS TESMAN (*with a little laugh*): That's right, so I do. (*Changing the subject.*) But we were talking about your trip. It must have cost a terrible amount of money.

TESMAN: Well, that big fellowship, you know — it took us a good part of the way.

MISS TESMAN: But I don't see how you could stretch it enough for two.

TESMAN: No, that's not so easy to see — uh?

MISS TESMAN: And especially traveling with a lady. For I hear tell that's much more expensive.

TESMAN: Yes, of course — it's a bit more expensive. But Hedda just had to have that trip. She *had* to. There was nothing else to be done.

MISS TESMAN: No, no, I guess not. A honeymoon abroad seems to be the thing nowadays. But tell me — have you had a good look around your house?

TESMAN: You can bet I have! I've been up since daybreak.

MISS TESMAN: And how does it strike you, all in all?

TESMAN: First-rate! Absolutely first-rate! Only I don't know what we'll do with the two empty rooms between the back parlor and Hedda's bedroom.

MISS TESMAN (*laughing again*): Oh, my dear George, I think you can use them — as time goes on.

TESMAN: Yes, you're quite right about that, Aunt Julie! In time, as I build up my library — uh?

MISS TESMAN: Of course, my dear boy. It was your library I meant.

TESMAN: I'm happiest now for Hedda's sake. Before we were engaged, she used to say so many times there was no place she'd rather live than here, in Secretary Falk's town house.

MISS TESMAN: Yes, and then to have it come on the market just after you'd sailed.

TESMAN: We really have had luck, haven't we?

MISS TESMAN: But expensive, George dear! You'll find it expensive, all this here.

TESMAN (*looks at her, somewhat crestfallen*): Yes, I suppose I will.

MISS TESMAN: Oh, Lord, yes!

TESMAN: How much do you think? Approximately? Hm?

MISS TESMAN: It's impossible to say till the bills are all in.

TESMAN: Well, fortunately Judge Brack has gotten me quite easy terms. That's what he wrote Hedda.

MISS TESMAN: Don't worry yourself about that, dear. I've also put up security to cover the carpets and furniture.

TESMAN: Security? Aunt Julie, dear — you? What kind of security could *you* give?

MISS TESMAN: I took out a mortgage on our pension.

TESMAN (*jumping up*): What! On your — and Auntie Rina's pension!

MISS TESMAN: I saw nothing else to do.

TESMAN (*standing in front of her*): But you're out of your mind, Aunt Julie! That pension — it's all Aunt Rina and you have to live on.

MISS TESMAN: Now, now — don't make so much of it. It's only a formality; Judge Brack said so. He was good enough to arrange the whole thing for me. Just a formality, he said.

TESMAN: That's all well enough. But still —

MISS TESMAN: You'll be drawing your own salary

now. And good gracious, if we have to lay out a bit, just now at the start — why, it's no more than a pleasure for us.

TESMAN: Oh, Aunt Julie — you never get tired of making sacrifices for me!

MISS TESMAN (*rises and places her hands on his shoulders*): What other joy do I have in this world than smoothing the path for you, my dear boy? You, without father or mother to turn to. And now we've come to the goal, George! Things may have looked black at times; but now, thank heaven, you've made it.

TESMAN: Yes, it's remarkable, really, how everything's turned out for the best.

MISS TESMAN: Yes — and those who stood against you — who wanted to bar your way — they've gone down. They've fallen, George. The one most dangerous to you — he fell farthest. And he's lying there now, in the bed he made — poor, misguided creature.

TESMAN: Have you heard any news of Eilert? I mean, since I went away.

MISS TESMAN: Only that he's supposed to have brought out a new book.

TESMAN: What's that? Eilert Løvborg? Just recently, uh?

MISS TESMAN: So they say. But considering everything, it can hardly amount to much. Ah, but when *your* new book comes out — it'll be a different story, George! What will it be about?

TESMAN: It's going to treat the domestic handicrafts of Brabant in the Middle Ages.

MISS TESMAN: Just imagine — that you can write about things like that!

TESMAN: Actually, the book may take quite a while yet. I have this tremendous collection of material to put in order, you know.

MISS TESMAN: Yes, collecting and ordering — you do that so well. You're not my brother's son for nothing.

TESMAN: I look forward so much to getting started. Especially now, with a comfortable home of my own to work in.

MISS TESMAN: And most of all, dear, now that you've won her, the wife of your heart.

TESMAN (*embracing her*): Yes, yes, Aunt Julie! Hedda — that's the most beautiful part of it all! (*Glancing toward the doorway.*) But I think she's coming — uh?

(*Hedda enters from the left through the inner room. She is a woman of twenty-nine. Her face and figure show breeding and distinction; her complexion is pallid and opaque. Her steel gray eyes express a cool,* unruffled calm. *Her hair is an attractive medium brown, but not particularly abundant. She wears a tasteful, rather loose-fitting gown.*)

MISS TESMAN (*going to meet Hedda*): Good morning, Hedda dear — how good to see you!

HEDDA (*holding out her hand*): Good morning, my dear Miss Tesman! Calling so early? This *is* kind of you.

MISS TESMAN (*slightly embarrassed*): Well — did the bride sleep well in her new home?

HEDDA: Oh yes, thanks. Quite adequately.

TESMAN: Adequately! Oh, I like that, Hedda! You were sleeping like a stone when I got up.

HEDDA: Fortunately. But of course one has to grow accustomed to anything new, Miss Tesman — little by little. (*Looking toward the left.*) Oh! That maid has left the door open — and the sunlight's just flooding in.

MISS TESMAN (*going toward the door*): Well, we can close it.

HEDDA: No, no — don't! (*To Tesman.*) There, dear, draw the curtains. It gives a softer light.

TESMAN (*by the glass door*): All right — all right. Look, Hedda — now you have shade and fresh air both.

HEDDA: Yes, we really need some fresh air here, with all these piles of flowers — But — won't you sit down, Miss Tesman?

MISS TESMAN: Oh no, thank you. Now that I know that everything's fine — thank goodness — I will have to run along home. My sister's lying there waiting, poor thing.

TESMAN: Give her my very, very best, won't you? And say I'll be looking in on her later today.

MISS TESMAN: Oh, you can be sure I will. But what do you know, George — (*Searching in her bag.*) — I nearly forgot. I have something here for you.

TESMAN: What's that, Aunt Julie? Hm?

MISS TESMAN (*brings out a flat package wrapped in newspaper and hands it to him*): There, dear. Look.

TESMAN (*opening it*): Oh, my — you kept them for me, Aunt Julie! Hedda! That's really touching! Uh?

HEDDA (*by the* étagère *on the right*): Yes, dear, what is it?

TESMAN: My old bedroom slippers! My slippers!

HEDDA: Oh yes. I remember how often you spoke of them during the trip.

TESMAN: Yes, I missed them terribly. (*Going over to her.*) Now you can see them, Hedda!

HEDDA (*moves toward the stove*): Thanks, but I really don't care to.

TESMAN (*following her*): Imagine — Auntie Rina lay and embroidered them, sick as she was. Oh, you couldn't believe how many memories are bound up in them.

HEDDA (*at the table*): But not for me.

MISS TESMAN: I think Hedda is right, George.

TESMAN: Yes, but I only thought, now that she's part of the family —

HEDDA (*interrupting*): We're never going to manage with this maid, Tesman.

MISS TESMAN: Not manage with Berta?

TESMAN: But dear — why do you say that? Uh?

HEDDA (*pointing*): See there! She's left her old hat lying out on a chair.

TESMAN (*shocked; dropping the slippers*): But Hedda —!

HEDDA: Suppose someone came in and saw it.

TESMAN: Hedda — that's Aunt Julie's hat!

HEDDA: Really?

MISS TESMAN (*picking it up*): That's right, it's mine. And what's more, it certainly is not old — Mrs. Tesman.

HEDDA: I really hadn't looked closely at it, Miss Tesman.

MISS TESMAN (*putting on the hat*): It's actually the first time I've had it on. The very first time.

TESMAN: And it's lovely, too. Most attractive!

MISS TESMAN: Oh, it's hardly all that, George. (*Looks about.*) My parasol —? Ah, here. (*Takes it.*) For that's mine too. (*Murmurs.*) Not Berta's.

TESMAN: New hat and new parasol! Just imagine, Hedda!

HEDDA: Quite charming, really.

TESMAN: Yes, aren't they, huh? But Auntie, take a good look at Hedda before you leave. See how charming *she* is!

MISS TESMAN: But George dear, there's nothing new in that. Hedda's been lovely all her life. (*She nods and starts out, right.*)

TESMAN (*following her*): But have you noticed how plump and buxom she's grown? How much she's filled out on the trip?

HEDDA (*crossing the room*): Oh, do be quiet —!

MISS TESMAN (*who has stopped and turned*): Filled out?

TESMAN: Of course, you can't see it so well when she has that dressing gown on. But I, who have the opportunity to —

HEDDA (*by the glass door, impatiently*): Oh, you have no opportunity for anything!

TESMAN: It must have been the mountain air, down in the Tyrol —

HEDDA (*brusquely interrupting*): I'm exactly as I was when I left.

TESMAN: Yes, that's your claim. But you certainly are not. Auntie, don't you agree?

MISS TESMAN (*gazing at her with folded hands*): Hedda is lovely — lovely — lovely. (*Goes up to her, takes her head in both hands, bends it down and kisses her hair.*) God bless and keep Hedda Tesman — for George's sake.

HEDDA (*gently freeing herself*): Oh —! Let me go.

MISS TESMAN (*with quiet feeling*): I won't let a day go by without looking in on you two.

TESMAN: Yes, please do that, Aunt Julie! Uh?

MISS TESMAN: Good-bye — good-bye!

(*She goes out by the hall door. Tesman accompanies her, leaving the door half open. He can be heard reiterating his greetings to Aunt Rina and his thanks for the slippers. At the same time, Hedda moves about the room, raising her arms and clenching her fists as if in a frenzy. Then she flings back the curtains from the glass door and stands there, looking out. A moment later Tesman comes back, closing the door after him.*)

TESMAN (*retrieving the slippers from the floor*): What are you standing and looking at, Hedda?

HEDDA (*again calm and controlled*): I'm just looking at the leaves — they're so yellow — and so withered.

TESMAN (*wraps up the slippers and puts them on the table*): Yes, well, we're into September now.

HEDDA (*once more restless*): Yes, to think — that already we're in — in September.

TESMAN: Didn't Aunt Julie seem a bit strange? A little — almost formal? What do you suppose was bothering her? Hm?

HEDDA: I hardly know her at all. Isn't that how she usually is?

TESMAN: No, not like this, today.

HEDDA (*leaving the glass door*): Do you think this thing with the hat upset her?

TESMAN: Oh, not very much. A little, just at the moment, perhaps —

HEDDA: But really, what kind of manners has she — to go throwing her hat about in a drawing room! It's just not proper.

TESMAN: Well, you can be sure Aunt Julie won't do it again.

HEDDA: Anyhow, I'll manage to smooth it over with her.

TESMAN: Yes, Hedda dear, I wish you would!

HEDDA: When you go in to see them later on, you might ask her out for the evening.

TESMAN: Yes, I'll do that. And there's something else you could do that would make her terribly happy.

HEDDA: Oh?

TESMAN: If only you could bring yourself to speak to

her warmly, by her first name. For my sake, Hedda? Uh?

HEDDA: No, no — don't ask me to do that. I told you this once before. I'll try to call her "Aunt." That should be enough.

TESMAN: Oh, all right. I was only thinking, now that you belong to the family —

HEDDA: Hm — I really don't know — (*She crosses the room to the doorway.*)

TESMAN (*after a pause*): Is something the matter, Hedda? Uh?

HEDDA: I'm just looking at my old piano. It doesn't really fit in with all these other things.

TESMAN: With the first salary I draw, we can see about trading it in on a new one.

HEDDA: No, not traded in. I don't want to part with it. We can put it there, in the inner room, and get another here in its place. When there's a chance, I mean.

TESMAN (*slightly cast down*): Yes, we could do that, of course.

HEDDA (*picks up the bouquet from the piano*): These flowers weren't here when we got in last night.

TESMAN: Aunt Julie must have brought them for you.

HEDDA (*examining the bouquet*): A visiting card. (*Takes it out and reads it.*) "Will stop back later today." Can you guess who this is from?

TESMAN: No. Who? Hm?

HEDDA: It says, "Mrs. Elvsted."

TESMAN: No, really? Sheriff Elvsted's wife. Miss Rysing, she used to be.

HEDDA: Exactly. The one with the irritating hair that she was always showing off. An old flame of yours, I've heard.

TESMAN (*laughing*): Oh, that wasn't for long. And it was before I knew you, Hedda. But imagine — that she's here in town.

HEDDA: It's odd that she calls on us. I've hardly seen her since we were in school.

TESMAN: Yes, I haven't seen her either — since God knows when. I wonder how she can stand living in such an out-of-the-way place. Hm?

HEDDA (*thinks a moment, then bursts out*): But wait — isn't it somewhere up in those parts that he — that Eilert Løvborg lives?

TESMAN: Yes, it's someplace right around there. (*Berta enters by the hall door.*)

BERTA: She's back again, ma'am — that lady who stopped by and left the flowers an hour ago. (*Pointing.*) The ones you have in your hand, ma'am.

HEDDA: Oh, is she? Good. Would you ask her to come in.

(*Berta opens the door for Mrs. Elvsted and goes out. Mrs. Elvsted is a slender woman with soft, pretty*

features. Her eyes are light blue, large, round, and somewhat prominent, with a startled, questioning look. Her hair is remarkably light, almost a white-gold, and unusually abundant and wavy. She is a couple of years younger than Hedda. She wears a dark visiting dress, tasteful, but not quite in the latest fashion.)

HEDDA (*going to greet her warmly*): Good morning, my dear Mrs. Elvsted. How delightful to see you again!

MRS. ELVSTED (*nervously; struggling to control herself*): Yes, it's a very long time since we last met.

TESMAN (*gives her his hand*): Or since *we* met, uh?

HEDDA: Thank you for your beautiful flowers —

MRS. ELVSTED: Oh, that's nothing — I would have come straight out here yesterday afternoon, but then I heard you weren't at home —

TESMAN: Have you just now come to town? Uh?

MRS. ELVSTED: I got in yesterday toward noon. Oh, I was in desperation when I heard that you weren't at home.

HEDDA: Desperation! Why?

TESMAN: But my dear Mrs. Rysing — Mrs. Elvsted, I mean —

HEDDA: You're not in some kind of trouble?

MRS. ELVSTED: Yes, I am. And I don't know another living soul down here I can turn to.

HEDDA (*putting the bouquet down on the table*): Come, then — let's sit here on the sofa —

MRS. ELVSTED: Oh, I can't sit down. I'm really too much on edge!

HEDDA: Why, of course you can. Come here.

(*She draws Mrs. Elvsted down on the sofa and sits beside her.*)

TESMAN: Well? What is it, Mrs. Elvsted?

HEDDA: Has anything particular happened at home?

MRS. ELVSTED: Yes, that's both it — and not it. Oh, I do want so much that you don't misunderstand me —

HEDDA: But then the best thing, Mrs. Elvsted, is simply to speak your mind.

TESMAN: Because I suppose that's why you've come. Hm?

MRS. ELVSTED: Oh yes, that's why. Well, then, I have to tell you — if you don't already know — that Eilert Løvborg's also in town.

HEDDA: Løvborg —!

TESMAN: What! Is Eilert Løvborg back! Just think, Hedda!

HEDDA: Good Lord, I can hear.

MRS. ELVSTED: He's been back all of a week's time

now. A whole week — in this dangerous town! Alone! With all the bad company that's around.

HEDDA: But my dear Mrs. Elvsted, what does *he* have to do with you?

MRS. ELVSTED (*glances anxiously at her and says quickly*): He was the children's tutor.

HEDDA: Your children's?

MRS. ELVSTED: My husband's. I have none.

HEDDA: Your stepchildren's, then.

MRS. ELVSTED: Yes.

TESMAN (*somewhat hesitantly*): But was he — I don't know quite how to put it — was he sufficiently — responsible in his habits for such a job? Uh?

MRS. ELVSTED: In these last two years, there wasn't a word to be said against him.

TESMAN: Not a word? Just think of that, Hedda!

HEDDA: I heard it.

MRS. ELVSTED: Not even a murmur, I can assure you! Nothing. But anyway — now that I know he's here — in this big city — and with so much money in his hands — then I'm just frightened to death for him.

TESMAN: But why didn't he stay up there where he was? With you and your husband? Uh?

MRS. ELVSTED: After the book came out, he just couldn't rest content with us.

TESMAN: Yes, that's right — Aunt Julie was saying he'd published a new book.

MRS. ELVSTED: Yes, a great new book, on the course of civilization — in all its stages. It's been out two weeks. And now it's been bought and read so much — and it's made a tremendous stir —

TESMAN: Has it really? It must be something he's had lying around from his better days.

MRS. ELVSTED: Years back, you mean?

TESMAN: I suppose.

MRS. ELVSTED: No, he's written it all up there with us. Now — in this last year.

TESMAN: That's marvelous to hear. Hedda! Just imagine!

MRS. ELVSTED: Yes, if only it can go on like this!

HEDDA: Have you seen him here in town?

MRS. ELVSTED: No, not yet. I had such trouble finding out his address. But this morning I got it at last.

HEDDA (*looks searchingly at her*): I must say it seems rather odd of your husband —

MRS. ELVSTED (*with a nervous start*): Of my husband —! What?

HEDDA: To send you to town on this sort of errand. Not to come and look after his friend himself.

MRS. ELVSTED: No, no, my husband hasn't the time for that. And then I had — some shopping to do.

HEDDA (*with a slight smile*): Oh, that's different.

MRS. ELVSTED (*getting up quickly and uneasily*): I beg you, please, Mr. Tesman — be good to Eilert Løvborg if he comes to you. And he will, I'm sure. You know — you were such good friends in the old days. And you're both doing the same kind of work. The same type of research — from what I can gather.

TESMAN: We were once, at any rate.

MRS. ELVSTED: Yes, and that's why I'm asking you, please — you too — to keep an eye on him. Oh, you will do that, Mr. Tesman — promise me that?

TESMAN: I'll be only too glad to, Mrs. Rysing —

HEDDA: Elvsted.

TESMAN: I'll certainly do everything in my power for Eilert. You can depend on that.

MRS. ELVSTED: Oh, how terribly kind of you! (*Pressing his hands.*) Many, many thanks! (*Frightened.*) He means so much to my husband, you know.

HEDDA (*rising*): You ought to write him, dear. He might not come by on his own.

TESMAN: Yes, that probably would be the best, Hedda? Hm?

HEDDA: And the sooner the better. Right now, I'd say.

MRS. ELVSTED (*imploringly*): Oh yes, if you could!

TESMAN: I'll write him this very moment. Have you got his address, Mrs. — Mrs. Elvsted?

MRS. ELVSTED: Yes. (*Takes a slip of paper from her pocket and hands it to him.*) Here it is.

TESMAN: Good, good. Then I'll go in — (*Looking about.*) But wait — my slippers? Ah! Here. (*Takes the package and starts to leave.*)

HEDDA: Write him a really warm, friendly letter. Nice and long, too.

TESMAN: Don't worry, I will.

MRS. ELVSTED: But please, not a word that I asked you to!

TESMAN: No, that goes without saying. Uh? (*Leaves by the inner room, to the right.*)

HEDDA (*goes over to Mrs. Elvsted, smiles, and speaks softly*): How's that! Now we've killed two birds with one stone.

MRS. ELVSTED: What do you mean?

HEDDA: Didn't you see that I wanted him out of the room?

MRS. ELVSTED: Yes, to write the letter —

HEDDA: But also to talk with you alone.

MRS. ELVSTED (*confused*): About this same thing?

HEDDA: Precisely.

MRS. ELVSTED (*upset*): But Mrs. Tesman, there's nothing more to say! Nothing!

HEDDA: Oh yes, but there is. There's a great deal more — I can see that. Come, sit here — and let's speak openly now, the two of us. (*She forces Mrs. Elvsted down into the armchair by the stove and sits on one of the taborets.*)

MRS. ELVSTED (*anxiously glancing at her watch*): But Mrs. Tesman, dear — I was just planning to leave.

HEDDA: Oh, you can't be in such a rush — Now! Tell me a little about how things are going at home.

MRS. ELVSTED: Oh, that's the last thing I'd ever want to discuss.

HEDDA: But with me, dear —? After all, we were in school together.

MRS. ELVSTED: Yes, but you were a class ahead of me. Oh, I was terribly afraid of you then!

HEDDA: Afraid of me?

MRS. ELVSTED: Yes, terribly. Because whenever we met on the stairs, you'd always pull my hair.

HEDDA: Did I really?

MRS. ELVSTED: Yes, and once you said you would burn it off.

HEDDA: Oh, that was just foolish talk, you know.

MRS. ELVSTED: Yes, but I was so stupid then. And, anyway, since then — we've drifted so far — far apart from each other. We've moved in such different circles.

HEDDA: Well, let's try now to come closer again. Listen, at school we were quite good friends, and we called each other by our first names —

MRS. ELVSTED: No, I'm sure you're mistaken.

HEDDA: Oh, I couldn't be! I remember it clearly. And that's why we have to be perfectly open, just as we were. (*Moves the stool nearer Mrs. Elvsted.*) There now! (*Kissing her cheek.*) You have to call me Hedda.

MRS. ELVSTED (*pressing and patting her hands*): Oh, you're so good and kind —! It's not at all what I'm used to.

HEDDA: There, there! And I'm going to call you my own dear Thora.

MRS. ELVSTED: My name is Thea.

HEDDA: Oh yes, of course. I meant Thea. (*Looks at her compassionately.*) So you're not much used to goodness or kindness, Thea? In your own home?

MRS. ELVSTED: If only I had a home! But I don't. I never have.

HEDDA (*glances quickly at her*): I thought it had to be something like that.

MRS. ELVSTED (*gazing helplessly into space*): Yes — yes — yes.

HEDDA: I can't quite remember now — but wasn't it as a housekeeper that you first came up to the Elvsteds?

MRS. ELVSTED: Actually as a governess. But his wife — his first wife — she was an invalid and mostly kept to her bed. So I had to take care of the house too.

HEDDA: But finally you became mistress of the house yourself.

MRS. ELVSTED (*heavily*): Yes, I did.

HEDDA: Let me see — about how long ago was that?

MRS. ELVSTED: That I was married?

HEDDA: Yes.

MRS. ELVSTED: It's five years now.

HEDDA: That's right. It must be.

MRS. ELVSTED: Oh, these five years —! Or the last two or three, anyway. Oh, if you only knew, Mrs. Tesman —

HEDDA (*gives her hand a little slap*): Mrs. Tesman! Now, Thea!

MRS. ELVSTED: I'm sorry; I'll try — Yes, if you could only understand — Hedda —

HEDDA (*casually*): Eilert Løvborg has lived up there about three years too, hasn't he?

MRS. ELVSTED (*looks at her doubtfully*): Eilert Løvborg? Yes — he has.

HEDDA: Had you already known him here in town?

MRS. ELVSTED: Hardly at all. Well, I mean — by name, of course.

HEDDA: But up there — I suppose he'd visit you both?

MRS. ELVSTED: Yes, he came to see us every day. He was tutoring the children, you know. Because, in the long run, I couldn't do it all myself.

HEDDA: No, that's obvious. And your husband —? I suppose he often has to be away?

MRS. ELVSTED: Yes, you can imagine, as sheriff, how much traveling he does around in the district.

HEDDA (*leaning against the chair arm*): Thea — my poor, sweet Thea — now you must tell me everything — just as it is.

MRS. ELVSTED: Well, then you have to ask the questions.

HEDDA: What sort of man is your husband, Thea? I mean — you know — to be with. Is he good to you?

MRS. ELVSTED (*evasively*): He believes he does everything for the best.

HEDDA: I only think he must be much too old for you. More than twenty years older, isn't he?

MRS. ELVSTED (*irritated*): That's true. Along with everything else. I just can't stand him! We haven't a single thought in common. Nothing at all — he and I.

HEDDA: But doesn't he care for you all the same — in his own way?

MRS. ELVSTED: Oh, I don't know what he feels. I'm no more than useful to him. And then it doesn't cost much to keep me. I'm inexpensive.

HEDDA: That's stupid of you.

MRS. ELVSTED (*shaking her head*): It can't be otherwise. Not with him. He really doesn't care for anyone but himself — and maybe a little for the children.

HEDDA: And for Eilert Løvborg, Thea.

MRS. ELVSTED (*looking at her*): Eilert Løvborg! Why do you think so?

HEDDA: But my dear — it seems to me, when he sends you all the way into town to look after him — (*Smiles almost imperceptibly.*) Besides, it's what you told my husband.

MRS. ELVSTED (*with a little nervous shudder*): Really? Yes, I suppose I did. (*In a quiet outburst.*) No — I might as well tell you here and now! It's bound to come out in time.

HEDDA: But my dear Thea —?

MRS. ELVSTED: All right, then! My husband never knew I was coming here.

HEDDA: What! Your husband never knew —

MRS. ELVSTED: Of course not. Anyway, he wasn't at home. Off traveling somewhere. Oh, I couldn't bear it any longer, Hedda. It was impossible! I would have been so alone up there now.

HEDDA: Well? What then?

MRS. ELVSTED: So I packed a few of my things together — the barest necessities — without saying a word. And I slipped away from the house.

HEDDA: Right then and there?

MRS. ELVSTED: Yes, and took the train straight into town.

HEDDA: But my dearest girl — that you could dare to do such a thing!

MRS. ELVSTED (*rising and walking about the room*): What else could I possibly do!

HEDDA: But what do you think your husband will say when you go back home?

MRS. ELVSTED (*by the table, looking at her*): Back to *him*?

HEDDA: Yes, of course.

MRS. ELVSTED: I'll never go back to him.

HEDDA (*rising and approaching her*): You mean you've left, in dead earnest, for good?

MRS. ELVSTED: Yes. There didn't seem anything else to do.

HEDDA: But — to go away so openly.

MRS. ELVSTED: Oh, you can't keep a thing like that secret.

HEDDA: But what do you think people will say about you, Thea?

MRS. ELVSTED: God knows they'll say what they please. (*Sitting wearily and sadly on the sofa.*) I only did what I had to do.

HEDDA (*after a short silence*): What do you plan on now? What kind of work?

MRS. ELVSTED: I don't know yet. I only know I have to live here, where Eilert Løvborg is — if I'm going to live at all.

HEDDA (*moves a chair over from the table, sits beside her, and strokes her hands*): Thea dear — how did this — this friendship — between you and Eilert Løvborg come about?

MRS. ELVSTED: Oh, it happened little by little. I got some kind of power, almost, over him.

HEDDA: Really?

MRS. ELVSTED: He gave up his old habits. Not because I'd asked him to. I never dared do that. But he could tell they upset me, and so he dropped them.

HEDDA (*hiding an involuntary, scornful smile*): My dear little Thea — just as they say — you rehabilitated him.

MRS. ELVSTED: Well, he says so, at any rate. And he — on his part — he's made a real human being out of me. Taught me to think — and understand so many things.

HEDDA: You mean he tutored you also?

MRS. ELVSTED: No, not exactly. But he'd talk to me — talk endlessly on about one thing after another. And then came the wonderful, happy time when I could share in his work! When I could help him!

HEDDA: Could you really?

MRS. ELVSTED: Yes! Whenever he wrote anything, we'd always work on it together.

HEDDA: Like two true companions.

MRS. ELVSTED (*eagerly*): Companions! You know, Hedda — that's what he said too! Oh, I ought to feel so happy — but I can't. I just don't know if it's going to last.

HEDDA: You're no more sure of him than that?

MRS. ELVSTED (*despondently*): There's a woman's shadow between Eilert Løvborg and me.

HEDDA (*looks at her intently*): Who could that be?

MRS. ELVSTED: I don't know. Someone out of his — his past. Someone he's really never forgotten.

HEDDA: What has he said — about this!

MRS. ELVSTED: It's only once — and just vaguely — that he touched on it.

HEDDA: Well! And what did he say!

MRS. ELVSTED: He said that when they broke off she was going to shoot him with a pistol.

HEDDA (*with cold constraint*): That's nonsense! Nobody behaves that way around here.

MRS. ELVSTED: No. And that's why I think it must have been that redheaded singer that at one time he —

HEDDA: Yes, quite likely.

MRS. ELVSTED: I remember they used to say about her that she carried loaded weapons.

HEDDA: Ah — then of course it must have been her.

MRS. ELVSTED (*wringing her hands*): But you know what, Hedda — I've heard that this singer — that she's in town again! Oh, it has me out of my mind —

HEDDA (*glancing toward the inner room*): Shh! Tesman's coming. (*Gets up and whispers.*) Thea — keep all this just between us.

MRS. ELVSTED (*jumping up*): Oh yes! In heaven's name —!

(*George Tesman, with a letter in his hand, enters from the right through the inner room.*)

TESMAN: There, now — the letter's signed and sealed.

HEDDA: That's fine. I think Mrs. Elvsted was just

leaving. Wait a minute. I'll go with you to the garden gate.

TESMAN: Hedda, dear — could Berta maybe look after this?

HEDDA (*taking the letter*): I'll tell her to.

(*Berta enters from the hall.*)

BERTA: Judge Brack is here and says he'd like to greet you and the Doctor, ma'am.

HEDDA: Yes, ask Judge Brack to come in. And, here — put this letter in the mail.

BERTA (*takes the letter*): Yes, ma'am.

(*She opens the door for Judge Brack and goes out. Brack is a man of forty-five, thickset, yet well built, with supple movements. His face is roundish, with a distinguished profile. His hair is short, still mostly black, and carefully groomed. His eyes are bright and lively. Thick eyebrows; a mustache to match, with neatly clipped ends. He wears a trimly tailored walking suit, a bit too youthful for his age. Uses a monocle, which he now and then lets fall.*)

JUDGE BRACK (*hat in hand, bowing*): May one dare to call so early?

HEDDA: Of course one may.

TESMAN (*shakes his hand*): You're always welcome here. (*Introducing him.*) Judge Brack — Miss Rysing —

HEDDA: Ah —!

BRACK (*bowing*): I'm delighted.

HEDDA (*looks at him and laughs*): It's really a treat to see you by daylight, Judge!

BRACK: You find me — changed?

HEDDA: Yes. A bit younger, I think.

BRACK: Thank you, most kindly.

TESMAN: But what do you say for Hedda, uh? Doesn't she look flourishing? She's actually —

HEDDA: Oh, leave me out of it! You might thank Judge Brack for all the trouble he's gone to —

BRACK: Nonsense — it was a pleasure —

HEDDA: Yes, you're a true friend. But here's Thea, standing here, aching to get away. Excuse me, Judge; I'll be right back.

(*Mutual good-byes. Mrs. Elvsted and Hedda go out by the hall door.*)

BRACK: So — is your wife fairly well satisfied, then —?

TESMAN: Yes, we can't thank you enough. Of course — I gather there's some rearrangement called for here and there. And one or two things are lacking. We still have to buy a few minor items.

BRACK: Really?

TESMAN: But that's nothing for you to worry about.

Hedda said she'd pick up those things herself. Why don't we sit down, hm?

BRACK: Thanks. Just for a moment. (*Sits by the table.*) There's something I'd like to discuss with you, Tesman.

TESMAN: What? Oh, I understand! (*Sitting.*) It's the serious part of the banquet we're coming to, uh?

BRACK: Oh, as far as money matters go, there's no great rush — though I must say I wish we'd managed things a bit more economically.

TESMAN: But that was completely impossible! Think about Hedda, Judge! You, who know her so well — I simply couldn't have her live like a grocer's wife.

BRACK: No, no — that's the trouble, exactly.

TESMAN: And then — fortunately — it can't be long before I get my appointment.

BRACK: Well, you know — these things can often hang fire.

TESMAN: Have you heard something further? Hm?

BRACK: Nothing really definite — (*Changing the subject.*) But incidentally — I do have one piece of news for you.

TESMAN: Well?

BRACK: Your old friend Eilert Løvborg is back in town.

TESMAN: I already know.

BRACK: Oh? How did you hear?

TESMAN: She told me. The lady that left with Hedda.

BRACK: I see. What was her name again? I didn't quite catch it —

TESMAN: Mrs. Elvsted.

BRACK: Aha — Sheriff Elvsted's wife. Yes — it's up near them he's been staying.

TESMAN: And, just think — what a pleasure to hear that he's completely stable again!

BRACK: Yes, that's what they claim.

TESMAN: And that he's published a new book, uh?

BRACK: Oh yes!

TESMAN: And it's created quite a sensation.

BRACK: An extraordinary sensation.

TESMAN: Just imagine — isn't that marvelous? He, with his remarkable talents — I was so very afraid that he'd really gone down for good.

BRACK: That's what everyone thought.

TESMAN: But I've no idea what he'll find to do now. How on earth can he ever make a living? Hm?

(*During the last words, Hedda comes in by the hall door.*)

HEDDA (*to Brack, laughing, with a touch of scorn*): Tesman always goes around worrying about how people are going to make a living.

TESMAN: My Lord — it's poor Eilert Løvborg we're talking of, dear.

HEDDA (*glancing quickly at him*): Oh, really? (*Sits in the armchair by the stove and asks casually.*) What's the matter with him?

TESMAN: Well — he must have run through his inheritance long ago. And he can't write a new book every year. Uh? So I was asking, really, what's going to become of him.

BRACK: Perhaps I can shed some light on that.

TESMAN: Oh?

BRACK: You must remember that he does have relatives with a great deal of influence.

TESMAN: Yes, but they've washed their hands of him altogether.

BRACK: They used to call him the family's white hope.

TESMAN: They used to, yes! But he spoiled all that himself.

HEDDA: Who knows? (*With a slight smile.*) He's been rehabilitated up at the Elvsteds —

BRACK: And then this book that he's published —

TESMAN: Oh, well, let's hope they really help him some way or other. I just now wrote to him. Hedda dear, I asked him out here this evening.

BRACK: But my dear fellow, you're coming to my stag party this evening. You promised down on the pier last night.

HEDDA: Had you forgotten, Tesman?

TESMAN: Yes, I absolutely had.

BRACK: For that matter, you can rest assured that he'd never come.

TESMAN: What makes you say that, hm?

BRACK (*hesitating, rising and leaning on the back of the chair*): My dear Tesman — and you too, Mrs. Tesman — I can't, in all conscience, let you go on without knowing something that — that —

TESMAN: Something involving Eilert —?

BRACK: Both you and him.

TESMAN: But my dear Judge, then tell us!

BRACK: You must be prepared that your appointment may not come through as quickly as you've wished or expected.

TESMAN (*jumping up nervously*): Has something gone wrong? Uh?

BRACK: It may turn out that there'll have to be a competition for the post —

TESMAN: A competition! Imagine, Hedda!

HEDDA (*leaning further back in the chair*): Ah, there — you see!

TESMAN: But with whom! You can't mean —?

BRACK: Yes, exactly. With Eilert Løvborg.

TESMAN (*striking his hands together*): No, no — that's completely unthinkable! It's impossible! Uh?

BRACK: Hm — but it may come about, all the same.

TESMAN: No, but, Judge Brack — that would just be incredibly inconsiderate toward me! (*Waving his arms.*) Yes, because — you know — I'm a married

man! We married on my prospects, Hedda and I. We went into debt. And even borrowed money from Aunt Julie. Because that job — my Lord, it was as good as promised to me, uh?

BRACK: Easy now — I'm sure you'll get the appointment. But you will have to compete for it.

HEDDA (*motionless in the armchair*): Just think, Tesman — it will be like a kind of championship match.

TESMAN: But Hedda dearest, how can you take it so calmly!

HEDDA (*as before*): I'm not the least bit calm. I can't wait to see how it turns out.

BRACK: In any case, Mrs. Tesman, it's well that you know now how things stand. I mean — with respect to those little purchases I hear you've been threatening to make.

HEDDA: This business can't change anything.

BRACK: I see! Well, that's another matter. Good-bye. (*To Tesman.*) When I take my afternoon walk, I'll stop by and fetch you.

TESMAN: Oh yes, please do — I don't know where I'm at.

HEDDA (*leaning back and reaching out her hand*): Good-bye, Judge. And come again soon.

BRACK: Many thanks. Good-bye now.

TESMAN (*accompanying him to the door*): Good-bye, Judge! You really must excuse me —

(*Brack goes out by the hall door.*)

TESMAN (*pacing about the room*): Oh, Hedda — one should never go off and lose oneself in dreams, uh?

HEDDA (*looks at him and smiles*): Do *you* do *that*?

TESMAN: No use denying it. It was living in dreams to go and get married and set up house on nothing but expectations.

HEDDA: Perhaps you're right about that.

TESMAN: Well, at least we have our comfortable home, Hedda! The home that we always wanted. That we both fell in love with, I could almost say. Hm?

HEDDA (*rising slowly and wearily*): It was part of our bargain that we'd live in society — that we'd keep a great house —

TESMAN: Yes, of course — how I'd looked forward to that! Imagine — seeing you as a hostess — in our own select circle of friends! Yes, yes — well, for a while, we two will just have to get on by ourselves, Hedda. Perhaps have Aunt Julie here now and then. Oh, you — for you I wanted to have things so — so utterly different —!

HEDDA: Naturally this means I can't have a butler now.

TESMAN: Oh no — I'm sorry, a butler — we can't even talk about that, you know.

HEDDA: And the riding horse I was going to have —

TESMAN (*appalled*): Riding horse!

HEDDA: I suppose I can't think of that anymore.

TESMAN: Good Lord, no — that's obvious!

HEDDA (*crossing the room*): Well, at least I have one thing left to amuse myself with.

TESMAN (*beaming*): Ah, thank heaven for that! What is it, Hedda? Uh?

HEDDA (*in the center doorway, looking at him with veiled scorn*): My pistols, George.

TESMAN (*in fright*): Your pistols!

HEDDA (*her eyes cold*): General Gabler's pistols. (*She goes through the inner room and out to the left.*)

TESMAN (*runs to the center doorway and calls after her*): No, for heaven's sake, Hedda darling — don't touch those dangerous things! For my sake, Hedda! Uh?

ACT II

(*The rooms at the Tesmans', same as in the first act, except that the piano has been moved out and an elegant little writing table with a bookcase put in its place. A smaller table stands by the sofa to the left. Most of the flowers have been removed. Mrs. Elvsted's bouquet stands on the large table in the foreground. It is afternoon.*)

(*Hedda, dressed to receive callers, is alone in the room. She stands by the open glass door, loading a revolver. The match to it lies in an open pistol case on the writing table.*)

HEDDA (*looking down into the garden and calling*): Good to see you again, Judge!

BRACK (*heard from below, at a distance*): Likewise, Mrs. Tesman!

HEDDA (*raises the pistol and aims*): And now, Judge, I'm going to shoot you!

BRACK (*shouting from below*): No-no-no! Don't point that thing at me!

HEDDA: That's what comes of sneaking in the back way. (*She fires.*)

BRACK (*nearer*): Are you out of your mind —!

HEDDA: Oh dear — I didn't hit you, did I?

BRACK (*still outside*): Just stop this nonsense!

HEDDA: All right, you can come in, Judge.

(*Judge Brack, dressed for a stag party, enters through the glass door. He carries a light overcoat on his arm.*)

BRACK: Good God! Are you still playing such games? What are you shooting at?

HEDDA: Oh, I was just shooting into the sky.

BRACK (*gently taking the pistol out of her hand*): Per- mit me. (*Looks at it.*) Ah, this one — I know it well. (*Glancing around.*) Where's the case? Ah, here. (*Puts the pistol away and shuts the case.*) We'll have no more of that kind of fun today.

HEDDA: Well, what in heaven's name do you want me to do with myself?

BRACK: You haven't had any visitors?

HEDDA (*closing the glass door*): Not a single one. All of our set are still in the country, I guess.

BRACK: And Tesman isn't home either?

HEDDA (*at the writing table, putting the pistol case away in a drawer*): No. Right after lunch he ran over to his aunts. He didn't expect you so soon.

BRACK: Hm — I should have realized. That was stupid of me.

HEDDA (*turning her head and looking at him*): Why stupid?

BRACK: Because in that case I would have stopped by a little bit — earlier.

HEDDA (*crossing the room*): Well, you'd have found no one here then at all. I've been up in my room dressing since lunch.

BRACK: And there's not the least little crack in the door we could have conferred through.

HEDDA: You forgot to arrange it.

BRACK: Also stupid of me.

HEDDA: Well, we'll just have to settle down here — and wait. Tesman won't be back for a while.

BRACK: Don't worry, I can be patient.

(*Hedda sits in the corner of the sofa. Brack lays his coat over the back of the nearest chair and sits down, keeping his hat in his hand. A short pause. They look at each other.*)

HEDDA: Well?

BRACK (*in the same tone*): Well?

HEDDA: I spoke first.

BRACK (*leaning slightly forward*): Then let's have a nice little cozy chat, Mrs. Hedda.

HEDDA (*leaning further back on the sofa*): Doesn't it seem like a whole eternity since the last time we talked together? Oh, a few words last night and this morning — but they don't count.

BRACK: You mean, like this — between ourselves? Just the two of us?

HEDDA: Well, more or less.

BRACK: There wasn't a day that I didn't wish you were home again.

HEDDA: And I was wishing exactly the same.

BRACK: You? Really, Mrs. Hedda? And I thought you were having such a marvelous time on this trip.

HEDDA: Oh, you can imagine!

BRACK: But that's what Tesman always wrote.

HEDDA: Oh, him! There's nothing he likes better than

grubbing around in libraries and copying out old parchments, or whatever you call them.

BRACK (*with a touch of malice*): But after all, it's his calling in life. In good part, anyway.

HEDDA: Yes, that's true. So there's nothing wrong with it — But what about *me*! Oh, Judge, you don't know — I've been so dreadfully bored.

BRACK (*sympathetically*): You really mean that? In all seriousness?

HEDDA: Well, you can understand —! To go for a whole six months without meeting a soul who knew the least bit about our circle. No one that one could talk to about our kind of things.

BRACK: Ah, yes — I think that would bother me too.

HEDDA: But then the most unbearable thing of all —

BRACK: What?

HEDDA: To be everlastingly together with — with one and the same person —

BRACK (*nodding in agreement*): Morning, noon, and night — yes. At every conceivable hour.

HEDDA: I said "everlastingly."

BRACK: All right. But with our good friend Tesman, I really should have thought —

HEDDA: My dear Judge, Tesman is — a specialist.

BRACK: Undeniably.

HEDDA: And specialists aren't at all amusing to travel with. Not in the long run, anyway.

BRACK: Not even — the specialist that one *loves*.

HEDDA: Ugh — don't use that syrupy word!

BRACK (*startled*): What's that, Mrs. Hedda!

HEDDA (*half laughing, half annoyed*): Well, just try it yourself! Try listening to the history of civilization morning, noon, and —

BRACK: Everlastingly.

HEDDA: Yes! Yes! And then all this business about domestic crafts in the Middle Ages —! That really is just too revolting!

BRACK (*looks searchingly at her*): But tell me — I can't see how it ever came about that —? Hm —

HEDDA: That George Tesman and I could make a match?

BRACK: All right, let's put it that way.

HEDDA: Good Lord, does it seem so remarkable?

BRACK: Well, yes — and no, Mrs. Hedda.

HEDDA: I really had danced myself out, Judge. My time was up. (*With a slight shudder.*) Ugh! No, I don't want to say that. Or think it, either.

BRACK: You certainly have no reason to.

HEDDA: Oh — reasons — (*Watching him carefully.*) And George Tesman — he is, after all, a thoroughly acceptable choice.

BRACK: Acceptable and dependable, beyond a doubt.

HEDDA: And I don't find anything especially ridiculous about him. Do you?

BRACK: Ridiculous? No-o-o, I wouldn't say that.

HEDDA: Hm. Anyway, he works incredibly hard on his research! There's every chance that, in time, he could still make a name for himself.

BRACK (*looking at her with some uncertainty*): I thought you believed, like everyone else, that he was going to be quite famous some day.

HEDDA (*wearily*): Yes, so I did. And then when he kept pressing and pleading to be allowed to take care of me — I didn't see why I ought to resist.

BRACK: No. From that point of view, of course not —

HEDDA: It was certainly more than my other admirers were willing to do for me, Judge.

BRACK (*laughing*): Well, I can't exactly answer for all the others. But as far as I'm concerned, you know that I've always cherished a — a certain respect for the marriage bond. Generally speaking, that is.

HEDDA (*bantering*): Oh, I never really held out any hopes for *you*.

BRACK: All I want is to have a warm circle of intimate friends, where I can be of use one way or another, with the freedom to come and go as — as a trusted friend —

HEDDA: Of the man of the house, you mean?

BRACK (*with a bow*): Frankly — I prefer the lady. But the man, too, of course, in his place. That kind of — let's say, triangular arrangement — you can't imagine how satisfying it can be all around.

HEDDA: Yes, I must say I longed for some third person so many times on that trip. Oh — those endless tête-à-têtes° in railway compartments —!

BRACK: Fortunately the wedding trip's over now.

HEDDA (*shaking her head*): The trip will go on — and on. I've only come to one stop on the line.

BRACK: Well, then what you do is jump out — and stretch yourself a little, Mrs. Hedda.

HEDDA: I'll never jump out.

BRACK: Never?

HEDDA: No. Because there's always someone on the platform who —

BRACK (*with a laugh*): Who looks at your legs, is that it?

HEDDA: Precisely.

BRACK: Yes, but after all —

HEDDA (*with a disdainful gesture*): I'm not interested. I'd rather keep my seat — right here, where I am. Tête-à-tête.

BRACK: Well, but suppose a third person came on board and joined the couple.

HEDDA: Ah! That's entirely different.

BRACK: A trusted friend, who understands —

HEDDA: And can talk about all kinds of lively things —

---

tête-à-têtes: Face-to-face conversations.

BRACK: Who's not in the least a specialist.

HEDDA (*with an audible sigh*): Yes, that would be a relief.

BRACK (*hearing the front door open and glancing toward it*): The triangle is complete.

HEDDA (*lowering her voice*): And the train goes on.

(*George Tesman, in a gray walking suit and a soft felt hat, enters from the hall. He has a good number of unbound books under his arm and in his pockets.*)

TESMAN (*going up to the table by the corner settee*): Phew! Let me tell you, that's hot work — carrying all these. (*Setting the books down.*) I'm actually sweating, Hedda. And what's this — you're already here, Judge? Hm? Berta didn't tell me.

BRACK (*rising*): I came in through the garden.

HEDDA: What are all these books you've gotten?

TESMAN (*stands leafing through them*): They're new publications in my special field. I absolutely need them.

HEDDA: Your special field?

BRACK: Of course. Books in his special field, Mrs. Tesman.

(*Brack and Hedda exchange a knowing smile.*)

HEDDA: You need still more books in your special field?

TESMAN: Hedda, my dear, it's impossible ever to have too many. You have to keep up with what's written and published.

HEDDA: Oh, I suppose so.

TESMAN (*searching among the books*): And look — I picked up Eilert Løvborg's new book too. (*Offering it to her.*) Maybe you'd like to have a look at it? Uh?

HEDDA: No, thank you. Or — well, perhaps later.

TESMAN: I skimmed through some of it on the way home.

HEDDA: Well, what do you think of it — as a specialist?

TESMAN: I think it's amazing how well it holds up. He's never written like this before. (*Gathers up the books.*) But I'll take these into the study now. I can't wait to cut the pages° —! And then I better dress up a bit. (*To Brack.*) We don't have to rush right off, do we? Hm?

BRACK: No, not at all. There's ample time.

TESMAN: Ah, then I'll be at my leisure. (*Starts out with the books, but pauses and turns in the doorway.*) Oh, incidentally, Hedda — Aunt Julie won't be by to see you this evening.

cut the pages: Book pages were printed on large sheets of paper that were folded and bound in groups of four. Readers had to trim the edges to separate the pages.

HEDDA: She won't? I suppose it's that business with the hat?

TESMAN: Don't be silly. How can you think that of Aunt Julie? Imagine —! No, it's Auntie Rina — she's very ill.

HEDDA: She always is.

TESMAN: Yes, but today she really took a turn for the worse.

HEDDA: Well, then it's only right for her sister to stay with her. I'll have to bear with it.

TESMAN: But you can't imagine how delighted Aunt Julie was all the same — because you'd filled out so nicely on the trip!

HEDDA (*under her breath; rising*): Oh, these eternal aunts!

TESMAN: What?

HEDDA (*going over to the glass door*): Nothing.

TESMAN: All right, then. (*He goes through the inner room and out, right.*)

BRACK: What were you saying about a hat?

HEDDA: Oh, it's something that happened with Miss Tesman this morning. She'd put her hat down over there on the chair. (*Looks at him and smiles.*) And I pretended I thought it was the maid's.

BRACK (*shaking his head*): But my dear Mrs. Hedda, how could you do that! Hurt that fine old lady!

HEDDA (*nervously, pacing the room*): Well, it's — these things come over me, just like that, suddenly. And I can't hold back. (*Throws herself down in the armchair by the stove.*) Oh, I don't know myself how to explain it.

BRACK (*behind the armchair*): You're not really happy — that's the heart of it.

HEDDA (*gazing straight ahead*): And I don't know why I ought to be — happy. Or maybe you can tell me why?

BRACK: Yes — among other things, because you've gotten just the home you've always wanted.

HEDDA (*looks up at him and laughs*): You believe that story too?

BRACK: You mean there's nothing to it?

HEDDA: Oh, yes — there's something to it.

BRACK: Well?

HEDDA: There's this much to it, that I used Tesman as my escort home from parties last summer —

BRACK: Unfortunately — I was going in another direction then.

HEDDA: How true. Yes, you had other directions to go last summer.

BRACK (*laughing*): For shame, Mrs. Hedda! Well — so you and Tesman —?

HEDDA: Yes, so one evening we walked by this place. And Tesman, poor thing, was writhing in torment, because he couldn't find anything to say. And I felt sorry for a man of such learning —

BRACK (*smiling skeptically*): Did you? Hm —

HEDDA: No, I honestly did. And so — just to help him off the hook — I came out with some rash remark about this lovely house being where I'd always wanted to live.

BRACK: No more than that?

HEDDA: No more that evening.

BRACK: But afterward?

HEDDA: Yes, my rashness had its consequences, Judge.

BRACK: I'm afraid our rashness all too often does, Mrs. Hedda.

HEDDA: Thanks! But don't you see, it was this passion for the old Falk mansion that drew George Tesman and me together! It was nothing more than that, that brought on our engagement and the marriage and the wedding trip and everything else. Oh yes, Judge — I was going to say, you make your bed and then you lie in it.

BRACK: But that's priceless! So actually you couldn't care less about all this?

HEDDA: God knows, not in the least.

BRACK: But even now? Now that we've made it somewhat comfortable for you here?

HEDDA: Ugh — all the rooms seem to smell of lavender and dried roses. But maybe that scent was brought in by Aunt Julie.

BRACK (*laughing*): No, I think it's a bequest from the late Mrs. Falk.

HEDDA: Yes, there's something in it of the odor of death. It's like a corsage — the day after the dance. (*Folds her hands behind her neck, leans back in her chair, and looks at him.*) Oh, my dear Judge — you can't imagine how horribly I'm going to bore myself here.

BRACK: But couldn't you find some goal in life to work toward? Others do, Mrs. Hedda.

HEDDA: A goal — that would really absorb me?

BRACK: Yes, preferably.

HEDDA: God only knows what that could be. I often wonder if — (*Breaks off.*) But that's impossible too.

BRACK: Who knows? Tell me.

HEDDA: I was thinking — if I could get Tesman to go into politics.

BRACK (*laughing*): Tesman! No, I can promise you — politics is absolutely out of his line.

HEDDA: No, I can believe you. But even so, I wonder if I could get him into it?

BRACK: Well, what satisfaction would you have in that, if he can't succeed? Why push him in that direction?

HEDDA: Because, I've told you, I'm bored! (*After a*

Marit Gronhaug as Hedda in the 1986 Rogaland Teater (Norway) production of *Hedda Gabler* in London.

pause.) Then you think it's really out of the question that he could ever be a cabinet minister?

BRACK: Hm — you see, Mrs. Hedda — to be anything like that, he'd have to be fairly wealthy to start with.

HEDDA (*rising impatiently*): Yes, there it is! It's this tight little world I've stumbled into — (*Crossing the room.*) That's what makes life so miserable! So utterly ludicrous! Because that's what it *is.*

BRACK: I'd say the fault lies elsewhere.

HEDDA: Where?

BRACK: You've never experienced anything that's really stirred you.

HEDDA: Anything serious, you mean.

BRACK: Well, you can call it that, if you like. But now perhaps it's on the way.

HEDDA (*tossing her head*): Oh, you mean all the fuss over that wretched professorship! But that's Tesman's problem. I'm not going to give it a single thought.

BRACK: No, that isn't — ah, never mind. But suppose you were to be confronted now by what — in rather elegant language — is called your most solemn responsibility. (*Smiling.*) A new responsibility, Mrs. Hedda.

HEDDA (*angrily*): Be quiet! You'll never see me like that!

BRACK (*delicately*): We'll discuss it again in a year's time — at the latest.

HEDDA (*curtly*): I have no talent for such things, Judge. I won't have responsibilities!

BRACK: Don't you think you've a talent for what almost every woman finds the most meaningful —

HEDDA (*over by the glass door*): Oh, I told you, be quiet! I often think I have talent for only one thing in life.

BRACK (*moving closer*): And what, may I ask, is that?

HEDDA (*stands looking out*): Boring myself to death. And that's the truth. (*Turns, looks toward the inner room, and laughs.*) See what I mean! Here comes the professor.

BRACK (*in a low tone of warning*): Ah-ah-ah, Mrs. Hedda!

(*George Tesman, dressed for the party, with hat and gloves in hand, enters from the right through the inner room.*)

TESMAN: Hedda — there's been no word from Eilert Løvborg, has there? Hm?

HEDDA: No.

TESMAN: Well, he's bound to be here soon then. You'll see.

BRACK: You really believe he'll come?

TESMAN: Yes, I'm almost positive of it. Because I'm

sure they're nothing but rumors, what you told us this morning.

BRACK: Oh?

TESMAN: Yes. At least Aunt Julie said she couldn't for the world believe that he'd stand in my way again. Can you imagine that!

BRACK: So, then everything's well and good.

TESMAN (*putting his hat with the gloves inside on a chair to the right*): Yes, but I really would like to wait for him as long as possible.

BRACK: We have plenty of time for that. There's no one due at my place till seven or half past.

TESMAN: Why, then we can keep Hedda company for a while. And see what turns up. Uh?

HEDDA (*taking Brack's hat and coat over to the settee*): And if worst comes to worst, Mr. Løvborg can sit and talk with me.

BRACK (*trying to take his things himself*): Ah, please, Mrs. Tesman —! What do you mean by "worst," in this case?

HEDDA: If he won't go with you and Tesman.

TESMAN (*looks doubtfully at her*): But Hedda dear — is it quite right that he stays with you here? Uh? Remember that Aunt Julie isn't coming.

HEDDA: No, but Mrs. Elvsted is. The three of us can have tea together.

TESMAN: Oh, well, that's all right.

BRACK (*smiling*): And that might be the soundest plan for him too.

HEDDA: Why?

BRACK: Well, really, Mrs. Tesman, you've made enough pointed remarks about my little bachelor parties. You've always said they're only fit for men of the strictest principles.

HEDDA: But Mr. Løvborg is surely a man of principle now. After all, a reformed sinner —

(*Berta appears at the hall door.*)

BERTA: Ma'am, there's a gentleman here who'd like to see you —

HEDDA: Yes, show him in.

TESMAN (*softly*): I'm sure it's him! Just think!

(*Eilert Løvborg enters from the hall. He is lean and gaunt, the same age as Tesman, but looks older and rather exhausted. His hair and beard are dark brown, his face long and pale, but with reddish patches over the cheekbones. He is dressed in a trim black suit, quite new, and holds dark gloves and a top hat in his hand. He hesitates by the door and bows abruptly. He seems somewhat embarrassed.*)

TESMAN (*crosses over and shakes his hand*): Ah, my dear Eilert — so at last we meet again!

EILERT LØVBORG (*speaking in a hushed voice*): Thanks for your letter, George! (*Approaching Hedda.*) May I shake hands with you too, Mrs. Tesman?

HEDDA (*taking his hand*): So glad to see you, Mr. Løvborg. (*Gesturing with her hand.*) I don't know if you two gentlemen —?

LØVBORG (*bowing slightly*): Judge Brack, I believe.

BRACK (*reciprocating*): Of course. It's been some years —

TESMAN (*to Løvborg, with his hands on his shoulders*): And now, Eilert, make yourself at home, completely! Right, Hedda? I hear you'll be settling down here in town again? Uh?

LØVBORG: I plan to.

TESMAN: Well, that makes sense. Listen — I just got hold of your new book. But I really haven't had time to read it yet.

LØVBORG: You can save yourself the bother.

TESMAN: Why? What do you mean?

LØVBORG: There's very little to it.

TESMAN: Imagine — you can say that!

BRACK: But it's won such high praise, I hear.

LØVBORG: That's exactly what I wanted. So I wrote a book that everyone could agree with.

BRACK: Very sound.

TESMAN: Yes, but my dear Eilert —!

LØVBORG: Because now I want to build up my position again — and try to make a fresh start.

TESMAN (*somewhat distressed*): Yes, that is what you want, I suppose. Uh?

LØVBORG (*smiling, puts down his hat and takes a thick manila envelope out of his pocket*): But when this comes out — George Tesman — you'll have to read it. Because this is the real book — the one that speaks for my true self.

TESMAN: Oh, really? What sort of book is that?

LØVBORG: It's the sequel.

TESMAN: Sequel? To what?

LØVBORG: To the book.

TESMAN: The one just out?

LØVBORG: Of course.

TESMAN: Yes, but my dear Eilert — that comes right down to our own time!

LØVBORG: Yes, it does. And this one deals with the future.

TESMAN: The future! But good Lord, there's nothing we know about that!

LØVBORG: True. But there are one or two things worth saying about it all the same. (*Opens the envelope.*) Here, take a look —

TESMAN: But that's not your handwriting.

LØVBORG: I dictated it. (*Paging through the manuscript.*) It's divided into two sections. The first is about the forces shaping the civilization of the fu-

ture. And the second part, here — (*paging further on*) suggests what lines of development it's likely to take.

TESMAN: How extraordinary! It never would have occurred to me to write about anything like that.

HEDDA (*at the glass door, drumming on the pane*): Hm — no, of course not.

LØVBORG (*puts the manuscript back in the envelope and lays it on the table*): I brought it along because I thought I might read you a bit of it this evening.

TESMAN: Ah, that's very good of you, Eilert; but this evening — (*Glancing at Brack.*) I'm really not sure that it's possible —

LØVBORG: Well, some other time, then. There's no hurry.

BRACK: I should explain, Mr. Løvborg — there's a little party at my place tonight. Mostly for Tesman, you understand.

LØVBORG (*looking for his hat*): Ah — then I won't stay —

BRACK: No, listen — won't you give me the pleasure of having you join us?

LØVBORG (*sharply and decisively*): No, I can't. Thanks very much.

BRACK: Oh, nonsense! Do that. We'll be a small, select group. And you can bet we'll have it "lively," as Mrs. Hed — Mrs. Tesman says.

LØVBORG: I don't doubt it. But nevertheless —

BRACK: You could bring your manuscript with you and read it to Tesman there, at my place. I have a spare room you could use.

TESMAN: Why, of course, Eilert — you could do that, couldn't you? Uh?

HEDDA (*intervening*): But dear, if Mr. Løvborg simply doesn't want to! I'm sure Mr. Løvborg would much prefer to settle down here and have supper with me.

LØVBORG (*looking at her*): With you, Mrs. Tesman!

HEDDA: And with Mrs. Elvsted.

LØVBORG: Ah. (*Casually.*) I saw her a moment this afternoon.

HEDDA: Oh, did you? Well, she'll be here soon. So it's almost essential for you to stay, Mr. Løvborg. Otherwise, she'll have no one to see her home.

LØVBORG: That's true. Yes, thank you, Mrs. Tesman — I'll be staying, then.

HEDDA: Then let me just tell the maid —

(*She goes to the hall door and rings. Berta enters. Hedda talks to her quietly and points toward the inner room. Berta nods and goes out again.*)

TESMAN (*at the same time, to Løvborg*): Tell me, Eilert — is it this new material — about the future — that you're going to be lecturing on?

LØVBORG: Yes.

TESMAN: Because I heard at the bookstore that you'll be giving a lecture series here this autumn.

LØVBORG: I intend to. I hope you won't be offended, Tesman.

TESMAN: Why, of course not! But —?

LØVBORG: I can easily understand that it makes things rather difficult for you.

TESMAN (*dispiritedly*): Oh, I could hardly expect that for my sake you'd —

LØVBORG: But I'm going to wait till you have your appointment.

TESMAN: You'll wait! Yes, but — but — you're not competing for it, then? Uh?

LØVBORG: No. I only want to win in the eyes of the world.

TESMAN: But, my Lord — then Aunt Julie was right after all! Oh yes — I knew it all along! Hedda! Can you imagine — Eilert Løvborg won't stand in our way!

HEDDA (*brusquely*): Our way? Leave me out of it.

(*She goes up toward the inner room where Berta is putting a tray with decanters and glasses on the table. Hedda nods her approval and comes back again. Berta goes out.*)

TESMAN (*at the same time*): But you, Judge — what do you say to all this? Uh?

BRACK: Well, I'd say that victory and honor — hm — after all, they're very sweet —

TESMAN: Yes, of course. But still —

HEDDA (*regarding Tesman with a cold smile*): You look as if you'd been struck by lightning.

TESMAN: Yes — something like it — I guess —

BRACK: That's because a thunderstorm just passed over us, Mrs. Tesman.

HEDDA (*pointing toward the inner room*): Won't you gentlemen please help yourselves to a glass of cold punch?

BRACK (*looking at his watch*): A parting cup? That's not such a bad idea.

TESMAN: Marvelous, Hedda! Simply marvelous! The way I feel now, with this weight off my mind —

HEDDA: Please, Mr. Løvborg, you too.

LØVBORG (*with a gesture of refusal*): No, thank you. Not for me.

BRACK: Good Lord, cold punch — it isn't poison, you know.

LØVBORG: Perhaps not for everyone.

HEDDA: I'll keep Mr. Løvborg company a while.

TESMAN: All right, Hedda dear, you do that.

(*He and Brack go into the inner room, sit down, drink punch, smoke cigarettes, and talk animatedly during the following. Løvborg remains standing by the stove. Hedda goes to the writing table.*)

HEDDA (*slightly raising her voice*): I can show you some photographs, if you like. Tesman and I traveled through the Tyrol on our way home.

(*She brings over an album and lays it on the table by the sofa, seating herself in the farthest corner. Eilert Løvborg comes closer, stops and looks at her. Then he takes a chair and sits down on her left, his back toward the inner room.*)

HEDDA (*opening the album*): You see this view of the mountains, Mr. Løvborg. That's the Ortler group. Tesman's labeled them underneath. Here it is: "The Ortler group, near Meran."

LØVBORG (*whose eyes have never left her, speaking in a low, soft voice*): Hedda — Gabler!

HEDDA (*with a quick glance at him*): Ah! Shh!

LØVBORG (*repeating softly*): Hedda Gabler!

HEDDA (*looks at the album*): Yes, I used to be called that. In those days — when we two knew each other.

LØVBORG: And from now on — for the rest of my life — I have to teach myself not to say Hedda Gabler.

HEDDA (*turning the pages*): Yes, you have to. And I think you ought to start practicing it. The sooner the better, I'd say.

LØVBORG (*resentment in his voice*): Hedda Gabler married? And to George Tesman!

HEDDA: Yes — that's how it goes.

LØVBORG: Oh, Hedda, Hedda — how could you throw yourself away like that!

HEDDA (*looks at him sharply*): All right — no more of that!

LØVBORG: What do you mean?

(*Tesman comes in and over to the sofa.*)

HEDDA (*hears him coming and says casually*): And this one, Mr. Løvborg, was taken from the Val d'Ampezzo. Just look at the peaks of those mountains. (*Looks warmly up at Tesman.*) Now what were those marvelous mountains called, dear?

TESMAN: Let me see. Oh, those are the Dolomites.

HEDDA: Why, of course! Those are the Dolomites, Mr. Løvborg.

TESMAN: Hedda dear — I only wanted to ask if we shouldn't bring in some punch anyway. At least for you, hm?

HEDDA: Yes, thank you. And a couple of *petits fours*, please.

TESMAN: No cigarettes?

HEDDA: No.

TESMAN: Right.

(*He goes through the inner room and out to the right. Brack remains sitting inside, keeping his eye from time to time on Hedda and Løvborg.*)

LØVBORG (*softly, as before*): Answer me, Hedda — how could you go and do such a thing?

HEDDA (*apparently immersed in the album*): If you keep on saying Hedda like that to me, I won't talk to you.

LØVBORG: Can't I say Hedda even when we're alone?

HEDDA: No. You can think it, but you mustn't say it like that.

LØVBORG: Ah, I understand. It offends your — love for George Tesman.

HEDDA (*glances at him and smiles*): Love? You *are* absurd!

LØVBORG: Then you don't love him!

HEDDA: I don't expect to be unfaithful, either. I'm not having any of that!

LØVBORG: Hedda, just answer me one thing —

HEDDA: Shh!

(*Tesman, carrying a tray, enters from the inner room.*)

TESMAN: Look out! Here come the goodies. (*He sets the tray on the table.*)

HEDDA: Why do you do the serving?

TESMAN (*filling the glasses*): Because I think it's such fun to wait on you, Hedda.

HEDDA: But now you've poured out two glasses. And you know Mr. Løvborg doesn't want —

TESMAN: Well, but Mrs. Elvsted will be along soon.

HEDDA: Yes, that's right — Mrs. Elvsted —

TESMAN: Had you forgotten her? Uh?

HEDDA: We've been so caught up in these. (*Showing him a picture.*) Do you remember this little village?

TESMAN: Oh, that's the one just below the Brenner Pass! It was there that we stayed overnight —

HEDDA: And met all those lively summer people.

TESMAN: Yes, that's the place. Just think — if we could have had *you* with us, Eilert! My! (*He goes back and sits beside Brack.*)

LØVBORG: Answer me just one thing, Hedda —

HEDDA: Yes?

LØVBORG: Was there no love with respect to me, either? Not a spark — not one glimmer of love at all?

HEDDA: I wonder, really, was there? To me it was as if we were two true companions — two very close friends. (*Smiling.*) You, especially, were so open with me.

LØVBORG: You wanted it that way.

HEDDA: When I look back on it now, there was really something beautiful and fascinating — and daring, it seems to me, about — about our secret closeness — our companionship that no one, not a soul, suspected.

LØVBORG: Yes, Hedda, that's true! Wasn't there? When I'd come over to your father's in the afternoon — and the general sat by the window reading his papers — with his back to us —

HEDDA: And we'd sit on the corner sofa —

LØVBORG: Always with the same illustrated magazine in front of us —

HEDDA: Yes, for the lack of an album.

LØVBORG: Yes, Hedda — and the confessions I used to make — telling you things about myself that no one else knew of then. About the way I'd go out, the drinking, the madness that went on day and night, for days at a time. Ah, what power was it in you, Hedda, that made me tell you such things?

HEDDA: You think it was some kind of power in me?

LØVBORG: How else can I explain it? And all those — those devious questions you asked me —

HEDDA: That you understood so remarkably well —

LØVBORG: To think you could sit there and ask such questions! So boldly.

HEDDA: Deviously, please.

LØVBORG: Yes, but boldly, all the same. Interrogating me about — all that kind of thing!

HEDDA: And to think you could answer, Mr. Løvborg.

LØVBORG: Yes, that's exactly what I don't understand — now, looking back. But tell me, Hedda — the root of that bond between us, wasn't it love? Didn't you feel, on your part, as if you wanted to cleanse and absolve me — when I brought those confessions to you? Wasn't that it?

HEDDA: No, not quite.

LØVBORG: What was your power, then?

HEDDA: Do you find it so very surprising that a young girl — if there's no chance of anyone knowing —

LØVBORG: Yes?

HEDDA: That she'd like some glimpse of a world that —

LØVBORG: That —?

HEDDA: That she's forbidden to know anything about.

LØVBORG: So that was it?

HEDDA: Partly. Partly that, I guess.

LØVBORG: Companionship in a thirst for life. But why, then, couldn't it have gone on?

HEDDA: But that was your fault.

LØVBORG: You broke it off.

HEDDA: Yes, when that closeness of ours threatened to grow more serious. Shame on you, Eilert Løvborg! How could you violate my trust when I'd been so — so bold with my friendship?

LØVBORG (*clenching his fists*): Oh, why didn't you do what you said! Why didn't you shoot me down!

HEDDA: I'm — much too afraid of scandal.

LØVBORG: Yes, Hedda, you're a coward at heart.

HEDDA: A terrible coward. (*Changing her tone.*) But that was lucky for you. And now you're so nicely consoled at the Elvsteds'.

LØVBORG: I know what Thea's been telling you.

HEDDA: And perhaps you've been telling her all about us?

LØVBORG: Not a word. She's too stupid for that sort of thing.

HEDDA: Stupid?

LØVBORG: When it comes to those things, she's stupid.

HEDDA: And I'm a coward. (*Leans closer, without looking him in the eyes, and speaks softly.*) But there *is* something now that I can tell you.

LØVBORG (*intently*): What?

HEDDA: When I didn't dare shoot you —

LØVBORG: Yes?

HEDDA: That wasn't my worst cowardice — that night.

LØVBORG (*looks at her a moment, understands, and whispers passionately*): Oh, Hedda! Hedda Gabler! Now I begin to see it, the hidden reason why we've been so close! You and I — ! . . . It was the hunger for *life* in you —

HEDDA (*quietly, with a sharp glance*): Careful! That's no way to think!

(*It has begun to grow dark. The hall door is opened from without by Berta.*)

HEDDA (*clapping the album shut and calling out with a smile*): Well, at last! Thea dear — please come in!

(*Mrs. Elvsted enters from the hall. She is in evening dress. The door is closed behind her.*)

HEDDA (*on the sofa, stretching her arms out toward her*): Thea, my sweet — I thought you were never coming!

(*In passing, Mrs. Elvsted exchanges light greetings with the gentlemen in the inner room, then comes over to the table and extends her hand to Hedda.*

Løvborg has gotten up. He and Mrs. Elvsted greet each other with a silent nod.)

MRS. ELVSTED: Perhaps I ought to go in and talk a bit with your husband?

HEDDA: Oh, nonsense. Let them be. They're leaving soon.

MRS. ELVSTED: They're leaving?

HEDDA: Yes, for a drinking party.

MRS. ELVSTED *(quickly, to Løvborg)*: But you're not?

LØVBORG: No.

HEDDA: Mr. Løvborg — is staying with us.

MRS. ELVSTED *(taking a chair, about to sit down beside him)*: Oh, it's so good to be here!

HEDDA: No, no, Thea dear! Not there! You have to come over here by me. I want to be in the middle.

MRS. ELVSTED: Any way you please.

(She goes around the table and sits on the sofa to Hedda's right. Løvborg resumes his seat.)

LØVBORG *(after a brief pause, to Hedda)*: Isn't she lovely to look at?

HEDDA *(lightly stroking her hair)*: Only to look at?

LØVBORG: Yes. Because we two — she and I — we really *are* true companions. We trust each other completely. We can talk things out together without any reservations —

HEDDA: Never anything devious, Mr. Løvborg?

LØVBORG: Well —

MRS. ELVSTED *(quietly, leaning close to Hedda)*: Oh, Hedda, you don't know how happy I am! Just think — he says that I've inspired him.

HEDDA *(regarding her with a smile)*: Really, dear; did he say that?

LØVBORG: And then the courage she has, Mrs. Tesman, when it's put to the test.

MRS. ELVSTED: Good heavens, me! Courage!

LØVBORG: Enormous courage — where I'm concerned.

HEDDA: Yes, courage — yes! If one only had that.

LØVBORG: Then what?

HEDDA: Then life might still be bearable. *(Suddenly changing her tone.)* But now, Thea dearest — you really must have a nice cold glass of punch.

MRS. ELVSTED: No, thank you. I never drink that sort of thing.

HEDDA: Well, then you, Mr. Løvborg.

LØVBORG: Thanks, not for me either.

MRS. ELVSTED: No, not for him either!

HEDDA *(looking intently at him)*: But if I insist?

LØVBORG: Makes no difference.

HEDDA *(with a laugh)*: Poor me, then I have no power over you at all?

LØVBORG: Not in that area.

HEDDA: But seriously, I think you ought to, all the same. For your own sake.

MRS. ELVSTED: But Hedda —!

LØVBORG: Why do you think so?

HEDDA: Or, to be more exact, for others' sakes.

LØVBORG: Oh?

HEDDA: Otherwise, people might get the idea that you're not very bold at heart. That you're not really sure of yourself at all.

MRS. ELVSTED *(softly)*: Oh, Hedda, don't —!

LØVBORG: People can think whatever they like, for all I care.

MRS. ELVSTED *(happily)*: Yes, that's right!

HEDDA: I saw it so clearly in Judge Brack a moment ago.

LØVBORG: What did you see?

HEDDA: The contempt in his smile when you didn't dare join them for a drink.

LØVBORG: Didn't dare! Obviously I'd rather stay here and talk with you.

MRS. ELVSTED: That's only reasonable, Hedda.

HEDDA: But how could the judge know that? And besides, I noticed him smile and glance at Tesman when you couldn't bring yourself to go to their wretched little party.

LØVBORG: Couldn't! Are you saying I couldn't?

HEDDA: *I'm* not. But that's the way Judge Brack sees it.

LØVBORG: All right, let him.

HEDDA: Then you won't go along?

LØVBORG: I'm staying here with you and Thea.

MRS. ELVSTED: Yes, Hedda — you can be sure he is!

HEDDA *(smiles and nods approvingly at Løvborg)*: I see. Firm as a rock. True to principle, to the end of time. There, that's what a man ought to be! *(Turning to Mrs. Elvsted and patting her.)* Well, now, didn't I tell you that, when you came here so distraught this morning —

LØVBORG *(surprised)*: Distraught?

MRS. ELVSTED *(terrified)*: Hedda —! But Hedda —!

HEDDA: Can't you see for yourself? There's no need at all for your going around so deathly afraid that — *(Changing her tone.)* There! Now we can all enjoy ourselves!

LØVBORG *(shaken)*: What is all this, Mrs. Tesman?

MRS. ELVSTED: Oh, God, oh, God, Hedda! What are you saying! What are you doing!

HEDDA: Not so loud. That disgusting judge is watching you.

LØVBORG: So deathly afraid? For my sake?

MRS. ELVSTED *(in a low moan)*: Oh, Hedda, you've made me so miserable!

LØVBORG *(looks intently at her a moment, his face drawn)*: So that's how completely you trusted me.

MRS. ELVSTED *(imploringly)*: Oh, my dearest — if you'll only listen —!

LØVBORG *(takes one of the glasses of punch, raises it,*

and says in a low, hoarse voice): Your health, Thea! (*He empties the glass, puts it down, and takes the other.*)

MRS. ELVSTED (*softly*): Oh, Hedda, Hedda — how could you want such a thing!

HEDDA: Want it? I? Are you crazy?

LØVBORG: And your health too, Mrs. Tesman. Thanks for the truth. Long live truth! (*Drains the glass and starts to refill it.*)

HEDDA (*laying her hand on his arm*): All right — no more for now. Remember, you're going to a party.

MRS. ELVSTED: No, no, no!

HEDDA: Shh! They're watching you.

LØVBORG (*putting down his glass*): Now, Thea — tell me honestly —

MRS. ELVSTED: Yes!

LØVBORG: Did your husband know that you followed me?

MRS. ELVSTED (*wringing her hands*): Oh, Hedda — listen to him!

LØVBORG: Did you have it arranged, you and he, that you should come down into town and spy on me? Or maybe he got you to do it himself? Ah, yes — I'm sure he needed me back in the office! Or maybe he missed my hand at cards?

MRS. ELVSTED (*softly, in anguish*): Oh, Eilert, Eilert —!

LØVBORG (*seizing his glass to fill it*): Skoal to the old sheriff, too!

HEDDA (*stopping him*): That's enough. Don't forget, you're giving a reading for Tesman.

LØVBORG (*calmly, setting down his glass*): That was stupid of me, Thea. I mean, taking it like this. Don't be angry at me, my dearest. You'll see — you and all the others — that if I stumbled and fell — I'm back on my feet again now! With your help, Thea.

MRS. ELVSTED (*radiant with joy*): Oh, thank God —!

(*Brack, in the meantime, has looked at his watch. He and Tesman stand up and enter the drawing room.*)

BRACK (*takes his hat and overcoat*): Well, Mrs. Tesman, our time is up.

HEDDA: I suppose it is.

LØVBORG (*rising*): Mine too, Judge.

MRS. ELVSTED (*softly pleading*): Oh, Eilert — don't!

HEDDA (*pinching her arm*): They can hear you!

MRS. ELVSTED (*with a small cry*): Ow!

LØVBORG (*to Brack*): You were kind enough to ask me along.

BRACK: Oh, then you *are* coming, after all?

LØVBORG: Yes, thank you.

BRACK: I'm delighted —

LØVBORG (*putting the manila envelope in his pocket, to Tesman*): I'd like to show you one or two things before I turn this in.

TESMAN: Just think — how exciting! But Hedda dear, how will Mrs. Elvsted get home? Uh?

HEDDA: Oh, we'll hit on something.

LØVBORG (*glancing toward the ladies*): Mrs. Elvsted? Don't worry, I'll stop back and fetch her. (*Coming nearer.*) Say about ten o'clock, Mrs. Tesman? Will that do?

HEDDA: Yes. That will do very nicely.

TESMAN: Well, then everything's all set. But you mustn't expect *me* that early, Hedda.

HEDDA: Dear, you stay as long — just as long as you like.

MRS. ELVSTED (*with suppressed anxiety*): Mr. Løvborg — I'll be waiting here till you come.

LØVBORG (*his hat in his hand*): Yes, I understand.

BRACK: So, gentlemen — the excursion train is leaving! I hope it's going to be lively, as a certain fair lady puts it.

HEDDA: Ah, if only that fair lady could be there, invisible —!

BRACK: Why invisible?

HEDDA: To hear a little of your unadulterated liveliness.

BRACK (*laughs*): I wouldn't advise the fair lady to try.

TESMAN (*also laughing*): Hedda, you are the limit! What an idea!

BRACK: Well, good night. Good night, ladies.

LØVBORG (*bowing*): About ten o'clock, then.

(*Brack, Løvborg, and Tesman go out the hall door. At the same time, Berta enters from the inner room with a lighted lamp, which she sets on the drawing room table, then goes out the same way.*)

MRS. ELVSTED (*having risen, moving restlessly about the room*): Hedda — Hedda — what's going to come of all this?

HEDDA: At ten o'clock — he'll be here. I can see him now — with vine leaves in his hair — fiery and bold —

MRS. ELVSTED: Oh, how good that would be!

HEDDA: And then, you'll see — he'll be back in control of himself. He'll be a free man, then, for the rest of his days.

MRS. ELVSTED: Oh, God — if only he comes as you see him now!

HEDDA: He'll come back like that, and no other way! (*Gets up and goes closer.*) Go on and doubt him as much as you like. *I* believe in him. And now we'll find out —

MRS. ELVSTED: There's something behind what you're doing, Hedda.

HEDDA: Yes, there is. For once in my life, I want to have power over a human being.

MRS. ELVSTED: But don't you have that?

HEDDA: I don't have it. I've never had it.

MRS. ELVSTED: Not with your husband?

HEDDA: Yes, what a bargain *that* was! Oh, if you only could understand how poor I am. And you're allowed to be so rich! (*Passionately throws her arms about her.*) I think I'll burn your hair off, after all!

MRS. ELVSTED: Let go! Let me go! I'm afraid of you, Hedda!

BERTA (*in the doorway to the inner room*): Supper's waiting in the dining room, ma'am.

HEDDA: All right, we're coming.

MRS. ELVSTED: No, no, no! I'd rather go home alone! Right away — now!

HEDDA: Nonsense! First you're going to have tea, you little fool. And then — ten o'clock — Eilert Løvborg comes — with vine leaves in his hair.

(*She drags Mrs. Elvsted, almost by force, toward the doorway.*)

ACT III

(*The same rooms at the Tesmans'. The curtains are down across the doorway to the inner room, and also across the glass door. The lamp, shaded and turned down low, is burning on the table. The door to the stove stands open; the fire has nearly gone out.*)

(*Mrs. Elvsted, wrapped in a large shawl, with her feet up on a footstool, lies back in the armchair close by the stove. Hedda, fully dressed, is asleep on the sofa, with a blanket over her. After a pause, Mrs. Elvsted suddenly sits straight up in the chair, listening tensely. Then she sinks wearily back again.*)

MRS. ELVSTED (*in a low moan*): Not yet — oh, God — oh, God — not yet!

(*Berta slips in cautiously by the hall door. She holds a letter in her hand.*)

MRS. ELVSTED (*turns and whispers anxiously*): Yes? Has anyone come?

BERTA (*softly*): Yes, a girl just now stopped by with this letter.

MRS. ELVSTED (*quickly, reaching out her hand*): A letter! Give it to me!

BERTA: No, it's for the Doctor, ma'am.

MRS. ELVSTED: Oh.

BERTA: It was Miss Tesman's maid that brought it. I'll leave it here on the table.

MRS. ELVSTED: Yes, do.

BERTA (*putting the letter down*): I think I'd best put out the lamp. It's smoking.

MRS. ELVSTED: Yes, put it out. It'll be daylight soon.

BERTA (*does so*): It's broad daylight already, ma'am.

MRS. ELVSTED: It's daylight! And still no one's come —!

BERTA: Oh, mercy — I knew it would go like this.

MRS. ELVSTED: You knew?

BERTA: Yes, when I saw that a certain gentleman was back here in town — and that he went off with them. We've heard plenty about that gentleman over the years.

MRS. ELVSTED: Don't talk so loud. You'll wake Mrs. Tesman.

BERTA (*looks toward the sofa and sighs*): Goodness me — yes, let her sleep, poor thing. Should I put a bit more on the fire?

MRS. ELVSTED: Thanks, not for me.

BERTA: All right. (*She goes quietly out the hall door.*)

HEDDA (*wakes as the door shuts and looks up*): What's that?

MRS. ELVSTED: It was just the maid —

HEDDA (*glancing about*): In here —? Oh yes, I remember now. (*Sits up on the sofa, stretches, and rubs her eyes.*) What time is it, Thea?

MRS. ELVSTED (*looking at her watch*): It's after seven.

HEDDA: When did Tesman get in?

MRS. ELVSTED: He isn't back.

HEDDA: Not back yet?

MRS. ELVSTED (*getting up*): No one's come in.

HEDDA: And we sat here and waited up for them till four o'clock —

MRS. ELVSTED (*wringing her hands*): And *how* I've waited for him!

HEDDA (*yawns, and speaks with her hand in front of her mouth*): Oh, dear — we could have saved ourselves the trouble.

MRS. ELVSTED: Did you get any sleep?

HEDDA: Oh yes. I slept quite well, I think. Didn't you?

MRS. ELVSTED: No, not at all. I couldn't, Hedda! It was just impossible.

HEDDA (*rising and going toward her*): There, there, now! There's nothing to worry about. It's not hard to guess what happened.

MRS. ELVSTED: Oh, what? Tell me!

HEDDA: Well, it's clear that the party must have gone on till all hours —

MRS. ELVSTED: Oh, Lord, yes — it must have. But even so —

HEDDA: And then, of course, Tesman didn't want to come home and make a commotion in the middle of the night. (*Laughs.*) Probably didn't care to show himself, either — so full of his party spirits.

MRS. ELVSTED: But where else could he have gone?

HEDDA: He must have gone up to his aunts' to sleep. They keep his old room ready.

MRS. ELVSTED: No, he can't be with them. Because he just now got a letter from Miss Tesman. It's over there.

HEDDA: Oh? (*Looking at the address.*) Yes, that's Aunt Julie's handwriting, all right. Well, then he must have stayed over at Judge Brack's. And Eilert Løvborg — he's sitting with vine leaves in his hair, reading away.

MRS. ELVSTED: Oh, Hedda, you say these things, and you really don't believe them at all.

HEDDA: You're such a little fool, Thea.

MRS. ELVSTED: That's true; I guess I am.

HEDDA: And you really look dead tired.

MRS. ELVSTED: Yes, I feel dead tired.

HEDDA: Well, you just do as I say, then. Go in my room and stretch out on the bed for a while.

MRS. ELVSTED: No, no — I still wouldn't get any sleep.

HEDDA: Why, of course you would.

MRS. ELVSTED: Well, but your husband's sure to be home now soon. And I've got to know right away —

HEDDA: I'll call you the moment he comes.

MRS. ELVSTED: Yes? Promise me, Hedda?

HEDDA: You can count on it. Just go and get some sleep.

MRS. ELVSTED: Thanks. I'll try. (*She goes out through the inner room.*)

(*Hedda goes over to the glass door and draws the curtains back. Bright daylight streams into the room. She goes over to the writing table, takes out a small hand mirror, regards herself and arranges her hair. She then goes to the hall door and presses the bell. After a moment, Berta enters.*)

BERTA: Did you want something, ma'am?

HEDDA: Yes, you can build up the fire. I'm freezing in here.

BERTA: Why, my goodness — we'll have it warm in no time. (*She rakes the embers together and puts some wood on, then stops and listens.*) There's the front doorbell, ma'am.

HEDDA: Go see who it is. I'll take care of the stove.

BERTA: It'll be burning soon. (*She goes out the hall door.*)

(*Hedda kneels on the footstool and lays more wood on the fire. After a moment, George Tesman comes in from the hall. He looks tired and rather serious. He tiptoes toward the doorway to the inner room and is about to slip through the curtains.*)

HEDDA (*at the stove, without looking up*): Good morning.

TESMAN (*turns*): Hedda! (*Approaching her.*) But what on earth —! You're up so early? Uh?

HEDDA: Yes, I'm up quite early today.

TESMAN: And I was so sure you were still in bed sleeping. Isn't that something, Hedda!

HEDDA: Not so loud. Mrs. Elvsted's resting in my room.

TESMAN: Was Mrs. Elvsted here all night?

HEDDA: Well, no one returned to take her home.

TESMAN: No, I guess that's right.

HEDDA (*shuts the door to the stove and gets up*): So — did you enjoy your party?

TESMAN: Were you worried about me? Hm?

HEDDA: No, that never occurred to me. I just asked if you'd had a good time.

TESMAN: Oh yes, I really did, for once. But more at the beginning, I'd say — when Eilert read to me out of his book. We got there more than an hour too soon — imagine! And Brack had so much to get ready. But then Eilert read to me.

HEDDA (*sitting at the right-hand side of the table*): Well? Tell me about it —

TESMAN (*sitting on a footstool by the stove*): Really, Hedda — you can't imagine what a book that's going to be! I do believe it's one of the most remarkable things ever written. Just think!

HEDDA: Yes, I don't mean the book —

TESMAN: But I have to make a confession, Hedda. When he'd finished reading — I had such a nasty feeling —

HEDDA: Nasty?

TESMAN: I found myself envying Eilert, that he was able to write such a book. Can you imagine, Hedda!

HEDDA: Oh yes, I can imagine!

TESMAN: And then how sad to see — that with all his gifts — he's still quite irreclaimable.

HEDDA: Don't you mean that he has more courage to live than the others?

TESMAN: Good Lord, no — I mean, he simply can't take his pleasures in moderation.

HEDDA: Well, what happened then — at the end?

TESMAN: I suppose I'd have to say it turned into an orgy, Hedda.

HEDDA: Were there vine leaves in his hair?

TESMAN: Vine leaves? Not that I noticed. But he gave a long, muddled speech in honor of the woman who'd inspired his work. Yes, that was his phrase for it.

HEDDA: Did he give her name?

TESMAN: No, he didn't. But it seems to me it has to be Mrs. Elvsted. Wait and see!

HEDDA: Oh? Where did you leave him?

TESMAN: On the way here. We broke up — the last of us — all together. And Brack came along with us too, to get a little fresh air. And then we did want to make sure that Eilert got home safe. Because he really had a load on, you know.

HEDDA: He must have.

TESMAN: But here's the curious part of it, Hedda. Or

perhaps I should say, the distressing part. Oh, I'm almost ashamed to speak of it — for Eilert's sake —

HEDDA: Yes, go on —

TESMAN: Well, as we were walking toward town, you see, I happened to drop back a little behind the others. Only for a minute or two — you follow me?

HEDDA: Yes, yes, so —?

TESMAN: And then when I was catching up with the rest of them, what do you think I found on the sidewalk? Uh?

HEDDA: Oh, how should I know!

TESMAN: You mustn't breathe a word to anyone, Hedda — you hear me? Promise me that, for Eilert's sake. (*Takes a manila envelope out of his coat pocket.*) Just think — I found this.

HEDDA: Isn't that what he had with him yesterday?

TESMAN: That's right. It's the whole of his precious, irreplaceable manuscript. And he went and lost it — without even noticing. Can you imagine, Hedda! How distressing —

HEDDA: But why didn't you give it right back to him?

TESMAN: No, I didn't dare do that — in the state he was in —

HEDDA: And you didn't tell any of the others you'd found it?

TESMAN: Of course not. I'd never do that, you know — for Eilert's sake.

HEDDA: Then there's no one who knows you have Eilert Løvborg's manuscript?

TESMAN: No. And no one must ever know, either.

HEDDA: What did you say to him afterwards?

TESMAN: I had no chance at all to speak with him. As soon as we reached the edge of town, he and a couple of others got away from us and disappeared. Imagine!

HEDDA: Oh? I expect they saw him home.

TESMAN: Yes, they probably did, I suppose. And also Brack went home.

HEDDA: And where've you been carrying on since then?

TESMAN: Well, I and some of the others — we were invited up by one of the fellows and had morning coffee at his place. Or a post-midnight snack, maybe — uh? But as soon as I've had a little rest — and given poor Eilert time to sleep it off, then I've got to take this back to him.

HEDDA (*reaching out for the envelope*): No — don't give it back! Not yet, I mean. Let me read it first.

TESMAN: Hedda dearest, no. My Lord, I can't do that.

HEDDA: You can't?

TESMAN: No. Why, you can just imagine the anguish he'll feel when he wakes up and misses the manuscript. He hasn't any copy of it, you know. He told me that himself.

HEDDA (*looks searchingly at him*): Can't such a work be rewritten? I mean, over again?

TESMAN: Oh, I don't see how it could. Because the inspiration, you know —

HEDDA: Yes, yes — that's the thing, I suppose. (*Casually.*) Oh, by the way — there's a letter for you.

TESMAN: No, really —?

HEDDA (*handing it to him*): It came early this morning.

TESMAN: Dear, from Aunt Julie! What could that be? (*Sets the envelope on the other taboret, opens the letter, skims through it, and springs to his feet.*) Oh, Hedda — she says poor Auntie Rina's dying!

HEDDA: It's no more than we've been expecting.

TESMAN: And if I want to see her one last time, I've got to hurry. I'll have to hop right over.

HEDDA (*suppressing a smile*): Hop?

TESMAN: Oh, Hedda dearest, if you could only bring yourself to come with me! Think of it!

HEDDA (*rises and dismisses the thought wearily*): No, no, don't ask me to do such things. I don't want to look on sickness and death. I want to be free of everything ugly.

TESMAN: Yes, all right, then — (*Dashing about.*) My hat —? My overcoat —? Oh, in the hall — I do hope I'm not there too late, Hedda! Hm?

HEDDA: Oh, if you hurry —

(*Berta appears at the hall door.*)

BERTA: Judge Brack's outside, asking if he might stop in.

TESMAN: At a time like this! No, I can't possibly see him now.

HEDDA: But I can. (*To Berta.*) Ask the judge to come in.

(*Berta goes out.*)

HEDDA (*quickly, in a whisper*): Tesman, the manuscript! (*She snatches it from the taboret.*)

TESMAN: Yes, give it here!

HEDDA: No, no, I'll keep it till you're back.

(*She moves over to the writing table and slips it in the bookcase. Tesman stands flustered, unable to get his gloves on. Brack enters from the hall.*)

HEDDA: Well, aren't you the early bird.

BRACK: Yes, wouldn't you say so? (*To Tesman.*) Are you off and away too?

TESMAN: Yes, I absolutely have to get over to my aunts'. Just think — the invalid one, she's dying.

BRACK: Good Lord, she is? But then you mustn't let me detain you. Not at a moment like this —

TESMAN: Yes, I really must run — Good-bye! Good-bye! (*He goes hurriedly out the hall door.*)

HEDDA: It would seem you had quite a time of it last night, Judge.

BRACK: I've not been out of my clothes yet, Mrs. Hedda.

HEDDA: Not you, either?

BRACK: No, as you can see. But what's Tesman been telling you about our night's adventures?

HEDDA: Oh, some tedious tale. Something about stopping up somewhere for coffee.

BRACK: Yes, I know all about the coffee party. Eilert Løvborg wasn't with them, I expect?

HEDDA: No, they'd already taken him home.

BRACK: Tesman, as well.

HEDDA: No, but he said some others had.

BRACK (smiles): George Tesman is really a simple soul, Mrs. Hedda.

HEDDA: God knows he's that. But was there something else that went on?

BRACK: Oh, you might say so.

HEDDA: Well, now! Let's sit down, Judge; you'll talk more easily then.

(She sits at the left-hand side of the table, with Brack at the long side, near her.)

HEDDA: So?

BRACK: I had particular reasons for keeping track of my guests — or, I should say, certain of my guests, last night.

HEDDA: And among them Eilert Løvborg, perhaps?

BRACK: To be frank — yes.

HEDDA: Now you really have me curious —

BRACK: You know where he and a couple of the others spent the rest of the night, Mrs. Hedda?

HEDDA: Tell me — if it's fit to be told.

BRACK: Oh, it's very much fit to be told. Well, it seems they showed up at a quite animated soiree.

HEDDA: Of the lively sort.

BRACK: Of the liveliest.

HEDDA: Do go on, Judge —

BRACK: Løvborg, and the others also, had advance invitations. I knew all about it. But Løvborg had begged off, because now, of course, he was supposed to have become a new man, as you know.

HEDDA: Up at the Elvsteds', yes. But he went anyway?

BRACK: Well, you see, Mrs. Hedda — unfortunately the spirit moved him up at my place last evening —

HEDDA: Yes, I hear that he *was* inspired there.

BRACK: To a very powerful degree, I'd say. Well, so his mind turned to other things, that's clear. We males, sad to say — we're not always so true to principle as we ought to be.

HEDDA: Oh, I'm sure you're an exception, Judge. But what about Løvborg —?

BRACK: Well, to cut it short — the result was that he wound up in Mademoiselle Diana's parlors.

HEDDA: Mademoiselle Diana's?

BRACK: It was Mademoiselle Diana who was holding

the soiree. For a select circle of lady friends and admirers.

HEDDA: Is she a red-haired woman?

BRACK: Precisely.

HEDDA: Sort of a — singer?

BRACK: Oh yes — she's that too. And also a mighty huntress — of men, Mrs. Hedda. You've undoubtedly heard about her. Løvborg was one of her ruling favorites — back there in his palmy° days.

HEDDA: And how did all this end?

BRACK: Less amicably, it seems. She gave him a most tender welcoming, with open arms, but before long she'd taken to fists.

HEDDA: Against Løvborg?

BRACK: That's right. He accused her or her friends of having robbed him. He claimed that his wallet was missing — along with some other things. In short, he must have made a frightful scene.

HEDDA: And what did it come to?

BRACK: It came to a regular free-for-all, the men and the women both. Luckily the police finally got there.

HEDDA: The police too?

BRACK: Yes. But it's likely to prove an expensive little romp for Eilert Løvborg. That crazy fool.

HEDDA: So?

BRACK: He apparently made violent resistance. Struck one of the officers on the side of the head and ripped his coat. So they took him along to the station house.

HEDDA: Where did you hear all this?

BRACK: From the police themselves.

HEDDA (gazing straight ahead): So that's how it went. Then he had no vine leaves in his hair.

BRACK: Vine leaves, Mrs. Hedda?

HEDDA (changing her tone): But tell me, Judge — just why do you go around like this, spying on Eilert Løvborg?

BRACK: In the first place, it's hardly a matter of no concern to me, if it's brought out during the investigation that he'd come direct from my house.

HEDDA: There'll be an investigation —?

BRACK: Naturally. Anyway, that takes care of itself. But I felt that as a friend of the family I owed you and Tesman a full account of his nocturnal exploits.

HEDDA: Why, exactly?

BRACK: Well, because I have a strong suspicion that he'll try to use you as a kind of screen.

HEDDA: Oh, how could you ever think such a thing!

BRACK: Good Lord — we're really not blind, Mrs. Hedda. You'll see! This Mrs. Elvsted, she won't be going home now so quickly.

HEDDA: Well, even supposing there were something

palmy: Prosperous.

between them, there are plenty of other places where they could meet.

BRACK: Not one single home. From now on, every decent house will be closed to Eilert Løvborg.

HEDDA: So mine ought to be too, is that what you mean?

BRACK: Yes. I'll admit I'd find it more than annoying if that gentleman were to have free access here. If he came like an intruder, an irrelevancy, forcing his way into —

HEDDA: Into the triangle?

BRACK: Precisely. It would almost be like turning me out of my home.

HEDDA (*looks at him with a smile*): I see. The one cock of the walk — that's what you want to be.

BRACK (*nodding slowly and lowering his voice*): Yes, that's what I want to be. And that's what I'll fight for — with every means at my disposal.

HEDDA (*her smile vanishing*): You can be a dangerous person, can't you — in a tight corner.

BRACK: Do you think so?

HEDDA: Yes, now I'm beginning to think so. And I'm thoroughly grateful — that you have no kind of hold over me.

BRACK (*with an ambiguous laugh*): Ah, yes, Mrs. Hedda — perhaps you're right about that. If I had, then who knows just what I might do?

HEDDA: Now you listen here, Judge! That sounds too much like a threat.

BRACK (*rising*): Oh, nothing of the kind! A triangle, after all — is best fortified and defended by volunteers.

HEDDA: There we're agreed.

BRACK: Well, now that I've said all I have to say, I'd better get back to town. Good-bye, Mrs. Hedda. (*He goes toward the glass door.*)

HEDDA (*rising*): Are you going through the garden?

BRACK: Yes, I find it's shorter.

HEDDA: Yes, and then it's the back way, too.

BRACK: How true. I have nothing against back ways. At certain times they can be rather piquant.

HEDDA: You mean, when somebody's sharpshooting?

BRACK (*in the doorway, laughing*): Oh, people don't shoot their tame roosters!

HEDDA (*also laughing*): I guess not. Not when there's only one —

(*Still laughing, they nod good-bye to each other. He goes. She shuts the door after him, then stands for a moment, quite serious, looking out. She then goes over and glances through the curtains to the inner room. Moves to the writing table, takes Løvborg's envelope from the bookcase, and is about to page through it, when Berta's voice is heard loudly in the hall. Hedda turns and listens. She hurriedly locks the envelope in* the drawer and lays the key on the inkstand. Eilert Løvborg, with his overcoat on and his hat in his hand, throws open the hall door. He looks confused and excited.)

LØVBORG (*turned toward the hall*): And I'm telling you, I have to go in! I will, you hear me! (*He shuts the door, turns, sees Hedda, immediately gains control of himself and bows.*)

HEDDA (*at the writing table*): Well, Mr. Løvborg, it's late to call for Thea.

LØVBORG: Or rather early to call on you. You must forgive me.

HEDDA: How did you know she was still with me?

LØVBORG: They said at her lodgings that she'd been out all night.

HEDDA (*goes to the center table*): Did you notice anything in their faces when they said that?

LØVBORG (*looking at her inquiringly*): Notice anything?

HEDDA: I mean, did it look like they had their own thoughts on the matter?

LØVBORG (*suddenly understanding*): Oh yes, that's true? I'm dragging her down with me! Actually, I didn't notice anything. Tesman — I don't suppose he's up yet?

HEDDA: No, I don't think so.

LØVBORG: When did he get in?

HEDDA: Very late.

LØVBORG: Did he tell you anything?

HEDDA: Well, I heard you'd had a high time of it out at Judge Brack's.

LØVBORG: Anything else?

HEDDA: No, I don't think so. As a matter of fact, I was terribly sleepy —

(*Mrs. Elvsted comes in through the curtains to the inner room.*)

MRS. ELVSTED (*running toward him*): Oh, Eilert! At last —!

LØVBORG: Yes, at last. And too late.

MRS. ELVSTED (*looking anxiously at him*): What's too late?

LØVBORG: Everything's too late now. It's over with me.

MRS. ELVSTED: Oh no, no — don't say that!

LØVBORG: You'll say the same thing when you've heard —

MRS. ELVSTED: I won't hear anything!

HEDDA: Maybe you'd prefer to talk with her alone. I can leave.

LØVBORG: No, stay — you too. Please.

MRS. ELVSTED: But I tell you, I don't want to hear anything!

LØVBORG: It's nothing about last night.

Mrs. Elvsted: What is it, then —?

Løvborg: It's simply this, that from now on, we separate.

Mrs. Elvsted: Separate!

Hedda (*involuntarily*): I knew it!

Løvborg: Because I have no more use for you, Thea.

Mrs. Elvsted: And you can stand there and say that! No more use for me! Then I'm not going to help you now, as I have? We're not going to go on working together?

Løvborg: I have no plans for any more work.

Mrs. Elvsted (*in desperation*): Then what will I do with my life?

Løvborg: You must try to go on living as if you'd never known me.

Mrs. Elvsted: But I can't do that!

Løvborg: You must try to, Thea. You'll have to go home again —

Mrs. Elvsted (*in a fury of protest*): Never! No! Where you are, that's where I want to be! I won't be driven away like this! I'm going to stay right here — and be together with you when the book comes out.

Hedda (*in a tense whisper*): Ah, yes — the book!

Løvborg (*looks at her*): My book and Thea's — for that's what it is.

Mrs. Elvsted: Yes, that's what I feel it is. And that's why I have the right, as well, to be with you when it comes out. I want to see you covered with honor and respect again. And the joy — I want to share the joy of it with you too.

Løvborg: Thea — our book's never coming out.

Hedda: Ah!

Mrs. Elvsted: Never coming out!

Løvborg: *Can* never come out.

Mrs. Elvsted (*with anguished foreboding*): Eilert — what have you done with the manuscript?

Hedda (*watching him intently*): Yes, the manuscript —?

Mrs. Elvsted: Where is it!

Løvborg: Oh, Thea — don't ask me that.

Mrs. Elvsted: Yes, yes, I have to know. I've got a right to know, this minute!

Løvborg: The manuscript — well, you see — I tore the manuscript into a thousand pieces.

Mrs. Elvsted (*screams*): Oh no, no —!

Hedda (*involuntarily*): But that just isn't —!

Løvborg (*looks at her*): Isn't so, you think?

Hedda (*composing herself*): All right. Of course; if you say it yourself. But it sounds so incredible —

Løvborg: It's true, all the same.

Mrs. Elvsted (*wringing her hands*): Oh, God — oh, God, Hedda — to tear his own work to bits!

Løvborg: I've torn my own life to bits. So why not tear up my life's work as well —

Mrs. Elvsted: And you did this thing last night!

Løvborg: Yes, you heard me. In a thousand pieces. And scattered them into the fjord. Far out. At least there, there's clean salt water. Let them drift out to sea — drift with the tide and the wind. And after a while, they'll sink. Deeper and deeper. As I will, Thea.

Mrs. Elvsted: Do you know, Eilert, this thing you've done with the book — for the rest of my life it will seem to me as if you'd killed a little child.

Løvborg: You're right. It was like murdering a child.

Mrs. Elvsted: But how could you do it —! It was my child too.

Hedda (*almost inaudible*): Ah, the child —

Mrs. Elvsted (*breathes heavily*): Then it *is* all over. Yes, yes, I'm going now, Hedda.

Hedda: But you're not leaving town, are you?

Mrs. Elvsted: Oh, I don't know myself what I'll do. Everything's dark for me now. (*She goes out the hall door.*)

Hedda (*stands waiting a moment*): You're not going to take her home, then, Mr. Løvborg?

Løvborg: I? Through the streets? So people could see that she'd been with me?

Hedda: I don't know what else may have happened last night. But is it so completely irredeemable?

Løvborg: It won't just end with last night — I know that well enough. But the thing is, I've lost all desire for that kind of life. I don't want to start it again, not now. It's the courage and daring for life — that's what she's broken in me.

Hedda (*staring straight ahead*): To think that pretty little fool could have a man's fate in her hands. (*Looks at him.*) But still, how could you treat her so heartlessly?

Løvborg: Oh, don't say it was heartless!

Hedda: To go ahead and destroy what's filled her whole being for months and years! That's not heartless?

Løvborg: To you, Hedda — I can tell the truth.

Hedda: The truth?

Løvborg: Promise me first — give me your word that what I tell you now, you'll never let Thea know.

Hedda: You have my word.

Løvborg: Good. I can tell you, then, that what I said here just now isn't true.

Hedda: About the manuscript?

Løvborg: Yes. I didn't tear it up — or throw it in the fjord.

Hedda: No, but — where is it, then?

Løvborg: I've destroyed it all the same, Hedda. Utterly destroyed it.

Hedda: I don't understand.

Løvborg: Thea said that what I've done, for her was like killing a child.

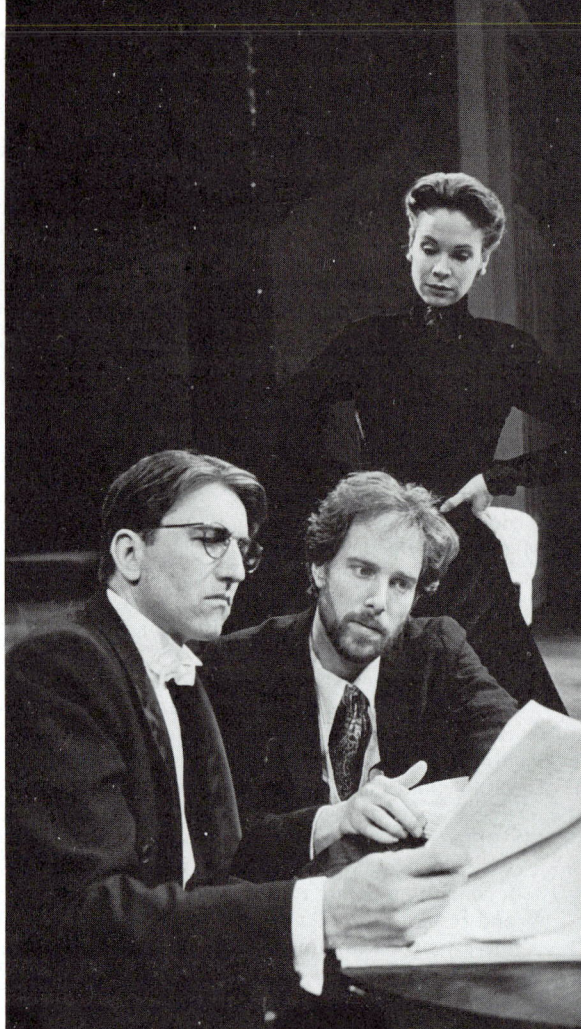

HEDDA: Yes — that's what she said.

LØVBORG: But killing his child — that's not the worst thing a father can do.

HEDDA: *That's* not the worst?

LØVBORG: No. I wanted to spare Thea the worst.

HEDDA: And what's that — the worst?

LØVBORG: Suppose now, Hedda, that a man — in the early morning hours, say — after a wild, drunken night, comes home to his child's mother and says: "Listen — I've been out to this place and that — here and there. And I had our child with me. In this place and that. And I lost the child. Just lost it. God only knows what hands it's come into. Or who's got hold of it."

HEDDA: Well — but when all's said and done — it was only a book —

LØVBORG: Thea's pure soul was in that book.

HEDDA: Yes, I understand.

LØVBORG: Well, then you can understand that for her and me there's no future possible any more.

HEDDA: What do you intend to do?

LØVBORG: Nothing. Just put an end to it all. The sooner the better.

HEDDA (*coming a step closer*): Eilert Løvborg — listen to me. Couldn't you arrange that — that it's done beautifully?

LØVBORG: Beautifully? (*Smiles.*) With vine leaves in my hair, as you used to dream in the old days —

HEDDA: No. I don't believe in vine leaves anymore. But beautifully, all the same. For this once —! Good-bye! You must go now — and never come here again.

LØVBORG: Good-bye, then. And give my best to George Tesman. (*He turns to leave.*)

HEDDA: No, wait. I want you to have a souvenir from me.

626

FAR LEFT: Hedda silhouetted near a portrait of her father, the General, in the Hartford Stage Company's 1988 production. NEAR LEFT: Tesman (Scott Wentworth), Løvborg (Richard Bekins), and Hedda (Mary Layne) discuss Løvborg's manuscript. RIGHT: Tesman and Mrs. Elvsted (Elisabeth Berridge) plan to rewrite Løvborg's lost manuscript. BELOW RIGHT: Judge Brack (William Duff-Griffin) examines Hedda's father's pistol.

(*She goes to the writing desk and opens the drawer and the pistol case, then comes back to Løvborg with one of the pistols.*)

LØVBORG (*looks at her*): That? Is that the souvenir?

HEDDA (*nods slowly*): Do you recognize it? It was aimed at you once.

LØVBORG: You should have used it then.

HEDDA: Here! Use it now.

LØVBORG (*puts the pistol in his breast pocket*): Thanks.

HEDDA: And beautifully, Eilert Løvborg. Promise me that!

LØVBORG: Good-bye, Hedda Gabler.

(*He goes out the hall door. Hedda listens a moment at the door. Then she goes over to the writing table, takes out the envelope with the manuscript, glances inside, pulls some of the sheets half out and looks at them. She then goes over to the armchair by the stove and sits, with the envelope in her lap. After a moment, she opens the stove door, then brings out the manuscript.*)

HEDDA (*throwing some of the sheets into the fire and whispering to herself*): Now I'm burning your child, Thea! You, with your curly hair! (*Throwing another sheaf in the stove.*) Your child and Eilert Løvborg's. (*Throwing in the rest.*) Now I'm burning — I'm burning the child.

ACT IV

(*The same rooms at the Tesmans'. It is evening. The drawing room is in darkness. The inner room is lit by the hanging lamp over the table. The curtains are drawn across the glass door. Hedda, dressed in black, is pacing back and forth in the dark room. She then enters the inner room, moving out of sight toward the left. Several chords are heard on the piano. She comes in view again, returning into the drawing room. Berta enters from the right through the inner room with a lighted lamp, which she puts on the table in front of the settee in the drawing room. Her eyes are red from crying, and she has black ribbons on her cap. She goes quietly and discreetly out to the right. Hedda moves to the glass door, lifts the curtains aside slightly, and gazes out into the darkness.*)

(*Shortly after, Miss Tesman, in mourning, with a hat and veil, comes in from the hall. Hedda goes toward her, extending her hand.*)

MISS TESMAN: Well, Hedda, here I am, all dressed in mourning. My poor sister's ordeal is finally over.

HEDDA: As you see, I've already heard. Tesman sent me a note.

MISS TESMAN: Yes, he promised he would. But all the same I thought that, to Hedda — here in the house of life — I ought to bear the news of death myself.

HEDDA: That was very kind of you.

MISS TESMAN: Ah, Rina ought not to have passed on just now. This is no time for grief in Hedda's house.

HEDDA (*changing the subject*): She had a peaceful death, then, Miss Tesman?

MISS TESMAN: Oh, she went so calmly, so beautifully. And so inexpressibly happy that she could see George once again. And say good-bye to him properly. Is it possible that he's still not home?

HEDDA: No, he wrote that I shouldn't expect him too early. But won't you sit down?

MISS TESMAN: No, thank you, my dear — blessed Hedda. I'd love to, but I have so little time. I want to see her dressed and made ready as best as I can. She should go to her grave looking her finest.

HEDDA: Can't I help you with something?

MISS TESMAN: Oh, you mustn't think of it. This is nothing for Hedda Tesman to put her hands to. Or let her thoughts dwell on, either. Not at a time like this, no.

HEDDA: Ah, thoughts — they're not so easy to control —

MISS TESMAN (*continuing*): Well, there's life for you. At my house now we'll be sewing a shroud for Rina. And here, too, there'll be sewing soon, I imagine. But a far different kind, praise God!

(*George Tesman enters from the hall.*)

HEDDA: Well, at last! It's about time.

TESMAN: Are you here, Aunt Julie? With Hedda? Think of that!

MISS TESMAN: I was just this minute leaving, dear boy. Well, did you get done all you promised you would?

TESMAN: No, I'm really afraid I've forgotten half. I'll have to run over and see you tomorrow. My brain's completely in a whirl today. I can't keep my thoughts together.

MISS TESMAN: But George dear, you mustn't take it that way.

TESMAN: Oh? Well, how should I, then?

MISS TESMAN: You should rejoice in your grief. Rejoice in everything that's happened, as I do.

TESMAN: Oh yes, of course. You're thinking of Auntie Rina.

HEDDA: It's going to be lonely for you, Miss Tesman.

MISS TESMAN: For the first few days, yes. But it won't be for long, I hope. I won't let dear Rina's little room stand empty.

TESMAN: No? Who would you want to have in it? Hm?

MISS TESMAN: Oh, there's always some poor invalid in need of care and attention.

HEDDA: Would you really take another burden like that on yourself?

MISS TESMAN: Burden! Mercy on you, child — it's been no burden for me.

HEDDA: But now, with a stranger —

MISS TESMAN: Oh, you soon make friends with an invalid. And I do so much need someone to live for — I, too. Well, thank God, in this house as well, there soon ought to be work that an old aunt can turn her hand to.

HEDDA: Oh, forget about us —

TESMAN: Yes, think how pleasant it could be for the three of us if —

HEDDA: If —?

TESMAN (*uneasily*): Oh, nothing. It'll all take care of itself. Let's hope so. Uh?

MISS TESMAN: Ah, yes. Well, I expect you two have things to talk about. (*Smiles.*) And perhaps Hedda has something to tell you, George. Good-bye. I'll have to get home now to Rina. (*Turning at the door.*) Goodness me, how strange! Now Rina's both with me and with poor dear Jochum as well.

TESMAN: Yes, imagine that, Aunt Julie! Hm?

(*Miss Tesman goes out the hall door.*)

HEDDA (*follows Tesman with a cold, probing look*): I almost think you feel this death more than she.

TESMAN: Oh, it's not just Auntie Rina's death. It's Eilert who has me worried.

HEDDA (*quickly*): Any news about him?

TESMAN: I stopped up at his place this afternoon, thinking to tell him that the manuscript was safe.

HEDDA: Well? Didn't you see him then?

TESMAN: No, he wasn't home. But afterward I met Mrs. Elvsted, and she said he'd been here early this morning.

HEDDA: Yes, right after you left.

TESMAN: And apparently he said he'd torn his manuscript up. Uh?

HEDDA: Yes, he claimed that he had.

TESMAN: But good Lord, then he must have been completely demented! Well, then I guess you didn't dare give it back to him, Hedda, did you?

HEDDA: No, he didn't get it.

TESMAN: But you did tell him we had it, I suppose?

HEDDA: No. (*Quickly.*) Did you tell Mrs. Elvsted anything?

TESMAN: No, I thought I'd better not. But you should have said something to him. Just think, if he goes off in desperation and does himself some harm! Give me the manuscript, Hedda! I'm taking it back to him right away. Where do you have it?

HEDDA (*cold and impassive, leaning against the armchair*): I don't have it anymore.

TESMAN: You don't have it! What on earth do you mean by that?

HEDDA: I burned it — the whole thing.

TESMAN (*with a start of terror*): Burned it! Burned Eilert Løvborg's manuscript!

HEDDA: Stop shouting. The maid could hear you.

TESMAN: Burned it! But my God in heaven —! No, no, no — that's impossible!

HEDDA: Yes, but it's true, all the same.

TESMAN: But do you realize what you've done, Hedda! It's illegal disposition of lost property. Just think! Yes, you can ask Judge Brack; he'll tell you.

HEDDA: It would be wiser not mentioning this — either to the judge or to anyone else.

TESMAN: But how could you go and do such an incredible thing! Whatever put it into your head? What got into you, anyway? Answer me! Well?

HEDDA (*suppressing an almost imperceptible smile*): I did it for your sake, George.

TESMAN: For my sake!

HEDDA: When you came home this morning and told about how he'd read to you —

TESMAN: Yes, yes, then what?

HEDDA: Then you confessed that you envied him this book.

TESMAN: Good Lord, I didn't mean it literally.

HEDDA: Never mind. I still couldn't bear the thought that anyone should eclipse you.

TESMAN (*in an outburst of mingled doubt and joy*): Hedda — is this true, what you say! Yes, but — but — I never dreamed you could show your love like this. Imagine!

HEDDA: Well, then it's best you know that — that I'm going to — (*Impatiently, breaking off.*) No, no — you ask your Aunt Julie. She's the one who can tell you.

TESMAN: Oh, I'm beginning to understand you, Hedda! (*Claps his hands together.*) Good heavens, no! Is it actually *that*! Can it be?

HEDDA: Don't shout so. The maid can hear you.

TESMAN: The maid! Oh, Hedda, you're priceless, really! The maid — but that's Berta! Why, I'll go out and tell her myself.

HEDDA (*clenching her fists in despair*): Oh, I'll die — I'll die of all this!

TESMAN: Of what, Hedda? Uh?

HEDDA: Of all these — absurdities — George.

TESMAN: Absurdities? What's absurd about my being so happy? Well, all right — I guess there's no point in my saying anything to Berta.

HEDDA: Oh, go ahead — why not that, too?

TESMAN: No, no, not yet. But Aunt Julie will have to hear. And then, that you've started to call me George, too! Imagine! Oh, Aunt Julie will be so glad — so glad!

HEDDA: When she hears that I burned Eilert Løvborg's book — for your sake?

TESMAN: Well, as far as that goes — this thing with the book — of course, no one's to know about that. But that you have a love that burns for me, Hedda — Aunt Julie can certainly share in that! You know, I wonder, really, if things such as this are common among young wives? Hm?

HEDDA: I think you should ask Aunt Julie about that, too.

TESMAN: Yes, I definitely will, when I have the chance.

(*Mrs. Elvsted, dressed as on her first visit, with hat and coat, comes in the hall door.*)

MRS. ELVSTED (*greets them hurriedly and speaks in agitation*): Oh, Hedda dear, don't be annoyed that I'm back again.

HEDDA: Has something happened, Thea?

TESMAN: Something with Eilert Løvborg? Uh?

MRS. ELVSTED: Yes, I'm so terribly afraid he's met with an accident.

HEDDA (*seizing her arm*): Ah — you think so!

TESMAN: But, Mrs. Elvsted, where did you get that idea?

MRS. ELVSTED: Well, because I heard them speaking of him at the boardinghouse, just as I came in. Oh, there are the most incredible rumors about him in town today.

TESMAN: Yes, you know, I heard them too! And yet I could swear that he went right home to bed last night. Imagine!

HEDDA: Well — what did they say at the boardinghouse?

MRS. ELVSTED: Oh, I couldn't get anything clearly. They either didn't know much themselves, or else — They stopped talking when they saw me. And I didn't dare to ask.

TESMAN (*restlessly moving about*): Let's hope — let's hope you misunderstood them, Mrs. Elvsted!

MRS. ELVSTED: No, no, I'm sure they were talking of him. And then I heard them say something or other about the hospital, or —

TESMAN: The hospital!

HEDDA: No — but that's impossible!

MRS. ELVSTED: Oh, I'm so deathly afraid for him now. And later I went up to his lodging to ask about him.

HEDDA: But was that very wise to do, Thea?

MRS. ELVSTED: What else could I do? I couldn't bear the uncertainty any longer.

TESMAN: But didn't you find him there either? Hm?

MRS. ELVSTED: No. And no one had any word of him. He hadn't been in since yesterday afternoon, they said.

TESMAN: Yesterday! Imagine them saying that!

MRS. ELVSTED: I think there can only be one reason — something terrible must have happened to him!

TESMAN: Hedda dear — suppose I went over and made a few inquiries —?

HEDDA: No, no — don't you get mixed up in this business.

(*Judge Brack, with hat in hand, enters from the hall, Berta letting him in and shutting the door after him. He looks grave and bows silently.*)

TESMAN: Oh, is that you, Judge? Uh?

BRACK: Yes, it's imperative that I see you this evening.

TESMAN: I can see that you've heard the news from Aunt Julie.

BRACK: Among other things, yes.

TESMAN: It's sad, isn't it? Uh?

BRACK: Well, my dear Tesman, that depends on how you look at it.

TESMAN (*eyes him doubtfully*): Has anything else happened?

BRACK: Yes, as a matter of fact.

HEDDA (*intently*): Something distressing, Judge?

BRACK: Again, that depends on how you look at it, Mrs. Tesman.

MRS. ELVSTED (*in an uncontrollable outburst*): Oh, it's something about Eilert Løvborg!

BRACK (*glancing at her*): Now how did you hit upon that, Mrs. Elvsted? Have you, perhaps, heard something already —?

MRS. ELVSTED (*in confusion*): No, no, nothing like that — but —

TESMAN: Oh, for heaven's sake, tell us!

BRACK (*with a shrug*): Well — I'm sorry, but — Eilert Løvborg's been taken to the hospital. He's dying.

MRS. ELVSTED (*crying out*): Oh, God, oh, God —!

TESMAN: To the hospital! And dying!

HEDDA (*involuntarily*): All so soon —!

MRS. ELVSTED (*wailing*): And we parted in anger, Hedda!

HEDDA (*in a whisper*): Thea — be careful, Thea!

MRS. ELVSTED (*ignoring her*): I have to see him! I have to see him alive!

BRACK: No use, Mrs. Elvsted. No one's allowed in to see him.

MRS. ELVSTED: Oh, but tell me, at least, what happened to him! What is it?

TESMAN: Don't tell me he tried to —! Uh?

HEDDA: Yes, he did, I'm sure of it.

TESMAN: Hedda — how can you say —!

BRACK (*his eyes steadily on her*): Unhappily, you've guessed exactly right, Mrs. Tesman.

MRS. ELVSTED: Oh, how horrible!

TESMAN: Did it himself! Imagine!

HEDDA: Shot himself!

BRACK: Again, exactly right, Mrs. Tesman.

MRS. ELVSTED (*trying to control herself*): When did it happen, Mr. Brack?

BRACK: This afternoon. Between three and four.

TESMAN: But good Lord — where did he do it, then? Hm?

BRACK (*hesitating slightly*): Where? Why — in his room, I suppose.

MRS. ELVSTED: No, that can't be right. I was there between six and seven.

BRACK: Well, somewhere else, then. I don't know exactly. I only know he was found like that. Shot — in the chest.

MRS. ELVSTED: What a horrible thought! That he should end that way!

HEDDA (*to Brack*): In the chest, you say.

BRACK: Yes — I told you.

HEDDA: Not the temple?

BRACK: In the chest, Mrs. Tesman.

HEDDA: Well — well, the chest is just as good.

BRACK: Why, Mrs. Tesman?

HEDDA (*evasively*): Oh, nothing — never mind.

TESMAN: And the wound is critical, you say? Uh?

BRACK: The wound is absolutely fatal. Most likely, it's over already.

MRS. ELVSTED: Yes, yes, I can feel that it is! It's over! All over! Oh, Hedda —!

TESMAN: But tell me now — how did you learn about this?

BRACK (*brusquely*): One of the police. Someone I talked to.

HEDDA (*in a clear, bold voice*): At last, something truly done!

TESMAN (*shocked*): My God, what are you saying, Hedda!

HEDDA: I'm saying there's beauty in all this.

BRACK: Hm, Mrs. Tesman —

TESMAN: Beauty! What an idea!

MRS. ELVSTED: Oh, Hedda, how can you talk about beauty in such a thing?

HEDDA: Eilert Løvborg's settled accounts with himself. He's had the courage to do what — what had to be done.

MRS. ELVSTED: Don't you believe it! It never happened like that. When he did this, he was in a delirium!

TESMAN: In despair, you mean.

HEDDA: No, he wasn't. I'm certain of that.

MRS. ELVSTED: But he was! In delirium! The way he was when he tore up our book.

BRACK (*startled*): The book? His manuscript, you mean? He tore it up?

MRS. ELVSTED: Yes. Last night.

TESMAN (*in a low whisper*): Oh, Hedda, we'll never come clear of all this.

BRACK: Hm, that's very strange.

TESMAN (*walking about the room*): To think Eilert could be gone like that! And then not to have left behind the one thing that could have made his name live on.

MRS. ELVSTED: Oh, if it could only be put together again!

TESMAN: Yes, imagine if that were possible! I don't know what I wouldn't give —

MRS. ELVSTED: Perhaps it can, Mr. Tesman.

TESMAN: What do you mean?

MRS. ELVSTED (*searching in the pockets of her dress*): Look here. I've kept all these notes that he used to dictate from.

HEDDA (*coming a step closer*): Ah —!

TESMAN: You've kept them, Mrs. Elvsted! Uh?

MRS. ELVSTED: Yes, here they are. I took them along when I left home. And they've stayed right here in my pocket —

TESMAN: Oh, let me look!

MRS. ELVSTED (*hands him a sheaf of small papers*): But they're in such a mess. All mixed up.

TESMAN: But just think, if we could decipher them, even so! Maybe the two of us could help each other —

MRS. ELVSTED: Oh yes! At least, we could try —

TESMAN: We can do it! We *must*! I'll give my whole life to this!

HEDDA: You, George. Your life?

TESMAN: Yes. Or, let's say, all the time I can spare. My own research will have to wait. You can understand, Hedda. Hm! It's something I owe to Eilert's memory.

HEDDA: Perhaps.

TESMAN: And so, my dear Mrs. Elvsted, let's see if we can't join forces. Good Lord, there's no use brooding over what's gone by. Uh? We must try to compose our thoughts as much as we can, in order that —

MRS. ELVSTED: Yes, yes, Mr. Tesman, I'll do the best I can.

TESMAN: Come on, then. Let's look over these notes right away. Where shall we sit? Here? No, in there, in the back room. Excuse us, Judge. You come with me, Mrs. Elvsted.

MRS. ELVSTED: Dear God — if only we can do this!

(*Tesman and Mrs. Elvsted go into the inner room. She takes off her hat and coat. They both sit at the table under the hanging lamp and become totally immersed in examining the papers. Hedda goes toward the stove and sits in the armchair. After a moment, Brack goes over by her.*)

HEDDA (*her voice lowered*): Ah, Judge — what a liberation it is, this act of Eilert Løvborg's.

BRACK: Liberation, Mrs. Hedda? Well, yes, for him; you could certainly say he's been liberated —

HEDDA: I mean for me. It's liberating to know that there can still actually be a free and courageous action in this world. Something that shimmers with spontaneous beauty.

BRACK (*smiling*): Hm — my dear Mrs. Hedda —

HEDDA: Oh, I already know what you're going to say. Because you're a kind of specialist too, you know, just like — Oh, well!

BRACK (*looking fixedly at her*): Eilert Løvborg meant more to you than you're willing to admit, perhaps even to yourself. Or am I wrong about that?

HEDDA: I won't answer that sort of question. I simply know that Eilert Løvborg's had the courage to live life after his own mind. And now — this last great act, filled with beauty! That he had the strength and the will to break away from the banquet of life — so young.

BRACK: It grieves me, Mrs. Hedda — but I'm afraid I have to disburden you of this beautiful illusion.

HEDDA: Illusion?

BRACK: One that, in any case, you'd soon be deprived of.

HEDDA: And what's that?

BRACK: He didn't shoot himself — of his own free will.

HEDDA: He didn't —!

BRACK: No. This whole affair didn't go off quite the way I described it.

HEDDA (*in suspense*): You've hidden something? What is it?

BRACK: For poor Mrs. Elvsted's sake, I did a little editing here and there.

HEDDA: Where?

BRACK: First, the fact that he's already dead.

HEDDA: In the hospital?

BRACK: Yes. Without regaining consciousness.

HEDDA: What else did you hide?

BRACK: That the incident didn't occur in his room.

HEDDA: Well, that's rather unimportant.

BRACK: Not entirely. Suppose I were to tell you that Eilert Løvborg was found shot in — in Mademoiselle Diana's boudoir.

HEDDA (*half rises, then sinks back again*): That's impossible, Judge! He wouldn't have gone there again today!

BRACK: He was there this afternoon. He went there, demanding something he said they'd stolen from him. Kept raving about a lost child —

HEDDA: Ah — so that was it —

BRACK: I thought perhaps that might be his manuscript. But, I hear now, he destroyed that himself. So it must have been his wallet.

HEDDA: I suppose so. Then, there — that's where they found him.

BRACK: Yes, there. With a discharged pistol in his breast pocket. The bullet had wounded him fatally.

HEDDA: In the chest — yes.

BRACK: No — in the stomach — more or less.

HEDDA (*stares up at him with a look of revulsion*): That too! What is it, this — this curse — that everything I touch turns ridiculous and vile?

BRACK: There's something else, Mrs. Hedda. Another ugly aspect to the case.

HEDDA: What's that?

BRACK: The pistol he was carrying —

HEDDA (*breathlessly*): Well! What about it!

BRACK: He must have stolen it.

HEDDA (*springs up*): Stolen! That's not true! He didn't!

BRACK: It seems impossible otherwise. He must have stolen it — shh!

(*Tesman and Mrs. Elvsted have gotten up from the table in the inner room and come into the drawing room.*)

TESMAN (*with both hands full of papers*): Hedda dear — it's nearly impossible to see in there under that overhead lamp. You know?

HEDDA: Yes, I know.

TESMAN: Do you think it would be all right if we used your table for a while? Hm?

HEDDA: Yes, I don't mind. (*Quickly.*) Wait! No, let me clear it off first.

TESMAN: Oh, don't bother, Hedda. There's plenty of room.

HEDDA: No, no, let me just clear it off, can't you? I'll put all this in by the piano. There!

(*She has pulled out an object covered with sheet music from under the bookcase, adds more music to it, and carries the whole thing into the inner room and off left. Tesman puts the scraps of paper on the writing table and moves the lamp over from the corner table. He and Mrs. Elvsted sit down and go on with their work. Hedda comes back.*)

HEDDA (*behind Mrs. Elvsted's chair, gently ruffling

her hair): Well, my sweet little Thea — how is it going with Eilert Løvborg's monument?

MRS. ELVSTED (*looking despondently up at her*): Oh, dear — it's going to be terribly hard to set these in order.

TESMAN: It's got to be done. There's just no alternative. Besides, setting other people's papers in order — it's exactly what I can do best.

(*Hedda goes over by the stove and sits on one of the taborets. Brack stands over her, leaning on the armchair.*)

HEDDA (*whispering*): What did you say about the pistol?

BRACK (*softly*): That he must have stolen it.

HEDDA: Why, necessarily, that?

BRACK: Because every other explanation would seem impossible, Mrs. Hedda.

HEDDA: I see.

BRACK (*glancing at her*): Of course, Eilert Løvborg was here this morning. Wasn't he?

HEDDA: Yes.

BRACK: Were you alone with him?

HEDDA: Yes, briefly.

BRACK: Did you leave the room while he was here?

HEDDA: No.

BRACK: Consider. You didn't leave, even for a moment?

HEDDA: Well, yes, perhaps, just for a moment — into the hall.

BRACK: And where did you have your pistol case?

HEDDA: I had it put away in —

BRACK: Yes, Mrs. Hedda?

HEDDA: It was lying over there, on the writing table.

BRACK: Have you looked since to see if both pistols are there?

HEDDA: No.

BRACK: No need to. I saw the pistol. Løvborg had it on him. I knew it immediately, from yesterday. And other days too.

HEDDA: Do you have it, maybe?

BRACK: No, the police have it.

HEDDA: What will they do with it?

BRACK: Try to trace it to the owner.

HEDDA: Do you think they'll succeed?

BRACK (*bending over her and whispering*): No, Hedda Gabler — as long as I keep quiet.

HEDDA (*looking at him anxiously*): And if you don't keep quiet — then what?

BRACK (*with a shrug*): Counsel could always claim that the pistol was stolen.

HEDDA (*decisively*): I'd rather die!

BRACK (*smiling*): People *say* such things. But they don't *do* them.

HEDDA (*without answering*): And what, then, if the pistol wasn't stolen. And they found the owner. What would happen?

BRACK: Well, Hedda — there'd be a scandal.

HEDDA: A scandal!

BRACK: A scandal, yes — the kind you're so deathly afraid of. Naturally, you'd appear in court — you and Mademoiselle Diana. She'd have to explain how the whole thing occurred. Whether it was an accident or homicide. Was he trying to pull the pistol out of his pocket to threaten her? Is that why it went off? Or had she torn the pistol out of his hand, shot him, and slipped it back in his pocket again? It's rather like her to do that, you know. She's a powerful woman, this Mademoiselle Diana.

HEDDA: But all that sordid business is no concern of mine.

BRACK: No. But you'll have to answer the question: Why did you give Eilert Løvborg the pistol? And what conclusions will people draw from the fact that you did give it to him?

HEDDA (*her head sinking*): That's true. I hadn't thought of that.

BRACK: Well, luckily there's no danger, as long as I keep quiet.

HEDDA: So I'm in your power, Judge. You have your hold over me from now on.

BRACK (*whispers more softly*): My dearest Hedda — believe me — I won't abuse my position.

HEDDA: All the same, I'm in your power. Tied to your will and desire. Not free. Not free, then! (*Rises impetuously.*) No — I can't bear the thought of it. Never!

BRACK (*looks at her half mockingly*): One usually manages to adjust to the inevitable.

HEDDA (*returning his look*): Yes, perhaps so. (*She goes over to the writing table. Suppressing an involuntary smile, she imitates Tesman's intonation.*) Well? Getting on with it, George? Uh?

TESMAN: Goodness knows, dear. It's going to mean months and months of work, in any case.

HEDDA (*as before*): Imagine that! (*Runs her hand lightly through Mrs. Elvsted's hair.*) Don't you find it strange, Thea? Here you are, sitting now beside Tesman — just as you used to sit with Eilert Løvborg.

MRS. ELVSTED: Oh, if I could only inspire your husband in the same way.

HEDDA: Oh, that will surely come — in time.

TESMAN: Yes, you know what, Hedda — I really think I'm beginning to feel something of the kind. But you go back and sit with Judge Brack.

HEDDA: Is there nothing the two of you need from me now?

TESMAN: No, nothing in the world. (*Turning his head.*) From now on, Judge, you'll have to be good enough to keep Hedda company.

BRACK (*with a glance at Hedda*): I'll take the greatest pleasure in that.

HEDDA: Thanks. But I'm tired this evening. I want to rest a while in there on the sofa.

TESMAN: Yes, do that, dear. Uh?

(*Hedda goes into the inner room, pulling the curtains closed after her. Short pause. Suddenly she is heard playing a wild dance melody on the piano.*)

MRS. ELVSTED (*starting up from her chair*): Oh — what's that?

TESMAN (*running to the center doorway*): But Hedda dearest — don't go playing dance music tonight! Think of Auntie Rina! And Eilert, too!

HEDDA (*putting her head out between the curtains*): And Auntie Julie. And all the rest of them. From now on I'll be quiet. (*She closes the curtains again.*)

TESMAN (*at the writing table*): She can't feel very happy seeing us do this melancholy work. You know what, Mrs. Elvsted — you must move in with Aunt Julie. Then I can come over evenings. And then we can sit and work *there*. Uh?

MRS. ELVSTED: Yes, perhaps that would be best —

HEDDA: I can hear everything you say, Tesman. But what will I do evenings over here?

TESMAN (*leafing through the notes*): Oh, I'm sure Judge Brack will be good enough to stop by and see you.

BRACK (*in the armchair, calling out gaily*): I couldn't miss an evening, Mrs. Tesman! We'll have great times here together, the two of us!

HEDDA (*in a clear, ringing voice*): Yes, you can hope so, Judge, can't you? You, the one cock of the walk —

(*A shot is heard within. Tesman, Mrs. Elvsted, and Brack start from their chairs.*)

TESMAN: Oh, now she's fooling with those pistols again.

(*He throws the curtains back and runs in. Mrs. Elvsted follows. Hedda lies, lifeless, stretched out on the sofa. Confusion and cries. Berta comes in, bewildered, from the right.*)

TESMAN (*shrieking to Brack*): Shot herself! Shot herself in the temple! Can you imagine!

BRACK (*in the armchair, prostrated*): But good God! People don't *do* such things!

COMMENTARIES

Ibsen wrote about his own work, both in his letters to producers and actors and in his notes describing the development of his plays. Such notes reveal his concern, his insights as he wrote the plays, and his motives. Sometimes he says things about the plays that do not completely square with modern interpretations. On the other hand, he explains in his notes that the circumstances of women in modern society were much on his mind when he was working on *A Doll House*.

Ibsen's "Notes for the Modern Tragedy" is remarkable for suggesting a separate sensibility (spiritual law) for men and for women. His observations about the society in which women live — and in which Nora is confounded — sound as if they could have been written a century later than they were. When Bernard Shaw wrote his comments on *A Doll House* the play was a popular shocker and Shaw's observations were designed to help audiences interpret the play's actions more carefully. He is one of the earliest critics of the play, and one must remember while reading Shaw that some productions of the play changed the ending to make it happy. Muriel Bradbrook's discussion of *A Doll House* focuses on the moral bankruptcy of Nora's situation, which is to say the situation of all wives of the period.

Ibsen's notes to *Hedda Gabler* show us what a complex process he went through to conceive the character and put her in action. One sees his method of sketching out the action of the play, then commenting to himself on what the action implies. Caroline Mayerson's extensive commentary gives us insight into the symbolic levels of meaning in the play. Since the play has been considered a masterpiece of realism, some critics have assumed that it has no symbolic texture. Mayerson counters that view with a detailed analysis. Jan Kott's interpretation of Hedda's pistols, which he sees as explicit sexual symbols, helps to expand Mayerson's claim that the drama, while realistic, does not ignore the deeper significance of its own imagery.

Henrik Ibsen (1828–1906)
NOTES FOR THE MODERN TRAGEDY   1878

TRANSLATED BY A. G. CHATER

Ibsen's first notes for A Doll House *were jotted down on October 19, 1878. They show that his thinking on the relations between men and women was considerably sophisticated at this time and that the material for the play had been gestating. His comments indicate that the essentially male society he knew was one of his central concerns in the play.*

There are two kinds of spiritual law, two kinds of conscience, one in man and another, altogether different, in woman. They do not understand each other; but in practical life the woman is judged by man's law, as though she were not a woman but a man.

The wife in the play ends by having no idea of what is right or wrong; natural feeling on the one hand and belief in authority on the other have altogether bewildered her.

A woman cannot be herself in the society of the present day, which is an exclusively masculine society, with laws framed by men and with a judicial system that judges feminine conduct from a masculine point of view.

She has committed forgery, and she is proud of it; for she did it out of love for her husband, to save his life. But this husband with his commonplace principles of honor is on the side of the law and looks at the question from the masculine point of view.

Spiritual conflicts. Oppressed and bewildered by the belief in authority, she loses faith in her moral right and ability to bring up her children. Bitterness. A mother in modern society, like certain insects who go away and die when she has done her duty in the propagation of the race. Love of life, of home, of husband and children and family. Now and then a womanly shaking off of her thoughts. Sudden return of anxiety and terror. She must bear it all alone.

The catastrophe approaches, inexorably, inevitably. Despair, conflict, and destruction.

(Krogstad has acted dishonorably and thereby become well-to-do; now his prosperity does not help him, he cannot recover his honor.)

Bernard Shaw (1856–1950)

A DOLL'S HOUSE   *1891*

One of the first English men of letters to pay close attention to Ibsen's work was Bernard Shaw. Shaw was beginning to write his own plays, but he also spent time in the theater as a critic. His landmark book The Quintessence of Ibsenism (1891; rev. ed. 1913), *in which this comment on* A Doll House *appears, is a thorough discussion not only of the individual plays that Ibsen had produced but of their implication for future literature. Shaw saw the significance of the new realism and its implications for the audiences of the later nineteenth century. He saw, too, that Ibsen's brand of realism would have an effect on the beliefs of his audiences, that Ibsen's drama was a drama of important ideas. In the following excerpt Shaw is especially sensitive to the feminist issues that are at the heart of the play and pays close attention to Nora's character development.*

Unfortunately, *Pillars of Society*, as a propagandist play, is disabled by the circumstance that the hero, being a fraudulent hypocrite in the ordinary police-court sense of the phrase, would hardly be accepted as a typical pillar of society by the class he represents. Accordingly, Ibsen took care next time to make his idealist irreproachable from the standpoint of the ordinary idealist morality. In the famous *Doll's House*, the pillar of society who owns the doll is a model husband, father, and citizen. In his little household, with the three darling children and the affectionate little wife, all on the most loving terms with one another, we have the sweet home, the womanly woman, the happy family life of the idealist's dream. Mrs. Nora Helmer is happy in the belief that she has attained a valid realization of all these illusions; that she is an ideal wife and mother; and that Helmer is an ideal husband who would, if the necessity arose, give his life to save her reputation. A few simply contrived incidents disabuse her effectually on all these points. One of her earliest acts of devotion to her husband has been the secret raising of a sum of money to enable him to make a tour which was necessary to restore his health. As he would have broken down sooner than go into debt, she has had to persuade him that the money was a gift from her father. It was really obtained from a moneylender, who refused to make her the loan unless she induced her father to endorse the promissory note. This being impossible, as her father was dying at the time, she took the shortest way out of the difficulty by writing the name herself, to the entire satisfaction of the moneylender, who, though not at all duped, knew that forged bills are often the surest to be paid. Since then she has slaved in secret at scrivener's work until she has nearly paid off the debt.

At this point Helmer is made manager of the bank in which he is employed; and the moneylender, wishing to obtain a post there, uses the forged bill to force Nora to exert her influence with Helmer on his behalf. But she, having a hearty contempt for the man, cannot be persuaded by him that there was any harm in putting her father's name on the bill, and ridicules the suggestion that the law would not recognize that she was right under the circumstances. It is her husband's own contemptuous denunciation of a forgery formerly committed by the moneylender himself that destroys her self-satisfaction and opens her eyes to her ignorance of the serious business of the world to which her husband belongs: the world outside the home he shares with her. When he goes on to tell her that commercial dishonesty is generally to be traced to the influence of bad mothers, she begins to perceive that the happy way in which she plays with the children, and the care she takes to dress them nicely, are not sufficient to constitute her a fit person to train them. To redeem the forged bill, she resolves to borrow the balance due upon it from an intimate friend of the family. She has learnt to coax her husband into giving her what she asks by appealing to his affection for her: that is, by playing all sorts of pretty tricks until he is wheedled into an amorous humor. This plan she has adopted without thinking about it, instinctively taking the line of least resistance with him. And now she naturally takes the same line with her husband's friend. An unexpected declaration of love from him is the result; and it at once explains to her the real nature of the domestic influence she has been so proud of.

All her illusions about herself are now shattered. She sees herself as an ignorant and silly woman, a dangerous mother, and a wife kept for her husband's pleasure merely; but she clings all the harder to her illusion about him: He is still the ideal husband who would make any sacrifice to rescue her from ruin. She resolves to kill herself rather than allow him to destroy his own career by taking the forgery on himself to save her reputation. The final disillusion comes when he, instead of at once proposing to pursue this ideal line of conduct when he hears of the forgery, naturally enough flies into a vulgar rage and heaps invective on her for disgracing him. Then she sees that their whole family life has been a fiction: their home a mere doll's house in which they have been playing at ideal husband and father, wife and mother. So she leaves him then and there and goes out into the real world to find out its reality for herself, and to gain some position not fundamentally false, refusing to see her children again until she is fit to be in charge of them, or to live with him until she and he become capable of a more honorable relation to one another. He at first cannot understand what has happened, and flourishes the shattered ideals over her as if they were as potent as ever. He presents the course most agreeable to him — that of her staying at home and avoiding a scandal — as her duty to her husband, to her children, and to her religion; but the magic of these disguises is gone; and at last even he understands what has really happened, and sits down alone to wonder whether that more honorable relation can ever come to pass between them.

Muriel C. Bradbrook
A DOLL'S HOUSE: IBSEN THE MORALIST   *1948*

> *In her important study of Ibsen,* Ibsen: The Norwegian, *Muriel Bradbrook discusses all the important plays, but she reserves a special place for* A Doll House. *In her analysis she suggests that Nora slowly discovers the fundamental bankruptcy of her marriage. Bradbrook calls it "eight years' prostitution." She*

also shows the true extent to which Torvald is both possessive and immature. As Bradbrook says, the true moment of recognition — in the Greek tragic sense — occurs when Nora sees both herself and Torvald in their true nature. Bradbrook also helps us see the full implication of Nora's leaving her home. She can never hope again for the comforts she has enjoyed as Torvald's wife.

Poor Nora, living by playing her tricks like a little pet animal, sensing how to manage Torvald by those pettinesses in his character she does not know she knows of, is too vulnerably sympathetic to find her life-work in reading John Stuart Mill. At the end she still does not understand the strange world in which she has done wrong by forging a signature. She does understand that she has lived by what Virginia Woolf called "the slow waterlogged sinking of her will into his." And this picture is built up for her and for us by the power of structural implication, a form of writing particularly suited to drama, where the latent possibilities of a long stretch of past time can be thrown into relief by a crisis. In *A Doll's House*, the past is not only lighted up by the present, as a transparency might be lit up with a lamp; the past is changed by the present so that it becomes a different thing. Nora's marriage becomes eight years' prostitution, as she gradually learns the true nature of her relations with Torvald and the true nature of Torvald's feelings for her.

In Act I, no less than six different episodes bring out the war that is secretly waged between his masculine dictatorship and her feminine wiles:

Her wheedling him for money with a simple transference: "Let us do as *you* suggest. . . ."

Her promise to Christine: "Just leave it to me: I will broach the matter very cleverly." She is evidently habituated to and aware of her own technique.

Her description of how she tried to coax Torvald into taking the holiday and how she was saving up the story of the bond "for when I am no longer as good-looking as I am now." She knows the precarious nature of her hold.

Her method of asking work for Christine by putting Christine also into a (completely bogus) position of worshiping subservience to Torvald.

Her boast to Krogstad about her influence. Whilst this may be a justifiable triumph over her tormentor, it is an unconscious betrayal of Torvald (witness his fury in Act II at the idea of being thought uxorious).

After this faceted exposition, the treatment grows much broader. Nora admits Torvald's jealousy: Yet she flirts with Rank, aware but not acknowledging the grounds of her control. The pressure of implication remains constant throughout: It is comparable with the effect of a dialect, coloring all that is said. To take a few lines at random from the dialogue of Nora and Rank in Act II:

> NORA (*putting her hand on his shoulder*): Dear, dear Dr. Rank! Death mustn't take you away from Torvald and me. [Nora is getting demonstrative as she senses Rank's responsiveness, and her hopes of obtaining a loan from him rise. Hence her warmth of feeling, purely seductive.]
>
> RANK: It is a loss you will easily recover from. Those who are gone away are soon forgotten. [Poor Rank is reminded by that "Torvald and me" how little he really counts to Nora.]
>
> NORA (*anxiously*): Do you believe that? [Rank has awakened her thoughts of what may happen if *she* has to go away.]

Her methods grow more desperate — the open appeal to Torvald to keep Krogstad and the frantic expedient of the tarantella. In the last act her fate is upon her; yet in spite of all her terror and Torvald's tipsy amorousness, she still believes in his chivalry and devotion. This extraordinary self-deception is perhaps the subtlest and most telling implication of all. Practice had left her theory unshaken: So when the crash comes, she cries, "I have been living with a strange man," yet it was but the kind of man her actions had always implied him to be. Her vanity had completely prevented her from recognizing what she was doing, even though she had become such an expert at doing it.

Torvald is more gradually revealed. In the first act he appears indulgent, perhaps a trifle inclined to nag about the macaroons and to preach, but virtually a more efficient David Copperfield curbing a rather better-trained Dora. In the second act, his resentment and his pleasure alike uncover the deeper bases of his dominance. His anger at the prospect of being thought under his wife's influence and his fury at the imputation of narrow-mindedness show that it is really based on his own cowardice, the need for something weaker to bully: This is confirmed when he gloats over Nora's panic as evidence of her love for him, and over her agitation in the tarantella ("you little helpless thing!"). His love of order and his fastidiousness, when joined to such qualities, betray a set personality; and the last act shows that he has neither control nor sympathy on the physical level. But he is no fool, and his integrity is not all cowardice. Doubtless, debt or forgery really was abhorrent to him.

The climax of the play comes when Nora sees Torvald and sees herself: It is an *anagnorisis,* a recognition. Her life is cored like an apple. For she has had no life apart from this. Behind the irrelevant program for self-education there stands a woman, pitifully inexperienced, numbed by emotional shock, but with a newfound will to face what has happened, to accept her bankruptcy, as, in a very different way, Peer Gynt had at last accepted his.

"Yes, I am beginning to understand. . . ." she says. "What you did," observes the now magnanimous Torvald, "you did out of love for me." "That is true," says Nora: And she calls him to a "settling of accounts," not in any spirit of hostility but in an attempt to organize vacancy. "I have made nothing of my life. . . . I must stand quite alone . . . it is necessary to me . . ." That is really the program. *Ainsi tout leur a craqué dans les mains.*°

The spare and laminated speech gains its effect by inference and riddle. But these are the characteristic virtues of Norse. Irony is its natural weapon. Ibsen was working with the grain of the language. It was no accident that it fell to a Norwegian to take that most finely tooled art, the drama, and bring it to a point and precision so nice that literally not a phrase is without its direct contribution to the structure. The unrelenting cohesion of *A Doll's House* is perhaps, like that of the *Oedipus the King,* too hard on the playgoer; he is allowed no relief. Nora cannot coo to her baby without saying: "My sweet little *baby doll!*" or play with her children without choosing, significantly, *Hide and Seek.* Ibsen will not allow the smallest action to escape from the psychopathology of everyday life. However, a play cannot be acted so that every moment is tense with significance, and, in practice, an actor, for the sake of light and shade, will probably slur some of Ibsen's points, deliberately or unconsciously. The tension between the characters is such that the slightest movement of one sets all the others quivering. But this is partly because they are

---

Ainsi . . . mains: Thus everything has shattered in their hands.

seen with such detachment, like a clear-cut intaglio. The play is, above all, articulated.

That is not to say that it is the mere dissection of a problem. Perhaps Rank and Mrs. Linde would have been more subtly wrought into the action at a later date; but the tight control kept over Nora and Torvald does not mean that they can be exhausted by analysis or staled by custom. They are so far in advance of the characters of *Pillars of Society* that they are capable of the surprising yet inevitable development that marks the character conceived "in the round," the character that is, in Ibsen's phrase, fully "seen."

Consider, for example, Torvald's soliloquy whilst Nora is taking off her masquerade dress. It recalls at one moment Dickens's most unctuous hypocrites — "Here I will protect you like a hunted dove that I have saved from the claws of the hawk!" — at another Meredith's Willoughby Patterne° — "Only be frank and open with me and I will be both will and conscience to you" — yet from broadest caricature to sharpest analysis, it remains the self-glorified strut of the one character, the bank clerk in his pride, cousin to Peer Gynt, that typical Norwegian, and to Hjalmer Ekdal, the toiling breadwinner of the studio.

Whilst the Ibsenites might have conceded that Torvald is Art, they would probably have contended that Nora is Truth. Nora, however, is much more than a Revolting Wife. She is not a sour misanthropist or a fighting suffragette, but a lovely young woman who knows that she still holds her husband firmly infatuated after eight years of marriage. . . .

In leaving her husband Nora is seeking a fuller life as a human being. She is emancipating herself. Yet the seeking itself is also a renunciation, a kind of death — "I must stand alone." No less than Falk, or the hero of *On the Vidda*, she gives up something that has been her whole life. She is as broken as Torvald in the end: But she is a strong character and he is a weak one. In the "happy ending" which Ibsen reluctantly allowed to be used, it was the sight of the children that persuaded her to stay, and unless it is remembered that leaving Torvald means leaving the children, the full measure of Nora's decision cannot be taken. An actress gets her chance to make this point in the reply to Torvald's plea that Nora should stay for the children's sake.

It should be remembered, too, that the seriousness of the step she takes is lost on the present generation. She was putting herself outside society, inviting insult, destitution, and loneliness. She went out into a very dark night.

Willoughby Patterne: The protagonist in George Meredith's novel *The Egoist* (1879), an arrogant aristocrat who lacks awareness of the needs and desires of the women in his life.

Henrik Ibsen (1828–1906)
NOTES FOR *HEDDA GABLER*   *1890*

TRANSLATED BY EVERT SPRINCHORN

Like most playwrights, Ibsen kept a notebook into which he jotted ideas as he was writing his plays. The notes that follow are some of those he gathered as he was writing Hedda Gabler. *They show how his mind worked on the material, how he considered alternatives to what he was doing, and how he permitted his material to grow and develop.*

¶ One talks about building railways and highways for the cause of progress. But no, no, that is not what is needed. Space must be cleared so that the spirit of man can make its great turnabout. For it has gone astray. The spirit of man has gone astray. . . .

¶ *Notes:* One evening as Hedda and Tesman, together with some others, were on their way home from a party, Hedda remarked as they walked by a charming house that was where she would like to live. She meant it, but she said it only to keep the conversation with Tesman going. "He simply cannot carry on a conversation."

The house was actually for rent or sale. Tesman had been pointed out as the coming young man. And later when he proposed, and let slip that he too had dreamed of living there, she accepted.

He too had liked the house very much.

They get married. And they rent the house.[1]

But when Hedda returns as a young wife, with a vague sense of responsibility, the whole thing seems distasteful to her. She conceives a kind of hatred for the house just because it has become her home. She confides this to Brack. She evades the question with Tesman.

¶ The play shall deal with "the impossible," that is, to aspire to and strive for something which is against all the conventions, against that which is acceptable to conscious minds — Hedda's included.

¶ The episode of the hat makes Aunt Rising° lose her composure. She leaves — That it could be taken for the maid's hat — no, that's going too far!

That my hat, which I've had for over nine years, could be taken for the maid's — no, that's really too much! . . .

¶ Very few true parents are to be found in the world. Most people grow up under the influence of aunts or uncles — either neglected and misunderstood or else spoiled. . . .

¶ Hedda feels herself demoniacally attracted by the tendencies of the times. But she lacks courage. Her thoughts remain theories, ineffective dreams.

¶ The feminine imagination is not active and independently creative like the masculine. It needs a bit of reality as a help.

¶ Løvborg has had inclinations toward "the bohemian life." Hedda is attracted in the same direction, but she does not dare to take the leap.

¶ Buried deep within Hedda there is a level of poetry. But the environment frightens her. Suppose she were to make herself ridiculous!

¶ Hedda realizes that she, much more than Thea, has abandoned her husband.

¶ The newly wedded couple return home in September — as the summer is dying. In the second act they sit in the garden — but with their coats on.

---

[1]Both of them, each in his and her own way, have seen in their common love for this house a sign of their mutual understanding. As if they sought and were drawn to a common home.

Then he rents the house. They get married and go abroad. He orders the house bought and his aunt furnishes it at his expense. Now it is their home. It is theirs and yet it is not, because it is not paid for. Everything depends on his getting the professorship. [Ibsen's note.]

Aunt Rising: Ibsen also spelled it *Rysing*. She became Aunt Juliana Tesman in the final version of the play.

¶ Being frightened by one's own voice. Something strange, foreign.

¶ NEWEST PLAN: The festivities in Tesman's garden — and Løvborg's defeat — already prepared for in the 1st act. Second act: the party —

¶ Hedda energetically refuses to serve as hostess. She will not celebrate their marriage because (in her opinion, it isn't a marriage) . . .

¶ Hedda is the type of woman in her position and with her character. She marries Tesman but she devotes her imagination to Eilert Løvborg. She leans back in her chair, closes her eyes, and dreams of his adventures. . . . This is the enormous difference: Mrs. Elvsted "works for his moral improvement." But for Hedda he is the object of cowardly, tempting daydreams. In reality she does not have the courage to be a part of anything like that. Then she realizes her condition. Caught! Can't comprehend it. Ridiculous! Ridiculous!

¶ The traditional delusion that one man and one woman are made for each other. Hedda has her roots in the conventional. She marries Tesman but she dreams of Eilert Løvborg. . . . She is disgusted by the latter's flight from life. He believes that this has raised him in her estimation. . . . Thea Elvsted is the conventional, sentimental, hysterical Philistine.

¶ Those Philistines, Mrs. E. and Tesman, explain my behavior by saying first I drink myself drunk and that the rest is done in insanity. It's a flight from reality which is an absolute necessity to me.

¶ *E. L.*: Give me something — a flower — at our parting. Hedda hands him the revolver.

Then Tesman arrives: Has he gone? "Yes." Do you think he will still compete against me? No, I don't think so. You can set your mind at rest.

¶ Tesman relates that when they were in Gratz she did not want to visit her relatives —

He misunderstands her real motives.

¶ In the last act as Tesman, Mrs. Elvsted, and Miss Rysing are consulting, Hedda plays in the small room at the back. She stops. The conversation continues. She appears in the doorway — Good night — I'm going now. Do you need me for anything? Tesman: No, nothing at all. Good night, my dear! . . . The shot is fired —

¶ CONCLUSION: All rush into the back room. Brack sinks as if paralyzed into a chair near the stove: But God have mercy — people don't *do* such things!

¶ When Hedda hints at her ideas to Brack, he says: Yes, yes, that's extraordinarily amusing — Ha ha ha! He does not understand that she is quite serious.

¶ Hedda is right in this: There is no love on Tesman's part. Nor on the aunt's part. However full of love she may be.

Eilert Løvborg has a double nature. It is a fiction that one loves only *one* person. He loves two — or many — alternately (to put it frivolously). But how can he explain his position? Mrs. Elvsted, who forces him to behave correctly, runs away from her husband. Hedda, who drives him beyond all limits, draws back at the thought of a scandal.

¶ Neither he nor Mrs. Elvsted understands the point. Tesman reads in the manuscript that was left behind about "the two ideals." Mrs. Elvsted can't explain to him what E. L. meant. Then comes the burlesque note: Both T. and Mrs. E. are going to devote their future lives to interpreting the mystery.

¶ Tesman thinks that Hedda hates E. L.

Mrs. Elvsted thinks so too.

Hedda sees their delusion but dares not disabuse them of it. There is something beautiful about having an aim in life. Even if it is a delusion —

She cannot do it. Take part in someone else's.

That is when she shoots herself.

The destroyed manuscript is entitled "The ~~Philosophy~~ Ethics of Future Society."

¶ Tesman is on the verge of losing his head. All this work meaningless. New thoughts! New visions! A whole new world! Then the two of them sit there, trying to find the meaning in it. Can't make any sense of it. . . .

¶ The greatest misery in this world is that so many have nothing to do but pursue happiness without being able to find it. . . .

¶ The simile: The journey of life = the journey on a train.

H.: One doesn't usually jump out of the compartment.

No, not when the train is moving.

Nor stand still when it is stationary. There's always someone on the platform, staring in.

¶ *Hedda*: Dream of a scandal — yes, I understand that well enough. But commit one — no, no, no.

¶ *Løvborg*: Now I understand. My ideal was an illusion. You aren't a bit better than I. Now I have nothing left to live for. Except pleasure — dissipation — as you call it . . . Wait, here's a present (The pistol)

¶ Tesman is nearsighted. Wears glasses. My, what a beautiful rose! Then he stuck his nose in the cactus. Ever since then —!

¶ NB: The mutual hatred of women. Women have no influence on external matters of government. Therefore they want to have an influence on souls. And then so many of them have no aim in life (the lack thereof is inherited) — . . .

¶ Men and women don't belong to the same century. . . . What a great prejudice that one should love only *one*! . . .

¶ The demoniacal element in Hedda is this: She wants to exert her influence on someone — But once she has done so, she despises him. . . . The manuscript?

¶ In the third act Hedda questions Mrs. Elvsted. But if he's like that, why is he worth holding on to. . . . Yes, yes, I know — . . .

¶ NB!! The reversal in the play occurs during the big scene between Hedda and E. L. *He*: What a wretched business it is to conform to the existing morals. It would be ideal if a man of the present could live the life of the future. What a miserable business it is to fight over a professorship!

Hedda — that lovely girl! *H.*: No! *E. L.*: Yes, I'm going to say it. That lovely, cold girl — cold as marble.

I'm not dissipated fundamentally. But the life of reality isn't livable — . . .

¶ Life becomes for Hedda a ridiculous affair that isn't "worth seeing through to the end."

¶ The happiest mission in life is to place the people of today in the conditions of the future.

L.: Never put a child in this world, H.!

¶ When Brack speaks of a "triangular affair," Hedda thinks about what is going to happen and refers ambiguously to it. Brack doesn't understand.

¶ Brack cannot bear to be in a house where there are small children. "Children shouldn't be allowed to exist until they are fourteen or fifteen. That is, girls. What about boys? Shouldn't be allowed to exist at all — or else they should be raised outside the house."

¶ H. admits that children have always been a horror to her too.

¶ Hedda is strongly but imprecisely opposed to the idea that one should love "the family." The aunts mean nothing to her.

¶ It liberated Hedda's spirit to serve as a confessor to E. L. Her sympathy has secretly been on his side — But it became ugly when the public found out everything. Then she backed out.

¶ MAIN POINTS: (1) They are not all made to be mothers. (2) They are passionate but they are afraid of scandal. (3) They perceive that the times are full of missions worth devoting one's life to, but they cannot discover them.

¶ And besides Tesman is not exactly a professional, but he is a specialist. The Middle Ages are dead —

¶ T.: Now there you see also the great advantages to my studies. I can lose manuscripts and rewrite them — no inspiration needed —

¶ Hedda is completely taken up by the child that is to come, but when it is born she dreads what is to follow —

¶ Hedda must say somewhere in the play that she did not like to get out of her compartment while on the trip. Why not? I don't like to show my legs. . . . Ah, Mrs. H., but they do indeed show themselves. Nevertheless, I don't.

¶ Shot herself! Shot herself!

Brack (collapsing in the easy chair): But great God — people don't *do* such things!

¶NB!! Eilert Løvborg believes that a comradeship must be formed between man and woman out of which the truly spiritual human being can arise. Whatever else the two of them do is of no concern. This is what the people around him do not understand. To them he is dissolute. Inwardly he is not.

¶ If a man can have several male friends, why can't he have several lady friends?

¶ It is precisely the sensual feelings that are aroused while in the company of his female "friends" or "comrades" that seek release in his excesses.

¶ Now I'm going. Don't you have some little remembrance to give me —? You have flowers — and so many other things — (The story of the pistol from before) — But you won't use it anyhow —

¶ In the fourth act when Hedda finds out that he has shot himself, she is jubilant. . . . He had courage.

Here is the rest of the manuscript.

¶ CONCLUSION: Life isn't tragic. . . . Life is ridiculous. . . . And that's what I can't bear.

¶ Do you know what happens in novels? All those who kill themselves — through the head — not in the stomach. . . . How ridiculous — how baroque — . . .

Caroline W. Mayerson (b. 1907)

THEMATIC SYMBOLS IN *HEDDA GABLER*   1965

Sometimes the designation of realism has been applied to Ibsen in such a way as to suggest that all we get in his plays is a slice of life, with details that are meaningless except that they are there. The fact is that, like Gustave Flaubert, James Joyce, August Strindberg, and other realistic writers of his time, Ibsen was a craftsman who tried to make every detail in his plays add up to something.

Caroline Mayerson shows us how loaded with significance certain otherwise innocent-looking objects are in Hedda Gabler. *She begins with Thea's hair, the manuscript that Løvborg loses, and General Gabler's pistols. By examining them, she shows us just how rich the surfaces of Ibsen's plays can be.*

During the course of the play, Ibsen places considerable emphasis upon Thea's hair, upon the manuscript as her "child," and upon General Gabler's pistols, and his treatment of these items suggests that he intended them to have symbolic significance. We shall be concerned in this essay with determining this significance and its effect upon the total meaning of the play. My analysis of the three symbols in their relationship to the theme, the characters, and the action will be based upon several broad assumptions which reflect views of Ibsen's concepts and methods implied or expressed by a number of previous commentators: (1) In *Hedda Gabler*, Ibsen examines the possibility of attaining freedom and fulfillment in modern society. (2) Hedda is a woman, not a monster; neurotic, but not psychotic. Thus, she may be held accountable for her behavior. But she is spiritually sterile. Her yearning for self-realization through exercise of her natural endowments is in conflict with her enslavement to a narrow standard of conduct. This conflict is complicated by her incomplete understanding of what freedom and fulfillment mean and how they may be achieved. She fails to realize that one must earn his inheritance in order to possess it, and she romanticizes the destructive and sensational aspects of Dionysiac ecstasy without perceiving that its true end is regeneration through sublimation of the ego in a larger unity. (3) Ibsen, as an experienced artist, was aware of the impact of minutiae and the need for integrating these with the general impression to be projected; therefore we may regard his descriptions, his stage directions, and his properties, no less than his dialogue, as means whereby intention and significance are conveyed.

While all the other characters in *Hedda Gabler* are implicitly compared to Hedda and serve, in one way or another, to throw light upon her personality, Thea Elvsted is the one with whom she is most obviously contrasted. Furthermore, their contest for the control of Loevborg is the most prominent external conflict in the play. The sterility-fertility antithesis from which central action proceeds is chiefly realized through the opposition of these two. Hedda is pregnant, and Thea is physically barren. But in emotionally repudiating her unborn child, Hedda rejects what Ibsen considered woman's opportunity to advance the march of progress.[1] The many other symptoms of her psychic sterility need little enlargement. Unwilling to give or even share herself, she maintains her independence at the price of complete frustration. Ibsen uses Thea, on the other hand, to indicate a way to freedom which Hedda never apprehends. Through her ability to extend herself in comradeship with Loevborg, Thea not only brings about the rebirth of his creative powers, but merges her own best self with his to produce a prophecy of the future, conceivably of the "Third Kingdom," in which Ibsen believed that the ideals of the past would coalesce in a new and more perfect unity. Having lost herself to find herself, she almost instinctively

[1] Cf. Ibsen's speech to the Norwegian Women's Rights League (1898): "It is women who are to solve the social problems. As mothers they are to do it. And only as such can they do it. Here lies a great task for woman" (*Speeches and New Letters of Henrik Ibsen*, trans. Arne Kildal [Boston, 1901], 66).

breaks with the mores of her culture in order to ensure continuance of function. Despite her palpitating femininity, she is the most truly emancipated person in the play. And it is she who wins at least a limited victory in the end. Although Loevborg has failed her, her fecundity is indefatigable; as Hedda kills herself, Thea is busily preparing to recreate her "child" with Tesman, thereby at once enabling him to realize his own little talents and weakening even further the tenuous bond which ties him to Hedda.

The contrast outlined above is reinforced by the procreative imagery of the play. The manuscript is Loevborg's and Thea's "child," the idea of progress born of a union between individuals who have freed themselves from the pre-conceptions of their environment.[2] This manuscript the sterile Hedda throws into the fire at the climax of her vindictive passion. Her impulse to annihilate by burning is directed both toward Thea's "child" and toward Thea's hair and calls attention to the relationship between them. Even without other indications that Ibsen was using hair as a symbol of fertility, such an inference might be made from the words which accompany the destruction of the manuscript:

> Now I am burning your child, Thea! Burning it, curly-locks! Your child and Eilert Loevborg's. I am burning — I am burning your child.

There is, however, considerable evidence, both before and after this scene, that Thea's hair is a sign of that potency which Hedda envies even while she ridicules and bullies its possessor. Ibsen, of course, had ample precedent for employing hair as a symbol of fertility. Perhaps the best support for the argument that he made a literary adaptation of this well-known, ancient idea in *Hedda Gabler* is a summary of the instances in which the hair is mentioned.

Although Ibsen's unobtrusive description of the hair of each of these women at her initial entrance may seem at the time only a casual stroke in the sketch, it assumes importance in retrospect. Hedda's hair is "not particularly abundant," whereas Thea's is "unusually abundant and wavy." Hedda's strongest impression of Thea is of that abundance: She recalls her as "the girl with the irritating hair, that she was always showing off." Moreover, Thea fearfully recollects Hedda's schoolgirl reaction to it: ". . . When we met on the stairs you used always to pull my hair. . . . Yes, and once you said you would burn it off my head." When Thea and Loevborg first meet in the play, Hedda seats herself, significantly, between them; the brief exchange of questions and answers which ensues is notable for its overtones: "Is not she [Thea] lovely to look at?" Loevborg asks. Hedda, lightly stroking Thea's hair, answers, "Only to look at?" Loevborg understands the innuendo, for he replies, "Yes. For we two — she and I — we two are real comrades." Later, when the women are alone, Hedda, now fully informed of the extent to which Thea has realized her generative powers, laments her own meager endowment and renews her threat in its adolescent terms:

> Oh, if you could only understand how poor I am, and fate has made you so rich! (*Clasps her passionately in her arms.*) I think I must burn your hair off after all.

Hedda's violent gesture and Thea's almost hysterical reaction ("Let me go! Let me go! I am afraid of you, Hedda!") indicate the dangerous seriousness of words

---

[2]Cf. Ibsen's statement: "I firmly believe in the capacity for procreation and development of ideals" (*Speeches and New Letters*, 57).

which otherwise might be mistaken for a joke; the threat prepares us for the burning of the manuscript, which follows in Act III. In the last tense scene of the play Hedda twice handles Thea's hair. The reader's imagination readily constructs the expressions and gestures whereby an actress could show Hedda's true attitude toward the hair which Ibsen directs her to ruffle "gently" and to pass her hands "softly through." The first gesture follows immediately upon an important action — Hedda has just removed the pistol to the inner room. The second accompanies dialogue which for the last time emphasizes Hedda's association of the hair with Thea's fertility and which brings home to Hedda her own predicament:

> HEDDA (*passes her hands softly through Mrs. Elvsted's hair*): Doesn't it seem strange to you, Thea? Here you are sitting with Tesman — just as you used to sit with Eilert Loevborg?
> MRS. ELVSTED: Ah, if I could only inspire your husband in the same way!
> HEDDA: Oh, that will come too — in time.
> TESMAN: Yes, do you know, Hedda — I really think I begin to feel something of the sort. But won't you go to sit with Brack again?
> HEDDA: Is there nothing I can do to help you two?
> TESMAN: No, nothing in the world.

These scenes in which the hair plays a part not only call attention to Hedda's limitations but show her reaction to her partial apprehension of them. In adapting a primitive symbol, Ibsen slightly altered its conventional meaning, substituting psychic for physical potency. Its primitivistic associations nevertheless pervade the fundamental relationships between the two women. The weapons Hedda uses against Thea are her hands and fire. The shock of the climactic scene results chiefly from seeing the savage emerge from behind her veneer of sophistication — the Hedda who feeds the manuscript to the flames is a naked woman engaged in a barbaric act. In contrast, the Hedda who handles her father's pistols is self-consciously cloaked in illusions of her hereditary participation in a chivalric tradition.

The pistols, like many other symbols used by Ibsen, quite obviously are not merely symbols, but have important plot function as well. Moreover, their symbolic significance cannot be reduced to a simple formula, but must be thought of in the light of the complex of associations which they carry as Hedda's legacy from General Gabler. Through Hedda's attitude toward and uses of the pistols, Ibsen constantly reminds us that Hedda "is to be regarded rather as her father's daughter than as her husband's wife."[3] Clearly the pistols are linked with certain values in her background which Hedda cherishes. Complete definition of these values is difficult without a more thorough knowledge of Ibsen's conception of a Norwegian general than the play or contemporary comment on it allows. Perhaps, as Brandes said, nineteenth-century audiences recognized that Hedda's pretensions to dignity and grandeur as a general's daughter were falsely based, "that a Norwegian general is a cavalry officer, who as a rule, has never smelt powder, and whose pistols are innocent of bloodshed."[4] Such a realization, however, by no means nullifies the *theoretical* attributes and privileges of gen-

[3]*The Correspondence of Henrik Ibsen*, trans. & ed. Mary Morison (London, 1905), 435.

[4]Georg Brandes, *Henrik Ibsen. Björnstjerne Björnson: Critical Studies* (New York, 1899), 94.

eralship to which Hedda aspires. Possibly Ibsen intended us to understand that Hedda is a member of a second generation of "ham actors" who betray their proud tradition by their melodramatic posturings. But it is this tradition, however ignoble its carrier, to which the pistols and Hedda (in her own mind) belong, and it is, after all, the general only as glimpsed through his daughter's ambitions and conceptions of worth that is of real importance in the play. These conceptions, as embodied in Hedda's romantic ideal of manhood, may be synthesized from the action and dialogue. The aristocrat possesses, above all, courage and self-control. He expresses himself through direct and independent action, living to capacity and scorning security and public opinion. Danger only piques his appetite, and death with honor is the victory to be plucked from defeat. But the recklessness of this Hotspur is tempered by a disciplined will, by means of which he "beautifully" orders both his own actions and those of others on whom his power is imposed. Such a one uses his pistols with deliberation, with calculated aim. He shoots straight — to defend his life or his honor, and to maintain his authority. Pistols, however, have no intrinsic glamor. Of the several possible accoutrements of a general, his pistols are those least likely to evoke thoughts of chivalric principles and most likely to recall the menace of the power vested in him. And such power, as *Hedda Gabler* shows us, delivered into the hands of a confused and irresponsible egotist, brings only meaningless destruction to all who come within its range.

The manipulation of the pistols throughout the play is a mockery of their traditional role. Except at target practice, Hedda does not even shoot straight until her suicide. Her potential danger is recognized by both men whom she threatens, but both understand (Brack, immediately; Loevborg, in Act II) that her threat is a theatrical gesture and that she has no real intention of acting directly, in defiance of the conventions which bid her "go roundabout." Her crass dishonesty in her sexual encounters is highlighted by this gun play. She uses the pistols, to be sure, to ward off or warn off encroachments upon her "honor." This honor, however, is rooted in social expedience rather than in a moral code. Having indirectly encouraged Loevborg by a succession of intimate *tête-à-têtes,* she poses as an outraged maiden when he makes amorous advances, thereby, as she later hints, thwarting her own emotional needs. Subsequently she sells her body to Tesman as cynically as (and far less honestly than) Madame Diana sells hers, then deliberately participates in the form, if not the substance, of marital infidelity with Brack in order to relieve her boredom. Both Hedda and Brack become aware of the cold ruthlessness of the other and the consequent danger to the loser if the delicate equilibrium of their relationship should be disturbed. But until the end Brack is so complacently convinced that Hedda is his female counterpart that he has no fear she will do more than shoot over his head; even as she lies dead, he can hardly believe that she has resorted to direct action — "People don't do such things."

The part the pistols play in Loevborg's death makes a central contribution to our understanding of the degree to which the ideals they represent are distorted by the clouded perspective from which Hedda views them. She has no real comprehension of, nor interest in, the vital creative powers Thea helps Loevborg to realize. Instead, she glorifies his weaknesses, mistaking bravado for courage, the indulgence of physical appetites for godlike participation in "the banquet of life," a flight from reality for a heroic quest for totality of experience. Even more important is the fact that as she inhibits her own instinctive urge for fulfillment, she romanticizes its converse. Thus, having instigated his ruin, she incites Loevborg to commit suicide with her pistol. This radical denial of the will to live she arbitrarily invests with the heroism and beauty one associates with a sacrificial death; Hedda is incapable of making the distinction between an exhibitionistic gesture which inflates the ego and the tragic death, in which the ego is sublimated in order that the values of life may be extended and reborn.

Her inability to perceive the difference between melodrama and tragedy accounts for the disparity between Hedda's presumptive view of her own suicide and our evaluation of its significance. Ibsen with diabolical irony arranged a situation which bears close superficial resemblance to the traditional tragic end. Symbolically withdrawing herself from the bourgeois environment into the inner chamber which contains the relics of her earlier life, Hedda plays a "wild dance" upon her piano and, beneath her father's portrait, shoots herself "beautifully" through the temple with her father's pistol. She dies to vindicate her heritage of independence; with disciplined and direct aim she at last defeats the Bogy, which hitherto she has unsuccessfully attempted to circumvent. So Hedda would see her death, we are led to believe, could she be both principal and spectator; and no doubt she would find high-sounding phrases with which to memorialize it. But of course it is Brack and Tesman who have the curtain lines, and these lines show how little of her intent Hedda has conveyed to her world. And we, having the opportunity to judge the act with relation to its full context, may properly interpret it as the final self-dramatization of the consistently sterile protagonist. Hedda gains no insight; her death affirms nothing of importance. She never understands why, at her touch, everything becomes "ludicrous and mean." She dies to escape a sordid situation that is largely of her own making; she will not face reality nor assume responsibility for the consequences of her acts. The pistols, having descended to a coward and a cheat, bring only death without honor.

It would appear, then, that the symbols, while they do not carry the whole thematic burden of *Hedda Gabler*, illuminate the meaning of the characters and the action with which they are associated. As Eric Bentley has suggested, the characters, like those in the other plays of Ibsen's last period, are the living dead who dwell in a waste-land that resembles T. S. Eliot's. And, like Eliot later, Ibsen emphasized the aridity of the present by contrasting it with the heroic past. Indeed, *Hedda Gabler* may be thought of as a mock-tragedy, a sardonically contrived travesty of tragic action, which Ibsen shows us is no longer possible in the world of the play. This world is sick with a disease less curable than that of Oedipus's Thebes or Hamlet's Denmark. For its hereditary leaders are shrunken in stature, maimed and paralyzed by their enslavement to the ideals of the dominant middle class. With the other hollow men, they despise but nonetheless worship the false gods of respectability and security, paying only lip service to their ancestral principles. Such geniuses as this society produces are, when left to themselves, too weak to do more than batter their own heads against constricting barriers. They dissipate their talents and so fail in their mission as prophets and disseminators of Western culture; its interpretation is left to the unimaginative pedant, picking over the dry bones of the past. Women, the natural seminal vesicles of that culture, the mothers of the future, are those most cruelly inhibited by the sterilizing atmosphere of their environment. At one extreme is Aunt Julia, the genteel spinster, overcompensating for her starved emotions with obsessive self-dedication. At the other is Diana, the harlot. Even Thea, the progenitive spirit, the girl with the abundant hair, is a frail and colorless repository for the seeds of generation. Her break with convention when it threatens her maternity is shown to be the one mode of escape from the fate that overtakes the others. But Ibsen gives her triumph, too, a ludicrous twist. Hardly having begun the mourning song for her Adonis, she brings forth her embryonic offspring from her pocket and proceeds to mold it into shape with the aid of a Tesman — an echo of the classic death and rebirth, to be sure, but one not likely to produce the glorious Third Kingdom of which Ibsen dreamed. And appropriately holding the center of the stage throughout is Hedda, in whom the shadows of the past still struggle in a losing battle with the sterile specter of the present. Her pistols are engraved with insignia which the others understand not at all and which she only dimly comprehends. Her colossal egotism, her lack of self-knowledge, her cowardice, render her search for fulfillment but a succession of futile blunders which culminate in the supreme futility of death. Like Peer Gynt, she is fit only for the ladle of the button-molder;° she fails to realize a capacity either for great good or for great evil. Her mirror-image wears the mask of tragedy, but Ibsen makes certain that we see the horns and pointed ears of the satyr protruding from behind it.

button-molder: At the end of Ibsen's play *Peer Gynt*, the Button Molder tries to melt Peer in his ladle, an action that symbolizes loss of identity.

Jan Kott (b. 1914)
On *Hedda Gabler*   1984

Jan Kott's sexual analysis of Hedda's pistols introduces important levels of metaphor into a play that is already laden with sexual imagery.

Chekhov wrote: "If in the first act a gun hangs on the wall, in the last act it must go off." In laying down this dramatic precept, he must surely have had *Hedda Gabler* in mind. Hedda inherits two pistols from her father. She fires the first one over Judge Brack's head when he approaches the house from the garden; and again at the end, when she shoots herself. The other pistol is fired offstage. It kills Eilert Loevborg. But the two pistols in *Hedda Gabler* are not only props exploited by Ibsen with iron-clad dramatic logic and preordained consequences; they also have sexual undertones. A Scandinavian Madame Bovary, well read in romantic novels, gives Loevborg a pistol: "use it now . . . and beautifully." But the fatal shot wounds him "in the stomach — more or less," and is fired in the parlor of the red-haired Mademoiselle Diana.

Ibsen's setting for *Hedda Gabler* is striking. The action takes place in a spacious salon with French windows which open out on a veranda and a garden in the "fashionable part of town," not a fjord. The windows are curtained; the theater had already learned the advantages of gaslight.

In the first scene, Hedda orders the curtains drawn. She can't stand sunlight. This is our first glimpse of her character. The salon is spacious and the furniture projects collapsed, and when that happened, they were left with little alternative but to produce whatever was left, which is how *Anywhere to Anywhere* (1985) ended up in the programme. The minutes record that some members of the company had reservations about the match between the group's politics and the show's content. As stated, the women who worked in the Air Transport Auxiliary were middle- and upper-class, and they were concerned that the only 'angle' on the play available was 'nostalgia' (Sphinx Archive, 1984a). The company was also discussing a play about miners' wives at the same time, a topic generally considered more 'apt' and topical. But eventually *Anywhere to Anywhere* was the only show ready to go, and so it went into production and, despite the company's initial reservations, was very successful (Sphinx Archive, 1984a).

Throughout the 1980s, it was increasingly clear to the company and ACGB personnel that WTG was struggling with the collective form. In 1986 the company voted to establish an Advisory Board because it wished 'to have a body which could provide an overview of the work of the company, give advice and bring to the attention of the Group areas for development' (Sphinx Archive 1986b). In the same year, the company was reviewed by the Arts Council, which had begun to shift to a more business-focused mode of operation, yet was keen to help WTG regain its reputation and bookings and assist its move into middle-scale touring. In 1989 the collective structure was wound down and a small management team was formed, along with a Board of Directors, whose expertize could help move the company towards developing and showcasing new writing and away from devised work.[6] Claire Grove was the first Artistic Director, quickly followed by Sue Parrish when Grove joined the BBC. Parrish had impeccable credentials: she had worked at the 'Half Moon Theatre, London' workshops and co-founded the Standing Conference of Women Theatre Directors and Administrators in 1979 and the Women's Playhouse Trust in 1980.

The company launched a concerted research campaign to find out what its audiences and peers in the theatre industry thought about WTG and used that work to provide feedback to a consultant, who worked on rebranding and repositioning. Part of the research was a survey to canvass public awareness of the company. The majority of those surveyed could not/did not distinguish the WTG from other women's companies and couldn't successfully identify its work. The survey results bore out on a grand scale what the group had learned on a smaller one. Collective identity, like collective working, had become

a weakness rather than a strength and the WTG needed a s[...] distinctive identity (Sphinx Archive, n.d.). WTG had wanted to [...] itself the National Women's Theatre Company, which both th[...] Council and the branding consultant were against (Sphinx A[...] n.d). WTG thought the problematic part of the name was 'gro[...] much of the evidence pointed to the fact that it was 'Women[...] Sphinx was born. The publicity explained:

Why The Sphinx?
As the original national touring women's theatre company, [...] Women's Theatre Group has been developing and commissioni[...] new theatre writing by women since 1973. Following a summer [...] extensive research into audience perceptions of the field, in whic[...] number of our mailing list members took part, the company mar[...] a new phase in its life with a new name, The Sphinx, and with th[...] artistic maturity to take its place in the mainstream of British theatr[...] The Sphinx reflects the work of the company in all her qualities: She is:

FEMALE – placing women's experience centre-stage;
CLASSICAL – proud of her past, developing the canon of women's writing;
STORY-TELLING – producing original, spectacular, high-quality theatre;
MULTIFORM – reflecting women in all their diversity and subjectivity;
DANGEROUS – challenging and risk-taking theatre;
ORGANIC – nurturing the development of women's writing.
She has:
A WOMAN'S HEAD – to be a leading voice in addressing the cultural disenfranchisement of women;
A LION'S BODY – to fight for the creative freedom of women artists. (Sphinx Archive, n.d)

Without wishing to sound unduly cynical, it is hard to see how th[...] elaborate reasoning could be apparent to the woman in the stree[...] The company may have aspired to reflect women in all their 'diversit[...] and subjectivity', but, in common with other alternative companie[...] members were mostly playing to constituencies like themselves [...] middle-class by education, if not by birth. The key point about the new name, however, is that by the 1990s it was unusual for companies to hav[...]

poems' (Sphinx Archive, THM/322/8/2, Flyer). Toured to Action Space and The Tricycle, London, 1980/81.

Breaking Through by Timberlake Wertenbaker, directed by Julie Holledge. Topic: a sci-fi musical exploring quantum physics and nuclear weapons, aimed at teenagers. Performed at The Cockpit and various schools in the London area, 1980/81.

New Anatomies by Timberlake Wertenbaker, directed by Nancy Duguid. Topic: 'New Anatomies is about women who escaped convention in order to lead exciting and creative lives.' (Sphinx Archive, THM/322/8/2 Flyer for *New Anatomies*.) Performed at the Edinburgh Theatre Workshop and the ICA in London. Published in *Wertenbaker Plays One*, London: Methuen, 1980/81.

Time Pieces devised by the company, directed by Lou Wakefield. Topic: the changing role of women over a century. Performed at Derby Hall Bury, BAC, and Oval House, 1982.

Double Vision devised by the company, directed by Libby Mason. Topic: clashing ideologies in a lesbian relationship. Performed at Ovalhouse, Brighton Pavilion and in schools and community centres around the country, 1982.

Love and Dissent by Elisabeth Bond, directed by Nona Shepphard. Part of WTG's project to look at the personal as political (the other plays were *Double Vision* and *Dear Girl*. Topic: the play combined WTG's core themes of the importance of educating young women, motherhood and the struggle for women's liberation. A progressive headmistress struggling to introduce a Women's Studies course at her school is haunted by nineteenth-century Marxist revolutionary Alexandra Kollontai. Performed at Ovalhouse, Croydon Warehouse and Tricycle, 1983.

Dear Girl by Libby Mason and Tierl Thompson, directed by Libby Mason. Topic: a documentary theatre piece exploring the friendship of four working-class women at the turn of the twentieth century. Performed at Theatre Workshop Edinburgh, Croydon Warehouse Theatre, Old Red Lion, then on to Bath, Manchester, Burnley, Preston, Bury, Newcastle Under Lyme, Droitwch, Stafford, Wolverhampton, Elsemere, Milton Keynes, Hull, Yorkshire, Brighton and back to London to the Ovalhouse, 1983.

Pax by Deborah Levy, directed by [Lily] Susan Todd and Anna Furse. Topic: the play deals obliquely with fear of nuclear war through an allegorical account of the history of Europe. Performed at the Oval House, Albany Centre Bristol, Derby Hall, Bury and Croydon Warehouse, 1984/85.

Anywhere to Anywhere by Joyce Halliday, directed by Kate Crutchley. Topic: 'a musical documentary about the women who flew the planes [during World War II] and the problems and contradictions they encountered' (*Anywhere to Anywhere* Flyer, Sphinx Company File, V&A). Performed at Derby Playhouse Studio; Nuffield Theatre Studio; Lancaster; Droitwich; Arts Centre; York; Norwich; Crucible Theatre; Sheffield; Albany Empire London and Albany Centre Bristol, 1985.

Witchcraze by Bryony Lavery, directed by Nonna Shepphard. Topic: a mask verse play analyzing the persecution of witches in history. A historical epic, the play begins with witchcraft's roots in pre-Christian religion and ends in contemporary Britain. Performed at Battersea Arts Centre, London, Albany Arts Centre Bristol, Warwick Arts Centre, Pavilion Theatre Brighton and Sheffield Crucible, 1985.

Fixed Deal by Paulette Randall and Tasha Fairbanks, directed by Decima Francis. Topic: 'the story of four women from different backgrounds and cultures. The one thing they have in common is that they are all, in their various ways, affected by drugs' (flyer for *Fixed Deal*, V&A). Performed at Ovalhouse, London, 1986.

Our Lady by Deborah Levy. Topic: 'Three women, two black and one white, from different cultures and experience of life all claim to be Our Lady. They are brought to trial for heresy by the Holy Inquisition, whose representative has been summoned from the fifteenth century' (Flyer for *Our Lady*, THM/322/5/17). Performed at Coventry Women's Festival; Edinburgh; Milton Keynes; Drill Hall; Brewhouse Taunton; Portsmouth Drama Centre; Havant Arts Centre; Bury Metro Arts; Durham Sixth Form Centre; Barton Live Arts; Basingstoke and New Milton. (Sponsored by Southern Arts and the West Midlands Arts Association on a six-week tour, 1986).

Lear's Daughters by the company with Elaine Feinstein, directed by Gwenda Hughes. Topic: a pre-herstory of *King Lear*. Performed at BAC, Gulbenkian studio Newcastle, Crewe, Leeds, York and Aberdeen during the first tour, 1987.

Picture Palace by Winsome Pinnock, directed by Gwenda Hughes. Topic: black ushers in a cinema dreaming of another life. Performed at Ovalhouse, Milton Keynes, Worcester, Worksop, Canterbury and Leicester, 1988.

Pinchdice & Co by Julie Wilkinson, directed by Claire Grove. Topic: a riff on *Mother Courage*; the herstory of women during the Crusades. Performed in Hemel Hempstead, Northampton, Coventry, Chesterfield and Wakefield in colleges, community centres and studio theatres, 1989.

Zerri's Choice by Sandra Yaw, directed by Joan Ann Maynard. Topic: a mother deciding whether or not to go back to Guyana. Performed at the Drill Hall, Birmingham Rep Studio, Northampton Arts Centre and community halls and colleges in Bristol, Sheffield, Leicester and Derby. Funded by London Borough Grants Scheme, 1989.

Her Aching Heart by Bryony Lavery, directed by Claire Grove. Topic: a lesbian romance. Performed at Ovalhouse, Jackson's Lane Community Centre, Windsor Arts Centre, Moat Community Centre Maidstone, 1991.

The Roaring Girl's Hamlet by William Shakespeare in a setting by Claire Luckham, directed by Sue Parrish. Topic: *Hamlet* performed by a company of women led by Roaring Girl Moll Cutpurse. Opened at Croydon Warehouse, 1992.

Every Bit of It by Jackie Kay directed by Sue Parrish. Topic: blues singer Bessie Smith and the impact of her music on two women. Opened at Warwick Arts Centre, 1992/93.

Playhouse Creatures by April de Angelis, directed by Sue Parrish. Topic: a black comedy about the struggles of the first generation of actresses on the Restoration stage. Opened at the Leicester Haymarket Studio and ended with a two-week run at the Hammersmith Lyric Studio, 1993.

Chapter 8

TALAWA

Kene Igweonu

Introduction

The good and great work from all cultures belongs to everyone.
(TTC/8/3/3/4, 1989)

From its earliest days, Talawa Theatre Company set out to challenge long-held perceptions about black theatre, culture and black people in general. From its emergence in 1985, Talawa has remained ambitious in their avowed commitment to promote the profile of black actors, theatre and culture in Britain in their firm belief of the ability of theatre to reflect and ultimately transform society. Talawa members quickly set themselves apart by taking on ambitious productions of West Indian, African and Western classics such as C. L. R. James's *The Black Jacobins* (1986), Oscar Wilde's *The Importance of Being Earnest* (1989), Ola Rotimi's *The Gods Are Not to Blame* (1989), Shakespeare's *Antony and Cleopatra* (1991) and *The Road* by Wole Soyinka (1992), to name but a few.

Even though the company is equally known for its developmental work and production of new writing, Talawa's continued reliance and attraction to classical texts can be seen to derive from the statement cited at the start of this essay that 'the good and great works from all cultures belongs to everyone' (TTC, 8/3/3/4, 1989). In other words, Talawa views these classical productions as opportunities to show that black–British actors can be judged by the same professional standards as their white counterparts. By so doing, Talawa poses a constant challenge to implied and long-standing discrimination against black–British actors, which for a long time made it impossible for them to play dominant roles in mainstream theatre productions. In fact, black–British actors often lose out to their African–American counterparts in the casting of existing major roles, as was the case with the London premiere of *The Black Jacobins* at the Westminster Theatre in 1936, with Paul Robeson playing the role of the military genius and leader of the Haitian Revolution, Toussaint Louverture.

Talawa provided the political platform for black people to ask questions about what it meant to be black and British. Moreover, this development is rendered all the more remarkable as Talawa's influence was not limited to blacks who were born or grew up in Britain (Igweonu, 2013, 89). This is a fact acknowledged by the American-born playwright and critic Bonnie Greer, who in a 2011 interview with Nosheen Iqbal of the *Guardian* recalled that:

> Talawa's 25th coincides with my own 25th anniversary living in London. And Talawa was one of the reasons I moved to the UK: I wanted to be a part of it, to work with the sparkling array of black directors and actors employed by these theatres. (Iqbal, 2011)

As I discuss later, Talawa's broad-based appeal came as a result of a deliberate shift in the company's artistic policy in 1989 that saw it move from producing only West Indian plays to 'the good and great work from all cultures' (TTC, 8/3/3/4, 1989). Moreover, Talawa's political will in projecting an image of black people and culture that is both mainstream and versatile is equally matched by audiences who, according to a later artistic director, Pat Cumper, saw their patronage of Talawa as a 'political act' (Allfree, 2011, 52). This was particularly the case in the company's earliest years, marked by a phenomenal rise in political awareness in 1980s Britain as evidenced by the violent riots that took place across several inner-London suburbs, with Brixton as the epicentre, and against the backdrop of the perceived inequalities experienced by black people in 1980s Britain (Igweonu, 2013, 89).

Moreover, the political climate of Britain in the 1980s was not favourable to blacks, particularly with regard to their articulation of Britishness through the medium of their African and/or Caribbean heritage. This period was marked by overwhelming political coercion to conform to white British stereotypes. Perhaps the greatest illustration of this pressure can be seen in the Conservative Party's ethnic election poster of 1983. The poster shows a young black man in a suit, with his arms folded across his chest. Below him, in bold print, is the inscription 'Labour says he's black. Tories say he's British' (Gilroy, 1987, 58). Paul Gilroy observes that the suit in this poster becomes a key signifier in the articulation of white Britishness and a representation of what it means to be British (Gilroy, 1987, 59). The spectre of the Conservative election poster, coupled with the Brixton riots, hung over the black–British community throughout the 1980s, and it was against this backdrop that Talawa's audiences saw their patronage of the company's work as a political act, even though Talawa never tackled these issues directly.

That Talawa never directly addressed the riots or the question of being a black Briton in any of its work does not suggest a contradiction of philosophy or commitment to project the black–British experience on to the mainstream arena. On the contrary, Talawa's approach is premised on the company's view of itself as one that provides the space for British peoples of all ethnicities to converge and explore their shared humanity and collective identity. Pat Cumper highlights this strategy in a 2011 interview when she emphasizes:

> The stuff that we want to do isn't about anger and it's not about opposition. It's actually about saying, 'this is where we are and this is what we do.' Sometimes it's a very hard position to hold because sometimes you are very angry ... That plays into – we were quite canny and always have been – the funders idea that actually they know they are not serving wide enough audiences, so a company like ours would be allowed into all sorts of spaces ... Sometimes we facilitate those relationships, sometimes it works, and sometimes it doesn't. (Cumper, 2011)

Seen from this perspective, Talawa's approach to issues such as the 1980s riots has been to symbolically stand in the gap between different racial communities in Britain and, from this position, lead them in the search for a collective identity that is British, as opposed to merely seeing themselves as black or white. In this way Talawa is able to help not only blacks but also whites to understand themselves better, because, as Cumper puts it, 'we know them better than they know themselves' (Cumper, 2011). Cumper's view of Talawa's position and the possibilities it presents for performing the 'other' is one that has, in the past, been put forward by Dimple Godiwala:

> The racial heterogeneity of contemporary Britain seems to be a subject tackled largely (and excellently) by the strangers in diaspora rather than the indigenous or 'ethnic English' dramatist or director. Furthermore, it is these very theatres which function as sites of

genuine interculturalism within the changing structures of British stages'. (Godiwala, 2006, 6)

In this chapter I examine the first decade of Talawa's existence as a black-led British theatre company, since its foundation in 1985 by the quartet of Yvonne Brewster, Carmen Munroe, Mona Hammond and Inigo Espejel. Subsequently, it has cemented its place in mainstream British theatre and prides itself as Britain's *primary* black-led theatre company. This chapter utilizes a range of sources, including material from the company archives held at the Victoria and Albert Museum in London, to construct a narrative of Talawa's development from 1985 to 1994 – a period of phenomenal rise for the company that contrasts sharply with a decline in the number of black and ethnic minorities (BAME) theatre companies in Britain.

This decline was largely a result of two debilitating factors, the first of which was the decision of the then Conservative government of Margaret Thatcher in 1986 to dissolve the Labour-run GLC, which had funded a significant number of BAME arts. Secondly, the introduction of the 1986 Arts and Ethnic Minorities Action Plan by the then Arts Council of Great Britain led to a significant reconfiguration of the way BAME theatre companies were funded, and attempted to further isolate them from the mainstream British theatre establishment through its insistence that 4 per cent of the subsidy offered to any theatre company classed as representing the black and ethnic minorities be dedicated to the development of work specifically for black artists (Johnson, 2001, 69). This situation, according to David Johnson, led to a decline in the number of subsidized black theatre companies in Britain in the late 1980s and early 1990s, with the few that retained or gained funding from the Arts Council 'held up as flagship[s] for the genre leaving no space for expansion within or, indeed, beyond the genre' (Johnson, 2001, 70).

However, what makes Talawa's rise in this particular period remarkable is that, while the two issues identified above led to either the demise or ghettoization of black theatre in Britain, Talawa – despite being held up as a flagship of black-British theatre by the *establishment* in order to continue enjoying Arts Council subsidies through the years – was canny in persistently pursuing a vision that has now seen them acknowledged as the premier *black-led* theatre company in Britain, as opposed to being seen as a *black–British* theatre company. As a black-led theatre company, Talawa is able to surmount the limitation of being considered simply as black–British – producing works considered as black – to become a producer of world classical theatre from all cultures, and thus enabling 'black performers to be seen in the widest possible range of performance work' (Johnson, 2001, 70).

History of the Company's Development

Talawa's inception can be seen to have come about due to the offer of culturally specific funding ... The production would be funded as part of the Greater London Council's (GLC) (Race Equality Unit) 'Black Experience Arts Programme' dedicated to enhancing the profile of black work. (Johnson, 2001, 71)

That Talawa's arrival on the British stage is inextricably linked to culturally specific funding could be seen to suggest a company that was 'essentially black and political' (Johnson, 2001, 71). However, as I have begun to argue, Talawa did not want to fall into the trap of being ghettoized as black–British, or even as a small-scale touring company, and set out to challenge and subvert the very establishment that nurtured and held it up as such. The name Talawa is derived from the Jamaican word *tallawah* (pronounced tàlawa), which is used to convey a basic sense of being materially strong and tough, but also 'goes beyond the physical to mean dangerous', as in the 'proverbial Jamaican phrase: "Me lickle but me Talawa": Don't underestimate me' (TTC, 1996a, 1/8/1). For Talawa, the choice of name can be seen as encapsulating a unique philosophy, which allows for the astute political and social positioning of the company as not wanting to be seen as part of the *establishment*, but of having the power associated with it in the event it needs to wield it.

This philosophical positioning enables the company to retain the possibility of mobility in many directions, and to be able to pick and choose its fights as well as *when* to fight. By adopting this approach Talawa is able to route backwards and forwards in all directions, to the West Indies, Africa and elsewhere, to contribute to a redefinition of the idea of Britishness to include not only black people but people of other races and ethnicities as well. Writing about the particular point in history from which Talawa emerged, Michael McMillan observes that:

The renaissance of a Black arts movement in the 1980s signified the coming of age of second-generation Blacks who had grown up in Britain and were exploring questions of identification and representation. Could being Black and British be reconciled, and what did this mean? (McMillan, 2006, 4)

However, the renaissance and 'coming of age of second-generation Blacks who had grown up in Britain' was, in essence, a reflection of the aspirations of black peoples living in Britain in general; led primarily by Caribbean émigrés. Lending his voice to this development, Johnson argues that:

> The history of black people on the British stage and their contemporary presence was seldom profiled or rarely discussed in the mainstream. The main change to this was in the development of black theatre companies in the 1980s. Talawa Theatre Company emerging in the midst of this and later becoming the longest running of these companies can be seen to have lent itself to the task of beginning to redress the balance. (Johnson, 2001, 4)

Talawa set about, from the outset, to convey the image of a company that was associated with the limited number of medium- to large-scale companies that received a substantial share of the Arts Council subsidies available to the sector – a position well served by the company's receipt of a level of funding from the GLC that was unprecedented for a BAME theatre company in 1986. Talawa drew particularly on Brewster's experience as a Drama Officer with the Arts Council from 1982 to 1984 to develop and articulate a comprehensive artistic policy that anticipated the ever-changing funding priorities of the Arts Council. Brewster had a good understanding of how funding structures worked, and was able to exploit this to Talawa's benefit for a long time. Consequently, Talawa's transition in 1989 from a company that relied solely on case-by-case project funding to one that received annual Arts Council revenue subsidies marked a crucial change in its status as a middle-scale producer on the mainstream British stage (TTC, 1989a, 9/1/1). Thus, the increase in culturally specific funding to Talawa, rather than encumbering it with the burden of representation, marked a momentous turning point in the company's existence, catapulting it into a new phase in its determined move into mainstream British theatre in defiance of the limitations often placed on black theatre by the very same establishment that funds it.

Talawa's founding vision was aptly summed up in its principal objectives of providing a viable platform for a) nurturing and showcasing black talents, b) giving voice to the black–British experience and

c) cultivating black theatre audiences, as well as developing mainstream audiences for black work (TTC, 1996b, 1/8/1). This vision was equally evident in Talawa's working methodologies, which has seen the group go through a number of developmental phases in its journey to the mainstream. In examining this journey, or more precisely its determined leap into the arena of mainstream British theatre, the period between 1985 and 1994 was significant as it marked three remarkable phases in Talawa's development, and heralded what Brewster declared as Talawa's 'eclectic phase' (TTC, 1994, 1/2/1). While it is beyond the scope of this chapter to offer a detailed discussion of the company's 'eclectic phase' from 1996 onwards, it is useful to highlight some of the significant developments that lend themselves to such a description before examining the three phases that preceded it.

The period from 1996 saw a more confident Talawa develop a much wider range of activities and interests: these included establishing a middle-scale touring circuit in London's West End and through a number of regional theatres in England promoting new writing with the debut of 'Zebra Crossing' in the same year. Effectively, the period from 1996 saw Talawa evolve a repertory style, which enabled the company to utilize the out-of-season months (from September to January) for developmental and educational outreach work. Zebra Crossing was central to Talawa's developmental and educational work in this period and allowed it to facilitate masterclasses to foster the development of new writing, performances and diverse artistic collaborations between young writers, performers and artists.

Funding and Company Structure

Talawa Theatre Company currently operates through a team of five employees, seven company directors and a company secretary. The staff includes an artistic director, executive producer, finance officer, company administrator and a participation and education officer. To date, Talawa has had a total of four artistic directors, arguably five if one considers Ben Thomas, a veteran actor with Talawa who was appointed as acting Artistic Director following the sudden resignation of Paulette Randall in 2004 (seven other staff and board members also resigned that year). Yvonne Brewster served as Artistic Director from the company's inception in 1985 until 2003, when she handed over to Randall. Pat Cumper was appointed to the post in 2005 and finally stepped down in the spring of 2012, having made tremendous progress with the company that she rescued from near-total collapse and from being placed under administration (Iqbal, 2011). Michael Buffong succeeded Cumper.

From its inception, Talawa had been recognized as a middle-scale theatre company. Talawa's mission statement and artistic policy are: 1) to use black culture and experience to further enrich British theatre; 2) to provide middle-/large-scale, high-quality productions that reflect the serious creative role that black theatre has within the UK as well as the wider world; 3) to enlarge theatre audiences from the black community (TTC (1989b), 1/8/1). This statement is analysed by Johnson, who notes:

> Talawa's first aim would add a new dimension to British theatre by presenting African and Caribbean cultures and societies in performance. European classical and modern texts would also be explored bringing to them relevant issues of black African/Caribbean and British life that may be ignored by the wider mainstream British theatre companies. (Johnson, 2001, 74)

While the company successfully continues to excel in promoting this socio-cultural dimension to its work, the exigencies of public funding have seen Talawa straddle the gap between small- and middle-scale, engaging in experimental and developmental work on the small-scale, while producing major shows that sit comfortably within the middle-scale. Talawa's tenacity in holding on to this position goes back to its very beginning as a theatre company. As mentioned previously, Talawa signalled this determination with its inaugural production of C. L. R. James's *The Black Jacobins*. With its large cast and ambitious scale, the production was a deliberate political and ideological statement in order to stake Talawa's place in British theatre. Cumper points out that her predecessor Yvonne Brewster 'felt very strongly that what we were not going to do was be pushed into studios and small venues – to be seen as an experimental theatre company. She wanted to occupy the mainstream' (Cumper, 2011).

Ultimately, this ambitious production was executed with a large cast size of 23 actors, and was made possible by a very generous grant of £86,251 from the GLC. These figures are contained in a financial report prepared by Brewster to outline the final costs of producing *The Black Jacobins*, in which she equally indicates that the company made a net profit of £8,250 from a total of 20 performances (TTC, 2/2/1). As a consequence of this level of project funding, Talawa was taken seriously by the Arts Council, who agreed to offer the company a grant of £70,000 in 1989 (TTC, 1989a, 9/1/1). Cumper acknowledges this strategy in Talawa's approach when she notes, 'It's about how you negotiate your relationship with the Arts Council. So they [the Arts Council] will give you different levels of funding according to what scale they think you are' (Cumper, 2013). As a result of this strategy, Talawa became a regular recipient of Arts Council revenue subsidy, which was later to increase substantially to £250,000 in 1993 (TTC, 1993a, 9/1/2).

From 1989, another source of funding for Talawa resulted from the company's recourse to co-productions. Crucially, these ventures were principally prudent sustainability strategies which allowed the group to expand its office and staff base (TTC, 1989a, 9/1/1). The company also began to actively solicit funding from alternative sources receiving, for example, British Council support for the Irish leg of their tour of *The Importance of Being Earnest* in 1989 (TTC, 1989c, 8/2/3). Talawa also sought commercial sponsorship for its work during this period, attaining relative success with receipt of funds from a range of organizations including the John Lewis Partnership, British Telecom and London Weekend Television (Johnson, 2001, 73).

These initiatives were a consequence of Talawa's ambition to expand yet, in doing so, during those early days it was spending about 50 per cent of total revenue on staff salaries and overheads, which reduced the amount available to mount independent productions (TTC, 1994, 1/2/1). By engaging in mutually beneficial co-production ventures and seeking corporate sponsorship, the company stood a better chance of sustaining its developmental aspirations while retaining the capacity to continue to produce works that served to advance the mission of providing 'high quality productions that reflect the significant creative roles that black theatre plays within the national and international arena' (TTC, 1989, 1/8/1). John Doyle, Artistic Director of Everyman Theatre, also articulates the mutual benefit of co-producing with Talawa:

> At a time when grants are at a standstill, it takes enormous energy and commitment from the organization to ensure that our output and scale is of the highest standard. The sharing of resources when working with Talawa means that we can look at different styles and new artistic inputs, at a time when the theatre would otherwise be having to conserve its energy. (TTC, 1991, 8/3/3/9)

After securing residency at the Cochrane Theatre, London from September 1991, as well as a significant increase in Arts Council subsidy from £70,000 to £250,000, Talawa was able to expand its operations to move into a third phase of development (1992–4). Its first production in this phase was Wole Soyinka's *The Road*, which played to audiences at the Cochrane Theatre from 26 February to 28 March 1992. *The Road* effectively opened the way to a period of unprecedented success that is evidenced in the number and range of productions that followed. In addition to about a dozen productions in this phase, its building-based status meant that Talawa could 'offer much needed training opportunities to young black performers, stage managers, designers, as well as a comprehensive education programme to serve the wider community' (TTC, 1993b, 8/2/12). Effectively, the residency at the Cochrane yielded a number of benefits including the convenience of a regular rehearsal and performance venue and the advantage of a central London location – both allowing the company to build a core-base of regular audiences. However, in 1994 the company took the decision to seek residency at another London theatre due to what it perceived as the poor quality of service delivered by the London Institute, which owned the Cochrane. Talawa is currently based in East London, where it operates out of an office and studio space, which they also hire out to generate additional income.

Key Works Produced in this Period

As already indicated, the period under discussion (1985–94) is marked by three distinct phases, each with different artistic choices. The first phase runs from 1985 to 1988, the second from 1989 to 1991 and third phase 1992 to 1994. Each respective period, as well as the works produced in it, reflects a strategic and idiosyncratic approach in the company's journey to the mainstream. The significance of these early years of Talawa's evolution and the key works produced in them cannot be overemphasized, as they very clearly highlight the company's determined leap into the mainstream, as well as the steep upward trajectory of the company's development in its first decade of existence.

The first distinct phase of the company's development (1985–8) was a period where Talawa did not have an office base or permanent personnel. Despite this, it was a period of boundless enthusiasm and ambition, which saw the company receive phenomenal project funding from the then GLC and later from the Arts Council of Great Britain (ACGB). During this time, Talawa produced three middle-scale shows, namely the aforementioned *The Black Jacobins* (1986), Dennis Scott's

An Echo in the Bone (1986) and *O Babylon!* (1988) by Derek Walcott and Galt McDermot. The choice of texts in this phase was borne out of the company's commitment to West Indian playwrights, which was largely a tacit acknowledgement of then Artistic Director Yvonne Brewster's background and politics. However, I will focus on the two plays produced by the company in 1986 to announce its entry into the British theatre arena, as these were key to understanding Talawa's impact on black people in Britain, as well as on British theatre and culture in general.

The Black Jacobins opened to the public on 21 February 1986 and ran until 15 March 1986 at London's Riverside Studios. James's play, which juxtaposes the Haitian revolution with the French revolution, tells the epic story of the first successful uprising by black slaves of San Domingue, who fought to establish Haiti as an independent republic at the end of the revolution in 1804. Talawa's production, directed by Yvonne Brewster, had an all-black cast, which included Norman Beaton playing the part of the charismatic Toussaint L'Ouverture, and Trevor Laird taking on the role of Dessalines, who succeeded Toussaint.

Significantly, Brewster's choice of *The Black Jacobins* to inaugurate the company is loaded with political symbolism. On the one hand, it was an audacious move by Brewster to 'bypass' the small-scale circuit and 'announce' Talawa as a direct contender for the mainstream space occupied by middle-scale theatre companies. In his review of the production, which he describes as 'a play on an epic scale' (Coveney, 1986, 27), Michael Coveney describes the production as 'ambitious, continuously interesting but rough around the edges'. He goes on to add, 'how marvellous to see a large-scale project – presented by the newly formed Talawa company ... this is the sort of show ... that lends dignity and credibility to the British black theatre movement' (Coveney, 1986, 27). The choice of play by Brewster came from her recognition that 'the politics of C. L. R. James were so immensely important to black people in this country [Britain] today' (Gardner, 1986, 7) and this view is echoed by Johnson, who concedes that 'the impact of Talawa's first performance ... meant that Talawa's work could not avoid becoming political' (Johnson, 2001, 71).

Talawa's second show, *An Echo in the Bone* by Dennis Scott, was produced in 1986 and played to audiences at the Drill Hall Arts Centre, London from 24 June to 19 July. The play, again directed by Brewster, had a cast of six male and four female actors and was set in the Jamaica in 1937 – a period in Jamaican political history that is marked by increasing agitation for better wages by farm workers, which ultimately culminated in the 1938 labour revolt. The play explores the history of slavery and the oppression of black people through re-enactments by family and friends at a Nine Nights service for its central character, Crew, who disappears and is assumed dead. The Nine Nights service is commonly attended by descendants of erstwhile slaves in the Caribbean to mourn the death of a loved one, and to celebrate his or her passing from the suffering and hardship of life to rest and freedom in the afterlife. During the service, stories about the life of the deceased are told and re-enacted by those present. In the play, Crew's story symbolizes that of black people, by taking the audience through their history of slavery, the Middle Passage, (a phase that refers to the liminal period for slaves on their enforced journey from Africa to the New World). Talawa's production of the play could be said to represent the experiences of black people at the margins of 1980s British society, rooted in their collective memory of racial discrimination and prejudice from which they, like the spirit of Crew, need to break free. However, it is worth noting that according to Laurel B. Ince, Talawa's production of *An Echo in the Bone* 'is not about confusion. It is not sentimentality; it is not about hate; it is not about anger. It is drama which touches the human soul, and it is brilliantly done' (Ince, 1986, 31), concluding, 'The Talawa Theatre Company justifies the "talawa" designation' (Ince, 1986, 31).

The second phase of Talawa's development (1989–91), can be considered as being significantly marked by co-productions – in fact, all four works presented in this period attest to this in one way or another. With the exception of Ola Rotimi's *The Gods Are Not to Blame* (1989), which the company describes as being produced 'in association' with Everyman Theatre Liverpool, the other three are clearly identified as co-productions. For instance, *The Importance of Being Earnest* (1989) by Oscar Wilde was a co-production with the Newcastle-based Tyne Theatre Company, *The Dragon Can't Dance* (1990) by Earl Lovelace was co-produced with The Theatre Royal Stratford East, while Shakespeare's *Antony and Cleopatra* (1991) was a co-production with Everyman Theatre Liverpool. This second phase also signified a departure from reliance on project funding to yearly revenue grants from the Arts Council. The development was significant in the life of the company as it enabled them to establish an office base in London and to employ two permanent staff, as well as cover operational overheads.

This second phase equally marked a major shift away from the company's focus on West Indian playwrights by the inclusion of three great works by Wilde, Rotimi and Shakespeare. This shift in Talawa's choice of works made it possible for the company to be seen as representing an aesthetic that was neither West Indian nor African, but black–British. This policy was effectively instituted by Brewster during Talawa's early years as a way of undoing a pattern that began to emerge following the company's successive production of three West Indian plays in its first phase of development. Cumper argues that identifying the company as black–British rather than West Indian or African allowed it to root back to both cultures, as well as to stake its presence in Britain in order to proclaim its Britishness and that of those it represents (Cumper, 2011).

Talawa's first co-production in this period was *The Importance of Being Earnest* (1989), also its first production outside London. The venues were the Tyne Theatre and Opera House Newcastle (19 April–13 May), the Bloomsbury Theatre London (15–27 May) and the Cork Opera House in Cork, Ireland (19–24 June). This was also the first non-West Indian play to be offered by Talawa. In the programme notes for the London production, the company set out the approach to its staging:

> In producing *The Importance of Being Earnest*, Talawa set out to be as truthful to the text as it was humanly possible to be, bearing in mind that an all-black production of *The Importance of Being Earnest* was probably very far from Wilde's wildest imagination ... We felt it was important to set the play in England in 1895, but not ever to disguise or trivialise the fact that we were black. This made certain decisions easier to make; having tea in the conservatory seemed a more likely possibility ... Mad dogs and Englishmen eat in the sun! (TTC, 1989b, 8/3/3/4)

Talawa's successful all-black productions of Wilde's play, and Shakespeare's *Antony and Cleopatra* in 1991, allowed Talawa to show how Western classical theatre could address the issues affecting the black–British community and, at the same time, provide a professional platform for black actors to be judged by the same standards as their white counterparts. In fact, Victor Ukaegbu contends that 'the *graduation* of Talawa actors and personnel onto mainstream theatres and their successes in other performance media demonstrate its growing status, influence and contributions to contemporary British theatre' (Ukaegbu, 2006, 124, emphasis original).

The Gods Are Not to Blame, the first work by an African playwright to be produced by Talawa, opened at the Riverside Studios, London on 31 October 1989. The play is Rotimi's reworking of Sophocles' Athenian tragedy *Oedipus the King* into a Yoruba (Nigerian) tragedy. It draws heavily on Yoruba rituals and myths to convey its narrative and, in a sense, embodied a realization of the company's ambition of staging black–British identity that is accepting of the various historical and cultural influences that shape it. This view derives in part from my argument elsewhere that black diaspora performance often addresses issues of identity 'through a continuous re/negotiation of the past, in relation to cultural origin, geographic origin and the debilitating experience of transatlantic slavery, in an effort to come to terms with, and make sense of, present realities' (Igweonu, 2011, 61). Going further, I contended in the same essay that African cultures feature prominently in this process, in tacit acknowledgement of their profound influence in shaping the black diaspora identity, which Talawa's work represents (Igweonu, 2011).

Talawa clearly sees itself as a company that represents the aspirations of black–British people, and a key part of this is their recognition that the black audience 'in London for example, [is] more Nigerian than it is Caribbean' (Cumper cited in Igweonu, 2013, 91). Seen from this perspective, Talawa's production of *The Gods Are Not to Blame* attests to the changing dynamic of the black population of London, which witnessed a demographic shift with a growth in the number of black African émigrés to Britain from mid-1980s. Extending the cultural reach of company's work to include African plays like *The Gods Are Not to Blame* made it possible for Talawa to be seen as representing and articulating a black–British aesthetic that roots back to both its Caribbean and African origins. Moreover, as noted in the programme for the production, Brewster's choice of *The Gods Are Not to Blame* was equally based on her desire 'to bring together the disparate elements from our three cultural horizons, Europe, the Caribbean and Africa and to integrate them into a new harmony' (TTC, 1989d, 8/3/3/6). Ukaegbu acknowledges this approach to Talawa's work when he observes:

> Talawa theatre company derives its cultural edge by creating and staging performances that when not contextualising and resisting cultural and historical stereotypes, reflect the contemporary experiences of black peoples. It achieves this purpose through a creative forum that draws from black and white people's [sic] historical and cultural experiences in and about the UK society. (Ukaegbu, 2006, 124)

Writing about this first production of an African play, Brewster notes, for instance, that 'with a brave company of actors, designers and technicians we attempted to excavate and make relevant for our times a stellar example of ritual theatre from the established canon of black plays, Ola Rotimi's *The Gods are Not to Blame*' (Brewster, 2008, 2).

Prior to directing *The Gods Are Not to Blame* Brewster undertook a trip to Nigeria to experience the Yoruba culture first hand and to meet with the playwright. Writing about her experience of this research trip, Brewster notes that she was

> heartened by the manner in which those in the business of inter-preting the mysteries of Yoruba culture in Nigeria, were happy, willing and eager to encourage experiment with the form when I pressed for explanations. Rotimi himself was eager to share in our 'British' exploration of the Yoruba rites of succession and responsi-bility. (Brewster, 2008, 2)

The outcome of this British exploration, according to Jillian Binns, was Rotimi's delight at the attention given by Talawa to the text, instead of merely focusing on theatrical spectacle as in most Nigerian produc-tions of the play (Binns, 1989, 4).

While the events of the second phase of Talawa's development were a major achievement for such a young company, the third phase (1992–4) saw it achieve the envied status of a building-based theatre company with residency at the Cochrane Theatre in London. The staff base of the company also grew to six members. With a significant increase in the subsidy it received from the Arts Council, from £70,000 in 1989 to £250,000 in 1992, Talawa ventured into independent touring with Trevor Rhone's *Smile Orange* (1992) and Shakespeare's *King Lear* (1994). Additionally, the company also produced a substantial number of shows, including Wole Soyinka's *The Road*, Ntozake Shange's *The Love Space Demands* (1992), Tariq Ali's *Necklaces* (1992), *Arawak Gold* written by Ted Dwyer and adapted by Yvonne Brewster (1993), Endesha Ida Mae Holland's *From the Mississippi Delta* (1993), Michael Abbensetts's *The Lion* (1993), Biyi Bandele's *Resurrections* (1994) and a production of John Ford's *'Tis Pity She's a Whore* (1994).

According to Brewster, programming in this period 'reflected (on hindsight) the pressures of the singularity of Talawa's position and the eruption of expectation which descended upon the Company and its new building based status' (TTC, 1994, 1/2/1). The number and range of productions in this period echoed the company's growing confidence arising from its residency status and witnessed a new shift that is evidenced by the production of two American plays, new writing, as well as increased educational and audience development activities. The first of the two American plays produced in the third phase of Talawa's development, entitled *The Love Space Demands*, described as a choreopoem, ran at the Cochrane Theatre from 1 to 21 October 1992. The second American play, *From the Mississippi Delta*, opened at the Cochrane Theatre on 1 April and ran until 1 May 1993, and transferred to the Contact Theatre Manchester from 12 May to 5 June of the same year. Both plays are written by black, female playwrights and focus on the exploration of experiences from the perspectives of African–American women, while equally drawing parallels to the shared experience of black-British women in general. However, it is worth noting that while these American plays address issues from a female perspective, Brewster did not necessarily see their production by Talawa as being defined by feminism, since this was 'not the primary concern of her work' (Goodman, 1993, 150).

From the Mississippi Delta, for instance, is an autobiographical play that chronicles the life experiences of the playwright, and is set in 1960s America, at the height of the civil rights movement. The play dramatizes Holland's struggles; her experience of being raped by a white man when she was 11 years old, her consequent life of prostitution and petty crime, involvement with the civil rights movement, the death of her mother in a suspicious fire at home and her eventual journey towards 'redemption' through education. These experiences were dramatized by the trio of Pauline Black, Joy Richardson and Josette Bushell-Mingo, with each taking turns to portray the various characters encountered in Holland's life journey, including her mother, Aunt Baby, a midwife who occasionally lodged local prostitutes in the shack she shared with her children in order to generate some much-needed income. In Talawa's production of the play all the male characters are also played by the three female performers, who give 'a passionate performance of each phase of Holland's life and throw themselves into their roles with jubilation and complete dedication' (Morgan, 1993, 11). Despite the all-female cast, the play succeeds in representing the black experience of disadvantage and social deprivation, out of which Holland's character is able to rise with dignity owing to her sheer doggedness – equally echoed in the many references to the civil rights movement. Moreover, as Johnson suggests, Talawa's choice of a play that presents

> the overt discussion of sex and violence and the plight of blacks attempting to take a fighting stance against white American society,

gave Talawa (at least momentarily) a more feisty and politically
militant identity than many of the Caribbean plays can be seen to
have done. (Johnson, 2001, 232)

Critical Reception

Talawa has not always received the sort of critical attention and acclaim
it deserves. While, in general, the company's productions often elicit
mixed responses from mainstream theatre critics, such attention is
rarely sustained in terms of critical engagement with what the company
stands for or has managed to achieve in its relatively short existence. In
fact, Johnson contends that the best critical reception of the company's
work in their first decade of existence was for the production of *The
Love Space Demands* and *From the Mississippi Delta* – the only two
American plays produced by Talawa during that decade. Writing
specifically about the latter, Johnson argues that the 'mainstream
theatre critics were all positive in their appreciation of the show in a
way that did not occur with any of the Caribbean or African productions' (Johnson, 2001, 231). For instance, Joy Morgan urged the British
public in no uncertain terms to 'make an exception for this Talawa
Theatre production' (Morgan, 1993, 11), while Deborah McLauchlan
demanded, 'if you can't afford it, save; and if you haven't got time,
cancel something else' (McLauchlan, 1993, 37). Similarly, Michael
Billington and Nick Curtis described *The Love Space Demands* respectively as 'impressive' (Billington, 1992, 36) and 'a remarkable, lyrical
experience of live poetry' (Curtis, 1992, 23). In Johnson's opinion,
however, the enthusiastic reception accorded Talawa's production of
the two American plays by mainstream theatre critics may well be

> a result of the critics having a better understanding of the genre as
> American culture has a firm place on British television. Another
> possibility is that on a linguistic level the critics found the play easier
> to understand. Perhaps the critics considered the performers to be
> *acting* rather than copying the voices of their parents as they may
> have been perceived to be doing in the Caribbean and African plays.
> (Johnson, 2001, 231, emphasis mine)

In articulating these possibilities in the attempt to try and understand
why mainstream, predominantly white, theatre critics seemed to be
unduly fixated on the two American productions in their praise of

Talawa's work, Johnson touches on a rather intriguing concept which may account for this attitude. The prejudiced assumption that Talawa performers were not merely 'copying the voices of their parents as they may have been perceived to be doing in the Caribbean and African plays' but were indeed *acting* could account for the enthusiasm of the critics. Johnson's claim that mainstream theatre critics did not offer the same sort of enthusiastic and blatantly positive review given to Talawa's production of the American plays to their Caribbean and African productions can be seen in some of the mixed, often scathing reviews in mainstream British press. A good example is Kate Bassett's review for *The Times* of Talawa's 1994 production of *Maskarade* by Sylvia Wynter, entitled 'Reviving a happy tradition'. Bassett contends:

> the company energy seems squashed already, not doing Sylvia Wynter's lively script justice. They are unanimated, some inaudible. The set, creating a town out of bamboo blinds, is pretty. However, energy seems to disperse into its spaciousness ... Isira Makuloluwe, the trained dancer of the company, is actually irritatingly incongruous, making earthily sexy movements effetely balletic. Cy Grant's Narrator is ill-at-ease: it is like watching Jacob Bronowski trying to get on down and be wizardy. Allister Bain as Driver, the ageing local with his eye on a girl, gives an unsure performance. (Bassett, 1994, 34)

Reading Bassett's analysis of the production, one can almost feel a sense of frustration that the performance did not meet a romanticized view of Caribbean performance, à la Notting Hill carnival, as can be inferred from her criticism of the '*trained dancer*' of the company as being '*effetely balletic*'.

Such concerns that Talawa might be copying instead of acting is not evidenced in reviews of its Caribbean and African productions by critics from these communities, opting instead to be far more objective in their criticism of Talawa. For instance, Talawa's 1986 production of *An Echo in the Bone* attracted criticism from Caryl Phillips, who disparaged the actors for not having 'uniformly Jamaican' accents and for putting on ritualistic actions that seemed laboured and acted, instead of being felt by the audience (Phillips, 1986, 26). Seen from the perspective of Johnson's statement about the role of language or dialect in determining whether the Talawa performers were acting or copying, Phillips' criticism of the actors' poor Jamaican accents highlights the point about Caribbean and African critics being more likely to offer arrangement makes it possible for two separate conversations to be carried on at the same time. The old-fashioned *a parte*° is no longer necessary. Chekhov borrowed this "contrapuntal" dialogue from Ibsen and masterfully refined it.

The crucial part of the stage design is the room in the background, with a huge portrait of "a handsome, elderly man in a general's uniform" hanging on the wall behind the sofa. In the last scene Hedda will enter this room, draw the curtains, and shoot herself in front of her father's portrait. Hedda Tesman, two months pregnant, kills Hedda Gabler. The inner room, whose only exit leads to the salon in the foreground, is at once the concrete and the symbolic setting of the conflict between the Father/superego and the id. By shooting herself, Hedda kills the shadow of her Father and the child she never wanted. The "shadow" of the father kills the daughter. In contrast to the earlier dramas [by Ibsen], *Lady from the Sea* and *Rosmersholm*, where the prehistory of the conflicts, traumas, and sexual complexes festers beneath the surface, and though continuing to grow they are never seen, in *Hedda Gabler* nothing remains unspoken.

In this case study of a neurosis, the mother's place is left empty. Hedda was raised by her father, who would have preferred a son. She rode horses and learned to shoot guns. In school, like a tomboy, she pulled her girlfriends' hair. She can barely resist pulling Thea's blond locks in Act II. In the last *Hedda Gabler* I saw, in Bochum in 1977, Peter Zadek directed the scene of Hedda's and Thea's drinking bout with distinct lesbian undertones. It is an extreme though not arbitrary reading of the text. In this record of sexual neurosis, the inversion and displacement of libido are intended. Thirty-year-old Hedda Gabler is frigid.

General Gabler's daughter not only wants to rule in a man's world. Unable to assume her female sexual role, she escapes by playing out the male one in her imagination. She demands that Loevborg initiate her into masculine rites and describe his visits to the red-haired Diana. Imaginary sex is vicarious. Hedda, rejecting the traditional roles of wife and mother, is condemned to live vicariously, full of the frustration and sense of emptiness which she calls deadly boredom. Madame Bovary's love affairs with shallow men were substitutions for the romantic ecstasies she read about in contemporary novels. For General Gabler's daughter these flights and escapes are ruled out. She has only her inner room "with its heavy curtains and her father's portrait."

It is not only sexual fulfillment that Hedda strives for through imagination. Until the very last scene, all her passions and hatreds are realized only by acts of substitution. The manuscript of Loevborg's new book is twice called his and Thea's "child"; Hedda commits a substitute "infanticide" by burning it in the fireplace. The pistol shot above Judge Brack's head was a substitute murder and a substitute sexual act. Fear paralyzed her twice before: once when she was afraid to shoot Loevborg for his aggressive advances, and then a second time when she was afraid to sleep with him. Handing the pistol to Loevborg is murder by intent: The shot that kills him, in keeping with the logic of the dramaturgy, symbolically castrates him as well.

In coded messages, myths, dreams, and unconscious acts, opposite terms are interchangeable: They assume the guise of their antitheses. As in Racine and

---

a parte: Keeping different conversations separate from one another as if in different spaces.

Chekhov (although in Chekhov it is deeply hidden), the appeal of death in Ibsen disguises itself as the pulse of life, the instinct toward self-destruction is masked as libido. *Hedda Gabler* appears to return to the realistic technique of the earlier dramas, but along with *Rosmersholm*, it marks the beginning of Ibsen's last cycle of plays, from *Little Eyolf* to *When We Dead Awaken*, each of which repeats the theme of sexual frustration leading to self-destruction. With the exception of his final masterpiece, *John Gabriel Borkman*, in all these plays the balance between the realistic world and its symbolic projection is broken.

In his biography of Ibsen (1957), Michael Meyer entitled his chapter on *Hedda Gabler* "Portrait of the Dramatist as a Young Woman." "*Madame Bovary — c'est moi*," Flaubert once wrote, and Hedda Gabler is in some sense Ibsen's alter ego. The psychoanalysis of Hedda would no doubt become the merciless psychoanalysis of her author. But in psychoanalytic interpretations of the author or of his work Ibsen's invention and artistic discoveries are usually neglected, and what is even more important, the historical context, the customs and atmospheric realism of the *fin de siècle*,° are altogether lost.

Ibsen never read a page of Freud. Neither did Strindberg. In the early 1890s Freud began his first methodical studies of hysteria; in 1895 he announced his first analysis of dreams; and he used the term "psychoanalysis" for the first time in 1896. The Scandinavian Miss Julies and Heddas were finding their dramatists in Strindberg and Ibsen while the Viennese Julies and Heddas were finding their analyst in Freud.

   fin de siècle: Turn of the century.

August Strindberg

The Swedish playwright August Strindberg (1849–1912) wrote fifty-eight plays, more than a dozen novels, and more than a hundred short stories, all collected now in fifty-five volumes. Much of the time he was producing this astonishing body of work, he was the victim of persistent paranoia, suffered the destruction of three marriages, and lived through a major nervous breakdown.

He was a man of enormous complexity whose work has traditionally been broken into two parts: The first comprises the work he wrote up to 1894, which includes *The Father* (1877), *Miss Julie* (1888), *The Creditors* (1889), and other naturalistic plays; the second comprises work he wrote after 1897, including *There Are Crimes and Crimes* (1899), *Easter*, and *The Dance of Death* (both 1901). These are largely expressionist plays. EXPRESSIONISM disregarded the strict demands of naturalism to present a "slice of life" without artistic shaping of plot and resolution. Instead, expressionist drama used materials that resembled dreams — or nightmares — and focused on symbolic actions and a subjective interpretation of the world. Strindberg's later drama is often symbolic, taut, and psychological. His novel *Inferno* (1897) not only marks the transition between his early and late work; it gives the period its name. Strindberg's Inferno period was a time of madness and paranoic behavior that virtually redirected his life for more than three years. During this time he was convinced that the secrets of life were wrapped in the occult, and his energies went into alchemical experiments and studies of cabalistic lore.

The first period of his dramatic career began with *Master Olof* (1872), a historical drama that he chose to write in prose, which he felt was a more natural medium than verse, the convention for such plays at the time. When he rewrote the play in verse in 1876, it was rejected for the second time by the Royal Dramatic Theater but was finally produced the following year. At that time, Strindberg recorded: "In 1877 Antoine opened his Théâtre Libre in Paris, and *Thérèse Raquin*, although nothing but an adapted novel, became the dominant model. It was the powerful theme and the concentrated form that showed innovation, although the unity of time was not yet observed, and curtain falls were retained. It was then I wrote my dramas: *Lady Julie*, *The Father*, and *Creditors*." *Thérèse Raquin*, Émile Zola's naturalistic play, inspired Strindberg to move further toward his own interpretation of naturalism, which is perhaps most evident in *Miss Julie*. Strindberg was more subjective in his approach to naturalism, less scientific and deterministic, than Zola. Whereas Zola's approach might be described as "photographic" realism, Strindberg's was more selective and impressionistic, but no less honest and true. He saw his characters operating out of "a whole series of deeply buried motives." His characters were not necessarily the product of their genes or their social circumstances, as the naturalists of Zola's stripe sometimes implied. Yet he saw clearly that class distinctions helped determine the behavior of many people. Strindberg seemed to accept the view that people were not created by their class but rather belonged to their class because of the kind of people they were. Strindberg probed deeply into the psychology of his characters, whose emotional lives, rather than outward social qualities, determined their actions.

Strindberg is often described as a woman-hater, a misogynist. For periods of his life he seems to have been misogynistic, but he was nonetheless extremely contradictory in both behavior and belief. There is no simple way to talk about Strindberg's attitude toward women. On the one hand, he is conventional in his thinking that women belong in the home. On the other hand, he married a highly successful actress, Siri von Essen. As he said in a letter in 1895, "Woman is to me the earth and all its glory, the bond that binds, and of all the evil the worst evil I have seen is the female sex." A decade later in *A Blue Book*, he wrote, "When I approach a woman as a lover, I look up to her, I see something of the mother in her, and this I respect. I assume a subordinate position, become childish and puerile and actually am subordinate, like most men. . . . I put her on a pedestal." As in many things, including his attitude toward dramatic techniques and style, Strindberg is a mass of contradictions and complexities of the sort sometimes associated with genius.

MISS JULIE

Miss Julie, the daughter of a Count, and Jean, the Count's valet, come from strikingly different social backgrounds. In ordinary circumstances, they might not have been on friendly terms, much less have become lovers, as they do. But the Count is away and it is Midsummer Eve, and Miss Julie and Jean are drawn into a sexual liaison marked by a struggle for dominance and control. Miss Julie's fiancé has been disposed of before the play begins because he refused to debase himself slavishly to her will. She is a free spirit, but her breeding is suspect because her mother, like her, took a lover and defied the Count. Miss Julie's mother rebelled against her husband and punished him by burning their house down after the insurance expired. As further punishment and abasement, she humiliated the Count by arranging to have her lover loan him the money to rebuild the house. Thus, Miss Julie's heritage is one of independence, rebellion, and unorthodoxy.

From her mother's tutelage, Miss Julie was raised to manipulate men, but she cannot accept them totally. She also seems to feel a mixture of contempt for herself as a woman along with her contempt for men. In his Preface to the play, Strindberg says that Julie is a modern "half-woman" "man-hater" who sells herself for honors of various kinds. (See the commentary on pp. 673–74.)

The play has a mysterious quality. It takes place on Midsummer Eve, when lovers are sometimes revealed to one another and when almost anything can happen. In primitive fertility rites it was a time associated with sexual awakening. Kristine mentions that it is the feast of St. John and alludes to his beheading for spurning Salome's advances. Jean (French for John) in one violent moment of the play beheads Julie's pet bird as a sign of the violence pent up in him. It also foreshadows Miss Julie's death.

The fairy-tale quality that creeps into the play — as in *A Midsummer Night's Dream*, set on the same day — may seem out of place in a realistic drama, but it is profoundly compelling. It is also typical of Strindberg, who often uses symbolism to suggest a dream quality and deepen the significance of the action. Dreams are a part of reality that modern playwrights have taken great pains to explore.

The Count himself, Julie's father, never appears in the play, but his presence is always ominous and intense, very much as in a fairy tale. Jean tells Miss Julie that he would willingly kill himself if the Count were to order it. The cook, Kristine, like a witch, demands retribution because she was spurned by Jean, who once was her lover. Near the end of the play she prevents Julie and Jean from running away from the Count by impounding the horses in the stable. She has her revenge on both of them.

Although Julie may be seen as the princess, Jean has very little claim to being Prince Charming of the play, especially since he has little strength of character. He feels superior to his station as a valet, and Strindberg in his Preface refers to him as a nobleman. However, like Kristine, he is coarse beneath his outwardly polished appearance. His highest ambition is to be the proprietor of a first-class hotel, a prospect he wants to share with Julie.

One of the most striking passages in the play is the story Jean tells Julie almost reluctantly. He tries to explain to her what it feels like to be "down below," where she has never been. When he was a boy he thought of the apple trees in her father's garden as part of the "Garden of Eden, guarded by angry angels." He entered this enchanted place with his mother to weed onions and wandered into the outhouse — a building like a Turkish pavilion whose function he could not guess. While he was exploring it, he heard someone coming and had to exit beneath the outhouse and hide himself under a pile of weeds and "wet dirt that stank." From his hiding place he saw Julie in a pink dress and white stockings. He rushed to the millpond and jumped in to wash the filth off himself. Ironically, only a few moments after he tells her this story he calls her a whore, and she, in response, says, "Oh, God in heaven, end my wretched life! Take me away from the filth I'm sinking into! Save me! Save me!"

Miss Julie has been compared with Beatrice-Joanna in Middleton's *The Changeling* because, like her, Julie falls into the power of her lover and cannot redirect her life. She sinks deeper and deeper into "filth." And, like Beatrice-Joanna, Miss Julie has few choices at the end of the play. The conclusion to *Miss Julie* is swift. The contrast between the willfulness of Julie and the caution of Jean makes their situation especially desperate. When Julie leaves at the end of the play to seal her fate, we sense the terrible weight of their society's values. Those values are symbolized by the return of the Count and the expectations he had of Julie's behavior while he was gone.

Miss Julie in Performance

The first planned professional production of *Miss Julie* was canceled at the last minute by censors in Copenhagen on March 1, 1889. Although it was performed privately on March 14, 1889, in Copenhagen University's Students' Union, it was not performed professionally in Stockholm until 1906. Some important early productions of the play were in Paris in Antoine's distinguished Théâtre Libre in 1893 and in Berlin in Max Reinhardt's Kleine Theater in 1904. Reinhardt produced seventeen of Strindberg's plays and was one of his great champions. In 1907 Strindberg produced the play in his own Intimate Theatre in Stockholm, where it ran intermittently for 134 showings. He even arranged a special performance for George Bernard Shaw. The first London production was in 1912, but since the 1930s it has been revived many times, with many distinguished actors in all three major roles.

Among the notable modern productions is the Old Vic's 1966 version directed by Michael Elliott, with Maggie Smith and Albert Finney starring. The Baxter Theatre of Johannesburg, South Africa, produced the play in 1985 with the black actor John Kani as Jean and the white Afrikaner actress Sandra Prinsloo as Julie. It was considered outrageous by some white audiences. The sensational Ingmar Bergman production at the Brooklyn Academy of Music in 1991 stretched the play to two hours and made it more of a domestic tragedy — as John Simon said, "more like us, more believable, and, therefore, more terrifying."

Miss Julie has been filmed at least five times, and it has been televised as well. It is one of the most produced of modern plays.

August Strindberg (1849–1912)

MISS JULIE   *1888*

TRANSLATED BY HARRY G. CARLSON

Characters

MISS JULIE, *25 years old*
JEAN, *her father's valet, 30 years old*
KRISTINE, *her father's cook, 35 years old*

(*The action takes place in the Count's kitchen on midsummer eve.*)

Setting: (*A large kitchen, the ceiling and side walls of which are hidden by draperies. The rear wall runs diagonally from down left to up right. On the wall down left are two shelves with copper, iron, and pewter utensils; the shelves are lined with scalloped paper. Visible to the right is most of a set of large, arched glass doors, through which can be seen a fountain with a statue of Cupid, lilac bushes in bloom, and the tops of some Lombardy poplars. At down left is the corner of a large tiled stove; a portion of its hood is showing. At right, one end of the servants' white pine dining table juts out; several chairs stand around it. The stove is decorated with birch branches; juniper twigs are strewn on the floor. On the end of the table stands a large Japanese spice jar, filled with lilac blossoms. An ice box, a sink, and a washstand. Above the door is an old-fashioned bell on a spring; to the left of the door, the mouthpiece of a speaking tube is visible.*)

(*Kristine is frying something on the stove. She is wearing a light-colored cotton dress and an apron. Jean enters. He is wearing livery and carries a pair of high riding boots with spurs, which he puts down on the floor where they can be seen by the audience.*)

JEAN: Miss Julie's crazy again tonight; absolutely crazy!

KRISTINE: So you finally came back?

JEAN: I took the Count to the station and when I returned past the barn I stopped in for a dance. Who do I see but Miss Julie leading off the dance with the gamekeeper! But as soon as she saw me she rushed over to ask me for the next waltz. And she's been waltzing ever since — I've never seen anything like it. She's crazy!

KRISTINE: She always has been, but never as bad as the last two weeks since her engagement was broken off.

JEAN: Yes, I wonder what the real story was there. He was a gentleman, even if he wasn't rich. Ah! These people have such romantic ideas. (*Sits at the end of the table.*) Still, it's strange, isn't it? I mean that she'd rather stay home with the servants on midsummer eve instead of going with her father to visit relatives?

KRISTINE: She's probably embarrassed after that row with her fiancé.

JEAN: Probably! He gave a good account of himself, though. Do you know how it happened, Kristine? I saw it, you know, though I didn't let on I had.

KRISTINE: No! You saw it?

JEAN: Yes, I did. ——— That evening they were out near the stable, and she was "training" him — as she called it. Do you know what she did? She made him jump over her riding crop, the way you'd teach a dog to jump. He jumped twice and she hit him each time. But the third time he grabbed the crop out of her hand, hit her with it across the cheek, and broke it in pieces. Then he left.

KRISTINE: So, that's what happened! I can't believe it!

JEAN: Yes, that's the way it went! ——— What have you got for me that's tasty, Kristine?

KRISTINE (*serving him from the pan*): Oh, it's only a piece of kidney I cut from the veal roast.

JEAN (*smelling the food*): Beautiful! That's my favorite *délice.*° (*Feeling the plate.*) But you could have warmed the plate!

KRISTINE: You're fussier than the Count himself, once you start! (*She pulls his hair affectionately.*)

JEAN (*angry*): Stop it, leave my hair alone! You know I'm touchy about that.

KRISTINE: Now, now, it's only love, you know that. (*Jean eats. Kristine opens a bottle of beer.*)

JEAN: Beer? On midsummer eve? No thank you! I can do better than that. (*Opens a drawer in the table and takes out a bottle of red wine with yellow sealing wax.*) See that? Yellow seal! Give me a glass! A wine glass! I'm drinking this *pur.*°

KRISTINE (*returns to the stove and puts on a small saucepan*): God help the woman who gets you for a husband! What a fussbudget.

---

délice: Delight.
pur: Pure; the first drink from the bottle.

JEAN: Nonsense! You'd be damned lucky to get a man like me. It certainly hasn't done you any harm to have people call me your sweetheart. (*Tastes the wine.*) Good! Very good! Just needs a little warming. (*Warms the glass between his hands.*) We bought this in Dijon. Four francs a liter, not counting the cost of the bottle, or the customs duty. ———— What are you cooking now? It stinks like hell!

KRISTINE: Oh, some slop Miss Julie wants to give Diana.

JEAN: Watch your language, Kristine. But why should you have to cook for that damn mutt on midsummer eve? Is she sick?

KRISTINE: Yes, she's sick! She sneaked out with the gatekeeper's dog — and now there's hell to pay. Miss Julie won't have it!

JEAN: Miss Julie has too much pride about some things and not enough about others, just like her mother was. The Countess was most at home in the kitchen and the cowsheds, but a *one*-horse carriage wasn't elegant enough for her. The cuffs of her blouse were dirty, but she had to have her coat of arms on her cufflinks. ———— And Miss Julie won't take proper care of herself either. If you ask me, she just isn't refined. Just now, when she was dancing in the barn, she pulled the gamekeeper away from Anna and made him dance with her. *We* wouldn't behave like that, but that's what happens when aristocrats pretend they're common people — they get *common*! ———— But she is quite a woman! Magnificent! What shoulders, and what — et cetera!

KRISTINE: Oh, don't overdo it! I've heard what Clara says, and she dresses her.

JEAN: Ha, Clara! You're all jealous of each other! I've been out riding with her. . . . And the way she dances!

KRISTINE: Listen, Jean! You're going to dance with me, when I'm finished here, aren't you?

JEAN: Of course I will.

KRISTINE: Promise?

JEAN: Promise? When I say I'll do something, I do it! By the way, the kidney was very good. (*Corks the bottle.*)

JULIE (*in the doorway to someone outside*): I'll be right back! You go ahead for now! (*Jean sneaks the bottle back into the table drawer and gets up respectfully. Miss Julie enters and crosses to Kristine by the stove.*) Well? Is it ready? (*Kristine indicates that Jean is present.*)

JEAN (*gallantly*): Are you ladies up to something secret?

JULIE (*flicking her handkerchief in his face*): None of your business!

JEAN: Hmm! I like the smell of violets!

JULIE (*coquettishly*): Shame on you! So you know about perfumes, too? You certainly know how to dance. Ah, ah! No peeking! Go away.

JEAN (*boldly but respectfully*): Are you brewing up a magic potion for midsummer eve? Something to prophesy by under a lucky star, so you'll catch a glimpse of your future husband!

JULIE (*caustically*): You'd need sharp eyes to see him! (*To Kristine.*) Pour out half a bottle and cork it well. ———— Come and dance a schottische° with me, Jean . . .

JEAN (*hesitating*): I don't want to be impolite to anyone, and I've already promised this dance to Kristine . . .

JULIE: Oh, she can have another one — can't you, Kristine? Won't you lend me Jean?

KRISTINE: It's not up to me, ma'am. (*To Jean.*) If the mistress is so generous, it wouldn't do for you to say no. Go on, Jean, and thank her for the honor.

JEAN: To be honest, and no offense intended, I wonder whether it's wise for you to dance twice running with the same partner, especially since these people are quick to jump to conclusions . . .

JULIE (*flaring up*): What's that? What sort of conclusions? What do you mean?

JEAN (*submissively*): If you don't understand, ma'am, I must speak more plainly. It doesn't look good to play favorites with your servants. . . .

JULIE: Play favorites! What an idea! I'm astonished! As mistress of the house, I honor your dance with my presence. And when I dance, I want to dance with someone who can lead, so I won't look ridiculous.

JEAN: As you order, ma'am! I'm at your service!

JULIE (*gently*): Don't take it as an order! On a night like this we're all just ordinary people having fun, so we'll forget about rank. Now, take my arm! ———— Don't worry, Kristine! I won't steal your sweetheart! (*Jean offers his arm and leads Miss Julie out.*)

Mime

(*The following should be played as if the actress playing Kristine were really alone. When she has to, she turns her back to the audience. She does not look toward them, nor does she hurry as if she were afraid they would grow impatient. Schottische music played on a fiddle sounds in the distance. Kristine hums along with the music. She clears the table, washes the dishes, dries them, and puts them away. She takes off her apron. From a table drawer she removes a small mirror and leans it against the bowl of lilacs on the table.*)

schottische: A Scottish round dance resembling a polka.

She lights a candle, heats a hairpin over the flame, and uses it to set a curl on her forehead. She crosses to the door and listens, then returns to the table. She finds the handkerchief Miss Julie left behind, picks it up, and smells it. Then, preoccupied, she spreads it out, stretches it, smoothes out the wrinkles, and folds it into quarters, and so forth.)

JEAN (*enters alone*): God, she really *is* crazy! What a way to dance! Everybody's laughing at her behind her back. What do you make of it, Kristine?

KRISTINE: Ah! It's that time of the month for her, and she always gets peculiar like that. Are you going to dance with me now?

JEAN: You're not mad at me, are you, for leaving . . . ?

KRISTINE: Of course not! —— Why should I be, for a little thing like that? Besides, I know my place . . .

JEAN (*puts his arm around her waist*): You're a sensible girl, Kristine, and you'd make a good wife . . .

JULIE (*entering; uncomfortably surprised; with forced good humor*): What a charming escort — running away from your partner.

JEAN: On the contrary, Miss Julie. Don't you see how I rushed back to the partner I abandoned!

JULIE (*changing her tone*): You know, you're a superb dancer! —— But why are you wearing livery on a holiday? Take it off at once!

JEAN: Then I must ask you to go outside for a moment. You see, my black coat is hanging over here . . . (*Gestures and crosses right.*)

JULIE: Are you embarrassed about changing your coat in front of me? Well, go in your room then. Either that or stay and I'll turn my back.

JEAN: With your permission, ma'am! (*He crosses right. His arm is visible as he changes his jacket.*)

JULIE (*to Kristine*): Tell me, Kristine — you two are so close —. Is Jean your fiancé?

KRISTINE: Fiancé? Yes, if you wish. We can call him that.

JULIE: What do you mean?

KRISTINE: You had a fiancé yourself, didn't you? So . . .

JULIE: Well, we were properly engaged . . .

KRISTINE: But nothing came of it, did it? (*Jean returns dressed in a frock coat and bowler hat.*)

JULIE: *Très gentil, monsieur Jean! Très gentil!*

JEAN: *Vous voulez plaisanter, madame!*

JULIE: *Et vous voulez parler français!°* Where did you learn that?

Très gentil . . . français!:
Very pleasing, Mr. Jean! Very pleasing.
You would trifle with me, madam!
And you want to speak French!

JEAN: In Switzerland, when I was wine steward in one of the biggest hotels in Lucerne!

JULIE: You look like a real gentleman in that coat! *Charmant!°* (*Sits at the table.*)

JEAN: Oh, you're flattering me!

JULIE (*offended*): Flattering you?

JEAN: My natural modesty forbids me to believe that you would really compliment someone like me, and so I took the liberty of assuming that you were exaggerating, which polite people call flattering.

JULIE: Where did you learn to talk like that? You must have been to the theater often.

JEAN: Of course. And I've done a lot of traveling.

JULIE: But you come from here, don't you?

JEAN: My father was a farmhand on the district attorney's estate nearby. I used to see you when you were little, but you never noticed me.

JULIE: No! Really?

JEAN: Sure. I remember one time especially . . . but I can't talk about that.

JULIE: Oh, come now! Why not? Just this once!

JEAN: No, I really couldn't, not now. Some other time, perhaps.

JULIE: Why some other time? What's so dangerous about now?

JEAN: It's not dangerous, but there are obstacles. —— Her, for example. (*Indicating Kristine, who has fallen asleep in a chair by the stove.*)

JULIE: What a pleasant wife she'll make! She probably snores, too.

JEAN: No, she doesn't, but she talks in her sleep.

JULIE (*cynically*): How do *you* know?

JEAN (*audaciously*): I've heard her! (*Pause, during which they stare at each other.*)

JULIE: Why don't you sit down?

JEAN: I couldn't do that in your presence.

JULIE: But if I order you to?

JEAN: Then I'd obey.

JULIE: Sit down, then. —— No, wait. Can you get me something to drink first?

JEAN: I don't know what we have in the ice box. I think there's only beer.

JULIE: Why do you say "only"? My tastes are so simple I prefer beer to wine. (*Jean takes a bottle of beer from the ice box and opens it. He looks for a glass and a plate in the cupboard and serves her.*)

JEAN: Here you are, ma'am.

JULIE: Thank you. Won't you have something yourself?

JEAN: I'm not partial to beer, but if it's an order . . .

JULIE: An order? —— Surely a gentleman can keep his lady company.

JEAN: You're right, of course. (*Opens a bottle and gets a glass.*)

Charmant: Charming.

JULIE: Now, drink to my health! (*He hesitates.*) What? A man of the world — and shy?

JEAN (*in mock romantic fashion, he kneels and raises his glass*): Skål to my mistress!

JULIE: Bravo! —— Now kiss my shoe, to finish it properly. (*Jean hesitates, then boldly seizes her foot and kisses it lightly.*) Perfect! You should have been an actor.

JEAN (*rising*): That's enough now, Miss Julie! Someone might come in and see us.

JULIE: What of it?

JEAN: People talk, that's what! If you knew how their tongues were wagging just now at the dance, you'd . . .

JULIE: What were they saying? Tell me! —— Sit down!

JEAN (*sits*): I don't want to hurt you, but they were saying things —— suggestive things, that, that . . . well, you can figure it out for yourself! You're not a child. If a woman is seen drinking alone with a man — let alone a servant — at night — then . . .

JULIE: Then what? Besides, we're not alone. Kristine is here.

JEAN: Asleep!

JULIE: Then I'll wake her up. (*Rising.*) Kristine! Are you asleep? (*Kristine mumbles in her sleep.*)

JULIE: Kristine! —— She certainly can sleep!

KRISTINE (*in her sleep*): The Count's boots are brushed — put the coffee on — right away, right away — uh, huh — oh!

JULIE (*grabbing Kristine's nose*): Will you wake up!

JEAN (*severely*): Leave her alone — let her sleep!

JULIE (*sharply*): What?

JEAN: Someone who's been standing over a stove all day has a right to be tired by now. Sleep should be respected . . .

JULIE (*changing her tone*): What a considerate thought — it does you credit — thank you! (*Offering her hand.*) Come outside and pick some lilacs for me! (*During the following, Kristine awakens and shambles sleepily off right to bed.*)

JEAN: Go with you?

JULIE: With me!

JEAN: We couldn't do that! Absolutely not!

JULIE: I don't understand. Surely you don't imagine . . .

JEAN: No, I don't, but the others might.

JULIE: What? That I've fallen in love with a servant?

JEAN: I'm not a conceited man, but such things happen — and for these people, nothing is sacred.

JULIE: I do believe you're an aristocrat!

JEAN: Yes, I am.

JULIE: And I'm stepping down . . .

JEAN: Don't step down, Miss Julie, take my advice. No one'll believe you stepped down voluntarily. People will always say you fell.

JULIE: I have a higher opinion of people than you. Come and see! —— Come! (*She stares at him broodingly.*)

JEAN: You're very strange, do you know that?

JULIE: Perhaps! But so are you! —— For that matter, everything is strange. Life, people, everything. Like floating scum, drifting on and on across the water, until it sinks down and down! That reminds me of a dream I have now and then. I've climbed up on top of a pillar. I sit there and see no way of getting down. I get dizzy when I look down, and I must get down, but I don't have the courage to jump. I can't hold on firmly, and I long to be able to fall, but I don't fall. And yet I'll have no peace until I get down, no rest unless I get down, down on the ground! And if I did get down to the ground, I'd want to be under the earth . . . Have you ever felt anything like that?

JEAN: No. I dream that I'm lying under a high tree in a dark forest. I want to get up, up on top, and look out over the bright landscape, where the sun is shining, and plunder the bird's nest up there, where the golden eggs lie. And I climb and climb, but the trunk's so thick and smooth, and it's so far to the first branch. But I know if I just reached that first branch, I'd go right to the top, like up a ladder. I haven't reached it yet, but I will, even if it's only in a dream!

JULIE: Here I am chattering with you about dreams. Come, let's go out! Just into the park! (*She offers him her arm, and they start to leave.*)

JEAN: We'll have to sleep on nine midsummer flowers, Miss Julie, to make our dreams come true! (*They turn at the door. Jean puts his hand to his eye.*)

JULIE: Did you get something in your eye?

JEAN: It's nothing — just a speck — it'll be gone in a minute.

JULIE: My sleeve must have brushed against you. Sit down and let me help you. (*She takes him by the arm and seats him. She tilts his head back and with the tip of a handkerchief tries to remove the speck.*) Sit still, absolutely still! (*She slaps his hand.*) Didn't you hear me? —— Why, you're trembling; the big, strong man is trembling! (*Feels his biceps.*) What muscles you have!

JEAN (*warning*): Miss Julie!

JULIE: Yes, *monsieur* Jean.

JEAN: *Attention! Je ne suis qu'un homme!*°

JULIE: Will you sit still! —— There! Now it's gone! Kiss my hand and thank me.

Attention! Je ne suis qu'un homme!: Watch out! I am only a man!

JEAN (*rising*): Miss Julie, listen to me! ——— Kristine has gone to bed! ——— Will you listen to me!

JULIE: Kiss my hand first!

JEAN: Listen to me!

JULIE: Kiss my hand first!

JEAN: All right, but you've only yourself to blame!

JULIE: For what?

JEAN: For what? Are you still a child at twenty-five? Don't you know that it's dangerous to play with fire?

JULIE: Not for me. I'm insured.

JEAN (*boldly*): No, you're not! But even if you were, there's combustible material close by.

JULIE: Meaning you?

JEAN: Yes! Not because it's me, but because I'm young ———

JULIE: And handsome — what incredible conceit! A Don Juan perhaps! Or a Joseph!° Yes, that's it, I do believe you're a Joseph!

JEAN: Do you?

JULIE: I'm almost afraid so. (*Jean boldly tries to put his arm around her waist and kiss her. She slaps his face.*) How dare you?

JEAN: Are you serious or joking?

JULIE: Serious.

JEAN: Then so was what just happened. You play games too seriously, and that's dangerous. Well, I'm tired of games. You'll excuse me if I get back to work. I haven't done the Count's boots yet and it's long past midnight.

JULIE: Put the boots down!

JEAN: No! It's the work I have to do. I never agreed to be your playmate, and never will. It's beneath me.

JULIE: You're proud.

JEAN: In certain ways, but not in others.

JULIE: Have you ever been in love?

JEAN: We don't use that word, but I've been fond of many girls, and once I was sick because I couldn't have the one I wanted. That's right, sick, like those princes in the Arabian Nights — who couldn't eat or drink because of love.

JULIE: Who was she? (*Jean is silent.*) Who was she?

JEAN: You can't force me to tell you that.

JULIE: But if I ask you as an equal, as a — friend! Who was she?

JEAN: You!

JULIE (*sits*): How amusing . . .

JEAN: Yes, if you like! It was ridiculous! ——— You see, that was the story I didn't want to tell you earlier. Maybe I will now. Do you know how the world looks from down below? ——— Of course you don't. Neither do hawks and falcons, whose backs we can't see because they're usually soaring up there above us. I grew up in a shack with seven brothers and sisters and a pig, in the middle of a wasteland, where there wasn't a single tree. But from our window I could see the tops of apple trees above the wall of your father's garden. That was the Garden of Eden, guarded by angry angels with flaming swords. All the same, the other boys and I managed to find our way to the Tree of Life. ——— Now you think I'm contemptible, I suppose.

JULIE: Oh, all boys steal apples.

JEAN: You say that, but you think I'm contemptible anyway. Oh well! One day I went into the Garden of Eden with my mother, to weed the onion beds. Near the vegetable garden was a small Turkish pavilion in the shadow of jasmine bushes and overgrown with honeysuckle. I had no idea what it was used for, but I'd never seen such a beautiful building. People went in and came out again, and one day the door was left open. I sneaked close and saw walls covered with pictures of kings and emperors, and red curtains with fringes at the windows — now you know the place I mean. I ——— (*Breaks off a sprig of lilac and holds it in front of Miss Julie's nose.*) ——— I'd never been inside the manor house, never seen anything except the church — but this was more beautiful. From then on, no matter where my thoughts wandered, they returned — there. And gradually I got a longing to experience, just once, the full pleasure of — *enfin*,° I sneaked in, saw, and marveled! But then I heard someone coming! There was only one exit for ladies and gentlemen, but for me there was another, and I had no choice but to take it! (*Miss Julie, who has taken the lilac sprig, lets it fall on the table.*) Afterwards, I started running. I crashed through a raspberry bush, flew over a strawberry patch, and came up onto the rose terrace. There I caught sight of a pink dress and a pair of white stockings — it was you. I crawled under a pile of weeds, and I mean under — under thistles that pricked me and wet dirt that stank. And I looked at you as you walked among the roses, and I thought: If it's true that a thief can enter heaven and be with the angels, then why can't a farmhand's son here on God's earth enter the manor house garden and play with the Count's daughter?

JULIE (*romantically*): Do you think all poor children would have thought the way you did?

Don Juan . . . Joseph: Don Juan in Spanish legend is a seducer of women; in Genesis, Joseph resists the advances of Potiphar's wife.

enfin: Finally.

JEAN (*at first hesitant, then with conviction*): If *all* poor — yes — of course. Of course!

JULIE: It must be terrible to be poor!

JEAN (*with exaggerated suffering*): Oh, Miss Julie! Oh! —— A dog can lie on the Countess's sofa, a horse can have his nose patted by a young lady's hand, but a servant —— (*Changing his tone.*) —— oh, I know — now and then you find one with enough stuff in him to get ahead in the world, but how often? —— Anyhow, do you know what I did then? —— I jumped in the millstream with my clothes on, was pulled out, and got a beating. But the following Sunday, when my father and all the others went to my grandmother's, I arranged to stay home. I scrubbed myself with soap and water, put on my best clothes, and went to church so that I could see you! I saw you and returned home, determined to die. But I wanted to die beautifully and pleasantly, without pain. And then I remembered that it was dangerous to sleep under an elder bush. We had a big one, and it was in full flower. I plundered its treasures and bedded down under them in the oat bin. Have you ever noticed how smooth oats are? — and soft to the touch, like human skin . . . ! Well, I shut the lid and closed my eyes. I fell asleep and woke up feeling very sick. But I didn't die, as you can see. What was I after? —— I don't know. There was no hope of winning you, of course. —— You were a symbol of the hopelessness of ever rising out of the class in which I was born.

JULIE: You're a charming storyteller. Did you ever go to school?

JEAN: A bit, but I've read lots of novels and been to the theater often. And then I've listened to people like you talk — that's where I learned most.

JULIE: Do you listen to what we say?

JEAN: Naturally! And I've heard plenty, too, driving the carriage or rowing the boat. Once I heard you and a friend . . .

JULIE: Oh? —— What did you hear?

JEAN: I'd better not say. But I was surprised a little. I couldn't imagine where you learned such words. Maybe at bottom there isn't such a great difference between people as we think.

JULIE: Shame on you! We don't act like you when we're engaged.

JEAN (*staring at her*): Is that true? —— You don't have to play innocent with me, Miss . . .

JULIE: The man I gave my love to was a swine.

JEAN: That's what you all say — afterwards.

JULIE: All?

JEAN: I think so. I know I've heard that phrase before, on similar occasions.

JULIE: What occasions?

JEAN: Like the one I'm talking about. The last time . . .

JULIE (*rising*): Quiet! I don't want to hear any more!

JEAN: That's interesting — that's what *she* said, too. Well, if you'll excuse me, I'm going to bed.

JULIE (*gently*): To bed? On midsummer eve?

JEAN: Yes! Dancing with the rabble out there doesn't amuse me much.

JULIE: Get the key to the boat and row me out on the lake. I want to see the sun come up.

JEAN: Is that wise?

JULIE: Are you worried about your reputation?

JEAN: Why not? Why should I risk looking ridiculous and getting fired without a reference, just when I'm trying to establish myself. Besides, I think I owe something to Kristine.

JULIE: So, now it's Kristine . . .

JEAN: Yes, but you, too. —— Take my advice, go up and go to bed!

JULIE: Am I to obey you?

JEAN: Just this once — for your own good! Please! It's very late. Drowsiness makes people giddy and liable to lose their heads! Go to bed! Besides — unless I'm mistaken — I hear the others coming to look for me. And if they find us together, you'll be lost!

(*The Chorus approaches, singing.*)

The swineherd found his true love
a pretty girl so fair,
The swineherd found his true love
but let the girl beware.

For then he saw the princess
the princess on the golden hill,
but then saw the princess,
so much fairer still.

So the swineherd and the princess
they danced the whole night through,
and he forgot his first love,
to her he was untrue.

And when the long night ended,
and in the light of day, of day,
the dancing too was ended,
and the princess could not stay.

Then the swineherd lost his true love,
and the princess grieves him still,
and never more she'll wander
from atop the golden hill.

JULIE: I know all these people and I love them, just as they love me. Let them come in and you'll see.

JEAN: No, Miss Julie, they don't love you. They take your food, but they spit on it! Believe me! Listen to them, listen to what they're singing! —— No, don't listen to them!

JULIE (*listening*): What are they singing?

JEAN: It's a dirty song! About you and me!

JULIE: Disgusting! Oh! How deceitful! ——

JEAN: The rabble is always cowardly! And in a battle like this, you don't fight; you can only run away!

JULIE: Run away? But where? We can't go out — or into Kristine's room.

JEAN: True. But there's my room. Necessity knows no rules. Besides, you can trust me. I'm your friend and I respect you.

JULIE: But suppose — suppose they look for you in there?

JEAN: I'll bolt the door, and if anyone tries to break in, I'll shoot! —— Come! (*On his knees.*) Come!

JULIE (*urgently*): Promise me . . . ?

JEAN: I swear! (*Miss Julie runs off right. Jean hastens after her.*)

Ballet

(*Led by a fiddler, the servants and farm people enter, dressed festively, with flowers in their hats. On the table they place a small barrel of beer and a keg of schnapps, both garlanded. Glasses are brought out, and the drinking starts. A dance circle is formed and "The Swineherd and the Princess" is sung. When the dance is finished, everyone leaves, singing.*)

(*Miss Julie enters alone. She notices the mess in the kitchen, wrings her hands, then takes out her powder puff and powders her nose.*)

JEAN (*enters, agitated*): There, you see? And you heard them. We can't possibly stay here now, you know that.

JULIE: Yes, I know. But what can we do?

JEAN: Leave, travel, far away from here.

JULIE: Travel? Yes, but where?

JEAN: To Switzerland, to the Italian lakes. Have you ever been there?

JULIE: No. Is it beautiful?

JEAN: Oh, an eternal summer — oranges growing everywhere, laurel trees, always green . . .

JULIE: But what'll we do there?

JEAN: I'll open a hotel — with first-class service for first-class people.

JULIE: Hotel?

JEAN: That's the life, you know. Always new faces, new languages. No time to worry or be nervous. No hunting for something to do — there's always work to be done: bells ringing night and day, train whistles blowing, carriages coming and going, and all the while gold rolling into the till! That's the life!

JULIE: Yes, it sounds wonderful. But what'll I do?

JEAN: You'll be mistress of the house: the jewel in our crown! With your looks . . . and your manner — oh — success is guaranteed! It'll be wonderful! You'll sit in your office like a queen and push an electric button to set your slaves in motion. The guests will file past your throne and timidly lay their treasures before you. —— You have no idea how people tremble when they get their bill. —— I'll salt the bills° and you'll sweeten them with your prettiest smile. —— Let's get away from here —— (*Takes a timetable out of his pocket.*) —— Right away, on the next train! —— We'll be in Malmö six-thirty tomorrow morning, Hamburg at eight-forty; from Frankfort to Basel will take a day, then on to Como by way of the St. Gotthard Tunnel, in, let's see, three days. Three days!

JULIE: That's all very well! But Jean — you must give me courage! —— Tell me you love me! Put your arms around me!

JEAN (*hesitating*): I want to — but I don't dare. Not in this house, not again. I love you — never doubt that — you don't doubt it, do you, Miss Julie?

JULIE (*shy; very feminine*): "Miss!" —— Call me Julie! There are no barriers between us anymore. Call me Julie!

JEAN (*tormented*): I can't! There'll always be barriers between us as long as we stay in this house. —— There's the past and there's the Count. I've never met anyone I had such respect for. —— When I see his gloves lying on a chair, I feel small. —— When I hear that bell up there ring, I jump like a skittish horse. —— And when I look at his boots standing there so stiff and proud, I feel like bowing! (*Kicking the boots.*) Superstitions and prejudices we learned as children — but they can easily be forgotten. If I can just get to another country, a republic, people will bow and scrape when they see my livery — *they'll* bow and scrape, you hear, not me! I wasn't born to cringe. I've got stuff in me, I've got character, and if I can only grab onto that first branch, you watch me climb! I'm a servant today, but next year I'll own my own hotel. In ten years I'll have enough to retire. Then I'll go to Rumania and be decorated. I could — mind you I said *could* — end up a count!

JULIE: Wonderful, wonderful!

JEAN: Ah, in Rumania you just buy your title, and so you'll be a countess after all. My countess!

JULIE: But I don't care about that — that's what I'm

---

salt the bills: Inflate or pad the bills.

putting behind me! Show me you love me, otherwise — otherwise, what am I?

JEAN: I'll show you a thousand times — afterwards! Not here! And whatever you do, no emotional outbursts, or we'll both be lost! We must think this through coolly, like sensible people. (*He takes out a cigar, snips the end, and lights it.*) You sit there, and I'll sit here. We'll talk as if nothing happened.

JULIE (*desperately*): Oh, my God! Have you no feelings?

JEAN: Me? No one has more feelings than I do, but I know how to control them.

JULIE: A little while ago you could kiss my shoe — and now!

JEAN (*harshly*): Yes, but that was before. Now we have other things to think about.

JULIE: Don't speak harshly to me!

JEAN: I'm not — just sensibly! We've already done one foolish thing, let's not have any more. The Count could return any minute, and by then we've got to decide what to do with our lives. What do you think of my plans for the future? Do you approve?

JULIE: They sound reasonable enough. I have only one question: For such a big undertaking you need capital — do you have it?

JEAN (*chewing on the cigar*): Me? Certainly! I have my professional expertise, my wide experience, and my knowledge of languages. That's capital enough, I should think!

JULIE: But all that won't even buy a train ticket.

JEAN: That's true. That's why I'm looking for a partner to advance me the money.

JULIE: Where will you find one quickly enough?

JEAN: That's up to you, if you want to come with me.

JULIE: But I can't; I have no money of my own. (*Pause.*)

JEAN: Then it's all off . . .

JULIE: And . . .

JEAN: Things stay as they are.

JULIE: Do you think I'm going to stay in this house as your lover? With all the servants pointing their fingers at me? Do you imagine I can face my father after this? No! Take me away from here, away from shame and dishonor ——— Oh, what have I done! My God, my God! (*She cries.*)

JEAN: Now, don't start that old song! ——— What have you done? The same as many others before you.

JULIE (*screaming convulsively*): And now you think I'm contemptible! ——— I'm falling, I'm falling!

JEAN: Fall down to my level and I'll lift you up again.

JULIE: What terrible power drew me to you? The attraction of the weak to the strong? The falling to

the rising? Or was it love? Was this love? Do you know what love is?

JEAN: Me? What do you take me for? You don't think this was my first time, do you?

JULIE: The things you say, the thoughts you think!

JEAN: That's the way I was taught, and that's the way I am! Now don't get excited and don't play the grand lady, because we're in the same boat now! ——— Come on, Julie, I'll pour you a glass of something special! (*He opens a drawer in the table, takes out a wine bottle, and fills two glasses already used.*)

JULIE: Where did you get that wine?

JEAN: From the cellar.

JULIE: My father's burgundy!

JEAN: That'll do for his son-in-law, won't it?

JULIE: And I drink beer! Beer!

JEAN: That only shows I have better taste.

JULIE: Thief!

JEAN: Planning to tell?

JULIE: Oh, oh! Accomplice of a common thief! Was I drunk? Have I been walking in a dream the whole evening? Midsummer eve! A time of innocent fun!

JEAN: Innocent, eh?

JULIE (*pacing back and forth*): Is there anyone on earth more miserable than I am at this moment?

JEAN: Why should you be? After such a conquest? Think of Kristine in there. Don't you think she has feelings, too?

JULIE: I thought so awhile ago, but not any more. No, a servant is a servant . . .

JEAN: And a whore is a whore!

JULIE (*on her knees, her hands clasped*): Oh, God in heaven, end my wretched life! Take me away from the filth I'm sinking into! Save me! Save me!

JEAN: I can't deny I feel sorry for you. When I lay in that onion bed and saw you in the rose garden, well . . . I'll be frank . . . I had the same dirty thoughts all boys have.

JULIE: And you wanted to die for me!

JEAN: In the oat bin? That was just talk.

JULIE: A lie, in other words!

JEAN (*beginning to feel sleepy*): More or less! I got the idea from a newspaper story about a chimney sweep who curled up in a firewood bin full of lilacs because he got a summons for not supporting his illegitimate child . . .

JULIE: So, that's what you're like . . .

JEAN: I had to think of something. And that's the kind of story women always go for.

JULIE: Swine!

JEAN: *Merde!*

JULIE: And now you've seen the hawk's back . . .

JEAN: Not exactly its *back* . . .

JULIE: And I was to be the first branch . . .

JEAN: But the branch was rotten . . .

JULIE: I was to be the sign on the hotel . . .

JEAN: And I the hotel . . .

JULIE: Sit at your desk, entice your customers, pad their bills . . .

JEAN: That I'd do myself . . .

JULIE: How can anyone be so thoroughly filthy?

JEAN: Better clean up then!

JULIE: You lackey, you menial, stand up, when I speak to you!

JEAN: Menial's strumpet, lackey's whore, shut up and get out of here! Who are you to lecture me on coarseness? None of my kind is ever as coarse as you were tonight. Do you think one of your maids would throw herself at a man the way you did? Have you ever seen any girl of my class offer herself like that? I've only seen it among animals and streetwalkers.

JULIE (*crushed*): You're right. Hit me, trample on me. I don't deserve any better. I'm worthless. But help me! If you see any way out of this, help me, Jean, please!

JEAN (*more gently*): I'd be lying if I didn't admit to a sense of triumph in all this, but do you think that a person like me would have dared even to look at someone like you if you hadn't invited it? I'm still amazed . . .

JULIE: And proud . . .

JEAN: Why not? Though I must say it was too easy to be really exciting.

JULIE: Go on, hit me, hit me harder!

JEAN (*rising*): No! Forgive me for what I've said! I don't hit a man when he's down, let alone a woman. I can't deny though, that I'm pleased to find out that what looked so dazzling to us from below was only tinsel, that the hawk's back was only gray, after all, that the lovely complexion was only powder, that those polished fingernails had black edges, and that a dirty handkerchief is still dirty, even if it smells of perfume . . . ! On the other hand, it hurts me to find out that what I was striving for wasn't finer, more substantial. It hurts me to see you sunk so low that you're inferior to your own cook. It hurts like watching flowers beaten down by autumn rains and turned into mud.

JULIE: You talk as if you were already above me.

JEAN: I am. You see, I could make you a countess, but you could never make me a count.

JULIE: But I'm the child of a count — something you could never be!

JEAN: That's true. But I could be the father of counts — if . . .

JULIE: But you're a thief. I'm not.

JEAN: There are worse things than being a thief! Besides, when I'm working in a house, I consider myself sort of a member of the family, like one of the children. And you don't call it stealing when a child snatches a berry off a full bush. (*His passion is aroused again.*) Miss Julie, you're a glorious woman, much too good for someone like me! You were drinking and you lost your head. Now you want to cover up your mistake by telling yourself that you love me! You don't. Maybe there was a physical attraction — but then your love is no better than mine. ———— I could never be satisfied to be no more than an animal to you, and I could never arouse real love in you.

JULIE: Are you sure of that?

JEAN: You're suggesting it's possible ———— Oh, I could fall in love with you, no doubt about it. You're beautiful, you're refined ———— (*approaching and taking her hand*) ———— cultured, lovable when you want to be, and once you start a fire in a man, it never goes out. (*Putting his arm around her waist.*) You're like hot, spicy wine, and one kiss from you . . . (*He tries to lead her out, but she slowly frees herself.*)

JULIE: Let me go!? ———— You'll never win me like that.

JEAN: *How* then? ———— Not like that? Not with caresses and pretty speeches. Not with plans about the future or rescue from disgrace! *How* then?

JULIE: How? How? I don't know! ———— I have no idea! ———— I detest you as I detest rats, but I can't escape from you.

JEAN: Escape with me!

JULIE (*pulling herself together*): Escape? Yes, we must escape! ———— But I'm so tired. Give me a glass of wine? (*Jean pours the wine. She looks at her watch.*) But we must talk first. We still have a little time. (*She drains the glass, then holds it out for more.*)

JEAN: Don't drink so fast. It'll go to your head.

JULIE: What does it matter?

JEAN: What does it matter? It's vulgar to get drunk! What did you want to tell me?

JULIE: We must escape! But first we must talk, I mean I must talk. You've done all the talking up to now. You told about your life, now I want to tell about mine, so we'll know all about each other before we go off together.

JEAN: Just a minute! Forgive me! If you don't want to regret it afterwards, you'd better think twice before revealing any secrets about yourself.

JULIE: Aren't you my friend?

JEAN: Yes, sometimes! But don't rely on me.

JULIE: You're only saying that. ———— Besides, everyone already knows my secrets. ———— You see, my mother was a commoner — very humble background. She was brought up believing in social equality, women's rights, and all that. The idea of marriage repelled her. So, when my father proposed, she replied that she would never become his wife, but he could be her lover. He insisted that he didn't want the woman he loved to be less respected than he. But his passion ruled him, and when she explained that the world's respect meant nothing to her, he accepted her conditions.

But now his friends avoided him and his life was restricted to taking care of the estate, which couldn't satisfy him. I came into the world — against my mother's wishes, as far as I can understand. She wanted to bring me up as a child of nature, and, what's more, to learn everything a boy had to learn, so that I might be an example of how a woman can be as good as a man. I had to wear boy's clothes and learn to take care of horses, but I was never allowed in the cowshed. I had to groom and harness the horses and go hunting — and even had to watch them slaughter animals — that was disgusting! On the estate men were put on women's jobs and women on men's jobs — with the result that the property became run down and we became the laughingstock of the district. Finally, my father must have awakened from his trance because he rebelled and changed everything his way. My parents were then married quietly. Mother became ill — I don't know what illness it was — but she often had convulsions, hid in the attic and in the garden, and sometimes stayed out all night. Then came the great fire, which you've heard about. The house, the stables, and the cowshed all burned down, under very curious circumstances, suggesting arson, because the accident happened the day after the insurance had expired. The quarterly premium my father sent in was delayed because of a messenger's carelessness and didn't arrive in time. *(She fills her glass and drinks.)*

JEAN: Don't drink any more!

JULIE: Oh, what does it matter. ——— We were left penniless and had to sleep in the carriages. My father had no idea where to find money to rebuild the house because he had so slighted his old friends that they had forgotten him. Then my mother suggested that he borrow from a childhood friend of hers, a brick manufacturer who lived nearby. Father got the loan without having to pay interest, which surprised him. And that's how the estate was rebuilt. ——— *(Drinks again.)* Do you know who started the fire?

JEAN: The Countess, your mother.

JULIE: Do you know who the brick manufacturer was?

JEAN: Your mother's lover?

JULIE: Do you know whose money it was?

JEAN: Wait a moment — no, I don't.

JULIE: It was my mother's.

JEAN: You mean the Count's, unless they didn't sign an agreement when they were married.

JULIE: They didn't. ——— My mother had a small inheritance which she didn't want under my father's control, so she entrusted it to her — friend.

JEAN: Who stole it!

JULIE: Exactly! He kept it. ——— All this my father found out, but he couldn't bring it to court, couldn't repay his wife's lover, couldn't prove it was his wife's money! It was my mother's revenge for being forced into marriage against her will. It nearly drove him to suicide — there was a rumor that he tried with a pistol, but failed. So, he managed to live through it and my mother had to suffer for what she'd done. You can imagine that those were a terrible five years for me. I loved my father, but I sided with my mother because I didn't know the circumstances. I learned from her to hate men — you've heard how she hated the whole male sex — and I swore to her I'd never be a slave to any man.

JEAN: But you got engaged to that lawyer.

JULIE: In order to make him my slave.

JEAN: And he wasn't willing?

JULIE: He was willing, all right, but I wouldn't let him. I got tired of him.

JEAN: I saw it — out near the stable.

JULIE: What did you see?

JEAN: I saw — how he broke off the engagement.

JULIE: That's a lie! I was the one who broke it off. Has he said that he did? That swine . . .

JEAN: He was no swine, I'm sure. So, you hate men, Miss Julie?

JULIE: Yes! ——— Most of the time! But sometimes — when the weakness comes, when passion burns! Oh, God, will the fire never die out?

JEAN: Do you hate me, too?

JULIE: Immeasurably! I'd like to have you put to death, like an animal . . .

JEAN: I see — the penalty for bestiality — the woman gets two years at hard labor and the animal is put to death. Right?

JULIE: Exactly!

JEAN: But there's no prosecutor here — and no animal. So, what'll we do?

JULIE: Go away!

JEAN: To torment each other to death?

JULIE: No! To be happy for — two days, a week, as long as we can be happy, and then — die . . .

JEAN: Die? That's stupid! It's better to open a hotel!

JULIE *(without listening)*: ——— on the shore of Lake Como, where the sun always shines, where the laurels are green at Christmas and the oranges glow.

JEAN: Lake Como is a rainy hole, and I never saw any oranges outside the stores. But tourists are attracted there because there are plenty of villas to be rented out to lovers, and that's a profitable business. —— Do you know why? Because they sign a lease for six months — and then leave after three weeks!

JULIE (*naively*): Why after three weeks?

JEAN: They quarrel, of course! But they still have to pay the rent in full! And so you rent the villas out again. And that's the way it goes, time after time. There's never a shortage of love — even if it doesn't last long!

JULIE: You don't want to die with me?

JEAN: I don't want to die at all! For one thing, I like living, and for another, I think suicide is a crime against the Providence which gave us life.

JULIE: You believe in God? *You?*

JEAN: Of course I do. And I go to church every other Sunday. —— To be honest, I'm tired of all this, and I'm going to bed.

JULIE: Are you? And do you think I can let it go at that? A man owes something to the woman he's shamed.

JEAN (*taking out his purse and throwing a silver coin on the table*): Here! I don't like owing anything to anybody.

JULIE (*pretending not to notice the insult*): Do you know what the law states . . .

JEAN: Unfortunately the law doesn't state any punishment for the woman who seduces a man!

JULIE (*as before*): Do you see any way out but to leave, get married, and then separate?

JEAN: Suppose I refuse such a *mésalliance?*°

JULIE: *Mésalliance* . . .

JEAN: Yes, for me! You see, I come from better stock than you. There's no arsonist in my family.

JULIE: How do you know?

JEAN: You can't prove otherwise. We don't keep charts on our ancestors — there's just the police records! But I've read about your family. Do you know who the founder was? He was a miller who let the king sleep with his wife one night during the Danish War. I don't have any noble ancestors like that. I don't have any noble ancestors at all, but I could become one myself.

JULIE: This is what I get for opening my heart to someone unworthy, for giving my family's honor . . .

mésalliance: Misalliance or mismatch, especially regarding relative social status.

JEAN: Dishonor! —— Well, I told you so: When people drink, they talk, and talk is dangerous!

JULIE: Oh, how I regret it! —— How I regret it! —— If you at least loved me.

JEAN: For the last time — what do you want? Shall I cry; shall I jump over your riding crop? Shall I kiss you and lure you off to Lake Como for three weeks, and then God knows what . . . ? What shall I do? What do you want? This is getting painfully embarrassing! But that's what happens when you stick your nose in women's business. Miss Julie! I see that you're unhappy. I know you're suffering, but I can't understand you. We don't have such romantic ideas; there's not this kind of hate between us. Love is a game we play when we get time off from work, but we don't have all day and night, like you. I think you're sick, really sick. Your mother was crazy, and her ideas have poisoned your life.

JULIE: Be kind to me. At least now you're talking like a human being.

JEAN: Be human yourself, then. You spit on me, and you won't let me wipe myself off ——

JULIE: Help me! Help me! Just tell me what to do, where to go!

JEAN: In God's name, if I only knew myself!

JULIE: I've been crazy, out of my mind, but isn't there any way out?

JEAN: Stay here and keep calm! No one knows anything!

JULIE: Impossible! The others know and Kristine knows.

JEAN: No they don't, and they'd never believe a thing like that!

JULIE (*hesitantly*): But — it could happen again!

JEAN: That's true!

JULIE: And then?

JEAN (*frightened*): Then? —— Why didn't I think about that? Yes, there is only one thing to do — get away from here! Right away! I can't come with you, then we'd be finished, so you'll have to go alone — away — anywhere!

JULIE: Alone? —— Where? —— I can't do that!

JEAN: You must! And before the Count gets back! If you stay, you know what'll happen. Once you make a mistake like this, you want to continue because the damage has already been done. . . . Then you get bolder and bolder — until finally you're caught! So leave! Later you can write to the Count and confess everything — except that it was me! He'll never guess who it was, and he's not going to be eager to find out, anyway.

JULIE: I'll go if you come with me.

JEAN: Are you out of your head? Miss Julie runs away

with her servant! In two days it would be in the newspapers, and that's something your father would never live through.

JULIE: I can't go and I can't stay! Help me! I'm so tired, so terribly tired. —— Order me! Set me in motion — I can't think or act on my own . . .

JEAN: What miserable creatures you people are! You strut around with your noses in the air as if you were the lords of creation! All right, I'll order you. Go upstairs and get dressed! Get some money for the trip, and then come back down!

JULIE (*in a half-whisper*): Come up with me!

JEAN: To your room? —— Now you're crazy again! (*Hesitates for a moment.*) No! Go, at once! (*Takes her hand to lead her out.*)

JULIE (*as she leaves*): Speak kindly to me, Jean!

JEAN: An order always sounds unkind — now you know how it feels. (*Jean, alone, sighs with relief. He sits at the table, takes out a notebook and pencil, and begins adding up figures, counting aloud as he works. He continues in dumb show until Kristine enters, dressed for church. She is carrying a white tie and shirt front.*)

KRISTINE: Lord Jesus, what a mess! What have you been up to?

JEAN: Oh, Miss Julie dragged everybody in here. You mean you didn't hear anything? You must have been sleeping soundly.

KRISTINE: Like a log.

JEAN: And dressed for church already?

KRISTINE: Of course! You remember you promised to come with me to communion today!

JEAN: Oh, yes, that's right. —— And you brought my things. Come on, then! (*He sits down. Kristine starts to put on his shirt front and tie. Pause. Jean begins sleepily.*) What's the gospel text for today?

KRISTINE: On St. John's Day? — the beheading of John the Baptist, I should think!

JEAN: Ah, that'll be a long one, for sure. —— Hey, you're choking me! —— Oh, I'm sleepy, so sleepy!

KRISTINE: Yes, what have you been doing, up all night? Your face is absolutely green.

JEAN: I've been sitting here gabbing with Miss Julie.

KRISTINE: She has no idea what's proper, that one! (*Pause.*)

JEAN: You know, Kristine . . .

KRISTINE: What?

JEAN: It's really strange when you think about it. —— Her!

KRISTINE: What's so strange?

JEAN: Everything! (*Pause.*)

KRISTINE (*looking at the half-empty glasses standing on the table*): Have you been drinking together, too?

JEAN: Yes.

KRISTINE: Shame on you! —— Look me in the eye!

JEAN: Well?

KRISTINE: Is it possible? Is it possible?

JEAN (*thinking it over for a moment*): Yes, it is.

KRISTINE: Ugh! I never would have believed it! No, shame on you, shame!

JEAN: You're not jealous of her, are you?

KRISTINE: No, not of her! If it had been Clara or Sofie I'd have scratched your eyes out! —— I don't know why, but that's the way I feel. —— Oh, it's disgusting!

JEAN: Are you angry at her, then?

KRISTINE: No, at you! That was an awful thing to do, awful! Poor girl! —— No, I don't care who knows it — I won't stay in a house where we can't respect the people we work for.

JEAN: Why should we respect them?

KRISTINE: You're so clever, you tell me! Do you want to wait on people who can't behave decently? Do you? You disgrace yourself that way, if you ask me.

JEAN: But it's a comfort to know they aren't any better than us.

KRISTINE: Not for me. If they're no better, what do we have to strive for to better ourselves. —— And think of the Count! Think of him! As if he hasn't had enough misery in his life! Lord Jesus! No, I won't stay in this house any longer! —— And it had to be with someone like you! If it had been that lawyer, if it had been a real gentleman . . .

JEAN: What do you mean?

KRISTINE: Oh, you're all right for what you are, but there are men and gentlemen, after all! —— No, this business with Miss Julie I can never forget. She was so proud, so arrogant with men, you wouldn't have believed she could just go and give herself — and to someone like you! And she was going to have poor Diana shot for running after the gatekeepers' mutt! —— Yes, I'm giving my notice, I mean it — I won't stay here any longer. On the twenty-fourth of October, I leave!

JEAN: And then?

KRISTINE: Well, since the subject has come up, it's about time you looked around for something since we're going to get married, in any case.

JEAN: Where am I going to look? I couldn't find a job like this if I was married.

KRISTINE: No, that's true. But you can find work as a porter or as a caretaker in some government office. The state doesn't pay much, I know, but it's secure, and there's a pension for the wife and children . . .

JEAN (*grimacing*): That's all very well, but it's a bit

early for me to think about dying for a wife and children. My ambitions are a little higher than that.

KRISTINE: Your ambitions, yes! Well, you have obligations, too! Think about them!

JEAN: Don't start nagging me about obligations. I know what I have to do! (*Listening for something outside.*) Besides, this is something we have plenty of time to think over. Go and get ready for church.

KRISTINE: Who's that walking around up there?

JEAN: I don't know, unless it's Clara.

KRISTINE (*going*): You don't suppose it's the Count, who came home without us hearing him?

JEAN (*frightened*): The Count? No, I don't think so. He'd have rung.

KRISTINE (*going*): Well, God help us! I've never seen anything like this before. (*The sun has risen and shines through the treetops in the park. The light shifts gradually until it slants in through the windows. Jean goes to the door and signals. Miss Julie enters, dressed in travel clothes and carrying a small bird cage, covered with a cloth, which she places on a chair.*)

JULIE: I'm ready now.

JEAN: Shh! Kristine is awake.

JULIE (*very nervous during the following*): Does she suspect something?

JEAN: She doesn't know anything. But my God, you look awful!

JULIE: Why? How do I look?

JEAN: You're pale as a ghost and — excuse me, but your face is dirty.

JULIE: Let me wash up then. ——— (*She goes to the basin and washes her hands and face.*) Give me a towel! ——— Oh — the sun's coming up.

JEAN: Then the goblins will disappear.

JULIE: Yes, there must have been goblins out last night! ——— Jean, listen, come with me! I have some money now.

JEAN (*hesitantly*): Enough?

JULIE: Enough to start with. Come with me! I just can't travel alone on a day like this — midsummer day on a stuffy train — jammed in among crowds of people staring at me. Eternal delays at every station, while I'd wish I had wings. No, I can't, I can't! And then there'll be memories, memories of midsummer days when I was little. The church — decorated with birch leaves and lilacs; dinner at the big table with relatives and friends; the afternoons in the park, dancing, music, flowers, and games. Oh, no matter how far we travel, the memories will follow in the baggage car, with remorse and guilt!

JEAN: I'll go with you — but right away, before it's too late. Right this minute!

JULIE: Get dressed, then! (*Picking up the bird cage.*)

JEAN: But no baggage! It would give us away!

JULIE: No, nothing! Only what we can have in the compartment with us.

JEAN (*has taken his hat*): What've you got there? What is it?

JULIE: It's only my greenfinch. I couldn't leave her behind.

JEAN: What? Bring a bird cage with us? You're out of your head! Put it down!

JULIE: It's the only thing I'm taking from my home — the only living being that loves me, since Diana was unfaithful. Don't be cruel! Let me take her!

JEAN: Put the cage down, I said! ——— And don't talk so loudly — Kristine will hear us!

JULIE: No, I won't leave her in the hands of strangers! I'd rather you killed her.

JEAN: Bring the thing here, then, I'll cut its head off!

JULIE: Oh! But don't hurt her! Don't . . . no, I can't.

JEAN: Bring it here! I can!

JULIE (*taking the bird out of the cage and kissing it*): Oh, my little Serena, must you die and leave your mistress?

JEAN: Please don't make a scene! Your whole future is at stake! Hurry up! (*He snatches the bird from her, carries it over to the chopping block, and picks up a meat cleaver. Miss Julie turns away.*) You should have learned how to slaughter chickens instead of how to fire pistols. (*He chops off the bird's head.*) Then you wouldn't feel faint at the sight of blood.

JULIE (*screaming*): Kill me, too! Kill me! You, who can slaughter an innocent animal without blinking an eye! Oh, how I hate, how I detest you! There's blood between us now! I curse the moment I set eyes on you! I curse the moment I was conceived in my mother's womb!

JEAN: What good does cursing do? Let's go!

JULIE (*approaching the chopping block, as if drawn against her will*): No, I don't want to go yet. I can't . . . until I see . . . Shh! I hear a carriage ——— (*She listens, but her eyes never leave the cleaver and the chopping block.*) Do you think I can't stand the sight of blood? You think I'm so weak . . . Oh — I'd like to see your blood and your brains on a chopping block! ——— I'd like to see your whole sex swimming in a sea of blood, like my little bird . . . I think I could drink from your skull! I'd like to bathe my feet in your open chest and eat your heart roasted whole! ——— You think I'm weak. You think I love you because my womb craved your seed. You think I want to carry your spawn under my heart and nourish it with my blood — bear your child and take your name! By the way, what is your family name? I've never heard it. —— Do you have one? I was to be Mrs. Bootblack — or Madame Pigsty. —— You dog, who wears my collar, you lackey, who bears my coat of arms on your buttons — do I have to share you with my cook, compete with my own servant? Oh! Oh! Oh! —— You think I'm a coward who wants to run away! No, now I'm staying — and let the storm break! My father will come home . . . to find his desk broken open . . . and his money gone! Then he'll ring — that bell . . . twice for his valet — and then he'll send for the police . . . and then I'll tell everything! Everything! Oh, what a relief it'll be to have it all end — if only it will end! —— And then he'll have a stroke and die . . . That'll be the end of all of us — and there'll be peace . . . quiet . . . eternal rest! —— And then our coat of arms will be broken against his coffin — the family title extinct — but the valet's line will go on in an orphanage . . . win laurels in the gutter, and end in jail!

JEAN: There's the blue blood talking! Very good, Miss Julie! Just don't let that miller out of the closet! (*Kristine enters, dressed for church, with a psalmbook in her hand.*)

JULIE (*rushing to Kristine and falling into her arms, as if seeking protection*): Help, Kristine! Help me against this man!

KRISTINE (*unmoved and cold*): What a fine way to behave on a Sunday morning! (*Sees the chopping block.*) And look at this mess! —— What does all this mean? Why all this screaming and carrying on?

JULIE: Kristine! You're a woman and my friend! Beware of this swine!

JEAN (*uncomfortable*): While you ladies discuss this, I'll go in and shave. (*Slips off right.*)

JULIE: You must listen to me so you'll understand!

KRISTINE: No, I could never understand such disgusting behavior! Where are you off to in your traveling clothes? —— And he had his hat on. —— Well? —— Well? ——

JULIE: Listen to me, Kristine! Listen, and I'll tell you everything ——

KRISTINE: I don't want to hear it . . .

JULIE: But you must listen to me . . .

KRISTINE: What about? If it's about this silliness with Jean, I'm not interested, because it's none of my business. But if you're thinking of tricking him into running out, we'll soon put a stop to that!

JULIE (*extremely nervous*): Try to be calm now, Kristine, and listen to me! I can't stay here, and neither can Jean — so we must go away . . .

KRISTINE: Hm, hm!

JULIE (*brightening*): You see, I just had an idea —— What if all three of us go — abroad — to Swit-

zerland and start a hotel together? —— I have money, you see — and Jean and I could run it — and I thought you, you could take care of the kitchen . . . Wouldn't that be wonderful? —— Say yes! And come with us, and then everything will be settled! —— Oh, do say yes! (*Embracing Kristine and patting her warmly.*)

KRISTINE (*coolly, thoughtfully*): Hm, hm!

JULIE (*presto tempo*):° You've never traveled, Kristine. —— You must get out and see the world. You can't imagine how much fun it is to travel by train — always new faces — new countries. —— And when we get to Hamburg, we'll stop off at the zoo — you'll like that. —— and then we'll go to the theater and the opera — and when we get to Munich, dear, there we have museums, with Rubens and Raphael, the great painters, as you know. —— You've heard of Munich, where King Ludwig lived — the king who went mad. —— And then we'll see his castles — they're still there and they're like castles in fairy tales. —— And from there it isn't far to Switzerland — and the Alps. —— Imagine — the Alps have snow on them even in the middle of summer! —— And oranges grow there and laurel trees that are green all year round —— (*Jean can be seen in the wings right, sharpening his razor on a strop which he holds with his teeth and his left hand. He listens to the conversation with satisfaction, nodding now and then in approval. Miss Julie continues tempo prestissimo.*)° And then we'll start a hotel — and I'll be at the desk, while Jean greets the guests . . . does the shopping . . . writes letters. —— You have no idea what a life it'll be — the train whistles blowing and the carriages arriving and the bells ringing in the rooms and down in the restaurant. —— And I'll make out the bills — and I know how to salt them! . . . You'll never believe how timid travelers are when they have to pay their bills! —— And you — you'll be in charge of the kitchen. —— Naturally, you won't have to stand over the stove yourself. —— And since you're going to be seen by people, you'll have to wear beautiful clothes. —— And you, with your looks — no, I'm not flattering you — one fine day you'll grab yourself a husband! —— You'll see! —— A rich Englishman — they're so easy to —— (*Slowing down.*) —— catch — and then we'll get rich — and build ourselves a villa on Lake Como. —— It's true it rains there a little now and then, but —— (*Dully.*) —— the

presto tempo: At a rapid pace.
tempo prestissimo: At a very rapid pace.

sun has to shine sometimes — although it looks dark — and then . . . of course we could always come back home again ——— (*Pause.*) ——— here — or somewhere else ———

KRISTINE: Listen, Miss Julie, do you believe all this?

JULIE (*crushed*): Do I believe it?

KRISTINE: Yes!

JULIE (*wearily*): I don't know. I don't believe in anything anymore. (*She sinks down on the bench and cradles her head in her arms on the table.*) Nothing! Nothing at all!

KRISTINE (*turning right to where Jean is standing*): So, you thought you'd run out?

JEAN (*embarrassed; puts the razor on the table*): Run out? That's no way to put it. You hear Miss Julie's plan, and even if she is tired after being up all night, it's still a practical plan.

KRISTINE: Now you listen to me! Did you think I'd work as a cook for that . . .

JEAN (*sharply*): You watch what you say in front of your mistress! Do you understand?

KRISTINE: Mistress!

JEAN: Yes!

KRISTINE: Listen to him! Listen to him!

JEAN: Yes, you listen! It'd do you good to listen more and talk less! Miss Julie is your mistress. If you despise her, you have to despise yourself for the same reason!

KRISTINE: I've always had enough self-respect ———

JEAN: ——— to be able to despise other people!

KRISTINE: ——— to stop me from doing anything that's beneath me. You can't say that the Count's cook has been up to something with the groom or the swineherd! Can you?

JEAN: No, you were lucky enough to get hold of a gentleman!

KRISTINE: Yes, a gentleman who sells the Count's oats from the stable.

JEAN: You should talk — taking a commission from the grocer and bribes from the butcher.

KRISTINE: What?

JEAN: And you say you can't respect your employers any longer. You, you, you!

KRISTINE: Are you coming to church with me, now? You could use a good sermon after your fine deed!

JEAN: No, I'm not going to church today. You'll have to go alone and confess what you've been up to.

KRISTINE: Yes, I'll do that, and I'll bring back enough forgiveness for you, too. The Savior suffered and died on the Cross for all our sins, and if we go to Him with faith and a penitent heart, He takes all our sins on Himself.

JEAN: Even grocery sins?

JULIE: And do you believe that, Kristine?

KRISTINE: It's my living faith, as sure as I stand here.

It's the faith I learned as a child, Miss Julie, and kept ever since. "Where sin abounded, grace did much more abound!"

JULIE: Oh, if I only had your faith. If only . . .

KRISTINE: Well, you see, we can't have it without God's special grace, and that isn't given to everyone ———

JULIE: Who is it given to then?

KRISTINE: That's the great secret of the workings of grace, Miss Julie, and God is no respecter of persons, for the last shall be the first . . .

JULIE: Then He does respect the last.

KRISTINE (*continuing*): . . . and it is easier for a camel to go through the eye of a needle, than for a rich man to enter the Kingdom of God. That's how it is, Miss Julie! Anyhow, I'm going now — alone, and on the way I'm going to tell the groom not to let any horses out, in case anyone wants to leave before the Count gets back! ——— Goodbye! (*Leaves.*)

JEAN: What a witch! ——— And all this because of a greenfinch! ———

JULIE (*dully*): Never mind the greenfinch! ——— Can you see any way out of this? Any end to it?

JEAN (*thinking*): No!

JULIE: What would you do in my place?

JEAN: In your place? Let's see — as a person of position, as a woman who had — fallen. I don't know — wait, now I know.

JULIE (*taking the razor and making a gesture*): You mean like this?

JEAN: Yes! But — understand — *I* wouldn't do it! That's the difference between us!

JULIE: Because you're a man and I'm a woman? What sort of difference is that?

JEAN: The usual difference — between a man and a woman.

JULIE (*with the razor in her hand*): I want to, but I can't! ——— My father couldn't either, the time he should have done it.

JEAN: No, he shouldn't have! He had to revenge himself first.

JULIE: And now my mother is revenged again, through me.

JEAN: Didn't you ever love your father, Miss Julie?

JULIE: Oh yes, deeply, but I've hated him, too. I must have done so without realizing it! It was he who brought me up to despise my own sex, making me half woman, half man. Whose fault is what's happened? My father's, my mother's, my own? My own? I don't have anything that's my own. I don't have a single thought that I didn't get from my father, not an emotion that I didn't get from my mother, and this last idea — that all people are equal — I got that from my fiancé. ——— That's why I called him a swine! How can it be my fault? Shall I let Jesus take on the blame, the way Kristine does? ——— No, I'm too proud to do that and too sensible — thanks to my father's teachings. ——— And as for someone rich not going to heaven, that's a lie. But Kristine won't get in — how will she explain the money she has in the savings bank? Whose fault is it? ——— What does it matter whose fault it is? I'm still the one who has to bear the blame, face the consequences . . .

JEAN: Yes, but . . . (*The bell rings sharply twice. Miss Julie jumps up. Jean changes his coat.*) The Count is back! Do you suppose Kristine — (*He goes to the speaking tube, taps the lid, and listens.*)

JULIE: He's been to his desk!

JEAN: It's Jean, sir! (*Listening; the audience cannot hear the Count's voice.*) Yes, sir! (*Listening.*) Yes, sir! Right away! (*Listening.*) At once, sir! (*Listening.*) I see, in half an hour!

JULIE (*desperately frightened*): What did he say? Dear Lord, what did he say?

JEAN: He wants his boots and his coffee in half an hour.

JULIE: So, in half an hour! Oh, I'm so tired. I'm not able to do anything. I can't repent, can't run away, can't stay, can't live — can't die! Help me now! Order me, and I'll obey like a dog! Do me this last service, save my honor, save his name! You know what I *should* do, but don't have the will to . . . You will it, you order me to do it!

JEAN: I don't know why ——— but now I can't either ——— I don't understand. ——— It's as if this coat made it impossible for me to order you to do anything. ——— And now, since the Count spoke to me — I — I can't really explain it — but — ah, it's the damn lackey in me! ——— I think if the Count came down here now — and ordered me to cut my throat, I'd do it on the spot.

JULIE: Then pretend you're he, and I'm you! ——— You gave such a good performance before when you knelt at my feet.——— You were a real nobleman. ——— Or — have you ever seen a hypnotist in the theater? (*Jean nods.*) He says to his subject: "Take the broom," and he takes it. He says: "Sweep," and he sweeps ———

JEAN: But the subject has to be asleep.

JULIE (*ecstatically*): I'm already asleep. ——— The whole room is like smoke around me . . . and you look like an iron stove . . . shaped like a man in black, with a tall hat — and your eyes glow like coals when the fire is dying — and your face is a white patch, like ashes ——— (*The sunlight has reached the floor and now shines on Jean.*) ——— it's so warm and good ——— (*She rubs her hands as if warming them before a fire.*) ——— and bright — and so peaceful!

JEAN (*taking the razor and putting it in her hand*): Here's the broom! Go now while it's bright — out to the barn — and . . . (*Whispers in her ear.*)

JULIE (*awake*): Thank you. I'm going now to rest! But just tell me — that those who are first can also receive the gift of grace. Say it, even if you don't believe it.

JEAN: The first? No, I can't ——— But wait — Miss Julie — now I know! You're no longer among the first — you're now among — the last!

JULIE: That's true. ——— I'm among the very last. I'm the last one of all! Oh! ——— But now I can't go! ——— Tell me once more to go!

JEAN: No, now I can't either! I can't!

JULIE: And the first shall be the last!

JEAN: Don't think, don't think! You're taking all my strength from me, making me a coward. ——— What was that? I thought the bell moved! ——— No! Shall we stuff paper in it? ——— To be so afraid of a bell! ——— But it isn't just a bell. ——— There's someone behind it — a hand sets it in motion — and something else sets the hand in motion. ——— Maybe if you cover your ears — cover your ears! But then it rings even louder! rings until someone answers. ——— And then it's too late! And then the police come — and — then ——— (*The bell rings twice loudly. Jean flinches, then straightens up.*) It's horrible! But there's no other way! ——— Go! (*Miss Julie walks firmly out through the door.*)

COMMENTARY

August Strindberg (1849–1912)
FROM THE PREFACE TO *MISS JULIE*   1888
TRANSLATED BY HARRY G. CARLSON

Strindberg's Preface sets out his intentions in writing Miss Julie, *a play concerned with the problem of "social climbing or falling, of higher or lower, better or worse, man or woman." He discusses the struggle for dominance between Miss Julie and Jean, and characterizes Miss Julie as a woman forced to "wreak vengeance" upon herself.*

Miss Julie is a modern character. Not that the man-hating half-woman has not existed in all ages but because now that she has been discovered, she has come out in the open to make herself heard. The half-woman is a type who pushes her way ahead, selling herself nowadays for power, decorations, honors, and diplomas, as formerly she used to do for money. The type implies a retrogressive step in evolution, an inferior species who cannot endure. Unfortunately, they are able to pass on their wretchedness; degenerate men seem unconsciously to choose their mates from among them. And so they breed, producing an indeterminate sex for whom life is a torture. Fortunately, the offspring go under either because they are out of harmony with reality or because their repressed instincts break out uncontrollably or because their hopes of achieving equality with men are crushed. The type is tragic, revealing the drama of a desperate struggle against Nature, tragic as the romantic heritage now being dissipated by naturalism, which has a contrary aim: happiness, and happiness belongs only to the strong and skillful species.

But Miss Julie is also: a relic of the old warrior nobility now giving way to a new nobility of nerve and intellect, a victim of her own flawed constitution, a victim of the discord caused in a family by a mother's "crime," a victim of the delusions and conditions of her age — and together these are the equivalent of the concept of Destiny, or Universal Law, of antiquity. Guilt has been abolished by the naturalist, along with God, but the consequences of an action — punishment, imprisonment or the fear of it — that he cannot erase, for the simple reason that they remain, whether he pronounces acquittal or not. Those who have been injured are not as kind and understanding as an unscathed outsider can afford to be. Even if her father felt constrained not to seek revenge, his daughter would wreak vengeance upon herself, as she does here, out of an innate or acquired sense of honor, which the upper classes inherit — from where? From barbarism, from the ancient Aryan home of the race, from medieval chivalry. It is a beautiful thing, but nowadays a hindrance to the survival of the race. It is the nobleman's harikari, which compels him to slit open his own stomach when someone insults him and which survives in a modified form in the duel, that privilege of the nobility. That is why Jean, the servant, lives, while Miss Julie cannot live without honor. The slave's advantage over the nobleman is that he lacks this fatal preoccupation with honor. But in all of us Aryans there is something of the nobleman, or a Don Quixote. And so we sympathize with the suicide, whose act means a loss of honor. We are noblemen enough to be pained when we see the mighty fallen and as superfluous as a corpse, yes, even if the fallen should rise again and make amends through an honorable act. The servant Jean is a race-founder, someone in whom the process of differentiation can be detected. Born the son of a tenant farmer, he has educated himself in the things a gentleman should know. He has been quick to learn, has finely developed senses (smell, taste, sight) and a feeling for what is beautiful. He is already moving up in the world and is not embarrassed about using other people's help. He is alienated from his fellow servants, despising them as parts of a past he has already put behind him. He fears and flees them because they know his secrets, pry into his intentions, envy his rise, and look forward eagerly to his fall. Hence his dual, indecisive nature, vacillating between sympathy for people in high social positions and hatred for those who currently occupy those positions. He is an aristocrat, as he himself says, has learned the secrets of good society, is polished on the surface but coarse beneath, wears a frock coat tastefully but without any guarantee that his body is clean.

He has respect for Miss Julie, but is afraid of Kristine because she knows his dangerous secrets. He is sufficiently callous not to let the night's events disturb his plans for the future. With both a slave's brutality and a master's lack of squeamishness, he can see blood without fainting and shake off misfortune easily. Consequently, he comes through the struggle unscathed and will probably end up an innkeeper. And even if *he* does not become a Rumanian count, his son will become a university student and possibly a county police commissioner. . . .

Apart from the fact that Jean is rising in the world, he is superior to Miss Julie because he is a man. Sexually, he is an aristocrat because of his masculine strength, his more keenly developed senses, and his capacity for taking the initiative. His sense of inferiority is mostly due to the social circumstances in which he happens to be living, and he can probably shed it along with his valet's jacket.

His slave mentality expresses itself in the fearful respect he has for the Count (the boots) and his religious superstition; but he respects the Count mainly as the occupant of the kind of high position to which he himself aspires; and the respect remains even after he has conquered the daughter of the house and seen how empty the lovely shell was.

I do not believe that love in any "higher" sense can exist between two people of such different natures, and so I have Miss Julie's love as something she fabricates in order to protect and excuse herself; and I have Jean suppose himself capable of loving her under other social circumstances. I think it is the same with love as with the hyacinth, which must take root in darkness *before* it can produce a sturdy flower. Here a flower shoots up, blooms, and goes to seed all at once, and that is why it dies so quickly.

Oscar Wilde

Oscar Fingal O'Flahertie Wills Wilde (1854–1900) was born to a famous eye surgeon who maintained a home in Dublin's most exclusive neighborhood. Wilde's mother, known by her literary name as Speranza, was noted for collecting Irish folk stories in the western hills in the late 1870s. Her work was important to later literature, but it was especially important for its timing, since most of the storytellers in Ireland were gone by the turn of the century.

Wilde was a brilliant classics scholar at Trinity College, Dublin, where his tutor was the legendary Mahaffy, who later traveled with him in France. After Trininy, he went to Magdalen College, Oxford, where he took a distinguished degree. Among his influences in Oxford was Slade Professor of Art John Ruskin, with whom Wilde had long walks and talks. Ruskin had published important books on northern Gothic art and on Italian art, especially the art of Venice. Art was one of Wilde's primary passions, and his special passion seems to have been for decoration and the decorative arts. He agreed with Walter Pater, a contemporary art critic, that art must best serve the needs of art. He felt, for example, that poetry did not serve religious, political, social, or biographical goals. Its ends were aesthetic and its pleasures were in its sounds, images, and thoughts.

Partly because of his brilliance and partly because he was one of the age's greatest conversationalists, he was soon in the company of the famous and amusing people of his generation. Some of his conversational gift is apparent in his plays.

By his own admission, his life was marked by an overindulgence in sensuality: "What paradox was to me in the sphere of thought, perversity became to me in the sphere of passion." He married Constance Lloyd in 1884 and soon had two sons. But by 1891 he had already had several homosexual liaisons, one of which was to bring him to ruin. His relationship with the much younger Lord Alfred Douglas ended with Douglas's father, the marquis of Queensberry, publicly denouncing Wilde as a sodomite. Wilde sued for libel but lost. As a result, in 1895 he was tried for sodomy, convicted, and sentenced to two years' hard labor. Wilde's actions have been seen as self-destructive, but they are also consistent with his efforts to force society to examine its own hypocrisy. Unfortunately, his efforts in court and prison ruined him and he died in exile in Paris three years after his release.

His best-known novel, *The Picture of Dorian Gray* (1890; expanded

1891), is the story of a young man whose sensual life eats away at him and eventually destroys him. The novel's failure led Wilde to try the stage, where he was a signal success. Remarkably, all his plays were written in the period between 1891 and his imprisonment in 1895. *Salomé* (1891), *Lady Windermere's Fan* (1892), *A Woman of No Importance* (1893), *An Ideal Husband* (1895), and *The Importance of Being Earnest* (1895) rank as witty, insightful, and sharp commentaries on the upper-class British society he knew best. They owe a great deal to eighteenth-century comedies, such as William Congreve's *The Way of the World*. But they also owe a great deal to English and European farces and comedies of his own time, many of which he seems to have studied closely. Unlike those plays — many have never been published and no longer exist — Wilde's are still funny and still seem pertinent even though the class he criticized has long vanished.

The Importance of Being Earnest was a remarkable success when it opened at St. James's Theatre on Valentine's Day 1895, but it closed in two months after fewer than one hundred performances when the scandal of Wilde's conviction became public. Wilde's reputation as playwright was made and broken in a matter of a few years, and it was not restored until after his death.

THE IMPORTANCE OF BEING EARNEST

The play was originally written in four acts, but because the producer requested it be cut, Wilde reworked it into three acts, agreeing that the excisions made the play stronger. Its subtitle, *A Trivial Comedy for Serious People*, has prompted commentators to think of the play as farcical fluff, a play about little or nothing that is nonetheless profoundly amusing. The *New York Times* commented after its first U.S. opening, "The thing is as slight in structure and as devoid of purpose as a paper balloon, but it is extraordinarily funny." Recent critics have challenged this view on the grounds that its subject matter centers on the questions of identity and reality. One current view is that its surfaces are slight but that beneath the surface is a commentary on a society that judges things only by appearance.

The primary characters are Algernon Moncrieff and Jack Worthing, young gentlemen of marriageable age. Among the women are Algernon's cousin Gwendolen Fairfax, who adores the name Ernest and is in love with Jack, and Lady Bracknell, her mother. Bunbury, referred to by

Algernon, seems to be a character, but is instead an invention. He is a convenience for Algernon, a country friend whose illnesses Algernon uses to avoid social events he dislikes, such as Lady Bracknell's dinners. Jack, who lives in the country, has created a similar figure to help him escape to town — an imaginary brother Ernest. In town, Jack pretends to be Ernest; and all his town acquaintances, including Algernon and Gwendolen, know Jack by that name.

The similarities with Congreve's *The Way of the World* are striking. The question of marriage is central in both plays, and they both deal with the question of a marriage contract. The latter aspect of marriage in Wilde's social class is one of the targets of his satire. When Lady Bracknell probes into Jack Worthing's background, she discovers the distressing news about his family "line": Jack is a foundling who had been left in a handbag in Victoria Station. His family "line" is the Brighton Line. Gwendolen could also have stepped from a Congreve comedy. She is determined to have Jack Worthing, and when he seems sluggish about proposing she prompts him, offering a critique of his proposal by telling him he seems inexperienced at it.

The play owes perhaps even more to the farces of the 1880s and 1890s and a great deal to the well-made play of Eugène Scribe and his successors. Critics often compare Wilde to Alexander Dumas, the author of *La Dame aux camélias* (*Camille*), because both writers fashioned their plays with a considerable degree of artificiality, planting information in the first act that would prove the solution to problems in the last act. They also play with questions of identity, disguise, and revelation at the last minute in much the way Wilde does here when he reveals the identity of Ernest.

In melodramas and well-made plays, the revelation at the end was not that the potential husband had the right name so much as that he had the right background: He was an aristocrat and not the commoner he seemed to be. Wilde has fun with this convention and many others. In an instant, he ridicules the trick of revealing the hero to be "marriageable" because of his birth by emphasizing the triviality of a name. Yet names are of great importance (as Shakespeare tells us in *Romeo and Juliet*), and the earnestness implied in Ernest is one ingredient that helps Jack Worthing succeed.

Kerry Powell has demonstrated that almost every device in *The Importance of Being Earnest* was drawn from a contemporary farce or comedy. The device of the child lost in a piece of luggage was used in *The Lost Child* (1863), and *The Foundling* (1894) actually takes place in Brighton. The name Bunbury and the concept of "Bunburying" come from *The Godpapa* (1891). Even the device of baptism was used in *Crimes and Christening* (1891). What this proves is not just that Wilde was a good audience but that he was adept at taking the theater conventions his audience was most familiar with and using them to his own ends — to entertain his audience, but at the same time to help him put an extra edge on his satire.

The Importance of Being Earnest in Performance

After the first production closed down in 1895, the play was revived in London in 1898 and 1902, but an even more successful production in 1909 saw 324 performances. The benchmark for a truly successful play in those days seems to have been one hundred performances, and Wilde would have felt vindicated by the 1909 production, had he lived to see it. *The Importance of Being Earnest* has been produced so often in England and the United States that only a few productions can be taken into account here. The first New York production was in 1902. John Gielgud and Edith Evans played in the 1939 London production, then again in 1942. In 1947 Gielgud played in New York with Clifton Webb and Estelle Winwood. The reviews were especially strong, calling the play "as insolently monocled in manner and as killingly high-toned in language as mischievous tomfoolery can make it."

The play inspired at least five musicals between 1927 and 1984. The 1979 production at Stratford, Ontario, was called "a perfect play in a perfect production." An unsuccessful production by the Berlin Play Actors used all men and relied on insights drawn from transvestite performers, but it was badly received. University productions of the play are fairly common, although, like the Yale Repertory production in 1986, they are not always able to pull off the comic demands of the play's exacting language. The original four-act version of the play, discovered in 1977 in the New York Public Library, was produced in Ohio in the John Carroll University's Marinello Theater in 1985. It was more a curiosity than a triumph.

The play is a witty tour de force of language. Its surfaces gleam, and the best productions play it straight.

Oscar Wilde (1854–1900)

THE IMPORTANCE OF BEING EARNEST   1895
A TRIVIAL COMEDY FOR SERIOUS PEOPLE

The Persons of the Play

JOHN WORTHING, J.P., *of the Manor House, Woolton, Hertfordshire*
ALGERNON MONCRIEFF, *his friend*
REV. CANON CHASUBLE, D.D., *rector of Woolton*
MERRIMAN, *butler to Mr. Worthing*
LANE, *Mr. Moncrieff's manservant*
LADY BRACKNELL
HON. GWENDOLEN FAIRFAX, *her daughter*
CECILY CARDEW, *John Worthing's ward*
MISS PRISM, *her governess*

The Scenes of the Play

Act I: *Algernon Moncrieff's Flat in Half Moon Street, W.*
Act II: *The Garden at the Manor House, Woolton*
Act III: *Morning Room at the Manor House, Woolton*

ACT I

(*Scene: Morning room in Algernon's flat in Half Moon Street. The room is luxuriously and artistically furnished. The sound of a piano is heard in the adjoining room. Lane is arranging afternoon tea on the table, and after the music has ceased, Algernon enters.*)

ALGERNON: Did you hear what I was playing, Lane?

LANE: I didn't think it polite to listen, sir.

ALGERNON: I'm sorry for that, for your sake. I don't play accurately — anyone can play accurately — but I play with wonderful expression. As far as the piano is concerned, sentiment is my forte. I keep science for Life.

LANE: Yes, sir.

ALGERNON: And, speaking of the science of Life, have you got the cucumber sandwiches cut for Lady Bracknell?

LANE: Yes, sir.   (*Hands them on a salver.*)

ALGERNON (*inspects them, takes two, and sits down on the sofa*): Oh! — by the way, Lane, I see from your book that on Thursday night, when Lord Shoreham and Mr. Worthing were dining with me, eight bottles of champagne are entered as having been consumed.

LANE: Yes, sir; eight bottles and a pint.

ALGERNON: Why is it that at a bachelor's establishment the servants invariably drink the champagne? I ask merely for information.

LANE: I attribute it to the superior quality of the wine, sir. I have often observed that in married households the champagne is rarely of a first-rate brand.

ALGERNON: Good heavens! Is marriage so demoralizing as that?

LANE: I believe it *is* a very pleasant state, sir. I have had very little experience of it myself up to the present. I have only been married once. That was in consequence of a misunderstanding between myself and a young person.

ALGERNON (*languidly*): I don't know that I am much interested in your family life, Lane.

LANE: No, sir; it is not a very interesting subject. I never think of it myself.

ALGERNON: Very natural, I am sure. That will do, Lane, thank you.

LANE: Thank you, sir.   (*Lane goes out.*)

ALGERNON: Lane's views on marriage seem somewhat lax. Really, if the lower orders don't set us a good example, what on earth is the use of them? They seem, as a class, to have absolutely no sense of moral responsibility.

(*Enter Lane.*)

LANE: Mr. Ernest Worthing.

(*Enter Jack. Lane goes out.*)

ALGERNON: How are you, my dear Ernest? What brings you up to town?

JACK: Oh, pleasure, pleasure! What else should bring one anywhere? Eating as usual, I see, Algy!

ALGERNON (*stiffly*): I believe it is customary in good society to take some slight refreshment at five o'clock. Where have you been since last Thursday?

JACK (*sitting down on the sofa*): In the country.

ALGERNON: What on earth do you do there?

JACK (*pulling off his gloves*): When one is in town one amuses oneself. When one is in the country one amuses other people. It is excessively boring.

ALGERNON: And who are the people you amuse?

JACK (*airily*): Oh, neighbors, neighbors.

ALGERNON: Got nice neighbors in your part of Shropshire?

JACK: Perfectly horrid! Never speak to one of them.

ALGERNON: How immensely you must amuse them! (*Goes over and takes sandwich.*) By the way, Shropshire is your county, is it not?

JACK: Eh? Shropshire? Yes, of course. Hallo! Why all these cups? Why cucumber sandwiches? Why such reckless extravagance in one so young? Who is coming to tea?

ALGERNON: Oh! merely Aunt Augusta and Gwendolen.

JACK: How perfectly delightful!

ALGERNON: Yes, that is all very well; but I am afraid Aunt Augusta won't quite approve of your being here.

JACK: May I ask why?

ALGERNON: My dear fellow, the way you flirt with Gwendolen is perfectly disgraceful. It is almost as bad as the way Gwendolen flirts with you.

JACK: I am in love with Gwendolen. I have come up to town expressly to propose to her.

ALGERNON: I thought you had come up for pleasure? — I call that business.

JACK: How utterly unromantic you are!

ALGERNON: I really don't see anything romantic in proposing. It is very romantic to be in love. But there is nothing romantic about a definite proposal. Why, one may be accepted. One usually is, I believe. Then the excitement is all over. The very essence of romance is uncertainty. If ever I get married, I'll certainly try to forget the fact.

JACK: I have no doubt about that, dear Algy. The Divorce Court was specially invented for people whose memories are so curiously constituted.

ALGERNON: Oh! there is no use speculating on that subject. Divorces are made in heaven — (*Jack puts out his hand to take a sandwich. Algernon at once interferes.*) Please don't touch the cucumber sandwiches. They are ordered specially for Aunt Augusta.   (*Takes one and eats it.*)

JACK: Well, you have been eating them all the time.

ALGERNON: That is quite a different matter. She is my aunt. (*Takes plate from below.*) Have some bread and butter. The bread and butter is for Gwendolen. Gwendolen is devoted to bread and butter.

JACK (*advancing to table and helping himself*): And very good bread and butter it is too.

ALGERNON: Well, my dear fellow, you need not eat as if you were going to eat it all. You behave as if you were married to her already. You are not married to her already, and I don't think you ever will be.

JACK: Why on earth do you say that?

ALGERNON: Well, in the first place, girls never marry the men they flirt with. Girls don't think it right.

JACK: Oh, that is nonsense!

ALGERNON: It isn't. It is a great truth. It accounts for the extraordinary number of bachelors that one sees all over the place. In the second place, I don't give my consent.

JACK: Your consent!

ALGERNON: My dear fellow, Gwendolen is my first cousin. And before I allow you to marry her, you will have to clear up the whole question of Cecily.   (*Rings bell.*)

JACK: Cecily! What on earth do you mean? What do you mean, Algy, by Cecily? I don't know anyone of the name of Cecily.

(*Enter Lane.*)

ALGERNON: Bring me that cigarette case Mr. Worthing left in the smoking room the last time he dined here.

LANE: Yes, sir.   (*Lane goes out.*)

JACK: Do you mean to say you have had my cigarette case all this time? I wish to goodness you had let me know. I have been writing frantic letters to Scotland Yard about it. I was very nearly offering a large reward.

ALGERNON: Well, I wish you would offer one. I happen to be more than usually hard up.

JACK: There is no good offering a large reward now that the thing is found.

(*Enter Lane with the cigarette case on a salver. Algernon takes it at once. Lane goes out.*)

ALGERNON: I think that is rather mean of you, Ernest, I must say. (*Opens case and examines it.*) However, it makes no matter, for, now that I look at the inscription inside, I find that the thing isn't yours after all.

JACK: Of course it's mine. (*Moving to him.*) You have seen me with it a hundred times, and you have no

right whatsoever to read what is written inside. It is a very ungentlemanly thing to read a private cigarette case.

ALGERNON: Oh! it is absurd to have a hard-and-fast rule about what one should read and what one shouldn't. More than half of modern culture depends on what one shouldn't read.

JACK: I am quite aware of the fact, and I don't propose to discuss modern culture. It isn't the sort of thing one should talk of in private. I simply want my cigarette case back.

ALGERNON: Yes; but this isn't your cigarette case. This cigarette case is a present from someone of the name of Cecily, and you said you didn't know anyone of that name.

JACK: Well, if you want to know, Cecily happens to be my aunt.

ALGERNON: Your aunt!

JACK: Yes. Charming old lady she is, too. Lives at Tunbridge Wells. Just give it back to me, Algy.

ALGERNON (*retreating to back of sofa*): But why does she call herself little Cecily if she is your aunt and lives at Tunbridge Wells? (*Reading.*) "From little Cecily with her fondest love."

JACK (*moving to sofa and kneeling upon it*): My dear fellow, what on earth is there in that? Some aunts are tall, some aunts are not tall. That is a matter that surely an aunt may be allowed to decide for herself. You seem to think that every aunt should be exactly like your aunt! That is absurd! For heaven's sake give me back my cigarette case. (*Follows Algernon round the room.*)

ALGERNON: Yes. But why does your aunt call you her uncle? "From little Cecily, with her fondest love to her dear Uncle Jack." There is no objection, I admit, to an aunt being a small aunt, but why an aunt, no matter what her size may be, should call her own nephew her uncle, I can't quite make out. Besides, your name isn't Jack at all; it is Ernest.

JACK: It isn't Ernest; it's Jack.

ALGERNON: You have always told me it was Ernest. I have introduced you to everyone as Ernest. You answer to the name of Ernest. You look as if your name was Ernest. You are the most earnest looking person I ever saw in my life. It is perfectly absurd your saying that your name isn't Ernest. It's on your cards. Here is one of them (*taking it from case*) "Mr. Ernest Worthing, B.4, The Albany." I'll keep this as a proof that your name is Ernest if ever you attempt to deny it to me, or to Gwendolen, or to anyone else.   (*Puts the card in his pocket.*)

JACK: Well, my name is Ernest in town and Jack in the country, and the cigarette case was given to me in the country.

ALGERNON: Yes, but that does not account for the fact that your small Aunt Cecily, who lives at Tunbridge Wells, calls you her dear uncle. Come, old boy, you had much better have the thing out at once.

JACK: My dear Algy, you talk exactly as if you were a dentist. It is very vulgar to talk like a dentist when one isn't a dentist. It produces a false impression.

ALGERNON: Well, that is exactly what dentists always do. Now, go on! Tell me the whole thing. I may mention that I have always suspected you of being a confirmed and secret Bunburyist; and I am quite sure of it now.

JACK: Bunburyist? What on earth do you mean by a Bunburyist?

ALGERNON: I'll reveal to you the meaning of that incomparable expression as soon as you are kind enough to inform me why you are Ernest in town and Jack in the country.

JACK: Well, produce my cigarette case first.

ALGERNON: Here it is. (*Hands cigarette case.*) Now produce your explanation, and pray make it improbable.   (*Sits on sofa.*)

JACK: My dear fellow, there is nothing improbable about my explanation at all. In fact it's perfectly ordinary. Old Mr. Thomas Cardew, who adopted me when I was a little boy, made me in his will guardian to his granddaughter, Miss Cecily Cardew. Cecily, who addresses me as her uncle from motives of respect that you could not possibly appreciate, lives at my place in the country under the charge of her admirable governess, Miss Prism.

ALGERNON: Where is that place in the country, by the way?

JACK: That is nothing to you, dear boy. You are not going to be invited — I may tell you candidly that the place is not in Shropshire.

ALGERNON: I suspected that, my dear fellow! I have Bunburyed all over Shropshire on two separate occasions. Now, go on. Why are you Ernest in town and Jack in the country?

JACK: My dear Algy, I don't know whether you will be able to understand my real motives. You are hardly serious enough. When one is placed in the position of guardian, one has to adopt a very high moral tone on all subjects. It's one's duty to do so. And as a high moral tone can hardly be said to conduce very much to either one's health or one's happiness, in order to get up to town I have always pretended to have a younger brother of the name of Ernest, who lives in the Albany, and gets into the most dreadful scrapes. That, my dear Algy, is the whole truth pure and simple.

ALGERNON: The truth is rarely pure and never simple. Modern life would be very tedious if it were either, and modern literature a complete impossibility!

JACK: That wouldn't be at all a bad thing.

ALGERNON: Literary criticism is not your forte, my dear fellow. Don't try it. You should leave that to people who haven't been at a university. They do it so well in the daily papers. What you really are is a Bunburyist. I was quite right in saying you were a Bunburyist. You are one of the most advanced Bunburyists I know.

JACK: What on earth do you mean?

ALGERNON: You have invented a very useful younger brother called Ernest, in order that you may be able to come up to town as often as you like. I have invented an invaluable permanent invalid called Bunbury, in order that I may be able to go down into the country whenever I choose. Bunbury is perfectly invaluable. If it wasn't for Bunbury's extraordinary bad health, for instance, I wouldn't be able to dine with you at Willis's tonight, for I have been really engaged to Aunt Augusta for more than a week.

JACK: I haven't asked you to dine with me anywhere tonight.

ALGERNON: I know. You are absurdly careless about sending out invitations. It is very foolish of you. Nothing annoys people so much as not receiving invitations.

JACK: You had much better dine with your Aunt Augusta.

ALGERNON: I haven't the smallest intention of doing anything of the kind. To begin with, I dined there on Monday, and once a week is quite enough to dine with one's own relations. In the second place, whenever I do dine there I am always treated as a member of the family, and sent down with° either no woman at all, or two. In the third place, I know perfectly well whom she will place me next to, tonight. She will place me next Mary Farquhar, who always flirts with her own husband across the dinner table. That is not very pleasant. Indeed, it is not even decent — and that sort of thing is enormously on the increase. The amount of women in London who flirt with their own husbands is perfectly scandalous. It looks so bad. It is simply washing one's clean linen in public. Besides, now that I know you to be a confirmed Bunburyist I naturally want to talk to you about Bunburying. I want to tell you the rules.

JACK: I'm not a Bunburyist at all. If Gwendolen accepts me, I am going to kill my brother, indeed I think I'll kill him in any case. Cecily is a little too

---

sent down with: Assigned a woman to escort into the dining room for dinner.

much interested in him. It is rather a bore. So I am going to get rid of Ernest. And I strongly advise you to do the same with Mr. — with your invalid friend who has the absurd name.

ALGERNON: Nothing will induce me to part with Bunbury, and if you ever get married, which seems to me extremely problematic, you will be very glad to know Bunbury. A man who marries without knowing Bunbury has a very tedious time of it.

JACK: That is nonsense. If I marry a charming girl like Gwendolen, and she is the only girl I ever saw in my life that I would marry, I certainly won't want to know Bunbury.

ALGERNON: Then your wife will. You don't seem to realize, that in married life three is company and two is none.

JACK (*sententiously*): That, my dear young friend, is the theory that the corrupt French drama has been propounding for the last fifty years.

ALGERNON: Yes; and that the happy English home has proved in half the time.

JACK: For heaven's sake, don't try to be cynical. It's perfectly easy to be cynical.

ALGERNON: My dear fellow, it isn't easy to be anything nowadays. There's such a lot of beastly competition about. (*The sound of an electric bell is heard.*) Ah! that must be Aunt Augusta. Only relatives, or creditors, ever ring in that Wagnerian° manner. Now, if I get her out of the way for ten minutes, so that you can have an opportunity for proposing to Gwendolen, may I dine with you tonight at Willis's?

JACK: I suppose so, if you want to.

ALGERNON: Yes, but you must be serious about it. I hate people who are not serious about meals. It is so shallow of them.

(*Enter Lane.*)

LANE: Lady Bracknell and Miss Fairfax.

(*Algernon goes forward to meet them. Enter Lady Bracknell and Gwendolen.*)

LADY BRACKNELL: Good afternoon, dear Algernon, I hope you are behaving very well.

ALGERNON: I'm feeling very well, Aunt Augusta.

LADY BRACKNELL: That's not quite the same thing. In fact the two things rarely go together.
(*Sees Jack and bows to him with icy coldness.*)

ALGERNON (*to Gwendolen*): Dear me, you are smart!

Wagnerian: Referring to the operas of Richard Wagner (1813–1883), whose music was popularly thought to be loud.

GWENDOLEN: I am always smart! Aren't I, Mr. Worthing?

JACK: You're quite perfect, Miss Fairfax.

GWENDOLEN: Oh! I hope I am not that. It would leave no room for developments, and I intend to develop in many directions.

(*Gwendolen and Jack sit down together in the corner.*)

LADY BRACKNELL: I'm sorry if we are a little late, Algernon, but I was obliged to call on dear Lady Harbury. I hadn't been there since her poor husband's death. I never saw a woman so altered; she looks quite twenty years younger. And now I'll have a cup of tea, and one of those nice cucumber sandwiches you promised me.

ALGERNON: Certainly, Aunt Augusta.
(*Goes over to tea table.*)

LADY BRACKNELL: Won't you come and sit here, Gwendolen?

GWENDOLEN: Thanks, Mama, I'm quite comfortable where I am.

ALGERNON (*picking up empty plate in horror*): Good heavens! Lane! Why are there no cucumber sandwiches? I ordered them specially.

LANE (*gravely*): There were no cucumbers in the market this morning, sir. I went down twice.

ALGERNON: No cucumbers!

LANE: No, sir. Not even for ready money.

ALGERNON: That will do, Lane, thank you.

LANE: Thank you, sir.   (*Goes out.*)

ALGERNON: I am greatly distressed, Aunt Augusta, about there being no cucumbers, not even for ready money.

LADY BRACKNELL: It really makes no matter, Algernon. I had some crumpets with Lady Harbury, who seems to me to be living entirely for pleasure now.

ALGERNON: I hear her hair has turned quite gold from grief.

LADY BRACKNELL: It certainly has changed its color. From what cause I, of course, cannot say. (*Algernon crosses and hands tea.*) Thank you. I've quite a treat for you tonight, Algernon. I am going to send you down with Mary Farquhar. She is such a nice woman, and so attentive to her husband. It's delightful to watch them.

ALGERNON: I am afraid, Aunt Augusta, I shall have to give up the pleasure of dining with you tonight after all.

LADY BRACKNELL (*frowning*): I hope not, Algernon. It would put my table completely out. Your uncle would have to dine upstairs. Fortunately he is accustomed to that.

ALGERNON: It is a great bore, and, I need hardly say, a terrible disappointment to me, but the fact is I have just had a telegram to say that my poor friend Bunbury is very ill again. (*Exchanges glances with Jack.*) They seem to think I should be with him.

LADY BRACKNELL: It is very strange. This Mr. Bunbury seems to suffer from curiously bad health.

ALGERNON: Yes; poor Bunbury is a dreadful invalid.

LADY BRACKNELL: Well, I must say, Algernon, that I think it is high time that Mr. Bunbury made up his mind whether he was going to live or to die. This shilly-shallying with the question is absurd. Nor do I in any way approve of the modern sympathy with invalids. I consider it morbid. Illness of any kind is hardly a thing to be encouraged in others. Health is the primary duty of life. I am always telling that to your poor uncle, but he never seems to take much notice — as far as any improvement in his ailments goes. I should be much obliged if you would ask Mr. Bunbury, from me, to be kind enough not to have a relapse on Saturday, for I rely on you to arrange my music for me. It is my last reception, and one wants something that will encourage conversation, particularly at the end of the season when everyone has practically said whatever they had to say, which, in most cases, was probably not much.

ALGERNON: I'll speak to Bunbury, Aunt Augusta, if he is still conscious, and I think I can promise you he'll be all right by Saturday. Of course the music is a great difficulty. You see, if one plays good music, people don't listen, and if one plays bad music people don't talk. But I'll run over the program I've drawn out, if you will kindly come into the next room for a moment.

LADY BRACKNELL: Thank you, Algernon. It is very thoughtful of you. (*Rising, and following Algernon.*) I'm sure the program will be delightful, after a few expurgations. French songs I cannot possibly allow. People always seem to think that they are improper, and either look shocked, which is vulgar, or laugh, which is worse. But German sounds a thoroughly respectable language, and indeed, I believe is so. Gwendolen, you will accompany me.

GWENDOLEN: Certainly, Mama.

(*Lady Bracknell and Algernon go into the music room. Gwendolen remains behind.*)

JACK: Charming day it has been, Miss Fairfax.

GWENDOLEN: Pray don't talk to me about the weather, Mr. Worthing. Whenever people talk to me about the weather, I always feel quite certain that they mean something else. And that makes me so nervous.

JACK: I do mean something else.

GWENDOLEN: I thought so. In fact, I am never wrong.

JACK: And I would like to be allowed to take advantage of Lady Bracknell's temporary absence —

GWENDOLEN: I would certainly advise you to do so. Mama has a way of coming back suddenly into a room that I have often had to speak to her about.

JACK (*nervously*): Miss Fairfax, ever since I met you I have admired you more than any girl — I have ever met since — I met you.

GWENDOLEN: Yes, I am quite aware of the fact. And I often wish that in public, at any rate, you had been more demonstrative. For me you have always had an irresistible fascination. Even before I met you I was far from indifferent to you. (*Jack looks at her in amazement.*) We live, as I hope you know, Mr. Worthing, in an age of ideals. The fact is constantly mentioned in the more expensive monthly magazines, and has reached the provincial pulpits I am told: And my ideal has always been to love someone of the name of Ernest. There is something in that name that inspires absolute confidence. The moment Algernon first mentioned to me that he had a friend called Ernest, I knew I was destined to love you.

JACK: You really love me, Gwendolen?

GWENDOLEN: Passionately!

JACK: Darling! You don't know how happy you've made me.

GWENDOLEN: My own Ernest!

JACK: But you don't mean to say that you couldn't love me if my name wasn't Ernest?

GWENDOLEN: But your name is Ernest.

JACK: Yes, I know it is. But supposing it was something else? Do you mean to say you couldn't love me then?

GWENDOLEN (*glibly*): Ah! that is clearly a metaphysical speculation, and like most metaphysical speculations has very little reference at all to the actual facts of real life, as we know them.

JACK: Personally, darling, to speak quite candidly, I don't much care about the name of Ernest — I don't think the name suits me at all.

GWENDOLEN: It suits you perfectly. It is a divine name. It has a music of its own. It produces vibrations.

JACK: Well, really, Gwendolen, I must say that I think there are lots of other much nicer names. I think Jack, for instance, a charming name.

GWENDOLEN: Jack? — No, there is very little music in the name Jack, if any at all, indeed. It does not thrill. It produces absolutely no vibrations — I have known several Jacks, and they all, without exception, were more than usually plain. Besides, Jack is a notorious domesticity for John! And I pity any woman who is married to a man called John. She would probably never be allowed to know the entrancing pleasure of a single moment's solitude. The only really safe name is Ernest.

JACK: Gwendolen, I must get christened at once — I mean we must get married at once. There is no time to be lost.

GWENDOLEN: Married, Mr. Worthing?

JACK (*astounded*): Well — surely. You know that I love you, and you led me to believe, Miss Fairfax, that you were not absolutely indifferent to me.

GWENDOLEN: I adore you. But you haven't proposed to me yet. Nothing has been said at all about marriage. The subject has not even been touched on.

JACK: Well — may I propose to you now?

GWENDOLEN: I think it would be an admirable opportunity. And to spare you any possible disappointment, Mr. Worthing, I think it only fair to tell you quite frankly beforehand that I am fully determined to accept you.

JACK: Gwendolen!

GWENDOLEN: Yes, Mr. Worthing, what have you got to say to me?

JACK: You know what I have got to say to you.

GWENDOLEN: Yes, but you don't say it.

JACK: Gwendolen, will you marry me?

(*Goes on his knees.*)

GWENDOLEN: Of course I will, darling. How long you have been about it! I am afraid you have had very little experience in how to propose.

JACK: My own one, I have never loved anyone in the world but you.

GWENDOLEN: Yes, but men often propose for practice. I know my brother Gerald does. All my girlfriends tell me so. What wonderfully blue eyes you have, Ernest! They are quite, quite blue. I hope you will always look at me just like that, especially when there are other people present.

(*Enter Lady Bracknell.*)

LADY BRACKNELL: Mr. Worthing! Rise, sir, from this semirecumbent posture. It is most indecorous.

GWENDOLEN: Mama! (*He tries to rise; she restrains him.*) I must beg you to retire. This is no place for you. Besides, Mr. Worthing has not quite finished yet.

LADY BRACKNELL: Finished what, may I ask?

GWENDOLEN: I am engaged to Mr. Worthing, Mama.

(*They rise together.*)

LADY BRACKNELL: Pardon me, you are not engaged to anyone. When you do become engaged to someone, I, or your father, should his health permit him, will inform you of the fact. An engagement should come on a young girl as a surprise, pleasant or unpleasant, as the case may be. It is hardly a matter that she could be allowed to arrange for herself — And now I have a few questions to put to you, Mr. Worthing. While I am making these inquiries, you, Gwendolen, will wait for me below in the carriage.

GWENDOLEN (*reproachfully*): Mama!

LADY BRACKNELL: In the carriage, Gwendolen! (*Gwendolen goes to the door. She and Jack blow kisses to each other behind Lady Bracknell's back. Lady Bracknell looks vaguely about as if she could not understand what the noise was. Finally turns round.*) Gwendolen, the carriage!

GWENDOLEN: Yes, Mama.

(*Goes out, looking back at Jack.*)

LADY BRACKNELL (*sitting down*): You can take a seat, Mr. Worthing.

(*Looks in her pocket for notebook and pencil.*)

JACK: Thank you, Lady Bracknell, I prefer standing.

LADY BRACKNELL (*pencil and notebook in hand*): I feel bound to tell you that you are not down on my list of eligible young men, although I have the same list as the dear Duchess of Bolton has. We work together, in fact. However, I am quite ready to enter your name, should your answers be what a really affectionate mother requires. Do you smoke?

JACK: Well, yes, I must admit I smoke.

LADY BRACKNELL: I am glad to hear it. A man should always have an occupation of some kind. There are far too many idle men in London as it is. How old are you?

JACK: Twenty-nine.

LADY BRACKNELL: A very good age to be married at. I have always been of opinion that a man who desires to get married should know either everything or nothing. Which do you know?

JACK (*after some hesitation*): I know nothing, Lady Bracknell.

LADY BRACKNELL: I am pleased to hear it. I do not approve of anything that tampers with natural ignorance. Ignorance is like a delicate exotic fruit; touch it and the bloom is gone. The whole theory of modern education is radically unsound. Fortunately in England, at any rate, education produces no effect whatsoever. If it did, it would prove a serious danger to the upper classes, and probably lead to acts of violence in Grosvenor Square. What is your income?

JACK: Between seven and eight thousand a year.

LADY BRACKNELL (*makes a note in her book*): In land, or in investments?

JACK: In investments, chiefly.

LADY BRACKNELL: That is satisfactory. What between the duties expected of one during one's lifetime, and the duties exacted from one after one's death, land has ceased to be either a profit or a pleasure. It gives one position, and prevents one from keeping it up. That's all that can be said about land.

JACK: I have a country house with some land, of course, attached to it, about fifteen hundred acres, I believe; but I don't depend on that for my real income. In fact, as far as I can make out, the poachers are the only people who make anything out of it.

LADY BRACKNELL: A country house! How many bedrooms? Well, that point can be cleared up afterwards. You have a town house, I hope? A girl with a simple, unspoiled nature, like Gwendolen, could hardly be expected to reside in the country.

JACK: Well, I own a house in Belgrave Square, but it is let by the year to Lady Bloxham. Of course, I can get it back whenever I like, at six months' notice.

LADY BRACKNELL: Lady Bloxham? I don't know her.

JACK: Oh, she goes about very little. She is a lady considerably advanced in years.

LADY BRACKNELL: Ah, nowadays that is no guarantee of respectability of character. What number in Belgrave Square?

JACK: 149.

LADY BRACKNELL (*shaking her head*): The unfashionable side. I thought there was something. However, that could easily be altered.

JACK: Do you mean the fashion, or the side?

LADY BRACKNELL (*sternly*): Both, if necessary, I presume. What are your politics?

JACK: Well, I am afraid I really have none. I am a Liberal Unionist.

LADY BRACKNELL: Oh, they count as Tories. They dine with us. Or come in the evening, at any rate. Now to minor matters. Are your parents living?

JACK: I have lost both my parents.

LADY BRACKNELL: Both? To lose one parent may be regarded as a misfortune — to lose *both* seems like carelessness. Who was your father? He was evidently a man of some wealth. Was he born in what the Radical papers call the purple of commerce, or did he rise from the ranks of the aristocracy?

JACK: I am afraid I really don't know. The fact is, Lady Bracknell, I said I had lost my parents. It would be nearer the truth to say that my parents seem to have lost me — I don't actually know who I am by birth. I was — well, I was found.

LADY BRACKNELL: Found!

JACK: The late Mr. Thomas Cardew, an old gentleman of a very charitable and kindly disposition, found me, and gave me the name of Worthing, because he happened to have a first-class ticket for Wor-

thing in his pocket at the time. Worthing is a place in Sussex. It is a seaside resort.

LADY BRACKNELL: Where did the charitable gentleman who had a first-class ticket for this seaside resort find you?

JACK (*gravely*): In a handbag.

LADY BRACKNELL: A handbag?

JACK (*very seriously*): Yes, Lady Bracknell. I was in a handbag — a somewhat large, black leather handbag, with handles to it — an ordinary handbag in fact.

LADY BRACKNELL: In what locality did this Mr. James, or Thomas, Cardew come across this ordinary handbag?

JACK: In the cloakroom at Victoria Station. It was given to him in mistake for his own.

LADY BRACKNELL: The cloakroom at Victoria Station?

JACK: Yes. The Brighton line.

LADY BRACKNELL: The line is immaterial. Mr. Worthing, I confess I feel somewhat bewildered by what you have just told me. To be born, or at any rate bred, in a handbag, whether it had handles or not, seems to me to display a contempt for the ordinary decencies of family life that reminds one of the worst excesses of the French Revolution. And I presume you know what that unfortunate movement led to? As for the particular locality in which the handbag was found, a cloakroom at a railway station might serve to conceal a social indiscretion — has probably, indeed, been used for that purpose before now — but it could hardly be regarded as an assured basis for a recognized position in good society.

JACK: May I ask you then what you would advise me to do? I need hardly say I would do anything in the world to ensure Gwendolen's happiness.

LADY BRACKNELL: I would strongly advise you, Mr. Worthing, to try and acquire some relations as soon as possible, and to make a definite effort to produce at any rate one parent of either sex, before the season is quite over.

JACK: Well, I don't see how I could possibly manage to do that. I can produce the handbag at any moment. It is in my dressing room at home. I really think that should satisfy you, Lady Bracknell.

LADY BRACKNELL: Me, sir! What has it to do with me? You can hardly imagine that I and Lord Bracknell would dream of allowing our only daughter — a girl brought up with the utmost care — to marry into a cloakroom, and form an alliance with a parcel? Good morning, Mr. Worthing!

(*Lady Bracknell sweeps out in majestic indignation.*)

JACK: Good morning! (*Algernon, from the other*

room, strikes up the Wedding March. Jack looks perfectly furious, and goes to the door.) For goodness' sake don't play that ghastly tune, Algy! How idiotic you are!

(*The music stops, and Algernon enters cheerily.*)

ALGERNON: Didn't it go off all right, old boy? You don't mean to say Gwendolen refused you? I know it is a way she has. She is always refusing people. I think it is most ill-natured of her.

JACK: Oh, Gwendolen is as right as a trivet. As far as she is concerned, we are engaged. Her mother is perfectly unbearable. Never met such a Gorgon° — I don't really know what a Gorgon is like, but I am quite sure that Lady Bracknell is one. In any case, she is a monster, without being a myth, which is rather unfair. I beg your pardon, Algy, I suppose I shouldn't talk about your own aunt in that way before you.

ALGERNON: My dear boy, I love hearing my relations abused. It is the only thing that makes me put up with them at all. Relations are simply a tedious pack of people, who haven't got the remotest knowledge of how to live, nor the smallest instinct about when to die.

JACK: Oh, that is nonsense!

ALGERNON: It isn't!

JACK: Well, I won't argue about the matter. You always want to argue about things.

ALGERNON: That is exactly what things were originally made for.

JACK: Upon my word, if I thought that, I'd shoot myself — (*A pause.*) You don't think there is any chance of Gwendolen becoming like her mother in about a hundred and fifty years, do you Algy?

ALGERNON: All women become like their mothers. That is their tragedy. No man does. That's his.

JACK: Is that clever?

ALGERNON: It is perfectly phrased! and quite as true as any observation in civilized life should be.

JACK: I am sick to death of cleverness. Everybody is clever nowadays. You can't go anywhere without meeting clever people. The thing has become an absolute public nuisance. I wish to goodness we had a few fools left.

ALGERNON: We have.

JACK: I should extremely like to meet them. What do they talk about?

ALGERNON: The fools? Oh! about the clever people, of course.

JACK: What fools!

ALGERNON: By the way, did you tell Gwendolen the

Gorgon: In Greek myth, one of three very ugly sisters who had, among other characteristics, serpents for hair.

---

truth about your being Ernest in town, and Jack in the country?

JACK (*in a very patronizing manner*): My dear fellow, the truth isn't quite the sort of thing one tells to a nice sweet refined girl. What extraordinary ideas you have about the way to behave to a woman!

ALGERNON: The only way to behave to a woman is to make love to her if she is pretty, and to someone else if she is plain.

JACK: Oh, that is nonsense.

ALGERNON: What about your brother? What about the profligate Ernest?

JACK: Oh, before the end of the week I shall have got rid of him. I'll say he died in Paris of apoplexy. Lots of people die of apoplexy, quite suddenly, don't they?

ALGERNON: Yes, but it's hereditary, my dear fellow. It's a sort of thing that runs in families. You had much better say a severe chill.

JACK: You are sure a severe chill isn't hereditary, or anything of that kind?

ALGERNON: Of course it isn't!

JACK: Very well, then. My poor brother Ernest is carried off suddenly in Paris, by a severe chill. That gets rid of him.

ALGERNON: But I thought you said that — Miss Cardew was a little too much interested in your poor brother Ernest? Won't she feel his loss a good deal?

JACK: Oh, that is all right. Cecily is not a silly romantic girl, I am glad to say. She has got a capital appetite, goes long walks, and pays no attention at all to her lessons.

ALGERNON: I would rather like to see Cecily.

JACK: I will take very good care you never do. She is excessively pretty, and she is only just eighteen.

ALGERNON: Have you told Gwendolen yet that you have an excessively pretty ward who is only just eighteen?

JACK: Oh! one doesn't blurt these things out to people. Cecily and Gwendolen are perfectly certain to be extremely great friends. I'll bet you anything you like that half an hour after they have met, they will be calling each other sister.

ALGERNON: Women only do that when they have called each other a lot of other things first. Now, my dear boy, if we want to get a good table at Willis's, we really must go and dress. Do you know it is nearly seven?

JACK (*irritably*): Oh! it always is nearly seven.

ALGERNON: Well, I'm hungry.

JACK: I never knew you when you weren't —

ALGERNON: What shall we do after dinner? Go to a theater?

JACK: Oh, no! I loathe listening.

ALGERNON: Well, let us go to the Club?

JACK: Oh, no! I hate talking.

ALGERNON: Well, we might trot round to the Empire° at ten?

JACK: Oh, no! I can't bear looking at things. It is so silly.

ALGERNON: Well, what shall we do?

JACK: Nothing!

ALGERNON: It is awfully hard work doing nothing. However, I don't mind hard work where there is no definite object of any kind.

(*Enter Lane.*)

LANE: Miss Fairfax.

(*Enter Gwendolen. Lane goes out.*)

ALGERNON: Gwendolen, upon my word!

GWENDOLEN: Algy, kindly turn your back. I have something very particular to say to Mr. Worthing.

ALGERNON: Really, Gwendolen, I don't think I can allow this at all.

GWENDOLEN: Algy, you always adopt a strictly immoral attitude towards life. You are not quite old enough to do that.

(*Algernon retires to the fireplace.*)

JACK: My own darling!

GWENDOLEN: Ernest, we may never be married. From the expression on Mama's face I fear we never shall. Few parents nowadays pay any regard to what their children say to them. The old-fashioned respect for the young is fast dying out. Whatever influence I ever had over Mama, I lost at the age of three. But although she may prevent us from becoming man and wife, and I may marry someone else, and marry often, nothing that she can possibly do can alter my eternal devotion to you.

JACK: Dear Gwendolen!

GWENDOLEN: The story of your romantic origin, as related to me by Mama, with unpleasing comments, has naturally stirred the deeper fibers of my nature. Your Christian name has an irresistible fascination. The simplicity of your character makes you exquisitely incomprehensible to me. Your town address at the Albany I have. What is your address in the country?

JACK: The Manor House, Woolton, Hertfordshire.

(*Algernon, who has been carefully listening, smiles to himself, and writes the address on his shirt cuff. Then picks up the Railway Guide.*)

GWENDOLEN: There is a good postal service, I suppose? It may be necessary to do something desperate. That of course will require serious consideration. I will communicate with you daily.

Empire: Empire Theatre, a London music hall that was also a rendezvous for prostitutes.

JACK: My own one!

GWENDOLEN: How long do you remain in town?

JACK: Till Monday.

GWENDOLEN: Good! Algy, you may turn round now.

ALGERNON: Thanks, I've turned round already.

GWENDOLEN: You may also ring the bell.

JACK: You will let me see you to your carriage, my own darling?

GWENDOLEN: Certainly.

JACK (*to Lane, who now enters*): I will see Miss Fairfax out.

LANE: Yes, sir.   (*Jack and Gwendolen go off.*)

(*Lane presents several letters on a salver to Algernon. It is to be surmised that they are bills, as Algernon, after looking at the envelopes, tears them up.*)

ALGERNON: A glass of sherry, Lane.

LANE: Yes, sir.

ALGERNON: Tomorrow, Lane, I'm going Bunburying.

LANE: Yes, sir.

ALGERNON: I shall probably not be back till Monday. You can put up my dress clothes, my smoking jacket, and all the Bunbury suits —

LANE: Yes, sir.   (*Handing sherry.*)

ALGERNON: I hope tomorrow will be a fine day, Lane.

LANE: It never is, sir.

ALGERNON: Lane, you're a perfect pessimist.

LANE: I do my best to give satisfaction, sir.

(*Enter Jack. Lane goes off.*)

JACK: There's a sensible, intellectual girl! the only girl I ever cared for in my life. (*Algernon is laughing immoderately.*) What on earth are you so amused at?

ALGERNON: Oh, I'm a little anxious about poor Bunbury, that is all.

JACK: If you don't take care, your friend Bunbury will get you into a serious scrape some day.

ALGERNON: I love scrapes. They are the only things that are never serious.

JACK: Oh, that's nonsense, Algy. You never talk anything but nonsense.

ALGERNON: Nobody ever does.

(*Jack looks indignantly at him, and leaves the room. Algernon lights a cigarette, reads his shirt cuff, and smiles.*)

ACT II

(*Scene: Garden at the Manor House. A flight of gray stone steps leads up to the house. The garden, an old-fashioned one, full of roses. Time of year, July. Basket chairs, and a table covered with books, are set under a large yew tree. Miss Prism discovered seated at the table. Cecily is at the back watering flowers.)*

MISS PRISM (*calling*): Cecily, Cecily! Surely such a utilitarian occupation as the watering of flowers is rather Moulton's duty than yours? Especially at a moment when intellectual pleasures await you. Your German grammar is on the table. Pray open it at page fifteen. We will repeat yesterday's lesson.

CECILY (*coming over very slowly*): But I don't like German. It isn't at all a becoming language. I know perfectly well that I look quite plain after my German lesson.

MISS PRISM: Child, you know how anxious your guardian is that you should improve yourself in every way. He laid particular stress on your German, as he was leaving for town yesterday. Indeed, he always lays stress on your German when he is leaving for town.

CECILY: Dear Uncle Jack is so very serious! Sometimes he is so serious that I think he cannot be quite well.

MISS PRISM (*drawing herself up*): Your guardian enjoys the best of health, and his gravity of demeanor is especially to be commended in one so comparatively young as he is. I know no one who has a higher sense of duty and responsibility.

CECILY: I suppose that is why he often looks a little bored when we three are together.

MISS PRISM: Cecily! I am surprised at you. Mr. Worthing has many troubles in his life. Idle merriment and triviality would be out of place in his conversation. You must remember his constant anxiety about that unfortunate young man his brother.

CECILY: I wish Uncle Jack would allow that unfortunate young man, his brother, to come down here sometimes. We might have a good influence over him, Miss Prism. I am sure you certainly would. You know German, and geology, and things of that kind influence a man very much.

(*Cecily begins to write in her diary.*)

MISS PRISM (*shaking her head*): I do not think that even I could produce any effect on a character that according to his own brother's admission is irretrievably weak and vacillating. Indeed I am not sure that I would desire to reclaim him. I am not in favor of this modern mania for turning bad people into good people at a moment's notice. As a man sows so let him reap. You must put away your diary, Cecily. I really don't see why you should keep a diary at all.

CECILY: I keep a diary in order to enter the wonderful secrets of my life. If I didn't write them down I should probably forget all about them.

MISS PRISM: Memory, my dear Cecily, is the diary that we all carry about with us.

CECILY: Yes, but it usually chronicles the things that have never happened, and couldn't possibly have happened. I believe that Memory is responsible for nearly all the three-volume novels that Mudie sends us.

MISS PRISM: Do not speak slightingly of the three-volume novel, Cecily. I wrote one myself in earlier days.

CECILY: Did you really, Miss Prism? How wonderfully clever you are! I hope it did not end happily? I don't like novels that end happily. They depress me so much.

MISS PRISM: The good ended happily, and the bad unhappily. That is what Fiction means.

CECILY: I suppose so. But it seems very unfair. And was your novel ever published?

MISS PRISM: Alas! no. The manuscript unfortunately was abandoned. I use the word in the sense of lost or mislaid. To your work, child, these speculations are profitless.

CECILY (*smiling*): But I see dear Dr. Chasuble coming up through the garden.

MISS PRISM (*rising and advancing*): Dr. Chasuble! This is indeed a pleasure.

(*Enter Canon Chasuble.*)

CHASUBLE: And how are we this morning? Miss Prism, you are, I trust, well?

CECILY: Miss Prism has just been complaining of a slight headache. I think it would do her so much good to have a short stroll with you in the park, Dr. Chasuble.

MISS PRISM: Cecily, I have not mentioned anything about a headache.

CECILY: No, dear Miss Prism, I know that, but I felt instinctively that you had a headache. Indeed I was thinking about that, and not about my German lesson, when the Rector came in.

CHASUBLE: I hope, Cecily, you are not inattentive.

CECILY: Oh, I am afraid I am.

CHASUBLE: That is strange. Were I fortunate enough to be Miss Prism's pupil, I would hang upon her lips. (*Miss Prism glares.*) I spoke metaphorically. — My metaphor was drawn from bees. Ahem! Mr. Worthing, I suppose, has not returned from town yet?

MISS PRISM: We do not expect him till Monday afternoon.

CHASUBLE: Ah yes, he usually likes to spend his Sunday in London. He is not one of those whose sole aim is enjoyment, as, by all accounts, that unfortunate young man his brother seems to be. But I must not disturb Egeria° and her pupil any longer.

Egeria: Roman goddess of water.

MISS PRISM: Egeria? My name is Laetitia, Doctor.

CHASUBLE (*bowing*): A classical allusion merely, drawn from the Pagan authors. I shall see you both no doubt at Evensong?

MISS PRISM: I think, dear Doctor, I will have a stroll with you. I find I have a headache after all, and a walk might do it good.

CHASUBLE: With pleasure, Miss Prism, with pleasure. We might go as far as the schools and back.

MISS PRISM: That would be delightful. Cecily, you will read your Political Economy in my absence. The chapter on the Fall of the Rupee° you may omit. It is somewhat too sensational. Even these metallic problems have their melodramatic side.

(*Goes down the garden with Dr. Chasuble.*)

CECILY (*picks up books and throws them back on table*): Horrid Political Economy! Horrid Geography! Horrid, horrid German!

(*Enter Merriman with a card on a salver.*)

MERRIMAN: Mr. Ernest Worthing has just driven over from the station. He has brought his luggage with him.

CECILY (*takes the card and reads it*): "Mr. Ernest Worthing, B.4, The Albany, W." Uncle Jack's brother! Did you tell him Mr. Worthing was in town?

MERRIMAN: Yes, Miss. He seemed very much disappointed. I mentioned that you and Miss Prism were in the garden. He said he was anxious to speak to you privately for a moment.

CECILY: Ask Mr. Ernest Worthing to come here. I suppose you had better talk to the housekeeper about a room for him.

MERRIMAN: Yes, Miss.   (*Merriman goes off.*)

CECILY: I have never met any really wicked person before. I feel rather frightened. I am so afraid he will look just like everyone else.

(*Enter Algernon, very gay and debonair.*)

He does!

ALGERNON (*raising his hat*): You are my little cousin Cecily, I'm sure.

CECILY: You are under some strange mistake. I am not little. In fact, I believe I am more than usually tall for my age (*Algernon is rather taken aback*). But I am your cousin Cecily. You, I see from your card, are Uncle Jack's brother, my cousin Ernest, my wicked cousin Ernest.

ALGERNON: Oh! I am not really wicked at all, Cousin Cecily. You mustn't think that I am wicked.

CECILY: If you are not, then you have certainly been deceiving us all in a very inexcusable manner. I hope you have not been leading a double life, pretending to be wicked and being really good all the time. That would be hypocrisy.

ALGERNON (*looks at her in amazement*): Oh! Of course I have been rather reckless.

CECILY: I am glad to hear it.

ALGERNON: In fact, now you mention the subject, I have been very bad in my own small way.

CECILY: I don't think you should be so proud of that, though I am sure it must have been very pleasant.

ALGERNON: It is much pleasanter being here with you.

CECILY: I can't understand how you are here at all. Uncle Jack won't be back till Monday afternoon.

ALGERNON: That is a great disappointment. I am obliged to go up by the first train on Monday morning. I have a business appointment that I am anxious — to miss.

CECILY: Couldn't you miss it anywhere but in London?

ALGERNON: No: the appointment is in London.

CECILY: Well, I know, of course, how important it is not to keep a business engagement, if one wants to retain any sense of the beauty of life, but still I think you had better wait till Uncle Jack arrives. I know he wants to speak to you about your emigrating.

ALGERNON: About my what?

CECILY: Your emigrating. He has gone up to buy your outfit.

ALGERNON: I certainly wouldn't let Jack buy my outfit. He has no taste in neckties at all.

CECILY: I don't think you will require neckties. Uncle Jack is sending you to Australia.

ALGERNON: Australia! I'd sooner die.

CECILY: Well, he said at dinner on Wednesday night, that you would have to choose between this world, the next world, and Australia.

ALGERNON: Oh, well! The accounts I have received of Australia and the next world are not particularly encouraging. This world is good enough for me, Cousin Cecily.

CECILY: Yes, but are you good enough for it?

ALGERNON: I'm afraid I'm not that. That is why I want you to reform me. You might make that your mission, if you don't mind, Cousin Cecily.

CECILY: I'm afraid I've no time, this afternoon.

ALGERNON: Well, would you mind my reforming myself this afternoon?

CECILY: It is rather quixotic° of you. But I think you should try.

Fall of the Rupee: Reference to the Indian rupee, whose steady deflation between 1873 and 1893 caused the Indian governments finally to close the mints.

quixotic: Foolishly impractical, from the idealistic hero of Cervantes' *Don Quixote*.

ALGERNON: I will. I feel better already.

CECILY: You are looking a little worse.

ALGERNON: That is because I am hungry.

CECILY: How thoughtless of me. I should have re-membered that when one is going to lead an en-tirely new life, one requires regular and wholesome meals. Won't you come in?

ALGERNON: Thank you. Might I have a buttonhole° first? I never have any appetite unless I have a buttonhole first.

CECILY: A Maréchal Niel?°

ALGERNON: No, I'd sooner have a pink rose.

CECILY: Why? (*Cuts a flower.*)

ALGERNON: Because you are like a pink rose, Cousin Cecily.

CECILY: I don't think it can be right for you to talk to me like that. Miss Prism never says such things to me.

ALGERNON: Then Miss Prism is a shortsighted old lady. (*Cecily puts the rose in his buttonhole.*) You are the prettiest girl I ever saw.

CECILY: Miss Prism says that all good looks are a snare.

ALGERNON: They are a snare that every sensible man would like to be caught in.

CECILY: Oh! I don't think I would care to catch a sensible man. I shouldn't know what to talk to him about.

(*They pass into the house. Miss Prism and Dr. Chasuble return.*)

MISS PRISM: You are too much alone, dear Dr. Cha-suble. You should get married. A misanthrope I can understand — a womanthrope, never!

CHASUBLE (*with a scholar's shudder*): Believe me, I do not deserve so neologistic a phrase. The precept as well as the practice of the Primitive Church was distinctly against matrimony.

MISS PRISM (*sententiously*): That is obviously the rea-son why the Primitive Church has not lasted up to the present day. And you do not seem to realize, dear Doctor, that by persistently remaining single, a man converts himself into a permanent public temptation. Men should be more careful; this very celibacy leads weaker vessels astray.

CHASUBLE: But is a man not equally attractive when married?

MISS PRISM: No married man is ever attractive except to his wife.

CHASUBLE: And often, I've been told, not even to her.

MISS PRISM: That depends on the intellectual sym-pathies of the woman. Maturity can always be depended on. Ripeness can be trusted. Young

buttonhole: Boutonniere.
Maréchal Niel: A yellow rose.

women are green. (*Dr. Chasuble starts.*) I spoke horticulturally. My metaphor was drawn from fruits. But where is Cecily?

CHASUBLE: Perhaps she followed us to the schools.

(*Enter Jack slowly from the back of the garden. He is dressed in the deepest mourning, with crepe hatband and black gloves.*)

MISS PRISM: Mr. Worthing!

CHASUBLE: Mr. Worthing?

MISS PRISM: This is indeed a surprise. We did not look for you till Monday afternoon.

JACK (*shakes Miss Prism's hand in a tragic manner*): I have returned sooner than I expected. Dr. Cha-suble, I hope you are well?

CHASUBLE: Dear Mr. Worthing, I trust this garb of woe does not betoken some terrible calamity?

JACK: My brother.

MISS PRISM: More shameful debts and extravagance?

CHASUBLE: Still leading his life of pleasure?

JACK (*shaking his head*): Dead!

CHASUBLE: Your brother Ernest dead?

JACK: Quite dead.

MISS PRISM: What a lesson for him! I trust he will profit by it.

CHASUBLE: Mr. Worthing, I offer you my sincere con-dolence. You have at least the consolation of know-ing that you were always the most generous and forgiving of brothers.

JACK: Poor Ernest! He had many faults, but it is a sad, sad blow.

CHASUBLE: Very sad indeed. Were you with him at the end?

JACK: No. He died abroad; in Paris, in fact. I had a telegram last night from the manager of the Grand Hotel.

CHASUBLE: Was the cause of death mentioned?

JACK: A severe chill, it seems.

MISS PRISM: As a man sows, so shall he reap.

CHASUBLE (*raising his hand*): Charity, dear Miss Prism, charity! None of us are perfect. I myself am peculiarly susceptible to drafts. Will the interment take place here?

JACK: No. He seemed to have expressed a desire to be buried in Paris.

CHASUBLE: In Paris! (*Shakes his head.*) I fear that hardly points to any very serious state of mind at the last. You would no doubt wish me to make some slight allusion to this tragic domestic afflic-tion next Sunday. (*Jack presses his hand convul-sively.*) My sermon on the meaning of the manna in the wilderness can be adapted to almost any occasion, joyful, or, as in the present case, dis-tressing. (*All sigh.*) I have preached it at harvest celebrations, christenings, confirmations, on days of humiliation and festal days. The last time I delivered it was in the Cathedral, as a charity sermon on behalf of the Society for the Prevention of Discontent among the Upper Orders. The Bishop, who was present, was much struck by some of the analogies I drew.

JACK: Ah! that reminds me, you mentioned christenings I think, Dr. Chasuble? I suppose you know how to christen all right? (*Dr. Chasuble looks astounded.*) I mean, of course, you are continually christening, aren't you?

MISS PRISM: It is, I regret to say, one of the Rector's most constant duties in this parish. I have often spoken to the poorer classes on the subject. But they don't seem to know what thrift is.

CHASUBLE: But is there any particular infant in whom you are interested, Mr. Worthing? Your brother was, I believe, unmarried, was he not?

JACK: Oh yes.

MISS PRISM (*bitterly*): People who live entirely for pleasure usually are.

JACK: But it is not for any child, dear Doctor. I am very fond of children. No! the fact is, I would like to be christened myself, this afternoon, if you have nothing better to do.

CHASUBLE: But surely, Mr. Worthing, you have been christened already?

JACK: I don't remember anything about it.

CHASUBLE: But have you any grave doubts on the subject?

JACK: I certainly intend to have. Of course I don't know if the thing would bother you in any way, or if you think I am a little too old now.

CHASUBLE: Not at all. The sprinkling, and, indeed, the immersion of adults is a perfectly canonical practice.

JACK: Immersion!

CHASUBLE: You need have no apprehensions. Sprinkling is all that is necessary, or indeed I think advisable. Our weather is so changeable. At what hour would you wish the ceremony performed?

JACK: Oh, I might trot round about five if that would suit you.

CHASUBLE: Perfectly, perfectly! In fact I have two similar ceremonies to perform at that time. A case of twins that occurred recently in one of the outlying cottages on your own estate. Poor Jenkins the carter, a most hardworking man.

JACK: Oh! I don't see much fun in being christened along with other babies. It would be childish. Would half-past five do?

CHASUBLE: Admirably! Admirably! (*Takes out watch.*) And now, dear Mr. Worthing, I will not intrude any longer into a house of sorrow. I would merely beg you not to be too much bowed down by grief.

What seem to us bitter trials are often blessings in disguise.

MISS PRISM: This seems to me a blessing of an extremely obvious kind.

(*Enter Cecily from the house.*)

CECILY: Uncle Jack! Oh, I am pleased to see you back. But what horrid clothes you have got on! Do go and change them.

MISS PRISM: Cecily!

CHASUBLE: My child! my child!

(*Cecily goes towards Jack; he kisses her brow in a melancholy manner.*)

CECILY: What is the matter, Uncle Jack? Do look happy! You look as if you had toothache, and I have got such a surprise for you. Who do you think is in the dining room? Your brother!

JACK: Who?

CECILY: Your brother Ernest. He arrived about half an hour ago.

JACK: What nonsense! I haven't got a brother.

CECILY: Oh, don't say that. However badly he may have behaved to you in the past he is still your brother. You couldn't be so heartless as to disown him. I'll tell him to come out. And you will shake hands with him, won't you, Uncle Jack?
(*Runs back into the house.*)

CHASUBLE: These are very joyful tidings.

MISS PRISM: After we had all been resigned to his loss, his sudden return seems to me peculiarly distressing.

JACK: My brother is in the dining room? I don't know what it all means. I think it is perfectly absurd.

(*Enter Algernon and Cecily hand in hand. They come slowly up to Jack.*)

JACK: Good heavens!   (*Motions Algernon away.*)

ALGERNON: Brother John, I have come down from town to tell you that I am very sorry for all the trouble I have given you, and that I intend to lead a better life in the future.
(*Jack glares at him and does not take his hand.*)

CECILY: Uncle Jack, you are not going to refuse your own brother's hand?

JACK: Nothing will induce me to take his hand. I think his coming down here disgraceful. He knows perfectly well why.

CECILY: Uncle Jack, do be nice. There is some good in everyone. Ernest has just been telling me about his poor invalid friend Mr. Bunbury whom he goes to visit so often. And surely there must be much good in one who is kind to an invalid, and leaves the pleasures of London to sit by a bed of pain.

JACK: Oh! he has been talking about Bunbury has he?

CECILY: Yes, he has told me all about poor Mr. Bunbury, and his terrible state of health.

JACK: Bunbury! Well, I won't have him talk to you about Bunbury or about anything else. It is enough to drive one perfectly frantic.

ALGERNON: Of course I admit that the faults were all on my side. But I must say that I think that Brother John's coldness to me is peculiarly painful. I expected a more enthusiastic welcome, especially considering it is the first time I have come here.

CECILY: Uncle Jack, if you don't shake hands with Ernest I will never forgive you.

JACK: Never forgive me?

CECILY: Never, never, never!

JACK: Well, this is the last time I shall ever do it.
        (*Shakes hands with Algernon and glares.*)

CHASUBLE: It's pleasant, is it not, to see so perfect a reconciliation? I think we might leave the two brothers together.

MISS PRISM: Cecily, you will come with us.

CECILY: Certainly, Miss Prism. My little task of reconciliation is over.

CHASUBLE: You have done a beautiful action today, dear child.

MISS PRISM: We must not be premature in our judgments.

CECILY: I feel very happy.   (*They all go off.*)

JACK: You young scoundrel, Algy, you must get out of this place as soon as possible. I don't allow any Bunburying here.

(*Enter Merriman.*)

MERRIMAN: I have put Mr. Ernest's things in the room next to yours, sir. I suppose that is all right?

JACK: What?

MERRIMAN: Mr. Ernest's luggage, sir. I have unpacked it and put it in the room next to your own.

JACK: His luggage?

MERRIMAN: Yes, sir. Three portmanteaus, a dressing case, two hatboxes, and a large luncheon basket.

ALGERNON: I am afraid I can't stay more than a week this time.

JACK: Merriman, order the dog cart at once. Mr. Ernest has been suddenly called back to town.

MERRIMAN: Yes, sir.   (*Goes back into the house.*)

ALGERNON: What a fearful liar you are, Jack. I have not been called back to town at all.

JACK: Yes, you have.

ALGERNON: I haven't heard anyone call me.

JACK: Your duty as a gentleman calls you back.

ALGERNON: My duty as a gentleman has never interfered with my pleasures in the smallest degree.

JACK: I can quite understand that.

ALGERNON: Well, Cecily is a darling.

JACK: You are not to talk of Miss Cardew like that. I don't like it.

ALGERNON: Well, I don't like your clothes. You look perfectly ridiculous in them. Why on earth don't you go up and change? It is perfectly childish to be in deep mourning for a man who is actually staying for a whole week in your house as a guest. I call it grotesque.

JACK: You are certainly not staying with me for a whole week as a guest or anything else. You have got to leave — by the four-five train.

ALGERNON: I certainly won't leave you so long as you are in mourning. It would be most unfriendly. If I were in mourning you would stay with me, I suppose. I should think it very unkind if you didn't.

JACK: Well, will you go if I change my clothes?

ALGERNON: Yes, if you are not too long. I never saw anybody take so long to dress, and with such little result.

JACK: Well, at any rate, that is better than being always overdressed as you are.

ALGERNON: If I am occasionally a little overdressed, I make up for it by being always immensely overeducated.

JACK: Your vanity is ridiculous, your conduct an outrage, and your presence in my garden utterly absurd. However, you have got to catch the four-five, and I hope you will have a pleasant journey back to town. This Bunburying, as you call it, has not been a great success for you.
        (*Goes into the house.*)

ALGERNON: I think it has been a great success. I'm in love with Cecily, and that is everything.

(*Enter Cecily at the back of the garden. She picks up the can and begins to water the flowers.*)

But I must see her before I go, and make arrangements for another Bunbury. Ah, there she is.

CECILY: Oh, I merely came back to water the roses. I thought you were with Uncle Jack.

ALGERNON: He's gone to order the dog cart for me.

CECILY: Oh, is he going to take you for a nice drive?

ALGERNON: He's going to send me away.

CECILY: Then have we got to part?

ALGERNON: I am afraid so. It's a very painful parting.

CECILY: It is always painful to part from people whom one has known for a very brief space of time. The absence of old friends one can endure with equanimity. But even a momentary separation from anyone to whom one has just been introduced is almost unbearable.

ALGERNON: Thank you.

(*Enter Merriman.*)

MERRIMAN: The dog cart is at the door, sir.
     (*Algernon looks appealingly at Cecily.*)
CECILY: It can wait, Merriman — for — five minutes.
MERRIMAN: Yes, miss.   (*Exit Merriman.*)
ALGERNON: I hope, Cecily, I shall not offend you if I state quite frankly and openly that you seem to me to be in every way the visible personification of absolute perfection.
CECILY: I think your frankness does you great credit, Ernest. If you will allow me I will copy your remarks into my diary.
     (*Goes over to table and begins writing in diary.*)
ALGERNON: Do you really keep a diary? I'd give anything to look at it. May I?
CECILY: Oh no. (*Puts her hand over it.*) You see, it is simply a very young girl's record of her own thoughts and impressions, and consequently meant for publication. When it appears in volume form I hope you will order a copy. But pray, Ernest, don't stop. I delight in taking down from dictation. I have reached "absolute perfection." You can go on. I am quite ready for more.
ALGERNON (*somewhat taken aback*): Ahem! Ahem!
CECILY: Oh, don't cough, Ernest. When one is dictating one should speak fluently and not cough. Besides, I don't know how to spell a cough.
     (*Writes as Algernon speaks.*)
ALGERNON (*speaking very rapidly*): Cecily, ever since I first looked upon your wonderful and incomparable beauty, I have dared to love you wildly, passionately, devotedly, hopelessly.
CECILY: I don't think that you should tell me that you love me wildly, passionately, devotedly, hopelessly. Hopelessly doesn't seem to make much sense, does it?
ALGERNON: Cecily!

(*Enter Merriman.*)

MERRIMAN: The dog cart is waiting, sir.
ALGERNON: Tell it to come round next week, at the same hour.
MERRIMAN (*looks at Cecily, who makes no sign*): Yes, sir.   (*Merriman retires.*)
CECILY: Uncle Jack would be very much annoyed if he knew you were staying on till next week, at the same hour.
ALGERNON: Oh, I don't care about Jack. I don't care for anybody in the whole world but you. I love you, Cecily. You will marry me, won't you?
CECILY: You silly boy! Of course. Why, we have been engaged for the last three months.
ALGERNON: For the last three months?
CECILY: Yes, it will be exactly three months on Thursday.

ALGERNON: But how did we become engaged?
CECILY: Well, ever since dear Uncle Jack first confessed to us that he had a younger brother who was very wicked and bad, you of course have formed the chief topic of conversation between myself and Miss Prism. And of course a man who is much talked about is always very attractive. One feels there must be something in him after all. I daresay it was foolish of me, but I fell in love with you, Ernest.
ALGERNON: Darling! And when was the engagement actually settled?
CECILY: On the 14th of February last. Worn out by your entire ignorance of my existence, I determined to end the matter one way or the other, and after a long struggle with myself I accepted you under this dear old tree here. The next day I bought this little ring in your name, and this is the little bangle with the true lovers' knot I promised you always to wear.
ALGERNON: Did I give you this? It's very pretty, isn't it?
CECILY: Yes, you've wonderfully good taste, Ernest. It's the excuse I've always given for your leading such a bad life. And this is the box in which I keep all your dear letters.

(*Kneels at table, opens box, and produces letters tied up with blue ribbon.*)

ALGERNON: My letters! But my own sweet Cecily, I have never written you any letters.
CECILY: You need hardly remind me of that, Ernest. I remember only too well that I was forced to write your letters for you. I wrote always three times a week, and sometimes oftener.
ALGERNON: Oh, do let me read them, Cecily!
CECILY: Oh, I couldn't possibly. They would make you far too conceited. (*Replaces box.*) The three you wrote me after I had broken off the engagement are so beautiful, and so badly spelled, that even now I can hardly read them without crying a little.
ALGERNON: But was our engagement ever broken off?
CECILY: Of course it was. On the 22nd of last March. You can see the entry if you like. (*Shows diary.*) "Today I broke off my engagement with Ernest. I feel it is better to do so. The weather still continues charming."
ALGERNON: But why on earth did you break it off? What had I done? I had done nothing at all. Cecily, I am very much hurt indeed to hear you broke it off. Particularly when the weather was so charming.
CECILY: It would hardly have been a really serious

engagement if it hadn't been broken off at least once. But I forgave you before the week was out.

ALGERNON (*crossing to her, and kneeling*): What a perfect angel you are, Cecily.

CECILY: You dear romantic boy. (*He kisses her; she puts her fingers through his hair.*) I hope your hair curls naturally, does it?

ALGERNON: Yes, darling, with a little help from others.

CECILY: I am so glad.

ALGERNON: You'll never break off our engagement again, Cecily?

CECILY: I don't think I could break it off now that I have actually met you. Besides, of course, there is the question of your name.

ALGERNON (*nervously*): Yes, of course.

CECILY: You must not laugh at me, darling, but it had always been a girlish dream of mine to love someone whose name was Ernest. (*Algernon rises, Cecily also.*) There is something in that name that seems to inspire absolute confidence. I pity any poor married woman whose husband is not called Ernest.

ALGERNON: But, my dear child, do you mean to say you could not love me if I had some other name?

CECILY: But what name?

ALGERNON: Oh, any name you like — Algernon — for instance —

CECILY: But I don't like the name of Algernon.

ALGERNON: Well, my own dear, sweet, loving little darling, I really can't see why you should object to the name of Algernon. It is not at all a bad name. In fact, it is rather an aristocratic name. Half of the chaps who get into the Bankruptcy Court are called Algernon. But seriously, Cecily — (*moving to her*) — if my name was Algy, couldn't you love me?

CECILY (*rising*): I might respect you, Ernest, I might admire your character, but I fear that I should not be able to give you my undivided attention.

ALGERNON: Ahem! Cecily! (*Picking up hat.*) Your Rector here is, I suppose, thoroughly experienced in the practice of all the rites and ceremonials of the Church?

CECILY: Oh yes. Dr. Chasuble is a most learned man. He has never written a single book, so you can imagine how much he knows.

ALGERNON: I must see him at once on a most important christening — I mean on most important business.

CECILY: Oh!

ALGERNON: I shan't be away more than half an hour.

CECILY: Considering that we have been engaged since February the 14th, and that I only met you today for the first time, I think it is rather hard that you should leave me for so long a period as half an hour. Couldn't you make it twenty minutes?

ALGERNON: I'll be back in no time.

(*Kisses her and rushes down the garden.*)

CECILY: What an impetuous boy he is! I like his hair so much. I must enter his proposal in my diary.

(*Enter Merriman.*)

MERRIMAN: A Miss Fairfax has just called to see Mr. Worthing. On very important business Miss Fairfax states.

CECILY: Isn't Mr. Worthing in his library?

MERRIMAN: Mr. Worthing went over in the direction of the Rectory some time ago.

CECILY: Pray ask the lady to come out here; Mr. Worthing is sure to be back soon. And you can bring tea.

MERRIMAN: Yes, miss.   (*Goes out.*)

CECILY: Miss Fairfax! I suppose one of the many good elderly women who are associated with Uncle Jack in some of his philanthropic work in London. I don't quite like women who are interested in philanthropic work. I think it is so forward of them.

(*Enter Merriman.*)

MERRIMAN: Miss Fairfax.

(*Enter Gwendolen. Exit Merriman.*)

CECILY (*advancing to meet her*): Pray let me introduce myself to you. My name is Cecily Cardew.

GWENDOLEN: Cecily Cardew? (*Moving to her and shaking hands.*) What a very sweet name! Something tells me that we are going to be great friends. I like you already more than I can say. My first impressions of people are never wrong.

CECILY: How nice of you to like me so much after we have known each other such a comparatively short time. Pray sit down.

GWENDOLEN (*still standing up*): I may call you Cecily, may I not?

CECILY: With pleasure!

GWENDOLEN: And you will always call me Gwendolen, won't you?

CECILY: If you wish.

GWENDOLEN: Then that is all quite settled, is it not?

CECILY: I hope so.

(*A pause. They both sit down together.*)

GWENDOLEN: Perhaps this might be a favorable opportunity for my mentioning who I am. My father is Lord Bracknell. You have never heard of Papa, I suppose?

CECILY: I don't think so.

GWENDOLEN: Outside the family circle, Papa, I am glad to say, is entirely unknown. I think that is quite as it should be. The home seems to me to be the proper sphere for the man. And certainly once a man begins to neglect his domestic duties he becomes painfully effeminate, does he not? And I don't like that. It makes men so very attractive. Cecily, Mama, whose views on education are remarkably strict, has brought me up to be extremely shortsighted; it is part of her system; so do you mind my looking at you through my glasses?

CECILY: Oh! not at all, Gwendolen. I am very fond of being looked at.

GWENDOLEN (*after examining Cecily carefully through a lorgnette*): You are here on a short visit I suppose?

CECILY: Oh no! I live here.

GWENDOLEN (*severely*): Really? Your mother, no doubt, or some female relative of advanced years, resides here also?

CECILY: Oh no! I have no mother, nor, in fact, any relations.

GWENDOLEN: Indeed?

CECILY: My dear guardian, with the assistance of Miss Prism, has the arduous task of looking after me.

GWENDOLEN: Your guardian?

CECILY: Yes, I am Mr. Worthing's ward.

GWENDOLEN: Oh! It is strange he never mentioned to me that he had a ward. How secretive of him! He grows more interesting hourly. I am not sure, however, that the news inspires me with feelings of unmixed delight. (*Rising and going to her.*) I am very fond of you, Cecily; I have liked you ever since I met you! But I am bound to state that now that I know that you are Mr. Worthing's ward, I cannot help expressing a wish you were — well just a little older than you seem to be — and not quite so very alluring in appearance. In fact, if I may speak candidly —

CECILY: Pray do! I think that whenever one has anything unpleasant to say, one should always be quite candid.

GWENDOLEN: Well, to speak with perfect candor, Cecily, I wish that you were fully forty-two, and more than usually plain for your age. Ernest has a strong upright nature. He is the very soul of truth and honor. Disloyalty would be as impossible to him as deception. But even men of the noblest possible moral character are extremely susceptible to the influence of the physical charms of others. Modern, no less than Ancient History, supplies us with many most painful examples of what I refer to. If it were not so, indeed, History would be quite unreadable.

CECILY: I beg your pardon, Gwendolen, did you say Ernest?

GWENDOLEN: Yes.

CECILY: Oh, but it is not Mr. Ernest Worthing who is my guardian. It is his brother — his elder brother.

GWENDOLEN (*sitting down again*): Ernest never mentioned to me that he had a brother.

CECILY: I am sorry to say they have not been on good terms for a long time.

GWENDOLEN: Ah! that accounts for it. And now that I think of it I have never heard any man mention his brother. The subject seems distasteful to most men. Cecily, you have lifted a load from my mind. I was growing almost anxious. It would have been terrible if any cloud had come across a friendship like ours, would it not? Of course you are quite, quite sure that it is not Mr. Ernest Worthing who is your guardian?

CECILY: Quite sure. (*A pause.*) In fact, I am going to be his.

GWENDOLEN (*inquiringly*): I beg your pardon?

CECILY (*rather shy and confidingly*): Dearest Gwendolen, there is no reason why I should make a secret of it to you. Our little county newspaper is sure to chronicle the fact next week. Mr. Ernest Worthing and I are engaged to be married.

GWENDOLEN (*quite politely, rising*): My darling Cecily, I think there must be some slight error. Mr. Ernest Worthing is engaged to me. The announcement will appear in the *Morning Post* on Saturday at the latest.

CECILY (*very politely, rising*): I am afraid you must be under some misconception. Ernest proposed to me exactly ten minutes ago.   (*Shows diary.*)

GWENDOLEN (*examines diary through her lorgnette carefully*): It is certainly very curious, for he asked me to be his wife yesterday afternoon at 5:30. If you would care to verify the incident, pray do so. (*Produces diary of her own.*) I never travel without my diary. One should always have something sensational to read in the train. I am so sorry, dear Cecily, if it is any disappointment to you, but I am afraid *I* have the prior claim.

CECILY: It would distress me more than I can tell you, dear Gwendolen, if it caused you any mental or physical anguish, but I feel bound to point out that since Ernest proposed to you he clearly has changed his mind.

GWENDOLEN (*meditatively*): If the poor fellow has been entrapped into any foolish promise I shall consider it my duty to rescue him at once, and with a firm hand.

CECILY (*thoughtfully and sadly*): Whatever unfortunate entanglement my dear boy may have got into, I will never reproach him with it after we are married.

GWENDOLEN: Do you allude to me, Miss Cardew, as

an entanglement? You are presumptuous. On an occasion of this kind it becomes more than a moral duty to speak one's mind. It becomes a pleasure.

CECILY: Do you suggest, Miss Fairfax, that I entrapped Ernest into an engagement? How dare you? This is no time for wearing the shallow mask of manners. When I see a spade I call it a spade.

GWENDOLEN (*satirically*): I am glad to say that I have never seen a spade. It is obvious that our social spheres have been widely different.

(*Enter Merriman, followed by the Footman. He carries a salver, tablecloth, and plate stand. Cecily is about to retort. The presence of the servants exercises a restraining influence, under which both girls chafe.*)

MERRIMAN: Shall I lay tea here as usual, miss?

CECILY (*sternly, in a calm voice*): Yes, as usual.

(*Merriman begins to clear table and lay cloth. A long pause. Cecily and Gwendolen glare at each other.*)

GWENDOLEN: Are there many interesting walks in the vicinity, Miss Cardew?

CECILY: Oh! Yes! a great many. From the top of one of the hills quite close one can see five counties.

GWENDOLEN: Five counties! I don't think I should like that. I hate crowds.

CECILY (*sweetly*): I suppose that is why you live in town?

(*Gwendolen bites her lip, and beats her foot nervously with her parasol.*)

GWENDOLEN (*looking round*): Quite a well-kept garden this is, Miss Cardew.

CECILY: So glad you like it, Miss Fairfax.

GWENDOLEN: I had no idea there were any flowers in the country.

CECILY: Oh, flowers are as common here, Miss Fairfax, as people are in London.

GWENDOLEN: Personally I cannot understand how anybody manages to exist in the country, if anybody who is anybody does. The country always bores me to death.

CECILY: Ah! This is what the newspapers call agricultural depression, is it not? I believe the aristocracy are suffering very much from it just at present. It is almost an epidemic amongst them, I have been told. May I offer you some tea, Miss Fairfax?

GWENDOLEN (*with elaborate politeness*): Thank you. (*Aside.*) Detestable girl! But I require tea!

CECILY (*sweetly*): Sugar?

GWENDOLEN (*superciliously*): No, thank you. Sugar is not fashionable anymore.

(*Cecily looks angrily at her, takes up the tongs, and puts four lumps of sugar into the cup.*)

CECILY (*severely*): Cake or bread and butter?

GWENDOLEN (*in a bored manner*): Bread and butter, please. Cake is rarely seen at the best houses nowadays.

CECILY (*cuts a very large slice of cake, and puts it on the tray*): Hand that to Miss Fairfax.

(*Merriman does so, and goes out with Footman. Gwendolen drinks the tea and makes a grimace. Puts down cup at once, reaches out her hand to the bread and butter, looks at it, and finds it is cake. Rises in indignation.*)

GWENDOLEN: You have filled my tea with lumps of sugar, and though I asked most distinctly for bread and butter, you have given me cake. I am known for the gentleness of my disposition, and the extraordinary sweetness of my nature, but I warn you, Miss Cardew, you may go too far.

CECILY (*rising*): To save my poor, innocent, trusting boy from the machinations of any other girl there are no lengths to which I would not go.

GWENDOLEN: From the moment I saw you I distrusted you. I felt that you were false and deceitful. I am never deceived in such matters. My first impressions of people are invariably right.

CECILY: It seems to me, Miss Fairfax, that I am trespassing on your valuable time. No doubt you have many other calls of a similar character to make in the neighborhood.

(*Enter Jack.*)

GWENDOLEN (*catching sight of him*): Ernest! My own Ernest!

JACK: Gwendolen! Darling! (*Offers to kiss her.*)

GWENDOLEN (*drawing back*): A moment! May I ask if you are engaged to be married to this young lady? (*Points to Cecily.*)

JACK (*laughing*): To dear little Cecily! Of course not! What could have put such an idea into your pretty little head?

GWENDOLEN: Thank you. You may! (*Offers her cheek.*)

CECILY (*very sweetly*): I knew there must be some misunderstanding, Miss Fairfax. The gentleman whose arm is at present round your waist is my dear guardian, Mr. John Worthing.

GWENDOLEN: I beg your pardon?

CECILY: This is Uncle Jack.

GWENDOLEN (*receding*): Jack! Oh!

(*Enter Algernon.*)

CECILY: Here is Ernest.

ALGERNON (*goes straight over to Cecily without noticing anyone else*): My own love! (*Offers to kiss her.*)

CECILY (*drawing back*): A moment, Ernest! May I ask you — are you engaged to be married to this young lady?

ALGERNON (*looking round*): To what young lady? Good heavens! Gwendolen!

CECILY: Yes! to good heavens, Gwendolen, I mean to Gwendolen.

ALGERNON (*laughing*): Of course not! What could have put such an idea into your pretty little head?

CECILY: Thank you. (*Presenting her cheek to be kissed.*) You may.   (*Algernon kisses her.*)

GWENDOLEN: I felt there was some slight error, Miss Cardew. The gentleman who is now embracing you is my cousin, Mr. Algernon Moncrieff.

CECILY (*breaking away from Algernon*): Algernon Moncrieff! Oh!

(*The two girls move towards each other and put their arms round each other's waists as if for protection.*)

CECILY: Are you called Algernon?

ALGERNON: I cannot deny it.

CECILY: Oh!

GWENDOLEN: Is your name really John?

JACK (*standing rather proudly*): I could deny it if I liked. I could deny anything if I liked. But my name certainly is John. It has been John for years.

CECILY (*to Gwendolen*): A gross deception has been practiced on both of us.

GWENDOLEN: My poor wounded Cecily!

CECILY: My sweet wronged Gwendolen!

GWENDOLEN (*slowly and seriously*): You will call me sister, will you not?

(*They embrace. Jack and Algernon groan and walk up and down.*)

CECILY (*rather brightly*): There is just one question I would like to be allowed to ask my guardian.

GWENDOLEN: An admirable idea! Mr. Worthing, there is just one question I would like to be permitted to put to you. Where is your brother Ernest? We are both engaged to be married to your brother Ernest, so it is a matter of some importance to us to know where your brother Ernest is at present.

JACK (*slowly and hesitatingly*): Gwendolen — Cecily — it is very painful for me to be forced to speak the truth. It is the first time in my life that I have ever been reduced to such a painful position, and I am really quite inexperienced in doing anything of the kind. However I will tell you quite frankly that I have no brother Ernest. I have no brother at all. I never had a brother in my life, and I certainly have not the smallest intention of ever having one in the future.

CECILY (*surprised*): No brother at all?

JACK (*cheerily*): None!

GWENDOLEN (*severely*): Had you never a brother of any kind?

JACK (*pleasantly*): Never. Not even of any kind.

GWENDOLEN: I am afraid it is quite clear, Cecily, that neither of us is engaged to be married to anyone.

CECILY: It is not a very pleasant position for a young girl suddenly to find herself in. Is it?

GWENDOLEN: Let us go into the house. They will hardly venture to come after us there.

CECILY: No, men are so cowardly, aren't they?

(*They retire into the house with scornful looks.*)

JACK: This ghastly state of things is what you call Bunburying, I suppose?

ALGERNON: Yes, and a perfectly wonderful Bunbury it is. The most wonderful Bunbury I have ever had in my life.

JACK: Well, you've no right whatsoever to Bunbury here.

ALGERNON: That is absurd. One has a right to Bunbury anywhere one chooses. Every serious Bunburyist knows that.

JACK: Serious Bunburyist! Good heavens!

ALGERNON: Well, one must be serious about something, if one wants to have any amusement in life. I happen to be serious about Bunburying. What on earth you are serious about I haven't got the remotest idea. About everything, I should fancy. You have such an absolutely trivial nature.

JACK: Well, the only small satisfaction I have in the whole of this wretched business is that your friend Bunbury is quite exploded. You won't be able to run down to the country quite so often as you used to do, dear Algy. And a very good thing too.

ALGERNON: Your brother is a little off color, isn't he, dear Jack? You won't be able to disappear to London quite so frequently as your wicked custom was. And not a bad thing either.

JACK: As for your conduct towards Miss Cardew, I must say that your taking in a sweet, simple, innocent girl like that is quite inexcusable. To say nothing of the fact that she is my ward.

ALGERNON: I can see no possible defense at all for your deceiving a brilliant, clever, thoroughly experienced young lady like Miss Fairfax. To say nothing of the fact that she is my cousin.

JACK: I wanted to be engaged to Gwendolen, that is all. I love her.

ALGERNON: Well, I simply wanted to be engaged to Cecily. I adore her.

JACK: There is certainly no chance of your marrying Miss Cardew.

ALGERNON: I don't think there is much likelihood, Jack, of you and Miss Fairfax being united.

JACK: Well, that is no business of yours.

ALGERNON: If it was my business, I wouldn't talk about it. (*Begins to eat muffins.*) It is very vulgar to talk about one's business. Only people like stockbrokers do that, and then merely at dinner parties.

JACK: How you can sit there, calmly eating muffins when we are in this horrible trouble. I can't make out. You seem to me to be perfectly heartless.

ALGERNON: Well, I can't eat muffins in an agitated manner. The butter would probably get on my cuffs. One should always eat muffins quite calmly. It is the only way to eat them.

JACK: I say it's perfectly heartless your eating muffins at all, under the circumstances.

ALGERNON: When I am in trouble, eating is the only thing that consoles me. Indeed, when I am in really great trouble, as anyone who knows me intimately will tell you, I refuse everything except food and drink. At the present moment I am eating muffins because I am unhappy. Besides, I am particularly fond of muffins. (*Rising.*)

JACK (*rising*): Well, that is no reason why you should eat them all in that greedy way.
(*Takes muffins from Algernon.*)

ALGERNON (*offering tea cake*): I wish you would have tea cake instead. I don't like tea cake.

JACK: Good heavens! I suppose a man may eat his own muffins in his own garden.

ALGERNON: But you have just said it was perfectly heartless to eat muffins.

JACK: I said it was perfectly heartless of you, under the circumstances. That is a very different thing.

ALGERNON: That may be, but the muffins are the same. (*He seizes the muffin dish from Jack.*)

JACK: Algy, I wish to goodness you would go.

ALGERNON: You can't possibly ask me to go without having some dinner. It's absurd. I never go without my dinner. No one ever does, except vegetarians and people like that. Besides I have just made arrangements with Dr. Chasuble to be christened at a quarter to six under the name of Ernest.

JACK: My dear fellow, the sooner you give up that nonsense the better. I made arrangements this morning with Dr. Chasuble to be christened myself at 5:30, and I naturally will take the name of Ernest. Gwendolen would wish it. We can't both be christened Ernest. It's absurd. Besides, I have a perfect right to be christened if I like. There is no evidence at all that I ever have been christened by anybody. I should think it extremely probable I never was, and so does Dr. Chasuble. It is entirely different in your case. You have been christened already.

ALGERNON: Yes, but I have not been christened for years.

JACK: Yes, but you have been christened. That is the important thing.

ALGERNON: Quite so. So I know my constitution can stand it. If you are not quite sure about your ever having been christened, I must say I think it rather dangerous your venturing on it now. It might make you very unwell. You can hardly have forgotten that someone very closely connected with you was very nearly carried off this week in Paris by a severe chill.

JACK: Yes, but you said yourself that a severe chill was not hereditary.

ALGERNON: It usen't to be, I know — but I daresay it is now. Science is always making wonderful improvements in things.

JACK (*picking up the muffin dish*): Oh, that is nonsense; you are always talking nonsense.

ALGERNON: Jack, you are at the muffins again! I wish you wouldn't. There are only two left. (*Takes them.*) I told you I was particularly fond of muffins.

JACK: But I hate tea cake.

ALGERNON: Why on earth then do you allow tea cake to be served up for your guests? What ideas you have of hospitality!

JACK: Algernon! I have already told you to go. I don't want you here. Why don't you go!

ALGERNON: I haven't quite finished my tea yet! and there is still one muffin left.

(*Jack groans, and sinks into a chair. Algernon still continues eating.*)

ACT III

(*Scene: Morning room at the Manor House. Gwendolen and Cecily are at the window, looking out into the garden.*)

GWENDOLEN: The fact that they did not follow us at once into the house, as anyone else would have done, seems to me to show that they have some sense of shame left.

CECILY: They have been eating muffins. That looks like repentance.

GWENDOLEN (*after a pause*): They don't seem to notice us at all. Couldn't you cough?

CECILY: But I haven't got a cough.

GWENDOLEN: They're looking at us. What effrontery!

CECILY: They're approaching. That's very forward of them.

GWENDOLEN: Let us preserve a dignified silence.

CECILY: Certainly. It's the only thing to do now.

(*Enter Jack followed by Algernon. They whistle some dreadful popular air from a British opera.*)

GWENDOLEN: This dignified silence seems to produce an unpleasant effect.

CECILY: A most distasteful one.

GWENDOLEN: But we will not be the first to speak.

CECILY: Certainly not.

GWENDOLEN: Mr. Worthing, I have something very particular to ask you. Much depends on your reply.

CECILY: Gwendolen, your common sense is invaluable. Mr. Moncrieff, kindly answer me the following question. Why did you pretend to be my guardian's brother?

ALGERNON: In order that I might have an opportunity of meeting you.

CECILY (to Gwendolen): That certainly seems a satisfactory explanation, does it not?

GWENDOLEN: Yes, dear, if you can believe him.

CECILY: I don't. But that does not affect the wonderful beauty of his answer.

GWENDOLEN: True. In matters of grave importance, style, not sincerity is the vital thing. Mr. Worthing, what explanation can you offer to me for pretending to have a brother? Was it in order that you might have an opportunity of coming up to town to see me as often as possible?

JACK: Can you doubt it, Miss Fairfax?

GWENDOLEN: I have the gravest doubts upon the subject. But I intend to crush them. This is not the moment for German skepticism. (Moving to Cecily.) Their explanations appear to be quite satisfactory, especially Mr. Worthing's. That seems to me to have the stamp of truth upon it.

CECILY: I am more than content with what Mr. Moncrieff said. His voice alone inspires one with absolute credulity.

GWENDOLEN: Then you think we should forgive them?

CECILY: Yes. I mean no.

GWENDOLEN: True! I had forgotten. There are principles at stake that one cannot surrender. Which of us should tell them? The task is not a pleasant one.

CECILY: Could we not both speak at the same time?

GWENDOLEN: An excellent idea! I nearly always speak at the same time as other people. Will you take the time from me?

CECILY: Certainly.
         (Gwendolyn beats time with uplifted finger.)

GWENDOLEN and CECILY (speaking together): Your Christian names are still an insuperable barrier. That is all!

JACK and ALGERNON (speaking together): Our Christian names! Is that all? But we are going to be christened this afternoon.

GWENDOLEN (to Jack): For my sake you are prepared to do this terrible thing?

JACK: I am!

CECILY (to Algernon): To please me you are ready to face this fearful ordeal?

ALGERNON: I am!

GWENDOLEN: How absurd to talk of the equality of the sexes! Where questions of self-sacrifice are concerned, men are infinitely beyond us.

JACK: We are! (Clasps hands with Algernon.)

CECILY: They have moments of physical courage of which we women know absolutely nothing.

GWENDOLEN (to Jack): Darling!

ALGERNON (to Cecily): Darling!
              (They fall into each other's arms.)

(Enter Merriman. When he enters he coughs loudly, seeing the situation.)

MERRIMAN: Ahem! Ahem! Lady Bracknell!

JACK: Good heavens!

(Enter Lady Bracknell. The couples separate, in alarm. Exit Merriman.)

LADY BRACKNELL: Gwendolen! What does this mean?

GWENDOLEN: Merely that I am engaged to be married to Mr. Worthing, Mama.

LADY BRACKNELL: Come here. Sit down. Sit down immediately. Hesitation of any kind is a sign of mental decay in the young, of physical weakness in the old. (Turns to Jack.) Apprised, sir, of my daughter's sudden flight by her trusty maid, whose confidence I purchased by means of a small coin, I followed her at once by a luggage train. Her unhappy father is, I am glad to say, under the impression that she is attending a more than usually lengthy lecture by the University Extension Scheme on the influence of a permanent income on thought. I do not propose to undeceive him. Indeed I have never undeceived him on any question. I would consider it wrong. But of course, you will clearly understand that all communication between yourself and my daughter must cease immediately from this moment. On this point, as indeed on all points, I am firm.

JACK: I am engaged to be married to Gwendolen, Lady Bracknell!

LADY BRACKNELL: You are nothing of the kind, sir. And now, as regards Algernon! — Algernon!

ALGERNON: Yes, Aunt Augusta.

LADY BRACKNELL: May I ask if it is in this house that your invalid friend Mr. Bunbury resides?

ALGERNON (stammering): Oh! No! Bunbury doesn't live here. Bunbury is somewhere else at present. In fact, Bunbury is dead.

LADY BRACKNELL: Dead! When did Mr. Bunbury die? His death must have been extremely sudden.

ALGERNON (airily): Oh! I killed Bunbury this afternoon. I mean poor Bunbury died this afternoon.

LADY BRACKNELL: What did he die of?

ALGERNON: Bunbury? Oh, he was quite exploded.

LADY BRACKNELL: Exploded! Was he the victim of a revolutionary outrage? I was not aware that Mr. Bunbury was interested in social legislation. If so, he is well punished for his morbidity.

ALGERNON: My dear Aunt Augusta, I mean he was found out! The doctors found out that Bunbury could not live, that is what I mean — so Bunbury died.

LADY BRACKNELL: He seems to have had great confidence in the opinion of his physicians. I am glad, however, that he made up his mind at the last to some definite course of action, and acted under proper medical advice. And now that we have finally got rid of this Mr. Bunbury, may I ask, Mr. Worthing, who is that young person whose hand my nephew Algernon is now holding in what seems to me a peculiarly unnecessary manner?

JACK: That lady is Miss Cecily Cardew, my ward.

(Lady Bracknell bows coldly to Cecily.)

ALGERNON: I am engaged to be married to Cecily, Aunt Augusta.

LADY BRACKNELL: I beg your pardon?

CECILY: Mr. Moncrieff and I are engaged to be married, Lady Bracknell.

LADY BRACKNELL (with a shiver, crossing to the sofa and sitting down): I do not know whether there is anything peculiarly exciting in the air of this particular part of Hertfordshire, but the number of engagements that go on seems to me considerably above the proper average that statistics have laid down for our guidance. I think some preliminary inquiry on my part would not be out of place. Mr. Worthing, is Miss Cardew at all connected with any of the larger railway stations in London? I merely desire information. Until yesterday I had no idea that there were any families or persons whose origin was a Terminus.

(Jack looks perfectly furious, but restrains himself.)

JACK (in a clear, cold voice): Miss Cardew is the granddaughter of the late Mr. Thomas Cardew of 149, Belgrave Square, S.W.; Gervase Park, Dorking, Surrey; and the Sporran, Fifeshire, N.B.

LADY BRACKNELL: That sounds not unsatisfactory. Three addresses always inspire confidence, even in tradesmen. But what proof have I of their authenticity?

JACK: I have carefully preserved the Court Guides of the period. They are open to your inspection, Lady Bracknell.

LADY BRACKNELL (grimly): I have known strange errors in that publication.

JACK: Miss Cardew's family solicitors are Messrs. Markby, Markby, and Markby.

LADY BRACKNELL: Markby, Markby, and Markby? A firm of the very highest position in their profession. Indeed I am told that one of the Mr. Markbys is occasionally to be seen at dinner parties. So far I am satisfied.

JACK (very irritably): How extremely kind of you, Lady Bracknell! I have also in my possession, you will be pleased to hear, certificates of Miss Cardew's birth, baptism, whooping cough, registration, vaccination, confirmation, and the measles; both the German and the English variety.

LADY BRACKNELL: Ah! A life crowded with incident, I see; though perhaps somewhat too exciting for a young girl. I am not myself in favor of premature experiences. (Rises, looks at her watch.) Gwendolen! the time approaches for our departure. We have not a moment to lose. As a matter of form, Mr. Worthing, I had better ask you if Miss Cardew has any little fortune?

JACK: Oh! about a hundred and thirty thousand pounds in the Funds. That is all. Good-bye, Lady Bracknell. So pleased to have seen you.

LADY BRACKNELL (sitting down again): A moment, Mr. Worthing. A hundred and thirty thousand pounds! And in the Funds! Miss Cardew seems to me a most attractive young lady, now that I look at her. Few girls of the present day have any really solid qualities, any of the qualities that last, and improve with time. We live, I regret to say, in an age of surfaces. (To Cecily.) Come over here, dear. (Cecily goes across.) Pretty child! your dress is sadly simple, and your hair seems almost as Nature might have left it. But we can soon alter all that. A thoroughly experienced French maid produces a really marvelous result in a very brief space of time. I remember recommending one to young Lady Lancing, and after three months her own husband did not know her.

JACK (aside): And after six months nobody knew her.

LADY BRACKNELL (glares at Jack for a few moments. Then bends, with a practiced smile, to Cecily): Kindly turn round, sweet child. (Cecily turns completely round.) No, the side view is what I want. (Cecily presents her profile.) Yes, quite as I expected. There are distinct social possibilities in your profile. The two weak points in our age are its want of principle and its want of profile. The chin a little higher, dear. Style largely depends on the way the chin is worn. They are worn very high, just at present. Algernon!

ALGERNON: Yes, Aunt Augusta!

LADY BRACKNELL: There are distinct social possibilities in Miss Cardew's profile.

ALGERNON: Cecily is the sweetest, dearest, prettiest girl in the whole world. And I don't care twopence about social possibilities.

LADY BRACKNELL: Never speak disrespectfully of Society, Algernon. Only people who can't get into it do that. (*To Cecily.*) Dear child, of course you know that Algernon has nothing but his debts to depend upon. But I do not approve of mercenary marriages. When I married Lord Bracknell I had no fortune of any kind. But I never dreamed for a moment of allowing that to stand in my way. Well, I suppose I must give my consent.

ALGERNON: Thank you, Aunt Augusta.

LADY BRACKNELL: Cecily, you may kiss me!

CECILY (*kisses her*): Thank you, Lady Bracknell.

LADY BRACKNELL: You may also address me as Aunt Augusta for the future.

CECILY: Thank you, Aunt Augusta.

LADY BRACKNELL: The marriage, I think, had better take place quite soon.

ALGERNON: Thank you, Aunt Augusta.

CECILY: Thank you, Aunt Augusta.

LADY BRACKNELL: To speak frankly, I am not in favor of long engagements. They give people the opportunity of finding out each other's character before marriage, which I think is never advisable.

JACK: I beg your pardon for interrupting you, Lady Bracknell, but this engagement is quite out of the question. I am Miss Cardew's guardian, and she cannot marry without my consent until she comes of age. That consent I absolutely decline to give.

LADY BRACKNELL: Upon what grounds may I ask? Algernon is an extremely, I may almost say an ostentatiously, eligible young man. He has nothing, but he looks everything. What more can one desire?

JACK: It pains me very much to have to speak frankly to you, Lady Bracknell, about your nephew, but the fact is that I do not approve at all of his moral character. I suspect him of being untruthful.

(*Algernon and Cecily look at him in indignant amazement.*)

LADY BRACKNELL: Untruthful! My nephew Algernon? Impossible! He is an Oxonian.°

JACK: I fear there can be no possible doubt about the matter. This afternoon, during my temporary absence in London on an important question of romance, he obtained admission to my house by means of the false pretense of being my brother. Under an assumed name he drank, I've just been informed by my butler, an entire pint bottle of my Perrier-Jouët, Brut, '89; a wine I was specially reserving for myself. Continuing his disgraceful deception, he succeeded in the course of the afternoon in alienating the affections of my only ward. He subsequently stayed to tea, and devoured every single muffin. And what makes his conduct all the more heartless is, that he was perfectly well aware from

the first that I have no brother, that I never had a brother, and that I don't intend to have a brother, not even of any kind. I distinctly told him so myself yesterday afternoon.

LADY BRACKNELL: Ahem! Mr. Worthing, after careful consideration I have decided entirely to overlook my nephew's conduct to you.

JACK: That is very generous of you, Lady Bracknell. My own decision, however, is unalterable. I decline to give my consent.

LADY BRACKNELL (*to Cecily*): Come here, sweet child. (*Cecily goes over.*) How old are you, dear?

CECILY: Well, I am really only eighteen, but I always admit to twenty when I go to evening parties.

LADY BRACKNELL: You are perfectly right in making some slight alteration. Indeed, no woman should ever be quite accurate about her age. It looks so calculating — (*In a meditative manner.*) Eighteen, but admitting to twenty at evening parties. Well, it will not be very long before you are of age and free from the restraints of tutelage. So I don't think your guardian's consent is, after all, a matter of any importance.

JACK: Pray excuse me, Lady Bracknell, for interrupting you again, but it is only fair to tell you that according to the terms of her grandfather's will Miss Cardew does not come legally of age till she is thirty-five.

LADY BRACKNELL: That does not seem to me to be a grave objection. Thirty-five is a very attractive age. London society is full of women of the very highest birth who have, of their own free choice, remained thirty-five for years. Lady Dumbleton is an instance in point. To my own knowledge she has been thirty-five ever since she arrived at the age of forty, which was many years ago now. I see no reason why our dear Cecily should not be even still more attractive at the age you mention than she is at present. There will be a large accumulation of property.

CECILY: Algy, could you wait for me till I was thirty-five?

ALGERNON: Of course I could, Cecily. You know I could.

CECILY: Yes, I felt it instinctively, but I couldn't wait all that time. I hate waiting even five minutes for anybody. It always makes me rather cross. I am not punctual myself, I know, but I do like punctuality in others, and waiting, even to be married, is quite out of the question.

ALGERNON: Then what is to be done, Cecily?

CECILY: I don't know, Mr. Moncrieff.

LADY BRACKNELL: My dear Mr. Worthing, as Miss Cardew states positively that she cannot wait till she is thirty-five — a remark which I am bound to say seems to me to show a somewhat impatient

---

Oxonian: Educated at Oxford University.

nature — I would beg of you to reconsider your decision.

JACK: But my dear Lady Bracknell, the matter is entirely in your own hands. The moment you consent to my marriage with Gwendolen, I will most gladly allow your nephew to form an alliance with my ward.

LADY BRACKNELL (*rising and drawing herself up*): You must be quite aware that what you propose is out of the question.

JACK: Then a passionate celibacy is all that any of us can look forward to.

LADY BRACKNELL: That is not the destiny I propose for Gwendolen. Algernon, of course, can choose for himself. (*Pulls out her watch.*) Come, dear; (*Gwendolen rises*) we have already missed five, if not six, trains. To miss any more might expose us to comment on the platform.

(*Enter Dr. Chasuble.*)

CHASUBLE: Everything is quite ready for the christenings.

LADY BRACKNELL: The christenings, sir! Is not that somewhat premature?

CHASUBLE (*looking rather puzzled, and pointing to Jack and Algernon*): Both these gentlemen have expressed a desire for immediate baptism.

LADY BRACKNELL: At their age? The idea is grotesque and irreligious! Algernon, I forbid you to be baptized. I will not hear of such excesses. Lord Bracknell would be highly displeased if he learned that that was the way in which you wasted your time and money.

CHASUBLE: Am I to understand then that there are to be no christenings at all this afternoon?

JACK: I don't think that, as things are now, it would be of much practical value to either of us, Dr. Chasuble.

CHASUBLE: I am grieved to hear such sentiments from you, Mr. Worthing. They savor of the heretical views of the Anabaptists,° views that I have completely refuted in four of my unpublished sermons. However, as your present mood seems to be one peculiarly secular, I will return to the church at once. Indeed, I have just been informed by the pew opener that for the last hour and a half Miss Prism has been waiting for me in the vestry.

LADY BRACKNELL (*starting*): Miss Prism! Did I hear you mention a Miss Prism?

CHASUBLE: Yes, Lady Bracknell. I am on my way to join her.

LADY BRACKNELL: Pray allow me to detain you for a moment. This matter may prove to be one of vital importance to Lord Bracknell and myself. Is this Miss Prism a female of repellent aspect, remotely connected with education?

CHASUBLE (*somewhat indignantly*): She is the most cultivated of ladies, and the very picture of respectability.

LADY BRACKNELL: It is obviously the same person. May I ask what position she holds in your household?

CHASUBLE (*severely*): I am a celibate, madam.

JACK (*interposing*): Miss Prism, Lady Bracknell, has been for the last three years Miss Cardew's esteemed governess and valued companion.

LADY BRACKNELL: In spite of what I hear of her, I must see her at once. Let her be sent for.

CHASUBLE (*looking off*): She approaches; she is nigh.

(*Enter Miss Prism hurriedly.*)

MISS PRISM: I was told you expected me in the vestry, dear Canon. I have been waiting for you there for an hour and three-quarters.

(*Catches sight of Lady Bracknell who has fixed her with a stony glare. Miss Prism grows pale and quails. She looks anxiously round as if desirous to escape.*)

LADY BRACKNELL (*in a severe, judicial voice*): Prism! (*Miss Prism bows her head in shame.*) Come here, Prism! (*Miss Prism approaches in a humble manner.*) Prism! Where is that baby? (*General consternation. The Canon starts back in horror. Algernon and Jack pretend to be anxious to shield Cecily and Gwendolen from hearing the details of a terrible public scandal.*) Twenty-eight years ago, Prism, you left Lord Bracknell's house, Number 104, Upper Grosvenor Street, in charge of a perambulator that contained a baby, of the male sex. You never returned. A few weeks later, through the elaborate investigations of the Metropolitan police, the perambulator was discovered at midnight, standing by itself in a remote corner of Bayswater. It contained the manuscript of a three-volume novel of more than usually revolting sentimentality. (*Miss Prism starts in involuntary indignation.*) But the baby was not there! (*Everyone looks at Miss Prism.*) Prism! Where is that baby?   (*A pause.*)

MISS PRISM: Lady Bracknell, I admit with shame that I do not know. I only wish I did. The plain facts of the case are these. On the morning of the day you mention, a day that is forever branded on my memory, I prepared as usual to take the baby out in its perambulator. I had also with me a somewhat old, but capacious handbag in which I had intended to place the manuscript of a work of fiction that

---

Anabaptists: A religious sect beginning in the sixteenth century and advocating adult baptism and church membership by adults only.

I had written during my few unoccupied hours. In a moment of mental abstraction, for which I never can forgive myself, I deposited the manuscript in the bassinette, and placed the baby in the handbag.

JACK (*who has been listening attentively*): But where did you deposit the handbag?

MISS PRISM: Do not ask me, Mr. Worthing.

JACK: Miss Prism, this is a matter of no small importance to me. I insist on knowing where you deposited the handbag that contained that infant.

MISS PRISM: I left it in the cloakroom of one of the larger railway stations in London.

JACK: What railway station?

MISS PRISM (*quite crushed*): Victoria. The Brighton line.   (*Sinks into a chair.*)

JACK: I must retire to my room for a moment. Gwendolen, wait here for me.

GWENDOLEN: If you are not too long, I will wait here for you all my life.

(*Exit Jack in great excitement.*)

CHASUBLE: What do you think this means, Lady Bracknell?

LADY BRACKNELL: I dare not even suspect, Dr. Chasuble. I need hardly tell you that in families of high position strange coincidences are not supposed to occur. They are hardly considered the thing.

(*Noises heard overhead as if someone was throwing trunks about. Everyone looks up.*)

CECILY: Uncle Jack seems strangely agitated.

CHASUBLE: Your guardian has a very emotional nature.

LADY BRACKNELL: This noise is extremely unpleasant. It sounds as if he was having an argument. I dislike arguments of any kind. They are always vulgar, and often convincing.

CHASUBLE (*looking up*): It has stopped now.

(*The noise is redoubled.*)

LADY BRACKNELL: I wish he would arrive at some conclusion.

GWENDOLEN: This suspense is terrible. I hope it will last.

(*Enter Jack with a handbag of black leather in his hand.*)

JACK (*rushing over to Miss Prism*): Is this the handbag, Miss Prism? Examine it carefully before you speak. The happiness of more than one life depends on your answer.

MISS PRISM (*calmly*): It seems to be mine. Yes, here is the injury it received through the upsetting of a Gower Street omnibus in younger and happier days. Here is the stain on the lining caused by the explosion of a temperance beverage, an incident that occurred at Leamington. And here, on the lock, are my initials. I had forgotten that in an extravagant mood I had had them placed there. The bag is undoubtedly mine. I am delighted to have it so unexpectedly restored to me. It has been a great inconvenience being without it all these years.

JACK (*in a pathetic voice*): Miss Prism, more is restored to you than this handbag. I was the baby you placed in it.

MISS PRISM (*amazed*): You?

JACK (*embracing her*): Yes — mother!

MISS PRISM (*recoiling in indignant astonishment*): Mr. Worthing! I am unmarried!

JACK: Unmarried! I do not deny that is a serious blow. But after all, who has the right to cast a stone against one who has suffered? Cannot repentance wipe out an act of folly? Why should there be one law for men, and another for women? Mother, I forgive you.   (*Tries to embrace her again.*)

MISS PRISM (*still more indignant*): Mr. Worthing, there is some error. (*Pointing to Lady Bracknell.*) There is the lady who can tell you who you really are.

JACK (*after a pause*): Lady Bracknell, I hate to seem inquisitive, but would you kindly inform me who I am?

LADY BRACKNELL: I am afraid that the news I have to give you will not altogether please you. You are the son of my poor sister, Mrs. Moncrieff, and consequently Algernon's elder brother.

JACK: Algy's elder brother! Then I have a brother after all. I knew I had a brother! I always said I had a brother! Cecily, — how could you have ever doubted that I had a brother. (*Seizes hold of Algernon.*) Dr. Chasuble, my unfortunate brother. Miss Prism, my unfortunate brother. Gwendolen, my unfortunate brother. Algy, you young scoundrel, you will have to treat me with more respect in the future. You have never behaved to me like a brother in all your life.

ALGERNON: Well, not till today, old boy, I admit. I did my best, however, though I was out of practice.

(*Shakes hands.*)

GWENDOLEN (*to Jack*): My own! But what own are you? What is your Christian name, now that you have become someone else?

JACK: Good heavens! — I had quite forgotten that point. Your decision on the subject of my name is irrevocable, I suppose?

GWENDOLEN: I never change, except in my affections.

CECILY: What a noble nature you have, Gwendolen!

JACK: Then the question had better be cleared up at once. Aunt Augusta, a moment. At the time when Miss Prism left me in the handbag, had I been christened already?

LADY BRACKNELL: Every luxury that money could buy, including christening, had been lavished upon you by your fond and doting parents.

JACK: Then I was christened! That is settled. Now, what name was I given? Let me know the worst.

LADY BRACKNELL: Being the eldest son you were naturally christened after your father.

JACK (*irritably*): Yes, but what was my father's Christian name?

LADY BRACKNELL (*meditatively*): I cannot at the present moment recall what the General's Christian name was. But I have no doubt he had one. He was eccentric, I admit. But only in later years. And that was the result of the Indian climate, and marriage, and indigestion, and other things of that kind.

JACK: Algy! Can't you recollect what our father's Christian name was?

ALGERNON: My dear boy, we were never even on speaking terms. He died before I was a year old.

JACK: His name would appear in the Army Lists of the period, I suppose, Aunt Augusta?

LADY BRACKNELL: The General was essentially a man of peace, except in his domestic life. But I have no doubt his name would appear in any military directory.

JACK: The Army Lists of the last forty years are here. These delightful records should have been my constant study. (*Rushes to bookcase and tears the books out.*) M. Generals — Mallam, Maxbohm, Magley, what ghastly names they have — Markby, Migsby, Mobbs, Moncrieff! Lieutenant 1840, Captain, Lieutenant-Colonel, Colonel, General 1869, Christian names, Ernest John. (*Puts book very quietly down and speaks quite calmly.*) I always told you, Gwendolen, my name was Ernest, didn't I? Well, it is Ernest after all. I mean it naturally is Ernest.

LADY BRACKNELL: Yes, I remember now that the General was called Ernest. I knew I had some particular reason for disliking the name.

GWENDOLEN: Ernest! My own Ernest! I felt from the first that you could have no other name!

JACK: Gwendolen, it is a terrible thing for a man to find out suddenly that all his life he has been speaking nothing but the truth. Can you forgive me?

GWENDOLEN: I can. For I feel that you are sure to change.

JACK: My own one!

CHASUBLE (*to Miss Prism*): Laetitia! (*Embraces her.*)

MISS PRISM (*enthusiastically*): Frederick! At last!

ALGERNON: Cecily! (*Embraces her.*) At last!

JACK: Gwendolen! (*Embraces her.*) At last!

LADY BRACKNELL: My nephew, you seem to be displaying signs of triviality.

JACK: On the contrary, Aunt Augusta, I've now realized for the first time in my life the vital Importance of Being Earnest.

Anton Chekhov

Anton Chekhov (1860–1904) spent most of his childhood in relative poverty. His family managed to set up its household in Moscow after years spent in remote Taganrog, six hundred miles to the south. He studied medicine in Moscow and eventually took his degree. He practiced medicine most of his life, but, as he said, if medicine was his wife, literature was his mistress. His earliest literary efforts were for the purpose of relieving his family's poverty, but it was not long before he earned more from his writing than he did from medicine. By 1896 he had written more than three hundred short stories, most of them published in newspapers. Many of them are classics.

His first theatrical works, apart from his short farces, were not successful. *Ivanov* (1887–1889), rushed to production, was a failure. Its revised 1889 version, reflecting much of his personal life, was successful. *The Wood Demon* (1889), also a failure, helped Chekhov eventually produce one of his great plays, *Uncle Vanya* (1897). His most important plays are *The Seagull* (1896); *Three Sisters* (1901); and his last, *The Cherry Orchard* (1903). These plays essentially reshaped modern drama and created a style that critic Richard Peace describes as a "subtle blend of naturalism and symbolism."

The Seagull attracted the attention of the Moscow Art Theatre, which planned a production of it in 1898. Konstantin Stanislavsky, the great Russian director and actor, played Trigorin, the lead character, but Chekhov felt he was overacting. They often had disagreements about the playwright's work, but the Moscow Art Theatre supported Chekhov fully.

The surfaces of Chekhov's plays are so lifelike that at times one feels his dramatic purposes are submerged, and to an extent that is true. Chekhov is the master of the SUBTEXT, a technique in which the surface of the dialogue seems innocuous or meandering, but deeper meanings are implied. Madame Ranevskaya's meanderings about her childhood in act I of *The Cherry Orchard* contrast with the purposeful dialogue of Lopakhin. Her long speeches in act III talking about the "millstone" she loves in Paris are also meanderings, but they reveal an idealistic character doomed to suffer at the hands of a new generation of realists who have no time for her ramblings and sentimentalism.

Because Chekhov's subtexts are always present, it is not a simple matter to read his work. One must constantly probe, analyze, ask what is implied by what is being said. Chekhov resists "explaining" his plays by having key characters give key thematic speeches. Instead, the meaning builds slowly. Our understanding of what a situation or circumstance finally means will change as we read and as we gather more understanding of the subtleties veiled by surfaces.

Chekhov's style is remarkable for its modernity. His approach to writing was direct, simple, and effective. Even his short stories have a clear dramatic center, and the characters he chose to observe are exceptionally modern in one important way: They are not heroes and not villains. The dramatic concept of a hero who, like Oedipus, is larger than life, or a villain, like De Flores in *The Changeling*, who is essentially a devil, is nowhere to be seen in his work. Chekhov's characters are limited, recognizable, and in many ways completely ordinary.

Chekhov's genius was in taking such characters and showing their ambitions, their pain, and their successes. He was quite aware of important social changes taking place in Russia, especially changes that saw the old aristocratic classes, who once owned serfs, being reduced to a genteel impoverishment while the children of former slaves were beginning to succeed in business and real estate ventures. Chekhov's grandfather had been a serf who bought his freedom in 1841, so it is likely that Chekhov was especially supportive of such social change. His best plays provide ample evidence of his concern for the changes taking place in Russia.

THE CHERRY ORCHARD

The Cherry Orchard (1903), premiered on Chekhov's birthday, January 17, in 1904. The Moscow Art Theatre performance was directed by Konstantin Stanislavsky, an actor-director who pioneered a new method of realistic acting. (Stanislavsky is still read and admired the world over. His techniques were modified in the United States and form the basis of METHOD ACTING.) However, when Chekhov saw him acting in his plays, he was alarmed. He found Stanislavsky too stagey, too flamboyant and melodramatic, for the effects he wanted. He and Stanislavsky argued hotly over what should happen in his plays, and often Stanislavsky prevailed.

They argued over whether *The Cherry Orchard* was a tragedy. Chekhov steadfastly called it a comedy, but Stanislavsky saw the ruin of Madame Ranevskaya and the destruction of the cherry orchard as tragic. Chekhov perhaps saw it the same way, but he also considered its potential as the beginning of a new, more realistic life for Madame Ranevskaya and Gayev. Their impracticality was an important cause of their having lost their wealth and estate.

How audiences interpret Lopakhin depends on how they view the ambition of the new class of businessmen whose zeal, work, and cleverness earn them the estates that previously they could only have hoped to work on. Social change is fueled by money, which replaces an inherited aristocracy with ambitious moneymakers who earn the power to force changes on the old, less flexible aristocrats. In Russia massive social change was eventually effected by revolution and the institution of communism. But *The Cherry Orchard* shows that change would have come to Russia in any event.

Perhaps Chekhov's peasant blood helped him see the play as more of a comedy than a tragedy even though he portrays the characters with greater complexity than we might expect in comedy. Lopakhin is not a simple unsympathetic character; Trofimov is not a simple dreamer. We need to look closely at what they do and why they do it. For example, when thinking about preserving the beauties of the cherry orchard, Trofimov reminds people that all of Russia is an orchard, that the world is filled with beautiful places. Such a view makes it difficult for him to feel nostalgia for aristocratic privilege.

Trofimov sounds a striking note about the practice of slavery in Russia. He tells Madame Ranevskaya and Gayev that they are living on credit, that they have debts that must be paid back to the Russian people. The cherry orchard is beautiful because each tree represents the soul of a serf. The beautiful class of people to which the impractical Madame Ranevskaya belongs owes its beauty and grace to the institution of slavery, and soon the note will be presented for payment. The sound of the breaking string in act I, repeated at the end of the play, is Chekhov's way of symbolizing the losses and the changes represented in the play.

Madame Ranevskaya, however, cannot change. Her habits of mind are fully formed before the play begins and nothing that Lopakhin can say will help change her. Even though she knows she is dangerously in debt, she gives a gold coin to a beggar. *Noblesse oblige* — the duty of the upper class to help the poor — is still part of her ethos, even if it also involves her own ruin.

A sense of tragedy is apparent in Madame Ranevskaya's feelings and her helplessness. She seems incapable of renovating herself, no matter how much she may wish to change. We see her as a victim of fate, a fate that is formed by her expectations and training. But the play also contains comic and nonsensical moments, as, for example, in the byplay of Varya, Yasha, and Yepikhodov over a game of billiards in act III. In his letters, Chekhov mentions that the play is happy and frivolous, "in places even a farce."

The Cherry Orchard in Performance

Since its first production in 1904, *The Cherry Orchard* has played to responsive audiences in Europe and abroad. It was produced in London in 1911, Berlin in 1919, and New York in 1923 (in Russian). Eva Le Gallienne produced it in New York in her English version in 1928. In 1968 she directed the play with Uta Hagen as Madame Ranevskaya. Tyrone Guthrie directed it at the Old Vic in 1933 and again in 1941. John Gielgud, Peggy Ashcroft, Judy Dench, and Dorothy Tutin performed in a powerful and well-reviewed version in London in 1961. An all-black *Cherry Orchard* was produced by Joseph Papp in 1973, and James Earl Jones was praised as a powerful Lopakhin.

Andrei Serban's 1977 production for Joseph Papp at Lincoln Center in New York was praised for its extraordinary stage effects. According to the reviewer at *Time* magazine,

> Serban's best images effectively magnify the play's conflict between the old order and the bright new world that is its doom: a frieze of peasants laboring beneath modern telegraph wires, a group of aristocrats watching the setting sun silhouette a factory on the horizon.

The American playwright Jean Claude van Italie has interpreted the text for contemporary audiences. His version, produced at the John Drew Theater of Guild Hall in East Hampton in July 1985, was directed by Elinor Renfield. Amanda Plummer played Anya and Joanna Merlin played Madame Ranevskaya. Peter Brook's 1987 New York production with Brian Dennehy as a notable Lopakhin had little scenery beyond a great number of Oriental rugs. It was played without intermissions at breakneck speed. *New York Times* critic Frank Rich said of it, "On this director's magic carpets, *The Cherry Orchard* flies."

Anton Chekhov (1860–1904)

THE CHERRY ORCHARD

1903

TRANSLATED BY ANN DUNNIGAN

Characters

RANEVSKAYA, LYUBOV ANDREYEVNA, *a landowner*
ANYA, *her daughter, seventeen years old*
VARYA, *her adopted daughter, twenty-four years old*
GAYEV, LEONID ANDREYEVICH, *Madame Ranevskaya's brother*
LOPAKHIN, YERMOLAI ALEKSEYEVICH, *a merchant*
TROFIMOV, PYOTR SERGEYEVICH, *a student*
SEMYONOV-PISHCHIK, BORIS BORISOVICH, *a landowner*
CHARLOTTA IVANOVNA, *a governess*

YEPIKHODOV, SEMYON PANTELEYEVICH, *a clerk*
DUNYASHA, *a maid*
FIRS, *an old valet, eighty-seven years old*
YASHA, *a young footman*
A STRANGER
THE STATIONMASTER
A POST OFFICE CLERK
GUESTS, SERVANTS

The action takes place on Madame Ranevskaya's estate.

ACT I

(A room that is still called the nursery. One of the doors leads into Anya's room. Dawn; the sun will soon rise. It is May, the cherry trees are in bloom, but it is cold in the orchard; there is a morning frost. The windows in the room are closed. Enter Dunyasha with a candle, and Lopakhin with a book in his hand.)

LOPAKHIN: The train is in, thank God. What time is it?

DUNYASHA: Nearly two. *(Blows out the candle.)* It's already light.

LOPAKHIN: How late is the train, anyway? A couple of hours at least. *(Yawns and stretches.)* I'm a fine one! What a fool I've made of myself! Came here on purpose to meet them at the station, and then overslept. . . . Fell asleep in the chair. It's annoying. . . . You might have waked me.

DUNYASHA: I thought you had gone. *(Listens.)* They're coming now, I think!

LOPAKHIN *(listens)*: No . . . they've got to get the luggage and one thing and another. *(Pause.)* Lyubov Andreyevna has lived abroad for five years, I don't know what she's like now. . . . She's a fine person. Sweet-tempered, simple. I remember when I was a boy of fifteen, my late father — he had a shop in the village then — gave me a punch in the face and made my nose bleed. . . . We had come into the yard here for some reason or other, and he'd had a drop too much. Lyubov Andreyevna — I remember as if it were yesterday — still young, and so slender, led me to the washstand in this very room, the nursery. "Don't cry, little peasant," she said, "it will heal in time for your wedding. . . ." *(Pause.)* Little peasant . . . my father was a peasant, it's true, and here I am in a white waistcoat and tan shoes. Like a pig in a pastry shop. . . . I may be rich, I've made a lot of money, but if you think about it, analyze it, I'm a peasant through and through. *(Turning pages of the book.)* Here I've been reading this book, and I didn't understand a thing. Fell asleep over it. *(Pause.)*

DUNYASHA: The dogs didn't sleep all night: They can tell that their masters are coming.

LOPAKHIN: What's the matter with you, Dunyasha, you're so . . .

DUNYASHA: My hands are trembling. I'm going to faint.

LOPAKHIN: You're much too delicate, Dunyasha. You dress like a lady, and do your hair like one, too. It's not right. You should know your place.

(Enter Yepikhodov with a bouquet; he wears a jacket and highly polished boots that squeak loudly. He drops the flowers as he comes in.)

YEPIKHODOV *(picking up the flowers)*: Here, the gardener sent these. He says you're to put them in the dining room. *(Hands the bouquet to Dunyasha.)*

LOPAKHIN: And bring me some kvas.°

DUNYASHA: Yes, sir. *(Goes out.)*

YEPIKHODOV: There's a frost this morning — three degrees — and the cherry trees are in bloom. I cannot approve of our climate. *(Sighs.)* I cannot. Our climate is not exactly conducive. And now, Yermolai Alekseyevich, permit me to append: The day before yesterday I bought myself a pair of boots, which, I venture to assure you, squeak so that it's quite infeasible. What should I grease them with?

LOPAKHIN: Leave me alone. You make me tired.

YEPIKHODOV: Every day some misfortune happens to me. But I don't complain, I'm used to it, I even smile.

(Dunyasha enters, serves Lopakhin the kvas.)

YEPIKHODOV: I'm going. *(Stumbles over a chair and upsets it.)* There! *(As if in triumph.)* Now you see, excuse the expression . . . the sort of circumstance, incidentally. . . . It's really quite remarkable! *(Goes out.)*

DUNYASHA: You know, Yermolai Alekseyich, I have to confess that Yepikhodov has proposed to me.

LOPAKHIN: Ah!

DUNYASHA: And I simply don't know. . . . He's a quiet man, but sometimes, when he starts talking, you can't understand a thing he says. It's nice, and full of feeling, only it doesn't make sense. I sort of like him. He's madly in love with me. But he's an unlucky fellow: Every day something happens to him. They tease him about it around here; they call him Two-and-twenty Troubles.

LOPAKHIN *(listening)*: I think I hear them coming . . .

DUNYASHA: They're coming! What's the matter with me? I'm cold all over.

LOPAKHIN: They're really coming. Let's go and meet them. Will she recognize me? It's five years since we've seen each other.

DUNYASHA *(agitated)*: I'll faint this very minute . . . oh, I'm going to faint!

(Two carriages are heard driving up to the house. Lopakhin and Dunyasha go out quickly. The stage is empty. There is a hubbub in the adjoining rooms. Firs hurriedly crosses the stage leaning on a stick. He has been to meet Lyubov Andreyevna and wears old-fashioned livery and a high hat. He mutters something to himself, not a word of which can be understood. The noise offstage grows louder and louder. A voice:

kvas: A Russian beer.

"Let's go through here. . . ." Enter Lyubov Andrey-
evna, Anya, Charlotta Ivanovna with a little dog on
a chain, all in traveling dress; Varya wearing a coat
and kerchief; Gayev, Semyonov-Pishchik, Lopakhin,
Dunyasha with a bundle and parasol; servants with
luggage — all walk through the room.)

ANYA: Let's go this way. Do you remember, Mama, what room this is?

LYUBOV ANDREYEVNA: (*joyfully, through tears*): The nursery!

VARYA: How cold it is! My hands are numb. (*To Lyubov Andreyevna.*) Your rooms, both the white one and the violet one, are just as you left them, Mama.

LYUBOV ANDREYEVNA: The nursery . . . my dear, lovely nursery. . . . I used to sleep here when I was little. . . . (*Weeps.*) And now, like a child, I . . . (*Kisses her brother, Varya, then her brother again.*) Varya hasn't changed; she still looks like a nun. And I recognized Dunyasha. . . . (*Kisses Dunyasha.*)

GAYEV: The train was two hours late. How's that? What kind of management is that?

CHARLOTTA (*to Pishchik*): My dog even eats nuts.

PISHCHIK (*amazed*): Think of that now!

(They all go out except Anya and Dunyasha.)

DUNYASHA: We've been waiting and waiting for you. . . . (*Takes off Anya's coat and hat.*)

ANYA: I didn't sleep for four nights on the road . . . now I feel cold.

DUNYASHA: It was Lent when you went away, there was snow and frost then, but now? My darling! (*Laughs and kisses her.*) I've waited so long for you, my joy, my precious . . . I must tell you at once, I can't wait another minute. . . .

ANYA (*listlessly*): What now?

DUNYASHA: The clerk, Yepikhodov, proposed to me just after Easter.

ANYA: You always talk about the same thing. . . . (*Straightening her hair.*) I've lost all my hairpins. . . . (*She is so exhausted she can hardly stand.*)

DUNYASHA: I really don't know what to think. He loves me — he loves me so!

ANYA (*looking through the door into her room, tenderly*): My room, my windows . . . it's just as though I'd never been away. I am home! Tomorrow morning I'll get up and run into the orchard. . . . Oh, if I could only sleep! I didn't sleep during the entire journey, I was so tormented by anxiety.

DUNYASHA: Pyotr Sergeich arrived the day before yesterday.

ANYA (*joyfully*): Petya!

DUNYASHA: He's asleep in the bathhouse, he's staying there. "I'm afraid of being in the way," he said. (*Looks at her pocket watch.*) I ought to wake him up, but Varvara Mikhailovna told me not to. "Don't you wake him," she said.

(Enter Varya with a bunch of keys at her waist.)

VARYA: Dunyasha, coffee, quickly . . . Mama's asking for coffee.

DUNYASHA: This very minute. (*Goes out.*)

VARYA: Thank God, you've come! You're home again. (*Caressing her.*) My little darling has come back! My pretty one is here!

ANYA: I've been through so much.

VARYA: I can imagine!

ANYA: I left in Holy Week, it was cold then. Charlotta never stopped talking and doing her conjuring tricks the entire journey. Why did you saddle me with Charlotta?

VARYA: You couldn't have traveled alone, darling. At seventeen!

ANYA: When we arrived in Paris, it was cold, snowing. My French is awful. . . . Mama was living on the fifth floor, and when I got there, she had all sorts of Frenchmen and ladies with her, and an old priest with a little book, and it was full of smoke, dismal. Suddenly I felt sorry for Mama, so sorry. I took her head in my arms and held her close and couldn't let her go. Afterward she kept hugging me and crying. . . .

VARYA (*through her tears*): Don't talk about it, don't talk about it. . . .

ANYA: She had already sold her villa near Mentone, and she had nothing left, nothing. And I hadn't so much as a kopeck left, we barely managed to get there. But Mama doesn't understand! When we had dinner in a station restaurant, she always ordered the most expensive dishes and tipped each of the waiters a ruble. Charlotta is the same. And Yasha also ordered a dinner, it was simply awful. You know, Yasha is Mama's footman; we brought him with us.

VARYA: I saw the rogue.

ANYA: Well, how are things? Have you paid the interest?

VARYA: How could we?

ANYA: Oh, my God, my God!

VARYA: In August the estate will be put up for sale.

ANYA: My God!

(Lopakhin peeps in at the door and moos like a cow.)

LOPAKHIN: Moo-o-o! (*Disappears.*)

VARYA (*through her tears*): What I couldn't do to him! (*Shakes her fist.*)

ANYA (*embracing Varya, softly*): Varya, has he proposed to you? (*Varya shakes her head.*) But he loves you. . . . Why don't you come to an understanding, what are you waiting for?

VARYA: I don't think anything will ever come of it. He's too busy, he has no time for me . . . he doesn't even notice me. I've washed my hands of him, it makes me miserable to see him. . . . Everyone talks of our wedding, they all congratulate me, and actually there's nothing to it — it's all like a dream. . . . (*In a different tone.*) You have a brooch like a bee.

ANYA (*sadly*): Mama bought it. (*Goes into her own room; speaks gaily, like a child.*) In Paris I went up in a balloon!

VARYA: My darling is home! My pretty one has come back!

(*Dunyasha has come in with the coffeepot and prepares coffee.*)

VARYA (*stands at the door of Anya's room*): You know, darling, all day long I'm busy looking after the house, but I keep dreaming. If we could marry you to a rich man I'd be at peace. I could go into a hermitage, then to Kiev, to Moscow, and from one holy place to another. . . . I'd go on and on. What a blessing!

ANYA: The birds are singing in the orchard. What time is it?

VARYA: It must be after two. Time you were asleep, darling. (*Goes into Anya's room.*) What a blessing!

(*Yasha enters with a lap robe and a traveling bag.*)

YASHA (*crosses the stage mincingly*): May one go through here?

DUNYASHA: A person would hardly recognize you, Yasha. Your stay abroad has done wonders for you.

YASHA: Hm. . . . And who are you?

DUNYASHA: When you left here I was only that high — (*indicating with her hand*). I'm Dunyasha, Fyodor Kozoyedov's daughter. You don't remember?

YASHA: Hm. . . . A little cucumber! (*Looks around, then embraces her; she cries out and drops a saucer. He quickly goes out.*)

VARYA (*in a tone of annoyance, from the doorway*): What's going on here?

DUNYASHA (*tearfully*): I broke a saucer.

VARYA: That's good luck.

ANYA: We ought to prepare Mama: Petya is here. . . .

VARYA: I gave orders not to wake him.

ANYA (*pensively*): Six years ago Father died, and a month later brother Grisha drowned in the river . . . a pretty little seven-year-old boy. Mama couldn't bear it and went away . . . went without looking back. . . . (*Shudders.*) How I understand her, if she only knew! (*Pause.*) And Petya Trofimov was Grisha's tutor, he may remind her. . . .

(*Enter Firs wearing a jacket and a white waistcoat.*)

FIRS (*goes to the coffeepot, anxiously*): The mistress will have her coffee here. (*Puts on white gloves.*) Is the coffee ready? (*To Dunyasha, sternly.*) You! Where's the cream?

DUNYASHA: Oh, my goodness! (*Quickly goes out.*)

FIRS (*fussing over the coffeepot*): Ah, what an addlepate! (*Mutters to himself.*) They've come back from Paris. . . . The master used to go to Paris . . . by carriage. . . . (*Laughs.*)

VARYA: What is it, Firs?

FIRS: If you please? (*Joyfully.*) My mistress has come home! At last! Now I can die. . . . (*Weeps with joy.*)

(*Enter Lyubov Andreyevna, Gayev, and Semyonov-Pishchik, the last wearing a sleeveless peasant coat of fine cloth and full trousers. Gayev, as he comes in, goes through the motions of playing billiards.*)

LYUBOV ANDREYEVNA: How does it go? Let's see if I can remember . . . cue ball into the corner! Double the rail to center table.

GAYEV: Cut shot into the corner! There was a time, sister, when you and I used to sleep here in this very room, and now I'm fifty-one, strange as it may seem. . . .

LOPAKHIN: Yes, time passes.

GAYEV: How's that?

LOPAKHIN: Time, I say, passes.

GAYEV: It smells of patchouli here.

ANYA: I'm going to bed. Good night, Mama. (*Kisses her mother.*)

LYUBOV ANDREYEVNA: My precious child. (*Kisses her hands.*) Are you glad to be home? I still feel dazed.

ANYA: Good night, Uncle.

GAYEV (*kisses her face and hands*): God bless you. How like your mother you are! (*To his sister.*) At her age you were exactly like her, Lyuba.

(*Anya shakes hands with Lopakhin and Pishchik and goes out, closing the door after her.*)

LYUBOV ANDREYEVNA: She's exhausted.

PISHCHIK: Must have been a long journey.

VARYA: Well, gentlemen? It's after two, high time you were going.

LYUBOV ANDREYEVNA (*laughs*): You haven't changed, Varya. (*Draws Varya to her and kisses her.*) I'll just drink my coffee and then we'll all go. (*Firs *places a cushion under her feet.*) Thank you, my dear. I've got used to coffee. I drink it day and night. Thanks, dear old man. (*Kisses him.*)

VARYA: I'd better see if all the luggage has been brought in.

LYUBOV ANDREYEVNA: Is this really me sitting here? (*Laughs.*) I feel like jumping about and waving my arms. (*Buries her face in her hands.*) What if it's only a dream! God knows I love my country, love it dearly. I couldn't look out the train window, I was crying so! (*Through tears.*) But I must drink my coffee. Thank you, Firs, thank you, my dear old friend. I'm so glad you're still alive.

FIRS: The day before yesterday.

GAYEV: He's hard of hearing.

LOPAKHIN: I must go now, I'm leaving for Kharkov about five o'clock. It's so annoying! I wanted to have a good look at you, and have a talk. You're as splendid as ever.

PISHCHIK (*breathing heavily*): Even more beautiful. . . . Dressed like a Parisienne. . . . There goes my wagon, all four wheels!

LOPAKHIN: Your brother here, Leonid Andreich, says I'm a boor, a moneygrubber, but I don't mind. Let him talk. All I want is that you should trust me as you used to, and that your wonderful, touching eyes should look at me as they did then. Merciful God! My father was one of your father's serfs, and your grandfather's, but you yourself did so much for me once, that I've forgotten all that and love you as if you were my own kin — more than my kin.

LYUBOV ANDREYEVNA: I can't sit still, I simply cannot. (*Jumps up and walks about the room in great excitement.*) I cannot bear this joy. . . . Laugh at me, I'm silly. . . . My dear little bookcase . . . (*kisses bookcase*) my little table . . .

GAYEV: Nurse died while you were away.

LYUBOV ANDREYEVNA (*sits down and drinks coffee*): Yes, God rest her soul. They wrote me.

GAYEV: And Anastasy is dead. Petrushka Kosoi left me and is now with the police inspector in town. (*Takes a box of hard candies from his pocket and begins to suck one.*)

PISHCHIK: My daughter, Dashenka . . . sends her regards . . .

LOPAKHIN: I wish I could tell you something very pleasant and cheering. (*Glances at his watch.*) I must go directly, there's no time to talk, but . . . well, I'll say it in a couple of words. As you know, the cherry orchard is to be sold to pay your debts. The auction is set for August twenty-second, but you need not worry, my dear, you can sleep in peace, there is a way out. This is my plan. Now, please listen! Your estate is only twenty versts° from town, the railway runs close by, and if the cherry orchard and the land along the river were cut up into lots and leased for summer cottages, you'd have, at the very least, an income of twenty-five thousand a year.

GAYEV: Excuse me, what nonsense!

LYUBOV ANDREYEVNA: I don't quite understand you, Yermolai Alekseich.

LOPAKHIN: You will get, at the very least, twenty-five rubles a year for a two-and-a-half-acre lot, and if you advertise now, I guarantee you won't have a single plot of ground left by autumn, everything will be snapped up. In short, I congratulate you, you are saved. The site is splendid, the river is deep. Only, of course, the ground must be cleared . . . you must tear down all the old outbuildings, for instance, and this house, which is worthless, cut down the old cherry orchard —

LYUBOV ANDREYEVNA: Cut it down? Forgive me, my dear, but you don't know what you are talking about. If there is one thing in the whole province that is interesting, not to say remarkable, it's our cherry orchard.

LOPAKHIN: The only remarkable thing about this orchard is that it is very big. There's a crop of cherries every other year, and then you can't get rid of them, nobody buys them.

GAYEV: This orchard is even mentioned in the *Encyclopedia.*

LOPAKHIN (*glancing at his watch*): If we don't think of something and come to a decision, on the twenty-second of August the cherry orchard, and the entire estate, will be sold at auction. Make up your minds! There is no other way out, I swear to you. None whatsoever.

FIRS: In the old days, forty or fifty years ago, the cherries were dried, soaked, marinated, and made into jam, and they used to —

GAYEV: Be quiet, Firs.

FIRS: And they used to send cartloads of dried cherries to Moscow and Kharkov. And that brought in money! The dried cherries were soft and juicy in those days, sweet, fragrant. . . . They had a method then . . .

LYUBOV ANDREYEVNA: And what has become of that method now?

FIRS: Forgotten. Nobody remembers. . . .

PISHCHIK: How was it in Paris? What's it like there? Did you eat frogs?

LYUBOV ANDREYEVNA: I ate crocodiles.

---

versts: A verst is approximately equal to a kilometer, a little more than half a mile.

PISHCHIK: Think of that now!

LOPAKHIN: There used to be only the gentry and the peasants living in the country, but now these summer people have appeared. All the towns, even the smallest ones, are surrounded by summer cottages. And it is safe to say that in another twenty years these people will multiply enormously. Now the summer resident only drinks tea on his porch, but it may well be that he'll take to cultivating his acre, and then your cherry orchard will be a happy, rich, luxuriant —

GAYEV (*indignantly*): What nonsense!

(*Enter Varya and Yasha.*)

VARYA: There are two telegrams for you, Mama. (*Picks out a key and with a jingling sound opens an old-fashioned bookcase.*) Here they are.

LYUBOV ANDREYEVNA: From Paris. (*Tears up the telegrams without reading them.*) That's all over....

GAYEV: Do you know, Lyuba, how old this bookcase is? A week ago I pulled out the bottom drawer, and what do I see? Some figures burnt into it. The bookcase was made exactly a hundred years ago. What do you think of that? Eh? We could have celebrated its jubilee. It's an inanimate object, but nevertheless, for all that, it's a bookcase.

PISHCHIK: A hundred years ... think of that now!

GAYEV: Yes ... that is something.... (*Feeling the bookcase.*) Dear, honored bookcase. I salute thy existence, which for over one hundred years has served the glorious ideals of goodness and justice; thy silent appeal to fruitful endeavor, unflagging in the course of a hundred years, tearfully sustaining through generations of our family, courage and faith in a better future, and fostering in us ideals of goodness and social consciousness....

(*A pause.*)

LOPAKHIN: Yes ...

LYUBOV ANDREYEVNA: You are the same as ever, Lyonya.

GAYEV (*somewhat embarrassed*): Carom into the corner, cut shot to center table.

LOPAKHIN (*looks at his watch*): Well, time for me to go.

YASHA (*hands medicine to Lyubov Andreyevna*): Perhaps you will take your pills now.

PISHCHIK: Don't take medicaments, dearest lady, they do neither harm nor good. Let me have them, honored lady. (*Takes the pillbox, shakes the pills into his hand, blows on them, puts them into his mouth, and washes them down with kvas.*) There!

LYUBOV ANDREYEVNA (*alarmed*): Why, you must be mad!

PISHCHIK: I've taken all the pills.

LOPAKHIN: What a glutton!

(*Everyone laughs.*)

FIRS: The gentleman stayed with us during Holy Week ... ate half a bucket of pickles.... (*Mumbles.*)

LYUBOV ANDREYEVNA: What is he saying?

VARYA: He's been muttering like that for three years now. We've grown used to it.

YASHA: He's in his dotage.

(*Charlotta Ivanovna, very thin, tightly laced, in a white dress with a lorgnette at her belt, crosses the stage.*)

LOPAKHIN: Forgive me, Charlotta Ivanovna, I haven't had a chance to say how do you do to you. (*Tries to kiss her hand.*)

CHARLOTTA (*pulls her hand away*): If I permit you to kiss my hand you'll be wanting to kiss my elbow next, then my shoulder.

LOPAKHIN: I have no luck today. (*Everyone laughs.*) Charlotta Ivanovna, show us a trick!

LYUBOV ANDREYEVNA: Charlotta, show us a trick!

CHARLOTTA: No. I want to sleep. (*Goes out.*)

LOPAKHIN: In three weeks we'll meet again. (*Kisses Lyubov Andreyevna's hand.*) Good-bye till then. Time to go. (*To Gayev.*) Good-bye. (*Kisses Pishchik.*) Good-bye. (*Shakes hands with Varya, then with Firs and Yasha.*) I don't feel like going. (*To Lyubov Andreyevna.*) If you make up your mind about the summer cottages and come to a decision, let me know; I'll get you a loan of fifty thousand or so. Think it over seriously.

VARYA (*angrily*): Oh, why don't you go!

LOPAKHIN: I'm going, I'm going. (*Goes out.*)

GAYEV: Boor. Oh, pardon. Varya's going to marry him, he's Varya's young man.

VARYA: Uncle dear, you talk too much.

LYUBOV ANDREYEVNA: Well, Varya, I shall be very glad. He's a good man.

PISHCHIK: A man, I must truly say ... most worthy. ... And my Dashenka ... says, too, that ... says all sorts of things. (*Snores but wakes up at once.*) In any case, honored lady, oblige me ... a loan of two hundred and forty rubles ... tomorrow the interest on my mortgage is due....

VARYA (*in alarm*): We have nothing, nothing at all!

LYUBOV ANDREYEVNA: I really haven't any money.

PISHCHIK: It'll turn up. (*Laughs.*) I never lose hope. Just when I thought everything was lost, that I was done for, lo and behold — the railway line ran through my land ... and they paid me for it. And before you know it, something else will turn up, if not today — tomorrow. . . . Dashenka will win two hundred thousand . . . she's got a lottery ticket.

LYUBOV ANDREYEVNA: The coffee is finished, we can go to bed.

FIRS (*brushing Gayev's clothes, admonishingly*): You've put on the wrong trousers again. What am I to do with you?

VARYA (*softly*): Anya's asleep. (*Quietly opens the window.*) The sun has risen, it's no longer cold. Look, Mama dear, what wonderful trees! Oh, Lord, the air! The starlings are singing!

GAYEV (*opens another window*): The orchard is all white. You haven't forgotten, Lyuba? That long avenue there that runs straight — straight as a stretched-out strap; it gleams on moonlight nights. Remember? You've not forgotten?

LYUBOV ANDREYEVNA (*looking out the window at the orchard*): Oh, my childhood, my innocence! I used to sleep in this nursery, I looked out from here into the orchard, happiness awoke with me each morning, it was just as it is now, nothing has changed. (*Laughing with joy.*) All, all white! Oh, my orchard! After the dark, rainy autumn and the cold winter, you are young again, full of happiness, the heavenly angels have not forsaken you. . . . If I could cast off this heavy stone weighing on my breast and shoulders, if I could forget my past!

GAYEV: Yes, and the orchard will be sold for our debts, strange as it may seem. . . .

LYUBOV ANDREYEVNA: Look, our dead mother walks in the orchard . . . in a white dress! (*Laughs with joy.*) It is she!

GAYEV: Where?

VARYA: God be with you, Mama dear.

LYUBOV ANDREYEVNA: There's no one there, I just imagined it. To the right, as you turn to the summerhouse, a slender white sapling is bent over . . . it looks like a woman.

(*Enter Trofimov wearing a shabby student's uniform and spectacles.*)

LYUBOV ANDREYEVNA: What a wonderful orchard! The white masses of blossoms, the blue sky —

TROFIMOV: Lyubov Andreyevna! (*She looks around at him.*) I only want to pay my respects, then I'll go at once. (*Kisses her hand ardently.*) I was told to wait until morning, but I hadn't the patience.

(*Lyubov Andreyevna looks at him, puzzled.*)

VARYA (*through tears*): This is Petya Trofimov.

TROFIMOV: Petya Trofimov, I was Grisha's tutor. . . . Can I have changed so much?

(*Lyubov Andreyevna embraces him, quietly weeping.*)

GAYEV (*embarrassed*): There, there, Lyuba.

VARYA (*crying*): Didn't I tell you, Petya, to wait till tomorrow?

LYUBOV ANDREYEVNA: My Grisha . . . my little boy . . . Grisha . . . my son. . . .

VARYA: What can we do, Mama dear? It's God's will.

TROFIMOV (*gently, through tears*): Don't, don't. . . .

LYUBOV ANDREYEVNA (*quietly weeping*): My little boy dead, drowned. . . . Why? Why, my friend? (*In a lower voice.*) Anya is sleeping in there, and I'm talking loudly . . . making all this noise. . . . But Petya, why do you look so bad? Why have you grown so old?

TROFIMOV: A peasant woman in the train called me a mangy gentleman.

LYUBOV ANDREYEVNA: You were just a boy then, a charming little student, and now your hair is thin — and spectacles! Is it possible you are still a student? (*Goes toward the door.*)

TROFIMOV: I shall probably be an eternal student.

LYUBOV ANDREYEVNA (*kisses her brother, then has Varya*): Now, go to bed. . . . You've grown older too, Leonid.

PISHCHIK (*follows her*): Well, seems to be time to sleep. . . . Oh, my gout! I'm staying the night. Lyubov Andreyevna, my soul, tomorrow morning . . . two hundred and forty rubles. . . .

GAYEV: He keeps at it.

PISHCHIK: Two hundred and forty rubles . . . to pay the interest on my mortgage.

LYUBOV ANDREYEVNA: I have no money, my friend.

PISHCHIK: My dear, I'll pay it back. . . . It's a trifling sum.

LYUBOV ANDREYEVNA: Well, all right, Leonid will give it to you. . . . Give it to him, Leonid.

GAYEV: Me give it to him! . . . Hold out your pocket!

LYUBOV ANDREYEVNA: It can't be helped, give it to him. . . . He needs it. . . . He'll pay it back.

(*Lyubov Andreyevna, Trofimov, Pishchik, and Firs go out. Gayev, Varya, and Yasha remain.*)

GAYEV: My sister hasn't yet lost her habit of squandering money. (*To Yasha.*) Go away, my good fellow, you smell of the henhouse.

YASHA (*with a smirk*): And you, Leonid Andreyevich, are just the same as ever.

GAYEV: How's that? (*To Varya.*) What did he say?

VARYA: Your mother has come from the village; she's been sitting in the servants' room since yesterday, waiting to see you. . . .

YASHA: Let her wait, for God's sake!

VARYA: Aren't you ashamed?

YASHA: A lot I need her! She could have come tomorrow. (*Goes out.*)

VARYA: Mama's the same as ever, she hasn't changed a bit. She'd give away everything, if she could.

GAYEV: Yes. . . . (*A pause.*) If a great many remedies are suggested for a disease, it means that the disease is incurable. I keep thinking, racking my brains, I have many remedies, a great many, and that means, in effect, that I have none. It would be good to receive a legacy from someone, good to marry our Anya to a very rich man, good to go to Yaroslav and try our luck with our aunt, the Countess. She is very, very rich, you know.

VARYA (*crying*): If only God would help us!

GAYEV: Stop bawling. Auntie's very rich, but she doesn't like us. In the first place, sister married a lawyer, not a nobleman . . . (*Anya appears in the doorway.*) She married beneath her, and it cannot be said that she has conducted herself very virtuously. She is good, kind, charming, and I love her dearly, but no matter how much you allow for extenuating circumstances, you must admit she leads a sinful life. You feel it in her slightest movement.

VARYA (*in a whisper*): Anya is standing in the doorway.

GAYEV: What? (*Pause.*) Funny, something got into my right eye . . . I can't see very well. And Thursday, when I was in the district court . . .

(*Anya enters.*)

VARYA: Why aren't you asleep, Anya?

ANYA: I can't get to sleep. I just can't.

GAYEV: My little one! (*Kisses Anya's face and hands.*) My child. . . . (*Through tears.*) You are not my niece, you are my angel, you are everything to me. Believe me, believe . . .

ANYA: I believe you, Uncle. Everyone loves you and respects you, but, Uncle dear, you must keep quiet, just keep quiet. What were you saying just now about my mother, about your own sister? What made you say that?

GAYEV: Yes, yes. . . . (*Covers his face with her hand.*) Really, it's awful! My God! God help me! And today I made a speech to the bookcase . . . so stupid! And it was only when I had finished that I realized it was stupid.

VARYA: It's true, Uncle dear, you ought to keep quiet. Just don't talk, that's all.

ANYA: If you could keep from talking, it would make things easier for you, too.

GAYEV: I'll be quiet. (*Kisses Anya's and Varya's hands.*) I'll be quiet. Only this is about business. On Thursday I was in the district court, well, a group of us gathered together and began talking about one thing and another, this and that, and it seems it might be possible to arrange a loan on a promissory note to pay the interest at the bank.

VARYA: If only God would help us!

GAYEV: On Tuesday I'll go and talk it over again. (*To Varya.*) Stop bawling. (*To Anya.*) Your mama will talk to Lopakhin; he, of course, will not refuse her. . . . And as soon as you've rested, you will go to Yaroslav to the Countess, your great-aunt. In that way we shall be working from three directions — and our business is in the hat. We'll pay the interest, I'm certain of it. . . . (*Puts a candy in his mouth.*) On my honor, I'll swear by anything you like, the estate shall not be sold. (*Excitedly.*) By my happiness, I swear it! Here's my hand on it, call me a worthless, dishonorable man if I let it come to auction! I swear by my whole being!

ANYA (*a calm mood returns to her, she is happy*): How good you are, Uncle, how clever! (*Embraces him.*) Now I am at peace! I'm at peace! I'm happy!

(*Enter Firs.*)

FIRS (*reproachfully*): Leonid Andreich, have you no fear of God? When are you going to bed?

GAYEV: Presently, presently. Go away, Firs. I'll . . . all right, I'll undress myself. Well, children, bye-bye. . . . Details tomorrow, and now go to sleep. (*Kisses Anya and Varya.*) I am a man of the eighties. . . . They don't think much of that period today, nevertheless, I can say that in the course of my life I have suffered not a little for my convictions. It is not for nothing that the peasant loves me. You have to know the peasant! You have to know from what —

ANYA: There you go again, Uncle!

VARYA: Uncle dear, do be quiet.

FIRS (*angrily*): Leonid Andreich!

GAYEV: I'm coming, I'm coming. . . . Go to bed. A clean double rail shot to center table. . . . (*Goes out; Firs hobbles after him.*)

ANYA: I'm at peace now. I would rather not go to Yaroslav, I don't like my great-aunt, but still, I'm at peace, thanks to Uncle. (*She sits down.*)

VARYA: We must get some sleep. I'm going now. Oh, something unpleasant happened while you were away. In the old servants' quarters, as you know, there are only the old people: Yefimushka, Polya, Yevstignei, and, of course, Karp. They began letting in all sorts of rogues to spend the night — I didn't say anything. But then I heard they'd been spreading a rumor that I'd given an order for them to be fed nothing but dried peas. Out of stinginess, you see. . . . It was all Yevstignei's doing. . . . Very well, I think, if that's how it is, you just wait. I send for Yevstignei . . . (*yawning*) he comes. . . . "How is it, Yevstignei," I say, "that you could be such a fool...." (*Looks at Anya.*) She's fallen asleep. (*Takes her by the arm.*) Come to your little bed. ... Come along. (*Leading her.*) My little darling fell asleep. Come.... (*They go.*)

(*In the distance, beyond the orchard, a shepherd is playing on a reed pipe. Trofimov crosses the stage and, seeing Varya and Anya, stops.*)

VARYA: Sh! She's asleep ... asleep.... Come along, darling.

ANYA (*softly, half-asleep*): I'm so tired.... Those bells ... Uncle ... dear ... Mama and Uncle ...

VARYA: Come, darling, come along. (*They go into Anya's room.*)

TROFIMOV (*deeply moved*): My sunshine! My spring!

ACT II

(*A meadow. An old, lopsided, long-abandoned little chapel; near it a well, large stones that apparently were once tombstones, and an old bench. A road to the Gayev manor house can be seen. On one side, where the cherry orchard begins, tall poplars loom. In the distance a row of telegraph poles, and far, far away, on the horizon, the faint outline of a large town, which is visible only in very fine, clear weather. The sun will soon set. Charlotta, Yasha, and Dunyasha are sitting on the bench; Yepikhodov stands near playing something sad on the guitar. They are all lost in thought. Charlotta wears an old forage cap; she has taken a gun from her shoulder and is adjusting the buckle on the sling.*)

CHARLOTTA (*reflectively*): I haven't got a real passport, I don't know how old I am, but it always seems to me that I'm quite young. When I was a little girl, my father and mother used to travel from one fair to another giving performances — very good ones. And I did the *salto mortale*° and all sorts of tricks. Then when Papa and Mama died, a German lady took me to live with her and began teaching me. Good. I grew up and became a governess. But where I come from and who I am — I do not know.... Who my parents were — perhaps they weren't even married — I don't know. (*Takes a cucumber out of her pocket and eats it.*) I don't know anything. (*Pause.*) One wants so much to talk, but there isn't anyone to talk to ... I have no one.

YEPIKHODOV (*plays the guitar and sings*): "What care

salto mortale: Somersault.

I for the clamorous world, what's friend or foe to me?" ... How pleasant it is to play a mandolin!

DUNYASHA: That's a guitar, not a mandolin. (*Looks at herself in a hand mirror and powders her face.*)

YEPIKHODOV: To a madman, in love, it is a mandolin. ... (*Sings.*) "Would that the heart were warmed by the flame of requited love ..."

(*Yasha joins in.*)

CHARLOTTA: How horribly these people sing! ... Pfui! Like jackals!

DUNYASHA (*to Yasha*): Really, how fortunate to have been abroad!

YASHA: Yes, to be sure. I cannot but agree with you there. (*Yawns, then lights a cigar.*)

YEPIKHODOV: It stands to reason. Abroad everything has long since been fully constituted.

YASHA: Obviously.

YEPIKHODOV: I am a cultivated man, I read all sorts of remarkable books, but I am in no way able to make out my own inclinations, what it is I really want, whether, strictly speaking, to live or to shoot myself; nevertheless, I always carry a revolver on me. Here it is. (*Shows revolver.*)

CHARLOTTA: Finished. Now I'm going. (*Slings the gun over her shoulder.*) You're a very clever man, Yepikhodov, and quite terrifying; women must be mad about you. Brrr! (*Starts to go.*) These clever people are all so stupid, there's no one for me to talk to.... Alone, always alone, I have no one ... and who I am, and why I am, nobody knows.... (*Goes out unhurriedly.*)

YEPIKHODOV: Strictly speaking, all else aside, I must state regarding myself, that fate treats me unmercifully, as a storm does a small ship. If, let us assume, I am mistaken, then why, to mention a single instance, do I wake up this morning, and there on my chest see a spider of terrifying magnitude? ... Like that. (*Indicates with both hands.*) And likewise, I take up some kvas to quench my thirst, and there see something in the highest degree unseemly, like a cockroach. (*Pause.*) Have you read Buckle?° (*Pause.*) If I may trouble you, Avdotya Fedorovna, I should like to have a word or two with you.

DUNYASHA: Go ahead.

YEPIKHODOV: I prefer to speak with you alone.... (*Sighs.*)

DUNYASHA (*embarrassed*): Very well ... only first

Buckle: Thomas Henry Buckle (1821–1862) was a radical historian who formulated a scientific basis for history emphasizing the interrelationship of climate, food production, population, and wealth.

bring me my little cape . . . you'll find it by the cupboard. . . . It's rather damp here. . . .

YEPIKHODOV: Certainly, ma'am . . . I'll fetch it, ma'am. . . . Now I know what to do with my revolver. . . . (*Takes the guitar and goes off playing it.*)

YASHA: Two-and-twenty Troubles! Between ourselves, a stupid fellow. (*Yawns.*)

DUNYASHA: God forbid that he should shoot himself. (*Pause.*) I've grown so anxious, I'm always worried. I was only a little girl when I was taken into the master's house, and now I'm quite unused to the simple life, and my hands are white as can be, just like a lady's. I've become so delicate, so tender and ladylike, I'm afraid of everything. . . . Frightfully so. And, Yasha, if you deceive me, I just don't know what will become of my nerves.

YASHA (*kisses her*): You little cucumber! Of course, a girl should never forget herself. What I dislike above everything is when a girl doesn't conduct herself properly.

DUNYASHA: I'm passionately in love with you, you're educated, you can discuss anything. (*Pause.*)

YASHA (*yawns*): Yes. . . . As I see it, it's like this: If a girl loves somebody, that means she's immoral. (*Pause.*) Very pleasant smoking a cigar in the open air. . . . (*Listens.*) Someone's coming this way. . . . It's the masters. (*Dunyasha impulsively embraces him.*) You go home, as if you'd been to the river to bathe; take that path, otherwise they'll see you and suspect me of having a rendezvous with you. I can't endure that sort of thing.

DUNYASHA (*with a little cough*): My head is beginning to ache from your cigar. . . . (*Goes out.*)

(*Yasha remains, sitting near the chapel. Lyubov Andreyevna, Gayev, and Lopakhin enter.*)

LOPAKHIN: You must make up your mind once and for all — time won't stand still. The question, after all, is quite simple. Do you agree to lease the land for summer cottages or not? Answer in one word: Yes or no? Only one word!

LYUBOV ANDREYEVNA: Who is it that smokes those disgusting cigars out here? (*Sits down.*)

GAYEV: Now that the railway line is so near, it's made things convenient. (*Sits down.*) We went to town and had lunch . . . cue ball to the center! I feel like going to the house first and playing a game.

LYUBOV ANDREYEVNA: Later.

LOPAKHIN: Just one word! (*Imploringly.*) Do give me an answer!

GAYEV (*yawning*): How's that?

LYUBOV ANDREYEVNA (*looks into her purse*): Yesterday I had a lot of money, and today there's hardly any left. My poor Varya tries to economize by feeding everyone milk soup, and in the kitchen the old people get nothing but dried peas, while I squander money foolishly. . . . (*Drops the purse, scattering gold coins.*) There they go. . . . (*Vexed.*)

YASHA: Allow me, I'll pick them up in an instant. (*Picks up the money.*)

LYUBOV ANDREYEVNA: Please do, Yasha. And why did I go to town for lunch? . . . That miserable restaurant of yours with its music, and tablecloths smelling of soap. . . . Why drink so much, Lyonya? Why eat so much? Why talk so much? Today in the restaurant again you talked too much, and it was all so pointless. About the seventies, about the decadents. And to whom? Talking to waiters about the decadents!

LOPAKHIN: Yes.

GAYEV (*waving his hand*): I'm incorrigible, that's evident. . . . (*Irritably to Yasha.*) Why do you keep twirling about in front of me?

YASHA (*laughs*): I can't help laughing when I hear your voice.

GAYEV (*to his sister*): Either he or I —

LYUBOV ANDREYEVNA: Go away, Yasha, run along.

YASHA (*hands Lyubov Andreyevna her purse*): I'm going, right away. (*Hardly able to contain his laughter.*) This very instant. . . . (*Goes out.*)

LOPAKHIN: That rich man, Deriganov, is prepared to buy the estate. They say he's coming to the auction himself.

LYUBOV ANDREYEVNA: Where did you hear that?

LOPAKHIN: That's what they're saying in town.

LYUBOV ANDREYEVNA: Our aunt in Yaroslav promised to send us something, but when and how much, no one knows.

LOPAKHIN: How much do you think she'll send? A hundred thousand? Two hundred?

LYUBOV ANDREYEVNA: Oh . . . ten or fifteen thousand, and we'll be thankful for that.

LOPAKHIN: Forgive me, but I have never seen such frivolous, such queer, unbusinesslike people as you, my friends. You are told in plain language that your estate is to be sold, and it's as though you don't understand it.

LYUBOV ANDREYEVNA: But what are we to do? Tell us what to do.

LOPAKHIN: I tell you every day. Every day I say the same thing. Both the cherry orchard and the land must be leased for summer cottages, and it must be done now, as quickly as possible — the auction is close at hand. Try to understand! Once you definitely decide on the cottages, you can raise as much money as you like, and then you are saved.

LYUBOV ANDREYEVNA: Cottages, summer people — forgive me, but it's so vulgar.

GAYEV: I agree with you, absolutely.

LOPAKHIN: I'll either burst into tears, start shouting, or fall into a faint! I can't stand it! You've worn me out! (*To Gayev.*) You're an old woman!

GAYEV: How's that?

LOPAKHIN: An old woman! (*Starts to go.*)

LYUBOV ANDREYEVNA (*alarmed*): No, don't go, stay, my dear. I beg you. Perhaps we'll think of something!

LOPAKHIN: What is there to think of?

LYUBOV ANDREYEVNA: Don't go away, please. With you here it's more cheerful somehow. . . . (*Pause.*) I keep expecting something to happen, like the house caving in on us.

GAYEV (*in deep thought*): Double rail shot into the corner. . . . Cross table to the center. . . .

LYUBOV ANDREYEVNA: We have sinned so much. . . .

LOPAKHIN: What sins could you have —

GAYEV (*puts a candy into his mouth*): They say I've eaten up my entire fortune in candies. . . . (*Laughs.*)

LYUBOV ANDREYEVNA: Oh, my sins. . . . I've always squandered money recklessly, like a madwoman, and I married a man who did nothing but amass debts. My husband died from champagne — he drank terribly — then, to my sorrow, I fell in love with another man, lived with him, and just at that time — that was my first punishment, a blow on the head — my little boy was drowned . . . here in the river. And I went abroad, went away for good, never to return, never to see this river. . . . I closed my eyes and ran, beside myself, and *he* after me . . . callously, without pity. I bought a villa near Mentone, because he fell ill there, and for three years I had no rest, day or night. The sick man wore me out, my soul dried up. Then last year, when the villa was sold to pay my debts, I went to Paris, and there he stripped me of everything, and left me for another woman; I tried to poison myself. . . . So stupid, so shameful. . . . And suddenly I felt a longing for Russia, for my own country, for my little girl. . . . (*Wipes away her tears.*) Lord, Lord, be merciful, forgive my sins! Don't punish me anymore! (*Takes a telegram out of her pocket.*) This came today from Paris. . . . He asks my forgiveness, begs me to return. . . . (*Tears up telegram.*) Do I hear music? (*Listens.*)

GAYEV: That's our famous Jewish band. You remember, four violins, a flute, and double bass.

LYUBOV ANDREYEVNA: It's still in existence? We ought to send for them sometime and give a party.

LOPAKHIN (*listens*): I don't hear anything. . . . (*Sings softly.*) "The Germans, for pay, will turn Russians into Frenchmen, they say." (*Laughs.*) What a play I saw yesterday at the theater — very funny!

LYUBOV ANDREYEVNA: There was probably nothing funny about it. Instead of going to see plays you ought to look at yourselves a little more often. How drab your lives are, how full of futile talk!

LOPAKHIN: That's true. I must say, this life of ours is stupid. . . . (*Pause.*) My father was a peasant, an idiot; he understood nothing, taught me nothing; all he did was beat me when he was drunk, and always with a stick. As a matter of fact, I'm as big a blockhead and idiot as he was. I never learned anything, my handwriting's disgusting, I write like a pig — I'm ashamed to have people see it.

LYUBOV ANDREYEVNA: You ought to get married, my friend.

LOPAKHIN: Yes . . . that's true.

LYUBOV ANDREYEVNA: To our Varya. She's a nice girl.

LOPAKHIN: Yes.

LYUBOV ANDREYEVNA: She's a girl who comes from simple people, works all day long, but the main thing is she loves you. Besides, you've liked her for a long time now.

LOPAKHIN: Well? I've nothing against it. . . . She's a good girl. (*Pause.*)

GAYEV: I've been offered a place in the bank. Six thousand a year. . . . Have you heard?

LYUBOV ANDREYEVNA: How could you! You stay where you are. . . .

(*Firs enters carrying an overcoat.*)

FIRS (*to Gayev*): If you please, sir, put this on, it's damp.

GAYEV (*puts on the overcoat*): You're a pest, old man.

FIRS: Never mind. . . . You went off this morning without telling me. (*Looks him over.*)

LYUBOV ANDREYEVNA: How you have aged, Firs!

FIRS: What do you wish, madam?

LOPAKHIN: She says you've grown very old!

FIRS: I've lived a long time. They were arranging a marriage for me before your papa was born. . . . (*Laughs.*) I was already head footman when the emancipation came. At that time I wouldn't consent to my freedom, I stayed with the masters. . . . (*Pause.*) I remember, everyone was happy, but what they were happy about, they themselves didn't know.

LOPAKHIN: It was better in the old days. At least they flogged them.

FIRS (*not hearing*): Of course. The peasants kept to the masters, the masters kept to the peasants; but now they have all gone their own ways, you can't tell about anything.

GAYEV: Be quiet, Firs. Tomorrow I must go to town. I've been promised an introduction to a certain general who might let us have a loan.

LOPAKHIN: Nothing will come of it. And you can rest assured, you won't even pay the interest.

LYUBOV ANDREYEVNA: He's raving. There is no such general.

(*Enter Trofimov, Anya, and Varya.*)

GAYEV: Here come our young people.

ANYA: There's Mama.

LYUBOV ANDREYEVNA (*tenderly*): Come, come along, my darlings. (*Embraces Anya and Varya.*) If you only knew how I love you both! Sit here beside me — there, like that.

(*They all sit down.*)

LOPAKHIN: Our eternal student is always with the young ladies.

TROFIMOV: That's none of your business.

LOPAKHIN: He'll soon be fifty, but he's still a student.

TROFIMOV: Drop your stupid jokes.

LOPAKHIN: What are you so angry about, you queer fellow?

TROFIMOV: Just leave me alone.

LOPAKHIN (*laughs*): Let me ask you something: What do you make of me?

TROFIMOV: My idea of you, Yermolai Alekseich, is this: You're a rich man, you will soon be a millionaire. Just as the beast of prey, which devours everything that crosses its path, is necessary in the metabolic process, so are you necessary.

(*Everyone laughs.*)

VARYA: Petya, you'd better tell us something about the planets.

LYUBOV ANDREYEVNA: No, let's go on with yesterday's conversation.

TROFIMOV: What was it about?

GAYEV: About the proud man.

TROFIMOV: We talked a long time yesterday, but we didn't get anywhere. In the proud man, in your sense of the word, there's something mystical. And you may be right from your point of view, but if you look at it simply, without being abstruse, why even talk about pride? Is there any sense in it if, physiologically, man is poorly constructed, if, in the vast majority of cases, he is coarse, ignorant, and profoundly unhappy? We should stop admiring ourselves. We should just work, and that's all.

GAYEV: You die, anyway.

TROFIMOV: Who knows? And what does it mean — to die? It may be that man has a hundred senses, and at his death only the five that are known to us perish, and the other ninety-five go on living.

LYUBOV ANDREYEVNA: How clever you are, Petya!

LOPAKHIN (*ironically*): Terribly clever!

TROFIMOV: Mankind goes forward, perfecting its powers. Everything that is now unattainable will some day be comprehensible and within our grasp, only we must work, and help with all our might those who are seeking the truth. So far, among us here in Russia, only a very few work. The great majority of the intelligentsia that I know seek nothing, do nothing, and as yet are incapable of work. They call themselves the intelligentsia, yet they belittle their servants, treat the peasants like animals, are wretched students, never read anything serious, and do absolutely nothing; they only talk about science and know very little about art. They all look serious, have grim expressions, speak of weighty matters, and philosophize; and meanwhile anyone can see that the workers eat abominably, sleep without pillows, thirty or forty to a room, and everywhere there are bedbugs, stench, dampness, and immorality. . . . It's obvious that all our fine talk is merely to delude ourselves and others. Show me the day nurseries they are always talking about — and where are the reading rooms? They only write about them in novels, but in reality they don't exist. There is nothing but filth, vulgarity, asiaticism.° . . . I'm afraid of those very serious countenances, I don't like them, I'm afraid of serious conversations. We'd do better to remain silent.

LOPAKHIN: You know, I get up before five in the morning, and I work from morning to night; now, I'm always handling money, my own and other people's, and I see what people around me are like. You have only to start doing something to find out how few honest, decent people there are. Sometimes, when I can't sleep, I think: "Lord, Thou gavest us vast forests, boundless fields, broad horizons, and living in their midst we ourselves ought truly to be giants. . . ."

LYUBOV ANDREYEVNA: Now you want giants! They're good only in fairy tales, otherwise they're frightening.

(*Yepikhodov crosses at the rear of the stage, playing the guitar.*)

LYUBOV ANDREYEVNA (*pensively*): There goes Yepikhodov . . .

ANYA (*pensively*): There goes Yepikhodov . . .

GAYEV: The sun has set, ladies and gentlemen.

TROFIMOV: Yes.

GAYEV (*in a low voice, as though reciting*): Oh, Nature, wondrous Nature, you shine with eternal radiance, beautiful and indifferent; you, whom we call mother, unite within yourself both life and death, giving life and taking it away. . . .

VARYA (*beseechingly*): Uncle dear!

---

asiaticism: Trofimov, expressing a common prejudice of the time, refers to Asian apathy.

ANYA: Uncle, you're doing it again!

TROFIMOV: You'd better cue ball into the center.

GAYEV: I'll be silent, silent.

(*All sit lost in thought. The silence is broken only by the subdued muttering of Firs. Suddenly a distant sound is heard, as if from the sky, like the sound of a snapped string mournfully dying away.*)

LYUBOV ANDREYEVNA: What was that?

LOPAKHIN: I don't know. Somewhere far off in a mine shaft a bucket's broken loose. But somewhere very far away.

GAYEV: It might be a bird of some sort . . . like a heron.

TROFIMOV: Or an owl . . .

LYUBOV ANDREYEVNA (*shudders*): It's unpleasant somehow. . . . (*Pause.*)

FIRS: The same thing happened before the troubles: An owl hooted and the samovar hissed continually.

GAYEV: Before what troubles?

FIRS: Before the emancipation.

LYUBOV ANDREYEVNA: Come along, my friends, let us go, evening is falling. (*To Anya.*) There are tears in your eyes — what is it, my little one?

(*Embraces her.*)

ANYA: It's all right, Mama. It's nothing.

TROFIMOV: Someone is coming.

(*A Stranger appears wearing a shabby white forage cap and an overcoat. He is slightly drunk.*)

STRANGER: Permit me to inquire, can I go straight through here to the station?

GAYEV: You can. Follow the road.

STRANGER: I am deeply grateful to you. (*Coughs.*) Splendid weather. . . . (*Reciting.*) "My brother, my suffering brother . . . come to the Volga, whose groans" . . . (*To Varya.*) Mademoiselle, will you oblige a hungry Russian with thirty kopecks?

(*Varya, frightened, cries out.*)

LOPAKHIN (*angrily*): There's a limit to everything.

LYUBOV ANDREYEVNA (*panic-stricken*): Here you are — take this. . . . (*Fumbles in her purse.*) I have no silver. . . . Never mind, here's a gold piece for you. . . .

STRANGER: I am deeply grateful to you. (*Goes off.*)

(*Laughter.*)

VARYA (*frightened*): I'm leaving . . . I'm leaving. . . . Oh, Mama, dear, there's nothing in the house for the servants to eat, and you give him a gold piece!

LYUBOV ANDREYEVNA: What's to be done with such a silly creature? When we get home I'll give you all I've got. Yermolai Alekseyevich, you'll lend me some more!

LOPAKHIN: At your service.

LYUBOV ANDREYEVNA: Come, my friends, it's time to go. Oh, Varya, we have definitely made a match for you. Congratulations!

VARYA (*through tears*): Mama, that's not something to joke about.

LOPAKHIN: "Aurelia, get thee to a nunnery . . ."°

GAYEV: Look, my hands are trembling: It's a long time since I've played a game of billiards.

LOPAKHIN: "Aurelia, O Nymph, in thy orisons, be all my sins remember'd!"

LYUBOV ANDREYEVNA: Let us go, my friends, it will soon be suppertime.

VARYA: He frightened me. My heart is simply pounding.

LOPAKHIN: Let me remind you, ladies and gentlemen: On the twenty-second of August the cherry orchard is to be sold. Think about that! — Think!

(*All go out except Trofimov and Anya.*)

ANYA (*laughs*): My thanks to the stranger for frightening Varya, now we are alone.

TROFIMOV: Varya is so afraid we might suddenly fall in love with each other that she hasn't left us alone for days. With her narrow mind she can't understand that we are above love. To avoid the petty and the illusory, which prevent our being free and happy — that is the aim and meaning of life. Forward! We are moving irresistibly toward the bright star that burns in the distance! Forward! Do not fall behind, friends!

ANYA (*clasping her hands*): How well you talk! (*Pause.*) It's marvelous here today!

TROFIMOV: Yes, the weather is wonderful.

ANYA: What have you done to me, Petya, that I no longer love the cherry orchard as I used to? I loved it so tenderly, it seemed to me there was no better place on earth than our orchard.

TROFIMOV: All Russia is our orchard. It is a great and beautiful land, and there are many wonderful places in it. (*Pause.*) Just think, Anya: Your grandfather, your great-grandfather, and all your ancestors were serf-owners, possessors of living souls. Don't you see that from every cherry tree, from every leaf and trunk, human beings are peering out at you? Don't you hear their voices? To possess living souls — that has corrupted all of you, those who lived before and you who are living now, so

"**Aurelia . . . nunnery**": From Hamlet's famous line rejecting Ophelia (Lopakhin's next line is also from Shakespeare's *Hamlet*).

that your mother, you, your uncle, no longer perceive that you are living in debt, at someone else's expense, at the expense of those whom you wouldn't allow to cross your threshold. . . . We are at least two hundred years behind the times, we have as yet absolutely nothing, we have no definite attitude toward the past, we only philosophize, complain of boredom, or drink vodka. Yet it's quite clear that to begin to live we must first atone for the past, be done with it, and we can atone for it only by suffering, only by extraordinary, unceasing labor. Understand this, Anya.

ANYA: The house we live in hasn't really been ours for a long time, and I shall leave it, I give you my word.

TROFIMOV: If you have the keys of the household, throw them into the well and go. Be as free as the wind.

ANYA (*in ecstasy*): How well you put that!

TROFIMOV: Believe me, Anya, believe me! I am not yet thirty, I am young, still a student, but I have already been through so much! As soon as winter comes, I am hungry, sick, worried, poor as a beggar, and — where has not fate driven me! Where have I not been? And yet always, every minute of the day and night, my soul was filled with inexplicable premonitions. I have a premonition of happiness, Anya, I can see it . . .

ANYA: The moon is rising.

(*Yepikhodov is heard playing the same melancholy song on the guitar. The moon rises. Somewhere near the poplars Varya is looking for Anya and calling: "Anya, where are you?"*)

TROFIMOV: Yes, the moon is rising. (*Pause.*) There it is — happiness . . . it's coming, nearer and nearer, I can hear its footsteps. And if we do not see it, if we do not recognize it, what does it matter? Others will see it.

VARYA'S VOICE: Anya! Where are you?

TROFIMOV: That Varya again! (*Angrily.*) It's revolting!

ANYA: Well? Let's go down to the river. It's lovely there.

TROFIMOV: Come on. (*They go.*)

VARYA'S VOICE: Anya! Anya!

ACT III

(*The drawing room, separated by an arch from the ballroom. The chandelier is lighted. The Jewish band that was mentioned in act II is heard playing in the hall. It is evening. In the ballroom they are dancing*

a grand rond. The voice of Semyonov-Pishchik: "Promenade à une paire!"° They all enter the drawing room: Pishchik and Charlotta Ivanovna are the first couple, Trofimov and Lyubov Andreyevna the second, Anya and the Post-Office Clerk the third, Varya and the Stationmaster the fourth, etc. Varya, quietly weeping, dries her tears as she dances. Dunyasha is in the last couple. As they cross the drawing room Pishchik calls: "Grand rond, balancez!" and "Les cavaliers à genoux et remercier vos dames!"° Firs, wearing a dress coat, brings in a tray with seltzer water. Pishchik and Trofimov come into the drawing room.)

PISHCHIK: I'm a full-blooded man, I've already had two strokes, and dancing's hard work for me, but as they say, "If you run with the pack, you can bark or not, but at least wag your tail." At that, I'm as strong as a horse. My late father — quite a joker he was, God rest his soul — used to say, talking about our origins, that the ancient line of Semyonov-Pishchik was descended from the very horse that Caligula had seated in the Senate.° . . . (*Sits down.*) But the trouble is — no money! A hungry dog believes in nothing but meat. . . . (*Snores but wakes up at once.*) It's the same with me — I can think of nothing but money. . . .

TROFIMOV: You know, there really is something equine about your figure.

PISHCHIK: Well, a horse is a fine animal. . . . You can sell a horse.

(*There is the sound of a billiard game in the next room. Varya appears in the archway.*)

TROFIMOV (*teasing her*): Madame Lopakhina! Madame Lopakhina!

VARYA (*angrily*): Mangy gentleman!

TROFIMOV: Yes, I am a mangy gentleman, and proud of it!

VARYA (*reflecting bitterly*): Here we've hired musicians, and what are we going to pay them with? (*Goes out.*)

TROFIMOV (*to Pishchik*): If the energy you have expended in the course of your life trying to find money to pay interest had gone into something else, ultimately, you might very well have turned the world upside down.

PISHCHIK: Nietzsche . . . the philosopher . . . the greatest, most renowned . . . a man of tremendous in-

---

"Promenade à une paire!": French for "Walk in pairs."
"Grand rond . . . dames!": Instructions in the dance: "Large circle!" and "Gentlemen, kneel down and thank your ladies!"
Caligula . . . Senate: Caligula (A.D. 12–41), a cavalry soldier, was Roman emperor (A.D. 37–41).

tellect . . . says in his works that it is possible to forge banknotes.

TROFIMOV: And have you read Nietzsche?

PISHCHIK: Well . . . Dashenka told me. I'm in such a state now that I'm just about ready for forging. . . . The day after tomorrow I have to pay three hundred and ten rubles . . . I've got a hundred and thirty. . . . (*Feels in his pocket, grows alarmed.*) The money is gone! I've lost the money! (*Tearfully.*) Where is my money? (*Joyfully.*) Here it is, inside the lining. . . . I'm all in a sweat. . . .

(*Lyubov Andreyevna and Charlotta Ivanovna come in.*)

LYUBOV ANDREYEVNA (*humming a* Lezginka):° Why does Leonid take so long? What is he doing in town? (*To Dunyasha.*) Dunyasha, offer the musicians some tea.

TROFIMOV: In all probability, the auction didn't take place.

LYUBOV ANDREYEVNA: It was the wrong time to have the musicians, the wrong time to give a dance. . . . Well, never mind. . . . (*Sits down and hums softly.*)

CHARLOTTA (*gives Pishchik a deck of cards*): Here's a deck of cards for you. Think of a card.

PISHCHIK: I've thought of one.

CHARLOTTA: Now shuffle the pack. Very good. And now, my dear Mr. Pishchik, hand it to me. *Ein, zwei, drei!*° Now look for it — it's in your side pocket.

PISHCHIK (*takes the card out of his side pocket*): The eight of spades — absolutely right! (*Amazed.*) Think of that, now!

CHARLOTTA (*holding the deck of cards in the palm of her hand, to Trofimov*): Quickly, tell me, which card is on top?

TROFIMOV: What? Well, the queen of spades.

CHARLOTTA: Right! (*To Pishchik.*) Now which card is on top?

PISHCHIK: The ace of hearts.

CHARLOTTA: Right! (*Claps her hands and the deck of cards disappears.*) What lovely weather we're having today! (*A mysterious feminine voice, which seems to come from under the floor, answers her: "Oh, yes, splendid weather, madam."*) You are so nice, you're my ideal. . . . (*The voice: "And I'm very fond of you, too, madam."*)

STATIONMASTER (*applauding*): Bravo, Madame Ventriloquist!

PISHCHIK (*amazed*): Think of that, now! Most enchanting Charlotta Ivanovna . . . I am simply in love with you. . . .

CHARLOTTA: In love? (*Shrugs her shoulders.*) Is it possible that you can love? *Guter Mensch, aber schlechter Musikant.*°

TROFIMOV (*claps Pishchik on the shoulder*): You old horse, you!

CHARLOTTA: Attention, please! One more trick. (*Takes a lap robe from a chair.*) Here's a very fine lap robe; I should like to sell it. (*Shakes it out.*) Doesn't anyone want to buy it?

PISHCHIK (*amazed*): Think of that, now!

CHARLOTTA: *Ein, zwei, drei!* (*Quickly raises the lap robe; behind it stands Anya, who curtsies, runs to her mother, embraces her, and runs back into the ballroom amid the general enthusiasm.*)

LYUBOV ANDREYEVNA (*applauding*): Bravo, bravo!

CHARLOTTA: Once again! *Ein, zwei, drei.* (*Raises the lap robe; behind it stands Varya, who bows.*)

PISHCHIK (*amazed*): Think of that, now!

CHARLOTTA: The end! (*Throws the robe at Pishchik, makes a curtsy, and runs out of the room.*)

PISHCHIK (*hurries after her*): The minx! . . . What a woman! What a woman! (*Goes out.*)

LYUBOV ANDREYEVNA: And Leonid still not here. What he is doing in town so long, I do not understand! It must be all over by now. Either the estate is sold, or the auction didn't take place — but why keep us in suspense so long!

VARYA (*trying to comfort her*): Uncle has bought it, I am certain of that.

TROFIMOV (*mockingly*): Yes.

VARYA: Great-aunt sent him power of attorney to buy it in her name and transfer the debt. She's doing it for Anya's sake. And I am sure, with God's help, Uncle will buy it.

LYUBOV ANDREYEVNA: Our great-aunt in Yaroslav sent fifteen thousand to buy the estate in her name — she doesn't trust us — but that's not even enough to pay the interest. (*Covers her face with her hands.*) Today my fate will be decided, my fate . . .

TROFIMOV (*teasing Varya*): Madame Lopakhina!

VARYA (*angrily*): Eternal student! Twice already you've been expelled from the university.

LYUBOV ANDREYEVNA: Why are you so cross, Varya? If he teases you about Lopakhin, what of it? Go ahead and marry Lopakhin if you want to. He's a nice man, he's interesting. And if you don't want to, don't. Nobody's forcing you, my pet.

VARYA: To be frank, Mama dear, I regard this matter seriously. He is a good man, I like him.

LYUBOV ANDREYEVNA: Then marry him. I don't know what you're waiting for!

Lezginka: A lively Russian tune for a dance.
Ein, zwei, drei!: "One, two, three" in German.

Guter Mensch, aber schlechter Musikant: "Good man, but poor musician" in German.

VARYA: Mama, I can't propose to him myself. For the last two years everyone's been talking to me about him; everyone talks, but he is either silent or he jokes. I understand. He's getting rich, he's absorbed in business, he has no time for me. If I had some money, no matter how little, if it were only a hundred rubles, I'd drop everything and go far away. I'd go into a nunnery.

TROFIMOV: A blessing!

VARYA (*to Trofimov*): A student ought to be intelligent! (*In a gentle tone, tearfully.*) How homely you have grown, Petya, how old! (*To Lyubov Andreyevna, no longer crying.*) It's just that I cannot live without work, Mama. I must be doing something every minute.

(*Yasha enters.*)

YASHA (*barely able to suppress his laughter*): Yepikhodov has broken a billiard cue! (*Goes out.*)

VARYA: But why is Yepikhodov here? Who gave him permission to play billiards? I don't understand these people. . . . (*Goes out.*)

LYUBOV ANDREYEVNA: Don't tease her, Petya. You can see she's unhappy enough without that.

TROFIMOV: She's much too zealous, always meddling in other people's affairs. All summer long she's given Anya and me no peace — afraid a romance might develop. What business is it of hers? Besides, I've given no occasion for it, I am far removed from such banality. We are above love!

LYUBOV ANDREYEVNA: And I suppose I am beneath love. (*In great agitation.*) Why isn't Leonid here? If only I knew whether the estate had been sold or not! The disaster seems to me so incredible that I don't even know what to think, I'm lost. . . . I could scream this very instant . . . I could do something foolish. Save me, Petya. Talk to me, say something. . . .

TROFIMOV: Whether or not the estate is sold today — does it really matter? That's all done with long ago; there's no turning back, the path is overgrown. Be calm, my dear. One must not deceive oneself; at least once in one's life one ought to look the truth straight in the eye.

LYUBOV ANDREYEVNA: What truth? You can see where there is truth and where there isn't, but I seem to have lost my sight, I see nothing. You boldly settle all the important problems, but tell me, my dear boy, isn't it because you are young and have not yet had to suffer for a single one of your problems? You boldly look ahead, but isn't it because you neither see nor expect anything dreadful, since life is still hidden from your young eyes? You're bolder, more honest, deeper than we are, but think about it, be just a little bit magnanimous, and spare me. You see, I was born here, my mother and father lived here, and my grandfather. I love this house, without the cherry orchard my life has no meaning for me, and if it must be sold, then sell me with the orchard. . . . (*Embraces Trofimov and kisses him on the forehead.*) And my son was drowned here. . . . (*Weeps.*) Have pity on me, you good, kind man.

TROFIMOV: You know I feel for you with all my heart.

LYUBOV ANDREYEVNA: But that should have been said differently, quite differently. . . . (*Takes out her handkerchief and a telegram falls to the floor.*) My heart is heavy today, you can't imagine. It's so noisy here, my soul quivers at every sound, I tremble all over, and yet I can't go to my room. When I am alone the silence frightens me. Don't condemn me, Petya . . . I love you as if you were my own. I would gladly let you marry Anya, I swear it, only you must study, my dear, you must get your degree. You do nothing, fate simply tosses you from place to place — it's so strange. . . . Isn't that true? Isn't it? And you must do something about your beard, to make it grow somehow. . . . (*Laughs.*) You're so funny!

TROFIMOV (*picks up the telegram*): I have no desire to be an Adonis.°

LYUBOV ANDREYEVNA: That's a telegram from Paris. I get them every day. One yesterday, one today. That wild man has fallen ill again, he's in trouble again. . . . He begs my forgiveness, implores me to come, and really, I ought to go to Paris to be near him. Your face is stern, Petya, but what can one do, my dear? What am I to do? He is ill, he's alone and unhappy, and who will look after him there, who will keep him from making mistakes, who will give him his medicine on time? And why hide it or keep silent, I love him, that's clear. I love him, love him. . . . It's a millstone round my neck, I'm sinking to the bottom with it, but I love that stone, I cannot live without it. (*Presses Trofimov's hand.*) Don't think badly of me, Petya, and don't say anything to me, don't say anything. . . .

TROFIMOV (*through tears*): For God's sake, forgive my frankness: You know that he robbed you!

LYUBOV ANDREYEVNA: No, no, no, you mustn't say such things! (*Covers her ears.*)

TROFIMOV: But he's a scoundrel! You're the only one who doesn't know it! He's a petty scoundrel, a nonentity —

LYUBOV ANDREYEVNA (*angry, but controlling herself*): You are twenty-six or twenty-seven years old, but you're still a schoolboy!

TROFIMOV: That may be!

Adonis: From Greek myth, a beautiful young man.

LYUBOV ANDREYEVNA: You should be a man, at your age you ought to understand those who love. And you ought to be in love yourself. (*Angrily.*) Yes, yes! It's not purity with you, it's simply prudery, you're a ridiculous crank, a freak —

TROFIMOV (*horrified*): What is she saying!

LYUBOV ANDREYEVNA: "I am above love!" You're not above love, you're just an addlepate, as Firs would say. Not to have a mistress at your age!

TROFIMOV (*in horror*): This is awful! What is she saying! . . . (*Goes quickly toward the ballroom.*) This is awful . . . I can't . . . I won't stay here. . . . (*Goes out, but immediately returns.*) All is over between us! (*Goes out to the hall.*)

LYUBOV ANDREYEVNA (*calls after him*): Petya, wait! You absurd creature, I was joking! Petya!

(*In the hall there is the sound of someone running quickly downstairs and suddenly falling with a crash. Anya and Varya scream, but a moment later laughter is heard.*)

LYUBOV ANDREYEVNA: What was that?

(*Anya runs in.*)

ANYA (*laughing*): Petya fell down the stairs! (*Runs out.*)

LYUBOV ANDREYEVNA: What a funny boy that Petya is!

(*The Stationmaster stands in the middle of the ballroom and recites A. Tolstoy's° "The Sinner." Everyone listens to him, but he has no sooner spoken a few lines than the sound of a waltz is heard from the hall and the recitation is broken off. They all dance. Trofimov, Anya, Varya, and Lyubov Andreyevna come in from the hall.*)

LYUBOV ANDREYEVNA: Come, Petya . . . come, you pure soul . . . please, forgive me. . . . Let's dance. . . . (*They dance.*)

(*Anya and Varya dance. Firs comes in, puts his stick by the side door. Yasha also comes into the drawing room and watches the dancers.*)

YASHA: What is it, grandpa?

FIRS: I don't feel well. In the old days, we used to have generals, barons, admirals, dancing at our balls, but now we send for the post office clerk and the stationmaster, and even they are none too eager to come. Somehow I've grown weak. The late master, their grandfather, dosed everyone with sealing wax, no matter what ailed them. I've been

A. Tolstoy: Aleksey Konstantinovich Tolstoy (1817–1875), Russian novelist, dramatist, and poet.

taking sealing wax every day for twenty years or more; maybe that's what's kept me alive.

YASHA: You bore me, grandpa. (*Yawns.*) High time you croaked.

FIRS: Ah, you . . . addlepate! (*Mumbles.*)

(*Trofimov and Lyubov Andreyevna dance from the ballroom into the drawing room.*)

LYUBOV ANDREYEVNA: *Merci.* I'll sit down a while. (*Sits.*) I'm tired.

(*Anya comes in.*)

ANYA (*excitedly*): There was a man in the kitchen just now saying that the cherry orchard was sold today.

LYUBOV ANDREYEVNA: Sold to whom?

ANYA: He didn't say. He's gone. (*Dances with Trofimov; they go into the ballroom.*)

YASHA: That was just some old man babbling. A stranger.

FIRS: Leonid Andreich is not back yet, still hasn't come. And he's wearing the light, between-seasons overcoat; like enough he'll catch cold. Ah, when they're young they're green.

LYUBOV ANDREYEVNA: This is killing me. Yasha, go and find out who it was sold to.

YASHA: But that old man left long ago. (*Laughs.*)

LYUBOV ANDREYEVNA (*slightly annoyed*): Well, what are you laughing at? What are you so happy about?

YASHA: That Yepikhodov is very funny! Hopeless! Two-and-twenty Troubles.

LYUBOV ANDREYEVNA: Firs, if the estate is sold, where will you go?

FIRS: Wherever you tell me to go, I'll go.

LYUBOV ANDREYEVNA: Why do you look like that? Aren't you well? You ought to go to bed.

FIRS: Yes. . . . (*With a smirk.*) Go to bed, and without me who will serve, who will see to things? I'm the only one in the whole house.

YASHA (*to Lyubov Andreyevna*): Lyubov Andreyevna! Permit me to make a request, be so kind! If you go back to Paris again, do me the favor of taking me with you. It is positively impossible for me to stay here. (*Looking around, then in a low voice.*) There's no need to say it, you can see for yourself, it's an uncivilized country, the people have no morals, and the boredom! The food they give us in the kitchen is unmentionable, and besides, there's this Firs who keeps walking about mumbling all sorts of inappropriate things. Take me with you, be so kind!

(*Enter Pishchik.*)

PISHCHIK: May I have the pleasure of a waltz with you, fairest lady? (*Lyubov Andreyevna goes with him.*) I really must borrow a hundred and eighty rubles from you, my charmer . . . I really must. . . . (*Dancing.*) Just a hundred and eighty rubles. . . . (*They pass into the ballroom.*)

YASHA (*softly sings*): "Wilt thou know my soul's unrest . . ."

(*In the ballroom a figure in a gray top hat and checked trousers is jumping about, waving its arms; there are shouts of "Bravo, Charlotta Ivanovna!"*)

DUNYASHA (*stopping to powder her face*): The young mistress told me to dance — there are lots of gentlemen and not enough ladies — but dancing makes me dizzy, and my heart begins to thump. Firs Nikolayevich, the post office clerk just said something to me that took my breath away.

(*The music grows more subdued.*)

FIRS: What did he say to you?
DUNYASHA: "You," he said, "are like a flower."
YASHA (*yawns*): What ignorance. . . . (*Goes out.*)
DUNYASHA: Like a flower. . . . I'm such a delicate girl, I just adore tender words.
FIRS: You'll get your head turned.

(*Enter Yepikhodov.*)

YEPIKHODOV: Avdotya Fyodorovna, you are not desirous of seeing me. . . . I might almost be some sort of insect. (*Sighs.*) Ah, life!
DUNYASHA: What is it you want?
YEPIKHODOV: Indubitably, you may be right. (*Sighs.*) But, of course, if one looks at it from a point of view, then, if I may so express myself, and you will forgive my frankness, you have completely reduced me to a state of mind. I know my fate, every day some misfortune befalls me, but I have long since grown accustomed to that; I look upon my fate with a smile. But you gave me your word, and although I —
DUNYASHA: Please, we'll talk about it later, but leave me in peace now. Just now I'm dreaming. . . . (*Plays with her fan.*)
YEPIKHODOV: Every day a misfortune, and yet, if I may so express myself, I merely smile, I even laugh.

(*Varya enters from the ballroom.*)

VARYA: Are you still here, Semyon? What a disrespectful man you are, really! (*To Dunyasha.*) Run along, Dunyasha. (*To Yepikhodov.*) First you play billiards and break a cue, then you wander about the drawing room as though you were a guest.
YEPIKHODOV: You cannot, if I may so express myself, penalize me.
VARYA: I am not penalizing you, I'm telling you. You do nothing but wander from one place to another,

and you don't do your work. We keep a clerk, but for what, I don't know.
YEPIKHODOV (*offended*): Whether I work, or wander about, or eat, or play billiards, these are matters to be discussed only by persons of discernment, and my elders.
VARYA: You dare say that to me! (*Flaring up.*) You dare? You mean to say I have no discernment? Get out of here! This instant!
YEPIKHODOV (*intimidated*): I beg you to express yourself in a more delicate manner.
VARYA (*beside herself*): Get out, this very instant! Get out! (*He goes to the door, she follows him.*) Two-and-twenty Troubles! Don't let me set eyes on you again!
YEPIKHODOV (*goes out, his voice is heard behind the door*): I shall lodge a complaint against you!
VARYA: Oh, you're coming back? (*Seizes the stick left near the door by Firs.*) Come, come on. . . . Come, I'll show you. . . . Ah, so you're coming, are you? Then take that — (*Swings the stick just as Lopakhin enters.*)
LOPAKHIN: Thank you kindly.
VARYA (*angrily and mockingly*): I beg your pardon.
LOPAKHIN: Not at all. I humbly thank you for your charming reception.
VARYA: Don't mention it. (*Walks away, then looks back and gently asks.*) I didn't hurt you, did I?
LOPAKHIN: No, it's nothing. A huge bump coming up, that's all.

(*Voices in the ballroom: "Lopakhin has come! Yermolai Alekseich!" Pishchik enters.*)

PISHCHIK: As I live and breathe! (*Kisses Lopakhin.*) There is a whiff of cognac about you, dear soul. And we've been making merry here, too.

(*Enter Lyubov Andreyevna.*)

LYUBOV ANDREYEVNA: Is that you, Yermolai Alekseich? What kept you so long? Where's Leonid?
LOPAKHIN: Leonid Andreich arrived with me, he's coming . . .
LYUBOV ANDREYEVNA (*agitated*): Well, what happened? Did the sale take place? Tell me!
LOPAKHIN (*embarrassed, fearing to reveal his joy*): The auction was over by four o'clock. . . . We missed the train, had to wait till half past nine. (*Sighing heavily.*) Ugh! My head is swimming. . . .

(*Enter Gayev; he carries his purchases in one hand and wipes away his tears with the other.*)

LYUBOV ANDREYEVNA: Lyonya, what happened? Well, Lyonya? (*Impatiently, through tears.*) Be quick, for God's sake!
GAYEV (*not answering her, simply waves his hand.*

To Firs, weeping): Here, take these. . . . There's anchovies, Kerch herrings. . . . I haven't eaten anything all day. . . . What I have been through! (*The click of billiard balls is heard through the open door to the billiard room, and Yasha's voice: "Seven and eighteen!" Gayev's expression changes, he is no longer weeping.*) I'm terribly tired. Firs, help me change. (*Goes through the ballroom to his own room, followed by Firs.*)

PISHCHIK: What happened at the auction? Come on, tell us!

LYUBOV ANDREYEVNA: Is the cherry orchard sold?

LOPAKHIN: It's sold.

LYUBOV ANDREYEVNA: Who bought it?

LOPAKHIN: I bought it. (*Pause.*)

(*Lyubov Andreyevna is overcome; she would fall to the floor if it were not for the chair and table near which she stands. Varya takes the keys from her belt and throws them on the floor in the middle of the drawing room and goes out.*)

LOPAKHIN: I bought it! Kindly wait a moment, ladies and gentlemen, my head is swimming. I can't talk. . . . (*Laughs.*) We arrived at the auction, Deriganov was already there. Leonid Andreich had only fifteen thousand, and straight off Deriganov bid thirty thousand over and above the mortgage. I saw how the land lay, so I got into the fight and bid forty. He bid forty-five. I bid fifty-five. In other words, he kept raising it by five thousand, and I by ten. Well, it finally came to an end. I bid ninety thousand above the mortgage, and it was knocked down to me. The cherry orchard is now mine! Mine! (*Laughs uproariously.*) Lord! God in heaven! The cherry orchard is mine! Tell me I'm drunk, out of my mind, that I imagine it. . . . (*Stamps his feet.*) Don't laugh at me! If my father and my grandfather could only rise from their graves and see all that has happened, how their Yermolai, their beaten, half-literate Yermolai, who used to run about barefoot in winter, how that same Yermolai has bought an estate, the most beautiful estate in the whole world! I bought the estate where my father and grandfather were slaves, where they weren't even allowed in the kitchen. I'm asleep, this is just some dream of mine, it only seems to be. . . . It's the fruit of your imagination, hidden in the darkness of uncertainty. . . . (*Picks up the keys, smiling tenderly.*) She threw down the keys, wants to show that she's not mistress here anymore. . . . (*Jingles the keys.*) Well, no matter. (*The orchestra is heard tuning up.*) Hey, musicians, play, I want to hear you! Come on, everybody, and see how Yermolai Lopakhin will lay the ax to the cherry orchard, how the trees will fall to the ground! We're going

to build summer cottages and our grandsons and great-grandsons will see a new life here. . . . Music! Strike up!

(*The orchestra plays. Lyubov Andreyevna sinks into a chair and weeps bitterly.*)

LOPAKHIN (*reproachfully*): Why didn't you listen to me, why? My poor friend, there's no turning back now. (*With tears.*) Oh, if only all this could be over quickly, if somehow our discordant, unhappy life could be changed!

PISHCHIK (*takes him by the arm; speaks in an undertone*): She's crying. Let's go into the ballroom, let her be alone. . . . Come on. . . . (*Leads him into the ballroom.*)

LOPAKHIN: What's happened? Musicians, play so I can hear you! Let everything be as I want it! (*Ironically.*) Here comes the new master, owner of the cherry orchard! (*Accidentally bumps into a little table, almost upsetting the candelabrum.*) I can pay for everything! (*Goes out with Pishchik.*)

(*There is no one left in either the drawing room or the ballroom except Lyubov Andreyevna, who sits huddled up and weeping bitterly. The music plays softly. Anya and Trofimov enter hurriedly. Anya goes to her mother and kneels before her. Trofimov remains in the doorway of the ballroom.*)

ANYA: Mama! . . . Mama, you're crying! Dear, kind, good Mama, my beautiful one, I love you . . . I bless you. The cherry orchard is sold, it's gone, that's true, true, but don't cry, Mama, life is still before you, you still have your good, pure soul. . . . Come with me, come, darling, we'll go away from here! . . . We'll plant a new orchard, more luxuriant than this one. You will see it and understand; and joy, quiet, deep joy, will sink into your soul, like the evening sun, and you will smile, Mama! Come, darling, let us go. . . .

ACT IV

(*The scene is the same as act I. There are neither curtains on the windows nor pictures on the walls, and only a little furniture piled up in one corner, as if for sale. There is a sense of emptiness. Near the outer door, at the rear of the stage, suitcases, traveling bags, etc., are piled up. Through the open door on the left the voices of Varya and Anya can be heard. Lopakhin stands waiting. Yasha is holding a tray with little glasses of champagne. In the hall, Yepikhodov is tying up a box. Offstage, at the rear, there is a hum of voices. It is the peasants who have come to say*) *good-bye. Gayev's voice: "Thanks, brothers, thank you."*)

YASHA: The peasants have come to say good-bye. In my opinion, Yermolai Alekseich, peasants are good-natured, but they don't know much.

(*The hum subsides. Lyubov Andreyevna enters from the hall with Gayev. She is not crying, but she is pale, her face twitches, and she cannot speak.*)

GAYEV: You gave them your purse, Lyuba. That won't do! That won't do!

LYUBOV ANDREYEVNA: I couldn't help it! I couldn't help it! (*They both go out.*)

LOPAKHIN (*in the doorway, calls after them*): Please, do me the honor of having a little glass at parting. I didn't think of bringing champagne from town, and at the station I found only one bottle. Please! What's the matter, friends, don't you want any? (*Walks away from the door.*) If I'd known that, I wouldn't have bought it. Well, then I won't drink any either. (*Yasha carefully sets the tray down on a chair.*) At least you have a glass, Yasha.

YASHA: To those who are departing! Good luck! (*Drinks.*) This champagne is not the real stuff, I can assure you.

LOPAKHIN: Eight rubles a bottle. (*Pause.*) It's devilish cold in here.

YASHA: They didn't light the stoves today; it doesn't matter, since we're leaving. (*Laughs.*)

LOPAKHIN: Why are you laughing?

YASHA: Because I'm pleased.

LOPAKHIN: It's October, yet it's sunny and still outside, like summer. Good for building. (*Looks at his watch, then calls through the door.*) Bear in mind, ladies and gentlemen, only forty-six minutes till train time! That means leaving for the station in twenty minutes. Better hurry up!

(*Trofimov enters from outside wearing an overcoat.*)

TROFIMOV: Seems to me it's time to start. The carriages are at the door. What the devil has become of my rubbers? They're lost. (*Calls through the door.*) Anya, my rubbers are not here. I can't find them.

LOPAKHIN: I've got to go to Kharkov. I'm taking the same train you are. I'm going to spend the winter in Kharkov. I've been hanging around here with you, and I'm sick and tired of loafing. I can't live without work, I don't know what to do with my hands; they dangle in some strange way, as if they didn't belong to me.

TROFIMOV: We'll soon be gone, then you can take up your useful labors again.

LOPAKHIN: Here, have a little drink.

TROFIMOV: No, I don't want any.

LOPAKHIN: So you're off for Moscow?

TROFIMOV: Yes, I'll see them into town, and tomorrow I'll go to Moscow.

LOPAKHIN: Yes. . . . Well, I expect the professors haven't been giving any lectures: They're waiting for you to come!

TROFIMOV: That's none of your business.

LOPAKHIN: How many years is it you've been studying at the university?

TROFIMOV: Can't you think of something new? That's stale and flat. (*Looks for his rubbers.*) You know, we'll probably never see each other again, so allow me to give you one piece of advice at parting: Don't wave your arms about! Get out of that habit — of arm-waving. And another thing, building cottages and counting on the summer residents in time becoming independent farmers — that's just another form of arm-waving. Well, when all's said and done, I'm fond of you anyway. You have fine, delicate fingers, like an artist; you have a fine delicate soul.

LOPAKHIN (*embraces him*): Good-bye, my dear fellow. Thank you for everything. Let me give you some money for the journey, if you need it.

TROFIMOV: What for? I don't need it.

LOPAKHIN: But you haven't any!

TROFIMOV: I have. Thank you. I got some money for a translation. Here it is in my pocket. (*Anxiously.*) But where are my rubbers?

VARYA (*from the next room*): Here, take the nasty things! (*Flings a pair of rubbers onto the stage.*)

TROFIMOV: What are you so cross about, Varya? Hm. . . . But these are not my rubbers.

LOPAKHIN: In the spring I sowed three thousand acres of poppies, and now I've made forty thousand rubles clear. And when my poppies were in bloom, what a picture it was! So, I'm telling you, I've made forty thousand, which means I'm offering you a loan because I can afford to. Why turn up your nose? I'm a peasant — I speak bluntly.

TROFIMOV: Your father was a peasant, mine was a pharmacist — which proves absolutely nothing. (*Lopakhin takes out his wallet.*) No, don't — even if you gave me two hundred thousand I wouldn't take it. I'm a free man. And everything that is valued so highly and held so dear by all of you, rich and poor alike, has not the slightest power over me — it's like a feather floating in the air. I can get along without you, I can pass you by, I'm strong and proud. Mankind is advancing toward the highest truth, the highest happiness attainable on earth, and I am in the front ranks!

LOPAKHIN: Will you get there?

TROFIMOV: I'll get there. (*Pause.*) I'll either get there or I'll show others the way to get there.

(*The sound of axes chopping down trees is heard in the distance.*)

LOPAKHIN: Well, good-bye, my dear fellow. It's time to go. We turn up our noses at one another, but life goes on just the same. When I work for a long time without stopping, my mind is easier, and it seems to me that I, too, know why I exist. But how many there are in Russia, brother, who exist nobody knows why. Well, it doesn't matter, that's not what makes the wheels go round. They say Leonid Andreich has taken a position in the bank, six thousand a year. . . . Only, of course, he won't stick it out, he's too lazy. . . .

ANYA (*in the doorway*): Mama asks you not to start cutting down the cherry orchard until she's gone.

TROFIMOV: Yes, really, not to have had the tact . . . (*Goes out through the hall.*)

LOPAKHIN: Right away, right away. . . . Ach, what people. . . . (*Follows Trofimov out.*)

ANYA: Has Firs been taken to the hospital?

YASHA: I told them this morning. They must have taken him.

ANYA (*to Yepikhodov, who is crossing the room*): Semyon Panteleich, please find out if Firs has been taken to the hospital.

YASHA (*offended*): I told Yegor this morning. Why ask a dozen times?

YEPIKHODOV: It is my conclusive opinion that the venerable Firs is beyond repair; it's time he was gathered to his fathers. And I can only envy him. (*Puts a suitcase down on a hatbox and crushes it.*) There you are! Of course! I knew it! (*Goes out.*)

YASHA (*mockingly*): Two-and-twenty Troubles!

VARYA (*through the door*): Has Firs been taken to the hospital?

ANYA: Yes, he has.

VARYA: Then why didn't they take the letter to the doctor?

ANYA: We must send it on after them. . . . (*Goes out.*)

VARYA (*from the adjoining room*): Where is Yasha? Tell him his mother has come to say good-bye to him.

YASHA (*waves his hand*): They really try my patience.

(*Dunyasha has been fussing with the luggage; now that Yasha is alone she goes up to him.*)

DUNYASHA: You might give me one little look, Yasha. You're going away . . . leaving me. . . . (*Cries and throws herself on his neck.*)

YASHA: What's there to cry about? (*Drinks champagne.*) In six days I'll be in Paris again. Tomorrow we'll take the express, off we go, and that's the last you'll see of us. I can hardly believe it. *Vive la France!* This place is not for me, I can't live

here. . . . It can't be helped. I've had enough of this ignorance — I'm fed up with it. (*Drinks champagne.*) What are you crying for? Behave yourself properly, then you won't cry.

DUNYASHA (*looks into a small mirror and powders her face*): Send me a letter from Paris. You know, I loved you, Yasha, how I loved you! I'm such a tender creature, Yasha!

YASHA: Here they come. (*Busies himself with the luggage, humming softly.*)

(*Enter Lyubov Andreyevna, Gayev, Charlotta Ivanovna.*)

GAYEV: We ought to be leaving. There's not much time now. (*Looks at Yasha.*) Who smells of herring?

LYUBOV ANDREYEVNA: In about ten minutes we should be getting into the carriages. (*Glances around the room.*) Good-bye, dear house, old grandfather. Winter will pass, spring will come, and you will no longer be here, they will tear you down. How much these walls have seen! (*Kisses her daughter warmly.*) My treasure, you are radiant, your eyes are sparkling like two diamonds. Are you glad? Very?

ANYA: Very! A new life is beginning, Mama!

GAYEV (*cheerfully*): Yes, indeed, everything is all right now. Before the cherry orchard was sold we were all worried and miserable, but afterward, when the question was finally settled once and for all, everybody calmed down and felt quite cheerful. . . . I'm in a bank now, a financier . . . cue ball into the center . . . and you, Lyuba, say what you like, you look better, no doubt about it.

LYUBOV ANDREYEVNA: Yes. My nerves are better, that's true. (*Her hat and coat are handed to her.*) I sleep well. Carry out my things, Yasha, it's time. (*To Anya.*) My little girl, we shall see each other soon. . . . I shall go to Paris and live there on the money your great-aunt sent to buy the estate — long live Auntie! — but that money won't last long.

ANYA: You'll come back soon, Mama, soon . . . won't you? I'll study hard and pass my high school examinations, and then I can work and help you. We'll read all sorts of books together, Mama. . . . Won't we? (*Kisses her mother's hand.*) We'll read in the autumn evenings, we'll read lots of books, and a new and wonderful world will open up before us. . . . (*Dreaming.*) Mama, come back. . . .

LYUBOV ANDREYEVNA: I'll come, my precious. (*Embraces her.*)

(*Enter Lopakhin, Charlotta Ivanovna is softly humming a song.*)

GAYEV: Happy Charlotta: She's singing!

CHARLOTTA (*picks up a bundle and holds it like a baby in swaddling clothes*): Bye, baby, bye. . . . (*A baby's crying is heard, "Wah! Wah!"*) Be quiet, my darling, my dear little boy. (*"Wah! Wah!"*) I'm so sorry for you! (*Throws the bundle down.*) You will find me a position, won't you? I can't go on like this.

LOPAKHIN: We'll find something, Charlotta Ivanovna, don't worry.

GAYEV: Everyone is leaving us, Varya's going away . . . all of a sudden nobody needs us.

CHARLOTTA: I have nowhere to go in town. I must go away. (*Hums.*) It doesn't matter . . .

(*Enter Pishchik.*)

LOPAKHIN: Nature's wonder!

PISHCHIK (*panting*): Ugh! Let me catch my breath. . . . I'm exhausted. . . . My esteemed friends. . . . Give me some water. . . .

GAYEV: After money, I suppose? Excuse me, I'm fleeing from temptation. . . . (*Goes out.*)

PISHCHIK: It's a long time since I've been to see you . . . fairest lady. . . . (*To Lopakhin*) So you're here. . . . Glad to see you, you intellectual giant. . . . Here . . . take it . . . four hundred rubles . . . I still owe you eight hundred and forty . . .

LOPAKHIN (*shrugs his shoulders in bewilderment*): I must be dreaming. . . . Where did you get it?

PISHCHIK: Wait . . . I'm hot. . . . A most extraordinary event. Some Englishmen came to my place and discovered some kind of white clay on my land. (*To Lyubov Andreyevna*) And four hundred for you . . . fairest, most wonderful lady. . . . (*Hands her the money.*) The rest later. (*Takes a drink of water.*) Just now a young man in the train was saying that a certain . . . great philosopher recommends jumping off roofs. . . . "Jump!" he says, and therein lies the whole problem. (*In amazement.*) Think of that, now! . . . Water!

LOPAKHIN: Who were those Englishmen?

PISHCHIK: I leased them the tract of land with the clay on it for twenty-four years. . . . And now, excuse me, I have no time . . . I must be trotting along . . . I'm going to Znoikov's . . . to Kardamanov's . . . I owe everybody. (*Drinks.*) Keep well . . . I'll drop in on Thursday . . .

LYUBOV ANDREYEVNA: We're just moving into town, and tomorrow I go abroad . . .

PISHCHIK: What? (*Alarmed.*) Why into town? That's why I see the furniture . . . suitcases. . . . Well, never mind. . . . (*Through tears.*) Never mind. . . . Men of the greatest intellect, those Englishmen. . . . Never mind. . . . Be happy . . . God will help you. . . . Never mind. . . . Everything in this world comes to an end. . . . (*Kisses Lyubov Andreyevna's hand.*)

And should the news reach you that my end has come, just remember this old horse, and say: "There once lived a certain Semyonov-Pishchik, God rest his soul." . . . Splendid weather. . . . Yes. . . . (*Goes out greatly disconcerted, but immediately returns and speaks from the doorway.*) Dashenka sends her regards. (*Goes out.*)

LYUBOV ANDREYEVNA: Now we can go. I am leaving with two things on my mind. First — that Firs is sick. (*Looks at her watch.*) We still have about five minutes. . . .

ANYA: Mama, Firs has already been taken to the hospital. Yasha sent him there this morning.

LYUBOV ANDREYEVNA: My second concern is Varya. She's used to getting up early and working, and now, with no work to do, she's like a fish out of water. She's grown pale and thin, and cries all the time, poor girl. . . . (*Pauses.*) You know very well, Yermolai Alekseich, that I dreamed of marrying her to you, and everything pointed to your getting married. (*Whispers to Anya, who nods to Charlotta, and they both go out.*) She loves you, you are fond of her, and I don't know — I don't know why it is you seem to avoid each other. I can't understand it!

LOPAKHIN: To tell you the truth, I don't understand it myself. The whole thing is strange, somehow. . . . If there's still time, I'm ready right now. . . . Let's finish it up — and *basta,*° but without you I feel I'll never be able to propose to her.

LYUBOV ANDREYEVNA: Splendid! After all, it only takes a minute. I'll call her in at once. . . .

LOPAKHIN: And we even have the champagne. (*Looks at the glasses.*) Empty! Somebody's already drunk it. (*Yasha coughs.*) That's what you call lapping it up.

LYUBOV ANDREYEVNA (*animatedly*): Splendid! We'll leave you. . . . Yasha, *allez!*° I'll call her. . . . (*At the door.*) Varya, leave everything and come here. Come! (*Goes out with Yasha.*)

LOPAKHIN (*looking at his watch*): Yes. . . . (*Pause.*)

(*Behind the door there is smothered laughter and whispering; finally Varya enters.*)

VARYA (*looking over the luggage for a long time*): Strange, I can't seem to find it . . .

LOPAKHIN: What are you looking for?

VARYA: I packed it myself, and I can't remember . . . (*Pause.*)

LOPAKHIN: Where are you going now, Varya Mikhailovna?

VARYA: I? To the Ragulins'. . . . I've agreed to go

basta: Italian for "enough."
allez: French for "go."

there to look after the house . . . as a sort of housekeeper.

LOPAKHIN: At Yashnevo? That would be about seventy versts from here. (*Pause.*) Well, life in this house has come to an end. . . .

VARYA (*examining the luggage*): Where can it be? . . . Perhaps I put it in the trunk. . . . Yes, life in this house has come to an end . . . there'll be no more . . .

LOPAKHIN: And I'm off for Kharkov . . . by the next train. I have a lot to do. I'm leaving Yepikhodov here . . . I've taken him on.

VARYA: Really!

LOPAKHIN: Last year at this time it was already snowing, if you remember, but now it's still and sunny. It's cold though. . . . About three degrees of frost.

VARYA: I haven't looked. (*Pause.*) And besides, our thermometer's broken. (*Pause.*)

(*A voice from the yard calls: "Yermolai Alekseich!"*)

LOPAKHIN (*as if he had been waiting for a long time for the call*): Coming! (*Goes out quickly.*)

(*Varya sits on the floor, lays her head on a bundle of clothes, and quietly sobs. The door opens and Lyubov Andreyevna enters cautiously.*)

LYUBOV ANDREYEVNA: Well? (*Pause.*) We must be going.

VARYA (*no longer crying, dries her eyes*): Yes, it's time, Mama dear. I can get to the Ragulins' today, if only we don't miss the train.

LYUBOV ANDREYEVNA (*in the doorway*): Anya, put your things on!

(*Enter Anya, then Gayev and Charlotta Ivanovna. Gayev wears a warm overcoat with a hood. The servants and coachmen come in. Yepikhodov bustles about the luggage.*)

LYUBOV ANDREYEVNA: Now we can be on our way.

ANYA (*joyfully*): On our way!

GAYEV: My friends, my dear, cherished friends! Leaving this house forever, can I pass over in silence, can I refrain from giving utterance, as we say farewell, to those feelings that now fill my whole being —

ANYA (*imploringly*): Uncle!

VARYA: Uncle dear, don't!

GAYEV (*forlornly*): Double the rail off the white to center table . . . yellow into the side pocket. . . . I'll be quiet. . . .

(*Enter Trofimov, then Lopakhin.*)

TROFIMOV: Well, ladies and gentlemen, it's time to go!

LOPAKHIN: Yepikhodov, my coat!

LYUBOV ANDREYEVNA: I'll sit here just one more minute. It's as though I had never before seen what the walls of this house were like, what the ceilings were like, and now I look at them hungrily, with such tender love . . .

GAYEV: I remember when I was six years old, sitting on this windowsill on Whitsunday, watching my father going to church . . .

LYUBOV ANDREYEVNA: Have they taken all the things?

LOPAKHIN: Everything, I think. (*Puts on his overcoat.*) Yepikhodov, see that everything is in order.

YEPIKHODOV (*in a hoarse voice*): Rest assured, Yermolai Alekseich!

LOPAKHIN: What's the matter with your voice?

YEPIKHODOV: Just drank some water . . . must have swallowed something.

YASHA (*contemptuously*): What ignorance!

LYUBOV ANDREYEVNA: When we go — there won't be a soul left here. . . .

LOPAKHIN: Till spring.

VARYA (*pulls an umbrella out of a bundle as though she were going to hit someone; Lopakhin pretends to be frightened*): Why are you — I never thought of such a thing!

TROFIMOV: Ladies and gentlemen, let's get into the carriages — it's time now! The train will soon be in!

VARYA: Petya, there they are — your rubbers, by the suitcase. (*Tearfully.*) And what dirty old things they are!

TROFIMOV (*putting on his rubbers*): Let's go, ladies and gentlemen!

GAYEV (*extremely upset, afraid of bursting into tears*): The train . . . the station. . . . Cross table to the center, double the rail . . . on the white into the corner.

LYUBOV ANDREYEVNA: Let us go!

GAYEV: Are we all here? No one in there? (*Locks the side door on the left.*) There are some things stored in there, we must lock up. Let's go!

ANYA: Good-bye, house! Good-bye, old life!

TROFIMOV: Hail to the new life! (*Goes out with Anya.*)

(*Varya looks around the room and slowly goes out. Yasha and Charlotta with her dog go out.*)

LOPAKHIN: And so, till spring. Come along, my friends. . . . Till we meet! (*Goes out.*)

(*Lyubov Andreyevna and Gayev are left alone. As though they had been waiting for this, they fall onto each other's necks and break into quiet, restrained sobs, afraid of being heard.*)

GAYEV (*in despair*): My sister, my sister. . . .

LYUBOV ANDREYEVNA: Oh, my dear, sweet, lovely orchard! . . . My life, my youth, my happiness, good-bye! . . . Good-bye!

ANYA'S VOICE (*gaily calling*): Mama!

TROFIMOV'S VOICE (*gay and excited*): Aa-oo!

LYUBOV ANDREYEVNA: One last look at these walls, these windows. . . . Mother loved to walk about in this room. . . .

GAYEV: My sister, my sister!

ANYA'S VOICE: Mama!

TROFIMOV'S VOICE: Aa-oo!

LYUBOV ANDREYEVNA: We're coming! (*They go out.*)

(*The stage is empty. There is the sound of doors being locked, then of the carriages driving away. It grows quiet. In the stillness there is the dull thud of an ax on a tree, a forlorn, melancholy sound. Footsteps are heard. From the door on the right Firs appears. He is dressed as always in a jacket and white waistcoat, and wears slippers. He is ill.*)

FIRS (*goes to the door and tries the handle*): Locked. They have gone. . . . (*Sits down on the sofa.*) They've forgotten me. . . . Never mind. . . . I'll sit here awhile. . . . I expect Leonid Andreich hasn't put on his fur coat and has gone off in his overcoat. (*Sighs anxiously.*) And I didn't see to it. . . . When they're young, they're green! (*Mumbles something which cannot be understood.*) I'll lie down awhile. . . . There's no strength left in you, nothing's left, nothing. . . . Ach, you . . . addlepate! (*Lies motionless.*)

(*A distant sound is heard that seems to come from the sky, the sound of a snapped string mournfully dying away. A stillness falls, and nothing is heard but the thud of the ax on a tree far away in the orchard.*)

COMMENTARIES

Anton Chekhov (1860–1904)
FROM CHEKHOV'S LETTERS

TRANSLATED BY MICHAEL HENRY HEIM WITH SIMON KARLINSKY

Chekhov, like Ibsen, was an inveterate letter writer. In letters to family members and colleagues, he spoke quite frankly about his hopes, expectations, and difficulties regarding his work. Chekhov's letters concerning his purpose as an artist and his play The Cherry Orchard *give us some insight into the anxieties and hopes that Chekhov had for his work. His awareness of the difficulties he faced in his writing helps us understand how his plays developed into complex and demanding works.*

October 4, 1888

The people I fear are those who look for tendentiousness between the lines and are determined to see me as either liberal or conservative. I am neither liberal, nor conservative, nor gradualist, nor monk, nor indifferentist. I should like to be a free artist and nothing else. That is why I cultivate no particular predilection for policemen, butchers, scientists, writers, or the younger generation. I look upon tags and labels as prejudices. My holy of holies is the human body, health, intelligence, talent, inspiration, love and the most absolute freedom imaginable, freedom from violence and lies.

November 25, 1892

Keep in mind that the writers we call eternal or simply good, the writers who intoxicate us, have one highly important trait in common: They are moving towards something definite and beckon you to follow, and you feel with your entire being, not only with your mind, that they have a certain goal, like the ghost of Hamlet's father, which had a motive for coming and stirring Hamlet's imagination. Depending on their caliber, some have immediate goals — the abolition of serfdom, the liberation of one's country, politics, beauty, or simply vodka . . . — while the goals of others are more remote — God, life after death, the happiness of mankind, etc. The best of them are realistic and describe life as it is, but because each line is saturated with the consciousness of its goal, you feel life as it should be in addition to life as it is, and you are captivated by it. But what about us? Us! We describe life as it is and stop dead right there. We wouldn't lift a hoof if you lit into us with a whip. We have neither immediate nor remote goals, and there is an emptiness in our souls. We have no politics, we don't believe in revolution, there is no God, we're not afraid of ghosts, and I personally am not even afraid of death or blindness. If you want nothing, hope for nothing, and fear nothing, you cannot be an artist.

To K. S. Stanislavsky°
Yalta. Oct. 30, 1903

When I was writing Lopakhin, I thought of it as a part for you. If for any reason you don't care for it, take the part of Gayev. Lopakhin is a merchant, of course, but he is a very decent person in every sense. He must behave with perfect decorum, like an educated man, with no petty ways or tricks of any sort, and it seemed to me this part, the central one of the play, would come out brilliantly in your hands. . . . In choosing an actor for the part you must remember that Varya, a serious and religious girl, is in love with Lopakhin; she wouldn't be in love with a mere moneygrubber. . . .

To Vl. I. Nemirovich-Danchenko°
Yalta. Nov. 2, 1903

. . . Pishchik is a Russian, an old man, worn out by the gout, age, and satiety; stout, dressed in a sleeveless undercoat (à la Simov [an actor in the Moscow Art Theatre], boots without heels. Lopakhin — a white waistcoat, yellow shoes; when walking, swings his arms, a broad stride, thinks deeply while walking, walks as if on a straight line. Hair not short, and therefore often throws back his head; while in thought he passes his hand through his beard, combing it from the back forward, i.e., from the neck toward the mouth. Trofimov, I think, is clear. Varya — black dress, wide belt.

Three years I spent writing "The Cherry Orchard," and for three years I have been telling you that it is necessary to invite an actress for the role of

K. S. Stanislavsky: Konstantin Stanislavsky (1863–1938), director with the Moscow Art Theatre, which produced most of Chekhov's plays.
Vl. I. Nemirovich-Danchenko: Vladimir Ivanovich Nemirovich-Danchenko, novelist and codirector of the Moscow Art Theatre.

Lyubov Andreyevna. And now you see you are trying to solve a puzzle that won't work out.

To K. S. Alekseyev (Stanislavsky)
Yalta. Nov. 5, 1903

The house in the play is two-storied, a large one. But in the third act does it not speak of a stairway leading down? Nevertheless, this third act worries me. . . . N. has it that the third act takes place in "some kind of hotel"; . . . evidently I made an error in the play. The action does not pass in "some kind of hotel," but in a *drawing-room*. If I mention a hotel in the play, which I cannot now doubt, after Vl. Iv.'s [Nemirovich-Danchenko] letter, please telegraph me. We must correct it; we cannot issue it thus, with grave errors distorting its meaning.

The house must be large, solid; wooden (like Aksakov's, which, I think, S. T. Morozov has seen) or stone, it is all the same. It is very old and imposing; country residents do not take such houses; such houses are usually wrecked and the material employed for the construction of a country house. The furniture is ancient, stylish, solid; ruin and debt have not affected the surroundings.

When they buy such a house, they reason thus: it is cheaper and easier to build a new and smaller one than to repair this old one.

Your shepherd played well. That was most essential.

Maxim Gorky (1868–1936)
FROM *RECOLLECTIONS*

Alexei Maximovitch Pyeshkov changed his name to Maxim Gorky, which in Russian means Maxim the Bitter. His childhood and early years gave him great reason for bitterness, because he was raised by a brutal grandfather who regularly beat Maxim and his mother. Once, when he was eight, he attacked his grandfather with a bread knife for beating his frail and sick mother. Gorky spent many years tramping through Russia and became a writer of the common people. He was introduced to the Moscow Art Theatre by Chekhov, and his first play, The Lower Depths *(1902), starred Chekhov's wife, Olga Knipper. It was a mercilessly realistic portrait of the homeless, impoverished castaways of Russian life. It established Gorky as a major dramatist, and after the Russian revolution he became the most revered of Soviet writers.*

Reading Anton Chekhov's stories, one feels oneself in a melancholy day of late autumn, when the air is transparent and the outline of naked trees, narrow houses, grayish people, is sharp. Everything is strange, lonely, motionless, helpless. The horizon, blue and empty, melts into the pale sky, and its breath is terribly cold upon the earth, which is covered with frozen mud. The author's mind, like the autumn sun, shows up in hard outline the monotonous roads, the crooked streets, the little squalid houses in which tiny, miserable people are stifled by boredom and laziness and fill the houses with an unintelligible, drowsy bustle. . . .

Here is the lachrymose Ranevskaya and the other owners of *The Cherry Orchard*, egotistical like children, with the flabbiness of senility. They missed the right moment for dying; they whine, seeing nothing of what is going on around them, understanding nothing, parasites without the power of again taking root in life. The wretched little student, Trofimov, speaks eloquently of the necessity of working — and does nothing but amuse himself, out of sheer boredom, with stupid mockery of Varya, who works ceaselessly for the good of idlers. . . .

There passes before one a long file of men and women, slaves of their love, of their stupidity and idleness, of their greed for the good things of life; there walk the slaves of the dark fear of life; they straggle anxiously along, filling life with incoherent words about the future, feeling that in the present there is no place for them.

At moments out of the gray mass of them one hears the sound of a shot: Ivanov [in *Ivanov*] or Treplev [in *The Seagull*] has guessed what he ought to do and has died.

Many of them have nice dreams of how pleasant life will be in three hundred years, but it occurs to none of them to ask themselves who will make life pleasant if we only dream.

In front of that dreary, gray crowd of helpless people there passed a great, wise, and observant man; he looked at all these dreary inhabitants of his country, and, with a sad smile, with a tone of gentle but deep reproach, with anguish in his face and in his heart, in a beautiful and sincere voice, he said to them:

"You live badly, my friends. It is shameful to live like that."

Virginia Woolf (1882–1941)
ON *THE CHERRY ORCHARD*

Virginia Woolf was one of the most important experimental writers of fiction in the first half of the twentieth century. Her best-known works include Mrs. Dalloway *(1925),* To the Lighthouse *(1927),* Orlando *(1928),* A Room of One's Own *(1930), and* The Waves *(1931). But in addition to these landmark works, she wrote a huge number of essays and commentaries, not to mention letters that have now been gathered into five large volumes. Her insight into literature is always keen and original. Her approach, for instance, to a 1920 production of* The Cherry Orchard *is through language. She is naturally sensitive to careful use of language, and it is therefore important for her to observe that out of the apparently disjointed use of sentences comes extraordinary drama. She ends her commentary with an interesting comparison that delves into the realm of music — or, more properly, into an imaginative realm in which the theatergoers themselves are musical instruments.*

It is, as a rule, when a critic does not wish to commit himself or to trouble himself, that he refers to atmosphere. And, given time, something might be said in greater detail of the causes which produced this atmosphere — the strange dislocated sentences, each so erratic and yet cutting out the shape so firmly, of the realism, of the humor, of the artistic unity. But let the word atmosphere be taken literally to mean that Chekhov has contrived to shed over us a luminous vapor in which life appears as it is, without veils, transparent and visible to the depths. Long before the play was over, we seemed to have sunk below the surface of things and to be feeling our way among submerged but recognizable emotions. "I have no proper passport. I don't know how old I am; I always feel I am still young" — how the words go sounding on in one's mind — how the whole play resounds with such sentences, which reverberate, melt into each other, and pass far away out beyond everything! In short, if it is permissible to use such vague language, I do not know how better to describe the sensation at the end of *The Cherry Orchard,* than by saying that it sends one into the street feeling like a piano played upon at last, not in the middle only but all over the keyboard and with the lid left open so that the sound goes on.

Peter Brook (b. 1925)
ON CHEKHOV

Peter Brook has established himself as one of the most distinguished modern directors. He was educated at Oxford University and has been a director of the Royal Shakespeare Company in England. In 1987 he directed The Cherry Orchard *at the Brooklyn Academy of Music. Some of his thoughts as he prepared to direct the play are presented here, showing his awareness of Chekhov's "film sense" in a play that was written just as film was emerging as a popular form. He is also aware of Chekhov's personal vision of death and sees it expressed in the circumstances of the play.*

Chekhov always looked for what's natural; he wanted performances and productions to be as limpid as life itself. Chekhov's writing is extremely concentrated, employing a minimum of words; in a way, it is similar to Pinter or Beckett. As with them, it is construction that counts, rhythm, the purely theatrical poetry that comes not from beautiful words but from the right word at the right moment. In the theater, someone can say "yes" in such a way that the "yes" is no longer ordinary — it can become a beautiful word, because it is the perfect expression of what cannot be expressed in any other way. With Chekhov, periods, commas, points of suspension are all of a fundamental importance, as fundamental as the "pauses" precisely indicated by Beckett. If one fails to observe them, one loses the rhythm and tensions of the play. In Chekhov's work, the punctuation represents a series of coded messages which record characters' relationships and emotions, the moments at which ideas come together or follow their own course. The punctuation enables us to grasp what the words conceal.

Chekhov is like a perfect filmmaker. Instead of cutting from one image to another — perhaps from one place to another — he switches from one emotion to another just before it gets too heavy. At the precise moment when the spectator risks becoming too involved in a character, an unexpected situation cuts across: Nothing is stable. Chekhov portrays individuals and a society in a state of perpetual change, he is the dramatist of life's movement, simultaneously smiling and serious, amusing and bitter — completely free from the "music," the Slav "nostalgia" that Paris nightclubs still preserve. He often stated that his plays were comedies — this was the central issue of his conflict with Stanislavsky.

But it's wrong to conclude that *The Cherry Orchard* should be performed as a vaudeville. Chekhov is an infinitely detailed observer of the human comedy. As a doctor, he knew the meaning of certain kinds of behavior, how to discern what was essential, to expose what he diagnosed. Although he shows tenderness and an attentive sympathy, he never sentimentalizes. One doesn't imagine a doctor shedding tears over the illnesses of his patients. He learns how to balance compassion with distance.

In Chekhov's work, death is omnipresent — he knew it well — but there is nothing negative or unsavory in its presence. The awareness of death is balanced with a desire to live. His characters possess a sense of the present moment, and the need to taste it fully. As in great tragedies, one finds a harmony between life and death.

Chekhov died young, having traveled, written, and loved enormously, having taken part in the events of his day, in great schemes of social reform. He died shortly after asking for some champagne, and his coffin was transported in a wagon bearing the inscription "Fresh Oysters." His awareness of death, and of the precious moments that could be lived, endow his work with a sense of the relative: in other words, a viewpoint from which the tragic is always a bit absurd.

In Chekhov's work, each character has its own existence: not one of them resembles another, particularly in *The Cherry Orchard,* which presents a microcosm of the political tendencies of the time. There are those who believe in social transformations, others attached to a disappearing past. None of them can achieve satisfaction or plenitude, and seen from outside, their existences might well appear empty, senseless. But they all burn with intense desires. They are not disillusioned, quite the contrary: In their own ways, they are all searching for a better quality of life, emotionally and socially. Their drama is that society — the outside world — blocks their energy. The complexity of their behavior is not indicated in the words, it emerges from the mosaic construction of an infinite number of details. What is essential is to see that these are not plays about lethargic people. They are hypervital people in a lethargic world, forced to dramatize the minutest happening out of a passionate desire to live. They have not given up.

Bernard Shaw

The Irish playwright Bernard Shaw (1856–1950) was astonishing not only for the range of his writing but for the length and vigor of his life. He was a public figure for most of his days, with an especially keen ability to catch public attention and make his presence felt. His early work was devoted to criticism in newspapers, then to a series of fairly successful novels. He began writing plays in his late thirties; once he began, he realized that he had discovered his vocation, and he continued to write more than fifty. Some of them, such as *Arms and the Man* (1894), *Candida* (1897), *Mrs. Warren's Profession* (1898), *Man and Superman* (1901–1903), *Pygmalion* (1913), *Heartbreak House* (1919), *Back to Methuselah* (1921), and *St. Joan* (1923), are among the most performed plays by any English language writer of his time.

Shaw's gift of analysis and philosophical reflection created in his works a new kind of drama that has sometimes been named for him — Shavian. The term implies a deep interest in ideas rather than character and a propensity for elaborate discourse between characters who represent different points of view. Shaw assumed that drama should amuse and entertain, but of much greater importance was his didactic motive. Drama should teach a lesson about something of great moral importance.

This is not to say that Shaw was unable to be entertaining. Some of his comedies, still played today, are light, bright, and witty. *You Never Can Tell* (1898), a comedy about male-female relationships whose main character is a dentist, and *Pygmalion* (1913), a comedy in which a man teaches a cockney girl how to speak with an upper-class accent and then falls in love with her, are both funny plays. *Pygmalion* was redone as a musical, *My Fair Lady*, and has been Shaw's most financially successful play.

However, Shaw was basically a philosophical writer. His plays can usually be seen as having a specific theme on which the characters constantly discourse. Whether it is on the relation of England to Ireland, on the state of the medical profession, on genetics and propagation, or on poverty, Shaw always focused on an issue. His concern for issues was so great that he once commented that Shakespeare's shortcoming was that his plays have no message.

Shaw frequently wrote elaborate and lengthy prefaces to his published plays. The Preface to *Major Barbara*, included as a commentary, is a representative exploration of the issues of morality and poverty in the play. In his other prefaces, Shaw takes time to explain — and fully explore — the messages of his plays. He discusses the questions of genetic planning and the improvement of the race in his Preface to *Man and Superman*; in the Preface to *Candida* he discusses the relationship of pity to love.

Shaw's lifelong socialism affected his work and his thinking. The Fabian Society, a political group to which he belonged, was the socialist conscience of British politics, and he himself was a socialist politician for a short period. Consequently, it is not uncommon to see political concerns expressed and debated in his plays.

His political ideas were shaped by his concern for economics as a discipline, beginning in 1882. In 1884 he joined the Fabian Society, established a year earlier as a group to study and promote socialism, and remained active until 1911. Fabianism, unlike Marxism or communism, believed that society need not be destroyed by revolution but could become an instrument of socialist reform. For this reason Fabianism was known as evolutionary socialism. *Fabian Essays* (1889), which Shaw edited, were used by study groups that sprouted up throughout England to spread Fabian socialist ideas through politics, religion, and society. The result of the movement was the organization of a new political party, the Labor Party (1893), which still exists. The socialist government of England in the 1960s and 1970s was a direct outgrowth of Fabian theories.

While Shaw studied economics he grew to believe that all social values were built on an economic base. He developed this idea in his Fabian essays and maintained it throughout his plays. He also maintained a presence as a critic of theater and accepted Ibsen as a major playwright when most London critics found his work unacceptable. Shaw's *Quintessence of Ibsenism* (1891; revised after Ibsen's death in 1913) is still a useful commentary on that playwright's work.

MAJOR BARBARA

Major Barbara (1905) centers on the question of poverty, which, as Shaw says in his Preface to the play, is a modern kind of crime. The play is not realistic in the way that Ibsen's or Strindberg's plays are, and yet it maintains a sense of naturalness, a suitably convincing surface of realism that works well enough within the limits of the drama.

It soon becomes clear that the extreme positions of Major Barbara of the Salvation Army and her father, Andrew Undershaft, the millionaire owner of the largest munitions factories in England, represent two sides of a debate. Andrew Undershaft wins easily, perhaps too easily. The Salvation Army cannot save souls without the cash needed to feed them. The cash comes from two sources: Bodger, the distiller who has provided liquor to most of the impoverished of the area, and Undershaft himself, who in effect buys the Salvation Army by giving it the wherewithal to continue operating.

The conflict is expressed through a series of oppositions. The most effective is the conflict between Major Barbara, the idealist who thinks that the munitions maker is evil, and Undershaft, who takes life as it is, seeing the munitions maker as neither good nor evil, but simply as an instrument of society. The creed of the munitions maker is simple: Sell weapons to anyone who can afford them. The outcome of that creed was illustrated the year before the play was produced, in the Russo-Japanese War, when better-equipped Japanese troops defeated a much larger Russian army.

If we can talk about realists in the play, then we must point to Andrew Undershaft and his constant reminders about what really counts in Europe. He attacks the idealists and reminds people of the harsh economic realities that rule their lives. The man who falls in love with Barbara, the professor of Greek Adolphus Cusins, turns out to be the perfect successor to Andrew Undershaft, who, according to tradition, must retire and pass his business on to a foundling. Adolphus qualifies on a technicality and, after some hard dealing, accepts the offer of the business with a clear understanding of what the power of the office means.

At the same time, he proposes to Major Barbara, who has left the Salvation Army with some of her ideals bruised. But she, too, is much more realistic about life than any mere idealist could be, and when Adolphus chooses to accept the job, Barbara is completely behind him. She can see that more good can be done from a position of power than from a position of weakness.

Major Barbara is more a drama of ideas than it is of character, so the characters are sometimes two-dimensional. But they are always interesting enough to carry the drama forward. Barbara may be enigmatic at the end, but Andrew is clear-thinking, warning Adolphus that he will be driven by the business, not just drive it.

Some of the questions the play raises center on issues of morality. The play opens with the Salvation Army attempting to do good and to maintain a high moral level among the people. But the fact that the Army's money comes from enterprises that, at root, contribute to immoral behavior — the sale of liquor and munitions manufacturing — points to a serious question about Major Barbara's behavior. Shaw asks whether she is realistic and knowledgeable about what she is doing. Is she aware of the contradictions that are already built into the pattern of behavior she has chosen?

Major Barbara learns a great many things in the course of the play, not the least of which is that Andrew Undershaft's money can buy not only things, but people. Somehow she thought that her work went beyond such banal facts. Her leaving the Salvation Army is her acknowledgment that in an indirect way even she had been bought by Undershaft's money.

From Shaw's position, the most important question of the play concerns poverty. It is unforgivable, a crime. Andrew Undershaft does his best to expose the myths of idealism and relate them to the horrors of poverty. In this sense the play has an extremely modern tone. We cannot help but reflect on the extent to which modern prosperity is built on the ideals of Andrew Undershaft more than on the ideals of Major Barbara. Shaw, in his Preface to the play, tells his readers that most of them refuse to look at the truth, that "the greatest of our crimes is poverty, and that our first duty, to which every other consideration should be sacrificed, is not to be poor." Those are very difficult words for an idealist like Major Barbara.

Major Barbara in Performance

Shaw called *Major Barbara* a "discussion," and the first production, in November 1905 in London, pleased the British prime minister and most of the audience. The critic of the London *Times* accused Shaw of not being very convincing as a dramatist, but of being a good thinker. Shaw considered the *Times*'s comment a compliment. Major productions followed in New York in 1915 and again in 1928, with a flapper Barbara. Both productions had splendid casts and received good reviews, although the length of the runs (under one hundred nights) was disappointing. All the early productions were praised for their wit and modernity.

Maurice Evans starred in the 1935 London performance, and Rex Harrison starred in the film version in 1941. The *New York Times* said of the film: "Wendy Hiller plays Barbara with more exaltation and grace, more anguish and eventual triumph than even Mr. Shaw, we feel sure, imagined for her." Charles Laughton, Glynis Johns, and Eli Wallach starred in a successful 1956 production that lasted 232 performances. It would have gone on if Laughton had not had to leave to produce a film. There were numerous undistinguished productions in New York and London in the 1970s. Lloyd Richards directed the 1983 production at the Yale Repertory Theatre. The play is a favorite with college and regional theaters and continues to be performed worldwide.

Bernard Shaw (1856–1950)
MAJOR BARBARA   1905

Characters

ANDREW UNDERSHAFT	RUMMY MITCHENS
LADY BRITOMART	SNOBBY PRICE
STEPHEN UNDERSHAFT	PETER SHIRLEY
BARBARA UNDERSHAFT°	BILL WALKER
SARAH UNDERSHAFT	JENNY HILL
ADOLPHUS CUSINS	MRS. BAINES
CHARLES LOMAX	BILTON
MORRISON	

ACT I

(*It is after dinner in January 1906, in the library in Lady Britomart Undershaft's house in Wilton Crescent. A large and comfortable settee is in the middle of the room, upholstered in dark leather. A person sitting on it (it is vacant at present) would have, on his right, Lady Britomart's writing table, with the lady herself busy at it; a smaller writing table behind him on his left; the door behind him on Lady Britomart's side; and a window with a window seat directly on his left. Near the window is an armchair.*)

(*Lady Britomart is a woman of fifty or thereabouts, well dressed and yet careless of her dress, well bred and quite reckless of her breeding, well mannered and yet appallingly outspoken and indifferent to the opinion of her interlocutors, amiable and yet peremptory, arbitrary, and high-tempered to the last bearable degree, and withal a very typical managing matron of the upper class, treated as a naughty child until she grew into a scolding mother, and finally settling down with plenty of practical ability and worldly experience, limited in the oddest way with domestic and class limitations, conceiving the universe exactly as if it were a large house in Wilton Crescent, though handling her corner of it very effectively on that assumption, and being quite enlightened and liberal as to the books in the library, the pictures on the walls, the music in the portfolios, and the articles in the papers.*)

(*Her son, Stephen, comes in. He is a gravely correct young man under 25, taking himself very seriously,* but still in some awe of his mother, from childish habit and bachelor shyness rather than from any weakness of character.*)

STEPHEN: Whats the matter?

LADY BRITOMART: Presently, Stephen.

(*Stephen submissively walks to the settee and sits down. He takes up a Liberal weekly called* The Speaker.)

LADY BRITOMART: Dont begin to read, Stephen. I shall require all your attention.

STEPHEN: It was only while I was waiting —

LADY BRITOMART: Dont make excuses, Stephen. (*He puts down* The Speaker.) Now! (*She finishes her writing; rises; and comes to the settee.*) I have not kept you waiting very long, I think.

STEPHEN: Not at all, mother.

LADY BRITOMART: Bring me my cushion. (*He takes the cushion from the chair at the desk and arranges it for her as she sits down on the settee.*) Sit down. (*He sits down and fingers his tie nervously.*) Dont fiddle with your tie, Stephen: there is nothing the matter with it.

STEPHEN: I beg your pardon. (*He fiddles with his watch chain instead.*)

LADY BRITOMART: Now are you attending to me, Stephen?

STEPHEN: Of course, mother.

LADY BRITOMART: No: it's not of course. I want something much more than your everyday matter-of-course attention. I am going to speak to you very seriously, Stephen. I wish you would let that chain alone.

STEPHEN (*hastily relinquishing the chain*): Have I done anything to annoy you, mother? If so, it was quite unintentional.

LADY BRITOMART (*astonished*): Nonsense! (*With some remorse.*) My poor boy, did you think I was angry with you?

STEPHEN: What is it, then, mother? You are making me very uneasy.

LADY BRITOMART (*squaring herself at him rather aggressively*): Stephen: may I ask how soon you intend to realize that you are a grown-up man, and that I am only a woman?

Barbara: St. Barbara is the patron saint of gunsmiths.

STEPHEN (*amazed*): Only a —

LADY BRITOMART: Dont repeat my words, please: it is a most aggravating habit. You must learn to face life seriously, Stephen. I really cannot bear the whole burden of our family affairs any longer. You must advise me: you must assume the responsibility.

STEPHEN: I!

LADY BRITOMART: Yes, you, of course. You were 24 last June. Youve been at Harrow and Cambridge. Youve been to India and Japan. You must know a lot of things, now; unless you have wasted your time most scandalously. Well, advise me.

STEPHEN (*much perplexed*): You know I have never interfered in the household —

LADY BRITOMART: No: I should think not. I dont want you to order the dinner.

STEPHEN: I mean in our family affairs.

LADY BRITOMART: Well, you must interfere now for they are getting quite beyond me.

STEPHEN (*troubled*): I have thought sometimes that perhaps I ought; but really, mother, I know so little about them; and what I do know is so painful! it is so impossible to mention some things to you — (*He stops, ashamed.*)

LADY BRITOMART: I suppose you mean your father.

STEPHEN (*almost inaudibly*): Yes.

LADY BRITOMART: My dear: we cant go on all our lives not mentioning him. Of course you were quite right not to open the subject until I asked you to; but you are old enough now to be taken into my confidence, and to help me to deal with him about the girls.

STEPHEN: But the girls are all right. They are engaged.

LADY BRITOMART (*complacently*): Yes: I have made a very good match for Sarah. Charles Lomax will be a millionaire at 35. But that is ten years ahead; and in the meantime his trustees cannot under the terms of his father's will allow him more than £800 a year.

STEPHEN: But the will says also that if he increases his income by his own exertions, they may double the increase.

LADY BRITOMART: Charles Lomax's exertions are much more likely to decrease his income than to increase it. Sarah will have to find at least another £800 a year for the next ten years; and even then they will be as poor as church mice. And what about Barbara? I thought Barbara was going to make the most brilliant career of all of you. And what does she do? Joins the Salvation Army; discharges her maid; lives on a pound a week and walks in one evening with a professor of Greek whom she has picked up in the street, and who pretends to be a Salvationist, and actually plays the big drum for her in public because he has fallen head over ears in love with her.

STEPHEN: I was certainly rather taken aback when I heard they were engaged. Cusins is a very nice fellow, certainly: nobody would ever guess that he was born in Australia; but —

LADY BRITOMART: Oh, Adolphus Cusins will make a very good husband. After all, nobody can say a word against Greek: it stamps a man at once as an educated gentleman. And my family, thank Heaven, is not a pig-headed Tory one. We are Whigs, and believe in liberty. Let snobbish people say what they please: Barbara shall marry, not the man they like, but the man *I* like.

STEPHEN: Of course I was thinking only of his income. However, he is not likely to be extravagant.

LADY BRITOMART: Dont be too sure of that, Stephen. I know your quiet, simple, refined, poetic people like Adolphus: quite content with the best of everything! They cost more than your extravagant people, who are always as mean as they are second rate. No: Barbara will need at least £2000 a year. You see it means two additional households. Besides, my dear, you must marry soon. I dont approve of the present fashion of philandering bachelors and late marriages; and I am trying to arrange something for you.

STEPHEN: It's very good of you, mother; but perhaps I had better arrange that for myself.

LADY BRITOMART: Nonsense! you are much too young to begin matchmaking: you would be taken in by some pretty little nobody. Of course I dont mean that you are not to be consulted: you know that as well as I do. (*Stephen closes his lips and is silent.*) Now dont sulk, Stephen.

STEPHEN: I am not sulking, mother. What has all this got to do with — with — with my father?

LADY BRITOMART: My dear Stephen: where is the money to come from? It is easy enough for you and the other children to live on my income as long as we are in the same house; but I cant keep four families in four separate houses. You know how poor my father is: he has barely seven thousand a year now; and really, if he were not the Earl of Stevenage, he would have to give up society. He can do nothing for us. He says, naturally enough, that it is absurd that he should be asked to provide for the children of a man who is rolling in money. You see, Stephen, your father must be fabulously wealthy, because there is always a war going on somewhere.

STEPHEN: You need not remind me of that, mother. I have hardly ever opened a newspaper in my life without seeing our name in it. The Undershaft torpedo! The Undershaft quick firers! The Undershaft ten inch! the Undershaft disappearing rampart gun!

the Undershaft submarine! and now the Undershaft aerial battleship! At Harrow they called me the Woolwich Infant.° At Cambridge it was the same. A little brute at King's who was always trying to get up revivals, spoilt my Bible — your first birthday present to me — by writing under my name, "Son and heir to Undershaft and Lazarus, Death and Destruction Dealers: address Christendom and Judea." But that was not so bad as the way I was kowtowed to everywhere because my father was making millions by selling cannons.

LADY BRITOMART: It is not only the cannons, but the war loans that Lazarus arranges under cover of giving credit for the cannons. You know, Stephen, it's perfectly scandalous. Those two men, Andrew Undershaft and Lazarus, positively have Europe under their thumbs. That is why your father is able to behave as he does. He is above the law. Do you think Bismarck or Gladstone or Disraeli° could have openly defied every social and moral obligation all their lives as your father has? They simply wouldnt have dared. I asked Gladstone to take it up. I asked *The Times* to take it up. I asked the Lord Chamberlain to take it up. But it was just like asking them to declare war on the Sultan. They wouldnt. They said they couldnt touch him. I believe they were afraid.

STEPHEN: What could they do? He does not actually break the law.

LADY BRITOMART: Not break the law! He is always breaking the law. He broke the law when he was born: his parents were not married.

STEPHEN: Mother! Is that true?

LADY BRITOMART: Of course it's true: that was why we separated.

STEPHEN: He married without letting you know that!

LADY BRITOMART (*rather taken aback by this inference*): Oh no. To do Andrew justice, that was not the sort of thing he did. Besides, you know the Undershaft motto: Unashamed. Everybody knew.

STEPHEN: But you said that was why you separated.

LADY BRITOMART: Yes, because he was not content with being a foundling himself: he wanted to disinherit you for another foundling. That was what I couldnt stand.

STEPHEN (*ashamed*): Do you mean for — for — for —

LADY BRITOMART: Dont stammer, Stephen. Speak distinctly.

Woolwich Infant: A term used for a class of heavy guns.
Bismarck or Gladstone or Disraeli: Otto von Bismarck (1815–98) was a powerful and influential German statesman; William Gladstone (1809–98) was four-time British prime minister; Benjamin Disraeli (1804–81) was also a British statesman and two-time prime minister. All were noted for their social reforms.

STEPHEN: But this is so frightful to me, mother. To have to speak to you about such things!

LADY BRITOMART: It's not pleasant for me, either, especially if you are still so childish that you must make it worse by a display of embarrassment. It is only in the middle classes, Stephen, that people get into a state of dumb helpless horror when they find that there are wicked people in the world. In our class, we have to decide what is to be done with wicked people; and nothing should disturb our self-possession. Now ask your question properly.

STEPHEN: Mother: have you no consideration for me? For Heaven's sake either treat me as a child, as you always do, and tell me nothing at all or tell me everything and let me take it as best I can.

LADY BRITOMART: Treat you as a child! What do you mean? It is most unkind and ungrateful of you to say such a thing. You know I have never treated any of you as children. I have always made you my companions and friends, and allowed you perfect freedom to do and say whatever you like, so long as you liked what I could approve of.

STEPHEN (*desperately*): I daresay we have been the very imperfect children of a very perfect mother; but I do beg you to let me alone for once, and tell me about this horrible business of my father wanting to set me aside for another son.

LADY BRITOMART (*amazed*): Another son! I never said anything of the kind. I never dreamt of such a thing. This is what comes of interrupting me.

STEPHEN: But you said —

LADY BRITOMART (*cutting him short*): Now be a good boy, Stephen, and listen to me patiently. The Undershafts are descended from a foundling in the parish of St. Andrew Undershaft in the city. That was long ago, in the reign of James the First. Well, this foundling was adopted by an armorer and gunmaker. In the course of time the foundling succeeded to the business; and from some notion of gratitude, or some vow or something, he adopted another foundling, and left the business to him. And that foundling did the same. Ever since that, the cannon business has always been left to an adopted foundling named Andrew Undershaft.

STEPHEN: But did they never marry? Were there no legitimate sons?

LADY BRITOMART: Oh yes: they married just as your father did; and they were rich enough to buy land for their own children and leave them well provided for. But they always adopted and trained some foundling to succeed them in the business; and of course they always quarreled with their wives furiously over it. Your father was adopted in that way and he pretends to consider himself bound to keep up the tradition and adopt somebody to leave the business to. Of course I was not going to stand that. There may have been some reason for it when the Undershafts could only marry women in their own class, whose sons were not fit to govern great estates. But there could be no excuse for passing over my son.

STEPHEN (*dubiously*): I am afraid I should make a poor hand of managing a cannon foundry.

LADY BRITOMART: Nonsense! you could easily get a manager and pay him a salary.

STEPHEN: My father evidently had no great opinion of my capacity.

LADY BRITOMART: Stuff, child! you were only a baby: it had nothing to do with your capacity. Andrew did it on principle, just as he did every perverse and wicked thing on principle. When my father remonstrated, Andrew actually told him to his face that history tells us of only two successful institutions: one the Undershaft firm and the other the Roman Empire under the Antonines. That was because the Antonine emperors all adopted their successors. Such rubbish! The Stevenages are as good as the Antonines, I hope: and you are a Stevenage. But that was Andrew all over. There you have the man! Always clever and unanswerable when he was defending nonsense and wickedness: always awkward and sullen when he had to behave sensibly and decently!

STEPHEN: Then it was on my account that your home life was broken up, mother. I am sorry.

LADY BRITOMART: Well, dear, there were other differences. I really cannot bear an immoral man. I am not a Pharisee, I hope; and I should not have minded his merely doing wrong things: we are none of us perfect. But your father didnt exactly do wrong things: he said them and thought them: that was what was so dreadful. He really had a sort of religion of wrongness. Just as one doesnt mind men practicing immorality so long as they own that they are in the wrong by preaching morality; so I couldnt forgive Andrew for preaching immorality while he practiced morality. You would all have grown up without principles, without any knowledge of right and wrong, if he had been in the house. You know, my dear, your father was a very attractive man in some ways. Children did not dislike him; and he took advantage of it to put the wickedest ideas into their heads, and make them quite unmanageable. I did not dislike him myself: very far from it; but nothing can bridge over moral disagreement.

STEPHEN: All this simply bewilders me, mother. People may differ about matters of opinion, or even about religion; but how can they differ about right and wrong? Right is right; and wrong is wrong; and if a man cannot distinguish them properly, he is either a fool or a rascal: thats all.

LADY BRITOMART (*touched*): Thats my own boy (*she pats his cheek*)! Your father never could answer that: he used to laugh and get out of it under cover of some affectionate nonsense. And now that you understand the situation, what do you advise me to do?

STEPHEN: Well, what can you do?

LADY BRITOMART: I must get the money somehow.

STEPHEN: We cannot take money from him. I had rather go and live in some cheap place like Bedford Square or even Hampstead than take a farthing of his money.

LADY BRITOMART: But after all, Stephen, our present income comes from Andrew.

STEPHEN (*shocked*): I never knew that.

LADY BRITOMART: Well, you surely didnt suppose your grandfather had anything to give me. The Stevenages could not do everything for you. We gave you social position. Andrew had to contribute something. He had a very good bargain, I think.

STEPHEN (*bitterly*): We are utterly dependent on him and his cannons, then?

LADY BRITOMART: Certainly not: the money is settled. But he provided it. So you see it is not a question of taking money from him or not: it is simply a question of how much. I dont want any more for myself.

STEPHEN: Nor do I.

LADY BRITOMART: But Sarah does; and Barbara does. That is, Charles Lomax and Adolphus Cusins will cost them more. So I must put my pride in my pocket and ask for it, I suppose. That is your advice, Stephen, is it not?

STEPHEN: No.

LADY BRITOMART (*sharply*): Stephen!

STEPHEN: Of course if you are determined —

LADY BRITOMART: I am not determined: I ask your advice; and I am waiting for it. I will not have all the responsibility thrown on my shoulders.

STEPHEN (*obstinately*): I would die sooner than ask him for another penny.

LADY BRITOMART (*resignedly*): You mean that I must ask him. Very well, Stephen: it shall be as you wish. You will be glad to know that your grandfather concurs. But he thinks I ought to ask Andrew to come here and see the girls. After all, he must have some natural affection for them.

STEPHEN: Ask him here!!!

LADY BRITOMART: Do not repeat my words, Stephen. Where else can I ask him?

STEPHEN: I never expected you to ask him at all.

LADY BRITOMART: Now dont tease, Stephen. Come!

you see that it is necessary that he should pay us a visit, dont you?

STEPHEN (*reluctantly*): I suppose so, if the girls cannot do without his money.

LADY BRITOMART: Thank you, Stephen: I knew you would give me the right advice when it was properly explained to you. I have asked your father to come this evening. (*Stephen bounds from his seat.*) Dont jump, Stephen: it fidgets me.

STEPHEN (*in utter consternation*): Do you mean to say that my father is coming here tonight — that he may be here at any moment?

LADY BRITOMART (*looking at her watch*): I said nine. (*He gasps. She rises.*) Ring the bell, please. (*Stephen goes to the smaller writing table; presses a button on it; and sits at it with his elbows on the table and his head in his hands, outwitted and overwhelmed.*) It is ten minutes to nine yet; and I have to prepare the girls. I asked Charles Lomax and Adolphus to dinner on purpose that they might be here. Andrew had better see them in case he should cherish any delusion as to their being capable of supporting their wives. (*The butler enters: Lady Britomart goes behind the settee to speak to him.*) Morrison: go up to the drawing room and tell everybody to come down here at once. (*Morrison withdraws. Lady Britomart turns to Stephen.*) Now remember, Stephen: I shall need all your countenance and authority. (*He rises and tries to recover some vestige of these attributes.*) Give me a chair, dear. (*He pushes a chair forward from the wall to where she stands, near the smaller writing table. She sits down; and he goes to the armchair, into which he throws himself.*) I dont know how Barbara will take it. Ever since they made her a major in the Salvation Army she has developed a propensity to have her own way and order people about which quite cows me sometimes. It's not ladylike: I'm not sure I dont know where she picked it up. Anyhow, Barbara shant bully me but still it's just as well that your father should be here before she has time to refuse to meet him or make a fuss. Dont look nervous, Stephen: it will only encourage Barbara to make difficulties. *I* am nervous enough, goodness knows; but I dont show it.

(*Sarah and Barbara come in with their respective young men, Charles Lomax and Adolphus Cusins. Sarah is slender, bored, and mundane. Barbara is robuster, jollier, much more energetic. Sarah is fashionably dressed: Barbara is in Salvation Army uniform. Lomax, a young man about town, is like many other young men about town. He is afflicted with a frivolous sense of humor which plunges him at the most inopportune moments into paroxysms of imperfectly suppressed laughter. Cusins is a spectacled student, slight, thin-haired, and sweet-voiced, with a more complex form of Lomax's complaint. His sense of humor is intellectual and subtle and is complicated by an appalling temper. The lifelong struggle of a benevolent temperament and a high conscience against impulses of inhuman ridicule and fierce impatience has set up a chronic strain which has visibly wrecked his constitution. He is a most implacable, determined, tenacious, intolerant person who by mere force of character presents himself as — and indeed actually is — considerate, gentle, explanatory, even mild and apologetic, capable possibly of murder, but not of cruelty or coarseness. By the operation of some instinct which is not merciful enough to blind him with the illusions of love, he is obstinately bent on marrying Barbara. Lomax likes Sarah and thinks it will be rather a lark to marry her. Consequently he has not attempted to resist Lady Britomart's arrangements to that end.*)

(*All four look as if they had been having a good deal of fun in the drawing room. The girls enter first, leaving the swains outside. Sarah comes to the settee. Barbara comes in after her and stops at the door.*)

BARBARA: Are Cholly and Dolly to come in?

LADY BRITOMART (*forcibly*): Barbara: I will not have Charles called Cholly: the vulgarity of it positively makes me ill.

BARBARA: It's all right, mother: Cholly is quite correct nowadays. Are they to come in?

LADY BRITOMART: Yes, if they will behave themselves.

BARBARA (*through the door*): Come in, Dolly; and behave yourself.

(*Barbara comes to her mother's writing table. Cusins enters smiling, and wanders towards Lady Britomart.*)

SARAH (*calling*): Come in, Cholly. (*Lomax enters, controlling his features very imperfectly, and places himself vaguely between Sarah and Barbara.*)

LADY BRITOMART (*peremptorily*): Sit down, all of you. (*They sit. Cusins crosses to the window and seats himself there. Lomax takes a chair. Barbara sits at the writing table and Sarah on the settee.*) I dont in the least know what you are laughing at, Adolphus. I am surprised at you, though I expected nothing better from Charles Lomax.

CUSINS (*in a remarkably gentle voice*): Barbara has been trying to teach me the West Ham Salvation March.

LADY BRITOMART: I see nothing to laugh at in that; nor should you if you are really converted.

CUSINS (*sweetly*): You were not present. It was really funny, I believe.

LOMAX: Ripping.

LADY BRITOMART: Be quiet, Charles. Now listen to me, children. Your father is coming here this evening.

(*General stupefaction. Lomax, Sarah, and Barbara rise: Sarah scared, and Barbara amused and expectant.*)

LOMAX (*remonstrating*): Oh I say!

LADY BRITOMART: You are not called on to say anything, Charles.

SARAH: Are you serious, mother?

LADY BRITOMART: Of course I am serious. It is on your account, Sarah, and also on Charles's. (*Silence, Sarah sits, with a shrug. Charles looks painfully unworthy.*) I hope you are not going to object, Barbara.

BARBARA: I! why should I? My father has a soul to be saved like everybody else. He's quite welcome as far as I am concerned. (*She sits on the table, and softly whistles "Onward, Christian Soldiers."*)

LOMAX (*still remonstrant*): But really, dont you know! Oh I say!

LADY BRITOMART (*frigidly*): What do you wish to convey, Charles?

LOMAX: Well, you must admit that this is a bit thick.

LADY BRITOMART (*turning with ominous suavity to Cusins*): Adolphus: you are a professor of Greek. Can you translate Charles Lomax's remarks into reputable English for us?

CUSINS (*cautiously*): If I may say so, Lady Brit, I think Charles has rather happily expressed what we feel. Homer, speaking of Autolycus, uses the same phrase. πυκινὸν δόμον ἐλθεῖν means a bit thick.

LOMAX (*handsomely*): Not that I mind, you know, if Sarah dont. (*He sits.*)

LADY BRITOMART (*crushingly*): Thank you. Have I your permission, Adolphus, to invite my own husband to my own house?

CUSINS (*gallantly*): You have my unhesitating support in everything you do.

LADY BRITOMART: Tush! Sarah: have you nothing to say?

SARAH: Do you mean that he is coming regularly to live here?

LADY BRITOMART: Certainly not. The spare room is ready for him if he likes to stay for a day or two and see a little more of you; but there are limits.

SARAH: Well, he cant eat us, I suppose. I dont mind.

LOMAX (*chuckling*): I wonder how the old man will take it.

LADY BRITOMART: Much as the old woman will, no doubt, Charles.

LOMAX (*abashed*): I didnt mean — at least —

LADY BRITOMART: You didnt think, Charles. You never do; and the result is, you never mean any-thing. And now please attend to me, children. Your father will be quite a stranger to us.

LOMAX: I suppose he hasnt seen Sarah since she was a little kid.

LADY BRITOMART: Not since she was a little kid, Charles, as you express it with that elegance of diction and refinement of thought that seem never to desert you. Accordingly — er — (*Impatiently.*) Now I have forgotten what I was going to say. That comes of your provoking me to be sarcastic, Charles. Adolphus: will you kindly tell me where I was.

CUSINS (*sweetly*): You were saying that as Mr. Undershaft has not seen his children since they were babies, he will form his opinion of the way you have brought them up from their behavior tonight, and that therefore you wish us all to be particularly careful to conduct ourselves well, especially Charles.

LADY BRITOMART (*with emphatic approval*): Precisely.

LOMAX: Look here, Dolly: Lady Brit didnt say that.

LADY BRITOMART (*vehemently*): I did, Charles. Adolphus's recollection is perfectly correct. It is most important that you should be good; and I do beg you for once not to pair off into opposite corners and giggle and whisper while I am speaking to your father.

BARBARA: All right, mother. We'll do you credit. (*She comes off the table and sits in her chair with ladylike elegance.*)

LADY BRITOMART: Remember, Charles, that Sarah will want to feel proud of you instead of ashamed of you.

LOMAX: Oh I say! theres nothing to be exactly proud of, dont you know.

LADY BRITOMART: Well, try and look as if there was.

(*Morrison, pale and dismayed, breaks into the room in unconcealed disorder.*)

MORRISON: Might I speak a word to you, my lady?

LADY BRITOMART: Nonsense! Show him up.

MORRISON: Yes, my lady. (*He goes.*)

LOMAX: Does Morrison know who it is?

LADY BRITOMART: Of course. Morrison has always been with us.

LOMAX: It must be a regular corker for him, dont you know.

LADY BRITOMART: Is this a moment to get on my nerves, Charles, with your outrageous expressions?

LOMAX: But this is something out of the ordinary, really —

MORRISON (*at the door*): The — er — Mr. Undershaft. (*He retreats in confusion.*)

(*Andrew Undershaft comes in. All rise. Lady Brito-*

mart meets him in the middle of the room behind the settee.)

(*Andrew is, on the surface, a stoutish, easygoing elderly man, with kindly patient manners and an engaging simplicity of character. But he has a watchful, deliberate, waiting, listening face and formidable reserves of power, both bodily and mental, in his capacious chest and long head. His gentleness is partly that of a strong man who has learnt by experience that his natural grip hurts ordinary people unless he handles them very carefully, and partly the mellowness of age and success. He is also a little shy in his present very delicate situation.*)

LADY BRITOMART: Good evening, Andrew.

UNDERSHAFT: How d'ye do, my dear.

LADY BRITOMART: You look a good deal older.

UNDERSHAFT (*apologetically*): I am somewhat older. (*Taking her hand with a touch of courtship.*) Time has stood still with you.

LADY BRITOMART (*throwing away his hand*): Rubbish! This is your family.

UNDERSHAFT (*surprised*): Is it so large? I am sorry to say my memory is failing very badly in some things. (*He offers his hand with paternal kindness to Lomax.*)

LOMAX (*jerkily shaking his hand*): Ahdedoo.

UNDERSHAFT: I can see you are my eldest. I am very glad to meet you again, my boy.

LOMAX (*remonstrating*): No, but look here dont you know — (*Overcome.*) Oh I say!

LADY BRITOMART (*recovering from momentary speechlessness*): Andrew: do you mean to say that you dont remember how many children you have?

UNDERSHAFT: Well, I am afraid I —. They have grown so much — er. Am I making any ridiculous mistake? I may as well confess: I recollect only one son. But so many things have happened since, of course — er —

LADY BRITOMART (*decisively*): Andrew: you are talking nonsense. Of course you have only one son.

UNDERSHAFT: Perhaps you will be good enough to introduce me, my dear.

LADY BRITOMART: That is Charles Lomax, who is engaged to Sarah.

UNDERSHAFT: My dear sir, I beg your pardon.

LOMAX: Notatall. Delighted, I assure you.

LADY BRITOMART: This is Stephen.

UNDERSHAFT (*bowing*): Happy to make your acquaintance, Mr. Stephen. Then (*going to Cusins*) you must be my son. (*Taking Cusins's hands in his.*) How are you, my young friend? (*To Lady Britomart.*) He is very like you, my love.

CUSINS: You flatter me, Mr. Undershaft. My name is Cusins: engaged to Barbara. (*Very explicitly.*) That

is Major Barbara Undershaft, of the Salvation Army. This is Sarah, your second daughter. This is Stephen Undershaft, your son.

UNDERSHAFT: My dear Stephen, I beg your pardon.

STEPHEN: Not at all.

UNDERSHAFT: Mr. Cusins: I am much indebted to you for explaining so precisely. (*Turning to Sarah.*) Barbara, my dear —

SARAH (*prompting him*): Sarah.

UNDERSHAFT: Sarah, of course. (*They shake hands. He goes over to Barbara.*) Barbara — I am right this time, I hope?

BARBARA: Quite right. (*They shake hands.*)

LADY BRITOMART (*resuming command*): Sit down, all of you. Sit down, Andrew. (*She comes forward and sits on the settee. Cusins also brings his chair forward on her left. Barbara and Stephen resume their seats. Lomax gives his chair to Sarah and goes for another.*)

UNDERSHAFT: Thank you, my love.

LOMAX (*conversationally, as he brings a chair forward between the writing table and the settee, and offers it to Undershaft*): Takes you some time to find out exactly where you are, dont it?

UNDERSHAFT (*accepting the chair, but remaining standing*): That is not what embarrasses me, Mr. Lomax. My difficulty is that if I play the part of a father, I shall produce the effect of an intrusive stranger; and if I play the part of a discreet stranger, I may appear a callous father.

LADY BRITOMART: There is no need for you to play any part at all, Andrew. You had much better be sincere and natural.

UNDERSHAFT (*submissively*): Yes, my dear: I daresay that will be best. (*He sits down comfortably.*) Well, here I am. Now what can I do for you all?

LADY BRITOMART: You need not do anything, Andrew. You are one of the family. You can sit with us and enjoy yourself.

(*A painfully conscious pause. Barbara makes a face at Lomax, whose too long suppressed mirth immediately explodes in agonized neighings.*)

LADY BRITOMART (*outraged*): Charles Lomax: if you can behave yourself, behave yourself. If not, leave the room.

LOMAX: I'm awfully sorry, Lady Brit; but really you know, upon my soul! (*He sits on the settee between Lady Britomart and Undershaft, quite overcome.*)

BARBARA: Why dont you laugh if you want to, Cholly? It's good for your inside.

LADY BRITOMART: Barbara: you have had the education of a lady. Please let your father see that; and dont talk like a street girl.

UNDERSHAFT: Never mind me, my dear. As you know, I am not a gentleman; and I was never educated.

LOMAX (*encouragingly*): Nobody'd know it, I assure you. You look all right, you know.

CUSINS: Let me advise you to study Greek, Mr. Undershaft. Greek scholars are privileged men. Few of them know Greek; and none of them know anything else; but their position is unchallengeable. Other languages are the qualifications of waiters and commercial travelers: Greek is to a man of position what the hallmark is to silver.

BARBARA: Dolly: dont be insincere. Cholly: fetch your concertina and play something for us.

LOMAX (*jumps up eagerly, but checks himself to remark doubtfully to Undershaft*): Perhaps that sort of thing isnt in your line, eh?

UNDERSHAFT: I am particularly fond of music.

LOMAX (*delighted*): Are you? Then I'll get it. (*He goes upstairs for the instrument.*)

UNDERSHAFT: Do you play, Barbara?

BARBARA: Only the tambourine. But Cholly's teaching me the concertina.

UNDERSHAFT: Is Cholly also a member of the Salvation Army?

BARBARA: No: he says it's bad form to be a dissenter. But I dont despair of Cholly. I made him come yesterday to a meeting at the dock gates, and take the collection in his hat.

UNDERSHAFT (*looks whimsically at his wife*): !!

LADY BRITOMART: It is not my doing, Andrew. Barbara is old enough to take her own way. She has no father to advise her.

BARBARA: Oh yes she has. There are no orphans in the Salvation Army.

UNDERSHAFT: Your father there has a great many children and plenty of experience, eh?

BARBARA (*looking at him with quick interest and nodding*): Just so. How did you come to understand that? (*Lomax is heard at the door trying the concertina.*)

LADY BRITOMART: Come in, Charles. Play us something at once.

LOMAX: Righto! (*He sits down in his former place, and preludes.*)

UNDERSHAFT: One moment, Mr. Lomax. I am rather interested in the Salvation Army. Its motto might be my own: Blood and Fire.

LOMAX (*shocked*): But not your sort of blood and fire, you know.

UNDERSHAFT: My sort of blood cleanses: my sort of fire purifies.

BARBARA: So do ours. Come down tomorrow to my shelter — the West Ham shelter — and see what we're doing. We're going to march to a great meeting in the Assembly Hall at Mile End. Come and see the shelter and then march with us: it will do you a lot of good. Can you play anything?

UNDERSHAFT: In my youth I earned pennies, and even shillings occasionally, in the streets and in public house parlors by my natural talent for stepdancing. Later on, I became a member of the Undershaft orchestral society, and performed passably on the tenor trombone.

LOMAX (*scandalized — putting down the concertina*): Oh I say!

BARBARA: Many a sinner has played himself into heaven on the trombone, thanks to the Army.

LOMAX (*to Barbara, still rather shocked*): Yes, but what about the cannon business, dont you know? (*To Undershaft.*) Getting into heaven is not exactly in your line, is it?

LADY BRITOMART: Charles!!!

LOMAX: Well; but it stands to reason, dont it? The cannon business may be necessary and all that: we cant get on without cannons; but it isnt right, you know. On the other hand, there may be a certain amount of tosh about the Salvation Army — I belong to the Established Church myself — but still you cant deny that it's religion; and you cant go against religion, can you? At least unless youre downright immoral, dont you know.

UNDERSHAFT: You hardly appreciate my position, Mr. Lomax —

LOMAX (*hastily*): I'm not saying anything against you personally —

UNDERSHAFT: Quite so, quite so. But consider for a moment. Here I am, a profiteer in mutilation and murder. I find myself in a specially amiable humor just now because, this morning, down at the foundry, we blew twenty-seven dummy soldiers into fragments with a gun which formerly destroyed only thirteen.

LOMAX (*leniently*): Well, the more destructive war becomes, the sooner it will be abolished, eh?

UNDERSHAFT: Not at all. The more destructive war becomes the more fascinating we find it. No, Mr. Lomax: I am obliged to you for making the usual excuse for my trade; but I am not ashamed of it. I am not one of those men who keep their morals and their business in watertight compartments. All the spare money my trade rivals spend on hospitals, cathedrals, and other receptacles for conscience money, I devote to experiments and researches in improved methods of destroying life and property. I have always done so; and I always shall. Therefore your Christmas card moralities of peace on earth and goodwill among men are of no use to me. Your Christianity, which enjoins you to resist not evil, and to turn the other cheek, would make me a bankrupt. My morality — my religion —

must have a place for cannons and torpedoes in it.

STEPHEN (*coldly — almost sullenly*): You speak as if there were half a dozen moralities and religions to choose from, instead of one true morality and one true religion.

UNDERSHAFT: For me there is only one true morality; but it might not fit you, as you do not manufacture aerial battleships. There is only one true morality for every man; but every man has not the same true morality.

LOMAX (*overtaxed*): Would you mind saying that again? I didnt quite follow it.

CUSINS: It's quite simple. As Euripides says, one man's meat is another man's poison morally as well as physically.

UNDERSHAFT: Precisely.

LOMAX: Oh, that! Yes, yes, yes. True. True.

STEPHEN: In other words, some men are honest and some are scoundrels.

BARBARA: Bosh! There are no scoundrels.

UNDERSHAFT: Indeed? Are there any good men?

BARBARA: No. Not one. There are neither good men nor scoundrels: there are just children of one Father; and the sooner they stop calling one another names the better. You neednt talk to me: I know them. Ive had scores of them through my hands: scoundrels, criminals, infidels, philanthropists, missionaries, county councillors, all sorts. Theyre all just the same sort of sinner; and theres the same salvation ready for them all.

UNDERSHAFT: May I ask have you ever saved a maker of cannons?

BARBARA: No. Will you let me try?

UNDERSHAFT: Well, I will make a bargain with you. If I go to see you tomorrow in your Salvation Shelter, will you come the day after to see me in my cannon works?

BARBARA: Take care. It may end in your giving up the cannons for the sake of the Salvation Army.

UNDERSHAFT: Are you sure it will not end in your giving up the Salvation Army for the sake of the cannons?

BARBARA: I will take my chance of that.

UNDERSHAFT: And I will take my chance of the other. (*They shake hands on it.*) Where is your shelter?

BARBARA: In West Ham. At the sign of the cross. Ask anybody in Canning Town. Where are your works?

UNDERSHAFT: In Perivale St. Andrews. At the sign of the sword. Ask anybody in Europe.

LOMAX: Hadnt I better play something?

BARBARA: Yes. Give us Onward, Christian Soldiers.

LOMAX: Well, thats rather a strong order to begin with, dont you know. Suppose I sing Thou't passing hence, my brother. It's much the same tune.

BARBARA: It's too melancholy. You get saved, Cholly; and youll pass hence, my brother, without making such a fuss about it.

LADY BRITOMART: Really, Barbara, you go on as if religion were a pleasant subject. Do have some sense of propriety.

UNDERSHAFT: I do not find it an unpleasant subject, my dear. It is the only one that capable people really care for.

LADY BRITOMART (*looking at her watch*): Well, if you are determined to have it, I insist on having it in a proper and respectable way. Charles: ring for prayers.

(*General amazement. Stephen rises in dismay.*)

LOMAX (*rising*): Oh I say!

UNDERSHAFT (*rising*): I am afraid I must be going.

LADY BRITOMART: You cannot go now, Andrew: it would be most improper. Sit down. What will the servants think?

UNDERSHAFT: My dear: I have conscientious scruples. May I suggest a compromise? If Barbara will conduct a little service in the drawing room, with Mr. Lomax as organist, I will attend it willingly. I will even take part, if a trombone can be procured.

LADY BRITOMART: Dont mock, Andrew.

UNDERSHAFT (*shocked — to Barbara*): You dont think I am mocking, my love, I hope.

BARBARA: No, of course not; and it wouldnt matter if you were: half the Army came to their first meeting for a lark. (*Rising.*) Come along. (*She throws her arm round her father and sweeps him out, calling to the others from the threshold.*) Come, Dolly. Come, Cholly.

LADY BRITOMART: I will not be disobeyed by everybody. Adolphus: sit down. (*He does not.*) Charles: you may go. You are not fit for prayers: you cannot keep your countenance.

LOMAX: Oh I say! (*He goes out.*)

LADY BRITOMART (*continuing*): But you, Adolphus, can behave yourself if you choose to. I insist on your staying.

CUSINS: My dear Lady Brit: there are things in the family prayer book that I couldnt bear to hear you say.

LADY BRITOMART: What things, pray?

CUSINS: Well, you would have to say before all the servants that we have done things we ought not to have done, and left undone things we ought to have done, and that there is no health in us. I cannot bear to hear you doing yourself such an injustice, and Barbara such an injustice. As for myself, I flatly deny it: I have done my best. I shouldnt dare to marry Barbara — I couldnt look you in the face — if it were true. So I must go to the drawing room.

LADY BRITOMART (*offended*): Well, go. (*He starts for the door.*) And remember this, Adolphus (*he turns to listen*): I have a very strong suspicion that you went to the Salvation Army to worship Barbara and nothing else. And I quite appreciate the very clever way in which you systematically humbug me. I have found you out. Take care Barbara doesnt. Thats all.

CUSINS (*with unruffled sweetness*): Dont tell on me. (*He steals out.*)

LADY BRITOMART: Sarah: if you want to go, go. Anything's better than to sit there as if you wished you were a thousand miles away.

SARAH (*languidly*): Very well, mamma. (*She goes.*)

(*Lady Britomart, with a sudden flounce, gives way to a little gust of tears.*)

STEPHEN (*going to her*): Mother: whats the matter?

LADY BRITOMART (*swishing away her tears with her handkerchief*): Nothing. Foolishness. You can go with him, too, if you like, and leave me with the servants.

STEPHEN: Oh, you mustnt think that, mother. I — I dont like him.

LADY BRITOMART: The others do. That is the injustice of a woman's lot. A woman has to bring up her children; and that means to restrain them, to deny them things they want, to set them tasks, to punish them when they do wrong, to do all the unpleasant things. And then the father, who has nothing to do but pet them and spoil them, comes in when all her work is done and steals their affection from her.

STEPHEN: He has not stolen our affection from you. It is only curiosity.

LADY BRITOMART (*violently*): I wont be consoled, Stephen. There is nothing the matter with me. (*She rises and goes towards the door.*)

STEPHEN: Where are you going, mother?

LADY BRITOMART: To the drawing room, of course. (*She goes out. Onward, Christian Soldiers, on the concertina, with tambourine accompaniment, is heard when the door opens.*) Are you coming, Stephen?

STEPHEN: No. Certainly not. (*She goes. He sits down on the settee, with compressed lips and an expression of strong dislike.*)

ACT II

(*The yard of the West Ham shelter of the Salvation Army is a cold place on a January morning. The building itself, an old warehouse, is newly whitewashed.*

Its gabled end projects into the yard in the middle, with a door on the ground floor, and another in the loft above it without any balcony or ladder, but with a pulley rigged over it for hoisting sacks. Those who come from this central gable end into the yard have the gateway leading to the street on their left, with a stone horse-trough just beyond it, and, on the right, a penthouse shielding a table from the weather. There are forms at the table; and on them are seated a man and a woman, both much down on their luck, finishing a meal of bread (one thick slice each, with margarine and golden syrup) and diluted milk.)

(*The man, a workman out of employment, is young, agile, a talker, a poser, sharp enough to be capable of anything in reason except honesty or altruistic considerations of any kind. The woman is a commonplace old bundle of poverty and hard-worn humanity. She looks sixty and probably is forty-five. If they were rich people, gloved and muffed and well wrapped up in furs and overcoats, they would be numbed and miserable; for it is a grindingly cold raw January day; and a glance at the background of grimy warehouses and leaden sky visible over the whitewashed walls of the yard would drive any idle rich person straight to the Mediterranean. But these two, being no more troubled with visions of the Mediterranean than of the moon, and being compelled to keep more of their clothes in the pawnshop, and less on their persons, in winter than in summer, are not depressed by the cold: rather are they stung into vivacity, to which their meal has just now given an almost jolly turn. The man takes a pull at his mug, and then gets up and moves about the yard with his hands deep in his pockets, occasionally breaking into a stepdance.*)

THE WOMAN: Feel better arter your meal, sir?

THE MAN: No. Call that a meal! Good enough for you, praps, but wot is it to me, an intelligent workin man.

THE WOMAN: Workin man! Wot are you?

THE MAN: Painter.

THE WOMAN (*skeptically*): Yus, I dessay.

THE MAN: Yus, you dessay! I know. Every loafer that cant do nothink calls isself a painter. Well, I'm a real painter: grainer, finisher, thirty-eight bob a week when I can get it.

THE WOMAN: Then why dont you go and get it?

THE MAN: I'll tell you why. Fust: I'm intelligent — fffff! it's rotten cold here (*He dances a step or two.*) — yes: intelligent beyond the station o life into which it has pleased the capitalists to call me: and they dont like a man that sees through em. Second, an intelligent bein needs a doo share of appiness; so I drink somethink cruel when I get the chawnce. Third, I stand by my class and do as little as I can so's to leave arf the job for me fellow workers. Fourth, I'm fly enough to know wots inside the law and wots outside it; and inside it I do as the capitalists do: pinch wot I can lay me ands on. In a proper state of society I am sober, industrious and honest: in Rome, so to speak, I do as the Romans do. Wots the consequence? When trade is bad — and it's rotten bad just now — and the employers az to sack arf their men, they generally start on me.

THE WOMAN: Whats your name?

THE MAN: Price. Bronterre O'Brien Price. Usually called Snobby Price, for short.

THE WOMAN: Snobby's a carpenter, aint it? You said you was a painter.

PRICE: Not that kind of snob, but the genteel sort. I'm too uppish, owing to my intelligence, and my father being a Chartist° and a reading, thinking man: a stationer, too. I'm none of your common hewers of wood and drawers of water; and dont you forget it. (*He returns to his seat at the table and takes up his mug.*) Wots your name?

THE WOMAN: Rummy Mitchens, sir.

PRICE (*quaffing the remains of his milk to her*): Your elth, Miss Mitchens.

RUMMY (*correcting him*): Missis Mitchens.

PRICE: Wot! Oh Rummy, Rummy! Respectable married woman, Rummy, gittin rescued by the Salvation Army by pretendin to be a bad un. Same old game!

RUMMY: What am I to do? I cant starve. Them Salvation lasses is dear good girls; but the better you are, the worse they likes to think you were before they rescued you. Why shouldnt they av a bit o credit, poor loves? theyre worn to rags by their work. And where would they get the money to rescue us if we was to let on we're no worse than other people? You know what ladies and gentlemen are.

PRICE: Thievin swine! Wish I ad their job, Rummy, all the same. Wot does Rummy stand for? Pet name praps?

RUMMY: Short for Romola.

PRICE: For wot!?

RUMMY: Romola. It was out of a new book. Somebody me mother wanted me to grow up like.

PRICE: We're companions in misfortune, Rummy. Both on us got names that nobody cawnt pronounce. Consequently I'm Snobby and youre Rummy because Bill and Sally wasnt good enough for our parents. Such is life!

Chartist: Member of the British working-class reform movement known as chartism (1838–1848).

RUMMY: Who saved you, Mr. Price? Was it Major Barbara?

PRICE: No: I come here on my own. I'm going to be Bronterre O'Brien Price, the converted painter. I know wot they like. I'll tell em how I blasphemed and gambled and wopped my poor old mother —

RUMMY (*shocked*): Used you to beat your mother?

PRICE: Not likely. She used to beat me. No matter: you come and listen to the converted painter, and youll hear how she was a pious woman that taught me me prayers at er knee, an how I used to come home drunk and drag her out o bed be er snow white airs, an lam into er with the poker.

RUMMY: Thats whats so unfair to us women. Your confessions is just as big lies as ours: you dont tell what you really done no more than us; but you men can tell your lies right out at the meetins and be made much of for it, while the sort o confessions we az to make az to be whispered to one lady at a time. It aint right, spite of all their piety.

PRICE: Right! Do you spose the Army'd be allowed if it went and did right? Not much. It combs our air and makes us good little blokes to be robbed and put upon. But I'll play the game as good as any of em. I'll see somebody struck by lightnin, or hear a voice sayin "Snobby Price: where will you spend eternity?" I'll av a time of it, I tell you.

RUMMY: You wont be let drink, though.

PRICE: I'll take it out in gorspellin, then. I dont want to drink if I can get fun enough any other way.

(*Jenny Hill, a pale, overwrought, pretty Salvation lass of 18, comes in through the yard gate, leading Peter Shirley, a half hardened, half worn-out elderly man, weak with hunger.*)

JENNY (*supporting him*): Come! pluck up. I'll get you something to eat. Youll be all right then.

PRICE (*rising and hurrying officiously to take the old man off Jenny's hands*): Poor old man! Cheer up, brother: youll find rest and peace and appiness ere. Hurry up with the food, miss: e's fair done. (*Jenny hurries into the shelter.*) Ere, buck up, daddy! she's fetchin y'a thick slice of breadn treacle, an a mug o skyblue. (*He seats him at the corner of the table.*)

RUMMY (*gaily*): Keep up your old art! Never say die!

SHIRLEY: I'm not an old man. I'm only forty-six. I'm as good as ever I was. The grey patch come in my hair before I was 30. All it wants is three pennorth o hair dye: am I to be turned on the streets to starve for it? Holy God! I've worked ten to twelve hours a day since I was thirteen, and paid my way all through; and now am I to be thrown into the gutter and my job given to a young man that can do it no better than me because Ive black hair that goes white at the first change?

PRICE (*cheerfully*): No good jawrin about it. Youre ony a jumped-up, jerked-off, orspittle-turned-out incurable of an ole workin man: who cares about you? Eh? Make the thievin swine give you a meal: theyve stole many a one from you. Get a bit o your own back. (*Jenny returns with the usual meal.*) There you are, brother. Awsk a blessin an tuck that into you.

SHIRLEY (*looking at it ravenously but not touching it, and crying like a child*): I never took anything before.

JENNY (*petting him*): Come, come! the Lord sends it to you: he wasn't above taking bread from his friends; and why should you be? Besides, when we find you a job you can pay us for it if you like.

SHIRLEY (*eagerly*): Yes, yes: thats true. I can pay you back: it's only a loan. (*Shivering.*) Oh Lord! oh Lord! (*He turns to the table and attacks the meal ravenously.*)

JENNY: Well, Rummy, are you more comfortable now?

RUMMY: God bless you, lovey! youve fed my body and saved my soul, havent you? (*Jenny, touched, kisses her.*) Sit down and rest a bit: you must be ready to drop.

JENNY: Ive been going hard since morning. But theres more work than we can do. I mustnt stop.

RUMMY: Try a prayer for just two minutes. Youll work all the better after.

JENNY (*her eyes lighting up*): Oh isnt it wonderful how a few minutes prayer revives you! I was quite lightheaded at twelve o'clock, I was so tired; but Major Barbara just sent me to pray for five minutes; and I was able to go on as if I had only just begun. (*To Price.*) Did you have a piece of bread?

PRICE (*with unaction*): Yes, miss; but Ive got the piece that I value more; and thats the peace that passeth hall hannerstennin.

RUMMY (*fervently*): Glory Hallelujah!

(*Bill Walker, a rough customer of about 25, appears at the yard gate and looks malevolently at Jenny.*)

JENNY: That makes me so happy. When you say that, I feel wicked for loitering here. I must get to work again.

(*She is hurrying to the shelter, when the newcomer moves quickly up to the door and intercepts her. His manner is so threatening that she retreats as he comes at her truculently, driving her down the yard.*)

BILL: Aw knaow you. Youre the one that took awy maw girl. Youre the one that set er agen me. Well, I'm gowin to ev er aht. Not that Aw care a carse for er or you: see? Bat Aw'll let er knaow; and Aw'll let you knaow. Aw'm gowing to give her a doin thatll teach er to cat awy from me. Nah in wiv you and tell er to cam aht afore Aw cam in and kick er aht. Tell er Bill Walker wants er. She'll knaow wot thet means; and if she keeps me witin itll be worse. You stop to jawr beck at me: and Aw'll stawt on you: d'ye eah? Theres your wy. In you gow. (*He takes her by the arm and slings her towards the door of the shelter. She falls on her hand and knee. Rummy helps her up again.*)

PRICE (*rising, and venturing irresolutely towards Bill*): Easy there, mate. She aint doin you no arm.

BILL: Oo are you callin mite? (*Standing over him threateningly.*) Youre gowin to stend ap for er, aw yer? Put ap your ends.

RUMMY (*running indignantly to him to scold him*): Oh, you great brute — (*He instantly swings his left hand back against her face. She screams and reels back to the trough, where she sits down, covering her bruised face with her hands and rocking herself and moaning with pain.*)

JENNY (*going to her*): Oh, God forgive you! How could you strike an old woman like that?

BILL (*seizing her by the hair so violently that she also screams, and tearing her away from the old woman*): You Gawd forgimme again an Aw'll Gawd forgive you one on the jawr thetll stop you pryin for a week. (*Holding her and turning fiercely on Price.*) Ev you ennything to sy agen it?

PRICE (*intimidated*): No, matey: she aint anything to do with me.

BILL: Good job for you! Aw'd pat two meals into you and fawt you with one finger arter, you stawved cur. (*To Jenny.*) Nah are you gowin to fetch aht Mog Ebbijem; or em Aw to knock your fice off you and fetch her meself?

JENNY (*writhing in his grasp*): Oh please someone go in and tell Major Barbara — (*She screams again as he wrenches her head down; and Price and Rummy flee into the shelter.*)

BILL: You want to gow in and tell your Mijor of me, do you?

JENNY: Oh please dont drag my hair. Let me go.

BILL: Do you or downt you? (*She stifles a scream.*) Yus or nao?

JENNY: God give me strength —

BILL (*striking her with his fist in the face*): Gow an shaow her thet, and tell her if she wants one lawk it to cam and interfere with me. (*Jenny, crying with pain, goes into the shed. He goes to the form and addresses the old man.*) Eah: finish your mess; an git aht o mah wy.

SHIRLEY (*springing up and facing him fiercely, with the mug in his hand*): You take a liberty with me, and I'll smash you over the face with the mug and cut your eye out. Aint you satisfied — young whelps like you — with takin the bread out o the mouths of your elders that have brought you up and slaved for you, but you must come shovin and cheekin and bullyin in here, where the bread o charity is sickenin in our stummicks?

BILL (*contemptuously, but backing a little*): Wot good are you, you aold palsy mag? Wot good are you?

SHIRLEY: As good as you and better. I'll do a day's work agen you or any fat young soaker of your age. Go and take my job at Horrockses, where I worked for ten year. They want young men there: they cant afford to keep men over forty-five. Theyre very sorry — give you a character and happy to help you to get anything suited to your years — sure a steady man wont be long out of a job. Well, let em try you. Theyll find the differ. What do you know? Not as much as how to beeyave yourself — layin your dirty fist across the mouth of a respectable woman!

BILL: Downt provowk me to ly it acrost yours: d'ye eah?

SHIRLEY (*with blighting contempt*): Yes: you like an old man to hit, dont you, when youve finished with the women. I ain't seen you hit a young one yet.

BILL (*stung*): You loy, you aold soupkitchener, you. There was a yang menn eah. Did Aw offer to itt him or did Aw not?

SHIRLEY: Was he starvin or was he not? Was he a man or only a crossed-eyed thief an a loafer? Would you hit my son-in-law's brother?

BILL: Oo's ee?

SHIRLEY: Todger Fairmile o Balls Pond. Him that won £20 off the Japanese wrastler at the music hall by standin out 17 minutes 4 seconds agen him.

BILL (*sullenly*): Aw'm nao music awl wrastler. Ken he box?

SHIRLEY: Yes: an you cant.

BILL: Wot! Aw cawnt, cawnt Aw? Wots thet you sy (*threatening him*)?

SHIRLEY (*not budging an inch*): Will you box Todger Fairmile if I put him on to you? Say the word.

BILL (*subsiding with a slouch*): Aw'll stend ap to enny menn alawv, if he was ten Todger Fairmawls. But Aw dont set ap to be a perfeshnal.

SHIRLEY (*looking down on him with unfathomable disdain*): You box! Slap an old woman with the back o your hand! You hadnt even the sense to hit her where the magistrate couldnt see the mark of it, you silly young lump of conceit and ignorance. Hit a girl in the jaw and ony make her cry! If Todger Fairmile's done it, she wouldnt a got up inside o ten minutes, no more than you would if he got on to you. Yah! I'd set about you myself if I had a week's feedin in me instead o two months' starvation. (*He turns his back on him and sits down moodily at the table.*)

BILL (*following him and stooping over him to drive the taunt in*): You loy! youve the bread and treacle in you that you cam eah to beg.

SHIRLEY (*bursting into tears*): Oh God! it's true: I'm only an old pauper on the scrap heap. (*Furiously.*) But youll come to it yourself; and then youll know. Youll come to it sooner than a teetotaller like me, fillin yourself with gin at this hour o the mornin!

BILL: Aw'm nao gin drinker, you oald lawr; but wen Aw want to give my girl a bloomin good awdin Aw lawk to ev a bit o devil in me: see? An eah Aw emm, talkin to a rotten aold blawter like you sted o givin her wot for. (*Working himself into a rage.*) Aw'm gowin in there to fetch her aht. (*He makes vengefully for the shelter door.*)

SHIRLEY: Youre goin to the station on a stretcher, more likely; and theyll take the gin and the devil out of you there when they get you inside. You mind what youre about: the major here is the Earl o Stevenage's granddaughter.

BILL (*checked*): Garn!

SHIRLEY: Youll see.

BILL (*his resolution oozing*): Well, Aw aint dan nathin to er.

SHIRLEY: Spose she said you did! who'd believe you?

BILL (*very uneasy, skulking back to the corner of the penthouse*): Gawd! theres no jastice in this cantry. To think wot them people can do! Aw'm as good as er.

SHIRLEY: Tell her so. It's just what a fool like you would do.

(*Barbara, brisk and businesslike, comes from the shelter with a notebook, and addresses herself to Shirley. Bill, cowed, sits down in the corner on a form, and turns his back on them.*)

BARBARA: Good morning.

SHIRLEY (*standing up and taking off his hat*): Good morning, miss.

BARBARA: Sit down: make yourself at home. (*He hesitates; but she puts a friendly hand on his shoulder and makes him obey.*) Now then! since youve made friends with us, we want to know all about you. Names and addresses and trades.

SHIRLEY: Peter Shirley. Fitter. Chucked out two months ago because I was too old.

BARBARA (*not at all surprised*): Youd pass still. Why didnt you dye your hair?

SHIRLEY: I did. Me age come out at a coroner's inquest on me daughter.

BARBARA: Steady?

SHIRLEY: Teetotaler. Never out of a job before. Good worker. And sent to the knackers like an old horse!

BARBARA: No matter: if you did your part God will do his.

SHIRLEY (*suddenly stubborn*): My religion's no concern of anybody but myself.

BARBARA (*guessing*): I know. Secularist?

SHIRLEY (*hotly*): Did I offer to deny it?

BARBARA: Why should you? My own father's a Secularist, I think. Our Father — yours and mine — fulfills himself in many ways; and I daresay he knew what he was about when he made a Secularist of you. So buck up, Peter! we can always find a job for a steady man like you. (*Shirley, disarmed and a little bewildered, touches his hat. She turns from him to Bill.*) Whats your name?

BILL (*insolently*): Wots thet to you?

BARBARA (*calmly making a note*): Afraid to give his name. Any trade?

BILL: Oo's afride to give is nime? (*Doggedly, with a sense of heroically defying the House of Lords in the person of Lord Stevenage.*) If you want to bring a chawge agen me, bring it. (*She waits, unruffled.*) Moy nime's Bill Walker.

BARBARA (*as if the name were familiar: trying to remember how*): Bill Walker? (*Recollecting.*) Oh, I know: youre the man that Jenny Hill was praying for inside just now. (*She enters his name in her notebook.*)

BILL: Oo's Jenny Ill? And wot call as she to pry for me?

BARBARA: I dont know. Perhaps it was you that cut her lip.

BILL (*defiantly*): Yus, it was me that cat her lip. Aw aint afride o you.

BARBARA: How could you be, since youre not afraid of God? Youre a brave man, Mr. Walker. It takes some pluck to do our work here; but none of us dare lift our hand against a girl like that, for fear of her father in heaven.

BILL (*sullenly*): I want nan o your kentin jawr. I spowse you think Aw cam eah to beg from you, like this demmiged lot eah. Not me. Aw downt want your bread and scripe and ketlep. Aw dont belive in your Gawd, no more than you do yourself.

BARBARA (*sunnily apologetic and ladylike, as on a new footing with him*): Oh, I beg your pardon for putting your name down, Mr. Walker. I didn't understand. I'll strike it out.

BILL (*taking this as a slight, and deeply wounded by it*): Eah! you let maw nime alown. Aint it good enaff to be in your book?

BARBARA (*considering*): Well, you see, theres no use putting down your name unless I can do something for you, is there? Whats your trade?

BILL (*still smarting*): Thets nao concern o yours.

BARBARA: Just so. (*Very businesslike.*) I'll put you down as (*writing*) the man who — struck — poor little Jenny Hill — in the mouth.

BILL (*rising threateningly*): See eah. Awve ed enaff o this.

BARBARA (*quite sunny and fearless*): What did you come to us for?

BILL: Aw cam for maw gel, see? Aw cam to tike her aht o this and to brike er jawr for er.

BARBARA (*complacently*): You see I was right about your trade. (*Bill, on the point of retorting furiously, finds himself, to his great shame and terror, in danger of crying instead. He sits down again suddenly.*) Whats her name?

BILL (*dogged*): Er nime's Mog Ebbijem: thets wot her nime is.

BARBARA: Mog Habbijam! Oh, she's gone to Canning Town, to our barracks there.

BILL (*fortified by his resentment of Mog's perfidy*): Is she? (*Vindictively.*) Then Aw'm gowin to Kennintahn arter her. (*He crosses to the gate; hesitates; finally comes back at Barbara.*) Are you loyin to me to git shat o me?

BARBARA: I dont want to get shut of you. I want to keep you here and save your soul. Youd better stay: youre going to have a bad time today, Bill.

BILL: Oo's gowin to give it to me? You, preps?

BARBARA: Someone you dont believe in. But youll be glad afterwards.

BILL (*slinking off*): Aw'll gow to Kennintahn to be aht o reach o your tangue. (*Suddenly turning on her with intense malice.*) And if Aw downt fawnd Mog there, Aw'll cam beck and do two years for you, selp me Gawd if Aw downt!

BARBARA (*a shade kindlier, if possible*): It's no use, Bill. She's got another bloke.

BILL: Wot!

BARBARA: One of her own converts. He fell in love with her when he saw her with her soul saved, and her face clean, and her hair washed.

BILL (*surprised*): Wottud she wash it for, the carroty slat? It's red.

BARBARA: It's quite lovely now, because she wears a new look in her eyes with it. It's a pity youre too late. The new bloke has put your nose out of joint, Bill.

BILL: Aw'll put his nowse aht o joint for him. Not that Aw care a carse for er, mawnd thet. But Aw'll teach her to drop me as if Aw was dirt. And Aw'll teach him to meddle with maw Judy. Wots iz bleedin nime?

BARBARA: Sergeant Todger Fairmile.

SHIRLEY (*rising with grim joy*): I'll go with him, miss. I want to see them two meet. I'll take him to the infirmary when it's over.

BILL (*to Shirley, with undissembled misgiving*): Is thet im you was speakin on?

SHIRLEY: Thats him.

BILL: Im that wrastled in the music awl?

SHIRLEY: The competitions at the National Sportin Club was worth nigh a hundred a year to him. He's gev em up now for religion; so he's a bit fresh for want of the exercise he was accustomed to. He'll be glad to see you. Come along.

BILL: Wots is wight?

SHIRLEY: Thirteen four.° (*Bill's last hope expires.*)

BARBARA: Go and talk to him, Bill. He'll convert you.

SHIRLEY: He'll convert your head into a mashed potato.

BILL (*sullenly*): Aw aint afride of im. Aw aint afride of ennybody. Bat e can lick me. She's dan me. (*He sits down moodily on the edge of the horse trough.*)

SHIRLEY: You aint going. I thought not. (*He resumes his seat.*)

BARBARA (*calling*): Jenny!

JENNY (*appearing at the shelter door with a plaster on the corner of her mouth*): Yes, Major.

BARBARA: Send Rummy Mitchens out to clear away here.

JENNY: I think she's afraid.

BARBARA (*her resemblance to her mother flashing out for a moment*): Nonsense! she must do as she's told.

JENNY (*calling into the shelter*): Rummy: the Major says you must come.

(*Jenny comes to Barbara, purposely keeping on the side next Bill, lest he should suppose that she shrank from him or bore malice.*)

BARBARA: Poor little Jenny! Are you tired? (*Looking at the wounded cheek.*) Does it hurt?

JENNY: No: it's all right now. It was nothing.

BARBARA (*critically*): It was as hard as he could hit, I expect. Poor Bill! You dont feel angry with him, do you?

JENNY: Oh no, no, no: indeed I dont, Major, bless his poor heart! (*Barbara kisses her; and she runs away merrily into the shelter. Bill writhes with an agonizing return of his new and alarming symptoms, but says nothing. Rummy Mitchens comes from the shelter.*)

BARBARA (*going to meet Rummy*): Now Rummy, bustle. Take in those mugs and plates to be washed; and throw the crumbs about for the birds.

(*Rummy takes the three plates and mugs; but Shirley takes back his mug from her, as there is still some milk left in it.*)

RUMMY: There aint any crumbs. This aint a time to waste good bread on birds.

Thirteen four: Thirteen stone, four pounds. (A stone is a British weight equal to fourteen pounds.)

PRICE (*appearing at the shelter door*): Gentleman come to see the shelter, Major. Says he's your father.

BARBARA: All right. Coming. (*Snobby goes back into the shelter, followed by Barbara.*)

RUMMY (*stealing across to Bill and addressing him in a subdued voice, but with intense conviction*): I'd av the lor of you, you flat eared pignosed potwalloper, if she'd let me. Youre no gentleman, to hit a lady in the face. (*Bill, with greater things moving in him, takes no notice.*)

SHIRLEY (*following her*): Here! in with you and dont get yourself into more trouble by talking.

RUMMY (*with hauteur*): I aint ad the pleasure o being hintroduced to you, as I can remember. (*She goes into the shelter with the plates.*)

SHIRLEY: Thats the —

BILL (*savagely*): Downt you talk to me, d'ye eah? You lea me alown, or Aw'll do you a mischief. Aw'm not dirt under your feet, ennywy.

SHIRLEY (*calmly*): Dont you be aferd. You aint such prime company that you need expect to be sought after. (*He is about to go into the shelter when Barbara comes out, with Undershaft on her right.*)

BARBARA: Oh, there you are, Mr. Shirley! (*Between them.*) This is my father: I told you he was a Secularist, didn't I? Perhaps youll be able to comfort one another.

UNDERSHAFT (*startled*): A Secularist! Not the least in the world: on the contrary, a confirmed mystic.

BARBARA: Sorry, I'm sure. By the way, papa, what is your religion? in case I have to introduce you again.

UNDERSHAFT: My religion? Well, my dear, I am a Millionaire. That is my religion.

BARBARA: Then I'm afraid you and Mr. Shirley wont be able to comfort one another after all. Youre not a Millionaire, are you, Peter?

SHIRLEY: No; and proud of it.

UNDERSHAFT (*gravely*): Poverty, my friend, is not a thing to be proud of.

SHIRLEY (*angrily*): Who made your millions for you? Me and my like. Whats kep us poor? Keepin you rich. I wouldnt have your conscience, not for all your income.

UNDERSHAFT: I wouldnt have your income, not for all your conscience, Mr. Shirley. (*He goes to the penthouse and sits down on a form.*)

BARBARA (*stopping Shirley adroitly as he is about to retort*): You wouldnt think he was my father, would you, Peter? Will you go into the shelter and lend the lasses a hand for a while: we're worked off our feet.

SHIRLEY (*bitterly*): Yes: I'm in their debt for a meal, aint I?

BARBARA: Oh, not because youre in their debt, but

for love of them, Peter, for love of them. (*He cannot understand, and is rather scandalized.*) There! dont stare at me. In with you; and give that conscience of yours a holiday. (*Bustling him into the shelter.*)

SHIRLEY (*as he goes in*): Ah! it's a pity you never was trained to use your reason, miss. Youd have been a very taking lecturer on Secularism.

(*Barbara turns to her father.*)

UNDERSHAFT: Never mind me, my dear. Go about your work; and let me watch it for a while.

BARBARA: All right.

UNDERSHAFT: For instance, whats the matter with that outpatient over there?

BARBARA (*looking at Bill, whose attitude has never changed, and whose expression of brooding wrath has deepened*): Oh, we shall cure him in no time. Just watch. (*She goes over to Bill and waits. He glances up at her and casts his eyes down again, uneasy, but grimmer than ever.*) It would be nice to just stamp on Mog Habbijam's face, wouldnt it, Bill?

BILL (*starting up from the trough in consternation*): It's a loy: Aw never said so. (*She shakes her head.*) Oo taold you wot was in moy mawnd?

BARBARA: Only your new friend.

BILL: Wot new friend?

BARBARA: The devil, Bill. When he gets round people they get miserable, just like you.

BILL (*with a heartbreaking attempt at devil-may-care cheerfulness*): Aw aint miserable. (*He sits down again and stretches his legs in an attempt to seem indifferent.*)

BARBARA: Well, if youre happy, why dont you look happy, as we do?

BILL (*his legs curling back in spite of him*): Aw'm eppy enaff, Aw tell you. Woy cawnt you lea me alown? Wot ev I dan to you? Aw aint smashed your fice, ev Aw?

BARBARA (*softly: wooing his soul*): It's not me thats getting at you, Bill.

BILL: Oo else is it?

BARBARA: Somebody that doesnt intend you to smash women's faces, I suppose. Somebody or something that wants to make a man of you.

BILL (*blustering*): Mike a menn o me! Aint Aw a menn? eh? Oo sez Aw'm not a menn?

BARBARA: Theres a man in you somewhere, I suppose. But why did he let you hit poor little Jenny Hill? That wasn't very manly of him, was it?

BILL (*tormented*): Ev dan wiv it, Aw tell you. Chack it. Aw'm sick o your Jenny Ill and er silly little fice.

BARBARA: Then why do you keep thinking about it?

Why does it keep coming up against you in your mind? Youre not getting converted, are you?

BILL (*with conviction*): Not ME. Not lawkly.

BARBARA: Thats right, Bill. Hold out against it. Put out your strength. Dont lets get you cheap. Todger Fairmile said he wrestled for three nights against his salvation harder than he ever wrestled with the Jap at the music hall. He gave in to the Jap when his arm was going to break. But he didnt give in to his salvation until his heart was going to break. Perhaps youll escape that. You havnt any heart, have you?

BILL: Wot d'ye mean? Woy aint Aw got a awt the sime as ennybody else?

BARBARA: A man with a heart wouldnt have bashed poor little Jenny's face, would he?

BILL (*almost crying*): Ow, will you lea me alown? Ev Aw ever offered to meddle with you, that you cam neggin and provowkin me lawk this? (*He writhes convulsively from his eyes to his toes.*)

BARBARA (*with a steady soothing hand on his arm and a gentle voice that never lets him go*): It's your soul thats hurting you, Bill, and not me. Weve been through it all ourselves. Come with us, Bill. (*He looks wildly round.*) To brave manhood on earth and eternal glory in heaven. (*He is on the point of breaking down.*) Come. (*A drum is heard in the shelter; and Bill, with a gasp, escapes from the spell as Barbara turns quickly. Adolphus enters from the shelter with a big drum.*) Oh! there you are, Dolly. Let me introduce a new friend of mine, Mr. Bill Walker. This is my bloke, Bill: Mr. Cusins. (*Cusins salutes with his drumstick.*)

BILL: Gowin to merry im?

BARBARA: Yes.

BILL (*fervently*): Gawd elp im! Gaw-aw-aw-awd elp him!

BARBARA: Why? Do you think he wont be happy with me?

BILL: Awve aony ed to stend it for a mawnin: e'll ev to stend it for a lawftawm.

CUSINS: That is a frightful reflection, Mr. Walker. But I cant tear myself away from her.

BILL: Well, Aw ken. (*To Barbara.*) Eah do you knaow where Aw'm gowin to, and wot Aw'm gowin to do?

BARBARA: Yes: youre going to heaven; and youre coming back here before the week's out to tell me so.

BILL: You loy. Aw'm gowin to Kennintahn, to spit in Todger Fairmawl's eye. Aw beshed Jenny Ill's fice; an nar Aw'll git me aown fice beshed and cam bec and shaow it to er. Ee'll itt me ardern Aw itt her. Thatll mike us square. (*To Adolphus.*) Is thet fair or is it not? Youre a genlmn: you oughter knaow.

BARBARA: Two black eyes wont make one white one, Bill.

BILL: Aw didnt awst you. Cawnt you never keep your mahth shat? Oy awst the genlmn.

CUSINS (*reflectively*): Yes: I think youre right, Mr. Walker. Yes: I should do it. It's curious: it's exactly what an ancient Greek would have done.

BARBARA: But what good will it do?

CUSINS: Well, it will give Mr. Fairmile some exercise; and it will satisfy Mr. Walker's soul.

BILL: Rot! there aint nao sach a thing as a saoul. Ah kin you tell wevver Awve a saoul or not? You never seen it.

BARBARA: Ive seen it hurting you when you went against it.

BILL (*with compressed aggravation*): If you was maw gel and took the word awt o me mahth lawk thet, Aw'd give you sathink youd feel urtin, Aw would. (*To Adolphus.*) You tike maw tip, mite. Stop er jawr or youll doy afoah your tawm (*With intense expression.*) Wore aht: thets wot youll be: wore aht. (*He goes away through the gate.*)

CUSINS (*looking after him*): I wonder!

BARBARA: Dolly! (*Indignant, in her mother's manner.*)

CUSINS: Yes, my dear, it's very wearing to be in love with you. If it lasts, I quite think I shall die young.

BARBARA: Should you mind?

CUSINS: Not at all. (*He is suddenly softened, and kisses her over the drum, evidently not for the first time, as people cannot kiss over a big drum without practice. Undershaft coughs.*)

BARBARA: It's all right, papa, weve not forgotten you. Dolly: explain the place to papa: I havnt time. (*She goes busily into the shelter.*)

(*Undershaft and Adolphus now have the yard to themselves. Undershaft, seated on a form, and still keenly attentive, looks hard at Adolphus. Adolphus looks hard at him.*)

UNDERSHAFT: I fancy you guess something of what is in my mind, Mr. Cusins. (*Cusins flourishes his drumsticks as if in the act of beating a lively rataplan, but makes no sound.*) Exactly so. But suppose Barbara finds you out!

CUSINS: You know, I do not admit that I am imposing on Barbara. I am quite genuinely interested in the views of the Salvation Army. The fact is, I am a sort of collector of religions; and the curious thing is that I find I can believe them all. By the way, have you any religion?

UNDERSHAFT: Yes.

CUSINS: Anything out of the common?

UNDERSHAFT: Only that there are two things necessary to Salvation.

CUSINS (*disappointed, but polite*): Ah, the Church Cat-echism. Charles Lomax also belongs to the Established Church.

UNDERSHAFT: The two things are —

CUSINS: Baptism and —

UNDERSHAFT: No. Money and gunpowder.

CUSINS (*surprised, but interested*): That is the general opinion of our governing classes. The novelty is in hearing any man confess it.

UNDERSHAFT: Just so.

CUSINS: Excuse me: is there any place in your religion for honor, justice, truth, love, mercy, and so forth?

UNDERSHAFT: Yes: they are the graces and luxuries of a rich, strong, and safe life.

CUSINS: Suppose one is forced to choose between them and money or gunpowder?

UNDERSHAFT: Choose money and gunpowder; for without enough of both you cannot afford the others.

CUSINS: That is your religion?

UNDERSHAFT: Yes.

(*The cadence of this reply makes a full close in the conversation. Cusins twists his face dubiously and contemplates Undershaft. Undershaft contemplates him.*)

CUSINS: Barbara wont stand that. You will have to choose between your religion and Barbara.

UNDERSHAFT: So will you, my friend. She will find out that that drum of yours is hollow.

CUSINS: Father Undershaft: you are mistaken: I am a sincere Salvationist. You do not understand the Salvation Army. It is the army of joy, of love, of courage: it has banished the fear and remorse and despair of the old hell-ridden evangelical sects: it marches to fight the devil with trumpet and drum, with music and dancing, with banner and palm, as becomes a sally from heaven by its happy garrison. It picks the waster out of the public house and makes a man of him: it finds a worm wriggling in a back kitchen, and lo! a woman! Men and women of rank too, sons and daughters of the Highest. It takes the poor professor of Greek, the most artificial and self-suppressed of human creatures, from his meal of roots, and lets loose the rhapsodist in him; reveals the true worship of Dionysos to him; sends him down the public street drumming dithyrambs. (*He plays a thundering flourish on the drum.*)

UNDERSHAFT: You will alarm the shelter.

CUSINS: Oh, they are accustomed to these sudden ecstasies. However, if the drum worries you — (*He pockets the drumsticks, unhooks the drum, and stands it on the ground opposite the gateway.*)

UNDERSHAFT: Thank you.

CUSINS: You remember what Euripides says about your money and gunpowder?°

UNDERSHAFT: No.

CUSINS (*declaiming*): One and another
In money and guns may outpass his brother;
And men in their millions float and flow
And seethe with a million hopes as leaven;
And they win their will; or they miss their will;
And their hopes are dead or are pined for still;
   But who'er can know
   As the long days go
That to live is happy, has found his heaven.

My translation: what do you think of it?

UNDERSHAFT: I think, my friend, that if you wish to know, as the long days go, that to live is happy, you must first acquire money enough for a decent life, and power enough to be your own master.

CUSINS: You are damnably discouraging. (*He resumes his declamation.*)
   Is it so hard a thing to see
   That the spirit of God — whate'er it be —
The law that abides and changes not, ages long,
The Eternal and Nature-born: these things be strong?
What else is Wisdom? What of Man's endeavor,
Of God's high grace so lovely and so great?
To stand from fear set free? to breathe and wait?
To hold a hand uplifted over Fate?
And shall not Barbara be loved for ever?

UNDERSHAFT: Euripides mentions Barbara, does he?

CUSINS: It is a fair translation. The word means Loveliness.

UNDERSHAFT: May I ask — as Barbara's father — how much a year she is to be loved for ever on?

CUSINS: As for Barbara's father, that is more your affair than mine. I can feed her by teaching Greek: that is about all.

UNDERSHAFT: Do you consider it a good match for her?

CUSINS (*with polite obstinacy*): Mr. Undershaft: I am in many ways a weak, timid, ineffectual person; and my health is far from satisfactory. But whenever I feel that I must have anything, I get it, sooner or later. I feel that way about Barbara. I dont like marriage: I feel intensely afraid of it; and I dont know what I shall do with Barbara or what she

will do with me. But I feel that I and nobody else must marry her. Please regard that as settled. — Not that I wish to be arbitrary; but why should I waste your time in discussing what is inevitable?

UNDERSHAFT: You mean that you will stick at nothing: not even the conversion of the Salvation Army to the worship of Dionysos.

CUSINS: The business of the Salvation Army is to save, not to wrangle about the name of the pathfinder. Dionysos or another: what does it matter?

UNDERSHAFT (*rising and approaching him*): Professor Cusins: you are a young man after my own heart.

CUSINS: Mr. Undershaft: you are, as far as I am able to gather, a most infernal old rascal; but you appeal very strongly to my sense of ironic humor.

(*Undershaft mutely offers his hand. They shake.*)

UNDERSHAFT (*suddenly concentrating himself*): And now to business.

CUSINS: Pardon me. We are discussing religion. Why go back to such an uninteresting and unimportant subject as business?

UNDERSHAFT: Religion is our business at present, because it is through religion alone that we can win Barbara.

CUSINS: Have you, too, fallen in love with Barbara?

UNDERSHAFT: Yes, with a father's love.

CUSINS: A father's love for a grown-up daughter is the most dangerous of all infatuations. I apologize for mentioning my own pale, coy, mistrustful fancy in the same breath with it.

UNDERSHAFT: Keep to the point. We have to win her; and we are neither of us Methodists.

CUSINS: That doesnt matter. The power Barbara wields here — the power that wields Barbara herself — is not Calvinism, not Presbyterianism, not Methodism —

UNDERSHAFT: Not Greek Paganism either, eh?

CUSINS: I admit that. Barbara is quite original in her religion.

UNDERSHAFT (*triumphantly*): Aha! Barbara Undershaft would be. Her inspiration comes from within herself.

CUSINS: How do you suppose it got there?

UNDERSHAFT (*in towering excitement*): It is the Undershaft inheritance. I shall hand on my torch to my daughter. She shall make my converts and preach my gospel —

CUSINS: What! Money and gunpowder!

UNDERSHAFT: Yes, money and gunpowder. Freedom and power. Command of life and command of death.

CUSINS (*urbanely: trying to bring him down to earth*): This is extremely interesting, Mr. Undershaft. Of course you know that you are mad.

N.B.: The Euripidean verses in the second act of *Major Barbara* are not by me, nor even directly by Euripides. They are by Professor Gilbert Murray, whose English version of *The Bacchae* came into our dramatic literature with all the impulsive power of an original work shortly before *Major Barbara* was begun. The play, indeed, stands indebted to him in more ways than one. B.S.

UNDERSHAFT (*with redoubled force*): And you?

CUSINS: Oh, mad as a hatter. You are welcome to my secret since I have discovered yours. But I am astonished. Can a madman make cannons?

UNDERSHAFT: Would anyone else than a madman make them? And now (*with surging energy*) question for question. Can a sane man translate Euripides?

CUSINS: No.

UNDERSHAFT (*seizing him by the shoulder*): Can a sane woman make a man of a waster or a woman of a worm?

CUSINS (*reeling before the storm*): Father Colossus — Mammoth Millionaire —

UNDERSHAFT (*pressing him*): Are there two mad people or three in this Salvation shelter today?

CUSINS: You mean Barbara is as mad as we are?

UNDERSHAFT (*pushing him lightly off and resuming his equanimity suddenly and completely*): Pooh, Professor! let us call things by their proper names. I am a millionaire; you are a poet: Barbara is a savior of souls. What have we three to do with the common mob of slaves and idolators? (*He sits down again with a shrug of contempt for the mob.*)

CUSINS: Take care! Barbara is in love with the common people. So am I. Have you never felt the romance of that love?

UNDERSHAFT (*cold and sardonic*): Have you ever been in love with Poverty, like St. Francis? Have you ever been in love with Dirt, like St. Simeon! Have you ever been in love with disease and suffering, like our nurses and philanthropists? Such passions are not virtues, but the most unnatural of all the vices. This love of the common people may please an earl's granddaughter and a university professor; but I have been a common man and a poor man; and it has no romance for me. Leave it to the poor to pretend that poverty is a blessing: leave it to the coward to make a religion of his cowardice by preaching humility: we know better than that. We three must stand together above the common people: how else can we help their children to climb up beside us? Barbara must belong to us, not to the Salvation Army.

CUSINS: Well, I can only say that if you think you will get her away from the Salvation Army by talking to her as you have been talking to me, you dont know Barbara.

UNDERSHAFT: My friend: I never ask for what I can buy.

CUSINS (*in a white fury*): Do I understand you to imply that you can buy Barbara?

UNDERSHAFT: No; but I can buy the Salvation Army.

CUSINS: Quite impossible.

UNDERSHAFT: You shall see. All religious organizations exist by selling themselves to the rich.

CUSINS: Not the Army. That is the Church of the poor.

UNDERSHAFT: All the more reason for buying it.

CUSINS: I dont think you quite know what the Army does for the poor.

UNDERSHAFT: Oh yes I do. It draws their teeth: that is enough for me as a man of business.

CUSINS: Nonsense! It makes them sober —

UNDERSHAFT: I prefer sober workmen. The profits are larger.

CUSINS: — honest —

UNDERSHAFT: Honest workmen are the most economical.

CUSINS: — attached to their homes —

UNDERSHAFT: So much the better: they will put up with anything sooner than change their shop.

CUSINS: — happy —

UNDERSHAFT: An invaluable safeguard against revolution.

CUSINS: — unselfish —

UNDERSHAFT: Indifferent to their own interests, which suits me exactly.

CUSINS: — with their thoughts on heavenly things —

UNDERSHAFT (*rising*): And not on Trade Unionism nor Socialism. Excellent.

CUSINS (*revolted*): You really are an infernal old rascal.

UNDERSHAFT (*indicating Peter Shirley, who has just come from the shelter and strolled dejectedly down the yard between them*): And this is an honest man!

SHIRLEY: Yes; and what av I got by it? (*He passes on bitterly and sits on the form, in the corner of the penthouse.*)

(*Snobby Price, beaming sanctimoniously, and Jenny Hill, with a tambourine full of coppers, come from the shelter and go to the drum, on which Jenny begins to count the money.*)

UNDERSHAFT (*replying to Shirley*): Oh, your employers must have got a good deal by it from first to last. (*He sits on the table, with one foot on the side form. Cusins, overwhelmed, sits down on the same form nearer the shelter. Barbara comes from the shelter to the middle of the yard. She is excited and a little overwrought.*)

BARBARA: Weve just had a splendid experience meeting at the other gate in Cripps's lane. Ive hardly ever seen them so much moved as they were by your confession, Mr. Price.

PRICE: I could almost be glad of my past wickedness if I could believe that it would elp to keep hathers stright.

BARBARA: So it will, Snobby. How much, Jenny?

JENNY: Four and tenpence, Major.

BARBARA: Oh Snobby, if you had given your poor mother just one more kick, we should have got the whole five shillings!

PRICE: If she heard you say that, miss, she'd be sorry I didnt. But I'm glad. Oh what a joy it will be to her when she hears I'm saved!

UNDERSHAFT: Shall I contribute the odd twopence, Barbara? The millionaire's mite, eh? (*He takes a couple of pennies from his pocket.*)

BARBARA: How did you make that twopence?

UNDERSHAFT: As usual. By selling cannons, torpedoes, submarines, and my new patent Grand Duke hand grenade.

BARBARA: Put it back in your pocket. You cant buy your salvation here for twopence: you must work it out.

UNDERSHAFT: Is twopence not enough? I can afford a little more, if you press me.

BARBARA: Two million millions would not be enough. There is bad blood on your hands; and nothing but good blood can cleanse them. Money is no use. Take it away. (*She turns to Cusins.*) Dolly: you must write another letter for me to the papers. (*He makes a wry face.*) Yes: I know you dont like it; but it must be done. The starvation this winter is beating us: everybody is unemployed. The General says we must close this shelter if we cant get more money. I force the collections at the meetings until I am ashamed: dont I, Snobby?

PRICE: It's a fair treat to see you work it, miss. The way you got them up from three-and-six to four-and-ten with that hymn, penny by penny and verse by verse, was a caution. Not a Cheap Jack on Mile End Waste could touch you at it.

BARBARA: Yes: but I wish we could do without it. I am getting at last to think more of the collection than of the people's souls. And what are those hatfuls of pence and halfpence? We want thousands! tens of thousands! hundreds of thousands! I want to convert people, not to be always begging for the Army in a way I'd die sooner than beg for myself.

UNDERSHAFT (*in profound irony*): Genuine unselfishness is capable of anything, my dear.

BARBARA (*unsuspectingly, as she turns away to take the money from the drum and put it in a cash bag she carries*): Yes, isnt it? (*Undershaft looks sardonically at Cusins.*)

CUSINS (*aside to Undershaft*): Mephistopheles! Machiavelli!°

BARBARA (*tears coming into her eyes as she ties the*

Mephistopheles! Machiavelli!: In the Faust legend Mephistopheles tempts Faust with worldly promises and strikes a bargain for Faust's soul. Niccolò Machiavelli (1469–1527) was an Italian political philosopher whose name became synonymous with political cynicism and treachery.

bag and pockets it): How are we to feed them? I cant talk religion to a man with bodily hunger in his eyes. (*Almost breaking down.*) It's frightful.

JENNY (*running to her*): Major, dear —

BARBARA (*rebounding*): No: dont comfort me. It will be all right. We shall get the money.

UNDERSHAFT: How?

JENNY: By praying for it, of course. Mrs. Baines says she prayed for it last night; and she has never prayed for it in vain: never once. (*She goes to the gate and looks out into the street.*)

BARBARA (*who has dried her eyes and regained her composure*): By the way, dad, Mrs. Baines has come to march with us to our big meeting this afternoon and she is very anxious to meet you, for some reason or other. Perhaps she'll convert you.

UNDERSHAFT: I shall be delighted, my dear.

JENNY (*at the gate: excitedly*): Major! Major! here's that man back again.

BARBARA: What man?

JENNY: The man that hit me. Oh, I hope he's coming back to join us.

(*Bill Walker, with frost on his jacket, comes through the gate, his hands deep in his pockets and his chin sunk between his shoulders, like a cleaned-out gambler. He halts between Barbara and the drum.*)

BARBARA: Hullo, Bill! Back already!

BILL (*nagging at her*): Bin talkin ever sence, ev you?

BARBARA: Pretty nearly. Well, has Todger paid you out for poor Jenny's jaw?

BILL: Nao e aint.

BARBARA: I thought your jacket looked a bit snowy.

BILL: Sao it is snaowy. You want to knaow where the snaow cam from, downt you?

BARBARA: Yes.

BILL: Well, it cam from orf the grahnd in Pawkinses Corner in Kennintahn. It got rabbed orf be maw shaoulders: see?

BARBARA: Pity you didnt rub some off with your knees, Bill! That would have done you a lot of good.

BILL (*with sour mirthless humor*): Aw was sivin anather menn's knees at the tawm. E was kneelin on moy ed, e was.

JENNY: Who was kneeling on your head?

BILL: Todger was. E was pryin for me: pryin comfortable wiv me as a cawpet. Sow was Mog. Sao was the aol bloomin meeting. Mog she sez "Ow Lawd brike is stabborn sperrit; bat downt urt is dear art." Thet was wot she said. "Downt urt is dear art"! An er blowk — thirteen stun four! — kneelin wiv all is wight on me. Fanny, aint it?

JENNY: Oh no. We're so sorry, Mr. Walker.

BARBARA (*enjoying it frankly*): Nonsense! of course

it's funny. Served you right, Bill! You must have done something to him first.

BILL (*doggedly*): Aw did wot Aw said Aw'd do. Aw spit in is eye. E looks ap at the skoy and sez, "Ow that Aw should be fahnd worthy to be spit upon for the gospel's sike!" e sez; an Mog sez "Glaory Allelloolier!"; and then e called me Braddher an dahned me as if Aw was a kid and he was me mather worshin me a Setterda nawt. Aw ednt jast nao shaow wiv im at all. Arf the street pryed; an the tather arf larfed fit to split theirselves. (*To Barbara.*) There are you settisfawd nah?

BARBARA (*her eyes dancing*): Wish I'd been there, Bill.

BILL: Yus: youd a got in a hextra bit o talk on me, wouldnt you?

JENNY: I'm so sorry, Mr. Walker.

BILL (*fiercely*): Downt you gow being sorry for me: youve no call. Listen eah. Aw browk your jawr.

JENNY: No, it didnt hurt me: indeed it didnt, except for a moment. It was only that I was frightened.

BILL: Aw downt want to be forgive you, or be ennybody. Wot Aw did Aw'll py for. Aw trawd to gat me aown jawr browk to settisfaw you —

JENNY (*distressed*): Oh no —

BILL (*impatiently*): Tell y' Aw did: cawnt you listen to wots being taold you? All Aw got be it was being mide a sawt of in the public street for me pines. Well, if Aw cawnt settisfaw you one wy, Aw ken another. Listen eah! Aw ed two quid sived agen the frost; an Awve a pahnd of it left. A mite o mawn last week ed words with the judy e's gowing to merry. E give er wot-for; an e's bin fawned fifteen bob. E ed a rawt to itt er cause they was gowin to be merrid; but Aw ednt nao rawt to itt you; sao put another fawv bob on an call it a pahnd's worth. (*He produces a sovereign.*) Eahs the manney. Tike it, and lets ev no more o your forgivin an prying and your Mijor jawrin me. Let wot Aw dan be dan an pide for; and let there be a end of it.

JENNY: Oh, I couldn't take it, Mr. Walker. But if you would give a shilling or two to poor Rummy Mitchens! you really did hurt her; and she's old.

BILL (*contemptuously*): Not lawkly. Aw'd give her anather as soon as look at er. Let her ev the lawr o me as she threatened! She aint forgiven me: not mach. Wot Aw dan to er is not on me mawnd — wot she (*indicating Barbara*) mawt call on me conscience — no more than stickin a pig. It's this Christian gime o yours that Aw wownt ev plyed agen me: this bloomin forgivin an neggin an jawrin that mikes a menn thet sore that iz lawf's a burdn to im. Aw wownt ev it, Aw tell you; sao tike your manney and stop thraowin your silly beshed fice hap agen me.

JENNY: Major: may I take a little of it for the Army?

BARBARA: No: the Army is not to be bought. We want your soul, Bill; and we'll take nothing less.

BILL (*bitterly*): Aw knaow. Me an maw few shillins is not good enaff for you. Youre a earl's grendorter, you are. Nathink less than a andered pahnd for you.

UNDERSHAFT: Come, Barbara! you could do a great deal of good with a hundred pounds. If you will set this gentleman's mind at ease by taking his pound, I will give the other ninety-nine.

(*Bill, dazed by such opulence, instinctively touches his cap.*)

BARBARA: Oh, youre too extravagant, papa. Bill offers twenty pieces of silver. All you need offer is the other ten. That will make the standard price to buy anybody who's for sale. I'm not; and the Army's not. (*To Bill.*) Youll never have another quiet moment, Bill, until you come around to us. You cant stand out against your salvation.

BILL (*sullenly*): Aw cawnt stend aht agen music awl wrastlers and awtful tangued women. Awve offered to py. Aw can do no more. Tike it or leave it. There it is. (*He throws the sovereign on the drum and sits down on the horse trough. The coin fascinates Snobby Price, who takes an early opportunity of dropping his cap on it.*)

(*Mrs. Baines comes from the shelter. She is dressed as a Salvation Army Commissioner. She is an earnest looking woman of about 40, with a caressing, urgent voice, and an appealing manner.*)

BARBARA: This is my father, Mrs. Baines. (*Undershaft comes from the table, taking his hat off with marked civility.*) Try what you can do with him. He wont listen to me, because he remembers what a fool I was when I was a baby. (*She leaves them together and chats with Jenny.*)

MRS. BAINES: Have you been shown over the shelter, Mr. Undershaft? You know the work we're doing, of course.

UNDERSHAFT (*very civilly*): The whole nation knows it, Mrs. Baines.

MRS. BAINES: No, sir: the whole nation does not know it, or we should not be crippled as we are for want of money to carry our work through the length and breadth of the land. Let me tell you that there would have been rioting this winter in London but for us.

UNDERSHAFT: You really think so?

MRS. BAINES: I know it. I remember 1886, when you rich gentlemen hardened your hearts against the cry of the poor. They broke the windows of your clubs in Pall Mall.

UNDERSHAFT (*gleaming with approval of their method*): And the Mansion House Fund went up next day from thirty thousand pounds to seventy-nine thousand! I remember quite well.

MRS. BAINES: Well, wont you help me to get at the people? They wont break windows then. Come here, Price. Let me show you to this gentleman (*Price comes to be inspected*). Do you remember the window breaking?

PRICE: My ole father thought it was the revolution, maam.

MRS. BAINES: Would you break windows now?

PRICE: Oh no, maam. The windows of eaven av bin opened to me. I know now that the rich man is a sinner like myself.

RUMMY (*appearing above at the loft door*): Snobby Price!

SNOBBY: Wot is it?

RUMMY: Your mother's askin for you at the other gate in Cripps's Lane. She's heard about your confession. (*Price turns pale.*)

MRS. BAINES: Go, Mr. Price; and pray with her.

JENNY: You can go through the shelter, Snobby.

PRICE (*to Mrs. Baines*): I couldnt face her now, maam, with all the weight of my sins fresh on me. Tell her she'll find her son at ome, waitin for her in prayer. (*He skulks off through the gate, incidentally stealing the sovereign on his way out by picking up his cap from the drum.*)

MRS. BAINES (*with swimming eyes*): You see how we take the anger and the bitterness against you out of their hearts, Mr. Undershaft.

UNDERSHAFT: It is certainly most convenient and gratifying to all large employers of labor, Mrs. Baines.

MRS. BAINES: Barbara: Jenny: I have good news: most wonderful news. (*Jenny runs to her.*) My prayers have been answered. I told you they would, Jenny, didnt I?

JENNY: Yes, yes.

BARBARA (*moving nearer to the drum*): Have we got money enough to keep the shelter open?

MRS. BAINES: I hope we shall have enough to keep all the shelters open. Lord Saxmundham has promised us five thousand pounds —

BARBARA: Hooray!

JENNY: Glory!

MRS. BAINES: — if —

BARBARA: "If!" If what?

MRS. BAINES: — if five other gentlemen will give a thousand each to make it up to ten thousand.

BARBARA: Who is Lord Saxmundham? I never heard of him.

UNDERSHAFT (*who has pricked up his ears at the peer's name, and is now watching Barbara curiously*): A new creation, my dear. You have heard of Sir Horace Bodger?

BARBARA: Bodger! Do you mean the distiller? Bodger's whisky!

UNDERSHAFT: That is the man. He is one of the greatest of our public benefactors. He restored the cathedral at Hakington. They made him a baronet for that. He gave half a million to the funds of his party: they made him a baron for that.

SHIRLEY: What will they give him for the five thousand?

UNDERSHAFT: There is nothing left to give him. So the five thousand, I should think, is to save his soul.

MRS. BAINES: Heaven grant it may! Oh Mr. Undershaft, you have some very rich friends. Cant you help us towards the other five thousand? We are going to hold a great meeting this afternoon at the Assembly Hall in the Mile End Road. If I could only announce that one gentleman had come forward to support Lord Saxmundham, others would follow. Dont you know somebody? couldnt you? wouldnt you? (*Her eyes fill with tears.*) Oh, think of those poor people, Mr. Undershaft: think of how much it means to them, and how little to a great man like you.

UNDERSHAFT (*sardonically gallant*): Mrs. Baines: you are irresistible. I cant disappoint you; and I cant deny myself the satisfaction of making Bodger pay up. You shall have your five thousand pounds.

MRS. BAINES: Thank God!

UNDERSHAFT: You dont thank me?

MRS. BAINES: Oh sir, dont try to be cynical: dont be ashamed of being a good man. The Lord will bless you abundantly; and our prayers will be like a strong fortification round you all the days of your life. (*With a touch of caution.*) You will let me have the check to show at the meeting, wont you? Jenny: go in and fetch a pen and ink. (*Jenny runs to the shelter door.*)

UNDERSHAFT: Do not disturb Miss Hill: I have a fountain pen. (*Jenny halts. He sits at the table and writes the check. Cusins rises to make room for him. They all watch him silently.*)

BILL (*cynically, aside to Barbara, his voice and accent horribly debased*): Wot prawce selvytion nah?

BARBARA: Stop. (*Undershaft stops writing: they all turn to her in surprise.*) Mrs. Baines: are you really going to take this money?

MRS. BAINES (*astonished*): Why not, dear?

BARBARA: Why not! Do you know what my father is? Have you forgotten that Lord Saxmundham is Bodger the whisky man? Do you remember how we implored the County Council to stop him from writing Bodger's Whisky in letters of fire against the sky; so that the poor drink-ruined creatures on the Embankment could not wake up from their snatches of sleep without being reminded of their deadly thirst by that wicked sky sign? Do you know that the worst thing I have had to fight here is not the devil, but Bodger, Bodger, Bodger, with his whisky, his distilleries, and his tied houses? Are you going to make our shelter another tied house for him, and ask me to keep it?

BILL: Rotten dranken whisky it is too.

MRS. BAINES: Dear Barbara: Lord Saxmundham has a soul to be saved like any of us. If heaven had found the way to make a good use of his money, are we to set ourselves up against the answer to our prayers?

BARBARA: I know he has a soul to be saved. Let him come down here; and I'll do my best to help him to his salvation. But he wants to send his check down to buy us, and go on being as wicked as ever.

UNDERSHAFT (*with a reasonableness which Cusins alone perceives to be ironical*): My dear Barbara: alcohol is a very necessary article. It heals the sick —

BARBARA: It does nothing of the sort.

UNDERSHAFT: Well, it assists the doctor: that is perhaps a less questionable way of putting it. It makes life bearable to millions of people who could not endure their existence if they were quite sober. It enables Parliament to do things at eleven at night that no sane person would do at eleven in the morning. Is it Bodger's fault that this inestimable gift is deplorably abused by less than one per cent of the poor? (*He turns again to the table; signs the check; and crosses it.*)

MRS. BAINES: Barbara: will there be less drinking or more if all those poor souls we are saving come tomorrow and find the doors of our shelters shut in their faces? Lord Saxmundham gives us the money to stop drinking — to take his own business from him.

CUSINS (*impishly*): Pure self-sacrifice on Bodger's part, clearly! Bless dear Bodger! (*Barbara almost breaks down as Adolphus, too, fails her.*)

UNDERSHAFT (*tearing out the check and pocketing the book as he rises and goes past Cusins to Mrs. Baines*): I also, Mrs. Baines, may claim a little disinterestedness. Think of my business! think of the widows and orphans! the men and lads torn to pieces with shrapnel and poisoned with lyddite! (*Mrs. Baines shrinks; but he goes on remorselessly.*) the oceans of blood, not one drop of which is shed in a really just cause! the ravaged crops! the peaceful peasants forced, women and men, to till their fields under the fire of opposing armies on pain of starvation! the bad blood of the fierce little cowards at home who egg on others to fight for the gratification of their national vanity! All this makes

money for me: I am never richer, never busier than when the papers are full of it. Well, it is your work to preach peace on earth and good will to men. (*Mrs. Baines's face lights up again.*) Every convert you make is a vote against war. (*Her lips move in prayer.*) Yet I give you this money to help you to hasten my own commercial ruin. (*He gives her the check.*)

CUSINS (*mounting the form in an ecstasy of mischief*): The millennium will be inaugurated by the unselfishness of Undershaft and Bodger. Oh be joyful! (*He takes the drumsticks from his pocket and flourishes them.*)

MRS. BAINES (*taking the check*): The longer I live the more proof I see that there is an Infinite Goodness that turns everything to the work of salvation sooner or later. Who would have thought that any good could have come out of war and drink? And yet their profits are brought today to the feet of salvation to do its blessed work. (*She is affected to tears.*)

JENNY (*running to Mrs. Baines and throwing her arms round her*): Oh dear! how blessed, how glorious it all is!

CUSINS (*in a convulsion of irony*): Let us seize this unspeakable moment. Let us march to the great meeting at once. Excuse me just an instant. (*He rushes into the shelter. Jenny takes her tambourine from the drum head.*)

MRS. BAINES: Mr. Undershaft: have you ever seen a thousand people fall on their knees with one impulse and pray? Come with us to the meeting. Barbara shall tell them that the Army is saved, and saved through you.

CUSINS (*returning impetuously from the shelter with a flag and a trombone, and coming between Mrs. Baines and Undershaft*): You shall carry the flag down the first street, Mrs. Baines. (*He gives her the flag.*) Mr. Undershaft is a gifted trombonist: he shall intone an Olympian diapason° to the West Ham Salvation March. (*Aside to Undershaft, as he forces the trombone on him.*) Blow, Machiavelli, blow.

UNDERSHAFT (*aside to him, as he takes the trombone*): The Trumpet in Zion! (*Cusins rushes to the drum, which he takes up and puts on. Undershaft continues, aloud.*) I will do my best. I could vamp a bass if I knew the tune.

CUSINS: It is a wedding chorus from one of Donizetti's operas; but we have converted it. We convert everything to good here, including Bodger. You remember the chorus. "For thee immense rejoicing — immenso giubilo — immenso giubilo." (*With

---

diapason: An outburst of harmonious sound.

drum obbligato.) Rum tum ti tum tum, tum tum ti ta —

BARBARA: Dolly: you are breaking my heart.

CUSINS: What is a broken heart more or less here? Dionysos° Undershaft has descended. I am possessed.

MRS. BAINES: Come, Barbara: I must have my dear Major to carry the flag with me.

JENNY: Yes, yes, Major darling.

CUSINS (*Snatches the tambourine out of Jenny's hand and mutely offers it to Barbara.*)

BARBARA (*coming forward a little as she puts the offer behind her with a shudder, while Cusins recklessly tosses the tambourine back to Jenny and goes to the gate*): I cant come.

JENNY: Not come!

MRS. BAINES (*with tears in her eyes*): Barbara: do you think I am wrong to take the money?

BARBARA (*impulsively going to her and kissing her*): No, no: God help you, dear, you must: you are saving the Army. Go; and may you have a great meeting!

JENNY: But arnt you coming?

BARBARA: No. (*She begins taking off the silver S brooch from her collar.*)

MRS. BAINES: Barbara: what are you doing?

JENNY: Why are you taking your badge off? You cant be going to leave us, Major.

BARBARA (*quietly*): Father: come here.

UNDERSHAFT (*coming to her*): My dear! (*Seeing that she is going to pin the badge on his collar, he retreats to the penthouse in some alarm.*)

BARBARA (*following him*): Don't be frightened. (*She pins the badge on and steps back towards the table, showing him to the others.*) There! It's not much for £5000, is it?

MRS. BAINES: Barbara: if you wont come and pray with us, promise me you will pray for us.

BARBARA: I cant pray now. Perhaps I shall never pray again.

MRS. BAINES: Barbara!

JENNY: Major!

BARBARA (*almost delirious*): I cant bear any more. Quick march!

CUSINS (*calling to the procession in the street outside*): Off we go. Play up, there! Immenso giubilo. (*He gives the time with his drum; and the band strikes up the march, which rapidly becomes more distant as the procession moves briskly away.*)

MRS. BAINES: I must go, dear. Youre overworked: you will be all right tomorrow. We'll never lose you.

Dionysos: The Greek god of wine and the symbol of life-giving power.

Now Jenny: step out with the old flag. Blood and Fire! (*She marches out through the gate with her flag.*)

JENNY: Glory Hallelujah! (*Flourishing her tambourine and marching.*)

UNDERSHAFT (*to Cusins, as he marches out past him easing the slide of his trombone*): "My ducats and my daughter"!°

CUSINS (*following him out*): Money and gunpowder!

BARBARA: Drunkenness and Murder! My God: why hast thou forsaken me?

(*She sinks on the form with her face buried in her hands. The march passes away into silence. Bill Walker steals across to her.*)

BILL (*taunting*): Wot prawce selvytion nah?

SHIRLEY: Don't you hit her when she's down.

BILL: She it me wen aw wiz dahn. Waw shouldnt Aw git a bit o me aown beck?

BARBARA (*raising her head*): I didnt take your money, Bill. (*She crosses the yard to the gate and turns her back on the two men to hide her face from them.*)

BILL (*sneering after her*): Naow, it warnt enaff for you. (*Turning to the drum, he misses the money.*) Ellow! If you aint took it sammun else ez. Weres it gorn? Bly me if Jenny Ill didnt tike it arter all!

RUMMY (*screaming at him from the loft*): You lie, you dirty blackguard! Snobby Price pinched it off the drum when he took up his cap. I was up here all the time an see im do it.

BILL: Wot! Stowl may manney! Waw didnt you call thief on him, you silly aold macker you?

RUMMY: To serve you aht for ittin me acrost the fice. It's cost y'pahnd, that az. (*Raising a paeon of squalid triumph.*) I done you. I'm even with you. Uve ad it aht o y — (*Bill snatches up Shirley's mug and hurls it at her. She slams the loft door and vanishes. The mug smashes against the door and falls in fragments.*)

BILL (*beginning to chuckle*): Tell us, aol menn, wot o'clock this mawnin was it wen im as they call Snobby Prawce was sived?

BARBARA (*turning to him more composedly, and with unspoiled sweetness*): About half past twelve, Bill. And he pinched your pound at a quarter to two. I know. Well, you cant afford to lose it. I'll send it to you.

"My . . . daughter"!: Shylock's line in Shakespeare's *Merchant of Venice*. When Shylock's daughter elopes, taking some of her father's money with her, Shylock is more concerned with the loss of his money (ducats) than with the loss of his daughter.

BILL (*his voice and accent suddenly improving*): Not if Aw wiz to stawve for it. Aw aint to be bought.

SHIRLEY: Aint you? Youd sell yourself to the devil for a pint o beer; only there aint no devil to make the offer.

BILL (*unashamed*): Sao Aw would, mite, and often ev, cheerful. But she cawnt baw me. (*Approaching Barbara.*) You wanted maw soul, did you? Well, you aint got it.

BARBARA: I nearly got it, Bill. But weve sold it back to you for ten thousand pounds.

SHIRLEY: And dear at the money!

BARBARA: No, Peter: it was worth more than money.

BILL (*salvationproof*): It's nao good: you cawnt get rahnd me nah. Aw downt blieve in it; and Awve seen tody that Aw was rawt. (*Going.*) Sao long, aol soupkitchener! Ta, ta, Mijor Earl's Grendorter! (*Turning at the gate.*) Wot prawce selvytion nah? Snobby Prawce! Ha! ha!

BARBARA (*offering her hand*): Goodbye, Bill.

BILL (*taken aback, half plucks his cap off; then shoves it on again defiantly*): Get aht. (*Barbara drops her hand, discouraged. He has a twinge of remorse.*) But thets aw rawt, you knaow. Nathink pasnl. Naow mellice. Sao long, Judy. (*He goes.*)

BARBARA: No malice. So long, Bill.

SHIRLEY (*shaking his head*): You make too much of him, miss, in your innocence.

BARBARA (*going to him*): Peter: I'm like you now. Cleaned out, and lost my job.

SHIRLEY: Youve youth an hope. Thats two better than me.

BARBARA: I'll get you a job, Peter. Thats hope for you: the youth will have to be enough for me. (*She counts her money.*) I have just enough left for two teas at Lockharts, a Rowton doss for you, and my tram and bus home. (*He frowns and rises with offended pride. She takes his arm.*) Dont be proud, Peter: it's sharing between friends. And promise me youll talk to me and not let me cry. (*She draws him towards the gate.*)

SHIRLEY: Well, I'm not accustomed to talk to the like of you —

BARBARA (*gently*): Yes, yes: you must talk to me. Tell me about Tom Paine's books and Bradlaugh's lectures.° Come along.

SHIRLEY: Ah, if you would only read Tom Paine in

Tom Paine's . . . Bradlaugh's lectures: Thomas Paine (1737–1809) was a political radical whose works urged revolution, particularly in France and the United States. Charles Bradlaugh (1833–91) was a social reformer and political free thinker who gave lectures under the pseudonym Iconoclast.

---

the proper spirit, miss! (*They go out through the gate together.*)

ACT III

(*Next day after lunch Lady Britomart is writing in the library in Wilton Crescent. Sarah is reading in the armchair near the window. Barbara, in ordinary fashionable dress, pale and brooding, is on the settee. Charles Lomax enters. He starts on seeing Barbara fashionably attired and in low spirits.*)

LOMAX: Youve left off your uniform!

(*Barbara says nothing; but an expression of pain passes over her face.*)

LADY BRITOMART (*warning him in low tones to be careful*): Charles!

LOMAX (*much concerned, coming behind the settee and bending sympathetically over Barbara*): I'm awfully sorry, Barbara. You know I helped you all I could with the concertina and so forth. (*Momentously.*) Still, I have never shut my eyes to the fact that there is a certain amount of tosh about the Salvation Army. Now the claims of the Church of England —

LADY BRITOMART: Thats enough, Charles. Speak of something suited to your mental capacity.

LOMAX: But surely the Church of England is suited to all our capacities.

BARBARA (*pressing his hand*): Thank you for your sympathy, Cholly. Now go and spoon with Sarah.

LOMAX (*dragging a chair from the writing table and seating himself affectionately by Sarah's side*): How is my ownest today?

SARAH: I wish you wouldnt tell Cholly to do things, Barbara. He always comes straight and does them. Cholly: we're going to the works this afternoon.

LOMAX: What works?

SARAH: The cannon works.

LOMAX: What? your governor's shop!

SARAH: Yes.

LOMAX: Oh I say!

(*Cusins enters in poor condition. He also starts visibly when he sees Barbara without her uniform.*)

BARBARA: I expected you this morning, Dolly. Didnt you guess that?

CUSINS (*sitting down beside her*): I'm sorry. I have only just breakfasted.

SARAH: But weve just finished lunch.

BARBARA: Have you had one of your bad nights?

CUSINS: No: I had rather a good night: in fact, one of the most remarkable nights I have ever passed.

BARBARA: The meeting?

CUSINS: No: after the meeting.

LADY BRITOMART: You should have gone to bed after the meeting. What were you doing?

CUSINS: Drinking.

LADY BRITOMART: Adolphus!
SARAH: Dolly!
BARBARA: Dolly!
LOMAX: Oh I say!

LADY BRITOMART: What were you drinking, may I ask?

CUSINS: A most devilish kind of Spanish burgundy, warranted free from added alcohol: a Temperance burgundy in fact. Its richness in natural alcohol made any addition superfluous.

BARBARA: Are you joking, Dolly?

CUSINS (patiently): No. I have been making a night of it with the nominal head of this household: that is all.

LADY BRITOMART: Andrew made you drunk!

CUSINS: No: he only provided the wine. I think it was Dionysos who made me drunk. (To Barbara.) I told you I was possessed.

LADY BRITOMART: Youre not sober yet. Go home to bed at once.

CUSINS: I have never before ventured to reproach you, Lady Brit; but how could you marry the Prince of Darkness?

LADY BRITOMART: It was much more excusable to marry him than to get drunk with him. That is a new accomplishment of Andrew's, by the way. He usent to drink.

CUSINS: He doesnt now. He only sat there and completed the wreck of my moral basis, the rout of my convictions, the purchase of my soul. He cares for you, Barbara. That is what makes him so dangerous to me.

BARBARA: That has nothing to do with it, Dolly. There are larger loves and diviner dreams than the fireside ones. You know that, dont you?

CUSINS: Yes: that is our understanding. I know it. I hold to it. Unless he can win me on that holier ground he may amuse me for a while; but he can get no deeper hold, strong as he is.

BARBARA: Keep to that; and the end will be right. Now tell me what happened at the meeting?

CUSINS: It was an amazing meeting. Mrs. Baines almost died of emotion. Jenny Hill simply gibbered with hysteria. The Prince of Darkness played his trombone like a madman: its brazen roarings were like the laughter of the damned. 117 conversions took place then and there. They prayed with the most touching sincerity and gratitude for Bodger, and for the anonymous donor of the £5000. Your father would not let his name be given.

LOMAX: That was rather fine of the old man, you know. Most chaps would have wanted the advertisement.

CUSINS: He said all the charitable institutions would be down on him like kites on a battlefield if he gave his name.

LADY BRITOMART: Thats Andrew all over. He never does a proper thing without giving an improper reason for it.

CUSINS: He convinced me that I have all my life been doing improper things for proper reasons.

LADY BRITOMART: Adolphus: now that Barbara has left the Salvation Army, you had better leave it too. I will not have you playing that drum in the streets.

CUSINS: Your orders are already obeyed, Lady Brit.

BARBARA: Dolly: were you ever really in earnest about it? Would you have joined if you had never seen me?

CUSINS (disingenuously): Well — er — well, possibly, as a collector of religions —

LOMAX (cunningly): Not as a drummer, though, you know. You are a very clearheaded brainy chap, Dolly; and it must have been apparent to you that there is a certain amount of tosh about —

LADY BRITOMART: Charles: if you must drivel, drivel like a grown-up man and not like a schoolboy.

LOMAX (out of countenance): Well, drivel is drivel, dont you know, whatever a man's age.

LADY BRITOMART: In good society in England, Charles, men drivel at all ages by repeating silly formulas with an air of wisdom. Schoolboys make their own formulas out of slang, like you. When they reach your age, and get political private secretaryships and things of that sort, they drop slang and get their formulas out of the *Spectator* or *The Times*. You had better confine yourself to *The Times*. You will find that there is a certain amount of tosh about *The Times*; but at least its language is reputable.

LOMAX (overwhelmed): You are so awfully strongminded, Lady Brit —

LADY BRITOMART: Rubbish! (Morrison comes in.) What is it?

MORRISON: If you please, my lady, Mr. Undershaft has just drove up to the door.

LADY BRITOMART: Well, let him in. (Morrison hesitates.) Whats the matter with you?

MORRISON: Shall I announce him, my lady; or is he at home here, so to speak, my lady?

LADY BRITOMART: Announce him.

MORRISON: Thank you, my lady. You wont mind my

asking, I hope. The occasion is in a manner of speaking new to me.

LADY BRITOMART: Quite right. Go and let him in.

MORRISON: Thank you, my lady. (*He withdraws.*)

LADY BRITOMART: Children: go and get ready. (*Sarah and Barbara go upstairs for their out-of-door wraps.*) Charles: go and tell Stephen to come down here in five minutes: you will find him in the drawing room. (*Charles goes.*) Adolphus: tell them to send round the carriage in about fifteen minutes. (*Adolphus goes.*)

MORRISON (*at the door*): Mr. Undershaft.

(*Undershaft comes in. Morrison goes out.*)

UNDERSHAFT: Alone! How fortunate!

LADY BRITOMART (*rising*): Dont be sentimental, Andrew. Sit down. (*She sits on the settee: he sits beside her, on her left. She comes to the point before he has time to breathe.*) Sarah must have £800 a year until Charles Lomax comes into his property. Barbara will need more, and need it permanently, because Adolphus hasnt any property.

UNDERSHAFT (*resignedly*): Yes, my dear: I will see to it. Anything else? for yourself, for instance?

LADY BRITOMART: I want to talk to you about Stephen.

UNDERSHAFT (*rather wearily*): Dont, my dear. Stephen doesnt interest me.

LADY BRITOMART: He does interest me. He is our son.

UNDERSHAFT: Do you really think so? He has induced us to bring him into the world; but he chose his parents very incongruously, I think. I see nothing of myself in him, and less of you.

LADY BRITOMART: Andrew: Stephen is an excellent son, and a most steady, capable, highminded young man. You are simply trying to find an excuse for disinheriting him.

UNDERSHAFT: My dear Biddy: the Undershaft tradition disinherits him. It would be dishonest of me to leave the cannon foundry to my son.

LADY BRITOMART: It would be most unnatural and improper of you to leave it to anyone else, Andrew. Do you suppose this wicked and immoral tradition can be kept up for ever? Do you pretend that Stephen could not carry on the foundry just as well as all the other sons of the big business houses?

UNDERSHAFT: Yes: he could learn the office routine without understanding the business, like all the other sons; and the firm would go by its own momentum until the real Undershaft — probably an Italian or a German — would invent a new method and cut him out.

LADY BRITOMART: There is nothing that any Italian or German could do that Stephen could not do. And Stephen at least has breeding.

UNDERSHAFT: The son of a foundling! Nonsense!

LADY BRITOMART: My son, Andrew! And even you may have good blood in your veins for all you know.

UNDERSHAFT: True. Probably I have. That is another argument in favor of a foundling.

LADY BRITOMART: Andrew: dont be aggravating. And dont be wicked. At present you are both.

UNDERSHAFT: This conversation is part of the Undershaft tradition, Biddy. Every Undershaft's wife has treated him to it ever since the house was founded. It is mere waste of breath. If the tradition be ever broken it will be for an abler man than Stephen.

LADY BRITOMART (*pouting*): Then go away.

UNDERSHAFT (*deprecatory*): Go away!

LADY BRITOMART: Yes: go away. If you will do nothing for Stephen, you are not wanted here. Go to your foundling, whoever he is; and look after him.

UNDERSHAFT: The fact is, Biddy —

LADY BRITOMART: Dont call me Biddy. I dont call you Andy.

UNDERSHAFT: I will not call my wife Britomart: it is not good sense. Seriously, my love, the Undershaft tradition has landed me in a difficulty. I am getting on in years; and my partner Lazarus has at last made a stand and insisted that the succession must be settled one way or the other; and of course he is quite right. You see, I havent found a fit successor yet.

LADY BRITOMART (*obstinately*): There is Stephen.

UNDERSHAFT: Thats just it: all the foundlings I can find are exactly like Stephen.

LADY BRITOMART: Andrew!

UNDERSHAFT: I want a man with no relations and no schooling: that is, a man who would be out of the running altogether if he were not a strong man. And I cant find him. Every blessed foundling nowadays is snapped up in his infancy by Barnardo homes, or School Board officers, or Boards of Guardians; and if he shows the least ability he is fastened on by schoolmasters; trained to win scholarships like a racehorse; crammed with secondhand ideas; drilled and disciplined in docility and what they call good taste; and lamed for life so that he is fit for nothing but teaching. If you want to keep the foundry in the family, you had better find an eligible foundling and marry him to Barbara.

LADY BRITOMART: Ah! Barbara! Your Pet! You would sacrifice Stephen to Barbara.

UNDERSHAFT: Cheerfully. And you, my dear, would boil Barbara to make soup for Stephen.

LADY BRITOMART: Andrew: this is not a question of our likings and dislikings: it is a question of duty. It is your duty to make Stephen your successor.

UNDERSHAFT: Just as much as it is your duty to submit

to your husband. Come, Biddy! these tricks of the governing class are of no use with me. I am one of the governing class myself; and it is waste of time giving tracts to a missionary. I have the power in this matter; and I am not to be humbugged into using it for your purposes.

LADY BRITOMART: Andrew: you can talk my head off; but you cant change wrong into right. And your tie is all on one side. Put it straight.

UNDERSHAFT (*disconcerted*): It won't stay unless it's pinned (*he fumbles at it with childish grimaces*) —

(*Stephen comes in.*)

STEPHEN (*at the door*): I beg your pardon. (*About to retire.*)

LADY BRITOMART: No: come in, Stephen. (*Stephen comes forward to his mother's writing table.*)

UNDERSHAFT (*not very cordially*): Good afternoon.

STEPHEN (*coldly*): Good afternoon.

UNDERSHAFT (*to Lady Britomart*): He knows all about the tradition, I suppose?

LADY BRITOMART: Yes. (*To Stephen.*) It is what I told you last night, Stephen.

UNDERSHAFT (*sulkily*): I understand you want to come into the cannon business.

STEPHEN: *I* go into trade! Certainly not.

UNDERSHAFT (*opening his eyes, greatly eased in mind and manner*): Oh! in that case —

LADY BRITOMART: Cannons are not trade, Stephen. They are enterprise.

STEPHEN: I have no intention of becoming a man of business in any sense. I have no capacity for business and no taste for it. I intend to devote myself to politics.

UNDERSHAFT (*rising*): My dear boy: this is an immense relief to me. And I trust it may prove an equally good thing for the country. I was afraid you would consider yourself disparaged and slighted. (*He moves towards Stephen as if to shake hands with him.*)

LADY BRITOMART (*rising and interposing*): Stephen: I cannot allow you to throw away an enormous property like this.

STEPHEN (*stiffly*): Mother: there must be an end of treating me as a child, if you please. (*Lady Britomart recoils, deeply wounded by his tone.*) Until last night I did not take your attitude seriously, because I did not think you meant it seriously. But I find now that you left me in the dark as to matters which you should have explained to me years ago. I am extremely hurt and offended. Any further discussion of my intentions had better take place with my father, as between one man and another.

LADY BRITOMART: Stephen! (*She sits down again, her eyes filling with tears.*)

UNDERSHAFT (*with grave compassion*): You see, my dear, it is only the big men who can be treated as children.

STEPHEN: I am sorry, mother, that you have forced me —

UNDERSHAFT (*stopping him*): Yes, yes, yes, yes: thats all right, Stephen. She wont interfere with you any more: your independence is achieved: you have won your latchkey. Dont rub it in; and above all, dont apologize. (*He resumes his seat.*) Now what about your future, as between one man and another — I beg your pardon, Biddy: as between two men and a woman.

LADY BRITOMART (*who has pulled herself together strongly*): I quite understand, Stephen. By all means go your own way if you feel strong enough. (*Stephen sits down magisterially in the chair at the writing table with an air of affirming his majority.*)

UNDERSHAFT: It is settled that you do not ask for the succession to the cannon business.

STEPHEN: I hope it is settled that I repudiate the cannon business.

UNDERSHAFT: Come, come! dont be so devilishly sulky: it's boyish. Freedom should be generous. Besides, I owe you a fair start in life in exchange for disinheriting you. You cant become prime minister all at once. Havent you a turn for something? What about literature, art, and so forth?

STEPHEN: I have nothing of the artist about me, either in faculty or character, thank Heaven!

UNDERSHAFT: A philosopher, perhaps? Eh?

STEPHEN: I make no such ridiculous pretension.

UNDERSHAFT: Just so. Well, there is the army, the navy, the Church, the Bar. The Bar requires some ability. What about the Bar?

STEPHEN: I have not studied law. And I am afraid I have not the necessary push — I believe that is the name barristers give to their vulgarity — for success in pleading.

UNDERSHAFT: Rather a difficult case, Stephen. Hardly anything left but the stage, is there? (*Stephen makes an impatient movement.*) Well, come! is there anything you know or care for?

STEPHEN (*rising and looking at him steadily*): I know the difference between right and wrong.

UNDERSHAFT (*hugely tickled*): You dont say so! What! no capacity for business, no knowledge of law, no sympathy with art, no pretension to philosophy; only a simple knowledge of the secret that has puzzled all the philosophers, baffled all the lawyers, muddled all the men of business, and ruined most of the artists: the secret of right and wrong. Why, man, youre a genius, a master of masters, a god! At twenty-four, too!

STEPHEN (*keeping his temper with difficulty*): You are

pleased to be facetious. I pretend to nothing more than any honorable English gentleman claims as his birthright. (*He sits down angrily.*)

UNDERSHAFT: Oh, thats everybody's birthright. Look at poor little Jenny Hill, the Salvation lassie! she would think you were laughing at her if you asked her to stand up in the street and teach grammar or geography or mathematics or even drawing room dancing; but it never occurs to her to doubt that she can teach morals and religion. You are all alike, you respectable people. You cant tell me the bursting strain of a ten-inch gun, which is a very simple matter; but you all think you can tell me the bursting strain of a man under temptation. You darent handle high explosives; but youre all ready to handle honesty and truth and justice and the whole duty of man, and kill one another at that game. What a country! What a world!

LADY BRITOMART (*uneasily*): What do you think he had better do, Andrew?

UNDERSHAFT: Oh, just what he wants to do. He knows nothing and he thinks he knows everything. That points clearly to a political career. Get him a private secretaryship to someone who can get him an Under Secretaryship; and then leave him alone. He will find his natural and proper place in the end on the Treasury Bench.

STEPHEN (*springing up again*): I am sorry, sir, that you force me to forget the respect due to you as my father. I am an Englishman and I will not hear the Government of my country insulted. (*He thrusts his hands in his pockets and walks angrily across to the window.*)

UNDERSHAFT (*with a touch of brutality*): The government of your country! *I* am the government of your country: I, and Lazarus. Do you suppose that you and half a dozen amateurs like you, sitting in a row in that foolish gabble shop, can govern Undershaft and Lazarus? No, my friend: you will do what pays *us.* You will make war when it suits us, and keep peace when it doesnt. You will find out that trade requires certain measures when we have decided on those measures. When I want anything to keep my dividends up, you will discover that my want is a national need. When other people want something to keep my dividends down, you will call out the police and military. And in return you shall have the support and applause of my newspapers, and the delight of imagining that you are a great statesman. Government of your country! Be off with you, my boy, and play with your caucuses and leading articles and historic parties and great leaders and burning questions and the rest of your toys. *I* am going back to my counting-house to pay the piper and call the tune.

STEPHEN (*actually smiling, and putting his hand on his father's shoulder with indulgent patronage*): Really, my dear father, it is impossible to be angry with you. You dont know how absurd all this sounds to me. You are very properly proud of having been industrious enough to make money; and it is greatly to your credit that you have made so much of it. But it has kept you in circles where you are valued for your money and deferred to for it, instead of in the doubtless very old-fashioned and behind-the-times public school and university where I formed my habits of mind. It is natural for you to think that money governs England; but you must allow me to think I know better.

UNDERSHAFT: And what does govern England, pray?

STEPHEN: Character, father, character.

UNDERSHAFT: Whose character? Yours or mine?

STEPHEN: Neither yours nor mine, father, but the best elements in the English national character.

UNDERSHAFT: Stephen: Ive found your profession for you. Youre a born journalist. I'll start you with a high-toned weekly review. There!

(*Before Stephen can reply Sarah, Barbara, Lomax, and Cusins come in ready for walking. Barbara crosses the room to the window and looks out. Cusins drifts amiably to the armchair. Lomax remains near the door, while Sarah comes to her mother.*)

(*Stephen goes to the smaller writing table and busies himself with his letters.*)

SARAH: Go and get ready, mamma: the carriage is waiting. (*Lady Britomart leaves the room.*)

UNDERSHAFT (*to Sarah*): Good day, my dear. Good afternoon, Mr. Lomax.

LOMAX (*vaguely*): Ahdedoo.

UNDERSHAFT (*to Cusins*): Quite well after last night, Euripides, eh?

CUSINS: As well as can be expected.

UNDERSHAFT: Thats right. (*To Barbara.*) So you are coming to see my death and devastation factory, Barbara?

BARBARA (*at the window*): You came yesterday to see my salvation factory. I promised you a return visit.

LOMAX (*coming forward between Sarah and Undershaft*): Youll find it awfully interesting. Ive been through the Woolwich Arsenal and it gives you a ripping feeling of security, you know, to think of the lot of beggars we could kill if it came to fighting. (*To Undershaft, with sudden solemnity.*) Still, it must be rather an awful reflection for you, from the religious point of view as it were. Youre getting on, you know, and all that.

SARAH: You dont mind Cholly's imbecility, papa, do you?

LOMAX (*much taken aback*): Oh I say!

UNDERSHAFT: Mr. Lomax looks at the matter in a very proper spirit, my dear.

LOMAX: Just so. Thats all I meant, I assure you.

SARAH: Are you coming, Stephen?

STEPHEN: Well, I am rather busy — er — (*Magnanimously.*) Oh well, yes: I'll come. That is, if there is room for me.

UNDERSHAFT: I can take two with me in a little motor I am experimenting with for field use. You wont mind its being rather unfashionable. It's not painted yet; but it's bulletproof.

LOMAX (*appalled at the prospect of confronting Wilton Crescent in an unpainted motor*): Oh I say!

SARAH: The carriage for me, thank you. Barbara doesnt mind what she's seen in.

LOMAX: I say, Dolly, old chap: do you really mind the car being a guy?° Because of course if you do I'll go in it. Still —

CUSINS: I prefer it.

LOMAX: Thanks awfully, old man. Come, my ownest. (*He hurries out to secure his seat in the carriage. Sarah follows him.*)

CUSINS (*moodily walking across to Lady Britomart's writing table*): Why are we two coming to this Works Department of Hell? that is what I ask myself.

BARBARA: I have always thought of it as a sort of pit where lost creatures with blackened faces stirred up smoky fires and were driven and tormented by my father. Is it like that, dad?

UNDERSHAFT (*scandalized*): My dear! It is a spotlessly clean and beautiful hillside town.

CUSINS: With a Methodist chapel? Oh do say theres a Methodist chapel.

UNDERSHAFT: There are two: a Primitive one and a sophisticated one. There is even an Ethical Society; but it is not much patronized, as my men are all strongly religious. In the High Explosives Sheds they object to the presence of Agnostics as unsafe.

CUSINS: And yet they dont object to you!

BARBARA: Do they obey all your orders?

UNDERSHAFT: I never give them any orders. When I speak to one of them it is "Well, Jones, is the baby doing well? and has Mrs. Jones made a good recovery?" "Nicely, thank you, sir." And thats all.

CUSINS: But Jones has to be kept in order. How do you maintain discipline among your men?

UNDERSHAFT: I dont. They do. You see, the one thing Jones wont stand is any rebellion from the man under him, or any assertion of social equality between the wife of the man with 4 shillings a week less than himself, and Mrs. Jones! Of course they all rebel against me, theoretically. Practically, every

guy: A person (or thing) of grotesque appearance.

man of them keeps the man just below him in his place. I never meddle with them. I never bully them. I dont even bully Lazarus. I say that certain things are to be done; but I dont order anybody to do them. I dont say, mind you, that there is no ordering about and snubbing and even bullying. The men snub the boys and order them about; the carmen snub the sweepers; the artisans snub the unskilled laborers; the foremen drive and bully both the laborers and artisans; the assistant engineers find fault with the foremen; the chief engineers drop on the assistants; the departmental managers worry the chiefs; and the clerks have tall hats and hymnbooks and keep up the social tone by refusing to associate on equal terms with anybody. The result is a colossal profit, which comes to me.

CUSINS (*revolted*): You really are a — well, what I was saying yesterday.

BARBARA: What was he saying yesterday?

UNDERSHAFT: Never mind, my dear. He thinks I have made you unhappy. Have I?

BARBARA: Do you think I can be happy in this vulgar silly dress? I! who have worn the uniform. Do you understand what you have done to me? Yesterday I had a man's soul in my hand. I set him in the way of life with his face to salvation. But when we took your money he turned back to drunkenness and derision. (*With intense conviction.*) I will never forgive you that. If I had a child, and you destroyed its body with your explosives — if you murdered Dolly with your horrible guns — I could forgive you if my forgiveness would open the gates of heaven to you. But to take a human soul from me, and turn it into the soul of a wolf! that is worse than any murder.

UNDERSHAFT: Does my daughter despair so easily? Can you strike a man to the heart and leave no mark on him?

BARBARA (*her face lighting up*): Oh, you are right: he can never be lost now: where was my faith?

CUSINS: Oh, clever clever devil!

BARBARA: You may be a devil; but God speaks through you sometimes. (*She takes her father's hands and kisses them.*) You have given me back my happiness: I feel it deep down now, though my spirit is troubled.

UNDERSHAFT: You have learnt something. That always feels at first as if you had lost something.

BARBARA: Well, take me to the factory of death; and let me learn something more. There must be some truth or other behind all this frightful irony. Come, Dolly. (*She goes out.*)

CUSINS: My guardian angel! (*To Undershaft.*) Avaunt! (*He follows Barbara.*)

STEPHEN (*quietly, at the writing table*): You must not

mind Cusins, father. He is a very amiable good fellow; but he is a Greek scholar and naturally a little eccentric.

UNDERSHAFT: Ah, quite so. Thank you, Stephen. Thank you. (*He goes out.*)

(*Stephen smiles patronizingly; buttons his coat responsibly; and crosses the room to the door. Lady Britomart, dressed for out of doors, opens it before he reaches it. She looks round for the others; looks at Stephen and turns to go without a word.*)

STEPHEN (*embarrassed*): Mother —

LADY BRITOMART: Dont be apologetic, Stephen. And dont forget that you have outgrown your mother. (*She goes out.*)

(*Perivale St. Andrews lies between two Middlesex hills, half climbing the northern one. It is an almost smokeless town of white walls, roofs of narrow green slates or red tiles, tall trees, domes, campaniles, and slender chimney shafts, beautifully situated and beautiful in itself. The best view of it is obtained from the crest of a slope about half a mile to the east, where the high explosives are dealt with. The foundry lies hidden in the depths between, the tops of its chimneys sprouting like huge skittles into the middle distance. Across the crest runs an emplacement of concrete, with a firestep, and a parapet which suggests a fortification, because there is a huge cannon of the obsolete Woolwich Infant pattern peering across it at the town. The cannon is mounted on an experimental gun carriage: possibly the original model of the Undershaft disappearing rampart gun alluded to by Stephen. The firestep, being a convenient place to sit, is furnished here and there with straw disc cushions; and at one place there is the additional luxury of a fur rug.*)

(*Barbara is standing on the firestep, looking over the parapet towards the town. On her right is the cannon; on her left the end of a shed raised on piles, with a ladder of three or four steps up to the door, which opens outwards and has a little wooden landing at the threshold, with a fire bucket in the corner of the landing. Several dummy soldiers more or less mutilated, with straw protruding from their gashes, have been shoved out of the way under the landing. A few others are nearly upright against the shed; and one has fallen forward and lies, like a grotesque corpse, on the emplacement. The parapet stops short of the shed, leaving a gap which is the beginning of the path down the hill through the foundry to the town. The rug is on the firestep near this gap. Down on the emplacement behind the cannon is a trolley carrying a huge conical bombshell with a red band painted on it. Further to the right is the door of an office, which, like the sheds, is of the lightest possible construction.*)

(*Cusins arrives by the path from the town.*)

BARBARA: Well?

CUSINS: Not a ray of hope. Everything perfect! wonderful! real! It only needs a cathedral to be a heavenly city instead of a hellish one.

BARBARA: Have you found out whether they have done anything for old Peter Shirley?

CUSINS: They have found him a job as gatekeeper and timekeeper. He's frightfully miserable. He calls the timekeeping brainwork, and says he isnt used to it; and his gate lodge is so splendid that he's ashamed to use the rooms, and skulks in the scullery.

BARBARA: Poor Peter!

(*Stephen arrives from the town. He carries a fieldglass.*)

STEPHEN (*enthusiastically*): Have you two seen the place? Why did you leave us?

CUSINS: I wanted to see everything I was not intended to see; and Barbara wanted to make the men talk.

STEPHEN: Have you found anything discreditable?

CUSINS: No. They call him Dandy Andy and are proud of his being a cunning old rascal; but it's all horribly, frightfully, immorally, unanswerably perfect.

(*Sarah arrives.*)

SARAH: Heavens! what a place! (*She crosses to the trolley.*) Did you see the nursing home? (*She sits down on the shell.*)

STEPHEN: Did you see the libraries and schools?

SARAH: Did you see the ballroom and the banqueting chamber in the Town Hall!?

STEPHEN: Have you gone into the insurance fund, the pension fund, the building society, the various applications of cooperation!?

(*Undershaft comes from the office, with a sheaf of telegrams in his hand.*)

UNDERSHAFT: Well, have you seen everything? I'm sorry I was called away. (*Indicating the telegrams.*) Good news from Manchuria.

STEPHEN: Another Japanese victory?

UNDERSHAFT: Oh, I dont know. Which side wins does not concern us here. No: the good news is that the aerial battleship is a tremendous success. At the first trial it has wiped out a fort with three hundred soldiers in it.

CUSINS (*from the platform*): Dummy soldiers?

UNDERSHAFT (*striding across to Stephen and kicking the prostrate dummy brutally out of his way*): No: the real thing.

(*Cusins and Barbara exchange glances. Then Cusins sits on the step and buries his face in his hands. Barbara gravely lays her hand on his shoulder. He looks up at her in whimsical desperation.*)

UNDERSHAFT: Well, Stephen, what do you think of the place?

STEPHEN: Oh, magnificent. A perfect triumph of modern industry. Frankly, my dear father, I have been a fool: I had no idea of what it all meant: of the wonderful forethought, the power of organization, the administrative capacity, the financial genius, the colossal capital it represents. I have been repeating to myself as I came through your streets "Peace hath her victories no less renowned than War." I have only one misgiving about it all.

UNDERSHAFT: Out with it.

STEPHEN: Well, I cannot help thinking that all this provision for every want of your workmen may sap their independence and weaken their sense of responsibility. And greatly as we enjoyed our tea at that splendid restaurant — how they gave us all that luxury and cake and jam and cream for threepence I really cannot imagine! — still you must remember that restaurants break up home life. Look at the continent, for instance! Are you sure so much pampering is really good for the men's characters?

UNDERSHAFT: Well you see, my dear boy, when you are organizing civilization you have to make up your mind whether trouble and anxiety are good things or not. If you decide that they are, then, I take it, you simply dont organize civilization; and there you are, with trouble and anxiety enough to make us all angels! But if you decide the other way, you may as well go through with it. However, Stephen, our characters are safe here. A sufficient dose of anxiety is always provided by the fact that we may be blown to smithereens at any moment.

SARAH: By the way, papa, where do you make the explosives?

UNDERSHAFT: In separate little sheds like that one. When one of them blows up, it costs very little, and only the people quite close to it are killed.

(Stephen, who is quite close to it, looks at it rather scaredly, and moves away quickly to the cannon. At the same moment the door of the shed is thrown abruptly open; and a foreman in overalls and list slippers comes out on the little landing and holds the door for Lomax, who appears in the doorway.)

LOMAX (with studied coolness): My good fellow: you neednt get into a state of nerves. Nothing's going to happen to you; and I suppose it wouldnt be the end of the world if anything did. A little bit of British pluck is what you want, old chap. (He descends and strolls across to Sarah.)

UNDERSHAFT (to the foreman): Anything wrong, Bilton?

BILTON (with ironic calm): Gentleman walked into the high explosives shed and lit a cigarette, sir: thats all.

UNDERSHAFT: Ah, quite so. (Going over to Lomax.) Do you happen to remember what you did with the match?

LOMAX: Oh come! I'm not a fool. I took jolly good care to blow it out before I chucked it away.

BILTON: The top of it was red hot inside, sir.

LOMAX: Well, suppose it was! I didnt chuck it into any of your messes.

UNDERSHAFT: Think no more of it, Mr. Lomax. By the way, would you mind lending me your matches.

LOMAX (offering his box): Certainly.

UNDERSHAFT: Thanks. (He pockets the matches.)

LOMAX (lecturing to the company generally): You know, these high explosives dont go off like gunpowder, except when theyre in a gun. When theyre spread loose, you can put a match to them without the least risk: they just burn quietly like a bit of paper. (Warming to the scientific interest of the subject.) Did you know that, Undershaft? Have you ever tried?

UNDERSHAFT: Not on a large scale, Mr. Lomax. Bilton will give you a sample of guncotton when you are leaving if you ask him. You can experiment with it at home. (Bilton looks puzzled.)

SARAH: Bilton will do nothing of the sort, papa. I suppose it's your business to blow up the Russians and Japs; but you might really stop short of blowing up poor Cholly. (Bilton gives it up and retires into the shed.)

LOMAX: My ownest, there is no danger. (He sits beside her on the shell.)

(Lady Britomart arrives from the town with a bouquet.)

LADY BRITOMART (impetuously): Andrew: you shouldnt have let me see this place.

UNDERSHAFT: Why, my dear?

LADY BRITOMART: Never mind why: you shouldnt have: thats all. To think of all that (indicating the town) being yours! and that you have kept it to yourself all these years!

UNDERSHAFT: It does not belong to me. I belong to it. It is the Undershaft inheritance.

LADY BRITOMART: It is not. Your ridiculous cannons and that noisy banking foundry may be the Undershaft inheritance; but all that plate and linen, all that furniture and those houses and orchards and gardens belong to us. They belong to me: they are not a man's business. I wont give them up. You must be out of your senses to throw them all away; and if you persist in such folly, I will call in a doctor.

UNDERSHAFT (*stooping to smell the bouquet*): Where did you get the flowers, my dear?

LADY BRITOMART: Your men presented them to me in your William Morris Labor Church.

CUSINS: Oh! It needed only that. A Labor Church! (*He mounts the firestep distractedly and leans with his elbows on the parapet, turning his back to them.*)

LADY BRITOMART: Yes, with Morris's words in mosaic letters ten feet high around the dome. NO MAN IS GOOD ENOUGH TO BE ANOTHER MAN'S MASTER. The cynicism of it!

UNDERSHAFT: It shocked the men at first, I am afraid. But now they take no more notice of it than of the ten commandments in church.

LADY BRITOMART: Andrew: you are trying to put me off the subject of the inheritance by profane jokes. Well, you shant. I dont ask it any longer for Stephen: he has inherited far too much of your perversity to be fit for it. But Barbara has rights as well as Stephen. Why should not Adolphus succeed to the inheritance? I could manage the town for him and he can look after the cannons, if they are really necessary.

UNDERSHAFT: I should ask nothing better if Adolphus were a foundling. He is exactly the sort of new blood that is wanted in English business. But he's not a foundling; and theres an end of it. (*He makes for the office door.*)

CUSINS (*turning to them*): Not quite. (*They all turn and stare at him.*) I think — Mind! I am not committing myself in any way as to my future course — but I think the foundling difficulty can be got over. (*He jumps down to the emplacement.*)

UNDERSHAFT (*coming back to him*): What do you mean?

CUSINS: Well, I have something to say which is in the nature of a confession.

SARAH:
LADY BRITOMART: ⎫
BARBARA: ⎬ Confession!
STEPHEN: ⎭

LOMAX: Oh I say!

CUSINS: Yes, a confession. Listen, all. Until I met Barbara I thought myself in the main an honorable, truthful man, because I wanted the approval of my conscience more than I wanted anything else. But the moment I saw Barbara, I wanted her far more than the approval of my conscience.

LADY BRITOMART: Adolphus!

CUSINS: It is true. You accused me yourself, Lady Brit, of joining the Army to worship Barbara; and so I did. She bought my soul like a flower at a street corner; but she bought it for herself.

UNDERSHAFT: What! Not for Dionysos or another?

CUSINS: Dionysos and all the others are in herself. I adored what was divine in her, and was therefore a true worshipper. But I was romantic about her too. I thought she was a woman of the people, and that a marriage with a professor of Greek would be far beyond the wildest social ambitions of her rank.

LADY BRITOMART: Adolphus!!

LOMAX: Oh I say!!!

CUSINS: When I learnt the horrible truth —

LADY BRITOMART: What do you mean by the horrible truth, pray?

CUSINS: That she was enormously rich; that her grandfather was an earl; that her father was the Prince of Darkness —

UNDERSHAFT: Chut!

CUSINS: — and that I was only an adventurer trying to catch a rich wife, then I stooped to deceive her about my birth.

BARBARA (*rising*): Dolly!

LADY BRITOMART: Your birth! Now Adolphus, dont dare to make up a wicked story for the sake of these wretched cannons. Remember: I have seen photographs of your parents; and the Agent General for South Western Australia knows them personally and has assured me that they are most respectable married people.

CUSINS: So they are in Australia; but here they are outcasts. Their marriage is legal in Australia, but not in England. My mother is my father's deceased wife's sister; and in this island I am consequently a foundling. (*Sensation.*)

BARBARA: Silly! (*She climbs to the cannon, and leans, listening, in the angle it makes with the parapet.*)

CUSINS: Is the subterfuge good enough, Machiavelli?

UNDERSHAFT (*thoughtfully*): Biddy: this may be a way out of the difficulty.

LADY BRITOMART: Stuff! A man cant make cannons any the better for being his own cousin instead of his proper self. (*She sits down on the rug with a bounce that expresses her downright contempt for their casuistry.*)

UNDERSHAFT (*to Cusins*): You are an educated man. That is against the tradition.

CUSINS: Once in ten thousand times it happens that the schoolboy is a born master of what they try to teach him. Greek has not destroyed my mind: it has nourished it. Besides, I did not learn it at an English public school.

UNDERSHAFT: Hm! Well, I cannot afford to be too particular: you have cornered the foundling market. Let it pass. You are eligible, Euripides: you are eligible.

BARBARA: Dolly: yesterday morning, when Stephen

told us all about the tradition, you became very silent, and you have been strange and excited ever since. Were you thinking of your birth then?

CUSINS: When the finger of Destiny suddenly points at a man in the middle of his breakfast, it makes him thoughtful.

UNDERSHAFT: Aha! You have had your eye on the business, my young friend, have you?

CUSINS: Take care! There is an abyss of moral horror between me and your accursed aerial battleships.

UNDERSHAFT: Never mind the abyss for the present. Let us settle the practical details and leave your final decision open. You know that you will have to change your name. Do you object to that?

CUSINS: Would any man named Adolphus — any man called Dolly! — object to be called something else?

UNDERSHAFT: Good. Now, as to money! I propose to treat you handsomely from the beginning. You shall start at a thousand a year.

CUSINS (*with sudden heat, his spectacles twinkling with mischief*): A thousand! You dare offer a miserable thousand to the son-in-law of a millionaire! No, by Heavens, Machiavelli! you shall not cheat me. You cannot do without me; and I can do without you. I must have two thousand five hundred a year for two years. At the end of that time, if I am a failure, I go. But if I am a success, and stay on, you must give me the other five thousand.

UNDERSHAFT: What other five thousand?

CUSINS: To make the two years up to five thousand a year. The two thousand five hundred is only half pay in case I should turn out a failure. The third year I must have ten percent on the profits.

UNDERSHAFT (*taken aback*): Ten percent! Why, man, do you know what my profits are?

CUSINS: Enormous, I hope: otherwise I shall require twenty-five percent.

UNDERSHAFT: But, Mr. Cusins, this is a serious matter of business. You are not bringing any capital into the concern.

CUSINS: What! no capital! Is my mastery of Greek no capital? Is my access to the subtlest thought, the loftiest poetry yet attained by humanity, no capital? My character! my intellect! my life! my career! what Barbara calls my soul! are these no capital? Say another word; and I double my salary.

UNDERSHAFT: Be reasonable —

CUSINS (*peremptorily*): Mr. Undershaft: you have my terms. Take them or leave them.

UNDERSHAFT (*recovering himself*): Very well, I note your terms; and I offer you half.

CUSINS (*disgusted*): Half!

UNDERSHAFT (*firmly*): Half.

CUSINS: You call yourself a gentleman; and you offer me half!!

UNDERSHAFT: I do not call myself a gentleman; but I offer you half.

CUSINS: This to your future partner! your successor! your son-in-law!

BARBARA: You are selling your own soul, Dolly, not mine. Leave me out of the bargain, please.

UNDERSHAFT: Come! I will go a step further for Barbara's sake. I will give you three-fifths; but that is my last word.

CUSINS: Done!

LOMAX: Done in the eye! Why, *I* get only eight hundred, you know.

CUSINS: By the way, Mac, I am a classical scholar not an arithmetical one. Is three-fifths more than half or less?

UNDERSHAFT: More, of course.

CUSINS: I would have taken two hundred and fifty. How you can succeed in business when you are willing to pay all that money to a University don who is obviously not worth a junior clerk's wages! — well! What will Lazarus say?

UNDERSHAFT: Lazarus is a gentle romantic Jew who cares for nothing but string quartets and stalls at fashionable theaters. He will be blamed for your rapacity in money matters, poor fellow! as he has hitherto been blamed for mine. You are a shark of the first order, Euripides. So much the better for the firm!

BARBARA: Is the bargain closed, Dolly? Does your soul belong to him now?

CUSINS: No: the price is settled: that is all. The real tug of war is still to come. What about the moral question?

LADY BRITOMART: There is no moral question in the matter at all, Adolphus. You must simply sell cannons and weapons to people whose cause is right and just, and refuse them to foreigners and criminals.

UNDERSHAFT (*determinedly*): No: none of that. You must keep the true faith of an Armorer, or you dont come in here.

CUSINS: What on earth is the true faith of an Armorer?

UNDERSHAFT: To give arms to all men who offer an honest price for them, without respect of persons or principles: to aristocrat and republican, to Nihilist and Tsar, to Capitalist and Socialist, to Protestant and Catholic, to burglar and policeman, to black man, white man, and yellow man, to all sorts and conditions, all nationalities, all faiths, all follies, all causes, and all crimes. The first Undershaft wrote up in his shop IF GOD GAVE THE HAND, LET NOT MAN WITHHOLD THE SWORD. The second wrote up ALL HAVE THE RIGHT TO FIGHT: NONE HAVE

THE RIGHT TO JUDGE. The third wrote up TO MAN THE WEAPON: TO HEAVEN THE VICTORY. The fourth had no literary turn; so he did not write up anything; but he sold cannons to Napoleon under the nose of George the Third. The fifth wrote up PEACE SHALL NOT PREVAIL SAVE WITH A SWORD IN HER HAND. The sixth, my master, was the best of all. He wrote up NOTHING IS EVER DONE IN THIS WORLD UNTIL MEN ARE PREPARED TO KILL ONE ANOTHER IF IT IS NOT DONE. After that, there was nothing left for the seventh to say. So he wrote up, simply, UNASHAMED.

CUSINS: My good Machiavelli. I shall certainly write something up on the wall; only, as I shall write it in Greek, you wont be able to read it. But as to your Armorer's faith, if I take my neck out of the noose of my own morality I am not going to put it into the noose of yours. I shall sell cannons to whom I please and refuse them to whom I please. So there!

UNDERSHAFT: From the moment when you become Andrew Undershaft, you will never do as you please again. Dont come here lusting for power, young man.

CUSINS: If power were my aim I should not come here for it. You have no power.

UNDERSHAFT: None of my own, certainly.

CUSINS: I have more power than you, more will. You do not drive this place: it drives you. And what drives the place?

UNDERSHAFT (*enigmatically*): A will of which I am a part.

BARBARA (*startled*): Father! Do you know what you are saying; or are you laying a snare for my soul?

CUSINS: Dont listen to his metaphysics, Barbara. The place is driven by the most rascally part of society, the money hunters, the pleasure hunters, the military promotion hunters; and he is their slave.

UNDERSHAFT: Not necessarily. Remember the Armorer's Faith. I will take an order from a good man as cheerfully as from a bad one. If you good people prefer preaching and shirking to buying my weapons and fighting the rascals, dont blame me. I can make cannons: I cannot make courage and conviction. Bah! you tire me, Euripides, with your morality mongering. Ask Barbara: she understands. (*He suddenly reaches up and takes Barbara's hands, looking powerfully into her eyes.*) Tell him, my love, what power really means.

BARBARA (*hypnotized*): Before I joined the Salvation Army, I was in my own power and the consequence was that I never knew what to do with myself. When I joined it, I had not time enough for all the things I had to do.

UNDERSHAFT (*approvingly*): Just so. And why was that, do you suppose?

BARBARA: Yesterday I should have said, because I was in the power of God. (*She resumes her self-possession, withdrawing her hands from his with a power equal to his own.*) But you came and showed me that I was in the power of Bodger and Undershaft. Today I feel — oh! how can I put it into words? Sarah: do you remember the earthquake at Cannes, when we were little children? — how little the surprise of the first shock mattered compared to the dread and horror of waiting for the second? That is how I feel in this place today. I stood on the rock I thought eternal; and without a word of warning it reeled and crumbled under me. I was safe with an infinite wisdom watching me, an army marching to Salvation with me; and in a moment, at a stroke of your pen in a check book, I stood alone; and the heavens were empty. That was the first shock of the earthquake: I am waiting for the second.

UNDERSHAFT: Come, come, my daughter! dont make too much of your little tinpot tragedy. What do we do here when we spend years of work and thought and thousands of pounds of solid cash on a new gun or an aerial battleship that turns out just a hairsbreadth wrong after all? Scrap it. Scrap it without wasting another hour or another pound on it. Well, you have made for yourself something that you call a morality or a religion or what not. It doesnt fit the facts. Well, scrap it. Scrap it and get one that does fit. That is what is wrong with the world at present. It scraps its obsolete steam engines and dynamos; but it wont scrap its old prejudices and its old moralities and its old religions and its old political constitutions. Whats the result? In machinery it does very well; but in morals and religion and politics it is working at a loss that brings it nearer bankruptcy every year. Dont persist in that folly. If your old religion broke down yesterday, get a newer and a better one for tomorrow.

BARBARA: Oh how gladly I would take a better one to my soul! But you offer me a worse one. (*Turning on him with sudden vehemence.*) Justify yourself: show me some light through the darkness of this dreadful place, with its beautifully clean workshops, and respectable workmen, and model homes.

UNDERSHAFT: Cleanliness and respectability do not need justification, Barbara: they justify themselves. I see no darkness here, no dreadfulness. In your Salvation shelter I saw poverty, misery, cold, and hunger. You gave them bread and treacle and dreams of heaven. I give from thirty shillings a week to twelve thousand a year. They find their own dreams but I look after the drainage.

BARBARA: And their souls?

UNDERSHAFT: I save their souls just as I saved yours.

BARBARA (*revolted*): You saved my soul! What do you mean?

UNDERSHAFT: I fed you and clothed you and housed you. I took care that you should have money enough to live handsomely — more than enough; so that you could be wasteful, careless, generous. That saved your soul from the seven deadly sins.

BARBARA (*bewildered*): The seven deadly sins!

UNDERSHAFT: Yes, the deadly seven. (*Counting on his fingers.*) Food, clothing, firing, rent, taxes, respectability, and children. Nothing can lift those seven millstones from Man's neck but money and the spirit cannot soar until the millstones are lifted. I lifted them from your spirit. I enabled Barbara to become Major Barbara; and I saved her from the crime of poverty.

CUSINS: Do you call poverty a crime?

UNDERSHAFT: The worst of crimes. All the other crimes are virtues beside it: all the other dishonors are chivalry itself by comparison. Poverty blights whole cities; spreads horrible pestilences; strikes dead the very souls of all who come within sight, sound, or smell of it. What you call crime is nothing: a murder here and a theft there, a blow now and a curse then: what do they matter? they are only the accidents and illnesses of life: there are not fifty genuine professional criminals in London. But there are millions of poor people, abject people, dirty people, ill fed, ill clothed people. They poison us morally and physically: they kill the happiness of society: they force us to do away with our own liberties and to organize unnatural cruelties for fear they should rise against us and drag us down into their abyss. Only fools fear crime: we all fear poverty. Pah! (*turning on Barbara*) you talk of your half-saved ruffian in West Ham: you accuse me of dragging his soul back to perdition. Well, bring him to me here; and I will drag his soul back again to salvation for you. Not by words and dreams; but by thirty-eight shillings a week, a sound house in a handsome street, and a permanent job. In three weeks he will have a fancy waistcoat; in three months a tall hat and a chapel sitting; before the end of the year he will shake hands with a duchess at a Primrose League meeting, and join the Conservative Party.

BARBARA: And will he be the better for that?

UNDERSHAFT: You know he will. Dont be a hypocrite, Barbara. He will be better fed, better housed, better clothed, better behaved; and his children will be pounds heavier and bigger. That will be better than

an American cloth mattress in a shelter, chopping firewood, eating bread and treacle, and being forced to kneel down from time to time to thank heaven for it: knee drill, I think you call it. It is cheap work converting starving men with a Bible in one hand and a slice of bread in the other. I will undertake to convert West Ham to Mahometanism° on the same terms. Try your hand on my men: their souls are hungry because their bodies are full.

BARBARA: And leave the east end to starve?

UNDERSHAFT (*his energetic tone dropping into one of bitter and brooding remembrance*): I was an east ender. I moralized and starved until one day I swore that I would be a full-fed free man at all costs; that nothing should stop me except a bullet, neither reason nor morals nor the lives of other men. I said "Thou shalt starve ere I starve"; and with that word I became free and great. I was a dangerous man until I had my will: now I am a useful, beneficent, kindly person. That is the history of most self-made millionaires, I fancy. When it is the history of every Englishman we shall have an England worth living in.

LADY BRITOMART: Stop making speeches, Andrew. This is not the place for them.

UNDERSHAFT (*punctured*): My dear: I have no other means of conveying my ideas.

LADY BRITOMART: Your ideas are nonsense. You got on because you were selfish and unscrupulous.

UNDERSHAFT: Not at all. I had the strongest scruples about poverty and starvation. Your moralists are quite unscrupulous about both: they make virtues of them. I had rather be a thief than a pauper. I had rather be a murderer than a slave. I dont want to be either; but if you force the alternative on me, then, by Heaven, I'll choose the braver and more moral one. I hate poverty and slavery worse than any other crimes whatsoever. And let me tell you this. Poverty and slavery have stood up for centuries to your sermons and leading articles: they will not stand up to my machine guns. Dont preach at them: dont reason with them. Kill them.

BARBARA: Killing. Is that your remedy for everything?

UNDERSHAFT: It is the final test of conviction, the only lever strong enough to overturn a social system, the only way of saying Must. Let six hundred and seventy fools loose in the streets; and three policemen can scatter them. But huddle them together in a certain house in Westminster; and let them go through certain ceremonies and call themselves certain names until at last they get the courage to kill; and your six hundred and seventy fools become a

---

Mahometanism: Islam.

government. Your pious mob fills up ballot papers and imagines it is governing its masters; but the ballot paper that really governs is the paper that has a bullet wrapped up in it.

CUSINS: That is perhaps why, like most intelligent people, I never vote.

UNDERSHAFT: Vote! Bah! When you vote, you only change the names of the cabinet. When you shoot, you pull down governments, inaugurate new epochs, abolish old orders, and set up new. Is that historically true, Mr. Learned Man, or is it not?

CUSINS: It is historically true. I loathe having to admit it. I repudiate your sentiments. I abhor your nature. I defy you in every possible way. Still, it is true. But it ought not to be true.

UNDERSHAFT: Ought! ought! ought! ought! ought! Are you going to spend your life saying ought, like the rest of our moralists? Turn your oughts into shalls, man. Come and make explosives with me. Whatever can blow men up can blow society up. The history of the world is the history of those who had courage enough to embrace this truth. Have you the courage to embrace it, Barbara?

LADY BRITOMART: Barbara: I positively forbid you to listen to your father's abominable wickedness. And you, Adolphus, ought to know better than to go about saying that wrong things are true. What does it matter whether they are true if they are wrong?

UNDERSHAFT: What does it matter whether they are wrong if they are true?

LADY BRITOMART (*rising*): Children: come home instantly. Andrew: I am exceedingly sorry I allowed you to call on us. You are wickeder than ever. Come at once.

BARBARA (*shaking her head*): It's no use running away from wicked people, mamma.

LADY BRITOMART: It is every use. It shows your disapprobation of them.

BARBARA: It does not save them.

LADY BRITOMART: I can see that you are going to disobey me. Sarah: are you coming home or are you not?

SARAH: I daresay it's very wicked of papa to make cannons; but I dont think I shall cut him on that account.

LOMAX (*pouring oil on the troubled waters*): The fact is, you know, there is a certain amount of tosh about this notion of wickedness. It doesnt work. You must look at facts. Not that I would say a word in favor of anything wrong; but then, you see, all sorts of chaps are always doing all sorts of things; and we have to fit them in somehow, dont you know. What I mean is that you cant go cutting everybody; and thats about what it comes to.

(*Their rapt attention to his eloquence makes him nervous.*) Perhaps I dont make myself clear.

LADY BRITOMART: You are lucidity itself, Charles. Because Andrew is successful and has plenty of money to give to Sarah, you will flatter him and encourage him in his wickedness.

LOMAX (*unruffled*): Well, where the carcase is, there will the eagles be gathered, dont you know. (*To Undershaft.*) Eh? What?

UNDERSHAFT: Precisely. By the way, may I call you Charles?

LOMAX: Delighted. Cholly is the usual ticket.

UNDERSHAFT (*to Lady Britomart*): Biddy —

LADY BRITOMART (*violently*): Dont dare call me Biddy. Charles Lomax: you are a fool. Adolphus Cusins: you are a Jesuit. Stephen: you are a prig. Barbara: you are a lunatic. Andrew: you are a vulgar tradesman. Now you all know my opinion; and my conscience is clear, at all events. (*She sits down with a vehemence that the rug fortunately softens.*)

UNDERSHAFT: My dear: you are the incarnation of morality. (*She snorts.*) Your conscience is clear and your duty done when you have called everybody names. Come, Euripides! it is getting late; and we all want to get home. Make up your mind.

CUSINS: Understand this, you old demon —

LADY BRITOMART: Adolphus!

UNDERSHAFT: Let him alone, Biddy. Proceed, Euripides.

CUSINS: You have me in a horrible dilemma. I want Barbara.

UNDERSHAFT: Like all young men, you greatly exaggerate the difference between one young woman and another.

BARBARA: Quite true, Dolly.

CUSINS: I also want to avoid being a rascal.

UNDERSHAFT (*with biting contempt*): You lust for personal righteousness, for self-approval, for what you call a good conscience, for what Barbara calls salvation, for what I call patronizing people who are not so lucky as yourself.

CUSINS: I do not: all the poet in me recoils from being a good man. But there are things in me that I must reckon with. Pity —

UNDERSHAFT: Pity! The scavenger of misery.

CUSINS: Well, love.

UNDERSHAFT: I know. You love the needy and the outcast: you love the oppressed races, the negro, the Indian ryot, the underdog everywhere. Do you love the Japanese? Do you love the French? Do you love the English?

CUSINS: No. Every true Englishman detests the English. We are the wickedest nation on earth; and our success is a moral horror.

UNDERSHAFT: That is what comes of your gospel of love, is it?

CUSINS: May I not love even my father-in-law?

UNDERSHAFT: Who wants your love, man? By what right do you take the liberty of offering it to me? I will have your due heed and respect, or I will kill you. But your love! Damn your impertinence!

CUSINS (grinning): I may not be able to control my affections, Mac.

UNDERSHAFT: You are fencing, Euripides. You are weakening: your grip is slipping. Come! try your last weapon. Pity and love have broken in your hand: forgiveness is still left.

CUSINS: No: forgiveness is a beggar's refuge. I am with you there: we must pay our debts.

UNDERSHAFT: Well said. Come! you will suit me. Remember the words of Plato.

CUSINS (starting): Plato! You dare quote Plato to me!

UNDERSHAFT: Plato says, my friend, that society cannot be saved until either the Professors of Greek take to making gunpowder, or else the makers of gunpowder become Professors of Greek.

CUSINS: Oh, tempter, cunning tempter!

UNDERSHAFT: Come! choose, man, choose.

CUSINS: But perhaps Barbara will not marry me if I make the wrong choice.

BARBARA: Perhaps not.

CUSINS (desperately perplexed): You hear!

BARBARA: Father: do you love nobody?

UNDERSHAFT: I love my best friend.

LADY BRITOMART: And who is that, pray?

UNDERSHAFT: My bravest enemy. That is the man who keeps me up to the mark.

CUSINS: You know, the creature is really a sort of poet in his way. Suppose he is a great man, after all!

UNDERSHAFT: Suppose you stop talking and make up your mind, my young friend.

CUSINS: But you are driving me against my nature. I hate war.

UNDERSHAFT: Hatred is the coward's revenge for being intimidated. Dare you make war on war? Here are the means: my friend Mr. Lomax is sitting on them.

LOMAX (springing up): Oh I say! You dont mean that this thing is loaded, do you? My ownest: come off it.

SARAH (sitting placidly on the shell): If I am to be blown up, the more thoroughly it is done the better. Dont fuss, Cholly.

LOMAX (to Undershaft, strongly remonstrant): Your own daughter, you know!

UNDERSHAFT: So I see. (To Cusins.) Well, my friend, may we expect you here at six tomorrow morning?

CUSINS (firmly): Not on any account. I will see the whole establishment blown up with its own dy-

namite before I will get up at five. My hours are healthy, rational hours: eleven to five.

UNDERSHAFT: Come when you please: before a week you will come at six and stay until I turn you out for the sake of your health. (Calling.) Bilton! (He turns to Lady Britomart, who rises.) My dear: let us leave these two young people to themselves for a moment. (Bilton comes from the shed.) I am going to take you through the guncotton shed.

BILTON (barring the way): You cant take anything explosive in here, sir.

LADY BRITOMART: What do you mean? Are you alluding to me?

BILTON (unmoved): No, maam. Mr. Undershaft has the other gentleman's matches in his pocket.

LADY BRITOMART (abruptly): Oh! I beg your pardon! (She goes into the shed.)

UNDERSHAFT: Quite right, Bilton, quite right: here you are. (He gives Bilton the box of matches.) Come, Stephen. Come, Charles. Bring Sarah. (He passes into the shed.)

(Bilton opens the box and deliberately drops the matches into the fire bucket.)

LOMAX: Oh! I say. (Bilton stolidly hands him the empty box.) Infernal nonsense! Pure scientific ignorance! (He goes in.)

SARAH: Am I all right, Bilton?

BILTON: Youll have to put on list slippers, miss: thats all. Weve got em inside. (She goes in.)

STEPHEN (very seriously to Cusins): Dolly, old fellow, think. Think before you decide. Do you feel that you are a sufficiently practical man? It is a huge undertaking, an enormous responsibility. All this mass of business will be Greek to you.

CUSINS: Oh, I think it will be much less difficult than Greek.

STEPHEN: Well, I just want to say this before I leave you to yourselves. Dont let anything I have said about right and wrong prejudice you against this great chance in life. I have satisfied myself that the business is one of the highest character and a credit to our country. (Emotionally.) I am very proud of my father. I — (Unable to proceed, he presses Cusins's hand and goes hastily into the shed, followed by Bilton.)

(Barbara and Cusins, left alone together, look at one another silently.)

CUSINS: Barbara: I am going to accept this offer.

BARBARA: I thought you would.

CUSINS: You understand, dont you, that I had to decide without consulting you. If I had thrown the burden of the choice on you, you would sooner or later have despised me for it.

BARBARA: Yes: I did not want you to sell your soul for me any more than for this inheritance.

CUSINS: It is not the sale of my soul that troubles me: I have sold it too often to care about that. I have sold it for a professorship. I have sold it for an income. I have sold it to escape being imprisoned for refusing to pay taxes for hangmen's ropes and unjust wars and things that I abhor. What is all human conduct but the daily and hourly sale of our souls for trifles? What I am now selling it for is neither money nor position nor comfort, but for reality and for power.

BARBARA: You know that you will have no power, and that he has none.

CUSINS: I know. It is not for myself alone. I want to make power for the world.

BARBARA: I want to make power for the world too; but it must be spiritual power.

CUSINS: I think all power is spiritual: these cannons will not go off by themselves. I have tried to make spiritual power by teaching Greek. But the world can never be really touched by a dead language and a dead civilization. The people must have power; and the people cannot have Greek. Now the power that is made here can be wielded by all men.

BARBARA: Power to burn women's houses down and kill their sons and tear their husbands to pieces.

CUSINS: You cannot have power for good without having power for evil too. Even mother's milk nourishes murderers as well as heroes. This power which only tears men's bodies to pieces has never been so horribly abused as the intellectual power, the imaginative power, the poetic, religious power that can enslave men's souls. As a teacher of Greek I gave the intellectual man weapons against the common man. I now want to give the common man weapons against the intellectual man. I love the common people. I want to arm them against the lawyers, the doctors, the priests, the literary men, the professors, the artists, and the politicians, who, once in authority, are more disastrous and tyrannical than all the fools, rascals, and impostors. I want a power simple enough for common men to use, yet strong enough to force the intellectual oligarchy to use its genius for the general good.

BARBARA: Is there no higher power than that (*pointing to the shell*)?

CUSINS: Yes; but that power can destroy the higher powers just as a tiger can destroy a man: therefore Man must master that power first. I admitted this when the Turks and Greeks were last at war. My best pupil went out to fight for Hellas. My parting gift to him was not a copy of Plato's *Republic*, but a revolver and a hundred Undershaft cartridges.

The blood of every Turk he shot — if he shot any — is on my head as well as on Undershaft's. That act committed me to this place for ever. Your father's challenge has beaten me. Dare I make war on war? I must. I will. And now, is it all over between us?

BARBARA (*touched by his evident dread of her answer*): Silly baby Dolly! How could it be!

CUSINS (*overjoyed*): Then you — you — you — Oh for my drum! (*He flourishes imaginary drumsticks.*)

BARBARA (*angered by his levity*): Take care, Dolly, take care. Oh, if only I could get away from you and from father and from it all! if I could have the wings of a dove and fly away to heaven!

CUSINS: And leave me!

BARBARA: Yes, you, and all the other naughty mischievous children of men. But I cant. I was happy in the Salvation Army for a moment. I escaped from the world into a paradise of enthusiasm and prayer and soul saving; but the moment our money ran short, it all came back to Bodger: it was he who saved our people: he, and the Prince of Darkness, my papa. Undershaft and Bodger: their hands stretch everywhere: when we feed a starving fellow creature, it is with their bread, because there is no other bread; when we tend the sick, it is in the hospitals they endow; if we turn from the churches they build, we must kneel on the stones of the streets they pave. As long as that lasts, there is no getting away from them. Turning our backs on Bodger and Undershaft is turning our backs on life.

CUSINS: I thought you were determined to turn your back on the wicked side of life.

BARBARA: There is no wicked side: life is all one. And I never wanted to shirk my share in whatever evil must be endured, whether it be sin or suffering. I wish I could cure you of middle-class ideas, Dolly.

CUSINS (*gasping*): Middle cl —! A snub! A social snub to me from the daughter of a foundling!

BARBARA: That is why I have no class, Dolly: I come straight out of the heart of the whole people. If I were middle class I should turn my back on my father's business; and we should both live in an artistic drawing room, with you reading the reviews in one corner, and I in the other at the piano, playing Schumann: both very superior persons, and neither of us a bit of use. Sooner than that, I would sweep out the guncotton shed, or be one of Bodger's barmaids. Do you know what would have happened if you had refused papa's offer?

CUSINS: I wonder!

BARBARA: I should have given you up and married the man who accepted it. After all, my dear old mother has more sense than any of you. I felt like her when I saw this place — felt that I must have it — that never, never, never could I let it go; only she thought it was the houses and the kitchen ranges and the linen and china, when it was really all the human souls to be saved: not weak souls in starved bodies, sobbing with gratitude for a scrap of bread and treacle, but fullfed, quarrelsome, snobbish, uppish creatures, all standing on their little rights and dignities, and thinking that my father ought to be greatly obliged to them for making so much money for him — and so he ought. That is where salvation is really wanted. My father shall never throw it in my teeth again that my converts were bribed with bread. (*She is transfigured.*) I have got rid of the bribe of bread. I have got rid of the bribe of heaven. Let God's work be done for its own sake: the work he had to create us to do because it cannot be done except by living men and women. When I die, let him be in my debt, not I in his; and let me forgive him as becomes a woman of my rank.

CUSINS: Then the way of life lies through the factory of death?

BARBARA: Yes, through the raising of hell to heaven and of man to God, through the unveiling of an eternal light in the Valley of The Shadow. (*Seizing him with both hands.*) Oh, did you think my courage would never come back? did you believe that I was a deserter? that I, who have stood in the streets, and taken my people to my heart, and talked of the holiest and greatest things with them, could ever turn back and chatter foolishly to fashionable people about nothing in a drawing room? Never, never, never, never: Major Barbara will die

with the colors. Oh! and I have my dear little Dolly boy still; and he has found me my place and my work. Glory Hallelujah! (*She kisses him.*)

CUSINS: My dearest: consider my delicate health. I cannot stand as much happiness as you can.

BARBARA: Yes: it is not easy work being in love with me, is it? But it's good for you. (*She runs to the shed, and calls, childlike.*) Mamma! Mamma! (*Bilton comes out of the shed, followed by Undershaft.*) I want Mamma.

UNDERSHAFT: She is taking off her list slippers, dear. (*He passes on to Cusins.*) Well? What does she say?

CUSINS: She has gone right up into the skies.

LADY BRITOMART (*coming from the shed and stopping on the steps, obstructing Sarah, who follows with Lomax. Barbara clutches like a baby at her mother's skirt*): Barbara: when will you learn to be independent and to act and think for yourself? I know, as well as possible what that cry of "Mamma, Mamma," means. Always running to me!

SARAH (*touching Lady Britomart's ribs with her fingertips and imitating a bicycle horn*): Pip! pip!

LADY BRITOMART (*highly indignant*): How dare you say Pip! pip! to me, Sarah? You are both very naughty children. What do you want, Barbara?

BARBARA: I want a house in the village to live in with Dolly. (*Dragging at the skirt.*) Come and tell me which one to take.

UNDERSHAFT (*to Cusins*): Six o'clock tomorrow morning, Euripides.

COMMENTARY

Bernard Shaw (1856–1950)
FROM THE PREFACE TO *MAJOR BARBARA*   1906

> *Shaw's plays were always about something important, and at times he indicated that the critics missed the point. In his preface to Major Barbara, Shaw gives the critics something to say by going through the play himself, talking about its situations and its characters as well as about its ideas and deepest*

concerns. His comments generally focus on the economic issues underlying the play. Shaw's socialist views come to the fore in his Preface as he condemns poverty as a crime and urges society to give every citizen a stipend on which to live. The moral issues of the play — concerning the ethics of making munitions — shift their ground in the Preface, since it is shown that moral issues involved in avoiding poverty far outweigh the question of how a person earns money.

The Gospel of St. Andrew Undershaft

In the millionaire Undershaft I have represented a man who has become intellectually and spiritually as well as practically conscious of the irrestible natural truth which we all abhor and repudiate; to wit, that the greatest of our evils, and the worst of our crimes is poverty, and that our first duty, to which every other consideration should be sacrificed, is not to be poor. "Poor but honest," "the respectable poor," and such phrases are as intolerable and as immoral as "drunken but amiable," "fraudulent but a good after-dinner speaker," "splendidly criminal," or the like. Security, the chief pretense of civilization, cannot exist where the worst of dangers, the danger of poverty, hangs over everyone's head, and where the alleged protection of our persons from violence is only an accidental result of the existence of a police force whose real business is to force the poor man to see his children starve whilst idle people overfeed pet dogs with the money that might feed and clothe them.

It is exceedingly difficult to make people realize that an evil is an evil. For instance, we seize a man and deliberately do him a malicious injury: say, imprison him for years. One would not suppose that it needed any exceptional clearness of wit to recognize in this an act of diabolical cruelty. But in England such a recognition provokes a stare of surprise, followed by an explanation that the outrage is punishment or justice or something else that is all right, or perhaps by a heated attempt to argue that we should all be robbed and murdered in our beds if such stupid villainies as sentences of imprisonment were not committed daily. It is useless to argue that even if this were true, which it is not, the alternative to adding crimes of our own to the crimes from which we suffer is not helpless submission. Chickenpox is an evil; but if I were to declare that we must either submit to it or else repress it sternly by seizing everyone who suffers from it and punishing them by inoculation with smallpox, I should be laughed at; for though nobody could deny that the result would be to prevent chickenpox to some extent by making people avoid it much more carefully, and to effect a further apparent prevention by making them conceal it very anxiously, yet people would have sense enough to see that the deliberate propagation of smallpox was a creation of evil, and must therefore be ruled out in favor of purely humane and hygienic measures. Yet in the precisely parallel case of a man breaking into my house and stealing my wife's diamonds I am expected as a matter of course to steal ten years of his life, torturing him all the time. If he tries to defeat that monstrous retaliation by shooting me, my survivors hang him. The net result suggested by the police statistics is that we inflict atrocious injuries on the burglars we catch in order to make the rest take effectual precautions against detection; so that instead of saving our wives' diamonds from burglary we only greatly decrease our chances of ever getting them back, and increase our chances of being shot by the robber if we are unlucky enough to disturb him at his work.

But the thoughtless wickedness with which we scatter sentences of imprisonment, torture in the solitary cell and on the plank bed, and flogging, on moral invalids and energetic rebels, is as nothing compared to the silly levity with which we tolerate poverty as if it were either a wholesome tonic for lazy people or else a virtue to be embraced as St Francis embraced it. If a man is indolent, let him be poor. If he is drunken, let him be poor. If he is not a gentleman, let him be poor. If he is addicted to the fine arts or to pure science instead of to trade and finance, let him be poor. If he chooses to spend his urban eighteen shillings a week or his agricultural thirteen shillings a week on his beer and his family instead of saving it up for his old age, let him be poor. Let nothing be done for "the undeserving": let him be poor. Serve him right! Also — somewhat inconsistently — blessed are the poor!

Now what does this Let Him Be Poor mean? It means let him be weak. Let him be ignorant. Let him become a nucleus of disease. Let him be a standing exhibition and example of ugliness and dirt. Let him have rickety children. Let him be cheap, and drag his fellows down to his own price by selling himself to do their work. Let his habitations turn our cities into poisonous congeries of slums. Let his daughters infect our young men with the diseases of the streets, and his sons revenge him by turning the nation's manhood into scrofula, cowardice, cruelty, hypocrisy, political imbecility, and all the other fruits of oppression and malnutrition. Let the undeserving become still less deserving; and let the deserving lay up for himself, not treasures in heaven, but horrors in hell upon earth. This being so, is it really wise to let him be poor? Would he not do ten times less harm as a prosperous burglar, incendiary, ravisher or murderer, to the utmost limits of humanity's comparatively negligible impulses in these directions? Suppose we were to abolish all penalties for such activities, and decide that poverty is the one thing we will not tolerate — that every adult with less than, say, £365 a year, shall be painlessly but inexorably killed, and every hungry half naked child forcibly fattened and clothed, would not that be an enormous improvement on our existing system, which has already destroyed so many civilizations, and is visibly destroying ours in the same way?

Is there any radicle of such legislation in our parliamentary system? Well, there are two measures just sprouting in the political soil, which may conceivably grow to something valuable. One is the institution of a Legal Minimum Wage. The other, Old Age Pensions. But there is a better plan than either of these. Some time ago I mentioned the subject of Universal Old Age Pensions to my fellow Socialist Cobden-Sanderson, famous as an artist-craftsman in bookbinding and printing. "Why not Universal Pensions for Life?" said Cobden-Sanderson. In saying this, he solved the industrial problem at a stroke. At present we say callously to each citizen "If you want money, earn it" as if his having or not having it were a matter that concerned himself alone. We do not even secure for him the opportunity of earning it: on the contrary, we allow our industry to be organized in open dependence on the maintenance of "a reserve army of unemployed" for the sake of "elasticity." The sensible course would be Cobden-Sanderson's: that is, to give every man enough to live well on, so as to guarantee the community against the possibility of a case of the malignant disease of poverty, and then (necessarily) to see that he earned it.

Undershaft, the hero of Major Barbara, is simply a man who, having grasped the fact that poverty is a crime, knows that when society offered him the alternative of poverty or a lucrative trade in death and destruction, it offered him, not a choice between opulent villainy and humble virtue, but between energetic enterprise and cowardly infamy. His conduct stands the Kantian test,° which Peter Shirley's does not. Peter Shirley is what we call the honest poor man. Undershaft is what we call the wicked rich one: Shirley is Lazarus, Undershaft Dives.° Well, the misery of the world is due to the fact that the great mass of men act and believe as Peter Shirley acts and believes. If they acted and believed as Undershaft acts and believes, the immediate result would be a revolution of incalculable beneficence. To be wealthy, says Undershaft, is with me a point of honor for which I am prepared to kill at the risk of my own life. This preparedness is, as he says, the final test of sincerity. Like Froissart's medieval hero, who saw that "to rob and pill was a good life," he is not the dupe of that public sentiment against killing which is propagated and endowed by people who would otherwise be killed themselves, or of the mouth-honor paid to poverty and obedience by rich and insubordinate do-nothings who want to rob the poor without courage and command them without superiority. Froissart's knight, in placing the achievement of a good life before all the other duties — which indeed are not duties at all when they conflict with it, but plain wickedness — behaved bravely, admirably, and, in the final analysis, public-spiritedly. Medieval society, on the other hand, behaved very badly indeed in organizing itself so stupidly that a good life could be achieved by robbing and pilling. If the knight's contemporaries had been all as resolute as he, robbing and pilling would have been the shortest way to the gallows, just as, if we were all as resolute and clearsighted as Undershaft, an attempt to live by means of what is called "an independent income" would be the shortest way to the lethal chamber. But as, thanks to our political imbecility and personal cowardice (fruits of poverty, both), the best imitation of a good life now procurable is life on an independent income, all sensible people aim at securing such an income, and are, of course, careful to legalize and moralize both it and all the actions and sentiments which lead to it and support it as an institution. What else can they do? They know, of course, that they are rich because others are poor. But they cannot help that: it is for the poor to repudiate poverty when they have had enough of it. The thing can be done easily enough: the demonstrations to the contrary made by the economists, jurists, moralists and sentimentalists hired by the rich to defend them, or even doing the work gratuitously out of sheer folly and abjectness, impose only on those who want to be imposed on.

The reason why the independent income-tax payers are not solid in defense of their position is that since we are not medieval rovers through a sparsely populated country, the poverty of those we rob prevents our having the good life for which we sacrifice them. Rich men or aristocrats with a developed sense of life — men like Ruskin and William Morris and Kropotkin — have enormous social appetites and very fastidious personal ones. They are not content with handsome houses: they want handsome cities. They are not content with be-diamonded wives and blooming daughters: they complain because the charwoman

Kantian test: Immanuel Kant (1724–1804) in the *Critique of Practical Reason* sets forth the "categorical imperative": "Act only according to a maxim by which you can at the same time will that it shall become universal law."

Shirley . . . Dives: In Luke 16:19–31 Jesus tells a parable about a poor man, Lazarus, who begs crumbs from a rich man, Dives. Lazarus is turned away. After they die, however, Lazarus receives a place in Abraham's bosom and Dives suffers in anguish.

is badly dressed, because the laundress smells of gin, because the sempstress is anemic, because every man they meet is not a friend and every woman not a romance. They turn up their noses at their neighbor's drains, and are made ill by the architecture of their neighbor's houses. Trade patterns made to suit vulgar people do not please them (and they can get nothing else): they cannot sleep nor sit at ease upon "slaughtered" cabinet makers' furniture. The very air is not good enough for them: there is too much factory smoke in it. They even demand abstract conditions: justice, honor, a noble moral atmosphere, a mystic nexus to replace the cash nexus. Finally they declare that though to rob and pill with your own hand on horseback and in steel coat may have been a good life, to rob and pill by the hands of the policeman, the bailiff, and the soldier, and to underpay them meanly for doing it, is not a good life, but rather fatal to all possibility of even a tolerable one. They call on the poor to revolt, and, finding the poor shocked at their ungentlemanliness, despairingly revile the proletariat for its "damned wantlessness" (*verdammte Bedürfnislosigkeit*).

So far, however, their attack on society has lacked simplicity. The poor do not share their tastes nor understand their art-criticisms. They do not want the simple life, nor the esthetic life; on the contrary, they want very much to wallow in all the costly vulgarities from which the elect souls among the rich turn away with loathing. It is by surfeit and not by abstinence that they will be cured of their hankering after unwholesome sweets. What they do dislike and despise and are ashamed of is poverty. To ask them to fight for the difference between the Christmas number of the Illustrated London News and the Kelmscott Chaucer is silly: they prefer the News. The difference between a stock-broker's cheap and dirty starched white shirt and collar and the comparatively costly and carefully dyed blue shirt of William Morris is a difference so disgraceful to Morris in their eyes that if they fought on the subject at all, they would fight in defense of the starch. "Cease to be slaves, in order that you may become cranks" is not a very inspiring call to arms; nor is it really improved by substituting saints for cranks. Both terms denote men of genius; and the common man does not want to live the life of a man of genius: he would much rather live the life of a pet collie if that were the only alternative. But he does want more money. Whatever else he may be vague about, he is clear about that. He may or may not prefer Major Barbara to the Drury Lane pantomime; but he always prefers five hundred pounds to five hundred shillings.

Now to deplore this preference as sordid, and teach children that it is sinful to desire money, is to strain towards the extreme possible limit of impudence in lying and corruption in hypocrisy. The universal regard for money is the one hopeful fact in our civilization, the one sound spot in our social conscience. Money is the most important thing in the world. It represents health, strength, honor, generosity and beauty as conspicuously and undeniably as the want of it represents illness, weakness, disgrace, meanness and ugliness. Not the least of its virtues is that it destroys base people as certainly as it fortifies and dignifies noble people. It is only when it is cheapened to worthlessness for some and made impossibly dear to others, that it becomes a curse. In short, it is a curse only in such foolish social conditions that life itself is a curse. For the two things are inseparable: money is the counter that enables life to be distributed socially: it *is* life as truly as sovereigns and bank notes are money. The first duty of every citizen is to insist on having money on reasonable terms; and this demand is not complied with by giving four men three shillings each for ten or twelve hours' drudgery and one man a thousand pounds for nothing. The crying need of the nation is not for better morals, cheaper bread, temperance, liberty, culture, redemption of fallen sisters and erring brothers, nor the grace, love and fellowship of the Trinity, but simply for enough money. And the evil to be attacked is not sin, suffering, greed, priestcraft, kingcraft, demagogy, monopoly, ignorance, drink, war, pestilence, nor any other of the scapegoats which reformers sacrifice, but simply poverty.

Once take your eyes from the ends of the earth and fix them on this truth just under your nose; and Andrew Undershaft's views will not perplex you in the least. Unless indeed his constant sense that he is only the instrument of a Will or Life Force which uses him for purposes wider than his own, may puzzle you. If so, that is because you are walking either in artificial Darwinian darkness, or in mere stupidity. All genuinely religious people have that consciousness. To them Undershaft the Mystic will be quite intelligible, and his perfect comprehension of his daughter the Salvationist and her lover the Euripidean republican natural and inevitable. That, however, is not new, even on the stage. What is new, as far as I know, is that article in Undershaft's religion which recognizes in Money the first need and in poverty the vilest sin of man and society.

This dramatic conception has not, of course, been attained *per saltum.*° Nor has it been borrowed from Nietzsche or from any man born beyond the Channel. The late Samuel Butler, in his own department the greatest English writer of the latter half of the XIX century, steadily inculcated the necessity and morality of a conscientious Laodiceanism in religion and of an earnest and constant sense of the importance of money. It drives one almost to despair of English literature when one sees so extraordinary a study of English life as Butler's posthumous *Way of All Flesh* making so little impression that when, some years later, I produce plays in which Butler's extraordinarily fresh, free and future-piercing suggestions have an obvious share, I am met with nothing but vague cacklings about Ibsen and Nietzsche, and am only too thankful that they are not about Alfred de Musset and Georges Sand. Really, the English do not deserve to have great men. They allowed Butler to die practically unknown, whilst I, a comparatively insignificant Irish journalist, was leading them by the nose into an advertisement of me which has made my own life a burden. In Sicily there is a Via Samuele Butler. When an English tourist sees it, he either asks "Who the devil was Samuele Butler?" or wonders why the Sicilians should perpetuate the memory of the author of *Hudibras*.

Well, it cannot be denied that the English are only too anxious to recognize a man of genius if somebody will kindly point him out to them. Having pointed myself out in this manner with some success, I now point out Samuel Butler, and trust that in consequence I shall hear a little less in future of the novelty and foreign origin of the ideas which are now making their way into the English theater through plays written by Socialists. There are living men whose originality and power are as obvious as Butler's and when they die that fact will be discovered. Meanwhile I recommend them to insist on their own merits as an important part of their own business.

per saltum: Latin for "by a leap," that is, all at once.

The Salvation Army

When *Major Barbara* was produced in London, the second act was reported in an important northern newspaper as a withering attack on the Salvation Army, and the despairing ejaculation of Barbara deplored by a London daily as a tasteless blasphemy. And they were set right, not by the professed critics of the theater, but by religious and philosophical publicists like Sir Oliver Lodge and Dr. Stanton Coit, and strenuous Nonconformist journalists like William Stead, who not only understood the act as well as the Salvationists themselves, but also saw it in its relation to the religious life of the nation, a life which seems to lie not only outside the sympathy of many of our theater critics, but actually outside their knowledge of society. Indeed nothing could be more ironically curious than the confrontation Major Barbara effected of the theater enthusiasts with the religious enthusiasts. On the one hand was the playgoer, always seeking pleasure, paying exorbitantly for it, suffering unbearable discomforts for it, and hardly ever getting it. On the other hand was the Salvationist, repudiating gaiety and courting effort and sacrifice, yet always in the wildest spirits, laughing, joking, singing, rejoicing, drumming, and tambourining: his life flying by in a flash of excitement, and his death arriving as a climax of triumph. And, if you please, the playgoer despising the Salvationist as a joyless person, shut out from the heaven of the theater, self-condemned to a life of hideous gloom; and the Salvationist mourning over the playgoer as over a prodigal with vine leaves in his hair, careering outrageously to hell amid the popping of champagne corks and the ribald laughter of sirens! Could misunderstanding be more complete, or sympathy worse misplaced?

Fortunately, the Salvationists are more accessible to the religious character of the drama than the playgoers to the gay energy and artistic fertility of religion. They can see, when it is pointed out to them, that a theater, as a place where two or three are gathered together, takes from that divine presence an inalienable sanctity of which the grossest and profanest farce can no more deprive it than a hypocritical sermon by a snobbish bishop can desecrate Westminster Abbey. But in our professional playgoers this indispensable preliminary conception of sanctity seems wanting. They talk of actors as mimes and mummers, and I fear, think of dramatic authors as liars and pandars, whose main business is the voluptuous soothing of the tired city speculator when what he calls the serious business of the day is over. Passion, the life of drama, means nothing to them but primitive sexual excitement: such phrases as "impassioned poetry" or "passionate love of truth" have fallen quite out of their vocabulary and been replaced by "passional crime" and the like. They assume, as far as I can gather, that people in whom passion has a larger scope are passionless and therefore uninteresting. Consequently they come to think of religious people as people who are not interesting and not amusing. And so, when Barbara cuts the regular Salvation Army jokes, and snatches a kiss from her lover across his drum, the devotees of the theater think they ought to appear shocked, and conclude that the whole play is an elaborate mockery of the Army. And then either hypocritically rebuke me for mocking, or foolishly take part in the supposed mockery!

Even the handful of mentally competent critics got into difficulties over my demonstration of the economic deadlock in which the Salvation Army finds itself. Some of them thought that the Army would not have taken money from a distiller and a cannon founder: others thought it should not have taken it: all assumed more or less definitely that it reduced itself to absurdity or hypocrisy by taking it. On the first point the reply of the Army itself was prompt and conclusive. As one of its officers said, they would take money from the devil himself and be only too glad to get it out of his hands and into God's. They gratefully acknowledged that publicans not only give them money but allow them to collect it in the bar — sometimes even when there is a Salvation meeting outside preaching teetotalism. In fact, they questioned the verisimilitude of the play, not because Mrs Baines took the money, but because Barbara refused it.

On the point that the Army ought not to take such money, its justification is obvious. It must take the money because it cannot exist without money, and there is no other money to be had. Practically all the spare money in the country consists of a mass of rent, interest, and profit, every penny of which is bound up with crime, drink, prostitution, disease, and all the evil fruits of poverty, as inextricably as with enterprise, wealth, commercial probity, and national prosperity. The notion that you can earmark certain coins as tainted is an unpractical individualist superstition. Nonetheless the fact that all our money is tainted gives a very severe shock to earnest young souls when some dramatic instance of the taint first makes them conscious of it. When an enthusiastic young clergyman of the Established Church first realizes that the Ecclesiastical Commissioners receive the rents of sporting public houses, brothels, and sweating dens; or that the most generous contributor at his last charity sermon was an employer trading in female labor cheapened by prostitution as unscrupulously as a hotel keeper trades in waiters' labor cheapened by tips, or commissionaires' labor cheapened by pensions; or that the only patron who can afford to rebuild his church or his schools or give his boys' brigade a gymnasium or a library is the son-in-law of a Chicago meat King, that young clergyman has, like Barbara, a very bad quarter hour. But he cannot help himself by refusing to accept money from anybody except sweet old ladies with independent incomes and gentle and lovely ways of life. He has only to follow up the income of the sweet ladies to its industrial source, and there he will find Mrs Warren's profession° and the poisonous canned meat and all the rest of it. His own stipend has the same root. He must either share the world's guilt or go to another planet. He must save the world's honor if he is to save his own. This is what all the Churches find just as the Salvation Army and Barbara find it in the play. Her discovery that she is her father's accomplice; that the Salvation Army is the accomplice of the distiller and the dynamite maker; that they can no more escape one another than they can escape the air they breathe; that there is no salvation for them through personal righteousness, but only through the redemption of the whole nation from its vicious, lazy, competitive anarchy: this discovery has been made by everyone except the Pharisees and (apparently) the professional playgoers, who still wear their Tom Hood shirts and underpay their washerwoman without the slightest misgiving as to the elevation of their private characters, the purity of their private atmospheres, and their right to repudiate as foreign to themselves the coarse depravity of the garret and the slum. Not that they mean any harm: they only desire to be, in their little private way, what they call gentlemen. They do not understand Barbara's lesson because they have not, like her, learnt it by taking their part in the larger life of the nation.

Mrs Warren's profession: Prostitution, as in his play *Mrs Warren's Profession*.

Barbara's Return to the Colors

Barbara's return to the colors may yet provide a subject for the dramatic historian of the future. To get back to the Salvation Army with the knowledge that even the Salvationists themselves are not saved yet; that poverty is not blessed, but a most damnable sin; and that when General Booth chose Blood and Fire for the emblem of Salvation instead of the Cross, he was perhaps better inspired than he knew: such knowledge, for the daughter of Andrew Undershaft, will clearly lead to something hopefuller than distributing bread and treacle at the expense of Bodger.

It is a very significant thing, this instinctive choice of the military form of organization, this substitution of the drum for the organ, by the Salvation Army. Does it not suggest that the Salvationists divine that they must actually fight the devil instead of merely praying at him? At present, it is true, they have not quite ascertained his correct address. When they do, they may give a very rude shock to that sense of security which he has gained from his experience of the fact that hard words, even when uttered by eloquent essayists and lecturers, or carried unanimously at enthusiastic public meetings on the motion of eminent reformers, break no bones. It has been said that the French Revolution was the work of Voltaire, Rousseau, and the Encyclopedists. It seems to me to have been the work of men who had observed that virtuous indignation, caustic criticism, conclusive argument, and instructive pamphleteering, even when done by the most earnest and witty literary geniuses, were as useless as praying, things going steadily from bad to worse whilst the Social Contract and the pamphlets of Voltaire were at the height of their vogue. Eventually, as we know, perfectly respectable citizens and earnest philanthropists connived at the September massacres because hard experience had convinced them that if they contented themselves with appeals to humanity and patriotism, the aristocracy, though it would read their appeals with the greatest enjoyment and appreciation, flattering and admiring the writers, would nonetheless continue to conspire with foreign monarchists to undo the revolution and restore the old system with every circumstance of savage vengeance and ruthless repression of popular liberties.

The nineteenth century saw the same lesson repeated in England. It had its Utilitarians, its Christian Socialists, its Fabians (still extant): it had Bentham, Mill, Dickens, Ruskin, Carlyle, Butler, Henry George, and Morris. And the end of all their efforts is in the Chicago described by Mr Upton Sinclair, and the London in which the people who pay to be amused by my dramatic representation of Peter Shirley turned out to starve at forty because there are younger slaves to be had for his wages, do not take, and have not the slightest intention of taking, any effective step to organize society in such a way as to make that everyday infamy impossible. I, who have preached and pamphleteered like any Encyclopedist, have to confess that my methods are no use, and would be no use if I were Voltaire, Rousseau, Bentham, Marx, Mill, Dickens, Carlyle, Ruskin, Butler, and Morris all rolled into one, with Euripides, More, Montaigne, Molière, Beaumarchais, Swift, Goethe, Ibsen, Tolstoy, Jesus, and the prophets all thrown in (as indeed in some sort I actually am, standing as I do on all their shoulders). The problem being to make heroes out of cowards, we paper apostles and artist-magicians have succeeded only in giving cowards all the sensations of heroes whilst they tolerate every abomination, accept every plunder, and submit to every oppression. Christianity, in making a merit of such submission, has marked only that depth in the abyss at which the very sense of shame is lost. The Christian has been like Dickens's doctor in the debtor's prison, who tells the newcomer of its ineffable peace and security: no duns; no tyrannical collectors of rates, taxes, and rent; no importunate hopes nor exacting duties; nothing but the rest and safety of having no farther to fall.

Yet in the poorest corner of this soul-destroying Christendom vitality suddenly begins to germinate again. Joyousness, a sacred gift long dethroned by the hellish laughter of derision and obscenity, rises like a flood miraculously out of the fetid dust and mud of the slums; rousing marches and impetuous dithyrambs rise to the heavens from people among whom the depressing noise called "sacred music" is a standing joke; a flag with Blood and Fire on it is unfurled, not in murderous rancor, but because fire is beautiful and blood a vital and splendid red; Fear, which we flatter by calling Self, vanishes; and transfigured men and women carry their gospel through a transfigured world, calling their leader General, themselves captains and brigadiers, and their whole body an Army: praying, but praying only for refreshment, for strength to fight, and for needful MONEY (a notable sign, that); preaching, but not preaching submission; daring ill-usage and abuse, but not putting up with more of it than is inevitable; and practicing what the world will let them practice, including soap and water, color and music. There is danger in such activity; and where there is danger there is hope. Our present security is nothing, and can be nothing, but evil made irresistible.

Weaknesses of the Salvation Army

For the present, however, it is not my business to flatter the Salvation Army. Rather must I point out to it that it has almost as many weaknesses as the Church of England itself. It is building up a business organization which will compel it eventually to see that its present staff of enthusiast-commanders shall be succeeded by a bureaucracy of men of business who will be no better than bishops, and perhaps a good deal more unscrupulous. That has always happened sooner or later to great orders founded by saints; and the order founded by St William Booth is not exempt from the same danger. It is even more dependent than the Church on rich people who would cut off supplies at once if it began to preach that indispensable revolt against poverty which must also be a revolt against riches. It is hampered by a heavy contingent of pious elders who are not really Salvationists at all, but Evangelicals of the old school. It still, as Commissioner Howard affirms, "sticks to Moses," which is flat nonsense at this time of day if the Commissioner means, as I am afraid he does, that the Book of Genesis contains a trustworthy scientific account of the origin of species, and that the god to whom Jephthah sacrificed his daughter is any less obviously a tribal idol than Dagon or Chemosh.

Further, there is still too much other-worldliness about the Army. Like Frederick's grenadier, the Salvationist wants to live forever (the most monstrous way of crying for the moon); and though it is evident to anyone who has ever heard General Booth and his best officers that they would work as hard for human salvation as they do at present if they believed that death would be the end of them individually, they and their followers have a bad habit of talking as if the Salvationists were heroically enduring a very bad time on earth as an investment which will bring them in dividends later on in the form, not of a better life to come for the whole world, but of an eternity spent by themselves personally in a sort of bliss which would bore any active person to a second death. Surely the truth is that the Salvationists are unusually happy people. And is it not the very diagnostic of true salvation that it shall overcome the fear of death? Now the man who has come to believe that there is no such thing as death, the change so called being merely the transition to an exquisitely happy and utterly careless life, has not overcome the fear of death at all: on the contrary, it has overcome him so completely that he refuses to die on any terms whatever. I do not call a Salvationist really saved until he is ready to lie down cheerfully on the scrap heap, having paid scot and lot and something over, and let his eternal life pass on to renew its youth in the battalions of the future.

Then there is the nasty lying habit called confession, which the Army encourages because it lends itself to dramatic oratory, with plenty of thrilling incident. For my part, when I hear a convert relating the violences and oaths and blasphemies he was guilty of before he was saved, making out that he was a very terrible fellow then and is the most contrite and chastened of Christians now, I believe him no more than I believe the millionaire who says he came up to London or Chicago as a boy with only three halfpence in his pocket. Salvationists have said to me that Barbara in my play would never have been taken in by so transparent a humbug as Snobby Price; and certainly I do not think Snobby could have taken in any experienced Salvationist on a point on which the Salvationist did not wish to be taken in. But on the point of conversion all Salvationists wish to be taken in; for the more obvious the sinner the more obvious the miracle of his conversion. When you advertise a converted burglar or reclaimed drunkard as one of the attractions at an experience meeting, your burglar can hardly have been too burglarious or your drunkard too drunken. As long as such attractions are relied on, you will have your Snobbies claiming to have beaten their mothers when they were as a matter of prosaic fact habitually beaten by them, and your Rummies of the tamest respectability pretending to a past of reckless and dazzling vice. Even when confessions are sincerely autobiographic we should beware of assuming that the impulse to make them was pious or that the interest of the hearers is wholesome. As well might we assume that the poor people who insist on showing disgusting ulcers to district visitors are convinced hygienists, or that the curiosity which sometimes welcomes such exhibitions is a pleasant and creditable one. One is often tempted to suggest that those who pester our police superintendents with confessions of murder might very wisely be taken at their word and executed, except in the few cases in which a real murderer is seeking to be relieved of his guilt by confession and expiation. For though I am not, I hope, an unmerciful person, I do not think that the inexorability of the deed once done should be disguised by any ritual, whether in the confessional or on the scaffold.

And here my disagreement with the Salvation Army, and with all propagandists of the Cross (which I loathe as I loathe all gibbets) becomes deep indeed. Forgiveness, absolution, atonement, are figments: punishment is only a pretense of canceling one crime by another; and you can no more have forgiveness without vindictiveness than you can have a cure without a disease. You will never get a high morality from people who conceive that their misdeeds are revocable and pardonable, or in a society where absolution and expiation are officially provided for us all. The demand may be very real; but the supply is spurious. Thus Bill Walker, in my play, having assaulted the Salvation Lass, presently finds himself overwhelmed with an intolerable conviction of sin under the skilled treatment of Barbara. Straightway he begins to try to unassault the lass and deruffianize his deed, first by getting punished for it in kind, and, when that relief is denied him, by fining himself a pound to compensate the girl. He is foiled both ways. He finds the Salvation Army is inexorable as fact itself. It will not punish him: it will not take his money. It will not tolerate a redeemed ruffian: it leaves him no means of salvation except ceasing to be a ruffian. In doing this, the Salvation Army instinctively grasps the central truth of Christianity, and discards its central superstition: that central truth being the vanity of revenge and punishment, and that central superstition the salvation of the world by the gibbet.

For, be it noted, Bill has assaulted an old and starving woman also; and for this worse offense he feels no remorse whatever, because she makes it clear that her malice is as great as his own. "Let her have the law of me, as she said she would," says Bill: "what I done to her is no more on what you might call my conscience than sticking a pig." This shows a perfectly natural and wholesome state of mind on his part. The old woman, like the law she threatens him with, is perfectly ready to play the game of retaliation with him: to rob him if he steals, to flog him if he strikes, to murder him if he kills. By example and precept the law and public opinion teach him to impose his will on others by anger, violence, and cruelty, and to wipe off the moral score by punishment. That is sound Crosstianity. But his Crosstianity has got entangled with something which Barbara calls Christianity, and which unexpectedly causes her to refuse to play the hangman's game of Satan casting out Satan. She refuses to prosecute a drunken ruffian; she converses on equal terms with a blackguard to whom no lady should be seen speaking in the public street: in short, she imitates Christ. Bill's conscience reacts to this just as naturally as it does to the old woman's threats. He is placed in a position of unbearable moral inferiority, and strives by every means in his power to escape from it, whilst he is still quite ready to meet the abuse of the old woman by attempting to smash a mug on her face. And that is the triumphant justification of Barbara's Christianity as against our system of judicial punishment and the vindictive villain-thrashings and "poetic justice" of the romantic stage.

For the credit of literature it must be pointed out that the situation is only partly novel. Victor Hugo long ago gave us the epic of the convict and the bishop's candlesticks, of the Crosstian policeman annihilated by his encounter with the Christian Valjean. But Bill Walker is not, like Valjean, romantically changed from a demon into an angel. There are millions of Bill Walkers in all classes of society today; and the point which I, as a professor of natural psychology, desire to demonstrate, is that Bill, without any change in his character or circumstances whatsoever, will react one way to one sort of treatment and another way to another.

In proof I might point to the sensational object lesson provided by our commercial millionaires today. They begin as brigands: merciless, unscrupulous, dealing out ruin and death and slavery to their competitors and employees, and facing desperately the worst that their competitors can do to them. The history of the English factories, the American Trusts, the exploitation of African gold, diamonds, ivory and rubber, outdoes in villainy the worst that has ever been imagined of the buccaneers of the Spanish Main. Captain Kidd would have marooned a modern Trust magnate for conduct unworthy of a gentleman of fortune. The law every day seizes on unsuccessful scoundrels of this type and punishes them with a cruelty worse than their own, with the result that they come out of the torture house more dangerous than they went in, and renew their evil doing (nobody will employ them at anything else) until they are again seized, again tormented, and again let loose, with the same result.

But the successful scoundrel is dealt with very differently, and very Christianly. He is not only forgiven: he is idolized, respected, made much of, all but worshiped. Society returns him good for evil in the most extravagant overmeasure. And with what result? He begins to idolize himself, to respect himself, to live up to the treatment he receives. He preaches sermons; he writes books of the most edifying advice to young men, and actually persuades himself that he got on by taking his own advice; he endows educational institutions; he supports charities; he dies finally in the odor of sanctity, leaving a will which is a monument of public spirit and bounty. And all this without any change in his character. The spots of the leopard and the stripes of the tiger are as brilliant as ever; but the conduct of the world towards him has changed; and his conduct has changed accordingly. You have only to reverse your attitude towards him — to lay hands on his property, revile him, assault him, and he will be a brigand again in a moment, as ready to crush you as you are to crush him, and quite as full of pretentious moral reasons for doing it.

In short, when Major Barbara says that there are no scoundrels, she is right: there are no absolute scoundrels, though there are impracticable people of whom I shall treat presently. Every reasonable man (and woman) is a potential scoundrel and a potential good citizen. What a man is depends on his character; but what he does, and what we think of what he does, depends on his circumstances. The characteristics that ruin a man in one class make him eminent in another. The characters that behave differently in different circumstances behave alike in similar circumstances. Take a common English character like that of Bill Walker. We meet Bill everywhere: on the judicial bench, on the episcopal bench, in the Privy Council, at the War Office and Admiralty, as well as in the Old Bailey dock or in the ranks of casual unskilled labor. And the morality of Bill's characteristics varies with these various circumstances. The faults of the burglar are the qualities of the financier: the manners and habits of a duke would cost a city clerk his situation. In short, though character is independent of circumstances, conduct is not; and our moral judgments of character are not: both are circumstantial. Take any condition of life in which the circumstances are for a mass of men practically alike: felony, the House of Lords, the factory, the stables, the gipsy encampment or where you please! In spite of diversity of character and temperament, the conduct and morals of the individuals in each group are as predicable and as alike in the main as if they were a flock of sheep, morals being mostly only social habits and circumstantial necessities. Strong people know this and count upon it. In nothing have the master-minds of the world been distinguished from the ordinary suburban season-ticket holder more than in their straightforward perception of the fact that mankind is practically a single species, and not a menagerie of gentlemen and bounders, villains and heroes, cowards and daredevils, peers and peasants, grocers and aristocrats, artisans and laborers, washerwomen and duchesses, in which all the grades of income and caste represent distinct animals who must not be introduced to one another or intermarry. Napoleon constructing a galaxy of generals and courtiers, and even of monarchs, out of his collection of social nobodies; Julius Caesar appointing as governor of Egypt the son of a freedman — one who but a short time before would have been legally disqualified for the post even of a private soldier in the Roman army; Louis XI making his barber his privy councillor:

all these had in their different ways a firm hold of the scientific fact of human equality, expressed by Barbara in the Christian formula that all men are children of one father. A man who believes that men are naturally divided into upper and lower and middle classes morally is making exactly the same mistake as the man who believes that they are naturally divided in the same way socially. And just as our persistent attempts to found political institutions on a basis of social inequality have always produced long periods of destructive friction relieved from time to time by violent explosions of revolution; so the attempt — will Americans please note — to found moral institutions on a basis of moral inequality can lead to nothing but unnatural Reigns of the Saints relieved by licentious Restorations; to Americans who have made divorce a public institution turning the face of Europe into one huge sardonic smile by refusing to stay in the same hotel with a Russian man of genius who has changed wives without the sanction of South Dakota; to grotesque hypocrisy, cruel persecution, and final utter confusion of conventions and compliances with benevolence and respectability. It is quite useless to declare that all men are born free if you deny that they are born good. Guarantee a man's goodness and his liberty will take care of itself. To guarantee his freedom on condition that you approve of his moral character is formally to abolish all freedom whatsoever, as every man's liberty is at the mercy of a moral indictment which any fool can trump up against everyone who violates custom, whether as a prophet or as a rascal. This is the lesson Democracy has to learn before it can become anything but the most oppressive of all the priesthoods.

Let us now return to Bill Walker and his case of conscience against the Salvation Army. Major Barbara, not being a modern Tetzel, or the treasurer of a hospital, refuses to sell absolution to Bill for a sovereign. Unfortunately, what the Army can afford to refuse in the case of Bill Walker, it cannot refuse in the case of Bodger. Bodger is master of the situation because he holds the purse strings. "Strive as you will," says Bodger, in effect: "me you cannot do without. You cannot save Bill Walker without my money." And the Army answers, quite rightly under the circumstances, "We will take money from the devil himself sooner than abandon the work of Salvation." So Bodger pays his conscience-money and gets the absolution that is refused to Bill. In real life Bill would perhaps never know this. But I, the dramatist whose business it is to show the connection between things that seem apart and unrelated in the haphazard order of events in real life, have contrived to make it known to Bill, with the result that the Salvation Army loses its hold of him at once.

But Bill may not be lost, for all that. He is still in the grip of the facts and of his own conscience, and may find his taste for blackguardism permanently spoiled. Still, I cannot guarantee that happy ending. Walk through the poorer quarters of our cities on Sunday when the men are not working, but resting and chewing the cud of their reflections. You will find one expression common to every mature face: the expression of cynicism. The discovery made by Bill Walker about the Salvation Army has been made by everyone there. They have found that every man has his price; and they have been foolishly or corruptly taught to mistrust and despise him for that necessary and salutary condition of social existence. When they learn that General Booth, too, has his price, they do not admire him because it is a high one, and admit the need of organizing society so that he shall get it in an honorable way: they conclude that his character is unsound and that all religious men are hypocrites and allies of their sweaters and oppressors. They know that the large subscriptions which help to support the Army are endowments, not of religion, but of the wicked doctrine of docility in poverty and humility under oppression; and they are rent by the most agonizing of all the doubts of the soul, the doubt whether their true salvation must not come from their most abhorrent passions, from murder, envy, greed, stubbornness, rage, and terrorism, rather than from public spirit, reasonableness, humanity, generosity, tenderness, delicacy, pity, and kindness. The confirmation of that doubt, at which our newspapers have been working so hard for years past, is the morality of militarism; and the justification of militarism is that circumstances may at any time make it the true morality of the moment. It is by producing such moments that we produce violent and sanguinary revolutions, such as the one now in progress in Russia and the one which Capitalism in England and America is daily and diligently provoking.

At such moments it becomes the duty of the Churches to evoke all the powers of destruction against the existing order. But if they do this, the existing order must forcibly suppress them. Churches are suffered to exist only on condition that they preach submission to the State as at present capitalistically organized. The Church of England itself is compelled to add to the thirty-six articles in which it formulates its religious tenets, three more in which it apologetically protests that the moment any of these articles comes in conflict with the State it is to be entirely renounced, abjured, violated, abrogated and abhorred, the policeman being a much more important person than any of the Persons of the Trinity. And this is why no tolerated Church nor Salvation Army can ever win the entire confidence of the poor. It must be on the side of the police and the military, no matter what it believes or disbelieves; and as the police and the military are the instruments by which the rich rob and oppress the poor (on legal and moral principles made for the purpose), it is not possible to be on the side of the poor and of the police at the same time. Indeed the religious bodies, as the almoners of the rich, become a sort of auxiliary police, taking off the insurrectionary edge of poverty with coals and blankets, bread and treacle, and soothing and cheering the victims with hopes of immense and inexpensive happiness in another world when the process of working them to premature death in the service of the rich is complete in this.

Christianity and Anarchism

Such is the false position from which neither the Salvation Army nor the Church of England nor any other religious organization whatever can escape except through a reconstition of society. Nor can they merely endure the State passively, washing their hands of its sins. The State is constantly forcing the consciences of men by violence and cruelty. Not content with exacting money from us for the maintenance of its soldiers and policemen, its jailers and executioners, it forces us to take an active personal part in its proceedings on pain of becoming ourselves the victims of its violence. As I write these lines, a sensational example is given to the world. A royal marriage has been celebrated, first by sacrament in a cathedral, and then by a bullfight having for its main amusement the spectacle of horses gored and disemboweled by the bull, after which, when the bull is so exhausted as to be no longer dangerous, he is killed by a cautious matador. But the ironic contrast between the bullfight and the sacrament of marriage does not move anyone. Another contrast — that between the splendor, the happiness, the atmosphere of kindly admiration surrounding the young couple, and the price paid for it under our abominable social arrangements in the misery, squalor and degradation of millions of other young couples — is drawn at the same moment by a novelist, Mr Upton Sinclair, who chips a corner of the veneering from the huge meat packing industries of Chicago, and shows it to us as a sample of what is going on all over the world underneath the top layer of prosperous plutocracy. One man is sufficiently moved by that contrast to pay his own life as the price of one terrible blow at the responsible parties. His poverty has left him ignorant enough to be duped by the pretense that the innocent young bride and bridegroom, put forth and crowned by plutocracy as the heads of a State in which they have less personal power than any policeman, and less influence than any Chairman of a Trust, are responsible. At them accordingly he launches his sixpennorth of fulminate, missing his mark, but scattering the bowels of as many horses as any bull in the arena, and slaying twenty-three persons, besides wounding ninety-nine. And of all these, the horses alone are innocent of the guilt he is avenging: had he blown all Madrid to atoms with every adult person in it, not one could have escaped the charge of being an accessory, before, at, and after the fact, to poverty and prostitution, to such wholesale massacre of infants as Herod never dreamt of, to plague, pestilence and famine, battle, murder and lingering death — perhaps not one who had not helped, through example, precept, connivance, and even clamor, to teach the dynamiter his well-learnt gospel of hatred and vengeance, by approving every day of sentences of years of imprisonment so infernal in their unnatural stupidity and panic-stricken cruelty, that their advocates can disavow neither the dagger nor the bomb without stripping the mask of justice and humanity from themselves also.

Be it noted that at this very moment there appears the biography of one of our dukes, who, being a Scot, could argue about politics, and therefore stood out as a great brain among our aristocrats. And what, if you please, was his grace's favorite historical episode, which he declared he never read without intense satisfaction? Why, the young General Bonaparte's pounding of the Paris mob to pieces in 1795, called in playful approval by our respectable classes "the whiff of grapeshot," though Napoleon, to do him justice, took a deeper view of it, and would fain have had it forgotten. And since the Duke of Argyll was not a demon, but a man of like passions with ourselves, by no means rancorous or cruel as men go, who can doubt that all over the world proletarians of the ducal kidney are now reveling in "the whiff of dynamite" (the flavor of the joke seems to evaporate a little, does it not?) because it was aimed at the class they hate even as our argute duke hated what he called the mob.

In such an atmosphere there can be only one sequel to the Madrid explosion. All Europe burns to emulate it. Vengeance! More blood! Tear "the Anarchist beast" to shreds. Drag him to the scaffold. Imprison him for life. Let all civilized States band together to drive his like off the face of the earth; and if any State refuses to join, make war on it. This time the leading London newspaper, anti-Liberal and therefore anti-Russian in politics, does not say "Serve you right" to the victims, as it did, in effect, when Bobrikoff, and De Plehve, and Grand Duke Sergius, were in the same manner unofficially fulminated into fragments. No: fulminate our rivals in Asia by all means, ye brave Russian revolutionaries; but to aim at an English princess! monstrous! hideous! hound down the wretch to his doom; and observe, please, that we are a civilized and merciful people, and, however much we may regret it, must not treat him as Ravaillac and Damiens were treated. And meanwhile, since we have not yet caught him, let us soothe our quivering nerves with the bullfight, and comment in a courtly way on the unfailing tact and good taste of the ladies of our royal houses, who, though presumably of full normal natural tenderness, have been so effectually broken in to fashionable routine that they can be taken to see the horses slaughtered as helplessly as they could no doubt be taken to a gladiator show, if that happened to be the mode just now.

Strangely enough, in the midst of this raging fire of malice, the one man who still has faith in the kindness and intelligence of human nature is the fulminator, now a hunted wretch, with nothing, apparently, to secure his triumph over all the prisons and scaffolds of infuriate Europe except the revolver in his pocket and his readiness to discharge it at a moment's notice into his own or any other head. Think of him setting out to find a gentleman and a Christian in the multitude of human wolves howling for his blood. Think also of this: that at the very first essay he finds what he seeks, a veritable grandee of Spain, a noble, high-thinking, unterrified, malice-void soul, in the guise — of all masquerades in the world! — of a modern editor. The Anarchist wolf, flying from the wolves of plutocracy, throws himself on the honor of the man. The man, not being a wolf (nor a London editor), and therefore not having enough sympathy with his exploit to be made bloodthirsty by it, does not throw him back to the pursuing wolves — gives him, instead, what help he can to escape, and sends him off acquainted at last with a force that goes deeper than dynamite, though you cannot buy so much of it for sixpence. That righteous and honorable high human deed is not wasted on Europe, let us hope, though it benefits the fugitive wolf only for a moment. The plutocratic wolves presently smell him out. The fugitive shoots the unlucky wolf whose nose is nearest; shoots himself; and then convinces the world, by his photograph, that he was no monstrous freak of reversion to the tiger, but a good looking young man with nothing abnormal about him except his appalling courage and resolution (that is why the terrified shriek Coward at him): one to whom murdering a happy young couple on their wedding morning would have been an unthinkably unnatural abomination under rational and kindly human circumstances.

Then comes the climax of irony and blind stupidity. The wolves, balked of their meal of fellow-wolf, turn on the man, and proceed to torture him, after their manner, by imprisonment, for refusing to fasten his teeth in the throat of the dynamiter and hold him down until they came to finish him.

Thus, you see, a man may not be a gentleman nowadays even if he wishes to. As to being a Christian, he is allowed some latitude in that matter, because, I repeat, Christianity has two faces. Popular Christianity has for its emblem a gibbet, for its chief sensation a sanguinary execution after torture, for its central mystery an insane vengeance bought off by a trumpery expiation. But there is a nobler and profounder Christianity which affirms the sacred mystery of Equality, and forbids the glaring futility and folly of vengeance, often politely called punishment or justice. The gibbet part of Christianity is tolerated. The other is criminal felony. Connoisseurs in irony are well aware of the fact that the only editor in England who denounces punishment as radically wrong, also repudiates Christianity; calls his paper The Freethinker; and has been imprisoned for "bad taste" under the law against blasphemy.

Sane Conclusions

And now I must ask the excited reader not to lose his head on one side or the other, but to draw a sane moral from these grim absurdities. It is not good sense to propose that laws against crime should apply to principals only and not to accessories whose consent, counsel, or silence may secure impunity to the principal. If you institute punishment as part of the law, you must punish people for refusing to punish. If you have a police, part of its duty must be to compel everybody to assist the police. No doubt if your laws are unjust, and your policemen agents of oppression, the result will be an unbearable violation of the private consciences of citizens. But that cannot be helped: the remedy is, not to license everybody to thwart the law if they please, but to make laws that will command the public assent, and not to deal cruelly and stupidly with lawbreakers. Everybody disapproves of burglars; but the modern burglar, when caught and overpowered by a householder, usually appeals, and often, let us hope, with success, to his captor not to deliver him over to the useless horrors of penal servitude. In other cases the law-breaker escapes because those who could give him up do not consider his breach of the law a guilty action. Sometimes, even, private tribunals are formed in opposition to the official tribunals; and these private tribunals employ assassins as executioners, as was done, for example, by Mahomet before he had established his power officially, and by the Ribbon lodges of Ireland in their long struggle with the landlords. Under such circumstances, the assassin goes free although everybody in the district knows who he is and what he has done. They do not betray him, partly because they justify him exactly as the regular Government justifies its official executioner, and partly because they would themselves be assassinated if they betrayed him: another method learnt from the official government. Given a tribunal employing a slayer who has no personal quarrel with the slain; and there is clearly no moral difference between official and unofficial killing.

In short, all men are anarchists with regard to laws which are against their consciences, either in the preamble or in the penalty. In London our worst anarchists are the magistrates, because many of them are so old and ignorant that when they are called upon to administer any law that is based on ideas or knowledge less than half a century old, they disagree with it, and being mere ordinary homebred private Englishmen without any respect for law in the abstract, naively set the example of violating it. In this instance the man lags behind the law; but when the law lags behind the man, he becomes equally an anarchist. When some huge change in social conditions, such as the industrial revolution of the eighteenth and nineteenth centuries, throws our legal and industrial institutions out of date, Anarchism becomes almost a religion. The whole force of the most energetic geniuses of the time in philosophy, economics, and art, concentrates itself on demonstrations and reminders that morality and law are only conventions, fallible and continually obsolescing. Tragedies in which the heroes are bandits, and comedies in which law-abiding and conventionally moral folk are compelled to satirize themselves by outraging the conscience of the spectators every time they do their duty, appear simultaneously with economic treatises entitled "What Is Property? Theft!" and with histories of "The Conflict Between Religion and Science."

Now this is not a healthy state of things. The advantages of living in society are proportionate, not to the freedom of the individual from a code, but to the complexity and subtlety of the code he is prepared not only to accept but to uphold as a matter of such vital importance that a law-breaker at large is hardly to be tolerated on any plea. Such an attitude becomes impossible when the only men who can make themselves heard and remembered throughout the world spend all their energy in raising our gorge against current law, current morality, current respectability, and legal property. The ordinary man, uneducated in social theory even when he is schooled in Latin verse, cannot be set against all the laws of his country and yet persuaded to regard law in the abstract as vitally necessary to society. Once he is brought to repudiate the laws and institutions he knows, he will repudiate the very conception of law and the very groundwork of institutions, ridiculing human rights, extolling brainless methods as "historical," and tolerating nothing except pure empiricism in conduct, with dynamite as the basis of politics and vivisection as the basis of science. That is hideous; but what is to be done? Here am I, for instance, by class a respectable man, by common sense a hater of waste and disorder, by intellectual constitution legally minded to the verge of pedantry, and by temperament apprehensive and economically disposed to the limit of old-maidishness; yet I am, and have always been, and shall now always be, a revolutionary writer, because our laws make law impossible; our liberties destroy all freedom; our property is organized robbery; our morality is an impudent hypocrisy; our wisdom is administered by inexperienced or malexperienced dupes, our power wielded by cowards and weaklings, and our honor false in all its points. I am an enemy of the existing order for good reasons; but that does not make my attacks any less encouraging or helpful to people who are its enemies for bad reasons. The existing order may shriek that if I tell the truth about it, some foolish person may drive it to become still worse by trying to assassinate it. I cannot help that, even if I could see what worse it could do than it is already doing. And the disadvantage of that worst even from its own point of view is that society, with all its prisons and bayonets and whips and ostracisms and starvations, is powerless in the face of the Anarchist who is prepared to sacrifice his own life in the battle with it. Our natural safety from the cheap and devastating explosives which every Russian student can make, and every Russian grenadier has learnt to handle in Manchuria, lies in the fact that brave and resolute men, when they are rascals, will not risk their skins for the good of humanity, and, when they are not, are sympathetic enough to care for humanity, abhorring murder, and never committing it until their consciences are outraged beyond endurance. The remedy is, then, simply not to outrage their consciences.

Do not be afraid that they will not make allowances. All men make very large allowances indeed before they stake their own lives in a war to the death with society. Nobody demands or expects the millennium. But there are two things that must be set right, or we shall perish, like Rome, of soul atrophy disguised as empire.

The first is, that the daily ceremony of dividing the wealth of the country among its inhabitants shall be so conducted that no crumb shall, save as a criminal's ration, go to any able-bodied adults who are not producing by their personal exertions not only a full equivalent for what they take, but a surplus sufficient to provide for their superannuation and pay back the debt due for their nurture.

The second is that the deliberate infliction of malicious injuries which now goes on under the name of punishment be abandoned; so that the thief, the ruffian, the gambler, and the beggar, may without inhumanity be handed over to the law, and made to understand that a State which is too humane to punish will also be too thrifty to waste the life of honest men in watching or restraining dishonest ones. That is why we do not imprison dogs. We even take our chance of their first bite. But if a dog delights to bark and bite, it goes to the lethal chamber. That seems to me sensible. To allow the dog to expiate his bite by a period of torment, and then let him loose in a much more savage condition (for the chain makes a dog savage) to bite again and expiate again, having meanwhile spent a great deal of human life and happiness in the task of chaining and feeding and tormenting him, seems to me idiotic and superstitious. Yet that is what we do to men who bark and bite and steal. It would be far more sensible to put up with their vices, as we put up with their illnesses, until they give more trouble than they are worth, at which point we should, with many apologies and expressions of sympathy, and some generosity in complying with their last wishes, place them in the lethal chamber and get rid of them. Under no circumstances should they be allowed to expiate their misdeeds by a manufactured penalty, to subscribe to a charity, or to compensate the victims. If there is to be no punishment there can be no forgiveness. We shall never have real moral responsibility until everyone knows that his deeds are irrevocable, and that his life depends on his usefulness. Hitherto, alas! humanity has never dared face these hard facts. We frantically scatter conscience money and invent systems of conscience banking, with expiatory penalties, atonements, redemptions, salvations, hospital subscription lists and what not, to enable us to contract-out of the moral code. Not content with the old scapegoat and sacrificial lamb, we deify human saviors, and pray to miraculous virgin intercessors. We attribute mercy to the inexorable; soothe our consciences after commiting murder by throwing ourselves on the bosom of divine love; and shrink even from our own gallows because we are forced to admit that it, at least, is irrevocable — as if one hour of imprisonment were not as irrevocable as any execution!

If a man cannot look evil in the face without illusion, he will never know what it really is, or combat it effectually. The few men who have been able (relatively) to do this have been called cynics, and have sometimes had an abnormal share of evil in themselves, corresponding to the abnormal strength of their minds; but they have never done mischief unless they intended to do it. That is why great scoundrels have been beneficent rulers whilst amiable and privately harmless monarchs have ruined their countries by trusting to the hocuspocus of innocence and guilt, reward and punishment, virtuous indignation and pardon, instead of standing up to the facts without either malice or mercy. Major Barbara stands up to Bill Walker in that way, with the result that the ruffian who cannot get hated, has to hate himself. To relieve this agony he tries to get punished; but the Salvationist whom he tries to provoke is as merciless as Barbara, and only prays for him. Then he tries to pay, but can get nobody to take his money. His doom is the doom of Cain, who, failing to find either a savior, a policeman, or an almoner to help him to pretend that his brother's blood no longer cried from the ground, had to live and die a murderer. Cain took care not to commit another murder, unlike our railway shareholders (I am one) who kill and maim shunters by hundreds to save the cost of automatic couplings, and make atonement by annual subscriptions to deserving charities. Had Cain been allowed to pay off his score, he might possibly have killed Adam and Eve for the mere sake of a second luxurious reconciliation with God afterwards. Bodger, who may depend on it, will go on to the end of his life poisoning people with bad whisky, because he can always depend on the Salvation Army or the Church of England to negotiate a redemption for him in consideration of a trifling percentage of his profits.

There is a third condition too, which must be fulfilled before the great teachers of the world will cease to scoff at its religions. Creeds must become intellectually honest. At present there is not a single credible established religion in the world. That is perhaps the most stupendous fact in the whole world-situation. This play of mine, *Major Barbara*, is, I hope, both true and inspired; but whoever says that it all happened, and that faith in it and understanding of it consist in believing that it is a record of an actual occurrence, is, to speak according to Scripture, a fool and a liar, and is hereby solemnly denounced and cursed as such by me, the author, to all posterity.

Drama in the Early and Mid-Twentieth Century

The realist tradition in drama had certain EXPRESSIONIST qualities, evident in the symbolic actions in Strindberg's *Miss Julie* and the romantic fantasies of Hedda in *Hedda Gabler*. But the surfaces of the plays appear realistic, consisting of a sequence of events that we might imagine happening in real life. The subject matter of these plays is also in the tradition of naturalism because it is drawn from life and not beautified or toned down for the middle-class audience.

But in the early to mid-twentieth century realistic drama took a new turn, incorporating distortions of reality that border on the unreal or *surreal*. From the time of John Millington Synge in 1905 to Samuel Beckett in the 1950s, drama exploited the possibilities of realism, anti-realism, and the poetic expansion of expressionism.

The Heritage of Realism

In the late nineteenth century realism was often perceived as too severe on an audience that had applauded melodrama with great approval. Realistic plays forced comfortable audiences to observe psychological and physical problems that their status as members of the middle class usually allowed them to avoid. It was a painful experience for these audiences, and they often protested loudly.

However, the technique of realism could be adapted for many different purposes, and eventually realism was reshaped to satisfy middle-class sensibilities by commercial playwrights, who produced popular, pleasant plays. It took a few decades for this to happen, but by the 1920s in Europe and the 1930s in America, theatergoing audiences expected plays to be realistic. Even the light comedies dominating the commercial stage were in a more or less realistic mode. Anything that disturbed the illusion of realism was thought to be a flaw.

Reactions to the comfortable use of realistic techniques were numerous, especially after the First World War. One extreme reaction was that of the Dadaists. Through the group's chief propagandist, Tristan Tzara (1896–1963), they promoted an art that was essentially enigmatic and incoherent to the average person. That was its point. The Dadaists blamed World War I on sensible, middle-class people who were logical and well intentioned. The brief plays that were performed in many Dadaist clubs in Europe often featured actors speaking simultaneously so that nothing they said could be understood. The purpose was to confound the normal expectations of theatergoers.

Other developments also were making it possible for playwrights to experiment and move away from a strict reliance on "comfortable" realism. By World War I motion pictures began to make melodramatic entertainment available to most people in the world. Even when films were silent, they relied on techniques that had been common on the nineteenth-century stage. Their growing domination of popular dramatic entertainment provided an outlet for the expectations of middle-class audiences and freed more imaginative playwrights to experiment and develop in different directions.

Realism and Myth

The incorporation of myth in drama offered new opportunities to expand the limits of realism. Sigmund Freud's theories of psychoanalysis at the turn of the century stimulated a new interest in myth and dreams as a psychological link between people. Freud studied Greek myths for clues to the psychic state of his patients, and he published a number of commentaries on Greek plays and on *Hamlet*. The psychologist Carl Jung, a follower of Freud who eventually split with him, helped give a powerful impetus to the interest in dreams and the symbolism of myth by suggesting that all members of a culture share an inborn knowledge of the basic myths of the culture. Jung postulated a collective unconscious, a repository of mythic material in the mind that all humans inherit as part of their birthright. This theory gave credence to the power of myth in everyday life, and it is, along with Freud's theories, one of the most important ideas empowering drama and other art forms in this century. Playwrights who used elements of myth in their plays produced a poetic form of realism that deals with a level of truth common to all humans.

Poetic Realism

The Abbey Theatre in Dublin, which functioned with distinction from the turn of the century, produced major works by John Millington Synge, W. B. Yeats, Sean O'Casey, and Lady Augusta Gregory. Lady Gregory's peasant plays concentrated on the charming, the amusing, and occasionally the grotesque. She tried to represent the dialect she heard in the west of Ireland, a dialect that was distinctive, poetic, and colorful. She also took advantage of local Irish myths and used some of them for her most powerful plays, such as *Dervorgilla* and *Grania*, both portraits of passionate women whose stories were told in Irish legend and ancient Irish myth.

John Millington Synge, like Lady Gregory, was interested in the twin forces of myth and peasant dialects. His plays are difficult to fit into a realist mold, although their surfaces are sometimes naturalistic. Some audiences reacted violently to his realistic portrayals of peasant life because they were unflattering.

Synge's plays were sometimes directly connected with ancient Irish myth, as in *Deirdre of the Sorrows* (1910), which concerns a willful Irish princess who runs off with a young warrior and his brothers on the eve of her wedding to an old king. The story ends sadly for Deirdre, and she is regarded as a fated heroine, almost a Greek figure. Synge's great short tragedy *Riders to the Sea* may also have derived from an anecdote or legend; it is an expressionist play in its use of unreal moments, such as Maurya's encounter with the ghost of her son Michael and her vision of her dead son Bartley.

In the United States, Eugene O'Neill experimented with realism, first by presenting stark, powerful, realistic plays that disturbed his audiences. *The Hairy Ape* (1922) portrayed a primitive coal stoker on a passenger liner who awakened base emotions in the more refined passengers. In *The Emperor Jones* (1921) O'Neill produced the first important American expressionist play. The shifting scenery, created by lighting, was dreamlike and at times frightening. The experience of the play reflected the frightening psychic experiences of the main character, Brutus Jones.

O'Neill also experimented with more poetic forms of realism. In *Desire Under the Elms* (1924), he explores the myth of Phaedra — centering on her incestuous love for her husband's son — but sets it in rural New England on a rock-hard farm. It is as close as O'Neill can get to a peasant reality drawing on myth in America.

In the tradition of realism, the play treats unpleasant themes: sons' distrust of their father and their dishonoring him; lust between a son and his stepmother; and the murder of a baby to "prove" love. But it is not simply realistic. Without its underpinning of myth, the play would be sordid. The myth helps us see things much more clearly: Fate operates even today, but not in terms of messages from the gods. Rather, it works in terms of messages from our hearts and bodies. Lust is a force in nature. It drives and it destroys.

Social Realism

Ten years after *Desire Under the Elms* enjoyed popularity, a new kind of play based on social realism developed. This was realism with a political conscience. Since the world was in the throes of a depression that reduced many people to absolute poverty and homelessness, drama began to aim at awakening governments to the consequences of unbridled capitalism and the depressions that freewheeling economies produced.

Plays like Jack Kirkland's *Tobacco Road* (1933), adapted from Erskine Caldwell's novel, presented a grim portrait of rural poverty in America. Sidney Kingsley's *Dead End* (1935) portrayed the life of virtually homeless boys on the Lower East Side of Manhattan. In the same year Maxwell Anderson produced a verse comedy, *Winterset*, with gangsters and gangsterism at its core. Also in 1935 Clifford Odets produced *Waiting for Lefty*, an openly leftist labor drama. These plays' realist credentials lay primarily in their effort to show audiences portraits of real life that might shock their middle-class sensibilities.

Meanwhile, in Fascist Spain, Federico García Lorca, also a poetic realist, was pointing to dark emotional centers of the psyche in his *House of Bernarda Alba* (1936), which explores erotic forces repressed and then set loose. Lorca was opposed to fascism and was murdered by a Fascist agent. His plays reveal a darkness of spirit that helps us imagine the darkness — moral and psychological — that enveloped Europe in the 1940s.

Realism and Expressionism

After Eugene O'Neill's experiments in combining myth and realism, later American dramatists looked for new ways to expand the resources of realism while retaining its power. The use of expressionism — often poetic in language and effect — was one solution that appealed to both Tennessee Williams and Arthur Miller.

Tennessee Williams's *The Glass Menagerie* (1944) and Arthur Miller's *Death of a Salesman* (1949) both use expressionist techniques. Williams's poetic stage directions make clear that he is drawing on nonrealistic dramatic devices. He describes the scene as "memory and . . . therefore nonrealistic." He calls for an interior "rather dim and poetic," and he uses a character who also steps outside the staged action to serve as a narrator — one who "takes whatever license with dramatic convention as is convenient to his purposes." As the narrator tells his story, the walls of the building seem to melt away, revealing the inside of a house and the lives and fantasies of his mother and sister, both caught in their own distorted visions of life.

Arthur Miller's original image for *Death of a Salesman* was the inside of Willy Loman's mind; Jo Mielziner's expressionist set represented his idea as a cross section of Loman's house. As the action in one room concluded, lights went up to begin action in another (Figure 9). This evocative staging influenced the production of numerous plays by later writers. *Death of a Salesman* examines the assumptions that led Willy and his family to their state of desperation. They are the assumptions that many American businesspeople hold: If you are well liked you will get ahead; petty crimes such as stealing and adultery are evidence of high spirits; being an athlete confers glory and privileges; being studious leads nowhere.

Figure 9. Expressionistic setting in Arthur Miller's *Death of a Salesman*

Miller used expressionist techniques to create the hallucinatory sequences in which Willy talks with Ben, the man who walked into the jungle poor and walked out a millionaire, and Biff recalls seeing Willy with the woman in Boston.

Lorraine Hansberry's *A Raisin in the Sun* (1959) uses basically realistic staging and dialogue to portray the difficulties of the members of one family who struggle to take advantage of their opportunity to overcome poverty. For Williams and Miller, expressionism offered a way to bring other worlds to bear on the staged action — the worlds of dream and fantasy. Hansberry does not use the expressionist techniques of Miller. She chooses another path to a similar end when she introduces an exotic touch in the visit of the African young man, Asagai, and offers a moment of cultural counterpoint that is as effective in bringing in another world as is a dream or hallucinatory sequence. Hansberry's realism is essentially conservative.

Antirealism

SURREALISM (literally, "beyond realism") in the early twentieth century was based originally on an interpretation of experience not through the lucid mind of the waking person but through the mind of the dreamer, the unconscious mind that Freud described. Surrealism augmented or, for some playwrights, supplanted realism and became a means of distorting reality for emotional purposes.

When Pirandello's six characters come onstage looking for their author in *Six Characters in Search of an Author* (1921), no one can believe that they are characters rather than actors. Least of all does the audience believe that. Pirandello's play is an examination of the realities we take for granted in drama. He turns the world of expectation in drama upside down. He reminds us that what we assume to be real is always questionable — we cannot be sure of anything; we must presume things are true, and in some cases we must take them on faith.

Pirandello's philosophy dominated his stories, plays, and novels. His questioning of the certainty of human knowledge was designed to undermine his audience's faith in an absolute reality. Modern physicists have concurred with philosophers, ancient and modern, who question everyday reality. Pirandello was influenced by the modern theories of relativity that physicists were developing, and he found in them validation of his own attack on certainty.

Epic Theater

Bertolt Brecht (1898–1956) began writing plays just after World War I. He was a political dramatist who rejected the theater of his day, which valued the realistic "well-made play," in which all the parts fit perfectly together and function like a machine. His feeling was that such plays were too mechanical, like a "clockwork mouse."

Brecht conceived a new style that he called EPIC THEATER. The term implies a sequence of actions or episodes of the kind found in Homer's *Iliad*. In epic theater the sense of dramatic illusion is constantly voided by reminders from the stage that one is watching a play. Stark, harsh lighting, blank stages, placards announcing changes of scenes, bands playing music onstage, and long, discomfiting pauses make it impossible for an audience to become totally immersed in a realistic illusion. Brecht wanted the audience to analyze the play's thematic content rather than sit back and be entertained. Brecht offered a genuine alternative to realistic drama. His complaints about realistic drama were focused on the power of such drama to convince audiences that their realism described not just things as they are, but things as they must be. He thought such drama helped maintain the social problems that they portrayed by reinforcing, rather than challenging, their realities.

Brecht's *Mother Courage* (1941) is an antiwar drama written early in World War II. The use of song, an unreal setting, and an unusual historical perspective (the Thirty Years War in the seventeenth century) help to achieve the "defamiliarization" that Brecht thought drama ought to produce in its audiences. The techniques of epic theater as developed in *Galileo* and also *The Good Woman of Setzuan* (1943), a study of the immoralities that prosper under capitalism, were imitated by playwrights in the 1950s. Hardly a major play in that period is free of Brecht's influence.

Absurdist Drama

The critic Martin Esslin coined the term THEATER OF THE ABSURD when describing the work of Samuel Beckett (1906–1989), the Irish playwright whose dramas often dispense with almost everything that makes the well-made play well made. Some of his plays have no actors onstage — amplified breathing is the only hint of human presence in one case. Some have little or no plot; others have no words. His theater is minimalist, offering a stage reality that seems cut to the bone, without the usual realistic devices of plot, character development, and intricate setting.

The theater of the absurd assumes that the world is meaningless, that meaning is a human concept, and that individuals must create significance and not rely on institutions or traditions to provide it. The absurdist movement grew out of existentialism, a postwar French philosophy that demanded that the individual face the emptiness of the universe and create meaning in a life that has no essential meaning within itself. *Waiting for Godot* (1952) captured the modern imagination and established a landmark in absurdist drama.

In *Waiting for Godot* two tramps, Vladimir and Estragon, meet near a tree where they expect Godot to arrive to talk with them. The play has two acts that both end with a small boy explaining that Godot cannot come today but will come tomorrow. Godot is not coming, and the tramps who wait for Godot will wait forever. While they wait they entertain themselves with vaudeville routines and eventually are met by a rich man, Pozzo, and his slave, Lucky. Lucky, on the command "Think, pig," speaks in a stream of garbled phrases that evoke Western philosophy and religion but that remain meaningless. Pozzo and Lucky have no interest in joining Vladimir and Estragon in waiting for Godot. They leave the two alone, waiting — afraid to leave for fear of missing Godot, but uncertain that Godot will ever arrive.

Beckett seems to be saying that in an absurd world, such gestures are necessary to create the sense of significance that people need to live. His stark lighting, his characters' awareness of an audience, and his refusal to create a drama in which an audience can "lose" itself in a comfortable surface of realistic illusion are all, in their own way, indebted to Brecht.

Beckett's *Krapp's Last Tape* (1958) places some extraordinary limitations on performance. Krapp is the only person onstage throughout the play, and his dialogues are with tapes of himself made many years before. The situation is absurd, but as Beckett reveals to us, the absurd has its own complexities, and situations such as Krapp's can sustain complex interpretations. Like Brecht, Beckett expects his audience to analyze the drama, not sit back and merely be entertained.

The illusion of reality is shed almost entirely in *Endgame*. Hamm cannot move. His parents, both legless, are in ashbins onstage. Clov performs all the play's movement on a barren, cellarlike stage. On the other hand, Beckett's *All That Fall* seems realistic in style, but it was written for the radio and was not meant to be staged realistically.

The great plays of this period reflect the values of the cultures from which they spring. They make comments on life in the modern world and question the values that the culture takes for granted. The drama of this part of the twentieth century is a drama of examination.

John Millington Synge

John Millington Synge (1871–1909) was one of the brilliant discoveries of the Irish Literary Renaissance, which was largely the product of Lady Isabella Augusta Gregory and William Butler Yeats, the codirectors of the Abbey Theatre in Dublin. The Abbey ranks as one of the most influential and successful national theaters in European history. From 1904 to the present, it has been devoted to producing plays by Irish writers, some of whom have gone on to be ranked among the greatest of their age. Besides Synge, Bernard Shaw, Lady Gregory, Yeats, Sean O'Casey, and Brian Friel are among the many whose names still loom impressively as having contributed to building the reputation of the Abbey.

Synge was gifted in languages, with a degree in German from Trinity College, Dublin. But he was also a violinist and went to Paris to study music and live the bohemian life of the artist. It was there in 1896 that Yeats and Lady Gregory met him and convinced him to return to Ireland and write plays for what was to become the Abbey. They convinced him to spend time in the Aran Islands, the wildest part of Ireland. It is there that he set his play *Riders to the Sea*. Yeats felt the Arans were an important source of the literary energy of the nation because the Islanders' colorful language sounded like English filtered through Irish Gaelic.

Synge wrote a number of important plays within less than ten years. Most of them remain in the repertory of modern drama: *In the Shadow of the Glen* (1903); *Riders to the Sea* (1904); *The Well of the Saints* (1905); *The Tinker's Wedding* (1907); *The Playboy of the Western World* (1907); and *Deirdre of the Sorrows* (1910). With the exception of *The Tinker's Wedding*, which is so anticlerical that it has never been given a production at the Abbey, they are all still regularly produced there.

Synge was not always a popular playwright in Ireland. He felt he faithfully represented peasant ways, but his Dublin audiences often protested that he insulted the Irish. Synge's kind of realism, while not especially harsh or critical, was an unvarnished view of the west of Ireland. The Abbey audiences wanted an idealized portrait of their countrymen and countrywomen, not straightforward and sometimes embarrassing portraits such as the one Synge offered them in *The Playboy of the Western World*. That play caused riots in the Abbey Theatre when it was first performed.

The Playboy of the Western World is about a young man who, thinking he has killed his father, arrives at a shebeen — a kind of tavern — in Mayo where the townfolk make a kind of hero of him rather than turning him in to the police. He joins in their games and wins all the prizes and woos and almost wins Pegeen Mike, the local beauty. The subject matter — Irish people lionizing a presumed murderer — and the frank language were departures from previous Irish drama, but neither the playwright nor his producers at the Abbey Theatre were prepared for the audience's reaction. At its first performance when Christy, the Playboy, actually hit his father (who was not really dead) late in the play, the audience could sit still no longer. Such an act was perceived as an offense against all the Irish.

But vocal protest finally erupted at a line that describes women standing in their slips in front of the hero. At that point the crowd was so noisy that no one could hear what was said onstage. For subsequent performances, Lady Gregory advised the actors to move their lips when the crowd roared, but not to waste their voices unless the crowd noise died down. Eventually, the police were called in to throw out trouble-makers and to keep the audience noise down. When the Abbey company toured the United States in 1909 and performed the play in Boston, riots ensued again, with the local chapter of the nationalist Irish organization Sinn Féin enlisted to make a deafening racket during the performances.

Synge was shocked at the uproar; he had never expected his play to stimulate such a response. The question of realism was probably not on Synge's mind at all. *Playboy* is less a realistic play than *Riders to the Sea*, and both are rooted not in any effort to force the audience to look at life as it is really lived but rather in the mythic and symbolic forces that underlie everyone's experiences of heroism, life, and death. The deep roots of both plays are in Irish myth and the Christian religion. Synge was amazed to think that audiences ignored those important aspects and focused on other, less significant issues.

Synge's early death robbed world drama of a figure who certainly would have been among the greatest writers of the century. As it is, his work is remarkable; but in his last play, *Deirdre of the Sorrows*, which he never finished, we can see the promise of a body of work that would have taken its place with the best plays of our time.

RIDERS TO THE SEA

Riders to the Sea (1904) was the first success that Synge produced for the Abbey Theatre. In some ways it is still one of the most impressive plays to come out of the Irish Literary Renaissance. It is a one-act play, which the Abbey found congenial for its early programs, but its brevity in no way diminishes its power.

The play is set in the west of Ireland, the part least touched by English influence. Aran Islanders speak both Gaelic and English, but their English is marked with a very expressive and idiosyncratic flavor, which Synge tries to replicate in this play. The syntax of Synge's peasants benefits from his musician's ear as well as from his having lived in an inn in Wicklow where he eavesdropped on the local Irish kitchen girls speaking naturally and unaffectedly.

Riders to the Sea owes much of its power to the local speech and the local way of life portrayed faithfully in the play. In his preface to *The Playboy of the Western World*, Synge credits Irish writers with the advantage of listening "for a few years more" to a language that is "rich as a nut." Maurya's long speeches at the end of *Riders to the Sea* are filled with the rhythms of the sea and the agony of someone who has suffered as much as the world can demand. Even the speeches of the lesser characters have an extraordinarily expressive flavor.

The drama depicts the sufferings of a superstitious peasant woman, yet it contains the same kinds of intensity of dramatic action found in Greek tragedies. It maintains a unity of time, place, character, and action, as well as an intense sense of fate and impending doom. Synge may well have begun developing a new genre of folk tragedy, just as Arthur Miller later began developing a genre of middle-class tragedy in *Death of a Salesman. Riders to the Sea* is permeated by a sense of fate, and Maurya, whose name is remarkably close in sound to *moira,* the Greek word for fate, senses the inevitability of the premature death of her last son on the sea. The feeling of inevitability is heightened by the discussion between the daughters about the son Michael, who has been feared lost at sea, by their identification of his sock that was recovered from the sea, and by the willful insistence of the last son, Bartley, to ride the mares across the sea to the mainland, knowingly risking his life. (In fact, men did swim their animals from the islands to the mainland, and they often went out to meet the large boats that came near. Even today those waters are difficult, and Aran Islanders still use the same black curraghs their ancestors used to ferry themselves, their goods, and their livestock between the mainland and their homes.) Maurya's horrifying vision of Michael and Bartley on the mares confirms her premonitions and fears. It also provides an element of supernatural intensity.

As in so many Irish plays, the women remain to suffer after the men have perished. The play ends with the sound of women keening for the dead, knowing that there are no men left to help them survive in a harsh environment. A question that begs to be asked is why Bartley dares the sea, knowing the risks he is taking. What drives him on, as it drove his father and brothers? Nothing Maurya can say will make him swerve from his progress.

Perhaps because of its tragic Greek pattern, *Riders to the Sea* has a mythic force. The sense of destiny that Maurya feels is built into her life. Her sense of resignation and deep faith help her grow in our imagination and give her a heroic dimension. Synge's approach to realism is much different from Ibsen's or Chekhov's. It is more elemental, based on the spiritual life of the folk as expressed in the eloquence of their language.

Riders to the Sea in Performance

All of Synge's plays were written for the early Abbey Theatre, founded in 1904 by Lady Isabella Augusta Gregory and William Butler Yeats to perform Irish plays. At that time all performances were in Molesworth Hall, leased facilities. Synge's *In the Shadow of the Glen* was one of the first plays to be performed by the company, then known as the Irish National Theatre. The play opened in October 1903, coinciding with an Irish holiday, Samhain. Although controversial, it was a success. *Riders to the Sea* was Synge's second play, produced in Molesworth Hall in February 1904. At this time the Abbey had already attracted some excellent actors. Bartley was played by W. G. Fay, who was instrumental in shaping the Abbey. Sarah Allgood, destined to become a standard player in American films in the 1930s and 1940s, played Cathleen. The production was well received by press and public.

Riders to the Sea has usually been paired with other Irish plays in production. The Abbey Theatre Company still produces the play regularly and often takes it on tour. One of the most memorable tours was in 1957 when the Abbey brought the play to the tiny Theatre East in New York. Despite the theater's small size, the effect of the play, which had not been seen in an Abbey performance in the United States since 1911, was electrifying. The finest Irish actress of the age, Siobhan McKenna, played Maurya.

The stage, essentially a tile floor, was simply set. The actors entered through the aisles. At the end of one performance, as the women began keening over Bartley's body, one of the daughters came onstage with glass milk bottles in her apron. She dropped them accidentally, and they broke in huge shards. All the actresses were barefoot and all continued the performance, walking through the glass as if it were not there. Another actor quickly swept it up without breaking the mood of the ending. No one was cut, but the audience held its breath.

Riders to the Sea enjoys frequent production both by high school and college students. Its brevity and power make it a strong vehicle for amateur productions.

John Millington Synge (1871–1909)
RIDERS TO THE SEA

1904

Persons in the Play

MAURYA (*an old woman*)
BARTLEY (*her son*)
CATHLEEN (*her daughter*)
NORA (*a younger daughter*)
MEN *and* WOMEN

Scene: *An Island off the West of Ireland.*

(*Cottage kitchen, with nets, oilskins, spinning wheel, some new boards standing by the wall, etc. Cathleen, a girl of about twenty, finishes kneading cake, and puts it down in the pot-oven by the fire; then wipes her hands, and begins to spin at the wheel. Nora, a young girl, puts her head in at the door.*)

NORA (*in a low voice*): Where is she?

CATHLEEN: She's lying down, God help her, and may be sleeping, if she's able.

(*Nora comes in softly and takes a bundle from under her shawl.*)

CATHLEEN (*spinning the wheel rapidly*): What is it you have?

NORA: The young priest is after bringing them. It's a shirt and a plain stocking were got off a drowned man in Donegal.

(*Cathleen stops her wheel with a sudden movement, and leans out to listen.*)

NORA: We're to find out if it's Michael's they are, some time herself will be down looking by the sea.

CATHLEEN: How would they be Michael's, Nora. How would he go the length of that way to the far north?

NORA: The young priest says he's known the like of it. "If it's Michael's they are," says he, "you can tell herself he's got a clean burial by the grace of God, and if they're not his, let no one say a word about them, for she'll be getting her death," says he, "with crying and lamenting."

(*The door which Nora half closed is blown open by a gust of wind.*)

CATHLEEN (*looking out anxiously*): Did you ask him would he stop Bartley going this day with the horses to the Galway fair?

NORA: "I won't stop him," says he, "but let you not be afraid. Herself does be saying prayers half

through the night, and the Almighty God won't leave her destitute," says he, "with no son living."

CATHLEEN: Is the sea bad by the white rocks, Nora?

NORA: Middling bad, God help us. There's a great roaring in the west, and it's worse it'll be getting when the tide's turned to the wind. (*She goes over to the table with the bundle.*) Shall I open it now?

CATHLEEN: Maybe she'd wake up on us, and come in before we'd done. (*Coming to the table.*) It's a long time we'll be, and the two of us crying.

NORA (*goes to the inner door and listens*): She's moving about on the bed. She'll be coming in a minute.

CATHLEEN: Give me the ladder, and I'll put them up in the turf-loft, the way she won't know of them at all, and maybe when the tide turns she'll be going down to see would he be floating from the east.

(*They put the ladder against the gable of the chimney; Cathleen goes up a few steps and hides the bundle in the turf-loft. Maurya comes from the inner room.*)

MAURYA (*looking up at Cathleen and speaking querulously*): Isn't it turf enough you have for this day and evening?

CATHLEEN: There's a cake baking at the fire for a short space (*throwing down the turf*) and Bartley will want it when the tide turns if he goes to Connemara.

(*Nora picks up the turf and puts it round the pot-oven.*)

MAURYA (*sitting down on a stool at the fire*): He won't go this day with the wind rising from the south and west. He won't go this day, for the young priest will stop him surely.

NORA: He'll not stop him, mother, and I heard Eamon Simon and Stephen Pheety and Colum Shawn saying he would go.

MAURYA: Where is he itself?

NORA: He went down to see would there be another boat sailing in the week, and I'm thinking it won't be long till he's here now, for the tide's turning at the green head, and the hooker's tacking from the east.

CATHLEEN: I hear some one passing the big stones.

NORA (*looking out*): He's coming now, and he in a hurry.

BARTLEY (*comes in and looks round the room. Speak-

ing sadly and quietly): Where is the bit of new rope, Cathleen, was bought in Connemara?

CATHLEEN (*coming down*): Give it to him, Nora; it's on a nail by the white boards. I hung it up this morning, for the pig with the black feet was eating it.

NORA (*giving him a rope*): Is that it, Bartley?

MAURYA: You'd do right to leave that rope, Bartley, hanging by the boards. (*Bartley takes the rope.*) It will be wanting in this place, I'm telling you, if Michael is washed up tomorrow morning, or the next morning, or any morning in the week, for it's a deep grave we'll make him by the grace of God.

BARTLEY (*beginning to work with the rope*): I've no halter the way I can ride down on the mare, and I must go now quickly. This is the one boat going for two weeks or beyond it, and the fair will be a good fair for horses I heard them saying below.

MAURYA: It's a hard thing they'll be saying below if the body is washed up and there's no man in it to make the coffin, and I after giving a big price for the finest white boards you'd find in Connemara.

(*She looks round at the boards.*)

BARTLEY: How would it be washed up, and we after looking each day for nine days, and a strong wind blowing a while back from the west and south?

MAURYA: If it wasn't found itself, that wind is raising the sea, and there was a star up against the moon, and it rising in the night. If it was a hundred horses, or a thousand horses you had itself, what is the price of a thousand horses against a son where there is one son only?

BARTLEY (*working at the halter, to Cathleen*): Let you go down each day, and see the sheep aren't jumping in on the rye, and if the jobber comes you can sell the pig with the black feet if there is a good price going.

MAURYA: How would the like of her get a good price for a pig?

BARTLEY (*to Cathleen*): If the west wind holds with the last bit of the moon let you and Nora get up weed enough for another cock for the kelp. It's hard set we'll be from this day with no one in it but one man to work.

MAURYA: It's hard set we'll be surely the day you're drownd'd with the rest. What way will I live and the girls with me, and I an old woman looking for the grave?

(*Bartley lays down the halter, takes off his old coat, and puts on a newer one of the same flannel.*)

BARTLEY (*to Nora*): Is she coming to the pier?

NORA (*looking out*): She's passing the green head and letting fall her sails.

BARTLEY (*getting his purse and tobacco*): I'll have half an hour to go down, and you'll see me coming again in two days, or in three days, or maybe in four days if the wind is bad.

MAURYA (*turning round to the fire, and putting her shawl over her head*): Isn't it a hard and cruel man won't hear a word from an old woman, and she holding him from the sea?

CATHLEEN: It's the life of a young man to be going on the sea, and who would listen to an old woman with one thing and she saying it over?

BARTLEY (*taking the halter*): I must go now quickly. I'll ride down on the red mare, and the gray pony 'll run behind me. . . . The blessing of God on you.

(*He goes out.*)

MAURYA (*crying out as he is in the door*): He's gone now, God spare us, and we'll not see him again. He's gone now, and when the black night is falling I'll have no son left me in the world.

CATHLEEN: Why wouldn't you give him your blessing and he looking round in the door? Isn't it sorrow enough is on every one in this house without your sending him out with an unlucky word behind him, and a hard word in his ear?

(*Maurya takes up the tongs and begins raking the fire aimlessly without looking round.*)

NORA (*turning toward her*): You're taking away the turf from the cake.

CATHLEEN (*crying out*): The Son of God forgive us, Nora, we're after forgetting his bit of bread.

(*She comes over to the fire.*)

NORA: And it's destroyed he'll be going till dark night, and he after eating nothing since the sun went up.

CATHLEEN (*turning the cake out of the oven*): It's destroyed he'll be, surely. There's no sense left on any person in a house where an old woman will be talking forever.

(*Maurya sways herself on her stool.*)

CATHLEEN (*cutting off some of the bread and rolling it in a cloth; to Maurya*): Let you go down now to the spring well and give him this and he passing. You'll see him then and the dark word will be broken, and you can say "God speed you," the way he'll be easy in his mind.

MAURYA (*taking the bread*): Will I be in it as soon as himself?

CATHLEEN: If you go now quickly.

MAURYA (*standing up unsteadily*): It's hard set I am to walk.

CATHLEEN (*looking at her anxiously*): Give her the stick, Nora, or maybe she'll slip on the big stones.

NORA: What stick?

CATHLEEN: The stick Michael brought from Connemara.

MAURYA (*taking a stick Nora gives her*): In the big world the old people do be leaving things after them for their sons and children, but in this place it is the young men do be leaving things behind for them that do be old.

(*She goes out slowly. Nora goes over to the ladder.*)

CATHLEEN: Wait, Nora, maybe she'd turn back quickly. She's that sorry, God help her, you wouldn't know the thing she'd do.

NORA: Is she gone round by the bush?

CATHLEEN (*looking out*): She's gone now. Throw it down quickly, for the Lord knows when she'll be out of it again.

NORA (*getting the bundle from the loft*): The young priest said he'd be passing tomorrow, and we might go down and speak to him below if it's Michael's they are surely.

CATHLEEN (*taking the bundle*): Did he say what way they were found?

NORA (*coming down*): "There were two men," says he, "and they rowing round with poteen before the cocks crowed, and the oar of one of them caught the body, and they passing the black cliffs of the north."

CATHLEEN (*trying to open the bundle*): Give me a knife, Nora, the string's perished with the salt water, and there's a black knot on it you wouldn't loosen in a week.

NORA (*giving her a knife*): I've heard tell it was a long way to Donegal.

CATHLEEN (*cutting the string*): It is surely. There was a man in here a while ago — the man sold us that knife — and he said if you set off walking from the rocks beyond, it would be seven days you'd be in Donegal.

NORA: And what time would a man take, and he floating?

(*Cathleen opens the bundle and takes out a bit of a stocking. They look at them eagerly.*)

CATHLEEN (*in a low voice*): The Lord spare us, Nora! isn't it a queer hard thing to say if it's his they are surely?

NORA: I'll get his shirt off the hook the way we can put the one flannel on the other. (*She looks through some clothes hanging in the corner.*) It's not with them, Cathleen, and where will it be?

CATHLEEN: I'm thinking Bartley put it on him in the morning, for his own shirt was heavy with the salt in it (*pointing to the corner*). There's a bit of a sleeve was of the same stuff. Give me that and it will do.

(*Nora brings it to her and they compare the flannel.*)

CATHLEEN: It's the same stuff, Nora; but if it is itself aren't there great rolls of it in the shops of Galway, and isn't it many another man may have a shirt of it as well as Michael himself?

NORA (*who has taken up the stocking and counted the stitches, crying out*): It's Michael, Cathleen, it's Michael; God spare his soul, and what will herself say when she hears this story, and Bartley on the sea?

CATHLEEN (*taking the stocking*): It's a plain stocking.

NORA: It's the second one of the third pair I knitted, and I put up three score stitches, and I dropped four of them.

CATHLEEN (*counts the stitches*): It's that number is in it. (*Crying out.*) Ah, Nora, isn't it a bitter thing to think of him floating that way to the far north, and no one to keen him but the black hags that do be flying on the sea?

NORA (*swinging herself round, and throwing out her arms on the clothes*): And isn't it a pitiful thing when there is nothing left of a man who was a great rower and fisher, but a bit of an old shirt and a plain stocking?

CATHLEEN (*after an instant*): Tell me is herself coming, Nora? I hear a little sound on the path.

NORA (*looking out*): She is, Cathleen. She's coming up to the door.

CATHLEEN: Put these things away before she'll come in. Maybe it's easier she'll be after giving her blessing to Bartley, and we won't let on we've heard anything the time he's on the sea.

NORA (*helping Cathleen to close the bundle*): We'll put them here in the corner.

(*They put them into a hole in the chimney corner. Cathleen goes back to the spinning wheel.*)

NORA: Will she see it was crying I was?

CATHLEEN: Keep your back to the door the way the light'll not be on you.

(*Nora sits down at the chimney corner, with her back to the door. Maurya comes in very slowly, without looking at the girls, and goes over to her stool at the other side of the fire. The cloth with the bread is still in her hand. The girls look at each other, and Nora points to the bundle of bread.*)

CATHLEEN (*after spinning for a moment*): You didn't give him his bit of bread?

(*Maurya begins to keen softly, without turning round.*)

CATHLEEN: Did you see him riding down?

(*Maurya goes on keening.*)

CATHLEEN (*a little impatiently*): God forgive you; isn't it a better thing to raise your voice and tell what you seen, than to be making lamentation for a thing that's done? Did you see Bartley, I'm saying to you.

MAURYA (*with a weak voice*): My heart's broken from this day.

CATHLEEN (*as before*): Did you see Bartley?

MAURYA: I seen the fearfulest thing.

CATHLEEN (*leaves her wheel and looks out*): God forgive you; he's riding the mare now over the green head, and the gray pony behind him.

MAURYA (*starts, so that her shawl falls back from her head and shows her white tossed hair. With a frightened voice*): The gray pony behind him.

CATHLEEN (*coming to the fire*): What is it ails you, at all?

MAURYA (*speaking very slowly*): I've seen the fearfulest thing any person has seen, since the day Bride Dara seen the dead man with the child in his arms.

CATHLEEN AND NORA: Uah.

(*They crouch down in front of the old woman at the fire.*)

NORA: Tell us what it is you seen.

MAURYA: I went down to the spring well, and I stood there saying a prayer to myself. Then Bartley came along, and he riding on the red mare with the gray pony behind him. (*She puts up her hands, as if to hide something from her eyes.*) The Son of God spare us, Nora!

CATHLEEN: What is it you seen.

MAURYA: I seen Michael himself.

CATHLEEN (*speaking softly*): You did not, mother. It wasn't Michael you seen, for his body is after being found in the far north, and he's got a clean burial by the grace of God.

MAURYA (*a little defiantly*): I'm after seeing him this day, and he riding and galloping. Bartley came first on the red mare; and I tried to say "God speed you," but something choked the words in my throat. He went by quickly; and "the blessing of God on you," says he, and I could say nothing. I looked up then, and I crying, at the gray pony, and there was Michael upon it — with fine clothes on him, and new shoes on his feet.

CATHLEEN (*begins to keen*): It's destroyed we are from this day. It's destroyed, surely.

NORA: Didn't the young priest say the Almighty God wouldn't leave her destitute with no son living?

MAURYA (*in a low voice, but clearly*): It's little the like of him knows of the sea. . . . Bartley will be lost now, and let you call in Eamon and make me a good coffin out of the white boards, for I won't live after them. I've had a husband, and a husband's father, and six sons in this house — six fine men, though it was a hard birth I had with every one

of them and they coming to the world — and some of them were found and some of them were not found, but they're gone now the lot of them. . . . There were Stephen, and Shawn, were lost in the great wind, and found after in the Bay of Gregory of the Golden Mouth, and carried up the two of them on the one plank, and in by that door.

(*She pauses for a moment, the girls start as if they heard something through the door that is half open behind them.*)

NORA (*in a whisper*): Did you hear that, Cathleen? Did you hear a noise in the northeast?

CATHLEEN (*in a whisper*): There's some one after crying out by the seashore.

MAURYA (*continues without hearing anything*): There was Sheamus and his father, and his own father again, were lost in a dark night, and not a stick or sign was seen of them when the sun went up. There was Patch after was drowned out of a curagh° that turned over. I was sitting here with Bartley, and he a baby, lying on my two knees, and I seen two women, and three women, and four women coming in, and they crossing themselves, and not saying a word. I looked out then, and there were men coming after them, and they holding a thing in the half of a red sail, and water dripping out of it — it was a dry day, Nora — and leaving a track to the door.

(*She pauses again with her hand stretched out toward the door. It opens softly and old women begin to come in, crossing themselves on the threshold, and kneeling down in front of the stage with red petticoats over their heads.*)

MAURYA (*half in a dream, to Cathleen*): Is it Patch, or Michael, or what is it at all?

CATHLEEN: Michael is after being found in the far north, and when he is found there how could he be here in this place?

MAURYA: There does be a power of young men floating round in the sea, and what way would they know if it was Michael they had, or another man like him, for when a man is nine days in the sea, and the wind blowing, it's hard set his own mother would be to say what man was it.

CATHLEEN: It's Michael, God spare him, for they're after sending us a bit of his clothes from the far north.

(*She reaches out and hands Maurya the clothes that belonged to Michael. Maurya stands up slowly and takes them in her hands. Nora looks out.*)

---

curagh: A small boat with a hide- or tarpaulin-covered frame.

NORA: They're carrying a thing among them and there's water dripping out of it and leaving a track by the big stones.

CATHLEEN (*in a whisper to the women who have come in*): Is it Bartley it is?

ONE OF THE WOMEN: It is surely, God rest his soul.

(*Two younger women come in and pull out the table. Then men carry in the body of Bartley, laid on a plank, with a bit of a sail over it, and lay it on the table.*)

CATHLEEN (*to the women, as they are doing so*): What way was he drowned?

ONE OF THE WOMEN: The gray pony knocked him into the sea, and he was washed out where there is a great surf on the white rocks.

(*Maurya has gone over and knelt down at the head of the table. The women are keening softly and swaying themselves with a slow movement. Cathleen and Nora kneel at the other end of the table. The men kneel near the door.*)

MAURYA (*raising her head and speaking as if she did not see the people around her*): They're all gone now, and there isn't anything more the sea can do to me. ... I'll have no call now to be up crying and praying when the wind breaks from the south, and you can hear the surf is in the east, and the surf is in the west, making a great stir with the two noises, and they hitting one on the other. I'll have no call now to be going down and getting Holy Water in the dark nights after Samhain,° and I won't care what way the sea is when the other women will be keening. (*To Nora.*) Give me the Holy Water, Nora, there's a small sup still on the dresser.

(*Nora gives it to her.*)

MAURYA (*drops Michael's clothes across Bartley's feet, and sprinkles the Holy Water over him*): It isn't that I haven't prayed for you, Bartley, to the Almighty God. It isn't that I haven't said prayers in the dark night till you wouldn't know what I'ld be saying; but it's a great rest I'll have now, and it's time surely. It's a great rest I'll have now, and great sleeping in the long nights after Samhain, if

Samhain: Feast of All Saints, November 1.

it's only a bit of wet flour we do have to eat, and maybe a fish that would be stinking.

(*She kneels down again, crossing herself, and saying prayers under her breath.*)

CATHLEEN (*to an old man*): Maybe yourself and Eamon would make a coffin when the sun rises. We have fine white boards herself bought, God help her, thinking Michael would be found, and I have a new cake you can eat while you'll be working.

THE OLD MAN (*looking at the boards*): Are there nails with them?

CATHLEEN: There are not, Colum; we didn't think of the nails.

ANOTHER MAN: It's a great wonder she wouldn't think of the nails, and all the coffins she's seen made already.

CATHLEEN: It's getting old she is, and broken.

(*Maurya stands up again very slowly and spreads out the pieces of Michael's clothes beside the body, sprinkling them with the last of the Holy Water.*)

NORA (*in a whisper to Cathleen*): She's quiet now and easy; but the day Michael was drowned you could hear her crying out from this to the spring well. It's fonder she was of Michael, and would any one have thought that?

CATHLEEN (*slowly and clearly*): An old woman will be soon tired with anything she will do, and isn't it nine days herself is after crying and keening, and making great sorrow in the house?

MAURYA (*puts the empty cup mouth downward on the table, and lays her hands together on Bartley's feet*): They're all together this time, and the end is come. May the Almighty God have mercy on Bartley's soul, and on Michael's soul, and on the souls of Sheamus and Patch, and Stephen and Shawn (*bending her head*); and may He have mercy on my soul, Nora, and on the soul of every one is left living in the world.

(*She pauses, and the keen rises a little more loudly from the women, then sinks away.*)

MAURYA (*continuing*): Michael has a clean burial in the far north, by the grace of the Almighty God. Bartley will have a fine coffin out of the white boards, and a deep grave surely. What more can we want than that? No man at all can be living forever, and we must be satisfied.

(*She kneels down again and the curtain falls slowly.*)

Luigi Pirandello

Luigi Pirandello (1867–1936) was a short-story writer and novelist, a secondary school teacher, and finally a playwright. His life was complicated by business failures that wiped out his personal income and threw his wife into a psychological depression that Pirandello quite bluntly described as madness. Out of his acquaintance with madness — he remained with his wife for fourteen years after she lost touch with reality — Pirandello claimed to have developed much of his attitude toward the shifting surfaces of appearances.

Pirandello's short stories and novels show the consistent pattern of his plays: a deep examination of what we know to be real and a questioning of our confidence in our beliefs. His novel *Shoot* (1915) questions the surfaces of cinema reality, to which contemporary Italy had yielded with great enthusiasm. His relentless examination of the paradoxes of experience has given him a reputation for pessimism. He himself said, "I think of life as a very sad piece of buffoonery," and he insisted that people bear within them a deep need to deceive themselves "by creating a reality . . . which . . . is discovered to be vain and illusory."

Pirandello was not a popular writer in Italy, and much of his dramatic work was first performed abroad. But he did win the Nobel Prize for literature in 1934, an indication that his particular brand of modernism was indeed influential. At that time Pirandello was a member of the Fascist party in Italy, although his participation was limited primarily to his work in the state-supported Art Theater of Rome, which he founded.

Pirandello's influence in modern theater resulted from his experimentation with the concept of realism that dominated drama from the time of Strindberg and Ibsen. The concept of the imaginary "fourth wall" of the stage through which the audience observed the action of characters in their living rooms had become the norm in theater. Pirandello, however, questioned all thought of norms by bringing the very idea of reality under philosophical scrutiny. His relentless questioning helped playwrights around the world open themselves up to new approaches to theater in the early part of the twentieth century. Pirandello was one of the first, and one of the best, experimentalists.

SIX CHARACTERS IN SEARCH OF AN AUTHOR

Pirandello's play is part of a trilogy: *Six Characters in Search of an Author* (1921); *Each in His Own Way* (1924); and *Tonight We Improvise* (1930). These plays all examine the impossibility of knowing reality. There is no objective truth to know, Pirandello tells us, and what we think of as reality is totally subjective, something that each of us maintains independently of other people and that none of us can communicate. We are, in other words, apart, sealed into our own limited world.

These ideas were hardly novel. Playwrights had dealt with them before, even during the Elizabethan age, at a time when — because of the Protestant Reformation — the absolute systems of reality promoted by the Roman Catholic church had crumbled. Pirandello's plays were also produced in a time — the 1920s — when his culture was uncertain, frightened, and still reeling in shock from the destruction of World War I. It was a depressed time, and in Pirandello's work his audience saw a reflection of their own dispirited, fearful selves.

In a sense, *Six Characters in Search of an Author* is about the relationship of art and life, and especially about the relationship of drama and life. The premise of the play is absurd. In the middle of a rehearsal of a Pirandello play, several characters appear and request that an author be present to cobble them into a play. The stage manager assumes they mean that they are actors come to be in a play, but they explain that they are not actors. They are real characters. This implies a paradox, that characters are independent of the actors who play them. However, we are used to the characters being only on paper. When they demand actors to represent them we know that one limit of impossibility has been reached.

The characters who appear are, in a sense, types: a father, a mother, a stepdaughter, a son, two silent figures — the boy and the child — and, finally, a milliner, Madame Pace. Besides these characters are the actors of the company who are rehearsing the Pirandello play *Mixing It Up*. The six characters have been abandoned by their creator, the author who has absconded, leaving them in search of a substitute. The stepdaughter, late in the play, surmises that their author abandoned them "in a fit of depression, of disgust for the ordinary theater as the public knows it and likes it."

Pirandello uses his characters and their situation to comment on the life of the theater in the 1920s, and he also uses them to begin a series of speculations on the relationship of a public to the actors they see in plays, the characters the actors play, and the authors who create them. To an extent, the relationship between an author and his or her characters will always imply a metaphor for the relationship between a creator and all creation, and it is tempting to think of Samuel Beckett years later in his *Waiting for Godot* imagining an "author" having abandoned his creations because they failed to satisfy him. The six characters — or creations — who invade the stage in Pirandello's play have a firm sense of themselves and their actions. They bring with them a story — as all characters in plays do — and they invite the manager to participate in their stories, just as characters invite audiences to become one with their narratives.

One of the more amusing scenes depicts the characters' reactions to seeing actors play their parts. Since they are "real" characters, they have the utmost authority in knowing how their parts should be played, and they end up laughing at the inept efforts of the actors in act II. When the manager disputes with them, wondering why they protest so vigorously, they explain that they want to make sure the truth is told. The truth. The concept seems so simple on the surface, but in the situation that Pirandello has conceived, it is loaded with complexities that the stage manager cannot fathom.

By the time the question of the truth has been raised, the manager has begun to get a sense of the poignancy of the story that these characters have to tell. He has also begun to see that he must let them continue to tell their story — except that they are not telling it; they are living it. When the climax of their story is reached in the last moments of the play, the line between what is acted and what is lived onstage has become almost completely blurred. When the play ends, there is no telling what has truly occurred and what has truly been acted out.

Six Characters in Search of an Author has endured because it still rings true in its examination of the relationship of art to life, illusion to reality. The very word *illusion* is rejected by the characters — since as characters they are part of the illusion of reality. They reject the thought that they are literature, asserting, "This is Life, this is passion!"

Six Characters in Search of an Author in Performance

The 1916 Italian production of *Six Characters in Search of an Author* established Pirandello as a dramatist of major importance. The first London production was in the Kingsway Theatre in March 1922. The reviews were positive, and the audiences, although at times puzzled, were responsive to what the *Christian Science Monitor* called "one of the freshest and most original productions seen for a long time." The first production in New York was directed by Brock Pemberton at the Princess Theater in October 1922 with the distinguished American actress Florence Eldridge as the stepdaughter. One newspaper critic said, "Pirandello turns a powerful microscope on the dramatist's mental workshop — the modus operandi of play production — and after having destroyed our illusion, like a prestidigitator who shows us how a trick is done, expects us to believe in him."

Pirandello directed the play in Italian in London in 1925, and despite the audience's general inability to understand the language, the New Oxford Theatre was filled for every night of its run. He brought the company to the United States after the British censor determined that the play was "unsuitable for English audiences" and closed the play in London. It was not officially licensed for performance in England until 1928.

Revivals of the play have been numerous. Three productions in New York in the 1930s preceded revivals in 1948 and 1955. London saw productions in February 1932 and November 1950. By the 1930s, audience confusion had simmered down, and in 1932 one London critic declared, "Repetition cannot dull the brilliance of the play's attack on theatrical shams." Sir Ralph Richardson performed in London's West End in 1963. In 1955, Tyrone Guthrie's Phoenix Theater used a translation and adaptation by Guthrie and Michael Wager. The production was not successful, although critics liked the translation. Robert Brustein received extraordinary praise for his American Repertory Theatre (ART) production in 1985. Instead of having the six characters interrupt a Pirandello play, they interrupt the rehearsal of a Molière play, *Sganarelle*, which has roots in Italian *commedia dell'arte*. *Sganarelle* had been a highly successful ART production. This self-reference — in Pirandellian fashion — helped to blur the line between the realities on and off the stage. Boston critic Kevin Kelly said of the performance, "Brustein immediately links the paradox in Pirandello's theme about reality in illusion/illusion in reality to . . . the pragmatic fantasy of theater itself."

Luigi Pirandello (1867–1936)

SIX CHARACTERS IN SEARCH OF AN AUTHOR   *1921*
A COMEDY IN THE MAKING

TRANSLATED BY EDWARD STORER

Characters of the Comedy in the Making

THE FATHER	THE BOY } *do not speak*
THE MOTHER	THE CHILD }
THE STEPDAUGHTER	MADAME PACE
THE SON	

Actors of the Company

THE MANAGER	L'INGÉNUE
LEADING LADY	JUVENILE LEAD
LEADING MAN	OTHER ACTORS
SECOND LADY LEAD	AND ACTRESSES

PROPERTY MAN   MANAGER'S SECRETARY
PROMPTER   DOOR-KEEPER
MACHINIST   SCENE-SHIFTERS

Scene: *Daytime. The stage of a theater.*

(N.B.: *The Comedy is without acts or scenes. The performance is interrupted once, without the curtain being lowered, when the Manager and the chief characters withdraw to arrange a scenario. A second interruption of the action takes place when, by mistake, the stage hands let the curtain down.*)

ACT I

(The spectators will find the curtain raised and the stage as it usually is during the daytime. It will be half dark, and empty, so that from the beginning the public may have the impression of an impromptu performance.)

(Prompter's box and a small table and chair for the Manager.)

(Two other small tables and several chairs scattered about as during rehearsals.)

(The Actors and Actresses of the company enter from the back of the stage: first one, then another, then two together; nine or ten in all. They are about to rehearse a Pirandello play: Mixing It Up. Some of the company move off toward their dressing rooms. The Prompter, who has the "book" under his arm, is waiting for the Manager in order to begin the rehearsal.)

(The Actors and Actresses, some standing, some sitting, chat and smoke. One perhaps reads a paper; another cons his part.)

(Finally, the Manager enters and goes to the table prepared for him. His Secretary brings him his mail, through which he glances. The Prompter takes his seat, turns on a light, and opens the "book.")

THE MANAGER *(throwing a letter down on the table)*: I can't see. *(To Property Man.)* Let's have a little light, please!

PROPERTY MAN: Yes, sir, yes, at once. *(A light comes down on to the stage.)*

THE MANAGER *(clapping his hands)*: Come along! Come along! Second act of "Mixing It Up." *(Sits down.)*

(The Actors and Actresses go from the front of the stage to the wings, all except the three who are to begin the rehearsal.)

THE PROMPTER *(reading the "book")*: "Leo Gala's house. A curious room serving as dining-room and study."

THE MANAGER *(to Property Man)*: Fix up the old red room.

PROPERTY MAN *(noting it down)*: Red set. All right!

THE PROMPTER *(continuing to read from the "book")*: "Table already laid and writing desk with books and papers. Bookshelves. Exit rear to Leo's bedroom. Exit left to kitchen. Principal exit to right."

THE MANAGER *(energetically)*: Well, you understand: The principal exit over there; here, the kitchen. *(Turning to actor who is to play the part of Socrates.)* You make your entrances and exits here. *(To Property Man.)* The baize doors at the rear, and curtains.

PROPERTY MAN *(noting it down)*: Right!

PROMPTER *(reading as before)*: "When the curtain rises, Leo Gala, dressed in cook's cap and apron, is busy beating an egg in a cup. Philip, also dressed as a cook, is beating another egg. Guidi Venanzi is seated and listening."

LEADING MAN *(to Manager)*: Excuse me, but must I absolutely wear a cook's cap?

THE MANAGER *(annoyed)*: I imagine so. It says so there anyway. *(Pointing to the "book.")*

LEADING MAN: But it's ridiculous!

THE MANAGER *(jumping up in a rage)*: Ridiculous? Ridiculous? Is it my fault if France won't send us any more good comedies, and we are reduced to putting on Pirandello's works, where nobody understands anything, and where the author plays the fool with us all? *(The Actors grin. The Manager goes to Leading Man and shouts.)* Yes sir, you put on the cook's cap and beat eggs. Do you suppose that with all this egg-beating business you are on an ordinary stage? Get that out of your head. You represent the shell of the eggs you are beating! *(Laughter and comments among the Actors.)* Silence! and listen to my explanations, please! *(To Leading Man.)* "The empty form of reason without the fullness of instinct, which is blind." — You stand for reason, your wife is instinct. It's a mixing up of the parts, according to which you who act your own part become the puppet of yourself. Do you understand?

LEADING MAN: I'm hanged if I do.

THE MANAGER: Neither do I. But let's get on with it. It's sure to be a glorious failure anyway. *(Confidentially.)* But I say, please face three-quarters. Otherwise, what with the abstruseness of the dialogue, and the public that won't be able to hear you, the whole thing will go to hell. Come on! come on!

PROMPTER: Pardon sir, may I get into my box? There's a bit of a draft.

THE MANAGER: Yes, yes, of course!

(At this point, the Door-Keeper has entered from the stage door and advances toward the Manager's table, taking off his braided cap. During this maneuver, the Six Characters enter, and stop by the door at back of stage, so that when the Door-Keeper is about to announce their coming to the Manager, they are already on the stage. A tenuous light surrounds them, almost as if irradiated by them — the faint breath of their fantastic reality.)

(This light will disappear when they come forward toward the actors. They preserve, however, something of the dream lightness in which they seem almost

suspended; but this does not detract from the essential reality of their forms and expressions.)

(He who is known as the Father is a man of about 50: hair, reddish in color, thin at the temples; he is not bald, however; thick mustaches, falling over his still fresh mouth, which often opens in an empty and uncertain smile. He is fattish, pale; with an especially wide forehead. He has blue, oval-shaped eyes, very clear and piercing. Wears light trousers and a dark jacket. He is alternatively mellifluous and violent in his manner.)

(The Mother seems crushed and terrified as if by an intolerable weight of shame and abasement. She is dressed in modest black and wears a thick widow's veil of crepe. When she lifts this, she reveals a waxlike face. She always keeps her eyes downcast.)

(The Stepdaughter is dashing, almost impudent, beautiful. She wears mourning too, but with great elegance. She shows contempt for the timid half-frightened manner of the wretched Boy (14 years old, and also dressed in black); on the other hand, she displays a lively tenderness for her little sister, the Child (about four), who is dressed in white, with a black silk sash at the waist.)

(The Son (22) is tall, severe in his attitude of contempt for the Father, supercilious and indifferent to the Mother. He looks as if he had come on the stage against his will.)

DOOR-KEEPER (*cap in hand*): Excuse me, sir . . .

THE MANAGER (*rudely*): Eh? What is it?

DOOR-KEEPER (*timidly*): These people are asking for you, sir.

THE MANAGER (*furious*): I am rehearsing, and you know perfectly well no one's allowed to come in during rehearsals! (*Turning to the Characters.*) Who are you, please? What do you want?

THE FATHER (*coming forward a little, followed by the others who seem embarrassed*): As a matter of fact . . . we have come here in search of an author . . .

THE MANAGER (*half angry, half amazed*): An author? What author?

THE FATHER: Any author, sir.

THE MANAGER: But there's no author here. We are not rehearsing a new piece.

THE STEPDAUGHTER (*vivaciously*): So much the better, so much the better! We can be your new piece.

AN ACTOR (*coming forward from the others*): Oh, do you hear that?

THE FATHER (*to Stepdaughter*): Yes, but if the author isn't here . . . (*To Manager.*) unless you would be willing . . .

THE MANAGER: You are trying to be funny.

THE FATHER: No, for Heaven's sake, what are you saying? We bring you a drama, sir.

THE STEPDAUGHTER: We may be your fortune.

THE MANAGER: Will you oblige me by going away? We haven't time to waste with mad people.

THE FATHER (*mellifluously*): Oh sir, you know well that life is full of infinite absurdities, which, strangely enough, do not even need to appear plausible, since they are true.

THE MANAGER: What the devil is he talking about?

THE FATHER: I say that to reverse the ordinary process may well be considered a madness: that is, to create credible situations, in order that they may appear true. But permit me to observe that if this be madness, it is the sole *raison d'être*° of your profession, gentlemen. (*The Actors look hurt and perplexed.*)

THE MANAGER (*getting up and looking at him*): So our profession seems to you one worthy of madmen then?

THE FATHER: Well, to make seem true that which isn't true . . . without any need . . . for a joke as it were . . . Isn't that your mission, gentlemen: to give life to fantastic characters on the stage?

THE MANAGER (*interpreting the rising anger of the Company*): But I would beg you to believe, my dear sir, that the profession of the comedian is a noble one. If today, as things go, the playwrights give us stupid comedies to play and puppets to represent instead of men, remember we are proud to have given life to immortal works here on these very boards! (*The Actors, satisfied, applaud their Manager.*)

THE FATHER (*interrupting furiously*): Exactly, perfectly, to living beings more alive than those who breathe and wear clothes: beings less real perhaps, but truer! I agree with you entirely. (*The Actors look at one another in amazement.*)

THE MANAGER: But what do you mean? Before, you said . . .

THE FATHER: No, excuse me, I meant it for you, sir, who were crying out that you had no time to lose with madmen, while no one better than yourself knows that nature uses the instrument of human fantasy in order to pursue her high creative purpose.

THE MANAGER: Very well, — but where does all this take us?

THE FATHER: Nowhere! It is merely to show you that one is born to life in many forms, in many shapes, as tree, or as stone, as water, as butterfly, or as woman. So one may also be born a character in a play.

THE MANAGER (*with feigned comic dismay*): So you and these other friends of yours have been born characters?

---

raison d'être: French for "reason to exist."

THE FATHER: Exactly, and alive as you see! (*Manager and Actors burst out laughing.*)

THE FATHER (*hurt*): I am sorry you laugh, because we carry in us a drama, as you can guess from this woman here veiled in black.

THE MANAGER (*losing patience at last and almost indignant*): Oh, chuck it! Get away please! Clear out of here! (*To Property Man.*) For Heaven's sake, turn them out!

THE FATHER (*resisting*): No, no, look here, we . . .

THE MANAGER (*roaring*): We come here to work, you know.

LEADING ACTOR: One cannot let oneself be made such a fool of.

THE FATHER (*determined, coming forward*): I marvel at your incredulity, gentlemen. Are you not accustomed to see the characters created by an author spring to life in yourselves and face each other? Just because there is no "book" (*pointing to the Prompter's box*) which contains us, you refuse to believe . . .

THE STEPDAUGHTER (*advances toward Manager, smiling and coquettish*): Believe me, we are really six most interesting characters, sir; sidetracked however.

THE FATHER: Yes, that is the word! (*To Manager all at once.*) In the sense, that is, that the author who created us alive no longer wished, or was no longer able, materially to put us into a work of art. And this was a real crime, sir; because he who has had the luck to be born a character can laugh even at death. He cannot die. The man, the writer, the instrument of the creation will die, but his creation does not die. And to live for ever, it does not need to have extraordinary gifts or to be able to work wonders. Who was Sancho Panza? Who was Don Abbondio?° Yet they live eternally because — live germs as they were — they had the fortune to find a fecundating matrix, a fantasy which could raise and nourish them: make them live for ever!

THE MANAGER: That is quite all right. But what do you want here, all of you?

THE FATHER: We want to live.

THE MANAGER (*ironically*): For Eternity?

THE FATHER: No, sir, only for a moment . . . in you.

AN ACTOR: Just listen to him!

LEADING LADY: They want to live, in us . . . !

JUVENILE LEAD (*pointing to the Stepdaughter*): I've no objection, as far as that one is concerned!

THE FATHER: Look here! look here! The comedy has to be made. (*To the Manager.*) But if you and your

actors are willing, we can soon concert it among ourselves.

THE MANAGER (*annoyed*): But what do you want to concert? We don't go in for concerts here. Here we play dramas and comedies!

THE FATHER: Exactly! That is just why we have come to you.

THE MANAGER: And where is the "book"?

THE FATHER: It is in us! (*The Actors laugh.*) The drama is in us, and we are the drama. We are impatient to play it. Our inner passion drives us on to this.

THE STEPDAUGHTER (*disdainful, alluring, treacherous, full of impudence*): My passion, sir! Ah, if you only knew! My passion for him! (*Points to the Father and makes a pretense of embracing him. Then she breaks out into a loud laugh.*)

THE FATHER (*angrily*): Behave yourself! And please don't laugh in that fashion.

THE STEPDAUGHTER: With your permission, gentlemen, I, who am a two months orphan, will show you how I can dance and sing. (*Sings and then dances Prenez garde à Tchou-Tchin-Tchou.*)

Les chinois sont un peuple malin,
De Shangaî à Pékin,
Ils ont mis des écriteaux partout:
Prenez garde à Tchou-Tchin-Tchou.°

ACTORS AND ACTRESSES: Bravo! Well done! Tip-top!

THE MANAGER: Silence! This isn't a café concert, you know! (*Turning to the Father in consternation.*) Is she mad?

THE FATHER: Mad? No, she's worse than mad.

THE STEPDAUGHTER (*to Manager*): Worse? Worse? Listen! Stage this drama for us at once! Then you will see that at a certain moment I . . . when this little darling here. . . . (*Takes the Child by the hand and leads her to the Manager.*) Isn't she a dear? (*Takes her up and kisses her.*) Darling! Darling! (*Puts her down again and adds feelingly.*) Well, when God suddenly takes this dear little child away from that poor mother there; and this imbecile here (*seizing hold of the Boy roughly and pushing him forward*) does the stupidest things, like the fool he is, you will see me run away. Yes, gentlemen, I shall be off. But the moment hasn't arrived yet. After what has taken place between him and me (*indicates the Father with a horrible wink*) I can't remain any longer in this society, to have to witness

---

Sancho Panza . . . Don Abbondio: Memorable characters in novels: the squire in Cervantes's *Don Quixote* and the priest in Manzoni's *I Promessi Sposi* (*The Betrothed*), respectively.

Prenez . . . Tchou: This French popular song is an adaptation of "Chu-Chin-Chow," an old Broadway show tune. "The Chinese are a sly people; / From Shanghai to Peking, / They've stuck up warning signs: / Beware of Tchou-Tchin-Tchou." (The words are funnier in French because *chou* means "cabbage.")

the anguish of this mother here for that fool. . . . (*Indicates the Son.*) Look at him! Look at him! See how indifferent, how frigid he is, because he is the legitimate son. He despises me, despises him (*pointing to the Boy*), despises this baby here; because . . . we are bastards. (*Goes to the Mother and embraces her.*) And he doesn't want to recognize her as his mother — she who is the common mother of us all. He looks down upon her as if she were only the mother of us three bastards. Wretch! (*She says all this very rapidly, excitedly. At the word "bastards" she raises her voice, and almost spits out the final "Wretch!"*)

THE MOTHER (*to the Manager, in anguish*): In the name of these two little children, I beg you. . . . (*She grows faint and is about to fall.*) Oh God!

THE FATHER (*coming forward to support her as do some of the Actors*): Quick, a chair, a chair for this poor widow!

THE ACTORS: Is it true? Has she really fainted?

THE MANAGER: Quick, a chair! Here!

(*One of the Actors brings a chair, the others proffer assistance. The Mother tries to prevent the Father from lifting the veil which covers her face.*)

THE FATHER: Look at her! Look at her!

THE MOTHER: No, no; stop it please!

THE FATHER (*raising her veil*): Let them see you!

THE MOTHER (*rising and covering her face with her hands, in desperation*): I beg you, sir, to prevent this man from carrying out his plan which is loathsome to me.

THE MANAGER (*dumbfounded*): I don't understand at all. What is the situation? (*To the Father.*) Is this lady your wife?

THE FATHER: Yes, gentlemen: my wife!

THE MANAGER: But how can she be a widow if you are alive? (*The Actors find relief for their astonishment in a loud laugh.*)

THE FATHER: Don't laugh! Don't laugh like that, for Heaven's sake. Her drama lies just here in this: she has had a lover, a man who ought to be here.

THE MOTHER (*with a cry*): No! No!

THE STEPDAUGHTER: Fortunately for her, he is dead. Two months ago as I said. We are in mourning, as you see.

THE FATHER: He isn't here, you see, not because he is dead. He isn't here — look at her a moment and you will understand — because her drama isn't a drama of the love of two men for whom she was incapable of feeling anything except possibly a little gratitude — gratitude not for me but for the other. She isn't a woman, she is a mother, and her drama — powerful, sir, I assure you — lies, as a matter of fact, all in these four children she has had by two men.

THE MOTHER: I had them? Have you got the courage to say that I wanted them? (*To the Company.*) It was his doing. It was he who gave me that other man, who forced me to go away with him.

THE STEPDAUGHTER: It isn't true.

THE MOTHER (*startled*): Not true, isn't it?

THE STEPDAUGHTER: No, it isn't true, it just isn't true.

THE MOTHER: And what can you know about it?

THE STEPDAUGHTER: It isn't true. Don't believe it. (*To Manager.*) Do you know why she says so? For that fellow there. (*Indicates the Son.*) She tortures herself, destroys herself on account of the neglect of that son there; and she wants him to believe that if she abandoned him when he was only two years old, it was because he (*indicates the Father*) made her do so.

THE MOTHER (*vigorously*): He forced me to it, and I call God to witness it. (*To the Manager.*) Ask him (*indicates Husband*) if it isn't true. Let him speak. You (*to Daughter*) are not in a position to know anything about it.

THE STEPDAUGHTER: I know you lived in peace and happiness with my father while he lived. Can you deny it?

THE MOTHER: No, I don't deny it. . . .

THE STEPDAUGHTER: He was always full of affection and kindness for you. (*To the Boy, angrily.*) It's true, isn't it? Tell them! Why don't you speak, you little fool?

THE MOTHER: Leave the poor boy alone. Why do you want to make me appear ungrateful, daughter? I don't want to offend your father. I have answered him that I didn't abandon my house and my son through any fault of mine, nor from any wilful passion.

THE FATHER: It is true. It was my doing.

LEADING MAN (*to the Company*): What a spectacle!

LEADING LADY: We are the audience this time.

JUVENILE LEAD: For once, in a way.

THE MANAGER (*beginning to get really interested*): Let's hear them out. Listen!

THE SON: Oh yes, you're going to hear a fine bit now. He will talk to you of the Demon of Experiment.

THE FATHER: You are a cynical imbecile. I've told you so already a hundred times. (*To the Manager.*) He tries to make fun of me on account of this expression which I have found to excuse myself with.

THE SON (*with disgust*): Yes, phrases! phrases!

THE FATHER: Phrases! Isn't everyone consoled when faced with a trouble or fact he doesn't understand, by a word, some simple word, which tells us nothing and yet calms us?

THE STEPDAUGHTER: Even in the case of remorse. In fact, especially then.

THE FATHER: Remorse? No, that isn't true. I've done more than use words to quiet the remorse in me.

THE STEPDAUGHTER: Yes, there was a bit of money too. Yes, yes, a bit of money. There were the hundred lire he was about to offer me in payment, gentlemen. . . . (*Sensation of horror among the Actors.*)

THE SON (*to the Stepdaughter*): This is vile.

THE STEPDAUGHTER: Vile? There they were in a pale blue envelope on a little mahogany table in the back of Madame Pace's shop. You know Madame Pace — one of those ladies who attract poor girls of good family into their ateliers, under the pretext of their selling *robes et manteaux*.°

THE SON: And he thinks he has bought the right to tyrannize over us all with those hundred lire he was going to pay; but which, fortunately — note this, gentlemen — he had no chance of paying.

THE STEPDAUGHTER: It was a near thing, though, you know! (*Laughs ironically.*)

THE MOTHER (*protesting*): Shame, my daughter, shame!

THE STEPDAUGHTER: Shame indeed! This is my revenge! I am dying to live that scene . . . The room . . . I see it . . . Here is the window with the mantles exposed, there the divan, the looking-glass, a screen, there in front of the window the little mahogany table with the blue envelope containing one hundred lire. I see it. I see it. I could take hold of it. . . . But you, gentlemen, you ought to turn your backs now: I am almost nude, you know. But I don't blush: I leave that to him. (*Indicating Father.*)

THE MANAGER: I don't understand this at all.

THE FATHER: Naturally enough. I would ask you, sir, to exercise your authority a little here, and let me speak before you believe all she is trying to blame me with. Let me explain.

THE STEPDAUGHTER: Ah yes, explain it in your own way.

THE FATHER: But don't you see that the whole trouble lies here? In words, words. Each one of us has within him a whole world of things, each man of us his own special world. And how can we ever come to an understanding if I put in the words I utter the sense and value of things as I see them; while you who listen to me must inevitably translate them according to the conception of things each one of you has within himself. We think we understand each other, but we never really do. Look here! This woman (*indicating the Mother*)

takes all my pity for her as a specially ferocious form of cruelty.

THE MOTHER: But you drove me away.

THE FATHER: Do you hear her? I drove her away! She believes I really sent her away.

THE MOTHER: You know how to talk, and I don't; but, believe me, sir (*to Manager*), after he had married me . . . who knows why? . . . I was a poor insignificant woman. . . .

THE FATHER: But, good Heavens! it was just for your humility that I married you. I loved this simplicity in you. (*He stops when he sees she makes signs to contradict him, opens his arms wide in sign of desperation, seeing how hopeless it is to make himself understood.*) You see she denies it. Her mental deafness, believe me, is phenomenal, the limit: (*touches his forehead*) deaf, deaf, mentally deaf! She has plenty of feeling. Oh yes, a good heart for the children; but the brain — deaf, to the point of desperation —!

THE STEPDAUGHTER: Yes, but ask him how his intelligence has helped us.

THE FATHER: If we could see all the evil that may spring from good, what should we do? (*At this point the Leading Lady, who is biting her lips with rage at seeing the Leading Man flirting with the Stepdaughter, comes forward and speaks to the Manager.*)

LEADING LADY: Excuse me, but are we going to rehearse today?

MANAGER: Of course, of course; but let's hear them out.

JUVENILE LEAD: This is something quite new.

L'INGÉNUE: Most interesting!

LEADING LADY: Yes, for the people who like that kind of thing. (*Casts a glance at Leading Man.*)

THE MANAGER (*to Father*): You must please explain yourself quite clearly. (*Sits down.*)

THE FATHER: Very well then: listen! I had in my service a poor man, a clerk, a secretary of mine, full of devotion, who became friends with her. (*Indicating the Mother.*) They understood one another, were kindred souls in fact, without, however, the least suspicion of any evil existing. They were incapable even of thinking of it.

THE STEPDAUGHTER: So he thought of it — for them!

THE FATHER: That's not true. I meant to do good to them — and to myself, I confess, at the same time. Things had come to the point that I could not say a word to either of them without their making a mute appeal, one to the other, with their eyes. I could see them silently asking each other how I was to be kept in countenance, how I was to be kept quiet. And this, believe me, was just about

---

robes et manteaux: French for "dresses and capes."

enough of itself to keep me in a constant rage, to exasperate me beyond measure.

THE MANAGER: And why didn't you send him away then — this secretary of yours?

THE FATHER: Precisely what I did, sir. And then I had to watch this poor woman drifting forlornly about the house like an animal without a master, like an animal one has taken in out of pity.

THE MOTHER: Ah yes . . . !

THE FATHER (*suddenly turning to the Mother*): It's true about the son anyway, isn't it?

THE MOTHER: He took my son away from me first of all.

THE FATHER: But not from cruelty. I did it so that he should grow up healthy and strong by living in the country.

THE STEPDAUGHTER (*pointing to him ironically*): As one can see.

THE FATHER (*quickly*): Is it my fault if he has grown up like this? I sent him to a wet nurse in the country, a peasant, as *she* did not seem to me strong enough, though she is of humble origin. That was, anyway, the reason I married her. Unpleasant all this may be, but how can it be helped? My mistake possibly, but there we are! All my life I have had these confounded aspirations towards a certain moral sanity. (*At this point the Stepdaughter bursts into a noisy laugh.*) Oh, stop it! Stop it! I can't stand it.

THE MANAGER: Yes, please stop it, for Heaven's sake.

THE STEPDAUGHTER: But imagine moral sanity from him, if you please — the client of certain ateliers like that of Madame Pace!

THE FATHER: Fool! That is the proof that I am a man! This seeming contradiction, gentlemen, is the strongest proof that I stand here a live man before you. Why, it is just for this very incongruity in my nature that I have had to suffer what I have. I could not live by the side of that woman (*indicating the Mother*) any longer; but not so much for the boredom she inspired me with as for the pity I felt for her.

THE MOTHER: And so he turned me out —.

THE FATHER: — well provided for! Yes, I sent her to that man, gentlemen . . . to let her go free of me.

THE MOTHER: And to free himself.

THE FATHER: Yes, I admit it. It was also a liberation for me. But great evil has come of it. I meant well when I did it; and I did it more for her sake than mine. I swear it. (*Crosses his arms on his chest; then turns suddenly to the Mother.*) Did I ever lose sight of you until that other man carried you off to another town, like the angry fool he was? And on account of my pure interest in you . . . my pure interest, I repeat, that had no base motive in it . . .

I watched with the tenderest concern the new family that grew up around her. She can bear witness to this. (*Points to the Stepdaughter.*)

THE STEPDAUGHTER: Oh yes, that's true enough. When I was a kiddie, so so high, you know, with plaits over my shoulders and knickers longer than my skirts, I used to see him waiting outside the school for me to come out. He came to see how I was growing up.

THE FATHER: This is infamous, shameful!

THE STEPDAUGHTER: No. Why?

THE FATHER: Infamous! infamous! (*Then excitedly to Manager, explaining.*) After she (*indicating the Mother*) went away, my house seemed suddenly empty. She was my incubus, but she filled my house. I was like a dazed fly alone in the empty rooms. This boy here (*indicating the Son*) was educated away from home, and when he came back, he seemed to me to be no more mine. With no mother to stand between him and me, he grew up entirely for himself, on his own, apart, with no tie of intellect or affection binding him to me. And then — strange but true — I was driven, by curiosity at first and then by some tender sentiment, towards her family, which had come into being through my will. The thought of her began gradually to fill up the emptiness I felt all around me. I wanted to know if she were happy in living out the simple daily duties of life. I wanted to think of her as fortunate and happy because far away from the complicated torments of my spirit. And so, to have proof of this, I used to watch that child coming out of school.

THE STEPDAUGHTER: Yes, yes. True. He used to follow me in the street and smiled at me, waved his hand, like this. I would look at him with interest, wondering who he might be. I told my mother, who guessed at once. (*The Mother agrees with a nod.*) Then she didn't want to send me to school for some days; and when I finally went back, there he was again — looking so ridiculous — with a paper parcel in his hands. He came close to me, caressed me, and drew out a fine straw hat from the parcel, with a bouquet of flowers — all for me!

THE MANAGER: A bit discursive this, you know!

THE SON (*contemptuously*): Literature! Literature!

THE FATHER: Literature indeed! This is life, this is passion!

THE MANAGER: It may be, but it won't act.

THE FATHER: I agree. This is only the part leading up. I don't suggest this should be staged. She (*pointing to the Stepdaughter*), as you see, is no longer the flapper with plaits down her back —

THE STEPDAUGHTER: — and knickers showing below the skirt!

THE FATHER: The drama is coming now, sir; something new, complex, most interesting.

THE STEPDAUGHTER: As soon as my father died . . .

THE FATHER: — there was absolute misery for them. They came back here, unknown to me. Through her stupidity! (*Pointing to the Mother.*) It is true she can barely write her own name; but she could anyhow have got her daughter to write to me that they were in need . . .

THE MOTHER: And how was I to divine all this sentiment in him?

THE FATHER: That is exactly your mistake, never to have guessed any of my sentiments.

THE MOTHER: After so many years apart, and all that had happened . . .

THE FATHER: Was it my fault if that fellow carried you away? It happened quite suddenly; for after he had obtained some job or other, I could find no trace of them; and so, not unnaturally, my interest in them dwindled. But the drama culminated unforeseen and violent on their return, when I was impelled by my miserable flesh that still lives. . . . Ah! what misery, what wretchedness is that of the man who is alone and disdains debasing *liaisons!* Not old enough to do without women, and not young enough to go and look for one without shame. Misery? It's worse than misery; it's a horror; for no woman can any longer give him love; and when a man feels this. . . . One ought to do without, you say? Yes, yes, I know. Each of us when he appears before his fellows is clothed in a certain dignity. But every man knows what unconfessable things pass within the secrecy of his own heart. One gives way to the temptation, only to rise from it again, afterwards, with a great eagerness to reestablish one's dignity, as if it were a tombstone to place on the grave of one's shame, and a monument to hide and sign the memory of our weaknesses. Everybody's in the same case. Some folks haven't the courage to say certain things, that's all!

THE STEPDAUGHTER: All appear to have the courage to do them though.

THE FATHER: Yes, but in secret. Therefore, you want more courage to say these things. Let a man but speak these things out, and folks at once label him a cynic. But it isn't true. He is like all the others, better indeed, because he isn't afraid to reveal with the light of the intelligence the red shame of human bestiality on which most men close their eyes so as not to see it.

Woman — for example, look at her case! She turns tantalizing inviting glances on you. You seize her. No sooner does she feel herself in your grasp than she closes her eyes. It is the sign of her mission, the sign by which she says to man: "Blind yourself, for I am blind."

THE STEPDAUGHTER: Sometimes she can close them no more: when she no longer feels the need of hiding her shame to herself, but dry-eyed and dispassionately, sees only that of the man who has blinded himself without love. Oh, all these intellectual complications make me sick, disgust me — all this philosophy that uncovers the beast in man, and then seeks to save him, excuse him . . . I can't stand it, sir. When a man seeks to "simplify" life bestially, throwing aside every relic of humanity, every chaste aspiration, every pure feeling, all sense of ideality, duty, modesty, shame . . . then nothing is more revolting and nauseous than a certain kind of remorse — crocodiles' tears, that's what it is.

THE MANAGER: Let's come to the point. This is only discussion.

THE FATHER: Very good, sir! But a fact is like a sack which won't stand up when it's empty. In order that it may stand up, one has to put into it the reason and sentiment which have caused it to exist. I couldn't possibly know that after the death of that man, they had decided to return here, that they were in misery, and that she (*pointing to the Mother*) had gone to work as a modiste,° and at a shop of the type of that of Madame Pace.

THE STEPDAUGHTER: A real high-class modiste, you must know, gentlemen. In appearance, she works for the leaders of the best society; but she arranges matters so that these elegant ladies serve her purpose . . . without prejudice to other ladies who are . . . well . . . only so so.

THE MOTHER: You will believe me, gentlemen, that it never entered my mind that the old hag offered me work because she had her eye on my daughter.

THE STEPDAUGHTER: Poor mamma! Do you know, sir, what that woman did when I brought her back the work my mother had finished? She would point out to me that I had torn one of my frocks, and she would give it back to my mother to mend. It was I who paid for it, always I; while this poor creature here believed she was sacrificing herself for me and these two children here, sitting up at night sewing Madame Pace's robes.

THE MANAGER: And one day you met there . . .

THE STEPDAUGHTER: Him, him. Yes sir, an old client. There's a scene for you to play! Superb!

THE FATHER: She, the Mother arrived just then . . .

THE STEPDAUGHTER (*treacherously*): Almost in time!

THE FATHER (*crying out*): No, in time! in time! Fortunately I recognized her . . . in time. And I took them back home with me to my house. You can

---

modiste: A person who makes fashionable clothing for women.

imagine now her position and mine; she, as you see her; and I who cannot look her in the face.

THE STEPDAUGHTER: Absurd! How can I possibly be expected — after that — to be a modest young miss, a fit person to go with his confounded aspirations for "a solid moral sanity"?

THE FATHER: For the drama lies all in this — in the conscience that I have, that each one of us has. We believe this conscience to be a single thing, but it is many-sided. There is one for this person, and another for that. Diverse consciences. So we have this illusion of being one person for all, of having a personality that is unique in all our acts. But it isn't true. We perceive this when, tragically perhaps, in something we do, we are as it were, suspended, caught up in the air on a kind of hook. Then we perceive that all of us was not in that act, and that it would be an atrocious injustice to judge us by that action alone, as if all our existence were summed up in that one deed. Now do you understand the perfidy of this girl? She surprised me in a place, where she ought not to have known me, just as I could not exist for her; and she now seeks to attach to me a reality such as I could never suppose I should have to assume for her in a shameful and fleeting moment of my life. I feel this above all else. And the drama, you will see, acquires a tremendous value from this point. Then there is the position of the others . . . his. . . . (*Indicating the Son.*)

THE SON (*shrugging his shoulders scornfully*): Leave me alone! I don't come into this.

THE FATHER: What? You don't come into this?

THE SON: I've got nothing to do with it, and don't want to have; because you know well enough I wasn't made to be mixed up in all this with the rest of you.

THE STEPDAUGHTER: We are only vulgar folk! He is the fine gentleman. You may have noticed, Mr. Manager, that I fix him now and again with a look of scorn while he lowers his eyes — for he knows the evil he has done me.

THE SON (*scarcely looking at her*): I?

THE STEPDAUGHTER: You! you! I owe my life on the streets to you. Did you or did you not deny us, with your behavior, I won't say the intimacy of home, but even that mere hospitality which makes guests feel at their ease? We were intruders who had come to disturb the kingdom of your legitimacy. I should like to have you witness, Mr. Manager, certain scenes between him and me. He says I have tyrannized over everyone. But it was just his behavior which made me insist on the reason for which I had come into the house, — this reason he calls "vile" — into his house, with my mother who is his mother too. And I came as mistress of the house.

THE SON: It's easy for them to put me always in the wrong. But imagine, gentlemen, the position of a son, whose fate it is to see arrive one day at his home a young woman of impudent bearing, a young woman who inquires for his father, with whom who knows what business she has. This young man has then to witness her return bolder than ever, accompanied by that child there. He is obliged to watch her treat his father in an equivocal and confidential manner. She asks for money of him in a way that lets one suppose he must give it to her, *must,* do you understand, because he has every obligation to do so.

THE FATHER: But I have, as a matter of fact, this obligation. I owe it to your mother.

THE SON: How should I know? When had I ever seen or heard of her? One day there arrive with her (*indicating Stepdaughter*) that lad and this baby here. I am told: "This is *your* mother too, you know." I divine from her manner (*indicating Stepdaughter again*) why it is they have come home. I had rather not say what I feel and think about it. I shouldn't even care to confess to myself. No action can therefore be hoped for from me in this affair. Believe me, Mr. Manager, I am an "unrealized" character, dramatically speaking; and I find myself not at all at ease in their company. Leave me out of it, I beg you.

THE FATHER: What? It is just because you are so that . . .

THE SON: How do you know what I am like? When did you ever bother your head about me?

THE FATHER: I admit it. I admit it. But isn't that a situation in itself? This aloofness of yours which is so cruel to me and to your mother, who returns home and sees you almost for the first time grown up, who doesn't recognize you but knows you are her son. . . . (*Pointing out the Mother to the Manager.*) See, she's crying!

THE STEPDAUGHTER (*angrily, stamping her foot*): Like a fool!

THE FATHER (*indicating Stepdaughter*): She can't stand him, you know. (*Then referring again to the Son.*) He says he doesn't come into the affair, whereas he is really the hinge of the whole action. Look at that lad who is always clinging to his mother, frightened and humiliated. It is on account of this fellow here. Possibly his situation is the most painful of all. He feels himself a stranger more than the others. The poor little chap feels mortified, humiliated at being brought into a home out of charity as it were. (*In confidence.*) He is the image of his father. Hardly talks at all. Humble and quiet.

THE MANAGER: Oh, we'll cut him out. You've no notion what a nuisance boys are on the stage. . . .

THE FATHER: He disappears soon, you know. And the baby too. She is the first to vanish from the scene. The drama consists finally in this: when that mother reenters my house, her family born outside of it, and shall we say superimposed on the original, ends with the death of the little girl, the tragedy of the boy and the flight of the elder daughter. It cannot go on, because it is foreign to its surroundings. So after much torment, we three remain: I, the mother, that son. Then, owing to the disappearance of that extraneous family, we too find ourselves strange to one another. We find we are living in an atmosphere of mortal desolation which is the revenge, as he (*indicating Son*) scornfully said of the Demon of Experiment, that unfortunately hides in me. Thus, sir, you see when faith is lacking, it becomes impossible to create certain states of happiness, for we lack the necessary humility. Vaingloriously, we try to substitute ourselves for this faith, creating thus for the rest of the world a reality which we believe after their fashion, while, actually, it doesn't exist. For each one of us has his own reality to be respected before God, even when it is harmful to one's very self.

THE MANAGER: There is something in what you say. I assure you all this interests me very much. I begin to think there's the stuff for a drama in all this, and not a bad drama either.

THE STEPDAUGHTER (*coming forward*): When you've got a character like me . . .

THE FATHER (*shutting her up, all excited to learn the decision of the Manager*): You be quiet!

THE MANAGER (*reflecting, heedless of interruption*): It's new . . . hem . . . yes. . . .

THE FATHER: Absolutely new!

THE MANAGER: You've got a nerve though, I must say, to come here and fling it at me like this . . .

THE FATHER: You will understand, sir, born as we are for the stage . . .

THE MANAGER: Are you amateur actors then?

THE FATHER: No, I say born for the stage, because . . .

THE MANAGER: Oh, nonsense. You're an old hand, you know.

THE FATHER: No sir, no. We act that role for which we have been cast, that role which we are given in life. And in my own case, passion itself, as usually happens, becomes a trifle theatrical when it is exalted.

THE MANAGER: Well, well, that will do. But you see, without an author. . . . I could give you the address of an author if you like . . .

THE FATHER: No, no. Look here! You must be the author.

THE MANAGER: I? What are you talking about?

THE FATHER: Yes, you, you! Why not?

THE MANAGER: Because I have never been an author: that's why.

THE FATHER: Then why not turn author now? Everybody does it. You don't want any special qualities. Your task is made much easier by the fact that we are all here alive before you. . . .

THE MANAGER: It won't do.

THE FATHER: What? When you see us live our drama . . .

THE MANAGER: Yes, that's all right. But you want someone to write it.

THE FATHER: No, no. Someone to take it down, possibly, while we play it, scene by scene! It will be enough to sketch it out at first, and then try it over.

THE MANAGER: Well . . . I am almost tempted. It's a bit of an idea. One might have a shot at it.

THE FATHER: Of course. You'll see what scenes will come out of it. I can give you one, at once . . .

THE MANAGER: By Jove, it tempts me. I'd like to have a go at it. Let's try it out. Come with me to my office. (*Turning to the Actors.*) You are at liberty for a bit, but don't step out of the theater for long. In a quarter of an hour, twenty minutes, all back here again! (*To the Father.*) We'll see what can be done. Who knows if we don't get something really extraordinary out of it?

THE FATHER: There's no doubt about it. They (*indicating the Characters*) had better come with us too, hadn't they?

THE MANAGER: Yes, yes. Come on! come on! (*Moves away and then turning to the Actors.*) Be punctual, please! (*Manager and the Six Characters cross the stage and go off. The other Actors remain, looking at one another in astonishment.*)

LEADING MAN: Is he serious? What the devil does he want to do?

JUVENILE LEAD: This is rank madness.

THIRD ACTOR: Does he expect to knock up a drama in five minutes?

JUVENILE LEAD: Like the improvisers!

LEADING LADY: If he thinks I'm going to take part in a joke like this. . . .

JUVENILE LEAD: I'm out of it anyway.

FOURTH ACTOR: I should like to know who they are. (*Alludes to Characters.*)

THIRD ACTOR: What do you suppose? Madmen or rascals!

JUVENILE LEAD: And he takes them seriously!

L'INGÉNUE: Vanity! He fancies himself as an author now.

LEADING MAN: It's absolutely unheard of. If the stage has come to this . . . well I'm . . .

FIFTH ACTOR: It's rather a joke.

THIRD ACTOR: Well, we'll see what's going to happen next.

(*Thus talking, the Actors leave the stage, some going out by the little door at the back, others retiring to their dressing rooms.*)
(*The curtain remains up.*)
(*The action of the play is suspended for twenty minutes.*)

ACT II

(*The stage call-bells ring to warn the company that the play is about to begin again.*)
(*The Stepdaughter comes out of the Manager's office along with the Child and the Boy. As she comes out of the office, she cries: —*)

Nonsense! nonsense! Do it yourselves! I'm not going to mix myself up in this mess. (*Turning to the Child and coming quickly with her on to the stage.*) Come on, Rosetta, let's run!

(*The Boy follows them slowly, remaining a little behind and seeming perplexed.*)

THE STEPDAUGHTER (*stops, bends over the Child and takes the latter's face between her hands*): My little darling! You're frightened, aren't you? You don't know where we are, do you? (*Pretending to reply to a question of the Child.*) What is the stage? It's a place, baby, you know, where people play at being serious, a place where they act comedies. We've got to act a comedy now, dead serious, you know; and you're in it also, little one. (*Embraces her, pressing the little head to her breast, and rocking the Child for a moment.*) Oh darling, darling, what a horrid comedy you've got to play! What a wretched part they've found for you! A garden . . . a fountain . . . look . . . just suppose, kiddie, it's here. Where, you say? Why, right here in the middle. It's all pretense you know. That's the trouble, my pet: it's all make-believe here. It's better to imagine it though, because if they fix it up for you, it'll only be painted cardboard, painted cardboard for the rockery, the water, the plants. . . . Ah, but I think a baby like this one would sooner have a make-believe fountain than a real one, so she could play with it. What a joke it'll be for the others! But for you, alas! not quite such a joke: you who are real, baby dear, and really play by a real fountain that is big and green and beautiful, with ever so many bamboos around it that are reflected in the water, and a whole lot of little ducks swimming about. . . . No, Rosetta, no, your mother

doesn't bother about you on account of that wretch of a son there. I'm in the devil of a temper, and as for that lad. . . . (*Seizes Boy by the arm to force him to take one of his hands out of his pockets.*) What have you got there? What are you hiding? (*Pulls his hand out of his pocket, looks into it, and catches the glint of a revolver.*) Ah! where did you get this? (*The Boy, very pale in the face, looks at her, but does not answer.*) Idiot! If I'd been in your place, instead of killing myself, I'd have shot one of those two, or both of them: father and son.

(*The Father enters from the office, all excited from his work. The Manager follows him.*)

THE FATHER: Come on, come on dear! Come here for a minute! We've arranged everything. It's all fixed up.

THE MANAGER (*also excited*): If you please, young lady, there are one or two points to settle still. Will you come along?

THE STEPDAUGHTER (*following him toward the office*): Ouff! what's the good, if you've arranged everything.

(*The Father, Manager, and Stepdaughter go back into the office again [off] for a moment. At the same time, the Son, followed by the Mother, comes out.*)

THE SON (*looking at the three entering office*): Oh this is fine, fine! And to think I can't even get away!

(*The Mother attempts to look at him, but lowers her eyes immediately when he turns away from her. She then sits down. The Boy and the Child approach her. She casts a glance again at the Son, and speaks with humble tones, trying to draw him into conversation.*)

THE MOTHER: And isn't my punishment the worst of all? (*Then seeing from the Son's manner that he will not bother himself about her.*) My God! Why are you so cruel? Isn't it enough for one person to support all this torment? Must you then insist on others seeing it also?

THE SON (*half to himself, meaning the Mother to hear, however*): And they want to put it on the stage! If there was at least a reason for it! He thinks he has got at the meaning of it all. Just as if each one of us in every circumstance of life couldn't find his own explanation of it! (*Pauses.*) He complains he was discovered in a place where he ought not to have been seen, in a moment of his life which ought to have remained hidden and kept out of the reach of that convention which he has to maintain for other people. And what about my case? Haven't I had to reveal what no son ought ever to reveal: how father and mother live and are man and wife for themselves quite apart from that idea of father and mother which we give them? When this idea is revealed, our life is then linked at one point only to that man and that woman; and as such it should shame them, shouldn't it?

(*The Mother hides her face in her hands. From the dressing rooms and the little door at the back of the stage the Actors and Stage Manager return, followed by the Property Man and the Prompter. At the same moment, the Manager comes out of his office, accompanied by the Father and the Stepdaughter.*)

THE MANAGER: Come on, come on, ladies and gentlemen! Heh! you there, machinist!

MACHINIST: Yes sir?

THE MANAGER: Fix up the parlor with the floral decorations. Two wings and a drop with a door will do. Hurry up!

(*The Machinist runs off at once to prepare the scene and arranges it while the Manager talks with the Stage Manager, the Property Man, and the Prompter on matters of detail.*)

THE MANAGER (*to Property Man*): Just have a look, and see if there isn't a sofa or a divan in the wardrobe . . .

PROPERTY MAN: There's the green one.

THE STEPDAUGHTER: No no! Green won't do. It was yellow, ornamented with flowers — very large! and most comfortable!

PROPERTY MAN: There isn't one like that.

THE MANAGER: It doesn't matter. Use the one we've got.

THE STEPDAUGHTER: Doesn't matter? It's most important!

THE MANAGER: We're only trying it now. Please don't interfere. (*To Property Man.*) See if we've got a shop window — long and narrowish.

THE STEPDAUGHTER: And the little table! The little mahogany table for the pale blue envelope!

PROPERTY MAN (*to Manager*): There's that little gilt one.

THE MANAGER: That'll do fine.

THE FATHER: A mirror.

THE STEPDAUGHTER: And the screen! We must have a screen. Otherwise how can I manage?

PROPERTY MAN: That's all right, Miss. We've got any amount of them.

THE MANAGER (*to the Stepdaughter*): We want some clothes pegs too, don't we?

THE STEPDAUGHTER: Yes, several, several!

THE MANAGER: See how many we've got and bring them all.

PROPERTY MAN: All right!

(*The Property Man hurries off to obey his orders.*

While he is putting the things in their places, the Manager talks to the Prompter and then with the Characters and the Actors.)

THE MANAGER (*to Prompter*): Take your seat. Look here: this is the outline of the scenes, act by act. (*Hands him some sheets of paper.*) And now I'm going to ask you to do something out of the ordinary.

PROMPTER: Take it down in shorthand?

THE MANAGER (*pleasantly surprised*): Exactly! Can you do shorthand?

PROMPTER: Yes, a little.

THE MANAGER: Good! (*Turning to a Stage Hand.*) Go and get some paper from my office, plenty, as much as you can find.

(*The Stage Hand goes off and soon returns with a handful of paper which he gives to the Prompter.*)

THE MANAGER (*to Prompter*): You follow the scenes as we play them, and try and get the points down, at any rate the most important ones. (*Then addressing the Actors.*) Clear the stage, ladies and gentlemen! Come over here (*pointing to the left*) and listen attentively.

LEADING LADY: But, excuse me, we . . .

THE MANAGER (*guessing her thought*): Don't worry! You won't have to improvise.

LEADING MAN: What have we to do then?

THE MANAGER: Nothing. For the moment you just watch and listen. Everybody will get his part written out afterwards. At present we're going to try the thing as best we can. They're going to act now.

THE FATHER (*as if fallen from the clouds into the confusion of the stage*): We? What do you mean, if you please, by a rehearsal?

THE MANAGER: A rehearsal for them. (*Points to the Actors.*)

THE FATHER: But since we are the characters . . .

THE MANAGER: All right: "characters" then, if you insist on calling yourselves such. But here, my dear sir, the characters don't act. Here the actors do the acting. The characters are there, in the "book" (*pointing toward Prompter's box*) — when there is a "book"!

THE FATHER: I won't contradict you; but excuse me, the actors aren't the characters. They want to be, they pretend to be, don't they? Now if these gentlemen here are fortunate enough to have us alive before them . . .

THE MANAGER: Oh, this is grand! You want to come before the public yourselves then?

THE FATHER: As we are. . . .

THE MANAGER: I can assure you it would be a magnificent spectacle!

LEADING MAN: What's the use of us here anyway then?

THE MANAGER: You're not going to pretend that you can act? It makes me laugh! (*The Actors laugh.*) There, you see, they are laughing at the notion. But, by the way, I must cast the parts. That won't be difficult. They cast themselves. (*To the Second Lady Lead.*) You play the Mother. (*To the Father.*) We must find her a name.

THE FATHER: Amalia, sir.

THE MANAGER: But that is the real name of your wife. We don't want to call her by her real name.

THE FATHER: Why ever not, if it is her name? ... Still, perhaps, if that lady must ... (*Makes a slight motion of the hand to indicate the Second Lady Lead.*) I see this woman here (*means the Mother*) as Amalia. But do as you like. (*Gets more and more confused.*) I don't know what to say to you. Already, I begin to hear my own words ring false, as if they had another sound ...

THE MANAGER: Don't you worry about it. It'll be our job to find the right tones. And as for her name, if you want her Amalia, Amalia it shall be; and if you don't like it, we'll find another! For the moment though, we'll call the characters in this way: (*To Juvenile Lead.*) You are the Son. (*To the Leading Lady.*) You naturally are the Stepdaughter. ...

THE STEPDAUGHTER (*excitedly*): What? what? I, that woman there? (*Bursts out laughing.*)

THE MANAGER (*angry*): What is there to laugh at?

LEADING LADY (*indignant*): Nobody has ever dared to laugh at me. I insist on being treated with respect; otherwise I go away.

THE STEPDAUGHTER: No, no, excuse me ... I am not laughing at you. ...

THE MANAGER (*to Stepdaughter*): You ought to feel honored to be played by ...

LEADING LADY (*at once, contemptuously*): "That woman there" ...

THE STEPDAUGHTER: But I wasn't speaking of you, you know. I was speaking of myself — whom I can't see at all in you! That is all. I don't know ... but ... you ... aren't in the least like me. ...

THE FATHER: True. Here's the point. Look here, sir, our temperaments, our souls. ...

THE MANAGER: Temperament, soul, be hanged! Do you suppose the spirit of the piece is in you? Nothing of the kind!

THE FATHER: What, haven't we our own temperaments, our own souls?

THE MANAGER: Not at all. Your soul or whatever you like to call it takes shape here. The actors give body and form to it, voice and gesture. And my actors — I may tell you — have given expression to much more lofty material than this little drama of yours, which may or may not hold up on the stage. But if it does, the merit of it, believe me, will be due to my actors.

THE FATHER: I don't dare contradict you, sir; but, believe me, it is a terrible suffering for us who are as we are, with these bodies of ours, these features to see. ...

THE MANAGER (*cutting him short and out of patience*): Good heavens! The make-up will remedy all that, man, the make-up. ...

THE FATHER: Maybe. But the voice, the gestures ...

THE MANAGER: Now, look here! On the stage, you as yourself, cannot exist. The actor here acts you, and that's an end to it!

THE FATHER: I understand. And now I think I see why our author who conceived us as we are, all alive, didn't want to put us on the stage after all. I haven't the least desire to offend your actors. Far from it! But when I think that I am to be acted by ... I don't know by whom. ...

LEADING MAN (*on his dignity*): By me, if you've no objection!

THE FATHER (*humbly, mellifluously*): Honored, I assure you, sir. (*Bows.*) Still, I must say that try as this gentleman may, with all his good will and wonderful art, to absorb me into himself. ...

LEADING MAN: Oh chuck it! "Wonderful art!" Withdraw that, please!

THE FATHER: The performance he will give, even doing his best with make-up to look like me. ...

LEADING MAN: It will certainly be a bit difficult! (*The Actors laugh.*)

THE FATHER: Exactly! It will be difficult to act me as I really am. The effect will be rather — apart from the make-up — according as to how he supposes I am, as he senses me — if he does sense me — and not as I inside of myself feel myself to be. It seems to me then that account should be taken of this by everyone whose duty it may become to criticize us. ...

THE MANAGER: Heavens! The man's starting to think about the critics now! Let them say what they like. It's up to us to put on the play if we can. (*Looking around.*) Come on! come on! Is the stage set? (*To the Actors and Characters.*) Stand back — stand back! Let me see, and don't let's lose any more time! (*To the Stepdaughter.*) Is it all right as it is now?

THE STEPDAUGHTER: Well, to tell the truth, I don't recognize the scene.

THE MANAGER: My dear lady, you can't possibly suppose that we can construct that shop of Madame Pace piece by piece here? (*To the Father.*) You said a white room with flowered wallpaper, didn't you?

THE FATHER: Yes.

THE MANAGER: Well then. We've got the furniture right more or less. Bring that little table a bit further forward. (*The Stage Hands obey the order. To Property Man.*) You go and find an envelope, if possible, a pale blue one; and give it to that gentleman. (*Indicates Father.*)

PROPERTY MAN: An ordinary envelope?

MANAGER AND FATHER: Yes, yes, an ordinary envelope.

PROPERTY MAN: At once, sir. (*Exit.*)

THE MANAGER: Ready, everyone! First scene — the Young Lady. (*The Leading Lady comes forward.*) No, no, you must wait. I meant her. (*Indicating the Stepdaughter.*) You just watch —

THE STEPDAUGHTER (*adding at once*): How I shall play it, how I shall live it! . . .

LEADING LADY (*offended*): I shall live it also, you may be sure, as soon as I begin!

THE MANAGER (*with his hands to his head*): Ladies and gentlemen, if you please! No more useless discussions! Scene I: the Young Lady with Madame Pace: Oh! (*Looks around as if lost.*) And this Madame Pace, where is she?

THE FATHER: She isn't with us, sir.

THE MANAGER: Then what the devil's to be done?

THE FATHER: But she is alive too.

THE MANAGER: Yes, but where is she?

THE FATHER: One minute. Let me speak! (*Turning to the Actresses.*) If these ladies would be so good as to give me their hats for a moment. . . .

THE ACTRESSES (*half surprised, half laughing, in chorus*): What? Why? Our hats? What does he say?

THE MANAGER: What are you going to do with the ladies' hats? (*The Actors laugh.*)

THE FATHER: Oh nothing. I just want to put them on these pegs for a moment. And one of the ladies will be so kind as to take off her mantle. . . .

THE ACTORS: Oh, what d'you think of that? Only the mantle? He must be mad.

SOME ACTRESSES: But why? Mantles as well?

THE FATHER: To hang them up here for a moment. Please be so kind, will you?

THE ACTRESSES (*taking off their hats, one or two also their cloaks, and going to hang them on the racks*): After all, why not? There you are! This is really funny. We've got to put them on show.

THE FATHER: Exactly; just like that, on show.

THE MANAGER: May we know why?

THE FATHER: I'll tell you. Who knows if, by arranging the stage for her, she does not come here herself, attracted by the very articles of her trade? (*Inviting the Actors to look toward the exit at back of stage.*) Look! Look!

(*The door at the back of stage opens and Madame Pace enters and takes a few steps forward. She is a fat, oldish woman with puffy oxygenated hair. She is rouged and powdered, dressed with a comical elegance in black silk. Round her waist is a long silver chain from which hangs a pair of scissors. The Stepdaughter runs over to her at once amid the stupor of the Actors.*)

THE STEPDAUGHTER (*turning toward her*): There she is! There she is!

THE FATHER (*radiant*): It's she! I said so, didn't I! There she is!

THE MANAGER (*conquering his surprise, and then becoming indignant*): What sort of a trick is this?

LEADING MAN (*almost at the same time*): What's going to happen next?

JUVENILE LEAD: Where does *she* come from?

L'INGÉNUE: They've been holding her in reserve, I guess.

LEADING LADY: A vulgar trick!

THE FATHER (*dominating the protests*): Excuse me, all of you! Why are you so anxious to destroy in the name of a vulgar, commonplace sense of truth, this reality which comes to birth attracted and formed by the magic of the stage itself, which has indeed more right to live here than you, since it is much truer than you — if you don't mind my saying so? Which is the actress among you who is to play Madame Pace? Well, here is Madame Pace herself. And you will allow, I fancy, that the actress who acts her will be less true than this woman here, who is herself in person. You see my daughter recognized her and went over to her at once. Now you're going to witness the scene!

(*But the scene between the Stepdaughter and Madame Pace has already begun despite the protest of the Actors and the reply of the Father. It has begun quietly, naturally, in a manner impossible for the stage. So when the Actors, called to attention by the Father, turn round and see Madame Pace, who has placed one hand under the Stepdaughter's chin to raise her head, they observe her at first with great attention, but hearing her speak in an unintelligible manner their interest begins to wane.*)

THE MANAGER: Well? well?

LEADING MAN: What does she say?

LEADING LADY: One can't hear a word.

JUVENILE LEAD: Louder! Louder please!

THE STEPDAUGHTER (*leaving Madame Pace, who smiles a Sphinx-like smile, and advancing toward the Actors*): Louder? Louder? What are you talking about? These aren't matters which can be shouted at the top of one's voice. If I have spoken them out loud, it was to shame him and have my revenge. (*Indicates Father.*) But for Madame it's quite a different matter.

THE MANAGER: Indeed? indeed? But here, you know, people have got to make themselves heard, my dear. Even we who are on the stage can't hear you. What will it be when the public's in the theater? And anyway, you can very well speak up now among yourselves, since we shan't be present to listen to you as we are now. You've got to pretend to be alone in a room at the back of a shop where no one can hear you.

(*The Stepdaughter coquettishly and with a touch of malice makes a sign of disagreement two or three times with her finger.*)

THE MANAGER: What do you mean by no?

THE STEPDAUGHTER (*sotto voce,° mysteriously*): There's someone who will hear us if she (*indicating Madame Pace*) speaks out loud.

THE MANAGER (*in consternation*): What? Have you got someone else to spring on us now? (*The Actors burst out laughing.*)

THE FATHER: No, no sir. She is alluding to me. I've got to be here — there behind that door, in waiting; and Madame Pace knows it. In fact, if you will allow me, I'll go there at once, so I can be quite ready. (*Moves away.*)

THE MANAGER (*stopping him*): No! wait! wait! We must observe the conventions of the theater. Before you are ready . . .

THE STEPDAUGHTER (*interrupting him*): No, get on with it at once! I'm just dying, I tell you, to act this scene. If he's ready, I'm more than ready.

THE MANAGER (*shouting*): But, my dear young lady, first of all, we must have the scene between you and this lady. . . . (*Indicates Madame Pace.*) Do you understand?

THE STEPDAUGHTER: Good Heavens! She's been telling me what you know already: that mama's work is badly done again, that the material's ruined; and that if I want her to continue to help us in our misery I must be patient. . . .

MADAME PACE (*coming forward with an air of great importance*): Yes indeed, sir, I no wanta take advantage of her, I no wanta be hard. . . .

(*Note: Madame Pace is supposed to talk in a jargon half Italian, half English.*)

THE MANAGER (*alarmed*): What? What? She talks like that? (*The Actors burst out laughing again.*)

THE STEPDAUGHTER (*also laughing*): Yes yes, that's

the way she talks, half English, half Italian! Most comical it is!

MADAME PACE: Itta seem not verra polite gentlemen laugha atta me eeff I trya best speaka English.

THE MANAGER: *Diamine!°* Of course! Of course! Let her talk like that! Just what we want. Talk just like that, Madame, if you please! The effect will be certain. Exactly what was wanted to put a little comic relief into the crudity of the situation. Of course she talks like that! Magnificent!

THE STEPDAUGHTER: Magnificent? Certainly! When certain suggestions are made to one in language of that kind, the effect is certain, since it seems almost a joke. One feels inclined to laugh when one hears her talk about an "old signore" "who wanta talka nicely with you." Nice old signore, eh, Madame?

MADAME PACE: Not so old my dear, not so old! And even if you no lika him, he won't make any scandal!

THE MOTHER (*jumping up amid the amazement and consternation of the Actors, who had not been noticing her. They move to restrain her*): You old devil! You murderess!

THE STEPDAUGHTER (*running over to calm her Mother*): Calm yourself, Mother, calm yourself! Please don't. . . .

THE FATHER (*going to her also at the same time*): Calm yourself! Don't get excited! Sit down now!

THE MOTHER: Well then, take that woman away out of my sight!

THE STEPDAUGHTER (*to Manager*): It is impossible for my mother to remain here.

THE FATHER (*to Manager*): They can't be here together. And for this reason, you see: that woman there was not with us when we came. . . . If they are on together, the whole thing is given away inevitably, as you see.

THE MANAGER: It doesn't matter. This is only a first rough sketch — just to get an idea of the various points of the scene, even confusedly. . . . (*Turning to the Mother and leading her to her chair.*) Come along, my dear lady, sit down now, and let's get on with the scene. . . .

(*Meanwhile, the Stepdaughter, coming forward again, turns to Madame Pace.*)

THE STEPDAUGHTER: Come on, Madame, come on!

MADAME PACE (*offended*): No, no, *grazie*. I do not do anything witha your mother present.

THE STEPDAUGHTER: Nonsense! Introduce this "old signore" who wants to talk nicely to me. (*Addressing the Company imperiously.*) We've got to

---

***sotto voce*:** In a soft voice or stage whisper.

***Diamine!*:** Italian for "Well, I'll be damned!"

do this scene one way or another, haven't we? Come on! (*To Madame Pace.*) You can go!

MADAME PACE: Ah yes! I go'way! I go'way! Certainly! (*Exits furious.*)

THE STEPDAUGHTER (*to the Father*): Now you make your entry. No, you needn't go over there. Come here. Let's suppose you've already come in. Like that, yes! I'm here with bowed head, modest like. Come on! Out with your voice! Say "Good morning, Miss" in that peculiar tone, that special tone. . . .

THE MANAGER: Excuse me, but are you the Manager, or am I? (*To the Father, who looks undecided and perplexed.*) Get on with it, man! Go down there to the back of the stage. You needn't go off. Then come right forward here.

(*The Father does as he is told, looking troubled and perplexed at first. But as soon as he begins to move, the reality of the action affects him, and he begins to smile and to be more natural. The Actors watch intently.*)

THE MANAGER (*sotto voce, quickly to the Prompter in his box*): Ready! ready! Get ready to write now.

THE FATHER (*coming forward and speaking in a different tone*): Good afternoon, Miss!

THE STEPDAUGHTER (*head bowed down slightly, with restrained disgust*): Good afternoon!

THE FATHER (*looks under her hat which partly covers her face. Perceiving she is very young, he makes an exclamation, partly of surprise, partly of fear lest he compromise himself in a risky adventure*): Ah . . . but . . . ah . . . I say . . . this is not the first time that you have come here, is it?

THE STEPDAUGHTER (*modestly*): No sir.

THE FATHER: You've been here before, eh? (*Then seeing her nod agreement.*) More than once? (*Waits for her to answer, looks under her hat, smiles, and then says:*) Well then, there's no need to be so shy, is there? May I take off your hat?

THE STEPDAUGHTER (*anticipating him and with veiled disgust*): No sir . . . I'll do it myself. (*Takes it off quickly.*)

(*The Mother, who watches the progress of the scene with the Son and the other two children who cling to her, is on thorns; and follows with varying expressions of sorrow, indignation, anxiety, and horror the words and actions of the other two. From time to time she hides her face in her hands and sobs.*)

THE MOTHER: Oh, my God, my God!

THE FATHER (*playing his part with a touch of gallantry*): Give it to me! I'll put it down. (*Takes hat from her hands.*) But a dear little head like yours

ought to have a smarter hat. Come and help me choose one from the stock, won't you?

L'INGÉNUE (*interrupting*): I say . . . those are our hats you know.

THE MANAGER (*furious*): Silence! silence! Don't try and be funny, if you please. . . . We're playing the scene now, I'd have you notice. (*To the Stepdaughter.*) Begin again, please!

THE STEPDAUGHTER (*continuing*): No thank you, sir.

THE FATHER: Oh, come now. Don't talk like that. You must take it. I shall be upset if you don't. There are some lovely little hats here; and then — Madame will be pleased. She expects it, anyway, you know.

THE STEPDAUGHTER: No, no! I couldn't wear it!

THE FATHER: Oh, you're thinking about what they'd say at home if they saw you come in with a new hat? My dear girl, there's always a way round these little matters, you know.

THE STEPDAUGHTER (*all keyed up*): No, it's not that. I couldn't wear it because I am . . . as you see . . . you might have noticed . . .

(*Showing her black dress.*)

THE FATHER: . . . in mourning! Of course: I beg your pardon: I'm frightfully sorry. . . .

THE STEPDAUGHTER (*forcing herself to conquer her indignation and nausea*): Stop! Stop! It's I who must thank you. There's no need for you to feel mortified or specially sorry. Don't think any more of what I've said. (*Tries to smile.*) I must forget that I am dressed so. . . .

THE MANAGER (*interrupting and turning to the Prompter*): Stop a minute! Stop! Don't write that down. Cut out that last bit. (*Then to the Father and Stepdaughter.*) Fine! it's going fine! (*To the Father only.*) And now you can go on as we arranged. (*To the Actors.*) Pretty good that scene, where he offers her the hat, eh?

THE STEPDAUGHTER: The best's coming now. Why can't we go on?

THE MANAGER: Have a little patience! (*To the Actors.*) Of course, it must be treated rather lightly.

LEADING MAN: Still, with a bit of go in it!

LEADING LADY: Of course! It's easy enough! (*To Leading Man.*) Shall you and I try it now?

LEADING MAN: Why, yes! I'll prepare my entrance. (*Exit in order to make his entrance.*)

THE MANAGER (*to Leading Lady*): See here! The scene between you and Madame Pace is finished. I'll have it written out properly after. You remain here . . . oh, where are you going?

LEADING LADY: One minute. I want to put my hat on again. (*Goes over to hatrack and puts her hat on her head.*)

THE MANAGER: Good! You stay here with your head bowed down a bit.

THE STEPDAUGHTER: But she isn't dressed in black.

LEADING LADY: But I shall be, and much more effectively than you.

THE MANAGER (*to Stepdaughter*): Be quiet please, and watch! You'll be able to learn something. (*Clapping his hands.*) Come on! come on! Entrance, please!

(*The door at rear of stage opens, and the Leading Man enters with the lively manner of an old gallant. The rendering of the scene by the Actors from the very first words is seen to be quite a different thing, though it has not in any way the air of a parody. Naturally, the Stepdaughter and the Father, not being able to recognize themselves in the Leading Lady and the Leading Man, who deliver their words in different tones and with a different psychology, express, sometimes with smiles, sometimes with gestures, the impression they receive.*)

LEADING MAN: Good afternoon, Miss . . .

THE FATHER (*at once unable to contain himself*): No! no!

(*The Stepdaughter, noticing the way the Leading Man enters, bursts out laughing.*)

THE MANAGER (*furious*): Silence! And you, please, just stop that laughing. If we go on like this, we shall never finish.

THE STEPDAUGHTER: Forgive me, sir, but it's natural enough. This lady (*indicating Leading Lady*) stands there still; but if she is supposed to be me, I can assure you that if I heard anyone say "Good afternoon" in that manner and in that tone, I should burst out laughing as I did.

THE FATHER: Yes, yes, the manner, the tone . . .

THE MANAGER: Nonsense! Rubbish! Stand aside and let me see the action.

LEADING MAN: If I've got to represent an old fellow who's coming into a house of an equivocal character . . .

THE MANAGER: Don't listen to them, for Heaven's sake! Do it again! It goes fine. (*Waiting for the Actors to begin again.*) Well?

LEADING MAN: Good afternoon, Miss.

LEADING LADY: Good afternoon.

LEADING MAN (*imitating the gesture of the Father when he looked under the hat, and then expressing quite clearly first satisfaction and then fear*): Ah, but . . . I say . . . this is not the first time that you have come here, is it?

THE MANAGER: Good, but not quite so heavily. Like this. (*Acts himself.*) "This isn't the first time that you have come here" . . . (*To Leading Lady.*) And you say: "No, sir."

LEADING LADY: No, sir.

LEADING MAN: You've been here before, more than once.

THE MANAGER: No, no, stop! Let her nod "yes" first. "You've been here before, eh?" (*The Leading Lady lifts up her head slightly and closes her eyes as though in disgust. Then she inclines her head twice.*)

THE STEPDAUGHTER (*unable to contain herself*): Oh my God! (*Puts a hand to her mouth to prevent herself from laughing.*)

THE MANAGER (*turning round*): What's the matter?

THE STEPDAUGHTER: Nothing, nothing!

THE MANAGER (*to Leading Man*): Go on!

LEADING MAN: You've been here before, eh? Well then, there's no need to be so shy, is there? May I take off your hat?

(*The Leading Man says this last speech in such a tone and with such gestures that the Stepdaughter, though she has her hand to her mouth, cannot keep from laughing.*)

LEADING LADY (*indignant*): I'm not going to stop here to be made a fool of by that woman there.

LEADING MAN: Neither am I! I'm through with it!

THE MANAGER (*shouting to Stepdaughter*): Silence! for once and all, I tell you!

THE STEPDAUGHTER: Forgive me! forgive me!

THE MANAGER: You haven't any manners: that's what it is! You go too far.

THE FATHER (*endeavoring to intervene*): Yes, it's true, but excuse her . . .

THE MANAGER: Excuse what? It's absolutely disgusting.

THE FATHER: Yes, sir, but believe me, it has such a strange effect when . . .

THE MANAGER: Strange? Why strange? Where is it strange?

THE FATHER: No, sir; I admire your actors — this gentleman here, this lady; but they are certainly not us!

THE MANAGER: I should hope not. Evidently they cannot be you, if they are actors.

THE FATHER: Just so: actors! Both of them act our parts exceedingly well. But, believe me, it produces quite a different effect on us. They want to be us, but they aren't, all the same.

THE MANAGER: What is it then anyway?

THE FATHER: Something that is . . . that is theirs — and no longer ours . . .

THE MANAGER: But naturally, inevitably, I've told you so already.

THE FATHER: Yes, I understand . . . I understand . . .

THE MANAGER: Well then, let's have no more of it! (*Turning to the Actors.*) We'll have the rehearsals by ourselves, afterwards, in the ordinary way. I never could stand rehearsing with the author present. He's never satisfied! (*Turning to Father and Stepdaughter.*) Come on! Let's get on with it again; and try and see if you can't keep from laughing.

THE STEPDAUGHTER: Oh, I shan't laugh any more. There's a nice little bit coming from me now: you'll see.

THE MANAGER: Well then: when she says "Don't think any more of what I've said, I must forget, etc.," you (*addressing the Father*) come in sharp with "I understand"; and then you ask her . . .

THE STEPDAUGHTER (*interrupting*): What?

THE MANAGER: Why she is in mourning.

THE STEPDAUGHTER: Not at all! See here: when I told him that it was useless for me to be thinking about my wearing mourning, do you know how he answered me? "Ah well," he said, "then let's take off this little frock."

THE MANAGER: Great! Just what we want, to make a riot in the theater!

THE STEPDAUGHTER: But it's the truth!

THE MANAGER: What does that matter? Acting is our business here. Truth up to a certain point, but no further.

THE STEPDAUGHTER: What do you want to do then?

THE MANAGER: You'll see, you'll see! Leave it to me.

THE STEPDAUGHTER: No sir! What you want to do is to piece together a little romantic sentimental scene out of my disgust, out of all the reasons, each more cruel and viler than the other, why I am what I am. He is to ask me why I'm in mourning; and I'm to answer with tears in my eyes, that it is just two months since papa died. No sir, no! He's got to say to me, as he did say, "Well, let's take off this little dress at once." And I, with my two months' mourning in my heart, went there behind that screen, and with these fingers tingling with shame . . .

THE MANAGER (*running his hands through his hair*): For Heaven's sake! What are you saying?

THE STEPDAUGHTER (*crying out excitedly*): The truth! The truth!

THE MANAGER: It may be. I don't deny it, and I can understand all your horror; but you must surely see that you can't have this kind of thing on the stage. It won't go.

THE STEPDAUGHTER: Not possible, eh? Very well! I'm much obliged to you — but I'm off.

THE MANAGER: Now be reasonable! Don't lose your temper!

THE STEPDAUGHTER: I won't stop here! I won't! I can see you fixed it all up with him in your office. All this talk about what is possible for the stage . . . I understand! He wants to get at his complicated "cerebral drama," to have his famous remorses and torments acted; but I want to act my part, *my part!*

THE MANAGER (*annoyed, shaking his shoulders*): Ah! Just *your* part! But, if you will pardon me, there are other parts than yours: His (*indicating the Father*) and hers (*indicating the Mother*)! On the stage you can't have a character becoming too prominent and overshadowing all the others. The thing is to pack them all into a neat little framework and then act what is actable. I am aware of the fact that everyone has his own interior life which he wants very much to put forward. But the difficulty lies in this fact: to set out just so much as is necessary for the stage, taking the other characters into consideration, and at the same time hint at the unrevealed interior life of each. I am willing to admit, my dear young lady, that from your point of view it would be a fine idea if each character could tell the public all his troubles in a nice monologue or a regular one hour lecture. (*Good humoredly.*) You must restrain yourself, my dear, and in your own interest, too; because this fury of yours, this exaggerated disgust you show, may make a bad impression, you know. After you have confessed to me that there were others before him at Madame Pace's and more than once . . .

THE STEPDAUGHTER (*bowing her head, impressed*): It's true. But remember those others mean him for me all the same.

THE MANAGER (*not understanding*): What? The others? What do you mean?

THE STEPDAUGHTER: For one who has gone wrong, sir, he who was responsible for the first fault is responsible for all that follow. He is responsible for my faults, was, even before I was born. Look at him, and see if it isn't true!

THE MANAGER: Well, well! And does the weight of so much responsibility seem nothing to you? Give him a chance to act it, to get it over!

THE STEPDAUGHTER: How? How can he act all his "noble remorses," all his "moral torments," if you want to spare him the horror of being discovered one day — after he had asked her what he did ask her — in the arms of her, that already fallen woman, that child, sir, that child he used to watch come out of school? (*She is moved.*)

(*The Mother at this point is overcome with emotion and breaks out into a fit of crying. All are touched. A long pause.*)

THE STEPDAUGHTER (*as soon as the Mother becomes a little quieter, adds resolutely and gravely*): At present, we are unknown to the public. Tomorrow, you will act us as you wish, treating us in your own manner. But do you really want to see drama, do you want to see it flash out as it really did?

THE MANAGER: Of course! That's just what I do want, so I can use as much of it as is possible.

THE STEPDAUGHTER: Well then, ask that Mother there to leave us.

THE MOTHER (*changing her low plaint into a sharp cry*): No! No! Don't permit, it, sir, don't permit it!

THE MANAGER: But it's only to try it.

THE MOTHER: I can't bear it. I can't.

THE MANAGER: But since it has happened already . . . I don't understand!

THE MOTHER: It's taking place now. It happens all the time. My torment isn't a pretended one. I live and feel every minute of my torture. Those two children there — have you heard them speak? They can't speak anymore. They cling to me to keep my torment actual and vivid for me. But for themselves, they do not exist, they aren't anymore. And she (*indicating the Stepdaughter*) has run away, she has left me, and is lost. If I now see her here before me, it is only to renew for me the tortures I have suffered for her too.

THE FATHER: The eternal moment! She (*indicating the Stepdaughter*) is here to catch me, fix me, and hold me eternally in the stocks for that one fleeting and shameful moment of my life. She can't give it up! And you, sir, cannot either fairly spare me it.

THE MANAGER: I never said I didn't want to act it. It will form, as a matter of fact, the nucleus of the whole first act right up to her surprise. (*Indicates the Mother.*)

THE FATHER: Just so! This is my punishment: the passion in all of us that must culminate in her final cry.

THE STEPDAUGHTER: I can hear it still in my ears. It's driven me mad, that cry! — You can put me on as you like; it doesn't matter. Fully dressed, if you like — provided I have at least the arm bare; because, standing like this (*she goes close to the Father and leans her head on his breast*) with my head so, and my arms round his neck, I saw a vein pulsing in my arm here; and then, as if that live vein had awakened disgust in me, I closed my eyes like this, and let my head sink on his breast. (*Turning to the Mother.*) Cry out, mother! Cry out! (*Buries head in Father's breast, and with her shoulders raised as if to prevent her hearing the cry, adds in tones of intense emotion.*) Cry out as you did then!

THE MOTHER (*coming forward to separate them*): No! My daughter, my daughter! (*And after having pulled her away from him.*) You brute! you brute!

She is my daughter! Don't you see she's my daughter?

THE MANAGER (*walking backward toward footlights*): Fine! fine! Damned good! And then, of course — curtain!

THE FATHER (*going toward him excitedly*): Yes, of course, because that's the way it really happened.

THE MANAGER (*convinced and pleased*): Oh, yes, no doubt about it. Curtain here, curtain!

(*At the reiterated cry of the Manager, the Machinist lets the curtain down, leaving the Manager and the Father in front of it before the footlights.*)

THE MANAGER: The darned idiot! I said "curtain" to show the act should end there, and he goes and lets it down in earnest. (*To the Father, while he pulls the curtain back to go on to the stage again.*) Yes, yes, it's all right. Effect certain! That's the right ending. I'll guarantee the first act at any rate.

ACT III

(*When the curtain goes up again, it is seen that the stage hands have shifted the bit of scenery used in the last part and have rigged up instead at the back of the stage a drop, with some trees, and one or two wings. A portion of a fountain basin is visible. The Mother is sitting on the right with the two children by her side. The Son is on the same side, but away from the others. He seems bored, angry, and full of shame. The Father and the Stepdaughter are also seated toward the right front. On the other side (left) are the Actors, much in the positions they occupied before the curtain was lowered. Only the Manager is standing up in the middle of the stage, with his hand closed over his mouth, in the act of meditating.*)

THE MANAGER (*shaking his shoulders after a brief pause*): Ah yes: the second act! Leave it to me, leave it all to me as we arranged, and you'll see! It'll go fine!

THE STEPDAUGHTER: Our entry into his house (*indicates Father*) in spite of him . . . (*Indicates the Son.*)

THE MANAGER (*out of patience*): Leave it to me, I tell you!

THE STEPDAUGHTER: Do let it be clear, at any rate, that it is in spite of my wishes.

THE MOTHER (*from her corner, shaking her head*): For all the good that's come of it . . .

THE STEPDAUGHTER (*turning toward her quickly*): It doesn't matter. The more harm done us, the more remorse for him.

THE MANAGER (*impatiently*): I understand! Good Heavens! I understand! I'm taking it into account.

THE MOTHER (*supplicatingly*): I beg you, sir, to let it appear quite plain that for conscience' sake I did try in every way . . .

THE STEPDAUGHTER (*interrupting indignantly and continuing for the Mother*): . . . to pacify me, to dissuade me from spiting him. (*To Manager.*) Do as she wants: satisfy her, because it is true! I enjoy it immensely. Anyhow, as you can see, the meeker she is, the more she tries to get at his heart, the more distant and aloof does he become.

THE MANAGER: Are we going to begin this second act or not?

THE STEPDAUGHTER: I'm not going to talk any more now. But I must tell you this: you can't have the whole action take place in the garden, as you suggest. It isn't possible!

THE MANAGER: Why not?

THE STEPDAUGHTER: Because he (*indicates the Son again*) is always shut up alone in his room. And then there's all the part of that poor dazed-looking boy there which takes place indoors.

THE MANAGER: Maybe! On the other hand, you will understand — we can't change scenes three or four times in one act.

LEADING MAN: They used to once.

THE MANAGER: Yes, when the public was up to the level of that child there.

LEADING LADY: It makes the illusion easier.

THE FATHER (*irritated*): The illusion! For Heaven's sake, don't say illusion. Please don't use that word, which is particularly painful for us.

THE MANAGER (*astounded*): And why, if you please?

THE FATHER: It's painful, cruel, really cruel; and you ought to understand that.

THE MANAGER: But why? What ought we to say then? The illusion, I tell you, sir, which we've got to create for the audience. . . .

THE LEADING MAN: With our acting.

THE MANAGER: The illusion of a reality.

THE FATHER: I understand; but you, perhaps, do not understand us. Forgive me! You see . . . here for you and your actors, the thing is only — and rightly so . . . a kind of game. . . .

THE LEADING LADY (*interrupting indignantly*): A game! We're not children here, if you please! We are serious actors.

THE FATHER: I don't deny it. What I mean is the game, or play, of your art, which has to give, as the gentleman says, a perfect illusion of reality.

THE MANAGER: Precisely —!

THE FATHER: Now, if you consider the fact that we (*indicates himself and the other five Characters*),

as we are, have no other reality outside of this illusion. . . .

THE MANAGER (*astonished, looking at his Actors, who are also amazed*): And what does that mean?

THE FATHER (*after watching them for a moment with a wan smile*): As I say, sir, that which is a game of art for you is our sole reality. (*Brief pause. He goes a step or two nearer the Manager and adds.*) But not only for us, you know, by the way. Just you think it over well. (*Looks him in the eyes.*) Can you tell me who you are?

THE MANAGER (*perplexed, half smiling*): What? Who am I? I am myself.

THE FATHER: And if I were to tell you that that isn't true, because you and I . . . ?

THE MANAGER: I should say you were mad —! (*The Actors laugh.*)

THE FATHER: You're quite right to laugh: because we are all making believe here. (*To Manager.*) And you can therefore object that it's only for a joke that that gentleman there (*indicates the Leading Man*), who naturally is himself, has to be me, who am on the contrary myself — this thing you see here. You see I've caught you in a trap! (*The Actors laugh.*)

THE MANAGER (*annoyed*): But we've had all this over once before. Do you want to begin again?

THE FATHER: No, no! That wasn't my meaning! In fact, I should like to request you to abandon this game of art (*looking at the Leading Lady as if anticipating her*) which you are accustomed to play here with your actors, and to ask you seriously once again: who are you?

THE MANAGER (*astonished and irritated, turning to his Actors*): If this fellow here hasn't got a nerve! A man who calls himself a character comes and asks me who I am!

THE FATHER (*with dignity, but not offended*): A character, sir, may always ask a man who he is. Because a character has really a life of his own, marked with his especial characteristics; for which reason he is always "somebody." But a man — I'm not speaking of you now — may very well be "nobody."

THE MANAGER: Yes, but you are asking these questions of me, the boss, the manager! Do you understand?

THE FATHER: But only in order to know if you, as you really are now, see yourself as you once were with all the illusions that were yours then, with all the things both inside and outside of you as they seemed to you — as they were then indeed for you. Well, sir, if you think of all those illusions that mean nothing to you now, of all those things which don't even *seem* to you to exist anymore, while once they *were* for you, don't you feel that — I won't say these boards — but the very earth under your feet is sinking away from you when you reflect that in the same way this *you* as you feel it today — all this present reality of yours — is fated to seem a mere illusion to you tomorrow?

THE MANAGER (*without having understood much, but astonished by the specious argument*): Well, well! And where does all this take us anyway?

THE FATHER: Oh, nowhere! It's only to show you that if we (*indicating the Characters*) have no other reality beyond the illusion, you too must not count overmuch on your reality as you feel it today, since, like that of yesterday, it may prove an illusion for you tomorrow.

THE MANAGER (*determining to make fun of him*): Ah, excellent! Then you'll be saying next that you, with this comedy of yours that you brought here to act, are truer and more real than I am.

THE FATHER (*with the greatest seriousness*): But of course; without doubt!

THE MANAGER: Ah, really?

THE FATHER: Why, I thought you'd understand that from the beginning.

THE MANAGER: More real than I?

THE FATHER: If your reality can change from one day to another. . . .

THE MANAGER: But everyone knows it can change. It is always changing, the same as anyone else's.

THE FATHER (*with a cry*): No, sir, not ours! Look here! That is the very difference! Our reality doesn't change: it can't change! It can't be other than what it is, because it is already fixed for ever. It's terrible. Ours is an immutable reality which should make you shudder when you approach us if you are really conscious of the fact that your reality is a mere transitory and fleeting illusion, taking this form today and that tomorrow, according to the conditions, according to your will, your sentiments, which in turn are controlled by an intellect that shows them to you today in one manner and tomorrow . . . who knows how? . . . Illusions of reality represented in this fatuous comedy of life that never ends, nor can ever end! Because if tomorrow it were to end . . . then why, all would be finished.

THE MANAGER: Oh for God's sake, will you *at least* finish with this philosophizing and let us try and shape this comedy which you yourself have brought me here? You argue and philosophize a bit too much, my dear sir. You know you seem to me almost, almost . . . (*Stops and looks him over from head to foot.*) Ah, by the way, I think you introduced yourself to me as a — what shall . . . we say — a "character," created by an author who

did not afterward care to make a drama of his own creations.

THE FATHER: It is the simple truth, sir.

THE MANAGER: Nonsense! Cut that out, please! None of us believes it, because it isn't a thing, as you must recognize yourself, which one can believe seriously. If you want to know, it seems to me you are trying to imitate the manner of a certain author whom I heartily detest — I warn you — although I have unfortunately bound myself to put on one of his works. As a matter of fact, I was just starting to rehearse it, when you arrived. (*Turning to the Actors.*) And this is what we've gained — out of the frying-pan into the fire!

THE FATHER: I don't know to what author you may be alluding, but believe me I feel what I think; and I seem to be philosophizing only for those who do not think what they feel, because they blind themselves with their own sentiment. I know that for many people this self-blinding seems much more "human"; but the contrary is really true. For man never reasons so much and becomes so introspective as when he suffers; since he is anxious to get at the cause of his sufferings, to learn who has produced them, and whether it is just or unjust that he should have to bear them. On the other hand, when he is happy, he takes his happiness as it comes and doesn't analyze it, just as if happiness were his right. The animals suffer without reasoning about their sufferings. But take the case of a man who suffers and begins to reason about it. Oh no! it can't be allowed! Let him suffer like an animal, and then — ah yes, he is "human"!

THE MANAGER: Look here! Look here! You're off again, philosophizing worse than ever.

THE FATHER: Because I suffer, sir! I'm not philosophizing: I'm crying aloud the reason of my sufferings.

THE MANAGER (*makes brusque movement as he is taken with a new idea*): I should like to know if anyone has ever heard of a character who gets right out of his part and perorates and speechifies as you do. Have you ever heard of a case? I haven't.

THE FATHER: You have never met such a case, sir, because authors, as a rule, hide the labor of their creations. When the characters are really alive before their author, the latter does nothing but follow them in their action, in other words, in the situations which they suggest to him; and he has to will them the way they will themselves — for there's trouble if he doesn't. When a character is born, he acquires at once such an independence, even of his own author, that he can be imagined by everybody even in many other situations where the author never dreamed of placing him; and so he acquires for himself a meaning which the author never thought of giving him.

THE MANAGER: Yes, yes, I know this.

THE FATHER: What is there then to marvel at in us? Imagine such a misfortune for characters as I have described to you: to be born of an author's fantasy, and be denied life by him; and then answer me if these characters left alive, and yet without life, weren't right in doing what they did do and are doing now, after they have attempted everything in their power to persuade him to give them their stage life. We've all tried him in turn, I, she (*indicating the Stepdaughter*) and she (*indicating the Mother*).

THE STEPDAUGHTER: It's true. I too have sought to tempt him, many, many times, when he has been sitting at his writing table, feeling a bit melancholy, at the twilight hour. He would sit in his armchair too lazy to switch on the light, and all the shadows that crept into his room were full of our presence coming to tempt him. (*As if she saw herself still there by the writing table, and was annoyed by the presence of the Actors.*) Oh, if you would only go away, go away and leave us alone — mother here with that son of hers — I with that child — that boy there always alone — and then I with him (*just hints at the Father*) — and then I alone, alone . . . in those shadows! (*Makes a sudden movement as if in the vision she has of herself illuminating those shadows she wanted to seize hold of herself.*) Ah! my life! my life! Oh, what scenes we proposed to him — and I tempted him more than any of the others!

THE FATHER: Maybe. But perhaps it was your fault that he refused to give us life: because you were too insistent, too troublesome.

THE STEPDAUGHTER: Nonsense! Didn't he make me so himself? (*Goes close to the Manager to tell him as if in confidence.*) In my opinion he abandoned us in a fit of depression, of disgust for the ordinary theater as the public knows it and likes it.

THE SON: Exactly what it was, sir; exactly that!

THE FATHER: Not at all! Don't believe it for a minute. Listen to me! You'll be doing quite right to modify, as you suggest, the excesses both of this girl here, who wants to do too much, and of this young man, who won't do anything at all.

THE SON: No, nothing!

THE MANAGER: You too get over the mark occasionally, my dear sir, if I may say so.

THE FATHER: I? When? Where?

THE MANAGER: Always! Continuously! Then there's this insistence of yours in trying to make us believe you are a character. And then too, you must really argue and philosophize less, you know, much less.

THE FATHER: Well, if you want to take away from me the possibility of representing the torment of my spirit which never gives me peace, you will be suppressing me: that's all. Every true man, sir, who is a little above the level of the beasts and plants does not live for the sake of living, without knowing how to live; but he lives so as to give a meaning and a value of his own to life. For me this is *everything*. I cannot give up this, just to represent a mere fact as she (*indicating the Stepdaughter*) wants. It's all very well for her, since her "vendetta" lies in the "fact." I'm not going to do it. It destroys my *raison d'être*.

THE MANAGER: Your *raison d'être*! Oh, we're going ahead fine! First she starts off, and then you jump in. At this rate, we'll never finish.

THE FATHER: Now, don't be offended! Have it your own way — provided, however, that within the limits of the parts you assign us each one's sacrifice isn't too great.

THE MANAGER: You've got to understand that you can't go on arguing at your own pleasure. Drama is action, sir, action and not confounded philosophy.

THE FATHER: All right. I'll do just as much arguing and philosophizing as everybody does when he is considering his own torments.

THE MANAGER: If the drama permits! But for Heaven's sake, man, let's get along and come to the scene.

THE STEPDAUGHTER: It seems to me we've got too much action with our coming into his house. (*Indicating Father.*) You said, before, you couldn't change the scene every five minutes.

THE MANAGER: Of course not. What we've got to do is to combine and group up all the facts in one simultaneous, close-knit action. We can't have it as you want, with your little brother wandering like a ghost from room to room, hiding behind doors and meditating a project which — what did you say it did to him?

THE STEPDAUGHTER: Consumes him, sir, wastes him away!

THE MANAGER: Well, it may be. And then at the same time, you want the little girl there to be playing in the garden . . . one in the house, and the other in the garden; isn't that it?

THE STEPDAUGHTER: Yes, in the sun, in the sun! That is my only pleasure: to see her happy and careless in the garden after the misery and squalor of the horrible room where we all four slept together. And I had to sleep with her — I, do you understand? — with my vile contaminated body next to hers; with her folding me fast in her loving little arms. In the garden, whenever she spied me, she would run to take me by the hand. She didn't care for the big flowers, only the little ones; and she loved to show me them and pet me.

THE MANAGER: Well then, we'll have it in the garden. Everything shall happen in the garden; and we'll group the other scenes there. (*Calls a Stage Hand.*) Here, a backcloth with trees and something to do as a fountain basin. (*Turning round to look at the back of the stage.*) Ah, you've fixed it up. Good! (*To Stepdaughter.*) This is just to give an idea, of course. The Boy, instead of hiding behind the doors, will wander about here in the garden, hiding behind the trees. But it's going to be rather difficult to find a child to do that scene with you where she shows you the flowers. (*Turning to the Boy.*) Come forward a little, will you please? Let's try it now! Come along! come along! (*Then seeing him come shyly forward, full of fear and looking lost.*) It's a nice business, this lad here. What's the matter with him? We'll have to give him a word or two to say. (*Goes close to him, puts a hand on his shoulders, and leads him behind one of the trees.*) Come on! come on! Let me see you a little! Hide here . . . yes, like that. Try and show your head just a little as if you were looking for someone. . . . (*Goes back to observe the effect, when the Boy at once goes through the action.*) Excellent! fine! (*Turning to Stepdaughter.*) Suppose the little girl there were to surprise him as he looks round, and run over to him, so we could give him a word or two to say?

THE STEPDAUGHTER: It's useless to hope he will speak, as long as that fellow there is here. . . . (*Indicates the Son.*) You must send him away first.

THE SON (*jumping up*): Delighted! Delighted! I don't ask for anything better. (*Begins to move away.*)

THE MANAGER (*at once stopping him*): No! No! Where are you going? Wait a bit!

(*The Mother gets up alarmed and terrified at the thought that he is really about to go away. Instinctively she lifts her arms to prevent him, without, however, leaving her seat.*)

THE SON (*to Manager, who stops him*): I've got nothing to do with this affair. Let me go, please! Let me go!

THE MANAGER: What do you mean by saying you've got nothing to do with this?

THE STEPDAUGHTER (*calmly, with irony*): Don't bother to stop him: he won't go away.

THE FATHER: He has to act the terrible scene in the garden with his mother.

THE SON (*suddenly resolute and with dignity*): I shall act nothing at all. I've said so from the very beginning. (*To the Manager.*) Let me go!

THE STEPDAUGHTER (*going over to the Manager*): Al-

low me? (*Puts down the Manager's arm which is restraining the Son.*) Well, go away then, if you want to! (*The Son looks at her with contempt and hatred. She laughs and says.*) You see, he can't, he can't go away! He is obliged to stay here, indissolubly bound to the chain. If I, who fly off when that happens which has to happen because I can't bear him — if I am still here and support that face and expression of his, you can well imagine that he is unable to move. He has to remain here, has to stop with that nice father of his, and that mother whose only son he is. (*Turning to the Mother.*) Come on, mother, come along! (*Turning to Manager to indicate her.*) You see, she was getting up to keep him back. (*To the Mother, beckoning her with her hand.*) Come on, come on! (*Then to Manager.*) You can imagine how little she wants to show these actors of yours what she really feels; but so eager is she to get near him that. . . . There, you see? She is willing to act her part. (*And in fact, the Mother approaches him; and as soon as the Stepdaughter has finished speaking, opens her arms to signify that she consents.*)

THE SON (*suddenly*): No! no! If I can't go away, then I'll stop here; but I repeat: I act nothing!

THE FATHER (*to Manager excitedly*): You can force him, sir.

THE SON: Nobody can force me.

THE FATHER: I can.

THE STEPDAUGHTER: Wait a minute, wait . . . First of all, the baby has to go to the fountain. . . . (*Runs to take the Child and leads her to the fountain.*)

THE MANAGER: Yes, yes of course; that's it. Both at the same time.

(*The Second Lady Lead and the Juvenile Lead at this point separate themselves from the group of Actors. One watches the Mother attentively; the other moves about studying the movements and manner of the Son whom he will have to act.*)

THE SON (*to Manager*): What do you mean by both at the same time? It isn't right. There was no scene between me and her. (*Indicates the Mother.*) Ask her how it was!

THE MOTHER: Yes, it's true. I had come into his room. . . .

THE SON: Into my room, do you understand? Nothing to do with the garden.

THE MANAGER: It doesn't matter. Haven't I told you we've got to group the action?

THE SON (*observing the Juvenile Lead studying him*): What do you want?

THE JUVENILE LEAD: Nothing! I was just looking at you.

THE SON (*turning toward the Second Lady Lead*):

Ah! she's at it too: to re-act her part! (*Indicating the Mother.*)

THE MANAGER: Exactly! And it seems to me that you ought to be grateful to them for their interest.

THE SON: Yes, but haven't you yet perceived that it isn't possible to live in front of a mirror which not only freezes us with the image of ourselves, but throws our likeness back at us with a horrible grimace?

THE FATHER: That is true, absolutely true. You must see that.

THE MANAGER (*to Second Lady Lead and Juvenile Lead*): He's right! Move away from them!

THE SON: Do as you like. I'm out of this!

THE MANAGER: Be quiet, you, will you? And let me hear your mother! (*To Mother.*) You were saying you had entered. . . .

THE MOTHER: Yes, into his room, because I couldn't stand it any longer. I went to empty my heart to him of all the anguish that tortures me. . . . But as soon as he saw me come in. . . .

THE SON: Nothing happened! There was no scene. I went away, that's all! I don't care for scenes!

THE MOTHER: It's true, true. That's how it was.

THE MANAGER: Well now, we've got to do this bit between you and him. It's indispensable.

THE MOTHER: I'm ready . . . when you are ready. If you could only find a chance for me to tell him what I feel here in my heart.

THE FATHER (*going to Son in a great rage*): You'll do this for your mother, for your mother, do you understand?

THE SON (*quite determined*): I do nothing!

THE FATHER (*taking hold of him and shaking him*): For God's sake, do as I tell you! Don't you hear your mother asking you for a favor? Haven't you even got the guts to be a son?

THE SON (*taking hold of the Father*): No! No! And for God's sake stop it, or else. . . . (*General agitation. The Mother, frightened, tries to separate them.*)

THE MOTHER (*pleading*): Please! please!

THE FATHER (*not leaving hold of the Son*): You've got to obey, do you hear?

THE SON (*almost crying from rage*): What does it mean, this madness you've got? (*They separate.*) Have you no decency, that you insist on showing everyone our shame? I won't do it! I won't! And I stand for the will of our author in this. He didn't want to put us on the stage, after all!

THE MANAGER: Man alive! You came here . . .

THE SON (*indicating Father*): He did! I didn't!

THE MANAGER: Aren't you here now?

THE SON: It was his wish, and he dragged us along with him. He's told you not only the things that did happen, but also things that have never happened at all.

THE MANAGER: Well, tell me then what did happen. You went out of your room without saying a word?

THE SON: Without a word, so as to avoid a scene!

THE MANAGER: And then what did you do?

THE SON: Nothing . . . walking in the garden. . . . (*Hesitates for a moment with expression of gloom.*)

THE MANAGER (*coming closer to him, interested by his extraordinary reserve*): Well, well . . . walking in the garden. . . .

THE SON (*exasperated*): Why on earth do you insist? It's horrible!

(*The Mother trembles, sobs, and looks toward the fountain.*)

THE MANAGER (*slowly observing the glance and turning toward the Son with increasing apprehension*): The baby?

THE SON: There in the fountain. . . .

THE FATHER (*pointing with tender pity to the Mother*): She was following him at the moment. . . .

THE MANAGER (*to the Son anxiously*): And then you. . . .

THE SON: I ran over to her; I was jumping in to drag her out when I saw something that froze my blood . . . the boy standing stock still, with eyes like a madman's, watching his little drowned sister, in the fountain! (*The Stepdaughter bends over the fountain to hide the Child. She sobs.*) Then. . . . (*A revolver shot rings out behind the trees where the Boy is hidden.*)

THE MOTHER (*with a cry of terror runs over in that direction together with several of the Actors amid general confusion*): My son! My son! (*Then amid the cries and exclamations one hears her voice.*) Help! Help!

THE MANAGER (*pushing the Actors aside while they lift up the Boy and carry him off*): Is he really wounded?

SOME ACTORS: He's dead! dead!

OTHER ACTORS: No, no, it's only make-believe, it's only pretense!

THE FATHER (*with a terrible cry*): Pretense? Reality, sir, reality!

THE MANAGER: Pretense? Reality? To hell with it all! Never in my life has such a thing happened to me. I've lost a whole day over these people, a whole day!

Eugene O'Neill

Eugene O'Neill (1888–1953) is today a major figure in American drama. His enormous output is in the tradition of realism established by Strindberg and Ibsen, and his early plays, such as *Anna Christie* (1921), introduced Americans to the techniques of the great European realists. Realism for Americans was a move away from the sentimental comedies, the pathetic dramas, and melodrama that dominated the American stage from before the Civil War to World War I. O'Neill rejected the theater in which his father had thrived. James O'Neill had long been a star, traveling across the country in his production of *The Count of Monte Cristo*, which had made him rich but also had made him a prisoner of a single role.

Eugene O'Neill won the Pulitzer Prize for drama three times in the 1920s and the Nobel Prize for literature in 1936, but he was rarely a popular success in his own day. His plays have been mainstays of the American theater since his death, partly because some were published posthumously and partly because some of America's finest actors have taken a strong interest in his work and have produced it and acted in it both on the stage and on television. From the 1950s to the 1990s, the late Colleen Dewhurst and Jason Robards, Jr., in particular, gave some magnificent performances and interpretations of O'Neill's work.

The young O'Neill was a romantic in the popular sense of the word. After a year at Princeton University, he began to travel on the sea. His jaunts took him to South America as a young man, and he once wound up virtually broke and without resources in Buenos Aires. When he returned to America he studied for a year with George Pierce Baker, the most famous drama teacher of his day. Eventually he took up residence in Provincetown, Massachusetts, where a group of people dedicated to theater — including the playwright Susan Glaspell — began to put on plays in their living rooms. When their audiences spilled over, they created the Provincetown Playhouse, the theater in which many of O'Neill's earliest pieces were first performed.

The subjects of many of O'Neill's plays were not especially appealing to general theater audiences. Those who hoped for light comedy and a good laugh or light comedy and a good cry found the intensity of his dark vision of the world to be overwhelming. They came for mere entertainment, and he was providing them with frightening visions of the soul's interior. The glum and painful surroundings of *Anna Christie* (1921) and the brutality of the lower-class coal stoker in *The Hairy*

Ape (1922) were foreign to the comfortable middle-class audiences who supported commercial theater in America. They found O'Neill's characters to be haunted by family agonies, affections never given, ambitions never realized, pains never assuaged. Despite his remarkable abilities and the power of his drama, audiences often did not know what to make of him. To a large extent, his acceptance came on waves of shock, as had the acceptance of the Scandinavian realists.

O'Neill's early work is marked by a variety of experiments with theatrical effects and moods. He tried to use the primary influences of Greek drama in such plays as *Desire Under the Elms* (1924), which has been described by critics as Greek tragedy, and *Mourning Becomes Electra* (1931), which in its original version took three days to perform. But many of his early plays now seem dated and strange. His most impressive plays are his later work, such as *Ah, Wilderness!* (1933), *The Iceman Cometh* (1939), *Long Day's Journey into Night* (1939–1941), *A Moon for the Misbegotten* (1943), and *A Touch of the Poet* (1935–1942), which was performed posthumously in 1957.

Desire Under the Elms

Desire Under the Elms (1924) is Eugene O'Neill's first effort at writing in the style of Greek tragedy. He did not follow the Greek tradition and choose a great figure of noble birth about whom the fates would unravel their mystery. Rather, he was deliberately democratic and American, choosing a New England farmer and his family as the protagonists of his drama. The powers of fate that would animate a Greek tragedy are expressed in the emotional forces of jealousy, resentment, lust, and incestuous love.

O'Neill chose to place his play on a typically rocky New England soil, which in many ways bears a striking resemblance to the rocky soil of Athens and the Greek coastline. The unyielding toughness of life on that land contrasts with the easy life to be made from gold mining in California. Ephraim Cabot, the seventy-five-year-old father, has been made hard and physically powerful by his work. He has just taken a young and scheming wife, Abbie. Eben Cabot, one of Ephraim's sons, has decided to stay on the farm while his two brothers go to California and try to put New England behind them.

The sense of having been dispossessed of his farm drives Eben to hate his new mother, who married the elder Cabot merely to inherit his farm when he died. Abbie knows that Cabot is not a satisfying sexual partner, but she sees Eben as a reasonable substitute. At first the sparring between Abbie and Eben is based on calculating self-interest, but eventually their feelings for each other become overpowering. Lust turns to love, and the desires and emotions they thought they could control are quite out of control. The son they produce is passed off as old Cabot's, although the townspeople have no illusion about whose child it is.

The farm itself is a powerful presence in the play. Whenever old Cabot thinks he should give up and follow the promise of easy money in California, he gets vibrations from God telling him to stay. God operates for Ephraim as the oracle in *Oedipus Rex* does, giving him a message that is painful but that he is compelled to obey. The rocks on the farm are unforgiving, and so is the fate that Abbie and Eben face. Theirs is an impossible love; everything they do to prove their love condemns them even more. The forces of fate center on the farm. When the play opens, Eben says of it, "God! Purty!" When the play ends, the sheriff praises the farm and says he surely would like to own it, striking a clear note of irony: The agony of the play is rooted in lust — lust for the farm that parallels the lust between Abbie and Eben.

The play is haunted by the ghost of Eben's mother, whom Ephraim married primarily for her farm. When the ghost of Eben's mother is exorcised it is only because the cycle of retribution has begun. Old Cabot has committed a crime against her, and now he must become the victim.

The language of the dialogue is that of New England in the mid-nineteenth century. O'Neill lived in New England and understood the ways and the language of its people. He seems to have imagined the "down-east" flavor of Maine in the language, and he has been careful to build the proper pronunciation into the dialogue. This folksy way of speaking helps emphasize the peasantlike qualities in these New England farmers. O'Neill's careful use of language is reminiscent of Synge's masterful representation of the Irish-English speech of the Aran Islanders in *Riders to the Sea*, a play that is also a kind of folk tragedy.

The language of O'Neill's characters has a rocky toughness at times. Characters are laconic — they often answer in a single word: "Ay-eh." Faithful to his vision of the simple speech of country folk, O'Neill avoids giving them elaborate poetic soliloquies. Instead, he shows how, despite their limited language, rural people feel profound emotions and act on them.

O'Neill carefully links Abbie with Queen Phaedra, who in Euripides' play *Hippolytus* and in Racine's seventeenth-century play *Phèdre* finds herself uncontrollably desiring her husband's son as a lover. Racine and Racine's audience could easily imagine such intense emotions overwhelming a noblewoman because they thought that nobility felt everything more intensely and lived more intensely than ordinary people. But

O'Neill is trying to make his audience see that even unlettered farm people can feel as deeply as tragic heroes of any age. The Cabots are victims of passion. They share their fate with the great families of the Greek tragedies.

Desire Under the Elms in Performance

Desire Under the Elms was first performed in Greenwich Village in 1924 under the auspices of the Provincetown Players. A year later it appeared on Broadway for thirty-six weeks, a long run for a tragedy. Its first reviewers were courteous but puzzled. They compared the play with earlier O'Neill works, remarking on its "tragic gloom and irony" and praising its language. At the Los Angeles production in 1926, the cast was arrested for "giving an obscene play." The sexual themes offended theatergoers in California, and even those who defended the play admitted that the text would be offensive to some members of the audience.

Because the English censor banned the play until 1938, its first European production was in Prague's National Theatre in 1925. Its Czech title translated as "The Farm Under the Elms." The director used a highly stylized set influenced by the Moscow Art Theatre and later described as "a sort of two-storied wooded edifice . . . rather like a log cabin multiplied by four."

Other earlier European productions followed in Moscow in 1932, in Stockholm in 1933, and finally in London in 1940. The 1952 New York revival was not successful. The 1963 revival at the Circle in the Square in New York starred George C. Scott and his wife Colleen Dewhurst. Jose Quintero, a notable interpreter of O'Neill, directed. Critics complained about "awkward" echoes of Greek tragedy while admitting that the play had an uncanny power despite its flaws. It ran for 380 performances.

The play has been revived often: in Boston in 1967; at the Berkshire Theater Festival in 1974; at the Roundabout Theater in New York, directed by Terry Schrieber, in 1984; and by numerous local theater groups. In 1978 Edward Thomas staged it at Connecticut College in New London as an opera. A creditable production, it emphasized the play's American folk qualities.

Eugene O'Neill (1888–1953)
Desire Under the Elms

1924

Characters

EPHRAIM CABOT
SIMEON ⎫
PETER   ⎬ *his sons*
EBEN   ⎭
ABBIE PUTNAM
YOUNG GIRL, TWO FARMERS, *the* FIDDLER, *a* SHERIFF, *and other folk from the neighboring farms.*

The action of the entire play takes place in, and immediately outside of, the Cabot farmhouse in New England, in the year 1850. The south end of the house faces front to a stone wall with a wooden gate at center opening on a country road. The house is in good condition but in need of paint. Its walls are a sickly grayish, the green of the shutters faded. Two enormous elms are on each side of the house. They bend their trailing branches down over the roof. They appear to protect and at the same time subdue. There is a sinister maternity in their aspect, a crushing, jealous absorption. They have developed from their intimate contact with the life of man in the house an appalling humaneness. They brood oppressively over the house. They are like exhausted women resting their sagging breasts and hands and hair on its roof, and when it rains their tears trickle down monotonously and rot on the shingles.

There is a path running from the gate around the right corner of the house to the front door. A narrow porch is on this side. The end wall facing us has two windows in its upper story, two larger ones on the floor below. The two upper are those of the father's bedroom and that of the brothers. On the left, ground floor, is the kitchen — on the right, the parlor, the shades of which are always drawn down.

PART I · Scene 1

(Exterior of the farmhouse. It is sunset of a day at the beginning of summer in the year 1850. There is no wind and everything is still. The sky above the roof is suffused with deep colors, the green of the elms glows, but the house is in shadow, seeming pale and washed out by contrast.)

(A door opens and Eben Cabot comes to the end of the porch and stands looking down the road to the right. He has a large bell in his hand and this he swings mechanically, awakening a deafening clangor. Then he puts his hands on his hips and stares up at the sky. He sighs with a puzzled awe and blurts out with halting appreciation.)

EBEN: God! Purty! (*His eyes fall and he stares about him frowningly. He is twenty-five, tall and sinewy. His face is well formed, good-looking, but its expression is resentful and defensive. His defiant, dark eyes remind one of a wild animal's in captivity. Each day is a cage in which he finds himself trapped but inwardly unsubdued. There is a fierce repressed vitality about him. He has black hair, mustache, a thin curly trace of beard. He is dressed in rough farm clothes.*)

(He spits on the ground with intense disgust, turns, and goes back into the house.)

(Simeon and Peter come in from their work in the fields. They are tall men, much older than their half-brother [Simeon is thirty-nine and Peter thirty-seven], built on a squarer, simpler model, fleshier in body, more bovine and homelier in face, shrewder and more practical. Their shoulders stoop a bit from years of farm work. They clump heavily along in their clumsy thick-soled boots caked with earth. Their clothes, their faces, hands, bare arms, and throats are earth-stained. They smell of earth. They stand together for a moment in front of the house and, as if with the one impulse, stare dumbly up at the sky, leaning on their hoes. Their faces have a compressed, unresigned expression. As they look upward, this softens.)

SIMEON (*grudgingly*): Purty.
PETER: Ay-eh.
SIMEON (*suddenly*): Eighteen year ago.
PETER: What?
SIMEON: Jenn. My woman. She died.
PETER: I'd fergot.
SIMEON: I rec'lect — now an' agin. Makes it lonesome. She'd hair long's a hoss' tail — an' yaller like gold!
PETER: Waal — she's gone. (*This with indifferent finality — then after a pause.*) They's gold in the West, Sim.

SIMEON (*still under the influence of sunset — vaguely*): In the sky?

PETER: Waal — in a manner o' speakin' — that's the promise. (*Growing excited.*) Gold in the sky — in the West — Golden Gate — Californi-a! — Goldest West! — fields o' gold!

SIMEON (*excited in his turn*): Fortunes layin' just atop o' the ground waitin' t' be picked! Solomon's mines, they says! (*For a moment they continue looking up at the sky — then their eyes drop.*)

PETER (*with sardonic bitterness*): Here — it's stones atop o' the ground — stones atop o' stones — makin' stone walls — year atop o' year — him 'n' yew 'n' me 'n' then Eben — makin' stone walls fur him to fence us in!

SIMEON: We've wuked. Give our strength. Give our years. Plowed 'em under in the ground — (*He stamps rebelliously.*) — rottin' — makin' soil for his crops! (*A pause.*) Waal — the farm pays good for hereabouts.

PETER: If we plowed in Californi-a, they'd be lumps o' gold in the furrow!

SIMEON: Californi-a's t'other side o' earth, a'most. We got t' calc'late —

PETER (*after a pause*): 'Twould be hard fur me, too, to give up what we've 'arned here by our sweat. (*A pause. Eben sticks his head out of the dining room window, listening.*)

SIMEON: Ay-eh. (*A pause.*) Mebbe — he'll die soon.

PETER (*doubtfully*): Mebbe.

SIMEON: Mebbe — fur all we knows — he's dead now.

PETER: Ye'd need proof.

SIMEON: He's been gone two months — with no word.

PETER: Left us in the fields an evenin' like this. Hitched up an' druv off into the West. That's plum on-nateral. He hain't never been off this farm 'ceptin' t' the village in thirty year or more, not since he married Eben's maw. (*A pause. Shrewdly.*) I calc'late we might git him declared crazy by the court.

SIMEON: He skinned 'em too slick. He got the best o' all on 'em. They'd never b'lieve him crazy. (*A pause.*) We got t' wait — till he's underground.

EBEN (*with a sardonic chuckle*): Honor thy father! (*They turn startled, and stare at him. He grins, then scowls.*) I pray he's died. (*They stare at him. He continues matter-of-factly.*) Supper's ready.

SIMEON AND PETER (*together*): Ayeh.

EBEN (*gazing up at the sky*): Sun's downin' purty.

SIMEON AND PETER (*together*): Ay-eh. They's gold in the West.

EBEN: Ay-eh. (*Pointing.*) Yonder atop o' the hill pasture, ye mean?

SIMEON AND PETER (*together*): In Californi-a!

EBEN: Hunh? (*Stares at them indifferently for a second, then drawls.*) Waal — supper's gittin' cold. (*He turns back into kitchen.*)

SIMEON (*startled — smacks his lips*): I air hungry!

PETER (*sniffing*): I smells bacon!

SIMEON (*with hungry appreciation*): Bacon's good!

PETER (*in same tone*): Bacon's bacon! (*They turn, shouldering each other, their bodies bumping and rubbing together as they hurry clumsily to their food, like two friendly oxen toward their evening meal. They disappear around the right corner of house and can be heard entering the door.*)

Scene II

(*The color fades from the sky. Twilight begins. The interior of the kitchen is now visible. A pine table is at center, a cook-stove in the right rear corner, four rough wooden chairs, a tallow candle on the table. In the middle of the rear wall is fastened a big advertising poster with a ship in full sail and the word "California" in big letters. Kitchen utensils hang from nails. Everything is neat and in order but the atmosphere is of a men's camp kitchen rather than that of a home.*)

(*Places for three are laid. Eben takes boiled potatoes and bacon from the stove and puts them on the table, also a loaf of bread and a crock of water. Simeon and Peter shoulder in, slump down in their chairs without a word. Eben joins them. The three eat in silence for a moment, the two elder as naturally unrestrained as beasts of the field, Eben picking at his food without appetite, glancing at them with a tolerant dislike.*)

SIMEON (*suddenly turns to Eben*): Looky here! Ye'd oughtn't t' said that, Eben.

PETER: 'Twa'n't righteous.

EBEN: What?

SIMEON: Ye prayed he'd died.

EBEN: Waal — don't yew pray it? (*A pause.*)

PETER: He's our Paw.

EBEN (*violently*): Not mine!

SIMEON (*dryly*): Ye'd not let no one else say that about yer Maw! Ha! (*He gives one abrupt sardonic guffaw. Peter grins.*)

EBEN (*very pale*): I meant — I hain't his'n — I hain't like him — he hain't me!

PETER (*dryly*): Wait till ye've growed his age!

EBEN (*intensely*): I'm Maw — every drop o' blood! (*A pause. They stare at him with indifferent curiosity.*)

PETER (*reminiscently*): She was good t' Sim 'n' me. A good Stepmaw's scurse.

SIMEON: She was good t' everyone.

EBEN (*greatly moved, gets to his feet and makes an awkward bow to each of them — stammering*): I be thankful t' ye. I'm her — her heir. (*He sits down in confusion.*)

PETER (*after a pause — judicially*): She was good even t' him.

EBEN (*fiercely*): An' fur thanks he killed her!

SIMEON (*after a pause*): No one never kills nobody. It's allus somethin'. That's the murderer.

EBEN: Didn't he slave Maw t' death?

PETER: He's slaved himself t' death. He's slaved Sim 'n' me 'n' yew t' death — on'y none o' us hain't died — yit.

SIMEON: It's somethin' — drivin' him — t' drive us!

EBEN (*vengefully*): Waal — I hold him t' jedgment! (*Then scornfully.*) Somethin'! What's somethin'?

SIMEON: Dunno.

EBEN (*sardonically*): What's drivin' yew to California, mebbe? (*They look at him in surprise.*) Oh, I've heerd ye! (*Then, after a pause.*) But ye'll never go t' the gold fields!

PETER (*assertively*): Mebbe!

EBEN: Whar'll ye git the money?

PETER: We kin walk. It's an a'mighty ways — California — but if yew was t' put all the steps we've walked on this farm end t' end we'd be in the moon!

EBEN: The Injuns'll skulp ye on the plains.

SIMEON (*with grim humor*): We'll mebbe make 'em pay a hair fur a hair!

EBEN (*decisively*): But t'aint that. Ye won't never go because ye'll wait here fur yer share o' the farm, thinkin' allus he'll die soon.

SIMEON (*after a pause*): We've a right.

PETER: Two-thirds belongs t'us.

EBEN (*jumping to his feet*): Ye've no right! She wa'n't yewr Maw! It was her farm! Didn't he steal it from her? She's dead. It's my farm.

SIMEON (*sardonically*): Tell that t' Paw — when he comes! I'll bet ye a dollar he'll laugh — fur once in his life. Ha! (*He laughs himself in one single mirthless bark.*)

PETER (*amused in turn, echoes his brother*): Ha!

SIMEON (*after a pause*): What've ye got held agin us, Eben? Year arter year it's skulked in yer eye — somethin'.

PETER: Ay-eh.

EBEN: Ay-eh. They's somethin'. (*Suddenly exploding.*) Why didn't ye never stand between him 'n' my Maw when he was slavin' her to her grave — t' pay her back fur the kindness she done t' yew? (*There is a long pause. They stare at him in surprise.*)

SIMEON: Waal — the stock'd got t' be watered.

PETER: 'R they was woodin' t' do.

SIMEON: 'R plowin'.

PETER: 'R hayin'.

SIMEON: 'R spreadin' manure.

PETER: 'R weedin'.

SIMEON: 'R prunin'.

PETER: 'R milkin'.

EBEN (*breaking in harshly*): An' makin' walls — stone atop o' stone — makin' walls till yer heart's a stone ye heft up out o' the way o' growth onto a stone wall t' wall in yer heart!

SIMEON (*matter-of-factly*): We never had no time t' meddle.

PETER (*to Eben*): Yew was fifteen afore yer Maw died — an' big fur yer age. Why didn't ye never do nothin'?

EBEN (*harshly*): They was chores t' do, wa'n't they? (*A pause — then slowly.*) It was on'y arter she died I come to think o' it. Me cookin' — doin' her work — that made me know her, suffer her sufferin' — she'd come back t' help — come back t' bile potatoes — come back t' fry bacon — come back t' bake biscuits — come back all cramped up t' shake the fire, an' carry ashes, her eyes weepin' an' bloody with smoke an' cinders same's they used t' be. She still comes back — stands by the stove thar in the evenin' — she can't find it nateral sleepin' an' restin' in peace. She can't git used t' bein' free — even in her grave.

SIMEON: She never complained none.

EBEN: She'd got too tired. She'd got too used t' bein' too tired. That was what she done. (*With vengeful passion.*) An' sooner'r later, I'll meddle. I'll say the thin's I didn't say then t' him! I'll yell 'em at the top o' my lungs. I'll see t' it my Maw gits some rest an' sleep in her grave! (*He sits down again, relapsing into a brooding silence. They look at him with a queer indifferent curiosity.*)

PETER (*after a pause*): Whar in tarnation d'ye s'pose he went, Sim?

SIMEON: Dunno. He druv off in the buggy, all spick an' span, with the mare all breshed an' shiny, druv off clackin' his tongue an' wavin' his whip. I remember it right well. I was finishin' plowin', it was spring an' May an' sunset, an' gold in the West, an' he druv off into it. I yells "Whar ye goin', Paw?" an' he hauls up by the stone wall a jiffy. His old snake's eyes was glitterin' in the sun like he'd been drinkin' a jugful an' he says with a mule's grin: "Don't ye run away till I come back!"

PETER: Wonder if he knowed we was wantin' fur California?

SIMEON: Mebbe. I didn't say nothin' and he says, lookin' kinder queer an' sick: "I been hearin' the hens cluckin' an' the roosters crowin' all the durn day. I been listenin' t' the cows lowin' an' everythin' else kickin' up till I can't stand it no more. It's spring an' I'm feelin' damned," he says. "Damned like an old bare hickory tree fit on'y fur burnin'," he says. An' then I calc'late I must've looked a mite hopeful, fur he adds real spry and vicious: "But don't git no fool idee I'm dead. I've sworn t' live a hundred an' I'll do it, if on'y t' spite yer sinful greed! An' now I'm ridin' out t' learn God's message t' me in the spring, like the prophets done. An' yew git back t' yer plowin'," he says. An' he druv off singin' a hymn. I thought he was drunk — 'r I'd stopped him goin'.

EBEN (*scornfully*): No, ye wouldn't! Ye're scared o' him. He's stronger — inside — than both o' ye put together!

PETER (*sardonically*): An' yew — be yew Samson?°

EBEN: I'm gittin' stronger. I kin feel it growin' in me — growin' an' growin' — till it'll bust out —! (*He gets up and puts on his coat and a hat. They watch him, gradually breaking into grins. Eben avoids their eyes sheepishly.*) I'm goin' out fur a spell — up the road.

PETER: T' the village.

SIMEON: T' see Minnie?

EBEN (*defiantly*): Ay-eh!

PETER (*jeeringly*): The Scarlet Woman!

SIMEON: Lust — that's what's growin' in ye!

EBEN: Waal — she's purty!

PETER: She's been purty fur twenty year.

SIMEON: A new coat o' paint'll make a heifer out of forty.

EBEN: She hain't forty!

PETER: If she hain't, she's teeterin' on the edge.

EBEN (*desperately*): What d'yew know —

PETER: All they is ... Sim knew her — an' then me arter —

SIMEON: An' Paw kin tell yew somethin' too! He was fust!

EBEN: D'ye mean t' say he ... ?

SIMEON (*with a grin*): Ay-eh! We air his heirs in everythin'!

EBEN (*intensely*): That's more to it! That grows on it! It'll bust soon! (*Then violently.*) I'll go smash my fist in her face! (*He pulls open the door in rear violently.*)

SIMEON (*with a wink at Peter — drawlingly*): Mebbe — but the night's wa'm — purty — by the time ye git thar mebbe ye'll kiss her instead!

PETER: Sart'n he will! (*They both roar with coarse laughter. Eben rushes out and slams the door — then the outside front door — comes around the*

Samson: A biblical hero known for his great physical strength.

---

corner of the house and stands still by the gate, staring up at the sky.*)

SIMEON (*looking after him*): Like his Paw.

PETER: Dead spit an' image!

SIMEON: Dog'll eat dog!

PETER: Ay-eh. (*Pause. With yearning.*) Mebbe a year from now we'll be in Californi-a.

SIMEON: Ay-eh. (*A pause. Both yawn.*) Let's git t'bed. (*He blows out the candle. They go out door in rear. Eben stretches his arms up to the sky — rebelliously.*)

EBEN: Waal — thar's a star, an' somewhar's they's him, an' here's me, an' thar's Min up the road — in the same night. What if I does kiss her? She's like t'night, she's soft 'n' wa'm, her eyes kin wink like a star, her mouth's wa'm, her arms're wa'm, she smells like a wa'm plowed field, she's purty ... Ay-eh! By God A'mighty she's purty, an' I don't give a damn how many sins she's sinned afore mine or who she's sinned 'em with, my sin's as purty as any one on 'em! (*He strides off down the road to the left.*)

Scene III

(*It is the pitch darkness just before dawn. Eben comes in from the left and goes around to the porch, feeling his way, chuckling bitterly and cursing half-aloud to himself.*)

EBEN: The cussed old miser! (*He can be heard going in the front door. There is a pause as he goes upstairs, then a loud knock on the bedroom door of the brothers.*) Wake up!

SIMEON (*startledly*): Who's thar?

EBEN (*Pushing open the door and coming in, a lighted candle in his hand. The bedroom of the brothers is revealed. Its ceiling is the sloping roof. They can stand upright only close to the center dividing wall of the upstairs. Simeon and Peter are in a double bed, front. Eben's cot is to the rear. Eben has a mixture of silly grin and vicious scowl on his face.*): I be!

PETER (*angrily*): What in hell's-fire ... ?

EBEN: I got news fur ye! Ha! (*He gives one abrupt sardonic guffaw.*)

SIMEON (*angrily*): Couldn't ye hold it 'til we'd got our sleep?

EBEN: It's nigh sunup. (*Then explosively.*) He's gone an' married agen!

SIMEON AND PETER (*explosively*): Paw?

EBEN: Got himself hitched to a female 'bout thirty-five — an' purty, they says ...

SIMEON (*aghast*): It's a durn lie!

PETER: Who says?

SIMEON: They been stringin' ye!

EBEN: Think I'm a dunce, do ye? The hull village says. The preacher from New Dover, he brung the news — told it t'our preacher — New Dover, that's whar the old loon got himself hitched — that's whar the woman lived —

PETER (*no longer doubting — stunned*): Waal . . . !

SIMEON (*the same*): Waal . . . !

EBEN (*sitting down on a bed — with vicious hatred*): Ain't he a devil out o' hell? It's jest t' spite us — the damned old mule!

PETER (*after a pause*): Everythin'll go t'her now.

SIMEON: Ay-eh. (*A pause — dully.*) Waal — if it's done —

PETER: It's done us. (*Pause — then persuasively.*) They's gold in the fields o' Californi-a, Sim. No good a-stayin' here now.

SIMEON: Jest what I was a-thinkin'. (*Then with decision.*) S'well fust's last! Let's light out and git this mornin'.

PETER: Suits me.

EBEN: Ye must like walkin'.

SIMEON (*sardonically*): If ye'd grow wings on us we'd fly thar!

EBEN: Ye'd like ridin' better — on a boat, wouldn't ye? (*Fumbles in his pocket and takes out a crumpled sheet of foolscap.*) Waal, if ye sign this ye kin ride on a boat. I've had it writ out an' ready in case ye'd ever go. It says fur three hundred dollars t' each ye agree yewr shares o' the farm is sold t' me. (*They look suspiciously at the paper. A pause.*)

SIMEON (*wonderingly*): But if he's hitched agen —

PETER: An' whar'd yew git that sum o' money, anyways?

EBEN (*cunningly*): I know whar it's hid. I been waitin' — Maw told me. She knew whar it lay fur years, but she was waitin' . . . It's her'n — the money he hoarded from her farm an' hid from Maw. It's my money by rights now.

PETER: Whar's it hid?

EBEN (*cunningly*): Whar yew won't never find it without me. Maw spied on him — 'r she'd never knowed. (*A pause. They look at him suspiciously, and he at them.*) Waal, is it fa'r trade?

SIMEON: Dunno.

PETER: Dunno.

SIMEON (*looking at window*): Sky's grayin'.

PETER: Ye better start the fire, Eben.

SIMEON: An' fix some vittles.

EBEN: Ay-eh. (*Then with a forced jocular heartiness.*) I'll git ye a good one. If ye're startin' t' hoof it t' Californi-a ye'll need somethin' that'll stick t' yer ribs. (*He turns to the door, adding meaningly.*) But

ye kin ride on a boat if ye'll swap. (*He stops at the door and pauses. They stare at him.*)

SIMEON (*suspiciously*): Whar was ye all night?

EBEN (*defiantly*): Up t' Min's. (*Then slowly.*) Walkin' thar, fust I felt 's if I'd kiss her; then I got a-thinkin' o' what ye'd said o' him an' her an' I says, I'll bust her nose fur that! Then I got t' the village an' heerd the news an' I got madder'n hell an' run all the way t' Min's not knowin' what I'd do — (*He pauses — then sheepishly but more defiantly.*) Waal — when I seen her, I didn't hit her — nor I didn't kiss her nuther — I begun t' beller like a calf an' cuss at the same time, I was so durn mad — an' she got scared — an' I jest grabbed holt an' tuk her! (*Proudly.*) Yes, sirree! I tuk her. She may've been his'n — an' your'n, too — but she's mine now!

SIMEON (*dryly*): In love, air yew?

EBEN (*with lofty scorn*): Love! I don't take no stock in sech slop!

PETER (*winking at Simeon*): Mebbe Eben's aimin' t' marry, too.

SIMEON: Min'd make a true faithful he'pmeet! (*They snicker.*)

EBEN: What do I care fur her — 'ceptin' she's round an' wa'm? The p'int is she was his'n — an' now she b'longs t' me! (*He goes to the door — then turns — rebelliously.*) An' Min hain't sech a bad un. They's worse'n Min in the world, I'll bet ye! Wait'll we see this cow the Old Man's hitched t'! She'll beat Min, I got a notion! (*He starts to go out.*)

SIMEON (*suddenly*): Mebbe ye'll try t' make her your'n, too?

PETER: Ha! (*He gives a sardonic laugh of relish at this idea.*)

EBEN (*spitting with disgust*): Her — here — sleepin' with him — stealin' my Maw's farm! I'd as soon pet a skunk 'r kiss a snake! (*He goes out. The two stare after him suspiciously. A pause. They listen to his steps receding.*)

PETER: He's startin' the fire.

SIMEON: I'd like t' ride t' Californi-a — but —

PETER: Min might o' put some scheme in his head.

SIMEON: Mebbe it's all a lie 'bout Paw marryin'. We'd best wait an' see the bride.

PETER: An' don't sign nothin' till we does!

SIMEON: Nor till we've tested it's good money! (*Then with a grin.*) But if Paw's hitched we'd be sellin' Eben somethin' we'd never git nohow!

PETER: We'll wait an' see. (*Then with sudden vindictive anger.*) An' till he comes, let's yew 'n' me not wuk a lick, let Eben tend to thin's if he's a mind t', let's us jest sleep an' eat an' drink likker, an' let the hull damned farm go t' blazes!

SIMEON (*excitedly*): By God, we've 'arned a rest! We'll play rich fur a change. I hain't a-going to stir outa bed till breakfast's ready.

PETER: An' on the table!

SIMEON (*after a pause — thoughtfully*): What d'ye calc'late she'll be like — our new Maw? Like Eben thinks?

PETER: More'n' likely.

SIMEON (*vindictively*): Waal — I hope she's a she-devil that'll make him wish he was dead an' livin' in the pit o' hell fur comfort!

PETER (*fervently*): Amen!

SIMEON (*imitating his father's voice*): "I'm ridin' out t' learn God's message t' me in the spring like the prophets done," he says. I'll bet right then an' thar he knew plumb well he was goin' whorin', the stinkin' old hypocrite!

Scene IV

(*Same as scene II — shows the interior of the kitchen with a lighted candle on table. It is gray dawn outside. Simeon and Peter are just finishing their breakfast. Eben sits before his plate of untouched food, brooding frowningly.*)

PETER (*glancing at him rather irritably*): Lookin' glum don't help none.

SIMEON (*sarcastically*): Sorrowin' over his lust o' the flesh!

PETER (*with a grin*): Was she yer fust?

EBEN (*angrily*): None o' yer business. (*A pause.*) I was thinkin' o' him. I got a notion he's gittin' near — I kin feel him comin' on like yew kin feel malaria chill afore it takes ye.

PETER: It's too early yet.

SIMEON: Dunno. He'd like t' catch us nappin' — jest t' have somethin' t' hoss us 'round over.

PETER (*Mechanically gets to his feet. Simeon does the same.*): Waal — let's git t'wuk. (*They both plod mechanically toward the door before they realize. Then they stop short.*)

SIMEON (*grinning*): Ye're a cussed fool, Pete — and I be wuss! Let him see we hain't wukin'! We don't give a durn!

PETER (*as they go back to the table*): Not a damned durn! It'll serve t' show him we're done with him. (*They sit down again. Eben stares from one to the other with surprise.*)

SIMEON (*grins at him*): We're aimin' t' start bein' lilies o' the field.

PETER: Nary a toil 'r spin 'r lick o' wuk do we put in!

SIMEON: Ye're sole owner — till he comes — that's what ye wanted. Waal, ye got t' be sole hand, too.

PETER: The cows air bellerin'. Ye better hustle at the milkin'.

EBEN (*with excited joy*): Ye mean ye'll sign the paper?

SIMEON (*dryly*): Mebbe.

PETER: Mebbe.

SIMEON: We're considerin'. (*Peremptorily.*) Ye better git t' wuk.

EBEN (*with queer excitement*): It's Maw's farm agen! It's my farm! Them's my cows! I'll milk my durn fingers off fur cows o' mine! (*He goes out door in rear, they stare after him indifferently.*)

SIMEON: Like his Paw.

PETER: Dead spit 'n' image!

SIMEON: Waal — let dog eat dog! (*Eben comes out of front door and around the corner of the house. The sky is beginning to grow flushed with sunrise. Eben stops by the gate and stares around him with glowing, possessive eyes. He takes in the whole farm with his embracing glance of desire.*)

EBEN: It's purty! It's damned purty! It's mine! (*He suddenly throws his head back boldly and glares with hard, defiant eyes at the sky.*) Mine, d'ye hear? Mine! (*He turns and walks quickly off left, rear, toward the barn. The two brothers light their pipes.*)

SIMEON (*putting his muddy boots up on the table, tilting back his chair, and puffing defiantly*): Waal — this air solid comfort — fur once.

PETER: Ay-eh. (*He follows suit. A pause. Unconsciously they both sigh.*)

SIMEON (*suddenly*): He never was much o' a hand at milkin', Eben wa'n't.

PETER (*with a snort*): His hands air like hoofs! (*A pause.*)

SIMEON: Reach down the jug thar! Let's take a swaller. I'm feelin' kind o' low.

PETER: Good idee! (*He does so — gets two glasses — they pour out drinks of whisky.*) Here's t' the gold in Californi-a!

SIMEON: An' luck t' find it! (*They drink — puff resolutely — sigh — take their feet down from the table.*)

PETER: Likker don't pear t' sot right.

SIMEON: We hain't used t' it this early. (*A pause. They become very restless.*)

PETER: Gittin' close in this kitchen.

SIMEON (*with immense relief*): Let's git a breath o' air. (*They arise briskly and go out rear — appear around house and stop by the gate. They stare up at the sky with a numbed appreciation.*)

PETER: Purty!

SIMEON: Ay-eh. Gold's t' the East now.

PETER: Sun's startin' with us fur the Golden West.

SIMEON (*staring around the farm, his compressed face tightened, unable to conceal his emotion*): Waal — it's our last mornin' — mebbe.

PETER (*the same*): Ay-eh.

SIMEON (*stamps his foot on the earth and addresses it desperately*): Waal — ye've thirty year o' me buried in ye — spread out over ye — blood an' bone an' sweat — rotted away — fertilizin' ye — richin' yer soul — prime manure, by God, that's what I been t' ye!

PETER: Ay-eh! An' me.

SIMEON: An' yew, Peter. (*He sighs — then spits.*) Waal — no use'n cryin' over spilt milk.

PETER: They's gold in the West — an' freedom, mebbe. We been slaves t' stone walls here.

SIMEON (*defiantly*): We hain't nobody's slaves from this out — nor nothin's slaves nuther. (*A pause — restlessly.*) Speaking o' milk, wonder how Eben's managin'?

PETER: I s'pose he's managin'.

SIMEON: Mebbe we'd ought t' help — this once.

PETER: Mebbe. The cows knows us.

SIMEON: An' likes us. They don't know him much.

PETER: An' the hosses, an' pigs, an' chickens. They don't know him much.

SIMEON: They knows us like brothers — an' likes us! (*Proudly.*) Hain't we raised 'em t' be fust-rate, number one prize stock?

PETER: We hain't — not no more.

SIMEON (*dully*): I was fergittin'. (*Then resignedly.*) Waal, let's go help Eben a spell an' git waked up.

PETER: Suits me. (*They are starting off down left, rear, for the barn when Eben appears from there hurrying toward them, his face excited.*)

EBEN (*breathlessly*): Waal — har they be! The old mule an' the bride! I seen 'em from the barn down below at the turnin'.

PETER: How could ye tell that far?

EBEN: Hain't I as far-sight as he's near-sight? Don't I know the mare 'n' buggy, an' two people settin' in it? Who else . . . ? An' I tell ye I kin feel 'em a-comin', too! (*He squirms as if he had the itch.*)

PETER (*beginning to be angry*): Waal — let him do his own unhitchin'!

SIMEON (*angry in his turn*): Let's hustle in an' git our bundles an' be a-goin' as he's a-comin'. I don't want never t' step inside the door agen arter he's back. (*They both start back around the corner of the house. Eben follows them.*)

EBEN (*anxiously*): Will ye sign it afore ye go?

PETER: Let's see the color o' the old skinflint's money an' we'll sign. (*They disappear left. The two brothers clump upstairs to get their bundles. Eben appears in the kitchen, runs to window, peers out, comes back and pulls up a strip of flooring in under*

stove, takes out a canvas bag and puts it on table, then sets the floorboard back in place. The two brothers appear a moment after. They carry old carpetbags.*)

EBEN (*puts his hand on bag guardingly*): Have ye signed?

SIMEON (*shows paper in his hand*): Ay-eh. (*Greedily.*) Be that the money?

EBEN (*opens bag and pours out pile of twenty-dollar gold pieces*): Twenty-dollar pieces — thirty on 'em. Count 'em. (*Peter does so, arranging them in stacks of five, biting one or two to test them.*)

PETER: Six hundred. (*He puts them in bag and puts it inside his shirt carefully.*)

SIMEON (*handing paper to Eben*): Har ye be.

EBEN (*after a glance, folds it carefully and hides it under his shirt — gratefully*): Thank yew.

PETER: Thank yew fur the ride.

SIMEON: We'll send ye a lump o' gold fur Christmas. (*A pause. Eben stares at them and they at him.*)

PETER (*awkwardly*): Waal — we're a-goin'.

SIMEON: Comin' out t' the yard?

EBEN: No. I'm waitin' in here a spell. (*Another silence. The brothers edge awkwardly to door in rear — then turn and stand.*)

SIMEON: Waal — good-by.

PETER: Good-by.

EBEN: Good-by. (*They go out. He sits down at the table, faces the stove and pulls out the paper. He looks from it to the stove. His face, lighted up by the shaft of sunlight from the window, has an expression of trance. His lips move. The two brothers come out to the gate.*)

PETER (*looking off toward barn*): Thar he be — unhitchin'.

SIMEON (*with a chuckle*): I'll bet ye he's riled!

PETER: An' thar she be.

SIMEON: Let's wait 'n' see what our new Maw looks like.

PETER (*with a grin*): An' give him our partin' cuss!

SIMEON (*grinning*): I feel like raisin' fun. I feel light in my head an' feet.

PETER: Me, too. I feel like laffin' till I'd split up the middle.

SIMEON: Reckon it's the likker?

PETER: No. My feet feel itchin' t' walk an' walk — an' jump high over thin's — an'. . . .

SIMEON: Dance? (*A pause.*)

PETER (*puzzled*): It's plumb onnateral.

SIMEON (*a light coming over his face*): I calc'late it's 'cause school's out. It's holiday. Fur once we're free!

PETER (*dazedly*): Free?

SIMEON: The halter's broke — the harness is busted — the fence bars is down — the stone walls air crumblin' an' tumblin'! We'll be kickin' up an' tearin' away down the road!

PETER (*drawing a deep breath — oratorically*): Anybody that wants this stinkin' old rock-pile of a farm kin hev it. T'ain't our'n, no sirree!

SIMEON (*takes the gate off its hinges and puts it under his arm*): We harby 'bolishes shet gates, an' open gates, an' all gates, by thunder!

PETER: We'll take it with us fur luck an' let 'er sail free down some river.

SIMEON (*as a sound of voices comes from left, rear*): Har they comes! (*The two brothers congeal into two stiff, grim-visaged statues. Ephraim Cabot and Abbie Putnam come in. Cabot is seventy-five, tall and gaunt, with great, wiry, concentrated power, but stoop-shouldered from toil. His face is as hard as if it were hewn out of a boulder, yet there is a weakness in it, a petty pride in its own narrow strength. His eyes are small, close together, and extremely near-sighted, blinking continually in the effort to focus on objects, their stare having a straining, ingrowing quality. He is dressed in his dismal black Sunday suit. Abbie is thirty-five, buxom, full of vitality. Her round face is pretty but marred by its rather gross sensuality. There is strength and obstinacy in her jaw, a hard determination in her eyes, and about her whole personality the same unsettled, untamed, desperate quality which is so apparent in Eben.*)

CABOT (*as they enter — a queer strangled emotion in his dry cracking voice*): Har we be t' hum, Abbie.

ABBIE (*with lust for the word*): Hum! (*Her eyes gloating on the house without seeming to see the two stiff figures at the gate.*) It's purty — purty! I can't b'lieve it's r'ally mine.

CABOT (*sharply*): Yewr'n? Mine! (*He stares at her penetratingly. She stares back. He adds relentingly.*) Our'n — mebbe! It was lonesome too long. I was growin' old in the spring. A hum's got t' hev a woman.

ABBIE (*her voice taking possession*): A woman's got t' hev a hum!

CABOT (*nodding uncertainly*): Ay-eh. (*Then irritably.*) Whar be they? Ain't thar nobody about — 'r wukin' — 'r nothin'?

ABBIE (*Sees the brothers. She returns their stare of cold appraising contempt with interest — slowly.*): Thar's two men loafin' at the gate an' starin' at me like a couple o' strayed hogs.

CABOT (*straining his eyes*): I kin see 'em — but I can't make out. . . .

SIMEON: It's Simeon.

PETER: It's Peter.

CABOT (*exploding*): Why hain't ye wukin'?

SIMEON (*dryly*): We're waitin' t' welcome ye hum — yew an' the bride!

CABOT (*confusedly*): Huh? Waal — this be yer new Maw, boys. (*She stares at them and they at her.*)

SIMEON (*turns away and spits contemptuously*): I see her!

PETER (*spits also*): An' I see her!

ABBIE (*with the conqueror's conscious superiority*): I'll go in an' look at *my* house. (*She goes slowly around to porch.*)

SIMEON (*with a snort*): *Her* house!

PETER (*calls after her*): Ye'll find Eben inside. Ye better not tell him it's *yewr* house.

ABBIE (*mouthing the name*): Eben. (*Then quietly.*) I'll tell Eben.

CABOT (*with a contemptuous sneer*): Ye needn't heed Eben. Eben's a dumb fool — like his Maw — soft an' simple!

SIMEON (*with his sardonic burst of laughter*): Ha! Eben's a chip o' yew — spit 'n' image — hard 'n' bitter's a hickory tree! Dog'll eat dog. He'll eat ye yet, old man!

CABOT (*commandingly*): Ye git t' wuk!

SIMEON (*as Abbie disappears in house — winks at Peter and says tauntingly*): So that thar's our new Maw, be it? Whar in hell did ye dig her up? (*He and Peter laugh.*)

PETER: Ha! Ye'd better turn her in the pen with the other sows. (*They laugh uproariously, slapping their thighs.*)

CABOT (*so amazed at their effrontery that he stutters in confusion*): Simeon! Peter! What's come over ye? Air ye drunk?

SIMEON: We're free, old man — free o' yew an' the hull damned farm! (*They grow more and more hilarious and excited.*)

PETER: An' we're startin' out fur the gold fields o' Californi-a!

SIMEON: Ye kin take this place an' burn it!

PETER: An' bury it — fur all we cares!

SIMEON: We're free, old man! (*He cuts a caper.*)

PETER: Free! (*He gives a kick in the air.*)

SIMEON (*in a frenzy*): Whoop!

PETER: Whoop! (*They do an absurd Indian war dance about the old man who is petrified between rage and the fear that they are insane.*)

SIMEON: We're free as Injuns! Lucky we don't skulp ye!

PETER: An' burn yer barn an' kill the stock!

SIMEON: An' rape yer new woman! Whoop! (*He and Peter stop their dance, holding their sides, rocking with wild laughter.*)

CABOT (*edging away*): Lust fur gold — fur the sinful, easy gold o' Californi-a! It's made ye mad!

SIMEON (*tauntingly*): Wouldn't ye like us to send ye back some sinful gold, ye old sinner?

PETER: They's gold besides what's in Californi-a! (*He retreats back beyond the vision of the old man and takes the bag of money and flaunts it in the air above his head, laughing.*)

SIMEON: And sinfuller, too!

PETER: We'll be voyagin' on the sea! Whoop! (*He leaps up and down.*)

SIMEON: Livin' free! Whoop! (*He leaps in turn.*)

CABOT (*suddenly roaring with rage*): My cuss on ye!

SIMEON: Take our'n in trade fur it! Whoop!

CABOT: I'll hev ye both chained up in the asylum!

PETER: Ye old skinflint! Good-by!

SIMEON: Ye old blood sucker! Good-by!

CABOT: Go afore I . . . !

PETER: Whoop! (*He picks a stone from the road. Simeon does the same.*)

SIMEON: Maw'll be in the parlor.

PETER: Ay-eh! One! Two!

CABOT (*frightened*): What air ye . . . ?

PETER: Three! (*They both throw, the stones hitting the parlor window with a crash of glass, tearing the shade.*)

SIMEON: Whoop!

PETER: Whoop!

CABOT (*in a fury now, rushing toward them*): If I kin lay hands on ye — I'll break yer bones fur ye! (*But they beat a capering retreat before him, Simeon with the gate still under his arm. Cabot comes back, panting with impotent rage. Their voices as they go off take up the song of the gold-seekers to the old tune of "Oh, Susannah!"*)

"I jumped aboard the Liza ship,
And traveled on the sea,
And every time I thought of home
I wished it wasn't me!
Oh! Californi-a,
That's the land fur me!
I'm off to Californi-a!
With my wash bowl on my knee."

(*In the meantime, the window of the upper bedroom on right is raised and Abbie sticks her head out. She looks down at Cabot — with a sigh of relief.*)

ABBIE: Waal — that's the last o' them two, hain't it? (*He doesn't answer. Then in possessive tones.*) This here's a nice bedroom, Ephraim. It's a r'al nice bed. Is it my room, Ephraim?

CABOT (*grimly — without looking up*): Our'n! (*She cannot control a grimace of aversion and pulls back her head slowly and shuts the window. A sudden horrible thought seems to enter Cabot's head.*) They been up to somethin'! Mebbe — mebbe they've pizened the stock — 'r somethin'! (*He al-most runs off down toward the barn. A moment later the kitchen door is slowly pushed open and Abbie enters. For a moment she stands looking at Eben. He does not notice her at first. Her eyes take him in penetratingly with a calculating appraisal of his strength as against hers. But under this her desire is dimly awakened by his youth and good looks. Suddenly he becomes conscious of her presence and looks up. Their eyes meet. He leaps to his feet, glowering at her speechlessly.*)

ABBIE (*in her most seductive tones which she uses all through this scene*): Be you — Eben? I'm Abbie — (*She laughs.*) I mean, I'm yer new Maw.

EBEN (*viciously*): No, damn ye!

ABBIE (*as if she hadn't heard — with a queer smile*): Yer Paw's spoke a lot o' yew. . . .

EBEN: Ha!

ABBIE: Ye mustn't mind him. He's an old man. (*A long pause. They stare at each other.*) I don't want t' pretend playin' Maw t' ye, Eben. (*Admiringly.*) Ye're too big an' too strong fur that. I want t' be frens with ye. Mebbe with me fur a fren ye'd find ye'd like livin' here better. I kin make it easy fur ye with him, mebbe. (*With a scornful sense of power.*) I calc'late I kin git him t' do most anythin' fur me.

EBEN (*with bitter scorn*): Ha! (*They stare again, Eben obscurely moved, physically attracted to her — in forced stilted tones.*) Yew kin go t' the devil!

ABBIE (*calmly*): If cussin' me does ye good, cuss all ye've a mind t'. I'm all prepared t' have ye agin me — at fust. I don't blame ye nuther. I'd feel the same at any stranger comin' t' take my Maw's place. (*He shudders. She is watching him carefully.*) Yew must've cared a lot fur yewr Maw, didn't ye? My Maw died afore I'd growed. I don't remember her none. (*A pause.*) But yew won't hate me long, Eben. I'm not the wust in the world — an' yew an' me've got a lot in common. I kin tell that by lookin' at ye. Waal — I've had a hard life, too — oceans o' trouble an' nuthin' but wuk fur reward. I was a orphan early an' had t' wuk fur others in other folks' hums. Then I married an' he turned out a drunken spreer an' so he had to wuk fur others an' me too agen in other folks' hums, an' the baby died, an' my husband got sick an' died too, an' I was glad sayin' now I'm free fur once, on'y I diskivered right away all I was free fur was t' wuk agen in other folks' hums, doin' other folks' wuk till I'd most give up hope o' ever doin' my own wuk in my own hum, an' then your Paw come. . . . (*Cabot appears returning from the barn. He comes to the gate and looks down the road the brothers have gone. A faint strain of their retreating voices is heard: "Oh, Californi-a! That's the place for me." He stands glowering, his fist clenched, his face grim with rage.)*

EBEN (*fighting against his growing attraction and sympathy — harshly*): An' bought yew — like a harlot! (*She is stung and flushes angrily. She has been sincerely moved by the recital of her troubles. He adds furiously.*) An' the price he's payin' ye — this farm — was my Maw's, damn ye! — an' mine now!

ABBIE (*with a cool laugh of confidence*): Yewr'n? We'll see 'bout that! (*Then strongly.*) Waal — what if I did need a hum? What else'd I marry an old man like him fur?

EBEN (*maliciously*): I'll tell him ye said that!

ABBIE (*smiling*): I'll say ye're lyin' a-purpose — an' he'll drive ye off the place!

EBEN: Ye devil!

ABBIE (*defying him*): This be my farm — this be my hum — this be my kitchen —!

EBEN (*furiously, as if he were going to attack her*): Shut up, damn ye!

ABBIE (*walks up to him — a queer coarse expression of desire in her face and body — slowly*): An' upstairs — that be my bedroom — an' my bed! (*He stares into her eyes, terribly confused and torn. She adds softly.*) I hain't bad nor mean — 'ceptin' fur an enemy — but I got t' fight fur what's due me out o' life, if I ever 'spect t' git it. (*Then putting her hand on his arm — seductively.*) Let's yew 'n' me be frens, Eben.

EBEN (*stupidly — as if hypnotized*): Ay-eh. (*Then furiously flinging off her arm.*) No, ye durned old witch! I hate ye! (*He rushes out the door.*)

ABBIE (*looks after him smiling satisfiedly — then half to herself, mouthing the word*): Eben's nice. (*She looks at the table, proudly.*) I'll wash up *my* dishes now. (*Eben appears outside, slamming the door behind him. He comes around corner, stops on seeing his father, and stands staring at him with hate.*)

CABOT (*raising his arms to heaven in the fury he can no longer control*): Lord God o' Hosts, smite the undutiful sons with Thy wust cuss!

EBEN (*breaking in violently*): Yew 'n' yewr God! Allus cussin' folks — allus naggin' 'em!

CABOT (*oblivious to him — summoningly*): God o' the old! God o' the lonesome!

EBEN (*mockingly*): Naggin' His sheep t' sin! T' hell with yewr God! (*Cabot turns. He and Eben glower at each other.*)

CABOT (*harshly*): So it's yew. I might've knowed it. (*Shaking his finger threateningly at him.*) Blasphemin' fool! (*Then quickly.*) Why hain't ye t' wuk?

EBEN: Why hain't yew? They've went. I can't wuk it all alone.

CABOT (*contemptuously*): Nor noways! I'm wuth ten o' ye yit, old's I be! Ye'll never be more'n half a man! (*Then, matter-of-factly.*) Waal — let's git t' the barn. (*They go. A last faint note of the "Californi-a" song is heard from the distance. Abbie is washing her dishes.*)

PART II • *Scene I*

(*The exterior of the farmhouse, as in part I — a hot Sunday afternoon two months later. Abbie, dressed in her best, is discovered sitting in a rocker at the end of the porch. She rocks listlessly, enervated by the heat, staring in front of her with bored, half-closed eyes.*)

(*Eben sticks his head out of his bedroom window. He looks around furtively and tries to see — or hear — if anyone is on the porch, but although he has been careful to make no noise, Abbie has sensed his movement. She stops rocking, her face grows animated and eager, she waits attentively. Eben seems to feel her presence, he scowls back his thoughts of her and spits with exaggerated disdain — then withdraws back into the room. Abbie waits, holding her breath as she listens with passionate eagerness for every sound within the house.*)

(*Eben comes out. Their eyes meet; his falter. He is confused, he turns away and slams the door resentfully. At this gesture, Abbie laughs tantalizingly, amused but at the same time piqued and irritated. He scowls, strides off the porch to the path and starts to walk past her to the road with a grand swagger of ignoring her existence. He is dressed in his store suit, spruced up, his face shines from soap and water. Abbie leans forward on her chair, her eyes hard and angry now, and, as he passes her, gives a sneering, taunting chuckle.*)

EBEN (*stung — turns on her furiously*): What air yew cacklin' 'bout?

ABBIE (*triumphant*): Yew!

EBEN: What about me?

ABBIE: Ye look all slicked up like a prize bull.

EBEN (*with a sneer*): Waal — ye hain't so durned purty yerself, be ye? (*They stare into each other's eyes, his held by hers in spite of himself, hers glowingly possessive. Their physical attraction becomes a palpable force quivering in the hot air.*)

ABBIE (*softly*): Ye don't mean that, Eben. Ye may think ye mean it, mebbe, but ye don't. Ye can't. It's agin nature, Eben. Ye been fightin' yer nature ever since the day I come — tryin' t' tell yerself I hain't purty t'ye. (*She laughs a low humid laugh without taking her eyes from his. A pause — her body squirms desirously — she murmurs languorously.*) Hain't the sun strong an' hot? Ye kin feel it burnin' into the earth — Nature — makin' thin's grow — bigger 'n' bigger — burnin' inside ye — makin' ye want t' grow — into somethin' else — till ye're jined with it — an' it's your'n — but it owns ye, too — an' makes ye grow bigger — like a tree — like them elums — (*She laughs again softly, holding his eyes. He takes a step toward her, compelled against his will.*) Nature'll beat ye, Eben. Ye might's well own up t' it fust 's last.

EBEN (*trying to break from her spell — confusedly*): If Paw'd hear ye goin' on. . . . (*Resentfully.*) But ye've made such a damned idjit out o' the old devil . . . ! (*Abbie laughs.*)

ABBIE: Waal — hain't it easier fur yew with him changed softer?

EBEN (*defiantly*): No. I'm fightin' him — fightin' yew — fightin' fur Maw's rights t' her hum! (*This breaks her spell for him. He glowers at her.*) An' I'm onto ye. Ye hain't foolin' me a mite. Ye're aimin' t' swaller up everythin' an' make it your'n. Waal, you'll find I'm a heap sight bigger hunk nor yew kin chew! (*He turns from her with a sneer.*)

ABBIE (*trying to regain her ascendancy — seductively*): Eben!

EBEN: Leave me be! (*He starts to walk away.*)

ABBIE (*more commandingly*): Eben!

EBEN (*stops — resentfully*): What d'ye want?

ABBIE (*trying to conceal a growing excitement*): Whar air ye goin'?

EBEN (*with malicious nonchalance*): Oh — up the road a spell.

ABBIE: T' the village?

EBEN (*airily*): Mebbe.

ABBIE (*excitedly*): T' see that Min, I s'pose?

EBEN: Mebbe.

ABBIE (*weakly*): What d'ye want t' waste time on her fur?

EBEN (*revenging himself now — grinning at her*): Ye can't beat Nature, didn't ye say? (*He laughs and again starts to walk away.*)

ABBIE (*bursting out*): An ugly old hake!

EBEN (*with a tantalizing sneer*): She's purtier'n yew be!

ABBIE: That every wuthless drunk in the country has. . . .

EBEN (*tauntingly*): Mebbe — but she's better'n yew. She owns up fa'r 'n' squar' t' her doin's.

ABBIE (*furiously*): Don't ye dare compare. . . .

EBEN: She don't go sneakin' an' stealin' — what's mine.

ABBIE (*savagely seizing on his weak point*): Your'n? Yew mean — my farm?

EBEN: I mean the farm yew sold yerself fur like any other old whore — my farm!

ABBIE (*stung — fiercely*): Ye'll never live t' see the day when even a stinkin' weed on it'll belong t' ye! (*Then in a scream.*) Git out o' my sight! Go on t' yer slut — disgracin' yer Paw 'n' me! I'll git yer Paw t' horsewhip ye off the place if I want t'! Ye're only livin' here 'cause I tolerate ye! Git along! I hate the sight o' ye! (*She stops, panting and glaring at him.*)

EBEN (*returning her glance in kind*): An' I hate the sight o' yew! (*He turns and strides off up the road. She follows his retreating figure with concentrated hate. Old Cabot appears coming up from the barn. The hard, grim expression of his face has changed. He seems in some queer way softened, mellowed. His eyes have taken on a strange, incongruous dreamy quality. Yet there is no hint of physical weakness about him — rather he looks more robust and younger. Abbie sees him and turns away quickly with unconcealed aversion. He comes slowly up to her.*)

CABOT (*mildly*): War yew an' Eben quarrelin' agen?

ABBIE (*shortly*): No.

CABOT: Ye was talkin' a'mighty loud. (*He sits down on the edge of porch.*)

ABBIE (*snappishly*): If ye heerd us they hain't no need askin' questions.

CABOT: I didn't hear what ye said.

ABBIE (*relieved*): Waal — it wa'n't nothin' t' speak on.

CABOT (*after a pause*): Eben's queer.

ABBIE (*bitterly*): He's the dead spit 'n' image o' yew!

CABOT (*queerly interested*): D'ye think so, Abbie? (*After a pause, ruminatingly.*) Me 'n' Eben's allus fit 'n' fit. I never could b'ar him noways. He's so thunderin' soft — like his Maw.

ABBIE (*scornfully*): Ay-eh! 'Bout as soft as yew be!

CABOT (*as if he hadn't heard*): Mebbe I been too hard on him.

ABBIE (*jeeringly*): Waal — ye're gittin' soft now — soft as slop! That's what Eben was sayin'.

CABOT (*his face instantly grim and ominous*): Eben was sayin'? Waal, he'd best not do nothin' t' try me 'r he'll soon diskiver. . . . (*A pause. She keeps her face turned away. His gradually softens. He stares up at the sky.*) Purty, hain't it?

ABBIE (*crossly*): I don't see nothin' purty.

CABOT: The sky. Feels like a wa'm field up thar.

ABBIE (*sarcastically*): Air yew aimin' t' buy up over the farm too? (*She snickers contemptuously.*)

CABOT (*strangely*): I'd like t' own my place up thar. (*A pause.*) I'm gittin' old, Abbie. I'm gittin' ripe on the bough. (*A pause. She stares at him mystified. He goes on.*) It's allus lonesome cold in the house — even when it's bilin' hot outside. Hain't yew noticed?

ABBIE: No.

CABOT: It's wa'm down t' the barn — nice smellin' an' warm — with the cows. (*A pause.*) Cows is queer.

ABBIE: Like yew?

CABOT: Like Eben. (*A pause.*) I'm gittin' t' feel resigned t' Eben — jest as I got t' feel 'bout his Maw. I'm gittin' t' learn to b'ar his softness — jest like her'n. I calc'late I c'd a'most take t' him — if he wa'n't sech a dumb fool! (*A pause.*) I s'pose it's old age a-creepin' in my bones.

ABBIE (*indifferently*): Waal — ye hain't dead yet.

CABOT (*roused*): No, I hain't, yew bet — not by a hell of a sight — I'm sound 'n' tough as hickory! (*Then moodily.*) But arter three score and ten the Lord warns ye t' prepare. (*A pause.*) That's why Eben's come in my head. Now that his cussed sinful brothers is gone their path t' hell, they's no one left but Eben.

ABBIE (*resentfully*): They's me, hain't they? (*Agitatedly.*) What's all this sudden likin' ye've tuk to Eben? Why don't ye say nothin' 'bout me? Hain't I yer lawful wife?

CABOT (*simply*): Ay-eh. Ye be. (*A pause — he stares at her desirously — his eyes grow avid — then with a sudden movement he seizes her hands and squeezes them, declaiming in a queer camp meeting preacher's tempo.*) Yew air my Rose o' Sharon! Behold, yew air fair; yer eyes air doves; yer lips air like scarlet; yer two breasts air like two fawns; yer navel be like a round goblet; yer belly be like a heap o' wheat. . . . (*He covers her hand with kisses. She does not seem to notice. She stares before her with hard angry eyes.*)

ABBIE (*jerking her hands away — harshly*): So ye're plannin' t' leave the farm t' Eben, air ye?

CABOT (*dazedly*): Leave . . . ? (*Then with resentful obstinacy.*) I hain't a-givin' it t' no one!

ABBIE (*remorselessly*): Ye can't take it with ye.

CABOT (*thinks a moment — then reluctantly*): No, I calc'late not. (*After a pause — with a strange passion.*) But if I could, I would, by the Eternal! 'R if I could, in my dyin' hour, I'd set it afire an' watch it burn — this house an' every ear o' corn an' every tree down t' the last blade o' hay! I'd sit an' know it was all a-dying with me an' no one else'd ever own what was mine, what I'd made out o' nothin' with my own sweat 'n' blood! (*A pause — then he adds with a queer affection.*) 'Ceptin' the cows. Them I'd turn free.

ABBIE (*harshly*): An' me?

CABOT (*with a queer smile*): Ye'd be turned free, too.

ABBIE (*furiously*): So that's the thanks I git fur marryin' ye — t' have ye change kind to Eben who hates ye, an' talk o' turnin' me out in the road.

CABOT (*hastily*): Abbie! Ye know I wa'n't. . . .

ABBIE (*vengefully*): Just let me tell ye a thing or two 'bout Eben! Whar's he gone? T' see that harlot, Min! I tried fur t' stop him. Disgracin' yew an' me — on the Sabbath, too!

CABOT (*rather guiltily*): He's a sinner — nateral-born. It's lust eatin' his heart.

ABBIE (*enraged beyond endurance — wildly vindictive*): An' his lust fur me! Kin ye find excuses fur that?

CABOT (*stares at her — after a dead pause*): Lust — fur yew?

ABBIE (*defiantly*): He was tryin' t' make love t' me — when ye heerd us quarrelin'.

CABOT (*stares at her — then a terrible expression of rage comes over his face — he springs to his feet shaking all over*): By the A'mighty God — I'll end him!

ABBIE (*frightened now for Eben*): No! Don't ye!

CABOT (*violently*): I'll git the shotgun an' blow his soft brains t' the top o' them elums!

ABBIE (*throwing her arms around him*): No, Ephraim!

CABOT (*pushing her away violently*): I will, by God!

ABBIE (*in a quieting tone*): Listen, Ephraim. 'Twa'n't nothin' bad — on'y a boy's foolin' — 'twa'n't meant serious — jest jokin' an' teasin'. . . .

CABOT: Then why did ye say — lust?

ABBIE: It must hev sounded wusser'n I meant. An' I was mad at thinkin' — ye'd leave him the farm.

CABOT (*quieter but still grim and cruel*): Waal then, I'll horsewhip him off the place if that much'll content ye.

ABBIE (*reaching out and taking his hand*): No. Don't think o' me! Ye mustn't drive him off. 'Tain't sensible. Who'll ye get to help ye on the farm? They's no one hereabouts.

CABOT (*considers this — then nodding his appreciation*): Ye got a head on ye. (*Then irritably.*) Waal, let him stay. (*He sits down on the edge of the porch. She sits beside him. He murmurs contemptuously.*) I oughtn't t' git riled so — at that 'ere fool calf. (*A pause.*) But har's the p'int. What son o' mine'll keep on here t' the farm — when the Lord does call me? Simeon an' Peter air gone t' hell — an' Eben's follerin' 'em.

ABBIE: They's me.

CABOT: Ye're on'y a woman.

ABBIE: I'm yewr wife.

CABOT: That hain't me. A son is me — my blood — mine. Mine ought t' git mine. An' then it's still mine — even though I be six foot under. D'ye see?

ABBIE (*giving him a look of hatred*): Ay-eh. I see. (*She becomes very thoughtful, her face growing shrewd, her eyes studying Cabot craftily.*)

CABOT: I'm gittin' old — ripe on the bough. (*Then with a sudden forced reassurance.*) Not but what I hain't a hard nut t' crack even yet — an' fur many a year t' come! By the Etarnal, I kin break most o' the young fellers' backs at any kind o' work any day o' the year!

ABBIE (*suddenly*): Mebbe the Lord'll give *us* a son.

CABOT (*turns and stares at her eagerly*): Ye mean — a son — t' me 'n' yew?

ABBIE (*with a cajoling smile*): Ye're a strong man yet, hain't ye? 'Tain't noways impossible, be it? We know that. Why d'ye stare so? Hain't ye never thought o' that afore? I been thinkin' o' it all along. Ay-eh — an' I been prayin' it'd happen, too.

CABOT (*his face growing full of joyous pride and a sort of religious ecstasy*): Ye been prayin', Abbie? — fur a son? — t' us?

ABBIE: Ay-eh. (*With a grim resolution.*) I want a son now.

CABOT (*excitedly clutching both of her hands in his*): It'd be the blessin' o' God, Abbie — the blessin' o' God A'mighty on me — in my old age — in my lonesomeness! They hain't nothin' I wouldn't do fur ye then, Abbie. Ye'd hev on'y t' ask it — anythin' ye'd a mind t'!

ABBIE (*interrupting*): Would ye will the farm t' me then — t' me an' it . . . ?

CABOT (*vehemently*): I'd do anythin' ye axed, I tell ye! I swar it! May I be everlastin' damned t' hell if I wouldn't! (*He sinks to his knees pulling her down with him. He trembles all over with the fervor of his hopes.*) Pray t' the Lord agen, Abbie. It's the Sabbath! I'll jine ye! Two prayers air better nor one. "An' God hearkened unto Rachel"! An' God hearkened unto Abbie! Pray, Abbie! Pray fur him to hearken! (*He bows his head, mumbling. She pretends to do likewise but gives him a side glance of scorn and triumph.*)

Scene II

(*About eight in the evening. The interior of the two bedrooms on the top floor is shown. Eben is sitting on the side of his bed in the room on the left. On account of the heat he has taken off everything but his undershirt and pants. His feet are bare. He faces front, brooding moodily, his chin propped on his hands, a desperate expression on his face.*)

(*In the other room Cabot and Abbie are sitting side by side on the edge of their bed, an old four-poster with feather mattress. He is in his nightshirt,* she *in her nightdress. He is still in the queer, excited mood into which the notion of a son has thrown him. Both rooms are lighted dimly and flickeringly by tallow candles.*)

CABOT: The farm needs a son.

ABBIE: I need a son.

CABOT: Ay-eh. Sometimes ye air the farm an' sometimes the farm be yew. That's why I clove t' ye in my lonesomeness. (*A pause. He pounds his knee with his fist.*) Me an' the farm has got t' beget a son!

ABBIE: Ye'd best go t' sleep. Ye're gittin' thin's all mixed.

CABOT (*with an impatient gesture*): No, I hain't. My mind's clear's a well. Ye don't know me, that's it. (*He stares hopelessly at the floor.*)

ABBIE (*indifferently*): Mebbe. (*In the next room Eben gets up and paces up and down distractedly. Abbie hears him. Her eyes fasten on the intervening wall with concentrated attention. Eben stops and stares. Their hot glances seem to meet through the wall. Unconsciously he stretches out his arms for her and she half rises. Then aware, he mutters a curse at himself and flings himself face downward on the bed, his clenched fists above his head, his face buried in the pillow. Abbie relaxes with a faint sigh but her eyes remain fixed on the wall; she listens with all her attention for some movement from Eben.*)

CABOT (*suddenly raises his head and looks at her — scornfully*): Will ye ever know me — 'r will any man 'r woman? (*Shaking his head.*) No. I calc'late wa'n't t' be. (*He turns away. Abbie looks at the wall. Then, evidently unable to keep silent about his thoughts, without looking at his wife, he puts out his hand and clutches her knee. She starts violently, looks at him, sees he is not watching her, concentrates again on the wall, and pays no attention to what he says.*) Listen, Abbie. When I come here fifty odd year ago — I was jest twenty an' the strongest an' hardest ye ever seen — ten times as strong an' fifty times as hard as Eben. Waal — this place was nothin' but fields o' stones. Folks laughed when I tuk it. They couldn't know what I knowed. When ye kin make corn sprout out o' stones, God's livin' in yew! They wa'n't strong enuf fur that! They reckoned God was easy. They laughed. They don't laugh no more. Some died hereabouts. Some went West an' died. They're all underground — fur follerin' arter an easy God. God hain't easy. (*He shakes his head slowly.*) An' I growed hard. Folks kept allus sayin' he's a hard man like 'twas sinful t' be hard, so's at last I said back at 'em: Waal then, by thunder, ye'll git me hard an' see how ye like it! (*Then suddenly.*) But I give in t' weakness once. 'Twas arter I'd been here two year. I got weak — despairful — they was so many stones. They was a party leavin', givin' up, goin' West. I jined 'em. We tracked on 'n' on. We come t' broad medders, plains, whar the soil was black an' rich as gold. Nary a stone. Easy. Ye'd on'y to plow an' sow an' then set an' smoke yer pipe an' watch thin's grow. I could o' been a rich man — but somethin' in me fit me an' fit me — the voice o' God sayin': "This hain't wuth nothin' t' Me. Git ye back t' hum!" I got afeerd o' that voice an' I lit out back t' hum here, leavin' my claim an' crops t' whoever'd a mind t' take 'em. Ay-eh. I actoolly give up what was rightful mine! God's hard, not easy! God's in the stones! Build my church on a rock — out o' stones an' I'll be in them! That's what He meant t' Peter! (*He sighs heavily — a pause.*) Stones. I picked 'em up an' piled 'em into walls. Ye kin read the years of my life in them walls, every day a hefted stone, climbin' over the hills up and down, fencin' in the fields that was mine, whar I'd made thin's grow out o' nothin' — like the will o' God, like the servant o' His hand. It wa'n't easy. It was hard an' He made me hard fur it. (*He pauses.*) All the time I kept gittin' lonesomer. I tuk a wife. She bore Simeon an' Peter. She was a good woman. She wuked hard. We was married twenty year. She never knowed me. She helped but she never knowed what she was helpin'. I was allus lonesome. She died. After that it wa'n't so lonesome fur a spell. (*A pause.*) I lost count o' the years. I had no time t' fool away countin' 'em. Sim an' Peter helped. The farm growed. It was all mine! When I thought o' that I didn't feel lonesome. (*A pause.*) But ye can't hitch yer mind t' one thin' day an' night. I tuk another wife — Eben's Maw. Her folks was contestin' me at law over my deeds t' the farm — my farm! That's why Eben keeps a-talkin' his fool talk o' this bein' his Maw's farm. She bore Eben. She was purty — but soft. She tried t' be hard. She couldn't. She never knowed me nor nothin'. It was lonesomer 'n hell with her. After a matter o' sixteen odd years, she died. (*A pause.*) I lived with the boys. They hated me 'cause I was hard. I hated them 'cause they was soft. They coveted the farm without knowin' what it meant. It made me bitter 'n wormwood. It aged me — them coveting what I'd made fur mine. Then this spring the call come — the voice o' God cryin' in my wilderness, in my lonesomeness — t' go out an' seek an' find! (*Turning to her with strange passion.*) I sought ye an' I found ye! Yew air my Rose o' Sharon! Yer eyes air like. . . . (*She has turned a*

blank face, resentful eyes to his. He stares at her for a moment — then harshly.*) Air ye any the wiser fur all I've told ye?

ABBIE (*confusedly*): Mebbe.

CABOT (*pushing her away from him — angrily*): Ye don't know nothin' — nor never will. If ye don't hev a son t' redeem ye. . . . (*This in a tone of cold threat.*)

ABBIE (*resentfully*): I've prayed, hain't I?

CABOT (*bitterly*): Pray agen — fur understandin'!

ABBIE (*a veiled threat in her tone*): Ye'll have a son out o' me, I promise ye.

CABOT: How kin ye promise?

ABBIE: I got second-sight mebbe. I kin foretell. (*She gives a queer smile.*)

CABOT: I believe ye have. Ye give me the chills sometimes. (*He shivers.*) It's cold in this house. It's oneasy. They's thin's pokin' about in the dark — in the corners. (*He pulls on his trousers, tucking in his nightshirt, and pulls on his boots.*)

ABBIE (*surprised*): Whar air ye goin'?

CABOT (*queerly*): Down whar it's restful — whar it's warm — down t' the barn. (*Bitterly.*) I kin talk t' the cows. They know. They know the farm an' me. They'll give me peace. (*He turns to go out the door.*)

ABBIE (*a bit frightenedly*): Air ye ailin' tonight, Ephraim?

CABOT: Growin'. Growin' ripe on the bough. (*He turns and goes, his boots clumping down the stairs. Eben sits up with a start, listening. Abbie is conscious of his movement and stares at the wall. Cabot comes out of the house around the corner and stands by the gate, blinking at the sky. He stretches up his hands in a tortured gesture.*) God A'mighty, call from the dark! (*He listens as if expecting an answer. Then his arms drop, he shakes his head and plods off toward the barn. Eben and Abbie stare at each other through the wall. Eben sighs heavily and Abbie echoes it. Both become terribly nervous, uneasy. Finally Abbie gets up and listens, her ear to the wall. He acts as if he saw every move she was making, he becomes resolutely still. She seems driven into a decision — goes out the door in rear determinedly. His eyes follow her. Then as the door of his room is opened softly, he turns away, waits in an attitude of strained fixity. Abbie stands for a second staring at him, her eyes burning with desire. Then with a little cry she runs over and throws her arms about his neck, she pulls his head back and covers his mouth with kisses. At first, he submits dumbly; then he puts his arms about her neck and returns her kisses, but finally, suddenly aware of his hatred, he hurls her away from him, springing to his feet. They stand speechless and breathless, panting like two animals.*)

ABBIE (*at last — painfully*): Ye shouldn't, Eben — ye shouldn't — I'd make ye happy!

EBEN (*harshly*): I don't want t' be happy — from yew!

ABBIE (*helplessly*): Ye do, Eben! Ye do! Why d'ye lie?

EBEN (*viciously*): I don't take t'ye, I tell ye! I hate the sight o' ye!

ABBIE (*with an uncertain troubled laugh*): Waal, I kissed ye anyways — an' ye kissed back — yer lips was burnin' — ye can't lie 'bout that! (*Intensely.*) If ye don't care, why did ye kiss me back — why was yer lips burnin'?

EBEN (*wiping his mouth*): It was like pizen on 'em. (*Then tauntingly.*) When I kissed ye back, mebbe I thought 'twas someone else.

ABBIE (*wildly*): Min?

EBEN: Mebbe.

ABBIE (*torturedly*): Did ye go t' see her? Did ye r'ally go? I thought ye mightn't. Is that why ye throwed me off jest now?

EBEN (*sneeringly*): What if it be?

ABBIE (*raging*): Then ye're a dog, Eben Cabot!

EBEN (*threateningly*): Ye can't talk that way t' me!

ABBIE (*with a shrill laugh*): Can't I? Did ye think I was in love with ye — a weak thin' like yew? Not much! I on'y wanted ye fur a purpose o' my own — an' I'll hev ye fur it yet 'cause I'm stronger'n yew be!

EBEN (*resentfully*): I knowed well it was on'y part o' yer plan t' swaller everythin'!

ABBIE (*tauntingly*): Mebbe!

EBEN (*furious*): Git out o' my room!

ABBIE: This air my room an' ye're on'y hired help!

EBEN (*threateningly*): Git out afore I murder ye!

ABBIE (*quite confident now*): I hain't a mite afeerd. Ye want me, don't ye? Yes, ye do! An' yer Paw's son'll never kill what he wants! Look at yer eyes! They's lust fur me in 'em, burnin' 'em up! Look at yer lips now! They're tremblin' an' longin' t' kiss me, an' yer teeth t' bite! (*He is watching her now with a horrible fascination. She laughs a crazy triumphant laugh.*) I'm a-goin' t' make all o' this hum my hum! They's one room hain't mine yet, but it's a-goin' t' be tonight. I'm a-goin' down now an' light up! (*She makes him a mocking bow.*) Won't ye come courtin' me in the best parlor, Mister Cabot?

EBEN (*staring at her — horribly confused — dully*): Don't ye dare! It hain't been opened since Maw died an' was laid out thar! Don't ye . . . ! (*But her eyes are fixed on his so burningly that his will seems to wither before hers. He stands swaying toward her helplessly.*)

ABBIE (*holding his eyes and putting all her will into*

her words as she backs out the door): I'll expect ye afore long, Eben.

EBEN (*Stares after her for a while, walking toward the door. A light appears in the parlor window. He murmurs.*): In the parlor? (*This seems to arouse connotations, for he comes back and puts on his white shirt, collar, half ties the tie mechanically, puts on coat, takes his hat, stands barefooted looking about him in bewilderment, mutters wonderingly.*) Maw! Whar air yew? (*Then goes slowly toward the door in rear.*)

Scene III

(*A few minutes later. The interior of the parlor is shown. A grim, repressed room like a tomb in which the family has been interred alive. Abbie sits on the edge of the horsehair sofa. She has lighted all the candles and the room is revealed in all its preserved ugliness. A change has come over the woman. She looks awed and frightened now, ready to run away.*)

(*The door is opened and Eben appears. His face wears an expression of obsessed confusion. He stands staring at her, his arms hanging disjointedly from his shoulders, his feet bare, his hat in his hand.*)

ABBIE (*after a pause — with a nervous, formal politeness*): Won't ye set?

EBEN (*dully*): Ay-eh. (*Mechanically he places his hat carefully on the floor near the door and sits stiffly beside her on the edge of the sofa. A pause. They both remain rigid, looking straight ahead with eyes full of fear.*)

ABBIE: When I fust come in — in the dark — they seemed somethin' here.

EBEN (*simply*): Maw.

ABBIE: I kin still feel — somethin'. . . .

EBEN: It's Maw.

ABBIE: At fust I was feered o' it. I wanted t' yell an' run. Now — since yew come — seems like it's growin' soft an' kind t' me. (*Addressing the air — queerly.*) Thank yew.

EBEN: Maw allus loved me.

ABBIE: Mebbe it knows I love yew, too. Mebbe that makes it kind t' me.

EBEN (*dully*): I dunno. I should think she'd hate ye.

ABBIE (*with certainty*): No. I kin feel it don't — not no more.

EBEN: Hate ye fur stealin' her place — here in her hum — settin' in her parlor whar she was laid — (*He suddenly stops, staring stupidly before him.*)

ABBIE: What is it, Eben?

EBEN (*in a whisper*): Seems like Maw didn't want me t' remind ye.

ABBIE (*excitedly*): I knowed, Eben! It's kind t' me! It don't b'ar me no grudges fur what I never knowed an' couldn't help!

EBEN: Maw b'ars him a grudge.

ABBIE: Waal, so does all o' us.

EBEN: Ay-eh. (*With passion.*) I does, by God!

ABBIE (*taking one of his hands in hers and patting it*): Thar! Don't git riled thinkin' o' him. Think o' yer Maw who's kind t' us. Tell me about yer Maw, Eben.

EBEN: They hain't nothin' much. She was kind. She was good.

ABBIE (*Putting one arm over his shoulder. He does not seem to notice — passionately.*): I'll be kind an' good t' ye!

EBEN: Sometimes she used t' sing fur me.

ABBIE: I'll sing fur ye!

EBEN: This was her hum. This was her farm.

ABBIE: This is my hum! This is my farm!

EBEN: He married her t' steal 'em. She was soft an' easy. He couldn't 'preciate her.

ABBIE: He can't 'preciate me!

EBEN: He murdered her with his hardness.

ABBIE: He's murderin' me!

EBEN: She died. (*A pause.*) Sometimes she used to sing fur me. (*He bursts into a fit of sobbing.*)

ABBIE (*both her arms around him — with wild passion*): I'll sing fur ye! I'll die fur ye! (*In spite of her overwhelming desire for him, there is a sincere maternal love in her manner and voice — a horribly frank mixture of lust and mother love.*) Don't cry, Eben! I'll take yer Maw's place! I'll be everythin' she was t' ye! Let me kiss ye, Eben! (*She pulls his head around. He makes a bewildered pretense of resistance. She is tender.*) Don't be afeered! I'll kiss ye pure, Eben — same 's if I was a Maw t' ye — an' ye kin kiss me back 's if yew was my son — my boy — sayin' good-night t' me! Kiss me, Eben. (*They kiss in restrained fashion. Then suddenly wild passion overcomes her. She kisses him lustfully again and again and he flings his arms about her and returns her kisses. Suddenly, as in the bedroom, he frees himself from her violently and springs to his feet. He is trembling all over, in a strange state of terror. Abbie strains her arms toward him with fierce pleading.*) Don't ye leave me, Eben! Can't ye see it hain't enuf — lovin' ye like a Maw — can't ye see it's got t' be that an' more — much more — a hundred times more — fur me t' be happy — fur yew t' be happy?

EBEN (*to the presence he feels in the room*): Maw! Maw! What d'ye want? What air ye tellin' me?

ABBIE: She's tellin' ye t' love me. She knows I love ye an' I'll be good t' ye. Can't ye feel it? Don't ye know? She's tellin' ye t' love me, Eben!

EBEN: Ay-eh. I feel — mebbe she — but — I can't figger out — why — when ye've stole her place — here in her hum — in the parlor whar she was —

ABBIE (*fiercely*): She knows I love ye!

EBEN (*his face suddenly lighting up with a fierce, triumphant grin*): I see it! I sees why. It's her vengeance on him — so's she kin rest quiet in her grave!

ABBIE (*wildly*): Vengeance o' God on the hull o' us! What d'we give a durn? I love ye, Eben! God knows I love ye! (*She stretches out her arms for him.*)

EBEN (*throws himself on his knees beside the sofa and grabs her in his arms — releasing all his pent-up passion*): An' I love ye, Abbie! — now I kin say it! I been dyin' fur want o' ye — every hour since ye come! I love ye! (*Their lips meet in a fierce, bruising kiss.*)

Scene IV

(*Exterior of the farmhouse. It is just dawn. The front door at right is opened and Eben comes out and walks around to the gate. He is dressed in his working clothes. He seems changed. His face wears a bold and confident expression, he is grinning to himself with evident satisfaction. As he gets near the gate, the window of the parlor is heard opening and the shutters are flung back and Abbie sticks her head out. Her hair tumbles over her shoulders in disarray, her face is flushed, she looks at Eben with tender, languorous eyes and calls softly.*)

ABBIE: Eben. (*As he turns — playfully.*) Jest one more kiss afore ye go. I'm goin' to miss ye fearful all day.

EBEN: An' me yew, ye kin bet! (*He goes to her. They kiss several times. He draws away, laughingly.*) Thar. That's enuf, hain't it? Ye won't hev none left fur next time.

ABBIE: I got a million o' 'em left fur yew! (*Then a bit anxiously.*) D'ye r'ally love me, Eben?

EBEN (*emphatically*): I like ye better'n any gal I ever knowed! That's gospel!

ABBIE: Likin' hain't lovin'.

EBEN: Waal then — I love ye. Now air yew satisfied?

ABBIE: Ay-eh, I be. (*She smiles at him adoringly.*)

EBEN: I better git t' the barn. The old critter's liable t' suspicion an' come sneakin' up.

ABBIE (*with a confident laugh*): Let him! I kin allus pull the wool over his eyes. I'm goin' t' leave the shutters open and let in the sun 'n' air. This room's been dead long enuf. Now it's goin' t' be my room!

EBEN (*frowning*): Ay-eh.

ABBIE (*hastily*): I meant — our room.

EBEN: Ay-eh.

ABBIE: We made it our'n last night, didn't we? We give it life — our lovin' did. (*A pause.*)

EBEN (*with a strange look*): Maw's gone back t' her grave. She kin sleep now.

ABBIE: May she rest in peace! (*Then tenderly rebuking.*) Ye oughtn't t' talk o' sad thin's — this mornin'.

EBEN: It jest come up in my mind o' itself.

ABBIE: Don't let it. (*He doesn't answer. She yawns.*) Waal, I'm a-goin' t' steal a wink o' sleep. I'll tell the Old Man I hain't feelin' pert. Let him git his own vittles.

EBEN: I see him comin' from the barn. Ye better look smart an' git upstairs.

ABBIE: Ay-eh. Good-by. Don't ferget me. (*She throws him a kiss. He grins — then squares his shoulders and awaits his father confidently. Cabot walks slowly up from the left, staring up at the sky with a vague face.*)

EBEN (*jovially*): Mornin', Paw. Star-gazin' in daylight?

CABOT: Purty, hain't it?

EBEN (*looking around him possessively*): It's a durned purty farm.

CABOT: I mean the sky.

EBEN (*grinning*): How d'ye know? Them eyes o' your'n can't see that fur. (*This tickles his humor and he slaps his thigh and laughs.*) Ho-ho! That's a good un!

CABOT (*grimly sarcastic*): Ye're feelin' right chipper, hain't ye? Whar'd ye steal the likker?

EBEN (*good-naturedly*): 'Tain't likker. Jest life. (*Suddenly holding out his hand — soberly.*) Yew 'n' me is quits. Let's shake hands.

CABOT (*suspiciously*): What's come over ye?

EBEN: Then don't. Mebbe it's jest as well. (*A moment's pause.*) What's come over me? (*Queerly.*) Didn't ye feel her passin' — goin' back t' her grave?

CABOT (*dully*): Who?

EBEN: Maw. She kin rest now an' sleep content. She's quit with ye.

CABOT (*confusedly*): I rested. I slept good — down with the cows. They know how t' sleep. They're teachin' me.

EBEN (*suddenly jovial again*): Good fur the cows! Waal — ye better git t' work.

CABOT (*grimly amused*): Air yew bossin' me, ye calf?

EBEN (*beginning to laugh*): Ay-eh! I'm bossin' yew! Ha-ha-ha! See how ye like it! Ha-ha-ha! I'm the prize rooster o' this roost. Ha-ha-ha! (*He goes off toward the barn laughing.*)

CABOT (*looks after him with scornful pity*): Soft-headed. Like his Maw. Dead spit 'n' image. No hope in him! (*He spits with contemptuous disgust.*)

A born fool! (*Then matter-of-factly.*) Waal — I'm gittin' peckish. (*He goes toward door.*)

PART III • *Scene I*

(*A night in late spring the following year. The kitchen and the two bedrooms upstairs are shown. The two bedrooms are dimly lighted by a tallow candle in each. Eben is sitting on the side of the bed in his room, his chin propped on his fists, his face a study of the struggle he is making to understand his conflicting emotions. The noisy laughter and music from below where a kitchen dance is in progress annoy and distract him. He scowls at the floor.*)

(*In the next room a cradle stands beside the double bed.*)

(*In the kitchen all is festivity. The stove has been taken down to give more room to the dancers. The chairs, with wooden benches added, have been pushed back against the walls. On these are seated, squeezed in tight against one another, farmers and their wives and their young folks of both sexes from the neighboring farms. They are all chattering and laughing loudly. They evidently have some secret joke in common. There is no end of winking, of nudging, of meaning nods of the head toward Cabot who, in a state of extreme hilarious excitement increased by the amount he has drunk, is standing near the rear door where there is a small keg of whisky and serving drinks to all the men. In the left corner, front, dividing the attention with her husband, Abbie is sitting in a rocking chair, a shawl wrapped about her shoulders. She is very pale, her face is thin and drawn, her eyes are fixed anxiously on the open door in rear as if waiting for someone.*)

(*The musician is tuning up his fiddle, seated in the far right corner. He is a lanky young fellow with a long, weak face. His pale eyes blink incessantly and he grins about him slyly with a greedy malice.*)

ABBIE (*suddenly turning to a young girl on her right*): Whar's Eben?

YOUNG GIRL (*eyeing her scornfully*): I dunno, Mrs. Cabot. I hain't seen Eben in ages. (*Meaningly.*) Seems like he's spent most o' his time t' hum since yew come.

ABBIE (*vaguely*): I tuk his Maw's place.

YOUNG GIRL: Ay-eh. So I've heerd. (*She turns away to retail this bit of gossip to her mother sitting next to her. Abbie turns to her left to a big stoutish middle-aged man whose flushed face and starting eyes show the amount of "likker" he has consumed.*)

ABBIE: Ye hain't seen Eben, hev ye?

MAN: No, I hain't. (*Then he adds with a wink.*) If yew hain't, who would?

ABBIE: He's the best dancer in the county. He'd ought t' come an' dance.

MAN (*with a wink*): Mebbe he's doin' the dutiful an' walkin' the kid t' sleep. It's a boy, hain't it?

ABBIE (*nodding vaguely*): Ay-eh — born two weeks back — purty's a picter.

MAN: They all is — t' their Maws. (*Then in a whisper, with a nudge and a leer.*) Listen, Abbie — if ye ever git tired o' Eben, remember me! Don't fergit now! (*He looks at her uncomprehending face for a second — then grunts disgustedly.*) Waal — guess I'll likker agin. (*He goes over and joins Cabot who is arguing noisily with an old farmer over cows. They all drink.*)

ABBIE (*this time appealing to nobody in particular*): Wonder what Eben's a-doin'? (*Her remark is repeated down the line with many a guffaw and titter until it reaches the fiddler. He fastens his blinking eyes on Abbie.*)

FIDDLER (*raising his voice*): Bet I kin tell ye, Abbie, what Eben's doin'! He's down t' the church offerin' up prayers o' thanksgivin'. (*They all titter expectantly.*)

A MAN: What fur? (*Another titter.*)

FIDDLER: 'Cause unto him a — (*He hesitates just long enough.*) brother is born! (*A roar of laughter. They all look from Abbie to Cabot. She is oblivious, staring at the door. Cabot, although he hasn't heard the words, is irritated by the laughter and steps forward, glaring about him. There is an immediate silence.*)

CABOT: What're ye all bleatin' about — like a flock o' goats? Why don't ye dance, damn ye? I axed ye here t' dance — t' eat, drink an' be merry — an' thar ye set cacklin' like a lot o' wet hens with the pip! Ye've swilled my likker an' guzzled my vittles like hogs, hain't ye? Then dance fur me, can't ye? That's fa'r an' squar', hain't it? (*A grumble of resentment goes around but they are all evidently in too much awe of him to express it openly.*)

FIDDLER (*slyly*): We're waitin' fur Eben. (*A suppressed laugh.*)

CABOT (*with a fierce exultation*): T'hell with Eben! Eben's done fur now! I got a new son! (*His mood switching with drunken suddenness.*) But ye needn't t' laugh at Eben, none o' ye! He's my blood, if he be a dumb fool. He's better nor any o' yew! He kin do a day's work a'most up t' what I kin — an' that'd put any o' yew pore critters t' shame!

FIDDLER: An' he kin do a good night's work, too! (*A roar of laughter.*)

CABOT: Laugh, ye damn fools! Ye're right jist the same, Fiddler. He kin work day an' night too, like I kin, if need be!

OLD FARMER (*from behind the keg where he is weaving drunkenly back and forth — with great simplicity*): They hain't many t' touch ye, Ephraim — a son at seventy-six. That's a hard man fur ye! I be on'y sixty-eight an' I couldn't do it. (*A roar of laughter in which Cabot joins uproariously.*)

CABOT (*slapping him on the back*): I'm sorry fur ye, Hi. I'd never suspicion sech weakness from a boy like yew!

OLD FARMER: An' I never reckoned yew had it in ye nuther, Ephraim. (*There is another laugh.*)

CABOT (*suddenly grim*): I got a lot in me — a hell of a lot — folks don't know on. (*Turning to the fiddler.*) Fiddle 'er up, durn ye! Give 'em somethin' t' dance t'! What air ye, an ornament? Hain't this a celebration? Then grease yer elbow an' go it!

FIDDLER (*seizes a drink which the Old Farmer holds out to him and downs it*): Here goes! (*He starts to fiddle "Lady of the Lake." Four young fellows and four girls form in two lines and dance a square dance. The Fiddler shouts directions for the different movements, keeping his words in the rhythm of the music and interspersing them with jocular personal remarks to the dancers themselves. The people seated along the walls stamp their feet and clap their hands in unison. Cabot is especially active in this respect. Only Abbie remains apathetic, staring at the door as if she were alone in a silent room.*)

FIDDLER: Swing your partner t' the right! That's it, Jim! Give her a b'ar hug. Her Maw hain't lookin'. (*Laughter.*) Change partners! That suits ye, don't it, Essie, now ye got Reub afore ye? Look at her redden up, will ye? Waal, life is short an' so's love, as the feller says. (*Laughter.*)

CABOT (*excitedly, stamping his foot*): Go it, boys! Go it, gals!

FIDDLER (*with a wink at the others*): Ye're the spryest seventy-six ever I sees, Ephraim! Now if ye'd on'y good eyesight . . . ! (*Suppressed laughter. He gives Cabot no chance to retort but roars.*) Promenade! Ye're walkin' like a bride down the aisle, Sarah! Waal, while they's life they's allus hope, I've heerd tell. Swing your partner to the left! Gosh A'mighty, look at Johnny Cook high-steppin'! They hain't goin' t' be much strength left fur howin' in the corn lot t'morrow. (*Laughter.*)

CABOT: Go it! Go it! (*Then suddenly, unable to restrain himself any longer, he prances into the midst of the dancers, scattering them, waving his arms about wildly.*) Ye're all hoofs! Git out o' my road! Give me room! I'll show ye dancin'. Ye're all too soft! (*He pushes them roughly away. They crowd *back toward the walls, muttering, looking at him resentfully.*)

FIDDLER (*jeeringly*): Go it, Ephraim! Go it! (*He starts "Pop, Goes the Weasel," increasing the tempo with every verse until at the end he is fiddling crazily as fast as he can go.*)

CABOT (*Starts to dance, which he does very well and with tremendous vigor. Then he begins to improvise, cuts incredibly grotesque capers, leaping up and cracking his heels together, prancing around in a circle with body bent in an Indian war dance, then suddenly straightening up and kicking as high as he can with both legs. He is like a monkey on a string. And all the while he intersperses his antics with shouts and derisive comments.*): Whoop! Here's dancin' fur ye! Whoop! See that! Seventy-six, if I'm a day! Hard as iron yet! Beatin' the young 'uns like I allus done! Look at me! I'd invite ye t' dance on my hundredth birthday on'y ye'll all be dead by then. Ye're a sickly generation! Yer hearts air pink, not red! Yer veins is full o' mud an' water! I be the on'y man in the county! Whoop! See that! I'm a Injun! I've killed Injuns in the West afore ye was born — an' skulped 'em too! They's a arrer wound on my backside I c'd show ye! The hull tribe chased me. I outrun 'em all — with the arrer stuck in me! An' I tuk vengeance on 'em. Ten eyes fur an eye, that was my motter! Whoop! Look at me! I kin kick the ceilin' off the room! Whoop!

FIDDLER (*stops playing — exhaustedly*): God A'mighty, I got enuf. Ye got the devil's strength in ye.

CABOT (*delightedly*): Did I beat yew, too? Waal, ye played smart. Hev a swig. (*He pours whisky for himself and Fiddler. They drink. The others watch Cabot silently with cold, hostile eyes. There is a dead pause. The Fiddler rests. Cabot leans against the keg, panting, glaring around him confusedly. In the room above, Eben gets to his feet and tiptoes out the door in rear, appearing a moment later in the other bedroom. He moves silently, even frightenedly, toward the cradle and stands there looking down at the baby. His face is as vague as his reactions are confused, but there is a trace of tenderness, of interested discovery. At the same moment that he reaches the cradle, Abbie seems to sense something. She gets up weakly and goes to Cabot.*)

ABBIE: I'm goin' up t' the baby.

CABOT (*with real solicitation*): Air ye able fur the stairs? D'ye want me t' help ye, Abbie?

ABBIE: No. I'm able. I'll be down agen soon.

CABOT: Don't ye git wore out! He needs ye, remember — our son does! (*He grins affectionately, patting her on the back. She shrinks from his touch.*)

ABBIE (*dully*): Don't — tech me. I'm goin' — up. (*She goes. Cabot looks after her. A whisper goes around the room. Cabot turns. It ceases. He wipes his forehead streaming with sweat. He is breathing pantingly.*)

CABOT: I'm a-goin' out t' git fresh air. I'm feelin' a mite dizzy. Fiddle up thar! Dance, all o' ye! Here's likker fur them as wants it. Enjoy yerselves. I'll be back. (*He goes, closing the door behind him.*)

FIDDLER (*sarcastically*): Don't hurry none on our account! (*A suppressed laugh. He imitates Abbie.*) Whar's Eben? (*More laughter.*)

A WOMAN (*loudly*): What's happened in this house is plain as the nose on yer face! (*Abbie appears in the doorway upstairs and stands looking in surprise and adoration at Eben who does not see her.*)

A MAN: Ssshh! He's li'ble t' be listenin' at the door. That'd be like him. (*Their voices die to an intensive whispering. Their faces are concentrated on this gossip. A noise as of dead leaves in the wind comes from the room. Cabot has come out from the porch and stands by the gate, leaning on it, staring at the sky blinkingly. Abbie comes across the room silently. Eben does not notice her until quite near.*)

EBEN (*starting*): Abbie!

ABBIE: Ssshh! (*She throws her arms around him. They kiss — then bend over the cradle together.*) Ain't he purty? — dead spit 'n' image o' yew!

EBEN (*pleased*): Air he? I can't tell none.

ABBIE: E-zactly like!

EBEN (*frowningly*): I don't like this. I don't like lettin' on what's mine's his'n. I been doin' that all my life. I'm gittin' t' the end o' b'arin' it!

ABBIE (*putting her finger on his lips*): We're doin' the best we kin. We got t' wait. Somethin's bound t' happen. (*She puts her arms around him.*) I got t' go back.

EBEN: I'm goin' out. I can't b'ar it with the fiddle playin' an' the laughin'.

ABBIE: Don't git feelin' low. I love ye, Eben. Kiss me. (*He kisses her. They remain in each other's arms.*)

CABOT (*at the gate, confusedly*): Even the music can't drive it out — somethin'. Ye kin feel it droppin' off the elums, climbin' up the roof, sneakin' down the chimney, pokin' in the corners! They's no peace in houses, they's no rest livin' with folks. Somethin's always livin' with ye. (*With a deep sigh.*) I'll go t' the barn an' rest a spell. (*He goes wearily toward the barn.*)

FIDDLER (*tuning up*): Let's celebrate the old skunk gittin' fooled! We kin have some fun now he's went. (*He starts to fiddle "Turkey in the Straw." There is real merriment now. The young folks get up to dance.*)

Scene II

(*A half hour later — exterior — Eben is standing by the gate looking up at the sky, an expression of dumb pain bewildered by itself on his face. Cabot appears, returning from the barn, walking wearily, his eyes on the ground. He sees Eben and his whole mood immediately changes. He becomes excited, a cruel, triumphant grin comes to his lips, he strides up and slaps Eben on the back. From within comes the whining of the fiddle and the noise of stamping feet and laughing voices.*)

CABOT: So har ye be!

EBEN (*startled, stares at him with hatred for a moment — then dully*): Ay-eh.

CABOT (*surveying him jeeringly*): Why hain't ye been in t' dance? They was all axin' fur ye.

EBEN: Let 'em ax!

CABOT: They's a hull passel o' purty gals.

EBEN: T' hell with 'em!

CABOT: Ye'd ought t' be marryin' one o' 'em soon.

EBEN: I hain't marryin' no one.

CABOT: Ye might 'arn a share o' a farm that way.

EBEN (*with a sneer*): Like yew did, ye mean? I hain't that kind.

CABOT (*stung*): Ye lie! 'Twas yer Maw's folks aimed t' steal my farm from me.

EBEN: Other folks don't say so. (*After a pause — defiantly.*) An' I got a farm, anyways!

CABOT (*derisively*): Whar?

EBEN (*stamps a foot on the ground*): Har!

CABOT (*throws his head back and laughs coarsely*): Ho-ho! Ye hev, hev ye? Waal, that's a good un!

EBEN (*controlling himself — grimly*): Ye'll see!

CABOT (*stares at him suspiciously, trying to make him out — a pause — then with scornful confidence*): Ay-eh. I'll see. So'll ye. It's ye that's blind — blind as a mole underground. (*Eben suddenly laughs, one short sardonic bark: "Ha." A pause. Cabot peers at him with renewed suspicion.*) What air ye hawin' 'bout? (*Eben turns away without answering. Cabot grows angry.*) God A'mighty, yew air a dumb dunce! They's nothin' in that thick skull o' your'n but noise — like an empty keg it be! (*Eben doesn't seem to hear. Cabot's rage grows.*) Yewr farm! God A'mighty! If ye wa'n't a born donkey ye'd know ye'll never own stick nor stone on it, specially now arter him bein' born. It's his'n, I tell ye — his'n arter I die — but I'll live a hundred jest t' fool ye all — an' he'll be growed then — yewr age a'most! (*Eben laughs again his sardonic "Ha." This drives Cabot into a fury.*) Ha? Ye think ye kin git 'round that someways, do ye? Waal, it'll be her'n, too — Abbie's — ye won't git 'round her — she knows yer tricks — she'll be too much fur ye — she wants the farm her'n — she was afeerd o' ye — she told me ye was sneakin' 'round tryin' t' make love t' her t' git her on yer side ... ye ... ye mad fool, ye! (*He raises his clenched fists threateningly.*)

EBEN (*is confronting him, choking with rage*): Ye lie, ye old skunk! Abbie never said no sech thing!

CABOT (*suddenly triumphant when he sees how shaken Eben is*): She did. An' I says, I'll blow his brains t' the top o' them elums — an' she says no, that hain't sense, who'll ye git t'help ye on the farm in his place — an' then she says yew'n me ought t' have a son — I know we kin, she says — an' I says, if we do, ye kin have anythin' I've got ye've a mind t'. An' she says, I wants Eben cut off so's this farm'll be mine when ye die! (*With terrible gloating.*) An' that's what's happened, hain't it? An' the farm's her'n! An' the dust o' the road — that's you'rn! Ha! Now who's hawin'?

EBEN (*has been listening, petrified with grief and rage — suddenly laughs wildly and brokenly*): Ha-ha-ha! So that's her sneakin' game — all along! — like I suspicioned at fust — t' swaller it all — an' me, too ...! (*Madly.*) I'll murder her! (*He springs toward the porch but Cabot is quicker and gets in between.*)

CABOT: No, ye don't!

EBEN: Git out o' my road! (*He tries to throw Cabot aside. They grapple in what becomes immediately a murderous struggle. The old man's concentrated strength is too much for Eben. Cabot gets one hand on his throat and presses him back across the stone wall. At the same moment, Abbie comes out on the porch. With a stifled cry she runs toward them.*)

ABBIE: Eben! Ephraim! (*She tugs at the hand on Eben's throat.*) Let go, Ephraim! Ye're chokin' him!

CABOT (*Removes his hand and flings Eben sideways full length on the grass, gasping and choking. With a cry, Abbie kneels beside him, trying to take his head on her lap, but he pushes her away. Cabot stands looking down with fierce triumph.*): Ye needn't t've fret, Abbie, I wa'n't aimin' t' kill him. He hain't wuth hangin' fur — not by a hell of a sight! (*More and more triumphantly.*) Seventy-six an' him not thirty yit — an' look whar he be fur thinkin' his Paw was easy! No, by God, I hain't easy! An' him upstairs, I'll raise him t' be like me! (*He turns to leave them.*) I'm goin' in an' dance! — sing an' celebrate! (*He walks to the porch — then turns with a great grin.*) I don't calc'late it's left in him, but if he gits pesky, Abbie, ye jest sing out. I'll come a-runnin' an' by the Eternal, I'll put him across my knee an' birch him! Ha-ha-ha! (*He goes into the house laughing. A moment later his loud "whoop" is heard.*)

ABBIE (*tenderly*): Eben. Air ye hurt? (*She tries to kiss him but he pushes her violently away and struggles to a sitting position.*)

EBEN (*gaspingly*): T'hell — with ye!

ABBIE (*not believing her ears*): It's me, Eben — Abbie — don't ye know me?

EBEN (*glowering at her with hatred*): Ay-eh — I know ye — now! (*He suddenly breaks down, sobbing weakly.*)

ABBIE (*fearfully*): Eben — what's happened t' ye — why did ye look at me 's if ye hated me?

EBEN (*violently, between sobs and gasps*): I do hate ye! Ye're a whore — a damn trickin' whore!

ABBIE (*shrinking back horrified*): Eben! Ye don't know what ye're sayin'!

EBEN (*scrambling to his feet and following her — accusingly*): Ye're nothin' but a stinkin' passel o' lies! Ye've been lyin' t' me every word ye spoke, day an' night, since we fust — done it. Ye've kept sayin' ye loved me. . . .

ABBIE (*frantically*): I do love ye! (*She takes his hand but he flings hers away.*)

EBEN (*unheeding*): Ye've made a fool o' me — a sick, dumb fool — a-purpose! Ye've been on'y playin' yer sneakin', stealin' game all along — gittin' me t' lie with ye so's ye'd hev a son he'd think was his'n, an' makin' him promise he'd give ye the farm and let me eat dust, if ye did git him a son! (*Staring at her with anguished, bewildered eyes.*) They must be a devil livin' in ye! T'ain't human t' be as bad as that be!

ABBIE (*stunned — dully*): He told yew . . . ?

EBEN: Hain't it true? It hain't no good in yew lyin'.

ABBIE (*pleadingly*): Eben, listen — ye must listen — it was long ago — afore we done nothin' — yew was scornin' me — goin' t' see Min — when I was lovin' ye — an' I said it t' him t' git vengeance on ye!

EBEN (*Unheedingly. With tortured passion.*): I wish ye was dead! I wish I was dead along with ye afore this come! (*Ragingly.*) But I'll git my vengeance too! I'll pray Maw t' come back t' help me — t' put her cuss on yew an' him!

ABBIE (*brokenly*): Don't ye, Eben! Don't ye! (*She throws herself on her knees before him, weeping.*) I didn't mean t' do bad t'ye! Fergive me, won't ye?

EBEN (*not seeming to hear her — fiercely*): I'll git squar' with the old skunk — an' yew! I'll tell him the truth 'bout the son he's so proud o'! Then I'll leave ye here t' pizen each other — with Maw comin' out o' her grave at nights — an' I'll go t' the gold fields o' Californi-a whar Sim an' Peter be!

ABBIE (*terrified*): Ye won't — leave me? Ye can't!

EBEN (*with fierce determination*): I'm a-goin', I tell ye! I'll git rich thar an' come back an' fight him fur the farm he stole — an' I'll kick ye both out in the road — t' beg an' sleep in the woods — an' yer son along with ye — t' starve an' die! (*He is hysterical at the end.*)

ABBIE (*with a shudder — humbly*): He's yewr son, too, Eben.

EBEN (*torturedly*): I wish he never was born! I wish he'd die this minit! I wish I'd never sot eyes on him! It's him — yew havin' him — a-purpose t' steal — that's changed everythin'!

ABBIE (*gently*): Did ye believe I loved ye — afore he come?

EBEN: Aye-eh — like a dumb ox!

ABBIE: An' ye don't believe no more?

EBEN: B'lieve a lyin' thief! Ha!

ABBIE (*shudders — then humbly*): An' did ye r'ally love me afore?

EBEN (*brokenly*): Ay-eh — an' ye was trickin' me!

ABBIE: An' ye don't love me now!

EBEN (*violently*): I hate ye, I tell ye!

ABBIE: An' ye're truly goin' West — goin' t' leave me — all account o' him being born?

EBEN: I'm a-goin' in the mornin' — or may God strike me t' hell!

ABBIE (*after a pause — with a dreadful cold intensity — slowly*): If that's what his comin's done t' me — killin' yewr love — takin' yew away — my on'y joy — the on'y joy I ever knowed — like heaven t' me — purtier'n heaven — then I hate him, too, even if I be his Maw!

EBEN (*bitterly*): Lies! Ye love him! He'll steal the farm fur ye! (*Brokenly.*) But t'ain't the farm so much — not no more — it's yew foolin' me — gittin' me t' love ye — lyin' yew loved me — jest t' git a son t' steal!

ABBIE (*distractedly*): He won't steal! I'd kill him fust! I do love ye! I'll prove t' ye . . . !

EBEN (*harshly*): T'ain't no use lyin' no more. I'm deaf t' ye! (*He turns away.*) I hain't seein' ye agen. Good-by!

ABBIE (*pale with anguish*): Hain't ye even goin' t' kiss me — not once — arter all we loved?

EBEN (*in a hard voice*): I hain't wantin' t' kiss ye never agen! I'm wantin' t' forgit I ever sot eyes on ye!

ABBIE: Eben! — ye mustn't — wait a spell — I want t' tell ye. . . .

EBEN: I'm a-goin' in t' git drunk. I'm a-goin' t' dance.

ABBIE (*clinging to his arm — with passionate earnestness*): If I could make it — 's if he'd never come up between us — if I could prove t' ye I wa'n't schemin' t' steal from ye — so's everythin' could be jest the same with us, lovin' each other jest the same, kissin' an' happy the same's we've been happy afore he come — if I could do it —

ye'd love me agen, wouldn't ye? Ye'd kiss me agen? Ye wouldn't never leave me, would ye?

EBEN (*moved*): I calc'late not. (*Then shaking her hand off his arm — with a bitter smile.*) But ye hain't God, be ye?

ABBIE (*exultantly*): Remember ye've promised! (*Then with strange intensity.*) Mebbe I kin take back one thin' God does!

EBEN (*peering at her*): Ye're gittin' cracked, hain't ye? (*Then going toward door.*) I'm a-goin' t' dance.

ABBIE (*calls after him intensely*): I'll prove t' ye! I'll prove I love ye better'n. . . . (*He goes in the door, not seeming to hear. She remains standing where she is, looking after him — then she finishes desperately.*) Better'n everythin' else in the world!

Scene III

(*Just before dawn in the morning — shows the kitchen and Cabot's bedroom. In the kitchen, by the light of a tallow candle on the table, Eben is sitting, his chin propped on his hands, his drawn face blank and expressionless. His carpetbag is on the floor beside him. In the bedroom, dimly lighted by a small whale-oil lamp, Cabot lies asleep. Abbie is bending over the cradle, listening, her face full of terror yet with an undercurrent of desperate triumph. Suddenly, she breaks down and sobs, appears about to throw herself on her knees beside the cradle; but the old man turns restlessly, groaning in his sleep, and she controls herself, and, shrinking away from the cradle with a gesture of horror, backs swiftly toward the door in rear and goes out. A moment later she comes into the kitchen and, running to Eben, flings her arms about his neck and kisses him wildly. He hardens himself, he remains unmoved and cold, he keeps his eyes straight ahead.*)

ABBIE (*hysterically*): I done it, Eben! I told ye I'd do it! I've proved I love ye — better'n everythin' — so's ye can't never doubt me no more!

EBEN (*dully*): Whatever ye done, it hain't no good now.

ABBIE (*wildly*): Don't ye say that! Kiss me, Eben, won't ye? I need ye t' kiss me arter what I done! I need ye t' say ye love me!

EBEN (*kisses her without emotion — dully*): That's fur good-by. I'm a-goin' soon.

ABBIE: No! No! Ye won't go — not now!

EBEN (*going on with his own thoughts*): I been a-thinkin' — an' I hain't goin' t' tell Paw nothin'. I'll leave Maw t' take vengeance on ye. If I told him, the old skunk'd jest be stinkin' mean enuf to take it out on that baby. (*His voice showing emotion in spite of him.*) An' I don't want nothin' bad

t' happen t' him. He hain't t' blame fur yew. (*He adds with a certain queer pride.*) An' he looks like me! An' by God, he's mine! An' some day I'll be a-comin' back an' . . . !

ABBIE (*too absorbed in her own thoughts to listen to him — pleadingly*): They's no cause fur ye t' go now — they's no sense — it's all the same's it was — they's nothin' come b'tween us now — arter what I done!

EBEN (*Something in her voice arouses him. He stares at her a bit frightenedly.*): Ye look mad, Abbie. What did ye do?

ABBIE: I — I killed him, Eben.

EBEN (*amazed*): Ye killed him?

ABBIE (*dully*): Ay-eh.

EBEN (*recovering from his astonishment — savagely*): An' serves him right! But we got t' do somethin' quick t' make it look s'if the old skunk'd killed himself when he was drunk. We kin prove by 'em all how drunk he got.

ABBIE (*wildly*): No! No! Not him! (*Laughing distractedly.*) But that's what I ought t' done, hain't it? I oughter killed him instead! Why didn't ye tell me?

EBEN (*appalled*): Instead? What d'ye mean?

ABBIE: Not him.

EBEN (*his face grown ghastly*): Not — not that baby!

ABBIE (*dully*): Ay-eh!

EBEN (*falls to his knees as if he'd been struck — his voice trembling with horror*): Oh, God A'mighty! A'mighty God! Maw, whar was ye, why didn't ye stop her?

ABBIE (*simply*): She went back t' her grave that night we fust done it, remember? I hain't felt her about since. (*A pause. Eben hides his head in his hands, trembling all over as if he had the ague. She goes on dully.*) I left the piller over his little face. Then he killed himself. He stopped breathin'. (*She begins to weep softly.*)

EBEN (*rage beginning to mingle with grief*): He looked like me. He was mine, damn ye!

ABBIE (*slowly and brokenly*): I didn't want t' do it. I hated myself fur doin' it. I loved him. He was so purty — dead spit 'n' image o' yew. But I loved yew more — an' yew was goin' away — far off whar I'd never see ye agen, never kiss ye, never feel ye pressed agin me agen — an' ye said ye hated me fur havin' him — ye said ye hated him an' wished he was dead — ye said if it hadn't been fur him comin' it'd be the same's afore between us.

EBEN (*unable to endure this, springs to his feet in a fury, threatening her, his twitching fingers seeming to reach out for her throat*): Ye lie! I never said — I never dreamed ye'd — I'd cut off my head afore I'd hurt his finger!

ABBIE (*piteously, sinking on her knees*): Eben, don't

ye look at me like that — hatin' me — not after what I done fur ye — fur us — so's we could be happy agen —

EBEN (*furiously now*): Shut up, or I'll kill ye! I see yer game now — the same old sneakin' trick — ye're aimin' t' blame me fur the murder ye done!

ABBIE (*moaning — putting her hands over her ears*): Don't ye, Eben! Don't ye! (*She grasps his legs.*)

EBEN (*his mood suddenly changing to horror, shrinks away from her*): Don't ye tech me! Ye're pizen! How could ye — t' murder a pore little critter — Ye must've swapped yer soul t' hell! (*Suddenly raging.*) Ha! I kin see why ye done it! Not the lies ye jest told — but 'cause ye wanted t' steal agen — steal the last thin' ye'd left me — my part o' him — no, the hull o' him — ye saw he looked like me — ye knowed he was all mine — an' ye couldn't b'ar it — I know ye! Ye killed him fur bein' mine! (*All this has driven him almost insane. He makes a rush past her for the door — then turns — shaking both fists at her, violently.*) But I'll take vengeance now! I'll git the Sheriff! I'll tell him everythin'! Then I'll sing "I'm off to California!" an' go — gold — Golden Gate — gold sun — fields o' gold in the West! (*This last he half shouts, half croons incoherently, suddenly breaking off passionately.*) I'm a-goin' fur the Sheriff t' come an' git ye! I want ye tuk away, locked up from me! I can't stand t' luk at ye! Murderer an' thief 'r not, ye still tempt me! I'll give ye up t' the Sheriff! (*He turns and runs out, around the corner of house, panting and sobbing, and breaks into a swerving sprint down the road.*)

ABBIE (*struggling to her feet, runs to the door, calling after him*): I love ye, Eben! I love ye! (*She stops at the door weakly, swaying, about to fall.*) I don't care what ye do — if ye'll on'y love me agen — (*She falls limply to the floor in a faint.*)

Scene IV

(*About an hour later. Same as scene III. Shows the kitchen and Cabot's bedroom. It is after dawn. The sky is brilliant with the sunrise. In the kitchen, Abbie sits at the table, her body limp and exhausted, her head bowed down over her arms, her face hidden. Upstairs, Cabot is still asleep but awakens with a start. He looks toward the window and gives a snort of surprise and irritation — throws back the covers and begins hurriedly pulling on his clothes. Without looking behind him, he begins talking to Abbie whom he supposes beside him.*)

CABOT: Thunder 'n' lightin', Abbie! I hain't slept this late in fifty year! Looks 's if the sun was full riz a'most. Must've been the dancin' an' likker. Must be gittin' old. I hope Eben's t' wuk. Ye might've tuk the trouble t' rouse me, Abbie. (*He turns — sees no one there — surprised.*) Waal — whar air she? Gittin' vittles, I calc'late. (*He tiptoes to the cradle and peers down — proudly.*) Mornin', sonny. Purty's a picter! Sleepin' sound. He don't beller all night like most o' 'em. (*He goes quietly out the door in rear — a few moments later enters kitchen — sees Abbie — with satisfaction.*) So thar ye be. Ye got any vittles cooked?

ABBIE (*without moving*): No.

CABOT (*coming to her, almost sympathetically*): Ye feelin' sick?

ABBIE: No.

CABOT (*Pats her on shoulder. She shudders.*): Ye'd best lie down a spell. (*Half jocularly.*) Yer son'll be needin' ye soon. He'd ought t' wake up with a gnashin' appetite, the sound way he's sleepin'.

ABBIE (*shudders — then in a dead voice*): He hain't never goin' t' wake up.

CABOT (*jokingly*): Takes after me this mornin'. I hain't slept so late in . . .

ABBIE: He's dead.

CABOT (*stares at her — bewilderedly*): What. . . .

ABBIE: I killed him.

CABOT (*stepping back from her — aghast*): Air ye drunk — 'r crazy — 'r . . . ?

ABBIE (*suddenly lifts her head and turns on him — wildly*): I killed him, I tell ye! I smothered him. Go up an' see if ye don't b'lieve me!

(*Cabot stares at her a second, then bolts out the rear door, can be heard bounding up the stairs, and rushes into the bedroom and over to the cradle. Abbie has sunk back lifelessly into her former position. Cabot puts his hand down on the body in the crib. An expression of fear and horror comes over his face.*)

CABOT (*shrinking away — tremblingly*): God A'mighty! God A'mighty. (*He stumbles out the door — in a short while returns to the kitchen — comes to Abbie, the stunned expression still on his face — hoarsely.*) Why did ye do it? Why? (*As she doesn't answer, he grabs her violently by the shoulder and shakes her.*) I ax ye why ye done it! Ye'd better tell me 'r . . . !

ABBIE (*gives him a furious push which sends him staggering back and springs to her feet — with wild rage and hatred*): Don't ye dare tech me! What right hev ye t' question me 'bout him? He wa'n't yewr son! Think I'd have a son by yew? I'd die fust! I hate the sight o' ye an' allus did! It's yew I should've murdered, if I'd had good sense! I hate ye! I love Eben. I did from the fust. An' he was Eben's son — mine an' Eben's — not your'n!

CABOT (*stands looking at her dazedly — a pause —*

finding his words with an effort — dully): That was it — what I felt — pokin' round the corners — while ye lied — holdin' yerself from me — sayin' ye'd a'ready conceived — (*He lapses into crushed silence — then with a strange emotion.*) He's dead, sart'n. I felt his heart. Pore little critter! (*He blinks back one tear, wiping his sleeve across his nose.*)

ABBIE (*hysterically*): Don't ye! Don't ye! (*She sobs unrestrainedly.*)

CABOT (*with a concentrated effort that stiffens his body into a rigid line and hardens his face into a stony mask — through his teeth to himself*): I got t' be — like a stone — a rock o' jedgment! (*A pause. He gets complete control over himself — harshly.*) If he was Eben's, I be glad he air gone! An' mebbe I suspicioned it all along. I felt they was somethin' onnateral — somewhars — the house got so lonesome — an' cold — drivin' me down t' the barn — t' the beasts o' the field. . . . Ay-eh. I must've suspicioned — somethin'. Ye didn't fool me — not altogether, leastways — I'm too old a bird — growin' ripe on the bough. . . . (*He becomes aware he is wandering, straightens again, looks at Abbie with a cruel grin.*) So ye'd liked t' hev murdered him 'stead o' him, would ye? Waal, I'll live to a hundred! I'll live t' see ye hung! I'll deliver ye up t' the jedgment o' God an' the law! I'll git the Sheriff now. (*Starts for the door.*)

ABBIE (*dully*): Ye needn't. Eben's gone fur him.

CABOT (*amazed*): Eben — gone fur the Sheriff?

ABBIE: Ay-eh.

CABOT: T' inform agen ye?

ABBIE: Ay-eh.

CABOT (*considers this — a pause — then in a hard voice*): Waal, I'm thankful fur him savin' me the trouble. I'll git t' wuk. (*He goes to the door — then turns — in a voice full of strange emotion.*) He'd ought t' been my son, Abbie. Ye'd ought t' loved me. I'm a man. If ye'd loved me, I'd never told no Sheriff on ye no matter what ye did, if they was t' brile me alive!

ABBIE (*defensively*): They's more to it nor yew know, makes him tell.

CABOT (*dryly*): Fur yewr sake, I hope they be. (*He goes out — comes around to the gate — stares up at the sky. His control relaxes. For a moment he is old and weary. He murmurs despairingly.*) God A'mighty, I be lonesomer'n ever! (*He hears running footsteps from the left, immediately is himself again. Eben runs in, panting exhaustedly, wild-eyed and mad looking. He lurches through the gate. Cabot grabs him by the shoulder. Eben stares at him dumbly.*) Did ye tell the Sheriff?

EBEN (*nodding stupidly*): Ay-eh.

CABOT (*gives him a push away that sends him sprawl-*

ing — laughing with withering contempt): Good fur ye! A prime chip o' yer Maw ye be! (*He goes toward the barn, laughing harshly. Eben scrambles to his feet. Suddenly Cabot turns — grimly threatening.*) Git off this farm when the Sheriff takes her — or, by God, he'll have t' come back an' git me fur murder, too! (*He stalks off. Eben does not appear to have heard him. He runs to the door and comes into the kitchen. Abbie looks up with a cry of anguished joy. Eben stumbles over and throws himself on his knees beside her sobbing brokenly.*)

EBEN: Fergive me!

ABBIE (*happily*): Eben! (*She kisses him and pulls his head over against her breast.*)

EBEN: I love ye! Fergive me!

ABBIE (*ecstatically*): I'd fergive ye all the sins in hell fur sayin' that! (*She kisses his head, pressing it to her with a fierce passion of possession.*)

EBEN (*brokenly*): But I told the Sheriff. He's comin' fur ye!

ABBIE: I kin b'ar what happens t' me — now!

EBEN: I woke him up. I told him. He says, wait 'til I git dressed. I was waiting. I got to thinkin' o' yew. I got to thinkin' how I'd loved ye. It hurt like somethin' was bustin' in my chest an' head. I got t' cryin'. I knowed sudden I loved ye yet, an' allus would love ye!

ABBIE (*caressing his hair — tenderly*): My boy, hain't ye?

EBEN: I begun t' run back. I cut across the fields an' through the woods. I thought ye might have time t' run away — with me — an' . . .

ABBIE (*shaking her head*): I got t' take my punishment — t' pay fur my sin.

EBEN: Then I want t' share it with ye.

ABBIE: Ye didn't do nothin'.

EBEN: I put it in yer head. I wisht he was dead! I as much as urged ye t' do it!

ABBIE: No. It was me alone!

EBEN: I'm as guilty as yew be! He was the child o' our sin.

ABBIE (*lifting her head as if defying God*): I don't repent that sin! I hain't askin' God t' fergive that!

EBEN: Nor me — but it led up t' the other — an' the murder ye did, ye did 'count o' me — an' it's my murder, too, I'll tell the Sheriff — an' if ye deny it, I'll say we planned it t'gether — an' they'll all b'lieve me, fur they suspicion everythin' we've done, an' it'll seem likely an' true to 'em. An' it is true — way down. I did help ye — somehow.

ABBIE (*laying her head on his — sobbing*): No! I don't want yew t' suffer!

EBEN: I got t' pay fur my part o' the sin! An' I'd suffer wuss leavin' ye, goin' West, thinkin' o' ye day an' night, bein' out when yew was in — (*lowering his voice*) 'r bein' alive when yew was dead. (*A pause.*) I want t' share with ye, Abbie — prison 'r death 'r hell 'r anythin'! (*He looks into her eyes and forces a trembling smile.*) If I'm sharin' with ye, I won't feel lonesome, leastways.

ABBIE (*weakly*): Eben! I won't let ye! I can't let ye!

EBEN (*kissing her — tenderly*): Ye can't he'p yerself. I got ye beat fur once!

ABBIE (*forcing a smile — adoringly*): I hain't beat — s'long's I got ye!

EBEN (*hears the sound of feet outside*): Ssshh! Listen! They've come t' take us!

ABBIE: No, it's him. Don't give him no chance to fight ye, Eben. Don't say nothin' — no matter what he says. An' I won't neither. (*It is Cabot. He comes up from the barn in a great state of excitement and strides into the house and then into the kitchen. Eben is kneeling beside Abbie, his arm around her, hers around him. They stare straight ahead.*)

CABOT (*Stares at them, his face hard. A long pause — vindictively.*): Ye make a slick pair o' murderin' turtle doves! Ye'd ought t' be both hung on the same limb an' left thar t' swing in the breeze an' rot — a warnin' t' old fools like me t' b'ar their lonesomeness alone — an' fur young fools like ye t' hobble their lust. (*A pause. The excitement returns to his face, his eyes snap, he looks a bit crazy.*) I couldn't work today. I couldn't take no interest. T' hell with the farm! I'm leavin' it! I've turned the cows an' other stock loose! I've druv 'em into the woods whar they kin be free! By freein' 'em, I'm freein' myself! I'm quittin' here today! I'll set fire t' house an' barn an' watch 'em burn, an' I'll leave yer Maw t' haunt the ashes, an' I'll will the fields back t' God, so that nothin' human kin never touch 'em! I'll be a-goin' to Californi-a — t' jine Simeon an' Peter — true sons o' mine if they be dumb fools — an' the Cabots'll find Solomon's Mines t'gether! (*He suddenly cuts a mad caper.*) Whoop! What was the song they sung? "Oh, Californi-a! That's the land fur me." (*He sings this — then gets on his knees by the floorboard under which the money was hid.*) An' I'll sail thar on one o' the finest clippers I kin find! I've got the money! Pity ye didn't know whar this was hidden so's ye could steal. . . . (*He has pulled up the board. He stares — feels — stares again. A pause of dead silence. He slowly turns, slumping into a sitting position on the floor, his eyes like those of a dead fish, his face the sickly green of an attack of nausea. He swallows painfully several times — forces a weak smile at last.*) So — ye did steal it!

EBEN (*emotionlessly*): I swapped it t' Sim an' Peter fur their share o' the farm — t' pay their passage t' Californi-a.

CABOT (*with one sardonic*): Ha! (*He begins to recover. Gets slowly to his feet — strangely.*) I calc'late God give it to 'em — not yew! God's hard, not easy! Mebbe they's easy gold in the West but it hain't God's gold. It hain't fur me. I kin hear His voice warnin' me agen t' be hard an' stay on my farm. I kin see his hand usin' Eben t' steal t' keep me from weakness. I kin feel I be in the palm o' His hand, His fingers guidin' me. (*A pause — then he mutters sadly.*) It's a-goin' t' be lonesomer now than ever it war afore — an' I'm gittin' old, Lord — ripe on the bough. . . . (*Then stiffening.*) Waal — what d'ye want? God's lonesome, hain't He? God's hard an' lonesome! (*A pause. The Sheriff with two men comes up the road from the left. They move cautiously to the door. The Sheriff knocks on it with the butt of his pistol.*)

SHERIFF: Open in the name o' the law! (*They start.*)

CABOT: They've come fur ye. (*He goes to the rear door.*) Come in, Jim! (*The three men enter. Cabot meets them in doorway.*) Jest a minit, Jim. I got 'em safe here. (*The Sheriff nods. He and his companions remain in the doorway.*)

EBEN (*suddenly calls*): I lied this mornin', Jim. I helped her to do it. Ye kin take me, too.

ABBIE (*brokenly*): No!

CABOT: Take 'em both. (*He comes forward — stares at Eben with a trace of grudging admiration.*) Purty good — fur yew! Waal, I got t' round up the stock. Good-by.

EBEN: Good-by.

ABBIE: Good-by. (*Cabot turns and strides past the men — comes out and around the corner of the house, his shoulders squared, his face stony, and stalks grimly toward the barn. In the meantime the Sheriff and men have come into the room.*)

SHERIFF (*embarrassedly*): Waal — we'd best start.

ABBIE: Wait. (*Turns to Eben.*) I love ye, Eben.

EBEN: I love ye, Abbie. (*They kiss. The three men grin and shuffle embarrassedly. Eben takes Abbie's hand. They go out the door in rear, the men following, and come from the house, walking hand in hand to the gate. Eben stops there and points to the sunrise sky.*) Sun's a-rizin'. Purty, hain't it?

ABBIE: Ay-eh. (*They both stand for a moment looking up raptly in attitudes strangely aloof and devout.*)

SHERIFF (*looking around at the farm enviously — to his companions*): It's a jim-dandy farm, no denyin'. Wished I owned it!

Bertolt Brecht

Among the most inventive and influential of modern playwrights, Bertolt Brecht (1898–1956) has left a legacy of important plays and theories about how those plays should be produced. His work is inextricably connected with politics. Throughout most of his career he felt that drama should inform and awaken sensibilities, not just entertain or anesthetize an audience. Most of his plays concern philosophical and political issues, and some of them so threatened the Nazi regime that his works were burned publicly in Germany during the Third Reich.

When he was nineteen, Brecht was an orderly in a hospital during the last months of World War I. He saw so much carnage and misery in the medical wards that he became a lifelong pacifist. After the war he began writing plays while he was a student in Munich. His first successes in the Munich theater took the form of commentary on returned war veterans, on the questions of duty and heroism — which he treated negatively. His materialistic attitude (his rejection of spiritual concepts) was influenced by his readings of Hegel and the doctrines of Marx's dialectical materialism. Marx's theories predicted class struggles and based most social values in economic realities. Brecht eventually moved to Berlin, the theatrical center of Germany, and by 1926 was on his way to becoming a Communist.

Brecht found the political pressures in early Nazi Germany too frightening and dangerous for his writing, and he went into exile in 1933. He lived for a time in Scandinavia and later in the United States. After World War II Brecht and his wife returned to Berlin where, in 1949, he founded the Berliner Ensemble, which produced most of his later work. Brecht chose East Berlin as his home, in part because he felt his work could best be understood in a Communist setting. One irony is that his work has been even more widely appreciated and accepted in the West than in the former Communist eastern bloc.

Brecht wrote his most popular play in 1928, a musical in collaboration with the German composer Kurt Weill: *The Threepenny Opera*. The model for this play, the English writer John Gay's 1728 opera-drama *The Beggar's Opera*, provided Brecht with a perfect platform on which to comment satirically on the political and economic circumstances in Germany two hundred years after Gay wrote. The success of the Brecht-Weill collaboration — the work is still performed regularly — is due in part to Brecht's capacity to create appealing underworld characters such as Polly Peachum and Macheath, known as Mackie the Knife.

Brecht's wife, Helene Weigel, played Mrs. Peachum, the madam of the brothel in which the action takes place. Kurt Weill's second wife, Lotte Lenya, was an overnight sensation in the part of Jenny, and she had a reprise in New York almost twenty-five years later when she was as highly acclaimed as she was in the original Berlin production.

Brecht's most successful plays are *Galileo* (1938–1939); *Mother Courage* (1941); *The Good Woman of Setzuan* (1943); *The Private Lives of the Master Race* (1945); and *The Caucasian Chalk Circle* (1948). But these represent only a tiny fraction of a mass of work, including plays, poetry, criticism, and fiction. His output is extraordinary in volume and quality. It includes plays borrowed not only from Gay but from Sophocles, Molière, Gorky, Shakespeare, and John Webster, among others.

Brecht developed a number of theories regarding drama. He defined the concept of epic theater as an alternative to the traditional Aristotelian theory. Brecht wanted his audience to be in a dialectical and sometimes alienated relationship with the drama. He expected his audience to observe, but to observe critically, to draw conclusions and participate in an intellectual argument with the work at hand. The confrontational relationship he intended was designed to engage the audience in analyzing what they saw rather than identifying with the main characters or enjoying a wash of sentimentality or emotion.

One of the ways in which Brecht hoped to achieve his ends was by making the production's props, lights, sets, and equipment visible, thereby reminding the audience that they were seeing a play. He hoped to alienate his audience from the drama to keep them emotionally detached and intellectually alert. He used the term ALIENATION to define the effect he wanted his theater to have on an audience. Brecht's theater was political. He saw a connection between a critical theater audience and an audience able to analyze reality critically and see that conditions were not fixed immutably, but could be changed.

Brecht's theories produced interesting results and helped stimulate audiences that expected to be entertained by realistic and often sentimental plays. His style spread rapidly throughout the world of theater, and it is still being used and developed by contemporary playwrights such as Heinz Werner Henze and performers such as Pina Bausch.

GALILEO

Galileo Galilei (1564–1642) was a brilliant astronomer and physicist whose theories shook the established ecclesiastical and scientific order of his day. In a society that believed in witches but was suspicious of anyone who asserted that the earth revolves around the sun, the seventeenth-century church was caretaker of the truth. It held steadfast to scientific views rooted in ancient Greek tradition, particularly the work of Aristotle, even in the face of mounting scientific evidence to the contrary. Galileo's theories and findings about astronomical phenomena, such as the motion of heavenly bodies, clashed with the church's views. Even though Pope Urban VIII was a scientist (and presumably sympathetic) and Clavius, his official astronomer, believed that Galileo's theories were accurate, the Pope was persuaded to allow Galileo to be interrogated by the Inquisition, which had already burned at the stake the anti-Aristotelian philosopher Giordano Bruno. Threatened with a similar fate, Galileo recanted his theories in 1633 and lived out his old age in relative silence. Brecht once said that if Galileo had held firm, the period of the Great Enlightenment would have come a hundred years sooner.

Brecht seems to have chosen Galileo for his subject because the astronomer was working with observable scientific evidence that pointed to an indisputable truth. Contemporary events also fueled Brecht's interest in this material. When he began work on the play during his exile in Denmark in 1938–1939 the Nazis had purged the scientific establishment of its Jewish scientists, implying that an "Aryan physics" was superior to a "Jewish physics." In fascist countries truth had to be kept, like Galileo's *Discorsi* in scene 13, under one's coat. Brecht attacked fascism, which he described as a historical development of capitalism. In the late 1930s, Soviet Russia conducted purges of its own and emulated the repressive policies of fascism. However, Brecht did not address the issue of Stalin's purges. He focused on fascism and the evils of repressing the truth.

The subject of Galileo's heroism is one of the most complex problems of the play. Brecht portrays Galileo as a hedonist who loves good wine, good food, and who moves from one position in Italy to another for the sake of money. He appropriates the invention of the telescope and displays considerable vanity. Once faced with the instruments of torture, he caves in almost immediately, as he himself admits. He also admits to Andrea, who had bitterly renounced his master, that his recantation was not part of a "plan" to allow him to continue his scientific work. He simply was frightened. Yet he wins back the admiration of Andrea by revealing that he has spent his years of exile secretly writing his last book, the *Discorsi* (*Discourse on Two New Sciences, Mechanics and Motion*, 1638), which he daringly gives to Andrea to smuggle to Holland for publication. No one understands better than Galileo himself the meaning of his actions. His mind is restless and his work cannot stop, no matter how closely he is kept under house arrest. At every turn, Galileo makes it difficult for the Little Monk or Andrea to ascribe to him high-minded motives. In a scene drawing parallels with contemporary science, such as the development of the atomic bomb (added in a 1947 revision), Brecht portrays Galileo as a seventeenth-century Robert Oppenheimer, the atomic scientist, when he tells his industrialist supporter Matti: "They will always claim me as their spiritual leader, particularly in places where it doesn't help me at all. I have written a book about the mechanics of the firmament, that is all. What they do or don't do with it is not my concern."

The obligation of the scientist to the truth may not always be the same as the obligation of the scientist to the best interests of the people. *Galileo* does not make simple pronouncements on this question any more than it clearly settles the question of Galileo's heroism. If anything, it makes us more aware of the complexity of making any such judgments in a world as fraught with conflicting political and scientific realities as ours has been since Galileo's momentous recantation in 1633.

The present text of *Galileo* was translated over a period of two years by Brecht and Charles Laughton, who played the title role in Beverly Hills in 1947. Laughton made some structural changes such as omitting the original scene 5, in which Galileo risks his life during a plague season to continue his research. Brecht reinstated that scene in a 1955 version. The Laughton translation remains the best known to English audiences.

Galileo in Performance

The first performance was the German version, *Leben Des Galilei* (*Life of Galileo*), in Zurich on September 9, 1943. The Beverly Hills production of July 31, 1947, starred Charles Laughton. John Houseman produced the play, to tepid reviews. Gladwin Hill, the *New York Times* critic, saw its theme as "the topical one of science's conflict with the public mind, slow to grasp the significance of momentous discoveries" (August 1, 1947). The New York production opened on December 7, 1947, and theater critic Brooks Atkinson complained that like most experimental plays it was "a good deal less than perfect" (*New York Times*, December 8, 1947). The San Francisco production, directed by Herbert Blau in January 1963, received praise in part because of the large and energetic cast. John Hirsch staged the play with Anthony Quayle as Galileo in April 1967 at the Vivian Beaumont Theatre in Lincoln Center. In this production the poetic introductions to each scene were sung, and a summary of each scene's action was recited as if by a stationmaster announcing the trains. Although the text was based on the Brecht-Laughton translation, Hirsch took certain liberties. The production was praised for its exceptional performances, but Brecht's technique of epic theater was not easily accepted by audiences. Walter Kerr criticized the play for having "a classroom tone" (*New York Times*, April 14, 1967), although he also praised it as being a production that gave new hope to Lincoln Center. Nina Vance chose *Galileo* as one of the first major productions at the Alley Theater in Houston in 1968, where it was a success in part because it capitalized on the extraordinary resources of the new theater.

Bertolt Brecht (*1898–1956*)

GALILEO

TRANSLATED BY CHARLES LAUGHTON

1938–1939

It is my opinion that the earth is very noble and admirable by reason of so many and so different alterations and generations which are incessantly made therein.

— GALILEO GALILEI

Characters

GALILEO GALILEI
ANDREA SARTI, *two actors: boy and man*
MRS. SARTI
LUDOVICO MARSILI
PRIULI, THE CURATOR
SAGREDO, *Galileo's friend*
VIRGINIA GALILEI
TWO SENATORS
MATTI, *an iron founder*
PHILOSOPHER, *later, Rector of the University*
ELDERLY LADY
YOUNG LADY
FEDERZONI, *assistant to Galileo*
MATHEMATICIAN
LORD CHAMBERLAIN
FAT PRELATE
TWO SCHOLARS
TWO MONKS
INFURIATED MONK
OLD CARDINAL

ATTENDANT MONK
CHRISTOPHER CLAVIUS
LITTLE MONK
TWO SECRETARIES
CARDINAL BELLARMIN
CARDINAL BARBERINI
CARDINAL INQUISITOR
YOUNG GIRL
HER FRIEND
GIUSEPPE
STREET SINGER
HIS WIFE
REVELLER
A LOUD VOICE
INFORMER
TOWN CRIER
OFFICIAL
PEASANT
CUSTOMS OFFICER
BOY
SENATORS, OFFICIALS, PROFESSORS, LADIES, GUESTS, CHILDREN

There are two wordless roles: The Doge in scene 2 and Prince Cosmo de Medici in scene 4. The ballad of scene 9 is filled out by a pantomime: among the individuals in the pantomimic crowd are three extras (including the "King of Hungary"), Cobbler's Boy, Three Children, Peasant Woman, Monk, Rich Couple, Dwarf, Beggar, and Girl.

SCENE 1

> *In the year sixteen hundred and nine*
> *Science' light began to shine.*
> *At Padua City, in a modest house*
> *Galileo Galilei set out to prove*
> *The sun is still, the earth is on the move.*

(*Galileo's scantily furnished study. Morning. Galileo is washing himself. A barefooted boy, Andrea, son of his housekeeper, Mrs. Sarti, enters with a big astronomical model.*)

GALILEO: Where did you get that thing?
ANDREA: The coachman brought it.
GALILEO: Who sent it?
ANDREA: It said "From the Court of Naples" on the box.

GALILEO: I don't want their stupid presents. Illuminated manuscripts, a statue of Hercules the size of an elephant — they never send money.

ANDREA: But isn't this an astronomical instrument, Mr. Galilei?

GALILEO: That is an antique too. An expensive toy.

ANDREA: What's it for?

GALILEO: It's a map of the sky according to the wise men of ancient Greece. Bosh! We'll try and sell it to the university. They still teach it there.

ANDREA: How does it work, Mr. Galilei?

GALILEO: It's complicated.

ANDREA: I think I could understand it.

GALILEO (*interested*): Maybe. Let's begin at the beginning. Description!

ANDREA: There are metal rings, a lot of them.

GALILEO: How many?

ANDREA: Eight.

GALILEO: Correct. And?

ANDREA: There are words painted on the bands.

GALILEO: What words?

ANDREA: The names of stars.

GALILEO: Such as?

ANDREA: Here is a band with the sun on it and on the inside band is the moon.

GALILEO: Those metal bands represent crystal globes, eight of them.

ANDREA: Crystal?

GALILEO: Like huge soap bubbles one inside the other and the stars are supposed to be tacked on to them. Spin the band with the sun on it. (*Andrea does.*) You see the fixed ball in the middle?

ANDREA: Yes.

GALILEO: That's the earth. For two thousand years man has chosen to believe that the sun and all the host of stars revolve about him. Well. The Pope, the Cardinals, the princes, the scholars, captains, merchants, housewives, have pictured themselves squatting in the middle of an affair like that.

ANDREA: Locked up inside?

GALILEO (*triumphant*): Ah!

ANDREA: It's like a cage.

GALILEO: So you sensed that. (*Against the model.*) I like to think the ships began it.

ANDREA: Why?

GALILEO: They used to hug the coasts and then all of a sudden they left the coasts and spread over the oceans. A new age was coming. I was on to it years ago. I was a young man, in Siena. There was a group of masons arguing. They had to raise a block of granite. It was hot. To help matters, one of them wanted to try a new arrangement of ropes. After five minutes' discussion, out went a method which had been employed for a thousand years. The millennium of faith is ended, said I, this is the millennium of doubt. And we are pulling out of that contraption. The sayings of the wise men won't wash anymore. Everybody, at last, is getting nosy. I predict that in our time astronomy will become the gossip of the marketplace and the sons of fishwives will pack the schools.

ANDREA: You're off again, Mr. Galilei. Give me the towel. (*He wipes some soap from Galileo's back.*)

GALILEO: By that time, with any luck, they will be learning that the earth rolls round the sun, and that their mothers, the captains, the scholars, the princes, and the Pope are rolling with it.

ANDREA: That turning-round-business is no good. I can see with my own eyes that the sun comes up in one place in the morning and goes down in a different place in the evening. It doesn't stand still, I can see it move.

GALILEO: You see nothing, all you do is gawk. Gawking is not seeing. (*He puts the iron washstand in the middle of the room.*) Now: that's the sun. Sit down. (*Andrea sits on a chair. Galileo stands behind him.*) Where is the sun, on your right or on your left?

ANDREA: Left.

GALILEO: And how will it get to the right?

ANDREA: By your putting it there, of course.

GALILEO: Of course? (*He picks Andrea up, chair and all, and carries him round to the other side of the washstand.*) Now where is the sun?

ANDREA: On the right.

GALILEO: And did it move?

ANDREA: I did.

GALILEO: Wrong. Stupid! The chair moved.

ANDREA: But I was on it.

GALILEO: Of course. The chair is the earth, and you're sitting on it.

(*Mrs. Sarti, who has come in with a glass of milk and a roll, has been watching.*)

MRS. SARTI: What are you doing with my son, Mr. Galilei?

ANDREA: Now, mother, you don't understand.

MRS. SARTI: You understand, don't you? Last night he tried to tell me that the earth goes round the sun. You'll soon have him saying that two times two is five.

GALILEO (*eating his breakfast*): Apparently we are on the threshold of a new era, Mrs. Sarti.

MRS. SARTI: Well, I hope we can pay the milkman in this new era. A young gentleman is here to take private lessons and he is well-dressed and don't you frighten him away like you did the others. Wasting your time with Andrea! (*To Andrea.*) How many times have I told you not to wheedle free lessons out of Mr. Galilei? (*Mrs. Sarti goes.*)

GALILEO: So you thought enough of the turning-round-business to tell your mother about it.

ANDREA: Just to surprise her.

GALILEO: Andrea, I wouldn't talk about our ideas outside.

ANDREA: Why not?

GALILEO: Certain of the authorities won't like it.

ANDREA: Why not, if it's the truth?

GALILEO (*laughs*): Because we are like the worms who are little and have dim eyes and can hardly see the stars at all, and the new astronomy is a framework of guesses or very little more — yet.

(*Mrs. Sarti shows in Ludovico Marsili, a presentable young man.*)

GALILEO: This house is like a marketplace. (*Pointing to the model.*) Move that out of the way! Put it down there!

(*Ludovico does.*)

LUDOVICO: Good morning, sir. My name is Ludovico Marsili.

GALILEO (*reading a letter of recommendation he has brought*): You came by way of Holland and your family lives in the Campagna? Private lessons, thirty scudi a month.

LUDOVICO: That's all right, of course, sir.

GALILEO: What is your subject?

LUDOVICO: Horses.

GALILEO: Aha.

LUDOVICO: I don't understand science, sir.

GALILEO: Aha.

LUDOVICO: They showed me an instrument like that in Amsterdam. You'll pardon me, sir, but it didn't make sense to me at all.

GALILEO: It's out of date now.

(*Andrea goes.*)

LUDOVICO: You'll have to be patient with me, sir. Nothing in science makes sense to me.

GALILEO: Aha.

LUDOVICO: I saw a brand new instrument° in Amsterdam. A tube affair. "See things five times as

---

brand new instrument: The telescope was thought erroneously to have been invented by Hans Lippershey, who made and sold telescopes in Middelburg, Netherlands, in 1608. When he applied for a patent, he was refused on the grounds that the idea was widespread. Telescopes were available for sale in Paris in 1609, then Germany, Italy, and London in the same year. Galileo reinvented the instrument by calculating the mathematical relationship of the focal lengths of lenses. His versions were on the order of ten times more powerful than those available, and they also permitted the viewer to see things right side up, which Lippershey's did not.

large as life!" It had two lenses, one at each end, one lens bulged and the other was like that. (*Gesture.*) Any normal person would think that different lenses cancel each other out. They didn't! I just stood and looked a fool.

GALILEO: I don't quite follow you. What does one see enlarged?

LUDOVICO: Church steeples, pigeons, boats. Anything at a distance.

GALILEO: Did you yourself — see things enlarged?

LUDOVICO: Yes, sir.

GALILEO: And the tube had two lenses? Was it like this? (*He has been making a sketch.*)

(*Ludovico nods.*)

GALILEO: A recent invention?

LUDOVICO: It must be. They only started peddling it on the streets a few days before I left Holland.

GALILEO (*starts to scribble calculations on the sketch; almost friendly*): Why do you bother your head with science? Why don't you just breed horses?

(*Enter Mrs. Sarti. Galileo doesn't see her. She listens to the following.*)

LUDOVICO: My mother is set on the idea that science is necessary nowadays for conversation.

GALILEO: Aha. You'll find Latin or philosophy easier. (*Mrs. Sarti catches his eye.*) I'll see you on Tuesday afternoon.

LUDOVICO: I shall look forward to it, sir.

GALILEO: Good morning. (*He goes to the window and shouts into the street.*) Andrea! Hey, Redhead, Redhead!

MRS. SARTI: The curator of the museum is here to see you.

GALILEO: Don't look at me like that. I took him, didn't I?

MRS. SARTI: I caught your eye in time.

GALILEO: Show the curator in.

(*She goes. He scribbles something on a new sheet of paper. The Curator comes in.*)

CURATOR: Good morning, Mr. Galilei.

GALILEO: Lend me a scudo. (*He takes it and goes to the window, wrapping the coin in the paper on which he has been scribbling.*) Redhead, run to the spectacle-maker and bring me two lenses; here are the measurements. (*He throws the paper out of the window. During the following scene Galileo studies his sketch of the lenses.*)

CURATOR: Mr. Galilei, I have come to return your petition for an honorarium. Unfortunately I am unable to recommend your request.

GALILEO: My good sir, how can I make ends meet on five hundred scudi?

CURATOR: What about your private students?

GALILEO: If I spend all my time with students, when am I to study? My particular science is on the threshold of important discoveries. (*He throws a manuscript on the table.*) Here are my findings on the laws of falling bodies. That should be worth two hundred scudi.

CURATOR: I am sure that any paper of yours is of infinite worth, Mr. Galilei. . . .

GALILEO: I was limiting it to two hundred scudi.

CURATOR (*cool*): Mr. Galilei, if you want money and leisure, go to Florence. I have no doubt Prince Cosmo de Medici will be glad to subsidize you, but eventually you will be forbidden to think — in the name of the Inquisition. (*Galileo says nothing.*) Now let us not make a mountain out of a molehill. You are happy here in the Republic of Venice but you need money. Well, that's human, Mr. Galilei, may I suggest a simple solution? You remember that chart you made for the army to extract cube roots without any knowledge of mathematics? Now that was practical!

GALILEO: Bosh!

CURATOR: Don't say bosh about something that astounded the Chamber of Commerce. Our city elders are businessmen. Why don't you invent something useful that will bring them a little profit?

GALILEO (*playing with the sketch of the lenses; suddenly*): I see. Mr. Priuli, I may have something for you.

CURATOR: You don't say so.

GALILEO: It's not quite there yet, but . . .

CURATOR: You've never let me down yet, Galilei.

GALILEO: You are always an inspiration to me, Priuli.

CURATOR: You are a great man: a discontented man, but I've always said you are a great man.

GALILEO (*tartly*): My discontent, Priuli, is for the most part with myself. I am forty-six years of age and have achieved nothing which satisfies me.

CURATOR: I won't disturb you any further.

GALILEO: Thank you. Good morning.

CURATOR: Good morning. And thank you.

(*He goes. Galileo sighs. Andrea returns, bringing lenses.*)

ANDREA: One scudo was not enough. I had to leave my cap with him before he'd let me take them away.

GALILEO: We'll get it back someday. Give them to me. (*He takes the lenses over to the window, holding them in the relation they would have in a telescope.*)

ANDREA: What are those for?

GALILEO: Something for the senate. With any luck, they will rake in two hundred scudi. Take a look!

ANDREA: My, things look close! I can read the copper letters on the bell in the Campanile. And the washerwomen by the river, I can see their washboards!

GALILEO: Get out of the way. (*Looking through the lenses himself.*) Aha!

SCENE 2

No one's virtue is complete:
Great Galileo liked to eat.
You will not resent, we hope,
The truth about his telescope.

(*The great arsenal of Venice, overlooking the harbor full of ships. Senators and Officials on one side, Galileo, his daughter Virginia, and his friend Sagredo on the other side. They are dressed in formal, festive clothes. Virginia is fourteen and charming. She carries a velvet cushion on which lies a brand new telescope. Behind Galileo are some Artisans from the arsenal. There are onlookers, Ludovico amongst them.*)

CURATOR (*announcing*): Senators, Artisans of the Great Arsenal of Venice; Mr. Galileo Galilei, professor of mathematics at your University of Padua.

(*Galileo steps forward and starts to speak.*)

GALILEO: Members of the High Senate! Gentlemen: I have great pleasure, as director of this institute, in presenting for your approval and acceptance an entirely new instrument originating from this our great arsenal of the Republic of Venice. As professor of mathematics at your University of Padua, your obedient servant has always counted it his privilege to offer you such discoveries and inventions as might prove lucrative to the manufacturers and merchants of our Venetian Republic. Thus, in all humility, I tender you this, my optical tube, or telescope, constructed, I assure you, on the most scientific and Christian principles, the product of seventeen years patient research at your University of Padua.

(*Galileo steps back. The Senators applaud.*)

SAGREDO (*aside to Galileo*): Now you will be able to pay your bills.

GALILEO: Yes. It will make money for them. But you realize that it is more than a money-making gadget? — I turned it on the moon last night . . .

CURATOR (*in his best chamber-of-commerce manner*): Gentlemen: Our Republic is to be congratulated not only because this new acquisition will be one more feather in the cap of Venetian culture . . . (*polite applause*) . . . not only because our own Mr. Galilei has generously handed this fresh product of his teeming brain entirely over to you, allowing you to manufacture as many of these highly salable articles as you please. . . . (*Considerable applause.*) But Gentlemen of the Senate, has it occurred to you that — with the help of this remarkable new instrument — the battle fleet of the enemy will be visible to us a full two hours before we are visible to him? (*Tremendous applause.*)

GALILEO (*aside to Sagredo*): We have been held up three generations for lack of a thing like this. I want to go home.

SAGREDO: What about the moon?

GALILEO: Well, for one thing, it doesn't give off its own light.

CURATOR (*continuing his oration*): And now, Your Excellency, and Members of the Senate, Mr. Galilei entreats you to accept the instrument from the hands of his charming daughter Virginia.

(*Polite applause. He beckons to Virginia who steps forward and presents the telescope to the Doge.*)

CURATOR (*during this*): Mr. Galilei gives his invention entirely into your hands, Gentlemen, enjoining you to construct as many of these instruments as you may please.

(*More applause. The Senators gather round the telescope, examining it, and looking through it.*)

GALILEO (*aside to Sagredo*): Do you know what the Milky Way is made of?

SAGREDO: No.

GALILEO: I do.

CURATOR (*interrupting*): Congratulations, Mr. Galilei. Your extra five hundred scudi a year are safe.

GALILEO: Pardon? What? Of course, the five hundred scudi! Yes!

(*A prosperous man is standing beside the Curator.*)

CURATOR: Mr. Galilei, Mr. Matti of Florence.

MATTI: You're opening new fields, Mr. Galilei. We could do with you at Florence.

CURATOR: Now, Mr. Matti, leave something to us poor Venetians.

MATTI: It is a pity that a great republic has to seek an excuse to pay its great men their right and proper dues.

CURATOR: Even a great man has to have an incentive. (*He joins the Senators at the telescope.*)

MATTI: I am an iron founder.

GALILEO: Iron founder!

MATTI: With factories at Pisa and Florence. I wanted to talk to you about a machine you designed for a friend of mine in Padua.

GALILEO: I'll put you on to someone to copy it for you, I am not going to have the time. — How are things in Florence?

(*They wander away.*)

FIRST SENATOR (*peering*): Extraordinary! They're having their lunch on that frigate. Lobsters! I'm hungry!

(*Laughter.*)

SECOND SENATOR: Oh, good heavens, look at her! I must tell my wife to stop bathing on the roof. When can I buy one of these things?

(*Laughter. Virginia has spotted Ludovico among the onlookers and drags him to Galileo.*)

VIRGINIA (*to Ludovico*): Did I do it nicely?

LUDOVICO: I thought so.

VIRGINIA: Here's Ludovico to congratulate you, father.

LUDOVICO (*embarrassed*): Congratulations, sir.

GALILEO: I improved it.

LUDOVICO: Yes, sir. I am beginning to understand science.

(*Galileo is surrounded.*)

VIRGINIA: Isn't father a great man?

LUDOVICO: Yes.

VIRGINIA: Isn't that new thing father made pretty?

LUDOVICO: Yes, a pretty red. Where I saw it first it was covered in green.

VIRGINIA: What was?

LUDOVICO: Never mind. (*A short pause.*) Have you ever been to Holland?

(*They go. All Venice is congratulating Galileo, who wants to go home.*)

SCENE 3

January ten, sixteen ten;
Galileo Galilei abolishes heaven.

(*Galileo's study at Padua. It is night. Galileo and Sagredo at a telescope.*)

SAGREDO (*softly*): The edge of the crescent is jagged. All along the dark part, near the shiny crescent, bright particles of light keep coming up, one after the other and growing larger and merging with the bright crescent.

GALILEO: How do you explain those spots of light?

SAGREDO: It can't be true . . .

GALILEO: Is *is* true: they are high mountains.

SAGREDO: On a star?

GALILEO: Yes. The shining particles are mountain peaks catching the first rays of the rising sun while the slopes of the mountains are still dark, and what you see is the sunlight moving down from the peaks into the valleys.

SAGREDO: But this gives the lie to all the astronomy that's been taught for the last two thousand years.

GALILEO: Yes. What you are seeing now has been seen by no other man beside myself.

SAGREDO: But the moon can't be an earth with mountains and valleys like our own any more than the earth can be a star.

GALILEO: The moon *is* an earth with mountains and valleys — and the earth *is* a star. As the moon appears to us, so we appear to the moon. From the moon, the earth looks something like a crescent, sometimes like a half-globe, sometimes a full globe, and sometimes it is not visible at all.

SAGREDO: Galileo, this is frightening.

(*An urgent knocking on the door.*)

GALILEO: I've discovered something else, something even more astonishing.

(*More knocking. Galileo opens the door and the Curator comes in.*)

CURATOR: There it is — your "miraculous optical tube." Do you know that this invention he so picturesquely termed "the fruit of seventeen years research" will be on sale tomorrow for two scudi apiece at every street corner in Venice? A shipload of them has just arrived from Holland.

SAGREDO: Oh, dear!

(*Galileo turns his back and adjusts the telescope.*)

CURATOR: When I think of the poor gentlemen of the senate who believed they were getting an invention they could monopolize for their own profit.... Why, when they took their first look through the glass, it was only by the merest chance that they didn't see a peddler, seven times enlarged, selling tubes exactly like it at the corner of the street.

SAGREDO: Mr. Priuli, with the help of this instrument, Mr. Galilei has made discoveries that will revolutionize our concept of the universe.

CURATOR: Mr. Galilei provided the city with a first rate water pump and the irrigation works he designed function splendidly. How was I to expect this?

GALILEO (*still at the telescope*): Not so fast, Priuli. I may be on the track of a very large gadget. Certain of the stars appear to have regular movements. If there were a clock in the sky, it could be seen from anywhere. That might be useful for your shipowners.

CURATOR: I won't listen to you. I listened to you before, and as a reward for my friendship you have made me the laughingstock of the town. You can laugh — you got your money. But let me tell you this: you've destroyed my faith in a lot of things, Mr. Galilei. I'm disgusted with the world. That's all I have to say. (*He storms out.*)

GALILEO (*embarrassed*): Businessmen bore me, they suffer so. Did you see the frightened look in his eyes when he caught sight of a world not created solely for the purpose of doing business?

SAGREDO: Did you know that telescopes had been made in Holland?

GALILEO: I'd heard about it. But the one I made for the Senators was twice as good as any Dutchman's. Besides, I needed the money. How can I work, with the tax collector on the doorstep? And my poor daughter will never acquire a husband unless she has a dowry, she's not too bright. And I like to buy books — all kinds of books. Why not? And what about my appetite? I don't think well unless I eat well. Can I help it if I get my best ideas over a good meal and a bottle of wine? They don't pay me as much as they pay the butcher's boy. If only I could have five years to do nothing but research! Come on. I am going to show you something else.

SAGREDO: I don't know that I want to look again.

GALILEO: This is one of the brighter nebulae of the Milky Way. What do you see?

SAGREDO: But it's made up of stars — countless stars.

GALILEO: Countless worlds.

SAGREDO (*hesitating*): What about the theory that the earth revolves round the sun? Have you run across anything about that?

GALILEO: No. But I noticed something on Tuesday that might prove a step towards even that. Where's Jupiter? There are four lesser stars near Jupiter. I happened on them on Monday but didn't take any particular note of their position. On Tuesday I looked again. I could have sworn they had moved. They have changed again. Tell me what you see.

SAGREDO: I only see three.

GALILEO: Where's the fourth? Let's get the charts and settle down to work.

(*They work and the lights dim. The lights go up again. It is near dawn.*)

GALILEO: The only place the fourth can be is round at the back of the larger star where we cannot see it. This means there are small stars revolving around a big star. Where are the crystal shells now that the stars are supposed to be fixed to?

SAGREDO: Jupiter can't be attached to anything: there are other stars revolving round it.

GALILEO: There is no support in the heavens. (*Sagredo*

laughs awkwardly.) Don't stand there looking at me as if it weren't true.

SAGREDO: I suppose it is true. I'm afraid.

GALILEO: Why?

SAGREDO: What do you think is going to happen to you for saying that there is another sun around which other earths revolve? And that there are only stars and no difference between earth and heaven? Where is God then?

GALILEO: What do you mean?

SAGREDO: God? Where is God?

GALILEO (*angrily*): Not there! Any more than he'd be here — if creatures from the moon came down to look for him!

SAGREDO: Then where is He?

GALILEO: I'm not a theologian: I'm a mathematician.

SAGREDO: You are a human being! (*Almost shouting.*) Where is God in your system of the universe?

GALILEO: Within ourselves. Or — nowhere.

SAGREDO: Ten years ago a man was burned at the stake for saying that.

GALILEO: Giordano Bruno° was an idiot: he spoke too soon. He would never have been condemned if he could have backed up what he said with proof.

SAGREDO (*incredulously*): Do you really believe proof will make any difference?

GALILEO: I believe in the human race. The only people that can't be reasoned with are the dead. Human beings are intelligent.

SAGREDO: Intelligent — or merely shrewd?

GALILEO: I know they call a donkey a horse when they want to sell it, and a horse a donkey when they want to buy it. But is that the whole story? Aren't they susceptible to truth as well? (*He fishes a small pebble out of his pocket.*) If anybody were to drop a stone . . . (*drops the pebble*) . . . and tell them that it didn't fall, do you think they would keep quiet? The evidence of your own eyes is a very seductive thing. Sooner or later everybody must succumb to it.

SAGREDO: Galileo, I am helpless when you talk.

(*A church bell has been ringing for some time, calling people to Mass. Enter Virginia, muffled up for Mass, carrying a candle, protected from the wind by a globe.*)

VIRGINIA: Oh, father, you promised to go to bed to-night, and it's five o'clock again.

Giordano Bruno: Bruno (1548–1600), one of the most distinguished Italian Renaissance thinkers, lectured in England, France, Germany, and other countries in Europe before being imprisoned for heresy by the Inquisition. After a period of confinement and a lengthy trial, he was burned at the stake. He believed, like Galileo, in the Copernican view of astronomy, which asserted that the earth rotated around the sun.

GALILEO: Why are you up at this hour?

VIRGINIA: I'm going to Mass with Mrs. Sarti. Ludovico is going too. How was the night, father?

GALILEO: Bright.

VIRGINIA: What did you find through the tube?

GALILEO: Only some little specks by the side of a star. I must draw attention to them somehow. I think I'll name them after the Prince of Florence. Why not call them the Medicean planets? By the way, we may move to Florence. I've written to His Highness, asking if he can use me as Court Mathematician.

VIRGINIA: Oh, father, we'll be at the court!

SAGREDO (*amazed*): Galileo!

GALILEO: My dear Sagredo, I must have leisure. My only worry is that His Highness after all may not take me. I'm not accustomed to writing formal letters to great personages. Here, do you think this is the right sort of thing?

SAGREDO (*reads and quotes*): "Whose sole desire is to reside in Your Highness' presence — the rising sun of our great age." Cosmo de Medici is a boy of nine.

GALILEO: The only way a man like me can land a good job is by crawling on his stomach. Your father, my dear, is going to take his share of the pleasures of life in exchange for all his hard work, and about time too. I have no patience, Sagredo, with a man who doesn't use his brains to fill his belly. Run along to Mass now.

(*Virginia goes.*)

SAGREDO: Galileo, do not go to Florence.

GALILEO: Why not?

SAGREDO: The monks are in power there.

GALILEO: Going to Mass is a small price to pay for a full belly. And there are many famous scholars at the court of Florence.

SAGREDO: Court monkeys.

GALILEO: I shall enjoy taking them by the scruff of the neck and making them look through the telescope.

SAGREDO: Galileo, you are traveling the road to disaster. You are suspicious and skeptical in science, but in politics you are as naive as your daughter! How can people in power leave a man at large who tells the truth, even if it be the truth about the distant stars? Can you see the Pope scribbling a note in his diary: "10th of January, 1610, Heaven abolished"? A moment ago, when you were at the telescope, I saw you tied to the stake, and when you said you believed in proof, I smelt burning flesh!

GALILEO: I am going to Florence.

Before the next scene a curtain with the following legend on it is lowered:

By setting the name of Medici in the sky, I am bestowing immortality upon the stars. I commend myself to you as your most faithful and devoted servant, whose sole desire is to reside in Your Highness' presence, the rising sun of our great age.
— GALILEO GALILEI

SCENE 4

(*Galileo's house at Florence. Well-appointed. Galileo is demonstrating his telescope to Prince Cosmo de Medici, a boy of nine, accompanied by his Lord Chamberlain, Ladies and Gentlemen of the Court, and an assortment of university Professors. With Galileo are Andrea and Federzoni, the new assistant (an old man). Mrs. Sarti stands by. Before the scene opens the voice of the Philosopher can be heard.*)

VOICE OF THE PHILOSOPHER: Quaedam miracula universi. Orbes mystice canorae, arcus crystallini, circulatio corporum coelestium. Cyclorum epicyclorumque intoxicatio, integritas tabulae chordarum et architectura elata globorum coelestium.
GALILEO: Shall we speak in everyday language? My colleague Mr. Federzoni does not understand Latin.
PHILOSOPHER: Is it necessary that he should?
GALILEO: Yes.
PHILOSOPHER: Forgive me. I thought he was your mechanic.
ANDREA: Mr. Federzoni is a mechanic and a scholar.
PHILOSOPHER: Thank you, young man. If Mr. Federzoni insists . . .
GALILEO: I insist.
PHILOSOPHER: It will not be as clear, but it's your house. Your Highness . . . (*The Prince is ineffectually trying to establish contact with Andrea.*) I was about to recall to Mr. Galilei some of the wonders of the universe as they are set down for us in the Divine Classics. (*The Ladies "ah."*) Remind him of the "mystically musical spheres, the crystal arches, the circulation of the heavenly bodies —"
ELDERLY LADY: Perfect poise!
PHILOSOPHER: "— the intoxication of the cycles and epicycles, the integrity of the tables of chords and the enraptured architecture of the celestial globes."
ELDERLY LADY: What diction!
PHILOSOPHER: May I pose the question: Why should we go out of our way to look for things that can only strike a discord in this ineffable harmony?

(*The Ladies applaud.*)

FEDERZONI: Take a look through here — you'll be interested.
ANDREA: Sit down here, please.

(*The Professors laugh.*)

MATHEMATICIAN: Mr. Galilei, nobody doubts that your brain child — or is it your adopted brain child? — is brilliantly contrived.
GALILEO: Your Highness, one can see the four stars as large as life, you know.

(*The Prince looks to the Elderly Lady for guidance.*)

MATHEMATICIAN: Ah. But has it occurred to you that an eyeglass through which one sees such phenomena might not be a too reliable eyeglass?
GALILEO: How is that?
MATHEMATICIAN: If one could be sure you would keep your temper, Mr. Galilei, I could suggest that what one sees in the eyeglass and what is in the heavens are two entirely different things.
GALILEO (*quietly*): You are suggesting fraud?
MATHEMATICIAN: No! How could I, in the presence of His Highness?
ELDERLY LADY: The gentlemen are just wondering if Your Highness' stars are really, really there!

(*Pause.*)

YOUNG LADY (*trying to be helpful*): Can one see the claws on the Great Bear?
GALILEO: And everything on Taurus the Bull.
FEDERZONI: Are you going to look through it or not?
MATHEMATICIAN: With the greatest of pleasure.

(*Pause. Nobody goes near the telescope. All of a sudden the boy Andrea turns and marches pale and erect past them through the whole length of the room. The Guests follow with their eyes.*)

MRS. SARTI (*as he passes her*): What is the matter with you?
ANDREA (*shocked*): They are wicked.
PHILOSOPHER: Your Highness, it is a delicate matter and I had no intention of bringing it up, but Mr. Galilei was about to demonstrate the impossible. His new stars would have broken the outer crystal sphere — which we know of on the authority of Aristotle. I am sorry.
MATHEMATICIAN: The last word.
FEDERZONI: He had no telescope.
MATHEMATICIAN: Quite.
GALILEO (*keeping his temper*): "Truth is the daughter of Time, not of Authority." Gentlemen, the sum of our knowledge is pitiful. It has been my singular good fortune to find a new instrument which brings a small patch of the universe a little bit closer. It is at your disposal.

PHILOSOPHER: Where is all this leading?

GALILEO: Are we, as scholars, concerned with where the truth might lead us?

PHILOSOPHER: Mr. Galilei, the truth might lead us anywhere!

GALILEO: I can only beg you to look through my eyeglass.

MATHEMATICIAN (*wild*): If I understand Mr. Galilei correctly, he is asking us to discard the teachings of two thousand years.

GALILEO: For two thousand years we have been looking at the sky and didn't see the four moons of Jupiter, and there they were all the time. Why defend shaken teachings? You should be doing the shaking. (*The Prince is sleepy.*) Your Highness! My work in the Great Arsenal of Venice brought me in daily contact with sailors, carpenters, and so on. These men are unread. They depend on the evidence of their senses. But they taught me many new ways of doing things. The question is whether these gentlemen here want to be found out as fools by men who might not have had the advantages of a classical education but who are not afraid to use their eyes. I tell you that our dockyards are stirring with that same high curiosity which was the true glory of Ancient Greece.

(*Pause.*)

PHILOSOPHER: I have no doubt Mr. Galilei's theories will arouse the enthusiasm of the dockyards.

CHAMBERLAIN: Your Highness, I find to my amazement that this highly informative discussion has exceeded the time we had allowed for it. May I remind Your Highness that the State Ball begins in three-quarters of an hour?

(*The Court bows low.*)

ELDERLY LADY: We would really have liked to look through your eyeglass, Mr. Galilei, wouldn't we, Your Highness?

(*The Prince bows politely and is led to the door. Galileo follows the Prince, Chamberlain, and Ladies towards the exit. The Professors remain at the telescope.*)

GALILEO (*almost servile*): All anybody has to do is look through the telescope, Your Highness.

(*Mrs. Sarti takes a plate with candies to the Prince as he is walking out.*)

MRS. SARTI: A piece of homemade candy, Your Highness?

ELDERLY LADY: Not now. Thank you. It is too soon before His Highness' supper.

PHILOSOPHER: Wouldn't I like to take that thing to pieces.

MATHEMATICIAN: Ingenious contraption. It must be quite difficult to keep clean. (*He rubs the lens with his handkerchief and looks at the handkerchief.*)

FEDERZONI: We did not paint the Medicean stars on the lens.

ELDERLY LADY (*to the Prince, who has whispered something to her*): No, no, no, there is nothing the matter with your stars!

CHAMBERLAIN (*across the stage to Galileo*): His Highness will of course seek the opinion of the greatest living authority: Christopher Clavius, Chief Astronomer to the Papal College in Rome.

SCENE 5

*Things take indeed a wondrous turn
When learned men do stoop to learn.
Clavius, we are pleased to say,
Upheld Galileo Galilei.*

(*A burst of laughter is heard and the curtains reveal a hall in the Collegium Romanum. High Churchmen, Monks, and Scholars standing about talking and laughing. Galileo by himself in a corner.*)

FAT PRELATE (*shaking with laughter*): Hopeless! Hopeless! Hopeless! Will you tell me something people won't believe?

A SCHOLAR: Yes, that you don't love your stomach!

FAT PRELATE: They'd believe that. They only do not believe what's good for them. They doubt the devil, but fill them up with some fiddle-de-dee about the earth rolling like a marble in the gutter and they swallow it hook, line, and sinker. Sancta simplicitas!

(*He laughs until the tears run down his cheeks. The others laugh with him. A group has formed whose members boisterously begin to pretend they are standing on a rolling globe.*)

A MONK: It's rolling fast, I'm dizzy. May I hold on to you, Professor? (*He sways dizzily and clings to one of the scholars for support.*)

THE SCHOLAR: Old Mother Earth's been at the bottle again. Whoa!

MONK: Hey! Hey! We're slipping off! Help!

SECOND SCHOLAR: Look! There's Venus! Hold me, lads. Whee!

SECOND MONK: Don't, don't hurl us off on to the moon. There are nasty sharp mountain peaks on the moon, brethren!

VARIOUSLY: Hold tight! Hold tight! Don't look down! Hold tight! It'll make you giddy!

FAT PRELATE: And we cannot have giddy people in Holy Rome.

(*They rock with laughter. An Infuriated Monk comes out from a large door at the rear holding a Bible in his hand and pointing out a page with his finger.*)

INFURIATED MONK: What does the Bible say — "Sun, stand thou still on Gideon and thou, moon, in the valley of Ajalon." Can the sun come to a standstill if it doesn't ever move? Does the Bible lie?

FAT PRELATE: How did Christopher Clavius, the greatest astronomer we have, get mixed up in an investigation of this kind?

INFURIATED MONK: He's in there with his eye glued to that diabolical instrument.

FAT PRELATE (*to Galileo, who has been playing with his pebble and has dropped it*): Mr. Galilei, something dropped down.

GALILEO: Monsignor, are you sure it didn't drop up?

INFURIATED MONK: As astronomers we are aware that there are phenomena which are beyond us, but man can't expect to understand everything!

(*Enter a very old Cardinal leaning on a Monk for support. Others move aside.*)

OLD CARDINAL: Aren't they out yet? Can't they reach a decision on that paltry matter? Christopher Clavius ought to know his astronomy after all these years. I am informed that Mr. Galilei transfers mankind from the center of the universe to somewhere on the outskirts. Mr. Galilei is therefore an enemy of mankind and must be dealt with as such. Is it conceivable that God would trust this most precious fruit of His labor to a minor frolicking star? Would He have sent His Son to such a place? How can there be people with such twisted minds that they believe what they're told by the slave of a multiplication table?

FAT PRELATE (*quietly to Cardinal*): The gentleman is over there.

OLD CARDINAL: So you are the man. You know my eyes are not what they were, but I can see you bear a striking resemblance to the man we burned. What was his name?

MONK: Your Eminence must avoid excitement the doctor said . . .

OLD CARDINAL (*disregarding him*): So you have degraded the earth despite the fact that you live by her and receive everything from her. I won't have it! I won't have it! I won't be a nobody on an inconsequential star briefly twirling hither and thither. I tread the earth, and the earth is firm beneath my feet, and there is no motion to the earth, and the earth is the center of all things, and I am the center of the earth, and the eye of the creator is upon me. About me revolve, affixed to their crystal shells, the lesser lights of the stars and the great light of the sun, created to give light upon me that God might see me — Man, God's greatest effort, the center of creation. "In the image of God created He him." Immortal . . . (*His strength fails him and he catches for the Monk for support.*)

MONK: You mustn't overtax your strength, Your Eminence.

(*At this moment the door at the rear opens and Christopher Clavius enters followed by his Astronomers. He strides hastily across the hall, looking neither to right nor left. As he goes by we hear him say —*)

CLAVIUS: He is right.

(*Deadly silence. All turn to Galileo.*)

OLD CARDINAL: What is it? Have they reached a decision?

(*No one speaks.*)

MONK: It is time that Your Eminence went home.

(*The hall is emptying fast. One little Monk who had entered with Clavius speaks to Galileo.*)

LITTLE MONK: Mr. Galilei, I heard Father Clavius say: "Now it's for the theologians to set the heavens right again." You have won.

Before the next scene a curtain with the following legend on it is lowered:
    . . . As these new astronomical charts enable us to determine longitudes at sea and so make it possible to reach the new continents by the shortest routes, we would beseech Your Excellency to aid us in reaching Mr. Galilei, mathematician to the Court of Florence, who is now in Rome . . .
            — From a letter written by a member of the Genoa Chamber of Commerce and Navigation to the Papal Legation

SCENE 6

*When Galileo was in Rome
A Cardinal asked him to his home
He wined and dined him as his guest
And only made one small request.*

(*Cardinal Bellarmin's house in Rome. Music is heard and the chatter of many guests. Two Secretaries are at the rear of the stage at a desk. Galileo, his daughter Virginia, now twenty-one, and Ludovico Marsili, who* has become her fiancé, are just arriving. A few Guests, standing near the entrance with masks in their hands, nudge each other and are suddenly silent. Galileo looks at them. They applaud him politely and bow.)

VIRGINIA: O father! I'm so happy. I won't dance with anyone but you, Ludovico.

GALILEO (to a Secretary): I was to wait here for His Eminence.

FIRST SECRETARY: His Eminence will be with you in a few minutes.

VIRGINIA: Do I look proper?

LUDOVICO: You are showing some lace.

(Galileo puts his arms around their shoulders.)

GALILEO (quoting mischievously): Fret not,
        daughter, if perchance
   You attract a wanton glance.
   The eyes that catch a trembling lace
   Will guess the heartbeat's quickened pace.
   Lovely woman still may be
   Careless with felicity.

VIRGINIA (to Galileo): Feel my heart.

GALILEO (to Ludovico): It's thumping.

VIRGINIA: I hope I always say the right thing.

LUDOVICO: She's afraid she's going to let us down.

VIRGINIA: Oh, I want to look beautiful.

GALILEO: You'd better. If you don't they'll start saying all over again that the earth doesn't turn.

LUDOVICO (laughing): It doesn't turn, sir.

(Galileo laughs.)

GALILEO: Go and enjoy yourselves. (He speaks to one of the Secretaries.) A large fête?

FIRST SECRETARY: Two hundred and fifty guests, Mr. Galilei. We have represented here this evening most of the great families of Italy, the Orsinis, the Villanis, the Nuccolis, the Soldanieris, the Canes, the Lecchis, the Estensis, the Colombinis, the . . .

(Virginia comes running back.)

VIRGINIA: Oh father, I didn't tell you: you're famous.

GALILEO: Why?

VIRGINIA: The hairdresser in the Via Vittorio kept four other ladies waiting and took me first. (Exit.)

GALILEO (at the stairway, leaning over the well): Rome!

(Enter Cardinal Bellarmin, wearing the mask of a lamb, and Cardinal Barberini, wearing the mask of a dove.)

SECRETARIES: Their Eminences, Cardinals Bellarmin and Barberini.

(The Cardinals lower their masks.)

GALILEO (to Bellarmin): Your Eminence.

BELLARMIN: Mr. Galilei, Cardinal Barberini.

GALILEO: Your Eminence.

BARBERINI: So you are the father of that lovely child!

BELLARMIN: Who is inordinately proud of being her father's daughter.

(They laugh.)

BARBERINI (points his finger at Galileo): "The sun riseth and setteth and returneth to its place," saith the Bible. What saith Galilei?

GALILEO: Appearances are notoriously deceptive, Your Eminence. Once when I was so high, I was standing on a ship that was pulling away from the shore and I shouted, "The shore is moving!" I know now that it was the ship which was moving.

BARBERINI (laughs): You can't catch that man. I tell you, Bellarmin, his moons around Jupiter are hard nuts to crack. Unfortunately for me I happened to glance at a few papers on astronomy once. It is harder to get rid of than the itch.

BELLARMIN: Let's move with the times. If it makes navigation easier for sailors to use new charts based on a new hypothesis let them have them. We only have to scotch doctrines that contradict Holy Writ.

(He leans over the balustrade of the well and acknowledges various Guests.)

BARBERINI: But Bellarmin, you haven't caught on to this fellow. The scriptures don't satisfy him. Copernicus does.

GALILEO: Copernicus? "He that withholdeth corn the people shall curse him." Book of Proverbs.

BARBERINI: "A prudent man concealeth knowledge." Also Book of Proverbs.

GALILEO: "Where no oxen are, the stable is clean, but much increase is by the strength of the ox."

BARBERINI: "He that ruleth his spirit is better than he that taketh a city."

GALILEO: "But a broken spirit drieth up the bones." (Pause.) "Doth not wisdom cry?"

BARBERINI: "Can one walk on hot coals and his feet not be scorched?" — Welcome to Rome, Friend Galileo. You recall the legend of our city's origin? Two small boys found sustenance and refuge with a she-wolf and from that day we have paid the price for the she-wolf's milk. But the place is not bad. We have everything for your pleasure — from a scholarly dispute with Bellarmin to ladies of high degree. Look at that woman flaunting herself. No? He wants a weighty discussion! All right! (To Galileo.) You people speak in terms of circles and ellipses and regular velocities — simple movements that the human mind can grasp — very convenient — but suppose Almighty God had taken it into his head to make the stars move like that . . . (*he describes an irregular motion with his fingers through the air*) . . . then where would you be?

GALILEO: My good man — the Almighty would have endowed us with brains like that . . . (*repeats the movement*) . . . so that we could grasp the movements . . . (*repeats the movement*) . . . like that. I believe in the brain.

BARBERINI: I consider the brain inadequate. He doesn't answer. He is too polite to tell me he considers *my* brain inadequate. What is one to do with him? Butter wouldn't melt in his mouth. All he wants to do is to prove that God made a few boners in astronomy. God didn't study his astronomy hard enough before he composed Holy Writ. (*To the Secretaries.*) Don't take anything down. This is a scientific discussion among friends.

BELLARMIN (*to Galileo*): Does it not appear more probable — even to you — that the Creator knows more about his work than the created?

GALILEO: In his blindness man is liable to misread not only the sky but also the Bible.

BELLARMIN: The interpretation of the Bible is a matter for the ministers of God. (*Galileo remains silent.*) At last you are quiet. (*He gestures to the Secretaries. They start writing.*) Tonight the Holy Office has decided that the theory according to which the earth goes around the sun is foolish, absurd, and a heresy. I am charged, Mr. Galilei, with cautioning you to abandon these teachings. (*To the First Secretary.*) Would you repeat that?

FIRST SECRETARY (*reading*): "His Eminence, Cardinal Bellarmin, to the aforesaid Galilei: The Holy Office has resolved that the theory according to which the earth goes around the sun is foolish, absurd, and a heresy. I am charged, Mr. Galilei, with cautioning you to abandon these teachings."

GALILEO (*rocking on his base*): But the facts!

BARBERINI (*consoling*): Your findings have been ratified by the Papal Observatory, Galilei. That should be most flattering to you . . .

BELLARMIN (*cutting in*): The Holy Office formulated the decree without going into details.

GALILEO (*to Barberini*): Do you realize, the future of all scientific research is . . .

BELLARMIN (*cutting in*): Completely assured, Mr. Galilei. It is not given to man to know the truth: it is granted to him to seek after the truth. Science is the legitimate and beloved daughter of the Church. She must have confidence in the Church.

GALILEO (*infuriated*): I would not try confidence by whistling her too often.

BARBERINI (*quickly*): Be careful what you're doing — you'll be throwing out the baby with the bath

water, friend Galilei. (*Serious.*) We need you more than you need us.

BELLARMIN: Well, it is time we introduced our distinguished friend to our guests. The whole country talks of him!

BARBERINI: Let us replace our masks, Bellarmin. Poor Galilei hasn't got one.

(*He laughs. They take Galileo out.*)

FIRST SECRETARY: Did you get his last sentence?

SECOND SECRETARY: Yes. Do you have what he said about believing in the brain?

(*Another cardinal — the Inquisitor — enters.*)

INQUISITOR: Did the conference take place?

(*The First Secretary hands him the papers and the Inquisitor dismisses the Secretaries. They go. The Inquisitor sits down and starts to read the transcription. Two or three Young Ladies skitter across the stage; they see the Inquisitor and curtsy as they go.*)

YOUNG GIRL: Who was that?

HER FRIEND: The Cardinal Inquisitor.

(*They giggle and go. Enter Virginia. She curtsies as she goes. The Inquisitor stops her.*)

INQUISITOR: Good evening, my child. Beautiful night. May I congratulate you on your betrothal? Your young man comes from a fine family. Are you staying with us here in Rome?

VIRGINIA: Not now, Your Eminence. I must go home to prepare for the wedding.

INQUISITOR: Ah. You are accompanying your father to Florence. That should please him. Science must be cold comfort in a home. Your youth and warmth will keep him down to earth. It is easy to get lost up there. (*He gestures to the sky.*)

VIRGINIA: He doesn't talk to me about the stars, Your Eminence.

INQUISITOR: No. (*He laughs.*) They don't eat fish in the fisherman's house. I can tell you something about astronomy. My child, it seems that God has blessed our modern astronomers with imaginations. It is quite alarming! Do you know that the earth — which we old fogies supposed to be so large — has shrunk to something no bigger than a walnut, and the new universe has grown so vast that prelates — and even cardinals — look like ants. Why, God Almighty might lose sight of a Pope! I wonder if I know your Father Confessor.

VIRGINIA: Father Christopherus, from Saint Ursula's at Florence, Your Eminence.

INQUISITOR: My dear child, your father will need you. Not so much now perhaps, but one of these days. You are pure, and there is strength in purity. Greatness is sometimes, indeed often, too heavy a burden for those to whom God has granted it. What man is so great that he has no place in a prayer? But I am keeping you, my dear. Your fiancé will be jealous of me, and I am afraid your father will never forgive me for holding forth on astronomy. Go to your dancing and remember me to Father Christopherus.

(*Virginia kisses his ring and runs off. The Inquisitor resumes his reading.*)

SCENE 7

Galileo, feeling grim,
A young monk came to visit him.
The monk was born of common folk.
It was of science that they spoke.

(*Garden of the Florentine Ambassador in Rome. Distant hum of a great city. Galileo and the Little Monk of scene 5 are talking.*)

GALILEO: Let's hear it. That robe you're wearing gives you the right to say whatever you want to say. Let's hear it.

LITTLE MONK: I have studied physics, Mr. Galilei.

GALILEO: That might help us if it enabled you to admit that two and two are four.

LITTLE MONK: Mr. Galilei, I have spent four sleepless nights trying to reconcile the decree that I have read with the moons of Jupiter that I have seen. This morning I decided to come to see you after I had said Mass.

GALILEO: To tell me that Jupiter has no moons?

LITTLE MONK: No, I found out that I think the decree a wise decree. It has shocked me into realizing that free research has its dangers. I have had to decide to give up astronomy. However, I felt the impulse to confide in you some of the motives which have impelled even a passionate physicist to abandon his work.

GALILEO: Your motives are familiar to me.

LITTLE MONK: You mean, of course, the special powers invested in certain commissions of the Holy Office? But there is something else. I would like to talk to you about my family. I do not come from the great city. My parents are peasants in the Campagna, who know about the cultivation of the olive tree, and not much about anything else. Too often these days when I am trying to concentrate on tracking down the moons of Jupiter, I see my parents. I see them sitting by the fire with my sister, eating their curded cheese. I see the beams of the ceiling above them, which the smoke of centuries

has blackened, and I can see the veins stand out on their toil-worn hands, and the little spoons in their hands. They scrape a living, and underlying their poverty there is a sort of order. There are routines. The routine of scrubbing the floors, the routine of the seasons in the olive orchard, the routine of paying taxes. The troubles that come to them are recurrent troubles. My father did not get his poor bent back all at once, but little by little, year by year, in the olive orchard; just as year after year, with unfailing regularity, childbirth has made my mother more and more sexless. They draw the strength they need to sweat with their loaded baskets up the stony paths, to bear children, even to eat, from the sight of the trees greening each year anew, from the reproachful face of the soil, which is never satisfied, and from the little church and Bible texts they hear there on Sunday. They have been told that God relies upon them and that the pageant of the world has been written around them that they may be tested in the important or unimportant parts handed out to them. How could they take it, were I to tell them that they are on a lump of stone ceaselessly spinning in empty space, circling around a second-rate star? What, then, would be the use of their patience, their acceptance of misery? What comfort, then, the Holy Scriptures, which have mercifully explained their crucifixion? The Holy Scriptures would then be proved full of mistakes. No, I see them begin to look frightened. I see them slowly put their spoons down on the table. They would feel cheated. "There is no eye watching over us, after all," they would say. "We have to start out on our own, at our time of life. Nobody has planned a part for us beyond this wretched one on a worthless star. There is no meaning in our misery. Hunger is just not having eaten. It is no test of strength. Effort is just stooping and carrying. It is not a virtue." Can you understand that I read into the decree of the Holy Office a noble motherly pity and a great goodness of the soul?

GALILEO (*embarrassed*): Hm, well at least you have found out that it is not a question of the satellites of Jupiter, but of the peasants of the Campagna! And don't try to break me down by the halo of beauty that radiates from old age. How does a pearl develop in an oyster? A jagged grain of sand makes its way into the oyster's shell and makes its life unbearable. The oyster exudes slime to cover the grain of sand and the slime eventually hardens into a pearl. The oyster nearly dies in the process. To hell with the pearl, give me the healthy oyster! And virtues are not exclusive to misery. If your parents were prosperous and happy, they might develop the virtues of happiness and prosperity. Today the virtues of exhaustion are caused by the exhausted land. For that my new water pumps could work more wonders than their ridiculous superhuman efforts. Be fruitful and multiply: for war will cut down the population, and our fields are barren! (*A pause.*) Shall I lie to your people?

LITTLE MONK: We must be silent from the highest of motives: the inward peace of less fortunate souls.

GALILEO: My dear man, as a bonus for not meddling with your parents' peace, the authorities are tendering me, on a silver platter, persecution-free, my share of the fat sweated from your parents, who, as you know, were made in God's image. Should I condone this decree, my motives might not be disinterested: easy life, no persecution, and so on.

LITTLE MONK: Mr. Galilei, I am a priest.

GALILEO: You are also a physicist. How can new machinery be evolved to domesticate the river water if we physicists are forbidden to study, discuss, and pool our findings about the greatest machinery of all, the machinery of the heavenly bodies? Can I reconcile my findings on the paths of falling bodies with the current belief in the tracks of witches on broom sticks? (*A pause.*) I am sorry — I shouldn't have said that.

LITTLE MONK: You don't think that the truth, if it is the truth, would make its way without us?

GALILEO: No! No! No! As much of the truth gets through as we push through. You talk about the Campagna peasants as if they were the moss on their huts. Naturally, if they don't get a move on and learn to think for themselves, the most efficient of irrigation systems cannot help them. I can see their divine patience, but where is their divine fury?

LITTLE MONK (*helpless*): They are old!

(*Galileo stands for a moment, beaten; he cannot meet the Little Monk's eyes. He takes a manuscript from the table and throws it violently on the ground.*)

LITTLE MONK: What is that?

GALILEO: Here is writ what draws the ocean when it ebbs and flows. Let it lie there. Thou shalt not read. (*Little Monk has picked up the manuscript.*) Already! An apple of the tree of knowledge, he can't wait, he wolfs it down. He will rot in hell for all eternity. Look at him, where are his manners? — Sometimes I think I would let them imprison me in a place a thousand feet beneath the earth where no light could reach me, if in exchange I could find out what stuff that is: "Light." The bad thing is that, when I find something, I have to boast about it like a lover or a drunkard or a traitor. That is a hopeless vice and leads to the abyss. I wonder how long I shall be content to discuss it with my dog!

LITTLE MONK (*immersed in the manuscript*): I don't understand this sentence.

GALILEO: I'll explain it to you, I'll explain it to you.

(*They are sitting on the floor.*)

SCENE 8

Eight long years with tongue in cheek
Of what he knew he did not speak.
Then temptation grew too great
And Galileo challenged fate.

(*Galileo's house in Florence again. Galileo is supervising his Assistants Andrea, Federzoni, and the Little Monk who are about to prepare an experiment. Mrs. Sarti and Virginia are at a long table sewing bridal linen. There is a new telescope, larger than the old one. At the moment it is covered with a cloth.*)

ANDREA (*looking up a schedule*): Thursday. Afternoon. Floating bodies again. Ice, bowl of water, scales, and it says here an iron needle. Aristotle.

VIRGINIA: Ludovico likes to entertain. We must take care to be neat. His mother notices every stitch. She doesn't approve of father's books.

MRS. SARTI: That's all a thing of the past. He hasn't published a book for years.

VIRGINIA: That's true. Oh Sarti, it's fun sewing a trousseau.

MRS. SARTI: Virginia, I want to talk to you. You are very young, and you have no mother, and your father is putting those pieces of ice in water, and marriage is too serious a business to go into blind. Now you should go to see a real astronomer from the university and have him cast your horoscope so you know where you stand. (*Virginia giggles.*) What's the matter?

VIRGINIA: I've been already.

MRS. SARTI: Tell Sarti.

VIRGINIA: I have to be careful for three months now because the sun is in Capricorn, but after that I get a favorable ascendant, and I can undertake a journey if I am careful of Uranus, as I'm a Scorpion.

MRS. SARTI: What about Ludovico?

VIRGINIA: He's a Leo, the astronomer said. Leos are sensual. (*Giggles.*)

(*There is a knock at the door, it opens. Enter the Rector of the University, the philosopher of scene 4, bringing a book.*)

RECTOR (*to Virginia*): This is about the burning issue of the moment. He may want to glance over it.

My faculty would appreciate his comments. No, don't disturb him now, my dear. Every minute one takes of your father's time is stolen from Italy. (*He goes.*)

VIRGINIA: Federzoni! The rector of the university brought this.

(*Federzoni takes it.*)

GALILEO: What's it about?
FEDERZONI (*spelling*): DE MACULIS IN SOLE.
ANDREA: Oh, it's on the sun spots!

(*Andrea comes one side, and the Little Monk the other, to look at the book.*)

ANDREA: A new one!

(*Federzoni resentfully puts the book into their hands and continues with the preparation of the experiment.*)

ANDREA: Listen to this dedication. (*Quotes.*) "To the greatest living authority on physics, Galileo Galilei." — I read Fabricius' paper the other day. Fabricius says the spots are clusters of planets between us and the sun.
LITTLE MONK: Doubtful.
GALILEO (*noncommittal*): Yes?
ANDREA: Paris and Prague hold that they are vapors from the sun. Federzoni doubts that.
FEDERZONI: Me? You leave me out. I said "hm," that was all. And don't discuss new things before me. I can't read the material, it's in Latin. (*He drops the scales and stands trembling with fury.*) Tell me, can I doubt anything?

(*Galileo walks over and picks up the scales silently. Pause.*)

LITTLE MONK: There is happiness in doubting, I wonder why.
ANDREA: Aren't we going to take this up?
GALILEO: At the moment we are investigating floating bodies.
ANDREA: Mother has baskets full of letters from all over Europe asking his opinion.
FEDERZONI: The question is whether you can afford to remain silent.
GALILEO: I cannot afford to be smoked on a wood fire like a ham.
ANDREA (*surprised*): Ah. You think the sun spots may have something to do with that again? (*Galileo does not answer.*)
ANDREA: Well, we stick to fiddling about with bits of ice in water. That can't hurt you.
GALILEO: Correct. — Our thesis!
ANDREA: All things that are lighter than water float, and all things that are heavier sink.
GALILEO: Aristotle says —

LITTLE MONK (*reading out of a book, translating*): "A broad and flat disk of ice, although heavier than water, still floats, because it is unable to divide the water."
GALILEO: Well. Now I push the ice below the surface. I take away the pressure of my hands. What happens?

(*Pause.*)

LITTLE MONK: It rises to the surface.
GALILEO: Correct. It seems to be able to divide the water as it's coming up, doesn't it?
LITTLE MONK: Could it be lighter than water after all?
GALILEO: Aha!
ANDREA: Then all things that are lighter than water float, and all things that are heavier sink. Q.e.d.°
GALILEO: Not at all. Hand me that iron needle. Heavier than water? (*They all nod.*) A piece of paper. (*He places the needle on a piece of paper and floats it on the surface of the water. Pause.*) Do not be hasty with your conclusion. (*Pause.*) What happens?
FEDERZONI: The paper has sunk, the needle is floating.
VIRGINIA: What's the matter?
MRS. SARTI: Every time I hear them laugh it sends shivers down my spine.

(*There is a knocking at the outer door.*)

MRS. SARTI: Who's that at the door?

(*Enter Ludovico. Virginia runs to him. They embrace. Ludovico is followed by a servant with baggage.*)

MRS. SARTI: Well!
VIRGINIA: Oh! Why didn't you write that you were coming?
LUDOVICO: I decided on the spur of the moment. I was over inspecting our vineyards at Bucciole. I couldn't keep away.
GALILEO: Who's that?
LITTLE MONK: Miss Virginia's intended. What's the matter with your eyes?
GALILEO (*blinking*): Oh yes, it's Ludovico, so it is. Well! Sarti, get a jug of that Sicilian wine, the old kind. We celebrate.

Q.e.d.: In Latin, *quod erat demonstrandum*, "which was to be demonstrated," the usual ending on a logical examination using Aristotelian logic. The point is that it is not demonstrated; the experiment with the needle and the paper demonstrates the power of surface tension, which contradicts Andrea's earlier statement. Experimentation, in other words, is the final arbiter of what is true, not rules such as Andrea establishes.

(*Everybody sits down. Mrs. Sarti has left, followed by Ludovico's Servant.*)

GALILEO: Well, Ludovico, old man. How are the horses?

LUDOVICO: The horses are fine.

GALILEO: Fine.

LUDOVICO: But those vineyards need a firm hand. (*To Virginia.*) You look pale. Country life will suit you. Mother's planning on September.

VIRGINIA: I suppose I oughtn't, but stay here, I've got something to show you.

LUDOVICO: What?

VIRGINIA: Never mind. I won't be ten minutes. (*She runs out.*)

LUDOVICO: How's life these days, sir?

GALILEO: Dull. — How was the journey?

LUDOVICO: Dull. — Before I forget, mother sends her congratulations on your admirable tact over the latest rumblings of science.

GALILEO: Thank her from me.

LUDOVICO: Christopher Clavius had all Rome on its ears. He said he was afraid that the turning-around-business might crop up again on account of these spots on the sun.

ANDREA: Clavius is on the same track! (*To Ludovico.*) My mother's baskets are full of letters from all over Europe asking Mr. Galilei's opinion.

GALILEO: I am engaged in investigating the habits of floating bodies. Any harm in that?

(*Mrs. Sarti reenters, followed by the Servant. They bring wine and glasses on a tray.*)

GALILEO (*hands out the wine*): What news from the Holy City, apart from the prospect of my sins?

LUDOVICO: The Holy Father is on his death bed. Hadn't you heard?

LITTLE MONK: My goodness! What about the succession?

LUDOVICO: All the talk is of Barberini.

GALILEO: Barberini?

ANDREA: Mr. Galilei knows Barberini.

LITTLE MONK: Cardinal Barberini is a mathematician.

FEDERZONI: A scientist in the chair of Peter!

(*Pause.*)

GALILEO (*cheering up enormously*): This means change. We might live to see the day, Federzoni, when we don't have to whisper that two and two are four. (*To Ludovico.*) I like this wine. Don't you, Ludovico?

LUDOVICO: I like it.

GALILEO: I know the hill where it is grown. The slope is steep and stony, the grape almost blue. I am fond of this wine.

LUDOVICO: Yes, sir.

GALILEO: There are shadows in this wine. It is almost sweet but just stops short. — Andrea, clear that stuff away, ice, bowl and needle. — I cherish the consolations of the flesh. I have no patience with cowards who call them weaknesses. I say there is a certain achievement in enjoying things.

(*The Pupils get up and go to the experiment table.*)

LITTLE MONK: What are we to do?

FEDERZONI: He is starting on the sun.

(*They begin with clearing up.*)

ANDREA (*singing in a low voice*): The Bible proves the earth stands still,
The Pope, he swears with tears:
The earth stands still. To prove it so
He takes it by the ears.

LUDOVICO: What's the excitement?

MRS. SARTI: You're not going to start those hellish goings-on again, Mr. Galilei?

ANDREA: And gentlefolk, they say so too.
Each learned doctor proves,
(If you grease his palm): The earth stands still.
And yet — and yet it moves.

GALILEO: Barberini is in the ascendant, so your mother is uneasy, and you're sent to investigate me. Correct me if I am wrong, Ludovico. Clavius is right: These spots on the sun interest me.

ANDREA: We might find out that the sun also revolves. How would you like that, Ludovico?

GALILEO: Do you like my wine, Ludovico?

LUDOVICO: I told you I did, sir.

GALILEO: You really like it?

LUDOVICO: I like it.

GALILEO: Tell me, Ludovico, would you consider going so far as to accept a man's wine or his daughter without insisting that he drop his profession? I have no wish to intrude, but have the moons of Jupiter affected Virginia's bottom?

MRS. SARTI: That isn't funny, it's just vulgar. I am going for Virginia.

LUDOVICO (*keeps her back*): Marriages in families such as mine are not arranged on a basis of sexual attraction alone.

GALILEO: Did they keep you back from marrying my daughter for eight years because I was on probation?

LUDOVICO: My future wife must take her place in the family pew.

GALILEO: You mean, if the daughter of a bad man sat in your family pew, your peasants might stop paying the rent?

LUDOVICO: In a sort of way.

GALILEO: When I was your age, the only person I allowed to rap me on the knuckles was my girl.

LUDOVICO: My mother was assured that you had undertaken not to get mixed up in this turning-around-business again, sir.

GALILEO: We had a conservative Pope then.

MRS. SARTI: Had! His Holiness is not dead yet!

GALILEO (with relish): Pretty nearly.

MRS. SARTI: That man will weigh a chip of ice fifty times, but when it comes to something that's convenient, he believes it blindly. "Is His Holiness dead?" — "Pretty nearly!"

LUDOVICO: You will find, sir, if His Holiness passes away, the new Pope, whoever he turns out to be, will respect the convictions held by the solid families of the country.

GALILEO (to Andrea): That remains to be seen. — Andrea, get out the screen. We'll throw the image of the sun on our screen to save our eyes.

LITTLE MONK: I thought you'd been working at it. Do you know when I guessed it? When you didn't recognize Mr. Marsili.

MRS. SARTI: If my son has to go to hell for sticking to you, that's my affair, but you have no right to trample on your daughter's happiness.

LUDOVICO (to his Servant): Giuseppe, take my baggage back to the coach, will you?

MRS. SARTI: This will kill her. (She runs out, still clutching the jug.)

LUDOVICO (politely): Mr. Galilei, if we Marsilis were to countenance teachings frowned on by the church, it would unsettle our peasants. Bear in mind: these poor people in their brute state get everything upside down. They are nothing but animals. They will never comprehend the finer points of astronomy. Why, two months ago a rumor went around, an apple had been found on a pear tree, and they left their work in the fields to discuss it.

GALILEO (interested): Did they?

LUDOVICO: I have seen the day when my poor mother has had to have a dog whipped before their eyes to remind them to keep their place. Oh, you may have seen the waving corn from the window of your comfortable coach. You have, no doubt, nibbled our olives, and absentmindedly eaten our cheese, but you can have no idea how much responsibility that sort of thing entails.

GALILEO: Young man, I do not eat my cheese absentmindedly. (To Andrea.) Are we ready?

ANDREA: Yes, sir.

GALILEO (leaves Ludovico and adjusts the mirror): You would not confine your whippings to dogs to remind your peasants to keep their places, would you, Marsili?

LUDOVICO (after a pause): Mr. Galilei, you have a wonderful brain, it's a pity.

LITTLE MONK (astonished): He threatened you.

GALILEO: Yes. And he threatened you too. We might unsettle his peasants. Your sister, Fulganzio, who works the lever of the olive press, might laugh out loud if she heard the sun is not a gilded coat of arms but a lever too. The earth turns because the sun turns it.

ANDREA: That could interest his steward too and even his money lender — and the seaport towns . . .

FEDERZONI: None of them speak Latin.

GALILEO: I might write in plain language. The work we do is exacting. Who would go through the strain for less than the population at large!

LUDOVICO: I see you have made your decision. It was inevitable. You will always be a slave of your passions. Excuse me to Virginia, I think it's as well I don't see her now.

GALILEO: The dowry is at your disposal at any time.

LUDOVICO: Good afternoon. (He goes followed by the Servant.)

ANDREA: Exit Ludovico. To hell with all Marsilis, Villanis, Orsinis, Canes, Nuccolis, Soldanieris . . .

FEDERZONI: . . . who ordered the earth stand still because their castles might be shaken loose if it revolves . . .

LITTLE MONK: . . . and who only kiss the Pope's feet as long as he uses them to trample on the people. God made the physical world, God made the human brain. God will allow physics.

ANDREA: They will try to stop us.

GALILEO: Thus we enter the observation of these spots on the sun in which we are interested, at our own risk, not counting on protection from a problematical new Pope . . .

ANDREA: . . . but with great likelihood of dispelling Fabrizius' vapors, and the shadows of Paris and Prague, and of establishing the rotation of the sun . . .

GALILEO: . . . and with some likelihood of establishing the rotation of the sun. My intention is not to prove that I was right but to find out whether I was right. "Abandon hope all ye who enter — an observation." Before assuming these phenomena are spots, which would suit us, let us first set about proving that they are not — fried fish. We crawl by inches. What we find today we will wipe from the blackboard tomorrow and reject it — unless it shows up again the day after tomorrow. And if we find anything which would suit us, that thing we will eye with particular distrust. In fact, we will approach this observing of the sun with the implacable determination to prove that the earth stands still and only if hopelessly defeated in this pious undertaking can we allow ourselves to wonder if we may not have been right all the time: the earth revolves. Take the cloth off the telescope and turn it on the sun.

(*Quietly they start work. When the corruscating image of the sun is focused on the screen, Virginia enters hurriedly, her wedding dress on, her hair disheveled, Mrs. Sarti with her, carrying her wedding veil. The two women realize what has happened. Virginia faints. Andrea, Little Monk, and Galileo rush to her. Federzoni continues working.*)

SCENE 9

> On April Fool's Day, thirty two,
> Of science there was much ado.
> People had learned from Galilei:
> They used his teaching in their way.

(*Around the corner from the marketplace a Street Singer and his Wife, who is costumed to represent the earth in a skeleton globe made of thin bands of brass, are holding the attention of a sprinkling of representative citizens, some in masquerade who were on their way to see the carnival procession. From the marketplace the noise of an impatient crowd.*)

BALLAD SINGER (*accompanied by his Wife on the guitar*): When the Almighty made the universe
He made the earth and then he made the sun.
Then round the earth he bade the sun to turn —
That's in the Bible, Genesis, Chapter One.
And from that time all beings here below
Were in obedient circles meant to go:

Around the Pope the cardinals
Around the cardinals the bishops
Around the bishops the secretaries
Around the secretaries the aldermen
Around the aldermen the craftsmen
Around the craftsmen the servants
Around the servants the dogs, the chickens, and
the beggars.

(*A conspicuous reveller — henceforth called the Spinner — has slowly caught on and is exhibiting his idea of spinning around. He does not lose dignity, he faints with mock grace.*)

BALLAD SINGER: Up stood the learned Galileo
Glanced briefly at the sun
And said: "Almighty God was wrong
In Genesis, Chapter One!"

Now that was rash, my friends, it is no matter
small

For heresy will spread today like foul diseases.
Change Holy Writ, forsooth? What will be left
at all?
Why: each of us would say and do just what he
pleases!

(*Three wretched Extras, employed by the chamber of commerce, enter. Two of them, in ragged costumes, moodily bear a litter with a mock throne. The third sits on the throne. He wears sacking, a false beard, a prop crown, he carries a prop orb and sceptre, and around his chest the inscription "*THE KING OF HUNGARY.*" The litter has a card with "No. 4" written on it. The litter bearers dump him down and listen to the Ballad Singer.*)

BALLAD SINGER: Good people, what will come to
pass
If Galileo's teachings spread?
No altar boy will serve the Mass
No servant girl will make the bed.

Now that is grave, my friends, it is no matter
small:
For independent spirit spreads like foul diseases!
(Yet life is sweet and man is weak and after
all —
How nice it is, for a little change, to do just as
one pleases!)

(*The Ballad Singer takes over the guitar. His Wife dances around him, illustrating the motion of the earth. A Cobbler's Boy with a pair of resplendent lacquered boots hung over his shoulder has been jumping up and down in mock excitement. There are three more children, dressed as grownups among the spectators, two together and a single one with mother. The Cobbler's Boy takes the three Children in hand, forms a chain, and leads it, moving to the music, in and out among the spectators, "whipping" the chain so that the last child bumps into people. On the way past a Peasant Woman, he steals an egg from her basket. She gestures to him to return it. As he passes her again he quietly breaks the egg over her head. The King of Hungary ceremoniously hands his orb to one of his bearers, marches down with mock dignity, and chastises the Cobbler's Boy. The parents remove the three Children. The unseemliness subsides.*)

BALLAD SINGER: The carpenters take wood and
build
Their houses — not the church's pews.
And members of the cobblers' guild
Now boldly walk the streets — in shoes.
The tenant kicks the noble lord
Quite off the land he owned — like that!
The milk his wife once gave the priest

Now makes (at last!) her children fat.

Ts, ts, ts, ts, my friends, this is no matter small
For independent spirit spreads like foul diseases
People must keep their place, some down and
    some on top!
(Though it is nice, for a little change, to do just
    as one pleases!)

(*The Cobbler's Boy has put on the lacquered boots he was carrying. He struts off. The Ballad Singer takes over the guitar again. His Wife dances around him in increased tempo. A Monk has been standing near a rich Couple, who are in subdued costly clothes, without masks: shocked at the song, he now leaves. A Dwarf in the costume of an astronomer turns his telescope on the departing Monk, thus drawing attention to the rich Couple. In imitation of the Cobbler's Boy, the Spinner forms a chain of grownups. They move to the music, in and out, and between the rich Couple. The Spinner changes the Gentleman's bonnet for the ragged hat of a Beggar. The Gentleman decides to take this in good part, and a Girl is emboldened to take his dagger. The Gentleman is miffed, throws the Beggar's hat back. The Beggar discards the Gentleman's bonnet and drops it on the ground. The King of Hungary has walked from his throne, taken an egg from the Peasant Woman, and paid for it. He now ceremoniously breaks it over the Gentleman's head as he is bending down to pick up his bonnet. The Gentleman conducts the Lady away from the scene. The King of Hungary, about to resume his throne, finds one of the Children sitting on it. The Gentleman returns to retrieve his dagger. Merriment. The Ballad Singer wanders off. This is part of his routine. His Wife sings to the Spinner.*)

WIFE: Now speaking for myself I feel
    That I could also do with a change.
    You know, for me . . . (*Turning to a reveller*)
        . . . *you* have appeal
    Maybe tonight we could arrange . . .

(*The Dwarf-Astronomer has been amusing the people by focusing his telescope on her legs. The Ballad Singer has returned.*)

BALLAD SINGER: No, no, no, no, no, stop, Galileo,
    stop!
    For independent spirit spreads like foul diseases
    People must keep their place, some down and
        some on top!
    (Though it is nice, for a little change, to do just
        as one pleases!)

(*The Spectators stand embarrassed. A Girl laughs loudly.*)

BALLAD SINGER AND HIS WIFE: Good people who
    have trouble here below
In serving cruel lords and gentle Jesus
Who bids you turn the other cheek just so . . .
    (*With mimicry.*)
While they prepare to strike the second blow:
Obedience will never cure your woe
So each of you wake up and do just as he
    pleases!

(*The Ballad Singer and his Wife hurriedly start to try to sell pamphlets to the spectators.*)

BALLAD SINGER: Read all about the earth going round
    the sun, two centesemi only. As proved by the great
    Galileo. Two centesimi only. Written by a local
    scholar. Understandable to one and all. Buy one
    for your friends, your children and your aunty
    Rosa, two centesimi only. Abbreviated but complete. Fully illustrated with pictures of the planets,
    including Venus, two centesimi only.

(*During the speech of the Ballad Singer we hear the carnival procession approaching followed by laughter. A Reveller rushes in.*)

REVELLER: The procession!

(*The litter bearers speedily joggle out the King of Hungary. The Spectators turn and look at the first float of the procession, which now makes its appearance. It bears a gigantic figure of Galileo, holding in one hand an open Bible with the pages crossed out. The other hand points to the Bible, and the head mechanically turns from side to side as if to say "No! No!"*)

A LOUD VOICE: Galileo, the Bible killer!

(*The laughter from the marketplace becomes uproarious. The Monk comes flying from the marketplace followed by delighted Children.*)

SCENE 10

The depths are hot, the heights are chill
The streets are loud, the court is still.

(*Antechamber and staircase in the Medicean palace in Florence. Galileo, with a book under his arm, waits with his Daughter to be admitted to the presence of the Prince.*)

VIRGINIA: They are a long time.
GALILEO: Yes.
VIRGINIA: Who is that funny-looking man? (*She indicates the Informer who has entered casually and*

seated himself in the background, taking no apparent notice of Galileo.)

GALILEO: I don't know.

VIRGINIA: It's not the first time I have seen him around. He gives me the creeps.

GALILEO: Nonsense. We're in Florence, not among robbers in the mountains of Corsica.

VIRGINIA: Here comes the Rector.

(*The Rector comes down the stairs.*)

GALILEO: Gaffone is a bore. He attaches himself to you.

(*The Rector passes, scarcely nodding.*)

GALILEO: My eyes are bad today. Did he acknowledge us?

VIRGINIA: Barely. (*Pause.*) What's in your book? Will they say it's heretical?

GALILEO: You hang around church too much. And getting up at dawn and scurrying to Mass is ruining your skin. You pray for me, don't you?

(*A Man comes down the stairs.*)

VIRGINIA: Here's Mr. Matti. You designed a machine for his iron foundries.

MATTI: How were the squabs, Mr. Galilei? (*Low.*) My brother and I had a good laugh the other day. He picked up a racy pamphlet against the Bible somewhere. It quoted you.

GALILEO: The squabs, Matti, were wonderful, thank you again. Pamphlets I know nothing about. The Bible and Homer are my favorite reading.

MATTI: No necessity to be cautious with me, Mr. Galilei. I am on your side. I am not a man who knows about the motions of the stars, but you have championed the freedom to teach new things. Take that mechanical cultivator they have in Germany which you described to me. I can tell you, it will never be used in this country. The same circles that are hampering you now will forbid the physicians at Bologna to cut up corpses for research. Do you know, they have such things as money markets in Amsterdam and in London? Schools for business, too. Regular papers with news. Here we are not even free to make money. I have a stake in your career. They are against iron foundries because they say the gathering of so many workers in one place fosters immorality! If you ever try anything, Mr. Galilei, remember you have friends in all walks of life including an iron founder. Good luck to you. (*He goes.*)

GALILEO: Good man, but need he be so affectionate in public? His voice carries. They will always claim me as their spiritual leader particularly in places where it doesn't help me at all. I have written a book about the mechanics of the firmament, that is all. What they do or don't do with it is not my concern.

VIRGINIA (*loud*): If people only knew how you disagreed with those goings-on all over the country last All Fools day.

GALILEO: Yes. Offer honey to a bear, and lose your arm if the beast is hungry.

VIRGINIA (*low*): Did the prince ask you to come here today?

GALILEO: I sent word I was coming. He will want the book, he has paid for it. My health hasn't been any too good lately. I may accept Sagredo's invitation to stay with him in Padua for a few weeks.

VIRGINIA: You couldn't manage without your books.

GALILEO: Sagredo has an excellent library.

VIRGINIA: We haven't had this month's salary yet —

GALILEO: Yes. (*The Cardinal Inquisitor passes down the staircase. He bows deeply in answer to Galileo's bow.*) What is he doing in Florence? If they try to do anything to me, the new Pope will meet them with an iron NO. And the Prince is my pupil, he would never have me extradited.

VIRGINIA: Psst. The Lord Chamberlain.

(*The Lord Chamberlain comes down the stairs.*)

LORD CHAMBERLAIN: His Highness had hoped to find time for you, Mr. Galilei. Unfortunately, he has to leave immediately to judge the parade at the Riding Academy. On what business did you wish to see His Highness?

GALILEO: I wanted to present my book to His Highness.

LORD CHAMBERLAIN: How are your eyes today?

GALILEO: So, so. With His Highness' permission, I am dedicating the book . . .

LORD CHAMBERLAIN: Your eyes are a matter of great concern to His Highness. Could it be that you have been looking too long and too often through your marvelous tube? (*He leaves without accepting the book.*)

VIRGINIA (*greatly agitated*): Father, I am afraid.

GALILEO: He didn't take the book, did he? (*Low and resolute.*) Keep a straight face. We are not going home, but to the house of the lens-grinder. There is a coach and horses in his backyard. Keep your eyes to the front, don't look back at that man.

(*They start. The Lord Chamberlain comes back.*)

LORD CHAMBERLAIN: Oh, Mr. Galilei! His Highness has just charged me to inform you that the Florentine Court is no longer in a position to oppose the request of the Holy Inquisition to interrogate you in Rome.

SCENE 11

The Pope

(*A chamber in the Vatican. The Pope, Urban VIII —
formerly Cardinal Barberini — is giving audience to
the Cardinal Inquisitor. The trampling and shuffling
of many feet is heard throughout the scene from the
adjoining corridors. During the scene the Pope is being
robed for the conclave he is about to attend: at the
beginning of the scene he is plainly Barberini, but as
the scene proceeds he is more and more obscured by
grandiose vestments.*)

POPE: No! No! No!

INQUISITOR (*referring to the owners of the shuffling
feet*): Doctors of all chairs from the universities,
representatives of the special orders of the church,
representatives of the clergy as a whole who have
come believing with childlike faith in the word of
God as set forth in the scriptures, who have come
to hear Your Holiness confirm their faith: and Your
Holiness is really going to tell them that the Bible
can no longer be regarded as the alphabet of truth?

POPE: I will not set myself up against the multiplication
table. No!

INQUISITOR: Ah, that is what these people say, that it
is the multiplication table. Their cry is, "The figures
compel us," but where do these figures come from?
Plainly they come from doubt. These men doubt
everything. Can society stand on doubt and not on
faith? "Thou art my master, but I doubt whether
it is for the best." "This is my neighbor's house
and my neighbor's wife, but why shouldn't they
belong to me?" After the plague, after the new
war, after the unparalleled disaster of the Reformation, your dwindling flock look to their shepherd, and now the mathematicians turn their tubes
on the sky and announce to the world that you
have not the best advice about the heavens either — up to now your only uncontested sphere
of influence. This Galilei started meddling in machines at an early age. Now that men in ships are
venturing on the great oceans — I am not against
that of course — they are putting their faith in a
brass bowl they call a compass and not in Almighty
God.

POPE: This man is the greatest physicist of our time.
He is the light of Italy, and not just any muddle-
head.

INQUISITOR: Would we have had to arrest him otherwise? This bad man knows what he is doing, not
writing his books in Latin, but in the jargon of the
marketplace.

POPE (*occupied with the shuffling feet*): That was not
in the best of taste. (*A pause.*) These shuffling feet
are making me nervous.

INQUISITOR: May they be more telling than my words,
Your Holiness. Shall all these go from you with
doubt in their hearts?

POPE: This man has friends. What about Versailles?°
What about the Viennese court? They will call Holy
Church a cesspool for defunct ideas. Keep your
hands off him.

INQUISITOR: In practice it will never get far. He is a
man of the flesh. He would soften at once.

POPE: He has more enjoyment in him than any man
I ever saw. He loves eating and drinking and thinking. To excess. He indulges in thinking bouts! He
cannot say no to an old wine or a new thought.
(*Furious.*) I do not want a condemnation of physical facts. I do not want to hear battle cries:
Church, church, church! Reason, reason, reason!
(*Pause.*) These shuffling feet are intolerable. Has
the whole world come to my door?

INQUISITOR: Not the whole world, Your Holiness. A
select gathering of the faithful.

(*Pause.*)

POPE (*exhausted*): It is clearly understood: he is not
to be tortured. (*Pause.*) At the very most, he may
be shown the instruments.

INQUISITOR: That will be adequate, Your Holiness.
Mr. Galilei understands machinery.

(*The eyes of Barberini look helplessly at the Cardinal
Inquisitor from under the completely assembled pan-
oply of Pope Urban VIII.*)

SCENE 12

*June twenty-second, sixteen thirty-three,
A momentous date for you and me.
Of all the days that was the one
An age of reason could have begun.*

(*Again the garden of the Florentine Ambassador at
Rome, where Galileo's assistants wait the news of the
trial. The Little Monk and Federzoni are attempting
to concentrate on a game of chess. Virginia kneels in
a corner, praying and counting her beads.*)

LITTLE MONK: The Pope didn't even grant him an
audience.

FEDERZONI: No more scientific discussions.

Versailles: This reference to the French court is an anach-
ronism. The palace housing the court had not yet been built
at Versailles. In Galileo's time, it was in Paris.

ANDREA: The "Discorsi" will never be finished. The sum of his findings. They will kill him.

FEDERZONI (*stealing a glance at him*): Do you really think so?

ANDREA: He will never recant.

(*Silence.*)

LITTLE MONK: You know when you lie awake at night how your mind fastens on to something irrelevant. Last night I kept thinking: if only they would let him take his little stone in with him, the appeal-to-reason-pebble that he always carries in his pocket.

FEDERZONI: In the room *they'll* take him to, he won't have a pocket.

ANDREA: But he will not recant.

LITTLE MONK: How can they beat the truth out of a man who gave his sight in order to see?

FEDERZONI: Maybe they can't.

(*Silence.*)

ANDREA (*speaking about Virginia*): She is praying that he will recant.

FEDERZONI: Leave her alone. She doesn't know whether she's on her head or on her heels since they got hold of her. They brought her Father Confessor from Florence.

(*The Informer of scene 10 enters.*)

INFORMER: Mr. Galilei will be here soon. He may need a bed.

FEDERZONI: Have they let him out?

INFORMER: Mr. Galilei is expected to recant at five o'clock. The big bell of Saint Marcus will be rung and the complete text of his recantation publicly announced.

ANDREA: I don't believe it.

INFORMER: Mr. Galilei will be brought to the garden gate at the back of the house, to avoid the crowds collecting in the streets. (*He goes.*)

(*Silence.*)

ANDREA: The moon is an earth because the light of the moon is not her own. Jupiter is a fixed star, and four moons turn around Jupiter, therefore we are not shut in by crystal shells. The sun is the pivot of our world, therefore the earth is not the center. The earth moves, spinning about the sun. And he showed us. You can't make a man unsee what he has seen.

(*Silence.*)

FEDERZONI: Five o'clock is one minute.

(*Virginia prays louder.*)

ANDREA: Listen all of you, they are murdering the truth.

(*He stops up his ears with his fingers. The two other pupils do the same. Federzoni goes over to the Little Monk, and all of them stand absolutely still in cramped positions. Nothing happens. No bell sounds. After a silence, filled with the murmur of Virginia's prayers, Federzoni runs to the wall to look at the clock. He turns around, his expression changed. He shakes his head. They drop their hands.*)

FEDERZONI: No. No bell. It is three minutes after.

LITTLE MONK: He hasn't.

ANDREA: He held true. It is all right, it is all right.

LITTLE MONK: He did not recant.

FEDERZONI: No.

(*They embrace each other, they are delirious with joy.*)

ANDREA: So force cannot accomplish everything. What has been seen can't be unseen. Man is constant in the face of death.

FEDERZONI: June 22, 1633: dawn of the age of reason. I wouldn't have wanted to go on living if he had recanted.

LITTLE MONK: I didn't say anything, but I was in agony. Oh, ye of little faith!

ANDREA: I was sure.

FEDERZONI: It would have turned our morning to night.

ANDREA: It would have been as if the mountain had turned to water.

LITTLE MONK (*kneeling down, crying*): Oh God, I thank Thee.

ANDREA: Beaten humanity can lift its head. A man has stood up and said "no."

(*At this moment the bell of Saint Marcus begins to toll. They stand like statues. Virginia stands up.*)

VIRGINIA: The bell of Saint Marcus. He is not damned.

(*From the street one hears the Town Crier reading Galileo's recantation.*)

TOWN CRIER: I, Galileo Galilei, Teacher of Mathematics and Physics, do hereby publicly renounce my teaching that the earth moves. I foreswear this teaching with a sincere heart and unfeigned faith and detest and curse this and all other errors and heresies repugnant to the Holy Scriptures.

(*The lights dim; when they come up again the bell of Saint Marcus is petering out. Virginia has gone but the Scholars are still there waiting.*)

ANDREA (*loud*): The mountain did turn to water.

(*Galileo has entered quietly and unnoticed. He is*

*changed, almost unrecognizable. He has heard An-
drea. He waits some seconds by the door for somebody to greet him. Nobody does. They retreat from
him. He goes slowly and, because of his bad sight,
uncertainly, to the front of the stage where he finds
a chair, and sits down.)*

ANDREA: I can't look at him. Tell him to go away.
FEDERZONI: Steady.
ANDREA (*hysterically*): He saved his big gut.
FEDERZONI: Get him a glass of water.

*(The Little Monk fetches a glass of water for Andrea.
Nobody acknowledges the presence of Galileo, who
sits silently on his chair listening to the voice of the
Town Crier, now in another street.)*

ANDREA: I can walk. Just help me a bit.

(They help him to the door.)

ANDREA (*in the door*): "Unhappy is the land that
breeds no hero."
GALILEO: No, Andrea: "Unhappy is the land that
needs a hero."

*Before the next scene a curtain with the following
legend on it is lowered:*

You can plainly see that if a horse were to fall
from a height of three or four feet, it could break
its bones, whereas a dog would not suffer injury.
The same applies to a cat from a height of as much
as eight or ten feet, to a grasshopper from the top
of a tower, and to an ant falling down from the
moon. Nature could not allow a horse to become
as big as twenty horses nor a giant as big as ten
men, unless she were to change the proportions of
all its members, particularly the bones. Thus the
common assumption that great and small structures are equally tough is obviously wrong.
— From the *Discorsi*

SCENE 13

*1633–1642.
Galileo Galilei remains a prisoner
of the Inquisition until his death.*

*(A country house near Florence. A large room simply
furnished. There is a huge table, a leather chair, a
globe of the world on a stand, and a narrow bed. A
portion of the adjoining anteroom is visible, and the
front door which opens into it.)*

*(An Official of the Inquisition sits on guard in the
anteroom.)*

(In the large room, Galileo is quietly experimenting

*with a bent wooden rail and a small ball of wood.
He is still vigorous but almost blind.)*

*(After a while there is a knocking at the outside
door. The Official opens it to a Peasant who brings
a plucked goose. Virginia comes from the kitchen. She
is past forty.)*

PEASANT (*handing the goose to Virginia*): I was told
to deliver this here.
VIRGINIA: I didn't order a goose.
PEASANT: I was told to say it's from someone who
was passing through.

*(Virginia takes the goose, surprised. The Official takes
it from her and examines it suspiciously. Then, reassured, he hands it back to her. The Peasant goes.
Virginia brings the goose in to Galileo.)*

VIRGINIA: Somebody who was passing through sent
you something.
GALILEO: What is it?
VIRGINIA: Can't you see it?
GALILEO: No. (*He walks over.*) A goose. Any name?
VIRGINIA: No.
GALILEO (*weighing the goose*): Solid.
VIRGINIA (*cautiously*): Will you eat the liver, if I have
it cooked with a little apple?
GALILEO: I had my dinner. Are you under orders to
finish me off with food?
VIRGINIA: It's not rich. And what is wrong with your
eyes again? You should be able to see it.
GALILEO: You were standing in the light.
VIRGINIA: I was not. — You haven't been writing
again?
GALILEO (*sneering*): What do you think?

*(Virginia takes the goose out into the anteroom and
speaks to the Official.)*

VIRGINIA: You had better ask Monsignor Carpula to
send the doctor. Father couldn't see this goose
across the room. — Don't look at me like that. He
has not been writing. He dictates everything to me,
as you know.
OFFICIAL: Yes?
VIRGINIA: He abides by the rules. My father's repentance is sincere. I keep an eye on him. (*She
hands him the goose.*) Tell the cook to fry the liver
with an apple and an onion. (*She goes back into
the large room.*) And you have no business to be
doing that with those eyes of yours, father.
GALILEO: You may read me some Horace.
VIRGINIA: We should go on with your weekly letter
to the Archbishop. Monsignor Carpula to whom
we owe so much was all smiles the other day because the Archbishop had expressed his pleasure
at your collaboration.

GALILEO: Where were we?

VIRGINIA (*sits down to take his dictation*): Paragraph four.

GALILEO: Read what you have.

VIRGINIA: "The position of the church in the matter of the unrest at Genoa. I agree with Cardinal Spoletti in the matter of the unrest among the Venetian ropemakers . . ."

GALILEO: Yes. (*Dictates.*) I agree with Cardinal Spoletti in the matter of the unrest among the Venetian ropemakers: it is better to distribute good nourishing food in the name of charity than to pay them more for their bellropes. It being surely better to strengthen their faith than to encourage their acquisitiveness. St. Paul says: Charity never faileth. — How is that?

VIRGINIA: It's beautiful, father.

GALILEO: It couldn't be taken as irony?

VIRGINIA: No. The Archbishop will like it. It's so practical.

GALILEO: I trust your judgment. Read it over slowly.

VIRGINIA: "The position of the Church in the matter of the unrest . . ."

(*There is a knocking at the outside door. Virginia goes into the anteroom. The Official opens the door. It is Andrea.*)

ANDREA: Good evening. I am sorry to call so late, I'm on my way to Holland. I was asked to look him up. Can I go in?

VIRGINIA: I don't know whether he will see you. You never came.

ANDREA: Ask him.

(*Galileo recognizes the voice. He sits motionless. Virginia comes in to Galileo.*)

GALILEO: Is that Andrea?

VIRGINIA: Yes. (*Pause.*) I will send him away.

GALILEO: Show him in.

(*Virginia shows Andrea in. Virginia sits, Andrea remains standing.*)

ANDREA (*cool*): Have you been keeping well, Mr. Galilei?

GALILEO: Sit down. What are you doing these days? What are you working on? I heard it was something about hydraulics in Milan.

ANDREA: As he knew I was passing through, Fabricius of Amsterdam asked me to visit you and inquire about your health.

(*Pause.*)

GALILEO: I am very well.

ANDREA (*formally*): I am glad I can report you are in good health.

GALILEO: Fabricius will be glad to hear it. And you might inform him that, on account of the depth of my repentance, I live in comparative comfort.

ANDREA: Yes, we understand that the church is more than pleased with you. Your complete acceptance has had its effect. Not one paper expounding a new thesis has made its appearance in Italy since your submission.

(*Pause.*)

GALILEO: Unfortunately there are countries not under the wing of the church. Would you not say the erroneous condemned theories are still taught — there?

ANDREA (*relentless*): Things are almost at a standstill.

GALILEO: Are they? (*Pause.*) Nothing from Descartes in Paris?

ANDREA: Yes. On receiving the news of your recantation, he shelved his treatise on the nature of light.

GALILEO: I sometimes worry about my assistants whom I led into error. Have they benefited by my example?

ANDREA: In order to work I have to go to Holland.

GALILEO: Yes.

ANDREA: Federzoni is grinding lenses again, back in some shop.

GALILEO: He can't read the books.

ANDREA: Fulganzio, our little monk, has abandoned research and is resting in peace in the church.

GALILEO: So. (*Pause.*) My superiors are looking forward to my spiritual recovery. I am progressing as well as can be expected.

VIRGINIA: You are doing well, father.

GALILEO: Virginia, leave the room.

(*Virginia rises uncertainly and goes out.*)

VIRGINIA (*to the Official*): He was his pupil, so now he is his enemy. — Help me in the kitchen.

(*She leaves the anteroom with the Official.*)

ANDREA: May I go now, sir?

GALILEO: I do not know why you came, Sarti. To unsettle me? I have to be prudent.

ANDREA: I'll be on my way.

GALILEO: As it is, I have relapses. I completed the "Discorsi."

ANDREA: You completed what?

GALILEO: My "Discorsi."

ANDREA: How?

GALILEO: I am allowed pen and paper. My superiors are intelligent men. They know the habits of a lifetime cannot be broken abruptly. But they protect me from any unpleasant consequences: they lock my pages away as I dictate them. And I should know better than to risk my comfort. I wrote the

"Discorsi" out again during the night. The manuscript is in the globe. My vanity has up to now prevented me from destroying it. If you consider taking it, you will shoulder the entire risk. You will say it was pirated from the original in the hands of the Holy Office.

(*Andrea, as in a trance, has gone to the globe. He lifts the upper half and gets the book. He turns the pages as if wanting to devour them. In the background the opening sentences of the* Discorsi *appear:*
MY PURPOSE IS TO SET FORTH A VERY NEW SCIENCE DEALING WITH A VERY ANCIENT SUBJECT — MOTION. . . . AND I HAVE DISCOVERED BY EXPERIMENT SOME PROPERTIES OF IT WHICH ARE WORTH KNOWING. . . .)

GALILEO: I had to employ my time somehow.

(*The text disappears.*)

ANDREA: Two new sciences! This will be the foundation stone of a new physics.
GALILEO: Yes. Put it under your coat.
ANDREA: And we thought you had deserted. (*In a low voice.*) Mr. Galilei, how can I begin to express my shame. Mine has been the loudest voice against you.
GALILEO: That would seem to have been proper. I taught you science and I decried the truth.
ANDREA: Did you? I think not. Everything is changed!
GALILEO: What is changed?
ANDREA: You shielded the truth from the oppressor. Now I see! In your dealings with the Inquisition you used the same superb common sense you brought to physics.
GALILEO: Oh!
ANDREA: We lost our heads. With the crowd at the street corners we said: "He will die, he will never surrender!" You came back: "I surrendered but I am alive." We cried: "Your hands are stained!" You say: "Better stained than empty."
GALILEO: "Better stained than empty." — It sounds realistic. Sounds like me.
ANDREA: And I of all people should have known. I was twelve when you sold another man's telescope to the Venetian Senate, and saw you put it to immortal use. Your friends were baffled when you bowed to the Prince of Florence: Science gained a wider audience. You always laughed at heroics. "People who suffer bore me," you said. "Misfortunes are due mainly to miscalculations." And: "If there are obstacles, the shortest line between two points may be the crooked line."
GALILEO: It makes a picture.
ANDREA: And when you stooped to recant in 1633,

I should have understood that you were again about your business.
GALILEO: My business being?
ANDREA: Science. The study of the properties of motion, mother of the machines which will themselves change the ugly face of the earth.
GALILEO: Aha!
ANDREA: You gained time to write a book that only you could write. Had you burned at the stake in a blaze of glory they would have won.
GALILEO: They have won. And there is no such thing as a scientific work that only one man can write.
ANDREA: Then why did you recant, tell me that!
GALILEO: I recanted because I was afraid of physical pain.
ANDREA: No!
GALILEO: They showed me the instruments.
ANDREA: It was not a plan?
GALILEO: It was not.

(*Pause.*)

ANDREA: But you have contributed. Science has only one commandment: contribution. And you have contributed more than any man for a hundred years.
GALILEO: Have I? Then welcome to my gutter, dear colleague in science and brother in treason: I sold out, you are a buyer. The first sight of the book! His mouth watered and his scoldings were drowned. Blessed be our bargaining, whitewashing, death-fearing community!
ANDREA: The fear of death is human.
GALILEO: Even the church will teach you that to be weak is not human. It is just evil.
ANDREA: The church, yes! But science is not concerned with our weaknesses.
GALILEO: No? My dear Sarti, in spite of my present convictions, I may be able to give you a few pointers as to the concerns of your chosen profession.

(*Enter Virginia with a platter.*)

In my spare time, I happen to have gone over this case. I have spare time. — Even a man who sells wool, however good he is at buying wool cheap and selling it dear, must be concerned with the standing of the wool trade. The practice of science would seem to call for valor. She trades in knowledge, which is the product of doubt. And this new art of doubt has enchanted the public. The plight of the multitude is old as the rocks, and is believed to be basic as the rocks. But now they have learned to doubt. They snatched the telescopes out of our hands and had them trained on their tormentors: prince, official, public moralist. The mechanism of the heavens was clearer, the mechanism of their courts was still murky. The battle to measure the heavens is won by doubt; by credulity the Roman housewife's battle for milk will always be lost. Word is passed down that this is of no concern to the scientist who is told he will only release such of his findings as do not disturb the peace, that is, the peace of mind of the well-to-do. Threats and bribes fill the air. Can the scientist hold out on the numbers? — For what reason do you labor? I take it the intent of science is to ease human existence. If you give way to coercion, science can be crippled, and your new machines may simply suggest new drudgeries. Should you then, in time, discover all there is to be discovered, your progress must then become a progress away from the bulk of humanity. The gulf might even grow so wide that the sound of your cheering at some new achievement would be echoed by a universal howl of horror. — As a scientist I had an almost unique opportunity. In my day astronomy emerged into the marketplace. At that particular time, had one man put up a fight, it could have had wide repercussions. I have come to believe that I was never in real danger; for some years I was as strong as the authorities, and I surrendered my knowledge to the powers that be, to use it, no, not *use* it, *abuse* it, as it suits their ends. I have betrayed my profession. Any man who does what I have done must not be tolerated in the ranks of science.

(*Virginia, who has stood motionless, puts the platter on the table.*)

VIRGINIA: You are accepted in the ranks of the faithful, father.
GALILEO (*sees her*): Correct. (*He goes over to the table.*) I have to eat now.
VIRGINIA: We lock up at eight.
ANDREA: I am glad I came. (*He extends his hand. Galileo ignores it and goes over to his meal.*)
GALILEO (*examining the plate; to Andrea*): Somebody who knows me sent me a goose. I still enjoy eating.
ANDREA: And your opinion is now that the "new age" was an illusion?
GALILEO: Well. — This age of ours turned out to be a whore, spattered with blood. Maybe, new ages look like blood-spattered whores. Take care of yourself.
ANDREA: Yes. (*Unable to go.*) With reference to your evaluation of the author in question — I do not know the answer. But I cannot think that your savage analysis is the last word.
GALILEO: Thank you, sir.

(*Official knocks at the door.*)

VIRGINIA (*showing Andrea out*): I don't like visitors from the past, they excite him.

(*She lets him out. The Official closes the iron door. Virginia returns.*)

GALILEO (*eating*): Did you try and think who sent the goose?
VIRGINIA: Not Andrea.
GALILEO: Maybe not. I gave Redhead his first lesson; when he held out his hand, I had to remind myself he is teaching now. — How is the sky tonight?
VIRGINIA (*at the window*): Bright.

(*Galileo continues eating.*)

SCENE 14

> The great book o'er the border went
> And, good folk, that was the end.
> But we hope you'll keep in mind
> You and I were left behind.

(*Before a little Italian customs house early in the morning. Andrea sits upon one of his traveling trunks at the barrier and reads Galileo's book. The window of a small house is still lit, and a big grotesque shadow, like an old witch and her cauldron, falls upon the house wall beyond. Barefoot Children in rags see it and point to the little house.*)

CHILDREN (*singing*): One, two, three, four, five, six,
Old Marina is a witch.
At night, on a broomstick she sits
And on the church steeple she spits.
CUSTOMS OFFICER (*to Andrea*): Why are you making this journey?
ANDREA: I am a scholar.
CUSTOMS OFFICER (*to his Clerk*): Put down under "reason for leaving the country": Scholar. (*He points to the baggage.*) Books! Anything dangerous in these books?
ANDREA: What is dangerous?
CUSTOMS OFFICER: Religion. Politics.
ANDREA: These are nothing but mathematical formulas.
CUSTOMS OFFICER: What's that?
ANDREA: Figures.
CUSTOMS OFFICER: Oh, figures. No harm in figures. Just wait a minute, sir, we will soon have your papers stamped. (*He exits with Clerk.*)

(*Meanwhile, a little council of war among the Children has taken place. Andrea quietly watches. One of the Boys, pushed forward by the others, creeps up to the little house from which the shadow comes and takes the jug of milk on the doorstep.*)

ANDREA (*quietly*): What are you doing with that milk?
BOY (*stopping in mid-movement*): She is a witch.

(*The other Children run away behind the customs house. One of them shouts, "Run, Paolo!"*)

ANDREA: Hmm! — And because she is a witch she mustn't have milk. Is that the idea?
BOY: Yes.
ANDREA: And how do you know she is a witch?
BOY (*points to shadow on house wall*): Look!
ANDREA: Oh! I see.
BOY: And she rides on a broomstick at night — and she bewitches the coachman's horses. My cousin Luigi looked through the hole in the stable roof, that the snowstorm made, and heard the horses coughing something terrible.
ANDREA: Oh! — How big was the hole in the stable roof?
BOY: Luigi didn't tell. Why?
ANDREA: I was asking because maybe the horses got sick because it was cold in the stable. You had better ask Luigi how big that hole is.
BOY: You are not going to say Old Marina isn't a witch, because you can't.
ANDREA: No, I can't say she isn't a witch. I haven't looked into it. A man can't know about a thing he hasn't looked into, or can he?
BOY: No! — But THAT! (*He points to the shadow.*) She is stirring hell-broth.
ANDREA: Let's see. Do you want to take a look? I can lift you up.
BOY: You lift me to the window, mister! (*He takes a sling shot out of his pocket.*) I can really bash her from there.

ANDREA: Hadn't we better make sure she is a witch before we shoot? I'll hold that.

(*The Boy puts the milk jug down and follows him reluctantly to the window. Andrea lifts the boy up so that he can look in.*)

ANDREA: What do you see?
BOY (*slowly*): Just an old girl cooking porridge.
ANDREA: Oh! Nothing to it then. Now look at her shadow, Paolo.

(*The Boy looks over his shoulder and back and compares the reality and the shadow.*)

BOY: The big thing is a soup ladle.
ANDREA: Ah! A ladle! You see, I would have taken it for a broomstick, but I haven't looked into the matter as you have, Paolo. Here is your sling.
CUSTOMS OFFICER (*returning with the Clerk and handing Andrea his papers*): All present and correct. Good luck, sir.

(*Andrea goes, reading Galileo's book. The Clerk starts to bring his baggage after him. The barrier rises. Andrea passes through, still reading the book. The Boy kicks over the milk jug.*)

BOY (*shouting after Andrea*): She *is* a witch! She *is* a witch!
ANDREA: You saw with your own eyes: think it over!

(*The Boy joins the others. They sing.*)

One, two, three, four, five, six,
Old Marina is a witch.
At night, on a broomstick she sits
And on the church steeple she spits.

(*The Customs Officers laugh. Andrea goes.*)

Tennessee Williams

Tennessee Williams (1911–1983) was one of a handful of post–World War II American playwrights to achieve an international reputation. He was born Thomas Lanier Williams in Columbus, Mississippi, the son of a traveling shoe salesman who eventually moved the family to a dark and dreary tenement in St. Louis. A precocious child, Williams was given a typewriter by his mother when he was eleven years old. The instrument helped him create fantasy worlds that seemed more real, more important to him than the dark and sometimes threatening world in which he lived. His parents, when they were expecting a third child, bought a house whose gloominess depressed virtually everyone in it. His mother and father found themselves arguing, and his sister, Rose, took refuge from the real world by closeting herself with a collection of glass animals.

Both Rose and Tennessee responded badly to their environment, and both had breakdowns. Tennessee was so ill that he suffered a partial paralysis of his legs, a disorder that made him a victim of bullies at school and a disappointment to his father at home. He could never participate in sports and was always somewhat frail; however, he was very advanced intellectually and published his first story when he was sixteen.

His education was sporadic. He attended the University of Missouri but failed ROTC because of his physical limitations and soon dropped out of school to work in a shoe company. Then he went to Washington University in St. Louis and dropped out again. Finally, he earned a bachelor's degree in playwriting at the State University of Iowa when he was twenty-four. During this time he was writing plays, some of which were produced at Washington University. Two years after he graduated, the Theatre Guild produced his first commercial play, *Battle of Angels* (1940), in Boston. It was such a distinct failure that he feared his career was stunted from the beginning. But he kept writing and managed to live for a few years on foundation grants. It was not until the production of *The Glass Menagerie* (1944 in Chicago, 1945 in New York) that he achieved the kind of notice he knew he deserved. His first real success, the play was given the New York Drama Critics' Circle Award, the sign of his having achieved a measure of professional recognition and financial independence.

Although he had tried his hand at many activities to make a living, including an unsuccessful attempt at screenwriting, he had no more worries about work after *The Glass Menagerie* ran on Broadway for 561 performances. In 1947 his second success, *A Streetcar Named Desire*, starring the then unknown Marlon Brando, was an even bigger box-office smash. It ran for 855 performances and won the Pulitzer Prize. By the time Tennessee Williams was thirty-six, he was thought of as one of the most important playwrights in America.

Williams followed these successes with a number of plays that were not all as well received as his first works. *Summer and Smoke* (1948), *The Rose Tattoo* (1951), and *Camino Real* (1953) were met with measured enthusiasm from the public, although the critics thought highly of Williams's work. These plays were followed by the saga of a southern family, *Cat on a Hot Tin Roof*, which won all the major drama prizes in 1955, including the Pulitzer.

Williams's energy was unfailing in the next several years. He authored a screenplay, *Baby Doll*, with the legendary producer Elia Kazan, in 1956. In 1958 he wrote a one-act play, *Suddenly Last Summer*, and in 1959 *Sweet Bird of Youth*. Some of his later plays are *The Night of the Iguana* (1961), *The Milk Train Doesn't Stop Here Anymore* (1963), and *Small Craft Warnings* (1972). He also wrote a novel and several volumes of short stories, establishing himself as an important writer in many genres. His accidental death in 1983 shocked the theater world.

THE GLASS MENAGERIE

Tennessee Williams has often been accused of exorcising his family demons in his plays and of therefore sometimes cloaking events in a personal symbolism that is impossible for an audience to penetrate totally. *The Glass Menagerie* (1944) certainly derives from his personal experience growing up in St. Louis in a tenement, the setting for the play. The characters are drawn from his own family, particularly the character Laura, who is based on his sister. But the symbolism in the play is not so obscure as to give an audience special difficulty.

In a way, Williams thought of the play as a tribute to his sister, Rose. Rose's depressions were so severe that eventually she received a lobotomy, which rendered her more passive and more hopeless than before. The operation did not achieve anything positive, and Williams felt somewhat responsible because he had not urged the family to refuse the treatment.

In the play, Amanda Wingfield is obsessed with finding gentleman callers and a suitable career for her daughter, Laura, who is partially lame and exceedingly shy. Amanda lives in a world of imagination, inventing stories about a glorious past she never lived and about all the suitors she could have had before she married. Amanda bullies Laura, whose only defense is to bury herself in her own fantasy world of spun-glass animals. Tom, the son and narrator of the play, is also a victim of Amanda's bullying, but he is more independent and better able to withstand her assaults.

Both children are great disappointments to Amanda. Tom is aloof, indolent, something like his father, present only in his picture on the wall. Laura calls herself a cripple and has no self-esteem or hope for a future such as the one her mother conceives for her. Laura's shyness is almost uncontrollable. It has ruined any hope of a business career, to Amanda's intense distress. When Tom brings home Jim, the one boy Laura remembers from high school, Laura is nearly too shy to come to the dinner table. And when it becomes clear that Jim is not the gentleman caller of Amanda's dreams, Amanda and Laura are left to face reality or to continue living in their fantasy worlds.

Amanda confronts Tom at the end of the play and asserts that he "live[s] in a dream" and "manufacture[s] illusions." She could be speaking about any character in the play, including Jim, who lives according to popular illusions about self-fulfillment. But the Wingfields in particular pay dearly for their illusions, perhaps Laura more than anyone because of her mother's inability to relinquish her intense but unrealistic hopes for her.

Williams's written presentation of the play provides more insights than usual for a reading audience. His stage directions are elaborate, poetic, and exceptionally evocative. Through Tom, as narrator, he says that the play is not realistic but rather is a memory play, an enactment of moments in Tom's memory.

Williams specifies a setting that is almost dreamlike, using Brechtian devices such as the visual images and screen legends flashed at appropriate moments. Like Brecht in certain plays, Williams also uses music to establish a mood or stimulate an association. These devices may be thought of as expressionistic, although they fall short of the fullness of expressionism, which usually involves a distortion of reality to express the feelings of the author.

Modern productions rarely follow Williams's directions, however, so the dreamlike quality is sometimes lost. In fact, ironically, modern productions of this play are often realistic rather than symbolic, although they usually maintain the mood that Williams hoped to achieve.

The Glass Menagerie in Performance

The first production of *The Glass Menagerie* opened in Chicago on December 26, 1944, during World War II. Audiences were not drawn to it at first, but the critics' positive reviews began to attract people to the theater. In March 1945, when it was playing to full houses, the play transferred to New York and began a run of 563 performances. It won the Drama Critics' Circle Award as the best American play of the 1944–1945 season. Two road companies then toured the play around the country. The first London performance, in the large and distinguished Theatre Royal in Haymarket in July 1948, was directed by John Gielgud and starred Helen Hayes as Amanda Wingfield. A film version followed in 1950.

Revivals of the play have been both numerous and successful. Laurette Taylor, who played Amanda in the original New York production, set a standard with her interpretation of Williams's poetic language. Maureen Stapleton, whose more vigorous approach contrasted sharply with Taylor's, took the role in the 1965 production in the Brooks Atkinson Theater in New York. The critic Howard Taubman said, "Maureen Stapleton does not cause one to forget Miss Taylor. . . . Through the magic of her own sensitivity, she gives Amanda a strong, binding thread of sadness and tenderness." Katharine Hepburn's first television performance was as Amanda in 1973. "She gives a brilliant, multifaceted performance that is surely the acting tour de force of the year," said Percy Shain. Jessica Tandy performed the role in 1983 at the Eugene O'Neill Theater in New York, with Amanda Plummer as Laura. *New York Times* critic Frank Rich declared, "This Amanda is tough, and even her most comic badgerings leave a bitter aftertaste." Interestingly, the British director of that production, John Dexter, used some of the flash cards that Williams specified in the original published version but that had been omitted from previous productions. They flashed important speeches on the scrim during the performance.

Joanne Woodward played Amanda in the 1986 revival at the Long Wharf Theater in New Haven in a version that had been performed at the Williamstown Theater Festival in 1982. Treat Williams was the son, James Naughton was the suitor, and the Long Wharf production was impressively dreamlike and powerful. Woodward's husband, Paul Newman, directed this version in the 1987 film of the play.

Tennessee Williams (1911–1983)

THE GLASS MENAGERIE   *1944*

nobody, not even the rain, has such small hands   — E. E. CUMMINGS

Production Notes by Tennessee Williams

Being a "memory play," *The Glass Menagerie* can be presented with unusual freedom of convention. Because of its considerably delicate or tenuous material, atmospheric touches and subtleties of direction play a particularly important part. Expressionism and all other unconventional techniques in drama have only one valid aim, and this is a closer approach to truth. When a play employs unconventional techniques, it is not, or certainly shouldn't be, trying to escape its responsibility of dealing with reality, or interpreting experience, but is actually or should be attempting to find a closer approach, or more penetrating and vivid expression of things as they are. The straight realistic play with its genuine frigidaire and authentic ice cubes, its characters that speak exactly as its audience speaks, corresponds to the academic landscape and has the same virtue of a photographic likeness. Everyone should know nowadays the unimportance of the photographic in art: that truth, life, or reality is an organic thing which the poetic imagination can represent or suggest, in essence, only through transformation, through changing into other forms than those which were merely present in appearance.

These remarks are not meant as a preface only to this particular play. They have to do with a conception of a new, plastic theatre which must take the place of the exhausted theatre of realistic conventions if the theatre is to resume vitality as a part of our culture.

The Screen Device. There is *only one important difference between the original and acting version of the play* and that is the *omission* in the latter of the device which I tentatively included in my *original* script. This device was the use of a screen on which were projected magic-lantern slides bearing images or titles. I do not regret the omission of this device from the present Broadway production. The extraordinary power of Miss Taylor's performance made it suitable to have the utmost simplicity in the physical production. But I think it may be interesting to some readers to see how this device was conceived. So I am putting it into the published manuscript. These images and legends, projected from behind, were cast on a section of wall between the front-room and dining-room areas, which should be indistinguishable from the rest when not in use.

The purpose of this will probably be apparent. It is to give accent to certain values in each scene. Each scene contains a particular point (or several) which is structurally the most important. In an episodic play, such as this, the basic structure or narrative line may be obscured from the audience; the effect may seem fragmentary rather than architectural. This may not be the fault of the play so much as a lack of attention in the audience. The legend or image upon the screen will strengthen the effect of what is merely allusion in the writing and allow the primary point to be made more simply and lightly than if the entire responsibility were on the spoken lines. Aside from this structural value, I think the screen will have a definite emotional appeal, less definable but just as important. An imaginative producer or director may invent many other uses for this device than those indicated in the present script. In fact the possibilities of the device seem much larger to me than the instance of this play can possibly utilize.

The Music. Another extra-literary accent in this play is provided by the use of music. A single recurring tune, "The Glass Menagerie," is used to give emotional emphasis to suitable passages. This tune is like circus music, not when you are on the grounds or in the immediate vicinity of the parade, but when you are at some distance and very likely thinking of something else. It seems under those circumstances to continue almost interminably and it weaves in and out of your preoccupied consciousness; then it is the lightest, most delicate music in the world and perhaps the saddest. It expresses the surface vivacity of life with the underlying strain of immutable and inexpressible sorrow. When you look at a piece of delicately spun glass you think of two things: how beautiful it is and how easily it can be broken. Both of those ideas should be woven into the recurring tune, which dips in and out of the play as if it were carried on a wind that changes. It serves as a thread of connection and allusion between the narrator with his separate point in time and space and the subject of his story. Between each episode it returns as reference to the emotion, nostalgia, which is the first condition of the play. It is primarily Laura's music and therefore comes out most clearly when the play focuses upon her and the lovely fragility of glass which is her image.

The Lighting. The lighting in the play is not realistic. In keeping with the atmosphere of memory, the stage is dim. Shafts of light are focused on selected areas or actors, sometimes in contradistinction to what is the apparent center. For instance, in the quarrel scene between Tom and Amanda, in which Laura has no active part, the clearest pool of light is on her figure. This is also true of the supper scene, when her silent figure on the sofa should remain the visual center. The light upon Laura should be distinct from the others, having a peculiar pristine clarity such as light used in early religious portraits of female saints or madonnas. A certain correspondence to light in religious paintings, such as El Greco's, where the figures are radiant in atmosphere that is relatively dusky, could be effectively used throughout the play. (It will also permit a more effective use of the screen.) A free, imaginative use of light can be of enormous value in giving a mobile, plastic quality to plays of a more or less static nature.

Characters

AMANDA WINGFIELD, *the mother. A little woman of great but confused vitality clinging frantically to another time and place. Her characterization must be carefully created, not copied from type. She is not paranoiac, but her life is paranoia. There is much to admire in Amanda, and as much to love and pity as there is to laugh at. Certainly she has endurance and a kind of heroism, and though her foolishness makes her unwittingly cruel at times, there is tenderness in her slight person.*

LAURA WINGFIELD, *her daughter. Amanda, having failed to establish contact with reality, continues to live vitally in her illusions, but Laura's situation is even graver. A childhood illness has left her crippled, one leg slightly shorter than the other, and held in a brace. This defect need not be more than suggested on the stage. Stemming from this, Laura's separation increases till she is like a piece of her own glass collection, too exquisitely fragile to move from the shelf.*

TOM WINGFIELD, *her son. And the narrator of the play. A poet with a job in a warehouse. His nature is not remorseless, but to escape from a trap he has to act without pity.*

JIM O'CONNOR, *the gentleman caller. A nice, ordinary, young man.*

Scene: *An alley in St. Louis.*
Part I: *Preparation for a Gentleman Caller.*
Part II: *The Gentleman Calls.*
Time: *Now and the Past.*

SCENE 1

(The Wingfield apartment is in the rear of the building, one of those vast hive-like conglomerations of cellular living-units that flower as warty growths in over-crowded urban centers of lower middle-class population and are symptomatic of the impulse of this largest and fundamentally enslaved section of American society to avoid fluidity and differentiation and to exist and function as one interfused mass of automatism.)

(The apartment faces an alley and is entered by a fire escape, a structure whose name is a touch of accidental poetic truth, for all of these huge buildings are always burning with the slow and implacable fires of human desperation. The fire escape is included in the set — that is, the landing of it and steps descending from it.)

(The scene is memory and is therefore nonrealistic. Memory takes a lot of poetic license. It omits some details; others are exaggerated, according to the emotional value of the articles it touches, for memory is seated predominantly in the heart. The interior is therefore rather dim and poetic.)

(At the rise of the curtain, the audience is faced with the dark, grim rear wall of the Wingfield tenement. This building, which runs parallel to the footlights, is flanked on both sides by dark, narrow alleys which run into murky canyons of tangled clotheslines, garbage cans, and the sinister latticework of neighboring fire escapes. It is up and down these side alleys that exterior entrances and exits are made, during the play. At the end of Tom's opening commentary, the dark tenement wall slowly reveals (by means of a transparency) the interior of the ground floor Wingfield apartment.)*

(Downstage is the living room, which also serves as a sleeping room for Laura, the sofa unfolding to make her bed. Upstage, center, and divided by a wide arch or second proscenium with transparent faded portieres (or second curtain), is the dining room. In an old-fashioned what-not in the living room are seen scores of transparent glass animals. A blown-up photograph of the father hangs on the wall of the living room, facing the audience, to the left of the archway. It is the face of a very handsome young man in a doughboy's First World War cap. He is gallantly smiling, ineluctably smiling, as if to say, "I will be smiling forever.")

(The audience hears and sees the opening scene in the dining room through both the transparent fourth wall of the building and the transparent gauze portieres of the dining-room arch. It is during this revealing scene that the fourth wall slowly ascends, out of sight. This transparent exterior wall is not brought down again until the very end of the play, during Tom's final speech.)

(The narrator is an undisguised convention of the play. He takes whatever license with dramatic convention as is convenient to his purposes.)

(Tom enters dressed as a merchant sailor from alley, stage left, and strolls across the front of the stage to the fire escape. There he stops and lights a cigarette. He addresses the audience.)

TOM: Yes, I have tricks in my pocket, I have things up my sleeve. But I am the opposite of a stage magician. He gives you illusion that has the appearance of truth. I give you truth in the pleasant disguise of illusion. To begin with, I turn back time. I reverse it to that quaint period, the thirties, when the huge middle class of America was matriculating in a school for the blind. Their eyes had failed them, or they had failed their eyes, and so they were having their fingers pressed forcibly down on the fiery Braille alphabet of a dissolving economy. In Spain there was revolution. Here there was only shouting and confusion. In Spain there was Guernica. Here there were disturbances of labor, sometimes pretty violent, in otherwise peaceful cities such as Chicago, Cleveland, Saint Louis. . . . This is the social background of the play.

(Music.)

The play is memory. Being a memory play, it is dimly lighted, it is sentimental, it is not realistic. In memory everything seems to happen to music. That explains the fiddle in the wings. I am the narrator of the play, and also a character in it. The other characters are my mother, Amanda, my sister, Laura, and a gentleman caller who appears in the final scenes. He is the most realistic character in the play, being an emissary from a world of reality that we were somehow set apart from. But since I have a poet's weakness for symbols, I am using this character also as a symbol; he is the long delayed but always expected something that we live for. There is a fifth character in the play who doesn't appear except in this larger-than-life photograph over the mantel. This is our father who left us a long time ago. He was a telephone man who fell in love with long distances; he gave up his job with the telephone company and skipped the light fantastic out of town . . . The last we heard of him was a picture postcard from Mazatlan, on the Pacific coast of Mexico, containing a message of two words — "Hello — Good-bye!" and no address. I think the rest of the play will explain itself. . . .

(*Amanda's voice becomes audible through the portieres.*)

(*Legend on Screen: "Où Sont les Neiges."*)°

(*He divides the portieres and enters the upstage area.*)

(*Amanda and Laura are seated at a drop-leaf table. Eating is indicated by gestures without food or utensils. Amanda faces the audience. Tom and Laura are seated in profile.*)

(*The interior has lit up softly and through the scrim we see Amanda and Laura seated at the table in the upstage area.*)

AMANDA (*calling*): Tom?

TOM: Yes, Mother.

AMANDA: We can't say grace until you come to the table!

TOM: Coming, Mother. (*He bows slightly and withdraws, reappearing a few moments later in his place at the table.*)

AMANDA (*to her son*): Honey, don't *push* with your *fingers*. If you have to push with something, the thing to push with is a crust of bread. And chew — chew! Animals have sections in their stomachs which enable them to digest food without mastication, but human beings are supposed to chew their food before they swallow it down. Eat food leisurely, son, and really enjoy it. A well-

Où Sont les Neiges: Where are the snows [of yesteryear].

cooked meal has lots of delicate flavors that have to be held in the mouth for appreciation. So chew your food and give your salivary glands a chance to function!

(*Tom deliberately lays his imaginary fork down and pushes his chair back from the table.*)

TOM: I haven't enjoyed one bite of this dinner because of your constant directions on how to eat it. It's you that makes me rush through meals with your hawk-like attention to every bite I take. Sickening — spoils my appetite — all this discussion of animals' secretion — salivary glands — mastication!

AMANDA (*lightly*): Temperament like a Metropolitan° star! (*He rises and crosses downstage.*) You're not excused from the table.

TOM: I'm getting a cigarette.

AMANDA: You smoke too much.

(*Laura rises.*)

LAURA: I'll bring in the blancmange.

(*He remains standing with his cigarette by the portieres during the following.*)

AMANDA (*rising*): No, sister, no, sister — you be the lady this time and I'll be the darky.

LAURA: I'm already up.

AMANDA: Resume your seat, little sister — I want you to stay fresh and pretty — for gentlemen callers!

LAURA: I'm not expecting any gentlemen callers.

AMANDA (*crossing out to kitchenette. Airily*): Sometimes they come when they are least expected! Why, I remember one Sunday afternoon in Blue Mountain — (*Enters kitchenette.*)

TOM: I know what's coming!

LAURA: Yes. But let her tell it.

TOM: Again?

LAURA: She loves to tell it.

(*Amanda returns with bowl of dessert.*)

AMANDA: One Sunday afternoon in Blue Mountain — your mother received — *seventeen!* — gentlemen callers! Why, sometimes there weren't chairs enough to accommodate them all. We had to send the nigger over to bring in folding chairs from the parish house.

TOM (*remaining at portieres*): How did you entertain those gentlemen callers?

AMANDA: I understood the art of conversation!

TOM: I bet you could talk.

AMANDA: Girls in those days *knew* how to talk, I can tell you.

Metropolitan: The Metropolitan Opera in New York City.

TOM: Yes?

(*Image: Amanda as a girl on a porch greeting callers.*)

AMANDA: They knew how to entertain their gentlemen callers. It wasn't enough for a girl to be possessed of a pretty face and a graceful figure — although I wasn't slighted in either respect. She also needed to have a nimble wit and a tongue to meet all occasions.

TOM: What did you talk about?

AMANDA: Things of importance going on in the world! Never anything coarse or common or vulgar. (*She addresses Tom as though he were seated in the vacant chair at the table though he remains by portieres. He plays this scene as though he held the book.*) My callers were gentlemen — all! Among my callers were some of the most prominent young planters of the Mississippi Delta — planters and sons of planters!

(*Tom motions for music and a spot of light on Amanda.*)

(*Her eyes lift, her face glows, her voice becomes rich and elegiac.*)

(*Screen legend: "Où Sont les Neiges."*)

There was young Champ Laughlin who later became vice-president of the Delta Planters Bank. Hadley Stevenson who was drowned in Moon Lake and left his widow one hundred and fifty thousand in Government bonds. There were the Cutrere brothers, Wesley and Bates. Bates was one of my bright particular beaux! He got in a quarrel with that wild Wainright boy. They shot it out on the floor of Moon Lake Casino. Bates was shot through the stomach. Died in the ambulance on his way to Memphis. His widow was also well-provided for, came into eight or ten thousand acres, that's all. She married him on the rebound — never loved her — carried my picture on him the night he died! And there was that boy that every girl in the Delta had set her cap for! That beautiful, brilliant young Fitzhugh boy from Greene County!

TOM: What did he leave his widow?

AMANDA: He never married! Gracious, you talk as though all of my old admirers had turned up their toes to the daisies!

TOM: Isn't this the first you mentioned that still survives?

AMANDA: That Fitzhugh boy went North and made a fortune — came to be known as the Wolf of Wall Street! He had the Midas touch, whatever he touched turned to gold! And I could have been Mrs. Duncan J. Fitzhugh, mind you! But — I picked your *father!*

LAURA (*rising*): Mother, let me clear the table.

AMANDA: No, dear, you go in front and study your typewriter chart. Or practice your shorthand a little. Stay fresh and pretty! — It's almost time for our gentlemen callers to start arriving. (*She flounces girlishly toward the kitchenette.*) How many do you suppose we're going to entertain this afternoon?

(*Tom throws down the paper and jumps up with a groan.*)

LAURA (*alone in the dining room*): I don't believe we're going to receive any, Mother.

AMANDA (*reappearing, airily*): What? No one — not one? You must be joking! (*Laura nervously echoes her laugh. She slips in a fugitive manner through the half-open portieres and draws them gently behind her. A shaft of very clear light is thrown on her face against the faded tapestry of the curtains. Music: "The Glass Menagerie" under faintly. Lightly.*) Not one gentleman caller? It can't be true! There must be a flood, there must have been a tornado!

LAURA: It isn't a flood, it's not a tornado, Mother. I'm just not popular like you were in Blue Mountain. . . . (*Tom utters another groan. Laura glances at him with a faint, apologetic smile. Her voice catching a little.*) Mother's afraid I'm going to be an old maid.

(*The scene dims out with "Glass Menagerie" music.*)

SCENE 2

(*"Laura, Haven't You Ever Liked Some Boy?"*)

(*On the dark stage the screen is lighted with the image of blue roses.*)

(*Gradually Laura's figure becomes apparent and the screen goes out.*)

(*The music subsides.*)

(*Laura is seated in the delicate ivory chair at the small clawfoot table.*)

(*She wears a dress of soft violet material for a kimono — her hair tied back from her forehead with a ribbon.*)

(*She is washing and polishing her collection of glass.*)

(*Amanda appears on the fire escape steps. At the sound of her ascent, Laura catches her breath, thrusts the bowl of ornaments away and seats herself stiffly before the diagram of the typewriter keyboard as though it held her spellbound. Something has happened to Amanda. It is written in her face as she climbs to the landing: a look that is grim and hopeless and a little absurd.*)

(*She has on one of those cheap or imitation velvety-looking cloth coats with imitation fur collar. Her hat is five or six years old, one of those dreadful cloche hats that were worn in the late twenties, and she is clasping an enormous black patent-leather pocketbook with nickel clasp and initials. This is her full-dress outfit, the one she usually wears to the D.A.R.°*)

(*Before entering she looks through the door.*)

(*She purses her lips, opens her eyes wide, rolls them upward and shakes her head.*)

(*Then she slowly lets herself in the door. Seeing her mother's expression Laura touches her lips with a nervous gesture.*)

LAURA: Hello, Mother, I was — (*She makes a nervous gesture toward the chart on the wall. Amanda leans against the shut door and stares at Laura with a martyred look.*)

AMANDA: Deception? Deception? (*She slowly removes her hat and gloves, continuing the swift suffering stare. She lets the hat and gloves fall on the floor — a bit of acting.*)

LAURA (*shakily*): How was the D.A.R. meeting? (*Amanda slowly opens her purse and removes a dainty white handkerchief which she shakes out delicately and delicately touches to her lips and nostrils.*) Didn't you go to the D.A.R. meeting, Mother?

AMANDA (*faintly, almost inaudibly*): — No. — No. (*Then more forcibly*). I did not have the strength — to go to the D.A.R. In fact, I did not have the courage! I wanted to find a hole in the ground and hide myself in it forever! (*She crosses slowly to the wall and removes the diagram of the typewriter keyboard. She holds it in front of her for a second, staring at it sweetly and sorrowfully — then bites her lips and tears it in two pieces.*)

LAURA (*faintly*): Why did you do that, Mother? (*Amanda repeats the same procedure with the chart of the Gregg Alphabet.*) Why are you —

AMANDA: Why? Why? How old are you, Laura?

LAURA: Mother, you know my age.

AMANDA: I thought that you were an adult; it seems that I was mistaken. (*She crosses slowly to the sofa and sinks down and stares at Laura.*)

LAURA: Please don't stare at me, Mother.

(*Amanda closes her eyes and lowers her head. Count ten.*)

D.A.R.: Daughters of the American Revolution, a conservative, patriotic organization for women whose ancestors were involved in the American Revolutionary War.

AMANDA: What are we going to do, what is going to become of us, what is the future?

(*Count ten.*)

LAURA: Has something happened, Mother? (*Amanda draws a long breath and takes out the handkerchief again. Dabbing process.*) Mother, has — something happened?

AMANDA: I'll be all right in a minute. I'm just bewildered — (*Count five.*) — by life. . . .

LAURA: Mother, I wish that you would tell me what's happened.

AMANDA: As you know, I was supposed to be inducted into my office at the D.A.R. this afternoon. (*Image: a swarm of typewriters.*) But I stopped off at Rubicam's Business College to speak to your teachers about your having a cold and ask them what progress they thought you were making down there.

LAURA: Oh. . . .

AMANDA: I went to the typing instructor and introduced myself as your mother. She didn't know who you were. Wingfield, she said. We don't have any such student enrolled at the school! I assured her she did, that you had been going to classes since early in January. "I wonder," she said, "if you could be talking about that terribly shy little girl who dropped out of school after only a few days' attendance?" "No," I said, "Laura, my daughter, has been going to school every day for the past six weeks!" "Excuse me," she said. She took the attendance book out and there was your name, unmistakably printed, and all the dates you were absent until they decided that you had dropped out of school. I still said, "No, there must have been some mistake! There must have been some mix-up in the records!" And she said, "No — I remember her perfectly now. Her hands shook so that she couldn't hit the right keys! The first time we gave a speed test, she broke down completely — was sick at the stomach and almost had to be carried into the wash-room! After that morning she never showed up any more. We phoned the house but never got any answer" — while I was working at Famous and Barr, I suppose, demonstrating those — Oh! I felt so weak I could barely keep on my feet! I had to sit down while they got me a glass of water! Fifty dollars' tuition, all of our plans — my hopes and ambitions for you — just gone up the spout, just gone up the spout like that. (*Laura draws a long breath and gets awkwardly to her feet. She crosses to the victrola and winds it up.*) What are you doing?

LAURA: Oh! (*She releases the handle and returns to her seat.*)

AMANDA: Laura, where have you been going when

you've gone out pretending that you were going to business college?

LAURA: I've just been going out walking.

AMANDA: That's not true.

LAURA: It is. I just went walking.

AMANDA: Walking? Walking? In winter? Deliberately courting pneumonia in that light coat? Where did you walk to, Laura?

LAURA: All sorts of places — mostly in the park.

AMANDA: Even after you'd started catching that cold?

LAURA: It was the lesser of two evils, Mother. (*Image: winter scene in park.*) I couldn't go back up. I — threw up — on the floor!

AMANDA: From half past seven till after five every day you mean to tell me you walked around in the park, because you wanted to make me think that you were still going to Rubicam's Business College?

LAURA: It wasn't as bad as it sounds. I went inside places to get warmed up.

AMANDA: Inside where?

LAURA: I went in the art museum and the bird houses at the Zoo. I visited the penguins every day! Sometimes I did without lunch and went to the movies. Lately I've been spending most of my afternoons in the Jewel-box, that big glass house where they raise the tropical flowers.

AMANDA: You did all this to deceive me, just for the deception? (*Laura looks down.*) Why?

LAURA: Mother, when you're disappointed, you get that awful suffering look on your face, like the picture of Jesus' mother in the museum!

AMANDA: Hush!

LAURA: I couldn't face it.

(*Pause. A whisper of strings.*)
(*Legend: "The Crust of Humility."*)

AMANDA (*hopelessly fingering the huge pocketbook*): So what are we going to do the rest of our lives? Stay home and watch the parades go by? Amuse ourselves with the glass menagerie, darling? Eternally play those worn-out phonograph records your father left as a painful reminder of him? We won't have a business career — we've given that up because it gave us nervous indigestion! (*Laughs wearily.*) What is there left but dependency all our lives? I know so well what becomes of unmarried women who aren't prepared to occupy a position. I've seen such pitiful cases in the South — barely tolerated spinsters living upon the grudging patronage of sister's husband or brother's wife! — stuck away in some little mousetrap of a room — encouraged by one in-law to visit another — little birdlike women without any nest — eating the crust of humility all their life! Is that the future that we've mapped out for ourselves? I swear it's the

only alternative I can think of! It isn't a very pleasant alternative, is it? Of course — some girls do *marry*. (*Laura twists her hands nervously.*) Haven't you ever liked some boy?

LAURA: Yes. I liked one once. (*Rises.*) I came across his picture a while ago.

AMANDA (*with some interest*): He gave you his picture?

LAURA: No, it's in the yearbook.

AMANDA (*disappointed*): Oh — a high-school boy.

(*Screen image: Jim as high school hero bearing a silver cup.*)

LAURA: Yes. His name was Jim. (*Laura lifts the heavy annual from the clawfoot table.*) Here he is in *The Pirates of Penzance*.

AMANDA (*absently*): The what?

LAURA: The operetta the senior class put on. He had a wonderful voice and we sat across the aisle from each other Mondays, Wednesdays, and Fridays in the Aud. Here he is with the silver cup for debating! See his grin?

AMANDA (*absently*): He must have had a jolly disposition.

LAURA: He used to call me — Blue Roses.

(*Image: blue roses.*)

AMANDA: Why did he call you such a name as that?

LAURA: When I had that attack of pleurosis — he asked me what was the matter when I came back. I said pleurosis — he thought that I said Blue Roses! So that's what he always called me after that. Whenever he saw me, he'd holler, "Hello, Blue Roses!" I didn't care for the girl that he went out with. Emily Meisenbach. Emily was the best-dressed girl at Soldan. She never struck me, though, as being sincere . . . It says in the Personal Section — they're engaged. That's — six years ago! They must be married by now.

AMANDA: Girls that aren't cut out for business careers usually wind up married to some nice man. (*Gets up with a spark of revival.*) Sister, that's what you'll do!

(*Laura utters a startled, doubtful laugh. She reaches quickly for a piece of glass.*)

LAURA: But, Mother —

AMANDA: Yes? (*Crossing to photograph.*)

LAURA (*in a tone of frightened apology*): I'm — crippled!

(*Image: screen.*)

AMANDA: Nonsense! Laura, I've told you never, never to use that word. Why, you're not crippled, you just have a little defect — hardly noticeable, even!

When people have some slight disadvantage like that, they cultivate other things to make up for it — develop charm — and vivacity — and — *charm!* That's all you have to do! (*She turns again to the photograph.*) One thing your father had *plenty of* — was *charm!*

(*Tom motions to the fiddle in the wings.*)
(*The scene fades out with music.*)

SCENE 3

(*Legend on screen: "After the Fiasco — "*)
(*Tom speaks from the fire escape landing.*)

TOM: After the fiasco at Rubicam's Business College, the idea of getting a gentleman caller for Laura began to play a more important part in Mother's calculations. It became an obsession. Like some archetype of the universal unconscious, the image of the gentleman caller haunted our small apartment. . . . (*Image: young man at door with flowers.*) An evening at home rarely passed without some allusion to this image, this specter, this hope. . . . Even when he wasn't mentioned, his presence hung in Mother's preoccupied look and in my sister's frightened, apologetic manner — hung like a sentence passed upon the Wingfields! Mother was a woman of action as well as words. She began to take logical steps in the planned direction. Late that winter and in the early spring — realizing that extra money would be needed to properly feather the nest and plume the bird — she conducted a vigorous campaign on the telephone, roping in subscribers to one of those magazines for matrons called *The Home-maker's Companion,* the type of journal that features the serialized sublimations of ladies of letters who think in terms of delicate cuplike breasts, slim, tapering waists, rich, creamy thighs, eyes like wood smoke in autumn, fingers that soothe and caress like strains of music, bodies as powerful as Etruscan sculpture.

(*Screen image: glamor magazine cover.*)
(*Amanda enters with phone on long extension cord. She is spotted in the dim stage.*)

AMANDA: Ida Scott? This is Amanda Wingfield! We *missed* you at the D.A.R. last Monday! I said to myself: She's probably suffering with that sinus condition! How is that sinus condition? Horrors! Heaven have mercy! — You're a Christian martyr, yes, that's what you are, a Christian martyr! Well, I just now happened to notice that your subscription to the *Companion's* about to expire! Yes, it expires with the next issue, honey! — just when that wonderful new serial by Bessie Mae Hopper is getting off to such an exciting start. Oh, honey, it's something that you can't miss! You remember how *Gone With the Wind* took everybody by storm? You simply couldn't go out if you hadn't read it. All everybody *talked* was Scarlett O'Hara. Well, this is a book that critics already compare to *Gone With the Wind.* It's the *Gone With the Wind* of the post–World War generation! — What? — Burning? — Oh, honey, don't let them burn, go take a look in the oven and I'll hold the wire! Heavens — I think she's hung up!

(*Dim out.*)
(*Legend on screen: "You Think I'm in Love with Continental Shoemakers?"*)
(*Before the stage is lighted, the violent voices of Tom and Amanda are heard.*)
(*They are quarreling behind the portieres. In front of them stands Laura with clenched hands and panicky expression.*)
(*A clear pool of light on her figure throughout this scene.*)

TOM: What in Christ's name am I —
AMANDA (*shrilly*): Don't you use that —
TOM: Supposed to do!
AMANDA: Expression! Not in my —
TOM: Ohhh!
AMANDA: Presence! Have you gone out of your senses?
TOM: I have, that's true, *driven* out!
AMANDA: What is the matter with you, you — big — big — IDIOT!
TOM: Look — I've got *no thing,* no single thing —
AMANDA: Lower your voice!
TOM: In my life here that I can call my OWN! Everything is —
AMANDA: Stop that shouting!
TOM: Yesterday you confiscated my books! You had the nerve to —
AMANDA: I took that horrible novel back to the library — yes! That hideous book by that insane Mr. Lawrence. (*Tom laughs wildly.*) I cannot control the output of diseased minds or people who cater to them — (*Tom laughs still more wildly.*) BUT I WON'T ALLOW SUCH FILTH BROUGHT INTO MY HOUSE! No, no, no, no, no!
TOM: House, house! Who pays rent on it, who makes a slave of himself to —
AMANDA (*fairly screeching*): Don't you DARE to —
TOM: No, no, *I* musn't say things! *I've* got to just —
AMANDA: Let me tell you —
TOM: I don't want to hear any more! (*He tears the*

portieres open. The upstage area is lit with a turgid smoky red glow.)

(*Amanda's hair is in metal curlers and she wears a very old bathrobe, much too large for her slight figure, a relic of the faithless Mr. Wingfield.*)

(*An upright typewriter and a wild disarray of manuscripts are on the dropleaf table. The quarrel was probably precipitated by Amanda's interruption of his creative labor. A chair lying overthrown on the floor.*)

(*Their gesticulating shadows are cast on the ceiling by the fiery glow.*)

AMANDA: You *will* hear more, you —

TOM: No, I won't hear more, I'm going out!

AMANDA: You come right back in —

TOM: Out, out out! Because I'm —

AMANDA: Come back here, Tom Wingfield! I'm not through talking to you!

TOM: Oh, go —

LAURA (*desperately*): Tom!

AMANDA: You're going to listen, and no more insolence from you! I'm at the end of my patience! (*He comes back toward her.*)

TOM: What do you think I'm at? Aren't I supposed to have any patience to reach the end of, Mother? I know, I know. It seems unimportant to you, what I'm *doing* — what I *want* to do — having a little *difference* between them! You don't think that —

AMANDA: I think you've been doing things that you're ashamed of. That's why you act like this. I don't believe that you go every night to the movies. Nobody goes to the movies night after night. Nobody in their right minds goes to the movies as often as you pretend to. People don't go to the movies at nearly midnight, and movies don't let out at two A.M. Come in stumbling. Muttering to yourself like a maniac! You get three hours' sleep and then go to work. Oh, I can picture the way you're doing down there. Moping, doping, because you're in no condition.

TOM (*wildly*): No, I'm in no condition!

AMANDA: What right have you got to jeopardize your job? Jeopardize the security of us all? How do you think we'd manage if you were —

TOM: Listen! You think I'm crazy *about the warehouse*? (*He bends fiercely toward her slight figure.*) You think I'm in love with the Continental Shoemakers? You think I want to spend fifty-five *years* down there in that — *celotex interior!* with — *fluorescent* — *tubes!* Look! I'd rather somebody picked up a crowbar and battered out my brains — than go back mornings! I *go!* Every time you come in yelling that God damn "*Rise and Shine!*" "*Rise and Shine!*" I say to myself, "How *lucky dead* people are!" But I get up. I *go!* For

sixty-five dollars a month I give up all that I dream of doing and being *ever!* And you say self — *self's* all I ever think of. Why, listen, if self is what I thought of, Mother, I'd be where he is — GONE! (*Pointing to father's picture.*) As far as the system of transportation reaches! (*He starts past her. She grabs his arm.*) Don't grab at me, Mother!

AMANDA: Where are you going?

TOM: I'm going to the *movies!*

AMANDA: I don't believe that lie!

TOM (*Crouching toward her, overtowering her tiny figure. She backs away, gasping.*): I'm going to opium dens! Yes, opium dens, dens of vice and criminals' hangouts, Mother. I've joined the Hogan gang, I'm a hired assassin, I carry a tommy-gun in a violin case! I run a string of cathouses in the Valley! They call me Killer, Killer Wingfield, I'm leading a double life, a simple, honest warehouse worker by day, by night, a dynamic *czar* of the *underworld, Mother.* I go to gambling casinos, I spin away fortunes on the roulette table! I wear a patch over one eye and a false mustache, sometimes I put on green whiskers. On those occasions they call me — *El Diablo!* Oh, I could tell you things to make you sleepless! My enemies plan to dynamite this place. They're going to blow us all sky-high some night! I'll be glad, very happy, and so will you! You'll go up, up on a broomstick, over Blue Mountain with seventeen gentlemen callers! You ugly — babbling old — *witch.* . . . (*He goes through a series of violent, clumsy movements, seizing his overcoat, lunging to the door, pulling it fiercely open. The women watch him, aghast. His arm catches in the sleeve of the coat as he struggles to pull it on. For a moment he is pinioned by the bulky garment. With an outraged groan he tears the coat off again, splitting the shoulders of it, and hurls it across the room. It strikes against the shelf of Laura's glass collection, there is a tinkle of shattering glass. Laura cries out as if wounded.*)

(*Music legend: "The Glass Menagerie."*)

LAURA (*shrilly*): My glass! — menagerie. . . . (*She covers her face and turns away.*)

(*But Amanda is still stunned and stupefied by the "ugly witch" so that she barely notices this occurrence. Now she recovers her speech.*)

AMANDA (*in an awful voice*): I won't speak to you — until you apologize! (*She crosses through portieres and draws them together behind her. Tom is left with Laura. Laura clings weakly to the mantel with her face averted. Tom stares at her stupidly for a moment. Then he crosses to shelf. Drops awkwardly to his knees to collect the fallen glass, glancing at Laura as if he would speak but couldn't.*)

("*The Glass Menagerie*" *steals in as the scene dims out.*)

SCENE 4

(*The interior is dark. Faint light in the alley.*)

(*A deep-voiced bell in a church is tolling the hour of five as the scene commences.*)

(*Tom appears at the top of the alley. After each solemn boom of the bell in the tower, he shakes a little noisemaker or rattle as if to express the tiny spasm of man in contrast to the sustained power and dignity of the Almighty. This and the unsteadiness of his advance make it evident that he has been drinking.*)

(*As he climbs the few steps to the fire escape landing light steals up inside. Laura appears in nightdress, observing Tom's empty bed in the front room.*)

(*Tom fishes in his pockets for the door key, removing a motley assortment of articles in the search, including a perfect shower of movie ticket stubs and an empty bottle. At last he finds the key, but just as he is about to insert it, it slips from his fingers. He strikes a match and crouches below the door.*)

TOM (*bitterly*): One crack — and it falls through!

(*Laura opens the door.*)

LAURA: Tom! Tom, what are you doing?
TOM: Looking for a door key.
LAURA: Where have you been all this time?
TOM: I have been to the movies.
LAURA: All this time at the movies?
TOM: There was a very long program. There was a Garbo picture and a Mickey Mouse and a travelogue and a newsreel and a preview of coming attractions. And there was an organ solo and a collection for the milk fund — simultaneously — which ended up in a terrible fight between a fat lady and an usher!
LAURA (*innocently*): Did you have to stay through everything?
TOM: Of course! And, oh, I forgot! There was a big stage show! The headliner on this stage show was Malvolio the Magician. He performed wonderful tricks, many of them, such as pouring water back and forth between pitchers. First it turned to wine and then it turned to beer and then it turned to whiskey. I know it was whiskey it finally turned into because he needed somebody to come up out of the audience to help him, and I came up — both shows! It was Kentucky Straight Bourbon. A very

generous fellow, he gave souvenirs. (*He pulls from his back pocket a shimmering rainbow-colored scarf.*) He gave me this. This is his magic scarf. You can have it, Laura. You wave it over a canary cage and you get a bowl of goldfish. You wave it over the goldfish bowl and they fly away canaries. . . . But the wonderfullest trick of all was the coffin trick. We nailed him into a coffin and he got out of the coffin without removing one nail. (*He has come inside.*) There is a trick that would come in handy for me — get me out of this 2 by 4 situation! (*Flops onto bed and starts removing shoes.*)
LAURA: Tom — Shhh!
TOM: What you shushing me for?
LAURA: You'll wake up Mother.
TOM: Goody, goody! Pay 'er back for all those "Rise an' Shines." (*Lies down, groaning.*) You know it don't take much intelligence to get yourself into a nailed-up coffin, Laura. But who in hell ever got himself out of one without removing one nail?

(*As if in answer, the father's grinning photograph lights up.*)

(*Scene dims out.*)

(*Immediately following: The church bell is heard striking six. At the sixth stroke the alarm clock goes off in Amanda's room, and after a few moments we hear her calling: "Rise and Shine! Rise and Shine! Laura, go tell your brother to rise and shine!"*)

TOM (*sitting up slowly*): I'll rise — but I won't shine.

(*The light increases.*)

AMANDA: Laura, tell your brother his coffee is ready.

(*Laura slips into front room.*)

LAURA: Tom! it's nearly seven. Don't make Mother nervous. (*He stares at her stupidly. Beseechingly.*) Tom, speak to Mother this morning. Make up with her, apologize, speak to her!
TOM: She won't to me. It's her that started not speaking.
LAURA: If you just say you're sorry she'll start speaking.
TOM: Her not speaking — is that such a tragedy?
LAURA: Please — please!
AMANDA (*calling from kitchenette*): Laura, are you going to do what I asked you to do, or do I have to get dressed and go out myself?
LAURA: Going, going — soon as I get on my coat! (*She pulls on a shapeless felt hat with nervous, jerky movement, pleadingly glancing at Tom. Rushes awkwardly for coat. The coat is one of Amanda's, inaccurately made over, the sleeves too short for Laura.*) Butter and what else?

AMANDA (*entering upstage*): Just butter. Tell them to charge it.

LAURA: Mother, they make such faces when I do that.

AMANDA: Sticks and stones may break my bones, but the expression on Mr. Garfinkel's face won't harm us! Tell your brother his coffee is getting cold.

LAURA (*at door*): Do what I asked you, will you, will you, Tom?

(*He looks sullenly away.*)

AMANDA: Laura, go now or just don't go at all!

LAURA (*rushing out*): Going — going! (*A second later she cries out. Tom springs up and crosses to the door. Amanda rushes anxiously in. Tom opens the door.*)

TOM: Laura?

LAURA: I'm all right. I slipped, but I'm all right.

AMANDA (*peering anxiously after her*): If anyone breaks a leg on those fire escape steps, the landlord ought to be sued for every cent he possesses! (*She shuts door. Remembers she isn't speaking and returns to other room.*)

(*As Tom enters listlessly for his coffee, she turns her back to him and stands rigidly facing the window on the gloomy gray vault of the areaway. Its light on her face with its aged but childish features is cruelly sharp, satirical as a Daumier print.*)

(*Music under: "Ave Maria."*)

(*Tom glances sheepishly but sullenly at her averted figure and slumps at the table. The coffee is scalding hot; he sips it and gasps and spits it back in the cup. At his gasp, Amanda catches her breath and half turns. Then catches herself and turns back to window.*)

(*Tom blows on his coffee, glancing sidewise at his mother. She clears her throat. Tom clears his. He starts to rise. Sinks back down again, scratches his head, clears his throat again. Amanda coughs. Tom raises his cup in both hands to blow on it, his eyes staring over the rim of it at his mother for several moments. Then he slowly sets the cup down and awkwardly and hesitantly rises from the chair.*)

TOM (*hoarsely*): Mother. I — I apologize. Mother. (*Amanda draws a quick, shuddering breath. Her face works grotesquely. She breaks into childlike tears.*) I'm sorry for what I said, for everything that I said, I didn't mean it.

AMANDA (*sobbingly*): My devotion has made me a witch and so I make myself hateful to my children!

TOM: *No,* you *don't.*

AMANDA: I worry so much, don't sleep, it makes me nervous!

TOM (*gently*): I understand that.

AMANDA: I've had to put up a solitary battle all these years. But you're my right-hand bower! Don't fall down, don't fail!

TOM (*gently*): I try, Mother.

AMANDA (*with great enthusiasm*). Try and you will SUCCEED! (*The notion makes her breathless.*) Why, you — you're just *full* of natural endowments! Both of my children — they're *unusual* children! Don't you think I know it? I'm so — *proud!* Happy and — feel I've — so much to be thankful for but — Promise me one thing, son!

TOM: What, Mother?

AMANDA: Promise, son, you'll — never be a drunkard!

TOM (*turns to her grinning*): I will never be a drunkard, Mother.

AMANDA: That's what frightened me so, that you'd be drinking! Eat a bowl of Purina!

TOM: Just coffee, Mother.

AMANDA: Shredded wheat biscuit?

TOM: No, no, Mother, just coffee.

AMANDA: You can't put in a day's work on an empty stomach. You've got ten minutes — don't gulp! Drinking too-hot liquids makes cancer of the stomach. . . . Put cream in.

TOM: No, thank you.

AMANDA: To cool it.

TOM: No! No, thank you, I want it black.

AMANDA: I know, but it's not good for you. We have to do all that we can to build ourselves up. In these trying times we live in, all that we have to cling to is — each other. . . . That's why it's so important to — Tom, I — I sent out your sister so I could discuss something with you. If you hadn't spoken I would have spoken to you. (*Sits down.*)

TOM (*gently*): What is it, Mother, that you want to discuss?

AMANDA: *Laura!*

(*Tom puts his cup down slowly.*)
(*Legend on screen: "Laura."*)
(*Music: "The Glass Menagerie."*)

TOM: — Oh. — Laura . . .

AMANDA (*touching his sleeve*): You know how Laura is. So quiet but — still water runs deep! She notices things and I think she — broods about them. (*Tom*

FAR LEFT: Laurette Taylor as Amanda in the original 1944 production of *The Glass Menagerie.* LEFT: Julie Haydon as Laura and Anthony Ross as the Gentleman Caller. RIGHT: Laura.

looks up.) A few days ago I came in and she was crying.

TOM: What about?

AMANDA: You.

TOM: Me?

AMANDA: She has an idea that you're not happy here.

TOM: What gave her that idea?

AMANDA: What gives her any idea? However, you do act strangely. I — I'm not criticizing, understand *that!* I know your ambitions do not lie in the warehouse, that like everybody in the whole wide world — you've had to — make sacrifices, but — Tom — Tom — life's not easy, it calls for — Spartan endurance! There's so many things in my heart that I cannot describe to you! I've never told you but I — *loved your father....*

TOM (*gently*): I know that, Mother.

AMANDA: And you — when I see you taking after his ways! Staying out late — and — well, you *had* been drinking the night you were in that — terrifying condition! Laura says that you hate the apartment and that you go out nights to get away from it! Is that true, Tom?

TOM: No. You say there's so much in your heart that you can't describe to me. That's true of me, too. There's so much in my heart that I can't describe to *you!* So let's respect each other's —

AMANDA: But, why — *why,* Tom — are you always so *restless?* Where do you go to, nights?

TOM: I — go to the movies.

AMANDA: Why do you go to the movies so much, Tom?

TOM: I go to the movies because — I like adventure. Adventure is something I don't have much of at work, so I go to the movies.

AMANDA: But, Tom, you go to the movies *entirely* too *much!*

TOM: I like a lot of adventure.

(*Amanda looks baffled, then hurt. As the familiar inquisition resumes he becomes hard and impatient again. Amanda slips back into her querulous attitude toward him.*)

(*Image on screen: sailing vessel with Jolly Roger.°*)

AMANDA: Most young men find adventure in their careers.

TOM: Then most young men are not employed in a warehouse.

AMANDA: The world is full of young men employed in warehouses and offices and factories.

TOM: Do all of them find adventure in their careers?

Jolly Roger: The black flag with white skull and crossbones used by pirates.

AMANDA: They do or they do without it! Not everybody has a craze for adventure.

TOM: Man is by instinct a lover, a hunter, a fighter, and none of those instincts are given much play at the warehouse!

AMANDA: Man is by instinct! Don't quote instinct to me! Instinct is something that people have got away from! It belongs to animals! Christian adults don't want it!

TOM: What do Christian adults want, then, Mother?

AMANDA: Superior things! Things of the mind and the spirit! Only animals have to satisfy instincts! Surely your aims are somewhat higher than theirs! Than monkeys — pigs —

TOM: I reckon they're not.

AMANDA: You're joking. However, that isn't what I wanted to discuss.

TOM (*rising*): I haven't much time.

AMANDA (*pushing his shoulders*): Sit down.

TOM: You want me to punch in red at the warehouse, Mother?

AMANDA: You have five minutes. I want to talk about Laura.

(*Legend: "Plans and Provisions."*)

TOM: All right! What about Laura?

AMANDA: We have to be making plans and provisions for her. She's older than you, two years, and nothing has happened. She just drifts along doing nothing. It frightens me terribly how she just drifts along.

TOM: I guess she's the type that people call home girls.

AMANDA: There's no such type, and if there is, it's a pity! That is unless the home is hers, with a husband!

TOM: What?

AMANDA: Oh, I can see the handwriting on the wall as plain as I see the nose in front of my face! It's terrifying! More and more you remind me of your father! He was out all hours without explanation — Then *left! Good-bye!* And me with a bag to hold. I saw that letter you got from the Merchant Marine. I know what you're dreaming of. I'm not standing here blindfolded. Very well, then. Then *do* it! But not till there's somebody to take your place.

TOM: What do you mean?

AMANDA: I mean that as soon as Laura has got somebody to take care of her, married, a home of her own, independent — why, then you'll be free to go wherever you please, on land, on sea, whichever way the wind blows you! But until that time you've got to look out for your sister. I don't say me because I'm old and don't matter! I say for your sister because she's young and dependent. I put her in business college — a dismal failure! Frightened her so it made her sick to her stomach. I took her over to the Young People's League at the church. Another fiasco. She spoke to nobody, nobody spoke to her. Now all she does is fool with those pieces of glass and play those worn-out records. What kind of a life is that for a girl to lead!

TOM: What can I do about it?

AMANDA: Overcome selfishness! Self, self, self is all that you ever think of! (*Tom springs up and crosses to get his coat. It is ugly and bulky. He pulls on a cap with earmuffs.*) Where is your muffler? Put your wool muffler on! (*He snatches it angrily from the closet and tosses it around his neck and pulls both ends tight.*) Tom! I haven't said what I had in mind to ask you.

TOM: I'm too late to —

AMANDA (*Catching his arms — very importunately. Then shyly*): Down at the warehouse, aren't there some — nice young men?

TOM: No!

AMANDA: There *must* be — *some* . . .

TOM: Mother —

(*Gesture.*)

AMANDA: Find out one that's clean-living — doesn't drink and — ask him out for sister!

TOM: What?

AMANDA: For *sister!* To *meet!* Get *acquainted!*

TOM (*stamping to door*): Oh, my go-osh!

AMANDA: Will you? (*He opens door. Imploringly.*) Will you? (*He starts down.*) Will you? *Will* you, dear?

TOM (*calling back*): YES!

(*Amanda closes the door hesitantly and with a troubled but faintly hopeful expression.*)
(*Screen image: glamor magazine cover.*)
(*Spot° Amanda at phone.*)

AMANDA: Ella Cartwright? This is Amanda Wingfield! How are you, honey? How is that kidney condition? (*Count five.*) *Horrors!* (*Count five.*) You're a Christian martyr, yes, honey, that's what you are, a Christian martyr! Well, I just happened to notice in my little red book that your subscription to the *Companion* has just run out! I knew that you wouldn't want to miss out on the wonderful serial starting in this new issue. It's by Bessie Mae Hopper, the first thing she's written since *Honeymoon for Three.* Wasn't that a strange and interesting story? Well, this one is even lovelier, I

___

Spot: Spotlight.

believe. It has a sophisticated society background. It's all about the horsey set on Long Island!

(*Fade out.*)

SCENE 5

(*Legend on screen: "Annunciation." Fade with music.*)
(*It is early dusk of a spring evening. Supper has just been finished in the Wingfield apartment. Amanda and Laura in light colored dresses are removing dishes from the table, in the upstage area, which is shadowy, their movements formalized almost as a dance or ritual, their moving forms as pale and silent as moths.*)
(*Tom, in white shirt and trousers, rises from the table and crosses toward the fire escape.*)

AMANDA (*as he passes her*): Son, will you do me a favor?

TOM: What?

AMANDA: Comb your hair! You look so pretty when your hair is combed! (*Tom slouches on sofa with evening paper. Enormous caption "Franco Triumphs."*) There is only one respect in which I would like you to emulate your father.

TOM: What respect is that?

AMANDA: The care he always took of his appearance. He never allowed himself to look untidy. (*He throws down the paper and crosses to fire escape.*) Where are you going?

TOM: I'm going out to smoke.

AMANDA: You smoke too much. A pack a day at fifteen cents a pack. How much would that amount to in a month? Thirty times fifteen is how much, Tom? Figure it out and you will be astounded at what you could save. Enough to give you a night school course in accounting at Washington U! Just think what a wonderful thing that would be for you, son!

(*Tom is unmoved by the thought.*)

TOM: I'd rather smoke. (*He steps out on landing, letting the screen door slam.*)

AMANDA (*sharply*): I know! That's the tragedy of it. . . . (*Alone, she turns to look at her husband's picture.*)

(*Dance music: "All the World is Waiting for the Sunrise!"*)

TOM (*to the audience*): Across the alley from us was the Paradise Dance Hall. On evenings in spring the windows and doors were open and the music came outdoors. Sometimes the lights were turned out except for a large glass sphere that hung from the ceiling. It would turn slowly about and filter the dusk with delicate rainbow colors. Then the orchestra played a waltz or a tango, something that had a slow and sensuous rhythm. Couples would come outside, to the relative privacy of the alley. You could see them kissing behind ash-pits and telephone poles. This was the compensation for lives that passed like mine, without any change or adventure. Adventure and change were imminent in this year. They were waiting around the corner for all these kids. Suspended in the mist over Berchtesgaden, caught in the folds of Chamberlain's umbrella — In Spain there was Guernica!° But here there was only hot swing music and liquor, dance halls, bars, and movies, and sex that hung in the gloom like a chandelier and flooded the world with brief, deceptive rainbows. . . . All the world was waiting for bombardments!

(*Amanda turns from the picture and comes outside.*)

AMANDA (*sighing*): A fire escape landing's a poor excuse for a porch. (*She spreads a newspaper on a step and sits down, gracefully and demurely as if she were settling into a swing on a Mississippi veranda.*) What are you looking at?
TOM: The moon.
AMANDA: Is there a moon this evening?
TOM: It's rising over Garfinkel's Delicatessen.
AMANDA: So it is! A little silver slipper of a moon. Have you made a wish on it yet?
TOM: Um-hum.
AMANDA: What did you wish for?
TOM: That's a secret.
AMANDA: A secret, huh? Well, I won't tell mine either. I will be just as mysterious as you.
TOM: I bet I can guess what yours is.
AMANDA: Is my head so transparent?
TOM: You're not a sphinx.
AMANDA: No, I don't have secrets. I'll tell you what I wished for on the moon. Success and happiness for my precious children! I wish for that whenever there's a moon, and when there isn't a moon, I wish for it, too.
TOM: I thought perhaps you wished for a gentleman caller.
AMANDA: Why do you say that?
TOM: Don't you remember asking me to fetch one?

Berchtesgaden . . . Chamberlain . . . Guernica: All references to the approach of World War II in Europe. Berchtesgaden was Hitler's summer home; Neville Chamberlain was the prime minister of England who signed the Munich Pact, which was regarded as a capitulation to Hitler; and the Spanish town Guernica was destroyed by German bombs during the Spanish Civil War in the late 1930s.

AMANDA: I remember suggesting that it would be nice for your sister if you brought home some nice young man from the warehouse. I think I've made that suggestion more than once.
TOM: Yes, you have made it repeatedly.
AMANDA: Well?
TOM: We are going to have one.
AMANDA: *What?*
TOM: A gentleman caller!

(*The annunciation is celebrated with music.*)
(*Amanda rises.*)
(*Image on screen: caller with bouquet.*)

AMANDA: You mean you have asked some nice young man to come over?
TOM: Yep. I've asked him to dinner.
AMANDA: You really did?
TOM: I did!
AMANDA: You did, and did he — *accept?*
TOM: He did!
AMANDA: Well, well — well, well! That's — lovely!
TOM: I thought that you would be pleased.
AMANDA: It's definite, then?
TOM: Very definite.
AMANDA: Soon?
TOM: Very soon.
AMANDA: For heaven's sake, stop putting on and tell me some things, will you?
TOM: What things do you want me to tell you?
AMANDA: *Naturally* I would like to know when he's *coming!*
TOM: He's coming tomorrow.
AMANDA: *Tomorrow?*
TOM: Yep. Tomorrow.
AMANDA: But, Tom!
TOM: Yes, Mother?
AMANDA: Tomorrow gives me no time!
TOM: Time for what?
AMANDA: Preparations! Why didn't you phone me at once, as soon as you asked him, the minute that he accepted? Then, don't you see, I could have been getting ready!
TOM: You don't have to make any fuss.
AMANDA: Oh, Tom, Tom, Tom, of course I have to make a fuss! I want things nice, not sloppy! Not thrown together. I'll certainly have to do some fast thinking, won't I?
TOM: I don't see why you have to think at all.
AMANDA: You just don't know. We can't have a gentleman caller in a pigsty! All my wedding silver has to be polished, the monogrammed table linen ought to be laundered! The windows have to be washed and fresh curtains put up. And how about clothes? We have to *wear* something, don't we?
TOM: Mother, this boy is no one to make a fuss over!

AMANDA: Do you realize he's the first young man we've introduced to your sister? It's terrible, dreadful, disgraceful that poor little sister has never received a single gentleman caller! Tom, come inside! (*She opens the screen door.*)

TOM: What for?

AMANDA: I want to ask you some things.

TOM: If you're going to make such a fuss, I'll call it off, I'll tell him not to come.

AMANDA: You certainly won't do anything of the kind. Nothing offends people worse than broken engagements. It simply means I'll have to work like a Turk! We won't be brilliant, but we'll pass inspection. Come on inside. (*Tom follows, groaning.*) Sit down.

TOM: Any particular place you would like me to sit?

AMANDA: Thank heavens I've got that new sofa! I'm also making payments on a floor lamp I'll have sent out! And put the chintz covers on, they'll brighten things up! Of course I'd hoped to have these walls repapered. . . . What is the young man's name?

TOM: His name is O'Connor.

AMANDA: That, of course, means fish — tomorrow is Friday!° I'll have that salmon loaf — with Durkee's dressing! What does he do? He works at the warehouse?

TOM: Of course! How else would I —

AMANDA: Tom, he — doesn't drink?

TOM: Why do you ask me that?

AMANDA: Your father *did*!

TOM: Don't get started on that!

AMANDA: He *does* drink, then?

TOM: Not that I know of!

AMANDA: Make sure, be certain! The last thing I want for my daughter's a boy who drinks!

TOM: Aren't you being a little premature? Mr. O'Connor has not yet appeared on the scene!

AMANDA: But will tomorrow. To meet your sister, and what do I know about his character? Nothing! Old maids are better off than wives of drunkards!

TOM: Oh, my God!

AMANDA: Be still!

TOM (*leaning forward to whisper*): Lots of fellows meet girls whom they don't marry!

AMANDA: Oh, talk sensibly, Tom — and don't be sarcastic! (*She has gotten a hairbrush.*)

TOM: What are you doing?

AMANDA: I'm brushing that cowlick down! What is this young man's position at the warehouse?

TOM (*submitting grimly to the brush and the interrogation*): This young man's position is that of a shipping clerk, Mother.

AMANDA: Sounds to me like a fairly responsible job, the sort of a job *you* would be in if you just had more *get-up*. What is his salary? Have you got any idea?

TOM: I would judge it to be approximately eighty-five dollars a month.

AMANDA: Well — not princely, but —

TOM: Twenty more than I make.

AMANDA: Yes, how well I know! But for a family man, eighty-five dollars a month is not much more than you can just get by on. . . .

TOM: Yes, but Mr. O'Connor is not a family man.

AMANDA: He might be, mightn't he? Some time in the future?

TOM: I see. Plans and provisions.

AMANDA: You are the only young man that I know of who ignores the fact that the future becomes the present, the present the past, and the past turns into everlasting regret if you don't plan for it!

TOM: I will think that over and see what I can make of it.

AMANDA: Don't be supercilious with your mother! Tell me some more about this — what do you call him?

TOM: James D. O'Connor. The D. is for Delaney.

AMANDA: Irish on *both* sides! *Gracious!* And doesn't drink?

TOM: Shall I call him up and ask him right this minute?

AMANDA: The only way to find out about those things is to make discreet inquiries at the proper moment. When I was a girl in Blue Mountain and it was suspected that a young man drank, the girl whose attentions he had been receiving, if any girl *was*, would sometimes speak to the minister of his church, or rather her father would if her father was living, and sort of feel him out on the young man's character. That is the way such things are discreetly handled to keep a young woman from making a tragic mistake!

TOM: Then how did you happen to make a tragic mistake?

AMANDA: That innocent look of your father's had everyone fooled! He *smiled* — the world was *enchanted*! No girl can do worse than put herself at the mercy of a handsome appearance! I hope that Mr. O'Connor is not too good-looking.

TOM: No, he's not too good-looking. He's covered with freckles and hasn't too much of a nose.

AMANDA: He's not right-down homely, though?

TOM: Not right-down homely. Just medium homely, I'd say.

AMANDA: Character's what to look for in a man.

---

fish . . . Friday: Until recent decades, Catholics were prohibited from eating meat on Fridays.

TOM: That's what I've always said, Mother.

AMANDA: You've never said anything of the kind and I suspect you would never give it a thought.

TOM: Don't be suspicious of me.

AMANDA: At least I hope he's the type that's up and coming.

TOM: I think he really goes in for self-improvement.

AMANDA: What reason have you to think so?

TOM: He goes to night school.

AMANDA (*beaming*): Splendid! What does he do, I mean study?

TOM: Radio engineering and public speaking!

AMANDA: Then he has visions of being advanced in the world! Any young man who studies public speaking is aiming to have an executive job some day! And radio engineering? A thing for the future! Both of these facts are very illuminating. Those are the sort of things that a mother should know concerning any young man who comes to call on her daughter. Seriously or — not.

TOM: One little warning. He doesn't know about Laura. I didn't let on that we had dark ulterior motives. I just said, why don't you come have dinner with us? He said okay and that was the whole conversation.

AMANDA: I bet it was! You're eloquent as an oyster. However, he'll know about Laura when he gets here. When he sees how lovely and sweet and pretty she is, he'll thank his lucky stars he was asked to dinner.

TOM: Mother, you mustn't expect too much of Laura.

AMANDA: What do you mean?

TOM: Laura seems all those things to you and me because she's ours and we love her. We don't even notice she's crippled anymore.

AMANDA: Don't say crippled! You know that I never allow that word to be used!

TOM: But face facts, Mother. She is and — that's not all —

AMANDA: What do you mean "not all"?

TOM: Laura is very different from other girls.

AMANDA: I think the difference is all to her advantage.

TOM: Not quite all — in the eyes of others — strangers — she's terribly shy and lives in a world of her own and those things make her seem a little peculiar to people outside the house.

AMANDA: Don't say peculiar.

TOM: Face the facts. She is.

(*The dance-hall music changes to a tango that has a minor and somewhat ominous tone.*)

AMANDA: In what way is she peculiar — may I ask?

TOM (*gently*): She lives in a world of her own — a world of — little glass ornaments, Mother. . . . (*Gets up. Amanda remains holding brush, looking*

at him, troubled.*) She plays old phonograph records and — that's about all — (*He glances at himself in the mirror and crosses to door.*)

AMANDA (*sharply*): Where are you going?

TOM: I'm going to the movies. (*Out screen door.*)

AMANDA: Not to the movies, every night to the movies! (*Follows quickly to screen door.*) I don't believe you always go to the movies! (*He is gone. Amanda looks worriedly after him for a moment. Then vitality and optimism return and she turns from the door. Crossing to portieres.*) Laura! Laura! (*Laura answers from kitchenette.*)

LAURA: Yes, Mother.

AMANDA: Let those dishes go and come in front! (*Laura appears with dish towel. Gaily.*) Laura, come here and make a wish on the moon!

LAURA (*entering*): Moon — moon?

AMANDA: A little silver slipper of a moon. Look over your left shoulder, Laura, and make a wish! (*Laura looks faintly puzzled as if called out of sleep. Amanda seizes her shoulders and turns her at an angle by the door.*) Now! Now, darling, *wish!*

LAURA: What shall I wish for, Mother?

AMANDA (*her voice trembling and her eyes suddenly filling with tears*): Happiness! Good Fortune!

(*The violin rises and the stage dims out.*)

SCENE 6

(*Image: high school hero.*)

TOM: And so the following evening I brought Jim home to dinner. I had known Jim slightly in high school. In high school Jim was a hero. He had tremendous Irish good nature and vitality with the scrubbed and polished look of white chinaware. He seemed to move in a continual spotlight. He was a star in basketball, captain of the debating club, president of the senior class and the glee club and he sang the male lead in the annual light operas. He was always running or bounding, never just walking. He seemed always at the point of defeating the law of gravity. He was shooting with such velocity through his adolescence that you would logically expect him to arrive at nothing short of the White House by the time he was thirty. But Jim apparently ran into more interference after his graduation from Soldan. His speed had definitely slowed. Six years after he left high school he was holding a job that wasn't much better than mine.

(*Image: clerk.*)

He was the only one at the warehouse with whom I was on friendly terms. I was valuable to him as someone who could remember his former glory, who had seen him win basketball games and the silver cup in debating. He knew of my secret practice of retiring to a cabinet of the washroom to work on poems when business was slack in the warehouse. He called me Shakespeare. And while the other boys in the warehouse regarded me with suspicious hostility, Jim took a humorous attitude toward me. Gradually his attitude affected the others, their hostility wore off and they also began to smile at me as people smile at an oddly fashioned dog who trots across their path at some distance.

I knew that Jim and Laura had known each other at Soldan, and I had heard Laura speak admiringly of his voice. I didn't know if Jim remembered her or not. In high school Laura had been as unobtrusive as Jim had been astonishing. If he did remember Laura, it was not as my sister, for when I asked him to dinner, he grinned and said, "You know, Shakespeare, I never thought of you as having folks!"

He was about to discover that I did. . . .

(*Light up stage.*)

(*Legend on screen: "The Accent of a Coming Foot."*)

(*Friday evening. It is about five o'clock of a late spring evening which comes "scattering poems in the sky."*)

(*A delicate lemony light is in the Wingfield apartment.*)

(*Amanda has worked like a Turk in preparation for the gentleman caller. The results are astonishing. The new floor lamp with its rose-silk shade is in place, a colored paper lantern conceals the broken light fixture in the ceiling, new billowing white curtains are at the windows, chintz covers are on chairs and sofa, a pair of new sofa pillows make their initial appearance.*)

(*Open boxes and tissue paper are scattered on the floor.*)

(*Laura stands in the middle with lifted arms while Amanda crouches before her, adjusting the hem of the new dress, devout and ritualistic. The dress is colored and designed by memory. The arrangement of Laura's hair is changed; it is softer and more becoming. A fragile, unearthly prettiness has come out in Laura: she is like a piece of translucent glass touched by light, given a momentary radiance, not actual, not lasting.*)

AMANDA (*impatiently*): Why are you trembling?
LAURA: Mother, you've made me so nervous!
AMANDA: How have I made you nervous?

LAURA: By all this fuss! You make it seem so important!
AMANDA: I don't understand you, Laura. You couldn't be satisfied with just sitting home, and yet whenever I try to arrange something for you, you seem to resist it. (*She gets up.*) Now take a look at yourself. No, wait! Wait just a moment — I have an idea!
LAURA: What is it now?

(*Amanda produces two powder puffs which she wraps in handkerchiefs and stuffs in Laura's bosom.*)

LAURA: Mother, what are you doing?
AMANDA: They call them "Gay Deceivers"!
LAURA: I won't wear them!
AMANDA: You will!
LAURA: Why should I?
AMANDA: Because, to be painfully honest, your chest is flat.
LAURA: You make it seem like we were setting a trap.
AMANDA: All pretty girls are a trap, a pretty trap, and men expect them to be. (*Legend: "A Pretty Trap."*) Now look at yourself, young lady. This is the prettiest you will ever be! I've got to fix myself now! You're going to be surprised by your mother's appearance! (*She crosses through portieres, humming gaily.*)

(*Laura moves slowly to the long mirror and stares solemnly at herself.*)

(*A wind blows the white curtains inward in a slow, graceful motion and with a faint, sorrowful sighing.*)

AMANDA (*offstage*): It isn't dark enough yet. (*She turns slowly before the mirror with a troubled look.*)

(*Legend on screen: "This Is My Sister: Celebrate Her with Strings!" Music.*)

AMANDA (*laughing, off*): I'm going to show you something. I'm going to make a spectacular appearance!
LAURA: What is it, Mother?
AMANDA: Possess your soul in patience — you will see! Something I've resurrected from that old trunk! Styles haven't changed so terribly much after all. . . . (*She parts the portieres.*) Now just look at your mother! (*She wears a girlish frock of yellowed voile with a blue silk sash. She carries a bunch of jonquils — the legend of her youth is nearly revived. Feverishly.*) This is the dress in which I led the cotillion. Won the cakewalk twice at Sunset Hill, wore one spring to the Governor's ball in Jackson! See how I sashayed around the ballroom, Laura? (*She raises her skirt and does a mincing step around the room.*) I wore it on Sundays for my gentlemen callers! I had it on the day I met your father — I had malaria fever all that spring.

The change of climate from East Tennessee to the Delta — weakened resistance — I had a little temperature all the time — not enough to be serious — just enough to make me restless and giddy! Invitations poured in — parties all over the Delta! — "Stay in bed," said Mother, "you have fever!" — but I just wouldn't. — I took quinine but kept on going, going! — Evenings, dances! — Afternoons, long, long rides! Picnics — lovely! — So lovely, that country in May. — All lacy with dogwood, literally flooded with jonquils! — That was the spring I had the craze for jonquils. Jonquils became an absolute obsession. Mother said, "Honey, there's no more room for jonquils." And still I kept on bringing in more jonquils. Whenever, wherever I saw them, I'd say, "Stop! Stop! I see jonquils!" I made the young men help me gather the jonquils! It was a joke, Amanda and her jonquils! Finally there were no more vases to hold them, every available space was filled with jonquils. No vases to hold them? All right, I'll hold them myself! And then I — (*She stops in front of the picture. Music.*) met your father! Malaria fever and jonquils and then — this — boy.... (*She switches on the rose-colored lamp.*) I hope they get here before it starts to rain. (*She crosses upstage and places the jonquils in bowl on table.*) I gave your brother a little extra change so he and Mr. O'Connor could take the service car home.

LAURA (*with altered look*): What did you say his name was?

AMANDA: O'Connor.

LAURA: What is his first name?

AMANDA: I don't remember. Oh, yes, I do. It was — Jim!

(*Laura sways slightly and catches hold of a chair.*)
(*Legend on screen: "Not Jim!"*)

LAURA (*faintly*): Not — Jim!

AMANDA: Yes, that was it, it was Jim! I've never known a Jim that wasn't nice!

(*Music: ominous.*)

LAURA: Are you sure his name is Jim O'Connor?

AMANDA: Yes. Why?

LAURA: Is he the one that Tom used to know in high school?

AMANDA: He didn't say so. I think he just got to know him at the warehouse.

LAURA: There was a Jim O'Connor we both knew in high school — (*Then, with effort.*) If that is the one that Tom is bringing to dinner — you'll have to excuse me, I won't come to the table.

AMANDA: What sort of nonsense is this?

LAURA: You asked me once if I'd ever liked a boy.

Don't you remember I showed you this boy's picture?

AMANDA: You mean the boy you showed me in the yearbook?

LAURA: Yes, that boy.

AMANDA: Laura, Laura, were you in love with that boy?

LAURA: I don't know, Mother. All I know is I couldn't sit at the table if it was him!

AMANDA: It won't be him! It isn't the least bit likely. But whether it is or not, you will come to the table. You will not be excused.

LAURA: I'll have to be, Mother.

AMANDA: I don't intend to humor your silliness, Laura. I've had too much from you and your brother, both! So just sit down and compose yourself till they come. Tom has forgotten his key so you'll have to let them in, when they arrive.

LAURA (*panicky*): Oh, Mother — *you* answer the door!

AMANDA (*lightly*): I'll be in the kitchen — busy!

LAURA: Oh, Mother, please answer the door, don't make me do it!

AMANDA (*crossing into kitchenette*): I've got to fix the dressing for the salmon. Fuss, fuss — silliness! — over a gentleman caller!

(*Door swings shut. Laura is left alone.*)
(*Legend: "Terror!"*)
(*She utters a low moan and turns off the lamp — sits stiffly on the edge of the sofa, knotting her fingers together.*)
(*Legend on screen: "The Opening of a Door!"*)
(*Tom and Jim appear on the fire escape steps and climb to landing. Hearing their approach, Laura rises with a panicky gesture. She retreats to the portieres.*)
(*The doorbell. Laura catches her breath and touches her throat. Low drums.*)

AMANDA (*calling*): Laura, sweetheart! The door!

(*Laura stares at it without moving.*)

JIM: I think we just beat the rain.

TOM: Uh-huh. (*He rings again, nervously. Jim whistles and fishes for a cigarette.*)

AMANDA (*very, very gaily*): Laura, that is your brother and Mr. O'Connor! Will you let them in, darling?

(*Laura crosses toward kitchenette door.*)

LAURA (*breathlessly*): Mother — you go to the door!

(*Amanda steps out of kitchenette and stares furiously at Laura. She points imperiously at the door.*)

LAURA: Please, please!

AMANDA (*in a fierce whisper*): What is the matter with you, you silly thing?

LAURA (*desperately*): Please, you answer it, *please!*

AMANDA: I told you I wasn't going to humor you, Laura. Why have you chosen this moment to lose your mind?

LAURA: Please, please, please, you go!

AMANDA: You'll have to go to the door because I can't!

LAURA (*despairingly*): I can't either!

AMANDA: *Why?*

LAURA: I'm *sick!*

AMANDA: I'm sick, too — of your nonsense! Why can't you and your brother be normal people? Fantastic whims and behavior! (*Tom gives a long ring.*) Preposterous goings on! Can you give me one reason — (*Calls out lyrically.*) COMING! JUST ONE SECOND! — why should you be afraid to open a door? Now you answer it, Laura!

LAURA: Oh, oh, oh . . . (*She returns through the portieres. Darts to the victrola and winds it frantically and turns it on.*)

AMANDA: Laura Wingfield, you march right to that door!

LAURA: Yes — yes, Mother!

(*A faraway, scratchy rendition of "Dardanella" softens the air and gives her strength to move through it. She slips to the door and draws it cautiously open.*)
(*Tom enters with the caller, Jim O'Connor.*)

TOM: Laura, this is Jim. Jim, this is my sister, Laura.

JIM (*stepping inside*): I didn't know that Shakespeare had a sister!

LAURA (*retreating stiff and trembling from the door*): How — how do you do?

JIM (*heartily extending his hand*): Okay!

(*Laura touches it hesitantly with hers.*)

JIM: Your hand's *cold*, Laura!

LAURA: Yes, well — I've been playing the victrola. . . .

JIM: Must have been playing classical music on it! You ought to play a little hot swing music to warm you up!

LAURA: Excuse me — I haven't finished playing the victrola. . . .

(*She turns awkwardly and hurries into the front room. She pauses a second by the victrola. Then catches her breath and darts through the portieres like a frightened deer.*)

JIM (*grinning*): What was the matter?

TOM: Oh — with Laura? Laura is — terribly shy.

JIM: Shy, huh? It's unusual to meet a shy girl nowadays. I don't believe you ever mentioned you had a sister.

TOM: Well, now you know. I have one. Here is the *Post Dispatch*. You want a piece of it?

JIM: Uh-huh.

TOM: What piece? The comics?

JIM: Sports! (*Glances at it.*) Ole Dizzy Dean is on his bad behavior.

TOM (*disinterest*): Yeah? (*Lights cigarette and crosses back to fire escape door.*)

JIM: Where are *you* going?

TOM: I'm going out on the terrace.

JIM (*goes after him*): You know, Shakespeare — I'm going to sell you a bill of goods!

TOM: What goods?

JIM: A course I'm taking.

TOM: Huh?

JIM: In public speaking! You and me, we're not the warehouse type.

TOM: Thanks — that's good news. But what has public speaking got to do with it?

JIM: It fits you for — executive positions!

TOM: Awww.

JIM: I tell you it's done a helluva lot for me.

(*Image: executive at desk.*)

TOM: In what respect?

JIM: In every! Ask yourself what is the difference between you an' me and men in the office down front? Brains? — No! — Ability? — No! Then what? Just one little thing —

TOM: What is that one little thing?

JIM: Primarily it amounts to — social poise! Being able to square up to people and hold your own on any social level!

AMANDA (*offstage*): Tom?

TOM: Yes, Mother?

AMANDA: Is that you and Mr. O'Connor?

TOM: Yes, Mother.

AMANDA: Well, you just make yourselves comfortable in there.

TOM: Yes, Mother.

AMANDA: Ask Mr. O'Connor if he would like to wash his hands.

JIM: Aw, — no — no — thank you — I took care of that at the warehouse. Tom —

TOM: Yes?

JIM: Mr. Mendoza was speaking to me about you.

TOM: Favorably?

JIM: What do you think?

TOM: Well —

JIM: You're going to be out of a job if you don't wake up.

TOM: I am waking up —

JIM: You show no signs.

TOM: The signs are interior.

(*Image on screen: the sailing vessel with Jolly Roger again.*)

TOM: I'm planning to change. (*He leans over the rail speaking with quiet exhilaration. The incandescent marquees and signs of the first-run movie houses light his face from across the alley. He looks like a voyager.*) I'm right at the point of committing myself to a future that doesn't include the warehouse and Mr. Mendoza or even a night school course in public speaking.

JIM: What are you gassing about?

TOM: I'm tired of the movies.

JIM: Movies!

TOM: Yes, movies! Look at them — (*A wave toward the marvels of Grand Avenue.*) All of those glamorous people — having adventures — hogging it all, gobbling the whole thing up! You know what happens? People go to the *movies* instead of *moving!* Hollywood characters are supposed to have all the adventures for everybody in America, while everybody in America sits in a dark room and watches them have them! Yes, until there's a war. That's when adventure becomes available to the masses! *Everyone's* dish, not only Gable's! Then the people in the dark room come out of the dark room to have some adventures themselves — Goody, goody! — It's our turn now, to go to the South Sea Island — to make a safari — to be exotic, far-off! — But I'm not patient. I don't want to wait till then. I'm tired of the *movies* and I am *about* to *move!*

JIM (*incredulously*): Move?

TOM: Yes.

JIM: When?

TOM: Soon!

JIM: Where? Where?

(*Theme three music seems to answer the question, while Tom thinks it over. He searches among his pockets.*)

TOM: I'm starting to boil inside. I know I seem dreamy, but inside — well, I'm boiling! Whenever I pick up a shoe, I shudder a little thinking how short life is and what I am doing! — Whatever that means. I know it doesn't mean shoes — except as something to wear on a traveler's feet! (*Finds paper.*) Look —

JIM: What?

TOM: I'm a member.

JIM (*reading*): The Union of Merchant Seamen.

TOM: I paid my dues this month, instead of the light bill.

JIM: You will regret it when they turn the lights off.

TOM: I won't be here.

JIM: How about your mother?

TOM: I'm like my father. The bastard son of a bastard!

FAR LEFT: Amanda (Ruby Dee) and Laura (Tonia Rowe) in the 1989 Arena Stage production of *The Glass Menagerie*, directed by Tazewell Thompson. LEFT: Laura, Amanda, and Tom (Jonathan Earl Peck). RIGHT: Scene from *The Glass Menagerie*.

See how he grins? And he's been absent going on sixteen years!

JIM: You're just talking, you drip. How does your mother feel about it?

TOM: Shhh! — Here comes Mother! Mother is not acquainted with my plans!

AMANDA (*enters portieres*): Where are you all?

TOM: On the terrace, Mother.

(*They start inside. She advances to them. Tom is distinctly shocked at her appearance. Even Jim blinks a little. He is making his first contact with girlish Southern vivacity and in spite of the night school course in public speaking is somewhat thrown off the beam by the unexpected outlay of social charm.*)

(*Certain responses are attempted by Jim but are swept aside by Amanda's gay laughter and chatter. Tom is embarrassed but after the first shock Jim reacts very warmly. Grins and chuckles, is altogether won over.*)

(*Image: Amanda as a girl.*)

AMANDA (*coyly smiling, shaking her girlish ringlets*): Well, well, well, so this is Mr. O'Connor. Introductions entirely unnecessary. I've heard so much about you from my boy. I finally said to him,

Tom — good gracious! — why don't you bring this paragon to supper? I'd like to meet this nice young man at the warehouse! — Instead of just hearing him sing your praises so much! I don't know why my son is so standoffish — that's not Southern behavior! Let's sit down and — I think we could stand a little more air in here! Tom, leave the door open. I felt a nice fresh breeze a moment ago. Where has it gone to? Mmm, so warm already! And not quite summer, even. We're going to burn up when summer really gets started. However, we're having — we're having a very light supper. I think light things are better fo' this time of year. The same as light clothes are. Light clothes an' light food are what warm weather calls fo'. You know our blood gets so thick during th' winter — it takes a while fo' us to *adjust* ou'selves! — when the season changes . . . It's come so quick this year. I wasn't prepared. All of a sudden — heavens! Already summer! — I ran to the trunk an' pulled out this light dress — Terribly old! Historical almost! But feels so good — so good an' co-ol, y'know. . . .

TOM: Mother —

AMANDA: Yes, honey?

TOM: How about — supper?

AMANDA: Honey, you go ask Sister if supper is ready! You know that Sister is in full charge of supper! Tell her you hungry boys are waiting for it. (*To Jim.*) Have you met Laura?

JIM: She —

AMANDA: Let you in? Oh, good, you've met already! It's rare for a girl as sweet an' pretty as Laura to be domestic! But Laura is, thank heavens, not only pretty but also very domestic. I'm not at all. I never was a bit. I never could make a thing but angel food cake. Well, in the South we had so many servants. Gone, gone, gone. All vestiges of gracious living! Gone completely! I wasn't prepared for what the future brought me. All of my gentlemen callers were sons of planters and so of course I assumed that I would be married to one and raise my family on a large piece of land with plenty of servants. But man proposes — and woman accepts the proposal! — To vary that old, old saying a little bit — I married no planter! I married a man who worked for the telephone company! — That gallantly smiling gentleman over there! (*Points to the picture.*) A telephone man who — fell in love with long distance! — Now he travels and I don't even know where! — But what am I going on for about my — tribulations! Tell me yours — I hope you don't have any! Tom?

TOM (*returning*): Yes, Mother?

AMANDA: Is supper nearly ready?

TOM: It looks to me like supper is on the table.

AMANDA: Let me look — (*She rises prettily and looks through portieres.*) Oh, lovely! — But where is Sister?

TOM: Laura is not feeling well and she says that she thinks she'd better not come to the table.

AMANDA: What? — Nonsense! — Laura? Oh, Laura!

LAURA (*offstage, faintly*): Yes, Mother.

AMANDA: You really must come to the table. We won't be seated until you come to the table! Come in, Mr. O'Connor. You sit over there, and I'll — Laura? Laura Wingfield! You're keeping us waiting, honey! We can't say grace until you come to the table!

(*The back door is pushed weakly open and Laura comes in. She is obviously quite faint, her lips trembling, her eyes wide and staring. She moves unsteadily toward the table.*)

(*Legend: "Terror!"*)

(*Outside a summer storm is coming abruptly. The white curtains billow inward at the windows and there is a sorrowful murmur and deep blue dusk.*)

(*Laura suddenly stumbles — she catches at a chair with a faint moan.*)

TOM: Laura!

AMANDA: Laura! (*There is a clap of thunder.*) (*Legend: "Ah!"*) (*Despairingly.*) Why, Laura, you *are* sick, darling! Tom, help your sister into the living room, dear! Sit in the living room, Laura — rest on the sofa. Well! (*To the gentleman caller.*) Standing over the hot stove made her ill! — I told her that it was just too warm this evening, but — (*Tom comes back in. Laura is on the sofa.*) Is Laura all right now?

TOM: Yes.

AMANDA: What *is* that? Rain? A nice cool rain has come up! (*She gives the gentleman caller a frightened look.*) I think we may — have grace — now . . . (*Tom looks at her stupidly.*) Tom, honey — you say grace!

TOM: Oh . . . "For these and all thy mercies — " (*They bow their heads, Amanda stealing a nervous glance at Jim. In the living room Laura, stretched on the sofa, clenches her hand to her lips, to hold back a shuddering sob.*) God's Holy Name be praised —

(*The scene dims out.*)

SCENE 7

(*A Souvenir*)

(*Half an hour later. Dinner is just being finished in the upstage area which is concealed by the drawn portieres.*)

(*As the curtain rises Laura is still huddled upon the sofa, her feet drawn under her, her head resting on a pale blue pillow, her eyes wide and mysteriously watchful. The new floor lamp with its shade of rose-colored silk gives a soft, becoming light to her face, bringing out the fragile, unearthly prettiness which usually escapes attention. There is a steady murmur of rain, but it is slackening and stops soon after the scene begins; the air outside becomes pale and luminous as the moon breaks out.*)

(*A moment after the curtain rises, the lights in both rooms flicker and go out.*)

JIM: Hey, there, Mr. Light Bulb!

(*Amanda laughs nervously.*)
(*Legend: "Suspension of a Public Service."*)

AMANDA: Where was Moses when the lights went out? Ha-ha. Do you know the answer to that one, Mr. O'Connor?
JIM: No, Ma'am, what's the answer?
AMANDA: In the dark! (*Jim laughs appreciably.*) Everybody sit still. I'll light the candles. Isn't it lucky we have them on the table? Where's a match? Which of you gentlemen can provide a match?
JIM: Here.
AMANDA: Thank you, sir.
JIM: Not at all, Ma'am!
AMANDA: I guess the fuse has burnt out. Mr. O'Connor, can you tell a burnt-out fuse? I know I can't and Tom is a total loss when it comes to mechanics. (*Sound: getting up: voices recede a little to kitchenette.*) Oh, be careful you don't bump into something. We don't want our gentleman caller to break his neck. Now wouldn't that be a fine howdy-do?
JIM: Ha-ha! Where is the fuse box?
AMANDA: Right here next to the stove. Can you see anything?
JIM: Just a minute.
AMANDA: Isn't electricity a mysterious thing? Wasn't it Benjamin Franklin who tied a key to a kite? We live in such a mysterious universe, don't we? Some people say that science clears up all the mysteries for us. In my opinion it only creates more! Have you found it yet?
JIM: No, Ma'am. All these fuses look okay to me.
AMANDA: Tom!
TOM: Yes, Mother?

AMANDA: That light bill I gave you several days ago. The one I told you we got the notices about?
TOM: Oh. — Yeah.

(*Legend: "Ha!"*)

AMANDA: You didn't neglect to pay it by any chance?
TOM: Why, I —
AMANDA: Didn't! I might have known it!
JIM: Shakespeare probably wrote a poem on that light bill, Mrs. Wingfield.
AMANDA: I might have known better than to trust him with it! There's such a high price for negligence in this world!
JIM: Maybe the poem will win a ten-dollar prize.
AMANDA: We'll just have to spend the remainder of the evening in the nineteenth century, before Mr. Edison made the Mazda lamp!
JIM: Candlelight is my favorite kind of light.
AMANDA: That shows you're romantic! But that's no excuse for Tom. Well, we got through dinner. Very considerate of them to let us get through dinner before they plunged us into everlasting darkness, wasn't it, Mr. O'Connor?
JIM: Ha-ha!
AMANDA: Tom, as a penalty for your carelessness you can help me with the dishes.
JIM: Let me give you a hand.
AMANDA: Indeed you will not!
JIM: I ought to be good for something.
AMANDA: Good for something? (*Her tone is rhapsodic.*) You? Why, Mr. O'Connor, nobody, *nobody's* given me this much entertainment in years — as you have!
JIM: Aw, now, Mrs. Wingfield!
AMANDA: I'm not exaggerating, not one bit! But Sister is all by her lonesome. You go keep her company in the parlor! I'll give you this lovely old candelabrum that used to be on the altar at the church of the Heavenly Rest. It was melted a little out of shape when the church burnt down. Lightning struck it one spring. Gypsy Jones was holding a revival at the time and he intimated that the church was destroyed because the Episcopalians gave card parties.
JIM: Ha-ha.
AMANDA: And how about coaxing Sister to drink a little wine? I think it would be good for her! Can you carry both at once?
JIM: Sure. I'm Superman!
AMANDA: Now, Thomas, get into this apron!

(*The door of kitchenette swings closed on Amanda's gay laughter; the flickering light approaches the portieres.*)

(*Laura sits up nervously as he enters. Her speech at first is low and breathless from the almost intolerable strain of being alone with a stranger.*)

(*The legend: "I Don't Suppose You Remember Me at All!"*)

(*In her first speeches in this scene, before Jim's warmth overcomes her paralyzing shyness, Laura's voice is thin and breathless as though she has just run up a steep flight of stairs.*)

(*Jim's attitude is gently humorous. In playing this scene it should be stressed that while the incident is apparently unimportant, it is to Laura the climax of her secret life.*)

JIM: Hello, there, Laura.

LAURA (*faintly*): Hello. (*She clears her throat.*)

JIM: How are you feeling now? Better?

LAURA: Yes. Yes, thank you.

JIM: This is for you. A little dandelion wine. (*He extends it toward her with extravagant gallantry.*)

LAURA: Thank you.

JIM: Drink it — but don't get drunk! (*He laughs heartily. Laura takes the glass uncertainly; laughs shyly.*) Where shall I set the candles?

LAURA: Oh — oh, anywhere . . .

JIM: How about here on the floor? Any objections?

LAURA: No.

JIM: I'll spread a newspaper under to catch the drippings. I like to sit on the floor. Mind if I do?

LAURA: Oh, no.

JIM: Give me a pillow?

LAURA: What?

JIM: A pillow!

LAURA: Oh . . . (*Hands him one quickly.*)

JIM: How about you? Don't you like to sit on the floor?

LAURA: Oh — yes.

JIM: Why don't you, then?

LAURA: I — will.

JIM: Take a pillow! (*Laura does. Sits on the other side of the candelabrum. Jim crosses his legs and smiles engagingly at her.*) I can't hardly see you sitting way over there.

LAURA: I can — see you.

JIM: I know, but that's not fair, I'm in the limelight. (*Laura moves her pillow closer.*) Good! Now I can see you! Comfortable?

LAURA: Yes.

JIM: So am I. Comfortable as a cow. Will you have some gum?

LAURA: No, thank you.

JIM: I think that I will indulge, with your permission. (*Musingly unwraps it and holds it up.*) Think of the fortune made by the guy that invented the first piece of chewing gum. Amazing, huh? The Wrigley Building is one of the sights of Chicago. — I saw it summer before last when I went up to the Century of Progress. Did you take in the Century of Progress?

LAURA: No, I didn't.

JIM: Well, it was quite a wonderful exposition. What impressed me most was the Hall of Science. Gives you an idea of what the future will be in America, even more wonderful than the present time is! (*Pause. Smiling at her.*) Your brother tells me you're shy. Is that right, Laura?

LAURA: I — don't know.

JIM: I judge you to be an old-fashioned type of girl. Well, I think that's a pretty good type to be. Hope you don't think I'm being too personal — do you?

LAURA (*hastily, out of embarrassment*): I believe I *will* take a piece of gum, if you — don't mind. (*Clearing her throat.*) Mr. O'Connor, have you — kept up with your singing?

JIM: Singing? Me?

LAURA: Yes. I remember what a beautiful voice you had.

JIM: When did you hear me sing?

(*Voice offstage in the pause.*)

VOICE (*offstage*): O blow, ye winds, heigh-ho,
    A-roving I will go!
      I'm off to my love
        With a boxing glove —
    Ten thousand miles away!

JIM: You say you've heard me sing?

LAURA: Oh, yes! Yes, very often . . . I — don't suppose you remember me — at all?

JIM (*smiling doubtfully*): You know I have an idea I've seen you before. I had that idea soon as you opened the door. It seemed almost like I was about to remember your name. But the name that I started to call you — wasn't a name! And so I stopped myself before I said it.

LAURA: Wasn't it — Blue Roses?

JIM (*Springs up. Grinning.*): Blue Roses! My gosh, yes — Blue Roses! That's what I had on my tongue when you opened the door! Isn't it funny what tricks your memory plays? I didn't connect you with the high school somehow or other. But that's where it was; it was high school. I didn't even know you were Shakespeare's sister! Gosh, I'm sorry.

LAURA: I didn't expect you to. You — barely knew me!

JIM: But we did have a speaking acquaintance, huh?

LAURA: Yes, we — spoke to each other.

JIM: When did you recognize me?

LAURA: Oh, right away!

JIM: Soon as I came in the door?

LAURA: When I heard your name I thought it was

probably you. I knew that Tom used to know you a little in high school. So when you came in the door — Well, then I was — sure.

JIM: Why didn't you *say* something, then?

LAURA (*breathlessly*): I didn't know what to say, I was — too surprised!

JIM: For goodness' sakes! You know, this sure is funny!

LAURA: Yes! Yes, isn't it, though . . .

JIM: Didn't we have a class in something together?

LAURA: Yes, we did.

JIM: What class was that?

LAURA: It was — singing — Chorus!

JIM: Aw!

LAURA: I sat across the aisle from you in the Aud.

JIM: Aw.

LAURA: Mondays, Wednesdays, and Fridays.

JIM: Now I remember — you always came in late.

LAURA: Yes, it was so hard for me, getting upstairs. I had that brace on my leg — it clumped so loud!

JIM: I never heard any clumping.

LAURA (*wincing at the recollection*): To me it sounded like — thunder!

JIM: Well, well, well, I never even noticed.

LAURA: And everybody was seated before I came in. I had to walk in front of all those people. My seat was in the back row. I had to go clumping all the way up the aisle with everyone watching!

JIM: You shouldn't have been self-conscious.

LAURA: I know, but I was. It was always such a relief when the singing started.

JIM: Aw, yes, I've placed you now! I used to call you Blue Roses. How was it that I got started calling you that?

LAURA: I was out of school a little while with pleurosis. When I came back you asked me what was the matter. I said I had pleurosis — you thought I said Blue Roses. That's what you always called me after that!

JIM: I hope you didn't mind.

LAURA: Oh, no — I liked it. You see, I wasn't acquainted with many — people. . . .

JIM: As I remember you sort of stuck by yourself.

LAURA: I — I — never had much luck at — making friends.

JIM: I don't see why you wouldn't.

LAURA: Well, I — started out badly.

JIM: You mean being —

LAURA: Yes, it sort of — stood between me —

JIM: You shouldn't have let it!

LAURA: I know, but it did, and —

JIM: You were shy with people!

LAURA: I tried not to be but never could —

JIM: Overcome it?

LAURA: No, I — I never could!

JIM: I guess being shy is something you have to work out of kind of gradually.

LAURA (*sorrowfully*): Yes — I guess it —

JIM: Takes time!

LAURA: Yes —

JIM: People are not so dreadful when you know them. That's what you have to remember! And everybody has problems, not just you, but practically everybody has got some problems. You think of yourself as having the only problems, as being the only one who is disappointed. But just look around you and you will see lots of people as disappointed as you are. For instance, I hoped when I was going to high school that I would be further along at this time, six years later, than I am now — You remember that wonderful write-up I had in *The Torch?*

LAURA: Yes! (*She rises and crosses to table.*)

JIM: It said I was bound to succeed in anything I went into! (*Laura returns with the annual.*) Holy Jeez! *The Torch!* (*He accepts it reverently. They smile across it with mutual wonder. Laura crouches beside him and they begin to turn through it. Laura's shyness is dissolving in his warmth.*)

LAURA: Here you are in *Pirates of Penzance!*

JIM (*wistfully*): I sang the baritone lead in that operetta.

LAURA (*rapidly*): So — *beautifully!*

JIM (*protesting*): Aw —

LAURA: Yes, yes — beautifully — beautifully!

JIM: You heard me?

LAURA: All three times!

JIM: No!

LAURA: Yes!

JIM: All three performances?

LAURA (*looking down*): Yes.

JIM: Why?

LAURA: I — wanted to ask you to — autograph my program.

JIM: Why didn't you ask me to?

LAURA: You were always surrounded by your own friends so much that I never had a chance to.

JIM: You should have just —

LAURA: Well, I — thought you might think I was —

JIM: Thought I might think you was — what?

LAURA: Oh —

JIM (*with reflective relish*): I was beleaguered by females in those days.

LAURA: You were terribly popular!

JIM: Yeah —

LAURA: You had such a — friendly way —

JIM: I was spoiled in high school.

LAURA: Everybody — liked you!

JIM: Including you?

LAURA: I — yes, I — I did, too — (*She gently closes the book in her lap.*)

JIM: Well, well, well! — Give me that program, Laura. (*She hands it to him. He signs it with a flourish.*) There you are — better late than never!

LAURA: Oh, I — what a — surprise!

JIM: My signature isn't worth very much right now. But some day — maybe — it will increase in value! Being disappointed is one thing and being discouraged is something else. I am disappointed but I am not discouraged. I'm twenty-three years old. How old are you?

LAURA: I'll be twenty-four in June.

JIM: That's not old age!

LAURA: No, but —

JIM: You finished high school?

LAURA (*with difficulty*): I didn't go back.

JIM: You mean you dropped out?

LAURA: I made bad grades in my final examinations. (*She rises and replaces the book and the program. Her voice strained.*) How is — Emily Meisenbach getting along?

JIM: Oh, that kraut-head!

LAURA: Why do you call her that?

JIM: That's what she was.

LAURA: You're not still — going with her?

JIM: I never see her.

LAURA: It said in the Personal Section that you were — engaged!

JIM: I know, but I wasn't impressed by that — propaganda!

LAURA: It wasn't — the truth?

JIM: Only in Emily's optimistic opinion!

LAURA: Oh —

(*Legend: "What Have You Done since High School?"*)

(*Jim lights a cigarette and leans indolently back on his elbows smiling at Laura with a warmth and charm which lights her inwardly with altar candles. She remains by the table and turns in her hands a piece of glass to cover her tumult.*)

JIM (*after several reflective puffs on a cigarette*): What have you done since high school? (*She seems not to hear him.*) Huh? (*Laura looks up.*) I said what have you done since high school, Laura?

LAURA: Nothing much.

JIM: You must have been doing something these six long years.

LAURA: Yes.

JIM: Well, then, such as what?

LAURA: I took a business course at business college —

JIM: How did that work out?

LAURA: Well, not very — well — I had to drop out, it gave me — indigestion —

(*Jim laughs gently.*)

JIM: What are you doing now?

LAURA: I don't do anything — much. Oh, please don't think I sit around doing nothing! My glass collection takes up a good deal of my time. Glass is something you have to take good care of.

JIM: What did you say — about glass?

LAURA: Collection I said — I have one — (*She clears her throat and turns away again, acutely shy.*)

JIM (*abruptly*): You know what I judge to be the trouble with you? Inferiority complex! Know what that is? That's what they call it when someone low-rates himself! I understand it because I had it, too. Although my case was not so aggravated as yours seems to be. I had it until I took up public speaking, developed my voice, and learned that I had an aptitude for science. Before that time I never thought of myself as being outstanding in any way whatsoever! Now I've never made a regular study of it, but I have a friend who says I can analyze people better than doctors that make a profession of it. I don't claim that to be necessarily true, but I can sure guess a person's psychology, Laura! (*Takes out his gum.*) Excuse me, Laura. I always take it out when the flavor is gone. I'll use this scrap of paper to wrap it in. I know how it is to get it stuck on a shoe. Yep — that's what I judge to be your principal trouble. A lack of confidence in yourself as a person. You don't have the proper amount of faith in yourself. I'm basing that fact on a number of your remarks and also on certain observations I've made. For instance that clumping you thought was so awful in high school. You say that you even dreaded to walk into class. You see what you did? You dropped out of school, you gave up an education because of a clump, which as far as I know was practically nonexistent! A little physical defect is what you have. Hardly noticeable even! Magnified thousands of times by imagination! You know what my strong advice to you is? Think of yourself as *superior* in some way!

LAURA: In what way would I think?

JIM: Why, man alive, Laura! Just look about you a little. What do you see? A world full of common people! All of 'em born and all of 'em going to die! Which of them has one-tenth of your good points! Or mine! Or anyone else's, as far as that goes — Gosh! Everybody excels in some one thing. Some in many! (*Unconsciously glances at himself in the mirror.*) All you've got to do is discover in *what!* Take me, for instance. (*He adjusts his tie at the mirror.*) My interest happens to lie in electro-dynamics. I'm taking a course in radio engineering at night school, Laura, on top of a fairly responsible job at the warehouse. I'm taking that course and studying public speaking.

LAURA: Ohhhh.

JIM: Because I believe in the future of television! (*Turning back to her.*) I wish to be ready to go up right along with it. Therefore I'm planning to get in on the ground floor. In fact, I've already made the right connections and all that remains is for the industry itself to get under way! Full steam — (*His eyes are starry.*) *Knowledge* — Zzzzzp! *Money* — Zzzzzzp! — *Power!* That's the cycle democracy is built on! (*His attitude is convincingly dynamic. Laura stares at him, even her shyness eclipsed in her absolute wonder. He suddenly grins.*) I guess you think I think a lot of myself!

LAURA: No — o-o-o, I —

JIM: Now how about you? Isn't there something you take more interest in than anything else?

LAURA: Well, I do — as I said — have my — glass collection —

(*A peal of girlish laughter from the kitchen.*)

JIM: I'm not right sure I know what you're talking about. What kind of glass is it?

LAURA: Little articles of it, they're ornaments mostly! Most of them are little animals made out of glass, the tiniest little animals in the world. Mother calls them a glass menagerie! Here's an example of one, if you'd like to see it! This one is one of the oldest. It's nearly thirteen. (*He stretches out his hand.*) (*Music: "The Glass Menagerie."*) Oh, be careful — if you breathe, it breaks!

JIM: I'd better not take it. I'm pretty clumsy with things.

LAURA: Go on, I trust you with him! (*Places it in his palm.*) There now — you're holding him gently! Hold him over the light, he loves the light! You see how the light shines through him?

JIM: It sure does shine!

LAURA: I shouldn't be partial, but he is my favorite one.

JIM: What kind of a thing is this one supposed to be?

LAURA: Haven't you noticed the single horn on his forehead?

JIM: A unicorn, huh?

LAURA: Mmm-hmmm!

JIM: Unicorns, aren't they extinct in the modern world?

LAURA: I know!

JIM: Poor little fellow, he must feel sort of lonesome.

LAURA (*smiling*): Well, if he does he doesn't complain about it. He stays on a shelf with some horses that don't have horns and all of them seem to get along nicely together.

JIM: How do you know?

LAURA (*lightly*): I haven't heard any arguments among them!

JIM (*grinning*): No arguments, huh? Well, that's a pretty good sign! Where shall I set him?

LAURA: Put him on the table. They all like a change of scenery once in a while!

JIM (*stretching*): Well, well, well, well — Look how big my shadow is when I stretch!

LAURA: Oh, oh, yes — it stretches across the ceiling!

JIM (*crossing to door*): I think it's stopped raining. (*Opens fire escape door.*) Where does the music come from?

LAURA: From the Paradise Dance Hall across the alley.

JIM: How about cutting the rug a little, Miss Wingfield?

LAURA: Oh, I —

JIM: Or is your program filled up? Let me have a look at it. (*Grasps imaginary card.*) Why, every dance is taken! I'll just have to scratch some out. (*Waltz music: "La Golondrina."*) Ahhh, a waltz! (*He executes some sweeping turns by himself then holds his arms toward Laura.*)

LAURA (*breathlessly*): I — can't dance!

JIM: There you go, that inferiority stuff!

LAURA: I've never danced in my life!

JIM: Come on, try!

LAURA: Oh, but I'd step on you!

JIM: I'm not made out of glass.

LAURA: How — how — how do we start?

JIM: Just leave it to me. You hold your arms out a little.

LAURA: Like this?

JIM: A little bit higher. Right. Now don't tighten up, that's the main thing about it — relax.

LAURA (*laughing breathlessly*): It's hard not to.

JIM: Okay.

LAURA: I'm afraid you can't budge me.

JIM: What do you bet I can't? (*He swings her into motion.*)

LAURA: Goodness, yes, you can!

JIM: Let yourself go, now, Laura, just let yourself go.

LAURA: I'm —

JIM: Come on!

LAURA: Trying!

JIM: Not so stiff — Easy does it!

LAURA: I know but I'm —

JIM: Loosen th' backbone! There now, that's a lot better.

LAURA: Am I?

JIM: Lots, lots better! (*He moves her about the room in a clumsy waltz.*)

LAURA: Oh, my!

JIM: Ha-ha!

LAURA: Oh, my goodness!

JIM: Ha-ha-ha! (*They suddenly bump into the table. Jim stops.*) What did we hit on?

LAURA: Table.

JIM: Did something fall off it? I think —

LAURA: Yes.

JIM: I hope that it wasn't the little glass horse with the horn!

LAURA: Yes.

JIM: Aw, aw, aw. Is it broken?

LAURA: Now it is just like all the other horses.

JIM: It's lost its —

LAURA: Horn! It doesn't matter. Maybe it's a blessing in disguise.

JIM: You'll never forgive me. I bet that that was your favorite piece of glass.

LAURA: I don't have favorites much. It's no tragedy, Freckles. Glass breaks so easily. No matter how careful you are. The traffic jars the shelves and things fall off them.

JIM: Still I'm awfully sorry that I was the cause.

LAURA (*smiling*): I'll just imagine he had an operation. The horn was removed to make him feel less — freakish! (*They both laugh.*) Now he will feel more at home with the other horses, the ones that don't have horns . . .

JIM: Ha-ha, that's very funny! (*Suddenly serious.*) I'm glad to see that you have a sense of humor. You know — you're — well — very different! Surprisingly different from anyone else I know! (*His voice becomes soft and hesitant with a genuine feeling.*) Do you mind me telling you that? (*Laura is abashed beyond speech.*) I mean it in a nice way . . . (*Laura nods shyly, looking away.*) You make me feel sort of — I don't know how to put it! I'm usually pretty good at expressing things, but — This is something that I don't know how to say! (*Laura touches her throat and clears it — turns the broken unicorn in her hands.*) (*Even softer.*) Has anyone ever told you that you were pretty? (*Pause: Music.*) (*Laura looks up slowly, with wonder, and shakes her head.*) Well, you are! In a very different way from anyone else. And all the nicer because of the difference, too. (*His voice becomes low and husky. Laura turns away, nearly faint with the novelty of her emotions.*) I wish that you were my sister. I'd teach you to have some confidence in yourself. The different people are not like other people, but being different is nothing to be ashamed of. Because other people are not such wonderful people. They're one hundred times one thousand. You're one times one! They walk all over the earth. You just stay here. They're common as — weeds, but — you — well, you're — *Blue Roses!*

(*Image on screen: blue roses.*)

(*Music changes.*)

LAURA: But blue is wrong for — roses . . .

JIM: It's right for you — You're — pretty!

LAURA: In what respect am I pretty?

JIM: In all respects — believe me! Your eyes — your hair — are pretty! Your hands are pretty! (*He catches hold of her hand.*) You think I'm making this up because I'm invited to dinner and have to be nice. Oh, I could do that! I could put on an act for you, Laura, and say lots of things without being very sincere. But this time I am. I'm talking to you sincerely. I happened to notice you had this inferiority complex that keeps you from feeling comfortable with people. Somebody needs to build your confidence up and make you proud instead of shy and turning away and — blushing — Somebody ought to — Ought to — *kiss* you, Laura! (*His hand slips slowly up her arm to her shoulder.*) (*Music swells tumultuously.*) (*He suddenly turns her about and kisses her on the lips. When he releases her Laura sinks on the sofa with a bright, dazed look. Jim backs away and fishes in his pocket for a cigarette.*) (*Legend on screen: "Souvenir."*) Stumble-john! (*He lights the cigarette, avoiding her look. There is a peal of girlish laughter from Amanda in the kitchen. Laura slowly raises and opens her hand. It still contains the little broken glass animal. She looks at it with a tender, bewildered expression.*) Stumble-john! I shouldn't have done that — That was way off the beam. You don't smoke, do you? (*She looks up, smiling, not hearing the question. He sits beside her a little gingerly. She looks at him speechlessly — waiting. He coughs decorously and moves a little farther aside as he considers the situation and senses her feelings, dimly, with perturbation. Gently.*) Would you — care for a — mint? (*She doesn't seem to hear him but her look grows brighter even.*) Peppermint — Life Saver? My pocket's a regular drugstore — wherever I go . . . (*He pops a mint in his mouth. Then gulps and decides to make a clean breast of it. He speaks slowly and gingerly.*) Laura, you know, if I had a sister like you, I'd do the same thing as Tom. I'd bring out fellows and — introduce her to them. The right type of boys of a type to — appreciate her. Only — well — he made a mistake about me. Maybe I've got no call to be saying this. That may not have been the idea in having me over. But what if it was? There's nothing wrong about that. The only trouble is that in my case — I'm not in a situation to — do the right thing. I can't take down your number and say I'll phone. I can't call up next week and — ask for a date. I thought I had better explain the situation in case you misunderstood it and — hurt your feelings. . . . (*Pause. Slowly, very slowly, Laura's look changes, her eyes returning slowly from his to the ornament in her palm.*)

(*Amanda utters another gay laugh in the kitchen.*)

LAURA (*faintly*): You — won't — call again?

JIM: No, Laura, I can't. (*He rises from the sofa.*) As I was just explaining, I've — got strings on me, Laura, I've — been going steady! I go out all the time with a girl named Betty. She's a home-girl like you, and Catholic, and Irish, and in a great many ways we — get along fine. I met her last summer on a moonlight boat trip up the river to Alton, on the *Majestic*. Well — right away from the start it was — love! (*Legend: Love!*) (*Laura sways slightly forward and grips the arm of the sofa. He fails to notice, now enrapt in his own comfortable being.*) Being in love has made a new man of me! (*Leaning stiffly forward, clutching the arm of the sofa, Laura struggles visibly with her storm. But Jim is oblivious, she is a long way off.*) The power of love is really pretty tremendous! Love is something that — changes the whole world, Laura! (*The storm abates a little and Laura leans back. He notices her again.*) It happened that Betty's aunt took sick, she got a wire and had to go to Centralia. So Tom — when he asked me to dinner — I naturally just accepted the invitation, not knowing that you — that he — that I — (*He stops awkwardly.*) Huh — I'm a stumble-john! (*He flops back on the sofa. The holy candles in the altar of Laura's face have been snuffed out! There is a look of almost infinite desolation. Jim glances at her uneasily.*) I wish that you would — say something. (*She bites her lip which was trembling and then bravely smiles. She opens her hand again on the broken glass ornament. Then she gently takes his hand and raises it level with her own. She carefully places the unicorn in the palm of his hand, then pushes his fingers closed upon it.*) What are you — doing that for? You want me to have him? — Laura? (*She nods.*) What for?

LAURA: A — souvenir . . .

(*She rises unsteadily and crouches beside the victrola to wind it up.*)

(*Legend on screen: "Things Have a Way of Turning out so Badly."*)

(*Or Image: "Gentleman Caller Waving Goodbye! — Gaily."*)

(*At this moment Amanda rushes brightly back in the front room. She bears a pitcher of fruit punch in an old-fashioned cut-glass pitcher and a plate of mac-aroons. The plate has a gold border and poppies painted on it.*)

AMANDA: Well, well, well! Isn't the air delightful after the shower? I've made you children a little liquid refreshment. (*Turns gaily to the gentleman caller.*) Jim, do you know that song about lemonade?

"Lemonade, lemonade
    Made in the shade and stirred with a spade —
Good enough for any old maid!"

JIM (*uneasily*): Ha-ha! No — I never heard it.

AMANDA: Why, Laura! You look so serious!

JIM: We were having a serious conversation.

AMANDA: Good! Now you're better acquainted!

JIM (*uncertainly*): Ha-ha! Yes.

AMANDA: You modern young people are much more serious-minded than my generation. I was so gay as a girl!

JIM: You haven't changed, Mrs. Wingfield.

AMANDA: Tonight I'm rejuvenated! The gaiety of the occasion, Mr. O'Connor! (*She tosses her head with a peal of laughter. Spills lemonade.*) Oooo! I'm baptizing myself!

JIM: Here — let me —

AMANDA (*setting the pitcher down*): There now. I discovered we had some maraschino cherries. I dumped them in, juice and all!

JIM: You shouldn't have gone to that trouble, Mrs. Wingfield.

AMANDA: Trouble, trouble? Why it was loads of fun! Didn't you hear me cutting up in the kitchen? I bet your ears were burning! I told Tom how outdone with him I was for keeping you to himself so long a time! He should have brought you over much, much sooner! Well, now that you've found your way, I want you to be a very frequent caller! Not just occasional but all the time. Oh, we're going to have a lot of gay times together! I see them coming! Mmm, just breathe that air! So fresh, and the moon's so pretty! I'll skip back out — I know where my place is when young folks are having a — serious conversation!

JIM: Oh, don't go out, Mrs. Wingfield. The fact of the matter is I've got to be going.

AMANDA: Going, now? You're joking! Why, it's only the shank of the evening, Mr. O'Connor!

JIM: Well, you know how it is.

AMANDA: You mean you're a young workingman and have to keep workingmen's hours. We'll let you off early tonight. But only on the condition that next time you stay later. What's the best night for you? Isn't Saturday night the best night for you workingmen?

JIM: I have a couple of time clocks to punch, Mrs. Wingfield. One at morning, another one at night!

AMANDA: My, but you *are* ambitious! You work at night, too?

JIM: No, Ma'am, not work but — Betty! (*He crosses deliberately to pick up his hat. The band at the Paradise Dance Hall goes into a tender waltz.*)

AMANDA: Betty? Betty? Who's — Betty! (*There is an ominous cracking sound in the sky.*)

JIM: Oh, just a girl. The girl I go steady with! (*He smiles charmingly. The sky falls.*)

(*Legend: "The Sky Falls."*)

AMANDA (*a long-drawn exhalation*): Ohhhh . . . Is it a serious romance, Mr. O'Connor?

JIM: We're going to be married the second Sunday in June.

AMANDA: Ohhhh — how nice! Tom didn't mention that you were engaged to be married.

JIM: The cat's not out of the bag at the warehouse yet. You know how they are. They call you Romeo and stuff like that. (*He stops at the oval mirror to put on his hat. He carefully shapes the brim and the crown to give a discreetly dashing effect.*) It's been a wonderful evening, Mrs. Wingfield. I guess this is what they mean by Southern hospitality.

AMANDA: It really wasn't anything at all.

JIM: I hope it don't seem like I'm rushing off. But I promised Betty I'd pick her up at the Wabash depot, an' by the time I get my jalopy down there her train'll be in. Some women are pretty upset if you keep 'em waiting.

AMANDA: Yes, I know — The tyranny of women! (*Extends her hand.*) Good-bye, Mr. O'Connor. I wish you luck — and happiness — and success! All three of them, and so does Laura! — Don't you, Laura?

LAURA: Yes!

JIM (*taking her hand*): Good-bye, Laura. I'm certainly going to treasure that souvenir. And don't you forget the good advice I gave you. (*Raises his voice to a cheery shout.*) So long, Shakespeare! Thanks again, ladies — Good night!

(*He grins and ducks jauntily out.*)

(*Still bravely grimacing, Amanda closes the door on the gentleman caller. Then she turns back to the room with a puzzled expression. She and Laura don't dare to face each other. Laura crouches beside the victrola to wind it.*)

AMANDA (*faintly*): Things have a way of turning out so badly. I don't believe that I would play the victrola. Well, well — well — Our gentleman caller was engaged to be married! Tom!

TOM (*from back*): Yes, Mother?

AMANDA: Come in here a minute. I want to tell you something awfully funny.

TOM (*enters with macaroon and a glass of the lemonade*): Has the gentleman caller gotten away already?

AMANDA: The gentleman caller has made an early departure. What a wonderful joke you played on us!

TOM: How do you mean?

AMANDA: You didn't mention that he was engaged to be married.

TOM: Jim? Engaged?

AMANDA: That's what he just informed us.

TOM: I'll be jiggered! I didn't know about that.

AMANDA: That seems very peculiar.

TOM: What's peculiar about it?

AMANDA: Didn't you call him your best friend down at the warehouse?

TOM: He is, but how did I know?

AMANDA: It seems extremely peculiar that you wouldn't know your best friend was going to be married!

TOM: The warehouse is where I work, not where I know things about people!

AMANDA: You don't know things anywhere! You live in a dream; you manufacture illusions! (*He crosses to door.*) Where are you going?

TOM: I'm going to the movies.

AMANDA: That's right, now that you've had us make such fools of ourselves. The effort, the preparations, all the expense! The new floor lamp, the rug, the clothes for Laura! All for what? To entertain some other girl's fiancé! Go to the movies, go! Don't think about us, a mother deserted, an unmarried sister who's crippled and has no job! Don't let anything interfere with your selfish pleasure! Just go, go, go — to the movies!

TOM: All right, I will! The more you shout about my selfishness to me the quicker I'll go, and I won't go to the movies!

AMANDA: Go, then! Then go to the moon — you selfish dreamer!

(*Tom smashes his glass on the floor. He plunges out on the fire escape, slamming the door. Laura screams — cut by door.*)

(*Dance hall music up. Tom goes to the rail and grips it desperately, lifting his face in the chill white moonlight penetrating the narrow abyss of the alley.*)

(*Legend on screen: "And so Good-bye . . ."*)

(*Tom's closing speech is timed with the interior pantomime. The interior scene is played as though viewed through soundproof glass. Amanda appears to be making a comforting speech to Laura who is huddled upon the sofa. Now that we cannot hear the mother's speech, her silliness is gone and she has dignity and tragic beauty. Laura's dark hair hides her face*) *until at the end of the speech she lifts it to smile at her mother. Amanda's gestures are slow and graceful, almost dancelike, as she comforts the daughter. At the end of her speech she glances a moment at the father's picture — then withdraws through the portieres. At close of Tom's speech, Laura blows out the candles, ending the play.*)

TOM: I didn't go to the moon, I went much further — for time is the longest distance between two places — Not long after that I was fired for writing a poem on the lid of a shoebox. I left Saint Louis. I descended the steps of this fire escape for a last time and followed, from then on, in my father's footsteps, attempting to find in motion what was lost in space — I traveled around a great deal. The cities swept about me like dead leaves, leaves that were brightly colored but torn away from the branches. I would have stopped, but I was pursued by something. It always came upon me unawares, taking me altogether by surprise. Perhaps it was a familiar bit of music. Perhaps it was only a piece of transparent glass — Perhaps I am walking along a street at night, in some strange city, before I have found companions. I pass the lighted window of a shop where perfume is sold. The window is filled with pieces of colored glass, tiny transparent bottles in delicate colors, like bits of a shattered rainbow. Then all at once my sister touches my shoulder. I turn around and look into her eyes . . . Oh, Laura, Laura, I tried to leave you behind me, but I am more faithful than I intended to be! I reach for a cigarette, I cross the street, I run into the movies or a bar, I buy a drink, I speak to the nearest stranger — anything that can blow your candles out! (*Laura bends over the candles.*) — for nowadays the world is lit by lightning! Blow out your candles, Laura — and so good-bye. . . .

(*She blows the candles out.*)
(*The scene dissolves.*)

CAT ON A HOT TIN ROOF

The title of the play comes from an offhand remark made by Tennessee Williams's father, Cornelius Williams, who told his wife that she sometimes made him "as nervous as a cat on a hot tin roof." In its first production, Williams said that he saw his father in the character of Big Daddy. Reminiscence and family memory are as apparent in this play as in most of his work. The secret ingredient in the play, the secret that haunts Brick and torments Maggie, is homosexuality and Brick's relationship with his now-dead friend Skipper. Maggie seduced Skipper to find out what his relation with Brick was, and when he was unable to perform sexually with her, she felt she knew the truth. The theme of homosexuality extends to the previous inhabitants of Maggie and Brick's bedroom, the bachelors Jack Straw and Peter Ochello, the original owners of the plantation. Williams's note that the two "shared this room all their lives together" implies that their relationship was that of lovers. Williams had already become fully aware of his own homosexuality, although he revealed that personal element only obliquely in works such as *Cat on a Hot Tin Roof* until he "came out" during a television interview with David Frost in 1970.

Williams said in his *Memoirs* that this play was his favorite: "I believe that in *Cat* I reached beyond myself, in the second act, to a kind of crude eloquence of expression in Big Daddy that I have managed to give no other character of my creation." Critics have said that one reason Williams liked the play is that he was able to observe the unities of time, place, and action. Brick is confined to his room because he has broken his ankle in a drunken competition at the high school track. The central action of the play, the celebration of Big Daddy's sixty-fifth birthday, is thus brought to the bedroom, which is also at the center of one of the principal tensions in the play.

Big Daddy owns a cotton plantation and both his sons are a disappointment to him. Gooper, with his ambitious wife and his five "no-neck monsters," is weak and unappealing. Even though Gooper has become a lawyer and produced children in an effort to please his father, Big Daddy sees him as possessing none of the masculine qualities he expects in his heir. Brick, a former football player and Big Daddy's favorite, slipped into debilitating alcoholism after Skipper's death. At the time of the play he has no career and few prospects. Maggie sees that the only way she can secure Big Daddy's blessing in the form of Brick's inheritance is by having a child. And with Brick keeping a sexual distance from her, she has to find a way to help him over his grief.

Because Williams made Brick's homosexuality more or less ambiguous, some critics felt the play's structure was inconclusive. For example, they reasoned that one sexual failure on the part of Skipper did not prove anything about his sexual preference. They also felt that Maggie and Brick's sexual efforts after the curtain falls on the last act may not be successful at all.

Williams's original version of the play — before it was performed — differed from his final version. Originally Big Daddy did not appear after act 2, and Maggie and Brick did not vow to have a child or to get together at all. The play was changed because its first director, Elia Kazan, felt that Big Daddy was too brilliant a character to leave out of act 3. He argued with Williams until, against his will, Williams revised act 3 to imply a more positive ending, to bring back Big Daddy — who tells an elephant joke that caused the censor to complain in 1955 — and to make Maggie a softer, less acerbic, and much more appealing character. Williams later said that he agreed that the revision made the play stronger, although he preferred his original ending. He later published the play with two act 3s so that regional and other theaters could choose the ending they preferred.

Cat on a Hot Tin Roof in Performance

The play premiered at the Morosco Theater in New York in March 1955 with Burl Ives, then known best as a folk singer, as Big Daddy, Barbara Bel Geddes as Maggie, Ben Gazzara as Brick, and Mildred Dunnock as Big Mama. This powerful cast made the play a huge success.

It played for 694 performances in New York and then toured for another 268 performances. It won Williams his second Pulitzer Prize and his third Drama Critics' Circle Award for best play of the season. Elia Kazan not only directed the play but worked hard to help Williams alter his conception. Williams felt that the play should have a realistic production, since in his mind it was a realistic play. Kazan saw it otherwise and introduced soft lighting and a dreamy setting which established the play as expressionistic.

London theaters were banned from performing the play as written, but a theater club produced it to mixed reviews in 1956. The film version originally was to have Grace Kelly as Maggie, but Elizabeth Taylor got the role, and Paul Newman played Brick. The film version removed all suggestions of homosexuality, focusing instead on Brick's immaturity and his need to grow up to the responsibilities of marriage. It was a highly successful film for its time.

Numerous revivals of the play have appeared in many countries, including a production in Tokyo in 1970. Williams revised the ending once more — putting back the elephant joke — for a restaging of the play in 1974 in Stratford, Connecticut, and then took it to New York for twenty weeks with Elizabeth Ashley as Maggie and Keir Dullea as Brick. That version (which we use in this book) was made into a television production in 1984 with Rip Torn as Big Daddy, Kim Stanley as Big Mama, Tommy Lee Jones as Brick, and Jessica Lange as Maggie. TV critic Richard Zoglin said, "The net effect is to retain the beefed-up dimensions of Maggie and Big Daddy from Broadway, but to leave Brick, at the end, a little more stuck in what Williams describes as a 'state of spiritual despair.'" *Newsweek* described the 1990 New York production, with Howard Davies directing Kathleen Turner as Maggie, as "one of the strongest Tennessee Williams revivals ever on Broadway." Charles Durning's Big Daddy was described as "a powerhouse performance."

Tennessee Williams (1911–1983)
CAT ON A HOT TIN ROOF   *1955*

Characters

MARGARET
BRICK
MAE, *sometimes called Sister Woman*
BIG MAMA
DIXIE, *a little girl*
BIG DADDY

REVEREND TOOKER
GOOPER, *sometimes called Brother Man*
DOCTOR BAUGH, *pronounced "Baw"*
LACEY, *a Negro servant*
SOOKEY, *another*
CHILDREN

Notes for the Designer

The set is the bed-sitting-room of a plantation home in the Mississippi Delta. It is along an upstairs gallery which probably runs around the entire house; it has two pairs of very wide doors opening onto the gallery, showing white balustrades against a fair summer sky that fades into dusk and night during the course of the play, which occupies precisely the time of its performance, excepting, of course, the fifteen minutes of intermission.

Perhaps the style of the room is not what you would expect in the home of the Delta's biggest cotton planter. It is Victorian with a touch of the Far East. It hasn't changed much since it was occupied by the original owners of the place, Jack Straw and Peter Ochello, a pair of old bachelors who shared this room all their lives together. In other words, the room must evoke some ghosts; it is gently and poetically haunted by a relationship that must have involved a tenderness which was uncommon. This may be irrelevant or unnecessary, but I once saw a reproduction of a faded photograph of the verandah of Robert Louis Stevenson's home on that Samoan Island where he spent his last years, and there was a quality of tender light on weathered wood, such as porch furniture made of bamboo and wicker, exposed to tropical suns and tropical rains, which came to mind when I thought about the set for this play, bringing also to mind the grace and comfort of light, the reassurance it gives, on a late and fair afternoon in summer, the way that no matter what, even dread of death, is gently touched and soothed by it. For the set is the background for a play that deals with human extremities of emotion, and it needs that softness behind it.

The bathroom door, showing only pale-blue tile and silver towel racks, is in one side wall; the hall door in the opposite wall. Two articles of furniture need mention: a big double bed which staging should make a functional part of the set as often as suitable, the surface of which should be slightly raked to make figures on it seen more easily; and against the wall space between the two huge double doors upstage: a monumental monstrosity peculiar to our times, a *huge* console combination of radio-phonograph (hi-fi with three speakers), TV set, *and* liquor cabinet, bearing and containing many glasses and bottles, all in one piece, which is a composition of muted silver tones, and the opalescent tones of reflecting glass, a chromatic link, this thing, between the sepia (tawny gold) tones of the interior and the cool (white and blue) tones of the gallery and sky. This piece of furniture (?!), this monument, is a very complete and compact little shrine to virtually all the comforts and illusions behind which we hide from such things as the characters in the play are faced with. . . .

The set should be far less realistic than I have so far implied in this description of it. I think the walls below the ceiling should dissolve mysteriously into air; the set should be roofed by the sky; stars and moon suggested by traces of milky pallor, as if they were observed through a telescope lens out of focus.

Anything else I can think of? Oh, yes, fanlights (transoms shaped like an open glass fan) above all the doors in the set, with panes of blue and amber, and above all, the designer should take as many pains to give the actors room to move about freely (to show their restlessness, their passion for breaking out) as if it were a set for a ballet.

An evening in summer. The action is continuous, with two intermissions.

ACT 1

(*At the rise of the curtain someone is taking a shower in the bathroom, the door of which is half open. A pretty young woman, with anxious lines in her face, enters the bedroom and crosses to the bathroom door.*)

MARGARET (*shouting above roar of water*): One of those no-neck monsters hit me with a hot buttered biscuit so I have t' change!

(*Margaret's voice is both rapid and drawling. In her long speeches she has the vocal tricks of a priest delivering a liturgical chant, the lines are almost sung, always continuing a little beyond her breath so she has to gasp for another. Sometimes she intersperses the lines with a little wordless singing, such as "Da-da-daaaa!"*)

(*Water turns off and Brick calls out to her, but is still unseen. A tone of politely feigned interest, masking indifference, or worse, is characteristic of his speech with Margaret.*)

BRICK: Wha'd you say, Maggie? Water was on s' loud I couldn't hearya. . . .

MARGARET: Well, I! — just remarked that! — one of th' no-neck monsters messed up m' lovely lace dress so I got t' — cha-a-ange. . . .

(*She opens and kicks shut drawers of the dresser.*)

BRICK: Why d'ya call Gooper's kiddies no-neck monsters?

MARGARET: Because they've got no necks! Isn't that a good enough reason?

BRICK: Don't they have any necks?

MARGARET: None visible. Their fat little heads are set on their fat little bodies without a bit of connection.

BRICK: That's too bad.

MARGARET: Yes, it's too bad because you can't wring their necks if they've got no necks to wring! Isn't that right, honey?

(*She steps out of her dress, stands in a slip of ivory satin and lace.*)

Yep, they're no-neck monsters, all no-neck people are monsters . . .

(*Children shriek downstairs.*)

Hear them? Hear them screaming? I don't know where their voice boxes are located since they don't have necks. I tell you I got so nervous at that table tonight I thought I would throw back my head and utter a scream you could hear across the Arkansas border an' parts of Louisiana an' Tennessee. I said to your charming sister-in-law, Mae, honey, couldn't you feed those precious little things at a separate table with an oilcloth cover? They make such a mess an' the lace cloth looks *so* pretty! She made enormous eyes at me and said, "Ohhh, noooooo! On Big Daddy's birthday? Why, he would never forgive me!" Well, I want you to know, Big Daddy hadn't been at the table two minutes with those five no-neck monsters slobbering and drooling over their food before he threw down his fork an' shouted, "Fo' God's sake, Gooper, why don't you put them pigs at a trough in th' kitchen?" — Well, I swear, I simply could have di-ieed!

Think of it, Brick, they've got five of them and number six is coming. They've brought the whole bunch down here like animals to display at a county fair. Why, they have those children doin' tricks all the time! "Junior, show Big Daddy how you do this, show Big Daddy how you do that, say your little piece fo' Big Daddy, Sister. Show your dimples, Sugar. Brother, show Big Daddy how you stand on your head!" — It goes on all the time, along with constant little remarks and innuendos about the fact that you and I have not produced any children, are totally childless and therefore totally useless! — Of course it's comical but it's also disgusting since it's so obvious what they're up to!

BRICK (*without interest*): What are they up to, Maggie?

MARGARET: Why, you know what they're up to!

BRICK (*appearing*): No, I don't know what they're up to.

(*He stands there in the bathroom doorway drying his hair with a towel and hanging onto the towel rack because one ankle is broken, plastered and bound. He is still slim and firm as a boy. His liquor hasn't started tearing him down outside. He has the additional charm of that cool air of detachment that people have who have given up the struggle. But now and then, when disturbed, something flashes behind it, like lightning in a fair sky, which shows that at some deeper level he is far from peaceful. Perhaps in a stronger light he would show some signs of deliquescence, but the fading, still warm light from the gallery treats him gently.*)

MARGARET: I'll tell you what they're up to, boy of mine! — They're up to cutting you out of your father's estate, and —

(*She freezes momentarily before her next remark. Her voice drops as if it were somehow a personally embarrassing admission.*)

— Now we know that Big Daddy's dyin' of — cancer. . . .

(*There are voices on the lawn below: long-drawn calls across distance. Margaret raises her lovely bare arms and powders her armpits with a light sigh.*)

(*She adjusts the angle of a magnifying mirror to straighten an eyelash, then rises fretfully saying:*)

There's so much light in the room it —

BRICK (*softly but sharply*): Do we?

MARGARET: Do we what?

BRICK: Know Big Daddy's dyin' of cancer?

MARGARET: Got the report today.

BRICK: Oh . . .

MARGARET (*letting down bamboo blinds which cast long, gold-fretted shadows over the room*): Yep, got th' report just now . . . it didn't surprise me, Baby. . . .

(*Her voice has range, and music; sometimes it drops low as a boy's and you have a sudden image of her playing boy's games as a child.*)

I recognized the symptoms soon's we got here last spring and I'm willin' to bet you that Brother Man and his wife were pretty sure of it, too. That more than likely explains why their usual summer migration to the coolness of the Great Smokies was passed up this summer in favor of — hustlin' down here ev'ry whipstitch with their whole screamin' tribe! And why so many allusions have been made to Rainbow Hill lately. You know what Rainbow Hill is? Place that's famous for treatin' alcoholics an' dope fiends in the movies!

BRICK: I'm not in the movies.

MARGARET: No, and you don't take dope. Otherwise you're a perfect candidate for Rainbow Hill, Baby, and that's where they aim to ship you — over my dead body! Yep, over my dead body they'll ship you there, but nothing would please them better. Then Brother Man could get a-hold of the purse strings and dole out remittances to us, maybe get power of attorney and sign checks for us and cut off our credit wherever, whenever he wanted! Son-of-a-bitch! — How'd you like that, Baby? — Well, you've been doin' just about ev'rything in your power to bring it about, you've just been doin' ev'rything you can think of to aid and abet them in this scheme of theirs! Quittin' work, devoting yourself to the occupation of drinkin'! — Breakin' your ankle last night on the high school athletic field: doin' what? Jumpin' hurdles? At two or three in the morning? Just fantastic! Got in the paper. *Clarksdale Register* carried a nice little item about it, human interest story about a well-known former athlete stagin' a one-man track meet on the Glorious Hill High School athletic field last night, but was slightly out of condition and didn't clear the first hurdle! Brother Man Gooper claims he exercised his influence t' keep it from goin' out over AP or UP or every goddam "P."

But, Brick? You still have one big advantage!

(*During the above swift flood of words, Brick has reclined with contrapuntal leisure on the snowy surface of the bed and has rolled over carefully on his side or belly.*)

BRICK (*wryly*): Did you *say* something, Maggie?

MARGARET: Big Daddy dotes on you, honey. And he can't stand Brother Man and Brother Man's wife, that monster of fertility, Mae. Know how I know? By little expressions that flicker over his face when that woman is holding fo'th on one of her choice topics such as — how she refused twilight sleep!° — when the twins were delivered! Because she feels motherhood's an experience that a woman ought to experience fully! — in order to fully appreciate the wonder and beauty of it! HAH! — and how she made Brother Man come in an' stand beside her in the delivery room so he would not miss out on the "wonder and beauty" of it either! — producin' those no-neck monsters. . . .

(*A speech of this kind would be antipathetic from almost anybody but Margaret; she makes it oddly funny, because her eyes constantly twinkle and her*

---

twilight sleep: Anesthesia.

---

voice shakes with laughter which is basically indulgent.*)

— Big Daddy shares my attitude toward those two! As for me, well — I give him a laugh now and then and he tolerates me. In fact! — I sometimes suspect that Big Daddy harbors a little unconscious "lech" fo' me. . . .

BRICK: What makes you think that Big Daddy has a lech for you, Maggie?

MARGARET: Way he always drops his eyes down my body when I'm talkin' to him, drops his eyes to my boobs an' licks his old chops! Ha ha!

BRICK: That kind of talk is disgusting.

MARGARET: Did anyone ever tell you that you're an ass-aching Puritan, Brick?

I think it's mighty fine that that ole fellow, on the doorstep of death, still takes in my shape with what I think is deserved appreciation!

And you wanta know something else? Big Daddy didn't know how many little Maes and Goopers had been produced! "How many kids have you got?" he asked at the table, just like Brother Man and his wife were new acquaintances to him! Big Mama said he was jokin', but that ole boy wasn't jokin', Lord, no!

And when they infawmed him that they had five already and were turning out number six! — the news seemed to come as a sort of unpleasant surprise . . .

(*Children yell below.*)

Scream, monsters!

(*Turns to Brick with a sudden, gay, charming smile which fades as she notices that he is not looking at her but into fading gold space with a troubled expression.*)

(*It is constant rejection that makes her humor "bitchy."*)

Yes, you should of been at that supper-table, Baby.

(*Whenever she calls him "baby" the word is a soft caress.*)

Y'know, Big Daddy, bless his ole sweet soul, he's the dearest ole thing in the world, but he does hunch over his food as if he preferred not to notice anything else. Well, Mae an' Gooper were side by side at the table, direckly across from Big Daddy, watchin' his face like hawks while they jawed an' jabbered about the cuteness an' brillance of th' no-neck monsters!

(*She giggles with a hand fluttering at her throat and her breast and her long throat arched.*)

(*She comes downstage and recreates the scene with voice and gesture.*)

And the no-neck monsters were ranged around the table, some in high chairs and some on th' *Books of Knowledge,* all in fancy little paper caps in honor of Big Daddy's birthday, and all through dinner, well, I want you to know that Brother Man an' his partner never once, for one moment, stopped exchanging pokes an' pinches an' kicks an' signs an' signals! — Why, they were like a couple of cardsharps fleecing a sucker. — Even Big Mama, bless her ole sweet soul, she isn't th' quickest an' brightest thing in the world, she finally noticed, at last, an' said to Gooper, "Gooper, what are you an' Mae makin' all these signs at each other about?" — I swear t' goodness, I nearly choked on my chicken!

(*Margaret, back at the dressing table, still doesn't see Brick. He is watching her with a look that is not quite definable — Amused? shocked? contemptuous? — part of those and part of something else.*)

Y'know — your brother Gooper still cherishes the illusion he took a giant step up on the social ladder when he married Miss Mae Flynn of the Memphis Flynns.

But I have a piece of Spanish news for Gooper. The Flynns never had a thing in this world but money and they lost that, they were nothing at all but fairly successful climbers. Of course, Mae Flynn came out in Memphis eight years before I made my debut in Nashville, but I had friends at Ward-Belmont who came from Memphis and they used to come to see me and I used to go to see them for Christmas and spring vacations, and so I know who rates an' who doesn't rate in Memphis society. Why, y'know ole Papa Flynn, he barely escaped doing time in the Federal pen for shady manipulations on th' stock market when his chain stores crashed, and as for Mae having been a cotton carnival queen, as they remind us so often, lest we forget, well, that's one honor that I don't envy her for! — Sit on a brass throne on a tacky float an' ride down Main Street, smilin', bowin', and blowin' kisses to all the trash on the street —

(*She picks out a pair of jeweled sandals and rushes to the dressing table.*)

Why, year before last, when Susan McPheeters was singled out fo' that honor, y'know what happened to her? Y'know what happened to poor little Susie McPheeters?

BRICK (*absently*): No. What happened to little Susie McPheeters?

MARGARET: Somebody spit tobacco juice in her face.

BRICK (*dreamily*): Somebody spit tobacco juice in her face?

MARGARET: That's right, some old drunk leaned out of a window in the Hotel Gayoso and yelled, "Hey, Queen, hey, hey, there, Queenie!" Poor Susie looked up and flashed him a radiant smile and he shot out a squirt of tobacco juice right in poor Susie's face.

BRICK: Well, what d'you know about that.

MARGARET (*gaily*): What do I know about it? I was there, I saw it!

BRICK (*absently*): Must have been kind of funny.

MARGARET: Susie didn't think so. Had hysterics. Screamed like a banshee. They had to stop th' parade an' remove her from her throne an' go on with —

(*She catches sight of him in the mirror, gasps slightly, wheels about to face him. Count ten.*)

— Why are you looking at me like that?

BRICK (*whistling softly, now*): Like what, Maggie?

MARGARET (*intensely, fearfully*): The way y' were lookin' at me just now, befo' I caught your eye in the mirror and you started t' whistle! I don't know how t' describe it but it froze my blood! — I've caught you lookin' at me like that so often lately. What are you thinkin' of when you look at me like that?

BRICK: I wasn't conscious of lookin' at you, Maggie.

MARGARET: Well, I was conscious of it! What were you thinkin'?

BRICK: I don't remember thinking of anything, Maggie.

MARGARET: Don't you think I know that —? Don't you —? — Think I know that —?

BRICK (*cooly*): Know *what,* Maggie?

MARGARET (*struggling for expression*): That I've gone through this — *hideous!* — *transformation,* become — *hard!* Frantic!

(*Then she adds, almost tenderly:*)

— cruel!!
That's what you've been observing in me lately. How could y' help but observe it? That's all right. I'm not — thin-skinned any more, can't afford t' be thin-skinned any more.

(*She is now recovering her power.*)

— But Brick? Brick?

BRICK: Did you say something?

MARGARET: I was *goin'* t' say something: that I get — lonely. Very!

BRICK: Ev'rybody gets that . . .

MARGARET: Living with someone you love can be

lonelier — than living entirely *alone!* — if the one that y' love doesn't love you. . . .

(*There is a pause. Brick hobbles downstage and asks, without looking at her:*)

BRICK: Would you like to live alone, Maggie?

(*Another pause: then — after she has caught a quick, hurt breath:*)

MARGARET: No! — God! — I wouldn't!

(*Another gasping breath. She forcibly controls what must have been an impulse to cry out. We see her deliberately, very forcibly, going all the way back to the world in which you can talk about ordinary matters.*)

Did you have a nice shower?
BRICK: Uh-huh.
MARGARET: Was the water cool?
BRICK: No.
MARGARET: But it made y' feel fresh, huh?
BRICK: Fresher. . . .
MARGARET: I know something would make y' feel *much* fresher!
BRICK: What?
MARGARET: An alcohol rub. Or cologne, a rub with cologne!
BRICK: That's good after a workout but I haven't been workin' out, Maggie.
MARGARET: You've kept in good shape, though.
BRICK (*indifferently*): You think so, Maggie?
MARGARET: I always thought drinkin' men lost their looks, but I was plainly mistaken.
BRICK (*wryly*): Why, thanks, Maggie.
MARGARET: You're the only drinkin' man I know that it never seems t' put fat on.
BRICK: I'm gettin' softer, Maggie.
MARGARET: Well, sooner or later it's bound to soften you up. It was just beginning to soften up Skipper when —

(*She stops short.*)

I'm sorry. I never could keep my fingers off a sore — I wish you *would* lose your looks. If you did it would make the martyrdom of Saint Maggie a little more bearable. But no such goddam luck. I actually believe you've gotten better looking since you've gone on the bottle. Yeah, a person who didn't know you would think you'd never had a tense nerve in your body or a strained muscle.

(*There are sounds of croquet on the lawn below: the click of mallets, light voices, near and distant.*)

Of course, you always had that detached quality as if you were playing a game without much con-cern over whether you won or lost, and now that you've lost the game, not lost but just quit playing, you have that rare sort of charm that usually only happens in very old or hopelessly sick people, the charm of the defeated. — You look so cool, so cool, so enviably cool.
REVEREND TOOKER (*offstage right*): Now looka here, boy, lemme show you how to get outa that!
MARGARET: They're playing croquet. The moon has appeared and it's white, just beginning to turn a little bit yellow. . . .
    You were a wonderful lover. . . .
    Such a wonderful person to go to bed with, and I think mostly because you were really indifferent to it. Isn't that right? Never had any anxiety about it, did it naturally, easily, slowly, with absolute confidence and perfect calm, more like opening a door for a lady or seating her at a table than giving expression to any longing for her. Your indifference made you wonderful at lovemaking — *strange?* — but true. . . .
REVEREND TOOKER: Oh! That's a beauty.
DOCTOR BAUGH: Yeah. I got you boxed.
MARGARET: You know, if I thought you would never, never, *never* make love to me again — I would go downstairs to the kitchen and pick out the longest and sharpest knife I could find and stick it straight into my heart, I swear that I would!
REVEREND TOOKER: Watch out, you're gonna miss it.
DOCTOR BAUGH: You just don't know me, boy!
MARGARET: But one thing I don't have is the charm of the defeated, my hat is still in the ring, and I am determined to win!

(*There is the sound of croquet mallets hitting croquet balls.*)

REVEREND TOOKER: Mmm — You're too slippery for me.
MARGARET: — What is the victory of a cat on a hot tin roof? — I wish I knew. . . .
    Just staying on it, I guess, as long as she can. . . .
DOCTOR BAUGH: Jus' like an eel, boy, jus' like an eel!

(*More croquet sounds.*)

MARGARET: Later tonight I'm going to tell you I love you an' maybe by that time you'll be drunk enough to believe me. Yes, they're playing croquet. . . .
    Big Daddy is dying of cancer. . . .
    What were you thinking of when I caught you looking at me like that? Were you thinking of Skipper?

(*Brick takes up his crutch, rises.*)

Oh, excuse me, forgive me, but laws of silence don't work! No, laws of silence don't work. . . .

ABOVE LEFT: Maggie (Elizabeth
Ashley) in the 1974 American
Shakespeare Theater production
of *Cat on a Hot Tin Roof*.
LEFT: Brick (Keir Dullea) and
Maggie. ABOVE: Maggie and
Big Daddy (Fred Gwynne).

(*Brick crosses to the bar, takes a quick drink, and rubs his head with a towel.*)

Laws of silence don't work. . . .

When something is festering in your memory or your imagination, laws of silence don't work, it's just like shutting a door and locking it on a house on fire in hope of forgetting that the house is burning. But not facing a fire doesn't put it out. Silence about a thing just magnifies it. It grows and festers in silence, becomes malignant. . . .

(*He drops his crutch.*)

BRICK: Give me my crutch.

(*He has stopped rubbing his hair dry but still stands hanging onto the towel rack in a white towel-cloth robe.*)

MARGARET: Lean on me.
BRICK: No, just give me my crutch.
MARGARET: Lean on my shoulder.
BRICK: *I don't want to lean on your shoulder, I want my crutch!*

(*This is spoken like sudden lightning.*)

Are you going to give me my crutch or do I have to get down on my knees on the floor and —
MARGARET: *Here, here, take it, take it!*

(*She has thrust the crutch at him.*)

BRICK (*hobbling out*): Thanks . . .
MARGARET: We mustn't scream at each other, the walls in this house have ears. . . .

(*He hobbles directly to liquor cabinet to get a new drink.*)

— but that's the first time I've heard you raise your voice in a long time, Brick. A crack in the wall? — Of composure?

— I think that's a good sign. . . .
A sign of nerves in a player on the defensive!

(*Brick turns and smiles at her coolly over his fresh drink.*)

BRICK: It just hasn't happened yet, Maggie.
MARGARET: What?
BRICK: The click I get in my head when I've had enough of this stuff to make me peaceful. . . .
Will you do me a favor?
MARGARET: Maybe I will. What favor?
BRICK: Just, just keep your voice down!
MARGARET (*in a hoarse whisper*): I'll do you that favor, I'll speak in a whisper, if not shut up completely, if *you* will do *me* a favor and make that drink your last one till after the party.

BRICK: What party?
MARGARET: Big Daddy's birthday party.
BRICK: Is this Big Daddy's birthday?
MARGARET: You know this is Big Daddy's birthday!
BRICK: No, I don't, I forgot it.
MARGARET: Well, I remembered it for you. . . .

(*They are both speaking as breathlessly as a pair of kids after a fight, drawing deep exhausted breaths and looking at each other with faraway eyes, shaking and panting together as if they had broken apart from a violent struggle.*)

BRICK: Good for you, Maggie.
MARGARET: You just have to scribble a few lines on this card.
BRICK: You scribble something, Maggie.
MARGARET: It's got to be your handwriting; it's your present, I've given him my present; it's got to be your handwriting!

(*The tension between them is building again, the voices becoming shrill once more.*)

BRICK: I didn't get him a present.
MARGARET: I got one for you.
BRICK: All right. You write the card, then.
MARGARET: And have him know you didn't remember his birthday?
BRICK: I didn't remember his birthday.
MARGARET: You don't have to prove you didn't!
BRICK: I don't want to fool him about it.
MARGARET: Just write "Love, Brick!" for God's —
BRICK: No.
MARGARET: You've *got* to!
BRICK: I don't have to do anything I don't want to do. You keep forgetting the conditions on which I agreed to stay on living with you.
MARGARET (*out before she knows it*): I'm not living with you. We occupy the same cage.
BRICK: You've got to remember the conditions agreed on.
SONNY (*offstage*): Mommy, give it to me. I had it first.
MAE: Hush.
MARGARET: They're impossible conditions!
BRICK: Then why don't you —?
SONNY: I want it, I want it!
MAE: Get away!
MARGARET: HUSH! Who is out there? Is somebody at the door?

(*There are footsteps in hall.*)

MAE (*outside*): May I enter a moment?
MARGARET: Oh, *you!* Sure. Come in, Mae.

(*Mae enters bearing aloft the bow of a young lady's archery set.*)

MAE: Brick, is this thing yours?

MARGARET: Why, Sister Woman — that's my Diana Trophy. Won it at the intercollegiate archery contest on the Ole Miss campus.

MAE: It's a mighty dangerous thing to leave exposed round a house full of nawmal rid-blooded children attracted t'weapons.

MARGARET: "Nawmal rid-blooded children attracted t'weapons" ought t'be taught to keep their hands off things that don't belong to them.

MAE: Maggie, honey, if you had children of your own you'd know how funny that is. Will you please lock this up and put the key out of reach?

MARGARET: Sister Woman, nobody is plotting the destruction of your kiddies. — Brick and I still have our special archers' license. We're goin' deer-huntin' on Moon Lake as soon as the season starts. I love to run with dogs through chilly woods, run, run leap over obstructions —

(*She goes into the closet carrying the bow.*)

MAE: How's the injured ankle, Brick?

BRICK: Doesn't hurt. Just itches.

MAE: Oh, my! Brick — Brick, you should've been downstairs after supper! Kiddies put on a show. Polly played the piano, Buster an' Sonny drums, an' then they turned out the lights an' Dixie an' Trixie puhfawmed a toe dance in fairy costume with *spahkluhs!* Big Daddy just beamed! He just beamed!

MARGARET (*from the closet with a sharp laugh*): Oh, I bet. It breaks my heart that we missed it!

(*She reenters.*)

But Mae? Why did y'give dawgs' names to all your kiddies?

MAE: *Dogs'* names?

MARGARET (*sweetly*): Dixie, Trixie, Buster, Sonny, Polly! — Sounds like four dogs and a parrot . . .

MAE: Maggie?

(*Margaret turns with a smile.*)

Why are you so catty?

MARGARET: Cause I'm a cat! But why can't *you* take a joke, Sister Woman?

MAE: Nothin' pleases me more than a joke that's funny. You know the real names of our kiddies. Buster's real name is Robert. Sonny's real name is Saunders. Trixie's real name is Marlene and Dixie's —

(*Gooper downstairs calls for her. "Hey, Mae! Sister Woman, intermission is over!" — She rushes to door, saying:*)

Intermission is over! See ya later!

MARGARET: I wonder what Dixie's real name is?

BRICK: Maggie, being catty doesn't help things any . . .

MARGARET: I know! *WHY!* — Am I so catty? — Cause I'm consumed with envy an' eaten up with longing? — Brick, I'm going to lay out your beautiful Shantung silk suit from Rome and one of your monogrammed silk shirts. I'll put your cuff links in it, those lovely star sapphires I get you to wear so rarely. . . .

BRICK: I can't get trousers on over this plaster cast.

MARGARET: Yes, you can, I'll help you.

BRICK: I'm not going to get dressed, Maggie.

MARGARET: Will you just put on a pair of white silk pajamas?

BRICK: Yes, I'll do that, Maggie.

MARGARET: *Thank* you, thank you so *much!*

BRICK: Don't mention it.

MARGARET: *Oh, Brick!* How long does it have t' go on? This punishment? Haven't I done time enough, haven't I served my term, can't I apply for a — pardon?

BRICK: Maggie, you're spoiling my liquor. Lately your voice always sounds like you'd been running upstairs to warn somebody that the house was on fire!

MARGARET: Well, no wonder, no wonder. Y'know what I feel like, Brick?

I feel all the time like a cat on a hot tin roof!

BRICK: Then jump off the roof, jump off it, cats can jump off roofs and land on their four feet uninjured!

MARGARET: Oh, yes!

BRICK: Do it! — fo' God's sake, do it . . .

MARGARET: Do what?

BRICK: Take a lover!

MARGARET: I can't see a man but you! Even with my eyes closed, I just see you! Why don't you get ugly, Brick, why don't you please get fat or ugly or something so I could stand it?

(*She rushes to hall door, opens it, listens.*)

The concert is still going on! Bravo, no-necks, bravo!

(*She slams and locks door fiercely.*)

BRICK: What did you lock the door for?

MARGARET: To give us a little privacy for a while.

BRICK: You know better, Maggie.

MARGARET: No, I don't know better. . . .

(*She rushes to gallery doors, draws the rose-silk drapes across them.*)

BRICK: Don't make a fool of yourself.

MARGARET: I don't mind makin' a fool of myself over you!

BRICK: I mind, Maggie. I feel embarrassed for you.

MARGARET: Feel embarrassed! But don't continue my torture. I can't live on and on under these circumstances.

BRICK: You agreed to —

MARGARET: I know but —

BRICK: — Accept that condition!

MARGARET: *I CAN'T! CAN'T! CAN'T!*

(*She seizes his shoulder.*)

BRICK: Let go!

(*He breaks away from her and seizes the small boudoir chair and raises it like a lion-tamer facing a big circus cat.*)

(*Count five. She stares at him with her fist pressed to her mouth, then bursts into shrill, almost hysterical laughter. He remains grave for a moment, then grins and puts the chair down.*)

(*Big Mama calls through closed door.*)

BIG MAMA: Son? Son? Son?

BRICK: What is it, Big Mama?

BIG MAMA (*outside*): Oh, son! We got the most wonderful news about Big Daddy. I just had t' run up an' tell you right this —

(*She rattles the knob.*)

— What's this door doin', locked, faw? You all think there's robbers in the house?

MARGARET: Big Mama, Brick is dressin', he's not dressed yet.

BIG MAMA: That's all right, it won't be the first time I've seen Brick not dressed. Come on, open this door!

(*Margaret, with a grimace, goes to unlock and open the hall door, as Brick hobbles rapidly to the bathroom and kicks the door shut. Big Mama has disappeared from the hall.*)

MARGARET: Big Mama?

(*Big Mama appears through the opposite gallery doors behind Margaret, huffing and puffing like an old bulldog. She is a short, stout woman; her sixty years and 170 pounds have left her somewhat breathless most of the time; she's always tensed like a boxer, or rather, a Japanese wrestler. Her "family" was maybe a little superior to Big Daddy's, but not much. She wears a black or silver lace dress and at least half a million in flashy gems. She is very sincere.*)

BIG MAMA (*loudly, startling Margaret*): Here — I come through Gooper's and Mae's gall'ry door. Where's Brick? *Brick* — Hurry on out of there, son, I just have a second and want to give you the news about Big Daddy. — I hate locked doors in a house. . . .

MARGARET (*with affected lightness*): I've noticed you do, Big Mama, but people have got to have *some* moments of privacy, don't they?

BIG MAMA: No, ma'am, not in *my* house. (*Without pause.*) Whacha took off you' dress faw? I thought that little lace dress was so sweet on yuh, honey.

MARGARET: I thought it looked sweet on me, too, but one of m' cute little table-partners used it for a napkin so —!

BIG MAMA (*picking up stockings on floor*): What?

MARGARET: You know, Big Mama, Mae and Gooper's so touchy about those children — thanks, Big Mama . . .

(*Big Mama has thrust the picked-up stockings in Margaret's hand with a grunt.*)

— that you just don't dare to suggest there's any room for improvement in their —

BIG MAMA: Brick, hurry out! — Shoot, Maggie, you just don't like children.

MARGARET: I do SO like children! Adore them! — well brought up!

BIG MAMA (*gentle — loving*): Well, why don't you have some and bring them up well, then, instead of all the time pickin' on Gooper's an' Mae's?

GOOPER (*shouting up the stairs*): Hey, hey, Big Mama, Betsy an' Hugh got to go, waitin' t' tell yuh g'by!

BIG MAMA: Tell 'em to hold their hawses, I'll be right down in a jiffy!

GOOPER: Yes ma'am!

(*She turns to the bathroom door and calls out.*)

BIG MAMA: Son? Can you hear me in there?

(*There is a muffled answer.*)

We just got the full report from the laboratory at the Ochsner Clinic, completely negative, son, ev'rything negative, right on down the line! Nothin' a-tall's wrong with him but some little functional thing called a spastic colon. Can you hear me, son?

MARGARET: He can hear you, Big Mama.

BIG MAMA: Then why don't he say something? God Almighty, a piece of news like that should make him shout. It made *me* shout, I can tell you. I shouted and sobbed and fell right down on my knees! — Look!

(*She pulls up her skirt.*)

See the bruises where I hit my kneecaps? Took both doctors to haul me back on my feet!

(*She laughs — she always laughs like hell at herself.*)

Big Daddy was furious with me! But ain't that wonderful news?

(*Facing bathroom again, she continues:*)

After all the anxiety we been through to git a report like that on Big Daddy's birthday? Big Daddy tried to hide how much of a load that news took off his mind, but didn't fool *me*. He was mighty close to crying about it *himself!*

(*Good-byes are shouted downstairs, and she rushes to door.*)

GOOPER: Big Mama!

BIG MAMA: *Hold those people down there, don't let them go!* — Now, git dressed, we're all comin' up to this room fo' Big Daddy's birthday party because of your ankle. — How's his ankle, Maggie?

MARGARET: Well, he broke it, Big Mama.

BIG MAMA: I know he broke it.

(*A phone is ringing in hall. A Negro voice answers: "Mistuh Polly's res'dence."*)

I mean does it hurt him much still.

MARGARET: I'm afraid I can't give you that information, Big Mama. You'll have to ask Brick if it hurts much still or not.

SOOKEY (*in the hall*): It's Memphis, Mizz Polly, it's Miss Sally in Memphis.

BIG MAMA: Awright, Sookey.

(*Big Mama rushes into the hall and is heard shouting on the phone:*)

Hello, Miss Sally. How are you, Miss Sally? — Yes, well, I was just gonna call you about it. *Shoot!* —

MARGARET: Brick, don't!

(*Big Mama raises her voice to a bellow.*)

BIG MAMA: Miss Sally? *Don't ever call me from the Gayoso Lobby, too much talk goes on in that hotel lobby, no wonder you can't hear me!* Now listen, Miss Sally. They's nothin' serious wrong with Big Daddy. We got the report just now, they's nothin' wrong but a thing called a — spastic! SPASTIC! — colon . . .

(*She appears at the hall door and calls to Margaret.*)

— Maggie, come out here and talk to that fool on the phone. I'm shouted breathless!

MARGARET (*goes out and is heard sweetly at phone*): Miss Sally? This is Brick's wife, Maggie. So nice to hear your voice. Can you hear *mine*? Well, good! — Big Mama just wanted you to know that they've got the report from the Ochsner Clinic and what Big Daddy has is a spastic colon. Yes. Spastic colon, Miss Sally. That's right, spastic colon. *G'bye, Miss Sally, hope I'll see you real soon!*

(*Hangs up a little before Miss Sally was probably ready to terminate the talk. She returns through the hall door.*)

She heard me perfectly. I've discovered with deaf people the thing to do is not shout at them but just enunciate clearly. My rich old Aunt Cornelia was deaf as the dead but I could make her hear me just by sayin' each word slowly, distinctly, close to her ear. I read her the *Commercial Appeal* ev'ry night, read her the classified ads in it, even, she never missed a word of it. But was she a mean ole thing! Know what I got when she died? Her unexpired subscriptions to five magazines and the Book-of-the-Month Club and a LIBRARY full of ev'ry dull book ever written! All else went to her hellcat of a sister . . . meaner than she was, even!

(*Big Mama has been straightening things up in the room during this speech.*)

BIG MAMA (*closing closet door on discarded clothes*): Miss Sally sure is a case! Big Daddy says she's always got her hand out fo' something. He's not mistaken. That poor ole thing always has her hand out fo' somethin'. I don't think Big Daddy gives her as much as he should.

GOOPER: Big Mama! Come on now! Betsy and Hugh can't wait no longer!

BIG MAMA (*shouting*): I'm comin'!

(*She starts out. At the hall door, turns and jerks a forefinger, first toward the bathroom door, then toward the liquor cabinet, meaning: "Has Brick been drinking?" Margaret pretends not to understand, cocks her head and raises her brows as if the pantomimic performance was completely mystifying to her.*)

(*Big Mama rushes back to Margaret:*)

Shoot! Stop playin' so dumb! — I mean has he been drinkin' that stuff much yet?

MARGARET (*with a little laugh*): Oh! I think he had a highball after supper.

BIG MAMA: Don't laugh about it! — Some single men stop drinkin' when they git married and others start! Brick never touched liquor before he —!

MARGARET (*crying out*): THAT'S NOT FAIR!

BIG MAMA: Fair or not fair I want to ask you a question, one question: D'you make Brick happy in bed?

MARGARET: Why don't you ask if he makes *me* happy in bed?

BIG MAMA: Because I know that —

MARGARET: *It works both ways!*

BIG MAMA: Something's not right! You're childless and my son drinks!

GOOPER: Come on, Big Mama!

(*Gooper has called her downstairs and she has rushed to the door on the line above. She turns at the door and points at the bed.*)

— When a marriage goes on the rocks, the rocks are *there*, right *there*!

MARGARET: *That's* —

(*Big Mama has swept out of the room and slammed the door.*)

— not — *fair* . . .

(*Margaret is alone, completely alone, and she feels it. She draws in, hunches her shoulders, raises her arms with fists clenched, shuts her eyes tight as a child about to be stabbed with a vaccination needle. When she opens her eyes again, what she sees is the long oval mirror and she rushes straight to it, stares into it with a grimace and says: "Who are you?" — Then she crouches a little and answers herself in a different voice which is high, thin, mocking: "I am Maggie the Cat!" — Straightens quickly as bathroom door opens a little and Brick calls out to her.*)

BRICK: Has Big Mama gone?

MARGARET: She's gone.

(*He opens the bathroom door and hobbles out, with his liquor glass now empty, straight to the liquor cabinet. He is whistling softly. Margaret's head pivots on her long, slender throat to watch him.*)

(*She raises a hand uncertainly to the base of her throat, as if it was difficult for her to swallow, before she speaks:*)

You know, our sex life didn't just peter out in the usual way, it was cut off short, long before the natural time for it to, and it's going to revive again, just as sudden as that. I'm confident of it. That's what I'm keeping myself attractive for. For the time when you'll see me again like other men see me. Yes, like other men see me. They still see me, Brick, and they like what they see. Uh-huh. Some of them would give their —
    Look, Brick!

(*She stands before the long oval mirror, touches her breast and then her hips with her two hands.*)

How high my body stays on me! — Nothing has fallen on me — not a fraction. . . .

(*Her voice is soft and trembling: a pleading child's. At this moment as he turns to glance at her — a look which is like a player passing a ball to another player,*

third down and goal to go — she has to capture the audience in a grip so tight that she can hold it till the first intermission without any lapse of attention.)

Other men still want me. My face looks strained, sometimes, but I've kept my figure as well as you've kept yours, and men admire it. I still turn heads on the street. Why, last week in Memphis everywhere that I went men's eyes burned holes in my clothes, at the country club and in restaurants and department stores, there wasn't a man I met or walked by that didn't just eat me up with his eyes and turn around when I passed him and look back at me. Why, at Alice's party for her New York cousins, the best-lookin' man in the crowd — followed me upstairs and tried to force his way in the powder room with me, followed me to the door and tried to force his way in!

BRICK: Why didn't you let him, Maggie?

MARGARET: Because I'm not that common, for one thing. Not that I wasn't almost tempted to. You like to know who it was? It was Sonny Boy Maxwell, that's who!

BRICK: Oh, yeah, Sonny Boy Maxwell, he was a good end-runner but had a little injury to his back and had to quit.

MARGARET: He has no injury now and has no wife and still has a lech for me!

BRICK: I see no reason to lock him out of a powder room in that case.

MARGARET: And have someone catch me at it? I'm not that stupid. Oh, I might sometime cheat on you with someone, since you're so insultingly eager to have me do it! — But if I do, you can be damned sure it will be in a place and a time where no one but me and the man could possibly know. Because I'm not going to give you any excuse to divorce me for being unfaithful or anything else. . . .

BRICK: Maggie, I wouldn't divorce you for being unfaithful or anything else. Don't you know that? Hell. I'd be relieved to know that you'd found yourself a lover.

MARGARET: Well, I'm taking no chances. No, I'd rather stay on this hot tin roof.

BRICK: A hot tin roof's 'n uncomfo'table place t' stay on. . . .

(*He starts to whistle softly.*)

MARGARET (*through his whistle*): Yeah, but I can stay on it just as long as I have to.

BRICK: You could leave me, Maggie.

(*He resumes whistle. She wheels about to glare at him.*)

MARGARET: *Don't want to and will not!* Besides if I

did, you don't have a cent to pay for it but what you get from Big Daddy and he's dying of cancer!

(*For the first time a realization of Big Daddy's doom seems to penetrate to Brick's consciousness, visibly, and he looks at Margaret.*)

BRICK: Big Mama just said he *wasn't*, that the report was okay.

MARGARET: That's what she thinks because she got the same story that they gave Big Daddy. And was just as taken in by it as he was, poor ole things. . . .

But tonight they're going to tell her the truth about it. When Big Daddy goes to bed, they're going to tell her that he is dying of cancer.

(*She slams the dresser drawer.*)

— It's malignant and it's terminal.

BRICK: Does Big Daddy know it?

MARGARET: Hell, do they *ever* know it? Nobody says, "You're dying." You have to fool them. They have to fool *themselves*.

BRICK: Why?

MARGARET: *Why?* Because human beings dream of life everlasting, that's the reason! But most of them want it on earth and not in heaven.

(*He gives a short, hard laugh at her touch of humor.*)

Well. . . . (*She touches up her mascara.*) That's how it is, anyhow. . . . (*She looks about.*) Where did I put down my cigarette? Don't want to burn up the home-place, at least not with Mae and Gooper and their five monsters in it!

(*She has found it and sucks at it greedily. Blows out smoke and continues:*)

So this is Big Daddy's last birthday. And Mae and Gooper, they know it, oh, *they* know it, all right. They got the first information from the Ochsner Clinic. That's why they rushed down here with their no-neck monsters. Because. Do you know something? Big Daddy's made no will? Big Daddy's never made out any will in his life, and so this campaign's afoot to impress him, forcibly as possible, with the fact that you drink and I've borne no children!

(*He continues to stare at her a moment, then mutters something sharp but not audible and hobbles rather rapidly out onto the long gallery in the fading, much faded, gold light.*)

MARGARET (*continuing her liturgical chant*): Y'know, I'm *fond* of Big Daddy, I am genuinely fond of that old man, I really *am*, you know. . . .

BRICK (*faintly, vaguely*): Yes, I know you are. . . .

MARGARET: I've always sort of admired him in spite of his coarseness, his four-letter words and so forth. Because Big Daddy *is* what he *is*, and he makes no bones about it. He hasn't turned gentleman farmer, he's still a Mississippi redneck, as much of a redneck as he must have been when he was just overseer here on the old Jack Straw and Peter Ochello place. But he got hold of it an' built it into th' biggest an' finest plantation in the Delta. — I've always *liked* Big Daddy. . . .

(*She crosses to the proscenium.*)

Well, this is Big Daddy's last birthday. I'm sorry about it. But I'm facing the facts. It takes money to take care of a drinker and that's the office that I've been elected to lately.

BRICK: You don't have to take care of me.

MARGARET: Yes, I do. Two people in the same boat have got to take care of each other. At least you want money to buy more Echo Spring when this supply is exhausted, or will you be satisfied with a ten-cent beer?

Mae an' Gooper are plannin' to freeze us out of Big Daddy's estate because you drink and I'm childless. But we can defeat that plan. We're *going* to defeat that plan!

Brick, y'know, I've been so God damn disgustingly poor all my life! — That's the *truth*, Brick!

BRICK: I'm not sayin' it isn't.

MARGARET: Always had to suck up to people I couldn't stand because they had money and I was poor as Job's turkey. You don't know what that's like. Well, I'll tell you, it's like you would feel a thousand miles away from Echo Spring! — And had to get back to it on that broken ankle . . . without a crutch!

That's how it feels to be as poor as Job's turkey and have to suck up to relatives that you hated because they had money and all you had was a bunch of hand-me-down clothes and a few old moldly three-percent government bonds. My daddy loved his liquor, he fell in love with his liquor the way you've fallen in love with Echo Spring! — And my poor Mama, having to maintain some semblance of social position, to keep appearances up, on an income of one hundred and fifty dollars a month on those old government bonds!

When I came out, the year that I made my debut, I had just two evening dresses! One Mother made me from a pattern in *Vogue*, the other a hand-me-down from a snotty rich cousin I hated!

— The dress that I married you in was my grandmother's weddin' gown. . . .

So that's why I'm like a cat on a hot tin roof!

(*Brick is still on the gallery. Someone below calls up to him in a warm Negro voice, "Hiya, Mistuh Brick, how yuh feelin'?" Brick raises his liquor glass as if that answered the question.*)

MARGARET: You can be young without money, but you can't be old without it. You've got to be old *with* money because to be old without it is just too awful, you've got to be one or the other, either *young* or *with money*, you can't be old and *without* it. — That's the *truth*, Brick....

(*Brick whistles softly, vaguely.*)

Well, now I'm dressed, I'm all dressed, there's nothing else for me to do.

(*Forlornly, almost fearfully.*)

I'm dressed, all dressed, nothing else for me to do....

(*She moves about restlessly, aimlessly, and speaks, as if to herself.*)

What am I —? Oh! — my bracelets....

(*She starts working a collection of bracelets over her hands onto her wrists, about six on each, as she talks.*)

I've thought a whole lot about it and now I know when I made my mistake. Yes, I made my mistake when I told you the truth about that thing with Skipper. Never should have confessed it, a fatal error, tellin' you about that thing with Skipper.
BRICK: Maggie, shut up about Skipper. I mean it, Maggie; you got to shut up about Skipper.
MARGARET: You ought to understand that Skipper and I —
BRICK: You don't think I'm serious, Maggie? You're fooled by the fact that I am saying this quiet? Look, Maggie. What you're doing is a dangerous thing to do. You're — you're — you're — foolin' with something that — nobody ought to fool with.
MARGARET: This time I'm going to finish what I have to say to you. Skipper and I made love, if love you could call it, because it made both of us feel a little bit closer to you. You see, you son of a bitch, you asked too much of people, of me, of him, of all the unlucky poor damned sons of bitches that happen to love you, and there was a whole pack of them, yes, there was a pack of them besides me and Skipper, you asked too goddam much of people that loved you, you — superior creature! — you godlike being! — And so we made love to each other to dream it was you, both of us! Yes, yes, yes! Truth, truth! What's so awful about it? I like it, I think the truth is — yeah! I shouldn't have told you....

BRICK (*holding his head unnaturally still and uptilted a bit*): It was Skipper that told me about it. Not you, Maggie.
MARGARET: I told you!
BRICK: After he told me!
MARGARET: What does it matter who —?
DIXIE: I got your mallet, I got your mallet.
TRIXIE: Give it to me, give it to me. IT's mine.

(*Brick turns suddenly out upon the gallery and calls:*)

BRICK: Little girl! Hey, little girl!
LITTLE GIRL (*at a distance*): What, Uncle Brick?
BRICK: Tell the folks to come up! — Bring everybody upstairs!
TRIXIE: It's mine, it's mine.
MARGARET: I can't stop myself! I'd go on telling you this in front of them all, if I had to!
BRICK: Little girl! Go on, go on, will you? Do what I told you, call them!
DIXIE: Okay.
MARGARET: Because it's got to be told and you, you! — you never let me!

(*She sobs, then controls herself, and continues almost calmly.*)

It was one of those beautiful, ideal things they tell about in the Greek legends, it couldn't be anything else, you being you, and that's what made it so sad, that's what made it so awful, because it was love that never could be carried through to anything satisfying or even talked about plainly.
BRICK: Maggie, you gotta stop this.
MARGARET: Brick, I tell you, you got to believe me, Brick, I *do* understand all about it! I — I think it was — *noble!* Can't you tell I'm sincere when I say I respect it? My only point, the only point that I'm making, is life has got to be allowed to continue even after the *dream* of life is — all — over....

(*Brick is without his crutch. Leaning on furniture, he crosses to pick it up as she continues as if possessed by a will outside herself:*)

Why I remember when we double-dated at college, Gladys Fitzgerald and I and you and Skipper, it was more like a date between you and Skipper. Gladys and I were just sort of tagging along as if it was necessary to chaperone you! — to make a good public impression —
BRICK (*turns to face her, half lifting his crutch*): Maggie, you want me to hit you with this crutch? Don't you know I could kill you with this crutch?
MARGARET: Good Lord, man, d' you think I'd care if you did?
BRICK: One man has one great good true thing in his

ABOVE: Kathleen Turner as Maggie in the 1990 Eugene O'Neill Theatre production of *Cat on a Hot Tin Roof*, directed by Howard Davies. BELOW: Brick (Daniel Hugh Kelly) and Maggie. (Photos by Michael Tighe.)

life. One great good thing which is true! — I had friendship with Skipper. — You are naming it dirty!

MARGARET: I'm not naming it dirty! I am naming it clean.

BRICK: Not love with you, Maggie, but friendship with Skipper was that one great true thing, and you are naming it dirty!

MARGARET: Then you haven't been listenin', not understood what I'm saying! I'm naming it so damn clean that it killed poor Skipper! — You two had something that had to be kept on ice, yes, incorruptible, yes! — and death was the only icebox where you could keep it. . . .

BRICK: I married you, Maggie. Why would I marry you, Maggie, if I was —?

MARGARET: Brick, let me finish! — I know, believe me I know, that it was only Skipper that harbored even any *unconscious* desire for anything not perfectly pure between you two! — Now let me skip a little. You married me early that summer we graduated out of Ole Miss, and we were happy, weren't we, we were blissful, yes, hit heaven together ev'ry time that we loved! But that fall you an' Skipper turned down wonderful offers of jobs in order to keep on bein' football heroes — pro-football heroes. You organized the Dixie Stars that fall, so you could keep on bein' teammates forever! But somethin' was not right with it! — *Me in-cluded!* — between you. Skipper began hittin' the bottle . . . you got a spinal injury — couldn't play the Thanksgivin' game in Chicago, watched it on TV from a traction bed in Toledo. I joined Skipper. The Dixie Stars lost because poor Skipper was drunk. We drank together that night all night in the bar of the Blackstone and when cold day was comin' up over the Lake an' we were comin' out drunk to take a dizzy look at it, I said, "SKIPPER! STOP LOVIN' MY HUSBAND OR TELL HIM HE'S GOT TO LET YOU ADMIT IT TO HIM!" — one way or another!

   HE SLAPPED ME HARD ON THE MOUTH! — then turned and ran without stopping once, I am sure, all the way back into his room at the Blackstone. . . .

   — When I came to his room that night, with a little scratch like a shy little mouse at his door, he made that pitiful, ineffectual little attempt to prove that what I had said wasn't true. . . .

(*Brick strikes at her with crutch, a blow that shatters the gemlike lamp on the table.*)

   — In this way, I destroyed him, by telling him truth that he and his world which he was born and raised in, yours and his world, had told him could not be told?

   — From then on Skipper was nothing at all but a receptacle for liquor and drugs. . . .

   — *Who shot cock robin? I with my —*

(*She throws back her head with tight shut eyes.*)

   — *merciful arrow!*

(*Brick strikes at her; misses.*)

   Missed me! — Sorry, — I'm not tryin' to whitewash my behavior, Christ, no! Brick, I'm not good. I don't know why people have to pretend to be good, nobody's good. The rich or the well-to-do can afford to respect moral patterns, conventional moral patterns, but I could never afford to, yeah, but — I'm honest! Give me credit for just that, will you *please?* — Born poor, raised poor, expect to die poor unless I manage to get us something out of what Big Daddy leaves when he dies of cancer! But Brick?! — *Skipper is dead! I'm alive!* Maggie the cat is —

(*Brick hops awkwardly forward and strikes at her again with his crutch.*)

   — *alive! I am alive, alive! I am . . .*

(*He hurls the crutch at her, across the bed she took refuge behind, and pitches forward on the floor as she completes her speech.*)

   — *alive!*

(*A little girl, Dixie, bursts into the room, wearing an Indian war bonnet and firing a cap pistol at Margaret and shouting: "Bang, bang, bang!"*)

(*Laughter downstairs floats through the open hall door. Margaret had crouched gasping to bed at child's entrance. She now rises and says with cool fury:*)

   Little girl, your mother or someone should teach you — (*gasping*) — to knock at a door before you come into a room. Otherwise people might think that you — lack — good breeding. . . .

DIXIE: Yanh, yanh, yanh, what is Uncle Brick doin' on th' floor?

BRICK: I tried to kill your Aunt Maggie, but I failed — and I fell. Little girl, give me my crutch so I can get up off th' floor.

MARGARET: Yes, give your uncle his crutch, he's a cripple, honey, he broke his ankle last night jumping hurdles on the high school athletic field!

DIXIE: What were you jumping hurdles for, Uncle Brick?

BRICK: Because I used to jump them, and people like to do what they used to do, even after they've stopped being able to do it. . . .

MARGARET: That's right, that's your answer, now go away, little girl.

(*Dixie fires cap pistol at Margaret three times.*)

Stop, you stop that, monster! You little no-neck monster!

(*She seizes the cap pistol and hurls it through gallery doors.*)

DIXIE (*with a precocious instinct for the cruelest thing*): You're *jealous!* — You're just jealous because you can't have babies!

(*She sticks out her tongue at Margaret as she sashays past her with her stomach stuck out, to the gallery. Margaret slams the gallery doors and leans panting against them. There is a pause. Brick has replaced his spilt drink and sits, faraway, on the great four-poster bed.*)

MARGARET: You see? — they gloat over us being childless, even in front of their five little no-neck monsters!

(*Pauses. Voices approach on the stairs.*)

Brick? — I've been to a doctor in Memphis, a — a gynecologist. . . .
    I've been completely examined, and there is no reason why we can't have a child whenever we want one. And this is my time by the calendar to conceive. Are you listening to me? Are you? Are you LISTENING TO ME!

BRICK: Yes. I hear you, Maggie.

(*His attention returns to her inflamed face.*)

— But how in hell on earth do you imagine — that you're going to have a child by a man that can't stand you?

MARGARET: That's a problem that I will have to work out.

(*She wheels about to face the hall door.*)

MAE (*offstage left*): Come on, Big Daddy. We're all goin' up to Brick's room.

(*From offstage left, voices: Reverend Tooker, Doctor Baugh, Mae.*)

MARGARET: *Here they come!*

(*The lights dim.*)

ACT 2

(*There is no lapse of time. Margaret and Brick are in the same positions they held at the end of act 1.*)

MARGARET (*at door*): *Here they come!*

(*Big Daddy appears first, a tall man with a fierce, anxious look, moving carefully not to betray his weakness even, or especially, to himself.*)

GOOPER: I read in the *Register* that you're getting a new memorial window.

(*Some of the people are approaching through the hall, others along the gallery: voices from both directions. Gooper and Reverend Tooker become visible outside gallery doors, and their voices come in clearly.*)
(*They pause outside as Gooper lights a cigar.*)

REVEREND TOOKER (*vivaciously*): Oh, but St. Paul's in Grenada has three memorial windows, and the latest one is a Tiffany stained-glass window that cost twenty-five hundred dollars, a picture of Christ the Good Shepherd with a Lamb in His arms.

MARGARET: Big Daddy.

BIG DADDY: Well, Brick.

BRICK: Hello Big Daddy. — Congratulations!

BIG DADDY: — Crap. . . .

GOOPER: Who give that window, Preach?

REVEREND TOOKER: Clyde Fletcher's widow. Also presented St. Paul's with a baptismal font.

GOOPER: Y'know what somebody ought t' give your church is a *coolin'* system, Preach.

MAE (*almost religiously*): — Let's see now, they've had their *tyyy*-phoid shots, and their tetanus shots, their diphtheria shots and their hepatitis shots and their polio shots, they got *those* shots every month from May through September, and — Gooper? Hey! Gooper! — What all have the kiddies been shot faw?

REVEREND TOOKER: Yes, siree, Bob! And y'know what Gus Hamma's family gave in his memory to the church at Two Rivers? A complete new stone parish-house with a basketball court in the basement and a —

BIG DADDY (*uttering a loud barking laugh which is far from truly mirthful*): Hey, Preach! What's all this talk about memorials, Preach? Y' think somebody's about t' kick off around here? 'S that it?

(*Startled by this interjection, Reverend Tooker decides to laugh at the question almost as loud as he can.*)
(*How he would answer the question we'll never know, as he's spared that embarrassment by the voice of Gooper's wife, Mae, rising high and clear as she appears with "Doc" Baugh, the family doctor, through the hall door.*)

MARGARET (*overlapping a bit*): Turn on the hi-fi, Brick! Let's have some music t' start off th' party with!

BRICK: You turn it on, Maggie.

(*The talk becomes so general that the room sounds

like a great aviary of chattering birds. Only Brick remains unengaged, leaning upon the liquor cabinet with his faraway smile, an ice cube in a paper napkin with which he now and then rubs his forehead. He doesn't respond to Margaret's command. She bounds forward and stoops over the instrument panel of the console.)

GOOPER: We gave 'em that thing for a third anniversary present, got three speakers in it.

(The room is suddenly blasted by the climax of a Wagnerian opera or a Beethoven symphony.)

BIG DADDY: *Turn that dam thing off!*

(Almost instant silence, almost instantly broken by the shouting charge of Big Mama, entering through hall door like a charging rhino.)

BIG MAMA: *Wha's my Brick, wha's mah precious baby!!*

BIG DADDY: *Sorry! Turn it back on!*

(Everyone laughs very loud. Big Daddy is famous for his jokes at Big Mama's expense, and nobody laughs louder at these jokes than Big Mama herself, though sometimes they're pretty cruel and Big Mama has to pick up or fuss with something to cover the hurt that the loud laugh doesn't quite cover.)
    (On this occasion, a happy occasion because the dread in her heart has also been lifted by the false report on Big Daddy's condition, she giggles, grotesquely, coyly, in Big Daddy's direction and bears down upon Brick, all very quick and alive.)

BIG MAMA: Here he is, here's my precious baby! What's that you've got in your hand? You put that liquor down, son, your hand was made fo' holdin' somethin' better than that!

GOOPER: Look at Brick put it down!

(Brick has obeyed Big Mama by draining the glass and handing it to her. Again everyone laughs, some high, some low.)

BIG MAMA: Oh, you bad boy, you, you're my bad little boy. Give Big Mama a kiss, you bad boy, you! — Look at him shy away, will you? Brick never liked bein' kissed or made a fuss over, I guess because he's always had too much of it!
    Son, you turn that thing off!

(Brick has switched on the TV set.)

I can't stand TV, radio was bad enough but TV has gone it one better, I mean — *(plops wheezing in chair)* — one worse, ha ha! Now what'm I sittin' down here faw? I want t' sit next to my sweetheart on the sofa, hold hands with him and love him up a little!

(Big Mama has on a black and white figured chiffon. The large irregular patterns, like the markings of some massive animal, the luster of her great diamonds and many pearls, the brilliants set in the silver frames of her glasses, her riotous voice, booming laugh, have dominated the room since she entered. Big Daddy has been regarding her with a steady grimace of chronic annoyance.)

BIG MAMA *(still louder)*: Preacher, Preacher, hey, Preach! Give me you' hand an' help me up from this chair!

REVEREND TOOKER: None of your tricks, Big Mama!

BIG MAMA: What tricks? You give me you' hand so I can get up an' —

(Reverend Tooker extends her his hand. She grabs it and pulls him into her lap with a shrill laugh that spans an octave in two notes.)

    Ever seen a preacher in a fat lady's lap? Hey, hey, folks! Ever seen a preacher in a fat lady's lap?

(Big Mama is notorious throughout the Delta for this sort of inelegant horseplay. Margaret looks on with indulgent humor, sipping Dubonnet "on the rocks" and watching Brick, but Mae and Gooper exchange signs of humorless anxiety over these antics, the sort of behavior which Mae thinks may account for their failure to quite get in with the smartest young married set in Memphis, despite all. One of the Negroes, Lacey or Sookey, peeks in, cackling. They are waiting for a sign to bring in the cake and champagne. But Big Daddy's not amused. He doesn't understand why, in spite of the infinite mental relief he's received from the doctor's report, he still has these same old fox teeth in his guts. "This spastic condition is something else," he says to himself, but aloud he roars at Big Mama:)

BIG DADDY: *BIG MAMA, WILL YOU QUIT HORSIN'?* — You're too old an' too fat fo' that sort of crazy kid stuff an' besides a woman with your blood pressure — she had two hundred last spring! — is riskin' a stroke when you mess around like that. . . .

(Mae blows on a pitch pipe.)

BIG MAMA: *Here comes Big Daddy's birthday!*

(Negroes in white jackets enter with an enormous birthday cake ablaze with candles and carrying buckets of champagne with satin ribbons about the bottle necks.)
    (Mae and Gooper strike up song, and everybody,

including the Negroes and Children, joins in. Only Brick remains aloof.)

EVERYONE: Happy birthday to you.
Happy birthday to you.
Happy birthday, Big Daddy —

(*Some sing: "Dear, Big Daddy!"*)

Happy birthday to you.

(*Some sing: "How old are you?"*)
(*Mae has come down center and is organizing her children like a chorus. She gives them a barely audible: "One, two, three!" and they are off in the new tune.*)

CHILDREN: Skinamarinka — dinka — dink
Skinamarinka — do
We love you.
Skinamarinka — dinka — dink
Skinamarinka — do.

(*All together, they turn to Big Daddy.*)

Big Daddy, you!

(*They turn back front, like a musical comedy chorus.*)

We love you in the morning;
We love you in the night.
We love you when we're with you,
And we love you out of sight.
Skinamarinka — dinka — dink
Skinamarinka — do.

(*Mae turns to Big Mama.*)

Big Mama, too!

(*Big Mama bursts into tears. The Negroes leave.*)

BIG DADDY: Now Ida, what the hell is the matter with you?
MAE: She's just so happy.
BIG MAMA: I'm just so happy, Big Daddy, I have to cry or something.

(*Sudden and loud in the hush:*)

Brick, do you know the wonderful news that Doc Baugh got from the clinic about Big Daddy? Big Daddy's one hundred percent!
MARGARET: Isn't that wonderful?
BIG MAMA: He's just one hundred percent. Passed the examination with flying colors. Now that we know there's nothing wrong with Big Daddy but a spastic colon, I can tell you something. I was worried sick, half out of my mind, for fear that Big Daddy might have a thing like —

(*Margaret cuts through this speech, jumping up and exclaiming shrilly:*)

MARGARET: Brick, honey, aren't you going to give Big Daddy his birthday present?

(*Passing by him, she snatches his liquor glass from him.*)
(*She picks up a fancily wrapped package.*)

Here it is, Big Daddy, this is from Brick!
BIG MAMA: This is the biggest birthday Big Daddy's ever had, a hundred presents and bushels of telegrams from —
MAE (*at same time*): What is it, Brick?
GOOPER: I bet 500 to 50 that Brick don't *know* what it is.
BIG MAMA: The fun of presents is not knowing what they are till you open the package. Open your present, Big Daddy.
BIG DADDY: Open it you'self. I want to ask Brick somethin! Come here, Brick.
MARGARET: Big Daddy's callin' you, Brick.

(*She is opening the package.*)

BRICK: Tell Big Daddy I'm crippled.
BIG DADDY: I see you're crippled. I want to know how you got crippled.
MARGARET (*making diversionary tactics*): Oh, look, oh, look, why, it's a cashmere robe!

(*She holds the robe up for all to see.*)

MAE: You sound surprised, Maggie.
MARGARET: I never saw one before.
MAE: That's funny. — *Hah!*
MARGARET (*turning on her fiercely, with a brilliant smile*): Why is it funny? All my family ever had was family — and luxuries such as cashmere robes still surprise me!
BIG DADDY (*ominously*): Quiet!
MAE (*heedless in her fury*): I don't see how you could be so surprised when you bought it yourself at Loewenstein's in Memphis last Saturday. You know how I know?
BIG DADDY: I said, Quiet!
MAE: — I know because the salesgirl that sold it to you waited on me and said, Oh, Mrs. Pollitt, your sister-in-law just bought a cashmere robe for your husband's father!
MARGARET: Sister Woman! Your talents are wasted as a housewife and mother, you really ought to be with the FBI or —
BIG DADDY: QUIET!

(*Reverend Tooker's reflexes are slower than the others'. He finishes a sentence after the bellow.*)

REVEREND TOOKER (*to Doc Baugh*): — the Stork and the Reaper are running neck and neck!

(*He starts to laugh gaily when he notices the silence and Big Daddy's glare. His laugh dies falsely.*)

BIG DADDY: Preacher, I hope I'm not butting in on more talk about memorial stained-glass windows, am I, Preacher?

(*Reverend Tooker laughs feebly, then coughs dryly in the embarrassed silence.*)

Preacher?

BIG MAMA: Now, Big Daddy, don't you pick on Preacher!

BIG DADDY (*raising his voice*): You ever hear that expression all hawk and no spit? You bring that expression to mind with that little dry cough of yours, all hawk an' no spit. . . .

(*The pause is broken only by a short startled laugh from Margaret, the only one there who is conscious of and amused by the grotesque.*)

MAE (*raising her arms and jangling her bracelets*): I wonder if the mosquitoes are active tonight?

BIG DADDY: What's that, Little Mama? Did you make some remark?

MAE: Yes, I said I wondered if the mosquitoes would eat us alive if we went out on the gallery for a while.

BIG DADDY: Well, if they do, I'll have your bones pulverized for fertilizer!

BIG MAMA (*quickly*): Last week we had an airplane spraying the place and I think it done some good, at least I haven't had a —

BIG DADDY (*cutting her speech*): Brick, they tell me, if what they tell me is true, that you done some jumping last night on the high school athletic field?

BIG MAMA: Brick, Big Daddy is talking to you, son.

BRICK (*smiling vaguely over his drink*): What was that, Big Daddy?

BIG DADDY: They said you done some jumping on the high school track field last night.

BRICK: That's what they told me, too.

BIG DADDY: Was it jumping or humping that you were doing out there? What were you doing out there at three A.M., layin' a woman on that cinder track?

BIG MAMA: Big Daddy, you are off the sick-list, now, and I'm not going to excuse you for talkin' so —

BIG DADDY: Quiet!

BIG MAMA: — nasty in front of Preacher and —

BIG DADDY: *QUIET!* — I ast you, Brick, if you was cuttin' you'self a piece o' poon-tang last night on that cinder track? I thought maybe you were chasin' poon-tang on that track an' tripped over something in the heat of the chase — 'sthat it?

(*Gooper laughs, loud and false, others nervously following suit. Big Mama stamps her foot, and purses*

her lips, crossing to Mae and whispering something to her as Brick meets his father's hard, intent, grinning stare with a slow, vague smile that he offers all situations from behind the screen of his liquor.*)

BRICK: No, sir, I don't think so. . . .

MAE (*at the same time, sweetly*): Reverend Tooker, let's you and I take a stroll on the widow's walk.

(*She and the preacher go out on the gallery as Big Daddy says:*)

BIG DADDY: Then what the hell were you doing out there at three o'clock in the morning?

BRICK: Jumping the hurdles, Big Daddy, runnin' and jumpin' the hurdles, but those high hurdles have gotten too high for me, now.

BIG DADDY: Cause you was drunk?

BRICK (*his vague smile fading a little*): Sober I wouldn't have tried to jump the *low* ones. . . .

BIG MAMA (*quickly*): Big Daddy, blow out the candles on your birthday cake!

MARGARET (*at the same time*): I want to propose a toast to Big Daddy Pollitt on his sixty-fifth birthday, the biggest cotton planter in —

BIG DADDY (*bellowing with fury and disgust*): *I told you to stop it, now stop it, quit this — !*

BIG MAMA (*coming in front of Big Daddy with the cake*): Big Daddy, I will not allow you to talk that way, not even on your birthday, I —

BIG DADDY: I'll talk like I want to on my birthday, Ida, or any other goddam day of the year and anybody here that don't like it knows what they can do!

BIG MAMA: You don't mean that!

BIG DADDY: What makes you think I don't mean it?

(*Meanwhile various discreet signals have been exchanged and Gooper has also gone out on the gallery.*)

BIG MAMA: I just know you don't mean it.

BIG DADDY: You don't know a goddam thing and you never did!

BIG MAMA: Big Daddy, you don't mean that.

BIG DADDY: Oh, yes, I do, oh, yes, I do, I mean it! I put up with a whole lot of crap around here because I thought I was dying. And you thought I was dying and you started taking over, well, you can stop taking over now, Ida, because I'm not gonna die, you can just stop now this business of taking over because you're not taking over because I'm not dying, I went through the laboratory and the goddam exploratory operation and there's nothing wrong with me but a spastic colon. And I'm not dying of cancer which you thought I was dying of. Ain't that so? Didn't you think that I was dying of cancer, Ida?

(*Almost everybody is out on the gallery but the two old people glaring at each other across the blazing cake.*)

(*Big Mama's chest heaves and she presses a fat fist to her mouth.*)

(*Big Daddy continues, hoarsely:*)

Ain't that so, Ida? Didn't you have an idea I was dying of cancer and now you could take control of this place and everything on it? I got that impression, I seemed to get that impression. Your loud voice everywhere, your fat old body butting in here and there!

BIG MAMA: Hush! The Preacher!

BIG DADDY: Fuck the goddam preacher!

(*Big Mama gasps loudly and sits down on the sofa which is almost too small for her.*)

Did you hear what I said? I said fuck the goddam preacher!

(*Somebody closes the gallery doors from outside just as there is a burst of fireworks and excited cries from the children.*)

BIG MAMA: I never seen you act like this before and I can't think what's got in you!

BIG DADDY: I went through all that laboratory and operation and all just so I would know if you or me was boss here! Well, now it turns out that I am and you ain't — and that's my birthday present — and my cake and champagne! — because for three years now you been gradually taking over. Bossing. Talking. Sashaying your fat old body around the place I made! I made this place! I was overseer on it! I was the overseer on the old Straw and Ochello plantation. I quit school at ten! I quit school at ten years old and went to work like a nigger in the fields. And I rose to be overseer of the Straw and Ochello plantation. And old Straw died and I was Ochello's partner and the place got bigger and bigger and bigger and bigger and bigger! I did all that myself with no goddam help from you, and now you think you're just about to take over. Well, I am just about to tell you that you are not just about to take over, you are not just about to take over a God damn thing. Is that clear to you, Ida? Is that very plain to you, now? Is that understood completely? I been through the laboratory from A to Z. I've had the goddam exploratory operation, and nothing is wrong with me but a spastic colon — made spastic, I guess, by *disgust*! By all the goddam lies and liars that I have had to put up with, and all the goddam hypocrisy that I lived with all these forty years that we been livin' together!

Hey! Ida!! Blow out the candles on the birthday cake! Purse up your lips and draw a deep breath and blow out the goddam candles on the cake!

BIG MAMA: Oh, Big Daddy, oh, oh, oh, Big Daddy!

BIG DADDY: What's the matter with you?

BIG MAMA: *In all these years you never believed that I loved you??*

BIG DADDY: Huh?

BIG MAMA: *And I did, I did so much, I did love you!* — I even loved your hate and your hardness, Big Daddy!

(*She sobs and rushes awkwardly out onto the gallery.*)

BIG DADDY (*to himself*): *Wouldn't it be funny if that was true. . . .*

(*A pause is followed by a burst of light in the sky from the fireworks.*)

BRICK! HEY, BRICK!

(*He stands over his blazing birthday cake.*)

(*After some moments, Brick hobbles in on his crutch, holding his glass.*)

(*Margaret follows him with a bright, anxious smile.*)

I didn't call you, Maggie. I called Brick.

MARGARET: I'm just delivering him to you.

(*She kisses Brick on the mouth which he immediately wipes with the back of his hand. She flies girlishly back out. Brick and his father are alone.*)

BIG DADDY: Why did you do that?

BRICK: Do what, Big Daddy?

BIG DADDY: Wipe her kiss off your mouth like she'd spit on you.

BRICK: I don't know. I wasn't conscious of it.

BIG DADDY: That woman of yours has a better shape on her than Gooper's but somehow or other they got the same look about them.

BRICK: What sort of look is that, Big Daddy?

BIG DADDY: I don't know how to describe it but it's the same look.

BRICK: They don't look peaceful, do they?

BIG DADDY: No, they sure in hell don't.

BRICK: They look nervous as cats?

BIG DADDY: That's right, they look nervous as cats.

BRICK: Nervous as a couple of cats on a hot tin roof?

BIG DADDY: That's right, boy, they look like a couple of cats on a hot tin roof. It's funny that you and Gooper being so different would pick out the same type of woman.

BRICK: Both of us married into society, Big Daddy.

BIG DADDY: Crap . . . I wonder what gives them both that look?

BRICK: Well. They're sittin' in the middle of a big piece of land, Big Daddy, twenty-eight thousand acres is a pretty big piece of land and so they're squaring off on it, each determined to knock off a bigger piece of it than the other whenever you let it go.

BIG DADDY: I got a surprise for those women. I'm not gonna let it go for a long time yet if that's what they're waiting for.

BRICK: That's right, Big Daddy. You just sit tight and let them scratch each other's eyes out. . . .

BIG DADDY: You bet your life I'm going to sit tight on it and let those sons of bitches scratch their eyes out, ha ha ha. . . .

But Gooper's wife's a good breeder, you got to admit she's fertile. Hell, at supper tonight she had them all at the table and they had to put a couple of extra leafs in the table to make room for them, she's got five head of them, now, and another one's comin'.

BRICK: Yep, number six is comin'. . . .

BIG DADDY: Six hell, she'll probably drop a litter next time. Brick, you know, I swear to God, I don't know the way it happens.

BRICK: The way what happens, Big Daddy?

BIG DADDY: You git you a piece of land, by hook or crook, an' things start growin' on it, things accumulate on it, and the first thing you know it's completely out of hand, completely out of hand!

BRICK: Well, they say nature hates a vacuum, Big Daddy.

BIG DADDY: That's what they say, but sometimes I think that a vacuum is a hell of a lot better than some of the stuff that nature replaces it with.

Is someone out there by that door?

GOOPER: Hey Mae.

BRICK: Yep.

BIG DADDY: Who?

(*He has lowered his voice.*)

BRICK: Someone int'rested in what we say to each other.

BIG DADDY: Gooper? — GOOPER!

(*After a discreet pause, Mae appears in the gallery door.*)

MAE: Did you call Gooper, Big Daddy?

BIG DADDY: Aw, it was you.

MAE: Do you want Gooper, Big Daddy?

BIG DADDY: No, and I don't want you. I want some privacy here, while I'm having a confidential talk with my son Brick. Now it's too hot in here to close them doors, but if I have to close those fuckin' doors in order to have a private talk with my son Brick, just let me know and I'll close 'em. Because I hate eavesdroppers, I don't like any kind of sneakin' an' spyin'.

MAE: Why, Big Daddy —

BIG DADDY: You stood on the wrong side of the moon, it threw your shadow!

MAE: I was just —

BIG DADDY: You was just nothing but *spyin'* an' you *know* it!

MAE (*begins to sniff and sob*): Oh, Big Daddy, you're so unkind for some reason to those that really love you!

BIG DADDY: Shut up, shut up, shut up! I'm going to move you and Gooper out of that room next to this! It's none of your goddam business what goes on in here at night between Brick an' Maggie. You listen at night like a couple of rutten peekhole spies and go and give a report on what you hear to Big Mama an' she comes to me and says they say such and such and so and so about what they heard goin' on between Brick an' Maggie, and Jesus, it makes me sick. I'm goin' to move you an' Gooper out of that room, I can't stand sneakin' an' spyin', it makes me puke. . . .

(*Mae throws back her head and rolls her eyes heavenward and extends her arms as if invoking God's pity for this unjust martyrdom; then she presses a handkerchief to her nose and flies from the room with a loud swish of skirts.*)

BRICK (*now at the liquor cabinet*): They listen, do they?

BIG DADDY: Yeah. They listen and give reports to Big Mama on what goes on in here between you and Maggie. They say that —

(*He stops as if embarrassed.*)

— You won't sleep with her, that you sleep on the sofa. Is that true or not true? If you don't like Maggie, get rid of Maggie! — What are you doin' there now?

BRICK: Fresh'nin' up my drink.

BIG DADDY: Son, you know you got a real liquor problem?

BRICK: Yes, sir, yes, I know.

BIG DADDY: Is that why you quit sports-announcing, because of this liquor problem?

BRICK: Yes, sir, yes, sir, I guess so.

(*He smiles vaguely and amiably at his father across his replenished drink.*)

BIG DADDY: Son, don't guess about it, it's too important.

BRICK (*vaguely*): Yes, sir.

BIG DADDY: And listen to me, don't look at the damn chandelier. . . .

(*Pause. Big Daddy's voice is husky.*)

— Somethin' else we picked up at th' big fire-sale in Europe.

(*Another pause.*)

Life is important. There's nothing else to hold onto. A man that drinks is throwing his life away. Don't do it, hold onto your life. There's nothing else to hold onto. . . .

Sit down over here so we don't have to raise our voices, the walls have ears in this place.

BRICK (*hobbling over to sit on the sofa beside him*): All right, Big Daddy.

BIG DADDY: Quit! — how'd that come about? Some disappointment?

BRICK: I don't know. Do you?

BIG DADDY: I'm askin' you, God damn it! How in hell would I know if you don't?

BRICK: I just got out there and found that I had a mouth full of cotton. I was always two or three beats behind what was goin' on on the field and so I —

BIG DADDY: Quit!

BRICK (*amiably*): Yes, quit.

BIG DADDY: Son?

BRICK: Huh?

BIG DADDY (*inhales loudly and deeply from his cigar; then bends suddenly a little forward, exhaling loudly and raising a hand to his forehead*): — Whew! — ha ha! — I took in too much smoke, it made me a little lightheaded. . . .

(*The mantel clock chimes.*)

Why is it so damn hard for people to talk?

BRICK: Yeah. . . .

(*The clock goes on sweetly chiming till it has completed the stroke of ten.*)

— Nice peaceful-soundin' clock, I like to hear it all night. . . .

(*He slides low and comfortable on the sofa; Big Daddy sits up straight and rigid with some unspoken anxiety. All his gestures are tense and jerky as he talks. He wheezes and pants and sniffs through his nervous speech, glancing quickly, shyly, from time to time, at his son.*)

BIG DADDY: We got that clock the summer we wint to Europe, me an' Big Mama on that damn Cook's Tour, never had such an awful time in my life, I'm tellin' you, son, those gooks over there, they gouge your eyeballs out in their grand hotels. And Big Mama bought more stuff than you could haul in a couple of boxcars, that's no crap. Everywhere she wint on this whirlwind tour, she bought, bought, bought. Why, half that stuff she bought is still crated up in the cellar, under water last spring!

(*He laughs.*)

That Europe is nothin' on earth but a great big auction, that's all it is, that bunch of old worn-out places, it's just a big fire-sale, the whole fuckin' thing, an' Big Mama wint wild in it, why, you couldn't hold that woman with a mule's harness! Bought, bought, bought! — lucky I'm a rich man, yes siree, Bob, an' half that stuff is mildewin' in th' basement. It's lucky I'm a rich man, it sure is lucky, well, I'm a rich man, Brick, yep, I'm a mighty rich man.

(*His eyes light up for a moment.*)

Y'know how much I'm worth? Guess, Brick! Guess how much I'm worth!

(*Brick smiles vaguely over his drink.*)

Close on ten million in cash an' blue-chip stocks, outside, mind you, of twenty-eight thousand acres of the richest land this side of the valley Nile!

But a man can't buy his life with it, he can't buy back his life with it when his life has been spent, that's one thing not offered in the Europe fire-sale or in the American markets or any markets on earth, a man can't buy his life with it, he can't buy back his life when his life is finished. . . .

That's a sobering thought, a very sobering thought, and that's a thought that I was turning over in my head, over and over and over — until today. . . .

I'm wiser and sadder, Brick, for this experience which I just gone through. They's one thing else that I remember in Europe.

BRICK: What is that, Big Daddy?

BIG DADDY: The hills around Barcelona in the country of Spain and the children running over those bare hills in their bare skins beggin' like starvin' dogs with howls and screeches, and how fat the priests are on the streets of Barcelona, so many of them and so fat and so pleasant, ha ha! — Y'know I could feed that country? I got money enough to feed that goddam country, but the human animal is a selfish beast and I don't reckon the money I passed out there to those howling children in the hills around Barcelona would more than upholster the chairs in this room, I mean pay to put a new cover on this chair!

Hell, I threw them money like you'd scatter feed corn for chickens, I threw money at them just to get rid of them long enough to climb back into th' car and — drive away. . . .

And then in Morocco, them Arabs, why, I remember one day in Marrakech, that old walled Arab city, I set on a broken-down wall to have a cigar, it was fearful hot there and this Arab woman stood in the road and looked at me till I was embarrassed, she stood stock still in the dusty hot road and looked at me till I was embarrassed. But listen to this. She had a naked child with her, a little naked girl with her, barely able to toddle, and after a while she set this child on the ground and give her a push and whispered something to her.

This child come toward me, barely able t' walk, come toddling up to me and —

Jesus, it makes you sick t' remember a thing like this! It stuck out its hand and tried to unbutton my trousers!

That child was not yet five! Can you believe me? Or do you think that I am making this up? I wint back to the hotel and said to Big Mama, Git packed! We're clearing out of this country. . . .

BRICK: Big Daddy, you're on a talkin' jag tonight.

BIG DADDY (*ignoring this remark*): Yes, sir, that's how it is, the human animal is a beast that dies but the fact that he's dying don't give him pity for others, no, sir, it —

— Did you say something?

BRICK: Yes.

BIG DADDY: What?

BRICK: Hand me over that crutch so I can get up.

BIG DADDY: Where you goin'?

BRICK: I'm takin' a little short trip to Echo Spring.

BIG DADDY: To where?

BRICK: Liquor cabinet. . . .

BIG DADDY: Yes, sir, boy —

(*He hands Brick the crutch.*)

— the human animal is a beast that dies and if he's got money he buys and buys and buys and I think the reason he buys everything he can buy is that in the back of his mind he has the crazy hope that one of his purchases will be life everlasting! — Which it never can be. . . . The human animal is a beast that —

BRICK (*at the liquor cabinet*): Big Daddy, you sure are shootin' th' breeze here tonight.

(*There is a pause and voices are heard outside.*)

BIG DADDY: I been quiet here lately, spoke not a word, just sat and stared into space. I had something heavy weighing on my mind but tonight that load was took off me. That's why I'm talking. — The sky looks diff'rent to me. . . .

BRICK: You know what I like to hear most?

BIG DADDY: What?

BRICK: Solid quiet. Perfect unbroken quiet.

BIG DADDY: Why?

BRICK: Because it's more peaceful.

BIG DADDY: Man, you'll hear a lot of that in the grave.

(*He chuckles agreeably.*)

BRICK: Are you through talkin' to me?

BIG DADDY: Why are you so anxious to shut me up?

BRICK: Well, sir, ever so often you say to me, Brick, I want to have a talk with you, but when we talk, it never materializes. Nothing is said. You sit in a chair and gas about this and that and I look like I listen. I try to look like I listen, but I don't listen, not much. Communication is — awful hard between people an' — somehow between you and me, it just don't — happen.

BIG DADDY: Have you ever been scared? I mean have you ever felt downright terror of something?

(*He gets up.*)

Just one moment.

(*He looks off as if he were going to tell an important secret.*)

Brick?

BRICK: What?

BIG DADDY: Son, I thought I had it!

BRICK: Had what? Had what, Big Daddy?

BIG DADDY: Cancer!

BRICK: Oh . . .

BIG DADDY: I thought the old man made out of bones had laid his cold and heavy hand on my shoulder!

BRICK: Well, Big Daddy, you kept a tight mouth about it.

BIG DADDY: A pig squeals. A man keeps a tight mouth about it, in spite of a man not having a pig's advantage.

BRICK: What advantage is that?

BIG DADDY: Ignorance — of mortality — is a comfort. A man don't have that comfort, he's the only living thing that conceives of death, that knows what it is. The others go without knowing which is the way that anything living should go, go without knowing, without any knowledge of it, and yet a pig squeals, but a man sometimes, he can keep a tight mouth about it. Sometimes he —

(*There is a deep, smoldering ferocity in the old man.*)

— can keep a tight mouth about it. I wonder if —

BRICK: What, Big Daddy?

BIG DADDY: A whiskey highball would injure this spastic condition?

BRICK: No, sir, it might do it good.

BIG DADDY (*grins suddenly, wolfishly*): Jesus, I can't tell you! The sky is open! Christ, it's open again! It's open, boy, it's open!

(*Brick looks down at his drink.*)

BRICK: You feel better, Big Daddy?

BIG DADDY: Better? Hell! I can breathe! — All of my life I been like a doubled up fist. . . .

(*He pours a drink.*)

— Poundin', smashin', drivin'! — now I'm going to loosen these doubled-up hands and touch things *easy* with them. . . .

(*He spreads his hands as if caressing the air.*)

You know what I'm contemplating?

BRICK (*vaguely*): No, sir. What are you contemplating?

BIG DADDY: Ha ha! — *Pleasure!* — pleasure with *women!*

(*Brick's smile fades a little but lingers.*)

— Yes, boy. I'll tell you something that you might not guess. I still have desire for women and this is my sixty-fifth birthday.

BRICK: I think that's mighty remarkable, Big Daddy.

BIG DADDY: Remarkable?

BRICK: *Admirable*, Big Daddy.

BIG DADDY: You're damn right it is, remarkable and admirable both. I realize now that I never had me enough. I let many chances slip by because of scruples about it, scruples, convention — crap. . . . All that stuff is bull, bull, bull! — It took the shadow of death to make me see it. Now that shadow's lifted, I'm going to cut loose and have, what is it they call it, have me a — ball!

BRICK: A ball, huh?

BIG DADDY: That's right, a ball, a ball! Hell! — I slept with Big Mama till, let's see, five years ago, till I was sixty and she was fifty-eight, and never even liked her, never did!

(*The phone has been ringing down the hall. Big Mama enters, exclaiming:*)

BIG MAMA: Don't you men hear that phone ring? I heard it way out on the gall'ry.

BIG DADDY: There's five rooms off this front gall'ry that you could go through. Why do you go through this one?

(*Big Mama makes a playful face as she bustles out the hall door.*)

Hunh! — Why, when Big Mama goes out of a room, I can't remember what that woman looks like —

BIG MAMA: Hello.

BIG DADDY: — But when Big Mama comes back into the room, boy, then I see what she looks like, and I wish I didn't!

(*Bends over laughing at this joke till it hurts his guts and he straightens with a grimace. The laugh subsides to a chuckle as he puts the liquor glass a little distrustfully down the table.*)

BIG MAMA: Hello, Miss Sally.

(*Brick has risen and hobbled to the gallery doors.*)

BIG DADDY: Hey! Where you goin'?

BRICK: Out for a breather.

BIG DADDY: Not yet you ain't. Stay here till this talk is finished, young fellow.

BRICK: I thought it was finished, Big Daddy.

BIG DADDY: It ain't even begun.

BRICK: My mistake. Excuse me. I just wanted to feel that river breeze.

BIG DADDY: Set back down in that chair.

(*Big Mama's voice rises, carrying down the hall.*)

BIG MAMA: Miss Sally, you're a case! You're a caution, Miss Sally.

BIG DADDY: Jesus, she's talking to my old maid sister again.

BIG MAMA: Why didn't you give me a chance to explain it to you?

BIG DADDY: Brick, this stuff burns me.

BIG MAMA: Well, good-bye, now, Miss Sally. You come down real soon. Big Daddy's dying to see you.

BIG DADDY: Crap!

BIG MAMA: Yaiss, good-bye, Miss Sally. . . .

(*She hangs up and bellows with mirth. Big Daddy groans and covers his ears as she approaches.*)
    (*Bursting in:*)

Big Daddy, that was Miss Sally callin' from Memphis again! You know what she done, Big Daddy? She called her doctor in Memphis to git him to tell her what that spastic thing is! Ha-*HAAAA!* — And called back to tell me how relieved she was that — Hey! Let me in!

(*Big Daddy has been holding the door half closed against her.*)

BIG DADDY: Naw I ain't. I told you not to come and go through this room. You just back out and go through those five other rooms.

BIG MAMA: Big Daddy? Big Daddy? Oh, Big Daddy! — You didn't mean those things you said to me, did you?

(*He shuts door firmly against her but she still calls.*)

Sweetheart? Sweetheart? Big Daddy? You didn't

Brick (Ben Gazzara) and Big Daddy (Burl Ives) in the original 1955 production of *Cat on a Hot Tin Roof*, directed by Elia Kazan.

mean those awful things you said to me? — I know you didn't. I know you didn't mean those things in your heart. . . .

(*The childlike voice fades with a sob and her heavy footsteps retreat down the hall. Brick has risen once more on his crutches and starts for the gallery again.*)

BIG DADDY: All I ask of that woman is that she leave me alone. But she can't admit to herself that she makes me sick. That comes of having slept with her too many years. Should of quit much sooner but that old woman she never got enough of it — and I was good in bed . . . I never should of wasted so much of it on her. . . . They say you got just so many and each one is numbered. Well, I got a few left in me, a few, and I'm going to pick me a good one to spend 'em on! I'm going to pick me a choice one, I don't care how much she costs, I'll smother her in — minks! Ha ha! I'll strip her naked

and smother her in minks and choke her with diamonds! Ha ha! I'll strip her naked and choke her with diamonds and smother her with minks and hump her from hell to breakfast. *Ha aha ha ha ha!*

MAE (*gaily at door*): Who's that laughin' in there?
GOOPER: Is Big Daddy laughin' in there?
BIG DADDY: Crap! — them two — *drips.* . . .

(*He goes over and touches Brick's shoulder.*)

Yes, son. Brick, boy. — I'm — *happy!* I'm happy, son, I'm happy!

(*He chokes a little and bites his under lip, pressing his head quickly, shyly against his son's head and then, coughing with embarrassment, goes uncertainly back to the table where he set down the glass. He drinks and makes a grimace as it burns his guts. Brick sighs and rises with effort.*)

What makes you so restless? Have you got ants in your britches?

BRICK: Yes, sir . . .

BIG DADDY: Why?

BRICK: — Something — hasn't — happened. . . .

BIG DADDY: Yeah? What is that!

BRICK (*sadly*): — the click. . . .

BIG DADDY: Did you say click?

BRICK: Yes, click.

BIG DADDY: What click?

BRICK: A click that I get in my head that makes me peaceful.

BIG DADDY: I sure in hell don't know what you're talking about, but it disturbs me.

BRICK: It's just a mechanical thing.

BIG DADDY: What is a mechanical thing?

BRICK: This click that I get in my head that makes me peaceful. I got to drink till I get it. It's just a mechanical thing, something like a — like a — like a —

BIG DADDY: Like a —

BRICK: Switch clicking off in my head, turning the hot light off and the cool night on and —

(*He looks up, smiling sadly.*)

— all of a sudden there's — peace!

BIG DADDY (*whistles long and soft with astonishment; he goes back to Brick and clasps his son's two shoulders*): Jesus! I didn't know it had gotten that bad with you. Why, boy, you're — *alcoholic*!

BRICK: That's the truth, Big Daddy. I'm alcoholic.

BIG DADDY: This shows how I — let things go!

BRICK: I have to hear that little click in my head that makes me peaceful. Usually I hear it sooner than this, sometimes as early as — noon, but —
— Today it's — dilatory. . . .
I just haven't got the right level of alcohol in my bloodstream yet!

(*This last statement is made with energy as he freshens his drink.*)

BIG DADDY: Uh — huh. Expecting death made me blind. I didn't have no idea that a son of mine was turning into a drunkard under my nose.

BRICK (*gently*): Well, now you do, Big Daddy, the news has penetrated.

BIG DADDY: UH-huh, yes, now I do, the news has — penetrated. . . .

BRICK: And so if you'll excuse me —

BIG DADDY: No, I won't excuse you.

BRICK: — I'd better sit by myself till I hear that click in my head, it's just a mechanical thing but it don't happen except when I'm alone or talking to no one. . . .

BIG DADDY: You got a long, long time to sit still, boy, and talk to no one, but now you're talkin' to me. At least I'm talking to you. And you set there and listen until I tell you the conversation is over!

BRICK: But this talk is like all the others we've ever had together in our lives! It's nowhere, nowhere! — it's — it's *painful*, Big Daddy. . . .

BIG DADDY: All right, then let it be painful, but don't you move from that chair! — I'm going to remove that crutch. . . .

(*He seizes the crutch and tosses it across room.*)

BRICK: I can hop on one foot, and if I fall, I can crawl!

BIG DADDY: If you ain't careful you're gonna crawl off this plantation and then, by Jesus, you'll have to hustle your drinks along Skid Row!

BRICK: That'll come, Big Daddy.

BIG DADDY: Naw, it won't. You're my son and I'm going to straighten you out; now that *I'm* straightened out, I'm going to straighten out you!

BRICK: Yeah?

BIG DADDY: Today the report come in from Ochsner Clinic. Y'know what they told me?

(*His face glows with triumph.*)

The only thing that they could detect with all the instruments of science in that great hospital is a little spastic condition of the colon! And nerves torn to pieces by all that worry about it.

(*A little girl bursts into room with a sparkler clutched in each fist, hops and shrieks like a monkey gone mad and rushes back out again as Big Daddy strikes at her.*)
(*Silence. The two men stare at each other. A woman laughs gaily outside.*)

I want you to know I breathed a sigh of relief almost as powerful as the Vicksburg tornado!

(*There is laughter outside, running footsteps, the soft, plushy sound and light of exploding rockets.*)
(*Brick stares at him soberly for a long moment; then makes a sort of startled sound in his nostrils and springs up on one foot and hops across the room to grab his crutch, swinging on the furniture for support. He gets the crutch and flees as if in horror for the gallery. His father seizes him by the sleeve of his white silk pajamas.*)

Stay here, you son of a bitch! — till I say go!

BRICK: I can't.

BIG DADDY: You sure in hell will, God damn it.

BRICK: No, I can't. We talk, you talk, in — circles! We get no where, no where! It's always the same, you say you want to talk to me and don't have a fuckin' thing to say to me!

BIG DADDY: Nothin' to say when I'm tellin' you I'm going to live when I thought I was dying?!

BRICK: Oh — *that!* — Is that what you have to say to me?

BIG DADDY: Why, you son of a bitch! Ain't that, ain't that — *important?!*

BRICK: Well, you said that, that's said, and now I —

BIG DADDY: Now you set back down.

BRICK: You're all balled up, you —

BIG DADDY: I ain't balled up!

BRICK: You are, you're all balled up!

BIG DADDY: Don't tell me what I am, you drunken whelp! I'm going to tear this coat sleeve off if you don't set down!

BRICK: Big Daddy —

BIG DADDY: Do what I tell you! I'm the boss here, now! I want you to know I'm back in the driver's seat now!

(*Big Mama rushes in, clutching her great heaving bosom.*)

BIG MAMA: Big Daddy!

BIG DADDY: What in hell do you want in here, Big Mama?

BIG MAMA: Oh, Big Daddy! Why are you shouting like that? I just cain't *stainnnnnnnnd* — it. . . .

BIG DADDY (*raising the back of his hand above his head*): GIT! — outa here.

(*She rushes back out, sobbing.*)

BRICK (*softly, sadly*): Christ. . . .

BIG DADDY (*fiercely*): Yeah! Christ! — is right. . . .

(*Brick breaks loose and hobbles toward the gallery.*)
(*Big Daddy jerks his crutch from under Brick so he steps with the injured ankle. He utters a hissing cry of anguish, clutches a chair and pulls it over on top of him on the floor.*)

Son of a — tub of — hog fat. . . .

BRICK: Big Daddy! Give me my crutch.

(*Big Daddy throws the crutch out of reach.*)

Give me that crutch, Big Daddy.

BIG DADDY: Why do you drink?

BRICK: Don't know, give me my crutch!

BIG DADDY: You better think why you drink or give up drinking!

BRICK: Will you please give me my crutch so I can get up off this floor?

BIG DADDY: First you answer my question. Why do you drink? Why are you throwing your life away, boy, like somethin' disgusting you picked up on the street?

BRICK (*getting onto his knees*): Big Daddy, I'm in pain, I stepped on that foot.

BIG DADDY: Good! I'm glad you're not too numb with the liquor in you to feel some pain!

BRICK: You — spilled my — drink . . .

BIG DADDY: I'll make a bargain with you. You tell me why you drink and I'll hand you one. I'll pour you the liquor myself and hand it to you.

BRICK: Why do I drink?

BIG DADDY: Yea! Why?

BRICK: Give me a drink and I'll tell you.

BIG DADDY: Tell me first!

BRICK: I'll tell you in one word.

BIG DADDY: What word?

BRICK: DISGUST!

(*The clock chimes softly, sweetly. Big Daddy gives it a short, outraged glance.*)

Now how about that drink?

BIG DADDY: What are you disgusted with? You got to tell me that, first. Otherwise being disgusted don't make no sense!

BRICK: Give me my crutch.

BIG DADDY: You heard me, you got to tell me what I asked you first.

BRICK: I told you, I said to kill my disgust!

BIG DADDY: DISGUST WITH WHAT!

BRICK: You strike a hard bargain.

BIG DADDY: What are you disgusted with? — an' I'll pass you the liquor.

BRICK: I can hop on one foot, and if I fall, I can crawl.

BIG DADDY: You want liquor that bad?

BRICK (*dragging himself up, clinging to bedstead*): Yeah, I want it that bad.

BIG DADDY: If I give you a drink, will you tell me what it is you're disgusted with, Brick?

BRICK: Yes, sir, I will try to.

(*The old man pours him a drink and solemnly passes it to him.*)
(*There is silence as Brick drinks.*)

Have you ever heard the word "mendacity"?

BIG DADDY: Sure. Mendacity is one of them five dollar words that cheap politicians throw back and forth at each other.

BRICK: You know what it means?

BIG DADDY: Don't it mean lying and liars?

BRICK: Yes, sir, lying and liars.

BIG DADDY: Has someone been lying to you?

CHILDREN (*chanting in chorus offstage*):
We want Big Dad-dee!
We want Big Dad-dee!

(*Gooper appears in the gallery door.*)

GOOPER: Big Daddy, the kiddies are shouting for you out there.

BIG DADDY (*fiercely*): Keep out, Gooper!

GOOPER: 'Scuse me!

(*Big Daddy slams the doors after Gooper.*)

BIG DADDY: Who's been lying to you, has Margaret been lying to you, has your wife been lying to you about something, Brick?

BRICK: Not her. That wouldn't matter.

BIG DADDY: Then who's been lying to you, and what about?

BRICK: No one single person and no one lie. . . .

BIG DADDY: Then what, what then, for Christ's sake?

BRICK: — The whole, the whole — thing. . . .

BIG DADDY: Why are you rubbing your head? You got a headache?

BRICK: No, I'm tryin' to —

BIG DADDY: — Concentrate, but you can't because your brain's all soaked with liquor, is that the trouble? Wet brain!

(*He snatches the glass from Brick's hand.*)

What do you know about this mendacity thing? Hell! I could write a book on it! Don't you know that? I could write a book on it and still not cover the subject? Well, I could, I could write a goddam book on it and still not cover the subject anywhere near enough!! — Think of all the lies I got to put up with! — Pretenses! Ain't that mendacity? Having to pretend stuff you don't think or feel or have any idea of? Having for instance to act like I care for Big Mama! — I haven't been able to stand the sight, sound, or smell of that woman for forty years now! — even when I *laid* her! — regular as a piston. . . .

Pretend to love that son of a bitch of a Gooper and his wife Mae and those five same screechers out there like parrots in a jungle? Jesus! Can't stand to look at 'em!

Church! — it bores the bejesus out of me but I go! — I go an' sit there and listen to the fool preacher!

Clubs! — Elks! Masons! Rotary! — *crap!*

(*A spasm of pain makes him clutch his belly. He sinks into a chair and his voice is softer and hoarser.*)

You I *do* like for some reason, did always have some kind of real feeling for — affection — respect — yes, always. . . .

You and being a success as a planter is all I ever had any devotion to in my whole life! — and that's the truth. . . .

I don't know why, but it is!

I've lived with mendacity! — Why can't *you*

live with it? Hell, you *got* to live with it, there's nothing *else* to *live* with except mendacity, is there?

BRICK: Yes, sir. Yes, sir there is something else that you can live with!

BIG DADDY: What?

BRICK (*lifting his glass*): This! — Liquor. . . .

BIG DADDY: That's not living, that's dodging away from life.

BRICK: I want to dodge away from it.

BIG DADDY: Then why don't you kill yourself, man?

BRICK: I like to drink. . . .

BIG DADDY: Oh, God, I can't talk to you. . . .

BRICK: I'm sorry, Big Daddy.

BIG DADDY: Not as sorry as I am. I'll tell you something. A little while back when I thought my number was up —

(*This speech should have torrential pace and fury.*)

— before I found out it was just this — spastic — colon. I thought about you. Should I or should I not, if the jig was up, give you this place when I go — since I hate Gooper an' Mae an' know that they hate me, and since all five same monkeys are little Maes an' Goopers. — And I thought, No! — Then I thought, Yes! — I couldn't make up my mind. I hate Gooper and his five same monkeys and that bitch Mae! Why should I turn over twenty-eight thousand acres of the richest land this side of the valley Nile to not my kind? — But why in hell, on the other hand, Brick — should I subsidize a goddam fool on the bottle? — Liked or not liked, well, maybe even — *loved!* — Why should I do that? — Subsidize worthless behavior? Rot? Corruption?

BRICK (*smiling*): I understand.

BIG DADDY: Well, if you do, you're smarter than I am, God damn it, because I don't understand. And this I will tell you frankly. I didn't make up my mind at all on that question and still to this day I ain't made out no will! — Well, now I don't *have* to. The pressure is gone. I can just wait and see if you pull yourself together or if you don't.

BRICK: That's right, Big Daddy.

BIG DADDY: You sound like you thought I was kidding.

BRICK (*rising*): No, sir, I know you're not kidding.

BIG DADDY: But you don't care —?

BRICK (*hobbling toward the gallery door*): No, sir, I don't care. . . .

(*He stands in the gallery doorway as the night sky turns pink and green and gold with successive flashes of light.*)

BIG DADDY: *WAIT!* — Brick. . . .

(*His voice drops. Suddenly there is something shy, almost tender, in his restraining gesture.*)

Don't let's — leave it like this, like them other talks we've had, we've always — talked around things, we've — just talked around things for some fuckin' reason, I don't know what, it's always like something was left not spoken, something avoided because neither of us was honest enough with the — other. . . .

BRICK: I never lied to you, Big Daddy.

BIG DADDY: Did I ever to *you?*

BRICK: No, sir. . . .

BIG DADDY: Then there is at least two people that never lied to each other.

BRICK: But we've never *talked* to each other.

BIG DADDY: We can *now.*

BRICK: Big Daddy, there don't seem to be anything much to say.

BIG DADDY: You say that you drink to kill your disgust with lying.

BRICK: You said to give you a reason.

BIG DADDY: Is liquor the only thing that'll kill this disgust?

BRICK: Now. Yes.

BIG DADDY: But not once, huh?

BRICK: Not when I was still young an' believing. A drinking man's someone who wants to forget he isn't still young an' believing.

BIG DADDY: Believing what?

BRICK: Believing. . . .

BIG DADDY: Believing *what?*

BRICK (*stubbornly evasive*): Believing. . . .

BIG DADDY: I don't know what the hell you mean by believing and I don't think you know what you mean by believing, but if you still got sports in your blood, go back to sports announcing and —

BRICK: Sit in a glass box watching games I can't play? Describing what I can't do while players do it? Sweating out their disgust and confusion in contests I'm not fit for? Drinkin' a coke, half bourbon, so I can stand it? That's no goddam good any more, no help — time just outran me, Big Daddy — got there first . . .

BIG DADDY: I think you're passing the buck.

BRICK: You know many drinkin' men?

BIG DADDY (*with a slight, charming smile*): I have known a fair number of that species.

BRICK: Could any of them tell you why he drank?

BIG DADDY: Yep, you're passin' the buck to things like time and disgust with "mendacity" and — crap! — if you got to use that kind of language about a thing, it's ninety-proof bull, and I'm not buying any.

BRICK: I had to give you a reason to get a drink!

BIG DADDY: You started drinkin' when your friend Skipper died.

(*Silence for five beats. Then Brick makes a startled movement, reaching for his crutch.*)

BRICK: What are you suggesting?

BIG DADDY: I'm suggesting nothing.

(*The shuffle and clop of Brick's rapid hobble away from his father's steady, grave attention.*)

— But Gooper an' Mae suggested that there was something not right exactly in your —

BRICK (*stopping short downstage as if backed to a wall*): "Not right"?

BIG DADDY: Not, well, exactly *normal* in your friendship with —

BRICK: They suggested that, too? I thought that was Maggie's suggestion.

(*Brick's detachment is at last broken through. His heart is accelerated; his forehead sweat-beaded; his breath becomes more rapid and his voice hoarse. The thing they're discussing, timidly and painfully on the side of Big Daddy, fiercely, violently on Brick's side, is the inadmissible thing that Skipper died to disavow between them. The fact that if it existed it had to be disavowed to "keep face" in the world they lived in, may be at the heart of the "mendacity" that Brick drinks to kill his disgust with. It may be the root of his collapse. Or maybe it is only a single manifestation of it, not even the most important. The bird that I hope to catch in the net of this play is not the solution of one man's psychological problem. I'm trying to catch the true quality of experience in a group of people, that cloudy, flickering, evanescent — fiercely charged! — interplay of live human beings in the thundercloud of a common crisis. Some mystery should be left in the revelation of character in a play, just as a great deal of mystery is always left in the revelation of character in life, even in one's own character to himself. This does not absolve the playwright of his duty to observe and probe as clearly and deeply as he legitimately can: But it should steer him away from "pat" conclusions, facile definitions which make a play just a play, not a snare for the truth of human experience.*)

(*The following scene should be played with great concentration, with most of the power leashed but palpable in what is left unspoken.*)

Who else's suggestion is it, is it *yours?* How many others thought that Skipper and I were —

BIG DADDY (*gently*): Now, hold on, hold on a minute, son. — I knocked around in my time.

BRICK: What's that got to do with —

BIG DADDY: I said "Hold on!" — I bummed, I bummed this country till I was —

BRICK: Whose suggestion, who else's suggestion is it?

BIG DADDY: Slept in hobo jungles and railroad Y's and flophouses in all cities before I —

BRICK: Oh, *you* think so, too, you call me your son and a queer. Oh! Maybe that's why you put Maggie and me in this room that was Jack Straw's and Peter Ochello's, in which that pair of old sisters slept in a double bed where both of 'em died!

BIG DADDY: *Now just don't go throwing rocks at —*

(*Suddenly Reverend Tooker appears in the gallery doors, his head slightly, playfully, fatuously cocked, with a practiced clergyman's smile, sincere as a bird-call blown on a hunter's whistle, the living embodiment of the pious, conventional lie.*)

(*Big Daddy gasps a little at this perfectly timed, but incongruous, apparition.*)

— What're you lookin' for, preacher?

REVEREND TOOKER: The gentleman's lavatory, ha ha! — heh, heh . . .

BIG DADDY (*with strained courtesy*): — Go back out and walk down to the other end of the gallery, Reverend Tooker, and use the bathroom connected with my bedroom, and if you can't find it, ask them where it is!

REVEREND TOOKER: Ah, thanks.

(*He goes out with a deprecatory chuckle.*)

BIG DADDY: It's hard to talk in this place . . .

BRICK: Son of a —!

BIG DADDY (*leaving a lot unspoken*): — I seen all things and understood a lot of them, till 1910. Christ, the year that — I had worn my shoes through, hocked my — I hopped off a yellow dog freight car half a mile down the road, slept in a wagon of cotton outside the gin — Jack Straw an' Peter Ochello took me in. Hired me to manage this place which grew into this one. — When Jack Straw died — why, old Peter Ochello quit eatin' like a dog does when its master's dead, and died, too!

BRICK: Christ!

BIG DADDY: I'm just saying I understand such —

BRICK (*violently*): Skipper is dead. I have not quit eating!

BIG DADDY: No, but you started drinking.

(*Brick wheels on his crutch and hurls his glass across the room shouting.*)

BRICK: YOU THINK SO, TOO?

(*Footsteps run on the gallery. There are women's calls.*)

(*Big Daddy goes toward the door.*)

(*Brick is transformed, as if a quiet mountain blew suddenly up in volcanic flame.*)

BRICK: You think so, too? You think so, too? You think me an' Skipper did, did, did! — *sodomy!* — together?

BIG DADDY: Hold —!

BRICK: That what you —

BIG DADDY: — *ON* — a minute!

BRICK: You think we did dirty things between us, Skipper an' —

BIG DADDY: Why are you shouting like that? Why are you —

BRICK: — Me, is that what you think of Skipper, is that —

BIG DADDY: — so excited? I don't think nothing. I don't know nothing. I'm simply telling you what —

BRICK: You think that Skipper and me were a pair of dirty old men?

BIG DADDY: Now that's —

BRICK: Straw? Ochello? A couple of —

BIG DADDY: Now just —

BRICK: — fucking sissies? Queers? Is that what you —

BIG DADDY: Shhh.

BRICK: — think?

(*He loses his balance and pitches to his knees without noticing the pain. He grabs the bed and drags himself up.*)

BIG DADDY: Jesus! — Whew. . . . Grab my hand!

BRICK: Naw, I don't want your hand. . . .

BIG DADDY: Well, I want yours. Git up!

(*He draws him up, keeps an arm about him with concern and affection.*)

You broken out in a sweat! You're panting like you'd run a race with —

BRICK (*freeing himself from his father's hold*): Big Daddy, you shock me, Big Daddy, you, you — *shock* me! Talkin' so —

(*He turns away from his father.*)

— casually! — about a — thing like that . . .

— Don't you know how people *feel* about things like that? How, how *disgusted* they are by things like that? Why, at Ole Miss when it was discovered a pledge to our fraternity, Skipper's and mine, did a, *attempted* to do a, unnatural thing with —

We not only dropped him like a hot rock! — We told him to git off the campus, and he did, he got! — All the way to —

(*He halts, breathless.*)

BIG DADDY: — Where?

BRICK: — North Africa, last I heard!

BIG DADDY: Well, I have come back from further away than that, I have just now returned from the other side of the moon, death's country, son, and I'm not easy to shock by anything here.

(*He comes downstage and faces out.*)

Always, anyhow, lived with too much space around me to be infected by ideas of other people. One thing you can grow on a big place more important than cotton! — is *tolerance!* — I grown it.

(*He returns toward Brick.*)

BRICK: Why can't exceptional friendship, *real, real, deep, deep friendship!* between two men be respected as something clean and decent without being thought of as —
BIG DADDY: It can, it is, for God's sake.
BRICK: — *Fairies.* . . .

(*In his utterance of this word, we gauge the wide and profound reach of the conventional mores he got from the world that crowned him with early laurel.*)

BIG DADDY: I told Mae an' Gooper —
BRICK: Frig Mae and Gooper, frig all dirty lies and liars! — Skipper and me had a clean, true thing between us! — had a clean friendship, practically all our lives, till Maggie got the idea you're talking about. Normal? No! — It was too rare to be normal, any true thing between two people is too rare to be normal. Oh, once in a while he put his hand on my shoulder or I'd put mine on his, oh, maybe even, when we were touring the country in profootball an' shared hotel rooms we'd reach across the space between the two beds and shake hands to say goodnight, yeah, one or two times we —
BIG DADDY: Brick, nobody thinks that that's not normal!
BRICK: Well, they're mistaken, it was! It was a pure an' true thing an' that's not normal.
MAE (*offstage*): Big Daddy, they're startin' the fireworks.

(*They both stare straight at each other for a long moment. The tension breaks and both turn away as if tired.*)

BIG DADDY: Yeah, it's — hard t' — talk. . . .
BRICK: All right, then, let's — let it go. . . .
BIG DADDY: Why did Skipper crack up? Why have you?

(*Brick looks back at his father again. He has already decided, without knowing that he mas made this decision, that he is going to tell his father that he is dying of cancer. Only this could even the score between them: one inadmissible thing in return for another.*)

BRICK (*ominously*): All right. You're asking for it, Big Daddy. We're finally going to have that real true talk you wanted. It's too late to stop it, now, we got to carry it through and cover every subject.

(*He hobbles back to the liquor cabinet.*)

Uh-huh.

(*He opens the ice bucket and picks up the silver tongs with slow admiration of their frosty brightness.*)

Maggie declares that Skipper and I went into profootball after we left Ole Miss because we were scared to grow up . . .

(*He moves downstage with the shuffle and clop of a cripple on a crutch. As Margaret did when her speech became "recitative," he looks out into the house, commanding its attention by his direct, concentrated gaze — a broken, "tragically elegant" figure telling simply as much as he knows of "the Truth":*)

— Wanted to — keep on tossing — those long, long! — high, high! — passes that — couldn't be intercepted except by time, the aerial attack that made us famous! And so we did, we did, we kept it up for one season, that aerial attack, we held it high! — Yeah, but —
— that summer, Maggie, she laid the law down to me, said, Now or never, and so I married Maggie. . . .
BIG DADDY: How was Maggie in bed?
BRICK (*wryly*): Great! the greatest!

(*Big Daddy nods as if he thought so.*)

She went on the road that fall with the Dixie Stars. Oh, she made a great show of being the world's best sport. She wore a — wore a — tall bearskin cap! A shako, they call it, a dyed moleskin coat, a moleskin coat dyed red! — Cut up crazy! Rented hotel ballrooms for victory celebrations, wouldn't cancel them when it — turned out — defeat. . . .
  MAGGIE THE CAT! Ha ha!

(*Big Daddy nods.*)

— But Skipper, he had some fever which came back on him which doctors couldn't explain and I got that injury — turned out to be just a shadow on the X-ray plate — and a touch of bursitis. . . .
  I lay in a hospital bed, watched our games on TV, saw Maggie on the bench next to Skipper when he was hauled out of a game for stumbles, fumbles! — Burned me up the way she hung on his arm! — Y'know, I think that Maggie had always

felt sort of left out because she and me never got any closer together than two people just get in bed, which is not much closer than two cats on a — fence humping. . . .

So! She took this time to work on poor dumb Skipper. He was a less than average student at Ole Miss, you know that, don't you?! — Poured in his mind the dirty, false idea that what we were, him and me, was a frustrated case of that ole pair of sisters that lived in this room, Jack Straw and Peter Ochello! — He, poor Skipper, went to bed with Maggie to prove it wasn't true, and when it didn't work out, he thought it *was* true! — Skipper broke in two like a rotten stick — nobody ever turned so fast to a lush — or died of it so quick. . . .

— Now are you satisfied?

(*Big Daddy has listened to this story, dividing the grain from the chaff. Now he looks at his son.*)

BIG DADDY: Are *you* satisfied?
BRICK: With what?
BIG DADDY: That half-ass story!
BRICK: What's half-ass about it?
BIG DADDY: Something's left out of that story. What did you leave out?

(*The phone has started ringing in the hall.*)

GOOPER (*offstage*): Hello.

(*As if it reminded him of something, Brick glances suddenly toward the sound and says:*)

BRICK: Yes! — I left out a long-distance call which I had from Skipper —
GOOPER: Speaking, go ahead.
BRICK: — In which he made a drunken confession to me and on which I hung up!
GOOPER: No.
BRICK: — Last time we spoke to each other in our lives . . .
GOOPER: No, sir.
BIG DADDY: You musta said something to him before you hung up.
BRICK: What could I say to him?
BIG DADDY: Anything. Something.
BRICK: Nothing.
BIG DADDY: Just hung up?
BRICK: Just hung up.
BIG DADDY: Uh-huh. Anyhow now! — we have tracked down the lie with which you're disgusted and which you are drinking to kill your disgust with, Brick. You been passing the buck. This disgust with mendacity is disgust with yourself.

You! — dug the grave of your friend and kicked him in it! — before you'd face truth with him!
BRICK: *His* truth, not *mine!*

BIG DADDY: His truth, okay! But you wouldn't face it with him!
BRICK: Who *can* face truth? Can *you?*
BIG DADDY: Now don't start passin' the rotten buck again, boy!
BRICK: How about these birthday congratulations, these many, many happy returns of the day, when ev'rybody knows there won't be any except you!

(*Gooper, who has answered the hall phone, lets out a high, shrill laugh; the voice becomes audible saying: "No, no, you got it all wrong! Upside down! Are you crazy?"*)

(*Brick suddenly catches his breath as he realizes that he has made a shocking disclosure. He hobbles a few paces, then freezes, and without looking at his father's shocked face says:*)

Let's, let's — go out, now, and — watch the fireworks. Come on, Big Daddy.

(*Big Daddy moves suddenly forward and grabs hold of the boy's crutch like it was a weapon for which they were fighting for possession.*)

BIG DADDY: Oh, no, no! No one's going out! What did you start to say?
BRICK: I don't remember.
BIG DADDY: "Many happy returns when they know there won't be any"?
BRICK: Aw, hell, Big Daddy, forget it. Come on out on the gallery and look at the fireworks they're shooting off for your birthday. . . .
BIG DADDY: First you finish that remark you were makin' before you cut off. "Many happy returns when they know there won't be any"? — Ain't that what you just said?
BRICK: Look, now. I can get around without that crutch if I have to but it would be a lot easier on the furniture an' glassware if I didn't have to go swinging along like Tarzan of th' —
BIG DADDY: FINISH! WHAT YOU WAS SAYIN'!

(*An eerie green glow shows in sky behind him.*)

BRICK (*sucking the ice in his glass, speech becoming thick*): Leave th' place to Gooper and Mae an' their five little same little monkeys. All I want is —
BIG DADDY: "LEAVE TH' PLACE," did you say?
BRICK (*vaguely*): All twenty-eight thousand acres of the richest land this side of the valley Nile.
BIG DADDY: Who said I was "leaving the place" to Gooper or anybody? This is my sixty-fifth birthday! I got fifteen years or twenty years left in me! I'll outlive *you!* I'll bury you an' have to pay for your coffin!
BRICK: Sure. Many happy returns. Now let's go watch the fireworks, come on, let's —

BIG DADDY: Lying, have they been lying? About the report from th' — clinic? Did they, did they — find something? — *Cancer.* Maybe?

BRICK: Mendacity is a system that we live in. Liquor is one way out an' death's the other. . . .

(*He takes the crutch from Big Daddy's loose grip and swings out on the gallery leaving the doors open.*)
(*A song, "Pick a Bale of Cotton," is heard.*)

MAE (*appearing in door*): Oh, Big Daddy, the field hands are singin' fo' you!

BRICK: I'm sorry, Big Daddy. My head don't work any more and it's hard for me to understand how anybody could care if he lived or died or was dying or cared about anything but whether or not there was liquor left in the bottle and so I said what I said without thinking. In some ways I'm no better than the others, in some ways worse because I'm less alive. Maybe it's being alive that makes them lie, and being almost *not* alive makes me sort of accidentally truthful — I don't know but — anyway — we've been friends . . .
— And being friends is telling each other the truth. . . .

(*There is a pause.*)

You told *me!* I told *you!*

BIG DADDY (*slowly and passionately*): CHRIST — DAMN —

GOOPER (*offstage*): Let her go!

(*Fireworks offstage right.*)

BIG DADDY: — ALL — LYING SONS OF — LYING BITCHES!

(*He straightens at last and crosses to the inside door. At the door he turns and looks back as if he had some desperate question he couldn't put into words. Then he nods reflectively and says in a hoarse voice:*)

Yes, all liars, all liars, all lying dying liars!

(*This is said slowly, slowly, with a fierce revulsion. He goes on out.*)

— Lying! Dying! Liars!

(*Brick remains motionless as the lights dim out and the curtain falls.*)

ACT 3

(*There is no lapse of time. Big Daddy is seen leaving as at the end of act 2.*)

BIG DADDY: ALL LYIN' — DYIN'! — LIARS! LIARS! — LIARS!

(*Margaret enters.*)

MARGARET: Brick, what in the name of God was goin' on in this room?

(*Dixie and Trixie enter through the doors and circle around Margaret shouting. Mae enters from the lower gallery window.*)

MAE: Dixie, Trixie, you quit that!

(*Gooper enters through the doors.*)

Gooper, will y' please get these kiddies to bed right now!

GOOPER: Mae, you seen Big Mama?

MAE: Not yet.

(*Gooper and kids exit through the doors. Reverend Tooker enters through the windows.*)

REVEREND TOOKER: Those kiddies are so full of vitality. I think I'll have to be starting back to town.

MAE: Not yet, Preacher. You know we regard you as a member of this family, one of our closest an' dearest, so you just got t' be with us when Doc Baugh gives Big Mama th' actual truth about th' report from the clinic.

MARGARET: Where do you think you're going?

BRICK: Out for some air.

MARGARET: Why'd Big Daddy shout "Liars"?

MAE: Has Big Daddy gone to bed, Brick?

GOOPER (*entering*): Now where is that old lady?

REVEREND TOOKER: I'll look for her.

(*He exits to the gallery.*)

MAE: Cain'tcha find her, Gooper?

GOOPER: She's avoidin' this talk.

MAE: I think she senses somethin'.

MARGARET (*going out on the gallery to Brick*): Brick, they're goin' to tell Big Mama the truth about Big Daddy and she's goin' to need you.

DOCTOR BAUGH: This is going to be painful.

MAE: Painful things caint always be avoided.

REVEREND TOOKER: I see Big Mama.

GOOPER: Hey, Big Mama, come here.

MAE: Hush, Gooper, don't holler.

BIG MAMA (*entering*): Too much smell of burnt fireworks makes me feel a little bit sick at my stomach. — Where is Big Daddy?

MAE: That's what I want to know, where has Big Daddy gone?

BIG MAMA: He must have turned in, I reckon he went to baid . . .

GOOPER: Well, then, now we can talk.

BIG MAMA: What *is* this talk, *what* talk?

(*Margaret appears on the gallery, talking to Doctor Baugh.*)

MARGARET (*musically*): My family freed their slaves ten years before abolition. My great-great-grand-father gave his slaves their freedom five years before the War between the States started!

MAE: Oh, for God's sake! Maggie's climbed back up in her family tree!

MARGARET (*sweetly*): What, Mae?

(*The pace must be very quick: great Southern animation.*)

BIG MAMA (*addressing them all*): I think Big Daddy was just worn out. He loves his family, he loves to have them around him, but it's a strain on his nerves. He wasn't himself tonight, Big Daddy wasn't himself, I could tell he was all worked up.

REVEREND TOOKER: I think he's remarkable.

BIG MAMA: Yaisss! Just remarkable. Did you all notice the food he ate at that table? Did you all notice the supper he put away? Why he ate like a hawss!

GOOPER: I hope he doesn't regret it.

BIG MAMA: What? Why that man — ate a huge piece of cawn bread with molasses on it! Helped himself twice to hoppin' John.

MARGARET: Big Daddy loves hoppin' John. — We had a real country dinner.

BIG MAMA (*overlapping Margaret*): Yaiss, he simply adores it! an' candied yams? Son? That man put away enough food at that table to stuff a *field* hand!

GOOPER (*with grim relish*): I hope he don't have to pay for it later on . . .

BIG MAMA (*fiercely*): What's *that*, Gooper?

MAE: Gooper says he hopes Big Daddy doesn't suffer tonight.

BIG MAMA: Oh, shoot, Gooper says, Gooper says! Why should Big Daddy suffer for satisfying a nor-mal appetite? There's nothin' wrong with that man but nerves, he's sound as a dollar! And now he knows he is an' that's why he ate such a supper. He had a big load off his mind, knowin' he wasn't doomed t' — what he thought he was doomed to . . .

MARGARET (*sadly and sweetly*): Bless his old sweet soul . . .

BIG MAMA (*vaguely*): Yais, bless his heart, where's Brick?

MAE: Outside.

GOOPER: — Drinkin' . . .

BIG MAMA: I know he's drinkin'. Cain't I see he's drinkin' without you continually tellin' me that boy's drinkin'?

MARGARET: Good for you, Big Mama!

(*She applauds.*)

BIG MAMA: Other people *drink* and *have* drunk an' will *drink,* as long as they make that stuff an' put it in bottles.

MARGARET: That's the truth. I never trusted a man that didn't drink.

BIG MAMA: *Brick? Brick!*

MARGARET: He's still on the gall'ry. I'll go bring him in so we can talk.

BIG MAMA (*worriedly*): I don't know what this mys-terious family conference is about.

(*Awkward silence. Big Mama looks from face to face, then belches slightly and mutters, "Excuse me . . ." She opens an ornamental fan suspended about her throat. A black lace fan to go with her black lace gown, and fans her wilting corsage, sniffing nervously and looking from face to face in the uncomfortable silence as Margaret calls "Brick?" and Brick sings to the moon on the gallery.*)

MARGARET: Brick, they're gonna tell Big Mama the truth an' she's gonna need you.

BIG MAMA: I don't know what's wrong here, you all have such long faces! Open that door on the hall and let some air circulate through here, will you please, Gooper?

MAE: I think we'd better leave that door closed, Big Mama, till after the talk.

MARGARET: Brick!

BIG MAMA: Reveren' Tooker, will *you* please open that door?

REVEREND TOOKER: I sure will, Big Mama.

MAE: I just didn't think we ought t' take any chance of Big Daddy hearin' a word of this discussion.

BIG MAMA: *I swan!* Nothing's going to be said in Big Daddy's house that he caint hear if he want to!

GOOPER: Well, Big Mama, it's —

(*Mae gives him a quick, hard poke to shut him up. He glares at her fiercely as she circles before him like a burlesque ballerina, raising her skinny bare arms over her head, jangling her bracelets, exclaiming:*)

MAE: *A breeze! A breeze!*

REVEREND TOOKER: I think this house is the coolest house in the Delta. — Did you all know that Halsey Banks's widow put air-conditioning units in the church and rectory at Friar's Point in memory of Halsey?

(*General conversation has resumed; everybody is chat-ting so that the stage sounds like a bird cage.*)

GOOPER: Too bad nobody cools your church off for you. I bet you sweat in that pulpit these hot Sun-days, Reverend Tooker.

REVEREND TOOKER: Yes, my vestments are drenched. Last Sunday the gold in my chasuble faded into the purple.

GOOPER: Reveren', you musta been preachin' hell's fire last Sunday.

MAE (*at the same time to Doctor Baugh*): You reckon those vitamin B12 injections are what they're cracked up t' be, Doc Baugh?

DOCTOR BAUGH: Well, if you want to be stuck with something I guess they're as good to be stuck with as anything else.

BIG MAMA (*at the gallery door*): *Maggie, Maggie, aren't you comin' with Brick?*

MAE (*suddenly and loudly, creating a silence*): I have a strange feeling, I have a peculiar feeling!

BIG MAMA (*turning from the gallery*): What feeling?

MAE: That Brick said somethin' he shouldn't of said t' Big Daddy.

BIG MAMA: Now what on earth could Brick of said t' Big Daddy that he shouldn't say?

GOOPER: Big Mama, there's somethin' —

MAE: NOW, WAIT!

(*She rushes up to Big Mama and gives her a quick hug and kiss. Big Mama pushes her impatiently off.*)

DOCTOR BAUGH: In my day they had what they call the Keeley cure for heavy drinkers.

BIG MAMA: Shoot!

DOCTOR BAUGH: But now I understand they just take some kind of tablets.

GOOPER: They call them "Annie Bust" tablets.

BIG MAMA: *Brick* don't need to take *nothin'*.

(*Brick and Margaret appear in gallery doors, Big Mama unaware of his presence behind her.*)

That boy is just broken up over Skipper's death. You know how poor Skipper died. They gave him a big, big dose of that sodium amytal stuff at his home and then they called the ambulance and give him another big, big dose of it at the hospital and that and all of the alcohol in his system fo' months an' months just proved too much for his heart . . . I'm scared of needles! I'm more scared of a needle than the knife . . . I think more people have been needled out of this world than —

(*She stops short and wheels about.*)

Oh — here's Brick! My precious baby —

(*She turns upon Brick with short, fat arms extended, at the same time uttering a loud, short sob, which is both comic and touching. Brick smiles and bows slightly, making a burlesque gesture of gallantry for Margaret to pass before him into the room. Then he hobbles on his crutch directly to the liquor cabinet and there is absolute silence, with everybody looking at Brick as everybody has always looked at Brick when he spoke or moved or appeared. One by one he drops ice cubes in his glass, then suddenly, but not quickly, looks back over his shoulder with a wry, charming smile, and says:*)

BRICK: I'm sorry! Anyone else?

BIG MAMA (*sadly*): No, son. I *wish* you wouldn't!

BRICK: I wish I didn't have to, Big Mama, but I'm still waiting for that click in my head which makes it all smooth out!

BIG MAMA: Ow, Brick, you — BREAK MY HEART!

MARGARET (*at same time*): Brick, go sit with Big Mama!

BIG MAMA: I just cain't staiiiiii-nnnnnnnd-it . . .

(*She sobs.*)

MAE: Now that we're all assembled —

GOOPER: We kin talk . . .

BIG MAMA: Breaks my heart . . .

MARGARET: Sit with Big Mama, Brick, and hold her hand.

(*Big Mama sniffs very loudly three times, almost like three drumbeats in the pocket of silence.*)

BRICK: You do that, Maggie. I'm a restless cripple. I got to stay on my crutch.

(*Brick hobbles to the gallery door; leans there as if waiting.*)
  (*Mae sits beside Big Mama, while Gooper moves in front and sits on the end of the couch, facing her. Reverend Tooker moves nervously into the space between them; on the other side, Doctor Baugh stands looking at nothing in particular and lights a cigar. Margaret turns away.*)

BIG MAMA: Why're you all *surroundin'* me — like this? Why're you all starin' at me like this an' makin' signs at each other?

(*Reverend Tooker steps back startled.*)

MAE: Calm yourself, Big Mama.

BIG MAMA: Calm you'self, *you'self*, Sister Woman. How could I calm myself with everyone starin' at me as if big drops of blood had broken out on m'face? What's this all about, annh! What?

(*Gooper coughs and takes a center position.*)

GOOPER: Now, Doc Baugh.

MAE: Doc Baugh?

GOOPER: Big Mama wants to know the complete truth about the report we got from the Ochsner Clinic.

MAE (*eagerly*): — on Big Daddy's condition!

GOOPER: Yais, on Big Daddy's condition, we got to face it.

DOCTOR BAUGH: Well . . .

BIG MAMA (*terrified, rising*): Is there? Something? Something that I? Don't — know?

(*In these few words, this startled, very soft, question, Big Mama reviews the history of her forty-five years with Big Daddy, her great, almost embarrassingly true-hearted and simple-minded devotion to Big Daddy, who must have had something Brick has, who made himself loved so much by the "simple expedient" of not loving enough to disturb his charming detachment, also once coupled, like Brick, with virile beauty.*)

(*Big Mama has a dignity at this moment; she almost stops being fat.*)

DOCTOR BAUGH (*after a pause, uncomfortably*): Yes? — Well —

BIG MAMA: I!!! — want to — *knowwwwww* . . .

(*Immediately she thrusts her fist to her mouth as if to deny that statement. Then for some curious reason, she snatches the withered corsage from her breast and hurls it on the floor and steps on it with her short, fat feet.*)

Somebody must be lyin'! — I want to know!

MAE: Sit down, Big Mama, sit down on this sofa.

MARGARET: Brick, go sit with Big Mama.

BIG MAMA: *What is it, what is it?*

DOCTOR BAUGH: I never have seen a more thorough examination than Big Daddy Pollitt was given in all my experience with the Ochsner Clinic.

GOOPER: It's one of the best in the country.

MAE: It's THE best in the country — bar *none!*

(*For some reason she gives Gooper a violent poke as she goes past him. He slaps at her hand without removing his eyes from his mother's face.*)

DOCTOR BAUGH: Of course they were ninety-nine and nine-tenths percent sure before they even started.

BIG MAMA: Sure of what, sure of what, sure of — what? — what?

(*She catches her breath in a startled sob. Mae kisses her quickly. She thrusts Mae fiercely away from her, staring at the Doctor.*)

MAE: Mommy, be a brave girl!

BRICK (*in the doorway, softly*): "By the light, by the light, Of the sil-ve-ry mo-oo-n . . ."

GOOPER: Shut up! — Brick.

BRICK: Sorry . . .

(*He wanders out on the gallery.*)

DOCTOR BAUGH: But now, you see, Big Mama, they cut a piece of this growth, a specimen of the tissue and —

BIG MAMA: Growth? You told Big Daddy —

DOCTOR BAUGH: Now wait.

BIG MAMA (*fiercely*): You told me and Big Daddy there wasn't a thing wrong with him but —

MAE: Big Mama, they always —

GOOPER: Let Doc Baugh talk, will yuh?

BIG MAMA: — little spastic condition of —

(*Her breath gives out in a sob.*)

DOCTOR BAUGH: Yes, that's what we told Big Daddy. But we had this bit of tissue run through the laboratory and I'm sorry to say the test was positive on it. It's — well — malignant . . .

(*Pause.*)

BIG MAMA: — Cancer?! Cancer?!

(*Doctor Baugh nods gravely. Big Mama gives a long gasping cry.*)

MAE AND GOOPER: Now, now, now, Big Mama, you had to know . . .

BIG MAMA: WHY DIDN'T THEY CUT IT OUT OF HIM? HANH? HANH?

DOCTOR BAUGH: Involved too much, Big Mama, too many organs affected.

MAE: Big Mama, the liver's affected and so's the kidneys, both! It's gone way past what they call a —

GOOPER: A surgical risk.

MAE: — Uh-huh . . .

(*Big Mama draws a breath like a dying gasp.*)

REVEREND TOOKER: Tch, tch, tch, tch, tch!

DOCTOR BAUGH: Yes it's gone past the knife.

MAE: *That's why he's turned yellow, Mommy!*

BIG MAMA: *Git away from me, git away from me, Mae!*

(*She rises abruptly.*)

I want Brick! Where's Brick? Where is my only son?

MAE: Mama! Did she say "*only* son"?

GOOPER: What does that make *me?*

MAE: A sober responsible man with five precious children! — *Six!*

BIG MAMA: I want Brick to tell me! Brick! Brick!

MARGARET (*rising from her reflections in a corner*): Brick was so upset he went back out.

BIG MAMA: *Brick!*

MARGARET: Mama, let *me* tell you!

BIG MAMA: No, no, leave me alone, you're not my blood!

GOOPER: *Mama, I'm your son!* Listen to *me!*

MAE: Gooper's your son, he's your first-born!

BIG MAMA: Gooper never liked Daddy.

MAE (*as if terribly shocked*): That's not TRUE!

(*There is a pause. The minister coughs and rises.*)

REVEREND TOOKER (*to Mae*): I think I'd better slip away at this point.

(*Discreetly.*)

Good night, good night, everybody, and God bless you all . . . on this place . . .

(*He slips out.*)
(*Mae coughs and points at Big Mama.*)

GOOPER: Well, Big Mama . . .

(*He sighs.*)

BIG MAMA: It's all a mistake, I know it's just a bad dream.

DOCTOR BAUGH: We're gonna keep Big Daddy as comfortable as we can.

BIG MAMA: Yes, it's just a bad dream, that's all it is, it's just an awful dream.

GOOPER: In my opinion Big Daddy is having some pain but won't admit that he has it.

BIG MAMA: Just a dream, a bad dream.

DOCTOR BAUGH: That's what lots of them do, they think if they don't admit they're having the pain they can sort of escape the fact of it.

GOOPER (*with relish*): Yes, they get sly about it, they get real sly about it.

MAE: Gooper and I think —

GOOPER: Shut up, Mae! Big Mama, I think — Big Daddy ought to be started on morphine.

BIG MAMA: Nobody's going to give Big Daddy morphine.

DOCTOR BAUGH: Now, Big Mama, when that pain strikes it's going to strike mighty hard and Big Daddy's going to need the needle to bear it.

BIG MAMA: I tell you, nobody's going to give him morphine.

MAE: Big Mama, you don't want to see Big Daddy suffer, you know you —

(*Gooper, standing beside her, gives her a savage poke.*)

DOCTOR BAUGH (*placing a package on the table*): I'm leaving this stuff here, so if there's a sudden attack you all won't have to send out for it.

MAE: I know how to give a hypo.

BIG MAMA: Nobody's gonna give Big Daddy morphine.

GOOPER: Mae took a course in nursing during the war.

MARGARET: Somehow I don't think Big Daddy would want Mae to give him a hypo.

MAE: You think he'd want *you* to do it?

DOCTOR BAUGH: Well . . .

(*Doctor Baugh rises.*)

GOOPER: Doctor Baugh is goin'.

DOCTOR BAUGH: Yes, I got to be goin'. Well, keep your chin up, Big Mama.

GOOPER (*with jocularity*): She's gonna keep *both* chins up, aren't you, Big Mama?

(*Big Mama sobs.*)

Now stop that, Big Mama.

GOOPER (*at the door with Doctor Baugh*): Well, Doc, we sure do appreciate all you done. I'm telling you, we're surely obligated to you for —

(*Doctor Baugh has gone out without a glance at him.*)

— I guess that doctor has got a lot on his mind but it wouldn't hurt him to act a little more human . . .

(*Big Mama sobs.*)

Now be a brave girl, Mommy.

BIG MAMA: It's not true, I know that it's just not true!

GOOPER: Mama, those tests are infallible!

BIG MAMA: Why are you so determined to see your father daid?

MAE: Big Mama!

MARGARET (*gently*): I know what Big Mama means.

MAE (*fiercely*): Oh, do you?

MARGARET (*quietly and very sadly*): Yes, I think I do.

MAE: For a newcomer in the family you sure do show a lot of understanding.

MARGARET: Understanding is needed on this place.

MAE: I guess you must have needed a lot of it in your family, Maggie, with your father's liquor problem and now you've got Brick with his!

MARGARET: Brick does not have a liquor problem at all. Brick is devoted to Big Daddy. This thing is a terrible strain on him.

BIG MAMA: Brick is Big Daddy's boy, but he drinks too much and it worries me and Big Daddy, and, Margaret, you've got to cooperate with us, you've got to cooperate with Big Daddy and me in getting Brick straightened out. Because it will break Big Daddy's heart if Brick don't pull himself together and take hold of things.

MAE: Take hold of *what* things, Big Mama?

BIG MAMA: The place.

(*There is a quick violent look between Mae and Gooper.*)

GOOPER: Big Mama, you've had a shock.

MAE: Yais, we've all had a shock, but . . .

GOOPER: Let's be realistic —

MAE: — Big Daddy would never, would *never*, be foolish enough to —

GOOPER: — put this place in irresponsible hands!

BIG MAMA: Big Daddy ain't going to leave the place

in anybody's hands; Big Daddy is *not* going to die. I want you to get that in your heads, all of you!

MAE: Mommy, Mommy, Big Mama, we're just as hopeful an' optimistic as you are about Big Daddy's prospects, we have faith in *prayer* — but nevertheless there are certain matters that have to be discussed an' dealt with, because otherwise —

GOOPER: Eventualities have to be considered and now's the time . . . Mae, will you please get my brief case out of our room?

MAE: Yes, honey.

(She rises and goes out through the hall door.)

GOOPER *(standing over Big Mama)*: Now, Big Mom. What you said just now was not at all true and you know it. I've always loved Big Daddy in my own quiet way. I never made a show of it, and I know that Big Daddy has always been fond of me in a quiet way, too, and he never made a show of it neither.

(Mae returns with Gooper's brief case.)

MAE: Here's your brief case, Gooper, honey.

GOOPER *(handing the brief case back to her)*: Thank you . . . Of cou'se, my relationship with Big Daddy is different from Brick's.

MAE: You're eight years older'n Brick an' always had t' carry a bigger load of th' responsibilities than Brick ever had t' carry. He never carried a thing in his life but a football or a highball.

GOOPER: Mae, will y' let me talk, please?

MAE: Yes, honey.

GOOPER: Now, a twenty-eight-thousand-acre plantation's a mighty big thing t' run.

MAE: Almost singlehanded.

(Margaret has gone out onto the gallery and can be heard calling softly to Brick.)

BIG MAMA: You never had to run this place! What are you talking about? As if Big Daddy was dead and in his grave, you had to run it? Why, you just helped him out with a few business details and had your law practice at the same time in Memphis!

MAE: Oh, Mommy, Mommy, Big Mommy! Let's be fair!

MARGARET: Brick!

MAE: Why, Gooper has given himself body and soul to keeping this place up for the past five years since Big Daddy's health started failing.

MARGARET: Brick!

MAE: Gooper won't say it, Gooper never thought of it as a duty, he just did it. And what did Brick do? Brick kept living in his past glory at college! Still a football player at twenty-seven!

MARGARET *(returning alone)*: Who are you talking

about now? Brick? A football player? He isn't a football player and you know it. Brick is a sports announcer on T.V. and one of the best-known ones in the country!

MAE: I'm talking about what he was.

MARGARET: Well, I wish you would just stop talking about my husband.

GOOPER: I've got a right to discuss my brother with other members of MY OWN family, which don't include *you*. Why don't you go out there and drink with Brick?

MARGARET: I've never seen such malice toward a brother.

GOOPER: How about his for me? Why, he can't stand to be in the same room with me!

MARGARET: This is a deliberate campaign of vilification for the most disgusting and sordid reason on earth, and I know what it is! It's *avarice, avarice, greed, greed!*

BIG MAMA: *Oh, I'll scream! I will scream in a moment unless this stops!*

(Gooper has stalked up to Margaret with clenched fists at his sides as if he would strike her. Mae distorts her face again into a hideous grimace behind Margaret's back.)

BIG MAMA *(sobs)*: Margaret. Child. Come here. Sit next to Big Mama.

MARGARET: Precious Mommy. I'm sorry, I'm sorry, I —!

(She bends her long graceful neck to press her forehead to Big Mama's bulging shoulder under its black chiffon.)

MAE: How beautiful, how touching, this display of devotion! Do you know why she's childless? She's childless because that big beautiful athlete husband of hers won't go to bed with her!

GOOPER: You jest won't let me do this in a nice way, will yah? Aw right — I don't give a goddam if Big Daddy likes me or don't like me or did or never did or will or will never! I'm just appealing to a sense of common decency and fair play. I'll tell you the truth. I've resented Big Daddy's partiality to Brick ever since Brick was born, and the way I've been treated like I was just barely good enough to spit on and sometimes not even good enough for that. Big Daddy is dying of cancer, and it's spread all through him and it's attacked all his vital organs including the kidneys and right now he is sinking into uremia, and you all know what uremia is, it's poisoning of the whole system due to the failure of the body to eliminate its poisons.

MARGARET *(to herself, downstage, hissingly)*: *Poisons,*

poisons! Venomous thoughts and words! In hearts and minds! — That's poisons!

GOOPER (*overlapping her*): I am asking for a square deal, and, by God, I expect to get one. But if I don't get one, if there's any peculiar shenanigans going on around here behind my back, well, I'm not a corporation lawyer for nothing, I know how to protect my own interests.

(*Brick enters from the gallery with a tranquil, blurred smile, carrying an empty glass with him.*)

BRICK: Storm coming up.
GOOPER: Oh! A late arrival!
MAE: Behold the conquering hero comes!
GOOPER: The fabulous Brick Pollitt! Remember him? — Who could forget him!
MAE: He looks like he's been injured in a game!
GOOPER: Yep, I'm afraid you'll have to warm the bench at the Sugar Bowl this year, Brick!

(*Mae laughs shrilly.*)

Or was it the Rose Bowl that he made that famous run in? —

(*Thunder.*)

MAE: The punch bowl, honey. It was in the punch bowl, the cut-glass punch bowl!
GOOPER: Oh, that's right, I'm getting the bowls mixed up!
MARGARET: Why don't you stop venting your malice and envy on a sick boy?
BIG MAMA: *Now you two hush, I mean it, hush, all of you, hush!*
DAISY, SOOKEY: Storm! Storm comin'! Storm! Storm!
LACEY: Brightie, close them shutters.
GOOPER: Lacey, put the top up on my Cadillac, will yuh?
LACEY: Yes, suh, Mistah Pollitt!
GOOPER (*at the same time*): Big Mama, you know it's necessary for me t' go back to Memphis in th' mornin' t' represent the Parker estate in a lawsuit.

(*Mae sits on the bed and arranges papers she has taken from the brief case.*)

BIG MAMA: Is it, Gooper?
MAE: Yaiss.
GOOPER: That's why I'm forced to — to bring up a problem that —
MAE: Somethin' that's too important t' be put off!
GOOPER: If Brick was sober, he ought to be in on this.
MARGARET: Brick is present; we're present.
GOOPER: Well, good. I will now give you this outline my partner, Tom Bullitt, an' me have drawn up — a sort of dummy — trusteeship.

MARGARET: Oh, that's it! You'll be in charge an' dole out remittances, will you?
GOOPER: This we did as soon as we got the report on Big Daddy from th' Ochsner Laboratories. We did this thing, I mean we drew up this dummy outline with the advice and assistance of the Chairman of the Boa'd of Directors of th' Southern Plantahs Bank and Trust Company in Memphis, C. C. Bellowes, a man who handles estates for all th' prominent fam'lies in West Tennessee and th' Delta.
BIG MAMA: Gooper?
GOOPER (*crouching in front of Big Mama*): Now this is not — not final, or anything like it. This is just a preliminary outline. But it does provide a basis — a design — a — possible, feasible — *plan!*
MARGARET: Yes, I'll bet it's a plan.

(*Thunder.*)

MAE: It's a plan to protect the biggest estate in the Delta from irresponsibility an' —
BIG MAMA: Now you listen to me, all of you, you listen here! They's not goin' to be any more catty talk in my house! And Gooper, you put that away before I grab it out of your hand and tear it right up! I don't know what the hell's in it, and I don't want to know what the hell's in it. I'm talkin' in Big Daddy's language now; I'm his *wife,* not his *widow,* I'm still his *wife!* And I'm talkin' to you in his language an' —
GOOPER: Big Mama, what I have here is —
MAE (*at the same time*): Gooper explained that it's just a plan . . .
BIG MAMA: I don't care what you got there. Just put it back where it came from, an' don't let me see it again, not even the outside of the envelope of it! Is that understood? Basis! Plan! Preliminary! Design! I say — what is it Big Daddy always says when he's disgusted?
BRICK (*from the bar*): Big Daddy says "crap" when he's disgusted.
BIG MAMA (*rising*): That's right — CRAP! I say CRAP too, like Big Daddy!

(*Thunder.*)

MAE: Coarse language doesn't seem called for in this —
GOOPER: Somethin' in me is *deeply outraged* by hearin' you talk like this.
BIG MAMA: *Nobody's goin' to take nothin'!* — till Big Daddy lets go of it — maybe, just possibly, not — not even then! No, not even then!

(*Thunder.*)

MAE: Sookey, hurry up an' git that po'ch furniture covahed; want th' paint to come off?

GOOPER: Lacey, put mah car away!

LACEY: Caint, Mistah Pollitt, you got the keys!

GOOPER: Naw, you got 'em, man. Where th' keys to th' car, honey?

MAE: You got 'em in your pocket!

BRICK: "You can always hear me singin' this song, Show me the way to go home."

(*Thunder distantly.*)

BIG MAMA: Brick! Come here, Brick, I need you. Tonight Brick looks like he used to look when he was a little boy, just like he did when he played wild games and used to come home when I hollered myself hoarse for him, all sweaty and pink cheeked and sleepy, with his — red curls shining . . .

(*Brick draws aside as he does from all physical contact and continues the song in a whisper, opening the ice bucket and dropping in the ice cubes one by one as if he were mixing some important chemical formula.*)
(*Distant thunder.*)

Time goes by so fast. Nothin' can outrun it. Death commences too early — almost before you're half acquainted with life — you meet the other . . . Oh, you know we just got to love each other an' stay together, all of us, just as close as we can, especially now that such a *black* thing has come and moved into this place without invitation.

(*Awkwardly embracing Brick, she presses her head to his shoulder.*)
(*A dog howls offstage.*)

Oh, Brick, son of Big Daddy, Big Daddy does so love you. Y'know what would be his fondest dream come true? If before he passed on, if Big Daddy has to pass on . . .

(*A dog howls.*)

. . . you give him a child of yours, a grandson as much like his son as his son is like Big Daddy . . .

MARGARET: I know that's Big Daddy's dream.

BIG MAMA: That's his dream.

MAE: Such a pity that Maggie and Brick can't oblige.

BIG DADDY (*off downstage right on the gallery*): Looks like the wind was takin' liberties with this place.

SERVANT (*offstage*): Yes, sir, Mr. Pollitt.

MARGARET (*crossing to the right door*): Big Daddy's on the gall'ry.

(*Big Mama has turned toward the hall door at the sound of Big Daddy's voice on the gallery.*)

BIG MAMA: I can't stay here. He'll see somethin' in my eyes.

(*Big Daddy enters the room from upstage right.*)

BIG DADDY: Can I come in?

(*He puts his cigar in an ash tray.*)

MARGARET: Did the storm wake you up, Big Daddy?

BIG DADDY: Which stawm are you talkin' about — th' one outside or th' hullballoo in here?

(*Gooper squeezes past Big Daddy.*)

GOOPER: 'Scuse me.

(*Mae tries to squeeze past Big Daddy to join Gooper, but Big Daddy puts his arm firmly around her.*)

BIG DADDY: I heard some mighty loud talk. Sounded like somethin' important was bein' discussed. What was the powwow about?

MAE (*flustered*): Why — nothin', Big Daddy . . .

BIG DADDY (*crossing to extreme left center, taking Mae with him*): What is that pregnant-lookin' envelope you're puttin' back in your brief case, Gooper?

GOOPER (*at the foot of the bed, caught, as he stuffs papers into envelope*): That? Nothin', suh — nothin' much of anythin' at all . . .

BIG DADDY: Nothin'? It looks like a whole lot of nothin'!

(*He turns upstage to the group.*)

You all know th' story about th' young married couple —

GOOPER: Yes, sir!

BIG DADDY: Hello, Brick —

BRICK: Hello, Big Daddy.

(*The group is arranged in a semicircle above Big Daddy, Margaret at the extreme right, then Mae and Gooper, then Big Mama, with Brick at the left.*)

BIG DADDY: Young married couple took Junior out to th' zoo one Sunday, inspected all of God's creatures in their cages, with satisfaction.

GOOPER: Satisfaction.

BIG DADDY (*crossing to upstage center, facing front*): This afternoon was a warm afternoon in spring an' that ole elephant had somethin' else on his mind which was bigger'n peanuts. You know this story, Brick?

(*Gooper nods.*)

BRICK: No, sir, I don't know it.

BIG DADDY: Y'see, in th' cage adjoinin' they was a young female elephant in heat!

BIG MAMA (*at Big Daddy's shoulder*): Oh, Big Daddy!

BIG DADDY: What's the matter, preacher's gone, ain't he? All right. That female elephant in the next cage was permeatin' the atmosphere about her with a powerful and excitin' odor of female fertility! Huh! Ain't that a nice way to put it, Brick?

BRICK: Yes, sir, nothin' wrong with it.

BIG DADDY: Brick says th's nothin' wrong with it!

BIG MAMA: Oh, Big Daddy!

BIG DADDY (*crossing to downstage center*): So this ole bull elephant still had a couple of fornications left in him. He reared back his trunk an' got a whiff of that elephant lady next door! — began to paw at the dirt in his cage an' butt his head against the separatin' partition and, first thing y'know, there was a conspicuous change in his *profile* — very *conspicuous*! Ain't I tellin' this story in decent language, Brick?

BRICK: Yes, sir, too fuckin' decent!

BIG DADDY: So, the little boy pointed at it and said, "What's that?" His mama said, "Oh, that's — nothin'!" — His papa said, "She's spoiled!"

(*Big Daddy crosses to Brick at left.*)

You didn't laugh at that story, Brick.

(*Big Mama crosses to downstage right crying. Margaret goes to her. Mae and Gooper hold upstage right center.*)

BRICK: No, sir, I didn't laugh at that story.

BIG DADDY: What is the smell in this room? Don't you notice it, Brick? Don't you notice a powerful and obnoxious odor of mendacity in this room?

BRICK: Yes, sir, I think I do, sir.

GOOPER: Mae, Mae . . .

BIG DADDY: There is nothing more powerful. Is there, Brick?

BRICK: No, sir. No, sir, there isn't, an' nothin' more obnoxious.

BIG DADDY: Brick agrees with me. The odor of mendacity is a powerful and obnoxious odor an' the stawm hasn't blown it away from this room yet. You notice it, Gooper?

GOOPER: What, sir?

BIG DADDY: How about you, Sister Woman? You notice the unpleasant odor of mendacity in this room?

MAE: Why, Big Daddy, I don't even know what that is.

BIG DADDY: You can smell it. Hell it smells like death!

(*Big Mama sobs. Big Daddy looks toward her.*)

What's wrong with that fat woman over there, loaded with diamonds? Hey, what's-you-name, what's the matter with you?

MARGARET (*crossing toward Big Daddy*): She had a slight dizzy spell, Big Daddy.

BIG DADDY: You better watch that, Big Mama. A stroke is a bad way to go.

MARGARET (*crossing to Big Daddy at center*): Oh, Brick, Big Daddy has on your birthday present to him, Brick, he has on your cashmere robe, the softest material I have ever felt.

BIG DADDY: Yeah, this is my soft birthday, Maggie . . . Not my gold or my silver birthday, but my soft birthday, everything's got to be soft for Big Daddy on this soft birthday.

(*Maggie kneels before Big Daddy at center.*)

MARGARET: Big Daddy's got on his Chinese slippers that I gave him, Brick. Big Daddy, I haven't given you my big present yet, but now I will, now's the time for me to present it to you! I have an announcement to make!

MAE: What? What kind of announcement?

GOOPER: A sports announcement, Maggie?

MARGARET: Announcement of life beginning! A child is coming, sired by Brick, and out of Maggie the Cat! I have Brick's child in my body, an' that's my birthday present to Big Daddy on this birthday!

(*Big Daddy looks at Brick who crosses behind Big Daddy to downstage portal, left.*)

BIG DADDY: Get up, girl, get up off your knees, girl.

(*Big Daddy helps Margaret to rise. He crosses above her, to her right, bites off the end of a fresh cigar, taken from his bathrobe pocket, as he studies Margaret.*)

Uh-huh, this girl has life in her body, that's no lie!

BIG MAMA: BIG DADDY'S DREAM COME TRUE!

BRICK: JESUS!

BIG DADDY (*crossing right below wicker stand*): Gooper, I want my lawyer in the mornin'.

BRICK: Where are you goin', Big Daddy?

BIG DADDY: Son, I'm goin' up on the roof, to the belvedere on th' roof to look over my kingdom before I give up my kingdom — twenty-eight thousand acres of th' richest land this side of the valley Nile!

(*He exits through right doors, and down right on the gallery.*)

BIG MAMA (*following*): Sweetheart, sweetheart, sweetheart — can I come with you?

(*She exits downstage right.*)
(*Margaret is downstage center in the mirror area. Mae has joined Gooper and she gives him a fierce poke, making a low hissing sound and a grimace of fury.*)

GOOPER (*pushing her aside*): Brick, could you possibly spare me one small shot of that liquor?

BRICK: Why, help yourself, Gooper boy.

GOOPER: I will.

MAE (*shrilly*): Of course we know that this is — a lie.

GOOPER: *Be still, Mae.*

MAE: I won't be still! I know she's made this up!

GOOPER: Goddam it, I said shut up!

MARGARET: Gracious! I didn't know that my little announcement was going to provoke such a storm!

MAE: *That* woman isn't *pregnant!*

GOOPER: Who said she was?

MAE: *She* did.

GOOPER: The doctor didn't. Doc Baugh didn't.

MARGARET: I haven't gone to Doc Baugh.

GOOPER: Then who'd you go to, Maggie?

MARGARET: One of the best gynecologists in the South.

GOOPER: Uh huh, uh huh! — I see . . .

(*He takes out a pencil and notebook.*)

 — May we have his name, please?

MARGARET: No, you may not, Mister Prosecuting Attorney!

MAE: He doesn't have any name, he doesn't exist!

MARGARET: Oh, he exists all right, and so does my child, Brick's baby!

MAE: You can't conceive a child by a man that won't sleep with you unless you think you're —

(*Brick has turned on the phonograph. A scat song cuts Mae's speech.*)

GOOPER: *Turn that off!*

MAE: We know it's a lie because we hear you in here; he won't sleep with you, we hear you! So don't imagine you're going to put a trick over on us, to fool a dying man with a —

(*A long drawn cry of agony and rage fills the house. Margaret turns the phonograph down to a whisper. The cry is repeated.*)

MAE: Did you hear that, Gooper, did you hear that?

GOOPER: Sounds like the pain has struck.

GOOPER: Come along and leave these lovebirds together in their nest!

(*He goes out first. Mae follows but turns at the door, contorting her face and hissing at Margaret.*)

MAE: *Liar!*

(*She slams the door.*)
    (*Margaret exhales with relief and moves a little unsteadily to catch hold of Brick's arm.*)

MARGARET: Thank you for — keeping still . . .

BRICK: O.K., Maggie.

MARGARET: It was gallant of you to save my face!

(*He now pours down three shots in quick succession*

and stands waiting, silent. All at once he turns with a smile and says:)

BRICK: *There!*

MARGARET: What?

BRICK: The *click* . . .

(*His gratitude seems almost infinite as he hobbles out on the gallery with a drink. We hear his crutch as he swings out of sight. Then, at some distance, he begins singing to himself a peaceful song. Margaret holds the big pillow forlornly as if it were her only companion, for a few moments, then throws it on the bed. She rushes to the liquor cabinet, gathers all the bottles in her arms, turns about undecidedly, then runs out of the room with them, leaving the door ajar on the dim yellow hall. Brick is heard hobbling back along the gallery, singing his peaceful song. He comes back in, sees the pillow on the bed, laughs lightly, sadly, picks it up. He has it under his arm as Margaret returns to the room. Margaret softly shuts the door and leans against it, smiling softly at Brick.*)

MARGARET: Brick, I used to think that you were stronger than me and I didn't want to be overpowered by you. But now, since you've taken to liquor — you know what? — I guess it's bad, but now I'm stronger than you and I can love you more truly! Don't move that pillow. I'll move it right back if you do! — Brick?

(*She turns out all the lamps but a single rose-silk-shaded one by the bed.*)

I really have been to a doctor and I know what to do and — Brick? — this is my time by the calendar to conceive?

BRICK: Yes, I understand, Maggie. But how are you going to conceive a child by a man in love with his liquor?

MARGARET: By locking his liquor up and making him satisfy my desire before I unlock it!

BRICK: Is that what you've done, Maggie?

MARGARET: Look and see. That cabinet's mighty empty compared to before!

BRICK: Well, I'll be a son of a —

(*He reaches for his crutch but she beats him to it and rushes out on the gallery, hurls the crutch over the rail, and comes back in, panting.*)

MARGARET: And so tonight we're going to make the lie true, and when that's done, I'll bring the liquor back here and we'll get drunk together, here, tonight, in this place that death has come into . . . — What do you say?

BRICK: I don't say anything. I guess there's nothing to say.

MARGARET: Oh, you weak people, you weak, beautiful people! — who give up with such grace. What you want is someone to —

(*She turns out the rose-silk lamp.*)

— take hold of you. — Gently, gently with love hand your life back to you, like somethin' gold you let go of. I *do* love you, Brick, I *do!*

BRICK (*smiling with charming sadness*): Wouldn't it be funny if that was true?

COMMENTARIES

Tennessee Williams has long been one of the fascinating figures of American drama. He was a forceful personality who charmed his friends and the public alike, although his life was often filled with uncertainties and unresolved problems. Some of his best work derived from his private agonies. His work was taken seriously almost from the first, and a body of criticism has developed around it, including biographies, personal reminiscences of collaborators, critical commentaries, and scholarship.

Among the commentaries included here is a sampling from his *Memoirs*, published in 1972, in which he discusses *The Glass Menagerie* and *Cat on a Hot Tin Roof*. Williams reflects on his role as author, what he calls "the professional side of my life." He talks about his reasons for liking *Cat on a Hot Tin Roof* best among his plays. His additional comments on what it is like to be a writer are brief, but loaded with meaning.

Donald Spoto, who wrote *The Kindness of Strangers: The Life of Tennessee Williams* (1985), tells about Laurette Taylor, who played the mother in the first production of *The Glass Menagerie*. Taylor, a powerful actress whose career had seemed finished when the part was offered to her, almost refused the role at first. But her interpretation established a point of reference to which later actresses had to pay homage. Spoto helps us understand the power of collaboration between actor and playwright that sometimes helps both expand their understanding of the work.

Benjamin Nelson explains that "*The Glass Menagerie* exhibits several of Williams's weaknesses as well as his strengths as a playwright." He discusses Williams's characterizations, especially of Laura and Amanda. He also points to "poetic passages" in the play that he feels are weaknesses. Ultimately, Nelson poses an interesting dramatic question: Is the play a tragedy? The search for an answer to this question involves a full consideration of the play's strengths and weaknesses, its success or failure.

Collaboration is the theme of Brenda Murphy's discussion of Williams's work with Elia Kazan, who directed *Cat on a Hot Tin Roof* and other works by Williams. She reveals that their collaboration was a clash of powerful personalities. Each had his own professional authority but different ideas. In the case of *Cat on a Hot Tin Roof*, their difficulties centered on Big Daddy, a character whose appeal and force onstage were so great that Kazan did not want him to disappear after act 2. Williams rewrote the ending under duress and much later admitted that Kazan was right. Murphy makes us aware of the extent to which theater is a collaboration, even when a play flows from the pen of a genius such as Williams.

Donald Spoto (b. 1941)
LAURETTE TAYLOR IN *THE GLASS MENAGERIE*   1985

When the part of Amanda Wingfield was offered to her, Laurette Taylor thought her career as an actress was over. Donald Spoto, the biographer of Tennessee Williams, gives us a vision of how persistence and devotion to someone of genuine talent produced a legend in American acting.

That month [December 1944], the details moved together swiftly. [Actor-producer-director Eddie] Dowling, who had directed actress Julie Haydon in *The Time of Your Life*,° convinced her that (although she was thirty-four) she would be credible as the lame, fragile Laura, a character at least a decade younger. She, in turn, took the play to her friend and mentor (later her husband), the formidable critic George Jean Nathan, whose approval she felt obligatory. At the same time, the forty-nine-year-old Dowling announced — without a smile — that he would play young (twentyish) Tom, the shoe-warehouse clerk and aspiring poet; for the role of the gentleman caller, Anthony Ross was hired. The remaining role to be cast was Amanda Wingfield — the "little woman of great but confused vitality," as Williams described her in the play, "clinging frantically to another time and place." The role demanded not mere competence, but the nuances of dramatic greatness. Nathan suggested Laurette Taylor. Dowling and [Audrey] Wood [Williams's agent] and Williams saw his wisdom; they also panicked.

Laurette Taylor, then sixty, had been up to the 1930s one of the great ladies of the American stage. Those who had seen her in *Peg O' My Heart* (in 1912) or *The Furies* (in 1928) or *Outward Bound* (in 1938) knew her gifts. But for almost ten years she had herself become a woman of great but confused vitality, and a confirmed alcoholic.

At that time, Taylor was living in sad withdrawal from the theater, at a hotel on East 60th Street, where she was daily attended by a drama student named Eloise Sheldon. In return for acting lessons, the young woman cared for the practical details of Taylor's life and offered devoted companionship. The

The Time of Your Life: A play (1939) by William Saroyan.

play reached Taylor by the circuitous route of Wood to Dowling to Haydon to Nathan to Sheldon to Taylor. It also bore a new title — *The Glass Menagerie*.

"Of course her first reaction was to turn it down," Eloise Sheldon Armen recalled years later; "she thought her career was over. But we prevailed on her to see that no one could bring this character to life the way she could." At last, with the loving encouragement of Eloise — "a small flame," as Laurette Taylor's daughter appreciatively wrote of the young student, "guiding [Taylor] back to the paths of everyday life" — she accepted the part. She did not, however, stop drinking, nor did she seem to give much attention to memorizing lines before or during rehearsals.

In November, Dowling (with, Williams insisted, Margo Jones as codirector) began rehearsals in New York prior to a scheduled Chicago tryout at the end of December. Terrified that something like the history of *Battle of Angels* would be repeated — not because of the new play's content (which could not have been more different) but because he no longer believed the play was anything but "rather dull, too nice" — Williams fled New York for St. Louis. There he was interviewed on his life and work and hopes by the drama critic of the *Star-Times*, a man named William Inge. The resulting article was full of inaccuracies, half-truths and Williams's typical alterations of personal history; the resulting friendship was much more intense and dramatic.

But Audrey and Dowling would not allow Williams to be an absentee author, and in December he was summoned to Chicago. The situation, he quickly realized, was as bleak as the fierce winter that had already descended.

First of all, Laurette Taylor — with only a week remaining before the December 26 premiere — attended the final rehearsals in what can only be called an alcoholic stupor, barely summarizing the dialogue and so broadly defining the woman's Southern accent and character that, as Williams wrote . . . , she made the play sound like the Aunt Jemima Pancake Hour. In addition, Jo Mielziner's stage designs were being followed with great difficulty, and the music Williams had commissioned from his old acquaintance Paul Bowles sounded harsh through the theater's crude sound system. Luggage had not arrived; a winter storm raged; the Civic Theatre was inconvenient to Chicago's main theater district; there was no budget for advertising or publicity; and everyone in the company (except Eddie Dowling and Julie Haydon) — cast, crew, author — submerged the fear of failure in strong drink. Margo Jones, Williams wrote . . . , was like a scoutmaster leading a wayward and desperate troop to their doom.

As late as Christmas Eve, the lines of the play had been neither "frozen" (fixed by the producer and playwright to be performed as written) nor completely memorized. Laurette Taylor managed only a martini mumble, Dowling was demanding rewrites, and the cast was stumbling into props and one another. "Mr. Dowling," Williams said quietly that night, "art is experience remembered in tranquillity. And I find no tranquillity in Chicago."

The night after Christmas, *The Glass Menagerie* was somehow performed for a small, diffident audience. By the afternoon of the twenty-seventh, the box office had taken in only four hundred dollars, and the producers prepared a closing notice. But then Audrey telephoned them to read two brief reviews: Critic Claudia Cassidy, writing in the *Chicago Daily Tribune*, said the play had "the stamina of success . . . [it] knows people and how they tick. . . . If it is your play, as it is mine, it reaches out . . . and you are caught in its spell." And

Ashton Stevens, in the *Herald American*, said *The Glass Menagerie* "has the courage of true poetry couched in colloquial prose."

Before the end of that day, the mayor of Chicago, at the urging of the Civic Theatre's management, authorized a fifty-percent ticket subsidy for municipal employees. On the third night, Laurette Taylor was not simply discharging a half-formed role, she was creating a legend; she had begun to draw a more wonderful portrait than anyone could have imagined — not Eddie Dowling (who resented the critics' subsequent raves about her), not Tennessee Williams nor Audrey Wood, not anyone connected with the play.

"Actually," according to the playwright, "she directed many of the scenes, particularly the ones between mother and daughter, and she did a top-notch job. She was continually working on her part, putting in little things and taking them out — almost every night in Chicago there was something new, but she never disturbed the central characterization. Everything she did was absolutely in character."

The closing notice was removed — not, however, because box-office business dramatically improved, but because Claudia Cassidy and Ashton Stevens had been championing the play, returning almost nightly and telling and writing about it almost daily. "It gripped players and audiences alike," Cassidy wrote on January 7, 1945, "and created one of those rare evenings in the theater that make 'stagestruck' an honorable word." By the middle of the month, no tickets were available. In an unusual example of journalistic salvation, a play was for once not lost but kept alive because of critical support.

Benjamin Nelson
PROBLEMS IN *THE GLASS MENAGERIE*   *1961*

Benjamin Nelson's analysis of Williams's play recognizes the power of the circumstances portrayed in the play. However, Nelson's concern is that the characters, especially Laura, are not as fully and carefully drawn as they need to be to make the play truly powerful. He also criticizes Williams for creating a universe that "does not allow tragedy."

The Glass Menagerie exhibits several of Williams' weaknesses as well as his strengths as a playwright. The great strength of the play is of course the delicate, sympathetic, yet objective creation of meaningful people in a meaningful situation. Williams has caught a decisive and desperate moment in the lives of four individuals and given it illumination and a sense of deep meaning — no small feat for any writer.

His characterizations are not equally realized. He has been unable to create Laura on more than a single dimension, while Amanda is overwhelming in her multi-faceted delineation. On a more technical level the play manifests a doubt on the part of its author toward the power of the written word. As a backdrop for *The Glass Menagerie*, Williams originally wished to use a screen to register emotions and present images from the past, present, and future. For example, when Jim O'Connor confesses to the family that he is going steady with another girl, the legend on the screen is to read, "The Sky Falls." Fortunately, [actor-director] Eddie Dowling deleted these touches of the poet from his production, but the play still abounds with a number of pretentious statements on the part of Tom as Narrator.

I assume that the final scene between Amanda and Laura is played in pantomime because Williams wished to portray Amanda's dignity through her gestures and her daughter's reaction, rather than through the mother's speech, which during the course of the drama has been either shrill, simpering, or saucy. But in relegating this scene to background silence while Tom makes a self-conscious statement about drifting like a dead leaf "attempting to find in motion what was lost in space," he has substituted a painfully pretentious narration for what could have been an intense and luminous moment between the two women.

Again, on the credit side of the author, his play presents genuine situation, motivation, and, as Joseph Wood Krutch has noted, "a hard substantial core of shrewd observation and deft, economical characterization." But Mr. Krutch also noted that "this hard core is enveloped in a fuzzy haze of pretentious, sentimental, pseudo-poetic verbiage." [1] In *The Glass Menagerie*, the strained lyricism runs parallel with dialogue that is fresh, alive, and highly characteristic, particularly in the speech of Amanda. This dialogue fortunately dominates the proceedings, but the excess of self-conscious "poetical" passages is quite apparent and is a fault of which Williams is to be guilty in much of his later work.

But the great weakness of *The Glass Menagerie* does not lie in its author's artistic or technical deficiencies. The weakness lies at the core of the play and evolves out of what is to become the playwright's hardening philosophical commitment. We can begin to comprehend this when we ask ourselves whether or not *The Glass Menagerie* is a tragedy. It presents a tragic situation and characters who, despite their moodiness and foolishness and self-deception, possess a sense of the tragic. With the possible exception of Laura, they are intensely genuine and the destruction of their dreams and aspirations bears the illusion of great importance. But the play is not a tragedy. The universe of *The Glass Menagerie* does not allow tragedy.

Everyone in the play is a failure and in the course of their drama they all perish a little. Amanda, the most heroic of the quartet, is pitiful but not tragic because from the outset she is doomed to failure despite her desperate struggle to right things. None of these people are given the opportunity to triumph against a fate which is as malignant as it is implacable. Their struggle is a rearguard action against life, a continuous retreat. This retreat may be moving, pathetic, melodramatic, or boisterous, but it is always a withdrawal. After all, what is the world outside the glass menagerie?

> There was only hot swing music and liquor, dance halls, bars, and movies, and sex that hung in the gloom like a chandelier and flooded the world with brief, deceptive rainbows. . . . All the world was waiting for bombardments! (p. 922)

The world outside the Wingfield apartment is a world of illusions, also, even more deceptive and destructive than those held by Amanda and Laura. It is the world of *Stairs to the Roof* and this time the escape is not to a new star but

---

[1]Joseph Wood Krutch, *The Nation* 14 April 1945:24.

into the individual and personal illusions fostered by each of the characters as his private defense against destruction. Jim waits for the day when his "zzzzzp!" will at last disperse his fear and uncertainty; Laura creates her own sparkling, cold world which gives the illusion of warmth but is as eternal in its unreality as the glass from which it is composed; Amanda strikes out with all her power against her fate by clinging to the past as to a shield; and Tom, recognizing the plight of his family, can do no more than drift away from them, rudderless, frightened, and never really as far from Amanda and Laura as he knows he should be.

Not one of these individuals can cope with his situation. They struggle and their hopes and the destruction of these hopes possess a sense of great importance because Williams has created genuine people in an intensely genuine situation, but they lack the completeness to truly cope with their dilemma. They are not responsible for what has happened to them and they are much too helpless to do more than delay the inevitable. And destruction is inevitable because it is implicit in the universe of Tennessee Williams.

> For the sins of the world are really only its partialities, and these are what sufferings must atone for. . . . The nature of man is full of such makeshift arrangements, devised by himself to cover his incompletion. He feels a part of himself to be like a missing wall or a room left unfurnished and he tries as well as he can to make up for it. The use of imagination, resorting to dreams or the loftier purpose of art, is a mask he devises to cover his incompletion. Or violence such as a war, between two men or among a number of nations, is also a blind and senseless compensation for that which is not yet formed in human nature. Then there is still another compensation. This one is found in the principle of atonement, the surrender of self to violent treatment by others with the idea of thereby cleansing one's self of his guilt.[2]

This statement emanates from the core of Williams' thought and is perhaps his most illuminating commentary about himself and his work. It represents a philosophy, or let us say an attitude toward man in his universe, which is to manifest itself in all his work. It is taken from his short story, "Desire and the Black Masseur," which deals with the final compensation cited in the above quotation: purification through violence. In this tale, a man atones for what the author feels is a cosmic fragmentation and guilt by allowing — and actually furthering — his destruction by a cannibal. In *Battle of Angels* and *The Purification*, we find this same kind of violent cleansing.

The Glass Menagerie is a far cry from any of these works; it is the most nonviolent drama written by Williams. Nevertheless it adheres to the belief set forth in the short story. The underlying belief in *The Glass Menagerie* is that there is very little, if any, reason for living. Man is by nature incomplete because his universe is fragmented. There is nothing to be done about this condition because nothing *can* be done about it. Human guilt becomes a corollary of universal guilt and man's life is an atonement for the human condition. In each character in *The Glass Menagerie* there is a part "like a missing wall or a room left unfurnished and he tries as well as he can to make up for it." The mask devised by Laura and Amanda and Tom and Jim is "the use of imagination, resorting to dreams." The Wingfields are broken, fragmented people because "the sins of the world are really only its partialities." They are really not at all

---

[2]Williams, "Desire and the Black Masseur," *One Arm and Other Stories* (New York, 1948), 85.

responsible for their condition, and thus are in no way able to cope with it. They are trapped in a determined universe. Without some kind of responsibility on the part of the protagonist there is opportunity neither for tragic elevation nor tragic fall. The Wingfields were doomed the moment they were born. At best their struggles will allow them to survive . . . for a time. They will never be allowed to triumph. Thus their struggles, their hopes, and even their eventual destruction can never move far beyond pathos. The beauty and magic of *The Glass Menagerie* is that this pathos is genuine, objective, and deeply moving.

Tennessee Williams (1911–1983)
MEMOIRS

1972

Tennessee Williams published Memoirs *in 1972, after establishing himself as one of the most successful American playwrights. The two excerpts included here concern his feelings about* Cat on a Hot Tin Roof *and his feelings about being a writer.*

Well, now, about plays, what about them? Plays are written and then, if they are lucky, they are performed, and if their luck still holds, which is not too frequently the case, their performance is so successful that both audience and critics at the first night are aware that they are being offered a dramatic work which is both honest and entertaining and also somehow capable of engaging their aesthetic appreciation.

I have never liked to talk about the professional side of my life. Am I afraid that it is a bird that will be startled away by discussion, as by a hawk's shadow? Something like that, I suppose.

People are always asking me, at those symposia to which I've been subjected in recent years, which is my favorite among the plays I have written, the number of which eludes my recollection, and I either say to them, "Always the latest" or I succumb to my instinct for the truth and say, "I suppose it must be the published version of *Cat on a Hot Tin Roof.*"

That play comes closest to being both a work of art and a work of craft. It is really very well put together, in my opinion, and all its characters are amusing and credible and touching. Also it adheres to the valuable edict of Aristotle that a tragedy must have unity of time and place and magnitude of theme.

The set in *Cat* never changes and its running time is exactly the time of its action, meaning that one act, timewise, follows directly upon the other, and I know of no other modern American play in which this is accomplished.

However my reasons for liking *Cat* best are deeper than that. I believe that in *Cat* I reached beyond myself, in the second act, to a kind of crude eloquence of expression in Big Daddy that I have managed to give no other character of my creation.

The story of *Cat*'s production in 1954 and the disaster that followed upon its enormous success must be told now.

[Director Elia] Kazan immediately shared Audrey's [Wood, Williams's agent] enthusiasm for *Cat* but he said that it was faulty in one act. I assumed that he meant the first act, but no, it was the third act. He wanted a more admirable heroine than the Maggie offered in the original script.

Inwardly I disagreed. I thought that in Maggie I had presented a very true and moving portrait of a young woman whose frustration in love and whose practicality drove her to the literal seduction of an unwilling young man. Seduction is too soft a word. Brick was literally forced back to bed by Maggie, when she confiscated his booze . . .

Then I also had to violate my own intuition by having Big Daddy re-enter the stage in Act Three. I saw nothing for him to do in that act when he re-entered and I did not think that it was dramatically proper that he should re-enter. Consequently I had him tell "the elephant story." This was assaulted by censors. I was told it must be removed. The material which I then had to put in its place was always offensive to me.

I would not tell you this except for the consequences to me as a writer after *Cat* had received its Critics' Award and its Pulitzer.

Even though I always go crazy on opening nights, the New York opening of *Cat* was particularly dreadful. I thought it was a failure, a distortion of what I had intended. After the show was over I thought I had heard coughs all during the performance. I suppose there weren't that many, probably the usual number. And it did become by biggest, my longest-running play. But after the show was over on opening night, Kazan said, "Let's go to my apartment until the reviews are out." He was totally confident that it would be a hit. I met Audrey Wood outside, and at the time I was totally dependent on her for any creative confidence; and so I said, "Audrey, we're all going up to the Kazans' to wait for the notices." She said, "Oh no, I have other plans." I was hurt, and said something mean. . . .

What is it like being a writer? I would say it is like being free.

I know that some writers aren't free, they are professionally employed, which is quite a different thing.

Professionally, they are probably better writers in the conventional sense of "better." They have an ear to the ground of best-seller demands: They please their publishers and presumably their public as well.

But they are not free and so they are not what I regard a true writer as being.

To be free is to have achieved your life.

It means any number of freedoms.

It means the freedom to stop when you please, to go where and when you please, it means to be voyager here and there, one who flees many hotels, sad or happy, without obstruction and without much regret.

It means the freedom of being. And someone has wisely observed, if you can't be yourself, what's the point of being anything at all?

I am not a frequent reader nor quoter of Scriptures and yet I love a piece of advice which occurs among them:

"Let thy light so shine among men that they see thy good works and glorify thy Father which is in heaven."

There is a New Journalism, there is a New Criticism, there is a new look and style of cinema and theater, of practically everything that we live with, but what I think we most need is a New Morality.

And I think we've arrived at a point where that is a necessity of continued and bearable existence.

Brenda Murphy (*b. 1950*)
TENNESSEE WILLIAMS AND ELIA KAZAN COLLABORATE ON *CAT*   1991

Theater is a collaborative art, and numerous plays have been altered because of suggestions of director or actor. The collaboration of Tennessee Williams and director Elia Kazan was special because both were powerful personalities and each respected the other. The Cat on a Hot Tin Roof *that we know is much different from the one Williams wrote because of Williams's willingness to make many of the creative changes suggested by Kazan.*

[Director Elia Kazan's] imagination stimulated by Big Daddy's rhetorical power, Kazan developed the production around the impetus of direct communication between the characters and the audience. At the beginning of Act 2, for example, he made a note to himself to have Big Daddy come downstage facing the audience and talk straight out to them while the others remained way upstage, even out on the gallery. Williams agreed with Kazan about the power of Big Daddy's character and the centrality of words in the play. In *Memoirs* he wrote, "In *Cat* I reached beyond myself, in the second act, to a kind of crude eloquence of expression in Big Daddy that I have managed to give no other character of my creation." [1]

Although Williams had incorporated the idea of addressing the audience in the "recitative" speeches of Maggie and Brick in the early scripts, he had not counted on what was in 1955 the radical concept that Kazan devised for the production. As Kazan noted in a later interview, the conventions of representational realism were so entrenched in the Broadway theater of the fifties that foregrounding the production's theatricality to the extent of having the characters address the audience directly had been considered anathema for many years. The last time he could remember it being done was in the production of *Our Town*° in 1938. [2]

Kazan's pride in this rejection of realistic convention and his continuing interest in subjectifying theatrical experience were evident in an interview he gave in the early sixties:

I was busting out of the goddamned proscenium theater uptown. In *Cat on a Hot Tin Roof* I had everybody address the audience continually. Every time they had one of those long speeches they'd turn and say it to the audience. Nobody thought anything of it once we opened. But there was a hell of a lot of bitching about it before. . . . The whole second act of *Cat* was a long address by Burl Ives to the audience. I had

---

[1] Williams, Tennessee, *Memoirs* (Garden City: Doubleday, 1975).

Our Town: In this play by Thornton Wilder, a character called the Stage Manager speaks to the audience throughout the play.

[2] Michel Ciment, *Kazan on Kazan* (New York: Viking, 1974) 47.

him address various members of the audience . . . "what would *you* do?" is implicit in this kind of staging. It sucks the audience into the experience and emotion of that moment.[3]

Kazan wrote in his autobiography that he had to convince Williams to accept his notion of how Burl Ives would play the part of Big Daddy. When Kazan said he was going to bring Ives right down to the edge of the forestage, have him "look the audience right in the eye, and speak it directly to them," Williams protested that *Cat* was a realistic play, and should be kept within the representational conventions. When pressed by Kazan to say whether old cotton planters actually talked that eloquently and that long without interruption, Williams replied that they did. After all, who would dare interrupt them?[4] Nonetheless Kazan pursued his concept for the production in the face of Williams's skepticism, if not his opposition.

The Design

When the central dynamic of the production had been established as direct communication between the characters and the audience, it had to imbue all the elements of the stage language. Here Kazan reports that he did run into opposition from Williams, who had a clear idea of what he thought the set should be like, an image that had evolved as he had revised the play. In the notes for the designer he prepared for the script preceding the November prerehearsal version, Williams described the basic plan of the set that was eventually used for the production: a bed–sitting room in a Mississippi Delta plantation, opening onto an upstairs gallery and showing white balustrades against a fair summer sky that fades into dusk and night during the course of the play. This is what is needed to support the action of the play which, as Williams was fond of pointing out, observed the unities of time and place, the action of the play being confined to the single set and occupying exactly the amount of time it took to enact on stage. The lighting was obviously crucial for this play, to show the passage of time that is a central thematic concern as well as a structural one.

Beyond this, however, Williams's original image of the set was strikingly different from the set Kazan and Jo Mielziner eventually devised between them. Williams described the room as Victorian, with a touch of the Far East, and poetically haunted by the tender relationship of Jack Straw and Peter Ochello. He noted that the room should not have changed much since Straw and Ochello's time. To suggest the style for the design, Williams referred the designer to the reproduction he had seen of a faded photograph of the verandah of Robert Louis Stevenson's home in Samoa: "There was a quality of tender light on weathered wood, such as porch-furniture made of bamboo and wicker, exposed to tropical suns and tropical rains, which came to mind when I thought about the set for this play" (RV xiii).° The photograph, he wrote, also brought to mind "the grace and comfort of light, the reassurance it gives, on a late and fair afternoon in summer, the way that no matter what, even dread of death,

[3]Quoted in Richard Schechner and Theodore Hoffman, " 'Look, There's the American Theatre': An Interview with Elia Kazan," *Tulane Drama Review*, 9 (Winter 1964): 71.
[4]Elia Kazan, *Elia Kazan: A Life* (New York: Knopf, 1988) 541–42.
RV: The reading version of the play (New York: New American Library, 1958), which has both versions of the third act.

is gently touched and soothed by it. For the set is the background for a play that deals with human extremities of emotion and needs that softness behind it" (RV xiii).

Williams described in detail the big, slightly raked, double bed and the "entertainment center" that were the most significant objects in the set, and then he cautioned the designer, lest he feel that the previous description confined him to literal realism. As in the published "Note for the Designer," Williams envisioned that "the set should be far less realistic than I have so far implied in this description of it": The walls should dissolve mysteriously into the air below the ceiling; the set should be roofed by the sky; stars and moon suggested by traces of milky pallor, as if they were observed through a telescope lens out of focus (RV xiv). The original note, however, added the idea that a spiral nebula might be faintly suggested in order to suggest the "mystery of the cosmos," which Williams thought should be a visible presence in the play, almost as present as an actor in it. He also thought that the cloud effects and the sound effects for the windstorm in Act 3 should be as unrealistic as the set. As he revised the script, however, Williams began to reconceptualize the set as well. In November he sent off a rewrite of the scene description suggesting that the room should appear to have been remodeled since Straw and Ochello's time, and now had an open, Japanese effect. The canopied bed, he suggested, could appear to have been removed from an Italian renaissance palazzo when Big Daddy and Big Mama raided Europe a few years previously.

When Kazan and Mielziner began talking about the design, their concept of a production that foregrounded the characters' rhetorical appeals to the audience became the central element in their discussion. Kazan has written:

> Jo Mielziner and I had read the play in the same way; we saw its great merit was its brilliant rhetoric and its theatricality. Jo didn't see the play as realistic any more than I did. If it was to be done realistically, I would have to contrive stage business to keep the old man talking those great second-act speeches turned out front and pretend that it was just another day in the life of the Pollitt family. This would, it seemed to me, amount to an apology to the audience for the glory of the author's language. It didn't seem like just another day in the life of a cotton planter's family to Jo or to me; it seemed like the best kind of theater, the kind we were interested in encouraging, the theater theatrical, not pretending any longer that an audience wasn't out there to be addressed but having a performer as great as Burl Ives acknowledge their presence at all times and even make eye contact with individuals.[5]

Accordingly, Kazan wrote, "I caused Jo to design our setting as I wished, a large, triangular platform, tipped toward the audience and holding only one piece of furniture, an ornate bed. This brought the play down to its essentials and made it impossible for it to be played any way except as I preferred."[6]

The set was not quite so spare as Kazan remembered it, but the central point of his statement, that the presentational impulse was the dominant aesthetic factor in creating the design, has been fully corroborated by Mielziner. In his memoir, Mielziner described their discussion about the design much as Kazan did. Asked how he thought the "elephant story" should be handled proxemically, Mielziner told Kazan that he thought it should receive as much emphasis as possible: "I suggested that we have an area of the stage on which Big Daddy could come down close to the audience and deliver the lines with dramatic

[5]Kazan 542–43.
[6]Kazan 543.

force." Mielziner wrote that Kazan was delighted with his answer, and "from this discussion grew the idea of creating a stage within the stage. It would be steeply raked toward the audience with one corner actually jutting out over the footlights. In its final form it turned out to be a sort of thrust stage." [7]

Mielziner's design was a departure from the subjective realism he had employed in *Menagerie*, *Streetcar*, and *Summer and Smoke*, in that he did not try to suggest through the material elements of the stage language that the events unfolding on stage were filtered through the mind of one of the characters. Instead, the design of the set projected the action out toward the audience, forcing it to become involved as though it were one of the characters. Extremely spare, the set was composed of two platforms, a large diamond-shaped one, a corner of which projected beyond the proscenium, and a smaller rectangle a foot lower at stage right. There were no doors, such actions as opening doors and looking into the mirror being mimed in this production. The only items of furniture Mielziner drew in his sketches were the primary material signifiers: the large bed, which signified both Maggie and Brick's failing marriage and the lingering memory of Straw and Ochello; the entertainment center, which signified both Brick's immediate goal of escape from reality and the vacuous materialism that Williams saw in the fifties; and the daybed, which signified Brick's withdrawal from Maggie, their marriage, and life in general. The actual set, however, also held a wicker night table and a large wicker armchair which could accommodate either Burl Ives or two of the other actors. The overall effect was of a large playing space down front where the actors could address the audience as if from a bare platform.

The lines of the design contributed to this effect. The perspective was such that the corner of the ceiling came down to a point slightly to the left of upstage center, helping to focus the audience's attention on the point of the diamond where the characters addressed the audience. Mielziner took Williams's hints to give lighting a central function in the play, running a scrim from floor to ceiling along two sides of the set with strips of black velour indicating the lines of the columns outside the windows of the room when the light of the moon was projected through them. To signify sunlight, slide projections of blinds were thrown on the scrims, while the gallery and the lawn beyond the windows were blocked out. When characters on the gallery or the lawn were to be seen, the lights behind the scrim were brought up, making the actors visible to the audience, as had been done with *Streetcar*.

Two follow-spots were used in the production. One, on the audience's left, highlighted Maggie throughout Act 1 and picked up Big Mama, Maggie, and Brick in Act 2, as they were in turn nominally being addressed by Big Daddy, who was downstage talking to the audience. In Act 3 the light again shone on Maggie almost without interruption. The follow-spot on the audience's right highlighted the characters Maggie was addressing in Act 1, chiefly Brick, as she had her turn at "recitative." It shone on Big Daddy throughout Act 2 and picked up Brick, Big Mama, Gooper, Mae, and Maggie at various times during Act 3, emphasizing a significant entrance or a significant reaction indexically as it occurred. Contributing to the generally "golden" look of the production's lighting, the follow-spots were amber except when a character went out onto the

[7]*Designing for Theatre: A Memoir and a Portfolio* (New York: Bram Hall House, 1965) 183.

gallery, when they were changed to blue. The follow-spots not only helped to avoid confusion by focusing the audience's attention where Kazan wanted it to be, they also contributed to the foregrounding of the theatricality in the production by "framing" specific characters and pieces of action. Kazan stylized the composition of his stage picture in *Cat*, and encoded a great deal of meaning through gesture, movement, and pose in the production. Using the follow-spots to highlight these formal compositions emphasized that what was happening onstage was not real life but theater.

In designing the furniture, both Kazan and Mielziner took their cue from Williams's earlier description of the set, emphasizing the qualities he had seen in the Robert Louis Stevenson photograph. Kazan had underlined elements of this description in his copy of the script. Listed together, they indicate quite well the direction Mielziner took with the design after their conferences:

Delta's biggest cotton planter
Far East
The room must evoke some ghosts
Gently . . . poetically haunted by a relationship . . . a tenderness which was uncommon
Samoan Island
tender light on weathered wood
Bamboo . . . wicker
[the entertainment center] monument . . . very complete . . . compact little shrine . . .
    all the comforts . . . illusions . . . hide [written in the margin, "Brick hides"] such
    things as the characters in the play are faced with (RV xii–xiv)

From these suggestions came the old wicker headboard with its huge and fantastically shaped design of two cornucopias, the matching wicker furniture, the carpet with its lushly fertile design of oversized flowers and vines, and the one object in the room that competed with the fertility symbol of the bed for the audience's attention, the oversized bar, hi-fi, radio, and television with its sleekly modern fifties lines. This object realized Williams's description of a compact modern shrine to all the comforts and illusions of contemporary life and signified Brick's retreat from human contact.

Kazan has said more than once that Williams did not like the set that Mielziner finally developed for *Cat* because he thought his play should be performed realistically. Kazan has also indicated that the set was a material signifier of his aesthetic vision in opposition to Williams's:

I had the setting I'd asked for; Jo had given me what I wanted. Tennessee had approved of it earlier, when he was ready to approve of damn near anything I asked for, because I was the director he wanted. Now the setting was up onstage, too late to change, and on that setting there was only one way for any human to conduct himself: "out front" it's called. Dear Tennessee was stuck with my vision, like it or not.[8]

---

[8]Kazan 543.

Arthur Miller

Arthur Miller (b. 1915) has been the dean of American playwrights since the opening of *Death of a Salesman* in 1949. His steady output as a writer and a playwright began with his first publications after college in 1939, when he worked in the New York Federal Theatre Project, a branch of the Work Projects Administration (WPA), Franklin D. Roosevelt's huge Depression effort to put Americans back to work.

Miller, the son of a Jewish immigrant, was born and raised during his early years in the Harlem section of Manhattan and later in Brooklyn after his father's business failed. In high school, Miller thought of himself more as an athlete than a student, and he had trouble getting teachers' recommendations for college. After considerable struggle and waiting, he entered the University of Michigan, where his talent as a playwright emerged under the tutelage of Kenneth Rowe, his playwriting professor. His undergraduate plays won important university awards and he became noticed by the Theatre Guild, a highly respected theater founded to present excellent plays (not necessarily commercial successes). His career was under way.

From 1939 to 1947, Miller wrote radio plays, screenplays, articles, stories, and a novel. His work covered a wide range of material, much of it growing out of his childhood memories of a tightly knit and somewhat eccentric family that provided him with a large gallery of characters. But he also dealt with political issues and problems of anti-Semitism, which was widespread in the 1930s and 1940s. Miller's political concerns have been a constant presence in his work since his earliest writings.

All My Sons (1947) was his first successful play. It ran on Broadway for 300 performances, a remarkable record for a serious drama. The story centers on a man who knowingly produces defective parts for airplanes and then blames the subsequent crashes on his business partner, who is ruined and imprisoned. When the man's son finds out the truth, he confronts his father and rebukes him. Ultimately, the man realizes not only that he has lost his son because of his deceit but that the dead pilots were also "all my sons." The play won the New York Drama Critics' Circle Award.

Miller's next play, *Death of a Salesman* (1949), was written in six weeks. Its concerns were rooted in the American ideal of business success, and its conclusions were a challenge to standard American business values. Willy Loman, first performed by Lee J. Cobb, became a symbol for Americans in the postwar period of growing wealth and affluence.

Miller's next play, *The Crucible* (1953), portrayed witch-hunts of seventeenth-century New England. However, it was clear to most people that the play had a subtext: It was about contemporary anti-Communist witch-hunts. In the late 1940s and early 1950s the House Un-American Activities Committee (HUAC) held hearings to flush out suspected Communists from all areas of American life, particularly the arts. Many writers, artists, and performers came under close, often unfair, scrutiny by HUAC for their own political views and allegiances and were often asked to testify against their friends. Many were blacklisted — prevented from working in commercial theaters and movie companies — some were imprisoned for not testifying at others' trials, and some had their reputations and careers destroyed.

Arthur Miller was fearless in facing down HUAC, and he was convicted of contempt of court for not testifying against his friends. For a time he too was blacklisted, but his contempt citation was reversed, and he was not imprisoned. Given his personal political stance during this dangerous time, it is not a surprise to find that his themes usually center on matters of social concern.

DEATH OF A SALESMAN

Death of a Salesman (1949) was a hit from its first performances and has remained at the center of modern American drama ever since. It has been successful in China, where there were no salesmen, and in Europe, where many salesmen dominate certain industries. Everywhere it has been seen it has touched the hearts and minds of its audiences. Its success is a phenomenon of American drama.

The play was first performed in an environment that must be called experimental. Miller had originally conceived of a model of a man's head as the stage setting. He has said: "The first image that occurred to me which was to result in *Death of a Salesman* was of an enormous face the height of the proscenium arch which would appear and then open up, and we would see the inside of a man's head. In fact, *The Inside of His Head* was the first title." This technique was not used, but when Miller worked with the director and producer of the first production, he helped develop a setting that became a model for the "American style" in drama. The multilevel set permitted the play to shift from Willy Loman and his wife, Linda, having a conversation in their kitchen to their son's bedroom on the second level of the house.

It permitted portions of the stage to be reserved for Willy's visions of his brother, Ben, and for scenes outside the house such as Willy's interlude with the woman in Boston.

In a way, the setup of the stage respected Miller's original plan, but instead of portraying a cross section of Willy's head, it presented a metaphor for a cross section of his life. The audience felt that they were looking in on more than a living room, as in the nineteenth-century Ibsenist approach; they were looking in on an entire house and an entire life.

Using a cross section of a house as a metaphor was an especially important device in this play because of the play's allusions to Greek tragedy. The great Greek tragedies usually portray the destruction of a house — such as the house of Atreus — as a way of making a metaphor for a whole family, not just an individual. When Hamlet dies, for example, his entire line dies with him. His family is gone at the end of act V. The death in *Death of a Salesman* implies the destruction of a family that has held certain beliefs that have been wrong from the start.

The life of the salesman has given Willy a sense of dignity and worth, and he imagines that the modern world has corrupted that sense by robbing salesmen of the value of their personality. He thinks the modern world has failed him, but he is wrong. His original belief that what counts is not *what* you know but *whom* you know and how well you are liked lies at the heart of his failure. When the play opens, he has failed. He cannot do the traveling salesman's job because he can no longer drive to the territory. He cannot sell what he needs to sell.

Willy has inculcated his beliefs in his sons, Happy and Biff, and both are as ineffectual as their father. Willy doted on Biff and encouraged him to become a high school football star at the expense of his studies. But when Biff cannot pass an important course, and when his plans to make up the work are subverted by his disillusionment in his father, his dreams of a college football career are gone. He cannot change, cannot recover from this defeat. Happy, like his father, builds castles in the air and assumes somehow that he will be successful when he has nothing to back himself up with. He wants the glory — and he spends time in fanciful imaginings, as Willy does — but he cannot do the basic work that makes it possible to achieve glory. Ironically, it is the "anemic" Bernard — who studies hard, stresses personal honesty and diligence, and never brags — who is successful.

Linda supports Willy's illusions, allowing him to be a fraud by believing — or pretending to believe — in his dream with him. Willy has permitted himself to feel that integrity, honesty, and fidelity are not so important as being well liked.

The play ends with Willy still unable to face the deceptions he has perpetuated. He commits suicide in the firm belief that his sons will be able to follow in his footsteps and succeed where he did not. He thinks that his insurance money will be just what they need to save the house and the family. What he does not realize is that they are no more capable than he is. They have been corrupted by his thinking, his values, his beliefs. And they cannot solve the problems that overwhelmed him.

Death of a Salesman has been given a privileged position in American drama because it is a modern tragedy. Aristotle felt that only characters of noble birth could be tragic heroes, but Miller confounds this theory, as John Millington Synge did, by showing the human integrity in even the lowliest characters. Miller's Willy Loman is not a peasant, nor is he noble in the savage way that Maurya is in *Riders to the Sea*. In fact, Miller took a frightening risk in producing a figure that we find hard to like. Willy wants to be well liked, but as an audience we find it difficult to like a person who whines, complains, and accepts petty immorality as a normal way of life. It is despite his character that we are awed by his fate.

One Chinese commentator said after the Chinese production that China is filled with such dreamers as Willy. Certainly America has been filled with them. Willy stands as an aspect of our culture, commercial and otherwise, that is at the center of our reflection of ourselves. Perhaps we react so strongly to Willy because we are afraid that we might easily become a Willy Loman if we are not vigilant about our moral views, our psychological well-being, and the limits of our commitment to success. Willy Loman has mesmerized audiences in America in many different economic circumstances: during prosperity, recession, rapid growth, and cautious development. No matter what those circumstances, we have looked at the play as if looking in a mirror. What we have seen has always involved us, although it may not always make us pleased with ourselves.

Death of a Salesman in Performance

Death of a Salesman opened on Broadway on February 10, 1949, and won virtually every prize available for drama, including the Pulitzer Prize and the New York Drama Critics' Circle Award for best play. It ran on Broadway for an incredible 742 performances. Elia Kazan, director, was instrumental in establishing the play's innovative staging. Lee J. Cobb was cast as Willy, Mildred Dunnock as Linda, Arthur Kennedy as Biff, and Cameron Mitchell as Happy. The London production in July 1949, with Paul Muni as Willy and Kevin McCarthy as Biff, lasted 204 performances. Robert Coleman said of the New York production: "An explosion of emotional dynamite was set off last evening in the Morosco [Theater]. . . . In fashioning *Death of a Salesman* for them, author Arthur Miller and director Elia Kazan have collaborated on as exciting and devastating a theatrical blast as the nerves of modern playgoers can stand." Of Cobb, Howard Barnes said, "Cobb contributes a mammoth and magnificent portrayal of the central character. In his hands the salesman's frustration and final suicide are a matter of tremendous import."

An all-black production was directed by Lee Sankowich in Baltimore in 1972. Miller, in the audience on that production's opening night, commented that the play had been well received in "many countries and cultures" and that the Baltimore production further underscored the universality of the play. George C. Scott was praised for the power of his performance as Willy in New York's Circle in the Square production in 1975. A Chinese production directed by Arthur Miller was enormously successful in the 1980s. In the most celebrated revival of the play Dustin Hoffman portrayed Willy, John Malkovich played Biff, and Michael Rudman directed at the Broadhurst Theatre in New York in 1984. The critic Benedict Nightingale said of that production: "Somewhere at the core of him [Willy] an elaborate battle is being fought between dishonesty and honesty, glitter and substance, appearance and reality, between the promises or supposed promises of society and the claims of the self, between what Willy professes to value and what, perhaps without knowing it, he actually does value." In 1985 Dustin Hoffman brought his production of Miller's play to television, where it was viewed by an estimated twenty-five million people.

Arthur Miller (b. 1915)

DEATH OF A SALESMAN   *1949*

Characters

WILLY LOMAN	UNCLE BEN
LINDA	HOWARD WAGNER
BIFF	JENNY
HAPPY	STANLEY
BERNARD	MISS FORSYTHE
THE WOMAN	LETTA
CHARLEY	

The action takes place in Willy Loman's house and yard and in various places he visits in the New York and Boston of today.

(Throughout the play, in the stage directions, left and right mean stage left and stage right.)

ACT I

(A melody is heard, played upon a flute. It is small and fine, telling of grass and trees and the horizon. The curtain rises.)

(Before us is the Salesman's house. We are aware of towering, angular shapes behind it, surrounding it on all sides. Only the blue light of the sky falls upon the house and forestage; the surrounding area shows an angry glow of orange. As more light appears, we see a solid vault of apartment houses around the small, fragile-seeming home. An air of the dream clings to the place, a dream rising out of reality. The kitchen at center seems actual enough, for there is a kitchen table with three chairs, and a refrigerator. But no other fixtures are seen. At the back of the kitchen there is a draped entrance, which leads to the living room. To the right of the kitchen, on a level raised two feet, is a bedroom furnished only with a brass bedstead and a straight chair. On a shelf over the bed a silver athletic trophy stands. A window opens onto the apartment house at the side.)

(Behind the kitchen, on a level raised six and a half feet, is the boys' bedroom, at present barely visible. Two beds are dimly seen, and at the back of the room a dormer window. [This bedroom is above the unseen living room.] At the left a stairway curves up to it from the kitchen.)

(*The entire setting is wholly or, in some places, partially transparent. The roofline of the house is one-dimensional; under and over it we see the apartment buildings. Before the house lies an apron, curving beyond the forestage into the orchestra. This forward area serves as the back yard as well as the locale of all Willy's imaginings and of his city scenes. Whenever the action is in the present the actors observe the imaginary wall-lines, entering the house only through its door at the left. But in the scenes of the past these boundaries are broken, and characters enter or leave a room by stepping "through" a wall onto the forestage.*)

(*From the right, Willy Loman, the Salesman, enters, carrying two large sample cases. The flute plays on. He hears but is not aware of it. He is past sixty years of age, dressed quietly. Even as he crosses the stage to the doorway of the house, his exhaustion is apparent. He unlocks the door, comes into the kitchen, and thankfully lets his burden down, feeling the soreness of his palms. A word-sigh escapes his lips — it might be "Oh, boy, oh, boy." He closes the door, then carries his cases out into the living room, through the draped kitchen doorway.*)

(*Linda, his wife, has stirred in her bed at the right. She gets out and puts on a robe, listening. Most often jovial, she has developed an iron repression of her exceptions to Willy's behavior — she more than loves him, she admires him, as though his mercurial nature, his temper, his massive dreams and little cruelties, served her only as sharp reminders of the turbulent longings within him, longings which she shares but lacks the temperament to utter and follow to their end.*)

LINDA (*hearing Willy outside the bedroom, calls with some trepidation*): Willy!

WILLY: It's all right. I came back.

LINDA: Why? What happened? (*Slight pause.*) Did something happen, Willy?

WILLY: No, nothing happened.

LINDA: You didn't smash the car, did you?

WILLY (*with casual irritation*): I said nothing happened. Didn't you hear me?

LINDA: Don't you feel well?

WILLY: I'm tired to the death. (*The flute has faded away. He sits on the bed beside her, a little numb.*) I couldn't make it. I just couldn't make it, Linda.

LINDA (*very carefully, delicately*): Where were you all day? You look terrible.

WILLY: I got as far as a little above Yonkers. I stopped for a cup of coffee. Maybe it was the coffee.

LINDA: What?

WILLY (*after a pause*): I suddenly couldn't drive any-more. The car kept going off onto the shoulder, y'know?

LINDA (*helpfully*): Oh. Maybe it was the steering again. I don't think Angelo knows the Studebaker.

WILLY: No, it's me, it's me. Suddenly I realize I'm goin' sixty miles an hour and I don't remember the last five minutes. I'm — I can't seem to — keep my mind to it.

LINDA: Maybe it's your glasses. You never went for your new glasses.

WILLY: No, I see everything. I came back ten miles an hour. It took me nearly four hours from Yonkers.

LINDA (*resigned*): Well, you'll just have to take a rest, Willy, you can't continue this way.

WILLY: I just got back from Florida.

LINDA: But you didn't rest your mind. Your mind is overactive, and the mind is what counts, dear.

WILLY: I'll start out in the morning. Maybe I'll feel better in the morning. (*She is taking off his shoes.*) These goddam arch supports are killing me.

LINDA: Take an aspirin. Should I get you an aspirin? It'll soothe you.

WILLY (*with wonder*): I was driving along, you understand? And I was fine. I was even observing the scenery. You can imagine, me looking at scenery, on the road every week of my life. But it's so beautiful up there, Linda, the trees are so thick, and the sun is warm. I opened the windshield and just let the warm air bathe over me. And then all of a sudden I'm goin' off the road! I'm tellin' ya, I absolutely forgot I was driving. If I'd've gone the other way over the white line I might've killed somebody. So I went on again — and five minutes later I'm dreamin' again, and I nearly — (*He presses two fingers against his eyes.*) I have such thoughts, I have such strange thoughts.

LINDA: Willy, dear. Talk to them again. There's no reason why you can't work in New York.

WILLY: They don't need me in New York. I'm the New England man. I'm vital in New England.

LINDA: But you're sixty years old. They can't expect you to keep traveling every week.

WILLY: I'll have to send a wire to Portland. I'm supposed to see Brown and Morrison tomorrow morning at ten o'clock to show the line. Goddammit, I could sell them! (*He starts putting on his jacket.*)

LINDA (*taking the jacket from him*): Why don't you go down to the place tomorrow and tell Howard you've simply got to work in New York? You're too accommodating, dear.

WILLY: If old man Wagner was alive I'd a been in charge of New York now! That man was a prince, he was a masterful man. But that boy of his, that Howard, he don't appreciate. When I went north the first time, the Wagner Company didn't know where New England was!

LINDA: Why don't you tell those things to Howard, dear?

WILLY (*encouraged*): I will, I definitely will. Is there any cheese?

LINDA: I'll make you a sandwich.

WILLY: No, go to sleep. I'll take some milk. I'll be up right away. The boys in?

LINDA: They're sleeping. Happy took Biff on a date tonight.

WILLY (*interested*): That so?

LINDA: It was so nice to see them shaving together, one behind the other, in the bathroom. And going out together. You notice? The whole house smells of shaving lotion.

WILLY: Figure it out. Work a lifetime to pay off a house. You finally own it, and there's nobody to live in it.

LINDA: Well, dear, life is a casting off. It's always that way.

WILLY: No, no, some people — some people accomplish something. Did Biff say anything after I went this morning?

LINDA: You shouldn't have criticized him, Willy, especially after he just got off the train. You mustn't lose your temper with him.

WILLY: When the hell did I lose my temper? I simply asked him if he was making any money. Is that a criticism?

LINDA: But, dear, how could he make any money?

WILLY (*worried and angered*): There's such an undercurrent in him. He became a moody man. Did he apologize when I left this morning?

LINDA: He was crestfallen, Willy. You know how he admires you. I think if he finds himself, then you'll both be happier and not fight any more.

WILLY: How can he find himself on a farm? Is that a life? A farmhand? In the beginning, when he was young, I thought, well, a young man, it's good for him to tramp around, take a lot of different jobs. But it's more than ten years now and he has yet to make thirty-five dollars a week!

LINDA: He's finding himself, Willy.

WILLY: Not finding yourself at the age of thirty-four is a disgrace!

LINDA: Shh!

WILLY: The trouble is he's lazy, goddammit!

LINDA: Willy, please!

WILLY: Biff is a lazy bum!

LINDA: They're sleeping. Get something to eat. Go on down.

WILLY: Why did he come home? I would like to know what brought him home.

LINDA: I don't know. I think he's still lost, Willy. I think he's very lost.

WILLY: Biff Loman is lost. In the greatest country in the world a young man with such — personal attractiveness, gets lost. And such a hard worker. There's one thing about Biff — he's not lazy.

LINDA: Never.

WILLY (*with pity and resolve*): I'll see him in the morning; I'll have a nice talk with him. I'll get him a job selling. He could be big in no time. My God! Remember how they used to follow him around in high school? When he smiled at one of them their faces lit up. When he walked down the street . . . (*He loses himself in reminiscences.*)

LINDA (*trying to bring him out of it*): Willy, dear, I got a new kind of American-type cheese today. It's whipped.

WILLY: Why do you get American when I like Swiss?

LINDA: I just thought you'd like a change —

WILLY: I don't want a change! I want Swiss cheese. Why am I always being contradicted?

LINDA (*with a covering laugh*): I thought it would be a surprise.

WILLY: Why don't you open a window in here, for God's sake?

LINDA (*with infinite patience*): They're all open, dear.

WILLY: The way they boxed us in here. Bricks and windows, windows and bricks.

LINDA: We should've bought the land next door.

WILLY: The street is lined with cars. There's not a breath of fresh air in the neighborhood. The grass don't grow anymore, you can't raise a carrot in the back yard. They should've had a law against apartment houses. Remember those two beautiful elm trees out there? When I and Biff hung the swing between them?

LINDA: Yeah, like being a million miles from the city.

WILLY: They should've arrested the builder for cutting those down. They massacred the neighborhood. (*Lost.*) More and more I think of those days, Linda. This time of year it was lilac and wisteria. And then the peonies would come out, and the daffodils. What fragrance in this room!

LINDA: Well, after all, people had to move somewhere.

WILLY: No, there's more people now.

LINDA: I don't think there's more people. I think —

WILLY: There's more people! That's what's ruining this country! Population is getting out of control. The competition is maddening! Smell the stink from that apartment house! And another one on the other side . . . How can they whip cheese?

(*On Willy's last line, Biff and Happy raise themselves up in their beds, listening.*)

LINDA: Go down, try it. And be quiet.

WILLY (*turning to Linda, guiltily*): You're not worried about me, are you, sweetheart?

BIFF: What's the matter?

HAPPY: Listen!

LINDA: You've got too much on the ball to worry about.

WILLY: You're my foundation and my support, Linda.

LINDA: Just try to relax, dear. You make mountains out of molehills.

WILLY: I won't fight with him any more. If he wants to go back to Texas, let him go.

LINDA: He'll find his way.

WILLY: Sure. Certain men just don't get started till later in life. Like Thomas Edison, I think. Or B. F. Goodrich. One of them was deaf. (*He starts for the bedroom doorway.*) I'll put my money on Biff.

LINDA: And Willy — if it's warm Sunday we'll drive in the country. And we'll open the windshield, and take lunch.

WILLY: No, the windshields don't open on the new cars.

LINDA: But you opened it today.

WILLY: Me? I didn't. (*He stops.*) Now isn't that peculiar! Isn't that a remarkable — (*He breaks off in amazement and fright as the flute is heard distantly.*)

LINDA: What, darling?

WILLY: That is the most remarkable thing.

LINDA: What, dear?

WILLY: I was thinking of the Chevvy. (*Slight pause.*) Nineteen twenty-eight ... when I had that red Chevvy — (*Breaks off.*) That funny? I coulda sworn I was driving that Chevvy today.

LINDA: Well, that's nothing. Something must've reminded you.

WILLY: Remarkable. Ts. Remember those days? The way Biff used to simonize that car? The dealer refused to believe there was eighty thousand miles on it. (*He shakes his head.*) Heh! (*To Linda.*) Close your eyes, I'll be right up. (*He walks out of the bedroom.*)

HAPPY (*to Biff*): Jesus, maybe he smashed up the car again!

LINDA (*calling after Willy*): Be careful on the stairs, dear! The cheese is on the middle shelf! (*She turns, goes over to the bed, takes his jacket, and goes out of the bedroom.*)

(*Light has risen on the boys' room. Unseen, Willy is heard talking to himself, "Eighty thousand miles," and a little laugh. Biff gets out of bed, comes downstage a bit, and stands attentively. Biff is two years older than his brother Happy, well built, but in these days bears a worn air and seems less self-assured. He has succeeded less, and his dreams are stronger and less*
acceptable than Happy's. Happy is tall, powerfully made. Sexuality is like a visible color on him, or a scent that many women have discovered. He, like his brother, is lost, but in a different way, for he has never allowed himself to turn his face toward defeat and is thus more confused and hard-skinned, although seemingly more content.*)

HAPPY (*getting out of bed*): He's going to get his license taken away if he keeps that up. I'm getting nervous about him, y'know, Biff?

BIFF: His eyes are going.

HAPPY: No, I've driven with him. He sees all right. He just doesn't keep his mind on it. I drove into the city with him last week. He stops at a green light and then it turns red and he goes. (*He laughs.*)

BIFF: Maybe he's color-blind.

HAPPY: Pop? Why he's got the finest eye for color in the business. You know that.

BIFF (*sitting down on his bed*): I'm going to sleep.

HAPPY: You're not still sour on Dad, are you, Biff?

BIFF: He's all right, I guess.

WILLY (*underneath them, in the living room*): Yes, sir, eighty thousand miles — eighty-two thousand!

BIFF: You smoking?

HAPPY (*holding out a pack of cigarettes*): Want one?

BIFF (*taking a cigarette*): I can never sleep when I smell it.

WILLY: What a simonizing job, heh!

HAPPY (*with deep sentiment*): Funny, Biff, y'know? Us sleeping in here again? The old beds. (*He pats his bed affectionately.*) All the talk that went across those two beds, huh? Our whole lives.

BIFF: Yeah. Lotta dreams and plans.

HAPPY (*with a deep and masculine laugh*): About five hundred women would like to know what was said in this room.

(*They share a soft laugh.*)

BIFF: Remember that big Betsy something — what the hell was her name — over on Bushwick Avenue?

HAPPY (*combing his hair*): With the collie dog!

BIFF: That's the one. I got you in there, remember?

HAPPY: Yeah, that was my first time — I think. Boy, there was a pig. (*They laugh, almost crudely.*) You taught me everything I know about women. Don't forget that.

BIFF: I bet you forgot how bashful you used to be. Especially with girls.

HAPPY: Oh, I still am, Biff.

BIFF: Oh, go on.

HAPPY: I just control it, that's all. I think I got less bashful and you got more so. What happened, Biff? Where's the old humor, the old confidence?

(*He shakes Biff's knee. Biff gets up and moves restlessly about the room.*) What's the matter?

BIFF: Why does Dad mock me all the time?

HAPPY: He's not mocking you, he —

BIFF: Everything I say there's a twist of mockery on his face. I can't get near him.

HAPPY: He just wants you to make good, that's all. I wanted to talk to you about Dad for a long time, Biff. Something's — happening to him. He — talks to himself.

BIFF: I noticed that this morning. But he always mumbled.

HAPPY: But not so noticeable. It got so embarrassing I sent him to Florida. And you know something? Most of the time he's talking to you.

BIFF: What's he say about me?

HAPPY: I can't make it out.

BIFF: What's he say about me?

HAPPY: I think the fact that you're not settled, that you're still kind of up in the air . . .

BIFF: There's one or two other things depressing him, Happy.

HAPPY: What do you mean?

BIFF: Never mind. Just don't lay it all to me.

HAPPY: But I think if you just got started — I mean — is there any future for you out there?

BIFF: I tell ya, Hap, I don't know what the future is. I don't know — what I'm supposed to want.

HAPPY: What do you mean?

BIFF: Well, I spent six or seven years after high school trying to work myself up. Shipping clerk, salesman, business of one kind or another. And it's a measly manner of existence. To get on that subway on the hot mornings in summer. To devote your whole life to keeping stock, or making phone calls, or selling or buying. To suffer fifty weeks of the year for the sake of a two-week vacation, when all you really desire is to be outdoors, with your shirt off. And always to have to get ahead of the next fella. And still — that's how you build a future.

HAPPY: Well, you really enjoy it on a farm? Are you content out there?

BIFF (*with rising agitation*): Hap, I've had twenty or thirty different kinds of jobs since I left home before the war, and it always turns out the same. I just realized it lately. In Nebraska when I herded cattle, and the Dakotas, and Arizona, and now in Texas. It's why I came home now, I guess, because I realized it. This farm I work on, it's spring there now, see? And they've got about fifteen new colts. There's nothing more inspiring or — beautiful than the sight of a mare and a new colt. And it's cool there now, see? Texas is cool now, and it's spring. And whenever spring comes to where I am, I suddenly get the feeling, my God, I'm not gettin' any-

where! What the hell am I doing, playing around with horses, twenty-eight dollars a week! I'm thirty-four years old, I oughta be makin' my future. That's when I come running home. And now, I get here, and I don't know what to do with myself. (*After a pause.*) I've always made a point of not wasting my life, and every time I come back here I know that all I've done is to waste my life.

HAPPY: You're a poet, you know that, Biff? You're a — you're an idealist!

BIFF: No, I'm mixed up very bad. Maybe I oughta get married. Maybe I oughta get stuck into something. Maybe that's my trouble. I'm like a boy. I'm not married, I'm not in business, I just — I'm like a boy. Are you content, Hap? You're a success, aren't you? Are you content?

HAPPY: Hell, no!

BIFF: Why? You're making money, aren't you?

HAPPY (*moving about with energy, expressiveness*): All I can do now is wait for the merchandise manager to die. And suppose I get to be merchandise manager? He's a good friend of mine, and he just built a terrific estate on Long Island. And he lived there about two months and sold it, and now he's building another one. He can't enjoy it once it's finished. And I know that's just what I would do. I don't know what the hell I'm workin' for. Sometimes I sit in my apartment — all alone. And I think of the rent I'm paying. And it's crazy. But then, it's what I always wanted. My own apartment, a car, and plenty of women. And still, goddammit, I'm lonely.

BIFF (*with enthusiasm*): Listen, why don't you come out West with me?

HAPPY: You and I, heh?

BIFF: Sure, maybe we could buy a ranch. Raise cattle, use our muscles. Men built like we are should be working out in the open.

HAPPY (*avidly*): The Loman Brothers, heh?

BIFF (*with vast affection*): Sure, we'd be known all over the counties!

HAPPY (*enthralled*): That's what I dream about, Biff. Sometimes I want to just rip my clothes off in the middle of the store and outbox that goddam merchandise manager. I mean I can outbox, outrun, and outlift anybody in that store, and I have to take orders from those common, petty sons-of-bitches till I can't stand it anymore.

BIFF: I'm tellin' you, kid, if you were with me I'd be happy out there.

HAPPY (*enthused*): See, Biff, everybody around me is so false that I'm constantly lowering my ideals . . .

BIFF: Baby, together we'd stand up for one another, we'd have someone to trust.

HAPPY: If I were around you —

BIFF: Hap, the trouble is we weren't brought up to grub for money. I don't know how to do it.

HAPPY: Neither can I!

BIFF: Then let's go!

HAPPY: The only thing is — what can you make out there?

BIFF: But look at your friend. Builds an estate and then hasn't the peace of mind to live in it.

HAPPY: Yeah, but when he walks into the store the waves part in front of him. That's fifty-two thousand dollars a year coming through the revolving door, and I got more in my pinky finger than he's got in his head.

BIFF: Yeah, but you just said —

HAPPY: I gotta show some of those pompous, self-important executives over there that Hap Loman can make the grade. I want to walk into the store the way he walks in. Then I'll go with you, Biff. We'll be together yet, I swear. But take those two we had tonight. Now weren't they gorgeous creatures?

BIFF: Yeah, yeah, most gorgeous I've had in years.

HAPPY: I get that any time I want, Biff. Whenever I feel disgusted. The only trouble is, it gets like bowling or something. I just keep knockin' them over and it doesn't mean anything. You still run around a lot?

BIFF: Naa. I'd like to find a girl — steady, somebody with substance.

HAPPY: That's what I long for.

BIFF: Go on! You'd never come home.

HAPPY: I would! Somebody with character, with resistance! Like Mom, y'know? You're gonna call me a bastard when I tell you this. That girl Charlotte I was with tonight is engaged to be married in five weeks. (*He tries on his new hat.*)

BIFF: No kiddin'!

HAPPY: Sure, the guy's in line for the vice-presidency of the store. I don't know what gets into me, maybe I just have an overdeveloped sense of competition or something, but I went and ruined her, and furthermore I can't get rid of her. And he's the third executive I've done that to. Isn't that a crummy characteristic? And to top it all, I go to their weddings! (*Indignantly, but laughing.*) Like I'm not supposed to take bribes. Manufacturers offer me a hundred-dollar bill now and then to throw an order their way. You know how honest I am, but it's like this girl, see. I hate myself for it. Because I don't want the girl, and, still, I take it and — I love it!

BIFF: Let's go to sleep.

HAPPY: I guess we didn't settle anything, heh?

BIFF: I just got one idea that I think I'm going to try.

HAPPY: What's that?

BIFF: Remember Bill Oliver?

HAPPY: Sure, Oliver is very big now. You want to work for him again?

BIFF: No, but when I quit he said something to me. He put his arm on my shoulder, and he said, "Biff, if you ever need anything, come to me."

HAPPY: I remember that. That sounds good.

BIFF: I think I'll go to see him. If I could get ten thousand or even seven or eight thousand dollars I could buy a beautiful ranch.

HAPPY: I bet he'd back you. 'Cause he thought highly of you, Biff. I mean, they all do. You're well liked, Biff. That's why I say to come back here, and we both have the apartment. And I'm tellin' you, Biff, any babe you want . . .

BIFF: No, with a ranch I could do the work I like and still be something. I just wonder though. I wonder if Oliver still thinks I stole that carton of basketballs.

HAPPY: Oh, he probably forgot that long ago. It's almost ten years. You're too sensitive. Anyway, he didn't really fire you.

BIFF: Well, I think he was going to. I think that's why I quit. I was never sure whether he knew or not. I know he thought the world of me, though. I was the only one he'd let lock up the place.

WILLY (*below*): You gonna wash the engine, Biff?

HAPPY: Shh!

(*Biff looks at Happy, who is gazing down, listening. Willy is mumbling in the parlor.*)

HAPPY: You hear that?

(*They listen. Willy laughs warmly.*)

BIFF (*growing angry*): Doesn't he know Mom can hear that?

WILLY: Don't get your sweater dirty, Biff!

(*A look of pain crosses Biff's face.*)

HAPPY: Isn't that terrible? Don't leave again, will you? You'll find a job here. You gotta stick around. I don't know what to do about him, it's getting embarrassing.

WILLY: What a simonizing job!

BIFF: Mom's hearing that!

WILLY: No kiddin', Biff, you got a date? Wonderful!

HAPPY: Go on to sleep. But talk to him in the morning, will you?

BIFF (*reluctantly getting into bed*): With her in the house. Brother!

HAPPY (*getting into bed*): I wish you'd have a good talk with him.

(*The light on their room begins to fade.*)

BIFF (*to himself in bed*): That selfish, stupid . . .

HAPPY: Sh . . . Sleep, Biff.

(*Their light is out. Well before they have finished speaking, Willy's form is dimly seen below in the darkened kitchen. He opens the refrigerator, searches in there, and takes out a bottle of milk. The apartment houses are fading out, and the entire house and surroundings become covered with leaves. Music insinuates itself as the leaves appear.*)

WILLY: Just wanna be careful with those girls, Biff, that's all. Don't make any promises. No promises of any kind. Because a girl, y'know, they always believe what you tell 'em, and you're very young, Biff, you're too young to be talking seriously to girls.

(*Light rises on the kitchen. Willy, talking, shuts the refrigerator door and comes downstage to the kitchen table. He pours milk into a glass. He is totally immersed in himself, smiling faintly.*)

WILLY: Too young entirely, Biff. You want to watch your schooling first. Then when you're all set, there'll be plenty of girls for a boy like you. (*He smiles broadly at a kitchen chair.*) That so? The girls pay for you? (*He laughs.*) Boy, you must really be makin' a hit.

(*Willy is gradually addressing — physically — a point offstage, speaking through the wall of the kitchen, and his voice has been rising in volume to that of a normal conversation.*)

WILLY: I been wondering why you polish the car so careful. Ha! Don't leave the hubcaps, boys. Get the chamois to the hubcaps. Happy, use newspaper on the windows, it's the easiest thing. Show him how to do it, Biff! You see, Happy? Pad it up, use it like a pad. That's it, that's it, good work. You're doin' all right, Hap. (*He pauses, then nods in approbation for a few seconds, then looks upward.*) Biff, first thing we gotta do when we get time is clip that big branch over the house. Afraid it's gonna fall in a storm and hit the roof. Tell you what. We get a rope and sling her around, and then we climb up there with a couple of saws and take her down. Soon as you finish the car, boys, I wanna see ya. I got a surprise for you, boys.
BIFF (*offstage*): Whatta ya got, Dad?
WILLY: No, you finish first. Never leave a job till you're finished — remember that. (*Looking toward the "big trees."*) Biff, up in Albany I saw a beautiful hammock. I think I'll buy it next trip, and we'll hang it right between those two elms. Wouldn't that be something? Just swingin' there under those branches. Boy, that would be . . .

(*Young Biff and Young Happy appear from the direction Willy was addressing. Happy carries rags and a pail of water. Biff, wearing a sweater with a block "S," carries a football.*)

BIFF (*pointing in the direction of the car offstage*): How's that, Pop, professional?
WILLY: Terrific. Terrific job, boys. Good work, Biff.
HAPPY: Where's the surprise, Pop?
WILLY: In the back seat of the car.
HAPPY: Boy! (*He runs off.*)
BIFF: What is it, Dad? Tell me, what'd you buy?
WILLY (*laughing, cuffs him*): Never mind, something I want you to have.
BIFF (*turns and starts off*): What is it, Hap?
HAPPY (*offstage*): It's a punching bag!
BIFF: Oh, Pop!
WILLY: It's got Gene Tunney's signature on it!

(*Happy runs onstage with a punching bag.*)

BIFF: Gee, how'd you know we wanted a punching bag?
WILLY: Well, it's the finest thing for the timing.
HAPPY (*lies down on his back and pedals with his feet*): I'm losing weight, you notice, Pop?
WILLY (*to Happy*): Jumping rope is good too.
BIFF: Did you see the new football I got?
WILLY (*examining the ball*): Where'd you get a new ball?
BIFF: The coach told me to practice my passing.
WILLY: That so? And he gave you the ball, heh?
BIFF: Well, I borrowed it from the locker room. (*He laughs confidentially.*)
WILLY (*laughing with him at the theft*): I want you to return that.
HAPPY: I told you he wouldn't like it!
BIFF (*angrily*): Well, I'm bringing it back!
WILLY (*stopping the incipient argument, to Happy*): Sure, he's gotta practice with a regulation ball, doesn't he? (*To Biff.*) Coach'll probably congratulate you on your initiative!
BIFF: Oh, he keeps congratulating my initiative all the time, Pop.
WILLY: That's because he likes you. If somebody else took that ball there'd be an uproar. So what's the report, boys, what's the report?
BIFF: Where'd you go this time, Dad? Gee we were lonesome for you.
WILLY (*pleased, puts an arm around each boy and they come down to the apron*): Lonesome, heh?
BIFF: Missed you every minute.
WILLY: Don't say? Tell you a secret, boys. Don't breathe it to a soul. Someday I'll have my own business, and I'll never have to leave home anymore.

HAPPY: Like Uncle Charley, heh?

WILLY: Bigger than Uncle Charley! Because Charley is not — liked. He's liked, but he's not — well liked.

BIFF: Where'd you go this time, Dad?

WILLY: Well, I got on the road, and I went north to Providence. Met the Mayor.

BIFF: The Mayor of Providence!

WILLY: He was sitting in the hotel lobby.

BIFF: What'd he say?

WILLY: He said, "Morning!" And I said, "You got a fine city here, Mayor." And then he had coffee with me. And then I went to Waterbury. Waterbury is a fine city. Big clock city, the famous Waterbury clock. Sold a nice bill there. And then Boston — Boston is the cradle of the Revolution. A fine city. And a couple of other towns in Mass., and on to Portland and Bangor and straight home!

BIFF: Gee, I'd love to go with you sometime, Dad.

WILLY: Soon as summer comes.

HAPPY: Promise?

WILLY: You and Hap and I, and I'll show you all the towns. America is full of beautiful towns and fine, upstanding people. And they know me, boys, they know me up and down New England. The finest people. And when I bring you fellas up, there'll be open sesame for all of us, 'cause one thing, boys: I have friends. I can park my car in any street in New England, and the cops protect it like their own. This summer, heh?

BIFF AND HAPPY (*together*): Yeah! You bet!

WILLY: We'll take our bathing suits.

HAPPY: We'll carry your bags, Pop!

WILLY: Oh, won't that be something! Me comin' into the Boston stores with you boys carryin' my bags. What a sensation!

(*Biff is prancing around, practicing passing the ball.*)

WILLY: You nervous, Biff, about the game?

BIFF: Not if you're gonna be there.

WILLY: What do they say about you in school, now that they made you captain?

HAPPY: There's a crowd of girls behind him every time the classes change.

BIFF (*taking Willy's hand*): This Saturday, Pop, this Saturday — just for you, I'm going to break through for a touchdown.

HAPPY: You're supposed to pass.

BIFF: I'm takin' one play for Pop. You watch me, Pop, and when I take off my helmet, that means I'm breakin' out. Then you watch me crash through that line!

WILLY (*kisses Biff*): Oh, wait'll I tell this in Boston!

(*Bernard enters in knickers. He is younger than Biff, earnest and loyal, a worried boy.*)

BERNARD: Biff, where are you? You're supposed to study with me today.

WILLY: Hey, looka Bernard. What're you lookin' so anemic about, Bernard?

BERNARD: He's gotta study, Uncle Willy. He's got Regents next week.

HAPPY (*tauntingly, spinning Bernard around*): Let's box, Bernard!

BERNARD: Biff! (*He gets away from Happy.*) Listen, Biff, I heard Mr. Birnbaum say that if you don't start studyin' math he's gonna flunk you, and you won't graduate. I heard him!

WILLY: You better study with him, Biff. Go ahead now.

BERNARD: I heard him!

BIFF: Oh, Pop, you didn't see my sneakers! (*He holds up a foot for Willy to look at.*)

WILLY: Hey, that's a beautiful job of printing!

BERNARD (*wiping his glasses*): Just because he printed University of Virginia on his sneakers doesn't mean they've got to graduate him, Uncle Willy!

WILLY (*angrily*): What're you talking about? With scholarships to three universities they're gonna flunk him?

BERNARD: But I heard Mr. Birnbaum say —

WILLY: Don't be a pest, Bernard! (*To his boys.*) What an anemic!

BERNARD: Okay, I'm waiting for you in my house, Biff.

(*Bernard goes off. The Lomans laugh.*)

WILLY: Bernard is not well liked, is he?

BIFF: He's liked, but he's not well liked.

HAPPY: That's right, Pop.

WILLY: That's just what I mean. Bernard can get the best marks in school, y'understand, but when he gets out in the business world, y'understand, you are going to be five times ahead of him. That's why I thank Almighty God you're both built like Adonises. Because the man who makes an appearance in the business world, the man who creates personal interest, is the man who gets ahead. Be liked and you will never want. You take me, for instance. I never have to wait in line to see a buyer. "Willy Loman is here!" That's all they have to know, and I go right through.

BIFF: Did you knock them dead, Pop?

WILLY: Knocked 'em cold in Providence, slaughtered 'em in Boston.

HAPPY (*on his back, pedaling again*): I'm losing weight, you notice, Pop?

(*Linda enters as of old, a ribbon in her hair, carrying a basket of washing.*)

LINDA (*with youthful energy*): Hello, dear!

WILLY: Sweetheart!

LINDA: How'd the Chevvy run?

WILLY: Chevrolet, Linda, is the greatest car ever built. (*To the boys.*) Since when do you let your mother carry wash up the stairs?

BIFF: Grab hold there, boy!

HAPPY: Where to, Mom?

LINDA: Hang them up on the line. And you better go down to your friends, Biff. The cellar is full of boys. They don't know what to do with themselves.

BIFF: Ah, when Pop comes home they can wait!

WILLY (*laughs appreciatively*): You better go down and tell them what to do, Biff.

BIFF: I think I'll have them sweep out the furnace room.

WILLY: Good work, Biff.

BIFF (*goes through wall-line of kitchen to doorway at back and calls down*): Fellas! Everybody sweep out the furnace room! I'll be right down!

VOICES: All right! Okay, Biff.

BIFF: George and Sam and Frank, come out back! We're hangin' up the wash! Come on, Hap, on the double! (*He and Happy carry out the basket.*)

LINDA: The way they obey him!

WILLY: Well, that's training, the training. I'm tellin' you, I was sellin' thousands and thousands, but I had to come home.

LINDA: Oh, the whole block'll be at that game. Did you sell anything?

WILLY: I did five hundred gross in Providence and seven hundred gross in Boston.

LINDA: No! Wait a minute, I've got a pencil. (*She pulls pencil and paper out of her apron pocket.*) That makes your commission . . . Two hundred — my God! Two hundred and twelve dollars!

WILLY: Well, I didn't figure it yet, but . . .

LINDA: How much did you do?

WILLY: Well, I — I did — about a hundred and eighty gross in Providence. Well, no — it came to — roughly two hundred gross on the whole trip.

LINDA (*without hesitation*): Two hundred gross. That's . . . (*She figures.*)

WILLY: The trouble was that three of the stores were half-closed for inventory in Boston. Otherwise I woulda broke records.

LINDA: Well, it makes seventy dollars and some pennies. That's very good.

WILLY: What do we owe?

LINDA: Well, on the first there's sixteen dollars on the refrigerator —

WILLY: Why sixteen?

LINDA: Well, the fan belt broke, so it was a dollar eighty.

WILLY: But it's brand new.

LINDA: Well, the man said that's the way it is. Till they work themselves in, y'know.

(*They move through the wall-line into the kitchen.*)

WILLY: I hope we didn't get stuck on that machine.

LINDA: They got the biggest ads of any of them!

WILLY: I know, it's a fine machine. What else?

LINDA: Well, there's nine-sixty for the washing machine. And for the vacuum cleaner there's three and a half due on the fifteenth. Then the roof, you got twenty-one dollars remaining.

WILLY: It don't leak, does it?

LINDA: No, they did a wonderful job. Then you owe Frank for the carburetor.

WILLY: I'm not going to pay that man! That goddam Chevrolet, they ought to prohibit the manufacture of that car!

LINDA: Well, you owe him three and a half. And odds and ends, comes to around a hundred and twenty dollars by the fifteenth.

WILLY: A hundred and twenty dollars! My God, if business don't pick up I don't know what I'm gonna do!

LINDA: Well, next week you'll do better.

WILLY: Oh, I'll knock 'em dead next week. I'll go to Hartford. I'm very well liked in Hartford. You know, the trouble is, Linda, people don't seem to take to me.

(*They move onto the forestage.*)

LINDA: Oh, don't be foolish.

WILLY: I know it when I walk in. They seem to laugh at me.

LINDA: Why? Why would they laugh at you? Don't talk that way, Willy.

(*Willy moves to the edge of the stage. Linda goes into the kitchen and starts to darn stockings.*)

WILLY: I don't know the reason for it, but they just pass me by. I'm not noticed.

LINDA: But you're doing wonderful, dear. You're making seventy to a hundred dollars a week.

WILLY: But I gotta be at it ten, twelve hours a day. Other men — I don't know — they do it easier. I don't know why — I can't stop myself — I talk too much. A man oughta come in with a few words. One thing about Charley. He's a man of few words, and they respect him.

LINDA: You don't talk too much, you're just lively.

WILLY (*smiling*): Well, I figure, what the hell, life is short, a couple of jokes. (*To himself.*) I joke too much! (*The smile goes.*)

LINDA: Why? You're —

WILLY: I'm fat. I'm very — foolish to look at, Linda. I didn't tell you, but Christmas time I happened to be calling on F. H. Stewarts, and a salesman I know, as I was going in to see the buyer I heard him say something about — walrus. And I — I cracked him right across the face. I won't take that. I simply will not take that. But they do laugh at me. I know that.

LINDA: Darling . . .

WILLY: I gotta overcome it. I know I gotta overcome it. I'm not dressing to advantage, maybe.

LINDA: Willy, darling, you're the handsomest man in the world —

WILLY: Oh, no, Linda.

LINDA: To me you are. (*Slight pause.*) The handsomest.

(*From the darkness is heard the laughter of a woman. Willy doesn't turn to it, but it continues through Linda's lines.*)

LINDA: And the boys, Willy. Few men are idolized by their children the way you are.

(*Music is heard as behind a scrim, to the left of the house, The Woman, dimly seen, is dressing.*)

WILLY (*with great feeling*): You're the best there is, Linda, you're a pal, you know that? On the road — on the road I want to grab you sometimes and just kiss the life outa you.

(*The laughter is loud now, and he moves into a brightening area at the left, where The Woman has come from behind the scrim and is standing, putting on her hat, looking into a "mirror" and laughing.*)

WILLY: 'Cause I get so lonely — especially when business is bad and there's nobody to talk to. I get the feeling that I'll never sell anything again, that I won't make a living for you, or a business, a business for the boys. (*He talks through The Woman's subsiding laughter; The Woman primps at the "mirror."*) There's so much I want to make for —

THE WOMAN: Me? You didn't make me, Willy. I picked you.

WILLY (*pleased*): You picked me?

THE WOMAN (*who is quite proper-looking, Willy's age*): I did. I've been sitting at that desk watching all the salesmen go by, day in, day out. But you've got such a sense of humor, and we do have such a good time together, don't we?

WILLY: Sure, sure. (*He takes her in his arms.*) Why do you have to go now?

THE WOMAN: It's two o'clock . . .

WILLY: No, come on in! (*He pulls her.*)

THE WOMAN: . . . my sisters'll be scandalized. When'll you be back?

WILLY: Oh, two weeks about. Will you come up again?

THE WOMAN: Sure thing. You do make me laugh. It's good for me. (*She squeezes his arm, kisses him.*) And I think you're a wonderful man.

WILLY: You picked me, heh?

THE WOMAN: Sure. Because you're so sweet. And such a kidder.

WILLY: Well, I'll see you next time I'm in Boston.

THE WOMAN: I'll put you right through to the buyers.

WILLY (*slapping her bottom*): Right. Well, bottoms up!

THE WOMAN (*slaps him gently and laughs*): You just kill me, Willy. (*He suddenly grabs her and kisses her roughly.*) You kill me. And thanks for the stockings. I love a lot of stockings. Well, good night.

WILLY: Good night. And keep your pores open!

THE WOMAN: Oh, Willy!

(*The Woman bursts out laughing, and Linda's laughter blends in. The Woman disappears into the dark. Now the area at the kitchen table brightens. Linda is sitting where she was at the kitchen table, but now is mending a pair of her silk stockings.*)

LINDA: You are, Willy. The handsomest man. You've got no reason to feel that —

WILLY (*coming out of The Woman's dimming area and going over to Linda*): I'll make it all up to you, Linda, I'll —

LINDA: There's nothing to make up, dear. You're doing fine, better than —

WILLY (*noticing her mending*): What's that?

LINDA: Just mending my stockings. They're so expensive —

WILLY (*angrily, taking them from her*): I won't have you mending stockings in this house! Now throw them out!

(*Linda puts the stockings in her pocket.*)

BERNARD (*entering on the run*): Where is he? If he doesn't study!

WILLY (*moving to the forestage, with great agitation*): You'll give him the answers!

BERNARD: I do, but I can't on a Regents! That's a state exam! They're liable to arrest me!

WILLY: Where is he? I'll whip him, I'll whip him!

LINDA: And he'd better give back that football, Willy, it's not nice.

WILLY: Biff! Where is he? Why is he taking everything?

LINDA: He's too rough with the girls, Willy. All the mothers are afraid of him!

WILLY: I'll whip him!

BERNARD: He's driving the car without a license!

(*The Woman's laugh is heard.*)

WILLY: Shut up!

LINDA: All the mothers —

WILLY: Shut up!

BERNARD (*backing quietly away and out*): Mr. Birnbaum says he's stuck up.

WILLY: Get outa here!

BERNARD: If he doesn't buckle down he'll flunk math! (*He goes off.*)

LINDA: He's right, Willy, you've gotta —

WILLY (*exploding at her*): There's nothing the matter with him! You want him to be a worm like Bernard? He's got spirit, personality . . .

(*As he speaks, Linda, almost in tears, exits into the living room. Willy is alone in the kitchen, wilting and staring. The leaves are gone. It is night again, and the apartment houses look down from behind.*)

WILLY: Loaded with it. Loaded! What is he stealing? He's giving it back, isn't he? Why is he stealing? What did I tell him? I never in my life told him anything but decent things.

(*Happy in pajamas has come down the stairs; Willy suddenly becomes aware of Happy's presence.*)

HAPPY: Let's go now, come on.

WILLY (*sitting down at the kitchen table*): Huh! Why did she have to wax the floors herself? Everytime she waxes the floors she keels over. She knows that!

HAPPY: Shh! Take it easy. What brought you back tonight?

WILLY: I got an awful scare. Nearly hit a kid in Yonkers. God! Why didn't I go to Alaska with my brother Ben that time! Ben! That man was a genius, that man was success incarnate! What a mistake! He begged me to go.

HAPPY: Well, there's no use in —

WILLY: You guys! There was a man started with the clothes on his back and ended up with diamond mines!

HAPPY: Boy, someday I'd like to know how he did it.

WILLY: What's the mystery? The man knew what he wanted and went out and got it! Walked into a jungle, and comes out, the age of twenty-one, and he's rich! The world is an oyster, but you don't crack it open on a mattress!

HAPPY: Pop, I told you I'm gonna retire you for life.

WILLY: You'll retire me for life on seventy goddam dollars a week? And your women and your car and your apartment, and you'll retire me for life! Christ's sake, I couldn't get past Yonkers today! Where are you guys, where are you? The woods are burning! I can't drive a car!

(*Charley has appeared in the doorway. He is a large*

man, *slow of speech, laconic, immovable. In all he says, despite what he says, there is pity, and, now, trepidation. He has a robe over pajamas, slippers on his feet. He enters the kitchen.*)

CHARLEY: Everything all right?

HAPPY: Yeah, Charley, everything's . . .

WILLY: What's the matter?

CHARLEY: I heard some noise. I thought something happened. Can't we do something about the walls? You sneeze in here, and in my house hats blow off.

HAPPY: Let's go to bed, Dad. Come on.

(*Charley signals to Happy to go.*)

WILLY: You go ahead, I'm not tired at the moment.

HAPPY (*to Willy*): Take it easy, huh? (*He exits.*)

WILLY: What're you doin' up?

CHARLEY (*sitting down at the kitchen table opposite Willy*): Couldn't sleep good. I had a heartburn.

WILLY: Well, you don't know how to eat.

CHARLEY: I eat with my mouth.

WILLY: No, you're ignorant. You gotta know about vitamins and things like that.

CHARLEY: Come on, let's shoot. Tire you out a little.

WILLY (*hesitantly*): All right. You got cards?

CHARLEY (*taking a deck from his pocket*): Yeah, I got them. Someplace. What is it with those vitamins?

WILLY (*dealing*): They build up your bones. Chemistry.

CHARLEY: Yeah, but there's no bones in a heartburn.

WILLY: What are you talkin' about? Do you know the first thing about it?

CHARLEY: Don't get insulted.

WILLY: Don't talk about something you don't know anything about.

(*They are playing. Pause.*)

CHARLEY: What're you doin' home?

WILLY: A little trouble with the car.

CHARLEY: Oh. (*Pause.*) I'd like to take a trip to California.

WILLY: Don't say.

CHARLEY: You want a job?

WILLY: I got a job, I told you that. (*After a slight pause.*) What the hell are you offering me a job for?

CHARLEY: Don't get insulted.

WILLY: Don't insult me.

CHARLEY: I don't see no sense in it. You don't have to go on this way.

WILLY: I got a good job. (*Slight pause.*) What do you keep comin' in here for?

CHARLEY: You want me to go?

WILLY (*after a pause, withering*): I can't understand

it. He's going back to Texas again. What the hell is that?

CHARLEY: Let him go.

WILLY: I got nothin' to give him, Charley, I'm clean, I'm clean.

CHARLEY: He won't starve. None a them starve. Forget about him.

WILLY: Then what have I got to remember?

CHARLEY: You take it too hard. To hell with it. When a deposit bottle is broken you don't get your nickel back.

WILLY: That's easy enough for you to say.

CHARLEY: That ain't easy for me to say.

WILLY: Did you see the ceiling I put up in the living room?

CHARLEY: Yeah, that's a piece of work. To put up a ceiling is a mystery to me. How do you do it?

WILLY: What's the difference?

CHARLEY: Well, talk about it.

WILLY: You gonna put up a ceiling?

CHARLEY: How could I put up a ceiling?

WILLY: Then what the hell are you bothering me for?

CHARLEY: You're insulted again.

WILLY: A man who can't handle tools is not a man. You're disgusting.

CHARLEY: Don't call me disgusting, Willy.

(*Uncle Ben, carrying a valise and an umbrella, enters the forestage from around the right corner of the house. He is a stolid man, in his sixties, with a mustache and an authoritative air. He is utterly certain of his destiny, and there is an aura of far places about him. He enters exactly as Willy speaks.*)

WILLY: I'm getting awfully tired, Ben.

(*Ben's music is heard. Ben looks around at everything.*)

CHARLEY: Good, keep playing; you'll sleep better. Did you call me Ben?

(*Ben looks at his watch.*)

WILLY: That's funny. For a second there you reminded me of my brother Ben.

BEN: I only have a few minutes. (*He strolls, inspecting the place. Willy and Charley continue playing.*)

CHARLEY: You never heard from him again, heh? Since that time?

WILLY: Didn't Linda tell you? Couple of weeks ago we got a letter from his wife in Africa. He died.

CHARLEY: That so.

BEN (*chuckling*): So this is Brooklyn, eh?

CHARLEY: Maybe you're in for some of his money.

WILLY: Naa, he had seven sons. There's just one opportunity I had with that man . . .

BEN: I must make a train, William. There are several properties I'm looking at in Alaska.

WILLY: Sure, sure! If I'd gone with him to Alaska that time, everything would've been totally different.

CHARLEY: Go on, you'd froze to death up there.

WILLY: What're you talking about?

BEN: Opportunity is tremendous in Alaska, William. Surprised you're not up there.

WILLY: Sure, tremendous.

CHARLEY: Heh?

WILLY: There was the only man I ever met who knew the answers.

CHARLEY: Who?

BEN: How are you all?

WILLY (*taking a pot, smiling*): Fine, fine.

CHARLEY: Pretty sharp tonight.

BEN: Is Mother living with you?

WILLY: No, she died a long time ago.

CHARLEY: Who?

BEN: That's too bad. Fine specimen of a lady, Mother.

WILLY (*to Charley*): Heh?

BEN: I'd hoped to see the old girl.

CHARLEY: Who died?

BEN: Heard anything from Father, have you?

WILLY (*unnerved*): What do you mean, who died?

CHARLEY (*taking a pot*): What're you talkin' about?

BEN (*looking at his watch*): William, it's half-past eight!

WILLY (*as though to dispel his confusion he angrily stops Charley's hand*): That's my build!

CHARLEY: I put the ace —

WILLY: If you don't know how to play the game I'm not gonna throw my money away on you!

CHARLEY (*rising*): It was my ace, for God's sake!

WILLY: I'm through, I'm through!

BEN: When did Mother die?

WILLY: Long ago. Since the beginning you never knew how to play cards.

CHARLEY (*picks up the cards and goes to the door*): All right! Next time I'll bring a deck with five aces.

WILLY: I don't play that kind of game!

CHARLEY (*turning to him*): You ought to be ashamed of yourself!

WILLY: Yeah?

CHARLEY: Yeah! (*He goes out.*)

WILLY (*slamming the door after him*): Ignoramus!

BEN (*as Willy comes toward him through the wall-line of the kitchen*): So you're William.

WILLY (*shaking Ben's hand*): Ben! I've been waiting for you so long! What's the answer? How did you do it?

BEN: Oh, there's a story in that.

(*Linda enters the forestage, as of old, carrying the wash basket.*)

LINDA: Is this Ben?

BEN (*gallantly*): How do you do, my dear.

LINDA: Where've you been all these years? Willy's always wondered why you —

WILLY (*pulling Ben away from her impatiently*): Where is Dad? Didn't you follow him? How did you get started?

BEN: Well, I don't know how much you remember.

WILLY: Well, I was just a baby, of course, only three or four years old —

BEN: Three years and eleven months.

WILLY: What a memory, Ben!

BEN: I have many enterprises, William, and I have never kept books.

WILLY: I remember I was sitting under the wagon in — was it Nebraska?

BEN: It was South Dakota, and I gave you a bunch of wild flowers.

WILLY: I remember you walking away down some open road.

BEN (*laughing*): I was going to find Father in Alaska.

WILLY: Where is he?

BEN: At that age I had a very faulty view of geography, William. I discovered after a few days that I was heading due south, so instead of Alaska, I ended up in Africa.

LINDA: Africa!

WILLY: The Gold Coast!

BEN: Principally diamond mines.

LINDA: Diamond mines!

BEN: Yes, my dear. But I've only a few minutes —

WILLY: No! Boys! Boys! (*Young Biff and Happy appear.*) Listen to this. This is your Uncle Ben, a great man! Tell my boys, Ben!

BEN: Why, boys, when I was seventeen I walked into the jungle, and when I was twenty-one I walked out. (*He laughs.*) And by God I was rich.

WILLY (*to the boys*): You see what I been talking about? The greatest things can happen!

BEN (*glancing at his watch*): I have an appointment in Ketchikan Tuesday week.

WILLY: No, Ben! Please tell about Dad. I want my boys to hear. I want them to know the kind of stock they spring from. All I remember is a man with a big beard, and I was in Mamma's lap, sitting around a fire, and some kind of high music.

BEN: His flute. He played the flute.

WILLY: Sure, the flute, that's right!

(*New music is heard, a high, rollicking tune.*)

BEN: Father was a very great and a very wild-hearted man. We would start in Boston, and he'd toss the whole family into the wagon, and then he'd drive the team right across the country; through Ohio, and Indiana, Michigan, Illinois, and all the Western

states. And we'd stop in the towns and sell the flutes that he'd made on the way. Great inventor, Father. With one gadget he made more in a week than a man like you could make in a lifetime.

WILLY: That's just the way I'm bringing them up, Ben — rugged, well liked, all-around.

BEN: Yeah? (*To Biff.*) Hit that, boy — hard as you can. (*He pounds his stomach.*)

BIFF: Oh, no, sir!

BEN (*taking boxing stance*): Come on, get to me! (*He laughs.*)

WILLY: Go to it, Biff! Go ahead, show him!

BIFF: Okay! (*He cocks his fists and starts in.*)

LINDA (*to Willy*): Why must he fight, dear?

BEN (*sparring with Biff*): Good boy! Good boy!

WILLY: How's that, Ben, heh?

HAPPY: Give him the left, Biff!

LINDA: Why are you fighting?

BEN: Good boy! (*Suddenly comes in, trips Biff, and stands over him, the point of his umbrella poised over Biff's eye.*)

LINDA: Look out, Biff!

BIFF: Gee!

BEN (*patting Biff's knee*): Never fight fair with a stranger, boy. You'll never get out of the jungle that way. (*Taking Linda's hand and bowing.*) It was an honor and a pleasure to meet you, Linda.

LINDA (*withdrawing her hand coldly, frightened*): Have a nice — trip.

BEN (*to Willy*): And good luck with your — what do you do?

WILLY: Selling.

BEN: Yes. Well . . . (*He raises his hand in farewell to all.*)

WILLY: No, Ben, I don't want you to think . . . (*He takes Ben's arm to show him.*) It's Brooklyn, I know, but we hunt too.

BEN: Really, now.

WILLY: Oh, sure, there's snakes and rabbits and — that's why I moved out here. Why, Biff can fell any one of these trees in no time! Boys! Go right over to where they're building the apartment house and get some sand. We're gonna rebuild the entire front stoop right now! Watch this, Ben!

BIFF: Yes, sir! On the double, Hap!

HAPPY (*as he and Biff run off*): I lost weight, Pop, you notice?

(*Charley enters in knickers, even before the boys are gone.*)

CHARLEY: Listen, if they steal any more from that building the watchman'll put the cops on them!

LINDA (*to Willy*): Don't let Biff . . .

(*Ben laughs lustily.*)

WILLY: You shoulda seen the lumber they brought home last week. At least a dozen six-by-tens worth all kinds a money.

CHARLEY: Listen, if that watchman —

WILLY: I gave them hell, understand. But I got a couple of fearless characters there.

CHARLEY: Willy, the jails are full of fearless characters.

BEN (*clapping Willy on the back, with a laugh at Charley*): And the stock exchange, friend!

WILLY (*joining in Ben's laughter*): Where are the rest of your pants?

CHARLEY: My wife bought them.

WILLY: Now all you need is a golf club and you can go upstairs and go to sleep. (*To Ben.*) Great athlete! Between him and his son Bernard they can't hammer a nail!

BERNARD (*rushing in*): The watchman's chasing Biff!

WILLY (*angrily*): Shut up! He's not stealing anything!

LINDA (*alarmed, hurrying off left*): Where is he? Biff, dear! (*She exits.*)

WILLY (*moving toward the left, away from Ben*): There's nothing wrong. What's the matter with you?

BEN: Nervy boy. Good!

WILLY (*laughing*): Oh, nerves of iron, that Biff!

CHARLEY: Don't know what it is. My New England man comes back and he's bleedin', they murdered him up there.

WILLY: It's contacts, Charley, I got important contacts!

CHARLEY (*sarcastically*): Glad to hear it, Willy. Come in later, we'll shoot a little casino. I'll take some of your Portland money. (*He laughs at Willy and exits.*)

WILLY (*turning to Ben*): Business is bad, it's murderous. But not for me, of course.

BEN: I'll stop by on my way back to Africa.

WILLY (*longingly*): Can't you stay a few days? You're just what I need, Ben, because I — I have a fine position here, but I — well, Dad left when I was such a baby and I never had a chance to talk to him and I still feel — kind of temporary about myself.

BEN: I'll be late for my train.

(*They are at opposite ends of the stage.*)

WILLY: Ben, my boys — can't we talk? They'd go into the jaws of hell for me, see, but I —

BEN: William, you're being first-rate with your boys. Outstanding, manly chaps!

WILLY (*hanging on to his words*): Oh, Ben, that's good to hear! Because sometimes I'm afraid that I'm not teaching them the right kind of — Ben, how should I teach them?

BEN (*giving great weight to each word, and with a certain vicious audacity*): William, when I walked into the jungle, I was seventeen. When I walked out I was twenty-one. And, by God, I was rich! (*He goes off into darkness around the right corner of the house.*)

WILLY: . . . was rich! That's just the spirit I want to imbue them with! To walk into a jungle! I was right! I was right! I was right!

(*Ben is gone, but Willy is still speaking to him as Linda, in nightgown and robe, enters the kitchen, glances around for Willy, then goes to the door of the house, looks out and sees him. Comes down to his left. He looks at her.*)

LINDA: Willy, dear? Willy?

WILLY: I was right!

LINDA: Did you have some cheese? (*He can't answer.*) It's very late, darling. Come to bed, heh?

WILLY (*looking straight up*): Gotta break your neck to see a star in this yard.

LINDA: You coming in?

WILLY: Whatever happened to that diamond watch fob? Remember? When Ben came from Africa that time? Didn't he give me a watch fob with a diamond in it?

LINDA: You pawned it, dear. Twelve, thirteen years ago. For Biff's radio correspondence course.

WILLY: Gee, that was a beautiful thing. I'll take a walk.

LINDA: But you're in your slippers.

WILLY (*starting to go around the house at the left*): I was right! I was! (*Half to Linda, as he goes, shaking his head.*) What a man! There was a man worth talking to. I was right!

LINDA (*calling after Willy*): But in your slippers, Willy!

(*Willy is almost gone when Biff, in his pajamas, comes down the stairs and enters the kitchen.*)

BIFF: What is he doing out there?

LINDA: Sh!

BIFF: God Almighty, Mom, how long has he been doing this?

LINDA: Don't, he'll hear you.

BIFF: What the hell is the matter with him?

LINDA: It'll pass by morning.

BIFF: Shouldn't we do anything?

LINDA: Oh, my dear, you should do a lot of things, but there's nothing to do, so go to sleep.

(*Happy comes down the stair and sits on the steps.*)

HAPPY: I never heard him so loud, Mom.

LINDA: Well, come around more often; you'll hear him. (*She sits down at the table and mends the lining of Willy's jacket.*)

BIFF: Why didn't you ever write me about this, Mom?

LINDA: How would I write to you? For over three months you had no address.

BIFF: I was on the move. But you know I thought of you all the time. You know that, don't you, pal?

LINDA: I know, dear, I know. But he likes to have a letter. Just to know that there's still a possibility for better things.

BIFF: He's not like this all the time, is he?

LINDA: It's when you come home he's always the worst.

BIFF: When I come home?

LINDA: When you write you're coming, he's all smiles, and talks about the future, and — he's just wonderful. And then the closer you seem to come, the more shaky he gets, and then, by the time you get here, he's arguing, and he seems angry at you. I think it's just that maybe he can't bring himself to — to open up to you. Why are you so hateful to each other? Why is that?

BIFF (evasively): I'm not hateful, Mom.

LINDA: But you no sooner come in the door than you're fighting!

BIFF: I don't know why. I mean to change. I'm tryin', Mom, you understand?

LINDA: Are you home to stay now?

BIFF: I don't know. I want to look around, see what's doin'.

LINDA: Biff, you can't look around all your life, can you?

BIFF: I just can't take hold, Mom. I can't take hold of some kind of a life.

LINDA: Biff, a man is not a bird, to come and go with the springtime.

BIFF: Your hair . . . (He touches her hair.) Your hair got so gray.

LINDA: Oh, it's been gray since you were in high school. I just stopped dyeing it, that's all.

BIFF: Dye it again, will ya? I don't want my pal looking old. (He smiles.)

LINDA: You're such a boy! You think you can go away for a year and . . . You've got to get it into your head now that one day you'll knock on this door and there'll be strange people here —

BIFF: What are you talking about? You're not even sixty, Mom.

LINDA: But what about your father?

BIFF (lamely): Well, I meant him too.

HAPPY: He admires Pop.

LINDA: Biff, dear, if you don't have any feeling for him, then you can't have any feeling for me.

BIFF: Sure I can, Mom.

LINDA: No. You can't just come to see me, because I love him. (With a threat, but only a threat, of tears.) He's the dearest man in the world to me, and I won't have anyone making him feel unwanted

and low and blue. You've got to make up your mind now, darling, there's no leeway any more. Either he's your father and you pay him that respect, or else you're not to come here. I know he's not easy to get along with — nobody knows that better than me — but . . .

WILLY (from the left, with a laugh): Hey, hey, Biffo!

BIFF (starting to go out after Willy): What the hell is the matter with him? (Happy stops him.)

LINDA: Don't — don't go near him!

BIFF: Stop making excuses for him! He always, always wiped the floor with you. Never had an ounce of respect for you.

HAPPY: He's always had respect for —

BIFF: What the hell do you know about it?

HAPPY (surlily): Just don't call him crazy!

BIFF: He's got no character — Charley wouldn't do this. Not in his own house — spewing out that vomit from his mind.

HAPPY: Charley never had to cope with what he's got to.

BIFF: People are worse off than Willy Loman. Believe me, I've seen them!

LINDA: Then make Charley your father, Biff. You can't do that, can you? I don't say he's a great man. Willy Loman never made a lot of money. His name was never in the paper. He's not the finest character that ever lived. But he's a human being, and a terrible thing is happening to him. So attention must be paid. He's not to be allowed to fall into his grave like an old dog. Attention, attention must be finally paid to such a person. You called him crazy —

BIFF: I didn't mean —

LINDA: No, a lot of people think he's lost his — balance. But you don't have to be very smart to know what his trouble is. The man is exhausted.

HAPPY: Sure!

LINDA: A small man can be just as exhausted as a great man. He works for a company thirty-six years this March, opens up unheard-of territories to their trademark, and now in his old age they take his salary away.

HAPPY (indignantly): I didn't know that, Mom.

LINDA: You never asked, my dear! Now that you get your spending money someplace else you don't trouble your mind with him.

HAPPY: But I gave you money last —

LINDA: Christmas time, fifty dollars! To fix the hot water it cost ninety-seven fifty! For five weeks he's been on straight commission, like a beginner, an unknown!

BIFF: Those ungrateful bastards!

LINDA: Are they any worse than his sons? When he brought them business, when he was young, they were glad to see him. But now his old friends, the old buyers that loved him so and always found some order to hand him in a pinch — they're all dead, retired. He used to be able to make six, seven calls a day in Boston. Now he takes his valises out of the car and puts them back and takes them out again and he's exhausted. Instead of walking he talks now. He drives seven hundred miles, and when he gets there no one knows him anymore, no one welcomes him. And what goes through a man's mind, driving seven hundred miles home without having earned a cent? Why shouldn't he talk to himself? Why? When he has to go to Charley and borrow fifty dollars a week and pretend to me that it's his pay? How long can that go on? How long? You see what I'm sitting here and waiting for? And you tell me he has no character? The man who never worked a day but for your benefit? When does he get the medal for that? Is this his reward — to turn around at the age of sixty-three and find his sons, who he loved better than his life, one a philandering bum —

HAPPY: Mom!

LINDA: That's all you are, my baby! (*To Biff.*) And you! What happened to the love you had for him? You were such pals! How you used to talk to him on the phone every night! How lonely he was till he could come home to you!

BIFF: All right, Mom. I'll live here in my room, and I'll get a job. I'll keep away from him, that's all.

LINDA: No, Biff. You can't stay here and fight all the time.

BIFF: He threw me out of this house, remember that.

LINDA: Why did he do that? I never knew why.

BIFF: Because I know he's a fake and he doesn't like anybody around who knows!

LINDA: Why a fake? In what way? What do you mean?

BIFF: Just don't lay it all at my feet. It's between me and him — that's all I have to say. I'll chip in from now on. He'll settle for half my pay check. He'll be all right. I'm going to bed. (*He starts for the stairs.*)

LINDA: He won't be all right.

BIFF (*turning on the stairs, furiously*): I hate this city and I'll stay here. Now what do you want?

LINDA: He's dying, Biff.

(*Happy turns quickly to her, shocked.*)

BIFF (*after a pause*): Why is he dying?

LINDA: He's been trying to kill himself.

BIFF (*with great horror*): How?

LINDA: I live from day to day.

BIFF: What're you talking about?

LINDA: Remember I wrote you that he smashed up the car again? In February?

BIFF: Well?

LINDA: The insurance inspector came. He said that they have evidence. That all these accidents in the last year — weren't — weren't — accidents.

HAPPY: How can they tell that? That's a lie.

LINDA: It seems there's a woman . . . (*She takes a breath as*)

BIFF (*sharply but contained*): What woman?
LINDA (*simultaneously*): . . . and this woman . . .

LINDA: What?

BIFF: Nothing. Go ahead.

LINDA: What did you say?

BIFF: Nothing. I just said what woman?

HAPPY: What about her?

LINDA: Well, it seems she was walking down the road and saw his car. She says that he wasn't driving fast at all, and that he didn't skid. She says he came to that little bridge, and then deliberately smashed into the railing, and it was only the shallowness of the water that saved him.

BIFF: Oh, no, he probably just fell asleep again.

LINDA: I don't think he fell asleep.

BIFF: Why not?

LINDA: Last month . . . (*With great difficulty.*) Oh, boys, it's so hard to say a thing like this! He's just a big stupid man to you, but I tell you there's more good in him than in many other people. (*She chokes, wipes her eyes.*) I was looking for a fuse. The lights blew out, and I went down the cellar. And behind the fuse box — it happened to fall out — was a length of rubber pipe — just short.

HAPPY: No kidding!

LINDA: There's a little attachment on the end of it. I knew right away. And sure enough, on the bottom of the water heater there's a new little nipple on the gas pipe.

HAPPY (*angrily*): That — jerk.

BIFF: Did you have it taken off?

LINDA: I'm — I'm ashamed to. How can I mention it to him? Every day I go down and take away that little rubber pipe. But, when he comes home, I put it back where it was. How can I insult him that way? I don't know what to do. I live from day to day, boys. I tell you, I know every thought in his mind. It sounds so old-fashioned and silly, but I tell you he put his whole life into you and you've turned your backs on him. (*She is bent over in the chair, weeping, her face in her hands.*) Biff, I swear to God! Biff, his life is in your hands!

HAPPY (*to Biff*): How do you like that damned fool!

BIFF (*kissing her*): All right, pal, all right. It's all settled now. I've been remiss. I know that, Mom. But now I'll stay, and I swear to you, I'll apply myself. (*Kneeling in front of her, in a fever of self-reproach.*) It's just — you see, Mom, I don't fit in business. Not that I won't try. I'll try, and I'll make good.

HAPPY: Sure you will. The trouble with you in business was you never tried to please people.

BIFF: I know, I —

HAPPY: Like when you worked for Harrison's. Bob Harrison said you were tops, and then you go and do some damn fool thing like whistling whole songs in the elevator like a comedian.

BIFF (*against Happy*): So what? I like to whistle sometimes.

HAPPY: You don't raise a guy to a responsible job who whistles in the elevator!

LINDA: Well, don't argue about it now.

HAPPY: Like when you'd go off and swim in the middle of the day instead of taking the line around.

BIFF (*his resentment rising*): Well, don't you run off? You take off sometimes, don't you? On a nice summer day?

HAPPY: Yeah, but I cover myself!

LINDA: Boys!

HAPPY: If I'm going to take a fade the boss can call any number where I'm supposed to be and they'll swear to him that I just left. I'll tell you something that I hate to say, Biff, but in the business world some of them think you're crazy.

BIFF (*angered*): Screw the business world!

HAPPY: All right, screw it! Great, but cover yourself!

LINDA: Hap, Hap!

BIFF: I don't care what they think! They've laughed at Dad for years, and you know why? Because we don't belong in this nuthouse of a city! We should be mixing cement on some open plain, or — or carpenters. A carpenter is allowed to whistle!

(*Willy walks in from the entrance of the house, at left.*)

WILLY: Even your grandfather was better than a carpenter. (*Pause. They watch him.*) You never grew up. Bernard does not whistle in the elevator, I assure you.

BIFF (*as though to laugh Willy out of it*): Yeah, but you do, Pop.

WILLY: I never in my life whistled in an elevator! And who in the business world thinks I'm crazy?

BIFF: I didn't mean it like that, Pop. Now don't make a whole thing out of it, will ya?

WILLY: Go back to the West! Be a carpenter, a cowboy, enjoy yourself!

LINDA: Willy, he was just saying —

WILLY: I heard what he said!

HAPPY (*trying to quiet Willy*): Hey, Pop, come on now . . .

WILLY (*continuing over Happy's line*): They laugh at me, heh? Go to Filene's, go to the Hub, go to Slattery's, Boston. Call out the name Willy Loman and see what happens! Big shot!

BIFF: All right, Pop.

WILLY: Big!

BIFF: All right!

WILLY: Why do you always insult me?

BIFF: I didn't say a word. (*To Linda.*) Did I say a word?

LINDA: He didn't say anything, Willy.

WILLY (*going to the doorway of the living room*): All right, good night, good night.

LINDA: Willy, dear, he just decided . . .

WILLY (*to Biff*): If you get tired hanging around tomorrow, paint the ceiling I put up in the living room.

BIFF: I'm leaving early tomorrow.

HAPPY: He's going to see Bill Oliver, Pop.

WILLY (*interestedly*): Oliver? For what?

BIFF (*with reserve, but trying, trying*): He always said he'd stake me. I'd like to go into business, so maybe I can take him up on it.

LINDA: Isn't that wonderful?

WILLY: Don't interrupt. What's wonderful about it? There's fifty men in the City of New York who'd stake him. (*To Biff.*) Sporting goods?

BIFF: I guess so. I know something about it and —

WILLY: He knows something about it! You know sporting goods better than Spalding, for God's sake! How much is he giving you?

BIFF: I don't know, I didn't even see him yet, but —

WILLY: Then what're you talkin' about?

BIFF (*getting angry*): Well, all I said was I'm gonna see him, that's all!

WILLY (*turning away*): Ah, you're counting your chickens again.

BIFF (*starting left for the stairs*): Oh, Jesus, I'm going to sleep!

WILLY (*calling after him*): Don't curse in this house!

BIFF (*turning*): Since when did you get so clean?

HAPPY (*trying to stop them*): Wait a . . .

WILLY: Don't use that language to me! I won't have it!

HAPPY (*grabbing Biff, shouts*): Wait a minute! I got an idea. I got a feasible idea. Come here, Biff, let's talk this over now, let's talk some sense here. When I was down in Florida last time, I thought of a great idea to sell sporting goods. It just came back to me. You and I, Biff — we have a line, the Loman Line. We train a couple of weeks, and put on a couple of exhibitions, see?

WILLY: That's an idea!

HAPPY: Wait! We form two basketball teams, see? Two water polo teams. We play each other. It's a million dollars' worth of publicity. Two brothers, see? The Loman Brothers. Displays in the Royal

Palms — all the hotels. And banners over the ring and the basketball court: "Loman Brothers." Baby, we could sell sporting goods!

WILLY: That is a one-million-dollar idea!

LINDA: Marvelous!

BIFF: I'm in great shape as far as that's concerned.

HAPPY: And the beauty of it is, Biff, it wouldn't be like a business. We'd be out playin' ball again . . .

BIFF (enthused): Yeah, that's . . .

WILLY: Million-dollar . . .

HAPPY: And you wouldn't get fed up with it, Biff. It'd be the family again. There'd be the old honor, and comradeship, and if you wanted to go off for a swim or somethin' — well, you'd do it! Without some smart cooky gettin' up ahead of you!

WILLY: Lick the world! You guys together could absolutely lick the civilized world.

BIFF: I'll see Oliver tomorrow. Hap, if we could work that out . . .

LINDA: Maybe things are beginning to —

WILLY (wildly enthused, to Linda): Stop interrupting! (To Biff.) But don't wear sport jacket and slacks when you see Oliver.

BIFF: No, I'll —

WILLY: A business suit, and talk as little as possible, and don't crack any jokes.

BIFF: He did like me. Always liked me.

LINDA: He loved you!

WILLY (to Linda): Will you stop! (To Biff.) Walk in very serious. You are not applying for a boy's job. Money is to pass. Be quiet, fine, and serious. Everybody likes a kidder, but nobody lends him money.

HAPPY: I'll try to get some myself, Biff. I'm sure I can.

WILLY: I see great things for you kids, I think your troubles are over. But remember, start big and you'll end big. Ask for fifteen. How much you gonna ask for?

BIFF: Gee, I don't know —

WILLY: And don't say "Gee." "Gee" is a boy's word. A man walking in for fifteen thousand dollars does not say "Gee!"

BIFF: Ten, I think, would be top though.

WILLY: Don't be so modest. You always started too low. Walk in with a big laugh. Don't look worried. Start off with a couple of your good stories to lighten things up. It's not what you say, it's how you say it — because personality always wins the day.

LINDA: Oliver always thought the highest of him —

WILLY: Will you let me talk?

BIFF: Don't yell at her, Pop, will ya?

WILLY (angrily): I was talking, wasn't I?

BIFF: I don't like you yelling at her all the time, and I'm tellin' you, that's all.

WILLY: What're you, takin' over this house?

LINDA: Willy —

WILLY (turning to her): Don't take his side all the time, goddammit!

BIFF (furiously): Stop yelling at her!

WILLY (suddenly pulling on his cheek, beaten down, guilt ridden): Give my best to Bill Oliver — he may remember me. (He exits through the living room doorway.)

LINDA (her voice subdued): What'd you have to start that for? (Biff turns away.) You see how sweet he was as soon as you talked hopefully? (She goes over to Biff.) Come up and say good night to him. Don't let him go to bed that way.

HAPPY: Come on, Biff, let's buck him up.

LINDA: Please, dear. Just say good night. It takes so little to make him happy. Come. (She goes through the living room doorway, calling upstairs from within the living room.) Your pajamas are hanging in the bathroom, Willy!

HAPPY (looking toward where Linda went out): What a woman! They broke the mold when they made her. You know that, Biff?

BIFF: He's off salary. My God, working on commission!

HAPPY: Well, let's face it: he's no hot-shot selling man. Except that sometimes, you have to admit, he's a sweet personality.

BIFF (deciding): Lend me ten bucks, will ya? I want to buy some new ties.

HAPPY: I'll take you to a place I know. Beautiful stuff. Wear one of my striped shirts tomorrow.

BIFF: She got gray. Mom got awful old. Gee, I'm gonna go in to Oliver tomorrow and knock him for a —

HAPPY: Come on up. Tell that to Dad. Let's give him a whirl. Come on.

BIFF (steamed up): You know, with ten thousand bucks, boy!

HAPPY (as they go into the living room): That's the talk, Biff, that's the first time I've heard the old confidence out of you! (From within the living room, fading off.) You're gonna live with me, kid, and any babe you want just say the word . . . (The last lines are hardly heard. They are mounting the stairs to their parents' bedroom.)

LINDA (entering her bedroom and addressing Willy, who is in the bathroom. She is straightening the bed for him.): Can you do anything about the shower? It drips.

WILLY (from the bathroom): All of a sudden everything falls to pieces. Goddam plumbing, oughta be sued, those people. I hardly finished putting it in and the thing . . . (His words rumble off.)

LINDA: I'm just wondering if Oliver will remember him. You think he might?

WILLY (coming out of the bathroom in his pajamas):

Remember him? What's the matter with you, you crazy? If he'd've stayed with Oliver he'd be on top by now! Wait'll Oliver gets a look at him. You don't know the average caliber any more. The average young man today — (*he is getting into bed*) — is got a caliber of zero. Greatest thing in the world for him was to bum around.

(*Biff and Happy enter the bedroom. Slight pause.*)

WILLY (*stops short, looking at Biff*): Glad to hear it, boy.

HAPPY: He wanted to say good night to you, sport.

WILLY (*to Biff*): Yeah. Knock him dead, boy. What'd you want to tell me?

BIFF: Just take it easy, Pop. Good night. (*He turns to go.*)

WILLY (*unable to resist*): And if anything falls off the desk while you're talking to him — like a package or something — don't you pick it up. They have office boys for that.

LINDA: I'll make a big breakfast —

WILLY: Will you let me finish? (*To Biff.*) Tell him you were in the business in the West. Not farm work.

BIFF: All right, Dad.

LINDA: I think everything —

WILLY (*going right through her speech*): And don't undersell yourself. No less than fifteen thousand dollars.

BIFF (*unable to bear him*): Okay. Good night, Mom. (*He starts moving.*)

WILLY: Because you got a greatness in you, Biff, remember that. You got all kinds of greatness . . . (*He lies back, exhausted. Biff walks out.*)

LINDA (*calling after Biff*): Sleep well, darling!

HAPPY: I'm gonna get married, Mom. I wanted to tell you.

LINDA: Go to sleep, dear.

HAPPY (*going*): I just wanted to tell you.

WILLY: Keep up the good work. (*Happy exits.*) God . . . remember that Ebbets Field game? The championship of the city?

LINDA: Just rest. Should I sing to you?

WILLY: Yeah. Sing to me. (*Linda hums a soft lullaby.*) When that team came out — he was the tallest, remember?

LINDA: Oh, yes. And in gold.

(*Biff enters the darkened kitchen, takes a cigarette, and leaves the house. He comes downstage into a golden pool of light. He smokes, staring at the night.*)

WILLY: Like a young god. Hercules — something like that. And the sun, the sun all around him. Remember how he waved to me? Right up from the field, with the representatives of three colleges standing by? And the buyers I brought, and the

cheers when he came out — Loman, Loman, Loman! God Almighty, he'll be great yet. A star like that, magnificent, can never really fade away!

(*The light on Willy is fading. The gas heater begins to glow through the kitchen wall, near the stairs, a blue flame beneath red coils.*)

LINDA (*timidly*): Willy dear, what has he got against you?

WILLY: I'm so tired. Don't talk anymore.

(*Biff slowly returns to the kitchen. He stops, stares toward the heater.*)

LINDA: Will you ask Howard to let you work in New York?

WILLY: First thing in the morning. Everything'll be all right.

(*Biff reaches behind the heater and draws out a length of rubber tubing. He is horrified and turns his head toward Willy's room, still dimly lit, from which the strains of Linda's desperate but monotonous humming rise.*)

WILLY (*staring through the window into the moonlight*): Gee, look at the moon moving between the buildings!

(*Biff wraps the tubing around his hand and quickly goes up the stairs.*)

ACT II

(*Music is heard, gay and bright. The curtain rises as the music fades away. Willy, in shirt sleeves, is sitting at the kitchen table, sipping coffee, his hat in his lap. Linda is filling his cup when she can.*)

WILLY: Wonderful coffee. Meal in itself.

LINDA: Can I make you some eggs?

WILLY: No. Take a breath.

LINDA: You look so rested, dear.

WILLY: I slept like a dead one. First time in months. Imagine, sleeping till ten on a Tuesday morning. Boys left nice and early, heh?

LINDA: They were out of here by eight o'clock.

WILLY: Good work!

LINDA: It was so thrilling to see them leaving together. I can't get over the shaving lotion in this house!

WILLY (*smiling*): Mmm —

LINDA: Biff was very changed this morning. His whole attitude seemed to be hopeful. He couldn't wait to get downtown to see Oliver.

WILLY: He's heading for a change. There's no question, there simply are certain men that take longer to get — solidified. How did he dress?

LINDA: His blue suit. He's so handsome in that suit. He could be a — anything in that suit!

(*Willy gets up from the table. Linda holds his jacket for him.*)

WILLY: There's no question, no question at all. Gee, on the way home tonight I'd like to buy some seeds.

LINDA (*laughing*): That'd be wonderful. But not enough sun gets back there. Nothing'll grow any more.

WILLY: You wait, kid, before it's all over we're gonna get a little place out in the country, and I'll raise some vegetables, a couple of chickens . . .

LINDA: You'll do it yet, dear.

(*Willy walks out of his jacket. Linda follows him.*)

WILLY: And they'll get married, and come for a weekend. I'd build a little guest house. 'Cause I got so many fine tools, all I'd need would be a little lumber and some peace of mind.

LINDA (*joyfully*): I sewed the lining . . .

WILLY: I could build two guest houses, so they'd both come. Did he decide how much he's going to ask Oliver for?

LINDA (*getting him into the jacket*): He didn't mention it, but I imagine ten or fifteen thousand. You going to talk to Howard today?

WILLY: Yeah. I'll put it to him straight and simple. He'll just have to take me off the road.

LINDA: And Willy, don't forget to ask for a little advance, because we've got the insurance premium. It's the grace period now.

WILLY: That's a hundred . . . ?

LINDA: A hundred and eight, sixty-eight. Because we're a little short again.

WILLY: Why are we short?

LINDA: Well, you had the motor job on the car . . .

WILLY: That goddam Studebaker!

LINDA: And you got one more payment on the refrigerator . . .

WILLY: But it just broke again!

LINDA: Well, it's old, dear.

WILLY: I told you we should've bought a well-advertised machine. Charley bought a General Electric and it's twenty years old and it's still good, that son-of-a-bitch.

LINDA: But, Willy —

WILLY: Whoever heard of a Hastings refrigerator? Once in my life I would like to own something outright before it's broken! I'm always in a race with the junkyard! I just finished paying for the car and it's on its last legs. The refrigerator con-

sumes belts like a goddamn maniac. They time those things. They time them so when you finally paid for them, they're used up.

LINDA (*buttoning up his jacket as he unbuttons it*): All told, about two hundred dollars would carry us, dear. But that includes the last payment on the mortgage. After this payment, Willy, the house belongs to us.

WILLY: It's twenty-five years!

LINDA: Biff was nine years old when we bought it.

WILLY: Well, that's a great thing. To weather a twenty-five year mortgage is —

LINDA: It's an accomplishment.

WILLY: All the cement, the lumber, the reconstruction I put in this house! There ain't a crack to be found in it anymore.

LINDA: Well, it served its purpose.

WILLY: What purpose? Some stranger'll come along, move in, and that's that. If only Biff would take this house, and raise a family . . . (*He starts to go.*) Good-by, I'm late.

LINDA (*suddenly remembering*): Oh, I forgot! You're supposed to meet them for dinner.

WILLY: Me?

LINDA: At Frank's Chop House on Forty-eighth near Sixth Avenue.

WILLY: Is that so! How about you?

LINDA: No, just the three of you. They're gonna blow you to a big meal!

WILLY: Don't say! Who thought of that?

LINDA: Biff came to me this morning, Willy, and he said, "Tell Dad, we want to blow him to a big meal." Be there six o'clock. You and your two boys are going to have dinner.

WILLY: Gee whiz! That's really somethin'. I'm gonna knock Howard for a loop, kid. I'll get an advance, and I'll come home with a New York job. Goddammit, now I'm gonna do it!

LINDA: Oh, that's the spirit, Willy!

WILLY: I will never get behind a wheel the rest of my life!

LINDA: It's changing, Willy, I can feel it changing!

WILLY: Beyond a question. G'by, I'm late. (*He starts to go again.*)

LINDA (*calling after him as she runs to the kitchen table for a handkerchief*): You got your glasses?

WILLY (*feels for them, then comes back in*): Yeah, yeah, got my glasses.

LINDA (*giving him the handkerchief*): And a handkerchief.

WILLY: Yeah, handkerchief.

LINDA: And your saccharine?

WILLY: Yeah, my saccharine.

LINDA: Be careful on the subway stairs.

(*She kisses him, and a silk stocking is seen hanging from her hand. Willy notices it.*)

WILLY: Will you stop mending stockings? At least while I'm in the house. It gets me nervous. I can't tell you. Please.

(*Linda hides the stocking in her hand as she follows Willy across the forestage in front of the house.*)

LINDA: Remember, Frank's Chop House.

WILLY (*passing the apron*): Maybe beets would grow out there.

LINDA (*laughing*): But you tried so many times.

WILLY: Yeah. Well, don't work hard today. (*He disappears around the right corner of the house.*)

LINDA: Be careful!

(*As Willy vanishes, Linda waves to him. Suddenly the phone rings. She runs across the stage and into the kitchen and lifts it.*)

LINDA: Hello? Oh, Biff! I'm so glad you called, I just . . . Yes, sure, I just told him. Yes, he'll be there for dinner at six o'clock, I didn't forget. Listen, I was just dying to tell you. You know that little rubber pipe I told you about? That he connected to the gas heater? I finally decided to go down the cellar this morning and take it away and destroy it. But it's gone! Imagine? He took it away himself, it isn't there! (*She listens.*) When? Oh, then you took it. Oh — nothing, it's just that I'd hoped he'd taken it away himself. Oh, I'm not worried, darling, because this morning he left in such high spirits, it was like the old days! I'm not afraid any more. Did Mr. Oliver see you? . . . Well, you wait there then. And make a nice impression on him, darling. Just don't perspire too much before you see him. And have a nice time with Dad. He may have big news too! . . . That's right, a New York job. And be sweet to him tonight, dear. Be loving to him. Because he's only a little boat looking for a harbor. (*She is trembling with sorrow and joy.*) Oh, that's wonderful, Biff, you'll save his life. Thanks, darling. Just put your arm around him when he comes into the restaurant. Give him a smile. That's the boy . . . Good-by, dear. . . . You got your comb? . . . That's fine. Good-by, Biff dear.

(*In the middle of her speech, Howard Wagner, thirty-six, wheels in a small typewriter table on which is a wire-recording machine and proceeds to plug it in. This is on the left forestage. Light slowly fades on Linda as it rises on Howard. Howard is intent on threading the machine and only glances over his shoulder as Willy appears.*)

WILLY: Pst! Pst!

HOWARD: Hello, Willy, come in.

WILLY: Like to have a little talk with you, Howard.

HOWARD: Sorry to keep you waiting. I'll be with you in a minute.

WILLY: What's that, Howard?

HOWARD: Didn't you ever see one of these? Wire recorder.

WILLY: Oh. Can we talk a minute?

HOWARD: Records things. Just got delivery yesterday. Been driving me crazy, the most terrific machine I ever saw in my life. I was up all night with it.

WILLY: What do you do with it?

HOWARD: I bought it for dictation, but you can do anything with it. Listen to this. I had it home last night. Listen to what I picked up. The first one is my daughter. Get this. (*He flicks the switch and "Roll out the Barrel" is heard being whistled.*) Listen to that kid whistle.

WILLY: That is lifelike, isn't it?

HOWARD: Seven years old. Get that tone.

WILLY: Ts, ts. Like to ask a little favor if you . . .

(*The whistling breaks off, and the voice of Howard's daughter is heard.*)

HIS DAUGHTER: "Now you, Daddy."

HOWARD: She's crazy for me! (*Again the same song is whistled.*) That's me! Ha! (*He winks.*)

WILLY: You're very good!

(*The whistling breaks off again. The machine runs silent for a moment.*)

HOWARD: Sh! Get this now, this is my son.

HIS SON: "The capital of Alabama is Montgomery; the capital of Arizona is Phoenix; the capital of Arkansas is Little Rock; the capital of California is Sacramento . . ." (*and on, and on.*)

HOWARD (*holding up five fingers*): Five years old, Willy!

WILLY: He'll make an announcer some day!

HIS SON (*continuing*): "The capital . . ."

HOWARD: Get that — alphabetical order! (*The machine breaks off suddenly.*) Wait a minute. The maid kicked the plug out.

WILLY: It certainly is a —

HOWARD: Sh, for God's sake!

HIS SON: "It's nine o'clock, Bulova watch time. So I have to go to sleep."

WILLY: That really is —

HOWARD: Wait a minute! The next is my wife.

(*They wait.*)

HOWARD'S VOICE: "Go on, say something." (*Pause.*) "Well, you gonna talk?"

HIS WIFE: "I can't think of anything."

HOWARD'S VOICE: "Well, talk — it's turning."

HIS WIFE (*shyly, beaten*): "Hello." (*Silence.*) "Oh, Howard, I can't talk into this . . ."

HOWARD (*snapping the machine off*): That was my wife.

WILLY: That is a wonderful machine. Can we —

HOWARD: I tell you, Willy, I'm gonna take my camera, and my bandsaw, and all my hobbies, and out they go. This is the most fascinating relaxation I ever found.

WILLY: I think I'll get one myself.

HOWARD: Sure, they're only a hundred and a half. You can't do without it. Supposing you wanna hear Jack Benny, see? But you can't be at home at that hour. So you tell the maid to turn the radio on when Jack Benny comes on, and this automatically goes on with the radio . . .

WILLY: And when you come home you . . .

HOWARD: You can come home twelve o'clock, one o'clock, any time you like, and you get yourself a Coke and sit yourself down, throw the switch, and there's Jack Benny's program in the middle of the night!

WILLY: I'm definitely going to get one. Because lots of times I'm on the road, and I think to myself, what I must be missing on the radio!

HOWARD: Don't you have a radio in the car?

WILLY: Well, yeah, but who ever thinks of turning it on?

HOWARD: Say, aren't you supposed to be in Boston?

WILLY: That's what I want to talk to you about, Howard. You got a minute? (*He draws a chair in from the wing.*)

HOWARD: What happened? What're you doing here?

WILLY: Well . . .

HOWARD: You didn't crack up again, did you?

WILLY: Oh, no. No . . .

HOWARD: Geez, you had me worried there for a minute. What's the trouble?

WILLY: Well, tell you the truth, Howard. I've come to the decision that I'd rather not travel anymore.

HOWARD: Not travel! Well, what'll you do?

WILLY: Remember, Christmas time, when you had the party here? You said you'd try to think of some spot for me here in town.

HOWARD: With us?

WILLY: Well, sure.

HOWARD: Oh, yeah, yeah. I remember. Well, I couldn't think of anything for you, Willy.

WILLY: I tell ya, Howard. The kids are all grown up, y'know. I don't need much anymore. If I could take home — well, sixty-five dollars a week, I could swing it.

HOWARD: Yeah, but Willy, see I —

WILLY: I tell ya why, Howard. Speaking frankly and between the two of us, y'know — I'm just a little tired.

HOWARD: Oh, I could understand that, Willy. But you're a road man, Willy, and we do a road business. We've only got a half-dozen salesmen on the floor here.

WILLY: God knows, Howard, I never asked a favor of any man. But I was with the firm when your father used to carry you in here in his arms.

HOWARD: I know that, Willy, but —

WILLY: Your father came to me the day you were born and asked me what I thought of the name Howard, may he rest in peace.

HOWARD: I appreciate that, Willy, but there just is no spot here for you. If I had a spot I'd slam you right in, but I just don't have a single solitary spot.

(*He looks for his lighter. Willy has picked it up and gives it to him. Pause.*)

WILLY (*with increasing anger*): Howard, all I need to set my table is fifty dollars a week.

HOWARD: But where am I going to put you, kid?

WILLY: Look, it isn't a question of whether I can sell merchandise, is it?

HOWARD: No, but it's business, kid, and everybody's gotta pull his own weight.

WILLY (*desperately*): Just let me tell you a story, Howard —

HOWARD: 'Cause you gotta admit, business is business.

WILLY (*angrily*): Business is definitely business, but just listen for a minute. You don't understand this. When I was a boy — eighteen, nineteen — I was already on the road. And there was a question in my mind as to whether selling had a future for me. Because in those days I had a yearning to go to Alaska. See, there were three gold strikes in one month in Alaska, and I felt like going out. Just for the ride, you might say.

HOWARD (*barely interested*): Don't say.

WILLY: Oh, yeah, my father lived many years in Alaska. He was an adventurous man. We've got quite a little streak of self-reliance in our family. I thought I'd go out with my older brother and try to locate him, and maybe settle in the North with the old man. And I was almost decided to go, when I met a salesman in the Parker House. His name was Dave Singleman. And he was eighty-four years old, and he'd drummed merchandise in thirty-one states. And old Dave, he'd go up to his room, y'understand, put on his green velvet slippers —

I'll never forget — and pick up his phone and call the buyers, and without ever leaving his room, at the age of eighty-four, he made his living. And when I saw that, I realized that selling was the greatest career a man could want. 'Cause what could be more satisfying than to be able to go, at the age of eighty-four, into twenty or thirty different cities, and pick up a phone, and be remembered and loved and helped by so many different people? Do you know? When he died — and by the way he died the death of a salesman, in his green velvet slippers in the smoker of the New York, New Haven and Hartford, going into Boston — when he died, hundreds of salesmen and buyers were at his funeral. Things were sad on a lotta trains for months after that. (*He stands up. Howard has not looked at him.*) In those days there was personality in it, Howard. There was respect, and comradeship, and gratitude in it. Today, it's all cut and dried, and there's no chance for bringing friendship to bear — or personality. You see what I mean? They don't know me any more.

HOWARD (*moving away, to the right*): That's just the thing, Willy.

WILLY: If I had forty dollars a week — that's all I'd need. Forty dollars, Howard.

HOWARD: Kid, I can't take blood from a stone, I —

WILLY (*desperation is on him now*): Howard, the year Al Smith was nominated, your father came to me and —

HOWARD (*starting to go off*): I've got to see some people, kid.

WILLY (*stopping him*): I'm talking about your father! There were promises made across this desk! You mustn't tell me you've got people to see — I put thirty-four years into this firm, Howard, and now I can't pay my insurance! You can't eat the orange and throw the peel away — a man is not a piece of fruit! (*After a pause.*) Now pay attention. Your father — in 1928 I had a big year. I averaged a hundred and seventy dollars a week in commissions.

HOWARD (*impatiently*): Now, Willy, you never averaged —

WILLY (*banging his hand on the desk*): I averaged a hundred and seventy dollars a week in the year of 1928! And your father came to me — or rather, I was in the office here — it was right over this desk — and he put his hand on my shoulder —

HOWARD (*getting up*): You'll have to excuse me, Willy, I gotta see some people. Pull yourself together. (*Going out.*) I'll be back in a little while.

(*On Howard's exit, the light on his chair grows very bright and strange.*)

WILLY: Pull myself together! What the hell did I say to him? My God, I was yelling at him! How could I? (*Willy breaks off, staring at the light, which occupies the chair, animating it. He approaches this chair, standing across the desk from it.*) Frank, Frank, don't you remember what you told me that time? How you put your hand on my shoulder, and Frank . . . (*He leans on the desk and as he speaks the dead man's name he accidentally switches on the recorder, and instantly*)

HOWARD'S SON: ". . . of New York is Albany. The capital of Ohio is Cincinnati, the capital of Rhode Island is . . ." (*The recitation continues.*)

WILLY (*leaping away with fright, shouting*): Ha! Howard! Howard! Howard!

HOWARD (*rushing in*): What happened?

WILLY (*pointing at the machine, which continues nasally, childishly, with the capital cities*): Shut it off! Shut it off!

HOWARD (*pulling the plug out*): Look, Willy . . .

WILLY (*pressing his hands to his eyes*): I gotta get myself some coffee. I'll get some coffee . . .

(*Willy starts to walk out. Howard stops him.*)

HOWARD (*rolling up the cord*): Willy, look . . .

WILLY: I'll go to Boston.

HOWARD: Willy, you can't go to Boston for us.

WILLY: Why can't I go?

HOWARD: I don't want you to represent us. I've been meaning to tell you for a long time now.

WILLY: Howard, are you firing me?

HOWARD: I think you need a good long rest, Willy.

WILLY: Howard —

HOWARD: And when you feel better, come back, and we'll see if we can work something out.

WILLY: But I gotta earn money, Howard. I'm in no position to —

HOWARD: Where are your sons? Why don't your sons give you a hand?

WILLY: They're working on a very big deal.

HOWARD: This is no time for false pride, Willy. You go to your sons and you tell them that you're tired. You've got two great boys, haven't you?

WILLY: Oh, no question, no question, but in the meantime . . .

HOWARD: Then that's that, heh?

WILLY: All right, I'll go to Boston tomorrow.

HOWARD: No, no.

WILLY: I can't throw myself on my sons. I'm not a cripple!

HOWARD: Look, kid, I'm busy this morning.

WILLY (*grasping Howard's arm*): Howard, you've got to let me go to Boston!

HOWARD (*hard, keeping himself under control*): I've got a line of people to see this morning. Sit down, take five minutes, and pull yourself together, and then go home, will ya? I need the office, Willy. (*He starts to go, turns, remembering the recorder, starts to push off the table holding the recorder.*) Oh, yeah. Whenever you can this week, stop by and drop off the samples. You'll feel better, Willy, and then come back and we'll talk. Pull yourself together, kid, there's people outside.

(*Howard exits, pushing the table off left. Willy stares into space, exhausted. Now the music is heard — Ben's music — first distantly, then closer, closer. As Willy speaks, Ben enters from the right. He carries valise and umbrella.*)

WILLY: Oh, Ben, how did you do it? What is the answer? Did you wind up the Alaska deal already?

BEN: Doesn't take much time if you know what you're doing. Just a short business trip. Boarding ship in an hour. Wanted to say good-by.

WILLY: Ben, I've got to talk to you.

BEN (*glancing at his watch*): Haven't the time, William.

WILLY (*crossing the apron to Ben*): Ben, nothing's working out. I don't know what to do.

BEN: Now, look here, William. I've bought timberland in Alaska and I need a man to look after things for me.

WILLY: God, timberland! Me and my boys in those grand outdoors!

BEN: You've got a new continent at your doorstep, William. Get out of these cities, they're full of talk and time payments and courts of law. Screw on your fists and you can fight for a fortune up there.

WILLY: Yes, yes! Linda, Linda!

(*Linda enters as of old, with the wash.*)

LINDA: Oh, you're back?

BEN: I haven't much time.

WILLY: No, wait! Linda, he's got a proposition for me in Alaska.

LINDA: But you've got — (*To Ben.*) He's got a beautiful job here.

WILLY: But in Alaska, kid, I could —

LINDA: You're doing well enough, Willy!

BEN (*to Linda*): Enough for what, my dear?

LINDA (*frightened of Ben and angry at him*): Don't say those things to him! Enough to be happy right here, right now. (*To Willy, while Ben laughs.*) Why must everybody conquer the world? You're well liked, and the boys love you, and someday — (*To Ben*) — why, old man Wagner told him just the other day that if he keeps it up he'll be a member of the firm, didn't he, Willy?

WILLY: Sure, sure. I am building something with this firm, Ben, and if a man is building something he must be on the right track, mustn't he?

BEN: What are you building? Lay your hand on it. Where is it?

WILLY (*hesitantly*): That's true, Linda, there's nothing.

LINDA: Why? (*To Ben.*) There's a man eighty-four years old —

WILLY: That's right, Ben, that's right. When I look at that man I say, what is there to worry about?

BEN: Bah!

WILLY: It's true, Ben. All he has to do is go into any city, pick up the phone, and he's making his living and you know why?

BEN (*picking up his valise*): I've got to go.

WILLY (*holding Ben back*): Look at this boy!

(*Biff, in his high school sweater, enters carrying suitcase. Happy carries Biff's shoulder guards, gold helmet, and football pants.*)

WILLY: Without a penny to his name, three great universities are begging for him, and from there the sky's the limit, because it's not what you do, Ben. It's who you know and the smile on your face! It's contacts, Ben, contacts! The whole wealth of Alaska passes over the lunch table at the Commodore Hotel, and that's the wonder, the wonder of this country, that a man can end with diamonds here on the basis of being liked! (*He turns to Biff.*) And that's why when you get out on that field today it's important. Because thousands of people will be rooting for you and loving you. (*To Ben, who has again begun to leave.*) And Ben! when he walks into a business office his name will sound out like a bell and all the doors will open to him! I've seen it, Ben, I've seen it a thousand times! You can't feel it with your hand like timber, but it's there!

BEN: Good-by, William.

WILLY: Ben, am I right? Don't you think I'm right? I value your advice.

BEN: There's a new continent at your doorstep, William. You could walk out rich. Rich! (*He is gone.*)

WILLY: We'll do it here, Ben! You hear me? We're gonna do it here!

(*Young Bernard rushes in. The gay music of the Boys is heard.*)

BERNARD: Oh, gee, I was afraid you left already!

WILLY: Why? What time is it?

BERNARD: It's half-past one!

WILLY: Well, come on, everybody! Ebbets Field next stop! Where's the pennants? (*He rushes through the wall-line of the kitchen and out into the living room.*)

LINDA (*to Biff*): Did you pack fresh underwear?

BIFF (*who has been limbering up*): I want to go!

BERNARD: Biff, I'm carrying your helmet, ain't I?

HAPPY: No, I'm carrying the helmet.

BERNARD: Oh, Biff, you promised me.

HAPPY: I'm carrying the helmet.

BERNARD: How am I going to get in the locker room?

LINDA: Let him carry the shoulder guards. (*She puts her coat and hat on in the kitchen.*)

BERNARD: Can I, Biff? 'Cause I told everybody I'm going to be in the locker room.

HAPPY: In Ebbets Field it's the clubhouse.

BERNARD: I meant the clubhouse. Biff!

HAPPY: Biff!

BIFF (*grandly, after a slight pause*): Let him carry the shoulder guards.

HAPPY (*as he gives Bernard the shoulder guards*): Stay close to us now.

(*Willy rushes in with the pennants.*)

WILLY (*handing them out*): Everybody wave when Biff comes out on the field. (*Happy and Bernard run off.*) You set now, boy?

(*The music has died away.*)

BIFF: Ready to go, Pop. Every muscle is ready.

WILLY (*at the edge of the apron*): You realize what this means?

BIFF: That's right, Pop.

WILLY (*feeling Biff's muscles*): You're comin' home this afternoon captain of the All-Scholastic Championship Team of the City of New York.

BIFF: I got it, Pop. And remember, pal, when I take off my helmet, that touchdown is for you.

WILLY: Let's go! (*He is starting out, with his arm around Biff, when Charley enters, as of old, in knickers.*) I got no room for you, Charley.

CHARLEY: Room? For what?

WILLY: In the car.

CHARLEY: You goin' for a ride? I wanted to shoot some casino.

WILLY (*furiously*): Casino! (*Incredulously.*) Don't you realize what today is?

LINDA: Oh, he knows, Willy. He's just kidding you.

WILLY: That's nothing to kid about!

CHARLEY: No, Linda, what's goin' on?

LINDA: He's playing in Ebbets Field.

CHARLEY: Baseball in this weather?

WILLY: Don't talk to him. Come on, come on! (*He is pushing them out.*)

CHARLEY: Wait a minute, didn't you hear the news?

WILLY: What?

CHARLEY: Don't you listen to the radio? Ebbets Field just blew up.

WILLY: You go to hell! (*Charley laughs. Pushing them out.*) Come on, come on! We're late.

CHARLEY (*as they go*): Knock a homer, Biff, knock a homer!

WILLY (*the last to leave, turning to Charley*): I don't think that was funny, Charley. This is the greatest day of his life.

CHARLEY: Willy, when are you going to grow up?

WILLY: Yeah, heh? When this game is over, Charley, you'll be laughing out of the other side of your face. They'll be calling him another Red Grange. Twenty-five thousand a year.

CHARLEY (*kidding*): Is that so?

WILLY: Yeah, that's so.

CHARLEY: Well, then, I'm sorry, Willy. But tell me something.

WILLY: What?

CHARLEY: Who is Red Grange?

WILLY: Put up your hands. Goddam you, put up your hands!

(*Charley, chuckling, shakes his head and walks away, around the left corner of the stage. Willy follows him. The music rises to a mocking frenzy.*)

WILLY: Who the hell do you think you are, better than everybody else? You don't know everything, you big, ignorant, stupid . . . Put up your hands!

(*Light rises, on the right side of the forestage, on a small table in the reception room of Charley's office. Traffic sounds are heard. Bernard, now mature, sits whistling to himself. A pair of tennis rackets and an overnight bag are on the floor beside him.*)

WILLY (*offstage*): What are you walking away for? Don't walk away! If you're going to say something say it to my face! I know you laugh at me behind my back. You'll laugh out of the other side of your goddam face after this game. Touchdown! Touchdown! Eighty thousand people! Touchdown! Right between the goal posts.

(*Bernard is a quiet, earnest, but self-assured young man. Willy's voice is coming from right upstage now. Bernard lowers his feet off the table and listens. Jenny, his father's secretary, enters.*)

JENNY (*distressed*): Say, Bernard, will you go out in the hall?

BERNARD: What is that noise? Who is it?

JENNY: Mr. Loman. He just got off the elevator.

BERNARD (*getting up*): Who's he arguing with?

JENNY: Nobody. There's nobody with him. I can't deal with him anymore, and your father gets all upset everytime he comes. I've got a lot of typing to do, and your father's waiting to sign it. Will you see him?

WILLY (*entering*): Touchdown! Touch — (*He sees*

Jenny.) Jenny, Jenny, good to see you. How're ya? Workin'? Or still honest?

JENNY: Fine. How've you been feeling?

WILLY: Not much any more, Jenny. Ha, ha! (*He is surprised to see the rackets.*)

BERNARD: Hello, Uncle Willy.

WILLY (*almost shocked*): Bernard! Well, look who's here! (*He comes quickly, guiltily, to Bernard and warmly shakes his hand.*)

BERNARD: How are you? Good to see you.

WILLY: What are you doing here?

BERNARD: Oh, just stopped by to see Pop. Get off my feet till my train leaves. I'm going to Washington in a few minutes.

WILLY: Is he in?

BERNARD: Yes, he's in his office with the accountant. Sit down.

WILLY (*sitting down*): What're you going to do in Washington?

BERNARD: Oh, just a case I've got there, Willy.

WILLY: That so? (*Indicating the rackets.*) You going to play tennis there?

BERNARD: I'm staying with a friend who's got a court.

WILLY: Don't say. His own tennis court. Must be fine people, I bet.

BERNARD: They are, very nice. Dad tells me Biff's in town.

WILLY (*with a big smile*): Yeah, Biff's in. Working on a very big deal, Bernard.

BERNARD: What's Biff doing?

WILLY: Well, he's been doing very big things in the West. But he decided to establish himself here. Very big. We're having dinner. Did I hear your wife had a boy?

BERNARD: That's right. Our second.

WILLY: Two boys! What do you know!

BERNARD: What kind of a deal has Biff got?

WILLY: Well, Bill Oliver — very big sporting-goods man — he wants Biff very badly. Called him in from the West. Long distance, carte blanche, special deliveries. Your friends have their own private tennis court?

BERNARD: You still with the old firm, Willy?

WILLY (*after a pause*): I'm — I'm overjoyed to see how you made the grade, Bernard, overjoyed. It's an encouraging thing to see a young man really — really — Looks very good for Biff — very — (*He breaks off, then.*) Bernard — (*He is so full of emotion, he breaks off again.*)

BERNARD: What is it, Willy?

WILLY (*small and alone*): What — what's the secret?

BERNARD: What secret?

WILLY: How — how did you? Why didn't he ever catch on?

BERNARD: I wouldn't know that, Willy.

WILLY (*confidentially, desperately*): You were his friend, his boyhood friend. There's something I don't understand about it. His life ended after that Ebbets Field game. From the age of seventeen nothing good ever happened to him.

BERNARD: He never trained himself for anything.

WILLY: But he did, he did. After high school he took so many correspondence courses. Radio mechanics; television; God knows what, and never made the slightest mark.

BERNARD (*taking off his glasses*): Willy, do you want to talk candidly?

WILLY (*rising, faces Bernard*): I regard you as a very brilliant man, Bernard. I value your advice.

BERNARD: Oh, the hell with the advice, Willy. I couldn't advise you. There's just one thing I've always wanted to ask you. When he was supposed to graduate, and the math teacher flunked him —

WILLY: Oh, that son-of-a-bitch ruined his life.

BERNARD: Yeah, but, Willy, all he had to do was go to summer school and make up that subject.

WILLY: That's right, that's right.

BERNARD: Did you tell him not to go to summer school?

WILLY: Me? I begged him to go. I ordered him to go!

BERNARD: Then why wouldn't he go?

WILLY: Why? Why! Bernard, that question has been trailing me like a ghost for the last fifteen years. He flunked the subject, and laid down and died like a hammer hit him!

BERNARD: Take it easy, kid.

WILLY: Let me talk to you — I got nobody to talk to. Bernard, Bernard, was it my fault? Y'see? It keeps going around in my mind, maybe I did something to him. I got nothing to give him.

BERNARD: Don't take it so hard.

WILLY: Why did he lay down? What is the story there? You were his friend!

BERNARD: Willy, I remember, it was June, and our grades came out. And he'd flunked math.

WILLY: That son-of-a-bitch!

BERNARD: No, it wasn't right then. Biff just got very angry, I remember, and he was ready to enroll in summer school.

WILLY (*surprised*): He was?

BERNARD: He wasn't beaten by it at all. But then, Willy, he disappeared from the block for almost a month. And I got the idea that he'd gone up to New England to see you. Did he have a talk with you then?

(*Willy stares in silence.*)

BERNARD: Willy?

WILLY (*with a strong edge of resentment in his voice*): Yeah, he came to Boston. What about it?

BERNARD: Well, just that when he came back — I'll never forget this, it always mystifies me. Because I'd thought so well of Biff, even though he'd always taken advantage of me. I loved him, Willy, y'know? And he came back after that month and took his sneakers — remember those sneakers with "University of Virginia" printed on them? He was so proud of those, wore them every day. And he took them down in the cellar, and burned them up in the furnace. We had a fist fight. It lasted at least half an hour. Just the two of us, punching each other down the cellar, and crying right through it. I've often thought of how strange it was that I knew he'd given up his life. What happened in Boston, Willy?

(*Willy looks at him as at an intruder.*)

BERNARD: I just bring it up because you asked me.
WILLY (*angrily*): Nothing. What do you mean, "What happened?" What's that got to do with anything?
BERNARD: Well, don't get sore.
WILLY: What are you trying to do, blame it on me? If a boy lays down is that my fault?
BERNARD: Now, Willy, don't get —
WILLY: Well, don't — don't talk to me that way! What does that mean, "What happened?"

(*Charley enters. He is in his vest, and he carries a bottle of bourbon.*)

CHARLEY: Hey, you're going to miss that train. (*He waves the bottle.*)
BERNARD: Yeah, I'm going. (*He takes the bottle.*) Thanks, Pop. (*He picks up his rackets and bag.*) Good-by, Willy, and don't worry about it. You know, "If at first you don't succeed . . ."
WILLY: Yes, I believe in that.
BERNARD: But sometimes, Willy, it's better for a man just to walk away.
WILLY: Walk away?
BERNARD: That's right.
WILLY: But if you can't walk away?
BERNARD (*after a slight pause*): I guess that's when it's tough. (*Extending his hand.*) Good-by, Willy.
WILLY (*shaking Bernard's hand*): Good-by, boy.
CHARLEY (*an arm on Bernard's shoulder*): How do you like this kid? Gonna argue a case in front of the Supreme Court.
BERNARD (*protesting*): Pop!
WILLY (*genuinely shocked, pained, and happy*): No! The Supreme Court!
BERNARD: I gotta run. 'By, Dad!
CHARLEY: Knock 'em dead, Bernard!

(*Bernard goes off.*)

WILLY (*as Charley takes out his wallet*): The Supreme Court! And he didn't even mention it!
CHARLEY (*counting out money on the desk*): He don't have to — he's gonna do it.
WILLY: And you never told him what to do, did you? You never took any interest in him.
CHARLEY: My salvation is that I never took any interest in anything. There's some money — fifty dollars. I got an accountant inside.
WILLY: Charley, look . . . (*With difficulty.*) I got my insurance to pay. If you can manage it — I need a hundred and ten dollars.

(*Charley doesn't reply for a moment; merely stops moving.*)

WILLY: I'd draw it from my bank but Linda would know, and I . . .
CHARLEY: Sit down, Willy.
WILLY (*moving toward the chair*): I'm keeping an account of everything, remember. I'll pay every penny back. (*He sits.*)
CHARLEY: Now listen to me, Willy.
WILLY: I want you to know I appreciate . . .
CHARLEY (*sitting down on the table*): Willy, what're you doin'? What the hell is goin' on in your head?
WILLY: Why? I'm simply . . .
CHARLEY: I offered you a job. You make fifty dollars a week. And I won't send you on the road.
WILLY: I've got a job.
CHARLEY: Without pay? What kind of a job is a job without pay? (*He rises.*) Now, look, kid, enough is enough. I'm no genius but I know when I'm being insulted.
WILLY: Insulted!
CHARLEY: Why don't you want to work for me?
WILLY: What's the matter with you? I've got a job.
CHARLEY: Then what're you walkin' in here every week for?
WILLY (*getting up*): Well, if you don't want me to walk in here —
CHARLEY: I'm offering you a job.
WILLY: I don't want your goddam job!
CHARLEY: When the hell are you going to grow up?
WILLY (*furiously*): You big ignoramus, if you say that to me again I'll rap you one! I don't care how big you are! (*He's ready to fight.*)

(*Pause.*)

CHARLEY (*kindly, going to him*): How much do you need, Willy?
WILLY: Charley, I'm strapped. I'm strapped. I don't know what to do. I was just fired.
CHARLEY: Howard fired you?
WILLY: That snotnose. Imagine that? I named him. I named him Howard.

CHARLEY: Willy, when're you gonna realize that them things don't mean anything? You named him Howard, but you can't sell that. The only thing you got in this world is what you can sell. And the funny thing is that you're a salesman, and you don't know that.

WILLY: I've always tried to think otherwise, I guess. I always felt that if a man was impressive, and well liked, that nothing —

CHARLEY: Why must everybody like you? Who liked J. P. Morgan?° Was he impressive? In a Turkish bath he'd look like a butcher. But with his pockets on he was very well liked. Now listen, Willy, I know you don't like me, and nobody can say I'm in love with you, but I'll give you a job because — just for the hell of it, put it that way. Now what do you say?

WILLY: I — I just can't work for you, Charley.

CHARLEY: What're you, jealous of me?

WILLY: I can't work for you, that's all, don't ask me why.

CHARLEY (angered, takes out more bills): You been jealous of me all your life, you dammed fool! Here, pay your insurance. (He puts the money in Willy's hand.)

WILLY: I'm keeping strict accounts.

CHARLEY: I've got some work to do. Take care of yourself. And pay your insurance.

WILLY (moving to the right): Funny, y'know? After all the highways, and the trains, and the appointments, and the years, you end up worth more dead than alive.

CHARLEY: Willy, nobody's worth nothin' dead. (After a slight pause.) Did you hear what I said?

(Willy stands still, dreaming.)

CHARLEY: Willy!

WILLY: Apologize to Bernard for me when you see him. I didn't mean to argue with him. He's a fine boy. They're all fine boys, and they'll end up big — all of them. Someday they'll all play tennis together. Wish me luck, Charley. He saw Bill Oliver today.

CHARLEY: Good luck.

WILLY (on the verge of tears): Charley, you're the only friend I got. Isn't that a remarkable thing? (He goes out.)

CHARLEY: Jesus!

(Charley stares after him a moment and follows. All light blacks out. Suddenly raucous music is heard, and

J. P. Morgan: (1837–1913), wealthy financier and art collector whose money was made chiefly in banking, railroads, and steel.

a red glow rises behind the screen at right. Stanley, a young waiter, appears, carrying a table, followed by Happy, who is carrying two chairs.)

STANLEY (putting the table down): That's all right, Mr. Loman, I can handle it myself. (He turns and takes the chairs from Happy and places them at the table.)

HAPPY (glancing around): Oh, this is better.

STANLEY: Sure, in the front there you're in the middle of all kinds of noise. Whenever you got a party, Mr. Loman, you just tell me and I'll put you back here. Y'know, there's a lotta people they don't like it private, because when they go out they like to see a lotta action around them because they're sick and tired to stay in the house by theirself. But I know you, you ain't from Hackensack. You know what I mean?

HAPPY (sitting down): So how's it coming, Stanley?

STANLEY: Ah, it's a dog life. I only wish during the war they'd a took me in the Army. I coulda been dead by now.

HAPPY: My brother's back, Stanley.

STANLEY: Oh, he come back, heh? From the Far West.

HAPPY: Yeah, big cattle man, my brother, so treat him right. And my father's coming too.

STANLEY: Oh, your father too!

HAPPY: You got a couple of nice lobsters?

STANLEY: Hundred percent, big.

HAPPY: I want them with the claws.

STANLEY: Don't worry, I don't give you no mice. (Happy laughs.) How about some wine? It'll put a head on the meal.

HAPPY: No. You remember, Stanley, that recipe I brought you from overseas? With the champagne in it?

STANLEY: Oh, yeah, sure. I still got it tacked up yet in the kitchen. But that'll have to cost a buck apiece anyways.

HAPPY: That's all right.

STANLEY: What'd you, hit a number or somethin'?

HAPPY: No, it's a little celebration. My brother is — I think he pulled off a big deal today. I think we're going into business together.

STANLEY: Great! That's the best for you. Because a family business, you know what I mean? — that's the best.

HAPPY: That's what I think.

STANLEY: 'Cause what's the difference? Somebody steals? It's in the family. Know what I mean? (Sotto voce.°) Like this bartender here. The boss is goin' crazy what kinda leak he's got in the cash register. You put it in but it don't come out.

Sotto voce: In a soft voice or stage whisper.

HAPPY (*raising his head*): Sh!

STANLEY: What?

HAPPY: You notice I wasn't lookin' right or left, was I?

STANLEY: No.

HAPPY: And my eyes are closed.

STANLEY: So what's the — ?

HAPPY: Strudel's comin'.

STANLEY (*catching on, looks around*): Ah, no, there's no —

(*He breaks off as a furred, lavishly dressed girl enters and sits at the next table. Both follow her with their eyes.*)

STANLEY: Geez, how'd ya know?

HAPPY: I got radar or something. (*Staring directly at her profile.*) Oooooooo . . . Stanley.

STANLEY: I think that's for you, Mr. Loman.

HAPPY: Look at that mouth. Oh, God. And the binoculars.

STANLEY: Geez, you got a life, Mr. Loman.

HAPPY: Wait on her.

STANLEY (*going to the girl's table*): Would you like a menu, ma'am?

GIRL: I'm expecting someone, but I'd like a —

HAPPY: Why don't you bring her — excuse me, miss, do you mind? I sell champagne, and I'd like you to try my brand. Bring her a champagne, Stanley.

GIRL: That's awfully nice of you.

HAPPY: Don't mention it. It's all company money. (*He laughs.*)

GIRL: That's a charming product to be selling, isn't it?

HAPPY: Oh, gets to be like everything else. Selling is selling, y'know.

GIRL: I suppose.

HAPPY: You don't happen to sell, do you?

GIRL: No, I don't sell.

HAPPY: Would you object to a compliment from a stranger? You ought to be on a magazine cover.

GIRL (*looking at him a little archly*): I have been.

(*Stanley comes in with a glass of champagne.*)

HAPPY: What'd I say before, Stanley? You see? She's a cover girl.

STANLEY: Oh, I could see, I could see.

HAPPY (*to the Girl*): What magazine?

GIRL: Oh, a lot of them. (*She takes the drink.*) Thank you.

HAPPY: You know what they say in France, don't you? "Champagne is the drink of the complexion" — Hya, Biff!

(*Biff has entered and sits with Happy.*)

BIFF: Hello, kid. Sorry I'm late.

HAPPY: I just got here. Uh, Miss — ?

GIRL: Forsythe.

HAPPY: Miss Forsythe, this is my brother.

BIFF: Is Dad here?

HAPPY: His name is Biff. You might've heard of him. Great football player.

GIRL: Really? What team?

HAPPY: Are you familiar with football?

GIRL: No, I'm afraid I'm not.

HAPPY: Biff is quarterback with the New York Giants.

GIRL: Well, that is nice, isn't it? (*She drinks.*)

HAPPY: Good health.

GIRL: I'm happy to meet you.

HAPPY: That's my name. Hap. It's really Harold, but at West Point they called me Happy.

GIRL (*now really impressed*): Oh, I see. How do you do? (*She turns her profile.*)

BIFF: Isn't Dad coming?

HAPPY: You want her?

BIFF: Oh, I could never make that.

HAPPY: I remember the time that idea would never come into your head. Where's the old confidence, Biff?

BIFF: I just saw Oliver —

HAPPY: Wait a minute. I've got to see that old confidence again. Do you want her? She's on call.

BIFF: Oh, no. (*He turns to look at the Girl.*)

HAPPY: I'm telling you. Watch this. (*Turning to the Girl*): Honey? (*She turns to him.*) Are you busy?

GIRL: Well, I am . . . but I could make a phone call.

HAPPY: Do that, will you, honey? And see if you can get a friend. We'll be here for a while. Biff is one of the greatest football players in the country.

GIRL (*standing up*): Well, I'm certainly happy to meet you.

HAPPY: Come back soon.

GIRL: I'll try.

HAPPY: Don't try, honey, try hard.

(*The Girl exits. Stanley follows, shaking his head in bewildered admiration.*)

HAPPY: Isn't that a shame now? A beautiful girl like that? That's why I can't get married. There's not a good woman in a thousand. New York is loaded with them, kid!

BIFF: Hap, look —

HAPPY: I told you she was on call!

BIFF (*strangely unnerved*): Cut it out, will ya? I want to say something to you.

HAPPY: Did you see Oliver?

BIFF: I saw him all right. Now look, I want to tell Dad a couple of things and I want you to help me.

HAPPY: What? Is he going to back you?

BIFF: Are you crazy? You're out of your goddam head, you know that?

HAPPY: Why? What happened?

BIFF (*breathlessly*): I did a terrible thing today, Hap. It's been the strangest day I ever went through. I'm all numb, I swear.

HAPPY: You mean he wouldn't see you?

BIFF: Well, I waited six hours for him, see? All day. Kept sending my name in. Even tried to date his secretary so she'd get me to him, but no soap.

HAPPY: Because you're not showin' the old confidence, Biff. He remembered you, didn't he?

BIFF (*stopping Happy with a gesture*): Finally, about five o'clock, he comes out. Didn't remember who I was or anything. I felt like such an idiot, Hap.

HAPPY: Did you tell him my Florida idea?

BIFF: He walked away. I saw him for one minute. I got so mad I could've torn the walls down! How the hell did I ever get the idea I was a salesman there? I even believed myself that I'd been a salesman for him! And then he gave me one look and — I realized what a ridiculous lie my whole life has been! We've been talking in a dream for fifteen years. I was a shipping clerk.

HAPPY: What'd you do?

BIFF (*with great tension and wonder*): Well, he left, see. And the secretary went out. I was all alone in the waiting room. I don't know what came over me, Hap. The next thing I know I'm in his office — paneled walls, everything. I can't explain it. I — Hap, I took his fountain pen.

HAPPY: Geez, did he catch you?

BIFF: I ran out. I ran down all eleven flights. I ran and ran and ran.

HAPPY: That was an awful dumb — what'd you do that for?

BIFF (*agonized*): I don't know, I just — wanted to take something, I don't know. You gotta help me, Hap. I'm gonna tell Pop.

HAPPY: You crazy? What for?

BIFF: Hap, he's got to understand that I'm not the man somebody lends that kind of money to. He thinks I've been spiting him all these years and it's eating him up.

HAPPY: That's just it. You tell him something nice.

BIFF: I can't.

HAPPY: Say you got a lunch date with Oliver tomorrow.

BIFF: So what do I do tomorrow?

HAPPY: You leave the house tomorrow and come back at night and say Oliver is thinking it over. And he thinks it over for a couple of weeks, and gradually it fades away and nobody's the worse.

BIFF: But it'll go on forever!

HAPPY: Dad is never so happy as when he's looking forward to something!

(*Willy enters.*)

HAPPY: Hello, scout!

WILLY: Gee, I haven't been here in years!

(*Stanley has followed Willy in and sets a chair for him. Stanley starts off but Happy stops him.*)

HAPPY: Stanley!

(*Stanley stands by, waiting for an order.*)

BIFF (*going to Willy with guilt, as to an invalid*): Sit down, Pop. You want a drink?

WILLY: Sure, I don't mind.

BIFF: Let's get a load on.

WILLY: You look worried.

BIFF: N-no. (*To Stanley.*) Scotch all around. Make it doubles.

STANLEY: Doubles, right. (*He goes.*)

WILLY: You had a couple already, didn't you?

BIFF: Just a couple, yeah.

WILLY: Well, what happened, boy? (*Nodding affirmatively, with a smile.*) Everything go all right?

BIFF (*takes a breath, then reaches out and grasps Willy's hand*): Pal . . . (*He is smiling bravely, and Willy is smiling too.*) I had an experience today.

HAPPY: Terrific, Pop.

WILLY: That so? What happened?

BIFF (*high, slightly alcoholic, above the earth*): I'm going to tell you everything from first to last. It's been a strange day. (*Silence. He looks around, composes himself as best he can, but his breath keeps breaking the rhythm of his voice.*) I had to wait quite a while for him, and —

WILLY: Oliver?

BIFF: Yeah, Oliver. All day, as a matter of cold fact. And a lot of — instances — facts, Pop, facts about my life came back to me. Who was it, Pop? Who ever said I was a salesman with Oliver?

WILLY: Well, you were.

BIFF: No, Dad, I was a shipping clerk.

WILLY: But you were practically —

BIFF (*with determination*): Dad, I don't know who said it first, but I was never a salesman for Bill Oliver.

WILLY: What're you talking about?

BIFF: Let's hold on to the facts tonight, Pop. We're not going to get anywhere bullin' around. I was a shipping clerk.

WILLY (*angrily*): All right, now listen to me —

BIFF: Why don't you let me finish?

WILLY: I'm not interested in stories about the past or any crap of that kind because the woods are burning, boys, you understand? There's a big blaze going on all around. I was fired today.

BIFF (*shocked*): How could you be?

WILLY: I was fired, and I'm looking for a little good news to tell your mother, because the woman has waited and the woman has suffered. The gist of it is that I haven't got a story left in my head, Biff. So don't give me a lecture about facts and aspects. I am not interested. Now what've you got to say to me?

(*Stanley enters with three drinks. They wait until he leaves.*)

WILLY: Did you see Oliver?
BIFF: Jesus, Dad!
WILLY: You mean you didn't go up there?
HAPPY: Sure he went up there.
BIFF: I did. I — saw him. How could they fire you?
WILLY (*on the edge of his chair*): What kind of a welcome did he give you?
BIFF: He won't even let you work on commission?
WILLY: I'm out! (*Driving.*) So tell me, he gave you a warm welcome?
HAPPY: Sure, Pop, sure!
BIFF (*driven*): Well, it was kind of —
WILLY: I was wondering if he'd remember you. (*To Happy.*) Imagine, man doesn't see him for ten, twelve years and gives him that kind of a welcome!
HAPPY: Damn right!
BIFF (*trying to return to the offensive*): Pop, look —
WILLY: You know why he remembered you, don't you? Because you impressed him in those days.
BIFF: Let's talk quietly and get this down to the facts, huh?
WILLY (*as though Biff had been interrupting*): Well, what happened? It's great news, Biff. Did he take you into his office or'd you talk in the waiting room?
BIFF: Well, he came in, see, and —
WILLY (*with a big smile*): What'd he say? Betcha he threw his arm around you.
BIFF: Well, he kinda —
WILLY: He's a fine man. (*To Happy.*) Very hard man to see, y'know.
HAPPY (*agreeing*): Oh, I know.
WILLY (*to Biff*): Is that where you had the drinks?
BIFF: Yeah, he gave me a couple of — no, no!
HAPPY (*cutting in*): He told him my Florida idea.
WILLY: Don't interrupt. (*To Biff.*) How'd he react to the Florida idea?
BIFF: Dad, will you give me a minute to explain?
WILLY: I've been waiting for you to explain since I sat down here! What happened? He took you into his office and what?
BIFF: Well — I talked. And — and he listened, see.
WILLY: Famous for the way he listens, y'know. What was his answer?
BIFF: His answer was — (*He breaks off, suddenly*

angry.) Dad, you're not letting me tell you what I want to tell you!
WILLY (*accusing, angered*): You didn't see him, did you?
BIFF: I did see him!
WILLY: What'd you insult him or something? You insulted him, didn't you?
BIFF: Listen, will you let me out of it, will you just let me out of it!
HAPPY: What the hell!
WILLY: Tell me what happened!
BIFF (*to Happy*): I can't talk to him!

(*A single trumpet note jars the ear. The light of green leaves stains the house, which holds the air of night and a dream. Young Bernard enters and knocks on the door of the house.*)

YOUNG BERNARD (*frantically*): Mrs. Loman, Mrs. Loman!
HAPPY: Tell him what happened!
BIFF (*to Happy*): Shut up and leave me alone!
WILLY: No, no! You had to go and flunk math!
BIFF: What math? What're you talking about?
YOUNG BERNARD: Mrs. Loman, Mrs. Loman!

(*Linda appears in the house, as of old.*)

WILLY (*wildly*): Math, math, math!
BIFF: Take it easy, Pop!
YOUNG BERNARD: Mrs. Loman!
WILLY (*furiously*): If you hadn't flunked you'd've been set by now!
BIFF: Now, look, I'm gonna tell you what happened, and you're going to listen to me.
YOUNG BERNARD: Mrs. Loman!
BIFF: I waited six hours —
HAPPY: What the hell are you saying?
BIFF: I kept sending in my name but he wouldn't see me. So finally he . . . (*He continues unheard as light fades low on the restaurant.*)
YOUNG BERNARD: Biff flunked math!
LINDA: No!
YOUNG BERNARD: Birnbaum flunked him! They won't graduate him!
LINDA: But they have to. He's gotta go to the university. Where is he? Biff! Biff!
YOUNG BERNARD: No, he left. He went to Grand Central.
LINDA: Grand — You mean he went to Boston!
YOUNG BERNARD: Is Uncle Willy in Boston?
LINDA: Oh, maybe Willy can talk to the teacher. Oh, the poor, poor boy!

(*Light on house area snaps out.*)

BIFF (*at the table, now audible, holding up a gold fountain pen*): . . . so I'm washed up with Oliver, you understand? Are you listening to me?

WILLY (*at a loss*): Yeah, sure. If you hadn't flunked —

BIFF: Flunked what? What're you talking about?

WILLY: Don't blame everything on me! I didn't flunk math — you did! What pen?

HAPPY: That was awful dumb, Biff, a pen like that is worth —

WILLY (*seeing the pen for the first time*): You took Oliver's pen?

BIFF (*weakening*): Dad, I just explained it to you.

WILLY: You stole Bill Oliver's fountain pen!

BIFF: I didn't exactly steal it! That's just what I've been explaining to you!

HAPPY: He had it in his hand and just then Oliver walked in, so he got nervous and stuck it in his pocket!

WILLY: My God, Biff!

BIFF: I never intended to do it, Dad!

OPERATOR'S VOICE: Standish Arms, good evening!

WILLY (*shouting*): I'm not in my room!

BIFF (*frightened*): Dad, what's the matter? (*He and Happy stand up.*)

OPERATOR: Ringing Mr. Loman for you!

WILLY: I'm not there, stop it!

BIFF (*horrified, gets down on one knee before Willy*): Dad, I'll make good, I'll make good. (*Willy tries to get to his feet. Biff holds him down.*) Sit down now.

WILLY: No, you're no good, you're no good for anything.

BIFF: I am, Dad, I'll find something else, you understand? Now don't worry about anything. (*He holds up Willy's face.*) Talk to me, Dad.

OPERATOR: Mr. Loman does not answer. Shall I page him?

WILLY (*attempting to stand, as though to rush and silence the Operator*): No, no, no!

HAPPY: He'll strike something, Pop.

WILLY: No, no . . .

BIFF (*desperately, standing over Willy*): Pop, listen! Listen to me! I'm telling you something good. Oliver talked to his partner about the Florida idea. You listening? He — he talked to his partner, and he came to me . . . I'm going to be all right, you hear? Dad, listen to me, he said it was just a question of the amount!

WILLY: Then you . . . got it?

HAPPY: He's gonna be terrific, Pop!

WILLY (*trying to stand*): Then you got it, haven't you? You got it! You got it!

BIFF (*agonized, holds Willy down*): No, no. Look, Pop. I'm supposed to have lunch with them tomorrow. I'm just telling you this so you'll know that I can still make an impression, Pop. And I'll make good somewhere, but I can't go tomorrow, see?

WILLY: Why not? You simply —

BIFF: But the pen, Pop!

WILLY: You give it to him and tell him it was an oversight!

HAPPY: Sure, have lunch tomorrow!

BIFF: I can't say that —

WILLY: You were doing a crossword puzzle and accidentally used his pen!

BIFF: Listen, kid, I took those balls years ago, now I walk in with his fountain pen? That clinches it, don't you see? I can't face him like that! I'll try elsewhere.

PAGE'S VOICE: Paging Mr. Loman!

WILLY: Don't you want to be anything?

BIFF: Pop, how can I go back?

WILLY: You don't want to be anything, is that what's behind it?

BIFF (*now angry at Willy for not crediting his sympathy*): Don't take it that way! You think it was easy walking into that office after what I'd done to him? A team of horses couldn't have dragged me back to Bill Oliver!

WILLY: Then why'd you go?

BIFF: Why did I go? Why did I go! Look at you! Look at what's become of you!

(*Off left, The Woman laughs.*)

WILLY: Biff, you're going to go to that lunch tomorrow, or —

BIFF: I can't go. I've got no appointment!

HAPPY: Biff, for . . . !

WILLY: Are you spiting me?

BIFF: Don't take it that way! Goddammit!

WILLY (*strikes Biff and falters away from the table*): You rotten little louse! Are you spiting me?

THE WOMAN: Someone's at the door, Willy!

BIFF: I'm no good, can't you see what I am?

HAPPY (*separating them*): Hey, you're in a restaurant! Now cut it out, both of you! (*The girls enter.*) Hello, girls, sit down.

(*The Woman laughs, off left.*)

MISS FORSYTHE: I guess we might as well. This is Letta.

THE WOMAN: Willy, are you going to wake up?

BIFF (*ignoring Willy*): How're ya, miss, sit down. What do you drink?

MISS FORSYTHE: Letta might not be able to stay long.

LETTA: I gotta get up very early tomorrow. I got jury duty. I'm so excited! Were you fellows ever on a jury?

BIFF: No, but I been in front of them! (*The girls laugh.*) This is my father.

LETTA: Isn't he cute? Sit down with us, Pop.

HAPPY: Sit him down, Biff!

BIFF (*going to him*): Come on, slugger, drink us under the table. To hell with it! Come on, sit down, pal.

(*On Biff's last insistence, Willy is about to sit.*)

THE WOMAN (*now urgently*): Willy, are you going to answer the door!

(*The Woman's call pulls Willy back. He starts right, befuddled.*)

BIFF: Hey, where are you going?

WILLY: Open the door.

BIFF: The door?

WILLY: The washroom ... the door ... where's the door?

BIFF (*leading Willy to the left*): Just go straight down.

(*Willy moves left.*)

THE WOMAN: Willy, Willy, are you going to get up, get up, get up, get up?

(*Willy exits left.*)

LETTA: I think it's sweet you bring your daddy along.

MISS FORSYTHE: Oh, he isn't really your father!

BIFF (*at left, turning to her resentfully*): Miss Forsythe, you've just seen a prince walk by. A fine, troubled prince. A hard-working, unappreciated prince. A pal, you understand? A good companion. Always for his boys.

LETTA: That's so sweet.

HAPPY: Well, girls, what's the program? We're wasting time. Come on, Biff. Gather round. Where would you like to go?

BIFF: Why don't you do something for him?

HAPPY: Me!

BIFF: Don't you give a damn for him, Hap?

HAPPY: What're you talking about? I'm the one who —

BIFF: I sense it, you don't give a good goddam about him. (*He takes the rolled-up hose from his pocket and puts it on the table in front of Happy.*) Look what I found in the cellar, for Christ's sake. How can you bear to let it go on?

HAPPY: Me? Who goes away? Who runs off and —

BIFF: Yeah, but he doesn't mean anything to you. You could help him — I can't! Don't you understand what I'm talking about? He's going to kill himself, don't you know that?

HAPPY: Don't I know it! Me!

BIFF: Hap, help him! Jesus ... help him ... Help me, help me, I can't bear to look at his face! (*Ready to weep, he hurries out, up right.*)

HAPPY (*starting after him*): Where are you going?

MISS FORSYTHE: What's he so mad about?

HAPPY: Come on, girls, we'll catch up with him.

MISS FORSYTHE (*as Happy pushes her out*): Say, I don't like that temper of his!

HAPPY: He's just a little overstrung, he'll be all right!

WILLY (*off left, as The Woman laughs*): Don't answer! Don't answer!

LETTA: Don't you want to tell your father —

HAPPY: No, that's not my father. He's just a guy. Come on, we'll catch Biff, and, honey, we're going to paint this town! Stanley, where's the check! Hey, Stanley!

(*They exit. Stanley looks toward left.*)

STANLEY (*calling to Happy indignantly*): Mr. Loman! Mr. Loman!

(*Stanley picks up a chair and follows them off. Knocking is heard off left. The Woman enters, laughing. Willy follows her. She is in a black slip; he is buttoning his shirt. Raw, sensuous music accompanies their speech.*)

WILLY: Will you stop laughing? Will you stop?

THE WOMAN: Aren't you going to answer the door? He'll wake the whole hotel.

WILLY: I'm not expecting anybody.

THE WOMAN: Whyn't you have another drink, honey, and stop being so damn self-centered?

WILLY: I'm so lonely.

THE WOMAN: You know you ruined me, Willy? From now on, whenever you come to the office, I'll see that you go right through to the buyers. No waiting at my desk anymore, Willy. You ruined me.

WILLY: That's nice of you to say that.

THE WOMAN: Gee, you are self-centered! Why so sad? You are the saddest, self-centeredest soul I ever did see-saw. (*She laughs. He kisses her.*) Come on inside, drummer boy. It's silly to be dressing in the middle of the night. (*As knocking is heard.*) Aren't you going to answer the door?

WILLY: They're knocking on the wrong door.

THE WOMAN: But I felt the knocking. And he heard us talking in here. Maybe the hotel's on fire!

WILLY (*his terror rising*): It's a mistake.

THE WOMAN: Then tell him to go away!

WILLY: There's nobody there.

THE WOMAN: It's getting on my nerves, Willy. There's somebody standing out there and it's getting on my nerves!

WILLY (*pushing her away from him*): All right, stay in the bathroom here, and don't come out. I think there's a law in Massachusetts about it, so don't come out. It may be that new room clerk. He looked very mean. So don't come out. It's a mistake, there's no fire.

(*The knocking is heard again. He takes a few steps*

away from her, and she vanishes into the wing. The light follows him, and now he is facing Young Biff, who carries a suitcase. Biff steps toward him. The music is gone.)

BIFF: Why didn't you answer?

WILLY: Biff! What are you doing in Boston?

BIFF: Why didn't you answer? I've been knocking for five minutes, I called you on the phone —

WILLY: I just heard you. I was in the bathroom and had the door shut. Did anything happen home?

BIFF: Dad — I let you down.

WILLY: What do you mean?

BIFF: Dad . . .

WILLY: Biffo, what's this about? (*Putting his arm around Biff.*) Come on, let's go downstairs and get you a malted.

BIFF: Dad, I flunked math.

WILLY: Not for the term?

BIFF: The term. I haven't got enough credits to graduate.

WILLY: You mean to say Bernard wouldn't give you the answers?

BIFF: He did, he tried, but I only got a sixty-one.

WILLY: And they wouldn't give you four points?

BIFF: Birnbaum refused absolutely. I begged him, Pop, but he won't give me those points. You gotta talk to him before they close the school. Because if he saw the kind of man you are, and you just talked to him in your way, I'm sure he'd come through for me. The class came right before practice, see, and I didn't go enough. Would you talk to him? He'd like you, Pop. You know the way you could talk.

WILLY: You're on. We'll drive right back.

BIFF: Oh, Dad, good work! I'm sure he'll change it for you!

WILLY: Go downstairs and tell the clerk I'm checkin' out. Go right down.

BIFF: Yes, sir! See, the reason he hates me, Pop — one day he was late for class so I got up at the blackboard and imitated him. I crossed my eyes and talked with a lithp.

WILLY (*laughing*): You did? The kids like it?

BIFF: They nearly died laughing!

WILLY: Yeah? What'd you do?

BIFF: The thquare root of thixty twee is . . . (*Willy bursts out laughing; Biff joins.*) And in the middle of it he walked in!

(*Willy laughs and The Woman joins in offstage.*)

WILLY (*without hesitation*): Hurry downstairs and —

BIFF: Somebody in there?

WILLY: No, that was next door.

(*The Woman laughs offstage.*)

BIFF: Somebody got in your bathroom!

WILLY: No, it's the next room, there's a party —

THE WOMAN (*enters, laughing. She lisps this.*): Can I come in? There's something in the bathtub, Willy, and it's moving!

(*Willy looks at Biff, who is staring open-mouthed and horrified at The Woman.*)

WILLY: Ah — you better go back to your room. They must be finished painting by now. They're painting her room so I let her take a shower here. Go back, go back . . . (*He pushes her.*)

THE WOMAN (*resisting*): But I've got to get dressed, Willy, I can't —

WILLY: Get out of here! Go back, go back . . . (*Suddenly striving for the ordinary.*) This is Miss Francis, Biff, she's a buyer. They're painting her room. Go back, Miss Francis, go back . . .

THE WOMAN: But my clothes, I can't go out naked in the hall!

WILLY (*pushing her offstage*): Get outa here! Go back, go back!

(*Biff slowly sits down on his suitcase as the argument continues offstage.*)

THE WOMAN: Where's my stockings? You promised me stockings, Willy!

WILLY: I have no stockings here!

THE WOMAN: You had two boxes of size nine sheers for me, and I want them!

WILLY: Here, for God's sake, will you get outa here!

THE WOMAN (*enters holding a box of stockings*): I just hope there's nobody in the hall. That's all I hope. (*To Biff.*) Are you football or baseball?

BIFF: Football.

THE WOMAN (*angry, humiliated*): That's me too. G'night. (*She snatches her clothes from Willy, and walks out.*)

WILLY (*after a pause*): Well, better get going. I want to get to the school first thing in the morning. Get my suits out of the closet. I'll get my valise. (*Biff doesn't move.*) What's the matter! (*Biff remains motionless, tears falling.*) She's a buyer. Buys for J. H. Simmons. She lives down the hall — they're painting. You don't imagine — (*He breaks off. After a pause.*) Now listen, pal, she's just a buyer. She sees merchandise in her room and they have to keep it looking just so . . . (*Pause. Assuming command.*) All right, get my suits. (*Biff doesn't move.*) Now stop crying and do as I say. I gave you an order. Biff, I gave you an order! Is that what you do when I give you an order? How dare you cry! (*Putting his arm around Biff.*) Now look, Biff, when you grow up you'll understand about these things. You mustn't — you mustn't overemphasize a thing like this. I'll see Birnbaum first thing in the morning.

BIFF: Never mind.

WILLY (*getting down beside Biff*): Never mind! He's going to give you those points. I'll see to it.

BIFF: He wouldn't listen to you.

WILLY: He certainly will listen to me. You need those points for the U. of Virginia.

BIFF: I'm not going there.

WILLY: Heh? If I can't get him to change that mark you'll make it up in summer school. You've got all summer to —

BIFF (*his weeping breaking from him*): Dad . . .

WILLY (*infected by it*): Oh, my boy . . .

BIFF: Dad . . .

WILLY: She's nothing to me, Biff. I was lonely, I was terribly lonely.

BIFF: You — you gave her Mama's stockings! (*His tears break through and he rises to go.*)

WILLY (*grabbing for Biff*): I gave you an order!

BIFF: Don't touch me, you — liar!

WILLY: Apologize for that!

BIFF: You fake! You phony little fake! You fake! (*Overcome, he turns quickly and weeping fully goes out with his suitcase. Willy is left on the floor on his knees.*)

WILLY: I gave you an order! Biff, come back here or I'll beat you! Come back here! I'll whip you!

(*Stanley comes quickly in from the right and stands in front of Willy.*)

WILLY (*shouts at Stanley*): I gave you an order . . .

STANLEY: Hey, let's pick it up, pick it up, Mr. Loman. (*He helps Willy to his feet.*) Your boys left with the chippies. They said they'll see you home.

(*A second waiter watches some distance away.*)

WILLY: But we were supposed to have dinner together.

(*Music is heard, Willy's theme.*)

STANLEY: Can you make it?

WILLY: I'll — sure, I can make it. (*Suddenly concerned about his clothes.*) Do I — I look all right?

STANLEY: Sure, you look all right. (*He flicks a speck off Willy's lapel.*)

WILLY: Here — here's a dollar.

STANLEY: Oh, your son paid me. It's all right.

WILLY (*putting it in Stanley's hand*): No, take it. You're a good boy.

STANLEY: Oh, no, you don't have to . . .

WILLY: Here — here's some more, I don't need it anymore. (*After a slight pause.*) Tell me — is there a seed store in the neighborhood?

STANLEY: Seeds? You mean like to plant?

(*As Willy turns, Stanley slips the money back into his jacket pocket.*)

WILLY: Yes. Carrots, peas . . .

STANLEY: Well, there's hardware stores on Sixth Avenue, but it may be too late now.

WILLY (*anxiously*): Oh, I'd better hurry. I've got to get some seeds. (*He starts off to the right.*) I've got to get some seeds, right away. Nothing's planted. I don't have a thing in the ground.

(*Willy hurries out as the light goes down. Stanley moves over to the right after him, watches him off. The other waiter has been staring at Willy.*)

STANLEY (*to the waiter*): Well, whatta you looking at?

(*The waiter picks up the chairs and moves off right. Stanley takes the table and follows him. The light fades on this area. There is a long pause, the sound of the flute coming over. The light gradually rises on the kitchen, which is empty. Happy appears at the door of the house, followed by Biff. Happy is carrying a large bunch of long-stemmed roses. He enters the kitchen, looks around for Linda. Not seeing her, he turns to Biff, who is just outside the house door, and makes a gesture with his hands, indicating "Not here, I guess." He looks into the living room and freezes. Inside, Linda, unseen, is seated, Willy's coat on her lap. She rises ominously and quietly and moves toward Happy, who backs up into the kitchen, afraid.*)

HAPPY: Hey, what're you doing up? (*Linda says nothing but moves toward him implacably.*) Where's Pop? (*He keeps backing to the right, and now Linda is in full view in the doorway to the living room.*) Is he sleeping?

LINDA: Where were you?

HAPPY (*trying to laugh it off*): We met two girls, Mom, very fine types. Here, we brought you some flowers. (*Offering them to her.*) Put them in your room, Ma.

(*She knocks them to the floor at Biff's feet. He has now come inside and closed the door behind him. She stares at Biff, silent.*)

HAPPY: Now what'd you do that for? Mom, I want you to have some flowers —

LINDA (*cutting Happy off, violently to Biff*): Don't you care whether he lives or dies?

HAPPY (*going to the stairs*): Come upstairs, Biff.

BIFF (*with a flare of disgust, to Happy*): Go away from me! (*To Linda.*) What do you mean, lives or dies? Nobody's dying around here, pal.

LINDA: Get out of my sight! Get out of here!

BIFF: I wanna see the boss.

LINDA: You're not going near him!

BIFF: Where is he? (*He moves into the living room and Linda follows.*)

LINDA (*shouting after Biff*): You invite him for dinner. He looks forward to it all day — (*Biff appears in his parents' bedroom, looks around, and exits*) — and then you desert him there. There's no stranger you'd do that to!

HAPPY: Why? He had a swell time with us. Listen, when I — (*Linda comes back into the kitchen*) — desert him I hope I don't outlive the day!

LINDA: Get out of here!

HAPPY: Now look, Mom . . .

LINDA: Did you have to go to women tonight? You and your lousy rotten whores!

(*Biff reenters the kitchen.*)

HAPPY: Mom, all we did was follow Biff around trying to cheer him up! (*To Biff.*) Boy, what a night you gave me!

LINDA: Get out of here, both of you, and don't come back! I don't want you tormenting him any more. Go on now, get your things together! (*To Biff.*) You can sleep in his apartment. (*She starts to pick up the flowers and stops herself.*) Pick up this stuff, I'm not your maid anymore. Pick it up, you bum, you!

(*Happy turns his back to her in refusal. Biff slowly moves over and gets down on his knees, picking up the flowers.*)

LINDA: You're a pair of animals! Not one, not another living soul would have had the cruelty to walk out on that man in a restaurant!

BIFF (*not looking at her*): Is that what he said?

LINDA: He didn't have to say anything. He was so humiliated he nearly limped when he came in.

HAPPY: But, Mom, he had a great time with us —

BIFF (*cutting him off violently*): Shut up!

(*Without another word, Happy goes upstairs.*)

LINDA: You! You didn't even go in to see if he was all right!

BIFF (*still on the floor in front of Linda, the flowers in his hand; with self-loathing*): No. Didn't. Didn't do a damned thing. How do you like that, heh? Left him babbling in a toilet.

LINDA: You louse. You . . .

BIFF: Now you hit it on the nose! (*He gets up, throws the flowers in the wastebasket.*) The scum of the earth, and you're looking at him!

LINDA: Get out of here!

BIFF: I gotta talk to the boss, Mom. Where is he?

LINDA: You're not going near him. Get out of this house!

BIFF (*with absolute assurance, determination*): No. We're gonna have an abrupt conversation, him and me.

LINDA: You're not talking to him.

(*Hammering is heard from outside the house, off right. Biff turns toward the noise.*)

LINDA (*suddenly pleading*): Will you please leave him alone?

BIFF: What's he doing out there?

LINDA: He's planting the garden!

BIFF (*quietly*): Now? Oh, my God!

(*Biff moves outside, Linda following. The light dies down on them and comes up on the center of the apron as Willy walks into it. He is carrying a flashlight, a hoe, and a handful of seed packets. He raps the top of the hoe sharply to fix it firmly, and then moves to the left, measuring off the distance with his foot. He holds the flashlight to look at the seed packets, reading off the instructions. He is in the blue of night.*)

WILLY: Carrots . . . quarter-inch apart. Rows . . . one-foot rows. (*He measures it off.*) One foot. (*He puts down a package and measures off.*) Beets. (*He puts down another package and measures again.*) Lettuce. (*He reads the package, puts it down.*) One foot — (*He breaks off as Ben appears at the right and moves slowly down to him.*) What a proposition, ts, ts. Terrific, terrific. 'Cause she's suffered, Ben, the woman has suffered. You understand me? A man can't go out the way he came in, Ben, a man has got to add up to something. You can't, you can't — (*Ben moves toward him as though to interrupt.*) You gotta consider, now. Don't answer so quick. Remember, it's a guaranteed twenty-thousand-dollar proposition. Now look, Ben, I want you to go through the ins and outs of this thing with me. I've got nobody to talk to, Ben, and the woman has suffered, you hear me?

BEN (*standing still, considering*): What's the proposition?

WILLY: It's twenty thousand dollars on the barrelhead. Guaranteed, gilt-edged, you understand?

BEN: You don't want to make a fool of yourself. They might not honor the policy.

WILLY: How can they dare refuse? Didn't I work like a coolie to meet every premium on the nose? And now they don't pay off? Impossible!

BEN: It's called a cowardly thing, William.

WILLY: Why? Does it take more guts to stand here the rest of my life ringing up a zero?

BEN (*yielding*): That's a point, William. (*He moves, thinking, turns.*) And twenty thousand — that *is* something one can feel with the hand, it is there.

WILLY (*now assured, with rising power*): Oh, Ben,

that's the whole beauty of it! I see it like a diamond, shining in the dark, hard and rough, that I can pick up and touch in my hand. Not like — like an appointment! This would not be another damned-fool appointment, Ben, and it changes all the aspects. Because he thinks I'm nothing, see, and so he spites me. But the funeral — (*Straightening up.*) Ben, that funeral will be massive! They'll come from Maine, Massachusetts, Vermont, New Hampshire! All the old-timers with the strange license plates — that boy will be thunderstruck, Ben, because he never realized — I am known! Rhode Island, New York, New Jersey — I am known, Ben, and he'll see it with his eyes once and for all. He'll see what I am, Ben! He's in for a shock, that boy!

BEN (*coming down to the edge of the garden*): He'll call you a coward.

WILLY (*suddenly fearful*): No, that would be terrible.

BEN: Yes. And a damned fool.

WILLY: No, no, he mustn't, I won't have that! (*He is broken and desperate.*)

BEN: He'll hate you, William.

(*The gay music of the Boys is heard.*)

WILLY: Oh, Ben, how do we get back to all the great times? Used to be so full of light, and comradeship, the sleigh-riding in winter, and the ruddiness on his cheeks. And always some kind of good news coming up, always something nice coming up ahead. And never even let me carry the valises in the house, and simonizing, simonizing that little red car! Why, why can't I give him something and not have him hate me?

BEN: Let me think about it. (*He glances at his watch.*) I still have a little time. Remarkable proposition, but you've got to be sure you're not making a fool of yourself.

(*Ben drifts off upstage and goes out of sight. Biff comes down from the left.*)

WILLY (*suddenly conscious of Biff, turns and looks up at him, then begins picking up the packages of seeds in confusion*): Where the hell is that seed? (*Indignantly.*) You can't see nothing out here! They boxed in the whole goddam neighborhood!

BIFF: There are people all around here. Don't you realize that?

WILLY: I'm busy. Don't bother me.

BIFF (*taking the hoe from Willy*): I'm saying good-by to you, Pop. (*Willy looks at him, silent, unable to move.*) I'm not coming back any more.

WILLY: You're not going to see Oliver tomorrow?

BIFF: I've got no appointment, Dad.

WILLY: He put his arm around you, and you've got no appointment?

BIFF: Pop, get this now, will you? Everytime I've left it's been a fight that sent me out of here. Today I realized something about myself and I tried to explain it to you and I — I think I'm just not smart enough to make any sense out of it for you. To hell with whose fault it is or anything like that. (*He takes Willy's arm.*) Let's just wrap it up, heh? Come on in, we'll tell Mom. (*He gently tries to pull Willy to left.*)

WILLY (*frozen, immobile, with guilt in his voice*): No, I don't want to see her.

BIFF: Come on! (*He pulls again, and Willy tries to pull away.*)

WILLY (*highly nervous*): No, no, I don't want to see her.

BIFF (*tries to look into Willy's face, as if to find the answer there*): Why don't you want to see her?

WILLY (*more harshly now*): Don't bother me, will you?

BIFF: What do you mean, you don't want to see her? You don't want them calling you yellow, do you? This isn't your fault; it's me, I'm a bum. Now come inside! (*Willy strains to get away.*) Did you hear what I said to you?

(*Willy pulls away and quickly goes by himself into the house. Biff follows.*)

LINDA (*to Willy*): Did you plant, dear?

BIFF (*at the door, to Linda*): All right, we had it out. I'm going and I'm not writing any more.

LINDA (*going to Willy in the kitchen*): I think that's the best way, dear. 'Cause there's no use drawing it out, you'll just never get along.

(*Willy doesn't respond.*)

BIFF: People ask where I am and what I'm doing, you don't know, and you don't care. That way it'll be off your mind and you can start brightening up again. All right? That clears it, doesn't it? (*Willy is silent, and Biff goes to him.*) You gonna wish me luck, scout? (*He extends his hand.*) What do you say?

LINDA: Shake his hand, Willy.

WILLY (*turning to her, seething with hurt*): There's no necessity to mention the pen at all, y'know.

BIFF (*gently*): I've got no appointment, Dad.

WILLY (*erupting fiercely*): He put his arm around . . . ?

BIFF: Dad, you're never going to see what I am, so what's the use of arguing? If I strike oil I'll send you a check. Meantime forget I'm alive.

WILLY (*to Linda*): Spite, see?

BIFF: Shake hands, Dad.

WILLY: Not my hand.

BIFF: I was hoping not to go this way.

WILLY: Well, this is the way you're going. Good-by.

(*Biff looks at him a moment, then turns sharply and goes to the stairs.*)

WILLY (*stops him with*): May you rot in hell if you leave this house!

BIFF (*turning*): Exactly what is it that you want from me?

WILLY: I want you to know, on the train, in the mountains, in the valleys, wherever you go, that you cut down your life for spite!

BIFF: No, no.

WILLY: Spite, spite, is the word of your undoing! And when you're down and out, remember what did it. When you're rotting somewhere beside the railroad tracks, remember, and don't you dare blame it on me!

BIFF: I'm not blaming it on you!

WILLY: I won't take the rap for this, you hear?

(*Happy comes down the stairs and stands on the bottom step, watching.*)

BIFF: That's just what I'm telling you!

WILLY (*sinking into a chair at a table, with full accusation*): You're trying to put a knife in me — don't think I don't know what you're doing!

BIFF: All right, phony! Then let's lay it on the line. (*He whips the rubber tube out of his pocket and puts it on the table.*)

HAPPY: You crazy . . .

LINDA: Biff! (*She moves to grab the hose, but Biff holds it down with his hand.*)

BIFF: Leave it there! Don't move it!

WILLY (*not looking at it*): What is that?

BIFF: You know goddam well what that is.

WILLY (*caged, wanting to escape*): I never saw that.

BIFF: You saw it. The mice didn't bring it into the cellar! What is this supposed to do, make a hero out of you? This supposed to make me sorry for you?

WILLY: Never heard of it.

BIFF: There'll be no pity for you, you hear it? No pity!

WILLY (*to Linda*): You hear the spite!

BIFF: No, you're going to hear the truth — what you are and what I am!

LINDA: Stop it!

WILLY: Spite!

HAPPY (*coming down toward Biff*): You cut it now!

BIFF (*to Happy*): The man don't know who we are! The man is gonna know! (*To Willy.*) We never told the truth for ten minutes in this house!

HAPPY: We always told the truth!

BIFF (*turning on him*): You big blow, are you the assistant buyer? You're one of the two assistants to the assistant, aren't you?

HAPPY: Well, I'm practically . . .

BIFF: You're practically full of it! We all are! and I'm through with it. (*To Willy.*) Now hear this, Willy, this is me.

WILLY: I know you!

BIFF: You know why I had no address for three months? I stole a suit in Kansas City and I was in jail. (*To Linda, who is sobbing.*) Stop crying. I'm through with it.

(*Linda turns away from them, her hands covering her face.*)

WILLY: I suppose that's my fault!

BIFF: I stole myself out of every good job since high school!

WILLY: And whose fault is that?

BIFF: And I never got anywhere because you blew me so full of hot air I could never stand taking orders from anybody! That's whose fault it is!

WILLY: I hear that!

LINDA: Don't, Biff!

BIFF: It's goddam time you heard that! I had to be boss big shot in two weeks, and I'm through with it!

WILLY: Then hang yourself! For spite, hang yourself!

BIFF: No! Nobody's hanging himself, Willy! I ran down eleven flights with a pen in my hand today. And suddenly I stopped, you hear me? And in the middle of that office building, do you hear this? I stopped in the middle of that building and I saw — the sky. I saw the things that I love in this world. The work and the food and time to sit and smoke. And I looked at the pen and said to myself, what the hell am I grabbing this for? Why am I trying to become what I don't want to be? What am I doing in an office, making a contemptuous, begging fool of myself, when all I want is out there, waiting for me the minute I say I know who I am! Why can't I say that, Willy? (*He tries to make Willy face him, but Willy pulls away and moves to the left.*)

WILLY (*with hatred, threateningly*): The door of your life is wide open!

BIFF: Pop! I'm a dime a dozen, and so are you!

WILLY (*turning on him now in an uncontrolled outburst*): I am not a dime a dozen! I am Willy Loman, and you are Biff Loman!

(*Biff starts for Willy, but is blocked by Happy. In his fury, Biff seems on the verge of attacking his father.*)

BIFF: I am not a leader of men, Willy, and neither are you. You were never anything but a hard-working drummer who landed in the ash can like all the rest of them! I'm one dollar an hour, Willy! I tried seven states and couldn't raise it. A buck an hour! Do you gather my meaning? I'm not bringing home any prizes any more, and you're going to stop waiting for me to bring them home!

WILLY (*directly to Biff*): You vengeful, spiteful mutt!

(*Biff breaks from Happy. Willy, in fright, starts up the stairs. Biff grabs him:*)

BIFF (*at the peak of his fury*): Pop, I'm nothing! I'm nothing, Pop. Can't you understand that? There's no spite in it any more. I'm just what I am, that's all.

(*Biff's fury has spent itself and he breaks down, sobbing, holding on to Willy, who dumbly fumbles for Biff's face.*)

WILLY (*astonished*): What're you doing? What're you doing? (*To Linda.*) Why is he crying?

BIFF (*crying, broken*): Will you let me go, for Christ's sake? Will you take that phony dream and burn it before something happens? (*Struggling to contain himself he pulls away and moves to the stairs.*) I'll go in the morning. Put him — put him to bed. (*Exhausted, Biff moves up the stairs to his room.*)

WILLY (*after a long pause, astonished, elevated*): Isn't that — isn't that remarkable? Biff — he likes me!

LINDA: He loves you, Willy!

HAPPY (*deeply moved*): Always did, Pop.

WILLY: Oh, Biff! (*Staring wildly.*) He cried! Cried to me. (*He is choking with his love, and now cries out his promise.*) That boy — that boy is going to be magnificent!

(*Ben appears in the light just outside the kitchen.*)

BEN: Yes, outstanding, with twenty thousand behind him.

LINDA (*sensing the racing of his mind, fearfully, carefully*): Now come to bed, Willy. It's all settled now.

WILLY (*finding it difficult not to rush out of the house*): Yes, we'll sleep. Come on. Go to sleep, Hap.

BEN: And it does take a great kind of a man to crack the jungle.

(*In accents of dread, Ben's idyllic music starts up.*)

HAPPY (*his arm around Linda*): I'm getting married, Pop, don't forget it. I'm changing everything. I'm gonna run that department before the year is up. You'll see, Mom. (*He kisses her.*)

BEN: The jungle is dark but full of diamonds, Willy.

(*Willy turns, moves, listening to Ben.*)

LINDA: Be good. You're both good boys, just act that way, that's all.

HAPPY: 'Night, Pop. (*He goes upstairs.*)

LINDA (*to Willy*): Come, dear.

BEN (*with greater force*): One must go in to fetch a diamond out.

WILLY (*to Linda, as he moves slowly along the edge of kitchen, toward the door*): I just want to get settled down, Linda. Let me sit alone for a little.

LINDA (*almost uttering her fear*): I want you upstairs.

WILLY (*taking her in his arms*): In a few minutes, Linda. I couldn't sleep right now. Go on, you look awful tired. (*He kisses her.*)

BEN: Not like an appointment at all. A diamond is rough and hard to the touch.

WILLY: Go on now. I'll be right up.

LINDA: I think this is the only way, Willy.

WILLY: Sure, it's the best thing.

BEN: Best thing!

WILLY: The only way. Everything is gonna be — go on, kid, get to bed. You look so tired.

LINDA: Come right up.

WILLY: Two minutes.

(*Linda goes into the living room, then reappears in her bedroom. Willy moves just outside the kitchen door.*)

WILLY: Loves me. (*Wonderingly.*) Always loved me. Isn't that a remarkable thing? Ben, he'll worship me for it!

BEN (*with promise*): It's dark there, but full of diamonds.

WILLY: Can you imagine that magnificence with twenty thousand dollars in his pocket?

LINDA (*calling from her room*): Willy! Come up!

WILLY (*calling into the kitchen*): Yes! yes. Coming! It's very smart, you realize that, don't you, sweetheart? Even Ben sees it. I gotta go, baby. 'By! 'By! (*Going over to Ben, almost dancing.*) Imagine? When the mail comes he'll be ahead of Bernard again!

BEN: A perfect proposition all around.

WILLY: Did you see how he cried to me? Oh, if I could kiss him, Ben!

BEN: Time, William, time!

WILLY: Oh, Ben, I always knew one way or another we were gonna make it, Biff and I!

BEN (*looking at his watch*): The boat. We'll be late. (*He moves slowly off into the darkness.*)

WILLY (*elegiacally, turning to the house*): Now when you kick off, boy, I want a seventy-yard boot, and get right down the field under the ball, and when you hit, hit low and hit hard, because it's important, boy. (*He swings around and faces the audience.*) There's all kinds of important people in the stands, and the first thing you know . . . (*Suddenly realizing he is alone.*) Ben! Ben, where do I . . . ?

(*He makes a sudden movement of search.*) Ben, how do I . . . ?

LINDA (*calling*): Willy, you coming up?

WILLY (*uttering a gasp of fear, whirling about as if to quiet her*): Sh! (*He turns around as if to find his way; sounds, faces, voices, seem to be swarming in upon him and he flicks at them, crying, Sh! Sh! Suddenly music, faint and high, stops him. It rises in intensity, almost to an unbearable scream. He goes up and down on his toes, and rushes off around the house.*) Shhh!

LINDA: Willy?

(*There is no answer. Linda waits. Biff gets up off his bed. He is still in his clothes. Happy sits up. Biff stands listening.*)

LINDA (*with real fear*): Willy, answer me! Willy!

(*There is the sound of a car starting and moving away at full speed.*)

LINDA: No!

BIFF (*rushing down the stairs*): Pop!

(*As the car speeds off, the music crashes down in a frenzy of sound, which becomes the soft pulsation of a single cello string. Biff slowly returns to his bedroom. He and Happy gravely don their jackets. Linda slowly walks out of her room. The music has developed into a dead march. The leaves of day are appearing over everything. Charley and Bernard, somberly dressed, appear and knock on the kitchen door. Biff and Happy slowly descend the stairs to the kitchen as Charley and Bernard enter. All stop a moment when Linda, in clothes of mourning, bearing a little bunch of roses, comes through the draped doorway into the kitchen. She goes to Charley and takes his arm. Now all move toward the audience, through the wall-line of the kitchen. At the limit of the apron, Linda lays down the flowers, kneels, and sits back on her heels. All stare down at the grave.*)

REQUIEM

CHARLEY: It's getting dark, Linda.

(*Linda doesn't react. She stares at the grave.*)

BIFF: How about it, Mom? Better get some rest, heh? They'll be closing the gate soon.

(*Linda makes no move. Pause.*)

HAPPY (*deeply angered*): He had no right to do that. There was no necessity for it. We would've helped him.

CHARLEY (*grunting*): Hmmm.

BIFF: Come along, Mom.

LINDA: Why didn't anybody come?

CHARLEY: It was a very nice funeral.

LINDA: But where are all the people he knew? Maybe they blame him.

CHARLEY: Naa. It's a rough world, Linda. They wouldn't blame him.

LINDA: I can't understand it. At this time especially. First time in thirty-five years we were just about free and clear. He only needed a little salary. He was even finished with the dentist.

CHARLEY: No man only needs a little salary.

LINDA: I can't understand it.

BIFF: There were a lot of nice days. When he'd come home from a trip; or on Sundays, making the stoop; finishing the cellar; putting on the new porch; when he built the extra bathroom; and put up the garage. You know something, Charley, there's more of him in that front stoop than in all the sales he ever made.

CHARLEY: Yeah. He was a happy man with a batch of cement.

LINDA: He was so wonderful with his hands.

BIFF: He had the wrong dreams. All, all, wrong.

HAPPY (*almost ready to fight Biff*): Don't say that!

BIFF: He never knew who he was.

CHARLEY (*stopping Happy's movement and reply. To Biff*): Nobody dast blame this man. You don't understand: Willy was a salesman. And for a salesman, there is no rock bottom to the life. He don't put a bolt to a nut, he don't tell you the law or give you medicine. He's a man way out there in the blue, riding on a smile and a shoeshine. And when they start not smiling back — that's an earthquake. And then you get yourself a couple of spots on your hat, and you're finished. Nobody dast blame this man. A salesman is got to dream, boy. It comes with the territory.

BIFF: Charley, the man didn't know who he was.

HAPPY (*infuriated*): Don't say that!

BIFF: Why don't you come with me, Happy?

HAPPY: I'm not licked that easily. I'm staying right in this city, and I'm gonna beat this racket! (*He looks at Biff, his chin set.*) The Loman Brothers!

BIFF: I know who I am, kid.

HAPPY: All right, boy. I'm gonna show you and everybody else that Willy Loman did not die in vain. He had a good dream. It's the only dream you can have — to come out number-one man. He fought it out here, and this is where I'm gonna win it for him.

BIFF (*with a hopeless glance at Happy, bends toward his mother*): Let's go, Mom.

LINDA: I'll be with you in a minute. Go on, Charley.

(*He hesitates.*) I want to, just for a minute. I never had a chance to say good-by.

(*Charley moves away, followed by Happy. Biff remains a slight distance up and left of Linda. She sits there, summoning herself. The flute begins, not far away, playing behind her speech.*)

LINDA: Forgive me, dear. I can't cry. I don't know what it is, but I can't cry. I don't understand it. Why did you ever do that? Help me, Willy, I can't cry. It seems to me that you're just on another trip. I keep expecting you. Willy, dear, I can't cry. Why did you do it? I search and search and I search, and I can't understand it, Willy. I made the last payment on the house today. Today, dear. And there'll be nobody home. (*A sob rises in her throat.*) We're free and clear. (*Sobbing more fully, released.*) We're free. (*Biff comes slowly toward her.*) We're free . . . We're free . . .

(*Biff lifts her to her feet and moves out up right with her in his arms. Linda sobs quietly. Bernard and Charley come together and follow them, followed by Happy. Only the music of the flute is left on the darkening stage as over the house the hard towers of the apartment buildings rise into sharp focus, and the curtain falls.*)

COMMENTARY

Arthur Miller (*b. 1915*)
TRAGEDY AND THE COMMON MAN   *1949*

One of the curious debates that arose around Death of a Salesman *was the question of whether or not it was a genuine tragedy. One of the requirements for traditional tragedy is that the hero be of noble birth; that is, that only a king or queen can suffice. Miller countered that notion with a clear statement of modern purpose regarding tragedy.*

In this age few tragedies are written. It has often been held that the lack is due to a paucity of heroes among us, or else that modern man has had the blood drawn out of his organs of belief by the skepticism of science, and the heroic attack on life cannot feed on an attitude of reserve and circumspection. For one reason or another, we are often held to be below tragedy — or tragedy above us. The inevitable conclusion is, of course, that the tragic mode is archaic, fit only for the very highly placed, the kings or the kingly, and where this admission is not made in so many words it is most often implied.

I believe that the common man is as apt a subject for tragedy in its highest sense as kings were. On the face of it this ought to be obvious in the light of modern psychiatry, which bases its analysis upon classic formulations, such as the Oedipus and Orestes complexes, for instance, which were enacted by royal beings, but which apply to everyone in similar emotional situations.

More simply, when the question of tragedy in art is not at issue, we never hesitate to attribute to the well-placed and the exalted the very same mental processes as the lowly. And finally, if the exaltation of tragic action were truly a property of the high-bred character alone, it is inconceivable that the mass of mankind should cherish tragedy above all other forms, let alone be capable of understanding it.

As a general rule, to which there may be exceptions unknown to me, I think the tragic feeling is evoked in us when we are in the presence of a character who is ready to lay down his life, if need be, to secure one thing — his sense of personal dignity. From Orestes to Hamlet, Medea to Macbeth, the underlying struggle is that of the individual attempting to gain his "rightful" position in his society.

Sometimes he is one who has been displaced from it, sometimes one who seeks to attain it for the first time, but the fateful wound from which the inevitable events spiral is the wound of indignity, and its dominant force is indignation. Tragedy, then, is the consequence of a man's total compulsion to evaluate himself justly.

In the sense of having been initiated by the hero himself, the tale always reveals what has been called his "tragic flaw," a failing that is not peculiar to grand or elevated characters. Nor is it necessarily a weakness. The flaw, or crack in the character, is really nothing — and need be nothing — but his inherent unwillingness to remain passive in the face of what he conceives to be a challenge to his dignity, his image of his rightful status. Only the passive, only those who accept their lot without active retaliation, are "flawless." Most of us are in that category.

But there are among us today, as there always have been, those who act against the scheme of things that degrades them, and in the process of action everything we have accepted out of fear or insensitivity or ignorance is shaken before us and examined, and from this total onslaught by an individual against the seemingly stable cosmos surrounding us — from this total examination of the "unchangeable" environment — comes the terror and the fear that is classically associated with tragedy.

More important, from this total questioning of what has previously been unquestioned, we learn. And such a process is not beyond the common man. In revolutions around the world, these past thirty years, he has demonstrated again and again this inner dynamic of all tragedy.

Insistence upon the rank of the tragic hero, or the so-called nobility of his character, is really but a clinging to the outward forms of tragedy. If rank or nobility of character was indispensable, then it would follow that the problems of those with rank were the particular problems of tragedy. But surely the right of one monarch to capture the domain from another no longer raises our passions, nor are our concepts of justice what they were to the mind of an Elizabethan king.

The quality in such plays that does shake us, however, derives from the underlying fear of being displaced, the disaster inherent in being torn away from our chosen image of what and who we are in this world. Among us today this fear is as strong, and perhaps stronger, than it ever was. In fact, it is the common man who knows this fear best.

Now, if it is true that tragedy is the consequence of a man's total compulsion to evaluate himself justly, his destruction in the attempt posits a wrong or an evil in his environment. And this is precisely the morality of tragedy and its lesson. The discovery of the moral law, which is what the enlightenment of tragedy consists of, is not the discovery of some abstract or metaphysical quantity.

The tragic right is a condition of life, a condition in which the human personality is able to flower and realize itself. The wrong is the condition which suppresses man, perverts the flowing out of his love and creative instinct. Tragedy enlightens — and it must, in that it points the heroic finger at the enemy of man's freedom. The thrust for freedom is the quality in tragedy which exalts. The revolutionary questioning of the stable environment is what terrifies. In no way is the common man debarred from such thoughts or such actions.

Seen in this light, our lack of tragedy may be partially accounted for by the turn which modern literature has taken toward the purely psychiatric view of life, or the purely sociological. If all our miseries, our indignities, are born and bred within our minds, then all action, let alone the heroic action, is obviously impossible.

And if society alone is responsible for the cramping of our lives, then the protagonist must needs be so pure and faultless as to force us to deny his validity as a character. From neither of these views can tragedy derive, simply because neither represents a balanced concept of life. Above all else, tragedy requires the finest appreciation by the writer of cause and effect.

No tragedy can therefore come about when its author fears to question absolutely everything, when he regards any institution, habit, or custom as being either everlasting, immutable, or inevitable. In the tragic view the need of man to wholly realize himself is the only fixed star, and whatever it is that hedges his nature and lowers it is ripe for attack and examination. Which is not to say that tragedy must preach revolution.

The Greeks could probe the very heavenly origin of their ways and return to confirm the rightness of laws. And Job could face God in anger, demanding his right and end in submission. But for a moment everything is in suspension, nothing is accepted, and in this stretching and tearing apart of the cosmos, in the very action of so doing, the character gains "size," the tragic stature which is spuriously attached to the royal or the highborn in our minds. The commonest of men may take on that stature to the extent of his willingness to throw all he has into the contest, the battle to secure his rightful place in his world.

There is a misconception of tragedy with which I have been struck in review after review, and in many conversations with writers and readers alike. It is the idea that tragedy is of necessity allied to pessimism. Even the dictionary says nothing more about the word than that it means a story with a sad or unhappy ending. This impression is so firmly fixed that I almost hesitate to claim that in truth tragedy implies more optimism in its author than does comedy, and that its final result ought to be the reinforcement of the onlooker's brightest opinions of the human animal.

For, if it is true to say that in essence the tragic hero is intent upon claiming his whole due as a personality, and if this struggle must be total and without reservation, then it automatically demonstrates the indestructible will of man to achieve his humanity.

The possibility of victory must be there in tragedy. Where pathos rules, where pathos is finally derived, a character has fought a battle he could not possibly have won. The pathetic is achieved when the protagonist is, by virtue of his witlessness, his insensitivity, or the very air he gives off, incapable of grappling with a much superior force.

Pathos truly is the mode for the pessimist. But tragedy requires a nicer balance between what is possible and what is impossible. And it is curious, although edifying, that the plays we revere, century after century, are the tragedies. In them, and in them alone, lies the belief — optimistic, if you will — in the perfectibility of man.

It is time, I think, that we who are without kings, took up this bright thread of our history and followed it to the only place it can possibly lead in our time — the heart and spirit of the average man.

Samuel Beckett

Samuel Beckett (1906–1989) was born into an upper-middle-class family in Dublin. His people were Protestants, and he received a privileged education at the Portora Royal School and then went to Trinity College, Dublin, where he studied French and Italian. He was an exceptionally good student and, in 1928 after graduation, went to Paris to teach English at the École Normale Supérieure, an unusual reward for good scholarship.

Beckett early on straddled two literary cultures: Irish and Anglo-Irish. Most of the literary energy in Ireland in the 1920s and 1930s was split between the essentially conservative Anglo-Irish Protestants, such as William Butler Yeats and Lady Isabella Augusta Gregory, and the more avant-garde Catholics, such as James Joyce, with whom Beckett formed an enduring personal and literary friendship in Paris. Although much younger than Joyce, Beckett developed a close artistic sympathy with him. Beckett's first published work (1929) was one of the earliest critical essays on Joyce's most radical literary composition, the not-yet-published *Finnegans Wake*.

When he was first in France, Beckett's reading of French philosophers, especially Descartes, exerted a strong influence on his work. Beckett's earliest writings appeared in Eugene Jolas's avant-garde literary journal *transition*, which put him in the center of Parisian literary activity in the late 1920s. After 1930, his series of short stories published under the title *More Pricks than Kicks* (1934) established him as an important writer. After settling in Paris in 1937, Beckett wrote the novel *Murphy* (1938), on a recognizably Irish theme of economic impoverishment, alienation, and inward meditation and spiritual complexity.

When World War II began in 1939 Beckett took up the cause of the French Resistance. His activity caught the eye of the Gestapo, and for two years he lay low in unoccupied France by working as a farmhand and also writing another novel, *Watt* (written in 1944 but published in 1953). After the war he took up residence again in Paris and began writing most of his work in French. His greatest novels were written in the five years after the war, and they are often referred to as his trilogy: *Molloy*, *Malone Dies*, and *The Unnamable*. These three novels are about men who have become disaffected with society and who have strange and compelling urgencies to be alone and to follow exacting and repetitive patterns of behavior. In a sense, they are archetypes of the kinds of heroes — if that word can be used for them — that Beckett created in most of his work.

Beckett's first published play, *Waiting for Godot* (1952), was produced in Paris in 1953, in London in 1955, and in Miami in 1956. From the first, its repetitive, whimsical, and sometimes nonsensical style established the play as a major postwar statement. In a barren setting, Vladimir and Estragon, two tramps who echo the comic vision of Charlie Chaplin, wait for Godot to come. They amuse themselves by doing vaudeville routines, but their loneliness and isolation are painfully apparent to the audience. Godot has promised to come, and as they wait, Vladimir and Estragon speculate on whether or not Godot will come.

The comic moments in the play, along with the enigma of Vladimir and Estragon's fruitless waiting, combined to capture the imagination of audiences and the press. They saw the play as a modern statement about the condition of humankind, although there was never any agreement on just what the statement was. Godot sends a boy to say that he will indeed come, but when the play ends, he has not arrived. The implication seems to be that he will never arrive. Most audiences saw Godot as a metaphor for God. Despite the critics' constant inquiries, Beckett was careful never to confirm the view that Godot was God and to keep Godot's identity open-ended.

The play itself was open-ended, as Beckett had hoped, and therefore could be interpreted in many ways. One was to see the play as a commentary on the futility of religion; another was to suggest that the play underscored the loneliness of humankind in an empty universe; yet a third implied that it was up to individuals, represented by the hapless Vladimir and Estragon, to shape the significance of their own lives, and their waiting represented that effort.

Many of the themes in *Waiting for Godot* are apparent in Beckett's later plays. The radio play *All That Fall* (1957) was followed by the very successful *Krapp's Last Tape* (1958). Also in 1957, *Endgame*, a play on the themes of the end of the world, was produced, followed in 1961 by *Happy Days*. Beckett experimented with minimalist approaches to drama, exemplified in *Act Without Words I* and *Act Without Words II*, both mime plays. Other plays experiment with minimalism in setting, props, and — in the mime plays — even words.

Beckett's plays reveal the deep influence of French postwar philosophers, such as Albert Camus and Jean-Paul Sartre, both existentialists. Their philosophy declares that people are not essentially good, bad, kind, or anything else, but what they make of themselves. Beckett's adaptation of existentialism sometimes borders on pessimism because his vision seems to negate many of the consolations of religious and secular philosophy. His style is antirealist, but the search for beliefs that are reasonable and plausible in a fundamentally absurd world and the plight of individuals who must make their own meanings is central to most of his work.

Beckett's view of the world is not cheerful. We are not cheered by Hamm or Mrs. Rooney. But his vision is consistent, honest, and sympathetic to the persistence of his characters, who endure even in the face of apparent defeat. The significance of Beckett's achievements was recognized in 1969 when he was awarded the Nobel Prize for literature.

ENDGAME

The title of this play derives from the game of chess, which has three different strategies to mark the opening, the middle game, and the endgame. The strategy of the endgame is based on the protection of the king and depends on there usually being very few pieces left on the board — the king and sometimes a rook and a pawn. The moves in the endgame are always restricted, often repetitive, and limited by the fact that the king, if it can move at all, cannot move more than one space at a time. In Beckett's *Endgame* Hamm is the king and the central character in the drama. However, he cannot move or even stand by himself. His parents, Nagg and Nell, stuck immobile in ashcans, resemble rooks, who protect the king by controlling spaces forward, backward, and side to side but have little reason themselves to move. Clov, who most closely resembles a pawn, cannot sit down and is the only character in the play who can move. He is also the only means by which Hamm can move. Beckett has described Hamm as "a king in the chess game lost from the start."

World politics in 1957, when the play was written, were dominated by the threat of nuclear war and the possible extinction of the human race. The circumstances of *Endgame* suggest that the play portrays a version of the end of the world. Clov's description of the world outside the window implies desolation and grief. At one point as Clov looks out the window, Hamm tells him to use his "glass," his telescope, and report back to him. Clov says all is "Zero," and Hamm asks, "All is what?" "In a word?" says Clov. "Is that what you want to know?" And in a moment he reports his one word: "Corpsed."

Unlike Hamm and Clov, who seem rooted only in the present, Nagg and Nell have a past. They remember rowing on Lake Como on an April afternoon after they were engaged. It was a moment in which Nell remembers she was happy. But they also remember the day they crashed on their tandem bicycle and lost their legs. Nagg recalls it was in the Ardennes forest on the road to Sedan. Beckett is making a distant allusion to the Ardennes, in France, which was the site of the most appalling and murderous fighting in World War I, and to Sedan, the place of the most decisive French defeat by the Germans in the war of 1879.

Ruby Cohn and other critics have noted that the characters' names echo associations with hammers and nails: Nell is a homophone for *nail*; Hamm is a shortened form of *hammer*; Nagg is from the German *nagel*, for *nail*; and Clov is from the French *clou*, also for *nail*. The characters thus seem to be equipped to rebuild their society, but they refuse to do so. By using English, French, and German versions of *nail* Beckett involves the principal combatants of modern European wars.

Some critics have observed that Beckett's drama often focuses on elements of play. Plays are play; life is play. In chess an endgame is played. In Beckett's drama characters' actions seem to be performed as if they were part of a game. Clov exercises great precision, for example, in placing Hamm exactly where he wishes to be. When Clov has done the rounds and moved Hamm's chair back to its position, Hamm says, "I feel a little too far to the left. Now I feel a little too far to the right." In a game of chess it would matter if he were too far to the left or right. In an endgame the king might move to one square and then move back again and again. The movements of Hamm and Clov are repetitious and meaningful only within the "system" of the drama and its space, just as all moves in an endgame are meaningful only within the "system" of the game of chess. Clov continually enters and exits with his ladder and looks out the windows, only to find that nothing has changed. He picks up the lids of Nagg and Nell's ashcans and replaces them several times. He pushes Hamm's chair along the wall, making minute adjustments, for no apparent reason, when he returns the chair to the center of the room. His moves are part of an endgame and *Endgame* is a play.

Beckett critic Ted Estess has said that "in Beckett's literature 'existence is play,'" implying a form of absurdity of the kind Martin Esslin talks about in his discussion of theater of the absurd. (See the commentary on page 1094.) The absurd implies a nonmeaning, such as the meaningless movements of Hamm by Clov. The meaning of those moves is in the action itself, which strikes those in the audience as absurd. Beckett's use of the absurd helps him move away from the well-made play with its clearly marked beginning, middle, and end. In the process, he pokes fun at that concept by embedding the end in the beginning of *Endgame*. As the lights go up and Clov removes the sheets from the ashcans and from Hamm in his chair, he intones to the audience: "Finished." The audience is meant to feel this irony: It is the endgame when the action — and the play — stop. Hamm says it clearly: "The end is in the beginning and yet you go on."

***Endgame* in Performance**

Endgame was first produced in 1957. The year before, *Waiting for Godot* had been produced in Miami and New York, establishing Beckett as an important figure in modern experimental drama. *Endgame*, his next major play, satisfied the critics but baffled the public. The first London production was in French, at the Royal Court Theatre, which was known for producing experimental plays. Roger Blin directed. The first Paris production began three weeks later, April 26, 1957, in the Studio des Champs-Élysées. The New York production, directed by Beckett's friend and interpreter Alan Schneider, opened on January 28, 1958. A number of important revivals of the play have attested to its continuing power. The Royal Shakespeare Company produced it in its theater, the Aldwych, in 1964. Beckett himself directed the play at the Schiller Theatre in Berlin in September 1967. In the 1970 Open Theater Production at the Loeb Theater in Cambridge, Massachusetts, Joseph Chaikin as Hamm created a richly nuanced performance:

> Joseph Chaikin as the chairbound Hamm, throws an eerie light over the play. . . . He is sensual, domineering, crafty, and infinitely tender; he prattles and tells macabre stories and his dominion over the dwindling lives of his family is like the last hoarse gasp of King Lear over the strangled body of Cordelia. (Samuel Hirsch, *Herald Traveler*, Boston, May 13, 1970)

Andre Gregory directed the play at the Manhattan Project in 1973. Clive Barnes noted the unusual staging of this production:

> Mr. Gregory has built himself a strange, bullring of a theater. It is hexagonal, and the audience is on two levels. The audience is placed in cubicles — each holding four chairs. Each cubicle is insulated from the stage and from the world by chicken wire. (*New York Times*, February 9, 1973)

The Royal Court played it in English during its Beckett Festival in 1976. Beckett directed the play again in London at the Young Vic in January 1980 and then in Chicago's Goodman Theater with the San Quentin Workshop in September 1980. In 1984 JoAnn Akalaitis staged a controversial *Endgame* at the American Repertory Theatre in Cambridge, Massachusetts. She set the play in a burned-out subway tunnel and commissioned an eerie musical score by minimalist composer Philip Glass. Grove Press, Beckett's representative, complained that the production disregarded "the playwright's sparse, rigorous scenic demands" and added uncalled-for music. As one critic noted, Akalaitis had "simply, vividly visualized and auralized *Endgame*'s nuclear-holocaustal implications, at the expense of its chess and theatrical imagery" (Carolyn Clay, *Boston Phoenix*, December 18, 1984). The production was allowed to continue after the American Repertory Theatre agreed to include a program insert, signed by Beckett, "decrying the interpretation."

Samuel Beckett (1906–1989)

ENDGAME   1957

A PLAY IN ONE ACT

The Characters

NAGG   HAMM
NELL   CLOV

(*Bare interior.*)
  (*Gray light.*)
  (*Left and right back, high up, two small windows, curtains drawn.*)
  (*Front right, a door. Hanging near door, its face to wall, a picture.*)
  (*Front left, touching each other, covered with an old sheet, two ashbins.*)
  (*Center, in an armchair on casters, covered with an old sheet, Hamm.*)
  (*Motionless by the door, his eyes fixed on Hamm, Clov. Very red face.*)
  (*Brief tableau.*)

(*Clov goes and stands under window left. Stiff, staggering walk. He looks up at window left. He turns and looks at window right. He goes and stands under window right. He looks up at window right. He turns and looks at window left. He goes out, comes back immediately with a small stepladder, carries it over and sets it down under window left, gets up on it, draws back curtain. He gets down, takes six steps (for example) towards window right, goes back for ladder, carries it over and sets it down under window right, gets up on it, draws back curtain. He gets down, takes three steps towards window left, goes back for ladder, carries it over and sets it down under window left, gets up on it, looks out of window. Brief laugh. He gets down, takes one step towards window right, goes back for ladder, carries it over and sets it down under window right, gets up on it, looks out of window. Brief laugh. He gets down, goes with ladder towards ashbins, halts, turns, carries back ladder and sets it down under window right, goes to ashbins, removes sheet covering them, folds it over his arm. He raises one lid, stoops and looks into bin. Brief laugh. He closes lid. Same with other bin. He goes to Hamm, removes sheet covering him, folds it over his arm. In a dressing gown, a stiff toque° on his head, a large bloodstained handkerchief over his face, a whistle*)

toque: A small, brimless, close-fitting hat.

hanging from his neck, a rug over his knees, thick socks on his feet, Hamm seems to be asleep. Clov looks over him. Brief laugh. He goes to door, halts, turns towards auditorium.*)

CLOV (*fixed gaze, tonelessly*): Finished, it's finished, nearly finished, it must be nearly finished.

(*Pause.*)

  Grain upon grain, one by one, and one day, suddenly, there's a heap, a little heap, the impossible heap.

(*Pause.*)

  I can't be punished anymore.

(*Pause.*)

  I'll go now to my kitchen, ten feet by ten feet by ten feet, and wait for him to whistle me.

(*Pause.*)

  Nice dimensions, nice proportions, I'll lean on the table, and look at the wall, and wait for him to whistle me.

(*He remains a moment motionless, then goes out. He comes back immediately, goes to window right, takes up the ladder and carries it out. Pause. Hamm stirs. He yawns under the handkerchief. He removes the handkerchief from his face. Very red face. Black glasses.*)

HAMM: Me — (*he yawns*) — to play.

(*He holds the handkerchief spread out before him.*)

  Old stancher!°

(*He takes off his glasses, wipes his eyes, his face, the glasses, puts them on again, folds the handkerchief and puts it back neatly in the breast pocket of his dressing gown. He clears his throat, joins the tips of his fingers.*)

  Can there be misery — (*he yawns*) — loftier than mine? No doubt. Formerly. But now?

stancher: The handkerchief, which stops, or stanches, the flow of blood.

(*Pause.*)

My father?

(*Pause.*)

My mother?

(*Pause.*)

My . . . dog?

(*Pause.*)

Oh I am willing to believe they suffer as much as such creatures can suffer. But does that mean their sufferings equal mine? No doubt.

(*Pause.*)

No, all is a — (*he yawns*) — bsolute, (*proudly*) the bigger a man is the fuller he is.

(*Pause. Gloomily.*)

And the emptier.

(*He sniffs.*)

Clov!

(*Pause.*)

No, alone.

(*Pause.*)

What dreams! Those forests!

(*Pause.*)

Enough, it's time it ended, in the shelter too.

(*Pause.*)

And yet I hesitate, I hesitate to . . . to end. Yes, there it is, it's time it ended and yet I hesitate to — (*he yawns*) — to end.

(*Yawns.*)

God, I'm tired, I'd be better off in bed.

(*He whistles. Enter Clov immediately. He halts beside the chair.*)

You pollute the air!

(*Pause.*)

Get me ready, I'm going to bed.

CLOV: I've just got you up.

HAMM: And what of it?

CLOV: I can't be getting you up and putting you to bed every five minutes, I have things to do.

(*Pause.*)

HAMM: Did you ever see my eyes?

CLOV: No.

HAMM: Did you never have the curiosity, while I was sleeping, to take off my glasses and look at my eyes?

CLOV: Pulling back the lids?

(*Pause.*)

No.

HAMM: One of these days I'll show them to you.

(*Pause.*)

It seems they've gone all white.

(*Pause.*)

What time is it?

CLOV: The same as usual.

HAMM (*gesture towards window right*): Have you looked?

CLOV: Yes.

HAMM: Well?

CLOV: Zero.

HAMM: It'd need to rain.

CLOV: It won't rain.

(*Pause.*)

HAMM: Apart from that, how do you feel?

CLOV: I don't complain.

HAMM: You feel normal?

CLOV (*irritably*): I tell you I don't complain.

HAMM: I feel a little queer.

(*Pause.*)

Clov!

CLOV: Yes.

HAMM: Have you not had enough?

CLOV: Yes!

(*Pause.*)

Of what?

HAMM: Of this . . . this . . . thing.

CLOV: I always had.

(*Pause.*)

Not you?

HAMM (*gloomily*): Then there's no reason for it to change.

CLOV: It may end.

(*Pause.*)

All life long the same questions, the same answers.

HAMM: Get me ready.

(*Clov does not move.*)

Go and get the sheet.

(*Clov does not move.*)

Clov!

CLOV: Yes.

HAMM: I'll give you nothing more to eat.

CLOV: Then we'll die.

HAMM: I'll give you just enough to keep you from dying. You'll be hungry all the time.

CLOV: Then we won't die.

(*Pause.*)

I'll go and get the sheet.

(*He goes towards the door.*)

HAMM: No!

(*Clov halts.*)

I'll give you one biscuit per day.

(*Pause.*)

One and a half.

(*Pause.*)

Why do you stay with me?

CLOV: Why do you keep me?

HAMM: There's no one else.

CLOV: There's nowhere else.

(*Pause.*)

HAMM: You're leaving me all the same.

CLOV: I'm trying.

HAMM: You don't love me.

CLOV: No.

HAMM: You loved me once.

CLOV: Once!

HAMM: I've made you suffer too much.

(*Pause.*)

Haven't I?

CLOV: It's not that.

HAMM (*shocked*): I haven't made you suffer too much?

CLOV: Yes!

HAMM (*relieved*): Ah you gave me a fright!

(*Pause. Coldly.*)

Forgive me.

(*Pause. Louder.*)

I said, Forgive me.

CLOV: I heard you.

(*Pause.*)

Have you bled?

HAMM: Less.

(*Pause.*)

Is it not time for my painkiller?

CLOV: No.

(*Pause.*)

HAMM: How are your eyes?

CLOV: Bad.

HAMM: How are your legs?

CLOV: Bad.

HAMM: But you can move.

CLOV: Yes.

HAMM (*violently*): Then move!

(*Clov goes to back wall, leans against it with his forehead and hands.*)

Where are you?

CLOV: Here.

HAMM: Come back!

(*Clov returns to his place beside the chair.*)

Where are you?

CLOV: Here.

HAMM: Why don't you kill me?

CLOV: I don't know the combination of the cupboard.

(*Pause.*)

HAMM: Go and get two bicycle wheels.

CLOV: There are no more bicycle wheels.

HAMM: What have you done with your bicycle?

CLOV: I never had a bicycle.

HAMM: The thing is impossible.

CLOV: When there were still bicycles I wept to have one. I crawled at your feet. You told me to go to hell. Now there are none.

HAMM: And your rounds? When you inspected my paupers. Always on foot?

CLOV: Sometimes on horse.

(*The lid of one of the bins lifts and the hands of Nagg appear, gripping the rim. Then his head emerges. Nightcap. Very white face. Nagg yawns, then listens.*)

I'll leave you, I have things to do.

HAMM: In your kitchen?

CLOV: Yes.

HAMM: Outside of here it's death.

(*Pause.*)

All right, be off.

(*Exit Clov. Pause.*)

We're getting on.

NAGG: Me pap!

HAMM: Accursed progenitor!

NAGG: Me pap!

HAMM: The old folks at home! No decency left! Guzzle, guzzle, that's all they think of.

(*He whistles. Enter Clov. He halts beside the chair.*)

Well! I thought you were leaving me.

CLOV: Oh not just yet, not just yet.

NAGG: Me pap!

HAMM: Give him his pap.

CLOV: There's no more pap.

HAMM (*to Nagg*): Do you hear that? There's no more pap. You'll never get any more pap.

NAGG: I want me pap!

HAMM: Give him a biscuit.

(*Exit Clov.*)

Accursed fornicator! How are your stumps?

NAGG: Never mind me stumps.

(*Enter Clov with biscuit.*)

CLOV: I'm back again, with the biscuit.

(*He gives biscuit to Nagg who fingers it, sniffs it.*)

NAGG (*plaintively*): What is it?

CLOV: Spratt's medium.

NAGG (*as before*): It's hard! I can't!

HAMM: Bottle him!

(*Clov pushes Nagg back into the bin, closes the lid.*)

CLOV (*returning to his place beside the chair*): If age but knew!

HAMM: Sit on him!

CLOV: I can't sit.

HAMM: True. And I can't stand.

CLOV: So it is.

HAMM: Every man his speciality.

(*Pause.*)

No phone calls?

(*Pause.*)

Don't we laugh?

CLOV (*after reflection*): I don't feel like it.

HAMM (*after reflection*): Nor I.

(*Pause.*)

Clov!

CLOV: Yes.

HAMM: Nature has forgotten us.

CLOV: There's no more nature.

HAMM: No more nature! You exaggerate.

CLOV: In the vicinity.

HAMM: But we breathe, we change! We lose our hair, our teeth! Our bloom! Our ideals!

CLOV: Then she hasn't forgotten us.

HAMM: But you say there is none.

CLOV (*sadly*): No one that ever lived ever thought so crooked as we.

HAMM: We do what we can.

CLOV: We shouldn't.

(*Pause.*)

HAMM: You're a bit of all right, aren't you?

CLOV: A smithereen.

(*Pause.*)

HAMM: This is slow work.

(*Pause.*)

Is it not time for my painkiller?

CLOV: No.

(*Pause.*)

I'll leave you, I have things to do.

HAMM: In your kitchen?

CLOV: Yes.

HAMM: What, I'd like to know.

CLOV: I look at the wall.

HAMM: The wall! And what do you see on your wall? Mene, mene?° Naked bodies?

CLOV: I see my light dying.

HAMM: Your light dying! Listen to that! Well, it can die just as well here, *your* light. Take a look at me and then come back and tell me what you think of *your* light.

(*Pause.*)

CLOV: You shouldn't speak to me like that.

(*Pause.*)

HAMM (*coldly*): Forgive me.

(*Pause. Louder.*)

I said, Forgive me.

CLOV: I heard you.

(*The lid of Nagg's bin lifts. His hands appear, gripping the rim. Then his head emerges. In his mouth the biscuit. He listens.*)

HAMM: Did your seeds come up?

CLOV: No.

HAMM: Did you scratch round them to see if they had sprouted?

CLOV: They haven't sprouted.

HAMM: Perhaps it's still too early.

CLOV: If they were going to sprout they would have sprouted.

(*Violently.*)

They'll never sprout!

(*Pause. Nagg takes biscuit in his hand.*)

Mene, mene: The handwriting on the wall in Daniel 5:25 indicating the end of King Belshazzar's reign: "MENE, MENE, TEKEL, and PARSIN."

HAMM: This is not much fun.

(*Pause.*)

But that's always the way at the end of the day, isn't it, Clov?

CLOV: Always.

HAMM: It's the end of the day like any other day, isn't it, Clov?

CLOV: Looks like it.

(*Pause.*)

HAMM (*anguished*): What's happening, what's happening?

CLOV: Something is taking its course.

(*Pause.*)

HAMM: All right, be off.

(*He leans back in his chair, remains motionless. Clov does not move, heaves a great groaning sigh. Hamm sits up.*)

I thought I told you to be off.

CLOV: I'm trying.

(*He goes to door, halts.*)

Ever since I was whelped.

(*Exit Clov.*)

HAMM: We're getting on.

(*He leans back in his chair, remains motionless. Nagg knocks on the lid of the other bin. Pause. He knocks harder. The lid lifts and the hands of Nell appear, gripping the rim. Then her head emerges. Lace cap. Very white face.*)

NELL: What is it, my pet?

(*Pause.*)

Time for love?

NAGG: Were you asleep?

NELL: Oh no!

NAGG: Kiss me.

NELL: We can't.

NAGG: Try.

(*Their heads strain towards each other, fail to meet, fall apart again.*)

NELL: Why this farce, day after day?

(*Pause.*)

NAGG: I've lost me tooth.

NELL: When?

NAGG: I had it yesterday.

NELL (*elegiac*): Ah yesterday!

(*They turn painfully towards each other.*)

NAGG: Can you see me?

NELL: Hardly. And you?

NAGG: What?

NELL: Can you see me?

NAGG: Hardly.

NELL: So much the better, so much the better.

NAGG: Don't say that.

(*Pause.*)

Our sight has failed.

NELL: Yes.

(*Pause. They turn away from each other.*)

NAGG: Can you hear me?

NELL: Yes. And you?

NAGG: Yes.

(*Pause.*)

Our hearing hasn't failed.

NELL: Our what?

NAGG: Our hearing.

NELL: No.

(*Pause.*)

Have you anything else to say to me?

NAGG: Do you remember —

NELL: No.

NAGG: When we crashed on our tandem and lost our shanks.

(*They laugh heartily.*)

NELL: It was in the Ardennes.

(*They laugh less heartily.*)

NAGG: On the road to Sedan.

(*They laugh still less heartily.*)

Are you cold?

NELL: Yes, perished. And you?

NAGG:

(*Pause.*)

I'm freezing.

(*Pause.*)

Do you want to go in?

NELL: Yes.

NAGG: Then go in.

(*Nell does not move.*)

Why don't you go in?

NELL: I don't know.

(*Pause.*)

NAGG: Has he changed your sawdust?
NELL: It isn't sawdust.

(*Pause. Wearily.*)

Can you not be a little accurate, Nagg?
NAGG: Your sand then. It's not important.
NELL: It is important.

(*Pause.*)

NAGG: It was sawdust once.
NELL: Once!
NAGG: And now it's sand.

(*Pause.*)

From the shore.

(*Pause. Impatiently.*)

Now it's sand he fetches from the shore.
NELL: Now it's sand.
NAGG: Has he changed yours?
NELL: No.
NAGG: Nor mine.

(*Pause.*)

I won't have it!

(*Pause. Holding up the biscuit.*)

Do you want a bit?
NELL: No.

(*Pause.*)

Of what?
NAGG: Biscuit. I've kept you half.

(*He looks at the biscuit. Proudly.*)

Three quarters. For you. Here.

(*He proffers the biscuit.*)

No?

(*Pause.*)

Do you not feel well?
HAMM (*wearily*): Quiet, quiet, you're keeping me awake.

(*Pause.*)

Talk softer.

(*Pause.*)

If I could sleep I might make love. I'd go into the woods. My eyes would see . . . the sky, the earth. I'd run, run, they wouldn't catch me.

(*Pause.*)

Nature!

(*Pause.*)

There's something dripping in my head.

(*Pause.*)

A heart, a heart in my head.

(*Pause.*)

NAGG (*soft*): Do you hear him? A heart in his head!

(*He chuckles cautiously.*)

NELL: One mustn't laugh at those things, Nagg. Why must you always laugh at them?
NAGG: Not so loud!
NELL (*without lowering her voice*): Nothing is funnier than unhappiness, I grant you that. But —
NAGG (*shocked*): Oh!
NELL: Yes, yes, it's the most comical thing in the world. And we laugh, we laugh, with a will, in the beginning. But it's always the same thing. Yes, it's like the funny story we have heard too often, we still find it funny, but we don't laugh anymore.

(*Pause.*)

Have you anything else to say to me?
NAGG: No.
NELL: Are you quite sure?

(*Pause.*)

Then I'll leave you.
NAGG: Do you not want your biscuit?

(*Pause.*)

I'll keep it for you.

(*Pause.*)

I thought you were going to leave me.
NELL: I am going to leave you.
NAGG: Could you give me a scratch before you go?
NELL: No.

(*Pause.*)

Where?
NAGG: In the back.
NELL: No.

(*Pause.*)

Rub yourself against the rim.
NAGG: It's lower down. In the hollow.
NELL: What hollow?
NAGG: The hollow!

(*Pause.*)

Could you not?

(*Pause.*)

Yesterday you scratched me there.

NELL (*elegiac*): Ah yesterday!

NAGG: Could you not?

(*Pause.*)

Would you like me to scratch you?

(*Pause.*)

Are you crying again?

NELL: I was trying.

(*Pause.*)

HAMM: Perhaps it's a little vein.

(*Pause.*)

NAGG: What was that he said?

NELL: Perhaps it's a little vein.

NAGG: What does that mean?

(*Pause.*)

That means nothing.

(*Pause.*)

Will I tell you the story of the tailor?

NELL: No.

(*Pause.*)

What for?

NAGG: To cheer you up.

NELL: It's not funny.

NAGG: It always made you laugh.

(*Pause.*)

The first time I thought you'd die.

NELL: It was on Lake Como.

(*Pause.*)

One April afternoon.

(*Pause.*)

Can you believe it?

NAGG: What?

NELL: That we once went out rowing on Lake Como.

(*Pause.*)

One April afternoon.

NAGG: We had got engaged the day before.

NELL: Engaged!

NAGG: You were in such fits that we capsized. By rights we should have been drowned.

NELL: It was because I felt happy.

NAGG (*indignant*): It was not, it was not, it was my story and nothing else. Happy! Don't you laugh at it still? Every time I tell it. Happy!

NELL: It was deep, deep. And you could see down to the bottom. So white. So clean.

NAGG: Let me tell it again.

(*Raconteur's voice.*)

An Englishman, needing a pair of striped trousers in a hurry for the New Year festivities, goes to his tailor who takes his measurements.

(*Tailor's voice.*)

"That's the lot, come back in four days, I'll have it ready." Good. Four days later.

(*Tailor's voice.*)

"So sorry, come back in a week, I've made a mess of the seat." Good, that's all right, a neat seat can be very ticklish. A week later.

(*Tailor's voice.*)

"Frightfully sorry, come back in ten days, I've made a hash of the crotch." Good, can't be helped, a snug crotch is always a teaser. Ten days later.

(*Tailor's voice.*)

"Dreadfully sorry, come back in a fortnight, I've made a balls of the fly." Good, at a pinch, a smart fly is a stiff proposition.

(*Pause. Normal voice.*)

I never told it worse.

(*Pause. Gloomy.*)

I tell this story worse and worse.

(*Pause. Raconteur's voice.*)

Well, to make it short, the bluebells are blowing and he ballockses the buttonholes.

(*Customer's voice.*)

"God damn you to hell, Sir, no, it's indecent, there are limits! In six days, do you hear me, six days, God made the world. Yes Sir, no less Sir, the WORLD! And you are not bloody well capable of making me a pair of trousers in three months!"

(*Tailor's voice, scandalized.*)

"But my dear Sir, my dear Sir, look — (*disdainful gesture, disgustedly*) — at the world — (*pause*) and look — (*loving gesture, proudly*) — at my TROUSERS!"

(*Pause. He looks at Nell who has remained impassive, her eyes unseeing, breaks into a high forced laugh, cuts it short, pokes his head towards Nell, launches his laugh again.*)

HAMM: Silence!

(*Nagg starts, cuts short his laugh.*)

NELL: You could see down to the bottom.

HAMM (*exasperated*): Have you not finished? Will you never finish?

(*With sudden fury.*)

Will this never finish?

(*Nagg disappears into his bin, closes the lid behind him. Nell does not move. Frenziedly.*)

My kingdom for a nightman!

(*He whistles. Enter Clov.*)

Clear away this muck! Chuck it in the sea!

(*Clov goes to bins, halts.*)

NELL: So white.

HAMM: What? What's she blathering about?

(*Clov stoops, takes Nell's hand, feels her pulse.*)

NELL (*to Clov*): Desert!

(*Clov lets go her hand, pushes her back in the bin, closes the lid.*)

CLOV (*returning to his place beside the chair*): She has no pulse.

HAMM: What was she driveling about?

CLOV: She told me to go away, into the desert.

HAMM: Damn busybody! Is that all?

CLOV: No.

HAMM: What else?

CLOV: I didn't understand.

HAMM: Have you bottled her?

CLOV: Yes.

HAMM: Are they both bottled?

CLOV: Yes.

HAMM: Screw down the lids.

(*Clov goes towards door.*)

Time enough.

(*Clov halts.*)

My anger subsides, I'd like to pee.

CLOV (*with alacrity*): I'll go and get the catheter.

(*He goes towards door.*)

HAMM: Time enough.

(*Clov halts.*)

Give me my painkiller.

CLOV: It's too soon.

(*Pause.*)

It's too soon on top of your tonic, it wouldn't act.

HAMM: In the morning they brace you up and in the evening they calm you down. Unless it's the other way round.

(*Pause.*)

That old doctor, he's dead naturally?

CLOV: He wasn't old.

HAMM: But he's dead?

CLOV: Naturally.

(*Pause.*)

You ask *me* that?

(*Pause.*)

HAMM: Take me for a little turn.

(*Clov goes behind the chair and pushes it forward.*)

Not too fast!

(*Clov pushes chair.*)

Right round the world!

(*Clov pushes chair.*)

Hug the walls, then back to the center again.

(*Clov pushes chair.*)

I was right in the center, wasn't I?

CLOV (*pushing*): Yes.

HAMM: We'd need a proper wheelchair. With big wheels. Bicycle wheels!

(*Pause.*)

Are you hugging?

CLOV (*pushing*): Yes.

HAMM (*groping for wall*): It's a lie! Why do you lie to me?

CLOV (*bearing closer to wall*): There! There!

HAMM: Stop!

(*Clov stops chair close to back wall. Hamm lays his hand against wall.*)

Old wall!

(*Pause.*)

Beyond is the . . . other hell.

(*Pause. Violently.*)

Closer! Closer! Up against!

CLOV: Take away your hand.

(*Hamm withdraws his hand. Clov rams chair against wall.*)

There!

(*Hamm leans towards wall, applies his ear to it.*)

HAMM: Do you hear?

(*He strikes the wall with his knuckles.*)

Do you hear? Hollow bricks!

(*He strikes again.*)

All that's hollow!

(*Pause. He straightens up. Violently.*)

That's enough. Back!
CLOV: We haven't done the round.
HAMM: Back to my place!

(*Clov pushes chair back to center.*)

Is that my place?
CLOV: Yes, that's your place.
HAMM: Am I right in the center?
CLOV: I'll measure it.
HAMM: More or less! More or less!
CLOV (*moving chair slightly*): There!
HAMM: I'm more or less in the center?
CLOV: I'd say so.
HAMM: You'd say so! Put me right in the center!
CLOV: I'll go and get the tape.
HAMM: Roughly! Roughly!

(*Clov moves chair slightly.*)

Bang in the center!
CLOV: There!

(*Pause.*)

HAMM: I feel a little too far to the left.

(*Clov moves chair slightly.*)

Now I feel a little too far to the right.

(*Clov moves chair slightly.*)

I feel a little too far forward.

(*Clov moves chair slightly.*)

Now I feel a little too far back.

(*Clov moves chair slightly.*)

Don't stay there, (*i.e., behind the chair*) you give me the shivers.

(*Clov returns to his place beside the chair.*)

CLOV: If I could kill him I'd die happy.

(*Pause.*)

HAMM: What's the weather like?
CLOV: As usual.
HAMM: Look at the earth.

CLOV: I've looked.
HAMM: With the glass?
CLOV: No need of the glass.
HAMM: Look at it with the glass.
CLOV: I'll go and get the glass.

(*Exit Clov.*)

HAMM: No need of the glass!

(*Enter Clov with telescope.*)

CLOV: I'm back again, with the glass.

(*He goes to window right, looks up at it.*)

I need the steps.
HAMM: Why? Have you shrunk?

(*Exit Clov with telescope.*)

I don't like that, I don't like that.

(*Enter Clov with ladder, but without telescope.*)

CLOV: I'm back again, with the steps.

(*He sets down ladder under window right, gets up on it, realizes he has not the telescope, gets down.*)

I need the glass.

(*He goes towards door.*)

HAMM (*violently*): But you have the glass!
CLOV (*halting, violently*): No, I haven't the glass!

(*Exit Clov.*)

HAMM: This is deadly.

(*Enter Clov with telescope. He goes towards ladder.*)

CLOV: Things are livening up.

(*He gets up on ladder, raises the telescope, lets it fall.*)

I did it on purpose.

(*He gets down, picks up the telescope, turns it on auditorium.*)

I see . . . a multitude . . . in transports . . . of joy.

(*Pause.*)

That's what I call a magnifier.

(*He lowers the telescope, turns towards Hamm.*)

Well? Don't we laugh?
HAMM (*after reflection*): I don't.
CLOV (*after reflection*): Nor I.

(*He gets up on ladder, turns the telescope on the without.*)

Let's see.

(*He looks, moving the telescope.*)

Zero . . . (*he looks*) . . . zero . . . (*he looks*) . . . and zero.

HAMM: Nothing stirs. All is —

CLOV: Zer —

HAMM (*violently*): Wait till you're spoken to!

(*Normal voice.*)

All is . . . all is . . . all is what?

(*Violently.*)

All is what?

CLOV: What all is? In a word? Is that what you want to know? Just a moment.

(*He turns the telescope on the without, looks, lowers the telescope, turns towards Hamm.*)

Corpsed.

(*Pause.*)

Well? Content?

HAMM: Look at the sea.

CLOV: It's the same.

HAMM: Look at the ocean!

(*Clov gets down, takes a few steps towards window left, goes back for ladder, carries it over and sets it down under window left, gets up on it, turns the telescope on the without, looks at length. He starts, lowers the telescope, examines it, turns it again on the without.*)

CLOV: Never seen anything like that!

HAMM (*anxious*): What? A sail? A fin? Smoke?

CLOV (*looking*): The light is sunk.

HAMM (*relieved*): Pah! We all knew that.

CLOV (*looking*): There was a bit left.

HAMM: The base.

CLOV (*looking*): Yes.

HAMM: And now?

CLOV (*looking*): All gone.

HAMM: No gulls?

CLOV (*looking*): Gulls!

HAMM: And the horizon? Nothing on the horizon?

CLOV (*lowering the telescope, turning towards Hamm, exasperated*): What in God's name could there be on the horizon?

(*Pause.*)

HAMM: The waves, how are the waves?

CLOV: The waves?

(*He turns the telescope on the waves.*)

Lead.

HAMM: And the sun?

CLOV (*looking*): Zero.

HAMM: But it should be sinking. Look again.

CLOV (*looking*): Damn the sun.

HAMM: Is it night already then?

CLOV (*looking*): No.

HAMM: Then what is it?

CLOV (*looking*): Gray.

(*Lowering the telescope, turning towards Hamm, louder.*)

Gray!

(*Pause. Still louder.*)

GRRAY!

(*Pause. He gets down, approaches Hamm from behind, whispers in his ear.*)

HAMM (*starting*): Gray! Did I hear you say gray?

CLOV: Light black. From pole to pole.

HAMM: You exaggerate.

(*Pause.*)

Don't stay there, you give me the shivers.

(*Clov returns to his place beside the chair.*)

CLOV: Why this farce, day after day?

HAMM: Routine. One never knows.

(*Pause.*)

Last night I saw inside my breast. There was a big sore.

CLOV: Pah! You saw your heart.

HAMM: No, it was living.

(*Pause. Anguished.*)

Clov!

CLOV: Yes.

HAMM: What's happening?

CLOV: Something is taking its course.

(*Pause.*)

HAMM: Clov!

CLOV (*impatiently*): What is it?

HAMM: We're not beginning to . . . to . . . mean something?

CLOV: Mean something! You and I, mean something!

(*Brief laugh.*)

Ah that's a good one!

HAMM: I wonder.

(*Pause.*)

Imagine if a rational being came back to earth, wouldn't he be liable to get ideas into his head if he observed us long enough.

(*Voice of rational being.*)

Ah, good, now I see what it is, yes, now I understand what they're at!

(*Clov starts, drops the telescope and begins to scratch his belly with both hands. Normal voice.*)

And without going so far as that, we ourselves . . . (*with emotion*) . . . we ourselves . . . at certain moments . . .

(*Vehemently.*)

To think perhaps it won't all have been for nothing!

CLOV (*anguished, scratching himself*): I have a flea!

HAMM: A flea! Are there still fleas?

CLOV: On me there's one.

(*Scratching.*)

Unless it's a crablouse.

HAMM (*very perturbed*): But humanity might start from there all over again! Catch him, for the love of God!

CLOV: I'll go and get the powder.

(*Exit Clov.*)

HAMM: A flea! This is awful! What a day!

(*Enter Clov with a sprinkling tin.*)

CLOV: I'm back again, with the insecticide.

HAMM: Let him have it!

(*Clov loosens the top of his trousers, pulls it forward and shakes powder into the aperture. He stoops, looks, waits, starts, frenziedly shakes more powder, stoops, looks, waits.*)

CLOV: The bastard!

HAMM: Did you get him?

CLOV: Looks like it.

(*He drops the tin and adjusts his trousers.*)

RIGHT: Hamm (Alvin Epstein), seated, and Clov (Peter Evans) in the 1984 Harold Clurman Theatre production of *Endgame,* directed by Alvin Epstein. FAR RIGHT: Nell (Alice Drummond), Nagg (James Greene), Hamm, and Clov.

Unless he's laying doggo.°

HAMM: Laying! Lying you mean. Unless he's *lying* doggo.

CLOV: Ah? One says lying? One doesn't say laying?

HAMM: Use your head, can't you. If he was laying we'd be bitched.

CLOV: Ah.

(*Pause.*)

What about that pee?

HAMM: I'm having it.

CLOV: Ah that's the spirit, that's the spirit!

(*Pause.*)

HAMM (*with ardor*): Let's go from here, the two of us! South! You can make a raft and the currents will carry us away, far away, to other ... mammals!

CLOV: God forbid!

HAMM: Alone, I'll embark alone! Get working on that raft immediately. Tomorrow I'll be gone forever.

CLOV (*hastening towards door*): I'll start straight away.

HAMM: Wait!

(*Clov halts.*)

Will there be sharks, do you think?

CLOV: Sharks? I don't know. If there are there will be.

(*He goes towards door.*)

HAMM: Wait!

(*Clov halts.*)

Is it not yet time for my painkiller?

CLOV (*violently*): No!

doggo: In hiding.

(*He goes towards door.*)

HAMM: Wait!

(*Clov halts.*)

How are your eyes?
CLOV: Bad.
HAMM: But you can see.
CLOV: All I want.
HAMM: How are your legs?
CLOV: Bad.
HAMM: But you can walk.
CLOV: I come . . . and go.
HAMM: In my house.

(*Pause. With prophetic relish.*)

One day you'll be blind, like me. You'll be sitting there, a speck in the void, in the dark, forever, like me.

(*Pause.*)

One day you'll say to yourself, I'm tired, I'll sit down, and you'll go and sit down. Then you'll say, I'm hungry, I'll get up and get something to eat. But you won't get up. You'll say, I shouldn't have sat down, but since I have I'll sit on a little longer, then I'll get up and get something to eat. But you won't get up and you won't get anything to eat.

(*Pause.*)

You'll look at the wall a while, then you'll say, I'll close my eyes, perhaps have a little sleep, after that I'll feel better, and you'll close them. And when you open them again there'll be no wall anymore.

(*Pause.*)

Infinite emptiness will be all around you, all the resurrected dead of all the ages wouldn't fill it, and there you'll be like a little bit of grit in the middle of the steppe.

(*Pause.*)

Yes, one day you'll know what it is, you'll be like me, except that you won't have anyone with you, because you won't have had pity on anyone and because there won't be anyone left to have pity on.

(*Pause.*)

CLOV: It's not certain.

(*Pause.*)

And there's one thing you forget.
HAMM: Ah?
CLOV: I can't sit down.
HAMM (*impatiently*): Well you'll lie down then, what

the hell! Or you'll come to a standstill, simply stop and stand still, the way you are now. One day you'll say, I'm tired, I'll stop. What does the attitude matter?

(*Pause.*)

CLOV: So you all want me to leave you.
HAMM: Naturally.
CLOV: Then I'll leave you.
HAMM: You can't leave us.
CLOV: Then I won't leave you.

(*Pause.*)

HAMM: Why don't you finish us?

(*Pause.*)

I'll tell you the combination of the cupboard if you promise to finish me.
CLOV: I couldn't finish you.
HAMM: Then you won't finish me.

(*Pause.*)

CLOV: I'll leave you, I have things to do.
HAMM: Do you remember when you came here?
CLOV: No. Too small, you told me.
HAMM: Do you remember your father?
CLOV (*wearily*): Same answer.

(*Pause.*)

You've asked me these questions millions of times.
HAMM: I love the old questions.

(*With fervor.*)

Ah the old questions, the old answers, there's nothing like them!

(*Pause.*)

It was I was a father to you.
CLOV: Yes.

(*He looks at Hamm fixedly.*)

You were that to me.
HAMM: My house a home for you.
CLOV: Yes.

(*He looks about him.*)

This was that for me.
HAMM (*proudly*): But for me, (*gesture towards himself*) no father. But for Hamm, (*gesture towards surroundings*) no home.

(*Pause.*)

CLOV: I'll leave you.
HAMM: Did you ever think of one thing?
CLOV: Never.

HAMM: That here we're down in a hole.

(*Pause.*)

But beyond the hills? Eh? Perhaps it's still green. Eh?

(*Pause.*)

Flora! Pomona!

(*Ecstatically.*)

Ceres!°

(*Pause.*)

Perhaps you won't need to go very far.
CLOV: I can't go very far.

(*Pause.*)

I'll leave you.
HAMM: Is my dog ready?
CLOV: He lacks a leg.
HAMM: Is he silky?
CLOV: He's a kind of Pomeranian.
HAMM: Go and get him.
CLOV: He lacks a leg.
HAMM: Go and get him!

(*Exit Clov.*)

We're getting on.

(*Enter Clov holding by one of its three legs a black toy dog.*)

CLOV: Your dogs are here.

(*He hands the dog to Hamm who feels it, fondles it.*)

HAMM: He's white, isn't he?
CLOV: Nearly.
HAMM: What do you mean, nearly? Is he white or isn't he?
CLOV: He isn't.

(*Pause.*)

HAMM: You've forgotten the sex.
CLOV (*vexed*): But he isn't finished. The sex goes on at the end.

(*Pause.*)

HAMM: You haven't put on his ribbon.
CLOV (*angrily*): But he isn't finished, I tell you! First you finish your dog and then you put on his ribbon!

(*Pause.*)

HAMM: Can he stand?

Flora ... Pomona ... Ceres: Goddesses of agricultural fertility.

CLOV: I don't know.
HAMM: Try.

(*He hands the dog to Clov who places it on the ground.*)

Well?
CLOV: Wait!

(*He squats down and tries to get the dog to stand on its three legs, fails, lets it go. The dog falls on its side.*)

HAMM (*impatiently*): Well?
CLOV: He's standing.
HAMM (*groping for the dog*): Where? Where is he?

(*Clov holds up the dog in a standing position.*)

CLOV: There.

(*He takes Hamm's hand and guides it towards the dog's head.*)

HAMM (*his hand on the dog's head*): Is he gazing at me?
CLOV: Yes.
HAMM (*proudly*): As if he were asking me to take him for a walk?
CLOV: If you like.
HAMM (*as before*): Or as if he were begging me for a bone.

(*He withdraws his hand.*)

Leave him like that, standing there imploring me.

(*Clov straightens up. The dog falls on its side.*)

CLOV: I'll leave you.
HAMM: Have you had your visions?
CLOV: Less.
HAMM: Is Mother Pegg's light on?
CLOV: Light! How could anyone's light be on?
HAMM: Extinguished!
CLOV: Naturally it's extinguished. If it's not on it's extinguished.
HAMM: No, I mean Mother Pegg.
CLOV: But naturally she's extinguished!

(*Pause.*)

What's the matter with you today?
HAMM: I'm taking my course.

(*Pause.*)

Is she buried?
CLOV: Buried! Who would have buried her?
HAMM: You.
CLOV: Me! Haven't I enough to do without burying people?
HAMM: But you'll bury me.
CLOV: No I won't bury you.

(*Pause.*)

HAMM: She was bonny once, like a flower of the field.

(*With reminiscent leer.*)

And a great one for the men!

CLOV: We too were bonny — once. It's a rare thing not to have been bonny — once.

(*Pause.*)

HAMM: Go and get the gaff.

(*Clov goes to door, halts.*)

CLOV: Do this, do that, and I do it. I never refuse. Why?

HAMM: You're not able to.

CLOV: Soon I won't do it anymore.

HAMM: You won't be able to anymore.

(*Exit Clov.*)

Ah the creatures, the creatures, everything has to be explained to them.

(*Enter Clov with gaff.*)

CLOV: Here's your gaff. Stick it up.

(*He gives the gaff to Hamm who, wielding it like a puntpole,° tries to move his chair.*)

HAMM: Did I move?

CLOV: No.

(*Hamm throws down the gaff.*)

HAMM: Go and get the oilcan.

CLOV: What for?

HAMM: To oil the casters.

CLOV: I oiled them yesterday.

HAMM: Yesterday! What does that mean? Yesterday!

CLOV (*violently*): That means that bloody awful day, long ago, before this bloody awful day. I use the words you taught me. If they don't mean anything anymore, teach me others. Or let me be silent.

(*Pause.*)

HAMM: I once knew a madman who thought the end of the world had come. He was a painter — and engraver. I had a great fondness for him. I used to go and see him, in the asylum. I'd take him by the hand and drag him to the window. Look! There! All that rising corn! And there! Look! The sails of the herring fleet! All that loveliness!

(*Pause.*)

puntpole: A pole used to propel a punt, a flat-bottomed boat, through the water.

He'd snatch away his hand and go back into his corner. Appalled. All he had seen was ashes.

(*Pause.*)

He alone had been spared.

(*Pause.*)

Forgotten.

(*Pause.*)

It appears the case is . . . was not so . . . so unusual.

CLOV: A madman? When was that?

HAMM: Oh way back, way back, you weren't in the land of the living.

CLOV: God be with the days!

(*Pause. Hamm raises his toque.*)

HAMM: I had a great fondness for him.

(*Pause. He puts on his toque again.*)

He was a painter — and engraver.

CLOV: There are so many terrible things.

HAMM: No, no, there are not so many now.

(*Pause.*)

Clov!

CLOV: Yes.

HAMM: Do you not think this has gone on long enough?

CLOV: Yes!

(*Pause.*)

What?

HAMM: This . . . this . . . thing.

CLOV: I've always thought so.

(*Pause.*)

You not?

HAMM (*gloomily*): Then it's a day like any other day.

CLOV: As long as it lasts.

(*Pause.*)

All life long the same inanities.

HAMM: I can't leave you.

CLOV: I know. And you can't follow me.

(*Pause.*)

HAMM: If you leave me how shall I know?

CLOV (*briskly*): Well you simply whistle me and if I don't come running it means I've left you.

(*Pause.*)

HAMM: You won't come and kiss me good-bye?

CLOV: Oh I shouldn't think so.

(Pause.)

HAMM: But you might be merely dead in your kitchen.
CLOV: The result would be the same.
HAMM: Yes, but how would I know, if you were merely dead in your kitchen?
CLOV: Well . . . sooner or later I'd start to stink.
HAMM: You stink already. The whole place stinks of corpses.
CLOV: The whole universe.
HAMM *(angrily)*: To hell with the universe.

(Pause.)

    Think of something.
CLOV: What?
HAMM: An idea, have an idea.

(Angrily.)

    A bright idea!
CLOV: Ah good.

(He starts pacing to and fro, his eyes fixed on the ground, his hands behind his back. He halts.)

    The pains in my legs! It's unbelievable! Soon I won't be able to think anymore.
HAMM: You won't be able to leave me.

(Clov resumes his pacing.)

    What are you doing?
CLOV: Having an idea.

(He paces.)

    Ah!

(He halts.)

HAMM: What a brain!

(Pause.)

    Well?
CLOV: Wait!

(He meditates. Not very convinced.)

    Yes . . .

(Pause. More convinced.)

    Yes!

(He raises his head.)

    I have it! I set the alarm.

(Pause.)

HAMM: This is perhaps not one of my bright days, but frankly —
CLOV: You whistle me. I don't come. The alarm rings. I'm gone. It doesn't ring. I'm dead.

(Pause.)

HAMM: Is it working?

(Pause. Impatiently.)

    The alarm, is it working?
CLOV: Why wouldn't it be working?
HAMM: Because it's worked too much.
CLOV: But it's hardly worked at all.
HAMM *(angrily)*: Then because it's worked too little!
CLOV: I'll go and see.

(Exit Clov. Brief ring of alarm off. Enter Clov with alarm clock. He holds it against Hamm's ear and releases alarm. They listen to it ringing to the end. Pause.)

    Fit to wake the dead! Did you hear it?
HAMM: Vaguely.
CLOV: The end is terrific!
HAMM: I prefer the middle.

(Pause.)

    Is it not time for my painkiller?
CLOV: No!

(He goes to door, turns.)

    I'll leave you.
HAMM: It's time for my story. Do you want to listen to my story?
CLOV: No.
HAMM: Ask my father if he wants to listen to my story.

(Clov goes to bins, raises the lid of Nagg's, stoops, looks into it. Pause. He straightens up.)

CLOV: He's asleep.
HAMM: Wake him.

(Clov stoops, wakes Nagg with the alarm. Unintelligible words. Clov straightens up.)

CLOV: He doesn't want to listen to your story.
HAMM: I'll give him a bonbon.

(Clov stoops. As before.)

CLOV: He wants a sugarplum.
HAMM: He'll get a sugarplum.

(Clov stoops. As before.)

CLOV: It's a deal.

(He goes towards door. Nagg's hands appear, gripping the rim. Then the head emerges. Clov reaches door, turns.)

    Do you believe in the life to come?
HAMM: Mine was always that.

(*Exit Clov.*)

Got him that time!
NAGG: I'm listening.
HAMM: Scoundrel! Why did you engender me?
NAGG: I didn't know.
HAMM: What? What didn't you know?
NAGG: That it'd be you.

(*Pause.*)

You'll give me a sugarplum?
HAMM: After the audition.
NAGG: You swear?
HAMM: Yes.
NAGG: On what?
HAMM: My honor.

(*Pause. They laugh heartily.*)

NAGG: Two.
HAMM: One.
NAGG: One for me and one for —
HAMM: One! Silence!

(*Pause.*)

Where was I?

(*Pause. Gloomily.*)

It's finished, we're finished.

(*Pause.*)

Nearly finished.

(*Pause.*)

There'll be no more speech.

(*Pause.*)

Something dripping in my head, ever since the fontanelles.°

(*Stifled hilarity of Nagg.*)

Splash, splash, always on the same spot.

(*Pause.*)

Perhaps it's a little vein.

(*Pause.*)

A little artery.

(*Pause. More animated.*)

Enough of that, it's story time, where was I?

(*Pause. Narrative tone.*)

The man crame crawling towards me, on his belly. Pale, wonderfully pale and thin, he seemed on the point of —

(*Pause. Normal tone.*)

No, I've done that bit.

(*Pause. Narrative tone.*)

I calmly filled my pipe — the meerschaum, lit it with . . . let us say a vesta,° drew a few puffs. Aah!

(*Pause.*)

Well, what is it *you* want?

(*Pause.*)

It was an extraordinarily bitter day, I remember, zero by the thermometer. But considering it was Christmas Eve there was nothing . . . extraordinary about that. Seasonable weather, for once in a way.

(*Pause.*)

Well, what ill wind blows you my way? He raised his face to me, black with mingled dirt and tears.

(*Pause. Normal tone.*)

That should do it.

(*Narrative tone.*)

No no, don't look at me, don't look at me. He dropped his eyes and mumbled something, apologies I presume.

(*Pause.*)

I'm a busy man, you know, the final touches, before the festivities, you know what it is.

(*Pause. Forcibly.*)

Come on now, what is the object of this invasion?

(*Pause.*)

It was a glorious bright day, I remember, fifty by the heliometer,° but already the sun was sinking down into the . . . down among the dead.

(*Normal tone.*)

Nicely·put, that.

(*Narrative tone.*)

Come on now, come on, present your petition and let me resume my labors.

---

since the fontanelles: Since his embryonic development, when the membranes formed linking his skull bones in his infant head.

vesta: A wooden match.
heliometer: A telescope for measuring the apparent diameter of the sun.

(*Pause. Normal tone.*)

There's English for you. Ah well . . .

(*Narrative tone.*)

It was then he took the plunge. It's my little one, he said. Tsstss, a little one, that's bad. My little boy, he said, as if the sex mattered. Where did he come from? He named the hole. A good half-day, on horse. What are you insinuating? That the place is still inhabited? No, no, not a soul, except himself and the child — assuming he existed. Good. I inquired about the situation at Kov, beyond the gulf. Not a sinner. Good. And you expect me to believe you have left your little one back there, all alone, and alive into the bargain? Come now!

(*Pause.*)

It was a howling wild day, I remember, a hundred by the anemometer.° The wind was tearing up the dead pines and sweeping them . . . away.

(*Pause. Normal tone.*)

A bit feeble, that.

(*Narrative tone.*)

Come on, man, speak up, what is you want from me, I have to put up my holly.

(*Pause.*)

Well to make it short it finally transpired that what he wanted from me was . . . bread for his brat? Bread? But I have no bread, it doesn't agree with me. Good. Then perhaps a little corn?

(*Pause. Normal tone.*)

That should do it.

(*Narrative tone.*)

Corn, yes, I have corn, it's true, in my granaries. But use your head. I give you some corn, a pound, a pound and a half, you bring it back to your child and you make him — if he's still alive — a nice pot of porridge, (*Nagg reacts*) a nice pot and a half of porridge, full of nourishment. Good. The colors come back into his little cheeks — perhaps. And then?

(*Pause.*)

I lost patience.

(*Violently.*)

Use your head, can't you, use your head, you're on earth, there's no cure for that!

anemometer: An instrument for measuring wind speed.

(*Pause.*)

It was an exceedingly dry day, I remember, zero by the hygrometer.° Ideal weather, for my lumbago.

(*Pause. Violently.*)

But what in God's name do you imagine? That the earth will awake in spring? That the rivers and seas will run with fish again? That there's manna in heaven still for imbeciles like you?

(*Pause.*)

Gradually I cooled down, sufficiently at least to ask him how long he had taken on the way. Three whole days. Good. In what condition he had left the child. Deep in sleep.

(*Forcibly.*)

But deep in what sleep, deep in what sleep already?

(*Pause.*)

Well to make it short I finally offered to take him into my service. He had touched a chord. And then I imagined already that I wasn't much longer for this world.

(*He laughs. Pause.*)

Well?

(*Pause.*)

Well? Here if you were careful you might die a nice natural death, in peace and comfort.

(*Pause.*)

Well?

(*Pause.*)

In the end he asked me would I consent to take in the child as well — if he were still alive.

(*Pause.*)

It was the moment I was waiting for.

(*Pause.*)

Would I consent to take in the child . . .

(*Pause.*)

I can see him still, down on his knees, his hands flat on the ground, glaring at me with his mad eyes, in defiance of my wishes.

(*Pause. Normal tone.*)

I'll soon have finished with this story.

hygrometer: Device for measuring humidity.

(*Pause.*)

Unless I bring in other characters.

(*Pause.*)

But where would I find them?

(*Pause.*)

Where would I look for them?

(*Pause. He whistles. Enter Clov.*)

Let us pray to God.
NAGG: Me sugarplum!
CLOV: There's a rat in the kitchen!
HAMM: A rat! Are there still rats?
CLOV: In the kitchen there's one.
HAMM: And you haven't exterminated him?
CLOV: Half. You disturbed us.
HAMM: He can't get away?
CLOV: No.
HAMM: You'll finish him later. Let us pray to God.
CLOV: Again!
NAGG: Me sugarplum!
HAMM: God first!

(*Pause.*)

Are you right?
CLOV (*resigned*): Off we go.
HAMM (*to Nagg*): And you?
NAGG (*clasping his hands, closing his eyes, in a gabble*): Our Father which art —
HAMM: Silence! In silence! Where are your manners?

(*Pause.*)

Off we go.

(*Attitudes of prayer. Silence. Abandoning his attitude, discouraged.*)

Well?
CLOV (*abandoning his attitude*): What a hope! And you?
HAMM: Sweet damn all!

(*To Nagg.*)

And you?
NAGG: Wait!

(*Pause. Abandoning his attitude.*)

Nothing doing!
HAMM: The bastard! He doesn't exist!
CLOV: Not yet.
NAGG: Me sugarplum!
HAMM: There are no more sugarplums!

(*Pause.*)

NAGG: It's natural. After all I'm your father. It's true if it hadn't been me it would have been someone else. But that's no excuse.

(*Pause.*)

Turkish Delight,° for example, which no longer exists, we all know that, there is nothing in the world I love more. And one day I'll ask you for some, in return for a kindness, and you'll promise it to me. One must live with the times.

(*Pause.*)

Whom did you call when you were a tiny boy, and were frightened, in the dark? Your mother? No. Me. We let you cry. Then we moved you out of earshot, so that we might sleep in peace.

(*Pause.*)

I was asleep, as happy as a king, and you woke me up to have me listen to you. It wasn't indispensable, you didn't really need to have me listen to you.

(*Pause.*)

I hope the day will come when you'll really need to have me listen to you, and need to hear my voice, any voice.

(*Pause.*)

Yes, I hope I'll live till then, to hear you calling me like when you were a tiny boy, and were frightened, in the dark, and I was your only hope.

(*Pause. Nagg knocks on lid of Nell's bin. Pause.*)

Nell!

(*Pause. He knocks louder. Pause. Louder.*)

Nell!

(*Pause. Nagg sinks back into his bin, closes the lid behind him. Pause.*)

HAMM: Our revels now are ended.

(*He gropes for the dog.*)

The dog's gone.
CLOV: He's not a real dog, he can't go.
HAMM (*groping*): He's not there.
CLOV: He's lain down.
HAMM: Give him up to me.

(*Clov picks up the dog and gives it to Hamm. Hamm holds it in his arms. Pause. Hamm throws away the dog.*)

Turkish Delight: A gummy candy.

Dirty brute!

(*Clov begins to pick up the objects lying on the ground.*)

What are you doing?
CLOV: Putting things in order.

(*He straightens up. Fervently.*)

I'm going to clear everything away!

(*He starts picking up again.*)

HAMM: Order!
CLOV (*straightening up*): I love order. It's my dream. A world where all would be silent and still and each thing in its last place, under the last dust.

(*He starts picking up again.*)

HAMM (*exasperated*): What in God's name do you think you are doing?
CLOV (*straightening up*): I'm doing my best to create a little order.
HAMM: Drop it!

(*Clov drops the objects he has picked up.*)

CLOV: After all, there or elsewhere.

(*He goes towards door.*)

HAMM (*irritably*): What's wrong with your feet?
CLOV: My feet?
HAMM: Tramp! Tramp!
CLOV: I must have put on my boots.
HAMM: Your slippers were hurting you?

(*Pause.*)

CLOV: I'll leave you.
HAMM: No!
CLOV: What is there to keep me here?
HAMM: The dialogue.

(*Pause.*)

I've got on with my story.

(*Pause.*)

I've got on with it well.

(*Pause. Irritably.*)

Ask me where I've got to.
CLOV: Oh, by the way, your story?
HAMM (*surprised*): What story?
CLOV: The one you've been telling yourself all your days.
HAMM: Ah you mean my chronicle?
CLOV: That's the one.

(*Pause.*)

HAMM (*angrily*): Keep going, can't you, keep going!
CLOV: You've got on with it, I hope.
HAMM (*modestly*): Oh not very far, not very far.

(*He sighs.*)

There are days like that, one isn't inspired.

(*Pause.*)

Nothing you can do about it, just wait for it to come.

(*Pause.*)

No forcing, no forcing, it's fatal.

(*Pause.*)

I've got on with it a little all the same.

(*Pause.*)

Technique, you know.

(*Pause. Irritably.*)

I say I've got on with it a little all the same.
CLOV (*admiringly*): Well I never! In spite of everything you were able to get on with it!
HAMM (*modestly*): Oh not very far, you know, not very far, but nevertheless, better than nothing.
CLOV: Better than nothing! Is it possible?
HAMM: I'll tell you how it goes. He comes crawling on his belly —
CLOV: Who?
HAMM: What?
CLOV: Who do you mean, he?
HAMM: Who do I mean! Yet another.
CLOV: Ah him! I wasn't sure.
HAMM: Crawling on his belly, whining for bread for his brat. He's offered a job as gardener. Before —

(*Clov bursts out laughing.*)

What is there so funny about that?
CLOV: A job as gardener!
HAMM: Is that what tickles you?
CLOV: It must be that.
HAMM: It wouldn't be the bread?
CLOV: Or the brat.

(*Pause.*)

HAMM: The whole thing is comical, I grant you that. What about having a good guffaw the two of us together?
CLOV (*after reflection*): I couldn't guffaw again today.
HAMM (*after reflection*): Nor I.

(*Pause.*)

I continue then. Before accepting with gratitude he asks if he may have his little boy with him.

CLOV: What age?
HAMM: Oh tiny.
CLOV: He would have climbed the trees.
HAMM: All the little odd jobs.
CLOV: And then he would have grown up.
HAMM: Very likely.

(*Pause.*)

CLOV: Keep going, can't you, keep going!
HAMM: That's all. I stopped there.

(*Pause.*)

CLOV: Do you see how it goes on.
HAMM: More or less.
CLOV: Will it not soon be the end?
HAMM: I'm afraid it will.
CLOV: Pah! You'll make up another.
HAMM: I don't know.

(*Pause.*)

I feel rather drained.

(*Pause.*)

The prolonged creative effort.

(*Pause.*)

If I could drag myself down to the sea! I'd make a pillow of sand for my head and the tide would come.
CLOV: There's no more tide.

(*Pause.*)

HAMM: Go and see is she dead.

(*Clov goes to bins, raises the lid of Nell's, stoops, looks into it. Pause.*)

CLOV: Looks like it.

(*He closes the lid, straightens up. Hamm raises his toque. Pause. He puts it on again.*)

HAMM (*with his hand to his toque*): And Nagg?

(*Clov raises lid of Nagg's bin, stoops, looks into it. Pause.*)

CLOV: Doesn't look like it.

(*He closes the lid, straightens up.*)

HAMM (*letting go his toque*): What's he doing?

(*Clov raises lid of Nagg's bin, stoops, looks into it. Pause.*)

CLOV: He's crying.

(*He closes lid, straightens up.*)

HAMM: Then he's living.

(*Pause.*)

Did you ever have an instant of happiness?
CLOV: Not to my knowledge.

(*Pause.*)

HAMM: Bring me under the window.

(*Clov goes towards chair.*)

I want to feel the light on my face.

(*Clov pushes chair.*)

Do you remember, in the beginning, when you took me for a turn? You used to hold the chair too high. At every step you nearly tipped me out.

(*With senile quaver.*)

Ah great fun, we had, the two of us, great fun.

(*Gloomily.*)

And then we got into the way of it.

(*Clov stops the chair under window right.*)

There already?

(*Pause. He tilts back his head.*)

Is it light?
CLOV: It isn't dark.
HAMM (*angrily*): I'm asking you is it light.
CLOV: Yes.

(*Pause.*)

HAMM: The curtain isn't closed?
CLOV: No.
HAMM: What window is it?
CLOV: The earth.
HAMM: I knew it!

(*Angrily.*)

But there's no light there! The other!

(*Clov pushes chair towards window left.*)

The earth!

(*Clov stops the chair under window left. Hamm tilts back his head.*)

That's what I call light!

(*Pause.*)

Feels like a ray of sunshine.

(*Pause.*)

No?
CLOV: No.
HAMM: It isn't a ray of sunshine I feel on my face?

RIGHT: Clov (John Bottoms) and Hamm (Ben Halley, Jr.), seated, in the 1984 American Repertory Theatre production of *Endgame*, directed by JoAnne Akalaitis. BELOW: Hamm and Clov.

CLOV: No.

(*Pause.*)

HAMM: Am I very white?

(*Pause. Angrily.*)

  I'm asking you am I very white!
CLOV: Not more so than usual.

(*Pause.*)

HAMM: Open the window.
CLOV: What for?
HAMM: I want to hear the sea.
CLOV: You wouldn't hear it.
HAMM: Even if you opened the window?
CLOV: No.
HAMM: Then it's not worthwhile opening it?
CLOV: No.
HAMM (*violently*): Then open it!

(*Clov gets up on the ladder, opens the window. Pause.*)

  Have you opened it?
CLOV: Yes.

(*Pause.*)

HAMM: You swear you've opened it?
CLOV: Yes.

(*Pause.*)

HAMM: Well . . . !

(*Pause.*)

  It must be very calm.

(*Pause. Violently.*)

  I'm asking you is it very calm!
CLOV: Yes.
HAMM: It's because there are no more navigators.

(*Pause.*)

  You haven't much conversation all of a sudden.
  Do you not feel well?
CLOV: I'm cold.
HAMM: What month are we?

(*Pause.*)

  Close the window, we're going back.

(*Clov closes the window, gets down, pushes the chair back to its place, remains standing behind it, head bowed.*)

  Don't stay there, you give me the shivers!

(*Clov returns to his place beside the chair.*)

  Father!

(*Pause. Louder.*)

  Father!

(*Pause.*)

  Go and see did he hear me.

(*Clov goes to Nagg's bin, raises the lid, stoops. Unintelligible words. Clov straightens up.*)

CLOV: Yes.
HAMM: Both times?

(*Clov stoops. As before.*)

CLOV: Once only.
HAMM: The first time or the second?

(*Clov stoops. As before.*)

CLOV: He doesn't know.
HAMM: It must have been the second.
CLOV: We'll never know.

(*He closes lid.*)

HAMM: Is he still crying?
CLOV: No.
HAMM: The dead go fast.

(*Pause.*)

  What's he doing?
CLOV: Sucking his biscuit.
HAMM: Life goes on.

(*Clov returns to his place beside the chair.*)

  Give me a rug,° I'm freezing.
CLOV: There are no more rugs.

(*Pause.*)

HAMM: Kiss me.

(*Pause.*)

  Will you not kiss me?
CLOV: No.
HAMM: On the forehead.
CLOV: I won't kiss you anywhere.

(*Pause.*)

HAMM (*holding out his hand*): Give me your hand at
  least.

(*Pause.*)

  Will you not give me your hand?
CLOV: I won't touch you.

(*Pause.*)

rug: A small blanket to cover the lap, legs, and feet.

HAMM: Give me the dog.

(*Clov looks round for the dog.*)

No!
CLOV: Do you not want your dog?
HAMM: No.
CLOV: Then I'll leave you.
HAMM (*head bowed, absently*): That's right.

(*Clov goes to door, turns.*)

CLOV: If I don't kill that rat he'll die.
HAMM (*as before*): That's right.

(*Exit Clov. Pause.*)

Me to play.

(*He takes out his handkerchief, unfolds it, holds it spread out before him.*)

We're getting on.

(*Pause.*)

You weep, and weep, for nothing, so as not to laugh, and little by little . . . you begin to grieve.

(*He folds the handkerchief, puts it back in his pocket, raises his head.*)

All those I might have helped.

(*Pause.*)

Helped!

(*Pause.*)

Saved.

(*Pause.*)

Saved!

(*Pause.*)

The place was crawling with them!

(*Pause. Violently.*)

Use your head, can't you, use your head, you're on earth, there's no cure for that!

(*Pause.*)

Get out of here and love one another! Lick your neighbor as yourself!

(*Pause. Calmer.*)

When it wasn't bread they wanted it was crumpets.

(*Pause. Violently.*)

Out of my sight and back to your petting parties!

(*Pause.*)

All that, all that!

(*Pause.*)

Not even a real dog!

(*Calmer.*)

The end is in the beginning and yet you go on.

(*Pause.*)

Perhaps I could go on with my story, end it and begin another.

(*Pause.*)

Perhaps I could throw myself out on the floor.

(*He pushes himself painfully off his seat, falls back again.*)

Dig my nails into the cracks and drag myself forward with my fingers.

(*Pause.*)

It will be the end and there I'll be, wondering what can have brought it on and wondering what can have . . . (*he hesitates*) . . . why it was so long coming.

(*Pause.*)

There I'll be, in the old shelter, alone against the silence and . . . (*he hesitates*) . . . the stillness. If I can hold my peace, and sit quiet, it will be all over with sound, and motion, all over and done with.

(*Pause.*)

I'll have called my father and I'll have called my . . . (*he hesitates*) . . . my son. And even twice, or three times, in case they shouldn't have heard me, the first time, or the second.

(*Pause.*)

I'll say to myself, He'll come back.

(*Pause.*)

And then?

(*Pause.*)

And then?

(*Pause.*)

He couldn't, he has gone too far.

(*Pause.*)

And then?

(*Pause. Very agitated.*)

All kinds of fantasies! That I'm being watched! A rat! Steps! Breath held and then . . .

(*He breathes out.*)

Then babble, babble, words, like the solitary child who turns himself into children, two, three, so as to be together, and whisper together, in the dark.

(*Pause.*)

Moment upon moment, pattering down, like the millet grains of . . . (*he hesitates*) . . . that old Greek, and all life long you wait for that to mount up to a life.

(*Pause. He opens his mouth to continue, renounces.*)

Ah let's get it over!

(*He whistles. Enter Clov with alarm clock. He halts beside the chair.*)

What? Neither gone nor dead?
CLOV: In spirit only.
HAMM: Which?
CLOV: Both.
HAMM: Gone from me you'd be dead.
CLOV: And vice versa.
HAMM: Outside of here it's death!

(*Pause.*)

And the rat?
CLOV: He's got away.
HAMM: He can't go far.

(*Pause. Anxious.*)

Eh?
CLOV: He doesn't need to go far.

(*Pause.*)

HAMM: Is it not time for my painkiller?
CLOV: Yes.
HAMM: Ah! At last! Give it to me! Quick!

(*Pause.*)

CLOV: There's no more painkiller.

(*Pause.*)

HAMM (*appalled*): Good . . . !

(*Pause.*)

No more painkiller!
CLOV: No more painkiller. You'll never get any more painkiller.

(*Pause.*)

HAMM: But the little round box. It was full!
CLOV: Yes. But now it's empty.

(*Pause. Clov starts to move about the room. He is looking for a place to put down the alarm clock.*)

HAMM (*soft*): What'll I do?

(*Pause. In a scream.*)

What'll I do?

(*Clov sees the picture, takes it down, stands it on the floor with its face to the wall, hangs up the alarm clock in its place.*)

What are you doing?
CLOV: Winding up.
HAMM: Look at the earth.
CLOV: Again!
HAMM: Since it's calling to you.
CLOV: Is your throat sore?

(*Pause.*)

Would you like a lozenge?

(*Pause.*)

No.

(*Pause.*)

Pity.

(*Clov goes, humming, towards window right, halts before it, looks up at it.*)

HAMM: Don't sing.
CLOV (*turning towards Hamm*): One hasn't the right to sing anymore?
HAMM: No.
CLOV: Then how can it end?
HAMM: You want it to end?
CLOV: I want to sing.
HAMM: I can't prevent you.

(*Pause. Clov turns towards window right.*)

CLOV: What did I do with that steps?

(*He looks around for ladder.*)

You didn't see that steps?

(*He sees it.*)

Ah, about time.

(*He goes towards window left.*)

Sometimes I wonder if I'm in my right mind. Then it passes over and I'm as lucid as before.

(*He gets up on ladder, looks out of window.*)

Christ, she's under water!

(*He looks.*)

How can that be?

(*He pokes forward his head, his hand above his eyes.*)

It hasn't rained.

(*He wipes the pane, looks. Pause.*)

Ah what a fool I am! I'm on the wrong side!

(*He gets down, takes a few steps towards window right.*)

Under water!

(*He goes back for ladder.*)

What a fool I am!

(*He carries ladder towards window right.*)

Sometimes I wonder if I'm in my right senses. Then it passes off and I'm as intelligent as ever.

(*He sets down ladder under window right, gets up on it, looks out of window. He turns towards Hamm.*)

Any particular sector you fancy? Or merely the whole thing?
HAMM: Whole thing.
CLOV: The general effect? Just a moment.

(*He looks out of window. Pause.*)

HAMM: Clov.
CLOV (*absorbed*): Mmm.
HAMM: Do you know what it is?
CLOV (*as before*): Mmm.
HAMM: I was never there.

(*Pause.*)

Clov!
CLOV (*turning towards Hamm, exasperated*): What is it?
HAMM: I was never there.
CLOV: Lucky for you.

(*He looks out of window.*)

HAMM: Absent, always. It all happened without me. I don't know what's happened.

(*Pause.*)

Do you know what's happened?

(*Pause.*)

Clov!
CLOV (*turning towards Hamm, exasperated*): Do you want me to look at this muckheap, yes or no?
HAMM: Answer me first.
CLOV: What?
HAMM: Do you know what's happened?
CLOV: When? Where?

HAMM (*violently*): When! What's happened? Use your head, can't you! What has happened?
CLOV: What for Christ's sake does it matter?

(*He looks out of window.*)

HAMM: I don't know.

(*Pause. Clov turns towards Hamm.*)

CLOV (*harshly*): When old Mother Pegg asked you for oil for her lamp and you told her to get out to hell, you knew what was happening then, no?

(*Pause.*)

You know what she died of, Mother Pegg? Of darkness.
HAMM (*feebly*): I hadn't any.
CLOV (*as before*): Yes, you had.

(*Pause.*)

HAMM: Have you the glass?
CLOV: No, it's clear enough as it is.
HAMM: Go and get it.

(*Pause. Clov casts up his eyes, brandishes his fists. He loses balance, clutches on to the ladder. He starts to get down, halts.*)

CLOV: There's one thing I'll never understand.

(*He gets down.*)

Why I always obey you. Can you explain that to me?
HAMM: No. . . . Perhaps it's compassion.

(*Pause.*)

A kind of great compassion.

(*Pause.*)

Oh you won't find it easy, you won't find it easy.

(*Pause. Clov begins to move about the room in search of the telescope.*)

CLOV: I'm tired of our goings on, very tired.

(*He searches.*)

You're not sitting on it?

(*He moves the chair, looks at the place where it stood, resumes his search.*)

HAMM (*anguished*): Don't leave me there!

(*Angrily Clov restores the chair to its place.*)

Am I right in the center?
CLOV: You'd need a microscope to find this —

(*He sees the telescope.*)

Ah, about time.

(*He picks up the telescope, gets up on the ladder, turns the telescope on the without.*)

HAMM: Give me the dog.
CLOV (*looking*): Quiet!
HAMM (*angrily*): Give me the dog!

(*Clov drops the telescope, clasps his hands to his head. Pause. He gets down precipitately, looks for the dog, sees it, picks it up, hastens towards Hamm and strikes him violently on the head with the dog.*)

CLOV: There's your dog for you!

(*The dog falls to the ground. Pause.*)

HAMM: He hit me!
CLOV: You drive me mad, I'm mad!
HAMM: If you must hit me, hit me with the axe.

(*Pause.*)

Or with the gaff, hit me with the gaff. Not with the dog. With the gaff. Or with the axe.

(*Clov picks up the dog and gives it to Hamm who takes it in his arms.*)

CLOV (*imploringly*): Let's stop playing!
HAMM: Never!

(*Pause.*)

Put me in my coffin.
CLOV: There are no more coffins.
HAMM: Then let it end!

(*Clov goes towards ladder.*)

With a bang!

(*Clov gets up on ladder, gets down again, looks for telescope, sees it, picks it up, gets up ladder, raises telescope.*)

Of darkness! And me? Did anyone ever have pity on me?
CLOV (*lowering the telescope, turning towards Hamm*): What?

(*Pause.*)

Is it me you're referring to?
HAMM (*angrily*): An aside, ape! Did you never hear an aside before?

(*Pause.*)

I'm warming up for my last soliloquy.
CLOV: I warn you. I'm going to look at this filth since it's an order. But it's the last time.

(*He turns the telescope on the without.*)

Let's see.

(*He moves the telescope.*)

Nothing . . . nothing . . . good . . . good . . . nothing . . . goo —

(*He starts, lowers the telescope, examines it, turns it again on the without. Pause.*)

Bad luck to it!
HAMM: More complications!

(*Clov gets down.*)

Not an underplot, I trust.

(*Clov moves ladder nearer window, gets up on it, turns telescope on the without.*)

CLOV (*dismayed*): Looks like a small boy!
HAMM (*sarcastic*): A small . . . boy!
CLOV: I'll go and see.

(*He gets down, drops the telescope, goes towards door, turns.*)

I'll take the gaff.

(*He looks for the gaff, sees it, picks it up, hastens towards door.*)

HAMM: No!

(*Clov halts.*)

CLOV: No? A potential procreator?
HAMM: If he exists he'll die there or he'll come here. And if he doesn't . . .

(*Pause.*)

CLOV: You don't believe me? You think I'm inventing?

(*Pause.*)

HAMM: It's the end, Clov, we've come to the end. I don't need you anymore.

(*Pause.*)

CLOV: Lucky for you.

(*He goes towards door.*)

HAMM: Leave me the gaff.

(*Clov gives him the gaff, goes towards door, halts, looks at alarm clock, takes it down, looks round for a better place to put it, goes to bins, puts it on lid of Nagg's bin. Pause.*)

CLOV: I'll leave you.

(*He goes towards door.*)

HAMM: Before you go . . .

(*Clov halts near door.*)

. . . say something.

CLOV: There is nothing to say.

HAMM: A few words . . . to ponder . . . in my heart.

CLOV: Your heart!

HAMM: Yes.

(*Pause. Forcibly.*)

Yes!

(*Pause.*)

With the rest, in the end, the shadows, the murmurs, all the trouble, to end up with.

(*Pause.*)

Clov. . . . He never spoke to me. Then, in the end, before he went, without my having asked him, he spoke to me. He said . . .

CLOV (*despairingly*): Ah . . . !

HAMM: Something . . . from your heart.

CLOV: My heart!

HAMM: A few words . . . from your heart.

(*Pause.*)

CLOV (*fixed gaze, tonelessly, towards auditorium*): They said to me, That's love, yes, yes, not a doubt, now you see how —

HAMM: Articulate!

CLOV (*as before*): How easy it is. They said to me, That's friendship, yes, yes, no question, you've found it. They said to me, Here's the place, stop, raise your head and look at all that beauty. That order! They said to me, Come now, you're not a brute beast, think upon these things and you'll see how all becomes clear. And simple! They said to me, What skilled attention they get, all these dying of their wounds.

HAMM: Enough!

CLOV (*as before*): I say to myself — sometimes, Clov, you must learn to suffer better than that if you want them to weary of punishing you — one day. I say to myself — sometimes, Clov, you must be there better than that if you want them to let you go — one day. But I feel too old, and too far, to form new habits. Good, it'll never end, I'll never go.

(*Pause.*)

Then one day, suddenly, it ends, it changes, I don't understand, it dies, or it's me, I don't understand, that either. I ask the words that remain — sleeping, waking, morning, evening. They have nothing to say.

(*Pause.*)

I open the door of the cell and go. I am so bowed I only see my feet, if I open my eyes, and between my legs a little trail of black dust. I say to myself that the earth is extinguished, though I never saw it lit.

(*Pause.*)

It's easy going.

(*Pause.*)

When I fall I'll weep for happiness.

(*Pause. He goes towards door.*)

HAMM: Clov!

(*Clov halts, without turning.*)

Nothing.

(*Clov moves on.*)

Clov!

(*Clov halts, without turning.*)

CLOV: This is what we call making an exit.

HAMM: I'm obliged to you, Clov. For your services.

CLOV (*turning, sharply*): Ah pardon, it's I am obliged to you.

HAMM: It's we are obliged to each other.

(*Pause. Clov goes towards door.*)

One thing more.

(*Clov halts.*)

A last favor.

(*Exit Clov.*)

Cover me with the sheet.

(*Long pause.*)

No? Good.

(*Pause.*)

Me to play.

(*Pause. Wearily.*)

Old endgame lost of old, play and lose and have done with losing.

(*Pause. More animated.*)

Let me see.

(*Pause.*)

Ah yes!

(*He tries to move the chair, using the gaff as before. Enter Clov, dressed for the road. Panama hat, tweed* coat, raincoat over his arm, umbrella, bag. He halts by the door and stands there, impassive and motionless, his eyes fixed on Hamm, till the end. Hamm gives up.)

Good.

(*Pause.*)

Discard.

(*He throws away the gaff, makes to throw away the dog, thinks better of it.*)

Take it easy.

(*Pause.*)

And now?

(*Pause.*)

Raise hat.

(*He raises his toque.*)

Peace to our . . . arses.

(*Pause.*)

And put on again.

(*He puts on his toque.*)

Deuce.

(*Pause. He takes off his glasses.*)

Wipe.

(*He takes out his handkerchief and, without unfolding it, wipes his glasses.*)

And put on again.

(*He puts on his glasses, puts back the handkerchief in his pocket.*)

We're coming. A few more squirms like that and I'll call.

(*Pause.*)

A little poetry.

(*Pause.*)

You prayed —

(*Pause. He corrects himself.*)

You CRIED for night; it comes —

(*Pause. He corrects himself.*)

It FALLS: now cry in darkness.

(*He repeats, chanting.*)

You cried for night; it falls: now cry in darkness.

(*Pause.*)

Nicely put, that.

(*Pause.*)

And now?

(*Pause.*)

Moments for nothing, now as always, time was never and time is over, reckoning closed and story ended.

(*Pause. Narrative tone.*)

If he could have his child with him. . . .

(*Pause.*)

It was the moment I was waiting for.

(*Pause.*)

You don't want to abandon him? You want him to bloom while you are withering? Be there to solace your last million last moments?

(*Pause.*)

He doesn't realize, all he knows is hunger, and cold, and death to crown it all. But you! You ought to know what the earth is like, nowadays. Oh I put him before his responsibilities!

(*Pause. Normal tone.*)

Well, there we are, there I am, that's enough.

(*He raises the whistle to his lips, hesitates, drops it. Pause.*)

Yes, truly!

(*He whistles. Pause. Louder. Pause.*)

Good.

(*Pause.*)

Father!

(*Pause. Louder.*)

Father!

(*Pause.*)

Good.

(*Pause.*)

We're coming.

(*Pause.*)

And to end up with?

(*Pause.*)

Discard.

(*He throws away the dog. He tears the whistle from his neck.*)

With my compliments.

(*He throws whistle towards auditorium. Pause. He sniffs. Soft.*)

Clov!

(*Long pause.*)

No? Good.

(*He takes out the handkerchief.*)

Since that's the way we're playing it . . . (*he unfolds handkerchief*) . . . let's play it that way . . . (*he unfolds*) . . . and speak no more about it . . . (*he finishes unfolding*) . . . speak no more.

(*He holds handkerchief spread out before him.*)

Old stancher!

(*Pause.*)

You . . . remain.

(*Pause. He covers his face with handkerchief, lowers his arms to armrests, remains motionless.*) (*Brief tableau.*)

ALL THAT FALL

Because it was commissioned by the BBC as a radio play and was broadcast in 1957, *All That Fall* posed unusual problems for Beckett while it also offered unusual opportunities. Since the action of a radio play must be imagined by an audience, the medium of sound must be used flexibly. Words, noises, and music all have their respective power and inform the imagination in special ways. Beckett recognized the opportunity, writing to his friend Nancy Cunard: "Never thought about a radio play technique . . . but in the dead of t'other night got a nice gruesome idea full of cartwheels and dragging feet and puffing and panting which may or may not lead to something." Critics have pointed out that certain effects were actually easier to achieve and more powerful in the medium of radio than they would have been onstage — Mrs. Rooney's huffing and puffing give us a full sense of the encumbrance of her voluminous girth. The audience's imagination has no bounds when listening to a radio play.

Almost ten years later, *All That Fall* was produced onstage in a version authorized by Beckett, who was always careful to supervise his plays in production when possible. One might expect that a full production of the drama would increase its realism, but instead symbolic aspects were emphasized in such a way as to intensify the play's unreality. Ruby Cohn's description (page 1101) of the conversion of *All That Fall* into a multimedia production gives us an insight into the problems and opportunities experienced by producers such as Christopher Hampton.

The title of the play derives from a biblical quotation: "The Lord

upholdeth all that fall and raiseth up all those that be bowed down."
It has been interpreted as meaning that those who fall will be helped
and somehow saved. By connecting with this quotation, Beckett imparts
a cosmic significance to the action. The play begins by implying a cycle
of falling and rising, of death and birth, the continuous cycle of life
itself. However, the images in the play center on the breaking of that
cycle. The Rooneys' only daughter, Minna, has been dead for forty
years. Mr. Tyler's daughter has had a hysterectomy, breaking his family's
cycle of regeneration. Mr. Slocum's mother is dying. Even the train's
unpunctuality implies a break in the cycle.

Repetitive patterns are often basic to Beckett's work. Just as repetition
of various kinds — verbal and gestural — dominates *Waiting for Godot*
and *Endgame, All That Fall* is marked by repetition. Mrs. Rooney's
coming to meet her husband at the train, the basic action of the drama,
is repetitive. The various modes of transportation imply repetition: Mr.
Slocum's car, in which Mrs. Rooney gets comically stuck; Christy's cart,
with the regenerative dung nobody wants; Mr. Tyler's bicycle; and the
train itself are all repetitive forms of transportation. All their wheels,
from the flat tire of the bicycle to the sleep-inducing bogeys (the wheel
assembly of the train carriage), reinforce the imagery of cycles.

Beckett's outlook in most of his plays is not bright and cheerful but
rather grim and sometimes bitter. By questioning the biblical quotation,
Beckett questions hopefulness. If *Endgame* is a political comment on
the way the world will end, *All That Fall* may be thought of as a
theological comment on the way the world could end.

All That Fall in Performance

The British Broadcasting Corporation first aired *All That Fall* on its
Third Programme on January 13, 1957. Although it was not originally
intended for the stage, it has been given several successful stage productions. One was in Santa Barbara, California, in 1965. But a more
important production was Deryk Mendel's 1966 version in the Schiller
Theatre in Berlin in January 1966. The play was translated into German
and Beckett authorized the production, which he later described as a
"stage reading." As Ruby Cohn notes (page 1100), the stage was barren,
black, white, and gray, and the vehicles were "invisible and their sound
effects smothered." Christopher Hampton's three productions in Calgary
in 1967 were multimedia events, with screens on which realistic and
abstract images were variously projected. Each of his three versions —
performed only two months apart — handled the slides and projection
screens in different ways to achieve different effects. In the end, Hampton
himself admitted that he thought his stage versions were inferior to the
original BBC radio production.

In 1986 the Poets' Audio Center in Boston began making a series of
tapes including *All That Fall* to celebrate Beckett's eightieth birthday.
It was a coproduction of Soundscape Incorporated and the West German

radio station RIAS-Berlin and was aired on WGBH in Boston over the American Public Radio network. Billie Whitelaw and David Warrilow, both well-known interpreters of Beckett's work, were the readers.

Samuel Beckett (1906–1989)

ALL THAT FALL

1957

The Characters

MRS. ROONEY (MADDY), *a lady in her seventies*
CHRISTY, *a carter*
MR. TYLER, *a retired bill-broker*
MR. SLOCUM, *Clerk of the Racecourse*
TOMMY, *a porter*
MR. BARRELL, *a stationmaster*
MISS FITT, *a lady in her thirties*
A FEMALE VOICE
DOLLY, *a small girl*
MR. ROONEY (DAN), *husband of Mrs. Rooney, blind*
JERRY, *a small boy*

(*Rural sounds. Sheep, bird, cow, cock, severally, then together.*)
    (*Silence.*)
    (*Mrs. Rooney advances along country road towards railway station. Sound of her dragging feet.*)
    (*Music faint from house by way. "Death and the Maiden." The steps slow down, stop.*)

MRS. ROONEY: Poor woman. All alone in that ruinous old house.

(*Music louder. Silence but for music playing.*)
    (*The steps resume. Music dies. Mrs. Rooney murmurs melody. Her murmur dies.*)
    (*Sound of approaching cartwheels. The cart stops. The steps slow down, stop.*)

MRS. ROONEY: Is that you, Christy?
CHRISTY: It is, Ma'am.
MRS. ROONEY: I thought the hinny° was familiar. How is your poor wife?
CHRISTY: No better, Ma'am.
MRS. ROONEY: Your daughter then?
CHRISTY: No worse, Ma'am.

(*Silence.*)

---

hinny: A donkey that is sterile and cannot procreate.

MRS. ROONEY: Why do you halt? (*Pause.*) But why do I halt?

(*Silence.*)

CHRISTY: Nice day for the races, Ma'am.
MRS. ROONEY: No doubt it is. (*Pause.*) But will it hold up? (*Pause. With emotion.*) Will it hold up?

(*Silence.*)

CHRISTY: I suppose you wouldn't —
MRS. ROONEY: Hist! (*Pause.*) Surely to goodness that cannot be the up mail I hear already?

(*Silence. The hinny neighs. Silence.*)

CHRISTY: Damn the mail.
MRS. ROONEY: Oh thank God for that! I could have sworn I heard it, thundering up the track in the far distance. (*Pause.*) So hinnies whinny. Well, it is not surprising.
CHRISTY: I suppose you wouldn't be in need of a small load of dung?
MRS. ROONEY: Dung? What class of dung?
CHRISTY: Stydung.
MRS. ROONEY: Stydung . . . I like your frankness, Christy. (*Pause.*) I'll ask the master. (*Pause.*) Christy.
CHRISTY: Yes, Ma'am.
MRS. ROONEY: Do you find anything . . . bizarre about my way of speaking? (*Pause.*) I do not mean the voice. (*Pause.*) No, I mean the words. (*Pause. More to herself.*) I use none but the simplest words, I hope, and yet I sometimes find my way of speaking very . . . bizarre. (*Pause.*) Mercy! What was that?
CHRISTY: Never mind her, Ma'am, she's very fresh in herself today.

(*Silence.*)

MRS. ROONEY: Dung? What would we want with dung, at our time of life? (*Pause.*) Why are you on your feet down on the road? Why do you not climb up on the crest of your manure and let yourself be carried along? Is it that you have no head for heights?

(*Silence.*)

CHRISTY (*to the hinny*): Yep! (*Pause. Louder.*) Yep wiyya to hell owwa that!

(*Silence.*)

MRS. ROONEY: She does not move a muscle. (*Pause.*) I too should be getting along, if I do not wish to arrive late at the station. (*Pause.*) But a moment ago she neighed and pawed the ground. And now she refuses to advance. Give her a good welt on the rump. (*Sound of welt. Pause.*) Harder! (*Sound of welt. Pause.*) Well! If someone were to do that for me I should not dally. (*Pause.*) How she gazes at me to be sure, with her great moist cleg-tormented° eyes! Perhaps if I were to move on, down the road, out of her field of vision . . . (*Sound of welt.*) No, no, enough! Take her by the snaffle and pull her eyes away from me. Oh this is awful! (*She moves on. Sound of her dragging feet.*) What have I done to deserve all this, what, what? (*Dragging feet.*) So long ago . . . No! No! (*Dragging feet. Quotes.*) "Sigh out a something something tale of things, Done long ago and ill done." (*She halts.*) How can I go on, I cannot. Oh let me just flop down flat on the road like a big fat jelly out of a bowl and never move again! A great big slop thick with grit and dust and flies, they would have to scoop me up with a shovel. (*Pause.*) Heavens, there is that up mail again, what will become of me! (*The dragging steps resume.*) Oh I am just a hysterical old hag I know, destroyed with sorrow and pining and gentility and churchgoing and fat and rheumatism and childlessness. (*Pause. Brokenly.*) Minnie! Little Minnie! (*Pause.*) Love, that is all I asked, a little love, daily, twice daily, fifty years of twice daily love like a Paris horse-butcher's regular, what normal woman wants affection? A peck on the jaw at morning, near the ear, and another at evening, peck, peck, till you grow whiskers on you. There is that lovely laburnum° again.

(*Dragging feet. Sound of bicycle bell. It is old Mr. Tyler coming up behind her on his bicycle, on his way to the station. Squeak of brakes. He slows down and rides abreast of her.*)

MR. TYLER: Mrs. Rooney! Pardon me if I do not doff my cap, I'd fall off. Divine day for the meeting.°
MRS. ROONEY: Oh, Mr. Tyler, you startled the life

cleg-tormented: Bothered by horseflies.
laburnum: A tree with bright yellow flowers.
meeting: Races.

out of me stealing up behind me like that like a deer stalker! Oh!
MR. TYLER (*playfully*): I rang my bell, Mrs. Rooney, the moment I sighted you I started tinkling my bell, now don't you deny it.
MRS. ROONEY: Your bell is one thing, Mr. Tyler, and you are another. What news of your daughter?
MR. TYLER: Fair, fair. They removed everything, you know, the whole . . . er . . . bag of tricks. Now I am grandchildless.

(*Dragging feet.*)

MRS. ROONEY: Gracious how you wobble! Dismount, for mercy's sake, or ride on.
MR. TYLER: Perhaps if I were to lay my hand lightly on your shoulder, Mrs. Rooney, how would that be? (*Pause.*) Would you permit that?
MRS. ROONEY: No, Mr. Rooney, Mr. Tyler I mean, I am tired of light old hands on my shoulders and other senseless places, sick and tired of them. Heavens, here comes Connolly's van! (*She halts. Sound of motor van. It approaches, passes with thunderous rattle, recedes.*) Are you all right, Mr. Tyler? (*Pause.*) Where is he? (*Pause.*) Ah there you are! (*The dragging steps resume.*) That was a narrow squeak.
MR. TYLER: I alit in the nick of time.
MRS. ROONEY: It is suicide to be abroad. But what is it to be at home, Mr. Tyler, what is it to be at home? A lingering dissolution. Now we are white with dust from head to foot. I beg your pardon?
MR. TYLER: Nothing, Mrs. Rooney, nothing, I was merely cursing, under my breath, God and man, under my breath, and the wet Saturday afternoon of my conception. My back tire has gone down again. I pumped it hard as iron before I set out. And now I am on the rim.
MRS. ROONEY: Oh what a shame!
MR. TYLER: Now if it were the front I should not so much mind. But the back. The back! The chain! The oil! The grease! The hub! The brakes! The gear! No! It is too much!

(*Dragging feet.*)

MRS. ROONEY: Are we very late, Mr. Tyler, I have not the courage to look at my watch.
MR. TYLER (*bitterly*): Late! I on my bicycle as I bowled along was already late. Now therefore we are doubly late, trebly, quadrupedly late. Would I had shot by you, without a word.

(*Dragging feet.*)

MRS. ROONEY: Whom are you meeting, Mr. Tyler?
MR. TYLER: Hardy. (*Pause.*) We used to climb to-

MR. SLOCUM: (*in position behind her*): Now, Mrs. Rooney, how shall we do this?

MRS. ROONEY: As if I were a bale, Mr. Slocum, don't be afraid. (*Pause. Sounds of effort.*) That's the way! (*Effort.*) Lower! (*Effort.*) Wait! (*Pause.*) No, don't let go! (*Pause.*) Suppose I do get up, will I ever get down?

MR. SLOCUM (*breathing hard*): You'll get down, Mrs. Rooney, you'll get down. We may not get you up, but I warrant you we'll get you down.

(*He resumes his efforts. Sound of these.*)

MRS. ROONEY: Oh! . . . Lower! . . . Don't be afraid! . . . We're past the age when . . . There! . . . Now! . . . Get your shoulder under it . . . Oh! . . . (*Giggles.*) Oh glory! . . . Up! Up! . . . Ah! . . . I'm in! (*Panting of Mr. Slocum. He slams the door. In a scream.*) My frock! You've nipped my frock! (*Mr. Slocum opens the door. Mrs. Rooney frees her frock. Mr. Slocum slams the door. His violent unintelligible muttering as he walks round to the other door. Tearfully.*) My nice frock! Look what you've done to my nice frock! (*Mr. Slocum gets into his seat, slams driver's door, presses starter. The engine does not start. He releases starter.*) What will Dan say when he sees me?

MR. SLOCUM: Has he then recovered his sight?

MRS. ROONEY: No, I mean when he knows, what will he say when he feels the hole? (*Mr. Slocum presses starter. As before. Silence.*) What are you doing, Mr. Slocum?

MR. SLOCUM: Gazing straight before me, Mrs. Rooney, through the windscreen, into the void.

MRS. ROONEY: Start her up, I beseech you, and let us be off. This is awful!

MR. SLOCUM: (*dreamily*): All morning she went like a dream and now she is dead. That is what you get for a good deed. (*Pause. Hopefully.*) Perhaps if I were to choke her. (*He does so, presses the starter. The engine roars. Roaring to make himself heard.*) She was getting too much air!

(*He throttles down, grinds in his first gear, moves off, changes up in a grinding of gears.*)

MRS. ROONEY (*in anguish*): Mind the hen! (*Scream of brakes. Squawk of hen.*) Oh mother, you have squashed her, drive on, drive on! (*The car accelerates. Pause.*) What a death! One minute picking happy at the dung, on the road, in the sun, with now and then a dust bath, and then — bang! — all her troubles over. (*Pause.*) All the laying and the hatching. (*Pause.*) Just one great squawk and then . . . peace. (*Pause.*) They would have slit her

weasand° in any case. (*Pause.*) Here we are, let me down. (*The car slows down, stops, engine running. Mr. Slocum blows his horn. Pause. Louder. Pause.*) What are you up to now, Mr. Slocum? We are at a standstill, all danger is past, and you blow your horn. Now if instead of blowing it now you had blown it at that unfortunate —

(*Horn violently. Tommy the porter appears at top of station steps.*)

MR. SLOCUM: (*calling*): Will you come down, Tommy, and help this lady out, she's stuck. (*Tommy descends the steps.*) Open the door, Tommy, and ease her out.

(*Tommy opens the door.*)

TOMMY: Certainly, Sir. Nice day for the races, Sir. What would you fancy for —

MRS. ROONEY: Don't mind me. Don't take any notice of me. I do not exist. The fact is well known.

MR. SLOCUM: Do as you're asked, Tommy, for the love of God.

TOMMY: Yessir. Now, Mrs. Rooney.

(*He starts pulling her out.*)

MRS. ROONEY: Wait, Tommy, wait now, don't bustle me, just let me wheel round and get my feet to the ground. (*Her efforts to achieve this.*) Now.

TOMMY (*pulling her out*): Mind your feather, Ma'am. (*Sounds of effort.*) Easy now, easy.

MRS. ROONEY: Wait, for God's sake, you'll have me beheaded.

TOMMY: Crouch down, Mrs. Rooney, crouch down, and get your head in the open.

MRS. ROONEY: Crouch down! At my time of life! This is lunacy!

TOMMY: Press her down, Sir.

(*Sounds of combined efforts.*)

MRS. ROONEY: Merde!

TOMMY: Now! She's coming! Straighten up, Ma'am! There!

(*Mr. Slocum slams the door.*)

MRS. ROONEY: Am I out?

(*The voice of Mr. Barrell, the stationmaster, raised in anger.*)

MR. BARRELL: Tommy! Tommy! Where the hell is he?

(*Mr. Slocum grinds in his gear.*)

TOMMY (*hurriedly*): You wouldn't have something for the Ladies Plate, Sir, I was given Flash Harry.

weasand: Throat.

MR. SLOCUM: (*scornfully*): Flash Harry! That carthorse!

MR. BARRELL (*at top of steps, roaring*): Tommy! Blast your bleeding bloody — (*He sees Mrs. Rooney.*) Oh, Mrs. Rooney . . . (*Mr. Slocum drives away in a grinding of gears.*) Who's that crucifying his gearbox, Tommy?

TOMMY: Old Cissy Slocum.

MRS. ROONEY: Cissy Slocum! That's a nice way to refer to your betters. Cissy Slocum! And you an orphan!

MR. BARRELL (*angrily to Tommy*): What are you doing stravaging° down here on the public road? This is no place for you at all! Nip up there on the platform now and whip out the truck! Won't the twelve thirty be on top of us before we can turn round?

TOMMY (*bitterly*): And that's the thanks you get for a Christian act.

MR. BARRELL (*violently*): Get on with you now before I report you! (*Slow feet of Tommy climbing steps.*) Do you want me to come down to you with the shovel? (*The feet quicken, recede, cease.*) Ah, God forgive me, it's a hard life. (*Pause.*) Well, Mrs. Rooney, it's nice to see you up and about again. You were laid up there a long time.

MRS. ROONEY: Not long enough, Mr. Barrell. (*Pause.*) Would I were still in bed, Mr. Barrell. (*Pause.*) Would I were lying stretched out in my comfortable bed, Mr. Barrell, just wasting slowly painlessly away, keeping up my strength with arrowroot and calves-foot jelly, till in the end you wouldn't see me under the blankets any more than a board. (*Pause.*) Oh no coughing or spitting or bleeding or vomiting, just drifting gently down into the higher life, and remembering, remembering . . . (*the voice breaks*) . . . all the silly unhappiness . . . as though . . . it had never happened . . . what did I do with that handerkerchief? (*Sound of handerkerchief loudly applied.*) How long have you been master of this station now, Mr. Barrell?

MR. BARRELL: Don't ask me, Mrs. Rooney, don't ask me.

MRS. ROONEY: You stepped into your father's shoes, I believe, when he took them off.

MR. BARRELL: Poor Pappy! (*Reverent pause.*) He didn't live long to enjoy his ease.

MRS. ROONEY: I remember him clearly. A small ferrety purple-faced widower, deaf as a doornail, very testy and snappy. (*Pause.*) I suppose you'll be retiring soon yourself, Mr. Barrell, and growing your roses. (*Pause.*) Did I understand you to say the twelve thirty would soon be upon us?

MR. BARRELL: Those were my words.

MRS. ROONEY: But according to my watch, which is more or less right — or was — by the eight o'clock news, the time is now coming up to twelve . . . (*pause as she consults her watch*) . . . thirty-six. (*Pause.*) And yet upon the other hand the up mail has not yet gone through. (*Pause.*) Or has it sped by unbeknown to me? (*Pause.*) For there was a moment there, I remember now, I was so plunged in sorrow I wouldn't have heard a steamroller go over me. (*Pause. Mr. Barrell turns to go.*) Don't go, Mr. Barrell! (*Mr. Barrell goes. Loud.*) Mr. Barrell! (*Pause. Louder.*) Mr. Barrell!

(*Mr. Barrell comes back.*)

MR. BARRELL (*testily*): What is it, Mrs. Rooney, I have my work to do.

(*Silence. Sound of wind.*)

MRS. ROONEY: The wind is getting up. (*Pause. Wind.*) The best of the day is over. (*Pause. Wind. Dreamily.*) Soon the rain will begin to fall and go on falling, all afternoon. (*Mr. Barrell goes.*) Then at evening the clouds will part, the setting sun will shine an instant, then sink, behind the hills. (*She realizes Mr. Barrell has gone.*) Mr. Barrell! Mr. Barrell! (*Silence.*) I estrange them all. They come towards me, uninvited, bygones bygones, full of kindness, anxious to help . . . (*the voice breaks*) . . . genuinely pleased . . . to see me again . . . looking so well . . . (*Handkerchief.*) A few simple words . . . from my heart . . . and I am all alone . . . once more . . . (*Handerkerchief. Vehemently.*) I should not be out at all! I should never leave the grounds! (*Pause.*) Oh there is that Fitt woman, I wonder will she bow to me. (*Sound of Miss Fitt approaching, humming a hymn. She starts climbing the steps.*) Miss Fitt! (*Miss Fitt halts, stops humming.*) Am I then invisible, Miss Fitt? Is this cretonne° so becoming to me that I merge into the masonry? (*Miss Fitt descends a step.*) That is right, Miss Fitt, look closely and you will finally distinguish a once female shape.

MISS FITT: Mrs. Rooney! I saw you, but I did not know you.

MRS. ROONEY: Last Sunday we worshiped together. We knelt side by side at the same altar. We drank from the same chalice. Have I so changed since then?

MISS FITT (*shocked*): Oh but in church, Mrs. Rooney, in church I am alone with my Maker. Are not you? (*Pause.*) Why, even the sexton himself, you know,

---

stravaging: Roaming.

cretonne: A heavy cloth usually used for curtains or upholstery.

when he takes up the collection, knows it is useless
to pause before me. I simply do not see the plate,
or bag, whatever it is they use, how could I?
(*Pause.*) Why even when all is over and I go out
into the sweet fresh air, why even then for the first
furlong or so I stumble in a kind of daze as you
might say, oblivious to my coreligionists. And they
are very kind, I must admit — the vast majority — very kind and understanding. They know
me now and take no umbrage. There she goes, they
say, there goes the dark Miss Fitt, alone with her
Maker, take no notice of her. And they step down
off the path to avoid my running into them.
(*Pause.*) Ah yes, I am distray, very distray, even
on weekdays. Ask Mother, if you do not believe
me. Hetty, she says, when I start eating my doily
instead of the thin bread and butter, Hetty, how
can you be so distray? (*Sighs.*) I suppose the truth
is I am not there, Mrs. Rooney, just not really there
at all. I see, hear, smell, and so on, I go through
the usual motions, but my heart is not in it, Mrs.
Rooney, but heart is in none of it. Left to myself,
with no one to check me, I would soon be flown
. . . home. (*Pause.*) So if you think I cut you just
now, Mrs. Rooney, you do me an injustice. All I
saw was a big pale blur, just another big pale blur.
(*Pause.*) Is anything amiss, Mrs. Rooney, you do
not look normal somehow. So bowed and bent.

MRS. ROONEY (*ruefully*): Maddy Rooney, née Dunne,
the big pale blur. (*Pause.*) You have piercing sight,
Miss Fitt, if you only knew it, literally piercing.

(*Pause.*)

MISS FITT: Well . . . is there anything I can do, now
that I am here?

MRS. ROONEY: If you would help me up the face of
this cliff, Miss Fitt, I have little doubt your Maker
would requite you, if no one else.

MISS FITT: Now now, Mrs. Rooney, don't put your
teeth in me. Requite! I make these sacrifices for
nothing — or not at all. (*Pause. Sound of her
descending steps.*) I take it you want to lean on
me, Mrs. Rooney.

MRS. ROONEY: I asked Mr. Barrell to give me his arm,
just give me his arm. (*Pause.*) He turned on his
heel and strode away.

MISS FITT: Is it my arm you want then? (*Pause. Impatiently.*) Is it my arm you want, Mrs. Rooney,
or what is it?

MRS. ROONEY (*exploding*): Your arm! Any arm! A
helping hand! For five seconds! Christ, what a
planet!

MISS FITT: Really . . . Do you know what it is, Mrs.
Rooney, I do not think it is wise of you to be going
about at all.

MRS. ROONEY (*violently*): Come down here, Miss Fitt,
and give me your arm, before I scream down the
parish!

(*Pause. Wind. Sound of Miss Fitt descending last steps.*)

MISS FITT (*resignedly*): Well, I suppose it is the Protestant thing to do.

MRS. ROONEY: Pismires° do it for one another.
(*Pause.*) I have seen slugs do it. (*Miss Fitt proffers
her arm.*) No, the other side, my dear, if it's all
the same to you, I'm left-handed on top of everything else. (*She takes Miss Fitt's right arm.*) Heavens, child, you're just a bag of bones, you need
building up. (*Sound of her toiling up steps on Miss
Fit's arm.*) This is worse than the Matterhorn, were
you ever up the Matterhorn, Miss Fitt, great honeymoon resort. (*Sound of toiling.*) Why don't they
have a handrail! (*Panting.*) Wait till I get some air.
(*Pause.*) Don't let me go! (*Miss Fitt hums her hymn.
After a moment Mrs. Rooney joins in with the
words.*) . . . the encircling gloo-oom (*Miss Fitt stops
humming*) . . . tum tum me on. (*Forte*) The night
is dark and I am far from ho-ome, tum tum —

MISS FITT (*hysterically*): Stop it, Mrs. Rooney, stop
it, or I'll drop you!

MRS. ROONEY: Wasn't it that they sung on the *Lusitania*? Or Rock of Ages? Most touching it must
have been. Or was it the *Titanic*?

(*Attracted by the noise a group, including Mr. Tyler,
Mr. Barrell, and Tommy, gathers at top of steps.*)

MR. BARRELL: What the —

(*Silence.*)

MR. TYLER: Lovely day for the fixture.

(*Loud titter from Tommy cut short by Mr. Barrell
with backhanded blow in the stomach. Appropriate
noise from Tommy.*)

FEMALE VOICE (*shrill*): Oh look, Dolly, look!
DOLLY: What, Mamma?
FEMALE VOICE: They are stuck! (*Cackling laugh.*) They
are stuck!

MRS. ROONEY: Now we are the laughingstock of the
twenty-six counties. Or is it thirty-six?

MR. TYLER: That is a nice way to treat your defenseless subordinates, Mr. Barrell, hitting them without
warning in the pit of the stomach.

MISS FITT: Has anybody seen my mother?
MR. BARRELL: Who is that?
TOMMY: The dark Miss Fitt.
MR. BARRELL: Where is her face?

Pismires: Ants.

MRS. ROONEY: Now, deary, I am ready if you are. (*They toil up remaining steps.*) Stand back, you cads!

(*Shuffle of feet.*)

FEMALE VOICE: Mind yourself, Dolly!

MRS. ROONEY: Thank you, Miss Fitt, thank you, that will do, just prop me up against the wall like a roll of tarpaulin and that will be all, for the moment. (*Pause.*) I am sorry for all this ramdam, Miss Fitt, had I known you were looking for your mother I should not have importuned you, I know what it is.

MR. TYLER (*in marveling aside*): Ramdam!

FEMALE VOICE: Come, Dolly darling, let us take up our stand before the first-class smokers. Give me your hand and hold me tight, one can be sucked under.

MR. TYLER: You have lost your mother, Miss Fitt?

MISS FITT: Good morning, Mr. Tyler.

MR. TYLER: Good morning, Miss Fitt.

MR. BARRELL: Good morning, Miss Fitt.

MISS FITT: Good morning, Mr. Barrell.

MR. TYLER: You have lost your mother, Miss Fitt?

MISS FITT: She said she would be on the last train.

MRS. ROONEY: Do not imagine, because I am silent, that I am not present, and alive, to all that is going on.

MR. TYLER (*to Miss Fitt*): When you say the last train —

MRS. ROONEY: Do not flatter yourselves for one moment, because I hold aloof, that my sufferings have ceased. No. The entire scene, the hills, the plain, the racecourse with its miles and miles of white rails and three red stands, the pretty little wayside station, even you yourselves, yes, I mean it, and over all the clouding blue, I see it all, I stand here and see it all with eyes . . . (*the voice breaks*) . . . through eyes . . . oh, if you had my eyes . . . you would understand . . . the things they have seen . . . and not looked away . . . this is nothing . . . nothing . . . what did I do with that handkerchief?

(*Pause.*)

MR. TYLER (*to Miss Fitt*): When you say the last train — (*Mrs. Rooney blows her nose violently and long*) — when you say the last train, Miss Fitt, I take it you mean the twelve thirty.

MISS FITT: What else could I mean, Mr. Tyler, what else could I *conceivably* mean?

MR. TYLER: Then you have no cause for anxiety, Miss Fitt, for the twelve thirty has not yet arrived. Look. (*Miss Fitt looks.*) No, up the line. (*Miss Fitt looks. Patiently.*) No, Miss Fitt, follow the direction of

my index. (*Miss Fitt looks.*) There. You see now. The signal. At the bawdy hour of nine. (*In rueful afterthought.*) Or three alas! (*Mr. Barrell stifles a guffaw.*) Thank you, Mr. Barrell.

MISS FITT: But the time is now getting on for —

MR. TYLER (*patiently*): We all know, Miss Fitt, we all know only too well what the time is now getting on for, and yet the cruel fact remains that the twelve thirty has not yet arrived.

MISS FITT: Not an accident, I trust! (*Pause.*) Do not tell me she has left the track! (*Pause.*) Oh darling mother! With the fresh sole for lunch!

(*Loud titter from Tommy, checked as before by Mr. Barrell.*)

MR. BARRELL: That's enough old guff out of you. Nip up to the box now and see has Mr. Case anything for me.

(*Tommy goes.*)

MRS. ROONEY (*sadly*): Poor Dan!

MISS FITT (*in anguish*): What terrible thing has happened?

MR. TYLER: Now now, Miss Fitt, do not —

MRS. ROONEY (*with vehement sadness*): Poor Dan!

MR. TYLER: Now now, Miss Fitt, do not give way . . . to despair, all will come right . . . in the end. (*Aside to Mr. Barrell.*) What *is* the situation, Mr. Barrell? Not a collision surely?

MRS. ROONEY (*enthusiastically*): A collision! Oh that would be wonderful!

MISS FITT (*horrified*): A collision! I knew it!

MR. TYLER: Come, Miss Fitt, let us move a little up the platform.

MRS. ROONEY: Yes, let us all do that. (*Pause.*) No? (*Pause.*) You have changed your mind? (*Pause.*) I quite agree, we are better here, in the shadow of the waiting room.

MR. BARRELL: Excuse me a moment.

MRS. ROONEY: Before you slink away, Mr. Barrell, please, a statement of some kind, I insist. Even the slowest train on this brief line is not ten minutes and more behind its scheduled time without good cause, one imagines. (*Pause.*) We all know your station is the best kept of the entire network, but there are times when that is not enough, just not enough. (*Pause.*) Now, Mr. Barrell, leave off chewing your whiskers, we are waiting to hear from you — we the unfortunate ticket holders' nearest if not dearest.

(*Pause.*)

MR. TYLER (*reasonably*): I do think we are owed some kind of explanation, Mr. Barrell, if only to set our minds at rest.

MR. BARRELL: I know nothing. All I know is there has been a hitch. All traffic is retarded.

MRS. ROONEY (*derisively*): Retarded! A hitch! Ah these celibates! Here we are eating our hearts out with anxiety for our loved ones and he calls that a hitch! Those of us like myself with heart and kidney trouble may collapse at any moment and he calls that a hitch! In our ovens the Saturday roast is burning to a shrivel and he calls that —

MR. TYLER: Here comes Tommy, running! I am glad I have been spared to see this.

TOMMY (*excitedly, in the distance*): She's coming. (*Pause. Nearer.*) She's at the level crossing!

(*Immediately exaggerated station sounds. Falling signals. Bells. Whistles, Crescendo of train whistle approaching. Sound of train rushing through station.*)

MRS. ROONEY (*above rush of train*): The up mail! The up mail! (*The up mail recedes, the down train approaches, enters the station, pulls up with great hissing of steam and clashing of couplings. Noise of passengers descending, doors banging, Mr. Barrell shouting "Boghill! Boghill!" etc. Piercingly.*) Dan! . . . Are you all right? . . . Where is he? . . . Dan! . . . Did you see my husband? . . . Dan! . . . (*Noise of station emptying. Guard's whistle. Train departing, receding. Silence.*) He isn't on it! The misery I have endured, to get here, and he isn't on it! . . . Mr. Barrell! . . . Was he not on it? (*Pause.*) Is anything the matter, you look as if you had seen a ghost. (*Pause.*) Tommy! . . . Did you see the master?

TOMMY: He'll be along, Ma'am, Jerry is minding him.

(*Mr. Rooney suddenly appears on platform, advancing on small boy Jerry's arm. He is blind, thumps the ground with his stick and pants incessantly.*)

MRS. ROONEY: Oh, Dan! There you are! (*Her dragging feet as she hastens towards him. She reaches him. They halt.*) Where in the world were you?

MR. ROONEY (*coolly*): Maddy.

MRS. ROONEY: Where were you all this time?

MR. ROONEY: In the men's.

MRS. ROONEY: Kiss me!

MR. ROONEY: Kiss you? In public? On the platform? Before the boy? Have you taken leave of your senses?

MRS. ROONEY: Jerry wouldn't mind. Would you, Jerry?

JERRY: No, Ma'am.

MRS. ROONEY: How is your poor father?

JERRY: They took him away, Ma'am.

MRS. ROONEY: Then you are all alone?

JERRY: Yes, Ma'am.

MR. ROONEY: Why are you here? You did not notify me.

MRS. ROONEY: I wanted to give you a surprise. For your birthday.

MR. ROONEY: My birthday?

MRS. ROONEY: Don't you remember? I wished you your happy returns in the bathroom.

MR. ROONEY: I did not hear you.

MRS. ROONEY: But I gave you a tie! You have it on!

(*Pause.*)

MR. ROONEY: How old am I now?

MRS. ROONEY: Now never mind about that. Come.

MR. ROONEY: Why did you not cancel the boy? Now we shall have to give him a penny.

MRS. ROONEY (*miserably*): I forgot! I had such a time getting here! Such horrid nasty people! (*Pause. Pleading.*) Be nice to me, Dan, be nice to me today!

MR. ROONEY: Give the boy a penny.

MRS. ROONEY: Here are two halfpennies, Jerry. Run along now and buy yourself a nice gobstopper.

JERRY: Yes, Ma'am.

MR. ROONEY: Come for me on Monday, if I am still alive.

JERRY: Yessir.

(*He runs off.*)

MR. ROONEY: We could have saved sixpence. We have saved fivepence. (*Pause.*) But at what cost?

(*They move off along platform arm in arm. Dragging feet, panting, thudding stick.*)

MRS. ROONEY: Are you not well?

(*They halt, on Mr. Rooney's initiative.*)

MR. ROONEY: Once and for all, do not ask me to speak and move at the same time. I shall not say this in this life again.

(*They move off. Dragging feet, etc. They halt at top of steps.*)

MRS. ROONEY: Are you not —

MR. ROONEY: Let us get this precipice over.

MRS. ROONEY: Put your arm round me.

MR. ROONEY: Have you been drinking again? (*Pause.*) You are quivering like a blancmange.° (*Pause.*) Are you in a condition to lead me? (*Pause.*) We shall fall into the ditch.

MRS. ROONEY: Oh, Dan! It will be like old times!

MR. ROONEY: Pull yourself together or I shall send Tommy for the cab. Then, instead of having saved sixpence, no, fivepence, we shall have lost . . . (*calculating mumble*) . . . two and three less six one

---

blancmange: A custardlike dessert.

and no plus one one and no plus three one and nine and one ten and three two and one . . . (*normal voice*) two and one, we shall be the poorer to the tune of two and one. (*Pause.*) Curse that sun, it has gone in. What is the day doing?

(*Wind.*)

MRS. ROONEY: Shrouding, shrouding, the best of it is past. (*Pause.*) Soon the first great drops will fall splashing in the dust.

MR. ROONEY: And yet the glass was firm. (*Pause.*) Let us hasten home and sit before the fire. We shall draw the blinds. You will read to me. I think Effie is going to commit adultery with the Major. (*Brief drag of feet.*) Wait! (*Feet cease. Stick tapping at steps.*) I have been up and down these steps five thousand times and still I do not know how many there are. When I think there are six there are four or five or seven or eight and when I remember there are five there are three or four or six or seven and when finally I realize there are seven there are five or six or eight or nine. Sometimes I wonder if they do not change them in the night. (*Pause. Irritably.*) Well? How many do you make them today?

MRS. ROONEY: Do not ask me to count, Dan, not now.

MR. ROONEY: Not count! One of the few satisfactions in life?

MRS. ROONEY: Not steps, Dan, please, I always get them wrong. Then you might fall on your wound and I would have that on my manure heap on top of everything else. No, just cling to me and all will be well.

(*Confused noise of their descent. Panting, stumbling, ejaculations, curses. Silence.*)

MR. ROONEY: Well! That is what you call well!

MRS. ROONEY: We are down. And little the worse. (*Silence. A donkey brays. Silence.*) That was a true donkey. Its father and mother were donkeys.

(*Silence.*)

MR. ROONEY: Do you know what it is, I think I shall retire.

MRS. ROONEY (*appalled*): Retire! And live at home? On your grant!

MR. ROONEY: Never tread these cursed steps again. Trudge this hellish road for the last time. Sit at home on the remnants of my bottom counting the hours — till the next meal. (*Pause.*) The very thought puts life in me! Forward, before it dies!

(*They move on. Dragging feet, panting, thudding stick.*)

MRS. ROONEY: Now mind, here is the path . . . Up! . . . Well done! Now we are in safety and a straight run home.

MR. ROONEY (*without halting, between gasps*): A straight . . . run! . . . She calls that . . . a straight . . . run! . . .

MRS. ROONEY: Hush! do not speak as you go along, you know it is not good for your coronary. (*Dragging steps, etc.*) Just concentrate on putting one foot before the next or whatever the expression is. (*Dragging feet, etc.*) That is the way, now we are doing nicely. (*Dragging feet, etc. They suddenly halt, on Mrs. Rooney's initiative.*) Heavens! I knew there was something! With all the excitement! I forgot!

MR. ROONEY (*quietly*): Good God.

MRS. ROONEY: But you must know, Dan, of course, you were on it. What ever happened? Tell me!

MR. ROONEY: I have never known anything to happen.

MRS. ROONEY: But you must —

MR. ROONEY (*violently*): All this stopping and starting again is devilish, devilish! I get a little way on me and begin to be carried along when suddenly you stop dead! Two hundred pounds of unhealthy fat! What possessed you to come out at all? Let go of me!

MRS. ROONEY (*in great agitation*): No, I must know, we won't stir from here till you tell me. Fifteen minutes late! On a thirty minute run! It's unheard of!

MR. ROONEY: I know nothing. Let go of me before I shake you off.

MRS. ROONEY: But you must know! You were on it! Was it at the terminus? Did you leave on time? Or was it on the line? (*Pause.*) Did something happen on the line? (*Pause.*) Dan! (*Brokenly.*) Why won't you tell me!

(*Silence. They move off. Dragging feet, etc.*)
(*They halt. Pause.*)

MR. ROONEY: Poor Maddy! (*Pause. Children's cries.*) What was that?

(*Pause for Mrs. Rooney to ascertain.*)

MRS. ROONEY: The Lynch twins jeering at us.

(*Cries.*)

MR. ROONEY: Will they pelt us with mud today, do you suppose?

(*Cries.*)

MRS. ROONEY: Let us turn and face them. (*Cries. They turn. Silence.*) Threaten them with your stick. (*Silence.*) They have run away.

(*Pause.*)

MR. ROONEY: Did you ever wish to kill a child? (*Pause.*) Nip some young doom in the bud. (*Pause.*) Many a time at night, in winter, on the black road home, I nearly attacked the boy. (*Pause.*) Poor Jerry! (*Pause.*) What restrained me then? (*Pause.*) Not fear of man. (*Pause.*) Shall we go on backwards now a little?

MRS. ROONEY: Backwards?

MR. ROONEY: Yes. Or you forwards and I backwards. The perfect pair. Like Dante's damned, with their faces arsy-versy. Our tears will water our bottoms.

MRS. ROONEY: What is the matter, Dan? Are you not well?

MR. ROONEY: Well! Did you ever know me to be well? The day you met me I should have been in bed. The day you proposed to me the doctors gave me up. You knew that, did you not? The night you married me they came for me with an ambulance. You have not forgotten that, I suppose? (*Pause.*) No, I cannot be said to be well. But I am no worse. Indeed I am better than I was. The loss of my sight was a great fillip.° If I could go deaf and dumb I think I might pant on to be a hundred. Or have I done so? (*Pause.*) Was I a hundred today? (*Pause.*) Am I a hundred, Maddy?

(*Silence.*)

MRS. ROONEY: All is still. No living soul in sight. There is no one to ask. The world is feeding. The wind — (*brief wind*) — scarcely stirs the leaves and the birds — (*brief chirp*) — are tired singing. The cows — (*brief moo*) — and sheep — (*brief baa*) — ruminate in silence. The dogs — (*brief bark*) — are hushed and the hens — (*brief cackle*) — sprawl torpid in the dust. We are alone. There is no one to ask.

(*Silence.*)

MR. ROONEY (*clearing his throat, narrative tone*): We drew out on the tick of time, I can vouch for that. I was —

MRS. ROONEY: How can you vouch for it?

MR. ROONEY (*normal tone, angrily*): I can vouch for it, I tell you! Do you want my relation or don't you? (*Pause. Narrative tone.*) On the tick of time. I had the compartment to myself, as usual. At least I hope so, for I made no attempt to restrain myself. My mind — (*Normal tone.*) But why do we not sit down somewhere? Are we afraid we should never rise again?

MRS. ROONEY: Sit down on what?

fillip: Boon; stroke of luck.

MR. ROONEY: On a bench, for example.

MRS. ROONEY: There is no bench.

MR. ROONEY: Then on a bank, let us sink down upon a bank.

MRS. ROONEY: There is no bank.

MR. ROONEY: Then we cannot. (*Pause.*) I dream of other roads, in other lands. Of another home, another — (*he hesitates*) — another home. (*Pause.*) What was I trying to say?

MRS. ROONEY: Something about your mind.

MR. ROONEY (*startled*): My mind? Are you sure. (*Pause. Incredulous.*) My mind? . . . (*Pause.*) Ah yes. (*Narrative tone.*) Alone in the compartment my mind began to work, as so often after office hours, on the way home, in the train, to the lilt of the bogeys.° Your season ticket, I said, costs you twelve pounds a year and you earn, on an average, seven and six a day, that is to say barely enough to keep you alive and twitching with the help of food, drink, tobacco, and periodicals until you finally reach home and fall into bed. Add to this — or subtract from it — rent, stationery, various subscriptions, tramfares to and fro, light and heat, permits and licenses, hair trims and shaves, tips to escorts, upkeep of premises and appearances, and a thousand unspecifiable sundries, and it is clear that by lying at home in bed, day and night, winter and summer, with a change of pajamas once a fortnight, you would add very considerably to your income. Business, I said — (*A cry. Pause. Again. Normal tone.*) Did I hear a cry?

MRS. ROONEY: Mrs. Tully, I fancy. Her poor husband is in constant pain and beats her unmercifully.

(*Silence.*)

MR. ROONEY: That was a short knock. (*Pause.*) What was I trying to get at?

MRS. ROONEY: Business.

MR. ROONEY: Ah yes, business. (*Narrative tone.*) Business, old man, I said, retire from business, it has retired from you. (*Normal tone.*) One has these moments of lucidity.

MRS. ROONEY: I feel very cold and weak.

MR. ROONEY (*narrative tone*): On the other hand, I said, there are the horrors of home life, the dusting, sweeping, airing, scrubbing, waxing, waning, washing, mangling, drying, mowing, clipping, raking, rolling, scuffling, shoveling, grinding, tearing, pounding, banging, and slamming. And the brats, the happy little hearty little howling neighbors' brats. Of all this and much more the weekend, the Saturday intermission and then the day of rest, have given you some idea. But what must it be like on

bogeys: Railway carriage wheels.

a working day? A Wednesday? A Friday! What must it be like on a Friday! And I fell to thinking of my silent, back-street, basement office, with its obliterated plate, rest couch, and velvet hangings, and what it means to be buried there alive, if only from ten to five, with convenient to the one hand a bottle of light pale ale and to the other a long ice-cold fillet of hake. Nothing, I said, not even fully certified death, can ever take the place of that. It was then I noticed we were at a standstill. (*Pause. Normal tone. Irritably.*) Why are you hanging out of me like that? Have you swooned away?

MRS. ROONEY: I feel very cold and faint. The wind — (*whistling wind*) — is whistling through my summer frock as if I had nothing on over my bloomers. I have had no solid food since my elevenses.

MR. ROONEY: You have ceased to care. I speak — and you listen to the wind.

MRS. ROONEY: No no, I am agog, tell me all, then we shall press on and never pause, never pause, till we come safe to haven.

(*Pause.*)

MR. ROONEY: Never pause . . . safe to haven. . . . Do you know, Maddy, sometimes one would think you were struggling with a dead language.

MRS. ROONEY: Yes indeed, Dan, I know full well what you mean, I often have that feeling, it is unspeakably excruciating.

MR. ROONEY: I confess I have it sometimes myself, when I happen to overhear what I am saying.

MRS. ROONEY: Well, you know, it will be dead in time, just like our own poor dear Gaelic, there is that to be said.

(*Urgent baa.*)

MR. ROONEY (*startled*): Good God!

MRS. ROONEY: Oh, the pretty little woolly lamb, crying to suck its mother! Theirs has not changed, since Arcady.

(*Pause.*)

MR. ROONEY: Where was I in my composition?

MRS. ROONEY: At a standstill.

MR. ROONEY: Ah yes. (*Clears his throat. Narrative tone.*) I concluded naturally that we had entered a station and would soon be on our way again, and I sat on, without misgiving. Not a sound. Things are very dull today, I said, nobody getting down, nobody getting on. Then as time flew by and nothing happened I realized my error. We had not entered a station.

MRS. ROONEY: Did you not spring up and poke your head out of the window?

MR. ROONEY: What good would that have done me?

MRS. ROONEY: Why to call out to be told what was amiss.

MR. ROONEY: I did not care what was amiss. No, I just sat on, saying, If this train were never to move again I should not greatly mind. Then gradually a — how shall I say — a growing desire to — er — you know — welled up within me. Nervous probably. In fact now I am sure. You know, the feeling of being confined.

MRS. ROONEY: Yes, yes, I have been through that.

MR. ROONEY: If we sit here much longer, I said, I really do not know what I shall do. I got up and paced to and fro between the seats, like a caged beast.

MRS. ROONEY: That is a help sometimes.

MR. ROONEY: After what seemed an eternity we simply moved off. And the next thing was Barrell bawling the abhorred name. I got down and Jerry led me to the men's, or Fir as they call it now, from Vir Viris° I suppose, the V becoming F, in accordance with Grimm's Law. (*Pause.*) The rest you know. (*Pause.*) You say nothing? (*Pause.*) Say something, Maddy. Say you believe me.

MRS. ROONEY: I remember once attending a lecture by one of these new mind doctors, I forget what you call them. He spoke —

MR. ROONEY: A lunatic specialist?

MRS. ROONEY: No no, just the troubled mind, I was hoping he might shed a little light on my lifelong preoccupation with horses' buttocks.

MR. ROONEY: A neurologist.

MRS. ROONEY: No no, just mental distress, the name will come back to me in the night. I remember his telling us the story of a little girl, very strange and unhappy in her ways, and how he treated her unsuccessfully over a period of years and was finally obliged to give up the case. He could find nothing wrong with her, he said. The only thing wrong with her as far as he could see was that she was dying. And she did in fact die, shortly after he washed his hands of her.

MR. ROONEY: Well? What is there so wonderful about that?

MRS. ROONEY: No, it was just something he said, and the way he said it, that have haunted me ever since.

MR. ROONEY: You lie awake at night, tossing to and fro and brooding on it.

MRS. ROONEY: On it and other . . . wretchedness. (*Pause.*) When he had done with the little girl he stood there motionless for some time, quite two minutes I should say, looking down at his table. Then he suddenly raised his head and exclaimed, as if he had had a revelation, The trouble with her

Vir Viris: Latin for "man, men."

was she had never been really born! (*Pause.*) He spoke throughout without notes. (*Pause.*) I left before the end.

MR. ROONEY: Nothing about your buttocks? (*Mrs. Rooney weeps. In affectionate remonstrance.*) Maddy!

MRS. ROONEY: There is nothing to be done for those people!

MR. ROONEY: For which is there? (*Pause.*) That does not sound right somehow. (*Pause.*) What way am I facing?

MRS. ROONEY: What?

MR. ROONEY: I have forgotten what way I am facing.

MRS. ROONEY: You have turned aside and are bowed down over the ditch.

MR. ROONEY: There is a dead dog down there.

MRS. ROONEY: No no, just the rotting leaves.

MR. ROONEY: In June? Rotting leaves in June?

MRS. ROONEY: Yes dear, from last year, and from the year before last, and from the year before that again. (*Silence. Rainy wind. They move on. Dragging steps, etc.*) There is that lovely laburnum again. Poor thing, it is losing all its tassels. (*Dragging steps, etc.*) There are the first drops. (*Rain. Dragging feet, etc.*) Golden drizzle. (*Dragging steps, etc.*) Do not mind me, dear, I am just talking to myself. (*Rain heavier. Dragging steps, etc.*) Can hinnies procreate, I wonder.

(*They halt, on Mr. Rooney's initiative.*)

MR. ROONEY: Say that again.

MRS. ROONEY: Come on, dear, don't mind me, we are getting drenched.

MR. ROONEY (*forcibly*): Can what what?

MRS. ROONEY: Hinnies procreate. (*Silence.*) You know, hinnies, or is it jinnies, aren't they barren, or sterile, or whatever it is? (*Pause.*) It wasn't an ass's colt at all, you know, I asked the Regius Professor.

(*Pause.*)

MR. ROONEY: He should know.

MRS. ROONEY: Yes, it was a hinny, he° rode into Jerusalem or wherever it was on a hinny. (*Pause.*) That must mean something. (*Pause.*) It's like the sparrows, of many of which we are of more value, they weren't sparrows at all.

MR. ROONEY: Than many of which. . . . You exaggerate, Maddy.

MRS. ROONEY (*with emotion*): They weren't sparrows at all!

MR. ROONEY: Does that put our price up?

he: Jesus, who rode into Jerusalem on a donkey.

(*Silence. They move on. Wind and rain. Dragging feet, etc. They halt.*)

MRS. ROONEY: Do you want some dung? (*Silence. They move on. Wind and rain, etc. They halt.*) Why do you stop? Do you want to say something?

MR. ROONEY: No.

MRS. ROONEY: Then why do you stop?

MR. ROONEY: It is easier.

MRS. ROONEY: Are you very wet?

MR. ROONEY: To the buff.

MRS. ROONEY: The buff?

MR. ROONEY: The buff. From buffalo.

MRS. ROONEY: We shall hang up all our things in the hot-cupboard and get into our dressing gowns. (*Pause.*) Put your arm round me. (*Pause.*) Be nice to me! (*Pause. Gratefully.*) Ah Dan! (*They move on. Wind and rain. Dragging feet, etc. Faintly same music as before. They halt. Music clearer. Silence but for music playing. Music dies.*) All day the same old record. All alone in that great empty house. She must be a very old woman now.

MR. ROONEY (*indistinctly*): Death and the Maiden.

(*Silence.*)

MRS. ROONEY: You are crying. (*Pause.*) Are you crying?

MR. ROONEY (*violently*): Yes! (*They move on. Wind and rain. Dragging feet, etc. They halt. They move on. Wind and rain. Dragging feet, etc. They halt.*) Who is the preacher tomorrow? The incumbent?

MRS. ROONEY: No.

MR. ROONEY: Thank God for that. Who?

MRS. ROONEY: Hardy.

MR. ROONEY: "How to Be Happy Though Married"?

MRS. ROONEY: No no, he died, you remember. No connection.

MR. ROONEY: Has he announced the text?

MRS. ROONEY: "The Lord upholdeth all that fall and raiseth up all those that be bowed down." (*Silence. They join in wild laughter. They move on. Wind and rain. Dragging feet, etc.*) Hold me tighter, Dan! (*Pause.*) Oh yes!

(*They halt.*)

MR. ROONEY: I hear something behind us.

(*Pause.*)

MRS. ROONEY: It looks like Jerry. (*Pause.*) It is Jerry.

(*Sound of Jerry's running steps approaching. He halts beside them, panting.*)

JERRY (*panting*): You dropped —

MRS. ROONEY: Take your time, my little man, you will burst a blood vessel.

JERRY (*panting*): You dropped something, Sir, Mr. Barrell told me to run after you.

MRS. ROONEY: Show. (*She takes the object.*) What is it? (*She examines it.*) What is this thing, Dan?

MR. ROONEY: Perhaps it is not mine at all.

JERRY: Mr. Barrell said it was, Sir.

MRS. ROONEY: It looks like a kind of ball. And yet it is not a ball.

MR. ROONEY: Give it to me.

MRS. ROONEY (*giving it*): What *is* it, Dan?

MR. ROONEY: It is a thing I carry about with me.

MRS. ROONEY: Yes, but what —

MR. ROONEY (*violently*): It is a thing I carry about with me!

(*Silence. Mrs. Rooney looks for a penny.*)

MRS. ROONEY: I have no small money. Have you?

MR. ROONEY: I have none of any kind.

MRS. ROONEY: We are out of change, Jerry. Remind Mr. Rooney on Monday and he will give you a penny for your pains.

JERRY: Yes, Ma'am.

MR. ROONEY: If I am alive.

JERRY: Yessir.

(*Jerry starts running back towards the station.*)

MRS. ROONEY: Jerry! (*Jerry halts.*) Did you hear what the hitch was? (*Pause.*) Did you hear what kept the train so late?

MR. ROONEY: How would he have heard? Come on.

MRS. ROONEY: What was it, Jerry?

JERRY: It was a —

MR. ROONEY: Leave the boy alone, he knows nothing! Come on!

MRS. ROONEY: What was it, Jerry?

JERRY: It was a little child, Ma'am.

(*Mr. Rooney groans.*)

MRS. ROONEY: What do you mean, it was a little child?

JERRY: It was a little child fell out of the carriage. On to the line, Ma'am. (*Pause.*) Under the wheels, Ma'am.

(*Silence. Jerry runs off. His steps die away. Tempest of wind and rain. It abates. They move on. Dragging steps, etc. They halt. Tempest of wind and rain.*)

COMMENTARIES

Samuel Beckett's plays are considered difficult, obscure, experimental, and — ever since critic Martin Esslin defined the term — absurd. Absurd literature might seem to require no commentary because absurdity ought to have no significant content, but one of the anomalies of absurdist literature is that it may require more commentary than other literature.

Martin Esslin's essay explains the term by which we describe works by Beckett as well as by some playwrights who are influenced by him, such as Harold Pinter and Suzan-Lori Parks. Esslin establishes the nature of absurd drama, its limits, and its importance. Audiences were baffled by Beckett's work, starting with *Waiting for Godot* and continuing through *Endgame, All That Fall,* and the late works. The very essence of these plays is restriction: of character, space, action. Esslin helps us interpret the force of these restrictions.

Sidney Homan discusses the ending of *Endgame,* a play that may rightly be said to be *all* about ending. Homan focuses on Hamm "in his bomb shelter, in his circumscribed, lonely, inner world." Hamm is facing death at the end of the play, and Homan raises the question of a life after death as he considers Hamm's isolation and realization that he is part of a small community — perhaps including the audience — and then goes on to link the "knowing" about death with Christ's sense of knowing. Homan's efforts enlarge the context of the play and demonstrate that the restriction of space in the play does not imply a restriction of meaning.

Alan Astro's analysis of *All That Fall* is useful for helping us understand the difference between a play that is designed to be staged and one that is designed to be heard on the radio. Beckett grew up at a time when radio plays were commonplace. In the 1930s and 1940s most people heard such plays regularly, since television was not widely available until the 1950s. Astro introduces some interesting interpretations as, for example, when he suggests that "Mr. Rooney may have taken the ball from a child he pushed onto the tracks." He also suggests that the play may be much closer in theme to *Endgame* than its very different surface might at first suggest. Finally, Astro reminds us of the function of sounds in the play, sounds that would have been extremely effective in a radio production but not, perhaps, in a staged version.

All That Fall was eventually staged, as Ruby Cohn explains in her commentary. She discusses the problems inherent in transferring a drama from radio to the stage. As she notes, a radio listener might have thought of the play as being generally realistic. However, in its staged versions, it has been in many ways quite fantastic. Cohn discusses eight staged versions of the play, focusing on the productions of Clas Zilliacus and Christopher Hampton, whose versions were done with Beckett's knowledge but with a strong caveat from the author: "I authorize you to try and stage the work in the way you describe," Beckett said to Hampton, "on the understanding that you will not insist if you find it doesn't work." Hampton was not sure, after three different versions, that it did work as a staged play. In the end, he felt that he had done little to improve it over the radio version.

Martin Esslin (b. 1918)
The Theater of the Absurd

Martin Esslin is a drama critic whose work has had wide currency. He was the first to write extensively about the theater of the absurd, a term that has come to describe the plays of Samuel Beckett and a number of other post–World War II playwrights such as Eugène Ionesco and Harold Pinter. The question of what use playwrights make of the absurd and why it is an appropriate term to reflect the achievement of Beckett is explored briefly in this excerpt.

The Theater of the Absurd shows the world as an incomprehensible place. The spectators see the happenings on the stage entirely from the outside, without ever understanding the full meaning of these strange patterns of events, as newly arrived visitors might watch life in a country of which they have not yet mastered the language. The confrontation of the audience with characters and happenings which they are not quite able to comprehend makes it impossible for them to share the aspirations and emotions depicted in the play. Brecht's famous "Verfremdungseffekt" (alienation effect), the inhibition of any identification between spectator and actor, which Brecht could never successfully achieve in his own highly rational theater, really comes into its own in the Theater of the Absurd. It is impossible to identify oneself with characters one does not understand or whose motives remain a closed book, and so the distance between the public and the happenings on the stage can be maintained. Emotional identification with the characters is replaced by a puzzled, critical attention. For while the happenings on the stage are absurd, they yet remain recognizable as somehow related to real life with *its* absurdity, so that eventually the spectators are brought face to face with the irrational side of their existence. Thus, the absurd and fantastic goings-on of the Theater of the Absurd will, in the end, be found to reveal the irrationality of the human condition and the illusion of what we thought was its apparent logical structure.

If the dialogue in these plays consists of meaningless clichés and the mechanical, circular repetition of stereotyped phrases — how many meaningless clichés and stereotyped phrases do we use in our day-to-day conversation? If the characters change their personality halfway through the action, how consistent and truly integrated are the people we meet in our real life? And if people in these plays appear as mere marionettes, helpless puppets without any will of their own, passively at the mercy of blind fate and meaningless circumstance, do we, in fact, in our overorganized world, still possess any genuine initiative or power to decide our own destiny? The spectators of the Theater of the Absurd are thus confronted with a grotesquely heightened picture of their own world: a world without faith, meaning, and genuine freedom of will. In this sense, the Theater of the Absurd is the true theater of our time.

The theater of most previous epochs reflected an accepted moral order, a world whose aims and objectives were clearly present to the minds of all its public, whether it was the audience of the medieval mystery plays with their solidly accepted faith in the Christian world order or the audience of the drama of Ibsen, Shaw, or Hauptmann with their unquestioned belief in evolution and progress. To such audiences, right and wrong were never in doubt, nor did they question the then accepted goals of human endeavor. Our own time, at least in the Western world, wholly lacks such a generally accepted and completely integrated world picture. The decline of religious faith, the destruction of the belief in automatic social and biological progress, the discovery of vast areas of irrational and unconscious forces within the human psyche, the loss of a sense of control over rational human development in an age of totalitarianism and weapons of mass destruction, have all contributed to the erosion of the basis for a dramatic convention in which the action proceeds within a fixed and self-evident framework of generally accepted values. Faced with the vacuum left by the destruction of a universally accepted and unified set of beliefs, most serious playwrights have felt the need to fit their work into the frame of values and objectives expressed in one of the contemporary ideologies: Marxism, psychoanalysis, aestheticism, or nature worship. But these, in the eyes of a writer like Adamov, are nothing but superficial rationalizations which try to hide the depth of man's predicament, his loneliness and his anxiety. Or, as Ionesco puts it:

> As far as I am concerned, I believe sincerely in the poverty of the poor, I deplore it; it is real; it can become a subject for the theatre; I also believe in the anxieties and serious troubles the rich may suffer from; but it is neither in the misery of the former nor in the melancholia of the latter, that I, for one, find my dramatic subject matter. Theatre is for me the outward projection onto the stage of an inner world; it is in my dreams, in my anxieties, in my obscure desires, in my internal contradictions that I, for one, reserve for myself the right of finding my dramatic subject matter. As I am not alone in the world, as each of us, in the depth of his being, is at the same time part and parcel of all others, my dreams, my desires, my anxieties, my obsessions do not belong to me alone. They form part of an ancestral heritage, a very ancient storehouse which is a portion of the common property of all mankind. It is this, which, transcending their outward diversity, reunites all human beings and constitutes our profound common patrimony, the universal language.[1]

In other words, the commonly acceptable framework of beliefs and values of former epochs which has now been shattered is to be replaced by the community of dreams and desires of a collective unconscious. And, to quote Ionesco again:

> ... the new dramatist is one ... who tries to link up with what is most ancient: new language and subject matter in a dramatic structure which aims at being clearer, more stripped of inessentials and more purely theatrical; the rejection of traditionalism to rediscover tradition; a synthesis of knowledge and invention, of the real and imaginary, of the particular and the universal, or as they say now, of the individual and the collective. ... By expressing my deepest obsessions, I express my deepest humanity. I become one with all others, spontaneously, over and above all the barriers of caste and different psychologies. I express my solitude and become one with all other solitudes.[2]

What is the tradition with which the Theater of the Absurd — at first sight the most revolutionary and radically new movement — is trying to link itself? It is in fact a very ancient and a very rich tradition, nourished from many and varied sources: the verbal exuberance and extravagant inventions of Rabelais, the age-old clowning of the Roman mimes and the Italian *Commedia dell'Arte*, the knock-about humor of circus clowns like Grock; the wild, archetypal symbolism of English nonsense verse, the baroque horror of Jacobean dramatists like Webster or Tourneur, the harsh, incisive, and often brutal tones of the German drama of Grabbe, Büchner, Kleist, and Wedekind with its delirious language and grotesque inventiveness; and the Nordic paranoia of the dreams and persecution fantasies of Strindberg.

[1]Eugène Ionesco, "L'Impromptu de l'Alma," *Théâtre II* (Paris, 1958).
[2]Ionesco, "The Avant-Garde Theatre," *World Theatre* 8.3 (Autumn 1959).

Sidney Homan (b. 1938)
THE ENDING OF *ENDGAME*   1984

Sidney Homan's book Beckett's Theaters: Interpretations for Performance *concentrates on the production of Beckett's plays. His discussion of* Endgame *focuses on the performance aspects of movement in the final moments of the play. The question of death is central to the question of* Endgame.

Despite its seeming chaos on the surface, Hamm's last speech, that string of short phrases and snatches of dialogue much like that of Winnie in *Happy Days*, provides the most sustained insight into his playwright's mentality. In the words of the Unnamable,° it is the "end of the joke," the aesthetic painkiller, if you will, as handy as that literal painkiller in the cupboard was not. Unseen, except by us, Clov constitutes the onstage audience of one. The speech itself is surely meant to contrast with Hamm's opening dialogue: This time Hamm is not discovered but rather constitutes *all* the stage, at least as far as he knows, and the speech is about endings rather than beginnings. The proper verbal constructions, in terms of his opening lines, would be something akin to "Me to play having played." No fear of mere "reveling" here.

Hamm's speech seems to be madness without matter. As with the scattered fragments in the closing lines of Eliot's *The Waste Land*, however, there is here an order and a depth of reference below the surface. Clov is absent, though he stands impassive upstage. The sheet with which he "discovered" Hamm at the opening is now useless. In a larger sense, Hamm has been revealed, the play itself representing his disclosure as a symbol. The removal of the sheet itself is thereby the stimulus for an aesthetic revelation. He is now moving toward the purely symbolic, and the chess metaphor comes to the fore, chess itself a symbolic enactment of literal battles and armies: "Me to play" and "Old endgame." Indeed, Hamm is moving toward the same sense of completeness found by Mr. Endon in *Murphy*. The King, the central piece, is now immobile at the center of the board, the word for both the theater and the field of chess pieces. Then "discard" the last life-support; the gaff is thrown away, though the dog, symbol of Hamm's artifice, is retained.

We see the artist now attempting to document the moment before human extinction. It is the process toward that movement, and not the actual event itself, defining the limits of our earthly inquiry.

Like Shakespeare, Beckett does not depict a hereafter. We may speculate on what will happen to Lear — can a pagan go to any sort of heaven? — but the Renaissance playwright, like the modern one, is content to show him approaching the end, promised or otherwise. There is a farewell here to the audience, obscene to be sure, and with that salute an identification with us as Hamm uses the plural possessive "our." The "You" who wants poetry, or the efficacy of prayer, or night to come is also the "you" that, in an absurdist or relative world, must cry in darkness. Again, we all die alone. Hamm's aesthetic consciousness, like that of the narrator in *Cascando*,° is now most acute: "Nicely put, that."

If relativity, both in terms of time itself and the mutability of all human things, relentlessly moves on, Hamm, now enveloped in his story, is about to make time run, to echo the Renaissance poet Marvell. The time is "over, reckoning closed and story ended." The wish for extinction, however, cannot hold as the life force, the final reference to the father and his starving son, is

---

Unnamable: Narrator of *The Unnamable* (1958), third in a trilogy of novels by Beckett.

Cascando: Beckett's radio play for voice and music (1962), first broadcast in English by the BBC in 1964.

sounded. Hamm cannot shake off that memory. An invasion of his world, the story irritates the aesthetic fiber he has so closely woven. It is another world, with a past, with characters, and involving those issues of life and the sustenance of life that Hamm has otherwise so assiduously blocked out in his bomb shelter, in his circumscribed, lonely, inner world. The "Oh I put him before his responsibilities" sounds as much neurotic as convincing. Then with a *calm* — again, one of Beckett's favorite words — returning, Hamm reverses himself in the recognition that he is not alone, that he is part and parcel of all humanity, including us, including the fictive, or seemingly fictive father and his son: "Well, there we are, there I am, that's enough." This is something "truly," though the aesthetic inner world is itself in flux, only a momentary stay against reality, and yet Hamm will now be able to sustain this playwright-actor's posture at least until the end.

He approaches death with the same sense of "knowing" his story that several modern biblical scholars have attributed to Christ, an "actor" who plays the parts of a visitor to earth, prophet, crucified savior, and risen spirit. We approach now the closest thing to transcendence in Beckett, undercut, of course, by the fact that Hamm "*remains motionless*" as the curtain closes (he can no more leave his stage than Vladimir and Estragon can leave theirs). The dog is discarded, the last vestige of his creation; and then in a brilliant gesture he throws the whistle toward us, the audience — the "*auditorium.*" Though the isolation is illusory — again, Clov is backstage, visible to us if not to Hamm — for Hamm it is a convincing illusion. He is approaching the nonbeing sought by Nell in her vision of a silent, white ocean bottom, an empty world where nothingness is a fact, not a conceit, where we can cease to be like those talkative "political" artists who, in giving form to nothing, are bound to fail. In essence, Hamm is trying to give up the last hold on life, even if that "life" be the illusory existence of the stage world.

The transcendence itself is aborted. However much he would later cut away at the time scheme or the plot or the place of his plays (witness *Breath*), Beckett cannot present us with nothing: "Nothing" itself can be spoken of but not enacted. A bare stage is only a bare stage and not a play. Here Beckett is like Emily Dickinson in "I heard a fly buzz when I died," as she tries poetically to cross the thin boundary line between life and death and is frustrated in that attempt when a fly intervenes between her eyes and the "light." Beckett is trying to go to the nonstate, if I may put it that way, of nonbeing. That is the way Hamm would "play it," so that he could "speak no more about it." I repeat his wish: "Speak no more." He seeks here not the failure of words, the very possibility that unnerves Winnie. Nor will he use words anymore to define nonbeing.

Now, without words and with the major character free of the tension in seeking physical life or death, we move to the level of mime. Our audience surrogate, the silent Clov, now sees Hamm hold the bloodied handkerchief before him and then cover his face. Two phrases act as glosses to the action. One is the descriptive "Old stancher," lest an audience member fail to identify properly the symbol, Hamm's Greek-like mask that is the physical correlative for his misery, for his suffering than which no one's is greater, as he reminds us early in the play. In effect, Hamm, like the figures in Greek myths, has passed through earthly existence and literally become a star. He has won his right to be a symbol, a symbol sustained by the play, a symbol that now wordlessly compresses all that he means, or has meant. This wretched piece of a costume, in effect, now equals the entire play. In Beckett, truly, the last shall be first. One also thinks of the handkerchief worn by Keaton in *Film*, and that used by Willie in *Happy Days*, though neither was so developed, nor so perfect a symbol of suffering.

The other phrase, a tantalizing one, is the closing "You . . . remain." Initially, it appears simply an appositive for "Old stancher," but I also take it as a reference to the audience. That is, Hamm has now *realized* his role; he has been elevated to a symbol. Our task has now just begun; we must leave the theater, refreshed by Beckett's mirror world, and must encounter the suffering anew. Outside of here it is hell, as the Beckett characters are fond of saying. We remain; we are the "mutes and audience" of the act to which Hamlet refers (V, II, 337).

The play closes beyond words, as Hamm covers his face with the handkerchief and, like the Auditor in *Not I*, lowers his arms and in a mockery of mime and its movements stops on the stage direction to remain "*motionless.*" Initiated by language, the play ends in silence, the "*Brief tableau,*" like that called for by Beckett in *The Unnamable. Curtain*. It will also start again; as Winnie observes, even if the glass breaks, it will be there whole tomorrow. Tomorrow the handkerchief will revert to the old sheet covering Hamm, that, with the bloodstained handkerchief, will in turn be removed, discovering another potential tragic hero — or "figure," if "hero" sounds too affirmative for some readers. The uncovering will allow theatrical life to flow again, the act of artistic creation, the long creative process to which Hamm himself refers, the informing of a vision and the production of a symbol — a symbol that, at the end, will remain with us, only to be undone the next day, the next performance. Curtain. . . .

Ruby Cohn (b. 1922)
Radio to Stage: *All That Fall*   1980

Ruby Cohn is among the leading Beckett scholars of our time. Her numerous books on Beckett have included careful discussions of performance and production. Here she discusses the interesting problems attendant on staging a play that was written for radio.

As *Waiting for Godot*, Beckett's first play to be produced, remains his most popular theater piece, so *All That Fall*, his first radio play, remains most popular on that medium. A mixture of realism and poetry, it occasions the longest chapter of Clas Zilliacus in his *Beckett and Broadcasting*; he sifts the manuscripts, analyzes form and substance, and summarizes the production history. The chapter "The Plays out of Their Element" is largely devoted to eight staged versions of *All That Fall*. Two of these were accorded Beckett's permission, although he subsequently (1968) refused permission to the British National Theatre when Laurence Olivier and Joan Plowright wished to play Dan and Maddy Rooney.

On its sound surface, *All That Fall* is the most realistic of Beckett's radio plays, and one might think that transfer to the stage would increase the realism, but this was not true either of Deryk Mendel's Berlin production of 1966, or of Christopher Hampton's production in Calgary, Canada, the following year, both authorized. Each director thought that staging would enhance the symbolic aspect of the play.

In 1966 Beckett had not yet directed at Berlin's Schiller Theater, but he had advised on his friend Deryk Mendel's *Godot* production, and he consented to Mendel's triple bill (which opened in January 1966) of *Act Without Words II*, the world premiere of *Come and Go* (in German), and the theater translation of *All That Fall*. Looking back on it in 1971, Beckett wrote Clas Zilliacus, "I must have known about and authorized Mendel's 'stage reading' of *All That Fall*. I would not consent to [it] today."[1] With Beckett's consent came the cooperation of Beckett's Paris-based designer friend Matias and of two well-known German actors, Bernhard Minetti and the late Lu Säuberlich. Wishing to eschew the surface realism of the radio script, Mendel had designer Matias strip the stage to black, white, and gray, while he worked only with words, susceptible to symbolic extension. The stage was encased in a bone-white box whose ground was dark. On it the characters moved, Maddy and Dan Rooney in their black smocklike coats, and the other characters in gray. The vehicles of the text were invisible, and their sound effects smothered.

The production emphasized the tripartite division of *All That Fall*: (1) Maddy moved painfully from stage left to right, meeting each neighbor in turn; (2) at stage right, in dim light, shadowy figures jostled one another at Boghill Station; (3) leading her blind husband, Maddy moved back from right to left, meeting no one. Through all their complaints and digressions, the old couple shared a dialogue.

Clas Zilliacus has aptly summarized Maddy's physical itinerary in *All That Fall*: "ruinous house by the road — laburnum — ascent of station steps — platform — descent of steps — laburnum — ruinous house. It ends where it began."[2] On stage the to-and-fro movement of the large dark figure against the white ground hinted at purposeless absurdity. Although a more somber voyage than the aural trip of the BBC broadcast, the visualization offered a few comic moments in the stance or gait of the Boghill dwellers — Christy, Mr. Tyler, Mr. Slocum, and especially stiff Miss Fitt (played by Sibylle Gilles). All that *fall* actually add up to zero, but the sporadic lack of equilibrium recalled clown pratfalls. Funny and far-reaching was Dan Rooney–Minetti as a bellowing statue: "Once and for all, do not ask me to speak and move at the same time." The director, Mendel, made no such request of Minetti, who groped his slow way, seeming to reach for more than his way but stopping to sputter phrases. An intellectual actor, Minetti delivered his lines with a Cartesian crankiness; neither thinking nor being brought him any pleasure. In contrast, Maddy–Säuberlich exhibited verbal zest even when she questioned her own words. As Zilliacus points out, "Beckett identifies uncertainties of language with epistemological uncertainty."[3] From both uncertainties Säuberlich evoked tender

---

[1]Clas Zilliacus, *Beckett and Broadcasting* (Abo: Acta Academiae Aboensis, Ser. A. Humaniora, 1976) 180.
[2]Zilliacus 39.
[3]Zilliacus 50.

laughter. The harmonized performances of the two veteran German actors left one certain of *un*certainty about the death of the child: accident or murder? And that uncertainty radiates to all death, always sudden, always mysterious.

Christopher Hampton (not to be confused with the British playwright) knew nothing of the German staging when he requested Beckett's permission for a multimedia production in 1967, and, surprisingly, Beckett consented: "Though I continue to think that ATF as written cannot survive even the dimmest light, I am impressed by your awareness of the problem and by your approach to it. I authorize you to try and stage the work in the way you describe, on the understanding that you will not insist if you find it doesn't work." [4]

Hampton had directed a professional stage *Endgame* in Canada, and the same actors volunteered for the experimental *All That Fall*, which local Calgary newspapers misbilled as a "world premiere." Hampton has summarized the play's theme: "*All That Fall* is about the human choice of love and the consequent suffering and the death implicit in that choice." [5] In staging, he wished "to suggest symbolic intent through light-projections and thereby head off realistic readings. The directorial metaphor, then, is based on paradox: We must guard against the verisimilitude implicit in the visibility of actor, set and prop, and at the same time we hope through visible projections to emphasize symbolic content." Maddy's visible and realistic journey was to be undertaken in an environment composed of symbolically suggestive slides.

All That Fall actually received three stage productions in Calgary's Studio Theater, at intervals of about two months. In the first production the performers were surrounded by screens on which were projected images of (1) actual people, places, objects; (2) forms based on scenes but moving toward nonrealism; and (3) abstract forms with colors expressing mood. Some three hundred slides overwhelmed the setting. When Hampton was asked how he felt about staging a world premiere, he answered that he was too busy trying to arrange three hundred slides to worry about premieres. The technical logistics may also have led to insufficient concern with acting, as he came to realize.

For the second attempt, then, Hampton toned the visuals down to avoid what he called "focal dispersion." Four large screens that had surrounded the audience were moved behind the performers, and scrims were interposed between actors and audience. Images were then allowed to slide from scrim to screen to cyclorama, so that they lost intensity as compared to the acting. In addition Hampton deployed lights and microphones to emphasize that the actors were at the center of the performance. "The combination of image shifts and screen shifts, together with greater intensity achieved for the actors, seemed to pull the show into a unity." [6]

For the third and last production, new research was undertaken into more variety in the nonrealistic slides. To reduce technology stealing from the actors even further, control of all projectors was centered in one experienced technician, who could coordinate scenic changes with acting rhythms. In his article on the production, Hampton states that it fell short of the BBC radio version, but his letter to Beckett summarizes what was gained. . . . [Hampton told Beckett that

---

[4]Beckett letter to Hampton, June 17, 1967.
[5]"Staging *All That Fall*," *Drama at Calgary* (November 1967): 48.
[6]Christopher Hampton, "*All That Fall*, Productions II and III, Final Report," *Drama at Calgary* (May 1968): 40.

he feared the projectors distracted from the actors but discovered that they helped dramatize the environment's sometimes "remote" and sometimes "actively cruel" aspect.] Hampton now feels that the experiment was successful, although in a letter to me he admits, "One loves one's own children."

Alan Astro
ALL THAT FALL: AN ANALYSIS   *1990*

Alan Astro's discussion of All That Fall *examines the aspects of the play that suit it to radio. The sounds and noises that Beckett felt were essential to the play and an emphasis on language demonstrate one of Beckett's gifts: his ability to exploit the limitations as well as the possibilities of a production venue and of a dramatic genre.*

It is strange to consider that Beckett's radio play *All That Fall* (1957), the first work he originally wrote in English since the novel *Watt* in 1944, was composed at approximately the same time as *Endgame*. *Endgame* presents an absurd world reduced to its last survivors, whereas *All That Fall* is a basically realistic play, taking place in Ireland in the 1930s. It follows Mrs. Maddy Rooney, an old middle-class woman, as she wends her way slowly through a village, going to meet her blind husband's train. She comes successively upon several men, as old and decrepit as herself, with whom she vaguely flirts; two laborers who help her along; and a prude named Miss Fitt. The train comes in late, her husband Dan finally arrives, and they begin their journey homeward. Their conversation takes many odd turns, of which the strangest is no doubt this remark by Mr. Rooney: "Did you ever wish to kill a child? (*Pause.*) Nip some young doom in the bud" (p. 1090). Just before the end of the play a young man who had guided Mr. Rooney on the train runs up with an object Mr. Rooney had left behind in the men's room: It seems to be a small ball, such as children play with. Thereupon Mrs. Rooney asks why the train came in late; the reason, of which Mr. Rooney claims total ignorance, is that a child had been run over. The play abruptly ends, and we are left with the suspicion that Mr. Rooney may have taken the ball from a child he pushed onto the tracks.

Reading or hearing the play a second time, we see how carefully Beckett prepares us for this ending. Childlessness and the death of children are recurrent themes. For example, a mother is overheard warning a child to stay far from the railroad tracks; Mrs. Rooney mentioned a daughter who died young, saying that she would now be in her forties, "getting ready for the change" of life, when she could no longer have children (p. 1083); the first man Mrs. Rooney meets on the way to the station, Mr. Tyler, has a daughter who is sterile because of a hysterectomy: "They removed everything, you know, the whole . . . er . . . bag of tricks. Now I am grandchildless" (p. 1082). Mr. Tyler even regrets his own birth, "cursing, under [his] breath, [. . .] the wet Saturday afternoon of [his] conception" (p. 1082). Later on, Mrs. Rooney tells the story of a famed medical specialist she heard speak on the case of a young girl who died because "she had never been really born" (p. 1092). Even animal infertility occupies Mrs. Rooney's mind. She wonders whether "hinnies" — animals similar to mules — "can procreate": "Aren't they barren, or sterile, or whatever it is?" (p. 1092); and she mourns the loss of the potential offspring of a chicken she sees run over.

Childlessness means lack of posthumous existence, but Mrs. Rooney throws into question even her present one. She says to one of the men she comes upon: "Don't mind me. Don't take any notice of me. I do not exist. The fact is well known" (p. 1084). To another she says, "I was so plunged in sorrow that I wouldn't have heard a steamroller go over me" (p. 1085). Mrs. Rooney does not exist for others as well. The prudish Miss Fitt fails to greet her, claiming to be so absorbed in her pious thoughts that she sees only an indistinct shape. Mrs. Rooney, perhaps only half-ironically, reflects upon herself in Miss Fitt's eyes: "Maddy Rooney, née Dunne, the big pale blur" (p. 1086). The names, as always in Beckett, are suggestive. "Maddy" indicates she might be a little off mentally: She calls herself "hysterical" (p. 1082), a word that suggests reproductive problems in that it derives from the same Greek root as *uterus*. Her name reminds us that she had been a mother (*Maddy*), and Mr. Rooney's, that he had been a father (*Dan*). Yet they are failed parents, their daughter having died; whence, perhaps, their deformed names, similar to those Molloy gave to his parents, Da and Mag.

It is significant that Maddy is "née Dunne," that is, born Dunne, born done for — like the patient whom the great specialist diagnosed as never having been properly born. Such a diagnosis is less rare than might appear, since it applies to all of us: We are never properly born into life, for life is a road to death. The name Rooney underscores such congenital *ruin*ation; in the very first line of the play the syllable *ruin* is uttered, as Maddy evokes a woman whose fate is no happier than her own: "Poor woman. All alone in that ruinous old house."

Not only are individual deaths evoked; so is mass catastrophe. Mrs. Rooney remarks how "touching" it must have been that passengers on the doomed ships *Lusitania* and *Titanic* sang hymns (p. 1086). The uselessness of such appeals to God motivates the play's title, for the words come from a psalm quoted by Maddy as the subject of a sermon by her preacher: "The Lord upholdeth all that fall and raiseth up all those that be bowed down" (p. 1092; see Psalm 145:14). The title mentions the falling and leaves out the raising up, as befits these souls moving toward childless deaths.

The degradation of the characters is accompanied by the wearing away of language. Mr. Rooney wonders about his wife's and his own ungainly grammar:

MRS. ROONEY: There is nothing to be done for those people!
MR. ROONEY: For which is there? (*Pause.*) That does not sound right somehow. (p. 1092)

MRS. ROONEY: It's like the sparrows, than many of which we are of more value [. . .].
MR. ROONEY: Than many of which. . . . You exaggerate, Maddy. (p. 1092)

Mrs. Rooney had already remarked that her speech is unusual, asking her helper Christy:

Do you find anything . . . bizarre about my way of speaking? (*Pause.*) I do not mean the voice. (*Pause.*) No, I mean the words. (*Pause. More to herself.*) I use none but the simplest words, I hope, and yet I sometimes find my way of speaking very . . . bizarre. (p. 1081)

This description corresponds not only to Maddy's speech but also to Beckett's style throughout his oeuvre, starting with the switch to French. The simplest words are used, but they are combined in the strangest ways. *All That Fall* contains the dialogue . . . where the characters, feeling the strangeness of their own English words, have the impression of speaking a dead language.

The themes of *All That Fall* — sterility of the old and the death of the young, the wearing away of language — show how close this play is to *Endgame*, despite the difference in setting: The seeds of destruction exist within everyday life. There is, however, a more apparent similarity between the two plays: In each the male protagonist, the one responsible for the tragedy (the sacrifice of a child or of an entire universe), is blind.

Hamm's and Dan's lack of vision relates them to the great tragic hero Oedipus. Sophocles' *Oedipus the King* portrays the aftermath of the plague at Thebes, and *Endgame* recounts what follows even more general destruction. Likewise, the ancient myth tells the story of Oedipus as a child, who was to be killed to avoid catastrophe (the fulfillment of the prophecy that he would kill his father and marry his mother); *All That Fall* reveals the murder of a child "in order to nip some young doom in the bud," in accordance with the classical wisdom evoked by Nietzsche at the beginning of *The Birth of Tragedy*: "What is best of all is . . . not to be born. . . . But the second best for you is — to die soon."[1]

In a radio play blindness corresponds to our situation as listeners, who cannot see what is going on; in this way we resemble not only the blind Mr. Rooney but also Mr. Slocum, a stalled motorist whom Mrs. Rooney observes "gazing straight [. . .] through the windscreen, into the void" (p. 1084).

The noise of the failing automobile, reflecting the sounds of the decrepit characters moving along, is one of the sources of vaudevillesque humor in *All That Fall*. As critic Linda Ben-Zvi has noted, in this radio play Beckett had to use sound to achieve the comical effects attained with stage numbers in *Waiting for Godot*.[2] Another critic, Robert Wilcher, has pointed to a more unusual use of sound in *All That Fall*.[3] Mrs. Rooney evokes natural phenomena *before* we hear the noises associated with them:

> The wind — (*brief wind*) — scarcely stirs the leaves and the birds — (*brief chirp*) — are tired singing. The cows — (*brief moo*) — and sheep — (*brief baa*) — ruminate in silence. The dogs — (*brief bark*) — are hushed and the hens — (*brief cackle*) — sprawl torpid in the dust. We are alone. There is no one to ask. (p. 1090)

Contrary to the myth that language originated when humans imitated the sounds of nature, here language appears as primary, calling forth natural sounds. As Beckett reminded us in his essay on Dante and Joyce, Genesis does not say that God gave language to man; rather, man invented language: " 'The animals were given names by Adam,' the man who 'first said goo to a goose.' "[4] We

[1]Nietzsche, *The Birth of Tragedy and the Case of Wagner*, trans. Walter Kaufmann (New York: Vintage, 1967) 42.

[2]Linda Ben-Zvi, *Samuel Beckett* (Boston: Twayne, 1986) 188.

[3]Robert Wilcher, " 'Out of the Dark': Beckett's Texts for Radio," *Beckett's Later Fiction and Drama*, ed. James Acheson and Kateryna Arthur (Hong Kong: Macmillan, 1987) 5.

[4]*Disjecta: Miscellaneous Writings and a Dramatic Fragment*, ed. Ruby Cohn (London: John Calder, 1983) 31.

project our own sounds onto the world, even onto beasts, as is proven by the fact that in the several languages different words denote the cries of the same animals. God is not the guarantor of language; man himself is. Hence Mrs. Rooney's last words in her speech above: "We are alone. There is no one to ask." That the absence of God is evoked in a radio play is significant. The divine voice that the prophets heard crashing from the heavens has been transformed in our time into the human voice traveling through the airwaves. We fall, and have not the God who will raise us up.

Lorraine Hansberry

Lorraine Hansberry (1930–1965), like John Millington Synge, died tragically young. Her loss to the American stage is incalculable; her successes were only beginning, and at her death she seemed on the verge of a remarkable career.

Hansberry grew up in a middle-class black family in Chicago. Her father, a successful real estate man, founded one of the first banks for blacks in Chicago. However, he spent much of his life trying to find a way to make a decent life for himself and his family in America. He eventually gave up on the United States and, when he died in 1945, he was scouting for a place in Mexico where he could move his family to live comfortably.

Lorraine Hansberry went to college after her father died, and her first ambition was to become a visual artist. She attended the Art Institute of Chicago and numerous other schools before moving to New York. Once there, she became interested in some drama groups and soon married the playwright Howard Nemiroff. She began writing, sharing parts of her first play with friends in her own living room. They helped raise money to stage the play and, with black director Lloyd Richards and little-known Sidney Poitier as Walter Lee Younger, *A Raisin in the Sun* (1959) thrust her into the drama spotlight.

In 1959, when she was twenty-nine years old, she was the most promising woman writing for the American stage. She was also the first black American to win the New York Drama Critics' Circle Award for the best play of the year. She died of cancer the day her second produced play, *The Sign in Sidney Brustein's Window*, closed. She had finished a third play, *Les Blancs*, which was brought to Broadway by Nemiroff in 1970. Neither of her other plays was as popular as *Raisin*, but the two later plays demonstrate a deepening concern for and understanding of some of the key issues of racial and sexual politics that interested her throughout her career.

The Sign in Sidney Brustein's Window's hero is a Jewish intellectual in the 1950s in Greenwich Village who feels that all the radical struggle of the 1930s has been lost. He agitates for personal involvement, for emotional and intellectual action. It is an especially idealistic play, considering that it anticipates the political agitation in the United States during the mid-1960s and early 1970s. *Les Blancs* takes as its central character a black African intellectual, Tshembe, and explores his relationship to both Europe and Africa. In his uneasiness with both cultures he discovers that he cannot live outside his own history. In this play, Hansberry reveals some of her deep interest in Pan-Africanism and the search for a personal heritage.

A last, posthumous work was put together by Howard Nemiroff from Hansberry's notes, letters, and early writings. Titled *To Be Young, Gifted, and Black* (1971), it has helped solidify her achievements. It is certainly impossible to know just how Hansberry's career would have developed had she lived, but her gifts were so remarkable that we can only lament that she is not writing for the stage today.

A Raisin in the Sun

When it was produced on Broadway in 1959, *A Raisin in the Sun* was somewhat prophetic. Lorraine Hansberry's themes of blacks pressing forward with legitimate demands and expressing interest in their African heritage were to become primary themes of black culture in the 1960s, 1970s, and, indeed, to this day. The title of her play is from a poem by Langston Hughes, one of the poets of the Harlem Renaissance. It warns of the social explosions that might occur if society permits blacks to remain unequal and unfree.

The play appeared at the beginning of renewed political activity on the part of blacks, and it reveals its historical position in the use of the word *Negro*, which black activists rejected in the 1960s as an enslaving euphemism. In a way, the term was used at the time out of the same politeness that asked blacks to understand the feelings of whites who did not want to share their neighborhoods with them.

This play illustrates the American dream as it is felt not just by blacks but by all Americans: If you work hard and save your money, if you hold to the proper values and hope, then you can one day buy your own home and have the kind of space and privacy that permit people to live with dignity. Yet this very theme has plagued the play from the beginning: its apparent emphasis on middle-class, bourgeois values. On the surface, it seems to celebrate a mild form of consumerism — the desire for the little house in the suburbs with the TV set inside to anesthetize its occupants. Hansberry was shocked when such criticisms, from black critics as well as white, were leveled against the play. She had written it very carefully to explore just those issues, but in a context that demonstrated that black families' needs paralleled white families' while also having a different dimension that most white families could not understand.

Hansberry was quick to admit that Walter Lee Younger was affected by the same craziness that affected all Americans who lusted after possessions and the power they might confer. Walter wants to take his father's insurance money and buy a liquor store, which he plans to do in partnership with a con man. Lena Younger argues against her son's plan as a profanation of her husband's memory as well as an abuse of the American dream: She believes that the product of a liquor store will further poison the community. What she wants is not a consumer product. She wants the emblem of identity and security that she feels her family deserves.

Hansberry is painfully honest in this play. Walter Lee's weaknesses are recognizable. His black male chauvinistic behavior undoes him. He is caught up in the old, failing pattern of male dominance over women. But none of the women in his life will tolerate his behavior. Hansberry also admits of the social distinctions between blacks. George Murchison is a young man from a wealthy black family, and when Beneatha tells Lena that she will not marry George, she says, "The only people in the world who are more snobbish than rich white people are rich colored people." Beneatha's desire to be a doctor is obviously not rooted in consumerism any more than in the middle-class need to be comfortable and rich.

The confusion in the family when the African Asagai enters is realistically portrayed. In the early days of the Pan-African movement in the 1960s, blacks were often bemused by the way Africans presented themselves. Interest in Africa on the part of the American blacks was distorted by Tarzan movies and National Geographic ethnographic studies, none of which presented black Africans as role models. Therefore, the adjustment to black African pride — while made swiftly — was not made without difficulties. The Youngers are presented as no more sophisticated about black Africans than the rest of black society.

The pride of the Younger family finally triumphs. When Walter Lee stands up for himself, he is not asserting his macho domination. He is asserting black manhood — a manhood that needs no domination over women. He is not expressing a desire for a big house — as he had done when he reflected on the possessions of his rich employer — but a desire to demonstrate to the Clybourne Park Improvement Association that the Youngers are not socially inferior and that they have a right to live wherever they choose.

A Raisin in the Sun in Performance

Lloyd Richards directed the first production at the Ethel Barrymore Theater in New York on March 11, 1959. The play won major prizes, and Sidney Poitier as a passionate Walter Lee Younger was a signal success. *New York Times* critic Brooks Atkinson said, "Since the performance is also honest and since Sidney Poitier is a candid actor, *A Raisin in the Sun* has vigor as well as veracity and is likely to destroy the complacency of any one who sees it." Critics were astonished that a first play could have the sophistication and depth they saw onstage.

The Theater Guild produced the play in 1960 in Boston with a different cast but with similar reviews. The film version, with most of the New York cast, was directed by Daniel Petrie in 1961. A revival in Chicago in 1983 at the Art Institute of Chicago — Hansberry's alma mater — was not altogether successful, but critics felt the text held up well. The Chicago revival, like the 1985 Merrimack Repertory Theater revival in Lowell, Massachusetts, demonstrated only that the play needs strong actors to have the desired impact. A twenty-fifth anniversary production was directed by Lloyd Richards at the Yale Repertory Theatre in 1983. The setting was a realistic interior, emphasizing the play's realistic style. Critic Mel Gussow felt the revival demonstrated that the play is "an enduring work of contemporary theater." The production also revealed that Hansberry's language had not become dated, nor had the social issues of the play become any less critical and important for the lapse of twenty-five years. Like the proletarian plays of Sean O'Casey, who inspired Lorraine Hansberry, this play continues to move us because its problems are serious and still with us.

Lorraine Hansberry (*1930–1965*)

A RAISIN IN THE SUN   *1959*

Harlem (A Dream Deferred)

What happens to a dream deferred?

> *Does it dry up*
> *like a raisin in the sun?*
> *Or fester like a sore —*
> *And then run?*
> *Does it stink like rotten meat?*

Or crust and sugar over —
like a syrupy sweet?

Maybe it just sags
like a heavy load.

Or does it explode?   — LANGSTON HUGHES

Characters

RUTH YOUNGER
TRAVIS YOUNGER
WALTER LEE YOUNGER (*brother*)
BENEATHA YOUNGER
LENA YOUNGER (*Mama*)
JOSEPH ASAGAI
GEORGE MURCHISON
MRS. JOHNSON

KARL LINDNER
BOBO
MOVING MEN

The action of the play is set in Chicago's Southside, sometime between World War II and the present.

Act I
Scene I: *Friday morning.*
Scene II: *The following morning.*

Act II

Scene I: *Later, the same day.*
Scene II: *Friday night, a few weeks later.*
Scene III: *Moving day, one week later.*

Act III

An hour later.

ACT I • *Scene I*

(*The Younger living room would be a comfortable and well-ordered room if it were not for a number of indestructible contradictions to this state of being. Its furnishings are typical and undistinguished and their primary feature now is that they have clearly had to accommodate the living of too many people for too many years — and they are tired. Still, we can see that at some time, a time probably no longer remembered by the family [except perhaps for Mama], the furnishings of this room were actually selected with care and love and even hope — and brought to this apartment and arranged with taste and pride.*)

(*That was a long time ago. Now the once loved pattern of the couch upholstery has to fight to show itself from under acres of crocheted doilies and couch covers which have themselves finally come to be more important than the upholstery. And here a table or a chair has been moved to disguise the worn places in the carpet; but the carpet has fought back by showing its weariness, with depressing uniformity, elsewhere on its surface.*)

(*Weariness has, in fact, won in this room. Everything has been polished, washed, sat on, used, scrubbed too often. All pretenses but living itself have long since vanished from the very atmosphere of this room.*)

(*Moreover, a section of this room, for it is not really a room unto itself, though the landlord's lease would make it seem so, slopes backward to provide a small kitchen area, where the family prepares the meals that are eaten in the living room proper, which must also serve as dining room. The single window that has been provided for these "two" rooms is located in this kitchen area. The sole natural light the family may enjoy in the course of a day is only that which fights its way through this little window.*)

(*At left, a door leads to a bedroom which is shared by Mama and her daughter, Beneatha. At right, opposite, is a second room [which in the beginning of the life of this apartment was probably a breakfast room] which serves as a bedroom for Walter and his wife, Ruth.*)

(*Time: Sometime between World War II and the present.*)

(*Place: Chicago's Southside.*)

(*At rise: It is morning dark in the living room. Travis is asleep on the make-down bed at center. An alarm clock sounds from within the bedroom at right, and presently Ruth enters from that room and closes the door behind her. She crosses sleepily toward the window. As she passes her sleeping son she reaches down and shakes him a little. At the window she raises the shade and a dusky Southside morning light comes in feebly. She fills a pot with water and puts it on to boil. She calls to the boy, between yawns, in a slightly muffled voice.*)

(*Ruth is about thirty. We can see that she was a pretty girl, even exceptionally so, but now it is apparent that life has been little that she expected, and disappointment has already begun to hang in her face. In a few years, before thirty-five even, she will be known among her people as a "settled woman."*)

(*She crosses to her son and gives him a good, final, rousing shake.*)

RUTH: Come on now, boy, it's seven thirty! (*Her son sits up at last, in a stupor of sleepiness.*) I say hurry up, Travis! You ain't the only person in the world got to use a bathroom! (*The child, a sturdy, handsome little boy of ten or eleven, drags himself out of the bed and almost blindly takes his towels and "today's clothes" from drawers and a closet and goes out to the bathroom, which is in an outside hall and which is shared by another family or families on the same floor. Ruth crosses to the bedroom door at right and opens it and calls in to her husband.*) Walter Lee! ... It's after seven thirty! Lemme see you do some waking up in there now! (*She waits.*) You better get up from there, man! It's after seven thirty I tell you. (*She waits again.*) All right, you just go ahead and lay there and next thing you know Travis be finished and Mr. Johnson'll be in there and you'll be fussing and cussing round here like a madman! And be late too! (*She waits, at the end of patience.*) Walter Lee — it's time for you to GET UP!

(*She waits another second and then starts to go into the bedroom, but is apparently satisfied that her husband has begun to get up. She stops, pulls the door to, and returns to the kitchen area. She wipes her face with a moist cloth and runs her fingers through her sleep-disheveled hair in a vain effort and ties an apron around her housecoat. The bedroom door at right opens and her husband stands in the doorway in his pajamas, which are rumpled and mismated. He is a lean, intense young man in his middle thirties, inclined to quick nervous movements and erratic speech habits — and always in his voice there is a quality of indictment.*)

WALTER: Is he out yet?

RUTH: What you mean *out?* He ain't hardly got in there good yet.

WALTER (*wandering in, still more oriented to sleep than to a new day*): Well, what was you doing all that yelling for if I can't even get in there yet? (*Stopping and thinking.*) Check coming today?

RUTH: They *said* Saturday and this is just Friday and I hopes to God you ain't going to get up here first thing this morning and start talking to me 'bout no money — 'cause I 'bout don't want to hear it.

WALTER: Something the matter with you this morning?

RUTH: No — I'm just sleepy as the devil. What kind of eggs you want?

WALTER: Not scrambled. (*Ruth starts to scramble eggs.*) Paper come? (*Ruth points impatiently to the rolled up Tribune on the table, and he gets it and spreads it out and vaguely reads the front page.*) Set off another bomb yesterday.

RUTH (*maximum indifference*): Did they?

WALTER (*looking up*): What's the matter with you?

RUTH: Ain't nothing the matter with me. And don't keep asking me that this morning.

WALTER: Ain't nobody bothering you. (*Reading the news of the day absently again.*) Say Colonel McCormick is sick.

RUTH (*affecting tea-party interest*): Is he now? Poor thing.

WALTER (*sighing and looking at his watch*): Oh, me. (*He waits.*) Now what is that boy doing in that bathroom all this time? He just going to have to start getting up earlier. I can't be being late to work on account of him fooling around in there.

RUTH (*turning on him*): Oh, no he ain't going to be getting up no earlier no such thing! It ain't his fault that he can't get to bed no earlier nights 'cause he got a bunch of crazy good-for-nothing clowns sitting up running their mouths in what is supposed to be his bedroom after ten o'clock at night . . .

WALTER: That's what you mad about, ain't it? The things I want to talk about with my friends just couldn't be important in your mind, could they?

(*He rises and finds a cigarette in her handbag on the table and crosses to the little window and looks out, smoking and deeply enjoying this first one.*)

RUTH (*almost matter of factly, a complaint too automatic to deserve emphasis*): Why you always got to smoke before you eat in the morning?

WALTER (*at the window*): Just look at 'em down there . . . Running and racing to work . . . (*He turns and faces his wife and watches her a moment at the stove, and then, suddenly.*) You look young this morning, baby.

RUTH (*indifferently*): Yeah?

WALTER: Just for a second — stirring them eggs. Just for a second it was — you looked real young again. (*He reaches for her; she crosses away. Then, drily.*) It's gone now — you look like yourself again!

RUTH: Man, if you don't shut up and leave me alone.

WALTER (*looking out to the street again*): First thing a man ought to learn in life is not to make love to no colored woman first thing in the morning. You all some eeeevil people at eight o'clock in the morning.

(*Travis appears in the hall doorway, almost fully dressed and quite wide awake now, his towels and pajamas across his shoulders. He opens the door and signals for his father to make the bathroom in a hurry.*)

TRAVIS (*watching the bathroom*): Daddy, come on!

(*Walter gets his bathroom utensils and flies out to the bathroom.*)

RUTH: Sit down and have your breakfast, Travis.

TRAVIS: Mama, this is Friday. (*Gleefully.*) Check coming tomorrow, huh?

RUTH: You get your mind off money and eat your breakfast.

TRAVIS (*eating*): This is the morning we supposed to bring the fifty cents to school.

RUTH: Well, I ain't got no fifty cents this morning.

TRAVIS: Teacher say we have to.

RUTH: I don't care what teacher say. I ain't got it. Eat your breakfast, Travis.

TRAVIS: I *am* eating.

RUTH: Hush up now and just eat!

(*The boy gives her an exasperated look for her lack of understanding and eats grudgingly.*)

TRAVIS: You think Grandmama would have it?

RUTH: No! And I want you to stop asking your grandmother for money, you hear me?

TRAVIS (*outraged*): Gaaaleee! I don't ask her, she just gimme it sometimes!

RUTH: Travis Willard Younger — I got too much on me this morning to be —

TRAVIS: Maybe Daddy —

RUTH: *Travis!*

(*The boy hushes abruptly. They are both quiet and tense for several seconds.*)

TRAVIS (*presently*): Could I maybe go carry some groceries in front of the supermarket for a little while after school then?

RUTH: Just hush, I said. (*Travis jabs his spoon into his cereal bowl viciously and rests his head in anger upon his fists.*) If you through eating, you can get over there and make up your bed.

(*The boy obeys stiffly and crosses the room, almost mechanically, to the bed and more or less folds the bedding into a heap, then angrily gets his books and cap.*)

TRAVIS (*sulking and standing apart from her unnaturally*): I'm gone.

RUTH (*looking up from the stove to inspect him automatically*): Come here. (*He crosses to her and she studies his head.*) If you don't take this comb and fix this here head, you better! (*Travis puts down his books with a great sigh of oppression and crosses to the mirror. His mother mutters under her breath about his "slubbornness."*) 'Bout to march out of here with that head looking just like chickens slept in it! I just don't know where you get your slubborn ways . . . And get your jacket, too. Looks chilly out this morning.

TRAVIS (*with conspicuously brushed hair and jacket*): I'm gone.

RUTH: Get carfare and milk money — (*waving one finger*) — and not a single penny for no caps, you hear me?

TRAVIS (*with sullen politeness*): Yes'm.

(*He turns in outrage to leave. His mother watches after him as in his frustration he approaches the door almost comically. When she speaks to him, her voice has become a very gentle tease.*)

RUTH (*mocking; as she thinks he would say it*): Oh, Mama makes me so mad sometimes, I don't know what to do! (*She waits and continues to his back as he stands stock-still in front of the door.*) I wouldn't kiss that woman good-bye for nothing in this world this morning! (*The boy finally turns around and rolls his eyes at her, knowing the mood has changed and he is vindicated; he does not, however, move toward her yet.*) Not for nothing in this world! (*She finally laughs aloud at him and holds out her arms to him and we see that it is a way between them, very old and practiced. He crosses to her and allows her to embrace him warmly but keeps his face fixed with masculine rigidity. She holds him back from her presently and looks at him and runs her fingers over the features of his face. With utter gentleness —*) Now — whose little old angry man are you?

TRAVIS (*the masculinity and gruffness start to fade at last*): Aw gaalee — Mama . . .

RUTH (*mimicking*): Aw — gaaaaalleeeee, Mama! (*She pushes him, with rough playfulness and finality, toward the door.*) Get on out of here or you going to be late.

TRAVIS (*in the face of love, new aggressiveness*): Mama, could I *please* go carry groceries?

RUTH: Honey, it's starting to get so cold evenings.

WALTER (*coming in from the bathroom and drawing a make-believe gun from a make-believe holster and shooting at his son*): What is it he wants to do?

RUTH: Go carry groceries after school at the supermarket.

WALTER: Well, let him go . . .

TRAVIS (*quickly, to the ally*): I have to — she won't gimme the fifty cents . . .

WALTER (*to his wife only*): Why not?

RUTH (*simply, and with flavor*): 'Cause we don't have it.

WALTER (*to Ruth only*): What you tell the boy things like that for? (*Reaching down into his pants with a rather important gesture.*) Here, son —

(*He hands the boy the coin, but his eyes are directed to his wife's. Travis takes the money happily.*)

TRAVIS: Thanks, Daddy.

(*He starts out. Ruth watches both of them with murder in her eyes. Walter stands and stares back at her with defiance and suddenly reaches into his pocket again on an afterthought.*)

WALTER (*without even looking at his son, still staring hard at his wife*): In fact, here's another fifty cents . . . Buy yourself some fruit today — or take a taxicab to school or something!

TRAVIS: Whoopee —

(*He leaps up and clasps his father around the middle with his legs, and they face each other in mutual appreciation; slowly Walter Lee peeks around the boy to catch the violent rays from his wife's eyes and draws his head back as if shot.*)

WALTER: You better get down now — and get to school, man.

TRAVIS (*at the door*): O.K. Good-bye.

(*He exits.*)

WALTER (*after him, pointing with pride*): That's *my* boy. (*She looks at him in disgust and turns back to her work.*) You know what I was thinking 'bout in the bathroom this morning?

RUTH: No.

WALTER: How come you always try to be so pleasant!

RUTH: What is there to be pleasant 'bout!

WALTER: You want to know what I was thinking 'bout in the bathroom or not!

RUTH: I know what you thinking 'bout.

WALTER (*ignoring her*): 'Bout what me and Willy Harris was talking about last night.

RUTH (*immediately — a refrain*): Willy Harris is a good-for-nothing loudmouth.

WALTER: Anybody who talks to me has got to be a good-for-nothing loudmouth, ain't he? And what you know about who is just a good-for-nothing loudmouth? Charlie Atkins was just a "good-for-nothing loudmouth" too, wasn't he! When he wanted me to go in the dry-cleaning business with him. And now — he's grossing a hundred thousand a year. A hundred thousand dollars a year! You still call *him* a loudmouth!

RUTH (*bitterly*): Oh, Walter Lee . . .

(*She folds her head on her arms over the table.*)

WALTER (*rising and coming to her and standing over her*): You tired, ain't you? Tired of everything. Me, the boy, the way we live — this beat-up hole — everything. Ain't you? (*She doesn't look up, doesn't answer.*) So tired — moaning and groaning all the time, but you wouldn't do nothing to help, would you? You couldn't be on my side that long for nothing, could you?

RUTH: Walter, please leave me alone.

WALTER: A man needs for a woman to back him up . . .

RUTH: Walter —

WALTER: Mama would listen to you. You know she listen to you more than she do me and Bennie. She think more of you. All you have to do is just sit down with her when you drinking your coffee one morning and talking 'bout things like you do and — (*He sits down beside her and demonstrates graphically what he thinks her methods and tone shoud be.*) — you just sip your coffee, see, and say easy like that you been thinking 'bout that deal Walter Lee is so interested in, 'bout the store and all, and sip some more coffee, like what you saying ain't really that important to you — And the next thing you know, she be listening good and asking you questions and when I come home — I can tell her the details. This ain't no fly-by-night proposition, baby. I mean we figured it out, me and Willy and Bobo.

RUTH (*with a frown*): Bobo?

WALTER: Yeah. You see, this little liquor store we got in mind cost seventy-five thousand and we figured the initial investment on the place be 'bout thirty thousand, see. That be ten thousand each. Course, there's a couple of hundred you got to pay so's you don't spend your life just waiting for them clowns to let your license get approved —

RUTH: You mean graft?

WALTER (*frowning impatiently*): Don't call it that. See there, that just goes to show you what women understand about the world. Baby, don't *nothing* happen for you in this world 'less you pay *some-body* off!

RUTH: Walter, leave me alone! (*She raises her head and stares at him vigorously — then says, more quietly.*) Eat your eggs, they gonna be cold.

WALTER (*straightening up from her and looking off*): That's it. There you are. Man say to his woman: I got me a dream. His woman say: Eat your eggs. (*Sadly, but gaining in power.*) Man say: I got to take hold of this here world, baby! And a woman will say: Eat your eggs and go to work. (*Passionately now.*) Man say: I got to change my life, I'm choking to death, baby! And his woman say — (*in utter anguish as he brings his fists down on his thighs*) — Your eggs is getting cold!

RUTH (*softly*): Walter, that ain't none of our money.

WALTER (*not listening at all or even looking at her*): This morning, I was lookin' in the mirror and thinking about it . . . I'm thirty-five years old; I been married eleven years and I got a boy who sleeps in the living room — (*very, very quietly*) — and all I got to give him is stories about how rich white people live . . .

RUTH: Eat your eggs, Walter.

WALTER (*slams the table and jumps up*): — DAMN MY EGGS — DAMN ALL THE EGGS THAT EVER WAS!

RUTH: Then go to work.

WALTER (*looking up at her*): See — I'm trying to talk to you 'bout myself — (*shaking his head with the repetition*) — and all you can say is eat them eggs and go to work.

RUTH (*wearily*): Honey, you never say nothing new. I listen to you every day, every night and every morning, and you never say nothing new. (*Shrugging.*) So you would rather *be* Mr. Arnold than his chauffeur. So — I would *rather* be living in Buckingham Palace.

WALTER: That is just what is wrong with the colored woman in this world . . . Don't understand about building their men up and making 'em feel like they somebody. Like they can do something.

RUTH (*drily, but to hurt*): There *are* colored men who do things.

WALTER: No thanks to the colored woman.

RUTH: Well, being a colored woman, I guess I can't help myself none.

(*She rises and gets the ironing board and sets it up and attacks a huge pile of rough-dried clothes, sprinkling them in preparation for the ironing and then rolling them into tight fat balls.*)

WALTER (*mumbling*): We one group of men tied to a race of women with small minds!

(*His sister Beneatha enters. She is about twenty, as slim and intense as her brother. She is not as pretty as her sister-in-law, but her lean, almost intellectual*) *face has a handsomeness of its own. She wears a bright red flannel nightie, and her thick hair stands wildly about her head. Her speech is a mixture of many things; it is different from the rest of the family's insofar as education has permeated her sense of English — and perhaps the Midwest rather than the South has finally — at last — won out in her inflection; but not altogether, because over all of it is a soft slurring and transformed use of vowels which is the decided influence of the Southside. She passes through the room without looking at either Ruth or Walter and goes to the outside door and looks, a little blindly, out to the bathroom. She sees that it has been lost to the Johnsons. She closes the door with a sleepy vengeance and crosses to the table and sits down a little defeated.)*

BENEATHA: I am going to start timing those people.

WALTER: You should get up earlier.

BENEATHA (*Her face in her hands. She is still fighting the urge to go back to bed.*): Really — would you suggest dawn? Where's the paper?

WALTER (*pushing the paper across the table to her as he studies her almost clinically, as though he has never seen her before*): You a horrible-looking chick at this hour.

BENEATHA (*drily*): Good morning, everybody.

WALTER (*senselessly*): How is school coming?

BENEATHA (*in the same spirit*): Lovely. Lovely. And you know, biology is the greatest. (*Looking up at him.*) I dissected something that looked just like you yesterday.

WALTER: I just wondered if you've made up your mind and everything.

BENEATHA (*gaining in sharpness and impatience*): And what did I answer yesterday morning — and the day before that?

RUTH (*from the ironing board, like someone disinterested and old*): Don't be so nasty, Bennie.

BENEATHA (*still to her brother*): And the day before that and the day before that!

WALTER (*defensively*): I'm interested in you. Something wrong with that? Ain't many girls who decide —

WALTER AND BENEATHA (*in unison*): — "to be a doctor."

(*Silence.*)

WALTER: Have we figured out yet just exactly how much medical school is going to cost?

RUTH: Walter Lee, why don't you leave that girl alone and get out of here to work?

BENEATHA (*exits to the bathroom and bangs on the door*): Come on out of there, please!

(*She comes back into the room.*)

WALTER (*looking at his sister intently*): You know the check is coming tomorrow.

BENEATHA (*turning on him with a sharpness all her own*): That money belongs to Mama, Walter, and it's for her to decide how she wants to use it. I don't care if she wants to buy a house or a rocket-ship or just nail it up somewhere and look at it. It's hers. Not ours — *hers.*

WALTER (*bitterly*): Now ain't that fine! You just got your mother's interest at heart, ain't you, girl? You such a nice girl — but if Mama got that money she can always take a few thousand and help you through school too — can't she?

BENEATHA: I have never asked anyone around here to do anything for me!

WALTER: No! And the line between asking and just accepting when the time comes is big and wide — ain't it!

BENEATHA (*with fury*): What do you want from me, Brother — that I quit school or just drop dead, which!

WALTER: I don't want nothing but for you to stop acting holy 'round here. Me and Ruth done made some sacrifices for you — why can't you do something for the family?

RUTH: Walter, don't be dragging me in it.

WALTER: You are in it — Don't you get up and go work in somebody's kitchen for the last three years to help put clothes on her back?

RUTH: Oh, Walter — that's not fair . . .

WALTER: It ain't that nobody expects you to get on your knees and say thank you, Brother; thank you, Ruth; thank you, Mama — and thank you, Travis, for wearing the same pair of shoes for two semesters —

BENEATHA (*dropping to her knees*): Well — I *do* — all right? — thank everybody! And forgive me for ever wanting to be anything at all! (*Pursuing him on her knees across the floor.*) FORGIVE ME, FORGIVE ME, FORGIVE ME!

RUTH: Please stop it! Your mama'll hear you.

WALTER: Who the hell told you you had to be a doctor? If you so crazy 'bout messing 'round with sick people — then go be a nurse like other women — or just get married and be quiet . . .

BENEATHA: Well — you finally got it said . . . It took you three years but you finally got it said. Walter, give up; leave me alone — it's Mama's money.

WALTER: *He was my father, too!*

BENEATHA: So what? He was mine, too — and Travis' grandfather — but the insurance money belongs to Mama. Picking on me is not going to make her give it to you to invest in any liquor stores — (*under breath, dropping into a chair*) — and I for one say, God bless Mama for that!

WALTER (*to Ruth*): See — did you hear? Did you hear!

RUTH: Honey, please go to work.

WALTER: Nobody in this house is ever going to understand me.

BENEATHA: Because you're a nut.

WALTER: Who's a nut?

BENEATHA: You — you are a nut. Thee is mad, boy.

WALTER (*looking at his wife and his sister from the door, very sadly*): The world's most backward race of people, and that's a fact.

BENEATHA (*turning slowly in her chair*): And then there are all those prophets who would lead us out of the wilderness — (*Walter slams out of the house*) — into the swamps!

RUTH: Bennie, why you always gotta be pickin' on your brother? Can't you be a little sweeter sometimes? (*Door opens. Walter walks in. He fumbles with his cap, starts to speak, clears throat, looks everywhere but at Ruth. Finally.*)

WALTER (*to Ruth*): I need some money for carfare.

RUTH (*looks at him, then warms; teasing, but tenderly*): Fifty cents? (*She goes to her bag and gets money.*) Here — take a taxi!

(*Walter exits. Mama enters. She is a woman in her early sixties, full-bodied and strong. She is one of those women of a certain grace and beauty who wear it so unobtrusively that it takes a while to notice. Her dark brown face is surrounded by the total whiteness of her hair, and, being a woman who has adjusted to many things in life and overcome many more, her face is full of strength. She has, we can see, wit and faith of a kind that keep her eyes lit and full of interest and expectancy. She is, in a word, a beautiful woman. Her bearing is perhaps most like the noble bearing of the women of the Hereros of Southwest Africa — rather as if she imagines that as she walks she still bears a basket or a vessel upon her head. Her speech, on the other hand, is as careless as her carriage is precise — she is inclined to slur everything — but her voice is perhaps not so much quiet as simply soft.*)

MAMA: Who that 'round here slamming doors at this hour?

(*She crosses through the room, goes to the window, opens it, and brings in a feeble little plant growing doggedly in a small pot on the window sill. She feels the dirt and puts it back out.*)

RUTH: That was Walter Lee. He and Bennie was at it again.

MAMA: My children and they tempers. Lord, if this little old plant don't get more sun than it's been getting it ain't never going to see spring again. (*She turns from the window.*) What's the matter with

you this morning, Ruth? You looks right peaked. You aiming to iron all them things? Leave some for me. I'll get to 'em this afternoon. Bennie honey, it's too drafty for you to be sitting 'round half dressed. Where's your robe?

BENEATHA: In the cleaners.

MAMA: Well, go get mine and put it on.

BENEATHA: I'm not cold, Mama, honest.

MAMA: I know — but you so thin . . .

BENEATHA (*irritably*): Mama, I'm not cold.

MAMA (*seeing the make-down bed as Travis has left it*): Lord have mercy, look at that poor bed. Bless his heart — he tries, don't he?

(*She moves to the bed Travis has sloppily made up.*)

RUTH: No — he don't half try at all 'cause he knows you going to come along behind him and fix everything. That's just how come he don't know how to do nothing right now — you done spoiled that boy so.

MAMA (*folding bedding*): Well — he's a little boy. Ain't supposed to know 'bout housekeeping. My baby, that's what he is. What you fix for his breakfast this morning?

RUTH (*angrily*): I feed my son, Lena!

MAMA: I ain't meddling — (*Under breath; busybody-ish.*) I just noticed all last week he had cold cereal, and when it starts getting this chilly in the fall a child ought to have some hot grits or something when he goes out in the cold —

RUTH (*furious*): I gave him hot oats — is that all right!

MAMA: I ain't meddling. (*Pause.*) Put a lot of nice butter on it? (*Ruth shoots her an angry look and does not reply.*) He likes lots of butter.

RUTH (*exasperated*): Lena —

MAMA (*To Beneatha. Mama is inclined to wander conversationally sometimes.*): What was you and your brother fussing 'bout this morning?

BENEATHA: It's not important, Mama.

(*She gets up and goes to look out at the bathroom, which is apparently free, and she picks up her towels and rushes out.*)

MAMA: What was they fighting about?

RUTH: Now you know as well as I do.

MAMA (*shaking her head*): Brother still worrying hisself sick about that money?

RUTH: You know he is.

MAMA: You had breakfast?

RUTH: Some coffee.

MAMA: Girl, you better start eating and looking after yourself better. You almost thin as Travis.

RUTH: Lena —

MAMA: Un-hunh?

RUTH: What are you going to do with it?

MAMA: Now don't you start, child. It's too early in the morning to be talking about money. It ain't Christian.

RUTH: It's just that he got his heart set on that store —

MAMA: You mean that liquor store that Willy Harris want him to invest in?

RUTH: Yes —

MAMA: We ain't no business people, Ruth. We just plain working folks.

RUTH: Ain't nobody business people till they go into business. Walter Lee say colored people ain't never going to start getting ahead till they start gambling on some different kinds of things in the world — investments and things.

MAMA: What done got into you, girl? Walter Lee done finally sold you on investing.

RUTH: No. Mama, something is happening between Walter and me. I don't know what it is — but he needs something — something I can't give him anymore. He needs this chance, Lena.

MAMA (*frowning deeply*): But liquor, honey —

RUTH: Well — like Walter say — I spec people going to always be drinking themselves some liquor —

MAMA: Well — whether they drinks it or not ain't none of my business. But whether I go into business selling it to 'em *is*, and I don't want that on my ledger this late in life. (*Stopping suddenly and studying her daughter-in-law.*) Ruth Younger, what's the matter with you today? You look like you could fall over right there.

RUTH: I'm tired.

MAMA: Then you better stay home from work today.

RUTH: I can't stay home. She'd be calling up the agency and screaming at them, "My girl didn't come in today — send me somebody! My girl didn't come in!" Oh, she just have a fit . . .

MAMA: Well, let her have it. I'll just call her up and say you got the flu —

RUTH (*laughing*): Why the flu?

MAMA: 'Cause it sounds respectable to 'em. Something white people get, too. They know 'bout the flu. Otherwise they think you been cut up or something when you tell 'em you sick.

RUTH: I got to go in. We need the money.

MAMA: Somebody would of thought my children done all but starved to death the way they talk about money here late. Child, we got a great big old check coming tomorrow.

RUTH (*sincerely, but also self-righteously*): Now that's your money. It ain't got nothing to do with me. We all feel like that — Walter and Bennie and me — even Travis.

MAMA (*thoughtfully, and suddenly very far away*): Ten thousand dollars —

RUTH: Sure is wonderful.

MAMA: Ten thousand dollars.

RUTH: You know what you should do, Miss Lena? You should take yourself a trip somewhere. To Europe or South America or someplace —

MAMA (*throwing up her hands at the thought*): Oh, child!

RUTH: I'm serious. Just pack up and leave! Go on away and enjoy yourself some. Forget about the family and have yourself a ball for once in your life —

MAMA (*drily*): You sound like I'm just about ready to die. Who'd go with me? What I look like wandering 'round Europe by myself?

RUTH: Shoot — these here rich white women do it all the time. They don't think nothing of packing up they suitcases and piling on one of them big steamships and — swoosh! — they gone, child.

MAMA: Something always told me I wasn't no rich white woman.

RUTH: Well — what are you going to do with it then?

MAMA: I ain't rightly decided. (*Thinking. She speaks now with emphasis.*) Some of it got to be put away for Beneatha and her schoolin' — and ain't nothing going to touch that part of it. Nothing. (*She waits several seconds, trying to make up her mind about something, and looks at Ruth a little tentatively before going on.*) Been thinking that we maybe could meet the notes on a little old two-story somewhere, with a yard where Travis could play in the summertime, if we use part of the insurance for a down payment and everybody kind of pitch in. I could maybe take on a little day work again, few days a week —

RUTH (*studying her mother-in-law furtively and concentrating on her ironing, anxious to encourage without seeming to*): Well, Lord knows, we've put enough rent into this here rat trap to pay for four houses by now . . .

MAMA (*looking up at the words "rat trap" and then looking around and leaning back and sighing — in a suddenly reflective mood —*): "Rat trap" — yes, that's all it is. (*Smiling.*) I remember just as well the day me and Big Walter moved in here. Hadn't been married but two weeks and wasn't planning on living here no more than a year. (*She shakes her head at the dissolved dream.*) We was going to set away, little by little, don't you know, and buy a little place out in Morgan Park. We had even picked out the house. (*Chuckling a little.*) Looks right dumpy today. But Lord, child, you should know all the dreams I had 'bout buying that house and fixing it up and making me a little garden in the back — (*She waits and stops smiling.*) And didn't none of it happen.

(*Dropping her hands in a futile gesture.*)

RUTH (*keeps her head down, ironing*): Yes, life can be a barrel of disappointments, sometimes.

MAMA: Honey, Big Walter would come in here some nights back then and slump down on that couch there and just look at the rug, and look at me and look at the rug and then back at me — and I'd know he was down then . . . really down. (*After a second very long and thoughtful pause; she is seeing back to times that only she can see.*) And then, Lord, when I lost that baby — little Claude — I almost thought I was going to lose Big Walter too. Oh, that man grieved hisself! He was one man to love his children.

RUTH: Ain't nothin' can tear at you like losin' your baby.

MAMA: I guess that's how come that man finally worked hisself to death like he done. Like he was fighting his own war with this here world that took his baby from him.

RUTH: He sure was a fine man, all right. I always liked Mr. Younger.

MAMA: Crazy 'bout his children! God knows there was plenty wrong with Walter Younger — hard-headed, mean, kind of wild with women — plenty wrong with him. But he sure loved his children. Always wanted them to have something — be something. That's where Brother gets all these notions, I reckon. Big Walter used to say, he'd get right wet in the eyes sometimes, lean his head back with the water standing in his eyes and say, "Seem like God didn't see fit to give the black man nothing but dreams — but He did give us children to make them dreams seem worthwhile." (*She smiles.*) He could talk like that, don't you know.

RUTH: Yes, he sure could. He was a good man, Mr. Younger.

MAMA: Yes, a fine man — just couldn't never catch up with his dreams, that's all.

(*Beneatha comes in, brushing her hair and looking up to the ceiling, where the sound of a vacuum cleaner has started up.*)

BENEATHA: What could be so dirty on that woman's rugs that she has to vacuum them every single day?

RUTH: I wish certain young women 'round here who I could name would take inspiration about certain rugs in a certain apartment I could also mention.

BENEATHA (*shrugging*): How much cleaning can a house need, for Christ's sakes.

MAMA (*not liking the Lord's name used thus*): Bennie!

RUTH: Just listen to her — just listen!

BENEATHA: Oh, God!

MAMA: If you use the Lord's name just one more time —

BENEATHA (*a bit of a whine*): Oh, Mama —

RUTH: Fresh — just fresh as salt, this girl!

BENEATHA (*drily*): Well — if the salt loses its savor —

MAMA: Now that will do. I just ain't going to have you 'round here reciting the scriptures in vain — you hear me?

BENEATHA: How did I manage to get on everybody's wrong side by just walking into a room?

RUTH: If you weren't so fresh —

BENEATHA: Ruth, I'm twenty years old.

MAMA: What time you be home from school today?

BENEATHA: Kind of late. (*With enthusiasm.*) Madeline is going to start my guitar lessons today.

(*Mama and Ruth look up with the same expression.*)

MAMA: Your *what* kind of lessons?

BENEATHA: Guitar.

RUTH: Oh, Father!

MAMA: How come you done taken it in your mind to learn to play the guitar?

BENEATHA: I just want to, that's all.

MAMA (*smiling*): Lord, child, don't you know what to do with yourself? How long it going to be before you get tired of this now — like you got tired of that little play-acting group you joined last year? (*Looking at Ruth.*) And what was it the year before that?

RUTH: The horseback-riding club for which she bought that fifty-five-dollar riding habit that's been hanging in the closet ever since!

MAMA (*to Beneatha*): Why you got to flit so from one thing to another, baby?

BENEATHA (*sharply*): I just want to learn to play the guitar. Is there anything wrong with that?

MAMA: Ain't nobody trying to stop you. I just wonders sometimes why you has to flit so from one thing to another all the time. You ain't never done nothing with all that camera equipment you brought home —

BENEATHA: I don't flit! I — I experiment with different forms of expression —

RUTH: Like riding a horse?

BENEATHA: — People have to express themselves one way or another.

MAMA: What is it you want to express?

BENEATHA (*angrily*): Me! (*Mama and Ruth look at each other and burst into raucous laughter.*) Don't worry — I don't expect you to understand.

MAMA (*to change the subject*): Who you going out with tomorrow night?

BENEATHA (*with displeasure*): George Murchison again.

MAMA (*pleased*): Oh — you getting a little sweet on him?

RUTH: You ask me, this child ain't sweet on nobody but herself — (*Under breath.*) Express herself!

(*They laugh.*)

BENEATHA: Oh — I like George all right, Mama. I mean I like him enough to go out with him and stuff, but —

RUTH (*for devilment*): What does *and stuff* mean?

BENEATHA: Mind your own business.

MAMA: Stop picking at her now, Ruth. (*She chuckles — then a suspicious sudden look at her daughter as she turns in her chair for emphasis.*) What DOES it mean?

BENEATHA (*wearily*): Oh, I just mean I couldn't ever really be serious about George. He's — he's so shallow.

RUTH: Shallow — what do you mean he's shallow? He's *Rich!*

MAMA: Hush, Ruth.

BENEATHA: I know he's rich. He knows he's rich, too.

RUTH: Well — what other qualities a man got to have to satisfy you, little girl?

BENEATHA: You wouldn't even begin to understand. Anybody who married Walter could not possibly understand.

MAMA (*outraged*): What kind of way is that to talk about your brother?

BENEATHA: Brother is a flip — let's face it.

MAMA (*to Ruth, helplessly*): What's a flip?

RUTH (*glad to add kindling*): She's saying he's crazy.

BENEATHA: Not crazy. Brother isn't really crazy yet — he — he's an elaborate neurotic.

MAMA: Hush your mouth!

BENEATHA: As for George. Well. George looks good — he's got a beautiful car and he takes me to nice places and, as my sister-in-law says, he is probably the richest boy I will ever get to know and I even like him sometimes — but if the Youngers are sitting around waiting to see if their little Bennie is going to tie up the family with the Murchisons, they are wasting their time.

RUTH: You mean you wouldn't marry George Murchison if he asked you someday? That pretty, rich thing? Honey, I knew you was odd —

BENEATHA: No I would not marry him if all I felt for him was what I feel now. Besides, George's family wouldn't really like it.

MAMA: Why not?

BENEATHA: Oh, Mama — The Murchisons are honest-to-God-real-*live*-rich colored people, and the only people in the world who are more snobbish than rich white people are rich colored people. I thought everybody knew that. I've met Mrs. Murchison. She's a scene!

MAMA: You must not dislike people 'cause they well off, honey.

BENEATHA: Why not? It makes just as much sense as disliking people 'cause they are poor, and lots of people do that.

RUTH (*A wisdom-of-the-ages manner. To Mama.*): Well, she'll get over some of this —

BENEATHA: Get over it? What are you talking about, Ruth? Listen, I'm going to be a doctor. I'm not worried about who I'm going to marry yet — if I ever get married.

MAMA AND RUTH: *If!*

MAMA: Now, Bennie —

BENEATHA: Oh, I probably will . . . but first I'm going to be a doctor, and George, for one, still thinks that's pretty funny. I couldn't be bothered with that. I am going to be a doctor and everybody around here better understand that!

MAMA (*kindly*): 'Course you going to be a doctor, honey, God willing.

BENEATHA (*drily*): God hasn't got a thing to do with it.

MAMA: Beneatha — that just wasn't necessary.

BENEATHA: Well — neither is God. I get sick of hearing about God.

MAMA: Beneatha!

BENEATHA: I mean it! I'm just tired of hearing about God all the time. What has He got to do with anything? Does he pay tuition?

MAMA: You 'bout to get your fresh little jaw slapped!

RUTH: That's just what she needs, all right!

BENEATHA: Why? Why can't I say what I want to around here, like everybody else?

MAMA: It don't sound nice for a young girl to say things like that — you wasn't brought up that way. Me and your father went to trouble to get you and Brother to church every Sunday.

BENEATHA: Mama, you don't understand. It's all a matter of ideas, and God is just one idea I don't accept. It's not important. I am not going out and be immoral or commit crimes because I don't believe in God. I don't even think about it. It's just that I get tired of Him getting credit for all the things the human race achieves through its own stubborn effort. There simply is no blasted God — there is only man and it is *he* who makes miracles!

(*Mama absorbs this speech, studies her daughter and rises slowly and crosses to Beneatha and slaps her powerfully across the face. After, there is only silence and the daughter drops her eyes from her mother's face, and Mama is very tall before her.*)

MAMA: Now — you say after me, in my mother's

house there is still God. (*There is a long pause and Beneatha stares at the floor wordlessly. Mama repeats the phrase with precision and cool emotion.*) In my mother's house there is still God.

BENEATHA: In my mother's house there is still God.

(*A long pause.*)

MAMA (*Walking away from Beneatha, too disturbed for triumphant posture. Stopping and turning back to her daughter.*): There are some ideas we ain't going to have in this house. Not long as I am at the head of this family.

BENEATHA: Yes, ma'am.

(*Mama walks out of the room.*)

RUTH (*almost gently, with profound understanding*): You think you a woman, Bennie — but you still a little girl. What you did was childish — so you got treated like a child.

BENEATHA: I see. (*Quietly.*) I also see that everybody thinks it's all right for Mama to be a tyrant. But all the tyranny in the world will never put a God in the heavens!

(*She picks up her books and goes out. Pause.*)

RUTH (*goes to Mama's door*): She said she was sorry.

MAMA (*coming out, going to her plant*): They frightens me, Ruth. My children.

RUTH: You got good children, Lena. They just a little off sometimes — but they're good.

MAMA: No — there's something come down between me and them that don't let us understand each other and I don't know what it is. One done almost lost his mind thinking 'bout money all the time and the other done commence to talk about things I can't seem to understand in no form or fashion. What is it that's changing, Ruth.

RUTH (*soothingly, older than her years*): Now . . . you taking it all too seriously. You just got strong-willed children and it takes a strong woman like you to keep 'em in hand.

MAMA (*looking at her plant and sprinkling a little water on it*): They spirited all right, my children. Got to admit they got spirit — Bennie and Walter. Like this little old plant that ain't never had enough sunshine or nothing — and look at it . . .

(*She has her back to Ruth, who has had to stop ironing and lean against something and put the back of her hand to her forehead.*)

RUTH (*trying to keep Mama from noticing*): You . . . sure . . . loves that little old thing, don't you? . . .

MAMA: Well, I always wanted me a garden like I used to see sometimes at the back of the houses down home. This plant is close as I ever got to having

one. (*She looks out of the window as she replaces the plant.*) Lord, ain't nothing as dreary as the view from this window on a dreary day, is there? Why ain't you singing this morning, Ruth? Sing that "No Ways Tired." That song always lifts me up so — (*She turns at last to see that Ruth has slipped quietly to the floor, in a state of semiconsciousness.*) Ruth! Ruth honey — what's the matter with you . . . Ruth!

Scene II

(*It is the following morning; a Saturday morning, and house cleaning is in progress at the Youngers'. Furniture has been shoved hither and yon and Mama is giving the kitchen-area walls a washing down. Beneatha, in dungarees, with a handkerchief tied around her face, is spraying insecticide into the cracks in the walls. As they work, the radio is on and a Southside disk jockey program is inappropriately filling the house with a rather exotic saxophone blues. Travis, the sole idle one, is leaning on his arms, looking out of the window.*)

TRAVIS: Grandmama, that stuff Bennie is using smells awful. Can I go downstairs, please?

MAMA: Did you get all them chores done already? I ain't seen you doing much.

TRAVIS: Yes'm — finished early. Where did Mama go this morning?

MAMA (*looking at Beneatha*): She had to go on a little errand.

(*The phone rings. Beneatha runs to answer it and reaches it before Walter, who has entered from bedroom.*)

TRAVIS: Where?

MAMA: To tend to her business.

BENEATHA: Haylo . . . (*Disappointed.*) Yes, he is. (*She tosses the phone to Walter, who barely catches it.*) It's Willie Harris again.

WALTER (*as privately as possible under Mama's gaze*): Hello, Willie. Did you get the papers from the lawyer? . . . No, not yet. I told you the mailman doesn't get here till ten-thirty . . . No, I'll come there . . . Yeah! Right away. (*He hangs up and goes for his coat.*)

BENEATHA: Brother, where did Ruth go?

WALTER (*as he exits*): How should I know!

TRAVIS: Aw come on, Grandma. Can I go outside?

MAMA: Oh, I guess so. You stay right in front of the house, though, and keep a good lookout for the postman.

TRAVIS: Yes'm. (*He darts into bedroom for stickball*

and bat, reenters, and sees Beneatha on her knees spraying under sofa with behind upraised. He edges closer to the target, takes aim, and lets her have it. She screams.) Leave them poor little cockroaches alone, they ain't bothering you none! *(He runs as she swings the spraygun at him viciously and playfully.)* Grandma! Grandma!

MAMA: Look out there, girl, before you be spilling some of that stuff on that child!

TRAVIS *(safely behind the bastion of Mama)*: That's right — look out, now! *(He exits.)*

BENEATHA *(drily)*: I can't imagine that it would hurt him — it has never hurt the roaches.

MAMA: Well, little boys' hides ain't as tough as South-side roaches. You better get over there behind the bureau. I seen one marching out of there like Napoleon yesterday.

BENEATHA: There's really only one way to get rid of them, Mama —

MAMA: How?

BENEATHA: Set fire to this building! Mama, where did Ruth go?

MAMA *(looking at her with meaning)*: To the doctor, I think.

BENEATHA: The doctor? What's the matter? *(They exchange glances.)* You don't think —

MAMA *(with her sense of drama)*: Now I ain't saying what I think. But I ain't never been wrong 'bout a woman neither.

(The phone rings.)

BENEATHA *(at the phone)*: Hay-lo . . . *(Pause, and a moment of recognition.)* Well — when did you get back! . . . And how was it? . . . Of course I've missed you — in my way . . . This morning? No . . . house cleaning and all that and Mama hates it if I let people come over when the house is like this . . . You *have?* Well, that's different . . . What is it — Oh, what the hell, come on over . . . Right, see you then. *Arrivederci.*

(She hangs up.)

MAMA *(who has listened vigorously, as is her habit)*: Who is that you inviting over here with this house looking like this? You ain't got the pride you was born with!

BENEATHA: Asagai doesn't care how houses look, Mama — he's an intellectual.

MAMA: *Who?*

BENEATHA: Asagai — Joseph Asagai. He's an African boy I met on campus. He's been studying in Canada all summer.

MAMA: What's his name?

BENEATHA: Asagai, Joseph. Ah-sah-guy . . . He's from Nigeria.

MAMA: Oh, that's the little country that was founded by slaves way back . . .

BENEATHA: No, Mama — that's Liberia.

MAMA: I don't think I never met no African before.

BENEATHA: Well, do me a favor and don't ask him a whole lot of ignorant questions about Africans. I mean, do they wear clothes and all that —

MAMA: Well, now, I guess if you think we so ignorant 'round here maybe you shouldn't bring your friends here —

BENEATHA: It's just that people ask such crazy things. All anyone seems to know about when it comes to Africa is Tarzan.

MAMA *(indignantly)*: Why should I know anything about Africa?

BENEATHA: Why do you give money at church for the missionary work?

MAMA: Well, that's to help save people.

BENEATHA: You mean save them from *heathenism* —

MAMA *(innocently)*: Yes.

BENEATHA: I'm afraid they need more salvation from the British and the French.

(Ruth comes in forlornly and pulls off her coat with dejection. They both turn to look at her.)

RUTH *(dispiritedly)*: Well, I guess from all the happy faces — everybody knows.

BENEATHA: You pregnant?

MAMA: Lord have mercy, I sure hope it's a little old girl. Travis ought to have a sister.

(Beneatha and Ruth give her a hopeless look for this grandmotherly enthusiasm.)

BENEATHA: How far along are you?

RUTH: Two months.

BENEATHA: Did you mean to? I mean did you plan it or was it an accident?

MAMA: What do you know about planning or not planning?

BENEATHA: Oh, Mama.

RUTH *(wearily)*: She's twenty years old, Lena.

BENEATHA: Did you plan it, Ruth?

RUTH: Mind your own business.

BENEATHA: It is my business — where is he going to live, on the *roof?* *(There is silence following the remark as the three women react to the sense of it.)* Gee — I didn't mean that, Ruth, honest. Gee, I don't feel like that at all. I — I think it is wonderful.

RUTH *(dully)*: Wonderful.

BENEATHA: Yes — really.

MAMA *(looking at Ruth, worried)*: Doctor say everything going to be all right?

RUTH *(far away)*: Yes — she says everything is going to be fine . . .

MAMA (*immediately suspicious*): "She" — What doctor you went to?

(*Ruth folds over, near hysteria.*)

MAMA (*worriedly hovering over Ruth*): Ruth honey — what's the matter with you — you sick?

(*Ruth has her fists clenched on her thighs and is fighting hard to suppress a scream that seems to be rising in her.*)

BENEATHA: What's the matter with her, Mama?

MAMA (*working her fingers in Ruth's shoulders to relax her*): She be all right. Women gets right depressed sometimes when they get her way. (*Speaking softly, expertly, rapidly.*) Now you just relax. That's right . . . just lean back, don't think 'bout nothing at all . . . nothing at all —

RUTH: I'm all right . . .

(*The glassy-eyed look melts and then she collapses into a fit of heavy sobbing. The bell rings.*)

BENEATHA: Oh, my God — that must be Asagai.

MAMA (*to Ruth*): Come on now, honey. You need to lie down and rest awhile . . . then have some nice hot food.

(*They exit, Ruth's weight on her mother-in-law. Beneatha, herself profoundly disturbed, opens the door to admit a rather dramatic-looking young man with a large package.*)

ASAGAI: Hello, Alaiyo —

BENEATHA (*holding the door open and regarding him with pleasure*): Hello . . . (*Long pause.*) Well — come in. And please excuse everything. My mother was very upset about my letting anyone come here with the place like this.

ASAGAI (*coming into the room*): You look disturbed too . . . Is something wrong?

BENEATHA (*still at the door, absently*): Yes . . . we've all got acute ghetto-itus. (*She smiles and comes toward him, finding a cigarette and sitting.*) So — sit down! No! Wait! (*She whips the spraygun off sofa where she had left it and puts the cushions back. At last perches on arm of sofa. He sits.*) So, how was Canada?

ASAGAI (*a sophisticate*): Canadian.

BENEATHA (*looking at him*): Asagai, I'm very glad you are back.

ASAGAI (*looking back at her in turn*): Are you really?

BENEATHA: Yes — very.

ASAGAI: Why? — you were quite glad when I went away. What happened?

BENEATHA: You went away.

ASAGAI: Ahhhhhhhh.

BENEATHA: Before — you wanted to be so serious before there was time.

ASAGAI: How much time must there be before one knows what one feels?

BENEATHA (*Stalling this particular conversation. Her hands pressed together, in a deliberately childish gesture.*): What did you bring me?

ASAGAI (*handing her the package*): Open it and see.

BENEATHA (*eagerly opening the package and drawing out some records and the colorful robes of a Nigerian woman*): Oh, Asagai! . . . You got them for me! . . . How beautiful . . . and the records too! (*She lifts out the robes and runs to the mirror with them and holds the drapery up in front of herself.*)

ASAGAI (*coming to her at the mirror*): I shall have to teach you how to drape it properly. (*He flings the material about her for the moment and stands back to look at her.*) Ah — Oh-pay-gay-day, oh-gbah-mu-shay. (*A Yoruba exclamation for admiration.*) You wear it well . . . very well . . . mutilated hair and all.

BENEATHA (*turning suddenly*): My hair — what's wrong with my hair?

ASAGAI (*shrugging*): Were you born with it like that?

BENEATHA (*reaching up to touch it*): No . . . of course not.

(*She looks back to the mirror, disturbed.*)

ASAGAI (*smiling*): How then?

BENEATHA: You know perfectly well how . . . as crinkly as yours . . . that's how.

ASAGAI: And it is ugly to you that way?

BENEATHA (*quickly*): Oh, no — not ugly . . . (*More slowly, apologetically.*) But it's so hard to manage when it's, well — raw.

ASAGAI: And so to accommodate that — you mutilate it every week?

BENEATHA: It's not mutilation!

ASAGAI (*laughing aloud at her seriousness*): Oh . . . please! I am only teasing you because you are so very serious about these things. (*He stands back from her and folds his arms across his chest as he watches her pulling at her hair and frowning in the mirror.*) Do you remember the first time you met me at school? . . . (*He laughs.*) You came up to me and you said — and I thought you were the most serious little thing I had ever seen — you said: (*He imitates her.*) "Mr. Asagai — I want very much to talk with you. About Africa. You see, Mr. Asagai, I am looking for my *identity!*"

(*He laughs.*)

BENEATHA (*turning to him, not laughing*): Yes —

(*Her face is quizzical, profoundly disturbed.*)

ASAGAI (*still teasing and reaching out and taking her face in his hands and turning her profile to him*): Well . . . it is true that this is not so much a profile of a Hollywood queen as perhaps a queen of the Nile — (*A mock dismissal of the importance of the question.*) But what does it matter? Assimilationism is so popular in your country.

BENEATHA (*wheeling, passionately, sharply*): I am not an assimilationist!

ASAGAI (*the protest hangs in the room for a moment and Asagai studies her, his laughter fading*): Such a serious one. (*There is a pause.*) So — you like the robes? You must take excellent care of them — they are from my sister's personal wardrobe.

BENEATHA (*with incredulity*): You — you sent all the way home — for me?

ASAGAI (*with charm*): For you — I would do much more . . . Well, that is what I came for. I must go.

BENEATHA: Will you call me Monday?

ASAGAI: Yes . . . We have a great deal to talk about. I mean about identity and time and all that.

BENEATHA: Time?

ASAGAI: Yes. About how much time one needs to know what one feels.

BENEATHA: You see! You never understood that there is more than one kind of feeling which can exist between a man and a woman — or, at least, there should be.

ASAGAI (*shaking his head negatively but gently*): No. Between a man and a woman there need be only one kind of feeling. I have that for you . . . Now even . . . right this moment . . .

BENEATHA: I know — and by itself — it won't do. I can find that anywhere.

ASAGAI: For a woman it should be enough.

BENEATHA: I know — because that's what it says in all the novels that men write. But it isn't. Go ahead and laugh — but I'm not interested in being someone's little episode in America or — (*with feminine vengeance*) — one of them! (*Asagai has burst into laughter again.*) That's funny as hell, huh!

ASAGAI: It's just that every American girl I have known has said that to me. White — black — in this you are all the same. And the same speech, too!

BENEATHA (*angrily*): Yuk, yuk, yuk!

ASAGAI: It's how you can be sure that the world's most liberated women are not liberated at all. You all talk about it too much!

(*Mama enters and is immediately all social charm because of the presence of a guest.*)

BENEATHA: Oh — Mama — this is Mr. Asagai.

MAMA: How do you do?

ASAGAI (*total politeness to an elder*): How do you do,

Mrs. Younger. Please forgive me for coming at such an outrageous hour on a Saturday.

MAMA: Well, you are quite welcome. I just hope you understand that our house don't always look like this. (*Chatterish.*) You must come again. I would love to hear all about — (*not sure of the name*) — your country. I think it's so sad the way our American Negroes don't know nothing about Africa 'cept Tarzan and all that. And all that money they pour into these churches when they ought to be helping you people over there drive out them French and Englishmen done taken away your land.

(*The mother flashes a slightly superior look at her daughter upon completion of the recitation.*)

ASAGAI (*taken aback by this sudden and acutely unrelated expression of sympathy*): Yes . . . yes . . .

MAMA (*smiling at him suddenly and relaxing and looking him over*): How many miles is it from here to where you come from?

ASAGAI: Many thousands.

MAMA (*looking at him as she would Walter*): I bet you don't half look after yourself, being away from your mama either. I spec you better come 'round here from time to time to get yourself some decent home-cooked meals . . .

ASAGAI (*moved*): Thank you. Thank you very much. (*They are all quiet, then —*) Well . . . I must go. I will call you Monday, Alaiyo.

MAMA: What's that he call you?

ASAGAI: Oh — "Alaiyo." I hope you don't mind. It is what you would call a nickname, I think. It is a Yoruba word. I am a Yoruba.

MAMA (*looking at Beneatha*): I — I thought he was from — (*Uncertain.*)

ASAGAI (*understanding*): Nigeria is my country. Yoruba is my tribal origin —

BENEATHA: You didn't tell us what Alaiyo means . . . for all I know, you might be calling me Little Idiot or something . . .

ASAGAI: Well . . . let me see . . . I do not know how just to explain it . . . The sense of a thing can be so different when it changes languages.

BENEATHA: You're evading.

ASAGAI: No — really it is difficult . . . (*Thinking.*) It means . . . it means One for Whom Bread — Food — Is Not Enough. (*He looks at her.*) Is that all right?

BENEATHA (*understanding, softly*): Thank you.

MAMA (*looking from one to the other and not understanding any of it*): Well . . . that's nice . . . You must come see us again — Mr. ——

ASAGAI: Ah-sah-guy . . .

MAMA: Yes . . . Do come again.

ASAGAI: Good-bye.

(*He exits.*)

MAMA (*after him*): Lord, that's a pretty thing just went out here! (*Insinuatingly, to her daughter.*) Yes, I guess I see why we done commence to get so interested in Africa 'round here. Missionaries my aunt Jenny!

(*She exits.*)

BENEATHA: Oh, Mama! . . .

(*She picks up the Nigerian dress and holds it up to her in front of the mirror again. She sets the headdress on haphazardly and then notices her hair again and clutches at it and then replaces the headdress and frowns at herself. Then she starts to wriggle in front of the mirror as she thinks a Nigerian woman might. Travis enters and stands regarding her.*)

TRAVIS: What's the matter, girl, you cracking up?
BENEATHA: Shut up.

(*She pulls the headdress off and looks at herself in the mirror and clutches at her hair again and squinches her eyes as if trying to imagine something. Then, suddenly, she gets her raincoat and kerchief and hurriedly prepares for going out.*)

MAMA (*coming back into the room*): She's resting now. Travis, baby, run next door and ask Miss Johnson to please let me have a little kitchen cleanser. This here can is empty as Jacob's kettle.
TRAVIS: I just came in.
MAMA: Do as you told. (*He exits and she looks at her daughter.*) Where you going?
BENEATHA (*halting at the door*): To become a queen of the Nile!

(*She exits in a breathless blaze of glory. Ruth appears in the bedroom doorway.*)

MAMA: Who told you to get up?
RUTH: Ain't nothing wrong with me to be lying in no bed for. Where did Bennie go?
MAMA (*drumming her fingers*): Far as I could make out — to Egypt. (*Ruth just looks at her.*) What time is it getting to?
RUTH: Ten twenty. And the mailman going to ring that bell this morning just like he done every morning for the last umpteen years.

(*Travis comes in with the cleanser can.*)

TRAVIS: She say to tell you that she don't have much.
MAMA (*angrily*): Lord, some people I could name sure is tight-fisted! (*Directing her grandson.*) Mark two cans of cleanser down on the list there. If she that

hard up for kitchen cleanser, I sure don't want to forget to get her none!
RUTH: Lena — maybe the woman is just short on cleanser —
MAMA (*not listening*): — Much baking powder as she done borrowed from me all these years, she could of done gone into the baking business!

(*The bell sounds suddenly and sharply and all three are stunned — serious and silent — mid-speech. In spite of all the other conversations and distractions of the morning, this is what they have been waiting for, even Travis, who looks helplessly from his mother to his grandmother. Ruth is the first to come to life again.*)

RUTH (*to Travis*): Get down them steps, boy!

(*Travis snaps to life and flies out to get the mail.*)

MAMA (*her eyes wide, her hand to her breast*): You mean it done really come?
RUTH (*excited*): Oh, Miss Lena!
MAMA (*collecting herself*): Well . . . I don't know what we all so excited about 'round here for. We known it was coming for months.
RUTH: That's a whole lot different from having it come and being able to hold it in your hands . . . a piece of paper worth ten thousand dollars . . . (*Travis bursts back into the room. He holds the envelope high above his head, like a little dancer, his face is radiant and he is breathless. He moves to his grandmother with sudden slow ceremony and puts the envelope into her hands. She accepts it, and then merely holds it and looks at it.*) Come on! Open it . . . Lord have mercy, I wish Walter Lee was here!
TRAVIS: Open it, Grandmama!
MAMA (*staring at it*): Now you all be quiet. It's just a check.
RUTH: Open it . . .
MAMA (*still staring at it*): Now don't act silly . . . We ain't never been no people to act silly 'bout no money —
RUTH (*swiftly*): We ain't never had none before — OPEN IT!

(*Mama finally makes a good strong tear and pulls out the thin blue slice of paper and inspects it closely. The boy and his mother study it raptly over Mama's shoulders.*)

MAMA: Travis! (*She is counting off with doubt.*) Is that the right number of zeros.
TRAVIS: Yes'm . . . ten thousand dollars. Gaalee, Grandmama, you rich.
MAMA (*She holds the check away from her, still looking at it. Slowly her face sobers into a mask of*

unhappiness.): Ten thousand dollars. (*She hands it to Ruth.*) Put it away somewhere, Ruth. (*She does not look at Ruth; her eyes seem to be seeing something somewhere very far off.*) Ten thousand dollars they give you. Ten thousand dollars.

TRAVIS (*to his mother, sincerely*): What's the matter with Grandmama — don't she want to be rich?

RUTH (*distractedly*): You go on out and play now, baby. (*Travis exits. Mama starts wiping dishes absently, humming intently to herself. Ruth turns to her, with kind exasperation.*) You've gone and got yourself upset.

MAMA (*not looking at her*): I spec if it wasn't for you all . . . I would just put that money away or give it to the church or something.

RUTH: Now what kind of talk is that. Mr. Younger would just be plain mad if he could hear you talking foolish like that.

MAMA (*stopping and staring off*): Yes . . . he sure would. (*Sighing.*) We got enough to do with that money, all right. (*She halts then, and turns and looks at her daughter-in-law hard; Ruth avoids her eyes and Mama wipes her hands with finality and starts to speak firmly to Ruth.*) Where did you go today, girl?

RUTH: To the doctor.

MAMA (*impatiently*): Now, Ruth . . . you know better than that. Old Doctor Jones is strange enough in his way but there ain't nothing 'bout him make somebody slip and call him "she" — like you done this morning.

RUTH: Well, that's what happened — my tongue slipped.

MAMA: You went to see that woman, didn't you?

RUTH (*defensively, giving herself away*): What woman you talking about?

MAMA (*angrily*): That woman who —

(*Walter enters in great excitement.*)

WALTER: Did it come?

MAMA (*quietly*): Can't you give people a Christian greeting before you start asking about money?

WALTER (*to Ruth*): Did it come? (*Ruth unfolds the check and lays it quietly before him, watching him intently with thoughts of her own. Walter sits down and grasps it close and counts off the zeros.*) Ten thousand dollars — (*He turns suddenly, frantically to his mother and draws some papers out of his breast pocket.*) Mama — look. Old Willy Harris put everything on paper.

MAMA: Son — I think you ought to talk to your wife . . . I'll go on out and leave you alone if you want —

WALTER: I can talk to her later — Mama, look —

MAMA: Son —

WALTER: WILL SOMEBODY PLEASE LISTEN TO ME TODAY!

MAMA (*quietly*): I don't 'low no yellin' in this house, Walter Lee, and you know it — (*Walter stares at them in frustration and starts to speak several times.*) And there ain't going to be no investing in no liquor stores.

WALTER: But, Mama, you ain't even looked at it.

MAMA: I don't aim to have to speak on that again.

(*A long pause.*)

WALTER: You ain't looked at it and you don't aim to have to speak on that again? You ain't even looked at it and *you* have decided — (*Crumpling his papers.*) Well, *you* tell that to my boy tonight when you put him to sleep on the living room couch . . . (*Turning to Mama and speaking directly to her.*) Yeah — and tell it to my wife, Mama, tomorrow when she has to go out of here to look after somebody else's kids. And tell it to *me*, Mama, every time we need a new pair of curtains and I have to watch *you* go out and work in somebody's kitchen. Yeah, you tell me then!

(*Walter starts out.*)

RUTH: Where you going?

WALTER: I'm going out!

RUTH: Where?

WALTER: Just out of this house somewhere —

RUTH (*getting her coat*): I'll come too.

WALTER: I don't want you to come!

RUTH: I got something to talk to you about, Walter.

WALTER: That's too bad.

MAMA (*still quietly*): Walter Lee — (*She waits and he finally turns and looks at her.*) Sit down.

WALTER: I'm a grown man, Mama.

MAMA: Ain't nobody said you wasn't grown. But you still in my house and my presence. And as long as you are — you'll talk to your wife civil. Now sit down.

RUTH (*suddenly*): Oh, let him go on out and drink himself to death! He makes me sick to my stomach! (*She flings his coat against him and exits to bedroom.*)

WALTER (*violently flinging the coat after her*): And you turn mine too, baby! (*The door slams behind her.*) That was my biggest mistake —

MAMA (*still quietly*): Walter, what is the matter with you?

WALTER: Matter with me? Ain't nothing the matter with *me*!

MAMA: Yes there is. Something eating you up like a crazy man. Something more than me not giving you this money. The past few years I been watching it happen to you. You get all nervous acting and kind of wild in the eyes — (*Walter jumps up im-*

patiently at her words.) I said sit there now, I'm talking to you!

WALTER: Mama — I don't need no nagging at me today.

MAMA: Seem like you getting to a place where you always tied up in some kind of knot about something. But if anybody ask you 'bout it you just yell at 'em and bust out the house and go out and drink somewheres. Walter Lee, people can't live with that. Ruth's a good, patient girl in her way — but you getting to be too much. Boy, don't make the mistake of driving that girl away from you.

WALTER: Why — what she do for me?

MAMA: She loves you.

WALTER: Mama — I'm going out. I want to go off somewhere and be by myself for a while.

MAMA: I'm sorry 'bout your liquor store, son. It just wasn't the thing for us to do. That's what I want to tell you about —

WALTER: I got to go out, Mama —

(*He rises.*)

MAMA: It's dangerous, son.

WALTER: What's dangerous?

MAMA: When a man goes outside his home to look for peace.

WALTER (*beseechingly*): Then why can't there never be no peace in this house then?

MAMA: You done found it in some other house?

WALTER: No — there ain't no woman! Why do women always think there's a woman somewhere when a man gets restless. (*Picks up the check.*) Do you know what this money means to me? Do you know what this money can do for us? (*Puts it back.*) Mama — Mama — I want so many things . . .

MAMA: Yes, son —

WALTER: I want so many things that they are driving me kind of crazy . . . Mama — look at me.

MAMA: I'm looking at you. You a good-looking boy. You got a job, a nice wife, a fine boy and —

WALTER: A job. (*Looks at her.*) Mama, a job? I open and close car doors all day long. I drive a man around in his limousine and I say, "Yes, sir; no, sir; very good, sir; shall I take the Drive, sir?" Mama, that ain't no kind of job . . . that ain't nothing at all. (*Very quietly.*) Mama, I don't know if I can make you understand.

MAMA: Understand what, baby?

WALTER (*quietly*): Sometimes it's like I can see the future stretched out in front of me — just plain as day. The future, Mama. Hanging over there at the edge of my days. Just waiting for me — a big, looming blank space — full of *nothing*. Just waiting for *me*. But it don't have to be. (*Pause. Kneeling*

beside her chair.) Mama — sometimes when I'm downtown and I pass them cool, quiet-looking restaurants where them white boys are sitting back and talking 'bout things . . . sitting there turning deals worth millions of dollars . . . sometimes I see guys don't look much older than me —

MAMA: Son — how come you talk so much 'bout money?

WALTER (*with immense passion*): Because it is life, Mama!

MAMA (*quietly*): Oh — (*Very quietly.*) So now it's life. Money is life. Once upon a time freedom used to be life — now it's money. I guess the world really do change . . .

WALTER: No — it was always money, Mama. We just didn't know about it.

MAMA: No . . . something has changed. (*She looks at him.*) You something new, boy. In my time we was worried about not being lynched and getting to the North if we could and how to stay alive and still have a pinch of dignity too . . . Now here come you and Beneatha — talking 'bout things we ain't never even thought about hardly, me and your daddy. You ain't satisfied or proud of nothing we done. I mean that you had a home; that we kept you out of trouble till you was grown; that you don't have to ride to work on the back of nobody's streetcar — You my children — but how different we done become.

WALTER (*A long beat. He pats her hand and gets up.*): You just don't understand, Mama, you just don't understand.

MAMA: Son — do you know your wife is expecting another baby? (*Walter stands, stunned, and absorbs what his mother has said.*) That's what she wanted to talk to you about. (*Walter sinks down into a chair.*) This ain't for me to be telling — but you ought to know. (*She waits.*) I think Ruth is thinking 'bout getting rid of that child.

WALTER (*slowly understanding*): — No — no — Ruth wouldn't do that.

MAMA: When the world gets ugly enough — a woman will do anything for her family. *The part that's already living.*

WALTER: You don't know Ruth, Mama, if you think she would do that.

(*Ruth opens the bedroom door and stands there a little limp.*)

RUTH (*beaten*): Yes I would too, Walter. (*Pause.*) I gave her a five-dollar down payment.

(*There is total silence as the man stares at his wife and the mother stares at her son.*)

MAMA (*presently*): Well — (*Tightly.*) Well — son, I'm

waiting to hear you say something . . . (*She waits.*)
I'm waiting to hear how you be your father's son.
Be the man he was . . . (*Pause. The silence shouts.*)
Your wife says she going to destroy your child.
And I'm waiting to hear you talk like him and say
we a people who give children life, not who destroys them — (*She rises.*) I'm waiting to see you
stand up and look like your daddy and say we
done give up one baby to poverty and that we ain't
going to give up nary another one . . . I'm waiting.
WALTER: Ruth — (*He can say nothing.*)
MAMA: If you a son of mine, tell her! (*Walter picks
up his keys and his coat and walks out. She continues, bitterly.*) You . . . you are a disgrace to your
father's memory. Somebody get me my hat!

ACT II • *Scene 1*

(*Time: Later the same day.*)
    (*At rise: Ruth is ironing again. She has the radio
going. Presently Beneatha's bedroom door opens and
Ruth's mouth falls and she puts down the iron in
fascination.*)

RUTH: What have we got on tonight!
BENEATHA (*emerging grandly from the doorway so
that we can see her thoroughly robed in the costume Asagai brought*): You are looking at what a
well-dressed Nigerian woman wears — (*She parades for Ruth, her hair completely hidden by the
headdress; she is coquettishly fanning herself with
an ornate oriental fan, mistakenly more like But-
terfly° than any Nigerian that ever was.*) Isn't it
beautiful? (*She promenades to the radio and, with
an arrogant flourish, turns off the good loud blues
that is playing.*) Enough of this assimilationist junk!
(*Ruth follows her with her eyes as she goes to the
phonograph and puts on a record and turns and
waits ceremoniously for the music to come up.
Then, with a shout —*) OCOMOGOSIAY!

(*Ruth jumps. The music comes up, a lovely Nigerian
melody. Beneatha listens, enraptured, her eyes far
away — "back to the past." She begins to dance. Ruth
is dumfounded.*)

RUTH: What kind of dance is that?
BENEATHA: A folk dance.
RUTH (*Pearl Bailey*): What kind of folks do that,
honey?
BENEATHA: It's from Nigeria. It's a dance of welcome.
RUTH: Who you welcoming?

Butterfly: Madame Butterfly, the title character in the opera
by Puccini.

BENEATHA: The men back to the village.
RUTH: Where they been?
BENEATHA: How should I know — out hunting or
something. Anyway, they are coming back now . . .
RUTH: Well, that's good.
BENEATHA (*with the record*): Alundi, alundi
    Alundi alunya
    Jop pu a jeepua
    Ang gu soooooooooo

    Ai yai yae . . .
    Ayehaye — alundi . . .

(*Walter comes in during this performance; he has obviously been drinking. He leans against the door heavily and watches his sister, at first with distaste. Then
his eyes look off — "back to the past" — as he lifts
both his fists to the roof, screaming.*)

WALTER: YEAH . . . AND ETHIOPIA STRETCH FORTH HER
HANDS AGAIN! . . .
RUTH (*drily, looking at him*): Yes — and Africa sure
is claiming her own tonight. (*She gives them both
up and starts ironing again.*)
WALTER (*all in a drunken, dramatic shout*): Shut up!
. . . I'm digging them drums . . . them drums move
me! . . . (*He makes his weaving way to his wife's
face and leans in close to her.*) In my *heart of
hearts* — (*he thumps his chest*) — I am much
warrior!
RUTH (*without even looking up*): In your heart of
hearts you are much drunkard.
WALTER (*coming away from her and starting to wander around the room, shouting*): Me and Jomo . . .
(*Intently, in his sister's face. She has stopped dancing to watch him in this unknown mood.*) That's
my man, Kenyatta. (*Shouting and thumping his
chest.*) FLAMING SPEAR! HOT DAMN! (*He is suddenly in possession of an imaginary spear and actively spearing enemies all over the room.*)
OCOMOGOSIAY . . .
BENEATHA (*to encourage Walter, thoroughly caught
up with this side of him*): OCOMOGOSIAY, FLAMING
SPEAR!
WALTER: THE LION IS WAKING . . . OWIMOWEH! (*He
pulls his shirt open and leaps up on the table and
gestures with his spear.*)
BENEATHA: OWIMOWEH!
WALTER (*On the table, very far gone, his eyes pure
glass sheets. He sees what we cannot, that he is a
leader of his people, a great chief, a descendant of
Chaka, and that the hour to march has come.*):
Listen, my black brothers —
BENEATHA: OCOMOGOSIAY!
WALTER: — Do you hear the waters rushing against
the shores of the coastlands —

BENEATHA: OCOMOGOSIAY!

WALTER: — Do you hear the screeching of the cocks in yonder hills beyond where the chiefs meet in council for the coming of the mighty war —

BENEATHA: OCOMOGOSIAY!

(*And now the lighting shifts subtly to suggest the world of Walter's imagination, and the mood shifts from pure comedy. It is the inner Walter speaking: the Southside chauffeur has assumed an unexpected majesty.*)

WALTER: — Do you hear the beating of the wings of the birds flying low over the mountains and the low places of our land —

BENEATHA: OCOMOGOSIAY!

WALTER: — Do you hear the singing of the women, singing the war songs of our fathers to the babies in the great houses? Singing the sweet war songs! (*The doorbell rings.*) OH, DO YOU HEAR, MY *BLACK BROTHERS!*

BENEATHA (*completely gone*): We hear you, Flaming Spear —

(*Ruth shuts off the phonograph and opens the door. George Murchison enters.*)

WALTER: Telling us to prepare for the GREATNESS OF THE TIME! (*Lights back to normal. He turns and sees George.*) Black Brother!

(*He extends his hand for the fraternal clasp.*)

GEORGE: Black Brother, hell!

RUTH (*having had enough, and embarrassed for the family*): Beneatha, you got company — what's the matter with you? Walter Lee Younger, get down off that table and stop acting like a fool . . .

(*Walter comes down off the table suddenly and makes a quick exit to the bathroom.*)

RUTH: He's had a little to drink . . . I don't know what her excuse is.

GEORGE (*to Beneatha*): Look honey, we're going *to* the theater — we're not going to be *in* it . . . so go change, huh?

(*Beneatha looks at him and slowly, ceremoniously, lifts her hands and pulls off the headdress. Her hair is close-cropped and unstraightened. George freezes mid-sentence and Ruth's eyes all but fall out of her head.*)

GEORGE: What in the name of —

RUTH (*touching Beneatha's hair*): Girl, you done lost your natural mind? Look at your head!

GEORGE: What have you done to your head — I mean your hair!

BENEATHA: Nothing — except cut it off.

RUTH: Now that's the truth — it's what ain't been done to it! You expect this boy to go out with you with your head all nappy like that?

BENEATHA (*looking at George*): That's up to George. If he's ashamed of his heritage —

GEORGE: Oh, don't be so proud of yourself, Bennie — just because you look eccentric.

BENEATHA: How can something that's natural be eccentric?

GEORGE: That's what being eccentric means — being natural. Get dressed.

BENEATHA: I don't like that, George.

RUTH: Why must you and your brother make an argument out of everything people say?

BENEATHA: Because I hate assimilationist Negroes!

RUTH: Will somebody please tell me what assimila-whoever means!

GEORGE: Oh, it's just a college girl's way of calling people Uncle Toms — but that isn't what it means at all.

RUTH: Well, what does it mean?

BENEATHA (*cutting George off and staring at him as she replies to Ruth*): It means someone who is willing to give up his own culture and submerge himself completely in the dominant, and in this case *oppressive* culture!

GEORGE: Oh, dear, dear, dear! Here we go! A lecture on the African past! On our Great West African Heritage! In one second we will hear all about the great Ashanti empires; the great Songhay civilizations; and the great sculpture of Bénin — and then some poetry in the Bantu — and the whole monologue will end with the word *heritage!* (*Nastily.*) Let's face it, baby, your heritage is nothing but a bunch of raggedy-assed spirituals and some grass huts!

BENEATHA: GRASS HUTS! (*Ruth crosses to her and forcibly pushes her toward the bedroom.*) See there . . . you are standing there in your splendid ignorance talking about people who were the first to smelt iron on the face of the earth! (*Ruth is pushing her through the door.*) The Ashanti were performing surgical operations when the English — (*Ruth pulls the door to, with Beneatha on the other side, and smiles graciously at George. Beneatha opens the door and shouts the end of the sentence defiantly at George*) — were still tatooing themselves with blue dragons! (*She goes back inside.*)

RUTH: Have a seat, George. (*They both sit. Ruth folds her hands rather primly on her lap, determined to demonstrate the civilization of the family.*) Warm, ain't it? I mean for September. (*Pause.*) Just like they always say about Chicago weather: If it's too hot or cold for you, just wait a minute and it'll change. (*She smiles happily at this cliché of clichés.*)

Everybody say it's got to do with them bombs and things they keep setting off. (*Pause.*) Would you like a nice cold beer?

GEORGE: No, thank you. I don't care for beer. (*He looks at his watch.*) I hope she hurries up.

RUTH: What time is the show?

GEORGE: It's an eight-thirty curtain. That's just Chicago, though. In New York standard curtain time is eight forty.

(*He is rather proud of this knowledge.*)

RUTH (*properly appreciating it*): You get to New York a lot?

GEORGE (*offhand*): Few times a year.

RUTH: Oh — that's nice. I've never been to New York.

(*Walter enters. We feel he has relieved himself, but the edge of unreality is still with him.*)

WALTER: New York ain't got nothing Chicago ain't. Just a bunch of hustling people all squeezed up together — being "Eastern."

(*He turns his face into a screw of displeasure.*)

GEORGE: Oh — you've been?

WALTER: *Plenty* of times.

RUTH (*shocked at the lie*): Walter Lee Younger!

WALTER (*staring her down*): Plenty! (*Pause.*) What we got to drink in this house? Why don't you offer this man some refreshment. (*To George.*) They don't know how to entertain people in this house, man.

GEORGE: Thank you — I don't really care for anything.

WALTER (*feeling his head; sobriety coming*): Where's Mama?

RUTH: She ain't come back yet.

WALTER (*looking Murchison over from head to toe, scrutinizing his carefully casual tweed sports jacket over cashmere V-neck sweater over soft eyelet shirt and tie, and soft slacks, finished off with white buckskin shoes*): Why all you college boys wear them faggoty-looking white shoes?

RUTH: Walter Lee!

(*George Murchison ignores the remark.*)

WALTER (*to Ruth*): Well, they look crazy as hell — white shoes, cold as it is.

RUTH (*crushed*): You have to excuse him —

WALTER: No he don't! Excuse me for what? What you always excusing me for! I'll excuse myself when I needs to be excused! (*A pause.*) They look as funny as them black knee socks Beneatha wears out of here all the time.

RUTH: It's the college *style*, Walter.

WALTER: Style, hell. She looks like she got burnt legs or something!

RUTH: Oh, Walter —

WALTER (*an irritable mimic*): Oh, Walter! Oh, Walter! (*To Murchison.*) How's your old man making out? I understand you all going to buy that big hotel on the Drive? (*He finds a beer in the refrigerator, wanders over to Murchison, sipping and wiping his lips with the back of his hand, and straddling a chair backward to talk to the other man.*) Shrewd move. Your old man is all right, man. (*Tapping his head and half winking for emphasis.*) I mean he knows how to operate. I mean he thinks *big*, you know what I mean, I mean for a *home*, you know? But I think he's kind of running out of ideas now. I'd like to talk to him. Listen, man, I got some plans that could turn this city upside down. I mean think like he does. *Big.* Invest big, gamble big, hell, lose *big* if you have to, you know what I mean. It's hard to find a man on this whole Southside who understands my kind of thinking — you dig? (*He scrutinizes Murchison again, drinks his beer, squints his eyes, and leans in close, confidential, man to man.*) Me and you ought to sit down and talk sometimes, man. Man, I got me some ideas . . .

MURCHISON (*with boredom*): Yeah — sometimes we'll have to do that, Walter.

WALTER (*understanding the indifference, and offended*): Yeah — well, when you get the time, man. I know you a busy little boy.

RUTH: Walter, please —

WALTER (*bitterly, hurt*): I know ain't nothing in this world as busy as you colored college boys with your fraternity pins and white shoes . . .

RUTH (*covering her face with humiliation*): Oh, Walter Lee —

WALTER: I see you all all the time — with the books tucked under your arms — going to your (*British A — a mimic*) "clahsses." And for what! What the hell you learning over there? Filling up your heads — (*counting off on his fingers*) — with the sociology and the psychology — but they teaching you how to be a man? How to take over and run the world? They teaching you how to run a rubber plantation or a steel mill? Naw — just to talk proper and read books and wear them faggoty-looking white shoes . . .

GEORGE (*looking at him with distaste, a little above it all*): You're all wacked up with bitterness, man.

WALTER (*intently, almost quietly, between the teeth, glaring at the boy*): And you — ain't you bitter, man? Ain't you just about had it yet? Don't you see no stars gleaming that you can't reach out and grab? You happy? — You contented son-of-a-bitch —

you happy? You got it made? Bitter? Man, I'm a volcano. Bitter? Here I am a giant — surrounded by ants! Ants who can't even understand what it is the giant is talking about.

RUTH (*passionately and suddenly*): Oh, Walter — ain't you with nobody!

WALTER (*violently*): No! 'Cause ain't nobody with me! Not even my own mother!

RUTH: Walter, that's a terrible thing to say!

(*Beneatha enters, dressed for the evening in a cocktail dress and earrings, hair natural.*)

GEORGE: Well — hey — (*Crosses to Beneatha; thoughtful, with emphasis, since this is a reversal.*) You look great!

WALTER (*seeing his sister's hair for the first time*): What's the matter with your head?

BENEATHA (*tired of the jokes now*): I cut it off, Brother.

WALTER (*coming close to inspect it and walking around her*): Well, I'll be damned. So that's what they mean by the African bush . . .

BENEATHA: Ha ha. Let's go, George.

GEORGE (*looking at her*): You know something? I like it. It's sharp. I mean it really is. (*Helps her into her wrap.*)

RUTH: Yes — I think so, too. (*She goes to the mirror and starts to clutch at her hair.*)

WALTER: Oh no! You leave yours alone, baby. You might turn out to have a pin-shaped head or something!

BENEATHA: See you all later.

RUTH: Have a nice time.

GEORGE: Thanks. Good night. (*Half out the door, he reopens it. To Walter.*) Good night, Prometheus!°

(*Beneatha and George exit.*)

WALTER (*to Ruth*): Who is Prometheus?

RUTH: I don't know. Don't worry about it.

WALTER (*in fury, pointing after George*): See there — they get to a point where they can't insult you man to man — they got to go talk about something ain't nobody never heard of!

RUTH: How do you know it was an insult? (*To humor him.*) Maybe Prometheus is a nice fellow.

WALTER: Prometheus! I bet there ain't even no such thing! I bet that simple-minded clown —

RUTH: Walter —

(*She stops what she is doing and looks at him.*)

WALTER (*yelling*): Don't start!

RUTH: Start what?

Prometheus: A shrewd and inventive god noted for stealing fire from the heavens and giving it to humans.

WALTER: Your nagging! Where was I? Who was I with? How much money did I spend?

RUTH (*plaintively*): Walter Lee — why don't we just try to talk about it . . .

WALTER (*not listening*): I been out talking with people who understand me. People who care about the things I got on my mind.

RUTH (*wearily*): I guess that means people like Willy Harris.

WALTER: Yes, people like Willy Harris.

RUTH (*with a sudden flash of impatience*): Why don't you all just hurry up and go into the banking business and stop talking about it!

WALTER: Why? You want to know why? 'Cause we all tied up in a race of people that don't know how to do nothing but moan, pray, and have babies!

(*The line is too bitter even for him and he looks at her and sits down.*)

RUTH: Oh, Walter . . . (*Softly.*) Honey, why can't you stop fighting me?

WALTER (*without thinking*): Who's fighting you? Who even cares about you?

(*This line begins the retardation of his mood.*)

RUTH: Well — (*She waits a long time, and then with resignation starts to put away her things.*) I guess I might as well go on to bed . . . (*More or less to herself.*) I don't know where we lost it . . . but we have . . . (*Then, to him.*) I — I'm sorry about this new baby, Walter. I guess maybe I better go on and do what I started . . . I guess I just didn't realize how bad things was with us . . . I guess I just didn't really realize — (*She starts out to the bedroom and stops.*) You want some hot milk?

WALTER: Hot milk?

RUTH: Yes — hot milk.

WALTER: Why hot milk?

RUTH: 'Cause after all that liquor you come home with you ought to have something hot in your stomach.

WALTER: I don't want no milk.

RUTH: You want some coffee then?

WALTER: No, I don't want no coffee. I don't want nothing hot to drink. (*Almost plaintively.*) Why you always trying to give me something to eat?

RUTH (*standing and looking at him helplessly*): What *else* can I give you, Walter Lee Younger?

(*She stands and looks at him and presently turns to go out again. He lifts his head and watches her going away from him in a new mood which began to emerge when he asked her "Who cares about you?"*)

WALTER: It's been rough, ain't it, baby? (*She hears and stops but does not turn around and he con-*

tinues to her back.) I guess between two people there ain't never as much understood as folks generally thinks there is. I mean like between me and you — (*She turns to face him.*) How we gets to the place where we scared to talk softness to each other. (*He waits, thinking hard himself.*) Why you think it got to be like that? (*He is thoughtful, almost as a child would be.*) Ruth, what is it gets into people ought to be close?

RUTH: I don't know, honey. I think about it a lot.

WALTER: On account of you and me, you mean? The way things are with us. The way something done come down between us.

RUTH: There ain't so much between us, Walter . . . Not when you come to me and try to talk to me. Try to be with me . . . a little even.

WALTER (*total honesty*): Sometimes . . . sometimes . . . I don't even know how to try.

RUTH: Walter —

WALTER: Yes?

RUTH (*coming to him, gently and with misgiving, but coming to him*): Honey . . . life don't have to be like this. I mean sometimes people can do things so that things are better . . . You remember how we used to talk when Travis was born . . . about the way we were going to live . . . the kind of house . . . (*She is stroking his head.*) Well, it's all starting to slip away from us . . .

(*He turns her to him and they look at each other and kiss, tenderly and hungrily. The door opens and Mama enters — Walter breaks away and jumps up. A beat.*)

WALTER: Mama, where have you been?

MAMA: My — them steps is longer than they used to be. Whew! (*She sits down and ignores him.*) How you feeling this evening, Ruth?

(*Ruth shrugs, disturbed at having been interrupted and watching her husband knowingly.*)

WALTER: Mama, where have you been all day?

MAMA (*still ignoring him and leaning on the table and changing to more comfortable shoes*): Where's Travis?

RUTH: I let him go out earlier and he ain't come back yet. Boy, is he going to get it!

WALTER: Mama!

MAMA (*as if she has heard him for the first time*): Yes, son?

WALTER: Where did you go this afternoon?

MAMA: I went downtown to tend to some business that I had to tend to.

WALTER: What kind of business?

MAMA: You know better than to question me like a child, Brother.

WALTER (*rising and bending over the table*): Where

were you, Mama? (*Bringing his fists down and shouting.*) Mama, you didn't go do something with that insurance money, something crazy?

(*The front door opens slowly, interrupting him, and Travis peeks his head in, less than hopefully.*)

TRAVIS (*to his mother*): Mama, I —

RUTH: "Mama I" nothing! You're going to get it, boy! Get on in that bedroom and get yourself ready!

TRAVIS: But I —

MAMA: Why don't you all never let the child explain hisself.

RUTH: Keep out of it now, Lena.

(*Mama clamps her lips together, and Ruth advances toward her son menacingly.*)

RUTH: A thousand times I have told you not to go off like that —

MAMA (*holding out her arms to her grandson*): Well — at least let me tell him something. I want him to be the first one to hear . . . Come here, Travis. (*The boy obeys, gladly.*) Travis — (*she takes him by the shoulder and looks into his face*) — you know that money we got in the mail this morning?

TRAVIS: Yes'm —

MAMA: Well — what you think your grandmama gone and done with that money?

TRAVIS: I don't know, Grandmama.

MAMA (*putting her finger on his nose for emphasis*): She went out and she bought you a house! (*The explosion comes from Walter at the end of the revelation and he jumps up and turns away from all of them in a fury. Mama continues, to Travis.*) You glad about the house? It's going to be yours when you get to be a man.

TRAVIS: Yeah — I always wanted to live in a house.

MAMA: All right, gimme some sugar then — (*Travis puts his arms around her neck as she watches her son over the boy's shoulder. Then, to Travis, after the embrace.*) Now when you say your prayers tonight, you thank God and your grandfather — 'cause it was him who give you the house — in his way.

RUTH (*taking the boy from Mama and pushing him toward the bedroom*): Now you get out of here and get ready for your beating.

TRAVIS: Aw, Mama —

RUTH: Get on in there — (*Closing the door behind him and turning radiantly to her mother-in-law.*) So you went and did it!

MAMA (*quietly, looking at her son with pain*): Yes, I did.

RUTH (*raising both arms classically*): PRAISE GOD! (*Looks at Walter a moment, who says nothing. She crosses rapidly to her husband.*) Please, honey — let me be glad . . . you be glad too. (*She has laid her hands on his shoulders, but he shakes himself free of her roughly, without turning to face her.*) Oh, Walter . . . a home . . . *a home.* (*She comes back to Mama.*) Well — where is it? How big is it? How much it going to cost?

MAMA: Well —

RUTH: When we moving?

MAMA (*smiling at her*): First of the month.

RUTH (*throwing back her head with jubilance*): Praise God!

MAMA (*tentatively, still looking at her son's back turned against her and Ruth*): It's — it's a nice house too . . . (*She cannot help speaking directly to him. An imploring quality in her voice, her manner, makes her almost like a girl now.*) Three bedrooms — nice big one for you and Ruth . . . Me and Beneatha still have to share our room, but Travis have one of his own — and (*with difficulty*) I figure if the — new baby — is a boy, we could get one of them double-decker outfits . . . And there's a yard with a little patch of dirt where I could maybe get to grow me a few flowers . . . And a nice big basement . . .

RUTH: Walter honey, be glad —

MAMA (*still to his back, fingering things on the table*): 'Course I don't want to make it sound fancier than it is . . . It's just a plain little old house — but it's made good and solid — and it will be *ours.* Walter Lee — it makes a difference in a man when he can walk on floors that belong to *him* . . .

RUTH: Where is it?

MAMA (*frightened at this telling*): Well — well — it's out there in Clybourne Park —

(*Ruth's radiance fades abruptly, and Walter finally turns slowly to face his mother with incredulity and hostility.*)

RUTH: Where?

MAMA (*matter-of-factly*): Four o six Clybourne Street, Clybourne Park.

RUTH: Clybourne Park? Mama, there ain't no colored people living in Clybourne Park.

MAMA (*almost idiotically*): Well, I guess there's going to be some now.

WALTER (*bitterly*): So that's the peace and comfort you went out and bought for us today!

MAMA (*raising her eyes to meet his finally*): Son — I just tried to find the nicest place for the least amount of money for my family.

RUTH (*trying to recover from the shock*): Well — well — 'course I ain't one never been 'fraid of no

crackers,° mind you — but — well, wasn't there no other houses nowhere?

MAMA: Them houses they put up for colored in them areas way out all seem to cost twice as much as other houses. I did the best I could.

RUTH (*struck senseless with the news, in its various degrees of goodness and trouble, she sits a moment, her fists propping her chin in thought, and then she starts to rise, bringing her fists down with vigor, the radiance spreading from cheek to cheek again*): Well — well — All I can say is — if this is my time in life — MY TIME — to say good-bye — (*and she builds with momentum as she starts to circle the room with an exuberant, almost tearfully happy release*) — to these Goddamned cracking walls! — (*she pounds the walls*) — and these marching roaches! — (*she wipes at an imaginary army of marching roaches*) — and this cramped little closet which ain't now or never was no kitchen! . . . then I say it loud and good, HALLELUJAH! AND GOOD-BYE MISERY . . . I DON'T NEVER WANT TO SEE YOUR UGLY FACE AGAIN! (*She laughs joyously, having practically destroyed the apartment, and flings her arms up and lets them come down happily, slowly, reflectively, over her abdomen, aware for the first time perhaps that the life therein pulses with happiness and not despair.*) Lena?

MAMA (*moved, watching her happiness*): Yes, honey?

RUTH (*looking off*): Is there — is there a whole lot of sunlight?

MAMA (*understanding*): Yes, child, there's a whole lot of sunlight.

(*Long pause.*)

RUTH (*collecting herself and going to the door of the room Travis is in*): Well — I guess I better see 'bout Travis. (*To Mama.*) Lord, I sure don't feel like whipping nobody today!

(*She exits.*)

MAMA (*the mother and son are left alone now and the mother waits a long time, considering deeply, before she speaks*): Son — you — you understand what I done, don't you? (*Walter is silent and sullen.*) I — I just seen my family falling apart today . . . just falling to pieces in front of my eyes . . . We couldn't of gone on like we was today. We was going backwards 'stead of forwards — talking 'bout killing babies and wishing each other was dead . . . When it gets like that in life — you just got to do something different, push on out and do something bigger . . . (*She waits.*) I wish you say

---

crackers: White people, often used to refer disparagingly to poor whites.

something, son . . . I wish you'd say how deep inside you you think I done the right thing —

WALTER (*crossing slowly to his bedroom door and finally turning there and speaking measuredly*): What you need me to say you done right for? *You* the head of this family. You run our lives like you want to. It was your money and you did what you wanted with it. So what you need for me to say it was all right for? (*Bitterly, to hurt her as deeply as he knows is possible.*) So you butchered up a dream of mine — you — who always talking 'bout your children's dreams . . .

MAMA: Walter Lee —

(*He just closes the door behind him. Mama sits alone, thinking heavily.*)

Scene II

(*Time: Friday night. A few weeks later.*)

(*At rise: Packing crates mark the intention of the family to move. Beneatha and George come in, presumably from an evening out again.*)

GEORGE: O.K. . . . O.K., whatever you say . . . (*They both sit on the couch. He tries to kiss her. She moves away.*) Look, we've had a nice evening; let's not spoil it, huh? . . .

(*He again turns her head and tries to nuzzle in and she turns away from him, not with distaste but with momentary lack of interest; in a mood to pursue what they were talking about.*)

BENEATHA: I'm *trying* to talk to you.

GEORGE: We always talk.

BENEATHA: Yes — and I love to talk.

GEORGE (*exasperated; rising*): I know it and I don't mind it sometimes . . . I want you to cut it out, see — The moody stuff, I mean. I don't like it. You're a nice-looking girl . . . all over. That's all you need, honey, forget the atmosphere. Guys aren't going to go for the atmosphere — they're going to go for what they see. Be glad for that. Drop the Garbo routine. It doesn't go with you. As for myself, I want a nice — (*groping*) — simple (*thoughtfully*) — sophisticated girl . . . not a poet — O.K.?

(*He starts to kiss her, she rebuffs him again, and he jumps up.*)

BENEATHA: Why are you angry, George?

GEORGE: Because this is stupid! I don't go out with you to discuss the nature of "quiet desperation" or to hear all about your thoughts — because

the world will go on thinking what it thinks regardless —

BENEATHA: Then why read books? Why go to school?

GEORGE (*with artificial patience, counting on his fingers*): It's simple. You read books — to learn facts — to get grades — to pass the course — to get a degree. That's all — it has nothing to do with thoughts.

(*A long pause.*)

BENEATHA: I see. (*He starts to sit.*) Good night, George.

(*George looks at her a little oddly and starts to exit. He meets Mama coming in.*)

GEORGE: Oh — hello, Mrs. Younger.

MAMA: Hello, George, how you feeling?

GEORGE: Fine — fine, how are you?

MAMA: Oh, a little tired. You know them steps can get you after a day's work. You all have a nice time tonight?

GEORGE: Yes — a fine time. A fine time.

MAMA: Well, good night.

GEORGE: Good night. (*He exits. Mama closes the door behind her.*)

MAMA: Hello, honey. What you sitting like that for?

BENEATHA: I'm just sitting.

MAMA: Didn't you have a nice time?

BENEATHA: No.

MAMA: No? What's the matter?

BENEATHA: Mama, George is a fool — honest. (*She rises.*)

MAMA (*Hustling around unloading the packages she has entered with. She stops.*): Is he, baby?

BENEATHA: Yes.

(*Beneatha makes up Travis's bed as she talks.*)

MAMA: You sure?

BENEATHA: Yes.

MAMA: Well — I guess you better not waste your time with no fools.

(*Beneatha looks up at her mother, watching her put groceries in the refrigerator. Finally she gathers up her things and starts into the bedroom. At the door she stops and looks back at her mother.*)

BENEATHA: Mama —

MAMA: Yes, baby —

BENEATHA: Thank you.

MAMA: For what?

BENEATHA: For understanding me this time.

(*She exits quickly and the mother stands, smiling a little, looking at the place where Beneatha just stood. Ruth enters.*)

RUTH: Now don't you fool with any of this stuff, Lena —

MAMA: Oh, I just thought I'd sort a few things out. Is Brother here?

RUTH: Yes.

MAMA (*with concern*): Is he —

RUTH (*reading her eyes*): Yes.

(*Mama is silent and someone knocks on the door. Mama and Ruth exchange weary and knowing glances and Ruth opens it to admit the neighbor, Mrs. Johnson,° who is a rather squeaky wide-eyed lady of no particular age, with a newspaper under her arm.*)

MAMA (*changing her expression to acute delight and a ringing cheerful greeting*): Oh — hello there, Johnson.

JOHNSON (*this is a woman who decided long ago to be enthusiastic about* EVERYTHING *in life and she is inclined to wave her wrist vigorously at the height of her exclamatory comments*): Hello there, yourself! H'you this evening, Ruth?

RUTH (*not much of a deceptive type*): Fine, Mis' Johnson, h'you?

JOHNSON: Fine. (*Reaching out quickly, playfully, and patting Ruth's stomach.*) Ain't you starting to poke out none yet! (*She mugs with delight at the over-familiar remark and her eyes dart around looking at the crates and packing preparation; Mama's face is a cold sheet of endurance.*) Oh, ain't we getting ready round here, though! Yessir! Lookathere! I'm telling you the Youngers is really getting ready to "move on up a little higher!" — Bless God!

MAMA (*a little drily, doubting the total sincerity of the Blesser*): Bless God.

JOHNSON: He's good, ain't He?

MAMA: Oh yes, He's good.

JOHNSON: I mean sometimes He works in mysterious ways . . . but He works, don't He!

MAMA (*the same*): Yes, he does.

JOHNSON: I'm just soooooo happy for y'all. And this here child — (*about Ruth*) looks like she could just pop open with happiness, don't she. Where's all the rest of the family?

MAMA: Bennie's gone to bed —

JOHNSON: Ain't no . . . (*the implication is pregnancy*) sickness done hit you — I hope . . . ?

MAMA: No — she just tired. She was out this evening.

JOHNSON (*all is a coo, an emphatic coo*): Aw — ain't that lovely. She still going out with the little Murchison boy?

MAMA (*drily*): Ummmm huh.

Mrs. Johnson: This character and the scene of her visit were cut from the original production and early editions of the play.

JOHNSON: That's lovely. You sure got lovely children, Younger. Me and Isaiah talks all the time 'bout what fine children you was blessed with. We sure do.

MAMA: Ruth, give Mis' Johnson a piece of sweet potato pie and some milk.

JOHNSON: Oh honey, I can't stay hardly a minute — I just dropped in to see if there was anything I could do. (*Accepting the food easily.*) I guess y'all seen the news what's all over the colored paper this week . . .

MAMA: No — didn't get mine yet this week.

JOHNSON (*lifting her head and blinking with the spirit of catastrophe*): You mean you ain't read 'bout them colored people that was bombed out their place out there?

(*Ruth straightens with concern and takes the paper and reads it. Johnson notices her and feeds commentary.*)

JOHNSON: Ain't it something how bad these here white folks is getting here in Chicago! Lord, getting so you think you right down in Mississippi! (*With a tremendous and rather insincere sense of melodrama.*) 'Course I thinks it's wonderful how our folks keeps on pushing out. You hear some of these Negroes round here talking 'bout how they don't go where they ain't wanted and all that — but not me, honey! (*This is a lie.*) Wilhemenia Othella Johnson goes anywhere, any time she feels like it! (*With head movement for emphasis.*) Yes I do! Why if we left it up to these here crackers, the poor niggers wouldn't have nothing — (*She clasps her hand over her mouth.*) Oh, I always forgets you don't 'low that word in your house.

MAMA (*quietly, looking at her*): No — I don't 'low it.

JOHNSON (*vigorously again*): Me neither! I was just telling Isaiah yesterday when he come using it in front of me — I said, "Isaiah, it's just like Mis' Younger says all the time —"

MAMA: Don't you want some more pie?

JOHNSON: No — no thank you; this was lovely. I got to get on over home and have my midnight coffee. I hear some people say it don't let them sleep but I finds I can't close my eyes right lessen I done had that laaaast cup of coffee . . . (*She waits. A beat. Undaunted.*) My Good-night coffee, I calls it!

MAMA (*with much eye-rolling and communication between herself and Ruth*): Ruth, why don't you give Mis' Johnson some coffee.

(*Ruth gives Mama an unpleasant look for her kindness.*)

JOHNSON (*accepting the coffee*): Where's Brother tonight?

MAMA: He's lying down.

JOHNSON: Mmmmmmm, he sure gets his beauty rest, don't he? Good-looking man. Sure is a good-looking man! (*Reaching out to pat Ruth's stomach again.*) I guess that's how come we keep on having babies around here. (*She winks at Mama.*) One thing 'bout Brother, he always know how to have a *good* time. And soooooo ambitious! I bet it was his idea y'all moving out to Clybourne Park. Lord — I bet this time next month y'all's names will have been in the papers plenty — (*Holding up her hands to mark off each word of the headline she can see in front of her.*) "NEGROES INVADE CLYBOURNE PARK — BOMBED!"

MAMA (*she and Ruth look at the woman in amazement*): We ain't exactly moving out there to get bombed.

JOHNSON: Oh, honey — you know I'm praying to God every day that don't nothing like that happen! But you have to think of life like it is — and these here Chicago peckerwoods is some baaaad peckerwoods.

MAMA (*wearily*): We done thought about all that Mis' Johnson.

(*Beneatha comes out of the bedroom in her robe and passes through to the bathroom. Mrs. Johnson turns.*)

JOHNSON: Hello there, Bennie!

BENEATHA (*crisply*): Hello, Mrs. Johnson.

JOHNSON: How is school?

BENEATHA (*crisply*): Fine, thank you. (*She goes out.*)

JOHNSON (*insulted*): Getting so she don't have much to say to nobody.

MAMA: The child was on her way to the bathroom.

JOHNSON: I know — but sometimes she act like ain't got time to pass the time of day with nobody ain't been to college. Oh — I ain't criticizing her none. It's just — you know how some of our young people gets when they get a little education. (*Mama and Ruth say nothing, just look at her.*) Yes — well. Well, I guess I better get on home. (*Unmoving.*) 'Course I can understand how she must be proud and everything — being the only one in the family to make something of herself. I know just being a chauffeur ain't never satisfied Brother none. He shouldn't feel like that, though. Ain't nothing wrong with being a chauffeur.

MAMA: There's plenty wrong with it.

JOHNSON: What?

MAMA: Plenty. My husband always said being any kind of a servant wasn't a fit thing for a man to have to be. He always said a man's hands was made to make things, or to turn the earth with —

not to drive nobody's car for 'em — or — (*she looks at her own hands*) carry they slop jars. And my boy is just like him — he wasn't meant to wait on nobody.

JOHNSON (*rising, somewhat offended*): Mmmmmmmmm. The Youngers is too much for me! (*She looks around.*) You sure one proud-acting bunch of colored folks. Well — I always thinks like Booker T. Washington said that time — "Education has spoiled many a good plow hand" —

MAMA: Is that what old Booker T. said?

JOHNSON: He sure did.

MAMA: Well, it sounds just like him. The fool.

JOHNSON (*indignantly*): Well — he was one of our great men.

MAMA: Who said so?

JOHNSON (*nonplussed*): You know, me and you ain't never agreed about some things, Lena Younger. I guess I better be going —

RUTH (*quickly*): Good night.

JOHNSON: Good night. Oh — (*Thrusting it at her.*) You can keep the paper! (*With a trill.*) 'Night.

MAMA: Good night, Mis' Johnson.

(*Mrs. Johnson exits.*)

RUTH: If ignorance was gold . . .

MAMA: Shush. Don't talk about folks behind their backs.

RUTH: You do.

MAMA: I'm old and corrupted. (*Beneatha enters.*) You was rude to Mis' Johnson, Beneatha, and I don't like it at all.

BENEATHA (*at her door*): Mama, if there are two things we, as a people, have got to overcome, one is the Klu Klux Klan — and the other is Mrs. Johnson. (*She exits.*)

MAMA: Smart aleck.

(*The phone rings.*)

RUTH: I'll get it.

MAMA: Lord, ain't this a popular place tonight.

RUTH (*at the phone*): Hello — Just a minute. (*Goes to door.*) Walter, it's Mrs. Arnold. (*Waits. Goes back to the phone. Tense.*) Hello. Yes, this is his wife speaking . . . He's lying down now. Yes . . . well, he'll be in tomorrow. He's been very sick. Yes — I know we should have called, but we were so sure he'd be able to come in today. Yes — yes, I'm very sorry. Yes . . . Thank you very much. (*She hangs up. Walter is standing in the doorway of the bedroom behind her.*) That was Mrs. Arnold.

WALTER (*indifferently*): Was it?

RUTH: She said if you don't come in tomorrow that they are getting a new man . . .

WALTER: Ain't that sad — ain't that crying sad.

RUTH: She said Mr. Arnold has had to take a cab for three days . . . Walter, you ain't been to work for three days! (*This is a revelation to her.*) Where you been, Walter Lee Younger? (*Walter looks at her and starts to laugh.*) You're going to lose your job.

WALTER: That's right . . . (*He turns on the radio.*)

RUTH: Oh, Walter, and with your mother working like a dog every day —

(*A steamy, deep blues pours into the room.*)

WALTER: That's sad too — Everything is sad.

MAMA: What you been doing for these three days, son?

WALTER: Mama — you don't know all the things a man what got leisure can find to do in this city . . . What's this — Friday night? Well — Wednesday I borrowed Willy Harris' car and I went for a drive . . . just me and myself and I drove and drove . . . Way out . . . way past South Chicago, and I parked the car and I sat and looked at the steel mills all day long. I just sat in the car and looked at them big black chimneys for hours. Then I drove back and I went to the Green Hat. (*Pause.*) And Thursday — Thursday I borrowed the car again and I got in it and I pointed it the other way and I drove the other way — for hours — way, way up to Wisconsin, and I looked at the farms. I just drove and looked at the farms. Then I drove back and I went to the Green Hat. (*Pause.*) And today — today I didn't get the car. Today I just walked. All over the Southside. And I looked at the Negroes and they looked at me and finally I just sat down on the curb at Thirty-ninth and South Parkway and I just sat there and watched the Negroes go by. And then I went to the Green Hat. You all sad? You all depressed? And you know where I am going right now —

(*Ruth goes out quietly.*)

MAMA: Oh, Big Walter, is this the harvest of our days?

WALTER: You know what I like about the Green Hat? I like this little cat they got there who blows a sax . . . He blows. He talks to me. He ain't but 'bout five feet tall and he's got a conked head and his eyes is always closed and he's all music —

MAMA (*rising and getting some papers out of her handbag*): Walter —

WALTER: And there's this other guy who plays the piano . . . and they got a sound. I mean they can work on some music . . . They got the best little combo in the world in the Green Hat . . . You can just sit there and drink and listen to them three men play and you realize that don't nothing matter worth a damn, but just being there —

MAMA: I've helped do it to you, haven't I, son? Walter I been wrong.

WALTER: Naw — you ain't never been wrong about nothing, Mama.

MAMA: Listen to me, now. I say I been wrong, son. That I been doing to you what the rest of the world been doing to you. (*She turns off the radio.*) Walter — (*She stops and he looks up slowly at her and she meets his eyes pleadingly.*) What you ain't never understood is that I ain't got nothing, don't own nothing, ain't never really wanted nothing that wasn't for you. There ain't nothing as precious to me . . . There ain't nothing worth holding on to, money, dreams, nothing else — if it means — if it means it's going to destroy my boy. (*She takes an envelope out of her handbag and puts it in front of him and he watches her without speaking or moving.*) I paid the man thirty-five hundred dollars down on the house. That leaves sixty-five hundred dollars. Monday morning I want you to take this money and take three thousand dollars and put it in a savings account for Beneatha's medical schooling. The rest you put in a checking account — with your name on it. And from now on any penny that come out of it or that go in it is for you to look after. For you to decide. (*She drops her hands a little helplessly.*) It ain't much, but it's all I got in the world and I'm putting it in your hands. I'm telling you to be the head of this family from now on like you supposed to be.

WALTER (*stares at the money*): You trust me like that, Mama?

MAMA: I ain't never stop trusting you. Like I ain't never stop loving you.

(*She goes out, and Walter sits looking at the money on the table. Finally, in a decisive gesture, he gets up and, in mingled joy and desperation, picks up the money. At the same moment, Travis enters for bed.*)

TRAVIS: What's the matter, Daddy? You drunk?

WALTER (*sweetly, more sweetly than we have ever known him*): No, Daddy ain't drunk. Daddy ain't going to never be drunk again . . .

TRAVIS: Well, good night, Daddy.

(*The father has come from behind the couch and leans over, embracing his son.*)

WALTER: Son, I feel like talking to you tonight.

TRAVIS: About what?

WALTER: Oh, about a lot of things. About you and what kind of man you going to be when you grow up. . . . Son — son, what do you want to be when you grow up?

TRAVIS: A bus driver.

WALTER (*laughing a little*): A what? Man, that ain't nothing to want to be!

TRAVIS: Why not?

WALTER: 'Cause, man — it ain't big enough — you know what I mean.

TRAVIS: I don't know then. I can't make up my mind. Sometimes Mama asks me that too. And sometimes when I tell her I just want to be like you — she says she don't want me to be like that and sometimes she says she does. . . .

WALTER (*gathering him up in his arms*): You know what, Travis? In seven years you going to be seventeen years old. And things is going to be very different with us in seven years, Travis. . . . One day when you are seventeen I'll come home — home from my office downtown somewhere —

TRAVIS: You don't work in no office, Daddy.

WALTER: No — but after tonight. After what your daddy gonna do tonight, there's going to be offices — a whole lot of offices. . . .

TRAVIS: What you gonna do tonight, Daddy?

WALTER: You wouldn't understand yet, son, but your daddy's gonna make a transaction . . . a business transaction that's going to change our lives. . . . That's how come one day when you 'bout seventeen years old I'll come home and I'll be pretty tired, you know what I mean, after a day of conferences and secretaries getting things wrong the way they do . . . 'cause an executive's life is hell, man — (*The more he talks the farther away he gets.*) And I'll pull the car up on the driveway . . . just a plain black Chrysler, I think, with white walls — no — black tires. More elegant. Rich people don't have to be flashy . . . though I'll have to get something a little sportier for Ruth — maybe a Cadillac convertible to do her shopping in. . . . And I'll come up the steps to the house and the gardener will be clipping away at the hedges and he'll say, "Good evening, Mr. Younger." And I'll say, "Hello, Jefferson, how are you this evening?" And I'll go inside and Ruth will come downstairs and meet me at the door and we'll kiss each other and she'll take my arm and we'll go up to your room to see you sitting on the floor with the catalogues of all the great schools in America around you. . . . All the great schools in the world! And — and I'll say, all right son — it's your seventeenth birthday, what is it you've decided? . . . Just tell me where you want to go to school and you'll *go*. Just tell me, what it is you want to be — and you'll *be* it. . . . Whatever you want to be — Yessir! (*He holds his arms open for Travis.*) You just name it, son . . . (*Travis leaps into them*) and I hand you the world!

(*Walter's voice has risen in pitch and hysterical promise and on the last line he lifts Travis high.*)

Scene III

(*Time: Saturday, moving day, one week later.*)

(*Before the curtain rises, Ruth's voice, a strident, dramatic church alto, cuts through the silence.*)

(*It is, in the darkness, a triumphant surge, a penetrating statement of expectation: "Oh, Lord, I don't feel no ways tired! Children, oh, glory hallelujah!"*)

(*As the curtain rises we see that Ruth is alone in the living room, finishing up the family's packing. It is moving day. She is nailing crates and tying cartons. Beneatha enters, carrying a guitar case, and watches her exuberant sister-in-law.*)

RUTH: Hey!

BENEATHA (*putting away the case*): Hi.

RUTH (*pointing at a package*): Honey — look in that package there and see what I found on sale this morning at the South Center. (*Ruth gets up and moves to the package and draws out some curtains.*) Lookahere — hand-turned hems!

BENEATHA: How do you know the window size out there?

RUTH (*who hadn't thought of that*): Oh — Well, they bound to fit something in the whole house. Anyhow, they was too good a bargain to pass up. (*Ruth slaps her head, suddenly remembering something.*) Oh, Bennie — I meant to put a special note on that carton over there. That's your mama's good china and she wants 'em to be very careful with it.

BENEATHA: I'll do it.

(*Beneatha finds a piece of paper and starts to draw large letters on it.*)

RUTH: You know what I'm going to do soon as I get in that new house?

BENEATHA: What?

RUTH: Honey — I'm going to run me a tub of water up to here . . . (*With her fingers practically up to her nostrils.*) And I'm going to get in it — and I am going to sit . . . and sit . . . and sit in that hot water and the first person who knocks to tell *me* to hurry up and come out —

BENEATHA: Gets shot at sunrise.

RUTH (*laughing happily*): You said it, sister! (*Noticing how large Beneatha is absent-mindedly making the note.*) Honey, they ain't going to read that from no airplane.

BENEATHA (*laughing herself*): I guess I always think things have more emphasis if they are big, somehow.

RUTH (*looking up at her and smiling*): You and your brother seem to have that as a philosophy of life. Lord, that man — done changed so 'round here.

You know — you know what we did last night? Me and Walter Lee?

BENEATHA: What?

RUTH (*smiling to herself*): We went to the movies. (*Looking at Beneatha to see if she understands.*) We went to the movies. You know the last time me and Walter went to the movies together?

BENEATHA: No.

RUTH: Me neither. That's how long it been. (*Smiling again.*) But we went last night. The picture wasn't much good, but that didn't seem to matter. We went — and we held hands.

BENEATHA: Oh, Lord!

RUTH: We held hands — and you know what?

BENEATHA: What?

RUTH: When we come out of the show it was late and dark and all the stores and things was closed up . . . and it was kind of chilly and there wasn't many people on the streets . . . and we was still holding hands, me and Walter.

BENEATHA: You're killing me.

(*Walter enters with a large package. His happiness is deep in him; he cannot keep still with his newfound exuberance. He is singing and wiggling and snapping his fingers. He puts his package in a corner and puts a phonograph record, which he has brought in with him, on the record player. As the music, soulful and sensuous, comes up he dances over to Ruth and tries to get her to dance with him. She gives in at last to his raunchiness and in a fit of giggling allows herself to be drawn into his mood. They dip and she melts into his arms in a classic, body-melding "slow drag."*)

BENEATHA (*regarding them a long time as they dance, then drawing in her breath for a deeply exaggerated comment which she does not particularly mean*): Talk about — oldddddddddd-fashioneddddddd — Negroes!

WALTER (*stopping momentarily*): What kind of Negroes?

(*He says this in fun. He is not angry with her today, nor with anyone. He starts to dance with his wife again.*)

BENEATHA: Old-fashioned.

WALTER (*as he dances with Ruth*): You know, when these *New Negroes* have their convention — (*pointing at his sister*) — that is going to be the chairman of the Committee on Unending Agitation. (*He goes on dancing, then stops.*) Race, race, race! . . . Girl, I do believe you are the first person in the history of the entire human race to successfully brainwash yourself. (*Beneatha breaks up and he goes on dancing. He stops again, enjoying his tease.*) Damn, even the N double A C P takes a

holiday sometimes! (*Beneatha and Ruth laugh. He dances with Ruth some more and starts to laugh and stops and pantomimes someone over an operating table.*) I can just see that chick someday looking down at some poor cat on an operating table and before she starts to slice him, she says . . . (*pulling his sleeves back maliciously*) "By the way, what are your views on civil rights down there? . . ."

(*He laughs at her again and starts to dance happily. The bell sounds.*)

BENEATHA: Sticks and stones may break my bones but . . . words will never hurt me!

(*Beneatha goes to the door and opens it as Walter and Ruth go on with the clowning. Beneatha is somewhat surprised to see a quiet-looking middle-aged white man in a business suit holding his hat and a briefcase in his hand and consulting a small piece of paper.*)

MAN: Uh — how do you do, miss. I am looking for a Mrs. — (*he looks at the slip of paper*) Mrs. Lena Younger? (*He stops short, struck dumb at the sight of the oblivious Walter and Ruth.*)

BENEATHA (*smoothing her hair with slight embarrassment*): Oh — yes, that's my mother. Excuse me. (*She closes the door and turns to quiet the other two.*) Ruth! Brother! (*Enunciating precisely but soundlessly: "There's a white man at the door!" They stop dancing, Ruth cuts off the phonograph, Beneatha opens the door. The man casts a curious quick glance at all of them.*) Uh — come in please.

MAN (*coming in*): Thank you.

BENEATHA: My mother isn't here just now. Is it business?

MAN: Yes . . . well, of a sort.

WALTER (*freely, the Man of the House*): Have a seat. I'm Mrs. Younger's son. I look after most of her business matters.

(*Ruth and Beneatha exchange amused glances.*)

MAN (*regarding Walter, and sitting*): Well — My name is Karl Lindner . . .

WALTER (*stretching out his hand*): Walter Younger. This is my wife — (*Ruth nods politely*) — and my sister.

LINDNER: How do you do.

WALTER (*amiably, as he sits himself easily on a chair, leaning forward on his knees with interest and looking expectantly into the newcomer's face*): What can we do for you, Mr. Lindner!

LINDNER (*some minor shuffling of the hat and briefcase on his knees*): Well — I am a representative of the Clybourne Park Improvement Association —

WALTER (*pointing*): Why don't you sit your things on the floor?

LINDNER: Oh — yes. Thank you. (*He slides the briefcase and hat under the chair.*) And as I was saying — I am from the Clybourne Park Improvement Association and we have had it brought to our attention at the last meeting that you people — or at least your mother — has bought a piece of residential property at — (*he digs for the slip of paper again*) — four o six Clybourne Street . . .

WALTER: That's right. Care for something to drink? Ruth, get Mr. Lindner a beer.

LINDNER (*upset for some reason*): Oh — no, really. I mean thank you very much, but no thank you.

RUTH (*innocently*): Some coffee?

LINDNER: Thank you, nothing at all.

(*Beneatha is watching the man carefully.*)

LINDNER: Well, I don't know how much you folks know about our organization. (*He is a gentle man; thoughtful and somewhat labored in his manner.*) It is one of these community organizations set up to look after — oh, you know, things like block upkeep and special projects and we also have what we call our New Neighbors Orientation Committee . . .

BENEATHA (*drily*): Yes — and what do they do?

LINDNER (*turning a little to her and then returning the main force to Walter*): Well — it's what you might call a sort of welcoming committee, I guess. I mean they, we — I'm the chairman of the committee — go around and see the new people who move into the neighborhood and sort of give them the lowdown on the way we do things out in Clybourne Park.

BENEATHA (*with appreciation of the two meanings, which escape Ruth and Walter*): Un-huh.

LINDNER: And we also have the category of what the association calls — (*he looks elsewhere*) — uh — special community problems . . .

BENEATHA: Yes — and what are some of those?

WALTER: Girl, let the man talk.

LINDNER (*with understated relief*): Thank you. I would sort of like to explain this thing in my own way. I mean I want to explain to you in a certain way.

WALTER: Go ahead.

LINDNER: Yes. Well. I'm going to try to get right to the point. I'm sure we'll all appreciate that in the long run.

BENEATHA: Yes.

WALTER: Be still now!

LINDNER: Well —

RUTH (*still innocently*): Would you like another chair — you don't look comfortable.

LINDNER (*more frustrated than annoyed*): No, thank you very much. Please. Well — to get right to the point I — (*a great breath, and he is off at last*) I am sure you people must be aware of some of the incidents which have happened in various parts of the city when colored people have moved into certain areas — (*Beneatha exhales heavily and starts tossing a piece of fruit up and down in the air.*) Well — because we have what I think is going to be a unique type of organization in American community life — not only do we deplore that kind of thing — but we are trying to do something about it. (*Beneatha stops tossing and turns with a new and quizzical interest to the man.*) We feel — (*gaining confidence in his mission because of the interest in the faces of the people he is talking to*) — we feel that most of the trouble in this world, when you come right down to it — (*he hits his knee for emphasis*) — most of the trouble exists because people just don't sit down and talk to each other.

RUTH (*nodding as she might in church, pleased with the remark*): You can say that again, mister.

LINDNER (*more encouraged by such affirmation*): That we don't try hard enough in this world to understand the other fellow's problem. The other guy's point of view.

RUTH: Now that's right.

(*Beneatha and Walter merely watch and listen with genuine interest.*)

LINDNER: Yes — that's the way we feel out in Clybourne Park. And that's why I was elected to come here this afternoon and talk to you people. Friendly like, you know, the way people should talk to each other and see if we couldn't find some way to work this thing out. As I say, the whole business is a matter of *caring* about the other fellow. Anybody can see that you are a nice family of folks, hard-working and honest I'm sure. (*Beneatha frowns slightly, quizzically, her head tilted regarding him.*) Today everybody knows what it means to be on the outside of *something*. And of course, there is always somebody who is out to take advantage of people who don't always understand.

WALTER: What do you mean?

LINDNER: Well — you see our community is made up of people who've worked hard as the dickens for years to build up that little community. They're not rich and fancy people; just hard-working, honest people who don't really have much but those little homes and a dream of the kind of community they want to raise their children in. Now, I don't say we are perfect and there is a lot wrong in some of the things they want. But you've got to admit that a man, right or wrong, has the right to want to have the neighborhood he lives in a certain kind of way. And at the moment the overwhelming majority of our people out there feel that people get along better, take more of a common interest in the life of the community, when they share a common background. I want you to believe me when I tell you that race prejudice simply doesn't enter into it. It is a matter of the people of Clybourne Park believing, rightly or wrongly, as I say, that for the happiness of all concerned that our Negro families are happier when they live in their *own* communities.

BENEATHA (*with a grand and bitter gesture*): This, friends, is the Welcoming Committee!

WALTER (*dumfounded, looking at Lindner*): Is this what you came marching all the way over here to tell us?

LINDNER: Well, now we've been having a fine conversation. I hope you'll hear me all the way through.

WALTER (*tightly*): Go ahead, man.

LINDNER: You see — in the face of all the things I have said, we are prepared to make your family a very generous offer . . .

BENEATHA: Thirty pieces and not a coin less!

WALTER: Yeah!

LINDNER (*putting on his glasses and drawing a form out of the briefcase*): Our association is prepared, through the collective effort of our people, to buy the house from you at a financial gain to your family.

RUTH: Lord have mercy, ain't this the living gall!

WALTER: All right, you through?

LINDNER: Well, I want to give you the exact terms of the financial arrangement —

WALTER: We don't want to hear no exact terms of no arrangements. I want to know if you got any more to tell us 'bout getting together?

LINDNER (*taking off his glasses*): Well — I don't suppose that you feel . . .

WALTER: Never mind how I feel — you got any more to say 'bout how people ought to sit down and talk to each other? . . . Get out of my house, man.

(*He turns his back and walks to the door.*)

LINDNER (*looking around at the hostile faces and reaching and assembling his hat and briefcase*): Well — I don't understand why you people are reacting this way. What do you think you are going to gain by moving into a neighborhood where you just aren't wanted and where some elements — well — people can get awful worked up when they feel that their whole way of life and everything they've ever worked for is threatened.

WALTER: Get out.

LINDNER (*at the door, holding a small card*): Well — I'm sorry it went like this.

WALTER: Get out.

LINDNER (*almost sadly regarding Walter*): You just can't force people to change their hearts, son.

(*He turns and put his card on a table and exits. Walter pushes the door to with stinging hatred, and stands looking at it. Ruth just sits and Beneatha just stands. They say nothing. Mama and Travis enter.*)

MAMA: Well — this all the packing got done since I left out of here this morning. I testify before God that my children got all the energy of the *dead!* What time the moving men due?

BENEATHA: Four o'clock. You had a caller, Mama.

(*She is smiling, teasingly.*)

MAMA: Sure enough — who?

BENEATHA (*her arms folded saucily*): The Welcoming Committee.

(*Walter and Ruth giggle.*)

MAMA (*innocently*): Who?

BENEATHA: The Welcoming Committee. They said they're sure going to be glad to see you when you get there.

WALTER (*devilishly*): Yeah, they said they can't hardly wait to see your face.

(*Laughter.*)

MAMA (*sensing their facetiousness*): What's the matter with you all?

WALTER: Ain't nothing the matter with us. We just telling you 'bout the gentleman who came to see you this afternoon. From the Clybourne Park Improvement Association.

MAMA: What he want?

RUTH (*in the same mood as Beneatha and Walter*): To welcome you, honey.

WALTER: He said they can't hardly wait. He said the one thing they don't have, that they just *dying* to have out there is a fine family of fine colored people! (*To Ruth and Beneatha.*) Ain't that right!

RUTH (*mockingly*): Yeah! He left his card —

BENEATHA (*handing card to Mama*): In case.

(*Mama reads and throws it on the floor — understanding and looking off as she draws her chair up to the table on which she has put her plant and some sticks and some cord.*)

MAMA: Father, give us strength. (*Knowingly — and without fun.*) Did he threaten us?

BENEATHA: Oh — Mama — they don't do it like that anymore. He talked Brotherhood. He said everybody ought to learn how to sit down and hate each other with good Christian fellowship.

(*She and Walter shake hands to ridicule the remark.*)

MAMA (*sadly*): Lord, protect us . . .

RUTH: You should hear the money those folks raised to buy the house from us. All we paid and then some.

BENEATHA: What they think we going to do — eat 'em?

RUTH: No, honey, marry 'em.

MAMA (*shaking her head*): Lord, Lord, Lord . . .

RUTH: Well — that's the way the crackers crumble. (*A beat.*) Joke.

BENEATHA (*laughingly noticing what her mother is doing*): Mama, what are you doing?

MAMA: Fixing my plant so it won't get hurt none on the way . . .

BENEATHA: Mama, you going to take *that* to the new house?

MAMA: Un-huh —

BENEATHA: That raggedy-looking old thing?

MAMA (*stopping and looking at her*): It expresses ME!

RUTH (*with delight, to Beneatha*): So there, Miss Thing!

(*Walter comes to Mama suddenly and bends down behind her and squeezes her in his arms with all his strength. She is overwhelmed by the suddenness of it and, though delighted, her manner is like that of Ruth and Travis.*)

MAMA: Look out now, boy! You make me mess up my thing here!

WALTER (*his face lit, he slips down on his knees beside her, his arms still about her*): Mama . . . you know what it means to climb up in the chariot?

MAMA (*gruffly, very happy*): Get on away from me now . . .

RUTH (*near the gift-wrapped package, trying to catch Walter's eye*): Psst —

WALTER: What the old song say, Mama . . .

RUTH: Walter — Now?

(*She is pointing at the package.*)

WALTER (*speaking the lines, sweetly, playfully, in his mother's face*): I got wings . . . you got wings . . .

All God's Children got wings . . .

MAMA: Boy — get out of my face and do some work . . .

WALTER: When I get to heaven gonna put on my wings,

Gonna fly all over God's heaven . . .

BENEATHA (*teasingly, from across the room*): Everybody talking 'bout heaven ain't going there!

WALTER (*to Ruth, who is carrying the box across to them*): I don't know, you think we ought to give her that . . . Seems to me she ain't been very appreciative around here.

MAMA (*eyeing the box, which is obviously a gift*): What is that?

WALTER (*taking it from Ruth and putting it on the table in front of Mama*): Well — what you all think? Should we give it to her?

RUTH: Oh — she was pretty good today.

MAMA: I'll good you —

(*She turns her eyes to the box again.*)

BENEATHA: Open it, Mama.

(*She stands up, looks at it, turns, and looks at all of them, and then presses her hands together and does not open the package.*)

WALTER (*sweetly*): Open it, Mama. It's for you. (*Mama looks in his eyes. It is the first present in her life without its being Christmas. Slowly she opens her package and lifts out, one by one, a brand-new sparkling set of gardening tools. Walter continues, prodding.*) Ruth made up the note — read it . . .

MAMA (*picking up the card and adjusting her glasses*): "To our own Mrs. Miniver — Love from Brother, Ruth and Beneatha." Ain't that lovely . . .

TRAVIS (*tugging at his father's sleeve*): Daddy, can I give her mine now?

WALTER: All right, son. (*Travis flies to get his gift.*)

MAMA: Now I don't have to use my knives and forks no more . . .

WALTER: Travis didn't want to go in with the rest of us, Mama. He got his own. (*Somewhat amused.*) We don't know what it is . . .

TRAVIS (*racing back in the room with a large hatbox and putting it in front of his grandmother*): Here!

MAMA: Lord have mercy, baby. You done gone and bought your grandmother a hat?

TRAVIS (*very proud*): Open it!

(*She does and lifts out an elaborate, but very elaborate, wide gardening hat, and all the adults break up at the sight of it.*)

RUTH: Travis, honey, what is that?

TRAVIS (*who thinks it is beautiful and appropriate*): It's a gardening hat! Like the ladies always have on in the magazines when they work in their gardens.

BENEATHA (*giggling fiercely*): Travis — we were trying to make Mama Mrs. Miniver — not Scarlett O'Hara!

MAMA (*indignantly*): What's the matter with you all! This here is a beautiful hat! (*Absurdly.*) I always wanted me one just like it!

(*She pops it on her head to prove it to her grandson, and the hat is ludicrous and considerably oversized.*)

RUTH: Hot dog! Go, Mama!

WALTER (*doubled over with laughter*): I'm sorry, Mama — but you look like you ready to go out and chop you some cotton sure enough!

(*They all laugh except Mama, out of deference to Travis's feelings.*)

MAMA (*gathering the boy up to her*): Bless your heart — this is the prettiest hat I ever owned — (*Walter, Ruth, and Beneatha chime in — noisily, festively, and insincerely congratulating Travis on his gift.*) What are we all standing around here for? We ain't finished packin' yet. Bennie, you ain't packed one book.

(*The bell rings.*)

BENEATHA: That couldn't be the movers . . . it's not hardly two good yet —

(*Beneatha goes into her room. Mama starts for door.*)

WALTER (*turning, stiffening*): Wait — wait — I'll get it.

(*He stands and looks at the door.*)

MAMA: You expecting company, son?

WALTER (*just looking at the door*): Yeah — yeah . . .

(*Mama looks at Ruth, and they exchange innocent and unfrightened glances.*)

MAMA (*not understanding*): Well, let them in, son.

BENEATHA (*from her room*): We need some more string.

MAMA: Travis — you run to the hardware and get me some string cord.

(*Mama goes out and Walter turns and looks at Ruth. Travis goes to a dish for money.*)

RUTH: Why don't you answer the door, man?

WALTER (*suddenly bounding across the floor to embrace her*): 'Cause sometimes it hard to let the future begin! (*Stooping down in her face.*) I got wings! You got wings! All God's children got wings! (*He crosses to the door and throws it open. Standing there is a very slight little man in a not too prosperous business suit and with haunted frightened eyes and a hat pulled down tightly, brim up, around his forehead. Travis passes between the*

men and exits. Walter leans deep in the man's face, still in his jubilance.*) When I get to heaven gonna put on my wings, Gonna fly all over God's heaven . . . (*The little man just stares at him.*) Heaven — (*Suddenly he stops and looks past the little man into the empty hallway.*) Where's Willy, man?

BOBO: He ain't with me.

WALTER (*not disturbed*): Oh — come on in. You know my wife.

BOBO (*dumbly, taking off his hat*): Yes — h'you, Miss Ruth.

RUTH (*quietly, a mood apart from her husband already, seeing Bobo*): Hello, Bobo.

WALTER: You right on time today . . . Right on time. That's the way! (*He slaps Bobo on his back.*) Sit down . . . lemme hear.

(*Ruth stands stiffly and quietly in back of them, as though somehow she senses death, her eyes fixed on her husband.*)

BOBO (*his frightened eyes on the floor, his hat in his hands*): Could I please get a drink of water, before I tell you about it, Walter Lee?

(*Walter does not take his eyes off the man. Ruth goes blindly to the tap and gets a glass of water and brings it to Bobo.*)

WALTER: There ain't nothing wrong, is there?

BOBO: Lemme tell you —

WALTER: Man — didn't nothing go wrong?

BOBO: Lemme tell you — Walter Lee. (*Looking at Ruth and talking to her more than to Walter.*) You know how it was. I got to tell you how it was. I mean first I got to tell you how it was all the way . . . I mean about the money I put in, Walter Lee . . .

WALTER (*with taut agitation now*): What about the money you put in?

BOBO: Well — it wasn't much as we told you — me and Willy — (*He stops.*) I'm sorry, Walter. I got a bad feeling about it. I got a real bad feeling about it . . .

WALTER: Man, what you telling me about all this for? . . . Tell me what happened in Springfield . . .

BOBO: Springfield.

RUTH (*like a dead woman*): What was supposed to happen in Springfield?

BOBO (*to her*): This deal that me and Walter went into with Willy — Me and Willy was going to go down to Springfield and spread some money 'round so's we wouldn't have to wait so long for the liquor license . . . That's what we were going to do. Everybody said that was the way you had to do, you understand, Miss Ruth?

WALTER: Man — what happened down there?

BOBO (*a pitiful man, near tears*): I'm trying to tell you, Walter.

WALTER (*screaming at him suddenly*): THEN TELL ME, GODDAMMIT . . . WHAT'S THE MATTER WITH YOU?

BOBO: Man . . . I didn't go to no Springfield, yesterday.

WALTER (*halted, life hanging in the moment*): Why not?

BOBO (*the long way, the hard way to tell*): 'Cause I didn't have no reasons to . . .

WALTER: Man, what are you talking about!

BOBO: I'm talking about the fact that when I got to the train station yesterday morning — eight o'clock like we planned . . . Man — *Willy didn't never show up.*

WALTER: Why . . . where was he . . . where is he?

BOBO: That's what I'm trying to tell you . . . I don't know . . . I waited six hours . . . I called his house . . . and I waited . . . six hours . . . I waited in that train station six hours . . . (*Breaking into tears.*) That was all the extra money I had in the world . . . (*Looking up at Walter with the tears running down his face.*) Man, *Willy is gone.*

WALTER: Gone, what you mean Willy is gone? Gone where? You mean he went by himself. You mean he went off to Springfield by himself — to take care of getting the license — (*Turns and looks anxiously at Ruth.*) You mean maybe he didn't want too many people in on the business down there? (*Looks to Ruth again, as before.*) You know Willy got his own ways. (*Looks back to Bobo.*) Maybe you was late yesterday and he just went on down there without you. Maybe — maybe — he's been callin' you at home tryin' to tell you what happened or something. Maybe — maybe — he just got sick. He's somewhere — he's got to be somewhere. We just got to find him — me and you got to find him. (*Grabs Bobo senselessly by the collar and starts to shake him.*) We got to!

BOBO (*in sudden angry, frightened agony*): What's the matter with you, Walter! *When a cat take off with your money he don't leave you no road maps!*

WALTER (*turning madly, as though he is looking for Willy in the very room*): Willy! . . . Willy . . . don't do it . . . Please don't do it . . . Man, not with that money . . . Man, please, not with that money . . . Oh, God . . . Don't let it be true . . . (*He is wandering around, crying out for Willy and looking for him or perhaps for help from God.*) Man . . . I trusted you . . . Man, I put my life in your hands . . . (*He starts to crumple down on the floor as Ruth just covers her face in horror. Mama opens the door and comes into the room, with Beneatha behind her.*) Man . . . (*He starts to pound the floor with his fists, sobbing wildly.*) THAT MONEY IS MADE OUT OF MY FATHER'S FLESH ——

BOBO (*standing over him helplessly*): I'm sorry, Walter . . . (*Only Walter's sobs reply. Bobo puts on his hat.*) I had my life staked on this deal, too . . .

(*He exits.*)

MAMA (*to Walter*): Son — (*She goes to him, bends down to him, talks to his bent head.*) Son . . . Is it gone? Son, I gave you sixty-five hundred dollars. Is it gone? All of it? Beneatha's money too?

WALTER (*lifting his head slowly*): Mama . . . I never . . . went to the bank at all . . .

MAMA (*not wanting to believe him*): You mean . . . your sister's school money . . . you used that too . . . Walter? . . .

WALTER: Yessss! All of it . . . It's all gone . . .

(*There is total silence. Ruth stands with her face covered with her hands; Beneatha leans forlornly against a wall, fingering a piece of red ribbon from the mother's gift. Mama stops and looks at her son without recognition and then, quite without thinking about it, starts to beat him senselessly in the face. Beneatha goes to them and stops it.*)

BENEATHA: Mama!

(*Mama stops and looks at both of her children and rises slowly and wanders vaguely, aimlessly away from them.*)

MAMA: I seen . . . him . . . night after night . . . come in . . . and look at that rug . . . and then look at me . . . the red showing in his eyes . . . the veins moving in his head . . . I seen him grow thin and old before he was forty . . . working and working and working like somebody's old horse . . . killing himself . . . and you — you give it all away in a day — (*She raises her arms to strike him again.*)

BENEATHA: Mama —

MAMA: Oh, God . . . (*She looks up to Him.*) Look down here — and show me the strength.

BENEATHA: Mama —

MAMA (*folding over*): Strength . . .

BENEATHA (*plaintively*): Mama . . .

MAMA: Strength!

ACT III

(*An hour later.*)

(*At curtain, there is a sullen light of gloom in the living room, gray light not unlike that which began the first scene of act I. At left we can see Walter within his room, alone with himself. He is stretched out on the bed, his shirt out and open, his arms under his head. He does not smoke, he does not cry out, he merely lies there, looking up at the ceiling, much as if he were alone in the world.)*

(In the living room Beneatha sits at the table, still surrounded by the now almost ominous packing crates. She sits looking off. We feel that this is a mood struck perhaps an hour before, and it lingers now, full of the empty sound of profound disappointment. We see on a line from her brother's bedroom the sameness of their attitudes. Presently the bell rings and Beneatha rises without ambition or interest in answering. It is Asagai, smiling broadly, striding into the room with energy and happy expectation and conversation.)

ASAGAI: I came over . . . I had some free time. I thought I might help with the packing. Ah, I like the look of packing crates! A household in preparation for a journey! It depresses some people . . . but for me . . . it is another feeling. Something full of the flow of life, do you understand? Movement, progress . . . It makes me think of Africa.

BENEATHA: Africa!

ASAGAI: What kind of a mood is this? Have I told you how deeply you move me?

BENEATHA: He gave away the money, Asagai . . .

ASAGAI: Who gave away what money?

BENEATHA: The insurance money. My brother gave it away.

ASAGAI: Gave it away?

BENEATHA: He made an investment! With a man even Travis wouldn't have trusted with his most worn-out marbles.

ASAGAI: And it's gone?

BENEATHA: Gone!

ASAGAI: I'm very sorry . . . And you, now?

BENEATHA: Me? . . . Me? . . . Me, I'm nothing . . . Me. When I was very small . . . we used to take our sleds out in the wintertime and the only hills we had were the ice-covered stone steps of some houses down the street. And we used to fill them in with snow and make them smooth and slide down them all day . . . and it was very dangerous, you know . . . far too steep . . . and sure enough one day a kid named Rufus came down too fast and hit the sidewalk and we saw his face just split open right there in front of us . . . And I remember standing there looking at his bloody open face thinking that was the end of Rufus. But the ambulance came and they took him to the hospital and they fixed the broken bones and they sewed it all up . . . and the next time I saw Rufus he just had a little line down the middle of his face . . . I never got over that . . .

ASAGAI: What?

BENEATHA: That that was what one person could do for another, fix him up — sew up the problem, make him all right again. That was the most marvelous thing in the world . . . I wanted to do that. I always thought it was the one concrete thing in the world that a human being could do. Fix up the sick, you know — and make them whole again. This was truly being God . . .

ASAGAI: You wanted to be God?

BENEATHA: No — I wanted to cure. It used to be so important to me. I wanted to cure. It used to matter. I used to care. I mean about people and how their bodies hurt . . .

ASAGAI: And you've stopped caring?

BENEATHA: Yes — I think so.

ASAGAI: Why?

BENEATHA (*bitterly*): Because it doesn't seem deep enough, close enough to what ails mankind! It was a child's way of seeing things — or an idealist's.

ASAGAI: Children see things very well sometimes — and idealists even better.

BENEATHA: I know that's what you think. Because you are still where I left off. You with all your talk and dreams about Africa! You still think you can patch up the world. Cure the Great Sore of Colonialism — (*loftily, mocking it*) with the Penicillin of Independence —!

ASAGAI: Yes!

BENEATHA: Independence *and then what?* What about all the crooks and thieves and just plain idiots who will come into power and steal and plunder the same as before — only now they will be black and do it in the name of the new Independence — WHAT ABOUT THEM?!

ASAGAI: That will be the problem for another time. First we must get there.

BENEATHA: And where does it end?

ASAGAI: End? Who even spoke of an end? To life? To living?

BENEATHA: An end to misery! To stupidity! Don't you see there isn't any real progress, Asagai, there is only one large circle that we march in, around and around, each of us with our own little picture in front of us — our own little mirage that we think is the future.

ASAGAI: That is the mistake.

BENEATHA: What?

ASAGAI: What you just said — about the circle. It isn't a circle — it is simply a long line — as in geometry, you know, one that reaches into infinity. And because we cannot see the end — we also cannot see how it changes. And it is very odd but those who see the changes — who dream, who will not give up — are called idealists . . . and those who see only the circle — we call *them* the "realists"!

BENEATHA: Asagai, while I was sleeping in that bed in there, people went out and took the future right out of my hands! And nobody asked me, nobody consulted me — they just went out and changed my life!

ASAGAI: Was it your money?

BENEATHA: What?

ASAGAI: Was it your money he gave away?

BENEATHA: It belonged to all of us.

ASAGAI: But did you earn it? Would you have had it at all if your father had not died?

BENEATHA: No.

ASAGAI: Then isn't there something wrong in a house — in a world — where all dreams, good or bad, must depend on the death of a man? I never thought to see *you* like this, Alaiyo. You! Your brother made a mistake and you are grateful to him so that now you can give up the ailing human race on account of it! You talk about what good is struggle, what good is anything! Where are we all going and why are we bothering!

BENEATHA: AND YOU CANNOT ANSWER IT!

ASAGAI (*shouting over her*): I LIVE THE ANSWER! (*Pause.*) In my village at home it is the exceptional man who can even read a newspaper . . . or who ever sees a book at all. I will go home and much of what I will have to say will seem strange to the people of my village. But I will teach and work and things will happen, slowly and swiftly. At times it will seem that nothing changes at all . . . and then again the sudden dramatic events which make history leap into the future. And then quiet again. Retrogression even. Guns, murder, revolution. And I even will have moments when I wonder if the quiet was not better than all that death and hatred. But I will look about my village at the illiteracy and disease and ignorance and I will not wonder long. And perhaps . . . perhaps I will be a great man . . . I mean perhaps I will hold on to the substance of truth and find my way always with the right course . . . and perhaps for it I will be butchered in my bed some night by the servants of empire . . .

BENEATHA: *The martyr!*

ASAGAI (*he smiles*): . . . or perhaps I shall live to be a very old man, respected and esteemed in my new nation . . . And perhaps I shall hold office and this is what I'm trying to tell you, Alaiyo: Perhaps the things I believe now for my country will be wrong and outmoded, and I will not understand and do terrible things to have things my way or merely to keep my power. Don't you see that there will be ~ung men and women — not British soldiers then,

but my own black countrymen — to step out of the shadows some evening and slit my then useless throat? Don't you see they have always been there . . . that they always will be. And that such a thing as my own death will be an advance? They who might kill me even . . . actually replenish all that I was.

BENEATHA: Oh, Asagai, I know all that.

ASAGAI: Good! Then stop moaning and groaning and tell me what you plan to do.

BENEATHA: Do?

ASAGAI: I have a bit of a suggestion.

BENEATHA: What?

ASAGAI (*rather quietly for him*): That when it is all over — that you come home with me —

BENEATHA (*staring at him and crossing away with exasperation*): Oh — Asagai — at this moment you decide to be romantic!

ASAGAI (*quickly understanding the misunderstanding*): My dear, young creature of the New World — I do not mean across the city — I mean across the ocean: home — to Africa.

BENEATHA (*slowly understanding and turning to him with murmured amazement*): To Africa?

ASAGAI: Yes! . . . (*Smiling and lifting his arms playfully.*) Three hundred years later the African Prince rose up out of the seas and swept the maiden back across the middle passage over which her ancestors had come —

BENEATHA (*unable to play*): To — to Nigeria?

ASAGAI: Nigeria. Home. (*Coming to her with genuine romantic flippancy.*) I will show you our mountains and our stars; and give you cool drinks from gourds and teach you the old songs and the ways of our people — and, in time, we will pretend that — (*very softly*) — you have only been away for a day. Say that you'll come — (*He swings her around and takes her full in his arms in a kiss which proceeds to passion.*)

BENEATHA (*pulling away suddenly*): You're getting me all mixed up —

ASAGAI: Why?

BENEATHA: Too many things — too many things have happened today. I must sit down and think. I don't know what I feel about anything right this minute.

(*She promptly sits down and props her chin on her fist.*)

ASAGAI (*charmed*): All right, I shall leave you. No — don't get up. (*Touching her, gently, sweetly.*) Just sit awhile and think . . . Never be afraid to sit awhile and think. (*He goes to door and looks at her.*) How often I have looked at you and said, "Ah — so this is what the New World hath finally wrought . . ."

(*He exits. Beneatha sits on alone. Presently Walter enters from his room and starts to rummage through things, feverishly looking for something. She looks up and turns in her seat.*)

BENEATHA (*hissingly*): Yes — just look at what the New World hath wrought! . . . Just look! (*She gestures with bitter disgust.*) There he is! *Monsieur le petit bourgeois noir°* — himself! There he is — Symbol of a Rising Class! Entrepreneur! Titan° of the system! (*Walter ignores her completely and continues frantically and destructively looking for something and hurling things to floor and tearing things out of their place in his search. Beneatha ignores the eccentricity of his actions and goes on with the monologue of insult.*) Did you dream of yachts on Lake Michigan, Brother? Did you see yourself on that Great Day sitting down at the Conference Table, surrounded by all the mighty bald-headed men in America? All halted, waiting, breathless, waiting for your pronouncements on industry? Waiting for you — Chairman of the Board! (*Walter finds what he is looking for — a small piece of white paper — and pushes it in his pocket and puts on his coat and rushes out without ever having looked at her. She shouts after him.*) I look at you and I see the final triumph of stupidity in the world!

(*The door slams and she returns to just sitting again. Ruth comes quickly out of Mama's room.*)

RUTH: Who was that?
BENEATHA: Your husband.
RUTH: Where did he go?
BENEATHA: Who knows — maybe he has an appointment at U.S. Steel.
RUTH (*anxiously, with frightened eyes*): You didn't say nothing bad to him, did you?
BENEATHA: Bad? Say anything bad to him? No — I told him he was a sweet boy and full of dreams and everything is strictly peachy keen, as the ofay° kids say!

(*Mama enters from her bedroom. She is lost, vague, trying to catch hold, to make some sense of her former command of the world, but it still eludes her. A sense of waste overwhelms her gait; a measure of apology rides on her shoulders. She goes to her plant, which has remained on the table, looks at it, picks it up and takes it to the window sill and sits it outside, and she stands and looks at it a long moment. Then she closes*)

Monsieur . . . noir: Mr. Black Middle Class.
Titan: Person of great power.
ofay: White person, usually used disparagingly.

the window, straightens her body with effort, and turns around to her children.)

MAMA: Well — ain't it a mess in here, though? (*A false cheerfulness, a beginning of something.*) I guess we all better stop moping around and get some work done. All this unpacking and everything we got to do. (*Ruth raises her head slowly in response to the sense of the line; and Beneatha in similar manner turns very slowly to look at her mother.*) One of you all better call the moving people and tell 'em not to come.
RUTH: Tell 'em not to come?
MAMA: Of course, baby. Ain't no need in 'em coming all the way here and having to go back. They charges for that too. (*She sits down, fingers to her brow, thinking.*) Lord, ever since I was a little girl, I always remembers people saying, "Lena — Lena Eggleston, you aims too high all the time. You needs to slow down and see life a little more like it is. Just slow down some." That's what they always used to say down home — "Lord, that Lena Eggleston is a high-minded thing. She'll get her due one day!"
RUTH: No, Lena . . .
MAMA: Me and Big Walter just didn't never learn right.
RUTH: Lena, no! We gotta go. Bennie — tell her . . . (*She rises and crosses to Beneatha with her arms outstretched. Beneatha doesn't respond.*) Tell her we can still move . . . the notes ain't but a hundred and twenty-five a month. We got four grown people in this house — we can work . . .
MAMA (*to herself*): Just aimed too high all the time —
RUTH (*turning and going to Mama fast — the words pouring out with urgency and desperation*): Lena — I'll work . . . I'll work twenty hours a day in all the kitchens in Chicago . . . I'll strap my baby on my back if I have to and scrub all the floors in America and wash all the sheets in America if I have to — but we got to MOVE! We got to get OUT OF HERE!!

(*Mama reaches out absently and pats Ruth's hand.*)

MAMA: No — I sees things differently now. Been thinking 'bout some of the things we could do to fix this place up some. I seen a second-hand bureau over on Maxwell Street just the other day that could fit right there. (*She points to where the new furniture might go. Ruth wanders away from her.*) Would need some new handles on it and then a little varnish and it look like something brand-new. And — we can put up them new curtains in the kitchen . . . Why this place be looking fine. Cheer us all up so that we forget trouble ever come . . . (*To Ruth.*) And you could get some nice screens to put up in your room round the baby's bassinet . . . (*She looks at both of them, pleadingly.*) Sometimes you just got to know when to give up some things . . . and hold on to what you got. . . .

(*Walter enters from the outside, looking spent and leaning against the door, his coat hanging from him.*)

MAMA: Where you been, son?

WALTER (*breathing hard*): Made a call.

MAMA: To who, son?

WALTER: To The Man. (*He heads for his room.*)

MAMA: What man, baby?

WALTER (*stops in the door*): The Man, Mama. Don't you know who The Man is?

RUTH: Walter Lee?

WALTER: *The Man.* Like the guys in the streets say — The Man. Captain Boss — Mistuh Charley . . . Old Cap'n Please Mr. Bossman . . .

BENEATHA (*suddenly*): Lindner!

WALTER: That's right! That's good. I told him to come right over.

BENEATHA (*fiercely, understanding*): For what? What do you want to see him for!

WALTER (*looking at his sister*): We going to do business with him.

MAMA: What you talking 'bout, son?

WALTER: Talking 'bout life, Mama. You all always telling me to see life like it is. Well — I laid in there on my back today . . . and I figured it out. Life just like it is. Who gets and who don't get. (*He sits down with his coat on and laughs.*) Mama, you know it's all divided up. Life is. Sure enough. Between the takers and the "tooken." (*He laughs.*) I've figured it out finally. (*He looks around at them.*) Yeah. Some of us always getting "tooken." (*He laughs.*) People like Willy Harris, they don't never get "tooken." And you know why the rest of us do? 'Cause we all mixed up. Mixed up bad. We get to looking 'round for the right and the wrong; and we worry about it and cry about it and stay up nights trying to figure out 'bout the wrong and the right of things all the time . . . And all the time, man, them takers is out there operating, just taking and taking. Willy Harris? Shoot — Willy Harris don't even count. He don't even count in the big scheme of things. But I'll say one thing for old Willy Harris . . . he's taught me something. He's taught me to keep my eye on what counts in this world. Yeah — (*Shouting out a little.*) Thanks, Willy!

RUTH: What did you call that man for, Walter Lee?

WALTER: Called him to tell him to come on over to the show. Gonna put on a show for the man. Just what he wants to see. You see, Mama, the man came here today and he told us that them people out there where you want us to move — well they so upset they willing to pay us *not* to move! (*He laughs again.*) And — and oh, Mama — you would of been proud of the way me and Ruth and Bennie acted. We told him to get out . . . Lord have mercy! We told the man to get out! Oh, we was some proud folks this afternoon, yeah. (*He lights a cigarette.*) We were still full of that old-time stuff . . .

RUTH (*coming toward him slowly*): You talking 'bout taking them people's money to keep us from moving in that house?

WALTER: I ain't just talking 'bout it, baby — I'm telling you that's what's going to happen!

BENEATHA: Oh, God! Where is the bottom! Where is the real honest-to-God bottom so he can't go any farther!

WALTER: See — that's the old stuff. You and that boy that was here today. You all want everybody to carry a flag and a spear and sing some marching songs, huh? You wanna spend your life looking into things and trying to find the right and the wrong part, huh? Yeah. You know what's going to happen to that boy someday — he'll find himself sitting in a dungeon, locked in forever — and the takers will have the key! Forget it, baby! There ain't no causes — there ain't nothing but taking in this world, and he who takes most is smartest — and it don't make a damn bit of difference *how.*

MAMA: You making something inside me cry, son. Some awful pain inside me.

WALTER: Don't cry, Mama. Understand. That white man is going to walk in that door able to write checks for more money than we ever had. It's important to him and I'm going to help him . . . I'm going to put on the show, Mama.

MAMA: Son — I come from five generations of people who was slaves and sharecroppers — but ain't nobody in my family never let nobody pay 'em no money that was a way of telling us we wasn't fit to walk the earth. We ain't never been that poor. (*Raising her eyes and looking at him.*) We ain't never been that — dead inside.

BENEATHA: Well — we are dead now. All the talk about dreams and sunlight that goes on in this house. It's all dead now.

WALTER: What's the matter with you all! I didn't make this world! It was give to me this way! Hell, yes, I want me some yachts someday! Yes, I want to hang some real pearls 'round my wife's neck. Ain't she supposed to wear no pearls? Somebody tell me — tell me, who decides which women is suppose to wear pearls in this world. I tell you I am a *man* — and I think my wife should wear some pearls in this world!

(*This last line hangs a good while and Walter begins to move about the room. The word "Man" has penetrated his consciousness; he mumbles it to himself repeatedly between strange agitated pauses as he moves about.*)

MAMA: Baby, how you going to feel on the inside?

WALTER: Fine! . . . Going to feel fine . . . a man . . .

MAMA: You won't have nothing left then, Walter Lee.

WALTER (*coming to her*): I'm going to feel fine, Mama. I'm going to look that son-of-a-bitch in the eyes and say — (*he falters*) — and say, "All right, Mr. Lindner — (*he falters even more*) — that's *your* neighborhood out there! You got the right to keep it like you want! You got the right to have it like you want! Just write the check and — the house is yours." And — and I am going to say — (*His voice almost breaks.*) "And you — you people just put the money in my hand and you won't have to live next to this bunch of stinking niggers! . . ." (*He straightens up and moves away from his mother, walking around the room.*) And maybe — maybe I'll just get down on my black knees . . . (*He does so; Ruth and Bennie and Mama watch him in frozen horror.*) "Captain, Mistuh, Boss-man — (*Groveling and grinning and wringing his hands in profoundly anguished imitation of the slow-witted movie stereotype.*) A-hee-hee-hee! Oh, yassuh boss! Yasssssuh! Great white — (*voice breaking, he forces himself to go on*) — Father, just gi' ussen de money, fo' God's sake, and we's — we's ain't gwine come out deh and dirty up yo' white folks neighborhood . . ." (*He breaks down completely.*) And I'll feel fine! Fine! FINE! (*He gets up and goes into the bedroom.*)

BENEATHA: That is not a man. That is nothing but a toothless rat.

MAMA: Yes — death done come in this here house. (*She is nodding, slowly, reflectively.*) Done come walking in my house on the lips of my children. You what supposed to be my beginning again. You — what supposed to be my harvest. (*To Beneatha.*) You — you mourning your brother?

BENEATHA: He's no brother of mine.

MAMA: What you say?

BENEATHA: I said that that individual in that room is no brother of mine.

MAMA: That's what I thought you said. You feeling like you better than he is today? (*Beneatha does not answer.*) Yes? What you tell him a minute ago? That he wasn't a man? Yes? You give him up for me? You done wrote his epitaph too — like the rest of the world? Well, who give you the privilege?

BENEATHA: Be on my side for once! You saw what he just did, Mama! You saw him — down on his knees. Wasn't it you who taught me to despise any man who would do that? Do what he's going to do?

MAMA: Yes — I taught you that. Me and your daddy. But I thought I taught you something else too . . . I thought I taught you to love him.

BENEATHA: Love him? There is nothing left to love.

MAMA: There is *always* something left to love. And if you ain't learned that, you ain't learned nothing. (*Looking at her.*) Have you cried for that boy today? I don't mean for yourself and for the family 'cause we lost the money. I mean for him: what he been through and what it done to him. Child, when do you think is the time to love somebody the most? When they done good and made things easy for everybody? Well then, you ain't through learning — because that ain't the time at all. It's when he's at his lowest and can't believe in hisself 'cause the world done whipped him so! When you starts measuring somebody, measure him right, child, measure him right. Make sure you done taken into account what hills and valleys he come through before he got to wherever he is.

(*Travis bursts into the room at the end of the speech, leaving the door open.*)

TRAVIS: Grandmama — the moving men are downstairs! The truck just pulled up.

MAMA (*turning and looking at him*): Are they, baby? They downstairs?

(*She sighs and sits. Lindner appears in the doorway. He peers in and knocks lightly, to gain attention, and comes in. All turn to look at him.*)

LINDNER (*hat and briefcase in hand*): Uh — hello . . .

(*Ruth crosses mechanically to the bedroom door and opens it and lets it swing open freely and slowly as the lights come up on Walter within, still in his coat, sitting at the far corner of the room. He looks up and out through the room to Lindner.*)

RUTH: He's here.

(*A long minute passes and Walter slowly gets up.*)

LINDNER (*coming to the table with efficiency, putting his briefcase on the table and starting to unfold papers and unscrew fountain pens*): Well, I certainly was glad to hear from you people. (*Walter has begun the trek out of the room, slowly and awkwardly, rather like a small boy, passing the back of his sleeve across his mouth from time to time.*) Life can really be so much simpler than people let it be most of the time. Well — with whom do I negotiate? You, Mrs. Younger, or your son here? (*Mama sits with her hands folded on her lap and her eyes closed as Walter advances. Travis goes closer to Lindner and looks at the papers curiously.*) Just some official papers, sonny.

RUTH: Travis, you go downstairs —

MAMA (*opening her eyes and looking into Walter's*): No. Travis, you stay right here. And you make him understand what you doing, Walter Lee. You teach him good. Like Willy Harris taught you. You show where our five generations done come to. (*Walter looks from her to the boy, who grins at him innocently.*) Go ahead, son — (*She folds her hands and closes her eyes.*) Go ahead.

WALTER (*at last crosses to Lindner, who is reviewing the contract*): Well, Mr. Lindner. (*Beneatha turns away.*) We called you — (*there is a profound, simple groping quality in his speech*) — because, well, me and my family (*he looks around and shifts from one foot to the other*) Well — we are very plain people . . .

LINDNER: Yes —

WALTER: I mean — I have worked as a chauffeur most of my life — and my wife here, she does domestic work in people's kitchens. So does my mother. I mean — we are plain people . . .

LINDNER: Yes, Mr. Younger —

WALTER (*really like a small boy, looking down at his shoes and then up at the man*): And — uh — well, my father, well, he was a laborer most of his life. . . .

LINDNER (*absolutely confused*): Uh, yes — yes, I understand. (*He turns back to the contract.*)

WALTER (*a beat; staring at him*): And my father — (*With sudden intensity.*) My father almost *beat a man to death* once because this man called him a bad name or something, you know what I mean?

LINDNER (*looking up, frozen*): No, no, I'm afraid I don't —

WALTER (*A beat. The tension hangs; then Walter steps back from it.*): Yeah. Well — what I mean is that we come from people who had a lot of *pride*. I mean — we are very proud people. And that's my sister over there and she's going to be a doctor — and we are very proud —

LINDNER: Well — I am sure that is very nice, but —

WALTER: What I am telling you is that we called you over here to tell you that we are very proud and that this — (*Signaling to Travis.*) Travis, come here. (*Travis crosses and Walter draws him before him facing the man.*) This is my son, and he makes the sixth generation of our family in this country. And we have all thought about your offer —

~~DNER:~~ Well, good . . . good —

~~R:~~ And we have decided to move into our house

because my father — my father — he earned it for us brick by brick. (*Mama has her eyes closed and is rocking back and forth as though she were in church, with her head nodding the Amen yes.*) We don't want to make no trouble for nobody or fight no causes, and we will try to be good neighbors. And that's *all* we got to say about that. (*He looks the man absolutely in the eyes.*) We don't want your money. (*He turns and walks away.*)

LINDNER (*looking around at all of them*): I take it then — that you have decided to occupy . . .

BENEATHA: That's what the man said.

LINDNER (*to Mama in her reverie*): Then I would like to appeal to you, Mrs. Younger. You are older and wiser and understand things better I am sure . . .

MAMA: I am afraid you don't understand. My son said we was going to move and there ain't nothing left for me to say. (*Briskly.*) You know how these young folks is nowadays, mister. Can't do a thing with 'em! (*As he opens his mouth, she rises.*) Goodbye.

LINDNER (*folding up his materials*): Well — if you are that final about it . . . there is nothing left for me to say. (*He finishes, almost ignored by the family, who are concentrating on Walter Lee. At the door Lindner halts and looks around.*) I sure hope you people know what you're getting into.

(*He shakes his head and exits.*)

RUTH (*looking around and coming to life*): Well, for God's sake — if the moving men are here — LET'S GET THE HELL OUT OF HERE!

MAMA (*into action*): Ain't it the truth! Look at all this here mess. Ruth, put Travis's good jacket on him . . . Walter Lee, fix your tie and tuck your shirt in, you look like somebody's hoodlum! Lord have mercy, where is my plant? (*She flies to get it amid the general bustling of the family, who are deliberately trying to ignore the nobility of the past moment.*) You all start on down . . . Travis child, don't go empty-handed . . . Ruth, where did I put that box with my skillets in it? I want to be in charge of it myself . . . I'm going to make us the biggest dinner we ever ate tonight . . . Beneatha, what's the matter with them stockings? Pull them things up, girl . . .

(*The family starts to file out as two moving men appear and begin to carry out the heavier pieces of furniture, bumping into the family as they move about.*)

BENEATHA: Mama, Asagai asked me to marry him today and go to Africa —

MAMA (*in the middle of her getting-ready activity*): He did? You ain't old enough to marry nobody — (*Seeing the moving men lifting one of her chairs precariously.*) Darling, that ain't no bale of cotton, please handle it so we can sit in it again! I had that chair twenty-five years . . .

(*The movers sigh with exasperation and go on with their work.*)

BENEATHA (*girlishly and unreasonably trying to pursue the conversation*): To go to Africa, Mama — be a doctor in Africa . . .

MAMA (*distracted*): Yes, baby —

WALTER: *Africa!* What he want you to go to Africa for?

BENEATHA: To practice there . . .

WALTER: Girl, if you don't get all them silly ideas out your head! You better marry yourself a man with some loot . . .

BENEATHA (*angrily, precisely as in the first scene of the play*): What have you got to do with who I marry!

WALTER: Plenty. Now I think George Murchison —

BENEATHA: *George Murchison!* I wouldn't marry him if he was Adam and I was Eve!

(*Walter and Beneatha go out yelling at each other vigorously and the anger is loud and real till their voices diminish. Ruth stands at the door and turns to Mama and smiles knowingly.*)

MAMA (*fixing her hat at last*): Yeah — they something all right, my children . . .

RUTH: Yeah — they're something. Let's go, Lena.

MAMA (*stalling, starting to look around at the house*): Yes — I'm coming. Ruth —

RUTH: Yes?

MAMA (*quietly, woman to woman*): He finally come into his manhood today, didn't he? Kind of like a rainbow after the rain . . .

RUTH (*biting her lip lest her own pride explode in front of Mama*): Yes, Lena.

(*Walter's voice calls for them raucously.*)

WALTER (*offstage*): Y'all come on! These people charges by the hour, you know!

MAMA (*waving Ruth out vaguely*): All right, honey — go on down. I be down directly.

(*Ruth hesitates, then exits. Mama stands, at last alone in the living room, her plant on the table before her as the lights start to come down. She looks around at all the walls and ceilings and suddenly, despite herself, while the children call below, a great heaving thing rises in her and she puts her fist to her mouth to stifle it, takes a final desperate look, pulls her coat about her, pats her hat, and goes out. The lights dim down. The door opens and she comes back in, grabs her plant, and goes out for the last time.*)

Contemporary Drama

The experimentation in drama in the first half of the twentieth century has continued in contemporary drama. The achievements of Tennessee Williams, Arthur Miller, Samuel Beckett, and other mid-century playwrights encouraged later playwrights to experiment more daringly. Mixing media such as film, video, opera, rock, and other music with live actors was and still is an option for playwrights at the end of the twentieth century. However, most plays that have been celebrated by critics and audiences have been relatively traditional, building on the achievement of nineteenth-century realism and twentieth-century expressionism.

Harold Pinter's distinctive style, developed in the late 1950s and early 1960s, is connected with Samuel Beckett's absurdist gestures in *Waiting for Godot* and other plays, such as *All That Fall* and *Endgame*. The claustrophobic atmosphere of *Endgame* seems replicated in the tiny room in which Gus and Ben wait in Pinter's *The Dumb Waiter*. A dumb waiter is a small hand-operated elevator that moves food or other objects upstairs or downstairs in a house. In Pinter's play it also moves messages. The conversation between Gus and Ben — laconic, repetitive, not obviously moving the action forward — is typical of Pinter's extraordinary approach to dialogue. It is based on his own experiences listening to people talk, but onstage is has a mesmerizing effect. The effect of *The Dumb Waiter* is intensified by the sense of ordinariness that permeates all of its action.

Most of the interesting experimental theater was done in groups such as Richard Schechner's Performance Group, which created what Schechner called ENVIRONMENTAL THEATER in New York City in the late 1960s, and Jerzy Grotowski's Polish Laboratory Theatre in Wroclaw, Poland, during the same period. Ensembles like the Bread and Puppet Theatre, San Francisco Mime Troupe, and El Teatro Campesino on the West Coast, combined a radical political message with theatrical experimentation. The work of these groups is effective primarily at the level of performance; their texts are not representative of their impact on audiences.

Environmental Theater

Schechner's most famous production, based on Euripides' *The Bacchae*, was *Dionysus in 69* (1969), in which Pentheus is torn to pieces in an impassioned frenzy. Part of the point of Schechner's production was to inspire the audience so much that they took the stage, becoming indistinguishable from the actors. *Dionysus in 69* was an effort to draw on the same spiritual energies tapped by Greek drama by connecting with the feasts of Dionysus, god of wine and ecstasy. The play was a spontaneous and partly improvised performance piece rather than a text meant to be read. At one point the audience and actors disrobed in a simulation of a Greek religious orgy. Ordinarily, only a few audience members held back, and Schechner's goal of involving audience and actors in a pagan ritual was realized night after night during the run.

In a similar way, Julian Beck and Judith Malina's Living Theatre maintained a special relationship with the audience. Beck's plays were designed to break down the absolutes of dramatic space and audience space by having the actors roam through the audience and interact apparently at random with audience members. *Paradise Now* (1968) is his best-known play. Like Schechner's *Dionysus in 69*, it was essentially a performance piece. Certain segments were improvised; therefore, as a reading text, it has relatively little power.

"Poor Theater"

Grotowski's theater was called the "poor theater" because it was meant to contrast with the "rich theater" of the commercial stage, with its expensive lighting, decorated stages, rich costumes, numerous props, and elaborate settings. Grotowski had none of these. He followed the views of Antonin Artaud, whose notion of a THEATER OF CRUELTY influenced much of the experimental theater of this period. Artaud rejected mere entertainment. He designed theater to be a total experience — a sensational spectacle that did not depend on coherent plot or development. He wanted his theater of cruelty to play out horrors so that they wouldn't have to be enacted on the stage of history.

Grotowski's Laboratory Theatre, begun in 1959, relied on preexisting texts but interpreted them broadly through a total reconception of their meaning. For example, Grotowski's *Akropolis* (1962; revised frequently from 1963 to 1975) adapted an older Polish drama by Stanisław Wyspiański (1904) and reset it in modern times in Auschwitz, with the actors, dressed in ragged sackcloth prison uniforms, looking wretched and starving. At the end of the play the prisoners follow a headless puppet-corpse, Christ, into an afterlife. They march in an eerie ritual procession offstage into the waiting prison camp ovens.

Grotowski's theater has been influential worldwide. When the Polish government clamped down on the Solidarity movement in the late 1970s, Grotowski left Poland. After 1970 Grotowski shifted his focus from public performances to small, intense group workshops and, more recently, to the ritual performances of cultures from all over the world. The first phase of his work with the Laboratory Theatre has remained the most influential. One of his actors, Richard Cieslak, traveled widely training people in Grotowski's methods.

Theater of Images

Robert Wilson has been experimenting in the 1970s, 1980s, and 1990s with repetitive narratives that sometimes take eight hours to perform. His multimedia dramas involve huge casts and ordinarily cover an immense historic range (Figure 10). One of his most extraordinary successes has been *Einstein on the Beach* (1976), an opera written in collaboration with composer Philip Glass. It is eight hours long and was originally produced in a conventional theater, but it uses dramatic techniques that involve extensive patterns of repetition, the creation of enigmatic and evocative images, and characters who are cartoonlike caricatures of historical people. The overall effect is hypnotic; one of the points of Wilson's work seems to be to induce a trancelike state in his audience.

New Ensembles

Some of the most energetic theater of the period beginning in the 1960s has come from groups who have been excluded at times from representation in mainstream theater. Gays, lesbians, and some black groups have been virtually ignored by commercial theater and as a result have formed their own collectives and groups.

The Ridiculous Theatrical Company, founded by Charles Ludlam (1940–1987) in 1969, produced a formidable body of work rooted in the homosexual community of New York. Its influence reached to many parts of the world. One of Ludlam's catchphrases was "plays without the stink of art." His plays were often ridiculously funny. *Bluebeard* (1970), for example, focused on creating a third gender by inventing a third genital. *Camille* (1973), starring Ludlam himself in the title role, hilariously spoofed not only Dumas's play but most of the "Hallmark card" conventions about romantic love. Ludlam was a gifted female impersonator and played Hedda Gabler at the American Ibsen Theatre in Pittsburgh. The Ridiculous Theatrical Company continues Ludlam's tradition, with his partner Everett Quinton producing Ludlam's plays as well as new plays in his tradition. One reason for the development of gay theater in the United States and Great Britain in the 1960s was the decriminalization of homosexuality beginning in 1967. Depiction of homosexual love onstage waited even longer, until the Gay Workshop's plays in London beginning in 1976.

Lesbian theatrical groups have developed in the United States and Great Britain. They often merge with women's theater groups and deal with issues such as male violence, societal restrictions on women, and women's opportunities. A number of important collectives, such as the Rhode Island Women's Theater and At the Foot of the Mountain in Minneapolis treated general women's issues in the 1970s. Groups such

Figure 10. Multimedia effects in Robert Wilson's *CIVIL warS*

as Medusa's Revenge (founded 1976) and Atlanta's Red Dyke Theater (1974) were more centered on lesbian experience. These last two groups disbanded after a few years of successful productions. Megan Terry's Omaha Magic Theater, founded with Joanne Schmidman, has been a long-lasting theater focusing on women's issues. Gay and lesbian theater groups have often been concerned with erasing stereotypes while also celebrating gay and lesbian lifestyles. Plays that once may have been thought appropriate only for such groups — such as Martin Sherman's (b. 1938) *Bent* (1977) and Larry Kramer's (b. 1936) *The Normal Heart* (1985) — are now shown in theaters worldwide.

Through the 1970s and 1980s numerous black theatrical groups developed in many parts of the world. An important Afro-Caribbean theater group was formed in the Keskidee Center in North London, with Edgar White (b. 1947) as one of its directors. White's plays are often centered in Caribbean mystical experiences, including Rastafarianism. *The Nine Night* (1983), produced in London, focuses on a

Jamaican funeral tradition designed to help the deceased enter the gates of heaven.

Experiments with Theater Space

Drama around the world has developed alternatives to the proscenium theater. Theater in the round, which seats audiences on all sides of the actors, has been exceptionally powerful for certain plays. Peter Weiss's *Persecution and Assassination of Jean-Paul Marat as Performed by the Inmates of the Asylum of Charenton Under the Direction of the Marquis de Sade* (1964) was especially effective in this format. Other theatrical experiments explored the power of spaces one would not have thought appropriate for drama. For example, Wladimir Pereira Cardoso designed an elaborate welded-steel set for a production of Jean Genet's *The Balcony* in the Ruth Escobar Theater in São Paulo, Brazil. The set was a huge suspended cone in which people sat looking inward while the actors were suspended in the spherical space before them. The production was first staged in 1969 and was seen through 1971 and most of 1972 by many thousands of people. The set was constructed of eighty tons of iron assembled like a trellis and requiring 500,000 welds. The entire insides of the theater were torn out to accommodate the new set. The audience of 250 was seated on circular platforms and the actors moved through the space on ramps, on suspended cables, and on moving platforms. The same theater produced *The Voyage*, an adaptation of an epic poem, *The Lusiads*, about the origin of Portuguese people. That set used open welded platforms suggesting ships' decks. In Dubrovnik, Yugoslavia, a replica of Columbus's *Santa Maria* — built much larger than the original — was used to stage Miroslav Krleza's expressionist play *Christopher Columbus*, written in 1917. The ship was docked in Dubrovnik Harbor for the performances.

Richard Foreman's Ontological-Hysteric Theatre performs in a loft in New York City with all audience members facing in the same direction. This is not fundamentally different from the traditional proscenium theater, but the open loft space and the visible movements of actors offstage create a new relationship to the action. Foreman's work, such as *Sophia = (Wisdom)* (1970 and later), which has been performed in many parts, has none of the usually accepted narrative clues to its action. However, it aims to explore hitherto hidden aspects of experience, such as sexual taboos and unorthodox relationships. The relationship of the author to the performance is also experimental in his theater, since he directs his actors, often using a loud buzzer, as if they were extensions of his will. His work, begun in the 1960s, continues into the 1990s.

Experimentation Within the Tradition

It is too soon to assess the direction in which current drama is heading, but playwrights still use traditional staging and traditional techniques. Within the Chekhovian/Brechtian traditions of modern drama, current playwrights have been finding considerable range of expression. Marsha

Norman, who wrote *'night, Mother*, has said that her plays are "wildly traditional. I'm a purist about structure. Plays are like plane rides. You [the audience] buy the ticket and you have to get where the ticket takes you. Or else you've been had."

Wole Soyinka's experimentation has spanned two traditions, modern European theater and modern ritual theater of the Yoruba people in Nigeria. Yoruba plays develop from religious celebrations and annual festivals and include music and dance. Soyinka's plays, including *The Strong Breed*, concern themselves with African traditions and African issues, but they often explore mythic forces that link European and African culture. His plays have been produced throughout the world and have demonstrated the universality of community and the individual anxiety it sometimes breeds. Soyinka has also written on Yoruba tragedy and has interpreted, translated, and produced Greek tragedy.

Sam Shepard, one of the most prolific modern playwrights, experiments with his material, much of which premiered in small theaters in Greenwich Village, such as the La Mama Experimental Theater. But his most widely known plays, among them *Buried Child* (1978), are produced easily on conventional stages. Shepard's work is wide-ranging and challenging. His language is coarse, a representation of the way he has heard people speak, and the violence he portrays onstage is strong enough to alienate many in the audience. Shepard, important as he is, has not found a popular commercial audience for his plays. At root, his work is always experimental.

Athol Fugard, a South African, writes powerful plays that also work well on conventional proscenium stages. Like Shepard's, his subject matter is not the kind that permits an audience to sit back relaxed and appreciate the drama with a sense of detachment. Instead, the plays usually disturb audiences. His primary subject matter is the devastation — for blacks and whites — caused by apartheid in South Africa. Fugard's work with black actors in South Africa produced a vital experimental theater out of which his best early work grew.

The Blood Knot (1961) and *Boesman and Lena* (1969), part of a trilogy on South Africa, are based on the theme of racial discrimination. But other plays, such as *A Lesson from Aloes* (1978) and *My Children! My Africa!* (1989), are involved with problems of individuals in relation to their political world. Fugard is in many ways a traditional playwright, except for his subject matter. His characters are thoroughly developed, but with great economy; in *"MASTER HAROLD" . . . and the boys*, for example, we are given a deep understanding of Hally and Sam, whose relationship, past, present, and future, is the center of the play. Fugard is not writing the well-made play, any more than the other contemporary playwrights in this collection are. There is nothing "mechanical" in Fugard's work but rather a sense of organic growth, of actions arising from perceptible conditions and historical circumstances. These contribute to the sense of integrity that his plays communicate.

Some of Caryl Churchill's plays, emphasizing themes of socialism, colonialism, and feminism, were developed in workshops and collaborations with actors and directors. When writing a play she experiments early in the first stages by spending time in the environments her plays depict. When she worked on *Top Girls* (1982) she came up with the idea of setting the action in an employment agency after talking with many people whose lives are wrapped up in business. For *Serious Money* (1987), she and the group developing the play spent time at the London Stock Exchange, absorbing the atmosphere of frenetic buying and selling.

Though she claims to be a traditionalist, Marsha Norman has written experimental plays. Her first success, *Getting Out* (1977), portrays the same character at two periods in her life — as an adolescent and as an adult — on separate parts of the stage at the same time. The effect is startling, but the structure of the play is clear and simple: Arlene is trying to start life over after leaving prison, while Arlie, her younger, rebellious self, is still with her, commenting on what she is doing. The play ends with a reconciliation of the two parts of the character.

Norman's *'night, Mother* is another traditionally structured play. It respects the Aristotelian unities of time, place, and action, and it is confrontational. Thelma and her daughter, Jessie, are in a power struggle over Jessie's right to commit suicide. The technique is naturalistic, and the play's subject matter, as in the plays of Strindberg and Ibsen, is discomforting to its contemporary audiences.

August Wilson has been working on a series of ten plays on the subject of black life in twentieth-century America. So far he has written five of those plays, and each of the first four won the New York Drama Critics' Circle Award for best play of the year. Wilson's plays show the pain endured by blacks in an America that is supposed to be the land of opportunity. Like Arthur Miller in *Death of a Salesman* and Lorraine Hansberry in *A Raisin in the Sun*, Wilson explores the nature and consequences of the American dream, especially for those effectively excluded from this dream. Blacks' frustration, exploitation, and suffering are presented in powerful characters such as Troy Maxson in *Fences* (1985). Troy is a garbage man who was a star baseball player at a time when blacks could play only in their own league. The major leagues were exclusively white until 1947, when Jackie Robinson joined the Brooklyn Dodgers and the game began to be integrated. The play centers on Maxson's anger, but it also shows his pride for his family and his concerns for his son's growing up into a world in which he must empower himself to achieve what he most wants for himself.

Cory, Troy's son, does not see the same kind of discrimination and has not felt the unfairness that was Troy's primary experience in growing up. He does not understand the world from Troy Maxson's point of view. Showing the world as Troy Maxson sees it is one of the functions of the play.

All of Wilson's plays have explored the heritage of blacks to help them live intelligently in the present, with understanding and dignity.

People in his plays have lost touch with the past and, for that reason, risk a loss of self-understanding.

Wilson's plays have a naturalistic surface, but they also allude to the supernatural. Some of the roots of this tradition are in the black church and some in African religion, a source shared by Soyinka and Wilson, among others. Wilson's effects are achieved in a proscenium theater, using traditional methods of DRAMATURGY, the craft or techniques of dramatic composition. Much of the powerful and lasting drama of the 1980s and 1990s has followed a similar technical path. Contemporary dramatists are by no means shy of experimentation, but they are also sensitive to the continuing resources of the traditional stage as it was conceived by Chekhov and Ibsen and modified by Brecht.

Brian Friel follows traditional dramatic patterns in his work, drawing on the realistic techniques of writers such as Ibsen, Chekhov, and Arthur Miller. However, he is also interested in blending this technique with expressionism, even if in a mild way. His historical play *Translations* (1980) recreates the Irish countryside of 1830 and works within the realities of that setting. He takes liberty with dialogue by having characters speak English onstage while implying that they are speaking Irish to one another. In *Dancing at Lughnasa* (1990) the main character, Michael, is present as a child in the eyes of the characters, his aunts — but present at those moments only in the audience's imagination. The only Michael who actually appears as a character onstage is Michael the adult interpreting the action, somewhat the way Tom does in *The Glass Menagerie*. The effects are similar, and the result is typical of the modern memory play.

Suzan-Lori Parks works in a more experimental tradition. *The Death of the Last Black Man in the Whole Entire World* (1990) is not realistic and not a typical narrative play, as Friel's plays are. The result is that Friel's plays are more likely than Parks's to be produced in large commercial theaters, such as those in the West End in London, and on Broadway; Parks's are more likely to be seen by a small but appreciative audience because they take more liberties with the audience's expectations. Her plays narrate events, but loosely; at any moment the audience is involved with an episode that can stand on its own but that also fits loosely into the whole. Characters are like musicians in a jazz group: Each gets a chance to solo and to clarify his or her theme, and then each goes back to the ensemble performance. The texts of Parks's plays merely hint at the power of their performance. She does not offer conventional stage directions because she expects her directors and actors to contribute the theatrical insight needed to transform the text into a dramatic reality. Her work is exciting and offers theatergoers new directions for enjoying modern drama.

Harold Pinter

Harold Pinter (b. 1930) has written plays for the commercial stage, radio, and television as well as film scripts produced by some of the best directors of his time. Pinter was born into relatively humble circumstances in East London, but his early schooling distinguished him, and he eventually enrolled in London's prestigious Royal Academy of Dramatic Arts, where he studied acting. When he finished his studies, he joined a company, toured for several years, and began to write for the stage. His previous writing efforts were in prose: He wrote short stories and a long novel, *The Dwarfs* (1956), purportedly autobiographical, but never finished and not published until 1990. Produced as a radio play in 1960, it expresses some of the themes of his best work: the disintegration of a mind and the cruelty of people to their fellow beings.

In 1957, Pinter turned to playwriting and wrote three important plays, the one-act *The Room* and *The Dumb Waiter* and the full-length *The Birthday Party* (finished in 1958). All these plays were well received. They established his method in dialogue and to a large extent the style that has dominated his work. The critic Martin Esslin, who coined the term "theater of the absurd," saw in Pinter's work an absurdist strain, especially in the nihilism — the belief in nothing — that sometimes shows up in his work. Pinter's characters usually reveal no spiritual awareness and no longing for spiritual values.

Pinter's dialogue sometimes has qualities of aimlessness, at least on the surface. But always the dialogue penetrates the unconsciousness of the audience and reveals the nature of the characters and their situation. Even the repetitious dialogue makes the audience more aware of the limitations and the pain of the circumstances in which Pinter's people find themselves.

Early reaction to the plays sometimes saw the aimless dialogue and the absurdist qualities as shortcomings rather than as indictments of the social order from which the plays arose. Yet the brutality of his characters to one another, their lack of sympathy for one another, and their demands for dominance have all become hallmarks of late-twentieth-century life.

The first of Pinter's plays to catch the attention of the general theater public was the commercially produced *The Caretaker* (1960), a play about two brothers, one of whom, Aston, invites a bewildered and all but mentally destroyed tramp, Davies, to become a caretaker in his room. Davies hardly knows who he is. His identity is essentially reduced to nothing by his aimless, soul-destroying life, and he speaks in broken language, especially when he is trying to explain that he left his identity papers in his beloved Sidcup — some fifteen years before — and that if they could find those papers, he would know where he was born and who he was. At the end of the play the younger brother, Mick, torments Davies, demanding that he leave, twisting his arm, verbally abusing him, but then relenting. The play ends with the shards of a life, as Davies says: "Listen . . . if I . . . go down . . . if I was to . . . get my papers . . . would you . . . would you let . . . would you . . . if I got down . . . and got my . . . (*Long silence.*)"

Pinter's *The Homecoming* (1965) has a brutal, shocking quality. A professor returns to England from America with his wife, and it becomes clear that he plans to return to America but that his wife will stay on as a mistress to his father and his brothers. The matter-of-factness with which the situation is treated and the relationships are portrayed provides part of the play's shock value.

Beginning in the late 1960s and continuing to the present, Pinter has been writing screenplays, some of which are adaptations of his own plays. His other screenwriting credits include *The Servant, The Quiller Memorandum, Accident, The Go-Between, The French Lieutenant's Woman,* and *The Trial.*

THE DUMB WAITER

The claustrophobic qualities of *The Dumb Waiter* (1957), with all its action taking place in a confined basement room, are typical of Pinter's plays, which are often constrained by limits of space. To an extent, such constraint is a metaphor for the constraints that life itself places on people and that people place upon themselves.

The title of the play refers to the machine that ferries clothing and messages from Gus and Ben's room to someone whose identity is unknown. It also refers to Gus and Ben themselves, who are waiting dumbly for a job. They do what they are told and follow orders.

There is an ironic hominess to the domestic scene at the beginning of the play. Ben reads the newspaper and retells the important bits with some relish. Gus's reaction is what we might expect of a wife — if one of them had a wife. The stories they read and analyze give a glimpse of sensationalism that is an appropriate preamble to their own story. Gus and Ben have a sense of propriety and order that is as banal as we would expect from thugs. They like things to be orderly and neat. They want the toilet to work, and they can't help but wonder who cleans up after their jobs.

Ben and Gus are masters of small talk. The language of the play has a meandering, aimless quality that characterizes much of Pinter's style. Ben says one thing, and Gus repeats it. Ben begins a sentence, and Gus finishes. After a point has been made, one hears silence, then the point is made again:

> BEN: We do the same.
> GUS: Exactly the same?
> BEN: Exactly.
> (*Pause.*)
> GUS: We don't do anything different?
> BEN: We do exactly the same.
> GUS: Oh.

This technique results in the buildup of tension and anticipation. The technique also contributes to creating a sense of enigma — the audience strains to make meaning out of what appear to be banal observations, and in the process those observations begin to take on more importance. And, indeed, from the accretion of banalities a deeper meaning grows until trivial matters become matters of life and death.

The only conflict that develops is limited to the trivial disagreements the two old hands have about things that are of no abiding importance. Certainly, this is not the kind of dramatic conflict that engages Ibsen's characters or characters of a more traditional stripe. The petty disagreements seem very natural, and the play itself seems naturalistic. But the improbable intrusion of the dumb waiter changes our sense of what is and is not realistic. The dumb waiter sends down messages virtually in the manner of the oracle at Delphi, and it is up to those who receive them to act on them.

When the play ends, with the next victim walking into the room out of the lavatory, we can only assume that Ben will act on the oracle. And if he does, the message that has come down from on high is terrifying indeed.

The Dumb Waiter in Performance

The Dumb Waiter premiered in Frankfurt-am-Main, Germany, in 1959. Its first London production was in 1960, with *The Room*. The first New York production was at the Cherry Lane Theatre in November 1962, with *The Collection*. That production was titled *The Pinter Plays*. The director, Alan Schneider, was a long-standing friend of Samuel Beckett and had helped direct some of his work. The New York reviewers were puzzled by Pinter's plays. Howard Taubman in the *New*

York Times assured his readers that Pinter does not have his characters move haphazardly but that indeed "his work is fiercely controlled." The reviewers did not observe what later critics pointed out: that *The Dumb Waiter* parodies American gangster movies and that *The Collection* parodies American soap operas. Nonetheless the early reviewers felt that *The Dumb Waiter* was a serious and important play, but they were not sure what made it so. Comparisons with Beckett established the play in an absurdist vein, and the waiting of Ben and Gus was immediately compared with Vladimir and Estragon's situation in Beckett's *Waiting for Godot.*

The Dumb Waiter has been revived often in the United States and abroad. Christopher Payton staged it at the Dinosaur Space in Boston in 1983. John Engstrom's approving review stated, "It's almost as if Laurel and Hardy had stumbled into *Endgame.*" John Travolta and Tom Conti starred in a one-hour television adaptation for ABC in 1987.

Harold Pinter (b. 1930)

THE DUMB WAITER

1957

Characters

BEN
GUS

Scene: *A basement room. Two beds, flat against the back wall. A serving hatch, closed, between the beds. A door to the kitchen and lavatory, left. A door to a passage, right. Ben is lying on a bed, left, reading a paper. Gus is sitting on a bed, right, tying his shoelaces, with difficulty. Both are dressed in shirts, trousers, and braces.*

Silence.

Gus ties his laces, rises, yawns, and begins to walk slowly to the door, left. He stops, looks down, and shakes his foot.

Ben lowers his paper and watches him. Gus kneels and unties his shoelace and slowly takes off the shoe. He looks inside it and brings out a flattened matchbox. He shakes it and examines it. Their eyes meet. Ben rattles his paper and reads. Gus puts the matchbox in his pocket and bends down to put on his shoe. He ties his lace, with difficulty. Ben lowers his paper and watches him. Gus walks to the door, left, stops, and shakes the other foot. He kneels, unties his shoelace, and slowly takes off the shoe. He looks inside it and brings out a flattened cigarette packet. He shakes it

and examines it. Their eyes meet. Ben rattles his paper and reads. Gus puts the packet in his pocket, bends down, puts on his shoe, and ties the lace.

He wanders off, left.

Ben slams the paper down on the bed and glares after him. He picks up the paper and lies on his back, reading.

Silence.

A lavatory chain is pulled twice, off left, but the lavatory does not flush.

Silence.

Gus reenters, left, and halts at the door, scratching his head.

Ben slams down the paper.

BEN: Kaw!

(*He picks up the paper.*)

What about this? Listen to this!

(*He refers to the paper.*)

A man of eighty-seven wanted to cross the road. But there was a lot of traffic, see? He couldn't see how he was going to squeeze through. So he crawled under a lorry.°

lorry: Truck.

GUS: He what?
BEN: He crawled under a lorry. A stationary lorry.
GUS: No?
BEN: The lorry started and ran over him.
GUS: Go on!
BEN: That's what it says here.
GUS: Get away.
BEN: It's enough to make you want to puke, isn't it?
GUS: Who advised him to do a thing like that?
BEN: A man of eighty-seven crawling under a lorry!
GUS: It's unbelievable.
BEN: It's down here in black and white.
GUS: Incredible.

(*Silence.*)

  (*Gus shakes his head and exits. Ben lies back and reads.*)
  (*The lavatory chain is pulled once off left, but the lavatory does not flush.*)
  (*Ben whistles at an item in the paper.*)
  (*Gus reenters.*)

  I want to ask you something.
BEN: What are you doing out there?
GUS: Well, I was just —
BEN: What about the tea?
GUS: I'm just going to make it.
BEN: Well, go on, make it.
GUS: Yes, I will. (*He sits in a chair. Ruminatively.*)
  He's laid on some very nice crockery this time, I'll say that. It's sort of striped. There's a white stripe.

(*Ben reads.*)

  It's very nice. I'll say that.

(*Ben turns the page.*)

  You know, sort of round the cup. Round the rim. All the rest of it's black, you see. Then the saucer's black, except for right in the middle, where the cup goes, where it's white.

(*Ben reads.*)

  Then the plates are the same, you see. Only they've got a black stripe — the plates — right across the middle. Yes, I'm quite taken with the crockery.
BEN (*still reading*): What do you want plates for? You're not going to eat.
GUS: I've brought a few biscuits.
BEN: Well, you'd better eat them quick.
GUS: I always bring a few biscuits. Or a pie. You know I can't drink tea without anything to eat.
BEN: Well, make the tea then, will you? Time's getting on.

(*Gus brings out the flattened cigarette packet and examines it.*)

GUS: You got any cigarettes? I think I've run out.

(*He throws the packet high up and leans forward to catch it.*)

  I hope it won't be a long job, this one.

(*Aiming carefully, he flips the packet under his bed.*)

  Oh, I wanted to ask you something.
BEN (*slamming his paper down*): Kaw!
GUS: What's that?
BEN: A child of eight killed a cat!
GUS: Get away.
BEN: It's a fact. What about that, eh? A child of eight killing a cat!
GUS: How did he do it?
BEN: It was a girl.
GUS: How did she do it?
BEN: She —

(*He picks up the paper and studies it.*)

  It doesn't say.
GUS: Why not?
BEN: Wait a minute. It just says — Her brother, aged eleven, viewed the incident from the toolshed.
GUS: Go on!
BEN: That's bloody ridiculous.

(*Pause.*)

GUS: I bet he did it.
BEN: Who?
GUS: The brother.
BEN: I think you're right.

(*Pause.*)

  (*Slamming down the paper.*) What about that, eh? A kid of eleven killing a cat and blaming it on his little sister of eight! It's enough to —

(*He breaks off in disgust and seizes the paper. Gus rises.*)

GUS: What time is he getting in touch?

(*Ben reads.*)

  What time is he getting in touch?
BEN: What's the matter with you? It could be any time. Any time.
GUS (*moves to the foot of Ben's bed*): Well, I was going to ask you something.
BEN: What?
GUS: Have you noticed the time that tank takes to fill?
BEN: What tank?
GUS: In the lavatory.
BEN: No. Does it?
GUS: Terrible.

BEN: Well, what about it?

GUS: What do you think's the matter with it?

BEN: Nothing.

GUS: Nothing?

BEN: It's got a deficient ballcock, that's all.

GUS: A deficient what?

BEN: Ballcock.

GUS: No? Really?

BEN: That's what I should say.

GUS: Go on! That didn't occur to me.

(*Gus wanders to his bed and presses the mattress.*)

I didn't have a very restful sleep today, did you? It's not much of a bed. I could have done with another blanket too. (*He catches sight of a picture on the wall.*) Hello, what's this? (*Peering at it.*) "The First Eleven."° Cricketers. You seen this, Ben?

BEN (*reading*): What?

GUS: The first eleven.

BEN: What?

GUS: There's a photo here of the first eleven.

BEN: What first eleven?

GUS (*studying the photo*): It doesn't say.

BEN: What about that tea?

GUS: They all look a bit old to me.

(*Gus wanders downstage, looks out front, then all about the room.*)

I wouldn't like to live in this dump. I wouldn't mind if you had a window, you could see what it looked like outside.

BEN: What do you want a window for?

GUS: Well, I like to have a bit of a view, Ben. It wiles away the time.

(*He walks about the room.*)

I mean, you come into a place when it's still dark, you come into a room you've never seen before, you sleep all day, you do your job, and then you go away in the night again.

(*Pause.*)

I like to get a look at the scenery. You never get the chance in this job.

BEN: You get your holidays, don't you?

GUS: Only a fortnight.

BEN (*lowering the paper*): You kill me. Anyone would think you're working every day. How often do we do a job? Once a week? What are you complaining about?

GUS: Yes, but we've got to be on tap though, haven't we? You can't move out of the house in case a call comes.

The First Eleven: A cricket team.

BEN: You know what your trouble is?

GUS: What?

BEN: You haven't got any interests.

GUS: I've got interests.

BEN: What? Tell me one of your interests.

(*Pause.*)

GUS: I've got interests.

BEN: Look at me. What have I got?

GUS: I don't know. What?

BEN: I've got my woodwork. I've got my model boats. Have you ever seen me idle? I'm never idle. I know how to occupy my time, to its best advantage. Then when a call comes, I'm ready.

GUS: Don't you ever get a bit fed up?

BEN: Fed up? What with?

(*Silence.*)

(*Ben reads. Gus feels in the pocket of his jacket, which hangs on the bed.*)

GUS: You got any cigarettes? I've run out.

(*The lavatory flushes off left.*)

There she goes.

(*Gus sits on his bed.*)

No, I mean, I say the crockery's good. It is. It's very nice. But that's about all I can say for this place. It's worse than the last one. Remember that last place we were in? Last time, where was it? At least there was a wireless there. No, honest. He doesn't seem to bother much about our comfort these days.

BEN: When are you going to stop jabbering?

GUS: You'd get rheumatism in a place like this, if you stay long.

BEN: We're not staying long. Make the tea, will you? We'll be on the job in a minute.

(*Gus picks up a small bag by his bed and brings out a packet of tea. He examines it and looks up.*)

GUS: Eh, I've been meaning to ask you.

BEN: What the hell is it now?

GUS: Why did you stop the car this morning, in the middle of that road?

BEN (*lowering the paper*): I thought you were asleep.

GUS: I was, but I woke up when you stopped. You did stop, didn't you?

(*Pause.*)

In the middle of that road. It was still dark, don't you remember? I looked out. It was all misty. I thought perhaps you wanted to kip,° but you were

kip: Nap.

sitting up dead straight, like you were waiting for something.

BEN: I wasn't waiting for anything.

GUS: I must have fallen asleep again. What was all that about then? Why did you stop?

BEN (*picking up the paper*): We were too early.

GUS: Early? (*He rises.*) What do you mean? We got the call, didn't we, saying we were to start right away. We did. We shoved out on the dot. So how could we be too early?

BEN (*quietly*): Who took the call, me or you?

GUS: You.

BEN: We were too early.

GUS: Too early for what?

(*Pause.*)

You mean someone had to get out before we got in?

(*He examines the bedclothes.*)

I thought these sheets didn't look too bright. I thought they ponged° a bit. I was too tired to notice when I got in this morning. Eh, that's taking a bit of a liberty, isn't it? I don't want to share my bed sheets. I told you things were going down the drain. I mean, we've always had clean sheets laid on up till now. I've noticed it.

BEN: How do you know those sheets weren't clean?

GUS: What do you mean?

BEN: How do you know they weren't clean? You've spent the whole day in them, haven't you?

GUS: What, you mean it might be my pong? (*He sniffs sheets.*) Yes. (*He sits slowly on bed.*) It could be my pong, I suppose. It's difficult to tell. I don't really know what I pong like, that's the trouble.

BEN (*referring to the paper*): Kaw!

GUS: Eh, Ben.

BEN: Kaw!

GUS: Ben.

BEN: What?

GUS: What town are we in? I've forgotten.

BEN: I've told you. Birmingham.

GUS: Go on!

(*He looks with interest about the room.*)

That's in the Midlands. The second biggest city in Great Britain. I'd never have guessed.

(*He snaps his fingers.*)

Eh, it's Friday today, isn't it? It'll be Saturday tomorrow.

BEN: What about it?

GUS (*excited*): We could go and watch the Villa.°

BEN: They're playing away.

GUS: No, are they? Caarr! What a pity.

BEN: Anyway, there's no time. We've got to get straight back.

GUS: Well, we have done in the past, haven't we? Stayed over and watched a game, haven't we? For a bit of relaxation.

BEN: Things have tightened up, mate. They've tightened up.

(*Gus chuckles to himself.*)

GUS: I saw the Villa get beat in a cup tie once. Who was it against now? White shirts. It was one-all at halftime. I'll never forget it. Their opponents won by a penalty. Talk about drama. Yes, it was a disputed penalty. Disputed. They got beat two-one, anyway, because of it. You were there yourself.

BEN: Not me.

GUS: Yes, you were there. Don't you remember that disputed penalty?

BEN: No.

GUS: He went down just inside the area. Then they said he was just acting. I didn't think the other bloke touched him myself. But the referee had the ball on the spot.

BEN: Didn't touch him! What are you talking about? He laid him out flat!

GUS: Not the Villa. The Villa don't play that sort of game.

BEN: Get out of it.

(*Pause.*)

GUS: Eh, that must have been here, in Birmingham.

BEN: What must?

GUS: The Villa. That must have been here.

BEN: They were playing away.

GUS: Because you know who the other team was? It was the Spurs. It was Tottenham Hotspur.

BEN: Well, what about it?

GUS: We've never done a job in Tottenham.

BEN: How do you know?

GUS: I'd remember Tottenham.

(*Ben turns on his bed to look at him.*)

BEN: Don't make me laugh, will you?

(*Ben turns back and reads. Gus yawns and speaks through his yawn.*)

GUS: When's he going to get in touch?

(*Pause.*)

---

ponged: Smelled.

Villa: A soccer team.

Yes, I'd like to see another football° match. I've always been an ardent football fan. Here, what about coming to see the Spurs tomorrow?

BEN (*tonelessly*): They're playing away.

GUS: Who are?

BEN: The Spurs.

GUS: Then they might be playing here.

BEN: Don't be silly.

GUS: If they're playing away they might be playing here. They might be playing the Villa.

BEN (*tonelessly*): But the Villa are playing away.

(*Pause. An envelope slides under the door, right. Gus sees it. He stands, looking at it.*)

GUS: Ben.

BEN: Away. They're all playing away.

GUS: Ben, look here.

BEN: What?

GUS: Look.

(*Ben turns his head and sees the envelope. He stands.*)

BEN: What's that?

GUS: I don't know.

BEN: Where did it come from?

GUS: Under the door.

BEN: Well, what is it?

GUS: I don't know.

(*They stare at it.*)

BEN: Pick it up.

GUS: What do you mean?

BEN: Pick it up!

(*Gus slowly moves toward it, bends, and picks it up.*)

What is it?

GUS: An envelope.

BEN: Is there anything on it?

GUS: No.

BEN: Is it sealed?

GUS: Yes.

BEN: Open it.

GUS: What?

BEN: Open it!

(*Gus opens it and looks inside.*)

What's in it?

(*Gus empties twelve matches into his hand.*)

GUS: Matches.

BEN: Matches?

GUS: Yes.

BEN: Show it to me.

(*Gus passes the envelope. Ben examines it.*)

football: Soccer.

Nothing on it. Not a word.

GUS: That's funny, isn't it?

BEN: It came under the door?

GUS: Must have done.

BEN: Well, go on.

GUS: Go on where?

BEN: Open the door and see if you can catch anyone outside.

GUS: Who, me?

BEN: Go on!

(*Gus stares at him; puts the matches in his pocket, goes to his bed, and brings a revolver from under the pillow. He goes to the door, opens it, looks out, and shuts it.*)

GUS: No one.

(*He replaces the revolver.*)

BEN: What did you see?

GUS: Nothing.

BEN: They must have been pretty quick.

(*Gus takes the matches from pocket and looks at them.*)

GUS: Well, they'll come in handy.

BEN: Yes.

GUS: Won't they?

BEN: Yes, you're always running out, aren't you?

GUS: All the time.

BEN: Well, they'll come in handy then.

GUS: Yes.

BEN: Won't they?

GUS: Yes, I could do with them. I could do with them too.

BEN: You could, eh?

GUS: Yes.

BEN: Why?

GUS: We haven't got any.

BEN: Well, you've got some now, haven't you?

GUS: I can light the kettle now.

BEN: Yes, you're always cadging° matches. How many have you got there?

GUS: About a dozen.

BEN: Well, don't lose them. Red too. You don't even need a box.

(*Gus probes his ear with a match.*)

(*Slapping his hand.*) Don't waste them! Go on, go and light it.

GUS: Eh?

BEN: Go and light it.

GUS: Light what?

BEN: The kettle.

cadging: Begging.

GUS: You mean the gas.

BEN: Who does?

GUS: You do.

BEN (*his eyes narrowing*): What do you mean, I mean the gas?

GUS: Well, that's what you mean, don't you? The gas.

BEN (*powerfully*): If I say go and light the kettle I mean go and light the kettle.

GUS: How can you light a kettle?

BEN: It's a figure of speech! Light the kettle. It's a figure of speech!

GUS: I've never heard it.

BEN: Light the kettle! It's common usage!

GUS: I think you've got it wrong.

BEN (*menacing*): What do you mean?

GUS: They say put on the kettle.

BEN (*taut*): Who says?

(*They stare at each other, breathing hard.*)

(*Deliberately.*) I have never in all my life heard anyone say put on the kettle.

GUS: I bet my mother used to say it.

BEN: Your mother? When did you last see your mother?

GUS: I don't know, about —

BEN: Well, what are you talking about your mother for?

(*They stare.*)

Gus, I'm not trying to be unreasonable. I'm just trying to point out something to you.

GUS: Yes, but —

BEN: Who's the senior partner here, me or you?

GUS: You.

BEN: I'm only looking after your interests, Gus. You've got to learn, mate.

GUS: Yes, but I've never heard —

BEN (*vehemently*): Nobody says light the gas! What does the gas light?

GUS: What does the gas —?

BEN (*grabbing him with two hands by the throat, at arm's length*): THE KETTLE, YOU FOOL!

(*Gus takes the hands from his throat.*)

GUS: All right, all right.

(*Pause.*)

BEN: Well, what are you waiting for?

GUS: I want to see if they light.

BEN: What?

GUS: The matches.

(*He takes out the flattened box and tries to strike.*)

No.

(*He throws the box under the bed.*)
(*Ben stares at him.*)
(*Gus raises his foot.*)

Shall I try it on here?

(*Ben stares. Gus strikes a match on his shoe. It lights.*)

Here we are.

BEN (*wearily*): Put on the bloody kettle, for Christ's sake.

(*Ben goes to his bed, but, realizing what he has said, stops and half turns. They look at each other. Gus slowly exits, left. Ben slams his paper down on the bed and sits on it, head in hands.*)

GUS (*entering*): It's going.

BEN: What?

GUS: The stove.

(*Gus goes to his bed and sits.*)

I wonder who it'll be tonight.

(*Silence.*)

Eh, I've been wanting to ask you something.

BEN (*putting his legs on the bed*): Oh, for Christ's sake.

GUS: No. I was going to ask you something.

(*He rises and sits on Ben's bed.*)

BEN: What are you sitting on my bed for?

(*Gus sits.*)

What's the matter with you? You're always asking me questions. What's the matter with you?

GUS: Nothing.

BEN: You never used to ask me so many damn questions. What's come over you?

GUS: No, I was just wondering.

BEN: Stop wondering. You've got a job to do. Why don't you just do it and shut up?

GUS: That's what I was wondering about.

BEN: What?

GUS: The job.

BEN: What job?

GUS (*tentatively*): I thought perhaps you might know something.

(*Ben looks at him.*)

I thought perhaps you — I mean — have you got any idea — who it's going to be tonight?

BEN: Who what's going to be?

(*They look at each other.*)

GUS (*at length*): Who it's going to be.

(*Silence.*)

BEN: Are you feeling all right?

GUS: Sure.

BEN: Go and make the tea.

GUS: Yes, sure.

(*Gus exits, left, Ben looks after him. He then takes his revolver from under the pillow and checks it for ammunition. Gus reenters.*)

The gas has gone out.

BEN: Well, what about it?

GUS: There's a meter.

BEN: I haven't got any money.

GUS: Nor have I.

BEN: You'll have to wait.

GUS: What for?

BEN: For Wilson.

GUS: He might not come. He might just send a message. He doesn't always come.

BEN: Well, you'll have to do without it, won't you?

GUS: Blimey.

BEN: You'll have a cup of tea afterwards. What's the matter with you?

GUS: I like to have one before.

(*Ben holds the revolver up to the light and polishes it.*)

BEN: You'd better get ready anyway.

GUS: Well, I don't know, that's a bit much, you know, for my money.

(*He picks up a packet of tea from the bed and throws it into the bag.*)

I hope he's got a shilling, anyway, if he comes. He's entitled to have. After all, it's his place, he could have seen there was enough gas for a cup of tea.

BEN: What do you mean, it's his place?

GUS: Well, isn't it?

BEN: He's probably only rented it. It doesn't have to be his place.

GUS: I know it's his place. I bet the whole house is. He's not even laying on any gas now either.

(*Gus sits on his bed.*)

It's his place all right. Look at all the other places. You go to this address, there's a key there, there's a teapot, there's never a soul in sight — (*He pauses.*) Eh, nobody ever hears a thing, have you ever thought of that? We never get any complaints, do we, too much noise or anything like that? You never see a soul, do you? — except the bloke who comes. You ever noticed that? I wonder if the walls are soundproof. (*He touches the wall above his bed.*) Can't tell. All you do is wait, eh? Half the

time he doesn't even bother to put in an appearance, Wilson.

BEN: Why should he? He's a busy man.

GUS (*thoughtfully*): I find him hard to talk to, Wilson. Do you know that, Ben?

BEN: Scrub round it, will you?

(*Pause.*)

GUS: There are a number of things I want to ask him. But I can never get round to it, when I see him.

(*Pause.*)

I've been thinking about the last one.

BEN: What last one?

GUS: That girl.

(*Ben grabs the paper, which he reads.*)

(*Rising, looking down at Ben.*) How many times have you read that paper?

(*Ben slams the paper down and rises.*)

BEN (*angrily*): What do you mean?

GUS: I was just wondering how many times you'd —

BEN: What are you doing, criticizing me?

GUS: No, I was just —

BEN: You'll get a swipe round your earhole if you don't watch your step.

GUS: Now look here, Ben —

BEN: I'm not looking anywhere! (*He addresses the room.*) How many times have I —! A bloody liberty!

GUS: I didn't mean that.

BEN: You just get on with it, mate. Get on with it, that's all.

(*Ben gets back on the bed.*)

GUS: I was just thinking about that girl, that's all.

(*Gus sits on his bed.*)

She wasn't much to look at, I know, but still. It was a mess though, wasn't it? What a mess. Honest, I can't remember a mess like that one. They don't seem to hold together like men, women. A looser texture, like. Didn't she spread, eh? She didn't half spread. Kaw! But I've been meaning to ask you.

(*Ben sits up and clenches his eyes.*)

Who clears up after we've gone? I'm curious about that. Who does the clearing up? Maybe they don't clear up. Maybe they just leave them there, eh? What do you think? How many jobs have we done? Blimey, I can't count them. What if they never clear anything up after we've gone.

BEN (*pityingly*): You mutt. Do you think we're the

only branch of this organization? Have a bit of common. They got departments for everything.

GUS: What cleaners and all?

BEN: You birk!°

GUS: No, it was that girl made me start to think —

(*There is a loud clatter and racket in the bulge of wall between the beds, of something descending. They grab their revolvers, jump up, and face the wall. The noise comes to a stop. Silence. They look at each other. Ben gestures sharply toward the wall. Gus approaches the wall slowly. He bangs it with his revolver. It is hollow. Ben moves to the head of his bed, his revolver cocked. Gus puts his revolver on his bed and pats along the bottom of the center panel. He finds a rim. He lifts the panel. Disclosed is a serving hatch, a "dumb waiter." A wide box is held by pulleys. Gus peers into the box. He brings out a piece of paper.*)

BEN: What is it?

GUS: You have a look at it.

BEN: Read it.

GUS (*reading*): Two braised steak and chips. Two sago puddings. Two teas without sugar.

BEN: Let me see that. (*He takes the paper.*)

GUS (*to himself*): Two teas without sugar.

BEN: Mmnn.

GUS: What do you think of that?

BEN: Well —

(*The box goes up. Ben levels his revolver.*)

GUS: Give us a chance? They're in a hurry, aren't they?

(*Ben rereads the note. Gus looks over his shoulder.*)

That's a bit — that's a bit funny, isn't it?

BEN (*quickly*): No. It's not funny. It probably used to be a café here, that's all. Upstairs. These places change hands very quickly.

GUS: A café?

BEN: Yes.

GUS: What, you mean this was the kitchen, down here?

BEN: Yes, they change hands overnight, these places. Go into liquidation. The people who run it, you know, they don't find it a going concern, they move out.

GUS: You mean the people who ran this place didn't find it a going concern and moved out?

BEN: Sure.

GUS: WELL, WHO'S GOT IT NOW?

(*Silence.*)

BEN: What do you mean, who's got it now?

birk: Fool.

GUS: Who's got it now? If they moved out, who moved in?

BEN: Well, that all depends —

(*The box descends with a clatter and bang. Ben levels his revolver. Gus goes to the box and brings out a piece of paper.*)

GUS (*reading*): Soup of the day. Liver and onions. Jam tart.

(*A pause. Gus looks at Ben. Ben takes the note and reads it. He walks slowly to the hatch. Gus follows. Ben looks into the hatch but not up it. Gus puts his hand on Ben's shoulder. Ben throws it off. Gus puts his finger to his mouth. He leans on the hatch and swiftly looks up it. Ben flings him away in alarm. Ben looks at the note. He throws his revolver on the bed and speaks with decision.*)

BEN: We'd better send something up.

GUS: Eh?

BEN: We'd better send something up.

GUS: Oh! Yes. Yes. Maybe you're right.

(*They are both relieved at the decision.*)

BEN (*purposefully*): Quick! What have you got in that bag?

GUS: Not much.

(*Gus goes to the hatch and shouts up it.*)

Wait a minute!

BEN: Don't do that!

(*Gus examines the contents of the bag and brings them out, one by one.*)

GUS: Biscuits. A bar of chocolate. Half a pint of milk.

BEN: That all?

GUS: Packet of tea.

BEN: Good.

GUS: We can't send the tea. That's all the tea we've got.

BEN: Well, there's no gas. You can't do anything with it, can you?

GUS: Maybe they can send us down a bob.°

BEN: What else is there?

GUS (*reaching into bag*): One Eccles cake.°

BEN: One Eccles cake?

GUS: Yes.

BEN: You never told me you had an Eccles cake.

GUS: Didn't I?

BEN: Why only one? Didn't you bring one for me?

GUS: I didn't think you'd be keen.

BEN: Well, you can't send up one Eccles cake, anyway.

bob: A shilling for the gas meter.
Eccles cake: A sugared pastry.

GUS: Why not?
BEN: Fetch one of those plates.
GUS: All right.

(*Gus goes toward the door, left, and stops.*)

Do you mean I can keep the Eccles cake then?
BEN: Keep it?
GUS: Well, they don't know we've got it, do they?
BEN: That's not the point.
GUS: Can't I keep it?
BEN: No, you can't. Get the plate.

(*Gus exits, left. Ben looks in the bag. He brings out a packet of crisps.° Enter Gus with a plate.*)

(*Accusingly, holding up the crisps.*) Where did these come from?
GUS: What?
BEN: Where did these crisps come from?
GUS: Where did you find them?
BEN (*hitting him on the shoulder*): You're playing a dirty game, my lad!
GUS: I only eat those with beer!
BEN: Well, where were you going to get the beer?
GUS: I was saving them till I did.
BEN: I'll remember this. Put everything on the plate.

(*They pile everything on to the plate. The box goes up without the plate.*)

Wait a minute!

(*They stand.*)

GUS: It's gone up.
BEN: It's all your stupid fault, playing about!
GUS: What do we do now?
BEN: We'll have to wait till it comes down.

(*Ben puts the plate on the bed, puts on his shoulder holster, and starts to put on his tie.*)

You'd better get ready.

(*Gus goes to his bed, puts on his tie, and starts to fix his holster.*)

GUS: Hey, Ben.
BEN: What?
GUS: What's going on here?

(*Pause.*)

BEN: What do you mean?
GUS: How can this be a café?
BEN: It used to be a café.
GUS: Have you seen the gas stove?
BEN: What about it?
GUS: It's only got three rings.

crisps: Potato chips.

BEN: So what?
GUS: Well, you couldn't cook much on three rings, not for a busy place like this.
BEN (*irritably*): That's why the service is slow!

(*Ben puts on his waistcoat.*)

GUS: Yes, but what happens when we're not here? What do they do then? All these menus coming down and nothing going up. It might have been going on like this for years.

(*Ben brushes his jacket.*)

What happens when we go?

(*Ben puts on his jacket.*)

They can't do much business.

(*The box descends. They turn about. Gus goes to the hatch and brings out a note.*)

GUS (*reading*): Macaroni Pastitsio. Ormitha Macarounada.
BEN: What was that?
GUS: Macaroni Pastitsio. Ormitha Macarounada.
BEN: Greek dishes.
GUS: No.
BEN: That's right.
GUS: That's pretty high class.
BEN: Quick before it goes up.

(*Gus puts the plate in the box.*)

GUS (*calling up the hatch*): Three McVitie and Price! One Lyons Red Label! One Smith's Crisps! One Eccles cake! One Fruit and Nut!
BEN: Cadbury's.
GUS (*up the hatch*): Cadbury's!
BEN (*handing the milk*): One bottle of milk.
GUS (*up the hatch*): One bottle of milk! Half a pint! (*He looks at the label.*) Express Dairy! (*He puts the bottle in the box.*)

(*The box goes up.*)

Just did it.
BEN: You shouldn't shout like that.
GUS: Why not?
BEN: It isn't done.

(*Ben goes to his bed.*)

Well, that should be all right, anyway, for the time being.
GUS: You think so, eh?
BEN: Get dressed, will you? It'll be any minute now.

(*Gus puts on his waistcoat. Ben lies down and looks up at the ceiling.*)

GUS: This is some place. No tea and no biscuits.

BEN: Eating makes you lazy, mate. You're getting lazy, you know that? You don't want to get slack on your job.

GUS: Who me?

BEN: Slack, mate, slack.

GUS: Who me? Slack?

BEN: Have you checked your gun? You haven't even checked your gun. It looks disgraceful, anyway. Why don't you ever polish it?

(*Gus rubs his revolver on the sheet. Ben takes out a pocket mirror and straightens his tie.*)

GUS: I wonder where the cook is. They must have had a few, to cope with that. Maybe they had a few more gas stoves. Eh! Maybe there's another kitchen along the passage.

BEN: Of course there is! Do you know what it takes to make an Ormitha Macarounada?

GUS: No, what?

BEN: An Ormitha —! Buck your ideas up,° will you?

GUS: Takes a few cooks, eh?

(*Gus puts his revolver in its holster.*)

The sooner we're out of this place the better.

(*He puts on his jacket.*)

Why doesn't he get in touch? I feel like I've been here years. (*He takes his revolver out of its holster to check the ammunition.*) We've never let him down though, have we? We've never let him down. I was thinking only the other day, Ben. We're reliable, aren't we?

(*He puts his revolver back in its holster.*)

Still, I'll be glad when it's over tonight.

(*He brushes his jacket.*)

I hope the bloke's not going to get excited tonight, or anything. I'm feeling a bit off. I've got a splitting headache.

(*Silence.*)
(*The box descends. Ben jumps up.*)
(*Gus collects the note.*)

(*Reading.*) One Bamboo Shoots, Water Chestnuts and Chicken. One Char Siu and Beansprouts.

BEN: Beansprouts?

GUS: Yes.

BEN: Blimey.

GUS: I wouldn't know where to begin.

(*He looks back at the box. The packet of tea is inside it. He picks it up.*)

Buck . . . up: Improve or smarten up.

They've sent back the tea.

BEN (*anxious*): What'd they do that for?

GUS: Maybe it isn't tea-time.

(*The box goes up. Silence.*)

BEN (*throwing the tea on the bed, and speaking urgently*): Look here. We'd better tell them.

GUS: Tell them what?

BEN: That we can't do it, we haven't got it.

GUS: All right then.

BEN: Lend us your pencil. We'll write a note.

(*Gus, turning for a pencil, suddenly discovers the speaking tube, which hangs on the right wall of the hatch facing his bed.*)

GUS: What's this?

BEN: What?

GUS: This.

BEN (*examining it*): This? It's a speaking tube.

GUS: How long has that been there?

BEN: Just the job. We should have used it before, instead of shouting up there.

GUS: Funny I never noticed it before.

BEN: Well, come on.

GUS: What do you do?

BEN: See that? That's a whistle.

GUS: What, this?

BEN: Yes, take it out. Pull it out.

(*Gus does so.*)

That's it.

GUS: What do we do now?

BEN: Blow into it.

GUS: Blow?

BEN: It whistles up there if you blow. Then they know you want to speak. Blow.

(*Gus blows. Silence.*)

GUS (*tube at mouth*): I can't hear a thing.

BEN: Now you speak! Speak into it!

(*Gus looks at Ben, then speaks into the tube.*)

GUS: The larder's bare!

BEN: Give me that!

(*He grabs the tube and puts it to his mouth.*)

(*Speaking with great deference.*) Good evening. I'm sorry to — bother you, but we just thought we'd better let you know that we haven't got anything left. We sent up all we had. There's no more food down here.

(*He brings the tube slowly to his ear.*)

What?

(*To mouth.*)

What?

(*To ear. He listens. To mouth.*)

No, all we had we sent up.

(*To ear. He listens. To mouth.*)

Oh, I'm very sorry to hear that.

(*To ear. He listens. To Gus.*)

The Eccles cake was stale.

(*He listens. To Gus.*)

The chocolate was melted.

(*He listens. To Gus.*)

The milk was sour.
GUS: What about the crisps?
BEN (*listening*): The biscuits were moldy.

(*He glares at Gus. Tube to mouth.*)

Well, we're very sorry about that.

(*Tube to ear.*)

What?

(*To mouth.*)

What?

(*To ear.*)

Yes. Yes.

(*To mouth.*)

Yes certainly. Certainly. Right away.

(*To ear. The voice has ceased. He hangs up the tube.*)

(*Excitedly.*) Did you hear that?
GUS: What?
BEN: You know what he said? Light the kettle! Not put on the kettle! Not light the gas! But light the kettle!
GUS: How can we light the kettle?
BEN: What do you mean?
GUS: There's no gas.
BEN (*clapping hand to head*): Now what do we do?
GUS: What did he want us to light the kettle for?
BEN: For tea. He wanted a cup of tea.
GUS: *He* wanted a cup of tea! What about me? I've been wanting a cup of tea all night!
BEN (*despairingly*): What do we do now?
GUS: What are we supposed to drink?

(*Ben sits on his bed, staring.*)

What about us?

(*Ben sits.*)

I'm thirsty too. I'm starving. And he wants a cup of tea. That beats the band, that does.

(*Ben lets his head sink on to his chest.*)

I could do with a bit of sustenance myself. What about you? You look as if you could do with something too.

(*Gus sits on his bed.*)

We send him up all we've got and he's not satisfied. No, honest, it's enough to make the cat laugh. Why did you send him up all that stuff? (*Thoughtfully.*) Why did I send it up?

(*Pause.*)

Who knows what he's got upstairs? He's probably got a salad bowl. They must have something up there. They won't get much from down here. You notice they didn't ask for any salads? They've probably got a salad bowl up there. Cold meat, radishes, cucumbers. Watercress. Roll mops.°

(*Pause.*)

Hardboiled eggs.

(*Pause.*)

The lot. They've probably got a crate of beer too. Probably eating my crisps with a pint of beer now. Didn't have anything to say about those crisps, did he? They do all right, don't worry about that. You don't think they're just going to sit there and wait for stuff to come up from down here, do you? That'll get them nowhere.

(*Pause.*)

They do all right.

(*Pause.*)

And he wants a cup of tea.

(*Pause.*)

That's past a joke, in my opinion.

(*He looks over at Ben, rises, and goes to him.*)

What's the matter with you? You don't look too bright. I feel like an Alka-Seltzer myself.

(*Ben sits up.*)

BEN (*in a low voice*): Time's getting on.
GUS: I know. I don't like doing a job on an empty stomach.

Roll mops: Skewered herring with pickles.

BEN (*wearily*): Be quiet a minute. Let me give you your instructions.
GUS: What for? We always do it the same way, don't we?
BEN: Let me give you your instructions.

(*Gus sighs and sits next to Ben on the bed. The instructions are stated and repeated automatically.*)

When we get the call, you go over and stand behind the door.
GUS: Stand behind the door.
BEN: If there's a knock on the door you don't answer it.
GUS: If there's a knock on the door I don't answer it.
BEN: But there won't be a knock on the door.
GUS: So I won't answer it.
BEN: When the bloke comes in —
GUS: When the bloke comes in —
BEN: Shut the door behind him.
GUS: Shut the door behind him.
BEN: Without divulging your presence.
GUS: Without divulging my presence.
BEN: He'll see me and come towards me.
GUS: He'll see you and come towards you.
BEN: He won't see you.
GUS (*absently*): Eh?
BEN: He won't see you.
GUS: He won't see me.
BEN: But he'll see me.
GUS: He'll see you.
BEN: He won't know you're there.
GUS: He won't know you're there.
BEN: He won't know *you're* there.
GUS: He won't know I'm there.
BEN: I take out my gun.
GUS: You take out your gun.
BEN: He stops in his tracks.
GUS: He stops in his tracks.
BEN: If he turns round —
GUS: If he turns round —
BEN: You're there.
GUS: I'm here.

(*Ben frowns and presses his forehead.*)

You've missed something out.
BEN: I know. What?
GUS: I haven't taken my gun out, according to you.
BEN: You take your gun out —
GUS: After I've closed the door.
BEN: After you've closed the door.
GUS: You've never missed that out before, you know that?
BEN: When he sees you behind him —
GUS: Me behind him —

BEN: And me in front of him —
GUS: And you in front of him —
BEN: He'll feel uncertain —
GUS: Uneasy.
BEN: He won't know what to do.
GUS: So what will he do?
BEN: He'll look at me and he'll look at you.
GUS: We won't say a word.
BEN: We'll look at him.
GUS: He won't say a word.
BEN: He'll look at us.
GUS: And we'll look at him.
BEN: Nobody says a word.

(*Pause.*)

GUS: What do we do if it's a girl?
BEN: We do the same.
GUS: Exactly the same?
BEN: Exactly.

(*Pause.*)

GUS: We don't do anything different?
BEN: We do exactly the same.
GUS: Oh.

(*Gus rises and shivers.*)

Excuse me.

(*He exits through the door on the left. Ben remains sitting on the bed, still.*)
(*The lavatory chain is pulled once off left, but the lavatory does not flush.*)
(*Silence.*)
(*Gus reenters and stops inside the door, deep in thought. He looks at Ben, then walks slowly across to his own bed. He is troubled. He stands, thinking. He turns and looks at Ben. He moves a few paces toward him.*)

(*Slowly in a low, tense voice.*) Why did he send us matches if he knew there was no gas?

(*Silence.*)
(*Ben stares in front of him. Gus crosses to the left side of Ben, to the foot of his bed, to get to his other ear.*)

Ben. Why did he send us matches if he knew there was no gas?

(*Ben looks up.*)

Why did he do that?
BEN: Who?
GUS: Who sent us those matches?
BEN: What are you talking about?

(*Gus stares down at him.*)

GUS (*thickly*): Who is it upstairs?
BEN (*nervously*): What's one thing to do with another?
GUS: Who is it, though?
BEN: What's one thing to do with another?

(*Ben fumbles for his paper on the bed.*)

GUS: I asked you a question.
BEN: Enough!
GUS (*with growing agitation*): I asked you before. Who moved in? I asked you. You said the people who had it before moved out. Well, who moved in?
BEN (*hunched*): Shut up.
GUS: I told you, didn't I?
BEN (*standing*): Shut up!
GUS (*feverishly*): I told you before who owned this place, didn't I? I told you.

(*Ben hits him viciously on the shoulder.*)

I told you who ran this place, didn't I?

(*Ben hits him viciously on the shoulder.*)

(*Violently.*) Well, what's he playing all these games for? That's what I want to know. What's he doing it for?
BEN: What games?
GUS (*passionately, advancing*): What's he doing it for? We've been through our tests, haven't we? We got right through our tests, years ago, didn't we? We took them together, don't you remember, didn't we? We've proved ourselves before now, haven't we? We've always done our job. What's he doing all this for? What's the idea? What's he playing these games for?

(*The box in the shaft comes down behind them. The noise is this time accompanied by a shrill whistle, as it falls. Gus rushes to the hatch and seizes the note.*)

(*Reading.*) Scampi!

(*He crumples the note, picks up the tube, takes out the whistle, blows, and speaks.*)

WE'VE GOT NOTHING LEFT! NOTHING! DO YOU UNDERSTAND?

(*Ben seizes the tube and flings Gus away. He follows Gus and slaps him hard, back-handed, across the chest.*)

BEN: Stop it! You maniac!
GUS: But you heard!
BEN (*savagely*): That's enough! I'm warning you!

(*Silence.*)

(*Ben hangs the tube. He goes to his bed and lies down. He picks up his paper and reads.*)

(*Silence.*)
(*The box goes up.*)
(*They turn quickly, their eyes meet. Ben turns to his paper.*)
(*Slowly Gus goes back to his bed, and sits.*)
(*Silence.*)
(*The hatch falls back into place.*)
(*They turn quickly, their eyes meet. Ben turns back to his paper.*)
(*Silence.*)
(*Ben throws his paper down.*)

BEN: Kaw!

(*He picks up the paper and looks at it.*)

Listen to this!

(*Pause.*)

What about that, eh?

(*Pause.*)

Kaw!

(*Pause.*)

Have you ever heard such a thing?
GUS (*dully*): Go on!
BEN: It's true.
GUS: Get away.
BEN: It's down here in black and white.
GUS (*very low*): Is that a fact?
BEN: Can you imagine it.
GUS: It's unbelievable.
BEN: It's enough to make you want to puke, isn't it?
GUS (*almost inaudible*): Incredible.

(*Ben shakes his head. He puts the paper down and rises. He fixes the revolver in his holster.*)
(*Gus stands up. He goes toward the door on the left.*)

BEN: Where are you going?
GUS: I'm going to have a glass of water.

(*He exits. Ben brushes dust off his clothes and shoes. The whistle in the speaking tube blows. He goes to it, takes the whistle out, and puts the tube to his ear. He listens. He puts it to his mouth.*)

BEN: Yes.

(*To ear. He listens. To mouth.*)

Straight away. Right.

(*To ear. He listens. To mouth.*)

Sure we're ready.

(*To ear. He listens. To mouth.*)

Understood. Repeat. He has arrived and will be coming in straight away. The normal method to be employed. Understood.

(*To ear. He listens. To mouth.*)

Sure we're ready.

(*To ear. He listens. To mouth.*)

Right.

(*He hangs the tube up.*)

Gus!

(*He takes out a comb and combs his hair, adjusts his jacket to diminish the bulge of the revolver. The lavatory flushes off left. Ben goes quickly to the door, left.*)

Gus!

(*The door right opens sharply. Ben turns, his revolver leveled at the door.*)
    (*Gus stumbles in.*)
    (*He is stripped of his jacket, waistcoat, tie, holster, and revolver.*)
    (*He stops, body stooping, his arms at his sides.*)
    (*He raises his head and looks at Ben.*)
    (*A long silence.*)
    (*They stare at each other.*)

Wole Soyinka

Wole Soyinka (b. 1934) is one of Nigeria's several important writers to achieve international fame, winning the Nobel Prize for literature in 1986. His work includes novels, poems, and plays, but he admits that "there is no question at all that I think the Nobel Prize is for my drama."

Soyinka studied at University College, Ibadan, Nigeria, and began his literary career as an undergraduate, publishing poetry in the distinguished African literary magazine *Black Orpheus*. His work, especially his drama, has been an investigation of the political, religious, and other forces in Nigerian culture. *The Swamp Dwellers* (1958) is a powerful play condemning African superstition. *The Lion and the Jewel* (1959) offers a comic view of Nigerian attitudes toward European values left over from the colonial period. Among his other plays are *The Trials of Brother Jero* (1960), about a corrupt evangelist, and *Kongi's Harvest* (1964). *A Dance of the Forests* (1960) was written to celebrate Nigerian independence, but it also alerted people to Nigeria's past violence and warned against its return.

Nigeria went through a bitter civil war in 1967, and Soyinka's political sympathies led to a term in prison, where he was placed in solitary confinement. He continued his writing, even smuggling poems out of prison to give hope to his political allies. Interestingly, he criticized his own tribe, the Yoruba, for murdering members of the Ibo during the war against Biafra.

Soyinka studied at the University of Leeds after his schooling in Ibadan, and most of his writing is in English. However, he still writes some of his poetry in his tribal language, Yoruba, and has recommended Swahili as the national language of Nigeria. He has spoken out against cultural parochialism, including its manifestation in the negritude movement, which rejects white culture as a form of pollution. He expressed his philosophy to another great African writer, Leopold Senghor: "A tiger is not forever shouting about his tigritude"; a duiker antelope does not have to "prove his duikertude; you will know him by his elegant leap."

Soyinka has been chairman of the drama department at Ife University as well as of his own University College, Ibadan. He has also lectured in Cambridge, England, and in universities in North America. One of his most recent works, *A Play of Giants* (1984), is a scathing attack on abuse of power, indicting African tyrants such as Idi Amin, Jean-Bedel Bokassa, and others.

For all of his criticism of Nigerian politics, Soyinka has rooted his work in the religion and folklore of the Yoruba people. Ifa, the Yoruba religion, depends on a complex cosmology that sees experience as layered in interactive animal, mineral, and vegetable spheres. African critic Femi Osofisan has described Yoruba cosmology as holding "coeval the three historical, actual and prospective planes of entity; . . . the animal and vegetable essences are correspondent; . . . the acknowledged deities are both anthropomorphic and symbiotic, each fusing in his personality a series of antinomies." Osofisan also notes "the comprehensive union of religious and secular intuition in the traditional Yoruba." Ifa plays a role in *The Strong Breed*, but the play is nonetheless understandable to those unfamiliar with the religion. Soyinka must be thought of as a traditional dramatist, writing in the tradition of his Yoruba people, but reaching a worldwide audience.

THE STRONG BREED

The Strong Breed (1962) examines the interrelationship of ritual and community in African culture, describing one process by which a society renews itself. The "strong breed" are those men capable of the sacrifice needed annually to purify the community of its sins and allow it to start over again. The community's sacrifice signals the beginning of a new year.

As the new year approaches, the elders of the community, Jaguna and Oroge, search for the appropriate "carrier" who can bear the burden of the community's guilt. The tradition in their community is to choose a stranger. Despite the elders' reluctance, Eman, one of the strong breed who has exiled himself from his own community, seems a logical choice until another outsider, the idiot Ifada, comes on the scene. Ifada seems heaven-sent to serve the community. However, when he is chosen and protests in terrified confusion, Eman explains to Jaguna and Oroge that no community should force a carrier to perform unwillingly. If he is unwilling, the guilt will not be carried away. Eman then offers himself as a willing sacrifice in Ifada's place.

The mythic pattern of sacrifice and renewal is basic to much Yoruba myth. Part of the tradition of Yoruba ritual drama is the reenactment of myths that resemble Eman's willing sacrifice. These are celebrated annually on the feast of Obatala, the god of creation. *The Strong Breed* has also been connected to ritual tragedies enacted in honor of Ogun, who suffers greatly for the good of the community.

The Strong Breed is also informed by Soyinka's studies of Greek tragedy. Like Greek tragic figures, Soyinka's strong breed are genetically linked — they are fathers and sons who inherit their fathers' power. Soyinka's *The Bacchae of Euripides* (1973) deals with inspiration, intoxication, and a form of hysteria that affects a mass of people. *Death and the King's Horseman* (1976), centering on death, also explores Greek themes of fate and inevitability. Soyinka demonstrates the universality of Greek themes in both European and African experience.

Certain patterns link Eman with Oedipus. Once Eman is identified by his father as one of the strong breed, he prepares himself for his mission by leaving his community. Like Oedipus, he unwittingly goes to another community where he ultimately must be sacrificed. Eman also resembles Christ: He is a teacher and healer; he refuses to exploit those around him; he lifts up the weak and has empathy for everyone, including the idiot Ifada. And, like Christ, those for whom he sacrifices himself do not hold him in high regard.

Despite its Greek and Christian overtones, the story is grounded in Yoruba tradition, with its initiation rites and concepts of heredity, community, and sacrifice. Soyinka's stagecraft includes traditional Yoruba music and dance as well as traditional Yoruba images, such as the effigy — the carrier doll — and the appearance of the human carrier in the form of Ifada. Soyinka demonstrates that everything in the past is part of the present by overlaying the ghosts of Omae, the woman Eman was to marry, his father (the Old Man), his tutor, and the priest. The past shapes the present just as his father's blood runs in his veins and shapes everything he does as a man.

The play leaves us wondering if Eman's sacrifice was wasteful or redeeming. Is the community led by Jaguna and Oroge worth dying for? Will Eman's death benefit Sunma, Ifada, and the Girl who betrayed him to his killers? Or does Eman die only because he is one of the strong breed, whose mission is to serve as the sacrifice for the community? Even the latter interpretation might imply a positive ending for the play, although it would be a different ending than suggesting that Eman has died *for* this village and thus has secured its renewal. Yoruba tradition implies that even if the community is unworthy, it shares in purification by the sacrifice of the willing. The subtlety of the issues in this play invites multiple interpretations.

The Strong Breed in Performance

The Strong Breed was written at a time of political uncertainty in Nigeria. In Ibadan, Nigeria, in 1963, Soyinka created a twenty-five-minute version that omitted the flashbacks at the end of the play when Eman's past returns to him. This was done for Esso World Theatre and was included in the film *Culture in Transition.* The play was produced in its full-length version in 1964 at the Greenwich Mews Theatre in New York, and it has been performed by theater groups in several African nations. An African university theater group produced the play in its full-length version in Malawi in 1976 with Anthony Nazombe as Eman.

Wole Soyinka (b. 1934)
THE STRONG BREED

1962

Characters

EMAN, *a stranger*
SUNMA, *Jaguna's daughter*
IFADA, *an idiot*
A GIRL
JAGUNA
OROGE
ATTENDANT STALWARTS, *the villagers*

From Eman's past:
OLD MAN, *his father*
OMAE, *his betrothed*
TUTOR
PRIEST
ATTENDANTS, *the villagers*

The scenes are described briefly, but very often a darkened stage with lit areas will not only suffice but is necessary. Except for the one indicated place, there can be no break in the action. A distracting scene change would be ruinous.

(*A mud house, with space in front of it. Eman, in light buba and trousers stands at the window, looking out. Inside, Sunma is clearing the table of what looks like a modest clinic, putting the things away in a cupboard. Another rough table in the room is piled with exercise books, two or three worn textbooks, etc. Sunma appears agitated. Outside, just below the window crouches Ifada. He looks up with a shy smile from time to time, waiting for Eman to notice him.*)

SUNMA (*hesitant*): You will have to make up your mind soon, Eman. The lorry leaves very shortly.

(*As Eman does not answer, Sunma continues her work, more nervously. Two villagers, obvious travelers, pass hurriedly in front of the house, the man has a small raffia sack, the woman a cloth-covered*

basket, the man enters first, turns and urges the woman who is just emerging to hurry.*)

SUNMA (*seeing them, her tone is more intense*): Eman, are we going or aren't we? You will leave it till too late.

EMAN (*quietly*): There is still time — if you want to go.

SUNMA: If I want to go . . . and you?

(*Eman makes no reply.*)

SUNMA (*bitterly*): You don't really want to leave here. You never want to go away — even for a minute.

(*Ifada continues his antics. Eman eventually pats him on the head and the boy grins happily. Leaps up suddenly and returns with a basket of oranges which he offers to Eman.*)

EMAN: My gift for today's festival enh?

(*Ifada nods, grinning.*)

EMAN: They look ripe — that's a change.

SUNMA (*she has gone inside the room. Looks round the door*): Did you call me?

EMAN: No. (*She goes back.*) And what will you do tonight, Ifada? Will you take part in the dancing? Or perhaps you will mount your own masquerade?

(*Ifada shakes his head, regretfully.*)

EMAN: You won't? So you haven't any? But you would like to own one.

(*Ifada nods eagerly.*)

EMAN: Then why don't you make your own?

(*Ifada stares, puzzled by this idea.*)

EMAN: Sunma will let you have some cloth you know. And bits of wool . . .

SUNMA (*coming out*): Who are you talking to, Eman?

EMAN: Ifada. I am trying to persuade him to join the young maskers.

SUNMA (*losing control*): What does he want here? Why is he hanging round us?

EMAN (*amazed*): What . . . ? I said Ifada, Ifada.

SUNMA: Just tell him to go away. Let him go and play somewhere else!

EMAN: What is this? Hasn't he always played here?

SUNMA: I don't want him here. (*Rushes to the window.*) Get away, idiot. Don't bring your foolish face here anymore, do you hear? Go on, go away from here . . .

EMAN (*restraining her*): Control yourself, Sunma. What on earth has got into you?

(*Ifada, hurt and bewildered, backs slowly away.*)

SUNMA: He comes crawling round here like some horrible insect. I never want to lay my eyes on him again.

EMAN: I don't understand. It *is* Ifada you know. Ifada! The unfortunate one who runs errands for you and doesn't hurt a soul.

SUNMA: I cannot bear the sight of him.

EMAN: You can't do what? It can't be two days since he last fetched water for you.

SUNMA: What else can he do except that? He is useless. Just because we have been kind to him . . . Others would have put him in an asylum.

EMAN: You are not making sense. He is not a madman, he is just a little more unlucky than other children. (*Looks keenly at her.*) But what is the matter?

SUNMA: It's nothing. I only wish we had sent him off to one of those places for creatures like him.

EMAN: He is quite happy here. He doesn't bother anyone and he makes himself useful.

SUNMA: Useful! Is that one of any use to anybody? Boys of his age are already earning a living but all he can do is hang around and drool at the mouth.

EMAN: But he does work. You know he does a lot for you.

SUNMA: Does he? And what about the farm you started for him! Does he ever work on it? Or have you forgotten that it was really for Ifada you cleared that bush. Now you have to go and work it yourself. You spend all your time on it and you have no room for anything else.

EMAN: That wasn't his fault. I should first have asked him if he was fond of farming.

SUNMA: Oh, so he can choose? As if he shouldn't be thankful for being allowed to live.

EMAN: Sunma!

SUNMA: He does not like farming but he knows how to feast his dumb mouth on the fruits.

EMAN: But I want him to. I encourage him.

SUNMA: Well keep him. I don't want to see him anymore.

EMAN (*after some moments*): But why? You cannot be telling all the truth. What has he done?

SUNMA: The sight of him fills me with revulsion.

EMAN (*goes to her and holds her*): What really is it? (*Sunma avoids his eyes.*) It is almost as if you are forcing yourself to hate him. Why?

SUNMA: That is not true. Why should I?

EMAN: Then what is the secret? You've even played with him before.

SUNMA: I have always merely tolerated him. But I cannot anymore. Suddenly my disgust won't take him anymore. Perhaps . . . perhaps it is the new year. Yes, yes, it must be the new year.

EMAN: I don't believe that.

SUNMA: It must be. I am a woman, and these things matter. I don't want a misshape near me. Surely for one day in the year, I may demand some wholesomeness.

EMAN: I do not understand you.

(*Sunma is silent.*)

It was cruel of you. And to Ifada who is so helpless and alone. We are the only friends he has.

SUNMA: No, just you. I have told you, with me it has always been only an act of kindness. And now I haven't any pity left for him.

EMAN: No. He is not a wholesome being.

(*He turns back to looking through the window.*)

SUNMA (*half-pleading*): Ifada can rouse your pity. And yet if anything, I need more kindness from you. Every time my weakness betrays me, you close your mind against me . . . Eman . . . Eman . . .

(*A Girl comes in view, dragging an effigy by a rope attached to one of its legs. She stands for a while gazing at Eman. Ifada, who has crept back shyly to his accustomed position, becomes somewhat excited when he sees the effigy. The Girl is unsmiling. She possesses in fact a kind of inscrutability which does not make her hard but is unsettling.*)

GIRL: Is the teacher in?

EMAN (*smiling*): No.

GIRL: Where is he gone?

EMAN: I don't really know. Shall I ask?

GIRL: Yes, do.

EMAN (*turning slightly*): Sunma, a girl outside wants to know . . .

(*Sunma turns away, goes into the inside room.*)

EMAN: Oh. (*Returns to the Girl, but his slight gaiety is lost.*) There is no one at home who can tell me.

GIRL: Why are you not in?

EMAN: I don't really know. Maybe I went somewhere.

GIRL: All right. I will wait until you get back.

(*She pulls the effigy to her, sits down.*)

EMAN (*slowly regaining his amusement*): So you are all ready for the new year.

GIRL (*without turning round*): I am not going to the festival.

EMAN: Then why have you got that?

GIRL: Do you mean my carrier? I am unwell you know. My mother says it will take away my sickness with the old year.

EMAN: Won't you share the carrier with your playmates?

GIRL: Oh, no. Don't you know I play alone? The other children won't come near me. Their mothers would beat them.

EMAN: But I have never seen you here. Why don't you come to the clinic?

GIRL: My mother said No.

(*Gets up, begins to move off.*)

EMAN: You are not going away?

GIRL: I must not stay talking to you. If my mother caught me . . .

EMAN: All right, tell me what you want before you go.

GIRL (*stops. For some moments she remains silent*): I must have some clothes for my carrier.

EMAN: Is that all? You wait a moment.

(*Sunma comes out as he takes down a buba from the wall. She goes to the window and glares almost with hatred at the Girl. The Girl retreats hastily, still impassive.*)

By the way, Sunma, do you know who that girl is?

SUNMA: I hope you don't really mean to give her that.

EMAN: Why not? I hardly ever use it.

SUNMA: Just the same, don't give it to her. She is not a child. She is as evil as the rest of them.

EMAN: What has got into you today?

SUNMA: All right, all right. Do what you wish.

(*She withdraws. Baffled, Eman returns to the window.*)

EMAN: Here . . . will this do? Come and look at it.

GIRL: Throw it.

EMAN: What is the matter? I am not going to eat you.

GIRL: No one lets me come near them.

EMAN: But I am not afraid of catching your disease.

GIRL: Throw it.

(*Eman shrugs and tosses the buba. She takes it without*

a word and slips it on the effigy, completely absorbed in the task. Eman watches for a while, then joins Sunma in the inner room.)

GIRL (*after a long, cool survey of Ifada*): You have a head like a spider's egg, and your mouth dribbles like a roof. But there is no one else. Would you like to play?

(*Ifada nods eagerly, quite excited.*)

GIRL: You will have to get a stick.

(*Ifada rushes around, finds a big stick, and whirls it aloft, bearing down on the carrier.*)

GIRL: Wait. I don't want you to spoil it. If it gets torn I shall drive you away. Now, let me see how you are going to beat it.

(*Ifada hits it gently.*)

GIRL: You may hit harder than that. As long as there is something left to hang at the end.

(*She appraises him up and down.*)

You are not very tall . . . will you be able to hang it from a tree?

(*Ifada nods, grinning happily.*)

GIRL: You will hang it up and I will set fire to it. (*Then, with surprising venom.*) But just because you are helping me, don't think it is going to cure you. I am the one who will get well at midnight, do you understand? It is my carrier and it is for me alone.

(*She pulls at the rope to make sure that it is well attached to the leg.*)

Well don't stand there drooling. Let's go.

(*She begins to walk off, dragging the effigy in the dust. Ifada remains where he is for some moments, seemingly puzzled. Then his face breaks into a large grin and he leaps after the procession, belaboring the effigy with all his strength. The stage remains empty for some moments. Then the horn of a lorry is sounded and Sunma rushes out. The hooting continues for some time with a rhythmic pattern. Eman comes out.*)

EMAN: I am going to the village . . . I shan't be back before nightfall.

SUNMA (*blankly*): Yes.

EMAN (*hesitates*): Well what do you want me to do?

SUNMA: The lorry was hooting just now.

EMAN: I didn't hear it.

SUNMA: It will leave in a few minutes. And you did promise we could go away.

EMAN: I promised nothing. Will you go home by your-self or shall I come back for you?

SUNMA: You don't even want me here?

EMAN: But you have to go home haven't you?

SUNMA: I had hoped we would watch the new year together — in some other place.

EMAN: Why do you continue to distress yourself?

SUNMA: Because you will not listen to me. Why do you continue to stay where nobody wants you?

EMAN: That is not true.

SUNMA: It is. You are wasting your life on people who really want you out of their way.

EMAN: You don't know what you are saying.

SUNMA: You think they love you? Do you think they care at all for what you — or I — do for them?

EMAN: *Them?* These are your own people. Sometimes you talk as if you were a stranger too.

SUNMA: I wonder if I really sprang from here. I know they are evil and I am not. From the oldest to the smallest child, they are nourished in evil and un-wholesomeness in which I have no part.

EMAN: You knew this when you returned?

SUNMA: You reproach me then for trying at all?

EMAN: I reproach you with nothing? But you must leave me out of your plans. I can have no part in them.

SUNMA (*nearly pleading*): Once I could have run away. I would have gone and never looked back.

EMAN: I cannot listen when you talk like that.

SUNMA: I swear to you, I do not mind what happens afterwards. But you must help me tear myself away from here. I can no longer do it by myself . . . It is only a little thing. And we have worked so hard this past year . . . surely we can go away for a week . . . even a few days would be enough.

EMAN: I have told you, Sunma . . .

SUNMA (*desperately*): Two days, Eman. Only two days.

EMAN (*distressed*): But I tell you I have no wish to go.

SUNMA (*suddenly angry*): Are you so afraid then?

EMAN: Me? Afraid of what?

SUNMA: You think you will not want to come back.

EMAN (*pitying*): You cannot dare me that way.

SUNMA: Then why won't you leave here, even for an hour? If you are so sure that your life is settled here, why are you afraid to do this thing for me? What is so wrong that you will not go into the next town for a day or two?

EMAN: I don't want to. I do not have to persuade you or myself about anything. I simply have no desire to go away.

SUNMA (*his quiet confidence appears to incense her*): You are afraid. You accuse me of losing my sense of mission, but you are afraid to put yours to the test.

EMAN: You are wrong, Sunma. I have no sense of mission. But I have found peace here and I am content with that.

SUNMA: I haven't. For a while I thought that too, but I found there could be no peace in the midst of so much cruelty. Eman, tonight at least, the last night of the old year . . .

EMAN: No, Sunma. I find this too distressing; you should go home now.

SUNMA: It is the time for making changes in one's life, Eman. Let's breathe in the new year away from here.

EMAN: You are hurting yourself.

SUNMA: Tonight. Only tonight. We will come back tomorrow, as early as you like. But let us go away for this one night. Don't let another year break on me in this place . . . you don't know how important it is to me, but I will tell you, I will tell you on the way . . . but we must not be here today, Eman, do this one thing for me.

EMAN (*sadly*): I cannot.

SUNMA (*suddenly calm*): I was a fool to think it would be otherwise. The whole village may use you as they will but for me there is nothing. Sometimes I think you believe that doing anything for me makes you unfaithful to some part of your life. If it was a woman then I pity her for what she must have suffered.

(*Eman winces and hardens slowly. Sunma notices nothing.*)

Keeping faith with so much is slowly making you inhuman. (*Seeing the change in Eman.*) Eman. What is it?

(*As she goes toward him, Eman goes into the house.*)

SUNMA (*apprehensive, follows him*): What did I say? Eman, forgive me, forgive me please.

(*Eman remains facing into the slow darkness of the room. Sunma, distressed, cannot decide what to do.*)

I swear I didn't know . . . I would not have said it for all the world.

(*A lorry is heard taking off somewhere nearby. The sound comes up and slowly fades away into the distance. Sunma starts visibly, goes slowly to the window.*)

SUNMA (*as the sound dies off, to herself*): What happens now?

EMAN (*joining her at the window*): What did you say?

SUNMA: Nothing.

EMAN: Was that not the lorry going off?

SUNMA: It was.

EMAN: I am sorry I couldn't help you.

(*Sunma, about to speak, changes her mind.*)

EMAN: I think you ought to go home now.

SUNMA: No, don't send me away. It's the least you can do for me. Let me stay here until all the noise is over.

EMAN: But are you not needed at home? You have a part in the festival.

SUNMA: I have renounced it; I am Jaguna's eldest daughter only in name.

EMAN: Renouncing one's self is not so easy — surely you know that.

SUNMA: I don't want to talk about it. Will you at least let us be together tonight?

EMAN: But . . .

SUNMA: Unless you are afraid my father will accuse you of harboring me.

EMAN: All right, we will go out together.

SUNMA: Go out? I want us to stay here.

EMAN: When there is so much going on outside?

SUNMA: Someday you will wish that you went away when I tried to make you.

EMAN: Are we going back to that?

SUNMA: No. I promise you I will not recall it again. But you must know that it was also for your sake that I tried to get us away.

EMAN: For me? How?

SUNMA: By yourself you can do nothing here. Have you not noticed how tightly we shut out strangers? Even if you lived here for a lifetime, you would remain a stranger.

EMAN: Perhaps that is what I like. There is peace in being a stranger.

SUNMA: For a while perhaps. But they would reject you in the end. I tell you it is only I who stand between you and contempt. And because of this you have earned their hatred. I don't know why I say this now, except that somehow, I feel that it no longer matters. It is only I who have stood between you and much humiliation.

EMAN: Think carefully before you say any more. I am incapable of feeling indebted to you. This will make no difference at all.

SUNMA: I ask for nothing. But you must know it all the same. It is true I hadn't the strength to go by myself. And I must confess this now, if you had come with me, I would have done everything to keep you from returning.

EMAN: I know that.

SUNMA: You see, I bare myself to you. For days I had thought it over, this was to be a new beginning for us. And I placed my fate wholly in your hands. Now the thought will not leave me, I have a feeling which will not be shaken off, that in some way, you have tonight totally destroyed my life.

EMAN: You are depressed, you don't know what you are saying.

SUNMA: Don't think I am accusing you. I say all this only because I cannot help it.

EMAN: We must not remain shut up here. Let us go and be part of the living.

SUNMA: No. Leave them alone.

EMAN: Surely you don't want to stay indoors when the whole town is alive with rejoicing.

SUNMA: Rejoicing! Is that what it seems to you? No, let us remain here. Whatever happens I must not go out until all this is over.

(*There is silence. It has grown much darker.*)

EMAN: I shall light the lamp.

SUNMA (*eager to do something*): No, let me do it.

(*She goes into the inner room.*)

(*Eman paces the room, stops by a shelf and toys with the seeds in an "ayo" board, takes down the whole board and places it on a table, playing by himself.*)

(*The Girl is now seen coming back, still dragging her "carrier." Ifada brings up the rear as before. As he comes round the corner of the house two men emerge from the shadows. A sack is thrown over Ifada's head, the rope is pulled tight rendering him instantly helpless. The Girl has reached the front of the house before she turns round at the sound of scuffle. She is in time to see Ifada thrown over the shoulders and borne away. Her face betraying no emotion at all, the Girl backs slowly away, turns and flees, leaving the "carrier" behind. Sunma enters, carrying two kerosene lamps. She hangs one up from the wall.*)

EMAN: One is enough.

SUNMA: I want to leave one outside.

(*She goes out, hangs the lamp from a nail just above the door. As she turns she sees the effigy and gasps. Eman rushes out.*)

EMAN: What is it? Oh, is that what frightened you?

SUNMA: I thought . . . I didn't really see it properly.

(*Eman goes towards the object, stoops to pick it up.*)

EMAN: It must belong to that sick girl.

SUNMA: Don't touch it.

EMAN: Let's keep it for her.

SUNMA: Leave it alone. Don't touch it, Eman.

EMAN (*shrugs and goes back*): You are very nervous.

SUNMA: Let's go in.

EMAN: Wait. (*He detains her by the door, under the lamp.*) I know there is something more than you've told me. What are you afraid of tonight?

SUNMA: I was only scared by that thing. There is nothing else.

EMAN: I am not blind, Sunma. It is true I would not run away when you wanted me to, but that doesn't mean I do not feel things. What does tonight really mean that it makes you so helpless?

SUNMA: It is only a mood. And your indifference to me . . . let's go in.

(*Eman moves aside and she enters; he remains there for a moment and then follows.*)

(*She fiddles with the lamp, looks vaguely round the room, then goes and shuts the door, bolting it. When she turns, it is to meet Eman's eyes, questioning.*)

SUNMA: There is a cold wind coming in.

(*Eman keeps his gaze on her.*)

SUNMA: It *was* getting cold.

(*She moves guiltily to the table and stands by the "ayo" board, rearranging the seeds. Eman remains where he is a few moments, then brings a stool and sits opposite her. She sits down also and they begin to play in silence.*)

SUNMA: What brought you here at all, Eman? And what makes you stay?

(*There is another silence.*)

SUNMA: I am not trying to share your life. I know you too well by now. But at least we have worked together since you came. Is there nothing at all I deserve to know?

EMAN: Let me continue a stranger — especially to you. Those who have much to give fulfill themselves only in total loneliness.

SUNMA: Then there is no love in what you do.

EMAN: There is. Love comes to me more easily with strangers.

SUNMA: That is unnatural.

EMAN: Not for me. I know I find consummation only when I have spent myself for a total stranger.

SUNMA: It seems unnatural to me. But then I am a woman. I have a woman's longings and weaknesses. And the ties of blood are very strong in me.

EMAN (*smiling*): You think I have cut loose from all these — ties of blood.

SUNMA: Sometimes you are so inhuman.

EMAN: I don't know what that means. But I am very much my father's son.

(*They play in silence. Suddenly Eman pauses, listening.*)

EMAN: Did you hear that?

SUNMA (*quickly*): I heard nothing . . . it's your turn.

EMAN: Perhaps some of the mummers are coming this way.

(*Eman, about to play, leaps up suddenly.*)

SUNMA: What is it? Don't you want to play anymore?

(*Eman moves to the door.*)

SUNMA: No. Don't go out, Eman.

EMAN: If it's the dancers, I want to ask them to stay. At least we won't have to miss everything.

SUNMA: No, no. Don't open the door. Let us keep out everyone tonight.

(*A terrified and disordered figure bursts suddenly round the corner, past the window, and begins hammering at the door. It is Ifada. Desperate with terror, he pounds madly at the door, dumb-moaning all the while.*)

EMAN: Isn't that Ifada?

SUNMA: They are only fooling about. Don't pay any attention.

EMAN (*looks round the window*): That is Ifada. (*Begins to unbolt the door.*)

SUNMA (*pulling at his hands*): It is only a trick they are playing on you. Don't take any notice, Eman.

EMAN: What are you saying? The boy is out of his senses with fear.

SUNMA: No, no. Don't interfere, Eman. For God's sake, don't interfere.

EMAN: Do you know something of this then?

SUNMA: You are a stranger here, Eman. Just leave us alone and go your own way. There is nothing you can do.

EMAN (*he tries to push her out of the way but she clings fiercely to him*): Have you gone mad? I tell you the boy must come in.

SUNMA: Why won't you listen to me, Eman? I tell you it's none of your business. For your own sake, do as I say.

(*Eman pushes her off, unbolts the door. Ifada rushes in, clasps Eman round the knees, dumb-moaning against his legs.*)

EMAN (*manages to rebolt the door*): What is it, Ifada? What is the matter?

(*Shouts and voices are heard coming nearer the house.*)

SUNMA: Before it's too late, let him go. For once, Eman, believe what I tell you. Don't harbor him or you will regret it all your life.

(*Eman tries to calm Ifada who becomes more and more abject as the outside voices get nearer.*)

EMAN: What have they done to him? At least tell me that. What is going on, Sunma?

SUNMA (*with sudden venom*): Monster! Could you not take yourself somewhere else?

EMAN: Stop talking like that.

SUNMA: He could have run into the bush couldn't he? Toad! Why must he follow us with his own disasters!

VOICES OUTSIDE: It's here . . . Round the back . . . Spread, spread . . . this way . . . no, head him off . . . use the bush path and head him off . . . get some more lights . . .

(*Eman listens. Lifts Ifada bodily and carries him into the inner room. Returns at once, shutting the door behind him.*)

SUNMA (*slumps into a chair, resigned*): You always follow your own way.

JAGUNA (*comes round the corner followed by Oroge and three men, one bearing a torch*): I knew he would come here.

OROGE: I hope our friend won't make trouble.

JAGUNA: He had better not. You, recall all the men and tell them to surround the house.

OROGE: But he may not be in the house after all.

JAGUNA: I know he is here . . . (*to the men*) . . . go on, do as I say.

(*He bangs on the door.*)

Teacher, open your door . . . you two, stay by the door. If I need you I will call you.

(*Eman opens the door.*)

JAGUNA (*speaks as he enters*): We know he is here.

EMAN: Who?

JAGUNA: Don't let us waste time. We are grown men, teacher. You understand me and I understand you. But we must take back the boy.

EMAN: This is my house.

JAGUNA: Daughter, you'd better tell your friend. I don't think he quite knows our ways. Tell him why he must give up the boy.

SUNMA: Father, I . . .

JAGUNA: Are you going to tell him or aren't you?

SUNMA: Father, I beg you, leave us alone tonight . . .

JAGUNA: I thought you might be a hindrance. Go home then if you will not use your sense.

SUNMA: But there are other ways . . .

JAGUNA (*turning to the men*): See that she gets home. I no longer trust her. If she gives trouble carry her. And see that the women stay with her until all this is over.

(*Sunma departs, accompanied by one of the men.*)

JAGUNA: Now, teacher . . .

OROGE (*restrains him*): You see, Mister Eman, it is like this. Right now, nobody knows that Ifada has taken refuge here. No one except us and our men — and they know how to keep their mouths shut. We don't want to have to burn down the house you see, but if the word gets around, we would have no choice.

JAGUNA: In fact, it may be too late ?lready. A carrier should end up in the bush, not in a house. Anyone who doesn't guard his door when the carrier goes by has himself to blame. A contaminated house should be burnt down.

OROGE: But we are willing to let it pass. Only, you must bring him out quickly.

EMAN: All right. But at least you will let me ask you something.

JAGUNA: What is there to ask? Don't you understand what we have told you?

EMAN: Yes. But why did you pick on a helpless boy. Obviously he is not willing.

JAGUNA: What is the man talking about? Ifada is a godsend. Does he have to be willing?

EMAN: In my home, we believe that a man should be willing.

OROGE: Mister Eman, I don't think you quite understand. This is not a simple matter at all. I don't know what you do, but here, it is not a cheap task for anybody. No one in his senses would do such a job. Why do you think we give refuge to idiots like him? We don't know where he came from. One morning, he is simply there, just like that. From nowhere at all. You see, there is a purpose in that.

JAGUNA: We only waste time.

OROGE: Jaguna, be patient. After all, the man has been with us for some time now and deserves to know. The evil of the old year is no light thing to load on any man's head.

EMAN: I know something about that.

OROGE: You do? (*Turns to Jaguna who snorts impatiently.*) You see I told you so didn't I? From the moment you came I saw you were one of the knowing ones.

JAGUNA: Then let him behave like a man and give back the boy.

EMAN: It is you who are not behaving like men.

JAGUNA (*advances aggressively*): That is a quick mouth you have . . .

OROGE: Patience, Jaguna . . . if you want the new year to cushion the land there must be no deeds of anger. What did you mean, my friend?

EMAN: It is a simple thing. A village which cannot produce its own carrier contains no men.

JAGUNA: Enough. Let there be no more talk or this business will be ruined by some rashness. You . . . come inside. Bring the boy out, he must be in the room there.

EMAN: Wait.

(*The men hesitate.*)

JAGUNA (*hitting the nearer one and propelling him forward*): Go on. Have you changed masters now that you listen to what he says?

OROGE (*sadly*): I am sorry you would not understand, Mister Eman. But you ought to know that no carrier may return to the village. If he does, the people will stone him to death. It has happened before. Surely it is too much to ask a man to give up his own soil.

EMAN: I know others who have done more.

(*Ifada is brought out, abjectly dumb-moaning.*)

EMAN: You can see him with your own eyes. Does it really have meaning to use one as unwilling as that.

OROGE (*smiling*): He shall be willing. Not only willing but actually joyous. I am the one who prepares them all, and I have seen worse. This one escaped before I began to prepare him for the event. But you will see him later tonight, the most joyous creature in the festival. Then perhaps you will understand.

EMAN: Then it is only a deceit. Do you believe the spirit of a new year is so easily fooled?

JAGUNA: Take him out. (*The men carry out Ifada.*) You see, it is so easy to talk. You say there are no men in this village because they cannot provide a willing carrier. And yet I heard Oroge tell you we only use strangers. There is only one other stranger in the village, but I have not heard him offer himself (*spits*). It is so easy to talk is it not?

(*He turns his back on him.*)

(*They go off, taking Ifada with them, limp and silent. The only sign of life is that he strains his neck to keep his eyes on Eman till the very moment that he disappears from sight. Eman remains where they left him, staring after the group.*)

(*A blackout lasting no more than a minute. The lights come up slowly and Ifada is seen returning to the house. He stops at the window and looks in. Seeing no one, he bangs on the sill. Appears surprised that there is no response. He slithers down on his favorite spot, then sees the effigy still lying where the Girl had dropped it in her flight. After some hesitation, he goes towards it, begins to strip it of the clothing. Just then the Girl comes in.*)

GIRL: Hey, leave that alone. You know it's mine.

(*Ifada pauses, then speeds up his action.*)

GIRL: I said it is mine. Leave it where you found it.

(*She rushes at him and begins to struggle for possession of the carrier.*)

GIRL: Thief! Thief! Let it go, it is mine. Let it go. You animal, just because I let you play with it. Idiot! Idiot!

(*The struggle becomes quite violent. The Girl is hanging to the effigy and Ifada lifts her with it, flinging her all about. The Girl hangs on grimly.*)

GIRL: You are spoiling it . . . why don't you get your own? Thief! Let it go, you thief!

(*Sunma comes in walking very fast, throwing apprehensive glances over her shoulder. Seeing the two children, she becomes immediately angry. Advances on them.*)

SUNMA: So you've made this place your playground. Get away, you untrained pigs. Get out of here.

(*Ifada flees at once, the Girl retreats also, retaining possession of the "carrier."*)
(*Sunma goes to the door. She has her hand on the door when the significance of Ifada's presence strikes her for the first time. She stands rooted to the spot, then turns slowly round.*)

SUNMA: Ifada! What are you doing here?

(*Ifada is bewildered. Sunma turns suddenly and rushes into the house, flying into the inner room and out again.*)

Eman! Eman! Eman!

(*She rushes outside.*)

Where did he go? Where did they take him?

(*Ifada distressed, points. Sunma seizes him by the arm, drags him off.*)

Take me there at once. God help you if we are too late. You loathsome thing, if you have let him suffer . . .

(*Her voice fades into other shouts, running footsteps, banged tins, bells, dogs, etc., rising in volume.*)

(*It is a narrow passageway between two mud houses. At the far end one man after another is seen running across the entry, the noise dying off gradually.*)
(*About halfway down the passage, Eman is crouching against the wall, tense with apprehension. As the noise dies off, he seems to relax, but the alert hunted look is still in his eyes, which are ringed in a reddish color. The rest of his body has been whitened with a floury substance. He is naked down to the waist, wears a baggy pair of trousers, calf-length, and around both feet are bangles.*)

EMAN: I will simply stay here till dawn. I have done enough.

(*A window is thrown open and a woman empties some slop from a pail. With a startled cry Eman leaps aside to avoid it and the woman puts out her head.*)

WOMAN: Oh, my head. What have I done! Forgive me, neighbor. . . . Eh, it's the carrier!

(*Very rapidly she clears her throat and spits on him, flings the pail at him, and runs off, shouting.*)

He's here. The carrier is hiding in the passage. Quickly, I have found the carrier!

(*The cry is taken up and Eman flees down the passage. Shortly afterwards his pursuers come pouring down the passage in full cry. After the last of them come Jaguna and Oroge.*)

OROGE: Wait, wait. I cannot go so fast.
JAGUNA: We will rest a little then. We can do nothing anyway.
OROGE: If only he had let me prepare him.
JAGUNA: They are the ones who break first, these fools who think they were born to carry suffering like a hat. What are we to do now?
OROGE: When they catch him I must prepare him.
JAGUNA: He? It will be impossible now. There can be no joy left in that one.
OROGE: Still, it took him by surprise. He was not expecting what he met.
JAGUNA: Why then did he refuse to listen? Did he think he was coming to sit down to a feast. He had not even gone through one compound before he bolted. Did he think he was taken round the people to be blessed? A woman, that is all he is.
OROGE: No, no. He took the beating well enough. I think he is the kind who would let himself be beaten from night till dawn and not utter a sound. He would let himself be stoned until he dropped dead.
JAGUNA: Then what made him run like a coward?
OROGE: I don't know. I don't really know. It is a night of curses, Jaguna. It is not many unprepared minds will remain unhinged under the load.
JAGUNA: We must find him. It is a poor beginning for a year when our own curses remain hovering over our homes because the carrier refused to take them.

(*They go. The scene changes. Eman is crouching beside some shrubs, torn and bleeding.*)

EMAN: They are even guarding my house . . . as if I would go there, but I need water . . . they could at least grant me that . . . I can be thirsty too . . . (*He pricks his ears.*) . . . there must be a stream nearby . . . (*As he looks round him, his eyes widen at a scene he encounters.*)

(*An Old Man, short and vigorous looking, is seated on a stool. He also is wearing calf-length baggy trousers, white. On his head, a white cap. An attendant is engaged in rubbing his body with oil. Round his eyes, two white rings have already been marked.*)

OLD MAN: Have they prepared the boat?
ATTENDANT: They are making the last sacrifice.
OLD MAN: Good. Did you send for my son?
ATTENDANT: He's on his way.
OLD MAN: I have never met the carrying of the boat with such a heavy heart. I hope nothing comes of it.
ATTENDANT: The gods will not desert us on that account.
OLD MAN: A man should be at his strongest when he takes the boat, my friend. To be weighed down inside and out is not a wise thing. I hope when the moment comes I shall have found my strength.

(*Enter Eman, a wrapper round his waist and a danski° over it.*)

OLD MAN: I meant to wait until after my journey to the river, but my mind is so burdened with my own grief and yours I could not delay it. You know I must have all my strength. But I sit here, feeling it all eaten slowly away by my unspoken grief. It helps to say it out. It even helps to cry sometimes.

(*He signals to the attendant to leave them.*)

Come nearer . . . we will never meet again, son. Not on this side of the flesh. What I do not know is whether you will return to take my place.
EMAN: I will never come back.
OLD MAN: Do you know what you are saying? Ours is a strong breed, my son. It is only a strong breed that can take this boat to the river year after year and wax stronger on it. I have taken down each year's evils for over twenty years. I hoped you would follow me.
EMAN: My life here died with Omae.
OLD MAN: Omae died giving birth to your child and you think the world is ended. Eman, my pain did not begin when Omae died. Since you sent her to stay with me, son, I lived with the burden of knowing that this child would die bearing your son.
EMAN: Father . . .
OLD MAN: Don't you know it was the same with you? And me? No woman survives the bearing of the strong ones. Son, it is not the mouth of the boaster that says he belongs to the strong breed.

danski: A brief Yoruba garment.

It is the tongue that is red with pain and black with sorrow. Twelve years you were away my son, and for those twelve years I knew the love of an old man for his daughter and the pain of a man helplessly awaiting his loss.

EMAN: I wish I had stayed away. I wish I never came back to meet her.

OLD MAN: It had to be. But you know now what slowly ate away my strength. I awaited your return with love and fear. Forgive me then if I say that your grief is light. It will pass. This grief may drive you now from home. But you must return.

EMAN: You do not understand. It is not grief alone.

OLD MAN: What is it then? Tell me, I can still learn.

EMAN: I was away twelve years. I changed much in that time.

OLD MAN: I am listening.

EMAN: I am unfitted for your work, father. I wish to say no more. But I am totally unfitted for your call.

OLD MAN: It is only time you need, son. Stay longer and you will answer the urge of your blood.

EMAN: That I stayed at all was because of Omae. I did not expect to find her waiting. I would have taken her away, but hard as you claim to be, it would have killed you. And I was a tired man. I needed peace. Because Omae was peace, I stayed. Now nothing holds me here.

OLD MAN: Other men would rot and die doing this task year after year. It is strong medicine which only we can take. Our blood is strong like no other. Anything you do in life must be less than this, son.

EMAN: That is not true, father.

OLD MAN: I tell you it is true. Your own blood will betray you, son, because you cannot hold it back. If you make it do less than this, it will rush to your head and burst it open. I say what I know, my son.

EMAN: There are other tasks in life, father. This one is not for me. There are even greater things you know nothing of.

OLD MAN: I am very sad. You only go to give to others what rightly belongs to us. You will use your strength among thieves. They are thieves because they take what is ours, they have no claim of blood to it. They will even lack the knowledge to use it wisely. Truth is my companion at this moment, my son. I know everything I say will surely bring the sadness of truth.

EMAN: I am going, father.

OLD MAN: Call my attendant. And be with me in your strength for this last journey. A-ah, did you hear that? It came out without my knowing it; this is indeed my last journey. But I am not afraid.

(Eman goes out. A few moments later, the attendant enters.)

ATTENDANT: The boat is ready.

OLD MAN: So am I.

(He sits perfectly still for several moments. Drumming begins somewhere in the distance, and the Old Man sways his head almost imperceptibly. Two men come in bearing a miniature boat, containing an indefinable mound. They rush it in and set it briskly down near the Old Man, and stand well back. The Old Man gets up slowly, the Attendant watching him keenly. He signs to the men, who lift the boat quickly onto the Old Man's head. As soon as it touches his head, he holds it down with both hands and runs off, the men give him a start, then follow at a trot.)

(As the last man disappears Oroge limps in and comes face to face with Eman — as carrier — who is now seen still standing beside the shrubs, staring into the scene he has just witnessed. Oroge, struck by the look on Eman's face, looks anxiously behind him to see what has engaged Eman's attention. Eman notices him then, and the pair stare at each other. Jaguna enters, sees him and shouts, "Here he is," rushes at Eman who is whipped back to the immediate and flees, Jaguna in pursuit. Three or four others enter and follow them. Oroge remains where he is, thoughtful.)

JAGUNA *(reenters)*: They have closed in on him now, we'll get him this time.

OROGE: It is nearly midnight.

JAGUNA: You were standing there looking at him as if he was some strange spirit. Why didn't you shout?

OROGE: You shouted didn't you? Did that catch him?

JAGUNA: Don't worry. We have him now. But things have taken a bad turn. It is no longer enough to drive him past every house. There is too much contamination about already.

OROGE *(not listening)*: He saw something. Why may I not know what it was?

JAGUNA: What are you talking about?

OROGE: Hm. What is it?

JAGUNA: I said there is too much harm done already. The year will demand more from this carrier than we thought.

OROGE: What do you mean?

JAGUNA: Do we have to talk with the full mouth?

OROGE: S-sh . . . look!

(Jaguna turns just in time to see Sunma fly at him, clawing at his face like a crazed tigress.)

SUNMA: Murderer! What are you doing to him. Murderer! Murderer!

(Jaguna finds himself struggling really hard to keep off his daughter; he succeeds in pushing her off and striking her so hard on the face that she falls to her knees. He moves on her to hit her again.)

OROGE (*comes between*): Think what you are doing, Jaguna, she is your daughter.

JAGUNA: My daughter! Does this one look like my daughter? Let me cripple the harlot for life.

OROGE: That is a wicked thought, Jaguna.

JAGUNA: Don't come between me and her.

OROGE: Nothing in anger — do you forget what to-night is?

JAGUNA: Can you blame me for forgetting?

(Draws his hand across his cheek — it is covered with blood.)

OROGE: This is an unhappy night for us all. I fear what is to come of it.

JAGUNA: Let's go. I cannot restrain myself in this creature's presence. My own daughter . . . and for a stranger . . .

(They go off, Ifada, who came in with Sunma and had stood apart, horror-stricken, comes shyly forward. He helps Sunma up. They go off, he holding Sunma bent and sobbing.)

(Enter Eman — as carrier. He is physically present in the bounds of this next scene, a side of a round thatched hut. A young girl, about fourteen, runs in, stops beside the hut. She looks carefully to see that she is not observed, puts her mouth to a little hole in the wall.)

OMAE: Eman . . . Eman . . .

(Eman — as carrier — responds, as he does throughout the scene, but they are unaware of him.)

EMAN (*from inside*): Who is it?

OMAE: It is me, Omae.

EMAN: How dare you come here!

(Two hands appear at the hole and pushing outwards, create a much larger hole through which Eman puts out his head. It is Eman as a boy, the same age as the girl.)

Go away at once. Are you trying to get me into trouble!

OMAE: What is the matter?

EMAN: You. Go away.

OMAE: But I came to see you.

EMAN: Are you deaf? I say I don't want to see you. Now go before my tutor catches you.

OMAE: All right. Come out.

EMAN: Do what!

OMAE: Come out.

EMAN: You must be mad.

OMAE (*sits on the ground*): All right, if you don't come out I shall simply stay here until your tutor arrives.

EMAN (*about to explode, thinks better of it and the head disappears. A moment later he emerges from behind the hut*): What sort of a devil has got into you?

OMAE: None. I just wanted to see you.

EMAN (*his mimicry is nearly hysterical*): "None. I just wanted to see you." Do you think this place is the stream where you can go and molest innocent people?

OMAE (*coyly*): Aren't you glad to see me?

EMAN: I am not.

OMAE: Why?

EMAN: Why? Do you really ask me why? Because you are a woman and a most troublesome woman. Don't you know anything about this at all. We are not meant to see any woman. So go away before more harm is done.

OMAE (*flirtatious*): What is so secret about it anyway? What do they teach you?

EMAN: Nothing any woman can understand.

OMAE: Ha ha. You think we don't know eh? You've all come to be circumcised.

EMAN: Shut up. You don't know anything.

OMAE: Just think, all this time you haven't been circumcised, and you dared make eyes at us women.

EMAN: Thank you — woman. Now go.

OMAE: Do they give you enough to eat?

EMAN (*testily*): No. We are so hungry that when silly girls like you turn up, we eat them.

OMAE (*feigning tears*): Oh, oh, oh, he's abusing me. He's abusing me.

EMAN (*alarmed*): Don't try that here. Go quickly if you are going to cry.

OMAE: All right, I won't cry.

EMAN: Cry or no cry, go away and leave me alone. What do you think will happen if my tutor turns up now?

OMAE: He won't.

EMAN (*mimicking*): "He won't." I suppose you are his wife and he tells you where he goes. In fact this is just the time he comes round to our huts. He could be at the next hut this very moment.

OMAE: Ha-ha. You're lying. I left him by the stream, pinching the girls' bottoms. Is that the sort of thing he teaches you?

EMAN: Don't say anything against him or I shall beat you. Isn't it you loose girls who tease him, wiggling your bottoms under his nose?

OMAE (*going tearful again*): A-ah, so I am one of the loose girls eh?

EMAN: Now don't start accusing me of things I didn't say.

OMAE: But you said it. You said it.

EMAN: I didn't. Look, Omae, someone will hear you and I'll be in disgrace. Why don't you go before anything happens.

OMAE: It's all right. My friends have promised to hold your old rascal tutor till I get back.

EMAN: Then you go back right now. I have work to do. (*Going in.*)

OMAE (*runs after and tries to hold him. Eman leaps back, genuinely scared*): What is the matter? I was not going to bite you.

EMAN: Do you know what you nearly did? You almost touched me!

OMAE: Well?

EMAN: Well! Isn't it enough that you let me set my eyes on you? Must you now totally pollute me with your touch? Don't you understand anything?

OMAE: Oh, that.

EMAN (*nearly screaming*): It is not "oh that." Do you think this is only a joke or a little visit like spending the night with your grandmother? This is an important period of my life. Look, these huts, we built them with our own hands. Every boy builds his own. We learn things, do you understand? And we spend much time just thinking. At least, I do. It is the first time I have had nothing to do except think. Don't you see, I am becoming a man. For the first time, I understand that I have a life to fulfill. Has that thought ever worried you?

OMAE: You are frightening me.

EMAN: There. That is all you can say. And what use will that be when a man finds himself alone — like that? (*Points to the hut.*) A man must go on his own, go where no one can help him, and test his strength. Because he may find himself one day sitting alone in a wall as round as that. In there, my mind could hold no other thought. I may never have such moments again to myself. Don't dare to come and steal any more of it.

OMAE (*this time, genuinely tearful*): Oh, I know you hate me. You only want to drive me away.

EMAN (*impatiently*): Yes, yes, I know I hate you — but go.

OMAE (*going, all tears. Wipes her eyes, suddenly all mischief*): Eman.

EMAN: What now?

OMAE: I only want to ask one thing . . . do you promise to tell me?

EMAN: Well, what is it?

OMAE (*gleefully*): Does it hurt?

(*She turns instantly and flees, landing straight into the arms of the returning tutor.*)

TUTOR: Te-he-he . . . what have we here? What little mouse leaps straight into the beak of the wise old owl eh?

(*Omae struggles to free herself, flies to the opposite side, grimacing with distaste.*)

TUTOR: I suppose you merely came to pick some fruits eh? You did not sneak here to see any of my children.

OMAE: Yes, I came to steal your fruits.

TUTOR: Te-he-he . . . I thought so. And that dutiful son of mine over there. He saw you and came to chase you off my fruit trees didn't he? Te-he-he . . . I'm sure he did, isn't that so, my young Eman?

EMAN: I was talking to her.

TUTOR: Indeed you were. Now be good enough to go into your hut until I decide your punishment. (*Eman withdraws.*) Te-he-he . . . now now, my little daughter, you need not be afraid of me.

OMAE (*spiritedly*): I am not.

TUTOR: Good. Very good. We ought to be friendly. (*His voice becomes leering.*) Now this is nothing to worry you, my daughter . . . a very small thing indeed. Although of course if I were to let it slip that your young Eman had broken a strong taboo, it might go hard on him you know. I am sure you would not like that to happen, would you?

OMAE: No.

TUTOR: Good. You are sensible, my girl. Can you wash clothes?

OMAE: Yes.

TUTOR: Good. If you will come with me now to my hut, I shall give you some clothes to wash, and then we will forget all about this matter eh? Well, come on.

OMAE: I shall wait here. You go and bring the clothes.

TUTOR: Eh? What is that? Now now, don't make me angry. You should know better than to talk back at your elders. Come now.

(*He takes her by the arm and tries to drag her off.*)

OMAE: No no, I won't come to your hut. Leave me. Leave me alone, you shameless old man.

TUTOR: If you don't come I shall disgrace the whole family of Eman, and yours too.

(*Eman reenters with a small bundle.*)

EMAN: Leave her alone. Let us go, Omae.

TUTOR: And where do you think you are going?

EMAN: Home.

TUTOR: Te-he-he . . . As easy as that eh? You think you can leave here any time you please? Get right back inside that hut!

(*Eman takes Omae by the arm and begins to walk off.*)

TUTOR: Come back at once.

(*He goes after him and raises his stick. Eman catches it, wrenches it from him, and throws it away.*)

OMAE (*hopping delightedly*): Kill him. Beat him to death.

TUTOR: Help! Help! He is killing me! Help!

(*Alarmed, Eman clamps his hand over his mouth.*)

EMAN: Old tutor, I don't mean you any harm, but you mustn't try to harm me either. (*He removes his hand.*)

TUTOR: You think you can get away with your crime. My report shall reach the elders before you ever get into town.

EMAN: You are afraid of what I will say about you? Don't worry. Only if you try to shame me, then I will speak. I am not going back to the village anyway. Just tell them I have gone, no more. If you say one word more than that I shall hear of it the same day and I shall come back.

TUTOR: You are telling me what to do? But don't think to come back next year because I will drive you away. Don't think to come back here even ten years from now. And don't send your children.

(*Goes off with threatening gestures.*)

EMAN: I won't come back.

OMAE: Smoked vulture! But Eman, he says you cannot return next year. What will you do?

EMAN: It is a small thing one can do in the big towns.

OMAE: I thought you were going to beat him that time. Why didn't you crack his dirty hide?

EMAN: Listen carefully, Omae . . . I am going on a journey.

OMAE: Come on. Tell me about it on the way.

EMAN: No, I go that way. I cannot return to the village.

OMAE: Because of that wretched man? Anyway you will first talk to your father.

EMAN: Go and see him for me. Tell him I have gone away for some time. I think he will know.

OMAE: But, Eman . . .

EMAN: I haven't finished. You will go and live with him till I get back. I have spoken to him about you. Look after him!

OMAE: But what is this journey? When will you come back?

EMAN: I don't know. But this is a good moment to go. Nothing ties me down.

OMAE: But, Eman, you want to leave me.

EMAN: Don't forget all I said. I don't know how long I will be. Stay in my father's house as long as you remember me. When you become tired of waiting, you must do as you please. You understand? You must do as you please.

OMAE: I cannot understand anything, Eman. I don't know where you are going or why. Suppose you never came back! Don't go, Eman. Don't leave me by myself.

EMAN: I must go. Now let me see you on your way.

OMAE: I shall come with you.

EMAN: Come with me! And who will look after you? Me? You will only be in my way, you know that! You will hold me back and I shall desert you in a strange place. Go home and do as I say. Take care of my father and let him take care of you.

(*He starts going but Omae clings to him.*)

OMAE: But, Eman, stay the night at least. You will only lose your way. Your father, Eman, what will he say? I won't remember what you said . . . come back to the village . . . I cannot return alone, Eman . . . come with me as far as the crossroads.

(*His face set, Eman strides off and Omae loses balance as he increases his pace. Falling, she quickly wraps her arms around his ankle, but Eman continues unchecked, dragging her along.*)

OMAE: Don't go, Eman . . . Eman, don't leave me, don't leave me . . . don't leave your Omae . . . don't go, Eman . . . don't leave your Omae . . .

(*Eman — as carrier — makes a nervous move as if he intends to go after the vanished pair. He stops but continues to stare at the point where he last saw them. There is stillness for a while. Then the Girl enters from the same place and remains looking at Eman. Startled, Eman looks apprehensively round him. The Girl goes nearer but keeps beyond arm's length.*)

GIRL: Are you the carrier?

EMAN: Yes. I am Eman.

GIRL: Why are you hiding?

EMAN: I really came for a drink of water . . . er . . . is there anyone in front of the house?

GIRL: No.

EMAN: But there might be people in the house. Did you hear voices?

GIRL: There is no one here.

EMAN: Good. Thank you. (*He is about to go, stops suddenly.*) Er . . . would you . . . you will find a cup on the table. Could you bring me the water out here? The water pot is in a corner.

(*The Girl goes. She enters the house, then, watching Eman carefully, slips out and runs off.*)

EMAN (*sitting*): Perhaps they have all gone home. It will be good to rest. (*He hears voices and listens hard.*) Too late. (*Moves cautiously nearer the house.*) Quickly, girl, I can hear people coming. Hurry up. (*Looks through the window.*) Where are you? Where is she? (*The truth dawns on him suddenly and he moves off, sadly.*)

(*Enter Jaguna and Oroge, led by the Girl.*)

GIRL (*pointing*): He was there.
JAGUNA: Ay, he's gone now. He is a sly one is your friend. But it won't save him forever.
OROGE: What was he doing when you saw him?
GIRL: He asked me for a drink of water.
JAGUNA: }
OROGE: } Ah! (*They look at each other.*)
OROGE: We should have thought of that.
JAGUNA: He is surely finished now. If only we had thought of it earlier.
OROGE: It is not too late. There is still an hour before midnight.
JAGUNA: We must call back all the men. Now we need only wait for him — in the right place.
OROGE: Everyone must be told. We don't want anyone heading him off again.
JAGUNA: And it works so well. This is surely the help of the gods themselves, Oroge. Don't you know at once what is on the path to the stream?
OROGE: The sacred trees.
JAGUNA: I tell you it is the very hand of the gods. Let us go.

(*An overgrown part of the village. Eman wanders in, aimlessly, seemingly uncaring of discovery. Beyond him, an area lights up, revealing a group of people clustered round a spot, all the heads are bowed. One figure stands away and separate from them. Even as Eman looks, the group breaks up and the people disperse, coming down and past him. Only three people are left, a man [Eman] whose back is turned, the village priest, and the isolated one. They stand on opposite sides of the grave, the man on the mound of earth. The Priest walks round to the man's side and lays a hand on his shoulder.*)

PRIEST: Come.
EMAN: I will. Give me a few moments here alone.
PRIEST: Be comforted.

(*They fall silent.*)

EMAN: I was gone twelve years but she waited. She whom I thought had too much of the laughing child in her. Twelve years I was a pilgrim, seeking the vain shrine of secret strength. And all the time, strange knowledge, this silent strength of my child-woman.
PRIEST: We all saw it. It was a lesson to us; we did not know that such goodness could be found among us.

EMAN: Then why? Why the wasted years if she had to perish giving birth to my child? (*They are both silent.*) I do not really know for what great meaning I searched. When I returned, I could not be certain I had found it. Until I reached my home and I found her a full-grown woman, still a child at heart. When I grew to believe it, I thought, this, after all, is what I sought. It was here all the time. And I threw away my new-gained knowledge. I buried the part of me that was formed in strange places. I made a home in my birthplace.
PRIEST: That was as it should be.
EMAN: Any truth of that was killed in the cruelty of her brief happiness.
PRIEST (*looks up and sees the figure standing away from them, the child in his arms. He is totally still*): Your father — he is over there.
EMAN: I knew he would come. Has he my son with him?
PRIEST: Yes.
EMAN: He will let no one take the child. Go and comfort him, priest. He loved Omae like a daughter, and you all know how well she looked after him. You see how strong we really are. In his heart of hearts the old man's love really awaited a daughter. Go and comfort him. His grief is more than mine.

(*The Priest goes. The Old Man has stood well away from the burial group. His face is hard and his gaze unswerving from the grave. The Priest goes to him, pauses, but sees that he can make no dent in the man's grief. Bowed, he goes on his way.*)
(*Eman, as carrier, walking towards the graveside, the other Eman having gone. His feet sink into the mound and he breaks slowly onto his knees, scooping up the sand in his hands and pouring it on his head. The scene blacks out slowly.*)

(*Enter Jaguna and Oroge.*)

OROGE: We have only a little time.
JAGUNA: He will come. All the wells are guarded. There is only the stream left him. The animal must come to drink.
OROGE: You are sure it will not fail — the trap, I mean.
JAGUNA: When Jaguna sets the trap, even elephants pay homage — their trunks downwards and one leg up in the sky. When the carrier steps on the fallen twigs, it is up in the sacred trees with him.
OROGE: I shall breathe again when this long night is over.

(*They go out.*)
(*Enter Eman — as carrier — from the same di-*

rection as the last two entered. In front of him is a still figure, the Old Man as he was, carrying the dwarf boat.)

EMAN (joyfully): Father.

(The figure does not turn round.)

EMAN: It is your son, Eman. (He moves nearer.) Don't you want to look at me? It is I, Eman. (He moves nearer still.)

OLD MAN: You are coming too close. Don't you know what I carry on my head?

EMAN: But, Father, I am your son.

OLD MAN: Then go back. We cannot give the two of us.

EMAN: Tell me first where you are going.

OLD MAN: Do you ask that? Where else but to the river?

EMAN (visibly relieved): I only wanted to be sure. My throat is burning. I have been looking for the stream all night.

OLD MAN: It is the other way.

EMAN: But you said . . .

OLD MAN: I take the longer way, you know how I must do this. It is quicker if you take the other way. Go now.

EMAN: No, I will only get lost again. I shall go with you.

OLD MAN: Go back, my son. Go back.

EMAN: Why? Won't you even look at me?

OLD MAN: Listen to your father. Go back.

EMAN: But, father!

(He makes to hold him. Instantly the old man breaks into a rapid trot. Eman hesitates, then follows, his strength nearly gone.)

EMAN: Wait, father. I am coming with you . . . wait . . . wait for me, father . . .

(There is a sound of twigs breaking, of a sudden trembling in the branches. Then silence.)

(The front of Eman's house. The effigy is hanging from the sheaves. Enter Sunma, still supported by Ifada, she stands transfixed as she sees the hanging figure. Ifada appears to go mad, rushes at the object, and tears it down. Sunma, her last bit of will gone, crumbles against the wall. Some distance away from them, partly hidden, stands the Girl, impassively watching. Ifada hugs the effigy to him, stands above Sunma. The Girl remains where she is, observing.)

(Almost at once, the villagers begin to return, subdued and guilty.)

(They walk across the front, skirting the house as widely as they can. No word is exchanged. Jaguna and Oroge eventually appear. Jaguna, who is leading, sees Sunma as soon as he comes in view. He stops at once, retreating slightly.)

OROGE (almost whispering): What is it?

JAGUNA: The viper.

(Oroge looks cautiously at the woman.)

OROGE: I don't think she will even see you.

JAGUNA: Are you sure? I am in no frame of mind for another meeting with her.

OROGE: Let's go home.

JAGUNA: I am sick to the heart of the cowardice I have seen tonight.

OROGE: That is the nature of men.

JAGUNA: Then it is a sorry world to live in. We did it for them. It was all for their own common good. What did it benefit me whether the man lived or died. But did you see them? One and all they looked up at the man and words died in their throats.

OROGE: It was no common sight.

JAGUNA: Women could not have behaved so shamefully. One by one they crept off like sick dogs. Not one could raise a curse.

OROGE: It was not only him they fled. Do you see how unattended we are?

JAGUNA: There are those who will pay for this night's work!

OROGE: Ay, let us go home.

(They go off. Sunma, Ifada, and the Girl remain as they are, the light fading slowly on them.)

COMMENTARY

Lewis Nkosi

INTERVIEW WITH WOLE SOYINKA 1962

This early interview with Soyinka was taped in Lagos, Nigeria, in August 1962, while The Strong Breed *was very fresh in his mind. In fact, it had not yet had its first publication, which in Nigeria was in 1963. Nkosi in the interview highlights the impact of Bertolt Brecht's theater on Soyinka's writing.*

Nkosi: Well, Wole Soyinka, could you tell us what set you off on this road to writing?

Soyinka: I suppose that requires really going back a bit. I would say I began writing seriously, or rather taking myself seriously, taking my *writing* seriously about three, four years ago, but I can only presume that I have always been interested in writing. In school I wrote the usual little sketches for production, the occasional verse, you know, the short story, etc., and I think about 1951 I had the great excitement of having a short story of mine broadcast on the Nigerian Broadcasting Service and that was sort of my first public performance.

Nkosi: What schools did you attend?

Soyinka: I went to Government School, Ibadan; after that I spent a couple of years in the University College, Ibadan.

Nkosi: You have now published drama or rather you've had some plays produced?

Soyinka: Yes, "produced" is the correct word. I haven't had any plays published although some are in print right now and will come out shortly.

Nkosi: Could you tell us what those plays are?

Soyinka: There is *The Lion and the Jewel* which was the first play I wrote.

Nkosi: No, the second.

Soyinka: The first one I sent up, I suppose like most people do, is the *A Dance of Forests* which I wrote in 1960 and timed it for the Independence Celebrations; there is the *House of Banigeji* which has never been performed. And I have written about four one-acts including *The Trials of Brother Jero* which was done quite recently in Nigeria.

Nkosi: The *A Dance of the Forests* won you a prize, didn't it?

Soyinka: Yes, Nigerian Independence competition prize 1960.

Nkosi: Have you got any particular authors that have influenced you most?

Soyinka: This is a very difficult question for me because I am not aware of any conscious influence on my work, but I can say that if I wanted to aim at any particular kind of theater, I think, however subconsciously, I might aim at Brecht's kind of theater, which I admire tremendously, just his complete freedom with the medium of the theater.

Nkosi: In your last play, *A Dance of the Forests*, which caused a lot of people a tremendous amount of agony trying to figure out just exactly what it was trying to do — they felt that there were some hidden meanings contained in lots of symbolism which they couldn't gather. Now as you're the author, we are lucky to have you here, and we think that you probably might enlighten us about just what you were trying to say in that work of yours.

Soyinka: Well, let me say first of all that I think that my prime duty as a playwright is to provide excellent theater; in other words, I think that I have only one commitment to the public, and that is to my audience and that is to make sure they do not leave the theater bored. I don't believe that I have any obligation to enlighten, to instruct, to teach: I don't possess that sense of duty or didacticism — very much unlike Brecht for instance, for, you see, what I like in Brecht is his sort of theater, its liveliness and freedom, not so much his purpose or intentions. I believe my primary duty is just to see that I provide excellent theater for the audience. But inevitably, it is just common sense to say that one just cannot write about just nothing. In *A Dance of the Forests*, I was very much conscious of all the potentialities of existing theatrical idioms in Nigeria and I only know that there was one thing which motivated, maybe, guided the form and the shape of the play or the eventual fate of the characters. I use this word "motivated" quite cautiously because I do not think I consciously tried to preach or bring out, you know, a series of symbolisms at all, but the main thing was the realization that human beings are just destructive all over the world. I think this is it — I have thought about this again and again but during the production — I produced it myself — and in trying to see the play take shape on the stage, I find that the main thing is my own personal conviction or observation that human beings are simply cannibals all over the world so that their main preoccupation seems to be eating up one another. This I think is the main thing I would say was in the back of my mind when I wrote it.

Nkosi: Yes, that sounds very much like Tennessee Williams's idea of the world conscious of the evil.

Soyinka: Well, I don't sort of regard it so much as . . .

Nkosi: The ferocity of human beings.

Soyinka: Yes, the carnivorous nature of. . . .

Nkosi: Yes, I wonder whether now — have you pursued this theme in the other plays or are the other plays different?

Soyinka: . . . Fundamentally, I think they're different. I think that sort of semiconsciously the moment I realize I'm pursuing a theme again, it seems to ring a bell warning that I have preceded myself somewhere; I have such a feeling about this that I shirk from it but I would say there are traces of it in my other plays — in, for instance, my favorite one-act play which is *The Strong Breed*. I think this one is also very much mixed up with the whole element of sacrifice, so contrasting the idea of selfishness with willing self-sacrifice as opposed to the other general cannibalism of human beings.

Sam Shepard

Samuel Shepard Rogers VII was born in Illinois in 1943, but his father was a career man in the army, and like most "army brats," Shepard found himself essentially uprooted, moving from base to base around the country. If he has roots as a writer, they are clearly in the American West, but not necessarily the West created by writers of westerns, comic books, and second-rate movies. Shepard's plays often have a surreal quality, as if they are set in a world of the imagination rather than in a real place like Paris, Texas.

Shepard is one of America's most important playwrights. He has won numerous awards, including ten Obie Awards (given to off-Broadway plays) between 1966 and 1979, an Obie Award for sustained achievement in 1980, the New York Drama Critics' Circle Award for *A Lie of the Mind* in 1985, and a Pulitzer Prize for *Buried Child* in 1979. His work has been produced primarily in the experimental theater of downtown New York in places such as La Mama and in regional theaters throughout the United States that are known for their artistic integrity but not for their capacity to reach a broad spectrum of theatergoers. In his way, Shepard has been an underground playwright who has won the respect of most theater people, including the best playwrights.

Shepard's love for and frustrations with music have found their way into a major theme of his work. He plays drums and guitar and has never realized an early desire for a career in rock music. But the subversive qualities of rock and jazz — their implicit critique of middle-class life — appear in his plays in his analyses of the middle-class family. His primary themes center on the family and its complications, the nature of the person alone, and the myth of the Old West. In each theme, Shepard expresses a deep sense of longing and of loss, emotions that his audiences have found significant.

Because his father began to drink and family life became intolerable, Shepard left home after a year at college and toured with the Bishops Company Repertory Players. At nineteen he wound up in New York working in one of the best jazz clubs of the day, the Village Gate. During this time in Greenwich Village he began to write one-act plays with extraordinary energy. Like Jack Kerouac, he almost never revised his work. He wrote it in a burst of energy and then had it performed to audiences whose admiration grew.

In the 1970s Shepard began acting in major motion pictures. One of the ironies of his life is that he has become a matinee idol after appearing in movies such as *The Right Stuff, Fool for Love, Country,* and *Crimes of the Heart.* The critic Harry Haun has said of him, "He is the Recluse as Superstar, the man who has arrived on his own terms, carefully sculpting a special myth for himself."

His output for the stage has been prodigious, with dozens of one-act plays, and he has a central body of work that has gained him an enviable reputation. *Operation Sidewinder* (1970) was performed at the Vivian Beaumont Theater — a public theater at Lincoln Center in New York City — to mixed reviews. The play, set in the West, involves a giant mechanical snake designed to make contact with outer space travelers and includes Hopi snake dances as well as military scenes. *The Tooth of Crime* (1972) is about turf wars between an aging rock star and an up-and-coming young star. It has a brutality and directness that make it intense, exciting, and revealing of the California rock-and-roll scene in the early 1970s.

Curse of the Starving Class (1977) and *Buried Child* (1978) both helped solidify Shepard's reputation. *Suicide in B-flat* (1976) and *True West* (1980) only made it clearer that his work was developing in a consistent vein of black humor and dark criticism of the sanctity of family life. *A Lie of the Mind* (1985), like *Buried Child,* is about disturbed family life. It is filled with secrets: incest, murder, and sin. *New York Times* critic Mel Gussow said it explores "the damage that one does to filial, fraternal, and marital bonds." Incest — or potential incest — is also a theme in *A Fool for Love* (1983), in which Shepard starred on film. The play is set in the West and contains all the themes for which his work is known.

Shepard began his work with a sense of the West drawn from popular literature, reshaped it, and produced it in a new form. If the American West has a reality that survived its mythicization in the dime novel and John Wayne's movies, then Shepard is partly responsible for the way we now see it.

BURIED CHILD

Buried Child won the Pulitzer Prize for drama in 1979. The play was developed in an intense collaborative effort with cast, crew, director, and playwright using a process of give-and-take that has generally pleased Sam Shepard. In some cases he has turned down offers of major commercial productions of his plays because they would preclude that kind of collaborative atmosphere.

Critics have seen this play as loosely related to *Curse of the Starving Class* (1977) and *True West* (1980), forming a "family" trilogy. The three plays are very different in style, but they all offer a view of the American family that is painfully distant from the sentimental idealism of popular magazines of the 1940s and 1950s. Shepard emphasizes the rootlessness of the family, its emotional chill, and its capacity for violence.

Buried Child is beguilingly ordinary at first glance. The simple interior is dominated by a television set and an old sofa. Vince's girlfriend Shelly, who is visiting for the first time, had imagined that the house would resemble a Norman Rockwell painting — that is, a stereotypical American home. It falls short of that, but the living room is nonetheless a recognizable, low-key, ordinary room that might be found anywhere in middle America. However, beginning with the ordinariness of the setting, the ordinariness of Tilden's walking in with an armful of corn, and Dodge's wracking cough, Shepard builds a portrait of an extraordinary family.

Dodge's one-track alcoholic mind seems a minor aberration at first. And Halie's nagging seems comparatively normal. Even Tilden's distant relationship with his father seems close to ordinary. But when Vince and Shelly walk in and Vince identifies himself first to his grandfather and then to his father — whom he does not expect to find here — we begin to see that something is odd and that the situation is anything but ordinary. Neither grandfather nor father recognizes him. Eventually, as we watch Shepard explore the family relationships, we begin to sense that the surface ordinariness hides a deeper structure, one that is built on myth.

The play draws on agricultural myth similar to that in *Oedipus Rex*, which begins with a curse on the land. The crops have failed and there has been no rain. Yet Tilden walks in with an armful of corn, which Halie thinks he must have stolen. Critics have compared Tilden with the corn god, a symbol of renewal. Shepard adds to that the sense of doom visited upon the family as if its genes carried destruction. As in Wole Soyinka's *The Strong Breed*, responsibility is transmitted from father to son. Those who are of the strong breed do not escape their fate. It is not clear at first how responsibility is transmitted in Shepard's family until we begin to see that Vince assumes the role of Tilden and Halie's offspring, the child who is buried on the arid land. In the terms of *The Strong Breed*, Vince can be thought of as a "carrier," willing or unwilling. When Dodge bequeaths the house to Vince, he seals Vince's fate.

Certainly during the course of the play we begin to see that a change is at hand. The rains have come. Halie, who doubted the existence of the corn, calls down at the end of the play: "It's like a paradise out there, Dodge. You oughta' take a look. A miracle." But the "old king," Dodge, is dead. Vince has come to take his place.

Buried Child in Performance

Buried Child was first produced at the Magic Theatre in San Francisco in June 1978. Later that year it was transferred to the Theater for the New City in Greenwich Village. In May 1979 it was awarded the Pulitzer Prize.

About the Yale Repertory Theatre production of 1979, *New York Times* critic Mel Gussow said, "The tone of the play is almost surrealistic. Like a figure out of Ionesco, the father brings in armloads of fresh vegetables from a garden that has been barren for years." In commenting on the New York and Yale productions of the play, he said they ended with "a dirge for the decline of traditional values, a wake for the American dream."

In 1980 the Trinity Repertory Company in Providence produced the play, directed by Adrian Hall, the director of the Yale production. It contrasted with the New York production in that the sets and lighting were "slicker," more detailed, and more subtle. One critic labeled the first production of *Buried Child* a "Gothic comedy," and that description has affected subsequent productions. For example, the MIT student production in 1985 aimed at Gothic effects: dark colors, suspense, and other staple ingredients of horror films. Productions of that sort remind us that on one level, at least, the play is about a haunted house.

Sam Shepard (b. 1943)

BURIED CHILD   1978

While the rain of your fingertips falls,
while the rain of your bones falls,

and your laughter and marrow fall down,
you come flying.   — PABLO NERUDA

Characters

DODGE, *in his seventies*
HALIE, *his wife, mid-sixties*
TILDEN, *their oldest son*
BRADLEY, *their next oldest son, an amputee*
VINCE, *Tilden's son*
SHELLY, *Vince's girlfriend*
FATHER DEWIS, *a Protestant minister*

ACT 1

Scene: *Day. Old wooden staircase down left with pale, frayed carpet laid down on the steps. The stairs lead offstage left up into the wings with no landing.*

Up right is an old, dark green sofa with the stuffing coming out in spots. Stage right of the sofa is an upright lamp with a faded yellow shade and a small night table with several small bottles of pills on it. Down right of the sofa, with the screen facing the sofa, is a large, old-fashioned brown TV. A flickering blue light comes from the screen, but no image, no sound. In the dark, the light of the lamp and the TV slowly brighten in the black space. The space behind the sofa, upstage, is a large, screened-in porch with a board floor. A solid interior door to stage right of the sofa, leading into the room onstage; and another screen door up left, leading from the porch to the outside. Beyond that are the shapes of dark elm trees.

Gradually the form of Dodge is made out, sitting on the couch, facing the TV, the blue light flickering on his face. He wears a well-worn T-shirt, suspenders, khaki work pants, and brown slippers. He's covered himself in an old brown blanket. He's very thin and sickly looking, in his late seventies. He just stares at the TV. More light fills the stage softly. The sound of light rain. Dodge slowly tilts his head back and stares at the ceiling for a while, listening to the rain. He lowers his head again and stares at the TV. He turns his head slowly to the left and stares at the cushion of the sofa next to the one he's sitting on. He pulls his left arm out from under the blanket, slides his hand under the cushion, and pulls out a bottle of whiskey. He looks down left toward the staircase, listens, then uncaps the bottle, takes a long swig, and caps it again. He puts the bottle back under the cushion and stares at the TV. He starts to cough slowly and softly. The coughing gradually builds. He holds one hand to his mouth and tries to stifle it. The coughing gets louder, then suddenly stops when he hears the sound of his wife's voice coming from the top of the staircase.

HALIE'S VOICE: Dodge?

(Dodge just stares at the TV. Long pause. He stifles two short coughs.)

HALIE'S VOICE: Dodge! You want a pill, Dodge?

(He doesn't answer. Takes the bottle out again and takes another long swig. Puts the bottle back, stares at TV, pulls blanket up around his neck.)

HALIE'S VOICE: You know what it is, don't you? It's the rain! Weather. That's it. Every time. Every time you get like this, it's the rain. No sooner does the rain start then you start. (*Pause.*) Dodge?

(He makes no reply. Pulls a pack of cigarettes out from his sweater and lights one. Stares at TV. Pause.)

HALIE'S VOICE: You should see it coming down up here. Just coming down in sheets. Blue sheets. The bridge is pretty near flooded. What's it like down there? Dodge?

(Dodge turns his head back over his left shoulder and takes a look out through the porch. He turns back to the TV.)

DODGE (*to himself*): Catastrophic.
HALIE'S VOICE: What? What'd you say, Dodge?
DODGE (*louder*): It looks like rain to me! Plain old rain!
HALIE'S VOICE: Rain? Of course it's rain! Are you having a seizure or something! Dodge? (*Pause.*) I'm coming down there in about five minutes if you don't answer me!
DODGE: Don't come down.
HALIE'S VOICE: What!

DODGE (*louder*): Don't come down!

(He has another coughing attack. Stops.)

HALIE'S VOICE: You should take a pill for that! I don't see why you just don't take a pill. Be done with it once and for all. Put a stop to it.

(He takes bottle out again. Another swig. Returns bottle.)

HALIE'S VOICE: It's not Christian, but it works. It's not necessarily Christian, that is. We don't know. There's some things the ministers can't even answer. I, personally, can't see anything wrong with it. Pain is pain. Pure and simple. Suffering is a different matter. That's entirely different. A pill seems as good an answer as any. Dodge? (*Pause.*) Dodge, are you watching baseball?
DODGE: No.
HALIE'S VOICE: What?
DODGE (*louder*): No!
HALIE'S VOICE: What're you watching? You shouldn't be watching anything that'll get you excited! No horse racing!
DODGE: They don't race on Sundays.
HALIE'S VOICE: What?
DODGE (*louder*): They don't race on Sundays!
HALIE'S VOICE: Well they shouldn't race on Sundays.
DODGE: Well they don't!
HALIE'S VOICE: Good. I'm amazed they still have that kind of legislation. That's amazing.
DODGE: Yeah, it's amazing.
HALIE'S VOICE: What?
DODGE (*louder*): It is amazing!
HALIE'S VOICE: It is. It truly is. I would've thought these days they'd be racing on Christmas even. A big flashing Christmas tree right down at the finish line.
DODGE (*shakes his head*): No.
HALIE'S VOICE: They used to race on New Year's! I remember that.
DODGE: They never raced on New Year's!
HALIE'S VOICE: Sometimes they did.
DODGE: They never did!
HALIE'S VOICE: Before we were married they did!

(Dodge waves his hand in disgust at the staircase. Leans back in sofa. Stares at TV.)

HALIE'S VOICE: I went once. With a man.
DODGE (*mimicking her*): Oh, a "man."
HALIE'S VOICE: What?
DODGE: Nothing!
HALIE'S VOICE: A wonderful man. A breeder.
DODGE: A what?
HALIE'S VOICE: A breeder! A horse breeder! Thoroughbreds.

DODGE: Oh, thoroughbreds. Wonderful.

HALIE'S VOICE: That's right. He knew everything there was to know.

DODGE: I bet he taught you a thing or two, huh? Gave you a good turn around the old stable!

HALIE'S VOICE: Knew everything there was to know about horses. We won bookoos of money that day.

DODGE: What?

HALIE'S VOICE: Money! We won every race I think.

DODGE: Bookoos?

HALIE'S VOICE: Every single race.

DODGE: Bookoos of money?

HALIE'S VOICE: It was one of those kind of days.

DODGE: New Year's!

HALIE'S VOICE: Yes! It might've been Florida. Or California! One of those two.

DODGE: Can I take my pick?

HALIE'S VOICE: It was Florida!

DODGE: Aha!

HALIE'S VOICE: Wonderful! Absolutely wonderful! The sun was just gleaming. Flamingos. Bougainvilleas. Palm trees.

DODGE (*to himself, mimicking her*): Bougainvilleas. Palm trees.

HALIE'S VOICE: Everything was dancing with life! There were all kinds of people from everywhere. Everyone was dressed to the nines. Not like today. Not like they dress today.

DODGE: When was this anyway?

HALIE'S VOICE: This was long before I knew you.

DODGE: Must've been.

HALIE'S VOICE: Long before. I was escorted.

DODGE: To Florida?

HALIE'S VOICE: Yes. Or it might've been California. I'm not sure which.

DODGE: All that way you were escorted?

HALIE'S VOICE: Yes.

DODGE: And he never laid a finger on you, I suppose? (*Long silence.*) Halie?

(*No answer. Long pause.*)

HALIE'S VOICE: Are you going out today?

DODGE (*gesturing toward rain*): In this?

HALIE'S VOICE: I'm just asking a simple question.

DODGE: I rarely go out in the bright sunshine, why would I go out in this?

HALIE'S VOICE: I'm just asking because I'm not doing any shopping today. And if you need anything you should ask Tilden.

DODGE: Tilden's not here!

HALIE'S VOICE: He's in the kitchen.

(*Dodge looks toward stage left, then back toward TV.*)

DODGE: All right.

HALIE'S VOICE: What?

DODGE (*louder*): All right!

HALIE'S VOICE: Don't scream. It'll only get your coughing started.

DODGE: All right.

HALIE'S VOICE: Just tell Tilden what you want and he'll get it. (*Pause.*) Bradley should be over later.

DODGE: Bradley?

HALIE'S VOICE: Yes. To cut your hair.

DODGE: My hair? I don't need my hair cut!

HALIE'S VOICE: It won't hurt!

DODGE: I don't need it!

HALIE'S VOICE: It's been more than two weeks Dodge.

DODGE: I don't need it!

HALIE'S VOICE: I have to meet Father Dewis for lunch.

DODGE: You tell Bradley that if he shows up here with those clippers, I'll kill him!

HALIE'S VOICE: I won't be very late. No later than four at the very latest.

DODGE: You tell him! Last time he left me almost bald! And I wasn't even awake! I was sleeping! I woke up and he'd already left!

HALIE'S VOICE: That's not my fault!

DODGE: You put him up to it!

HALIE'S VOICE: I never did!

DODGE: You did too! You had some fancy, stupid meeting planned! Time to dress up the corpse for company! Lower the ears a little! Put up a little front! Surprised you didn't tape a pipe to my mouth while you were at it! That woulda' looked nice! Huh? A pipe? Maybe a bowler hat! Maybe a copy of the *Wall Street Journal* casually placed on my lap!

HALIE'S VOICE: You always imagine the worst things of people!

DODGE: That's not the worst! That's the least of the worst!

HALIE'S VOICE: I don't need to hear it! All day long I hear things like that and I don't need to hear more.

DODGE: You better tell him!

HALIE'S VOICE: You tell him yourself! He's your own son. You should be able to talk to your own son.

DODGE: Not while I'm sleeping! He cut my hair while I was sleeping!

HALIE'S VOICE: Well, he won't do it again.

DODGE: There's no guarantee.

HALIE'S VOICE: I promise he won't do it without your consent.

DODGE (*after pause*): There's no reason for him to even come over here.

HALIE'S VOICE: He feels responsible.

DODGE: For my hair?

HALIE'S VOICE: For your appearance.

DODGE: My appearance is out of his domain! It's even

out of mine! In fact, it's disappeared! I'm an invisible man!

HALIE'S VOICE: Don't be ridiculous.

DODGE: He better not try it. That's all I've got to say.

HALIE'S VOICE: Tilden will watch out for you.

DODGE: Tilden won't protect me from Bradley!

HALIE'S VOICE: Tilden's the oldest. He'll protect you.

DODGE: Tilden can't even protect himself!

HALIE'S VOICE: Not so loud! He'll hear you. He's right
in the kitchen.

DODGE (*yelling off left*): Tilden!

HALIE'S VOICE: Dodge, what are you trying to do?

DODGE (*yelling off left*): Tilden, get in here!

HALIE'S VOICE: Why do you enjoy stirring things up?

DODGE: I don't enjoy anything!

HALIE'S VOICE: That's a terrible thing to say.

DODGE: Tilden!

HALIE'S VOICE: That's the kind of statement that leads
people right to the end of their rope.

DODGE: Tilden!

HALIE'S VOICE: It's no wonder people turn to Christ!

DODGE: TILDEN!!

HALIE'S VOICE: It's no wonder the messengers of God's
word are shouted down in public places!

DODGE: TILDEN!!!!

(*Dodge goes into a violent, spasmodic coughing attack
as Tilden enters from stage left, his arms loaded with
fresh ears of corn. Tilden is Dodge's oldest son, late
forties, wears heavy construction boots, covered with
mud, dark green work pants, a plaid shirt, and a faded
brown windbreaker. He has a butch haircut, wet from
the rain. Something about him is profoundly burned
out and displaced. He stops center stage with the ears
of corn in his arms and just stares at Dodge until he
slowly finishes his coughing attack. Dodge looks up
at him slowly. He stares at the corn. Long pause as
they watch each other.*)

HALIE'S VOICE: Dodge, if you don't take that pill nobody's going to force you.

(*The two men ignore the voice.*)

DODCE (*to Tilden*): Where'd you get that?

TILDEN: Picked it.

DODGE: You picked all that?

(*Tilden nods.*)

DODGE: You expecting company?

TILDEN: No.

DODGE: Where'd you pick it from?

TILDEN: Right out back.

DODGE: Out back where!

TILDEN: Right out in back.

DODGE: There's nothing out there!

TILDEN: There's corn.

DODGE: There hasn't been corn out there since about
nineteen thirty-five! That's the last time I planted
corn out there!

TILDEN: It's out there now.

DODGE (*yelling at stairs*): Halie!

HALIE'S VOICE: Yes dear!

DODGE: Tilden's brought a whole bunch of corn in
here! There's no corn out in back is there?

TILDEN (*to himself*): There's tons of corn.

HALIE'S VOICE: Not that I know of!

DODGE: That's what I thought.

HALIE'S VOICE: Not since about nineteen thirty-five!

DODGE (*to Tilden*): That's right. Nineteen thirty-five.

TILDEN: It's out there now.

DODGE: You go and take that corn back to wherever
you got it from!

TILDEN (*after pause, staring at Dodge*): It's picked. I
picked it all in the rain. Once it's picked you can't
put it back.

DODGE: I haven't had trouble with neighbors here for
fifty-seven years. I don't even know who the neighbors are! And I don't wanna know! Now go put
that corn back where it came from!

(*Tilden stares at Dodge, then walks slowly over to
him and dumps all the corn on Dodge's lap and steps
back. Dodge stares at the corn, then back to Tilden.
Long pause.*)

DODGE: Are you having trouble here, Tilden? Are you
in some kind of trouble?

TILDEN: I'm not in any trouble.

DODGE: You can tell me if you are. I'm still your
father.

TILDEN: I know you're still my father.

DODGE: I know you had a little trouble back in New
Mexico. That's why you came out here.

TILDEN: I never had any trouble.

DODGE: Tilden, your mother told me all about it.

TILDEN: What'd she tell you?

(*Tilden pulls some chewing tobacco out of his jacket
and bites off a plug.*)

DODGE: I don't have to repeat what she told me! She
told me all about it!

TILDEN: Can I bring my chair in from the kitchen?

DODGE: What?

TILDEN: Can I bring in my chair from the kitchen?

DODGE: Sure. Bring your chair in.

(*Tilden exits left. Dodge pushes all the corn off his
lap onto the floor. He pulls the blanket off angrily
and tosses it at one end of the sofa, pulls out the
bottle and takes another swig. Tilden enters again
from left with a milking stool and a pail. Dodge hides
the bottle quickly under the cushion before Tilden sees*)

it. Tilden sets the stool down by the sofa, sits on it, puts the pail in front of him on the floor. Tilden starts picking up the ears of corn one at a time and husking them. He throws the husks and silk in the center of the stage and drops the ears into the pail each time he cleans one. He repeats this process as they talk.)

DODGE (*after pause*): Sure is nice looking corn.

TILDEN: It's the best.

DODGE: Hybrid?

TILDEN: What?

DODGE: Some kinda fancy hybrid?

TILDEN: You planted it. I don't know what it is.

DODGE (*pause*): Tilden, look, you can't stay here forever. You know that, don't you?

TILDEN (*spits in spittoon*): I'm not.

DODGE: I know you're not. I'm not worried about that. That's not the reason I brought it up.

TILDEN: What's the reason?

DODGE: The reason is I'm wondering what you're gonna do.

TILDEN: You're not worried about me, are you?

DODGE: I'm not worried about you.

TILDEN: You weren't worried about me when I wasn't here. When I was in New Mexico.

DODGE: No, I wasn't worried about you then either.

TILDEN: You shoulda worried about me then.

DODGE: Why's that? You didn't do anything down there, did you?

TILDEN: I didn't do anything.

DODGE: Then why should I have worried about you?

TILDEN: Because I was lonely.

DODGE: Because you were lonely?

TILDEN: Yeah. I was more lonely than I've ever been before.

DODGE: Why was that?

TILDEN (*pause*): Could I have some of that whiskey you've got?

DODGE: What whiskey? I haven't got any whiskey.

TILDEN: You've got some under the sofa.

DODGE: I haven't got anything under the sofa! Now mind your own damn business! Jesus God, you come into the house outa the middle of nowhere, haven't heard or seen you in twenty years and suddenly you're making accusations.

TILDEN: I'm not making accusations.

DODGE: You're accusing me of hoarding whiskey under the sofa!

TILDEN: I'm not accusing you.

DODGE: You just got through telling me I had whiskey under the sofa!

HALIE'S VOICE: Dodge?

DODGE (*to Tilden*): Now she knows about it!

TILDEN: She doesn't know about it.

HALIE'S VOICE: Dodge, are you talking to yourself down there?

DODGE: I'm talking to Tilden!

HALIE'S VOICE: Tilden's down there?

DODGE: He's right here!

HALIE'S VOICE: What?

DODGE (*louder*): He's right here!

HALIE'S VOICE: What's he doing?

DODGE (*to Tilden*): Don't answer her.

TILDEN (*to Dodge*): I'm not doing anything wrong.

DODGE: I know you're not.

HALIE'S VOICE: What's he doing down there!

DODGE (*to Tilden*): Don't answer.

TILDEN: I'm not.

HALIE'S VOICE: Dodge!

(The men sit in silence. Dodge lights a cigarette. Tilden keeps husking corn, spits tobacco now and then in spittoon.)

HALIE'S VOICE: Dodge! He's not drinking anything, is he? You see to it that he doesn't drink anything! You've gotta watch out for him. It's our responsibility. He can't look after himself anymore, so we have to do it. Nobody else will do it. We can't just send him away somewhere. If we had lots of money we could sent him away. But we don't. We never will. That's why we have to stay healthy. You and me. Nobody's going to look after us. Bradley can't look after us. Bradley can hardly look after himself. I was always hoping that Tilden would look out for Bradley when they got older. After Bradley lost his leg. Tilden's the oldest. I always thought he'd be the one to take responsibility. I had no idea in the world that Tilden would be so much trouble. Who would've dreamed. Tilden was an All-American, don't forget. Don't forget that. Fullback. Or quarterback. I forget which.

TILDEN (*to himself*): Fullback. (*Still husking.*)

HALIE'S VOICE: Then when Tilden turned out to be so much trouble, I put all my hopes on Ansel. Of course Ansel wasn't as handsome, but he was smart. He was the smartest probably. I think he probably was. Smarter than Bradley, that's for sure. Didn't go and chop his leg off with a chain saw. Smart enough not to go and do that. I think he was smarter than Tilden too. Especially after Tilden got in all that trouble. Doesn't take brains to go to jail. Anybody knows that. Course then when Ansel died that left us all alone. Same as being alone. No different. Same as if they'd all died. He was the smartest. He could've earned lots of money. Lots and lots of money.

(Halie enters slowly from the top of the staircase as she continues talking. Just her feet are seen at first as

she makes her way down the stairs, a step at a time. She appears dressed completely in black, as though in mourning. Black handbag, hat with a veil, and pulling on elbow-length black gloves. She is about sixty-five with pure white hair. She remains absorbed in what she's saying as she descends the stairs and doesn't really notice the two men who continue sitting there as they were before she came down, smoking and husking.)

HALIE: He would've took care of us, too. He would've seen to it that we were repaid. He was like that. He was a hero. Don't forget that. A genuine hero. Brave. Strong. And very intelligent. Ansel could've been a great man. One of the greatest. I only regret that he didn't die in action. It's not fitting for a man like that to die in a motel room. A soldier. He could've won a medal. He could've been decorated for valor. I've talked to Father Dewis about putting up a plaque for Ansel. He thinks it's a good idea. He agrees. He knew Ansel when he used to play basketball. Went to every game. Ansel was his favorite player. He even recommended to the City Council that they put up a statue of Ansel. A big, tall statue with a basketball in one hand and a rifle in the other. That's how much he thinks of Ansel.

(Halie reaches the stage and begins to wander around, still absorbed in pulling on her gloves, brushing lint off her dress, and continuously talking to herself as the men just sit.)

HALIE: Of course, he'd still be alive today if he hadn't married into the Catholics. The Mob. How in the world he never opened his eyes to that is beyond me. Just beyond me. Everyone around him could see the truth. Even Tilden. Tilden told him time and again. Catholic women are the Devil incarnate. He wouldn't listen. He was blind with love. Blind. I knew. Everyone knew. The wedding was more like a funeral. You remember? All those Italians. All that horrible black, greasy hair. The smell of cheap cologne. I think even the priest was wearing a pistol. When he gave her the ring I knew he was a dead man. I knew it. As soon as he gave her the ring. But then it was the honeymoon that killed him. The honeymoon. I knew he'd never come back from the honeymoon. I kissed him and he felt like a corpse. All white. Cold. Icy blue lips. He never used to kiss like that. Never before. I knew then that she'd cursed him. Taken his soul. I saw it in her eyes. She smiled at me with that Catholic sneer of hers. She told me with her eyes that she'd murder him in his bed. Murder my son. She told me. And there was nothing I could do. Absolutely nothing.

He was going with her, thinking he was free. Thinking it was love. What could I do? I couldn't tell him she was a witch. I couldn't tell him that. He'd have turned on me. Hated me. I couldn't stand him hating me and then dying before he ever saw me again. Hating me in his death bed. Hating me and loving her! How could I do that? I had to let him go. I had to. I watched him leave. I watched him throw gardenias as he helped her into the limousine. I watched his face disappear behind the glass.

(She stops abruptly and stares at the corn husks. She looks around the space as though just waking up. She turns and looks hard at Tilden and Dodge who continue sitting calmly. She looks again at the corn husks.)

HALIE *(pointing to the husks)*: What's this in my house! *(Kicks husks.)* What's all this!

(Tilden stops husking and stares at her.)

HALIE *(to Dodge)*: And you encourage him!

(Dodge pulls blanket over him again.)

DODGE: You're going out in the rain?
HALIE: It's not raining.

(Tilden starts husking again.)

DODGE: Not in Florida it's not.
HALIE: We're not in Florida!
DODGE: It's not raining at the race track.
HALIE: Have you been taking those pills? Those pills always make you talk crazy. Tilden, has he been taking those pills?
TILDEN: He hasn't took anything.
HALIE *(to Dodge)*: What've you been taking?
DODGE: It's not raining in California or Florida or the race track. Only in Illinois. This is the only place it's raining. All over the rest of the world it's bright golden sunshine.

(Halie goes to the night table next to the sofa and checks the bottle of pills.)

HALIE: Which ones did you take? Tilden, you must've seen him take something.
TILDEN: He never took a thing.
HALIE: Then why's he talking crazy?
TILDEN: I've been here the whole time.
HALIE: Then you've both been taking something!
TILDEN: I've just been husking the corn.
HALIE: Where'd you get that corn anyway? Why is the house suddenly full of corn?
DODGE: Bumper crop!
HALIE *(moving center)*: We haven't had corn here for over thirty years.

TILDEN: The whole back lot's full of corn. Far as the eye can see.

DODGE (*to Halie*): Things keep happening while you're upstairs, ya know. The world doesn't stop just because you're upstairs. Corn keeps growing. Rain keeps raining.

HALIE: I'm not unaware of the world around me! Thank you very much. It so happens that I have an overall view from the upstairs. The back yard's in plain view of my window. And there's no corn to speak of. Absolutely none!

DODGE: Tilden wouldn't lie. If he says there's corn, there's corn.

HALIE: What's the meaning of this corn, Tilden!

TILDEN: It's a mystery to me. I was out in back there. And the rain was coming down. And I didn't feel like coming back inside. I didn't feel the cold so much. I didn't mind the wet. So I was just walking. I was muddy but I didn't mind the mud so much. And I looked up. And I saw this stand of corn. In fact I was standing in it. So, I was standing in it.

HALIE: There isn't any corn outside, Tilden! There's no corn! Now, you must've either stolen this corn or you bought it.

DODGE: He doesn't have any money.

HALIE (*to Tilden*): So you stole it!

TILDEN: I didn't steal it. I don't want to get kicked out of Illinois. I was kicked out of New Mexico and I don't want to get kicked out of Illinois.

HALIE: You're going to get kicked out of this house, Tilden, if you don't tell me where you got that corn!

(*Tilden starts crying softly to himself but keeps husking corn. Pause.*)

DODGE (*to Halie*): Why'd you have to tell him that? Who cares where he got the corn? Why'd you have to go and tell him that?

HALIE (*to Dodge*): It's your fault you know! You're the one that's behind all this! I suppose you thought it'd be funny! Some joke! Cover the house with corn husks. You better get this cleaned up before Bradley sees it.

DODGE: Bradley's not getting in the front door!

HALIE (*kicking husks, striding back and forth*): Bradley's going to be very upset when he sees this. He doesn't like to see the house in disarray. He can't stand it when one thing is out of place. The slightest thing. You know how he gets.

DODGE: Bradley doesn't even live here!

HALIE: It's his home as much as ours. He was born in this house!

DODGE: He was born in a hog wallow.

HALIE: Don't you say that! Don't you ever say that!

DODGE: He was born in a goddamn hog wallow!

That's where he was born and that's where he belongs! He doesn't belong in this house!

HALIE (*she stops*): I don't know what's come over you, Dodge. I don't know what in the world's come over you. You've become an evil man. You used to be a good man.

DODGE: Six of one, a half dozen of another.

HALIE: You sit here day and night, festering away! Decomposing! Smelling up the house with your putrid body! Hacking your head off till all hours of the morning! Thinking up mean, evil, stupid things to say about your own flesh and blood!

DODGE: He's not my flesh and blood! My flesh and blood's buried in the back yard!

(*They freeze. Long pause. The men stare at her.*)

HALIE (*quietly*): That's enough, Dodge. That's quite enough. I'm going out now. I'm going to have lunch with Father Dewis. I'm going to ask him about a monument. A statue. At least a plaque.

(*She crosses to the door up right. She stops.*)

HALIE: If you need anything, ask Tilden. He's the oldest. I've left some money on the kitchen table.

DODGE: I don't need anything.

HALIE: No, I suppose not. (*She opens the door and looks out through porch.*) Still raining. I love the smell just after it stops. The ground. I won't be too late.

(*She goes out door and closes it. She's still visible on the porch as she crosses toward stage left screen door. She stops in the middle of the porch, speaks to Dodge but doesn't turn to him.*)

HALIE: Dodge, tell Tilden not to go out in the back lot anymore. I don't want him back there in the rain.

DODGE: You tell him. He's sitting right here.

HALIE: He never listens to me, Dodge. He's never listened to me in the past.

DODGE: I'll tell him.

HALIE: We have to watch him just like we used to now. Just like we always have. He's still a child.

DODGE: I'll watch him.

HALIE: Good.

(*She crosses to screen door, left, takes an umbrella off a hook, and goes out the door. The door slams behind her. Long pause. Tilden husks corn, stares at pail. Dodge lights a cigarette, stares at TV.*)

TILDEN (*still husking*): You shouldn't a told her that.

DODGE (*staring at TV*): What?

TILDEN: What you told her. You know.

DODGE: What do you know about it?

TILDEN: I know. I know all about it. We all know.

DODGE: So what difference does it make? Everybody knows, everybody's forgot.

TILDEN: She hasn't forgot.

DODGE: She should've forgot.

TILDEN: It's different for a woman. She couldn't forget that. How could she forget that?

DODGE: I don't want to talk about it!

TILDEN: What do you want to talk about?

DODGE: I don't want to talk about anything! I don't want to talk about troubles or what happened fifty years ago or thirty years ago or the race track or Florida or the last time I seeded the corn! I don't want to talk!

TILDEN: You don't wanna die, do you?

DODGE: No, I don't wanna die either.

TILDEN: Well, you gotta talk or you'll die.

DODGE: Who told you that?

TILDEN: That's what I know. I found that out in New Mexico. I thought I was dying but I just lost my voice.

DODGE: Were you with somebody?

TILDEN: I was alone. I thought I was dead.

DODGE: Might as well have been. What'd you come back here for?

TILDEN: I didn't know where to go.

DODGE: You're a grown man. You shouldn't be needing your parents at your age. It's unnatural. There's nothing we can do for you now anyway. Couldn't you make a living down there? Couldn't you find some way to make a living? Support yourself? What'd'ya come back here for? You expect us to feed you forever?

TILDEN: I didn't know where else to go.

DODGE: I never went back to my parents. Never. Never even had the urge. I was independent. Always independent. Always found a way.

TILDEN: I didn't know what to do. I couldn't figure anything out.

DODGE: There's nothing to figure out. You just forge ahead. What's there to figure out?

(*Tilden stands.*)

TILDEN: I don't know.

DODGE: Where are you going?

TILDEN: Out back.

DODGE: You're not supposed to go out there. You heard what she said. Don't play deaf with me!

TILDEN: I like it out there.

DODGE: In the rain?

TILDEN: Especially in the rain. I like the feeling of it. Feels like it always did.

DODGE: You're supposed to watch out for me. Get me things when I need them.

TILDEN: What do you need?

DODGE: I don't need anything! But I might. I might

need something any second. Any second now. I can't be left alone for a minute!

(*Dodge starts to cough.*)

TILDEN: I'll be right outside. You can just yell.

DODGE (*between coughs*): No! It's too far! You can't go out there! It's too far! You might not ever hear me!

TILDEN (*moving to pills*): Why don't you take a pill? You want a pill?

(*Dodge coughs more violently, throws himself back against sofa, clutches his throat. Tilden stands by helplessly.*)

DODGE: Water! Get me some water!

(*Tilden rushes off left. Dodge reaches out for the pills, knocking some bottles to the floor, coughing in spasms. He grabs a small bottle, takes out pills, and swallows them. Tilden rushes back on with a glass of water. Dodge takes it and drinks, his coughing subsides.*)

TILDEN: You all right now?

(*Dodge nods. Drinks more water. Tilden moves in closer to him. Dodge sets glass of water on the night table. His coughing is almost gone.*)

TILDEN: Why don't you lay down for a while? Just rest a little.

(*Tilden helps Dodge lay down on the sofa. Covers him with blanket.*)

DODGE: You're not going outside, are you?

TILDEN: No.

DODGE: I don't want to wake up and find you not here.

TILDEN: I'll be here.

(*Tilden tucks blanket around Dodge.*)

DODGE: You'll stay right here?

TILDEN: I'll stay in my chair.

DODGE: That's not a chair. That's my old milking stool.

TILDEN: I know.

DODGE: Don't call it a chair.

TILDEN: I won't.

(*Tilden tries to take Dodge's baseball cap off.*)

DODGE: What're you doing! Leave that on me! Don't take that offa me! That's my cap!

(*Tilden leaves the cap on Dodge.*)

TILDEN: I know.

DODGE: Bradley'll shave my head if I don't have that on. That's my cap.

TILDEN: I know it is.

DODGE: Don't take my cap off.

TILDEN: I won't.

DODGE: You stay right here now.

TILDEN (*sits on stool*): I will.

DODGE: Don't go outside. There's nothing out there.

TILDEN: I won't.

DODGE: Everything's in here. Everything you need. Money's on the table. TV. Is the TV on?

TILDEN: Yeah.

DODGE: Turn it off! Turn the damn thing off! What's it doing on?

TILDEN (*shuts off TV, light goes out*): You left it on.

DODGE: Well, turn it off.

TILDEN (*sits on stool again*): It's off.

DODGE: Leave it off.

TILDEN: I will.

DODGE: When I fall asleep you can turn it on.

TILDEN: Okay.

DODGE: You can watch the ball game. Red Sox. You like the Red Sox don't you?

TILDEN: Yeah.

DODGE: You can watch the Red Sox. Pee Wee Reese. Pee Wee Reese. You remember Pee Wee Reese?

TILDEN: No.

DODGE: Was he with the Red Sox?

TILDEN: I don't know.

DODGE: Pee Wee Reese. (*Falling asleep.*) You can watch the Cardinals. You remember Stan Musial.

TILDEN: No.

DODGE: Stan Musial. (*Falling into sleep.*) Bases loaded. Top a' the sixth. Bases loaded. Runner on first and third. Big fat knuckle ball. Floater. Big as a blimp. Cracko! Ball just took off like a rocket. Just pulverized. I marked it. Marked it with my eyes. Straight between the clock and the Burma Shave ad. I was the first kid out there. First kid. I had to fight hard for that ball. I wouldn't give it up. They almost tore the ears right off me. But I wouldn't give it up.

(*Dodge falls into deep sleep. Tilden just sits staring at him for a while. Slowly he leans toward the sofa, checking to see if Dodge is well asleep. He reaches slowly under the cushion and pulls out the bottle of booze. Dodge sleeps soundly. Tilden stands quietly, staring at Dodge as he uncaps the bottle and takes a long drink. He caps the bottle and sticks it in his hip pocket. He looks around at the husks on the floor and then back to Dodge. He moves center stage and gathers an armload of corn husks then crosses back to the sofa. He stands holding the husks over Dodge and looking down at him he gently spreads the corn husks over the whole length of Dodge's body. He stands back and looks at Dodge. Pulls out bottle, takes an-*

other drink, returns bottle to his hip pocket. He gathers more husks and repeats the procedure until the floor is clean of corn husks and Dodge is completely covered in them except for his head. Tilden takes another long drink, stares at Dodge sleeping, then quietly exits stage left. Long pause as the sound of rain continues. Dodge sleeps on. The figure of Bradley appears up left, outside the screen porch door. He holds a wet newspaper over his head as a protection from the rain. He seems to be struggling with the door, then slips and almost falls to the ground. Dodge sleeps on, undisturbed.)

BRADLEY: Sonuvabitch! Sonuvagoddamnbitch!

(*Bradley recovers his footing and makes it through the screen door onto the porch. He throws the newspaper down, shakes the water out of his hair, and brushes the rain off of his shoulders. He is a big man dressed in a gray sweatshirt, black suspenders, baggy dark blue pants, and black janitor's shoes. His left leg is wooden, having been amputated above the knee. He moves with an exaggerated, almost mechanical limp. The squeaking sounds of leather and metal accompany his walk coming from the harness and hinges of the false leg. His arms and shoulders are extremely powerful and muscular due to a lifetime dependency on the upper torso doing all the work for the legs. He is about five years younger than Tilden. He moves laboriously to the stage right door and enters, closing the door behind him. He doesn't notice Dodge at first. He moves toward the staircase.*)

BRADLEY (*calling to upstairs*): Mom!

(*He stops and listens. Turns upstage and sees Dodge sleeping. Notices corn husks. He moves slowly toward sofa. Stops next to pail and looks into it. Looks at husks. Dodge stays asleep. Talks to himself.*)

BRADLEY: What in the hell is this?

(*He looks at Dodge's sleeping face and shakes his head in disgust. He pulls out a pair of black electric hair clippers from his pocket. Unwinds the cord and crosses to the lamp. He jabs his wooden leg behind the knee, causing it to bend at the joint and awkwardly kneels to plug the cord into a floor outlet. He pulls himself to his feet again by using the sofa as leverage. He moves to Dodge's head and again jabs his false leg. Goes down on one knee. He violently knocks away some of the corn husks, and then jerks off Dodge's baseball cap and throws it down center stage. Dodge stays asleep. Bradley switches on the clippers. Lights start dimming. Bradley cuts Dodge's hair while he sleeps. Lights dim slowly to black with the sound of clippers and rain.*)

ACT 2

Scene: *Same set as act 1. Night. Sound of rain. Dodge still asleep on sofa. His hair is cut extremely short and in places the scalp is cut and bleeding. His cap is still center stage. All the corn and husks, pail and milking stool have been cleared away. The lights come up to the sound of a young girl laughing offstage left. Dodge remains asleep. Shelly and Vince appear up left outside the screen porch door sharing the shelter of Vince's overcoat above their heads. Shelly is about nineteen, black hair, very beautiful. She wears tight jeans, high heels, purple T-shirt, and a short rabbit fur coat. Her makeup is exaggerated and her hair has been curled. Vince is Tilden's son, about twenty-two, wears a plaid shirt, jeans, dark glasses, cowboy boots and carries a black saxophone case. They shake the rain off themselves as they enter the porch through the screen door.*

SHELLY (*laughing, gesturing to house*): This is it? I don't believe this is it!
VINCE: This is it.
SHELLY: This is the house?
VINCE: This is the house.
SHELLY: I don't believe it!
VINCE: How come?
SHELLY: It's like a Norman Rockwell cover or something.
VINCE: What's a' matter with that? It's American.
SHELLY: Where's the milkman and the little dog? What's the little dog's name? Spot. Spot and Jane. Dick and Jane and Spot.
VINCE: Knock it off.
SHELLY: Dick and Jane and Spot and Mom and Dad and Junior and Sissy!

(*She laughs. Slaps her knee.*)

VINCE: Come on! It's my heritage. What dya' expect?

(*She laughs more hysterically, out of control.*)

SHELLY: "And Tuffy and Toto and Dooda and Bonzo all went down one day to the corner grocery store to buy a big bag of licorice for Mr. Marshall's pussy cat!"

(*She laughs so hard she falls to her knees holding her stomach. Vince stands there looking at her.*)

VINCE: Shelly, will you get up!

(*She keeps laughing. Staggers to her feet. Turning in circles holding her stomach.*)

SHELLY (*continuing her story in kid's voice*): "Mr. Marshall was on vacation. He had no idea that the four little boys had taken such a liking to his little kitty cat."
VINCE: Have some respect, would ya'!
SHELLY (*trying to control herself*): I'm sorry.
VINCE: Pull yourself together.
SHELLY (*salutes him*): Yes, sir.

(*She giggles.*)

VINCE: Jesus Christ, Shelly.
SHELLY (*pause, smiling*): And Mr. Marshall —
VINCE: Cut it out.

(*She stops. Stands there staring at him. Stifles a giggle.*)

VINCE (*after pause*): Are you finished?
SHELLY: Oh brother!
VINCE: I don't wanna go in there with you acting like an idiot.
SHELLY: Thanks.
VINCE: Well, I don't.
SHELLY: I won't embarrass you. Don't worry.
VINCE: I'm not worried.
SHELLY: You are too.
VINCE: Shelly, look, I just don't wanna go in there with you giggling your head off. They might think something's wrong with you.
SHELLY: There is.
VINCE: There is not!
SHELLY: Something's definitely wrong with me.
VINCE: There is not!
SHELLY: There's something wrong with you too.
VINCE: There's nothing wrong with me either!
SHELLY: You wanna know what's wrong with you?
VINCE: What?

(*Shelly laughs.*)

VINCE (*crosses back left toward screen door*): I'm leaving!
SHELLY (*stops laughing*): Wait! Stop. Stop! (*Vince stops.*) What's wrong with you is that you take the situation too seriously.
VINCE: I just don't want to have them think that I've suddenly arrived out of the middle of nowhere completely deranged.
SHELLY: What do you want them to think then?
VINCE (*pause*): Nothing. Let's go in.

(*He crosses porch toward stage right interior door. Shelly follows him. The stage right door opens slowly. Vince sticks his head in, doesn't notice Dodge sleeping. Calls out toward staircase.*)

VINCE: Grandma!

(*Shelly breaks into laughter, unseen behind Vince. Vince pulls his head back outside and pulls door shut. We hear their voices again without seeing them.*)

SHELLY'S VOICE (*stops laughing*): I'm sorry. I'm sorry, Vince. I really am. I really am sorry. I won't do it again. I couldn't help it.

VINCE'S VOICE: It's not all that funny.

SHELLY'S VOICE: I know it's not. I'm sorry.

VINCE'S VOICE: I mean this is a tense situation for me! I haven't seen them for over six years. I don't know what to expect.

SHELLY'S VOICE: I know. I won't do it again.

VINCE'S VOICE: Can't you bite your tongue or something?

SHELLY'S VOICE: Just don't say "Grandma," okay? (*She giggles, stops.*) I mean if you say "Grandma," I don't know if I can stop myself.

VINCE'S VOICE: Well try!

SHELLY'S VOICE: Okay. Sorry.

(*Door opens again. Vince sticks his head in then enters. Shelly follows behind him. Vince crosses to staircase, sets down saxophone case and overcoat, looks up staircase. Shelly notices Dodge's baseball cap. Crosses to it. Picks it up and puts it on her head. Vince goes up the stairs and disappears at the top. Shelly watches him, then turns and sees Dodge on the sofa. She takes off the baseball cap.*)

VINCE'S VOICE (*from above stairs*): Grandma!

(*Shelly crosses over to Dodge slowly and stands next to him. She stands at his head, reaches out slowly, and touches one of the cuts. The second she touches his head, Dodge jerks up to a sitting position on the sofa, eyes open. Shelly gasps. Dodge looks at her, sees his cap in her hands, quickly puts his hand to his bare head. He glares at Shelly, then whips the cap out of her hands and puts it on. Shelly backs away from him. Dodge stares at her.*)

SHELLY: I'm uh — with Vince.

(*Dodge just glares at her.*)

SHELLY: He's upstairs.

(*Dodge looks at the staircase, then back to Shelly.*)

SHELLY (*calling upstairs*): Vince!

VINCE'S VOICE: Just a second!

SHELLY: You better get down here!

VINCE'S VOICE: Just a minute! I'm looking at the pictures.

(*Dodge keeps staring at her.*)

SHELLY (*to Dodge*): We just got here. Pouring rain on the freeway so we thought we'd stop by. I mean Vince was planning on stopping anyway. He wanted to see you. He said he hadn't seen you in a long time.

(*Pause. Dodge just keeps staring at her.*)

SHELLY: We were going all the way through to New Mexico. To see his father. I guess his father lives out there. We thought we'd stop by and see you on the way. Kill two birds with one stone, you know? (*She laughs, Dodge stares, she stops laughing.*) I mean Vince has this thing about his family now. I guess it's a new thing with him. I kind of find it hard to relate to. But he feels it's important. You know. I mean he feels he wants to get to know you all again. After all this time.

(*Pause, Dodge just stares at her. She moves nervously to staircase and yells up to Vince.*)

SHELLY: Vince, will you come down here please!

(*Vince comes halfway down the stairs.*)

VINCE: I guess they went out for a while.

(*Shelly points to sofa and Dodge. Vince turns and sees Dodge. He comes all the way down staircase and crosses to Dodge. Shelly stays behind near staircase, keeping her distance.*)

VINCE: Grandpa?

(*Dodge looks up at him, not recognizing him.*)

DODGE: Did you bring the whiskey?

(*Vince looks back at Shelly, then back to Dodge.*)

VINCE: Grandpa, it's Vince. I'm Vince. Tilden's son. You remember?

(*Dodge stares at him.*)

DODGE: You didn't do what you told me. You didn't stay here with me.

VINCE: Grandpa, I haven't been here until just now. I just got here.

DODGE: You left. You went outside like we told you not to do. You went out there in back. In the rain.

(*Vince looks back at Shelly. She moves slowly toward sofa.*)

SHELLY: Is he okay?

VINCE: I don't know. (*Takes off his shades.*) Look, Grandpa, don't you remember me? Vince. Your Grandson.

(*Dodge stares at him, then takes off his baseball cap.*)

DODGE (*points to his head*): See what happens when you leave me alone? See that? That's what happens.

(*Vince looks at his head. Vince reaches out to touch his head. Dodge slaps his hand away with the cap and puts it back on his head.*)

VINCE: What's going on, Grandpa? Where's Halie?

DODGE: Don't worry about her. She won't be back for days. She says she'll be back but she won't be. (*He starts laughing.*) There's life in the old girl yet! (*Stops laughing.*)

VINCE: How did you do that to your head?

DODGE: I didn't do it! Don't be ridiculous!

VINCE: Well, who did then?

(*Pause. Dodge stares at Vince.*)

DODGE: Who do you think did it? Who do you think?

(*Shelly moves toward Vince.*)

SHELLY: Vince, maybe we oughta' go. I don't like this. I mean this isn't my idea of a good time.

VINCE (*to Shelly*): Just a second. (*To Dodge.*) Grandpa, look, I just got here. I just now got here. I haven't been here for six years. I don't know anything that's happened.

(*Pause. Dodge stares at him.*)

DODGE: You don't know anything?

VINCE: No.

DODGE: Well, that's good. That's good. It's much better not to know anything. Much, much better.

VINCE: Isn't there anybody here with you?

(*Dodge turns slowly and looks off to stage left.*)

DODGE: Tilden's here.

VINCE: No, Grandpa, Tilden's in New Mexico. That's where I was going. I'm going out there to see him.

(*Dodge turns slowly back to Vince.*)

DODGE: Tilden's here.

(*Vince backs away and joins Shelly. Dodge stares at them.*)

SHELLY: Vince, why don't we spend the night in a motel and come back in the morning? We could have breakfast. Maybe everything would be different.

VINCE: Don't be scared. There's nothing to be scared of. He's just old.

SHELLY: I'm not scared!

DODGE: You two are not my idea of the perfect couple!

SHELLY (*after pause*): Oh really? Why's that?

VINCE: Shh! Don't aggravate him.

DODGE: There's something wrong between the two of you. Something not compatible.

VINCE: Grandpa, where did Halie go? Maybe we should call her.

DODGE: What are you talking about? Do you know what you're talking about? Are you just talking for the sake of talking? Lubricating the gums?

VINCE: I'm trying to figure out what's going on here!

DODGE: Is that it?

VINCE: Yes. I mean I expected everything to be different.

DODGE: Who are you to expect anything? Who are you supposed to be?

VINCE: I'm Vince! Your Grandson!

DODGE: Vince. My Grandson.

VINCE: Tilden's son.

DODGE: Tilden's son, Vince.

VINCE: You haven't seen me for a long time.

DODGE: When was the last time?

VINCE: I don't remember.

DODGE: You don't remember?

VINCE: No.

DODGE: You don't remember. How am I supposed to remember if you don't remember?

SHELLY: Vince, come on. This isn't going to work out.

VINCE (*to Shelly*): Just take it easy.

SHELLY: I'm taking it easy! He doesn't even know who you are!

VINCE (*crossing toward Dodge*): Grandpa, look —

DODGE: Stay where you are! Keep your distance!

(*Vince stops. Looks back at Shelly, then to Dodge.*)

SHELLY: Vince, this is really making me nervous. I mean he doesn't even want us here. He doesn't even like us.

DODGE: She's a beautiful girl.

VINCE: Thanks.

DODGE: Very Beautiful Girl.

SHELLY: Oh my God.

DODGE (*to Shelly*): What's your name?

SHELLY: Shelly.

DODGE: Shelly. That's a man's name isn't it?

SHELLY: Not in this case.

DODGE (*to Vince*): She's a smart-ass too.

SHELLY: Vince! Can we go?

DODGE: She wants to go. She just got here and she wants to go.

VINCE: This is kind of strange for her.

DODGE: She'll get used to it. (*To Shelly.*) What part of the country do you come from?

SHELLY: Originally?

DODGE: That's right. Originally. At the very start.

SHELLY: L.A.

DODGE: L.A. Stupid country.

SHELLY: I can't stand this, Vince! This is really unbelievable!

DODGE: It's stupid! L.A. is stupid! So is Florida! All those Sunshine States. They're all stupid! Do you know why they're stupid?

SHELLY: Illuminate me.

DODGE: I'll tell you why. Because they're full of smart-asses! That's why.

(*Shelly turns her back to Dodge, crosses to staircase, and sits on bottom step.*)

DODGE (*to Vince*): Now she's insulted.
VINCE: Well, you weren't very polite.
DODGE: She's insulted! Look at her! In my house she's insulted! She's over there sulking because I insulted her!
SHELLY (*to Vince*): This is really terrific. This is wonderful. And you were worried about me making the right first impression!
DODGE (*to Vince*): She's a fireball, isn't she? Regular fireball. I had some a' them in my day. Temporary stuff. Never lasted more than a week.
VINCE: Grandpa —
DODGE: Stop calling me Grandpa will ya'! It's sickening. "Grandpa." I'm nobody's Grandpa!

(*Dodge starts feeling around under the cushion for the bottle of whiskey. Shelly gets up from the staircase.*)

SHELLY (*to Vince*): Maybe you've got the wrong house. Did you ever think of that? Maybe this is the wrong address!
VINCE: It's not the wrong address! I recognize the yard.
SHELLY: Yeah, but do you recognize the people? He says he's not your Grandfather.
DODGE (*digging for bottle*): Where's that bottle!
VINCE: He's just sick of something. I don't know what's happened to him.
DODGE: Where's my goddamn bottle!

(*Dodge gets up from sofa and starts tearing the cushions off it and throwing them downstage, looking for the whiskey.*)

SHELLY: Can't we just drive on to New Mexico? This is terrible, Vince! I don't want to stay here. In this house. I thought it was going to be turkey dinners and apple pie and all that kinda stuff.
VINCE: Well, I hate to disappoint you!
SHELLY: I'm not disappointed! I'm fuckin' terrified! I wanna' go!

(*Dodge yells toward stage left.*)

DODGE: Tilden! Tilden!

(*Dodge keeps ripping away at the sofa looking for his bottle, he knocks over the night stand with the bottles. Vince and Shelly watch as he starts ripping the stuffing out of the sofa.*)

VINCE (*to Shelly*): He's lost his mind or something. I've got to try to help him.
SHELLY: You help him! I'm leaving!

(*Shelly starts to leave. Vince grabs her. They struggle as Dodge keeps ripping away at the sofa and yelling.*)

DODGE: Tilden! Tilden, get your ass in here! Tilden!
SHELLY: Let go of me!
VINCE: You're not going anywhere! You're going to stay right here!
SHELLY: Let go of me, you sonuvabitch! I'm not your property!

(*Suddenly Tilden walks on from stage left just as he did before. This time his arms are full of carrots. Dodge, Vince, and Shelly stop suddenly when they see him. They all stare at Tilden as he crosses slowly center stage with the carrots and stops. Dodge sits on sofa, exhausted.*)

DODGE (*panting, to Tilden*): Where in the hell have you been?
TILDEN: Out back.
DODGE: Where's my bottle?
TILDEN: Gone.

(*Tilden and Vince stare at each other. Shelly backs away.*)

DODGE (*to Tilden*): You stole my bottle!
VINCE (*to Tilden*): Dad?

(*Tilden just stares at Vince.*)

DODGE: You had no right to steal my bottle! No right at all!
VINCE (*to Tilden*): It's Vince. I'm Vince.

(*Tilden stares at Vince, then looks at Dodge, then turns to Shelly.*)

TILDEN (*after pause*): I picked these carrots. If anybody wants any carrots, I picked 'em.
SHELLY (*to Vince*): This is your father?
VINCE (*to Tilden*): Dad, what're you doing here?

(*Tilden just stares at Vince, holding carrots, Dodge pulls the blanket back over himself.*)

DODGE (*to Tilden*): You're going to have to get me another bottle! You gotta get me a bottle before Halie comes back! There's money on the table. (*Points to stage left kitchen.*)
TILDEN (*shaking his head*): I'm not going down there. Into town.

(*Shelly crosses to Tilden. Tilden stares at her.*)

SHELLY (*to Tilden*): Are you Vince's father?
TILDEN (*to Shelly*): Vince?
SHELLY (*pointing to Vince*): This is supposed to be your son! Is he your son? Do you recognize him? I'm just along for the ride here. I thought everybody knew each other!

(Tilden stares at Vince. Dodge wraps himself up in the blanket and sits on sofa staring at the floor.)

TILDEN: I had a son once but we buried him.

(Dodge quickly looks at Tilden. Shelly looks to Vince.)

DODGE: You shut up about that! You don't know anything about that!

VINCE: Dad, I thought you were in New Mexico. We were going to drive down there and see you.

TILDEN: Long way to drive.

DODGE (*to Tilden*): You don't know anything about that! That happened before you were born! Long before!

VINCE: What's happened, Dad? What's going on here? I thought everything was all right. What's happened to Halie?

TILDEN: She left.

SHELLY (*to Tilden*): Do you want me to take those carrots for you?

(Tilden stares at her. She moves in close to him. Holds out her arms. Tilden stares at her arms then slowly dumps the carrots into her arms. Shelly stands there holding the carrots.)

TILDEN (*to Shelly*): You like carrots?

SHELLY: Sure. I like all kinds of vegetables.

DODGE (*to Tilden*): You gotta get me a bottle before Halie comes back!

(Dodge hits sofa with his fist. Vince crosses up to Dodge and tries to console him. Shelly and Tilden stay facing each other.)

TILDEN (*to Shelly*): Back yard's full of carrots. Corn. Potatoes.

SHELLY: You're Vince's father, right?

TILDEN: All kinds of vegetables. You like vegetables?

SHELLY (*laughs*): Yeah. I love vegetables.

TILDEN: We could cook these carrots, ya' know. You could cut 'em up and we could cook 'em.

SHELLY: All right.

TILDEN: I'll get you a pail and a knife.

SHELLY: Okay.

TILDEN: I'll be right back. Don't go.

(Tilden exits offstage left. Shelly stands center, arms full of carrots. Vince stands next to Dodge. Shelly looks toward Vince, then down at the carrots.)

DODGE (*to Vince*): You could get me a bottle. (*Pointing off left.*) There's money on the table.

VINCE: Grandpa, why don't you lay down for a while?

DODGE: I don't wanna lay down for a while! Every time I lay down something happens! (*Whips off his cap, points at his head.*) Look what happens! That's what happens! (*Pulls his cap back on.*) You

go lie down and see what happens to you! See how you like it! They'll steal your bottle! They'll cut your hair! They'll murder your children! That's what'll happen.

VINCE: Just relax for a while.

DODGE (*pause*): You could get me a bottle, ya' know. There's nothing stopping you from getting me a bottle.

SHELLY: Why don't you get him a bottle, Vince? Maybe it would help everybody identify each other.

DODGE (*pointing to Shelly*): There, see? She thinks you should get me a bottle.

(Vince crosses to Shelly.)

VINCE: What're you doing with those carrots?

SHELLY: I'm waiting for your father.

DODGE: She thinks you should get me a bottle!

VINCE: Shelly, put the carrots down, will ya'! We gotta deal with the situation here! I'm gonna need your help.

SHELLY: I'm helping.

VINCE: You're only adding to the problem! You're making things worse! Put the carrots down!

(Vince tries to knock the carrots out of her arms. She turns away from him, protecting the carrots.)

SHELLY: Get away from me! Stop it!

(Vince stands back from her. She turns to him still holding the carrots.)

VINCE (*to Shelly*): Why are you doing this! Are you trying to make fun of me? This is my family, you know!

SHELLY: You coulda' fooled me! I'd just as soon not be here myself. I'd just as soon be a thousand miles from here. I'd rather be anywhere but here. You're the one who wants to stay. So I'll stay. I'll stay and I'll cut the carrots. And I'll cook the carrots. And I'll do whatever I have to do to survive. Just to make it through this.

VINCE: Put the carrots down, Shelly.

(Tilden enters from left with pail, milking stool, and a knife. He sets the stool and pail center stage for Shelly. Shelly looks at Vince, then sits down on stool, sets the carrots on the floor, and takes the knife from Tilden. She looks at Vince again, then picks up a carrot, cuts the ends off, scrapes it, and drops it in pail. She repeats this; Vince glares at her. She smiles.)

DODGE: She could get me a bottle. She's the type a' girl that could get me a bottle. Easy. She'd go down there. Slink up to the counter. They'd probably give her two bottles for the price of one. She could do that.

(*Shelly laughs. Keeps cutting carrots. Vince crosses up to Dodge, looks at him. Tilden watches Shelly's hands. Long pause.*)

VINCE (*to Dodge*): I haven't changed that much. I mean physically. Physically I'm just about the same. Same size. Same weight. Everything's the same.

(*Dodge keeps staring at Shelly while Vince talks to him.*)

DODGE: She's a beautiful girl. Exceptional.

(*Vince moves in front of Dodge to block his view of Shelly. Dodge keeps craning his head around to see her as Vince demonstrates tricks from his past.*)

VINCE: Look. Look at this. Do you remember this? I used to bend my thumb behind my knuckles. You remember? I used to do it at the dinner table.

(*Vince bends a thumb behind his knuckles for Dodge and holds it out to him. Dodge takes a short glance then looks back at Shelly. Vince shifts position and shows him something else.*)

VINCE: What about this?

(*Vince curls his lips back and starts drumming on his teeth with his fingernails making little tapping sounds. Dodge watches awhile. Tilden turns toward the sound. Vince keeps it up. He sees Tilden taking notice and crosses to Tilden as he drums on his teeth. Dodge turns TV on, watches it.*)

VINCE: You remember this, Dad?

(*Vince keeps on drumming for Tilden. Tilden watches awhile, fascinated, then turns back to Shelly. Vince keeps up the drumming on his teeth, crosses back to Dodge doing it. Shelly keeps working on carrots, talking to Tilden.*)

SHELLY (*to Tilden*): He drives me crazy with that sometimes.

VINCE (*to Dodge*): I know! Here's one you'll remember. You used to kick me out of the house for this one.

(*Vince pulls his shirt out of his belt and holds it tucked under his chin with his stomach exposed. He grabs the flesh on either side of his belly button and pushes it in and out to make it look like a mouth talking. He watches his belly button and makes a deep sounding cartoon voice to synchronize with the movement. He demonstrates it to Dodge, then crosses down to Tilden doing it. Both Dodge and Tilden take short, uninterested glances then ignore him.*)

VINCE (*deep cartoon voice*): "Hello. How are you? I'm fine. Thank you very much. It's so good to see you looking well this fine Sunday morning. I was going down to the hardware store to fetch a pail of water."

SHELLY: Vince, don't be pathetic, will ya'!

(*Vince stops. Tucks his shirt back in.*)

SHELLY: Jesus Christ. They're not gonna play. Can't you see that?

(*Shelly keeps cutting carrots. Vince slowly moves toward Tilden. Tilden keeps watching Shelly. Dodge watches TV.*)

VINCE (*to Shelly*): I don't get it. I really don't get it. Maybe it's me. Maybe I forgot something.

DODGE (*from sofa*): You forgot to get me a bottle! That's what you forgot. Anybody in this house could get me a bottle. Anybody! But nobody will. Nobody understands the urgency! Peelin carrots is more important. Playin piano on your teeth! Well I hope you all remember this when you get up in years. When you find yourself immobilized. Dependent on the whims of others.

(*Vince moves up toward Dodge. Pause as he looks at him.*)

VINCE: I'll get you a bottle.

DODGE: You will?

VINCE: Sure.

(*Shelly stands holding knife and carrot.*)

SHELLY: You're not going to leave me here, are you?

VINCE (*moving to her*): You suggested it! You said, "Why don't I go get him a bottle?" So I'll go get him a bottle!

SHELLY: But I can't stay here.

VINCE: What is going on! A minute ago you were ready to cut carrots all night!

SHELLY: That was only if you stayed. Something to keep me busy, so I wouldn't be so nervous. I don't want to stay here alone.

DODGE: Don't let her talk you out of it! She's a bad influence. I could see it the minute she stepped in here.

SHELLY (*to Dodge*): You were asleep!

TILDEN (*to Shelly*): Don't you want to cut carrots anymore?

SHELLY: Sure. Sure I do.

(*Shelly sits back down on stool and continues cutting carrots. Pause. Vince moves around, stroking his hair, staring at Dodge and Tilden. Vince and Shelly exchange glances. Dodge watches TV.*)

VINCE: Boy! This is amazing. This is truly amazing. (*Keeps moving around.*) What is this anyway? Am I in a time warp or something? Have I committed an unpardonable offense? It's true, I'm not married. (*Shelly looks at him, then back to carrots.*) But I'm also not divorced. I have been known to plunge into sinful infatuation with the Alto Saxophone. Sucking on number 5 reeds deep into the wee wee hours.

SHELLY: Vince, what are you doing that for? They don't care about any of that. They just don't recognize you, that's all.

VINCE: How could they not recognize me! How in the hell could they not recognize me! I'm their son!

DODGE (*watching TV*): You're no son of mine. I've had sons in my time and you're not one of 'em.

(*Long pause. Vince stares at Dodge, then looks at Tilden. He turns to Shelly.*)

VINCE: Shelly, I gotta go out for a while. I just gotta go out. I'll get a bottle and I'll come right back. You'll be okay here. Really.

SHELLY: I don't know if I can handle this, Vince.

VINCE: I just gotta think or something. I don't know. I gotta put this all together.

SHELLY: Can't we just go?

VINCE: No! I gotta find out what's going on.

SHELLY: Look, you think you're bad off, what about me? Not only don't they recognize me but I've never seen them before in my life. I don't know who these guys are. They could be anybody!

VINCE: They're not anybody!

SHELLY: That's what you say.

VINCE: They're my family for Christ's sake! I should know who my own family is! Now give me a break. It won't take that long. I'll just go out and I'll come right back. Nothing'll happen. I promise.

(*Shelly stares at him. Pause.*)

SHELLY: All right.

VINCE: Thanks. (*He crosses up to Dodge.*) I'm gonna go out now, Grandpa, and I'll pick you up a bottle. Okay?

DODGE: Change of heart huh? (*Pointing off left.*) Money's on the table. In the kitchen.

(*Vince moves toward Shelly.*)

VINCE (*to Shelly*): You be all right?

SHELLY (*cutting carrots*): Sure. I'm fine. I'll just keep real busy while you're gone.

(*Vince looks at Tilden who keeps staring down at Shelly's hands.*)

DODGE: Persistence, see? That's what it takes. Persistence. Persistence, fortitude, and determination. Those are the three virtues. You stick with those three and you can't go wrong.

VINCE (*to Tilden*): You want anything, Dad?

TILDEN (*looks up at Vince*): Me?

VINCE: From the store? I'm gonna get Grandpa a bottle.

TILDEN: He's not supposed to drink. Halie wouldn't like it.

VINCE: He wants a bottle.

TILDEN: He's not supposed to drink.

DODGE (*to Vince*): Don't negotiate with him! Don't make any transactions until you've spoken to me first! He'll steal you blind!

VINCE (*to Dodge*): Tilden says you're not supposed to drink.

DODGE: Tilden's lost his marbles! Look at him! He's around the bend. Take a look at him.

(*Vince stares at Tilden. Tilden watches Shelly's hands as she keeps cutting carrots.*)

DODGE: Now look at me. Look here at me!

(*Vince looks back to Dodge.*)

DODGE: Now, between the two of us, who do you think is more trustworthy? Him or me? Can you trust a man who keeps bringing in vegetables from out of nowhere? Take a look at him.

(*Vince looks back at Tilden.*)

SHELLY: Go get the bottle, Vince.

VINCE (*to Shelly*): You sure you'll be all right?

SHELLY: I'll be fine. I feel right at home now.

VINCE: You do?

SHELLY: I'm fine. Now that I've got the carrots everything is all right.

VINCE: I'll be right back.

(*Vince crosses stage left.*)

DODGE: Where are you going?

VINCE: I'm going to get the money.

DODGE: Then where are you going?

VINCE: Liquor store.

DODGE: Don't go anyplace else. Don't go off some place and drink. Come right back here.

VINCE: I will.

(*Vince exits stage left.*)

DODGE (*calling after Vince*): You've got responsibility now! And don't go out the back way either! Come out through this way! I wanna' see you when you leave! Don't go out the back!

VINCE'S VOICE (*off left*): I won't!

(*Dodge turns and looks at Tilden and Shelly.*)

DODGE: Untrustworthy. Probably drown himself if he went out the back. Fall right in a hole. I'd never get my bottle.

SHELLY: I wouldn't worry about Vince. He can take care of himself.

DODGE: Oh he can, huh? Independent.

(*Vince comes on again from stage left with two dollars in his hand. He crosses stage right past Dodge.*)

DODGE (*to Vince*): You got the money?

VINCE: Yeah. Two bucks.

DODGE: Two bucks. Two bucks is two bucks. Don't sneer.

VINCE: What kind do you want?

DODGE: Whiskey! Gold Star Sour Mash. Use your own discretion.

VINCE: Okay.

(*Vince crosses to stage right door. Opens it. Stops when he hears Tilden.*)

TILDEN (*to Vince*): You drove all the way from New Mexico?

(*Vince turns and looks at Tilden. They stare at each other. Vince shakes his head, goes out the door, crosses porch, and exits out screen door. Tilden watches him go. Pause.*)

SHELLY: You really don't recognize him? Either one of you?

(*Tilden turns again and stares at Shelly's hands as she cuts carrots.*)

DODGE (*watching TV*): Recognize who?

SHELLY: Vince.

DODGE: What's to recognize?

(*Dodge lights a cigarette, coughs slightly, and stares at TV.*)

SHELLY: It'd be cruel if you recognized him and didn't tell him. Wouldn't be fair.

(*Dodge just stares at TV, smoking.*)

TILDEN: I thought I recognized him. I thought I recognized something about him.

SHELLY: You did?

TILDEN: I thought I saw a face inside his face.

SHELLY: Well, it was probably that you saw what he used to look like. You haven't seen him for six years.

TILDEN: I haven't?

SHELLY: That's what he says.

(*Tilden moves around in front of her as she continues with carrots.*)

TILDEN: Where was it I saw him last?

SHELLY: I don't know. I've only known him for a few months. He doesn't tell me everything.

TILDEN: He doesn't?

SHELLY: Not stuff like that.

TILDEN: What does he tell you?

SHELLY: You mean in general?

TILDEN: Yeah.

(*Tilden moves around behind her.*)

SHELLY: Well, he tells me all kinds of things.

TILDEN: Like what?

SHELLY: I don't know! I mean I can't just come right out and tell you how he feels.

TILDEN: How come?

(*Tilden keeps moving around her slowly in a circle.*)

SHELLY: Because it's stuff he told me privately!

TILDEN: And you can't tell me?

SHELLY: I don't even know you!

DODGE: Tilden, go out in the kitchen and make me some coffee! Leave the girl alone.

SHELLY (*to Dodge*): He's all right.

(*Tilden ignores Dodge, keeps moving around Shelly. He stares at her hair and coat. Dodge stares at TV.*)

TILDEN: You mean you can't tell me anything?

SHELLY: I can tell you some things. I mean we can have a conversation.

TILDEN: We can?

SHELLY: Sure. We're having a conversation right now.

TILDEN: We are?

SHELLY: Yes. That's what we're doing.

TILDEN: But there's certain things you can't tell me, right?

SHELLY: Right.

TILDEN: There's certain things I can't tell you either.

SHELLY: How come?

TILDEN: I don't know. Nobody's supposed to hear it.

SHELLY: Well, you can tell me anything you want to.

TILDEN: I can?

SHELLY: Sure.

TILDEN: It might not be very nice.

SHELLY: That's all right. I've been around.

TILDEN: It might be awful.

SHELLY: Well, can't you tell me anything nice?

(*Tilden stops in front of her and stares at her coat. Shelly looks back at him. Long pause.*)

TILDEN (*after pause*): Can I touch your coat?

SHELLY: My coat? (*She looks at her coat then back to Tilden.*) Sure.

TILDEN: You don't mind?

SHELLY: No. Go ahead.

(*Shelly holds her arm out for Tilden to touch. Dodge stays fixed on TV. Tilden moves in slowly toward Shelly, staring at her arm. He reaches out very slowly and touches her arm, feels the fur gently, then draws his hand back. Shelly keeps her arm out.)*

SHELLY: It's rabbit.
TILDEN: Rabbit.

(He reaches out again very slowly and touches the fur on her arm then pulls back his hand again. Shelly drops her arm.)

SHELLY: My arm was getting tired.
TILDEN: Can I hold it?
SHELLY (*pause*): The coat? Sure.

(Shelly takes off her coat and hands it to Tilden. Tilden takes it slowly, feels the fur, then puts it on. Shelly watches as Tilden strokes the fur slowly. He smiles at her. She goes back to cutting carrots.)

SHELLY: You can have it if you want.
TILDEN: I can?
SHELLY: Yeah. I've got a raincoat in the car. That's all I need.
TILDEN: You've got a car?
SHELLY: Vince does.

(Tilden walks around stroking the fur and smiling at the coat. Shelly watches him when he's not looking. Dodge sticks with TV, stretches out on sofa wrapped in blanket.)

TILDEN (*as he walks around*): I had a car once! I had a white car! I drove. I went everywhere. I went to the mountains. I drove in the snow.
SHELLY: That must've been fun.
TILDEN (*still moving, feeling coat*): I drove all day long sometimes. Across the desert. Way out across the desert. I drove past towns. Anywhere. Past palm trees. Lightning. Anything. I would drive through it. I would drive through it and I would stop and I would look around and I would drive on. I would get back in and drive! I loved to drive. There was nothing I loved more. Nothing I dreamed of was better than driving.
DODGE (*eyes on TV*): Pipe down, would ya'!

(Tilden stops. Stares at Shelly.)

SHELLY: Do you do much driving now?
TILDEN: Now? Now? I don't drive now.
SHELLY: How come?
TILDEN: I'm grown up now.
SHELLY: Grown up?
TILDEN: I'm not a kid.
SHELLY: You don't have to be a kid to drive.
TILDEN: It wasn't driving then.
SHELLY: What was it?
TILDEN: Adventure. I went everywhere.
SHELLY: Well, you can still do that.

TILDEN: Not now.
SHELLY: Why not?
TILDEN: I just told you. You don't understand anything. If I told you something you wouldn't understand it.
SHELLY: Told me what?
TILDEN: Told you something that's true.
SHELLY: Like what?
TILDEN: Like a baby. Like a little tiny baby.
SHELLY: Like when you were little?
TILDEN: If I told you you'd make me give your coat back.
SHELLY: I won't. I promise. Tell me.
TILDEN: I can't. Dodge won't let me.
SHELLY: He won't hear you. It's okay.

(Pause. Tilden stares at her. Moves slightly toward her.)

TILDEN: We had a baby. (*Motioning to Dodge.*) He did. Dodge did. Could pick it up with one hand. Put it in the other. Little baby. Dodge killed it.

(Shelly stands.)

TILDEN: Don't stand up. Don't stand up!

(Shelly sits again. Dodge sits up on sofa and looks at them.)

TILDEN: Dodge drowned it.
SHELLY: Don't tell me anymore! Okay?

(Tilden moves closer to her. Dodge takes more interest.)

DODGE: Tilden? You leave that girl alone!
TILDEN (*pays no attention*): Never told Halie. Never told anybody. Just drowned it.
DODGE (*shuts off TV*): Tilden!
TILDEN: Nobody could find it. Just disappeared. Cops looked for it. Neighbors. Nobody could find it.

(Dodge struggles to get up from sofa.)

DODGE: Tilden, what're you telling her! Tilden!

(Dodge keeps struggling until he's standing.)

TILDEN: Finally everybody just gave up. Just stopped looking. Everybody had a different answer. Kidnap. Murder. Accident. Some kind of accident.

(Dodge struggles to walk toward Tilden and falls. Tilden ignores him.)

DODGE: Tilden, you shut up! You shut up about it!

(Dodge starts coughing on the floor. Shelly watches him from the stool.)

TILDEN: Little tiny baby just disappeared. It's not hard. It's so small. Almost invisible.

(*Shelly makes a move to help Dodge. Tilden firmly pushes her back down on the stool. Dodge keeps coughing.*)

TILDEN: He said he had his reasons. Said it went a long way back. But he wouldn't tell anybody.

DODGE: Tilden! Don't tell her anything! Don't tell her!

TILDEN: He's the only one who knows where it's buried. The only one. Like a secret buried treasure. Won't tell any of us. Won't tell me or mother or even Bradley. Especially Bradley. Bradley tried to force it out of him but he wouldn't tell. Wouldn't even tell why he did it. One night he just did it.

(*Dodge's coughing subsides. Shelly stays on stool staring at Dodge. Tilden slowly takes Shelly's coat off and holds it out to her. Long pause. Shelly sits there trembling.*)

TILDEN: You probably want your coat back now.

(*Shelly stares at coat but doesn't move to take it. The sound of Bradley's leg squeaking is heard off left. The others on stage remain still. Bradley appears up left outside the screen door wearing a yellow rain slicker. He enters through screen door, crosses porch to stage right door and enters stage. Closes door. Takes off rain slicker and shakes it out. He sees all the others and stops. Tilden turns to him. Bradley stares at Shelly. Dodge remains on floor.*)

BRADLEY: What's going on here? (*Motioning to Shelly.*) Who's that?

(*Shelly stands, moves back away from Bradley as he crosses toward her. He stops next to Tilden. He sees coat in Tilden's hand and grabs it away from him.*)

BRADLEY: Who's she supposed to be?
TILDEN: She's driving to New Mexico.

(*Bradley stares at her. Shelly is frozen. Bradley limps over to her with the coat in his fist. He stops in front of her.*)

BRADLEY (*to Shelly, after pause*): Vacation?

(*Shelly shakes her head "no," trembling.*)

BRADLEY (*to Shelly, motioning to Tilden*): You taking him with you?

(*Shelly shakes her head "no." Bradley crosses back to Tilden.*)

BRADLEY: You oughta'. No use leaving him here. Doesn't do a lick a' work. Doesn't raise a finger. (*Stopping, to Tilden.*) Do ya'. (*To Shelly.*) 'Course he used to be an All-American. Quarterback or fullback or somethin'. He tell you that?

(*Shelly shakes her head "no."*)

BRADLEY: Yeah, he used to be a big deal. Wore lettermen's sweaters. Had medals hanging all around his neck. Real purty. Big deal. (*He laughs to himself, notices Dodge on floor, crosses to him, stops.*) This one too. (*To Shelly.*) You'd never think it to look at him, would ya'? All bony and wasted away.

(*Shelly shakes her head again. Bradley stares at her, crosses back to her, clenching the coat in his fist. He stops in front of Shelly.*)

BRADLEY: Women like that kinda' thing, don't they?
SHELLY: What?
BRADLEY: Importance. Importance in a man?
SHELLY: I don't know.
BRADLEY: Yeah. You know, you know. Don't give me that. (*Moves closer to Shelly.*) You're with Tilden?
SHELLY: No.
BRADLEY (*turning to Tilden*): Tilden! She with you?

(*Tilden doesn't answer. Stares at floor.*)

BRADLEY: Tilden!

(*Tilden suddenly bolts and runs off up stage left. Bradley laughs. Talks to Shelly. Dodge starts moving his lips silently as though talking to someone invisible on the floor.*)

BRADLEY (*laughing*): Scared to death! He was always scared!

(*Bradley stops laughing. Stares at Shelly.*)

BRADLEY: You're scared too, right? (*Laughs again.*) You're scared and you don't even know me. (*Stops laughing.*) You don't gotta be scared.

(*Shelly looks at Dodge on the floor.*)

SHELLY: Can't we do something for him?
BRADLEY (*looking at Dodge*): We could shoot him. (*Laughs.*) We could drown him! What about drowning him?
SHELLY: Shut up!

(*Bradley stops laughing. Moves in closer to Shelly. She freezes. Bradley speaks slowly and deliberately.*)

BRADLEY: Hey! Missus. Don't talk to me like that. Don't talk to me in that tone a' voice. There was a time when I had to take that tone a' voice from pretty near everyone. (*Motioning to Dodge.*) Him, for one! Him and that half brain that just ran outa' here. They don't talk to me like that now. Not anymore. Everything's turned around now. Full circle. Isn't that funny?
SHELLY: I'm sorry.
BRADLEY: Open your mouth.

SHELLY: What?

BRADLEY (*motioning for her to open her mouth*): Open up.

(*She opens her mouth slightly.*)

BRADLEY: Wider.

(*She opens her mouth wider.*)

BRADLEY: Keep it like that.

(*She does. Stares at Bradley. With his free hand he puts his fingers into her mouth. She tries to pull away.*)

BRADLEY: Just stay put!

(*She freezes. He keeps his fingers in her mouth. Stares at her. Pause. He pulls his hand out. She closes her mouth, keeps her eyes on him. Bradley smiles. He looks at Dodge on the floor and crosses over to him. Shelly watches him closely. Bradley stands over Dodge and smiles at Shelly. He holds her coat up in both hands over Dodge, keeps smiling at Shelly. He looks down at Dodge, then drops the coat so that it lands on Dodge and covers his head. Bradley keeps his hands up in the position of holding the coat, looks over at Shelly, and smiles. The lights black out.*)

ACT 3

Scene: *Same set. Morning. Bright sun. No sound of rain. Everything has been cleared up again. No sign of carrots. No pail. No stool. Vince's saxophone case and overcoat are still at the foot of the staircase. Bradley is asleep on the sofa under Dodge's blanket. His head toward stage left. Bradley's wooden leg is leaning against the sofa right by his head. The shoe is left on it. The harness hangs down. Dodge is sitting on the floor, propped up against the TV set facing stage left wearing his baseball cap. Shelly's rabbit fur coat covers his chest and shoulders. He stares off toward stage left. He seems weaker and more disoriented. The lights rise slowly to the sound of birds and remain for a while in silence on the two men. Bradley sleeps very soundly. Dodge hardly moves. Shelly appears from stage left with a big smile, slowly crossing toward Dodge balancing a steaming cup of broth in a saucer. Dodge just stares at her as she gets close to him.*

SHELLY (*as she crosses*): This is going to make all the difference in the world, Grandpa. You don't mind me calling you Grandpa, do you? I mean I know you minded when Vince called you that but you don't even know him.

DODGE: He skipped town with my money, ya' know. I'm gonna hold you as collateral.

SHELLY: He'll be back. Don't you worry.

(*She kneels down next to Dodge and puts the cup and saucer in his lap.*)

DODGE: It's morning already! Not only didn't I get my bottle but he's got my two bucks!

SHELLY: Try to drink this, okay? Don't spill it.

DODGE: What is it?

SHELLY: Beef bouillon. It'll warm you up.

DODGE: Bouillon! I don't want any goddamn bouillon! Get that stuff away from me!

SHELLY: I just got through making it.

DODGE: I don't care if you just spent all week making it! I ain't drinking it!

SHELLY: Well, what am I supposed to do with it then? I'm trying to help you out. Besides, it's good for you.

DODGE: Get it away from me!

(*Shelly stands up with cup and saucer.*)

DODGE: What do you know what's good for me anyway?

(*She looks at Dodge, then turns away from him, crossing to staircase, sits on bottom step, and drinks the bouillon. Dodge stares at her.*)

DODGE: You know what'd be good for me?

SHELLY: What?

DODGE: A little massage. A little contact.

SHELLY: Oh no. I've had enough contact for a while. Thanks anyway.

(*She keeps sipping bouillon, stays sitting. Pause as Dodge stares at her.*)

DODGE: Why not? You got nothing better to do. That fella's not gonna be back here. You're not expecting him to show up again, are you?

SHELLY: Sure. He'll show up. He left his horn here.

DODGE: His horn? (*Laughs.*) You're his horn?

SHELLY: Very funny.

DODGE: He's run off with my money! He's not coming back here.

SHELLY: He'll be back.

DODGE: You're a funny chicken, you know that?

SHELLY: Thanks.

DODGE: Full of faith. Hope. Faith and hope. You're all alike, you hopers. If it's not God then it's a man. If it's not a man then it's a woman. If its not a woman then it's the land or the future of some kind. Some kind of future.

(*Pause.*)

SHELLY (*looking toward porch*): I'm glad it stopped raining.
DODGE (*looks toward porch then back to her*): That's what I mean. See, you're glad it stopped raining. Now you think everything's gonna be different. Just 'cause the sun comes out.
SHELLY: It's already different. Last night I was scared.
DODGE: Scared a' what?
SHELLY: Just scared.
DODGE: Bradley? (*Looks at Bradley.*) He's a pushover. 'Specially now. All ya' gotta do is take his leg and throw it out the back door. Helpless. Totally helpless.

(*Shelly turns and stares at Bradley's wooden leg, then looks at Dodge. She sips bouillon.*)

SHELLY: You'd do that?
DODGE: Me? I've hardly got the strength to breathe.
SHELLY: But you'd actually do it if you could?
DODGE: Don't be so easily shocked, girlie. There's nothing a man can't do. You dream it up and he can do it. Anything.
SHELLY: You've tried I guess.
DODGE: Don't sit there sippin' your bouillon and judging me! This is my house!
SHELLY: I forgot.
DODGE: You forgot? Whose house did you think it was?
SHELLY: Mine.

(*Dodge just stares at her. Long pause. She sips from cup.*)

SHELLY: I know it's not mine but I had that feeling.
DODGE: What feeling?
SHELLY: The feeling that nobody lives here but me. I mean everybody's gone. You're here, but it doesn't seem like you're supposed to be. (*Pointing to Bradley.*) Doesn't seem like he's supposed to be here either. I don't know what it is. It's the house or something. Something familiar. Like I know my way around here. Did you ever get that feeling?

(*Dodge stares at her in silence. Pause.*)

DODGE: No. No, I never did.

(*Shelly gets up. Moves around space holding cup.*)

SHELLY: Last night I went to sleep up there in that room.
DODGE: What room?
SHELLY: That room up there with all the pictures. All the crosses on the wall.
DODGE: Halie's room?
SHELLY: Yeah. Whoever "Halie" is.
DODGE: She's my wife.
SHELLY: So you remember her?

DODGE: Whad'ya mean! 'Course I remember her! She's only been gone for a day — half a day. However long it's been.
SHELLY: Do you remember her when her hair was bright red? Standing in front of an apple tree?
DODGE: What is this, the third degree or something! Who're you to be askin' me personal questions about my wife!
SHELLY: You never look at those pictures up there?
DODGE: What pictures!
SHELLY: Your whole life's up there hanging on the wall. Somebody who looks just like you. Somebody who looks just like you used to look.
DODGE: That isn't me! That never was me! This is me. Right here. This is it. The whole shootin' match, sittin' right in front of you.
SHELLY: So the past never happened as far as you're concerned?
DODGE: The past? Jesus Christ. The past. What do you know about the past?
SHELLY: Not much. I know there was a farm.

(*Pause.*)

DODGE: A farm?
SHELLY: There's a picture of a farm. A big farm. A bull. Wheat. Corn.
DODGE: Corn?
SHELLY: All the kids are standing out in the corn. They're all waving these big straw hats. One of them doesn't have a hat.
DODGE: Which one was that?
SHELLY: There's a baby. A baby in a woman's arms. The same woman with the red hair. She looks lost standing out there. Like she doesn't know how she got there.
DODGE: She knows! I told her a hundred times it wasn't gonna' be the city! I gave her plenty a' warning.
SHELLY: She's looking down at the baby like it was somebody else's. Like it didn't even belong to her.
DODGE: That's about enough outa' you! You got some funny ideas. Some damn funny ideas. You think just because people propagate they have to love their offspring? You never seen a bitch eat her puppies? Where are you from anyway?
SHELLY: L.A. We already went through that.
DODGE: That's right, L.A. I remember.
SHELLY: Stupid country.
DODGE: That's right! No wonder.

(*Pause.*)

SHELLY: What's happened to this family anyway?
DODGE: You're in no position to ask! What do you care? You some kinda' Social Worker?
SHELLY: I'm Vince's friend.

DODGE: Vince's friend! That's rich. That's really rich. "Vince"! "Mr. Vince"! "Mr. Thief" is more like it! His name doesn't mean a hoot in hell to me. Not a tinkle in the well. You know how many kids I've spawned? Not to mention Grand kids and Great Grand kids and Great Great Grand kids after them?

SHELLY: And you don't remember any of them?

DODGE: What's to remember? Halie's the one with the family album. She's the one you should talk to. She'll set you straight on the heritage if that's what you're interested in. She's traced it all the way back to the grave.

SHELLY: What do you mean?

DODGE: What do you think I mean? How far back can you go? A long line of corpses! There's not a living soul behind me. Not a one. Who's holding me in their memory? Who gives a damn about bones in the ground?

SHELLY: Was Tilden telling the truth?

(*Dodge stops short. Stares at Shelly. Shakes his head. He looks off stage left.*)

SHELLY: Was he?

(*Dodge's tone changes drastically.*)

DODGE: Tilden? (*Turns to Shelly, calmly.*) Where is Tilden?

SHELLY: Last night. Was he telling the truth about the baby?

(*Pause.*)

DODGE (*turns toward stage left*): What's happened to Tilden? Why isn't Tilden here?

SHELLY: Bradley chased him out.

DODGE (*looking at Bradley asleep*): Bradley? Why is he on my sofa? (*Turns back to Shelly.*) Have I been here all night? On the floor?

SHELLY: He wouldn't leave. I hid outside until he fell asleep.

DODGE: Outside? Is Tilden outside? He shouldn't be out there in the rain. He'll get himself into trouble. He doesn't know his way around here anymore. Not like he used to. He went out West and got himself into trouble. Got himself into bad trouble. We don't want any of that around here.

SHELLY: What did he do?

(*Pause.*)

DODGE (*quietly stares at Shelly*): Tilden? He got mixed up. That's what he did. We can't afford to leave him alone. Not now.

(*Sound of Halie laughing comes from off left. Shelly stands, looking in direction of voice, holding cup and saucer, doesn't know whether to stay or run.*)

DODGE (*motioning to Shelly*): Sit down! Sit back down!

(*Shelly sits. Sound of Halie's laughter again.*)

DODGE (*to Shelly in a heavy whisper, pulling coat up around him*): Don't leave me alone now! Promise me? Don't go off and leave me alone. I need somebody here with me. Tilden's gone now and I need someone. Don't leave me! Promise!

SHELLY (*sitting*): I won't.

(*Halie appears outside the screen porch door, up left with Father Dewis. She is wearing a bright yellow dress, no hat, white gloves and her arms are full of yellow roses. Father Dewis is dressed in traditional black suit, white clerical collar, and shirt. He is a very distinguished gray-haired man in his sixties. They are both slightly drunk and feeling giddy. As they enter the porch through the screen door, Dodge pulls the rabbit fur coat over his head and hides. Shelly stands again. Dodge drops the coat and whispers intensely to Shelly. Neither Halie nor Father Dewis are aware of the people inside the house.*)

DODGE (*to Shelly in a strong whisper*): You promised!

(*Shelly sits on stairs again. Dodge pulls coat back over his head. Halie and Father Dewis talk on the porch as they cross toward stage right interior door.*)

HALIE: Oh, Father! That's terrible! That's absolutely terrible. Aren't you afraid of being punished?

(*She giggles.*)

DEWIS: Not by the Italians. They're too busy punishing each other.

(*They both break out in giggles.*)

HALIE: What about God?

DEWIS: Well, prayerfully, God only hears what he wants to. That's just between you and me of course. In our heart of hearts we know we're every bit as wicked as the Catholics.

(*They giggle again and reach the stage right door.*)

HALIE: Father, I never heard you talk like this in Sunday sermon.

DEWIS: Well, I save all my best jokes for private company. Pearls before swine, you know.

(*They enter the room laughing and stop when they see Shelly. Shelly stands. Halie closes the door behind Father Dewis. Dodge's voice is heard under the coat, talking to Shelly.*)

DODGE (*under coat, to Shelly*): Sit down, sit down! Don't let 'em buffalo you!

(*Shelly sits on stair again. Halie looks at Dodge on the floor, then looks at Bradley asleep on sofa and sees his wooden leg. She lets out a shriek of embarrassment for Father Dewis.*)

HALIE: Oh my gracious! What in the name of Judas Priest is going on in this house!

(*She hands over the roses to Father Dewis.*)

HALIE: Excuse me, Father.

(*Halie crosses to Dodge, whips the coat off him, and covers the wooden leg with it. Bradley stays asleep.*)

HALIE: You can't leave this house for a second without the Devil blowing in through the front door!
DODGE: Gimme back that coat! Gimme back that goddamn coat before I freeze to death!
HALIE: You're not going to freeze! The sun's out in case you hadn't noticed!
DODGE: Gimme back that coat! That coat's for live flesh not dead wood!

(*Halie whips the blanket off Bradley and throws it on Dodge. Dodge covers his head again with blanket. Bradley's amputated leg can be faked by having half of it under a cushion of the sofa. He's fully clothed. Bradley sits up with a jerk when the blanket comes off him.*)

HALIE (*as she tosses blanket*): Here! Use this! It's yours anyway! Can't you take care of yourself for once!
BRADLEY (*yelling at Halie*): Gimme that blanket! Gimme back that blanket! That's my blanket!

(*Halie crosses back toward Father Dewis who just stands there with the roses. Bradley thrashes helplessly on the sofa trying to reach blanket. Dodge hides himself deeper in blanket. Shelly looks on from staircase, still holding cup and saucer.*)

HALIE: Believe me, Father, this is not what I had in mind when I invited you in.
DEWIS: Oh, no apologies please. I wouldn't be in the ministry if I couldn't face real life.

(*He laughs self-consciously. Halie notices Shelly again and crosses over to her. Shelly stays sitting. Halie stops and stares at her.*)

BRADLEY: I want my blanket back! Gimme my blanket!

(*Halie turns toward Bradley and silences him.*)

HALIE: Shut up, Bradley! Right this minute! I've had enough!

(*Bradley slowly recoils, lies back down on sofa, turns his back toward Halie and whimpers softly. Halie directs her attention to Shelly again. Pause.*)

HALIE (*to Shelly*): What're you doing with my cup and saucer?
SHELLY (*looking at cup, back to Halie*): I made some bouillon for Dodge.
HALIE: For Dodge?
SHELLY: Yeah.
HALIE: Well, did he drink it?
SHELLY: No.
HALIE: Did you drink it?
SHELLY: Yes.

(*Halie stares at her. Long pause. She turns abruptly away from Shelly and crosses back to Father Dewis.*)

HALIE: Father, there's a stranger in my house. What would you advise? What would be the Christian thing?
DEWIS (*squirming*): Oh, well. . . . I. . . . I really —
HALIE: We still have some whiskey, don't we?

(*Dodge slowly pulls the blanket down off his head and looks toward Father Dewis. Shelly stands.*)

SHELLY: Listen, I don't drink or anything. I just —

(*Halie turns toward Shelly viciously.*)

HALIE: You sit back down!

(*Shelly sits again on stair. Halie turns again to Dewis.*)

HALIE: I think we have plenty of whiskey left! Don't we, Father?
DEWIS: Well, yes. I think so. You'll have to get it. My hands are full.

(*Halie giggles. Reaches into Dewis's pockets, searching for bottle. She smells the roses as she searches. Dewis stands stiffly. Dodge watches Halie closely as she looks for bottle.*)

HALIE: The most incredible things, roses! Aren't they incredible, Father?
DEWIS: Yes. Yes, they are.
HALIE: They almost cover the stench of sin in this house. Just magnificent! The smell. We'll have to put some at the foot of Ansel's statue. On the day of the unveiling.

(*Halie finds a silver flask of whiskey in Dewis's vest pocket. She pulls it out. Dodge looks on eagerly. Halie crosses to Dodge, opens the flask, and takes a sip.*)

HALIE (*to Dodge*): Ansel's getting a statue, Dodge. Did you know that? Not a plaque but a real live statue. A full bronze. Tip to toe. A basketball in one hand and a rifle in the other.

BRADLEY (*his back to Halie*): He never played basketball!

HALIE: You shut up, Bradley! You shut up about Ansel! Ansel played basketball better than anyone! And you know it! He was an All-American! There's no reason to take the glory away from others.

(*Halie turns away from Bradley, crosses back toward Dewis, sipping on the flask and smiling.*)

HALIE (*to Dewis*): Ansel was a great basketball player. One of the greatest.

DEWIS: I remember Ansel.

HALIE: Of course! You remember. You remember how he could play. (*She turns toward Shelly.*) Of course, nowadays they play a different brand of basketball. More vicious. Isn't that right, dear?

SHELLY: I don't know.

(*Halie crosses to Shelly, sipping on flask. She stops in front of Shelly.*)

HALIE: Much, much more vicious. They smash into each other. They knock each other's teeth out. There's blood all over the court. Savages.

(*Halie takes the cup from Shelly and pours whiskey into it.*)

HALIE: They don't train like they used to. Not at all. They allow themselves to run amuck. Drugs and women. Women mostly.

(*Halie hands the cup of whiskey back to Shelly slowly. Shelly takes it.*)

HALIE: Mostly women. Girls. Sad, pathetic little girls. (*She crosses back to Father Dewis.*) It's just a reflection of the times, don't you think, Father? An indication of where we stand?

DEWIS: I suppose so, yes.

HALIE: Yes. A sort of bad omen. Our youth becoming monsters.

DEWIS: Well, I uh —

HALIE: Oh you can disagree with me if you want to, Father. I'm open to debate. I think argument only enriches both sides of the question don't you? (*She moves toward Dodge.*) I suppose, in the long run, it doesn't matter. When you see the way things deteriorate before your very eyes. Everything running downhill. It's kind of silly to even think about youth.

DEWIS: No, I don't think so. I think it's important to believe in certain things.

HALIE: Yes. Yes, I know what you mean. I think that's right. I think that's true. (*She looks at Dodge.*) Certain basic things. We can't shake certain basic things. We might end up crazy. Like my husband.

You can see it in his eyes. You can see how mad he is.

(*Dodge covers his head with the blanket again. Halie takes a single rose from Dewis and moves slowly over to Dodge.*)

HALIE: We can't not believe in something. We can't stop believing. We just end up dying if we stop. Just end up dead.

(*Halie throws the rose gently onto Dodge's blanket. It lands between his knees and stays there! Long pause as Halie stares at the rose. Shelly stands suddenly. Halie doesn't turn to her but keeps staring at rose.*)

SHELLY (*to Halie*): Don't you wanna' know who I am! Don't you wanna know what I'm doing here! I'm not dead!

(*Shelly crosses toward Halie. Halie turns slowly toward her.*)

HALIE: Did you drink your whiskey?

SHELLY: No! And I'm not going to either!

HALIE: Well, that's a firm stand. It's good to have a firm stand.

SHELLY: I don't have any stand at all. I'm just trying to put all this together.

(*Halie laughs and crosses back to Dewis.*)

HALIE (*to Dewis*): Surprises, surprises! Did you have any idea we'd be returning to this?

SHELLY: I came here with your grandson for a little visit! A little innocent friendly visit.

HALIE: My grandson?

SHELLY: Yes! That's right. The one no one remembers.

HALIE (*to Dewis*): This is getting a little far-fetched.

SHELLY: I told him it was stupid to come back here. To try to pick up from where he left off.

HALIE: Where was that?

SHELLY: Wherever he was when he left here! Six years ago! Ten years ago! Whenever it was. I told him nobody cares.

HALIE: Didn't he listen?

SHELLY: No! No, he didn't. We had to stop off at every tiny little meatball town that he remembered from his boyhood! Every stupid little donut shop he ever kissed a girl in. Every drive-in. Every drag strip. Every football field he ever broke a bone on.

HALIE (*suddenly alarmed, to Dodge*): Where's Tilden?

SHELLY: Don't ignore me!

HALIE: Dodge! Where's Tilden gone?

(*Shelly moves violently toward Halie.*)

SHELLY (*to Halie*): I'm talking to you!

(*Bradley sits up fast on the sofa, Shelly backs away.*)

BRADLEY (*to Shelly*): Don't you yell at my mother!

HALIE: Dodge! (*She kicks Dodge.*) I told you not to let Tilden out of your sight! Where's he gone to?

DODGE: Gimme a drink and I'll tell ya'.

DEWIS: Halie, maybe this isn't the right time for a visit.

(*Halie crosses back to Dewis.*)

HALIE (*to Dewis*): I never should've left. I never, never should've left! Tilden could be anywhere by now! Anywhere! He's not in control of his faculties. Dodge knew that. I told him when I left here. I told him specifically to watch out for Tilden.

(*Bradley reaches down, grabs Dodge's blanket, and yanks it off him. He lays down on sofa and pulls the blanket over his head.*)

DODGE: He's got my blanket again! He's got my blanket!

HALIE (*turning to Bradley*): Bradley! Bradley, put that blanket back!

(*Halie moves toward Bradley. Shelly suddenly throws the cup and saucer against the stage right door. Dewis ducks. The cup and saucer smash into pieces. Halie stops, turns toward Shelly. Everyone freezes. Bradley slowly pulls his head out from under blanket, looks toward stage right door, then to Shelly. Shelly stares at Halie. Dewis cowers with roses. Shelly moves slowly toward Halie. Long pause. Shelly speaks softly.*)

SHELLY (*to Halie*): I don't like being ignored. I don't like being treated like I'm not here. I didn't like it when I was a kid and I still don't like it.

BRADLEY (*sitting up on sofa*): We don't have to tell you anything, girl. Not a thing. You're not the police, are you? You're not the government. You're just some prostitute that Tilden brought in here.

HALIE: Language! I won't have that language in my house!

SHELLY (*to Bradley*): You stuck your hand in my mouth and you call me a prostitute!

HALIE: Bradley! Did you put your hand in her mouth? I'm ashamed of you. I can't leave you alone for a minute.

BRADLEY: I never did. She's lying!

DEWIS: Halie, I think I'll be running along now. I'll just put the roses in the kitchen.

(*Dewis moves toward stage left. Halie stops him.*)

HALIE: Don't go now, Father! Not now.

BRADLEY: I never did anything, Mom! I never touched her! She propositioned me! And I turned her down. I turned her down flat!

(*Shelly suddenly grabs her coat off the wooden leg and takes both the leg and coat downstage, away from Bradley.*)

BRADLEY: Mom! Mom! She's got my leg! She's taken my leg! I never did anything to her! She's stolen my leg!

(*Bradley reaches pathetically in the air for his leg. Shelly sets it down for a second, puts on her coat fast, and picks the leg up again. Dodge starts coughing softly.*)

HALIE (*to Shelly*): I think we've had about enough of you, young lady. Just about enough. I don't know where you came from or what you're doing here but you're no longer welcome in this house.

SHELLY (*laughs, holds leg*): No longer welcome!

BRADLEY: Mom! That's my leg! Get my leg back! I can't do anything without my leg.

(*Bradley keeps making whimpering sounds and reaching for his leg.*)

HALIE: Give my son back his leg. Right this very minute!

(*Dodge starts laughing softly to himself in between coughs.*)

HALIE (*to Dewis*): Father, do something about this, would you! I'm not about to be terrorized in my own house!

BRADLEY: Gimme back my leg!

HALIE: Oh, shut up, Bradley! Just shut up! You don't need your leg now! Just lay down and shut up!

(*Bradley whimpers. Lays down and pulls blanket around him. He keeps one arm outside blanket, reaching out toward his wooden leg. Dewis cautiously approaches Shelly with the roses in his arms. Shelly clutches the wooden leg to her chest as though she's kidnaped it.*)

DEWIS (*to Shelly*): Now, honestly dear, wouldn't it be better to try to talk things out? Try to use some reason?

SHELLY: There isn't any reason here! I can't find a reason for anything.

DEWIS: There's nothing to be afraid of. These are all good people. All righteous people.

SHELLY: I'm not afraid!

DEWIS: But this isn't your house. You have to have some respect.

SHELLY: You're the strangers here, not me.

HALIE: This has gone far enough!

DEWIS: Halie, please. Let me handle this.

SHELLY: Don't come near me! Don't anyone come near me. I don't need any words from you. I'm not threatening anybody. I don't even know what I'm doing here. You all say you don't remember Vince, okay, maybe you don't. Maybe it's Vince that's crazy. Maybe he's made this whole family thing up. I don't even care anymore. I was just coming along for the ride. I thought it'd be a nice gesture. Besides, I was curious. He made all of you sound familiar to me. Every one of you. For every name, I had an image. Every time he'd tell me a name, I'd see the person. In fact, each of you was so clear in my mind that I actually believed it was you. I really believed when I walked through that door that the people who lived here would turn out to be the same people in my imagination. But I don't recognize any of you. Not one. Not even the slightest resemblance.

DEWIS: Well, you can hardly blame others for not fulfilling your hallucination.

SHELLY: It was no hallucination! It was more like a prophecy. You believe in prophecy, don't you?

HALIE: Father, there's no point in talking to her any further. We're just going to have to call the police.

BRADLEY: No! Don't get the police in here. We don't want the police in here. This is our home.

SHELLY: That's right. Bradley's right. Don't you usually settle your affairs in private? Don't you usually take them out in the dark? Out in the back?

BRADLEY: You stay out of our lives! You have no business interfering!

SHELLY: I don't have any business period. I got nothing to lose.

(*She moves around, staring at each of them.*)

BRADLEY: You don't know what we've been through. You don't know anything!

SHELLY: I know you've got a secret. You've all got a secret. It's so secret in fact, you're all convinced it never happened.

(*Halie moves to Dewis.*)

HALIE: Oh, my God, Father!

DODGE (*laughing to himself*): She thinks she's going to get it out of us. She thinks she's going to uncover the truth of the matter. Like a detective or something.

BRADLEY: I'm not telling her anything! Nothing's wrong here! Nothin's ever been wrong! Everything's the way it's supposed to be! Nothing ever happened that's bad! Everything is all right here! We're all good people!

DODGE: She thinks she's gonna suddenly bring everything out into the open after all these years.

DEWIS (*to Shelly*): Can't you see that these people want to be left in peace? Don't you have any mercy? They haven't done anything to you.

DODGE: She wants to get to the bottom of it. (*To Shelly.*) That's it, isn't it? You'd like to get right down to bedrock? You want me to tell ya'? You want me to tell ya' what happened? I'll tell ya'. I might as well.

BRADLEY: No! Don't listen to him. He doesn't remember anything!

DODGE: I remember the whole thing from start to finish. I remember the day he was born.

(*Pause.*)

HALIE: Dodge, if you tell this thing — if you tell this, you'll be dead to me. You'll be just as good as dead.

DODGE: That won't be such a big change, Halie. See this girl, this girl here, she wants to know. She wants to know something more. And I got this feeling that it doesn't make a bit a' difference. I'd sooner tell it to a stranger than anybody else.

BRADLEY (*to Dodge*): We made a pact! We made a pact between us! You can't break that now!

DODGE: I don't remember any pact.

BRADLEY (*to Shelly*): See, he doesn't remember anything. I'm the only one in the family who remembers. The only one. And I'll never tell you!

SHELLY: I'm not so sure I want to find out now.

DODGE (*laughing to himself*): Listen to her! Now she's runnin' scared!

SHELLY: I'm not scared!

(*Dodge stops laughing, long pause. Dodge stares at her.*)

DODGE: You're not, huh? Well, that's good. Because I'm not either. See, we were a well-established family once. Well-established. All the boys were grown. The farm was producing enough milk to fill Lake Michigan twice over. Me and Halie here were pointed toward what looked like the middle part of our life. Everything was settled with us. All we had to do was ride it out. Then Halie got pregnant again. Outa' the middle a' nowhere, she got pregnant. We weren't planning on havin' any more boys. We had enough boys already. In fact, we hadn't been sleepin' in the same bed for about six years.

HALIE (*moving toward stairs*): I'm not listening to this! I don't have to listen to this!

DODGE (*stops Halie*): Where are you going! Upstairs! You'll just be listenin' to it upstairs! You go outside, you'll be listenin' to it outside. Might as well stay here and listen to it.

(*Halie stays by stairs.*)

BRADLEY: If I had my leg you wouldn't be saying this. You'd never get away with it if I had my leg.

DODGE (*pointing to Shelly*): She's got your leg. (*Laughs.*) She's gonna keep your leg too. (*To Shelly.*) She wants to hear this. Don't you?

SHELLY: I don't know.

DODGE: Well even if ya' don't I'm gonna' tell ya'. (*Pause.*) Halie had this kid. This baby boy. She had it. I let her have it on her own. All the other boys I had had the best doctors, best nurses, everything. This one I let her have by herself. This one hurt real bad. Almost killed her, but she had it anyway. It lived, see. It lived. It wanted to grow up in this family. It wanted to be just like us. It wanted to pretend that I was its father. She wanted me to believe in it. Even when everyone around us knew. Everyone. All our boys knew. Tilden knew.

HALIE: You shut up! Bradley, make him shut up!

BRADLEY: I can't.

DODGE: Tilden was the one who knew. Better than any of us. He'd walk for miles with that kid in his arms. Halie let him take it. All night sometimes. He'd walk all night out there in the pasture with it. Talkin' to it. Singin' to it. Used to hear him singing to it. He'd make up stories. He'd tell that kid all kinds a' stories. Even when he knew it couldn't understand him. Couldn't understand a word he was sayin'. Never would understand him. We couldn't let a thing like that continue. We couldn't allow that to grow up right in the middle of our lives. It made everything we'd accomplished look like it was nothin'. Everything was canceled out by this one mistake. This one weakness.

SHELLY: So you killed him?

DODGE: I killed it. I drowned it. Just like the runt of a litter. Just drowned it.

(*Halie moves toward Bradley.*)

HALIE (*to Bradley*): Ansel would've stopped him! Ansel would've stopped him from telling these lies! He was a hero! A man! A whole man! What's happened to the men in this family! Where are the men!

(*Suddenly Vince comes crashing through the screen porch door up left, tearing it off its hinges. Everyone but Dodge and Bradley back away from the porch and stare at Vince who has landed on his stomach on the porch in a drunken stupor. He is singing loudly to himself and hauls himself slowly to his feet. He has a paper shopping bag full of empty booze bottles. He takes them out one at a time as he sings and smashes them at the opposite end of the porch, behind the solid interior door, stage right. Shelly moves slowly toward stage right, holding wooden leg and watching Vince.*)

VINCE (*singing loudly as he hurls bottles*): "From the Halls of Montezuma to the Shores of Tripoli. We will fight our country's battles on the land and on the sea."

(*He punctuates the words "Montezuma," "Tripoli," "battles," and "sea" with a smashed bottle each. He stops throwing for a second, stares toward stage right of the porch, shades his eyes with his hand as though looking across to a battlefield, then cups his hands around his mouth and yells across the space of the porch to an imaginary army. The others watch in terror and expectation.*)

VINCE (*to imagined army*): Have you had enough over there! 'Cause there's a lot more here where that came from! (*Pointing to paper bag full of bottles.*) A helluva lot more! We got enough over here to blow ya' from here to Kingdomcome!

(*He takes another bottle, makes high whistling sound of a bomb, and throws it toward stage right porch. Sound of bottle smashing against wall. This should be the actual smashing of bottles and not tape sound. He keeps yelling and heaving bottles one after another.*)

(*Vince stops for a while, breathing heavily from exhaustion. Long silence as the others watch him. Shelly approaches tentatively in Vince's direction, still holding Bradley's wooden leg.*)

SHELLY (*after silence*): Vince?

(*Vince turns toward her. Peers through screen.*)

VINCE: Who? What? Vince who? Who's that in there?

(*Vince pushes his face against the screen from the porch and stares in at everyone.*)

DODGE: Where's my goddamn bottle!

VINCE (*looking in at Dodge*): What? Who is that?

DODGE: It's me! Your Grandfather! Don't play stupid with me! Where's my two bucks!

VINCE: Your two bucks?

(*Halie moves away from Dewis, upstage, peers out at Vince, trying to recognize him.*)

HALIE: Vincent? Is that you, Vincent?

(*Shelly stares at Halie, then looks out at Vince.*)

VINCE (*from porch*): Vincent who? What is this! Who are you people?

SHELLY (*to Halie*): Hey, wait a minute. Wait a minute! What's going on?

HALIE (*moving closer to porch screen*): We thought you were a murderer or something. Barging in through the door like that.

VINCE: I am a murderer! Don't underestimate me for

a minute! I'm the Midnight Strangler! I devour whole families in a single gulp!

(*Vince grabs another bottle and smashes it on the porch. Halie backs away.*)

SHELLY (*approaching Halie*): You mean you know who he is?

HALIE: Of course I know who he is! That's more than I can say for you.

BRADLEY (*sitting up on sofa*): You get off our front porch, you creep! What're you doing out there breaking bottles? Who are these foreigners anyway! Where did they come from?

VINCE: Maybe I should come in there and break them!

HALIE (*moving toward porch*): Don't you dare! Vincent, what's got into you! Why are you acting like this?

VINCE: Maybe I should come in there and usurp your territory!

(*Halie turns back toward Dewis and crosses to him.*)

HALIE (*to Dewis*): Father, why are you just standing around here when everything's falling apart? Can't you rectify this situation?

(*Dodge laughs, coughs.*)

DEWIS: I'm just a guest here, Halie. I don't know what my position is exactly. This is outside my parish anyway.

(*Vince starts throwing more bottles as things continue.*)

BRADLEY: If I had my leg I'd rectify! I'd rectify him all over the goddamn highway! I'd pull his ears out if I could reach him!

(*Bradley sticks his fist through the screening of the porch and reaches out for Vince, grabbing at him and missing. Vince jumps away from Bradley's hand.*)

VINCE: Aaaah! Our lines have been penetrated! Tentacles animals! Beasts from the deep!

(*Vince strikes out at Bradley's hand with a bottle. Bradley pulls his hand back inside.*)

SHELLY: Vince! Knock it off, will ya'! I want to get out of here!

(*Vince pushes his face against screen, looks in at Shelly.*)

VINCE (*to Shelly*): Have they got you prisoner in there, dear? Such a sweet young thing too. All her life in front of her. Nipped in the bud.

SHELLY: I'm coming out there, Vince! I'm coming out there and I want us to get in the car and drive away from here. Anywhere. Just away from here.

(*Shelly moves toward Vince's saxophone case and overcoat. She sets down the wooden leg, downstage left, and picks up the saxophone case and overcoat. Vince watches her through the screen.*)

VINCE (*to Shelly*): We'll have to negotiate. Make some kind of a deal. Prisoner exchange or something. A few of theirs for one of ours. Small price to pay if you ask me.

(*Shelly crosses toward stage right door with overcoat and case.*)

SHELLY: Just go and get the car! I'm coming out there now. We're going to leave.

VINCE: Don't come out here! Don't you dare come out here!

(*Shelly stops short of the door, stage right.*)

SHELLY: How come?

VINCE: Off limits! Verboten! This is taboo territory. No man or woman has ever crossed the line and lived to tell the tale!

SHELLY: I'll take my chances.

(*Shelly moves to stage right door and opens it. Vince pulls out a big folding hunting knife and pulls open the blade. He jabs the blade into the screen and starts cutting a hole big enough to climb through. Bradley cowers in a corner of the sofa as Vince rips at the screen.*)

VINCE (*as he cuts screen*): Don't come out here! I'm warning you! You'll disintegrate!

(*Dewis takes Halie by the arm and pulls her toward staircase.*)

DEWIS: Halie, maybe we should go upstairs until this blows over.

HALIE: I don't understand it. I just don't understand it. He was the sweetest little boy!

(*Dewis drops the roses beside the wooden leg at the foot of the staircase, then escorts Halie quickly up the stairs. Halie keeps looking back at Vince as they climb the stairs.*)

HALIE: There wasn't a mean bone in his body. Everyone loved Vincent. Everyone. He was the perfect baby.

DEWIS: He'll be all right after a while. He's just had a few too many that's all.

HALIE: He used to sing in his sleep. He'd sing. In the middle of the night. The sweetest voice. Like an angel. (*She stops for a moment.*) I used to lie awake listening to it. I used to lie awake thinking it was all right if I died. Because Vincent was an angel.

A guardian angel. He'd watch over us. He'd watch over all of us.

(*Dewis takes her all the way up the stairs. They disappear above. Vince is now climbing through the porch screen onto the sofa. Bradley crashes off the sofa, holding tight to his blanket, keeping it wrapped around him. Shelly is outside on the porch. Vince holds the knife in his teeth once he gets the hole wide enough to climb through. Bradley starts crawling slowly toward his wooden leg, reaching out for it.*)

DODGE (*to Vince*): Go ahead! Take over the house! Take over the whole goddamn house! You can have it! It's yours. It's been a pain in the neck ever since the very first mortgage. I'm gonna die any second now. Any second. You won't even notice. So I'll settle my affairs once and for all.

(*As Dodge proclaims his last will and testament, Vince climbs into the room, knife in mouth, and strides slowly around the space, inspecting his inheritance. He casually notices Bradley as he crawls toward his leg. Vince moves to the leg and keeps pushing it with his foot so that it's out of Bradley's reach, then goes on with his inspection. He picks up the roses and carries them around smelling them. Shelly can be seen outside on the porch, moving slowly center and staring in at Vince. Vince ignores her.*)

DODGE: The house goes to my Grandson, Vincent. All the furnishings, accoutrements, and paraphernalia therein. Everything tacked to the walls or otherwise resting under this roof. My tools — namely my band saw, my skill saw, my drill press, my chain saw, my lathe, my electric sander, all go to my eldest son, Tilden. That is, if he ever shows up again. My shed and gasoline powered equipment, namely my tractor, my dozer, my hand tiller plus all the attachments and riggings for the above mentioned machinery, namely my spring tooth harrow, my deep plows, my disk plows, my automatic fertilizing equipment, my reaper, my swathe, my seeder, my John Deere Harvester, my post hole digger, my jackhammer, my lathe — (*to himself*) Did I mention my lathe? I already mentioned my lathe — my Bennie Goodman records, my harnesses, my bits, my halters, my brace, my rough rasp, my forge, my welding equipment, my shoeing nails, my levels and bevels, my milking stool — no, not my milking stool — my hammers and chisels, my hinges, my cattle gates, my barbed wire, self-tapping augers, my horse hair ropes, and all related materials are to be pushed into a gigantic heap and set ablaze in the very center of my fields. When the blaze is at its highest, preferably on a cold, windless night, my body is to be pitched into the middle of it and burned till nothing remains but ash.

(*Pause. Vince takes the knife out of his mouth and smells the roses. He's facing toward audience and doesn't turn around to Shelly. He folds up knife and pockets it.*)

SHELLY (*from porch*): I'm leaving, Vince. Whether you come or not, I'm leaving.

VINCE (*smelling roses*): Just put my horn on the couch there before you take off.

SHELLY (*moving toward hole in screen*): You're not coming?

(*Vince stays downstage, turns, and looks at her.*)

VINCE: I just inherited a house.

SHELLY (*through hole, from porch*): You want to stay here?

VINCE (*as he pushes Bradley's leg out of reach*): I've gotta carry on the line. I've gotta see to it that things keep rolling.

(*Bradley looks up at him from floor, keeps pulling himself toward his leg. Vince keeps moving it.*)

SHELLY: What happened to you, Vince? You just disappeared.

VINCE (*pause, delivers speech front*): I was gonna run last night. I was gonna run and keep right on running. I drove all night. Clear to the Iowa border. The old man's two bucks sitting right on the seat beside me. It never stopped raining the whole time. Never stopped once. I could see myself in the windshield. My face. My eyes. I studied my face. Studied everything about it. As though I was looking at another man. As though I could see his whole race behind him. Like a mummy's face. I saw him dead and alive at the same time. In the same breath. In the windshield, I watched him breathe as though he was frozen in time. And every breath marked him. Marked him forever without him knowing. And then his face changed. His face became his father's face. Same bones. Same eyes. Same nose. Same breath. And his father's face changed to his grandfather's face. And it went on like that. Changing. Clear on back to faces I'd never seen before but still recognized. Still recognized the bones underneath. The eyes. The breath. The mouth. I followed my family clear into Iowa. Every last one. Straight into the Corn Belt and further. Straight back as far as they'd take me. Then it all dissolved. Everything dissolved.

(*Shelly stares at him for a while then reaches through the hole in the screen and sets the saxophone case and*

Vince's overcoat on the sofa. She looks at Vince again.)

SHELLY: Bye, Vince.

(She exits left off the porch. Vince watches her go. Bradley tries to make a lunge for his wooden leg. Vince quickly picks it up and dangles it over Bradley's head like a carrot. Bradley keeps making desperate grabs at the leg. Dewis comes down the staircase and stops halfway, staring at Vince and Bradley. Vince looks up at Dewis and smiles. He keeps moving backwards with the leg toward upstage left as Bradley crawls after him.)

VINCE *(to Dewis as he continues torturing Bradley)*: Oh, excuse me, Father. Just getting rid of some of the vermin in the house. This is my house now, ya' know? All mine. Everything. Except for the power tools and stuff. I'm gonna get all new equipment anyway. New plows, new tractor, everything. All brand new. *(Vince teases Bradley closer to the up left corner of the stage.)* Start right off on the ground floor.

(Vince throws Bradley's wooden leg far offstage left. Bradley follows his leg offstage, pulling himself along on the ground, whimpering. As Bradley exits, Vince pulls the blanket off him and throws it over his own shoulder. He crosses toward Dewis with the blanket and smells the roses. Dewis comes to the bottom of the stairs.)

DEWIS: You'd better go up and see your Grandmother.

VINCE *(looking up stairs, back to Dewis)*: My Grandmother? There's nobody else in this house. Except for you. And you're leaving, aren't you?

(Dewis crosses toward stage right door. He turns back to Vince.)

DEWIS: She's going to need someone. I can't help her. I don't know what to do. I don't know what my position is. I just came in for some tea. I had no idea there was any trouble. No idea at all.

(Vince just stares at him. Dewis goes out the door, crosses porch, and exits left. Vince listens to him leaving. He smells roses, looks up the staircase, then smells roses again. He turns and looks upstage at Dodge.)

He crosses up to him and bends over looking at Dodge's open eyes. Dodge is dead. His death should have come completely unnoticed by the audience. Vince covers Dodge's body with the blanket, then covers his head. He sits on the sofa, smelling roses and staring at Dodge's body. Long pause. Vince places the roses on Dodge's chest, then lays down on the sofa, arms folded behind his head, staring at the ceiling. His body is in the same relationship to Dodge's After a while Halie's voice is heard coming from above the staircase. The lights start to dim almost imperceptibly as Halie speaks. Vince keeps staring at the ceiling.)

HALIE'S VOICE: Dodge? Is that you, Dodge? Tilden was right about the corn, you know. I've never seen such corn. Have you taken a look at it lately? Tall as a man already. This early in the year. Carrots too. Potatoes. Peas. It's like a paradise out there, Dodge. You oughta' take a look. A miracle. I've never seen it like this. Maybe the rain did something. Maybe it was the rain.

(As Halie keeps talking offstage, Tilden appears from stage left, dripping with mud from the knees down. His arms and hands are covered with mud. In his hands he carries the corpse of a small child at chest level, staring down at it. The corpse mainly consists of bones wrapped in muddy, rotten cloth. He moves slowly downstage toward the staircase, ignoring Vince on the sofa. Vince keeps staring at the ceiling as though Tilden wasn't there. As Halie's voice continues, Tilden slowly makes his way up the stairs. His eyes never leave the corpse of the child. The lights keep fading.)

HALIE'S VOICE: Good hard rain. Takes everything straight down deep to the roots. The rest takes care of itself. You can't force a thing to grow. You can't interfere with it. It's all hidden. It's all unseen. You just gotta wait till it pops up out of the ground. Tiny little shoot. Tiny little white shoot. All hairy and fragile. Strong though. Strong enough to break the earth even. It's a miracle, Dodge. I've never seen a crop like this in my whole life. Maybe it's the sun. Maybe that's it. Maybe it's the sun.

(Tilden disappears above. Silence. Lights go to black.)

Athol Fugard

Athol Fugard (b. 1932) was an actor before becoming a playwright. In 1956, he began working with a theater group called the Serpent Company in Cape Town, South Africa. The group included both black and white actors as participants at a time when racial mixing was illegal. Fugard's wife, the actress Sheila Meiring, stimulated his interest in theater in 1956 and in developing the theater company, which sustained itself to produce fine plays and to make a contribution to world drama.

Fugard, who is white, met Zakes Mokae, a black musician and actor, in the early days of the Serpent players, and the two collaborated on several works. Mokae has said that the tradition in Africa was not so much for a solitary playwright to compose a work that others would act out as it was for people to develop a communal approach to drama, crafting a dramatic piece through their interaction. To some extent, Fugard in his early efforts did just that. He worked with actors, watched how things developed, and then shaped the drama around them.

In 1960, he began to write a two-person play called *The Blood Knot* while he was in England trying to establish a theater group there. This play was part of a trilogy called *The Family*, with *Hello and Goodbye* (1965) and *Boesman and Lena* (1969). *The Blood Knot* was given its first performance in Dorkay House in Johannesburg late in 1961. As Fugard has said, the entire production, which starred Fugard and Mokae, was put together so quickly that the government never had time to stop it. The play is about two brothers, one black, the other light-skinned enough to pass for white. It is exceptionally powerful, and in its first performances in Johannesburg, it was a sensation. As a result of its success, it toured South Africa and had a revival in New Haven and in New York in 1984 and 1985.

While they toured South Africa, Fugard and Mokae were victims of the country's apartheid policies. They could not travel in the same train car: Fugard went first class and Mokae had to go in the special cars for blacks. After *The Blood Knot*'s success the government passed laws making it all but impossible to have black and white actors working together on the stage.

Fugard has had a considerable number of plays produced in New York and London in recent years. *Sizwe Banzi Is Dead* (1972), written with John Kani and Winston Ntshona, which is about a man who exchanges identity with a corpse as a way of avoiding the racial laws of South Africa, was well received. *The Island* (1975), also written with Kani and Ntshona, starred the latter two black actors, who have become associated with Fugard and his work. They portray prisoners who are putting on *Antigone* and who become immersed in the political themes of the play, seeing it as an example of the political repression they experience in their own lives.

His plays *A Lesson from Aloes* (1978) and *The Road to Mecca* (1984) were successful in their first American productions at the Yale Repertory Theatre and on Broadway. Fugard's works are not always concerned with racial problems, but they usually center on political issues and the stress that individuals feel in trying to be themselves in an intolerant society.

Fugard is now in a somewhat anomalous position in South Africa. Blacks have criticized him for dealing with themes that they feel are more properly developed by black writers. At the same time, he is ostracized by white South African society because of his sympathies toward blacks. He himself feels he is writing what he knows about, and he does not apologize for its revealing his own limitations and his own point of view. And his attachment and commitment to South Africa remain deep and lifelong. He always returns to his homeland from his travels abroad because, as he says, he learned in South Africa everything he knows about how to develop deep feelings. His gravesite is in South Africa, a fact that he says gives him great pleasure.

"MASTER HAROLD"
. . . AND THE BOYS

Athol Fugard has said that *"MASTER HAROLD" . . . and the boys* (1982) is a very personal play in which he exorcises personal guilt (Fugard's entire name is Athol Harold Lannigan Fugard). As a white South African he has written numerous plays that represent the racial circumstances of life in that troubled nation. This play has won international distinction and has made a reputation for its stars, especially Zakes Mokae, with whom Fugard has worked for more than thirty years.

Hally reveals throughout the play (which is set in 1950) that he is more attached emotionally to Sam, the black waiter in his parents' restaurant who has befriended him, than he is even to his own parents. His attitude toward his father is complicated by his father's alcoholism and confinement. Even such an alcoholic is considered, in South Africa, automatically superior to a black man such as Sam, who is intelligent, quick, thoughtful, and generous. When Hally reveals his anxiety about his father, Sam warns him that it is dishonorable to treat one's father the way he does, but Sam's presumption in admonishing Hally triggers Hally's mean outburst toward him.

Zakes Mokae, who created the role of Sam in the first performance of the play at the Yale Repertory Theatre, has commented extensively about his role and the character of Sam. He has observed that some black audience members called out during a performance that he should beat Hally up the minute Hally demands that Sam call him Master Harold. But other black audience members spoke with him after the performance and agreed that, because Sam had never taken that kind of stand against Harold or his father, he was getting what he deserved. Mokae himself has pointed out that Sam is probably not living in Port Elizabeth legally and that to have taken action, even if he wanted to, would have ended with his removal from the town into exile.

Zakes Mokae understands the character from his perspective as a black South African, and he realizes Sam's limits. But he has said that if he had written the play Sam would give Hally a beating and "suffer the consequences." He points out, however, that he is an urban South African, unlike Sam, and his attitude is quite different from anything that Sam would have understood. As an urban black, Mokae could not have been sent into exile, although he could certainly have been punished, for beating a white boy.

About the question of whether the play made a positive contribution to white-black relations in South Africa, Mokae feels that a play cannot change people's minds. Audiences were not likely to seek to change the government of South Africa simply because they had seen a play. But at the same time, he feels that it was productive to talk about the apartheid and racial distrust in South Africa.

Unfortunately, the government of South Africa decided that the play was too inflammatory for performance in its country, and the play was banned for a brief period from performance in Johannesburg and other theatrical centers in South Africa. This suggests that while Zakes Mokae does not feel that one play will have much impact on injustices in South Africa, it is likely that the government feared otherwise.

In an important way, *"MASTER HAROLD" . . . and the boys* is a personal statement by Fugard that establishes the extent to which apartheid can damage even a person sympathetic to black rights. It is astonishing in retrospect to think, as his interviewer, Heinrich von Staden, once said, that Hally could grow up to be Athol himself. If this is true, then it is also true that the play is hopeful.

One sign of hope is that the violence in the play is restrained. Sam does not beat Hally for his humiliation of him, although he probably would like to. And no one in the play makes a move to be physically threatening to Sam. Faint as they are, such signs are signs of hope. And as Zakes Mokae has said about the situation in his homeland, "One is always optimistic. It can't go on forever." Now it is finally coming to an end.

"MASTER HAROLD" . . . and the boys in Performance

The world premiere of *"MASTER HAROLD" . . . and the boys* was at the Yale Repertory Theatre in March 1982. Fugard himself directed the play, with Zakes Mokae as Sam, Danny Glover as Willie, and Željko Ivanek as Hally. It was the first of his plays to premiere outside South Africa. Fugard chose New Haven in part because the play's setting was so personal that he feared it might disturb his brother and sister if it were produced first in South Africa. The setting was a bright tea room — a restaurant that serves light meals — interpreted to look like the tea room Fugard's mother actually ran in Port Elizabeth when he was a child. The space was open, the walls a whitish hue, everything simple and plain in decoration.

New York Times critic Frank Rich reviewed the premiere, saying, "*'MASTER HAROLD' . . . and the boys* is only an anecdote, really, and it's often as warm and musical as the men's dance. But somewhere along the way it rises up and breaks over the audience like a storm." Alan Stern of the *Boston Phoenix* linked the play with Greek tragedy:

> One reason for the play's potency is that, as in Greek tragedy, the events seem preordained — they're the by-product of social forces and human nature. Even as he spits in Sam's face, Hally realizes the magnitude of his action, that he is the one who will be harmed by it. And yet he can't help himself. Power corrupts, and in a society that sanctions the domination of one man — or set of men — over another, all relationships, even the promising ones, are poisoned.

Zakes Mokae and Danny Glover starred in the Broadway production in May 1982. After a brief period in which it was banned, the play was produced in Johannesburg, South Africa, in March 1983 with a South African cast. Joseph Lelyveld, in the *New York Times*, said of that production: "Athol Fugard's confessional drama about a white adolescent's initiation in the uses of racial power has come home to South Africa, and it left its multiracial audience . . . visibly shaken and stunned. . . . Many, blacks and whites, were crying."

The play was televised in 1984 with Matthew Broderick as Hally. It has had revivals in 1985 by the Trinity Repertory Company in Providence, in 1986 by the Boston Shakespeare Company in Boston, and in 1987 at the American Stage Festival in Milford, New Hampshire. These productions, although without Fugard's direction and without a "star" cast, had the same effect on their audiences as the major productions in New York and Johannesburg. Clifford Gallo in the *Boston Globe* called the American Stage production "a devastating look at the loss of racial innocence in a nation where political and social inequality are the norm."

Athol Fugard (b. 1932)
"MASTER HAROLD" . . . AND THE BOYS   1982

Characters

WILLIE
SAM
HALLY

(*The St. George's Park Tea Room on a wet and windy Port Elizabeth afternoon.*)

(*Tables and chairs have been cleared and are stacked on one side except for one which stands apart with a single chair. On this table a knife, fork, spoon and side plate in anticipation of a simple meal, together with a pile of comic books.*)

(*Other elements: a serving counter with a few stale cakes under glass and a not very impressive display of sweets, cigarettes and cool drinks, etc.; a few cardboard advertising handouts — Cadbury's Chocolate, Coca-Cola — and a blackboard on which an untrained hand has chalked up the prices of Tea, Coffee, Scones, Milkshakes — all flavors — and Cool Drinks; a few sad ferns in pots; a telephone; an old-style jukebox.*)

(*There is an entrance on one side and an exit into a kitchen on the other.*)

(*Leaning on the solitary table, his head cupped in one hand as he pages through one of the comic books, is Sam. A black man in his mid-forties. He wears the white coat of a waiter. Behind him on his knees, mopping down the floor with a bucket of water and a rag, is Willie. Also black and about the same age as Sam. He has his sleeves and trousers rolled up.*)

(*The year: 1950.*)

WILLIE (*singing as he works*): "She was scandalizin' my name,
She took my money
She called me honey
But she was scandalizin' my name.
Called it love but was playin' a game. . . ."

(*He gets up and moves the bucket. Stands thinking for a moment, then, raising his arms to hold an imag-*inary partner, he launches into an intricate ballroom dance step. Although a mildly comic figure, he reveals a reasonable degree of accomplishment.*)

Hey, Sam.

(*Sam, absorbed in the comic book, does not respond.*)

Hey, Boet° Sam!

(*Sam looks up.*)

I'm getting it. The quickstep. Look now and tell me. (*He repeats the step.*) Well?
SAM (*encouragingly*): Show me again.
WILLIE: Okay, count for me.
SAM: Ready?
WILLIE: Ready.
SAM: Five, six, seven, eight. . . . (*Willie starts to dance.*) A-n-d one two three four . . . and one two three four. . . . (*Ad libbing as Willie dances.*) Your shoulders, Willie . . . your shoulders! Don't look down! Look happy, Willie! Relax, Willie!
WILLIE (*desperate but still dancing*): I am relax.
SAM: No, you're not.
WILLIE (*he falters*): Ag no man, Sam! Mustn't talk. You make me make mistakes.
SAM: But you're stiff.
WILLIE: Yesterday I'm not straight . . . today I'm too stiff!
SAM: Well, you are. You asked me and I'm telling you.
WILLIE: Where?
SAM: Everywhere. Try to glide through it.
WILLIE: Glide?
SAM: Ja, make it smooth. And give it more style. It must look like you're enjoying yourself.
WILLIE (*emphatically*): I wasn't.
SAM: Exactly.
WILLIE: How can I enjoy myself? Not straight, too

Boet: Brother.

stiff and now it's also glide, give it more style, make it smooth. . . . Haai! Is hard to remember all those things, Boet Sam.

SAM: That's your trouble. You're trying too hard.

WILLIE: I try hard because it *is* hard.

SAM: But don't let me see it. The secret is to make it look easy. Ballroom must look happy, Willie, not like hard work. It must. . . . Ja! . . . it must look like romance.

WILLIE: Now another one! What's romance?

SAM: Love story with happy ending. A handsome man in tails, and in his arms, smiling at him, a beautiful lady in evening dress!

WILLIE: Fred Astaire, Ginger Rogers.

SAM: You got it. Tapdance or ballroom, it's the same. Romance. In two weeks' time when the judges look at you and Hilda, they must see a man and a woman who are dancing their way to a happy ending. What I saw was you holding her like you were frightened she was going to run away.

WILLIE: Ja! Because that is what she wants to do! I got no romance left for Hilda anymore, Boet Sam.

SAM: Then pretend. When you put your arms around Hilda, imagine she is Ginger Rogers.

WILLIE: With no teeth? You try.

SAM: Well, just remember, there's only two weeks left.

WILLIE: I know, I know! (*To the jukebox.*) I do it better with music. You got sixpence for Sarah Vaughan?

SAM: That's a slow foxtrot. You're practicing the quickstep.

WILLIE: I'll practice slow foxtrot.

SAM (*shaking his head*): It's your turn to put money in the jukebox.

WILLIE: I only got bus fare to go home. (*He returns disconsolately to his work.*) Love story and happy ending! She's doing it all right, Boet Sam, but is not me she's giving happy endings. Fuckin' whore! Three nights now she doesn't come practice. I wind up gramophone, I get record ready and I sit and wait. What happens? Nothing. Ten o'clock I start dancing with my pillow. You try and practice romance by yourself, Boet Sam. Struesgod, she doesn't come tonight I take back my dress and ballroom shoes and I find me new partner. Size twenty-six. Shoes size seven. And now she's also making trouble for me with the baby again. Reports me to Child Wellfed, that I'm not giving her money. She lies! Every week I am giving her money for milk. And how do I know is my baby? Only his hair looks like me. She's fucking around all the time I turn my back. Hilda Samuels is a bitch! (*Pause.*) Hey, Sam!

SAM: Ja.

WILLIE: You listening?

SAM: Ja.

WILLIE: So what you say?

SAM: About Hilda?

WILLIE: Ja.

SAM: When did you last give her a hiding?

WILLIE (*reluctantly*): Sunday night.

SAM: And today is Thursday.

WILLIE (*he knows what's coming*): Okay.

SAM: Hiding on Sunday night, then Monday, Tuesday, and Wednesday she doesn't come to practice . . . and you are asking me why?

WILLIE: I said okay, Boet Sam!

SAM: You hit her too much. One day she's going to leave you for good.

WILLIE: So? She makes me the hell-in too much.

SAM (*emphasizing his point*): *Too* much and *too* hard. You had the same trouble with Eunice.

WILLIE: Because she also make the hell-in, Boet Sam. She never got the steps right. Even the waltz.

SAM: Beating her up every time she makes a mistake in the waltz? (*Shaking his head.*) No, Willie! That takes the pleasure out of ballroom dancing.

WILLIE: Hilda is not too bad with the waltz, Boet Sam. Is the quickstep where the trouble starts.

SAM (*teasing him gently*): How's your pillow with the quickstep?

WILLIE (*ignoring the tease*): Good! And why? Because it got no legs. That's her trouble. She can't move them quick enough, Boet Sam. I start the record and before halfway Count Basie is already winning. Only time we catch up with him is when gramophone runs down. (*Sam laughs.*) Haaikona, Boet Sam, is not funny.

SAM (*snapping his fingers*): I got it! Give her a handicap.

WILLIE: What's that?

SAM: Give her a ten-second start and then let Count Basie go. Then I put my money on her. Hot favorite in the Ballroom Stakes: Hilda Samuels ridden by Willie Malopo.

WILLIE (*turning away*): I'm not talking to you no more.

SAM (*relenting*): Sorry, Willie. . . .

WILLIE: It's finish between us.

SAM: Okay, okay . . . I'll stop.

WILLIE: You can also fuck off.

SAM: Willie, listen! I want to help you!

WILLIE: No more jokes?

SAM: I promise.

WILLIE: Okay. Help me.

SAM (*his turn to hold an imaginary partner*): Look and learn. Feet together. Back straight. Body relaxed. Right hand placed gently in the small of her back and wait for the music. Don't start worrying about making mistakes or the judges or the other competitors. It's just you, Hilda and the music, and you're going to have a good time. What Count Basie do you play?

WILLIE: "You the cream in my coffee, you the salt in my stew."

SAM: Right. Give it to me in strict tempo.

WILLIE: Ready?

SAM: Ready.

WILLIE: A-n-d . . . (*Singing.*)
"You the cream in my coffee.
You the salt in my stew.
You will always be my necessity.
I'd be lost without you. . . ." (*etc.*)

(*Sam launches into the quickstep. He is obviously a much more accomplished dancer than Willie. Hally enters. A seventeen-year-old white boy. Wet raincoat and school case. He stops and watches Sam. The demonstration comes to an end with a flourish. Applause from Hally and Willie.*)

HALLY: Bravo! No question about it. First place goes to Mr. Sam Semela.

WILLIE (*in total agreement*): You was gliding with style, Boet Sam.

HALLY (*cheerfully*): How's it, chaps?

SAM: Okay, Hally.

WILLIE (*springing to attention like a soldier and saluting*): At your service, Master Harold!

HALLY: Not long to the big event, hey!

SAM: Two weeks.

HALLY: You nervous?

SAM: No.

HALLY: Think you stand a chance?

SAM: Let's just say I'm ready to go out there and dance.

HALLY: It looked like it. What about you, Willie?

(*Willie groans.*)

What's the matter?

SAM: He's got leg trouble.

HALLY (*innocently*): Oh, sorry to hear that, Willie.

WILLIE: Boet Sam! You promised. (*Willie returns to his work.*)

(*Hally deposits his school case and takes off his raincoat. His clothes are a little neglected and untidy: black blazer with school badge, gray flannel trousers in need of an ironing, khaki shirt and tie, black shoes. Sam has fetched a towel for Hally to dry his hair.*)

HALLY: God, what a lousy bloody day. It's coming down cats and dogs out there. Bad for business, chaps. . . . (*Conspiratorial whisper.*) . . . but it also means we're in for a nice quiet afternoon.

SAM: You can speak loud. Your Mom's not here.

HALLY: Out shopping?

SAM: No. The hospital.

HALLY: But it's Thursday. There's no visiting on Thursday afternoons. Is my Dad okay?

SAM: Sounds like it. In fact, I think he's going home.

HALLY (*stopped short by Sam's remark*): What do you mean?

SAM: The hospital phoned.

HALLY: To say what?

SAM: I don't know. I just heard your Mom talking.

HALLY: So what makes you say he's going home?

SAM: It sounded as if they were telling her to come and fetch him.

(*Hally thinks about what Sam has said for a few seconds.*)

HALLY: When did she leave?

SAM: About an hour ago. She said she would phone you. Want to eat?

(*Hally doesn't respond.*)

Hally, want your lunch?

HALLY: I suppose so. (*His mood has changed.*) What's on the menu? . . . as if I don't know.

SAM: Soup, followed by meat pie and gravy.

HALLY: Today's?

SAM: No.

HALLY: And the soup?

SAM: Nourishing pea soup.

HALLY: Just the soup. (*The pile of comic books on the table.*) And these?

SAM: For your Dad. Mr. Kempston brought them.

HALLY: You haven't been reading them, have you?

SAM: Just looking.

HALLY (*examining the comics*): Jungle Jim . . . Batman and Robin . . . Tarzan . . . God, what rubbish! Mental pollution. Take them away.

(*Sam exits waltzing into the kitchen. Hally turns to Willie.*)

HALLY: Did you hear my Mom talking on the telephone, Willie?

WILLIE: No, Master Hally. I was at the back.

HALLY: And she didn't say anything to you before she left?

WILLIE: She said I must clean the floors.

HALLY: I mean about my Dad.

WILLIE: She didn't say nothing to me about him, Master Hally.

HALLY (*with conviction*): No! It can't be. They said he needed at least another three weeks of treatment.

Sam's definitely made a mistake. (*Rummages through his school case, finds a book and settles down at the table to read.*) So, Willie!

WILLIE: Yes, Master Hally! Schooling okay today?

HALLY: Yes, okay. . . . (*He thinks about it.*) . . . No, not really. Ag, what's the difference? I don't care. And Sam says you've got problems.

WILLIE: Big problems.

HALLY: Which leg is sore?

(*Willie groans.*)

Both legs.

WILLIE: There is nothing wrong with my legs. Sam is just making jokes.

HALLY: So then you *will* be in the competition.

WILLIE: Only if I can find a partner.

HALLY: But what about Hilda?

SAM (*returning with a bowl of soup*): She's the one who's got trouble with her legs.

HALLY: What sort of trouble, Willie?

SAM: From the way he describes it, I think the lady has gone a bit lame.

HALLY: Good God! Have you taken her to see a doctor?

SAM: I think a vet would be better.

HALLY: What do you mean?

SAM: What do you call it again when a racehorse goes very fast?

HALLY: Gallop?

SAM: That's it!

WILLIE: Boet Sam!

HALLY: "A gallop down the homestretch to the winning post." But what's that got to do with Hilda?

SAM: Count Basie always gets there first.

(*Willie lets fly with his slop rag. It misses Sam and hits Hally.*)

HALLY (*furious*): For Christ's sake, Willie! What the hell do you think you're doing?

WILLIE: Sorry, Master Hally, but it's him. . . .

HALLY: Act your bloody age! (*Hurls the rag back at Willie.*) Cut out the nonsense now and get on with your work. And you too, Sam. Stop fooling around.

(*Sam moves away.*)

No. Hang on. I haven't finished! Tell me exactly what my Mom said.

SAM: I have. "When Hally comes, tell him I've gone to the hospital and I'll phone him."

HALLY: She didn't say anything about taking my Dad home?

SAM: No. It's just that when she was talking on the phone. . . .

HALLY (*interrupting him*): No, Sam. They can't be discharging him. She would have said so if they

were. In any case, we saw him last night and he wasn't in good shape at all. Staff nurse even said there was talk about taking more X-rays. And now suddenly today he's better? If anything, it sounds more like a bad turn to me . . . which I sincerely hope it isn't. Hang on . . . how long ago did you say she left?

SAM: Just before two . . . (*His wrist watch.*) . . . hour and a half.

HALLY: I know how to settle it. (*Behind the counter to the telephone. Talking as he dials.*) Let's give her ten minutes to get to the hospital, ten minutes to load him up, another ten, at the most, to get home, and another ten to get him inside. Forty minutes. They should have been home for at least half an hour already. (*Pause — he waits with the receiver to his ear.*) No reply, chaps. And you know why? Because she's at his bedside in hospital helping him pull through a bad turn. You definitely heard wrong.

SAM: Okay.

(*As far as Hally is concerned, the matter is settled. He returns to his table, sits down, and divides his attention between the book and his soup. Sam is at his school case and picks up a textbook.*)

Modern Graded Mathematics for Standards Nine and Ten. (*Opens it at random and laughs at something he sees.*) Who is this supposed to be?

HALLY: Old fart-face Prentice.

SAM: Teacher?

HALLY: Thinks he is. And believe me, that is not a bad likeness.

SAM: Has he seen it?

HALLY: Yes.

SAM: What did he say?

HALLY: Tried to be clever, as usual. Said I was no Leonardo da Vinci and that bad art had to be punished. So, six of the best, and his are bloody good.

SAM: On your bum?

HALLY: Where else? The days when I got them on my hands are gone forever, Sam.

SAM: With your trousers down!

HALLY: No. He's not quite that barbaric.

SAM: That's the way they do it in jail.

HALLY (*flicker of morbid interest*): Really?

SAM: Ja. When the magistrate sentences you to "strokes with a light cane."

HALLY: Go on.

SAM: They make you lie down on a bench. One policeman pulls down your trousers and holds your ankles, another one pulls your shirt over your head and holds your arms. . . .

HALLY: Thank you! That's enough.

SAM: . . . and the one that gives you the strokes talks to you gently and for a long time between each one. (*He laughs.*)

HALLY: I've heard enough, Sam! Jesus! It's a bloody awful world when you come to think of it. People can be real bastards.

SAM: That's the way it is, Hally.

HALLY: It doesn't *have* to be that way. There is something called progress, you know. We don't exactly burn people at the stake anymore.

SAM: Like Joan of Arc.

HALLY: Correct. If she was captured today, she'd be given a fair trial.

SAM: And then the death sentence.

HALLY (*a world-weary sigh*): I know, I know! I oscillate between hope and despair for this world as well, Sam. But things will change, you wait and see. One day somebody is going to get up and give history a kick up the backside and get it going again.

SAM: Like who?

HALLY (*after thought*): They're called social reformers. Every age, Sam, has got its social reformer. My history book is full of them.

SAM: So where's ours?

HALLY: Good question. And I hate to say it, but the answer is: I don't know. Maybe he hasn't even been born yet. Or is still only a babe in arms at his mother's breast. God, what a thought.

SAM: So we just go on waiting.

HALLY: Ja, looks like it. (*Back to his soup and the book.*)

SAM (*reading from the textbook*): "Introduction: In some mathematical problems only the magnitude. . . ." (*He mispronounces the word "magnitude."*)

HALLY (*correcting him without looking up*): Magnitude.

SAM: What's it mean?

HALLY: How big it is. The size of the thing.

SAM (*reading*): ". . . magnitude of the quantities is of importance. In other problems we need to know whether these quantities are negative or positive. For example, whether there is a debit or credit bank balance . . ."

HALLY: Whether you're broke or not.

SAM: ". . . whether the temperature is above or below Zero. . . ."

HALLY: Naught degrees. Cheerful state of affairs! No cash and you're freezing to death. Mathematics won't get you out of that one.

SAM: "All these quantities are called . . ." (*spelling the word*) . . . s-c-a-l. . . .

HALLY: Scalars.

SAM: Scalars! (*Shaking his head with a laugh.*) You understand all that?

HALLY (*turning a page*): No. And I don't intend to try.

SAM: So what happens when the exams come?

HALLY: Failing a maths exam isn't the end of the world, Sam. How many times have I told you that examination results don't measure intelligence?

SAM: I would say about as many times as you've failed one of them.

HALLY (*mirthlessly*): Ha, ha, ha.

SAM (*simultaneously*): Ha, ha, ha.

HALLY: Just remember Winston Churchill didn't do particularly well at school.

SAM: You've also told me that one many times.

HALLY: Well, it just so happens to be the truth.

SAM (*enjoying the word*): Magnitude! Magnitude! Show me how to use it.

HALLY (*after thought*): An intrepid social reformer will not be daunted by the magnitude of the task he has undertaken.

SAM (*impressed*): Couple of jaw-breakers in there!

HALLY: I gave you three for the price of one. Intrepid, daunted, and magnitude. I did that once in an exam. Put five of the words I had to explain in one sentence. It was half a page long.

SAM: Well, I'll put my money on you in the English exam.

HALLY: Piece of cake. Eighty percent without even trying.

SAM (*another textbook from Hally's case*): And history?

HALLY: So-so. I'll scrape through. In the fifties if I'm lucky.

SAM: You didn't do too badly last year.

HALLY: Because we had World War One. That at least has some action. You try to find that in the South African Parliamentary system.

SAM (*reading from the history textbook*): "Napoleon and the principle of equality." Hey! This sounds interesting. "After concluding peace with Britain in 1802, Napoleon used a brief period of calm to in-sti-tute . . ."

HALLY: Introduce.

SAM: ". . . many reforms. Napoleon regarded all people as equal before the law and wanted them to have equal opportunities for advancement. All ves-ti-ges of the feu-dal sys-tem with its oppression of the poor were abol-ished." Vestiges, feudal system, and abolished. I'm all right on oppression.

HALLY: I'm thinking. He swept away . . . abolished . . . the last remains . . . vestiges . . . of the bad old days . . . feudal system.

SAM: Ha! There's the social reformer we're waiting for. He sounds like a man of some magnitude.

HALLY: I'm not so sure about that. It's a damn good title for a book, though. A man of magnitude!

SAM: He sounds pretty big to me, Hally.

HALLY: Don't confuse historical significance with greatness. But maybe I'm being a bit prejudiced. Have a look in there and you'll see he's two chapters long. And hell! . . . has he only got dates, Sam, all of which you've got to remember! This campaign and that campaign, and then, because of all the fighting, the next thing is we get Peace Treaties all over the place. And what's the end of the story? Battle of Waterloo, which he loses. Wasn't worth it. No, I don't know about him as a man of magnitude.

SAM: Then who would you say was?

HALLY: To answer that, we need a definition of greatness, and I suppose that would be somebody who . . . somebody who benefited all mankind.

SAM: Right. But like who?

HALLY (*he speaks with total conviction*): Charles Darwin. Remember him? That big book from the library. *The Origin of the Species.*

SAM: Him?

HALLY: Yes. For his Theory of Evolution.

SAM: You didn't finish it.

HALLY: I ran out of time. I didn't finish it because my two weeks was up. But I'm going to take it out again after I've digested what I read. It's safe. I've hidden it away in the Theology section. Nobody ever goes in there. And anyway who are you to talk? You hardly even looked at it.

SAM: I tried. I looked at the chapters in the beginning and I saw one called "The Struggle for an Existence." Ah ha, I thought. At last! But what did I get? Something called the mistiltoe which needs the apple tree and there's too many seeds and all are going to die except one . . . ! No, Hally.

HALLY (*intellectually outraged*): What do you mean, No! The poor man had to start somewhere. For God's sake, Sam, he revolutionized science. Now we know.

SAM: What?

HALLY: Where we come from and what it all means.

SAM: And that's a benefit to mankind? Anyway, I still don't believe it.

HALLY: God, you're impossible. I showed it to you in black and white.

SAM: Doesn't mean I got to believe it.

HALLY: It's the likes of you that kept the Inquisition in business. It's called bigotry. Anyway, that's my man of magnitude. Charles Darwin! Who's yours?

SAM (*without hesitation*): Abraham Lincoln.

HALLY: I might have guessed as much. Don't get sentimental, Sam. You've never been a slave, you know. And anyway we freed your ancestors here in South Africa long before the Americans. But if you want to thank somebody on their behalf, do it to Mr. William Wilberforce.° Come on. Try again. I want a real genius.

(*Now enjoying himself, and so is Sam. Hally goes behind the counter and helps himself to a chocolate.*)

SAM: William Shakespeare.

HALLY (*no enthusiasm*): Oh. So you're also one of them, are you? You're basing that opinion on only one play, you know. You've only read my *Julius Caesar* and even I don't understand half of what they're talking about. They should do what they did with the old Bible: bring the language up to date.

SAM: That's all you've got. It's also the only one *you've* read.

HALLY: I know. I admit it. That's why I suggest we reserve our judgment until we've checked up on a few others. I've got a feeling, though, that by the end of this year one is going to be enough for me, and I can give you the names of twenty-nine other chaps in the Standard Nine class of the Port Elizabeth Technical College who feel the same. But if you want him, you can have him. My turn now. (*Pacing.*) This is a damned good exercise, you know! It started off looking like a simple question and here it's got us really probing into the intellectual heritage of our civilization.

SAM: So who is it going to be?

HALLY: My next man . . . and he gets the title on two scores: social reform and literary genius . . . is Leo Nikolaevich Tolstoy.

SAM: That Russian.

HALLY: Correct. Remember the picture of him I showed you?

SAM: With the long beard.

HALLY (*trying to look like Tolstoy*): And those burning, visionary eyes. My God, the face of a social prophet if ever I saw one! And remember my words when I showed it to you? Here's a *man,* Sam!

SAM: Those were words, Hally.

HALLY: Not many intellectuals are prepared to shovel manure with the peasants and then go home and write a "little book" called *War and Peace.* Incidentally, Sam, he was somebody else who, to quote, ". . . did not distinguish himself scholastically."

SAM: Meaning?

HALLY: He was also no good at school.

SAM: Like you and Winston Churchill.

HALLY (*mirthlessly*): Ha, ha, ha.

Mr. William Wilberforce: (1759–1833), British statesman who supported a bill outlawing the slave trade and suppressing slavery in the British Empire.

SAM (*simultaneously*): Ha, ha, ha.

HALLY: Don't get clever, Sam. That man freed his serfs of his own free will.

SAM: No argument. He was a somebody, all right. I accept him.

HALLY: I'm sure Count Tolstoy will be very pleased to hear that. Your turn. Shoot. (*Another chocolate from behind the counter.*) I'm waiting, Sam.

SAM: I've got him.

HALLY: Good. Submit your candidate for examination.

SAM: Jesus.

HALLY (*stopped dead in his tracks*): Who?

SAM: Jesus Christ.

HALLY: Oh, come on, Sam!

SAM: The Messiah.

HALLY: Ja, but still . . . No, Sam. Don't let's get started on religion. We'll just spend the whole afternoon arguing again. Suppose I turn around and say Mohammed?

SAM: All right.

HALLY: You can't have them both on the same list!

SAM: Why not? You like Mohammed, I like Jesus.

HALLY: I *don't* like Mohammed. I never have. I was merely being hypothetical. As far as I'm concerned, the Koran is as bad as the Bible. No. Religion is out! I'm not going to waste my time again arguing with you about the existence of God. You know perfectly well I'm an atheist . . . and I've got homework to do.

SAM: Okay, I take him back.

HALLY: You've got time for one more name.

SAM (*after thought*): I've got one I know we'll agree on. A simple straightforward great Man of Magnitude . . . and no arguments. And *he* really *did* benefit all mankind.

HALLY: I wonder. After your last contribution I'm beginning to doubt whether anything in the way of an intellectual agreement is possible between the two of us. Who is he?

SAM: Guess.

HALLY: Socrates? Alexandre Dumas? Karl Marx, Dostoevsky? Nietzsche?

(*Sam shakes his head after each name.*)

Give me a clue.

SAM: The letter *P* is important. . . .

HALLY: Plato!

SAM: . . . and his name begins with an *F*.

HALLY: I've got it. Freud and Psychology.

SAM: No. I didn't understand him.

HALLY: That makes two of us.

SAM: Think of moldy apricot jam.

HALLY (*after a delighted laugh*): Penicillin and Sir Alexander Fleming! And the title of the book: The

Microbe Hunters. (*Delighted.*) Splendid, Sam! Splendid. For once we are in total agreement. The major breakthrough in medical science in the Twentieth Century. If it wasn't for him, we might have lost the Second World War. It's deeply gratifying, Sam, to know that I haven't been wasting my time in talking to you. (*Strutting around proudly.*) Tolstoy may have educated his peasants, but I've educated you.

SAM: Standard Four to Standard Nine.

HALLY: Have we been at it as long as that?

SAM: Yep. And my first lesson was geography.

HALLY (*intrigued*): Really? I don't remember.

SAM: My room there at the back of the old Jubilee Boarding House. I had just started working for your Mom. Little boy in short trousers walks in one afternoon and asks me seriously: "Sam, do you want to see South Africa?" Hey man! Sure I wanted to see South Africa!

HALLY: Was that me?

SAM: . . . So the next thing I'm looking at a map you had just done for homework. It was your first one and you were very proud of yourself.

HALLY: Go on.

SAM: Then came my first lesson. "Repeat after me, Sam: Gold in the Transvaal, mealies in the Free State, sugar in Natal, and grapes in the Cape." I still know it!

HALLY: Well, I'll be buggered. So that's how it all started.

SAM: And your next map was one with all the rivers and the mountains they came from. The Orange, the Vaal, the Limpopo, the Zambezi. . . .

HALLY: You've got a phenomenal memory!

SAM: You should be grateful. That is why you started passing your exams. You tried to be better than me.

(*They laugh together. Willie is attracted by the laughter and joins them.*)

HALLY: The old Jubilee Boarding House. Sixteen rooms with board and lodging, rent in advance and one week's notice. I haven't thought about it for donkey's years . . . and I don't think that's an accident. God, was I glad when we sold it and moved out. Those years are not remembered as the happiest ones of an unhappy childhood.

WILLIE (*knocking on the table and trying to imitate a woman's voice*): "Hally, are you there?"

HALLY: Who's that supposed to be?

WILLIE: "What you doing in there, Hally? Come out at once!"

HALLY (*to Sam*): What's he talking about?

SAM: Don't you remember?

WILLIE: "Sam, Willie . . . is he in there with you boys?"

SAM: Hiding away in our room when your mother was looking for you.

HALLY (*another good laugh*): Of course! I used to crawl and hide under your bed! But finish the story, Willie. Then what used to happen? You chaps would give the game away by telling her I was in there with you. So much for friendship.

SAM: We couldn't lie to her. She knew.

HALLY: Which meant I got another rowing for hanging around the "servants' quarters." I think I spent more time in there with you chaps than anywhere else in that dump. And do you blame me? Nothing but bloody misery wherever you went. Somebody was always complaining about the food, or my mother was having a fight with Micky Nash because she'd caught her with a petty officer in her room. Maud Meiring was another one. Remember those two? They were prostitutes, you know. Soldiers and sailors from the troopships. Bottom fell out of the business when the war ended. God, the flotsam and jetsam that life washed up on our shores! No joking, if it wasn't for your room, I would have been the first certified ten-year-old in medical history. Ja, the memories are coming back now. Walking home from school and thinking: "What can I do this afternoon?" Try out a few ideas, but sooner or later I'd end up in there with you fellows. I bet you I could still find my way to your room with my eyes closed. (*He does exactly that.*) Down the corridor ... telephone on the right, which my Mom keeps locked because somebody is using it on the sly and not paying ... past the kitchen and unappetizing cooking smells ... around the corner into the backyard, hold my breath again because there are more smells coming when I pass your lavatory, then into that little passageway, first door on the right and into your room. How's that?

SAM: Good. But, as usual, you forgot to knock.

HALLY: Like that time I barged in and caught you and Cynthia ... at it. Remember? God, was I embarrassed! I didn't know what was going on at first.

SAM: Ja, that taught you a lesson.

HALLY: And about a lot more than knocking on doors, I'll have you know, and I don't mean geography either. Hell, Sam, couldn't you have waited until it was dark?

SAM: No.

HALLY: Was it that urgent?

SAM: Yes, and if you don't believe me, wait until your time comes.

HALLY: No, thank you. I am not interested in girls. (*Back to his memories. ... Using a few chairs he re-creates the room as he lists the items.*) A gray little room with a cold cement floor. Your bed against that wall ... and I now know why the mattress sags so much! ... Willie's bed ... it's propped up on bricks because one leg is broken ... that wobbly little table with the washbasin and jug of water ... Yes! ... stuck to the wall above it are some pin-up pictures from magazines. Joe Louis. ...

WILLIE: Brown Bomber. World Title. (*Boxing pose.*) Three rounds and knockout.

HALLY: Against who?

SAM: Max Schmeling.

HALLY: Correct. I can also remember Fred Astaire and Ginger Rogers, and Rita Hayworth in a bathing costume which always made me hot and bothered when I looked at it. Under Willie's bed is an old suitcase with all his clothes in a mess, which is why I never hide there. Your things are neat and tidy in a trunk next to your bed, and on it there is a picture of you and Cynthia in your ballroom clothes, your first silver cup for third place in a competition and an old radio which doesn't work anymore. Have I left out anything?

SAM: No.

HALLY: Right, so much for the stage directions. Now the characters. (*Sam and Willie move to their appropriate positions in the bedroom.*) Willie is in bed, under his blankets with his clothes on, complaining nonstop about something, but we can't make out a word of what he's saying because he's got his head under the blankets as well. You're on your bed trimming your toenails with a knife — not a very edifying sight — and as for me. ... What am I doing?

SAM: You're sitting on the floor giving Willie a lecture about being a good loser while you get the checkerboard and pieces ready for a game. Then you go to Willie's bed, pull off the blankets and make him play with you first because you know you're going to win, and that gives you the second game with me.

HALLY: And you certainly were a bad loser, Willie!

WILLIE: Haai!

HALLY: Wasn't he, Sam? And so slow! A game with you almost took the whole afternoon. Thank God I gave up trying to teach you how to play chess.

WILLIE: You and Sam cheated.

HALLY: I never saw Sam cheat, and mine were mostly the mistakes of youth.

WILLIE: Then how is it you two was always winning?

HALLY: Have you ever considered the possibility, Willie, that it was because we were better than you?

WILLIE: Every time better?

HALLY: Not every time. There were occasions when we deliberately let you win a game so that you would stop sulking and go on playing with us. Sam used to wink at me when you weren't looking to show me it was time to let you win.

WILLIE: So then you two didn't play fair.

HALLY: It was for your benefit, Mr. Malopo, which is more than being fair. It was an act of self-sacrifice. (*To Sam.*) But you know what my best memory is, don't you?

SAM: No.

HALLY: Come on, guess. If your memory is so good, you must remember it as well.

SAM: We got up to a lot of tricks in there, Hally.

HALLY: This one was special, Sam.

SAM: I'm listening.

HALLY: It started off looking like another of those useless nothing-to-do afternoons. I'd already been down to Main Street looking for adventure, but nothing had happened. I didn't feel like climbing trees in the Donkin Park or pretending I was a private eye and following a stranger . . . so as usual: See what's cooking in Sam's room. This time it was you on the floor. You had two thin pieces of wood and you were smoothing them down with a knife. It didn't look particularly interesting, but when I asked you what you were doing, you just said, "Wait and see, Hally. Wait . . . and see" . . . in that secret sort of way of yours, so I knew there was a surprise coming. You teased me, you bugger, by being deliberately slow and not answering my questions!

(*Sam laughs.*)

And whistling while you worked away! God, it was infuriating! I could have brained you! It was only when you tied them together in a cross and put that down on the brown paper that I realized what you were doing. "Sam is making a kite?" And when I asked you and you said, "Yes" . . . ! (*Shaking his head with disbelief.*) The sheer audacity of it took my breath away. I mean, seriously, what the hell does a black man know about flying a kite? I'll be honest with you, Sam, I had no hopes for it. If you think I was excited and happy, you got another guess coming. In fact, I was shit-scared that we were going to make fools of ourselves. When we left the boarding house to go up onto the hill, I was praying quietly that there wouldn't be any other kids around to laugh at us.

SAM (*enjoying the memory as much as Hally*): Ja, I could see that.

HALLY: I made it obvious, did I?

SAM: Ja. You refused to carry it.

HALLY: Do you blame me? Can you remember what the poor thing looked like? Tomato-box wood and brown paper! Flour and water for glue! Two of my mother's old stockings for a tail, and then all those bits and pieces of string you made me tie together so that we could fly it! Hell, no, that was now only asking for a miracle to happen.

SAM: Then the big argument when I told you to hold the string and run with it when I let go.

HALLY: I was prepared to run, all right, but straight back to the boarding house.

SAM (*knowing what's coming*): So what happened?

HALLY: Come on, Sam, you remember as well as I do.

SAM: I want to hear it from you.

(*Hally pauses. He wants to be as accurate as possible.*)

HALLY: You went a little distance from me down the hill, you held it up ready to let it go. . . . "This is it," I thought. "Like everything else in my life, here comes another fiasco." Then you shouted, "Go, Hally!" and I started to run. (*Another pause.*) I don't know how to describe it, Sam. Ja! The miracle happened! I was running, waiting for it to crash to the ground, but instead suddenly there was something alive behind me at the end of the string, tugging at it as if it wanted to be free. I looked back . . . (*Shakes his head.*) . . . I still can't believe my eyes. It was flying! Looping around and trying to climb even higher into the sky. You shouted to me to let it have more string. I did, until there was none left and I was just holding that piece of wood we had tied it to. You came up and joined me. You were laughing.

SAM: So were you. And shouting, "It works, Sam! We've done it!"

HALLY: And we had! I was so proud of us! It was the most splendid thing I had ever seen. I wished there were hundreds of kids around to watch us. The part that scared me, though, was when you showed me how to make it dive down to the ground and then just when it was on the point of crashing, swoop up again!

SAM: You didn't want to try yourself.

HALLY: Of course not! I would have been suicidal if anything had happened to it. Watching you do it made me nervous enough. I was quite happy just to see it up there with its tail fluttering behind it. You left me after that, didn't you? You explained how to get it down, we tied it to the bench so that I could sit and watch it, and you went away. I wanted you to stay, you know. I was a little scared of having to look after it by myself.

SAM (*quietly*): I had work to do, Hally.

HALLY: It was sort of sad bringing it down, Sam. And it looked sad again when it was lying there on the ground. Like something that had lost its soul. Just tomato-box wood, brown paper and two of my mother's old stockings! But, hell, I'll never forget that first moment when I saw it up there. I had a stiff neck the next day from looking up so much.

(*Sam laughs. Hally turns to him with a question he never thought of asking before.*)

Why did you make that kite, Sam?

SAM (*evenly*): I can't remember.

HALLY: Truly?

SAM: Too long ago, Hally.

HALLY: Ja, I suppose it was. It's time for another one, you know.

SAM: Why do you say that?

HALLY: Because it feels like that. Wouldn't be a good day to fly it, though.

SAM: No. You can't fly kites on rainy days.

HALLY (*He studies Sam. Their memories have made him conscious of the man's presence in his life.*): How old are you, Sam?

SAM: Two score and five.

HALLY: Strange, isn't it?

SAM: What?

HALLY: Me and you.

SAM: What's strange about it?

HALLY: Little white boy in short trousers and a black man old enough to be his father flying a kite. It's not every day you see that.

SAM: But why strange? Because the one is white and the other black?

HALLY: I don't know. Would have been just as strange, I suppose, if it had been me and my Dad . . . cripple man and a little boy! Nope! There's no chance of me flying a kite without it being strange. (*Simple statement of fact — no self-pity.*) There's a nice little short story there. "The Kite-Flyers." But we'd have to find a twist in the ending.

SAM: Twist?

HALLY: Yes. Something unexpected. The way it ended with us was too straightforward . . . me on the bench and you going back to work. There's no drama in that.

WILLIE: And me?

HALLY: You?

WILLIE: Yes me.

HALLY: You want to get into the story as well, do you? I got it! Change the title: "Afternoons in Sam's Room" . . . expand it and tell all the stories. It's on its way to being a novel. Our days in the old Jubilee. Sad in a way that they're over. I almost wish we were still in that little room.

SAM: We're still together.

HALLY: That's true. It's just that life felt the right size in there . . . not too big and not too small. Wasn't so hard to work up a bit of courage. It's got so bloody complicated since then.

(*The telephone rings. Sam answers it.*)

SAM: St. George's Park Tea Room . . . Hello, Madam . . . Yes, Madam, he's here. . . . Hally, it's your mother.

HALLY: Where is she phoning from?

SAM: Sounds like the hospital. It's a public telephone.

HALLY (*relieved*): You see! I told you. (*The telephone.*) Hello, Mom . . . Yes . . . Yes no fine. Everything's under control here. How's things with poor old Dad? . . . Has he had a bad turn? . . . What? . . . Oh, God! . . . Yes, Sam told me, but I was sure he'd made a mistake. But what's this all about, Mom? He didn't look at all good last night. How can he get better so quickly? . . . Then very obviously you must say no. Be firm with him. You're the boss. . . . You know what it's going to be like if he comes home. . . . Well then, don't blame me when I fail my exams at the end of the year. . . . Yes! How am I expected to be fresh for school when I spend half the night massaging his gammy leg? . . . So am I! . . . So tell him a white lie. Say Dr. Colley wants more X-rays of his stump. Or bribe him. We'll sneak in double tots of brandy in future. . . . What? . . . Order him to get back into bed at once! If he's going to behave like a child, treat him like one. . . . All right, Mom! I was just trying to . . . I'm sorry. . . . I said I'm sorry. . . . Quick, give me your number. I'll phone you back. (*He hangs up and waits a few seconds.*) Here we go again! (*He dials.*) I'm sorry, Mom. . . . Okay. . . . But now listen to me carefully. All it needs is for you to put your foot down. Don't take no for an answer. . . . Did you hear me? And whatever you do, don't discuss it with him. . . . Because I'm frightened you'll give in to him. . . . Yes, Sam gave me lunch. . . . I ate all of it! . . . No, Mom not a soul. It's still raining here. . . . Right, I'll tell them. I'll just do some homework and then lock up. . . . But remember now, Mom. Don't listen to anything he says. And phone me back and let me know what happens. . . . Okay. Bye, Mom. (*He hangs up. The men are staring at him.*) My Mom says that when you're finished with the floors you must do the windows. (*Pause.*) Don't misunderstand me, chaps. All I want is for him to get better. And if he was, I'd be the first person to say: "Bring him home." But he's not, and we can't give him the medical care and attention he needs at home. That's what hospitals are there for. (*Brusquely.*) So don't just stand there! Get on with it!

(*Sam clears Hally's table.*)

You heard right. My Dad wants to go home.

SAM: Is he better?

HALLY (*sharply*): No! How the hell can he be better when last night he was groaning with pain? This is not an age of miracles!

SAM: Then he should stay in hospital.

HALLY (*seething with irritation and frustration*): Tell me something I don't know, Sam. What the hell do you think I was saying to my Mom? All I can say is fuck-it-all.

SAM: I'm sure he'll listen to your Mom.

HALLY: You don't know what she's up against. He's already packed his shaving kit and pajamas and is sitting on his bed with his crutches, dressed and ready to go. I know him when he gets in that mood. If she tries to reason with him, we've had it. She's no match for him when it comes to a battle of words. He'll tie her up in knots. (*Trying to hide his true feelings.*)

SAM: I suppose it gets lonely for him in there.

HALLY: With all the patients and nurses around? Regular visits from the Salvation Army? Balls! It's ten times worse for him at home. I'm at school and my mother is here in the business all day.

SAM: He's at least got you at night.

HALLY (*before he can stop himself*): And we've got him! Please! I don't want to talk about it anymore. (*Unpacks his school case, slamming down books on the table.*) Life is just a plain bloody mess, that's all. And people are fools.

SAM: Come on, Hally.

HALLY: Yes, they are! They bloody well deserve what they get.

SAM: Then don't complain.

HALLY: Don't try to be clever, Sam. It doesn't suit you. Anybody who thinks there's nothing wrong with this world needs to have his head examined. Just when things are going along all right, without fail someone or something will come along and spoil everything. Somebody should write that down as a fundamental law of the Universe. The principle of perpetual disappointment. If there is a God who created this world, he should scrap it and try again.

SAM: All right, Hally, all right. What you got for homework?

HALLY: Bullshit, as usual. (*Opens an exercise book and reads.*) "Write five hundred words describing an annual event of cultural or historical significance."

SAM: That should be easy enough for you.

HALLY: And also plain bloody boring. You know what he wants, don't you? One of their useless old ceremonies. The commemoration of the landing of the 1820 Settlers, or if it's going to be culture, Carols by Candlelight every Christmas.

SAM: It's an impressive sight. Make a good descrip-tion, Hally. All those candles glowing in the dark and the people singing hymns.

HALLY: And it's called religious hysteria. (*Intense irritation.*) Please, Sam! Just leave me alone and let me get on with it. I'm not in the mood for games this afternoon. And remember my Mom's orders . . . you're to help Willie with the windows. Come on now, I don't want any more nonsense in here.

SAM: Okay, Hally, okay.

(*Hally settles down to his homework; determined preparations . . . pen, ruler, exercise book, dictionary, another cake . . . all of which will lead to nothing.*)

(*Sam waltzes over to Willie and starts to replace tables and chairs. He practices a ballroom step while doing so. Willie watches. When Sam is finished, Willie tries.*)

Good! But just a little bit quicker on the turn and only move in to her after she's crossed over. What about this one?

(*Another step. When Sam is finished, Willie again has a go.*)

Much better. See what happens when you just relax and enjoy yourself? Remember that in two weeks' time and you'll be all right.

WILLIE: But I haven't got partner, Boet Sam.

SAM: Maybe Hilda will turn up tonight.

WILLIE: No, Boet Sam. (*Reluctantly.*) I gave her a good hiding.

SAM: You mean a bad one.

WILLIE: Good bad one.

SAM: Then you mustn't complain either. Now you pay the price for losing your temper.

WILLIE: I also pay two pounds ten shilling entrance fee.

SAM: They'll refund you if you withdraw now.

WILLIE (*appalled*): You mean, don't dance?

SAM: Yes.

WILLIE: No! I wait too long and I practice too hard. If I find me new partner, you think I can be ready in two weeks? I ask Madam for my leave now and we practice every day.

SAM: Quickstep nonstop for two weeks. World record, Willie, but you'll be mad at the end.

WILLIE: No jokes, Boet Sam.

SAM: I'm not joking.

WILLIE: So then what?

SAM: Find Hilda. Say you're sorry and promise you won't beat her again.

WILLIE: No.

SAM: Then withdraw. Try again next year.

WILLIE: No.

SAM: Then I give up.

WILLIE: Haaikona, Boet Sam, you can't.

SAM: What do you mean, I can't? I'm telling you: I give up.

WILLIE (*adamant*): No! (*Accusingly.*) It was you who start me ballroom dancing.

SAM: So?

WILLIE: Before that I use to be happy. And is you and Miriam who bring me to Hilda and say here's partner for you.

SAM: What are you saying, Willie?

WILLIE: You!

SAM: But me what? To blame?

WILLIE: Yes.

SAM: Willie . . . ? (*Bursts into laughter.*)

WILLIE: And now all you do is make jokes at me. You wait. When Miriam leaves you is my turn to laugh. Ha! Ha! Ha!

SAM (*he can't take Willie seriously any longer*): She can leave me tonight! I know what to do. (*Bowing before an imaginary partner.*) May I have the pleasure? (*He dances and sings.*)
"Just a fellow with his pillow . . .
Dancin' like a willow . . .
In an autumn breeze. . . ."

WILLIE: There you go again!

(*Sam goes on dancing and singing.*)

Boet Sam!

SAM: There's the answer to your problem! Judges' announcement in two weeks' time: "Ladies and gentlemen, the winner in the open section . . . Mr. Willie Malopo and his pillow!"

(*This is too much for a now really angry Willie. He goes for Sam, but the latter is too quick for him and puts Hally's table between the two of them.*)

HALLY (*exploding*): For Christ's sake, you two!

WILLIE (*still trying to get at Sam*): I donner you, Sam! Struesgod!

SAM (*still laughing*): Sorry, Willie . . . Sorry. . . .

HALLY: Sam! Willie! (*Grabs his ruler and gives Willie a vicious whack on the bum.*) How the hell am I supposed to concentrate with the two of you behaving like bloody children!

WILLIE: Hit him too!

HALLY: Shut up, Willie.

WILLIE: He started jokes again.

HALLY: Get back to your work. You too, Sam. (*His ruler.*) Do you want another one, Willie?

(*Sam and Willie return to their work. Hally uses the opportunity to escape from his unsuccessful attempt at homework. He struts around like a little despot, ruler in hand, giving vent to his anger and frustration.*)

Suppose a customer had walked in then? Or the Park Superintendent. And seen the two of you be-
having like a pair of hooligans. That would have been the end of my mother's license, you know. And your jobs? Well, this is the end of it. From now on there will be no more of your ballroom nonsense in here. This is a business establishment, not a bloody New Brighton dancing school. I've been far too lenient with the two of you. (*Behind the counter for a green cool drink and a dollop of ice cream. He keeps up his tirade as he prepares it.*) But what really makes me bitter is that I allow you chaps a little freedom in here when business is bad and what do you do with it? The foxtrot! Specially you, Sam. There's more to life than trotting around a dance floor and I thought at least you knew it.

SAM: It's a harmless pleasure, Hally. It doesn't hurt anybody.

HALLY: It's also a rather simple one, you know.

SAM: You reckon so? Have you ever tried?

HALLY: Of course not.

SAM: Why don't you? Now.

HALLY: What do you mean? Me dance?

SAM: Yes. I'll show you a simple step — the waltz — then you try it.

HALLY: What will that prove?

SAM: That it might not be as easy as you think.

HALLY: I didn't say it was easy. I said it was simple — like in simple-minded, meaning mentally retarded. You can't exactly say it challenges the intellect.

SAM: It does other things.

HALLY: Such as?

SAM: Make people happy.

HALLY (*the glass in his hand*): So do American cream sodas with ice cream. For God's sake, Sam, you're not asking me to take ballroom dancing serious, are you?

SAM: Yes.

HALLY (*sigh of defeat*): Oh, well, so much for trying to give you a decent education. I've obviously achieved nothing.

SAM: You still haven't told me what's wrong with admiring something that's beautiful and then trying to do it yourself.

HALLY: Nothing. But we happen to be talking about a foxtrot, not a thing of beauty.

SAM: But that is just what I'm saying. If you were to see two champions doing, two masters of the art . . . !

HALLY: Oh God, I give up. So now it's also art!

SAM: Ja.

HALLY: There's a limit, Sam. Don't confuse art and entertainment.

SAM: So then what is art?

HALLY: You want a definition?

SAM: Ja.

HALLY (*He realizes he has got to be careful. He gives the matter a lot of thought before answering.*): Philosophers have been trying to do that for centuries. What is Art? What is Life? But basically I suppose it's . . . the giving of meaning to matter.

SAM: Nothing to do with beautiful?

HALLY: It goes beyond that. It's the giving of form to the formless.

SAM: Ja, well, maybe it's not art, then. But I still say it's beautiful.

HALLY: I'm sure the word you mean to use is entertaining.

SAM (*adamant*): No. Beautiful. And if you want proof come along to the Centenary Hall in New Brighton in two weeks' time.

(*The mention of the Centenary Hall draws Willie over to them.*)

HALLY: What for? I've seen the two of you prancing around in here often enough.

SAM (*he laughs*): This isn't the real thing, Hally. We're just playing around in here.

HALLY: So? I can use my imagination.

SAM: And what do you get?

HALLY: A lot of people dancing around and having a so-called good time.

SAM: That all?

HALLY: Well, basically it is that, surely.

SAM: No, it isn't. Your imagination hasn't helped you at all. There's a lot more to it than that. We're getting ready for the championships, Hally, not just another dance. There's going to be a lot of people, all right, and they're going to have a good time, but they'll only be spectators, sitting around and watching. It's just the competitors out there on the dance floor. Party decorations and fancy lights all around the walls! The ladies in beautiful evening dresses!

HALLY: My mother's got one of those, Sam, and, quite frankly, it's an embarrassment every time she wears it.

SAM (*undeterred*): Your imagination left out the excitement.

(*Hally scoffs.*)

Oh, yes. The finalists are not going to be out there just to have a good time. One of those couples will be the 1950 Eastern Province Champions. And your imagination left out the music.

WILLIE: Mr. Elijah Gladman Guzana and his Orchestral Jazzonions.

SAM: The sound of the big band, Hally. Trombone, trumpet, tenor and alto sax. And then, finally, your imagination also left out the climax of the evening when the dancing is finished, the judges have stopped whispering among themselves and the Master of Ceremonies collects their scorecards and goes up onto the stage to announce the winners.

HALLY: All right. So you make it sound like a bit of a do. It's an occasion. Satisfied?

SAM (*victory*): So you admit that!

HALLY: Emotionally yes, intellectually no.

SAM: Well, I don't know what you mean by that, all I'm telling you is that it is going to be *the* event of the year in New Brighton. It's been sold out for two weeks already. There's only standing room left. We've got competitors coming from Kingwilliamstown, East London, Port Alfred.

(*Hally starts pacing thoughtfully.*)

HALLY: Tell me a bit more.

SAM: I thought you weren't interested . . . intellectually.

HALLY (*mysteriously*): I've got my reasons.

SAM: What do you want to know?

HALLY: It takes place every year?

SAM: Yes. But only every third year in New Brighton. It's East London's turn to have the championships next year.

HALLY: Which, I suppose, makes it an even more significant event.

SAM: Ah ha! We're getting somewhere. Our "occasion" is now a "significant event."

HALLY: I wonder.

SAM: What?

HALLY: I wonder if I would get away with it.

SAM: But what?

HALLY (*to the table and his exercise book*): "Write five hundred words describing an annual event of cultural or historical significance." Would I be stretching poetic license a little too far if I called your ballroom championships a cultural event?

SAM: You mean . . . ?

HALLY: You think we could get five hundred words out of it, Sam?

SAM: Victor Sylvester has written a whole book on ballroom dancing.

WILLIE: You going to write about it, Master Hally?

HALLY: Yes, gentlemen, that is precisely what I am considering doing. Old Doc Bromely — he's my English teacher — is going to argue with me, of course. He doesn't like natives. But I'll point out to him that in strict anthropological terms the culture of a primitive black society includes its dancing and singing. To put my thesis in a nutshell: The war-dance has been replaced by the waltz. But it still amounts to the same thing: the release of primitive emotions through movement. Shall we give it a go?

SAM: I'm ready.

WILLIE: Me also.

HALLY: Ha! This will teach the old bugger a lesson. (*Decision taken.*) Right. Let's get ourselves organized. (*This means another cake on the table. He sits.*) I think you've given me enough general atmosphere, Sam, but to build the tension and suspense I need facts. (*Pencil poised.*)

WILLIE: Give him facts, Boet Sam.

HALLY: What you called the climax . . . how many finalists?

SAM: Six couples.

HALLY (*making notes*): Go on. Give me the picture.

SAM: Spectators seated right around the hall. (*Willie becomes a spectator.*)

HALLY: . . . and it's a full house.

SAM: At one end, on the stage, Gladman and his Orchestral Jazzonions. At the other end is a long table with the three judges. The six finalists go onto the dance floor and take up their positions. When they are ready and the spectators have settled down, the Master of Ceremonies goes to the microphone. To start with, he makes some jokes to get people laughing. . . .

HALLY: Good touch. (*As he writes.*) ". . . creating a relaxed atmosphere which will change to one of tension and drama as the climax is approached."

SAM (*onto a chair to act out the M.C.*): "Ladies and gentlemen, we come now to the great moment you have all been waiting for this evening. . . . The finals of the 1950 Eastern Province Open Ballroom Dancing Championships. But first let me introduce the finalists! Mr. and Mrs. Welcome Tchabalala from Kingwilliamstown . . ."

WILLIE (*he applauds after every name*): Is when the people clap their hands and whistle and make a lot of noise, Master Hally.

SAM: "Mr. Mulligan Njikelane and Miss Nomhle Nkonyeni of Grahamstown; Mr. and Mrs. Norman Nchinga from Port Alfred; Mr. Fats Bokolane and Miss Dina Plaatjies from East London; Mr. Sipho Dugu and Mrs. Mable Magada from Peddie; and from New Brighton our very own Mr. Willie Malopo and Miss Hilda Samuels."

(*Willie can't believe his ears. He abandons his role as spectator and scrambles into position as a finalist.*)

WILLIE: Relaxed and ready to romance!

SAM: The applause dies down. When everybody is silent, Gladman lifts up his sax, nods at the Orchestral Jazzonions. . . .

WILLIE: Play the jukebox please, Boet Sam!

SAM: I also only got bus fare, Willie.

HALLY: Hold it, everybody. (*Heads for the cash register behind the counter.*) How much is in the till, Sam?

SAM: Three shillings. Hally . . . Your Mom counted it before she left.

(*Hally hesitates.*)

HALLY: Sorry, Willie. You know how she carried on the last time I did it. We'll just have to pool our combined imaginations and hope for the best. (*Returns to the table.*) Back to work. How are the points scored, Sam?

SAM: Maximum of ten points each for individual style, deportment, rhythm, and general appearance.

WILLIE: Must I start?

HALLY: Hold it for a second, Willie. And penalties?

SAM: For what?

HALLY: For doing something wrong. Say you stumble or bump into somebody . . . do they take off any points?

SAM (*aghast*): Hally . . . !

HALLY: When you're dancing. If you and your partner collide into another couple.

(*Hally can get no further. Sam has collapsed with laughter. He explains to Willie.*)

SAM: If me and Miriam bump into you and Hilda. . . .

(*Willie joins him in another good laugh.*)

Hally, Hally . . . !

HALLY (*perplexed*): Why? What did I say?

SAM: There's no collisions out there, Hally. Nobody trips or stumbles or bumps into anybody else. That's what that moment is all about. To be one of those finalists on that dance floor is like . . . like being in a dream about a world in which accidents don't happen.

HALLY (*genuinely moved by Sam's image*): Jesus, Sam! That's beautiful!

WILLIE (*can endure waiting no longer*): I'm starting!

(*Willie dances while Sam talks.*)

SAM: Of course it is. That's what I've been trying to say to you all afternoon. And it's beautiful because that is what we want life to be like. But instead, like you said, Hally, we're bumping into each other all the time. Look at the three of us this afternoon: I've bumped into Willie, the two of us have bumped into you, you've bumped into your mother, she bumping into your Dad. . . . None of us knows the steps and there's no music playing. And it doesn't stop with us. The whole world is doing it all the time. Open a newspaper and what do you read? America has bumped into Russia, England is bumping into India, rich man bumps into poor man. Those are big collisions, Hally. They make for a lot of bruises. People get hurt in all that bumping, and we're sick and tired of it now. It's been going on for too long. Are we never going to get it right? . . . Learn to dance life like champions instead of always being just a bunch of beginners at it?

HALLY (*deep and sincere admiration of the man*): You've got a vision, Sam!

SAM: Not just me. What I'm saying to you is that everybody's got it. That's why there's only standing room left for the Centenary Hall in two weeks' time. For as long as the music lasts, we are going to see six couples get it right, the way we want life to be.

HALLY: But is that the best we can do, Sam . . . watch six finalists dreaming about the way it should be?

SAM: I don't know. But it starts with that. Without the dream we won't know what we're going for. And anyway I reckon there are a few people who have got past just dreaming about it and are trying for something real. Remember that thing we read once in the paper about the Mahatma Gandhi? Going without food to stop those riots in India?

HALLY: You're right. He certainly was trying to teach people to get the steps right.

SAM: And the Pope.

HALLY: Yes, he's another one. Our old General Smuts° as well, you know. He's also out there dancing. You know, Sam, when you come to think of it, that's what the United Nations boils down to . . . a dancing school for politicians!

SAM: And let's hope they learn.

HALLY (*a little surge of hope*): You're right. We mustn't despair. Maybe there's some hope for mankind after all. Keep it up, Willie. (*Back to his table with determination.*) This is a lot bigger than I thought. So what have we got? Yes, our title: "A World Without Collisions."

SAM: That sounds good! "A World Without Collisions."

HALLY: Subtitle: "Global Politics on the Dance Floor." No. A bit too heavy, hey? What about "Ballroom Dancing as a Political Vision"?

(*The telephone rings. Sam answers it.*)

SAM: St. George's Park Tea Room . . . Yes, Madam . . . Hally, it's your Mom.

HALLY (*back to reality*): Oh, God, yes! I'd forgotten all about that. Shit! Remember my words, Sam?

General Smuts: (1870–1950), South African statesman who fought the British in the Boer War in 1899, was instrumental in forming the Union of South Africa in 1910, and was active in the creation of the United Nations.

Just when you're enjoying yourself, someone or something will come along and wreck everything.

SAM: You haven't heard what she's got to say yet.

HALLY: Public telephone?

SAM: No.

HALLY: Does she sound happy or unhappy?

SAM: I couldn't tell. (*Pause.*) She's waiting, Hally.

HALLY (*to the telephone*): Hello, Mom . . . No, everything is okay here. Just doing my homework. . . . What's your news? . . . You've what? . . . (*Pause. He takes the receiver away from his ear for a few seconds. In the course of Hally's telephone conversation, Sam and Willie discreetly position the stacked tables and chairs. Hally places the receiver back to his ear.*) Yes, I'm still here. Oh, well, I give up now. Why did you do it, Mom? . . . Well, I just hope you know what you've let us in for. . . . (*Loudly.*) I said I hope you know what you've let us in for! It's the end of the peace and quiet we've been having. (*Softly.*) Where is he? (*Normal voice.*) He can't hear us from in there. But for God's sake, Mom, what happened? I told you to be firm with him. . . . Then you and the nurses should have held him down, taken his crutches away. . . . I know only too well he's my father! . . . I'm not being disrespectful, but I'm sick and tired of emptying stinking chamber pots full of phlegm and piss. . . . Yes, I do! When you're not there, he asks *me* to do it. . . . If you really want to know the truth, that's why I've got no appetite for my food. . . . Yes! There's a lot of things you don't know about. For your information, I still haven't got that science textbook I need. And you know why? He borrowed the money you gave me for it. . . . Because I didn't want to start another fight between you two. . . . He says that every time. . . . All right, Mom! (*Viciously.*) Then just remember to start hiding your bag away again, because he'll be at your purse before long for money for booze. And when he's well enough to come down here, you better keep an eye on the till as well, because that is also going to develop a leak. . . . Then don't complain to me when he starts his old tricks. . . . Yes, you do. I get it from you on one side and from him on the other, and it makes life hell for me. I'm not going to be the peacemaker anymore. I'm warning you now: when the two of you start fighting again, I'm leaving home. . . . Mom, if you start crying, I'm going to put down the receiver. . . . Okay. . . . (*Lowering his voice to a vicious whisper.*) Okay, Mom. I heard you. (*Desperate.*) No. . . . Because I don't want to. I'll see him when I get home! Mom! . . . (*Pause. When he speaks again, his tone changes completely. It is not simply pretense. We sense a genuine emotional conflict.*) Welcome home, chum!

. . . What's that? . . . Don't be silly, Dad. You being home is just about the best news in the world. . . . I bet you are. Bloody depressing there with everybody going on about their ailments, hey! . . . How you feeling? . . . Good. . . . Here as well, pal. Coming down cats and dogs. . . . That's right. Just the day for a kip° and a toss in your old Uncle Ned. . . . Everything's just hunky-dory on my side, Dad. . . . Well, to start with, there's a nice pile of comics for you on the counter. . . . Yes, old Kemple brought them in. *Batman and Robin, Submariner* . . . just your cup of tea. . . . I will. . . . Yes, we'll spin a few yarns tonight. . . . Okay, chum, see you in a little while. . . . No, I promise. I'll come straight home. . . . (*Pause — his mother comes back on the phone.*) Mom? Okay. I'll lock up now. . . . What? . . . Oh, the brandy . . . Yes, I'll remember! . . . I'll put it in my suitcase now, for God's sake. I know well enough what will happen if he doesn't get it. . . . (*Places a bottle of brandy on the counter.*) I *was* kind to him, Mom. I didn't say anything nasty! . . . All right. Bye. (*End of telephone conversation. A desolate Hally doesn't move. A strained silence.*)

SAM (*quietly*): That sounded like a bad bump, Hally.

HALLY (*Having a hard time controlling his emotions. He speaks carefully.*): Mind your own business, Sam.

SAM: Sorry. I wasn't trying to interfere. Shall we carry on? Hally? (*He indicates the exercise book. No response from Hally.*)

WILLIE (*also trying*): Tell him about when they give out the cups, Boet Sam.

SAM: Ja! That's another big moment. The presentation of the cups after the winners have been announced. You've got to put that in.

(*Still no response from Hally.*)

WILLIE: A big silver one, Master Hally, called floating trophy for the champions.

SAM: We always invite some big-shot personality to hand them over. Guest of honor this year is going to be His Holiness Bishop Jabulani of the All African Free Zionist Church.

(*Hally gets up abruptly, goes to his table, and tears up the page he was writing on.*)

HALLY: So much for a bloody world without collisions.

SAM: Too bad. It was on its way to being a good composition.

HALLY: Let's stop bullshitting ourselves, Sam.

SAM: Have we been doing that?

kip: Nap.

HALLY: Yes! That's what all our talk about a decent world has been . . . just so much bullshit.

SAM: We did say it was still only a dream.

HALLY: And a bloody useless one at that. Life's a fuckup and it's never going to change.

SAM: Ja, maybe that's true.

HALLY: There's no maybe about it. It's a blunt and brutal fact. All we've done this afternoon is waste our time.

SAM: Not if we'd got your homework done.

HALLY: I don't give a shit about my homework, so, for Christ's sake, just shut up about it. (*Slamming books viciously into his school case.*) Hurry up now and finish your work. I want to lock up and get out of here. (*Pause.*) And then go where? Home-sweet-fucking-home. Jesus, I hate that word.

(*Hally goes to the counter to put the brandy bottle and comics in his school case. After a moment's hesitation, he smashes the bottle of brandy. He abandons all further attempts to hide his feelings. Sam and Willie work away as unobtrusively as possible.*)

Do you want to know what is really wrong with your lovely little dream, Sam? It's not just that we are all bad dancers. That does happen to be perfectly true, but there's more to it than just that. You left out the cripples.

SAM: Hally!

HALLY (*now totally reckless*): Ja! Can't leave them out, Sam. That's why we always end up on our backsides on the dance floor. They're also out there dancing . . . like a bunch of broken spiders trying to do the quickstep! (*An ugly attempt at laughter.*) When you come to think of it, it's a bloody comical sight. I mean, it's bad enough on two legs . . . but one and a pair of crutches! Hell, no, Sam. That's guaranteed to turn that dance floor into a shambles. Why you shaking your head? Picture it, man. For once this afternoon let's use our imaginations sensibly.

SAM: Be careful, Hally.

HALLY: Of what? The truth? I seem to be the only one around here who is prepared to face it. We've had the pretty dream, it's time now to wake up and have a good long look at the way things really are. Nobody knows the steps, there's no music, the cripples are also out there tripping up everybody and trying to get into the act, and it's all called the All-Comers-How-to-Make-a-Fuckup-of-Life Championships. (*Another ugly laugh.*) Hang on, Sam! The best bit is still coming. Do you know what the winner's trophy is? A beautiful big chamber pot with roses on the side, and it's full to the brim with piss. And guess who I think is going to be this year's winner.

SAM (*almost shouting*): Stop now!

HALLY (*suddenly appalled by how far he has gone*): Why?

SAM: Hally? It's your father you're talking about.

HALLY: So?

SAM: Do you know what you've been saying?

(*Hally can't answer. He is rigid with shame. Sam speaks to him sternly.*)

No, Hally, you mustn't do it. Take back those words and ask for forgiveness! It's a terrible sin for a son to mock his father with jokes like that. You'll be punished if you carry on. Your father is your father, even if he is a . . . cripple man.

WILLIE: Yes, Master Hally. Is true what Sam say.

SAM: I understand how you are feeling, Hally, but even so. . . .

HALLY: No, you don't!

SAM: I think I do.

HALLY: And I'm telling you you don't. Nobody does. (*Speaking carefully as his shame turns to rage at Sam.*) It's your turn to be careful, Sam. Very careful! You're treading on dangerous ground. Leave me and my father alone.

SAM: I'm not the one who's been saying things about him.

HALLY: What goes on between me and my Dad is none of your business!

SAM: Then don't tell me about it. If that's all you've got to say about him, I don't want to hear.

(*For a moment Hally is at loss for a response.*)

HALLY: Just get on with your bloody work and shut up.

SAM: Swearing at me won't help you.

HALLY: Yes, it does! Mind your own fucking business and shut up!

SAM: Okay. If that's the way you want it, I'll stop trying.

(*He turns away. This infuriates Hally even more.*)

HALLY: Good. Because what you've been trying to do is meddle in something you know nothing about. All that concerns you in here, Sam, is to try and do what you get paid for — keep the place clean and serve the customers. In plain words, just get on with your job. My mother is right. She's always warning me about allowing you to get too familiar. Well, this time you've gone too far. It's going to stop right now.

(*No response from Sam.*)

You're only a servant in here, and don't forget it.

(*Still no response. Hally is trying hard to get one.*)

And as far as my father is concerned, all you need to remember is that he is your boss.

SAM (*needled at last*): No, he isn't. I get paid by your mother.

HALLY: Don't argue with me, Sam!

SAM: Then don't say he's my boss.

HALLY: He's a white man and that's good enough for you.

SAM: I'll try to forget you said that.

HALLY: Don't! Because you won't be doing me a favor if you do. I'm telling you to remember it.

(*A pause. Sam pulls himself together and makes one last effort.*)

SAM: Hally, Hally . . . ! Come on now. Let's stop before it's too late. You're right. We *are* on dangerous ground. If we're not careful, somebody is going to get hurt.

HALLY: It won't be me.

SAM: Don't be so sure.

HALLY: I don't know what you're talking about, Sam.

SAM: Yes, you do.

HALLY (*furious*): Jesus, I wish you would stop trying to tell me what I do and what I don't know.

(*Sam gives up. He turns to Willie.*)

SAM: Let's finish up.

HALLY: Don't turn your back on me! I haven't finished talking.

(*He grabs Sam by the arm and tries to make him turn around. Sam reacts with a flash of anger.*)

SAM: Don't do that, Hally! (*Facing the boy.*) All right, I'm listening. Well? What do you want to say to me?

HALLY (*pause as Hally looks for something to say*): To begin with, why don't you also start calling me Master Harold, like Willie.

SAM: Do you mean that?

HALLY: Why the hell do you think I said it?

SAM: And if I don't?

HALLY: You might just lose your job.

SAM (*quietly and very carefully*): If you make me say it once, I'll never call you anything else again.

HALLY: So? (*The boy confronts the man.*) Is that meant to be a threat?

SAM: Just telling you what will happen if you make me do that. You must decide what it means to you.

HALLY: Well, I have. It's good news. Because that is exactly what Master Harold wants from now on. Think of it as a little lesson in respect, Sam, that's long overdue, and I hope you remember it as well as you do your geography. I can tell you now that somebody who will be glad to hear I've finally given it to you will be my Dad. Yes! He agrees with my

Mom. He's always going on about it as well. "You must teach the boys to show you more respect, my son."

SAM: So now you can stop complaining about going home. Everybody is going to be happy tonight.

HALLY: That's perfectly correct. You see, you mustn't get the wrong idea about me and my Dad, Sam. We also have our good times together. Some bloody good laughs. He's got a marvelous sense of humor. Want to know what our favorite joke is? He gives out a big groan, you see, and says: "It's not fair, is it, Hally?" Then I have to ask: "What, chum?" And then he says: "A nigger's arse" ... and we both have a good laugh.

(*The men stare at him with disbelief.*)

What's the matter, Willie? Don't you catch the joke? You always were a bit slow on the uptake. It's what is called a pun. You see, fair means both light in color and to be just and decent. (*He turns to Sam.*) I thought *you* would catch it, Sam.

SAM: Oh ja, I catch it all right.

HALLY: But it doesn't appeal to your sense of humor.

SAM: Do you really laugh?

HALLY: Of course.

SAM: To please him? Make him feel good?

HALLY: No, for heavens sake! I laugh because I think it's a bloody good joke.

SAM: You're really trying hard to be ugly, aren't you? And why drag poor old Willie into it? He's done nothing to you except show you the respect you want so badly. That's also not being fair, you know ... and *I* mean just or decent.

WILLIE: It's all right, Sam. Leave it now.

SAM: It's me you're after. You should just have said "Sam's arse" ... because that's the one you're trying to kick. Anyway, how do you know it's not fair? You've never seen it. Do you want to? (*He drops his trousers and underpants and presents his backside for Hally's inspection.*) Have a good look. A real Basuto arse ... which is about as nigger as they can come. Satisfied? (*Trousers up.*) Now you can make your Dad even happier when you go home tonight. Tell him I showed you my arse and he is quite right. It's not fair. And if it will give him an even better laugh next time, I'll also let *him* have a look. Come, Willie, let's finish up and go.

(*Sam and Willie start to tidy up the tea room. Hally doesn't move. He waits for a moment when Sam passes him.*)

HALLY (*quietly*): Sam ...

(*Sam stops and looks expectantly at the boy. Hally*

spits in his face. A long and heartfelt groan from Willie. For a few seconds Sam doesn't move.)

SAM (*taking out a handkerchief and wiping his face*): It's all right, Willie.

(*To Hally.*)

Ja, well, you've done it ... Master Harold. Yes, I'll start calling you that from now on. It won't be difficult anymore. You've hurt yourself, Master Harold. I saw it coming. I warned you, but you wouldn't listen. You've just hurt yourself *bad*. And you're a coward, Master Harold. The face you should be spitting in is your father's ... but you used mine, because you think you're safe inside your fair skin ... and this time I don't mean just or decent. (*Pause, then moving violently toward Hally.*) Should I hit him, Willie?

WILLIE (*stopping Sam*): No, Boet Sam.

SAM (*violently*): Why not?

WILLIE: It won't help, Boet Sam.

SAM: I don't want to help! I want to hurt him.

WILLIE: You also hurt yourself.

SAM: And if he had done it to you, Willie?

WILLIE: Me? Spit at me like I was a dog? (*A thought that had not occurred to him before. He looks at Hally.*) Ja. Then I want to hit him. I want to hit him hard!

(*A dangerous few seconds as the men stand staring at the boy. Willie turns away, shaking his head.*)

But maybe all I do is go cry at the back. He's little boy, Boet Sam. Little *white* boy. Long trousers now, but he's still little boy.

SAM (*his violence ebbing away into defeat as quickly as it flooded*): You're right. So go on, then: groan again, Willie. You do it better than me. (*To Hally.*) You don't know all of what you've just done ... Master Harold. It's not just that you've made me feel dirtier than I've ever been in my life ... I mean, how do I wash off yours and your father's filth? ... I've also failed. A long time ago I promised myself I was going to try and do something, but you've just shown me ... Master Harold ... that I've failed. (*Pause.*) I've also got a memory of a little white boy when he was still wearing short trousers and a black man, but they're not flying a kite. It was the old Jubilee days, after dinner one night. I was in my room. You came in and just stood against the wall, looking down at the ground, and only after I'd asked you what you wanted, what was wrong, I don't know how many times, did you speak and even then so softly I almost didn't hear you. "Sam, please help me to go and fetch my Dad." Remember? He was dead drunk on the floor of the Central Hotel Bar. They'd phoned for your Mom, but you were the only one at home. And do you remember how we did it? You went in first by yourself to ask permission for me to go into the bar. Then I loaded him onto my back like a baby and carried him back to the boarding house with you following behind carrying his crutches. (*Shaking his head as he remembers.*) A crowded Main Street with all the people watching a little white boy following his drunk father on a nigger's back! I felt for that little boy . . . Master Harold. I felt for him. After that we still had to clean him up, remember? He'd messed in his trousers, so we had to clean him up and get him into bed.

HALLY (*great pain*): I love him, Sam.

SAM: I know you do. That's why I tried to stop you from saying these things about him. It would have been so simple if you could have just despised him for being a weak man. But he's your father. You love him and you're ashamed of him. You're ashamed of so much! . . . And now that's going to include yourself. That was the promise I made to myself: to try and stop that happening. (*Pause.*) After we got him to bed you came back with me to my room and sat in a corner and carried on just looking down at the ground. And for days after that! You hadn't done anything wrong, but you went around as if you owed the world an apology for being alive. I didn't like seeing that! That's not the way a boy grows up to be a man! . . . But the one person who should have been teaching you what that means was the cause of your shame. If you really want to know, that's why I made you that kite. I wanted you to look up, be proud of something, of yourself . . . (*bitter smile at the memory*) . . . and you certainly were that when I left you with it up there on the hill. Oh, ja . . . something else! . . . If you ever do write it as a short story, there *was* a twist in our ending. I couldn't sit down there and stay with you. It was a "Whites Only" bench. You were too young, too excited to notice then. But not anymore. If you're not careful . . . Master Harold . . . you're going to be sitting up there by yourself for a long time to come, and there won't be a kite in the sky. (*Sam has got nothing more to say. He exits into the kitchen, taking off his waiter's jacket.*)

WILLIE: Is bad. Is all bad in here now.

HALLY (*books into his school case, raincoat on*): Willie . . . (*It is difficult to speak.*) Will you lock up for me and look after the keys?

WILLIE: Okay.

(*Sam returns. Hally goes behind the counter and collects the few coins in the cash register. As he starts to leave. . . .*)

SAM: Don't forget the comic books.

(*Hally returns to the counter and puts them in his case. He starts to leave again.*)

SAM (*to the retreating back of the boy*): Stop . . . Hally. . . .

(*Hally stops, but doesn't turn to face him.*)

Hally . . . I've got no right to tell you what being a man means if I don't behave like one myself, and I'm not doing so well at that this afternoon. Should we try again, Hally?

HALLY: Try what?

SAM: Fly another kite, I suppose. It worked once, and this time I need it as much as you do.

HALLY: It's still raining, Sam. You can't fly kites on rainy days, remember.

SAM: So what do we do? Hope for better weather tomorrow?

HALLY (*helpless gesture*): I don't know. I don't know anything anymore.

SAM: You sure of that, Hally? Because it would be pretty hopeless if that was true. It would mean nothing has been learnt in here this afternoon, and there was a hell of a lot of teaching going on . . . one way or the other. But anyway, I don't believe you. I reckon there's one thing you know. You don't *have* to sit up there by yourself. You know what that bench means now, and you can leave it any time you choose. All you've got to do is stand up and walk away from it.

(*Hally leaves. Willie goes up quietly to Sam.*)

WILLIE: Is okay, Boet Sam. You see. Is . . . (*he can't find any better words*) . . . is going to be okay tomorrow. (*Changing his tone.*) Hey, Boet Sam! (*He is trying hard.*) You right. I think about it and you right. Tonight I find Hilda and say sorry. And make promise I won't beat her no more. You hear me, Boet Sam?

SAM: I hear you, Willie.

WILLIE: And when we practice I relax and romance with her from beginning to end. Nonstop! You watch! Two weeks' time: "First prize for promising newcomers: Mr. Willie Malopo and Miss Hilda Samuels." (*Sudden impulse.*) To hell with it! I walk home. (*He goes to the jukebox, puts in a coin and selects a record. The machine comes to life in the gray twilight, blushing its way through a spectrum of soft, romantic colors.*) How did you say it, Boet Sam? Let's dream. (*Willie sways with the music and gestures for Sam to dance.*)

(Sarah Vaughan sings.)

"Little man you're crying,
I know why you're blue,
Someone took your kiddy car away;
Better go to sleep now,
Little man you've had a busy day." *(etc., etc.)*
You lead. I follow.

(The men dance together.)

"Johnny won your marbles,
Tell you what we'll do;
Dad will get you new ones right away;
Better go to sleep now,
Little man you've had a busy day."

COMMENTARIES

Heinrich von Staden (b. 1939)
INTERVIEW WITH ATHOL FUGARD   *1982*

When "MASTER HAROLD" . . . and the boys was first produced at the Yale Repertory Theatre, Athol Fugard had the chance to respond to some questions about its significance to him. He revealed that the play was deeply personal and that through it he had been able to exorcise a demon that had haunted him for some time. In this interview, Fugard detailed his involvement with South African drama and black actors in South Africa. He also commented on the extent to which censorship and other political pressures in South Africa have made it difficult for his work to be produced in his own country.

von Staden: The bombs of fiction — Athol, aren't they more explosive than TNT?

Fugard: I'd like to believe that. You understand I've got to be careful about that one. I've got to be careful about flattering myself about the potency of the one area of activity which I've got, which is theater and being a writer.

von Staden: How often have there been productions of your plays for non-segregated audiences in South Africa?

Fugard: I've had to change my tactics in terms of that over the years. At a period when the policy on segregated audiences in South Africa was rigid and very strictly enforced, I had to make a decision whether to take on an act of silence, just be silent because I couldn't go into a theater that was decent in my terms, or whether to take on the compromising circumstances of segregated audiences simply because I felt that if a play has got something to say, at least say it. And there were years when I decided to do the latter. I did perform before segregated audiences. In a sense I regret that decision now. I think I might possibly have looked after myself — and maybe the situation — better by not accepting that compromise. But I did.

von Staden: But do you think you had a genuine choice at that time?

Fugard: I had a choice between silence or being heard.

von Staden: Let me ask you along similar lines, when you are writing a play or a novel like *Tsotsi*, do you sense constraints on the way you are writing in view of the fact that certain things are anathema to the government, also in fiction?

Fugard: I would like to believe that I have operated at the table at which I sit and write, that I have operated totally without self-censorship. Maybe some awareness of what is possible and is not possible has operated subconsciously and is deciding choices I make in terms of what I favor. I think it may be pertinent to the conversation we are having, that *"MASTER HAROLD"* . . . *and the boys* is the first play of mine in twenty-four years of writing that will have its premiere outside of South Africa. And one of the reasons why I'm doing that this time is that there are elements in *"MASTER HAROLD"* . . . *and the boys* that might have run into censorship problems. . . .

von Staden: Here you are, a person who, critics say, has achieved exceptional insight into human nature, and you never obtained a university degree. What institutions, what processes do you think contributed most to the insights you have?

Fugard: Well, I think to be a South African is in a way to be at a university that teaches you about that. The South African experience is certainly one in which, if you're prepared to keep your eyes open and look, you're going to see a lot of suffering. But then, in terms of personal specifics, I suppose for me there was a very, very important relationship, a friendship, with a black man in what I suppose is any person's most formative and definitive years, the age between eleven, ten up until the age of twenty-one. It was a black man in Port Elizabeth, and my play *"MASTER HAROLD"* . . . *and the boys* reflects something of that friendship, tries to talk about it, look at it. I left South Africa, hitchhiked through the African continent, ended up as a sailor on a ship which, apart from the officers and engineers, had a totally nonwhite, had a totally black crew, and I was a sailor in a totally black crew. There was that, I think I can't nail down any one specific traumatic incident as being totally decisive. But I could be certain that *"MASTER HAROLD"* . . . *and the boys* deals with one specific moment which I'm trying to exorcise out of my soul.

von Staden: In all of your plays and in the novel you always have a South African setting. Yet your plays and your novels, though so rooted in the specifics of the South African situation, seem to have a tremendous appeal to audiences that are largely ignorant of the situation there. To what do you ascribe that?

Fugard: You take a chance. As a storyteller one year ago, I took a chance . . . I realized that it was finally time to deal with the story of a seventeen-year-old boy and his friendship with two black men. And it's a gamble. There's no formula. There is no way that you can make or decide or guarantee before the event that that story is going to resonate outside of its specific context. You just take a bloody chance.

Athol Fugard (*b. 1932*)
From NOTEBOOKS 1960–1977

Like most playwrights, Athol Fugard is a journal writer. In his notebooks, he has written scraps of memory that have special meaning to him. In one entry for March 1961, long before he began to write "MASTER HAROLD" . . . and the boys *(1982), he describes one of his childhood memories. It concerns the real-life Sam, and it reveals — very painfully — exactly what the personal crime was that his play deals with. His gesture of contempt for the man who was like a grandfather to him became a demon that had to be exorcised.*

Sam Semela — Basuto — with the family fifteen years. Meeting him again when he visited Mom set off string of memories.

The kite which he produced for me one day during those early years when Mom ran the Jubilee Hotel and he was a waiter there. He had made it himself: brown paper, its ribs fashioned from thin strips of tomato-box plank which he had smoothed down, a paste of flour and water for glue. I was surprised and bewildered that he had made it for me.

I vaguely recall shyly "haunting" the servants' quarters in the well of the hotel — cold, cement-gray world — the pungent mystery of the dark little rooms — a world I didn't understand. Frightened to enter any of the rooms. Sam, broad-faced, broader based — he smelled of woodsmoke. The "kaffir smell" of South Africa is the smell of poverty — woodsmoke and sweat.

Later, when he worked for her at the Park café, Mom gave him the sack: ". . . he became careless. He came late for work. His work went to hell. He didn't seem to care no more." I was about thirteen and served behind the counter while he waited on table.

Realize now he was the most significant — the only — friend of my boyhood years. On terrible windy days when no one came to swim or walk in the park, we would sit together and talk. Or I was reading — Introductions to Eastern Philosophy or Plato and Socrates — and when I had finished he would take the book back to New Brighton.

Can't remember now what precipitated it, but one day there was a rare quarrel between Sam and myself. In a truculent silence we closed the café, Sam set off home to New Brighton on foot and I followed a few minutes later on my bike. I saw him walking ahead of me and, coming out of a spasm of acute loneliness, as I rode up behind him I called his name, he turned in mid-stride to look back and, as I cycled past, I spat in his face. Don't suppose I will ever deal with the shame that overwhelmed me the second after I had done that.

Now he is thin. We had a long talk. He told about the old woman ("Ma") whom he and his wife have taken in to look after their house while he goes to work — he teaches ballroom dancing. "Ma" insists on behaving like a domestic — making Sam feel guilty and embarrassed. She brings him an early morning cup of coffee. Sam: "No, Ma, you mustn't, man." Ma: "I must." Sam: "Look, Ma, if I want it, I can make it." Ma: "No, I must."

Occasionally, when she is doing something, Sam feels like a cup of tea but is too embarrassed to ask her, and daren't make one for himself. Similarly, with his washing. After three days or a week away in other towns, giving dancing lessons, he comes back with underclothes that are very dirty. He is too shy to give them out to be washed so washes them himself. When Ma sees this she goes and complains to Sam's wife that he doesn't trust her, that it's all wrong for him to do the washing.

Of tsotsis, he said: "They grab a old man, stick him with a knife, and ransack him. And so he must go to hospital and his kids is starving with hungry." Of others: "He's got some little moneys. So he is facing starvation for the weekend."

Of township snobs, he says there are the educational ones: "If you haven't been to the big school, like Fort Hare, what you say isn't true." And the money ones: "If you aren't selling shops or got a business or a big car, man, you're nothing."

Sam's incredible theory about the likeness of those "with the true seed of love." Starts with Plato and Socrates — they were round. "Man is being shrinking all the time. An Abe Lincoln, him too, taller, but that's because man is shrinking." Basically, those with the true seed of love look the same — "It's in the eyes."

He spoke admiringly of one man, a black lawyer in East London, an educated man — university background — who was utterly without snobbery, looking down on no one — any man, educated or ignorant, rich or poor, was another *man* to him, another human being, to be respected, taken seriously, to be talked to, listened to.

"They" won't allow Sam any longer to earn a living as a dancing teacher. "You must get a job!" One of his fellow teachers was forced to work at Fraser's Quarries.

Marsha Norman

Marsha Norman was born in Louisville, Kentucky, in 1947. Because her mother was a deeply religious woman, she did not allow television in her house, and radios, though available, were never used. Movies were also forbidden. But Norman explains that her mother "did not know the dangers of books because she didn't read," so books were Marsha Norman's world for most of her childhood.

But they were not the only influence. Norman spent much of her youth playing the piano, and she enjoyed the children's productions of the Actors' Theatre of Louisville. The Actors' Theatre and its director, Jon Jory, later became influential on Norman's early career as a writer.

Norman has said many times that the best thing for a writer is to be able to see drama during childhood. She has intense memories of *The Glass Menagerie*, Peter Shaffer's *The Royal Hunt of the Sun*, which is about the last day of Montezuma's life, and Archibald MacLeish's *J.B.*, an adaptation of the Book of Job. The vigor and the violence of these plays were explicitly attractive to her. Some of the excitement of that kind of theatricality is present in her first play, *Getting Out* (1977), which had its first performance at the Actors' Theatre.

Norman was a philosophy major at Agnes Scott College in Georgia, but she spent a good deal of her energy in theater there. Yet when she left college she did not expect to do any writing. As she said, she was sure that she would have to work for a living. But a combination of circumstances changed that.

Norman had worked with disturbed teenagers in a Kentucky state hospital and had met a thirteen-year-old girl who was violent, reckless, and frightening. Later when she was working in children's TV in Louisville, Jon Jory offered to commission her to write a play, but initially she was not interested. When she talked over her feelings, Jory advised her to reflect on a moment when she was truly frightened. It was then that she remembered the thirteen-year-old girl, and thus began the gestation of *Getting Out*.

Her unusual approach in that play was to present two views of the same woman: Arlie as an imprisoned adolescent and Arlene as an adult trying to begin a reasonable life for herself in a shabby apartment. The two parts of the character share the stage simultaneously. The ultimate problem is how Arlene will learn to integrate the separate parts of her personality. It is a very effective work and ran for eight months off Broadway after a successful opening with the Actors' Theatre.

Norman also wrote some one-act plays for the Actors' Theatre — *The Laundromat* and *The Pool Hall* — and a full-length play, *Circus Valentine* (1979). She won the Pulitzer Prize for *'night, Mother* (1983), currently her most internationally successful play. *Traveler in the Dark* (1984) premiered at the American Repertory Theatre in Cambridge, Massachusetts, starring Sam Waterston as a cancer surgeon suffering from the strain of guilt. She also wrote the book (or script) for *The Secret Garden* (1990), a prize-winning Broadway musical.

Norman has frequently talked about the structure of her plays, which follow a very traditional pattern. She has linked them often to a "ski lift. When you get in it, you must feel absolutely secure; you must know that this thing can hold you up." Her sense of the play as resembling a machine is based in part on her awareness of the audience's needs and expectations. She has said that a good play should follow several simple rules: "You must state the issue at the beginning of the play. The audience must know what is at stake; they must know when they will be able to go home."

Norman is deeply concerned with giving language to those who are inarticulate. The most important characters in her best plays have been women who would not have been able to express themselves clearly without someone like Marsha Norman to give them a voice. Such an ambition may owe something to her youthful desire "to save the world," the same desire that led her to work in the Kentucky hospital that provided the material for her first play.

'NIGHT, MOTHER

Marsha Norman's best-known and most successful play, *'night, Mother* (1983), has won numerous awards including the Pulitzer Prize. Its subject — a middle-aged woman's determination to commit suicide and leave her mother behind — is not the uplifting fare usually offered to Broadway audiences. Such a play would seem to spell horror for a New York theater, and while it ran for ten months after a shaky start, Norman had to accept a fifty percent reduction in her standard royalties to keep the play open.

Her strategy in the play was to face the issue of suicide squarely and directly. She chose not to have Jessie deal with her decision alone and merely leave a note, as had been done in many such plays in the past. Rather, she chose to make the play a dialogue, with Jessie having to confront the one person who loves her most and who most wants her to live and to give up her thoughts of killing herself.

Norman also made the play more difficult for popular audiences because she did not take the obvious path of giving Jessie a terminal disease, as some plays had done. She felt it was imperative that the issues of life and death, of personal choice and motive, be explored directly onstage, with the characters facing as squarely as possible the ramifications of their choices.

The ethical issues that suicide raises are naturally complex, and the play does not broach them directly. But such issues are always in the minds of the audience. In no sense does the play offer anyone reasons for committing suicide. Jessie's discussion with her mother is not equivalent to a debate: She has made up her mind based on her personal feelings about life, and she makes her decision seem inevitable. Nothing Thelma can say will change it.

Jessie is not a deep thinker, not a reflective person, and she does not concern herself with spiritual issues in making her decision. Her last evening's concerns are limited to the physical, material, and psychological comfort of her mother.

'night, Mother in Performance

'night, Mother opened on March 31, 1983, at New York's Golden Theater. Kathy Bates played the daughter, Jessie, and Anne Pitoniak played Thelma, her mother. Not only was the play awarded the Pulitzer Prize, Bates and Pitoniak were voted best actresses of the year by the Critics' Outer Circle. The play ran for 388 performances.

Before its New York opening, the play premiered at the American Repertory Theatre under Robert Brustein's aegis in January 1983. Of that production Frank Rich, *New York Times* critic, said, " *'night, Mother* . . . is one of the most disturbing American plays of recent seasons. You can pick at it and argue with it, but you can't hide from its bruising impact." The fact that it premiered in Boston distinguished the play because it was the first time a playwright received a Pulitzer for a non–New York production. When the play moved to New York, Rich also reviewed it for the *Times*, praising "the superb actresses" and "the brilliant, unerring choreographic hand of the director Tom Moore."

In 1986 the film version appeared, with Tom Moore directing, Sissy Spacek as Jessie, and Anne Bancroft as Thelma. Some reviews complained of Moore's "busy-ness."

As of 1986, the play had appeared in productions in thirty-six countries in Europe, South America, Scandinavia, and Africa. Marsha Norman has commented on the differences in the languages and the actresses in various national productions in her interview with David Savran on p. 1277. *'night, Mother* has become a universal play, one that absorbs cultural differences and speaks to people everywhere.

Marsha Norman (*b. 1947*)

'NIGHT, MOTHER

1983

Characters

JESSIE CATES, *in her late thirties or early forties, is pale and vaguely unsteady physically. It is only in the last year that Jessie has gained control of her mind and body, and tonight she is determined to hold on to that control. She wears pants and a long black sweater with deep pockets, which contain scraps of paper, and there may be a pencil behind her ear or a pen clipped to one of the pockets of the sweater.*

As a rule, Jessie doesn't feel much like talking. Other people have rarely found her quirky sense of humor amusing. She has a peaceful energy on this night, a sense of purpose, but is clearly aware of the time passing moment by moment. Oddly enough, Jessie has never been as communicative or as enjoyable as she is on this evening, but we must know she has not always been this way. There is a familiarity between these two women that comes from having lived together for a long time. There is a shorthand to the talk and a sense of routine comfort in the way they relate to each other physically. Naturally, there are also routine aggravations.

THELMA CATES, "MAMA," *is Jessie's mother, in her late fifties or early sixties. She has begun to feel her age and so takes it easy when she can, or when it serves her purpose to let someone help her. But she speaks quickly and enjoys talking. She believes that things are what she says they are. Her sturdiness is more a mental quality than a physical one, finally. She is chatty and nosy, and this is her house.*

(*The play takes place in a relatively new house built way out on a country road, with a living room and connecting kitchen, and a center hall that leads off to the bedrooms. A pull cord in the hall ceiling releases a ladder which leads to the attic. One of these bedrooms opens directly onto the hall, and its entry should be visible to everyone in the audience. It should be, in fact, the focal point of the entire set, and the lighting should make it disappear completely at times and draw the entire set into it at others. It is a point of both threat and promise. It is an ordinary door that opens onto absolute nothingness. That door is the point of all the action, and the utmost care should be given to its design and construction.*)

(*The living room is cluttered with magazines and needlework catalogues, ashtrays and candy dishes. Examples of Mama's needlework are everywhere — pillows, afghans, and quilts, doilies and rugs, and they are quite nice examples. The house is more comfortable than messy, but there is quite a lot to keep in place here. It is more personal than charming. It is not quaint. Under no circumstances should the set and its dressing make a judgment about the intelligence or taste of Jessie and Mama. It should simply indicate that they are very specific real people who happen to live in a particular part of the country. Heavy accents, which would further distance the audience from Jessie and Mama, are also wrong.*)

(*The time is the present, with the action beginning about 8:15. Clocks onstage in the kitchen and on a table in the living room should run throughout the performance and be visible to the audience.*)

(*Mama stretches to reach the cupcakes in a cabinet in the kitchen. She can't see them, but she can feel around for them, and she's eager to have one, so she's working pretty hard at it. This may be the most serious exercise Mama ever gets. She finds a cupcake, the coconut-covered, raspberry-and-marshmallow-filled kind known as a snowball, but sees that there's one missing from the package. She calls to Jessie, who is apparently somewhere else in the house.*)

MAMA (*unwrapping the cupcake*): Jessie, it's the last snowball, sugar. Put it on the list, O.K.? And we're out of Hershey bars, and where's that peanut brittle? I think maybe Dawson's been in it again. I ought to put a big mirror on the refrigerator door. That'll keep him out of my treats, won't it? You hear me, honey? (*Then more to herself.*) I hate it when the coconut falls off. Why does the coconut fall off?

(*Jessie enters from her bedroom, carrying a stack of newspapers.*)

JESSIE: We got any old towels?
MAMA: There you are!
JESSIE (*holding a towel that was on the stack of newspapers*): Towels you don't want anymore. (*Picking up Mama's snowball wrapper.*) How about this

swimming towel Loretta gave us? Beach towel, that's the name of it. You want it? (*Mama shakes her head no.*)

MAMA: What have you been doing in there?

JESSIE: And a big piece of plastic like a rubber sheet or something. Garbage bags would do if there's enough.

MAMA: Don't go making a big mess, Jessie. It's eight o'clock already.

JESSIE: Maybe an old blanket or towels we got in a soap box sometime?

MAMA: I said don't make a mess. You hair is black enough, hon.

JESSIE (*continuing to search the kitchen cabinets, finding two or three more towels to add to her stack*): It's not for my hair, Mama. What about some old pillows anywhere, or a foam cushion out of a yard chair would be real good.

MAMA: You haven't forgot what night it is, have you? (*Holding up her fingernails.*) They're all chipped, see? I've been waiting all week, Jess. It's Saturday night, sugar.

JESSIE: I know. I got it on the schedule.

MAMA (*crossing to the living room*): You want me to wash 'em now or are you making your mess first? (*Looking at the snowball.*) We're out of these. Did I say that already?

JESSIE: There's more coming tomorrow. I ordered you a whole case.

MAMA (*checking the TV Guide*): A whole case will go stale, Jessie.

JESSIE: They can go in the freezer till you're ready for them. Where's Daddy's gun?

MAMA: In the attic.

JESSIE: Where in the attic? I looked your whole nap and couldn't find it anywhere.

MAMA: One of his shoeboxes, I think.

JESSIE: Full of shoes. I looked already.

MAMA: Well, you didn't look good enough, then. There's that box from the ones he wore to the hospital. When he died, they told me I could have them back, but I never did like those shoes.

JESSIE (*pulling them out of her pocket*): I found the bullets. They were in an old milk can.

MAMA (*as Jessie starts for the hall*): Dawson took the shotgun, didn't he? Hand me that basket, hon.

JESSIE (*getting the basket for her*): Dawson better not've taken that pistol.

MAMA (*stopping her again*): Now my glasses, please. (*Jessie returns to get the glasses.*) I told him to take those rubber boots, too, but he said they were for fishing. I told him to take up fishing.

(*Jessie reaches for the cleaning spray and cleans Mama's glasses for her*)

JESSIE: He's just too lazy to climb up there, Mama. Or maybe he's just being smart. That floor's not very steady.

MAMA (*getting out a piece of knitting*): It's not a floor at all, hon, it's a board now and then. Measure this for me. I need six inches.

JESSIE (*as she measures*): Dawson could probably use some of those clothes up there. Somebody should have them. You ought to call the Salvation Army before the whole thing falls in on you. Six inches exactly.

MAMA: It's plenty safe! As long as you don't go up there.

JESSIE (*turning to go again*): I'm careful.

MAMA: What do you want the gun for, Jess?

JESSIE (*Not returning this time. Opening the ladder in the hall.*): Protection. (*She steadies the ladder as Mama talks.*)

MAMA: You take the TV way too serious, hon. I've never seen a criminal in my life. This is way too far to come for what's out here to steal. Never seen a one.

JESSIE (*taking her first step up*): Except for Ricky.

MAMA: Ricky is mixed up. That's not a crime.

JESSIE: Get your hands washed. I'll be right back. And get 'em real dry. You dry your hands till I get back or it's no go, all right?

MAMA: I thought Dawson told you not to go up those stairs.

JESSIE (*going up*): He did.

MAMA: I don't like the idea of a gun, Jess.

JESSIE (*calling down from the attic*): Which shoebox, do you remember?

MAMA: Black.

JESSIE: The box was black?

MAMA: The shoes were black.

JESSIE: That doesn't help much, Mother.

MAMA: I'm not trying to help, sugar. (*No answer.*) We don't have anything anybody'd want, Jessie. I mean, I don't even want what we got, Jessie.

JESSIE: Neither do I. Wash your hands. (*Mama gets up and crosses to stand under the ladder.*)

MAMA: You come down from there before you have a fit. I can't come up and get you, you know.

JESSIE: I know.

MAMA: We'll just hand it over to them when they come, how's that? Whatever they want, the criminals.

JESSIE: That's a good idea, Mama.

MAMA: Ricky will grow out of this and be a real fine boy, Jess. But I have to tell you, I wouldn't want Ricky to know we had a gun in the house.

JESSIE: Here it is. I found it.

MAMA: It's just something Ricky's going through. Maybe he's in with some bad people. He just needs some time, sugar. He'll get back in school or get a job or one day you'll get a call and he'll say he's sorry for all the trouble he's caused and invite you out for supper someplace dress-up.

JESSIE (*coming back down the steps*): Don't worry. It's not for him, it's for me.

MAMA: I didn't think you would shoot your own boy, Jessie. I know you've felt like it, well, we've all felt like shooting somebody, but we don't do it. I just don't think we need . . .

JESSIE (*interrupting*): Your hands aren't washed. Do you want a manicure or not?

MAMA: Yes, I do, but . . .

JESSIE (*crossing to the chair*): Then wash your hands and don't talk to me anymore about Ricky. Those two rings he took were the last valuable things *I* had, so now he's started in on other people, door to door. I hope they put him away sometime. I'd turn him in myself if I knew where he was.

MAMA: You don't mean that.

JESSIE: Every word. Wash your hands and that's the last time I'm telling you.

(*Jessie sits down with the gun and starts cleaning it, pushing the cylinder out, checking to see that the chambers and barrel are empty, then putting some oil on a small patch of cloth and pushing it through the barrel with the push rod that was in the box. Mama goes to the kitchen and washes her hands, as instructed, trying not to show her concern about the gun.*)

MAMA: I shoulda got you to bring down that milk can. Agnes Fletcher sold hers to somebody with a flea market for forty dollars apiece.

JESSIE: I'll go back and get it in a minute. There's a wagon wheel up there, too. There's even a churn. I'll get it all if you want.

MAMA (*coming over, now, taking over now*): What are you doing?

JESSIE: The barrel has to be clean, Mama. Old powder, dust gets in it . . .

MAMA: What for?

JESSIE: I told you.

MAMA (*reaching for the gun*): And I told you, we don't get criminals out here.

JESSIE (*quickly pulling it to her*): And I told you . . . (*Then trying to be calm.*) The gun is for me.

MAMA: Well, you can have it if you want. When I die, you'll get it all, anyway.

JESSIE: I'm going to kill myself, Mama.

MAMA (*returning to the sofa*): Very funny. Very funny.

JESSIE: I am.

MAMA: You are not! Don't even say such a thing, Jessie.

JESSIE: How would you know if I didn't say it? You want it to be a surprise? You're lying there in your bed or maybe you're just brushing your teeth and you hear this . . . noise down the hall?

MAMA: Kill yourself.

JESSIE: Shoot myself. In a couple of hours.

MAMA: It must be time for your medicine.

JESSIE: Took it already.

MAMA: What's the matter with you?

JESSIE: Not a thing. Feel fine.

MAMA: You feel fine. You're just going to kill yourself.

JESSIE: Waited until I felt good enough, in fact.

MAMA: Don't make jokes, Jessie. I'm too old for jokes.

JESSIE: It's not a joke, Mama.

(*Mama watches for a moment in silence.*)

MAMA: That gun's no good, you know. He broke it right before he died. He dropped it in the mud one day.

JESSIE: Seems O.K. (*She spins the chamber, cocks the pistol, and pulls the trigger. The gun is not yet loaded, so all we hear is the click, but it will definitely work. It's also obvious that Jessie knows her way around a gun. Mama cannot speak.*) I had Cecil's all ready in there, just in case I couldn't find this one, but I'd rather use Daddy's.

MAMA: Those bullets are at least fifteen years old.

JESSIE (*pulling out another box*): These are from last week.

MAMA: Where did you get those?

JESSIE: Feed store Dawson told me about.

MAMA: Dawson!

JESSIE: I told him I was worried about prowlers. He said he thought it was a good idea. He told me what kind to ask for.

MAMA: If he had any idea . . .

JESSIE: He took it as a compliment. He thought I might be taking an interest in things. He got through telling me all about the bullets and then he said we ought to talk like this more often.

MAMA: And where was I while this was going on?

JESSIE: On the phone with Agnes. About the milk can, I guess. Anyway, I asked Dawson if he thought they'd send me some bullets and he said he'd just call for me, because he knew they'd send them if he told them to. And he was absolutely right. Here they are.

MAMA: How could he do that?

JESSIE: Just trying to help, Mama.

MAMA: And then I told you where the gun was.

JESSIE (*smiling, enjoying this joke*): See? Everybody's doing what they can.

MAMA: You told me it was for protection!

JESSIE: It *is*! I'm still doing your nails, though. Want to try that new Chinaberry color?

MAMA: Well, I'm calling Dawson right now. We'll just see what he has to say about this little stunt.

JESSIE: Dawson doesn't have any more to do with this.

MAMA: He's your brother.

JESSIE: And that's all.

MAMA (*stands up, moves toward the phone*): Dawson will put a stop to this. Yes he will. He'll take the gun away.

JESSIE: If you call him, I'll just have to do it before he gets here. Soon as you hang up the phone, I'll just walk in the bedroom and lock the door. Dawson will get here just in time to help you clean up. Go ahead, call him. Then call the police. Then call the funeral home. Then call Loretta and see if *she'll* do your nails.

MAMA: You will not! This is crazy talk, Jessie!

(*Mama goes directly to the telephone and starts to dial, but Jessie is fast, coming up behind her and taking the receiver out of her hand, putting it back down.*)

JESSIE (*firm and quiet*): I said no. This is private. Dawson is not invited.

MAMA: Just me.

JESSIE: I don't want anybody else over here. Just you and me. If Dawson comes over, it'll make me feel stupid for not doing it ten years ago.

MAMA: I think we better call the doctor. Or how about the ambulance. You like that one driver, I know. What's his name, Timmy? Get you somebody to talk to.

JESSIE (*going back to her chair*): I'm through talking, Mama. You're it. No more.

MAMA: We're just going to sit around like every other night in the world and then you're going to kill yourself? (*Jessie doesn't answer.*) You'll miss. (*Again there is no response.*) You'll just wind up a vegetable. How would you like that? Shoot your ear off? You know what the doctor said about getting excited. You'll cock the pistol and have a fit.

JESSIE: I think I can kill myself, Mama.

MAMA: You're not going to kill yourself, Jessie. You're not even upset! (*Jessie smiles, or laughs quietly, and Mama tries a different approach.*) People don't really kill themselves, Jessie. No, mam, doesn't make sense, unless you're retarded or deranged, and you're as normal as they come, Jessie, for the most part. We're all *afraid* to die.

JESSIE: I'm not, Mama. I'm cold all the time, anyway.

MAMA: That's ridiculous.

JESSIE: It's exactly what I want. It's dark and quiet.

MAMA: So is the back yard, Jessie! Close your eyes. Stuff cotton in your ears. Take a nap! It's quiet in your room. I'll leave the TV off all night.

JESSIE: So quiet I don't know it's quiet. So nobody can get me.

MAMA: You don't know what dead is like. It might not be quiet at all. What if it's like an alarm clock and you can't wake up so you can't shut it off. Ever.

JESSIE: Dead is everybody and everything I ever knew, gone. Dead is dead quiet.

MAMA: It's a sin. You'll go to hell.

JESSIE: Uh-huh.

MAMA: You will!

JESSIE: Jesus was a suicide, if you ask me.

MAMA: You'll go to hell just for saying that. Jessie!

JESSIE (*with genuine surprise*): I didn't know I thought that.

MAMA: Jessie!

(*Jessie doesn't answer. She puts the now-loaded gun back in the box and crosses to the kitchen. But Mama is afraid she's headed for the bedroom.*)

MAMA (*in a panic*): You can't use my towels! They're my towels. I've had them for a long time. I like my towels.

JESSIE: I asked you if you wanted that swimming towel and you said you didn't.

MAMA: And you can't use your father's gun, either. It's mine now, too. And you can't do it in my house.

JESSIE: Oh, come on.

MAMA: No. You can't do it. I won't let you. The house is in my name.

JESSIE: I have to go in the bedroom and lock the door behind me so they won't arrest you for killing me. They'll probably test your hands for gunpowder, anyway, but you'll pass.

MAMA: Not in my house!

JESSIE: If I'd known you were going to act like this, I wouldn't have told you.

MAMA: How am I supposed to act? Tell you to go ahead? O.K. by me, sugar? Might try it myself. What took you so long?

JESSIE: There's just no point in fighting me over it, that's all. Want some coffee?

MAMA: Your birthday's coming up, Jessie. Don't you want to know what we got you?

JESSIE: You got me dusting powder, Loretta got me a new housecoat, pink probably, and Dawson got me new slippers, too small, but they go with the robe, he'll say. (*Mama cannot speak.*) Right? (*Apparently Jessie is right.*) Be back in a minute.

(*Jessie takes the gun box, puts it on top of the stack of towels and garbage bags, and takes them into her bedroom. Mama, alone for a moment, goes to the phone, picks up the receiver, looks toward the bed-*

room, starts to dial, and then replaces the receiver in its cradle as Jessie walks back into the room. Jessie wonders, silently. They have lived together for so long there is very rarely any reason for one to ask what the other was about to do.)

MAMA: I started to, but I didn't. I didn't call him.

JESSIE: Good. Thank you.

MAMA (*starting over, a new approach*): What's this all about, Jessie?

JESSIE: About?

(Jessie now begins the next task she had "on the schedule," which is refilling all the candy jars, taking the empty papers out of the boxes of chocolates, etc. Mama generally snitches when Jessie does this. Not tonight, though. Nevertheless, Jessie offers.)

MAMA: What did I do?

JESSIE: Nothing. Want a caramel?

MAMA (*ignoring the candy*): You're mad at me.

JESSIE: Not a bit. I am worried about you, but I'm going to do what I can before I go. We're not just going to sit around tonight. I made a list of things.

MAMA: What things?

JESSIE: How the washer works. Things like that.

MAMA: I know how the washer works. You put the clothes in. You put the soap in. You turn it on. You wait.

JESSIE: You do something else. You don't just wait.

MAMA: Whatever else you find to do, you're still mainly waiting. The waiting's the worst part of it. The waiting's what you pay somebody else to do, if you can.

JESSIE (*nodding*): O.K. Where do we keep the soap?

MAMA: I could find it.

JESSIE: See?

MAMA: If you're mad about doing the wash, we can get Loretta to do it.

JESSIE: Oh now, that might be worth staying to see.

MAMA: She'd never in her life, would she?

JESSIE: Nope.

MAMA: What's the matter with her?

JESSIE: She thinks she's better than we are. She's not.

MAMA: Maybe if she didn't wear that yellow all the time.

JESSIE: The washer repair number is on a little card taped to the side of the machine.

MAMA: Loretta doesn't ever have to come over here again. Dawson can just leave her at home when he comes. And we don't ever have to see Dawson either if he bothers you. Does he bother you?

JESSIE: Sure he does. Be sure you clean out the lint tray every time you use the dryer. But don't ever put your house shoes in, it'll melt the soles.

MAMA: What does Dawson do, that bothers you?

JESSIE: He just calls me Jess like he knows who he's talking to. He's always wondering what I do all day. I mean, I wonder that myself, but it's my day, so it's mine to wonder about, not his.

MAMA: Family is just accident, Jessie. It's nothing personal, hon. They don't mean to get on your nerves. They don't even mean to be your family, they just are.

JESSIE: They know too much.

MAMA: About what?

JESSIE: They know things about you, and they learned it before you had a chance to say whether you wanted them to know it or not. They were there when it happened and it don't belong to them, it belongs to you, only they got it. Like my mail-order bra got delivered to their house.

MAMA: By accident!

JESSIE: All the same . . . they opened it. They saw the little rosebuds on it. (*Offering her another candy.*) Chewy mint?

MAMA (*shaking her head no*): What do they know about you? I'll tell them never to talk about it again. Is it Ricky or Cecil or your fits or your hair is falling out or you drink too much coffee or you never go out of the house or what?

JESSIE: I just don't like their talk. The account at the grocery is in Dawson's name when you call. The number's on a whole list of numbers on the back cover of the phone book.

MAMA: Well! Now we're getting somewhere. They're none of them ever setting foot in this house again.

JESSIE: It's not them, Mother. I wouldn't kill myself just to get away from them.

MAMA: You leave the room when they come over, anyway.

JESSIE: I stay as long as I can. Besides, it's you they come to see.

MAMA: That's because I stay in the room when they come.

JESSIE: It's not them.

MAMA: Then what is it?

JESSIE (*checking the list on her note pad*): The grocery won't deliver on Saturday anymore. And if you want your order the same day, you have to call before ten. And they won't deliver less than fifteen dollars' worth. What I do is tell them what we need and tell them to add on cigarettes until it gets to fifteen dollars.

MAMA: It's Ricky. You're trying to get through to him.

JESSIE: If I thought I could do that, I would stay.

MAMA: Make him sorry he hurt you, then. That's it, isn't it?

JESSIE: He's hurt me, I've hurt him. We're about even.

MAMA: You'll be telling him killing is O.K. with you,

you know. Want him to start killing next? Nothing wrong with it. Mom did it.

JESSIE: Only a matter of time, anyway, Mama. When the call comes, you let Dawson handle it.

MAMA: Honey, nothing says those calls are always going to be some new trouble he's into. You could get one that he's got a job, that he's getting married, or how about he's joined the army, wouldn't that be nice?

JESSIE: If you call the Sweet Tooth before you call the grocery, that Susie will take your fudge next door to the grocery and it'll all come out together. Be sure you talk to Susie, though. She won't let them put it in the bottom of a sack like that one time, remember?

MAMA: Ricky could come over, you know. What if he calls us?

JESSIE: It's not Ricky, Mama.

MAMA: Or anybody could call us, Jessie.

JESSIE: Not on Saturday night, Mama.

MAMA: Then what is it? Are you sick? If your gums are swelling again, we can get you to the dentist in the morning.

JESSIE: No. Can you order your medicine or do you want Dawson to? I've got a note to him. I'll add that to it if you want.

MAMA: Your eyes don't look right. I thought so yesterday.

JESSIE: That was just the ragweed. I'm not sick.

MAMA: Epilepsy is sick, Jessie.

JESSIE: It won't kill me. (*A pause.*) If it would, I wouldn't have to.

MAMA: You don't *have* to.

JESSIE: No, I don't. That's what I like about it.

MAMA: Well, I won't let you!

JESSIE: It's not up to you.

MAMA: Jessie!

JESSIE: I want to hang a big sign around my neck, like Daddy's on the barn. GONE FISHING.

MAMA: You don't like it here.

JESSIE (*smiling*): Exactly.

MAMA: I meant here in my house.

JESSIE: I know you did.

MAMA: You never should have moved back in here with me. If you'd kept your little house or found another place when Cecil left you, you'd have made some new friends at least. Had a life to lead. Had your own things around you. Give Ricky a place to come see you. You never should've come here.

JESSIE: Maybe.

MAMA: But I didn't force you, did I?

JESSIE: If it was a mistake, we made it together. You took me in. I appreciate that.

MAMA: You didn't have any business being by your-

self right then, but I can see how you might want a place of your own. A grown woman should . . .

JESSIE: Mama . . . I'm just not having a very good time and I don't have any reason to think it'll get anything but worse. I'm tired. I'm hurt. I'm sad. I feel used.

MAMA: Tired of what?

JESSIE: It all.

MAMA: What does that mean?

JESSIE: I can't say it any better.

MAMA: Well, you'll have to say it better because I'm not letting you alone till you do. What were those other things? Hurt . . . (*Before Jessie can answer.*) You had this all ready to say to me, didn't you? Did you write this down? How long have you been thinking about this?

JESSIE: Off and on, ten years. On all the time, since Christmas.

MAMA: What happened at Christmas?

JESSIE: Nothing.

MAMA: So why Christmas?

JESSIE: That's it. On the nose.

(*A pause. Mama knows exactly what Jessie means. She was there, too, after all.*)

JESSIE (*putting the candy sacks away*): See where all this is? Red hots up front, sour balls and horehound mixed together in this one sack. New packages of toffee and licorice right in back there.

MAMA: Go back to your list. You're hurt by what?

JESSIE (*Mama knows perfectly well*): Mama . . .

MAMA: O.K. Sad about what? There's nothing real sad going on right now. If it was after your divorce or something, that would make sense.

JESSIE (*looking at her list, then opening the drawer*): Now, this drawer has everything in it that there's no better place for. Extension cords, batteries for the radio, extra lighters, sandpaper, masking tape, Elmer's glue, thumbtacks, that kind of stuff. The mousetraps are under the sink, but you call Dawson if you've got one and let him do it.

MAMA: Sad about what?

JESSIE: The way things are.

MAMA: Not good enough. What things?

JESSIE: Oh, everything from you and me to Red China.

MAMA: I think we can leave the Chinese out of this.

JESSIE (*crosses back into the living room*): There's extra light bulbs in a box in the hall closet. And we've got a couple of packages of fuses in the fuse box. There's candles and matches in the top of the broom closet, but if the lights go out, just call Dawson and sit tight. But don't open the refrigerator door. Things will stay cool in there as long as you keep the door shut.

MAMA: I asked you a question.

JESSIE: I read the paper. I don't like how things are. And they're not any better out there than they are in here.

MAMA: If you're doing this because of the newspapers, I can sure fix that!

JESSIE: There's just more of it on TV.

MAMA (*kicking the television set*): Take it out, then!

JESSIE: You wouldn't do that.

MAMA: Watch me.

JESSIE: What would you do all day?

MAMA (*desperately*): Sing. (*Jessie laughs.*) I would, too. You want to watch? I'll sing till morning to keep you alive, Jessie, please!

JESSIE: No. (*Then affectionately.*) It's a funny idea, though. What do you sing?

MAMA (*has no idea how to answer this*): We've got a good life here!

JESSIE (*going back into the kitchen*): I called this morning and canceled the papers, except for Sunday, for your puzzles; you'll still get that one.

MAMA: Let's get another dog, Jessie! You liked a big dog, now, didn't you? That King dog, didn't you?

JESSIE (*washing her hands*): I did like that King dog, yes.

MAMA: I'm so dumb. He's the one run under the tractor.

JESSIE: That makes him dumb, not you.

MAMA: For bringing it up.

JESSIE: It's O.K. Handi-Wipes and sponges under the sink.

MAMA: We could get a new dog and keep him in the house. Dogs are cheap!

JESSIE (*getting big pill jars out of the cabinet*): No.

MAMA: Something for you to take care of.

JESSIE: I've had you, Mama.

MAMA (*frantically starting to fill pill bottles*): You do too much for me. I can fill pill bottles all day, Jessie, and change the shelf paper and wash the floor when I get through. You just watch me. You don't have to do another thing in this house if you don't want to. You don't have to take care of me, Jessie.

JESSIE: I know that. You've just been letting me do it so I'll have something to do, haven't you?

MAMA (*realizing this was a mistake*): I don't do it as well as you. I just meant if it tires you out or makes you feel used . . .

JESSIE: Mama, I know you used to ride the bus. Riding the bus and it's hot and bumpy and crowded and too noisy and more than anything in the world you want to get off and the only reason in the world you don't get off is it's still fifty blocks from where you're going? Well, I can get off right now if I want to, because even if I ride fifty more years and get off then, it's the same place when I step

down to it. Whenever I feel like it, I can get off. As soon as I've had enough, it's my stop. I've had enough.

MAMA: You're feeling sorry for yourself!

JESSIE: The plumber's helper is under the sink, too.

MAMA: You're not having a good time! Whoever promised you a good time? Do you think I've had a good time?

JESSIE: I think you're pretty happy, yeah. You have things you like to do.

MAMA: Like what?

JESSIE: Like crochet.

MAMA: I'll teach you to crochet.

JESSIE: I can't do any of that nice work, Mama.

MAMA: Good time don't come looking for you, Jessie. You could work some puzzles or put in a garden or go to the store. Let's call a taxi and go to the A&P!

JESSIE: I shopped you up for about two weeks already. You're not going to need toilet paper till Thanksgiving.

MAMA (*interrupting*): You're acting like some little brat, Jessie. You're mad and everybody's boring and you don't have anything to do and you don't like me and you don't like going out and you don't like staying in and you never talk on the phone and you don't watch TV and you're miserable and it's your own sweet fault.

JESSIE: And it's time I did something about it.

MAMA: Not something like killing yourself. Something like . . . buying us all new dishes! I'd like that. Or maybe the doctor would let you get a driver's license now, or I know what let's do right this minute, let's rearrange the furniture.

JESSIE: I'll do that. If you want. I always thought if the TV was somewhere else, you wouldn't get such a glare on it during the day. I'll do whatever you want before I go.

MAMA (*badly frightened by those words*): You could get a job!

JESSIE: I took that telephone sales job and I didn't even make enough money to pay the phone bill, and I tried to work at the gift shop at the hospital and they said I made people real uncomfortable smiling at them the way I did.

MAMA: You could keep books. You kept your dad's books.

JESSIE: But nobody ever checked them.

MAMA: When he died, they checked them.

JESSIE: And that's when they took the books away from me.

MAMA: That's because without him there wasn't any business, Jessie!

JESSIE (*putting the pill bottles away*): You know I couldn't work. I can't do anything. I've never been around people my whole life except when I went to the hospital. I could have a seizure any time. What good would a job do? The kind of job I could get would make me feel worse.

MAMA: Jessie!

JESSIE: It's true!

MAMA: It's what you think is true!

JESSIE (*struck by the clarity of that*): That's right. It's what I think is true.

MAMA (*hysterically*): But I can't do anything about that!

JESSIE (*quietly*): No. You can't. (*Mama slumps, if not physically, at least emotionally.*) And I can't do anything either, about my life, to change it, make it better, make me feel better about it. Like it better, make it work. But I can stop it. Shut it down, turn it off like the radio when there's nothing on I want to listen to. It's all I really have that belongs to me and I'm going to say what happens to it. And it's going to stop. And I'm going to stop it. So. Let's just have a good time.

MAMA: Have a good time.

JESSIE: We can't go on fussing all night. I mean, I could ask you things I always wanted to know and you could make me some hot chocolate. The old way.

MAMA (*in despair*): It takes cocoa, Jessie.

JESSIE (*gets it out of the cabinet*): I bought cocoa, Mama. And I'd like to have a caramel apple and do your nails.

MAMA: You didn't eat a bite of supper.

JESSIE: Does that mean I can't have a caramel apple?

MAMA: Of course not. I mean . . . (*Smiling a little.*) Of course you can have a caramel apple.

JESSIE: I thought I could.

MAMA: I make the best caramel apples in the world.

JESSIE: I know you do.

MAMA: Or used to. And you don't get cocoa like mine anywhere anymore.

JESSIE: It takes time, I know, but . . .

MAMA: The salt is the trick.

JESSIE: Trouble and everything.

MAMA (*backing away toward the stove*): It's no trouble. What trouble? You put it in the pan and stir it up. All right. Fine. Caramel apples. Cocoa. O.K.

(*Jessie walks to the counter to retrieve her cigarettes as Mama looks for the right pan. There are brief near-smiles, and maybe Mama clears her throat. We have a truce, for the moment. A genuine but nevertheless uneasy one. Jessie, who has been in constant motion since the beginning, now seems content to sit.*)

(*Mama starts looking for a pan to make the cocoa, getting out all the pans in the cabinets in the process.*

It looks like she's making a mess on purpose so Jessie will have to put them all away again. Mama is buying time, or trying to, and entertaining.)

JESSIE: You talk to Agnes today?

MAMA: She's calling me from a pay phone this week. God only knows why. She has a perfectly good Trimline at home.

JESSIE (*laughing*): Well, how is she?

MAMA: How is she every day, Jessie? Nuts.

JESSIE: Is she really crazy or just silly?

MAMA: No, she's really crazy. She was probably using the pay phone because she had another little fire problem at home.

JESSIE: Mother . . .

MAMA: I'm serious! Agnes Fletcher's burned down every house she ever lived in. Eight fires, and she's due for a new one any day now.

JESSIE (*laughing*): No!

MAMA: Wouldn't surprise me a bit.

JESSIE (*laughing*): Why didn't you tell me this before? Why isn't she locked up somewhere?

MAMA: 'Cause nobody ever got hurt, I guess. Agnes woke everybody up to watch the fires as soon as she set 'em. One time she set out porch chairs and served lemonade.

JESSIE (*shaking her head*): Real lemonade?

MAMA: The houses they lived in, you knew they were going to fall down anyway, so why wait for it, is all I could ever make out about it. Agnes likes a feeling of accomplishment.

JESSIE: Good for her.

MAMA (*finding the pan she wants*): Why are you asking about Agnes? One cup or two?

JESSIE: One. She's your friend. No marshmallows.

MAMA (*getting the milk, etc.*): You have to have marshmallows. That's the old way, Jess. Two or three? Three is better.

JESSIE: Three, then. Her whole house burns up? Her clothes and pillows and everything? I'm not sure I believe this.

MAMA: When she was a girl, Jess, not now. Long time ago. But she's still got it in her, I'm sure of it.

JESSIE: She wouldn't burn her house down now. Where would she go? She can't get Buster to build her a new one, he's dead. How could she burn it up?

MAMA: Be exciting, though, if she did. You never know.

JESSIE: You do too know, Mama. She wouldn't do it.

MAMA (*forced to admit, but reluctant*): I guess not.

JESSIE: What else? Why does she wear all those whistles around her neck?

MAMA: Why does she have a house full of birds?

JESSIE: I didn't know she had a house full of birds!

MAMA: Well, she does. And she says they just follow

her home. Well, I know for a fact she's still paying on the last parrot she bought. You gotta keep your life filled up, she says. She says a lot of stupid things. (*Jessie laughs, Mama continues, convinced she's getting somewhere.*) It's all that okra she eats. You can't just willy-nilly eat okra two meals a day and expect to get away with it. Made her crazy.

JESSIE: She really eats okra twice a day? Where does she get it in the winter?

MAMA: Well, she eats it a lot. Maybe not two meals, but . . .

JESSIE: More than the average person.

MAMA (*beginning to get irritated*): I don't know how much okra the average person eats.

JESSIE: Do you know how much okra Agnes eats?

MAMA: No.

JESSIE: How many birds does she have?

MAMA: Two.

JESSIE: Then what are the whistles for?

MAMA: They're not real whistles. Just little plastic ones on a necklace she won playing Bingo, and I only told you about it because I thought I might get a laugh out of you for once even if it wasn't the truth, Jessie. Things don't have to be true to talk about 'em, you know.

JESSIE: Why won't she come over here?

(*Mama is suddenly quiet, but the cocoa and milk are in the pan now, so she lights the stove and starts stirring.*)

MAMA: Well now, what a good idea. We should've had more cocoa. Cocoa is perfect.

JESSIE: Except you don't like milk.

MAMA (*another attempt, but not as energetic*): I hate milk. Coats your throat as bad as okra. Something just downright disgusting about it.

JESSIE: It's because of me, isn't it?

MAMA: No, Jess.

JESSIE: Yes, Mama.

MAMA: O.K. Yes, then, but she's crazy. She's as crazy as they come. She's a lunatic.

JESSIE: What is it exactly? Did I say something, sometime? Or did she see me have a fit and's afraid I might have another one if she came over, or what?

MAMA: I guess.

JESSIE: You guess what? What's she ever said? She must've given you some reason.

MAMA: Your hands are cold.

JESSIE: What difference does that make?

MAMA: "Like a corpse," she says, "and I'm gonna be one soon enough as it is."

JESSIE: That's crazy.

MAMA: That's Agnes. "Jessie's shook the hand of death and I can't take the chance it's catching, Thelma, so I ain't comin' over, and you can un-

derstand or not, but I ain't comin'. I'll come up the driveway, but that's as far as I go."

JESSIE (*laughing, relieved*): I thought she didn't like me! She's scared of me! How about that! Scared of me.

MAMA: I could make her come over here, Jessie. I could call her up right now and she could bring the birds and come visit. I didn't know you ever thought about her at all. I'll tell her she just has to come and she'll come, all right. She owes me one.

JESSIE: No, that's all right. I just wondered about it. When I'm in the hospital, does she come over here?

MAMA: Her kitchen is just a tiny thing. When she comes over here, she feels like . . . (*Toning it down a little.*) Well, we all like a change of scene, don't we?

JESSIE (*playing along*): Sure we do. Plus there's no birds diving around.

MAMA: I hate those birds. She says I don't understand them. What's there to understand about birds?

JESSIE: Why Agnes likes them, for one thing. Why they stay with her when they could be outside with the other birds. What their singing means. How they fly. What they think Agnes is.

MAMA: Why do you have to know so much about things, Jessie? There's just not that much *to* things that I could ever see.

JESSIE: That you could ever *tell*, you mean. You didn't have to lie to me about Agnes.

MAMA: I didn't lie. You never asked before!

JESSIE: You lied about setting fire to all those houses and about how many birds she has and how much okra she eats and why she won't come over here. If I have to keep dragging the truth out of you, this is going to take all night.

MAMA: That's fine with me. I'm not a bit sleepy.

JESSIE: Mama . . .

MAMA: All right. Ask me whatever you want. Here.

(*They come to an awkward stop, as the cocoa is ready and Mama pours it into the cups Jessie has set on the table.*)

JESSIE (*as Mama takes her first sip*): Did you love Daddy?

MAMA: No.

JESSIE (*pleased that Mama understands the rules better now*): I didn't think so. Were you really fifteen when you married him?

MAMA: The way he told it? I'm sitting in the mud, he comes along, drags me in the kitchen, "She's been there ever since"?

JESSIE: Yes.

MAMA: No. It was a big fat lie, the whole thing. He

just thought it was funnier that way. God, this milk in here.

JESSIE: The cocoa helps.

MAMA (*pleased that they agree on this, at least*): Not enough, though, does it? You can still taste it, can't you?

JESSIE: Yeah, it's pretty bad. I thought it was my memory that was bad, but it's not. It's the milk, all right.

MAMA: It's a real waste of chocolate. You don't have to finish it.

JESSIE (*putting her cup down*): Thanks, though.

MAMA: I should've known not to make it. I knew you wouldn't like it. You never did like it.

JESSIE: You didn't ever love him, or he did something and you stopped loving him, or what?

MAMA: He felt sorry for me. He wanted a plain country woman and that's what he married, and then he held it against me the rest of my life like I was supposed to change and surprise him somehow. Like I remember this one day he was standing on the porch and I told him to get a shirt on and he went in and got one and then he said, real peaceful, but to the point, "You're right, Thelma. If God had meant for people to go around without any clothes on, they'd have been born that way."

JESSIE (*sees Mama's hurt*): He didn't mean anything by that, Mama.

MAMA: He never said a word he didn't have to, Jessie. That was probably all he'd said to me all day, Jessie. So if he said it, there was something to it, but I never did figure that one out. What did that mean?

JESSIE: I don't know. I liked him better than you did, but I didn't know him any better.

MAMA: How could I love him, Jessie. I didn't have a thing he wanted. (*Jessie doesn't answer.*) He got his share, though. You loved him enough for both of us. You followed him around like some . . . Jessie, all the man ever did was farm and sit . . . and try to think of somebody to sell the farm to.

JESSIE: Or make me a boyfriend out of pipe cleaners and sit back and smile like the stick man was about to dance and wasn't I going to get a kick out of that. Or sit up with a sick cow all night and leave me a chain of sleepy stick elephants on my bed in the morning.

MAMA: Or just sit.

JESSIE: I liked him sitting. Big old faded blue man in the chair. Quiet.

MAMA: Agnes gets more talk out of her birds than I got from the two of you. He could've had that GONE FISHING sign around his neck in that chair. I saw him stare off at the water. I saw him look at the weather rolling in. I got where I could prac-

tically see the boat myself. But you, you knew what he was thinking about and you're going to tell me.

JESSIE: I don't know, Mama! His life, I guess. His corn. His boots. Us. Things. You know.

MAMA: No, I don't know, Jessie! You had those quiet little conversations after supper every night. What were you whispering about?

JESSIE: We weren't whispering, you were just across the room.

MAMA: What did you talk about?

JESSIE: We talked about why black socks are warmer than blue socks. Is that something to go tell Mother? You were just jealous because I'd rather talk to him than wash the dishes with you.

MAMA: I was jealous because you'd rather talk to him than anything! (*Jessie reaches across the table for the small clock and starts to wind it.*) If I had died instead of him, he wouldn't have taken you in like I did.

JESSIE: I wouldn't have expected him to.

MAMA: Then what would you have done?

JESSIE: Come visit.

MAMA: Oh, I see. He died and left you stuck with me and you're mad about it.

JESSIE (*getting up from the table*): Not anymore. He didn't mean to. I didn't have to come here. We've been through this.

MAMA: He felt sorry for you, too, Jessie, don't kid yourself about that. He said you were a runt and he said it from the day you were born and he said you didn't have a chance.

JESSIE (*getting the canister of sugar and starting to refill the sugar bowl*): I know he loved me.

MAMA: What if he did? It didn't change anything.

JESSIE: It didn't have to. I miss him.

MAMA: He never really went fishing, you know. Never once. His tackle box was full of chewing tobacco and all he ever did was drive out to the lake and sit in his car. Dawson told me. And Bennie at the bait shop, he told Dawson. They all laughed about it. And he'd come back from fishing and all he'd have to show for it was . . . a whole pipe-cleaner *family* — chickens, pigs, a dog with a bad leg — it was creepy strange. It made me sick to look at them and I hid his pipe cleaners a couple of times but he always had more somewhere.

JESSIE: I thought it might be better for you after he died. You'd get interested in things. Breathe better. Change somehow.

MAMA: Into what? The Queen? A clerk in a shoe store? Why should I? Because he said to? Because you said to? (*Jessie shakes her head.*) Well I wasn't here for his entertainment and I'm not here for yours either, Jessie. I don't know what I'm here for, but then I don't think about it. (*Realizing what all this means.*) But I bet you wouldn't be killing yourself if he were still alive. That's a fine thing to figure out, isn't it?

JESSIE (*filling the honey jar now*): That's not true.

MAMA: Oh no? Then what were you asking about him for? Why did you want to know if I loved him?

JESSIE: I didn't think you did, that's all.

MAMA: Fine then. You were right. Do you feel better now?

JESSIE (*cleaning the honey jar carefully*): It feels good to be right about it.

MAMA: It didn't matter whether I loved him. It didn't matter to me and it didn't matter to him. And it didn't mean we didn't get along. It wasn't important. We didn't talk about it. (*Sweeping the pots off the cabinet.*) Take all these pots out to the porch!

JESSIE: What for?

MAMA: Just leave me this one pan. (*She jerks the silverware drawer open.*) Get me one knife, one fork, one big spoon, and the can opener, and put them out where I can get them. (*Starts throwing knives and forks in one of the pans.*)

JESSIE: Don't do that! I just straightened that drawer!

MAMA (*throwing the pan in the sink*): And throw out all the plates and cups. I'll use paper. Loretta can have what she wants and Dawson can sell the rest.

JESSIE (*calmly*): What are you doing?

MAMA: I'm not going to cook. I never liked it, anyway. I like candy. Wrapped in plastic or coming in sacks. And tuna. I like tuna. I'll eat tuna, thank you.

JESSIE (*taking the pan out of the sink*): What if you want to make apple butter. You can't make apple butter in that little pan. What if you leave carrots on cooking and burn up that pan?

MAMA: I don't like carrots.

JESSIE: What if the strawberries are good this year and you want to go picking with Agnes.

MAMA: I'll tell her to bring a pan. You said you would do whatever I wanted! I don't want a bunch of pans cluttering up my cabinets I can't get down to, anyway. Throw them out. Every last one.

JESSIE (*gathering up the pots*): I'm putting them all back in. I'm not taking them to the porch. If you want them, they'll be here. You'll bend down and get them, like you got the one for the cocoa. And if somebody else comes over here to cook, they'll have something to cook in, and that's the end of it!

MAMA: Who's going to come cook here?

JESSIE: Agnes.

MAMA: In my pots. Not on your life.

JESSIE: There's no reason why the two of you couldn't just live here together. Be cheaper for both of you and somebody to talk to. And if the birds bothered you, well, one day when Agnes is out getting her hair done, you could take them all for a walk!

MAMA (*as Jessie straightens the silverware*): So that's why you're pestering me about Agnes. You think you can rest easy if you get me a new babysitter? Well, I don't want to live with Agnes. I barely want to talk with Agnes. She's just around. We go back, that's all. I'm not letting Agnes near this place. You don't get off as easy as that, child.

JESSIE: O.K., then. It's just something to think about.

MAMA: I don't like things to think about. I like things to go on.

JESSIE (*closing the silverware drawer*): I want to know what Daddy said to you the night he died. You came storming out of his room and said I could wait it out with him if I wanted to, but you were going to watch *Gunsmoke*. What did he say to you?

MAMA: He didn't have *anything* to say to me, Jessie. That's why I left. He didn't say a thing. It was his last chance not to talk to me and he took full advantage of it.

JESSIE (*after a moment*): I'm sorry you didn't love him. Sorry for you, I mean. He seemed like a nice man.

MAMA (*as Jessie walks to the refrigerator*): Ready for your apple now?

JESSIE: Soon as I'm through here, Mama.

MAMA: You won't like the apple, either. It'll be just like the cocoa. You never liked eating at all, did you? Any of it! What have you been living on all these years, toothpaste?

JESSIE (*as she starts to clean out the refrigerator*): Now, you know the milkman comes on Wednesdays and Saturdays, and he leaves the order blank in an egg box, and you give the bills to Dawson once a month.

MAMA: Do they still make that orangeade?

JESSIE: It's not orangeade, it's just orange.

MAMA: I'm going to get some. I thought they stopped making it. You just stopped ordering it.

JESSIE: You should drink milk.

MAMA: Not anymore, I'm not. That hot chocolate was the last. Hooray.

JESSIE (*getting the garbage can from under the sink*): I told them to keep delivering a quart a week no matter what you said. I told them you'd run out of Cokes and you'd have to drink it. I told them I knew you wouldn't pour it on the ground . . .

MAMA (*finishing her sentence*): And you told them you weren't going to be ordering anymore?

JESSIE: I told them I was taking a little holiday and to look after you.

MAMA: And they didn't think something was funny about that? You who doesn't go to the front steps?

You, who only sees the driveway looking down from a stretcher passed out cold?

JESSIE (*enjoying this, but not laughing*): They said it was about time, but why didn't I take you with me? And I said I didn't think you'd want to go, and they said, "Yeah, everybody's got their own idea of vacation."

MAMA: I guess you think that's funny.

JESSIE (*pulling jars out of the refrigerator*): You know there never was any reason to call the ambulance for me. All they ever did for me in the emergency room was let me wake up. I could've done that here. Now, I'll just call them out and you say yes or no. I know you like pickles. Ketchup?

MAMA: Keep it.

JESSIE: We've had this since last Fourth of July.

MAMA: Keep the ketchup. Keep it all.

JESSIE: Are you going to drink ketchup from the bottle or what? How can you want your food and not want your pots to cook it in? This stuff will all spoil in here, Mother.

MAMA: Nothing I ever did was good enough for you and I want to know why.

JESSIE: That's not true.

MAMA: And I want to know why you've lived here this long feeling the way you do.

JESSIE: You have no earthly idea how I feel.

MAMA: Well, how could I? You're real far back there, Jessie.

JESSIE: Back where?

MAMA: What's it like over there, where you are? Do people always say the right thing or get whatever they want, or what?

JESSIE: What are you talking about?

MAMA: Why do you read the newspaper? Why don't you wear that sweater I made for you? Do you remember how I used to look, or am I just any old woman now? When you have a fit, do you see stars or what? How did you fall off the horse, really? Why did Cecil leave you? Where did you put my old glasses?

JESSIE (*stunned by Mama's intensity*): They're in the bottom drawer of your dresser in an old Milk of Magnesia box. Cecil left me because he made me choose between him and smoking.

MAMA: Jessie, I know he wasn't that dumb.

JESSIE: I never understood why he hated it so much when it's so good. Smoking is the only thing I know that's always just what you think it's going to be. Just like it was the last time, right there when you want it and real quiet.

MAMA: Your fits made him sick and you know it.

JESSIE: Say seizures, not fits. Seizures.

MAMA: It's the same thing. A seizure in the hospital is a fit at home.

JESSIE: They didn't bother him at all. Except he did feel responsible for it. It *was* his idea to go horseback riding that day. It was his idea I could do *anything* if I just made up my mind to. I fell off the horse because I didn't know how to hold on. Cecil left for pretty much the same reason.

MAMA: He had a girl, Jessie. I walked right in on them in the toolshed.

JESSIE (*after a moment*): O.K. That's fair. (*Lighting another cigarette.*) Was she very pretty?

MAMA: She was Agnes's girl, Carlene. Judge for yourself.

JESSIE (*as she walks to the living room*): I guess you and Agnes had a good talk about that, huh?

MAMA: I never thought he was good enough for you. They moved here from Tennessee, you know.

JESSIE: What are you talking about? You liked him better than I did. You flirted him out here to build your porch or I'd never even met him at all. You thought maybe he'd help you out around the place, come in and get some coffee and talk to you. God knows what you thought. All that curly hair.

MAMA: He's the best carpenter I ever saw. That little house of yours will still be standing at the end of the world, Jessie.

JESSIE: You didn't need a porch, Mama.

MAMA: All right! I wanted you to have a husband.

JESSIE: And I couldn't get one on my own, of course.

MAMA: How were you going to get a husband never opening your mouth to a living soul?

JESSIE: So I was quiet about it, so what?

MAMA: So I should have let you just sit here? Sit like your daddy? Sit here?

JESSIE: Maybe.

MAMA: Well, I didn't think so.

JESSIE: Well, what did you know?

MAMA: I never said I knew much. How was I supposed to learn anything living out here? I didn't know enough to do half the things I did in my life. Things happen. You do what you can about them and you see what happens next. I married you off to the wrong man, I admit that. So I took you in when he left. I'm sorry.

JESSIE: He wasn't the wrong man.

MAMA: He didn't love you, Jessie, or he wouldn't have left.

JESSIE: He wasn't the wrong man, Mama. I loved Cecil so much. And I tried to get more exercise and I tried to stay awake. I tried to learn to ride a horse. And I tried to stay outside with him, but he always knew I was trying, so it didn't work.

MAMA: He was a selfish man. He told me once he hated to see people move into his houses after he built them. He knew they'd mess them up.

JESSIE: I loved that bridge he built over the creek in

back of the house. It didn't have to be anything special, a couple of boards would have been just fine, but he used that yellow pine and rubbed it so smooth . . .

MAMA: He had responsibilities here. He had a wife and son here and he failed you.

JESSIE: Or that baby bed he built for Ricky. I told him he didn't have to spend so much time on it, but he said it had to last, and the thing ended up weighing two hundred pounds and I couldn't move it. I said, "How long does a baby bed have to last, anyway?" But maybe he thought if it was strong enough, it might keep Ricky a baby.

MAMA: Ricky is too much like Cecil.

JESSIE: He is not. Ricky is as much like me as it's possible for any human to be. We even wear the same size pants. These are his, I think.

MAMA: That's just the same size. That's not you're the same person.

JESSIE: I see it on his face. I hear it when he talks. We look out at the world and we see the same thing: Not Fair. And the only difference between us is Ricky's out there trying to get even. And he knows not to trust anybody and he got it straight from me. And he knows not to try to get work, and guess where he got that. He walks around like there's loose boards in the floor, and you know who laid that floor, I did.

MAMA: Ricky isn't through yet. You don't know how he'll turn out!

JESSIE (*going back to the kitchen*): Yes I do and so did Cecil. Ricky is the two of us together for all time in too small a space. And we're tearing each other apart, like always, inside that boy, and if you don't see it, then you're just blind.

MAMA: Give him time, Jess.

JESSIE: Oh, he'll have plenty of that. Five years for forgery, ten years for armed assault . . .

MAMA (*furious*): Stop that! (*Then pleading.*) Jessie, Cecil might be ready to try it again, honey, that happens sometimes. Go downtown. Find him. Talk to him. He didn't know what he had in you. Maybe he sees things different now, but you're not going to know that till you go see him. Or call him up! Right now! He might be home.

JESSIE: And say what? Nothing's changed, Cecil, I'd just like to look at you, if you don't mind? No. He loved me, Mama. He just didn't know how things fall down around me like they do. I think he did the right thing. He gave himself another chance, that's all. But I did beg him to take me with him. I did tell him I would leave Ricky and you and everything I loved out here if only he would take me with him, but he couldn't and I understood that. (*Pause.*) I wrote that note I

showed you. I wrote it. Not Cecil. I said "I'm sorry, Jessie, I can't fix it all for you." I said I'd always love me, not Cecil. But that's how he felt.

MAMA: Then he should've taken you with him!

JESSIE (*picking up the garbage bag she has filled*): Mama, you don't pack your garbage when you move.

MAMA: You will not call yourself garbage, Jessie.

JESSIE (*taking the bag to the big garbage can near the back door*): Just a way of saying it, Mama. Thinking about my list, that's all. (*Opening the can, putting the garbage in, then securing the lid.*) Well, a little more than that. I was trying to say it's all right that Cecil left. It was . . . a relief in a way. I never was what he wanted to see, so it was better when he wasn't looking at me all the time.

MAMA: I'll make your apple now.

JESSIE: No thanks. You get the manicure stuff and I'll be right there.

(*Jessie ties up the big garbage bag in the can and replaces the small garbage bag under the sink, all the time trying desperately to regain her calm. Mama watches, from a distance, her hand reaching unconsciously for the phone. Then she has a better idea. Or rather she thinks of the only other thing left and is willing to try it. Maybe she is even convinced it will work.*)

MAMA: Jessie, I think your daddy had little . . .

JESSIE (*interrupting her*): Garbage night is Tuesday. Put it out as late as you can. The Davises' dogs get in it if you don't. (*Replacing the garbage bag in the can under the sink.*) And keep ordering the heavy black bags. It doesn't pay to buy the cheap ones. And I've got all the ties here with the hammers and all. Take them out of the box as soon as you open a new one and put them in this drawer. They'll get lost if you don't, and rubber bands or something else won't work.

MAMA: I think your daddy had fits, too. I think he sat in his chair and had little fits. I read this a long time ago in a magazine, how little fits go, just little blackouts where maybe their eyes don't even close and people just call them "thinking spells."

JESSIE (*getting the slipcover out of the laundry basket*): I don't think you want this manicure we've been looking forward to. I washed this cover for the sofa, but it'll take both of us to get it back on.

MAMA: I watched his eyes. I know that's what it was. The magazine said some people don't even know they've had one.

JESSIE: Daddy would've known if he'd had fits, Mama.

MAMA: The lady in this story had kept track of hers and she'd had eighty thousand of them in the last eleven years.

JESSIE: Next time you wash this cover, it'll dry better if you put it on wet.

MAMA: Jessie, listen to what I'm telling you. This lady had anywhere between five and five hundred fits a day and they lasted maybe fifteen seconds apiece, so that out of her life, she'd only lost about two weeks altogether, and she had a full-time secretary job and an IQ of 120.

JESSIE (*amused by Mama's approach*): You want to talk about fits, is that it?

MAMA: Yes. I do. I want to say . . .

JESSIE (*interrupting*): Most of the time I wouldn't even know I'd had one, except I wake up with different clothes on, feeling like I've been run over. Sometimes I feel my head start to turn around or hear myself scream. And sometimes there *is* this dizzy stupid feeling a little before it, but if the TV's on, well, it's easy to miss.

(*As Jessie and Mama replace the slipcover on the sofa and the afghan on the chair, the physical struggle somehow mirrors the emotional one in the conversation.*)

MAMA: I can tell when you're about to have one. Your eyes get this big! But, Jessie, you haven't . . .

JESSIE (*taking charge of this*): What do they look like? The seizures.

MAMA (*reluctant*): Different each time, Jess.

JESSIE: O.K. Pick one, then. A good one. I think I want to know now.

MAMA: There's not much to tell. You just . . . crumple, in a heap, like a puppet and somebody cut the strings all at once, or like the firing squad in some Mexican movie, you just slide down the wall, you know. You don't know what happens? How can you not know what happens?

JESSIE: I'm busy.

MAMA: That's not funny.

JESSIE: I'm not laughing. My head turns around and I fall down and then what?

MAMA: Well, your chest squeezes in and out, and you sound like you're gagging, sucking air in and out like you can't breathe.

JESSIE: Do it for me. Make the sound for me.

MAMA: I will not. It's awful-sounding.

JESSIE: Yeah. It felt like it might be. What's next?

MAMA: Your mouth bites down and I have to get your tongue out of the way fast, so you don't bite yourself.

JESSIE: Or you. I bite you, too, don't I?

MAMA: You got me once real good. I had to get a tetanus! But I know what to watch for now. And then you turn blue and the jerks start up. Like I'm standing there poking you with a cattle prod or

you're sticking your finger in a light socket as fast as you can . . .

JESSIE: Foaming like a mad dog the whole time.

MAMA: It's bubbling, Jess, not foam like the washer overflowed, for God's sake; it's bubbling like a baby spitting up. I go get a wet washcloth, that's all. And then the jerks slow down and you wet yourself and it's over. Two minutes tops.

JESSIE: How do I get to the bed?

MAMA: How do you think?

JESSIE: I'm too heavy for you now. How do you do it?

MAMA: I call Dawson. But I get you cleaned up before he gets here and I make him leave before you wake up.

JESSIE: You could just leave me on the floor.

MAMA: I want you to wake up someplace nice, O.K.? (*Then making a real effort.*) But, Jessie, and this is the reason I even brought this up! You haven't had a seizure for a solid year. A whole year, do you realize that?

JESSIE: Yeah, the phenobarb's about right now, I guess.

MAMA: You bet it is. You might never have another one, ever! You might be through with it for all time!

JESSIE: Could be.

MAMA: You are. I know you are!

JESSIE: I sure am feeling good. I really am. The double vision's gone and my gums aren't swelling. No rashes or anything. I'm feeling as good as I ever felt in my life. I'm even feeling like worrying or getting mad and I'm not afraid it will start a fit if I do, I just go ahead.

MAMA: Of course you do! You can even scream at me, if you want to. I can take it. You don't have to act like you're just visiting here, Jessie. This is your house, too.

JESSIE: The best part is, my memory's back.

MAMA: Your memory's always been good. When couldn't you remember things? You're always reminding me what . . .

JESSIE: Because I've made lists for everything. But now I remember what things mean on my lists. I see "dish towels," and I used to wonder whether I was supposed to wash them, buy them, or look for them because I wouldn't remember where I put them after I washed them, but now I know it means wrap them up, they're a present for Loretta's birthday.

MAMA (*finished with the sofa now*): You used to go looking for your lists, too, I've noticed that. You always know where they are now! (*Then suddenly worried.*) Loretta's birthday isn't coming up, is it?

JESSIE: I made a list of all the birthdays for you. I even

put yours on it. (*A small smile.*) So you can call Loretta and remind her.

MAMA: Let's take Loretta to Howard Johnson's and have those fried clams. I *know* you love that clam roll.

JESSIE (*slight pause*): I won't be here, Mama.

MAMA: What have we just been talking about? You'll be here. You're well, Jessie. You're starting all over. You said it yourself. You're remembering things and . . .

JESSIE: I won't be here. If I'd ever had a year like this, to think straight and all, before now, I'd be gone already.

MAMA (*not pleading, commanding*): No, Jessie.

JESSIE (*folding the rest of the laundry*): Yes, Mama. Once I started remembering, I could see what it all added up to.

MAMA: The fits are over!

JESSIE: It's not the fits, Mama.

MAMA: Then it's me for giving them to you, but I didn't do it!

JESSIE: It's not the fits! You said it yourself, the medicine takes care of the fits.

MAMA (*interrupting*): Your daddy gave you those fits, Jessie. He passed it down to you like your green eyes and your straight hair. It's not my fault!

JESSIE: So what if he had little fits? It's not inherited. I fell off the horse. It was an accident.

MAMA: The horse wasn't the first time, Jessie. You had a fit when you were five years old.

JESSIE: I did not.

MAMA: You did! You were eating a popsicle and down you went. He gave it to you. It's *his* fault, not mine.

JESSIE: Well, you took your time telling me.

MAMA: How do you tell that to a five-year-old?

JESSIE: What did the doctor say?

MAMA: He said kids have them all the time. He said there wasn't anything to do but wait for another one.

JESSIE: But I didn't have another one.

(*Now there is a real silence.*)

JESSIE: You mean to tell me I had fits all the time as a kid and you just told me I fell down or something and it wasn't till I had the fit when Cecil was looking that anybody bothered to find out what was the matter with me?

MAMA: It wasn't *all the time,* Jessie. And they changed when you started to school. More like your daddy's. Oh, that was some swell time, sitting here with the two of you turning off and on like light bulbs some nights.

JESSIE: How many fits did I have?

MAMA: You never hurt yourself. I never let you out of my sight. I caught you every time.

JESSIE: But you didn't tell anybody.

MAMA: It was none of their business.

JESSIE: You were ashamed.

MAMA: I didn't want anybody to know. Least of all you.

JESSIE: Least of all me. Oh, right. That was mine to know, Mama, not yours. Did Daddy know?

MAMA: He thought you were . . . you fell down a lot. That's what he thought. You were careless. Or maybe he thought I beat you. I don't know what he thought. He didn't think about it.

JESSIE: Because you didn't tell him!

MAMA: If I told him about you, I'd have to tell him about him!

JESSIE: I don't like this. I don't like this one bit.

MAMA: I didn't think you'd like it. That's why I didn't tell you.

JESSIE: If I'd known I was an epileptic, Mama, I wouldn't have ridden any horses.

MAMA: Make you feel like a freak, is that what I should have done?

JESSIE: Just get the manicure tray and sit down!

MAMA (*throwing it to the floor*): I don't want a manicure!

JESSIE: Doesn't look like you do, no.

MAMA: Maybe I did drop you, you don't know.

JESSIE: If you say you didn't, you didn't.

MAMA (*beginning to break down*): Maybe I fed you the wrong thing. Maybe you had a fever sometime and I didn't know it soon enough. Maybe it's a punishment.

JESSIE: For what?

MAMA: I don't know. Because of how I felt about your father. Because I didn't want any more children. Because I smoked too much or didn't eat right when I was carrying you. It has to be something I did.

JESSIE: It does not. It's just a sickness, not a curse. Epilepsy doesn't mean anything. It just is.

MAMA: I'm not talking about the fits here, Jessie! I'm talking about this killing yourself. It has to be me that's the matter here. You wouldn't be doing this if it wasn't. I didn't tell you things or I married you off to the wrong man or I took you in and let your life get away from you or all of it put together. I don't know what I did, but I did it, I know. This is all my fault, Jessie, but I don't know what to do about it now!

JESSIE (*exasperated at having to say this again*): It doesn't have anything to do with you!

MAMA: Everything you do has to do with me, Jessie. You can't do *anything,* wash your face or cut your finger, without doing it to me. That's right! You might as well kill me as you, Jessie, it's the same thing. This has to do with me, Jessie.

JESSIE: Then what if it does! What if it has everything to do with you! What if you are all I have and you're not enough? What if I could take all the rest of it if only I didn't have you here? What if the only way I can get away from you for good is to kill myself? What if it is? I can *still* do it!

MAMA (*in desperate tears*): Don't leave me, Jessie! (*Jessie stands for a moment, then turns for the bedroom.*) No! (*She grabs Jessie's arm.*)

JESSIE (*carefully taking her arm away*): I have a box of things I want people to have. I'm just going to go get it for you. You . . . just rest a minute.

(*Jessie is gone. Mama heads for the telephone, but she can't even pick up the receiver this time and, instead, stoops to clean up the bottles that have spilled out of the manicure tray.*)

(*Jessie returns, carrying a box that groceries were delivered in. It probably says Hershey Kisses or Starkist Tuna. Mama is still down on the floor cleaning up, hoping that maybe if she just makes it look nice enough, Jessie will stay.*)

MAMA: Jessie, how can I live here without you? I need you! You're supposed to tell me to stand up straight and say how nice I look in my pink dress, and drink my milk. You're supposed to go around and lock up so I know we're safe for the night, and when I wake up, you're supposed to be out there making the coffee and watching me get older every day, and you're supposed to help me die when the time comes. I can't do that by myself, Jessie. I'm not like you, Jessie. I hate the quiet and I don't want to die and I don't want you to go, Jessie. How can I . . . (*Has to stop a moment.*) How can I get up every day knowing you had to kill yourself to make it stop hurting and I was here all the time and I never even saw it. And then you gave me this chance to make it better, convince you to stay alive, and I couldn't do it. How can I live with myself after this, Jessie?

JESSIE: I only told you so I could explain it, so you wouldn't blame yourself, so you wouldn't feel bad. There wasn't anything you could say to change my mind. I didn't want you to save me. I just wanted you to know.

MAMA: Stay with me just a little longer. Just a few more years. I don't have that many more to go, Jessie. And as soon as I'm dead, you can do whatever you want. Maybe with me gone, you'll have all the quiet you want, right here in the house. And maybe one day you'll put in some begonias up the walk and get just the right rain for them all summer. And Ricky will be married by then and he'll

bring your grandbabies over and you can sneak them a piece of candy when their daddy's not looking and then be real glad when they've gone home and left you to your quiet again.

JESSIE: Don't you see, Mama, everything I do winds up like this. How could I think you would understand? How could I think you would want a manicure? We could hold hands for an hour and then I could go shoot myself? I'm sorry about tonight, Mama, but it's exactly why I'm doing it.

MAMA: If you've got the guts to kill yourself, Jessie, you've got the guts to stay alive.

JESSIE: I know that. So it's really just a matter of where I'd rather be.

MAMA: Look, maybe I can't think of what you should do, but that doesn't mean there isn't something that would help. *You* find it. *You* think of it. You can keep trying. You can get brave and try some more. You don't have to give up!

JESSIE: I'm *not* giving up! This *is* the other thing I'm trying. And I'm sure there are some other things that might work, but *might* work isn't good enough anymore. I need something that *will* work. *This* will work. That's why I picked it.

MAMA: But something might happen. Something that could change everything. Who knows what it might be, but it might be worth waiting for! (*Jessie doesn't respond.*) Try it for two more weeks. We could have more talks like tonight.

JESSIE: No, Mama.

MAMA: I'll pay more attention to you. Tell the truth when you ask me. Let you have your say.

JESSIE: No, Mama! We wouldn't have more talks like tonight, because it's this next part that's made this last part so good, Mama. No, Mama. *This* is how I have my say. This is how I say what I thought about it *all* and I say no. To Dawson and Loretta and the Red Chinese and epilepsy and Ricky and Cecil and you. And me. And hope. I say no! (*Then going to Mama on the sofa.*) Just let me go easy, Mama.

MAMA: How can I let you go?

JESSIE: You can because you have to. It's what you've always done.

MAMA: You are my child!

JESSIE: I am what became of your child. (*Mama cannot answer.*) I found an old baby picture of me. And it was somebody else, not me. It was somebody pink and fat who never heard of sick or lonely, somebody who cried and got fed, and reached up and got held and kicked but didn't hurt anybody, and slept whenever she wanted to, just by closing her eyes. Somebody who mainly just laid there and laughed at the colors waving around over her head and chewed on a polka-dot whale and woke up knowing some new trick nearly every day, and rolled over and drooled on the sheet and felt your hand pulling my quilt back up over me. That's who I started out and this is who is left. (*There is no self-pity here.*) That's what this is about. It's somebody I lost, all right, it's my own self. Who I never was. Or who I tried to be and never got there. Somebody I waited for who never came. And never will. So, see, it doesn't much matter what else happens in the world or in this house, even. I'm what was worth waiting for and I didn't make it. Me . . . who might have made a difference to me . . . I'm not going to show up, so there's no reason to stay, except to keep you company, and that's . . . not reason enough because I'm not . . . very good company. (*Pause.*) Am I.

MAMA (*knowing she must tell the truth*): No. And neither am I.

JESSIE: I had this strange little thought, well, maybe it's not so strange. Anyway, after Christmas, after I decided to do this, I would wonder, sometimes, what might keep me here, what might be worth staying for, and you know what it was? It was maybe if there was something I really liked, like maybe if I really liked rice pudding or cornflakes for breakfast or something, that might be enough.

MAMA: Rice pudding is good.

JESSIE: Not to me.

MAMA: And you're not afraid?

JESSIE: Afraid of what?

MAMA: I'm afraid of it, for me, I mean. When my time comes. I know it's coming, but . . .

JESSIE: You don't know when. Like in a scary movie.

MAMA: Yeah, sneaking up on me like some killer on the loose, hiding out in the back yard just waiting for me to have my hands full someday and how am I supposed to protect myself anyhow when I don't know what he looks like and I don't know how he sounds coming up behind me like that or if it will hurt or take very long or what I don't get done before it happens.

JESSIE: You've got plenty of time left.

MAMA: I forget what for, right now.

JESSIE: For whatever happens, I don't know. For the rest of your life. For Agnes burning down one more house or Dawson losing his hair or . . .

MAMA (*quickly*): Jessie, I can't just sit here and say O.K., kill yourself if you want to.

JESSIE: Sure you can. You just did. Say it again.

MAMA (*really startled*): Jessie! (*Quiet horror.*) How dare you! (*Furious.*) How dare you! You think you can just leave whenever you want, like you're watching television here? No, you can't, Jessie. You make me feel like a fool for being alive, child, and you are so wrong! I like it here, and I will stay here until they make me go, until they drag me screaming and I mean screeching into my grave, and you're real smart to get away before then because, I mean, honey, you've never heard noise like that in your life. (*Jessie turns away.*) Who am I talking to? You're gone already, aren't you? I'm looking right through you! I can't stop you because you're already gone! I guess you think they'll all have to talk about you now! I guess you think this will really confuse them. Oh yes, ever since Christmas you've been laughing to yourself and thinking, "Boy, are they all in for a surprise." Well, nobody's going to be a bit surprised, sweetheart. This is just like you. Do it the hard way, that's my girl, all right. (*Jessie gets up and goes into the kitchen, but Mama follows her.*) You know who they're going to feel sorry for? Me! How about that! Not you, me! They're going to be *ashamed* of you. Yes. *Ashamed!* If somebody asks Dawson about it, he'll change the subject as fast as he can. He'll talk about how much he has to pay to park his car these days.

JESSIE: Leave me alone.

MAMA: It's the truth!

JESSIE: I should've just left you a note!

MAMA (*screaming*): Yes! (*Then suddenly understanding what she has said, nearly paralyzed by the thought of it, she turns slowly to face Jessie, nearly whispering.*) No. No. I . . . might not have thought of all the things you've said.

JESSIE: It's O.K., Mama.

(*Mama is nearly unconscious from the emotional devastation of these last few moments. She sits down at the kitchen table, hurt and angry and desperately afraid. But she looks almost numb. She is so far beyond what is known as pain that she is virtually unreachable and Jessie knows this, and talks quietly, watching for signs of recovery.*)

JESSIE (*washes her hands in the sink*): I remember you liked that preacher who did Daddy's, so if you want to ask him to do the service, that's O.K. with me.

MAMA (*not an answer, just a word*): What.

JESSIE (*putting on hand lotion as she talks*): And pick some songs you like or let Agnes pick, she'll know exactly which ones. Oh, and I had your dress cleaned that you wore to Daddy's. You looked real good in that.

MAMA: I don't remember, hon.

JESSIE: And it won't be so bad once your friends start coming to the funeral home. You'll probably see people you haven't seen for years, but I thought about what you should say to get you over that nervous part when they first come in.

MAMA (*simply repeating*): Come in.

JESSIE: Take them up to see their flowers, they'd like that. And when they say, "I'm so sorry, Thelma," you just say, "I appreciate your coming, Connie." And then ask how their garden was this summer or what they're doing for Thanksgiving or how their children . . .

MAMA: I don't think I should ask about their children. I'll talk about what they have on, that's always good. And I'll have some crochet work with me.

JESSIE: And Agnes will be there, so you might not have to talk at all.

MAMA: Maybe if Connie Richards does come, I can get her to tell me where she gets that Irish yarn, she calls it. I know it doesn't come from Ireland. I think it just comes with a green wrapper.

JESSIE: And be sure to invite enough people home afterward so you get enough food to feed them all and have some left for you. But don't let anybody take anything home, especially Loretta.

MAMA: Loretta will get all the food set up, honey. It's only fair to let her have some macaroni or something.

JESSIE: No, Mama. You have to be more selfish from now on. (*Sitting at the table with Mama.*) Now, somebody's bound to ask you why I did it and you just say you don't know. That you loved me and you know I loved you and we just sat around tonight like every other night of our lives, and then I came over and kissed you and said, " 'Night, Mother," and you heard me close my bedroom door and the next thing you heard was the shot. And whatever reasons I had, well, you guess I just took them with me.

MAMA (*quietly*): It was something personal.

JESSIE: Good. That's good, Mama.

MAMA: That's what I'll say, then.

JESSIE: Personal. Yeah.

MAMA: Is that what I tell Dawson and Loretta, too? We sat around, you kissed me, " 'Night, Mother"? They'll want to know more, Jessie. They won't believe it.

JESSIE: Well, then, tell them what we did. I filled up the candy jars. I cleaned out the refrigerator. We made some hot chocolate and put the cover back on the sofa. You had no idea. All right? I really think it's better that way. If they know we talked about it, they really won't understand how you let me go.

MAMA: I guess not.

JESSIE: It's private. Tonight is private, yours and mine, and I don't want anybody else to have any of it.

MAMA: O.K., then.

JESSIE (*standing behind Mama now, holding her shoulders*): Now, when you hear the shot, I don't want you to come in. First of all, you won't be able to get in by yourself, but I don't want you trying. Call Dawson, then call the police, and then call Agnes. And then you'll need something to do till somebody gets here, so wash the hot-chocolate pan. You wash that pan till you hear the doorbell ring and I don't care if it's an hour, you keep washing that pan.

MAMA: I'll make my calls and then I'll just sit. I won't need something to do. What will the police say?

JESSIE: They'll do that gunpowder test, I guess, and ask you what happened, and by that time, the ambulance will be here and they'll come in and get me and you know how that goes. You stay out here with Dawson and Loretta. You keep Dawson out here. I want the police in the room first, not Dawson, O.K.?

MAMA: What if Dawson and Loretta want me to go home with them?

JESSIE (*returning to the living room*): That's up to you.

MAMA: I think I'll stay here. All they've got is Sanka.

JESSIE: Maybe Agnes could come stay with you for a few days.

MAMA (*standing up, looking into the living room*): I'd rather be by myself, I think. (*Walking toward the box Jessie brought in earlier.*) You want me to give people those things?

JESSIE (*they sit down on the sofa, Jessie holding the box on her lap*): I want Loretta to have my little calculator. Dawson bought it for himself, you know, but then he saw one he liked better and he couldn't bring both of them home with Loretta counting every penny the way she does, so he gave the first one to me. Be funny for her to have it now, don't you think? And all my house slippers are in a sack for her in my closet. Tell her I know they'll fit and I've never worn any of them, and make sure Dawson hears you tell her that. I'm glad he loves Loretta so much, but I wish he knew not everybody has her size feet.

MAMA (*taking the calculator*): O.K.

JESSIE (*reaching into the box again*): This letter is for Dawson, but it's mostly about you, so read it if you want. There's a list of presents for you for at least twenty more Christmases and birthdays, so if you want anything special you better add it to this list before you give it to him. Or if you want to be surprised, just don't read that page. This Christmas, you're getting mostly stuff for the house, like a new rug in your bathroom and needlework, but next Christmas, you're really going to cost him next Christmas. I think you'll like it a lot and you'd never think of it.

MAMA: And you think he'll go for it?

JESSIE: I think he'll feel like a real jerk if he doesn't. Me telling him to, like this and all. Now, this number's where you call Cecil. I called it last week and he answered, so I know he still lives there.

MAMA: What do you want me to tell him?

JESSIE: Tell him we talked about him and I only had good things to say about him, but mainly tell him to find Ricky and tell him what I did, and tell Ricky you have something for him, out here, from me, and to come get it. (*Pulls a sack out of the box.*)

MAMA (*the sack feels empty*): What is it?

JESSIE (*taking it off*): My watch. (*Putting it in the sack and taking a ribbon out of the sack to tie around the top of it.*)

MAMA: He'll sell it!

JESSIE: That's the idea. I appreciate him not stealing it already. I'd like to buy him a good meal.

MAMA: He'll buy dope with it!

JESSIE: Well, then, I hope he gets some good dope with it, Mama. And the rest of this is for you. (*Handing Mama the box now. Mama picks up the things and looks at them.*)

MAMA (*surprised and pleased*): When did you do all this? During my naps, I guess.

JESSIE: I guess. I tried to be quiet about it. (*As Mama is puzzled by the presents.*) Those are just little presents. For whenever you need one. They're not bought presents, just things I thought you might like to look at, pictures or things you think you've lost. Things you didn't know you had, even. You'll see.

MAMA: I'm not sure I want them. They'll make me think of you.

JESSIE: No they won't. They're just things, like a free tube of toothpaste I found hanging on the door one day.

MAMA: Oh. All right, then.

JESSIE: Well, maybe there's one nice present in there somewhere. It's Granny's ring she gave me and I thought you might like to have it, but I didn't think you'd wear it if I gave it to you right now.

MAMA (*taking the box to a table nearby*): No. Probably not. (*Turning back to face her.*) I'm ready for my manicure, I guess. Want me to wash my hands again?

JESSIE (*standing up*): It's time for me to go, Mama.

MAMA (*starting for her*): No, Jessie, you've got all night!

JESSIE (*as Mama grabs her*): No, Mama.

MAMA: It's not even ten o'clock.

JESSIE (*very calm*): Let me go, Mama.

MAMA: I can't. You can't go. You can't do this. You didn't say it would be so soon, Jessie. I'm scared. I love you.

JESSIE (*takes her hands away*): Let go of me, Mama. I've said everything I had to say.

MAMA (*standing still a minute*): You said you wanted to do my nails.

JESSIE (*taking a small step backward*): I can't. It's too late.

MAMA: It's not too late!

JESSIE: I don't want you to wake Dawson and Loretta when you call. I want them to still be up and dressed so they can get right over.

MAMA (*as Jessie backs up, Mama moves in on her, but carefully*): They wake up fast, Jessie, if they have to. They don't matter here, Jessie. You do. I do. We're not through yet. We've got a lot of things to take care of here. I don't know where my prescriptions are and you didn't tell me what to tell Dr. Davis when he calls or how much you want me to tell Ricky or who I call to rake the leaves or . . .

JESSIE: Don't try and stop me, Mama, you can't do it.

MAMA (*grabbing her again, this time hard*): I can too! I'll stand in front of this hall and you can't get past me. (*They struggle.*) You'll have to knock me down to get away from me, Jessie. I'm not about to let you . . .

(*Mama struggles with Jessie at the door and in the struggle Jessie gets away from her and —*)

JESSIE (*almost a whisper*): 'Night, Mother. (*She vanishes into her bedroom and we hear the door lock just as Mama gets to it.*)

MAMA (*screams*): Jessie! (*Pounding on the door.*) Jessie, you let me in there. Don't you do this, Jessie. I'm not going to stop screaming until you open this door, Jessie. Jessie! Jessie! What if I don't do any of the things you told me to do! I'll tell Cecil what a miserable man he was to make you feel the way he did and I'll give Ricky's watch to Dawson if I feel like it and the only way you can make sure I do what you want is you come out here and make me, Jessie! (*Pounding again.*) Jessie! Stop this! I didn't know! I was here with you all the time. How could I know you were so alone?

(*And Mama stops for a moment, breathless and frantic, putting her ear to the door, and when she doesn't hear anything, she stands up straight again and screams once more.*)

Jessie! Please!

(*And we hear the shot, and it sounds like an answer, it sounds like No.*)

(*Mama collapses against the door, tears streaming down her face, but not screaming anymore. In shock now.*)

Jessie, Jessie, child ... Forgive me. (*Pause.*) I thought you were mine.

(*And she leaves the door and makes her way through the living room, around the furniture, as though she didn't know where it was, not knowing what to do. Finally, she goes to the stove in the kitchen and picks* up *the hot-chocolate pan and carries it with her to the telephone and holds on to it while she dials the number. She looks down at the pan, holding it tight like her life depended on it. She hears Loretta answer.*)

MAMA: Loretta, let me talk to Dawson, honey.

COMMENTARY

David Savran (b. 1950)
INTERVIEW WITH MARSHA NORMAN   *1988*

As Marsha Norman said during an interview, her dissatisfaction with other plays about suicide led her to be very direct in her own play and to confront the issue directly. Here she discusses how that decision changed her entire concept of the play and helped her shape the dramatic action.

Savran: How do you begin a play? With an outline, a character, a line of dialogue?

Norman: ... With *'night, Mother* I knew I wanted to tell the story of this woman who kills herself, but I didn't have any idea how. At the time, in '81, there were a number of other plays on the subject. But I kept saying that these plays — particularly *Whose Life Is It Anyway?* — are tantrums. I wanted to put somebody in the room with this woman, somebody who cares deeply, wildly, madly, who will fight this person to the death to save her own life. This is a gladiator contest where the point is to keep the other person alive. And once I had that, I had all these parallels — gladiators and world heavyweight boxing championships — and I understood immediately how this has to work. You have to have a closed ring, nobody can get out or in, you can have only two people.

I knew going into *'night, Mother* that it was going to be the most treacherous act of my writing life. So I went to the world of music. I was in a mad Glenn Gould state at the time — I've spent my life at the piano. Okay, I thought, what if I do a little sonata form, a three-act play with no intermission? You can actually feel the moment when the orchestra stops and the conductor raises his hands and Jessie says, "You talked to Agnes today," and the second movement starts. The second movement ends when Jessie goes in to get the box of presents, Mama just having said, "Don't leave me, Jessie." The actors would come on stage knowing, "We don't have to go all the way to the end. We just have to get to the Agnes section." And then you start in on Agnes and think,

"Great, I'll just get to 'Don't leave me, Jessie,' then I can take a breath" — this is from Mama's point of view — "and get down and wash the floor." And then all they have to do is go to the end. *'Night, Mother* would be undoable if it weren't for that. People would fall out of it all the time. But they don't. So I think that if you don't have structure, you might as well not have anything to put in it. If you don't have the bookshelves, you don't have the books.

I have a great trick during that period of thinking about the play. I say, "I'm not writing until I absolutely have to, till I can no longer contain it." I build up the piece in a pressure cooker, as it were. All that time I'm writing myself notes in the form of questions. What did Daddy do? How long ago did he die? Where did he die? What did he ever do for Jessie? Those kinds of questions. Curiously enough, you'll find that just from asking the questions, you'll get all the answers during the next weeks. It's internal research into the lives of these people. From those questions will come lines of dialogue — you begin to hear the voicing, what they can talk about, what they think is funny. The first line of dialogue I wrote for *'night, Mother* was Jessie's line "We got any old towels?" As soon as I wrote it down, I understood that it was a ritual piece, that Jessie was coming in to celebrate this requiem mass, that she has these stacks of towels: here are the witnesses, the household objects. She comes in as though she is the altar boy.

I wait until I cannot avoid it anymore and by that time, I already know what the beginning is, because of all this scribbling down. Then it's really very easy. I keep two kinds of notebooks, one that has structure and information in it and the other that has my own thoughts — "Can we really have this? What about that? What would happen if this?" I have a wonderful piece of paper upstairs that says, "Have I written something that anybody will want to see? Have I written something that will last? Have I written something that will humiliate me?" This comes from a pretty grim moment in the writing of *'night, Mother*. I thought, "What is this that I've written?" Humiliation is easily a possibility.

Savran: What is the European reaction to *'night, Mother*?

Norman: *'Night, Mother* is done all over the world. Any list that New Guinea is on is a long list. It's still running in Spain, four and a half years later, with all of the jokes taken out. Curiously enough, my work has always been popular in Eastern Europe. But this time I've caught the Mediterranean crowd. What strikes you as you watch it in a foreign country, in another language, is that the play seems to contain this other culture. In Italy you get enormous "Mama mia" Mamas, and the Jessies are always Ariels, little sprites. In Scandinavian countries it's quite the opposite. The mothers are really small, like the old woman who lived in the shoe, and the daughters are Valkyries, towering over these little Mamas. In the Latin American countries Mama and Jessie look like sisters.

August Wilson

August Wilson was born in Pittsburgh in 1945, the son of a white father who never lived with his family and a black mother who had come from North Carolina to a Pittsburgh slum where she worked to keep her family together. Wilson's early childhood was spent in an environment very similar to that of his play *Fences*, and Troy Maxson seems to be patterned somewhat on Wilson's stepfather.

Wilson's writing is rooted to a large extent in music, specifically the blues. As a poet, writing over several years, Wilson found himself interested in the speech patterns and rhythms that were familiar to him from black neighborhoods, but the value of those patterns became clearer to him when he grew older and moved from Pittsburgh to Minneapolis. From a distance, he was able to see more clearly what had attracted him to the language and to begin to use the language more fully in his work.

In the 1960s and 1970s Wilson became involved in the civil rights movement and began to describe himself as a black nationalist, a term he has said he feels comfortable with. He began writing plays in the 1960s in Pittsburgh and then took a job in St. Paul writing dramatic skits for the Science Museum of Minnesota. He founded the Playwrights Center in Minneapolis and began writing a play, *Jitney*, about a gypsy cab station, which was produced in 1982. *Fullerton Street*, about Pittsburgh, was another play written in this early period. Wilson's first commercial success, *Ma Rainey's Black Bottom*, eventually premiered at the Yale Repertory Theatre in 1984 and then went to Broadway, where it enjoyed 275 performances and won the New York Drama Critics' Circle Award.

Ma Rainey's Black Bottom is the first of a planned sequence of ten plays based on the black American experience. As Wilson has said, "I think the black Americans have the most dramatic story of all mankind to tell." The concept of such a vast project echoes O'Neill's projected group of eleven plays based on the Irish-American experience. Unfortunately, O'Neill destroyed all but *A Touch of the Poet* in his series. Wilson's project, however, is ongoing and intense and so far has produced some of the most successful plays in the recent American theater.

Ma Rainey is about the legendary black blues singer who preceded Bessie Smith and Billie Holiday. The play is about the way in which she was exploited by white managers and recording executives and the way in which she knowingly dealt with her exploitation. In the cast of the play are several black musicians in the backup band. Levee, the trumpet player, has a dream of leading his own band and establishing himself as an important jazz musician. But he is haunted by memories of seeing his mother raped by a gang of white men when he was a boy. He wants to "improve" the session he's playing by making the old jazz tune "Black Bottom" swing in the new jazz style, but Ma Rainey keeps him in tow and demands that they play the tune in the old way. Levee finally cracks under the pressure, and the play ends painfully.

Fences opened at the Yale Repertory Theatre in 1985 and in New York in early 1987, where it won the Pulitzer Prize as well as the New York Drama Critics' Circle Award. This long-running success established Wilson firmly as an important writer. *Joe Turner's Come and Gone* opened at the Yale Repertory Theatre in late 1986 and moved to New York in early 1988, where it too has been hailed as an important play, winning its author the New York Drama Critics' Circle Award. *Joe Turner* is set in a rooming house in Pittsburgh in 1911 and is a study of the children of former slaves. They have come North to find work and some of them have been found by the legendary bounty hunter Joe Turner. As a study of a people in transition, the play is a quiet masterpiece. It incorporates a number of important African traditions, especially religious rituals of healing as performed by Bynum, the "bone man," a seer and a medicine man. In this play and others, Wilson makes a special effort to highlight the elements of African heritage that white society strips away from blacks.

The next play in Wilson's projected series, *The Piano Lesson*, which premiered at the Yale Repertory Theatre in 1987, also portrays the complexity of black attitudes toward the past and black heritage. The piano represents two kinds of culture: the white culture that produced it and the black culture, in the form of Papa Boy Willie, who carved into it images from black Africa. The central question in the play is whether Boy Willie should sell the piano and use the money for a down payment on a house and therefore on the future. Or should he follow his sister Berneice's advice and keep it because it is too precious to sell? The conflict is deep and the play ultimately focuses on a profound moment of spiritual exorcism. How one exorcises the past — how one lives with it or without it — is a central theme in Wilson's work.

Two Trains Running, the latest play in the series, is set in 1969, in the decade that saw the Vietnam War, racial and political riots, and the assassinations of both Kennedys, Malcolm X, and Martin Luther King, Jr. The play premiered at the Yale Repertory Theatre in 1990 and opened on Broadway at the Walter Kerr Theater in April 1992, directed by Lloyd Richards. The characters remain in Memphis Lee's diner — scheduled for demolition — throughout the play. The two trains in the title are heading to Africa and to the old South, but the characters seem indifferent to both of them. Wilson moved away from the careful structure of the well-made play in this work and produced an open-ended conclusion, leaving the racial and philosophical tensions unresolved.

FENCES

Fences (1985), like most of August Wilson's recent plays, was directed by Lloyd Richards, who also directed the first production of Lorraine Hansberry's *A Raisin in the Sun*. Richards was, until 1991, the dean of the School of Drama at Yale University and ran the Yale Repertory Theatre, where he directed all of the plays Wilson has written in his projected ten-play cycle about black American life.

Fences presents a slice of life in a black tenement in Pittsburgh in the 1950s. Its main character, Troy Maxson, is a garbage collector who has taken great pride in keeping his family together and providing for them. When the play opens he and his friend Bono are talking about Troy's challenge to the company and the union about blacks' ability to do the same "easy" work as whites. Troy's rebellion and frustration set the tone of the entire play: He is looking for his rights and, at age fifty-three, he has missed many opportunities to get what he deserves.

Troy's struggle for fairness becomes virtually mythic as he describes his wrestling with death during a bout with pneumonia in 1941. He describes a three-day struggle in which he eventually overcame his foe. Troy — a good baseball player who was relegated to the Negro leagues — sees death as nothing but a fastball, and he could always deal with a fastball. Both Bono and Troy's wife, Rose, show an intense admiration for him as he describes his ordeal.

The father-son relationship that begins to take a central role in the drama is complicated by strong feelings of pride and independence on both sides. Troy's son Cory wants to play football and Troy wants him to work on the fence he's mending. Cory's youthful enthusiasm probably echoes Troy's own youthful innocence, but Troy resents it in Cory, seeing it as partly responsible for his own predicament. Cory cannot see his father's point of view and feels that he is exempt from the kind of prejudice his father suffered.

The agony of the father-son relationship, their misperceptions of each other, persist through the play. Rose's capacity to cope with the deepest of Troy's anxieties — his fear of death — is one of her most important achievements in the play. At the end of the play Rose demands that Cory give Troy the respect he deserves, although Cory's anger and inexperience make it all but impossible for him to see his father as anything other than an oppressor. Cory feels that he must say no to his father once, but Rose will not let him deny his father. When the play ends with Gabe's fantastic ritualistic dance, the audience feels a sense of closure, of spiritual finish and a final seal.

Fences
in Performance

Like many of America's best plays, *Fences* began in a workshop production. Its first version was performed in a reading without full production — no sets, no full lighting, actors working "on book" instead of fully memorizing the play — in the summer of 1983 at the Eugene O'Neill Center in Waterford, Connecticut. This early version was four hours long.

Once Wilson found the focus of his play, it premiered in 1985 at the Yale Repertory Theatre in New Haven. Lloyd Richards, then dean of Yale Drama School, directed this as well as the New York production. The New York opening on March 27, 1987, starred Mary Alice, James Earl Jones, and Ray Anranha, the cast from New Haven. Frank Rich in the *New York Times* praised James Earl Jones, congratulating him on finding "what may be the best role of his career." He also said, "*Fences* leaves no doubt that Mr. Wilson is a major writer, combining a poet's ear for vernacular with a robust sense of humor (political and sexual), a sure instinct for crackling dramatic incident and a passionate commitment to a great subject."

From the first, *Fences* was recognized as an important play. It won four Tony Awards: best play, best actor, best supporting actress, and best director. It also won the New York Drama Critics' Circle Award for best play. Before the New York production, it had traveled to Chicago, San Francisco, and Seattle. It has been performed numerous times since, with the 1990 StageWest production in Springfield, Massachusetts, among the most recent. The film, with James Earl Jones, was released in 1992.

August Wilson (b. 1946)
FENCES

1987

Characters

TROY MAXSON
JIM BONO, *Troy's friend*
ROSE, *Troy's wife*
LYONS, *Troy's oldest son by previous marriage*
GABRIEL, *Troy's brother*

CORY, *Troy and Rose's son*
RAYNELL, *Troy's daughter*

Setting: *The setting is the yard which fronts the only entrance to the Maxson household, an ancient two-story brick house set back off a small alley in a big-*

city neighborhood. The entrance to the house is gained by two or three steps leading to a wooden porch badly in need of paint.

A relatively recent addition to the house and running its full width, the porch lacks congruence. It is a sturdy porch with a flat roof. One or two chairs of dubious value sit at one end where the kitchen window opens onto the porch. An old-fashioned icebox stands silent guard at the opposite end.

The yard is a small dirt yard, partially fenced, except for the last scene, with a wooden sawhorse, a pile of lumber, and other fence-building equipment set off to the side. Opposite is a tree from which hangs a ball made of rags. A baseball bat leans against the tree. Two oil drums serve as garbage receptacles and sit near the house at right to complete the setting.

The Play: *Near the turn of the century, the destitute of Europe sprang on the city with tenacious claws and an honest and solid dream. The city devoured them. They swelled its belly until it burst into a thousand furnaces and sewing machines, a thousand butcher shops and bakers' ovens, a thousand churches and hospitals and funeral parlors and money-lenders. The city grew. It nourished itself and offered each man a partnership limited only by his talent, his guile, and his willingness and capacity for hard work. For the immigrants of Europe, a dream dared and won true.*

The descendants of African slaves were offered no such welcome or participation. They came from places called the Carolinas and the Virginias, Georgia, Alabama, Mississippi, and Tennessee. They came strong, eager, searching. The city rejected them and they fled and settled along the riverbanks and under bridges in shallow, ramshackle houses made of sticks and tarpaper. They collected rags and wood. They sold the use of their muscles and their bodies. They cleaned houses and washed clothes, they shined shoes, and in quiet desperation and vengeful pride, they stole, and lived in pursuit of their own dream. That they could breathe free, finally, and stand to meet life with the force of dignity and whatever eloquence the heart could call upon.

By 1957, the hard-won victories of the European immigrants had solidified the industrial might of America. War had been confronted and won with new energies that used loyalty and patriotism as its fuel. Life was rich, full, and flourishing. The Milwaukee Braves won the World Series, and the hot winds of change that would make the sixties a turbulent, racing, dangerous, and provocative decade had not yet begun to blow full.

ACT I • Scene 1

(It is 1957. Troy and Bono enter the yard, engaged in conversation. Troy is fifty-three years old, a large man with thick, heavy hands; it is this largeness that he strives to fill out and make an accommodation with. Together with his blackness, his largeness informs his sensibilities and the choices he has made in his life.)

(Of the two men, Bono is obviously the follower. His commitment to their friendship of thirty-odd years is rooted in his admiration of Troy's honesty, capacity for hard work, and his strength, which Bono seeks to emulate.)

(It is Friday night, payday, and the one night of the week the two men engage in a ritual of talk and drink. Troy is usually the most talkative and at times he can be crude and almost vulgar, though he is capable of rising to profound heights of expression. The men carry lunch buckets and wear or carry burlap aprons and are dressed in clothes suitable to their jobs as garbage collectors.)

BONO: Troy, you ought to stop that lying!

TROY: I ain't lying! The nigger had a watermelon this big.

(He indicates with his hands.)

Talking about . . . "What watermelon, Mr. Rand?" I liked to fell out! "What watermelon, Mr. Rand?" . . . And it sitting there big as life.

BONO: What did Mr. Rand say?

TROY: Ain't said nothing. Figure if the nigger too dumb to know he carrying a watermelon, he wasn't gonna get much sense out of him. Trying to hide that great big old watermelon under his coat. Afraid to let the white man see him carry it home.

BONO: I'm like you . . . I ain't got no time for them kind of people.

TROY: Now what he look like getting mad cause he see the man from the union talking to Mr. Rand?

BONO: He come to me talking about . . . "Maxson gonna get us fired." I told him to get away from me with that. He walked away from me calling you a troublemaker. What Mr. Rand say?

TROY: Ain't said nothing. He told me to go down the Commissioner's office next Friday. They called me down there to see them.

BONO: Well, as long as you got your complaint filed, they can't fire you. That's what one of them white fellows tell me.

TROY: I ain't worried about them firing me. They gonna fire me cause I asked a question? That's all I did. I went to Mr. Rand and asked him, "Why? Why you got the white mens driving and the colored lifting?" Told him, "what's the matter, don't I count? You think only white fellows got sense enough to drive a truck. That ain't no paper job! Hell, anybody can drive a truck. How come you got all whites driving and the colored lifting?" He told me "take it to the union." Well, hell, that's what I done! Now they wanna come up with this pack of lies.

BONO: I told Brownie if the man come and ask him any questions . . . just tell the truth! It ain't nothing but something they done trumped up on you cause you filed a complaint on them.

TROY: Brownie don't understand nothing. All I want them to do is change the job description. Give everybody a chance to drive the truck. Brownie can't see that. He ain't got that much sense.

BONO: How you figure he be making out with that gal be up at Taylors' all the time . . . that Alberta gal?

TROY: Same as you and me. Getting just as much as we is. Which is to say nothing.

BONO: It is, huh? I figure you doing a little better than me . . . and I ain't saying what I'm doing.

TROY: Aw, nigger, look here . . . I know you. If you had got anywhere near that gal, twenty minutes later you be looking to tell somebody. And the first one you gonna tell . . . that you gonna want to brag to . . . is gonna be me.

BONO: I ain't saying that. I see where you be eyeing her.

TROY: I eye all the women. I don't miss nothing. Don't never let nobody tell you Troy Maxson don't eye the women.

BONO: You been doing more than eyeing her. You done bought her a drink or two.

TROY: Hell yeah, I bought her a drink! What that mean? I bought you one, too. What that mean cause I buy her a drink? I'm just being polite.

BONO: It's all right to buy her one drink. That's what you call being polite. But when you wanna be buying two or three . . . that's what you call eyeing her.

TROY: Look here, as long as you known me . . . you ever known me to chase after women?

BONO: Hell yeah! Long as I done known you. You forgetting I knew you when.

TROY: Naw, I'm talking about since I been married to Rose?

BONO: Oh, not since you been married to Rose. Now, that's the truth, there. I can say that.

TROY: All right then! Case closed.

BONO: I see you be walking up around Alberta's house. You supposed to be at Taylors' and you be walking up around there.

TROY: What you watching where I'm walking for? I ain't watching after you.

BONO: I seen you walking around there more than once.

TROY: Hell, you liable to see me walking anywhere! That don't mean nothing cause you see me walking around there.

BONO: Where she come from anyway? She just kinda showed up one day.

TROY: Tallahassee. You can look at her and tell she one of them Florida gals. They got some big healthy women down there. Grow them right up out the ground. Got a little bit of Indian in her. Most of them niggers down in Florida got some Indian in them.

BONO: I don't know about that Indian part. But she damn sure big and healthy. Woman wear some big stockings. Got them great big old legs and hips as wide as the Mississippi River.

TROY: Legs don't mean nothing. You don't do nothing but push them out of the way. But them hips cushion the ride!

BONO: Troy, you ain't got no sense.

TROY: It's the truth! Like you riding on Goodyears!

(*Rose enters from the house. She is ten years younger than Troy, her devotion to him stems from her recognition of the possibilities of her life without him: a succession of abusive men and their babies, a life of partying and running the streets, the Church, or aloneness with its attendant pain and frustration. She recognizes Troy's spirit as a fine and illuminating one and she either ignores or forgives his faults, only some of which she recognizes. Though she doesn't drink, her presence is an integral part of the Friday night rituals. She alternates between the porch and the kitchen, where supper preparations are under way.*)

ROSE: What you all out here getting into?

TROY: What you worried about what we getting into for? This is men talk, woman.

ROSE: What I care what you all talking about? Bono, you gonna stay for supper?

BONO: No, I thank you, Rose. But Lucille say she cooking up a pot of pigfeet.

TROY: Pigfeet! Hell, I'm going home with you! Might even stay the night if you got some pigfeet. You got something in there to top them pigfeet, Rose?

ROSE: I'm cooking up some chicken. I got some chicken and collard greens.

TROY: Well, go on back in the house and let me and Bono finish what we was talking about. This is men talk. I got some talk for you later. You know what kind of talk I mean. You go on and powder it up.

ROSE: Troy Maxson, don't you start that now!

TROY (*puts his arm around her*): Aw, woman . . . come here. Look here, Bono . . . when I met this woman . . . I got out that place, say, "Hitch up my pony, saddle up my mare . . . there's a woman out there for me somewhere. I looked here. Looked there. Saw Rose and latched on to her." I latched on to her and told her — I'm gonna tell you the truth — I told her, "Baby, I don't wanna marry, I just wanna be your man." Rose told me . . . tell him what you told me, Rose.

ROSE: I told him if he wasn't the marrying kind, then move out the way so the marrying kind could find me.

TROY: That's what she told me. "Nigger, you in my way. You blocking the view! Move out the way so I can find me a husband." I thought it over two or three days. Come back —

ROSE: Ain't no two or three days nothing. You was back the same night.

TROY: Come back, told her . . . "Okay, baby . . . but I'm gonna buy me a banty rooster and put him out there in the backyard . . . and when he see a stranger come, he'll flap his wings and crow . . ." Look here, Bono, I could watch the front door by myself . . . it was that back door I was worried about.

ROSE: Troy, you ought not talk like that. Troy ain't doing nothing but telling a lie.

TROY: Only thing is . . . when we first got married . . . forget the rooster . . . we ain't had no yard!

BONO: I hear you tell it. Me and Lucille was staying down there on Logan Street. Had two rooms with the outhouse in the back. I ain't mind the outhouse none. But when that goddamn wind blow through there in the winter . . . that's what I'm talking about! To this day I wonder why in the hell I ever stayed down there for six long years. But see, I didn't know I could do no better. I thought only white folks had inside toilets and things.

ROSE: There's a lot of people don't know they can do no better than they doing now. That's just something you got to learn. A lot of folks still shop at Bella's.

TROY: Ain't nothing wrong with shopping at Bella's. She got fresh food.

ROSE: I ain't said nothing about if she got fresh food. I'm talking about what she charge. She charge ten cents more than the A&P.

TROY: The A&P ain't never done nothing for me. I spends my money where I'm treated right. I go down to Bella, say, "I need a loaf of bread, I'll pay you Friday." She give it to me. What sense that make when I got money to go and spend it somewhere else and ignore the person who done right by me? That ain't in the Bible.

ROSE: We ain't talking about what's in the Bible. What sense it make to shop there when she overcharge?

TROY: You shop where you want to. I'll do my shopping where the people been good to me.

ROSE: Well, I don't think it's right for her to overcharge. That's all I was saying.

BONO: Look here . . . I got to get on. Lucille going be raising all kind of hell.

TROY: Where you going, nigger? We ain't finished this pint. Come here, finish this pint.

BONO: Well, hell, I am . . . if you ever turn the bottle loose.

TROY (*hands him the bottle*): The only thing I say about the A&P is I'm glad Cory got that job down there. Help him take care of his school clothes and things. Gabe done moved out and things getting tight around here. He got that job. . . . He can start to look out for himself.

ROSE: Cory done went and got recruited by a college football team.

TROY: I told that boy about that football stuff. The white man ain't gonna let him get nowhere with that football. I told him when he first come to me with it. Now you come telling me he done went and got more tied up in it. He ought to go and get recruited in how to fix cars or something where he can make a living.

ROSE: He ain't talking about making no living playing football. It's just something the boys in school do. They gonna send a recruiter by to talk to you. He'll tell you he ain't talking about making no living playing football. It's a honor to be recruited.

TROY: It ain't gonna get him nowhere. Bono'll tell you that.

BONO: If he be like you in the sports . . . he's gonna be all right. Ain't but two men ever played baseball as good as you. That's Babe Ruth and Josh Gibson.° Them's the only two men ever hit more home runs than you.

TROY: What it ever get me? Ain't got a pot to piss in or a window to throw it out of.

ROSE: Times have changed since you was playing baseball, Troy. That was before the war. Times have changed a lot since then.

TROY: How in hell they done changed?

ROSE: They got lots of colored boys playing ball now. Baseball and football.

BONO: You right about that, Rose. Times have changed, Troy. You just come along too early.

TROY: There ought not never have been no time called too early! Now you take that fellow . . . what's that fellow they had playing right field for the Yan-

Josh Gibson: (1911–1947), powerful black baseball player known in the 1930s as the Babe Ruth of the Negro leagues.

kees back then? You know who I'm talking about, Bono. Used to play right field for the Yankees.

ROSE: Selkirk?

TROY: Selkirk! That's it! Man batting .269, understand? .269. What kind of sense that make? I was hitting .432 with thirty-seven home runs! Man batting .269 and playing right field for the Yankees! I saw Josh Gibson's daughter yesterday. She walking around with raggedy shoes on her feet. Now I bet you Selkirk's daughter ain't walking around with raggedy shoes on her feet! I bet you that!

ROSE: They got a lot of colored baseball players now. Jackie Robinson was the first. Folks had to wait for Jackie Robinson.

TROY: I done seen a hundred niggers play baseball better than Jackie Robinson. Hell, I know some teams Jackie Robinson couldn't even make! What you talking about Jackie Robinson. Jackie Robinson wasn't nobody. I'm talking about if you could play ball then they ought to have let you play. Don't care what color you were. Come telling me I come along too early. If you could play . . . then they ought to have let you play.

(Troy takes a long drink from the bottle.)

ROSE: You gonna drink yourself to death. You don't need to be drinking like that.

TROY: Death ain't nothing. I done seen him. Done wrassled with him. You can't tell me nothing about death. Death ain't nothing but a fastball on the outside corner. And you know what I'll do to that! Lookee here, Bono . . . am I lying? You get one of them fastballs, about waist high, over the outside corner of the plate where you can get the meat of the bat on it . . . and good god! You can kiss it goodbye. Now, am I lying?

BONO: Naw, you telling the truth there. I seen you do it.

TROY: If I'm lying . . . that 450 feet worth of lying!

(Pause.)

That's all death is to me. A fastball on the outside corner.

ROSE: I don't know why you want to get on talking about death.

TROY: Ain't nothing wrong with talking about death. That's part of life. Everybody gonna die. You gonna die, I'm gonna die. Bono's gonna die. Hell, we all gonna die.

ROSE: But you ain't got to talk about it. I don't like to talk about it.

TROY: You the one brought it up. Me and Bono was talking about baseball . . . you tell me I'm gonna drink myself to death. Ain't that right, Bono? You know I don't drink this but one night out of the week. That's Friday night. I'm gonna drink just enough to where I can handle it. Then I cuts it loose. I leave it alone. So don't you worry about me drinking myself to death. 'Cause I ain't worried about Death. I done seen him. I done wrestled with him.

Look here, Bono . . . I looked up one day and Death was marching straight at me. Like Soldiers on Parade! The Army of Death was marching straight at me. The middle of July, 1941. It got real cold just like it be winter. It seem like Death himself reached out and touched me on the shoulder. He touch me just like I touch you. I got cold as ice and Death standing there grinning at me.

ROSE: Troy, why don't you hush that talk.

TROY: I say . . . What you want, Mr. Death? You be wanting me? You done brought your army to be getting me? I looked him dead in the eye. I wasn't fearing nothing. I was ready to tangle. Just like I'm ready to tangle now. The Bible say be ever vigilant. That's why I don't get but so drunk. I got to keep watch.

ROSE: Troy was right down there in Mercy Hospital. You remember he had pneumonia? Laying there with a fever talking plumb out of his head.

TROY: Death standing there staring at me . . . carrying that sickle in his hand. Finally he say, "You want bound over for another year?" See, just like that . . . "You want bound over for another year?" I told him, "Bound over hell! Let's settle this now!"

It seem like he kinda fell back when I said that, and all the cold went out of me. I reached down and grabbed that sickle and threw it just as far as I could throw it . . . and me and him commenced to wrestling.

We wrestled for three days and three nights. I can't say where I found the strength from. Every time it seemed like he was gonna get the best of me, I'd reach way down deep inside myself and find the strength to do him one better.

ROSE: Every time Troy tell that story he find different ways to tell it. Different things to make up about it.

TROY: I ain't making up nothing. I'm telling you the facts of what happened. I wrestled with Death for three days and three nights and I'm standing here to tell you about it.

(Pause.)

All right. At the end of the third night we done weakened each other to where we can't hardly move. Death stood up, throwed on his robe . . . had him a white robe with a hood on it. He throwed on that robe and went off to look for his sickle. Say, "I'll be back." Just like that. "I'll be back." I told him, say, "Yeah, but ... you gonna have to find me!" I wasn't no fool. I wan't going looking for him. Death ain't nothing to play with. And I know he's gonna get me. I know I got to join his army ... his camp followers. But as long as I keep my strength and see him coming ... as long as I keep up my vigilance ... he's gonna have to fight to get me. I ain't going easy.

BONO: Well, look here, since you got to keep up your vigilance ... let me have the bottle.

TROY: Aw hell, I shouldn't have told you that part. I should have left out that part.

ROSE: Troy be talking that stuff and half the time don't even know what he be talking about.

TROY: Bono know me better than that.

BONO: That's right. I know you. I know you got some Uncle Remus° in your blood. You got more stories than the devil got sinners.

TROY: Aw hell, I done seen him too! Done talked with the devil.

ROSE: Troy, don't nobody wanna be hearing all that stuff.

(Lyons enters the yard from the street. Thirty-four years old, Troy's son by a previous marriage, he sports a neatly trimmed goatee, sport coat, white shirt, tieless and buttoned at the collar. Though he fancies himself a musician, he is more caught up in the rituals and "idea" of being a musician than in the actual practice of the music. He has come to borrow money from Troy, and while he knows he will be successful, he is uncertain as to what extent his lifestyle will be held up to scrutiny and ridicule.)

LYONS: Hey, Pop.

TROY: What you come "Hey, Popping" me for?

LYONS: How you doing, Rose?

(He kisses her.)

Mr. Bono. How you doing?

BONO: Hey, Lyons ... how you been?

TROY: He must have been doing all right. I ain't seen him around here last week.

ROSE: Troy, leave your boy alone. He come by to see you and you wanna start all that nonsense.

TROY: I ain't bothering Lyons.

(Offers him the bottle.)

Here ... get you a drink. We got an understanding. I know why he come by to see me and he know I know.

LYONS: Come on, Pop ... I just stopped by to say hi ... see how you was doing.

Uncle Remus: Black storyteller who recounts traditional black tales in the book by Joel Chandler Harris.

TROY: You ain't stopped by yesterday.

ROSE: You gonna stay for supper, Lyons? I got some chicken cooking in the oven.

LYONS: No, Rose ... thanks. I was just in the neighborhood and thought I'd stop by for a minute.

TROY: You was in the neighborhood all right, nigger. You telling the truth there. You was in the neighborhood cause it's my payday.

LYONS: Well, hell, since you mentioned it ... let me have ten dollars.

TROY: I'll be damned! I'll die and go to hell and play blackjack with the devil before I give you ten dollars.

BONO: That's what I wanna know about ... that devil you done seen.

LYONS: What ... Pop done seen the devil? You too much, Pops.

TROY: Yeah, I done seen him. Talked to him too!

ROSE: You ain't seen no devil. I done told you that man ain't had nothing to do with the devil. Anything you can't understand, you want to call it the devil.

TROY: Look here, Bono ... I went down to see Hertzberger about some furniture. Got three rooms for two-ninety-eight. That what it say on the radio. "Three rooms ... two-ninety-eight." Even made up a little song about it. Go down there ... man tell me I can't get no credit. I'm working every day and can't get no credit. What to do? I got an empty house with some raggedy furniture in it. Cory ain't got no bed. He's sleeping on a pile of rags on the floor. Working every day and can't get no credit. Come back here — Rose'll tell you — madder than hell. Sit down ... try to figure what I'm gonna do. Come a knock on the door. Ain't been living here but three days. Who know I'm here? Open the door ... devil standing there bigger than life. White fellow ... got on good clothes and everything. Standing there with a clipboard in his hand. I ain't had to say nothing. First words come out of his mouth was ... "I understand you need some furniture and can't get no credit." I liked to fell over. He say, "I'll give you all the credit you want, but you got to pay the interest on it." I told him, "Give me three rooms worth and charge whatever you want." Next day a truck pulled up here and two men unloaded them three rooms. Man what drove the truck give me a book. Say send ten dollars, first of every month to the address in the book and everything will be all right. Say if I miss a payment the devil was coming back and it'll be hell to pay. That was fifteen years ago. To this day ... the first of the month I send my ten dollars, Rose'll tell you.

ROSE: Troy lying.

TROY: I ain't never seen that man since. Now you tell me who else that could have been but the devil? I ain't sold my soul or nothing like that, you understand. Naw, I wouldn't have truck with the devil about nothing like that. I got my furniture and pays my ten dollars the first of the month just like clockwork.

BONO: How long you say you been paying this ten dollars a month?

TROY: Fifteen years!

BONO: Hell, ain't you finished paying for it yet? How much the man done charged you.

TROY: Ah hell, I done paid for it. I done paid for it ten times over! The fact is I'm scared to stop paying it.

ROSE: Troy lying. We got that furniture from Mr. Glickman. He ain't paying no ten dollars a month to nobody.

TROY: Aw hell, woman. Bono know I ain't that big a fool.

LYONS: I was just getting ready to say . . . I know where there's a bridge for sale.

TROY: Look here, I'll tell you this . . . it don't matter to me if he was the devil. It don't matter if the devil give credit. Somebody has got to give it.

ROSE: It ought to matter. You going around talking about having truck with the devil . . . God's the one you gonna have to answer to. He's the one gonna be at the Judgment.

LYONS: Yeah, well, look here, Pop . . . let me have that ten dollars. I'll give it back to you. Bonnie got a job working at the hospital.

TROY: What I tell you, Bono? The only time I see this nigger is when he wants something. That's the only time I see him.

LYONS: Come on, Pop, Mr. Bono don't want to hear all that. Let me have the ten dollars. I told you Bonnie working.

TROY: What that mean to me? "Bonnie working." I don't care if she working. Go ask her for the ten dollars if she working. Talking about "Bonnie working." Why ain't you working?

LYONS: Aw, Pop, you know I can't find no decent job. Where am I gonna get a job at? You know I can't get no job.

TROY: I told you I know some people down there. I can get you on the rubbish if you want to work. I told you that the last time you came by here asking me for something.

LYONS: Naw, Pop . . . thanks. That ain't for me. I don't wanna be carrying nobody's rubbish. I don't wanna be punching nobody's time clock.

TROY: What's the matter, you too good to carry people's rubbish? Where you think that ten dollars you talking about come from? I'm just supposed to haul people's rubbish and give my money to you cause you too lazy to work. You too lazy to work and wanna know why you ain't got what I got.

ROSE: What hospital Bonnie working at? Mercy?

LYONS: She's down at Passavant working in the laundry.

TROY: I ain't got nothing as it is. I give you that ten dollars and I got to eat beans the rest of the week. Naw . . . you ain't getting no ten dollars here.

LYONS: You ain't got to be eating no beans. I don't know why you wanna say that.

TROY: I ain't got no extra money. Gabe done moved over to Miss Pearl's paying her the rent and things done got tight around here. I can't afford to be giving you every payday.

LYONS: I ain't asked you to give me nothing. I asked you to loan me ten dollars. I know you got ten dollars.

TROY: Yeah, I got it. You know why I got it? Cause I don't throw my money away out there in the streets. You living the fast life . . . wanna be a musician . . . running around in them clubs and things . . . then, you learn to take care of yourself. You ain't gonna find me going and asking nobody for nothing. I done spent too many years without.

LYONS: You and me is two different people, Pop.

TROY: I done learned my mistake and learned to do what's right by it. You still trying to get something for nothing. Life don't owe you nothing. You owe it to yourself. Ask Bono. He'll tell you I'm right.

LYONS: You got your way of dealing with the world . . . I got mine. The only thing that matters to me is the music.

TROY: Yeah, I can see that! It don't matter how you gonna eat . . . where your next dollar is coming from. You telling the truth there.

LYONS: I know I got to eat. But I got to live too. I need something that gonna help me to get out of the bed in the morning. Make me feel like I belong in the world. I don't bother nobody. I just stay with my music cause that's the only way I can find to live in the world. Otherwise there ain't no telling what I might do. Now I don't come criticizing you and how you live. I just come by to ask you for ten dollars. I don't wanna hear all that about how I live.

TROY: Boy, your mamma did a hell of a job raising you.

LYONS: You can't change me, Pop. I'm thirty-four years old. If you wanted to change me, you should have been there when I was growing up. I come by to see you . . . ask for ten dollars and you want to talk about how I was raised. You don't know nothing about how I was raised.

ROSE: Let the boy have ten dollars, Troy.

TROY (*to Lyons*): What the hell you looking at me for? I ain't got no ten dollars. You know what I do with my money.

(*To Rose.*)

Give him ten dollars if you want him to have it.

ROSE: I will. Just as soon as you turn it loose.

TROY (*handing Rose the money*): There it is. Seventy-six dollars and forty-two cents. You see this, Bono? Now, I ain't gonna get but six of that back.

ROSE: You ought to stop telling that lie. Here, Lyons. (*She hands him the money.*)

LYONS: Thanks, Rose. Look . . . I got to run . . . I'll see you later.

TROY: Wait a minute. You gonna say, "thanks, Rose" and ain't gonna look to see where she got that ten dollars from? See how they do me, Bono?

LYONS: I know she got it from you, Pop. Thanks. I'll give it back to you.

TROY: There he go telling another lie. Time I see that ten dollars . . . he'll be owing me thirty more.

LYONS: See you, Mr. Bono.

BONO: Take care, Lyons!

LYONS: Thanks, Pop. I'll see you again.

(*Lyons exits the yard.*)

TROY: I don't know why he don't go and get him a decent job and take care of that woman he got.

BONO: He'll be all right, Troy. The boy is still young.

TROY: The *boy* is thirty-four years old.

ROSE: Let's not get off into all that.

BONO: Look here . . . I got to be going. I got to be getting on. Lucille gonna be waiting.

TROY (*puts his arm around Rose*): See this woman, Bono? I love this woman. I love this woman so much it hurts. I love her so much . . . I done run out of ways of loving her. So I got to go back to basics. Don't you come by my house Monday morning talking about time to go to work . . . 'cause I'm still gonna be stroking!

ROSE: Troy! Stop it now!

BONO: I ain't paying him no mind, Rose. That ain't nothing but gin-talk. Go on, Troy. I'll see you Monday.

TROY: Don't you come by my house, nigger! I done told you what I'm gonna be doing.

(*The lights go down to black.*)

Scene II

(*The lights come up on Rose hanging up clothes. She hums and sings softly to herself. It is the following morning.*)

ROSE (*sings*): Jesus, be a fence all around me every day
Jesus, I want you to protect me as I travel on my way.
Jesus, be a fence all around me every day.

(*Troy enters from the house.*)

Jesus, I want you to protect me
As I travel on my way.
(*To Troy.*) 'Morning. You ready for breakfast? I can fix it soon as I finish hanging up these clothes?

TROY: I got the coffee on. That'll be all right. I'll just drink some of that this morning.

ROSE: That 651 hit yesterday. That's the second time this month. Miss Pearl hit for a dollar . . . seem like those that need the least always get lucky. Poor folks can't get nothing.

TROY: Them numbers don't know nobody. I don't know why you fool with them. You and Lyons both.

ROSE: It's something to do.

TROY: You ain't doing nothing but throwing your money away.

ROSE: Troy, you know I don't play foolishly. I just play a nickel here and a nickel there.

TROY: That's two nickels you done thrown away.

ROSE: Now I hit sometimes . . . that makes up for it. It always comes in handy when I do hit. I don't hear you complaining then.

TROY: I ain't complaining now. I just say it's foolish. Trying to guess out of six hundred ways which way the number gonna come. If I had all the money niggers, these Negroes, throw away on numbers for one week — just one week — I'd be a rich man.

ROSE: Well, you wishing and calling it foolish ain't gonna stop folks from playing numbers. That's one thing for sure. Besides . . . some good things come from playing numbers. Look where Pope done bought him that restaurant off of numbers.

TROY: I can't stand niggers like that. Man ain't had two dimes to rub together. He walking around with his shoes all run over bumming money for cigarettes. All right. Got lucky there and hit the numbers . . .

ROSE: Troy, I know all about it.

TROY: Had good sense, I'll say that for him. He ain't throwed his money away. I seen niggers hit the numbers and go through two thousand dollars in four days. Man bought him that restaurant down there . . . fixed it up real nice . . . and then didn't want nobody to come in it! A Negro go in there and can't get no kind of service. I seen a white fellow come in there and order a bowl of stew. Pope picked all the meat out the pot for him. Man ain't had nothing but a bowl of meat! Negro come behind him and ain't got nothing but the potatoes and carrots. Talking about what numbers do for people, you picked a wrong example. Ain't done nothing but make a worser fool out of him than he was before.

ROSE: Troy, you ought to stop worrying about what happened at work yesterday.

TROY: I ain't worried. Just told me to be down there at the Commissioner's office on Friday. Everybody think they gonna fire me. I ain't worried about them firing me. You ain't got to worry about that.

(*Pause.*)

Where's Cory? Cory in the house? (*Calls.*) Cory?

ROSE: He gone out.

TROY: Out, huh? He gone out 'cause he know I want him to help me with this fence. I know how he is. That boy scared of work.

(*Gabriel enters. He comes halfway down the alley and, hearing Troy's voice, stops.*)

TROY (*continues*): He ain't done a lick of work in his life.

ROSE: He had to go to football practice. Coach wanted them to get in a little extra practice before the season start.

TROY: I got his practice . . . running out of here before he get his chores done.

ROSE: Troy, what is wrong with you this morning? Don't nothing set right with you. Go on back in there and go to bed . . . get up on the other side.

TROY: Why something got to be wrong with me? I ain't said nothing wrong with me.

ROSE: You got something to say about everything. First it's the numbers . . . then it's the way the man runs his restaurant . . . then you done got on Cory. What's it gonna be next? Take a look up there and see if the weather suits you . . . or is it gonna be how you gonna put up the fence with the clothes hanging in the yard.

TROY: You hit the nail on the head then.

ROSE: I know you like I know the back of my hand. Go on in there and get you some coffee . . . see if that straighten you up. 'Cause you ain't right this morning.

(*Troy starts into the house and sees Gabriel. Gabriel starts singing. Troy's brother, he is seven years younger than Troy. Injured in World War II, he has a metal plate in his head. He carries an old trumpet tied around his waist and believes with every fiber of his being that he is the Archangel Gabriel. He carries a chipped basket with an assortment of discarded fruits and vegetables he has picked up in the strip district and which he attempts to sell.*)

GABRIEL (*singing*): Yes, ma'am, I got plums
You ask me how I sell them
Oh ten cents apiece
Three for a quarter
Come and buy now
'Cause I'm here today
And tomorrow I'll be gone

(*Gabriel enters.*)

Hey, Rose!

ROSE: How you doing, Gabe?

GABRIEL: There's Troy . . . Hey, Troy!

TROY: Hey, Gabe.

(*Exit into kitchen.*)

ROSE (*to Gabriel*): What you got there?

GABRIEL: You know what I got, Rose. I got fruits and vegetables.

ROSE (*looking in basket*): Where's all these plums you talking about?

GABRIEL: I ain't got no plums today, Rose. I was just singing that. Have some tomorrow. Put me in a big order for plums. Have enough plums tomorrow for St. Peter and everybody.

(*Troy reenters from kitchen, crosses to steps.*)
(*To Rose.*)

Troy's mad at me.

TROY: I ain't mad at you. What I got to be mad at you about? You ain't done nothing to me.

GABRIEL: I just moved over to Miss Pearl's to keep out from in your way. I ain't mean no harm by it.

TROY: Who said anything about that? I ain't said anything about that.

GABRIEL: You ain't mad at me, is you?

TROY: Naw . . . I ain't mad at you, Gabe. If I was mad at you I'd tell you about it.

GABRIEL: Got me two rooms. In the basement. Got my own door too. Wanna see my key?

(*He holds up a key.*)

That's my own key! Ain't nobody else got a key like that. That's my key! My two rooms!

TROY: Well, that's good, Gabe. You got your own key . . . that's good.

ROSE: You hungry, Gabe? I was just fixing to cook Troy his breakfast.

GABRIEL: I'll take some biscuits. You got some biscuits? Did you know when I was in heaven . . . every morning me and St. Peter would sit down by the gate and eat some big fat biscuits? Oh, yeah! We had us a good time. We'd sit there and eat us them biscuits and then St. Peter would go off to sleep and tell me to wake him up when it's time to open the gates for the judgment.

ROSE: Well, come on ... I'll make up a batch of biscuits.

(*Rose exits into the house.*)

GABRIEL: Troy ... St. Peter got your name in the book. I seen it. It say ... Troy Maxson. I say ... I know him! He got the same name like what I got. That's my brother!

TROY: How many times you gonna tell me that, Gabe?

GABRIEL: Ain't got my name in the book. Don't have to have my name. I done died and went to heaven. He got your name though. One morning St. Peter was looking at his book ... marking it up for the judgment ... and he let me see your name. Got it in there under M. Got Rose's name ... I ain't seen it like I seen yours ... but I know it's in there. He got a great big book. Got everybody's name what was ever been born. That's what he told me. But I seen your name. Seen it with my own eyes.

TROY: Go on in the house there. Rose going to fix you something to eat.

GABRIEL: Oh, I ain't hungry. I done had breakfast with Aunt Jemimah. She come by and cooked me up a whole mess of flapjacks. Remember how we used to eat them flapjacks?

TROY: Go on in the house and get you something to eat now.

GABRIEL: I got to go sell my plums. I done sold some tomatoes. Got me two quarters. Wanna see?

(*He shows Troy his quarters.*)

I'm gonna save them and buy me a new horn so St. Peter can hear me when it's time to open the gates.

(*Gabriel stops suddenly. Listens.*)

Hear that? That's the hellhounds. I got to chase them out of here. Go on get out of here! Get out!

(*Gabriel exits singing.*)

Better get ready for the judgment
Better get ready for the judgment
My Lord is coming down

(*Rose enters from the house.*)

TROY: He gone off somewhere.

GABRIEL (*offstage*): Better get ready for the judgment
Better get ready for the judgment morning
Better get ready for the judgment
My God is coming down

ROSE: He ain't eating right. Miss Pearl say she can't get him to eat nothing.

TROY: What you want me to do about it, Rose? I done did everything I can for the man. I can't make him get well. Man got half his head blown away ... what you expect?

ROSE: Seem like something ought to be done to help him.

TROY: Man don't bother nobody. He just mixed up from that metal plate he got in his head. Ain't no sense for him to go back into the hospital.

ROSE: Least he be eating right. They can help him take care of himself.

TROY: Don't nobody wanna be locked up, Rose. What you wanna lock him up for? Man go over there and fight the war ... messin' around with them Japs, get half his head blown off ... and they give him a lousy three thousand dollars. And I had to swoop down on that.

ROSE: Is you fixing to go into that again?

TROY: That's the only way I got a roof over my head ... cause of that metal plate.

ROSE: Ain't no sense you blaming yourself for nothing. Gabe wasn't in no condition to manage that money. You done what was right by him. Can't nobody say you ain't done what was right by him. Look how long you took care of him ... till he wanted to have his own place and moved over there with Miss Pearl.

TROY: That ain't what I'm saying, woman! I'm just stating the facts. If my brother didn't have that metal plate in his head ... I wouldn't have a pot to piss in or a window to throw it out of. And I'm fifty-three years old. Now see if you can understand that!

(*Troy gets up from the porch and starts to exit the yard.*)

ROSE: Where you going off to? You been running out of here every Saturday for weeks. I thought you was gonna work on this fence.

TROY: I'm gonna walk down to Taylors'. Listen to the ball game. I'll be back in a bit. I'll work on it when I get back.

(*He exits the yard. The lights go to black.*)

Scene III

(*The lights come up on the yard. It is four hours later. Rose is taking down the clothes from the line. Cory enters carrying his football equipment.*)

ROSE: Your daddy like to had a fit with you running

out of here this morning without doing your
chores.

CORY: I told you I had to go to practice.

ROSE: He say you were supposed to help him with
this fence.

CORY: He been saying that the last four or five Saturdays, and then he don't never do nothing but go
down to Taylors'. Did you tell him about the
recruiter?

ROSE: Yeah, I told him.

CORY: What he say?

ROSE: He ain't said nothing too much. You get in
there and get started on your chores before he gets
back. Go on and scrub down them steps before he
gets back here hollering and carrying on.

CORY: I'm hungry. What you got to eat, Mama?

ROSE: Go on and get started on your chores. I got
some meat loaf in there. Go on and make you a
sandwich . . . and don't leave no mess in there.

(*Cory exits into the house. Rose continues to take
down the clothes. Troy enters the yard and sneaks up
and grabs her from behind.*)

Troy! Go on, now. You liked to scared me to death.
What was the score of the game? Lucille had me
on the phone and I couldn't keep up with it.

TROY: What I care about the game? Come here,
woman. (*He tries to kiss her.*)

ROSE: I thought you went down Taylors' to listen to
the game. Go on, Troy! You supposed to be putting
up this fence.

TROY (*attempting to kiss her again*): I'll put it up when
I finish with what is at hand.

ROSE: Go on, Troy. I ain't studying you.

TROY (*chasing after her*): I'm studying you . . . fixing
to do my homework!

ROSE: Troy, you better leave me alone.

TROY: Where's Cory? That boy brought his butt home
yet?

ROSE: He's in the house doing his chores.

TROY (*calling*): Cory! Get your butt out here, boy!

(*Rose exits into the house with the laundry. Troy goes
over to the pile of wood, picks up a board, and starts
sawing. Cory enters from the house.*)

TROY: You just now coming in here from leaving this
morning?

CORY: Yeah, I had to go to football practice.

TROY: Yeah, what?

CORY: Yessir.

TROY: I ain't but two seconds off you noway. The
garbage sitting in there overflowing . . . you ain't
done none of your chores . . . and you come in
here talking about "Yeah."

CORY: I was just getting ready to do my chores now,
Pop . . .

TROY: Your first chore is to help me with this fence
on Saturday. Everything else come after that. Now
get that saw and cut them boards.

(*Cory takes the saw and begins cutting the boards.
Troy continues working. There is a long pause.*)

CORY: Hey, Pop . . . why don't you buy a TV?

TROY: What I want with a TV? What I want one of
them for?

CORY: Everybody got one. Earl, Ba Bra . . . Jesse!

TROY: I ain't asked you who had one. I say what I
want with one?

CORY: So you can watch it. They got lots of things
on TV. Baseball games and everything. We could
watch the World Series.

TROY: Yeah . . . and how much this TV cost?

CORY: I don't know. They got them on sale for around
two hundred dollars.

TROY: Two hundred dollars, huh?

CORY: That ain't that much, Pop.

TROY: Naw, it's just two hundred dollars. See that
roof you got over your head at night? Let me tell
you something about that roof. It's been over ten
years since that roof was last tarred. See now . . .
the snow come this winter and sit up there on that
roof like it is . . . and it's gonna seep inside. It's
just gonna be a little bit . . . ain't gonna hardly
notice it. Then the next thing you know, it's gonna
be leaking all over the house. Then the wood rot
from all that water and you gonna need a whole
new roof. Now, how much you think it cost to get
that roof tarred?

CORY: I don't know.

TROY: Two hundred and sixty-four dollars . . . cash
money. While you thinking about a TV, I got to
be thinking about the roof . . . and whatever else
go wrong around here. Now if you had two
hundred dollars, what would you do . . . fix the
roof or buy a TV?

CORY: I'd buy a TV. Then when the roof started to
leak . . . when it needed fixing . . . I'd fix it.

TROY: Where you gonna get the money from? You
done spent it for a TV. You gonna sit up and watch
the water run all over your brand new TV.

CORY: Aw, Pop. You got money. I know you do.

TROY: Where I got it at, huh?

CORY: You got it in the bank.

TROY: You wanna see my bankbook? You wanna see
that seventy-three dollars and twenty-two cents I
got sitting up in there.

CORY: You ain't got to pay for it all at one time. You
can put a down payment on it and carry it on
home with you.

TROY: Not me. I ain't gonna owe nobody nothing if I can help it. Miss a payment and they come and snatch it right out your house. Then what you got? Now, soon as I get two hundred dollars clear, then I'll buy a TV. Right now, as soon as I get two hundred and sixty-four dollars, I'm gonna have this roof tarred.

CORY: Aw . . . Pop!

TROY: You go on and get you two hundred dollars and buy one if ya want it. I got better things to do with my money.

CORY: I can't get no two hundred dollars. I ain't never seen two hundred dollars.

TROY: I'll tell you what . . . you get you a hundred dollars and I'll put the other hundred with it.

CORY: All right, I'm gonna show you.

TROY: You gonna show me how you can cut them boards right now.

(*Cory begins to cut the boards. There is a long pause.*)

CORY: The Pirates won today. That makes five in a row.

TROY: I ain't thinking about the Pirates. Got an all-white team. Got that boy . . . that Puerto Rican boy . . . Clemente. Don't even half-play him. That boy could be something if they give him a chance. Play him one day and sit him on the bench the next.

CORY: He gets a lot of chances to play.

TROY: I'm talking about playing regular. Playing every day so you can get your timing. That's what I'm talking about.

CORY: They got some white guys on the team that don't play every day. You can't play everybody at the same time.

TROY: If they got a white fellow sitting on the bench . . . you can bet your last dollar he can't play! The colored guy got to be twice as good before he get on the team. That's why I don't want you to get all tied up in them sports. Man on the team and what it get him? They got colored on the team and don't use them. Same as not having them. All them teams the same.

CORY: The Braves got Hank Aaron and Wes Covington. Hank Aaron hit two home runs today. That makes forty-three.

TROY: Hank Aaron ain't nobody. That's what you supposed to do. That's how you supposed to play the game. Ain't nothing to it. It's just a matter of timing . . . getting the right follow-through. Hell, I can hit forty-three home runs right now!

CORY: Not off no major-league pitching, you couldn't.

TROY: We had better pitching in the Negro leagues. I hit seven home runs off of Satchel Paige.° You can't get no better than that!

CORY: Sandy Koufax. He's leading the league in strikeouts.

TROY: I ain't thinking of no Sandy Koufax.

CORY: You got Warren Spahn and Lew Burdette. I bet you couldn't hit no home runs off of Warren Spahn.

TROY: I'm through with it now. You go on and cut them boards.

(*Pause.*)

Your mama tell me you done got recruited by a college football team? Is that right?

CORY: Yeah. Coach Zellman say the recruiter gonna be coming by to talk to you. Get you to sign the permission papers.

TROY: I thought you supposed to be working down there at the A&P. Ain't you suppose to be working down there after school?

CORY: Mr. Stawicki say he gonna hold my job for me until after the football season. Say starting next week I can work weekends.

TROY: I thought we had an understanding about this football stuff? You suppose to keep up with your chores and hold that job down at the A&P. Ain't been around here all day on a Saturday. Ain't none of your chores done . . . and now you telling me you done quit your job.

CORY: I'm gonna be working weekends.

TROY: You damn right you are! And ain't no need for nobody coming around here to talk to me about signing nothing.

CORY: Hey, Pop . . . you can't do that. He's coming all the way from North Carolina.

TROY: I don't care where he coming from. The white man ain't gonna let you get nowhere with that football noway. You go on and get your book-learning so you can work yourself up in that A&P or learn how to fix cars or build houses or something, get you a trade. That way you have something can't nobody take away from you. You go on and learn how to put your hands to some good use. Besides hauling people's garbage.

CORY: I get good grades, Pop. That's why the recruiter wants to talk with you. You got to keep up your grades to get recruited. This way I'll be going to college. I'll get a chance . . .

TROY: First you gonna get your butt down there to the A&P and get your job back.

CORY: Mr. Stawicki done already hired somebody else 'cause I told him I was playing football.

Satchel Paige: (1906?–1982), legendary black pitcher in the Negro leagues.

TROY: You a bigger fool than I thought . . . to let somebody take away your job so you can play some football. Where you gonna get your money to take out your girlfriend and whatnot? What kind of foolishness is that to let somebody take away your job?

CORY: I'm still gonna be working weekends.

TROY: Naw . . . naw. You getting your butt out of here and finding you another job.

CORY: Come on, Pop! I got to practice. I can't work after school and play football too. The team needs me. That's what Coach Zellman say . . .

TROY: I don't care what nobody else say. I'm the boss . . . you understand? I'm the boss around here. I do the only saying what counts.

CORY: Come on, Pop!

TROY: I asked you . . . did you understand?

CORY: Yeah . . .

TROY: What?!

CORY: Yessir.

TROY: You go on down there to that A&P and see if you can get your job back. If you can't do both . . . then you quit the football team. You've got to take the crookeds with the straights.

CORY: Yessir.

(*Pause.*)

Can I ask you a question?

TROY: What the hell you wanna ask me? Mr. Stawicki the one you got the questions for.

CORY: How come you ain't never liked me?

TROY: Liked you? Who the hell say I got to like you? What law is there say I got to like you? Wanna stand up in my face and ask a damn fool-ass question like that. Talking about liking somebody. Come here, boy, when I talk to you.

(*Cory comes over to where Troy is working. He stands slouched over and Troy shoves him on his shoulder.*)

Straighten up, goddammit! I asked you a question . . . what law is there say I got to like you?

CORY: None.

TROY: Well, all right then! Don't you eat every day?

(*Pause.*)

Answer me when I talk to you! Don't you eat every day?

CORY: Yeah.

TROY: Nigger, as long as you in my house, you put that sir on the end of it when you talk to me!

CORY: Yes . . . sir.

TROY: You eat every day.

CORY: Yessir!

TROY: Got a roof over your head.

CORY: Yessir!

TROY: Got clothes on your back.

CORY: Yessir.

TROY: Why you think that is?

CORY: Cause of you.

TROY: Ah, hell I know it's 'cause of me . . . but why do you think that is?

CORY (*hesitant*): Cause you like me.

TROY: Like you? I go out of here every morning . . . bust my butt . . . putting up with them crackers° every day . . . cause I like you? You about the biggest fool I ever saw.

(*Pause.*)

It's my job. It's my responsibility! You understand that? A man got to take care of his family. You live in my house . . . sleep you behind on my bedclothes . . . fill you belly up with my food . . . cause you my son. You my flesh and blood. Not 'cause I like you! Cause it's my duty to take care of you. I owe a responsibility to you! Let's get this straight right here . . . before it go along any further . . . I ain't got to like you. Mr. Rand don't give me my money come payday cause he likes me. He gives me cause he owe me. I done give you everything I had to give you. I gave you your life! Me and your mama worked that out between us. And liking your black ass wasn't part of the bargain. Don't you try and go through life worrying about if somebody like you or not. You best be making sure they doing right by you. You understand what I'm saying, boy?

CORY: Yessir.

TROY: Then get the hell out of my face, and get on down to that A&P.

(*Rose has been standing behind the screen door for much of the scene. She enters as Cory exits.*)

ROSE: Why don't you let the boy go ahead and play football, Troy? Ain't no harm in that. He's just trying to be like you with the sports.

TROY: I don't want him to be like me! I want him to move as far away from my life as he can get. You the only decent thing that ever happened to me. I wish him that. But I don't wish him a thing else from my life. I decided seventeen years ago that boy wasn't getting involved in no sports. Not after what they did to me in the sports.

ROSE: Troy, why don't you admit you was too old to play in the major leagues? For once . . . why don't you admit that?

TROY: What do you mean too old? Don't come telling me I was too old. I just wasn't the right color.

crackers: White people, often used to refer disparagingly to poor whites.

Hell, I'm fifty-three years old and can do better than Selkirk's .269 right now!

ROSE: How's was you gonna play ball when you were over forty? Sometimes I can't get no sense out of you.

TROY: I got good sense, woman. I got sense enough not to let my boy get hurt over playing no sports. You been mothering that boy too much. Worried about if people like him.

ROSE: Everything that boy do . . . he do for you. He wants you to say "Good job, son." That's all.

TROY: Rose, I ain't got time for that. He's alive. He's healthy. He's got to make his own way. I made mine. Ain't nobody gonna hold his hand when he get out there in that world.

ROSE: Times have changed from when you was young, Troy. People change. The world's changing around you and you can't even see it.

TROY (slow, methodical): Woman . . . I do the best I can do. I come in here every Friday. I carry a sack of potatoes and a bucket of lard. You all line up at the door with your hands out. I give you the lint from my pockets. I give you my sweat and my blood. I ain't got no tears. I done spent them. We go upstairs in that room at night . . . and I fall down on you and try to blast a hole into forever. I get up Monday morning . . . find my lunch on the table. I go out. Make my way. Find my strength to carry me through to the next Friday.

(Pause.)

That's all I got, Rose. That's all I got to give. I can't give nothing else.

(Troy exits into the house. The lights go down to black.)

Scene IV

(It is Friday. Two weeks later. Cory starts out of the house with his football equipment. The phone rings.)

CORY (calling): I got it!

(He answers the phone and stands in the screen door talking.)

Hello? Hey, Jesse. Naw . . . I was just getting ready to leave now.

ROSE (calling): Cory!

CORY: I told you, man, them spikes is all tore up. You can use them if you want, but they ain't no good. Earl got some spikes.

ROSE (calling): Cory!

CORY (calling to Rose): Mam? I'm talking to Jesse.

(Into phone.)

When she say that? (Pause.) Aw, you lying, man. I'm gonna tell her you said that.

ROSE (calling): Cory, don't you go nowhere!

CORY: I got to go to the game, Ma!

(Into the phone.)

Yeah, hey, look, I'll talk to you later. Yeah, I'll meet you over Earl's house. Later. Bye, Ma.

(Cory exits the house and starts out the yard.)

ROSE: Cory, where you going off to? You got that stuff all pulled out and thrown all over your room.

CORY (in the yard): I was looking for my spikes. Jesse wanted to borrow my spikes.

ROSE: Get up there and get that cleaned up before your daddy get back in here.

CORY: I got to go to the game! I'll clean it up when I get back.

(Cory exits.)

ROSE: That's all he need to do is see that room all messed up.

(Rose exits into the house. Troy and Bono enter the yard. Troy is dressed in clothes other than his work clothes.)

BONO: He told him the same thing he told you. Take it to the union.

TROY: Brownie ain't got that much sense. Man wasn't thinking about nothing. He wait until I confront them on it . . . then he wanna come crying seniority.

(Calls.)

Hey, Rose!

BONO: I wish I could have seen Mr. Rand's face when he told you.

TROY: He couldn't get it out of his mouth! Liked to bit his tongue! When they called me down there to the Commissioner's office . . . he thought they was gonna fire me. Like everybody else.

BONO: I didn't think they was gonna fire you. I thought they was gonna put you on the warning paper.

TROY: Hey, Rose!

(To Bono.)

Yeah, Mr. Rand like to bit his tongue.

(Troy breaks the seal on the bottle, takes a drink, and hands it to Bono.)

BONO: I see you run right down to Taylors' and told that Alberta gal.

TROY (*calling*): Hey, Rose! (*To Bono.*) I told everybody. Hey, Rose! I went down there to cash my check.

ROSE (*entering from the house*): Hush all that hollering, man! I know you out here. What they say down there at the Commissioner's office?

TROY: You supposed to come when I call you, woman. Bono'll tell you that.

(*To Bono.*)

Don't Lucille come when you call her?

ROSE: Man, hush your mouth. I ain't no dog . . . talk about "come when you call me."

TROY (*puts his arm around Rose*): You hear this, Bono? I had me an old dog used to get uppity like that. You say, "C'mere, Blue!" . . . and he just lay there and look at you. End up getting a stick and chasing him away trying to make him come.

ROSE: I ain't studying you and your dog. I remember you used to sing that old song.

TROY (*he sings*): Hear it ring! Hear it ring! I had a dog his name was Blue.

ROSE: Don't nobody wanna hear you sing that old song.

TROY (*sings*): You know Blue was mighty true.

ROSE: Used to have Cory running around here singing that song.

BONO: Hell, I remember that song myself.

TROY (*sings*): You know Blue was a good old dog. Blue treed a possum in a hollow log.
That was my daddy's song. My daddy made up that song.

ROSE: I don't care who made it up. Don't nobody wanna hear you sing it.

TROY (*makes a song like calling a dog*): Come here, woman.

ROSE: You come in here carrying on, I reckon they ain't fired you. What they say down there at the Commissioner's office?

TROY: Look here, Rose . . . Mr. Rand called me into his office today when I got back from talking to them people down there . . . it come from up top . . . he called me in and told me they was making me a driver.

ROSE: Troy, you kidding!

TROY: No I ain't. Ask Bono.

ROSE: Well, that's great, Troy. Now you don't have to hassle them people no more.

(*Lyons enters from the street.*)

TROY: Aw hell, I wasn't looking to see you today. I thought you was in jail. Got it all over the front page of the *Courier* about them raiding Sefus' place . . . where you be hanging out with all them thugs.

LYONS: Hey, Pop . . . that ain't got nothing to do with me. I don't go down there gambling. I go down there to sit in with the band. I ain't got nothing to do with the gambling part. They got some good music down there.

TROY: They got some rogues . . . is what they got.

LYONS: How you been, Mr. Bono? Hi, Rose.

BONO: I see where you playing down at the Crawford Grill tonight.

ROSE: How come you ain't brought Bonnie like I told you. You should have brought Bonnie with you, she ain't been over in a month of Sundays.

LYONS: I was just in the neighborhood . . . thought I'd stop by.

TROY: Here he come . . .

BONO: Your daddy got a promotion on the rubbish. He's gonna be the first colored driver. Ain't got to do nothing but sit up there and read the paper like them white fellows.

LYONS: Hey, Pop . . . if you knew how to read you'd be all right.

BONO: Naw . . . naw . . . you mean if the nigger knew how to *drive* he'd be all right. Been fighting with them people about driving and ain't even got a license. Mr. Rand know you ain't got no driver's license?

TROY: Driving ain't nothing. All you do is point the truck where you want it to go. Driving ain't nothing.

BONO: Do Mr. Rand know you ain't got no driver's license? That's what I'm talking about. I ain't asked if driving was easy. I asked if Mr. Rand know you ain't got no driver's license.

TROY: He ain't got to know. The man ain't got to know my business. Time he find out, I have two or three driver's licenses.

LYON (*going into his pocket*): Say, look here, Pop . . .

TROY: I knew it was coming. Didn't I tell you, Bono? I know what kind of "Look here, Pop" that was. The nigger fixing to ask me for some money. It's Friday night. It's my payday. All them rogues down there on the avenue . . . the ones that ain't in jail . . . and Lyons is hopping in his shoes to get down there with them.

LYONS: See, Pop . . . if you give somebody else a chance to talk sometime, you'd see that I was fixing to pay you back your ten dollars like I told you. Here . . . I told you I'd pay you when Bonnie got paid.

TROY: Naw . . . you go ahead and keep that ten dollars. Put it in the bank. The next time you feel like you wanna come by here and ask me for something . . . you go on down there and get that.

LYONS: Here's your ten dollars, Pop. I told you I don't want you to give me nothing. I just wanted to borrow ten dollars.

TROY: Naw . . . you go on and keep that for the next time you want to ask me.

LYONS: Come on, Pop . . . here go your ten dollars.

ROSE: Why don't you go on and let the boy pay you back, Troy?

LYONS: Here you go, Rose. If you don't take it I'm gonna have to hear about it for the next six months.

(*He hands her the money.*)

ROSE: You can hand yours over here too, Troy.

TROY: You see this, Bono. You see how they do me.

BONO: Yeah, Lucille do me the same way.

(*Gabriel is heard singing offstage. He enters.*)

GABRIEL: Better get ready for the Judgment! Better get ready for . . . Hey! . . . Hey! . . . There's Troy's boy!

LYONS: How are you doing, Uncle Gabe?

GABRIEL: Lyons . . . The King of the Jungle! Rose . . . hey, Rose. Got a flower for you.

(*He takes a rose from his pocket.*)

Picked it myself. That's the same rose like you is!

ROSE: That's right nice of you, Gabe.

LYONS: What you been doing, Uncle Gabe?

GABRIEL: Oh, I been chasing hellhounds and waiting on the time to tell St. Peter to open the gates.

LYONS: You been chasing hellhounds, huh? Well . . . you doing the right thing, Uncle Gabe. Somebody got to chase them.

GABRIEL: Oh, yeah . . . I know it. The devil's strong. The devil ain't no pushover. Hellhounds snipping at everybody's heels. But I got my trumpet waiting on the judgment time.

LYONS: Waiting on the Battle of Armageddon, huh?

GABRIEL: Ain't gonna be too much of a battle when God get to waving that Judgment sword. But the people's gonna have a hell of a time trying to get into heaven if them gates ain't open.

LYONS (*putting his arm around Gabriel*): You hear this, Pop. Uncle Gabe, you all right!

GABRIEL (*laughing with Lyons*): Lyons! King of the Jungle.

ROSE: You gonna stay for supper, Gabe. Want me to fix you a plate?

GABRIEL: I'll take a sandwich, Rose. Don't want no plate. Just wanna eat with my hands. I'll take a sandwich.

ROSE: How about you, Lyons? You staying? Got some short ribs cooking.

LYONS: Naw, I won't eat nothing till after we finished playing.

(*Pause.*)

You ought to come down and listen to me play, Pop.

TROY: I don't like that Chinese music. All that noise.

ROSE: Go on in the house and wash up, Gabe . . . I'll fix you a sandwich.

GABRIEL (*to Lyons, as he exits*): Troy's mad at me.

LYONS: What you mad at Uncle Gabe for, Pop.

ROSE: He thinks Troy's mad at him cause he moved over to Miss Pearl's.

TROY: I ain't mad at the man. He can live where he want to live at.

LYONS: What he move over there for? Miss Pearl don't like nobody.

ROSE: She don't mind him none. She treats him real nice. She just don't allow all that singing.

TROY: She don't mind that rent he be paying . . . that's what she don't mind.

ROSE: Troy, I ain't going through that with you no more. He's over there cause he want to have his own place. He can come and go as he please.

TROY: Hell, he could come and go as he please here. I wasn't stopping him. I ain't put no rules on him.

ROSE: It ain't the same thing, Troy. And you know it.

(*Gabriel comes to the door.*)

Now, that's the last I wanna hear about that. I don't wanna hear nothing else about Gabe and Miss Pearl. And next week . . .

GABRIEL: I'm ready for my sandwich, Rose.

ROSE: And next week . . . when that recruiter come from that school . . . I want you to sign that paper and go on and let Cory play football. Then that'll be the last I have to hear about that.

TROY (*to Rose as she exits into the house*): I ain't thinking about Cory nothing.

LYONS: What . . . Cory got recruited? What school he going to?

TROY: That boy walking around here smelling his piss . . . thinking he's grown. Thinking he's gonna do what he want, irrespective of what I say. Look here, Bono . . . I left the Commissioner's office and went down to the A&P . . . that boy ain't working down there. He lying to me. Telling me he got his job back . . . telling me he working weekends . . . telling me he working after school . . . Mr. Stawicki tell me he ain't working down there at all!

LYONS: Cory just growing up. He's just busting at the seams trying to fill out your shoes.

TROY: I don't care what he's doing. When he get to the point where he wanna disobey me . . . then it's time for him to move on. Bono'll tell you that. I bet he ain't never disobeyed his daddy without paying the consequences.

BONO: I ain't never had a chance. My daddy came

on through . . . but I ain't never knew him to see him . . . or what he had on his mind or where he went. Just moving on through. Searching out the New Land. That's what the old folks used to call it. See a fellow moving around from place to place . . . woman to woman . . . called it searching out the New Land. I can't say if he ever found it. I come along, didn't want no kids. Didn't know if I was gonna be in one place long enough to fix on them right as their daddy. I figured I was going searching too. As it turned out I been hooked up with Lucille near about as long as your daddy been with Rose. Going on sixteen years.

TROY: Sometimes I wish I hadn't known my daddy. He ain't cared nothing about no kids. A kid to him wasn't nothing. All he wanted was for you to learn how to walk so he could start you to working. When it come time for eating . . . he ate first. If there was anything left over, that's what you got. Man would sit down and eat two chickens and give you the wing.

LYONS: You ought to stop that, Pop. Everybody feed their kids. No matter how hard times is . . . everybody care about their kids. Make sure they have something to eat.

TROY: The only thing my daddy cared about was getting them bales of cotton in to Mr. Lubin. That's the only thing that mattered to him. Sometimes I used to wonder why he was living. Wonder why the devil hadn't come and got him. "Get them bales of cotton in to Mr. Lubin" and find out he owe him money . . .

LYONS: He should have just went on and left when he saw he couldn't get nowhere. That's what I would have done.

TROY: How he gonna leave with eleven kids? And where he gonna go? He ain't knew how to do nothing but farm. No, he was trapped and I think he knew it. But I'll say this for him . . . he felt a responsibility toward us. Maybe he ain't treated us the way I felt he should have . . . but without that responsibility he could have walked off and left us . . . made his own way.

BONO: A lot of them did. Back in those days what you talking about . . . they walk out their front door and just take on down one road or another and keep on walking.

LYONS: There you go! That's what I'm talking about.

BONO: Just keep on walking till you come to something else. Ain't you never heard of nobody having the walking blues? Well, that's what you call it when you just take off like that.

TROY: My daddy ain't had them walking blues! What you talking about? He stayed right there with his family. But he was just as evil as he could be. My mama couldn't stand him. Couldn't stand that evilness. She run off when I was about eight. She sneaked off one night after he had gone to sleep. Told me she was coming back for me. I ain't never seen her no more. All his women run off and left him. He wasn't good for nobody.

When my turn come to head out, I was fourteen and got to sniffing around Joe Canewell's daughter. Had us an old mule we called Greyboy. My daddy sent me out to do some plowing and I tied up Greyboy and went to fooling around with Joe Canewell's daughter. We done found us a nice little spot, got real cozy with each other. She about thirteen and we done figured we was grown anyway . . . so we down there enjoying ourselves . . . ain't thinking about nothing. We didn't know Greyboy had got loose and wandered back to the house and my daddy was looking for me. We down there by the creek enjoying ourselves when my daddy come up on us. Surprised us. He had them leather straps off the mule and commenced to whupping me like there was no tomorrow. I jumped up, mad and embarrassed. I was scared of my daddy. When he commenced to whupping on me . . . quite naturally I run to get out of the way.

(*Pause.*)

Now I thought he was mad cause I ain't done my work. But I see where he was chasing me off so he could have the gal for himself. When I see what the matter of it was, I lost all fear of my daddy. Right there is where I become a man . . . at fourteen years of age.

(*Pause.*)

Now it was my turn to run him off. I picked up them same reins that he had used on me. I picked up them reins and commenced to whupping on him. The gal jumped up and run off . . . and when my daddy turned to face me, I could see why the devil had never come to get him . . . cause he was the devil himself. I don't know what happened. When I woke up, I was laying right there by the creek, and Blue . . . this old dog we had . . . was licking my face. I thought I was blind. I couldn't see nothing. Both my eyes were swollen shut. I layed there and cried. I didn't know what I was gonna do. The only thing I knew was the time had come for me to leave my daddy's house. And right there the world suddenly got big. And it was a long time before I could cut it down to where I could handle it.

Part of that cutting down was when I got to the place where I could feel him kicking in my blood and knew that the only thing that separated us was the matter of a few years.

(*Gabriel enters from the house with a sandwich.*)

LYONS: What you got there, Uncle Gabe?

GABRIEL: Got me a ham sandwich. Rose gave me a ham sandwich.

TROY: I don't know what happened to him. I done lost touch with everybody except Gabriel. But I hope he's dead. I hope he found some peace.

LYONS: That's a heavy story, Pop. I didn't know you left home when you was fourteen.

TROY: And didn't know nothing. The only part of the world I knew was the forty-two acres of Mr. Lubin's land. That's all I knew about life.

LYONS: Fourteen's kinda young to be out on your own. (*Phone rings.*) I don't even think I was ready to be out on my own at fourteen. I don't know what I would have done.

TROY: I got up from the creek and walked on down to Mobile. I was through with farming. Figured I could do better in the city. So I walked the two hundred miles to Mobile.

LYONS: Wait a minute . . . you ain't walked no two hundred miles, Pop. Ain't nobody gonna walk no two hundred miles. You talking about some walking there.

BONO: That's the only way you got anywhere back in them days.

LYONS: Shhh. Damn if I wouldn't have hitched a ride with somebody!

TROY: Who you gonna hitch it with? They ain't had no cars and things like they got now. We talking about 1918.

ROSE (*entering*): What you all out here getting into?

TROY (*to Rose*): I'm telling Lyons how good he got it. He don't know nothing about this I'm talking.

ROSE: Lyons, that was Bonnie on the phone. She say you supposed to pick her up.

LYONS: Yeah, okay, Rose.

TROY: I walked on down to Mobile and hitched up with some of them fellows that was heading this way. Got up here and found out . . . not only couldn't you get a job . . . you couldn't find no place to live. I thought I was in freedom. Shhh. Colored folks living down there on the riverbanks in whatever kind of shelter they could find for themselves. Right down there under the Brady Street Bridge. Living in shacks made of sticks and tarpaper. Messed around there and went from bad to worse. Started stealing. First it was food. Then I figured, hell, if I steal money I can buy me some food. Buy me some shoes too! One thing led to another. Met your mama. I was young and anxious to be a man. Met your mama and had you. What

I do that for? Now I got to worry about feeding you and her. Got to steal three times as much. Went out one day looking for somebody to rob . . . that's what I was, a robber. I'll tell you the truth. I'm ashamed of it today. But it's the truth. Went to rob this fellow . . . pulled out my knife . . . and he pulled out a gun. Shot me in the chest. It felt just like somebody had taken a hot branding iron and laid it on me. When he shot me I jumped at him with my knife. They told me I killed him and they put me in the penitentiary and locked me up for fifteen years. That's where I met Bono. That's where I learned how to play baseball. Got out that place and your mama had taken you and went on to make life without me. Fifteen years was a long time for her to wait. But that fifteen years cured me of that robbing stuff. Rose'll tell you. She asked me when I met her if I had gotten all that foolishness out of my system. And I told her, "Baby, it's you and baseball all what count with me." You hear me, Bono? I meant it too. She say, "Which one comes first?" I told her, "Baby, ain't no doubt it's baseball . . . but you stick and get old with me and we'll both outlive this baseball." Am I right, Rose? And it's true.

ROSE: Man, hush your mouth. You ain't said no such thing. Talking about, "Baby, you know you'll always be number one with me." That's what you was talking.

TROY: You hear that, Bono. That's why I love her.

BONO: Rose'll keep you straight. You get off the track, she'll straighten you up.

ROSE: Lyons, you better get on up and get Bonnie. She waiting on you.

LYONS (*gets up to go*): Hey, Pop, why don't you come on down to the Grill and hear me play?

TROY: I ain't going down there. I'm too old to be sitting around in them clubs.

BONO: You got to be good to play down at the Grill.

LYONS: Come on, Pop . . .

TROY: I got to get up in the morning.

LYONS: You ain't got to stay long.

TROY: Naw, I'm gonna get my supper and go on to bed.

LYONS: Well, I got to go. I'll see you again.

TROY: Don't you come around my house on my payday.

ROSE: Pick up the phone and let somebody know you coming. And bring Bonnie with you. You know I'm always glad to see her.

LYONS: Yeah, I'll do that, Rose. You take care now. See you, Pop. See you, Mr. Bono. See you, Uncle Gabe.

GABRIEL: Lyons! King of the Jungle!

(*Lyons exits.*)

TROY: Is supper ready, woman? Me and you got some business to take care of. I'm gonna tear it up too.

ROSE: Troy, I done told you now!

TROY (*puts his arm around Bono*): Aw hell, woman . . . this is Bono. Bono like family. I done known this nigger since . . . how long I done know you?

BONO: It's been a long time.

TROY: I done known this nigger since Skippy was a pup. Me and him done been through some times.

BONO: You sure right about that.

TROY: Hell, I done know him longer than I known you. And we still standing shoulder to shoulder. Hey, look here, Bono . . . a man can't ask for no more than that.

(*Drinks to him.*)

I love you, nigger.

BONO: Hell, I love you too . . . but I got to get home see my woman. You got yours in hand. I got to go get mine.

(*Bono starts to exit as Cory enters the yard, dressed in his football uniform. He gives Troy a hard, uncompromising look.*)

CORY: What you do that for, Pop?

(*He throws his helmet down in the direction of Troy.*)

ROSE: What's the matter? Cory . . . what's the matter?

CORY: Papa done went up to the school and told Coach Zellman I can't play football no more. Wouldn't even let me play the game. Told him to tell the recruiter not to come.

ROSE: Troy . . .

TROY: What you Troying me for. Yeah, I did it. And the boy know why I did it.

CORY: Why you wanna do that to me? That was the one chance I had.

ROSE: Ain't nothing wrong with Cory playing football, Troy.

TROY: The boy lied to me. I told the nigger if he wanna play football . . . to keep up his chores and hold down that job at the A&P. That was the conditions. Stopped down there to see Mr. Stawicki . . .

CORY: I can't work after school during the football season, Pop! I tried to tell you that Mr. Stawicki's holding my job for me. You don't never want to listen to nobody. And then you wanna go and do this to me!

TROY: I ain't done nothing to you. You done it to yourself.

CORY: Just cause you didn't have a chance! You just scared I'm gonna be better than you, that's all.

TROY: Come here.

ROSE: Troy . . .

(*Cory reluctantly crosses over to Troy.*)

TROY: All right! See. You done made a mistake.

CORY: I didn't even do nothing!

TROY: I'm gonna tell you what your mistake was. See . . . you swung at the ball and didn't hit it. That's strike one. See, you in the batter's box now. You swung and you missed. That's strike one. Don't you strike out!

(*Lights fade to black.*)

ACT II • Scene 1

(*The following morning. Cory is at the tree hitting the ball with the bat. He tries to mimic Troy, but his swing is awkward, less sure. Rose enters from the house.*)

ROSE: Cory, I want you to help me with this cupboard.

CORY: I ain't quitting the team. I don't care what Poppa say.

ROSE: I'll talk to him when he gets back. He had to go see about your Uncle Gabe. The police done arrested him. Say he was disturbing the peace. He'll be back directly. Come on in here and help me clean out the top of this cupboard.

(*Cory exits into the house. Rose sees Troy and Bono coming down the alley.*)

Troy . . . what they say down there?

TROY: Ain't said nothing. I give them fifty dollars and they let him go. I'll talk to you about it. Where's Cory?

ROSE: He's in there helping me clean out these cupboards.

TROY: Tell him to get his butt out here.

(*Troy and Bono go over to the pile of wood. Bono picks up the saw and begins sawing.*)

TROY (*to Bono*): All they want is the money. That makes six or seven times I done went down there and got him. See me coming they stick out their *hands.*

BONO: Yeah. I know what you mean. That's all they care about . . . that money. They don't care about what's right.

(*Pause.*)

Nigger, why you got to go and get some hard wood? You ain't doing nothing but building a little old fence. Get you some soft pine wood. That's all you need.

TROY: I know what I'm doing. This is outside wood. You put pine wood inside the house. Pine wood is inside wood. This here is outside wood. Now you tell me where the fence is gonna be?

BONO: You don't need this wood. You can put it up with pine wood and it'll stand as long as you gonna be here looking at it.

TROY: How you know how long I'm gonna be here, nigger? Hell, I might just live forever. Live longer than old man Horsely.

BONO: That's what Magee used to say.

TROY: Magee's a damn fool. Now you tell me who you ever heard of gonna pull their own teeth with a pair of rusty pliers.

BONO: The old folks . . . my granddaddy used to pull his teeth with pliers. They ain't had no dentists for the colored folks back then.

TROY: Get clean pliers! You understand? Clean pliers! Sterilize them! Besides we ain't living back then. All Magee had to do was walk over to Doc Goldblum's.

BONO: I see where you and that Tallahassee gal . . . that Alberta . . . I see where you all done got tight.

TROY: What you mean "got tight"?

BONO: I see where you be laughing and joking with her all the time.

TROY: I laughs and jokes with all of them, Bono. You know me.

BONO: That ain't the kind of laughing and joking I'm talking about.

(*Cory enters from the house.*)

CORY: How you doing, Mr. Bono?

TROY: Cory? Get that saw from Bono and cut some wood. He talking about the wood's too hard to cut. Stand back there, Jim, and let that young boy show you how it's done.

BONO: He's sure welcome to it.

(*Cory takes the saw and begins to cut the wood.*)

Whew-e-e! Look at that. Big old strong boy. Look like Joe Louis. Hell, must be getting old the way I'm watching that boy whip through that wood.

CORY: I don't see why Mama want a fence around the yard noways.

TROY: Damn if I know either. What the hell she keeping out with it? She ain't got nothing nobody want.

BONO: Some people build fences to keep people out . . . and other people build fences to keep people in. Rose wants to hold on to you all. She loves you.

TROY: Hell, nigger, I don't need nobody to tell me my wife loves me, Cory . . . go on in the house and see if you can find that other saw.

CORY: Where's it at?

TROY: I said find it! Look for it till you find it!

(*Cory exits into the house.*)

What's that supposed to mean? Wanna keep us in?

BONO: Troy . . . I done known you seem like damn near my whole life. You and Rose both. I done know both of you all for a long time. I remember when you met Rose. When you was hitting them baseball out the park. A lot of them old gals was after you then. You had the pick of the litter. When you picked Rose, I was happy for you. That was the first time I knew you had any sense. I said . . . My man Troy knows what he's doing . . . I'm gonna follow this nigger . . . he might take me somewhere. I been following you too. I done learned a whole heap of things about life watching you. I done learned how to tell where the shit lies. How to tell it from the alfalfa. You done learned me a lot of things. You showed me how to not make the same mistakes . . . to take life as it comes along and keep putting one foot in front of the other.

(*Pause.*)

Rose a good woman, Troy.

TROY: Hell, nigger, I know she a good woman. I been married to her for eighteen years. What you got on your mind, Bono?

BONO: I just say she a good woman. Just like I say anything. I ain't got to have nothing on my mind.

TROY: You just gonna say she a good woman and leave it hanging out there like that? Why you telling me she a good woman?

BONO: She loves you, Troy. Rose loves you.

TROY: You saying I don't measure up. That's what you trying to say. I don't measure up cause I'm seeing this other gal. I know what you trying to say.

BONO: I know what Rose means to you, Troy. I'm just trying to say I don't want to see you mess up.

TROY: Yeah, I appreciate that, Bono. If you was messing around on Lucille I'd be telling you the same thing.

BONO: Well, that's all I got to say. I just say that because I love you both.

TROY: Hell, you know me . . . I wasn't out there looking for nothing. You can't find a better woman than Rose. I know that. But seems like this woman just stuck onto me where I can't shake her loose. I done wrestled with it, tried to throw her off me . . . but she just stuck on tighter. Now she's stuck on for good.

BONO: You's in control . . . that's what you tell me all the time. You responsible for what you do.

TROY: I ain't ducking the responsibility of it. As long

as it sets right in my heart . . . then I'm okay. Cause that's all I listen to. It'll tell me right from wrong every time. And I ain't talking about doing Rose no bad turn. I love Rose. She done carried me a long ways and I love and respect her for that.

BONO: I know you do. That's why I don't want to see you hurt her. But what you gonna do when she find out? What you got then? If you try and juggle both of them . . . sooner or later you gonna drop one of them. That's common sense.

TROY: Yeah, I hear what you saying, Bono. I been trying to figure a way to work it out.

BONO: Work it out right, Troy. I don't want to be getting all up between you and Rose's business . . . but work it so it come out right.

TROY: Ah hell, I get all up between you and Lucille's business. When you gonna get that woman that refrigerator she been wanting? Don't tell me you ain't got no money now. I know who your banker is. Mellon don't need that money bad as Lucille want that refrigerator. I'll tell you that.

BONO: Tell you what I'll do . . . when you finish building this fence for Rose . . . I'll buy Lucille that refrigerator.

TROY: You done stuck your foot in your mouth now!

(Troy grabs up a board and begins to saw. Bono starts to walk out the yard.)

Hey, nigger . . . where you going?

BONO: I'm going home. I know you don't expect me to help you now. I'm protecting my money. I wanna see you put that fence up by yourself. That's what I want to see. You'll be here another six months without me.

TROY: Nigger, you ain't right.

BONO: When it comes to my money . . . I'm right as fireworks on the Fourth of July.

TROY: All right, we gonna see now. You better get out your bankbook.

(Bono exits, and Troy continues to work. Rose enters from the house.)

ROSE: What they say down there? What's happening with Gabe?

TROY: I went down there and got him out. Cost me fifty dollars. Say he was disturbing the peace. Judge set up a hearing for him in three weeks. Say to show cause why he shouldn't be recommitted.

ROSE: What was he doing that cause them to arrest him?

TROY: Some kids was teasing him and he run them off home. Say he was howling and carrying on. Some folks seen him and called the police. That's all it was.

ROSE: Well, what's you say? What'd you tell the judge?

TROY: Told him I'd look after him. It didn't make no sense to recommit the man. He stuck out his big greasy palm and told me to give him fifty dollars and take him on home.

ROSE: Where's he at now? Where'd he go off to?

TROY: He's gone on about his business. He don't need nobody to hold his hand.

ROSE: Well, I don't know. Seem like that would be the best place for him if they did put him into the hospital. I know what you're gonna say. But that's what I think would be best.

TROY: The man done had his life ruined fighting for what? And they wanna take and lock him up. Let him be free. He don't bother nobody.

ROSE: Well, everybody got their own way of looking at it I guess. Come on and get your lunch. I got a bowl of lima beans and some cornbread in the oven. Come on get something to eat. Ain't no sense you fretting over Gabe.

(Rose turns to go into the house.)

TROY: Rose . . . got something to tell you.

ROSE: Well, come on . . . wait till I get this food on the table.

TROY: Rose!

(She stops and turns around.)

I don't know how to say this.

(Pause.)

I can't explain it none. It just sort of grows on you till it gets out of hand. It starts out like a little bush . . . and the next thing you know it's a whole forest.

ROSE: Troy . . . what is you talking about?

TROY: I'm talking, woman, let me talk. I'm trying to find a way to tell you . . . I'm gonna be a daddy. I'm gonna be somebody's daddy.

ROSE: Troy . . . you're not telling me this? You're gonna be . . . what?

TROY: Rose . . . now . . . see . . .

ROSE: You telling me you gonna be somebody's daddy? You telling your *wife* this?

(Gabriel enters from the street. He carries a rose in his hand.)

GABRIEL: Hey, Troy! Hey, Rose!

ROSE: I have to wait eighteen years to hear something like this.

GABRIEL: Hey, Rose . . . I got a flower for you.

(He hands it to her.)

That's a rose. Same rose like you is.

ROSE: Thanks, Gabe.

GABRIEL: Troy, you ain't mad at me is you? Them bad mens come and put me away. You ain't mad at me is you?

TROY: Naw, Gabe, I ain't mad at you.

ROSE: Eighteen years and you wanna come with this.

GABRIEL (*takes a quarter out of his pocket*): See what I got? Got a brand new quarter.

TROY: Rose . . . it's just . . .

ROSE: Ain't nothing you can say, Troy. Ain't no way of explaining that.

GABRIEL: Fellow that give me this quarter had a whole mess of them. I'm gonna keep this quarter till it stop shining.

ROSE: Gabe, go on in the house there. I got some watermelon in the frigidaire. Go on and get you a piece.

GABRIEL: Say, Rose . . . you know I was chasing hellhounds and them bad mens come and get me and take me away. Troy helped me. He come down there and told them they better let me go before he beat them up. Yeah, he did!

ROSE: You go on and get you a piece of watermelon, Gabe. Them bad mens is gone now.

GABRIEL: Okay, Rose . . . gonna get me some watermelon. The kind with the stripes on it.

(*Gabriel exits into the house.*)

ROSE: Why, Troy? Why? After all these years to come dragging this in to me now. It don't make no sense at your age. I could have expected this ten or fifteen years ago, but not now.

TROY: Age ain't got nothing to do with it, Rose.

ROSE: I done tried to be everything a wife should be. Everything a wife could be. Been married eighteen years and I got to live to see the day you tell me you been seeing another woman and done fathered a child by her. And you know I ain't never wanted no half nothing in my family. My whole family is half. Everybody got different fathers and mothers . . . my two sisters and my brother. Can't hardly tell who's who. Can't never sit down and talk about Papa and Mama. It's your papa and your mama and my papa and my mama . . .

TROY: Rose . . . stop it now.

ROSE: I ain't never wanted that for none of my children. And now you wanna drag your behind in here and tell me something like this.

TROY: You ought to know. It's time for you to know.

ROSE: Well, I don't want to know, goddamn it!

TROY: I can't just make it go away. It's done now. I can't wish the circumstance of the thing away.

ROSE: And you don't want to either. Maybe you want to wish me and my boy away. Maybe that's what you want? Well, you can't wish us away. I've got eighteen years of my life invested in you. You ought to have stayed upstairs in my bed where you belong.

TROY: Rose . . . now listen to me . . . we can get a handle on this thing. We can talk this out . . . come to an understanding.

ROSE: All of a sudden it's "we." Where was "we" at when you was down there rolling around with some godforsaken woman? "We" should have come to an understanding before you started making a damn fool of yourself. You're a day late and a dollar short when it comes to an understanding with me.

TROY: It's just . . . She gives me a different idea . . . a different understanding about myself. I can step out of this house and get away from the pressures and problems . . . be a different man. I ain't got to wonder how I'm gonna pay the bills or get the roof fixed. I can just be a part of myself that I ain't never been.

ROSE: What I want to know . . . is do you plan to continue seeing her. That's all you can say to me.

TROY: I can sit up in her house and laugh. Do you understand what I'm saying. I can laugh out loud . . . and it feels good. It reaches all the way down to the bottom of my shoes.

(*Pause.*)

Rose, I can't give that up.

ROSE: Maybe you ought to go on and stay down there with her . . . if she's a better woman than me.

TROY: It ain't about nobody being a better woman or nothing. Rose, you ain't the blame. A man couldn't ask for no woman to be a better wife than you've been. I'm responsible for it. I done locked myself into a pattern trying to take care of you all that I forgot about myself.

ROSE: What the hell was I there for? That was my job, not somebody else's.

TROY: Rose, I done tried all my life to live decent . . . to live a clean . . . hard . . . useful life. I tried to be a good husband to you. In every way I knew how. Maybe I come into the world backwards, I don't know. But . . . you born with two strikes on you before you come to the plate. You got to guard it closely . . . always looking for the curve ball on the inside corner. You can't afford to let none get past you. You can't afford a call strike. If you going down . . . you going down swinging. Everything lined up against you. What you gonna do. I fooled them, Rose. I bunted. When I found you and Cory and a halfway decent job . . . I was safe. Couldn't nothing touch me. I wasn't gonna strike out no more. I wasn't going back to the penitentiary. I wasn't gonna lay in the streets with a bottle of wine. I was safe. I had me a family. A job. I wasn't gonna get that last strike. I was on first looking for one of them boys to knock me in. To get me home.

ROSE: You should have stayed in my bed, Troy.

TROY: Then when I saw that gal . . . she firmed up my backbone. And I got to thinking that if I tried . . . I just might be able to steal second. Do you understand after eighteen years I wanted to steal second.

ROSE: You should have held me tight. You should have grabbed me and held on.

TROY: I stood on first base for eighteen years and I thought . . . well, goddamn it . . . go on for it!

ROSE: We're not talking about baseball! We're talking about you going off to lay in bed with another woman . . . and then bring it home to me. That's what we're talking about. We ain't talking about no baseball.

TROY: Rose, you're not listening to me. I'm trying the best I can to explain it to you. It's not easy for me to admit that I been standing in the same place for eighteen years.

ROSE: I been standing with you! I been right here with you, Troy. I got a life too. I gave eighteen years of my life to stand in the same spot with you. Don't you think I ever wanted other things? Don't you think I had dreams and hopes? What about my life? What about me. Don't you think it ever crossed my mind to want to know other men? That I wanted to lay up somewhere and forget about my responsibilities? That I wanted someone to make me laugh so I could feel good? You not the only one who's got wants and needs. But I held on to you, Troy. I took all my feelings, my wants and needs, my dreams . . . and I buried them inside you. I planted a seed and watched and prayed over it. I planted myself inside you and waited to bloom. And it didn't take me no eighteen years to find out the soil was hard and rocky and it wasn't never gonna bloom.

But I held on to you, Troy. I held you tighter. You was my husband. I owed you everything I had. Every part of me I could find to give you. And upstairs in that room . . . with the darkness falling in on me . . . I gave everything I had to try and erase the doubt that you wasn't the finest man in the world. And wherever you was going . . . I wanted to be there with you. Cause you was my husband. Cause that's the only way I was gonna survive as your wife. You always talking about what you give . . . and what you don't have to give. But you take too. You take . . . and don't even know nobody's giving!

(*Rose turns to exit into the house; Troy grabs her arm.*)

TROY: You say I take and don't give!

ROSE: Troy! You're hurting me!

TROY: You say I take and don't give.

ROSE: Troy . . . you're hurting my arm! Let go!

TROY: I done give you everything I got. Don't you tell that lie on me.

ROSE: Troy!

TROY: Don't you tell that lie on me!

(*Cory enters from the house.*)

CORY: Mama!

ROSE: Troy. You're hurting me.

TROY: Don't you tell me about no taking and giving.

(*Cory comes up behind Troy and grabs him. Troy, surprised, is thrown off balance just as Cory throws a glancing blow that catches him on the chest and knocks him down. Troy is stunned, as is Cory.*)

ROSE: Troy. Troy. No!

(*Troy gets to his feet and starts at Cory.*)

Troy . . . no. Please! Troy!

(*Rose pulls on Troy to hold him back. Troy stops himself.*)

TROY (*to Cory*): All right. That's strike two. You stay away from around me, boy. Don't you strike out. You living with a full count. Don't you strike out.

(*Troy exits out the yard as the lights go down.*)

Scene II

(*It is six months later, early afternoon. Troy enters from the house and starts to exit the yard. Rose enters from the house.*)

ROSE: Troy, I want to talk to you.

TROY: All of a sudden, after all this time, you want to talk to me, huh? You ain't wanted to talk to me for months. You ain't wanted to talk to me last night. You ain't wanted no part of me then. What you wanna talk to me about now?

ROSE: Tomorrow's Friday.

TROY: I know what day tomorrow is. You think I don't know tomorrow's Friday? My whole life I ain't done nothing but look to see Friday coming and you got to tell me it's Friday.

ROSE: I want to know if you're coming home.

TROY: I always come home, Rose. You know that. There ain't never been a night I ain't come home.

ROSE: That ain't what I mean . . . and you know it.

I want to know if you're coming straight home after work.

TROY: I figure I'd cash my check . . . hang out at Taylors' with the boys . . . maybe play a game of checkers . . .

ROSE: Troy, I can't live like this. I won't live like this. You livin' on borrowed time with me. It's been going on six months now you ain't been coming home.

TROY: I be here every night. Every night of the year. That's 365 days.

ROSE: I want you to come home tomorrow after work.

TROY: Rose . . . I don't mess up my pay. You know that now. I take my pay and I give it to you. I don't have no money but what you give me back. I just want to have a little time to myself . . . a little time to enjoy life.

ROSE: What about me? When's my time to enjoy life?

TROY: I don't know what to tell you, Rose. I'm doing the best I can.

ROSE: You ain't been home from work but time enough to change your clothes and run out . . . and you wanna call that the best you can do?

TROY: I'm going over to the hospital to see Alberta. She went into the hospital this afternoon. Look like she might have the baby early. I won't be gone long.

ROSE: Well, you ought to know. They went over to Miss Pearl's and got Gabe today. She said you told them to go ahead and lock him up.

TROY: I ain't said no such thing. Whoever told you that is telling a lie. Pearl ain't doing nothing but telling a big fat lie.

ROSE: She ain't had to tell me. I read it on the papers.

TROY: I ain't told them nothing of the kind.

ROSE: I saw it right there on the papers.

TROY: What it say, huh?

ROSE: It said you told them to take him.

TROY: Then they screwed that up, just the way they screw up everything. I ain't worried about what they got on the paper.

ROSE: Say the government send part of his check to the hospital and the other part to you.

TROY: I ain't got nothing to do with that if that's the way it works. I ain't made up the rules about how it work.

ROSE: You did Gabe just like you did Cory. You wouldn't sign the paper for Cory . . . but you signed for Gabe. You signed that paper.

(*The telephone is heard ringing inside the house.*)

TROY: I told you I ain't signed nothing, woman! The only thing I signed was the release form. Hell, I can't read, I don't know what they had on that paper! I ain't signed nothing about sending Gabe away.

ROSE: I said send him to the hospital . . . you said let him be free . . . now you done went down there and signed him to the hospital for half his money. You went back on yourself, Troy. You gonna have to answer for that.

TROY: See now . . . you been over there talking to Miss Pearl. She done got mad cause she ain't getting Gabe's rent money. That's all it is. She's liable to say anything.

ROSE: Troy, I seen where you signed the paper.

TROY: You ain't seen nothing I signed. What she doing got papers on my brother anyway? Miss Pearl telling a big fat lie. And I'm gonna tell her about it too! You ain't seen nothing I signed. Say . . . you ain't seen nothing I signed.

(*Rose exits into the house to answer the telephone. Presently she returns.*)

ROSE: Troy . . . that was the hospital. Alberta had the baby.

TROY: What she have? What is it?

ROSE: It's a girl.

TROY: I better get on down to the hospital to see her.

ROSE: Troy . . .

TROY: Rose . . . I got to go see her now. That's only right . . . what's the matter . . . the baby's all right, ain't it?

ROSE: Alberta died having the baby.

TROY: Died . . . you say she's dead? Alberta's dead?

ROSE: They said they done all they could. They couldn't do nothing for her.

TROY: The baby? How's the baby?

ROSE: They say it's healthy. I wonder who's gonna bury her.

TROY: She had family, Rose. She wasn't living in the world by herself.

ROSE: I know she wasn't living in the world by herself.

TROY: Next thing you gonna want to know if she had any insurance.

ROSE: Troy, you ain't got to talk like that.

TROY: That's the first thing that jumped out your mouth. "Who's gonna bury her?" Like I'm fixing to take on that task for myself.

ROSE: I am your wife. Don't push me away.

TROY: I ain't pushing nobody away. Just give me some space. That's all. Just give me some room to breathe.

(*Rose exits into the house. Troy walks about the yard.*)

TROY (*with a quiet rage that threatens to consume him*): All right . . . Mr. Death. See now . . . I'm gonna tell you what I'm gonna do. I'm gonna take and build me a fence around this yard. See? I'm gonna build me a fence around what belongs to me. And then I want you to stay on the other side. See? You stay over there until you're ready for me. Then you come on. Bring your army. Bring your sickle. Bring your wrestling clothes. I ain't gonna fall down on my vigilance this time. You ain't gonna sneak up on me no more. When you ready for me . . . when the top of your list say Troy Maxson . . . that's when you come around here. You come up and knock on the front door. Ain't nobody else got nothing to do with this. This is between you and me. Man to man. You stay on the other side of that fence until you ready for me. Then you come up and knock on the front door. Anytime you want. I'll be ready for you.

(*The lights go down to black.*)

Scene III

(*The lights come up on the porch. It is late evening three days later. Rose sits listening to the ball game waiting for Troy. The final out of the game is made and Rose switches off the radio. Troy enters the yard carrying an infant wrapped in blankets. He stands back from the house and calls.*)

(*Rose enters and stands on the porch. There is a long, awkward silence, the weight of which grows heavier with each passing second.*)

TROY: Rose . . . I'm standing here with my daughter in my arms. She ain't but a wee bittie little old thing. She don't know nothing about grownups' business. She innocent . . . and she ain't got no mama.

ROSE: What you telling me for, Troy?

(*She turns and exits into the house.*)

TROY: Well . . . I guess we'll just sit out here on the porch.

(*He sits down on the porch. There is an awkward indelicateness about the way he handles the baby. His largeness engulfs and seems to swallow it. He speaks loud enough for Rose to hear.*)

A man's got to do what's right for him. I ain't sorry for nothing I done. It felt right in my heart.

(*To the baby.*)

What you smiling at? Your daddy's a big man. Got these great big old hands. But sometimes he's scared. And right now your daddy's scared cause we sitting out here and ain't got no home. Oh, I been homeless before. I ain't had no little baby with me. But I been homeless. You just be out on

the road by your lonesome and you see one of them trains coming and you just kinda go like this . . .

(*He sings as a lullaby.*)

Please, Mr. Engineer let a man ride the line
Please, Mr. Engineer let a man ride the line
I ain't got no ticket please let me ride the blinds

(*Rose enters from the house. Troy hearing her steps behind him, stands and faces her.*)

She's my daughter, Rose. My own flesh and blood. I can't deny her no more than I can deny them boys.

(*Pause.*)

You and them boys is my family. You and them and this child is all I got in the world. So I guess what I'm saying is . . . I'd appreciate it if you'd help me take care of her.

ROSE: Okay, Troy . . . you're right. I'll take care of your baby for you . . . cause . . . like you say . . . she's innocent . . . and you can't visit the sins of the father upon the child. A motherless child has got a hard time.

(*She takes the baby from him.*)

From right now . . . this child got a mother. But you a womanless man.

(*Rose turns and exits into the house with the baby. Lights go down to black.*)

Scene IV

(*It is two months later. Lyons enters from the street. He knocks on the door and calls.*)

LYONS: Hey, Rose! (*Pause.*) Rose!

ROSE (*from inside the house*): Stop that yelling. You gonna wake up Raynell. I just got her to sleep.

LYONS: I just stopped by to pay Papa this twenty dollars I owe him. Where's Papa at?

ROSE: He should be here in a minute. I'm getting ready to go down to the church. Sit down and wait on him.

LYONS: I got to go pick up Bonnie over her mother's house.

ROSE: Well, sit it down there on the table. He'll get it.

LYONS (*enters the house and sets the money on the table*): Tell Papa I said thanks. I'll see you again.

ROSE: All right, Lyons. We'll see you.

(*Lyons starts to exit as Cory enters.*)

CORY: Hey, Lyons.

LYONS: What's happening, Cory. Say man, I'm sorry I missed your graduation. You know I had a gig and couldn't get away. Otherwise, I would have been there, man. So what you doing?

CORY: I'm trying to find a job.

LYONS: Yeah I know how that go, man. It's rough out here. Jobs are scarce.

CORY: Yeah, I know.

LYONS: Look here, I got to run. Talk to Papa . . . he know some people. He'll be able to help get you a job. Talk to him . . . see what he say.

CORY: Yeah . . . all right, Lyons.

LYONS: You take care. I'll talk to you soon. We'll find some time to talk.

(*Lyons exits the yard. Cory wanders over to the tree, picks up the bat, and assumes a batting stance. He studies an imaginary pitcher and swings. Dissatisfied with the result, he tries again. Troy enters. They eye each other for a beat. Cory puts the bat down and exits the yard. Troy starts into the house as Rose exits with Raynell. She is carrying a cake.*)

TROY: I'm coming in and everybody's going out.

ROSE: I'm taking this cake down to the church for the bake sale. Lyons was by to see you. He stopped by to pay you your twenty dollars. It's laying in there on the table.

TROY (*going into his pocket*): Well . . . here go this money.

ROSE: Put it in there on the table, Troy. I'll get it.

TROY: What time you coming back?

ROSE: Ain't no use in you studying me. It don't matter what time I come back.

TROY: I just asked you a question, woman. What's the matter . . . can't I ask you a question?

ROSE: Troy, I don't want to go into it. Your dinner's in there on the stove. All you got to do is heat it up. And don't you be eating the rest of them cakes in there. I'm coming back for them. We having a bake sale at the church tomorrow.

(*Rose exits the yard. Troy sits down on the steps, takes a pint bottle from his pocket, opens it, and drinks. He begins to sing.*)

TROY: Hear it ring! Hear it ring!
Had an old dog his name was Blue
You know Blue was mighty true
You know Blue as a good old dog
Blue trees a possum in a hollow log
You know from that he was a good old dog

(*Bono enters the yard.*)

BONO: Hey, Troy.

TROY: Hey, what's happening, Bono?

BONO: I just thought I'd stop by to see you.

TROY: What you stop by and see me for? You ain't stopped by in a month of Sundays. Hell, I must owe you money or something.

BONO: Since you got your promotion I can't keep up with you. Used to see you every day. Now I don't even know what route you working.

TROY: They keep switching me around. Got me out in Greentree now . . . hauling white folks' garbage.

BONO: Greentree, huh? You lucky, at least you ain't got to be lifting them barrels. Damn if they ain't getting heavier. I'm gonna put in my two years and call it quits.

TROY: I'm thinking about retiring myself.

BONO: You got it easy. You can *drive* for another five years.

TROY: It ain't the same, Bono. It ain't like working the back of the truck. Ain't got nobody to talk to . . . feel like you working by yourself. Naw, I'm thinking about retiring. How's Lucille?

BONO: She all right. Her arthritis get to acting up on her sometime. Saw Rose on my way in. She going down to the church, huh?

TROY: Yeah, she took up going down there. All them preachers looking for somebody to fatten their pockets.

(*Pause.*)

Got some gin here.

BONO: Naw, thanks. I just stopped by to say hello.

TROY: Hell, nigger . . . you can take a drink. I ain't never known you to say no to a drink. You ain't got to work tomorrow.

BONO: I just stopped by. I'm fixing to go over to Skinner's. We got us a domino game going over his house every Friday.

TROY: Nigger, you can't play no dominoes. I used to whup you four games out of five.

BONO: Well, that learned me. I'm getting better.

TROY: Yeah? Well, that's all right.

BONO: Look here . . . I got to be getting on. Stop by sometime, huh?

TROY: Yeah, I'll do that, Bono. Lucille told Rose you bought her a new refrigerator.

BONO: Yeah, Rose told Lucille you had finally built your fence . . . so I figured we'd call it even.

TROY: I knew you would.

BONO: Yeah . . . okay. I'll be talking to you.

TROY: Yeah, take care, Bono. Good to see you. I'm gonna stop over.

BONO: Yeah. Okay, Troy.

(*Bono exits. Troy drinks from the bottle.*)

TROY: Old Blue died and I dig his grave
Let him down with a golden chain

Every night when I hear old Blue bark
I know Blue treed a possum in Noah's Ark.
Hear it ring! Hear it ring!

(*Cory enters the yard. They eye each other for a beat. Troy is sitting in the middle of the steps. Cory walks over.*)

CORY: I got to get by.

TROY: Say what? What's you say?

CORY: You in my way. I got to get by.

TROY: You got to get by where? This is my house. Bought and paid for. In full. Took me fifteen years. And if you wanna go in my house and I'm sitting on the steps . . . you say excuse me. Like your mama taught you.

CORY: Come on, Pop . . . I got to get by.

(*Cory starts to maneuver his way past Troy. Troy grabs his leg and shoves him back.*)

TROY: You just gonna walk over top of me?

CORY: I live here too!

TROY (*advancing toward him*): You just gonna walk over top of me in my own house?

CORY: I ain't scared of you.

TROY: I ain't asked if you was scared of me. I asked you if you was fixing to walk over top of me in my own house? That's the question. You ain't gonna say excuse me? You just gonna walk over top of me?

CORY: If you wanna put it like that.

TROY: How else am I gonna put it?

CORY: I was walking by you to go into the house cause you sitting on the steps drunk, singing to yourself. You can put it like that.

TROY: Without saying excuse me???

(*Cory doesn't respond.*)

I asked you a question. Without saying excuse me???

CORY: I ain't got to say excuse me to you. You don't count around here no more.

TROY: Oh, I see . . . I don't count around here no more. You ain't got to say excuse me to your daddy. All of a sudden you done got so grown that your daddy don't count around here no more . . . Around here in his own house and yard that he done paid for with the sweat of his brow. You done got so grown to where you gonna take over. You gonna take over my house. Is that right? You gonna wear my pants. You gonna go in there and stretch out on my bed. You ain't got to say excuse me cause I don't count around here no more. Is that right?

CORY: That's right. You always talking this dumb stuff. Now, why don't you just get out my way.

TROY: I guess you got someplace to sleep and something to put in your belly. You got that, huh? You got that? That's what you need. You got that, huh?

CORY: You don't know what I got. You ain't got to worry about what I got.

TROY: You right! You one hundred percent right! I done spent the last seventeen years worrying about what you got. Now it's your turn, see? I'll tell you what to do. You grown . . . we done established that. You a man. Now, let's see you act like one. Turn your behind around and walk out this yard. And when you get out there in the alley . . . you can forget about this house. See? 'Cause this is my house. You go on and be a man and get your own house. You can forget about this. 'Cause this is mine. You go on and get yours 'cause I'm through with doing for you.

CORY: You talking about what you did for me . . . what'd you ever give me?

TROY: Them feet and bones! That pumping heart, nigger! I give you more than anybody else is ever gonna give you.

CORY: You ain't never gave me nothing! You ain't never done nothing but hold me back. Afraid I was gonna be better than you. All you ever did was try and make me scared of you. I used to tremble every time you called my name. Every time I heard your footsteps in the house. Wondering all the time . . . what's Papa gonna say if I do this? . . . What's he gonna say if I do that? . . . What's Papa gonna say if I turn on the radio? And Mama, too . . . she tries . . . but she's scared of you.

TROY: You leave your mama out of this. She ain't got nothing to do with this.

CORY: I don't know how she stand you . . . after what you did to her.

TROY: I told you to leave your mama out of this!

(*He advances toward Cory.*)

CORY: What you gonna do . . . give me a whupping? You can't whup me no more. You're too old. You just an old man.

TROY (*shoves him on his shoulder*): Nigger! That's what you are. You just another nigger on the street to me!

CORY: You crazy! You know that?

TROY: Go on now! You got the devil in you. Get on away from me!

CORY: You just a crazy old man . . . talking about I got the devil in me.

TROY: Yeah, I'm crazy! If you don't get on the other side of that yard . . . I'm gonna show you how crazy I am! Go on . . . get the hell out of my yard.

CORY: It ain't your yard. You took Uncle Gabe's

money he got from the army to buy this house and then you put him out.

TROY (*Troy advances on Cory*): Get your black ass out of my yard!

(*Troy's advance backs Cory up against the tree. Cory grabs up the bat.*)

CORY: I ain't going nowhere! Come on . . . put me out! I ain't scared of you.

TROY: That's my bat!

CORY: Come on!

TROY: Put my bat down!

CORY: Come on, put me out.

(*Cory swings at Troy, who backs across the yard.*)

What's the matter? You so bad . . . put me out!

(*Troy advances toward Cory.*)

CORY (*backing up*): Come on! Come on!

TROY: You're gonna have to use it! You wanna draw that bat back on me . . . you're gonna have to use it.

CORY: Come on! . . . Come on!

(*Cory swings the bat at Troy a second time. He misses. Troy continues to advance toward him.*)

TROY: You're gonna have to kill me! You wanna draw that bat back on me. You're gonna have to kill me.

(*Cory, backed up against the tree, can go no farther. Troy taunts him. He sticks out his head and offers him a target.*)

Come on! Come on!

(*Cory is unable to swing the bat. Troy grabs it.*)

TROY: Then I'll show you.

(*Cory and Troy struggle over the bat. The struggle is fierce and fully engaged. Troy ultimately is the stronger and takes the bat from Cory and stands over him ready to swing. He stops himself.*)

Go on and get away from around my house.

(*Cory, stung by his defeat, picks himself up, walks slowly out of the yard and up the alley.*)

CORY: Tell Mama I'll be back for my things.

TROY: They'll be on the other side of that fence.

(*Cory exits.*)

TROY: I can't taste nothing. Helluljah! I can't taste nothing no more. (*Troy assumes a batting posture and begins to taunt Death, the fastball on the outside corner.*) Come on! It's between you and me

now! Come on! Anytime you want! Come on! I be ready for you . . . but I ain't gonna be easy.

(*The lights go down on the scene.*)

Scene V

(*The time is 1965. The lights come up in the yard. It is the morning of Troy's funeral. A funeral plaque with a light hangs beside the door. There is a small garden plot off to the side. There is noise and activity in the house as Rose, Gabriel, and Bono have gathered. The door opens and Raynell, seven years old, enters dressed in a flannel nightgown. She crosses to the garden and pokes around with a stick. Rose calls from the house.*)

ROSE: Raynell!

RAYNELL: Mam?

ROSE: What you doing out there?

RAYNELL: Nothing.

(*Rose comes to the door.*)

ROSE: Girl, get in here and get dressed. What you doing?

RAYNELL: Seeing if my garden growed.

ROSE: I told you it ain't gonna grow overnight. You got to wait.

RAYNELL: It don't look like it never gonna grow. Dag!

ROSE: I told you a watched pot never boils. Get in here and get dressed.

RAYNELL: This ain't even no pot, Mama.

ROSE: You just have to give it a chance. It'll grow. Now you come on and do what I told you. We got to be getting ready. This ain't no morning to be playing around. You hear me?

RAYNELL: Yes, mam.

(*Rose exits into the house. Raynell continues to poke at her garden with a stick. Cory enters. He is dressed in a Marine corporal's uniform, and carries a duffel bag. His posture is that of a military man, and his speech has a clipped sternness.*)

CORY (*to Raynell*): Hi.

(*Pause.*)

I bet your name is Raynell.

RAYNELL: Uh huh.

CORY: Is your mama home?

(*Raynell runs up on the porch and calls through the screen door.*)

RAYNELL: Mama . . . there's some man out here. Mama?

(*Rose comes to the door.*)

ROSE: Cory? Lord have mercy! Look here, you all!

(*Rose and Cory embrace in a tearful reunion as Bono and Lyons enter from the house dressed in funeral clothes.*)

BONO: Aw, looka here . . .

ROSE: Done got all grown up!

CORY: Don't cry, Mama. What you crying about?

ROSE: I'm just so glad you made it.

CORY: Hey Lyons. How you doing, Mr. Bono.

(*Lyons goes to embrace Cory.*)

LYONS: Look at you, man. Look at you. Don't he look good, Rose. Got them Corporal stripes.

ROSE: What took you so long.

CORY: You know how the Marines are, Mama. They got to get all their paperwork straight before they let you do anything.

ROSE: Well, I'm sure glad you made it. They let Lyons come. Your Uncle Gabe's still in the hospital. They don't know if they gonna let him out or not. I just talked to them a little while ago.

LYONS: A Corporal in the United States Marines.

BONO: Your daddy knew you had it in you. He used to tell me all the time.

LYONS: Don't he look good, Mr. Bono?

BONO: Yeah, he remind me of Troy when I first met him.

(*Pause.*)

Say, Rose, Lucille's down at the church with the choir. I'm gonna go down and get the pallbearers lined up. I'll be back to get you all.

ROSE: Thanks, Jim.

CORY: See you, Mr. Bono.

LYONS (*with his arm around Raynell*): Cory . . . look at Raynell. Ain't she precious? She gonna break a whole lot of hearts.

ROSE: Raynell, come and say hello to your brother. This is your brother, Cory. You remember Cory.

RAYNELL: No, Mam.

CORY: She don't remember me, Mama.

ROSE: Well, we talk about you. She heard us talk about you. (*To Raynell.*) This is your brother, Cory. Come on and say hello.

RAYNELL: Hi.

CORY: Hi. So you're Raynell. Mama told me a lot about you.

ROSE: You all come on into the house and let me fix you some breakfast. Keep up your strength.

CORY: I ain't hungry, Mama.

LYONS: You can fix me something, Rose. I'll be in there in a minute.

ROSE: Cory, you sure you don't want nothing. I know they ain't feeding you right.

CORY: No, Mama . . . thanks. I don't feel like eating. I'll get something later.

ROSE: Raynell . . . get on upstairs and get that dress on like I told you.

(*Rose and Raynell exit into the house.*)

LYONS: So . . . I hear you thinking about getting married.

CORY: Yeah, I done found the right one, Lyons. It's about time.

LYONS: Me and Bonnie been split up about four years now. About the time Papa retired. I guess she just got tired of all them changes I was putting her through.

(*Pause.*)

I always knew you was gonna make something out yourself. Your head was always in the right direction. So . . . you gonna stay in . . . make it a career . . . put in your twenty years?

CORY: I don't know. I got six already, I think that's enough.

LYONS: Stick with Uncle Sam and retire early. Ain't nothing out here. I guess Rose told you what happened with me. They got me down the workhouse. I thought I was being slick cashing other people's checks.

CORY: How much time you doing?

LYONS: They give me three years. I got that beat now. I ain't got but nine more months. It ain't so bad. You learn to deal with it like anything else. You got to take the crookeds with the straights. That's what Papa used to say. He used to say that when he struck out. I seen him strike out three times in a row . . . and the next time up he hit the ball over the grandstand. Right out there in Homestead Field. He wasn't satisfied hitting in the seats . . . he want to hit it over everything! After the game he had two hundred people standing around waiting to shake his hand. You got to take the crookeds with the straights. Yeah, Papa was something else.

CORY: You still playing?

LYONS: Cory . . . you know I'm gonna do that. There's some fellows down there we got us a band . . . we gonna try and stay together when we get out . . . but yeah, I'm still playing. It still helps me to get out of bed in the morning. As long as it do that I'm gonna be right there playing and trying to make some sense out of it.

ROSE (*calling*): Lyons, I got these eggs in the pan.

LYONS: Let me go on and get these eggs, man. Get ready to go bury Papa.

(*Pause.*)

How you doing? You doing all right?

(*Cory nods. Lyons touches him on the shoulder and they share a moment of silent grief. Lyons exits into the house. Cory wanders about the yard. Raynell enters.*)

RAYNELL: Hi.

CORY: Hi.

RAYNELL: Did you used to sleep in my room?

CORY: Yeah . . . that used to be my room.

RAYNELL: That's what Papa call it. "Cory's room." It got your football in the closet.

(*Rose comes to the door.*)

ROSE: Raynell, get in there and get them good shoes on.

RAYNELL: Mama, can't I wear these. Them other one hurt my feet.

ROSE: Well, they just gonna have to hurt your feet for a while. You ain't said they hurt your feet when you went down to the store and got them.

RAYNELL: They didn't hurt then. My feet done got bigger.

ROSE: Don't you give me no backtalk now. You get in there and get them shoes on.

(*Raynell exits into the house.*)

Ain't too much changed. He still got that piece of rag tied to that tree. He was out here swinging that bat. I was just ready to go back in the house. He swung that bat and then he just fell over. Seem like he swung it and stood there with this grin on his face . . . and then he just fell over. They carried him on down to the hospital, but I knew there wasn't no need . . . why don't you come on in the house?

CORY: Mama . . . I got something to tell you. I don't know how to tell you this . . . but I've got to tell you . . . I'm not going to Papa's funeral.

ROSE: Boy, hush your mouth. That's your daddy you talking about. I don't want hear that kind of talk this morning. I done raised you to come to this? You standing there all healthy and grown talking about you ain't going to your daddy's funeral?

CORY: Mama . . . listen . . .

ROSE: I don't want to hear it, Cory. You just get that thought out of your head.

CORY: I can't drag Papa with me everywhere I go. I've got to say no to him. One time in my life I've got to say no.

ROSE: Don't nobody have to listen to nothing like that. I know you and your daddy ain't seen eye to eye, but I ain't got to listen to that kind of talk

this morning. Whatever was between you and your daddy . . . the time has come to put it aside. Just take it and set it over there on the shelf and forget about it. Disrespecting your daddy ain't gonna make you a man, Cory. You got to find a way to come to that on your own. Not going to your daddy's funeral ain't gonna make you a man.

CORY: The whole time I was growing up . . . living in his house . . . Papa was like a shadow that followed you everywhere. It weighed on you and sunk into your flesh. It would wrap around you and lay there until you couldn't tell which one was you anymore. That shadow digging in your flesh. Trying to crawl in. Trying to live through you. Everywhere I looked, Troy Maxson was staring back at me . . . hiding under the bed . . . in the closet. I'm just saying I've got to find a way to get rid of that shadow, Mama.

ROSE: You just like him. You got him in you good.

CORY: Don't tell me that, Mama.

ROSE: You Troy Maxson all over again.

CORY: I don't want to be Troy Maxson. I want to be me.

ROSE: You can't be nobody but who you are, Cory. That shadow wasn't nothing but you growing into yourself. You either got to grow into it or cut it down to fit you. But that's all you got to make life with. That's all you got to measure yourself against that world out there. Your daddy wanted you to be everything he wasn't . . . and at the same time he tried to make you into everything he was. I don't know if he was right or wrong . . . but I do know he meant to do more good than he meant to do harm. He wasn't always right. Sometimes when he touched he bruised. And sometimes when he took me in his arms he cut.

When I first met your daddy I thought . . . Here is a man I can lay down with and make a baby. That's the first thing I thought when I seen him. I was thirty years old and had done seen my share of men. But when he walked up to me and said, "I can dance a waltz that'll make you dizzy," I thought, Rose Lee, here is a man that you can open yourself up to and be filled to bursting. Here is a man that can fill all them empty spaces you been tipping around the edges of. One of them empty spaces was being somebody's mother.

I married your daddy and settled down to cooking his supper and keeping clean sheets on the bed. When your daddy walked through the house he was so big he filled it up. That was my first mistake. Not to make him leave some room for me. For my part in the matter. But at that time I wanted that. I wanted a house that I could sing in. And that's what your daddy gave me. I didn't know to keep up his strength I had to give up little pieces of mine. I did that. I took on his life as mine and mixed up the pieces so that you couldn't hardly tell which was which anymore. It was my choice. It was my life and I didn't have to live it like that. But that's what life offered me in the way of being a woman and I took it. I grabbed hold of it with both hands.

By the time Raynell came into the house, me and your daddy had done lost touch with one another. I didn't want to make my blessing off of nobody's misfortune . . . but I took on to Raynell like she was all them babies I had wanted and never had.

(*The phone rings.*)

Like I'd been blessed to relive a part of my life. And if the Lord see fit to keep up my strength . . . I'm gonna do her just like your daddy did you . . . I'm gonna give her the best of what's in me.
RAYNELL (*entering, still with her old shoes*): Mama . . . Reverend Tollivier on the phone.

(*Rose exits into the house.*)

RAYNELL: Hi.
CORY: Hi.
RAYNELL: You in the Army or the Marines?
CORY: Marines.
RAYNELL: Papa said it was the Army. Did you know Blue?
CORY: Blue? Who's Blue?
RAYNELL: Papa's dog what he sing about all the time.
CORY (*singing*): Hear it ring! Hear it ring!
   I had a dog his name was Blue
   You know Blue was mighty true
   You know Blue was a good old dog
   Blue treed a possum in a hollow log
   You know from that he was a good old dog.
   Hear it ring! Hear it ring!

(*Raynell joins in singing.*)

CORY AND RAYNELL: Blue treed a possum out on a
   limb
   Blue looked at me and I looked at him
   Grabbed that possum and put him in a sack
   Blue stayed there till I came back
   Old Blue's feets was big and round
   Never allowed a possum to touch the ground.

   Old Blue died and I dug his grave
   I dug his grave with a silver spade
   Let him down with a golden chain
   And every night I call his name
   Go on Blue, you good dog you
   Go on Blue, you good dog you

RAYNELL: Blue laid down and died like a man
   Blue laid down and died . . .
BOTH: Blue laid down and died like a man
   Now he's treeing possums in the Promised Land
   I'm gonna tell you this to let you know
   Blue's gone where the good dogs go
   When I hear old Blue bark
   When I hear old Blue bark
   Blue treed a possum in Noah's Ark
   Blue treed a possum in Noah's Ark.

(*Rose comes to the screen door.*)

ROSE: Cory, we gonna be ready to go in a minute.
CORY (*to Raynell*): You go on in the house and change them shoes like Mama told you so we can go to Papa's funeral.
RAYNELL: Okay, I'll be back.

(*Raynell exits into the house. Cory gets up and crosses over to the tree. Rose stands in the screen door watching him. Gabriel enters from the alley.*)

GABRIEL (*calling*): Hey, Rose!
ROSE: Gabe?
GABRIEL: I'm here, Rose. Hey Rose, I'm here!

(*Rose enters from the house.*)

ROSE: Lord . . . Look here, Lyons!
LYONS: See, I told you, Rose . . . I told you they'd let him come.
CORY: How you doing, Uncle Gabe?
LYONS: How you doing, Uncle Gabe?
GABRIEL: Hey, Rose. It's time. It's time to tell St. Peter to open the gates. Troy, you ready? You ready, Troy. I'm gonna tell St. Peter to open the gates. You get ready now.

(*Gabriel, with great fanfare, braces himself to blow. The trumpet is without a mouthpiece. He puts the end of it into his mouth and blows with great force, like a man who has been waiting some twenty-odd years for this single moment. No sound comes out of the trumpet. He braces himself and blows again with the same result. A third time he blows. There is a weight of impossible description that falls away and leaves him bare and exposed to a frightful realization. It is a trauma that a sane and normal mind would be unable to withstand. He begins to dance. A slow, strange dance, eerie and life-giving. A dance of atavistic signature and ritual. Lyons attempts to embrace him. Gabriel pushes Lyons away. He begins to howl in what is an attempt at song, or perhaps a song turning back into itself in an attempt at speech. He finishes his dance and the gates of heaven stand open as wide as God's closet.*)

That's the way that go!

COMMENTARY

David Savran (b. 1950)
INTERVIEW WITH AUGUST WILSON

August Wilson is interested not only in the characters in his plays but also in their political circumstances. One of his primary efforts has been to help strip away the black male stereotypes so that his audiences can see his people as he sees them. In this interview, he discusses the social conditions of black Americans and the relationship between Troy Maxson and his son Cory. Wilson's views about their relationship may be surprising, since he interprets it in a way that differs from many of the critics' interpretations.

Savran: In reading *Fences*, I came to view Troy more and more critically as the play progressed, sharing Rose's point of view. We see that Troy has been crippled by his father. That's being replayed in Troy's relationship with Cory. Do you think there's a way out of that cycle?

Wilson: Surely. First of all, we're all like our parents. The things we are taught early in life, how to respond to the world, our sense of morality — everything, we get from them. Now you can take that legacy and do with it anything you want to do. It's in your hands. Cory is Troy's son. How can he be Troy's son without sharing Troy's values? I was trying to get at why Troy made the choices he made, how they have influenced his values and how he attempts to pass those along to his son. Each generation gives the succeeding generation what they think they need. One question in the play is "Are the tools we are given sufficient to compete in a world that is different from the one our parents knew?" I think they are — it's just that we have to do different things with the tools. That's all Troy has to give. Troy's flaw is that he does not recognize that the world was changing. That's because he spent fifteen years in a penitentiary.

As African-Americans, we should demand to participate in society as Africans. That's the way out of the vicious cycle of poverty and neglect that exists in 1987 in America, where you have a huge percentage of blacks living in the equivalent of South African townships, in housing projects. No one is inviting these people to participate in society. Look at the poverty levels — $8,500 for a family of four, if you have $8,501 you're not counted. Those statistics would go up enormously if we had an honest assessment of the cost of living in America. I don't know how anybody can support a family of four on $8,500. What I'm saying is that 85 or 90 percent of blacks in America are living in abject poverty and, for the most part, are crowded into what amount to concentration camps. The situation for blacks in America is worse than it was forty years ago. Some sociologists will tell you about the tremendous progress we've made. They didn't put me out when I walked in the door. And you can always point to someone who works on Wall Street, or is a doctor. But they don't count in the larger scheme of things.

Savran: Do you have any idea how these political changes could take place?

Wilson: I'm not sure. I know that blacks must be allowed their cultural differences. I think the process of assimilation to white American society was a big mistake. We don't want to be like you. Blacks living in housing projects are isolated from the society, for the most part — living as they choose, as Africans. Only they don't realize the value in what they're doing because they have accepted their victimization. They've marked themselves as victims. Once they recognize that, they can begin to move through society in a different manner, from a stronger position, and claim what is theirs.

Savran: A project of yours is to point up what happens when oppression is internalized.

Wilson: Yes, transfer of aggression to the wrong target. I think it's interesting that the two roads open to blacks for "full participation" are entertainment and sports. *Ma Rainey* and *Fences*, and I didn't plan it that way. I don't think that they're the correct roads. I think Troy's right. Now with the benefit of historical perspective, I can say that the athletic scholarship was actually a way of exploiting. Now you've got two million kids who think they're going to play in the NBA. In the sixties the universities made a lot of money off of athletics. You had kids playing for free who, by and large, were not getting educated, were taking courses in basketweaving. Some of them could barely read.

Savran: Troy may be right about that issue, but it seems that he has passed on certain destructive traits in spite of himself. Take the hostility between father and son.

Wilson: I think every generation says to the previous generation: you're in my way, I've got to get by. The father-son conflict is actually a normal generational conflict that happens all the time.

Savran: So it's a healthy and a good thing?

Wilson: Oh, sure. Troy is seeing this boy walk around, smelling his piss. Two men cannot live in the same household. Troy would have been tremendously disappointed if Cory had not challenged him. Troy knows that this boy has to go out and do battle with that world: "So I had best prepare him because I know that's a harsh, cruel place out there. But that's going to be easy compared to what he's getting here. Ain't nobody gonna whip your ass like I'm gonna whip it." He has a tremendous love for the kid. But he's not going to say, "I love you," he's going to demonstrate it. He's carrying garbage for seventeen years just for the kid. The only world Troy knows is the one that he made. Cory's going to go on to find another one, he's going to arrive at the same place as Troy. I think one of the most important lines in the play is when Troy is talking about his father: "I got to the place where I could feel him kicking in my blood and knew that the only thing that separated us was the matter of a few years."

Hopefully, Cory will do things a bit differently with his son. For Troy, sports was not the way to go, the white man wouldn't let him get away with that. "Get you a job, with your hands, something that nobody can take away from you." The idea of school — he doesn't know what that is. That's for white folks. Very few blacks had paperwork jobs. But if you knew how to fix cars, you could always make some money. That's what Troy wants for Cory. There aren't many people who ever jumped up in Troy's face. So he's proud of the kid at the same time that he expresses a hurt that all men feel. You got to cut your kid loose at some point. There's that sense of loss and separation. You find out how Troy left his father's house and you see how Cory leaves his house. I suspect with Cory it will repeat with some differences and maybe, after five or six generations, they'll find a different way to do it.

Savran: Where Cory ends up is very ambiguous, as a marine in 1965.

Wilson: Yes. For the average black kid on the street, that was an alternative. You went into the army because you could learn how to do something. I can remember my parents talking about the son of some friends: "He's in the navy. He *did* something" — as opposed to standing on the street corner, shooting drugs, drinking wine, and robbing stores. Lyons says to Cory, "I always knew you were going to make something out of yourself." It really wounds me. He's a corporal in the marines. For blacks, that is a sense of accomplishment. Therein lies one of the tragedies of blacks in America. Cory says, "I don't know. I put in six years. That's enough." Anyone who goes into the army and makes a career out of it is a loser. They sit there and are nurtured by the army and they don't have to confront life. Then they get out of the army and find there's nothing to do. They didn't learn any skills. And if they did, they can't find a job. Four months later, they're shooting dope. In the sixties a whole bunch of blacks went over, fought and died in the Vietnam War. The survivors came back to the same street corners and found out nothing had changed. They still couldn't get a job.

At the end of *Fences* every person, with the exception of Raynell, is institutionalized. Rose is in a church. Lyons is in a penitentiary. Gabriel's in a mental hospital and Cory's in the marines. The only free person is the girl, Troy's daughter, the hope for the future. That was conscious on my part because in '57 that's what I saw. Blacks have relied on institutions which are really foreign — except for the black church, which has been our saving grace. I have some problems with it but I recognize it as a central social organization and sometimes an economic organization for the black community. I would like to see blacks develop their own institutions that respond to their needs.

Brian Friel

Born in County Tyrone, Northern Ireland, in 1929, Brian Friel has become Ireland's major playwright. His distinction has grown in recent years with dramatic successes in Ireland, London, and New York. From 1950 to 1960 he was a schoolteacher, but since 1960 he has been a full-time writer. His first well-received play was *Philadelphia, Here I Come!* (1964), which tells the story of Gar O'Donnell, who is about to emigrate to the United States from his tiny hamlet of Ballybeg, County Donegal, the village Friel usually uses for his settings. Ballybeg is tiny, depressed, unable to offer work or dignity to its young men, and those with spirit find that their choices are circumscribed by the limitations of the economy. America offers the most hope, and that is where Gar decides to go. The play captured the imagination of many Irish Americans because of their response to the theme of emigration, but it transcends ethnic concerns. In many ways it has a universal theme — the story of all young men who grow up and realize they must break with their home and set out on their own.

The Loves of Cass McGuire (1966) was first broadcast as a radio play and then produced in New York, Belfast, and London. It tells the story of an old woman whose hopes in life have been dashed by circumstances, none of which improve during the play. Friel developed several strains in his work after demonstrating an interest in the pathos of individual lives such as those of Gar O'Donnell and Cass McGuire. He showed a satirical streak in the political play *The Mundy Scheme* (1969), which focuses on a crazy plan of Irish politicians to capitalize on the Irish specialty of holding wakes for the dead. Mundy's proposal is to convert Ireland into the graveyard of all Europe, thus turning much unarable land to good account. *Freedom of the City* was produced in Dublin, London, and Chicago in 1973 and in New York the following year. It tells the story of three very different people — Michael, twenty-two, and Skinner, twenty-one, both with differing social attitudes, and Lily, forty-three, mother of eleven — who occupy the mayor's office in the Guildhall (town hall) of Derry City during a student protest march. Eventually the three discover common political ground and through a series of unexpected incidents find themselves facing death at the hands of surrounding soldiers.

The Faith Healer (1979) ostensibly portrays a wandering man who heals people in a miraculous way. But the deep structure of the play is about art and the artist's responsibility for healing society. It played in New York and London to considerable acclaim. The most highly regarded of Friel's plays, until *Dancing at Lughnasa,* was *Translations* (1980). Produced in Derry, London, and New York to appreciative crowds, it is set in 1833 in Baile Beg (Ballybeg) and follows the efforts of English surveyors to rename Irish places while making survey maps. These maps translate Irish place names in high-handed, arbitrary fashion. For example, they choose Burnfoot for Bun na hAbbann, which in Irish means "mouth of the river," because Burnfoot is the closest they can get to the Irish word in English. Throughout the play Irish characters speak Irish — or at least we are to understand that they do — while the English speak English.

Much of Friel's work has concerned Irish political issues, but plays such as *Translations* are easy for non-Irish audiences to understand and appreciate. Despite its portraying the English as unconscious oppressors, audiences in London's National Theatre were wildly enthusiastic about it during its extensive 1981 run. *Making History* (1989), set in Elizabethan Ireland, again concerns English oppression and is part of a historical cycle of plays. Friel's most recent play is *Dancing at Lughnasa* (1990), a personal examination of a childhood in Ballybeg in the 1930s.

Brian Friel has never been an actor, but he brings to the stage a keen ear for language in the Irish tradition of William Congreve, Bernard Shaw, Oscar Wilde, Lady Gregory, John Millington Synge, Sean O'Casey, and Samuel Beckett. He makes his characters' speeches rich with the rhythms of everyday Irish country life and the color and metaphor of people whose joy in language is intense and satisfying. At the moment he is a member — along with critic Seamus Deane, poets Seamus Heaney and Tom Paulin, and actor Stephen Rea — of an Irish literary group called Field Day, which has its own press and publishes poetry, fiction, and drama and has recently (1991) produced an ambitious three-volume anthology of Irish literature. He has published *Selected Stories* (1979) and *The Diviner* (1983), a book of short stories. In addition to all this, he has also translated Chekhov's *Three Sisters* (1981) and adapted Turgenev's *Fathers and Sons* (1987) for the stage. He is a prodigious figure in contemporary literature.

DANCING AT LUGHNASA

Dancing at Lughnasa (1990) is a memory play told from the point of view of Michael, an older man who recalls the year 1936, when he was seven years old living in Ballybeg with his unwed mother and his aunts. Lughnasa *"loo'-na-sa"* — Gaelic for August — is the name of a festival on August 1 that has been celebrated in Ireland since pagan times. Lugh, a corn god, was expected to guarantee a good harvest. In modern times Lá Lughnasa was celebrated by a dance at the beginning of harvest in early August in which young men and women courted each other. The dances, like the other ritual aspects of the celebration, were held on hilltops throughout Ireland. The best dancing couple was chosen at each of the ceremonies. In Ganiamore in County Donegal — where the action of this play takes place — the reward for the best male dancer was his choice of a bride from all the eligible women at the celebration.

In addition to dancing, which is central to the celebration, people picked the dark blue bilberries that marked the harvest time. It was essential that everyone, including the old and the infirm, should eat the bilberries so as to participate in the reward of a rich harvest.

The play is a demonstration of the value of memory. Michael does not appear onstage as a child of seven, although his mother and aunts talk to an imaginary Michael as if he were there at that age. The setting is a typical Irish cottage — its walls cut away so we can peer inside — and the immediate areas outside its door. In the background is a stand of wheat, as high as one's waist, with a path cut through it to the town. Michael the man is present to our eyes, but the rest of the characters do not see him. He wanders among his mother, his father, his aunts, and his uncle and tenderly observes their efforts at regulating each other's lives.

His mother, Chris, has demonstrated an unusual spirit and independence in giving herself to a man, a ne'er-do-well who cannot afford to marry but who cuts a dashing figure and demonstrates, onstage, a remarkable skill as a dancer. Her sisters Agnes and the simple-minded Rose are not adventurous. They have made a life in the cottage occupation of knitting gloves to be sold elsewhere. They make very little money, and late in the play we discover that their little bit will be taken from them when the mill develops new machinery and hires only younger women. Kate, biting, strong, and critical, is a schoolteacher earning the living for all of them. Aunt Maggie acts as their housekeeper, using her wit and humor as well as her skills at keeping things tidy.

Among these women Gerry, Michael's father, is an exotic. He comes to visit, bringing excuses and promises — little more — but he has a charm that all the women except Kate respond to. Father Jack is one of Friel's most interesting characters. Friel usually includes a character who is an outsider to Ballybeg, and in this play Father Jack is that character. He was born in Ballybeg but has been in Africa in a leper colony for twenty-five years, where he has spoken little English. He becomes not just an outsider in the community, but an outsider whose language needs reconstruction — providing some of the humor of the play — and whose beliefs have been touched deeply, and much to Kate's horror, by his sympathies for African religion. We realize soon enough that this Irish Catholic priest will not be allowed to say Mass again, not because he is infirm and ill but because he has shifted his faith so far as to absorb the religious beliefs of the people he lived with for so many years. The ritual celebration of Lá Lughnasa is close in character to the celebrations Father Jack remembers in Uganda.

The spirit of the play is marked by a deep affection for all these characters. Friel is working from personal experience in the play — the Mundys, if not his own family, are very close to them. Donal Donnelly, the actor who has worked with Friel for thirty years and who played the part of Father Jack in the New York production, said, "Brian has not talked to me about this, but two of his aunts *did* die homeless in London. And, recently, two elderly nuns came to the theatre with a special request to meet 'Aunt Kate' — the actress — because they had both been taught by the real Aunt Kate."

Dancing at Lughnasa in Performance

The play premiered at the Abbey Theatre in Dublin on April 24, 1990. Barry McGovern created the role of Father Jack, and Alec McCowen took the role to London's National Theatre in October 1990, where the play enjoyed such a successful run that it transferred to a West End theater (the London equivalent of Broadway) and enjoyed a striking commercial success. Its run in New York, at the Plymouth Theater beginning in October 1991, enjoyed an equal success.

The actors and actresses in the New York production were mostly brought from the Abbey production, and consequently the American audience was given a strong and insightful performance whose language — including the sonority of English as it is spoken by the rural Irish — was authentic and powerful. The setting, emphasizing as it did the wheat field ready for harvest, was somewhat enigmatic, especially as the elaborately constructed path in the field was used only once. The style of the play mixes realism with ritual tableau — as at the beginning and end — and the imaginative observations of Michael as he watches his family. The overall effect is powerful.

Brian Friel (b. 1929)

DANCING AT LUGHNASA

1990

Characters

MICHAEL, *young man, narrator*
KATE, *forty, schoolteacher*
MAGGIE, *thirty-eight, housekeeper*
AGNES, *thirty-five, knitter*
ROSE, *thirty-two, knitter*

CHRIS, *twenty-six, Michael's mother*
GERRY, *thirty-three, Michael's father*
JACK, *fifty-three, missionary priest*

MICHAEL, who narrates the story, also speaks the lines of the boy, i.e., himself when he was seven.

Act 1: *A warm day in early August 1936.*

Act 2: *Three weeks later.*

The home of the Mundy family, two miles outside the village of Ballybeg, County Donegal, Ireland.

Set: *Slightly more than half the area of the stage is taken up by the kitchen on the right. (Left and right from the point of view of the audience.) The rest of the stage — i.e., the remaining area stage left — is the garden adjoining the house. The garden is neat but not cultivated.*

Upstage center is a garden seat.

The (unseen) boy has been making two kites in the garden and pieces of wood, paper, cord, etc., are lying on the ground close to the garden seat. One kite is almost complete.

There are two doors leading out of the kitchen. The front door leads to the garden and the front of the house. The second in the top right-hand corner leads to the bedrooms and to the area behind the house.

One kitchen window looks out front. A second window looks on to the garden.

There is a sycamore tree off right. One of its branches reaches over part of the house.

The room has the furnishings of the usual country kitchen of the thirties: a large iron range, large turf box beside it, table and chairs, dresser, oil lamp, buckets with water at the back door, etc., etc. But because this is the home of five women the austerity of the furnishings is relieved by some gracious touches — flowers, pretty curtains, an attractive dresser arrangement, etc.

Dress: *Kate, the teacher, is the only wage-earner. Agnes and Rose make a little money knitting gloves at home. Chris and Maggie have no income. So the clothes of all the sisters reflect their lean circumstances. Rose wears Wellingtons even though the day is warm. Maggie wears large boots with long, untied laces. Rose, Maggie, and Agnes all wear the drab, wraparound overalls/aprons of the time.*

In the opening tableau Father Jack is wearing the uniform of a British army officer chaplain — a magnificent and immaculate uniform of dazzling white; gold epaulettes and gold buttons, tropical hat, clerical collar, military cane. He stands stiffly to attention. As the text says, he is "resplendent," "magnificent." So resplendent that he looks almost comic opera.

In this tableau, too, Gerry is wearing a spotless white tricorn hat with splendid white plumage. (Soiled and shabby versions of Jack's uniform and Gerry's ceremonial hat are worn at the end of the play, i.e., in the final tableau.)

Rose is "simple." All her sisters are kind to her and protective of her. But Agnes has taken on the role of special protector.

ACT 1

(When the play opens Michael is standing downstage left in a pool of light. The rest of the stage is in darkness. Immediately Michael begins speaking, slowly bring up the lights on the rest of the stage.)

(Around the stage and at a distance from Michael the other characters stand motionless in formal tableau. Maggie is at the kitchen window (right). Chris is at the front door. Kate at extreme stage right. Rose and Gerry sit on the garden seat. Jack stands beside Rose. Agnes is upstage left. They hold these positions while Michael talks to the audience.)

MICHAEL: When I cast my mind back to that summer of 1936 different kinds of memories offer themselves to me. We got our first wireless set that summer — well, a sort of a set; and it obsessed us. And because it arrived as August was about to begin, my Aunt Maggie — she was the joker of the family — she suggested we give it a name. She wanted to call it Lugh after the old Celtic God of the Harvest. Because in the old days August the First was *Lá Lughnasa*, the feast day of the pagan god Lugh; and the days and weeks of harvesting that followed were called the Festival of Lughnasa. But Aunt Kate — she was a national schoolteacher and a very proper woman — she said it would be sinful to christen an inanimate object with any kind of name, not to talk of a pagan god. So we just called it Marconi because that was the name emblazoned on the set.

And about three weeks before we got that wireless, my mother's brother, my Uncle Jack, came home from Africa for the first time ever. For twenty-five years he had worked in a leper colony there, in a remote village called Ryanga in Uganda. The only time he ever left that village was for about six months during World War One when he was chaplain to the British army in East Africa. Then back to that grim hospice where he worked without a break for a further eighteen years. And now in his early fifties and in bad health he had come home to Ballybeg — as it turned out — to die.

And when I cast my mind back to that summer of 1936, these two memories — of our first wireless and of Father Jack's return — are always linked. So that when I recall my first shock at Jack's appearance, shrunken and jaundiced with malaria, at the same time I remember my first delight, indeed my awe, at the sheer magic of that radio. And when I remember the kitchen throbbing with the beat of Irish dance music beamed to us all the way from Dublin, and my mother and her sisters suddenly catching hands and dancing a spontaneous step-dance and laughing — screaming! — like excited schoolgirls, at the same time I see that forlorn figure of Father Jack shuffling from room to room as if he were searching for something but couldn't remember what. And even though I was only a child of seven at the time I know I had a sense of unease, some awareness of a widening breach between what seemed to be and what was, of things changing too quickly before my eyes, of becoming what they ought not to be. That may have been because Uncle Jack hadn't turned out at all like the resplendent figure in my head. Or maybe because I had witnessed Marconi's voodoo derange those kind, sensible women and transform them into shrieking strangers. Or maybe it was because during those Lughnasa weeks of 1936 we were visited on two occasions by my father, Gerry Evans, and for the first time in my life I had a chance to observe him.

(*The lighting changes. The kitchen and garden are now lit as for a warm summer afternoon.*)

(*Michael, Kate, Gerry, and Father Jack go off. The others busy themselves with their tasks. Maggie makes a mash for hens. Agnes knits gloves. Rose carries a basket of turf into the kitchen and empties it into the large box beside the range. Chris irons at the kitchen table. They all work in silence. Then Chris stops ironing, goes to the tiny mirror on the wall, and scrutinizes her face.*)

CHRIS: When are we going to get a decent mirror to see ourselves in?

MAGGIE: You can see enough to do you.

CHRIS: I'm going to throw this aul cracked thing out.

MAGGIE: Indeed you're not, Chrissie. I'm the one that broke it and the only way to avoid seven years bad luck is to keep on using it.

CHRIS: You can see nothing in it.

AGNES: Except more and more wrinkles.

CHRIS: D'you know what I think I might do? I think I just might start wearing lipstick.

AGNES: Do you hear this, Maggie?

MAGGIE: Steady on, girl. Today it's lipstick; tomorrow it's the gin bottle.

CHRIS: I think I just might.

AGNES: As long as Kate's not around. "Do you want to make a pagan of yourself?"

(*Chris puts her face up close to the mirror and feels it.*)

CHRIS: Far too pale. And the aul mousy hair. Need a bit of color.

AGNES: What for?

CHRIS: What indeed. (*She shrugs and goes back to her ironing. She holds up a surplice.°*) Make a nice dress that, wouldn't it? . . . God forgive me . . .

(*Work continues. Nobody speaks. Then suddenly and unexpectedly Rose bursts into raucous song.*)

ROSE: "Will you come to Abyssinia, will you come? Bring your own cup and saucer and a bun . . ."

(*As she sings the next two lines she dances — a gauche, graceless shuffle that defies the rhythm of the song.*)

"Mussolini will be there with his airplanes in the air, Will you come to Abyssinia, will you come?" Not bad, Maggie — eh?

(*Maggie is trying to light a very short cigarette butt.*)

MAGGIE: You should be on the stage, Rose.

(*Rose continues to shuffle and now holds up her apron skirt.*)

ROSE: And not a bad bit of leg, Maggie — eh?

MAGGIE: Rose Mundy! Where's your modesty!

(*Maggie now hitches her own skirt even higher than Rose's and does a similar shuffle.*)

Is that not more like it?

ROSE: Good, Maggie — good — good! Look, Agnes, look!

AGNES: A right pair of pagans, the two of you.

ROSE: Turn on Marconi, Chrissie.

CHRIS: I've told you a dozen times: The battery's dead.

ROSE: It is not. It went for me a while ago.

(*She goes to the set and switches it on. There is a sudden, loud three-second blast of "The British Grenadiers."*)

You see! Takes aul Rosie!

(*She is about to launch into a dance — and the music suddenly dies.*)

CHRIS: Told you.

ROSE: That aul set's useless.

AGNES: Kate'll have a new battery back with her.

CHRIS: If it's the battery that's wrong.

ROSE: Is Abyssinia in Africa, Aggie?

AGNES: Yes.

ROSE: Is there a war there?

AGNES: Yes. I've told you that.

---

surplice: A loose-fitting, white garment worn by a priest over his black robe.

ROSE: But that's not where Father Jack was, is it?

AGNES (*patiently*): Jack was in Uganda, Rosie. That's a different part of Africa. You know that.

ROSE (*unhappily*): Yes, I do . . . I do . . . I know that . . .

(*Maggie catches her hand and sings softly into her ear to the same melody as the "Abyssinia" song.*)

MAGGIE: "Will you vote for De Valera,° will you vote? If you don't, we'll be like Gandhi with his goat."

(*Rose and Maggie now sing the next two lines together.*)

"Uncle Bill from Baltinglass has a wireless up his —"

(*They dance as they sing the final line of the song.*)

"Will you vote for De Valera, will you vote?"

MAGGIE: I'll tell you something, Rosie: The pair of us should be on the stage.

ROSE: The pair of us should be on the stage, Aggie!

(*They return to their tasks. Agnes goes to the cupboard for wool. On her way back to her seat she looks out the window that looks on to the garden.*)

AGNES: What's that son of yours at out there?

CHRIS: God knows. As long as he's quiet.

AGNES: He's making something. Looks like a kite.

(*She taps on the window, calls "Michael!" and blows a kiss to the imaginary child.*)

Oh, that was the wrong thing to do! He's going to have your hair, Chris.

CHRIS: Mine's like a whin-bush. Will you wash it for me tonight, Maggie?

MAGGIE: Are we all for a big dance somewhere?

CHRIS: After I've put Michael to bed. What about then?

MAGGIE: I'm your man.

AGNES (*at window*): Pity there aren't some boys about to play with.

MAGGIE: Now you're talking. Couldn't we all do with that?

AGNES (*leaving window*): Maggie!

MAGGIE: Wouldn't it be just great if we had a — (*Breaks off.*) Shhh.

CHRIS: What is it?

MAGGIE: Thought I heard Father Jack at the back door. I hope Kate remembers his quinine.

AGNES: She'll remember. Kate forgets nothing.

(*Pause.*)

De Valera: Eamon De Valera (1882–1975) was from 1937 to 1948 the leader of the Irish government.

ROSE: There's going to be pictures in the hall next Saturday, Aggie. I think maybe I'll go.

AGNES (*guarded*): Yes?

ROSE: I might be meeting somebody there.

AGNES: Who's that?

ROSE: I'm not saying.

CHRIS: Do we know him?

ROSE: I'm not saying.

AGNES: You'll enjoy that, Rosie. You loved the last picture we saw.

ROSE: And he wants to bring me up to the back hills next Sunday — up to Lough Anna. His father has a boat there. And I'm thinking maybe I'll bring a bottle of milk with me. And I've enough money saved to buy a packet of chocolate biscuits.

CHRIS: Danny Bradley is a scut, Rose.

ROSE: I never said it was Danny Bradley!

CHRIS: He's a married man with three young children.

ROSE: And that's just where you're wrong, missy — so there! (*To Agnes.*) She left him six months ago, Aggie, and went to England.

MAGGIE: Rose, love, we just want —

ROSE (*to Chris*): And who are you to talk, Christina Mundy! Don't you dare lecture me!

MAGGIE: Everybody in the town knows that Danny Bradley is —

ROSE (*to Maggie*): And you're jealous, too! That's what's wrong with the whole of you — you're jealous of me! (*To Agnes.*) He calls me his Rosebud. He waited for me outside the chapel gate last Christmas morning and he gave me this.

(*She opens the front of her apron. A charm and a medal are pinned to her jumper.*)

"That's for my Rosebud," he said.

AGNES: Is it a fish, Rosie?

ROSE: Isn't it lovely? It's made of pure silver. And it brings you good luck.

AGNES: It is lovely.

ROSE: I wear it all the time — besides my miraculous medal.° (*Pause.*) I love him, Aggie.

AGNES: I know.

CHRIS (*softly*): Bastard.

(*Rose closes the front of her apron. She is on the point of tears. Silence. Now Maggie lifts her hen bucket and using it as a dancing partner she does a very fast and very exaggerated tango across the kitchen floor as she sings in her parodic style the words from "The Isle of Capri."*)

MAGGIE: "Summer time was nearly over; Blue Italian skies above.

miraculous medal: A religious medal depicting the Virgin Mary.

I said, 'Mister, I'm a rover.
Can't you spare a sweet word of love?'"

(*And without pausing for breath she begins calling her hens as she exits by the back door.*)

Tchook-tchook-tchook-tchook-tchook-tchook-tchook-tchookeeeeeee . . .

(*Michael enters and stands stage left. Rose takes the lid off the range and throws turf into the fire.*)

CHRIS: For God's sake, I have an iron in there!
ROSE: How was I to know that?
CHRIS: Don't you see me ironing? (*Fishing with tongs.*) Now you've lost it. Get out of my road, will you!
AGNES: Rosie, love, would you give me a hand with this. (*Of wool.*) If we don't work a bit faster we'll never get two dozen pairs finished this week.

(*The convention must now be established that the [imaginary] Boy Michael is working at the kite materials lying on the ground. No dialogue with the Boy Michael must ever be addressed directly to adult Michael, the narrator. Here, for example, Maggie has her back to the narrator. Michael responds to Maggie in his ordinary narrator's voice. Maggie enters the garden from the back of the house.*)

MAGGIE: What are these supposed to be?
BOY: Kites.
MAGGIE: Kites! God help your wit!
BOY: Watch where you're walking, Aunt Maggie — you're standing on a tail.
MAGGIE: Did it squeal? — haaaa! I'll make a deal with you, cub: I'll give you a penny if those things ever leave the ground. Right?
BOY: You're on.

(*She now squats down beside him.*)

MAGGIE: I've new riddles for you.
BOY: Give up.
MAGGIE: What goes round the house and round the house and sits in the corner? (*Pause.*) A broom! Why is a river like a watch?
BOY: You're pathetic.
MAGGIE: Because it never goes far without winding! Hairy out and hairy in, lift your foot and stab it in — what is it?

(*Pause.*)

BOY: Give up.
MAGGIE: Think!
BOY: Give up.
MAGGIE: Have you even one brain in your head?
BOY: Give up.
MAGGIE: A sock!
BOY: A what?

MAGGIE: A sock — a sock! You know — lift your foot and stab it —

(*She demonstrates. No response.*)

D'you know what your trouble is, cub? You-are-buck-stupid!
BOY: Look out — there's a rat!

(*She screams and leaps to her feet in terror.*)

MAGGIE: Where? — where? — where? — Jesus, Mary, and Joseph, where is it?
BOY: Caught you again, Aunt Maggie.
MAGGIE: You evil wee brat — God forgive you! I'll get you for that, Michael! Don't you worry — I won't forget that!

(*She picks up her bucket and moves off towards the back of the house. Stops.*)

And I had a barley sugar sweet for you.
BOY: Are there bits of cigarette tobacco stuck to it?
MAGGIE: Jesus Christ! Some day you're going to fill some woman's life full of happiness. (*Moving off.*) Tchook-tchook-tchook-tchook . . .

(*Again she stops and throws him a sweet.*)

There. I hope it chokes you. (*Exits.*) Tchook-tchook-tchook-tchook-tchookeeeee . . .
MICHAEL: When I saw Uncle Jack for the first time the reason I was so shocked by his appearance was that I expected — well, I suppose, the hero from a schoolboy's book. Once I had seen a photograph of him radiant and splendid in his officer's uniform. It had fallen out of Aunt Kate's prayer book and she snatched it from me before I could study it in detail. It was a picture taken in 1917 when he was a chaplain to the British forces in East Africa and he looked — magnificent. But Aunt Kate had been involved locally in the War of Independence; so Father Jack's brief career in the British army was never referred to in that house. All the same the wonderful Father Jack of that photo was the image of him that lodged in my mind.

But if he was a hero to me, he was a hero and a saint to my mother and to my aunts. They pored over his occasional letters. They prayed every night for him and for his lepers and for the success of his mission. They scraped and saved for him — sixpence here, a shilling there — sacrifices they made willingly, joyously, so that they would have a little money to send to him at Christmas and for his birthday. And every so often when a story would appear in the *Donegal Enquirer* about "our own leper priest," as they called him — because Ballybeg was proud of him, the whole of Donegal was proud of him — it was only natural that our family would enjoy a small share of that fame — it gave us that little bit of status in the eyes of the parish. And it must have helped my aunts to bear the shame Mother brought on the household by having me — as it was called then — out of wedlock.

(*Kate enters left, laden with shopping bags. When she sees the Boy working at his kites her face lights up with pleasure. She watches him for a few seconds. Then she goes to him.*)

KATE: Well, that's what I call a busy man. Come here and give your Aunt Kate a big kiss.

(*She catches his head between her hands and kisses the crown of his head.*)

And what's all this? It's a kite, is it?

BOY: It's two kites.

KATE (*inspecting them*): It certainly is two kites. And they're the most wonderful kites I've ever seen. And what are these designs?

(*She studies the kite faces which the audience cannot see.*)

BOY: They're faces. I painted them.

KATE (*pretended horror*): Oh, good Lord, they put the heart across me! You did those? Oh, God bless us, those are scarifying! What are they? Devils? Ghosts? I wouldn't like to see those lads up in the sky looking down at me! Hold on now . . . (*She searches in her bags and produces a small, wooden spinning-top and whip.*) Do you know what this is? Of course you do — a spinning-top. Good boy. And this — this is the whip. You know how to use it? Indeed you do. What do you say?

BOY: Thanks.

KATE: Thank you, Aunt Kate. And do you know what I have in here? A new library book! With colored pictures! We'll begin reading it at bedtime.

(*Again she kisses the top of his head. She gets to her feet.*)

Call me the moment you're ready to fly them. I wouldn't miss that for all the world.

(*She goes into the kitchen.*)

D'you know what he's at out there? Did you see, Christina? Making two kites!

CHRIS: Some kites he'll make.

KATE: All by himself. No help from anybody.

AGNES: You always said he was talented, Kate.

KATE: No question about that. And very mature for his years.

CHRIS: Very cheeky for his years.

ROSE: I think he's beautiful, Chris. I wish he was mine.

CHRIS: Is that a spinning-top he has?

KATE: It's nothing.

(*Michael exits left.*)

CHRIS: Oh, Kate, you have him spoiled. Where did you get it?

KATE: Morgan's Arcade.

CHRIS: And I'm sure he didn't even thank you.

ROSE: I know why you went into Morgan's!

KATE: He did indeed. He's very mannerly.

ROSE: You wanted to see Austin Morgan!

KATE: Every field along the road — they're all out at the hay and the corn.

ROSE: Because you have a notion of that aul Austin Morgan!

KATE: Going to be a good harvest by the look of it.

ROSE: I know you have! She's blushing! Look! Isn't she blushing?

(*Chris holds up a skirt she is ironing.*)

CHRIS: You'd need to put a stitch in that hem, Rosie.

ROSE: (*to Kate*): But what you don't know is that he's going with a wee young thing from Carrickfad.

KATE: Rose, what Austin Morgan does or doesn't do with —

ROSE: Why are you blushing then? She's blushing, isn't she? Why-why-why, Kate?

KATE (*sudden anger*): For God's sake, Rose, shut up, would you!

ROSE: Anyhow we all know you always had a —

AGNES: Rosie, pass me those steel needles — would you, please?

(*Pause.*)

CHRIS (*to Kate*): Are you tired?

(*Kate flops into a seat.*)

KATE: That road from the town gets longer every day. You can laugh if you want but I *am* going to get that old bike fixed up and I *am* going to learn to ride this winter.

AGNES: Many about Ballybeg?

KATE: Ballybeg's off its head. I'm telling you. Everywhere you go — everyone you meet — it's the one topic: Are you going to the harvest dance? Who are you going with? What are you wearing? This year's going to be the biggest ever and the best ever.

AGNES: All the same I remember some great harvest dances.

CHRIS: Don't we all.

KATE (*unpacking*): Another of those riveting Annie M. P. Smithson novels for you, Agnes.

AGNES: Ah. Thanks.

KATE: *The Marriage of Nurse Harding* — oh, dear!

For you, Christina. One teaspoonful every morning before breakfast.

CHRIS: What's this?

KATE: Cod-liver oil. You're far too pale.

CHRIS: Thank you, Kate.

KATE: Because you take no exercise. Anyhow I'm in the chemist's shop and this young girl — a wee slip of a thing, can't even remember her name — her mother's the knitting agent that buys your gloves, Agnes —

AGNES: Vera McLaughlin.

KATE: Her daughter whatever you call her.

ROSE: Sophia.

KATE: Miss Sophia, who must be all of fifteen; she comes up to me and she says, "I hope you're not going to miss the harvest dance, Miss Mundy. It's going to be just *supreme* this year." And honest to God, if you'd seen the delight in her eyes, you'd think it was heaven she was talking about. I'm telling you — off its head — like a fever in the place. That's the quinine. The doctor says it won't cure the malaria but it might help to contain it. Is he in his room?

CHRIS: He's wandering about out the back somewhere.

KATE: I told the doctor you thought him very quiet, Agnes.

(*Agnes had stopped knitting and is looking abstractedly into the middle distance.*)

AGNES: Yes?

KATE: Well, didn't you? And the doctor says we must remember how strange everything here must be to him after so long. And on top of that Swahili has been his language for twenty-five years; so that it's not that his mind is confused — it's just that he has difficulty finding the English words for what he wants to say.

CHRIS: No matter what the doctor says, Kate, his mind is a bit confused. Sometimes he doesn't know the difference between us. I've heard him calling you Rose and he keeps calling me some strange name like —

KATE: Okawa.

CHRIS: That's it! Aggie, you've heard him, haven't you?

KATE: Okawa was his house boy. He was very attached to him. (*Taking off her shoe.*) I think I'm getting corns in this foot. I hope to God I don't end up crippled like poor mother, may she rest in peace.

AGNES: Wouldn't it be a good one if we all went?

CHRIS: Went where?

AGNES: To the harvest dance.

CHRIS: Aggie!

AGNES: Just like we used to. All dressed up. I think I'd go.

ROSE: I'd go, too, Aggie! I'd go with you!

KATE: For heaven's sake you're not serious, Agnes — are you?

AGNES: I think I am.

KATE: Hah! There's more than Ballybeg off its head.

AGNES: I think we should all go.

KATE: Have you any idea what it'll be like? — Crawling with cheeky young brats that I taught years ago.

AGNES: I'm game.

CHRIS: We couldn't, Aggie — could we?

KATE: And all the riff-raff of the countryside.

AGNES: I'm game.

CHRIS: Oh God, you know how I loved dancing, Aggie.

AGNES (*to Kate*): What do you say?

KATE (*to Chris*): You have a seven-year-old child — have you forgotten that?

AGNES (*to Chris*): You could wear that blue dress of mine — you have the figure for it and it brings out the color of your eyes.

CHRIS: Can I have it? God, Aggie, I could dance nonstop all night — all week — all month!

KATE: And who'd look after Father Jack?

AGNES (*to Kate*): And you look great in that cotton dress you got for confirmation last year. You're beautiful in it, Kate.

KATE: What sort of silly talk is —

AGNES (*to Kate*): And you can wear my brown shoes with the crossover straps.

KATE: This is silly talk. We can't, Agnes. How can we?

ROSE: Will Maggie go with us?

CHRIS: Will Maggie what! Try to stop her!

KATE: Oh God, Agnes, what do you think?

AGNES: We're going.

KATE: Are we?

ROSE: We're off! We're away!

KATE: Maybe we're mad — are we mad?

CHRIS: It costs four and six to get in.

AGNES: I've five pounds saved. I'll take you. I'll take us all.

KATE: Hold on now —

AGNES: How many years has it been since we were at the harvest dance? — at any dance? And I don't care how young they are, how drunk and dirty and sweaty they are. I want to dance, Kate. It's the Festival of Lughnasa. I'm only thirty-five. I want to dance.

KATE (*wretched*): I know, I know, Agnes, I know. All the same — oh my God — I don't know if it's —

AGNES: It's settled. We're going — the Mundy girls — all five of us together.

CHRIS: Like we used to.

AGNES: Like we used to.

ROSE: I love you, Aggie! I love you more than chocolate biscuits!

(*Rose kisses Agnes impetuously, flings her arms above her head, begins singing "Abyssinia," and does the first steps of a bizarre and abandoned dance. At this Kate panics.*)

KATE: No, no, no! We're going nowhere!

CHRIS: If we all want to go —

KATE: Look at yourselves, will you! Just look at yourselves! Dancing at our time of day? That's for young people with no duties and no responsibilities and nothing in their heads but pleasure.

AGNES: Kate, I think we —

KATE: Do you want the whole countryside to be laughing at us? — women of our years? — mature women, *dancing*? What's come over you all? And this is Father Jack's home — we must never forget that — ever. No, no, we're going to no harvest dance.

ROSE: But you just said —

KATE: And there'll be no more discussion about it. The matter's over. I don't want it mentioned again.

(*Silence. Maggie returns to the garden from the back of the house. She has the hen bucket on her arm and her hands are cupped as if she were holding something fragile between them. She goes to the kite materials.*)

MAGGIE: The fox is back.

BOY: Did you see him?

MAGGIE: He has a hole chewed in the henhouse door.

BOY: Did you get a look at him, Aunt Maggie?

MAGGIE: Wasn't I talking to him. He was asking for you.

BOY: Ha-ha. What's that you have in your hands?

MAGGIE: Something I found.

BOY: What?

MAGGIE: Sitting very still at the foot of the holly tree.

BOY: Show me.

MAGGIE: Say please three times.

BOY: Please-please-please.

MAGGIE: In Swahili.

BOY: Are you going to show it to me or are you not?

MAGGIE (*crouching down beside him*): Now, cub, put your ear over here. Listen. Shhh. D'you hear it?

BOY: I think so . . . yes.

MAGGIE: What do you hear?

BOY: Something.

MAGGIE: Are you sure?

BOY: Yes, I'm sure. Show me, Aunt Maggie.

MAGGIE: All right. Ready? Get back a bit. Bit further. Right?

BOY: Yes.

(*Suddenly she opens her hands and her eyes follow the rapid and imaginary flight of something up to the sky and out of sight. She continues staring after it. Pause.*)

What was it?

MAGGIE: Did you see it?

BOY: I think so . . . yes.

MAGGIE: Wasn't it wonderful?

BOY: Was it a bird?

MAGGIE: The colors are so beautiful. (*She gets to her feet.*) Trouble is — just one quick glimpse — that's all you ever get. And if you miss that . . .

(*She moves off towards the back door of the kitchen.*)

BOY: What was it, Aunt Maggie?

MAGGIE: Don't you know what it was? It was all in your mind. Now we're quits.

KATE (*unpacking*): Tea . . . soap . . . Indian meal . . . jelly . . .

MAGGIE: I'm sick of that white rooster of yours, Rosie. Some pet that. Look at the lump he took out of my arm.

ROSE: You don't speak to him right.

MAGGIE: I know the speaking he'll get from me — the weight of my boot. Would you put some turf on that fire, Chrissie; I'm going to make some soda bread.

(*Maggie washes her hands and begins baking.*)

ROSE (*privately*): Watch out. She's in one of her cranky moods.

KATE: Your ten Wild Woodbine, Maggie.

MAGGIE: Great. The tongue's out a mile.

ROSE (*privately*): You missed it all, Maggie.

MAGGIE: What did I miss this time?

ROSE: We were all going to go to the harvest dance — like the old days. And then Kate —

KATE: Your shoes, Rose. The shoemaker says, whatever kind of feet you have, only the insides of the soles wear down.

ROSE: Is that a bad thing?

KATE: That is neither a bad thing nor a good thing, Rose. It's just — distinctive, as might be expected.

(*Rose grimaces behind Kate's back.*)

Cornflour . . . salt . . . tapioca — it's gone up a penny for some reason . . . sugar for the bilberry jam — if we ever get the bilberries . . .

(*Agnes and Rose exchange looks.*)

MAGGIE (*privately to Rose*): Look at the packet of Wild Woodbine she got me.

ROSE: What's wrong with it?

MAGGIE: Only nine cigarettes in it. They're so wild one of them must have escaped on her.

(*They laugh secretly.*)

CHRIS: Doesn't Jack sometimes call you Okawa, too, Maggie?

MAGGIE: Yes. What does it mean?

CHRIS: Okawa was his house boy, Kate says.

MAGGIE: Dammit. I thought it was Swahili for gorgeous.

AGNES: Maggie!

MAGGIE: That's the very thing we could do with here — a house boy.

KATE: And the battery. The man in the shop says we go though these things quicker than anyone in Ballybeg.

CHRIS: Good for us.

(*Chris takes the battery and leaves it beside Marconi.*)

KATE: I met the parish priest. I don't know what has happened to that man. But ever since Father Jack came home he can hardly look me in the eye.

MAGGIE: That's because you keep winking at him, Kate.

CHRIS: He was always moody, that man.

KATE: Maybe that's it . . . The paper . . . candles . . . matches . . . The word's not good on that young Sweeney boy from the back hills. He was anointed° last night.

MAGGIE: I didn't know he was dying?

KATE: Not an inch of his body that isn't burned.

AGNES: Does anybody know what happened?

KATE: Some silly prank up in the hills. He knows he's dying, the poor boy. Just lies there, moaning.

CHRIS: What sort of prank?

KATE: How would I know?

CHRIS: What are they saying in the town?

KATE: I know no more than I've told you, Christina.

(*Pause.*)

ROSE (*quietly, resolutely*): It was last Sunday week, the first night of the Festival of Lughnasa; and they were doing what they do every year up there in the back hills.

KATE: Festival of Lughnasa! What sort of —

ROSE: First they light a bonfire beside a spring well. Then they dance round it. Then they drive their cattle through the flames to banish the devil out of them.

KATE: Banish the —! You don't know the first thing about what —

ROSE: And this year there was an extra big crowd of boys and girls. And they were off their heads with

---

anointed: Given the "last rites," a sacrament for the dying.

---

drink. And young Sweeney's trousers caught fire and he went up like a torch. That's what happened.

KATE: Who filled your head with that nonsense?

ROSE: They do it every Lughnasa. I'm telling you. That's what happened.

KATE (*very angry, almost shouting*): And they're savages! I know those people from the back hills! I've taught them! Savages — that's what they are! And what pagan practices they have are no concern of ours — none whatever! It's a sorry day to hear talk like that in a Christian home, a Catholic home! All I can say is that I'm shocked and disappointed to hear you repeating rubbish like that, Rose!

ROSE (*quietly, resolutely*): That's what happened. I'm telling you.

(*Pause.*)

MAGGIE: All the same it would be very handy in the wintertime to have a wee house boy to feed the hens: "Tchook-tchook-tchook-tchook-tchook-tchook-tchook-tchookeeee . . ."

(*Father Jack enters by the back door. He looks frail and older than his fifty-three years. Broad-brimmed black hat. Heavy gray top coat. Woolen trousers that stop well short of his ankles. Heavy black boots. Thick woolen socks. No clerical collar. He walks — shuffles quickly — with his hands behind his back. He seems uneasy, confused. Scarcely any trace of an Irish accent.*)

JACK: I beg your pardon . . . the wrong apartment . . . forgive me . . .

KATE: Come in and join us, Jack.

JACK: May I?

MAGGIE: You're looking well, Jack.

JACK: Yes? I expected to enter my bedroom through that . . . what I am missing — what I require . . . I had a handkerchief in my pocket and I think perhaps I —

CHRIS (*taking one from the ironing pile*): Here's a handkerchief.

JACK: I thank you. I am grateful. It is so strange: I don't remember the — the architecture? — the planning? — what's the word? — the layout! — I don't recollect the layout of this home . . . scarcely. That is strange, isn't it? I thought the front door was there. (*To Kate.*) You walked to the village to buy stores, Agnes?

KATE: It's Kate. And dozens of people were asking for you.

JACK: They remember me?

KATE: Of course they remember you! And when you're feeling stronger they're going to have a great public welcome for you — flags, bands, speeches, everything!

JACK: Why would they do this?

KATE: Because they're delighted you're back.

JACK: Yes?

KATE: Because they're delighted you're home.

JACK: I'm afraid I don't remember them. I couldn't name ten people in Ballybeg now.

CHRIS: It will all come back to you. Don't worry.

JACK: You think so?

AGNES: Yes, it will.

JACK: Perhaps . . . I feel the climate so cold . . . if you'll forgive me . . .

AGNES: Why don't you lie down for a while?

JACK: I may do that . . . thank you . . . you are most kind . . .

(*He shuffles off. Pause. A sense of unease, almost embarrassment.*)

KATE (*briskly*): It will be a slow process but he'll be fine. Apples . . . butter . . . margarine . . . flour . . . And wait till you hear! Who did I meet in the post office! Maggie, are you listening to me?

MAGGIE: Yes?

KATE: You'll never believe it — your old pal, Bernie O'Donnell! Home from London! First time back in twenty years!

MAGGIE: Bernie . . .

KATE: Absolutely gorgeous. The figure of a girl of eighteen. Dressed to kill from head to foot. And the hair! — as black and as curly as the day she left. I can't tell you — a film star!

MAGGIE: Bernie O'Donnell . . .

KATE: And beside her two of the most beautiful children you ever laid eyes on. Twins. They'll be fourteen next month. And to see the three of them together — like sisters, I'm telling you.

MAGGIE: Twin girls.

KATE: Identical.

MAGGIE: Identical.

KATE: Nora and Nina.

ROSE: Mother used to say twins are a double blessing.

MAGGIE: Bernie O'Donnell . . . oh my goodness . . .

KATE: And wait till you hear — they are pure blond! "Where in the name of God did the blond hair come from?" I asked her. "The father. Eric," she says. "He's from Stockholm."

AGNES: Stockholm!

ROSE: Where's Stockholm, Aggie?

KATE: So there you are. Bernie O'Donnell married to a Swede. I couldn't believe my eyes. But the same bubbly, laughing, happy Bernie. Asking about everybody by name.

(*Maggie goes to the window and looks out so that the others cannot see her face. She holds her hands, covered with flour, out from her body.*)

CHRIS: She remembered us all?

KATE: Knew all about Michael; had his age to the very month. Was Agnes still the quickest knitter in Ballybeg? Were none of us thinking of getting married? — and weren't we wise!

ROSE: Did she remember me?

KATE: "Rose had the sweetest smile I ever saw."

ROSE: There!

KATE: But asking specially for you, Maggie: how you were doing — what you were doing — how were you looking — were you as lighthearted as ever? Every time she thinks of you, she says, she has the memory of the two of you hiding behind the turf stack, passing a cigarette between you and falling about laughing about some boy called — what was it? — Curley somebody?

MAGGIE: Curley McDaid. An eejit of a fella. Bald as an egg at seventeen. Bernie O'Donnell . . . oh my goodness . . .

(*Pause.*)

AGNES: Will she be around for a while?

KATE: Leaving tomorrow.

AGNES: We won't see her so. That's a pity.

CHRIS: Nice names, aren't they? — Nina and Nora.

KATE: I like Nora. Nice name. Strong name.

AGNES: Not so sure about Nina. (*To Chris.*) Do you like Nina for a name?

CHRIS: Nina? No, not a lot.

KATE: Well, if there's a Saint Nina, I'm afraid she's not in my prayer book.

AGNES: Maybe she's a Swedish saint.

KATE: Saints in Sweden! What'll it be next!

ROSE: Mother used to say twins are a double blessing.

KATE (*sharply*): You've offered us that cheap wisdom already, Rose.

(*Pause.*)

CHRIS: You've got some flour on your nose, Maggie.

MAGGIE: When I was sixteen I remember slipping out one Sunday night — it was this time of year, the beginning of August — and Bernie and I met at the gate of the workhouse and the pair of us off to a dance in Ardstraw. I was being pestered by a fellow called Tim Carlin at the time but it was really Brian McGuinness that I was — that I was keen on. Remember Brian with the white hands and the longest eyelashes you ever saw? But of course he was crazy about Bernie. Anyhow the two boys took us on the bar of their bikes and off the four of us headed to Ardstraw, fifteen miles each way. If Daddy had known, may he rest in peace . . .

And at the end of the night there was a competition for the Best Military Two-step. And it was down to three couples: the local pair from Ardstraw; wee Timmy and myself — he was up to there on me; and Brian and Bernie . . .

And they were just so beautiful together, so stylish; you couldn't take your eyes off them. People just stopped dancing and gazed at them . . .

And when the judges announced the winners — they were probably blind drunk — naturally the local couple came first; and Timmy and myself came second; and Brian and Bernie came third.

Poor Bernie was stunned. She couldn't believe it. Couldn't talk. Wouldn't speak to any of us for the rest of the night. Wouldn't even cycle home with us. She was right, too: They should have won; they were just so beautiful together . . .

And that's the last time I saw Brian McGuinness — remember Brian with the . . . ? And the next thing I heard he had left for Australia . . .

She was right to be angry, Bernie. I know it wasn't fair — it wasn't fair at all. I mean they must have been blind drunk, those judges, whoever they were . . .

(*Maggie stands motionless, staring out of the window, seeing nothing. The others drift back to their tasks: Rose and Agnes knit; Kate puts the groceries away; Chris connects the battery. Pause.*)

KATE: Is it working now, Christina?
CHRIS: What's that?
KATE: Marconi.
CHRIS: Marconi? Yes, yes . . . should be . . .

(*She switches the set on and returns to her ironing. The music, at first scarcely audible, is Irish dance music — "The Mason's Apron," played by a ceili band. Very fast; very heavy beat; a raucous sound. At first we are aware of the beat only. Then, as the volume increases slowly, we hear the melody. For about ten seconds — until the sound has established itself — the women continue with their tasks. Then Maggie turns round. Her head is cocked to the beat, to the music. She is breathing deeply, rapidly. Now her features become animated by a look of defiance, of aggression; a crude mask of happiness. For a few seconds she stands still, listening, absorbing the rhythm, surveying her sisters with her defiant grimace. Now she spreads her fingers (which are covered with flour), pushes her hair back from her face, pulls her hands down her cheeks and patterns her face with an instant mask. At the same time she opens her mouth and emits a wild, raucous "Yaaaah!" — and immediately begins to dance, arms, legs, hair, long bootlaces flying. And as she dances she lilts — sings — shouts and calls, "Come on and join me! Come on! Come on!" For about ten seconds she dances alone — a white-faced, frantic dervish. Her sisters watch her.*)

(*Then Rose's face lights up. Suddenly she flings away her knitting, leaps to her feet, shouts, grabs Maggie's hand. They dance and sing — shout together; Rose's Wellingtons pounding out their own erratic rhythm. Now after another five seconds Agnes looks around, leaps up, joins Maggie and Rose. Of all the sisters she moves most gracefully, most sensuously. Then after the same interval Chris, who has been folding Jack's surplice, tosses it quickly over her head and joins in the dance. The moment she tosses the vestment over her head Kate cries out in remonstration, "Oh, Christina —!" But her protest is drowned. Agnes and Rose, Chris and Maggie, are now all doing a dance that is almost recognizable. They meet — they retreat. They form a circle and wheel round and round. But the movements seem caricatured; and the sound is too loud; and the beat is too fast; and the almost recognizable dance is made grotesque because — for example — instead of holding hands, they have their arms tightly around one another's neck, one another's waist. Finally Kate, who has been watching the scene with unease, with alarm, suddenly leaps to her feet, flings her head back, and emits a loud "Yaaaah!"*)

(*Kate dances alone, totally concentrated, totally private; a movement that is simultaneously controlled and frantic; a weave of complex steps that takes her quickly round the kitchen, past her sisters, out to the garden, round the summer seat, back to the kitchen; a pattern of action that is out of character and at the same time ominous of some deep and true emotion. Throughout the dance Rose, Agnes, Maggie, and Chris shout — call — sing to each other. Kate makes no sound.*)

(*With this too loud music, this pounding beat, this shouting — calling — singing, this parodic reel, there is a sense of order being consciously subverted, of the women consciously and crudely caricaturing themselves, indeed of near-hysteria being induced. The music stops abruptly in mid-phrase. But because of the noise they are making the sisters do not notice and continue dancing for a few seconds. Then Kate notices — and stops. Then Agnes. Then Chris and Maggie. Now only Rose is dancing her graceless dance by herself. Then finally she, too, notices and stops. Silence. For some time they stand where they have stopped. There is no sound but their gasping for breath and short bursts of static from the radio. They look at each other obliquely; avoid looking at each other; half smile in embarrassment; feel and look slightly ashamed and slightly defiant. Chris moves first. She goes to the radio.*)

CHRIS: It's away again, that aul thing. Sometimes you're good with it, Aggie.
AGNES: Feel the top. Is it warm?

CHRIS: Roasting.

AGNES: Turn it off till it cools down.

(*Chris turns it off — and slaps it.*)

CHRIS: Bloody useless set, that.

KATE: No need for corner-boy language, Christina.

AGNES: There must be some reason why it overheats.

CHRIS: Because it's a goddamn, bloody useless set — that's why.

ROSE: Goddamn bloody useless.

KATE: Are Wellingtons absolutely necessary on a day like this, Rose?

ROSE: I've only my Wellingtons and my Sunday shoes, Kate. And it's not Sunday, is it?

KATE: Oh, dear, we're suddenly very logical, aren't we?

MAGGIE (*lighting a cigarette*): I'll tell you something, girls: This Ginger Rogers has seen better days.

KATE: It's those cigarettes are killing you.

MAGGIE (*exhaling*): Wonderful Wild Woodbine. Next best thing to a wonderful, wild man. Want a drag, Kitty?

KATE: Go and wash your face, Maggie. And for goodness' sake tie those laces.

MAGGIE: Yes, miss. (*At window.*) Where's Michael, Chrissie?

CHRIS: Working at those kites, isn't he?

MAGGIE: He's not there. He's gone.

CHRIS: He won't go far.

MAGGIE: He was there ten minutes ago.

CHRIS: He'll be all right.

MAGGIE: But if he goes down to the old well —

CHRIS: Just leave him alone for once, will you, please?

(*Maggie shrugs and goes out the back door. Pause.*)

KATE: Who's making the tea this evening?

AGNES: Who makes the tea every evening?

CHRIS (*at radio*): The connections seem to be all right.

KATE: Please take that surplice off, Christina.

CHRIS: Maybe a valve has gone — if I knew what a valve looked like.

KATE: Have you no sense of propriety?

CHRIS: If you ask me we should throw it out.

AGNES: I'd be all for that. It's junk, that set.

ROSE: Goddamn and bloody useless.

KATE (*to Agnes*): And you'll buy a new one, will you?

AGNES: It was never any good.

KATE: You'll buy it out of your glove money, will you? I thought what you and Rose earned knitting gloves was barely sufficient to clothe the pair of you.

AGNES: This isn't your classroom, Kate.

KATE: Because I certainly don't see any of it being offered for the upkeep of the house.

AGNES: Please, Kate —

KATE: But now it stretches to buying a new wireless. Wonderful!

AGNES: I make every meal you sit down to every day of the week —

KATE: Maybe I should start knitting gloves?

AGNES: I wash every stitch of clothes you wear. I polish your shoes. I make your bed. We both do — Rose and I. Paint the house. Sweep the chimney. Cut the grass. Save the turf. What you have here, Kate, are two unpaid servants.

ROSE: And d'you know what your nickname at school is? The Gander! Everybody calls you the Gander!

(*Maggie runs on and goes straight to the window.*)

MAGGIE: Come here till you see! Look who's coming up the lane!

AGNES: Who's coming?

MAGGIE: I only got a glimpse of him — but I'm almost certain it's —

AGNES: Who? Who is it?

MAGGIE (*to Chris*): It's Gerry Evans, Chrissie.

CHRIS: Christ Almighty.

MAGGIE: He's at the bend in the lane.

CHRIS: Oh, Jesus Christ Almighty.

(*The news throws the sisters into chaos. Only Chris stands absolutely still, too shocked to move. Agnes picks up her knitting and works with excessive concentration. Rose and Maggie change their footwear. Everybody dashes about in confusion — peering into the tiny mirror, bumping into one another, peeping out the window, combing hair. During all this hectic activity they talk over each other and weave around the immobile Chris. The lines overlap.*)

KATE: How dare Mr. Evans show his face here.

MAGGIE: He wants to see his son, doesn't he?

KATE: There's no welcome for that creature here.

ROSE: Who hid my Sunday shoes?

MAGGIE: We'll have to give him his tea.

KATE: I don't see why we should.

MAGGIE: And there's nothing in the house.

KATE: No business at all coming here and upsetting everybody.

ROSE: You're right, Kate. I hate him!

MAGGIE: Has anybody got spare shoelaces?

KATE: Look at the state of that floor.

MAGGIE: Maybe he just wants to meet Father Jack.

KATE: Father Jack may have something to say to Mr. Evans. (*Of the ironing.*) Agnes, put those clothes away.

(*Agnes does not hear her, so apparently engrossed is she in her knitting.*)

MAGGIE: My Woodbine! Where's my Woodbine?

ROSE: He won't stay the night, Kate, will he?

KATE: He most certainly won't stay the night in this
house!

MAGGIE: Have you a piece of cord, Aggie? Anybody
got a bit of twine?

KATE: Behave quite normally. Be very calm and very
dignified. Stop peeping out, Rose!

ROSE: (*at window*): There's nobody coming at all.

(*Silence. Then Agnes puts down her knitting, rushes
to the window, pushes Rose aside, and looks out.*)

AGNES: Let me see.

ROSE: You imagined it, Maggie.

CHRIS: Oh God.

ROSE: He's not there at all.

AGNES (*softly*): Yes, he is. Maggie's right. There he
is.

ROSE: Show me.

KATE: Has he a walking stick?

ROSE: Yes.

KATE: And a straw hat?

ROSE: Yes.

KATE: It's Mr. Evans all right.

AGNES: Yes. There he is.

CHRIS: Oh sweet God — look at the state of me —
what'll I say to him? — how close is he?

ROSE: I couldn't look that man in the face. I just hate
him — hate him!

KATE: That's a very unchristian thing to say, Rose.
(*As Rose rushes off.*) There's no luck in talk like
that!

CHRIS: Look at my hands, Kate — I'm shaking.

(*Kate catches her shoulders.*)

KATE: You are not shaking. You are perfectly calm
and you are looking beautiful and what you are
going to do is this. You'll meet him outside. You'll
tell him his son is healthy and happy. And then
you'll send him packing — yourself and Michael
are managing quite well without him — as you
always have.

(*Chris does not move. She is about to cry. Kate now
takes her in her arms.*)

Of course ask him in. And give the creature his
tea. And stay the night if he wants to. (*Firm again.*)
But in the outside loft. And alone.
    Now. I brought a newspaper home with me.
Did anybody see where I left it?

(*Chris now rushes to the mirror and adroitly adjusts
her hair and her clothes.*)

AGNES: Where is he, Maggie?

MAGGIE: In the garden.

KATE: Agnes, did you see where I left the paper?

MAGGIE: It's on the turf box, Kate.

(*Kate reads the paper — or pretends to. Agnes sits
beside the radio and knits with total concentration.
Maggie stands at the side of the garden window. Gerry
Evans enters left, his step jaunty, swinging his cane,
his straw hat well back on his head. He knows he is
being watched. Although he is very ill at ease the smile
never leaves his face. Chris goes out to the garden
where they meet. Gerry has an English accent.*)

GERRY: How are you, Chrissie? Great to see you.

CHRIS: Hello, Gerry.

GERRY: And how have you been for the past six
months?

CHRIS: Thirteen months.

GERRY: Thirteen? Never!

CHRIS: July last year; July the seventh.

GERRY: Wow-wow-wow-wow. Where does the time
go? Thirteen months? Phew! A dozen times — two
dozen times I planned a visit and then something
turned up and I couldn't get away.

CHRIS: Well, you're here now.

GERRY: Certainly am. And that was a bit of good
fortune. Last night in a bar in Sligo. Bump into
this chappie with a brand new Morris Cowley who
lets slip that he's heading for Ballybeg in the morning. Ballybeg? Something familiar about that name!
So. Here I am. In the flesh. As a matter of interest.
Bit of good luck that, wasn't it?

CHRIS: Yes.

GERRY: He just let it slip. And here I am. Oh, yes,
wonderful luck.

CHRIS: Yes.

(*Pause.*)

MAGGIE: Looks terrified, the poor fella.

KATE: Terrified, my foot.

MAGGIE: Come here till you see him. Aggie.

AGNES: Not just now.

MAGGIE: I'm sure he could do with a good meal.

KATE: I'll give him three minutes. Then if she doesn't
hunt him, I will.

GERRY: You're looking wonderful, Chrissie. Really
great. Terrific.

CHRIS: My hair's like a whin-bush.

GERRY: Looks lovely to me.

CHRIS: Maggie's going to wash it tonight.

GERRY: And how's Maggie?

CHRIS: Fine.

GERRY: And Rose and Kate?

CHRIS: Grand.

GERRY: And Agnes?

CHRIS: Everybody's well, thanks.

GERRY: Tell her I was asking for her — Agnes.

CHRIS: I would ask you in but the place is —

GERRY: No, no, some other time; thanks all the same.

The old schedule's a bit tight today. And the chappie who gave me the lift tells me Father Jack's home.

CHRIS: Just a few weeks ago.

GERRY: All the way from Africa.

CHRIS: Yes.

GERRY: Safe and sound.

CHRIS: Yes.

GERRY: Terrific.

CHRIS: Yes.

GERRY: Lucky man.

CHRIS: Yes.

(*Gerry uses the cane as a golf club and swings.*)

GERRY: Must take up some exercise. Putting on too much weight.

KATE: He's not still there, is he?

MAGGIE: Yes.

KATE: Doing what, in God's name?

MAGGIE: Talking.

KATE: Would someone please tell me what they have to say to each other?

MAGGIE: He's Michael's father, Kate.

KATE: That's a responsibility never burdened Mr. Evans.

CHRIS: A commercial traveler called into Kate's school last Easter. He had met you somewhere in Dublin. He had some stupid story about you giving dancing lessons up there.

GERRY: He was right.

CHRIS: He was not, Gerry!

GERRY: Cross the old ticker.

CHRIS: Real lessons?

GERRY: All last winter.

CHRIS: What sort of dancing?

GERRY: Strictly ballroom. You're the one should have been giving them — you were always far better than me. Don't you remember? (*He does a quick step and a pirouette.*) Oh, that was fun while it lasted. I enjoyed that.

CHRIS: And people came to you to be taught?

GERRY: Don't look so surprised! Everybody wants to dance. I had thousands of pupils — millions!

CHRIS: Gerry —

GERRY: Fifty-three. I'm a liar. Fifty-one. And when the good weather came, they all drifted away. Shame, really. Yes, I enjoyed that. But I've just started a completely new career, as a matter of interest. Never been busier. Gramophone salesman. Agent for the whole country, if you don't mind. "Minerva Gramophones — The Wise Buy."

CHRIS: Sounds good, Gerry.

GERRY: Fabulous. All I have to do is get the orders and pass them on to Dublin. A big enterprise, Chrissie; oh, one very big enterprise.

CHRIS: And it's going all right for you?

GERRY: Unbelievable. The wholesaler can't keep up with me. Do you see this country? This country is gramophone crazy. Give you an example. Day before yesterday; just west of Oughterard; spots this small house up on the side of a hill. Something seemed just right about it — you know? Off the bike; up the lane; knocks. Out comes this enormous chappie with red hair — what are you laughing at?

CHRIS: Gerry —

GERRY: I promise you. I show him the brochures; we talk about them for ten minutes; and just like that he takes four — one for himself and three for the married daughters.

CHRIS: He took four gramophones?

GERRY: Four brochures!

(*They both laugh.*)

But he'll buy. I promise you he'll buy. Tell you this, Chrissie: People thought gramophones would be a thing of the past when radios came in. But they were wrong. In my experience . . . Don't turn round; but he's watching us from behind that bush.

CHRIS: Michael?

GERRY: Pretend you don't notice. Just carry on. This all his stuff?

CHRIS: He's making kites if you don't mind.

GERRY: Unbelievable. Got a glimpse of him down at the foot of the lane. He is just enormous.

CHRIS: He's at school, you know.

GERRY: Never! Wow-wow-wow-wow. Since when?

CHRIS: Since Christmas. Kate got him in early.

GERRY: Fabulous. And he likes it?

CHRIS: He doesn't say much.

GERRY: He loves it. He adores it. They all love school nowadays. And he'll be brilliant at school. Actually I intended bringing him something small —

CHRIS: No, no; his aunts have him —

GERRY: Just a token, really. As a matter of interest I was looking at a bicycle in Kilkenny last Monday. But they only had it in blue and I thought black might be more — you know — manly. They took my name and all. Call next time I'm down there. Are you busy yourself?

CHRIS: Oh, the usual — housework — looking after his lordship.

GERRY: Wonderful.

CHRIS: Give Agnes and Rose a hand at their knitting. The odd bit of sewing. Pity you don't sell sewing machines.

GERRY: That's an idea! Do the two jobs together! Make an absolute fortune. You have the most unbelievable business head, Chrissie. Never met anything like it.

(*She laughs.*)

What are you laughing at?

MAGGIE: You should see the way she's looking at him — you'd think he was the biggest toff in the world.

KATE: Tinker, more likely! Loafer! Wastrel!

MAGGIE: She knows all that, too.

KATE: Too? That's all there is.

MAGGIE: Come over till you see them, Agnes.

AGNES: Not just now.

GERRY: You'd never guess what I met on the road out from the town. Talk about good luck! A cow with a single horn coming straight out of the middle of its forehead.

CHRIS: You never did!

GERRY: As God is my judge. Walking along by itself. Nobody near it.

CHRIS: Gerry —

GERRY: And just as I was passing it, it stopped and looked me straight in the eye.

CHRIS: That was no cow you met — that was a unicorn.

GERRY: Go ahead and mock. A unicorn has the body of a horse. This was a cow — a perfectly ordinary brown cow except that it had a single horn just here. Would I tell you a lie?

(*Chris laughs.*)

Go ahead. Laugh. But that's what I saw. Wasn't that a spot of good luck?

CHRIS: Was it?

GERRY: A cow with a single horn? Oh, yes, that must be a good omen. How many cows like that have you ever met?

CHRIS: Thousands. Millions.

GERRY: Stop that! I'm sure it's the only one in Ireland; maybe the only one in the world. And I met it on the road to Ballybeg. And it winked at me.

CHRIS: You never mentioned that.

GERRY: What?

CHRIS: That it winked at you.

GERRY: Unbelievable. That's what made it all so mysterious. Oh, yes, that must be a fabulous omen. Maybe this week I'm going to sell a gramophone or two after all.

CHRIS: But I thought you —?

GERRY: Look! A single magpie! That's definitely a bad omen — one for sorrow. (*His stick as a gun.*) Bang! Missed. (*Mock serious.*) Where's my lucky cow? Come back, brown cow, come back!

(*They both laugh.*)

KATE: They're not *still* talking, are they?

MAGGIE: Laughing. She laughs all the time with him. D'you hear them, Aggie?

AGNES: Yes.

KATE: Laughing? Absolutely beyond my comprehension.

AGNES: Like so many things, Kate.

KATE: Two more minutes and Mr. Evans is going to talk to me. Laughing? Hah!

GERRY: Thinking of going away for a while, Chrissie.

CHRIS: Where to?

GERRY: But I'll come back to say good-bye first.

CHRIS: Are you going home to Wales?

GERRY: Wales isn't my home anymore. My home is here — well, Ireland. To Spain — as a matter of interest. Just for a short while.

CHRIS: To sell gramophones?

GERRY: Good God, no! (*Laughs.*) You'll never believe this — to do a spot of fighting. With the International Brigade. A company leaves in a few weeks. Bit ridiculous, isn't it? But you know old Gerry when the blood's up — bang-bang-bang! — missing everybody.

CHRIS: Are you serious?

GERRY: Bit surprised myself — as a matter of interest.

CHRIS: What do you know about Spain?

GERRY: Not a lot. A little. Enough, maybe. Yes, I know enough. And I thought I should try my hand at something worthy for a change. Give Evans a Big Cause and he won't let you down. It's only everyday stuff he's not so successful at. Anyhow I've still to enlist . . . He's still watching us. He thinks we don't see him. I wouldn't mind talking to him.

CHRIS: He's a bit shy.

GERRY: Naturally. And I'm a stranger to him practically . . . does he know my name?

CHRIS: Of course he knows your name.

GERRY: Good. Thanks. Well, maybe not so good. He's a very handsome child. With your eyes. Lucky boy.

(*"Dancing in the Dark" softly from the radio.*)

MAGGIE: Good for you, Aggie. What did you do to it?

AGNES: I didn't touch it.

KATE: Turn that thing off, Aggie, would you?

(*Agnes does not.*)

GERRY: You have a gramophone! I could have got it for you wholesale.

CHRIS: It's a wireless set.

GERRY: Oh, very posh.

CHRIS: It doesn't go half the time. Aggie says it's a heap of junk.

GERRY: I know nothing about radios but I'll take a look at it if you —

CHRIS: Some other time. When you come back.

(*Pause.*)

GERRY: And Agnes is well?

CHRIS: Fine — fine.

GERRY: Of all your sisters Agnes was the one that seemed to object least to me. Tell her I was asking for her.

CHRIS: I'll tell her.

(*They listen to the music.*)

GERRY: Good tune.

(*Suddenly he takes her in his arms and dances.*)

CHRIS: Gerry —

GERRY: Don't talk.

CHRIS: What are you at?

GERRY: Not a word.

CHRIS: Oh God, Gerry —

GERRY: Shhh.

CHRIS: They're watching us.

GERRY: Who is?

CHRIS: Maggie and Aggie. From the kitchen window.

GERRY: Hope so. And Kate.

CHRIS: And Father Jack.

GERRY: Better still! Terrific!

(*He suddenly swings her round and round and dances her lightly, elegantly across the garden. As he does he sings the song to her.*)

MAGGIE (*quietly*): They're dancing.

KATE: What!

MAGGIE: They're dancing together.

KATE: God forgive you!

MAGGIE: He has her in his arms.

KATE: He has not! The animal!

(*She flings the paper aside and joins Maggie at the window.*)

MAGGIE: They're dancing round the garden, Aggie.

KATE: Oh God, what sort of fool is she?

MAGGIE: He's a beautiful dancer, isn't he?

KATE: He's leading her astray again, Maggie.

MAGGIE: Look at her face — she's easy led. Come here till you see, Aggie.

AGNES: I'm busy! For God's sake can't you see I'm busy!

(*Maggie turns and tooks at her in amazement.*)

KATE: That's the only thing that Evans creature could ever do well — was dance. (*Pause.*) And look at her, the fool. For God's sake, would you look at that fool of a woman? (*Pause.*) Her whole face alters when she's happy, doesn't it? (*Pause.*) They dance so well together. They're such a beautiful couple. (*Pause.*) She's as beautiful as Bernie O'Donnell any day, isn't she?

(*Maggie moves slowly away from the window and sits motionless.*)

GERRY: Do you know the words?

CHRIS: I never know any words.

GERRY: Neither do I. Doesn't matter. This is more important. (*Pause.*) Marry me, Chrissie. (*Pause.*) Are you listening to me?

CHRIS: I hear you.

GERRY: Will you marry me when I come back in two weeks?

CHRIS: I don't think so, Gerry.

GERRY: I'm mad about you. You know I am. I've always been mad about you.

CHRIS: When you're with me.

GERRY: Leave this house and come away with —

CHRIS: But you'd walk out on me again. You wouldn't intend to but that's what would happen because that's your nature and you can't help yourself.

GERRY: Not this time, Chrissie. This time it will be —

CHRIS: Don't talk anymore; no more words. Just dance me down the lane and then you'll leave.

GERRY: Believe me, Chrissie; this time the omens are terrific! The omens are unbelievable this time!

(*They dance off. After they have exited the music continues for a few seconds and then stops suddenly in mid-phrase. Maggie goes to the set, slaps it, turns it off. Kate moves away from the window.*)

KATE: They're away. Dancing.

MAGGIE: Whatever's wrong with it, that's all it seems to last — a few minutes at a time. Something to do with the way it heats up.

KATE: We probably won't see Mr. Evans for another year — until the humor suddenly takes him again.

AGNES: He has a Christian name.

KATE: And in the meantime it's Christina's heart that gets crushed again. That's what I mind. But what really infuriates me is that the creature has no sense of ordinary duty. Does he ever wonder how she clothes and feeds Michael? Does he ask her? Does he care?

(*Agnes rises and goes to the back door.*)

AGNES: Going out to get my head cleared. Bit of a headache all day.

KATE: Seems to me the beasts of the field have more concern for their young than that creature has.

AGNES: Do you ever listen to yourself, Kate? You are such a damned righteous bitch! And his name is Gerry! — Gerry! — Gerry!

(*Now on the point of tears, she runs off.*)

KATE: And what was that all about?

MAGGIE: Who's to say?

KATE: Don't I know his name is Gerry? What am I calling him? — St. Patrick?

MAGGIE: She's worried about Chris, too.

KATE: You see, that's what a creature like Mr. Evans does: appears out of nowhere and suddenly poisons the atmosphere in the whole house — God forgive him, the bastard! There! That's what I mean! God forgive me!

(*Maggie begins putting on her long-laced boots again. As she does she sings listlessly, almost inaudibly.*)

MAGGIE: " 'Twas on the Isle of Capri that he found her
Beneath the shade of an old walnut tree.
Oh, I can still see the flowers blooming round her,
Where they met on the Isle of Capri."

KATE: If you knew your prayers as well as you know the words of those aul pagan songs! . . . She's right: I am a righteous bitch, amn't I?

MAGGIE: "She was as sweet as a rose at the dawning
But somehow fate hadn't meant it to be,
And though he sailed with the tide in the morning,
Still his heart's in the Isle of Capri."

(*Maggie now stands up and looks at her feet.*)

Now. Who's for a fox-trot?

KATE: You work hard at your job. You try to keep the home together. You perform your duties as best you can — because you believe in responsibilities and obligations and good order. And then suddenly, suddenly you realize that hair cracks are appearing everywhere; that control is slipping away; that the whole thing is so fragile it can't be held together much longer. It's all about to collapse, Maggie.

MAGGIE (*wearily*): Nothing's about to collapse, Kate.

KATE: That young Sweeney boy from the back hills — the boy who was anointed — his trousers didn't catch fire, as Rose said. They were doing some devilish thing with a goat — some sort of sacrifice for the Lughnasa Festival; and Sweeney was so drunk he toppled over into the middle of the bonfire. Don't know why that came into my head . . .

MAGGIE: Kate . . .

(*Maggie goes to her and sits beside her.*)

KATE: And Mr. Evans is off again for another twelve months and next week or the week after Christina'll collapse into one of her depressions. Remember last winter? — all that sobbing and lamenting in the middle of the night. I don't think I could go through that again. And the doctor says he doesn't think Father Jack's mind is confused but that his superiors probably had no choice but send him home. Whatever he means by that, Maggie. And the parish priest did talk to me today. He said the numbers in the school are falling and that there may not be a job for me after the summer. But the numbers aren't falling, Maggie. Why is he telling me lies? Why does he want rid of me? And why has he never come out to visit Father Jack? (*She tries to laugh.*) If he gives me the push, all five of us will be at home together all day long — we can spend the day dancing to Marconi.

(*Now she cries. Maggie puts her arm around her. Michael enters left.*)

But what worries me most of all is Rose. If I died — if I lost my job — if this house were broken up — what would become of our Rosie?

MAGGIE: Shhh.

KATE: I must put my trust in God, Maggie, mustn't I? He'll look after her, won't he? You believe that, Maggie, don't you?

MAGGIE: Kate . . . Kate . . . Kate, love . . .

KATE: I believe that, too . . . I believe that . . . I do believe that . . .

(*Maggie holds her and rocks her.*)
(*Chris enters quickly left, hugging herself. She sees the Boy at his kites, goes to him, and gets down beside him. She speaks eagerly, excitedly, confidentially.*)

CHRIS: Well. Now you've had a good look at him. What do you think of him? Do you remember him?

BOY (*bored*): I never saw him before.

CHRIS: Shhh. Yes, you did; five or six times. You've forgotten. And he saw you at the foot of the lane. He thinks you've got very big. And he thinks you're handsome!

BOY: Aunt Kate got me a spinning-top that won't spin.

CHRIS: He's handsome. Isn't he handsome?

BOY: Give up.

CHRIS: I'll tell you a secret. The others aren't to know. He has got a great new job! And he's wonderful at it!

BOY: What does he do?

CHRIS: Shhh. And he has bought a bicycle for you — a black bike — a man's bike and he's going to bring it with him the next time he comes.

(*She suddenly embraces him and hugs him.*)

BOY: Is he coming back soon?

CHRIS (*eyes closed*): Maybe — maybe. Yes! Yes, he is!

BOY: How soon?

CHRIS: Next week — the week after — soon — soon —

soon! Oh, yes, you have a handsome father. You are a lucky boy and I am a very, very lucky woman.

(*She gets to her feet, then bends down again and kisses him lightly.*)

And another bit of good news for you, lucky boy: You have your mother's eyes!

(*She laughs, pirouettes flirtatiously before him, and dances into the kitchen.*)

And what's the good news here?

MAGGIE: The good news here is . . . that's the most exciting turf we've ever burned!

KATE: Gerry's not gone, is he?

CHRIS: Just this minute.

(*Agnes enters through the back door. She is carrying some roses.*)

He says to thank you very much for the offer of the bed.

KATE: Next time he's back.

CHRIS: That'll be in a week or two — depending on his commitments.

KATE: Well, if the outside loft happens to be empty.

CHRIS: And he sends his love to you all. His special love to you, Aggie; and a big kiss.

AGNES: For me?

CHRIS: Yes! For you!

MAGGIE (*quickly*): Those are beautiful, Aggie. Would Jack like some in his room? Put them on his windowsill with a wee card — "ROSES" — so that the poor man's head won't be demented looking for the word. And now, girls, the daily dilemma: What's for the tea?

CHRIS: Let me make the tea, Maggie.

MAGGIE: We'll both make the tea. Perhaps something thrilling with tomatoes? We've got two, I think. Or if you're prepared to wait, I'll get that soda bread made.

AGNES: I'm making the tea, Maggie.

CHRIS: Let me, please. Just today.

AGNES (*almost aggressively*): I make the tea every evening, don't I? Why shouldn't I make it this evening as usual?

MAGGIE: No reason at all. Aggie's the chef. (*Sings raucously.*)

"Everybody's doing it, doing it, doing it.
Picking their noses and chewing it, chewing it, chewing it . . ."

KATE: Maggie, please!

MAGGIE: If she knew her prayers half as well as she knows the words of those aul pagan songs . . .
(*Now at the radio.*) Marconi, my friend, you're not still asleep, are you?

(*Father Jack enters. He shuffles quickly across the kitchen floor, hands behind his back, eyes on the ground, as if he were intent on some engagement elsewhere. Now he becomes aware of the others.*)

JACK: If anybody is looking for me, I'll be down at the bank of the river for the rest of the . . .

(*He tails off and looks around. Now he knows where he is. He smiles.*)

I beg your pardon. My mind was . . . It's Kate.

KATE: It's Kate.

JACK: And Agnes. And Margaret.

MAGGIE: How are you, Jack?

JACK: And this is —?

CHRIS: Chris — Christina.

JACK: Forgive me, Chris. You were only a baby when I went away. I remember Mother lifting you up as the train was pulling out of the station and catching your hand and waving it at me. You were so young you had scarcely any hair but she had managed to attach a tiny pink — a tiny pink — what's the word? — a bow! — a bow! — just about here; and as she waved your hand, the bow fell off. It's like a — a picture? — a camera picture — a photograph! — it's like a photograph in my mind.

CHRIS: The hair isn't much better even now, Jack.

JACK: And I remember you crying, Margaret.

MAGGIE: Was I?

JACK: Yes; your face was all blotchy with tears.

MAGGIE: You may be sure — beautiful as ever.

JACK (*to Agnes*): And you and Kate were on Mother's right and Rose was between you; you each had a hand. And Mother's face, I remember, showed nothing. I often wondered about that afterwards.

CHRIS: She knew she would never see you again in her lifetime.

JACK: I know that. But in the other life. Do you think perhaps Mother didn't believe in the ancestral spirits?

KATE: Ancestral —! What are you blathering about, Jack? Mother was a saintly woman who knew she was going straight to heaven. And don't you forget to take your medicine again this evening. You're supposed to take it three times a day.

JACK: One of our priests took so much quinine that he became an addict and almost died. A German priest; Father Sharpeggi. He was rushed to hospital in Kampala but they could do nothing for him. So Okawa and I brought him to our local medicine man and Karl Sharpeggi lived until he was eighty-eight! There was a strange white bird on my windowsill when I woke up this morning.

AGNES: That's Rosie's pet rooster. Keep away from that thing.

MAGGIE: Look what it did to my arm, Jack. One of these days I'm going to wring its neck.

JACK: That's what we do in Ryanga when we want to please the spirits — or to appease them: We kill a rooster or a young goat. It's a very exciting exhibition — that's not the word, is it? — demonstration? — no — show? No, no; what's the word I'm looking for? Spectacle? That's not it. The word to describe a sacred and mysterious . . . ? (*Slowly, deliberately.*) You have a ritual killing. You offer up sacrifice. You have dancing and incantations. What is the name for that whole — for that —? Gone. Lost it. My vocabulary has deserted me. Never mind. Doesn't matter . . . I think perhaps I should put on more clothes . . .

(*Pause.*)

MAGGIE: Did you speak Swahili all the time out there, Jack?

JACK: All the time. Yes. To the people. Swahili. When Europeans call, we speak English. Or if we have a — a visitor? — a visitation! — from the district commissioner. The present commissioner knows Swahili but he won't speak it. He's a stubborn man. He and I fight a lot but I like him. The Irish Outcast, he calls me. He is always inviting me to spend a weekend with him in Kampala — to keep me from "going native," as he calls it. Perhaps when I go back. If you cooperate with the English they give you lots of money for churches and schools and hospitals. And he gets so angry with me because I won't take his money. Reported me to my superiors in Head House last year; and they were very cross — oh, very cross. But I like him. When I was saying good-bye to him — he thought this was very funny! — he gave me a present of the last governor's ceremonial hat to take home with — Ceremony! That's the word! How could I have forgotten that? The offering, the ritual, the dancing — a ceremony! Such a simple word. What was I telling you?

AGNES: The district commissioner gave you this present.

JACK: Yes; a wonderful triangular hat with three enormous white ostrich plumes rising up out of the crown. I have it in one of my trunks. I'll show it to you later. Ceremony! I'm so glad I got that. Do you know what I found very strange? Coming back in the boat there were days when I couldn't remember even the simplest words. Not that anybody seemed to notice. And you can always point, Margaret, can't you?

MAGGIE: Or make signs.

JACK: Or make signs.

MAGGIE: Or dance.

KATE: What you must do is read a lot — books, papers, magazines, anything. I read every night with young Michael. It's great for his vocabulary.

JACK: I'm sure you're right, Kate. I'll do that. (*To Chris.*) I haven't seen young Michael today, Agnes.

KATE: Christina, Jack.

JACK: Sorry, I —

CHRIS: He's around there somewhere. Making kites, if you don't mind.

JACK: And I have still to meet your husband.

CHRIS: I'm not married.

JACK: Ah.

KATE: Michael's father was here a while ago . . . Gerry Evans . . . Mr. Evans is a Welshman . . . not that that's relevant to . . .

JACK: You were never married?

CHRIS: Never.

MAGGIE: We're all in the same boat, Jack. We're hoping that you'll hunt about and get men for all of us.

JACK (*to Chris*): So Michael is a love-child?

CHRIS: I — yes — I suppose so . . .

JACK: He's a fine boy.

CHRIS: He's not a bad boy.

JACK: You're lucky to have him.

AGNES: We're all lucky to have him.

JACK: In Ryanga women are eager to have love-children. The more love-children you have, the more fortunate your household is thought to be. Have you other love-children?

KATE: She certainly has not, Jack; and strange as it may seem to you, neither has Agnes nor Rose nor Maggie nor myself. No harm to Ryanga but you're home in Donegal now and much as we cherish love-children here they are not exactly the norm. And the doctor says if you don't take exercise your legs will seize up on you; so I'm going to walk you down to the main road and up again three times and then you'll get your tea and then you'll read the paper from front to back and then you'll take your medicine and then you'll go to bed. And we'll do the same thing tomorrow and the day after and the day after that until we have you back to what you were. You start off and I'll be with you in a second. Where's my cardigan?

(*Jack goes out to the garden. Kate gets her cardigan.*)

MICHAEL: Some of Aunt Kate's forebodings weren't all that inaccurate. Indeed some of them were fulfilled before the Festival of Lughnasa was over.

She was right about Uncle Jack. He had been sent home by his superiors, not because his mind was confused, but for reasons that became clearer as the summer drew to a close.

And she was right about losing her job in the

local school. The parish priest didn't take her back when the new term began; although that had more to do with Father Jack than with falling numbers.

And she had good reason for being uneasy about Rose — and, had she known, about Agnes, too. But what she couldn't have foreseen was that the home would break up quite so quickly and that when she would wake up one morning in early September both Rose and Agnes would have left forever.

(*At this point in Michael's speech Jack picks up two pieces of wood, portions of the kites, and strikes them together. The sound they make pleases him. He does it again — and again — and again. Now he begins to beat out a structured beat whose rhythm gives him pleasure. And as Michael continues his speech, Jack begins to shuffle — dance in time to his tattoo — his body slightly bent over, his eyes on the ground, his feet moving rhythmically. And as he dances — shuffles, he mutters — sings — makes occasional sounds that are incomprehensible and almost inaudible. Kate comes out to the garden and stands still, watching him. Rose enters. Now Rose and Maggie and Agnes are all watching him — some at the front door, some through the window. Only Chris has her eyes closed, her face raised, her mouth slightly open; remembering. Michael continues without stopping.*)

But she was wrong about my father. I suppose their natures were so out of tune that she would always be wrong about my father. Because he did come back in a couple of weeks as he said he would. And although my mother and he didn't go through a conventional form of marriage, once more they danced together, witnessed by the unseen sisters. And this time it was a dance without music; just there, in ritual circles round and round that square and then down the lane and back up again; slowly, formally, with easy deliberation. My mother with her head thrown back, her eyes closed, her mouth slightly open. My father holding her just that little distance away from him so that he could regard her upturned face. No singing, no melody, no words. Only the swish and whisper of their feet across the grass.

I watched the ceremony from behind that bush. But this time they were conscious only of themselves and of their dancing. And when he went off to fight with the International Brigade, my mother grieved as any bride would grieve. But this time there was no sobbing, no lamenting, no collapse into a depression.

(*Kate now goes to Jack and gently takes the sticks from him. She places them on the ground.*)

KATE: We'll leave these back where we found them, Jack. They aren't ours. They belong to the child.

(*She takes his arm and leads him off.*)

Now we'll go for our walk.

(*The others watch with expressionless faces.*)

ACT 2

(*Early September; three weeks later. Ink bottle and some paper on the kitchen table. Two finished kites — their artwork still unseen — lean against the garden seat.*)

(*Michael stands downstage left, listening to Maggie as she approaches, singing. Now she enters left carrying two zinc buckets of water. She is dressed as she was in act 1. She sings in her usual parodic style.*)

MAGGIE: "Oh play to me, Gypsy;
    The moon's high above.
    Oh, play me your serenade,
    The song I love . . ."

(*She goes into the kitchen and from her zinc buckets she fills the kettle and the saucepan on the range. She looks over at the writing materials.*)

Are you getting your books ready for school again?
BOY: School doesn't start for another ten days.
MAGGIE: God, I always hated school.

(*She hums the next line of the song. Then she remembers.*)

You and I have a little financial matter to discuss. (*Pause.*) D'you hear me, cub?
BOY: I'm not listening.
MAGGIE: You owe me money.
BOY: I do not.
MAGGIE: Oh, yes, you do. Three weeks ago I bet you a penny those aul kites would never get off the ground. And they never did.
BOY: Because there was never enough wind; that's why.
MAGGIE: Enough wind! Would you listen to him. A hurricane wouldn't shift those things. Anyhow a debt is a debt. One penny please at your convenience. Or the equivalent in kind: one Wild Woodbine.
(*Sings.*) "Beside your caravan
    The campfire's bright . . ."

(*She dances her exaggerated dance across to the table and tousles the Boy's hair.*)

BOY: Leave me alone, Aunt Maggie.

MAGGIE: "I'll be your vagabond
  Just for tonight . . ."
BOY: Now look at what you made me do! The page
  is all blotted!
MAGGIE: Your frank opinion, cub: Am I vagabond
  material?
BOY: Get out of my road, will you? I'm trying to write
  a letter.
MAGGIE: Who to? That's for me to know and you to
  find out. Whoever it is, he'd need to be smart to
  read that scrawl.

(*She returns to her buckets.*)

BOY: It's to Santa Claus.
MAGGIE: In September? Nothing like getting in before
  the rush. What are you asking for?
BOY: A bell.
MAGGIE: A bell.
BOY: For my bicycle.
MAGGIE: For your bicycle.
BOY: The bike my daddy has bought me — stupid!
MAGGIE: Your daddy has bought you a bicycle?
BOY: He told me today. He bought it in Kilkenny. So
  there!

(*Her manner changes. She returns to the table.*)

MAGGIE (*softly*): Your daddy told you that?
BOY: Ask him yourself. It's coming next week. It's a
  black bike — a man's bike.
MAGGIE: Aren't you the lucky boy?
BOY: It's going to be delivered here to the house. He
  promised me.
MAGGIE: Well, if he promised you . . . (*Very brisk.*)
  Now! Who can we get to teach you to ride?
BOY: I know how to ride!
MAGGIE: You don't.
BOY: I learned at school last Easter. So there! But you
  can't ride.
MAGGIE: I can so.
BOY: I know you can't.
MAGGIE: Maybe not by myself. But put me on the
  bar, cub — magnificent!
BOY: You never sat on the bar of a bike in your life,
  Aunt Maggie!
MAGGIE: Oh yes, I did, Michael. Oh yes, indeed I did.
  (*She gathers up the papers.*) Now away and write
  to Santa some other time. On a day like this you
  should be out running about the fields like a young
  calf. Hold on — a new riddle for you.
BOY: Give up.
MAGGIE: A man goes to an apple tree with two apples
  on it. He doesn't take apples off it. He doesn't
  leave apples on it. How does he do that?
BOY: Give up.
MAGGIE: Think, will you!

BOY: Give up.
MAGGIE: Well, since you don't know, I will tell you.
  He takes *one* apple off! Get it? He doesn't take
  apples off! He doesn't leave *apples* on!
BOY: God!
MAGGIE: You might as well be talking to a turf stack.

(*Jack enters. He looks much stronger and is very
sprightly and alert. He is not wearing the top coat or
the hat but instead a garish-colored — probably a
sister's — sweater. His dress looks now even more
bizarre.*)

JACK: Did I hear the church bell ringing?
MAGGIE: A big posh wedding today.
JACK: Not one of my sisters?
MAGGIE: No such luck. A man called Austin Morgan
  and a girl from Carrickfad.
JACK: Austin Morgan — should I know that name?
MAGGIE: I don't think so. They own the Arcade in
  the town. And how are you today?
JACK: Cold as usual, Maggie. And complaining about
  it as usual.

(*Michael exits.*)

MAGGIE: Complain away — why wouldn't you? And
  it is getting colder. But you're looking stronger
  every day, Jack.
JACK: I feel stronger, too. Now! Off for my last walk
  of the day.
MAGGIE: Number three?
JACK: Number four! Down past the clothes line; across
  the stream; round the old well; and up through the
  meadow. And when that's done Kate won't have
  to nag at me — nag? — nag? — sounds funny —
  something wrong with that — nag? — that's not
  a word, is it?
MAGGIE: Nag — yes; to keep on at somebody.
JACK: Yes? Nag. Good. So my English vocabulary is
  coming back, too. Great. Nag. Still sounds a bit
  strange.

(*Kate enters with an armful of clothes from the clothes
line.*)

KATE: Time for another walk, Jack.
JACK: Just about to set out on number four, Kate.
  And thank you for keeping at me.
KATE: No sign of Rose and Agnes yet?
MAGGIE: They said they'd be back for tea. (*To Jack.*)
  They're away picking bilberries.
KATE (*to Jack*): You used to pick bilberries. Do you
  remember?
JACK: Down beside the old quarry?
MAGGIE: The very place.
JACK: Mother and myself; every Lughnasa; the annual
  ritual. Of course I remember. And then she'd make

the most wonderful jam. And that's what you took to school with you every day all through the winter: a piece of soda bread and bilberry jam.

MAGGIE: But no butter.

JACK: Except on special occasions when you got scones and for some reason they were always buttered. I must walk down to that old quarry one of these days.

> "O ruddier than the cherry,
> O sweeter than the berry,
> O nymph more bright,
> Than moonshine night,
> Like kidlings blithe and merry."

(*Laughs.*) Where on earth did that come from? You see, Kate, it's all coming back to me.

KATE: So you'll soon begin saying Mass again?

JACK: Yes, indeed.

MAGGIE: Here in the house?

JACK: Why not? Perhaps I'll start next Monday. The neighbors would join us, wouldn't they?

KATE: They surely would. A lot of them have been asking me already.

JACK: How will we let them know?

MAGGIE: I wouldn't worry about that. Word gets about very quickly.

JACK: What Okawa does — you know Okawa, don't you?

MAGGIE: Your house boy?

JACK: My friend — my mentor — my counselor — and yes, my house boy as well; anyhow Okawa summons our people by striking a huge iron gong. Did you hear that wedding bell this morning, Kate?

KATE: Yes.

JACK: Well, Okawa's gong would carry four times as far as that. But if it's one of the bigger ceremonies, he'll spend a whole day going round all the neighboring villages, blowing on this enormous flute he made himself.

MAGGIE: And they all meet in your church?

JACK: When I had a church. Now we gather in the common in the middle of the village. If it's an important ceremony, you would have up to three or four hundred people.

KATE: All gathered together for Mass?

JACK: Maybe. Or maybe to offer sacrifice to Obi, our Great Goddess of the Earth, so that the crops will flourish. Or maybe to get in touch with our departed fathers for their advice and wisdom. Or maybe to thank the spirits of our tribe if they have been good to us; or to appease them if they're angry. I complain to Okawa that our calendar of ceremonies gets fuller every year. Now at this time of year over there — at the Ugandan harvest time — we have two very wonderful ceremonies: the Festival of the New Yam and the

Festival of the Sweet Cassava; and they're both dedicated to our Great Goddess, Obi —

KATE: But these aren't Christian ceremonies, Jack, are they?

JACK: Oh, no. They Ryangans have always been faithful to their own beliefs — like these two festivals I'm telling you about; and they are very special, really magnificent ceremonies. I haven't described those two festivals to you before, have I?

KATE: Not to me.

JACK: Well, they begin very formally, very solemnly with the ritual sacrifice of a fowl or a goat or a calf down at the bank of the river. Then the ceremonial cutting and anointing of the first yams and the first cassava; and we pass these round in huge wooden bowls. Then the incantation — a chant, really — that expresses our gratitude and that also acts as a rhythm or percussion for the ritual dance. And then, when the thanksgiving is over, the dance continues. And the interesting thing is that it grows naturally into a secular celebration; so that almost imperceptibly the religious ceremony ends and the community celebration takes over. And that part of the ceremony is a real spectacle. We light fires round the periphery of the circle; and we paint our faces with colored powders; and we sing local songs; and we drink palm wine. And then we dance — and dance — and dance — children, men, women, most of them lepers, many of them with misshapen limbs, with missing limbs — dancing, believe it or not, for days on end! It is the most wonderful sight you have ever seen! (*Laughs.*) That palm wine! They dole it out in horns! You lose all sense of time . . . !

Oh, yes, the Ryangans are a remarkable people: There is no distinction between the religious and the secular in their culture. And of course their capacity for fun, for laughing, for practical jokes — they've such open hearts! In some respects they're not unlike us. You'd love them, Maggie. You should come back with me!

How did I get into all that? You must stop me telling these long stories. Exercise time! I'll be back in ten minutes; and only last week it took me half an hour to do number four. You've done a great job with me, Kate. So please do keep nagging at me.

(*He moves off — then stops.*)

It's not Gilbert and Sullivan, is it?

KATE: Sorry?

JACK: That quotation.

KATE: What's that, Jack?

JACK: "O ruddier than the cherry / O sweeter than the berry" — no, it's not Gilbert and Sullivan. But it'll come back to me, I promise you. It's all coming back.

(*Again he moves off.*)

KATE: Jack.

JACK: Yes?

KATE: You are going to start saying Mass again?

JACK: We've agreed on next Monday, haven't we? Haven't we, Maggie?

MAGGIE: Yes.

JACK: At first light. The moment Rose's white cock crows. A harvest ceremony. You'll have to find a big gong somewhere, Kate.

(*He leaves. Pause. Kate and Maggie stare at each other in concern, in alarm. They speak in hushed voices.*)

KATE: I told you — you wouldn't believe me — I told you.

MAGGIE: Shhh.

KATE: What do you think?

MAGGIE: He's not back a month yet.

KATE: Yesterday I heard about their medicine man who brought a woman back from death —

MAGGIE: He needs more time.

KATE: And this morning it was "the spirits of the tribe"! And when I mentioned Mass to him you saw how he dodged about.

MAGGIE: He said he'd say Mass next Monday, Kate.

KATE: No, he won't. You know he won't. He's changed, Maggie.

MAGGIE: In another month, he'll be —

KATE: Completely changed. He's not our Jack at all. And it's what he's changed into that frightens me.

MAGGIE: Doesn't frighten me.

KATE: If you saw your face . . . of course it does . . . Oh, dear God —

(*Maggie now drifts back to the range. Kate goes to the table and with excessive vigor wipes it with a damp cloth. Then she stops suddenly, slumps into a seat, and covers her face with her hands. Maggie watches her, then goes to her. She stands behind her and holds her shoulders with her hands. Kate grasps Maggie's hands in hers.*)

MAGGIE: All the same, Kitty, I don't think it's a sight I'd like to see.

KATE: What sight?

MAGGIE: A clatter of lepers trying to do the Military Two-step.

KATE: God forgive you, Maggie Mundy! The poor creatures are as entitled to —

(*She breaks off because Chris's laughter is heard off. Kate jumps to her feet.*)

This must be kept in the family, Maggie! Not a

word of this must go outside these walls — d'you hear? — not a syllable!

(*Chris and Gerry enter left. He enters backways, pulling Chris who holds the end of his walking stick. Throughout the scene he keeps trying to embrace her. She keeps avoiding him.*)

GERRY: No false modesty. You know you're a great dancer, Chrissie.

CHRIS: No, I'm not.

GERRY: You should be a professional dancer.

CHRIS: You're talking rubbish.

GERRY: Let's dance round the garden again.

CHRIS: We've done that; and down the lane and up again — without music. And that's enough for one day. Tell me about signing up. Was it really in a church?

GERRY: I'm telling you — it was unbelievable.

CHRIS: It was a real church?

GERRY: A Catholic church as a matter of interest.

CHRIS: I don't believe a word of it.

GERRY: Would I tell you a lie? And up at the end — in the sanctuary? — there were three men, two of them with trench coats; and between them, behind this lectern and wearing a sort of military cap, this little chappie who spoke in an accent I could hardly understand. Naturally I thought he was Spanish. From Armagh, as it turned out.

CHRIS: I'm sure he couldn't understand you either.

GERRY: He described himself as the recruiting officer. "Take it from me, comrade, nobody joins the Brigade without my unanimity."

(*She laughs — and avoids his embrace.*)

CHRIS: It's a wonder he accepted you.

GERRY: "Do you offer your allegiance and your loyalty and your full endeavors to the Popular Front?"

CHRIS: What's the Popular Front?

GERRY: The Spanish government that I'm going to keep in power. "I take it you are a Syndicalist?" "No." "An Anarchist?" "No." "A Marxist?" "No." "A Republican, a Socialist, a Communist?" "No." "Do you speak Spanish?" "No." "Can you make explosives?" "No." "Can you ride a motorbike?" "Yes." "You're in. Sign here."

CHRIS: So you'll be a dispatch rider?

(*Gerry imitates riding a motorbike.*)

And you leave on Saturday?

GERRY: First tide.

CHRIS: How long will you be away?

GERRY: As long as it takes to sort the place out.

CHRIS: Seriously, Gerry.

GERRY: Maybe a couple of months. Everybody says it will be over by Christmas.

CHRIS: They always say it will be over by Christmas. I still don't know why you're going.
GERRY: Not so sure I know either. Who wants salesmen that can't sell? And there's bound to be *something* right about the cause, isn't there? And it's somewhere to go — isn't it? Maybe that's the important thing for a man: a *named* destination — democracy, Ballybeg, heaven. Women's illusions aren't so easily satisfied — they make better drifters. (*Laughs.*) Anyhow he held out a pen to sign on the dotted line and it was only when I was writing my name that I glanced over the lectern and saw the box.
CHRIS: What box?
GERRY: He was standing on a box. The chappie was a midget!
CHRIS: Gerry!
GERRY: No bigger than three feet.
CHRIS: Gerry, I —
GERRY: Promise you! And when we were having a drink afterwards he told me he was invaluable to the Brigade — because he was a master at disguising himself!
CHRIS: Gerry Evans, you are —
GERRY: Let's go down to the old well.
CHRIS: We're going nowhere. Come inside and take a look at this wireless. It stops and starts whenever it feels like it.
GERRY: I told you: I know nothing about radios.
CHRIS: I've said you're a genius at them.
GERRY: Chrissie, I don't even know how to —
CHRIS: You can try, can't you? Come on. Michael misses it badly.

(*She runs into the kitchen. He follows.*)

You should see Jack striding through the meadow. He looks like a new man.
KATE (*to Gerry*): Were you talking to him?
GERRY: He wants to do a swap with me: I'm to give him this hat and he's to give me some sort of a three-cornered hat with feathers that the district commissioner gave him. Sounds a fair exchange.
MAGGIE: Chrissie says you're great with radios, Gerry.
GERRY: I'll take a look at it — why not?
MAGGIE: All I can tell you is that it's not the battery. I got a new one yesterday.
GERRY: Let me check the aerial first. Very often that's where the trouble lies. Then I'll have a look at the ignition and sparking plugs. Leave it to Gerry.

(*He winks at Chris as he goes out the front door and off right.*)

MAGGIE: He sounds very knowledgeable.
CHRIS: It may be something he can't fix.
KATE: I know you're not responsible for Gerry's de-

cisions, Christina. But it would be on my conscience if I didn't tell you how strongly I disapprove of this International Brigade caper. It's a sorry day for Ireland when we send young men off to Spain to fight for godless communism.
CHRIS: For democracy, Kate.
KATE: I'm not going to argue. I just want to clear my conscience.
CHRIS: That's the important thing, of course. And now you've cleared it.

(*Gerry runs on and calls through the window.*)

GERRY: Turn the radio on, Chrissie, would you?
MAGGIE: It's on.
GERRY: Right.

(*He runs off again.*)

CHRIS: Just as we were coming out of the town we met Vera McLaughlin, the knitting agent. (*Softly.*) Agnes and Rose aren't back yet?
MAGGIE: They'll be here soon.
CHRIS: She says she'll call in tomorrow and tell them herself. The poor woman was very distressed.
KATE: Tell them what?
CHRIS: She's not buying any more handmade gloves.
MAGGIE: Why not?
CHRIS: Too dear, she says.
KATE: Too dear! She pays them a pittance!
CHRIS: There's a new factory started up in Donegal Town. They make machine gloves more quickly there and far more cheaply. The people Vera used to supply buy their gloves direct from the factory now.
MAGGIE: That's awful news, Chrissie.
CHRIS: She says they're organizing buses to bring the workers to the factory and back every day. Most of the people who used to work at home have signed on. She tried to get a job there herself. They told her she was too old. She's forty-one. The poor woman could hardly speak.
MAGGIE: Oh God . . . poor Aggie . . . poor Rose . . . what'll they do?

(*Agnes enters the garden. Kate sees her.*)

KATE: Shhh. They're back. Let them have their tea in peace. Tell them later.

(*They busy themselves with their tasks. Agnes is carrying two small pails of blackberries which she leaves outside the door of the house. Just as she is about to enter the kitchen a voice off calls her.*)

GERRY (*off*): Who is that beautiful woman!

(*She looks around, puzzled.*)

AGNES: Gerry?

GERRY: Up here, Aggie!
AGNES: Where?
GERRY: On top of the sycamore.

(*Now she sees him. The audience does not see him.*)

AGNES: Mother of God!
GERRY: Come up and join me!
AGNES: What are you doing up there?
GERRY: You can see into the future from here, Aggie!
AGNES: The tree isn't safe, Gerry. Please come down.
GERRY: Come up and see what's going to happen to you!
AGNES: That branch is dead, Gerry. I'm telling you.

(*The branch begins to sway.*)

GERRY: Do you think I could get a job in a circus? Wow-wow-wow-wow!
AGNES: Gerry —!
GERRY (*sings*): "He flies through the air with the greatest of ease —" Wheeeeeeeeee!

(*She covers her eyes in terror.*)

AGNES: Stop it, Gerry, stop it, stop it!
GERRY: "That daring young man on the flying trapeze . . ."
AGNES: You're going to fall! I'm not looking! I'm not watching!

(*She dashes into the house.*)

That clown of a man is up on top of the sycamore. Go out and tell him to come down, Chrissie.
MAGGIE: He's fixing the aerial.
AGNES: He's going to break his neck — I'm telling you!
MAGGIE: As long as he fixes the wireless first.
KATE: How are the bilberries, Agnes?
AGNES: Just that bit too ripe. We should have picked them a week ago.
CHRIS: Is that a purple stain on your gansey?
AGNES: I know. I'd only begun when I fell into a bush. And look at my hands — all scrabbed with briars. For all the sympathy I got from Rosie. Nearly died laughing at me. How is she now? (*Pause.*) Is she still in bed?
CHRIS: Bed?
AGNES: She wasn't feeling well. She left me and went home to lie down. (*Pause.*) She's here, isn't she?

(*Maggie rushes off to the bedroom.*)

KATE: I haven't seen her. (*To Chris.*) Have you?
CHRIS: No.
KATE: When did she leave you?
AGNES: Hours ago — I don't know — almost immediately after we got to the old quarry. She said she felt out of sorts.

CHRIS: And she went off by herself?
AGNES: Yes.
KATE: To come home?
AGNES: That's what she said.

(*Maggie enters.*)

MAGGIE: She's not in her bed.
AGNES: Oh God! Where could she —
KATE: Start at the beginning, Agnes. What exactly happened?
AGNES: Nothing "happened" — nothing at all. We left here together — when was it? — just after one o'clock —
CHRIS: That means she's missing for over three hours.
AGNES: We walked together to the quarry. She was chatting away as usual. I had my two buckets and she had —
KATE: Go on — go on!
AGNES: And just after we got there she said she wasn't feeling well. I told her not to bother about the bilberries — just to sit in the sun. And that's what she did.
KATE: For how long?
AGNES: I don't know — five — ten minutes. And then I fell into the bush. And that was when she laughed. And then she said — she said — I've forgotten what she said — something about a headache and her stomach being sick and she'd go home and sleep for a while. (*To Maggie.*) You're sure she's not in her bed?

(*Maggie shakes her head.*)

KATE: Then what?

(*Agnes begins to cry.*)

AGNES: Where is she? What's happened to our Rosie?
KATE: What direction did she go when she left you?
AGNES: Direction?
KATE: Stop sniveling, Agnes! Did she go towards home?
AGNES: I think so . . . yes . . . I don't know . . . Maggie —
MAGGIE: She may have gone into the town.
CHRIS: She wouldn't have gone into town in her Wellingtons.
AGNES: She was wearing her good shoes.
KATE: Are you sure?
AGNES: Yes; and her blue cardigan and her good skirt. I said to her — I said, "You're some lady to go picking bilberries with." And she just laughed and said, "I'm some toff, Aggie, amn't I some toff?"
MAGGIE: Had she a bottle of milk with her?
AGNES: I think so — yes — in one of her cans.
MAGGIE: Had she any money with her?
AGNES: She had half-a-crown. That's all she has.

MAGGIE (*softly*): Danny Bradley.

KATE: What? — who?

MAGGIE: Danny Bradley . . . Lough Anna . . . up in the back hills.

CHRIS: Oh God, no.

KATE: What? — what's this? — what about the back hills?

CHRIS: She has some silly notion about that scamp, Bradley. She believes he's in love with her. He gave her a present last Christmas — she says.

KATE (*to Agnes*): What do you know about this Bradley business?

AGNES: I know no more than Chris has —

KATE: I've often seen you and Rose whispering together. What plot has been hatched between Rose and Mr. Bradley?

AGNES: No plot . . . please, Kate —

KATE: You're lying to me, Agnes! You're withholding! I want the truth!

AGNES: Honest to God, all I know is what Chris has just —

KATE: I want to know everything you know! Now! I want to —

MAGGIE: That'll do, Kate! Stop that at once! (*Calmly.*) She may be in the town. She may be on her way home now. She may have taken a weak turn on her way back from the quarry. We're going to find her. (*To Chris.*) You search the fields on the upper side of the lane. (*To Agnes.*) You take the lower side, down as far as the main road. (*To Kate.*) You go to the old well and search all around there. I'm going into the town to tell the police.

KATE: You're going to no police, Maggie. If she's mixed up with that Bradley creature, I'm not going to have it broadcast all over —

MAGGIE: I'm going to the police and you'll do what I told you to do.

CHRIS: There she is! Look — look! There she is!

(*She has seen Rose through the window and is about to rush out to greet her. Maggie catches her arm and restrains her. The four sisters watch Rose as she crosses the garden — Chris and Kate from the window, Maggie and Agnes from the door. Rose is unaware of their anxious scrutiny. She is dressed in the "good" clothes described by Agnes and they have changed her appearance. Indeed, had we not seen the Rose of act 1, we might not now be immediately aware of her disability. At first look this might be any youngish country woman, carefully dressed, not unattractive, returning from a long walk on a summer day. She walks slowly, lethargically, towards the house. From her right hand hangs a red poppy that she plucked casually along the road. Her face reveals nothing — but nothing is being deliberately concealed. She sees Agnes's cans of fruit. She stops beside them and*

looks at them. Then she puts her hand into one of the cans, takes a fistful of berries, and thrusts the fistful into her mouth. Then she wipes her mouth with her sleeve and the back of her hand. As she chews she looks at her stained fingers. She wipes them on her skirt. All of these movements — stopping, eating, wiping — are done not dreamily, abstractedly, but calmly, naturally. Now she moves towards the house. As she approaches the door Agnes rushes to meet her. Instead of hugging her, as she wants to, she catches her arm.)

AGNES: Rosie, love, we were beginning to get worried about you.

ROSE: They're nice, Aggie. They're sweet. And you got two canfuls. Good for you.

(*Agnes leads her into the house.*)

AGNES: Is your stomach settled?

ROSE: My stomach?

AGNES: You weren't feeling well — remember? — when we were at the quarry?

ROSE: Oh, yes. Oh, I'm fine now, thanks.

AGNES: You left me there and you said you were coming home to lie down. D'you remember that?

ROSE: Yes.

CHRIS: But you didn't come home, Rosie.

ROSE: That's right.

AGNES: And we were very worried about you.

ROSE: Well . . . here I am.

CHRIS: Were you in the town?

AGNES: That's why you're all dressed up, isn't it?

CHRIS: You went into Ballybeg, didn't you?

(*Pause. Rose looks from one to the other.*)

MAGGIE (*briskly*): She's home safe and sound and that's all that matters. Now I don't know about you girls but I can tell you this chicken is weak with hunger. Let me tell you what's on the menu this evening. Our beverage is the usual hot, sweet tea. There is a choice between caraway-seed bread and soda bread, both fresh from the chef's oven. But now we come to the difficulty: There's only three eggs between the seven of us — I wish to God you'd persuade that white rooster of yours to lay eggs, Rosie.

CHRIS: There are eight of us, Maggie.

MAGGIE: How are there —? Of course — the soldier up the sycamore! Not a great larder but a nice challenge to someone like myself. Right. My suggestion is . . . Eggs Ballybeg; in other words scrambled and served on lightly toasted caraway-seed bread. Followed — for those so inclined — by one magnificent Wild Woodbine. Everybody happy?

CHRIS: Excellent, Margaret!

MAGGIE: Settled.

(*Rose has taken off her shoe and is examining it carefully.*)

AGNES: We'll go and pick some more bilberries next Sunday, Rosie.

ROSE: All right.

AGNES: Remember the cans you had? You had your own two cans — remember? Did you take them with you?

ROSE: Where to, Aggie?

AGNES: Into the town . . . wherever you went . . .

ROSE: I hid them at the quarry behind a stone wall. They're safe there. I'll go back and pick them up later this evening. Does anybody know where my overall is?

MAGGIE: It's lying across your bed. And you'd need to bring some turf in, Rosie.

ROSE: I'll change first, Maggie.

MAGGIE: Be quick about it.

CHRIS: How many pieces of toast do you want?

MAGGIE: All that loaf. And go easy on the butter — that's all we have. Now. Parsley. And just a whiff of basil. I don't want you to be too optimistic, girls, but you should know I feel very creative this evening.

(*Rose moves towards the bedroom door. Just as she is about to exit.*)

KATE: I want to know where you have been, Rose.

(*Rose stops. Pause.*)

You have been gone for the entire afternoon. I want you to tell me where you've been.

AGNES: Later, Kate; after —

KATE: Where have you been for the past three hours?

ROSE: (*inaudible*): Lough Anna.

KATE: I didn't hear what you said, Rose.

ROSE: Lough Anna.

CHRIS: Kate, just leave —

KATE: You walked from the quarry to Lough Anna?

ROSE: Yes.

KATE: Did you meet somebody there?

ROSE: Yes.

KATE: Had you arranged to meet somebody there?

ROSE: I had arranged to meet Danny Bradley there, Kate. He brought me out in his father's blue boat. (*To Maggie.*) I don't want anything to eat, Maggie. I brought a bottle of milk and a packet of chocolate biscuits with me and we had a picnic on the lake. (*To Agnes.*) Then the two of us went up through the back hills. He showed me what was left of the Lughnasa fires. A few of them are still burning away up there. (*To Kate.*) We passed young Sweeney's house — you know, the boy who got burned, the boy you said was dying. Well, he's on the mend, Danny says. His legs will be scarred but he'll be

all right. (*To all.*) It's a very peaceful place up there. There was nobody there but Danny and me. (*To Agnes.*) He calls me his Rosebud, Aggie. I told you that before, didn't I? (*To all.*) Then he walked me down as far as the workhouse gate and I came on home by myself. (*To Kate.*) And that's all I'm going to tell you. (*To all.*) That's all any of you are going to hear.

(*She exits, her shoes in one hand, the poppy in the other. Michael enters.*)

KATE: What has happened to this house? Mother of God, will we ever be able to lift our heads ever again . . . ?

(*Pause.*)

MICHAEL: The following night Vera McLaughlin arrived and explained to Agnes and Rose why she couldn't buy their hand-knitted gloves anymore. Most of her home knitters were already working in the new factory and she advised Agnes and Rose to apply immediately. The Industrial Revolution had finally caught up with Ballybeg.

They didn't apply, even though they had no other means of making a living, and they never discussed their situation with their sisters. Perhaps Agnes made the decision for both of them because she knew Rose wouldn't have got work there anyway. Or perhaps, as Kate believed, because Agnes was too notionate° to work in a factory. Or perhaps the two of them just wanted . . . away.

Anyhow, on my first day back at school, when we came into the kitchen for breakfast, there was a note propped up against the milk jug: "We are gone for good. This is best for all. Do not try to find us." It was written in Agnes's resolute hand.

Of course they did try to find them. So did the police. So did our neighbors who had a huge network of relatives all over England and America. But they had vanished without trace. And by the time I tracked them down — twenty-five years later, in London — Agnes was dead and Rose was dying in a hospice for the destitute in Southwark.

The scraps of information I gathered about their lives during those missing years were too sparse to be coherent. They had moved about a lot. They had worked as cleaning women in public toilets, in factories, in the Underground. Then, when Rose could no longer get work, Agnes tried to support them both — but couldn't. From then on, I gathered, they gave up. They took to drink; slept in parks, in doorways, on the Thames Embankment. Then Agnes died of exposure. And two days after

---

notionate: Strong-willed, stubborn.

I found Rose in that grim hospice — she didn't recognize me, of course — she died in her sleep.

Father Jack's health improved quickly and he soon recovered his full vocabulary and all his old bounce and vigor. But he didn't say Mass that following Monday. In fact he never said Mass again. And the neighbors stopped inquiring about him. And his name never again appeared in the *Donegal Enquirer*. And of course there was never a civic reception with bands and flags and speeches.

But he never lost his determination to return to Uganda and he still talked passionately about his life with the lepers there. And each new anecdote contained more revelations. And each new revelation startled — shocked — stunned poor Aunt Kate. Until finally she hit on a phrase that appeased her: "his own distinctive spiritual search." "Leaping around a fire and offering a little hen to Uka or Ito or whoever is not religion as I was taught it and indeed know it," she would say with a defiant toss of her head. "But then Jack must make his own distinctive search." And when he died suddenly of a heart attack — within a year of his homecoming, on the very eve of the following Lá Lughnasa — my mother and Maggie mourned him sorely. But for months Kate was inconsolable.

My father sailed for Spain that Saturday. The last I saw of him was dancing down the lane in imitation of Fred Astaire, swinging his walking stick, Uncle Jack's ceremonial tricorn at a jaunty angle over his left eye. When he got to the main road he stopped and turned and with both hands blew a dozen theatrical kisses back to Mother and me.

He was wounded in Barcelona — he fell off his motorbike — so that for the rest of his life he walked with a limp. The limp wasn't disabling but it put an end to his dancing days; and that really distressed him. Even the role of maimed veteran, which he loved, could never compensate for that.

He still visited us occasionally, perhaps once a year. Each time he was on the brink of a new career. And each time he proposed to Mother and promised me a new bike. Then the war came in 1939; his visits became more infrequent; and finally he stopped coming altogether.

Sometime in the mid-fifties I got a letter from a tiny village in the south of Wales; a curt note from a young man of my own age and also called Michael Evans. He had found my name and address among the belongings of his father, Gerry Evans. He introduced himself as my half-brother and he wanted me to know that Gerry Evans, the father we shared, had died peacefully in the family home the previous week. Throughout his final ill-

ness he was nursed by his wife and his three grown children who all lived and worked in the village.

My mother never knew of that letter. I decided to tell her — decided not to — vacillated for years as my father would have done; and eventually, rightly or wrongly, kept the information to myself.

(*Maggie, Chris, Kate, and Agnes now resume their tasks.*)

CHRIS: Well, at least that's good news.
MAGGIE: What's that?
CHRIS: That the young Sweeney boy from the back hills is going to live.
MAGGIE: Good news indeed.

(*Chris goes to the door and calls.*)

CHRIS: Michael! Where are you? We need some turf brought in!

(*She now goes outside and calls up to Gerry. Michael exits.*)

Are you still up there?
GERRY (*off*): Don't stand there. I might fall on top of you.
CHRIS: Have you any idea what you're doing?
GERRY (*off*): Come on up here to me.
CHRIS: I'm sure I will.
GERRY (*off*): We never made love on top of a sycamore tree.

(*She looks quickly around: Did her sisters hear that?*)

CHRIS: If you fall and break your neck it'll be too good for you. (*She goes inside.*) Nobody can vanish quicker than that Michael fellow when you need him.
MAGGIE (*to Agnes*): I had a brilliant idea when I woke up this morning, Aggie. I thought to myself: What is it that Ballybeg badly needs and that Ballybeg hasn't got?
AGNES: A riddle. Give up.
MAGGIE: A dressmaker! So why doesn't Agnes Mundy who has such clever hands, why doesn't she dressmake?
AGNES: Clever hands!

(*Maggie looks around for her cigarettes.*)

MAGGIE: She'd get a pile of work. They'd come to her from far and wide. She'd make a fortune.
AGNES: Some fortune in Ballybeg.
MAGGIE: And not only would the work be interesting but she wouldn't be ruining her eyes staring at gray wool eight hours a day. Did you notice how Rosie squints at things now? It's the job for you, Aggie; I'm telling you. Ah, holy God, girls, don't tell me I'm out of fags! How could that have happened?

(*Chris goes to the mantelpiece and produces a single cigarette.*) Chrissie, you are one genius. Look, Kate. (*Scowls.*) Misery. (*Lights cigarette.*) Happiness! Want a drag?

KATE: What's keeping those wonderful Eggs Ballybeg?

MAGGIE: If I had to choose between one Wild Woodbine and a man of — say — fifty-two — widower — plump, what would I do, Kate? I'd take fatso, wouldn't I? God, I really am getting desperate.

(*Jack enters through the garden.*)

Maybe I should go to Ryanga with you, Jack.

JACK: I know you won't but I know you'd love it.

MAGGIE: Could you guarantee a man for each of us?

JACK: I couldn't promise four men but I should be able to get one husband for all of you.

MAGGIE: Would we settle for that?

CHRIS: One between the four of us?

JACK: That's our system and it works very well. One of you would be his principal wife and live with him in his largest hut —

MAGGIE: That'd be you, Kate.

KATE: Stop that, Maggie!

JACK: And the other three of you he'd keep in his enclosure. It would be like living on the same small farm.

MAGGIE: Snug enough, girls, isn't it? (*To Jack.*) And what would be — what sort of duties would we have?

JACK: Cooking, sewing, helping with the crops, washing — the usual housekeeping tasks.

MAGGIE: Sure that's what we do anyway.

JACK: And looking after his children.

MAGGIE: That he'd have by Kate.

KATE: Maggie!

JACK: By all four of you! And what's so efficient about that system is that the husband and his wives and his children make up a small commune where everybody helps everybody else and cares for them. I'm completely in favor of it.

KATE: It may be efficient and you may be in favor of it, Jack, but I don't think it's what Pope Pius XI considers to be the holy sacrament of matrimony. And it might be better for you if you paid just a bit more attention to our Holy Father and a bit less to the Great Goddess . . . Iggie.

(*Music of "Anything Goes" very softly on the radio.*)

CHRIS: Listen.

MAGGIE: And they have hens there, too, Jack?

JACK: We're overrun with hens.

MAGGIE: Don't dismiss it, girls. It has its points. Would you be game, Kate?

KATE: Would you give my head peace, Maggie.

CHRIS: Gerry has it going!

MAGGIE: Tell me this, Jack: What's the Swahili for "tchook-tchook-tchook-tchook-tchook"?

JACK: You'd love the climate, too, Kate.

KATE: I'm not listening to a word you're saying.

(*Gerry runs on.*)

GERRY: Well? Any good?

CHRIS: Listen.

GERRY: Aha. Leave it to the expert.

JACK: I have something for you, Gerry.

GERRY: What's that?

JACK: The plumed hat — the ceremonial hat — remember? We agreed to swap. With you in a second.

(*He goes to his bedroom.*)

MAGGIE: Good work, Gerry.

GERRY: Thought it might be the aerial. That's the end of your troubles. (*Listens. Sings a line of the song.*) Dance with me, Agnes.

AGNES: Have a bit of sense, Gerry Evans.

GERRY: Dance with me. Please. Come on.

MAGGIE: Dance with him, Aggie.

GERRY (*sings*): "In olden times a glimpse of stocking
    Was looked on as something shocking —"
    Give me your hand.

MAGGIE: Go on, Aggie.

AGNES: Who wants to dance at this time of —

(*Gerry pulls her to her feet and takes her in his arms.*)

GERRY (*sings*): ". . . anything goes.
    Good authors, too, who once knew better words
    Now only use four-letter words
    Writing prose,
    Anything goes . . ."

(*Bring up the sound. With style and with easy elegance they dance once around the kitchen and then out to the garden — Gerry singing the words directly to her face.*)

    "If driving fast cars you like,
    If low bars you like,
    If old hymns you like,
    If bare limbs you like,
    If Mae West you like,
    Or me undressed you like,
    Why, nobody will oppose.
    When ev'ry night, the set that's smart is
        intruding in nudist parties in
    Studios,
    Anything goes . . ."

(*They are now in the far corner of the garden.*)

    You're a great dancer, Aggie.

AGNES: No, I'm not.

GERRY: You're a superb dancer.
AGNES: No, I'm not.
GERRY: You should be a professional dancer.
AGNES: Too late for that.
GERRY: You could teach dancing in Ballybeg.
AGNES: That's all they need.
GERRY: Maybe it is!

(*He bends down and kisses her on the forehead. All this is seen — but not heard — by Chris at the kitchen window. Immediately after this kiss Gerry bursts into song again, turns Agnes four or five times very rapidly, and dances her back to the kitchen.*)

There you are. Safe and sound.
MAGGIE: I wish to God I could dance like you, Aggie.
AGNES: I haven't a breath.
GERRY: Doesn't she dance elegantly?
MAGGIE: Always did, our Aggie.
GERRY: Unbelievable. Now, Chrissie — you and I.
CHRIS (*sharply*): Not now. I wonder where Michael's got to?
GERRY: Come on, Chrissie. Once round the floor.
CHRIS: Not now, I said. Are you thick?
MAGGIE: I'll dance with you, Gerry! (*She kicks her Wellingtons off.*) Do you want to see real class?
GERRY: Certainly do, Maggie.
MAGGIE: Stand back there, girls. Shirley Temple needs a lot of space.
GERRY: Wow-wow-wow-wow!
MAGGIE: Hold me close, Gerry. The old legs aren't too reliable.

(*She and Gerry sing and dance.*)

"In olden times a glimpse of stocking
Was looked on as something shocking
But now —"

(*Chris suddenly turns the radio off.*)

CHRIS: Sick of that damned thing.
GERRY: What happened?
MAGGIE: What are you at there, Chrissie?
CHRIS: We're only wasting the battery and we won't get a new one until the weekend.
MAGGIE: It wasn't to be, Gerry. But there'll be another day.
GERRY: That's a promise, Maggie.

(*He goes to Chris at the radio.*)

Not a bad little set, that.
KATE: Peace, thanks be to God! D'you know what that thing has done? Killed all Christian conversation in this country.
CHRIS (*to Agnes, icily*): Vera McLaughlin's calling here tomorrow. She wants to talk to you and Rose.

AGNES: What about?
KATE (*quickly*): I didn't tell you, did I? — her daughter's got engaged!
MAGGIE: Which of them?
KATE: "The harvest dance is going to be just supreme this year, Miss Mundy" — that wee brat!
MAGGIE: Sophia. Is she not still at school?
KATE: Left last year. She's fifteen. And the lucky man is sixteen.
MAGGIE: Holy God. We may pack it in, girls.
KATE: It's indecent, I'm telling you. Fifteen and sixteen! Don't tell me that's not totally improper. It's the poor mother I feel sorry for.
AGNES: What does she want to talk to us about?
CHRIS (*relenting*): Something about wool. Didn't sound important. She proably won't call at all.

(*Chris turns the radio on again. No sound.*)

(*To Maggie.*) Go ahead and dance, you two.
MAGGIE: Artistes like Margaret Mundy can't perform on demand, Chrissie. We need to be in touch with other forces first, don't we, Gerry?
GERRY: Absolutely. Why is there no sound?
KATE: Maggie, are we never going to eat?
MAGGIE: Indeed we are — outside in the garden! Eggs Ballybeg al fresco.° Lughnasa's almost over, girls. There aren't going to be many warm evenings left.
KATE: Good idea, Maggie.
AGNES: I'll get the cups and plates.
GERRY (*with Chris at radio*): Are you all right?
CHRIS: It's not gone again, is it?
GERRY: Have I done something wrong?
CHRIS: I switched it on again — that's all I did.
MAGGIE: Take out those chairs, Gerry.
GERRY: What about the table?
MAGGIE: We'll just spread a cloth on the ground.

(*Maggie exits with the cloth which she spreads in the middle of the garden. Gerry kisses Chris lightly on the back of the neck.*)

GERRY: At least we know it's not the aerial.
CHRIS: According to you.
GERRY: And if it's not the aerial the next thing to check is the ignition.
CHRIS: Ignition! Listen to that bluffer!
GERRY: Bluffer? (*To Agnes as she passes.*) Did you hear what she called me? That's unfair, Agnes, isn't it?

(*Agnes smiles and shrugs.*)

Let's take the back off and see what's what.

---

al fresco: In the open air.

(*Rose enters the garden from the back of the house. At first nobody notices her. She is dressed as in act 1. In her right hand she holds the dead rooster by the feet. Its feathers are ruffled and it is stained with blood. Rose is calm, almost matter-of-fact. Agnes sees her first and goes to her. Chris and Gerry join the others in the garden.*)

AGNES: Rosie, what is it, Rosie?
ROSE: My rooster's dead.
AGNES: Oh Rosie . . .
ROSE (*holding the dead bird up*): Look at him. He's dead.
AGNES: What happened to him?
ROSE: The fox must have got him.
AGNES: Oh, poor Rosie . . .
ROSE: Maggie warned me the fox was about again. (*To all.*) That's the end of my pet rooster. The fox must have got him. You were right, Maggie.

(*She places it carefully on the tablecloth in the middle of the garden.*)

MAGGIE: Did he get at the hens?
ROSE: I don't think so.
MAGGIE: Was the door left open?
ROSE: They're all right. They're safe.
MAGGIE: That itself.
AGNES: We'll get another white rooster for you, Rosie.
ROSE: Doesn't matter.
MAGGIE: And I'll put manners on him early on.
ROSE: I don't want another.
MAGGIE (*quick hug*): Poor old Rosie. (*As she moves away.*) We can hardly expect him to lay for us now . . .
CHRIS: Where's that Michael fellow got to? Michael! He hears me rightly, you know. I'm sure he's jouking° about out there somewhere, watching us. Michael!

(*Rose sits on the garden seat.*)

MAGGIE: All right, girls, what's missing? Knives, forks, plates —

(*She sees Jack coming through the kitchen.*)

Jesus, Mary, and Joseph!

(*Jack is wearing a very soiled, very crumpled white uniform — a version of the uniform we saw him in at the very beginning of the play. One of the epaulettes is hanging by a thread and the gold buttons are tarnished. The uniform is so large that it looks as if it were made for a much larger man: His hands are lost in the sleeves and the trousers trail on the ground.*)

jouking: Hiding.

On his head he wears a tricorn, ceremonial hat; once white like the uniform but now grubby, the plumage broken and tatty. He carries himself in military style, his army cane under his arm.*)

JACK: Gerry, my friend, where are you?
GERRY: Out here, Jack.
JACK: There you are. (*To all.*) I put on my ceremonial clothes for the formal exchange. There was a time when it fitted me — believe it or not. Wonderful uniform, isn't it?
GERRY: Unbelievable. I could do with that for Spain.
JACK: It was my uniform when I was chaplain to the British army during the Great War.
KATE: We know only too well what it is, Jack.
JACK: Isn't it splendid? Well, it was splendid. Needs a bit of a clean up. Okawa's always dressing up in it. I really must give it to him to keep.
KATE: It's not at all suitable for this climate, Jack.
JACK: You're not right, Kate. Just for the ceremony — then I'll change back. Now, if I were at home, what we do when we swap or barter is this. I place my possession on the ground —

(*He and Gerry enact this ritual.*)

Go ahead. (*Of hat.*) Put it on the grass — anywhere — just at your feet. Now take three steps away from it — yes? — a symbolic distancing of yourself from what you once possessed. Good. Now turn round once — like this — yes, a complete circle — and that's the formal rejection of what you once had — you no longer lay claim to it. Now I cross over to where you stand — right? And you come over to the position I have left. So. Excellent. The exchange is now formally and irrevocably complete. This is my straw hat. And that is your tricorn hat. Put it on. Splendid! And it suits you! Doesn't it suit him?
CHRIS: His head's too big.
GERRY (*adjusting hat*): What about that? (*To Agnes.*) Is that better, Agnes?
AGNES: You're lovely.

(*Gerry does a Charlie Chaplin walk across the garden, his feet spread, his cane twirling. As he does he sings.*)

GERRY: "In olden times a glimpse of stocking
　　Was looked on as something shocking . . ."
JACK (*adjusting his hat*): And what about this? Or like this? Or further back on my head?
MAGGIE: Would you look at them! Strutting about like a pair of peacocks! Now — teatime!
AGNES: I'll make the tea.
MAGGIE: You can start again tomorrow. Let me finish off Lughnasa. Chrissie, put on Marconi.
CHRIS: I think it's broken again.

AGNES: Gerry fixed it. Didn't you?

GERRY: Then Chrissie got at it again.

CHRIS: Possessed that thing, if you ask me.

KATE: I wish you wouldn't use words like that, Christina. There's still great heat in that sun.

MAGGIE: Great harvest weather.

KATE: I love September.

MAGGIE (*not moving*): Cooking time, girls.

KATE: Wait a while, Maggie. Enjoy the bit of heat that's left.

(*Agnes moves beside Rose.*)

AGNES: Next Sunday, then. Is that all right?

ROSE: What's next Sunday?

AGNES: We'll get some more bilberries.

ROSE: Yes. Yes. Whatever you say, Aggie.

(*Gerry examines the kites.*)

GERRY: Not bad for a kid of seven. Very neatly made.

KATE: Look at the artwork.

GERRY: Wow-wow-wow-wow! That is unbelievable!

KATE: I keep telling his mother — she has a very talented son.

CHRIS: So there, Mr. Evans.

GERRY: Have you all seen these?

MAGGIE: I hate them.

GERRY: I think they're just wonderful. Look, Jack.

(*For the first time we all see the images. On each kite is painted a crude, cruel, grinning face, primitively drawn, garishly painted.*)

I'll tell you something: This boy isn't going to end up selling gramophones.

CHRIS: Michael! He always vanishes when there's work to be done.

MAGGIE: I've a riddle for you. Why is a gramophone like a parrot?

KATE: Maggie!

MAGGIE: Because it . . . because it always . . . because a parrot . . . God, I've forgotten!

(*Maggie moves into the kitchen. Michael enters. The characters are now in positions similar to their positions at the beginning of the play — with some changes; Agnes and Gerry are on the garden seat. Jack stands stiffly to attention at Agnes's elbow. One kite, facing boldly out front, stands between Gerry and Agnes; the other between Agnes and Jack. Rose is upstage left. Maggie is at the kitchen window. Kate is downstage right. Chris is at the front door. During Michael's speech Kate cries quietly. As Michael begins to speak the stage is lit in a very soft, golden light so that the tableau we see is almost, but not quite, in a haze.*)

MICHAEL: As I said, Father Jack was dead within twelve months. And with him and Agnes and Rose all gone, the heart seemed to go out of the house.

Maggie took on the tasks Rose and Agnes had done and pretended to believe that nothing had changed. My mother spent the rest of her life in the knitting factory — and hated every day of it. And after a few years doing nothing Kate got the job of tutoring the young family of Austin Morgan of the Arcade. But much of the spirit and fun had gone out of their lives; and when my time came to go away, in the selfish way of young men I was happy to escape.

(*Now fade in very softly, just audible, the music — "It is Time to Say Goodnight" [not from the radio speaker]. And as Michael continues everybody sways very slightly from side to side — even the grinning kites. The movement is so minimal that we cannot be quite certain if it is happening or if we imagine it.*)

And so, when I cast my mind back to that summer of 1936, different kinds of memories offer themselves to me.

But there is one memory of that Lughnasa time that visits me most often; and what fascinates me about that memory is that it owes nothing to fact. In that memory atmosphere is more real than incident and everything is simultaneously actual and illusory. In that memory, too, the air is nostalgic with the music of the thirties. It drifts in from somewhere far away — a mirage of sound — a dream music that is both heard and imagined; that seems to be both itself and its own echo; a sound so alluring and so mesmeric that the afternoon is bewitched, maybe haunted, by it. And what is so strange about that memory is that everybody seems to be floating on those sweet sounds, moving rhythmically, languorously, in complete isolation; responding more to the mood of the music than to its beat. When I remember it, I think of it as dancing. Dancing with eyes half closed because to open them would break the spell. Dancing as if language had surrendered to movement — as if this ritual, this wordless ceremony, was now the way to speak, to whisper private and sacred things, to be in touch with some otherness. Dancing as if the very heart of life and all its hopes might be found in those assuaging notes and those hushed rhythms and in those silent and hypnotic movements. Dancing as if language no longer existed because words were no longer necessary . . .

(*Slowly bring up the music. Slowly bring down the lights.*)

Suzan-Lori Parks

Suzan-Lori Parks (b. 1964) was named by Mel Gussow in the *New York Times* as the "year's most promising playwright" in 1989. She lives in New York City and teaches as writer-in-residence at the New School for Social Research. Her work has been supported by grants from numerous agencies, including the Rockefeller and Ford foundations and the National Endowment for the Arts, from which she has received a playwriting fellowship twice. Her work has been seen primarily in small off-Broadway theaters in New York as well as important regional theaters.

Parks was the child of an army officer and therefore grew up in several different locations. She says, "I've heard horrible stories about 12-step groups for Army people. But I had a great childhood. My parents were really into experiencing the places we lived." She lived, for example, in a small town in Germany and attended German schools, studying in German. She went to Hampshire College, where she studied writing with James Baldwin. After that experience, she went to London for a year to study acting. "It really made a difference in my writing. It dawned on me that a lot of people write with ideas in mind. . . . But I never really have ideas, per se. I have these movements, these gestures. Then I figure out how to put those gestures into words."

She is aware of being influenced by a number of important literary figures, among them Gertrude Stein, James Joyce, William Faulkner, and Samuel Beckett, but there are echoes of other writers such as Shakespeare and Richard Wright in *The Death of the Last Black Man in the Whole Entire World*. Parks's approach to language is partly vernacular as she attempts to reproduce speech both as it is spoken and as her audience assumes it may be spoken. But she is interested in the hypnotic and musical value of words, which accounts for much of the patterning of repetition that marks her work.

Her plays have been performed in the BACA (Brooklyn Academy of Arts) Downtown Theater, Manhattan Theater Club, and small theaters south of 14th Street in Manhattan. Her early short plays are *Betting on the Dust Commander*, *Fishes*, *The Sinners' Place*, and *The America Play*. Her full-length play *Imperceptible Mutabilities in the Third Kingdom*, directed by her long-time collaborator Liz Diamond, won the Obie Award for the best off-Broadway play of 1990. One section of *Mutabilities* takes place on Emancipation Day in 1865 and is played in whiteface by African American actors. Another section, Greeks, makes reference to her own family, with a character called Mr. Sergeant Smith. Parts of the play have been described as "like a choral poem."

Parks has produced a film, *Anemone Me* (1990), that has been shown in New York. Her newest play, *Devotees in the Garden of Love* (1992), premiered at the Actors Theatre of Louisville, Kentucky. Parks, who is only at the beginning of her career, is an energetic, carefully focused, and clearly directed playwright with a special interest in the language of speech and the language of gesture — in almost equal measure.

THE DEATH OF THE LAST BLACK MAN IN THE WHOLE ENTIRE WORLD

The Death of the Last Black Man in the Whole Entire World (1990) is not a straight-line narrative, nor is it situational in the manner of the Scribean well-made play. It consists of several sections:

Overture

Panel I: Thuh Holy Ghost

Panel II: First Chorus

Panel III: Thuh Lonesome 3some

Panel IV: Second Chorus

Panel V: In thuh Garden of HooDoo It

Final Chorus

The first production of the play, at the Brooklyn Academy of the Arts (BACA) Downtown Theater, was directed by Liz Diamond in close collaboration with Suzan-Lori Parks. Although Parks's text provides no conventional stage directions, the BACA production created very powerful visual images in the staging and costuming. In Panels I, III, and IV the name of the panel was projected on the back of the stage, lighted brightly enough to be read, like the caption of a cartoon panel. The visual emblems that dominated the panels were powerful: an electric chair in "Thuh Holy Ghost," with Black Man, wearing only a pair of white jockey shorts, rising from a black catafalque to find himself seated in the chair with a metal helmet to facilitate the flow of electricity through his body. This emblem was duplicated: While one actor sat in the chair, another played his part downstage getting solace from Black Woman, who anointed him and washed his feet in the traditional Christian fashion.

In "Thuh Lonesome 3some" the emblem was three watermelons borne by Black Man with Watermelon, who struggles to understand the role these melons play in his life. The biblical references to melons in paradise ironically underpin this section. In "In thuh Garden of HooDoo It," another emblem of death, the lynched man, dangled over the action. Again, the Black Man was duplicated downstage with a noose around his neck and with a dead tree limb dragged onto the stage. In each instance the Black Man dies a different death, but he cannot die without the accompanying spirits telling their story.

Liz Diamond, the director, explained, "These are figures, not characters, and their function as figures must be understood." One of Diamond's greatest challenges was in bringing these figures onstage so the audience would understand that they are not "realistic" characters. They are epic types that Diamond calls spirits who will not let Black Man die before he hears them impart their wisdom. The figures come from many sources: And Bigger and Bigger and Bigger from Richard Wright's *Native Son*; Ham from the Bible; Black Man with Watermelon and Black Woman with Fried Drumstick from black folklore; Queen-then-Pharaoh Hatshepsut from history; Prunes and Prisms, an image of the black prom queen; and Voice on thuh Tee V, a contemporary image.

Each of these figures was costumed appropriately in the Diamond production. Hatshepsut wore the squared-off headdress found on the Sphinx with a gold pleated full-length dress. Black Man with Watermelon wore overalls; Black Woman wore a black matronly dress and later a black veil of mourning. Bigger wore a gold zoot suit; Voice on thuh Tee V wore a trench coat and carried a microphone. Ham, one of the most compelling figures, wore a multicolored shawl and headdress and carried a long staff. The inspiration for his character, as Parks and Diamond observed, was the "Times Square Prophet," a homeless wanderer who rants as if he were a holy man.

Ham's major section, Panel IV, is dominated by his biblical "voice." In the Bible, when Ham saw his father Noah's nakedness, he was condemned, and his progeny were forever black as a result. As Parks has said, "Ham doesn't get a chance to respond" in the Bible. But Parks provides Ham's response with a parody of the Bible's series of "begats." The figure Before Columbus was costumed like an African villager in an abbadan obie, an African tunic, and comments on the world when it was "flat." These figures are the stereotypes of blacks as created in the Western European imagination, beginning with the Bible.

Parks hears language as much as she sees it. Therefore in her text she spells words as she wants them to be heard and signifies meanings that sometimes transcend the limits of individual words. She adds the syllable *-ed* to a word such as *died,* and the result is a new word, in this case *dieded.* The effect is both ironic and rhythmically powerful and reinforcing. That kind of syllabic repetition also complements the repetition of important phrases, such as "You should write that down. You should write that down and hide it under uh rock." Much of history has been written down and hidden under rocks only to be discovered and deciphered by later generations. The point is to get it down in language somehow, to tell the story so that the future will know.

Music was used judiciously throughout the Yale performance, including a saxophone with a jazz riff, but no songs. A gong sounded to signal important moments like the string breaking in *The Cherry Orchard.* Subtle rhythmic effects are achieved with the repetition of words and phrases, and time becomes as plastic as space. The time of the play encompasses ancient Egypt, biblical Judea, the coming of Columbus, slavery in the American South, lynchings in the post–Civil War era, and contemporary electrocutions of blacks. *Last Black Man* is nothing if not inclusive.

The Death of the Last Black Man in the Whole Entire World in Performance

The Death of the Last Black Man in the Whole Entire World premiered in the BACA Downtown Theater in New York in September 1990. It was revived in a larger, full-scale production at the Yale Repertory Theatre Winterfest Program in early 1992. Audiences responded positively to a production that was more avant-garde than most drama being shown in regional theaters, and reviewers hailed Parks as an exciting new voice in theater.

Suzan-Lori Parks (*b. 1964*)

THE DEATH OF THE LAST BLACK MAN IN THE WHOLE ENTIRE WORLD

1990

When I die
I wont stay
Dead. — BOB KAUFMAN

The Figures

BLACK MAN WITH WATERMELON
BLACK WOMAN WITH FRIED DRUMSTICK
LOTS OF GREASE AND LOTS OF PORK
YES AND GREENS BLACK-EYED PEAS CORNBREAD
QUEEN-THEN-PHARAOH HATSHEPSUT

BEFORE COLUMBUS
OLD MAN RIVER JORDAN
HAM
AND BIGGER AND BIGGER AND BIGGER
PRUNES AND PRISMS
VOICE ON THUH TEE V

The Sections

The action takes place in the present.

OVERTURE

BLACK MAN WITH WATERMELON: The black man moves his hands.

(*a bell sounds twice*)

LOTS OF GREASE AND LOTS OF PORK: Lots of grease and lots of pork.

QUEEN-THEN-PHARAOH HATSHEPSUT: Queen-then-Pharaoh Hatshepsut.

AND BIGGER AND BIGGER AND BIGGER: And Bigger and Bigger and Bigger.

PRUNES AND PRISMS: Prunes and Prisms.

HAM: Ham.

VOICE ON THUH TEE V: Voice on thuh Tee V.

OLD MAN RIVER JORDAN: Old Man River Jordan.

YES AND GREENS BLACK-EYED PEAS CORNBREAD: Yes and Greens Black-Eyed Peas Cornbread.

BEFORE COLUMBUS: Before Columbus.

(*a bell sounds once*)

BLACK MAN WITH WATERMELON: The black man moves his hands.

QUEEN-THEN-PHARAOH HATSHEPSUT: Not yet. Let Queen-then-Pharaoh Hatshepsut tell you when.

LOTS OF GREASE AND LOTS OF PORK: This is the death of the last black man in the whole entire world.

(*a bell sounds three times*)

BLACK WOMAN WITH FRIED DRUMSTICK: Yesterday today next summer tomorrow just uh moment uhgoh in 1317 dieded thuh last black man in thuh whole entire world. Uh! Oh. Don't be uhlarmed. Do not be afeared. It was painless. Uh painless passin. He falls twenty-three floors to his death. 23 floors from uh passin ship from space tuh splat on thuh pavement. He have uh head he been keepin under thuh Tee V. On his bottom pantry shelf. He have uh head that hurts. Don't fit right. Put it on tuh go tuh thuh store and it pinched him when he walks his thoughts don't got room. Why dieded he huh?

Where he gonna go now that he done dieded? Where he gonna go tuh wash his hands?

YES AND GREENS BLACK-EYED PEAS CORNBREAD: You should write that down and you should hide it under a rock. This is the death of the last black man in the whole entire world.

LOTS OF GREASE AND LOTS OF PORK/PRUNES AND PRISMS: Not yet —

BLACK MAN WITH WATERMELON: The black man moves. His hands —

QUEEN-THEN-PHARAOH HATSHEPSUT: You are too young to move. Let me move it for you.

BLACK MAN WITH WATERMELON: The black man moves his hands. — He moves his hands round. Back. Back. Back tuh that.

LOTS OF GREASE AND LOTS OF PORK: (Not dat).

BLACK MAN WITH WATERMELON: When thuh worl usta be roun. Thuh worl usta be *roun.*

BLACK WOMAN WITH FRIED DRUMSTICK: Uh roun worl. Uh roun? Thuh worl? When was this.

QUEEN-THEN-PHARAOH HATSHEPSUT: Columbus. Before.

BEFORE COLUMBUS: Before. Columbus.

YES AND GREENS BLACK-EYED PEAS CORNBREAD: Before Columbus.

BLACK MAN WITH WATERMELON: HHH. HA!

QUEEN-THEN-PHARAOH HATSHEPSUT: Before Columbus thuh worl usta be *roun* they put uh /d/ on thuh end of roun makin round. Thusly they set in motion thuh end. Without that /d/ we coulda gone on spinnin for ever. Thuh /d/ thing ended things ended.

YES AND GREENS BLACK-EYED PEAS CORNBREAD: Before Columbus:

(*a bell sounds twice*)

BEFORE COLUMBUS: The popular thinking of the day back in them days was that the world was flat. They thought the world was flat. Back then when they thought the world was flat they were afeared and stayed at home. They wanted to go out back then when they thought the world was flat but the water had in it dragons of which meaning these dragons they were afeared back then when they thought the world was flat. They stayed at home. Them thinking the world was flat kept it roun. Them thinking the sun revolved around the earth kept them satellite-like. They figured out the truth and scurried out. Figuring out the truth put them in their place and they scurried out to put us in ours.

YES AND GREENS BLACK-EYED PEAS CORNBREAD: Mmmm. Yes. You should write this down. You should hide this under a rock.

LOTS OF GREASE AND LOTS OF PORK/PRUNES AND PRISMS: Not yet —

BLACK MAN WITH WATERMELON: The black man bursts into flames. The black man bursts into blames. Whose fault is it?

ALL: Ain't mines.

BLACK MAN WITH WATERMELON: Whose fault is it?

ALL: Ain't mines.

BLACK WOMAN WITH FRIED DRUMSTICK: I can't remember back that far.

QUEEN-THEN-PHARAOH HATSHEPSUT: And besides, I wasn't even there.

BLACK MAN WITH WATERMELON: Ha ha ha. The black man laughs out loud.

ALL (except Ham): HAM-BONE-HAM-BONE-WHERE - YOU - BEEN - ROUN - THUH - WORL - N-BACK-UH-GAIN.

YES AND GREENS BLACK-EYED PEAS CORNBREAD: Whatcha seen hambone girl?

BLACK WOMAN WITH FRIED DRUMSTICK: Didn't see you. I saw thuh worl.

QUEEN-THEN-PHARAOH HATSHEPSUT: I was there.

LOTS OF GREASE AND LOTS OF PORK: Didn't see you.

BLACK WOMAN WITH FRIED DRUMSTICK: I was there.

BLACK MAN WITH WATERMELON: Didn't see you. The black man moves his hands.

QUEEN-THEN-PHARAOH HATSHEPSUT: We are too young to see. Let them see it for you. We are too young to rule. Let them rule it for you. We are too young to have. Let them have it for you. You are too young to write. Let them — let them. Do it. Before you.

BLACK MAN WITH WATERMELON: The black man moves his hands.

YES AND GREENS BLACK-EYED PEAS CORNBREAD: You should write it down because if you dont write it down then they will come along and tell the future that we did not exist. You should write it down and you should hide it under a rock. You should write down the past and you should write down the present and in what in the future you should write it down. It will be of us but you should mention them from time to time so that in the future when they come along and know that they exist. You should hide it all under a rock so that in the future when they come along they will say that the rock did not exist.

BLACK WOMAN WITH FRIED DRUMSTICK: We getting somewheres. We getting down. Down down down down down down down —

QUEEN-THEN-PHARAOH HATSHEPSUT: I saw Columbus comin. / I saw Columbus comin goin over tuh visit you. "To borrow a cup of sugar," so he said. I waved my hands in warnin. You waved back. I aint seen you since.

LOTS OF GREASE AND LOTS OF PORK: In the future when they came along I meeting them. On thuh coast. Uh! Thuh Coast! I — was — so — polite. But in thuh dirt, I wrote: "Ha. Ha. Ha."

ALL: Ha. Ha. Ha. Ha. Ha. Ha. Ha. Ha. Ha. Ha. Ha. Ha. Ha. Ha. Ha. Ha. HHHHHHHHHHHHHHHH.

BLACK MAN WITH WATERMELON: Thuh black man he move. He move he hans.

(a bell sounds once)

PANEL I: THUH HOLY GHOST

BLACK MAN WITH WATERMELON: Saint mines. Saint mines. Iduhnt it Nope: iduhnt. Saint mines cause everythin I calls mines got uh print uh me someway on it in it dont got uh print uh me someway on it so saint mines. Duhduhnt so saint: huh.

BLACK WOMAN WITH FRIED DRUMSTICK: Hen.

BLACK MAN WITH WATERMELON: Huh. Huh?

BLACK WOMAN WITH FRIED DRUMSTICK: Hen. Hen?

BLACK MAN WITH WATERMELON: Who gived birth tuh this I wonder. Who gived birth tuh this. I wonder.

BLACK WOMAN WITH FRIED DRUMSTICK: You comed back. Comin backs somethin in itself. You comed back.

BLACK MAN WITH WATERMELON: This does not belong tuh me. Somebody planted this on me. On me in my hands.

BLACK WOMAN WITH FRIED DRUMSTICK: Cold compress. Cold compress then some hen. Lean back. You comed back. Lean back.

BLACK MAN WITH WATERMELON: Who gived birth tuh this I wonder who.

BLACK WOMAN WITH FRIED DRUMSTICK: Comin for you. Came for you: that they done did. Comin for tuh take you. Told me tuh pack up your clothes. Told me tuh cut my bed in 2 from double tuh single. Cut off thuh bed-foot where your feets had rested. Told me tuh do that too. Burry your ring in his hidin spot under thuh porch! That they told me too to do. Didnt have uh ring so I didnt do diddly. They told and told and told: proper instructions for thuh burial proper attire for thuh mournin. They told and told and told: I didnt do squat. Awe on that. You comed back. You got uhway. Knew you would. Hen?

BLACK MAN WITH WATERMELON: Who gived birth tuh this I wonder. Who? Not me. Saint mines.

BLACK WOMAN WITH FRIED DRUMSTICK: Killed every hen on thuh block. You comed back. Knew you would. Knew you would came back. Knew you will wanted uh good big hen dinner in waitin. Every hen on thuh block.

BLACK MAN WITH WATERMELON: Saint mines.

BLACK WOMAN WITH FRIED DRUMSTICK: Strutted down on up thuh road with my axe. By-myself-with-my-axe. Got tuh thuh street top 93 dyin hen din hand. Dropped thuh axe. Tooked tuh stranglin. 93 dyin hen din hand with no heads let em loose tuh run down tuh towards home infront of me. Flipped thuh necks of thuh next 23 more odd. Slinged um over my shoulders. Hens of thuh neighbors now in my pots. Feathers of thuh hens of thuh neighbors stucked in our mattress. They told and told and told. On me. Huh. Awe on that. Hen? You got uhway. Knew you would.

BLACK MAN WITH WATERMELON: Who gived birth tuh me I wonder.

BLACK WOMAN WITH FRIED DRUMSTICK: They dont speak tuh us no more. They pass by our porch but they dont nod. You been comed back goin on 9 years not even heard from thuh neighbors uh congratulation. Uh alienationed dum. Uh guess. Huh. Hen? *WE AINT GOT NO FRIENDS,* — sweetheart.

BLACK MAN WITH WATERMELON: *SWEET-HEART.*

BLACK WOMAN WITH FRIED DRUMSTICK: Hen!!

BLACK MAN WITH WATERMELON: Aint hungry.

BLACK WOMAN WITH FRIED DRUMSTICK: Hen.

BLACK MAN WITH WATERMELON: Aint eaten in years.

BLACK WOMAN WITH FRIED DRUMSTICK: Hen?

BLACK MAN WITH WATERMELON: Last meal I had was my last-mans-meal.

BLACK WOMAN WITH FRIED DRUMSTICK: You got uhway. Knew you would.

BLACK MAN WITH WATERMELON: This thing dont look like me!

BLACK WOMAN WITH FRIED DRUMSTICK: It dont. Do it. Should it? Hen: eat it.

BLACK MAN WITH WATERMELON: I kin tell whats mines by whats gots my looks. Ssmymethod. Try it by testin it and it turns out true. Every time. Fool proofly. Look down at my foot and wonder if its mine. Foot mine? I kin ask it and foot answers back with uh "yes Sir" — not like you and me say "yes Sir" but uh "yes Sir" peculiar tuh thuh foot. Foot mine? I kin ask it and through uh look that looks like my looks thuh foot gives me back uh "yes Sir." Ssmymethod. Try by thuh test tuh pass for true. Move on tuh thuh uther foot. Foot mine? And uh nother "yes Sir" so feets mine is understood. Got uh forearm thats up for question check myself out teeth by tooth. Melon mine? —. Dont look like me.

BLACK WOMAN WITH FRIED DRUMSTICK: Hen mine? Gobble it up and it will be. You got uhway. Fixed

uh good big hen dinner for you. Get yourself uh mouthful afore it rots.

BLACK MAN WITH WATERMELON: Was we green and stripe-dly when we first comed out?

BLACK WOMAN WITH FRIED DRUMSTICK: Uh huhn. Thuh features comes later. Later comes after now.

BLACK MAN WITH WATERMELON: Oh. Later comes now: melon mine?

BLACK WOMAN WITH FRIED DRUMSTICK: They comed for you and tooked you. That was yesterday. Today you sit in your chair where you sat yesterday and thuh day afore yesterday afore they comed and tooked you. Things today is just as they are yesterday cept nothin is familiar cause it was such uh long time uhgoh.

BLACK MAN WITH WATERMELON: Later oughta be now by now huh?: melon mine?

BLACK WOMAN WITH FRIED DRUMSTICK: Thuh chair was portable. They take it from county tuh county. Only got one. Can only eliminate one at uh time. Woulda fried you right here on thuh front porch but we dont got enough electric. No onessgot enough electric. Not on our block. Dont believe in havin enough. Put thuh Chair in thuh middle of thuh City. Outdoors. In thuh square. Folks come tuh watch with picnic baskets. — Hen?

BLACK MAN WITH WATERMELON: Sweetheart?

BLACK WOMAN WITH FRIED DRUMSTICK: They juiced you some, huh?

BLACK MAN WITH WATERMELON: Just uh squirt. Sweetheart.

BLACK WOMAN WITH FRIED DRUMSTICK: Humpty Dumpty.

BLACK MAN WITH WATERMELON: Melon mines?

BLACK WOMAN WITH FRIED DRUMSTICK: Humpty damn Dumpty actin like thuh Holy Ghost. You got uhway. Thuh lights dimmed but you got uhway. Knew you would.

BLACK MAN WITH WATERMELON: They juiced me some.

BLACK WOMAN WITH FRIED DRUMSTICK: Just uh squirt.

BLACK MAN WITH WATERMELON: They had theirselves uh extender chord. Fry uh man in thuh town square needs uh extender tuh reach em thuh electric Hook up thuh chair tuh thuh power. Extender: 49 foot in length. Closer tuh thuh power I never been. Flip on up thuh go switch. Huh! Juice begins its course.

BLACK WOMAN WITH FRIED DRUMSTICK: Humpty damn Dumpty.

BLACK MAN WITH WATERMELON: Thuh straps they have on me are leathern. See thuh cord waggin full with uh jump-juice try me tuh wiggle from thuh waggin but belt leathern straps: width thickly. One round each forearm. Forearm mines? 2 cross thuh chest. Chest is mines: and it explodin. One for my left hand fingers left strapted too. Right was done thuh same. Jump-juice meets me-mine juices I do uh slow soft shoe like on water. Town crier cries uh moan. Felt my nappy head go frizzly. Town follows thuh crier in uh sorta sing-uhlong-song.

BLACK WOMAN WITH FRIED DRUMSTICK: Then you got uhway. Got uhway in comed back.

BLACK MAN WITH WATERMELON: Uh extender chord 49 foot in length. Turned on thuh up switch in I started runnin. First 49 foot I was runnin they was still juicin.

BLACK WOMAN WITH FRIED DRUMSTICK: And they chase-ted you.

BLACK MAN WITH WATERMELON: — Melon mines?

BLACK WOMAN WITH FRIED DRUMSTICK: When you broked tuh seek your freedom they followed after, huh?

BLACK MAN WITH WATERMELON: Later oughta be now by now, huh?

BLACK WOMAN WITH FRIED DRUMSTICK: You comed back.

BLACK MAN WITH WATERMELON: — Not exactly.

BLACK WOMAN WITH FRIED DRUMSTICK: They comed for you tuh take you. Tooked you uhway: that they done did. You got uhway. Thuh lights dimmed. Had us uh brownout. You got past that. You comed back.

BLACK MAN WITH WATERMELON: Turned on thuh juice on me in me in I started runnin. First just runnin then runnin towards home. Couldnt find us. Think I got lost. Saw us on up uhhead but I flew over thuh yard. Couldnt stop. Think I overshot.

BLACK WOMAN WITH FRIED DRUMSTICK: Killed every hen on thuh block. Made you uh —

BLACK MAN WITH WATERMELON: Make me uh space 6 feet by 6 feet by 6. Make it big and mark it so as I wont miss it. If you would please, sweetness, uh mass grave-site. Theres company comin soonish. I would like tuh get up and go. I would like tuh move my hands.

BLACK WOMAN WITH FRIED DRUMSTICK: You comed back.

BLACK MAN WITH WATERMELON: Overshot. Overshot. I would like tuh move my hands.

BLACK WOMAN WITH FRIED DRUMSTICK: Cold compress?

BLACK MAN WITH WATERMELON: Sweetheart.

BLACK WOMAN WITH FRIED DRUMSTICK: How uhbout uh hen leg?

BLACK MAN WITH WATERMELON: Nothanks. Justate.

BLACK WOMAN WITH FRIED DRUMSTICK: Just ate?

BLACK MAN WITH WATERMELON: Justate. Thatsright. 6 by 6 by 6. Thatsright.

BLACK WOMAN WITH FRIED DRUMSTICK: Oh. —. They eat their own yuh know.

BLACK MAN WITH WATERMELON: HooDoo.

BLACK WOMAN WITH FRIED DRUMSTICK: Hen do. Saw it on thuh Tee V.

BLACK MAN WITH WATERMELON: Aint that nice.

(a bell sounds once)

PANEL II: FIRST CHORUS

BLACK MAN WITH WATERMELON: 6 by 6 by 6.

ALL: THATS RIGHT.

BLACK WOMAN WITH FRIED DRUMSTICK: Oh. They eat their own you know.

ALL: HOODOO.

BLACK WOMAN WITH FRIED DRUMSTICK: Hen do. Saw it on thuh Tee V.

ALL: Aint that nice.

AND BIGGER AND BIGGER AND BIGGER: WILL SOMEBODY TAKE THESE STRAPS OFF UH ME PLEASE? I WOULD LIKE TUH MOVE MY HANDS.

PRUNES AND PRISMS: Prunes and prisms will begin: prunes and prisms prunes and prisms prunes and prisms and prunes and prisms: 23.

VOICE ON THUH TEE V: Good evening. I'm Broad Caster. Headlining tonight: the news: is Gamble Major, the absolutely last living negro man in the whole entire known world — is dead. Major Gamble, born a slave, taught himself the rudiments of education to become a spearhead in the Civil Rights Movement. He was 38 years old. News of Major's death sparked controlled displays of jubilation in all corners of the world.

PRUNES AND PRISMS: Oh no no: world is roun.

AND BIGGER AND BIGGER AND BIGGER: WILL SOMEBODY TAKE THESE STRAPS OFF UH ME PLEASE? I WOULD LIKE TUH MOVE MY HANDS.

(a bell sounds 4 times)

LOTS OF GREASE AND LOTS OF PORK: This is the death of the last black man in the whole entire world.

PRUNES AND PRISMS: Not yet —

VOICE ON THUH TEE V: Good evening. Broad Caster. Head line tonight: Gamble Major, the absolutely last living negro man in the whole known entire world is dead. Gamble Major born a slave rose to become a spearhead in the Civil Rights Movement. He was 38 years old. The Civil Rights Movement. He was 38 years old.

AND BIGGER AND BIGGER AND BIGGER: WILL SOME-

BODY TAKE THESE STRAPS OFF UH ME PLEASE? I WOULD LIKE TUH MOVE MY HANDS.

LOTS OF GREASE AND LOTS OF PORK: This is the death of the last black man in the whole entire world.

(*a bell sounds 3 times*)

PRUNES AND PRISMS: Prunes and prisms prunes and prisms prunes and prisms prunes and prisms.

QUEEN-THEN-PHARAOH HATSHEPSUT: Yesterday tuhday next summer tuhmorrow just uh moment uhgoh in 1317 dieded thuh last black man in thuh whole entire world. Uh! Oh. Dont be uhlarmed. Do not be afeared. It was painless. Uh painless passin. He falls 23 floors to his death.

PRUNES AND PRISMS: No.

QUEEN-THEN-PHARAOH HATSHEPSUT: 23 floors from uh passin ship from space tuh splat on thuh pavement.

PRUNES AND PRISMS: No.

QUEEN-THEN-PHARAOH HATSHEPSUT: He have uh head he been keepin under thuh Tee V. On his bottom pantry shelf.

PRUNES AND PRISMS: No.

QUEEN-THEN-PHARAOH HATSHEPSUT: He have uh head that hurts. Dont fit right. Put it on tuh go tuh thuh store in it pinched him when he walks his thoughts dont got room. Why dieded he huh?

PRUNES AND PRISMS: No.

QUEEN-THEN-PHARAOH HATSHEPSUT: Where he gonna go now that he done dieded?

PRUNES AND PRISMS: No.

BLACK WOMAN WITH FRIED DRUMSTICK: Where he gonna go tuh wash his hands?

CHORUS: You should write that down. You should write that down and you should hide it under uh rock.

VOICE ON THUH TEE V: Good evening. Broad Caster. Headlinin tonight: thuh news:

OLD MAN RIVER JORDAN: Tell you of uh news. Last news. Last news of thuh last man. Last man had last words say hearin it. He spoked uh speech spoked hisself uh chatter-tooth babble "ya-oh-may/chuh-naw" dribblin down his lips tuh puddle in his lap. Dribblin by dropplets. Drop by drop. Last news. News flashes with drops. Thuh last drop was uh all uhlone drop. Singular. Thuh last drop started it off it all. Started off with uh drop. Started off with uh jungle. Started sproutin in his spittle growin leaves off of his mines and thuh vines say drippin doin it. Last news leads tuh thuh first news. He is dead he crosses thuh river. He jumps in thuh puddle have his clothing: ON. On thuh other side thuh mountin yo he dripply wet with soppin. Do drop be dripted? I say "yes."

BLACK MAN WITH WATERMELON: Dont leave me hear. Dont leave me. Hear?

QUEEN-THEN-PHARAOH HATSHEPSUT: Where he gonna go tuh wash his dribblin hands?

PRUNES AND PRISMS: Where he gonna go tuh dry his dripplin clothes?

YES AND GREENS BLACK-EYED PEAS CORNBREAD: Did you write it down? On uh little slip uh paper stick thuh slip in thuh river afore you slip in that way you keep your clothes dry, man.

PRUNES AND PRISMS: Aintcha heard uh that trick?

BEFORE COLUMBUS: That tricks thuh method.

QUEEN-THEN-PHARAOH HATSHEPSUT: They used it on uhlong uhgoh still works every time.

OLD MAN RIVER JORDAN: He jumped in thuh water without uh word for partin come out drippley wet with soppin. Do drop be dripted? I say "do."

BLACK MAN WITH WATERMELON: In you all theres kin. You all kin. Kin gave thuh first permission kin be givin it now still. Some things is all thuh ways gonna be uh continuin sort of uh some thing. Some things go on and on till they dont stop. I am soppin wet. I left my scent behind in uh bundle of old clothing that was not thrown out. Left thuh scent in thuh clothin in thuh clothin on uh rooftop. Dogs surround my house and laugh. They are mockin thuh scent that I left behind. I jumped in thuh water without uh word. I jumped in thuh water without uh smell. I am in thuh river and in my skin is soppin wet. I would like tuh stay afloat now. I would like tuh move my hands.

AND BIGGER AND BIGGER AND BIGGER: Would somebody take these straps off uh me please? I would like tuh move my hands.

BLACK MAN WITH WATERMELON: Now kin kin I move my hands?

QUEEN-THEN-PHARAOH HATSHEPSUT: My black man my subject man my man uh all mens my my my no no not yes no not yes thuh hands. Let Queen-then-Pharaoh Hatshepsut tell you when. She is I am. An I am she passing by with her train. Pulling it behind her on uh plastic chain. Ooooh who! Ooooooh who! Where you gonna go now, now that you done dieded?

CHORUS: Ha ha ha.

PRUNES AND PRISMS: Say "prunes and prisms" 40 times each day and you'll cure your big lips. Prunes and prisms prunes and prisms prunes and prisms: 19.

QUEEN-THEN-PHARAOH HATSHEPSUT: An I am Sheba-like she be me am passin on by she with her train. Pullin it behind / he on uh plastic chain. Oooh who! Oooh who! Come uhlong. Come uhlong.

BLACK WOMAN WITH FRIED DRUMSTICK: Say he was waitin on the right time.

1360

LEFT: Panel II: Prunes and Prisms (Karen A. Bishop), Black Woman with Fried Drumstick (Fanni Green), And Bigger and Bigger and Bigger (Michael Potts), Yes and Greens Black-Eyed Peas Cornbread (Melody J. Garrett), Old Man River Jordan (Ron Brice), and Black Man with Watermelon (Leon Addison Brown) in the 1992 Yale Repertory Theatre Winterfest production of *Last Black Man*. BELOW LEFT: Final Chorus: Black Man with Watermelon and And Bigger and Bigger and Bigger. RIGHT: Panel III: Black Man with Watermelon and Black Woman with Fried Drumstick.

AND BIGGER AND BIGGER AND BIGGER: Say he was waitin in thuh wrong line.

BLACK MAN WITH WATERMELON: I jumped in thuh river without a word. My kin are soppin wet.

QUEEN-THEN-PHARAOH HATSHEPSUT: Come uhlong. Come uhlong.

PRUNES AND PRISMS: Prunes and prisms prunes and prisms.

LOTS OF GREASE AND LOTS OF PORK: This is the death of the last black man in the whole entire world.

PRUNES AND PRISMS: Not yet.

LOTS OF GREASE AND LOTS OF PORK: Back tuh when thuh worl usta be roun.

QUEEN-THEN-PHARAOH HATSHEPSUT: Come uhlong come uhlong get on board come uhlong.

OLD MAN RIVER JORDAN: Back tuh that. Yes.

YES AND GREENS BLACK-EYED PEAS CORNBREAD: Back tuh then thuh worl usta be roun.

OLD MAN RIVER JORDAN: Uhcross thuh river in back tuh that. Yes. Do in diddly dip didded thuh drop.

Out to thuh river uhlong to thuh sea. Long thuh long coast. Skirtin. Yes. Skirtin back tuh that. Come up back flip take uhway like thuh waves do. Far uhway. Uhway tuh where they dont speak thuh language and where they dont want tuh. Huh. Go on back tuh that.

YES AND GREENS BLACK-EYED PEAS CORNBREAD: Awe on uh interior before uh demarcation made it mapped. Awe on uh interior with out uh road-word called macadam. Awe onin uh interior that was uh whole was once. Awe on uh whole roun worl uh roun worl with uh river.

OLD MAN RIVER JORDAN: In thuh interior was uh river. Huh. Back tuh that.

CHORUS: The river was roun as thuh worl was. Roun.

OLD MAN RIVER JORDAN: He hacks his way through thuh tall grass. Tall grass scratch. Width: thickly. Grasses thickly comin from all angles at it. He runs along thuh path worn out by uh 9 million paddin bare footed feet. Uh path overgrown cause it aint as all as happened as of yet. Tuh be extracted from thuh jungle first he gotta go in hide.

BLACK MAN WITH WATERMELON: Chaseted me outa thuh trees now they tree me. Thuh dogs come out from their hidin spots under thuh porch and give me uhway. Thuh hidin spot was under thuh porch of uh house that werent there as of yet. Thuh dogs give me uhway by uh laugh aimed at my scent.

AND BIGGER AND BIGGER AND BIGGER: HA HA HA. Thats how thuh laugh sorta like be wentin.

PRUNES AND PRISMS: Where he gonna go now now that he done dieded?

QUEEN-THEN-PHARAOH HATSHEPSUT: Where he gonna go tuh move his hands?

BLACK MAN WITH WATERMELON: I. I. I would like tuh move my hands.

YES AND GREENS BLACK-EYED PEAS CORNBREAD: Back tuh when thuh worl usta be roun.

LOTS OF GREASE AND LOTS OF PORK: Uh roun. Thuh worl? Uh roun worl? When was this?

OLD MAN RIVER JORDAN: Columbus. Before.

PRUNES AND PRISMS: Before Columbus?

AND BIGGER AND BIGGER AND BIGGER: Ha!

QUEEN-THEN-PHARAOH HATSHEPSUT: Before Columbus thuh worl usta be roun. They put uh /d/ on thuh end of roun makin round. Thusly they set in motion thuh enduh. Without that /d/ we could uh gone on spinnin forever. Thuh /d/ thing endiduh things endiduh.

BEFORE COLUMBUS: Before Columbus.

(a bell sounds once)

BEFORE COLUMBUS: Thuh popular thinkin kin of thuh day back then in them days was that thuh worl was flat. They thought thuh worl was flat. Back then kin in them days when they thought thuh worl was flat they were afeared and stayed at home. They wanted tuh go out back then when they thought thuh worl was flat but thuh water had in it dragons.

AND BIGGER AND BIGGER AND BIGGER: Not lurkin in thuh sea but lurkin in thuh street, see? Sir name Tom-us and Bigger be my christian name. Rise up out of uh made up story in grown Bigger and Bigger. Too big for my own name. Nostrils: flarin. Width: thickly. Breath: fire-laden and smellin badly.

BLACK WOMAN WITH FRIED DRUMSTICK: Huh. Whiffit.

BEFORE COLUMBUS: Dragons, of which meanin these dragons they were afeared back then. When they thought thuh worl was flat. They stayed at home. Them thinkin thuh worl was flat kept it roun. Them thinkin thuh sun revolved uhroun thuh earth kin kept them satellite-like. They figured out thuh truth and scurried out. Figurin out thuh truth kin put them in their place and they scurried out tuh put us in ours.

YES AND GREENS BLACK-EYED PEAS CORNBREAD: Mmmmm. Yes. You should write that down. You should write that down and you should hide it under uh rock.

BEFORE COLUMBUS: Thuh earthsgettin level with thuh land land HO and thuh lands gettin level with thuh sea.

PRUNES AND PRISMS: Not yet —

QUEEN-THEN-PHARAOH HATSHEPSUT: An I am Sheba she be me. Youll mutter thuh words and part thuh waves and come uhlong come uhlong.

AND BIGGER AND BIGGER AND BIGGER: I would like tuh fit in back in thuh storybook from which I camed.

BLACK MAN WITH WATERMELON: My text was writ in water. I would like tuh drink it down.

QUEEN-THEN-PHARAOH HATSHEPSUT: Down tuh float drown tuh float down. My son erased his mothers mark.

AND BIGGER AND BIGGER AND BIGGER: I am grown too big for thuh word thats me.

PRUNES AND PRISMS: Prunes and prisms prunes and prisms prunes and prisms: 14.

QUEEN-THEN-PHARAOH HATSHEPSUT: An I am Sheba me am (She be doo be wah waaaah doo wah). Come uhlong come on uhlong on.

BEFORE COLUMBUS: Before Columbus directs thuh traffic: left right left right.

PRUNES AND PRISMS: Prunes and prisms prunes and prisms.

QUEEN-THEN-PHARAOH HATSHEPSUT: I left my mark on all I made. My son erase his mothers mark.

BLACK WOMAN WITH FRIED DRUMSTICK: Where you gonna go now now that you done dieded?

AND BIGGER AND BIGGER AND BIGGER: Would somebody take these straps offuh me please? Gaw. I would like tuh drink in drown —

BEFORE COLUMBUS: There is uh tiny land mass just above my reach.

LOTS OF GREASE AND LOTS OF PORK: There is uh tiny land mass just outside of my vocabulary.

OLD MAN RIVER JORDAN: Do in dip diddly did-did thuh drop? Drop do it be dripted? Uh huh.

BEFORE COLUMBUS: Land:

AND BIGGER AND BIGGER AND BIGGER: HO!

QUEEN-THEN-PHARAOH HATSHEPSUT: I saw Columbus comin Before Columbus comin/goin over tuh meet you —

BEFORE COLUMBUS: Thuh first time I saw it. It was huge. Thuh green sea becomes uh hillside. Uh hillside populated with some peoples I will name. Thuh first time I saw it it was uh was-huge once one. Huh. It has been gettin smaller ever since.

QUEEN-THEN-PHARAOH HATSHEPSUT: Land:
BLACK MAN WITH WATERMELON: HO!

(a bell sounds once)

PANEL III: THUH LONESOME 3SOME

(NOTE: * *indicates a glottal stop and choking sound*)

BLACK MAN WITH WATERMELON: It must have rained. Gaw.* Must-uh-rained-on-down-us-why. Aint that somethin. Must uh rained! Gaw. Our crops have prospered. Must uh rained why aint that somethin why aint that somethin-somethin gaw somethin: nice.

BLACK WOMAN WITH FRIED DRUMSTICK: Funny.

BLACK MAN WITH WATERMELON: Gaw. Callin on it spose we did: gaw — thuh uhrainin gaw huh? Gaw gaw. Lookie look-see gaw: where there were rivlets now there are some. Gaw. Cement tuh mudment accomplished with uh gaw uh flick of my wrist gaw. Huh. Look here now there is uh gaw uh wormlett. Came out tuhday. In my stools gaw gaw gaw gaw they all out tuhday. Come out tuh breathe gaw dontcha? Sure ya dontcha sure gaw ya dontcha sure ya dontcha do yall gaw. Gaw. Our one melon has given intuh 3. Callin what it gived birth callin it gaw. 3 August hams out uh my hands now surroundin me an is all of um mines? GAW. Uh huhn. Gaw gaw. Cant breathe.

BLACK WOMAN WITH FRIED DRUMSTICK: Funny how they break when I dropped em. Thought they was past that. Huh. 3 broke in uh row. Guess mmm on uh roll uh some sort, huh. Hell. Huh. Whiffit.

BLACK MAN WITH WATERMELON: Gaw. Gaw. Cant breathe.

BLACK WOMAN WITH FRIED DRUMSTICK: Some things still hold. Huh. Uh old layed eggull break after droppin most likely. Huh. 4 in uh row. Awe on that.

BLACK MAN WITH WATERMELON: Gaw. Cant breathe you.

BLACK WOMAN WITH FRIED DRUMSTICK: You dont need to. No need for breathin for you no more, huh? 5. 6. Mm making uh history. 7-hhh 8-hhh mm makin uh mess. Huh. Whiffit.

BLACK MAN WITH WATERMELON: Gaw. Gaw loosen my collar. No air in here.

BLACK WOMAN WITH FRIED DRUMSTICK: 7ssgot uh red dot. Awe on that.

BLACK MAN WITH WATERMELON: Sweetheart —. SWEETHEART?!

BLACK WOMAN WITH FRIED DRUMSTICK: 9. Chuh. Funny. Funny. Somethin still holdin on. Let me

loosen your collar for you you comed home after uh hard days work. Your suit: tied. Days work was runnin from them we know aint chase-ted you. You comed back home after uh hard days work such uh hard days work that now you cant breathe, you. Now.

BLACK MAN WITH WATERMELON: Dont take it off just loosen it. Dont move thuh tree branch let thuh tree branch be.

BLACK WOMAN WITH FRIED DRUMSTICK: Your days work aint like any others day work: you bring your tree branch home. Let me loosen thuh tie let me loosen thuh neck-lace let me loosen up thuh noose that stringed him up let me leave thuh tree branch be. Let me rub your wrists.

BLACK MAN WITH WATERMELON: Gaw. Gaw.

BLACK WOMAN WITH FRIED DRUMSTICK: Some things still hold. Wrung thuh necks of them hens and they still give eggs. Huh: Like you. Still sproutin feathers even after they fried. Huh: like you too. 10. Chuh. Eggs still break. Thuh mess makes uh stain. Thuh stain makes uh mark. Whiffit. Whiffit.

BLACK MAN WITH WATERMELON: Put me on uh platform tuh wait for uh train. Uh who who uh who who uh where ya gonna go now — . Platform hitched with horses/steeds. Steeds runned off in left me there swingin. It had begun tuh rain. Hands behind my back. This time tied. I had heard of uh word called scaffold and thought that perhaps they just might build me one of um but uh uhn naw just outa my vocabulary but uh uhn naw trees come cheaply.

BLACK WOMAN WITH FRIED DRUMSTICK: 8. 9. I aint hungry. 9. 10. You dont eat. Dont need to.

BLACK MAN WITH WATERMELON: Swingin from front tuh back uhgain. Back tuh — back tuh that was how I be wentin. Chin on my chest hangin down in restin eyes each on eyein my 2 feets. Left on thuh right one right one on thuh left. Crossed eyin. It was difficult tuh breathe. Toes uncrossin then crossin for luck. With my eyes. Gaw. It had begun tuh rain. Oh. Gaw. Ever so lightly. Blood came on up. you know: tough. Like riggamartins-stifly only — isolated. They some of em pointed they summoned uh laughed they some looked quick in an then they looked uhway. It had begun tuh rain. I hung on out tuh dry. They puttin uhway their picnic baskets. Ever so lightly gaw gaw it had begun tuh rain. They pullin out their umbrellas in hidedid up their eyes. Oh.

BLACK WOMAN WITH FRIED DRUMSTICK: I aint hungry you dont eat 12 13 and thuh floor will shine. Look: there we are. You in me. Reflectin. Hello! Dont move —

BLACK MAN WITH WATERMELON: It had begun tuh

rain. Now: huh. Sky flew open and thuh light went ZAP. Tree bowed over till thuh branch said BROKE. Uhround my necklace my neck uhround my neck my tree branch. In full bloom. It had begun tuh rain. Feet hit thuh ground in I started runnin. I was wet right through intuh through. I was uh wet that dont get dry. Draggin on my tree branch on back tuh home.

BLACK WOMAN WITH FRIED DRUMSTICK: On back tuh that.

BLACK MAN WITH WATERMELON: Gaw. What was that?

BLACK WOMAN WITH FRIED DRUMSTICK: "On back tuh that?" Huh. Somethin I figured. Huh. Chuh. Lord. Who! Whiffit.

BLACK MAN WITH WATERMELON: When I dieded they cut me down. Didnt have no need for me no more. They let me go.

BLACK WOMAN WITH FRIED DRUMSTICK: Thuh lights dimmed in thats what saved you. Lightnin comed down zappin trees from thuh sky. You got uhway.

BLACK MAN WITH WATERMELON: Not exactly.

BLACK WOMAN WITH FRIED DRUMSTICK: Oh. I see.

BLACK MAN WITH WATERMELON: They tired of me. Pulled me out of thuh trees then treed me then tired of me. Thats how it has gone. Thats how it be wentin.

BLACK WOMAN WITH FRIED DRUMSTICK: Oh. I see. Youve been dismissed. But-where-to? Must be somewhere else tuh go aside from just go gone. Huh. Whiffit: huh. You smell.

BLACK MAN WITH WATERMELON: Maybe I should bathe.

BLACK WOMAN WITH FRIED DRUMSTICK: I call those 3 thuh lonesome 3some. Maybe we should pray.

BLACK MAN WITH WATERMELON: Thuh lonesome 3some. Spose theyll do.

(*a bell sounds twice*)

PANEL IV: SECOND CHORUS

OLD MAN RIVER JORDAN: Come in look tuh look-see.

VOICE ON THUH TEE V: Good evening this is thuh news. A small sliver of uh tree branch has been found in *The Death of the Last Black Man*. Upon careful examination thuh small sliver of thuh treed branch what was found has been found tuh be uh fosilized bone fragment. With this finding authorities claim they are hot on his tail.

PRUNES AND PRISMS: Uh small sliver of uh treed branch growed from-tuh uh bone.

AND BIGGER AND BIGGER AND BIGGER: WILL SOME-BODY WILL THIS ROPE FROM ROUND MY NECK GOD DAMN I WOULD LIKE TUH TAKE MY BREATH BY RIGHTS GAW GAW.

LOTS OF GREASE AND LOTS OF PORK: This is the death of the last black man in the whole entire world.

(*a bell sounds slowly twice*)

BLACK MAN WITH WATERMELON: I had heard of uh word called scaffold and had hopes they just might maybe build me one by uh uh naw gaw —

HAM: There was uh tree with your name on it.

BLACK MAN WITH WATERMELON: Jumpin out of uh tree they chase me tree me back tuh thuh tree. Thats where I be came from. Thats where I be wentin.

YES AND GREENS BLACK-EYED PEAS CORNBREAD: Someone ought tuh. Write that down.

LOTS OF GREASE AND LOTS OF PORK: There is a page dog eared at "Histree" hidin just outside my word hoard. Wheres he gonna come to now that he done gone from.

QUEEN-THEN-PHARAOH HATSHEPSUT: Wheres he gonna go come to now that he gonna go gone on?

OLD MAN RIVER JORDAN: For that you must ask Ham.

BLACK WOMAN WITH FRIED DRUMSTICK: Hen?

LOTS OF GREASE AND LOTS OF PORK: HAM.

QUEEN-THEN-PHARAOH HATSHEPSUT: Ham.

PRUNES AND PRISMS: Hmmmm.

(*a bell sounds twice*)

HAM: Ham's Begotten Tree (catchin up to um *in media res* that is we takin off from where we stopped up last time). Huh. NOW: She goned begotten One who in turn begotten Ours. Ours laughed one day uhloud in from thuh sound hittin thuh air smakity sprung up I, you, n He, She, It. They turned in engaged in simple multiplication thus tuh spawn of theirselves one We one You and one called They (They in certain conversation known as "Them" and in other certain conversation a.k.a. "Us"). Now very simply: Wassername she finally gave in-tuh It and tugether they broughted forth uh wildish one called simply Yo. Yo gone be wentin much too long without hisself uh comb in from thuh frizzly that resulted comed one called You (polite form). You (polite) birthed herself Mister, Miss, Maam and Sir who in his later years with That brought forth Yuh Fathuh. Thuh fact that That was uh mother tuh Yuh Fathuh didnt stop them 2 relations from havin relations. Those strange relations between That thuh mother and Yuh Fathuh thuh son brought forth uh odd lot: called: Yes Massuh, Yes Missy, Yes Maam n Yes Suh Mistuh Suh which goes tuh show that relations with your relations produces complications. Thuh children of That and Yuh Fathuh aside from being plain peculiar was all cross-eyed. This defect enhanced their multiplicative possibilities, for example. Yes Suh Mistuh Suh breeded with hisself n gived us Wassername (thuh 2nd), and Wassernickname (2 twins in birth joindid at thuh lip). Thuh 2 twins lived next door tuh one called Uhnother bringin forth Themuhns, She (thuh 2nd) Auntie, Cousin, and Bro who makeshifted continuous compensations for his loud and odiforous bodily emissions by all thuh time saying excuse me n through his graciousness brought forth They (polite) who had mixed feelins with She (thuh 2nd) thus bringin forth Ussin who then went on tuh have MeMines.

YES AND GREENS BLACK-EYED PEAS CORNBREAD: Thuh list goes on in on.

HAM: MeMines gived out 2 offspring one she called Mines after herself thuh uther she called Themuhns named after all them who comed before. Themuhns married outside thuh tribe joinin herself with uh man they called WhoDat. Themuhns n WhoDat brough forth only one child called WhoDatDere. Mines joined up with Wasshisname and from that union come AllYall.

BEFORE COLUMBUS: All us?

HAM: No. AllYall.

LOTS OF GREASE AND LOTS OF PORK: This list goes on in on.

HAM: Ah yes: Yo suddenly if by majic again became productive in after uh lapse of some great time came back intuh circulation to wiggled uhbout with Yes Missy (one of thuh cross-eyed daughters of That and Yuh Fathuh). Yo in Yes Missy begottin ThissunRightHere, Us, ThatOne, She (thuh 3rd) and one called Uncle (who from birth was gifted with great singin and dancin capabilities which helped him make his way in life but tended tuh bring shame on his family).

BEFORE COLUMBUS/BLACK MAN WITH WATERMELON: Shame on his family.

LOTS OF GREASE/BLACK MAN WITH WATERMELON: Shame on his family.

AND BIGGER AND BIGGER/BLACK MAN WITH WATERMELON: Shamed on his family gaw.

YES AND GREENS BLACK-EYED PEAS CORNBREAD: Write that down.

OLD MAN RIVER JORDAN: (Ham seed his daddy Noah neckked. From that seed, comed AllYall.)

(*a bell sounds twice*)

AND BIGGER AND BIGGER AND BIGGER: (Will somebody please will this rope —)

VOICE ON THUH TEE V: Good evening. This is thuh news: Whose fault is it?

BLACK MAN WITH WATERMELON: Saint mines.

VOICE ON THUH TEE V: Whose fault iszit??!

CHORUS: Saint mines!

OLD MAN RIVER JORDAN: I cant re-member back that far. (Ham can — but uh uh naw gaw — Ham wuduhnt there, huh.)

CHORUS: HAM BONE HAM BONE WHERE YOU BEEN ROUN THUH WORL N BACK A-GAIN.

QUEEN-THEN-PHARAOH HATSHEPSUT: Whatcha seen. Hambone girl?

BLACK WOMAN WITH FRIED DRUMSTICK: Didnt see you. I saw thuh worl.

HAM: I was there.

PRUNES AND PRISMS: Didnt see you.

HAM: I WAS THERE.

VOICE ON THUH TEE V: Didnt see you.

BLACK MAN WITH WATERMELON/AND BIGGER: THUH BLACK MAN. HE MOOOVE.

CHORUS: HAM BONE HAM BONE WHATCHA DO? GOT UH CHANCE N FAIRLY FLEW.

BLACK WOMAN WITH FRIED DRUMSTICK: Over thuh front yard.

BLACK MAN WITH WATERMELON: Overshot.

CHORUS: 6 BY 6 BY 6.

BLACK MAN WITH WATERMELON: Thats right.

AND BIGGER AND BIGGER AND BIGGER: WILL SOMEBODY WILL THIS ROPE —

CHORUS: Good evening. This is the news.

VOICE ON THUH TEE V: Whose fault is it?

ALL: Saint mines!

VOICE ON THUH TEE V: Whose fault iszit?

HAM: SAINT MINES!

(*a bell rings twice*)

—. Ham. Is. Not. Tuh. BLAME! WhoDatDere joinded with one called Sir 9th generation of thuh first Sir son of You (polite) thuh first daughter of You WhoDatDere with thuh 9th Sir begettin forth him —

BLACK MAN WITH WATERMELON: Ham?!

ALL (*except Ham*): HIM!

BLACK WOMAN WITH FRIED DRUMSTICK: sold.

HAM: SOLD! allyall[9°] not tuh be confused w/allus[12] joined w/allthem[3] in from that union comed forth wasshisname[21] SOLD wassername[19] still by thuh reputation uh thistree one uh thuh 2 twins loses her sight through fiddlin n falls w/ugly old yuhfathuh[4] given she[8] SOLD whodat[33] pairs w/you[23] (still polite) of which nothinmuch comes nothinmuch now nothinmuch[6] pairs with yessuhmistuhsuh[17] tuh drop one called yo now yo[9-0] still who gone be wentin now w/elle gived us el

---

[9]: The numbers in Ham's speech are chanted by several actors together as if they were auction prices or verses of the Bible.

RIGHT: Panel IV: Black Woman with Fried Drumstick, Before Columbus (Leo V. Finnie III), And Bigger and Bigger and Bigger (top), Ham (Reg E. Cathey) (center), Black Man with Watermelon (bottom), Yes and Greens Black-Eyed Peas Cornbread, and Lots of Grease and Lots of Pork (Darryl Theirse). MIDDLE RIGHT: Final Chorus: Queen-then-Pharaoh Hatshepsut (Pamala Tyson). FAR RIGHT: Final Chorus: Black Woman with Fried Drumstick.

SOLD let us not forget ye[1-2-5] w/ thee[3] givin us thou[9-2] who w/thuh they who switches their designation in certain conversation yes they[10] broughted forth onemore[2] at thuh same time in thuh same row right next door we have datone[12] w/ disone[14] droppin off duhutherone[2-2] SOLD let us not forget du and sie let us not forget yesssuhmassuhsuh[38] w/thou[8] who gived up memines[3-0] SOLD we are now rollin through thuh long division gimmie uh gimmie uh gimmie uh squared off route round it off round it off n round it out w/sistuh[4-3] who lives with one called saintmines[9] givin forth one uh year how it got there callin it jessgrew callin it saintmines callin it whatdat whatdat whatdat SOLD.

BLACK MAN WITH WATERMELON: Thuh list goes on and on. Dont it.

CHORUS: Ham Bone Ham Bone Ham Bone Ham Bone

BEFORE COLUMBUS: Left right left right.

QUEEN-THEN-PHARAOH HATSHEPSUT: Left left left whose left . . . ?

(a bell sounds twice)

LOTS OF GREASE AND LOTS OF PORK: This is the death of the last black man in the whole entire world.

PANEL V: IN THUH GARDEN OF HOODOO IT

BLACK WOMAN WITH FRIED DRUMSTICK: Somethins turnin. Huh. Whatizit. — Mercy. Mercy. Huh. Chew on this. Ssuh feather. Sswhatchashud be eatin now ya no. Ssuhfeather: stuffin. Chew on it. Huh. Feathers sprouted from thuh fried hens — dont ask me how. Somethins out uh whack. Somethins out uh rights. Your arms still on your elbows. I'm still here. Whensit gonna end. Soon. Huh. Mercy. Thuh Tree. Springtime. And harvest. Huh. Somethins turnin. So many melons. Huh. From one tuh 3 tuh many. Must be nature. Gnaw on this. Gnaw on this, huh? Gnaw on this awe on that.

BLACK MAN WITH WATERMELON: Aint eatable.

BLACK WOMAN WITH FRIED DRUMSTICK: I know.

BLACK MAN WITH WATERMELON: Aint eatable aint it. Nope. Nope.

BLACK WOMAN WITH FRIED DRUMSTICK: Somethins turnin. Huh. Whatizit.

BLACK MAN WITH WATERMELON: Aint eatable so I out in out ought not aint be eatin it aint that right. Yep. Nope. Yep. Uh huhn.

BLACK WOMAN WITH FRIED DRUMSTICK: Huh. Whatizit.

BLACK MAN WITH WATERMELON: I remember what I like. I remember what my likes tuh eat when I be in thuh eatin mode.

BLACK WOMAN WITH FRIED DRUMSTICK: Chew on this.

BLACK MAN WITH WATERMELON: When I be in thuh eatin mode.

BLACK WOMAN WITH FRIED DRUMSTICK: Swallow it down. I know. Gimmie your pit. Needs bathin.

BLACK MAN WITH WATERMELON: Choice between peas and corns — my feets —. Choice: peas. Choice between peas and greens choice: greens. Choice between greens and potatoes choice: potatoes. Yams. Boiled or mashed choice: mashed. Aaah. Mmm. My likenesses.

BLACK WOMAN WITH FRIED DRUMSTICK: Mercy. Turns —

BLACK MAN WITH WATERMELON: My likenesses! My feets! Aaah! SWEET-HEART. Aaah! SPRING-TIME!

BLACK WOMAN WITH FRIED DRUMSTICK: Spring-time.

BLACK MAN WITH WATERMELON: SPRING-TIME!

BLACK WOMAN WITH FRIED DRUMSTICK: Mercy. Turns —

BLACK MAN WITH WATERMELON: I remembers what I likes. I remembers what I likes tuh eat when I bein in had been in thuh eatin mode. Bein in had been: now in then. I be eatin hen. Hen.

BLACK WOMAN WITH FRIED DRUMSTICK: Huh?

BLACK MAN WITH WATERMELON: HEN!

BLACK WOMAN WITH FRIED DRUMSTICK: Hen?

BLACK MAN WITH WATERMELON: Hen. Huh. My meals. Aaaah: my meals. BRACH-A-LEE.

BLACK WOMAN WITH FRIED DRUMSTICK: Whatizit. Huh. — GNAW ON THIS! Good. Uhther pit?

BLACK MAN WITH WATERMELON: We sittin on this porch right now aint we. Uh huhn. Aaah. Yes. Sittin right here right now on it in it ainthuh first time either iduhnt it. Yep. Nope. Once we was here once wuhduhnt we. Yep. Yep. Once we being here. Uh huhn. Huh. There is uh Now and there is uh Then. Ssall there is. (I bein in uh Now: uh Now bein in uh Then; I bein, in Now in Then, in I will be. I was be too but that uh Then thats past. That me that was be is uh me-has-been. Thuh Then that was be is uh has-been-Then too. Thuh me-has-been sits in thuh be-me: we sit on this porch. Same porch. Same me. Thuh Then that been somehow sits in thuh Then that will be: same Thens. I swing from uh tree. You cut me down and bring me back. Home. Here. I fly over thuh yard. I fly over thuh yard in all over. Them thens stays fixed. Fixed Thens. Thuh Thems stays fixed too. Thuh Thems that come and take me and thuh Thems that greet me and then them Thems that send me back here. Home. Stays fixed. Them do.)

BLACK WOMAN WITH FRIED DRUMSTICK: Your feets.

BLACK MAN WITH WATERMELON: I: be. You: is. It: be. He, She: thats us. (Thats it.) We: thats he in she: you aroun me: us be here. You: still is. They:

be. Melon. Melon. Melon: mines. I remember all my lookuhlikes. You. You. Remember me.

BLACK WOMAN WITH FRIED DRUMSTICK: Gnaw on this then swallow it down. Youll have your fill then we'll put you in your suit coat.

BLACK MAN WITH WATERMELON: Thuh suit coat I picked out? Thuh stripely one? HA! Peas. Choice: BRACH-A-LEE.

BLACK WOMAN WITH FRIED DRUMSTICK: Chew and swallow please.

BLACK MAN WITH WATERMELON: Thuh stripely one with thuh fancy patch pockets!

BLACK WOMAN WITH FRIED DRUMSTICK: Sweetheart.

BLACK MAN WITH WATERMELON: SPRING-TIME.

BLACK WOMAN WITH FRIED DRUMSTICK: Sweetheart.

BLACK MAN WITH WATERMELON: SPRING-TIME.

BLACK WOMAN WITH FRIED DRUMSTICK: This could go on forever.

BLACK MAN WITH WATERMELON: Lets. Hope. Not.

BLACK WOMAN WITH FRIED DRUMSTICK: — Sweetheart.

BLACK MAN WITH WATERMELON: SPRING-TIME.

BLACK WOMAN WITH FRIED DRUMSTICK: Sweetheart.

BLACK MAN WITH WATERMELON: SPRING-TIME.

BLACK WOMAN WITH FRIED DRUMSTICK: This could go on forever.

BLACK MAN WITH WATERMELON: Lets. Hope. Not.

BLACK WOMAN WITH FRIED DRUMSTICK: Must be somewhere else tuh go aside from just go gone.

BLACK MAN WITH WATERMELON: 6 by 6 by 6.

BLACK WOMAN WITH FRIED DRUMSTICK: Thats right.

BLACK MAN WITH WATERMELON: Rock reads "HooDoo."

BLACK WOMAN WITH FRIED DRUMSTICK: Now you know. Know now dontcha. Somethins turnin —.

BLACK MAN WITH WATERMELON: Who do? Them do. Aint that nice. Huh. Miss me. Remember me. Missmemissmewhatsmyname.

BLACK WOMAN WITH FRIED DRUMSTICK: Aaaaaah?

BLACK MAN WITH WATERMELON: Remember me. AAAH.

BLACK WOMAN WITH FRIED DRUMSTICK: Thats it. Open wide. Here it comes. Stuffin.

BLACK MAN WITH WATERMELON: Yeeeech.

BLACK WOMAN WITH FRIED DRUMSTICK: Eat uhnother. Hear. I eat one. You eat one more.

BLACK MAN WITH WATERMELON: Stuffed. Time tuh go.

BLACK WOMAN WITH FRIED DRUMSTICK: Not yet!

BLACK MAN WITH WATERMELON: I got uhway?

BLACK WOMAN WITH FRIED DRUMSTICK: Huh?

BLACK MAN WITH WATERMELON: I got uhway?

BLACK WOMAN WITH FRIED DRUMSTICK: Nope. Yep. Nope. Nope.

BLACK MAN WITH WATERMELON: Miss me.

BLACK WOMAN WITH FRIED DRUMSTICK: Miss me.

BLACK MAN WITH WATERMELON: Re-member me.

BLACK WOMAN WITH FRIED DRUMSTICK: Re-member me.

BLACK MAN WITH WATERMELON: My hands are on my wrists. Arms on elbows. Looks: old fashioned. Nothin fancy there. Toes curl up not down. My feets-now clean. Still got all my teeth. Re-member me.

BLACK WOMAN WITH FRIED DRUMSTICK: Re-member me.

BLACK MAN WITH WATERMELON: Call on me sometime.

BLACK WOMAN WITH FRIED DRUMSTICK: Call on me sometime. Hear? Hear? Thuh dirt itself turns itself. So many melons. From one tuh 3 tuh many. Look at um all. Ssuh garden. Awe on that. Winter processin back tuh back with spring-time. They roll on by us that way. Uh whole line gone roun. Chuh. Thuh worl be roun. Moves that way so they say. You comed back. Yep. Nope. Well. Well. Build uh well.

(a bell sounds twice)

FINAL CHORUS

ALL: "YES. OH, ME? CHUH, NO —"

VOICE ON THUH TEE V: Good morning. This is thuh news:

BLACK WOMAN WITH FRIED DRUMSTICK: Somethins turnin. Thuh page.

(a bell sounds twice)

LOTS OF GREASE AND LOTS OF PORK: This is the death of the last black man in the whole entire worl

PRUNES AND PRISMS: 19.

OLD MAN RIVER JORDAN: Uh blank page turnin with thuh sound of it. Thuh sound of movin hands.

BLACK WOMAN WITH FRIED DRUMSTICK: Yesterday to-day next summer tomorrow just uh moment uhgoh in 1317 diedid thuh last black man in thuh whole entire world. Uh! Oh. Dont be uhlarmed. Do not be afeared. It was painless. Uh painless passin. He falls twenty-three floors to his death.

CHORUS: yes.

BLACK WOMAN WITH FRIED DRUMSTICK: 23 floors from uh passin ship from space tuh splat on thuh pavement.

CHORUS: yes.

BLACK WOMAN WITH FRIED DRUMSTICK: He have uh head he been keepin under thuh Tee V.

CHORUS: yes.

BLACK WOMAN WITH FRIED DRUMSTICK: On his bottom pantry shelf.

CHORUS: yes.

BLACK WOMAN WITH FRIED DRUMSTICK: He have uh head that hurts. Dont fit right. Put it on tuh go tuh thuh store in it pinched him when he walks his thoughts dont got room. He diediduh he did, huh.

CHORUS: yes.

BLACK WOMAN WITH FRIED DRUMSTICK: Where he gonna go now now now now now that he done diediduh?

CHORUS: yes.

BLACK WOMAN WITH FRIED DRUMSTICK: Where he gonna go tuh. WASH.

PRUNES AND PRISMS: Somethins turnin. Thuh page.

AND BIGGER AND BIGGER AND BIGGER: Somethins burnin. Thuh tongue.

BLACK MAN WITH WATERMELON: Thuh tongue itself burns.

OLD MAN RIVER JORDAN: He jumps in thuh river. These words for partin.

YES AND GREENS BLACK-EYED PEAS CORNBREAD: And you will write them down.

(a bell sounds 3 times)

BEFORE COLUMBUS: All these boats passed by my coast.

PRUNES AND PRISMS: Somethins turnin. Thuh page.

QUEEN-THEN-PHARAOH HATSHEPSUT: I saw Columbus comin / I saw Columbus comin goin —

QUEEN-THEN-PHARAOH HATSHEPSUT/BEFORE COLUMBUS: Left left left whose left ... ?

AND BIGGER AND BIGGER/BLACK MAN WITH WATERMELON: Somethins turnin. Thuh page.

BEFORE COLUMBUS: All those boats passed by me. My coast fell in-to-the-sea. All thuh boats. They stopped for me.

OLD MAN RIVER JORDAN: Land: HO!

QUEEN-THEN-PHARAOH HATSHEPSUT: I waved my hands in warnin. You waved back.

BLACK WOMAN WITH FRIED DRUMSTICK: Somethins burnin. Thuh page.

QUEEN-THEN-PHARAOH HATSHEPSUT: I have-not seen you since.

ALL: oh!

LOTS OF GREASE AND LOTS OF PORK: This is the death of the last black man in the whole entire worl

OLD MAN RIVER JORDAN: Do in diddley dip die-die thuh drop. Do drop be dripted? Why, of course.

AND BIGGER AND BIGGER AND BIGGER: Somethins burnin. Thuh tongue.

BLACK MAN WITH WATERMELON: The tongue itself burns itself.

HAM: ... And from that seed comed All Us.

BLACK WOMAN WITH FRIED DRUMSTICK: Thuh page.
ALL: 6 BY 6 BY 6.
BLACK WOMAN WITH FRIED DRUMSTICK: Thats right.

(*a bell sounds twice*)

BEFORE COLUMBUS: LAND: HO!
YES AND GREENS BLACK-EYED PEAS CORNBREAD: You will write it down because if you dont write it down then we will come along and tell the future that we did not exist. You will write it down and you will carve it out of a rock.

(*pause*)

You will write down thuh past and you will write down thuh present and in what in thuh future. You will write it down.

(*pause*)

It will be of us but you will mention them from time to time so that in the future when they come along theyll know how they exist.

(*pause*)

It will be for us but you will mention them from time to time so that in the future when they come along theyll know why they exist.

(*pause*)

You will carve it all out of a rock so that in the future when they come along we will know that the rock did yes exist.
BLACK WOMAN WITH FRIED DRUMSTICK: Down down down down down down down down —
LOTS OF GREASE AND LOTS OF PORK: This is the death of the last black man in the whole entire worl
PRUNES AND PRISMS: Somethins turnin. Thuh page.
OLD MAN RIVER JORDAN: Thuh last news of thuh last man:
VOICE ON THUH TEE V: Good mornin. This is thuh last news:
BLACK MAN WITH WATERMELON: Miss me.
BLACK WOMAN WITH FRIED DRUMSTICK: Miss me.
BLACK MAN WITH WATERMELON: Re-member me.
BLACK WOMAN WITH FRIED DRUMSTICK: Re-member me. Call on me sometime. Call on me sometime. Hear? Hear?
HAM: In thuh future when they came along I meeting them. On thuh coast. Uuuuhh! My coast! I — was — so — po-lite! But. In thuh rock. I wrote: ha ha ha.
ALL: Ha. Ha. Ha. Ha. Ha. Ha. Ha. Ha. Ha. Ha. Ha. Ha. Ha. Ha. HHHHHHHHHHHH. HA!
BLACK WOMAN WITH FRIED DRUMSTICK: Thuh black man he move. He move. He hans.

(*a bell sounds once*)

ALL: Hold it. Hold it. Hold it. Hold it. Hold it. Hold it. Hold it.

COMMENTARIES

The following interviews with Suzan-Lori Parks and Liz Diamond resulted from a meeting following the Yale production of *The Last Black Man* in February 1992. After discussing the play in production, I asked the author and director to respond to a number of questions that would give them a chance to explore issues of interest to those who would read the play but probably not see it in production. I gave them the questions to consider at home, and they returned their responses. Both interviews give us insight into the issues of space and time and of theme and style in this play and into the opportunities available to playwright and director when approaching a fresh script in a style that is innovative and exciting.

Lee A. Jacobus (b. 1935)
INTERVIEW WITH SUZAN-LORI PARKS   *1992*

Jacobus: Your play takes a long view of history and in a way has a profound narrative scope. But the play also avoids the beginning-middle-end approach to storytelling. How would you describe your approach to narrative structure — particularly in relation to time — in *The Death of the Last Black Man in the Whole Entire World*?

Parks: I start with "knowns" and I get to thinking — not merely sitting at my desk and scratching my head — but I get to listening, I get to watching, hearing, seeing. If time is more curved than flat, then a plot line of a play can be more curved. Then we can refigure "plot." Things may happen over and over again with slight changes. Words may come back to us again and again. Jazz musicians have been doing this for years. They call it "repetition and revision."

Jacobus: You describe the sections of your play as "Panels" and "Choruses." What do these terms mean to you and what should they mean to your audience?

Parks: "Panels" and "Choruses" are two different words that I use to denote two different kinds of experience or attack. In a Panel there are only the two of them, the Black Man with Watermelon and the Black Woman with Fried Drumstick; during the Panels we see them at various points of confusion — which are the same points of confusion over and over again refigured with different variables. The idea of this comes partly from the Stations of the Cross — the tableaux of Christ which hang in churches. The Choruses are the spaces between those tableaux — if you've seen those Stations hanging in a church you know that between them hangs — nothing. A blank space. So the Choruses are figuring the blank space between. That's why the Choruses are so weird. They're coming out of that blank, unspoken, unfigured space and all eleven figures are onstage.

There are Greek choruses. There are choruses in pop songs. Unlike the choruses in most songs, however, my Choruses work differently. Think of a well-known song — "America the Beautiful" for example. The verses contain the information or meat, the choruses the fun, the fat, the gravy. The power of the chorus comes not from the presentation of new information but from its repeating. In *Last Black Man* this is what I'm exploring with certain speeches such as the "Yesterday today next summer tomorrow . . ." speech or the "You should write that down . . ." line. In terms of the Panels and Choruses, where you'd expect the Chorus to simply repeat, Liz [Diamond, the director] discovered early in rehearsal that it is in the Panels where actions are repeated (the Black Man comes back; he is dead; the Black Woman must manage; she is alive), and the Choruses were where the really new information is presented, where the action really happens. With *Last Black Man* I'm using elements of traditional song structure and inverting, subverting, converting those elements.

Jacobus: Your figures have some interesting names, such as Lots of Grease and Lots of Pork. Could you tell us how you visualized some of them onstage?

Parks: I saw them as human — I didn't imagine that Lots of Grease and Lots of Pork would go through the play dressed up as a pork chop — that *would* be avant-garde, wouldn't it? The most important thing about the figures is that they are *figures* and not *characters*. They are *signs* of something and not people just like people we know. *Figures* help to cue the shape of the play. This is epic theater. This is a play where one stands for a thousand. Epic is a state of existence which, I think, comes very naturally out of the day-to-day African American existence — we're a people who are often honored or damned because of the actions of one of our group. One of us stands for all of us. Those are epic stakes.

Also important is where these figures come from: Prunes and Prisms comes from a line in Joyce's *Ulysses*; And Bigger and Bigger and Bigger spins out of Wright's *Native Son*; Ham is the biblical Ham; Queen-then-Pharaoh Hatshepsut really was once.

So. The figures aren't real people but they're voices briefly embodied — embodied for the duration of the play. Part of Liz's preset [the stage setting before the play begins] was an audio track of the figures whispering their names. Those whispers helped create the feeling of *Last Black Man* as a visitation.

Jacobus: You've got a new play in production and you have been very productive in the last several years. What are the sources of your inspiration as a playwright? What directions do you feel yourself heading in?

Parks: What inspires? *Inspirare:* to breathe. What keeps me breathing? What keeps me going? I have good friends. Good friends who read my work and encourage me. Working with Liz Diamond is always a joy — we've done five shows together now and we both keep getting better. What else? I listen to music: Ornette Coleman, Sarah Vaughan, Bach, Wagner, Dionne Warwick. I do karate. Read read read all the time. I work hard. I play with words. Spelling casts a spell. I think the world is telling us. Telling us telling us something that is present but not written down. As a child I wanted to be a geologist. Writing is like digging. So in this play they write it down and they lower him down. Into the ground. I have often thought that I could read the shape of my whole life through this play. So where am I heading? Well. I've done about ten plays now. I finished writing this play in 1990. I've written three more since then. None of the new plays are like this one. So much for predictable trajectory. In all of my work I'm concerned with space and time and the phenomenon of moving through them. Hopefully I'll write more. Hopefully stay sharp. *Awake.* Looking at this play — it's such an extravaganza, such a pageant — you'd figure the writer's next work would be maybe an opera. Yep. She would either write an opera or move to Las Vegas.

Lee A. Jacobus (b. 1935)
INTERVIEW WITH LIZ DIAMOND   1992

Jacobus: Some people have commented on the fact that Suzan-Lori Parks provided no stage directions for *The Last Black Man in the Whole Entire World.* What were the problems — and the opportunities — that resulted from her decision?

Diamond: It is somewhat misleading to say that Suzan-Lori wrote no stage directions. In a conventional sense it is true that the director will not find acres of parenthetical notes describing the stage setting and stage action as envisioned by the playwright. Nevertheless, a close reading of the text reveals that Suzan-Lori has some very specific ideas about how the dramatic action of the text should be played. "In thuh Garden of HooDoo It," Panel V of the play, begins with a speech by Black Woman with Fried Drumstick, who observes:

> Somethins turnin. Huh. Whatizit. — Mercy. Mercy. Huh. Chew on this. Ssuh feather. Sswhatchashud be eatin now ya no. Ssuhfeather: stuffin. Chew on it. Huh. Feathers sprouted from thuh fried hens — dont ask me how. Somethins out uh whack. Somethins out uh rights. Your arms still on your elbows. I'm still here. Whensit gonna end. Soon. Huh. Mercy. Thuh Tree. Springtime. And harvest. Huh. Somethins turnin. So many melons. Huh. From one tuh 3 tuh many. Must be nature. Gnaw on this. Gnaw on this, huh? Gnaw on this awe on that.

At the top of the speech Black Woman senses that something is different . . . the atmosphere, the emotional temperature of the play has changed. She senses it has something to do with mercy. Has it been bestowed? Does she sense a new atmosphere of forgiveness is in the air? She gives up trying to articulate what she senses for the moment with a "huh." And then moves on to the task at hand, which is, quite simply, to feed her beloved Black Man feathers which have mysteriously appeared. She must stuff him. Now, a director may or may not feel obliged to follow the stage direction that, I would argue, is quite explicitly embedded in the text. Nevertheless, it is there, and, I think, well worth exploring in rehearsal. In our production at the Yale Repertory Theatre, we did in fact have the Black Woman gently feed the Black Man feathers, then bathe him, in preparation for his final burial. These simple activities, in the context of the larger dramatic action of the text — to tell the Black Man's story and then to lay him to rest — achieved a metaphorical resonance that reinforced the text itself.

There is no doubt that I enjoyed and exercised a great deal of creative control over the visual and aural landscape of *The Death of the Last Black Man* by virtue of the fact that Suzan-Lori chose not to dictate details of set, costume, lighting, and sound. But the major design decisions I made — for example, to set the play in a highly ceremonial, ecclesiastical setting, a sort of surreal cathedral/burial ground, with a treelike pulpit and a huge black sarcophagus at the center that served as both coffin and altar, scaffold and auction block — all grew out of my reading of the play. I saw *Last Black Man* as a highly ritualized and presentational mourning and celebration of the death of the last black man in the whole entire world. Another director may well come along whose reading makes entirely different visual demands.

I do not believe that one reading is as good as another; a director's reading of the play not only must be internally coherent but must serve to open up the text to the spectator's understanding. The importance — or possibility — of honoring authorial intention in a stage production is a thorny issue better left to the critics. But a close reading of the text, a passionate hunt for every visual, aural clue the text has to offer — from its layout on the page, to punctuation (or lack of it), to scene titles, to spelling, to character names — all of this must be sharply observed for clues as to rhythm, tempo, and potential meaning.

Jacobus: One of your jobs as director was to help audiences see that the figures who appeared onstage to the Black Man and Black Woman were spirits. How did you solve the problem?

Diamond: Of course, one might first ask: Are those "figures," as they are called in the text, spirits? It doesn't explicitly state anywhere that Queen-then-Pharaoh Hatshepsut, Ham, etc. are any less real than the Black Man or Black Woman. But an offhand remark made by Suzan-Lori during one of our script conferences — "By the way, you could say that the only living human being onstage is the Black Woman. Everyone else is dead, some more than others, but dead" — suggested that something might be called for to help the audience discover that there is indeed a hierarchy of the dead in this play, moving in descending order from the biblical Ham, who "died" thousands of years ago, to the Voice on thuh Tee V, who perhaps died yesterday. But visually insisting on ghosts can get a bit silly in a play as stylistically unbound by the conventions of naturalism as is *The Death of the Last Black Man in the Whole Entire World.* So we decided (the costume designer, Caryn Neman, and myself) on "celestial" versions of each figure's own earthly dress. We put them all in what we called high church drag — the gold and glitter of the ultimate high mass, but kept each figure's costume pieces specific to the historic period or social role implied by their title. Thus Yes and Greens Black-Eyed Peas Cornbread wore the rags and pigtails of the pickaninny to be found in the racist cartoons and caricatures of the slave period but glowed with the gold and the glitter of the Promised Land. In contrast, the Black Woman wore a quite conventional black dress, the sort of garment any widow might wear to her husband's funeral.

Jacobus: Could you talk about your collaboration with Suzan-Lori in directing this play? Is it more or less difficult for the director when the playwright is in rehearsal?

Diamond: One of the many reasons Suzan-Lori and I love collaborating on a production is that we don't mess around in each other's business. She writes the play; I direct it. At the same time, we talk constantly. Before rehearsals begin, we read the play aloud together, with Suzan-Lori pointing out specific rhythmic requirements as they come up. She helps me decode the many and rich historic and fictional references woven into the text. She suggests books to read, artworks to examine, music to listen to. I try to avoid asking what a passage means, because I prefer to make those discoveries myself. I share with her my initial impressions, early hints as to where it all might take place, and obsessions begin to emerge as I read the play over and over. I listen carefully to her responses and to her elaborations on ideas I propose for setting, sound, action, etc. We cast the play together and I keep her abreast of the evolving design decisions. She attends the first read-through of the play. And then she does an amazing thing: She leaves us alone until the first run-through, which may be two or three weeks later. I consider the space she gives me and the actors — to make our own discoveries — an incredible gift, a little scary, and very smart. She understands our need to ask whatever comes into our heads, to try out all kinds of crazy solutions, and that it will be easier on everyone if the playwright is absent. By the time she comes back, of course, there is something reasonably coherent for her to respond to. She and I are likely to be in close touch by phone throughout the process, with me proposing textual changes as they come up in rehearsal, and with Suzan-Lori helping me untangle whatever staging knots I may be struggling with. It should be clear that what I am describing is an ongoing dialogue, one that thrives, I think, because we trust each other's judgment and taste, because we have so much fun tossing ideas back and forth and because we both get such a huge kick out of sitting in the back of the theater watching this *thing* we've created actually come to life.

Having a playwright come to rehearsal, in particular to that first run-through, is, of course, a terrifying moment for everyone. The writer is wondering: Will this play hold up? The director is wondering: Will this staging hold up? The actor is wondering: Am I about to be fired? But this atmosphere of near total paranoia is broken with the uttering of the first line of text, as private anxieties give way to this immense, collective rooting for the play to fly. The joy of working with Suzan-Lori is that when it's over, we collectively celebrate what works and collectively get to work on what doesn't. It is usually abundantly clear where the problems are, if not how to solve them, and very little ego gets in the way of just diving in and fixing them.

Alisa Solomon
LANGUAGE IN *LAST BLACK MAN*   *1990*

Alisa Solomon focuses on Suzan-Lori Parks's use of language, particularly repetition. She also focuses on influences from jazz, which also depends on choruses, verses, and refrains of the kind Parks has written. The connection between American jazz and African ritual is one of Parks's most important inspirations.

Parks's plays look like long, dialogic poems. There are no stage directions and little in the way of moorings for the unsuspecting director. But, Parks insists, movement is contained in the speech itself. Often leaving out punctuation that would delineate formal pauses, she lets words run together to find their own rhythms. And with a nod to Zora Neale Hurston's seamless welding of the "folkloric" and the "literary," Parks makes music of everyday usage. Even the way a word is spelled can imply stage action: "Thuh," she says, slumping, "makes the body do something very different" — and here she straightens up — "than 'The.'"

What's more, for African-Americans, the difference can mean the difference between work and unemployment, even between life and death. . . .

Parks goes even further in her experiments with language in her second major play, *The Death of the Last Black Man in the Whole Entire World*. If *Imperceptible Mutabilities* showed African-Americans in a perpetual state of middle passage, their identity hidden somewhere in the ocean-sized, centuries-old hyphen separating African from American, *Death of the Last Black Man*, with humor and pointedness, takes on the American side of the divide, confronting stereotypes and dismantling cultural myths.

Here, again, Parks addresses the themes of self-narration, the way language can confer autonomy, the gaps between image and reality, white America's denial of African-American history. But this play is even more complex in approach, more inventive in style, and, surprisingly — because its experiments are so formal — more passionate.

There's little that could be called plot here. Indeed, the idea of sequence is subverted again and again. Time itself is subverted, past and future conflated into the simultaneity of the theatrical present. When did the last black man die? "Yesterday tuhday next summer tuhmorrow just a moment ughoh in 1317."

Instead of relying on logical sequence, Parks creates a sense of progression through repetition. Her language gathers momentum through what Gertrude Stein called "the natural way to count . . . not that one and one make two but to go on counting by one and one. . . . One and one and one and one and one." Parks does not drive her plays with the mechanism of suspense: if there's any eagerness to find out what will happen next, it comes not from the hurtling forward of an event into its consequences, but from the variations she builds on established patterns.

Stein is one clear influence on this style; the other is jazz. Through listening to jazz, with its solos sculpted around revisions of a repeated theme, Parks says she's recently realized "how much this method is an integral part of the African and African-American literary and oral traditions."

In a note to other members of BACA's New Works Project — a workshop for writers and directors — Parks explains what intrigues her about this technique:

> Repetition — we accept it in poetry and call it incremental refrain. For the most part incremental refrain creates a weight and a rhythm. In dramatic writing it does the same — yes, but we want to get to the CLIMAX. Where does repetition fit? First, it's not just repetition, but repetition with *revision*. And in drama, change is the thing. Characters refigure their words. Secondly, a text based on the concept of repetition and revision is one which breaks from the text which we are told to write — the text which cleanly ARCS. Thirdly, Rep and Rev texts create a real challenge for the actor and director as they create a physical life appropriate to the text. In such pieces we are not moving from A–B but rather, for example, from A–A–A–B–A. Through such movement, we refigure A. And if we wish to continue to call this movement FORWARD PROGRESSION, which I think it is, then we refigure the concept of forward progression.

Subverting sequence changes the meaning of consequence. The teleological nature of naturalistic drama virtually requires some kind of huge event that brings on catastrophe — or at least consequences that the action of the play seeks to expose and explain. "If you stick to that kind of writing," Parks says, "then all you can write is plays about black men being killed by policemen, as if to indict society, you need a Big Event. But on stage, as in physics, an event doesn't have to be big to be a big deal. In the theater, someone can simply turn their hand palm up and that is an event."

In *Death of the Last Black Man*, history itself refuses to be linear or sequential. For Parks, history is round — or perhaps, roun'. "The worl usta be *roun*," the Black Man with Watermelon says, "before Columbus." And then, Queen-then-Pharaoh Hatshepsut explains, "they put uh 'd' on thuh end of roun making round. Thusly they set in motion thuh end. Without that 'd' we coulda gone on spinnin for ever. The 'd' thing ended things ended." More than that, [Before Columbus] replies, "Them thinking the world was flat kept it roun. Them thinking the sun revolved around the earth kept them satellite-like. They figured out the truth and scurried out. Figuring out the truth put them in their place and they scurried out to put us in ours. [Yes and Greens Black-Eyed Peas Cornbread adds] Mmm. Yes. You should write this down. You should hide this under a rock."

The consequences Parks is concerned with are those that resulted from that "d" being appended to the roun worl. In one sequence, the Black Man appears with a noose around his neck, dragging a tree branch behind him. Over and over in the play this last black man *almost* dies: We hear of him falling from a ship, bursting into flames, being plucked from his homeland, being auctioned at the block. And in another extended sequence, he tells the Black Woman how he escaped from electrocution, even after "Jump-juice meets me-mine juices I do uh slow soft shoe like on water. Town crier cries uh moan. Felt my nappy head go frizzly." All these deaths — or near-deaths — are offset by a celebration of births, presented as a ritualized series of begats: "MeMines gived out 2 offspring one she called Mines after herself thuh uther she called Themuhns named after all them who comed before." But these generically named offspring are a dubious blessing; this resurgence is given theatrical extension by an onstage proliferation of watermelons.

Still, the play implies, the greatest death of the Black Man is his being written out of history. Over and over, speakers advise each other, "You should write it down because if you don't write it down then they will come along and tell the future that we did not exist." Gradually, it seems the characters learn this lesson. By the play's end, they have gathered into "uh multitude," recognizing the pull of their own "Nature, History, Gravity." In a triumphant finale, the chorus's "And we will lay us down" gives way to the Black Man and Black Woman's "And we will write us down."

This, of course, is precisely what Suzan-Lori Parks, young, gifted, and African-American, has been doing, capturing the contradictions and crises contained in her own project. As she is increasingly recognized, she too — as she well knows — will run the risk of seeing white institutions want to fix that flattening -d onto her roun writing. In the *New York Times*, Mel Gussow called Parks the most promising playwright of the year; *Imperceptible Mutabilities* won an Obie Award from *The Village Voice* last spring. . . . Meanwhile, the Women's Project has commissioned a play from Parks, and regional theaters are considering productions of *Imperceptible Mutabilities* — though, Parks quips, "If they decide to do it, it will have to be in February so people can have an explanation for it." She's referring, of course, to Black History Month.

Writing About Drama

Why Write About Drama?

The act of writing involves making a commitment to ideas, and that commitment helps clarify your thinking. Your writing forces you to examine the details, the elements of a play that might otherwise pass unnoticed, and it helps you develop creative interpretations that enrich your appreciation of the plays you read. On one level, you can expect that your writing will deepen your understanding, and on another level you can hope that your writing can help deepen the understanding of your peers and readers, as the commentaries in this book are meant to do.

Since every reader of plays has a unique experience and background, every reader can contribute something to the experience and awareness of others. You will see things that others do not. You will interpret things in a way that others will not. Naturally, every reader's aim is to respect the text, but it is not reasonable to think that there is only one way to interpret a text. Nor is it reasonable to think that only a few people can give "correct" interpretations. One of the most interesting aspects of writing about drama is that it is usually preceded by discussion, through which a range of possible interpretations begins to appear. When you start to write, you commit yourself to working with certain ideas, and you begin to deepen your thinking about those ideas as you write.

Conventions in Writing Criticism About Drama

Ordinarily, when you are asked to write about a play, you are expected to produce a critical and analytical study. A critical essay will go beyond any subjective experience and include a discussion of what the play achieves and how it does so. If you have a choice, you should choose a play that you admire and enjoy. If you have special background material on that play, such as a playbill or newspaper article, or if you have seen a production, it will be especially useful to you in writing.

For a critical study you will need to go far beyond retelling the events of the play. You may have to describe what you feel happens in a given scene or moment in a play, but simply rewriting the plot of the play in your own words does not constitute an interpretation. A critical reading of the play demands that you isolate evidence and comment on it. For example, you may want to quote passages of dialogue or stage direction to point out an idea that plays a key role in the drama. When you do so, quote in moderation. A critical essay that is merely a string of quotations linked together with a small amount of your commentary will not suffice. Further, make sure that the quotations you use are illustrations of the point you are making or that you explain clearly what their importance to your discussion is.

Approaches to Criticism

Many critical approaches are available to the reader of drama. One approach might emphasize the response of audience members or readers, recognizing that the audience brings a great deal to the play even before the action begins. The audience's or reader's previous experience with drama influences expectations about what will happen onstage and about how the central characters will behave. Personal and cultural biases also influence how an audience member reacts to the unfolding drama. Reader response criticism pays close attention to these responses and to what causes them.

Another critical approach might treat the play as the coherent work of a playwright who intends the audience to perceive certain meanings in the play. This approach assumes that a careful analysis, or close reading, of the play will reveal the author's meanings. Either approach can lead to engaging essays on drama. In the pages that follow, you will find directions on how to pay attention to your responses as an audience member or reader and advice about how to read a play with close attention to dialogue, images, and patterns of action.

Reader Response Criticism

Response criticism depends on a full experience of the text — a good understanding of its meaning as well as of its conventions of staging and performance.

Your responses to various elements of the drama, whether to the characters, the setting, the theme, or the dialogue, may change and grow as you see a play or read it through. You might have a very different reaction to a play during a second reading or viewing of it. Keeping a careful record of your responses as you read is a first step in response criticism.

However, there is a big difference between recording your responses and examining them. Douglas Atkins of the University of Kansas speaks not only of reader response in criticism, but of reader responsibility, by which he means that readers have the responsibility to respond on more than a superficial level when they read drama. This book helps you reach deeper critical levels because it informs you about the history of drama so that you can read each play in light of its historical development. The book also gives you important background material and commentary from the playwrights and from professional critics. Reading such criticism helps you understand what the critic's role is and what a critic can say about drama.

Reading drama in a historical perspective is important because it can highlight similarities between plays of different eras. Anyone who has read *Oedipus Rex* and *Antigone* will be better prepared to respond to *Hamlet*. In addition to the history and criticism of drama presented in this book, the variety of style, subject matter, and scope of the plays in this volume gives you the opportunity to read and respond to a broad range of drama. The more plays you read carefully, the better you will become at responding to drama and writing about it.

When you write response criticism, keep these guidelines in mind:

1. As you read, make note of the important effects the text has on you. Annotate in the margins moments that are especially effective. Do you find yourself alarmed, disturbed, sympathetic, or unsympathetic to a character? Do you sense suspense, or are you confused about what is happening? Do you feel personally involved with the action, or is it very distant? Do you find the situation funny? What overall response do you find yourself giving the play?

2. By analyzing the following two elements of your response, establish why the play had the effects you observe. Do you think it would have those effects on others? Have you observed that it does?

First, determine what it is about the play that causes you to have the response you do. Is it the structure of the play, the way the characters behave, their talk? Is it an unusual use of language, allusions to literature you know (or don't know)? Is the society portrayed especially familiar (or especially unfamiliar) to you? What does the author seem to expect the audience to know before the play begins?

Second, determine what it is about you the reader that causes you to respond as you do. Were you prepared for the dramatic conventions of the play, in terms of its genre as tragedy, comedy, tragicomedy or in terms of its place in the history of drama? How does your preparation affect your response? Did you have difficulty interpreting the language of the play because of unfamiliarity? Are you especially responsive to certain kinds of plays because of familiarity?

3. What do your responses to the play tell you about your own limitations, your own expertise, your own values, and your own attitudes toward social behavior, uses of language, and your sense of what is "normal"? Be sure to be willing to face your limitations as well as your strengths.[1]

---

[1]Adapted from Kathleen McCormick, "Theory in the Reader: Bleich, Holland, and Beyond," *College English* 47 (1985): 838.

Reader response criticism is flexible and useful in the way it allows you to explore possible interpretations of a text. Everyone is capable of responding to drama and everyone's response will differ depending on his or her preparation and background.

Close Reading

The method of analyzing a play by close reading involves examining the text in detail, looking for patterns that imply a meaning that might not be evident with a less attentive approach to the text. Annotation is the key to close reading, since the critic's job is to keep track of elements in the play that, innocent though they may seem alone, imply a greater significance when seen together.

Close reading implies rereading, since you do not know the first time through a text just what will be meaningful as the play unfolds, and you will want to read it again to confirm and deepen your impressions. You will usually make only a few discoveries the first time through. However, it is important to annotate the text even the first time you read it.

The following guidelines will be helpful for annotating a play:

1. Underline all the speeches and images you think are important. Look for dialogue that you think reveals the play's themes, the true nature of the characters, and the position of the playwright.

2. Watch for repetition of imagery (such as the garden and weed imagery in *Hamlet*) and keep track of it through annotation. Do the same for repeated ideas in the dialogue, repeated comments on government or religion or psychology. Such repetitions will reveal their importance to the playwright.

3. Color-code or number-code various patterns in the text and then gather them either in photocopies or in lists for examination before you begin to plan your essay.

Criticism that uses the techniques of close reading pays very careful attention to the elements of drama — plot, characterization, setting, dialogue (use of language), movement, and theme — which were discussed earlier in relation to Lady Gregory's *The Rising of the Moon*. As you read a play, keep track of its chief elements because often they will give you useful ideas for your paper. You may find it helpful to refer to the earlier discussion of the elements in *The Rising of the Moon* since a short critical essay about that play is presented here.

Annotation of the special use of any of the elements will help you decide how important they are and whether a close study of them can contribute to an interesting interpretation of the play. You may not want to discuss all the elements in an essay, or if you do, only one may be truly dominant, but you should be aware of them in any play you write about.

From Prewriting to Final Draft: A Sample Essay on *The Rising of the Moon*

Most good writing results from good planning. When you write criticism about drama, consider these important stages:

1. When possible, choose a play that you enjoy.
2. Annotate the play very carefully.
3. Spend time prewriting.
4. Write a good first draft, then revise for content, organization, style, and mechanics.

The essay on Lady Gregory's *The Rising of the Moon* at the end of this section involved several stages of writing. First, the writer read and annotated the play. In the process of doing so, she noticed the unusual stage direction beginning the play, *Moonlight,* and noticed also that when the two policemen leave the Sergeant they take the lantern, but the Sergeant reminds them that it is very lonely waiting there "with nothing but the moon." Second, she used the stage directions regarding moonlight to guide her in several important techniques of prewriting, including brainstorming, clustering, freewriting, drafting a trial thesis, and outlining.

The first stage, brainstorming, involved listing ideas, words, or phrases suggested by reading the play. The idea of moonlight and the moon recurred often. Then the writer practiced clustering: beginning with

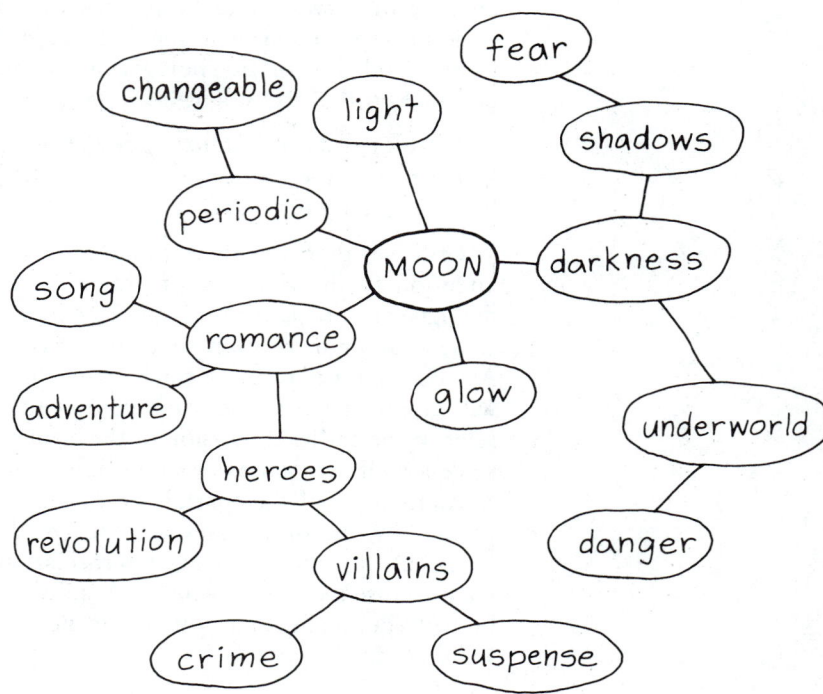

moon, a key term developed from brainstorming, then radiating from it all the associations that naturally suggested themselves.

Next the student chose the term *romance,* because it had generated a number of responses, and performed a freewriting exercise around that term. Freewriting is a technique in which a writer takes four or five minutes to write whatever comes to mind. The technique is designed to be done quickly so the conscious censor has to be turned off. Anything you write in freewriting may be useful because you may produce ideas you did not know you had.

The following passage is part of the freewriting exercise the student wrote using *romance* as a key term. The passage is also an example of invisible writing because the writing was done on a computer and the writer turned off the monitor so that she could not censor or erase what she was writing. The writer could only go forward, as fast as possible.

```
The setting of the play is completely romantic.  In a
lot of ways the play wouldn't work in a different set-
ting.  When you think about it the moon in the title is
what makes all the action possible.  Moon associated
with darkness, underworld, world of fairies, so the moon
is what makes all the action possible.  Moon makes Ser-
geant look at things differently.  The moon is the rebel
moon--that's what title means.  Rebel moon is rising,
always rising.  So the world the policeman lives in--sun
lights up everything in practical and nonromantic way--
is like lantern that second policeman brings to dock-
side.  It shows things in a harsh light.  Moon shows
things in soft light.  Without the moon there would be a
different play.
```

The freewriting gave the writer a new direction — discussing the setting of the play, especially the role of light. The clustering began with the moon, veered off to the concept of the romantic elements in the play, and then came back to the way the moon and the lantern function in the play. The writer was now ready to work up a trial thesis:

```
Lady Gregory uses light to create a romantic setting
that helps us understand the relationship between the
rebel and the Sergeant and the values that they each
stand for.
```

Because the thesis is drafted before the essay is written, the thesis is like a trial balloon. It may work or it may not. At this point it gives the writer direction.

Next the student outlined the essay. Since the writer did not know the outcome of the essay yet, her outline was necessarily sketchy:

```
I.   Moonlight is associated with romance and
     rebellion; harsh light of lantern is associated
     with repressiveness of police.
     A.  Rebel is associated with romance.
     B.  Sergeant is associated with practicality and
         the law.
II.  Without the lantern, the Sergeant is under the
     influence of the romantic moon and the rebel.
     A.  Sergeant feels resentment about his job.
     B.  Rebel sings forbidden song, and Sergeant
         reveals his former sympathies.
     C.  Sergeant admits he was romantic when young.
III. Sergeant must choose between moon and lantern.
     A.  Sergeant seems ready to arrest rebel.
     B.  When police return with lantern, the Sergeant
         sends them away.
     C.  Rebel escapes and Sergeant remains in
         moonlight.
```

The prewriting strategies of brainstorming, clustering, freewriting, drafting a thesis, and outlining helped the student generate ideas and material for her first draft. After writing this draft, she revised it carefully for organization, clarity of ideas, expression, punctuation, and format. What follows is her final draft.

```
Andrea James
Professor Jacobus
English 233
19 October 1992
          The Use of Light in The Rising of the Moon
     Lady Gregory uses light imagery in The Rising of
the Moon to contrast rebellion and repressiveness.  Her
```

initial stage direction is basic: <u>Moonlight</u>. She
suggests some of the values associated with moonlight,
such as rebellion and romance, caution and secrecy,
daring exploits, and even the underworld. All these are
set against the policemen, who are governed not by the
moon, which casts shadows and makes the world look
magical, but by the lantern, which casts a harsh light
that even the Sergeant eventually rejects.

The ballad singer, the rebel, is associated with
romance from the start: "Dark hair--dark eyes, smooth
face. . . . There isn't another man in Ireland would
have broken jail the way he did" (27-28). He is dark,
handsome, and recklessly brave. The Sergeant, by
contrast, is a practical man, no romantic. He sees that
he might have a chance to arrest the rebel and gain the
reward for his capture if he stays right on the quay, a
likely place for the rebel to escape from. But he
unknowingly spoils his chances by refusing to keep the
lantern the policemen offer. He tells the policemen,
"You can take the lantern. Don't be too long now. It's
very lonesome here with nothing but the moon" (28).
What he does not realize is that with the lantern as his
guiding light, he will behave like a proper Sergeant.
But with the moon to guide him, he will side with the
rebel.

It takes only a few minutes for the rebel to show
up on the scene. At first, the Sergeant is very tough
and abrupt with the rebel, who is disguised as "Jimmy
Walsh, a ballad singer." The rebel tells the Sergeant
that he is a traveler, that he is from Ennis, and that
he has been to Cork. Unlike the Sergeant, who has
stayed in one place and is a family man, the ballad
singer appears to be a romantic figure, in the sense
that he follows his mind to go where he wants to, sings
what he wants to, and does what he wants to.

When the ballad singer begins singing, the Sergeant
reacts badly, telling the singer, "Stop that noise"
(28). Maybe he is envious of the ballad singer's
freedom. When the Sergeant tries to make the rebel
leave, the rebel instead begins telling stories about
the man the Sergeant is looking for. He reminds the
Sergeant of deeds done that would frighten anyone. "It
was after the time of the attack on the police barrack
at Kilmallock. . . . Moonlight . . . just like this"
(29). The moonlight of the tale and the moonlight of
the setting combine to add mystery and suspense to the
situation.

The effect of the rebel's talk—and of the
moonlight—is to make the Sergeant feel sorry for
himself in a thankless job. "It's little we get but
abuse from the people, and no choice but to obey our
orders," he says bitterly while sitting on the barrel
sharing a pipe with the singer (29). When the rebel
sings an illegal song, the Sergeant corrects a few
words, revealing his former sympathies with the people.
The rebel realizes this, telling the Sergeant, "It was
with the people you were, and not with the law you were,
when you were a young man" (30). The Sergeant admits
that when he was young he too was a romantic, but now
that he is older he is practical and law-abiding:
"Well, if I was foolish then, that time's gone. . . . I
have my duties and I know them" (30).

Pulled by his past and his present, the Sergeant is
suddenly forced to choose when the ballad singer's
signal to his friend reveals the singer's identity to
the Sergeant. He must decide whether his heart is with
the world of moonlight or the world of the lantern. He
seizes the rebel's hat and wig and seems about to arrest
him when the policemen, with their lantern, come back.
The Sergeant orders the policemen back to the station,

and they offer to leave the lantern with him. But the
Sergeant refuses. We know that he will not turn the
rebel in. He has chosen the world of moonlight, of the
rebel.

Before they leave the policemen try to make the
world of the lantern seem the right choice. Policeman B
says:

> Well, I thought it might be a comfort to you.
> I often think when I have it in my hand and
> can be flashing it about into every dark
> corner (<u>doing so</u>) that it's the same as being
> beside the fire at home, and the bits of
> bogwood blazing up now and again.
> (<u>Flashes it about, now on the barrel, now on</u>
> <u>Sergeant</u>.) (31)

The Sergeant reacts furiously and tells them to get
out--"yourselves and your lantern!"

The play ends with the Sergeant giving the hat and
wig back to the rebel, obviously having chosen the side
of the people. When the rebel leaves, the Sergeant
wonders if he himself was crazy for losing his chance at
the reward. But as the curtain goes down, the Sergeant
is still in the moonlight.

Glossary of Dramatic Terms

Absurd, theater of the. A type of twentieth-century drama presenting the human condition as meaningless, absurd, and illogical. An example of the genre is Samuel Beckett's *Waiting for Godot*.

Act. A major division in the action of a play. Most plays from the Elizabethan era until the nineteenth century were divided into five acts by the playwrights or by later editors. In the nineteenth century many writers began to write four-act plays. Today one-, two-, and three-act plays are most common.

Action. What happens in a play; the events that make up the **plot**.

Agon. The Greek word for contest. In Greek tragedy the *agon* was often a formal debate in which the **chorus** divided and took the sides of the disputants.

Alienation effect. In his **epic theater**, Bertolt Brecht (1898–1956) tried to make the familiar unfamiliar (or to alienate it) to show the audience that familiar, seemingly "natural," and therefore unalterable social conditions could be changed. Different devices achieved the alienation effect by calling attention to the theater as theater — stage lights brought in front of the curtain, musicians put onstage instead of hidden in an orchestra pit, placards indicating scene changes and interrupting the linear flow of the action, actors distancing themselves from their characters to invite the audience to analyze and criticize the characters instead of empathizing with them. These alienating devices prevented the audience from losing itself in the illusion of reality. (See **epic theater**.)

Allegory. A literary work that is coherent on at least two levels simultaneously: a literal level consisting of recognizable characters and events and an allegorical level in which the literal characters and events represent moral, political, religious, or other ideas and meanings.

Anagnorisis. Greek term for a character's discovery or recognition of someone or something previously unknown. *Anagnorisis* often paves the way for a reversal of fortune (see **peripeteia**). An example in *Oedipus Rex* is Oedipus's discovery of his true identity.

Antagonist. A character or force in conflict with the **protagonist**. The antagonist is often another character but may also be an intangible force such as nature or society. The dramatic conflict can also take the form of a struggle with the protagonist's own character.

Anticlimax. See **plot**.

Antimasque. See **masque**.

Antistrophe. The second of the three parts of the verse ode sung by the **chorus** in Greek drama. While singing the **strophe** the chorus moves in a dance rhythm from right to left; during the antistrophe it moves from left to right back to its original position. The third part, the **epode**, was sung standing still.

Apron stage. The apron is the part of the stage extending in front of the **proscenium arch**. A stage is an apron stage if all or most of it is in front of any framing structures. The Elizabethan stage, which the audience surrounded on three sides, is an example of an apron stage.

Arena stage. A stage surrounded on all sides by the audience; actors make exits and entrances through the aisles. Usually used in **theater in the round**.

Arras. A curtain hung at the back of the Elizabethan

playhouse to partition off an alcove or booth. The curtain could be pulled back to reveal a room or a cave.

Aside. A short speech made by a character to the audience which, by **convention**, the other characters onstage cannot hear.

Atellan farce. Broad and sometimes coarse popular humor indigenous to the town of Atella in Italy. By the third century B.C., the Romans had imported the Atellan farce, which they continued to modify and develop.

Blank verse. An unrhymed verse form often used in writing drama. Blank verse is composed of ten-syllable lines accented on the second, fourth, sixth, eighth, and tenth syllables (**iambic pentameter**).

Bombast. A loud, pompous speech whose inflated diction is disproportionate to the subject matter it expresses.

Bourgeois drama. Drama that treats middle-class subject matter or characters rather than the lives of the rich and powerful.

Braggart soldier. A **stock character** in comedy who is usually cowardly, parasitical, pompous, and easily victimized by practical jokers. Sir John Falstaff in Shakespeare's *Henry IV* (parts 1, 2) is an example of this type.

Burla (plural, *burle*). Jests or practical jokes that were part of the comic **stage business** in the *commedia dell'arte.*

Buskin. A thick-soled boot worn by Greek tragedians to increase their stature. Later called a *cothurnes.*

Catastrophe. See **plot.**

Catharsis. The feeling of emotional purgation or release that, according to Aristotle, an audience should feel after watching a tragedy.

Ceremonial drama. Egyptian passion play about the god Osiris.

Character. Any person appearing in a drama or narrative.

Stock character. A stereotypical character type whose behavior, qualities, or beliefs conform to familiar dramatic **conventions,** such as the clever servant or the **braggart soldier.** (Also called *type character.*)

Chiton. Greek tunic worn by Roman actors.

Choragos. An influential citizen chosen to pay for the training and costuming of the **chorus** in Greek drama competitions. He probably also paid for the musicians and met other financial production demands not paid for by the state. *Choragos* also refers to the leader of the chorus.

Chorus. A masked group that sang and danced in Greek tragedy. The chorus usually chanted in unison, offering advice and commentary on the action but rarely participating. See also **strophe, antistrophe,** and **epode.**

City Dionysia. See **Dionysus.**

Climax. See **plot.**

Closet drama. A drama, usually in verse, meant for reading rather than for performance. Percy Bysshe Shelley's *Prometheus Unbound* and John Milton's *Samson Agonistes* are examples.

Comedy. A type of drama intended to interest and amuse rather than to concern the audience deeply. Although characters experience various discomfitures, the audience feels confident that they will overcome their ill fortune and find happiness at the end.

Comedy of humors. Form of comedy developed by Ben Jonson in the seventeenth century in which characters' actions are determined by the preponderance in their systems of one of the four bodily fluids or humors — blood, phlegm, choler (yellow bile), and melancholy (black bile). Characters' dispositions are exaggerated and stereotyped; common types are the melancholic and the belligerent bully.

Comedy of manners. Realistic, often satiric comedy concerned with the manners and conventions of high society. Usually refers to the Restoration comedies of late seventeenth-century England, which feature witty dialogue or **repartee.** An example is William Congreve's *The Way of the World.*

Drawing room comedy. A type of comedy of manners concerned with life in polite society. The action generally takes place in a drawing room.

Farce. A short dramatic work that depends on exaggerated, improbable situations, incongruities, coarse wit, and horseplay for its comic effect.

High comedy. Comedy that appeals to the intellect, often focusing on the pretensions, foolishness, and incongruity of human behavior. **Comedy of manners** with its witty dialogue is a type of high comedy.

Low comedy. Comedy that lacks the intellectual appeal of **high comedy,** depending instead on boisterous buffoonery, "gags," and jokes for its comic effect.

New Comedy. Emerging between the fourth and third centuries B.C. in ancient Greece, New Comedy replaced the farcical **Old Comedy.** New Comedy, usually associated with Menander, is witty and intellectually engaging; it is often thought of as the first **high comedy**.

Old Comedy. Greek comedy of the fifth century B.C. that uses stock characters and bawdy farce to attack satirically social, religious, and political institutions. Old Comedy is usually associated with Aristophanes.

Sentimental comedy. Comedy populated by stereotypical virtuous **protagonists** and villainous **antagonists** that resolves the domestic trials of middle-class people in a pat, happy ending.

Slapstick. Low comedy that involves little plot or character development but consists of physical horseplay or practical jokes.

Comic relief. The use of humorous characters, speeches, or scenes in an otherwise serious or tragic drama.

Commedia dell'arte. Italian **low comedy** dating from around the mid-sixteenth century in which professional actors playing **stock characters** improvised dialogue to fit a given **scenario**.

Complication. See **plot**.

Conflict. See **plot**.

Convention. Any feature of a literary work that has become standardized over time, such as the **aside** or the **stock character**. Often refers to an unrealistic device (such as Danish characters speaking English in *Hamlet*) that the audience tacitly agrees to accept.

Coryphaeus. See *koryphaios*.

Cosmic irony. See **irony**.

Cothurnes. See **buskin**.

Craft play. Medieval sacred drama based on Old and New Testament stories. Craft plays were performed outside the church by members of a particular trade guild, and their subject matter often reflected the guild's trade. The fisherman's guild, for example, might present the story of Noah and the flood.

Crisis. Same as **climax**. See **plot**.

Cruelty, theater of. A type of drama created by Antonin Artaud in the 1930s that uses shock techniques to expose the audience's primitive obsessions with cruelty and sexuality. The purpose was to overwhelm spectators' rational minds, leading them to understand and even participate in the cycle of cruelty and ritual purgation dramatized in the performance.

Cycle. A group of medieval **mystery plays** written in the vernacular (in English rather than Latin) for performance outside the church. Cycles, each of which treated biblical stories from creation through

the last judgment, are named after the town in which they were produced. Most extant mystery plays are from the York, Chester, Wakefield (Towneley), and N-Town cycles.

Decorum. A quality that exists when the style of a work is appropriate to the speaker, the occasion, and the subject matter. Kings should speak in a "high style" and clowns in a "low style," according to many Renaissance authors. Decorum was a guiding critical principle in **neoclassicism**.

Defamiliarization effect (*Verfremdung*). See **alienation effect**.

Denouement. See **plot**.

Deus ex machina. Latin for "a god out of a machine." In Greek drama, a mechanical device that could lower "gods" onto the stage to solve the seemingly unsolvable problems of mortal characters. Also used to describe a playwright's use of a forced or improbable solution to plot complications — for example, the discovery of a lost will or inheritance that will pay off the evil landlord.

Dialogue. Spoken interchange or conversation between two or more characters. Also see **soliloquy**.

Diction. A playwright's choice of words or the match between language and subject matter. Also refers collectively to an actor's phrasing, enunciation, and manner of speaking.

Dionysus. Greek nature god of wine, mystic revelry, and irrational impulse. Greek tragedy probably sprang from dramatized ritual choral celebrations in his honor.

City Dionysia. (Also called Great or Greater Dionysia.) The most important of the four Athenian festivals in honor of Dionysus. This spring festival sponsored the first tragedy competitions; comedy was associated with the winter festival, the Lenaea.

Director. The person responsible for a play's interpretation and staging and for the guidance of the actors.

Disguising. Medieval entertainment featuring a masked procession of actors performing short plays in pantomime; probably the origin of the court **masque**.

Dithyramb. Ancient Greek choral hymn sung and danced to honor **Dionysus**; originally divided into an improvised story sung by a choral leader and a traditional refrain sung by the **chorus**. Believed to be the origin of Greek tragedy.

Domestic tragedy. A serious play usually focusing on the family and depicting the fall of a middle-class **protagonist** rather than of a powerful or noble hero. Also called *bourgeois tragedy*. An example is Arthur Miller's *Death of a Salesman*, which traces the emotional collapse and eventual suicide of Willy Loman, a traveling salesman.

Double plot. See **plot**.

Drama. A play written in prose or verse that tells a story through **dialogue** and actions performed by actors impersonating the characters of the story.

Dramatic illusion. The illusion of reality created by drama and accepted by the audience for the duration of the play.

Dramatic irony. See **irony**.

Dramatist. The author of a play; playwright.

Dramaturg. One who represents the playwright and guides the production. In some cases, the dramaturg researches different aspects of the production or earlier productions of the play.

Dramaturgy. The art of writing plays.

Drawing room comedy. See **comedy**.

Empathy. The sense of feeling *with* a character. (Distinct from sympathy, which is feeling *for* a character.)

Ensemble acting. Performance by a group of actors, usually members of a **repertory** company, in which the integrated acting of all members is emphasized over individual star performances. The famous nineteenth-century director Konstantin Stanislavsky promoted this type of acting in the Moscow Art Theatre.

Environmental theater. A term used by Richard Schechner, director of the Performance Group in the late 1960s and early 1970s, to describe his work and the work of other theater companies, including the Bread and Puppet Theatre, Open Theatre, and Living Theatre. He also used the term to describe the indigenous theater of Africa and Asia. Environmental theater occupies the whole of a performance space; it is not confined to a stage separated from the audience. Action can take place in and around the audience, and audience members are often encouraged to participate in the theater event.

Epic theater. A type of theater first associated with German director Erwin Piscator (1893–1966). Bertolt Brecht (1898–1956) used the term to distinguish his own theater from the "dramatic" theater that created the illusion of reality and invited the audience to identify and empathize with the characters. Brecht criticized the dramatic theater for encouraging the audience to believe that social conditions were "natural" and therefore unalterable. According to Brecht, the theater should show human beings as dependent on certain political and economic factors and at the same time as capable of altering them. "The spectator is given the chance to criticize human behavior from a social point of view, and the scene is played as a piece of history," he wrote. Epic theater calls attention to itself as theater, bringing the stage lights in front of the curtain and interrupting the linear flow of the action to help the audience analyze the action and characters onstage. (See **alienation effect**.)

Epilogue. A final speech added to the end of a play. An example is Puck's "If we shadows have offended . . ." speech that ends Shakespeare's *A Midsummer Night's Dream*.

Epitasis. Ancient term for the **rising action** of a **plot**. (See also **plot**.)

Epode. The third of three parts of the verse ode sung by the **chorus** in a Greek drama. The epode follows the **strophe** and **antistrophe**.

Exodos. The concluding scene, which includes the exit of all characters and the **chorus**, of a Greek drama.

Exposition. See **plot**.

Expressionism. Early twentieth-century literary movement in Germany that posited that art should represent powerful emotional states and moods. Expressionists abandon **realism** and **verisimilitude**, producing distorted, nightmarish images of the individual unconscious.

Falling action. See **plot**.

Farce. See **comedy**.

First Folio. The first collected edition of thirty-six of Shakespeare's plays, collected by two of his fellow actors and published posthumously in 1623.

Foil. A character who, through difference or similarity, brings out a particular aspect of another character. Laertes, reacting to the death of his father, acts as a foil for Hamlet.

Foreshadowing. Ominous hints of events to come that help to create an air of suspense in a drama.

Frons scaena. The elaborately decorated facade of the *scaena* or stage house used in presenting Roman drama. (Also called *scaena frons*.)

Hamartia. An error or wrong act through which the fortunes of the **protagonist** are reversed in a tragedy.

High comedy. See **comedy**.

History play. A drama set in a time other than that in which it was written. The term usually refers to late Elizabethan drama, such as Shakespeare's Henry plays, that draws its plots from English historical materials such as Holinshed's *Chronicles*.

Hubris (or *hybris*). Excessive pride or ambition. In

ancient Greek tragedy *hubris* often causes the **protagonist**'s fall.

Humor character. A stereotyped character in the **comedy of humors** (see **comedy**). Clever plots often play on the character's personality distortions (caused by an imbalance of humors), revealing his or her absurdity.

Iambic pentameter. A poetic meter that divides a line into five parts (or feet), each part containing an unaccented syllable followed by an accented syllable. The line "When I consider everything that grows" is an example of iambic pentameter verse.

Imitation. See *mimesis*.

Impressionism. A highly personal style of writing in which the author presents characters, scenes, or moods as they appear to him or her at a particular moment rather than striving for an objectively realistic description.

Interlude. A short play, usually either farcical or moralistic, performed between the courses of a feast or between the acts of a longer play. The interlude thrived during the late fifteenth and early sixteenth centuries in England.

Irony. The use of words to suggest a meaning that is the opposite of the literal meaning, as in "I can't wait to take the exam." Irony is present in a literary work that gives expression to contradictory attitudes or impulses to entertain ambiguity or maintain detachment.

Cosmic irony. Irony present when destiny or the gods seem to be in favor of the **protagonist** but are actually engineering his or her downfall. (Same as *irony of fate*.)

Dramatic irony. Irony present when the outcome of an event or situation is the opposite of what a character expects.

Tragic irony. Irony that exists when a character's lack of complete knowledge or understanding (which the audience possesses) results in his or her fall or has tragic consequences for loved ones. An example from *Oedipus Rex* is Oedipus's declaration that he will stop at nothing to banish King Laios's murderer, whom the audience knows to be Oedipus himself.

Jongleur. A French term for early medieval musical entertainers who recited lyrics, ballads, and stories. Forerunners of the minstrel.

Koryphaios. The leader of the **chorus** in Greek drama.

Kothurnus. See **buskin**.

Lazzo (plural, *lazzi*). Comic routines or **stage business** associated with the stock situations and characters of the Italian *commedia dell'arte*. A scenario might, for example, call for the *lazzo* of fear.

Liturgical drama. Short dramatized sections of the medieval church service. Some scholars believe that these playlets evolved into the vernacular **mystery plays**, which were performed outside the church by lay people.

Low comedy. See **comedy**.

Mansion. Scenic structures used in medieval drama to indicate the locale or scene of the action. Mansions were areas inside the church used for performing liturgical drama; later more elaborate structures were built on pageant wagons to present **mystery plays** outside the church.

Mask. A covering used to disguise or ornament the face; used by actors in Greek drama and revived in the later *commedia dell'arte* and court **masque** to heighten dramatic effect.

Masque. (also **mask**). A short but elaborately staged court drama, often mythological and allegorical, principally acted and danced by masked courtiers. (Professional actors often performed the major speaking and singing roles.) Popular in England during the late sixteenth and early seventeenth centuries, masques were often commissioned to honor a particular person or occasion. Ben Jonson was the most important masque writer; the genre's most elaborate sets and costumes were designed by Jonson's occasional partner Inigo Jones.

Antimasque. A parody of the court **masque** developed by Ben Jonson featuring broad humor, grotesque characters, and ludicrous actions.

Melodrama. A suspenseful play filled with situations that appeal excessively to the audience's emotions. Justice triumphs in a happy ending: the good characters (completely virtuous) are rewarded and the bad characters (thoroughly villainous) are punished.

Method acting. A naturalistic technique of acting developed by the Russian director Konstantin Stanislavsky and adapted for American actors by Lee Strasberg, among others. The Method actor identifies with the **character** he or she portrays and experiences the emotions called for by the play in an effort to render the character with emotional **verisimilitude**.

Mimesis. The Greek word for imitation. Aristotle used the term to define the role of art as an "imitation of nature."

Miracle play. A type of medieval sacred drama that

depicts the lives of saints, focusing especially on the miracles performed by saints. The term is often used interchangeably with **mystery play.**

Mise-en-scène. The stage setting of a play, including the use of scenery and props.

Moira. Greek word for fate.

Morality play. Didactic late medieval drama (flourishing in England c. 1400–1550) that uses **allegory** to dramatize some aspects of the Christian moral life. Abstract qualities or entities such as Virtue, Vice, Good Deeds, Knowledge, and Death are cast as characters who discuss with the **protagonist** issues related to salvation and the afterlife. *Everyman* is an example.

Motivation. The reasons for a character's actions in a drama. For drama to be effective, the audience must believe that a character's actions are justified and plausible given what they know about him or her.

Mouth of hell. A stage prop in medieval drama suggesting the entrance to hell. Often in the shape of an open-mouthed monster's head, the mouth of hell was positioned over a smoke-and-fire-belching pit in the stage that appeared to swallow up sinners.

Mystery play. A sacred medieval play dramatizing biblical events such as the creation, the fall of Adam and Eve, and Christ's birth and resurrection. The genre probably evolved from **liturgical drama**; mystery plays were often incorporated into larger **cycles** of plays.

Naturalism. Literary philosophy popularized during the nineteenth century that casts art's role as the scientifically accurate reflection of a "slice of life." Naturalism is aligned with the belief that each person is a product of heredity and environment driven by internal and external forces beyond his or her control. August Strindberg's *Miss Julie,* with its focus on reality's sordidness and humankind's powerlessness, draws on naturalism.

Neoclassicism. A movement in sixteenth-century France to revive and emulate classical attitudes toward art based on principles of order, harmony, unity, restrained wit, and **decorum.** The neoclassical movement in France gave rise to a corresponding movement in England during the late seventeenth and eighteenth centuries.

New Comedy. See **comedy.**

Ode. A dignified Greek three-part song sung by the **chorus** in Greek drama. The parts are the **strophe,** the **antistrophe,** and the **epode.**

Old Comedy. See **comedy.**

Orchestra. Literally the "dancing place"; the circular stage where the Greek **chorus** performed.

Pageant. A movable stage or wagon (often called a pageant wagon) on which a set was built for the performance of medieval drama. The term can also refer to the spectacle itself.

Pallium. Long white cloak or mantle worn by Roman actors.

Pantomime. Silent acting using facial expression, body movement, and gesture to convey the plot and the characters' feelings.

Parodos. The often stately entrance song of the **chorus** in Greek drama. The term also refers to the aisles (plural, *paradoi*) on either side of the orchestra by which the chorus entered the Greek theater.

Pastoral drama. A dramatic form glorifying shepherds and rural life in an idealized natural setting; usually implies a negative comparison to urban life.

Pathos. The quality of evoking pity.

Peripeteia. A reversal of fortune, for better or worse, for the **protagonist.** Used especially to describe the main character's fall in Greek tragedy.

Phallus. An appendage added to the front of blatantly comic male characters' costumes in some Greek comedy; associated chiefly with the Greek **satyr play.**

Play. A literary genre whose plot is usually presented dramatically by actors portraying characters before an audience.

Play-within-the-play. A brief secondary drama presented to or by the characters of a play that reflects or comments on the larger work. An example is the Pyramus and Thisby episode in Shakespeare's *A Midsummer Night's Dream.*

Plot. The events of a play or narrative. The sequence and relative importance a **dramatist** assigns to these events.

Anticlimax. An unexpectedly trivial or significant conclusion to a series of significant events; an unsatisfying resolution that often occurs in place of a conventional **climax.**

Catastrophe. The outcome or conclusion of a play; usually applied specifically to tragedy. (**Denouement** is a parallel term applied to both comedy and tragedy.)

Climax. The turning point in a drama's action, preceded by the **rising action** and followed by the **falling action.** Same as *crisis.*

Complication. The part of the plot preceding the **climax** that establishes the entanglements to be untangled in the **denouement.** Part of the **rising action.**

Conflict. The struggle between the **protagonist** and the **antagonist** that propels the **rising action** of the plot and is resolved in the **denouement**.

Denouement. The "unknotting" of the plot's **complication**; the resolution of a drama's action. See **catastrophe**.

Double plot. A dramatic structure in which two related plots function simultaneously.

Exposition. The presentation of essential information, especially about events that have occurred prior to the first scene of a play. The exposition appears early in the play and initiates the **rising action**.

Falling action. The events of the plot following the **climax** and ending in the **castastrophe** or resolution.

Rising action. The events of the plot leading up to the **climax**.

Subplot. A secondary plot intertwined with the main plot, often reflecting or commenting on the main plot.

Underplot. Same as **subplot**.

Problem play. A drama that argues a point or presents a problem (usually a social problem). Ibsen is a notable writer of problem plays.

Prologos. In Greek drama, an introductory scene for actor or actors that precedes the entrance of the **chorus**. This **convention**, invented by Euripides, has evolved into the modern dramatic introductory monologue or **prologue**.

Prologue. A preface or introduction preceding the play proper.

Proscaena. The space in front of the *scaena* in a Roman theater.

Proscenium arch. An arched structure over the front of the stage from which a curtain often hangs. The arch frames the action onstage and separates the audience from the action.

Proskenion. The facade of the *skene* or scene house in Greek drama. May also have referred to the playing space in front of the building.

Protagonist. The main character in a drama. This character is usually the most interesting and sympathetic and is the person involved in the **conflict** driving the **plot**.

Protasis. Classical term for the introductory act or **exposition** of a drama.

Psychomachia. Psychological struggle; a war of souls.

Quem Quaeritis **trope.** A brief dramatized section of the medieval church's Easter liturgy. The oldest extant **trope** and the probable origin of liturgical drama, it enacts the visit of the three Marys to Christ's empty tomb (*quem quaeritis* means "whom do you seek?" in Latin).

Rising action. See **plot**.

Realism. The literary philosophy that holds that art should accurately reproduce an image of life. Avoids the use of dramatic **conventions** such as asides and soliloquies to depict ordinary people in ordinary situations. Ibsen's *A Doll House* is an example of realism in drama.

Recognition. See *anagnorisis*.

Repartee. Witty and pointed verbal exchanges usually found in the **comedy of manners**.

Repertory. A theater company or group of actors that presents a set of plays alternately throughout a season. The term also refers to the set of plays itself.

Restoration comedy. A type of **comedy of manners** that developed in England in the late seventeenth century. Often features **repartee** in the service of complex romantic plots. William Congreve's *The Way of the World* is an example.

Revenge tragedy. Sensational tragedy popularized during the Elizabethan age that is notable for bloody plots involving such elements as murder, ghosts, insanity, and crimes of lust.

Reversal. See *peripeteia*.

Riposte. A quick or sharp reply; similar to **repartee**.

Rising action. See **plot**.

Ritual. Repeated formalized or ceremonial practices, many of which have their roots in primitive cultures. Certain theorists hold that primitive ritual evolved into drama.

Satire. A work that makes fun of a social institution or human foible, often in an intellectually sophisticated way, to persuade the audience to share the author's views. Molière's *The Misanthrope* contains social satire.

Satyr play. A comic play performed after the tragic trilogy in Greek tragedy competitions. The satyr play provided **comic relief** and was usually a farcical, boisterous treatment of mythological material.

Scaena. The stage house in Roman drama; the facade of the *scaena* (called the **frons scaena**) was often elaborately ornamented.

Scenario. The plot outline around which professional actors of the *commedia dell'arte* improvised their plays. Most scenarios specified the action's sequence and the entrances of the main characters.

Scene. Division of an **act** in a drama. By traditional definition a scene has no major shift in place or time frame, and it is performed by a static group of actors onstage (if an actor enters or exits, the group is altered and the scene, technically, should change). The term also refers to the physical surroundings or locale in which a play's action is set.

Scenery. The backdrop and set (furniture and so on) onstage that suggest to the audience the surroundings in which a play's **action** takes place.

Scenography. Painting of backdrops and hangings.

Senecan tragedy. Tragic drama modeled on plays written by Seneca. The genre usually has five acts and features a chorus; it is notable for its thematic concern with bloodshed, revenge, and unnatural crimes. (See also **revenge tragedy**.)

Sentimental. Refers to tender emotions in excess of what the situation calls for.

Setting. All details of time, location, and environment relating to a play.

Skene. The building or scene house in the Greek theater that probably began as a dressing room and eventually was incorporated into the action as part of the scenery.

Slapstick. See **comedy**.

Slice of life. See **naturalism**.

Social problem play. Same as **problem play**.

Sock. Derived from the Latin *soccus,* the term refers to a light slipper or sock worn by Roman comic actors.

Soliloquy. A speech in which an actor, usually alone onstage, utters his or her thoughts aloud, revealing personal feelings. Hamlet's "To be, or not to be" speech is an example.

Spectacle. In Aristotle's terms, the costumes and scenery in a drama — the elements that appeal to the eye.

Stage business. Minor physical action, including an actor's posture and facial expression, and the use of props, all of which make up a particular interpretation of a character.

Stichomythia. Dialogue in which two speakers engage in a verbal duel in alternating lines.

Stock character. See **character**.

Strophe. The first of three parts of the verse **ode** sung by the Greek **chorus**. While singing the strophe the chorus moves in a dancelike pattern from right to left. See also **antistrophe** and **epode**.

Subplot. See **plot**.

Subtext. A level of meaning implicit in or underlying the surface meaning of a text.

Surrealism. A literary movement flourishing in France during the early twentieth century that valued the unwilled expression of the unconscious (usually as revealed in dreams) over a rendering of "reality" structured by the conscious mind.

Suspense. The sense of tension aroused by an audience's uncertainty about the resolution of dramatic conflicts.

Suspension of disbelief. An audience's willingness to accept the world of the drama as reality during the course of a play.

Symbolism. A literary device in which an object, event, or action is used to suggest a meaning beyond its literal meaning. The guns in *Hedda Gabler* have a symbolic function.

Theater. The building in which a play is performed. Also used to refer to drama as an art form.

Theater in the round. The presentation of a play on an **arena stage** surrounded by the audience.

Three unities. Aristotle specified that a play's action should occur within one day (unity of time) and in a single locale (unity of place) and should reveal clearly ordered actions and plot incidents moving toward the plot's resolution (unity of action). Later scholars and critics, especially those in the neoclassical tradition, interpreted Aristotle's ideas as rules and established them as standards for drama.

Thrust stage. A stage extending beyond the **proscenium arch,** usually surrounded on three sides by the audience.

Tiring house. From "attiring house," the backstage space in Elizabethan public theaters used for storage and possibly as a dressing room. The term also refers to the changing space beneath the medieval pageant wagon.

Total theater. A concept of the theater as an experience synthesizing all the expressive arts including music, dance, lighting, and so on.

Tragedy. Serious drama in which a **protagonist,** traditionally of noble position, suffers a series of unhappy events culminating in a **catastrophe** such as death or spiritual breakdown. Shakespeare's *Hamlet*, which ends with the prince's death, is an example of Elizabethan tragedy.

Tragicomedy. A play that combines elements of tragedy and comedy. Chekhov's *The Cherry Orchard* is an example. Tragicomedies often include a serious plot in which the expected tragic **catastrophe** is replaced by a happy ending.

Trope. Interpolation into or expansion of an existing medieval liturgical text. These expansions, such as the *Quem Quaeritis* trope, gave rise to **liturgical drama**.

Type character. See **character**.

Underplot. See **plot**.

Unity. The sense that the events of a play and the actions of the characters follow one another naturally to form one complete action. Unity is present when characters' behavior seems **motivated** and the work is perceived to be a connected artistic whole. See also **three unities**.

Verfremdung. German term coined by Bertolt Brecht to mean "alienation." See also **alienation effect**.

Verisimilitude. The degree to which a dramatic representation approximates an appearance of reality.

Well-made play. Drama that relies for effect on the suspense generated by its logical, cleverly constructed plot rather than on characterization. Plots often involve a withheld secret, a battle of wits between hero and villain, and a resolution in which the secret is revealed and the **protagonist** saved. The plays of Eugène Scribe (1791–1861) have defined the type.

Selected Bibliography

Selected References for Periods of Drama

GREEK DRAMA

Aylen, Leo. *The Greek Theater*. Rutherford: Fairleigh Dickinson UP, 1985.

Bieber, Margaret. *The History of the Greek and Roman Theater*. 2nd ed. Princeton: Princeton UP, 1961.

Hamilton, Edith. *The Greek Way*. New York: Norton, 1983.

Havelock, Eric. "The Double Vision of Greek Tragedy." *Hudson Review* 37 (1984): 244–70.

Kitto, H. D. F. *Greek Tragedy: A Literary Study*. 3rd ed. London: Methuen, 1966.

———. *Form and Meaning in Drama: A Study of Six Greek Plays and of "Hamlet."* 2nd ed. New York: Barnes, 1968.

Knox, Bernard M. *Word and Action: Essays on the Ancient Theater*. Baltimore: Johns Hopkins UP, 1979.

Pickard-Cambridge, Arthur W. *Dramatic Festivals of Athens*. 2nd ed. Revised by John Gould and D. M. Lewis. Oxford: Clarendon, 1962.

Steiner, George. *The Death of Tragedy*. New York: Knopf, 1961.

Taplin, Oliver. *Greek Tragedy in Action*. Berkeley: U of California P, 1978.

Trendall, A. D., and T. B. L. Webster. *Illustrations of Greek Drama*. London: Phaidon, 1971.

Vickers, Brian. *Towards Greek Tragedy: Drama, Myth, Society*. London: Longman, 1973.

Walcot, Peter. *Greek Drama in Its Theatrical and Social Context*. Cardiff: U of Wales P, 1976.

Walton, Michael J. *Living Greek Theater: A Handbook of Classical Performance and Modern Production*. New York: Greenwood, 1987.

Webster, T. B. L. *Greek Theater Production*. 2nd ed. London: Methuen, 1970.

Winkler, John J., and Froma I. Zeitlin. *Nothing to Do with Dionysus?: Athenian Drama in Its Social Context*. Princeton: Princeton UP, 1990.

ROMAN DRAMA

Beare, William. *The Roman Stage*. 3rd ed. London: Methuen, 1969.

Bieber, Margaret. *The History of the Greek and Roman Theater*. 2nd ed. Princeton: Princeton UP, 1961.

Duckworth, George E. *The Nature of Roman Comedy: A Study in Popular Entertainment*. Princeton: Princeton UP, 1952.

Hunter, R. L. *The New Comedy of Greece and Rome*. New York: Cambridge UP, 1985.

Kenney, E. J., ed. *The Cambridge History of Classical Literature*. 2 vols. New York: Cambridge UP, 1982.

Konstan, David. *Roman Comedy*. Ithaca: Cornell UP, 1983.

Segal, Erich. *Roman Laughter*. Cambridge: Harvard UP, 1968.

Wiles, David. *The Masks of Menander: Sign and Meaning in Greek and Roman Performances*. New York: Cambridge UP, 1991.

MEDIEVAL DRAMA

Axton, Richard. *European Drama of the Early Middle Ages*. London: Hutchinson, 1974.

Bevington, David, ed. *Medieval Drama*. Boston: Houghton, 1975.

Briscoe, Marianne G., and John C. Coldewey. *Contexts for Early English Drama*. Bloomington: Indiana UP, 1989.

Chambers, Edmund K. *English Literature at the Close of the Middle Ages*. Oxford: Clarendon, 1945.

———. *The Medieval Stage*. 2 vols. London: Oxford UP, 1967.

Craig, Hardin. *English Religious Drama of the Middle Ages*. 1968. Westport: Greenwood, 1978.

Davidson, Clifford, et al., eds. *Drama in the Middle Ages*. New York: Aims, 1982.

Elliott, John R. *Playing God: Medieval Mysteries on the Modern Stage*. Toronto: U Toronto P, 1989.

Gassner, John, ed. *Medieval and Tudor Drama*. New York: Bantam, 1971.

Hardison, O. B., Jr. *Christian Rite and Christian Drama in the Middle Ages: Essays in the Origin and Early History of Modern Drama*. Baltimore: Johns Hopkins UP, 1965.

Spinrad, Phoebe. *The Summons of Death on the Medieval and Renaissance English Stage*. Columbus: Ohio State UP, 1987.

Vince, Ronald W. *Ancient and Medieval Theatre: A Historiographical Handbook*. Westport: Greenwood, 1984.

Wickham, Glynne. *The Medieval Theatre*. 3rd ed. New York: Cambridge UP, 1987.

Woolf, Rosemary. *The English Mystery Plays*. Berkeley: U of California P, 1972.

Renaissance Drama

Adams, John C. *The Globe Playhouse*. 2nd ed. New York: Barnes, 1961.

Altman, Joel B. *The Tudor Play of Mind: Rhetorical Inquiry and the Development of Elizabethan Drama*. Berkeley: U of California P, 1978.

Bevington, David. *From Mankind to Marlowe: Growth of Structure in the Popular Drama of Tudor England*. Cambridge: Harvard UP, 1962.

Bradbrook, Muriel C. *The Growth and Structure of Elizabethan Comedy*. London: Chatto, 1955.

Braunmuller, A. R., and Michael Hattaway. *The Cambridge Companion to Renaissance Drama*. New York: Cambridge UP, 1990.

Bush, Douglas. *The Renaissance and English Humanism*. Toronto: U of Toronto P, 1939.

Bushnell, Rebecca W. *Tragedies of Tyrants: Political Thought and Theater in the English Renaissance*. Ithaca: Cornell UP, 1990.

Chambers, E. K. *The Elizabethan Stage*. 4 vols. Oxford: Clarendon, 1923.

Farnham, W. *The Medieval Heritage of Elizabethan Tragedy*. Berkeley: U of California P, 1936.

Hussey, Maurice. *The World of Shakespeare and His*

Contemporaries: A Visual Approach. New York: Viking, 1972.

Kernodle, George. *From Art to Theatre: Form and Convention in the Renaissance*. Chicago: U of Chicago P, 1944.

Lea, Kathleen M. *Italian Popular Comedy: A Study of the Commedia dell'Arte, 1560–1620*. 2 vols. Oxford: Clarendon, 1934.

Loomba, Ania. *Gender, Race, and Renaissance Drama*. New York: Manchester UP, 1989.

McLuskie, Kathleen. *Renaissance Dramatists*. Atlantic Highlands: Humanities Intl., 1989.

Nicoll, Allardyce. *The World of Harlequin*. Cambridge: Cambridge UP, 1963.

Rose, Mary Beth. *The Expense of Spirit: Love and Sexuality in English Renaissance Drama*. Ithaca: Cornell UP, 1988.

Waith, Eugene M. *Patterns and Perspectives in English Renaissance Drama*. Newark: U of Delaware P, 1988.

Welsford, Enid. *The Court Masque*. Cambridge: Cambridge UP, 1927.

Wind, Edgar. *Pagan Mysteries in the Renaissance*. New Haven: Yale UP, 1958.

Woodbridge, Linda. *Woman and the English Renaissance: Literature and the Nature of Womankind, 1540–1620*. Urbana: U of Illinois P, 1984.

Yates, Frances A. *Theatre of the World*. Chicago: U of Chicago P, 1969.

Late Seventeenth- and Eighteenth-Century Drama

Barber, Charles L. *The Idea of Honour in the English Drama, 1591–1700*. Stockholm: Göteborg, 1957.

Cox, Jeffrey N. *In the Shadows of Romance*. Athens: Ohio UP, 1987.

Grene, Nicholas. *Shakespeare, Jonson, Molière: The Comic Contract*. Totowa: Barnes, 1980.

Holland, Norman N. *The First Modern Comedies: The Significance of Etherege, Wycherley, and Congreve*. Cambridge: Harvard UP, 1959.

Hume, Robert. *The Rakish Stage: Studies in English Drama, 1660–1800*. Carbondale: Southern Illinois UP, 1983.

Loftis, John, ed. *Restoration Drama*. New York: Oxford UP, 1966.

Lynch, Kathleen M. *The Social Mode of Restoration Comedy*. New York: Farrar, 1975.

Marshall, Geoffrey. *Restoration Serious Drama*. Norman: U of Oklahoma P, 1975.

Nicoll, Allardyce. *A History of Restoration Drama, 1600–1700*. New York: Cambridge UP, 1923.

Peters, Julie Stone. "'Things Govern'd by Words':

Late 17th-Century Comedy and the Reformers." *English Studies* 68 (1987): 142–53.

Powell, Jocelyn. *Restoration Theatre Production*. Boston: Routledge, 1984.

Price, Cecil. *Theatre in the Age of Garrick*. Oxford: Oxford UP, 1973.

Richards, K. R., ed. *Essays on the Eighteenth Century English Stage*. London: Methuen, 1972.

Rothstein, Eric. *The Designs of Carolean Comedy*. Carbondale: Southern Illinois UP, 1988.

Stynan, J. L. *Restoration Comedy in Performance*. New York: Cambridge UP, 1986.

Turnell, Martin. *The Classical Movement: Studies in Corneille, Molière, and Racine*. New York: New Directions, 1948.

NINETEENTH-CENTURY DRAMA
TO THE TURN OF THE CENTURY

Bentley, Eric. *The Playwright as Thinker: A Study of Drama in Modern Times*. New York: Harcourt, 1967.

Bogard, Travis, ed. *Modern Drama: Essays in Criticism*. New York: Oxford UP, 1965.

Booth, Michael. *English Melodrama*. London: Jenkins, 1965.

Brustein, Robert. *The Theatre of Revolt*. Boston: Little, 1964.

Cole, Toby, ed. *Playwrights on Playwriting: The Meaning and Making of Modern Drama from Ibsen to Ionesco*. New York: Hill, 1960.

Driver, Tom Faw. *Romantic Quest and Modern Query: A History of the Modern Theatre*. New York: Delacorte, 1970.

Finney, Gail. *Women in Modern Drama: Freud, Feminism, and European Theater at the Turn of the Century*. Ithaca: Cornell UP, 1989.

Fisher, Judith L., and Stephen Watt, eds. *When They Weren't Doing Shakespeare: Essays on Nineteenth-century British and American Theatre*. Athens: U of Georgia P, 1989.

Gilman, Richard. *The Making of Modern Drama: A Study of Buchner, Ibsen, Strindberg, Chekhov, Pirandello, Brecht, Beckett, Handke*. New York: Farrar, 1974.

Stynan, J. L. *Modern Drama in Theory and Practice*. 3 vols. New York: Cambridge UP, 1980.

Valency, Maurice Jacques. *The Flower and the Castle: An Introduction to Modern Drama*. New York: Schocken, 1982.

Whitaker, Thomas R. *Fields of Play in Modern Drama*. Princeton: Princeton UP, 1977.

Williams, Raymond. *Drama from Ibsen to Eliot*. New York: Oxford UP, 1953.

DRAMA IN THE EARLY AND
MID-TWENTIETH CENTURY

Artaud, Antonin. *The Theatre and Its Double*. Trans. Mary C. Richards. New York: Grove, 1958.

Bentley, Eric. *The Theatre of Commitment and Other Essays on Drama in Our Society*. New York: Atheneum, 1967.

Blau, Herbert, *The Impossible Theatre: A Manifesto*. New York: Macmillan, 1964.

Brater, Enoch, and Ruby Cohn, eds. *Around the Absurd: Essays on Modern and Postmodern Drama*. Ann Arbor: U of Michigan P, 1990.

Bogard, Travis, and William I. Oliver, eds. *Modern Drama: Essays in Criticism*. New York: Oxford UP, 1965.

Brockett, Oscar G. *History of the Theatre*. 5th ed. Boston: Allyn, 1987.

Brook, Peter. *The Empty Space*. New York: Avon, 1968.

Cohn, Ruby. *From Desire to Godot: Pocket Theater of Postwar Paris*. Berkeley: U of California P, 1987.

Davidson, Clifford, C. J. Gianakaris, and John H. Stroupe, eds. *Drama in the Twentieth Century: Comparative and Critical Essays*. New York: AMS, 1984.

Esslin, Martin. *The Theatre of the Absurd*. Woodstock, NY: Overlook, 1973.

Gassner, John. *Theatre at the Crossroads*. New York: Holt, 1960.

Goldberg, RosaLee. *Performance: Live Art 1909 to the Present*. New York: Abrams, 1979.

Kernan, Alvin B., ed. *The Modern American Theater: A Collection of Critical Essays*. Englewood Cliffs: Prentice, 1967.

Kirby, Michael. *A Formalist Theatre*. Philadelphia: U of Pennsylvania P, 1987.

Orr, John. *Tragic Drama and Modern Society: Studies in Social and Literary Theory of Drama from 1870 to the Present*. New York: Macmillan, 1981.

Piscator, Erwin. *The Political Theatre: A History, 1914–1929*. Trans. Hugh Rorrison. London: Eyre Methuen, 1980.

Roose-Evans, James. *Experimental Theatre: From Stanislavsky to Today*. Rev. ed. London: Studio Vista, 1973.

Smith, Wendy. *Real Life Drama: The Group Theatre and America, 1931–1940*. New York: Knopf, 1990.

Szilassy, Zolt N. *American Theater of the 1960s*. Carbondale: U of Illinois P, 1986.

CONTEMPORARY DRAMA

Betsko, Kathleen, and Rachel Koenig. *Interviews with Contemporary Women Playwrights*. New York: Beech Tree, 1987.

Blau, Herbert. *Eye of Prey: Subversions of the Postmodern.* Bloomington: Indiana UP, 1987.

Blumenthal, Eileen. *Joseph Chaikin: Exploring at the Boundaries of Theatre.* New York: Cambridge UP, 1984.

Brecht, Stefan. *The Theatre of Visions: Robert Wilson.* Frankfurt am Main: Suhrkamp, 1978.

Cheney, Sheldon. *New Movement in the Theatre.* Westport: Greenwood, 1971.

The Drama Review [journal]. New York U.

Grotowski, Jerzy. *Towards a Poor Theatre.* New York: Simon, 1968.

Hart, Lynda, ed. *Making a Spectacle: Feminist Essays on Contemporary Women's Theatre.* Ann Arbor: U of Michigan P, 1989.

Hayman, Ronald. *Theatre and Anti-Theatre: New Movements Since Beckett.* New York: Oxford UP, 1979.

Hill, Errol, ed. *The Theatre of Black Americans.* 2 vols. Englewood Cliffs: Prentice, 1980.

Inverso, MaryBeth. *The Gothic Impulse in Contemporary Drama.* Ann Arbor: U of Michigan P, 1990.

Lahr, John. *Up Against the Fourth Wall: Essays on Modern Theatre.* New York: Grove, 1968.

Marranca, Bonnie, ed. *The Theatre of Images.* New York: Drama Book Specialists, 1977.

Orr, John. *Tragicomedy and Contemporary Culture: Play and Performance from Beckett to Shepard.* Ann Arbor: U of Michigan P, 1990.

Parker, Dorothy. *Essays on Modern American Drama: Williams, Miller, Albee, and Shepard.* Toronto: U of Toronto P, 1987.

Savran, David. *In Their Own Words: Contemporary American Playwrights.* New York: Theatre Communications Group, 1988.

Schechner, Richard. *Environmental Theater.* New York: Hawthorn, 1973.

Wellworth, George E. *The Theater of Protest and Paradox.* New York: New York UP, 1971.

Selected References for Playwrights and Plays

ARISTOPHANES

Dane, Joseph A. *Parody: Critical Concepts Versus Literary Practices, Aristophanes to Sterne.* Norman: U of Oklahoma P, 1988.

Deardon, C. W. *The Stage of Aristophanes.* London: Athlone, 1976.

Dover, K. J. *Aristophanic Comedy.* Berkeley: U of California P, 1972.

Gruber, William E. "The Wild Men of Comedy: Transformations in the Comic Hero from Aristophanes to Pirandello." *Genre* 14.2 (1981): 207–27.

Harriott, Rosemary. *Aristophanes: Poet and Dramatist.* Baltimore: Johns Hopkins UP, 1986.

Henderson, Jeffrey. *Aristophanes' "Lysistrata."* New York: Oxford UP, 1987.

McLeish, Kenneth. *The Theatre of Aristophanes.* New York: Taplinger, 1980.

Murray, Gilbert. *Aristophanes.* Oxford: Clarendon, 1933.

Reckford, Kenneth. *Aristophanes' Old-and-New Comedy.* Chapel Hill: U of North Carolina P, 1987.

Ussher, Robert Glenn. *Aristophanes.* New York: Oxford UP, 1979.

SAMUEL BECKETT

List of Plays

Waiting for Godot, 1952
All That Fall, 1957
Endgame, 1958
Act Without Words: A Mime for One Player, 1958
Krapp's Last Tape, 1958
Embers, 1959
Act Without Words II, 1959
Happy Days, 1961
Words and Music, 1962
Cascando, 1963
Play, 1963
Come and Go: Dramaticule, 1965
Film, 1965
Breath, 1970
Not I, 1973
That Time, 1976
Footfalls, 1976
Rough for Theatre I, 1976
Rough for Theatre II, 1976
A Piece of Monologue, 1979
Rockaby, 1981
Ohio Impromptu, 1981
Catastrophe, 1982
What Where, 1984

Astro, Alan. *Understanding Beckett.* Columbia: U of South Carolina P, 1990.

Ben-Zvi, Linda, ed. *Women in Beckett: Performance and Critical Perspectives.* Urbana: U of Illinois P, 1990.

Brater, Enoch, ed. *Beckett at 80: Beckett in Context.* New York: Oxford UP, 1986.

———. *Why Beckett: With 122 Illustrations.* New York: Thames, 1989.

Butler, Lance S., and Robin J. Davis, eds. *Rethinking Beckett: A Collection of Critical Essays.* New York: St. Martin's, 1990.

Cohn, Ruby. *Just Play: Beckett's Theater.* Princeton: Princeton UP, 1980.

———, ed. *Samuel Beckett: A Collection of Criticism.* New York: McGraw, 1975.

Dearlove, J. E. *Accommodating the Chaos: Samuel Beckett's Nonrelational Art.* Durham: Duke UP, 1982.

Doll, Mary Aswell. *Beckett and Myth: An Archetypal Approach.* Syracuse: Syracuse UP, 1988.

Esslin, Martin, ed. *Samuel Beckett: A Collection of Critical Essays.* Englewood Cliffs: Prentice, 1965.

Fletcher, Beryl S., et al. *A Student's Guide to the Plays of Samuel Beckett.* 2nd ed. Boston: Faber, 1985.

Fletcher, John. *Beckett, the Playwright.* New York: Hill, 1985.

Gidal, Peter. *Understanding Beckett.* New York: St. Martin's, 1986.

Gontarski, S. E. *On Beckett: Essays and Criticism.* New York: Grove, 1986.

Kenner, Hugh. *A Reader's Guide to Samuel Beckett.* New York: Farrar, 1973.

Lyons, Charles R. *Samuel Beckett.* New York: Grove, 1983.

Rosen, Steven J. *Samuel Beckett and the Pessimistic Tradition.* New Brunswick: Rutgers UP, 1976.

Beckett's *All That Fall*

Poutney, Rosemary. *Theatre of Shadows: Samuel Beckett's Drama from* All That Fall *to* Footfalls, *with Commentaries on the Latest Plays.* Totowa: Barnes, 1988.

Schirmer, Gregory A. "The Irish Connection: Ambiguity of Language in *All That Fall.*" *College Literature* 8.3 (1981): 283–91.

Van Laan, Thomas F. "*All That Fall* as 'a Play for Radio.'" *Modern Drama* 28 (1985): 38–47.

Beckett's *Endgame*

Beja, Morris, S. E. Gontarski, and Pierre Astier, eds. *Samuel Beckett: Humanistic Perspectives.* Columbus: Ohio State UP, 1983.

Bloom, Harold. *Samuel Beckett's "Endgame."* New York: Chelsea, 1988.

Bryden, Mary. "The Sacrificial Victim of Beckett's *Endgame.*" *Literature and Theology* 4.2 (1990): 219–25.

Lawley, Paul. "Adoption in *Endgame.*" *Modern Drama* 31 (1988): 529–35.

Noguchi, Rei. "Style and Strategy in *Endgame.*" *Journal of Beckett Studies* 9 (1984): 101–11.

O'Dair, Sharon K. "'The Contentless Passion of an Unfruitful Wind': Irony and Laughter in *Endgame.*" *Criticism* 28.2 (1986): 165–78.

APHRA BEHN

List of Plays

The Forced Marriage, 1651
The Amorous Prince, 1671
The Dutch Lover, 1677
ABDELAZER, 1677
The Town Fop, 1677
The Rover, 1677
Sir Patient Fancy, 1678
The Feigned Courtesans, 1679
The Rover, Part 2, 1681
The False Count, 1682
The Roundheads, 1682
The City Heiress, 1682
The Young King, 1683
The Lucky Chance, 1687
The Emperor of the Moon, 1687
The Widow Ranter, 1690
The Younger Brother, 1696

Armistid, J. M. *Four Restoration Playwrights: A Reference Guide to Thomas Shadwell, Aphra Behn, Nathaniel Lee, and Thomas Otway.* Boston: Hall, 1984.

DeRitter, Jones. "*The Gypsy, The Rover,* and the Wanderer: Aphra Behn's Revision of Thomas Killigrew." *Restoration: Studies in English Literary Culture, 1660–1700* 10.2 (1986): 82–92.

Gallagher, Catherine. "Who Was That Masked Woman? The Prostitute and the Playwright in the Comedies of Aphra Behn." *Last Laughs.* Ed. Gina Barreca. New York: Gordon, 1989. 23–42.

Goreau, Angeline. "'Last Night's Rambles': Restoration Literature and the War Between the Sexes." *The Sexual Dimension in Literature.* Ed. Alan Bold. Totowa: Barnes, 1982.

Jones, Jane. "New Light on the Background and Early Life of Aphra Behn." *Notes and Queries* 37 (1990): 288–93.

Link, Frederick M. *Aphra Behn.* Boston: Twayne, 1969.

Lussier, Mark. "'The Vile Mercandize of Fortune': Women, Economy, and Desire in Aphra Behn." *Women's Studies* 18.4 (1991): 379–93.

Mendelson, Sara Heller. *The Mental World of Stuart Women: Three Studies.* Amherst: U of Massachusetts P, 1987.

Munns, Jessica. "'I by a Double Right Thy Bounties

Claim': Aphra Behn and Sexual Space." *Curtain Calls: British and American Women and the Theater, 1660–1820.* Ed. Mary Anne Schofield and Cecilia Macheski. Athens: Ohio UP, 1991.

Musser, Joseph F., Jr. "'Imposing Nought but Constancy in Love': Aphra Behn Snares *The Rover.*" *Restoration: Studies in English Literary Culture, 1660–1700* 3.1 (1979): 17–25.

Wheatley, Christopher. "Romantic Love and Social Necessities: Reconsidering Justifications for Marriage in Restoration Comedy." *Restoration: Studies in English Literary Culture, 1660–1700* 14 (1990): 58–70.

BERTOLT BRECHT

Brecht, Bertolt. *Brecht on Theatre: The Development of an Aesthetic.* Ed. and trans. John Willett. New York: Hill, 1964.

Brown, Russell E. *Intimacy and Intimidation: Three Essays on Bertolt Brecht.* Stuttgart: Steiner, 1990.

Demetz, Peter, ed. *Brecht: A Collection of Critical Essays.* Englewood Cliffs: Prentice, 1962.

Esslin, Martin. *Brecht: The Man and His Works.* Garden City: Doubleday, 1971.

Ewen, Frederick. *Bertolt Brecht: His Life, His Art and His Times.* New York: Citadel, 1967.

Feugi, John. *Bertolt Brecht: Chaos, According to Plan.* New York: Cambridge UP, 1987.

Gray, Ronald. *Bertolt Brecht.* New York: Grove, 1967.

Hill, Claude. *Bertolt Brecht.* New York: Twayne, 1975.

Spalter, Max. *Brecht's Tradition.* Baltimore: Johns Hopkins UP, 1967.

Speirs, Ronald. *Bertolt Brecht.* New York: St. Martin's, 1987.

Willett, John. *Brecht in Context: Contemporary Approaches.* London: Methuen, 1984.

———. *The Theatre of Bertolt Brecht.* New York, 1959.

ANTON CHEKHOV

List of Plays

Platonov, 1881?
On the High Road, 1887
The Swan Song, 1887
The Bear, 1888
The Proposal, 1889
A Tragic Role, 1889
The Wedding, 1889

Ivanov, 1889
The Wood Demon, 1889
The Seagull, 1896
Uncle Vanya, 1899
Three Sisters, 1901
The Cherry Orchard, 1903

Barricelli, Jean-Pierre, ed. *Chekhov's Great Plays: A Critical Anthology.* New York: New York UP, 1981.

———. "Counterpoint of the Snapping String: Chekhov's *The Cherry Orchard.*" *Chekhov's Great Plays: A Critical Anthology.* New York: New York UP, 1981. 111–28.

Bely, Andrei. "The Cherry Orchard." *Russian Dramatic Theory from Pushkin to the Symbolists: An Anthology.* Ed. and trans. L. Senelick. Austin: U of Texas P, 1981. 89–92.

Deer, Irving. "Speech as Action in Chekhov's *The Cherry Orchard.*" *Educational Theatre Journal* 10 (1959): 30–34.

Eekman, Thomas A. *Critical Essays on Anton Chekhov.* Boston: Hall, 1989.

Emeljanow, Victor. *Chekhov: The Critical Heritage.* Boston: Routledge, 1981.

Hahn, Beverly. "Chekhov's *The Cherry Orchard.*" *Critical Review* 16 (1973): 56–72.

Hingley, Ronald. *Chekhov: A Biographical and Critical Study.* New York: Barnes, 1966.

Jackson, Robert Louis. *Chekhov: A Collection of Critical Essays.* Englewood Cliffs: Prentice, 1967.

Karlinsky, Simon, and Michael Heim, eds. *Anton Chekhov's Life and Thought: Selected Letters and Commentary.* Berkeley: U of California P, 1975.

Magarshak, David. *Chekhov the Dramatist.* New York: Hill, 1960.

Meister, Charles. *Chekhov Criticism 1880 through 1986.* New York: McFarland, 1988.

Peace, Richard. *Chekhov: A Study of the Four Major Plays.* New Haven: Yale UP, 1983.

Remaley, Peter B. "Chekhov's *The Cherry Orchard.*" *South Atlantic Bulletin* 38 (1973): 16–20.

Russell, Robert, and Andrew Barratt, eds. *Russian Theatre in the Age of Modernism.* New York: St. Martin's, 1990.

Stanislavsky, Konstantin. *My Life in Art.* Boston, 1924.

Stynan, J. L. *Chekhov in Performance.* Cambridge: Cambridge UP, 1971.

Toumanova, Princess Nina Andronikova. *Anton Chekhov: The Voice of Twilight Russia.* New York: Columbia UP, 1960.

Valency, Maurice. *The Breaking String: The Plays of Anton Chekhov.* New York: Oxford UP, 1966.

Welleck, Rene, and Nonna D. Welleck, eds. *Chekhov:*

New Perspectives. Englewood Cliffs: Prentice, 1984.

Williams, Lee J. *Anton Chekhov, the Iconoclast.* Scranton: U of Scranton P, 1989.

WILLIAM CONGREVE

Braverman, Richard. "Capital Relations and *The Way of the World.*" *ELH* 52.1 (1985): 133–58.

Dobree, Bonamy. *Congreve.* London: British Council, 1963.

Hodges, John C. *Congreve the Man: A Biography.* London: Oxford UP, 1941.

Kroll, Richard. "Discourse and Power in *The Way of the World.*" *ELH* 53.4 (1986): 727–58.

Love, Harold. *Congreve.* Oxford: Blackwell, 1974.

Lynch, Kathleen M. *The Social Mode of Restoration Comedy.* New York: Macmillan, 1926.

Markley, Robert. *Two-Edged Weapons: Style and Ideology in the Comedies of Etherege, Wycherley, and Congreve.* New York: Oxford UP, 1988.

Morris, Brian, ed. *Congreve: A Collection of Critical Studies.* London: Benn, 1972.

Mueschke, Paul and Carol. *A New View of Congreve's The Way of the World.* Ann Arbor: U of Michigan P, 1958.

Novak, Maximilian. *William Congreve.* Boston: Twayne, 1971.

Peters, Julie Stone. *Congreve: The Drama, and the Printed Word.* Stanford: Stanford UP, 1990.

Van Voris, W. *The Cultivated Stance: The Designs of Congreve's Plays.* Dublin: Dolmen, 1965.

Williams, Aubrey Lake. *An Approach to Congreve.* New Haven: Yale UP, 1979.

EURIPIDES

Barlow, Shirley Anne. "Stereotype and Reversal in Euripides' *Medea.*" *Greece & Rome* 36 (1989): 158–71.

Burian, Peter, ed. *Directions in Euripidean Criticism.* Durham: Duke UP, 1985.

Collard, Christopher. *Euripides.* New York: Oxford UP, 1981.

Foley, Helene P. "Medea's Divided Self." *Classical Antiquity* 8 (1989): 61–85.

———. *Ritual Irony: Poetry and Sacrifice in Euripides.* Ithaca: Cornell UP, 1985.

Halleran, Michael P. *Stagecraft in Euripides.* Totowa: Barnes, 1985.

Keane, Ellen Marie, Judith P. Saunders, and Ellen S. Silber. "Female Outlaws: Exploring Ethical Choice Through Literature." *Women's Voices.* Ed. Lorna D. Edmundson. Littleton, MA: Copley, 1987.

Meagher, Robert E. *Mortal Vision: The Wisdom of Euripides.* New York: St. Martin's, 1989.

Michelini, Ann N. *Euripides and the Tragic Tradition.* Madison: U of Wisconsin P, 1987.

O'Connor, E. A. M. E. *Aspects of Human Sacrifice in the Tragedies of Euripides.* Amsterdam: Grner, 1987.

Pucci, Pietro. *The Violence of Pity in Euripides' "Medea."* Ithaca: Cornell UP, 1980.

Segal, Erich, ed. *Euripides: A Collection of Critical Essays.* Englewood Cliffs: Prentice, 1968.

Stoeckl, Ula. "The Medea Myth in Contemporary Cinema." *Film Criticism* 10 (1985): 47–51.

Tuana, Nancy. "Medea: With the Eyes of the Lost Goddess." *Soundings: An Interdisciplinary Journal* 68.2 (1985): 253–72.

Whitman, Cedric Hubbel. *Euripides and the Full Circle of Myth.* Cambridge: Harvard UP, 1974.

EVERYMAN

Bevington, David M. *From Mankind to Marlowe: Growth of Structure in the Popular Drama of Tudor England.* Cambridge: Harvard UP, 1962.

Cawley, A. C. *Everyman.* Manchester: Manchester UP, 1977.

———, ed. *"Everyman" and Medieval Miracle Plays.* New York: Dutton, 1977.

Garner, Stanton B., Jr. "Theatricality in Mankind and *Everyman.*" *Studies in Philology* 84.3 (1987): 272–85.

Gilman, Donald, ed. *"Everyman" and Company: Essays on the Theme and Structure of the European Moral Play.* New York: AMS, 1989.

Munson, William. "Knowing and Doing in *Everyman.*" *The Chaucer Review* 19.3 (1985): 252–71.

Ryan, Lawrence V. "Doctrine and Dramatic Structure in *Everyman,*" *Mississippi Quarterly* 14 (1961): 3–13.

Spinrad, Phoebe S. "The Last Temptation of Everyman." *Philological Quarterly* 64.2 (1985): 185–94.

Tanner, Ron. "Humor in *Everyman* and the Middle English Morality Play." *Philological Quarterly* 70 (1991): 149–61.

White, D. Jerry. *Early English Drama: "Everyman" to 1580, A Reference Guide.* Boston: Hall, 1986.

BRIAN FRIEL

Ahrens, Ruediger. "National Myths and Stereotypes in Modern Irish Drama: Sean O'Casey, Brendan Behan, Brian Friel." *Fu Jen Studies: Literature & Linguistics* 21 (1988): 89–110.

Blake, Ann. "Brian Friel and the Irish Theatre." *Australasian Drama Studies* 10 (1987): 107–17.

Dantanus, Ulf. *Brian Friel: The Growth of an Irish*

Dramatist. Göteborg, Sweden: Acta Universitatis Gothoburgensis, 1985.

————. *Brian Friel: A Study.* Boston: Faber, 1988.

Etherton, Michael. *Contemporary Irish Dramatists.* New York: St. Martin's, 1989.

Kearney, Richard. "Friel and the Politics of Language Play." *Massachusetts Review* 28 (1987): 510–15.

Leary, Daniel. "The Romanticism of Brian Friel." *Contemporary Irish Writing.* Ed. James D. Brophy and Raymond J. Porter. Boston: Twayne, 1983. 127–41.

Maxwell, D. E. S. *Brian Friel.* Lewisburg: Bucknell UP, 1973.

McGrath, F. C. "Brian Friel and the Politics of the Anglo-Irish Language." *Colby Quarterly* 26.4 (1990): 241–48.

————. "Language, Myth, and History in the Later Plays of Brian Friel." *Contemporary Literature* 30.4 (1989): 534–45.

O'Brien, George. *Brian Friel.* Boston: Twayne, 1990.

Pine, Richard. *Brian Friel and Ireland's Drama.* New York: Routledge, 1990.

Rabey, David Ian. *British and Irish Political Drama in the Twentieth Century.* New York: St. Martin's, 1986.

Verstaeta, Ginette. "Brian Friel's Drama and the Limits of Language." *History and Violence in Anglo-Irish Literature.* Ed. Joris Duytschaever and Geert Lernout. Amsterdam: Rodopi, 1988. 85–96.

ATHOL FUGARD

Benson, Mary. "Keeping an Appointment with the Future: The Theatre of Athol Fugard." *Theatre Quarterly* 7 (1977/78): 77–83.

Bragg, Melvyn. "Athol Fugard, Playwright — a Conversation with Melvyn Bragg." *Listener* 5 Dec. 1974: 734.

Fugard, Athol. "Fugard on Actors, Actors on Fugard." *Theatre Quarterly* 7 (1977/78): 83–87.

————. "Fugard on Fugard." *Yale Theatre* 1 (Winter 1973): 41–54.

————. "Letter from Athol Fugard." *Classic* 1 (1966): 78–80.

————. *Notebooks 1960–1977.* New York: Knopf, 1983.

Gray, Stephen, ed. *Athol Fugard.* Southern Africa Literature Series 1. Johannesburg: McGraw, 1982.

Heywood, Christopher. *Aspects of South African Literature.* London: Heinemann, 1976.

Kavanagh, Robert Mshengu. *Theatre and Cultural Struggle in South Africa.* London: Zed, 1985.

Post, Robert M. "Racism in Athol Fugard's 'MASTER HAROLD' . . . and the boys." *World Literature Written in English* 30.1 (1990): 97–102.

Seidenspinner, Margarete. *Exploring the Labyrinth: Athol Fugard's Approach to South African Drama.* Essen: Verlag Die Blaue Eule, 1986.

Vandenbrouke, Russell. *Truths the Hand Can Touch: The Theatre of Athol Fugard.* New York: Theatre Communications Group, 1985.

Walder, Dennis. *Athol Fugard.* New York: Grove, 1985.

Wertheim, Albert. "Ballroom Dancing, Kites and Politics: Athol Fugard's 'MASTER HAROLD' . . . and the boys." *SPAN* 30 (1990): 141–55.

LADY GREGORY (ISABELLA AUGUSTA GREGORY)

Adams, Hazard. *Lady Gregory.* Lewisburg: Bucknell UP, 1973.

Coxhead, Elizabeth. *Lady Gregory: A Literary Portrait.* New York: Harcourt, 1961.

Gregory, Isabella Augusta. *Lady Gregory's Journals, 1910–1930.* New York: Oxford UP, 1978.

————. *Our Irish Theatre.* Gerrards Cross: Smythe, 1972.

Kohfeldt, Mary Lou. *Lady Gregory: The Woman Behind the Irish Renaissance.* New York: Atheneum, 1985.

Kopper, E. A., Jr. "Lady Gregory's *The Rising of the Moon.*" *Explicator* 47 (1989): 29–31.

Maxwell, D. E. S. *A Critical History of Modern Irish Drama: 1891–1980.* New York: Cambridge UP, 1984.

O'Connor, Ulick. *All the Olympians.* New York: Atheneum, 1984.

Owens, C'il'n D., and Joan N. Radner. *Irish Drama: 1900–1980.* Washington: Catholic U of America P, 1990.

Saddlemyer, Ann. *In Defense of Lady Gregory, Playwright.* Dublin: Dolmen, 1966.

————. *Lady Gregory, Fifty Years After.* Totowa: Barnes, 1987.

LORRAINE HANSBERRY

Brown, Lloyd W. "Lorraine Hansberry as Ironist: A Reappraisal of *A Raisin in the Sun.*" *Journal of Black Studies* 4 (March 1974): 237–47.

Carter, Steven R. *Hansberry's Drama: Commitment and Complexity.* Urbana: U of Illinois P, 1991.

Cheney, Anne. *Lorraine Hansberry.* Boston: Twayne, 1984.

Freedman, Morris. *American Drama in Social Context.* Carbondale: Southern Illinois UP, 1971.

Keyssar, Helene. "Rites and Responsibilities: The Drama of Black American Women." *The New Women Playwrights.* Ed. Enoch Brater. Oxford: Oxford UP, 1989. 226–40.

Miller, Jeanne-Marie A. "Images of Black Women in Plays by Black Playwrights." *CLA Journal* 20 (June 1977): 498–99.

Nemiroff, Robert. *To Be Young, Gifted, and Black: A Portrait of Lorraine Hansberry in Her Own Words.* Englewood Cliffs: Prentice, 1969.

Scheader, Catherine. *They Found a Way: Lorraine Hansberry.* Chicago: Children's, 1978.

Washington, J. Charles. "*A Raisin in the Sun* Revisited." *Black American Literature Forum* 22.1 (1988): 109–24.

Weales, Gerald. "Lorraine Hansberry." *Contemporary Dramatists.* Ed. D. L. Kirkpatrick. 4th ed. Chicago: St. James, 1988. 653–54.

Wilkerson, Margaret B. "Excavating Our History: The Importance of Biographies of Women of Color." *Black American Forum* 24.1 (1990): 73–84.

Williams, Mance. *Black Theatre in the 1960s and 1970s.* Westport: Greenwood, 1985.

HENRIK IBSEN

List of Plays

Catiline, 1850
Grouse in Justedal, 1850
The Burial Mound, 1850
Norma, 1851
St. John's Eve, 1853
Lady Inger of Østraat, 1855
The Feast at Solhoug, 1856
Olaf Liljekrans, 1857
The Vikings at Helgeland, 1857
Love's Comedy, 1862
The Pretenders, 1864
Brand, 1866
Peer Gynt, 1867
The League of Youth, 1869
Emperor and Galilean, 1873
The Pillars of Society, 1877
A Doll House, 1879
Quicksands, 1880
Ghosts, 1881
The Child Wife, 1882
An Enemy of the People, 1882
The Wild Duck, 1884
Rosmersholm, 1886
The Lady from the Sea, 1888
Hedda Gabler, 1890
The Master Builder, 1892
Little Eyolf, 1894
John Gabriel Borkman, 1896
When We Dead Awaken, 1899

Ackerman, Gretchen P. *Ibsen and the English Stage, 1889–1903.* New York: Garland, 1987.

Chamberlain, John S. *Ibsen: The Open Vision.* London: Athlone, 1982.

Egan, Michael, ed. *Ibsen: The Critical Heritage.* London: Routledge, 1972.

Fjelde, Rolf, ed. *Ibsen: A Collection of Critical Essays.* Englewood Cliffs: Prentice, 1965.

Gaskell, Ronald. *Drama and Reality: The European Theatre Since Ibsen.* London: Routledge, 1972.

Lebowitz, Naomi. *Ibsen and the Great World.* Baton Rouge: Louisiana UP, 1990.

McFarlane, James, ed. *Discussions of Henrik Ibsen.* Boston: Heath, 1962.

Marker, Frederick J. *Ibsen's Lively Art: A Performance Study of the Major Plays.* New York: Cambridge UP, 1989.

Meyer, Michael, *Henrik Ibsen: A Biography.* 3 vols. Garden City: Doubleday, 1971.

Noreng, Harald, et al., eds. *Contemporary Approaches to Ibsen.* Oslo: Universitetsforlaget, 1977.

Northam, John. *Ibsen: A Critical Study.* Cambridge: Cambridge UP, 1973.

Shaw, Bernard. *The Quintessence of Ibsenism.* New York: Hill, 1957.

Thomas, David. *Henrik Ibsen.* New York: Grove, 1984.

Ibsen's *A Doll House*

Andreas-Salomé, Lou. *Ibsen's Heroines.* Ed. and trans. Siegfried Mandel. Austrian/German Culture Series. Redding Ridge, CT: Black Swan, 1985.

Bradbrook, M. C. "*A Doll's House* and the Unweaving of the Web." *Women and Literature, 1779–1982.* Vol. 2. Totowa: Barnes, 1982. 81–92. 2 vols.

Downs, R. B. "Birth of the New Woman." *Molders of the Modern Mind.* New York: Barnes, 1961. 311–14.

Durbach, Errol. "*A Doll's House*": *Ibsen's Myth of Transformation.* Boston: Twayne, 1991.

Gassner, John. "An Ibsen Revival: Too Much Doll." *Dramatic Soundings.* New York: Crown, 1968. 290–94.

Hardwick, Elizabeth. "*A Doll's House.*" *Seduction and Betrayal.* New York: Random, 1974. 33–48.

Ibsen, Henrik. "*Doll's House*" [Ibsen's notes on *A Doll House*]. *Playwrights on Playwriting.* Ed. Toby Cole. New York: Hill, 1960. 151–54.

Sprinchorn, E. M. "Ibsen and the Actors." *Ibsen and the Theatre.* Ed. Errol Durbach. New York: New York UP, 1980. 118–30.

Ibsen's *Hedda Gabler*

Ackley, Katherine Anne. "A Rage to Live: The Violent Life and Death of Hedda Gabler." *Women and Violence in Literature: An Essay Collection.* Ed. Katherine Anne Ackley. New York: Garland, 1990. 163–73.

Braunmuller, A. R. "Hedda Gabler and the Sources of Symbolism." *Drama and Symbolism.* Ed. James Redmond. New York: Cambridge UP, 1982. 57–70.

Fuchs, Elinor. "Mythic Structure in *Hedda Gabler*: The Mask Behind the Face." *Comparative Drama* 19.3 (1985): 209–21.

Ibsen, Henrik. "*Hedda Gabler*" [Ibsen's notes on *Hedda Gabler*]. *Playwrights on Playwriting.* Ed. Toby Cole. New York: Hill, 1960. 156–70.

Low, Lisa Elaine. "In Defense of Hedda." *Massachusetts Studies in English* 8.3 (1982): 43–49.

Lyons, Charles R. "*Hedda Gabler*": *Gender, Role, and World.* Boston: Twayne, 1991.

Mayer, H. "Judith as Bourgeois Heroine." *Outsiders.* Cambridge: MIT P, 1982. 53–75.

Olsen, Stein Haugom. "Why Does Hedda Gabler Marry Jorgen Tesman?" *Modern Drama* 28 (1985): 591–610.

Suzman, Janet. "*Hedda Gabler*: The Play in Performance." *Ibsen and the Theatre.* Ed. Errol Durbach. New York: New York UP, 1980. 83–104.

Tynan, Kenneth. "*Hedda Gabler.*" *Curtains.* New York: Atheneum, 1961. 77–78.

Watson, George J. "Ibsen and Miller: The Individual and Society." *Drama: An Introduction.* New York: St. Martin's, 1983. 112–31.

THOMAS MIDDLETON AND WILLIAM ROWLEY

Baines, Barbara J. *The Lust Motif in the Plays of Thomas Middleton.* Salzburg: Institute for English Language and Literature, 1973.

Britten, Norman. *Thomas Middleton.* New York: Twayne, 1972.

Bromhan, Tony. *"The Changeling" and the Years of Crisis, 1619–1624: A Hieroglyph of Britain.* New York: Pinter, 1990.

Bueler, Lois E. "The Rhetoric of Change in *The Changeling.*" *English Literary Renaissance* 14.1 (1984): 95–113.

Cherry, Caroline Lockett. *The Most Unvaluedst Purchase: Women in the Plays of Thomas Middleton.* Salzburg: Institute for English Language and Literature, 1973.

Covatta, Anthony. *Thomas Middleton's City Comedies.* Lewisburg: Bucknell UP, 1973.

Daalder, Joost. "Folly and Madness in *The Changeling.*" *Essays in Criticism* 38 (1988): 1–21.

Dunkel, Wilbur Dwight. *The Dramatic Technique of Thomas Middleton in His Comedies of London Life.* New York: Russell, 1967.

Friedenreich, Kenneth. *Accompaninge the Players: Essays Celebrating Thomas Middleton, 1580–1980.* New York: AMS, 1983.

Heinemann, Margot. *Puritanism and Theatre: Thomas Middleton and Opposition Drama Under the Early Stuarts.* New York: Cambridge UP, 1980.

Hubert, Ronald. "Middleton's Nameless Art." *Sewanee Review* 95 (1987): 591–609.

Kistner, A. L., and M. K. Kistner. "The Five Structures of *The Changeling.*" *Modern Language Studies* 11 (1981): 40–53.

Kistner, A. L. *Middleton's Tragic Themes.* New York: Lang, 1984.

Lake, David J. *The Canon of Thomas Middleton's Plays: Internal Evidence for the Major Problems of Authorship.* London: Cambridge UP, 1975.

Levay, John. "Middleton and Rowley's *The Changeling.*" *Explicator* 45 (1987): 11–13.

Middleton, Thomas. *A Game at Chess.* New York: Oxford UP, 1990.

———. *The Selected Plays.* Ed. David L. Frost. New York: Cambridge UP, 1978.

———. *The Works of Thomas Middleton.* Ed. A. H. Bullen. London: Nimmo, 1886.

Randall, Dale B. J. "Some Observations on the Theme of Chastity in *The Changeling.*" *English Literary Renaissance* 14.3 (1984): 347–66.

Rowe, George. *Thomas Middleton and the New Comedy Tradition.* Lincoln: U of Nebraska P, 1979.

ARTHUR MILLER

Anderson, M. C. "*Death of a Salesman*: A Consideration of Willy Loman's Role in Twentieth-Century Tragedy." *CRUX* 20.2 (1986): 25–29.

August, Eugene R. "*Death of a Salesman*: A Men's Studies Approach." *Western Ohio Journal* 7.1 (1986): 53–71.

Bloom, Harold, ed. *Arthur Miller's "Death of a Salesman."* New York: Chelsea, 1988.

———. *Willy Loman.* New York: Chelsea, 1990.

Brucher, Richard T. "Willy Loman and the Soul of a New Machine: Technology and the Common Man." *Journal of American Studies* 17.3 (1983): 325–36.

Carson, Neil. *Arthur Miller.* London: Macmillan, 1982.

Corrigan, Robert W., ed. *Arthur Miller: A Collection*

of Critical Essays. Englewood Cliffs: Prentice, 1969.

Gelb, Phillip. "*Death of a Salesman*: A Symposium." *Tulane Drama Review* 2 (1958): 20–21.

Hagopian, John V. "Arthur Miller: The Salesman's Two Cases." *Modern Drama* 6 (1963): 117–25.

Hayman, Ronald. *Arthur Miller.* New York: Ungar, 1972.

Huftel, Sheila. *Arthur Miller: The Burning Glass.* New York: Citadel, 1965.

Koon, Helene Wickham. *Twentieth Century Interpretations of "Death of a Salesman."* Englewood Cliffs: Prentice, 1983.

Martin, Robert A., ed. *Arthur Miller: New Perspectives.* Englewood Cliffs: Prentice, 1982.

Miller, Arthur. *Collected Plays.* New York: Viking, 1957.

——. *The Theater Essays of Arthur Miller.* Ed. and intro. Robert A. Martin. New York: Viking, 1978.

——. *Timebends: A Life.* New York: Grove, 1987.

Roudane, Matthew C., ed. *Conversations with Arthur Miller.* Jackson: UP of Mississippi, 1987.

Schlueter, June, and James K. Flanagan. *Arthur Miller.* New York: Ungar, 1987.

Stanton, Kay. "Women and the American Dream of *Death of a Salesman.*" *Feminist Rereadings of Modern American Drama.* Ed. June Schlueter. Rutherford: Fairleigh Dickinson UP, 1989.

Vidal, Gore, et al. "*Death of a Salesman*: A Symposium." *Tulane Drama Review* 2 (May 1958): 63–69.

MOLIÈRE (JEAN BAPTISTE POQUELIN)

Bermel, Albert. *Molière's Theatrical Bounty: A New View of the Plays.* Carbondale: Southern Illinois UP, 1990.

Gaines, James F. *Molière's Theater.* Columbus: Ohio State UP, 1984.

Gross, Nathan. *From Gesture to Idea: Esthetics and Ethics in Molière's Comedy.* New York: Columbia UP, 1982.

Guicharnaud, Jacques. *Molière: A Collection of Critical Essays.* Englewood Cliffs: Prentice, 1964.

Hall, H. Gaston. *Comedy in Context: Essays on Molière.* Jackson: UP of Mississippi, 1984.

Jagendorf, Zvi. *The Happy End of Comedy: Jonson, Molière, and Shakespeare.* Newark: U of Delaware P, 1984.

Knutson, Harold C. *The Triumph of Wit: Molière and Restoration Comedy.* Columbus: Ohio State UP, 1988.

Molière. *Tartuffe: Comedy in Five Acts.* Trans. Richard Wilbur. New York: Harcourt, 1963.

Walker, Hallam. *Molière.* Rev. ed. Boston: Twayne, 1990.

MARSHA NORMAN

Betsko, Kathleen, and Rachel Koenig. "Marsha Norman." *Interviews with Contemporary Women Playwrights.* New York: Beech Tree, 1987.

Browder, Sally. " 'I Thought You Were Mine': Marsha Norman's *'night, Mother.*" *Mother Puzzles: Daughters and Mothers in Contemporary American Literature.* Ed. Mickey Pearlman. Westport: Greenwood, 1989.

Brustein, Robert. "Robert Brustein on Theater." *New Republic* 2 May 1983: 25–26.

Burkman, Katherine H. "The Demeter Myth and Doubling in Marsha Norman's *'night, Mother.*" *Modern American Drama: The Female Canon.* Ed. June Schlueter. Rutherford: Fairleigh Dickinson UP, 1990. 254–63.

Denby, David. "Stranger in a Strange Land." *Atlantic* Jan. 1985: 44–45.

Gill, Brendan. "The Theatre." *New Yorker* 11 April 1983: 109+.

Gilman, Richard. "Theater." *Nation* 7 May 1983: 586.

Greiff, Louis K. "Fathers, Daughters, and Spiritual Sisters: Marsha Norman's *'night, Mother* and Tennessee Williams's *The Glass Menagerie.*" *Text and Performance Quarterly* 9.3 (1989): 224–28.

Gussow, Mel. "Women Playwrights: New Voices in the Theatre." *New York Times Magazine* 1 May 1983: 22–40.

Hart, Lynda. "Doing Time: Hunger for Power in Marsha Norman's Plays." *Southern Quarterly* 25.3 (1987): 67–69.

Kane, Leslie. "The Way Out, the Way In: Paths to Self in the Plays of Marsha Norman." *Feminine Focus: The New Women Playwrights.* Ed. Enoch Brater. Oxford: Oxford UP, 1989. 255–74.

Kauffmann, Stanley. "More Trick than Tragedy." *Saturday Review* Oct. 1983: 47–48.

Sauvage, Leo. "Different Kinds of Kin." *New Leader* 18 April 1983: 21–22.

Savran, David. *In Their Own Words.* New York: Theater Communications Group, 1988.

Spencer, Jenny S. "Norman's *'night, Mother*: Psychodrama of Female Identity." *Modern Drama* 30.3 (1987): 364–75.

Stone, Elizabeth. "Playwright Marsha Norman: An Optimist Writes About Suicide, Confinement, and Despair." *Ms.* July 1983: 56–59.

Weales, Gerald. "Really 'Going On.' " *Commonweal* 17 June 1983: 370–71.

Wolfe, Irmgard H. "Marsha Norman: A Classified Bibliography." *Studies in American Drama, 1945–Present* 3 (1988): 148–75.

EUGENE O'NEILL

Ahuja, Chaman. *Tragedy, Modern Temper, and O'Neill*. Atlantic Highlands: Humanities, 1984.

Berlin, Normand. *Eugene O'Neill*. New York: Grove, 1987.

Bogard, Travis. *Contour in Time: The Plays of Eugene O'Neill*. New York: Oxford UP, 1988.

Cargill, Oscar, N. Bryllion Fagan, and William J. Fisher, eds. *O'Neill and His Plays: Four Decades of Criticism*. New York: New York UP, 1961.

Gassner, John, ed. *O'Neill: A Collection of Critical Essays*. Englewood Cliffs: Prentice, 1964.

Floyd, Virginia. *The Plays of Eugene O'Neill: A New Assessment*. New York: Ungar, 1985.

Leech, Clifford. *Eugene O'Neill*. New York: Grove, 1963.

Maufort, Marc, ed. *Eugene O'Neill and the Emergence of American Drama*. Atlanta: Rodopi, 1989.

Miller, Jordan Yale. *Eugene O'Neill and American Criticism: A Bibliographical Checklist*. 2nd ed. Hamden: Anchor, 1973.

Moorton, Richard F., Jr. *Eugene O'Neill's Century: Centennial Views on America's Foremost Critic*. New York: Greenwood, 1991.

O'Neill, Eugene. *The Plays of Eugene O'Neill*. 3 vols. New York: Modern Library, 1982.

———. *Long Day's Journey into Night*. New Haven: Yale UP, 1956.

Porter, Laurin. *The Banished Prince: Time, Memory, and Ritual in the Late Plays of Eugene O'Neill*. Ann Arbor: UMI Research, 1988.

Ranald, Margaret Loftus. *The Eugene O'Neill Companion*. Westport: Greenwood, 1984.

Wainscott, Ronald Harold. *Staging O'Neill: The Experimental Years, 1920–1934*. New Haven: Yale UP, 1988.

SUZAN-LORI PARKS

Carr, C. Rev. of *Imperceptible Mutabilities in the Third Kingdom*. *Artforum* Nov. 1989: 154.

Gussow, Mel. Rev. of *The Death of the Last Black Man in the Whole Entire World*. *New York Times* 25 Sept. 1990: C15.

———. Rev. of *Imperceptible Mutabilities in the Third Kingdom*. *New York Times* 20 Sept. 1989: C24.

Holden, Stephen. Rev. of *Betting on the Dust Commander*. *New York Times* 26 June 1991: C12.

HAROLD PINTER

Bloom, Harold, ed. *Harold Pinter*. New York: Chelsea, 1987.

Bold, Alan, ed. *Harold Pinter: You Never Heard Such Silence*. Critical Studies Series. Totowa: Barnes, 1985.

Burkman, Katherine H. *The Dramatic World of Harold Pinter*. Columbia: Ohio State UP, 1971.

Diamond, Elin. *Pinter's Comic Play*. Lewisburg: Bucknell UP, 1985.

Dukore, Bernard F. *Harold Pinter*. 2nd ed. New York: Macmillan, 1988.

Esslin, Martin. *Pinter: The Playwright*. New York: Methuen. 1984.

Gale, Steven H., ed. *Critical Essays on Harold Pinter*. Boston: Hall, 1990.

———. *Harold Pinter: Critical Approaches*. Rutherford: Fairleigh Dickinson UP, 1986.

Ganz, Arthur F., ed. *Pinter: A Collection of Critical Essays*. Englewood Cliffs: Prentice, 1979.

Hayman, Ronald. *Harold Pinter*. New York: Ungar, 1973.

Hinchliffe, Arnold P. *Harold Pinter*. Boston: Twayne, 1981.

Kerr, Walter. *Harold Pinter*. New York: Columbia UP, 1967.

Mayberry, Bob. *Theatre of Discord: Dissonance in Beckett, Albee, and Pinter*. Rutherford: Fairleigh Dickinson UP, 1989.

Pinter, Harold. *Complete Works*. 3 vols. New York: Grove, 1977–78.

Quigley, Austin E. *The Pinter Problem*. Princeton: Princeton UP, 1975.

Strunk, Volker. *Harold Pinter: Towards a Poetics of His Plays*. New York: Lang, 1989.

Sykes, Arlene. *Harold Pinter*. New York: Humanities, 1970.

LUIGI PIRANDELLO

Bassnett, Susan. *File on Pirandello*. London: Methuen, 1989.

Bassnett-McGuire, Susan. *Luigi Pirandello*. New York: Grove, 1983.

Bentley, Eric. *The Pirandello Commentaries*. Evanston: Northwestern UP, 1986.

Bloom, Harold. *Luigi Pirandello*. New York: Chelsea, 1989.

Büdel, Oscar. *Pirandello*. New York: Hillary, 1969.

Cambon, Glauco, ed. *Pirandello: A Collection of Critical Essays*. Englewood Cliffs: Prentice, 1967.

Caputi, Anthony. *Pirandello and the Crisis of Modern Consciousness*. Urbana: U of Illinois P, 1988.

Guidice, Gaspare. *Pirandello: A Biography*. Trans. Alastair Hamilton. New York: Oxford UP, 1975.

Mariani, Umberto. "The 'Pirandellian' Character." *Canadian Journal of Italian Studies* 12.38–39 (1989): 1–9.

Oliver, Roger W. *Dreams of Passion: The Theater of Luigi Pirandello*. New York: New York UP, 1979.

Paolucci, Anne. *Pirandello's Theater*. Carbondale: Southern Illinois UP, 1974.

Pirandello, Luigi. *Naked Masks, Five Plays*. Ed. Eric Bentley. New York: Dutton, 1952.

———. *Short Stories*. Ed. and trans. Frederick May. New York: Oxford UP, 1965.

Ragusa, Olga. "Comparative Perspectives on Pirandello." *Atenea* 8.1 (1988): 19–36.

Starkie, Walter. *Luigi Pirandello, 1867–1936*. 3rd ed. Berkeley: U of California P, 1965.

Stone, Jennifer. *Pirandello's Naked Prompt: The Structure of Repetition in Modernism*. Ravenna: Longo Editore, 1989.

PLAUTUS

Segal, Erich. *Roman Laughter: The Comedy of Plautus*. New York: Oxford UP, 1987.

Slater, Niall W. *Plautus in Performance: The Theater of the Mind*. Princeton: Princeton UP, 1985.

SENECA

Fairweather, Janet. *Seneca the Elder*. New York: Cambridge UP, 1981.

Tarrant, R. J. *Seneca's "Thyestes."* Atlanta: Scholars, 1985.

WILLIAM SHAKESPEARE

List of Plays

Comedies
The Comedy of Errors, 1592–94
The Taming of the Shrew, 1593–94
The Two Gentlemen of Verona, 1594
Love's Labor's Lost, 1594–95
A Midsummer Night's Dream, 1595–96
The Merchant of Venice, 1596–97
The Merry Wives of Windsor, 1597
Much Ado About Nothing, 1598–99
As You Like It, 1599
Twelfth Night, or What You Will, 1601–02
All's Well That Ends Well, 1602–03
Measure for Measure, 1604
Histories
Henry the Sixth, Part One, 1589–90
Henry the Sixth, Part Two, 1590–91
Henry the Sixth, Part Three, 1590–91
Richard the Third, 1592–93
King John, 1594–96
Richard the Second, 1595
Henry the Fourth, Part One, 1596–97
Henry the Fourth, Part Two, 1598
Henry the Fifth, 1599
Henry the Eighth, 1612–13
Tragedies
The Tragedy of Titus Andronicus, 1593
The Tragedy of Romeo and Juliet, 1595–96
The Tragedy of Julius Caesar, 1599
The Tragedy of Hamlet, 1600–01
The History of Troilus and Cressida, 1601–02
The Tragedy of Othello, the Moor of Venice, 1604
The Tragedy of King Lear, 1605
The Tragedy of Macbeth, 1606
The Tragedy of Antony and Cleopatra, 1606
The Tragedy of Coriolanus, 1607
The Life of Timon of Athens, 1607
Romances
Pericles, Prince of Tyre, 1607–08
Cymbeline, 1609–10
The Winter's Tale, 1610–11
The Tempest, 1611
Two Noble Kinsmen, 1613

Bamber, Linda. *Comic Women, Tragic Men: A Study of Gender and Genre in Shakespeare*. Stanford: Stanford UP, 1982.

Barber, C. L. *Shakespeare's Festive Comedy*. Princeton: Princeton UP, 1968.

Bradley, A. C. *Shakespearean Tragedy*. New York: Meridian, 1955.

Bullough, Geoffrey, ed. *Narrative and Dramatic Sources of Shakespeare*. 8 vols. New York: Columbia UP, 1957–75.

Chute, Marchette. *Shakespeare of London*. New York: Dutton, 1949.

Doran, Madeleine. *Shakespeare's Dramatic Language*. Madison: U of Wisconsin P, 1976.

Drakakis, John, ed. *Alternative Shakespeares*. New York: Methuen, 1985.

Dusinberre, Juliet. *Shakespeare and the Nature of Women*. London: Macmillan, 1975.

Dutton, Richard. *Shakespeare: A Literary Life*. New York: St. Martin's, 1989.

Eagleton, Terry. *William Shakespeare*. New York: Blackwell, 1986.

Erikson, Peter. *Rewriting Shakespeare, Rewriting Ourselves*. Berkeley: U of California P, 1991.

Frye, Northrop. *On Shakespeare*. New Haven: Yale UP, 1986.

Goddard, Harold C. *The Meaning of Shakespeare.* Chicago: U of Chicago P, 1951.

Grady, Hugh. *The Modernist Shakespeare: Critical Texts in a Material World.* New York: Oxford UP, 1991.

Granville-Barker, H. *Prefaces to Shakespeare.* Princeton: Princeton UP, 1946.

Greene, G., et al., eds. *The Women's Part: Feminist Criticism of Shakespeare.* Urbana: U of Illinois P, 1980.

Ioppolo, Grace. *Revising Shakespeare.* Cambridge: Harvard UP, 1991.

Jardine, Lisa. *Still Harping on Daughters: Women and Drama in the Age of Shakespeare.* Totowa: Barnes, 1983.

Kermode, Frank, ed. *Four Centuries of Shakespearean Criticism.* New York: Avon, 1974.

Kott, Jan. *Shakespeare Our Contemporary.* New York: Norton, 1974.

Righter, Anne. *Shakespeare and the Idea of the Play.* London: Chatto, 1962.

Schoenbaum, Samuel. *William Shakespeare: A Documentary Life.* New York: Oxford UP, 1975.

Schwartz, Murray M., and Coppelia Kahn, eds. *Representing Shakespeare: New Psychoanalytic Essays.* Baltimore: Johns Hopkins UP, 1981.

Scott, Michael. *Shakespeare and the Modern Dramatist.* New York: St. Martin's, 1989.

Shakespeare Quarterly. Annual Bibliography.

Shakespeare Survey.

Shakespeare's *Hamlet*

Berkoff, Steven. *I Am Hamlet.* New York: Grove, 1990.

Bloom, Harold, ed. *William Shakespeare's "Hamlet."* New York: Chelsea, 1986.

Calderwood, James. *To Be and Not to Be: Negation and Metadrama in "Hamlet."* New York: Columbia UP, 1983.

Cantor, Paul A. *Shakespeare, Hamlet.* New York: Cambridge UP, 1989.

Charney, Maurice. *Hamlet's Fictions.* New York: Routledge, 1988.

Cohen, Michael. *"Hamlet" in My Mind's Eye.* Athens: U of Georgia P, 1989.

Frye, Northrop. *Fools of Time: Studies in Shakespearean Tragedy.* Buffalo: U of Toronto P, 1973.

Jones, Ernest. *Hamlet and Oedipus.* New York: Norton, 1976.

Lacan, Jacques. "Desire and the Interpretation of Desire in *Hamlet*." *Literature and Psychoanalysis: The Question of Reading Otherwise.* Ed. Shoshana Felman. Baltimore: Johns Hopkins UP, 1982.

Levin, Harry. *The Question of Hamlet.* New York: Oxford UP, 1959.

Mack, Maynard. "The World of Hamlet." *Yale Review* 41 (1952): 502–23.

Mills, John A. *"Hamlet" on Stage: The Great Tradition.* Westport: Greenwood, 1985.

Prosser, Eleanor. *Hamlet and Revenge.* Stanford, CT: Stanford UP, 1967.

Ribner, Irving. *Patterns in Shakespearean Tragedy.* New York: Barnes, 1960.

Shakespeare Survey 9 (1956).

Showalter, Elaine. "Representing Ophelia: Women, Madness, and the Responsibilities of Feminist Criticism." *Shakespeare and the Question of Theory.* Ed. Patricia Parker and Geoffrey Hartman. New York: Methuen, 1985.

Trewin, J. C. *Five and Eighty Hamlets.* New York: New Amsterdam, 1987.

Wilson, John Dover. *What Happens in "Hamlet."* Cambridge: Cambridge UP, 1967.

Shakespeare's *A Midsummer Night's Dream*

Bevington, David. "But We Are Spirits of Another Sort: The Dark of Love and Magic in *A Midsummer Night's Dream*." *Medieval and Renaissance Studies* 7 (1975): 80–92.

Bloom, Harold, ed. *William Shakespeare's "A Midsummer Night's Dream."* New York: Chelsea, 1987.

Brown, John Russell. *Shakespeare and His Comedies.* London: Methuen, 1968.

Doran, Madeleine. "Pyramus and Thisbe Once More." *Essays on Shakespeare and Elizabethan Drama in Honor of Hardin Craig.* Ed. Richard Hosley. Columbia: U of Missouri P, 1962. 449–62.

Garber, Marjorie. *Dream in Shakespeare: From Metaphor to Metamorphosis.* New Haven: Yale UP, 1974.

Girard, Rene. "Myth and Ritual in Shakespeare: *A Midsummer Night's Dream*." *Textual Strategies: Perspectives in Post-Structuralist Criticism.* Ithaca: Cornell UP, 1979.

Kermode, Frank. "The Mature Comedies." *Early Shakespeare.* Ed. John Russell Brown and Bernard Harris. Stratford-upon-Avon Studies 3. London: Edward Arnold, 1961. 211–27.

Latham, Minor White. *The Elizabethan Fairies: The Fairies of Folklore and the Fairies of Shakespeare.* New York: Columbia UP, 1930.

Legatt, Alexander. *"A Midsummer Night's Dream": Shakespeare's Comedy of Love.* London: Methuen, 1974.

Montrose, Louis Adrian. "'Shaping Fantasies': Figurations of Gender and Power in Elizabethan Culture." *Representations* 1.2 (1983): 61–94.

Schanzer, Ernest. "The Central Theme of *A Midsummer Night's Dream.*" *University of Toronto Quarterly* 20 (1957): 233–38.

Shelbourne, David. *The Making of "A Midsummer Night's Dream."* London: Methuen, 1982.

Young, David P. *Something of Great Constancy: The Art of "A Midsummer Night's Dream."* New Haven: Yale UP, 1966.

Shakespeare's *The Tempest*

Brockbank, J. Philip. "*The Tempest*: Conventions of Art and Empire." *Later Shakespeare.* Ed. John Russell Brown and Bernard Harris. Stratford-upon-Avon Studies 8. New York: St. Martin's, 1966.

Brown, Paul. " 'This Thing of Darkness I Acknowledge Mine': *The Tempest* and the Discourse of Colonialism." *Political Shakespeare: New Essays.* Ed. Jonathan Dollimore and Alan Sinfield. Manchester: Manchester UP, 1985.

Felperin, Howard. "Undream's Shores: *The Tempest.*" *Shakespearean Romance.* Princeton: Princeton UP, 1972.

Fiedler, Leslie A. "The New World Savage as Stranger; or, 'Tis New to Thee.' " *The Stranger in Shakespeare.* New York: Stein, 1972.

Frye, Northrop. *A Natural Perspective: The Development of Shakespeare's Comedy and Romance.* New York: Columbia UP, 1965.

Griffiths, Trevor R. " 'This Island's Mine': Caliban and Colonialism." *Yearbook of English Studies* 13 (1983): 159–80.

James, D. G. *The Dream of Prospero.* Oxford: Clarendon, 1967.

Kermode, Frank. "*The Tempest.*" *William Shakespeare: The Final Plays.* London: Longman, 1963.

Kernan, Alvin B. " 'The Great Globe Itself': The Public Playhouse and the Ideal Theater of *The Tempest.*" *The Playwright as Magician: Shakespeare's Image of the Poet in the English Public Theater.* New Haven: Yale UP, 1979.

Marbane, John S. *Renaissance Magic and the Return of the Golden Age: The Occult Tradition and Marlowe, Jonson, and Shakespeare.* Lincoln: U of Nebraska P, 1989.

Orgel, Stephen. "New Uses of Adversity: Tragic Experience in *The Tempest.*" *Essays in Shakespearean Criticism.* Ed. James L. Calderwood and Harold Toliver. Englewood Cliffs: Prentice, 1970.

———. "Prospero's Wife." *Rewriting the Renaissance: The Discourse of Sexual Difference in Early Modern Europe.* Ed. Margaret W. Ferguson, Maureen Quilligan, and Catherine R. Stimpson. Chicago: U of Chicago P, 1986.

Payne, Michael. "Magic and Politics in *The Tempest.*" *Shakespeare and the Triple Play: From Study to Stage to Classroom.* Ed. Sidney Homan. Lewisburg: Bucknell UP, 1988.

Skura, Meredith Anne. "Discourse and the Individual: The Case of Colonialism in *The Tempest.*" *Shakespeare Quarterly* 40 (1989): 42–69.

Summers, Joseph. *Dreams of Love and Power.* Oxford: Clarendon, 1984.

Schwartz, Murray M., and Coppelia Kahn, eds. *Representing Shakespeare: New Psychoanalytic Essays.* Baltimore: Johns Hopkins UP, 1980.

William, David. "*The Tempest* on Stage." *Jacobean Theater.* Ed. John Russell Brown and Bernard Harris. Stratford-upon-Avon Studies 1. New York: St. Martin's, 1960.

BERNARD SHAW

Albrecht, Michael von. "Fate or Hate? A Textual Problem in Shaw's *Major Barbara.*" *Notes and Queries* 36 (1989): 196–97.

Bentley, Eric. *Bernard Shaw.* 2nd ed. London: Methuen, 1967.

Berst, Charles A. *Bernard Shaw and the Art of Drama.* Urbana: U of Illinois P, 1973.

Bloomfield, Zachary. "America's Response to George Bernard Shaw: A Study of Professional Productions." *Theatre Studies* 36 (1991): 5–17.

Bosha, Francis J. "William James's Unpublished Correspondence with Bernard Shaw." *Notes and Queries* 37 (1990): 432–33.

Brown, John Ivor. *Shaw in His Time.* London: Nelson, 1965.

Evans, T. F. *Shaw: The Critical Heritage.* Boston: Routledge, 1976.

Gainor, J. Ellen. "*G. B. S.* and the New Woman." *New England Theatre Journal* 1.1 (1990): 1–17.

Ganz, Arthur F. *George Bernard Shaw.* New York: Grove, 1983.

Gibbs, A. M. *The Art and Mind of Shaw: Essays in Criticism.* New York: St. Martin's, 1983.

———, ed. *Shaw: Interviews and Recollections.* Iowa City: U of Iowa P, 1990.

Gordon, David J. *Bernard Shaw and the Comic Sublime.* New York: St. Martin's, 1990.

Greene, Nicholas. *Bernard Shaw: A Critical View.* New York: St. Martin's, 1984.

Kaufman, R. J., ed. *G. B. Shaw: A Collection of Critical Essays.* Englewood Cliffs: Prentice, 1965.

May, Keith M. *Ibsen and Shaw.* New York: St. Martin's, 1985.

Shaw, Bernard. *An Autobiography*. Ed. Stanley Weintraub. 2 vols. New York: Weybright, 1969.

———. *Collected Letters*. Ed. Dan H. Laurence. New York: Dodd, 1972.

———. *Complete Plays with Prefaces*. New York: Dodd, 1962.

———. *Plays and Players: Essays on the Theatre*. Ed. A. C. Ward, New York: Oxford UP, 1963.

———. *Shaw on Shakespeare: An Anthology of Bernard Shaw's Writings on the Plays and Production of Shakespeare*. Ed. Edwin Wilson. New York: Dutton, 1961.

Zimbardo, Rose, ed. *Twentieth Century Interpretations of "Major Barbara."* Englewood Cliffs: Prentice, 1970.

SAM SHEPARD

Auerbach, Doris. *Sam Shepard, Arthur Kopit, and the Off-Broadway Theatre*. Twayne's United States Author Series 432. Boston: Twayne, 1982.

Cima, Gay Gibson. *"Buried Child." Theatre Journal* 35 (Dec. 1983): 559–60.

Cohn, Ruby. *New American Dramatists: 1960–1980*. New York: Grove, 1982.

Cott, Jonathan. "The Rolling Stone Interview: Sam Shepard." *Rolling Stone* 18 Dec. 1986–1 Jan. 1987: 166–72+.

Falk, Florence. "The Role of Performance in Sam Shepard's Plays." *Theatre Journal* May 1981: 182–98.

Gilman, Richard. Introduction. *Sam Shepard: Seven Plays*. New York: Bantam, 1981. ix–xiv.

Hart, Lynda. *Sam Shepard's Metaphorical Stages*. Westport: Greenwood, 1987.

King, Kimball, ed. *Sam Shepard: A Casebook*. New York: Garland, 1988.

Marranca, Bonnie, ed. *American Dreams: The Imagination of Sam Shepard*. New York: Performing Arts Journal, 1981.

Mottram, Ron. *Inner Landscapes: The Theater of Sam Shepard*. Columbia: U of Missouri P, 1984.

Nash, Thomas. "Sam Shepard's *Buried Child*: The Ironic Use of Folklore." *Modern Drama* 26 (1983): 486–91.

Orbison, Tucker. "Mythic Levels in Sam Shepard's *True West*." *Modern Drama* 27 (Dec. 1984): 506–19.

Oumano, Ellen. *Sam Shepard: The Life and Work of an American Dreamer*. New York: St. Martin's, 1986.

Sessums, Kevin. "Geography of a Horse Dreamer: Playwright, Actor, and Movie Director Sam Shepard." *Interview* Sept. 1988: 70–78.

Shepard, Sam. "Metaphors, Mad Dogs, and Old-Time Cowboys." *Theatre Quarterly* 15 (Aug.–Oct. 1974): 3–16.

———. "Visualization, Language, and the Inner Library." *Drama Review* 4 (Dec. 1977): 49–58.

Shewey, Don. *Sam Shepard*. New York: Dell, 1985.

SOPHOCLES

List of Plays (Sophocles wrote in the fifth century B.C. The exact dates for his plays are unknown.)

Oedipus Rex
Antigone
Oedipus at Colonus
Philoctetes
Ajax
Trachiniae
Elektra
Ichneutai
Aleadae

Bloom, Harold, ed. *Sophocles*. New York: Chelsea, 1990.

Bowra, Sir Maurice. *Sophoclean Tragedy*. Oxford: Clarendon, 1944.

Burton, Reginald William Boteler. *The Chorus in Sophocles' Tragedies*. New York: Oxford UP, 1980.

Bushnell, Rebecca. *Prophesying Tragedy: Sign and Voice in Sophocles' Theban Plays*. Ithaca: Cornell UP, 1988.

Buxton, R. G. A. *Sophocles*. New York: Clarendon, 1984.

Gardiner, Cynthia P. *The Sophoclean Chorus: A Study of Character and Function*. Iowa City: U of Iowa P, 1987.

Kitto, H. D. F. *Sophocles: Dramatist and Philosopher*. London: Oxford UP, 1958.

Knox, Bernard M. *Sophocles at Thebes: Sophocles' Tragic Hero and His Time*. New York: Norton, 1971.

Reinhardt, Karl. *Sophokles*. Trans. D. and H. Harvey. New York: Barnes, 1978.

Scodel, Ruth. *Sophocles*. Boston: Twayne, 1984.

Segal, Charles. *Tragedy and Civilization: An Interpretation of Sophocles*. Cambridge: Harvard UP, 1981.

Waldock, A. J. A. *Sophocles the Dramatist*. Cambridge: Cambridge UP, 1951.

Wiles, David. *The Masks of Menander: Sign and Meaning in Greek and Roman Performances*. Cambridge: Cambridge UP, 1991.

Winnington-Ingram, R. P. *Sophocles: An Interpretation*. New York: Cambridge UP, 1980.

Woodard, T. M., ed. *Sophocles: A Collection of Critical Essays*. Englewood Cliffs: Prentice, 1966.

Sophocles' *Oedipus Rex*

Bloom, Harold. *Sophocles' "Oedipus Rex."* New York: Chelsea, 1988.
Cameron, Alister. *The Identity of Oedipus the King: Five Essays on the "Oedipus Tyrannus."* New York: New York UP, 1968.
Edmonds, Lowell. *Oedipus: The Ancient Legend and Its Later Analogues*. Baltimore: Johns Hopkins UP, 1985.
Fergusson, Francis. *The Idea of a Theater*. Princeton: Princeton UP, 1949.
O'Brien, M. J., ed. *Twentieth Century Interpretations of "Oedipus Rex."* Englewood Cliffs: Prentice, 1968.
Rudnytsky, Peter L. *Freud and Oedipus*. New York: Columbia UP, 1987.
Tonelli, Franco. *Sophocles' Oedipus and the Tale of the Theatre."* Speculum Artium Series 12. Ravenna: Longo Editore, 1983.
Verhoeff, Han, and Harly Sonne. "Does Oedipus Have His Complex?" *Style* 18.3 (1984): 261–83.

Sophocles' *Antigone*

Brown, Andrew. *A New Companion to Greek Tragedy*. Totowa: Barnes, 1983.
Goheen, R. F. *The Imagery of Sophocles' "Antigone": A Study of Poetic Language and Structure*. Princeton: Princeton UP, 1951.
Joseph, Gerhard. "The *Antigone* as Cultural Touchstone: Matthew Arnold, Hegel, George Eliot, Virginia Woolf, and Margaret Drabble." *PMLA* 96 (1981): 22–35.
Linforth, I. M. *Antigone and Creon*. Berkeley: U of California P, 1961.
Steiner, George. *Antigones*. New York: Clarendon, 1984.

Wole Soyinka

Gibbs, James. "The BBC Became a Glutton for Punishment: Wole Soyinka's Dealings with the BBC (1953–1959)." *Crisis and Creativity in the New Literatures in English: Cross/Cultures*. Ed. Geoffrey Davis and Hena Maes-Jelinek. Amsterdam: Rodopi, 1990. 205–17.
———. *Critical Perspectives on Wole Soyinka*. Washington: Three Continents, 1980.
———. "'Marrying Earth to Heaven': A Nobel Laureate at the End of the Eighties." *International Literature in English: Essays on the Major Writers*. Ed. Robert L. Ross. New York: Garland, 1991.

———. *Wole Soyinka*. New York: Grove, 1986.
Jones, Eldred D. *The Writing of Wole Soyinka*. Portsmouth: Heinemann, 1988.
Katrak, Ketu H. *Wole Soyinka and Modern Tragedy: A Study of Dramatic Theory and Practice*. Westport: Greenwood, 1986.
Larsen, Stephan. *A Writer and His Gods: A Study of the Importance of Yoruba Myths and Religious Ideas to the Writing of Wole Soyinka*. Stockholm: U of Stockholm P, 1983.
Lindfors, Bernth. "Beating the White Man at His Own Game: Nigerian Reactions to the Nobel Prize in Literature." *Literary Criterion* 25.1 (1990: 43–59.
Maduakor, Obi. *Wole Soyinka: An Introduction to His Writings*. New York: Garland, 1987.
Soyinka, Wole. *Ake: The Years of Childhood*. New York: Random, 1981.
———. *Isara: A Voyage Round Essay*. New York: Random, 1989.
———. *The Man Died: The Prison Notes of Wole Soyinka*. London: Collings, 1972.

August Strindberg

Carlson, Harry Gilbert. *Strindberg and the Poetry of Myth*. Berkeley: U of California P, 1982.
Lally, M. L. K. "Strindberg's *Miss Julie*." *Explicator* 48.3 (1990): 196–98.
Lucas, F. L. *The Drama of Ibsen and Strindberg*. London: Cassell, 1962.
Parker, Brian. "Strindberg's *Miss Julie* and the Legend of Salome." *Modern Drama* 32 (1989): 469–84.
Reinert, Otto, ed. *Strindberg: A Collection of Critical Essays*. Englewood Cliffs: Prentice, 1971.
Robinson, Michael. "August Strindberg: His True Life?" *Scandinavica* 28.2 (1989): 185–91.
Shideler, Ross. "The Absent Authority: From Darwin to Nora and Julie." *Space and Boundaries in Literature*. Proc. of the 12th Congress of the Intl. Comparative Lit. Assn. Ed. Roger Bauer and Douwe Fokkema. Munich: Iudicium, 1990.
Sprinchorn, Evert. *Strindberg as Dramatist*. New Haven: Yale UP, 1982.
Steene, Birgitta. *The Greatest Fire: A Study of August Strindberg*. Carbondale: Southern Illinois UP, 1973.
Stockenstrom, Goran, ed. *Strindberg's Dramaturgy*. Minneapolis: U of Minnesota P, 1988.
Tornqvist, Egil. *Strindberg's "Miss Julie": A Play and Its Transpositions*. Norwich, Eng.: Norvik, 1988.

John Millington Synge

Benson, Eugene. *J. M. Synge*. New York: Grove, 1983.
Corkery, Daniel. *Synge and Anglo-Irish Literature*. Cork: Cork UP, 1955.

Gerstenberger, Donna Lorine. *John Millington Synge.* Rev. ed. Boston: Twayne, 1990.

Greene, David H., and Edward M. Stephens. *John Millington Synge, 1871–1909.* Rev. ed. New York: New York UP, 1989.

Kiberd, Declan. *Synge and the Irish Language.* London: Macmillan, 1979.

King, Mary C. *The Drama of J. M. Synge.* Syracuse: Syracuse UP, 1985.

Kopper, Edward A. *A John Millington Synge Literary Companion.* New York: Greenwood, 1988.

Price, Alan. *Synge and Anglo-Irish Drama.* London: Methuen, 1961.

Skelton, Robin. *J. M. Synge and His World.* New York: Viking, 1971.

———. *The Writings of J. M. Synge.* London: Thames, 1971.

TERENCE

Forehand, Walter. *Terence.* Boston: Twayne, 1985.

Goldberg, Sander M. *Understanding Terence.* Princeton: Princeton UP, 1986.

OSCAR WILDE

Bloom, Harold. *Oscar Wilde's "The Importance of Being Earnest."* New York: Chelsea, 1988.

Byrne, Patrick. *The Wildes of Merrion Square: The Family of Oscar Wilde.* New York: Staples, 1953.

Cohen, Ed. "Writing Gone Wild: Homoerotic Desire in the Closet of Representation." *PMLA* 102 (1987): 801–13.

Cohen, Philip K. *The Moral Vision of Oscar Wilde.* Rutherford: Fairleigh Dickinson UP, 1978.

Ellmann, Richard. *Oscar Wilde.* New York: Knopf, 1988.

———. *Oscar Wilde: A Collection of Critical Essays.* Englewood Cliffs: Prentice, 1969.

Erikson, Donald. *Oscar Wilde.* Boston: Twayne, 1977.

Gagnier, Regenia. *Idylls of the Marketplace: Oscar Wilde and the Victorian Public.* Stanford: Stanford UP, 1986.

Haley, Bruce. "Wilde's 'Decadence' and the Positivist Tradition." *Victorian Studies* 28 (1985): 215–29.

Hart-Davis, Rupert, ed. *Letters of Oscar Wilde.* New York: Harcourt, 1962.

———. *More Letters of Oscar Wilde.* New York: Vanguard, 1985.

Hodge, James H. *Famous Trials.* Baltimore: Penguin, 1963.

Mikhail, E. H. *Oscar Wilde: Interviews and Recollections.* New York: Barnes, 1979.

Miller, Robert Keith. *Oscar Wilde.* New York: Ungar, 1982.

Poznar, Walter. "Life and Play in Wilde's *The Importance of Being Earnest.*" *Midwest Quarterly* 30.4 (1989): 515–28.

San Juan, Epifanio. *The Art of Oscar Wilde.* Princeton: Princeton UP, 1963.

Smith, Philip E., and Michael S. Heffland, eds. *Oscar Wilde's Oxford Notebooks.* New York: Oxford UP, 1989.

Sullivan, Kevin. *Oscar Wilde.* Columbia Essays on Modern Writers 64. New York: Columbia UP, 1972.

Weintraub, Stanley. *The Literary Criticism of Oscar Wilde.* Lincoln: U of Nebraska P, 1968.

Wilde, Oscar. *The Complete Works.* New York: Doubleday, 1923.

———. *The Plays of Oscar Wilde.* New York: Random, 1980.

TENNESSEE WILLIAMS

List of Plays

American Blues, 1939 (published 1948)
Battle of Angels, 1940 (published 1945)
The Glass Menagerie, 1944
A Streetcar Named Desire, 1947
Summer and Smoke, 1947
The Rose Tatoo, 1950
Camino Real, 1953
Cat on a Hot Tin Roof, 1955
Orpheus Descending, 1957
Suddenly Last Summer, 1958
Sweet Bird of Youth, 1959
Period of Adjustment, 1960
The Night of the Iguana, 1962
The Milk Train Doesn't Stop Here Anymore, 1963
The Eccentricities of a Nightingale, 1965
The Seven Descents of Myrtle, 1968
In the Bar of a Tokyo Hotel, 1969
Small Craft Warnings, 1972
A Lovely Sunday for Creve Coeur, 1979
Clothes for a Summer Hotel, 1980

Aisbong, Emmanuel B. *Tennessee Williams: The Tragic Tension.* Elms Court: Stockwell, 1978.

Boxill, Roger. *Tennessee Williams.* New York: St. Martin's, 1987.

Devlin, Albert J., ed. *Conversations with Tennessee Williams.* Jackson: UP of Mississippi, 1986.

Donahue, Francis. *The Dramatic World of Tennessee Williams.* New York: Ungar, 1964.

Falk, Signi Lenea. *Tennessee Williams.* 2nd ed. Boston: Twayne, 1978.

Leavitt, Richard Freeman, ed. *The World of Tennessee Williams.* New York: Putnam's, 1978.

Parker, R. B., ed. *"The Glass Menagerie": A Collection of Critical Essays.* Englewood Cliffs: Prentice, 1983.

Savran, David. "'By coming suddenly into a room that I thought was empty': Mapping the Closet with Tennessee Williams." *Studies in the Literary Imagination* 24.2 (1991): 57–74.

Spoto, Donald. *The Kindness of Strangers: The Life of Tennessee Williams.* Boston: Little, 1985.

Stanton, Stephen, ed. *Tennessee Williams: A Collection of Critical Essays.* Englewood Cliffs: Prentice, 1977.

Thompson, Judith. *Tennessee Williams' Plays: Memory, Myth, and Symbol.* New York: Lang, 1987.

Williams, Dakin, with Shepherd Mead. *Tennessee Williams: An Intimate Biography.* New York: Arbor, 1983.

Williams, Tennessee. *Memoirs.* Garden City: Doubleday, 1975.

Williams's *Cat on a Hot Tin Roof*

Atkinson, Brooks. "Williams' 'Tin Roof.'" *New York Times* 3 Apr. 1955: B1.

Huzzard, Jere. "Williams' *Cat on a Hot Tin Roof.*" *Explicator* 43.2 (1985): 46–47.

Kalem, T. E. "Fate Strikes the Delta." *Time* 6 Dec. 1976: 97–98.

"London Sees Cat; Opinion Is Divided." *New York Times* 31 Jan. 1958: 24.

Mayberry, Susan Neal. "A Study of Illusion and the Grotesque in Tennessee Williams' *Cat on a Hot Tin Roof.*" *Southern Studies* 22.4 (1983): 359–65.

Rev. of *Cat on a Hot Tin Roof. New York Theatre Critics' Reviews* 20 Mar. 1955: 342–43.

Rev. of *Cat on a Hot Tin Roof. New York Theatre Critics' Reviews* 25 Sept. 1974: 242–46.

Williams's *The Glass Menagerie*

Beaurline, Lester A. "*The Glass Menagerie* from Story to Play." *Modern Drama* 8 (1965): 143–49.

Bloom, Harold. *Tennessee Williams's "The Glass Menagerie."* New York: Chelsea, 1988.

Greiff, Louis K. "Fathers, Daughters, and Spiritual Sisters: Marsha Norman's *'night, Mother* and Tennessee Williams's *The Glass Menagerie.*" *Text and Performance Quarterly* 9.3 (1989): 224–28.

Jones, John H. "The Missing Link: The Father in *The Glass Menagerie.*" *Notes on Mississippi Writers* 20.1 (1988): 29–38.

Parker, R. B. "The Circle Closed: A Psychological Reading of *The Glass Menagerie* and the *Two Character Play.*" *Modern Drama* 28 (1985): 517–34.

Presley, Delma Eugene. *"The Glass Menagerie": An American Memory.* Boston: Twayne, 1990.

Thierfelder, William R. "Williams's *The Glass Menagerie.*" *Explicator* 48.4 (1990): 284–85.

AUGUST WILSON

Freedman, Samuel G. "A Voice from the Streets." *New York Times Magazine* 15 Mar. 1987: 33+.

———. "Wilson's New *Fences* Nurtures a Partnership." *New York Times* 5 May 1985: sec. I: 80.

Gerard, Jeremy. "Waterford to Broadway: Well-Traveled *Fences.*" *New York Times* 9 Apr. 1987, sec. III: 21.

Henderson, Heather. "Building *Fences*: An Interview with Mary Alice and James Earl Jones." *Yale Theater* 12 (Summer/Fall 1985): 67–70.

Kelley, Kevin. "August Wilson an Heir to O'Neill." *Boston Globe* 24 Jan. 1988: A1+.

Rich, Frank. "Theater: Family Ties in Wilson's *Fences.*" *New York Times* 27 Mar. 1987, sec. II: 1.

Selected List of Film, Video, and Audiocassette Resources

The following is a list of audiovisual resources to supplement the teaching of plays in *The Bedford Introduction to Drama*. The resources are listed alphabetically by playwright.

The films and videos marked with an asterisk (*) are available for rental from member institutions of the Consortium of College and University Media Centers. For further information, consult the *Educational Film & Video Locator*, published by R. R. Bowker.

Many of the videos are available for rental from local video outlets. Others are available through a distributor. Check the Directory of Distributors at the end of this list for information.

ANONYMOUS

*Anonymous, *Everyman*
25 min., color, 1971.
16 mm film.
Abridged by H. Frances Clark.
Distributed by Coronet/MTI Film & Video.

Anonymous, *Everyman*
53 min., color, 1991.
VHS.
Produced in conjunction with medieval literature scholar Howard Schless of Columbia University. Authentically staged in period costume.
Distributed by Insight Media.

Anonymous, *Everyman* [recording]
1 cassette.
Dramatization performed by Burgess Meredith and Terrence Kilburn.
Distributed by Caedmon/HarperAudio.

ARISTOPHANES

Aristophanes, *Lysistrata*
97 min., color, 1987.
VHS.
A contemporary adaptation, shot on location at the Acropolis. In Greek with English subtitles.
Distributed by Insight Media.

Aristophanes, *Lysistrata* [recording]
2 cassettes.
Dramatization of Dudley Fitts's translation. Performed by Hermione Gingold and Stanley Holloway.
Distributed by Caedmon/HarperAudio.

SAMUEL BECKETT

Samuel Beckett, *Beckett Festival of Radio Plays* [recording]
1989.
Features a collection of five plays written for the radio: *All That Fall, Embers, Words and Music, Cascando,* and *Rough for Radio II.*
Distributed by National Public Radio.

Samuel Beckett
80 min., color, 1989.
Beta, VHS, 3/4″ U-matic cassette.
An autobiographical portrait of Beckett's artistic life through his work.
Distributed by Films for the Humanities and Sciences.

BERTOLT BRECHT

Bertolt Brecht
55 min., color, 1989.

Beta, VHS, 3/4″ U-matic cassette.
A biographical portrait of Brecht through his
works.
Distributed by Films for the Humanities and
Sciences.

Gisela May: Reflections on the Theater of Brecht
30 min., color, 1979.
Beta, VHS, 1/2″ open reel (EIAJ), 3/4″ U-matic cassette, 2″ quadraplex open reel.
Gisela May of the Berliner Ensemble performs excerpts from Brecht's plays.
Distributed by the New York State Education
Department.

ANTON CHEKHOV

*Anton Chekhov, *The Cherry Orchard, Part I:
Chekhov, Innovator of Modern Drama*
21 min., color and B/W, 1968.
Beta, VHS, 3/4″ U-matic cassette, 16 mm film.
Important scenes with discussion led by Norris
Houghton.
Distributed by Britannica Films.

*Anton Chekhov, *The Cherry Orchard, Part II:
Comedy or Tragedy?*
21 min., color and B/W, 1967.
Beta, VHS, 3/4″ U-matic cassette, 16 mm film.
Important scenes with discussion led by Norris
Houghton. Covers Chekhov's technique of dramatization of interior actions and examines the
notion of subtext.
Distributed by Britannica Films.

Anton Chekhov, *The Cherry Orchard* [recording]
3 cassettes.
Translated by Leonid Kipnis and performed by Jessica Tandy and Hume Cronyn.
Distributed by Caedmon/HarperAudio.

Anton Chekhov: A Writer's Life
37 min., B/W, 1974.
Beta, VHS, 3/4″ U-matic cassette.
A biographical portrait of the playwright.
Distributed by Films for the Humanities and
Sciences.

Chekhov [recording]
12 cassettes (90 min. each), 1989.
By Henri Troyat, read by Wolfram Kandinsky. A
biography of the writer.
Distributed by Books on Tape.

Chekhov: Humanity's Advocate [recording]
1 cassette (46 min.), 1968.

By Ernest J. Simmons. Explores various facets of
Chekhov's works and his artistic principles.
Classics of Russian Literature Series.
Distributed by Audio-Forum.

Chekhov and the Moscow Art Theatre
13 min., color.
Beta, VHS, 16 mm film.
Yuri Zavadsky uses the Stanislavsky Method in directing scenes from *The Cherry Orchard*.
Distributed by IASTA.

WILLIAM CONGREVE

*William Congreve, *The Way of the World*
60 min., color, 1978.
Beta, VHS, 3/4″ U-matic cassette.
Hosted by José Ferrer and Anna Russell. Focuses
on main characters and eliminates some
subplots.
Distributed by Films, Inc.

William Congreve, *The Way of the World*
[recording]
3 cassettes.
Performed by Helen Burns and Edward Hardwicke.
Distributed by Caedmon/HarperAudio.

*Aspects of 18th Century Comedy:
Congreve/Marivaux*
12 min., color.
Beta, VHS, 16 mm film.
Shows rehearsals of productions of Congreve's *The
Way of the World* and Marivaux's *The False
Confessions*. Actors learn the vocal style, diction,
postures, and gestures of eighteenth-century
comedy.
Distributed by IASTA.

EURIPIDES

*Euripides, *Medea*
118 min., color, 1970.
Beta, VHS.
With Maria Callas, Guiseppi Gentile, and Laurent
Tarzieff. Directed by Pier Paolo Passolini. In Italian with English subtitles.
Distributed by Video Artists International.

Euripides, *Medea*
110 min., 1979.
Beta, VHS.
With Maria Callas and Guiseppi Gentile. Directed
by Pier Paolo Passolini. In Greek with English
subtitles.
Distributed by Drama Classics Video.

Euripides, *Medea*
70 min., color, 1979.
Beta, VHS.
With Marina Goderdzishvili and Vladimir Julu-
khadze. A free adaptation for ballet.
Distributed by Kultur.

*Euripides, *Medea*
90 min., color, 1982.
Beta, VHS, 3/4″ U-matic cassette.
With Zoe Caldwell and Judith Anderson. A Ken-
nedy Center production based on poet Robinson
Jeffers's version.
Distributed by Films for the Humanities and
Sciences.

*Euripides, *Medea*
100 min., color, 1986.
VHS.
Performed by the New York Greek Drama Company in ancient Greek with English subtitles.

Euripides, *Medea* [recording]
2 cassettes.
Translated by Rex Warner. Performed by Judith
Anderson and Anthony Quayle.
Distributed by Caedmon/HarperAudio.

ATHOL FUGARD

Athol Fugard, *"MASTER HAROLD" . . . and the
boys*
90 min., color, 1984.
Beta, VHS.
With Matthew Broderick. A made-for-cable
production.
Distributed by Lorimar Home Video.

LORRAINE HANSBERRY

*Lorraine Hansberry, *A Raisin in the Sun*
128 min., B/W, 1961.
Beta, VHS.
With Sidney Poitier, Claudia McNeil, and Ruby
Dee. Directed by Daniel Petrie.
Distributed by RCA/Columbia Pictures Home
Video.

Lorraine Hansberry, *A Raisin in the Sun*
171 min., color, 1989.
Beta, VHS.
With Danny Glover, Esther Rolle, and Starletta
DuPois. Directed by Bill Duke. An American
Playhouse, made-for-television production.
Distributed by Fries Home Video.

Lorraine Hansberry, *A Raisin in the Sun* [recording]
3 cassettes.
Dramatization performed by Ossie Davis and Ruby
Dee.
Distributed by Caedmon/HarperAudio.

*Black Theatre Movement from "A Raisin in the
Sun" to the Present*
130 min., color, 1979.
16 mm film.
Traces the Black Theatre Movement from its roots
in Hansberry's play to the black plays and musicals on Broadway in the late 1970s. Includes interviews with performers, writers, and directors
as well as footage from plays and theater pieces
from around the country.

Lorraine Hansberry: *The Black Experience in the
Creation of Drama*
35 min., color, 1975.
Beta, VHS, 3/4″ U-matic cassette.
With Sidney Poitier, Ruby Dee, and Al Freeman, Jr.
Narrated by Claudia McNeil.
A profile of the playwright's life and work.
Distributed by Films for the Humanities and
Sciences.

Lorraine Hansberry Speaks Out: *Art and the Black
Revolution* [recording]
1 cassette.
By Lorraine Hansberry, edited by Robert Nemiroff.
Distributed by Caedmon/HarperAudio.

**A Raisin in the Sun*
9 min., color, 1969.
16 mm film.
An introduction to the racial problems dealt with in
the play.
Distributed by Phoenix/BFA Films.

**To Be Young, Gifted, and Black*
90 min., color, 1972.
Beta, VHS, 1/2″ open reel (EIAJ), 3/4″ U-matic cas-
sette, 16 mm film.
With Ruby Dee, Al Freeman, Jr., Claudia McNeil,
Barbara Barrie, Lauren Jones, Roy Scheider, and
Blythe Danner. A play about the life of Lorraine
Hansberry.
Distributed by the Indiana University Center for
Media and Teaching Resources.

HENRIK IBSEN

Henrik Ibsen, *A Doll's House*
89 min., B/W, 1959.

Beta, VHS, 3/4″ U-matic cassette.
With Julie Harris, Christopher Plummer, Jason Robards, Hume Cronyn, Eileen Heckart, and Richard Thomas. An original television production.
Distributed by MGM/UA Home Video.

*Henrik Ibsen, *A Doll's House*
98 min., color, 1973.
VHS, 16 mm film.
With Jane Fonda, Edward Fox, Trevor Howard, and David Warner. Screenplay by David Mercer.
Distributed by Prism (video) and the Learning Corporation of America (film).

Henrik Ibsen, *A Doll's House*
39 min., color, 1977.
Beta, VHS, 3/4″ U-matic cassette.
With Claire Bloom.
Distributed by AIMS.

Henrik Ibsen, *A Doll's House*
96 min., color, 1989.
Beta, VHS.
With Claire Bloom, Anthony Hopkins, Ralph Richardson, Denholm Elliott, Anna Massey, and Edith Evans. Directed by Patrick Garland. A Canadian production.
Distributed by Southgate Entertainment.

Henrik Ibsen, *A Doll's House* [recording]
3 cassettes.
Translated by Christopher Hampton and performed by Claire Bloom and Donald Madden.
Distributed by Caedmon/HarperAudio.

A Doll's House, Part I: The Distinction of Illusion
34 min., color, 1968.
Beta, VHS, 3/4″ U-matic cassette, 16 mm film.
Norris Houghton discusses the subsurface tensions in the play.
Distributed by Britannica Films.

A Doll's House, Part II: Ibsen's Themes
29 min., color, 1968.
Beta, VHS, 3/4″ U-matic cassette, 16 mm film.
Norris Houghton examines the cast of characters and the themes in the play.
Distributed by Britannica Films.

Henrik Ibsen, *Hedda*
102 min., color, 1975.
Beta, VHS.
With Glenda Jackson, Peter Eyre, and Timothy West. Directed by Trevor Nunn.
Distributed by Fox Video.

Henrik Ibsen, *Hedda Gabler*
(Also known as *The Theater of Social Problems*)
60 min., color, 1976.
VHS, 3/4″ U-matic cassette, 16 mm film.
Narrated by Irene Worth.
Distributed by Films for the Humanities and Sciences.

Henrik Ibsen, *Hedda Gabler* [recording]
3 cassettes.
Translated by Michael Meyer. Performed by Joan Plowright and Anthony Quayle.
Distributed by Caedmon/HarperAudio.

Henrik Ibsen, *Hedda Gabler* [recording]
3 cassettes.
Unabridged version. Performed by Eva Le Gallienne.
Distributed by Random Audiobooks.

Ibsen's Life and Times, Part I: Youth and Self-Imposed Exile
28 min., color.
VHS.
The conflict between individual and society is illustrated in scenes from *Ghosts*, featuring Beatrice Straight as Mrs. Alving. Includes a biographical segment on the playwright.
Distributed by Insight Media and IASTA.

Ibsen's Life and Times, Part II: The Later Years
24 min., color.
VHS.
Includes scenes from *The Master Builder* and *Lady from the Sea*, emphasizing the realism in Ibsen's plays. A biographical segment includes on-location footage.
Distributed by Insight Media and IASTA.

THOMAS MIDDLETON AND WILLIAM ROWLEY

Thomas Middleton and William Rowley, *The Changeling* [recording]
1 cassette.
Adapted by Dickon Reed. Performed by Martin Jarvis and Barry Foster.
Distributed by Audio-Forum.

ARTHUR MILLER

Arthur Miller, *Death of a Salesman*
135 min., color, 1985.
Beta, VHS.
With Dustin Hoffman, John Malkovich, Charles

Durning, and Stephen Lang. Directed by Volker Schlondorff.

A made-for-television adaptation of the play.

Distributed by Lorimar Home Video.

Arthur Miller, *Death of a Salesman* [recording]
3 cassettes.
Performed by Lee J. Cobb and Mildred Dunnock.
Distributed by Caedmon/HarperAudio.

Arthur Miller, *Death of a Salesman* [recording]
1 cassette, 1986.
Dramatization performed by Paul Douglas.
Distributed by the Mind's Eye.

Private Conversations on the Set of Death of a Salesman
82 min., color, 1985.
Beta, VHS.
With Arthur Miller, Dustin Hoffman, Volker Schlondorff, and John Malkovich. This PBS documentary presents heated discussions among actors, director, and playwright. Various interpretations of the play emerge and viewers gain insight into how each party contributed to the final production.
Distributed by Lorimar Home Video.

MOLIÈRE

Molière, *Le Misanthrope*
160 min., color, 1986.
Beta, VHS, 3/4″ U-matic cassette.
In French with English subtitles.
Distributed by Films for the Humanities and Sciences.

Molière, *The Misanthrope* [recording]
2 cassettes.
Translated by Richard Wilbur. Performed by Richard Easton and Sydney Walker.
Distributed by Caedmon/HarperAudio.

Molière
112 min., color, 1990.
Beta, VHS.
With Anthony Sher. Mikhail Bulgakov's comedy/drama of the playwright's life.
Distributed by Turner Home Entertainment.

Molière and the Comédie Française
17 min., color.
Beta, VHS, 16 mm film.
Film provides an overview of the Comédie fran-

çaise. Jacques Charon directs scenes from *The Misanthrope* and *Tartuffe*.
Distributed by IASTA.

MARSHA NORMAN

Marsha Norman, *'night, Mother*
97 min., color, 1986.
Beta, VHS, laser optical videodisc.
With Sissy Spacek and Anne Bancroft. Directed by Tom Moore.
Distributed by MCA/Universal Home Video.

EUGENE O'NEILL

Eugene O'Neill, *Desire Under the Elms*
114 min., B/W, 1958.
Beta, VHS.
With Sophia Loren, Anthony Perkins, and Burl Ives.
Distributed by Kartes Video Communications.

HAROLD PINTER

Harold Pinter, *The Dumb Waiter*
60 min., color, 1987.
With John Travolta and Tom Conti. Directed by Robert Altman.
Distributed by Prism Entertainment.

LUIGI PIRANDELLO

*Luigi Pirandello, *Six Characters in Search of an Author*
52 min., color, 1976.
Beta, VHS, 3/4″ U-matic cassette, 16mm film.
Joseph Heller discusses the boundaries between reality and fiction.
Distributed by Films for the Humanities and Sciences.

Luigi Pirandello, *Six Characters in Search of an Author*
60 min., color, 1978.
Beta, VHS, 3/4″ U-matic cassette.
Hosted by José Ferrer. As an accompaniment to the play, Ossie Davis discusses Pirandello's work in the theater.
Distributed by Films, Inc.

WILLIAM SHAKESPEARE

Hamlet
*William Shakespeare, *Hamlet*
153 min., B/W, 1948.
VHS and 16 mm film.

With Laurence Olivier, Basil Sydney, Felix Aylmer, Jean Simmons, Stanley Holloway, Peter Cushing, and Christopher Lee. Voice of John Gielgud. Directed by Olivier. Photographed in Denmark. Cut scenes include all of Rosencrantz and Guildenstern. Emphasizes Oedipal implications in the play.
Distributed by Paramount Home Video (video) and the Learning Corporation of America (film).

*William Shakespeare, *Hamlet*
115 min., color, 1969.
Beta, VHS, 16 mm film.
With Nicol Williamson. Directed by Tony Richardson.
Distributed by the Learning Corporation of America.

William Shakespeare, *Hamlet*
150 min., color, 1979.
Beta, VHS, 3/4″ U-matic cassette, other formats by arrangement.
Directed by Derek Jacobi.
Distributed by Time-Life Video.

William Shakespeare, *Hamlet*
135 min., color, 1990.
VHS.
With Mel Gibson, Glenn Close, Alan Bates, Paul Scofield, Ian Holm, and Helena Bonham-Carter. Directed by Franco Zeffirelli.
Distributed by Warner Home Video.

William Shakespeare, *Hamlet* [recording]
4 cassettes.
Performed by Paul Scofield and Diana Wynyard.
Distributed by Caedmon/HarperAudio.

William Shakespeare, *Hamlet* [recording]
1 cassette (60 min.), 1985.
Performed by Michael Redgrave. Living Shakespeare Series.
Distributed by Crown Publishers.

William Shakespeare, *Hamlet* [recording]
4 cassettes.
Performed by Ronald Pickup and Robert Lang.
Distributed by Audio-Forum.

William Shakespeare, *Hamlet* [recording]
2 cassettes (180 min.), 1988.
With Ronald Pickup and Angela Pleasance. Music by Malcolm Clarke, BBC Audio Collection.
Distributed by the Mind's Eye.

William Shakespeare, *Hamlet* [recording]
2 cassettes (120 min.)
With John Gielgud and the Old Vic Company.
Distributed by Durkin Hayes Publishing.

Approaches to Hamlet
45 min., color, 1979.
Beta, VHS, 3/4″ U-matic cassette, 16 mm film.
Includes footage of the four greatest Hamlets of this century: John Barrymore, Laurence Olivier, John Gielgud, and Nicol Williamson. Shows a young actor learning the role. Narrated by Gielgud.
Distributed by Films for the Humanities and Sciences.

Hamlet: The Age of Elizabeth, I
30 min., color, 1959.
Beta, VHS, 3/4″ U-matic cassette, 16 mm film.
An introduction to Elizabethan theater.
Distributed by Britannica Films.

Hamlet: What Happens in Hamlet, II
30 min., color, B/W, 1959.
Beta, VHS, 3/4″ U-matic cassette, 16 mm film.
Analyzes the play as a ghost story, a detective story, and a revenge story. Uses scenes from acts I, III, and V to introduce the principal characters and present the structure of each substory.
Distributed by Britannica Films.

Hamlet: The Poisoned Kingdom, III
30 min., color, 1959.
Beta, VHS, 3/4″ U-matic cassette, 16 mm film.
Observes that poisoning in the play is both literal and figurative and affects all the characters.
Distributed by Britannica Films.

Hamlet: The Readiness Is All, IV
30 min., color, 1959.
Beta, VHS, 3/4″ U-matic cassette, 16 mm film.
Hamlet is presented as a coming-of-age story.
Distributed by Britannica Films.

Hamlet: The Trouble with Hamlet
23 min., color, 1969.
16 mm film.
Emphasizes Hamlet's existential dilemma.
Distributed by the National Broadcasting Company.

The Tragedie of Hamlet: Prince of Denmark
22 min., color, 1988.
VHS.
Actors depict Shakespeare and his contemporary Richard Burbage rehearsing the play. "Shake-

speare" gives a line-by-line analysis of scenes from the play along with insight into plot and character. Part of the Shakespeare in Rehearsal Series.
Distributed by Coronet/MTI Film & Video.

A Midsummer Night's Dream
William Shakespeare, *A Midsummer Night's Dream*
117 min., B/W, 1935.
VHS.
With James Cagney, Mickey Rooney, Olivia de Havilland, Dick Powell, and Joe E. Brown. Directed by William Dieterle and Max Reinhardt.
Distributed by Key Video.

William Shakespeare, *A Midsummer Night's Dream*
111 min., B/W, 1963.
Beta, VHS.
With Patrick Allen, Eira Heath, Cyril Luckham, Tony Bateman, Jill Bennett. A live BBC-TV performance, with Mendelssohn's incidental music.
Distributed by Video Yesteryear.

*William Shakespeare, *A Midsummer Night's Dream*
120 min., 1968.
Beta, VHS, 16 mm film.
With Diana Rigg and David Warner. Directed by Peter Hall. A Royal Shakespeare Company performance.
Distributed by Drama Classics Video.

*William Shakespeare, *A Midsummer Night's Dream*
120 min., color, 1982.
Beta, VHS.
With Helen Mirren, Peter McEnery, and Brian Glover.
Distributed by Key Video and Time-Life Video.

*William Shakespeare, *A Midsummer Night's Dream*
165 min., color, 1983.
Beta, VHS, 3/4″ U-matic cassette.
With William Hurt and Michelle Shay. A lively interpretation by Joseph Papp.
Distributed by Films for the Humanities and Sciences.

William Shakespeare, *A Midsummer Night's Dream*
120 min., color, 1983.
Beta, VHS.
Available in two one-hour segments.
Distributed by King Features Entertainment.

William Shakespeare, *A Midsummer Night's Dream*
194 min., color, 1987.
Beta, VHS.
With Ileana Cotrubas, James Bowman, and Curt Appelgren. Directed by Peter Hall. A performance of the Benjamin Britten opera, taped at the Glyndebourne Festival Opera.
Distributed by Home Vision.

William Shakespeare, *A Midsummer Night's Dream* [recording]
1 cassette.
Dramatization performed by the Folio Theatre Players.
Distributed by Spoken Arts.

William Shakespeare, *A Midsummer Night's Dream* [recording]
3 cassettes (text included).
Dramatization performed by Paul Scofield and Joy Parker.
Distributed by Caedmon/HarperAudio.

William Shakespeare, *A Midsummer Night's Dream* [recording]
1 cassette (60 min.), 1985.
Dramatization performed by Stanley Holloway and Sarah Churchill. Living Shakespeare Series.
Distributed by Crown Publishers.

William Shakespeare, *A Midsummer Night's Dream* [recording]
2 cassettes (120 min.)
Performed by Robert Helpmann and Moira Shearer. An Old Vic production.
Distributed by Durkin Hayes Publishing.

A Midsummer Night's Dream: Introduction to the Play
14 min., B/W, 1954.
Key scenes from the play, with a discussion of characters and language.
Distributed by Coronet/MTI Film & Video.

The Tempest
*William Shakespeare, *The Tempest*
76 min., color, 1963.
Beta, VHS, 3/4″ U-matic cassette.
With Maurice Evans, Richard Burton, Roddy McDowall, Lee Remick, and Tom Poston. Directed by George Schaefer.
Distributed by Films for the Humanities and Sciences.

*William Shakespeare, *The Tempest*
150 min., color, 1980.
Beta, VHS, 3/4″ U-matic cassette, other formats by
   arrangement.
Distributed by Time-Life Video.

*William Shakespeare, *The Tempest*
126 min., color, 1983. Two cassettes.
Beta, VHS, 3/4″ U-matic cassette.
With Efrem Zimbalist, Jr., William H. Basset, Ted
   Sorrel, Kay E. Kuter, Edward Edwards, Nicholas
   Hammond, and Ron Palillo. Directed by William
   Woodman. Puts American actors on an artist's
   re-creation of the Globe Theatre stage.
Distributed by Kultur and Britannica Films.

William Shakespeare, *The Tempest* [recording]
1 cassette.
Dramatization performed by the Folio Theatre
   Players.
Distributed by Spoken Arts.

William Shakespeare, *The Tempest* [recording]
3 cassettes (text included).
Dramatization performed by Michael Redgrave and
   Vanessa Redgrave.
Distributed by Caedmon/HarperAudio.

Tempest
140 min., color, 1982.
Beta, VHS (stereo).
A modern version with John Cassavetes, Gena
   Rowlands, Susan Sarandon, Vittorio Gassman,
   and Raul Julia. Directed by Paul Mazursky. A
   New York architect abandons city life to go live
   on a barren Greek island with his daughter.
Distributed by RCA/Columbia Pictures Home
   Video.

Prospero's Books
130 min., color, 1992.
With John Gielgud, Erland Josephson, Michael
   Clark, Tom Bell, and Kenneth Cranham. Directed by Peter Greenaway. A loose interpretation of *The Tempest* with sumptuous visuals.

The Tempest
29 min., B/W, 1961.
3/4″ U-matic cassette, other formats by
   arrangement.
Examines three major interpretations of the play.
Distributed by Michigan Media.

The Tempest: O Brave New World
23 min., color, 1969.

16 mm film.
Explores the problem of evil in the play.
Distributed by the National Broadcasting Company.

General
*Behind the Scenes Views of Shakespeare: Shake-
   speare and His Theater* [recording]
1 cassette (60 min.)
Read by Daniel Seltzer. Explores Shakespeare and
   the characteristics of his works, suggesting how
   to watch a play.
Distributed by National Public Radio.

*Behind the Scenes Views of Shakespeare: Shake-
   speare in Our Time* [recording]
1 cassette (60 min.)
Read by Maynard Mack, Jr. Discusses Shakespeare
   from a modern perspective and considers to
   what extent he is and is not our contemporary.
Distributed by National Public Radio.

*Behind the Scenes Views of Shakespeare: Shake-
   speare the Man* [recording]
1 cassette (60 min.)
Portrays Shakespeare as reflected in his work and in
   the facts and myths about his life that have
   survived.
Distributed by National Public Radio.

*The Life and Times of William Shakespeare 1:
   The Historical Setting*
25 min., color, 1978.
VHS.
An overview of Elizabethan England.
Distributed by the University of Wyoming Audio-
   Visual Services.

*The Life and Times of William Shakespeare 2:
   English Drama*
20 min., color, 1978.
VHS.
History of drama from the Greeks to Shakespeare's
   time.
Distributed by the University of Wyoming Audio-
   Visual Services.

*The Life and Times of William Shakespeare 3:
   Stratford Years*
18 min., color, 1978.
VHS.
Deals with Shakespeare's early life.
Distributed by the University of Wyoming Audio-
   Visual Services.

*The Life and Times of William Shakespeare 4:
    London Years
33 min., color, 1978.
VHS.
A history of the center of the English-speaking
    world.
Distributed by the University of Wyoming Audio-
    Visual Services.

*The Life and Times of William Shakespeare 5:
    Globe Theatre
27 min., color, 1978.
VHS.
A study of the Globe and Elizabethan theater.
Distributed by the University of Wyoming Audio-
    Visual Services.

*Shakespeare and the Globe
31 min., color, 1985.
VHS.
A survey of Shakespeare's life, work, and cultural
    milieu.
Distributed by Films for the Humanities and
    Sciences.

*Shakespeare and His Stage
46 min., color, 1975.
VHS, 16 mm film.
Provides a montage of Shakespearean background,
    including scenes from Hamlet and the prepara-
    tion of various actors for the role.
Distributed by Films for the Humanities and
    Sciences.

*Shakespeare and His Theatre
55 min., color.
VHS, 16 mm film.
A history of Shakespeare's life and times.
Distributed by Media Guild.

*Shakespeare's Heritage
29 min., color, 1988.
16 mm film.
Narrated by Anthony Quayle. Explores Stratford
    and the life of the playwright.
Distributed by Britannica Films.

*Shakespeare's Theater
13 min., color, 1946.
16 mm film.
Re-creates the experience of going to a play at the
    Globe Theatre in Shakespeare's time.
Distributed by the Indiana University Center for
    Media and Teaching Resources.

*Shakespeare's Theater
28 min., B/W, 1952.
16 mm film.
Hosted by Frank Baxter. A discussion of the evolu-
    tion of Elizabethan theater and the original stag-
    ing of Shakespeare's plays.

*Shakespeare's Theater: The Globe Playhouse
18 min., B/W, 1953.
16 mm film.
Provides a model of the Globe Theatre and a dis-
    cussion of original staging of some of Shake-
    speare's plays.
Distributed by the University of California Exten-
    sion Media Center.

*Shakespeare's World and Shakespeare's London
29 min., B/W, 1952.
16 mm film.
Hosted by Frank Baxter. Re-creates the climate of
    Elizabethan England that allowed Shakespeare's
    genius to flourish.
Distributed by Films, Inc.

The Two Traditions
50 min., color, 1983.
VHS.
Deals with the problem of overcoming barriers of
    time and culture to make Shakespeare relevant
    today. Examples from Hamlet, Coriolanus, The
    Merchant of Venice, and Othello. Part of the
    Playing Shakespeare Series.
Distributed by Films for the Humanities and
    Sciences.

*Understanding Shakespeare: His Sources
20 min., color, 1972.
Beta, VHS, 3/4" U-matic cassette, 16 mm film,
    other formats by arrangement.
Examines how Shakespeare's plays grew out of
    sources available to him and how he enhanced
    the material with his own imagination.
Distributed by Coronet/MTI Film & Video.

The World of William Shakespeare [recording]
8 cassettes.
Dramatized version of Shakespeare's life.
Distributed by Cassette Book Company.

BERNARD SHAW

Bernard Shaw, Major Barbara
145 min., B/W, 1941.
Beta, VHS, 3/4" U-matic cassette.

With Wendy Hiller, Rex Harrison, Robert Morley, and Sybil Thorndike.
Distributed by the Learning Corporation of America.

Bernard Shaw, *Major Barbara* [recording]
4 cassettes.
Dramatization performed by Maggie Smith and Robert Morley.
Distributed by Caedmon/HarperAudio.

*George Bernard Shaw
16 min., B/W, 1956.
16 mm film.
A biographical tribute, with anecdotes and comments by Dame Sybil Thorndike, Wendy Hiller, and Colin Wilson; sketches by Felix Topolski; highlights from Shaw's plays and opinions; and interviews with the playwright.
Distributed by Phoenix/BFA Films.

*George Bernard Shaw
26 min., B/W, 1964.
16 mm film.
Narrated by Mike Wallace. A biographical portrait of Shaw the playwright and Shaw the man.
Distributed by CRM Films.

The Seven Ages of George Bernard Shaw [recording]
4 cassettes.
Unabridged version read by Margaret Webster. Discusses Shaw as comedian, satirist, iconoclast, social reformer, crusader, philosopher, and critic.
Distributed by Random Audiobooks.

SOPHOCLES

Sophocles, *Antigone*
88 min., B/W, 1962.
16 mm film.
With Irene Papas. Directed by George Tzavellas. In Greek with English subtitles.
Distributed by Films, Inc.

*Sophocles, Antigone
120 min., 1987.
Beta, VHS, 3/4″ U-matic cassette.
With Juliet Stevenson, John Shrapnel, and John Gielgud. Staged version.
Distributed by Films for the Humanities and Sciences.

Sophocles, *Antigone* [recording]
2 cassettes.
Dramatization of the Fitts and Fitzgerald translation. Performed by Dorothy Tutin and Max Adrian.
Distributed by Caedmon/HarperAudio.

Sophocles, *Antigone* [recording]
2 cassettes (60 min.)
Translated and adapted by Bernard Mayes.
Distributed by the Mind's Eye.

Antigone: Rights of Passion
85 min., color, 1990.
With Amy Greenfield and Bertram Ross. Directed by Amy Greenfield.
Distributed by Evergreen Video.

Sophocles, *Oedipus Rex*
20 min., color, 1957.
Beta, VHS, 3/4″ U-matic cassette.
A performance in which all the actors are deaf.
Distributed by Gallaudet University Library.

*Sophocles, Oedipus Rex
87 min., color, 1957.
VHS, 16 mm film.
With Douglas Campbell, Douglas Rain, Eric House, and Eleanor Stuart. Based on William Butler Yeats's translation. Directed by Tyrone Guthrie. Contained and highly structured rendering by the Stratford (Ontario) Festival Players.
Distributed by Water Bearer Films.

Sophocles, *Oedipus the King*
97 min., color, 1967.
VHS.
With Donald Sutherland, Christopher Plummer, Lilli Palmer, Orson Welles, Cyril Cusack, Richard Johnson, and Roger Livesey. Directed by Philip Saville. Simplified version of the play, filmed in Greece using an old amphitheater as background for much of the action.
Distributed by Crossroads Video.

*Sophocles, Oedipus the King
45 min., color, 1975.
Beta, VHS, 3/4″ U-matic cassette, 16 mm film.
With Anthony Quayle, James Mason, Claire Bloom, and Ian Richardson. A production by the Athens Classical Theatre Company, with an English soundtrack.
Distributed by Films for the Humanities and Sciences.

Sophocles, *Oedipus Tyrannus*
60 min., color, 1978.
Beta, VHS, 3/4" U-matic cassette.
Hosted by José Ferrer. Begins when Oedipus is informed of the death of his father. Expository portion shows scenes of Greek theaters and recounts Aristotle's definition of tragedy.
Distributed by Films, Inc.

Sophocles, *Oedipus the King*
120 min., color, 1987.
VHS.
With John Gielgud, Michael Pennington, and Claire Bloom.
Distributed by Films for the Humanities and Sciences.

Sophocles, *Oedipus Rex* [recording]
2 cassettes.
Translated by William Butler Yeats. Performed by Douglas Campbell and Eric House.
Distributed by Caedmon/HarperAudio.

Sophocles, *Oedipus Rex* [recording]
2 cassettes (100 min.).
Translated and adapted by Bernard Mayes.
Distributed by the Mind's Eye.

*Sophocles, *Oedipus at Colonus*
120 min., color, 1987.
Beta, VHS, 3/4" U-matic cassette.
With Anthony Quayle, Juliet Stevenson, and Kenneth Haigh. Staged version.
Distributed by Films for the Humanities and Sciences.

Oedipus Rex: Age of Sophocles, I
31 min., color and B/W, 1959.
Beta, VHS, 3/4" U-matic cassette, 16 mm film.
Discusses Greek civilization, the classic Greek theater, and the theme of fundamental human nature.
Distributed by Britannica Films.

Oedipus Rex: The Character of Oedipus, II
31 min., color and B/W, 1959.
Beta, VHS, 3/4" U-matic cassette, 16 mm film.
Debates whether Oedipus's trouble is a result of character flaws or of fate.
Distributed by Britannica Films.

Oedipus Rex: Man and God, III
30 min., color and B/W, 1959.
Beta, VHS, 3/4" U-matic cassette, 16 mm film.
Deals with the idea that Oedipus, although a

worldly ruler, cannot overcome the gods and his destiny.
Distributed by Britannica Films.

Oedipus Rex: Recovery of Oedipus, IV
30 min., color and B/W, 1959.
Beta, VHS, 3/4" U-matic cassette, 16 mm film.
Deals with human existence between God and beast.
Distributed by Britannica Films.

WOLE SOYINKA

Wole Soyinka
50 min., color, 1985.
VHS, 3/4" U-matic cassette.
An interview with the playwright, who discusses political and cultural life in Africa and the United States and what it means to be an artist.
Distributed by the Roland Collection.

AUGUST STRINDBERG

*August Strindberg, *Miss Julie*
90 min., B/W, 1950.
Beta, VHS.
With Anita Bjork and Ulf Palme. In Swedish with English subtitles.
Distributed by Nelson Entertainment.

*August Strindberg, *Miss Julie*
60 min., color, 1978.
Beta, VHS, 3/4" U-matic cassette. Ancillary materials available.
With Patrick Stewart and Lisa Harrow. Hosted by José Ferrer. Opens with a crucial scene rehearsal and closes with a full-dress version of the work. In between, the actors show different ways of playing a scene.
Distributed by Films, Inc.

August Strindberg, *Strindberg's "Miss Julie": Royal Shakespeare Company*
120 min., color, 1990.
Beta, VHS.
Distributed by Mastervision, Inc.

JOHN MILLINGTON SYNGE

John Millington Synge, *Riders to the Sea* [recording]
1 cassette.
Recorded with *In the Shadow of the Glen*.
Distributed by Spoken Arts.

OSCAR WILDE

*Oscar Wilde, *The Importance of Being Earnest*
95 min., color, 1952.
Beta, VHS.
With Michael Redgrave, Edith Evans, Margaret
  Rutherford, Michael Dennison, and Joan Green-
  wood. Directed by Anthony Asquith. Staged
  version.
Distributed by Paramount Home Video.

Oscar Wilde, *The Importance of Being Earnest*
99 min., color, 1980.
3/4" U-matic cassette.
A BBC production.
Distributed by Time-Life Video.

Oscar Wilde, *The Importance of Being Earnest*
  [recording]
2 cassettes (120 min.), 1980.
Unabridged dramatization performed by John Gielgud and Edith Evans.
Distributed by Durkin Hayes Publishing.

Oscar Wilde, *The Importance of Being Earnest*
  [recording]
2 cassettes.
Performed by Lynn Redgrave and Gladys Cooper.
Distributed by Caedmon/HarperAudio.

TENNESSEE WILLIAMS

*Tennessee Williams, *Cat on a Hot Tin Roof*
108 min., color, 1958.
With Paul Newman, Burl Ives, Elizabeth Taylor,
  and Jack Carson. Directed by Richard Brooks.
Distributed by MGM/UA Home Video.

Tennessee Williams, *Cat on a Hot Tin Roof*
148 min., color, 1984.
With Jessica Lange, Tommy Lee Jones, and Rip
  Torn. Directed by Jack Hofsiss.
Distributed by Vestron Video.

Tennessee Williams, *The Glass Menagerie*
134 min., color, 1987.
With Joanne Woodward, Karen Allen, John Mal-
  kovich, and James Naughton. Directed by Paul
  Newman.
Distributed by MCA/Universal Home Video.

Tennessee Williams, *The Glass Menagerie*
  [recording]
1 cassette (60 min.), 1980.

Abridged dramatization performed by Helen Hayes
  and Montgomery Clift. Radio Series.
Distributed by the Mind's Eye.

Tennessee Williams, *The Glass Menagerie*
  [recording]
2 cassettes.
Performed by Montgomery Clift and Julie Harris.
Distributed by Caedmon/HarperAudio.

Tennessee Williams, *The Glass Menagerie*
  [recording]
Read by Tennessee Williams. Includes "The Yellow
  Bird" (short story) and poems.
Distributed by the American Audio Prose Library.

Tennessee Williams, *Tennessee Williams Reads
  "The Glass Menagerie" and Others* [recording]
1 cassette.
Read by Tennessee Williams. Includes *The Glass
  Menagerie* (opening monologue and closing
  scene); "Cried the Fox"; "The Eyes"; "The
  Summer Belvedere"; "Some Poems Meant for
  Music: Little Horse"; "Which Is My Little Boy";
  "Little One"; "Gold-Tooth Blues"; "Kitchen-
  Door Blues"; "Heavenly Grass"; and "The Yel-
  low Bird."
Distributed by Caedmon/HarperAudio.

In the Country of Tennessee Williams
30 min., color, 1977.
Beta, VHS, 1/2" reel, 3/4" U-matic cassette, 2"
  Quad.
A one-act play about how Williams developed as a
  writer.
Distributed by the New York State Education
  Department.

General Resources

A Day at the Globe
30 min., color.
VHS.
Starts with a brief overview of early drama and of
  seventeenth-century England and then discusses
  the Globe Theatre, using still images. Explains
  how actors, artisans, and other company members prepared for performances. Also presents
  dramatic readings, period costumes, music and
  sound effects, helping students envision how
  Shakespearean drama actually looked.
Distributed by Insight Media.

*Drama Comes of Age
30 min., B/W, 1957.
16 mm film.
Discusses the Shakespearean theater and neoclassical drama. Demonstrates early realism with a scene from *Hedda Gabler*.
Distributed by the Indiana University Center for Media and Teaching Resources.

*Drama: How It Began
30 min., B/W, 1957.
16 mm film.
Discusses the early beginnings of the theater. Explains the techniques of the Greek theater and how playwriting developed. Illustrates the chorus technique with a scene from *Oedipus the King*.
Distributed by the Indiana University Center for Media and Teaching Resources.

The Elizabethan Age
30 min., color.
VHS.
A discussion of the resurgence of enthusiasm for the arts and letters that swept seventeenth-century England. Uses original sources.
Distributed by Insight Media.

*The Greek Theater: Greece 478–336 B.C.
26 min., color, 1979.
16 mm film.
Professor Eric Handley of University College and the Institute for Classical Studies, London, discusses the classical Greek theater, focusing on the theaters at Epidaurus and Athens. Contrasts the ancient and modern theatrical experiences and discusses such aspects of drama as costume, acting, and the function of the chorus.
Distributed by Media Guild.

Greek Tragedy [recording]
1 cassette.
Works of Euripides and Sophocles. Performed by Katina Paxinou and Alexis Minotis.
Distributed by Caedmon/HarperAudio.

*Irish Theatre & Juno and the Paycock
16 min., color.
Beta, VHS, 16 mm film.
Depicts the emergence of William Butler Yeats, John Millington Synge, and Sean O'Casey, all writing for the Abbey Theatre. Scenes from O'Casey's *Juno and the Paycock*.
Distributed by IASTA.

Old Globe: A Theatre Reborn
30 min., color, 1984.
Beta, VHS, 3/4″ U-matic cassette.
With Bing Crosby and Bob Hope. A documentary following the travels of the old theater, from Elizabethan England to the present. Features USO footage from World War II.
Distributed by San Diego State University.

*Roman Comedy, Part I: Platus/Shakespeare
22 min., color.
Beta, VHS, 16 mm film.
Shows Shakespeare's indebtedness to Plautus as a source for his works. Scenes from Plautus's *Amphityron* are contrasted with Shakespeare's *A Comedy of Errors*. The film demonstrates the power of the oversized Roman masks used in Plautus's theater. On-location footage places Plautus in the Rome of his day.
Distributed by IASTA.

*Roman Comedy, Part II: Terence/Molière
24 min., color.
Beta, VHS, 16 mm film.
Demonstrates that Molière relied on Terence for many of his sophisticated plots. The latter's *Phormio* is contrasted with Molière's *Scapin*. The actors use traditional, oversized Roman masks.
Distributed by IASTA.

The Theatre in Ancient Greece
26 min., color, 1989.
Beta, VHS, 3/4″ U-matic cassette.
Program explores ancient theater design, the origins of tragedy, the audience, the comparative roles of the writer/director and actors, and the use of landscape in many plays. Examines the theaters of Herodus, Atticus, Epidaurus, Corinth, and numerous others.
Distributed by Films for the Humanities and Sciences.

Directory of Distributors

AIMS Media Inc.
9710 DeSoto Ave.
Chatsworth, CA 91311-9409
(818) 773-4300
(800) 367-2467

American Audio Prose Library
P.O. Box 842
Columbia, MO 65205
(314) 443-0361
(800) 447-2275

Applause Productions
85-A Fernwood Lane
Roslyn, NY 11576
(516) 979-6670
(800) 253-5351

Audio Book Contractors
P.O. Box 40115
Washington, DC 20016
(202) 363-3429

Audio-Forum
Jeffrey Norton Publishers
96 Broad St.
Guilford, CT 06437
(203) 453-9794
(800) 243-1234

Books on Tape
P.O. Box 7900
Newport Beach, CA 92658
(714) 548-5525
(800) 626-3333

Britannica Films
310 South Michigan Ave.
Chicago, IL 60604
(800) 621-3900

Caedmon/HarperAudio
P.O. Box 588
Dunmore, PA 18512
(717) 343-4761
(800) 242-7737
(800) 982-4377 (in Pennsylvania)

Coronet/MTI Film & Video
108 Wilmot Rd.
Deerfield, IL 60015-9990
(708) 940-1260
(800) 621-2131

CRM Films
2215 Faraday Ave.
Carlsbad, CA 92008-7295
(619) 431-9800
(800) 421-0833

Crossroads Video
15 Buckminster Lane
Manhasset, NY 11030
(516) 365-3715
(516) 741-2155

Crown Publishers
See Random Audiobooks

Drama Classics Video
P.O. Box 2128
Manorhaven, NY 11050
(516) 767-7576

Durkin Hayes Publishing
1 Colomba Dr.
Niagara Falls, NY 14305
(716) 298-5150
(800) 962-5200
Canadian address:
3312 Mainway
Burlington, ON
CN L7M 7A7
(416) 335-0393

Evergreen Video
228 W. Houston St.
New York, NY 10014
(212) 691-7362
(800) 225-7783

Films for the Humanities and Sciences
743 Alexander Rd.
Princeton, NJ 08540
(609) 452-1128
(800) 257-5126

Films, Inc.
5547 North Ravenswood Ave.
Chicago, IL 60640-1199
(312) 878-2600
(800) 323-4222

Fox Video
See local retailer

Fries Home Video
6922 Hollywood Blvd., 12th floor
Los Angeles, CA 90028
(213) 466-2266

Gallaudet University Library
Gallaudet Media Distribution
800 Florida Ave. NE

Washington, DC 20002
(202) 651-5579
(202) 651-5580

Home Vision
See Films, Inc.

IASTA
310 West 56th St., #1B
New York, NY 10019
(212) 581-3133

Indiana University
Center for Media and Teaching Resources
Bloomington, IN 47405-5901
(812) 855-2853

Insight Media
121 West 85th St.
New York, NY 10024
(212) 721-6316

Kartes Video Communications
8500 Keystone Crossing, Suite 540
Indianapolis, IN 46240
(317) 254-4540
(800) 582-2000
(800) 523-5851 (in Indiana)

Key Video
See local retailer

King Features Entertainment
Ted Troll, librarian
235 East 45th St.
New York, NY 10017
(212) 455-4494

Kultur
121 Highway #36
West Long Branch, NJ 07764
(201) 229-2343
(800) 458-5887

Learning Corporation of America
See Coronet/MTI Film & Video

Lorimar Home Video
15838 North 62nd St.
Scottsdale, AZ 85254
(714) 474-0355
(800) 345-1441

Mastervision, Inc.
969 Park Ave.

New York, NY 10028
(212) 879-0448

MCA/Universal Home Video
See local retailer

Media Guild
11722 Sorrento Valley Rd., Suite E
San Diego, CA 92121
(619) 755-9191

MGM/UA Home Video
See local retailer

Michigan Media
University of Michigan
400 Fourth St.
Ann Arbor, MI 48109
(313) 764-8228

The Mind's Eye
Box 1060
Petaluma, CA 94953
(415) 883-7701
(800) 227-2020

National Broadcasting Company
30 Rockefeller Plaza
New York, NY 10020
(212) 664-4444

National Public Radio
2025 M St. NW
Washington, DC 20036
(202) 822-2323

Nelson Entertainment
See local retailer

New York State Education Department
Center for Learning Technologies
Media Distribution Network
Room C-7, Concourse Level
Cultural Education Center
Albany, NY 12230
(518) 474-1265

Paramount Home Video
See local retailer

Phoenix/BFA Films
468 Park Ave. South
New York, NY 10016
(212) 684-5910
(800) 221-1274

Prism Entertainment
See local retailer

Random Audiobooks
400 Hahn Rd.
Westminster, MD 21157
(800) 733-3000

RCA/Columbia Pictures Home Video
See local retailer

The Roland Collection
3120 Pawtucket Rd.
Northbrook, IL 60062
(708) 291-2230

San Diego State University
Learning Resources Center
San Diego, CA 92182
(714) 265-5726

Southgate Entertainment
See local retailer

Spoken Arts
10100 SBF Drive
Pinellas Park, FL 34666
(813) 578-7600
(800) 726-8090

Sterling Educational Films
241 East 34th St.
New York, NY 10016
(212) 262-9433

Time-Life Video
Customer Service
1450 East Parham Rd.
Richmond, VA 23280
(800) 621-7026

Turner Home Entertainment Co.
1608 Broadway and 49th St.
New York, NY 10019
(800) 942-4144

University of California Extension Media Center
2176 Shattuck Ave.
Berkeley, CA 94704
(510) 642-0460

University of Wyoming Audio-Visual Services
Box 3273 University Station
Room 14 Knight Hall
Laramie, WY 82071
(307) 766-3184

Vestron Video
See local retailer

Video Artists International
P.O. Box 158
Linwood Plaza
Suite 301
Fort Lee, NJ 07024
(201) 944-0099
(800) 477-7146

Video Yesteryear
Box C
Sandy Hook, CT 06482
(203) 426-2574
(800) 243-0987

Warner Home Video
See local retailer

Water Bearer Films
205 West End Ave.
Suite 24H
New York, NY 10023
(212) 580-8185
(800) 551-8304

Acknowledgments (*continued from p. iv*)

The Oedipus Rex of Sophocles, translated by Dudley Fitts and Robert Fitzgerald. Copyright 1949 by Harcourt Brace Jovanovich, Inc.; renewed 1977 by Cornelia Fitts and Robert Fitzgerald. Reprinted by permission of the publisher. CAUTION: All rights, including professional, amateur, motion picture, recitation, lecturing, performance, public reading, radio broadcasting, and television, are strictly reserved. Inquiries on all rights should be addressed to Harcourt Brace Jovanovich, Inc., Orlando, Florida 32887. *Photos:* Henry S. Kranzler, all rights reserved (pp. 48–49); The Guthrie Theater (p. 64).

The Antigone of Sophocles, translated by Dudley Fitts and Robert Fitzgerald. Copyright 1939 by Harcourt Brace Jovanovich, Inc.; renewed 1967 by Dudley Fitts and Robert Fitzgerald. Reprinted by permission of the publisher. CAUTION: All rights, including professional, amateur, motion picture, recitation, lecturing, performance, public reading, radio broadcasting, and television, are strictly reserved. Inquiries on all rights should be addressed to Harcourt Brace Jovanovich, Inc., Orlando, Florida 32887. *Photos:* © 1992 Martha Swope (pp. 74–75, 80–81).

"Poetics: Comedy and Epic and Tragedy" by Aristotle, from *Poetics,* translated by Gerald F. Else, (1967). Reprinted by permission of The University of Michigan Press.

Excerpt from "The Structural Study of Myth" by Claude Lévi-Strauss. Reprinted from *The Bibliographical and Special Series of the American Folklore Society, Vol. 5,* (1955) by permission of The American Folklore Society.

"Emotion and Meaning in Greek Tragedy," excerpt from *Greek Tragedy in Action* by Oliver Taplin. Reprinted by permission of Methuen & Co.

"Principal Constants of Conflict in *Antigone,*" excerpt from *Antigones* by George Steiner. Copyright © 1984 by George Steiner. Reprinted by permission of Oxford University Press.

Excerpt from *Antigone* by Jean Anouilh, adapted and translated by Lewis Galantière. Copyright 1946 by Random House, Inc. and renewed 1974 by Lewis Galantière. Reprinted by permission of Random House, Inc.

Medea is reprinted from *Three Plays of Euripides: Alcestis, Medea, The Bacchae,* translated by Paul Roche, with the permission of W. W. Norton & Company, Inc. Copyright © 1974 by Paul Roche.

Lysistrata, translated by Dudley Fitts. Copyright 1954 by Harcourt Brace Jovanovich, Inc. and renewed 1982 by Cornelia Fitts, Daniel H. Fitts, and Deborah W. Fitts. Reprinted by permission of the publisher. CAUTION: All rights, including professional, amateur, motion picture, recitation, lecturing, performance, public reading, radio broadcasting, and television, are strictly reserved. Inquiries on all rights should be addressed to Harcourt Brace Jovanovich, Inc., Orlando, Florida 32887.

Roman Drama

Figure 2. Theater of Marcellus from *The History of the Greek and Roman Theater* by Margarete Bieber. Copyright 1939, 1961 by Princeton University Press. Fig. 641 (after Peruzzi; redrawn by Mrs. Wadhams). Reprinted by permission of Princeton University Press.

Excerpt from *The Twin Menaechmi* from *Six Plays of Plautus* by Plautus, translated by Lionel Casson. Used by permission of Doubleday, a division of Bantam Doubleday Dell Publishing Group.

Excerpt from *The Brothers* by Terence from *The Comedies of Terence,* edited and with a foreword by Robert Graves. Reprinted by permission of Curtis Brown Ltd. Copyright © 1962 by Robert Graves.

Excerpt from *Thyestes* by Seneca from *The Complete Roman Drama* by George E. Duckworth. Copyright 1942 and renewed 1970 by Random House, Inc. Reprinted by permission of Random House, Inc.

Medieval Drama

Figure 3. Pageant wagon from *Early English Stages 1300 to 1660* by Glynne William Gladstone Wickham. Reprinted by permission of Columbia University Press and Routledge & Kegan Paul Ltd.

Everyman, edited by A. C. Cawley. Reprinted from the Everyman's Library edition, 1974, with footnotes by A. C. Cawley, by permission of David Campbell Publishers Ltd.

Renaissance Drama

Figure 4. Teatro Olimpico in Vicenza, Italy, Alinari/Art Resource New York.

Figure 5. Perspective setting designed by Peruzzi, Scala/Art Resource New York.

Figure 6. Swan Theatre from *Essai sur L'Histoire du Théâtre* by Germain Bapst. Reprinted by courtesy of the Trustees of the Boston Public Library.

Footnotes to accompany *A Midsummer Night's Dream, Hamlet,* and *The Tempest* from *The Complete Works of Shakespeare* by David Bevington. Copyright © 1980, 1973 by Scott, Foresman and Company. Reprinted by permission of HarperCollins Publishers, Inc. *Photos:* Richard M. Feldman (pp. 226–27, 272–73, 334); © 1992 Martha Swope (pp. 238–39, 324–25); © Donald Cooper/Photostage (pp. 288–89).

"Masque Elements in *A Midsummer Night's Dream*" by Enid Welsford, from *The Court Masque* by Enid Welsford. Cambridge: Cambridge University Press; New York: The Macmillan Company, 1927. Reprinted by permission of Cambridge University Press.

"Broken Nuptials," excerpt from *Broken Nuptials in Shakespeare's Plays* by Carol Thomas Neely. Reprinted by permission of Yale University Press.

"On *A Midsummer Night's Dream*" by Linda Bamber. Reprinted from *Comic Women, Tragic Men: A Study of Gender and Genre in Shakespeare* by Linda Bamber with the permission of the publishers, Stanford University Press. © 1982 by the Board of Trustees of the Leland Stanford Junior University.

"The Play Is the Message . . . " by Peter Brook from *The Shifting Point* by Peter Brook. Copyright © 1987 by Peter Brook. Reprinted by permission of HarperCollins Publishers, Inc.

"Hamlet and His Problems" from "Hamlet" in *Selected Essays* by T. S. Eliot, copyright 1950 by Harcourt Brace Jovanovich, Inc., renewed 1978 by Esme Valerie Eliot, reprinted by permission of Harcourt Brace Jovanovich, Inc., and Faber and Faber Ltd.

"Shakespeare in the Bush" by Laura Bohannon from *Natural History*, 75 (1966), pp. 28–33. Reprinted by permission of the author.

"Hamlet's Ghost," illustration of "Suggested Elizabethan Staging of the Ghost Scenes" by C. Walter Hodges from *The New Cambridge Shakespeare: Hamlet*, edited by Philip Edwards (Cambridge University Press). Reprinted by permission of C. Walter Hodges.

"*The Tempest* and the New World" by Stephen J. Greenblatt from *Learning to Curse* by Stephen J. Greenblatt. Reprinted by permission of Routledge.

The Changeling from *The Selected Plays of Thomas Middleton*, edited by David L. Frost. Copyright © 1978 by Cambridge University Press. Reprinted by permission of the author and Cambridge University Press.

"Tragicomedy and *The Changeling*," excerpt from *Tragicomedy* by David L. Hirst. Reprinted by permission of Methuen & Co.

Late Seventeenth- and Eighteenth-Century Drama

Figure 7. Early Restoration Theater, illustration by Peter Kahn. From *The Frolicks; or, The Lawyer Cheated* by Elizabeth Polwhele, edited by Judith Milhous and Robert D. Hume, Cornell University Press, 1977. Used by permission of the publisher, Cornell University Press.

The Misanthrope translated by Richard Wilbur. Copyright © 1955 and renewed 1983 by Richard Wilbur. Reprinted by permission of Harcourt Brace Jovanovich, Inc. CAUTION: Professionals and amateurs are hereby warned that this translation, being fully protected under the copyright laws of the United States, the British Commonwealth, including Canada, and all other countries which are signatories to the Universal Copyright Convention, is subject to royalty. All rights, including professional, amateur, motion picture, recitation, lecturing, public reading, radio broadcasting, and television, are strictly reserved. Particular emphasis is laid on the question of readings, permission for which must be secured from the author's agent in writing. Inquiries on professional rights (except for amateur rights) should be addressed to Mr. Gilbert Parker, Curtis Brown, Ltd., Ten Astor Place, New York, NY 10003. The amateur acting rights of *The Misanthrope* are controlled exclusively by the Dramatists Play Service, Inc., 440 Park Avenue South, New York, NY 10016. No amateur performance of the play may be given without obtaining in advance the written permission of the Dramatists Play Service, Inc. and paying the requisite fee. Translation rights should be addressed to Harcourt Brace Jovanovich, Inc., Permissions Department, Orlando, Florida 32887.

"Alceste's Love for Célimène," excerpt from *Men and Masks* by Lionel Gossman. Reprinted by permission of the author and Johns Hopkins University Press.

"On Aphra Behn," excerpt from *A Room of One's Own* by Virginia Woolf. Copyright © 1929 by Harcourt Brace Jovanovich, Inc. and renewed 1957 by Leonard Woolf. Reprinted by permission of the publisher.

"Courtship and Marriage in *The Rover*," excerpt from *Virtue of Necessity: English Women's Writing* by Elaine Hobby. Copyright © Elaine Hobby 1988. Published by Virago Press Ltd. 1988.

Nineteenth-Century Drama to the Turn of the Century

Figure 8. Realistic setting in Anton Chekhov's *The Cherry Orchard*, Harvard Theatre Collection.

A Doll House and *Hedda Gabler* from *The Complete Major Prose Plays of Henrik Ibsen* by Henrik Ibsen, translated by Rolf Fjelde. Translation copyright © 1965, 1970, 1978, by Rolf Fjelde. Used by permission of New American Library, a division of Penguin Books USA Inc. Photos: © 1992 Martha Swope (pp. 572–73); © Donald Cooper/Photostage (pp. 580–81, 611, 616–17); © T. Charles Erickson (pp. 626–27).

"*A Doll's House*: Ibsen the Moralist" by Muriel C. Bradbrook from *Ibsen: The Norwegian* by Muriel C. Bradbrook. Reprinted by permission of Random Century.

"Notes for *Hedda Gabler*," selection from Ibsen's Notes on *Hedda Gabler* translated by Evert Sprinchorn, from *Playwrights on Playwriting*, edited by Toby Cole. Copyright © 1960 and renewal copyright © 1988 by Toby Cole. Reprinted by permission of Hill and Wang, a division of Farrar, Straus and Giroux, Inc.

"Thematic Symbols in *Hedda Gabler*" by Caroline Mayerson. Reprinted by permission of the author.

"On *Hedda Gabler*," excerpt from "Ibsen Read Anew" by Jan Kott from *The Theatre of Essence and Other Essays* by Jan Kott, © 1984 by Jan Kott. Reprinted by permission of the author.

Miss Julie by August Strindberg and excerpt from the Preface to *Miss Julie*, from *Strindberg: Five Plays*, Harry Carlson, editor and translator. Copyright © 1983 The Regents of the University of California. Reprinted by permission of the University of California Press.

The Cherry Orchard by Anton Chekhov from *The Major Plays of Anton Chekhov,* translated by Ann Dunnigan. Translation copyright © 1964 by Ann Dunnigan. Used by permission of New American Library, a division of Penguin Books USA Inc.

"From Chekhov's Letters," two letters from *Letters of Anton Chekhov* translated by Michael Henry Heim with Simon Karlinsky. Copyright © 1973 by Harper & Row, Publishers, Inc. Reprinted by permission of HarperCollins Publishers, Inc.

Excerpt from "Recollections" by Maxim Gorky from *Reminiscences of Tolstoy, Chekhov and Andreyev* by Maxim Gorky. Reprinted by permission of Random Century.

"On Chekhov" by Peter Brook from *The Shifting Point* by Peter Brook. Copyright © 1987 by Peter Brook. Reprinted by permission of HarperCollins Publishers, Inc.

Major Barbara and the "Preface to *Major Barbara*" by Bernard Shaw. Copyright 1907, 1913, 1930, 1941 George Bernard Shaw. Copyright: 1957 The Public Trustees as Executor of the Estate of George Bernard Shaw. Reprinted by permission of The Society of Authors on behalf of the Estate of Bernard Shaw.

Drama in the Early and Mid-Twentieth Century

Figure 9. Expressionistic setting in Arthur Miller's *Death of a Salesman,* the Billy Rose Theatre Collection of New York Public Library for the Performing Arts/Astor, Lenox, and Tilden Foundations.

Six Characters in Search of an Author by Luigi Pirandello. Copyright 1922 by E. P. Dutton. Renewed 1950 in the names of Stefano, Fausto, and Lietta Pirandello. From *Naked Masks: Five Plays* by Luigi Pirandello, edited by Eric Bentley. Translation copyright 1922, 1952 by E. P. Dutton. Renewed 1950 in the names of Stefano, Fausto, and Lietta Pirandello. Introduction copyright 1952, © renewed 1980 by Eric Bentley. Used by permission of the publisher, Dutton, an imprint of New American Library, a division of Penguin Books USA Inc.

Desire Under the Elms by Eugene O'Neill. Copyright 1924 and renewed 1952 by Eugene O'Neill. Reprinted from *The Plays of Eugene O'Neill* by Eugene O'Neill by permission of Random House, Inc.

Galileo by Bertolt Brecht, translated by Charles Laughton from *From the Modern Repertoire,* Series Two (pp. 425–76), edited by Eric Bentley, © 1952. Reprinted by permission of Indiana University Press.

The Glass Menagerie by Tennessee Williams. Copyright 1945 by Tennessee Williams and Edwina D. Williams and renewed 1973 by Tennessee Williams. Reprinted by permission of Random House, Inc. *Photos:* The Billy Rose Theatre Collection of the New York Public Library for the Performing Arts/Astor, Lenox, and Tilden Foundations (pp. 918–19); Joan Marcus/Arena Stage (pp. 928–29).

Cat on a Hot Tin Roof by Tennessee Williams. Copyright © 1954, 1955, 1971, 1975 by Tennessee Williams. Reprinted by permission of New Directions Publishing Corporation. *Photos:* © 1992 Martha Swope (p. 947); © Michael Tighe/Visages 1992 (p. 955); Fred Fehl/The Billy Rose Theatre Collection of the New York Public Library for the Performing Arts/Astor, Lenox, and Tilden Foundations (p. 966).

"Laurette Taylor in *The Glass Menagerie*," excerpt from *The Kindness of Strangers: The Life of Tennessee Williams* by Donald Spoto. Copyright © 1985 by Donald Spoto. By permission of Little, Brown and Company.

"Problems in *The Glass Menagerie*," by Benjamin Nelson, excerpt from *Tennessee Williams: The Man and His Work* by Benjamin Nelson (New York: 1961). Reprinted by permission of the author.

"Memoirs," excerpt from *Tennessee Williams: Memoirs* by Tennessee Williams. Copyright © 1972, 1975 by Tennessee Williams. Used by permission of Doubleday, a division of Bantam Doubleday Dell Publishing Group, Inc.

"Tennessee Williams and Elia Kazan Collaborate on *Cat*," excerpt from *Tennessee Williams and Elia Kazan: A Collaboration in the Theatre* by Brenda Murphy. Copyright © 1991 by Cambridge University Press. Reprinted by permission of Cambridge University Press.

Death of a Salesman by Arthur Miller. Copyright 1949, renewed © 1977 by Arthur Miller. All rights reserved. Used by permission of Viking Penguin, a division of Penguin Books USA Inc.

"Tragedy and the Common Man," excerpt from *The Theatre Essays of Arthur Miller* by Arthur Miller, edited by Robert A. Martin. Copyright 1949, renewed © 1977 by Arthur Miller. Used by permission of Viking Penguin, a division of Penguin Books USA Inc.

Endgame by Samuel Beckett. Copyright © 1958 by Grove Press, Inc.; copyright renewed © 1986 by Samuel Beckett. Used by permission of Grove Press, Inc. *Photos:* © 1992 Martha Swope (pp. 1060–61); Richard M. Feldman (p. 1071).

All That Fall by Samuel Beckett. Copyright © 1957 by Samuel Beckett. Used by permission of Grove Press, Inc.

Excerpt from "The Theatre of the Absurd" by Martin Esslin. Reprinted by permission of the author.

"The Ending of *Endgame*," excerpt from *Beckett's Theaters: Interpretations for Performance* by Sidney Homan. Reprinted by permission of Bucknell University Press.

"Radio to Stage: *All That Fall*," excerpt from *Just Play: Beckett's Theater* by Ruby Cohn. Copyright © 1980 by Princeton University Press. Reprinted by permission. Letters written by Samuel Beckett quoted in this excerpt are reprinted by permission of Grove Press.

ACKNOWLEDGMENTS 1435

"All That Fall: An Analysis," excerpt from *Understanding Samuel Beckett* by Alan Astro. Reprinted by permission of the University of South Carolina Press.

A Raisin in the Sun by Lorraine Hansberry. Copyright © 1958 by Robert Nemiroff, as an unpublished work. Copyright © 1959, 1966, 1984 by Robert Nemiroff. Reprinted by permission of Random House, Inc. "Harlem (A Dream Deferred)" from *The Panther and the Lash* by Langston Hughes. Copyright 1951 by Langston Hughes. Reprinted by permission of Alfred A. Knopf, Inc.

Contemporary Drama

Figure 10. Multimedia effects in Robert Wilson's *CIVIL warS,* Richard M. Feldman.

The Dumb Waiter by Harold Pinter. Copyright © 1960 by Harold Pinter. Copyright renewed © 1988 by Harold Pinter. Reprinted by permission of Grove Press and Faber and Faber Ltd.

The Strong Breed by Wole Soyinka. © 1964 Oxford University Press. Reprinted from Wole Soyinka: *Collected Plays 1* (1973) by permission of Oxford University Press.

"Interview with Wole Soyinka" by Lewis Nkosi from *African Writers Talking: A Collection of Radio Interviews,* edited by Cosmo Pieterse and Dennis Duerden (New York: Holmes & Meier, 1972). Copyright © 1972 by Dennis Duerden and Cosmo Pieterse. Reproduced by permission of Holmes & Meier Publishers, Inc. and Heinemann Publishers (Oxford) Ltd.

Buried Child by Sam Shepard, copyright © 1979 by Sam Shepard from *Seven Plays* by Sam Shepard. Used by permission of Bantam Books, a division of Bantam Doubleday Dell Publishing Group, Inc.

"MASTER HAROLD" ... and the boys by Athol Fugard. Copyright © 1982 by Athol Fugard. Reprinted by permission of Alfred A. Knopf, Inc.

"Interview with Athol Fugard" by Heinrich von Staden from *Theater* (Yale) Vol. 14, No. 1, Winter 1982. Reprinted by permission of the author.

Excerpt from *Notebooks 1960–1977* by Athol Fugard. Copyright © 1983 by Athol Fugard. Reprinted by permission of Alfred A. Knopf, Inc.

'night, Mother by Marsha Norman. Copyright © 1983 by Marsha Norman. Reprinted by permission of Hill and Wang, a division of Farrar, Straus and Giroux, Inc. CAUTION: Professionals and amateurs are hereby warned that *'night, Mother,* being fully protected under the Copyright Laws of the United States of America and all other countries of the Berne and Universal Copyright Conventions, is subject to a royalty. All rights including, but not limited to, professional, amateur, recording, motion picture, recitation, lecturing, public reading, radio and television broadcasting, and the rights of translation into foreign languages are expressly reserved. All inquiries concerning rights (other than stock and amateur rights) should be addressed to author's agent, William Morris Agency, Inc., Attention: Samuel Liff, 1350 Avenue of the Americas, New York, NY 10019. The stock and amateur production rights for *'night, Mother* are controlled exclusively by the Dramatists Play Service, Inc., 440 Park Avenue South, New York, NY 10016. No amateur performance of the play may be given without obtaining prior written permission of the Dramatists Play Service, Inc., and paying the requisite fee.

"Interview with Marsha Norman" and "Interview with August Wilson" by David Savran from *In Their Own Voices* by David Savran. Reprinted by permission of Theatre Communications Group.

Fences by August Wilson. Copyright © 1986 August Wilson. Used by permission of New American Library, a division of Penguin Books USA Inc.

Dancing at Lughnasa by Brian Friel. Copyright © 1990 by Brian Friel. Reprinted by permission of Faber and Faber, Inc. Publishers.

The Death of the Last Black Man in the Whole Entire World by Suzan-Lori Parks. Copyright © 1990 by Suzan-Lori Parks. All rights reserved. Reprinted by permission of Wiley Hausam at International Creative Management. *Photos:* © 1992 Gerry Goodstein (pp. 1360–61, 1366–67).

"Interview with Suzan-Lori Parks" by Lee A. Jacobus. Reprinted by permission of Wiley Hausam at International Creative Management.

"Interview with Liz Diamond" by Lee A. Jacobus. Reprinted by permission of Liz Diamond.

"Language in *Last Black Man,*" excerpt from "Signifying on the Signifyin" by Alisa Solomon, *Theater* Vol. 21, No. 3, 1990, pp. 76, 79–80. Reprinted by permission of *Theater.*